2010/11
RULES GOVERNING THE COURTS OF OHIO

INCLUDING THE LATEST AMENDMENTS THROUGH JULY 1, 2010

VOLUME 1: STATE

LexisNexis®

QUESTIONS ABOUT THIS PUBLICATION?

For CUSTOMER SERVICE ASSISTANCE concerning replacement pages, shipments, billing, reprint permission, or other matters,

    please call Customer Service Department at 800-833-9844

    email *customer.support@lexisnexis.com*

    or visit our interactive customer service website at *www.lexisnexis.com/printcdsc*

For EDITORIAL **content questions** concerning this publication,

    please call 800-446-3410 ext. 7447

    or email: *Michael.Oechsler@lexisnexis.com*

For **information on other LEXISNEXIS MATTHEW BENDER publications,**

    please call us at 800-223-1940

    or visit our online bookstore at *www.lexisnexis.com/bookstore*

ISBN: 9781422465691 (3 Volume Set)

Matthew Bender & Company, Inc.
Editorial Offices
701 E. Water St.
Charlottesville, VA 22902
800-446-3410
www.lexisnexis.com

Product Number 4344018 (3 Volume Set)

LexisNexis®

CONTENTS

SUMMARY OF RULE CHANGES

July 2, 2009 through July 1, 2010

STATEWIDE OHIO RULES

Civil Rules
Rule 84, Domestic Relations Forms (effective 7-1-10)

Rules of Criminal Procedure
Rules 12, 16, 41, and 59 (effective 7-1-10)

Rules of Appellate Procedure
Rules 14, 15, 25, 26, and 43 (effective 7-1-10)

Rules of Superintendence for the Courts of Ohio
Rule 17 (effective 12-1-09)

Rules of Traffic
MUTT, Rules 2, 3, 4, 10, 12, 13, 17 (effective 1-1-10)

Rules of Superintendence for the Courts of Ohio
Rule 17 (effective 12-1-09)
Rules 51, 80-87, Appendix H, Probate Forms 18.0, 18.2, 18.4, 21.5, 23.0, 23.1, 23.2, 23.3, 23.4, 23.6, 23.7 (effective 1-1-10)
Rules 20, 20.01, 20.02, 20.03, 20.04, 20.05 (effective 3-1-10)
Rules 10, 10.01, 10.03, Domestic Violence Forms (effective 7-1-10)

Rules of Practice of the Suprmeme Court of Ohio
S.Ct.Prac.R. XV (effective 10-16-09)
Full Set Rewrite (effective 1-1-10)
S.Ct.Prac.R. 2.2 (effective 7-1-10)

Rules for the Government of the Bar of Ohio
Rule II, Sections 1, 2, 3, 4, 5, 6, 7 (effective 8-1-09)
Rule XX, Section 2 (effective 8-1-09)
Appendix II, Section 20 (effective 1-1-10)
Rule I, Section 11 (effective 5-1-10)
Rule XII, Sections 1, 2, 3, 4, 5, 6, 7 (effective 1-1-11)

Rules of Professional Conduct
Rule 1.15, Form of Citation (effective 1-1-10)

PUBLISHER'S NOTE

On the Relationship Between Statutes and Court Rules

In 1968, with the adoption of the modern courts amendments to the Ohio Constitution, a whole new dimension was added to the "law" of Ohio. Article IV, § 5(B) of the Ohio Constitution now provides that, "The supreme court shall prescribe rules governing practice and procedure in all courts of the state, which rules shall not abridge, enlarge, or modify any *substantive* right ... All laws *in conflict with* such rules shall be of no further force or effect after such rules have taken effect." (Emphasis added.) The Supreme Court of Ohio has exercised this authority by promulgating Rules of Civil Procedure, Rules of Criminal Procedure, Rules of Appellate Procedure, Rules of Juvenile Procedure and Rules of Evidence.

Thus the state "law" applicable to a particular situation must often be determined by consulting the Ohio Constitution, the Ohio Revised Code, the Ohio Administrative Code and court-prescribed Rules. The principle that, in instances of conflict, a jurisdiction's constitution prevails over its legislatively-enacted statutory law has been well settled since *Marbury v. Madison* (1803), 5 U.S. 137. The relationship between statutes and court Rules is less familiar because such Rules, on both the state and federal levels, are of more recent vintage.

At first glance Article IV, § 5(B), as quoted above, appears to dispose of any question as to the relationship between statutes and Rules. The italicized words, however, create two definite and recurrent issues.

"Substantive"

The first problem is to determine what is a substantive right and what is merely a matter of procedure. The complexity of this issue is well known. In *Erie Railroad Co. v. Tompkins* (1938), 304 U.S. 65, the United States Supreme Court declared that in diversity cases the federal court must apply state substantive law and federal procedural law. Since then, federal courts have often grappled with this distinction. Thus it cannot be predicted with certainty whether a court will find that a particular provision is "substantive" or "procedural."

The Supreme Court of Ohio, per Justice William B. Brown, commented at some length on the elusive nature of this distinction in *State v. Slatter* (1981), 66 Ohio St. 2d 452. The Court stated, at pp. 454, 455 that, "The application of the substantive-procedural distinction to a statute or rule is not without difficulty, as the substantive and procedural laws are not always mutually exclusive."

The Court also quoted, at pp. 455, 456 one of its earlier opinions to the effect that, "[M]any courts have erred in proceeding upon an assumption that the supposed dividing line between the two categories has some kind of objective existence upon one side or the other of which a set of facts must always fall. Decisions, expressed in terms of locating a pre-existing line instead of where the line ought to be drawn, have lent themselves immeasurably to the confusion which reigns in this whole area of law.... 'The precise meaning to be given to "substance" and to "procedure" ought, therefore, to be determined in the light of this underlying purpose to be fair to the individuals concerned....' "

In *State ex. rel. Silcott v. Spahr* (1990), 50 Ohio St. 3d 110, the Court held that a valid procedural rule can be invalidated only by a resolution of disapproval under Section 5(B), Article IV and once in effect, rules governing practice and procedure cannot be later invalidated by a purported withhold of "jurisdiction" to follow them.

In *State ex rel. Ohio Academy of Trial Lawyers v. Sheward* (1999), 86 Ohio St. 3d 451, the Court asserted that by amending or enacting a statute, the legislature cannot resurrect a statutory provision that has been held to be invalid under Section 5(B), Article IV.

Other cases on point are: *Proctor v. Kardassilaris* (2007), 115 Ohio St. 3d 71, *Seger v. For Women, Inc.* (2006), 110 Ohio St.3d 451; *State ex rel. Loyd v. Lovelady* (2006) 108 Ohio St.3d 86 *Fraiberg v. Cuyahoga Cty. Court of Common Pleas, Domestic Relations Div.* (1996), 76 Ohio St. 3d 374; *State ex rel. Botkins v. Laws* (1994), 69 Ohio St. 3d 383; *Hiatt v. S. Health Facilities, Inc.* (1994), 68 Ohio St. 3d 236; *State ex rel. Beacon Journal Publishing Co. v. Waters* (193), 67 Ohio St. 3d 321; and *In re Coy* (1993), 67 Ohio St. 3d 215. Additional, and subsequent, cases may be found in *Anderson's Ohio Case Locator* under "COURTS" or in the Appendix Volume to *Page's Ohio Revised Code Annotated.*

"In conflict with"

Even though a previously enacted statute and a Rule may cover essentially the same territory, they may not be completely overlapping. In that instance, some portions of the statute may survive since the Rule is silent on the particular point and the statute and the Rule are not, to that extent, "in conflict."

In *State v. Tate* (1979), 59 Ohio St. 2d 50, 391 N.E.2d 738, for example, the Court was confronted with a situation in which the defendant in a petty offense case had filed a jury demand but then proceeded to be tried, without objection, by the court without a jury. The Court noted that Crim. R. 23(A), as then in effect, did not directly address this situation. To resolve the issue of how such a jury demand could be withdrawn, the Court then turned to R.C. § 2945.05 and held that, in that specific situation, the statute remained effective as prescribing the procedure for the waiver.

Finally, it should be noted that not all rules promulgated by the Supreme Court of Ohio are issued under the authority of Article IV, § 5(B). Rules not issued pursuant to that article are not subject to the limitations imposed by the article.

The Rules of Professional Conduct are an example of the Ohio Supreme Court's other rule-making powers. This code of attorney conduct and discipline was issued pursuant to the Court's power, under Article IV, § 2 and R.C. Chapter 4705, to regulate the practice of law in this state.

Michael C. Oechsler, J.D.
of the Publisher's Staff
August 2010

PREFACE

The 2010/11 edition of Rules Governing the Courts of Ohio is divided into three volumes for ease of use.

Volume 1 contains rules of statewide application prescribed by the Supreme Court of Ohio. These rules include annotations from opinions issued by the Supreme Court of Ohio from the past three years. It also includes a Publisher's Note concerning the authority to promulgate those rules and on the relationship of court rules to statutory law in Ohio. Volume 2 contains the local rules of the twelve Ohio courts of appeals and of selected courts of common pleas. Volume 3 contains rules applicable to the Sixth Circuit Court of Appeals and the two federal district courts located in Ohio. See the Table of Contents for more specific information for each volume.

OHIO RULES OF CIVIL PROCEDURE

TIME TABLE UNDER THE CIVIL RULES

TITLE I
SCOPE OF RULES — ONE FORM OF ACTION

RULE 1.   Scope of rules: applicability; construction; exceptions

(A) **Applicability.** These rules prescribe the procedure to be followed in all courts of this state in the exercise of civil jurisdiction at law or in equity, with the exceptions stated in subdivision (C) of this rule.

(B) **Construction.** These rules shall be construed and applied to effect just results by eliminating delay, unnecessary expense and all other impediments to the expeditious administration of justice.

(C) **Exceptions.** These rules, to the extent that they would by their nature be clearly inapplicable, shall not apply to procedure (1) upon appeal to review any judgment, order or ruling, (2) in the appropriation of property, (3) in forcible entry and detainer, (4) in small claims matters under Chapter 1925, Revised Code, (5) in uniform reciprocal support actions, (6) in the commitment of the mentally ill, (7) in all other special statutory proceedings; provided, that where any statute provides for procedure by a general or specific reference to the statutes governing procedure in civil actions such procedure shall be in accordance with these rules.

History: Amended, eff 7-1-71; 7-1-75.

NOTES TO DECISIONS

ANALYSIS

Amendment
Applicability generally
Arbitration
Construction
Juvenile courts
Removal of public official
Small claims litigation

Amendment

Spirit of the Ohio Rules of Civil Procedure is the resolution of cases upon their merits, not upon pleading deficiencies, as Ohio R. Civ. P. 1(B) requires that the Rules be applied "to effect just results," and pleadings are simply an end to that objective, so the mandate of Oho R. Civ. P. 15(A) as to amendments requiring leave of court, is that leave "shall be freely given when justice so requires," and, while the grant or denial of leave to amend a pleading is discretionary, where it is possible that the plaintiff, by an amended complaint, may set forth a claim upon which relief can be granted, and it is tendered timely and in good faith and no reason is apparent or disclosed for denying leave, the denial of leave to file such amended complaint is an abuse of discretion. Hoskinson v. Lambert, — Ohio App. 3d —, 2006 Ohio 6940, — N.E. 2d —, 2006 Ohio App. LEXIS 6848 (Dec. 26, 2006).

Applicability generally

Although a city had no standing under Ohio R. App. P. 4(A) to appeal from a judgment in the trial court that was in favor of a union in the union's administrative appeal of a decision by the State Employment Relations Board, as the trial court had adopted a magistrate's decision to deny the city's motion to intervene in the trial court proceedings, and the Board could not assert as error on appeal that the trial court had improperly denied intervention to the city, as it was not "aggrieved" by that decision, the city could seek to intervene on the appellate level pursuant to Ohio R. Civ. P. 24 and 1(C); the city could not be substituted for the Board on appeal pursuant to Ohio R. App. P. 29(B), as such substitution was not "necessary." Queen City Lodge No. 69 v. State Empl. Rels. Bd., — Ohio App. 3d —, 2007 Ohio 170, — N.E. 2d —, 2007 Ohio App. LEXIS 173 (Jan. 19, 2007).

Where a city employee "certified" the authenticity of ordinances attached to referendum petitions and it was undisputed that the documents attached to those petitions were in fact true and accurate copies of the ordinances, such was sufficient under RC § 731.32, as the statute did not required a "certified copy" of the ordinance to be signed by the city clerk of council as the official custodian of the applicable records; although Ohio R. Civ. P. 44 and Ohio R. Evid. 901(B) set out requirements for establishing the authenticity of public records, such was applicable to litigation, pursuant to Ohio R. Civ. P. 1(A), and as they were not specifically referenced in Ohio's election law statutes, they were not the only required method pursuant to RC § 731.32. Rankin v. Underwood, — Ohio App. 3d —, 2006 Ohio 1237, — N.E. 2d —, 2006 Ohio App. LEXIS 1098 (Mar. 17, 2006).

Arbitration

Trial court did not err in overruling appellant's motion for a more definite statement and did not err in prohibiting discovery in appellee's action requesting that the trial court confirm an arbitration award because the proceedings before the trial court were limited to confirmation of the arbitration award, and the civil rules pertaining to discovery and to motions for a more definite statement are, pursuant to Ohio R. Civ. P. 1(C)(7), inapplicable to a proceeding under RC § 2711.09. MBNA America Bank, N.A. v. Anthony, — Ohio App. 3d —, 2006 Ohio 2032, — N.E. 2d —, 2006 Ohio App. LEXIS 1856 (Apr. 18, 2006).

Construction

When homeowners said a developer negligently misrepresented to them that a home they wanted to build would fit on two lots he proposed to sell them, it was not error for the trial court to decline to apply a negligent misrepresentation claim to the second of the two lots because the homeowners' complaint did not raise such a claim, even under a liberal interpretation of the complaint, pursuant to Ohio R. Civ. P. 8(F) and 1(B), nor did the parties impliedly consent to try such a claim, under Ohio R. Civ. P. 15(B). Brothers v. Morrone-O'Keefe Dev. Co., — Ohio App. 3d —, 2007 Ohio 1942, — N.E. 2d —, 2007 Ohio App. LEXIS 1762 (Apr. 24, 2007).

Juvenile courts

Trial court does not abuse its discretion when, after a minor parent or parents involved in a custody proceeding and who were minors at the onset reach the age of majority, the court removes as parties to the action the child's grandparents, who have no independent legal interest or rights in the proceeding: In re H.W., 114 Ohio St. 3d 65, 2007 Ohio 2879, 868 N.E.2d 261, 2007 Ohio LEXIS 1573 (2007).

Removal of public official

There is no good reason why CivR 12(B) should not apply in actions to remove a public official: Belle v. Carr, 169 Ohio App. 3d 286, 2006 Ohio 5689, 862 N.E.2d 847, 2006 Ohio App. LEXIS 5684 (2006).

Small claims litigation

Motions for summary judgment are permissible in small claims actions: Norwalk MK, Inc. v. McCormick, 170 Ohio App. 3d 147, 2006 Ohio 4640, 866 N.E.2d 516, 2006 Ohio App. LEXIS 4560 (2006).

Under RC § 1925.16 and Ohio R. Civ. P. 1, it was proper to file a summary judgment motion in small claims court. Norwalk MK, Inc. v. McCormick, 170 Ohio App. 3d 147, 2006 Ohio 4640, 866 N.E.2d 516, 2006 Ohio App. LEXIS 4560 (2006).

RULE 2. One form of action

There shall be only one form of action, and it shall be known as a civil action.

TITLE II
COMMENCEMENT OF ACTION AND VENUE; SERVICE OF PROCESS; SERVICE AND FILING OF PLEADINGS AND OTHER PAPERS SUBSEQUENT TO THE ORIGINAL COMPLAINT; TIME

RULE 3. Commencement of action; venue

(A) **Commencement.** A civil action is commenced by filing a complaint with the court, if service is obtained within one year from such filing upon a named defendant, or upon an incorrectly named defendant whose name is later corrected pursuant to Civ. R. 15(C), or upon a defendant identified by a fictitious name whose name is later corrected pursuant to Civ. R. 15(D).

(B) **Venue: where proper.** Any action may be venued, commenced, and decided in any court in any county. When applied to county and municipal courts, "county," as used in this rule, shall be construed, where appropriate, as the territorial limits of those courts. Proper venue lies in any one or more of the following counties:

(1) The county in which the defendant resides;

(2) The county in which the defendant has his or her principal place of business;

(3) A county in which the defendant conducted activity that gave rise to the claim for relief;

(4) A county in which a public officer maintains his or her principal office if suit is brought against the officer in the officer's official capacity;

(5) A county in which the property, or any part of the property, is situated if the subject of the action is real property or tangible personal property;

(6) The county in which all or part of the claim for relief arose; or, if the claim for relief arose upon a river, other watercourse, or a road, that is the boundary of the state, or of two or more counties, in any county bordering on the river, watercourse, or road, and opposite to the place where the claim for relief arose;

(7) In actions described in Civ. R. 4.3, in the county where plaintiff resides;

(8) In an action against an executor, administrator, guardian, or trustee, in the county in which the executor, administrator, guardian, or trustee was appointed;

(9) In actions for divorce, annulment, or legal separation, in the county in which the plaintiff is and has been a resident for at least ninety days immediately preceding the filing of the complaint;

(10) In actions for a civil protection order, in the county in which the petitioner currently or temporarily resides;

(11) In tort actions involving asbestos claims, silicosis claims, or mixed dust disease claims, only in the county in which all of the exposed plaintiffs reside, a county where all of the exposed plaintiffs were exposed to asbestos, silica, or mixed dust, or the county in which the defendant has his or her principal place of business.

(12) If there is no available forum in divisions (B)(1) to (B)(10) of this rule, in the county in which plaintiff resides, has his or her principal place of business, or regularly and systematically conducts business activity;

(13) If there is no available forum in divisions (B)(1) to (B)(11) of this rule:

(a) In a county in which defendant has property or debts owing to the defendant subject to attachment or garnishment;

(b) In a county in which defendant has appointed an agent to receive service of process or in which an agent has been appointed by operation of law.

(C) **Change of venue.**

(1) When an action has been commenced in a county other than stated to be proper in division (B) of this rule, upon timely assertion of the defense of improper venue as provided in Civ. R. 12, the court shall transfer the action to a county stated to be proper in division (B) of this rule.

(2) When an action is transferred to a county which is proper, the court may assess costs, including reasonable attorney fees, to the time of transfer against the party who commenced the action in a county other than stated to be proper in division (B) of this rule.

(3) Before entering a default judgment in an action in which the defendant has not appeared, the court, if it finds that the action has been commenced in a county other than stated to be proper in division (B) of this rule, may transfer the action to a county that is proper. The clerk of the court to which the action is transferred shall notify the defendant of the transfer, stating in the notice that the defendant shall have twenty-eight days from the receipt of the notice to answer in the transferred action.

(4) Upon motion of any party or upon its own motion the court may transfer any action to an adjoining county within this state when it appears that a fair and impartial trial cannot be had in the county in which the suit is pending.

(D) **Venue: no proper forum in Ohio.** When a court, upon motion of any party or upon its own motion, determines: (1) that the county in which the action is brought is not a proper forum; (2) that there is no other proper forum for trial within this state; and (3) that there exists a proper forum for trial in another jurisdiction outside this state, the court shall stay the action upon condition that all defendants consent to the jurisdiction, waive venue, and agree that the date of commencement of the action in Ohio shall be the date of commencement for the application of the statute of limitations to the action in that forum in another jurisdiction which the court deems to be the proper forum. If all defendants agree to the conditions, the court shall not dismiss the action, but the action shall be stayed until the court receives notice by affidavit that plaintiff has recommenced the action in the out-of-state forum within sixty days after the effective date of the order staying the original action. If the plaintiff fails to recommence the action in the out-of-state forum within the sixty day period, the court shall dismiss the action without prejudice. If all defendants do not agree to or comply with the conditions, the court shall hear the action.

If the court determines that a proper forum does not exist in another jurisdiction, it shall hear the action.

(E) **Venue: multiple defendants and multiple claims for relief.** In any action, brought by one or more plaintiffs against one or more defendants involving one or more claims for relief, the forum shall be deemed a proper forum, and venue in the forum shall be proper, if the venue is proper as to any one party other than a nominal party, or as to any one claim for relief.

Neither the dismissal of any claim nor of any party except an indispensable party shall affect the jurisdiction of the court over the remaining parties.

(F) **Venue: notice of pending litigation; transfer of judgments.**

(1) When an action affecting the title to or possession of real property or tangible personal property is commenced in a county other than the county in which all of the real property or tangible personal property is situated, the plaintiff shall cause a certified copy of the complaint to be filed with the clerk of the court of common pleas in each county or additional county in which the real property or tangible personal property affected by the action is situated. If the plaintiff fails to file a certified copy of the complaint, third persons will not be charged with notice of the pendency of the action.

To the extent authorized by the laws of the United States, division (F)(1) of this rule also applies to actions, other than proceedings in bankruptcy, affecting title to or possession of real property in this state commenced in a United States District Court whenever the real property is situated wholly or partly in a county other than the county in which the permanent records of the court are kept.

(2) After final judgment, or upon dismissal of the action, the clerk of the court that issued the judgment shall transmit a certified copy of the judgment or dismissal to the clerk of the court of common pleas in each county or additional county in which real or tangible personal property affected by the action is situated.

(3) When the clerk has transmitted a certified copy of the judgment to another county in accordance with division (F)(2) of this rule, and the judgment is later appealed, vacated or modified, the appellant or the party at whose instance the judgment was vacated or modified must cause a certified copy of the notice of appeal or order of vacation or modification to be filed with the clerk of the court of common pleas of each county or additional county in which the real property or tangible personal property is situated. Unless a

certified copy of the notice of appeal or order of vacation or modification is so filed, third persons will not be charged with notice of the appeal, vacation, or modification.

(4) The clerk of the court receiving a certified copy filed or transmitted in accordance with the provisions of division (F) of this rule shall number, index, docket, and file it in the records of the receiving court. The clerk shall index the first certified copy received in connection with a particular action in the indices to the records of actions commenced in the clerk's own court, but may number, docket, and file it in either the regular records of the court or in a separate set of records. When the clerk subsequently receives a certified copy in connection with that same action, the clerk need not index it, but shall docket and file it in the same set of records under the same case number previously assigned to the action.

(5) When an action affecting title to registered land is commenced in a county other than the county in which all of such land is situated, any certified copy required or permitted by this division (F) of this rule shall be filed with or transmitted to the county recorder, rather than the clerk of the court of common pleas, of each county or additional county in which the land is situated.

(G) **Venue: collateral attack; appeal.** The provisions of this rule relate to venue and are not jurisdictional. No order, judgment, or decree shall be void or subject to collateral attack solely on the ground that there was improper venue; however, nothing here shall affect the right to appeal an error of court concerning venue.

(H) As used in division (B)(11) of this rule:

(1) "Asbestos claim" has the same meaning as in section 2307.91 of the Revised Code;

(2) "Silicosis claim" and "mixed dust disease claim" have the same meaning as in section 2307.84 of the Revised Code;

(3) In reference to an asbestos claim, "tort action" has the same meaning as in section 2307.91 of the Revised Code;

(4) In reference to a silicosis claim or a mixed dust disease claim, "tort action" has the same meaning as in section 2307.84 of the Revised Code.

History: Amended, eff 7-1-71; 7-1-86; 7-1-91; 7-1-98; 7-1-05.

NOTES TO DECISIONS

ANALYSIS

Amendment
Forum selection clause
Forum non conveniens
Forum selection clause
Time for commencement of action
— Estoppel
Unknown defendants
Venue selection clause
Waiver of insufficiency of service

Amendment

Ohio R. Civ. P. 3(A) and 15(C) are read in pari materia to mean that notice to a new defendant of a claim, where amendment of a complaint to include the new defendant is sought, must occur within one year of the filing of the complaint if the statute of limitations has run and that such notice does not require service, so notice need not be received before the statute of limitations has run and eventual service need not be completed within one year of filing of the original complaint. Reighard v. Cleveland Elec. Illuminating, — Ohio App. 3d —, 2006 Ohio 1283, — N.E. 2d —, 2006 Ohio App. LEXIS 1179 (Mar. 16, 2006).

Forum selection clause

Fact that the agreement is embodied in a boilerplate form does not automatically defeat the validity of a forum selection clause. Allowing a third-party beneficiary to avoid an otherwise enforceable contract provision is inconsistent with contract law: Bohl v. Hauke, 180 Ohio App. 3d 526, 2009 Ohio 150, 906 N.E.2d 450, 2009 Ohio App. LEXIS 154 (2009).

Forum non conveniens

Common pleas court's overall balancing of the forum non conveniens factors amounted to an abuse of discretion inasmuch as its reasons for granting the railroad's motion to dismiss a railroad worker's suit on the ground of forum non conveniens were not especially weighty, and the balance, even if slightly favoring the railroad, clearly did not weigh strongly enough to justify the extreme remedy of dismissal for forum non conveniens. The common pleas court's finding that the distance of the Indiana accident site from the location of trial in Ohio weighed in favor of a trial in Indiana was faulty since the 140-mile distance could just as easily have been construed as a relatively short distance, and in determining the location of the witnesses, the common pleas court recognized that about half of the potential witnesses were located closer to Ohio. Omans v. Norfolk Southern Ry., 165 Ohio App. 3d 146, 2006 Ohio 325, 844 N.E. 2d 1259, 2006 Ohio App. LEXIS 295 (Jan. 27, 2006).

Forum selection clause

In a contract between two commercial entities, a forum selection clause with no reference to a specific jurisdiction or jurisdictions is valid absent a finding of fraud or overreaching or a finding that enforcement of the clause would be unreasonable and unjust. A forum selection clause may be held to be unreasonable if it would be against public policy to enforce it. Preferred Capital, Inc. v. Power Eng'g Group, Inc., 112 Ohio St. 3d 429, 2007 Ohio 257, 860 N.E.2d 741, 2007 Ohio LEXIS 231 (2006).

Time for commencement of action

As plaintiffs filed a multi-count tort action against assorted "John Doe" defendants and they thereafter filed an amended complaint pursuant to Ohio R. Civ. P. 15(D) to actually name two defendants in place of the John Doe designation, the certified mail service on them was sufficient and timely, such that a trial court's dismissal under Ohio R. Civ. P. 12(B)(6) due to the action being time-barred was error. The original complaint was filed within the time limitations period of RC § 2305.10, the amended complaint was filed within the one-year period of Ohio R. Civ. P. 3(A), which was the equivalent of a voluntary dismissal and refiling that made the savings statute, RC § 2305.19(A), applicable, and the service on defendants was timely made within the next one-year period. LaNeve v. Atlas Recycling, Inc., 172 Ohio App. 3d 44, 2007 Ohio 2856, 872 N.E.2d 1277, 2007 Ohio App. LEXIS 2615 (2007).

Executor's complaint against a dog owner was properly dismissed because of failure of service of process as the tolling provisions of the savings statutes could not be used to extend the limitation for service of process under Ohio R. Civ. P. 3(A). Since the executor did not appeal the court's previous ruling that the owner's participation in the action did not waive the defense of insufficiency of service of process, the issue was res judicata. Franklin v. Bear, — Ohio App. 3d —, 2007 Ohio 385, — N.E. 2d —, 2007 Ohio App. LEXIS 332 (Jan. 30, 2007).

In suit brought against property owner and John Doe defendants, since the one year period for service on the John Doe defendants, specified in Ohio R. Civ. P. 3(A), had not expired before the trial court entered judgment for the owner and since the entry granting summary judgment to the owner did not include Ohio R. Civ. P. 54(B) language, the trial court's order was not an appealable order. Mosley v. 131 Foods, Inc., — Ohio App. 3d —, 2006 Ohio 5719, — N.E. 2d —, 2006 Ohio App. LEXIS 5732 (Nov. 2, 2006).

As a city employee who was initially a "John Doe" defendant raised the lack of personal service and insufficiency of process as defenses in his answer to an amended complaint, the trial court properly granted him summary judgment on the basis of the statute of limitations once the one-year period provided for service under Ohio R. Civ. P. 3(A) had run; personal service of the original summons and complaint should have been made on the city employee pursuant to Ohio R. Civ. P. 15(D), and such defenses were clearly not waived under Ohio R. Civ. P. 12(G) and (H)(1). Burya v. Lake Metroparks Bd. of Park Comm'rs, — Ohio App. 3d —, 2006 Ohio 5192, — N.E. 2d —, 2006 Ohio App. LEXIS 5136 (Sept. 29, 2006).

— Estoppel

Because a passenger was married to a driver named as the defendant in the passenger's personal injury suit, the driver was estopped from claiming untimely service where the driver incorrectly told the passenger that he had received certified mail service within one year as required by Ohio R. Civ. P. 3(A), and, based on this, the passenger did not arrange for timely personal service on the driver. Elliott v. Elliott, 168 Ohio App. 3d 218, 2006 Ohio 3797, 859 N.E.2d 575, 2006 Ohio App. LEXIS 3769 (2006).

Under the circumstances, the defendant was equitably estopped from claiming that service was not accomplished within the statutory period of time. Elliott v. Elliott, 168 Ohio App. 3d 218, 2006 Ohio 3797, 859 N.E.2d 575, 2006 Ohio App. LEXIS 3769 (2006).

Unknown defendants

Where service on former John Doe defendants was improper under CivR 15(D), the amended complaint did not relate back pursuant to CivR 15(C). However, where the original complaint was filed within the applicable period of limitation, pursuant to RC § 2305.19 plaintiffs had one year to perfect service on those defendants: LaNeve v. Atlas Recycling, Inc., 172 Ohio App. 3d 44, 2007 Ohio 2856, 872 N.E.2d 1277, 2007 Ohio App. LEXIS 2615 (2007).

Venue selection clause

Parties' venue selection clause did not confer subject matter jurisdiction on the Franklin County Municipal Court. However, that court had subject matter jurisdiction where the contract claims culminated from "enumerated events" occurring within that county: Cheap Escape Co. v. Tri-State Constr., LLC, 173 Ohio App. 3d 683, 2007 Ohio 6185, 880 N.E.2d 122, 2007 Ohio App. LEXIS 5425 (2007).

Waiver of insufficiency of service

When the affirmative defense of insufficiency of service of process is properly raised and properly preserved, a party's active participation in the litigation of a case does not constitute waiver of that defense: Gliozzo v. Univ. Urologists of Cleveland, Inc., 114 Ohio St. 3d 141, 2007 Ohio 3762, 870 N.E.2d 714, 2007 Ohio LEXIS 1869 (2007).

RULE 4. Process: Summons

(A) **Summons: issuance.** Upon the filing of the complaint the clerk shall forthwith issue a summons for service upon each defendant listed in the caption. Upon request of the plaintiff separate or additional summons shall issue at any time against any defendant.

(B) **Summons: form; copy of complaint.** The summons shall be signed by the clerk, contain the name and address of the court and the names and addresses of the parties, be directed to the defendant, state the name and address of the plaintiff's attorney, if any, otherwise the plaintiff's address, and the times within which these rules or any statutory provision require the defendant to appear and defend, and shall notify the defendant that in case of failure to do so, judgment by default will be rendered against the defendant for the relief demanded in the complaint. Where there are multiple plaintiffs or multiple defendants, or both, the summons may contain, in lieu of the names and addresses of all parties, the name of the first party on each side and the name and address of the party to be served.

A copy of the complaint shall be attached to each summons. The plaintiff shall furnish the clerk with sufficient copies.

(C) **Summons: plaintiff and defendant defined.** For the purpose of issuance and service of summons "plaintiff" shall include any party seeking the issuance and service of summons, and "defendant" shall include any party upon whom service of summons is sought.

(D) **Waiver of service of summons.** Service of summons may be waived in writing by any person entitled thereto under Rule 4.2 who is at least eighteen years of age and not under disability.

(E) **Summons: time limit for service.** If a service of the summons and complaint is not made upon a defendant within six months after the filing of the complaint and the party on whose behalf such service was required cannot show good cause why such service was not made within that period, the action shall be dismissed as to that defendant without prejudice upon the court's own initiative with notice to such party or upon motion. This division shall not apply to out-of-state service pursuant to Rule 4.3 or to service in a foreign country pursuant to Rule 4.5.

(F) **Summons: revivor of dormant judgment** Upon the filing of a motion to revive a dormant judgment the clerk shall forthwith issue a summons for service upon each judgment debtor. The summons, with a copy of the motion attached, shall be in the same form and served in the same manner as provided in these rules for service of summons with complaint attached, shall command the judgment debtor to serve and file a response to the motion within the same time as provided by these rules for service and filing of an answer to a complaint, and shall notify the judgment debtor that in case of failure to respond the judgment will be revived.

History: Amended, eff 7-1-71; 7-1-73; 7-1-75; 7-1-84; 7-1-08.

NOTES TO DECISIONS

ANALYSIS

Dismissal for lack of service
Ineffective service
Modification of child support

Dismissal for lack of service

Where an unsolicited facsimile recipient filed an action against the out-of-state facsimile sender but her attempts at certified and ordinary mail service on the sender were unsuccessful, the trial court's dismissal for failure to perfect service within six months pursuant to Ohio R. Civ. P. 4(E) was error, as the recipient had acted with diligence in attempting service and then in applying for service by publication pursuant to Ohio R. Civ. P. 4.4(A); accordingly, the trial court should have afforded her an opportunity to show good cause why dismissal was not warranted in the circumstances. Ambrose v. Advanced Wireless Cellular Comm. Inc., — Ohio App. 3d —, 2007 Ohio 988, — N.E. 2d —, 2007 Ohio App. LEXIS 919 (Mar. 8, 2007).

Ineffective service

When it was alleged that a default judgment was improperly entered against an excavating company because the company was never served with process, the company did not have to satisfy the requirements of Ohio R. Civ. P. 60(B) because a lack of service deprived the trial court of jurisdiction to consider the complaint, so that any judgment entered on that complaint was void ab initio. Tractor Serv. & Supply v. Excavating, — Ohio App. 3d —, 2007 Ohio 5255, — N.E. 2d —, 2007 Ohio App. LEXIS 4643 (Sept. 19, 2007).

It did not appear that a note maker ever properly served his cross-claim upon the third-party plaintiff that the maker had joined because the certificate of service indicated that it was served upon the third-party plaintiff by regular U.S. Mail, and since the third-party plaintiff was in default for failure to appear, Ohio R. Civ. P. 5(A) required that service of summons be served in the manner provided for service in Ohio R. Civ. P. 4 through Ohio R. Civ. P. 4.6. Irion v. Incomm Electronics, — Ohio App. 3d —, 2006 Ohio 362, — N.E. 2d —, 2006 Ohio App. LEXIS 297 (Jan. 24, 2006).

Modification of child support

Trial court properly concluded that a father had failed to invoke the continuing jurisdiction of the trial court pursuant to Ohio R. Civ. P. 75(J) on the father's motion or modification and/or termination of child support where, while the father requested service of his motions by certified mail upon the Lake County Child Support Enforcement Agency and Ohio Child Support Payment Central, neither of which was currently a party to the action, there was no evidence that the father perfected or even attempted service upon the opposing party, the mother. Corrao v. Corrao, — Ohio App. 3d —, 2006 Ohio 1686, — N.E. 2d —, 2006 Ohio App. LEXIS 1545 (Mar. 31, 2006).

RULE 4.1.   Process: methods of service

All methods of service within this state, except service by publication as provided in Civ. R. 4.4(A) are described in this rule. Methods of out-of-state service and for service in a foreign country are described in Civ. R. 4.3 and 4.5.

(A) **Service by certified or express mail.** Evidenced by return receipt signed by any person, service of any process shall be by certified or express mail unless otherwise permitted by these rules. The clerk shall place a copy of the process and complaint or other document to be served in an envelope. The clerk shall address the envelope to the person to be served at the address set forth in the caption or at the address set forth in written instructions furnished to the clerk with instructions to forward. The clerk shall affix adequate postage and place the sealed envelope in the United States mail as certified or express mail return receipt requested with instructions to the delivering postal employee to show to whom delivered, date of delivery, and address where delivered.

The clerk shall forthwith enter the fact of mailing on the appearance docket and make a similar entry when the return receipt is received. If the envelope is returned with an endorsement showing failure of delivery, the clerk shall forthwith notify, by mail, the attorney of record or, if there is no attorney of record, the party at whose instance process was issued and enter the fact of notification on the appearance docket. The clerk shall file the return receipt or returned envelope in the records of the action.

All postage shall be charged to costs. If the parties to be served by certified or express mail are numerous and the clerk determines there is insufficient security for costs, the clerk may require the party requesting service to advance an amount estimated by the clerk to be sufficient to pay the postage.

(B) **Personal service.** When the plaintiff files a written request with the clerk for personal service, service of process shall be made by that method.

When process issued from the Supreme Court, a court of appeals, a court of common pleas or a county court is to be served personally, the clerk of the court shall deliver the process and sufficient copies of the process and complaint, or other document to be served, to the sheriff of the county in which the party to be served resides or may be found. When process issues from the municipal court, delivery shall be to the bailiff of the court for service on all defendants who reside or may be found within the county or counties in which that court has territorial jurisdiction and to the sheriff of any other county in this state for service upon a defendant who resides in or may be found in that other county. In the alternative, process issuing from any of these courts may be delivered by the clerk to any person not less than eighteen years of age, who is not a party and who has been designated by order of the court to make service of process. The person serving process shall locate the person to be served and shall tender a copy of the process and accompanying documents to the person to be served. When the copy of the process has been served, the person serving process shall endorse that fact on the process and return it to the clerk who shall make the appropriate entry on the appearance docket.

When the person serving process is unable to serve a copy of the process within twenty-eight days, the person shall endorse that fact and the reasons therefore on the process and return the process and copies to the clerk who shall make the appropriate entry on the appearance docket. In the event of failure of service, the clerk shall follow the notification procedure set forth in division (A) of this rule. Failure to make service within the twenty-eight day period and failure to make proof of service do not affect the validity of the service.

(C) **Residence service.** When the plaintiff files a written request with the clerk for residence service, service of process shall be made by that method.

Residence service shall be effected by leaving a copy of the process and the complaint, or other document to be served, at the usual place of residence of the person to be served with some person of suitable age and discretion then residing therein. The clerk of the court shall issue the process, and the process server shall return it, in the same manner as prescribed in division (B) of this rule. When the person serving process is unable to serve a copy of the process within twenty-eight days, the person shall endorse that fact and the reasons therefore on the process and return the process and copies to the clerk who shall make the appropriate entry on the appearance docket. In the event of failure of service, the clerk shall follow the notification procedure set forth in division (A) of this rule. Failure to make service within the twenty-eight day period and failure to make proof of service do not affect the validity of service.

History: Amended, eff 7-1-71; 7-1-80; 7-1-97.

NOTES TO DECISIONS

ANALYSIS

Business address service
Certified or express mail service
Failure of service
Ineffective service
Modification of child support
Personal service
Presumption of proper service
Residence service
Service by mail

Business address service

Service of process on an individual and on the individual's corporation was proper where the defendant's wife was served at the defendant's home, which was also listed as the address of the corporation's statutory agent: New v. All Transp. Solution, Inc., 177 Ohio App. 3d 620, 2008 Ohio 3949, 895 N.E.2d 606, 2008 Ohio App. LEXIS 3312 (2007).

Trial court's summary denial of a loan officer's motion to vacate a judgment against him pursuant to Ohio R. Civ. P. 60(B) was an abuse of discretion where no hearing was held despite the officer's having rebutted the presumption of effective service on him pursuant to Ohio R. Civ. P. 4.1 and 4.6. An issue was created as to whether service had been attempted at the proper business address for the loan officer, and where such issue was raised, it was reversible error to fail to hold a hearing in order to resolve the issue as to effective service. Money Tree Loan Co. v. Williams, 169 Ohio App. 3d 336, 2006 Ohio 5568, 862 N.E.2d 885, 2006 Ohio App. LEXIS 5553 (2006).

Trial court's grant of individual debtors' motion under Ohio R. Civ. P. 60(B)(5) to vacate a default judgment obtained against them by a creditor, based on their claim that they were not properly served by certified mail at their business address pursuant to Ohio R. Civ. P. 4.1(1), was error where the creditor was not given an opportunity to respond to the motion and an evidentiary hearing was not held for the trial court's factual determination regarding whether the debtors had a physical presence at the business address for purposes of finding that their due process rights under Ohio Const. art. I, § 16 were not violated by such service. Carter-Jones Lumber Co. v. Meyers, — Ohio App. 3d —, 2006 Ohio 5380, — N.E. 2d —, 2006 Ohio App. LEXIS 5336 (Oct. 13, 2006).

Certified or express mail service

Judgment entered against children of judgment debtors was not void ab initio for lack of personal service on them, as the complaint was sent by certified mail to their permanent addresses and it was accepted by their grandmother, who was

over the age of 16 years and was competent. Service was properly made under Ohio R. Civ. P. 4.1(A) and 4.2(A), and the trial court did not err in denying the children's motion for relief from judgment under Ohio R. Civ. P. 60(B). Tube City, Inc. v. Halishak, — Ohio App. 3d —, 2007 Ohio 2118, — N.E. 2d —, 2007 Ohio App. LEXIS 1976 (May 3, 2007).

When a party submitted unrebutted evidence that he was never properly served with process, under Ohio R. Civ. P. 4.1(A), in an action filed against him, because service was directed to the home of his parents, where he did not live and had not lived since the filing of the action, the action was never properly commenced, pursuant to Ohio R. Civ. P. 3(A), as service of process was not obtained within one year of filing, so a default judgment entered against the party had to be vacated. Jacobs v. Szakal, — Ohio App. 3d —, 2006 Ohio 1312, — N.E. 2d —, 2006 Ohio App. LEXIS 1196 (Mar. 22, 2006).

Failure of service

Where an insurer never perfected service on its insured for purposes of its declaratory judgment action under RC § 2721.03 in order to establish its coverage and defense obligations, as the certified mail pursuant to Ohio R. Civ. P. 4.1(A) was returned unclaimed and service under Ohio R. Civ. P. 4.6(D) was also unsuccessful, the action was never commenced within Ohio R. Civ. P. 3(A), and the summary judgment granted by the trial court to the insurer was void ab initio. Earl v. Nelson, — Ohio App. 3d —, 2006 Ohio 3341, — N.E. 2d —, 2006 Ohio App. LEXIS 3270 (June 30, 2006).

Trial court errs in summarily overruling a defendant's motion to set aside a judgment for lack of service, when the defendant submits a sworn statement that he or she did not receive service of process, without affording the defendant a hearing: Money Tree Loan Co. v. Williams, 169 Ohio App. 3d 336, 2006 Ohio 5568, 862 N.E.2d 885, 2006 Ohio App. LEXIS 5553 (2006).

Ineffective service

Juvenile court erred in modifying a father's child support pursuant to RC §§ 3105.21, 3109.05 because service on the mother had to be by personal service pursuant to CivR 4.1(A) where the father requested personal service; the residential service effected was inadequate for notice because the mother had moved from the residence. Any failure by the mother to notify the juvenile court promptly of any change in her address could not justify ineffective service of process when the juvenile court's continuing jurisdiction was invoked, because those service requirements were rooted in the mother's constitutional due process right to notice and an opportunity to be heard. In re Alexander-segar, — Ohio App. 3d —, 2008 Ohio 1580, — N.E. 2d —, 2008 Ohio App. LEXIS 1325 (Mar. 28, 2008).

Modification of child support

Trial court properly concluded that a father had failed to invoke the continuing jurisdiction of the trial court pursuant to Ohio R. Civ. P. 75(J) on the father's motion or modification and/or termination of child support where, while the father requested service of his motions by certified mail upon the Lake County Child Support Enforcement Agency and Ohio Child Support Payment Central, neither of which was currently a party to the action, there was no evidence that the father perfected or even attempted service upon the opposing party, the mother. Corrao v. Corrao, — Ohio App. 3d —, 2006 Ohio 1686, — N.E. 2d —, 2006 Ohio App. LEXIS 1545 (Mar. 31, 2006).

Personal service

As a process server went to a husband's residence, asked the children who answered the door for him, and the individual who matched the appearance of the husband from a photograph responded and indicated initially that he was in fact the husband, personal service pursuant to Ohio R. Civ. P. 3(A) and

4.1 was properly effected on the husband in a divorce action. The husband's claim to the contrary was not supported by the evidence, which included testimony from the process server. Torres v. Torres, — Ohio App. 3d —, 2007 Ohio 4443, — N.E. 2d —, 2007 Ohio App. LEXIS 4007 (Aug. 30, 2007).

Presumption of proper service

When a party submitted unrebutted evidence that he was never properly served with process, under Ohio R. Civ. P. 4.1(A), in an action filed against him, because service was directed to the home of his parents, where he did not live and had not lived since the filing of the action, the presumption that he had been properly served was rebutted, and the default judgment entered against him had to be vacated. Jacobs v. Szakal, — Ohio App. 3d —, 2006 Ohio 1312, — N.E. 2d —, 2006 Ohio App. LEXIS 1196 (Mar. 22, 2006).

As a motorist and the trial court clerk complied with the Ohio Civil Rules when certified mail was sent of the motorist's complaint to a driver, arising from a vehicle accident between the parties, a rebuttable presumption arose that service was proper pursuant to Ohio R. Civ. P. 4.1(A) and 4.6, and such presumption was not rebutted by the driver's claim that she did not have to answer until the service was docketed in the trial court. Such claim also did not satisfy the driver's burden of showing excusable neglect in order to avoid a default judgment against her and to allow her to file her answer instanter, pursuant to Ohio R. Civ. P. 12(A) and 6(B)(2). Sokol v. Spigiel, — Ohio App. 3d —, 2006 Ohio 4408, — N.E. 2d —, 2006 Ohio App. LEXIS 4345 (Aug. 28, 2006).

Residence service

Where a copy of a forcible entry and detainer summons and complaint were left with a person of "suitable age and discretion" at the tenants' residence, and a copy of the pleadings where thereafter mailed to the address, pursuant to RC § 1923.06(D)(1)(b) and (C), proper service was made pursuant to Ohio R. Civ. P. 4.1(C). Litman v. McLaughlin, — Ohio App. 3d —, 2006 Ohio 433, — N.E. 2d —, 2006 Ohio App. LEXIS 376 (Feb. 1, 2006).

Service by mail

When an agency moved for permanent custody of the children of a father who had been incarcerated at the beginning of the case, the father did not show that the father was not properly served with process, under Ohio R. Civ. P. 4.1(A) and 4.2(D), when the case started because the record reflected that a summons and complaint were sent to the father in care of the institution where the father was incarcerated by certified mail and a return receipt showed they were received. In re D.C., — Ohio App. 3d —, 2007 Ohio 2344, — N.E. 2d —, 2007 Ohio App. LEXIS 2205 (May 16, 2007).

When it was alleged that a father was in contempt for failing to obey an order to pay child support, service by certified mail of notice of a motion to show cause why the father should not be held in contempt was proper because the father was alleged to be in indirect civil contempt, so the Ohio Rules of Civil Procedure applied, and Ohio R. Civ. P. 4 and 4.1 were complied with. Bierce v. Howell, — Ohio App. 3d —, 2007 Ohio 3050, — N.E. 2d —, 2007 Ohio App. LEXIS 2793 (June 15, 2007).

RULE 4.2. Process: who may be served

Service of process, except service by publication as provided in Civ. R. 4.4(A), pursuant to Civ. R. 4 through Civ. R. 4.6 shall be made as follows:

(A) Upon an individual, other than a person under sixteen years of age or an incompetent person, by serving the individual;

(B) Upon a person under sixteen years of age by serving either the person's guardian or any one of the following persons with whom the person to be served lives or resides: father, mother, or the individual having the care of the person; or by serving the person if the person neither has a guardian nor lives or resides with a parent or a person having his or her care;

(C) Upon an incompetent person by serving either the incompetent's guardian or the person designated in division (E) of this rule, but if no guardian has been appointed and the incompetent is not under confinement or commitment, by serving the incompetent;

(D) Upon an individual, confined to a penal institution of this state or of a subdivision of this state, by serving the individual, except that when the individual to be served is a person under sixteen years of age, the provisions of division (B) of this rule shall be applicable;

(E) Upon an incompetent person who is confined in any institution for the mentally ill or mentally deficient or committed by order of court to the custody of some other institution or person by serving the superintendent or similar official of the institution to which the incompetent is confined or committed or the person to whose custody the incompetent is committed;

(F) Upon a corporation either domestic or foreign: by serving the agent authorized by appointment or by law to receive service of process; or by serving the corporation by certified or express mail at any of its usual places of business; or by serving an officer or a managing or general agent of the corporation;

(G) Upon a limited liability company by serving the agent authorized by appointment or by law to receive service of process; or by serving the limited liability company by certified or express mail at any of its usual places of business; or by serving a manager or member;

(H) Upon a partnership, a limited partnership, or a limited partnership association by serving the entity by certified or express mail at any of its usual places of business or by serving a partner, limited partner, manager, or member;

(I) Upon an unincorporated association by serving it in its entity name by certified or express mail at any of its usual places of business or by serving an officer of the unincorporated association;

(J) Upon a professional association by serving the association in its corporate name by certified or express mail at the place where the corporate offices are maintained or by serving a shareholder;

(K) Upon this state or any one of its departments, offices and institutions as defined in division (C) of section 121.01 of the Revised Code, by serving the officer responsible for the administration of the department, office or institution or by serving the attorney general of this state;

(L) Upon a county or upon any of its offices, agencies, districts, departments, institutions or administrative units, by serving the officer responsible for the administration of the office, agency, district, department, institution or unit or by serving the prosecuting attorney of the county;

(M) Upon a township by serving one or more of the township trustees or the township clerk or by serving the prosecuting attorney of the county in which the township is located, unless the township is organized under Chapter 504. of the Revised Code, in which case service may be made upon the township law director;

(N) Upon a municipal corporation or upon any of its offices, departments, agencies, authorities, institutions or administrative units by serving the officer responsible for the administration of the office, department, agency, authority, institution or unit or by serving the city solicitor or comparable legal officer;

(O) Upon any governmental entity not mentioned above by serving the person, officer, group or body responsible for the administration of that entity or by serving the appropriate legal officer, if any, representing the entity. Service upon any person who is a member of the "group" or "body" responsible for the administration of the entity shall be sufficient.

History: Amended, eff 7-1-71; 7-1-96; 7-1-97; 7-1-09.

NOTES TO DECISIONS

ANALYSIS

Municipal corporations
Service by mail
Service upon corporation

Municipal corporations

Village was not bound by the judgment entered against its former police chief because the common pleas court never obtained jurisdiction over the village in that case: State ex rel. Estate of Miles v. Piketon, 121 Ohio St. 3d 231, 2009 Ohio 786, 903 N.E.2d 311, 2009 Ohio LEXIS 550 (2009).

Service by mail

Judgment entered against children of judgment debtors was not void ab initio for lack of personal service on them, as the complaint was sent by certified mail to their permanent addresses and it was accepted by their grandmother, who was over the age of 16 years and was competent. Service was properly made under Ohio R. Civ. P. 4.1(A) and 4.2(A), and the trial court did not err in denying the children's motion for relief from judgment under Ohio R. Civ. P. 60(B). Tube City, Inc. v. Halishak, — Ohio App. 3d —, 2007 Ohio 2118, — N.E. 2d —, 2007 Ohio App. LEXIS 1976 (May 3, 2007).

When an agency moved for permanent custody of the children of a father who had been incarcerated at the beginning of the case, the father did not show that the father was not properly served with process, under Ohio R. Civ. P. 4.1(A) and 4.2(D), when the case started because the record reflected that a summons and complaint were sent to the father in care of the institution where the father was incarcerated by certified mail and a return receipt showed they were received. In re D.C., — Ohio App. 3d —, 2007 Ohio 2344, — N.E. 2d —, 2007 Ohio App. LEXIS 2205 (May 16, 2007).

When it was undisputed that a complaint filed against a restaurant was served on it in its business name at its business address, the fact that the individual who signed a certified mail receipt for the complaint was not authorized to do so did not demonstrate that the complaint was not properly served. Kemer v. Glass, — Ohio App. 3d —, 2006 Ohio 2979, — N.E. 2d —, 2006 Ohio App. LEXIS 2865 (June 14, 2006).

Service upon corporation

Service of process on an individual and on the individual's corporation was proper where the defendant's wife was served at the defendant's home, which was also listed as the address of the corporation's statutory agent: New v. All Transp.

Solution, Inc., 177 Ohio App. 3d 620, 2008 Ohio 3949, 895 N.E.2d 606, 2008 Ohio App. LEXIS 3312 (2007).

When a fertilizer company sued the manufacturer of a fertilizer tank that ruptured, the company diligently attempted to serve the manufacturer by mail and substituted service, as shown by the fact that when the company was allowed to serve the manufacturer by publication, under Ohio R. Civ. P. 4.4, the manufacturer filed an answer, and the fact that the company did not attempt substituted service on the Secretary of State, under RC § 1701.07(H), until after the case was moved to a different county did not mean the company's efforts were not diligent, as substituted service was not the required method of service following failed attempts to serve process by certified mail or through an appointed corporate agent. Land O'Lakes, Inc. v. Nationwide Tanks, Inc., — Ohio App. 3d —, 2006 Ohio 4327, — N.E. 2d —, 2006 Ohio App. LEXIS 4252 (Aug. 21, 2006).

Trial court properly determined that service on a corporation was not "reasonably calculated" to apprise it of a lawsuit pursuant to Ohio R. Civ. P. 4.2(F), as there was no showing that an attempt to serve the corporation at its address was made or that the statutory agent served was in fact the agent of the corporation. Madorsky v. Radiant Telecom, Inc., — Ohio App. 3d —, 2006 Ohio 6409, — N.E. 2d —, 2006 Ohio App. LEXIS 6375 (Dec. 7, 2006).

RULE 4.3.   Process: out-of-state service

(A) **When service permitted.** Service of process may be made outside of this state, as provided in this rule, in any action in this state, upon a person who, at the time of service of process, is a nonresident of this state or is a resident of this state who is absent from this state. "Person" includes an individual, an individual's executor, administrator, or other personal representative, or a corporation, partnership, association, or any other legal or commercial entity, who, acting directly or by an agent, has caused an event to occur out of which the claim that is the subject of the complaint arose, from the person's:

(1) Transacting any business in this state;

(2) Contracting to supply services or goods in this state;

(3) Causing tortious injury by an act or omission in this state, including, but not limited to, actions arising out of the ownership, operation, or use of a motor vehicle or aircraft in this state;

(4) Causing tortious injury in this state by an act or omission outside this state if the person regularly does or solicits business, engages in any other persistent course of conduct, or derives substantial revenue from goods used or consumed or services rendered in this state;

(5) Causing injury in this state to any person by breach of warranty expressly or impliedly made in the sale of goods outside this state when the person to be served might reasonably have expected the person who was injured to use, consume, or be affected by the goods in this state, provided that the person to be served also regularly does or solicits business, engages in any other persistent course of conduct, or derives substantial revenue from goods used or consumed or services rendered in this state;

(6) Having an interest in, using, or possessing real property in this state;

(7) Contracting to insure any person, property, or

risk located within this state at the time of contracting;

(8) Living in the marital relationship within this state notwithstanding subsequent departure from this state, as to all obligations arising for spousal support, custody, child support, or property settlement, if the other party to the marital relationship continues to reside in this state;

(9) Causing tortious injury in this state to any person by an act outside this state committed with the purpose of injuring persons, when the person to be served might reasonably have expected that some person would be injured by the act in this state;

(10) Causing tortious injury to any person by a criminal act, any element of which takes place in this state, that the person to be served commits or in the commission of which the person to be served is guilty of complicity.

(B) **Methods of service.**

(1) Service by certified or express mail. Evidenced by return receipt signed by any person, service of any process shall be by certified or express mail unless otherwise permitted by these rules. The clerk shall place a copy of the process and complaint or other document to be served in an envelope. The clerk shall address the envelope to the person to be served at the address set forth in the caption or at the address set forth in written instructions furnished to the clerk with instructions to forward. The clerk shall affix adequate postage and place the sealed envelope in the United States mail as certified or express mail return receipt requested with instructions to the delivering postal employee to show to whom delivered, date of delivery, and address where delivered.

The clerk shall forthwith enter the fact of mailing on the appearance docket and make a similar entry when the return receipt is received. If the envelope is returned with an endorsement showing failure of delivery, the clerk shall forthwith notify, by mail, the attorney of record or, if there is no attorney of record, the party at whose instance process was issued and enter the fact of notification on the appearance docket. The clerk shall file the return receipt or returned envelope in the records of the action. If the envelope is returned with an endorsement showing failure of delivery, service is complete when the attorney or serving party, after notification by the clerk, files with the clerk an affidavit setting forth facts indicating the reasonable diligence utilized to ascertain the whereabouts of the party to be served.

All postage shall be charged to costs. If the parties to be served by certified or express mail are numerous and the clerk determines there is insufficient security for costs, the clerk may require the party requesting service to advance an amount estimated by the clerk to be sufficient to pay the postage.

(2) Personal service. When ordered by a court, a "person" as defined in division (A) of this rule may be personally served with a copy of the process and complaint or other document to be served. Service under this division may be made by any person not less than eighteen years of age who is not a party and who has been designated by order of the court. On request, the clerk shall deliver the summons to the plaintiff for transmission to the person who will make service.

Proof of service may be made as prescribed by Civ. R. 4.1(B) or by order of the court.

History: Amended, eff 7-1-71; 7-1-80; 7-1-88; 7-1-91; 7-1-97.

NOTES TO DECISIONS

ANALYSIS

Appeals
Default judgments
Disseminating financial information
Jurisdiction
— Lack of personal jurisdiction
Marital relationship
Minimum contacts
Practicing law
Securities laws
Tobacco manufacturers
Transacting business in Ohio

Appeals

Dismissal for lack of personal jurisdiction, which prevents refiling in the trial court, is a final appealable order: Nat'l City Commer. Capital Corp. v. AAAA at Your Serv., Inc., 114 Ohio St. 3d 82, 2007 Ohio 2942, 868 N.E.2d 663, 2007 Ohio LEXIS 1603 (2007).

Default judgments

Trial court did not err in denying the motion to vacate the default judgment for want of service because the trial court file contained the returned addressee signature card with the driver's name signed and the transcript of the hearing on the driver's motion contained no testimony by her or other evidence as to the veracity of her apparent signature. She waived her right to appeal reliance on the Hague Convention or any other international agreements regarding service of legal documents as she did not invoke them in the trial court. Linquist v. Drossel, — Ohio App. 3d —, 2006 Ohio 5712, — N.E. 2d —, 2006 Ohio App. LEXIS 5698 (Oct. 30, 2006).

Disseminating financial information

Disseminating financial information to Ohio investors constitutes transacting business in Ohio. The defendant had sufficient contacts with Ohio that the suit in Ohio did not offend traditional notions of justice and fair play: Greene v. Whiteside, 181 Ohio App. 3d 253, 2009 Ohio 741, 908 N.E.2d 975, 2009 Ohio App. LEXIS 627.

Jurisdiction

Trial court properly held that the Ohio Department of Commerce, Division of Securities lacked personal jurisdiction over an oil and natural gas company which was not within Ohio, as there was no purposeful availment for due process purposes under U.S. Const. amend. XIV by the mere maintenance of a passive website by the company. Ohio's long-arm statute, RC § 2307.382, and Ohio R. Civ. P. 4.3(A) did not apply to regulatory actions or adjudicatory proceedings before administrative agencies. Blue Flame Energy Corp. v. Ohio Dep't of Commerce, 171 Ohio App. 3d 514, 2006 Ohio 6892, 871 N.E.2d 1227, 2006 Ohio App. LEXIS 6809 (2006).

— Lack of personal jurisdiction

Where an out-of-state defendant filed an answer without raising the defense of lack of personal jurisdiction, he waived personal jurisdiction and voluntarily assented to the jurisdiction of the Ohio court: Snyder Computer Sys. v. Stives, 175 Ohio App. 3d 653, 2008 Ohio 1192, 888 N.E.2d 1117, 2008 Ohio App. LEXIS 997 (2008).

Dismissal of claims against a Florida corporation was proper as the corporation did not engage in substantial activities in

Ohio that would have caused it to reasonably anticipate being haled into court in Ohio; its principal place of business was in Florida, it had no employees, agents, or independent contractors in Ohio, it never derived any substantial income from Ohio and with regard to its actions in investigating a driver from an auto accident, the only contact it had with Ohio was in the form of several telephone calls to an Ohio bowling alley. West v. Trace America, Inc., — Ohio App. 3d —, 2007 Ohio 3311, — N.E. 2d —, 2007 Ohio App. LEXIS 3037 (June 29, 2007).

Trial court erred in exercising personal jurisdiction over an action by a Canadian law firm against clients, alleging fraud, fraudulent transfer of real property, and breach of contract for failure to pay the firm's fees for services rendered, as the clients' ownership of real property was unconnected to the contract for legal services and accordingly, it violated due process under U.S. Const. amend. XIV to allow the trial court to confer jurisdiction on that basis alone pursuant to RC § 2307.382 and Ohio R. Civ. P. 4.3(A)(6). Prouse v. Dimarco, — Ohio App. 3d —, 2006 Ohio 1538, — N.E. 2d —, 2006 Ohio App. LEXIS 1405 (Mar. 30, 2006).

Complaint for a partnership accounting that arose out of a putative Ohio resident's cohabitation with an out-of-state resident in a different county than the one in which the action was filed was properly dismissed for improper venue and lack of jurisdiction. Neither service nor venue was proper under Ohio R. Civ. P. 3(B)(7), 4.3 because there was no verification in the pleadings that the putative Ohio resident who filed the action lived in the county where it was filed. Stoughton v. Ryan, — Ohio App. 3d —, 2006 Ohio 5277, — N.E. 2d —, 2006 Ohio App. LEXIS 5250 (Oct. 2, 2006).

Marital relationship

As an Ohio divorce complaint filed by a husband and served on the wife was "commenced" pursuant to Ohio R. Civ. P. 3(A) prior to the wife's Florida dissolution petition having been commenced, as the Florida action was filed earlier than the husband's Ohio action but served afterwards, and the filing of the Florida action and the service thereof pursuant to Fla. R. Civ. P. 1.050 and 1.070(i)(1) did not waive any objection to personal jurisdiction issues, the Ohio court acquired jurisdiction first; pursuant to Ohio R. Civ. P. 4.3(A)(8), personal jurisdiction was properly exerted over a non-resident spouse and accordingly, a trial court erred in dismissing the Ohio divorce complaint when it upheld the Florida dissolution decree, which had been obtained on default against the husband. Lanzer v. Lanzer, — Ohio App. 3d —, 2006 Ohio 1387, — N.E. 2d —, 2006 Ohio App. LEXIS 1254 (Mar. 20, 2006).

Minimum contacts

In an action by a consultant and a consulting service alleging tortious interference with business relationships arising from a non-compete clause in a terminated contract with a management company and its president, the consultant entities made a sufficient prima facie showing of personal jurisdiction of the management entities, both non-residents of Ohio, to survive a motion to dismiss for lack of personal jurisdiction, as minimum contacts in Ohio were shown for purposes of Ohio R. Civ. P. 4.3 and RC § 2307.382. It was shown that the assertion of jurisdiction over the parties would not offend traditional notions of fair play and substantial justice. Mellino Consulting, Inc. v. Synchronous Mgmt. Sarasota, — Ohio App. 3d —, 2007 Ohio 541, — N.E. 2d —, 2007 Ohio App. LEXIS 485 (Feb. 8, 2007).

Trial court properly adopted a decision by a magistrate to grant a wife and her minor daughter a civil protection order pursuant to RC § 3113.31 against her nonresident husband upon finding that the trial court had personal jurisdiction over him under Ohio R. Civ. P. 4.3(A)(9) and RC § 2307.382 based on his repeated visits to Ohio to visit the wife and his threatening phone call to her while she was in Ohio. The

exercise of personal jurisdiction over him satisfied the due process requirements of U.S. Const. amend. XIV and Ohio Const. art. I, § 16. Haas v. Semrad, — Ohio App. 3d —, 2007 Ohio 2828, — N.E. 2d —, 2007 Ohio App. LEXIS 2636 (June 8, 2007).

Practicing law

When an Ohio client sued, in Ohio, a Rhode Island law firm, which represented him in a lawsuit in Rhode Island, Ohio Const. art. I, § 16 did not require an Ohio trial court to exercise personal jurisdiction over the law firm because art. I, § 16 did not give the client unlimited access to the courts, as that access was limited by the jurisdictional requirements and geographical boundaries of the State of Ohio, under Ohio R. Civ. P. 4.3 and RC § 2307.382, and the Ohio Constitution did not control the actions of residents of the State of Rhode Island, and the fact that an Ohio court did not have personal jurisdiction over the firm and its lawyer did not deprive the client of a legal remedy, as he could sue in Rhode Island or in federal court. Gerber v. Blish & Cavanagh, — Ohio App. 3d —, 2006 Ohio 2252, — N.E. 2d —, 2006 Ohio App. LEXIS 2097 (May 8, 2006).

When an Ohio client sued, in Ohio, a Rhode Island law firm, which represented him in a lawsuit in Rhode Island, the Ohio trial court did not have personal jurisdiction over the law firm or its lawyer because the firm's only contacts with Ohio were its contacts with the client, in the course of its representation and efforts to collect fees from the client, and this was insufficient to establish personal jurisdiction over the firm under Ohio R. Civ. P. 4.3(A) or RC § 2307.382. Gerber v. Blish & Cavanagh, — Ohio App. 3d —, 2006 Ohio 2252, — N.E. 2d —, 2006 Ohio App. LEXIS 2097 (May 8, 2006).

Securities laws

RC § 2307.382 and CivR 4.3 do not apply to regulatory actions of the Ohio securities division. Maintenance of a passive website by a nonresident did not amount to purposeful availment of the privilege of doing business in Ohio for due process purposes. Filing of Form Ds with the division constituted a sufficient contact with Ohio purposes of personal jurisdiction over the corporations and the corporate officer who signed and filed the forms. Federal preemption did not apply where the defendants engaged in general advertising and solicitation via their website: Blue Flame Energy Corp. v. Ohio Dep't of Commerce, 171 Ohio App. 3d 514, 2006 Ohio 6892, 871 N.E.2d 1227, 2006 Ohio App. LEXIS 6809 (2006).

Tobacco manufacturers

Tobacco manufacturer's actions, including steps to market its products in the United States and the use of a closely affiliated distributor, resulting in millions of cigarettes being shipped into Ohio for sale, constituted transacting business in Ohio for purposes of RC § 2307.382. For due process purposes, the manufacturer purposely availed itself of conducting business in Ohio, and the assertion of jurisdiction in Ohio would be fair and reasonable: State ex rel. AG. v. Grand Tobacco, 171 Ohio App. 3d 551, 2007 Ohio 418, 871 N.E.2d 1255, 2007 Ohio App. LEXIS 363 (2007).

Trial court's grant of summary judgment and dismissal of an action by the Ohio Attorney General against a foreign tobacco company (TC) due to lack of personal jurisdiction was error under RC § 2307.382(A)(1) and Ohio R. Civ. P. 4.3(A)(1), as a prima facie showing was made that personal jurisdiction existed for transacting business based on the company's relationship with American distributors, the volume of cigarettes sold in Ohio, the company's involvement in the packaging of tobacco products, and the satisfaction of due process principles; as no evidentiary hearing was held, the trial court should not have considered evidence offered by the company in support of its claim of no jurisdiction. Ohio Ex Rel. Dann

v. Bulgartabac Holding Group, — Ohio App. 3d —, 2007 Ohio 6777, — N.E. 2d —, 2007 Ohio App. LEXIS 5928 (Dec. 18, 2007).

Transacting business in Ohio

Trial court properly exercised personal jurisdiction over a seller in a dispute arising out of a buyer's purchase of a car from the seller because the buyer transacted business in Ohio, within the meaning of RC § 2307.382(A)(1) and Ohio R. Civ. P. 4.3(A)(1), and the exercise of personal jurisdiction over the seller comported with U.S. Const. amend. XIV. While the seller resided in Kentucky and the car was picked up and paid for in Kentucky, negotiation for the purchase of the car was in Ohio and was completed by the seller's Ohio agent, and the seller should have reasonably anticipated that, if a dispute arose, he could be haled into an Ohio court. Muzzin v. Brooks, 168 Ohio App. 3d 231, 2006 Ohio 3844, 859 N.E.2d 584, 2006 Ohio App. LEXIS 3811 (2006).

Trial court erred in denying an asset purchaser's motion to dismiss a claim on account asserted against it by the asset seller, as the mere fact of the purchaser, a Montana corporation, having sent five checks to the seller, an Ohio corporation, did not constitute "transacting business" in Ohio under RC § 2307.382(A)(1) for purposes of establishing personal jurisdiction over the purchaser; accordingly, service was improperly made under Ohio R. Civ. P. 4.3(A)(1). Communication Exhibits, Inc. v. Windstone Med. Packaging, Inc., — Ohio App. 3d —, 2006 Ohio 4998, — N.E.2d —, 2006 Ohio App. LEXIS 4942 (Sept. 26, 2006).

Ohio court lacked personal jurisdiction over a Minnesota resident where he obtained a line of credit from an Ohio corporation in conjunction with a mortgage relating to real property he owned in Minnesota and executed the agreement in that state. Defendant's only performance in Ohio was to remit payment to the plaintiff in Ohio: Nat'l City Bank v. Yevu, 178 Ohio App. 3d 382, 898 N.E.2d 52, 2008 Ohio App. LEXIS 3955 (2008).

RULE 4.4.   Process: service by publication

(A) Residence unknown.

(1) Except in an action governed by division (A)(2) of this rule, if the residence of a defendant is unknown, service shall be made by publication in actions where such service is authorized by law. Before service by publication can be made, an affidavit of a party or his counsel shall be filed with the court. The affidavit shall aver that service of summons cannot be made because the residence of the defendant is unknown to the affiant, all of the efforts made on behalf of the party to ascertain the residence of the defendant, and that the residence of the defendant cannot be ascertained with reasonable diligence.

Upon the filing of the affidavit, the clerk shall cause service of notice to be made by publication in a newspaper of general circulation in the county in which the complaint is filed. If no newspaper is published in that county, then publication shall be in a newspaper published in an adjoining county. The publication shall contain the name and address of the court, the case number, the name of the first party on each side, and the name and last known address, if any, of the person or persons whose residence is unknown. The publication also shall contain a summary statement of the object of the complaint and demand for relief, and shall notify the person to be served that he or she is required to answer within twenty-eight days after the publication. The publication shall be published at least once a

week for six successive weeks unless publication for a lesser number of weeks is specifically provided by law. Service shall be complete at the date of the last publication.

After the last publication, the publisher or its agent shall file with the court an affidavit showing the fact of publication together with a copy of the notice of publication. The affidavit and copy of the notice shall constitute proof of service.

(2) In a divorce, annulment, or legal separation action, if the plaintiff is proceeding in forma pauperis and if the residence of the defendant is unknown, service by publication shall be made by posting and mail. Before service by posting and mail can be made, an affidavit of a party or the party's counsel shall be filed with the court. The affidavit shall contain the same averments required by division (A)(1) of this rule and, in addition, shall set forth the defendant's last known address.

Upon the filing of the affidavit, the clerk shall cause service of notice to be made by posting in a conspicuous place in the courthouse or courthouses in which the general and domestic relations divisions of the court of common pleas for the county are located and in two additional public places in the county that have been designated by local rule for the posting of notices pursuant to this rule. The notice shall contain the same information required by division (A)(1) of this rule to be contained in a newspaper publication. The notice shall be posted in the required locations for six successive weeks.

The clerk shall also cause the complaint and summons to be mailed by ordinary mail, address correction requested, to the defendant's last known address. The clerk shall obtain a certificate of mailing from the United States Postal Service. If the clerk is notified of a corrected or forwarding address of the defendant within the six-week period that notice is posted pursuant to division (A)(2) of this rule, the clerk shall cause the complaint and summons to be mailed to the corrected or forwarding address. The clerk shall note the name, address, and date of each mailing in the docket.

After the last week of posting, the clerk shall note on the docket where and when notice was posted. Service shall be complete upon the entry of posting.

(B) Residence known.

If the residence of a defendant is known, and the action is one in which service by publication is authorized by law, service of process shall be effected by a method other than by publication as provided by:

(1) Rule 4.1, if the defendant is a resident of this state,

(2) Rule 4.3(B), if defendant is not a resident of this state, or

(3) Rule 4.5, in the alternative, if service on defendant is to be effected in a foreign country.

If service of process cannot be effected under the provisions of this subdivision or Rule 4.6(C) or Rule 4.6(D), service of process shall proceed by publication.

History: Amended, eff 7-1-71; 7-1-91.

NOTES TO DECISIONS

ANALYSIS

Juvenile courts
Publication
Reasonable diligence

Juvenile courts

RC § 2705.031(D) suggests that service in accordance with JuvR 16, rather than CivR 4.4, may be used in contempt actions in juvenile court, as long as such service comports with due process. In re I.U., — Ohio App. 3d —, 2007 Ohio 6264, — N.E. 2d —, 2007 Ohio App. LEXIS 5518 (Nov. 21, 2007).

Publication

Trial court's entry of a default judgment against an attorney in a client's legal malpractice action was a nullity where the action was never properly commenced pursuant to Ohio R. Civ. P. 3, as service of the summons was never perfected on the attorney pursuant to Ohio R. Civ. P. 4 and he had asserted the defense of lack of personal jurisdiction in his answer. An attempt at certified mail sevice was returned "unclaimed" and attempts at service by the client's private investigator pursuant to Ohio R. Civ. P. 4.4 were unsuccessful. Abuhilwa v. O'Brien, — Ohio App. 3d —, — N.E. 2d —, 2007 Ohio App. LEXIS 3879 (Aug. 24, 2007).

Trial court's dismissal pursuant to Ohio R. Civ. P. 12(B)(5) of a personal injury action by a motorist and his wife, arising from a vehicle collision with two drivers, was proper where the affidavit submitted by the motorist and his wife in support of service by publication did not meet the requirements of Ohio R. Civ. P. 3(A) and 4.4(A) because it did not specify the efforts made to locate the drivers; accordingly, there was insufficient service of process. Lewis v. Buxton, — Ohio App. 3d —, 2007 Ohio 5986, — N.E. 2d —, 2007 Ohio App. LEXIS 5259 (Nov. 9, 2007).

Reasonable diligence

Children's services board exercised reasonable diligence in attempting to serve the father notice of the permanent custody proceeding because neither Ohio R. Civ. P. 4.6(D) nor the Due Process Clause required ordinary mail service when the postal authorities returned certified mail with the endorsement "Attempted Not Known" before a party attempted service by publication. The board complied with the rules by attempting to personally serve the father at one address, by attempting to serve him by certified mail at another address, and by publishing a notice in a newspaper; because the returned certified letter, endorsed "Attempted Not Known" clearly demonstrated that the father did not reside and was not known at that address, any ordinary mail addressed to him at that address could not have been reasonably calculated to give him notice and an opportunity to be heard at the permanent custody proceeding. In re Thompkins, 115 Ohio St. 3d 409, 2007 Ohio 5238, 875 N.E.2d 582, 2007 Ohio LEXIS 2523 (2007).

Where an unsolicited facsimile recipient filed an action against the out-of-state facsimile sender but her attempts at certified and ordinary mail service on the sender were unsuccessful, the trial court's dismissal for failure to perfect service within six months pursuant to Ohio R. Civ. P. 4(E) was error, as the recipient had acted with diligence in attempting service and then in applying for service by publication pursuant to Ohio R. Civ. P. 4.4(A); accordingly, the trial court should have afforded her an opportunity to show good cause why dismissal was not warranted in the circumstances. Ambrose v. Advanced Wireless Cellular Comm. Inc., — Ohio App. 3d —, 2007 Ohio 988, — N.E. 2d —, 2007 Ohio App. LEXIS 919 (Mar. 8, 2007).

When a fertilizer company sued the manufacturer of a fertilizer tank that ruptured, the company diligently attempted to serve the manufacturer by mail and substituted service, as shown by the fact that when the company was allowed to serve the manufacturer by publication, under Ohio R. Civ. P. 4.4, the manufacturer filed an answer, and the fact that the company did not attempt substituted service on the Secretary of State, under RC § 1701.07(H), until after the case was moved to a different county did not mean the company's efforts were not diligent, as substituted service was not the required method of service following failed attempts to serve process by certified mail or through an appointed corporate agent. Land O'Lakes, Inc. v. Nationwide Tanks, Inc., — Ohio App. 3d —, 2006 Ohio 4327, — N.E. 2d —, 2006 Ohio App. LEXIS 4252 (Aug. 21, 2006).

RULE 4.5. Process: alternative provisions for service in a foreign country

(A) **Manner.** When Civ. R. 4.3 or Civ. R. 4.4 or both allow service upon a person outside this state and service is to be effected in a foreign country, service of the summons and complaint may also be made:

(1) In the manner prescribed by the law of the foreign country for service in that country in an action in any of its courts of general jurisdiction when service is calculated to give actual notice;

(2) As directed by the foreign authority in response to a letter rogatory when service is calculated to give actual notice;

(3) Upon an individual by delivery to him personally;

(4) Upon a corporation or partnership or association by delivery to an officer, a managing or general agent;

(5) By any form of mail requiring a signed receipt, when the clerk of the court addresses and dispatches this mail to the party to be served;

(6) As directed by order of the court.

Service under division (A)(3) or (A)(6) of this rule may be made by any person not less than eighteen years of age who is not a party and who has been designated by order of the court, or by the foreign court. On request the clerk shall deliver the summons to the plaintiff for transmission to the person or the foreign court or officer who will make the service.

(B) **Return.** Proof of service may be made as prescribed by Civ. R. 4.1(B), or by the law of the foreign country, or by order of the court. When mail service is made pursuant to division (A)(5) of this rule, proof of service shall include a receipt signed by the addressee or other evidence of delivery to the addressee satisfactory to the court.

History: Amended, eff 7-1-97.

NOTES TO DECISIONS

ANALYSIS

Service by mail
Service ineffective

Service by mail

When an agency moved for permanent custody of the children of a father who had been deported to Italy, service of the permanent custody motion by registered mail at an address the father had provided to the agency satisfied the requirements of Ohio R. Civ. P. 4.3 and 4.5 and the Hague Convention on the Service Abroad of Judicial and Extrajudicial Documents in Civil and Commercial Matters art. 10(a),

Nov. 15, 1965, 20 U.S.T. 361, 658 U.N.T.S. 163 because (1) registered mail satisfied Ohio R. Civ. P. 4.3' s certified mail requirement, under RC 1.02(G), and (2) the Hague Convention on the Service Abroad of Judicial and Extrajudicial Documents in Civil and Commercial Matters art. 10(a), Nov. 15, 1965, 20 U.S.T. 361, 658 U.N.T.S. 163 allowed service by mail because Italy had not objected to such service and the permanent custody was a subsequent judicial document. In re D.C., — Ohio App. 3d —, 2007 Ohio 2344, — N.E. 2d —, 2007 Ohio App. LEXIS 2205 (May 16, 2007).

Service ineffective

Trial court's grant of a wife's motion for relief from judgment, pursuant to Ohio R. Civ. P. 60(B), with respect to the prior grant of a divorce to the husband, including provisions as to spousal support and property division pursuant to RC §§ 3105.18 and 3105.171, was proper with respect to the property and support determinations, as the wife, who was a German citizen and still resided in Germany, was not properly served with the divorce complaint pursuant to the provisions of the Hague Convention; as those service provisions had to be complied with pursuant to the supremacy principles under U.S. Const. art. VI, the service was insufficient under Ohio R. Civ. P. 4.5(A) in order to give the trial court jurisdiction over the wife, and as such, the financial awards could not be made because the trial court lacked jurisdiction. Collins v. Collins, 165 Ohio App. 3d 71, 2006 Ohio 181, 844 N.E. 2d 910, 2006 Ohio App. LEXIS 159 (Jan. 20, 2006).

RULE 4.6. Process: limits; amendment; service refused; service unclaimed

(A) **Limits of effective service.** All process may be served anywhere in this state and, when authorized by law or these rules, may be served outside this state.

(B) **Amendment.** The court within its discretion and upon such terms as are just, may at any time allow the amendment of any process or proof of service thereof, unless the amendment would cause material prejudice to the substantial rights of the party against whom the process was issued.

(C) **Service refused.** If service of process is refused, and the certified or express mail envelope is returned with an endorsement showing such refusal, or the return of the person serving process states that service of process has been refused, the clerk shall forthwith notify, by mail, the attorney of record or, if there is no attorney of record, the party at whose instance process was issued. If the attorney, or serving party, after notification by the clerk, files with the clerk a written request for ordinary mail service, the clerk shall send by ordinary mail a copy of the summons and complaint or other document to be served to the defendant at the address set forth in the caption, or at the address set forth in written instructions furnished to the clerk. The mailing shall be evidenced by a certificate of mailing which shall be completed and filed by the clerk. Answer day shall be twenty-eight days after the date of mailing as evidenced by the certificate of mailing. The clerk shall endorse this answer date upon the summons which is sent by ordinary mail. Service shall be deemed complete when the fact of mailing is entered of record. Failure to claim certified or express mail service is not refusal of service within the meaning of division (C) of this rule.

(D) **Service unclaimed.** If a certified or express mail envelope is returned with an endorsement show-

ing that the envelope was unclaimed, the clerk shall forthwith notify, by mail, the attorney of record or, if there is no attorney of record, the party at whose instance process was issued. If the attorney, or serving party, after notification by the clerk, files with the clerk a written request for ordinary mail service, the clerk shall send by ordinary mail a copy of the summons and complaint or other document to be served to the defendant at the address set forth in the caption, or at the address set forth in written instructions furnished to the clerk. The mailing shall be evidenced by a certificate of mailing which shall be completed and filed by the clerk. Answer day shall be twenty-eight days after the date of mailing as evidenced by the certificate of mailing. The clerk shall endorse this answer date upon the summons which is sent by ordinary mail. Service shall be deemed complete when the fact of mailing is entered of record, provided that the ordinary mail envelope is not returned by the postal authorities with an endorsement showing failure of delivery. If the ordinary mail envelope is returned undelivered, the clerk shall forthwith notify the attorney, or serving party, by mail.

(E) **Duty of attorney of record or serving party** . The attorney of record or the serving party shall be responsible for determining if service has been made and shall timely file written instructions with the clerk regarding completion of service notwithstanding the provisions in Civ. R. 4.1 through 4.6 which instruct a clerk to notify the attorney of record or the serving party of failure of service of process.

History: Amended, eff 7-1-71; 7-1-78; 7-1-97.

NOTES TO DECISIONS

ANALYSIS

Generally
Business address
Presumption of proper service
Service by ordinary mail
Service returned "Attempted Not Known"
Termination of parental rights

Generally

Where an insurer never perfected service on its insured for purposes of its declaratory judgment action under RC § 2721.03 in order to establish its coverage and defense obligations, as the certified mail pursuant to Ohio R. Civ. P. 4.1(A) was returned unclaimed and service under Ohio R. Civ. P. 4.6(D) was also unsuccessful, the action was never commenced within Ohio R. Civ. P. 3(A), and the summary judgment granted by the trial court to the insurer was void ab initio. Earl v. Nelson, — Ohio App. 3d —, 2006 Ohio 3341, — N.E. 2d —, 2006 Ohio App. LEXIS 3270 (June 30, 2006).

Business address

Trial court's denial of a motion by a business and guarantors, seeking either relief from a default judgment or to vacate the default judgment, pursuant to Ohio R. Civ. P. 60(B), was proper where the seller who obtained the default judgment had originally pursued service through certified mail, which was returned "unclaimed," and thereafter, service by ordinary mail was authorized, which was not returned to the court. The guarantors had another business only one mile away, they had the same postal carrier for both businesses who informed them when their business mailbox was full, they received utility bills and customer payments at the mailbox, and the circumstances indicated that the service by ordinary mail was reasonably calculated to reach them pursuant to Ohio R. Civ. P. 4.6(D). Seal Master Industries, Inc. v. Bay Area Seal Coating & Stripping, — Ohio App. 3d —, 2006 Ohio 3610, — N.E. 2d —, 2006 Ohio App. LEXIS 3547 (July 14, 2006).

Trial court's summary denial of a loan officer's motion to vacate a judgment against him pursuant to Ohio R. Civ. P. 60(B) was an abuse of discretion where no hearing was held despite the officer's having rebutted the presumption of effective service on him pursuant to Ohio R. Civ. P. 4.1 and 4.6. An issue was created as to whether service had been attempted at the proper business address for the loan officer, and where such issue was raised, it was reversible error to fail to hold a hearing in order to resolve the issue as to effective service. Money Tree Loan Co. v. Williams, 169 Ohio App. 3d 336, 2006 Ohio 5568, 862 N.E.2d 885, 2006 Ohio App. LEXIS 5553 (2006).

Presumption of proper service
In a law firm's suit against a former client for past due fees, in which the trial court had entered a default judgment against the client, the trial court's judgment vacating that default judgment, based on the client's letter to the court stating that the client was not served with process, was not disturbed on appeal because, while it was presumed, under Ohio R. Civ. P. 4.6(D), that service was proper, since process was sent to the client by ordinary mail and not returned, the firm did not file a transcript of the hearing at which the trial court decided to vacate the judgment, so the appellate court had to presume that the hearing was properly conducted and affirm the trial court's decision. Bringman v. Smith, — Ohio App. 3d —, 2007 Ohio 4684, — N.E. 2d —, 2007 Ohio App. LEXIS 4214 (Sept. 12, 2007).

As a motorist and the trial court clerk complied with the Ohio Civil Rules when certified mail was sent of the motorist's complaint to a driver, arising from a vehicle accident between the parties, a rebuttable presumption arose that service was proper pursuant to Ohio R. Civ. P. 4.1(A) and 4.6, and such presumption was not rebutted by the driver's claim that she did not have to answer until the service was docketed in the trial court. Such claim also did not satisfy the driver's burden of showing excusable neglect in order to avoid a default judgment against her and to allow her to file her answer instanter, pursuant to Ohio R. Civ. P. 12(A) and 6(B)(2). Sokol v. Spigiel, — Ohio App. 3d —, 2006 Ohio 4408, — N.E. 2d —, 2006 Ohio App. LEXIS 4345 (Aug. 28, 2006).

Denial of the driver's Ohio R. Civ. P. 60(B) motion to vacate the default judgment was proper because he failed to set forth a meritorious defense; the docket reflected that regular mail service was issued to the driver in response to the unclaimed certified mail service and that service was "deemed complete." Further, the driver's assertions did not refute the presumption of proper service that arose after the victim followed the procedure outlined in Ohio R. Civ. P. 4.6(D) because the driver presented no affidavit, deposition testimony, stipulations, or other evidence that would have demonstrated that service was improper. Harless v. Sprague, — Ohio App. 3d —, 2006 Ohio 4472, — N.E. 2d —, 2006 Ohio App. LEXIS 4391 (Aug. 30, 2006).

Motion under Ohio R. Civ. P. 60(B) for relief from default judgment was properly denied. Since the record did not indicate that the complaint sent to appellant by regular mail was returned, a presumption arose under Ohio R. Civ. P. 4.6(D) that service was properly completed, and appellant failed to rebut the presumption, presenting no evidence before the trial court to support his assertion that he never received the complaint. Erie Ins. v. Williams, — Ohio App. 3d —, 2006 Ohio 6754, — N.E. 2d —, 2006 Ohio App. LEXIS 6661 (Dec. 20, 2006).

Service by ordinary mail
Trial court did not err in denying a property owner's motion to set aside a default judgment pursuant to Ohio R. Civ. P. 60(B) in a tax foreclosure action, as multiple certified mail attempts came back, but the two that were marked as "unclaimed" led to service by ordinary mail at those addresses, one of which was not returned; pursuant to Ohio R. Civ. P. 4.6(D), the presumption that service was accomplished was not overcome, as the owner did not present any evidence that he did not actually receive service or notice of the complaint. Kapszukiewicz v. Samuel, — Ohio App. 3d —, 2007 Ohio 2152, — N.E. 2d —, 2007 Ohio App. LEXIS 1996 (May 4, 2007).

When an attempt to serve an excavating company by certified mail was returned unclaimed, service by ordinary mail, under Ohio R. Civ. P. 4.6(D), was presumed complete when it was mailed, but an affidavit filed on behalf of the company alleging that service of process was never received required an oral hearing to determine if sufficient competent, credible evidence of nonservice existed, to show that a default judgment against the company was void ab initio, due to a lack of service and resulting lack of jurisdiction. Tractor Serv. & Supply v. Excavating, — Ohio App. 3d —, 2007 Ohio 5255, — N.E. 2d —, 2007 Ohio App. LEXIS 4643 (Sept. 19, 2007).

Service returned "Attempted Not Known"
Neither Ohio R. Civ. P. 4.6(D) nor the Due Process Clause require ordinary mail service when the postal authorities return certified mail with the endorsement "Attempted Not Known" before a party attempts service by publication. In re Thompkins, 115 Ohio St. 3d 409, 2007 Ohio 5238, 875 N.E.2d 582, 2007 Ohio LEXIS 2523 (2007).

Children's services board exercised reasonable diligence in attempting to serve the father notice of the permanent custody proceeding because neither Ohio R. Civ. P. 4.6(D) nor the Due Process Clause required ordinary mail service when the postal authorities returned certified mail with the endorsement "Attempted Not Known" before a party attempted service by publication. The board complied with the rules by attempting to personally serve the father at one address, by attempting to serve him by certified mail at another address, and by publishing a notice in a newspaper; because the returned certified letter, endorsed "Attempted Not Known" clearly demonstrated that the father did not reside and was not known at that address, any ordinary mail addressed to him at that address could not have been reasonably calculated to give him notice and an opportunity to be heard at the permanent custody proceeding. In re Thompkins, 115 Ohio St. 3d 409, 2007 Ohio 5238, 875 N.E.2d 582, 2007 Ohio LEXIS 2523 (2007).

Termination of parental rights
County children service board exercised reasonable diligence in attempting to serve the father in a proceeding to terminate parental rights. Neither CivR 4.6(D) nor the due process clause requires ordinary mail service when postal authorities return certified mail with the endorsement "attempted not known" before a party attempts service by publication: In re Thompkins, 115 Ohio St. 3d 409, 2007 Ohio 5238, 875 N.E.2d 582, 2007 Ohio LEXIS 2523 (2007).

RULE 5.   Service and filing of pleadings and other papers subsequent to the original complaint

(A) **Service: when required.** Except as otherwise provided in these rules, every order required by its terms to be served, every pleading subsequent to the original complaint unless the court otherwise orders because of numerous defendants, every paper relating to discovery required to be served upon a party unless the court otherwise orders, every written motion other than one which may be heard ex parte, and every written notice, appearance, demand, offer of judgment, and similar paper shall be served upon each of the parties. Service is not required on parties in default for failure to appear except that pleadings asserting new or additional claims for relief or for additional damages against them shall be served upon them in the manner provided for service of summons in Civ. R. 4 through Civ. R. 4.6.

(B) **Service: how made.** Whenever under these rules service is required or permitted to be made upon a party who is represented by an attorney of record in the proceedings, the service shall be made upon the attorney unless service upon the party is ordered by the court. Service upon the attorney or party shall be made by delivering a copy to the person to be served, transmitting it to the office of the person to be served by facsimile transmission, mailing it to the last known address of the person to be served or, if no address is known, leaving it with the clerk of the court. The served copy shall be accompanied by a completed copy of the proof of service required by division (D) of this rule. "Delivering a copy" within this rule means: handing it to the attorney or party; leaving it at the office of the person to be served with a clerk or other person in charge; if there is no one in charge, leaving it in a conspicuous place in the office; or, if the office is closed or the person to be served has no office, leaving it at the dwelling house or usual place of abode of the person to be served with some person of suitable age and discretion then residing in the dwelling house or usual place of abode. Service by mail is complete upon mailing. Service by facsimile transmission is complete upon transmission.

(C) **Service: numerous defendants.** In any action in which there are unusually large numbers of defendants, the court, upon motion or of its own initiative, may order that service of the pleadings of the defendants and replies thereto need not be made as between the defendants and that any cross-claim, counterclaim, or matter constituting an avoidance or affirmative defense contained therein shall be deemed to be denied or avoided by all other parties and that the filing of any such pleading and service thereof upon the plaintiff constitutes due notice of it to the parties. A copy of every such order shall be served upon the parties in such manner and form as the court directs.

(D) **Filing.** All papers, after the complaint, required to be served upon a party shall be filed with the court within three days after service, but depositions upon oral examination, interrogatories, requests for documents, requests for admission, and answers and responses thereto shall not be filed unless on order of the court or for use as evidence or for consideration of a motion in the proceeding. Papers filed with the court shall not be considered until proof of service is endorsed thereon or separately filed. The proof of service shall state the date and manner of service and shall be signed in accordance with Civ. R. 11.

(E) **Filing with the court defined.** The filing of documents with the court, as required by these rules, shall be made by filing them with the clerk of court, except that the judge may permit the documents to be filed with the judge, in which event the judge shall note the filing date on the documents and transmit them to the clerk. A court may provide, by local rules adopted pursuant to the Rules of Superintendence, for the filing of documents by electronic means. If the court adopts such local rules, they shall include all of the following:

(1) Any signature on electronically transmitted documents shall be considered that of the attorney or party it purports to be for all purposes. If it is established that the documents were transmitted without authority, the court shall order the filing stricken.

(2) A provision shall specify the days and hours during which electronically transmitted documents will be received by the court, and a provision shall specify when documents received electronically will be considered to have been filed.

(3) Any document filed electronically that requires a filing fee may be rejected by the clerk of court unless the filer has complied with the mechanism established by the court for the payment of filing fees.

History: Amended, eff 7-1-71; 7-1-84; 7-1-91; 7-1-94; 7-1-01.

NOTES TO DECISIONS

Analysis

Contempt motion
Continuance
Custody matters
Default of answer
Filing
Magistrate's decision
Motion for continuance
new heading
Notice issued by court
— Notice of entry of judgment
Notice of appeal
Parties in default
Presumption of receipt
Receipt of notice
Service by mail
Service on attorney

Contempt motion

When it was alleged that a father was in contempt for failing to obey an order to pay child support, service by regular mail of notice of a hearing on a motion to show cause why the father should not be held in contempt was proper because the father had previously been served by certified mail with the motion to show cause, and he was alleged to be in indirect civil contempt, so the Ohio Rules of Civil Procedure applied, and Ohio R. Civ. P. 5(B) was complied with. Bierce v. Howell, — Ohio App. 3d —, 2007 Ohio 3050, — N.E. 2d —, 2007 Ohio App. LEXIS 2793 (June 15, 2007).

When a trial court, in a personal injury case, ordered the parties to attend a mediation conference and specifically required the attendance of clients and insurance representatives with authority to settle the case, an insurance adjustor who did not attend the conference was given sufficient notice of the order when it was served on her employer's counsel, pursuant to Civ. R. 5(B), so she could be held in contempt. Scarnecchia v. Rebhan, — Ohio App. 3d —, 2006 Ohio 7053, — N.E. 2d —, 2006 Ohio App. LEXIS 6974 (Dec. 14, 2006).

Continuance

As a trial of a lender's action against a debtor, seeking recovery for amounts due under her three defaulted loans, was continued multiple times and on the last such occasion, the trial court advised the parties that any further continuances would not be permitted, the trial court did not abuse its discretion under Franklin County, Ohio, Ct. C.P. R. 79, Ohio R. Civ. P. 5(A), and Ohio Superintendence Ct. R. 41(A) in holding the trial despite the debtor's absence and in denying her counsel's request for a continuance. Kemba Fin. Credit Union v. Fish, — Ohio App. 3d —, 2007 Ohio 43, — N.E. 2d —, 2007 Ohio App. LEXIS 33 (Jan. 9, 2007).

Custody matters

Juvenile court's order granting legal custody in the absence of a motion violated the mandatory statutory and procedural requirements of RC § 2151.353 and Ohio R. Juv. P. 34, and also was in direct contravention of Ohio R. Juv. P. 19, mandating that requests for relief be made by motion, Ohio R. Juv. P. 22(E), requiring that prehearing motions be filed at least seven days prior to the proceeding, Ohio R. Juv. P. 20, establishing filing and service requirements for written motions and other papers, and Ohio R. Civ. P. 5(D), imposing a proof of service requirement. In re L.R.T., 165 Ohio App. 3d 77, 2006 Ohio 207, 844 N.E. 2d 914, 2006 Ohio App. LEXIS 173 (Jan. 23, 2006).

Default of answer

Trial court properly denied an insurer's motion under Ohio R. Civ. P. 60(B)(3) for relief from a default judgment, as there was no fraud, misrepresentation, or misconduct by a movant's counsel's failure to notify the insurer's counsel that a default judgment was forthcoming where the insurer had not appeared in the action pursuant to Ohio R. Civ. P. 5(A) and 55(A). Linquist v. Allstate, — Ohio App. 3d —, 2007 Ohio 4587, — N.E. 2d —, 2007 Ohio App. LEXIS 4121 (Aug. 27, 2007).

Filing

Attorney who was sued for legal malpractice and who moved for leave to file a motion for summary judgment instanter sufficiently complied with the filing requirement of Ohio R. Civ. P. 5(E) where the actual summary judgment motion was directly field with the clerk of courts as an attachment to the motion for leave to file, such that the entirey of the filing was, in essence, accepted and time stamped by the clerk's office. Lee v. Norton, — Ohio App. 3d —, 2007 Ohio 534, — N.E. 2d —, 2007 Ohio App. LEXIS 473 (Feb. 8, 2007).

Magistrate's decision

Proper service of notice of a magistrate's decision includes service on a party's attorney of record in accordance with CivR 5(B) unless the court expressly orders otherwise: Roberts v. Skaggs, 176 Ohio App. 3d 251, 2008 Ohio 1954, 891 N.E.2d 827, 2008 Ohio App. LEXIS 1674 (2008).

In a divorce case, the trial court did not abuse its discretion in dismissing the husband's motion objecting to the magistrate's decision, a brief supporting the husband's opposition, and a proposed judgment entry; the pleading was not signed in violation of Ohio R. Civ. P. 11, and it was not served on opposing counsel in violation of Ohio R. Civ. P. 5, and amendment was, again, not served on the wife's representative. Havel v. Havel, — Ohio App. 3d —, 2006 Ohio 1692, — N.E. 2d —, 2006 Ohio App. LEXIS 1547 (Mar. 31, 2006).

Motion for continuance

Counsel's oral motion to continue, made on the day of the trial, failed to comply with filing requirements of motion for continuance and was properly denied. Pinson v. Lytle, — Ohio App. 3d —, 2006 Ohio 5441, — N.E. 2d —, 2006 Ohio App. LEXIS 5423 (Oct. 19, 2006).

new heading

RC § 2744.02(C) permits a political subdivision to appeal a trial court order that denies it the benefit of an alleged immunity from liability under RC Chapter 2744, even when the order makes no determination pursuant to CivR 54(B):

Sullivan v. Anderson Twp., 122 Ohio St. 3d 83, 2009 Ohio 1971, 909 N.E.2d 88, 2009 Ohio LEXIS 1170 (2009).

Notice issued by court

In a foreclosure action which was stayed when the mortgagor filed for bankruptcy, the trial court did not violate Ohio R. Civ. P. 5(A) by not notifying the mortgagor when the case was returned to the active docket, because the mortgagor had adequate notice of the proceedings against the mortgagor because the mortgagor received the mortgagee's motion to vacate the stay and for summary judgment, as well as the trial court's order establishing a time limit for discovery. Ameriquest Mortg. Co. v. Wilson, — Ohio App. 3d —, 2007 Ohio 2576, — N.E. 2d —, 2007 Ohio App. LEXIS 2395 (May 25, 2007).

— Notice of entry of judgment

As a trial court record indicated that within three days of entry of the trial court's summary judgment ruling in favor of an employee, the clerk of the trial court served the notice of final judgment on the counsel for the parties in a manner provided by Ohio R. Civ. P. 5 and the service was recorded in the court's docket, the requirements of Ohio R. Civ. P. 58(B) were met and due process under Ohio Const. art. I, § 16 was satisfied, such that the clerk was deemed to have issued proper service of the notice even if the employer's counsel did not actually receive it. There was no abuse of discretion in the trial court's denial of the employer's motion under Ohio R. Civ. P. 60(B)(5) for relief from judgment based on lack of service, as it did not meet the first prong of the GTE test because it sought to reargue issues raised and decided in the summary judgment motion, such that there was no showing of a meritorious defense if relief from judgment was granted. Leonard v. Consulting, — Ohio App. 3d —, 2007 Ohio 1846, — N.E. 2d —, 2007 Ohio App. LEXIS 1671 (Apr. 19, 2007).

Notice of appeal

Where a notation in a trial court's appearance docket did not comply with the requirements of Ohio R. Civ. P. 58(B) with respect to indicating the method of service of the appealed order on the parties by the court clerk, pursuant to Ohio R. Civ. P. 5(B), the time to file a notice of appeal had not yet begun to run pursuant to Ohio R. App. P. 4(A); accordingly, a motion by appellee to dismiss the appeal as untimely was denied. Carter-Jones Lumber Co. v. Willard, — Ohio App. 3d —, 2006 Ohio 1980, — N.E. 2d —, 2006 Ohio App. LEXIS 1822 (Apr. 17, 2006).

Parties in default

It did not appear that a note maker ever properly served his cross-claim upon the third-party plaintiff that the maker had joined because the certificate of service indicated that it was served upon the third-party plaintiff by regular U.S. Mail, and since the third-party plaintiff was in default for failure to appear, Ohio R. Civ. P. 5(A) required that service of summons be served in the manner provided for service in Ohio R. Civ. P. 4 through Ohio R. Civ. P. 4.6. Irion v. Incomm Electronics, — Ohio App. 3d —, 2006 Ohio 362, — N.E. 2d —, 2006 Ohio App. LEXIS 297 (Jan. 24, 2006).

Presumption of receipt

Doctor was not under some heightened legal obligation to serve the patient, due to her pro se status, above and beyond the requirements of Ohio R. Civ. P. 5, which provided that service of motions and discovery by regular mail was effective. The certificate of service attached to the doctor's request for admissions demonstrated that an original and copy of the request were served by regular mail to the patient at her home address and the presumption was that she received the requests; there was nothing in the record to indicate otherwise. Jackson-Summers v. Brooks, — Ohio App. 3d —, 2006 Ohio 1357, — N.E. 2d —, 2006 Ohio App. LEXIS 1233 (Mar. 23, 2006).

Receipt of notice

When an individual's motion to vacate an arbitration award was served on her opponent's counsel over a year after the arbitration award was mailed to her, she did not file her motion within the three-month period required by RC § 2711.13, as the arbitration award contained a proper certificate of service, in compliance with Ohio R. Civ. P. 5(A), showing it was mailed to her, so it was not error to find that her motion was untimely. CACV of Colorado v. Kogler, — Ohio App. 3d —, 2006 Ohio 5124, — N.E. 2d —, 2006 Ohio App. LEXIS 5053 (Sept. 29, 2006).

Service by mail

Trial court did not err in denying the landlord an extension of time to object to the magistrate's decision as it appropriately chose to serve the landlord by ordinary mail, even though he claimed to have been out of the country, and did not err in finding that his motion to extend time to filed objections to be untimely. Tidwell v. Quaglieri, — Ohio App. 3d —, 2007 Ohio 569, — N.E. 2d —, 2007 Ohio App. LEXIS 530 (Feb. 9, 2007).

Service on attorney

Appellant failed to demonstrate how he was prejudiced by a trial court's failure to provide notice of the deadline to file a brief in opposition to appellee's summary judgment motion before ruling on the motion as appellant, who had been given three months to respond to appellee's motion, had filed a brief in opposition to the motion, which the trial court considered in deciding the motion. The certificate of service attached to appellee's motion, wherein counsel for appellee attested that counsel for appellant had been served a copy of the motion via U.S. mail evidenced proper service of the motion under Ohio R. Civ. P. 5(B). Marino v. Oriana House, Inc., — Ohio App. 3d —, 2007 Ohio 1823, — N.E. 2d —, 2007 Ohio App. LEXIS 1664 (Apr. 18, 2007).

Trial court erred in allowing a bank to continually serve papers on an attorney who represented a debtor in a prior action, although the debtor had responded in the instant matter by appearing pro se and filing his own motions and counterclaims, as the trial court's practice was in violation of Ohio R. Civ. P. 5 and did not allow the debtor to review and respond to various significant motions, such as dismissal of his counterclaim seeking to confirm an arbitration award between the parties. Citibank v. Wood, — Ohio App. 3d —, 2006 Ohio 5755, — N.E. 2d —, 2006 Ohio App. LEXIS 5711 (Oct. 27, 2006).

City's motion to dismiss an individual's appeal was denied as, despite the notation on the appearance docket that the clerk served the individual with notice of the judgment by mail on November 22, 2005, the envelope that the clerk mailed to the individual's counsel containing the final appealable order was mailed on November 28, 2005. Service of the final judgment was not made until November 28, 2005, as service was complete upon mailing under Ohio R. Civ. P. 5(B), and the notice of appeal, which was filed on December 23, 2005, was timely filed under Ohio R. App. P. 4(A). Muranyi v. City of Oregon, — Ohio App. 3d —, 2006 Ohio 203, — N.E. 2d —, 2006 Ohio App. LEXIS 172 (Jan. 23, 2006).

RULE 6.   Time

(A) **Time: computation.** In computing any period of time prescribed or allowed by these rules, by the local rules of any court, by order of court, or by any applicable statute, the date of the act, event, or default from which the designated period of time begins to run shall not be included. The last day of the period so computed shall be included, unless it is a Saturday, a Sunday, or a legal holiday, in which event the period runs until the end of the next day which is not a Saturday, a Sunday, or a legal holiday. When the period of time prescribed or allowed is less than seven days, intermediate Saturdays, Sundays, and legal holidays shall be excluded in the computation. When a public office in which an act, required by law, rule, or order of court, is to be performed is closed to the public for the entire day which constitutes the last day for doing such an act, or before its usual closing time on such day, then such act may be performed on the next succeeding day which is not a Saturday, a Sunday, or a legal holiday.

(B) **Time: extension.** When by these rules or by a notice given thereunder or by order of court an act is required or allowed to be done at or within a specified time, the court for cause shown may at any time in its discretion (1) with or without motion or notice order the period enlarged if request therefore is made before the expiration of the period originally prescribed or as extended by a previous order, or (2) upon motion made after the expiration of the specified period permit the act to be done where the failure to act was the result of excusable neglect; but it may not extend the time for taking any action under Rule 50(B), Rule 59(B), Rule 59(D) and Rule 60(B), except to the extent and under the conditions stated in them.

(C) **Time: unaffected by expiration of term.** The period of time provided for the doing of any act or the taking of any proceeding is not affected or limited by the continued existence or expiration of a term of court. The existence or expiration of a term of court in no way affects the power of a court to do any act or take any proceeding in any civil action consistent with these rules.

(D) **Time: motions.** A written motion, other than one which may be heard ex parte, and notice of the hearing thereof shall be served not later than seven days before the time fixed for the hearing, unless a different period is fixed by these rules or by order of the court. Such an order may for cause shown be made on ex parte application. When a motion is supported by affidavit, the affidavit shall be served with the motion; and, except as otherwise provided in Rule 59(C), opposing affidavits may be served not later than one day before the hearing, unless the court permits them to be served at some other time.

(E) **Time: additional time after service by mail** . Whenever a party has the right or is required to do some act or take some proceedings within a prescribed period after the service of a notice or other paper upon him and the notice or paper is served upon him by mail, three days shall be added to the prescribed period. This subdivision does not apply to responses to service of summons under Rule 4 through Rule 4.6.

History: Amended, eff 7-1-78.

NOTES TO DECISIONS

ANALYSIS

Notice
Time limitations

_____

Applicability

Trial court did not err in denying a customer's motion for prejudgment interest because the customer failed to file her motion within 14 days of the trial court's judgment ordering the payment of money. The customer's contention that Ohio R. Civ. P. 6(E) allotted her an additional three days to file her motion was rejected because Ohio R. Civ. P. 6(E) applies only to an action that is to be taken after the service of summons, and RC § 1343.03(C) clearly states that the triggering event for filing a motion for prejudgment interest is the date of the judgment entry. Abbott v. Marshalls of Ma, Inc., — Ohio App. 3d —, 2007 Ohio 1146, — N.E. 2d —, 2007 Ohio App. LEXIS 1056 (Mar. 15, 2007).

Trial court did not err in denying a customer's motion for prejudgment interest because the customer failed to file her motion within 14 days of the trial court's judgment ordering the payment of money. The customer's contention that Ohio R. Civ. P. 6(E) allotted her an additional three days to file her motion was rejected because Ohio R. Civ. P. 6(E) applies only to an action that is to be taken after the service of summons, and RC § 1343.03(C) clearly states that the triggering event for filing a motion for prejudgment interest is the date of the judgment entry. Abbott v. Marshalls of Ma, Inc., — Ohio App. 3d —, 2007 Ohio 1146, — N.E. 2d —, 2007 Ohio App. LEXIS 1056 (Mar. 15, 2007).

As the time-extension provisions of Ohio R. Civ. P. 6(B) were not applicable to the Ohio saving statute, RC § 2305.19, where an employee in an employer's workers' compensation appeal pursuant to RC § 4123.512 voluntarily dismissed her complaint without prejudice pursuant to Ohio R. Civ. P. 41(A)(1)(a), her failure to re-file within the one-year period pursuant to RC § 2305.19 justified the trial court's grant of a judgment on the pleadings to the employer. Hughes v. Federal Mogul Ignition Co., — Ohio App. 3d —, 2007 Ohio 2021, — N.E. 2d —, 2007 Ohio App. LEXIS 1891 (Apr. 26, 2007).

Authority to extend time

As a father's objections to a magistrate's decision involving the date that child support was to commence were clearly untimely under Ohio R. Juv. P. 40(E)(3)(a) and Ohio R. Civ. P. 53(E)(3), warranting dismissal thereof by the juvenile court, and the father he did not seek to enlarge the time within which to file objections pursuant to Ohio R. Juv. P. 18(B) and Ohio R. Civ. P. 6(B), his time to appeal was not extended by the objections. His failure to appeal within 30 days of the juvenile court's adoption of the magistrate's decision did not preserve his merit issue for appellate review under Ohio R. App. P. 4(A). In re D.K.K., — Ohio App. 3d —, 2006 Ohio 5576, — N.E. 2d —, 2006 Ohio App. LEXIS 5590 (Oct. 20, 2006).

Death of a party

When, after a citizen and his wife sued a city and "unnamed police officers" for entering their home without a warrant, the wife died, her claims did not survive, under Ohio R. Civ. P. 25(A), because the citizen did not file a motion to substitute himself as her representative within 90 days of the city's filing of a suggestion of her death, nor did he seek additional time to do so, under Ohio R. Civ. P. 6(B). Maggio v. City of Warren, — Ohio App. 3d —, 2006 Ohio 6880, — N.E. 2d —, 2006 Ohio App. LEXIS 6801 (Dec. 22, 2006).

Excusable neglect

Proper standard by which a trial court was required to analyze a request for leave to plead out of rule was, as set forth in Ohio R. Civ. P. 6, that of excusable neglect, and it had to appear from the record that the successfully moving party made a showing of excusable neglect sufficient to support the

trial court's finding to that effect, and a determination of whether neglect was excusable or inexcusable had to take into consideration all the surrounding facts and circumstances, and courts had to be mindful that cases should be decided on their merits, where possible, rather than procedural grounds. Graham v. Nigh, — Ohio App. 3d —, 2007 Ohio 2161, — N.E. 2d —, 2007 Ohio App. LEXIS 2021 (May 7, 2007).

When an alleged offender sued his alleged rape victim for defamation for making a report to law enforcement, it was not an abuse of discretion for a trial court to grant the victim an extension of time, under Ohio R. Civ. P. 6(B)(2), within which to file an answer to the offender's complaint, or to deny the offender's motion to strike the victim's answer, because the victim's neglect of the matter, which resulted in her failure to file a timely answer, was excusable as (1) she had recently completed a pregnancy, and (2) her failure to defend was not due to a disregard of the court, but was due to her lack of understanding of the system, her lack of resources with which to obtain counsel or advice, and her fear of the legal system. Graham v. Nigh, — Ohio App. 3d —, 2007 Ohio 2161, — N.E. 2d —, 2007 Ohio App. LEXIS 2021 (May 7, 2007).

Trial court properly granted a default judgment pursuant to Ohio R. Civ. P. 55(A) to business purchasers in their action against the business seller, as the seller had failed to file a timely answer and counterclaim to the purchasers' amended complaint and he failed to show excusable neglect pursuant to Ohio R. Civ. P. 6(B)(2) for the untimely filing for purposes of his motion to file the answer and counterclaim instanter. As the seller also failed to show excusable neglect for the lack of reasonable diligence in filing the answer in a timely manner, as well as a meritorious defense to the complaint, his motion to vacate under Ohio R. Civ. P. 60(B) was properly denied. Ear v. Phnom Penh Rest., — Ohio App. 3d —, 2007 Ohio 3069, — N.E. 2d —, 2007 Ohio App. LEXIS 2811 (June 21, 2007).

Even assuming, arguendo, that the dentist was not on notice that the trial court had ruled on his motion to quash until he received the motion for default judgment, the trial court did not err in denying his motion for leave; it acted within its discretion in finding that the dentist's belated explanation did not constitute excusable neglect. The facts as set forth in the dentist's affidavit would have been known to him at the time that he initially sought leave and he could have informed the trial court, at that first opportunity, of the reason for missing the deadline, which he failed to do, resulting in further delay which was within his control to prevent. R.J. Donovan Co. v. Sohi, — Ohio App. 3d —, 2007 Ohio 3620, — N.E. 2d —, 2007 Ohio App. LEXIS 3316 (July 17, 2007).

In a legal malpractice case, a client's untimely motion for an extension of time within which to file a supplemental expert report, filed 18 days before trial was scheduled to begin, was properly denied because the motion did not attempt to show any excusable neglect, under Ohio R. Civ. P. 6(B), resulting in the motion being untimely, as the motion merely stated that the motion was filed in good faith and arose from information discovered in the discovery process. Welch v. Ziccarelli, — Ohio App. 3d —, 2007 Ohio 4374, — N.E. 2d —, 2007 Ohio App. LEXIS 3947 (Aug. 24, 2007).

Although a guardian of an incompetent did not receive a copy of a probate court judgment, adopting a magistrate's decision to remove her from that position, until after the expiration of the 14-day period within which to file objections, pursuant to Ohio R. Civ. P. 53, the probate court did not abuse its discretion in denying her motion for leave to file late objections, pursuant to Ohio R. Civ. P. 6(B), as there was no excusable neglect on the part of the guardian where she waited another 19 days after receiving the judgment before filing her motion for leave. In re Riccardi, — Ohio App. 3d —, 2006 Ohio 24, — N.E. 2d —, 2006 Ohio App. LEXIS 13 (Jan. 6, 2006).

Trial court did not abuse its discretion in concluding that appellant failed to establish excusable neglect for his failure to timely file an answer by his assertion that he was unaware of the 28-day time limitation for filing an answer. The summons specifically stated the time limitations; thus, appellant's motion under Ohio R. Civ. P. 6(B)(2) for leave to file an answer was properly denied. United Bank & Trust v. Kaufman, — Ohio App. 3d —, 2006 Ohio 2346, — N.E. 2d —, 2006 Ohio App. LEXIS 2229 (May 12, 2006).

Trial court did not err in denying debtors' motion for default judgment on their counterclaim against a creditor because, while the creditor did not respond within the time permitted by the Ohio Rules of Civil Procedure, it was within the trial court's discretion to grant the creditor leave to plead and to denying the debtors' motion for default judgment upon a finding that the creditor had shown excusable neglect for its delay, in that the creditor's counsel inadvertently failed to timely reply to the counterclaim due to a death in counsel's immediate family that required counsel's presence out-of-state for an extended period of time. Under Ohio R. Civ. P. 6(B)(2), the trial court had the discretion to allow for an extension of time to file a late pleading upon the showing of excusable neglect. Bank v. Damsel, — Ohio App. 3d —, 2006 Ohio 4071, — N.E. 2d —, 2006 Ohio App. LEXIS 3991 (Aug. 8, 2006).

As a motorist and the trial court clerk complied with the Ohio Civil Rules when certified mail was sent of the motorist's complaint to a driver, arising from a vehicle accident between the parties, a rebuttable presumption arose that service was proper pursuant to Ohio R. Civ. P. 4.1(A) and 4.6, and such presumption was not rebutted by the driver's claim that she did not have to answer until the service was docketed in the trial court. Such claim also did not satisfy the driver's burden of showing excusable neglect in order to avoid a default judgment against her and to allow her to file her answer instanter, pursuant to Ohio R. Civ. P. 12(A) and 6(B)(2). Sokol v. Spigiel, — Ohio App. 3d —, 2006 Ohio 4408, — N.E. 2d —, 2006 Ohio App. LEXIS 4345 (Aug. 28, 2006).

There was no abuse of discretion in the trial court's refusal to grant the father's motion for leave when the reason given for the late objections was due to a problem with the calendar program in the attorney's office; it was entirely within the trial court's discretion to determine whether a calendar problem was "excusable neglect." The trial court found that filing the objections one day late was not excusable and amending the proof of service did not correct the fact that it was originally filed late. Hale v. Hale, — Ohio App. 3d —, 2006 Ohio 5164, — N.E. 2d —, 2006 Ohio App. LEXIS 5123 (Sept. 29, 2006).

Trial court properly concluded that a city's deletion of an email transmission of a property owners' requests for admission for lack of an identifiable sender constituted excusable neglect that would justify an extension of time under Ohio R. Civ. P. 6 to respond to the requests for admission. Grano v. City of Mentor, — Ohio App. 3d —, 2006 Ohio 6104, — N.E. 2d —, 2006 Ohio App. LEXIS 6029 (Nov. 17, 2006).

—— Clerical error

Magistrate did not err in granting a judge's request under Ohio R. Civ. P. 6(B) that he be granted leave to file his responsive pleading to a request for a writ of mandamus instanter because the responsive pleading was not timely filed due to a clerical error and because no default motion was pending at the time that the judge's request was filed. State Ex Rel. Rutan v. Bessey, — Ohio App. 3d —, 2007 Ohio 6856, — N.E. 2d —, 2007 Ohio App. LEXIS 6021 (Dec. 20, 2007).

Extension of time

Medical malpractice claim was properly dismissed because, since the affidavit of merit was to be filed along with the complaint (before discovery), the patient's argument that she needed the doctor's deposition testimony in order to secure an affidavit of merit was without merit. Even if the doctor had been evading service, it would not have eliminated the patient's burden of submitting an affidavit of merit with her complaint; she had access to the requisite medical records and the trial court granted her a 90-day extension to file her affidavit, but it was not until five months later that the trial court finally dismissed the case. Colon v. Fortune, — Ohio App. 3d —, 2008 Ohio 576, — N.E. 2d —, 2008 Ohio App. LEXIS 488 (Feb. 14, 2008).

Where a court closed early due to Election Day, which was the last day under CivR 53(D)(2)(b)(i) for landlords to file objections to a magistrate's decision in a dispute with tenants, the time for filing the objections was extended to the next succeeding day under CivR 6(A), such that an attempt to file the objections at that time should have been accepted as timely. Sharla v. Yates, — Ohio App. 3d —, 2008 Ohio 616, — N.E. 2d —, 2008 Ohio App. LEXIS 534 (Feb. 15, 2008).

As an employee failed to oppose an employer's request for an extension of time to file a summary judgment motion, and no prejudice was shown by the granting of the extension pursuant to Ohio R. Civ. P. 6(B)(2), the trial court did not abuse its discretion; further, the court acted in line with the principle of attempting to resolve disputes on the merits, rather than on procedural grounds. Duffy v. Nourse Family of Dealerships-Chillicothe, Inc., — Ohio App. 3d —, 2006 Ohio 2057, — N.E. 2d —, 2006 Ohio App. LEXIS 1887 (Apr. 24, 2006).

Patient's motion under Ohio R. Civ. P. 6(B) for an extension of time to file an affidavit of merit under Ohio R. Civ. P. 10(D)(2) should have been granted because the motion was supported with an affidavit showing that the patient had been trying to obtain necessary medical records from a hospital and that the records had not been received until two weeks before the affidavit of merit was due. Under the circumstances, the patient should have been granted additional time to obtain a medical expert to review the records and prepare the affidavit of merit. Ervin v. Cleveland Clinic Found., — Ohio App. 3d —, 2007 Ohio 818, — N.E. 2d —, 2007 Ohio App. LEXIS 764 (Mar. 1, 2007).

Patient's motion under Ohio R. Civ. P. 6(B) for an extension of time to file an affidavit of merit under Ohio R. Civ. P. 10(D)(2) should have been granted because the motion was supported with an affidavit showing that the patient had been trying to obtain necessary medical records from a hospital and that the records had not been received until two weeks before the affidavit of merit was due. Under the circumstances, the patient should have been granted additional time to obtain a medical expert to review the records and prepare the affidavit of merit. Ervin v. Cleveland Clinic Found., — Ohio App. 3d —, 2007 Ohio 818, — N.E. 2d —, 2007 Ohio App. LEXIS 764 (Mar. 1, 2007).

After a former prosecutor was granted an initial extension to file his response to a city's motion to strike his complaint, the trial court did not abuse its discretion in denying his second request for an extension pursuant to Ohio R. Civ. P. 6(B), as the prosecutor's bald reference to his schedule conflict without further facts was not given much weight, he failed to comply with the requirement of Montgomery County, Ohio, Ct. C.P. R. 2.05 that he submit a "brief written memorandum" with the motion, and he had already had two months to file a response to the city's motion. Scaccia v. Lemmie, — Ohio App. 3d —, 2007 Ohio 1055, — N.E. 2d —, 2007 Ohio App. LEXIS 991 (Mar. 9, 2007).

When a husband sought relief from a trial court's order under Ohio R. Civ. P. 60(B)(1), Ohio R. Civ. P. 6(E) did not extend the one-year period within which he was required to file his motion because Ohio R. Civ. P. 60(B) did not trigger the running of this one-year limitation period with a service of notice requirement. Williams v. Williams, — Ohio App. 3d —, 2006 Ohio 2566, — N.E. 2d —, 2006 Ohio App. LEXIS 2420 (May 18, 2006).

Mortgagors' claim that the trial court erred by denying their motion for additional time to respond to the mortgagee's motion to appoint a receiver in his foreclosure action pursuant to Lucas County, Ohio, Ct. C.P. R. 5.04(D) and Ohio R. Civ. P. 6(E) was deemed moot, as the initial appointment of the receiver was stayed pending an evidentiary hearing and an appeal was taken from the original appointment, which later resulted in a consolidated appeal, such that there was ample time to have responded to the issues raised in the motion to appoint a receiver. As the issue was already determined and was being reviewed on appeal, the decision to deny the extension of time was moot. Harajli Mgmt. & Inv. v. A&M Inv. Strategies, 167 Ohio App. 3d 546, 2006 Ohio 3052, 855 N.E. 2d 1262, 2006 Ohio App. LEXIS 2927 (June 16, 2006).

Trial court abused its discretion by ignoring an attorney's failure to comply with the Ohio Rules of Civil Procedure, effectively overruling the client's motion for a default judgment, and entertaining the attorney's motion for summary judgment as the attorney did not file a request for an extension of time to answer a client's legal malpractice complaint under Ohio R. Civ. P. 6(B)(1) and filed his answer one week after the client filed a motion for default judgment, but did not file a motion showing excusable neglect and requesting leave of court to file his untimely answer. Rowe v. Stillpass, — Ohio App. 3d —, 2006 Ohio 3789, — N.E. 2d —, 2006 Ohio App. LEXIS 3748 (July 13, 2006).

In a medical malpractice action, a trial court did not abuse its discretion under Ohio R. Civ. P. 6(B) in denying a patient's motion for an extension of time to pursue further discovery in opposition to summary judgment motions filed by a hospital and other defendants because the patient did not explain why discovery involved in the hospital's appeal from a discovery order was necessary in order to formulate his opposition and, in fact, he did not need such discovery. In addition, he failed to provide an affidavit in support of his motion as required by Ohio R. Civ. P. 56(F). Cook v. Toledo Hosp., — Ohio App. 3d —, 2006 Ohio 5278, — N.E. 2d —, 2006 Ohio App. LEXIS 5266 (Oct. 6, 2006).

Magistrate's decision

Court declined to review the merits of a trial court's judgment adopting a magistrate's decision overruling a father's motion to modify child support obligations because the father did not timely object to magistrate's decision and, thus, under Ohio R. Civ. P. 53(E)(3)(d), could not assign as error on appeal the trial court's adoption of the magistrate's decision. Further, the father did not timely request an extension of time to file objections to the magistrate's decision before his prior extension expired, as required by Ohio R. Civ. P. 6(B)(1). Grubic v. Grubic, — Ohio App. 3d —, 2006 Ohio 172, — N.E. 2d —, 2006 Ohio App. LEXIS 146 (Jan. 19, 2006).

Husband's objections to a magistrate's order were timely filed, under Ohio R. Civ. P. 53(C)(3)(b), because the tenth day after the order was journalized was a Sunday, so, under Ohio R. Civ. P. 6(A), he had an additional day to file them, and he filed them on the following Monday. Rinkel v. Rinkel, — Ohio App. 3d —, 2006 Ohio 2560, — N.E. 2d —, 2006 Ohio App. LEXIS 2407 (May 24, 2006).

Mail rule did not apply to the time for filing objections to a magistrate's decision because the event that triggered the period for filing objections was not the service of the decision, as provided in Ohio R. Civ. P. 6(E), but the "filing" of the magistrate's decision, so the three-day mail rule did not extend the time for filing objections to a magistrate's decision. In re Estate of Jaric, — Ohio App. 3d —, 2006 Ohio 7066, — N.E. 2d —, 2006 Ohio App. LEXIS 6979 (Dec. 28, 2006).

Notice

It was not an abuse of discretion for the trial court to grant the husband's Ohio R. Civ. P. 60(B) motion for relief from judgment because the motion fulfilled each of the requirements; it presented a meritorious claim, as well as a reason upon which relief could be granted, in asserting that he had not received a seven-day notice, pursuant to Ohio R. Civ. P. 6(D). It was also made within a reasonable time and the trial

court held a hearing to verify operative facts set forth in the motion prior to ruling on the motion. Murphy v. Murphy, — Ohio App. 3d —, 2006 Ohio 4876, — N.E. 2d —, 2006 Ohio App. LEXIS 4791 (Sept. 1, 2006).

Time limitations

Although a trial court erred in accepting a party's late filing of proposed findings of fact and conclusions of law where no request for an extension of time was made pursuant to Ohio R. Civ. P. 6(B)(2), the late filing did not cause prejudice, as only the findings and conclusions made by the court became part of the record and accordingly, pursuant to Ohio R. Civ. P. 52, the parties' proposed findings and conclusions did not even comprise part of the record. The findings of fact and conclusions of law were supported by competent, credible evidence and were not contrary to law. Kimbler v. Kimbler, — Ohio App. 3d —, 2006 Ohio 2695, — N.E. 2d —, 2006 Ohio App. LEXIS 2516 (May 23, 2006).

TITLE III
PLEADINGS AND MOTIONS

RULE 7. Pleadings and motions

(A) **Pleadings.** There shall be a complaint and an answer; a reply to a counterclaim denominated as such; an answer to a cross-claim, if the answer contains a cross-claim; a third-party complaint, if a person who was not an original party is summoned under the provisions of Rule 14; and a third-party answer, if a third-party complaint is served. No other pleading shall be allowed, except that the court may order a reply to an answer or a third-party answer.

(B) **Motions.**

(1) An application to the court for an order shall be by motion which, unless made during a hearing or a trial, shall be made in writing. A motion, whether written or oral, shall state with particularity the grounds therefore, and shall set forth the relief or order sought. The requirement of writing is fulfilled if the motion is stated in a written notice of the hearing of the motion.

(2) To expedite its business, the court may make provision by rule or order for the submission and determination of motions without oral hearing upon brief written statements of reasons in support and opposition.

(3) The rules applicable to captions, signing, and other matters of form of pleading apply to all motions and other papers provided for by these rules.

(4) All motions shall be signed in accordance with Rule 11.

(C) **Demurrers abolished.** Demurrers shall not be used.

History: Amended, eff 7-1-84.

NOTES TO DECISIONS
Analysis

Default judgment

Trial court abused its discretion in granting judgment to an employee in her action under RC § 4123.512(D), as the employer's counsel's failure to appear at a pretrial conference could not have resulted in a default judgment under Ohio R. Civ. P. 7(A) and 55(A) because the employee did not offer evidence in an ex parte hearing to support her claims and further, the employer had filed an answer; the judgment could not have been based on a dismissal under Ohio R. Civ. P. 41(B) as a sanction, as the employer was never notified that such a sanction could be imposed if it failed to appear and further, counsel's 15-minute delay due to long elevator lines did not warrant such a harsh sanction in the circumstances. Baur v. Co-Ax Tech., — Ohio App. 3d —, 2007 Ohio 3910, — N.E. 2d —, 2007 Ohio App. LEXIS 3565 (Aug. 2, 2007).

Trial court erred in granting an employer's oral request for a default judgment, made on the day of the trial, as an employee's counsel was not afforded sufficient time to show good cause as to his failure to answer a counterclaim within 28 days of the service of the counterclaim and why leave to plead was appropriate. Absent seven days' written notice, the employee's ability to show cause under Ohio R. Civ. P. 55(A) was emasculated. Shikner v. Solutions, — Ohio App. 3d —, 2006 Ohio 127, — N.E. 2d —, 2006 Ohio App. LEXIS 104 (Jan. 13, 2006).

Hearings

Although a trial court could have held a hearing on a legal guardian's motions regarding jurisdiction over custody and visitation issues involving a child, the court acted properly under Ohio R. Civ. P. 7(B)(2) where it ruled on motions without an oral hearing upon submission of briefs in support of and in opposition to the motions. In re D.H., — Ohio App. 3d —, 2007 Ohio 4069, — N.E. 2d —, 2007 Ohio App. LEXIS 3683 (Aug. 9, 2007).

Motion

When, in a real estate contract dispute, the trial court found a contract to be enforceable and found the seller's brokers were entitled to a commission on the resulting sale, it was not error to deny pre-judgment interest, even though an award of pre-judgment interest in a contract case was not discretionary, because the brokers waived pre-judgment interest by failing to file a written motion for it, as required by Ohio R. Civ. P. 7. Peirce v. J.C. Meyer Co., — Ohio App. 3d —, 2006 Ohio 4065, — N.E. 2d —, 2006 Ohio App. LEXIS 4019 (Aug. 8, 2006).

Motion for intervention

Property owners met the requirements for intervention as of right under Ohio R. Civ. P. 24(A) in a quiet title and adverse possession action, as they filed a timely motion to intervene under Rule 24(C) and they indicated that they would file an adverse possession claim; although no pleading under Ohio R. Civ. P. 7(A) was included with their motion, the basis of their claim was known to the trial court, they did not have to show lack of access to their property for purposes of the claim, and no objection to the lack of pleading was filed. Korenko v. Kelleys Island Park Dev. Co., — Ohio App. 3d —, 2007 Ohio 2145, — N.E. 2d —, 2007 Ohio App. LEXIS 2004 (May 4, 2007).

Motion for relief from judgment

Where a car lessee who was involved in a dispute with a car dealership and a lender on her car lease filed a motion, seeking relief from the trial court's judgment which dismissed her third-party complaint for failure to prosecute, and she asserted grounds under Ohio R. Civ. P. 60(B)(1) and (3), the trial court erred in granting the relief from judgment on other grounds under Rule 60(B)(5), as such amounted to a sua sponte action by the trial court and it lacked that authority. Such a ruling did not afford the dealership due process under Ohio Const. art. I, § 16, in that it did not provide it with an ample opportunity to respond to the unasserted grounds for relief, and it violated the requirement of Ohio R. Civ. P. 7(B)(1) of setting out the grounds for a motion with particularity. First Merit Bank v. Crouse, — Ohio App. 3d —, 2007 Ohio 2440, — N.E. 2d —, 2007 Ohio App. LEXIS 2278 (May 21, 2007).

Prejudice

Employee's failure to contest damages after a default judgment was entered against him on a counterclaim was irrelevant to the issue of the lack of proper notice of a motion for default judgment as the default judgment effectively admitted the averments of the counterclaim and precluded the employee from asserting any affirmative defense that would have been considered an avoidance of the counterclaim. The prejudice resulting from the lack of notice lies in the admission of the counterclaim averments and preclusion of an affirmative defense, not the issue of damages. Shikner v. Solutions, — Ohio App. 3d —, 2006 Ohio 127, — N.E. 2d —, 2006 Ohio App. LEXIS 104 (Jan. 13, 2006).

Trial court's disciplinary rule improper

Order that a trial court would not consider any future pleadings filed by a bank's lawyers unless they began appearing for "the hearing they have ordered" was, in effect, a "disciplinary rule" as the promulgation of disciplinary rules was within the exclusive jurisdiction of the Supreme Court of Ohio, the trial court exceeded its authority and, thus, abused its discretion when it issued a punitive order. MBNA America Bank v. Bailey, — Ohio App. 3d —, 2006 Ohio 1550, — N.E. 2d —, 2006 Ohio App. LEXIS 1436 (Mar. 31, 2006).

RULE 8.   General rules of pleading

(A) **Claims for relief.** A pleading that sets forth a claim for relief, whether an original claim, counterclaim, cross-claim, or third-party claim, shall contain (1) a short and plain statement of the claim showing that the party is entitled to relief, and (2) a demand for judgment for the relief to which the party claims to be entitled. If the party seeks more than twenty-five thousand dollars, the party shall so state in the pleading but shall not specify in the demand for judgment the amount of recovery sought, unless the claim is based upon an instrument required to be attached pursuant to Civ. R. 10. At any time after the pleading is filed and served, any party from whom monetary recovery is sought may request in writing that the party seeking recovery provide the requesting party a written statement of the amount of recovery sought. Upon motion, the court shall require the party to respond to the request. Relief in the alternative or of several different types may be demanded.

(B) **Defenses; form of denials.** A party shall state in short and plain terms the party's defenses to each claim asserted and shall admit or deny the averments upon which the adverse party relies. If the party is without knowledge or information sufficient to form a belief as to the truth of an averment, the party shall so state and this has the effect of a denial. Denials shall fairly meet the substance of the averments denied. When a pleader intends in good faith to deny only a part or a qualification of an averment, the pleader shall specify so much of it as is true and material and shall deny the remainder. Unless the pleader intends in good faith to controvert all the averments of the preceding pleading, the pleader may make the denials as specific denials or designated averments or paragraphs, or the pleader may generally deny all the averments except the designated averments or paragraphs as the pleader expressly admits; but, when the pleader does intend to controvert all its averments, including averments of the grounds upon which the court's jurisdiction depends, the pleader may do so by general denial subject to the obligations set forth in Civ. R. 11.

(C) **Affirmative defenses.** In pleading to a preceding pleading, a party shall set forth affirmatively accord and satisfaction, arbitration and award, assumption of risk, contributory negligence, discharge in bankruptcy, duress, estoppel, failure of consideration, want of consideration for a negotiable instrument, fraud, illegality, injury by fellow servant, laches, license, payment, release, res judicata, statute of frauds, statute of limitations, waiver, and any other matter constituting an avoidance or affirmative defense. When a party has mistakenly designated a defense as a counterclaim or a counterclaim as a defense, the court, if justice so requires, shall treat the pleading as if there had been a proper designation.

(D) **Effect of failure to deny.** Averments in a pleading to which a responsive pleading is required, other than those as to the amount of damage, are admitted when not denied in the responsive pleading. Averments in a pleading to which no responsive pleading is required or permitted shall be taken as denied or avoided.

(E) **Pleading to be concise and direct; consistency.**

(1) Each averment of a pleading shall be simple, concise, and direct. No technical forms of pleading or motions are required.

(2) A party may set forth two or more statements of a claim or defense alternatively or hypothetically, either in one count or defense or in separate counts or defenses. When two or more statements are made in the alternative and one of them if made independently would be sufficient, the pleading is not made insufficient by the insufficiency of one or more of the alternative statements. A party may also state as many separate claims or defenses as he has regardless of consistency and whether based on legal or equitable grounds. All statements shall be made subject to the obligations set forth in Rule 11.

(F) **Construction of pleadings.** All pleadings shall be so construed as to do substantial justice.

(G) **Pleadings shall not be read or submitted.** Pleadings shall not be read or submitted to the jury, except insofar as a pleading or portion thereof is used in evidence.

(H) **Disclosure of minority or incompetency.** Every pleading or motion made by or on behalf of a minor or an incompetent shall set forth such fact unless the fact of minority or incompetency has been disclosed in a prior pleading or motion in the same action or proceeding.

History: Amended, eff 7-1-94.

NOTES TO DECISIONS

Analysis

Conditions precedent
Damages
Failure to comply
Failure to deny
Federal civil rights claims
Laches
Management theory of insurer's liability to insured
Piercing the corporate veil
Pleading
— Fair notice of action
— Pleading insufficient
Pro se litigants

Conditions precedent
Where the complaint in a foreclosure action did not allege that the lender complied with conditions precedent to enforcement of the note, including notice of default and an opportunity to cure, CivR 8(D) did not require the borrower to specifically deny such compliance. Where a cause of action is contingent upon satisfaction of some condition precedent, CivR 9(C) requires a plaintiff to plead that the condition has been satisfied, and permits the plaintiff to aver generally that any conditions precedent to recovery have been satisfied, rather than requiring the plaintiff to detail specifically how each condition has been satisfied: Nat'l City Mortg. Co. v. Richards, 182 Ohio App. 3d 534, 2009 Ohio 2556, 913 N.E.2d 1007, 2009 Ohio App. LEXIS 2123 (2009).

Damages
Trial court erred in entering judgment for the insurer for $18,567.03 because, in its complaint, the insurer only sought the amount of $9,309.69, incurred by the victim in medical bills. Thus, the insurer was limited at trial to recovering $9,309.69, the amount that it claimed it had paid on behalf of the victim. Qualchoice, Inc. v. Paige-Thompson, — Ohio App. 3d —, 2007 Ohio 1712, — N.E. 2d —, 2007 Ohio App. LEXIS 1568 (Apr. 12, 2007).

Failure to comply
In a legal malpractice action, if the first former client's motion for reconsideration of an involuntary dismissal of the action with prejudice could be considered a motion for relief from judgment under Ohio R. Civ. P. 60(B), it was insufficient to grant the relief requested as the age (90), inter alia, of the first client's counsel could not excuse the first client's failure to file a complaint that complied with Ohio R. Civ. P. 8(A) requirements or to comply with court-ordered deadlines. McGee v. Lynch, — Ohio App. 3d —, 2007 Ohio 3954, — N.E. 2d —, 2007 Ohio App. LEXIS 3619 (Aug. 3, 2007).

First former client's legal malpractice action was properly dismissed with prejudice under Ohio R. Civ. P. 41(B)(1) because despite numerous extensions, the first client failed to file a complaint that complied with Ohio R. Civ. P. 8(A) and failed to comply with several court-ordered deadlines McGee v. Lynch, — Ohio App. 3d —, 2007 Ohio 3954, — N.E. 2d —, 2007 Ohio App. LEXIS 3619 (Aug. 3, 2007).

Failure to deny
In homeowners' claims against mortgage brokers and the brokers' principal for violations of the Mortgage Broker Act, RC § 1322.01 et seq., and civil conspiracy, a trial court improperly denied the homeowners' motion for a default judgment against one broker because the broker did not answer the complaint served on the broker, and, under Ohio R. Civ. P. 8(D), the allegations against the broker should have been construed as admitted. Roark v. Rydell, 174 Ohio App. 3d 186, 2007 Ohio 6873, 881 N.E. 2d 333, 2007 Ohio App. LEXIS 6043 (Dec. 21, 2007).

Federal civil rights claims
Ohio courts consistently held that a complaint alleging an action under 42 U.S.C.S. § 1983 had to meet two requirements: (1) there had to be an allegation that the conduct in question was performed by a person acting under color of state law; and (2) the complaint had to sufficiently allege that

the conduct deprived the plaintiff of a federal right, so a plaintiff who asserted a federal civil rights action under § 1983 usually stated, for instance, that the defendant acted under color of state law and violated the Fourteenth Amendment by depriving plaintiff of property without due process. Maine v. Boardman Police Dep't, — Ohio App. 3d —, 2006 Ohio 4954, — N.E. 2d —, 2006 Ohio App. LEXIS 4891 (Sept. 20, 2006).

Laches

Although property owners did not waive their affirmative defense of laches pursuant to Ohio R. Civ. P. 8(C) against a builder for its failure to have submitted a bill to them for construction of a patio and porch on the owners' residence, they did not establish laches for purposes of barring the builder's claim due to the owners' alleged lack of payment, as they failed to establish they were materially prejudiced by the delay in the billing procedure. W. R. Martin, Inc. v. Zukowski, — Ohio App. 3d —, 2006 Ohio 6866, — N.E. 2d —, 2006 Ohio App. LEXIS 6785 (Dec. 22, 2006).

Management theory of insurer's liability to insured

Insured did not sufficiently plead a claim of the liability of certain companies of which the issuer of the insured's policy was a subsidiary, under a management theory of liability, because (1) as to one company, the insured only alleged that this company generally decided if a medical procedure was investigational, but the insured did not allege that this company decided specific coverage, and (2) as to another company, the insured only alleged that this company controlled the company's subsidiaries to the point that those subsidiaries did not have a separate mind, will or existence, alleging a claim for piercing the corporate veil, rather than a management theory of liability. Dombroski v. WellPoint, Inc., 173 Ohio App. 3d 508, 2007 Ohio 5054, 879 N.E.2d 225, 2007 Ohio App. LEXIS 4440 (2007).

Piercing the corporate veil

Insured sufficiently pled a claim for piercing the corporate veil against certain companies of which the issuer of the insured's policy was a subsidiary because the insured alleged that (1) the issuer of the insured's policy had no separate mind, will or existence due to the control exercised by the parent companies, (2) the parent companies committed the tort of an insurer's duty to act in good faith by claiming the parents' control was exercised so as to violate that duty, and (3) the insured suffered various injuries due to the "control and wrong" of the parent companies through their subsidiaries due to the corporate medical policy under which the insured's claim was denied. Dombroski v. WellPoint, Inc., 173 Ohio App. 3d 508, 2007 Ohio 5054, 879 N.E.2d 225, 2007 Ohio App. LEXIS 4440 (2007).

Party seeking to pierce the corporate veil is not required to relate that specific intention in the complaint in order to proceed under the doctrine of piercing the corporate veil: Dombroski v. WellPoint, Inc., 173 Ohio App. 3d 508, 2007 Ohio 5054, 879 N.E.2d 225, 2007 Ohio App. LEXIS 4440 (2007).

Pleading

When litigants sued the Ohio Attorney General and various courts and judicial officers, alleging violations of their civil, statutory, and constitutional rights, the complaint was properly dismissed, under Ohio R. Civ. P. 12(B)(6) because the factual basis for the litigants' claims could not be discerned, so they did not comply with the pleading requirements of Ohio R. Civ. P. 8(A), and, to the extent they asserted claims against state courts for acts performed within the scope of the duties of judicial officers, the courts and the officers were absolutely immune. Phelps v. Office of the AG, — Ohio App. 3d —, 2007 Ohio 14, — N.E. 2d —, 2007 Ohio App. LEXIS 3 (Jan. 4, 2007).

Trial court properly granted summary judgment to a city in an action by home owners, alleging that the city had undertaken to manage a storm water system on an adjacent property that had been developed into a subdivision in a negligent manner, as there was nothing in the owners' complaint, as required by Ohio R. Civ. P. 8(A), which adequately alleged that the city had acted negligently in that regard. Sexton v. City of Mason, — Ohio App. 3d —, 2007 Ohio 38, — N.E. 2d —, 2007 Ohio App. LEXIS 30 (Jan. 8, 2007).

As a debtor failed to assert a claim that a lender had violated RC ch. 1309 in her counterclaim, she did not meet the requirements of Ohio R. Civ. P. 8(A) and her claim on appeal was not reviewable. Even if it was reviewed, it lacked merit, as there was sufficient evidence that the lender's agent did not breach the peace in violation of RC § 1309.609 when he repossessed the debtor's vehicle. Kemba Fin. Credit Union v. Fish, — Ohio App. 3d —, 2007 Ohio 43, — N.E. 2d —, 2007 Ohio App. LEXIS 33 (Jan. 9, 2007).

Trial court's grant of a city's motion under Ohio R. Civ. P. 12(B)(6) to dismiss a complaint by a union and laid-off, full-time employees, seeking mandamus relief, injunctive relief, and contempt arising from the city's alleged violation of an arbitration award, was error, as the union and employees established that the city was required to engage in an affirmative act under the award by laying off employees in conformance with the parties' collective bargaining agreement, and that it failed to take such action; the requirements for notice-pleading under Ohio R. Civ. P. 8(A)(1) were met, as mandamus was sufficiently pled under RC § 2731.04, contempt by violation of the order was sufficiently pled under RC § 2705.02(A), and a request for injunctive relief was also properly asserted based on the elements thereof under Ohio R. Civ. P. 65. State ex rel. Malloy v. City of Girard, — Ohio App. 3d —, 2007 Ohio 338, — N.E. 2d —, 2007 Ohio App. LEXIS 304 (Jan. 26, 2007).

Where a former prosecutor's complaint covered 70 pages and contained 19 causes of action against a city and some of its employees, the trial court did not abuse its discretion in granting the city's motion to strike the complaint, as it did not constitute a short and plain statement of the prosecutor's claims and his entitlement to relief, and it contained numerous redundancies and irrelevant allegations, such that striking the complaint and ordering the prosecutor to file an amended complaint was proper under Ohio R. Civ. P. 8(A), (E)(1), and 12(F). Scaccia v. Lemmie, — Ohio App. 3d —, 2007 Ohio 1055, — N.E. 2d —, 2007 Ohio App. LEXIS 991 (Mar. 9, 2007).

Pursuant to the pleading requirements under Ohio R. Civ. P. 8(A), where former employees failed to allege violations of the Ohio Minimum Fair Wage Standards Act, RC ch. 4111, they were not entitled to an award of attorney fees pursuant to RC § 4111.10(A). A trial court's grant of summary judgment in favor of the former employer in the employees' breach of contract claims on the issue of attorney fees was proper. Meisler v. Toledo Sleep Disorders Center, Ltd., — Ohio App. 3d —, 2007 Ohio 1325, — N.E. 2d —, 2007 Ohio App. LEXIS 1234 (Mar. 23, 2007).

Pursuant to the pleading requirements under Ohio R. Civ. P. 8(A), where former employees failed to allege violations of the Ohio Minimum Fair Wage Standards Act, RC ch. 4111, they were not entitled to an award of attorney fees pursuant to RC § 4111.10(A). A trial court's grant of summary judgment in favor of the former employer in the employees' breach of contract claims on the issue of attorney fees was proper. Meisler v. Toledo Sleep Disorders Center, Ltd., — Ohio App. 3d —, 2007 Ohio 1325, — N.E. 2d —, 2007 Ohio App. LEXIS 1234 (Mar. 23, 2007).

In litigation between trustees, in which the parties settled their dispute and agreed to the appointment of a special master to promulgate rules for the future administration of the trust and to determine the validity and effect of existing rules, the failure of a beneficiary and her father, who was a general trustee, to raise the father's removal or reinstatement as a trustee in their complaint did not bar the master from recommending his reinstatement because (1) the master and the trial court had the authority to consider the issue under the authority the parties' agreed to grant them to promulgate rules and decide the validity of existing ones, and (2) the issue fell within the trial court's continuing jurisdiction to further administer the trust. Conway v. Conway, — Ohio App. 3d —, 2007 Ohio 1377, — N.E. 2d —, 2007 Ohio App. LEXIS 1247 (Mar. 23, 2007).

In litigation between trustees, in which the parties settled their dispute and agreed to the appointment of a special master to promulgate rules for the future administration of the trust and to determine the validity and effect of existing rules, the failure of a beneficiary and her father, who was a general trustee, to raise the father's removal or reinstatement as a trustee in their complaint did not bar the master from recommending his reinstatement because (1) the master and the trial court had the authority to consider the issue under the authority the parties' agreed to grant them to promulgate rules and decide the validity of existing ones, and (2) the issue fell within the trial court's continuing jurisdiction to further administer the trust. Conway v. Conway, — Ohio App. 3d —, 2007 Ohio 1377, — N.E. 2d —, 2007 Ohio App. LEXIS 1247 (Mar. 23, 2007).

Sister of a sole beneficiary of their aunt's estate failed to sufficiently allege facts to support a constructive trust in her complaint, pursuant to Ohio R. Civ. P. 8(A), as she failed to properly allege that a confidential relationship existed between the parties and she did not allege that the sole beneficiary did anything wrong that would have justified the imposition of the trust. Varee v. Holzinger, — Ohio App. 3d —, 2007 Ohio 1924, — N.E. 2d —, 2007 Ohio App. LEXIS 1733 (Apr. 20, 2007).

Trial court's grant of a judgment on the pleadings pursuant to Ohio R. Civ. P. 12(C) to a sole beneficiary under her aunt's will in an action by the beneficiary's sister, alleging a breach of contract claim, was proper, as the allegations of the complaint pursuant to Ohio R. Civ. P. 8(A) failed to show consideration for the alleged promise, which was a material element of any enforceable contract. As any contract therein could have potentially been performed within one year, the Statute of Frauds, RC § 1335.05, was not a bar to enforcement of a contract in the circumstances. Varee v. Holzinger, — Ohio App. 3d —, 2007 Ohio 1924, — N.E. 2d —, 2007 Ohio App. LEXIS 1733 (Apr. 20, 2007).

When homeowners said a developer negligently misrepresented to them that a home they wanted to build would fit on two lots he proposed to sell them, it was not error for the trial court to decline to apply a negligent misrepresentation claim to the second of the two lots because the homeowners' complaint did not raise such a claim, even under a liberal interpretation of the complaint, pursuant to Ohio R. Civ. P. 8(F) and 1(B), nor did the parties impliedly consent to try such a claim, under Ohio R. Civ. P. 15(B). Brothers v. Morrone-O'Keefe Dev. Co., — Ohio App. 3d —, 2007 Ohio 1942, — N.E. 2d —, 2007 Ohio App. LEXIS 1762 (Apr. 24, 2007).

Trial court erred in granting an employer's motion to dismiss an employee's complaint for failure to state a claim pursuant to Ohio R. Civ. P. 12(B)(6), as the allegations in the complaint were sufficient under Ohio R. Civ. P. 8 to apprise the employer and its agent of the basis for the causes of action of breach of contract and promissory estoppel, arising from the employer's withdrawal of its written offer of employment after the employee had quit her job in reliance thereon; her attachment of the written contract pursuant to Ohio R. Civ. P. 10(C) was deemed a part of the pleading, and as the terms thereof did not preclude relief under the claims, as she asserted exceptions to the at-will employment doctrine, dis-

missal was error. Mesek v. Roberts Communs., Inc., — Ohio App. 3d —, 2006 Ohio 3339, — N.E. 2d —, 2006 Ohio App. LEXIS 3268 (June 30, 2006).

Although an ambulance patron's complaint was sufficient to provide the ambulance company with notice of the circumstances of a false representation in its billing in order that it could prepare a defense, but the complaint did not provide any indication of what was obtained or given as a consequence of the alleged fraud, the required elements necessary to plead a claim of fraud with sufficient particularity pursuant to Ohio R. Civ. P. 8 and 9(B) were not satisfied. The patron failed to show justifiable reliance on the bill given to her for services provided by the company, as she refused to pay the bill on the basis that it was unreasonable, and accordingly, she was not entitled to compensatory and punitive damages on the fraud claim. Hailey v. Medcorp, Inc., — Ohio App. 3d —, 2006 Ohio 4804, — N.E. 2d —, 2006 Ohio App. LEXIS 4706 (Sept. 15, 2006).

When a citizen claimed that a police officer wrongfully confiscated the citizen's boat, and the citizen sought damages from the officer and the police department, the citizen could not avoid the immunity to which the officer and department were entitled, under RC § 2744.02(A)(1), by raising, on appeal, 42 U.S.C.S. § 1983, thereby attempting to avoid immunity under RC § 2744.09, because his complaint did not mention 42 U.S.C.S. § 1983, nor the constitution, nor the deprivation of a federal right, even generally, so it did not comply with the requirements of notice pleading to give the opposing parties notice that such a claim was asserted against them, as the complaint only gave notice of the assertion of a state tort claim. Maine v. Boardman Police Dep't, — Ohio App. 3d —, 2006 Ohio 4954, — N.E. 2d —, 2006 Ohio App. LEXIS 4891 (Sept. 20, 2006).

Where an employee sufficiently pleaded the elements of his claims for race and disability discrimination under RC §§ 4112.02(A) and 4112.99, he met the pleading requirements of Ohio R. Civ. P. 8(A) and the trial court erred in granting the employer's motion to dismiss the complaint for failure to state a claim. The "prima facie case" requirement was an evidentiary standard for purposes of RC § 4112.02(A) and not a pleading standard. Jackson v. Int'l Fiber, 169 Ohio App. 3d 395, 2006 Ohio 5799, 863 N.E.2d 189, 2006 Ohio App. LEXIS 5750 (2006).

— **Fair notice of action**

When homeowners sued a power company for recission of the homeowners' contract granting the company an easement over the homeowners' property, the homeowners sufficiently alleged, under Ohio R. Civ. P. 8(A), the mutual mistake of the homeowners and the company when the contract was entered into because the homeowners' complaint alleged the existence of a contract, that the contract was entered into to provide electric power to the homeowners' neighbor, that the company could not provide power to that neighbor, and that the blame for that mistake was with the company, rather than the homeowners, because the company later found the company could not provide power to the neighbor. Thomas v. Ohio Power Co., — Ohio App. 3d —, 2007 Ohio 5350, — N.E. 2d —, 2007 Ohio App. LEXIS 4715 (Sept. 27, 2007).

— **Pleading insufficient**

Former employee's complaint was properly dismissed under Ohio R. Civ. P. 12(B)(6) for failure to state a claim because the complaint did not place the employer on notice of a civil rights claim showing entitlement to relief as required by Ohio R. Civ. P. 8(A). The complaint only placed the employer on notice that there was a wrongful discharge in violation of public policy claim against it; because the employee was subject to a collective bargaining agreement, he was not an at-will employee and thus, could not file an action for wrongful discharge in violation of public policy. Williams v. W.

Reserve Transit Auth., — Ohio App. 3d —, 2007 Ohio 4747, — N.E. 2d —, 2007 Ohio App. LEXIS 4274 (Sept. 14, 2007).

Pro se litigants

When the factual basis for claims asserted by pro se litigants alleging violations of their civil, statutory, and constitutional rights could not be discerned, the fact that they were not represented did not protect them from dismissal of their complaint, under Ohio R. Civ. P. 12(B)(6), for failing to comply with the pleading requirements of Ohio R. Civ. P. 8(A). Phelps v. Office of the AG, — Ohio App. 3d —, 2007 Ohio 14, — N.E. 2d —, 2007 Ohio App. LEXIS 3 (Jan. 4, 2007).

RULE 9.   Pleading special matters

(A) **Capacity.** It is not necessary to aver the capacity of a party to sue or be sued or the authority of a party to sue or be sued in a representative capacity or the legal existence of an organized association of persons that is made a party. When a party desires to raise an issue as to the legal existence of any party or the capacity of any party to sue or be sued or the authority of a party to sue or be sued in a representative capacity, he shall do so by specific negative averment, which shall include such supporting particulars as are peculiarly within the pleader's knowledge.

(B) **Fraud, mistake, condition of the mind.** In all averments of fraud or mistake, the circumstances constituting fraud or mistake shall be stated with particularity. Malice, intent, knowledge, and other condition of mind of a person may be averred generally.

(C) **Conditions precedent.** In pleading the performance or occurrence of conditions precedent, it is sufficient to aver generally that all conditions precedent have been performed or have occurred. A denial of performance or occurrence shall be made specifically and with particularity.

(D) **Official document or act.** In pleading an official document or official act it is sufficient to aver that the document was issued or the act done in compliance with law.

(E) **Judgment.** In pleading a judgment or decision of a court of this state or a foreign court, judicial or quasi-judicial tribunal, or of a board or officer, it is sufficient to aver the judgment or decision without setting forth matter showing jurisdiction to render it.

(F) **Time and place.** For the purpose of testing the sufficiency of a pleading, averments of time and place are material and shall be considered like all other averments of material matter.

(G) **Special damage.** When items of special damage are claimed, they shall be specifically stated.

NOTES TO DECISIONS

ANALYSIS

Capacity
Condition precedent
Mistake
Special damages

Capacity

When a daughter sued an attorney for malpractice both in the daughter's capacity as executrix of the daughter's father's decedent's estate and as trustee of the beneficiary of the father's will, and the attorney's answer claimed the daughter was not the real party in interest, under Ohio R. Civ. P. 17(A),

the attorney waived the affirmative defense of lack of capacity to sue, under Ohio R. Civ. P. 9(A) because the affirmative defense of real party in interest did not also raise the affirmative defense of lack of capacity to sue, and lack of capacity required a specific negative averment, which the attorney did not make. Wanamaker v. Davis, — Ohio App. 3d —, 2007 Ohio 4340, — N.E. 2d —, 2007 Ohio App. LEXIS 3878 (Aug. 24, 2007).

Ohio R. Civ. P. 9(A) places the pleading burden upon a defendant to deny, by specific negative averment or with particularity, a plaintiff's capacity to sue, and the defense of lack of capacity to sue is typically waived when an answer only contains a general denial and when the defense is not raised by specific negative averment. Wanamaker v. Davis, — Ohio App. 3d —, 2007 Ohio 4340, — N.E. 2d —, 2007 Ohio App. LEXIS 3878 (Aug. 24, 2007).

When a widow sued an air conditioner installer for wrongful death and negligent infliction of emotional distress, and she was allowed to amend her complaint after judgment to substitute the installer personally for his defunct corporation, this was not error because the installer did not raise a defense challenging the capacity of his corporation to be sued by a specific negative averment. Estate of Heintzelman v. Air Experts, Inc., — Ohio App. 3d —, 2006 Ohio 4832, — N.E. 2d —, 2006 Ohio App. LEXIS 4741 (Sept. 14, 2006).

Condition precedent

Where the complaint in a foreclosure action did not allege that the lender complied with conditions precedent to enforcement of the note, including notice of default and an opportunity to cure, CivR 8(D) did not require the borrower to specifically deny such compliance. Where a cause of action is contingent upon satisfaction of some condition precedent, CivR 9(C) requires a plaintiff to plead that the condition has been satisfied, and permits the plaintiff to aver generally that any conditions precedent to recovery have been satisfied, rather than requiring the plaintiff to detail specifically how each condition has been satisfied: Nat'l City Mortg. Co. v. Richards, 182 Ohio App. 3d 534, 2009 Ohio 2556, 913 N.E.2d 1007, 2009 Ohio App. LEXIS 2123 (2009).

Where prior notice of default and/or acceleration was required by a provision in a note or mortgage instrument as a condition to seeking foreclosure, the provision of notice was a condition precedent subject to the specific pleading requirements of Ohio R. Civ. P. 9(C). First Fin. Bank v. Doellman, — Ohio App. 3d —, 2007 Ohio 222, — N.E. 2d —, 2007 Ohio App. LEXIS 200 (Jan. 22, 2007).

In a foreclosure suit, mortgagors did not plead that they did not receive a required notice of their default with the specificity required by Ohio R. Civ. P. 9(C), but, because the bank seeking foreclosure did not allege, even generally, that it complied with conditions precedent to recovery, such as the required notice, the mortgagors did not have to plead lack of notice with specificity, and their allegation that the bank did not state a claim upon which relief could be granted raised the issue sufficiently to allow them to assert it in their response to the bank's summary judgment motion. First Fin. Bank v. Doellman, — Ohio App. 3d —, 2007 Ohio 222, — N.E. 2d —, 2007 Ohio App. LEXIS 200 (Jan. 22, 2007).

Where a cause of action was contingent upon the satisfaction of some condition precedent, Ohio R. Civ. P. 9(C) required a plaintiff to plead that the condition was satisfied, and permitted the plaintiff to aver generally that any conditions precedent to recovery were satisfied, rather than requiring the plaintiff to detail specifically how each condition precedent was satisfied, but, in contrast to the liberal pleading standard for a party alleging the satisfaction of conditions precedent, a party denying the performance or occurrence of a condition precedent had to do so specifically and with particularity, under Rule 9(C), so a general denial of performance of conditions precedent was not sufficient to place performance of a condition precedent in issue, and the effect of a failure to deny conditions precedent in the manner provided by Rule 9(C) was that they were deemed admitted. First Fin. Bank v. Doellman, — Ohio App. 3d —, 2007 Ohio 222, — N.E. 2d —, 2007 Ohio App. LEXIS 200 (Jan. 22, 2007).

When, in a foreclosure, a mortgagor alleged that the mortgagor was not given notice of the mortgagee's acceleration of the mortgage, the mortgagor did not have to specifically plead this defense, under Ohio R. Civ. P. 9(C), because the mortgagee did not plead, even generally, that all conditions precedent were satisfied, and the mortgagor's general reservation in the mortgagor's answer was sufficient to preserve the matter. Wash. Mut. Bank v. Cowles, — Ohio App. 3d —, 2007 Ohio 4771, — N.E. 2d —, 2007 Ohio App. LEXIS 4259 (Sept. 14, 2007).

When, in a foreclosure, a mortgagor alleged that the mortgagor was not given notice of the mortgagee's acceleration of the mortgage, while the mortgagor did not have to specifically plead this defense, under Ohio R. Civ. P. 9(C), the mortgagor could not rely on the defense because the defense was raised in a motion to vacate an adverse summary judgment which the mortgagor did not allow the trial court to rule on before the mortgagor appealed the summary judgment, and the appellate court would not consider an issue the trial court did not rule on. Wash. Mut. Bank v. Cowles, — Ohio App. 3d —, 2007 Ohio 4771, — N.E. 2d —, 2007 Ohio App. LEXIS 4259 (Sept. 14, 2007).

When a plaintiff fails to allege, even generally, the occurrence of conditions precedent in a foreclosure action, a defendant need not comply with the particularity requirement of Ohio R. Civ. P. 9(C) by pleading the conditions' nonoccurrence, but, rather, the defense of failure to state a claim on which relief may be granted will suffice. Wash. Mut. Bank v. Cowles, — Ohio App. 3d —, 2007 Ohio 4771, — N.E. 2d —, 2007 Ohio App. LEXIS 4259 (Sept. 14, 2007).

Mistake

Ohio R. Civ. P. 9(B), requiring, inter alia, that mistake be pled with particularity, should not be strictly applied, even where pleadings are vague, as long as a defendant has notice of the matters about which the plaintiff complains, and, fundamentally, the general principle governing pleadings remains that pleadings must give fair notice of the nature of the action. Thomas v. Ohio Power Co., — Ohio App. 3d —, 2007 Ohio 5350, — N.E. 2d —, 2007 Ohio App. LEXIS 4715 (Sept. 27, 2007).

When homeowners sued a power company for recission of the homeowners' contract granting the company an easement over the homeowners' property, the homeowners sufficiently alleged the mutual mistake of the homeowners and the company by alleging the existence of a contract, that the contract was entered into to provide electric power to the homeowners' neighbor, that the company could not provide power to that neighbor, and that the blame for that mistake was with the company, rather than the homeowners, because the company later found the company could not provide power to the neighbor, and the requirement of Ohio R. Civ. P. 9(B) to plead mistake with particularity was satisfied when the contract was attached and incorporated into the complaint, pursuant to Ohio R. Civ. P. 10(C). Thomas v. Ohio Power Co., — Ohio App. 3d —, 2007 Ohio 5350, — N.E. 2d —, 2007 Ohio App. LEXIS 4715 (Sept. 27, 2007).

When a buyer and seller orally agreed to the sale of certain personalty for a specified price, and the buyer claimed the contract was unenforceable due to mutual mistake, the buyer did not sufficiently plead this affirmative defense, under Ohio R. Civ. P. 8(C) or 9(B), so it was waived. Fox v. Craftsmen Home Improvement Inc., — Ohio App. 3d —, 2006 Ohio 1427, — N.E. 2d —, 2006 Ohio App. LEXIS 1321 (Mar. 24, 2006).

Special damages

Appellant did not state a claim for defamation per quod as he did not adequately plead special damages, in compliance with Ohio R. Civ. P. 9(G). Whiteside v. Williams, — Ohio App. 3d —, 2007 Ohio 1100, — N.E. 2d —, 2007 Ohio App. LEXIS 1017 (Mar. 12, 2007).

Appellant did not state a claim for defamation per quod as he did not adequately plead special damages, in compliance with Ohio R. Civ. P. 9(G). Whiteside v. Williams, — Ohio App. 3d —, 2007 Ohio 1100, — N.E. 2d —, 2007 Ohio App. LEXIS 1017 (Mar. 12, 2007).

RULE 10. Form of pleadings

(A) **Caption; names of parties.** Every pleading shall contain a caption setting forth the name of the court, the title of the action, the case number, and a designation as in Rule 7(A). In the complaint the title of the action shall include the names and addresses of all the parties, but in other pleadings it is sufficient to state the name of the first party on each side with an appropriate indication of other parties.

(B) **Paragraphs; separate statements.** All averments of claim or defense shall be made in numbered paragraphs, the contents of each of which shall be limited as far as practicable to a statement of a single set of circumstances; and a paragraph may be referred to by number in all succeeding pleadings. Each claim founded upon a separate transaction or occurrence and each defense other than denials shall be stated in a separate count or defense whenever a separation facilitates the clear presentation of the matters set forth.

(C) **Adoption by reference; exhibits.** Statements in a pleading may be adopted by reference in a different part of the same pleading or in another pleading or in any motion. A copy of any written instrument attached to a pleading is a part of the pleading for all purposes.

(D) **Attachments to pleadings.**

(1) *Account or written instrument.* When any claim or defense is founded on an account or other written instrument, a copy of the account or written instrument must be attached to the pleading. If the account or written instrument is not attached, the reason for the omission must be stated in the pleading.

(2) *Affidavit of merit; medical liability claim.*

(a) Except as provided in division (D)(2)(b) of this rule, a complaint that contains a medical claim, dental claim, optometric claim, or chiropractic claim, as defined in section 2305.113 of the Revised Code, shall include one or more affidavits of merit relative to each defendant named in the complaint for whom expert testimony is necessary to establish liability. Affidavits of merit shall be provided by an expert witness pursuant to Rules 601(D) and 702 of the Ohio Rules of Evidence. Affidavits of merit shall include all of the following:

(i) A statement that the affiant has reviewed all medical records reasonably available to the plaintiff concerning the allegations contained in the complaint;

(ii) A statement that the affiant is familiar with the applicable standard of care;

(iii) The opinion of the affiant that the standard of care was breached by one or more of the defendants to the action and that the breach caused injury to the plaintiff.

(b) The plaintiff may file a motion to extend the period of time to file an affidavit of merit. The motion shall be filed by the plaintiff with the complaint. For good cause shown and in accordance with division (c) of this rule, the court shall grant the plaintiff a reasonable period of time to file an affidavit of merit, not to exceed ninety days, except the time may be extended beyond ninety days if the court determines that a defendant or non-party has failed to cooperate with discovery or that other circumstances warrant extension.

(c) In determining whether good cause exists to extend the period of time to file an affidavit of merit, the court shall consider the following:

(i) A description of any information necessary in order to obtain an affidavit of merit;

(ii) Whether the information is in the possession or control of a defendant or third party;

(iii) The scope and type of discovery necessary to obtain the information;

(iv) What efforts, if any, were taken to obtain the information;

(v) Any other facts or circumstances relevant to the ability of the plaintiff to obtain an affidavit of merit.

(d) An affidavit of merit is required to establish the adequacy of the complaint and shall not otherwise be admissible as evidence or used for purposes of impeachment. Any dismissal for the failure to comply with this rule shall operate as a failure otherwise than on the merits.

(e) If an affidavit of merit as required by this rule has been filed as to any defendant along with the complaint or amended complaint in which claims are first asserted against that defendant, and the affidavit of merit is determined by the court to be defective pursuant to the provisions of division (D)(2)(a) of this rule, the court shall grant the plaintiff a reasonable time, not to exceed sixty days, to file an affidavit of merit intended to cure the defect.

(E) **Size of paper filed.** All pleadings, motions, briefs, and other papers filed with the clerk, including those filed by electronic means, shall be on paper not exceeding 8 ½ x 11 inches in size without backing or cover.

History: Amended, eff 7-1-85; 7-1-91; 7-1-05; 7-1-07.

NOTES TO DECISIONS

ANALYSIS

Action on account
Addresses of parties
Affidavit of merit
—— Failure to file
Attachments
Caption
Contract
Medical malpractice
Parties
Unnamed parties
Written instruments

Action on account

Trial court did not err in concluding that the parties had an ongoing account relationship because, in its answer to the complaint, the corporation admitted that the supply company provided parts to the corporation pursuant to an ongoing account and that the corporation thereafter supplied the parts to two other companies and then collected on its own account with those companies. The supply company's complaint was limited to an action on account, pursuant to Ohio R. Civ. P. 10(D), and the trial court properly treated it as such. FCMP, Inc. v. Alegre, Inc., — Ohio App. 3d —, 2007 Ohio 132, — N.E. 2d —, 2007 Ohio App. LEXIS 123 (Jan. 12, 2007).

When a printer sued newspapers on a past due account and the newspapers moved to dismiss, under Ohio R. Civ. P. 41(B)(2), because the printer did not attach a statement of the account to the printer's complaint, as required by Ohio R. Civ. P. 10(D), it was not an abuse of discretion to deny the newspapers' motion because the newspapers had not moved for a definitive statement, under Ohio R. Civ. P. 12(E), before seeking dismissal. Marysville v. Del. Gazette Co., — Ohio App. 3d —, 2007 Ohio 4365, — N.E. 2d —, 2007 Ohio App. LEXIS 3943 (Aug. 27, 2007).

Addresses of parties

Court dismissed an inmate's mandamus action pursuant to RC § 2731.04, wherein he sought to compel a judge to rule on motions to correct sentence in underlying criminal matters, as the criminal motions had not yet been pending for 120 days and accordingly, there was no unreasonable delay under Ohio Superintendence Ct. R. 40(A)(3). There was no procedural compliance by the inmate with the certified statement requirement of RC § 2969.25(C), the inclusion of party addresses as required by Ohio R. Civ. P. 10(A), and the specifications of the claim pursuant to Ohio Eighth Dist. Ct. App. R. 45, and lastly, the request lacked substantive merit because the sentences imposed were proper under RC § 2929.14(E)(1)(a). State ex rel. Smith v. Court of Common Pleas, — Ohio App. 3d —, 2007 Ohio 89, — N.E. 2d —, 2007 Ohio App. LEXIS 83 (Jan. 10, 2007).

Defendant's habeas corpus petition was denied where he failed to have it verified pursuant to RC § 2725.04, he did not include the supporting affidavits as required by RC § 2969.25(A) and Ohio Eighth Dist. Ct. App. R. 45(B)(1)(a), and he did not include the address of the parties in the caption of the petition pursuant to Ohio R. Civ. P. 10(A). Although the affidavit of indigency included a list of civil filings during the prior five years as well as a sheet identified as his trust acocunt with the sheriff's office, they were not notarized or certified. Griffin v. McFaul, — Ohio App. 3d —, 2007 Ohio 2125, — N.E. 2d —, 2007 Ohio App. LEXIS 1980 (May 2, 2007).

Several procedural defects in an inmate's mandamus complaint, seeking an order requiring a trial court judge to resentence him in his criminal matter, supported dismissal of the action, including that the caption was wrong and did not include the inmate's address pursuant to RC § 2731.04 and Ohio R. Civ. P. 10(A), and that the inmate had failed to include the required documentation of his prison account balance pursuant to RC § 2969.25(C). As the judge had attached a copy of the resentencing order which indicated that the matter was moot, the matter warranted dismissal on substantive grounds as well. Walker v. Russo, — Ohio App. 3d —, 2007 Ohio 2912, — N.E. 2d —, 2007 Ohio App. LEXIS 2694 (June 12, 2007).

Mandamus complaint was sua sponte dismissed by a court where it was not pled with sufficient specificity to allow the court to review the request for the writ of mandamus on the merits, as it was unclear what the status of the underlying case was and what exact relief was requested. The complaint was procedurally defective where it was improperly captioned pursuant to RC § 2731.04, the addresses of the parties were not included as required by Ohio R. Civ. P. 10(A), and the affidavit that specified the details of the claim was not included as required by Ohio Eighth Dist. Ct. App. R. 45(B)(1)(a). Sultaana v. Giant Eagle, — Ohio App. 3d —, 2007 Ohio 3769, — N.E. 2d —, 2007 Ohio App. LEXIS 3444 (July 24, 2007).

Relator's petition for a writ of mandamus pursuant to RC § 2731.04 required dismissal due to procedural defects, as he failed to file the necessary affidavit pursuant to RC § 2969.25 and Ohio Eighth Dist. Ct. App. R. 45(B)(1)(a), his purported affidavit of indigency was not notarized, and he did not include the addresses of the parties in the caption of the matter pursuant to Ohio R. Civ. P. 10(A). Jarrett v. Cuyahoga County Common Pleas Court, — Ohio App. 3d —, 2006 Ohio 2220, — N.E. 2d —, 2006 Ohio App. LEXIS 2056 (May 2, 2006).

When a former client sought a writ of prohibition to keep a trial court from enforcing a charging lien against her, she improperly did not include the addresses of the parties, as required by Ohio R. Civ. P. 10(A), and she did not support her complaint with an affidavit "specifying the details of the claim," as required by Ohio Eighth Dist. Ct. App. R. 45(B)(1)(a). Tyus v. Grand Pointe Health Community, — Ohio App. 3d —, 2006 Ohio 2298, — N.E. 2d —, 2006 Ohio App. LEXIS 2164 (May 9, 2006).

Affidavit of merit

Medical malpractice claim was properly dismissed since the affidavit of merit was to be filed along with the complaint (before discovery), the patient's argument that she needed the doctor's deposition testimony in order to secure an affidavit of merit was without merit. Even if the doctor had been evading service, it would not have eliminated the patient's burden of submitting an affidavit of merit with her complaint; she had access to the requisite medical records and the trial court granted her a 90-day extension to file her affidavit, but it was not until five months later that the trial court finally dismissed the case. Colon v. Fortune, — Ohio App. 3d —, 2008 Ohio 576, — N.E. 2d —, 2008 Ohio App. LEXIS 488 (Feb. 14, 2008).

Patient's motion under Ohio R. Civ. P. 6(B) for an extension of time to file an affidavit of merit under Ohio R. Civ. P. 10(D)(2) should have been granted because the motion was supported with an affidavit showing that the patient had been trying to obtain necessary medical records from a hospital and that the records had not been received until two weeks before the affidavit of merit was due. Under the circumstances, the patient should have been granted additional time to obtain a medical expert to review the records and prepare the affidavit of merit. Ervin v. Cleveland Clinic Found., — Ohio App. 3d —, 2007 Ohio 818, — N.E. 2d —, 2007 Ohio App. LEXIS 764 (Mar. 1, 2007).

Proper remedy for failure to attach the required affidavit(s) of merit for a medical claim, pursuant to Ohio R. Civ. P. 10(D)(2)(c), is for a defendant to request a more definite statement. If a plaintiff fails to comply with an order to provide a more definite statement, a court may strike the pleading to which the motion was directed, or make any other orders as it deems just, which would include involuntary dismissal with prejudice pursuant to Ohio R. Civ. P. 41(B)(1). Fletcher v. Univ. Hosps. of Cleveland, 172 Ohio App. 3d 153, 2007 Ohio 2778, 873 N.E.2d 365, 2007 Ohio App. LEXIS 2568 (2007).

Trial court erred by dismissing with prejudice the complaint for failure to state a claim because, although the administratrix's wrongful death complaint presented a medical claim, as defined by RC § 2305.113(E)(3), which required the administratrix to supply an affidavit of merit pursuant to Ohio R. Civ. P. 10(D)(2), the proper remedy for failure to attach the required affidavit was for defendants to request a more definite statement. Fletcher v. Univ. Hosps. of Cleveland, 172

Ohio App. 3d 153, 2007 Ohio 2778, 873 N.E.2d 365, 2007 Ohio App. LEXIS 2568 (2007).

Under the language of Ohio R. Civ. P. 10(D)(2)(c), the purpose of an affidavit of merit required in a medical claim is solely to establish the adequacy of the complaint, and it is not otherwise admissible as evidence or used for purposes of impeachment, so the requirement of the affidavit is to winnow out utterly frivolous claims; its purpose is not to test the sufficiency of the plaintiff's evidence on the ultimate issue of the defendant's liability. Mike L. Tranter v. Mercy Franciscan Hosp. W. Hills, — Ohio App. 3d —, 2007 Ohio 5132, — N.E. 2d —, 2007 Ohio App. LEXIS 4514 (Sept. 28, 2007).

When a special administrator sued a hospital for medical malpractice, alleging that the negligence of nurses caused a now deceased patient to fall, it was error to dismiss the complaint with prejudice because, while a nurse whose affidavit was submitted in support of the complaint was not qualified to opine whether the patient's fall caused the patient's death over a year later, the nurse was qualified to opine about whether the nurses' negligence caused injury to the patient, within the meaning of Ohio R. Civ. P. 10(D)(2)(a)(iii). Mike L. Tranter v. Mercy Franciscan Hosp. W. Hills, — Ohio App. 3d —, 2007 Ohio 5132, — N.E. 2d —, 2007 Ohio App. LEXIS 4514 (Sept. 28, 2007).

When a special administrator sued a hospital for medical malpractice, alleging that the negligence of nurses caused a now deceased patient to fall, it was error to dismiss the complaint with prejudice because a nurse's affidavit submitted by the administrator satisfied the requirements of Ohio R. Civ. P. 10(D)(2) as the nurse was qualified to opine about the standard of care applicable to nurses and whether the nurses breached that standard, and it was unnecessary for the nurse to offer an opinion on the issue of proximate cause because that was within the trial court's common knowledge. Mike L. Tranter v. Mercy Franciscan Hosp. W. Hills, — Ohio App. 3d —, 2007 Ohio 5132, — N.E. 2d —, 2007 Ohio App. LEXIS 4514 (Sept. 28, 2007).

When a patient sued a medical practice, a physician, and a hospital for medical malpractice, it was premature for the trial court to dismiss the patient's complaint for a failure to attach an affidavit of merit required by Ohio R. Civ. P. 10(D)(2) because (1) the parties sued should have moved for a more definite statement, under Ohio R. Civ. P. 12(E), instead of dismissal, under Ohio R. Civ. P. 12(B)(6), and (2) the trial court did not rule on the patient's Ohio R. Civ. P. 10(D)(2)(b) motion for more time within which to file the affidavit, and it was not proper to presume that the trial court's failure to rule on the motion was a denial of the motion because the failure to rule on the motion ultimately resulted in dismissal of the case. Stewart v. Forum Health, — Ohio App. 3d —, 2007 Ohio 6922, — N.E. 2d —, 2007 Ohio App. LEXIS 6069 (Dec. 12, 2007).

After a patient's medical malpractice complaint was dismissed for failure to file an affidavit of merit along with her complaint, the patient's motion for relief from judgment on the ground of excusable neglect under Civ. R. 60(B) was properly granted because the evidence showed that the patient's attorney had diligently researched whether an affidavit of merit was required in filing a medical malpractice complaint but had missed the new version of Civ. R. 10, which required such an affidavit but had become effective only 27 days before patient's complaint was filed. The attorney had tried to be in compliance with the relevant law instead of choosing to be willfully ignorant of whether he was in compliance. Banfield v. Brodell, — Ohio App. 3d —, 2006 Ohio 5267, — N.E. 2d —, 2006 Ohio App. LEXIS 5262 (Sept. 27, 2006).

———— **Failure to file**

Proper response to the failure to file the affidavit required by CivR 10(D)(2) is a motion to dismiss pursuant to CivR

12(B)(6). A dismissal of a complaint for failure to file the affidavit required by CivR 10(D)(2) is an adjudication otherwise than on the merits. The dismissal, therefore, is without prejudice: Fletcher v. Univ. Hosps. of Cleveland, 120 Ohio St. 3d 167, 2008 Ohio 5379, 897 N.E.2d 147, 2008 Ohio LEXIS 2917 (2008).

Attachments

Although a real property purchaser's claim that a bank breached a short-sale contract to purchase a parcel of real estate was sufficient under RC § 1335.05 although it did not specifically state that the parties had entered into a written contract, as under the bank's motion to dismiss pursuant to Ohio R. Civ. P. 12(B)(6) the complaint was construed in favor of the purchaser, he failed to attach a copy of the contract to the complaint or to explain the absence thereof, as required by Ohio R. Civ. P. 10(D)(1); however, such failure of attachment did not warrant a dismissal of the complaint with prejudice. Maguire v. Nat'l City Bank, — Ohio App. 3d —, 2007 Ohio 4570, — N.E. 2d —, 2007 Ohio App. LEXIS 4117 (Aug. 31, 2007).

When a credit card issuer's assignee sued a debtor for breach of contract for not making payments required by a credit card agreement, the assignee's failure to file a supplemental folder referenced in the credit card agreement, in response to the debtor's motion for a more definite statement, was a violation of Ohio R. Civ. P. 10(D), but this violation did not require dismissal of the assignee's complaint, under Ohio R. Civ. P. 12(B)(6), because the assignee could still be entitled to the relief it sought, despite the violation, as it pled the elements of a breach of contract by alleging that its assignor extended credit to the debtor and the debtor did not repay the credit extended, pursuant to the terms of the debtor's credit card agreement with the assignor. National Check Bur. v. Buerger, — Ohio App. 3d —, 2006 Ohio 6673, — N.E. 2d —, 2006 Ohio App. LEXIS 6576 (Dec. 18, 2006).

Motion to dismiss for failure to state a claim under Ohio R. Civ. P. 12(B)(6), a motion for a more definite statement pursuant to Ohio R. Civ. P. 12(E), and the requirement to attach a written contract to a complaint when a claim was founded on that written contract, under Ohio R. Civ. P. 10(D), were all separate and distinct procedural rules under the Ohio Civil Rules, and a violation of one was not necessarily indicative of a violation of another. National Check Bur. v. Buerger, — Ohio App. 3d —, 2006 Ohio 6673, — N.E. 2d —, 2006 Ohio App. LEXIS 6576 (Dec. 18, 2006).

When a credit card issuer's assignee sued a debtor for breach of contract for not making payments required by a credit card agreement, and the assignee failed to file a supplemental folder referenced in the credit card agreement, in response to the debtor's motion for a more definite statement, in violation of Ohio R. Civ. P. 10(D), this violation did not require dismissal of the assignee's complaint, under Ohio R. Civ. P. 12(B)(6), because it had to be assumed, for purposes of the motion to dismiss, that the supplemental folder provided a way to calculate the damages to which the assignee claimed to be entitled, so the assignee pled the elements of a breach of contract. National Check Bur. v. Buerger, — Ohio App. 3d —, 2006 Ohio 6673, — N.E. 2d —, 2006 Ohio App. LEXIS 6576 (Dec. 18, 2006).

Failure to provide a document in violation of Ohio R. Civ. P. 10(D), in a suit based on a written contract, was not a basis for relief under Ohio R. Civ. P. 12(B)(6). National Check Bur. v. Buerger, — Ohio App. 3d —, 2006 Ohio 6673, — N.E. 2d —, 2006 Ohio App. LEXIS 6576 (Dec. 18, 2006).

In the event a party failed to obey an order of a trial court to provide a more definite statement, the court could strike the pleading to which the motion was directed, or make any other orders as it deemed just, which would include involuntary dismissal with prejudice pursuant to Ohio R. Civ. P. 41(B)(1), but it did not follow that because a plaintiff violated

Ohio R. Civ. P. 10(D), requiring it to attach to its complaint the written instrument on which it sued, its complaint did not state a claim upon which relief could be granted. National Check Bur. v. Buerger, — Ohio App. 3d —, 2006 Ohio 6673, — N.E. 2d —, 2006 Ohio App. LEXIS 6576 (Dec. 18, 2006).

Where a writing was attached to a complaint pursuant to Ohio R. Civ. P. 10(D), dismissal under Ohio R. Civ. P. 12(B)(6) was proper only when the language of the writing precluded any possibility of recovery by the plaintiff. National Check Bur. v. Buerger, — Ohio App. 3d —, 2006 Ohio 6673, — N.E. 2d —, 2006 Ohio App. LEXIS 6576 (Dec. 18, 2006).

Caption

Prisoner's petition for a writ of habeas corpus was dismissed because the prisoner had improperly captioned his petition by failing to identify the parties as petitioner or respondent and by failing to include the address of the sheriff, as required by Ohio R. Civ. P. 10(A). He had not verified his petition, as required by RC § 2725.04; he had failed to support his petition with a sworn affidavit specifying the details of the claim, as required by Ohio 8th Dist. Ct. App. R. 45(B)(1)(a); and he had failed to file an affidavit describing each civil action or appeal of a civil action that had been docketed in the previous five years, as required by RC § 2969.25(A). Notwithstanding the procedural defects, the prisoner had failed to substantively demonstrate that his bail was excessive as he did not address the factors as enumerated within Ohio R. Crim. P. 46(A). State v. Thomas, — Ohio App. 3d —, 2007 Ohio 1692, — N.E. 2d —, 2007 Ohio App. LEXIS 1555 (Apr. 10, 2007).

Inmate's habeas petition was dismissed because: (1) the caption did not identify the respondent, and the inmate had failed to include the address of the respondent as required by Civ. R. 10(A); (2) the inmate had failed to comply with the mandatory requirements of RC § 2725.04 as he failed to verify the petition; (3) the inmate failed to comply with Ohio 8th Dist. Ct. App. R. 45(B)(1)(a) by failing to support his petition with a sworn affidavit specifying the details of the claim; (4) the inmate had failed to comply with the mandatory requirements of RC § 2969.25(A) by failing to file an affidavit describing each civil action or appeal of a civil action that had been docketed in the previous five years; and (5) an appeal, rather than the extraordinary writ of habeas corpus, was the appropriate remedy to use when challenging a claimed violation of the right to a speedy trial. Hopkins v. State, — Ohio App. 3d —, 2007 Ohio 1855, — N.E. 2d —, 2007 Ohio App. LEXIS 1684 (Apr. 16, 2007).

Petition for a writ of mandamus by defendant was dismissed due to its procedural defects, as it was not properly captioned under RC § 2731.04 or Ohio R. Civ. P. 10 because it was not brought in the name of the state on relation of defendant, it was not brought against any judge or court as respondent, it did not list the addresses for service, and it did not include the necessary affidavit pursuant to RC § 2969.25. Cousino v. State, — Ohio App. 3d —, 2007 Ohio 2142, — N.E. 2d —, 2007 Ohio App. LEXIS 2008 (May 1, 2007).

Inmate's mandamus petition was procedurally defective where he did not caption it on relation of the State as required by RC § 2731.04, he failed to include the addresses of the parties in the caption pursuant to Ohio R. Civ. P. 10(A), and he failed to file the necessary affidavits pursuant to RC § 2969.25 and Ohio Eighth Dist. Ct. App. R. 45(B)(1)(a). Mauer v. Cuyahoga Co. Court of Common Pleas, — Ohio App. 3d —, 2007 Ohio 3641, — N.E. 2d —, 2007 Ohio App. LEXIS 3348 (July 18, 2007).

Contract

When homeowners sued a power company for recission of the homeowners' contract granting the company an easement over the homeowners' property, the homeowners sufficiently alleged the mutual mistake of the homeowners and the company by alleging the existence of a contract, that the contract was entered into to provide electric power to the homeowners' neighbor, that the company could not provide power to that neighbor, and that the blame for that mistake was with the company, rather than the homeowners, because the company later found the company could not provide power to the neighbor, and the requirement of Ohio R. Civ. P. 9(B) to plead mistake with particularity was satisfied when the contract was attached and incorporated into the complaint, pursuant to Ohio R. Civ. P. 10(C). Thomas v. Ohio Power Co., — Ohio App. 3d —, 2007 Ohio 5350, — N.E. 2d —, 2007 Ohio App. LEXIS 4715 (Sept. 27, 2007).

Trial court erred in granting an employer's motion to dismiss an employee's complaint for failure to state a claim pursuant to Ohio R. Civ. P. 12(B)(6), as the allegations in the complaint were sufficient under Ohio R. Civ. P. 8 to apprise the employer and its agent of the basis for the causes of action of breach of contract and promissory estoppel, arising from the employer's withdrawal of its written offer of employment after the employee had quit her job in reliance thereon; her attachment of the written contract pursuant to Ohio R. Civ. P. 10(C) was deemed a part of the pleading, and as the terms thereof did not preclude relief under the claims, as she asserted exceptions to the at-will employment doctrine, dismissal was error. Mesek v. Roberts Communs., Inc., — Ohio App. 3d —, 2006 Ohio 3339, — N.E. 2d —, 2006 Ohio App. LEXIS 3268 (June 30, 2006).

Medical malpractice

Trial court's order denying a motion to dismiss for the procedural pleading error of not filing an affidavit of merit contemporaneously with a complaint as required by CivR 10(D)(2) does not arise from an ancillary proceeding, does not deny a provisional remedy pursuant to RC § 2505.02(A)(3), and is not final and appealable under RC § 2505.02(B)(4): Manley v. Marsico, 116 Ohio St. 3d 85, 2007 Ohio 5543, 876 N.E.2d 910, 2007 Ohio LEXIS 2571 (2007).

Wrongful death claim was in fact a medical claim as defined in RC § 2305.113. A defendant's proper remedy for a failure to attach a required affidavit of merit is a motion for a more definite statement: Fletcher v. Univ. Hosps. of Cleveland, 172 Ohio App. 3d 153, 2007 Ohio 2778, 873 N.E.2d 365, 2007 Ohio App. LEXIS 2568 (2007).

Parties

Ohio R. Civ. P. 54(B) language and certification was not necessary for purposes of making a denial of an insurer's motion to intervene, pursuant to Ohio R. Civ. P. 24(A)(2), a final appealable order pursuant to RC § 2505.02(B), as the language of Ohio R. Civ. P. 54(B) connoted that claims or rights and liabilities of parties was involved, and the insurer was clearly not a party if it had to seek intervention to participate in the action. It was not included in the pleadings pursuant to Ohio R. Civ. P. 10(A), wherein a patient of the insured, a doctor, filed a civil tort action arising from the doctor's inappropriate conduct during a gynecological examination, and the insurer's intent in seeking intervention was to secure a specific, rather than general, verdict in order to deny the coverage to the doctor, which was provided under a reservation of rights. Filippi v. Ahmed, — Ohio App. 3d —, 2006 Ohio 4368, — N.E. 2d —, 2006 Ohio App. LEXIS 4290 (Aug. 24, 2006).

Unnamed parties

Where a resolution of default agreement named assorted defendant entities, plaintiff's claim that defendants breached their contractual obligations thereunder should not have been dismissed for failure to name those entities in the complaint, as the default agreement attached to the complaint and incorporated therein pursuant to Ohio R. Civ. P. 10(C) and such was sufficient for purposes of listing those defendants. Castle Hill Holdings v. Al Hut, Inc., — Ohio App. 3d —, 2006 Ohio 1353, — N.E. 2d —, 2006 Ohio App. LEXIS 1239 (Mar. 23, 2006).

Written instruments

When a purported franchisee sought a declaration that he was the true franchisee and that the franchisor was estopped from denying the purported franchisee's right to the franchise, the franchise agreement attached to the purported franchisee's complaint, pursuant to Ohio R. Civ. P. 10(D), was an insuperable bar to the purported franchisee's recovery because that agreement explicitly stated that another was the true franchisee. Iskander Abi Abdallah v. Doctor's Assocs., — Ohio App. 3d —, 2007 Ohio 6065, — N.E. 2d —, 2007 Ohio App. LEXIS 5335 (Nov. 15, 2007).

When a lender filed an answer and counter-claim in a foreclosure action brought by a bank, to which the lender attached a mortgage and promissory note in its favor regarding the subject property, pursuant to Ohio R. Civ. P. 10(D), it could not rely on these documents to show that it had an interest in the property which was superior to that of the bank because these documents were not, in and of themselves, evidence, and the lender did not seek to have them admitted into evidence. Park Nat'l Bank v. Chauvin, — Ohio App. 3d —, 2006 Ohio 5158, — N.E. 2d —, 2006 Ohio App. LEXIS 5060 (Oct. 2, 2006).

RULE 11. Signing of pleadings, motions, or other documents

Every pleading, motion, or other document of a party represented by an attorney shall be signed by at least one attorney of record in the attorney's individual name, whose address, attorney registration number, telephone number, telefax number, if any, and business e-mail address, if any, shall be stated. A party who is not represented by an attorney shall sign the pleading, motion, or other document and state the party's address. Except when otherwise specifically provided by these rules, pleadings need not be verified or accompanied by affidavit. The signature of an attorney or pro se party constitutes a certificate by the attorney or party that the attorney or party has read the document; that to the best of the attorney's or party's knowledge, information, and belief there is good ground to support it; and that it is not interposed for delay. If a document is not signed or is signed with intent to defeat the purpose of this rule, it may be stricken as sham and false and the action may proceed as though the document had not been served. For a willful violation of this rule, an attorney or pro se party, upon motion of a party or upon the court's own motion, may be subjected to appropriate action, including an award to the opposing party of expenses and reasonable attorney fees incurred in bringing any motion under this rule. Similar action may be taken if scandalous or indecent matter is inserted.

History: Amended, eff 7-1-94; 7-1-95; 7-1-01.

NOTES TO DECISIONS

ANALYSIS

Appeal
Attorney fees
Failure to sign brief
Filing groundless complaint
Findings
Groundless claims
Sanctions
— Generally
— Good faith belief

— Hearing on sanctions
— Motion for sanctions
— Not warranted
— Warranted
— Willful violation required
Violation of rule

Appeal

Where plaintiff had sufficient notice that defendant was seeking to impose sanctions against him for a frivolous filing under Ohio R. Civ. P. 11 and RC § 2323.51, although no motion for sanctions was actually ever filed, and plaintiff never filed an objection or sought clarification or limitation at any time during discussions, hearings, or filing of proposed findings and conclusions which indicated that such sanctions were being sought, plaintiff waived his right to raise an objection thereto on appeal. Neubauer v. Ohio Remcon, Inc., — Ohio App. 3d —, 2006 Ohio 1481, — N.E. 2d —, 2006 Ohio App. LEXIS 1335 (Mar. 28, 2006).

When a trial court awarded sanctions against an attorney and his former client, under Ohio R. Civ. P. 11 and RC § 2323.51, for frivolous conduct, the appellate court could not consider the attorney's assignments of error because he did not file a transcript of the trial court's proceedings. Peterman v. Stewart, — Ohio App. 3d —, 2006 Ohio 4671, — N.E. 2d —, 2006 Ohio App. LEXIS 4611 (Sept. 6, 2006).

Attorney fees

Because it was evident from the record that the trial court awarded the applicant attorney fees pursuant to RC § 2323.51 or Ohio R. Civ. P. 11, based on frivolous conduct, and not RC § 2335.39 for the prevailing party, the trial court had the legal authority to award the Medicaid applicant attorney fees. However, based on the law and the somewhat incomplete record, the trial court abused its discretion in awarding attorney fees without first providing the agency a hearing to explain the legal basis upon which its decisions and arguments were based and an opportunity to challenge the reasonableness of the fee request. Roe v. Ohio Dep't of Job & Family Servs., — Ohio App. 3d —, 2007 Ohio 4639, — N.E. 2d —, 2007 Ohio App. LEXIS 4177 (Sept. 7, 2007).

There was no error in the trial court's refusal to award the client attorney fees and expenses because, although the attorney dismissed his counterclaim prior to trial, he informed the trial court below that he did so not because the counterclaim was meritless but because he wanted to facilitate bringing the litigation to a close. The trial court reasonably could have concluded that the counterclaim was not frivolous and that no sanctions were warranted under RC § 2323.51 or Ohio R. Civ. P. 11. Nunn v. Cornyn, — Ohio App. 3d —, 2007 Ohio 5894, — N.E. 2d —, 2007 Ohio App. LEXIS 5185 (Nov. 5, 2007).

Trial court properly granted the guardian ad litem attorney fees under Ohio R. Civ. P. 11 and RC § 2323.51 because the father's complaint lacked merit. The guardian was immune from suit in his function as guardian ad litem for the father's son and, since the father failed to establish an attorney-client relationship between himself and the guardian, his legal malpractice claim was without merit. Because the father presented no evidence that the guardian's actions were other than in the performance of services as guardian ad litem, his multiple claims were not warranted under existing law. Kellogg v. Daulton, — Ohio App. 3d —, 2006 Ohio 4115, — N.E. 2d —, 2006 Ohio App. LEXIS 4044 (Aug. 10, 2006).

Trial court did not abuse its discretion in awarding attorney fees to an attorney for his representation of himself, his law firm, and his law clients against an action that was deemed frivolous under Ohio R. Civ. P. 11 and RC § 2323.51 although the trial court's reliance on "opportunity cost" theory for inability of the lawyer to have worked on other matters was

not relied on, as the attorney was not only acting as a pro se litigant because he represented the interests of others as well as himself in seeking the fee award. Recovery of "reasonably incurred" fees in defending the litigation was allowable despite the fact that the attorney did not choose to collect any fees from the clients or his firm, as he "incurred" fees through his work on behalf of the clients and his firm and was entitled to charge them for those fees if he chose to do so. Mikhael v. Gallup, — Ohio App. 3d —, 2006 Ohio 3917, — N.E. 2d —, 2006 Ohio App. LEXIS 3884 (Aug. 2, 2006).

When an attorney sought workers' compensation death benefits for a widow, due to the death of her husband, in violation of Ohio R. Civ. P. 11, because he filed a claim for those benefits five months after the widow died, using a form the widow did not sign or date, it was not an abuse of discretion to award attorney fees to an employer, under Rule 11, because of the attorney's willful violation of the Rule, but it was error to award fees under RC § 2323.51 because the widow's purported executrix voluntarily dismissed an appeal of the denial of the claim the attorney filed, under Ohio R. Civ. P. 41(A), which established the date of the final judgment in the case, and the employer did not seek sanctions within 21 days of that date, as required by the statute. Baker v. AK Steel Corp., — Ohio App. 3d —, 2006 Ohio 3895, — N.E. 2d —, 2006 Ohio App. LEXIS 3854 (July 31, 2006).

Failure to sign brief

In a divorce case, the trial court did not abuse its discretion in dismissing the husband's motion objecting to the magistrate's decision, a brief supporting the husband's opposition, and a proposed judgment entry; the pleading was not signed in violation of Ohio R. Civ. P. 11, and it was not served on opposing counsel in violation of Ohio R. Civ. P. 5, and amendment was, again, not served on the wife's representative. Havel v. Havel, — Ohio App. 3d —, 2006 Ohio 1692, — N.E. 2d —, 2006 Ohio App. LEXIS 1547 (Mar. 31, 2006).

Filing groundless complaint

Trial court properly found that the attorney engaged in sanctionable conduct under RC § 2323.51 and Ohio R. Civ. P. 11 for (1) bringing a loss of consortium claim, (2) including all defendants in the allegation that the patient was called a drug addict and told to leave the hospital because she did not have insurance, (3) failing to dismiss the case after learning that the case totally lacked merit and that his clients did not want to proceed, and (4) alleging punitive damages in the refiled complaint without any basis. Sigmon v. Southwest Gen. Health Ctr., — Ohio App. 3d —, 2007 Ohio 2117, — N.E. 2d —, 2007 Ohio App. LEXIS 1983 (May 3, 2007).

RC § 2323.51 and Ohio R. Civ. P. 11 did not conflict and thus, RC § 2323.51 did not violate Ohio Const. art. IV, §§ 5 and 2. A plain reading of RC § 2323.51 and Ohio R. Civ. P. 11 revealed that, although different language was used, both the statute and the rule imposed the same requirement on an attorney: to prosecute only claims having merit under existing law. Sigmon v. Southwest Gen. Health Ctr., — Ohio App. 3d —, 2007 Ohio 2117, — N.E. 2d —, 2007 Ohio App. LEXIS 1983 (May 3, 2007).

Trial court properly awarded attorney fees to parties pursuant to RC § 2323.51 and Ohio R. Civ. P. 11 as a sanction based on a finding that a lawsuit against them, alleging that they were involved in a civil conspiracy that included overcharges and kickbacks, was frivolous to an egregious degree, but the additional awards for "stress and lost time" and "miscellaneous" required reversal where there was no statutory provision for such awards. Orbit Electronics, Inc. v. Helm Instrument Co., Inc., 167 Ohio App. 3d 301, 2006 Ohio 2317, 855 N.E. 2d 91, 2006 Ohio App. LEXIS 2172 (May 11, 2006).

Trial court erred in granting the motion for attorney fees based on a finding that the subcontractor had filed a legally groundless claim because, at the time that the subcontractor and its attorney filed the complaint, they had no proof that payment had actually been made. Thus, under the circumstances, the actions in filing the suit were not frivolous under Ohio R. Civ. P. 11 or RC § 2323.51. Mainly Masonry/Land Builders, Inc. v. Sydlowski, — Ohio App. 3d —, 2006 Ohio 6809, — N.E. 2d —, 2006 Ohio App. LEXIS 6728 (Dec. 22, 2006).

Findings

Although a trial court's findings of fact and conclusion of law did not find that plaintiff willfully violated Ohio R. Civ. P. 11 for purposes of its imposition of sanctions against him due to a frivolous complaint, any error was inconsequential because the decision was also based on RC § 2323.51 which was broader and supported the sanctions pursuant to the trial court's court's findings. Neubauer v. Ohio Remcon, Inc., — Ohio App. 3d —, 2006 Ohio 1481, — N.E. 2d —, 2006 Ohio App. LEXIS 1335 (Mar. 28, 2006).

Groundless claims

Attorney engaged in frivolous conduct, for purposes of RC § 2323.51 and CivR 11, where he filed and maintained causes of action when it was subjectively and objectively clear that they were all beyond their respective statutes of limitations: Stafford v. Columbus Bonding Ctr., 177 Ohio App. 3d 799, 2008 Ohio 3948, 896 N.E.2d 191, 2008 Ohio App. LEXIS 3316 (2008).

As a billboard parts manufacturer had a right to seek an Ohio declaratory judgment pursuant to RC § 2721.04 regarding a determination of its rights under a contract with a parts user, although the parties' contract indicated that Virginia was the forum selected for resolving disputes and the user had filed a breach of contract action in Virginia, the declaratory judgment action was not frivolous pursuant to Ohio R. Civ. P. 11 and RC § 2323.51 even though it was dismissed. Upon dismissal due to lack of jurisdiction, a second action filed in Ohio by the manufacturer became frivolous, as the same jurisdictional ruling applied, such that an award of fees and costs as sanctions was proper, although it should only have been calculated from the time of the declaratory judgment dismissal until the dismissal of the second action. The Northern Mfg. Co., Inc. v. New Mkt. Metalcraft, Inc., — Ohio App. 3d —, 2007 Ohio 1873, — N.E. 2d —, 2007 Ohio App. LEXIS 1709 (Apr. 20, 2007).

Sanctions

Even if a former client's reply to an attorney's counterclaim in the client's legal malpractice action was not signed by the client's attorney in violation of CivR 11, there was no requirement that the pleading be stricken, as there was no showing that it was a fraud or a sham and no showing that the attorney's substantial rights were affected by the failure to have signed the reply. Goldberg v. Mittman, — Ohio App. 3d —, 2007 Ohio 6599, — N.E. 2d —, 2007 Ohio App. LEXIS 5768 (Dec. 11, 2007).

— Generally

Although an attorney for a county child support enforcement agency erred under Ohio R. Civ. P. 75(B)(1) and (I)(2) in filing motions to join a former husband's attorneys who represented him in a federal civil lawsuit into the support arrearage action, and to have restraining orders issued against the attorneys and the husband, as the motions were filed in good faith and there was no willful violation of Ohio R. Civ. P. 11 shown, the trial court did not abuse its discretion in denying a request by one of the attorneys for imposition of sanctions under Rule 11 against the attorney for the agency. Ransom v. Ransom, — Ohio App. 3d —, 2007 Ohio 457, — N.E. 2d —, 2007 Ohio App. LEXIS 411 (Feb. 5, 2007).

Store was awarded costs and attorney fees against a store patron and his attorney pursuant to Ohio R. App. P. 23 and Ohio R. Civ. P. 11 where the action brought against the store, alleging statutory violations due to the store's receipt indicating the patron's credit card expiration date, was completely frivolous and the attorney had no good ground to support the filing of an appeal, much less the complaint. The store patron and his attorney were both aware that an actual injury was required in order to assert a statutory claim for recovery, which did not exist in the circumstances. Burdge v. Supervalu Holdings, — Ohio App. 3d —, 2007 Ohio 1318, — N.E. 2d —, 2007 Ohio App. LEXIS 1205 (Mar. 23, 2007).

Store was awarded costs and attorney fees against a store patron and his attorney pursuant to Ohio R. App. P. 23 and Ohio R. Civ. P. 11 where the action brought against the store, alleging statutory violations due to the store's receipt indicating the patron's credit card expiration date, was completely frivolous and the attorney had no good ground to support the filing of an appeal, much less the complaint. The store patron and his attorney were both aware that an actual injury was required in order to assert a statutory claim for recovery, which did not exist in the circumstances. Burdge v. Supervalu Holdings, — Ohio App. 3d —, 2007 Ohio 1318, — N.E. 2d —, 2007 Ohio App. LEXIS 1205 (Mar. 23, 2007).

Trial court properly found that an attorney engaged in frivolous conduct and violated Ohio R. Civ. P. 11 and RC § 2323.51 as the evidence showed that the attorney filed a slander action against defense counsel based solely on the attorney's assumptions and suspicions without good ground to believe that defense counsel had made slanderous statements about the attorney's client and that the attorney maintained the action for several months after the attorney's only witness told the attorney that the attorney had no evidence to support her allegations. Moreover, the attorney's conduct was willful, in that the individual, whom the attorney alleged overheard the statements, never told the attorney that defense counsel made the slanderous comments nor did the individual ever tell the attorney that two female attorneys did. The attorney did not have reasonable grounds to believe that defense counsel made the statements. Stevenson v. Bernard, — Ohio App. 3d —, 2007 Ohio 3192, — N.E. 2d —, 2007 Ohio App. LEXIS 2921 (June 22, 2007).

When a former employee, having sued his former employer for compensation, did not comply with the employer's request for production of the former employee's W-2 forms and tax returns, or with the trial court's order to produce the documents, the former employee was not entitled to a hearing on the issue of whether he should be ordered to pay the former employer's attorney fees, under Ohio R. Civ. P. 37(D), because neither Ohio R. Civ. P. 11 nor RC 2323.51(B)(2)(c), regarding awards of attorney fees for frivolous conduct, under which a hearing was required, applied. Shikner v. Solutions, — Ohio App. 3d —, 2006 Ohio 1339, — N.E. 2d —, 2006 Ohio App. LEXIS 1220 (Mar. 23, 2006).

When customers sued a shipping company, it was an abuse of discretion for the trial court to sanction the company's counsel, under Ohio R. Civ. P. 11, for arguing that 49 U.S.C.S. § 14706 preempted the customers state law claims against the company, or for not mentioning that the statute had been amended or that the trial court had concurrent jurisdiction of claims under this statute, because the claims the customers filed against the company were the types of claims which were preempted under the statute, and the authority counsel relied on had not been overruled. Bowersmith v. UPS, 166 Ohio App. 3d 22, 2006 Ohio 1417, 848 N.E. 2d 919, 2006 Ohio App. LEXIS 1297 (Mar. 27, 2006).

Trial court's imposition of a damage award to a village as a sanction against property owners pursuant to Ohio R. Civ. P. 11 was proper, as the owners engaged in a consistent pattern of improper conduct, including voluminous baseless objections, motions, and allegations which were purposely made for delay and confusion. Village of Ottawa Hills v. Abdollah, — Ohio App. 3d —, 2006 Ohio 2618, — N.E. 2d —, 2006 Ohio App. LEXIS 2461 (May 26, 2006).

When a trial court awarded sanctions against an attorney and his former client, under Ohio R. Civ. P. 11 and RC

§ 2323.51, for frivolous conduct, the fact that the client voluntarily dismissed her suit did not preclude such an award. Peterman v. Stewart, — Ohio App. 3d —, 2006 Ohio 4671, — N.E. 2d —, 2006 Ohio App. LEXIS 4611 (Sept. 6, 2006).

When a trial court awarded sanctions against an attorney and his former client, under Ohio R. Civ. P. 11 and RC § 2323.51, for frivolous conduct, the fact that the attorney had withdrawn from representing the client did not preclude such an award. Peterman v. Stewart, — Ohio App. 3d —, 2006 Ohio 4671, — N.E. 2d —, 2006 Ohio App. LEXIS 4611 (Sept. 6, 2006).

Evidence supported a trial court's finding that an attorney, who represented the mother in a grandparent visitation case, had engaged in "frivolous conduct," under RC § 2323.51 and Ohio R. Civ. P. 11. While the parties had settled the issue of grandparent visitation three months after the complaint was filed, the client had deliberately failed to comply with visitation order, and the attorney had facilitated the client's conduct by moving to vacate almost every order. Butts v. Johnson, — Ohio App. 3d —, 2006 Ohio 5077, — N.E. 2d —, 2006 Ohio App. LEXIS 5011 (Sept. 29, 2006).

There was no abuse of discretion in a trial court's refusal to impose sanctions against a prosecutor pursuant to Ohio R. Civ. P. 11 in defendant's criminal action, arising from his claim that the prosecutor had intentionally misstated facts and law in replying to defendant's objections to a magistrate's denial of his suppression motion, as there was no evidence in the record to support the claim that the prosecutor made intentional misstatements of law or fact, or that admitted errors by him were egregious. State v. Keggan, — Ohio App. 3d —, 2006 Ohio 6663, — N.E. 2d —, 2006 Ohio App. LEXIS 6561 (Dec. 15, 2006).

— Good faith belief

There was no abuse of discretion in the denial of a request by a county prosecutor for sanctions against attorneys who filed a mandamus action on behalf of a county board of elections, as there was no evidence that the attorneys who filed the action engaged in any bad faith or a willful violation; rather, the evidence supported a determination that the attorneys made their argument that the board was entitled to disclosure of certain election records in good faith. State Ex Rel. Dreamer v. Mason, 115 Ohio St. 3d 190, 2007 Ohio 4789, 874 N.E. 2d 510, 2007 Ohio LEXIS 2216 (Sept. 20, 2007).

— Hearing on sanctions

Trial court erred in granting opposing counsels' Ohio R. Civ. P. 11 motion for sanctions because, although there was no agreement to submit the motion for sanctions through written materials, the trial court granted the motion without first holding a hearing and without even allowing the attorney to respond to the motion before imposing sanctions. The error was not waived by the attorney's failure to file a motion for reconsideration before the damages hearing because a motion for reconsideration is not required as a predicate for a later appeal, but even if such a motion were required, the trial court's action granting sanctions without a hearing constituted plain error. Sandberg v. John T. Crouch Co., — Ohio App. 3d —, 2006 Ohio 4519, — N.E. 2d —, 2006 Ohio App. LEXIS 4481 (Sept. 1, 2006).

Granting sanctions against a party without permitting a response seriously affects the basic fairness of the judicial process. Sandberg v. John T. Crouch Co., — Ohio App. 3d —, 2006 Ohio 4519, — N.E. 2d —, 2006 Ohio App. LEXIS 4481 (Sept. 1, 2006).

— Motion for sanctions

When an attorney voluntarily dismissed his action against an expert witness, under Ohio R. Civ. P. 41(A)(1), and refiled it in another court, the court in which the action was first filed had jurisdiction to consider the expert's motion for sanctions against the attorney, under Ohio R. Civ. P. 11, because it could

consider collateral issues not related to the merits of the action, so the attorney was not entitled to a writ of prohibition to bar the first trial court from proceeding with a consideration of the motion for sanctions because the court did not patently and unambiguously lack jurisdiction. State ex rel. Stifel v. Stokes, — Ohio App. 3d —, 2007 Ohio 997, — N.E. 2d —, 2007 Ohio App. LEXIS 986 (Mar. 2, 2007).

Although appellant voluntarily dismissed his action pursuant to Ohio R. Civ. P. 41(A)(1)(a), appellees' motion for sanctions and recovery of attorney fees and costs under Ohio R. Civ. P. 11 and RC § 2323.51, which had been filed prior to the dismissal, was properly ruled on by the trial court, as the motion involved a collateral issue that was not based on the merits of the case and accordingly, the trial court had jurisdiction to consider it; the trial court also had authority to assess costs for a voluntarily dismissed action under Ohio R. Civ. P. 41(A)(1)(D). Williams v. Thamann, 173 Ohio App. 3d 426, 2007 Ohio 4320, 878 N.E.2d 1070, 2007 Ohio App. LEXIS 3863 (2007).

Probate court erred in refusing to consider the merits of the guardian's motion for sanctions under Civ. R. 11 because, while Civ. R. 11 generally did not apply to conduct in the appellate court, appellees, in appealing the probate court's judgment, were required to file a notice of appeal in the probate court, signed by the attorney. Because Civ. R. 11 applied to every pleading, motion, or other document of a party represented by an attorney, there was no reason Civ. R. 11 should not have applied to the notice of appeal filed in the probate court. In re Wernick, — Ohio App. 3d —, 2006 Ohio 5950, — N.E. 2d —, 2006 Ohio App. LEXIS 5877 (Nov. 9, 2006).

— Not warranted

When a company sued a college for violating the Telephone Consumer Protection Act, 47 U.S.C.S. § 227, by sending the company an unsolicited facsimile, the company's filing of a motion in limine seeking to bar the college from arguing that the company had to ask the college to refrain from sending further facsimiles before the company could recover did not warrant the imposition of sanctions against the company because there was a legal basis for the motion, as the company did not have to make such a request, it was anticipated that the college would try to raise this as a defense, and the sending of one unsolicited facsimile was sufficient to violate the statute. Omerza v. Bryant & Stratton, — Ohio App. 3d —, 2007 Ohio 5216, — N.E. 2d —, 2007 Ohio App. LEXIS 4590 (Sept. 28, 2007).

When a company sued a college for violating the Telephone Consumer Protection Act, 47 U.S.C.S. § 227, by sending the company an unsolicited facsimile, and also stated a claim under the Consumer Sales Practices Act (CSPA), RC ch. 1345, the company's filing of a motion for attorney fees did not warrant the imposition of sanctions against the company because, had the company pursued and been successful on the company's CSPA claim, the company could have been entitled to attorney fees, and, while the motion was premature, there was no evidence that the company willfully violated Ohio R. Civ. P. 11. Omerza v. Bryant & Stratton, — Ohio App. 3d —, 2007 Ohio 5216, — N.E. 2d —, 2007 Ohio App. LEXIS 4590 (Sept. 28, 2007).

Trial court did not err in denying plaintiff's motion for sanctions without a hearing because the terms of Ohio R. Civ. P. 11 do not require the holding a hearing before denying a request for sanctions. Sat Adlaka v. Giannini, — Ohio App. 3d —, 2006 Ohio 4611, — N.E. 2d —, 2006 Ohio App. LEXIS 4574 (Sept. 1, 2006).

Plaintiff's motion for sanctions against the attorney he filed suit against was properly denied because, while the attorney filed his motion for summary judgment before even being served with the complaint, this was not grounds for sanctions. Even if the attorney's memorandum in opposition to plaintiff's request for leave should have been struck due to the lack of a signature, the end result was the same since the court had determined that plaintiff's complaint was properly dismissed. Sat Adlaka v. Giannini, — Ohio App. 3d —, 2006 Ohio 4611, — N.E. 2d —, 2006 Ohio App. LEXIS 4574 (Sept. 1, 2006).

— Warranted

Trial court abused its discretion in failing to award the surgical assistant sanctions (such as attorney fees) for the administratrix's frivolous conduct because at no point in the trial court proceedings did the administratrix obtain any evidence to support a claim of medical malpractice against the surgical assistant and yet, the administratrix took no action to remove the surgical assistant from the litigation. Instead, the administratrix required the surgical assistant to file a motion for summary judgment on the claim against him and then did not oppose such a motion. Ponder v. Kamienski, — Ohio App. 3d —, 2007 Ohio 5035, — N.E. 2d —, 2007 Ohio App. LEXIS 4453 (Sept. 26, 2007).

When parties agreed, on the record, not to file post-trial briefs and a trial court, as a result, directed that the court would not receive further briefs, it was error for the court to decline to impose sanctions when a party subsequenly filed "supplemental authorities," because (1) the filing was a brief, because the filing went beyond merely supplying the court with copies of additonal cases, (2) the filing was unjustified because the cases cited in the filing did little to support the filer's position, and (3) the cases cited had been available before trial, so it was not urgent that the cases be brought to the court's attention. Omerza v. Bryant & Stratton, — Ohio App. 3d —, 2007 Ohio 5216, — N.E. 2d —, 2007 Ohio App. LEXIS 4590 (Sept. 28, 2007).

— Willful violation required

Without a willful violation, it was error to sanction the attorneys under Civ. R. 11. Although the trial court found that the attorneys did not have a good faith basis to support the filing of the RICO claim, it did not make any specific findings that their failure amounted to a willful violation, as opposed to a merely negligent, violation. Wilson v. Marino, — Ohio App. 3d —, 2007 Ohio 1048, — N.E. 2d —, 2007 Ohio App. LEXIS 982 (Mar. 9, 2007).

Given the highly technical arguments that the administratrix made regarding the alleged medical malpractice, it could not be said that the administratrix lacked reasonable grounds for filing suit against the surgical assistant. Moreover, even if it were assumed that it was improper to name the surgical assistant, there was no evidence that the filing of the complaint was a willful violation of Ohio R. Civ. P. 11. Ponder v. Kamienski, — Ohio App. 3d —, 2007 Ohio 5035, — N.E. 2d —, 2007 Ohio App. LEXIS 4453 (Sept. 26, 2007).

Violation of rule

When an attorney was retained to seek workers' compensation death benefits for a widow, due to the death of her husband, he violated Ohio R. Civ. P. 11 because he filed a claim for those benefits five months after the widow died, using a form the widow did not sign or date, and he could not claim there was a good faith basis to claim benefits for the time between the death of the widow's husband and the death of the widow because no estate was opened to pursue such a claim, and, even if one had been opened, there was no claim to pursue because the claim was filed after the death of the widow, who was the person who had authority to pursue the claim, under RC § 4123.59. Baker v. AK Steel Corp., — Ohio App. 3d —, 2006 Ohio 3895, — N.E. 2d —, 2006 Ohio App. LEXIS 3854 (July 31, 2006).

RULE 12. Defenses and objections — when and how presented — by pleading or motion — motion for judgment on the pleadings

(A) **When answer presented.**

(1) **Generally.** The defendant shall serve his answer within twenty-eight days after service of the summons and complaint upon him; if service of notice has been made by publication, he shall serve his answer within twenty-eight days after the completion of service by publication.

(2) **Other responses and motions.** A party served with a pleading stating a cross-claim against him shall serve an answer thereto within twenty-eight days after the service upon him. The plaintiff shall serve his reply to a counterclaim in the answer within twenty-eight days after service of the answer or, if a reply is ordered by the court, within twenty-eight days after service of the order, unless the order otherwise directs. The service of a motion permitted under this rule alters these periods of time as follows, unless a different time is fixed by order of the court: (a) if the court denies the motion, a responsive pleading, delayed because of service of the motion, shall be served within fourteen days after notice of the court's action; (b) if the court grants the motion, a responsive pleading, delayed because of service of the motion, shall be served within fourteen days after service of the pleading which complies with the court's order.

(B) **How presented.** Every defense, in law or fact, to a claim for relief in any pleading, whether a claim, counterclaim, cross-claim, or third-party claim, shall be asserted in the responsive pleading thereto if one is required, except that the following defenses may at the option of the pleader be made by motion: (1) lack of jurisdiction over the subject matter, (2) lack of jurisdiction over the person, (3) improper venue, (4) insufficiency of process, (5) insufficiency of service of process, (6) failure to state a claim upon which relief can be granted, (7) failure to join a party under Rule 19 or Rule 19.1. A motion making any of these defenses shall be made before pleading if a further pleading is permitted. No defense or objection is waived by being joined with one or more other defenses or objections in a responsive pleading or motion. If a pleading sets forth a claim for relief to which the adverse party is not required to serve a responsive pleading, he may assert at the trial any defense in law or fact to that claim for relief. When a motion to dismiss for failure to state a claim upon which relief can be granted presents matters outside the pleading and such matters are not excluded by the court, the motion shall be treated as a motion for summary judgment and disposed of as provided in Rule 56. Provided, however, that the court shall consider only such matters outside the pleadings as are specifically enumerated in Rule 56. All parties shall be given reasonable opportunity to present all materials made pertinent to such a motion by Rule 56.

(C) **Motion for judgment on the pleadings.** After the pleadings are closed but within such times as not to delay the trial, any party may move for judgment on the pleadings.

(D) **Preliminary hearings.** The defenses specifically enumerated (1) to (7) in subdivision (B) of this rule, whether made in a pleading or by motion, and the motion for judgment mentioned in subdivision (C) of this rule shall be heard and determined before trial on application of any party.

(E) **Motion for definite statement.** If a pleading to which a responsive pleading is permitted is so vague or ambiguous that a party cannot reasonably be required to frame a responsive pleading, he may move for a definite statement before interposing his responsive pleading. The motion shall point out the defects complained of and the details desired. If the motion is granted and the order of the court is not obeyed within fourteen days after notice of the order or within such other time as the court may fix, the court may strike the pleading to which the motion was directed or make such order as it deems just.

(F) **Motion to strike.** Upon motion made by a party before responding to a pleading, or if no responsive pleading is permitted by these rules, upon motion made by a party within twenty-eight days after the service of the pleading upon him or upon the court's own initiative at any time, the court may order stricken from any pleading an insufficient claim or defense or any redundant, immaterial, impertinent or scandalous matter.

(G) **Consolidation of defenses and objections.** A party who makes a motion under this rule must join with it the other motions herein provided for and then available to him. If a party makes a motion under this rule and does not include therein all defenses and objections then available to him which this rule permits to be raised by motion, he shall not thereafter assert by motion or responsive pleading, any of the defenses or objections so omitted, except as provided in subdivision (H) of this rule.

(H) **Waiver of defenses and objections.**

(1) A defense of lack of jurisdiction over the person, improper venue, insufficiency of process, or insufficiency of service of process is waived (a) if omitted from a motion in the circumstances described in subdivision (G), or (b) if it is neither made by motion under this rule nor included in a responsive pleading or an amendment thereof permitted by Rule 15(A) to be made as a matter of course.

(2) A defense of failure to state a claim upon which relief can be granted, a defense of failure to join a party indispensable under Rule 19, and an objection of failure to state a legal defense to a claim may be made in any pleading permitted or ordered under Rule 7(A), or by motion for judgment on the pleadings, or at the trial on the merits.

(3) Whenever it appears by suggestion of the parties or otherwise that the court lacks jurisdiction of the subject matter, the court shall dismiss the action.

History: Amended, eff 7-1-83.

NOTES TO DECISIONS

Analysis

Applicability

Purported debtor's claim that he was an innocent third party with the same name as the actual judgment debtor went beyond the face of the complaint, so a trial court could not have resolved that issue by means of a Ohio R. Civ. P. 12(B)(6) motion to dismiss; rather, the purported debtor was entitled to a hearing pursuant to RC § 2716.13(C)(2). State Dep't of Taxation v. Banks, — Ohio App. 3d —, 2006 Ohio 3785, — N.E. 2d —, 2006 Ohio App. LEXIS 3725 (July 21, 2006).

Extension of time to answer

Even assuming, arguendo, that the dentist was not on notice that the trial court had ruled on his motion to quash until he received the motion for default judgment, the trial court did not err in denying his motion for leave; it acted within its discretion in finding that the dentist's belated explanation did not constitute excusable neglect. The facts as set forth in the dentist's affidavit would have been known to him at the time that he initially sought leave and he could have informed the trial court, at that first opportunity, of the reason for missing the deadline, which he failed to do, resulting in further delay which was within his control to prevent. R.J. Donovan Co. v. Sohi, — Ohio App. 3d —, 2007 Ohio 3620, — N.E. 2d —, 2007 Ohio App. LEXIS 3316 (July 17, 2007).

Trial court abused its discretion by ignoring an attorney's failure to comply with the Ohio Rules of Civil Procedure, effectively overruling the client's motion for a default judgment, and entertaining the attorney's motion for summary judgment as the attorney did not file a request for an extension of time to answer a client's legal malpractice complaint under Ohio R. Civ. P. 6(B)(1) and filed his answer one week after the client filed a motion for default judgment, but did not file a motion showing excusable neglect and requesting leave of court to file his untimely answer. Rowe v. Stillpass, — Ohio App. 3d —, 2006 Ohio 3789, — N.E. 2d —, 2006 Ohio App. LEXIS 3748 (July 13, 2006).

Failure to state a claim

Client did not demonstrate any error in the trial court's dismissal of the claims against the attorney for the apartment complex. In granting an Ohio R. Civ. P. 12(B)(6) motion for the attorney, the trial court properly found that the attorney was immune from liability because she was acting in her capacity as counsel. Nunn v. Cornyn, — Ohio App. 3d —, 2007 Ohio 5894, — N.E. 2d —, 2007 Ohio App. LEXIS 5185 (Nov. 5, 2007).

Failure to state claim

Trial court's ruling on an Ohio R. Civ. P. 12(B)(6) motion obviated the need for an answer, so the trial court did not err in failing to grant the buyer's motion for default judgment. Suarez Corp. Indus. v. Biern, — Ohio App. 3d —, 2006 Ohio 1510, — N.E. 2d —, 2006 Ohio App. LEXIS 1410 (Mar. 27, 2006).

—Piercing corporate veil

Party seeking to pierce the corporate veil is not required to relate that specific intention in the complaint in order to proceed under the doctrine of piercing the corporate veil: Dombroski v. WellPoint, Inc., 173 Ohio App. 3d 508, 2007 Ohio 5054, 879 N.E.2d 225, 2007 Ohio App. LEXIS 4440 (2007).

Motion for definite statement

When a patient sued a medical practice, a physician, and a hospital for medical malpractice, it was premature for the trial court to dismiss the patient's complaint for a failure to attach an affidavit of merit required by Ohio R. Civ. P. 10(D)(2) because (1) the parties sued should have moved for a more definite statement, under Ohio R. Civ. P. 12(E), instead of dismissal, under Ohio R. Civ. P. 12(B)(6), and (2) the trial court did not rule on the patient's Ohio R. Civ. P. 10(D)(2)(b) motion for more time within which to file the affidavit, and it was not proper to presume that the trial court's failure to rule on the motion was a denial of the motion because the failure to rule on the motion ultimately resulted in dismissal of the case. Stewart v. Forum Health, — Ohio App. 3d —, 2007 Ohio 6922, — N.E. 2d —, 2007 Ohio App. LEXIS 6069 (Dec. 12, 2007).

Trial court did not err in denying debtors' Ohio R. Civ. P. 12(E) motion for a definitive statement, seeking a more definitive statement from the creditor in its reply to the debtors' counterclaim filed in the creditor's foreclosure action, since the motion can only be used against a pleading to which a responsive pleading is permitted, and a responsive pleading is not permitted against a reply to a counterclaim. Bank v. Damsel, — Ohio App. 3d —, 2006 Ohio 4071, — N.E. 2d —, 2006 Ohio App. LEXIS 3991 (Aug. 8, 2006).

Motion to dismiss

Trial court erred in granting a motion to dismiss pursuant to CivR 12(B)(6) because such a motion was not pending before the court. The complaint was not frivolous, and it did not appear that the plaintiff could not prevail on the alleged facts: Concord Health Care, Inc. v. Schroeder, 177 Ohio App. 3d 228, 2008 Ohio 3392, 894 N.E.2d 351, 2008 Ohio App. LEXIS 2874 (2008).

— Conversion to motion for summary judgment

Trial court erred by converting the CivR 12(B)(6) motion into a motion for summary judgment and then granting that motion without notice to the parties of the conversion. None of the materials submitted was supported or opposed by affidavits made on personal knowledge as required by CivR 56(E): Ihenacho v. Coverall of S. Ohio, 173 Ohio App. 3d 13, 2007 Ohio 4206, 877 N.E.2d 351, 2007 Ohio App. LEXIS 3801 (2007).

Employer's contention that a trial court properly considered matters outside the pleadings in ruling on the employer's motion to dismiss was rejected as there was no evidence that the trial court provided notice to the parties that it intended to convert the employer's motion to dismiss into a motion for summary judgment. Goss v. Kmart Corp., — Ohio App. 3d —, 2007 Ohio 3200, — N.E. 2d —, 2007 Ohio App. LEXIS 2923 (June 22, 2007).

While the trial court should have converted a manufacturer's motion to dismiss appellants' complaint to a motion for summary judgment as it considered materials and evidence outside of the complaint to determine whether the complaint was barred by the doctrine of res judicata, the error was harmless because the trial court afforded both parties a reasonable opportunity to present matters outside the pleadings at the oral hearing on the manufacturer's motion to dismiss. Hutchinson v. Beazer East, Inc., — Ohio App. 3d —, 2006 Ohio 6761, — N.E. 2d —, 2006 Ohio App. LEXIS 6672 (Dec. 21, 2006).

Court rejected plaintiff's contention that a trial court improperly converted an attorney's motion for summary judgment into a motion to dismiss without notice of conversion under Ohio R. Civ. P. 12(B). When a motion for summary judgment is converted into a motion to dismiss, notice of conversion does not have to be given. Sat Adlaka v. Giannini, — Ohio App. 3d —, 2006 Ohio 4611, — N.E. 2d —, 2006 Ohio App. LEXIS 4574 (Sept. 1, 2006).

Ohio R. Civ. P. 12(B)(6) motion based on res judicata was procedurally inappropriate as the prior civil actions did not appear in the complaint, and the procedural course required was to convert the motion to a summary judgment motion. The trial court's ruling on the Ohio R. Civ. P. 12(B)(6) motion obviated the need for an answer, so the trial court did not err in failing to grant the buyer's motion for default judgment. Suarez Corp. Indus. v. Biern, — Ohio App. 3d —, 2006 Ohio 1510, — N.E. 2d —, 2006 Ohio App. LEXIS 1410 (Mar. 27, 2006).

Notice

Trial court erred in granting an employer's oral request for a default judgment, made on the day of the trial, as an employee's counsel was not afforded sufficient time to show good cause as to his failure to answer a counterclaim within 28 days of the service of the counterclaim and why leave to plead was appropriate. Absent seven days' written notice, the employee's ability to show cause under Ohio R. Civ. P. 55(A) was emasculated. Shikner v. Solutions, — Ohio App. 3d —, 2006 Ohio 127, — N.E. 2d —, 2006 Ohio App. LEXIS 104 (Jan. 13, 2006).

Procedure

Even if the trial court was allowed to take judicial notice of the arbitrator's decision, it was not allowed to do so when ruling on a Ohio R. Civ. P. 12(B)(6) motion as the arbitrator's decision constituted matters outside of the pleadings. Also, because the trial court did not provide notice to the parties, it was not allowed to convert the motion to dismiss into a motion for summary judgment. State Bd. of Educ., — Ohio App. 3d —, 2007 Ohio 5053, — N.E. 2d —, 2007 Ohio App. LEXIS 4442 (Sept. 20, 2007).

Trial court erred in granting default judgment to plaintiff as defendants were not in default of an answer. Without an order of the trial court overruling the Civ. R. 12(B)(6) motion to dismiss, as ordered on remand, the time for defendants to file their answer to the complaint did not begin to run. Bridge v. Park Nat'l Bank, 169 Ohio App. 3d 384, 2006 Ohio 5691, 863 N.E.2d 180, 2006 Ohio App. LEXIS 5691 (2006).

Removal of public official

There is no good reason why CivR 12(B) should not apply in actions to remove a public official: Belle v. Carr, 169 Ohio App. 3d 286, 2006 Ohio 5689, 862 N.E.2d 847, 2006 Ohio App. LEXIS 5684 (2006).

Statute of limitations

Although summary judgment is often used to resolve statute of limitations issues, a court may resolve the matter in a CivR 12(B)(6) motion when the relevant facts are pleaded in the complaint. The trial court could determine whether RC § 2305.15 applied from the allegations in the amended complaint: Grover v. Bartsch, 170 Ohio App. 3d 188, 2006 Ohio 6115, 866 N.E.2d 547, 2006 Ohio App. LEXIS 6086 (2006).

Time limitations

Once the appellate court reversed the judgment of the trial court and issued a mandate directing the trial court to act, it was the responsibility of the trial court to comply with the mandate and issue an order overruling the motion to dismiss. The trial court's order then triggers the 14-day response time of CivR 12(A)(2): Bridge v. Park Nat'l Bank, 169 Ohio App. 3d 384, 2006 Ohio 5691, 863 N.E.2d 180, 2006 Ohio App. LEXIS 5691 (2006).

RULE 13.   Counterclaim and cross-claim

(A) **Compulsory counterclaims.** A pleading shall state as a counterclaim any claim which at the time of serving the pleading the pleader has against any opposing party, if it arises out of the transaction or occurrence that is the subject matter of the opposing party's claim and does not require for its adjudication the presence of third parties of whom the court cannot acquire jurisdiction. But the pleader need not state the claim if (1) at the time the action was commenced the claim was the subject of another pending action, or (2) the opposing party brought suit upon his claim by attachment or other process by which the court did not acquire jurisdiction to render a personal judgment on that claim, and the pleader is not stating any counterclaim under this Rule 13.

(B) **Permissive counterclaims.** A pleading may state as a counterclaim any claim against an opposing party not arising out of the transaction or occurrence that is the subject matter of the opposing party's claim.

(C) **Counterclaim exceeding opposing claim.** A counterclaim may or may not diminish or defeat the recovery sought by the opposing party. It may claim relief exceeding in amount or different in kind from that sought in the pleading of the opposing party.

(D) **Counterclaim against this state.** These rules shall not be construed to enlarge beyond the limits now fixed by law the right to assert counterclaims or to claim credits against this state, a political subdivision or an officer in his representative capacity or agent of either.

(E) **Counterclaim maturing or acquired after pleading.** A claim which either matured or was acquired by the pleader after serving his pleading may, with the permission of the court, be presented as a counterclaim by supplemental pleadings.

(F) **Omitted counterclaim.** When a pleader fails to set up a counterclaim through oversight, inadvertence, or excusable neglect, or when justice requires, he may by leave of court set up the counterclaim by amendment.

(G) **Cross-claim against co-party.** A pleading may state as a cross-claim any claim by one party against a co-party arising out of the transaction or occurrence that is the subject matter either of the original action or of a counterclaim therein or relating to any property that is the subject matter of the original action. Such cross-claim may include a claim that the party against whom it is asserted is or may be liable to the cross-claimant for all or part of a claim asserted in the action against the cross-claimant.

(H) **Joinder of additional parties.** Persons other than those made parties to the original action may be made parties to a counterclaim or cross-claim in accordance with the provisions of Rule 19, Rule 19.1, and Rule 20. Such persons shall be served pursuant to Rule 4 through Rule 4.6

(I) **Separate trials; separate judgments.** If the court orders separate trials as provided in Rule 42(B), judgment on a counterclaim or cross-claim may be rendered in accordance with the terms of Rule 54(B) when the court has jurisdiction so to do, even if the claims of the opposing party have been dismissed or otherwise disposed of.

(J) **Certification of proceedings.** In the event that a counterclaim, cross-claim, or third-party claim exceeds the jurisdiction of the court, the court shall certify the proceedings in the case to the court of common pleas.

History: Amended, eff 7-1-71.

NOTES TO DECISIONS

ANALYSIS

Compulsory counterclaims
Conflict with statute
Joinder
Res judicata

Compulsory counterclaims

Purpose of CivR 13(A) is to promote judicial economy and avoid multiple lawsuits between the same parties arising from the same event or events. Pursuant to the "first in time" rule, the common pleas court should have dismissed the plaintiff's subsequent action filed in that court where the plaintiff had filed an earlier action in the municipal court that essentially involved the same parties and claims: Lewis v. Harding, 182 Ohio App. 3d 588, 2009 Ohio 3071, 913 N.E.2d 1048, 2009 Ohio App. LEXIS 2606 (2009).

In a multi-claim action involving multiple parties arising from a boat accident, a boat occupant was barred from asserting a claim for coverage against the boat owner's insurer regarding a claim by an injured passenger on the boat, as the occupant had not provided the insurer with notice of the claim for coverage based on an accusation of permissive use until four years after the incident, and the occupant failed to assert a compulsory counterclaim in earlier litigation pursuant to Ohio R. Civ. P. 13(A). Nationwide Mut. Fire Ins. Co. v. State Auto Ins. Cos., — Ohio App. 3d —, 2008 Ohio 573, — N.E. 2d —, 2008 Ohio App. LEXIS 505 (Feb. 14, 2008).

Trial court did not err in allowing a lender to file a counterclaim regarding an unpaid credit-card debt by a debtor in her action, alleging that the lender had engaged in unfair lending practices with respect to cross-collateralization of a credit card agreement and a car loan, as the unpaid credit card debt claim arose "from the transaction or occurrence" and accordingly, it was a compulsory counterclaim under Ohio R. Civ. P. 13(A). The credit card debt arose from the transaction that was the subject of the debtor's claim and it did not require the presence of any party outside of the trial court's jurisdiction. Wooding v. Cinfed Emples. Fed. Credit Union, — Ohio App. 3d —, 2007 Ohio 728, — N.E. 2d —, 2007 Ohio App. LEXIS 664 (Feb. 23, 2007).

When, in a partnership dispute, majority partners claimed, after judgment was entered against them in a prior suit for reducing a minority partner's partnership interest through a wrongful contribution call the minority partner could not pay, that the minority partner had to pay the minority partner's proportionate share of the contribution to maintain the minority partner's reduced interest in the partnership, the majority partners' claim was not a compulsory counterclaim in the prior suit, under CivR 13(A), because the claim did not exist when the minority partner filed the complaint in the prior case, as the claim did not exist until the minority partner prevailed in the prior case. Schafer v. RMS Realty, — Ohio App. 3d —, 2007 Ohio 7155, — N.E. 2d —, 2007 Ohio App. LEXIS 6273 (Dec. 28, 2007).

When a father sued his son to have a real estate purchase contract between them, and various related documents, voided and rescinded, and obtained a judgment voiding the deed evidencing the transfer, but did not obtain a judgment rescinding the contract, and he then filed a second suit against the son for rent for the period when the son was record owner of the real estate, the son's counterclaim, in the second suit, for breach of contract, was not a compulsory counterclaim in the first suit, because the contract had not been breached at the time of the son's pleadings in the first suit, and it was not breached until the father subsequently transferred a portion of the realty to another, so such a claim could not have been raised at that time, and it, thus, was not barred in the second suit, under Ohio R. Civ. P. 13(A). Shaffer v. Shaffer, — Ohio App. 3d —, 2006 Ohio 1997, — N.E. 2d —, 2006 Ohio App. LEXIS 1857 (Apr. 24, 2006).

First filed rule was not applicable to a bank's cognovit judgment action, which was commenced after a debtor had commenced her action against the bank in a different county, as the bank had strict requirements jurisdictionally under RC § 2323.13(A) as to where the action could be brought. It was not required to bring a compulsory counterclaim to the debor's action pursuant to Ohio R. Civ. P. 13(A), as such was not required until such time as a "pleading" was filed, the bank's motion to dismiss pursuant to Ohio R. Civ. P. 12(B)(6) in the debtor's action was not a pleading, and the matter was ultimately dismissed prior to a pleading having been entered therein. Fifth Third Bank v. Labate, — Ohio App. 3d —, 2006 Ohio 4239, — N.E. 2d —; 2006 Ohio App. LEXIS 4168 (Aug. 14, 2006).

Conflict with statute

Because RC § 5501.22 is a substantive law, it controls over the procedural rules in CivR 13(A) and (B) concerning counterclaims: Proctor v. Kardassilaris, 115 Ohio St. 3d 71, 2007 Ohio 4838, 873 N.E.2d 872, 2007 Ohio LEXIS 2404 (2007).

Joinder

Trial court committed no error in refusing to allow a debtor to join his wife as a party in an action between the debtor and a bank, arising from an arbitration between them involving a credit card account, as joinder was not required under Ohio R. Civ. P. 13(H), 19, 19.1, and 20 because the wife was not listed as a party to the arbitration decision. There was no reason that she should have been made a party to the action that involved the bank's request to vacate the arbitration award. Citibank v. Wood, — Ohio App. 3d —, 2006 Ohio 5755, — N.E. 2d —, 2006 Ohio App. LEXIS 5711 (Oct. 27, 2006).

Res judicata

Where a property owner voluntarily dismissed his counterclaim against a builder pursuant to Ohio R. Civ. P. 41(A)(1) in a prior action by the builder, arising from a dispute between the parties over payment due under a construction contract, RC § 2305.19 was not applicable for purposes of the owner's refiling of the counterclaim in a subsequent action, as the counterclaim had not been deemed time-barred in the first action. As the counterclaim was deemed compulsory pursuant to Ohio R. Civ. P. 13(A) in the first action, res judicata operated to bar the second action and dismissal by the trial court was proper. Carlton v. Alar Dev. Co., — Ohio App. 3d —, 2006 Ohio 6877, — N.E. 2d —, 2006 Ohio App. LEXIS 6797 (Dec. 22, 2006).

RULE 14. Third-party practice

(A) **When defendant may bring in third party.** At any time after commencement of the action a defending party, as a third-party plaintiff, may cause a summons and complaint to be served upon a person not a party to the action who is or may be liable to him for all or part of the plaintiff's claim against him. The third-party plaintiff need not obtain leave to make the service if he files the third-party complaint not later than fourteen days after he serves his original answer. Otherwise he must obtain leave on motion upon notice to all parties to the action. The person served with the summons and third-party complaint, hereinafter called the third-party defendant, shall make his defenses to the third-party plaintiff's claim as provided in Rule 12 and his counterclaims against the third-party plaintiff and cross-claims against other third-party defendants as provided in Rule 13. The third-party defendant may assert against the plaintiff any defenses which the third-party plaintiff has to the plaintiff's claim. The third-party defendant may also assert any claim against the plaintiff arising out of the transaction or occurrence that is the subject matter of the plaintiff's claim against the third-party plaintiff. The plaintiff may assert any claim against the third-party defendant arising out of the transaction or occurrence that is the subject matter of the plaintiff's claim against the third-party plaintiff, and the third-party defendant thereupon shall assert his defenses as provided in Rule 12 and his counterclaims and cross-claims as provided in Rule 13. Any party may move to strike the third-party claim, or for its severance or separate trial. If the third-party defendant is an employee, agent, or servant of the third-party plaintiff, the court shall order a separate trial upon the motion of any plaintiff. A third-party defendant may proceed under this rule against any person not a party to the action who is or may be liable to him for all or part of the claim made in the action against the third-party defendant.

(B) **When plaintiff may bring in third party.** When a counterclaim is asserted against a plaintiff, he may cause a third party to be brought in under circumstances which under this rule would entitle a defendant to do so.

NOTES TO DECISIONS

ANALYSIS

Third-party complaint

Third-party complaint

Trial court abused its discretion in denying the tortfeasor's motion to join the victim's attorney and his law firm as third-party defendants because the tortfeasor's claim against the attorney stemmed directly from the primary suit and was, in essence, a claim for indemnity. The tortfeasor's right to enforce the original settlement agreement, including the indemnification provision, arose only upon the successful prosecution by the victim's insurer of its claim against the tortfeasor. Qualchoice, Inc. v. Paige-Thompson, — Ohio App. 3d —, 2007 Ohio 1712, — N.E. 2d —, 2007 Ohio App. LEXIS 1568 (Apr. 12, 2007).

Probate court did not abuse its discretion in adopting a magistrate's decision denying an estate beneficiary's motion to file a third-party complaint pursuant to Ohio R. Civ. P. 14 in a pending probate proceeding against her, wherein she was accused of concealing and embezzling estate assets, as her third-party action was based on a separate and independent claim, and it was resolved by summary judgment for defendants. Randle v. Randle, — Ohio App. 3d —, 2007 Ohio 1156, — N.E. 2d —, 2007 Ohio App. LEXIS 1084 (Mar. 15, 2007).

When a real estate buyer sued the seller for fraud and breach of contract, and the seller filed a third-party complaint against his real estate agent, a third-party claim was appropriate, under Ohio R. Civ. P. 14(A), because the seller's claims were derivative of the buyer's action against him because, if the buyer was not successful, there would be no injury to the seller for which to seek to impose liability on the agent. Carter v. Bernard, — Ohio App. 3d —, 2006 Ohio 7058, — N.E. 2d —, 2006 Ohio App. LEXIS 6986 (Dec. 28, 2006).

RULE 15.   Amended and supplemental pleadings

(A) **Amendments.** A party may amend his pleading once as a matter of course at any time before a responsive pleading is served or, if the pleading is one to which no responsive pleading is permitted and the action has not been placed upon the trial calendar, he may so amend it at any time within twenty-eight days after it is served. Otherwise a party may amend his pleading only by leave of court or by written consent of the adverse party. Leave of court shall be freely given when justice so requires. A party shall plead in response to an amended pleading within the time remaining for response to the original pleading or within fourteen days after service of the amended pleading, whichever period may be the longer, unless the court otherwise orders.

(B) **Amendments to conform to the evidence.** When issues not raised by the pleadings are tried by express or implied consent of the parties, they shall be treated in all respects as if they had been raised in the pleadings. Such amendment of the pleadings as may be necessary to cause them to conform to the evidence and to raise these issues may be made upon motion of any party at any time, even after judgment. Failure to amend as provided herein does not affect the result of the trial of these issues. If evidence is objected to at the trial on the ground that it is not within the issues made by the pleadings, the court may allow the pleadings to be amended and shall do so freely when the presentation of the merits of the action will be subserved thereby and the objecting party fails to satisfy the court that the admission of such evidence would prejudice him in maintaining his action or defense upon the merits. The court may grant a continuance to enable the objecting party to meet such evidence.

(C) **Relation back of amendments.** Whenever the claim or defense asserted in the amended pleading arose out of the conduct, transaction, or occurrence set forth or attempted to be set forth in the original pleading, the amendment relates back to the date of the original pleading. An amendment changing the party against whom a claim is asserted relates back if the foregoing provision is satisfied and, within the period provided by law for commencing the action against him, the party to be brought in by amendment (1) has received such notice of the institution of the action that he will not be prejudiced in maintaining his defense on the merits, and (2) knew or should have known that, but for a mistake concerning the identity of the proper party, the action would have been brought against him.

The delivery or mailing of process to this state, a municipal corporation or other governmental agency,

or the responsible officer of any of the foregoing, subject to service of process under Rule 4 through Rule 4.6, satisfies the requirements of clauses (1) and (2) of the preceding paragraph if the above entities or officers thereof would have been proper defendants upon the original pleading. Such entities or officers thereof or both may be brought into the action as defendants.

(D) **Amendments where name of party unknown.** When the plaintiff does not know the name of a defendant, that defendant may be designated in a pleading or proceeding by any name and description. When the name is discovered, the pleading or proceeding must be amended accordingly. The plaintiff, in such case, must aver in the complaint the fact that he could not discover the name. The summons must contain the words "name unknown," and a copy thereof must be served personally upon the defendant.

(E) **Supplemental pleadings.** Upon motion of a party the court may, upon reasonable notice and upon such terms as are just, permit him to serve a supplemental pleading setting forth transactions or occurrences or events which have happened since the date of the pleading sought to be supplemented. Permission may be granted even though the original pleading is defective in its statement of a claim for relief or defense. If the court deems it advisable that the adverse party plead to the supplemental pleading, it shall so order, specifying the time therefore.

NOTES TO DECISIONS
ANALYSIS

Abuse of discretion
Amendment
— Generally
— Addition of party
— Amending complaint
— Amendment to conform to evidence
— Failure to raise issue
— Failure to support allegations
— Fictitious name of party
— Misnomer
— Name unknown
— Time for filing motions
Amendment denied
Amendment not required
Denial of amendment
— Not abuse of discretion
Dismissal of single claim
Negligence
Relation back
— Generally
— Fictitious name
Service on previously unknown defendant
Settlement agreement
Supplemental pleadings

Abuse of discretion
When a feed supplier sued farmers on account and the farmers responded with a recoupment defense and asserted counterclaims against the supplier and another supplier, it was an abuse of discretion for a trial court to allow the suppliers, under Ohio R. Civ. P. 15(A), to amend their answer to the farmers' counterclaims one week before trial to raise a statute of limitations defense because that defense was apparent in the counterclaims but the suppliers waited over 25 months after the counterclaims were filed and over 14 months after

they admitted they knew such a defense was available to them before they sought to amend their answer, and they did not offer an explanation for their delay, and the statement in their answers that they "reserved all the affirmative defenses available" was insufficient, under Ohio R. Civ. P. 8, which required them to expressly state affirmative defenses. L. E. Sommer Kidron, Inc. v. Kohler, — Ohio App. 3d —, 2007 Ohio 885, — N.E. 2d —, 2007 Ohio App. LEXIS 821 (Mar. 5, 2007).

Due to the determination that a trial court erred in granting an Ohio R. Civ. P. 12(B)(6) motion, the appellate court found no abuse of discretion in the denial of the station's motion for leave to amend the complaint "in lieu" of that dismissal. Lin TV Corp. v. Roth Ins. Agency, — Ohio App. 3d —, 2007 Ohio 4474, — N.E. 2d —, 2007 Ohio App. LEXIS 4030 (Aug. 31, 2007).

Trial court abused its discretion in dismissing a city's amended appropriation petition without allowing the city to file a second amended petition; the second amended petition corrected errors in the city's amended petition, it conformed to the requirements of R.C. 163.05, there was bad faith or undue delay on the part of the city, and the owners of the subject property would not suffer undue prejudice if the second amended petition was filed. City of Wadsworth v. Ross, — Ohio App. 3d —, 2007 Ohio 6684, — N.E. 2d —, 2007 Ohio App. LEXIS 5864 (Dec. 17, 2007).

In a case in which opposing parties filed competing quiet title claims to the same land, and one party's answer to the other party's counterclaim mistakenly admitted that her opponents were the owners of the land, after her complaint had contested this, a trial court abused its discretion when it denied her motion to amend her answer, under Ohio R. Civ. P. 15(A), to correct this mistake, due to her delay in filing her answer, because there was no evidence that her opponents would be prejudiced, as they already knew from her complaint that she contested their ownership claim, so they could not have been surprised by the amendment she requested. Hoskinson v. Lambert, — Ohio App. 3d —, 2006 Ohio 6940, — N.E. 2d —, 2006 Ohio App. LEXIS 6848 (Dec. 26, 2006).

Leave to file an amended complaint lies in a trial court's sound discretion, and in order to find an abuse of that discretion, an appellate court must determine the trial court's decision was unreasonable, arbitrary or unconscionable and not merely an error of law or judgment. Hoskinson v. Lambert, — Ohio App. 3d —, 2006 Ohio 6940, — N.E. 2d —, 2006 Ohio App. LEXIS 6848 (Dec. 26, 2006).

Spirit of the Ohio Rules of Civil Procedure is the resolution of cases upon their merits, not upon pleading deficiencies, as Ohio R. Civ. P. 1(B) requires that the Rules be applied "to effect just results," and pleadings are simply an end to that objective, so the mandate of Oho R. Civ. P. 15(A) as to amendments requiring leave of court, is that leave "shall be freely given when justice so requires," and, while the grant or denial of leave to amend a pleading is discretionary, where it is possible that the plaintiff, by an amended complaint, may set forth a claim upon which relief can be granted, and it is tendered timely and in good faith and no reason is apparent or disclosed for denying leave, the denial of leave to file such amended complaint is an abuse of discretion. Hoskinson v. Lambert, — Ohio App. 3d —, 2006 Ohio 6940, — N.E. 2d —, 2006 Ohio App. LEXIS 6848 (Dec. 26, 2006).

Amendment

City's demolition of a building constituting an alleged nuisance did not render the owner's claim for wrongful demolition moot, despite the owner's failure to obtain a stay. The trial court should have permitted the owner to amend her complaint to raise constitutional claims for a "taking" of property without due process and to seek a declaratory judgment that the lien filed under RC § 715.261 was invalid. Plaintiff's claims were exempted from RC Chapter 2744 pursuant to RC § 2744.09(E): City of Englewood v. Turner, 178 Ohio App. 3d 179, 2008 Ohio 4637, 897 N.E.2d 213, 2008 Ohio App. LEXIS 3885 (2008).

— Generally

When a mortgagee filed a supplemental complaint in a foreclosure action, which named an additional party defendant, it was inconsequential whether the complaint was filed pursuant to Ohio R. Civ. P. 15(A) or 15(E) because the other parties had notice of the new complaint and ample time to respond. Charter One Bank v. Tutin, — Ohio App. 3d —, 2007 Ohio 999, — N.E. 2d —, 2007 Ohio App. LEXIS 985 (Mar. 8, 2007).

Ohio R. Civ. P. 15 permits a litigant to change a pleading to adjust to factual changes, and whether such changes are made pursuant to Ohio R. Civ. P. 15(A) or 15(E) is inconsequential so long as the recipient of the changed complaint receives adequate notice, has a reasonable opportunity to respond, and is not otherwise prejudiced. Charter One Bank v. Tutin, — Ohio App. 3d —, 2007 Ohio 999, — N.E. 2d —, 2007 Ohio App. LEXIS 985 (Mar. 8, 2007).

Trial court's grant of a judgment on the pleadings pursuant to Ohio R. Civ. P. 12(C) to a subcontractor in a trip-and fall sidewalk pedestrian's negligence action was error, as the subcontractor was originally a fictitiously-named defendant that was later identified, and it was properly personally served with the original summons and complaint pursuant to Ohio R. Civ. P. 15(D) and 3(A) within the requisite time for purposes of the amended complaint relating back to the original complaint. Easter v. Complete Gen. Constr. Co., — Ohio App. 3d —, 2007 Ohio 1297, — N.E. 2d —, 2007 Ohio App. LEXIS 1175 (Mar. 22, 2007).

Trial court's grant of a judgment on the pleadings pursuant to Ohio R. Civ. P. 12(C) to a subcontractor in a trip-and fall sidewalk pedestrian's negligence action was error, as the subcontractor was originally a fictitiously-named defendant that was later identified, and it was properly personally served with the original summons and complaint pursuant to Ohio R. Civ. P. 15(D) and 3(A) within the requisite time for purposes of the amended complaint relating back to the original complaint. Easter v. Complete Gen. Constr. Co., — Ohio App. 3d —, 2007 Ohio 1297, — N.E. 2d —, 2007 Ohio App. LEXIS 1175 (Mar. 22, 2007).

As a land installment contract vendee did not raise the affirmative defense of abandonment of the contracts in his answer or by means of an amended pleading pursuant to Ohio R. Civ. P. 8(C) and 15, and he did not seek to raise the defense in a motion prior to entering his responsive pleading pursuant to Ohio R. Civ. P. 12(B), he waived the right to utilize the abandonment defense in a foreclosure action against him. Bradford v. B & P Wrecking Co., — Ohio App. 3d —, 2007 Ohio 1732, — N.E. 2d —, 2007 Ohio App. LEXIS 1599 (Apr. 13, 2007).

When a bank sued a towing company for conversion of a vehicle in which the bank had a security interest, and the towing company counterclaimed for the vehicle's towing and storage fees, it was not an abuse of discretion for a trial court to allow the towing company to amend its counterclaim one month before trial, under Ohio R. Civ. P. 15(A), when the bank did not move the trial court to continue the trial. Wesbanco Bank, Inc. v. Hays, — Ohio App. 3d —, 2007 Ohio 1825, — N.E. 2d —, 2007 Ohio App. LEXIS 1654 (Apr. 17, 2007).

In a foreclosure action in which a second lienholder was named as a party, in which the lienholder sought to amend the lienholder's answer to state affirmative defenses of fraud and equitable estoppel, the lienholder had to seek leave to amend because the lienholder was moving to amend nearly 10 months after filing the lienholder's answer. 2007 Ohio 2198, — N.E. 2d —, 2007 Ohio App. LEXIS 2054 (May 9, 2007).

When a lender sold a consumer a vehicle and financed the sale, and then repossessed and disposed of the vehicle when the consumer defaulted, after which the lender sought to collect on the lender's contract with the consumer, it was no abuse of discretion to grant the lender summary judgment without ruling on the consumer's motion to amend the consumer's counterclaim because not ruling on the motion implicitly denied it and, under Ohio R. Civ. P. 15(A), granting the motion would have prejudiced the lender. Columbus Mortg., Inc. v. Morton, — Ohio App. 3d —, 2007 Ohio 3057, — N.E. 2d —, 2007 Ohio App. LEXIS 2799 (June 19, 2007).

When sellers sued a partnership and others for defaulting on promissory notes, and the sellers moved to replace certain deceased or incompetent sellers with representatives, under Ohio R. Civ. P. 15(A), it was an abuse of discretion to deny the motion because the motion sought to add parties to represent the claims of parties who were privy to the relevant agreements because the parties to be replaced had either passed away or become incompetent, even though the case had been litigated for approximately 20 months and the parties had engaged in a great deal of pretrial discovery. Howick v. Lakewood Village, — Ohio App. 3d —, 2007 Ohio 4370, — N.E. 2d —, 2007 Ohio App. LEXIS 3944 (Aug. 27, 2007).

When a motorist sued the Ohio Bureau of Motor Vehicles for having incorrect information about the status of the motorist's insurance coverage and driver's license, and the motorist sought to amend the motorist's complaint, under Ohio R. Civ. P. 15(A), to include a claim for lost wages, the motion was properly denied because the Bureau had previously filed its investigation report, pursuant to court order, and the motorist did not obtain the Bureau's written consent to the amendment. Chaney v. BMV, — Ohio Misc. 2d —, 2007 Ohio 2697, — N.E. 2d —, 2007 Ohio Misc. LEXIS 168 (May 1, 2007).

Trial court did not err in striking a client's amended legal malpractice complaint because the amended complaint alleged no new causes of action and did not contain any allegation that there was another act of legal malpractice that extended the relevant statute of limitations. Further, the only difference between the original complaint and the amended complaint was that the amended complaint listed the social security numbers of two parties and failed to assert any reason for including such immaterial, impertinent, and harassing items on the caption. North Shore Auto Sales v. Weston, — Ohio App. 3d —, 2006 Ohio 456, — N.E. 2d —, 2006 Ohio App. LEXIS 393 (Feb. 2, 2006).

Bank was permitted by Ohio R. Civ. P. 15(A) to amend its original foreclosure complaint by adding to the document 13 days later when it filed a signed lost note affidavit, because it was still within the time period before the debtor's responsive pleading was served. Citifinancial Mortg. Co. v. Yoel, — Ohio App. 3d —, 2006 Ohio 331, — N.E.2d —, 2006 Ohio App. LEXIS 284 (Jan. 27, 2006).

Ohio R. Civ. P. 3(A) and 15(C) are read in pari materia to mean that notice to a new defendant of a claim, where amendment of a complaint to include the new defendant is sought, must occur within one year of the filing of the complaint if the statute of limitations has run and that such notice does not require service, so notice need not be received before the statute of limitations has run and eventual service need not be completed within one year of filing of the original complaint. Reighard v. Cleveland Elec. Illuminating, — Ohio App. 3d —, 2006 Ohio 1283, — N.E. 2d —, 2006 Ohio App. LEXIS 1179 (Mar. 16, 2006).

When an injured party filed a personal injury claim involving the electric lines running into her house against a company, which she incorrectly said was "formerly known as" the company responsible for those lines, it was error to deny her motion to amend her complaint, under Ohio R. Civ. P. 15(A), because (1) the company she sued was not prejudiced, as she proposed to dismiss it, (2) her bad faith was not shown,

(3) her delay in filing her motion was, in part, a result of the company she sued, and its parent, giving the impression that she had sued the correct company, and (4) the company she proposed suing, which likely had notice of her claim within the statute of limitations, as it and the company she sued were both subsidiaries of the same parent, could argue, once it was a party, any prejudice resulting from granting her motion to amend. Reighard v. Cleveland Elec. Illuminating, — Ohio App. 3d —, 2006 Ohio 1283, — N.E. 2d —, 2006 Ohio App. LEXIS 1179 (Mar. 16, 2006).

When an injured party filed a personal injury claim involving the electric lines running into her house against a company, which she incorrectly said was "formerly known as" the company responsible for those lines, that company did not have standing to oppose her motion to amend her complaint, under Ohio R. Civ. P. 15(A), because it claimed (1) it was unrelated to the company responsible for those lines, (2) it was not involved in the lines at issue in any way, and (3) the injured party did not contest that it was not liable. Reighard v. Cleveland Elec. Illuminating, — Ohio App. 3d —, 2006 Ohio 1283, — N.E. 2d —, 2006 Ohio App. LEXIS 1179 (Mar. 16, 2006).

Because the patient made no amendment pursuant to Ohio R. Civ. P. 15(D) and did not serve the John Doe defendants with a summons and copy of the complaint within one year of the filing of the complaint, the medical malpractice action against them was never commenced within the meaning of Ohio R. Civ. P. 3(A). Therefore, the judgment of the trial court adjudicated all pending claims, and the order from which the patient appealed was final and appealable pursuant to RC § 2505.02. Jackson-Summers v. Brooks, — Ohio App. 3d —, 2006 Ohio 1357, — N.E. 2d —, 2006 Ohio App. LEXIS 1233 (Mar. 23, 2006).

When a decedent's former wife, who was also the administrator of his estate, sued his brother, claiming that the decedent's transfers of property to the brother were fraudulent, it was proper for the trial court, under Ohio R. Civ. P. 15(A), to allow the brother to amend his answer to the wife's complaint, because (1) the answer mistakenly admitted a central allegation of the wife's complaint, so accepting that admission without allowing an amendment would have established that issue, (2) the wife did not claim or show that she would be prejudiced by an amendment, (3) the wife did not show the brother's bad faith, and (4) the wife did not show the brother's delay, as, when he was presented with the issue of his admission in the wife's summary judgment motion, he immediately sought to amend his answer. Lamar v. Washington, — Ohio App. 3d —, 2006 Ohio 1414, — N.E. 2d —, 2006 Ohio App. LEXIS 1298 (Mar. 27, 2006).

When an investor was denied leave to file a second amended complaint in his suit against an alleged joint venture partner, the investor's remedy was to appeal, and, when he, instead, filed a new action which essentially alleged the claims of his proposed second amended complaint, it was not error for the trial court to dismiss that second action, with prejudice, because he had already specifically been denied leave to raise those claims, allowing him to proceed would negate the trial court's actions, and the long-standing procedure that review of a trial court's ruling was to take place only after a final judgment would be undermined. Cusack v. ICS Holdings, — Ohio App. 3d —, 2006 Ohio 2536, — N.E. 2d —, 2006 Ohio App. LEXIS 2395 (May 23, 2006).

Trial court did not abuse its discretion in refusing to consider a policyholder's untimely second amended complaint because the complaint was not timely filed within the time period set by the trial court. Additionally, the policyholder failed to seek an extension of time in which the file the second amended complaint. MacConnell v. Safeco Prop., — Ohio App. 3d —, 2006 Ohio 2910, — N.E. 2d —, 2006 Ohio App. LEXIS 2735 (June 9, 2006).

Appellant's motion for relief from judgment under Ohio R. Civ. P. 60(B) was properly denied because it did not set forth any meritorious claim, and appellant failed to set forth any basis to support a finding that one of the five enumerated reasons set out in Ohio R. Civ. P. 60(B) would support relief from judgment. Appellant's motion to amend pleadings was also properly denied because there was no active, pending case in which there were pleadings to amend; instead, the motion to amend could have been granted only if appellant first prevailed on his motion for relief from judgment. Riser v. Wade, — Ohio App. 3d —, 2006 Ohio 3552, — N.E. 2d —, 2006 Ohio App. LEXIS 3503 (July 11, 2006).

Abandonment is an affirmative defense to a breach of contract action; because an ambulance service did not raise the affirmative defense of abandonment either in its answer to a breach of contract complaint or by means of an amended pleading, the ambulance service waived the abandonment defense. Buckeye Telesystem, Inc. v. Medcorp, Inc., — Ohio App. 3d —, 2006 Ohio 3798, — N.E. 2d —, 2006 Ohio App. LEXIS 3781 (July 21, 2006).

Where a city employee responded to a motion to dismiss his complaint with an amended complaint and a motion to declare the dismissal motion moot prior to the time that the initial dismissal motion was ruled upon by the trial court, the amended complaint properly replaced the original complaint under Ohio R. Civ. P. 15(A). The trial court's dismissal of the original complaint pursuant to the motion was error, as that complaint was no longer before the court. Barnes v. City of Beachwood, — Ohio App. 3d —, 2006 Ohio 3948, — N.E. 2d —, 2006 Ohio App. LEXIS 3906 (Aug. 3, 2006).

When a widow sued an air conditioner installer for wrongful death and negligent infliction of emotional distress, and she was allowed to amend her complaint after judgment to substitute the installer personally for his defunct corporation, this was not error because Ohio R. Civ. P. 15 permitted substitution of parties as long as the opposing party was not prejudiced, and the installer did not show prejudice. Estate of Heintzelman v. Air Experts, Inc., — Ohio App. 3d —, 2006 Ohio 4832, — N.E. 2d —, 2006 Ohio App. LEXIS 4741 (Sept. 14, 2006).

When a widow sued an air conditioner installer for wrongful death and negligent infliction of emotional distress, and she was allowed to amend her complaint after judgment to substitute the installer personally for his defunct corporation, this was not error because, under Ohio R. Civ. P. 15(B), the trial court could amend the pleadings to conform to the evidence presented at trial. Estate of Heintzelman v. Air Experts, Inc., — Ohio App. 3d —, 2006 Ohio 4832, — N.E. 2d —, 2006 Ohio App. LEXIS 4741 (Sept. 14, 2006).

There was no abuse of discretion in a trial court's denial, by its failure to rule, on a construction company's motion under Ohio R. Civ. P. 15(A) to amend its complaint to add an indemnification claim against an insurer, arising out of damage that occurred to a building that the company was working on, as the insurance policy clearly did not cover the damages caused by the collapse of the roof trusses installed by the company and there was no other provision in the insurance policy which provided a right of indemnification against the insurer. Journeyman Professionals, Inc. v. American Family Ins. Co., — Ohio App. 3d —, 2006 Ohio 5624, — N.E. 2d —, 2006 Ohio App. LEXIS 5611 (Oct. 27, 2006).

Trial court properly denied a passenger's Ohio R. Civ. P. 15 motion to amend her complaint to add a negligence claim against appellee because the motion was filed under Ohio R. Civ. P. 15(B), which involved amending a complaint during trial, and there was no trial in the case. Even if the motion were actually requested under Ohio R. Civ. P. 15(A), the trial court properly denied the motion because the passenger had waited until after the summary judgment hearing to make the request, which was 19 months after the complaint had been filed, and she based her request on appellee's deposition

transcript, which she had in her possession six months prior to filing her motion to amend. Suriano v. NAACP, — Ohio App. 3d —, 2006 Ohio 6131, — N.E. 2d —, 2006 Ohio App. LEXIS 6102 (Nov. 16, 2006).

Trial court's denial of a car occupant's motion under Ohio R. Civ. P.15(C) to add her name as a party-plaintiff to a timely-filed lawsuit by other occupants against a vehicle driver who had caused a vehicle collision was proper, as the statute of limitations had already expired and accordingly, the relation back doctrine did not apply; rather, to add her name, a new cause of action was created for limitations purposes. Bykova v. Szucs, — Ohio App. 3d —, 2006 Ohio 6424, — N.E. 2d —, 2006 Ohio App. LEXIS 6383 (Dec. 7, 2006).

Trial court did not err in denying a motion to amend the complaint by a patient and her husband, in a negligence action against a physician. No affidavits, dates, or deposition testimony was appended to the motion, no transcript of any oral or evidentiary hearing was filed by the patient and her husband, and as noted by the trial court, the matter had previously been filed and voluntarily dismissed and all discovery had been completed. Gregory v. Kodz, — Ohio App. 3d —, 2006 Ohio 6794, — N.E. 2d —, 2006 Ohio App. LEXIS 6717 (Dec. 18, 2006).

When a citizen and his wife sued a city and "unnamed police officers" for entering their home without a warrant, they never initiated any action against a named police officer, under Ohio R. Civ. P. 3(A) and 15(D), because they never identified an officer, nor was there any evidence that they served any officer with a summons and complaint. Maggio v. City of Warren, — Ohio App. 3d —, 2006 Ohio 6880, — N.E. 2d —, 2006 Ohio App. LEXIS 6801 (Dec. 22, 2006).

Ohio R. Civ. P. 15(A) favors a liberal amendment policy, so a motion for leave to amend should be granted absent a finding of bad faith, undue delay or undue prejudice to the opposing party, and prejudice to an opposing party is the most critical factor to be considered in determining whether to grant leave to amend; timeliness of the request is another factor to consider; but delay, in itself, should not operate to preclude an amendment. Hoskinson v. Lambert, — Ohio App. 3d —, 2006 Ohio 6940, — N.E. 2d —, 2006 Ohio App. LEXIS 6848 (Dec. 26, 2006).

— Addition of party
Trial court abused its discretion by vacating its order granting an amendment to add an additional defendant in a medical malpractice case where the alleged role of the additional defendant was revealed in a deposition of a defense expert witness: Christ v. Konski, 181 Ohio App. 3d 682, 2009 Ohio 1460, 910 N.E.2d 520, 2009 Ohio App. LEXIS 1225 (2009).

— Amending complaint
Trial court abused its discretion under Ohio R. Civ. P. 15 when it denied an employee's request to amend his complaint in order to add spoliation claims in his employment discrimination action, arising from the employer-city's failure to have retained multiple documents regarding its interview process for a superintendent position that was denied to the employee; the employee had made numerous requests for the documents, he did not unduly delay his request to amend, he did not engage in bad faith, there would have been no undue prejudice to the employer, and the records from hiring and promotion decisions would have presumably been within the definition of public records under RC § 149.011(G) for purposes of RC § 149.39. Mitchell v. Lemmie, — Ohio App. 3d —, 2007 Ohio 5757, — N.E. 2d —, 2007 Ohio App. LEXIS 5060 (Oct. 26, 2007).

— Amendment to conform to evidence
In tenants' appeal from a judgment granting a directed verdict to a landlord in the tenants' suit alleging claims of wrongful eviction and breach of contract, the court reviewed

the propriety of the trial court's decision pursuant to the standard set forth in Ohio R. Civ. P. 41(B)(2) and found that the evidence supported the trial court's action in granting a directed verdict to the landlord on the ground that the rental agreement between the parties was unenforceable because it was impossible to perform as the village in which the property was located had ordered the mobile home removed from the property and refused to grant a variance to allow its placement on the property. Though the landlord did not explicitly raise impossibility or illegality as an affirmative defense, as required by Ohio R. Civ. P. 8(C), the parties implicitly consented to try the issue at trial; thus, pursuant to Ohio R. Civ. P. 15(B), the pleadings were amended to conform to the evidence at trial. Mitchell v. Thompson, — Ohio App. 3d —, 2007 Ohio 5362, — N.E. 2d —, 2007 Ohio App. LEXIS 4710 (Oct. 1, 2007).

Although the girlfriend's complaint did not request partition, that remedy could still have been afforded to her as an alternative form of relief because both parties testified concerning joint property, and the boyfriend raised the issue of partition in his post-trial brief. The boyfriend could not complain at that point that the partition remedy was treated as if it had been pled and awarded as an alternative remedy to the girlfriend. McCall v. Sexton, — Ohio App. 3d —, 2007 Ohio 3982, — N.E. 2d —, 2007 Ohio App. LEXIS 3589 (June 28, 2007).

Pleadings were sufficiently amended to conform to the evidence presented at trial. Because the father's position was that he did not know the status of the child's alleged adoption, it would not have been prudent for him to totally abandon his statements in his pleadings where he sought parental rights and responsibilities for the child. Mendiola v. Mendiola, — Ohio App. 3d —, 2007 Ohio 466, — N.E. 2d —, 2007 Ohio App. LEXIS 419 (Feb. 2, 2007).

When homeowners said a developer negligently misrepresented to them that a home they wanted to build would fit on two lots he proposed to sell them, it was not error for the trial court to decline to apply a negligent misrepresentation claim to the second of the two lots because the homeowners' complaint did not raise such a claim, even under a liberal interpretation of the complaint, pursuant to Ohio R. Civ. P. 8(F) and 1(B), nor did the parties impliedly consent to try such a claim, under Ohio R. Civ. P. 15(B). Brothers v. Morrone-O'Keefe Dev. Co., — Ohio App. 3d —, 2007 Ohio 1942, — N.E. 2d —, 2007 Ohio App. LEXIS 1762 (Apr. 24, 2007).

Although a mortgagee did not specifically plead personal liability of mortgagors on a note and mortgage, the trial court properly adopted the magistrate's finding on that issue pursuant to Ohio R. Civ. P. 15(B) as there was no substantial prejudice that resulted to the mortgagors in the successor to the first mortgagee's foreclosure action upon its discovery that the debt was reaffirmed during one mortgagor's bankruptcy. The mortgagors had notice that they could be personally liable, they had ample opportunity to address the issue during discovery, admissions, summary judgment, and in a trial on the merits, and they had an opportunity to cross-examine witnesses. C&W Asset Acquistion, LLC v. Forster, — Ohio App. 3d —, 2007 Ohio 2081, — N.E. 2d —, 2007 Ohio App. LEXIS 1942 (Apr. 30, 2007).

In a foreclosure action in which a second lienholder was named as a party, in which the lienholder sought to amend the lienholder's answer to state affirmative defenses of fraud and equitable estoppel, Ohio R. Civ. P. 15(B) did not apply to the lienholder's motion to amend because no trial had taken place at which the opposing party's express or implied consent to try these affirmative defenses could have occurred. 2007 Ohio 2198, — N.E. 2d —, 2007 Ohio App. LEXIS 2054 (May 9, 2007).

Evidence supported a trial court's grant of a domestic violence civil protection order pursuant to RC § 3113.31(D) upon finding that a former wife threatened to kill her former husband and to kidnap the parties' daughter, that the parties were engaged in multiple actions regarding bitter custody disputes over their daughter, that the wife had previously failed to return the daughter after obtaining custody of her for a visitation period, and that the husband reasonably experienced fear from the threats. Although the date he provided as to the threat made by the wife was erroneous in the petition, the trial court acted properly when it sua sponte allowed an amendment of the pleadings to conform to the proof offered at trial regarding the correct date that the threat was made pursuant to Ohio R. Civ. P. 15(B). McGuire v. Sprinkle, — Ohio App. 3d —, 2007 Ohio 2705, — N.E. 2d —, 2007 Ohio App. LEXIS 2504 (June 4, 2007).

When an ex-wife and an ex-husband took out a line of credit, on which they defaulted, the ex-wife could not claim, on appeal, that the ex-husband was liable to her for contribution because she did not plead such a claim in her complaint, nor did she move, pursuant to Ohio R. Civ. P. 15(B), to amend her complaint to conform to the evidence to state such a claim, so she waived any contribution she might have been entitled to from the ex-husband. Eland v. Cleversy, — Ohio App. 3d —, 2006 Ohio 3416, — N.E. 2d —, 2006 Ohio App. LEXIS 3341 (June 30, 2006).

Trial court did not abuse its discretion when it amended the pleadings in the battery and intentional infliction of emotional distress case by instructing the jury on trespass because, although the terms "trespasser" or "trespass" were not used during the testimony, the defense of trespass was tried by the implied consent of the parties. Thus, under Ohio R. Civ. P. 15(B), the issue had to be treated as if it had been raised in the pleadings. Stafford v. Aces & Eights Harley-Davidson, — Ohio App. 3d —, 2006 Ohio 1780, — N.E. 2d —, 2006 Ohio App. LEXIS 1636 (Apr. 10, 2006).

When a printer sued a magazine publisher on account for amounts the publisher had not paid, it was error for the trial court to effectively enter judgment against the publisher's senior manager on a promissory note the manager signed with the publisher because (1) the printer sued only on the account, (2) the promissory note was a separate contract, and (3) the parties did not try the promissory note by consent, under Ohio R. Civ. P. 15(B), because the publisher's counsel did not acquiesce as such and the printer acquiesced, on appeal, that it had made it clear at trial that it was not suing on the note. Gray Printing Co. v. Brides, — Ohio App. 3d —, 2006 Ohio 1656, — N.E. 2d —, 2006 Ohio App. LEXIS 1435 (Mar. 31, 2006).

Trial court acted reasonably in denying a radiologist and her employer ("appellants") leave to amend the pleadings to include the affirmative defense of patient contributory negligence because appellants did not move to amend the pleadings until three months after the jury had returned its verdict, thereby virtually eliminating any opportunity that the administrator had to address the issue of patient negligence during the trial. Moreover, the record showed that the affirmative defense was specifically abandoned by appellants, that the issue of patient negligence was not tried with the express or implied consent of the parties, and that the affirmative defense was inconsistent with appellants' theory of the case. Viox v. Weinberg, — Ohio App. 3d —, 2006 Ohio 5075, — N.E. 2d —, 2006 Ohio App. LEXIS 5010 (Sept. 29, 2006).

Trial court did not abuse its discretion when it denied the administratrix's motion to amend her case, under Ohio R. Civ. P. 15(B), to include a claim of breach of patient confidentiality because an amendment to the pleadings to conform to the evidence was inappropriate under the circumstances of the case. The parties did not know what medical chart or document the doctor had allegedly reviewed, or whether he did so without authorization, and the additional claim presented questions substantially different from those at issue, gave rise the need for extra discovery, and created a real potential for new parties, counterclaims and cross-claims, and damages.

Simpson v. Kuchipudi, — Ohio App. 3d —, 2006 Ohio 5163, — N.E. 2d —, 2006 Ohio App. LEXIS 5103 (Oct. 2, 2006).

In an action for breach of an option-to-purchase contract filed by a lessee against lessors, the trial court did not abuse its discretion in considering an affidavit on facts relating to title pursuant to RC § 5301.22 that the lessee filed separately against the lessors, even though the affidavit was not filed until after the lessee had filed his complaint and the lessors had filed their answer and counterclaim. Under Ohio R. Civ. P. 15(B) the evidence was treated as if it had been raised by the pleadings because the lessee did not object to the admission of the affidavit into evidence or to any trial testimony concerning the affidavit. Weatherspoon v. Kuhlman, — Ohio App. 3d —, 2006 Ohio 5903, — N.E. 2d —, 2006 Ohio App. LEXIS 5866 (Nov. 9, 2006).

In a landlord's suit against a tenant for unpaid rent after the tenant prematurely vacated the landlord's apartment, the tenant's failure to file an answer raising the affirmative defense of mitigation of damages, under Ohio R. Civ. P. 8(C), did not bar the trial court from considering the issue because the landlord raised it in the trial court by presenting evidence on the issue, so it was tried with the landlord's implied consent, and was properly before the trial court for determination, under Ohio R. Civ. P. 15(B). Manor Park Apts. v. Delfosse, — Ohio App. 3d —, 2006 Ohio 6867, — N.E. 2d —, 2006 Ohio App. LEXIS 6799 (Dec. 22, 2006).

— Failure to raise issue

As a terminated anesthesiologist who sued the remaining anesthesiologists in the parties' practice never asserted a claim based on the practice's payment of the remaining anesthesiologists' attorney fees as an alleged basis for a breach of fiduciary duties to the terminated anesthesiologist, and the claim was not pled or tried with the express or implied consent of the remaining anesthesiologists pursuant to Ohio R. Civ. P. 15(B), the trial court did not err in failing to fashion relief on such a spurious claim. Mulchin v. Zzz Anesthesia, Inc., — Ohio App. 3d —, 2006 Ohio 5773, — N.E. 2d —, 2006 Ohio App. LEXIS 5757 (Nov. 3, 2006).

— Failure to support allegations

Trial court did not abuse its discretion in denying the employee's motion to amend the pleadings because the employee failed to comply with the minimal amendment requirements in that he failed to introduce any evidence to the trial court of the new matters sought to be pled. The employee offered no argument whatsoever to show that he could support his new claim, and he did not establish that the amendment was not simply a delaying tactic, nor one that would cause prejudice to the former employer. Williams v. W. Reserve Transit Auth., — Ohio App. 3d —, 2007 Ohio 4747, — N.E. 2d —, 2007 Ohio App. LEXIS 4274 (Sept. 14, 2007).

— Fictitious name of party

Arrestee who commenced a tort-based action against unnamed deputy sheriffs who allegedly mistreated her upon her arrest and who were thereafter properly identified and named by amendment to the pleading, failed to strictly comply with the specific requirements of Ohio R. Civ. P. 15(D) for purposes of the name amendment; however, summary judgment was granted to the sheriffs due to the lack of proof of service on them. Batchelder v. Young, — Ohio App. 3d —, 2006 Ohio 6097, — N.E. 2d —, 2006 Ohio App. LEXIS 6057 (Nov. 17, 2006).

— Misnomer

Where a mortgagee incorrectly named one of the defendants in its foreclosure action, the complaint did not mandate dismissal, as the trial court had granted the mortgagee's motion under Ohio R. Civ. P. 15(A) for leave to file an amended complaint, wherein the corrected defendants were properly added, and the mortgagee thereafter dismissed improper defendants pursuant to Ohio R. Civ. P. 41(A)(1). Lasalle Nat'l Bank v. Ingle, — Ohio App. 3d —, 2007 Ohio 77, — N.E. 2d —, 2007 Ohio App. LEXIS 71 (Jan. 11, 2007).

— Name unknown

As a traffic report which showed that a city-owned dump truck was involved in a traffic accident with motorists was not attached to a complaint or an amended complaint, it could not be considered for purposes of the city's dismissal motion under Ohio R. Civ. P. 12(B)(6) based on a claim that the limitations period had expired prior to the filing of an amended complaint which added the city as a party defendant; the city was deemed substituted for a John Doe defendant where the requirements of Ohio R. Civ. P. 15(C), (D), and 3(A) were satisfied, such that the complaint was deemed timely filed because it related back to the original complaint. Alcala v. Autullo, — Ohio App. 3d —, 2007 Ohio 5309, — N.E. 2d —, 2007 Ohio App. LEXIS 4674 (Sept. 28, 2007).

Where a mental health professional was served with an administratrix's amended complaint along with a summons, the summons failed to contain the words "name unknown" and the professional was not identified by name, the service was by certified mail rather than by personal service, and the professional raised as affirmative defenses the improper service of process and the bar of the statute of limitations, the requirements of Ohio R. Civ. P. 15(D) were not met, and accordingly, Rule 15(C) did not cause the amended complaint to relate back to the original filing date. Although summary judgment was granted on grounds of immunity to others, the amended complaint was time-barred as to the claim against the professional. Stewart v. North Coast Ctr., — Ohio App. 3d —, 2006 Ohio 2392, — N.E. 2d —, 2006 Ohio App. LEXIS 2247 (May 12, 2006).

— Time for filing motions

Trial court did not abuse its discretion in overruling a co-owner's motion for leave to file an amended complaint in a business dispute between the co-owners, as the motion was filed subsequent to the issuance of a magistrate's decision and after the co-owner had filed his objections to the magistrate's decision, and accordingly, it was untimely. Although the trial court did not rule on the motion, it was presumed to have been overruled where it was not discussed or ruled upon prior to the trial. Stumpff v. Harris, — Ohio App. 3d —, 2006 Ohio 4796, — N.E. 2d —, 2006 Ohio App. LEXIS 4691 (Sept. 15, 2006).

Amendment denied

There was no abuse of discretion in the denial of leave to file a third amended complaint because, although delay alone generally would not have justified denying leave to amend, the client previously had amended his original complaint two times. Moreover, denial of the motion was justified based on the fact that substantial discovery already had occurred, the fact that the client could have asserted his claims earlier, and the fact that allowing the amendment likely would have necessitated additional discovery and motion practice, thereby resulting in actual prejudice to defendants. Nunn v. Cornyn, — Ohio App. 3d —, 2007 Ohio 5894, — N.E. 2d —, 2007 Ohio App. LEXIS 5185 (Nov. 5, 2007).

Amendment not required

Despite the fact that an insureds' complaint, alleging claims for uninsured/underinsured motorists coverage and bad faith, did not base its bad faith claim specifically on the insurer's refusal to pay med-pay benefits, the trial court could have properly considered the insurer's delay in paying med-pay benefits in its analysis of the insurer's entitlement to summary judgment as the insurer did not object to the insureds' assertions in their response to the insurer's motion for summary judgment in which the insureds argued that the insurer's failure to pay med-pay benefits created a genuine issue of material fact as to whether the insurer acted in bad faith. In the absence of such an objection, and in accordance with the spirit of Ohio R. Civ. P. 15(B), the insurer implicitly consented to the trial court's consideration of the insurer's failure to pay med-pay benefits in the trial court's analysis of the insurer's entitlement to summary judgment. Zaychek v. Nationwide Mut. Ins. Co., — Ohio App. 3d —, 2007 Ohio 3297, — N.E. 2d —, 2007 Ohio App. LEXIS 3065 (June 29, 2007).

Court rejected an insurer's assertion that only conduct prior to the insureds' filing of its complaint seeking uninsured/underinsured motorists coverage and alleging a claim of bad faith could be considered as evidence of bad faith on the ground that the insureds did not supplement their complaint based on Ohio R. Civ. P. 15(E). The insurer's conduct after the complaint was filed in seeking medical records despite already having them in their possession and continuing to delay paying the claims after the complaint was filed was the same conduct that was alleged in the complaint. There was no need to supplement the insureds' pleadings with additional instances of the same conduct. Zaychek v. Nationwide Mut. Ins. Co., — Ohio App. 3d —, 2007 Ohio 3297, — N.E. 2d —, 2007 Ohio App. LEXIS 3065 (June 29, 2007).

Denial of amendment

Trial court did not err in denying a lien holder's Ohio R. Civ. P. 15 motion to amend his complaint against the clerk of courts and a deputy clerk, alleging that the clerks breached a duty by failing to properly record his lien, because the holder could not cure the defect in his complaint by amending in that it sought recovery from parties entitled to judicial immunity. Petho v. Cuyahoga County Court, — Ohio App. 3d —, 2007 Ohio 5710, — N.E. 2d —, 2007 Ohio App. LEXIS 5028 (Oct. 25, 2007).

Trial court did not abuse its discretion in denying a former husband's motion to amend his complaint in order to add a defamation claim against his former wife in a multi-count action against her and others, arising from his arrest and charge of domestic violence due to an allegation that he hit the parties' daughter, as the motion was made 18 months after he filed his original complaint, the period for discovery was closed, and summary judgment motions had already been pending for almost two months. Crosset v. Marquette, — Ohio App. 3d —, 2007 Ohio 550, — N.E. 2d —, 2007 Ohio App. LEXIS 508 (Feb. 9, 2007).

Trial court did not abuse its discretion in denying a motion under Ohio R. Civ. P. 15(A) to amend a complaint in order to add a claim of respondeat superior by temporary employment agency assignees against the agency, arising from their injuries suffered in a vehicle accident when another worker for the agency was driving them all to a job. If the worker was acting within the scope of his employment for purposes of respondeat superior liability on the agency, then the other assignees were also within the scope of their employment, and accordingly, they would have been barred from seeking relief other than through the workers' compensation system pursuant to Ohio Const. art. II, § 35 and RC § 4123.74. Heard v. Dubose, — Ohio App. 3d —, 2007 Ohio 551, — N.E. 2d —, 2007 Ohio App. LEXIS 510 (Feb. 9, 2007).

When a feed supplier sued farmers on account and the farmers responded with a recoupment defense and asserted counterclaims against the supplier and another supplier, it was not an abuse of discretion for a trial court to deny the farmers motion to amend their fraud counterclaim to state fraud with particularity because such an amendment would have been futile, as the farmers still did not sufficiently alleged that the suppliers knowingly or recklessly made a false representation to the farmers. L. E. Sommer Kidron, Inc. v. Kohler, — Ohio App. 3d —, 2007 Ohio 885, — N.E. 2d —, 2007 Ohio App. LEXIS 821 (Mar. 5, 2007).

Trial court did not abuse its discretion in denying the land buyer's motion to amend its second complaint because the seller's deposition was taken before the builder filed its first and second amended complaint and months before summary judgment motions had been filed. Therefore, the buyer had ample opportunities to amend its pleadings to accurately frame its allegations but delayed in doing so. Rockford Homes, Inc. v. Handel, — Ohio App. 3d —, 2007 Ohio 2581, — N.E. 2d —, 2007 Ohio App. LEXIS 2405 (May 25, 2007).

Trial court abused its discretion in denying appellants' leave to amend their refiled medical malpractice complaint to comply with Ohio R. Civ. P. 10(D)(2) because it was undisputed the refiled complaint was sufficient, except for the lack of the affidavit of merit and the doctor would not have incurred prejudice since he had knowledge of the experts' testimony from the depositions taken in the original action. The record demonstrated that leave was requested in the early stages of the proceedings, and that the doctor would not have been prejudiced by the trial court allowing appellants to amend their complaint and proceed with the case on the merits. Campbell v. Aepli, — Ohio App. 3d —, 2007 Ohio 3688, — N.E. 2d —, 2007 Ohio App. LEXIS 3358 (July 16, 2007).

When a church was sued on a mortgage the church granted to secure a trust indenture agreement, it was not an abuse of discretion to deny the church's motion, under Ohio R. Civ. P. 15(A), to amend the church's answer and file a counterclaim because most of the issues the church wanted to raise had been previously decided in ruling on the church's summary judgment motion, and the remaining issue was subsequently determined in a damages hearing. First Fin. Servs. v. Cross Tabernacle Deliverance Church, — Ohio App. 3d —, 2007 Ohio 4274, — N.E. 2d —, 2007 Ohio App. LEXIS 3937 (Aug. 21, 2007).

In a foreclosure action, a trial court properly determined that the amendment of the debtor's answer to include the equitable defense of unclean hands was unwarranted because the defense would not have affected the outcome of the case. Park Mill Run v. Garden Ridge Hilliard Delaware, — Ohio App. 3d —, 2006 Ohio 1535, — N.E. 2d —, 2006 Ohio App. LEXIS 1398 (Mar. 30, 2006).

— Not abuse of discretion

Trial court did not abuse its discretion in overruling the motion for leave to amend. Because plaintiffs failed to make the amended complaint and the supporting documents part of the record, there was only the motion for leave to amend for review and the proposed amendments would not have cured the problems of the original complaint. Moore v. Householder, — Ohio App. 3d —, 2006 Ohio 5682, — N.E. 2d —, 2006 Ohio App. LEXIS 5669 (Oct. 27, 2006).

Trial court did not abuse its discretion in denying debtors' motion for leave to file an amended answer under Ohio R. Civ. P. 15(A) and a third-party complaint. The trial court's finding of undue prejudice to the opposing party and undue delay was supported by the fact that the debtors sought to assert an independent cause of action against a third party in the foreclosure action brought by a creditor, and a third-party complaint cannot be founded upon an independent cause of action even if the cause of action arises out of the same occurrence as the original complaint. Bank v. Damsel, — Ohio App. 3d —, 2006 Ohio 4071, — N.E. 2d —, 2006 Ohio App. LEXIS 3991 (Aug. 8, 2006).

As a hardware company failed to show any prejudice that resulted from the trial court's refusal to accept its out-of-rule counterclaim pursuant to Ohio R. Civ. P. 15(A), and it did not cite to any issues that would have been raised in the counterclaim that were not considered and resolved by the trial court in its declaratory judgment ruling, there was no abuse of discretion in the trial court's ruling. Even if the trial court's denial of the counterclaim was an abuse of discretion, it was deemed harmless where no prejudice resulting from the denial was shown. Automated Solutions Corp. v. Paragon Data Sys., 167 Ohio App. 3d 685, 2006 Ohio 3492, 856 N.E. 2d 1008, 2006 Ohio App. LEXIS 3446 (July 6, 2006).

Dismissal of single claim

In order for a party's voluntary dismissal of one claim in a multi-count action to have been valid, it should have sought to amend the complaint under Ohio R. Civ. P. 15(A); the voluntary dismissal by stipulation pursuant to Ohio R. Civ. P. 41(A) was deemed a nullity where the entire action was not dismissed. Savage v. Cody-Zeigler, Inc., — Ohio App. 3d —, 2006 Ohio 2760, — N.E. 2d —, 2006 Ohio App. LEXIS 2601 (May 25, 2006).

Negligence

Corporation did not assert comparative or contributory negligence in its pleadings, and thus, the corporation waived the right to this defense; therefore, the trial court did not err when it denied the corporation's request for a jury instruction on comparative negligence. Barker v. Geotech Servs., — Ohio App. 3d —, 2006 Ohio 3814, — N.E. 2d —, 2006 Ohio App. LEXIS 3787 (July 26, 2006).

Relation back

Where motorists' insurer filed a subrogation action against a driver, alleging that the driver's negligence caused a motor vehicle accident for which the insurer had to pay various coverage expenses to the motorists, the motorists' intervening complaint should have been deemed timely filed pursuant to Ohio R. Civ. P. 15(C) and 19(A) and (B), as the motorists were necessary parties and their claims related back; the motorists and the insurer's claims had common questions of law and facts, and a determination regarding the driver's negligence and liability in the insurer's subrogation action was determinative with respect to the motorists' claims. Owens v. Smith, — Ohio App. 3d —, 2007 Ohio 6766, — N.E. 2d —, 2007 Ohio App. LEXIS 5916 (Dec. 14, 2007).

— Generally

Refiled complaint relates back to the original filing if the requirements of CivR 15(C) are met: Krieger v. Cleveland Indians Baseball Co., 176 Ohio App. 3d 410, 2008 Ohio 2183, 892 N.E.2d 461, 2008 Ohio App. LEXIS 1873 (2008).

Where service on former John Doe defendants was improper under CivR 15(D), the amended complaint did not relate back pursuant to CivR 15(C). However, where the original complaint was filed within the applicable period of limitation, pursuant to RC § 2305.19 plaintiffs had one year to perfect service on those defendants: LaNeve v. Atlas Recycling, Inc., 172 Ohio App. 3d 44, 2007 Ohio 2856, 872 N.E.2d 1277, 2007 Ohio App. LEXIS 2615 (2007).

Because the limitations period expired before the complaint was filed, there could be no relation back to salvage the claims as to the John Doe defendants. Bradigan v. Strongsville City Schs., — Ohio App. 3d —, 2007 Ohio 2773, — N.E. 2d —, 2007 Ohio App. LEXIS 2571 (June 7, 2007).

Trial court properly granted summary judgment to an employer and co-workers in a terminated employee's action, alleging invasion of privacy by the inadvertent recording of a phone conversation that the employee had with a competitor of the employer, wherein the employee made negative comments about the employer, as the claim was barred by the limitations period under RC § 2305.09, the relation back doctrine under Ohio R. Civ. P. 15(C) was inapplicable because there was no mistake about the parties involved, and there was no merit to the claim. There was no evidence that the recording of the conversation was anything but unintentional and there was no showing that the employee's privacy had been invaded. Roberts v. Murawski, — Ohio App. 3d —, 2007 Ohio 3555, — N.E. 2d —, 2007 Ohio App. LEXIS 3275 (July 13, 2007).

When a defendant's name was changed in a complaint, the amendment was governed by Ohio R. Civ. P. 15(C). Reighard v. Cleveland Elec. Illuminating, — Ohio App. 3d —, 2006 Ohio 1283, — N.E. 2d —, 2006 Ohio App. LEXIS 1179 (Mar. 16, 2006).

Where the statute of limitations has run as to a claim, Ohio R. Civ. P. 15(C) provides the test for determining if the amendment of a pleading relates back to the date of the original pleading, and first, the rule states that if the claim asserted in the amended pleading arose out of the conduct, transaction or occurrence set forth or attempted to be set forth in the original pleading, then the amendment relates back, but where the amendment changes the party against whom the claim is asserted, relation back also requires satisfaction of an additional test that within the period provided by law for commencing the action against him, the party to be brought in by amendment (1) has received such notice of the institution of the action that he will not be prejudiced in maintaining his defense on the merits, and (2) knew or should have known that, but for a mistake concerning the identity of the proper party, the action would have been brought against him. Reighard v. Cleveland Elec. Illuminating, — Ohio App. 3d —, 2006 Ohio 1283, — N.E. 2d —, 2006 Ohio App. LEXIS 1179 (Mar. 16, 2006).

— Fictitious name

When the specific requirements of CivR 15(D) for commencing an action are not met, an amendment does not relate back to the date of the original complaint under CivR 15(C) and CivR 3(A) and the saving statute of RC § 2305.19 does not apply: Laneve v. Atlas Recycling, 119 Ohio St. 3d 324, 2008 Ohio 3921, 894 N.E.2d 25, 2008 Ohio LEXIS 2240 (2008).

Service on previously unknown defendant

As plaintiffs filed a multi-count tort action against assorted "John Doe" defendants and they thereafter filed an amended complaint pursuant to Ohio R. Civ. P. 15(D) to actually name two defendants in place of the John Doe designation, the certified mail service on them was sufficient and timely, such that a trial court's dismissal under Ohio R. Civ. P. 12(B)(6) due to the action being time-barred was error. The original complaint was filed within the time limitations period of RC § 2305.10, the amended complaint was filed within the one-year period of Ohio R. Civ. P. 3(A), which was the equivalent of a voluntary dismissal and refiling that made the savings statute, RC § 2305.19(A), applicable, and the service on defendants was timely made within the next one-year period. LaNeve v. Atlas Recycling, Inc., 172 Ohio App. 3d 44, 2007 Ohio 2856, 872 N.E.2d 1277, 2007 Ohio App. LEXIS 2615 (2007).

As a city employee who was initially a "John Doe" defendant raised the lack of personal service and insufficiency of process as defenses in his answer to an amended complaint, the trial court properly granted him summary judgment on the basis of the statute of limitations once the one-year period provided for service under Ohio R. Civ. P. 3(A) had run; personal service of the original summons and complaint should have been made on the city employee pursuant to Ohio R. Civ. P. 15(D), and such defenses were clearly not waived under Ohio R. Civ. P. 12(G) and (H)(1). Burya v. Lake Metroparks Bd. of Park Comm'rs, — Ohio App. 3d —, 2006 Ohio 5192, — N.E. 2d —, 2006 Ohio App. LEXIS 5136 (Sept. 29, 2006).

Settlement agreement

Party could seek to enforce a settlement agreement through the filing of an independent action sounding in breach of contract, or it could be sought in the same action as the dispute settled through a supplemental pleading filed pursuant to Ohio R. Civ. P. 15(E), setting out the alleged agreement and breach. Cembex Care Solutions v. Gockerman, — Ohio App. 3d —, 2006 Ohio 3173, — N.E. 2d —, 2006 Ohio App. LEXIS 3028 (June 23, 2006).

In a former employer's suit against a former employee for breach of a confidentiality agreement, the parties' settlement agreement was properly enforced, under Ohio R. Civ. P. 15(E), because the agreement proposed to the court by the employee, which the trial court adopted, sufficiently stated the parties' intent that the agreement's release of the employee was limited to the breach currently alleged, and did not apply to any future breach, so the trial court's factual findings on this issue were supported by some competent, credible evidence. Cembex Care Solutions v. Gockerman, — Ohio App. 3d —, 2006 Ohio 3173, — N.E. 2d —, 2006 Ohio App. LEXIS 3028 (June 23, 2006).

Supplemental pleadings

In a foreclosure, a mortgagee's complaint was properly filed as a supplemental complaint, under Ohio R. Civ. P. 15(E), because its only difference from the original complaint was that it named an additional party defendant, so the mortgagee was not required to obtain leave to file it, under Ohio R. Civ. P. 15(A). Charter One Bank v. Tutin, — Ohio App. 3d —, 2007 Ohio 999, — N.E. 2d —, 2007 Ohio App. LEXIS 985 (Mar. 8, 2007).

Trial court abused its discretion in allowing home owners to supplement their complaint against a window and door seller which originally asserted a claim of slander of title in order to add claims for negligence and fraud pursuant to Ohio R. Civ. P. 15(E), as the supplemental pleading was more than a mere addition to, or continuation of, the original complaint and the new causes of action were different from the original claim. Gilson v. Windows & Doors Showcase, — Ohio App. 3d —, 2006 Ohio 2921, — N.E. 2d —, 2006 Ohio App. LEXIS 2807 (June 9, 2006).

In a workers' compensation claimant's appeal from the Industrial Commission of Ohio's denial of his workers' compensation claim, the employer's motion to supplement its answer so as to allege, as an affirmative defense, that the claimant, since the time that the appeal was filed, had executed a settlement agreement covering the claims at issue in the appeal was properly granted. The employer followed the appropriate procedure in raising its affirmative defenses, and since the supplemental answer raised an affirmative defense that could bar the claims, the trial court did not abuse its discretion in allowing the employer to file its motion for summary judgment even though the motion was not made until after the case was set for pretrial. Zestos v. Powertrain Div., GMC, — Ohio App. 3d —, 2006 Ohio 4545, — N.E. 2d —, 2006 Ohio App. LEXIS 4511 (Sept. 5, 2006).

RULE 16. Pretrial procedure

In any action, the court may schedule one or more conferences before trial to accomplish the following objectives:

(1) The possibility of settlement of the action;

(2) The simplification of the issues;

(3) Itemizations of expenses and special damages;

(4) The necessity of amendments to the pleadings;

(5) The exchange of reports of expert witnesses expected to be called by each party;

(6) The exchange of medical reports and hospital records;

(7) The number of expert witnesses;

(8) The timing, methods of search and production, and the limitations, if any, to be applied to the discovery of documents and electronically stored information;

(9) The adoption of any agreements by the parties for asserting claims of privilege or for protecting designated materials after production;

(10) The imposition of sanctions as authorized by Civ. R. 37;

(11) The possibility of obtaining:

(a) Admissions of fact;

(b) Agreements on admissibility of documents and other evidence to avoid unnecessary testimony or other proof during trial.

(12) Other matters which may aid in the disposition of the action.

The production by any party of medical reports or hospital records does not constitute a waiver of the privilege granted under section 2317.02 of the Revised Code.

The court may, and on the request of either party shall, make a written order that recites the action taken at the conference. The court shall enter the order and submit copies to the parties. Unless modified, the order shall control the subsequent course of action.

Upon reasonable notice to the parties, the court may require that parties, or their representatives or insurers, attend a conference or participate in other pretrial proceedings.

History: Amended, eff 7-1-08.

NOTES TO DECISIONS

ANALYSIS

Expert witness
Pretrial order
Prohibition

Expert witness

In the second trial in a patient's dental malpractice action, held because the patient's motion for a new trial was granted after a defense verdict was rendered in the first trial, the trial court did not abuse its discretion in precluding the dentist from calling an expert witness whose testimony had been precluded as a discovery sanction in the first trial. The preclusion order did not improperly change a separate discovery order that had set a deadline for the identification of expert witnesses because that order was not final and the preclusion order did not necessarily contradict it, trial courts could exclude the presentation of expert witnesses by parties who failed to comply with pretrial orders and, under Ohio R. Civ. P. 16(7), could reasonably limit the number of expert witnesses, and the dentist showed no prejudice to the defense caused by the preclusion of the expert's testimony. Scibelli v. Pannunzio, — Ohio App. 3d —, 2006 Ohio 5652, — N.E. 2d —, 2006 Ohio App. LEXIS 5650 (Oct. 26, 2006).

Pretrial order

Although an inmate who brought a civil action contended that certain events occurred at the pre-trial conference which were not listed in the pretrial order, and that certain events which were listed did not in fact occur, he failed to point to any evidence to support his claim that the order was inaccurate pursuant to Civ. R. 16. Brown v. Weidner, — Ohio App. 3d —, 2006 Ohio 6852, — N.E. 2d —, 2006 Ohio App. LEXIS 6765 (Dec. 26, 2006).

Prohibition

Prohibition was not available to prevent the trial court in a capital case from enforcing an order requiring the prosecuting attorney to provide all police reports and witness statements to defense counsel. The state had a right to appeal under RC § 2945.67 by leave of the court of appeals: State Ex Rel. Mason v. Burnside, 117 Ohio St. 3d 1, 2007 Ohio 6754, 881 N.E. 2d 224, 2007 Ohio LEXIS 3332 (Dec. 20, 2007).

TITLE IV
PARTIES

RULE 17. Parties plaintiff and defendant; capacity

(A) **Real party in interest.** Every action shall be prosecuted in the name of the real party in interest. An executor, administrator, guardian, bailee, trustee of an express trust, a party with whom or in whose name a contract has been made for the benefit of another, or a party authorized by statute may sue in his name as such representative without joining with him the party for whose benefit the action is brought. When a statute of this state so provides, an action for the use or benefit of another shall be brought in the name of this state. No action shall be dismissed on the ground that it is not prosecuted in the name of the real party in interest until a reasonable time has been allowed after objection for ratification of commencement of the action by, or joinder or substitution of, the real party in interest. Such ratification, joinder, or substitution shall have the same effect as if the action had been commenced in the name of the real party in interest.

(B) **Minors or incompetent persons.** Whenever a minor or incompetent person has a representative, such as a guardian or other like fiduciary, the representative may sue or defend on behalf of the minor or incompetent person. If a minor or incompetent person does not have a duly appointed representative the minor may sue by a next friend or defend by a guardian ad litem. When a minor or incompetent person is not otherwise represented in an action the court shall appoint a guardian ad litem or shall make such other order as it deems proper for the protection of such minor or incompetent person.

History: Amended, eff 7-1-75; 7-1-85.

NOTES TO DECISIONS

ANALYSIS

Bankruptcy
Decedents' estates
Incompetent
—— Divorce
Real party in interest
— Dismissal
— Insurance company
—— Mortgagee

___

Bankruptcy

Where the lawsuit did not include the trustee of the plaintiff's bankruptcy estate as a party, the action was not subject to dismissal on the basis that it was not brought in the name of the real party in interest. After becoming aware of the action, the trustee ratified its commencement: Krieger v. Cleveland Indians Baseball Co., 176 Ohio App. 3d 410, 2008 Ohio 2183, 892 N.E.2d 461, 2008 Ohio App. LEXIS 1873 (2008).

Where the bankruptcy trustee abandoned the petitioners legal malpractice claim against their original bankruptcy attorney, the petitioners had standing to pursue the malpractice claim: Newman v. Enriquez, 171 Ohio App. 3d 117, 2007 Ohio 1934, 869 N.E.2d 735, 2007 Ohio App. LEXIS 1741 (2007).

Decedents' estates

Decedent's daughter was not a real property in interest pursuant to Ohio R. Civ. P. 17(A) with respect to asserting a right to the decedent's father's estate, as the decedent's estate was the real party in interest where no estate had been filed for that particular decedent, such that it was unknown whether he died testate or intestate for purposes of determining his daughter's interest. Long v. Long, — Ohio App. 3d —, 2007 Ohio 5909, — N.E. 2d —, 2007 Ohio App. LEXIS 5207 (Nov. 2, 2007).

Incompetent

Decision refusing to allow a ward's personal representative to prosecute the ward's claims for relief was proper because the representative did not appear in the matter as Ohio R. Civ. P. 17(A) required when it was commenced, and thus, she was not entitled to prosecute the action at all because she was not a party and had not filed a motion to intervene as the ward's personal representative pursuant to Ohio R. Civ. P. 24(A). Neither could the representative appear as the ward's attorney or legal representative because she had not been admitted to the practice of law in Ohio, as required by RC § 4795.01. Brown v. Wright, — Ohio App. 3d —, 2006 Ohio 38, — N.E. 2d —, 2006 Ohio App. LEXIS 47 (Jan. 6, 2006).

—— Divorce

Pursuant to CivR 17(B) and 75(A), a guardian may sue for divorce on behalf of an incompetent spouse unless an exception under CivR 75 applies: Broach v. Broach, 177 Ohio App. 3d 664, 2008 Ohio 4132, 895 N.E.2d 640, 2008 Ohio App. LEXIS 3496 (2008).

Real party in interest

Current holder of the note and mortgage is the real party in interest in foreclosure actions. Various sections of the Uniform Commercial Code support the conclusion that the owner of a promissory note should be recognized as the owner of the related mortgage: U.S. Bank N.A. v. Marcino, 181 Ohio App. 3d 328, 2009 Ohio 1178, 908 N.E.2d 1032, 2009 Ohio App. LEXIS 1021 (2009).

Trial court did not abuse its discretion in denying a motion to vacate a void judgment under Ohio R. Civ. P. 60(B) by a promissory note debtor in a bank's foreclosure action, wherein the debtor claimed that the bank was not the real party in interest pursuant to Ohio R. Civ. P. 17. The real party in interest claim was not raised within a "reasonable time," such that it was deemed waived, and the debtor failed to show any evidence to support that claim or to support his request for relief from judgment based on the necessary showing required under Ohio R. Civ. P. 60(B). Washington Mutual Bank v. Novak, — Ohio App. 3d —, 2007 Ohio 996, — N.E. 2d —, 2007 Ohio App. LEXIS 990 (Mar. 8, 2007).

When a creditor sued a debtor for the balance due on a credit card account, the record sufficiently showed it was the real party in interest, even though the debtor said it was not the entity that issued the credit card, because no payments on the account were made to the issuer, and all payments were made to the creditor. Discover Bank v. Brockmeier, — Ohio App. 3d —, 2007 Ohio 1552, — N.E. 2d —, 2007 Ohio App. LEXIS 1419 (Apr. 2, 2007).

When clients filed a legal malpractice claim against their attorney after they had filed for bankruptcy, assuming that claim was an asset of their bankruptcy estate, only the bankruptcy trustee had standing to pursue it because he was the real party in interest, but, when he abandoned the claim after the statute of limitations expired, this ratified it, under

Ohio R. Civ. P. 17(A), and the ratification related back to the original filing of the claim, which was timely, under RC § 2305.11(A), so the clients were not time-barred from pursuing it. Newman v. Enriquez, 171 Ohio App. 3d 117, 2007 Ohio 1934, 869 N.E.2d 735, 2007 Ohio App. LEXIS 1741 (2007).

When clients timely filed a legal malpractice claim against their attorney after they had filed for bankruptcy, after which the bankruptcy trustee abandoned the claim, the clients became the real parties in interest as to the claim, as if no bankruptcy was ever filed, and the trustee's abandonment, after the statute of limitations expired, ratified the claim, under Ohio R. Civ. P. 17(A), and the ratification related back to its original filing, so the clients were not time-barred from pursuing it, because (1) the claim failed otherwise than on its merits, when they voluntarily dismissed it, under Ohio R. Civ. P. 41(A)(1)(a), (2) when they refiled the claim, the parties to the original and refiled claims were identical, and (3) the refiled claim was refiled one minute after the initial claim was dismissed, so the savings statute, RC § 2305.19(A), applied. Newman v. Enriquez, 171 Ohio App. 3d 117, 2007 Ohio 1934, 869 N.E.2d 735, 2007 Ohio App. LEXIS 1741 (2007).

As an insurer became subrogated to the rights of its insureds when it paid them for their claims that arose from a multi-vehicle collision, wherein they were passengers in one of the vehicles, it became a real party in interest in the action pursuant to Ohio R. Civ. P. 17(A). The failure to name a real party in interest or to join the insurer as a necessary party pursuant to Ohio R. Civ. P. 19(A) was waived where it was not promptly raised, and it was curable by any number of procedural devices, such as joinder, substitution, ratification, or amendment of the pleading. Goldney v. Byrd, — Ohio App. 3d —, 2007 Ohio 1985, — N.E. 2d —, 2007 Ohio App. LEXIS 1828 (Apr. 26, 2007).

When an entity with which a lender was associated entered into a contract with certain debtors, and then an assignment was executed which purportedly assigned the entity's rights in that contract to the lender, the lender had no standing to bring suit against the debtors pursuant to that assignment, nor was he a real party in interest, under Ohio R. Civ. P. 17(A), because the entity which purportedly assigned its rights in the original contract to the lender was not named in that original contract, so it had nothing to assign to the lender, and the lender's suit based on that assignment was properly dismissed with prejudice. Haley v. Hunter, — Ohio App. 3d —, 2006 Ohio 2975, — N.E. 2d —, 2006 Ohio App. LEXIS 2863 (June 14, 2006).

Where property owners held the real property in trust, and they were the sole trustees and beneficiaries thereof, the fact that they brought a breach of sale contract action in their individual capacities was not error under Ohio R. Civ. P. 17(A), as there was no danger that the property purchaser would face a subsequent similar action regarding the subject property or that the trial court judgment would not have the proper res judicata effect. In the circumstances, the owners were the real party in interest regardless of their designation as the trustees or not. Reitz v. Giltz & Assocs., — Ohio App. 3d —, 2006 Ohio 4175, — N.E. 2d —, 2006 Ohio App. LEXIS 4120 (Aug. 11, 2006).

In a dispute over funding and possible rescission of a contract pursuant to RC §§ 3314.02(D) and 3314.03 with respect to a community school formed under RC § 3314.01, the court of claims erred in not giving preclusive effect to a determination from prior litigation between the same school entity and a separate agency of the State of Ohio, wherein the governing authority of the school was recognized as the real party in interest pursuant to Ohio R. Civ. P. 17, as collateral estoppel precluded the decision by the court of claims that the educators who had sued the Ohio Department of Education lacked standing as the real parties in interest to bring the action because actions on behalf of state agencies were actions on behalf of the State and were binding pursuant to RC § 2743.01(A). Alternatives Unlimited-Special, Inc. v. Ohio Dep't of Educ., — Ohio App. 3d —, 2006 Ohio 4779, — N.E. 2d —, 2006 Ohio App. LEXIS 4656 (Sept. 14, 2006).

When a daughter sued an attorney for malpractice both in the daughter's capacity as executrix of the daughter's father's decedent's estate and as trustee of the beneficiary of the father's will, and the attorney's answer claimed the daughter was not the real party in interest, under Ohio R. Civ. P. 17(A), the attorney waived the affirmative defense of lack of capacity to sue, under Ohio R. Civ. P. 9(A) because the affirmative defense of real party in interest did not also raise the affirmative defense of lack of capacity to sue, and lack of capacity required a specific negative averment, which the attorney did not make. Wanamaker v. Davis, — Ohio App. 3d —, 2007 Ohio 4340, — N.E. 2d —, 2007 Ohio App. LEXIS 3878 (Aug. 24, 2007).

— Dismissal

In general, dismissal of an action because one of the parties is not a real party in interest is not a dismissal on the merits for purposes of res judicata: State ex rel. Coles v. Granville, 116 Ohio St. 3d 231, 2007 Ohio 6057, 877 N.E.2d 968, 2007 Ohio LEXIS 2878 (2007).

— Insurance company

When an insurer has paid all of the damages other than a deductible and is subrogated to the insured's rights, the insurer is the real party in interest in an action to recover amounts paid by the insurer. Where an insurer was not properly joined, CivR 19 required the court to determine whether the insurer should be joined: Ohio Cent. R.R. Sys. v. Mason Law Firm Co., LPA, 182 Ohio App. 3d 814, 2009 Ohio 3238, 915 N.E.2d 397, 2009 Ohio App. LEXIS 2769 (2009).

There was no error in the failure to join an insurer of a home owner in the owner's action against a party guest, alleging that she caused a fire in the home by her negligent disposal of her smoking materials, as the insurer was the real party in interest under Ohio R. Civ. P. 17(A) and it executed an affidavit indicating that it was bound by any decision in the owner's action, such that there was no concern about multiple lawsuits or judgments against the party guest; the insurer had become subrogated to the owner's rights insofar as it made payments to her pursuant to her insurance policy. Morelli v. Walker, — Ohio App. 3d —, 2007 Ohio 4832, — N.E. 2d —, 2007 Ohio App. LEXIS 4327 (Sept. 20, 2007).

—— Mortgagee

Where the mortgagee's title insurer had not yet reimbursed it for its loss, the mortgagee had standing, as an aggrieved party, to bring the appeal: Guernsey Bank v. Milano Sports Enters., LLC, 177 Ohio App. 3d 314, 2008 Ohio 2420, 894 N.E.2d 715, 2008 Ohio App. LEXIS 2066 (2008).

RULE 18.   Joinder of claims and remedies

(A) **Joinder of claims.** A party asserting a claim to relief as an original claim, counterclaim, cross-claim, or third-party claim, may join, either as independent or as alternate claims, as many claims, legal or equitable, as he has against an opposing party.

(B) **Joinder of remedies; fraudulent conveyances.** Whenever a claim is one heretofore cognizable only after another claim has been prosecuted to a conclusion, the two claims may be joined in a single action; but the court shall grant relief in that action only in accordance with the relative substantive rights of the parties. In particular, a plaintiff may state a claim for money and a claim to have set aside a conveyance fraudulent as to him, without first having obtained a judgment establishing the claim for money.

NOTES TO DECISIONS

ANALYSIS

Joinder of claims

Joinder of claims

Although a hospital's breach of contract action against a hospital patient for her failure to have paid for treatment on two occasions could have included claims for the patient's failure to pay for treatment on 12 other occasions, all of which arose from injuries the patient sustained in a motor vehicle accident, such joinder under Ohio R. Civ. P. 18 was not required and the fact that such would have caused the claims to exceed the trial court's jurisdiction would have been cured by certification of the case under RC § 1901.22(E), such that the jurisdictional limit would not have been a basis to apply the res judicata bar; however, as the claims were based on different treatment dates, involved different services and different bills, and they did not share a common nucleus of facts, application of the res judicata defense to the second set of claims was improper. Miami Valley Hosp. v. Purvis, — Ohio App. 3d —, 2007 Ohio 4721, — N.E. 2d —, 2007 Ohio App. LEXIS 4230 (Sept. 14, 2007).

When an assignee's assignor had a contract with a landowner allowing the assignor to deposit waste in a landfill on the landowner's property, and a foreclosure action was filed regarding that property, the assignee could properly, under Ohio R. Civ. P. 13(G), raise a cross-claim for breach of contract in the foreclosure action, because both the foreclosure action and the breach of contract claim concerned the same real property, and the assignee could, under Ohio R. Civ. P. 18(A), assert as many legal or equitable claims as he had against the landowner. LFL Logistics Co. v. Minerva Enterprises, Inc., — Ohio App. 3d —, 2006 Ohio 6398, — N.E. 2d —, 2006 Ohio App. LEXIS 6347 (Dec. 4, 2006).

RULE 19. Joinder of persons needed for just adjudication

(A) **Persons to be joined if feasible.** A person who is subject to service of process shall be joined as a party in the action if (1) in his absence complete relief cannot be accorded among those already parties, or (2) he claims an interest relating to the subject of the action and is so situated that the disposition of the action in his absence may (a) as a practical matter impair or impede his ability to protect that interest or (b) leave any of the persons already parties subject to a substantial risk of incurring double, multiple, or otherwise inconsistent obligations by reason of his claimed interest, or (3) he has an interest relating to the subject of the action as an assignor, assignee, subrogor, or subrogee. If he has not been so joined, the court shall order that he be made a party upon timely assertion of the defense of failure to join a party as provided in Rule 12(B)(7). If the defense is not timely asserted, waiver is applicable as provided in Rule 12(G) and (H). If he should join as a plaintiff but refuses to do so, he may be made a defendant, or, in a proper case, an involuntary plaintiff. In the event that such joinder causes the relief sought to exceed the jurisdiction of the court, the court shall certify the proceedings in the action to the court of common pleas.

(B) **Determination by court whenever joinder**

not feasible. If a person as described in subdivision (A)(1), (2), or (3) hereof cannot be made a party, the court shall determine whether in equity and good conscience the action should proceed among the parties before it, or should be dismissed, the absent person being thus regarded as indispensable. The factors to be considered by the court include: first, to what extent a judgment rendered in the person's absence might be prejudicial to him or those already parties; second, the extent to which, by protective provisions in the judgment, by the shaping of relief, or other measures, the prejudice can be lessened or avoided; third, whether a judgment rendered in the person's absence will be adequate; fourth, whether the plaintiff will have an adequate remedy if the action is dismissed for nonjoinder.

(C) **Pleading reasons for nonjoinder.** A pleading asserting a claim for relief shall state the names, if known to the pleader, of any persons as described in subdivision (A)(1), (2), or (3) hereof who are not joined, and the reasons why they are not joined.

(D) **Exception of class actions.** This rule is subject to the provisions of Rule 23.

NOTES TO DECISIONS

ANALYSIS

Business records
Declaratory judgments
Dismissal of action
Insurance
Intervention
Joinder
— Not required
Necessary party
Release
Waiver

Business records

Possessory interest of the plaintiffs, for purposes of RC § 1923.02(A)(5), could not be adjudicated where a decision would affect potential property rights of an absent party. That party should have been given an opportunity to assert its rights: Venture Props. of Boardman, Inc. v. Boardman Steel, Inc., 177 Ohio App. 3d 572, 2008 Ohio 3088, 895 N.E.2d 569, 2008 Ohio App. LEXIS 2601 (2008).

Declaratory judgments

Trial court's declaratory judgment, determining that an oral contract for real property purchasers to buy a real property owner's land existed and was to be enforced, was void ab initio where the owner had allegedly deeded a one-half interest in the property to his then-wife, such that she was a necessary party under Ohio R. Civ. P. 19(A)(2); although her interest could have been deemed invalid upon analysis, the trial court could not proceed to determine the matter under RC § 2721.12(A) without her having been joined, as it lacked subject matter jurisdiction. Young v. Wells, — Ohio App. 3d —, 2007 Ohio 4568, — N.E. 2d —, 2007 Ohio App. LEXIS 4094 (Aug. 28, 2007).

Dismissal of action

Ohio courts eschew the harsh result of dismissing an action because an indispensable party was not joined, electing instead to order that the party be joined pursuant to Ohio R. Civ. P. 19(A) (joinder if feasible) or that leave to amend the complaint be granted, and dismissal due to a party's failure to join a necessary party is warranted only where the defect cannot be cured. Congress Lake Club v. Witte, — Ohio App. 3d —, 2006 Ohio 59, — N.E. 2d —, 2006 Ohio App. LEXIS 34 (Jan. 3, 2006).

Insurance

When an insurer has paid all of the damages other than a deductible and is subrogated to the insured's rights, the insurer is the real party in interest in an action to recover amounts paid by the insurer. Where an insurer was not properly joined, CivR 19 required the court to determine whether the insurer should be joined: Ohio Cent. R.R. Sys. v. Mason Law Firm Co., LPA, 182 Ohio App. 3d 814, 2009 Ohio 3238, 915 N.E.2d 397, 2009 Ohio App. LEXIS 2769 (2009).

Intervention

Where motorists' insurer filed a subrogation action against a driver, alleging that the driver's negligence caused a motor vehicle accident for which the insurer had to pay various coverage expenses to the motorists, the motorists' intervening complaint should have been deemed timely filed pursuant to Ohio R. Civ. P. 15(C) and 19(A) and (B), as the motorists were necessary parties and their claims related back; the motorists and the insurer's claims had common questions of law and facts, and a determination regarding the driver's negligence and liability in the insurer's subrogation action was determinative with respect to the motorists' claims. Owens v. Smith, — Ohio App. 3d —, 2007 Ohio 6766, — N.E. 2d —, 2007 Ohio App. LEXIS 5916 (Dec. 14, 2007).

Joinder

Because there was no prejudice to the historical society by the formal addition of the genealogy society as an unincorporated association, the trial court did not abuse its discretion to allow the joinder. Everyone knew that the real plaintiff in interest was the genealogical society, either in its corporate or its unincorporated capacity and defendant historical society either knew, or should have known, that the genealogical society's unincorporated association status would arise. Gallia Co. Genealogical Society v. Gallia Co. Historical Society, — Ohio App. 3d —, 2007 Ohio 3882, — N.E. 2d —, 2007 Ohio App. LEXIS 3518 (July 24, 2007).

— Not required

Trial court committed no error in refusing to allow a debtor to join his wife as a party in an action between the debtor and a bank, arising from an arbitration between them involving a credit card account, as joinder was not required under Ohio R. Civ. P. 13(H), 19, 19.1, and 20 because the wife was not listed as a party to the arbitration decision. There was no reason that she should have been made a party to the action that involved the bank's request to vacate the arbitration award. Citibank v. Wood, — Ohio App. 3d —, 2006 Ohio 5755, — N.E. 2d —, 2006 Ohio App. LEXIS 5711 (Oct. 27, 2006).

Necessary party

As an insurer became subrogated to the rights of its insureds when it paid them for their claims that arose from a multi-vehicle collision, wherein they were passengers in one of the vehicles, it became a real party in interest in the action pursuant to Ohio R. Civ. P. 17(A). The failure to name a real party in interest or to join the insurer as a necessary party pursuant to Ohio R. Civ. P. 19(A) was waived where it was not promptly raised, and it was cured by any number of procedural devices, such as joinder, substitution, ratification, or amendment of the pleading. Goldney v. Byrd, — Ohio App. 3d —, 2007 Ohio 1985, — N.E. 2d —, 2007 Ohio App. LEXIS 1828 (Apr. 26, 2007).

Trust beneficiaries were not necessary parties to a declaratory judgment action brought by the beneficiaries' mother, as a co-trustee, against the beneficiaries' father, who was the other co-trustee, challenging self-dealing transfers of property made by the father to himself, since as grantors of the inter vivos revocable trust, the mother and the father had the right to add or withdraw assets from the trust or even to fully revoke the trust at any time; accordingly, although the beneficiaries had an interest in the trust, that interest was subject to complete defeasance, and the beneficiaries thus had no real interest in the trust to protect. Sredniawa v. Sredniawa, — Ohio App. 3d —, 2006 Ohio 1597, — N.E. 2d —, 2006 Ohio App. LEXIS 1499 (Mar. 30, 2006).

Trial court did not err in denying a motor vehicle driver's motion to dismiss an insurer's subrogation action, arising from a collision between the driver and the insurer's insured's vehicle, as the fact that the driver's vehicle was hit by a third-party vehicle, which then caused the driver's vehicle to have collided with the insured's vehicle did not result in a determination that the third-party driver was a necessary party pursuant to Ohio R. Civ. P. 19(A). The motor vehicle driver could have commenced a third-party action against him if he desired, he had ample opportunity during trial to show that the third-party driver was responsible for the accident because that individual testified at trial, and complete relief was available to the parties without joinder. State Farm Mut. Auto. Ins. Co. v. Swartz, — Ohio App. 3d —, 2006 Ohio 2096, — N.E. 2d —, 2006 Ohio App. LEXIS 1927 (Apr. 25, 2006).

In appellees' breach of contract action arising out of a transaction between appellees and the company in which a father, a son, and their respective wives were stockholders, the trial court did not err by failing to join the two wives as indispensable parties under Ohio R. Civ. P. 19 because the father and the son raised this issue in their answer in a vague manner and did not affirmatively identify the "indispensable parties" to the action. Moreover, the wives were not indispensable parties because, while they held stock in the company, they were not part of the agreement at issue. Loop v. Hall, — Ohio App. 3d —, 2006 Ohio 4363, — N.E. 2d —, 2006 Ohio App. LEXIS 4275 (Aug. 8, 2006).

Duty should fall on those who assert the absence of indispensable parties to identify those parties and to explain why they are indispensable to the action. Loop v. Hall, — Ohio App. 3d —, 2006 Ohio 4363, — N.E. 2d —, 2006 Ohio App. LEXIS 4275 (Aug. 8, 2006).

As RC § 2950.031(A) was only concerned with sex offenders and the remedies available for those offenders who lived within 1,000 feet of a school, an action by the State of Ohio that sought injunctive relief against a sex offender's wife, who owned the premises that the offender was residing in and which was located within the 1,000-foot restricted limit, failed to state a claim for relief against her pursuant to Ohio R. Civ. P. 12(B)(6), as the State could not seek to enjoin her from allowing the offender to live in the premises; she was not a necessary party to the action under Ohio R. Civ. P. 19(A). State ex rel. White v. Billings, 139 Ohio Misc. 2d 76, 2006 Ohio 4743, 860 N.E. 2d 831, 2006 Ohio Misc. LEXIS 215 (Aug. 10, 2006).

When a lessor sued a lessee in forcible entry and detainer regarding certain property which the lessee had purportedly conveyed to her son by a general warranty deed, the son claimed an interest relating to the subject matter of the action, and a disposition of the action in his absence might impair or impede his ability to protect that interest, under Ohio R. Civ. P. 19(A)(2). Congress Lake Club v. Witte, — Ohio App. 3d —, 2006 Ohio 59, — N.E. 2d —, 2006 Ohio App. LEXIS 34 (Jan. 3, 2006).

When a lessor sued a lessee in forcible entry and detainer regarding certain property which the lessee had purportedly conveyed to her son by a general warranty deed, it was an abuse of discretion for the trial court to deny the lessee's motion to dismiss due to the lessor's failure to join the son as a necessary party, because the son claimed an interest in the subject property which he had to be given an opportunity to protect. Congress Lake Club v. Witte, — Ohio App. 3d —, 2006 Ohio 59, — N.E. 2d —, 2006 Ohio App. LEXIS 34 (Jan. 3, 2006).

Release

Release in a related action against a vehicle manufacturer did not bar a buyer's claims against the seller alleging fraud and violations of the Ohio Consumer Sales Practices Act because the buyer only released warranty claims, which he withdrew in the instant action, and retained the other claims, and pursuant to Ohio R. Civ. P. 19, the seller was not considered an indispensable party to the related action. Hedrick v. Spitzer Motor City, Inc., — Ohio App. 3d —, 2007 Ohio 6820, — N.E. 2d —, 2007 Ohio App. LEXIS 5971 (Dec. 20, 2007).

Waiver

Trial court did not lack jurisdiction under RC § 1923.01(A) to decide a forcible entry and detainer action because, while the individual who signed the lease was not made a party, his exact status did not need to be determined since the only pertinent subject in such an action was that person or entity in immediate possession of the property in question. While appellant appeared to advance an argument that the individual was an indispensable ecessary party under Ohio R. Civ. P. 19, it raised this argument by failing to raise this issue to the trial court. Obermeyer v. Starship Enterprises, — Ohio App. 3d —, 2006 Ohio 4081, — N.E. 2d —, 2006 Ohio App. LEXIS 4038 (Aug. 9, 2006).

RULE 19.1. Compulsory joinder

(A) **Persons to be joined.** A person who is subject to service of process shall be joined as a party in the action, except as provided in division (B) of this rule, if the person has an interest in or a claim arising out of the following situations:

(1) Personal injury or property damage to the person or property of the decedent which survives the decedent's death and a claim for wrongful death to the same decedent if caused by the same wrongful act;

(2) Personal injury or property damage to a husband or wife and a claim of the spouse for loss of consortium or expenses or property damage if caused by the same wrongful act;

(3) Personal injury or property damage to a minor and a claim of the parent or guardian of the minor for loss of consortium or expenses or property damage if caused by the same wrongful act;

(4) Personal injury or property damage to an employee or agent and a claim of the employer or principal for property damage if caused by the same wrongful act.

If he has not been so joined, the court, subject to subdivision (B) hereof, shall order that he be made a party upon timely assertion of the defense of failure to join a party as provided in Rule 12(B)(7). If the defense is not timely asserted, waiver is applicable as provided in Rule 12(G) and (H). If he should join as a plaintiff but refuses to do so, he may be made a defendant, or, in a proper case, an involuntary plaintiff. In the event that such joinder causes the relief sought to exceed the jurisdiction of the court, the court shall certify the proceedings in the action to the court of common pleas.

(B) **Exception to compulsory joinder.** If a party to the action or a person described in subdivision (A) shows good cause why that person should not be joined, the court shall proceed without requiring joinder.

(C) **Pleading reasons for nonjoinder.** A pleading asserting a claim for relief shall state the names, if known to the pleader, of any persons as described in subdivision (A)(1), (2), (3), or (4) hereof who are not joined, and the reasons why they are not joined.

(D) **Exception to class actions.** This rule is subject to the provisions of Rule 23.

History: Amended, eff 7-1-96.

NOTES TO DECISIONS

ANALYSIS

Joinder

———

Joinder

Trial court committed no error in refusing to allow a debtor to join his wife as a party in an action between the debtor and a bank, arising from an arbitration between them involving a credit card account, as joinder was not required under Ohio R. Civ. P. 13(H), 19, 19.1, and 20 because the wife was not listed as a party to the arbitration decision. There was no reason that she should have been made a party to the action that involved the bank's request to vacate the arbitration award. Citibank v. Wood, — Ohio App. 3d —, 2006 Ohio 5755, — N.E. 2d —, 2006 Ohio App. LEXIS 5711 (Oct. 27, 2006).

RULE 20. Permissive joinder of parties

(A) **Permissive joinder.** All persons may join in one action as plaintiffs if they assert any right to relief jointly, severally, or in the alternative in respect of or arising out of the same transaction, occurrence, or succession or series of transactions or occurrences and if any question of law or fact common to all these persons will arise in the action. All persons may be joined in one action as defendants if there is asserted against them jointly, severally, or in the alternative, any right to relief in respect of or arising out of the same transaction, occurrence, or succession or series of transactions or occurrences and if any question of law or fact common to all defendants will arise in the action. A plaintiff or defendant need not be interested in obtaining or defending against all the relief demanded. Judgment may be given for one or more of the plaintiffs according to their respective rights to relief, and against one or more defendants according to their respective liabilities.

(B) **Separate trials.** The court may make such orders as will prevent a party from being prejudiced, delayed, or put to expense by the inclusion of a party against whom he asserts no claim and who asserts no claim against him, and may order separate trials or make other orders to prevent prejudice or delay.

NOTES TO DECISIONS

ANALYSIS

Joinder after judgment
Permissive joinder

———

Joinder after judgment

Joinder may be ordered after judgment is entered, and a trial court abuses its discretion if it denies such a request when the party seeking joinder lacks alternative remedies to obtain the relief for which joinder is requested: N. Side Bank & Trust

Co. v. Performance Home Buyers, LLC, 181 Ohio App. 3d 344, 2009 Ohio 1277, 908 N.E.2d 1044, 2009 Ohio App. LEXIS 1085 (2009).

Permissive joinder

Trial court committed no error in refusing to allow a debtor to join his wife as a party in an action between the debtor and a bank, arising from an arbitration between them involving a credit card account, as joinder was not required under Ohio R. Civ. P. 13(H), 19, 19.1, and 20 because the wife was not listed as a party to the arbitration decision. There was no reason that she should have been made a party to the action that involved the bank's request to vacate the arbitration award. Citibank v. Wood, — Ohio App. 3d —, 2006 Ohio 5755, — N.E. 2d —, 2006 Ohio App. LEXIS 5711 (Oct. 27, 2006).

RULE 21.   Misjoinder and nonjoinder of parties

Misjoinder of parties is not ground for dismissal of an action. Parties may be dropped or added by order of the court on motion of any party or of its own initiative at any stage of the action and on such terms as are just. Any claim against a party may be severed and proceeded with separately.

NOTES TO DECISIONS

ANALYSIS

Juvenile courts
Severance of claims

Juvenile courts

Trial court does not abuse its discretion when, after a minor parent or parents involved in a custody proceeding and who were minors at the onset reach the age of majority, the court removes as parties to the action the child's grandparents, who have no independent legal interest or rights in the proceeding: In re H.W., 114 Ohio St. 3d 65, 2007 Ohio 2879, 868 N.E.2d 261, 2007 Ohio LEXIS 1573 (2007).

Severance of claims

In a case in which a widow alleged her husband died from mesothelioma caused, in part, by asbestos in gaskets made by a manufacturer and supplied by a supplier, the manufacturer did not show that it was error for the trial court to grant the supplier's motion to sever the claims against it from those against the manufacturer, especially when the manufacturer did not raise the issue until the day of trial, so granting the manufacturer's motion to join the supplier would have been unfairly prejudicial to the supplier, or would have caused a significant delay, prejudicing the widow. Blandford v. A Best Prods. Co., — Ohio App. 3d —, 2006 Ohio 1332, — N.E. 2d —, 2006 Ohio App. LEXIS 1226 (Mar. 23, 2006).

RULE 22.   Interpleader

Persons having claims against the plaintiff may be joined as defendants and required to interplead when their claims are such that the plaintiff is or may be exposed to double or multiple liability. It is not ground for objection to the joinder that the claims of the several claimants or the titles on which their claims depend do not have a common origin or are not identical but are adverse to and independent of one another, or that the plaintiff avers that he is not liable in whole or in part to any or all of the claimants. A defendant exposed to similar liability may obtain such interpleader by way of cross-claim or counterclaim.

The provisions of this rule supplement and do not in any way limit the joinder of parties permitted in Rule 20.

In such an action in which any part of the relief sought is a judgment for a sum of money or the disposition of a sum of money or the disposition of any other thing capable of delivery, a party may deposit all or any part of such sum or thing with the court upon notice to every other party and leave of court. The court may make an order for the safekeeping, payment or disposition of such sum or thing.

NOTES TO DECISIONS

ANALYSIS

Requirements

Requirements

Potential lienholder's nominal interpleader complaints were properly dismissed because the lienholder's pleadings asserted that the lienholder had a lien against certain property owners rather than that the lienholder had funds subject to the claims of two or more claimants as required by Ohio R. Civ. P. 22; however, the case was remanded to determine whether a motion to intervene could be construed from the pleadings under Ohio R. Civ. P. 24. Sprouse v. Miller, — Ohio App. 3d —, 2007 Ohio 4397, — N.E. 2d —, 2007 Ohio App. LEXIS 3962 (Aug. 22, 2007).

RULE 23.   Class actions

(A) **Prerequisites to a class action.** One or more members of a class may sue or be sued as representative parties on behalf of all only if (1) the class is so numerous that joinder of all members is impracticable, (2) there are questions of law or fact common to the class, (3) the claims or defenses of the representative parties are typical of the claims or defenses of the class, and (4) the representative parties will fairly and adequately protect the interests of the class.

(B) **Class actions maintainable.** An action may be maintained as a class action if the prerequisites of subdivision (A) are satisfied, and in addition:

(1) the prosecution of separate actions by or against individual members of the class would create a risk of

(a) inconsistent or varying adjudications with respect to individual members of the class which would establish incompatible standards of conduct for the party opposing the class; or

(b) adjudications with respect to individual members of the class which would as a practical matter be dispositive of the interests of the other members not parties to the adjudications or substantially impair or impede their ability to protect their interests; or

(2) the party opposing the class has acted or refused to act on grounds generally applicable to the class, thereby making appropriate final injunctive relief or corresponding declaratory relief with respect to the class as a whole; or

(3) the court finds that the questions of law or fact common to the members of the class predominate over any questions affecting only individual members, and that a class action is superior to other available methods for the fair and efficient adjudication of the controversy. The matters pertinent to the findings include: (a)

the interest of members of the class in individually controlling the prosecution or defense of separate actions; (b) the extent and nature of any litigation concerning the controversy already commenced by or against members of the class; (c) the desirability or undesirability of concentrating the litigation of the claims in the particular forum; (d) the difficulties likely to be encountered in the management of a class action.

(C) **Determination by order whether class action to be maintained; notice; judgment; actions conducted partially as class actions.**

(1) As soon as practicable after the commencement of an action brought as a class action, the court shall determine by order whether it is to be so maintained. An order under this subdivision may be conditional, and may be altered or amended before the decision on the merits.

(2) In any class action maintained under subdivision (B)(3), the court shall direct to the members of the class the best notice practicable under the circumstances, including individual notice to all members who can be identified through reasonable effort. The notice shall advise each member that (a) the court will exclude him from the class if he so requests by a specified date; (b) the judgment, whether favorable or not, will include all members who do not request exclusion; and (c) any member who does not request exclusion may, if he desires, enter an appearance through his counsel.

(3) The judgment in an action maintained as a class action under subdivision (B)(1) or (B)(2), whether or not favorable to the class, shall include and describe those whom the court finds to be members of the class. The judgment in an action maintained as a class action under subdivision (B)(3), whether or not favorable to the class, shall include and specify or describe those to whom the notice provided in subdivision (C)(2) was directed, and who have not requested exclusion, and whom the court finds to be members of the class.

(4) When appropriate (a) an action may be brought or maintained as a class action with respect to particular issues, or (b) a class may be divided into subclasses and each subclass treated as a class, and the provisions of this rule shall then be construed and applied accordingly.

(D) **Orders in conduct of actions.** In the conduct of actions to which this rule applies, the court may make appropriate orders: (1) determining the course of proceedings or prescribing measure to prevent undue repetition or complication in the presentation of evidence or argument; (2) requiring, for the protection of the members of the class or otherwise for the fair conduct of the action, that notice be given in such manner as the court may direct to some or all of the members of any step in the action, or of the proposed extent of the judgment, or of the opportunity of members to signify whether they consider the representation fair and adequate, to intervene and present claims or defenses, or otherwise to come into the action; (3) imposing conditions on the representative parties or on intervenors; (4) requiring that the pleadings be amended to eliminate therefrom allegations as to representation of absent persons, and that the action proceed accordingly; (5) dealing with similar proce-

dural matters. The orders may combine with an order under Rule 16, and may be altered or amended as may be desirable from time to time.

(E) **Dismissal or compromise.** A class action shall not be dismissed or compromised without the approval of the court, and notice of the proposed dismissal or compromise shall be given to all members of the class in such manner as the court directs.

(F) **Aggregation of claims.** The claims of the class shall be aggregated in determining the jurisdiction of the court.

NOTES TO DECISIONS

Analysis

Generally
Ambiguous definition of class
Amendment of complaint
Appeal
Class representative
Consumer claims
Consumer fraud actions
Definition of class
Determination as class action
Findings
Injunctive or declaratory relief
Partial certification
Standing

Generally

Trial courts must carefully apply the class action requirements and conduct a rigorous analysis into whether the prerequisites of CivR 23 have been satisfied. A trial court's failure to provide a rationale for granting certification constitutes an abuse of discretion, and the cause will be remanded: Dunkelman v. Cincinnati Bengals, 170 Ohio App. 3d 224, 2006 Ohio 6825, 866 N.E.2d 576, 2006 Ohio App. LEXIS 6737 (2006).

Ambiguous definition of class

Trial court did not abuse its discretion in finding that the Ohio R. Civ. P. 23(A) requirements for a class action were not met in a home buyer's action against the seller of the home. An identifiable class did not exist, and the class was ambiguous, as it would require an individualized determination of each case prior to determining if the party was a member of the class. Lasson v. Coleman, — Ohio App. 3d —, 2007 Ohio 3443, — N.E. 2d —, 2007 Ohio App. LEXIS 3151 (June 29, 2007).

Amendment of complaint

Neither res judicata nor the law of the case precluded the trial court from granting class certification as to the amended complaint where additional named plaintiffs were added in the amended complaint: Rimedio v. Summacare, 172 Ohio App. 3d 639, 2007 Ohio 3244, 876 N.E.2d 986, 2007 Ohio App. LEXIS 2991 (2007).

Appeal

Where funeral home defendants opposed class certification that was requested by an estate throughout trial court proceedings, but the funeral home did not present any specific arguments opposing certification under Ohio R. Civ. P. 23(B)(2), it waived the issue for purposes of appeal after the trial court granted certification thereunder. Reed Estate v. Hadley, — Ohio App. 3d —, 2007 Ohio 5462, — N.E. 2d —, 2007 Ohio App. LEXIS 4799 (Oct. 9, 2007).

Appellate court had jurisdiction to review an appeal from a trial court order that granted class certification pursuant to Ohio R. Civ. P. 23, as it was a final appealable order under RC

§ 2505.02. Phillips v. Andy Buick, Inc., — Ohio App. 3d —, 2006 Ohio 5832, — N.E. 2d —, 2006 Ohio App. LEXIS 5766 (Nov. 3, 2006).

Where an action sat dormant for three years due to failed settlement attempts and then inaction by a trial court, the visiting judge who was then assigned to the matter abused his discretion when he certified the matter as a class action without providing reasons in support of the decision and where the record was devoid of evidence in support of a meaningful determination. Although a motion or hearing was not required prior to a certification decision, absent a viable explanation from the trial judge as to the reason for granting certification, it was concluded that the decision was arbitrary and unreasonable. Ward v. Nationsbanc Mortg. Corp., — Ohio App. 3d —, 2006 Ohio 2766, — N.E. 2d —, 2006 Ohio App. LEXIS 2599 (June 2, 2006).

Class representative

Adequacy of representation requirement under Ohio R. Civ. P. 23(A)(4) was satisfied for purposes of class certification in an action by truck dealers against a truck manufacturer, as the representative's claims were not antagonistic to other class members, and it was informed and supportive of the basic elements of the class claim. Although the claim asserted that a discount and concession program by the manufacturer was administered in an unfair manner to various dealers, such issues were merely a question of damages but all dealers allegedly suffered a breach of their franchise agreement with the manufacturer. Westgate Ford Truck Sales v. Ford Motor Co., — Ohio App. 3d —, 2007 Ohio 4013, — N.E. 2d —, 2007 Ohio App. LEXIS 3655 (Aug. 9, 2007).

Consumer claims

Where a cellular telephone service provider's contract prohibited the filing by customers of a class action under Ohio R. Civ. P. 23, it hindered the consumer protection purposes of the Ohio Consumer Sales Practices Act, RC § 1345.01 et seq., and it also prohibited an award of attorney fees in violation of those statutorily authorized under RC § 1345.09(F)(2). The arbitration clause was substantively unconscionable and the trial court did not err in denying the provider's motion to stay proceedings pending arbitration pursuant to RC § 2711.02(C). Schwartz v. Alltel Corp., — Ohio App. 3d —, 2006 Ohio 3353, — N.E. 2d —, 2006 Ohio App. LEXIS 3280 (June 29, 2006).

Consumer fraud actions

Because the trial court had sufficient information before it to rule on the question of class certification, it did not abuse its discretion by failing to hold an evidentiary hearing. In consumer fraud actions, the predominance test is satisfied where the existence of common misrepresentations obviates the need to elicit individual testimony as to each element of a fraud or misrepresentation claim. Trial court did not abuse its discretion in limiting class membership to Ohio residents: Ritt v. Billy Blanks Enters., 171 Ohio App. 3d 204, 2007 Ohio 1695, 870 N.E.2d 212, 2007 Ohio App. LEXIS 1552 (2007).

Definition of class

Trial court properly excluded members of a class who were outside of the State of Ohio for purposes of defining the class in its certification order, as Ohio choice of law principles used the place of injury, which would have required analysis of varying states' laws. Ritt v. Billy Blanks Enters., 171 Ohio App. 3d 204, 2007 Ohio 1695, 870 N.E.2d 212, 2007 Ohio App. LEXIS 1552 (2007).

As an unsolicited facsimile recipient failed to request modification of a proposed class and a trial court had no obligation to sua sponte modify a class definition, there was no abuse of discretion by a trial court's denial of certification without attempting a modification of the class in order to find a certifiable class. Cicero v. U.S. Four, Inc., — Ohio App. 3d —, 2007 Ohio 6600, — N.E. 2d —, 2007 Ohio App. LEXIS 5777 (Dec. 11, 2007).

Determination as class action

Trial court did not err in failing to make a determination regarding class certification in an action by inmates prior to the trial court's grant of a motion for judgment on the pleadings, as there was no request by the inmates for certification, such that the issue was not formally before the trial court for consideration. Ridenour v. Wilkinson, — Ohio App. 3d —, 2007 Ohio 5965, — N.E. 2d —, 2007 Ohio App. LEXIS 5238 (Nov. 8, 2007).

Findings

When a consumer sued the administrator of automobile extended service plans sold throughout the state, and the trial court found he was not entitled to the certification of a class, under Ohio R. Civ. P. 23(B)(3), because questions common to the class did not predominate over questions affecting individual class members, the trial court was not required to address other factors under Ohio R. Civ. P. 23, after finding the requirements of Ohio R. Civ. P. 23(B)(3) were not met. Cannon v. Fid. Warranty Servs., — Ohio App. 3d —, 2006 Ohio 4995, — N.E. 2d —, 2006 Ohio App. LEXIS 4944 (Sept. 19, 2006).

Injunctive or declaratory relief

Although class members sought monetary damages, they also and primarily sought declaratory and injunctive relief, such that the latter forms of relief were appropriate to the class as a whole and satisfied the requirements for certification under Ohio R. Civ. P. 23(B)(2). Maas v. Penn Cent. Corp., — Ohio App. 3d —, 2007 Ohio 2055, — N.E. 2d —, 2007 Ohio App. LEXIS 1922 (Apr. 27, 2007).

Partial certification

Trial court did not abuse its discretion by certifying one proposed class of cell phone customers, but denying certification of another proposed class. Nationwide certification was properly granted on the breach of contract claims: Cowit v. Cellco P'ship, 181 Ohio App. 3d 809, 2009 Ohio 1596, 911 N.E.2d 300, 2009 Ohio App. LEXIS 1891 (2009).

Standing

When two medical provider associations sued two state agencies regarding the insolvency of a Medicaid managed care plan, the associations had standing to represent their members in a class action because (1) individual members of the associations had standing to sue in their own right, (2) the litigation involved interests germane to the associations' purposes to advocate the interests of their members, and (3) while some relief requested might require the participation of individual members, the requirement that neither the claim asserted nor the relief requested required the participation of individual members was met by the provision of notice to individual members and their right to opt out of the class. OHA: The Ass'n for Hosps. & Health Sys. v. Dep't of Human Servs., — Ohio App. 3d —, 2006 Ohio 67, — N.E.2d —, 2006 Ohio App. LEXIS 42 (Jan. 10, 2006).

RULE 23.1.   Derivative actions by shareholders

In a derivative action brought by one or more legal or equitable owners of shares to enforce a right of a corporation, the corporation having failed to enforce a right which may properly be asserted by it, the complaint shall be verified and shall allege that the plaintiff was a shareholder at the time of the transaction of which he complains or that his share thereafter devolved on him by operation of law. The complaint shall also allege with particularity the efforts, if any, made by the plaintiff to obtain the action he desires from the directors and, if necessary, from the shareholders and the reasons for his failure to obtain the action or for not making the effort. The derivative action may not be maintained if it appears that the plaintiff does not fairly and adequately represent the interests of the shareholders similarly situated in enforcing the right of the corporation. The action shall not be dismissed or compromised without the approval of the court, and notice of the proposed dismissal or compromise shall be given to shareholders in such manner as the court directs.

NOTES TO DECISIONS

ANALYSIS

Direct cause of action

Direct cause of action

Generally, causes of action alleging negligence, fraud or breach of fiduciary duty by corporate directors and officers were to be brought in the form of shareholder derivative suits, under Ohio R. Civ. P. 23.1, because only a corporation and not its shareholders could complain of an injury sustained by, or a wrong done to, a corporation, but this general principle did not apply where the wrongful acts were not only against the corporation but were also violations of a duty arising from contract or otherwise owed directly by the wrongdoer to the shareholder, but where the defendant's wrongdoing caused direct damage to corporate worth, the cause of action accrued to the corporation, not to the shareholders, even though in an economic sense real harm might well be sustained by the shareholders as a result of reduced earnings, diminution in the value of ownership, or accumulation of personal debt and liabilities from the company's financial decline. Barr v. Lauer, — Ohio App. 3d —, 2007 Ohio 156, — N.E. 2d —, 2007 Ohio App. LEXIS 154 (Jan. 18, 2007).

When a shareholder filed a direct action against the officers of the corporation in which he owned stock, instead of filing a derivative action, he could not properly allege claims for breach of fiduciary duty, corporate waste, or reckless egligent hiring and retention because he did not allege facts showing that he was owed a duty in these areas beyond that owed by the officers to all shareholders, and his alleged injury from those claims was loss of his stock's value, which was an injury shared with all other shareholders. Barr v. Lauer, — Ohio App. 3d —, 2007 Ohio 156, — N.E. 2d —, 2007 Ohio App. LEXIS 154 (Jan. 18, 2007).

Shareholder brings a direct action against corporate officers when the shareholder is injured in a way that is separate and distinct from the injury to the corporation. Barr v. Lauer, — Ohio App. 3d —, 2007 Ohio 156, — N.E. 2d —, 2007 Ohio App. LEXIS 154 (Jan. 18, 2007).

RULE 24.   Intervention

(A) **Intervention of right.** Upon timely application anyone shall be permitted to intervene in an action: (1) when a statute of this state confers an unconditional right to intervene; or (2) when the applicant claims an interest relating to the property or transaction that is the subject of the action and the applicant is so situated that the disposition of the action may as a practical matter impair or impede the applicant's ability to protect that interest, unless the applicant's interest is adequately represented by existing parties.

(B) **Permissive intervention.** Upon timely appli-

cation anyone may be permitted to intervene in an action: (1) when a statute of this state confers a conditional right to intervene; or (2) when an applicant's claim or defense and the main action have a question of law or fact in common. When a party to an action relies for ground of claim or defense upon any statute or executive order administered by a federal or state governmental officer or agency or upon any regulation, order, requirement or agreement issued or made pursuant to the statute or executive order, the officer or agency upon timely application may be permitted to intervene in the action. In exercising its discretion the court shall consider whether the intervention will unduly delay or prejudice the adjudication of the rights of the original parties.

(C) **Procedure.** A person desiring to intervene shall serve a motion to intervene upon the parties as provided in Civ.R. 5. The motion and any supporting memorandum shall state the grounds for intervention and shall be accompanied by a pleading, as defined in Civ.R. 7(A), setting forth the claim or defense for which intervention is sought. The same procedure shall be followed when a statute of this state gives a right to intervene.

History: Amended, eff 7-1-99.

NOTES TO DECISIONS

ANALYSIS

Adequate representation
Administrative appeals
Adoption
Appellate intervention
Final order
Forfeiture proceedings
Insurance
Intervention
Motion to intervene
Permissive intervention
Post-judgment intervention
Prerequisites
Standing
Time for intervention

Adequate representation

Motion by the attorney for the beneficiaries of the restitution acted as a motion to intervene because neither the attorney nor the beneficiaries of the estate of one of the victims were actual parties to defendant's underlying criminal case. The attorney did not provide any case law or other authority to support his presumed ability to intervene in the case to request that the trial court determine the outstanding restitution balance (the attorney also did not comply with Ohio R. Civ. P. 24(C) as he did not serve a copy of his motion on the county prosecutor's office); the attorney and the beneficiaries should not have been permitted to request that the trial court continue restitution payments and determine the balance of restitution due as their interests were adequately represented by existing parties. Ohio v. Dillon, — Ohio App. 3d —, 2007 Ohio 4934, — N.E. 2d —, 2007 Ohio App. LEXIS 4619 (Sept. 24, 2007).

When a charity sought to intervene, under Ohio R. Civ. P. 24(A)(1), upon a transferee of land which had been bequeated to the charity seeking to remove charitable deed restrictions imposed on the property, and its motion was denied as to this issue, the charity did not show that its interests were not adequately represented by the attorney general, who was a party to the proceedings pursuant to RC § 109.25, because it did not explain how or why its interest was not sufficiently represented, as it pointed to no shortcomings in the representation of its rights by the attorney general's office or explain what it would have done to litigate the matter differently. Kayatin v. Petro, — Ohio App. 3d —, 2007 Ohio 334, — N.E. 2d —, 2007 Ohio App. LEXIS 294 (Jan. 29, 2007).

Administrative appeals

In the context of administrative appeals, more specific sections of the Revised Code may apply, and if they do, RC Chapter 2505 is superseded. Under the circumstances, the board of tax appeals' denial of intervention constituted a final, appealable order because it affect a substantial right and was made in a special proceeding. Southside Cmty. Dev. Corp. v. Levin, 116 Ohio St. 3d 1463, 2008 Ohio 3, 878 N.E.2d 640, 2008 Ohio LEXIS 5 (2007).

Adoption

Paternal grandfather only had standing to appeal the trial court's denial of his request to intervene pursuant to Ohio R. Civ. P. 24 in an adoption proceeding involving his grandchild. As he had no recognized right to participate in the proceeding pursuant to RC §§ 3107.11 and 3107.06, and he had not sought to adopt the child, denial of his intervention request was proper. In re T.B.S., — Ohio App. 3d —, 2007 Ohio 3559, — N.E. 2d —, 2007 Ohio App. LEXIS 3289 (July 5, 2007).

Appellate intervention

Although a city had no standing under Ohio R. App. P. 4(A) to appeal from a judgment in the trial court that was in favor of a union in the union's administrative appeal of a decision by the State Employment Relations Board, as the trial court had adopted a magistrate's decision to deny the city's motion to intervene in the trial court proceedings, and the Board could not assert as error on appeal that the trial court had improperly denied intervention to the city, as it was not "aggrieved" by that decision, the city could seek to intervene on the appellate level pursuant to Ohio R. Civ. P. 24 and 1(C). The city could not be substituted for the Board on appeal pursuant to Ohio R. App. P. 29(B), as such substitution was not "necessary." Queen City Lodge No. 69 v. State Empl. Rels. Bd., — Ohio App. 3d —, 2007 Ohio 170, — N.E. 2d —, 2007 Ohio App. LEXIS 173 (Jan. 19, 2007).

Final order

Although a trial court's adoption of a magistrate's decision to deny a city's motion to intervene pursuant to Ohio R. Civ. P. 24(A)(2) in an adminstrative appeal by a union from a decision of the State Employment Relations Board affected a substantial right of the city, effectively determined the action as to it, and prevented a judgment for it for purposes of being a "final order" under RC § 2505.02(B)(1), (2), or (4), as the trial court failed to include the language of Ohio R. Civ. P. 54(B) and the substantive claims of the parties remained outstanding, the appellate court lacked jurisdiction over the appealed order pursuant to Ohio Const. art. IV, § 3(B)(2). Queen City Lodge No. 69 v. State Empl. Rels. Bd., — Ohio App. 3d —, 2007 Ohio 170, — N.E. 2d —, 2007 Ohio App. LEXIS 173 (Jan. 19, 2007).

Lacking CivR 54(B) language, the order denying the motion to intervene was not a final appealable order. Under the circumstances, the motion to intervene was untimely: Davis v. Border, 170 Ohio App. 3d 758, 2007 Ohio 692, 869 N.E.2d 46, 2007 Ohio App. LEXIS 613 (2007).

Trial court's denial of a former attorney's motion to intervene in a personal injury proceeding was not a final appealable order under Ohio Const. art. IV, § 3(B)(2) and RC § 2505.02 where the attorney's purpose in intervening was to secure future standing in order to assert a claim for fees, such that there was no provisional remedy because it was not ancillary to the underlying action; further, a substantial right that determined the action and prevented judgment pursuant to

§ 2505.02(B)(1) was not involved. Luna v. Allstate Ins. Co., — Ohio App. 3d —, 2007 Ohio 6597, — N.E. 2d —, 2007 Ohio App. LEXIS 5770 (Dec. 11, 2007).

Trial court was not required to issue findings of fact and conclusions of law pursuant to Ohio R. Civ. P. 52 relating to its decision to grant a bank the right to intervene in a pending action pursuant to Ohio R. Civ. P. 24(A)(2), as the determination was based on mainly legal issues and no "trial" took place in making the decision thereon. The fact that the request for findings and conclusions was not complied with did not impair the ability to appeal another ruling in the matter, nor did it toll the time for appealing under Ohio R. App. P. 4(B)(2). Savage v. Cody-Zeigler, Inc., — Ohio App. 3d —, 2006 Ohio 2760, — N.E. 2d —, 2006 Ohio App. LEXIS 2601 (May 25, 2006).

While an order granting a motion to intervene was not generally final and appealable, under RC § 2505.02, a trial court's order granting intervention, under Ohio R. Civ. P. 24(A)(2) and (B)(2), was final and appealable, under RC § 2505.02(B)(3), because it implicitly granted the movant's motion to vacate a default judgment. State Farm Mut. Ins. Cos. v. Young, — Ohio App. 3d —, 2006 Ohio 3812, — N.E. 2d —, 2006 Ohio App. LEXIS 3784 (July 26, 2006).

Denial of a motion to intervene as of right, pursuant to Ohio R. Civ. P. 24(A), is a final appealable order. PNC Bank, N.A. v. Sedivy, — Ohio App. 3d —, 2006 Ohio 6694, — N.E. 2d —, 2006 Ohio App. LEXIS 6604 (Dec. 15, 2006).

Forfeiture proceedings

It was error for a trial court to deny the motion of the participants in a "Las Vegas night," whose money was seized by police, to intervene in forfeiture proceedings governed by RC § 2933.43(C) (repealed), because the participants had a legitimate interest in the property that was seized, and a defendant who pled guilty to operating a gambling house, under RC § 2915.03, could not assent to the forfeiture of property that did not belong to defendant. Dep't of Pub. Safety v. Buckley, — Ohio App. 3d —, 2007 Ohio 4628, — N.E. 2d —, 2007 Ohio App. LEXIS 4168 (Sept. 7, 2007).

Insurance

When an insurer filed a declaratory judgment action seeking a declaration that it was not obligated to indemnify its insureds due to an alleged injured party's suit against them, and a default judgment was entered in the insurer's favor, after which the alleged injured party moved to set aside that default, and subsequently moved to intervene, it was proper to grant the motion to intervene because (1) RC § 3929.06(C)(2) precluded the alleged injured party from otherwise litigating the existence of insurance coverage for his injuries, (2) the alleged injured party had an interest in the existence of such coverage, and (3) the insurer's insureds did not represent the alleged injured party's interests in the declaratory judgment action because they did not defend it. State Farm Mut. Ins. Cos. v. Young, — Ohio App. 3d —, 2006 Ohio 3812, — N.E. 2d —, 2006 Ohio App. LEXIS 3784 (July 26, 2006).

Ohio R. Civ. P. 54(B) language and certification was not necessary for purposes of making a denial of an insurer's motion to intervene, pursuant to Ohio R. Civ. P. 24(A)(2), a final appealable order pursuant to RC § 2505.02(B), as the language of Ohio R. Civ. P. 54(B) connoted that claims or rights and liabilities of parties was involved, and the insurer was clearly not a party if it had to seek intervention to participate in the action. It was not included in the pleadings pursuant to Ohio R. Civ. P. 10(A), wherein a patient of the insured, a doctor, filed a civil tort action arising from the doctor's inappropriate conduct during a gynecological examination, and the insurer's intent in seeking intervention was to secure a specific, rather than general, verdict in order to deny the coverage to the doctor, which was provided under a reservation of rights. Filippi v. Ahmed, — Ohio App. 3d —, 2006 Ohio 4368, — N.E. 2d —, 2006 Ohio App. LEXIS 4290 (Aug. 24, 2006).

Trial court abused its discretion in denying an insurer's motion to intervene pursuant to Ohio R. Civ. P. 24(A)(2) in an action by a patient against a doctor, who was an insured, alleging that the doctor committed inappropriate conduct during a gynecological examination, as intervention would not have caused any delay or disruption to the existing trial proceedings, the insurer's participation at trial would have been limited, there was no apparent prejudice that would have resulted from granting the intervention request, and it would have benefited the resolution of the issues of whether the insurer was obligated to provide coverage. Filippi v. Ahmed, — Ohio App. 3d —, 2006 Ohio 4368, — N.E. 2d —, 2006 Ohio App. LEXIS 4290 (Aug. 24, 2006).

Even though a liability insurer's motion to intervene as of right in a patient's action alleging that a physician over-prescribed addictive medication was filed three years after the action was commenced and five months before trial, the motion was entitled to consideration consistent with a liberal construction of Ohio R. Civ. P. 24(A) and the insurer was entitled to intervene. Ample time remained to prepare for trial, the insurer had a limited purpose of submitting jury interrogatories to determine factual coverage issues, the trial court could impose restrictions to avoid any further delay, the insurer's exposure in the action depended on the basis of the verdict, and only the insurer had an interest in identifying that basis. Doe v. Ramos, — Ohio App. 3d —, 2006 Ohio 5435, — N.E. 2d —, 2006 Ohio App. LEXIS 5432 (Oct. 19, 2006).

Intervention

Decision refusing to allow a ward's personal representative to prosecute the ward's claims for relief was proper because the representative did not appear in the matter as Ohio R. Civ. P. 17(A) required when it was commenced, and thus, she was not entitled to prosecute the action at all because she was not a party and had not filed a motion to intervene as the ward's personal representative pursuant to Ohio R. Civ. P. 24(A). Neither could the representative appear as the ward's attorney or legal representative because she had not been admitted to the practice of law in Ohio, as required by RC § 4795.01. Brown v. Wright, — Ohio App. 3d —, 2006 Ohio 38, — N.E. 2d —, 2006 Ohio App. LEXIS 47 (Jan. 6, 2006).

Trial court did not err in adopting a magistrate's decision to deny maternal grandparents' motion to intervene in an action commenced by their minor grandchild's biological father, seeking a determination of paternity, custody, visitation, and child support pursuant to RC § 2151.23(A)(2), as they did not establish an in loco parentis relationship with the minor child merely because they cared for the child during a period of time when the complaint was filed, and accordingly, they were not within the scope of the parties defined under Ohio R. Juv. R. 2(Y) and they did not have a right to intervene in the matter pursuant to Ohio R. Civ. P. 24(A); there was no cause to review the issue of parental unsuitability or the constitutional right of parents in the care, custody, and management of their children at that juncture of the matter. Brokaw v. Haser, — Ohio App. 3d —, 2006 Ohio 5171, — N.E. 2d —, 2006 Ohio App. LEXIS 5134 (Sept. 29, 2006).

Motion to intervene

City's motion to intervene in proceedings on a petition for a writ of mandamus to required that a proposed ordinance be placed on a ballot was denied because the city did not file a pleading with the city's motion, as required by Ohio R. Civ. P. 24(C), and the city filed the city's motion after the parties submitted the parties' evidence and briefs. Hamilton County Bd. of Elections, — Ohio St. 3d —, 2007 Ohio 5379, — N.E. 2d —, 2007 Ohio LEXIS 2514 (Oct. 8, 2007).

Potential lienholder's nominal interpleader complaints were properly dismissed because the lienholder's pleadings asserted that the lienholder had a lien against certain property owners rather than that the lienholder had funds subject to the claims of two or more claimants as required by Ohio R. Civ. P. 22; however, the case was remanded to determine whether a motion to intervene could be construed from the pleadings under Ohio R. Civ. P. 24. Sprouse v. Miller, — Ohio App. 3d —, 2007 Ohio 4397, — N.E. 2d —, 2007 Ohio App. LEXIS 3962 (Aug. 22, 2007).

Trial court did not err in denying the grandmother's motion to intervene because the grandmother failed to demonstrate that she was prejudiced by her inability to participate in the permanent custody proceedings. The grandmother did not challenge the validity of the parents' waiver of their parental rights, nor did she contend that she would have impacted their decision to surrender their rights if she had been permitted to participate in the proceedings; after the parents voluntarily relinquished their rights, it was unnecessary for the trial court to hold further permanent custody proceedings. In re A. P. & K., — Ohio App. 3d —, 2007 Ohio 5413, — N.E. 2d —, 2007 Ohio App. LEXIS 4768 (Oct. 10, 2007).

Probate court's denial of a motion under Ohio R. Civ. P. 24(A) to intervene in a ward's guardianship in order to assert a claim for recovery of legal services rendered by the attorney on behalf of the ward was error, as the attorney had a right to intervene in order to seek reimbursement out of settlement proceeds from the ward's bodily injury claim; although the attorney failed to properly attach the pleading, as required by Ohio R. Civ. P. 24(C) and 7(A), it was clear that the claim involved recovery of legal services provided to the ward's parents regarding the bodily injury claim, for which a proposed settlement was pending before the court for approval. In re Guardianship of Jerry L. Chambers, — Ohio App. 3d —, 2007 Ohio 6881, — N.E. 2d —, 2007 Ohio App. LEXIS 5996 (Dec. 21, 2007).

When an insurer filed a declaratory judgment action seeking a declaration that it was not obligated to indemnify its insureds due to an alleged injured party's suit against them, and a default judgment was entered in the insurer's favor, after which the alleged injured party moved to set aside that default, and subsequently moved to intervene, it was not error for the trial court to grant the motion to set aside the default judgment, even though it was technically filed by a non-party, because the trial court's order implicitly granting the motion to set the judgment aside also allowed the alleged injured party to intervene. State Farm Mut. Ins. Cos. v. Young, — Ohio App. 3d —, 2006 Ohio 3812, — N.E. 2d —, 2006 Ohio App. LEXIS 3784 (July 26, 2006).

Permissive intervention

Trial court erred by denying a motion to intervene pursuant to CivR 24(A)(2) where the movant's lien existed prior to the foreclosure sale and the sale proceeds were still in the custody of the court: Rokakis v. Martin, 180 Ohio App. 3d 696, 2009 Ohio 369, 906 N.E.2d 1200, 2009 Ohio App. LEXIS 320 (2009).

Trial court's denial of a maternal grandfather's motion to intervene pursuant to Ohio R. Civ. P. 24(B) in a custody and visitation matter involving his grandchild was not an abuse of discretion, as the parents had objected to his visitation request and their wishes and concerns were entitled to "special weight." In re Sadie Elizabeth S., — Ohio App. 3d —, 2006 Ohio 2928, — N.E. 2d —, 2006 Ohio App. LEXIS 2800 (June 9, 2006).

Post-judgment intervention

As a trial court had the authority to permit a neighbor to intervene as long as he met the requirements for intervention pursuant to Ohio R. Civ. P. 24 in an action between a village and a property owner regarding the owner's failure to cease his unauthorized excavation business operations, the trial court had jurisdiction to grant the neighbor's motion to intervene. The fact that the trial court had entered a final order in the matter prior to the filing of the motion to intervene did not preclude such intervention due to jurisdictional constraints. Village of Boston Hts. v. Cerny, — Ohio App. 3d —, 2007 Ohio 2886, — N.E. 2d —, 2007 Ohio App. LEXIS 2680 (June 13, 2007).

Prerequisites

Property owners met the requirements for intervention as of right under Ohio R. Civ. P. 24(A) in a quiet title and adverse possession action, as they filed a timely motion to intervene under Rule 24(C) and they indicated that they would file an adverse possession claim; although no pleading under Ohio R. Civ. P. 7(A) was included with their motion, the basis of their claim was known to the trial court, they did not have to show lack of access to their property for purposes of the claim, and no objection to the lack of pleading was filed. Korenko v. Kelleys Island Park Dev. Co., — Ohio App. 3d —, 2007 Ohio 2145, — N.E. 2d —, 2007 Ohio App. LEXIS 2004 (May 4, 2007).

It was not an abuse of discretion for a trial court to deny the motion of a child protection agency, under Ohio R. Civ. P. 24(A)(2), to intervene in proceedings concerning certain children because the agency had not had custody of the children since the agency had been ordered to provide temporary care for the children in the past, and the children's supervision had been properly transferred to another agency, so the moving agency had no interest which actions related to the case could impair. In re R.A., — Ohio App. 3d —, 2007 Ohio 2997, — N.E. 2d —, 2007 Ohio App. LEXIS 2761 (June 18, 2007).

Tenant had a right to intervene in the declaratory judgment proceedings under Ohio R. Civ. P. 24(A) because the tenant had a direct interest in the action to determine whether the previous owner's insurance policy covered the alleged tort (fire); under the amended Declaratory Judgment Act, RC § 2721.12(B), the declaratory judgment would have been binding on the tenant even if she was not a party to the declaratory judgment proceeding; and the tenant established that the previous owners may not have adequately represented her interests in the declaratory judgment action. Moreover, the tenant should have at least been granted a permissive intervention under Ohio R. Civ. P. 24(B) as the two cases had common questions of fact and there would have been no prejudice and RC § 2721.02(B) did not preclude the tenant from intervening in the declaratory judgment litigation. Indiana Ins. Co. v. Murphy, 165 Ohio App. 3d 812, 2006 Ohio 1264, 848 N.E. 2d 889, 2006 Ohio App. LEXIS 1163 (Mar. 20, 2006).

Trial court did not abuse its discretion in granting an injured passenger's motion to intervene in a declaratory judgment action commenced by an insurer against its insured, a driver, arising from an automobile accident caused by the driver which resulted in serious physical injuries to the passenger, as the requirements of Ohio R. Civ. P. 24(A) were met and RC § 2721.02(B) did not preclude such intervention, as the insurer "commenced" the action; the passenger showed that he maintained an interest in the litigation due to his injuries, the failure to allow intervention would have impaired or impeded his rights, the insurer would not have adequately represented his interests, and he sought intervention in a timely manner. Pfeiffer v. State Auto. Mut. Ins. Co., — Ohio App. 3d —, 2006 Ohio 5074, — N.E. 2d —, 2006 Ohio App. LEXIS 5009 (Sept. 29, 2006).

Standing

Person who has not filed an application to be appointed guardian, or who otherwise has not been made a party to the guardianship proceedings, has no standing to appeal: In re Guardianship of Santrucek, 120 Ohio St. 3d 67, 2008 Ohio 4915, 896 N.E.2d 683, 2008 Ohio LEXIS 2593 (2008).

As a paternal great-grandmother had not sought intervention in an adoption proceeding of her grandchild, she had no standing to assert assignments of error on appeal from the trial court's grant of the stepfather's adoption petition. In re T.B.S., — Ohio App. 3d —, 2007 Ohio 3559, — N.E. 2d —, 2007 Ohio App. LEXIS 3289 (July 5, 2007).

In a probate proceeding that resolved title to a decedent's real property, the fact that appellants were not parties to that proceeding and they failed to intervene therein pursuant to Ohio R. Civ. P. 24(A) and (C), they lacked any right or standing to appeal the probate court's order that denied their motion to dismiss and dissolve the probate proceedings. In re Markovich, — Ohio App. 3d —, 2006 Ohio 6064, — N.E. 2d —, 2006 Ohio App. LEXIS 6054 (Nov. 20, 2006).

When a mortgagor transferred any interest she had in foreclosed property to a recipient, by quit-claim deed, and, almost two years after a judgment of foreclosure was entered as to the property, the recipient moved to intervene in the foreclosure proceedings, under Ohio R. Civ. P. 24(A)(2), he had no standing to appeal the denial of his motion because, while he claimed an interest in the property, he could not show that a disposition of it by a sheriff's sale impaired or impeded his ability to protect that interest, because it had already been foreclosed on, and the mortgagor, who was already a party to the foreclosure, adequately represented the interest he claimed in the property. PNC Bank, N.A. v. Sedivy, — Ohio App. 3d —, 2006 Ohio 6694, — N.E. 2d —, 2006 Ohio App. LEXIS 6604 (Dec. 15, 2006).

Time for intervention

By any reasonable standard, the insurer's motion to intervene filed 14 months after the complaint was filed and two weeks before the trial date was untimely because the insurer was on notice from the time its insured was served with the complaint and it provided defense counsel for him at that time. If the motion to intervene had been granted, it would have necessarily interfered with the trial date and the insurer provided no reason for its delay in filing the motion. Davis v. Border, 170 Ohio App. 3d 758, 2007 Ohio 692, 869 N.E.2d 46, 2007 Ohio App. LEXIS 613 (2007).

When an insurer filed a declaratory judgment action seeking a declaration that it was not obligated to indemnify its insureds due to an alleged injured party's suit against them, and a default judgment was entered in the insurer's favor, after which the alleged injured party moved to set aside that default, and subsequently moved to intervene, the alleged injured party's motion was not timely, as it was filed 139 days after the default judgment, 109 after the expiration of the time to appeal that judgment, and more than 80 days after the alleged injured party admittedly had notice of it. It was not error to grant the motion, as the injured party's timely motion to vacate the default judgment gave the insurer notice of the injured party's intent to seek to intervene, and timeliness was only one factor to consider in deciding whether to allow the injured party to seek to intervene after judgment was entered. State Farm Mut. Ins. Cos. v. Young, — Ohio App. 3d —, 2006 Ohio 3812, — N.E. 2d —, 2006 Ohio App. LEXIS 3784 (July 26, 2006).

RULE 25.   Substitution of parties

(A) Death.

(1) If a party dies and the claim is not thereby extinguished, the court shall, upon motion, order substitution of the proper parties. The motion for substitution may be made by any party or by the successors or representatives of the deceased party and, together with the notice of hearing, shall be served on the parties as provided in Rule 5 and upon persons not parties in the manner provided in Rule 4 through Rule 4.6 for the service of summons. Unless the motion for substitution is made not later than ninety days after the

death is suggested upon the record by service of a statement of the fact of the death as provided herein for the service of the motion, the action shall be dismissed as to the deceased party.

(2) In the event of the death of one or more of the plaintiffs or of one or more of the defendants in an action in which the right sought to be enforced survives only to the surviving plaintiffs or only against the surviving defendants, the action does not abate. The death shall be suggested upon the record and the action shall proceed in favor of or against the surviving parties.

(B) **Incompetency.** If a party is adjudged incompetent, the court upon motion served as provided in subdivision (A) of this rule shall allow the action to be continued by or against his representative.

(C) **Transfer of interest.** In case of any transfer of interest, the action may be continued by or against the original party, unless the court upon motion directs the person to whom the interest is transferred to be substituted in the action or joined with the original party. Service of the motion shall be made as provided in subdivision (A) of this rule.

(D) **Public officers; death or separation from office.**

(1) When a public officer is a party to an action in his official capacity and during its pendency dies, resigns, or otherwise ceases to hold office, the action does not abate and his successor is automatically substituted as a party. Proceedings following the substitution shall be in the name of the substituted party, but any misnomer not affecting the substantial rights of the parties shall be disregarded. An order of substitution may be entered at any time, but the omission to enter such an order shall not affect the substitution.

(2) When a public officer sues or is sued in his official capacity, he may be described as a party by his official title rather than by name. The court however may require the addition of his name.

(E) **Suggestion of death or incompetency.** Upon the death or incompetency of a party it shall be the duty of the attorney of record for that party to suggest such fact upon the record within fourteen days after he acquires actual knowledge of the death or incompetency of that party. The suggestion of death or incompetency shall be served on all other parties as provided in Rule 5.

NOTES TO DECISIONS

ANALYSIS

Death of party
— Failure to substitute representative
Incompetency
—Failure to suggest

Death of party

Although a decedent brought an asbestos products action against assorted manufacturers while she was still alive, and after her death a suggestion of death was not filed and a substitution of the estate as the party was not made pursuant to Ohio R. Civ. P. 25(E) and (A), such failure of substitution only affected personal jurisdiction, which was waived pursuant to Ohio R. Civ. P. 12(H) where it was not challenged. Vince v. Crane Co., — Ohio App. 3d —, 2007 Ohio 1155, — N.E. 2d —, 2007 Ohio App. LEXIS 1083 (Mar. 15, 2007).

Although a decedent brought an asbestos products action against assorted manufacturers while she was still alive, and after her death a suggestion of death was not filed and a substitution of the estate as the party was not made pursuant to Ohio R. Civ. P. 25(E) and (A), such failure of substitution only affected personal jurisdiction, which was waived pursuant to Ohio R. Civ. P. 12(H) where it was not challenged. Vince v. Crane Co., — Ohio App. 3d —, 2007 Ohio 1155, — N.E. 2d —, 2007 Ohio App. LEXIS 1083 (Mar. 15, 2007).

— Failure to substitute representative

When, after a citizen and his wife sued a city and "unnamed police officers" for entering their home without a warrant, the wife died, her claims did not survive, under Ohio R. Civ. P. 25(A), because the citizen did not file a motion to substitute himself as her representative within 90 days of the city's filing of a suggestion of her death, nor did he seek additional time to do so, under Ohio R. Civ. P. 6(B). Maggio v. City of Warren, — Ohio App. 3d —, 2006 Ohio 6880, — N.E. 2d —, 2006 Ohio App. LEXIS 6801 (Dec. 22, 2006).

Incompetency

Although an apartment visitor filed a suggestion of incompetency pursuant to Ohio R. Civ. P. 25(E) in his negligence action against an apartment complex, as he failed to file a motion for substitution under Rule 25(A) in a timely manner, the trial court had nothing to issue a ruling on. Watts v. Forest Ridge Apts. & Town Homes, — Ohio App. 3d —, 2007 Ohio 1176, — N.E. 2d —, 2007 Ohio App. LEXIS 1091 (Mar. 16, 2007).

Although an apartment visitor filed a suggestion of incompetency pursuant to Ohio R. Civ. P. 25(E) in his negligence action against an apartment complex, as he failed to file a motion for substitution under Rule 25(A) in a timely manner, the trial court had nothing to issue a ruling on. Watts v. Forest Ridge Apts. & Town Homes, — Ohio App. 3d —, 2007 Ohio 1176, — N.E. 2d —, 2007 Ohio App. LEXIS 1091 (Mar. 16, 2007).

Trial court's granting of the wife's motion to substitute the party did not cause prejudice to the husband, and the wife demonstrated excusable neglect for filing a late suggestion of incompetency. It was the husband himself who initiated the suggestion of an incompetency proceeding. Banez v. Banez, — Ohio App. 3d —, 2007 Ohio 4584, — N.E. 2d —, 2007 Ohio App. LEXIS 4124 (Sept. 4, 2007).

—Failure to suggest

Attorney's failure to notify the court of a party's incompetency under Ohio R. Civ. P. 25(E) was not attributed to that party where the attorney had been removed and thereafter disbarred. Summit Gardens Ass'n v. Lemongelli, — Ohio App. 3d —, 2007 Ohio 6720, — N.E. 2d —, 2007 Ohio App. LEXIS 5891 (Dec. 14, 2007).

TITLE V
DISCOVERY

RULE 26. General provisions governing discovery

(A) **Policy; discovery methods.** It is the policy of these rules (1) to preserve the right of attorneys to prepare cases for trial with that degree of privacy necessary to encourage them to prepare their cases thoroughly and to investigate not only the favorable but the unfavorable aspects of such cases and (2) to prevent an attorney from taking undue advantage of an adversary's industry or efforts.

Parties may obtain discovery by one or more of the following methods: deposition upon oral examination or written questions; written interrogatories; production of documents, electronically stored information, or things or permission to enter upon land or other property, for inspection and other purposes; physical and mental examinations; and requests for admission. Unless the court orders otherwise, the frequency of use of these methods is not limited.

(B) **Scope of discovery.** Unless otherwise ordered by the court in accordance with these rules, the scope of discovery is as follows:

(1) **In General.** Parties may obtain discovery regarding any matter, not privileged, which is relevant to the subject matter involved in the pending action, whether it relates to the claim or defense of the party seeking discovery or to the claim or defense of any other party, including the existence, description, nature, custody, condition and location of any books, documents, electronically stored information, or other tangible things and the identity and location of persons having knowledge of any discoverable matter. It is not ground for objection that the information sought will be inadmissible at the trial if the information sought appears reasonably calculated to lead to the discovery of admissible evidence.

(2) **Insurance agreements.** A party may obtain discovery of the existence and contents of any insurance agreement under which any person carrying on an insurance business may be liable to satisfy part or all of a judgment which may be entered in the action or to indemnify or reimburse for payments made to satisfy the judgment. Information concerning the insurance agreement is not by reason of disclosure subject to comment or admissible in evidence at trial.

(3) **Trial preparation: materials.** Subject to the provisions of subdivision (B)(5) of this rule, a party may obtain discovery of documents, electronically stored information and tangible things prepared in anticipation of litigation or for trial by or for another party or by or for that other party's representative (including his attorney, consultant, surety, indemnitor, insurer, or agent) only upon a showing of good cause therefor. A statement concerning the action or its subject matter previously given by the party seeking the statement may be obtained without showing good cause. A statement of a party is (a) a written statement signed or otherwise adopted or approved by the party, or (b) a stenographic, mechanical, electrical, or other recording, or a transcription thereof, which is a substantially verbatim recital of an oral statement which was made by the party and contemporaneously recorded.

(4) **Electronically stored information.** A party need not provide discovery of electronically stored information when the production imposes undue burden or expense. On motion to compel discovery or for a protective order, the party from whom electronically stored information is sought must show that the information is not reasonably accessible because of undue burden or expense. If a showing of undue burden or expense is made, the court may nonetheless order production of electronically stored information if the

requesting party shows good cause. The court shall consider the following factors when determining if good cause exists:

(a) whether the discovery sought is unreasonably cumulative or duplicative;

(b) whether the information sought can be obtained from some other source that is less burdensome, or less expensive;

(c) whether the party seeking discovery has had ample opportunity by discovery in the action to obtain the information sought; and

(d) whether the burden or expense of the proposed discovery outweighs the likely benefit, taking into account the relative importance in the case of the issues on which electronic discovery is sought, the amount in controversy, the parties' resources, and the importance of the proposed discovery in resolving the issues.

In ordering production of electronically stored information, the court may specify the format, extent, timing, allocation of expenses and other conditions for the discovery of the electronically stored information.

(5) **Trial preparation: experts.**

(a) Subject to the provisions of subdivision (B)(5)(b) of this rule and Rule 35(B), a party may discover facts known or opinions held by an expert retained or specially employed by another party in anticipation of litigation or preparation for trial only upon a showing that the party seeking discovery is unable without undue hardship to obtain facts and opinions on the same subject by other means or upon a showing of other exceptional circumstances indicating that denial of discovery would cause manifest injustice.

(b) As an alternative or in addition to obtaining discovery under subdivision (B)(5)(a) of this rule, a party by means of interrogatories may require any other party (i) to identify each person whom the other party expects to call as an expert witness at trial, and (ii) to state the subject matter on which the expert is expected to testify. Thereafter, any party may discover from the expert or the other party facts known or opinions held by the expert which are relevant to the stated subject matter. Discovery of the expert's opinions and the grounds therefor is restricted to those previously given to the other party or those to be given on direct examination at trial.

(c) The court may require that the party seeking discovery under subdivision (B)(5)(b) of this rule pay the expert a reasonable fee for time spent in responding to discovery, and, with respect to discovery permitted under subdivision (B)(5)(a) of this rule, may require a party to pay another party a fair portion of the fees and expenses incurred by the latter party in obtaining facts and opinions from the expert.

(6) **Claims of Privilege or Protection of Trial-Preparation Materials.**

(a) **Information Withheld.** When information subject to discovery is withheld on a claim that it is privileged or subject to protection as trial preparation materials, the claim shall be made expressly and shall be supported by a description of the nature of the documents, communications, or things not produced that is sufficient to enable the demanding party to contest the claim.

(b) **Information Produced.** If information is produced in discovery that is subject to a claim of privilege or of protection as trial preparation material, the party making the claim may notify any party that received the information of the claim and the basis for it. After being notified, a receiving party must promptly return, sequester, or destroy the specified information and any copies within the party's possession, custody or control. A party may not use or disclose the information until the claim is resolved. A receiving party may promptly present the information to the court under seal for a determination of the claim of privilege or of protection as trial preparation material. If the receiving party disclosed the information before being notified, it must take reasonable steps to retrieve it. The producing party must preserve the information until the claim is resolved.

(C) **Protective orders.** Upon motion by any party or by the person from whom discovery is sought, and for good cause shown, the court in which the action is pending may make any order that justice requires to protect a party or person from annoyance, embarrassment, oppression, or undue burden or expense, including one or more of the following: (1) that the discovery not be had; (2) that the discovery may be had only on specified terms and conditions, including a designation of the time or place; (3) that the discovery may be had only by a method of discovery other than that selected by the party seeking discovery; (4) that certain matters not be inquired into or that the scope of the discovery be limited to certain matters; (5) that discovery be conducted with no one present except persons designated by the court; (6) that a deposition after being sealed be opened only by order of the court; (7) that a trade secret or other confidential research, development, or commercial information not be disclosed or be disclosed only in a designated way; (8) that the parties simultaneously file specified documents or information enclosed in sealed envelopes to be opened as directed by the court.

If the motion for a protective order is denied in whole or in part, the court, on terms and conditions as are just, may order that any party or person provide or permit discovery. The provisions of Civ. R. 37(A)(4) apply to the award of expenses incurred in relation to the motion.

Before any person moves for a protective order under this rule, that person shall make a reasonable effort to resolve the matter through discussion with the attorney or unrepresented party seeking discovery. A motion for a protective order shall be accompanied by a statement reciting the effort made to resolve the matter in accordance with this paragraph.

(D) **Sequence and timing of discovery.** Unless the court upon motion, for the convenience of parties and witnesses and in the interests of justice, orders otherwise, methods of discovery may be used in any sequence and the fact that a party is conducting discovery, whether by deposition or otherwise, shall not operate to delay any other party's discovery.

(E) **Supplementation of responses.** A party who has responded to a request for discovery with a response that was complete when made is under no duty to supplement his response to include information thereafter acquired, except as follows:

(1) A party is under a duty seasonably to supplement his response with respect to any question directly addressed to (a) the identity and location of persons having knowledge of discoverable matters, and (b) the identity of each person expected to be called as an expert witness at trial and the subject matter on which he is expected to testify.

(2) A party who knows or later learns that his response is incorrect is under a duty seasonably to correct the response.

(3) A duty to supplement responses may be imposed by order of the court, agreement of the parties, or at any time prior to trial through requests for supplementation of prior responses.

History: Amended, 7-1-94; 7-1-08.

NOTES TO DECISIONS

ANALYSIS

Appeal
Attorney-client privilege
— Work product
Construction
Discovery
Expert witness
— Fees
Finality of orders
Mass toxic torts
Medical records, nonparties
Minors, abuse and abortion records
Motion to compel
Privilege
— Medical records
— Trade secrets
Protective orders
— Proper
Statement of efforts to resolve matter
Stay of discovery
Supplementation
— Scope of information

Appeal

Home owners' appeal involving certain discovery orders pursuant to Ohio R. Civ. P. 26 in a foreclosure action was not reviewable because the discovery orders were interlocutory, rather than being final and appealable under RC § 2505.02. Miles Landing Homeowners Ass'n v. Bikkani, — Ohio App. 3d —, 2006 Ohio 3328, — N.E. 2d —, 2006 Ohio App. LEXIS 3244 (June 29, 2006).

Attorney-client privilege

Trial court's order that required an attorney to disclose various discovery logs was error where it encompassed documents that were protected by the attorney-client privilege or the work product doctrine under RC § 2317.02(A)(1), Ohio R. Prof. Conduct 1.6, and Ohio R. Civ. P. 26(B)(3); the only discoverable items related to a party's correspondence with a third-party that was within the attorney's file. Aultcare v. Roach, — Ohio App. 3d —, 2007 Ohio 5686, — N.E. 2d —, 2007 Ohio App. LEXIS 4995 (Oct. 22, 2007).

Doctor's motions to compel discovery, requesting that a medical practice's attorney produce two letters and answers to certain questions posed to him at a deposition, were properly denied. The materials were protected by the attorney-client privilege, and although the doctor contended that the attorney committed acts constituting a waiver of the privilege, only the practice could waive the privilege. Cecil v. Orthopedic Multispecialty Network, — Ohio App. 3d —, 2006 Ohio 4454, — N.E. 2d —, 2006 Ohio App. LEXIS 4380 (Aug. 28, 2006).

Since the requested information could have fallen under the umbrella of either opinion work product or ordinary fact work product, the possibility of two differing forms of protection under the attorney-client privilege necessitated an evidentiary hearing. Any blanket grant compelling discovery, under Ohio R. Civ. P. 26, 37(A)(2), and 34, was an abuse of discretion because the trial court had to first conduct a hearing to determine the nature of the privilege. Miller v. Bassett, — Ohio App. 3d —, 2006 Ohio 3590, — N.E. 2d —, 2006 Ohio App. LEXIS 3536 (July 13, 2006).

Where appellants claimed that certain documents were voluntarily, inadvertently, and unintentionally disclosed to opposing parties in the course of discovery, the trial court's determination of whether the attorney-client privilege had been waived with respect to motions by both sides regarding disclosure of the documents was to be made on a case-by-case basis, with consideration given to factors such as the reasonableness of disclosure prevention precautions, time taken to rectify the error, scope and nature of discovery, extent of disclosure, and fairness. The Court of Appeals of Ohio, Tenth Appellate District, Franklin County, holds that the law in Ohio shall be that a trial court, in addressing inadvertent disclosure of allegedly privileged documents in the course of discovery, must hold a hearing and consider various factors before determining to what extent, if any, waiver has occurred with respect to the contested materials. Miles-McClellan Constr. Co. v. Board of Educ. Westerville City Sch. Bd., — Ohio App. 3d —, 2006 Ohio 3439, — N.E. 2d —, 2006 Ohio App. LEXIS 3366 (June 30, 2006).

— Work product

Tenants' motion to compel the production of expert reports regarding an investigation of the causes of a fire was improperly granted. The trial court erred in failing to conduct a hearing or an in camera inspection to make the determinations as to whether the documents were privileged work product under Ohio R. Civ. P. 26 generated in anticipation of litigation or merely investigative business reports related to the processing of the landlords' insurance claim. Stegman v. Nickels, — Ohio App. 3d —, 2006 Ohio 4918, — N.E. 2d —, 2006 Ohio App. LEXIS 4843 (Sept. 22, 2006).

In order to obtain discovery of attorney work-product, a proponent had to show both substantial need and undue hardship. Where the work-product involved the attorney's mental impressions, conclusions, opinions or legal theories, such a showing would not suffice, since this "opinion work-product" enjoyed a nearly absolute immunity and could be discovered only in very rare and extraordinary circumstances. Stanton v. University Hosps. Health Sys., 166 Ohio App. 3d 758, 2006 Ohio 2297, 853 N.E. 2d 343, 2006 Ohio App. LEXIS 2166 (May 11, 2006).

Construction

Ohio R. Civ. P. 26 is not integral to Ohio R. Civ. P. 56 determinations. An owner's claim that a trial court improperly entered summary judgment in favor of the State on the State's forfeiture complaint because no discovery had been ordered was without merit. In re Forfeiture of John Deere Tractor, — Ohio App. 3d —, 2006 Ohio 388, — N.E. 2d —, 2006 Ohio App. LEXIS 329 (Jan. 18, 2006).

Discovery

Trial court, after an in camera review, properly ordered a hospital to produce certain peer review records to a patient in a negligent credentialing suit under former RC § 2305.251,

which was in effect at the time of the ruling on the patient's discovery requests. The amendment to former § 2305.251, which eradicated the patient's right to have an in camera review of the disputed documents, did not apply retroactively as the change was substantive and the litigation was pending at the time of the amendment. Tenan v. Huston, 165 Ohio App. 3d 185, 2006 Ohio 131, 845 N.E. 2d 549, 2006 Ohio App. LEXIS 125 (Jan. 13, 2006).

Expert witness

Trial court did not abuse its discretion when it precluded a patient's treating surgeon from testifying as an expert on the issues of standard of care and proximate cause in the patient's medical malpractice action against several other physicians, and in precluding the surgeon's recall in order to provide rebuttal evidence on those issues, as exclusion was a proper sanction in the circumstances under Ohio R. Civ. P. 26(E)(1) and 37 where the disclosure by the patient that the surgeon was going to testify as an expert was untimely and constituted unfair surprise. The case was filed in 1996, discovery was to have been completed in 2001, and the patient did not disclose his intent to call the surgeon as an expert until 10 days prior to the trial in 2003. Nead v. Brown County Gen. Hosp., — Ohio App. 3d —, 2007 Ohio 2443, — N.E. 2d —, 2007 Ohio App. LEXIS 2259 (May 21, 2007).

That the medical expert testified that he did not know what the mechanism was that caused the baby's brachial plexus injury, in the medical malpractice case, was not the same as him testifying that he did not know of other potential causes of the baby's injury. Thus, his testimony as to other potential causes was not inconsistent, nor a "surprise." Wasmire v. O'Dear, — Ohio App. 3d —, 2007 Ohio 736, — N.E. 2d —, 2007 Ohio App. LEXIS 674 (Feb. 20, 2007).

Trial court did not abuse its discretion in allowing an expert to testify in an asbestos litigation action commenced by a decedent's executor, as the expert witness had responded to a very generic question during his deposition and then at trial, he was provided with a more specific question to respond to, and his answer at trial was not a surprise opinion pursuant to Ohio R. Civ. P. 26(E)(1)(b). Barone v. GATX Corp., 167 Ohio App. 3d 744, 2006 Ohio 3221, 857 N.E. 2d 155, 2006 Ohio App. LEXIS 3146 (June 23, 2006).

In conjunction with Ohio R. Civ. P. 26(C), Cuyahoga County, Ohio, Ct. C.P. R. 21.1, entitled "Trial Witness," required that each counsel had to exchange with all other counsel written reports of medical and non-party expert witnesses expected to testify in advance of the trial, under Cuyahoga County, Ohio, Ct. C.P. R. 21.1(A), so the testifying experts and the bases of their opinions had to be disclosed in compliance both with Ohio R. Civ. P. 26(C) and Cuyahoga County, Ohio, Ct. C.P. R. 21.1. Stanton v. University Hosps. Health Sys., 166 Ohio App. 3d 758, 2006 Ohio 2297, 853 N.E. 2d 343, 2006 Ohio App. LEXIS 2166 (May 11, 2006).

Injured person was not entitled to additional financial information from a doctor who had performed an independent medical examination (IME) on the injured person, and the injured person's motion to compel disclosure of that information was properly denied, where the doctor had already provided, inter alia, the number of IMEs conducted by the doctor during a period of over six years, the price range for IMEs, the number of depositions provided by the doctor for the same period, and the charges typically associated with such depositions; additionally, the cross-examination portion of the doctor's video deposition, which was played at trial, dealt extensively with the doctor's medical-legal practice and the economic aspects thereof. Stinchcomb v. Mammone, 166 Ohio App. 3d 45, 2006 Ohio 1276, 849 N.E. 2d 54, 2006 Ohio App. LEXIS 1167 (Mar. 13, 2006).

In situations where a party deposes a witness, whom it has not identified as an expert, but from whom the party attempts to elicit expert opinion, the trial court has inherent authority under Ohio R. Civ. P. 26(B)(4)(c) to impose reasonable fees on that party for the expert testimony. Such a rule allows the trial court flexibility to control discovery, and discourages a party from obtaining expert testimony without notifying the opposition. Vance v. Marion Gen. Hosp., Inc., — Ohio App. 3d —, 2006 Ohio 146, — N.E. 2d —, 2006 Ohio App. LEXIS 116 (Jan. 17, 2006).

Doctor was properly awarded an expert witness fee of $1,500 for his testimony at a deposition under the trial court's inherent authority under Ohio R. Civ. P. 26(B)(4)(c) where an injured party did not identify the doctor as an expert witness, but attempted to elicit expert testimony from him on the symptoms the injured party showed, the cause of her injury, the connection between her condition and her treatment at a hospital, medical terminology, medical procedures, and the patient's likely pain. The fee was a reasonable compromise between the $2,500 requested by the doctor and the $500, plus $350 per hour of testimony initially offered by the injured party. Vance v. Marion Gen. Hosp., Inc., — Ohio App. 3d —, 2006 Ohio 146, — N.E. 2d —, 2006 Ohio App. LEXIS 116 (Jan. 17, 2006).

— Fees

In a malpractice case, the trial court did not err in denying a patient's motion to reduce discovery deposition fees demanded by a defense expert witness pursuant to Ohio R. Civ. P. 26(b)(4)(C); regardless of the reasonableness of a $ 650 per hour fee, the patient only timely moved to reduce a fee which ultimately cost the patient just $ 325 per hour. Such fee was not unreasonable on its face when reviewing for abuse of discretion. Duponty v. Kasamias, — Ohio App. 3d —, — N.E. 2d —, 2007 Ohio App. LEXIS 4441 (Sept. 19, 2007).

Finality of orders

In the second trial in a patient's dental malpractice action, held because the patient's motion for a new trial was granted after a defense verdict was rendered in the first trial, the trial court did not abuse its discretion in precluding the dentist from calling an expert witness whose testimony had been precluded as a discovery sanction in the first trial. The preclusion order did not improperly change a separate discovery order that had set a deadline for the identification of expert witnesses because that order was not final and the preclusion order did not necessarily contradict it, trial courts could exclude the presentation of expert witnesses by parties who failed to comply with pretrial orders and, under Ohio R. Civ. P. 16(7), could reasonably limit the number of expert witnesses, and the dentist showed no prejudice to the defense caused by the preclusion of the expert's testimony. Scibelli v. Pannunzio, — Ohio App. 3d —, 2006 Ohio 5652, — N.E. 2d —, 2006 Ohio App. LEXIS 5650 (Oct. 26, 2006).

Mass toxic torts

Lone Pine Order is a type of case management order that has been used in other jurisdictions to expedite claims and increase judicial efficiency in mass toxic tort litigation. The trial court's issuance of a Lone Pine order at a stage in the proceedings when there had yet to be any meaningful discovery, followed by the dismissal of the case with prejudice for failure to comply with the order, was an abuse of discretion under the circumstances of the case: Simeone v. Girard City Bd. of Educ., 171 Ohio App. 3d 633, 2007 Ohio 1775, 872 N.E.2d 344, 2007 Ohio App. LEXIS 1610 (2007).

Medical records, nonparties

Balancing test in Biddle v. Warren Gen. Hosp. (1999), 86 Ohio St.3d 395, 1999 Ohio 115, 715 N.E.2d 518, 1999 Ohio LEXIS 2925, applies only as a defense to the tort of unauthorized disclosure of confidential medical information and does not create a right to discover confidential medical records of nonparties in a private lawsuit: Roe v. Planned Parenthood Southwest Ohio Region, 122 Ohio St. 3d 399, 2009 Ohio 2973, 912 N.E.2d 61, 2009 Ohio LEXIS 1832 (2009).

Minors, abuse and abortion records

Abuse reports and medical records of minors receiving abortions are not discoverable, even in an identity-cloaking format, by private civil plaintiffs when the records are not necessary to develop the plaintiffs' claims: Roe v. Planned Parenthood Southwest Ohio Region, 173 Ohio App. 3d 414, 2007 Ohio 4318, 878 N.E.2d 1061, 2007 Ohio App. LEXIS 3868 (2007).

Motion to compel

When a trial court did not comply with the court's local rules by granting a motion to compel discovery four days after the motion was filed, there was no abuse of discretion because the trial court could choose to deviate from the court's local rules, and the court's order merely required a party to provide the discovery the party was already required to provide under Ohio R. Civ. P. 26. Flatt v. Atwood, — Ohio App. 3d —, 2007 Ohio 5387, — N.E. 2d —, 2007 Ohio App. LEXIS 4735 (Oct. 9, 2007).

Privilege

When there is a dispute about whether records are privileged, and when a party reasonably asserts that records should remain privileged, a trial court must conduct an in camera inspection of the records to determine if they are discoverable: Cargile v. Barrow, 182 Ohio App. 3d 55, 2009 Ohio 371, 911 N.E.2d 911, 2009 Ohio App. LEXIS 310 (2009).

Plaintiff waived the physician-patient privilege as to a former treating physician where he filed a legal malpractice claim and the physician's testimony was relevant to the defense of the action: Smalley v. Friedman, Damiano & Smith Co., L.P.A., 172 Ohio App. 3d 108, 2007 Ohio 2646, 873 N.E.2d 331, 2007 Ohio App. LEXIS 2475 (2007).

Trial court abused its discretion by compelling discovery of the entire case file without holding an evidentiary hearing or conducting an in camera review because the record was insufficiently developed to determine whether compelling discovery of the case file violated the attorney-client privilege or the work-product doctrine. The request to discover the entire attorney case file necessarily implicated an umbrella of protection under the attorney-client privilege and the work-product doctrine. Grace v. Mastruserio, — Ohio App. 3d —, 2007 Ohio 3942, — N.E. 2d —, 2007 Ohio App. LEXIS 3580 (Aug. 3, 2007).

Trial court erred in ordering disclosure under Ohio R. Civ. P. 26 by a clinic of 10 years' of minors' abortion records in an identity-concealing format, as they were covered by the patient-physician privilege under RC § 2317.02(B) and any possible probative value of the records was far outweighed by the potential invasion of privacy rights of the patients. The parents of a minor abortion patient's claims did not require disclosure thereof, as the clinic had acted in good faith in attempting to comply with the parental notification requirement of former RC § 2919.12 and the enforcement of RC § 2919.121 was enjoined at the time of the procedure, punitive damages were obtainable upon a showing of a single violation of either RC §§ 2919.12 or 2317.56, such that additional patient records were not necessary, and any duty to report suspected child abuse under RC § 2151.421 was confidential and was not admissible as evidence. Roe v. Planned Parenthood Southwest Ohio Region, 173 Ohio App. 3d 414, 2007 Ohio 4318, 878 N.E.2d 1061, 2007 Ohio App. LEXIS 3868 (2007).

— Medical records

Plaintiff filing a personal injury claim does not open herself to exposure, without limitation, of all her medical records. Rather, RC § 2317.02(B)(3)(a) limits discovery in such a case to medical records that are causally or historically related to the physical or mental injuries that are relevant to the issues in the case. The trial court had authority, without a request from the plaintiff, to order an in camera inspection of the requested medical records and determine which records were discoverable: Wooten v. Westfield Ins. Co., 181 Ohio App. 3d 59, 2009 Ohio 494, 907 N.E.2d 1219, 2009 Ohio App. LEXIS 418 (2009).

Trial court did not abuse its discretion in an action by a patient and her husband against a hospital, alleging that it breached its duty to protect her from another patient who sexually assaulted her because the hospital was aware of that patient's dangerous propensities and assaultive conduct, when it required the hospital to disclose the patient's medical records from before and after the assaultive incident, as the scope of discovery was within the trial court's discretion and such information was relevant under Ohio R. Civ. P. 26(B)(1) in determining the patient's prior actions and hence, the hospital's knowledge thereof. Alcorn v. Franciscan Hosp. Mt. Airy Campus, — Ohio App. 3d —, 2006 Ohio 5896, — N.E. 2d —, 2006 Ohio App. LEXIS 5840 (Nov. 9, 2006).

Trial court's decision to compel production of discovery as to two of the interrogatories was reversed as the answers sought were protected by the physician-patient privilege, pursuant to RC § 2317.02(B)(1), and the order to compel discovery as to one interrogatory was affirmed as to any request for the mental health information that the owner had directly put at issue through his claim for severe emotional distress. However, an evidentiary hearing was required to determine the appropriate look-back time frame of the discovery request. Miller v. Bassett, — Ohio App. 3d —, 2006 Ohio 3590, — N.E. 2d —, 2006 Ohio App. LEXIS 3536 (July 13, 2006).

— Trade secrets

Once a trade secret objection was raised, the trial court had an obligation, before compelling disclosure, to determine whether the materials requested were privileged trade secrets. To make this determination, the court is required to hold a hearing and conduct an in camera inspection of the information and documents. Mulkerin v. Cho, — Ohio App. 3d —, 2007 Ohio 6550, — N.E. 2d —, 2007 Ohio App. LEXIS 5714 (Dec. 10, 2007).

Motion for discovery of trade secrets was properly denied where the movant failed to present the kind of need that is so compelling as to warrant the risk that the trade secrets would be disseminated to a direct competitor: Splater v. Thermal Ease Hydronic Sys., Inc., 169 Ohio App. 3d 514, 2006 Ohio 5452, 863 N.E.2d 1060, 2006 Ohio App. LEXIS 5438 (2006).

Protective orders

When a client sued a lawyer for legal malpractice arising from the lawyer's representation of the client in the client's claim for negligent infliction of emotional distress under the Federal Employers' Liability Act, 45 U.S.C.S. § 51 et seq., the client was not entitled to a protective order, under Ohio R. Civ. P. 26(C), barring the client's physician from testifying as an expert witness for the lawyer because (1) the physician's testimony was not privileged, even though it was derived from the physician's treatment of the client, because, when the client filed a civil action involving the physician's treatment of the client, the client waived the client's physician-patient privilege, under RC § 2317.02(B)(1)(a)(iii), and (2) the physician's testimony was relevant, under RC § 2317.02(B)(3)(a) because it related causally or historically to physical injuries that were relevant to the client's claim. Smalley v. Friedman, Damiano & Smith Co., L.P.A., 172 Ohio App. 3d 108, 2007 Ohio 2646, 873 N.E.2d 331, 2007 Ohio App. LEXIS 2475 (2007).

When a client sued a lawyer for legal malpractice arising from the lawyer's representation of the client in the client's claim for negligent infliction of emotional distress under the Federal Employers' Liability Act, 45 U.S.C.S. § 51 et seq., a trial court's denial of the client's motion for a protective order, under Ohio R. Civ. P. 26(C), by which the client sought to keep the client's physician from testifying as an expert witness

for the lawyer, was final and appealable, under RC § 2505.02(B)(4)(a) and (b), because the motion concerned discovery of a potentially privileged matter, so it involved a provisional remedy, under RC § 2505.02(A)(3). Smalley v. Friedman, Damiano & Smith Co., L.P.A., 172 Ohio App. 3d 108, 2007 Ohio 2646, 873 N.E.2d 331, 2007 Ohio App. LEXIS 2475 (2007).

Trial court abused its discretion under Ohio R. Civ. P. 26(C) and 45(C) when it denied a former customer's motions to quash subpoenas and for a protective order with respect to requested documents that the customer claimed contained proprietary information and trade secrets, as there was no indication that the trial court considered whether the requesting party, a former supplier, had a substantial need for the discovery. Further, the trial court failed to provide any safeguards to protect the customer's trade secrets and confidential information. Lambda Research v. Jacobs, 170 Ohio App. 3d 750, 2007 Ohio 309, 869 N.E.2d 39, 2007 Ohio App. LEXIS 280 (2007).

To properly address whether communications or material sought in pre-trial discovery are subject to the attorney-client privilege, it is, at a minimum, necessary to ask the questions first and for the privilege rule to be invoked, after which a trial court then can, at hearing, determine if, in fact, privileged matters may be disclosed. Riggs v. Richard, — Ohio App. 3d —, 2007 Ohio 490, — N.E. 2d —, 2007 Ohio App. LEXIS 437 (Jan. 22, 2007).

When a trial court denied a lawyer's motion for a protective order, under Ohio R. Civ. P. 26(C), seeking to limit the lawyer's deposition to matters not protected by the attorney-client privilege in RC § 2317.02(A), the lawyer's appeal of that denial was premature until the deposition occurred, at which time the lawyer could state her objection to specific questions, fully developing the record for purposes of appeal. Riggs v. Richard, — Ohio App. 3d —, 2007 Ohio 490, — N.E. 2d —, 2007 Ohio App. LEXIS 437 (Jan. 22, 2007).

Trial court erred in granting a protective order under Ohio R. Civ. P. 26(C) based only on the finding that the motion for same was unopposed, as a grant of such a motion was to be based on a showing of "good cause," which was not made. Mellino Consulting, Inc. v. Synchronous Mgmt. Sarasota, — Ohio App. 3d —, 2007 Ohio 541, — N.E. 2d —, 2007 Ohio App. LEXIS 485 (Feb. 8, 2007).

Trial court did not abuse its discretion under Ohio R. Civ. P. 26(C)(7) in ordering a cleaning solvent manufacturer to disclose the ingredients in a solvent that caused injuries to an employee who was working as an electrician in a high school restoration project for purposes of further medical treatment and to prosecute his claim that inadequate warnings were provided by the manufacturer, as the trial court also provided a protective order that limited the release of that information which was undisputedly a trade secret under RC §§ 1333.61(D) and 1333.65. The trial court properly employed the balancing test in reaching its decision. Blackburn v. Coon Restoration & Sealants, Inc., — Ohio App. 3d —, 2007 Ohio 558, — N.E. 2d —, 2007 Ohio App. LEXIS 516 (Feb. 7, 2007).

It was an abuse of discretion to enter a corporation's default judgment based on the failure of the corporation's chief executive officer to appear at a deposition because the corporation's pending motion for a protective order, pursuant to Ohio R. Civ. P. 26(C), could be an excuse for the failure to appear, so the corporation could not have been found to have violated Ohio R. Civ. P. 37(D) because the motion for protective order, if granted, would excuse the corporation's duty to comply. Johnson Controls, Inc. v. Cadle Co., — Ohio App. 3d —, 2007 Ohio 3382, — N.E. 2d —, 2007 Ohio App. LEXIS 3100 (June 29, 2007).

Because individuals named as defendants in a fraudulent transfer claim were neither transferors nor transferees in the alleged fraudulent conveyance, residents were not entitled to discovery of the individuals' financial records because their financial condition was immaterial to the fraudulent conveyance issue. An LLC named as a defendant was the alleged transferee, so its financial condition was also irrelevant and the residents were not entitled to discovery of its records. Finally, because the trial court had not made a determination that the residents had a valid pending claim against a corporation, they were not creditors of the corporation, thus were not entitled to the financial records of the corporation at the present time, and the denial of the corporation's motion for a protective order was premature. Non-Employees of Chateau Estates Resident Ass'n v. Chateau Estates, Ltd., — Ohio App. 3d —, 2006 Ohio 3742, — N.E.2d —, 2006 Ohio App. LEXIS 3674 (July 21, 2006).

When, in a wrongful death action, two experts testified in their depositions that a nurse paralegal for plaintiff's counsel assisted them in the creation of their expert reports, it was proper to deny a request, under Ohio R. Civ. P. 26(C), for a protective order barring the deposition of the nurse paralegal because the nurse paralegal's deposition was only allowed on the narrow issue of the assistance she provided to the experts in the creation of their reports and did not invade the province of counsel's opinion work product. Stanton v. University Hosps. Health Sys., 166 Ohio App. 3d 758, 2006 Ohio 2297, 853 N.E. 2d 343, 2006 Ohio App. LEXIS 2166 (May 11, 2006).

Probate court did not abuse its discretion in denying an estate beneficiary's motion for a protective order pursuant to Ohio R. Civ. P. 26(A) in an estate matter, as the estate executrix had a right to depose the beneficiary, who was a "person" under Ohio R. Civ. P. 30(A), because the beneficiary had filed objections to the executrix's final account and he claimed that he had knowledge of alleged assets other than those listed therein; accordingly, the executrix was entitled to depose the beneficiary to discover and review the source and nature of those assets. In re Estate of Osborne, 166 Ohio App. 3d 732, 2006 Ohio 1952, 853 N.E. 2d 323, 2006 Ohio App. LEXIS 1806 (Apr. 17, 2006).

Trial court did not abuse its discretion under Ohio R. Civ. P. 26(C)(7), 34(C), and 45(C)(3)(b) in denying a product user's motion to compel disclosure of a nonparty manufacturer's formulae for polyethylene tubing in the user's products liability action, as the formulae were clearly trade secrets pursuant to RC § 1333.61(D) and the user did not show such a compelling need for the disclosure that it outweighed the manufacturer's interests in maintaining confidentiality of the information. It was noted that one of the opposing parties in the action was the manufacturer's direct competitor, which would have had access to that confidential information, and the user's expert only opined that the disclosure would have been "helpful" in his determination as to why the tubing had failed, which was not sufficiently compelling to require the requested disclosure. Splater v. Thermal Ease Hydronic Sys., Inc., 169 Ohio App. 3d 514, 2006 Ohio 5452, 863 N.E.2d 1060, 2006 Ohio App. LEXIS 5438 (2006).

— Proper

Trial court did not abuse its discretion in granting an author a protective order under Ohio R. Civ. P. 26(C) to stay proceedings in a defamation action pending determination by the trial court of the author's dismissal motion, as the matter had not been converted to one for summary judgment and accordingly, any discovery prior to ruling on the dismissal motion was premature and possibly unnecessary if the motion was granted. A limited opportunity to respond, which was deemed sufficient in the circumstances, was provided in order to resolve the issue of the stay prior to the date set for the deposition. Grover v. Bartsch, 170 Ohio App. 3d 188, 2006 Ohio 6115, 866 N.E.2d 547, 2006 Ohio App. LEXIS 6086 (2006).

Statement of efforts to resolve matter

Failure to comply with CivR 26(C) by filing a statement of efforts to resolve the matter constitutes a sufficient reason to vacate a protective order: State ex rel. Citizens for Open, Responsive & Accountable Gov't v. Register, 116 Ohio St. 3d 88, 2007 Ohio 5542, 876 N.E.2d 913, 2007 Ohio LEXIS 2569 (2007).

Stay of discovery

Considering that the motion to dismiss was based on the allegations in the complaint and might dispose of the litigation, the trial court acted within its discretion when it granted the defendant's motion for a stay of discovery: Grover v. Bartsch, 170 Ohio App. 3d 188, 2006 Ohio 6115, 866 N.E.2d 547, 2006 Ohio App. LEXIS 6086 (2006).

Supplementation

When a railroad sued a utility company for damages to the railroad's equipment caused by fallen electric lines, exhibits reflecting charges which the railroad did not present to the company until several days before trial were properly admitted, and the charges were properly included in an award of damages against the company, despite the railroad's duty of supplementation, in CivR 26(E), because the company had prior notice, from depositions of the railroad's employees, that invoices which the railroad had sent to the company did not include all of the damages the railroad claimed, so it was not appropriate to sanction the railroad. Norfolk S. Ry. v. Toledo Edison Co., — Ohio App. 3d —, 2008 Ohio 1572, — N.E. 2d —, 2008 Ohio App. LEXIS 1371 (Mar. 31, 2008).

— Scope of information

Trial court did not abuse its discretion under Ohio R. Civ. P. 59(A)(1) and (3) when it denied a patient's new trial motion after a jury entered a unanimous verdict in favor of a doctor in the patient's medical malpractice action, as an inconsistency in the doctor's testimony at his deposition and at trial was not objected to by the patient and was the subject of a jury instruction; although the doctor failed to apprise the patient of the change in his opinion with respect to the inconsistencies of his testimony, as required by Ohio R. Civ. P. 26(E), the patient was not prejudiced by the change in his testimony, as the statements did not involve the critical issue in the case. Garbers v. Rachwal, — Ohio App. 3d —, 2007 Ohio 4903, — N.E. 2d —, 2007 Ohio App. LEXIS 4361 (Sept. 21, 2007).

RULE 27. Perpetuation of testimony — depositions before action or pending appeal

(A) Before action.

(1) Petition. A person who desires to perpetuate his own testimony or the testimony of another person regarding any matter that may be cognizable in any court may file a petition in the court of common pleas in the county of the residence of any expected adverse party. The petitioner shall verify that he believes the facts stated in the petition are true. The petition shall be entitled in the name of the petitioner and shall show:

(a) That the petitioner or his personal representatives, heirs, beneficiaries, successors, or assigns may be parties to an action or proceeding cognizable in a court but is presently unable to bring or defend it;

(b) The subject matter of the expected action or proceeding and his interest therein (if the validity or construction of any written instrument connected with the subject matter of the deposition may be called in question a copy shall be attached to the petition);

(c) The facts which he desires to establish by the

proposed testimony and his reasons for desiring to perpetuate it;

(d) The names or, if the names are unknown, a description of the persons he expects will be adverse parties and their addresses so far as known;

(e) The names and addresses of the persons to be examined and the subject matter of the testimony which he expects to elicit from each.

The petition shall then ask for an order authorizing the petitioner to take the depositions of the persons to be examined named in the petition, for the purpose of perpetuating their testimony.

(2) **Notice and service.** The petitioner shall thereafter serve a notice upon each person named in the petition as an expected adverse party, together with a copy of the petition, stating that the petitioner will apply to the court, at a time and place named therein, for the order described in the petition. At least twenty-eight days before the date of hearing, unless the court upon application and showing of extraordinary circumstances prescribes a hearing on shorter notice, the notice shall be served either within or outside of this state by a method provided in Rule 4 through Rule 4.6 for service of summons, or in any other manner affording actual notice, as directed by order of the court. But if it appears to the court that an expected adverse party cannot be given actual notice, the court shall appoint a competent attorney to cross-examine the deponent; such attorney shall be allowed reasonable fees therefore which shall be taxed as costs. If any expected adverse party is a minor or incompetent the provisions of Rule 17(B) apply.

(3) **Order and examination.** If the court is satisfied that the allowance of the petition may prevent a failure or delay of justice, and that the petitioner is unable to bring or defend the contemplated action, the court shall order the testimony perpetuated, designating the deponents, the subject matter of the examination, when, where, and before whom their deposition shall be taken, and whether orally or upon written questions. The depositions may then be taken in accordance with these rules; and the court may make orders of the character provided for by Rule 34, Rule 35 and Rule 37. For the purpose of applying these rules to depositions for perpetuating testimony, each reference therein to the court in which the action is pending shall be deemed to refer to the court in which the petition for such deposition was filed.

(4) **Use of deposition.** Subject to the same limitations and objections as though the deponent were testifying at the trial in person, and to the provisions of Rule 26 and Rule 32(A) a deposition taken in accordance with this rule may be used as evidence in any action subsequently brought in any court, where the deposition is that of a party to the action, or where the issue is such that an interested party in the proceedings in which the deposition was taken had the right and opportunity for cross-examination with an interest and motive similar to that which the adverse party has in the action in which the deposition is offered. But, except where the deposition is that of a party to the action and is offered against the party, the deposition may not be used as evidence unless the deponent is unavailable as a witness at the trial.

(B) **Pending appeal.** If an appeal has been taken from a judgment of any court, a party who desires to perpetuate testimony may make a motion in the court where the action was tried, for leave to take depositions upon the same notice and service thereof as provided in (A)(2) of this rule. The motion shall show the names and addresses of the persons to be examined, the subject matter of the testimony which he expects to elicit from each, and the reasons for perpetuating their testimony. If the court is satisfied that the motion is proper to avoid a failure or delay of justice, it may make an order allowing the deposition to be taken and may make orders of the character provided for by Rule 34, Rule 35, and Rule 37. The depositions may be taken and used in the same manner and under the same conditions as are prescribed for depositions in Rule 26 and Rule 32(A).

(C) **Perpetuation by actions.** This rule does not limit the inherent power of a court to entertain an action to perpetuate testimony.

(D) **Filing of depositions.** Depositions taken under this rule shall be filed with the court in which the petition is filed or the motion is made.

(E) **Costs of deposition.** The party taking any deposition under this rule shall pay the costs thereof and of all proceedings hereunder, unless otherwise ordered by the court.

(F) **Depositions taken in other states.** A deposition taken under similar procedure of another jurisdiction is admissible in this state to the same extent as a deposition taken under this rule.

(G) **Construction of rule.** This rule shall be so construed as to effectuate the general purpose to make uniform the law of those states which have similar rules or statutes.

History: Amended, eff 7-1-72.

NOTES TO DECISIONS

ANALYSIS

Attorney-client privilege

Attorney-client privilege
Decedent's petition, under Ohio R. Civ. P. 27, to perpetuate his testimony, did not expressly or impliedly waive his attorney-client privilege, under RC § 2317.02(A), because the petition did not place any of decedent's communications with his attorney in issue, so the decedent's niece and nephew were not entitled to depose the decedent's attorney regarding his representation of the decedent. Wallace v. McElwain, — Ohio App. 3d —, 2006 Ohio 5226, — N.E. 2d —, 2006 Ohio App. LEXIS 5205 (Sept. 27, 2006).

RULE 28.   Persons before whom depositions may be taken

(A) **Depositions within state.** Depositions may be taken in this state before: a person authorized to administer any oath by the laws of this state, a person appointed by the court in which the action is pending, or a person agreed upon by written stipulation of all the parties.

(B) **Depositions outside state.** Depositions may

be taken outside this state before: a person authorized to administer oaths in the place where the deposition is taken, a person appointed by the court in which the action is pending, a person agreed upon by written stipulation of all the parties, or, in any foreign country, by any consular officer of the United States within his consular district.

(C) **Disqualification for interest.** Unless the parties agree otherwise as provided in Civ. R. 29, depositions shall not be taken before a person who:

(1) is a relative or employee of or attorney for any of the parties, or

(2) is a relative or employee of an attorney for any of the parties, or

(3) is financially interested in the action.

(D) **Prohibited contracts.**

(1) Any blanket contract for private court reporting services, not related to a particular case or reporting incident, shall be prohibited between a private court reporter or any other person with whom a private court reporter has a principal and agency relationship, and any attorney, party to an action, party having a financial interest in an action, or any entity providing the services of a shorthand reporter.

(2) "Blanket contract" means a contract under which a court reporter, court recorder, or court reporting firm agrees to perform all court reporting or court recording services for a client for two or more cases at a rate of compensation fixed in the contract.

(3) Negotiating or bidding reasonable fees, equal to all parties, on a case-by-case basis is not prohibited.

(4) Division (D) of this rule does not apply to the courts or the administrative tribunals of this state.

History: Amended, eff 7-1-01.

RULE 29. Stipulations regarding discovery procedure

Unless the court orders otherwise, the parties may by written stipulation (1) provide that depositions may be taken before any person, at any time or place, upon any notice, and in any manner and when so taken may be used like other depositions; and (2) modify the procedures provided by these rules for other methods of discovery.

RULE 30. Depositions upon oral examination

(A) **When depositions may be taken.** After commencement of the action, any party may take the testimony of any person, including a party, by deposition upon oral examination. The attendance of a witness deponent may be compelled by the use of subpoena as provided by Civ.R. 45. The attendance of a party deponent may be compelled by the use of notice of examination as provided by division (B) of this rule. The deposition of a person confined in prison may be taken only by leave of court on such terms as the court prescribes.

(B) **Notice of examination; general requirements; nonstenographic recording; production of** documents and things; deposition of organization; deposition by telephone.

(1) A party desiring to take the deposition of any person upon oral examination shall give reasonable notice in writing to every other party to the action. The notice shall state the time and place for taking the deposition and the name and address of each person to be examined, if known, and, if the name is not known, a general description sufficient to identify the person or the particular class or group to which the person belongs. If a subpoena duces tecum is to be served on the person to be examined, a designation of the materials to be produced shall be attached to or included in the notice.

(2) If any party shows that when the party was served with notice the party was unable, through the exercise of diligence, to obtain counsel to represent the party at the taking of the deposition, the deposition may not be used against the party.

(3) If a party taking a deposition wishes to have the testimony recorded by other than stenographic means, the notice shall specify the manner of recording, preserving, and filing the deposition. The court may require stenographic taking or make any other order to ensure that the recorded testimony will be accurate and trustworthy.

(4) The notice to a party deponent may be accompanied by a request made in compliance with Civ.R. 34 for the production of documents and tangible things at the taking of the deposition.

(5) A party, in the party's notice, may name as the deponent a public or private corporation, a partnership, or an association and designate with reasonable particularity the matters on which examination is requested. The organization so named shall choose one or more of its proper employees, officers, agents, or other persons duly authorized to testify on its behalf. The persons so designated shall testify as to matters known or available to the organization. Division (B)(5) does not preclude taking a deposition by any other procedure authorized in these rules.

(6) The parties may stipulate in writing or the court may upon motion order that a deposition be taken by telephone. For purposes of this rule, Civ. R. 28, and Civ. R. 45(C), a deposition taken by telephone is taken in the county and at the place where the deponent is to answer questions propounded to the deponent.

(C) **Examination and cross-examination; record of examination; oath; objections.** Examination and cross-examination of witnesses may proceed as permitted at the trial. The officer before whom the deposition is to be taken shall put the witness on oath or affirmation and personally, or by someone acting under the officer's direction and in the officer's presence, shall record the testimony of the witness. The testimony shall be taken stenographically or recorded by any other means designated in accordance with division (B)(3) of this rule. If requested by one of the parties, the testimony shall be transcribed.

All objections made at the time of the examination to the qualifications of the officer taking the deposition, or to the manner of taking it, or to the evidence presented, or to the conduct of any party, and any other objection to the proceedings, shall be noted by the officer upon the deposition. Evidence objected to shall be taken subject to the objections. In lieu of participating in the oral examination, parties may serve written questions on the party taking the deposition and require him to transmit them to the officer, who shall propound them to the witness and record the answers verbatim.

(D) **Motion to terminate or limit examinations.** At any time during the taking of the deposition, on motion of any party or of the deponent and upon a showing that the examination is being conducted in bad faith or in such manner as unreasonably to annoy, embarrass, or oppress the deponent or party, the court in which the action is pending may order the officer conducting the examination to cease forthwith from taking the deposition, or may limit the scope and manner of the taking of the deposition as provided in Civ. R. 26(C). If the order made terminates the examination, it shall be resumed thereafter only upon the order of the court in which the action is pending. Upon demand of the objecting party or deponent, the taking of the deposition shall be suspended for the time necessary to make a motion for an order. The provisions of Civ. R. 37 apply to the award of expenses incurred in relation to the motion.

(E) **Submission to witness; changes; signing.** When the testimony is fully transcribed, the deposition shall be submitted to the witness for examination and shall be read to or by the witness, unless examination and reading are waived by the witness and by the parties. Any changes in form or substance that the witness desires to make shall be entered upon the deposition by the officer with a statement of the reasons given by the witness for making them. The deposition shall then be signed by the witness, unless the parties by stipulation waive the signing or the witness is ill, cannot be found, or refuses to sign. The witness shall have thirty days from submission of the deposition to the witness to review and sign the deposition. If the deposition is taken within thirty days of a trial or hearing, the witness shall have seven days from submission of the deposition to the witness to review and sign the deposition. If the trial or hearing is scheduled to commence less than seven days before the deposition is submitted to the witness, the court may establish a deadline for the witness to review and sign the deposition. If the deposition is not signed by the witness during the period prescribed in this division, the officer shall sign it and state on the record the fact of the waiver or of the illness or absence of the witness or the fact of the refusal to sign together with the reason, if any, given therefor; and the deposition may then be used as fully as though signed, unless on a motion to suppress the court holds that the reasons given for the refusal to sign require rejection of the deposition in whole or in part.

(F) **Certification and filing by officer; exhibits; copies; notice of filing.**

(1)(a) Upon request of any party or order of the court, the officer shall transcribe the deposition. Provided the officer has retained an archival-quality copy of the officer's notes, the officer shall have no duty to retain paper notes of the deposition testimony. The officer shall certify on the transcribed deposition that the witness was fully sworn or affirmed by the officer and that the transcribed deposition is a true record of the testimony given by the witness. If any of the parties request or the court orders, the officer shall seal the transcribed deposition in an envelope endorsed with the title of the action and marked "Deposition of (here insert name of witness)" and, upon payment of the officer's fees, promptly shall file it with the court in which the action is pending or send it by certified or express mail to the clerk of the court for filing.

(b) Unless objection is made to their production for inspection during the examination of the witness, documents and things shall be marked for identification and annexed to and returned with the deposition. The materials may be inspected and copied by any party, except that the person producing the materials may substitute copies to be marked for identification, if the person affords to all parties fair opportunity to verify the copies by comparison with the originals. If the person producing the materials requests their return, the officer shall mark them, give each party an opportunity to inspect and copy them, and return them to the person producing them, and the materials may then be used in the same manner as if annexed to and returned with the deposition.

(2) Upon payment, the officer shall furnish a copy of the deposition to any party or to the deponent.

(3) The party requesting the filing of the deposition shall forthwith give notice of its filing to all other parties.

(G) **Failure to attend or to serve subpoena; expenses.**

(1) If the party giving the notice of the taking of a deposition fails to attend and proceed with the deposition and another party attends in person or by attorney pursuant to the notice, the court may order the party giving the notice to pay to the other party the amount of the reasonable expenses incurred by the other party and the other party's attorney in so attending, including reasonable attorney's fees.

(2) If the party giving the notice of the taking of a deposition of a witness fails to serve a subpoena upon the witness and the witness because of the failure does not attend, and another party attends in person or by attorney because the other party expects the deposition of that witness to be taken, the court may order the party giving the notice to pay to the other party the amount of the reasonable expenses incurred by the other party and the other party's attorney in so attending, including reasonable attorney's fees.

History: Amended, eff 7-1-76; 7-1-85; 7-1-92; 7-1-94; 7-1-97; 7-1-06.

NOTES TO DECISIONS

ANALYSIS

Appearance at deposition
Audio recording
Deposition conducted in bad faith
Sanctions

Appearance at deposition

Evidence supported the trial court's conclusion that counsel for the employee had engaged in frivolous conduct in connection with the deposition of the employee's daughter. The evidence showed that counsel provided an incorrect name for the witness to be deposed and then let opposing counsel fly to Illinois to conduct a deposition that he knew was most likely not to take place. Kinnison v. Advance Stores Co., — Ohio App. 3d —, 2006 Ohio 222, — N.E. 2d —, 2006 Ohio App. LEXIS 192 (Jan. 20, 2006).

Audio recording

There was no error in finding that counsel for the employee had violated Ohio R. Civ. P. 30(B)(3) as there was no dispute that he failed to give notice that he would be making an audio recording of the deposition and, in fact, there was evidence that he attempted to conceal the audio recording. In addition, even after opposing counsel objected, counsel persisted in making audio recordings for his own "private" use until a court reporter objected. Kinnison v. Advance Stores Co., — Ohio App. 3d —, 2006 Ohio 222, — N.E. 2d —, 2006 Ohio App. LEXIS 192 (Jan. 20, 2006).

Deposition conducted in bad faith

Trial court did not abuse its discretion in holding that counsel for the employee used the deposition of the manager's daughter to harass her and badger her with irrelevant and inadmissible material. Counsel went far beyond the scope authorized by the trial court. Kinnison v. Advance Stores Co., — Ohio App. 3d —, 2006 Ohio 222, — N.E. 2d —, 2006 Ohio App. LEXIS 192 (Jan. 20, 2006).

Sanctions

Trial court's imposition of attorney fees and travel expenses as a discovery sanction pursuant to Ohio R. Civ. P. 30(G)(1) and 37 was reasonable in the circumstances and not an abuse of discretion, as appellant's counsel had scheduled a deposition to be held at his office but he had failed to secure a court reporter, which required the rescheduling of the deposition, and he was aware that appellee's counsel had to travel from out of town. The fees and expenses for travel were deemed reasonable in the circumstances. McKowen v. United Church Homes, Inc., — Ohio App. 3d —, 2006 Ohio 6607, — N.E. 2d —, 2006 Ohio App. LEXIS 6519 (Dec. 8, 2006).

RULE 31. Depositions of witnesses upon written questions

(A) **Serving questions; notice.** After commencement of the action, any party may take the testimony of any person, including a party, by deposition upon written questions. The attendance of witnesses may be compelled by the use of subpoena as provided by Rule 45. The deposition of a person confined in prison may be taken only by leave of court on such terms as the court prescribes.

A party desiring to take a deposition upon written questions shall serve them upon every other party with a notice stating (1) the name and address of the person who is to answer them, if known, and if the name is not known, a general description sufficient to identify him or the particular class or group to which he belongs, and (2) the name and descriptive title and address of the officer before whom the deposition is to be taken. A deposition upon written questions may be taken of a public or private corporation or a partnership or association in accordance with the provisions of Rule 30(B)(5).

Within twenty-one days after the notice and written questions are served, a party may serve cross questions upon all other parties. Within fourteen days after being served with cross questions, a party may serve redirect questions upon all other parties. Within fourteen days after being served with redirect questions, a party may serve recross questions upon all other parties. The court may for cause shown enlarge or shorten the time.

(B) **Officer to take responses and prepare record.** A copy of the notice and copies of all questions served shall be delivered by the party taking the deposition to the officer designated in the notice, who shall proceed promptly, in the manner provided by Rule 30(C), (E), and (F), to take the testimony of the witness in response to the questions and to prepare, certify, and file or mail the deposition, attaching thereto the copy of the notice and the questions received by him.

(C) **Notice of filing.** The party requesting the filing of the deposition shall forthwith give notice of its filing to all other parties.

RULE 32. Use of depositions in court proceedings

(A) **Use of depositions.** Every deposition intended to be presented as evidence must be filed at least one day before the day of trial or hearing unless for good cause shown the court permits a later filing.

At the trial or upon the hearing of a motion or an interlocutory proceeding, any part or all of a deposition, so far as admissible under the rules of evidence applied as though the witness were then present and testifying, may be used against any party who was present or represented at the taking of the deposition or who had reasonable notice thereof, in accordance with any one of the following provisions:

(1) Any deposition may be used by any party for the purpose of contradicting or impeaching the testimony of deponent as a witness.

(2) The deposition of a party or of anyone who at the time of taking the deposition was an officer, director, or managing agent, or a person designated under Rule 30(B)(5) or Rule 31(A) to testify on behalf of a public or private corporation, partnership or association which is a party may be used by an adverse party for any purpose.

(3) The deposition of a witness, whether or not a party, may be used by any party for any purpose if the court finds: (a) that the witness is dead; or (b) that the witness is beyond the subpoena power of the court in which the action is pending or resides outside of the county in which the action is pending unless it appears that the absence of the witness was procured by the party offering the deposition; or (c) that the witness is unable to attend or testify because of age, sickness, infirmity, or imprisonment; or (d) that the party offering the deposition has been unable to procure the attendance of the witness by subpoena; or (e) that the witness is an attending physician or medical expert, although residing within the county in which the action is heard; or (f) that the oral examination of a witness is not required; or (g) upon application and notice, that such exceptional circumstances exist as to make it desirable, in the interest of justice and with due regard

to the importance of presenting the testimony of witnesses orally in open court, to allow the deposition to be used.

(4) If only part of a deposition is offered in evidence by a party, an adverse party may require him to introduce all of it which is relevant to the part introduced, and any party may introduce any other parts.

Substitution of parties pursuant to Rule 25 does not affect the right to use depositions previously taken. When another action involving the same subject matter is or has been brought between the same parties or their representatives or successors in interest, all depositions lawfully taken in the one action may be used in the other as if originally taken therefore.

(B) **Objections to admissibility.** Subject to the provisions of subdivision (D)(3) of this rule, objection may be made at the trial or hearing to receiving in evidence any deposition or part thereof for any reason which would require the exclusion of the evidence if the witness were then present and testifying. Upon the motion of a party, or upon its own initiative, the court shall decide such objections before the deposition is read in evidence.

(C) **Effect of taking or using depositions.** A party does not make a person his own witness for any purpose by taking his deposition. The introduction in evidence of the deposition or any part thereof for any purpose other than that of contradicting or impeaching the deponent makes the deponent the witness of the party introducing the deposition, but this shall not apply to the use by an adverse party of a deposition as described in subdivision (A)(2) of this rule. The use of subdivision (A)(3)(e) of this rule does not preclude any party from calling such a witness to appear personally at the trial nor does it preclude the taking and use of any deposition otherwise provided by law. At the trial or hearing any party may rebut any relevant evidence contained in a deposition whether introduced by him or by any other party.

(D) **Effect of errors and irregularities in depositions.**

(1) **As to notice.** All errors and irregularities in the notice for taking a deposition are waived unless written objection stating the grounds therefore, is promptly served upon the party giving the notice.

(2) **As to disqualification of officer.** Objection to taking a deposition because of disqualification of the officer before whom it is to be taken is waived unless made before the taking of the deposition begins or as soon thereafter as the disqualification becomes known or could be discovered with reasonable diligence.

(3) **As to taking of depositions.**

(a) Objections to the competency of a witness or to the competency, relevancy, or materiality of testimony are not waived by failure to make them before or during the taking of the deposition, unless the ground of the objection is one which might have been obviated or removed if presented at that time.

(b) Errors and irregularities occurring at the oral examination in the manner of taking the deposition, in the form of the questions or answers, in the oath or affirmation, or in the conduct of parties and errors of any kind which might be obviated, removed, or cured if promptly presented, are waived unless reasonable objection thereto is made at the taking of the deposition.

(c) Objections to the form of written questions submitted under Rule 31 are waived unless served in writing upon the party propounding them within the time allowed for serving the succeeding cross or other questions and within seven days after service of the last questions authorized.

(4) **As to completion and return of deposition.** Errors and irregularities in the manner in which the testimony is transcribed or the deposition is prepared, signed, certified, sealed, indorsed, transmitted, filed, or otherwise dealt with by the officer under Rule 30 and Rule 31 are waived unless a motion to suppress the deposition or some part thereof is made with reasonable promptness after such defect is, or with due diligence might have been, ascertained.

History: Amended, eff 7-1-72.

NOTES TO DECISIONS

ANALYSIS

Admissibility
Deposition of adverse party
Deposition testimony excluded
Filing and authentication
Harmless error
Notice
Summary judgment

Admissibility

Relevant evidence indicative of the sellers' knowledge of the alleged defects in the home presented by the buyer to oppose the motion for summary judgment was not admissible either under Ohio R. Civ. P. 32, in a deposition, or under Ohio R. Civ. P. 56, as an affidavit, because any evidence (what the neighbors told the buyer) that could even remotely have been construed as creating an inference that the sellers were or should have been aware of the defects in the residence was hearsay, pursuant to Ohio R. Evid. 801, because it was offered to prove the truth of the matter asserted (knowledge of defects). Therefore, the buyer did not meet his burden of production to overcome the motion for summary judgment. Reardon v. Hale, — Ohio App. 3d —, 2007 Ohio 4351, — N.E. 2d —, 2007 Ohio App. LEXIS 3906 (Aug. 27, 2007).

Deposition of adverse party

In homeowners' claims against mortgage brokers and the brokers' principal for violations of the Mortgage Broker Act, RC § 1322.01 et seq., and civil conspiracy, a trial court did not commit error by considering the principal's deposition as substantive evidence because Ohio R. Civ. P. 32(A) allowed a party to use an adverse party's deposition for any purpose, including as substantive evidence. Roark v. Rydell, 174 Ohio App. 3d 186, 2007 Ohio 6873, 881 N.E. 2d 333, 2007 Ohio App. LEXIS 6043 (Dec. 21, 2007).

Deposition testimony excluded

Exclusion at trial of the deposition testimony of an independent witness to an accident was an appropriate exercise of discretion under Ohio. R. Civ. P. 32 where the proponent of the deposition knew where the witness could be located, attempted to persuade the witness to testify, had the witness in counsel's office on the Friday before the Monday negligence trial, but failed to serve the witness with a subpoena to appear at trial. Johnson v. Eitle, — Ohio App. 3d —, 2007 Ohio 3315, — N.E. 2d —, 2007 Ohio App. LEXIS 3062 (June 29, 2007).

Filing and authentication

Depositions submitted by a property owner in support of its motion for summary judgment were not filed with the trial court, pursuant to Ohio R. Civ. P. 32(A) and, thus, could not be considered. Moore v. Tall Timbers Banquet & Conf. Ctr., — Ohio App. 3d —, 2006 Ohio 3249, — N.E. 2d —, 2006 Ohio App. LEXIS 3135 (June 22, 2006).

Harmless error

Although there was no evidence that an expert was unavailable for a dispositional hearing in a dependency matter and there was no indication that any of the criteria in Ohio R. Civ. P. 32(A)(3) applied for purposes of using the deposition in lieu of live hearing testimony, there was nothing that indicated that the trial court relied on the deposition in rendering its decision. As the record led to the conclusion that the juvenile court would have made the same disposition even if had not relied on the deposition, any potential error was harmless. In re Brown, — Ohio App. 3d —, 2006 Ohio 3189, — N.E. 2d —, 2006 Ohio App. LEXIS 3090 (June 23, 2006).

Notice

Trial court did not abuse its discretion when it precluded the administratrix from reading the deposition because it did not include testimony sufficient to establish that the expert was licensed to practice medicine and that he devoted the appropriate amount of his professional time to active clinical practice or teaching, under Ohio R. Evid. 601(D). Further, since the administratrix dismissed the second doctor from the initial proceeding before she deposed the expert, that doctor did not have reasonable notice of the taking of the deposition, pursuant to Ohio R. Civ. P. 32(A). Simpson v. Kuchipudi, — Ohio App. 3d —, 2006 Ohio 5163, — N.E. 2d —, 2006 Ohio App. LEXIS 5103 (Oct. 2, 2006).

Summary judgment

Party's deposition taken in another case could properly be considered as just as good as an affidavit for purposes of summary judgment: Hastings Mut. Ins. v. Halatek, 174 Ohio App. 3d 252, 2007 Ohio 6923, 881 N.E. 2d 897, 2007 Ohio App. LEXIS 6070 (Dec. 11, 2007).

Trial court properly considered a party's deposition that was taken in another matter for purposes of determining whether there was a genuine issue of material fact to preclude summary judgment in a separate declaratory judgment action, as pursuant to Ohio R. Civ. P. 32(A) and 56(C), the deposition was just as good as an affidavit, which was permissible; the deposition was based on personal knowledge, the deponent was available to testify at trial, and it was only used for summary judgment purposes. Hastings Mut. Ins. v. Halatek, 174 Ohio App. 3d 252, 2007 Ohio 6923, 881 N.E. 2d 897, 2007 Ohio App. LEXIS 6070 (Dec. 11, 2007).

RULE 33. Interrogatories to parties

(A) Availability; procedures for use. Any party, without leave of court, may serve upon any other party up to forty written interrogatories to be answered by the party served. A party serving interrogatories shall provide the party served with both a printed and an electronic copy of the interrogatories. The electronic copy shall be reasonably useable for word processing and provided on computer disk, by electronic mail, or by other means agreed to by the parties. A party who is unable to provide an electronic copy of the interrogatories may seek leave of court to be relieved of this requirement. A party shall not propound more than forty interrogatories to any other party without leave of court. Upon motion, and for good cause shown, the court may extend the number of interrogatories that a party may serve upon another party. For purposes of this rule, any subpart propounded under an interrogatory shall be considered a separate interrogatory.

(1) If the party served is a public or private corporation or a partnership or association, the organization shall choose one or more of its proper employees, officers, or agents to answer the interrogatories, and the employee, officer, or agent shall furnish information as is known or available to the organization.

(2) Interrogatories, without leave of court, may be served upon the plaintiff after commencement of the action and upon any other party with or after service of the summons and complaint upon the party.

(3) Each interrogatory shall be answered separately and fully in writing under oath, unless it is objected to, in which event the reasons for objection shall be stated in lieu of an answer. The party upon whom the interrogatories have been served shall quote each interrogatory immediately preceding the corresponding answer or objection. When the number of interrogatories exceeds forty without leave of court, the party upon whom the interrogatories have been served need only answer or object to the first forty interrogatories. The answers are to be signed by the person making them, and the objections signed by the attorney making them. The party upon whom the interrogatories have been served shall serve a copy of the answers and objections within a period designated by the party submitting the interrogatories, not less than twenty-eight days after the service of a printed copy of the interrogatories or within such shorter or longer time as the court may allow. Failure to provide an electronic copy does not alter the designated period for response, but shall constitute good cause for the court to order the period enlarged if request therefor is made pursuant to Rule 6(B) before the expiration of the designated period. If so ordered, the court may require that the party submitting the interrogatories provide an electronic copy as required by this rule unless relieved from this obligation.

(B) Scope and use at trial. Interrogatories may relate to any matters that can be inquired into under Civ. R. 26(B), and the answers may be used to the extent permitted by the rules of evidence.

The party calling for such examination shall not thereby be concluded but may rebut it by evidence.

An interrogatory otherwise proper is not objectionable merely because an answer to the interrogatory involves an opinion, contention, or legal conclusion, but the court may order that such an interrogatory be answered at a later time, or after designated discovery has been completed, or at a pretrial conference.

(C) Option to produce business records. Where the answer to an interrogatory may be derived or ascertained from the business records, including electronically stored information, of the party upon whom the interrogatory has been served or from an examination, audit, or inspection of the business records, or from a compilation, abstract, or summary based on the business records, and the burden of deriving or ascertaining the answer is substantially the same for the party serving the interrogatory as for the party served, it is a sufficient answer to the interrogatory to specify the records from which the answer may be derived or ascertained and to afford to the party serving the interrogatory reasonable opportunity to examine, audit, or inspect the records and to make copies of the records or compilations, abstracts, or summaries from the records.

History: Amended, eff 7-1-72; 7-1-89; 7-1-99; 7-1-04; 7-1-08; 7-1-09.

NOTES TO DECISIONS

ANALYSIS

Unduly burdensome interrogatores

Unduly burdensome interrogatores
Trial court properly ordered a husband to pay part of the husband's former wife's attorney fees because (1) the wife's counsel had to respond to interrogatories that were much more burdensome than provided for in Ohio R. Civ. P. 33(A), as the husband propounded 384 interrogatories to the wife, many of which were not designed to provide discoverable evidence or resolve potentially disputed issues, (2) the husband's "fault oriented position" prolonged the litigation, and (3) the husband was better able to pay the fees and obtain credit to assist in paying them. Doody v. Doody, — Ohio App. 3d —, 2007 Ohio 2567, — N.E. 2d —, 2007 Ohio App. LEXIS 2387 (May 25, 2007).

RULE 34. Production of documents and things for inspection, copying, testing and entry upon land for inspection and other purposes

(A) **Scope.** Subject to the scope of discovery provisions of Civ. R. 26(B), any party may serve on any other party a request to produce and permit the party making the request, or someone acting on the requesting party's behalf (1) to inspect and copy any designated documents or electronically stored information, including writings, drawings, graphs, charts, photographs, sound recordings, images, and other data or data compilations stored in any medium from which information can be obtained that are in the possession, custody, or control of the party upon whom the request is served; (2) to inspect and copy, test, or sample any tangible things that are in the possession, custody, or control of the party upon whom the request is served; (3) to enter upon designated land or other property in the possession or control of the party upon whom the request is served for the purpose of inspection and measuring, surveying, photographing, testing, or sampling the property or any designated object or operation on the property.

(B) **Procedure.** Without leave of court, the request may be served upon the plaintiff after commencement of the action and upon any other party with or after service of the summons and complaint upon that party. The request shall set forth the items to be inspected either by individual item or by category and describe each item and category with reasonable particularity. The request shall specify a reasonable time, place, and manner of making the inspection and performing the related acts. The request may specify the form or forms in which electronically stored information is to be produced, but may not require the production of the same information in more than one form.

(1) The party upon whom the request is served shall serve a written response within a period designated in the request that is not less than twenty-eight days after the service of the request or within a shorter or longer time as the court may allow. With respect to each item or category, the response shall state that inspection and related activities will be permitted as requested, unless it is objected to, including an objection to the requested form or forms for producing electronically stored information, in which event the reasons for objection shall be stated. If objection is made to part of an item or category, the part shall be specified. If objection is made to the requested form or forms for producing electronically stored information, or if no form was specified in the request, the responding party must state the form or forms it intends to use. The party submitting the request may move for an order under Civ. R. 37 with respect to any objection to or other failure to respond to the request or any part of the request, or any failure to permit inspection as requested.

(2) A party who produces documents for inspection shall, at its option, produce them as they are kept in the usual course of business or organized and labeled to correspond with the categories in the request.

(3) If a request does not specify the form or forms for producing electronically stored information, a responding party may produce the information in a form or forms in which the information is ordinarily maintained if that form is reasonably useable, or in any form that is reasonably useable. Unless ordered by the court or agreed to by the parties, a party need not produce the same electronically stored information in more than one form.

(C) **Persons not parties.** Subject to the scope of discovery provisions of Civ. R. 26(B) and 45(F), a person not a party to the action may be compelled to produce documents, electronically stored information or tangible things or to submit to an inspection as provided in Civ. R. 45.

(D) **Prior to filing of action.**

(1) Subject to the scope of discovery provisions of Civ.R. 26(B) and 45(F), a person who claims to have a potential cause of action may file a petition to obtain discovery as provided in this rule. Prior to filing a petition for discovery, the person seeking discovery shall make reasonable efforts to obtain voluntarily the information from the person from whom the discovery is sought. The petition shall be captioned in the name of the person seeking discovery and be filed in the court of common pleas in the county in which the person from whom the discovery is sought resides, the person's principal place of business is located, or the potential action may be filed. The petition shall include all of the following:

(a) A statement of the subject matter of the petitioner's potential cause of action and the petitioner's interest in the potential cause of action;

(b) A statement of the efforts made by the petitioner to obtain voluntarily the information from the person from whom the discovery is sought;

(c) A statement or description of the information sought to be discovered with reasonable particularity;

(d) The names and addresses, if known, of any person the petitioner expects will be an adverse party in the potential action;

(e) A request that the court issue an order authorizing the petitioner to obtain the discovery.

(2) The petition shall be served upon the person from whom discovery is sought and, if known, any person the petitioner expects will be an adverse party in the potential action, by one of the methods provided in these rules for service of summons.

(3) The court shall issue an order authorizing the petitioner to obtain the requested discovery if the court finds all of the following:

(a) The discovery is necessary to ascertain the identity of a potential adverse party;

(b) The petitioner is otherwise unable to bring the contemplated action;

(c) The petitioner made reasonable efforts to obtain voluntarily the information from the person from whom the discovery is sought.

History: Amended, eff 7-1-93; 7-1-94; 7-1-05; 7-1-08

NOTES TO DECISIONS

ANALYSIS

Arbitration
Privilege
Production of documents
Trade secrets

Arbitration

Complaint or petition for discovery pursuant to CivR 34(D) and/or RC § 2317.48 does not present an issue referable to arbitration for purposes of RC § 2711.02. An action for discovery is an auxiliary proceeding, separate from substantive claims referable to arbitration: White v. Equity, Inc., 178 Ohio App. 3d 604, 2008 Ohio 5226, 899 N.E.2d 205, 2008 Ohio App. LEXIS 4381 (2008).

Privilege

Trial court's decision to compel production of discovery as to two of the interrogatories was reversed as the answers sought were protected by the physician-patient privilege, pursuant to RC § 2317.02(B)(1), and the order to compel discovery as to one interrogatory was affirmed as to any request for the mental health information that the owner had directly put at issue through his claim for severe emotional distress. However, an evidentiary hearing was required to determine the appropriate look-back time frame of the discovery request. Miller v. Bassett, — Ohio App. 3d —, 2006 Ohio 3590, — N.E. 2d —, 2006 Ohio App. LEXIS 3536 (July 13, 2006).

Since the requested information could have fallen under the umbrella of either opinion work product or ordinary fact work product, the possibility of two differing forms of protection under the attorney-client privilege necessitated an evidentiary hearing. Any blanket grant compelling discovery, under Ohio R. Civ. P. 26, 37(A)(2), and 34, was an abuse of discretion because the trial court had to first conduct a hearing to determine the nature of the privilege. Miller v. Bassett, — Ohio App. 3d —, 2006 Ohio 3590, — N.E. 2d —, 2006 Ohio App. LEXIS 3536 (July 13, 2006).

Production of documents

When a former employee, having sued his former employer for compensation, did not comply with the employer's request for production of the former employee's W-2 forms and tax returns, or with the trial court's order to produce the documents, the former employee was not entitled to a hearing on the issue of whether he should be ordered to pay the former employer's attorney fees, under Ohio R. Civ. P. 37(D), because neither Ohio R. Civ. P. 11 nor RC 2323.51(B)(2)(c), regarding awards of attorney fees for frivolous conduct, under which a hearing was required, applied. Shikner v. Solutions, — Ohio App. 3d —, 2006 Ohio 1339, — N.E. 2d —, 2006 Ohio App. LEXIS 1220 (Mar. 23, 2006).

When a former employee sued his former employer for compensation, and the employer served a request for production of the former employee's W-2 forms and tax returns, and, upon his failure to comply, a trial court ordered the employee to produce the documents, when the former employee still did not comply, the trial court was required, under Ohio R. Civ. P. 37(D), to award the employer attorney fees, as it did not find the former employee's resistance to discovery was warranted or that an award of attorney fees would be unjust. Shikner v. Solutions, — Ohio App. 3d —, 2006 Ohio 1339, — N.E. 2d —, 2006 Ohio App. LEXIS 1220 (Mar. 23, 2006).

Trade secrets

Trial court did not abuse its discretion under Ohio R. Civ. P. 26(C)(7), 34(C), and 45(C)(3)(b) in denying a product user's motion to compel disclosure of a nonparty manufacturer's formulae for polyethylene tubing in the user's products liability action, as the formulae were clearly trade secrets pursuant to RC § 1333.61(D) and the user did not show such a compelling need for the disclosure that it outweighed the manufacturer's interests in maintaining confidentiality of the information. It was noted that one of the opposing parties in the action was the manufacturer's direct competitor, which would have had access to that confidential information, and the user's expert only opined that the disclosure would have been "helpful" in his determination as to why the tubing had failed, which was not sufficiently compelling to require the requested disclosure. Splater v. Thermal Ease Hydronic Sys., Inc., 169 Ohio App. 3d 514, 2006 Ohio 5452, 863 N.E.2d 1060, 2006 Ohio App. LEXIS 5438 (2006).

RULE 35. Physical and mental examination of persons

(A) **Order for examination.** When the mental or physical condition (including the blood group) of a party, or of a person in the custody or under the legal control of a party, is in controversy, the court in which the action is pending may order the party to submit himself to a physical or mental examination or to produce for such examination the person in the party's custody or legal control. The order may be made only on motion for good cause shown and upon notice to the person to be examined and to all parties and shall specify the time, place, manner, conditions, and scope of the examination and the person or persons by whom it is to be made.

(B) **Examiner's report.**

(1) If requested by the party against whom an order is made under Rule 35(A) or the person examined, the party causing the examination to be made shall deliver to such party or person a copy of the detailed written report submitted by the examiner to the party causing the examination to be made. The report shall set out the examiner's findings, including results of all tests made, diagnoses and conclusions, together with like

reports of all earlier examinations of the same condition. After delivery, the party causing the examination shall be entitled upon request to receive from the party against whom the order is made a like report of any examination, previously or thereafter made, of the same condition, unless, in the case of a report of examination of a person not a party, the party shows that he is unable to obtain it. The court on motion may make an order against a party to require delivery of a report on such terms as are just. If an examiner fails or refuses to make a report, the court on motion may order, at the expense of the party causing the examination, the taking of the deposition of the examiner if his testimony is to be offered at trial.

(2) By requesting and obtaining a report of the examination so ordered or by taking the deposition of the examiner, the party examined waives any privilege he may have in that action or any other involving the same controversy, regarding the testimony of every other person who has examined or may thereafter examine him in respect of the same mental or physical condition.

(3) This subdivision 35(B), applies to examinations made by agreement of the parties, unless the agreement expressly provides otherwise.

NOTES TO DECISIONS

ANALYSIS

Generally
Appeal
Child custody matters
Order for medical examination
Scope of exam

Generally

Both RC § 3109.04(C) and CivR 35(A) placed the decision to order an investigation of the psychological condition of the parties and their children within the trial court's sound discretion. Neither the statute nor the rule affords the party seeking such an examination the right to select the professional who will conduct the examination. Thus there was no final appealable order: Yazdani-Isfehani v. Yazdani-Isfehani, 170 Ohio App. 3d 1, 2006 Ohio 7105, 865 N.E.2d 924, 2006 Ohio App. LEXIS 7059 (2006).

Appeal

Trial court's order requiring the former spouses and their minor child to submit to a psychological examination, pursuant to CivR 35(A), was not a final appealable order under RC § 2505.02(B)(2): Prakash v. Prakash, 181 Ohio App. 3d 584, 2009 Ohio 1324, 910 N.E.2d 30, 2009 Ohio App. LEXIS 1121 (2009).

Child custody matters

Because the father did not have a right to have the expert of his choice conduct the psychological evaluations in the divorce proceeding, pursuant to RC § 3109.04(C) and Ohio R. Civ. P. 35(A), the order appealed from did not affect a substantial right within the meaning of RC § 2505.02(A)(1), and therefore, was not a final appealable order under RC § 2502(B)(2). Accordingly, the requisite jurisdiction to determine the merits of the father's argument was lacking for review. Yazdani-Isfehani v. Yazdani-Isfehani, 170 Ohio App. 3d 1, 2006 Ohio 7105, 865 N.E.2d 924, 2006 Ohio App. LEXIS 7059 (2006).

Order for medical examination

Order compelling an alleged injured party to submit to an independent medical examination, under Ohio R. Civ. P. 35(A), was final and appealable, under RC § 2505.02, because it was a provisional remedy which precluded a contrary order in favor of the alleged injured party, and the unlimited scope of the order created a risk of an unwarranted invasion of the alleged injured party's privacy. Stratman v. Sutantio, — Ohio App. 3d —, 2006 Ohio 4712, — N.E. 2d —, 2006 Ohio App. LEXIS 4631 (Sept. 12, 2006).

Order assessing the costs of obtaining an order against an alleged injured party compelling her to attend an independent medical examination was not, in itself, final and appealable, under RC § 2505.02, because it did not affect a substantial right, nor was the personal injury case in which it was issued a special proceeding, but, because it was arguably part of the appealable order compelling the alleged injured party to attend the examination, it was also appealable. Stratman v. Sutantio, — Ohio App. 3d —, 2006 Ohio 4712, — N.E. 2d —, 2006 Ohio App. LEXIS 4631 (Sept. 12, 2006).

Order compelling an alleged injured party to submit to an independent medical examination, under Ohio R. Civ. P. 35(A), was proper without a specific finding that her medical condition was in controversy or that there was good cause for the examination because her personal injury complaint alleging her injuries and seeking damages placed her medical condition in controversy and established good cause for the examination. Stratman v. Sutantio, — Ohio App. 3d —, 2006 Ohio 4712, — N.E. 2d —, 2006 Ohio App. LEXIS 4631 (Sept. 12, 2006).

Scope of exam

When an order compelling an alleged injured party to submit to an independent medical examination, under Ohio R. Civ. P. 35(A), was unlimited in scope, it was improper because there was a risk of an unwarranted invasion of the alleged injured party's privacy, so the order had to be remanded to the trial court to define the order's scope so that it would protect the alleged injured party from such an invasion while preserving the right of the motorist requesting the examination to such an exam. Stratman v. Sutantio, — Ohio App. 3d —, 2006 Ohio 4712, — N.E. 2d —, 2006 Ohio App. LEXIS 4631 (Sept. 12, 2006).

RULE 36.   Requests for admission

(A) **Availability; procedures for use.** A party may serve upon any other party a written request for the admission, for purposes of the pending action only, of the truth of any matters within the scope of Civ. R. 26(B) set forth in the request, that relate to statements or opinions of fact or of the application of law to fact, including the genuineness of any documents described in the request. Copies of documents shall be served with the request unless they have been or are otherwise furnished or made available for inspection and copying. The request may, without leave of court, be served upon the plaintiff after commencement of the action and upon any other party with or after service of the summons and complaint upon that party. A party serving a request for admission shall provide the party served with both a printed and an electronic copy of the request for admission. The electronic copy shall be reasonably useable for word processing and provided on computer disk, by electronic mail, or by other means agreed to by the parties. A party who is unable to provide an electronic copy of a request for admission may seek leave of court to be relieved of this requirement.

(1) Each matter of which an admission is requested shall be separately set forth. The party to whom the requests for admissions have been directed shall quote each request for admission immediately preceding the corresponding answer or objection. The matter is admitted unless, within a period designated in the request, not less than twenty-eight days after service of a printed copy of the request or within such shorter or longer time as the court may allow, the party to whom the request is directed serves upon the party requesting the admission a written answer or objection addressed to the matter, signed by the party or by the party's attorney. Failure to provide an electronic copy does not alter the designated period for response, but shall constitute good cause for the court to order the period enlarged if request therefor is made pursuant to Rule 6(B) before the expiration of the designated period. If so ordered, the court may require that the party requesting the admission provide an electronic copy as required by this rule unless relieved from this obligation.

(2) If objection is made, the reasons therefor shall be stated. The answer shall specifically deny the matter or set forth in detail the reasons why the answering party cannot truthfully admit or deny the matter. A denial shall fairly meet the substance of the requested admission, and when good faith requires that a party qualify his or her answer, or deny only a part of the matter of which an admission is requested, the party shall specify so much of it as is true and qualify or deny the remainder. An answering party may not give lack of information or knowledge as a reason for failure to admit or deny unless the party states that the party has made reasonable inquiry and that the information known or readily obtainable by the party is insufficient to enable the party to admit or deny. A party who considers that a matter of which an admission has been requested presents a genuine issue for trial may not, on that ground alone, object to the request; the party may, subject to the provisions of Civ. R. 37(C), deny the matter or set forth reasons why the party cannot admit or deny it.

(3) The party who has requested the admissions may move for an order with respect to the answers or objections. Unless the court determines that an objection is justified, it shall order that an answer be served. If the court determines that an answer does not comply with the requirements of this rule, it may order either that the matter is admitted or that an amended answer be served. The court may, in lieu of these orders, determine that final disposition of the request be made at a pretrial conference or at a designated time prior to trial. The provisions of Civ. R. 37(A)(4) apply to the award of expenses incurred in relation to the motion.

(B) **Effect of admission.** Any matter admitted under this rule is conclusively established unless the court on motion permits withdrawal or amendment of the admission. Subject to the provisions of Rule 16 governing modification of a pretrial order, the court may permit withdrawal or amendment when the presentation of the merits of the action will be subserved thereby and the party who obtained the admission fails to satisfy the court that withdrawal or amendment will prejudice the party in maintaining his action or defense on the merits. Any admission made by a party under this rule is for the purpose of the pending action only and is not an admission by him for any other purpose nor may it be used against the party in any other proceeding.

(C) **Document containing request for admission.** If a party includes a request for admission in a document containing any other form of discovery, the party shall include a caption on the document that indicates the document contains a request for admission. A party is not required to respond to requests for admission that are not made in compliance with this division.

History: Amended, eff 7-1-72; 7-1-76; 7-1-04; 7-1-05; 7-1-08; 7-1-09.

NOTES TO DECISIONS

ANALYSIS

Generally
Amendment or withdrawal of admission
Failure to answer request for admission
Failure to respond to request
Failure to respond to request for admissions
Late response to request for admission
Self-incrimination
Summary judgment
—Based on responses to discovery requests
— Procedure
Time to respond

Generally

CivR 36 is self-enforcing, and a trial court has no discretion whether to deem the matters admitted. If requests are not answered, they are admitted and conclusively established, and a trial court must recognize them as so: Martin v. Martin, 179 Ohio App. 3d 805, 2008 Ohio 6336, 903 N.E.2d 1243, 2008 Ohio App. LEXIS 5279 (2008).

Amendment or withdrawal of admission

Summary judgment was properly granted to a steel supplier in its action, seeking payment for supplies delivered to a steel purchaser, as the purchaser had failed to respond to the supplier's request for admissions pursuant to Ohio R. Civ. P. 36(A), and the purchaser's implied motion to amend or withdraw his admissions under Rule 36(B) by his summary judgment response was denied. He could not claim a de facto corporation was the purchaser without showing good faith efforts to incorporate that entity. Jade Sterling Steel Co. v. Stacey, — Ohio App. 3d —, 2007 Ohio 532, — N.E. 2d —, 2007 Ohio App. LEXIS 480 (Feb. 8, 2007).

Trial court did not err by allowing an insurer to withdraw a request for admission pursuant to Ohio R. Civ. P. 36 relating to the insured's cooperation with the insurer's investigation process because the insured was not surprised at trial, in that, he had the opportunity to question the insurer's representative on the point at issue in advance of trial, and because he did not rely solely upon the admission to establish his cooperation. Farmers Ins. of Columbus v. Lister, — Ohio App. 3d —, 2006 Ohio 142, — N.E. 2d —, 2006 Ohio App. LEXIS 109 (Jan. 9, 2006).

In a creditor's suit to recover money due on account, the trial court should have allowed the debtor to withdraw or modify his admission under Ohio R. Civ. P. 36 occurring when he did not respond to the creditor's requests for admission because the debtor stated his objection to the request and was consistent in arguing that the bill was not correct. Also, the creditor could not produce an itemized bill or other documentation as proof. Asset Acceptance, LLC v. Lemon, — Ohio App. 3d —, 2006 Ohio 4451, — N.E. 2d —, 2006 Ohio App. LEXIS 4381 (Aug. 25, 2006).

Trial court did not abuse its discretion by allowing an employer to file its responses to an administrator's requests for admission in an untimely manner because the withdrawal of the admissions did not prejudice the administrator, in that he did not rely upon the admissions in contesting the employer's motion for summary judgment, and the employer had made it clear that it was contesting the issues relevant to the first two admissions from the very early stages of the case. Moreover, the employer explained that it had completed the responses in a timely manner but had inadvertently failed to send the completed responses. Patidar v. Tri-state Renovations, Inc., — Ohio App. 3d —, 2006 Ohio 4631, — N.E. 2d —, 2006 Ohio App. LEXIS 4476 (Aug. 31, 2006).

Where an inmate's request for admissions pursuant to Ohio R. Civ. P. 36 did not contain a required date of response, the trial court did not abuse its discretion in granting the opposing parties' motion to withdraw admissions, as such motion was made prior to trial, which was the time that responses without a set deadline were required by. Brown v. Weidner, — Ohio App. 3d —, 2006 Ohio 6852, — N.E. 2d —, 2006 Ohio App. LEXIS 6765 (Dec. 26, 2006).

Failure to answer request for admission
Trial court did not abuse its discretion by rejecting the excuse proffered by a company and its owner for failing to respond to a bank's request for admissions, and by deeming the requested admissions admitted because the owner's affidavit established that, though he was ill, his illness occurred after the time for responding to the requests for admission had expired. Further, the matters deemed admitted by virtue of the failure of the company and the owner to respond to the bank's request for admission were competent evidence to support a motion for summary judgment. Jpmorgan v. Indus. Power Generation, — Ohio App. 3d —, 2007 Ohio 6008, — N.E. 2d —, 2007 Ohio App. LEXIS 5293 (Nov. 9, 2007).

Failure to respond to request
In an insurer's suit against an insured, the trial court did not err by considering the insurer's Ohio R. Civ. P. 36 request for admission, to which the insured never responded, in reaching its decision in favor of the insurer. While the insurer did not formally offer the admissions into evidence, the document was part of the record, and once the trial court deemed the request admitted, the matters contained in the request were conclusively established. Auto Owners Ins. v. Foxfire Golf Club, Inc., — Ohio App. 3d —, 2007 Ohio 1101, — N.E. 2d —, 2007 Ohio App. LEXIS 1024 (Mar. 8, 2007).

In an insurer's suit against an insured, the trial court did not err by considering the insurer's Ohio R. Civ. P. 36 request for admission, to which the insured never responded, in reaching its decision in favor of the insurer. While the insurer did not formally offer the admissions into evidence, the document was part of the record, and once the trial court deemed the request admitted, the matters contained in the request were conclusively established. Auto Owners Ins. v. Foxfire Golf Club, Inc., — Ohio App. 3d —, 2007 Ohio 1101, — N.E. 2d —, 2007 Ohio App. LEXIS 1024 (Mar. 8, 2007).

Due to a perpetrator's failure, despite numerous opportunities, to have fully responded to an insurer's requests for admissions in its subrogation action, a trial court properly entered judgment for the insurer by deeming the requests admitted under Ohio R. Civ. P. 36(A). As the perpetrator failed to show that the requests were objectionable, not of substantial importance, or that there was a good reason for his failure to have responded, the imposition of costs pursuant to Ohio R. Civ. P. 37(C) was proper. Progressive Cas. Ins. Co. v. Harrison, — Ohio App. 3d —, 2007 Ohio 579, — N.E. 2d —, 2007 Ohio App. LEXIS 536 (Feb. 9, 2007).

In a collection action, when a debtor did not respond to a creditor's requests for admission, its deemed admissions of the requests for admission conclusively established the facts deemed admitted, under Ohio R. Civ. P. 36(A) and (B), and they were properly the basis for a summary judgment motion. Carmel Fin. Corp. v. Leal, — Ohio App. 3d —, 2006 Ohio 5618, — N.E. 2d —, 2006 Ohio App. LEXIS 5608 (Oct. 27, 2006).

Consequence of a debtor's failure to respond to a second request for admissions under Ohio R. Civ. P. 36(A) was that there was no genuine issue as to the validity of the bank's claim; the trial court did not err in entering summary judgment in favor of the bank on its claim against the debtor. Capital One Bank v. James, — Ohio App. 3d —, 2006 Ohio 3190, — N.E. 2d —, 2006 Ohio App. LEXIS 3079 (June 23, 2006).

Where a credit card holder failed to respond to a credit card company's requests for admission under Ohio R. Civ. P. 36(A) in the company's action, seeking payment on an unpaid account, the matters therein were conclusively deemed admitted, and the trial court properly granted summary judgment where there were no disputed issues. Great Seneca Fin. Corp. v. Lee, — Ohio App. 3d —, 2006 Ohio 2123, — N.E. 2d —, 2006 Ohio App. LEXIS 1968 (Apr. 28, 2006).

Collector was entitled to summary judgment in its action seeking payment of a credit card balance. The debtor, by failing to respond to the collector's request for admissions, admitted, pursuant to Ohio R. Civ. P. 36, that the debtor owed the collector the amount sought and that every allegation in the complaint was true and correct. National Check Bur., Inc. v. Woodgeard, — Ohio App. 3d —, 2006 Ohio 140, — N.E. 2d —, 2006 Ohio App. LEXIS 110 (Jan. 9, 2006).

Failure to respond to request for admissions
As an attorney failed to respond to a former client's request for admissions pursuant to CivR 36(A), they were deemed admitted and constituted sufficient evidence to satisfy the requirement that the client show that there was a colorable defense to an underlying matter that had been resolved against the client due to the attorney's alleged malpractice, such that the element of causation was satisfied for purposes of the trial court's grant of summary judgment to the client. Goldberg v. Mittman, — Ohio App. 3d —, 2007 Ohio 6599, — N.E. 2d —, 2007 Ohio App. LEXIS 5768 (Dec. 11, 2007).

Late response to request for admission
Trial court could have reasonably found that the reasons stated in the motion for leave to file an untimely response to a request for admissions were insufficient to establish good cause for granting the motion: Ramos v. Khawli, 181 Ohio App. 3d 176, 2009 Ohio 798, 908 N.E.2d 495, 2009 Ohio App. LEXIS 661 (2009).

When an alleged injured party did not respond to requests for admissions served on his counsel within the time provided in the request or by the dates to which that time was extended, it was not an abuse of discretion for a trial court to find that the requests were deemed admitted, under Ohio R. Civ. P. 36(A), because counsel did not seek a protective order or other relief from the duty to respond to the requests, nor did she seek leave to file an untimely response or withdrawal of the deemed admissions, under Ohio R. Civ. P. 36(B). Farah v. Chatman, — Ohio App. 3d —, 2007 Ohio 697, — N.E. 2d —, 2007 Ohio App. LEXIS 629 (Feb. 20, 2007).

When an alleged injured party did not respond to requests for admissions served on his counsel within the time provided in the request or by the dates to which that time was extended, it was not an abuse of discretion for a trial court to find that the requests were deemed admitted, under Ohio R. Civ. P. 36(A), because, when counsel alleged that she had surgery which caused her to be unable to timely respond, that surgery did not occur until after a response was initiallly due and after the date to which that due date was first extended, so the surgery did not prohibit a timely response. Farah v. Chatman, — Ohio App. 3d —, 2007 Ohio 697, — N.E. 2d —, 2007 Ohio App. LEXIS 629 (Feb. 20, 2007).

When an alleged injured party did not respond to requests for admissions served on his counsel within the time provided in the request or by the dates to which that time was extended, it was not an abuse of discretion for a trial court to find that the requests were deemed admitted, under Ohio R. Civ. P. 36(A), because, when counsel alleged that she had difficulty communicating with her client due to his unfamiliarity with the English language, she obviously knew that this might be a problem when she agreed to represent him but, apparently, took no steps to remedy the problem. Farah v. Chatman, — Ohio App. 3d —, 2007 Ohio 697, — N.E. 2d —, 2007 Ohio App. LEXIS 629 (Feb. 20, 2007).

When an alleged injured party did not respond to requests for admissions served on his counsel within the time provided in the request or by the dates to which that time was extended, it was not an abuse of discretion for a trial court to find that the requests were deemed admitted, under Ohio R. Civ. P. 36(A), because (1) the record did not support his claim that he filed a late response to the requests, and (2) if he filed a response when he said he did, the response was untimely because it occurred after the date to which his duty to respond had been extended and the requests were deemed admitted when he did not timely respond, with a request to confirm those admissions being a mere formality. Farah v. Chatman, — Ohio App. 3d —, 2007 Ohio 697, — N.E. 2d —, 2007 Ohio App. LEXIS 629 (Feb. 20, 2007).

When a feed supplier sued farmers on account and the farmers responded with a recoupment defense and asserted counterclaims against the supplier and another supplier, it was an abuse of discretion for a trial court to allow one of the suppliers who had not responded to the farmers' request for admissions to belatedly respond one week before trial because (1) the supplier's claim that it never received the request was not credible, (2) the farmers were prejudiced by the late response because their expert relied on the admissions to form his opinion, (3) the other supplier's response was not made on behalf of the non-responding supplier because, while related, the two suppliers were separate entities separately named as counterclaim-defendants, and the non-responding supplier's owner said the other supplier did not speak for his company, and (4) there was a significant delay between the time the non-responding supplier learned that the farmers intended to use its admissions and its belated response. L. E. Sommer Kidron, Inc. v. Kohler, — Ohio App. 3d —, 2007 Ohio 885, — N.E. 2d —, 2007 Ohio App. LEXIS 821 (Mar. 5, 2007).

Trial court properly concluded that a city's deletion of an email transmission of a property owners' requests for admission for lack of an identifiable sender constituted excusable neglect that would justify an extension of time under Ohio R. Civ. P. 6 to respond to the requests for admission. Grano v. City of Mentor, — Ohio App. 3d —, 2006 Ohio 6104, — N.E. 2d —, 2006 Ohio App. LEXIS 6029 (Nov. 17, 2006).

Self-incrimination

When a consumer sued a company and its sole proprietor, and the proprietor also faced criminal charges arising from the same incident, the proprietor could not assert, on appeal, that he was not required to respond to the consumer's request for admissions, under Ohio R. Civ. P. 36(A), because the proprietor did not raise this in a timely objection to the request, and, because the proprietor chose not to respond in any way to the request, the Fifth Amendment was not violated by operation of the proprietor's default admissions to the request as he was not deprived of his choice to admit, deny, or refuse to answer the request. Vilardo v. Sheets, — Ohio App. 3d —, 2006 Ohio 3473, — N.E. 2d —, 2006 Ohio App. LEXIS 3415 (July 3, 2006).

Summary judgment

When an alleged injured party claimed the negligence of the parties he sued but did not respond to their requests for admissions served on his counsel, resulting in the requests being deemed admitted, under Ohio R. Civ. P. 36(A), he could not avoid the facts that were conclusively established by his deemed admissions by filing contradictory affidavits because those facts established that his negligence caused the accident in which he was injured, so the parties he sued were entitled to judgment as a matter of law. Farah v. Chatman, — Ohio App. 3d —, 2007 Ohio 697, — N.E. 2d —, 2007 Ohio App. LEXIS 629 (Feb. 20, 2007).

In an action on an account by a creditor bank against a debtor, the trial court erred in denying the debtor's motion under Ohio R. Civ. P. 12(E) for a more definite statement due to the creditor's failure to have attached a copy of the account pursuant to Ohio R. Civ. P. 10(D), and as the debtor was entitled to await that decision prior to responding to the creditor's request for admissions pursuant to Ohio R. Civ. P. 36(A), which decision was not properly served and filed as required by Ohio R. Civ. P. 58(B), the trial court erred in relying on the debtor's failure to respond to the discovery requests as support for the creditor's summary judgment motion under Ohio R. Civ. P. 56(C). As the creditor's motion to file summary judgment instanter was granted and the debtor was not thereafter given proper notice and time to file his response to the summary judgment motion, the trial court erred in granting summary judgment to the creditor four days later. Capital One Bank v. Toney, — Ohio App. 3d —, 2007 Ohio 1571, — N.E. 2d —, 2007 Ohio App. LEXIS 1443 (Mar. 28, 2007).

Trial court properly granted summary judgment to a roof material supplier in its breach of contract action against a contractor due to the contractor's failure to pay for the supplies, as the contractor failed to respond in a timely manner to the supplier's request for admissions pursuant to Ohio R. Civ. P. 36(A), and the conclusive establishment of the facts therein supported the finding that the supplier was entitled to judgment. Although the contractor had transferred the matter from a municipal court to a common pleas court due to the amount sought in its counterclaim, it failed to pay the security costs pursuant to RC § 2323.31, which caused the matter to be remanded back to the municipal court, and the contractor's claim that no court had jurisdiction for that period of time did not excuse its failure to timely respond to the admissions under the invited error doctrine. Palmer-Donavin v. Hanna, — Ohio App. 3d —, 2007 Ohio 2242, — N.E. 2d —, 2007 Ohio App. LEXIS 2081 (May 10, 2007).

In a customer's suit to recover for injuries she sustained on a property owner's property, the trial court properly considered a photograph attached to the owner's motion for summary judgment because, pursuant to Ohio R. Evid. 901(B)(1) and Ohio R. Civ. P. 36(B), the photograph was properly authenticated by the customer in her answer to a request for admission. It was not required to be marked as an exhibit to have evidentiary value. Haymond v. BP America, — Ohio App. 3d —, 2006 Ohio 2732, — N.E. 2d —, 2006 Ohio App. LEXIS 2585 (June 1, 2006).

Trial court's grant of summary judgment to staffing agency clients was proper where appellants failed to respond to discovery requests of the clients, despite having been granted an extension of time to do so, and they failed to respond to a request for admissions under Ohio R. Civ. P. 36(A), such that there were no genuine issues in dispute in appellants' action for services rendered that were not paid. Solutions v. Somerset Care Ctr., — Ohio App. 3d —, 2006 Ohio 3297, — N.E. 2d —, 2006 Ohio App. LEXIS 3212 (June 26, 2006).

—Based on responses to discovery requests

When summary judgment was granted in favor of a mortgagee in a foreclosure action, a mortgagor could not claim there was a genuine issue of material fact as to the mortgagor's counterclaim because that counterclaim was disposed of, under Ohio R. Civ. P. 36(A), by the mortgagor's deemed admissions when the mortgagor did not respond to the mortgagee's requests for admissions. Ameriquest Mortg. Co. v. Wilson, — Ohio App. 3d —, 2007 Ohio 2576, — N.E. 2d —, 2007 Ohio App. LEXIS 2395 (May 25, 2007).

When a consumer sued a company and its sole proprietor, and the proprietor did not respond to the consumer's request for admissions, under Ohio R. Civ. P. 36(A), the proprietor was properly deemed to have admitted the admissions propounded by the consumer, which conclusively established them, so the consumer was properly granted summary judgment based on the admissions. Vilardo v. Sheets, — Ohio App. 3d —, 2006 Ohio 3473, — N.E. 2d —, 2006 Ohio App. LEXIS 3415 (July 3, 2006).

— Procedure

In a suit between a creditor and a debtor, it was an abuse of discretion to grant the creditor's motion, under Ohio R. Civ. P. 36(B), to deem facts admitted because (1) it appeared that the debtor might have complied with discovery, as the debtor furnished the trial court with a copy of the responses the debtor said the debtor sent to the creditor, and (2) given a dispute regarding the facts, the trial court and/or its magistrate should have held an evidentiary hearing. Arrow Fin. Servs. v. Kuzniak, — Ohio App. 3d —, 2007 Ohio 2191, — N.E. 2d —, 2007 Ohio App. LEXIS 2049 (Apr. 24, 2007).

Time to respond

Because the tenant did not designate a period within which the landlord was required to respond to the requests for admissions, the requests for admissions did not comply with CivR 36(A), and, even assuming that the landlord was properly served, he was entitled to respond to the requests for admissions any time prior to trial. Thus, the trial court erred in deeming the matters set forth therein admitted and in denying the landlord's motion for leave to answer the requests or to amend or withdraw the admissions. McGreevy v. Bassler, — Ohio App. 3d —, 2008 Ohio 328, — N.E. 2d —, 2008 Ohio App. LEXIS 265 (Jan. 31, 2008).

RULE 37.   Failure to make discovery: sanctions

(A) **Motion for order compelling discovery.** Upon reasonable notice to other parties and all persons affected thereby, a party may move for an order compelling discovery as follows:

(1) Appropriate court. A motion for an order to a party or a deponent shall be made to the court in which the action is pending.

(2) Motion. If a deponent fails to answer a question propounded or submitted under Rule 30 or Rule 31, or a party fails to answer an interrogatory submitted under Rule 33, or if a party, in response to a request for inspection submitted under Rule 34, fails to respond that inspection will be permitted as requested or fails to permit inspection as requested, the discovering party may move for an order compelling an answer or an order compelling inspection in accordance with the request. On matters relating to a deposition on oral examination, the proponent of the question may complete or adjourn the examination before he applies for an order.

(3) Evasive or incomplete answer. For purposes of this subdivision an evasive or incomplete answer is a failure to answer.

(4) Award of expenses of motion. If the motion is granted, the court shall, after opportunity for hearing, require the party or deponent who opposed the motion or the party or attorney advising such conduct or both of them to pay to the moving party the reasonable expenses incurred in obtaining the order, including attorney's fees, unless the court finds that the opposition to the motion was substantially justified or that other circumstances make an award of expenses unjust.

If the motion is denied, the court shall, after opportunity for hearing, require the moving party or the attorney advising the motion or both of them to pay to the party or deponent who opposed the motion the reasonable expenses incurred in opposing the motion, including attorney's fees, unless the court finds that the making of the motion was substantially justified or that other circumstances make an award of expenses unjust.

If the motion is granted in part and denied in part, the court may apportion the reasonable expenses incurred in relation to the motion among the parties and persons in a just manner.

(B) **Failure to comply with order.**

(1) If a deponent fails to be sworn or to answer a question after being directed to do so by the court, the failure may be considered a contempt of that court.

(2) If any party or an officer, director, or managing agent of a party or a person designated under Rule 30(B)(5) or Rule 31(A) to testify on behalf of a party fails to obey an order to provide or permit discovery, including an order made under subdivision (A) of this rule and Rule 35, the court in which the action is pending may make such orders in regard to the failure as are just, and among others the following:

(a) An order that the matters regarding which the order was made or any other designated facts shall be taken to be established for the purposes of the action in accordance with the claim of the party obtaining the order;

(b) An order refusing to allow the disobedient party to support or oppose designated claims or defenses, or prohibiting him from introducing designated matters in evidence;

(c) An order striking out pleadings or parts thereof, or staying further proceedings until the order is obeyed, or dismissing the action or proceeding or any part thereof, or rendering a judgment by default against the disobedient party;

(d) In lieu of any of the foregoing orders or in addition thereto, an order treating as a contempt of court the failure to obey any orders except an order to submit to a physical or mental examination;

(e) Where a party has failed to comply with an order under Rule 35(A) requiring him to produce another for examination, such orders as are listed in subsections (a), (b), and (c) of this subdivision, unless the party failing to comply shows that he is unable to produce such person for examination.

In lieu of any of the foregoing orders or in addition thereto, the court shall require the party failing to obey the order or the attorney advising him or both to pay the reasonable expenses, including attorney's fees, caused by the failure, unless the court expressly finds that the failure was substantially justified or that other circumstances make an award of expenses unjust.

(C) **Expenses on failure to admit.** If a party, after being served with a request for admission under Rule 36, fails to admit the genuineness of any documents or the truth of any matter as requested, and if the party requesting the admissions thereafter proves the genuineness of the document or the truth of the matter, he may apply to the court for an order requiring the other party to pay him the reasonable expenses incurred in making that proof, including reasonable attorney's fees. Unless the request had been held objectionable under Rule 36(A) or the court finds that there was good reason for the failure to admit or that the admission sought was of no substantial importance, the order shall be made.

(D) **Failure of party to attend at own deposition or serve answers to interrogatories or respond to request for inspection.** If a party or an officer, director, or a managing agent of a party or a person designated under Rule 30(B)(5) or Rule 31(A) to testify on behalf of a party fails (1) to appear before the officer who is to take his deposition after being served with a proper notice, or (2) to serve answers or objections to interrogatories submitted under Rule 33, after proper service of the interrogatories, or (3) to serve a written response to a request for inspection submitted under Rule 34, after proper service of the request, the court in which the action is pending on motion and notice may make such orders in regard to the failure as are just, and among others it may take any action authorized under subsections (a), (b), and (c) of subdivision (B)(2) of this rule. In lieu of any order or in addition thereto, the court shall require the party failing to act or the attorney advising him or both to pay the reasonable expenses, including attorney's fees, caused by the failure, unless the court expressly finds that the failure was substantially justified or that other circumstances make an award of expenses unjust.

The failure to act described in this subdivision may not be excused on the ground that the discovery sought is objectionable unless the party failing to act has applied for a protective order as provided by Rule 26(C).

(E) **Duty to resolve.** Before filing a motion authorized by this rule, the party shall make a reasonable effort to resolve the matter through discussion with the attorney, unrepresented party, or person from whom discovery is sought. The motion shall be accompanied by a statement reciting the efforts made to resolve the matter in accordance with this section.

(F) **Electronically Stored Information** Absent exceptional circumstances, a court may not impose sanctions under these rules on a party for failing to provide electronically stored information lost as a result of the routine, good-faith operation of an electronic information system. The court may consider the following factors in determining whether to impose sanctions under this division:

(1) Whether and when any obligation to preserve the information was triggered;

(2) Whether the information was lost as a result of the routine alteration or deletion of information that attends the ordinary use of the system in issue;

(3) Whether the party intervened in a timely fashion to prevent the loss of information;

(4) Any steps taken to comply with any court order or party agreement requiring preservation of specific information;

(5) Any other facts relevant to its determination under this division.

History: Amended, eff 7-1-94; 7-1-08.

NOTES TO DECISIONS

ANALYSIS

Abuse of discretion
Appellate review
Attorney fees
Default judgment
Depositions
Disclosure of expert witness
Discovery orders
Dismissal
— With prejudice
Duty to resolve
Excuses for noncompliance
Insurance matters
Interrogatories
Jurisdiction
Motion to compel discovery
Order to compel discovery
— Willful noncompliance
Sanctions
Spoliation of evidence

Abuse of discretion

Where an action was stayed pending settlement negotiations, which failed, and the matter did not move forward thereafter due to the trial court's inaction for several years despite repeated attempts by appellant to conduct a scheduling conference, the trial court's imposition of discovery sanctions against appellant pursuant to Ohio R. Civ. P. 37 was an abuse of discretion, as it was unreasonable in the circumstances. Ward v. Nationsbanc Mortg. Corp., — Ohio App. 3d —, 2006 Ohio 2766, — N.E. 2d —, 2006 Ohio App. LEXIS 2599 (June 2, 2006).

Appellate review

Although the trial court did not specifically rule on all of a promisee's pending discovery motions, there was no abuse of discretion by the trial court under Ohio R. Civ. P. 37, as the motions were deemed overruled when the trial court entered summary judgment in favor of the promisor. Cote v. Eisinger, — Ohio App. 3d —, 2006 Ohio 4020, — N.E. 2d —, 2006 Ohio App. LEXIS 3989 (Aug. 7, 2006).

There was no abuse of discretion in a trial court's denial of an inmate's request to hold his sister and her husband in contempt for failing to comply with a trial court discovery order, as the inmate engaged in multiple motion practice and the sister and her husband sought withdawal of admissions in a timely manner. Brown v. Weidner, — Ohio App. 3d —, 2006 Ohio 6852, — N.E. 2d —, 2006 Ohio App. LEXIS 6765 (Dec. 26, 2006).

Attorney fees

Plaintiff did not prove that he incurred any additional expenses or attorneys fees as a result of the defendant's responses to discover requests: Desai v. Franklin, 177 Ohio App. 3d 679, 2008 Ohio 3957, 895 N.E.2d 875, 2008 Ohio App. LEXIS 3335 (2008).

When a former employee, having sued his former employer for compensation, did not comply with the employer's request for production of the former employee's W-2 forms and tax returns, or with the trial court's order to produce the documents, the former employee was not entitled to a hearing on the issue of whether he should be ordered to pay the former employer's attorney fees, under Ohio R. Civ. P. 37(D), because neither Ohio R. Civ. P. 11 nor RC 2323.51(B)(2)(c), regarding awards of attorney fees for frivolous conduct, under which a hearing was required, applied. Shikner v. Solutions, — Ohio App. 3d —, 2006 Ohio 1339, — N.E. 2d —, 2006 Ohio App. LEXIS 1220 (Mar. 23, 2006).

When a former employee sued his former employer for compensation, and the employer served a request for production of the former employee's W-2 forms and tax returns, and, upon his failure to comply, a trial court ordered the employee to produce the documents, when the former employee still did not comply, the trial court was required, under Ohio R. Civ. P. 37(D), to award the employer attorney fees, as it did not find the former employee's resistance to discovery was warranted or that an award of attorney fees would be unjust. Shikner v. Solutions, — Ohio App. 3d —, 2006 Ohio 1339, — N.E. 2d —, 2006 Ohio App. LEXIS 1220 (Mar. 23, 2006).

Default judgment

Default judgment was properly granted, under Ohio R. Civ. P. 37(B)(2)(c), against a party who did not comply with discovery or with an order compelling discovery because (1) the opponent who sought the default judgment attempted to gain compliance for six months before seeking a default judgment, (2) the party obligated to provide discovery, after initially providing inadequate discovery responses, made absolutely no further effort to comply, did not object to the order compelling discovery, and offered no reason for the failure to comply, and (3) the discovery sought was not of sensitive or prejudicial material. Flatt v. Atwood, — Ohio App. 3d —, 2007 Ohio 5387, — N.E. 2d —, 2007 Ohio App. LEXIS 4735 (Oct. 9, 2007).

Trial court did not abuse its discretion when it granted customers' motion under Ohio R. Civ. P. 60(B) for relief from a default judgment entered against them by a window and door company in its non-payment action, as the customers had no notice that the trial court might enter a default judgment as a potential sanction pursuant to Ohio R. Civ. P. 37(B) for their discovery non-compliance and no hearing was held on the issue of damages; although the docket incorrectly reflected that the default was entered due to lack of answer, such did not change the outcome of the matter where the right result was reached for the wrong reason. Gunton Corp. v. Architectural Concepts, — Ohio App. 3d —, 2007 Ohio 6805, — N.E. 2d —, 2007 Ohio App. LEXIS 5970 (Dec. 20, 2007).

As a note debtor failed to comply with a note holder's discovery request for the production of documents, a trial court's entry of a default judgment in favor of the holder pursuant to Ohio R. Civ. P. 37 as a discovery sanction was warranted, and as the debtor failed to establish any meritorious defense or claim if relief under Ohio R. Civ. P. 60(B) was granted, and the debtor also failed to show entitlement to relief thereunder, denial of the debtor's motion for relief from the default judgment was not an abuse of discretion; the debtor had failed to respond timely to the discovery request, had not responded to two additional letter requests for the discovery, and the debtor also failed to comply with a trial court order that set a date for the response to the discovery. Paparodis v. Snively, — Ohio App. 3d —, 2007 Ohio 6910, — N.E. 2d —, 2007 Ohio App. LEXIS 6064 (Dec. 12, 2007).

Although the time for answering plaintiff's amended complaint had not run when plaintiff filed his motion for default judgment, the trial court did not err in rendering default judgment against defendants because plaintiff's motion was based upon defendants' failure to comply with various discovery orders, in accordance with Ohio R. Civ. P. 37(B)(2)(c), not on defendants' failure to file a timely answer under Ohio R. Civ. P. 55(A). Sparks v. Gray's Used Tractors, — Ohio App. 3d —, 2006 Ohio 2658, — N.E. 2d —, 2006 Ohio App. LEXIS 2489 (May 19, 2006).

Default judgment as a discovery sanction pursuant to Ohio R. Civ. P. 37(B)(2) was proper where a lawyer, a defendant in a declaratory judgment suit, failed to appear for his scheduled deposition twice, the second time disobeying the trial court's order that he appear, and failed to appear at a records deposition which he had scheduled himself. Ohio Bar Liab. Ins. Co. v. Silverman, — Ohio App. 3d —, 2006 Ohio 3016, — N.E. 2d —, 2006 Ohio App. LEXIS 2881 (June 15, 2006).

Depositions

CivR 37(D) permitted an award only of fees "caused by the failure" to attend the deposition: Wrinch v. Miller, 183 Ohio App. 3d 445, 2009 Ohio 3862, 917 N.E.2d 349, 2009 Ohio App. LEXIS 3296 (2009).

Counsel received reasonable notice of the deposition for purposes of imposing sanctions pursuant to CivR 37(D) for the failure to appear. The amount of expenses was properly proven, but there was no evidence that attorney fees were actually incurred: State ex rel. Citizens for Open, Responsive & Accountable Gov't v. Register, 116 Ohio St. 3d 88, 2007 Ohio 5542, 876 N.E.2d 913, 2007 Ohio LEXIS 2569 (2007).

Disclosure of expert witness

Trial court did not abuse its discretion when it precluded a patient's treating surgeon from testifying as an expert on the issues of standard of care and proximate cause in the patient's medical malpractice action against several other physicians, and in precluding the surgeon's recall in order to provide rebuttal evidence on those issues, as exclusion was a proper sanction in the circumstances under Ohio R. Civ. P. 26(E)(1) and 37 where the disclosure by the patient that the surgeon was going to testify as an expert was untimely and constituted unfair surprise. The case was filed in 1996, discovery was to have been completed in 2001, and the patient did not disclose his intent to call the surgeon as an expert until 10 days prior to the trial in 2003. Nead v. Brown County Gen. Hosp., — Ohio App. 3d —, 2007 Ohio 2443, — N.E. 2d —, 2007 Ohio App. LEXIS 2259 (May 21, 2007).

Discovery orders

Due to a perpetrator's failure, despite numerous opportunities, to have fully responded to an insurer's requests for admissions in its subrogation action, a trial court properly entered judgment for the insurer by deeming the requests admitted under Ohio R. Civ. P. 36(A). As the perpetrator failed to show that the requests were objectionable, not of substantial importance, or that there was a good reason for his failure to have responded, the imposition of costs pursuant to Ohio R. Civ. P. 37(C) was proper. Progressive Cas. Ins. Co. v. Harrison, — Ohio App. 3d —, 2007 Ohio 579, — N.E. 2d —, 2007 Ohio App. LEXIS 536 (Feb. 9, 2007).

Dismissal

When a company asserted that a corporation which sued the company committed discovery violations, and the corporation specifically denied that allegation, it was an abuse of discretion for a trial court to enter the corporation's default judgment based on the alleged violations because the trial court did not conduct an evidentiary hearing. Johnson Controls, Inc. v. Cadle Co., — Ohio App. 3d —, 2007 Ohio 3382, — N.E. 2d —, 2007 Ohio App. LEXIS 3100 (June 29, 2007).

Appellant's failure to timely file any responses to appellee's discovery requests, which had been pending for about two years, was a proper ground for dismissal under Ohio R. Civ. P. 37(B)(2). Appellant had not shown any reason justifying his lack of compliance with the trial court's orders, and he had received notice from the trial court that failure to comply with the deadline would lead to dismissal of his case. Spragling v.

Oriana House, — Ohio App. 3d —, 2007 Ohio 3245, — N.E. 2d —, 2007 Ohio App. LEXIS 2993 (June 27, 2007).

Sanctions for failure to provide discovery under Ohio R. Civ. P. 37, including dismissal of a former bank employee's counterclaims under Rule 37(B)(2), were appropriate because the bank's motion for sanctions specifically requested dismissal of the counterclaims and a judgment in its favor in its action for, inter alia, breach of contract as a remedy for the employee's discovery misconduct. First Nat'l Bank of Southwestern Ohio v. Doellman, — Ohio App. 3d —, 2007 Ohio 2292, — N.E. 2d —, 2007 Ohio App. LEXIS 2157 (May 14, 2007).

Trial court's dismissal, pursuant to Ohio R. Civ. P. 41(B)(1), of an administrator's fraudulent concealment and bad faith claims against an insurance agency was not an abuse of discretion because (1) the administrator had notice of the administrator's discovery violations on which the dismissal was based, and (2) Ohio R. Civ. P. 37(B)(2)(c) expressly allowed a trial court to dismiss a claim for a discovery violation. Coe v. Grange Mut. Cas. Co., — Ohio App. 3d —, 2007 Ohio 2823, — N.E. 2d —, 2007 Ohio App. LEXIS 2632 (June 8, 2007).

Patient's medical malpractice claim was properly dismissed due to counsel's failure to comply with Ohio Ct. Cl. R. 7(E), requiring the production of expert witness reports, because (1) counsel had a history, in this case, of repeatedly failing to provide this information, (2) the information counsel eventually provided did not satisfy Rule 7(E) because it did not identify the person who allegedly misdiagnosed the patient, (3) the trial court had repeatedly unsuccessfully tried to remedy counsel's noncompliance, (4) the patient was on notice that the trial court was inclined to dismiss the case, and (5) Rule 7(E) authorized the trial court to employ the sanctions provided in Ohio R. Civ. P. 37, which included dismissal. Thompson v. Ohio State Univ. Hosps., — Ohio App. 3d —, 2007 Ohio 4668, — N.E. 2d —, 2007 Ohio App. LEXIS 4206 (Sept. 11, 2007).

Where a trial court indicated that it was holding an action between an employee and his father's company in abeyance pending the company's disclosure of corporate records in order to help the trial court ascertain whether the employee had any interest in the company and at such time that the records were disclosed, the final hearing would be scheduled and the claims between the parties determined, the trial court's subsequent sua sponte dismissal of the employee's claims and the entry of judgment for the company without the necessary disclosure and hearing was error; there was no basis under Ohio R. Civ. P. 12(B) and (C), 56, 37(B)(2)(c), and 41(B)(1) and (2) for the dismissal, nor was it based on the court's "inherent powers." Boccia v. Boccia, — Ohio App. 3d —, 2006 Ohio 2384, — N.E. 2d —, 2006 Ohio App. LEXIS 2251 (May 12, 2006).

When judgment in a personal injury suit was appealed, the party in whose favor judgment was entered could not claim that the matter had been dismissed, under Ohio R. Civ. P. 37(D), due to a discovery violation because that party had filed no statement, pursuant to Ohio R. Civ. P. 37(E), reciting an effort to resolve the matter through discussion, so dismissal could not have been sought or granted. Reighard v. Cleveland Elec. Illuminating, — Ohio App. 3d —, 2006 Ohio 1283, — N.E. 2d —, 2006 Ohio App. LEXIS 1179 (Mar. 16, 2006).

When a bank sued an attorney and the attorney filed counterclaims, it was not error for the trial court to dismiss the counterclaims, under Ohio R. Civ. P. 37(B)(2)(c), due to the attorney's failure to respond to discovery, because the attorney had notice, in the bank's motion for sanctions, that it would seek such relief, and this notice was sufficient, under Ohio R. Civ. P. 41(B)(1). First Nat'l Bank of Southwestern Ohio v. Doellman, — Ohio App. 3d —, 2006 Ohio 1663, — N.E. 2d —, 2006 Ohio App. LEXIS 1564 (Apr. 3, 2006).

— With prejudice

Although parties failed to comply with the trial court's directive to file expert witness reports by specified dates as required by Cuyahoga County, Ohio, Ct. C.P. R. 21.1(B) where such reports were required to prove causation for purposes of civil assault claims against each other, the trial court's dismissal was not based on discovery misconduct under Ohio R. Civ. P. 37, but rather, on failure to prosecute pursuant to Ohio R. Civ. P. 41(B)(1), and accordingly, the trial court did not have to consider less restrictive alternatives to the dismissal sanction; as the party objecting to the dismissal of his complaint had received adequate notice by the trial court and he had a reasonable opportunity to defend against dismissal, there was no abuse of discretion in the trial court's dismissal with prejudice. Badri v. Averbach, — Ohio App. 3d —, 2006 Ohio 3602, — N.E. 2d —, 2006 Ohio App. LEXIS 3556 (July 13, 2006).

Duty to resolve

Although appellant argued that appellee's outline of the discovery dispute between the parties did not comply with Ohio R. Civ. P. 37(E), there was no useful purpose in invoking Ohio R. Civ. P. 37(E) when a trial court had gone to the trouble of conducting a hearing on a motion to compel or to dismiss as a sanction for failing to respond to discovery and issuing a decision resolving the parties' dispute. Spragling v. Oriana House, — Ohio App. 3d —, 2007 Ohio 3245, — N.E. 2d —, 2007 Ohio App. LEXIS 2993 (June 27, 2007).

Since a trial court granted plaintiff's motion to compel defendants' discovery responses one week before defendants' memorandum was due under Clark County, Ohio, Mun. Ct. R. 2.27(C) and since plaintiff failed to comply with Ohio R. Civ. P. 37(E) concerning his efforts to resolve the dispute without the trial court's intervention, the trial court erred in granting the motion to compel. Cooper v. Drukker, — Ohio App. 3d —, 2007 Ohio 3702, — N.E. 2d —, 2007 Ohio App. LEXIS 3380 (July 20, 2007).

Excuses for noncompliance

It was an abuse of discretion to enter a corporation's default judgment based on the failure of the corporation's chief executive officer to appear at a deposition because the corporation's pending motion for a protective order, pursuant to Ohio R. Civ. P. 26(C), could be an excuse for the failure to appear, so the corporation could not have been found to have violated Ohio R. Civ. P. 37(D) because the motion for protective order, if granted, would excuse the corporation's duty to comply. Johnson Controls, Inc. v. Cadle Co., — Ohio App. 3d —, 2007 Ohio 3382, — N.E. 2d —, 2007 Ohio App. LEXIS 3100 (June 29, 2007).

Insurance matters

Claims file materials that show an insurer's lack of good faith in denying coverage are unworthy of protection, and claims-file materials showing an insurer's lack of good faith in processing, evaluating, or refusing to pay a claim are unworthy of the protection afforded by the attorney-client or work-product privilege, regardless of whether the insurer ever denied the claim outright. Unklesbay v. Fenwick, 167 Ohio App. 3d 408, 2006 Ohio 2630, 855 N.E. 2d 516, 2006 Ohio App. LEXIS 2515 (May 19, 2006).

When an insured sued an insurer for bad faith, it was not error for the trial court to consider the insured's motion to compel the production of the insurer's claims file, even though the insured had not strictly complied with the provisions of Ohio R. Civ. P. 37(E), because Rule 37(E) was designed for the benefit of trial courts, in an effort to avoid their involvement in discovery disputes, but, once the trial court conducted a hearing on the motion and issued a decision resolving the dispute, there was no useful purpose in invoking

Rule 37(E). Unklesbay v. Fenwick, 167 Ohio App. '3d 408, 2006 Ohio 2630, 855 N.E. 2d 516, 2006 Ohio App. LEXIS 2515 (May 19, 2006).

In an action alleging bad faith denial of insurance coverage, the insured was entitled to discover claims file materials containing attorney-client communications related to the issue of coverage that were created prior to the denial of coverage, as claims file materials that showed an insurer's lack of good faith in denying coverage were unworthy of protection, and the only documents that would contain information related to the bad faith claim, and, thus, be unworthy of protection, would have been created prior to the denial of coverage. This applied to discovery of attorney-client communications and work-product materials on a bad-faith denial-of-coverage claim. Unklesbay v. Fenwick, 167 Ohio App. 3d 408, 2006 Ohio 2630, 855 N.E. 2d 516, 2006 Ohio App. LEXIS 2515 (May 19, 2006).

When an insurer sued an insurer for bad faith, the insured was entitled to discover those parts of the claims file that were relevant to the claim of bad faith, even if the insurer had paid the insured benefits, but the trial court had to conduct an in camera inspection of the file. Unklesbay v. Fenwick, 167 Ohio App. 3d 408, 2006 Ohio 2630, 855 N.E. 2d 516, 2006 Ohio App. LEXIS 2515 (May 19, 2006).

If the defense, in a bad-faith claim against an insurer, asserted the attorney-client privilege with regard to the contents of a claims file, a trial court had to determine by in camera inspection which portions of the file, if any, were so privileged, and the plaintiff then had to be granted access to the non-privileged portions of the file. Unklesbay v. Fenwick, 167 Ohio App. 3d 408, 2006 Ohio 2630, 855 N.E. 2d 516, 2006 Ohio App. LEXIS 2515 (May 19, 2006).

Interrogatories

It was an abuse of discretion to enter a corporation's default judgment based on the corporation's submission of unsigned answers to interrogatories because this was not evidence of the corporation's bad faith because the corporation supplemented the unsigned answers with signed answers. Johnson Controls, Inc. v. Cadle Co., — Ohio App. 3d —, 2007 Ohio 3382, — N.E. 2d —, 2007 Ohio App. LEXIS 3100 (June 29, 2007).

Jurisdiction

Trial court had jurisdiction to award a seller attorney's fees associated with the refusal of buyers it sued to answer questions in a deposition, despite the buyers' notice of appeal, because nothing showed the refusal was substantially justified, and the trial court retained jurisdiction to rule on the seller's motion for sanctions, under Ohio R. Civ. P. 37(A)(4), because the trial court's decision on that motion did not affect the appellate court's power to review and decide the appeal. MSC Walbridge Coatings, Inc. v. Harmeyer, — Ohio App. 3d —, 2006 Ohio 3181, — N.E. 2d —, 2006 Ohio App. LEXIS 3065 (June 23, 2006).

Motion to compel discovery

As a property purchaser had failed to comply with Ohio R. Civ. P. 37(E) for purposes of his motion to compel discovery in a bank's foreclosure action, and the trial court had already granted him several extensions of time to respond to the bank's summary judgment motion, there was no abuse of discretion in the trial court's denial of the purchaser's motion for a continuance until after the bank had complied with all of his voluminous discovery requests pursuant to Ohio R. Civ. P. 56(F). Liberty Sav. Bank v. Jones, — Ohio App. 3d —, 2007 Ohio 198, — N.E. 2d —, 2007 Ohio App. LEXIS 189 (Jan. 19, 2007).

When an inmate sought a declaratory judgment that his sentence was unlawfully amended and sought to compel responses to his interrogatories, it was proper to deny his motion to compel because his interrogatories largely sought information about the knowledge and experience of the Ohio Department of Rehabilitation and Correction's Chief Counsel, and such information had no bearing on the issues presented by the inmate's complaint, nor would it have assisted him in responding to a summary judgment motion, particularly because he had responded to that motion before propounding his interrogatories. Way v. Ohio Dep't of Rehabilitation & Correction, — Ohio App. 3d —, 2007 Ohio 235, — N.E. 2d —, 2007 Ohio App. LEXIS 217 (Jan. 23, 2007).

Order to compel discovery

It was an abuse of discretion to enter a corporation's default judgment based on the corporation's alleged discovery violations because the record was devoid of any court orders, under Ohio R. Civ. P. 37(B)(2), requiring the corporation to comply with the discovery requests of the company against which the corporation filed suit, because Ohio R. Civ. P. 37 only permitted default judgment as a sanction for failing to comply with a prior court order. Johnson Controls, Inc. v. Cadle Co., — Ohio App. 3d —, 2007 Ohio 3382, — N.E. 2d —, 2007 Ohio App. LEXIS 3100 (June 29, 2007).

Since the requested information could have fallen under the umbrella of either opinion work product or ordinary fact work product, the possibility of two differing forms of protection under the attorney-client privilege necessitated an evidentiary hearing. Any blanket grant compelling discovery, under Ohio R. Civ. P. 26, 37(A)(2), and 34, was an abuse of discretion because the trial court had to first conduct a hearing to determine the nature of the privilege. Miller v. Bassett, — Ohio App. 3d —, 2006 Ohio 3590, — N.E. 2d —, 2006 Ohio App. LEXIS 3536 (July 13, 2006).

Trial court's decision to compel production of discovery as to two of the interrogatories was reversed as the answers sought were protected by the physician-patient privilege, pursuant to RC § 2317.02(B)(1), and the order to compel discovery as to one interrogatory was affirmed as to any request for the mental health information that the owner had directly put at issue through his claim for severe emotional distress. However, an evidentiary hearing was required to determine the appropriate look-back time frame of the discovery request. Miller v. Bassett, — Ohio App. 3d —, 2006 Ohio 3590, — N.E. 2d —, 2006 Ohio App. LEXIS 3536 (July 13, 2006).

— Willful noncompliance

Nothing in CivR 37(B)(2)(d) indicates that a court must comply with the procedural requirements of RC § 2705.03 before it treats a party's noncompliance with a discovery order as a contempt of court: Bank One Trust Co., N.A. v. Scherer, 176 Ohio App. 3d 694, 2008 Ohio 2952, 893 N.E.2d 542, 2008 Ohio App. LEXIS 2463 (2008).

Sanctions

In a suit between a creditor and a debtor, the debtor was not entitled to relief for the creditor's alleged failure to respond to the debtor's discovery requests because the debtor did not move to compel the creditor to respond, as required by Ohio R. Civ. P. 37(B)(2). Arrow Fin. Servs. v. Kuzniak, — Ohio App. 3d —, 2007 Ohio 2191, — N.E. 2d —, 2007 Ohio App. LEXIS 2049 (Apr. 24, 2007).

Party generally may not be sanctioned for discovery violations unless he or she has failed to comply with a court order compelling him or her to provide the requested discovery, under Ohio R. Civ. P. 37(B)(2). Arrow Fin. Servs. v. Kuzniak, — Ohio App. 3d —, 2007 Ohio 2191, — N.E. 2d —, 2007 Ohio App. LEXIS 2049 (Apr. 24, 2007).

Judicially-imposed waiver of attorney-client privilege is not a just order in regard to discovery failures. Beck v. First Fin. Ins. Co., — Ohio App. 3d —, 2006 Ohio 3463, — N.E. 2d —, 2006 Ohio App. LEXIS 3396 (July 3, 2006).

Trial court abused its discretion when it ordered the waiver of attorney-client privilege as a sanction, pursuant to Ohio R.

Civ. P. 37(B)(2), for appellant's discovery violations. The attorney-client privilege is inviolate. Beck v. First Fin. Ins. Co., — Ohio App. 3d —, 2006 Ohio 3463, — N.E. 2d —, 2006 Ohio App. LEXIS 3396 (July 3, 2006).

As a former wife had to expend substantial time, energy, and money to obtain requested discovery from her former husband for purposes of motions relating to his child support obligation, his gross income determination, and the amount of arrears that he owed, based on the husband's misconduct during discovery, an award of expenses and costs, including attorney fees, to the wife was proper under Ohio R. Civ. P. 37(B)(2). Glassman v. Offenberg, — Ohio App. 3d —, 2006 Ohio 3837, — N.E. 2d —, 2006 Ohio App. LEXIS 3801 (July 27, 2006).

When a trial court issued an order compelling an alleged injured party to attend an independent medical examination, it could not assess the costs of obtaining that order against the alleged injured party under Ohio R. Civ. P. 37(B), because the alleged injured party did not fail to comply with a court order, as the court's order compelled her to submit to an examination which was set six days before the order was filed. Stratman v. Sutantio, — Ohio App. 3d —, 2006 Ohio 4712, — N.E. 2d —, 2006 Ohio App. LEXIS 4631 (Sept. 12, 2006).

When a trial court issued an order compelling an alleged injured party to attend an independent medical examination, it did not have authority, under Ohio R. Civ. P. 37(A)(4), to assess the costs of obtaining that order against the alleged injured party because its authority to award expenses under that provision was limited to motions made in regard to Ohio R. Civ. P. 30, 31, 33 or 34, but Ohio R. Civ. P. 35 was not mentioned. Stratman v. Sutantio, — Ohio App. 3d —, 2006 Ohio 4712, — N.E. 2d —, 2006 Ohio App. LEXIS 4631 (Sept. 12, 2006).

Trial court's imposition of attorney fees and travel expenses as a discovery sanction pursuant to Ohio R. Civ. P. 30(G)(1) and 37 was reasonable in the circumstances and not an abuse of discretion, as appellant's counsel had scheduled a deposition to be held at his office but he had failed to secure a court reporter, which required the rescheduling of the deposition, and he was aware that appellee's counsel had to travel from out of town. The fees and expenses for travel were deemed reasonable in the circumstances. McKowen v. United Church Homes, Inc., — Ohio App. 3d —, 2006 Ohio 6607, — N.E. 2d —, 2006 Ohio App. LEXIS 6519 (Dec. 8, 2006).

When an insurer continued not to obey an order compelling discovery of its claims files, even after the order was affirmed and the time for seeking further review had expired, the insurer's arguments that sanctions against it should not be assessed for the period after the insurer's new counsel entered an appearance or that sanctions should not be assessed for time spent in productive efforts to resolve a confidentiality agreement regarding the files were not persuasive. National Union Fire Ins. Co. v. Ohio State Univ. Bd. of Trustees, — Ohio Misc. 2d —, 2006 Ohio 2541, — N.E. 2d —, 2006 Ohio Misc. LEXIS 89 (Apr. 6, 2006).

Insurer's appeal of an order compelling it to provide discovery of its claims files was not frivolous, but, once that order was affirmed and the time to appeal that affirmance expired, the insurer was not substantially justified in continuing to withhold discovery, so the party seeking discovery was entitled to its reasonable fees and expenses incurred between the time the appellate court's decision became final and the time discovery was actually provided. National Union Fire Ins. Co. v. Ohio State Univ. Bd. of Trustees, — Ohio Misc. 2d —, 2006 Ohio 2541, — N.E. 2d —, 2006 Ohio Misc. LEXIS 89 (Apr. 6, 2006).

When an insurer continued not to obey an order compelling discovery of its claims files, even after the order was affirmed and the time for seeking further review had expired, the insurer's argument in support of a subsequent motion for a protective order, claiming a need to insure the files' confiden-

tiality, was not persuasive. National Union Fire Ins. Co. v. Ohio State Univ. Bd. of Trustees, — Ohio Misc. 2d —, 2006 Ohio 2541, — N.E. 2d —, 2006 Ohio Misc. LEXIS 89 (Apr. 6, 2006).

Spoliation of evidence

In a mass toxic tort case in which alleged injured parties moved for sanctions due to the opposing parties' alleged spoliation of evidence, it was an abuse of discretion for a trial court to deny the motion because it was unclear if the court actually considered the motion or if evidence had been destroyed and the opposing parties had provided no discovery and did not deny the spoliation allegation. Simeone v. Girard City Bd. of Educ., 171 Ohio App. 3d 633, 2007 Ohio 1775, 872 N.E.2d 344, 2007 Ohio App. LEXIS 1610 (2007).

Motion for sanctions for spoliation of evidence was properly filed under Ohio R. Civ. P. 37, and the proponent had to first establish that: (1) the evidence was relevant; (2) the offending party's expert had an opportunity to examine the unaltered evidence; and (3) even though the offending party was put on notice of impending litigation, this evidence was intentionally or negligently destroyed or altered without providing an opportunity for inspection by the proponent. Simeone v. Girard City Bd. of Educ., 171 Ohio App. 3d 633, 2007 Ohio 1775, 872 N.E.2d 344, 2007 Ohio App. LEXIS 1610 (2007).

TITLE VI
TRIALS

RULE 38. Jury trial of right

(A) **Right preserved.** The right to trial by jury shall be preserved to the parties inviolate.

(B) **Demand.** Any party may demand a trial by jury on any issue triable of right by a jury by serving upon the other parties a demand therefore at any time after the commencement of the action and not later than fourteen days after the service of the last pleading directed to such issue. Such demand shall be in writing and may be indorsed upon a pleading of the party. If the demand is indorsed upon a pleading the caption of the pleading shall state "jury demand endorsed hereon." In an action for appropriation of a right of way brought by a corporation pursuant to Article XIII, Section 5, of the Ohio Constitution, the jury shall be composed of twelve members unless the demand specifies a lesser number; and in the event of timely demand by more than one party in such action the jury shall be composed of the greater number not to exceed twelve. In all other civil actions the jury shall be composed of eight members unless the demand specifies a lesser number; and in the event of timely demand by more than one party in such actions the jury shall be composed of the greater number not to exceed eight.

(C) **Specification of issues.** In his demand a party may specify the issues which he wishes so tried; otherwise he shall be deemed to have demanded trial by jury for all the issues so triable. If he has demanded trial by jury for only some of the issues, any other party within fourteen days after service of the demand or such lesser time as the court may order, may serve a demand for trial by jury of any other or all of the issues of fact in the action.

(D) **Waiver.** The failure of a party to serve a demand as required by this rule and to file it as required by Rule 5(D) constitutes a waiver by him of trial by jury. A demand for trial by jury made as herein provided may not be withdrawn without the consent of the parties.

History: Amended, eff 7-1-72; 7-1-76.

NOTES TO DECISIONS

ANALYSIS

Costs of jury trial
Counterclaims
Demand for jury trial
Failure to make timely jury demand
Validity of rule
Waiver

Costs of jury trial

Trial court did not err in striking the jury demand where a party did not pay the required fee or deposit: Arlington Natural Gas Co. v. Martens, 173 Ohio App. 3d 450, 2007 Ohio 5479, 878 N.E.2d 1088, 2007 Ohio App. LEXIS 4829 (2007).

Counterclaims

When a utility company sued a property owner for gas supplied to the property, the owner's Ohio R. Civ. P. 38(B) demand for a jury trial was properly stricken because (1) the demand was only made in the owner's counterclaim, which was properly stricken due to the owner's failure to pay a required filing fee, and (2) the owner did not pay a jury fee required by the trial court's local rules and authorized by RC § 1901.26(A)(3), which was a sufficient reason to strike the jury demand. Arlington Natural Gas Co. v. Martens, 173 Ohio App. 3d 450, 2007 Ohio 5479, 878 N.E.2d 1088, 2007 Ohio App. LEXIS 4829 (2007).

Demand for jury trial

Trial court's adoption of a magistrate's decision which granted parties a divorce did not merge the wife's claim of assault against the husband into that divorce judgment pursuant to Ohio R. Civ. P. 53(E)(3)(d) and (E)(4)(a), as the trial court's failure or refusal to consider the tort claim was not a "final disposition of the claim" and further, the wife had not been provided an opportunity to exercise her right to trial by jury of the assault claim, pursuant to Ohio R. Civ. P. 38(A). Reimund v. Hanna, — Ohio App. 3d —, 2006 Ohio 6848, — N.E. 2d —, 2006 Ohio App. LEXIS 6762 (Dec. 26, 2006).

Incompetent's daughter properly filed a jury demand pursuant to Ohio R. Civ. P. 38, as the failure to include the exact phrase "jury demand endorsed herein" did not negate the assertion of that right where no prejudice to the guardian of the incompetent or to the court's administrative practice was shown in an action between the parties regarding the daughter's tenancy in the incompetent's home, which the guardian sought to have her vacate, and she did not waive such right by any of the methods specified in Ohio R. Civ. P. 39. Her failure to attend a non-final hearing to consolidate two related cases and her appearance before a magistrate in a municipal court matter did not constitute a waiver thereof. Mickens v. Smith, — Ohio App. 3d —, 2006 Ohio 4300, — N.E. 2d —, 2006 Ohio App. LEXIS 4224 (Aug. 18, 2006).

Failure to make timely jury demand

In a law firm's suit against a former client for past due fees, a trial court properly found that the firm did not timely demand a jury trial, under Ohio R. Civ. P. 38(B), because the demand was not filed within 14 days of the filing of the former client's answer, and the client's subsequent filing of an amended answer did not initiate a new 14-day period because the amended answer did not allege any new facts. Bringman v. Smith, — Ohio App. 3d —, 2007 Ohio 4684, — N.E. 2d —, 2007 Ohio App. LEXIS 4214 (Sept. 12, 2007).

Validity of rule

When a body shop sued by a customer in municipal court demanded a jury trial, that demand was not effective unless and until the deposit was paid because (1) the deposit was required by Sandusky County, Ohio, Mun. Ct. R. 7(C) and 18(B), (2) Ohio Const. art. IV, § 5 allowed Ohio courts to adopt local rules that did not conflict with the Civil Rules of Procedure, (3) RC § 1901.26(A)(3), governing procedure in municipal courts, expressly permitted a municipal court to adopt a local rule requiring the deposit, and (4) as a result, Sandusky County, Ohio, Mun. Ct. R. 7(C) and 18(B) complemented, and did not conflict with, Ohio R. Civ. P. 38(B), allowing a party to a civil case to demand a jury trial. Hanson v. Moore, — Ohio App. 3d —, 2007 Ohio 2829, — N.E. 2d —, 2007 Ohio App. LEXIS 2634 (June 8, 2007).

Waiver

Where a tenant who was sued by her landlord filed an answer and later made a jury demand that included an affidavit asserting that she could not afford the jury deposit fee, which request to proceed in forma pauperis was denied, but she thereafter failed to appear for the trial involving the landlord's second cause of action and the tenant's counterclaims, she was deemed to have waived her right to a trial by jury pursuant to Ohio R. Civ. P. 38(A) and 39(A). Valente v. Johnson, — Ohio App. 3d —, 2007 Ohio 2664, — N.E. 2d —, 2007 Ohio App. LEXIS 2482 (May 29, 2007).

RULE 39.   Trial by jury or by the court

(A) **By jury.** When trial by jury has been demanded as provided in Rule 38, the action shall be designated upon the docket as a jury action. The trial of all issues so demanded shall be by jury, unless (1) the parties or their attorneys of record, by written stipulation filed with the court or by an oral stipulation made in open court and entered in the record, consent to trial by the court sitting without a jury or (2) the court upon motion or of its own initiative finds that a right of trial by jury of some or all of those issues does not exist. The failure of a party or his attorney of record either to answer or appear for trial constitutes a waiver of trial by jury by such party and authorizes submission of all issues to the court.

(B) **By the court.** Issues not demanded for trial by jury as provided in Rule 38 shall be tried by the court; but, notwithstanding the failure of a party to demand a jury in an action in which such a demand might have been made of right, the court in its discretion upon motion may order a trial by a jury of any or all issues.

(C) **Advisory jury and trial by consent.** In all actions not triable of right by a jury (1) the court upon motion or on its own initiative may try any issue with an advisory jury or (2) the court, with the consent of both parties, may order a trial of any issue with a jury, whose verdict has the same effect as if trial by jury had been a matter of right.

History: Amended, eff 7-1-71.

NOTES TO DECISIONS

ANALYSIS

Demand for jury trial
Waiver of jury demand

Demand for jury trial

Incompetent's daughter properly filed a jury demand pursuant to Ohio R. Civ. P. 38, as the failure to include the exact phrase "jury demand endorsed herein" did not negate the assertion of that right where no prejudice to the guardian of the incompetent or to the court's administrative practice was shown in an action between the parties regarding the daughter's tenancy in the incompetent's home, which the guardian sought to have her vacate, and she did not waive such right by any of the methods specified in Ohio R. Civ. P. 39; her failure to attend a non-final hearing to consolidate two related cases and her appearance before a magistrate in a municipal court matter did not constitute a waiver thereof. Mickens v. Smith, — Ohio App. 3d —, 2006 Ohio 4300, — N.E. 2d —, 2006 Ohio App. LEXIS 4224 (Aug. 18, 2006).

Trial court did not abuse its discretion when it allowed the driver to pay the jury fee after the deadline as it clearly understood the potential problems posed by Lucas County, Ohio, Ct. C.P. R. 5.07(F) and did not act arbitrarily by ordering a jury trial. The couple's interpretation of Rule 5.07(F) would have improperly conflicted with Ohio R. Civ. P. 39(B), which vested discretion with the trial court to order a jury trial. Ogdahl v. Drown, 168 Ohio App. 3d 49, 2006 Ohio 3376, 858 N.E.2d 824, 2006 Ohio App. LEXIS 3303 (2006).

Waiver of jury demand

Where a tenant who was sued by her landlord filed an answer and later made a jury demand that included an affidavit asserting that she could not afford the jury deposit fee, which request to proceed in forma pauperis was denied, but she thereafter failed to appear for the trial involving the landlord's second cause of action and the tenant's counterclaims, she was deemed to have waived her right to a trial by jury pursuant to Ohio R. Civ. P. 38(A) and 39(A). Valente v. Johnson, — Ohio App. 3d —, 2007 Ohio 2664, — N.E. 2d —, 2007 Ohio App. LEXIS 2482 (May 29, 2007).

When a bank sued an attorney and the attorney filed counterclaims on which he demanded a jury trial, it was not error, under Ohio R. Civ. P. 39(A), for the trial court to conduct a bench trial when the attorney did not appear for trial, as this waived his jury demand, and the bank waived a jury. First Nat'l Bank of Southwestern Ohio v. Doellman, — Ohio App. 3d —, 2006 Ohio 1663, — N.E. 2d —, 2006 Ohio App. LEXIS 1564 (Apr. 3, 2006).

RULE 40. Pre-recorded testimony

All of the testimony and such other evidence as may be appropriate may be presented at a trial by videotape, subject to the provisions of the Rules of Superintendence.

History: New, eff 7-1-72.

NOTES TO DECISIONS

ANALYSIS

Ordering prerecorded videotape trial

Ordering prerecorded videotape trial

After a trial court ordered, pursuant to Ohio Superintendence Ct. R. 13, Lorain County, Ohio, Ct. C.P. R. 23, and Ohio R. Civ. P. 40, that trial in a personal injury case would be conducted by videotape, it was an abuse of discretion for the trial court to deny the request of the alleged injured party to testify in person at the trial and then to grant the party's request to allow a third party to read a physician's deposition at the trial, without providing an explanation for the different orders, as the trial court did not consult counsel or consider the factors required by Ohio Superintendence Ct. R. 13(B) in issuing its orders. Armbruster v. Hampton, — Ohio App. 3d —, 2006 Ohio 4530, — N.E. 2d —, 2006 Ohio App. LEXIS 4518 (Sept. 5, 2006).

RULE 41. Dismissal of actions

(A) Voluntary dismissal: effect thereof.

(1) By plaintiff; by stipulation. Subject to the provisions of Civ. R. 23(E), Civ. R. 23.1, and Civ. R. 66, a plaintiff, without order of court, may dismiss all claims asserted by that plaintiff against a defendant by doing either of the following:

(a) filing a notice of dismissal at any time before the commencement of trial unless a counterclaim which cannot remain pending for independent adjudication by the court has been served by that defendant;

(b) filing a stipulation of dismissal signed by all parties who have appeared in the action.

Unless otherwise stated in the notice of dismissal or stipulation, the dismissal is without prejudice, except that a notice of dismissal operates as an adjudication upon the merits of any claim that the plaintiff has once dismissed in any court.

(2) By order of court. Except as provided in division (A)(1) of this rule, a claim shall not be dismissed at the plaintiff's instance except upon order of the court and upon such terms and conditions as the court deems proper. If a counterclaim has been pleaded by a defendant prior to the service upon that defendant of the plaintiff's motion to dismiss, a claim shall not be dismissed against the defendant's objection unless the counterclaim can remain pending for independent adjudication by the court. Unless otherwise specified in the order, a dismissal under division (A)(2) of this rule is without prejudice.

(B) Involuntary dismissal: effect thereof.

(1) Failure to prosecute. Where the plaintiff fails to prosecute, or comply with these rules or any court order, the court upon motion of a defendant or on its own motion may, after notice to the plaintiff's counsel, dismiss an action or claim.

(2) Dismissal; non-jury action. After the plaintiff, in an action tried by the court without a jury, has completed the presentation of the plaintiff's evidence, the defendant, without waiving the right to offer evidence in the event the motion is not granted, may move for a dismissal on the ground that upon the facts and the law the plaintiff has shown no right to relief. The court as trier of the facts may then determine them and render judgment against the plaintiff or may decline to render any judgment until the close of all the evidence. If the court renders judgment on the merits against the plaintiff, the court shall make findings as provided in Civ. R. 52 if requested to do so by any party.

(3) Adjudication on the merits; exception. A dismissal under division (B) of this rule and any dismissal not provided for in this rule, except as provided in division (B)(4) of this rule, operates as an adjudication upon the merits unless the court, in its order for dismissal, otherwise specifies.

(4) Failure other than on the merits. A dismissal for either of the following reasons shall operate as a failure otherwise than on the merits:

(a) lack of jurisdiction over the person or the subject matter;

(b) failure to join a party under Civ. R. 19 or Civ. R. 19.1.

(C) **Dismissal of counterclaim, cross-claim, or third-party claim.** The provisions of this rule apply to the dismissal of any counterclaim, cross-claim, or third-party claim. A voluntary dismissal by the claimant alone pursuant to division (A)(1) of this rule shall be made before the commencement of trial.

(D) **Costs of previously dismissed action.** If a plaintiff who has once dismissed a claim in any court commences an action based upon or including the same claim against the same defendant, the court may make such order for the payment of costs of the claim previously dismissed as it may deem proper and may stay the proceedings in the action until the plaintiff has complied with the order.

History: Amended, eff 7-1-71; 7-1-72; 7-1-01.

NOTES TO DECISIONS

ANALYSIS

Appeal
Applicability
Arbitration
Continuance
Costs and attorney fees
Directed verdict in bench trial
Discovery misconduct
Dismissal after plaintiff's case
Dismissal for failure to prove damages
Double dismissal rule
Evidence sufficient
Final appealable order
Involuntary dismissal
Jurisdiction
Mass toxic torts
Motion for directed verdict
Motion for dismissal
— Reasonable opportunity to contest
Non-jury actions
Notice
Procedure
Relation back
Res judicata
Sanctions for misconduct
Saving statute
Standing
Stipulation of dismissal
Two-dismissal rule
Voluntary dismissal
— Before trial
Workers' compensation

Appeal

Whether a trial court has properly dismissed a case with prejudice under Ohio R. Civ. P. 41(B)(1) is reviewed under an abuse of discretion standard, and since dismissal with prejudice is a particularly harsh sanction, a "heightened abuse of discretion standard" is used because decisions that forever deny a plaintiff a review of a claim's merits are being reviewed. Simeone v. Girard City Bd. of Educ., 171 Ohio App. 3d 633, 2007 Ohio 1775, 872 N.E.2d 344, 2007 Ohio App. LEXIS 1610 (2007).

As a trial court's denial of a real property seller's motion for summary judgment was accompanied by a dismissal of the seller's claims with prejudice pursuant to Ohio R. Civ. P. 41, the dismissed action was in effect adjudicated on the merits and it was appealable under RC § 2505.03. Because the trial court decided the seller's motion in a way that effectively determined the action in the purchaser's alleged agent's favor and prevented a judgment in the seller's favor, the decision was a final order under RC § 2505.02. Functional Furnishing, Inc. v. White, — Ohio App. 3d —, — N.E. 2d —, 2007 Ohio 3284, 2007 Ohio App. LEXIS 3005 (June 28, 2007).

Litigant's appeal of an opponent's Ohio R. Civ. P. 41(A)(1)(a) voluntary dismissal had to be filed within 30 days of the date the dismissal was filed, rather than within 30 days of the trial court's approval of the dismissal because the dismissal was self-executing, and the trial court's approval was an unnecessary nullity. Stern v. Stern, — Ohio App. 3d —, 2007 Ohio 3473, — N.E. 2d —, 2007 Ohio App. LEXIS 3202 (July 6, 2007).

Appeal from a trial court's order noting that "it is so ordered," filed after appellee submitted notice of voluntary dismissal under Ohio R. Civ. P. 41(A)(1)(a), was dismissed as untimely because a notice of voluntary dismissal under Ohio R. Civ. P. 41(A)(1)(a) was self-executing, and as a result, the time for filing the notice of appeal began to run from the time that appellee filed the notice of voluntary dismissal, not when the trial court made the notation. Since appellant had not complied with the thirty-day rule in App. R. 4(A) nor had it alleged that there was a failure by the trial court clerk to comply with Ohio R. Civ. P. 58(B), as specified in Ohio 11th Dist. Ct. App. R. 3(D)(2), the appeal was untimely. Thorton v. Montville Plastics & Rubber, — Ohio App. 3d —, 2007 Ohio 3475, — N.E. 2d —, 2007 Ohio App. LEXIS 3204 (July 6, 2007).

Dismissal with prejudice constituted a final appealable order where it left a party with no pending claims, thereby denying the party the right to redress injury and determined the action in favor of the opposing party. CivR 54(B) certification was not required where the court's action effectively resolved the only remaining claims: Sunkin v. Collision Pro, Inc., 174 Ohio App. 3d 56, 2007 Ohio 6046, 880 N.E.2d 947, 2007 Ohio App. LEXIS 5323 (2007).

As a contractor's claims that alleged breaches of implied warranties by suppliers were voluntarily dismissed by it pursuant to Ohio R. Civ. P. 41(A)(1)(a), there could be no noncontractual indemnification claim based on implied warranties under the Uniform Commercial Code pursuant to RC § 1302.65(E). Demarco, Inc. v. Johns-Manville Corp., — Ohio App. 3d —, 2006 Ohio 3587, — N.E. 2d —, 2006 Ohio App. LEXIS 3527 (July 13, 2006).

Where a trial court granted summary judgment to various entities who were involved in the care and control of a parking lot in an action by an injured pedestrian and his wife, alleging that the entities' negligence resulted in his having been struck while walking through the parking lot, but the pedestrian and his wife immediately filed a voluntary dismissal of their action under Ohio R. Civ. P. 41(A)(1)(a) prior to the summary judgment order having been time-stamped on the docket, there was no final appealable order in the matter under RC § 2505.02, and an appeal taken from the summary judgment was dismissed. It was noted that such a practice was abusive, but it was allowed by Rule 41 until such time as a legislative change was implemented. Witt v. Lamson, — Ohio App. 3d —, 2006 Ohio 3963, — N.E. 2d —, 2006 Ohio App. LEXIS 3912 (Aug. 3, 2006).

Applicability

Trial court's dismissal of appellee's claims against appellant was a granting of a directed verdict under Ohio R. Civ. P. 50, not a dismissal under Ohio R. Civ. P. 41(B)(2) because a jury had been empaneled at the time that the trial court entered its dismissal, and Ohio R. Civ. P. 41(B)(2) applies only to dismissals in non-jury actions. As a result, the order dismissing the complaint was a final, appealable order, and appellee's challenge to the propriety of the order after a trial was held on appellant's counterclaims that had been later reinstated was dismissed as untimely. Nelson Jewellery Arts Co. v. Fein Designs Co., — Ohio App. 3d —, 2006 Ohio 2276, — N.E. 2d —, 2006 Ohio App. LEXIS 2120 (May 10, 2006).

Where a class of asbestos claimants admittedly could not produce the evidence necessary to comply with RC § 2307.93(C) when it filed its complaint, a trial court erred when it dismissed the action with prejudice, as the statute provided that the court "shall" administratively dismiss the action, not dismiss the action with prejudice. As the class did not fail to prosecute or fail to comply with the Ohio Rules of Civil Procedure, or with any court order, Ohio R. Civ. P. 41(B)(1) was inapplicable. Lambert v. Anchor Packing Co., — Ohio App. 3d —, 2006 Ohio 7098, — N.E. 2d —, 2006 Ohio App. LEXIS 7048 (Dec. 20, 2006).

Arbitration

Because appellees voluntarily dismissed their complaints without prejudice, pursuant to Ohio R. Civ. P. 41, they were permitted to demand arbitration, which was analogous to refiling the action. Bhole, Inc. v. D&A Plumbing & Heating, Inc., — Ohio App. 3d —, 2007 Ohio 3635, — N.E. 2d —, 2007 Ohio App. LEXIS 3323 (July 16, 2007).

Continuance

Trial court's denial of a tenant's motion for a continuance pursuant to Ohio R. Civ. P. 41(A) in a small claims matter initiated by a landlord, seeking recovery of unpaid rent, was an abuse of the trial court's discretion, as the trial court's indication that medical documentation of the tenant's illness was required was error where there was only short notice of the situation, the trial court engaged in ex parte communications in violation of Ohio Code Jud. Conduct Canon 3(B) in making its determination, and there was no pressing need to expedite the matter; there had been no prior continuances, the landlord was not represented by counsel whose schedule would be inconvenienced, and the original trial date was set outside of the time limits under RC § 1925.04(B). Frampton v. Mike & Betty Sekula, — Ohio App. 3d —, 2007 Ohio 5039, — N.E. 2d —, 2007 Ohio App. LEXIS 4461 (Sept. 20, 2007).

Costs and attorney fees

Trial court was without authority to impose court costs on a motorist who voluntarily dismissed his action pursuant to Ohio R. Civ. P. 41(A)(1)(a) against a motor vehicle occupant, arising from an accident between the parties' vehicles, as the motorist had not yet refiled his action and accordingly, the imposition of such costs and the trial court's directive that payment of the costs was a prerequisite to refiling was premature. Under the circumstances, the imposition of court costs was an abuse of discretion. Hanson v. Riccardi, — Ohio App. 3d —, 2007 Ohio 449, — N.E. 2d —, 2007 Ohio App. LEXIS 402 (Feb. 2, 2007).

Although appellant voluntarily dismissed his action pursuant to Ohio R. Civ. P. 41(A)(1)(a), appellees' motion for sanctions and recovery of attorney fees and costs under Ohio R. Civ. P. 11 and RC § 2323.51, which had been filed prior to the dismissal, was properly ruled on by the trial court, as the motion involved a collateral issue that was not based on the merits of the case and accordingly, the trial court had jurisdiction to consider it. The trial court also had authority to assess costs for a voluntarily dismissed action under Ohio R. Civ. P. 41(A)(1)(D). Williams v. Thamann, 173 Ohio App. 3d 426, 2007 Ohio 4320, 878 N.E.2d 1070, 2007 Ohio App. LEXIS 3863 (2007).

Upon appellant's dismissal pursuant to Ohio R. Civ. P. 41(A)(1)(a) of her negligence action against appellee, even though it was the day before trial was set to commence, the trial court no longer had jurisdiction over the matter and accordingly, it abused its discretion in granting appellee's subsequent motion for costs under Rule 41(D) in the event

that appellant refiled her action. Stiriz v. Nissen, — Ohio App. 3d —, 2006 Ohio 3986, — N.E. 2d —, 2006 Ohio App. LEXIS 3959 (Aug. 4, 2006).

When an attorney sought workers' compensation death benefits for a widow, due to the death of her husband, in violation of Ohio R. Civ. P. 11, because he filed a claim for those benefits five months after the widow died, using a form the widow did not sign or date, it was not an abuse of discretion to award attorney fees to an employer, under Rule 11, because of the attorney's willful violation of the Rule, but it was error to award fees under RC § 2323.51 because the widow's purported executrix voluntarily dismissed an appeal of the denial of the claim the attorney filed, under Ohio R. Civ. P. 41(A), which established the date of the final judgment in the case, and the employer did not seek sanctions within 21 days of that date, as required by the statute. Baker v. AK Steel Corp., — Ohio App. 3d —, 2006 Ohio 3895, — N.E. 2d —, 2006 Ohio App. LEXIS 3854 (July 31, 2006).

Directed verdict in bench trial

When a trial court grants a "directed verdict" in a bench trial, an appellate court must first determine whether evidence of substantial, probative value supports each element of a plaintiff's claims. If the plaintiff has presented such evidence and the trial court nevertheless granted a "directed verdict" without weighing the evidence and determining the credibility of the witnesses, then an appellate court cannot treat the directed verdict as a CivR 41(B)(2) involuntary dismissal. The appellate court must remand so the trial court can fulfill its role as trier of fact: Jarupan v. Hanna, 173 Ohio App. 3d 284, 2007 Ohio 5081, 878 N.E.2d 66, 2007 Ohio App. LEXIS 4498 (2007).

Discovery misconduct

As an insurer and a rental car company each filed motions to dismiss an action for failure of an appellant to comply with discovery orders, appellant thereby had notice of the possibility that his action could be dismissed. Such a dismissal for discovery misconduct was necessarily "with prejudice" pursuant to Ohio R. Civ. P. 41(B)(3). Garnett v. Nationwide Prop. Ins., — Ohio App. 3d —, 2007 Ohio 2774, — N.E. 2d —, 2007 Ohio App. LEXIS 2574 (June 7, 2007).

Trial court's dismissal, pursuant to Ohio R. Civ. P. 41(B)(1), of an administrator's fraudulent concealment and bad faith claims against an insurance agency was not an abuse of discretion because (1) the administrator had notice of the administrator's discovery violations on which the dismissal was based, and (2) Ohio R. Civ. P. 37(B)(2)(c) expressly allowed a trial court to dismiss a claim for a discovery violation. Coe v. Grange Mut. Cas. Co., — Ohio App. 3d —, 2007 Ohio 2823, — N.E. 2d —, 2007 Ohio App. LEXIS 2632 (June 8, 2007).

Dismissal after plaintiff's case

Trial court's dismissal pursuant to Ohio R. Civ. P. 41(B)(2) of an alleged assault victim's claim of civil assault was proper where there was a lack of proof regarding the damages suffered; any claims on appeal regarding alleged erroneous evidentiary rulings by the trial court with respect to the alleged assailant's credibility were accordingly harmless, as any change therein would not have cured the failure of proof as to damages. Rieger v. Podeweltz, 2007 Ohio 5988, 2007 Ohio App. LEXIS 5264 (Nov. 9, 2007).

Dismissal for failure to prove damages

Trial court correctly dismissed the case under Ohio R. Civ. P. 41(B)(2) for failure of proof on the issue of damages. Although the alleged victim's proof at trial sufficed to show that the individual had shoved him, or pushed him away, thereby causing him to spill on himself the beer in the cup he was holding, there was no proof of any of the damages he claimed in his complaint, whether relating to embarrassment, mental anguish, pain, or suffering. Rieger v. Podeweltz, 2007 Ohio 5988, 2007 Ohio App. LEXIS 5264 (Nov. 9, 2007).

Double dismissal rule

Grant of a worker's motion under CivR 60(B)(1) for relief from judgment with respect to a second voluntary dismissal that the worker had filed pursuant to CivR 41(A)(1)(a) in an action involving a workers' compensation claim dispute was an abuse of discretion where the worker failed to show entitlement to relief; the worker made a unilateral allegation that the second filing was "in error," but there were no facts or evidence in the record to determine the reasonableness thereof. Smith v. Laidlaw Transp., Inc., — Ohio App. 3d —, 2008 Ohio 1642, — N.E. 2d —, 2008 Ohio App. LEXIS 1409 (Apr. 4, 2008).

Double-dismissal rule of CivR 41(A)(1) applies only when both dismissals were notice dismissals under CivR 41(A)(1)(a): Olynyk v. Scoles, 114 Ohio St. 3d 56, 2007 Ohio 2878, 868 N.E.2d 254, 2007 Ohio LEXIS 1576 (2007).

Evidence sufficient

Trial court properly denied publishing companies' motion under Ohio R. Civ. P. 41(B)(2) to dismiss a printing plant's action for recovery of money due under an account, as the plant properly proved the claim by a preponderance of the evidence where it presented billing records to support its claim of an outstanding debt. Marysville Newspapers, Inc. v. Del. Gazette Co., — Ohio App. 3d —, 2007 Ohio 3838, — N.E. 2d —, 2007 Ohio App. LEXIS 3485 (July 30, 2007).

Final appealable order

When a plaintiff has asserted multiple claims against one defendant, and some of those claims have been ruled upon but not converted into a final order through CivR 54(B), the plaintiff may not create a final order by voluntarily dismissing pursuant to CivR 41(A) the remaining claims against the same defendant: Pattison v. W.W. Grainger, Inc., 120 Ohio St. 3d 142, 2008 Ohio 5276, 897 N.E.2d 126, 2008 Ohio LEXIS 2785 (2008).

After alleged injured parties had dismissed the alleged injured parties' complaints, under Ohio R. Civ. P. 41(A)(2), and refiled the complaints, under the savings statute in RC § 2305.19, a trial court's order dismissing the complaints, which were consolidated, without prejudice for failure to prosecute, was a final, appealable order because the savings statute would not apply if the alleged injured parties tried to file the alleged injured parties' case yet again, even though the case was involuntarily dismissed without prejudice, so the alleged injured parties' claims would be barred by the applicable statutes of limitation, and, thus, the dismissal without prejudice did not leave the alleged injured parties in the same position as the alleged injured parties were in before the alleged injured parties filed the alleged injured parties' action, because the alleged injured parties could not refile. Maxwell v. Forest Fair Mall, — Ohio App. 3d —, 2007 Ohio 3087, — N.E. 2d —, 2007 Ohio App. LEXIS 2834 (June 22, 2007).

Trial court's dismissal of a patient's medical malpractice complaint, under Ohio R. Civ. P. 41(B)(1), was a final appealable order, under RC § 2505.02(B)(1), because the patient could not refile the complaint since the patient had previously dismissed and refiled the complaint after the expiration of the statute of limitations in RC § 2305.113, pursuant to RC § 2305.19(A), so, if the patient were allowed to again refile the patient's complaint, the patient would be refiling a complaint that had been filed after the statute of limitations expired, which was not allowed by § 2305.19(A). Thompson v. Ohio State Univ. Hosps., — Ohio App. 3d —, 2007 Ohio 4668, — N.E. 2d —, 2007 Ohio App. LEXIS 4206 (Sept. 11, 2007).

In a divorce action, the wife was permitted to appeal under RC § 2505.02(B)(1) an involuntary dismissal without prejudice under Ohio R. Civ. P. 41(B)(1) for want of prosecution because if the wife refiled her action, the wife would lose her right to collect the ordered but unpaid child and spousal support payments that had accumulated during the pendency of the divorce. Lippus v. Lippus, — Ohio App. 3d —, 2007 Ohio 6886, — N.E. 2d —, 2007 Ohio App. LEXIS 6001 (Dec. 20, 2007).

Involuntary dismissal

When an assignee suing a consumer for a deficiency judgment related to the consumer's purchase of a used car in another state moved for a directed verdict as to the consumer's counterclaims, the motion was properly viewed as a motion for involuntary dismissal, under Ohio R. Civ. P. 41(B)(2), because the matter was tried to the court, without a jury. D.A.N. Joint Venture III v. Armstrong, — Ohio App. 3d —, 2007 Ohio 898, — N.E. 2d —, 2007 Ohio App. LEXIS 805 (Mar. 2, 2007).

When an assignee suing a consumer for a deficiency judgment related to the consumer's purchase of a used car in another state moved for a directed verdict as to the consumer's counterclaims, the motion was properly viewed as a motion for involuntary dismissal, under Ohio R. Civ. P. 41(B)(2), because the matter was tried to the court, without a jury. D.A.N. Joint Venture III v. Armstrong, — Ohio App. 3d —, 2007 Ohio 898, — N.E. 2d —, 2007 Ohio App. LEXIS 805 (Mar. 2, 2007).

Proper factors for consideration in an Ohio R. Civ. P. 41(B)(1) dismissal with prejudice include the drawn-out history of the litigation, including a plaintiff's failure to respond to interrogatories until threatened with dismissal, and other evidence that a plaintiff is deliberately proceeding in dilatory fashion or has done so in a previously filed and voluntarily dismissed action. Simeone v. Girard City Bd. of Educ., 171 Ohio App. 3d 633, 2007 Ohio 1775, 872 N.E.2d 344, 2007 Ohio App. LEXIS 1610 (2007).

Where a trial court granted a former wife's request to conduct an in camera interview with the parties' child pursuant to RC § 3109.04(B)(2)(b) in furtherance of the wife's request for modification of the parties' shared parenting order, but the trial court never set a date for the interview and thereafter it granted the former husband's motion to involuntarily dismiss the wife's claim pursuant to Ohio R. Civ. P. 41(B)(2) after she concluded her case-in-chief at the merits hearing, such was error because the trial court was required to hold the interview once a request by a party for such an interview was made. Hill v. Hill, — Ohio App. 3d —, 2006 Ohio 5809, — N.E. 2d —, 2006 Ohio App. LEXIS 5782 (Nov. 6, 2006).

Jurisdiction

Once a trial court dismissed an action between the parties with prejudice, based upon their having entered into a settlement of the matter, it no longer had jurisdiction to entertain a motion by one of the parties to enforce the settlement agreement. Bugeja v. Luzik, — Ohio App. 3d —, 2007 Ohio 733, — N.E. 2d —, 2007 Ohio App. LEXIS 682 (Feb. 8, 2007).

Trial court improperly granted a summary judgment to tanning salon owners in a negligence case because a client and her spouse filed a Ohio R. Civ. P. 41(A)(1)(a) dismissal prior to the trial court's ruling on the summary judgment motion; thus, the trial court had no jurisdiction to enter the summary judgment order. Railing v. Shilot, — Ohio App. 3d —, 2007 Ohio 4989, — N.E. 2d —, 2007 Ohio App. LEXIS 4398 (Sept. 18, 2007).

Where a trial court granted summary judgment to a son in a multi-count action by his father, arising from the son's use of a power of attorney that the father had given him during a particular point in time, and thereafter the son voluntarily dismissed his counterclaim pursuant to Ohio R. Civ. P. 41(A)(1)(a), wherein he sought a determination as to the ownership of two wells, the trial court's further amended summary judgment ruling which determined the ownership thereof was error. After the initial grant of summary judgment based on the limitations bar and the son's dismissal of the counterclaim, the matter was resolved in toto and the trial court no longer had jurisdiction to rule on the matter. Emmert v. Emmert, — Ohio App. 3d —, 2006 Ohio 6456, — N.E. 2d —, 2006 Ohio App. LEXIS 6411 (Dec. 5, 2006).

Mass toxic torts

Lone Pine Order is a type of case management order that has been used in other jurisdictions to expedite claims and increase judicial efficiency in mass toxic tort litigation. The trial court's issuance of a Lone Pine order at a stage in the proceedings when there had yet to be any meaningful discovery, followed by the dismissal of the case with prejudice for failure to comply with the order, was an abuse of discretion under the circumstances of the case: Simeone v. Girard City Bd. of Educ., 171 Ohio App. 3d 633, 2007 Ohio 1775, 872 N.E.2d 344, 2007 Ohio App. LEXIS 1610 (2007).

Motion for directed verdict

When, in a bench trial of a suit for breach of contract, a trial court granted one party's motion for a directed verdict, under Ohio R. Civ. P. 50(A), the motion was properly reviewed, on appeal, as one for involuntary dismissal, under Ohio R. Civ. P. 41(B)(2), because a motion for a directed verdict did not apply in a non-jury trial. U.S. Constr. Corp. v. Harbor Bay Estates, — Ohio App. 3d —, 2007 Ohio 3823, — N.E. 2d —, 2007 Ohio App. LEXIS 3496 (July 27, 2007).

Because the standard for a directed verdict under Ohio R. Civ. P. 50(A) was much more rigorous than the standard for dismissal under Ohio R. Civ. P. 41(B)(2), the trial court's dismissal of the complaint under the directed verdict standard satisfied the standard for a Rule 41 dismissal and thus, there was no error. Whitestone Co. v. Stittsworth, — Ohio App. 3d —, 2007 Ohio 233, — N.E. 2d —, 2007 Ohio App. LEXIS 216 (Jan. 23, 2007).

In tenants' appeal from a judgment granting a directed verdict to a landlord in the tenants' suit alleging claims of wrongful eviction and breach of contract, the court reviewed the propriety of the trial court's decision pursuant to the standard set forth in Ohio R. Civ. P. 41(B)(2) and found that the evidence supported the trial court's action in granting a directed verdict to the landlord on the ground that the rental agreement between the parties was unenforceable because it was impossible to perform as the village in which the property was located had ordered the mobile home removed from the property and refused to grant a variance to allow its placement on the property. Though the landlord did not explicitly raise impossibility or illegality as an affirmative defense, as required by Ohio R. Civ. P. 8(C), the parties implicitly consented to try the issue at trial; thus, pursuant to Ohio R. Civ. P. 15(B), the pleadings were amended to conform to the evidence at trial. Mitchell v. Thompson, — Ohio App. 3d —, 2007 Ohio 5362, — N.E. 2d —, 2007 Ohio App. LEXIS 4710 (Oct. 1, 2007).

In tenants' appeal from a judgment granting a directed verdict to a landlord and a mover in the tenants' suit alleging a claim of conversion, the court reviewed the propriety of the trial court's decision pursuant to the standard set forth in Ohio R. Civ. P. 41(B)(2) and found that the evidence supported the trial court's action in granting a directed verdict to the landlord and the mover. The evidence showed that the tenants' property was removed from the landlord's property only after the tenants failed to respond to the landlord's request to remove their property. Mitchell v. Thompson, — Ohio App. 3d —, 2007 Ohio 5362, — N.E. 2d —, 2007 Ohio App. LEXIS 4710 (Oct. 1, 2007).

In tenants' appeal from a judgment granting a directed verdict to a landlord in the tenants' suit alleging a claim of unjust enrichment, the court reviewed the propriety of the trial court's decision pursuant to the standard set forth in Ohio R. Civ. P. 41(B)(2) and found that the evidence supported the trial court's action in granting a directed verdict to the landlord. Some evidence supported the trial court's finding that the tenants and the landlord did not have an agreement

regarding improvements to the land and that the tenant gratuitously improved the land; thus, the trial court's findings that it would not be unjust for the landlord to retain the benefits of the improvements made by the tenants to the landlord's land was appropriate. Mitchell v. Thompson, — Ohio App. 3d —, 2007 Ohio 5362, — N.E. 2d —, 2007 Ohio App. LEXIS 4710 (Oct. 1, 2007).

Motion for dismissal

There was no error in denying the former director's motion for dismissal on the breach of contract claim because it was clear from the record that the only breach of contract claim asserted against the director by the education board was voluntarily dismissed; thus, there was no breach of contract claim remaining against the director at the time of trial. To the extent that the director's Ohio R. Civ. P. 41 motion, made at trial, may have been a general assertion that the board had shown no right to relief, there was no error in the court's decision to decline to render judgment in the declaratory action until the close of all of the evidence. Butler County Joint Voc. Sch. Dist. Bd. of Educ. v. Andrews, — Ohio App. 3d —, 2007 Ohio 5896, — N.E. 2d —, 2007 Ohio App. LEXIS 5184 (Nov. 5, 2007).

— Reasonable opportunity to contest

Trial court's dismissal of appellant's complaint for want of prosecution under Ohio R. Civ. P. 41(B) was improper because, though the trial court provided appellant and his counsel with notice that the case could be dismissed for failure to appear at the final pretrial, it did not provide appellant or his counsel with a reasonable opportunity to defend against dismissal before dismissing the case. Monea v. Lanci, — Ohio App. 3d —, 2007 Ohio 6791, — N.E. 2d —, 2007 Ohio App. LEXIS 5944 (Dec. 17, 2007).

Non-jury actions

Under CivR 41(B)(2), a trial court is not required to construe the evidence in favor of a non-moving party, but rather may weigh the evidence and render judgment. Thus it is within the sound discretion of the court as to whether a case should be dismissed or judgment reserved until the close of all evidence: Hack v. Sand Beach Conservancy Dist., 176 Ohio App. 3d 309, 2008 Ohio 1858, 891 N.E.2d 1228, 2008 Ohio App. LEXIS 1581 (2008).

Notice

Trial court abused its discretion when it dismissed the case without prejudice without first providing notice pursuant to CivR 41(B)(1). Thus the plaintiff was entitled to relief pursuant to CivR 60(B)(5): Montgomery v. Tenneco Auto. Operating, Inc., 183 Ohio App. 3d 164, 2009 Ohio 3394, 916 N.E.2d 530, 2009 Ohio App. LEXIS 2925 (2009).

Trial court erred in dismissing foster parents' adoption petition under Ohio R. Civ. P. 41(B)(1) when the foster parents' counsel did not file a brief requested by the trial court but, instead, filed a motion to withdraw on the date that the brief was due because the foster parents were never notified, either expressly or impliedly, of the possibility that the petition would be dismissed with prejudice if the brief was not timely filed. The trial court should have afforded the foster parents additional time to secure new counsel to file the brief due in the matter. In re C.L.W., — Ohio App. 3d —, 2007 Ohio 3971, — N.E. 2d —, 2007 Ohio App. LEXIS 3592 (Aug. 3, 2007).

It was reversible error for a trial court to dismiss alleged injured parties' consolidated complaints without prejudice for failure to prosecute because the trial court gave no notice of the trial court's intention to dismiss and the applicable rule, which was Ohio R. Civ. P. 41(B)(1), explicitly required the trial court to provide the alleged injured parties with notice and an opportunity to be heard prior to dismissal. Maxwell v. Forest Fair Mall, — Ohio App. 3d —, 2007 Ohio 3087, — N.E. 2d —, 2007 Ohio App. LEXIS 2834 (June 22, 2007).

Trial court abused its discretion in dismissing plaintiff's complaint with prejudice under Ohio R. Civ. P. 41(B) because the record disclosed no notice to plaintiff or its counsel that the action was subject to dismissal with prejudice, and Ohio R. Civ. P. 41(B)(1) required notice before dismissal. Palisades Collection, LLC v. Person, — Ohio App. 3d —, 2007 Ohio 2362, — N.E. 2d —, 2007 Ohio App. LEXIS 2197 (May 11, 2007).

Trial court erred in denying a landlord's motion for summary judgment in a tenant's refiled personal injury action, arising from her fall on unlit stairs, as the tenant had filed a notice of dismissal of her original action and pursuant to Ohio R. Civ. P. 41(A)(1), that dismissal became effective on the date that it was filed rather than on the date that the trial court entered judgment thereon. As the refiled action was not filed within one year pursuant to RC § 2305.19(A) and the applicable limitations period under RC § 2305.10 had expired, the action was time-barred. Hawkins v. Innovative Prop. Mgmt., — Ohio App. 3d —, 2006 Ohio 6153, — N.E. 2d —, 2006 Ohio App. LEXIS 6123 (Nov. 22, 2006).

Review of a dismissal for failure to prosecute involved two assessments: first, an appellate court had to determine if the trial court provided the plaintiff with sufficient notice prior to dismissal, and, second, an appellate court had to determine whether the dismissal constituted an abuse of discretion. Carmel Fin. Corp. v. Leal, — Ohio App. 3d —, 2006 Ohio 5618, — N.E. 2d —, 2006 Ohio App. LEXIS 5608 (Oct. 27, 2006).

Generally, notice was a prerequisite to dismissal for failure to prosecute under Ohio R. Civ. P. 41(B)(1), and the purpose of notice was to provide the party who was in default an opportunity to explain the default or to correct it, or to explain why the case should not be dismissed with prejudice, and failure to give notice under the Rule constituted reversible error. Carmel Fin. Corp. v. Leal, — Ohio App. 3d —, 2006 Ohio 5618, — N.E. 2d —, 2006 Ohio App. LEXIS 5608 (Oct. 27, 2006).

When, in a collection action, a trial court denied a creditor's motion for a continuance and dismissed the case for failure to prosecute, it could properly vacate that dismissal because it had not given the creditor notice, under Ohio R. Civ. P. 41(B)(1), of its intention to dismiss the case, so the creditor had no opportunity to respond, and the dismissal was, thus, reversible. Carmel Fin. Corp. v. Leal, — Ohio App. 3d —, 2006 Ohio 5618, — N.E. 2d —, 2006 Ohio App. LEXIS 5608 (Oct. 27, 2006).

Trial court's dismissal pursuant to Ohio R. Civ. P. 41(B)(1) of an employer's appeal of an order from the Industrial Commission of Ohio, wherein an employee was awarded workers' compensation benefits, was too harsh where due process notice under Ohio Const. art. I, § 16 to the employee was not provided; the trial court had not indicated to the employee that it intended to enter a dismissal due to the employee's failure to have filed a timely petition under RC § 4123.512(D), there was no indication that the employee was even aware of his filing obligation, the trial court's entry of a scheduling order with respect to discovery, motions, and a trial date belied its intent to dismiss the matter, and the employee was not given an opportunity to explain why dismissal would not be proper. Franklin v. DaimlerChrysler Corp., — Ohio App. 3d —, 2006 Ohio 5620, — N.E.2d —, 2006 Ohio App. LEXIS 5607 (Oct. 27, 2006).

When, in a bank's suit against a debtor on a credit card, the trial court sent the parties notice of an "evidentiary hearing," without calling it a trial, and, at that hearing, the bank was not prepared to proceed with trial, it was improper for the trial court to consider that hearing as a commencement of trial, for purposes of voluntary dismissal, under Ohio R. Civ. P. 41(A), but, whether or not the hearing properly commenced trial, it was not an abuse of discretion for the trial court to deny the bank's oral motion to voluntarily dismiss, under Ohio R. Civ.

P. 41(A)(1), because that rule required written notice of dismissal which the bank did not provide, nor did it seek leave of the trial court to file such a written notice. Capital One Bank v. Woten, — Ohio App. 3d —, 2006 Ohio 4848, — N.E. 2d —, 2006 Ohio App. LEXIS 4755 (Sept. 18, 2006).

Plaintiff's absolute right to voluntarily dismiss under Ohio R. Civ. P. 41(A)(1) required filing of a written notice of dismissal, and an oral motion would not suffice. Capital One Bank v. Woten, — Ohio App. 3d —, 2006 Ohio 4848, — N.E. 2d —, 2006 Ohio App. LEXIS 4755 (Sept. 18, 2006).

Trial commenced in a civil trial, for purposes of Ohio R. Civ. P. 41(A)(1), when a jury was impaneled and sworn, or, in a bench trial, at opening statements. Capital One Bank v. Woten, — Ohio App. 3d —, 2006 Ohio 4848, — N.E. 2d —, 2006 Ohio App. LEXIS 4755 (Sept. 18, 2006).

Trial court's sua sponte striking of a mortgagee's notice of dismissal pursuant to Ohio R. Civ. P. 41(A)(1)(a) was an abuse of discretion in the mortgagee's foreclosure action, as a trial was not held and although a foreclosure sale was held and the property purchased through a bid, the sale was not completed because it had not been confirmed by the trial court and title had not been transferred. The mortgagee's unilaterally self-executing notice of voluntary dismissal was not invalidated by the unconfirmed sheriff's sale. Northern Ohio Inv. Co. v. Yarger, — Ohio App. 3d —, 2006 Ohio 4658, — N.E. 2d —, 2006 Ohio App. LEXIS 4589 (Sept. 8, 2006).

Trial court erred in dismissing, pursuant to Civ. R. 41(B)(1), appellant's complaint for failure to prosecute when he did not appear on the date set for trial because the record did not indicate that appellant received any notice that the case would be dismissed if he failed to appear. Smith v. Ramsey, — Ohio App. 3d —, 2006 Ohio 4859, — N.E. 2d —, 2006 Ohio App. LEXIS 4775 (Sept. 8, 2006).

Trial court did not err in dismissing the attorneys claims for defamation and civil conspiracy against defendants, under Ohio R. Civ. P. 41, because, since the attorney had knowledge that dismissal of his claims was a possibility and had ample opportunity to oppose dismissal, the trial court's dismissal of his claims, as requested by defendants, did not violate due process. Additionally, the interplay of the appellate court's two previous opinions entitled defendants to judgment as a matter of law. Cooke v. United Dairy Farmers, Inc., — Ohio App. 3d —, 2006 Ohio 4365, — N.E. 2d —, 2006 Ohio App. LEXIS 4276 (Aug. 24, 2006).

Trial court abused its discretion by denying a landlord's motion to vacate an order awarding summary judgment to a tenant and dismissing the landlord's counterclaim following the landlord's absence from the initial pretrial conference because the oversight of the landlord's counsel in noting an incorrect time for the pretrial conference did not exhibit a deliberate act of ignoring a judicial directive such as constituted excusable neglect, the landlord asserted a meritorious defense, and filed the motion in a timely manner. The trial court also erred in granting the tenant's oral motion for summary judgment because the landlord never had a chance to respond and in dismissing the counterclaim because the trial court failed to give the landlord the notice required by Ohio R. Civ. P. 41(B)(1) prior to dismissal of the counterclaim. Maddox v. Ward, — Ohio App. 3d —, 2006 Ohio 4099, — N.E. 2d —, 2006 Ohio App. LEXIS 4073 (Aug. 10, 2006).

Although a trial court may have dismissed a vexatious litigator's action without notice pursuant to Ohio R. Civ. P. 41(B)(1), his mandamus action under RC § 2731.04, seeking to compel the judge to reinstate and rule on the case was denied where the dismissal without notice was appropriate, regardless of RC § 2323.52, because the complaint was frivolous. Grundstein v Greene, — Ohio App. 3d —, 2006 Ohio 2205, — N.E. 2d —, 2006 Ohio App. LEXIS 2064 (Apr. 28, 2006).

When a bank sued an attorney and the attorney filed counterclaims, it was not error for the trial court to dismiss the counterclaims, under Ohio R. Civ. P. 37(B)(2)(c), due to the attorney's failure to respond to discovery, because the attorney had notice, in the bank's motion for sanctions, that it would seek such relief, and this notice was sufficient, under Ohio R. Civ. P. 41(B)(1). First Nat'l Bank of Southwestern Ohio v. Doellman, — Ohio App. 3d —, 2006 Ohio 1663, — N.E. 2d —, 2006 Ohio App. LEXIS 1564 (Apr. 3, 2006).

Procedure

In a bench trial, a trial court erred in entering a "directed verdict" under Ohio R. Civ. P. 50(A)(4) for a contractor in an owner's breach of contract action, as she provided evidence on each element of the claims with respect to the breaches of two contracts and the damages that she incurred thereby, and as such, the trial court could only have denied her claim if it weighed the evidence or judged the credibility of it and determined that the owner's testimony and exhibits was not believable; however, that was done under an involuntary dismissal standard pursuant to Ohio R. Civ. P. 41(B)(2), which should have been the proper procedural vehicle used by the trial court, such that its improper standard of review resulted in an erroneous determination. Jarupan v. Hanna, 173 Ohio App. 3d 284, 2007 Ohio 5081, 878 N.E.2d 66, 2007 Ohio App. LEXIS 4498 (2007).

Relation back

When clients timely filed a legal malpractice claim against their attorney after they had filed for bankruptcy, after which the bankruptcy trustee abandoned the claim, the clients became the real parties in interest as to the claim, as if no bankruptcy was ever filed, and the trustee's abandonment, after the statute of limitations expired, ratified the claim, under Ohio R. Civ. P. 17(A), and the ratification related back to its original filing, so the clients were not time-barred from pursuing it, because (1) the claim failed otherwise than on its merits, when they voluntarily dismissed it, under Ohio R. Civ. P. 41(A)(1)(a), (2) when they refiled the claim, the parties to the original and refiled claims were identical, and (3) the refiled claim was refiled one minute after the initial claim was dismissed, so the savings statute, RC § 2305.19(A), applied. Newman v. Enriquez, 171 Ohio App. 3d 117, 2007 Ohio 1934, 869 N.E.2d 735, 2007 Ohio App. LEXIS 1741 (2007).

Res judicata

Prior dismissal for lack of subject matter jurisdiction is not a prior final judgment for purposes of res judicata under Ohio law: Sheridan v. Metro. Life Ins. Co., 182 Ohio App. 3d 107, 2009 Ohio 1808, 911 N.E.2d 950, 2009 Ohio App. LEXIS 1524 (2009).

Appellants' second suit against a manufacturer was improperly dismissed on the basis of res judicata because, although the trial court had granted summary judgment to the manufacturer in the first suit, the order was not a final appealable order under RC § 2505.02 as claims remained pending against other defendants and the order did not contain Ohio R. Civ. P. 54(B) language. Appellants' subsequent Ohio R. Civ. P. 41(A) dismissal of the entire case dissolved all interlocutory orders, including the order granting summary judgment. Hutchinson v. Beazer East, Inc., — Ohio App. 3d —, 2006 Ohio 6761, — N.E. 2d —, 2006 Ohio App. LEXIS 6672 (Dec. 21, 2006).

Where a property owner voluntarily dismissed his counterclaim against a builder pursuant to Ohio R. Civ. P. 41(A)(1) in a prior action by the builder, arising from a dispute between the parties over payment due under a construction contract, RC § 2305.19 was not applicable for purposes of the owner's refiling of the counterclaim in a subsequent action, as the counterclaim had not been deemed time-barred in the first action. As the counterclaim was deemed compulsory pursuant to Ohio R. Civ. P. 13(A) in the first action, res judicata operated to bar the second action and dismissal by the trial

court was proper. Carlton v. Alar Dev. Co., — Ohio App. 3d —, 2006 Ohio 6877, — N.E. 2d —, 2006 Ohio App. LEXIS 6797 (Dec. 22, 2006).

Sanctions for misconduct

When an attorney voluntarily dismissed his action against an expert witness, under Ohio R. Civ. P. 41(A)(1), and refiled it in another court, the court in which the action was first filed had jurisdiction to consider the expert's motion for sanctions against the attorney, under Ohio R. Civ. P. 11, because it could consider collateral issues not related to the merits of the action, so the attorney was not entitled to a writ of prohibition to bar the first trial court from proceeding with a consideration of the motion for sanctions because the court did not patently and unambiguously lack jurisdiction. State ex rel. Stifel v. Stokes, — Ohio App. 3d —, 2007 Ohio 997, — N.E. 2d —, 2007 Ohio App. LEXIS 986 (Mar. 2, 2007).

Saving statute

As the time-extension provisions of Ohio R. Civ. P. 6(B) were not applicable to the Ohio saving statute, RC § 2305.19, where an employee in an employer's workers' compensation appeal pursuant to RC § 4123.512 voluntarily dismissed her complaint without prejudice pursuant to Ohio R. Civ. P. 41(A)(1)(a), her failure to re-file within the one-year period pursuant to RC § 2305.19 justified the trial court's grant of a judgment on the pleadings to the employer. Hughes v. Federal Mogul Ignition Co., — Ohio App. 3d —, 2007 Ohio 2021, — N.E. 2d —, 2007 Ohio App. LEXIS 1891 (Apr. 26, 2007).

Where an employer initiated an appeal from an award of workers' compensation to an injured employee and the employee filed his complaint pursuant to RC § 4123.512(D), but the employee thereafter filed a voluntary dismissal of the complaint under Ohio R. Civ. P. 41(A) and he failed to refile the action within the one-year savings provision of RC § 2305.19, the trial court properly granted judgment for the employer. Robinson v. Kokosing Constr. Co., — Ohio App. 3d —, 2006 Ohio 1532, — N.E. 2d —, 2006 Ohio App. LEXIS 1396 (Mar. 30, 2006).

When claimants against a decedent's estate timely filed those claims and timely filed an action in the trial court to enforce them, under RC § 2117.06, which they voluntarily dismissed, under Ohio R. Civ. P. 41(A)(1), they could refile the claims, despite the limitations in RC § 2117.12, because nothing in the savings statute, RC § 2305.19, indicated that it did not apply to claims against an estate, and nothing in RC § 2117.12 indicated that the savings statute did not apply to their claims. Vitantonio, Inc. v. Baxter, — Ohio App. 3d —, 2006 Ohio 1685, — N.E. 2d —, 2006 Ohio App. LEXIS 1543 (Mar. 31, 2006).

Standing

In a probate dispute between a decedent's executrix and the mother of the decedent's illegitimate grandchildren, when the executrix voluntarily dismissed her claims against the mother, under Ohio R. Civ. P. 41(A), this did not deprive the mother of standing, because the mother had filed claims against the executrix, and the mother was the guardian of the decedent's lineal descendants. Kasapis v. High Point Furniture Co., — Ohio App. 3d —, 2006 Ohio 255, — N.E. 2d —, 2006 Ohio App. LEXIS 211 (Jan. 25, 2006).

Stipulation of dismissal

As an employer who appealed pursuant to RC § 4123.512 from a decision by the Industrial Commission of Ohio, and an employee who filed a complaint in the trial court based on the same issue, entered into a joint notice of voluntary dismissal pursuant to Ohio R. Civ. P. 41(A)(1)(b), both of their documents were dismissed; as neither one re-filed their appeal or complaint within the one-year period of the savings statute, RC § 2305.19, the employer's motion for judgment on the pleadings pursuant to Ohio R. Civ. P. 12(C), which was filed more than four years after the dismissal, was properly stricken because the trial court lacked jurisdiction. Feckner v. Donley's, — Ohio App. 3d —, 2007 Ohio 5335, — N.E. 2d —, 2007 Ohio App. LEXIS 4694 (Oct. 4, 2007).

Two-dismissal rule

When a plaintiff files an instruction for a clerk to attempt service of a complaint that was filed more than a year prior, the instruction, by operation of law, is a notice dismissal of the claims, and if the plaintiff had previously filed a notice dismissing a complaint making the same claim, the instruction, by operation of law, is a second notice dismissal, resulting in dismissal with prejudice of the claims: Sisk & Assocs. v. Comm. to Elect Timothy Grendell, 123 Ohio St. 3d 447, 2009 Ohio 5591, 917 N.E.2d 271, 2009 Ohio LEXIS 2994 (2009).

In a matter where an employee appealed the decision of the Industrial Commission of Ohio to disallow his workers' compensation claim, the double dismissal rule under Ohio R. Civ. P. 41(A)(1)(a) was inapplicable to bar the employee's filing of a third notice of appeal therefrom. The first dismissal was by court order under Rule 41(B)(1) for the employee's failure to prosecute and the second dismissal was by stipulation of the parties under Rule 41(A)(1)(b), such that neither constituted a "notice" dismissal for purposes of the double dismissal rule. Conway v. RPM, Inc., et al., — Ohio App. 3d —, 2007 Ohio 1007, — N.E. 2d —, 2007 Ohio App. LEXIS 989 (Mar. 8, 2007).

Mortgagee's two prior foreclosure actions against a mortgagor, which it voluntarily dismissed pursuant to Ohio R. Civ. P. 41(A)(1), did not bar it from bringing a third foreclosure action against the mortgagor, as the two-dismissal rule and res judicata were inapplicable because the third foreclosure action listed a default date that was subsequent to the second action's dismissal and accordingly, covered different months and stated a new claim. As the mortgagor had failed to attach the prior two complaints to his summary judgment motion, the appellate court could not consider them pursuant to Ohio R. App. P. 9(A) in order to determine if the third action stated a new claim, although they were included in the mortgagor's brief on appeal. United States Bank Nat'l Ass'n v. Gullotta, — Ohio App. 3d —, 2007 Ohio 2085, — N.E. 2d —, 2007 Ohio App. LEXIS 1935 (Apr. 30, 2007).

Mortgage company's failure to appeal the denial of its first motion for relief from judgment did not bar its subsequent motion, given the subsequent events that provided the basis for the motion under Ohio R. Civ. P. 60(B)(4). At the time that the trial court denied the first motion for relief from judgment, the court had already rejected the debtor's argument that the two-dismissal rule barred the third foreclosure action; thus, the company's claims remained pending in the third foreclosure action. Chase Manhattan Bank v. Jenkins, — Ohio App. 3d —, 2007 Ohio 3622, — N.E. 2d —, 2007 Ohio App. LEXIS 3314 (July 17, 2007).

Home purchaser was subject to double dismissal rule in Ohio R. Civ. P. 41(A)(1)(a) because while the purchaser's initial fraud complaint was filed in the small claims division of municipal court, her dismissal without prejudice was not a nullity in that case as the small claims division only lacked subject matter jurisdiction under RC § 1925.02(A)(2) over punitive damages. Fromer v. DeVictor, — Ohio App. 3d —, — N.E. 2d —, 2007 Ohio App. LEXIS 4489 (Sept. 27, 2007).

Even if the student had timely filed her claims against the university, the claims had been adjudicated on the merits and thus, the doctrine of res judicata barred any further action on such claims. Her second notice of dismissal of her fourth complaint operated as an adjudication on the merits, pursuant to the two-dismissal rule set forth in Ohio R. Civ. P. 41(A)(1), and her filing of her third complaint prior to her dismissal of her fourth complaint did not affect the preclusive effect of the fourth complaint's dismissal. Boozer v. University of Cincinnati Sch. of Law, — Ohio App. 3d —, 2006 Ohio 2610, — N.E. 2d —, 2006 Ohio App. LEXIS 2426 (May 25, 2006).

Voluntary dismissal

When, in a dispute between a home builder and home owners, the builder waived its contractual right to arbitration by engaging in conduct inconsistent with the assertion of that right, its purported voluntary dismissal of its claim against the homeowners, under Ohio R. Civ. P. 41(A)(2), did not revoke this waiver because the trial court properly denied the builder's motion to dismiss as the builder's claims were inextricably intertwined with the owners' counterclaim against the builder, so there was no dismissal and, hence, no revocation. G.A. White Enterprises Custom Homes v. Black, — Ohio App. 3d —, 2007 Ohio 802, — N.E. 2d —, 2007 Ohio App. LEXIS 726 (Feb. 23, 2007).

When, in a dispute between a home builder and home owners, the builder waived its contractual right to arbitration by engaging in conduct inconsistent with the assertion of that right, its purported voluntary dismissal of its claim against the homeowners, under Ohio R. Civ. P. 41(A)(2), did not revoke this waiver because the trial court properly denied the builder's motion to dismiss as the builder's claims were inextricably intertwined with the owners' counterclaim against the builder, so there was no dismissal and, hence, no revocation. G.A. White Enterprises Custom Homes v. Black, — Ohio App. 3d —, 2007 Ohio 802, — N.E. 2d —, 2007 Ohio App. LEXIS 726 (Feb. 23, 2007).

After a child support enforcement agency determined that there were no public monies due and owing as a result of the birth of two children, for which a father's paternity had just been established, its withdrawal of the claim for maternity expenses and past care was not a dismissal of the entire action and did not amount to a voluntary dismissal under Ohio R. Civ. P. 41(A); it had also sought other support on behalf of the children. S/O, CSEA, ex rel., K.S. v. T.M., — Ohio App. 3d —, 2007 Ohio 984, — N.E. 2d —, 2007 Ohio App. LEXIS 925 (Mar. 8, 2007).

When an employee sued an employer for wrongful discharge and the employer filed various counterclaims, prompting the employee to claim the counterclaims were retaliatory, after which the employer voluntarily dismissed its counterclaims, under Ohio R. Civ. P. 41(A)(1), summary judgment dismissing the employee's claims that the counterclaims were retaliatory was error because (1) this allowed the employer to refile its counterclaims, as no judgment on the merits of those claims had been rendered, while barring the employee, under the doctrine of res judicata, from refiling the employee's responsive claims, and (2) the fact that the counterclaims were withdrawn did not change the fact that they were filed and that the employee suffered additional expense as a result, so there was a genuine issue of material fact as to whether the counterclaims were retaliatory and whether the employee was entitled to damages. Feurer v. Ohio Heartland Community Action Comm'n, — Ohio App. 3d —, 2007 Ohio 2278, — N.E. 2d —, 2007 Ohio App. LEXIS 2115 (May 14, 2007).

Appeal filed by appellant from a trial court's decision granting in part and denying in part appellees' motion to dismiss and motion for judgment on the pleadings was dismissed because appellant's notice of dismissal, stating that appellant voluntarily dismissed "this action, including all remaining claims," constituted a dismissal of the entire case pursuant to Ohio R. Civ. P. 41(A)(1)(a) and not just the remaining claims; thus, the court lacked jurisdiction to consider the appeal. Wilson v. Vaccariello, — Ohio App. 3d —, 2007 Ohio 2688, — N.E. 2d —, 2007 Ohio App. LEXIS 2491 (June 1, 2007).

Appeal filed by appellant from a trial court's decision granting in part and denying in part appellees' motion to dismiss and motion for judgment on the pleadings was dismissed because appellant's notice of dismissal, stating that appellant voluntarily dismissed "this action, including all remaining claims," constituted a dismissal of the entire case pursuant to Ohio R. Civ. P. 41(A)(1)(a) and not just the remaining claims; thus, the court lacked jurisdiction to consider the appeal. Wilson v. Vaccariello, — Ohio App. 3d —, 2007 Ohio 2694, — N.E. 2d —, 2007 Ohio App. LEXIS 2496 (June 1, 2007).

After summary judgment was granted to appellees on employee's age discrimination claim, the employee acted properly in voluntarily dismissing his remaining public policy claim, instead of amending his complaint to dismiss both of the claims in the multi-count complaint. A plaintiff could, under Ohio R. Civ. P. 41(A)(1)(a), voluntarily dismiss a single cause of action or multiple causes of action in a multi-count complaint in order to create a final order. Pattison v. Grainger, — Ohio App. 3d —, 2007 Ohio 3081, — N.E. 2d —, 2007 Ohio App. LEXIS 2860 (June 21, 2007).

Employee's appeal from a grant of summary judgment on his age discrimination claim was dismissed as untimely. When the employee voluntarily dismissed his other claim under Ohio R. Civ. P. 41(A)(1)(a), he converted the non-final summary judgment into a final order, and since the dismissal became effective upon filing, the notice of appeal, filed more than 30 days later, was untimely under Ohio R. App. P. 4(A). Pattison v. Grainger, — Ohio App. 3d —, 2007 Ohio 3081, — N.E. 2d —, 2007 Ohio App. LEXIS 2860 (June 21, 2007).

As an employee, through his counsel, filed a voluntary dismissal pursuant to Ohio R. Civ. P. 41(A)(1) of his personal injury action against his employer, which dismissal did not indicate that a refiling was required within one year, the trial court did not err in denying the employee's later motion for relief from the dismissal judgment pursuant to Ohio R. Civ. P. 60(B), as the voluntary dismissal was not a final order within Rule 60, such that the trial court lacked jurisdiction to grant relief from it. The employee had refiled his action within one year but it was during a bankruptcy of the employer, such that any litigation was stayed, and the stay was lifted prior to the termination of the limitations period. Lowenborg v. Oglebay Norton Co., — Ohio App. 3d —, 2007 Ohio 3408, — N.E. 2d —, 2007 Ohio App. LEXIS 3177 (July 5, 2007).

Appellant's voluntary dismissal of "the above captioned case," filed after the trial court dismissed appellant's claims as to certain defendants but provided that the case was to proceed as to the remaining claims, constituted a dismissal of the entire case pursuant to Ohio R. Civ. P. 41(A)(1)(a), not just the remaining claims. The court lacked jurisdiction to consider the appeal. Cregar v. City of Warren, — Ohio App. 3d —, 2007 Ohio 3970, — N.E. 2d —, 2007 Ohio App. LEXIS 3584 (Aug. 3, 2007).

As appellant voluntarily dismissed his original action under Ohio R. Civ. P. 41(A)(1)(a) and then he refiled the action one month later, the trial court's dismissal with prejudice of both actions pursuant to Rule 41(B)(1) was error, as the original action was no longer pending and accordingly, the trial court lacked jurisdiction to rule on the merits thereof or to dismiss it for any reason. As the first action was not pending, the second action was not prematurely filed and that basis for dismissal by the trial court was also error. Williams v. Thamann, 173 Ohio App. 3d 426, 2007 Ohio 4320, 878 N.E.2d 1070, 2007 Ohio App. LEXIS 3863 (2007).

Trial court's dismissal with prejudice for failure to prosecute was a legal nullity because the voluntary dismissal had already terminated the trial court's jurisdiction to rule on the merits of the original case. The court's denial of fees and costs as a sanction was not an abuse of discretion because the trial court maintained jurisdiction over this collateral issue: Williams v. Thamann, 173 Ohio App. 3d 426, 2007 Ohio 4320, 878 N.E.2d 1070, 2007 Ohio App. LEXIS 3863 (2007).

Voluntary dismissal under CivR 41(A) requires unequivocal action by the plaintiff, either in the form of a motion that complies with the specificity requirements of CivR 7 or in a notice that expresses the plaintiff's intentions clearly from the form and content of the document: Sunkin v. Collision Pro,

Inc., 174 Ohio App. 3d 56, 2007 Ohio 6046, 880 N.E.2d 947, 2007 Ohio App. LEXIS 5323 (2007).

When a construction company sued a corporation for breach of contract, a prompt payment statute violation, and unjust enrichment, and was granted summary judgment and damages on its breach of contract claim, but it was not found that there was no just reason to delay an appeal, under Ohio R. Civ. P. 54(B), nor were the other claims properly voluntarily dismissed, under Ohio R. Civ. P. 41(A) by a notice of dismissal, stipulation, or journalized court order, those claims remained pending and an appellate court had no jurisdiction, under Ohio R. App. P. 12(A)(1)(a), or RC § 2505.02, to hear an appeal of the breach of contract judgment. Spano Bros. Constr. Co. v. Adolph Johnson & Son Co., — Ohio App. 3d —, 2006 Ohio 4083, — N.E. 2d —, 2006 Ohio App. LEXIS 4039 (Aug. 9, 2006).

— Before trial

When a landlord sued tenants for possession, back rent, damages to the leased premises, and punitive damages and attorney fees, and an insurer intervened to assert a subrogation claim, the insurer's voluntary dismissal of its claim, pursuant to Ohio R. Civ. P. 41(A)(1)(a), was not improper because it was filed before the "commencement of trial" on the subrogation issue. Love Props., Inc. v. Kyles, — Ohio App. 3d —, 2007 Ohio 1966, — N.E. 2d —, 2007 Ohio App. LEXIS 1772 (Apr. 23, 2007).

Workers' compensation

Second voluntary dismissal under CivR 41(A)(1)(a) by an employee-claimant filed after the parties had agreed to settle a claim in an employer-initiated workers' compensation appeal pursuant to RC § 4123.512 is not a final judicial determination that payments made to the employee should not have been made, when the court of common pleas has not entered judgment to that effect: State ex rel. Dillard Dep't Stores v. Ryan, 122 Ohio St. 3d 241, 2009 Ohio 2683, 910 N.E.2d 438, 2009 Ohio LEXIS 1604 (2009).

RULE 42. Consolidation; separate trials

(A) Consolidation.

(1) *Generally.* When actions involving a common question of law or fact are pending before a court, that court after a hearing may order a joint hearing or trial of any or all the matters in issue in the actions; it may order some or all of the actions consolidated; and it may make such orders concerning proceedings therein as may tend to avoid unnecessary costs or delay.

(2) *Asbestos, silicosis, or mixed dust disease actions.* In tort actions involving an asbestos claim, a silicosis claim, or a mixed dust disease claim, the court may consolidate pending actions for case management purposes. For purposes of trial, the court may consolidate pending actions only with the consent of all parties. Absent the consent of all parties, the court may consolidate, for purposes of trial, only those pending actions relating to the same exposed person and members of the exposed person's household.

(3) As used in division (A)(2) of this rule:

(a) "Asbestos claim" has the same meaning as in section 2307.91 of the Revised Code;

(b) "Silicosis claim" and "mixed dust disease claim" have the same meaning as in section 2307.84 of the Revised Code;

(c) In reference to an asbestos claim, "tort action" has the same meaning as in section 2307.91 of the Revised Code;

(d) In reference to a silicosis claim or a mixed dust disease claim, "tort action" has the same meaning as in section 2307.84 of the Revised Code.

(B) **Separate trials.** The court, after a hearing, in furtherance of convenience or to avoid prejudice, or when separate trials will be conducive to expedition and economy, may order a separate trial of any claim, cross-claim, counterclaim, or third-party claim, or of any separate issue or of any number of claims, cross-claims, counterclaims, or third-party claims, or issues, always preserving inviolate the right to trial by jury.

History: Amended, eff 7-1-05.

NOTES TO DECISIONS

ANALYSIS

Bifurcation
Final order
Separate trials

Bifurcation

There was no abuse of discretion in the trial court's decision to bifurcate the trial to determine the questions of law at a bench trial and preserve any remaining issues of fact for a jury trial because determination of the competing declaratory actions rested on the court's interpretation of the agreement between the education board and the corporation. As the threshold questions presented were questions of law relating to contract interpretation, bifurcation of the case for a determination of the questions of law at a bench trial was not only appropriate, but necessary. Butler County Joint Voc. Sch. Dist. Bd. of Educ. v. Andrews, — Ohio App. 3d —, 2007 Ohio 5896, — N.E. 2d —, 2007 Ohio App. LEXIS 5184 (Nov. 5, 2007).

Although the timing of both the filing of the motion to bifurcate and the ruling on the motion was distasteful considering the preparation and associated costs for that type of litigation; the timing alone was not enough to rise to the level of an abuse of discretion. The parents could not show any clear correlation between the timing and the presentation of their case as resulting in a negative outcome. Spencer v. Lakeview Sch. Dist., — Ohio App. 3d —, 2006 Ohio 3429, — N.E. 2d —, 2006 Ohio App. LEXIS 3370 (June 30, 2006).

Final order

Trial court's denial of a property management company's motion under Ohio R. Civ. P. 42(B) to bifurcate the liability and punitive damage issues in a matter against it brought by apartment complex tenants was not a final appealable order pursuant to RC § 2505.02, as it did not affect any of the company's substantial rights which determined the action or prevented a judgment, and it was not a special proceeding. The appellate court lacked jurisdiction over the matter pursuant to Ohio Const. art. IV, § 3(B)(2). Finley v. First Realty Prop. Managment, Ltd., — Ohio App. 3d —, 2007 Ohio 2888, — N.E. 2d —, 2007 Ohio App. LEXIS 2686 (June 13, 2007).

Separate trials

Trial court did not abuse its discretion in denying a guarantor's motion under Ohio R. Civ. P. 42 to consolidate two cases, as the cases involved two different types of instruments signed at different times; one case was based on a default on a cognovit note which was guaranteed, and the other case involved a more general credit guaranty for a merchant with no confession of judgment. World Tire Corp. v. Webb, — Ohio App. 3d —, 2007 Ohio 5135, — N.E. 2d —, 2007 Ohio App. LEXIS 4517 (Sept. 27, 2007).

RULE 43. [Reserved]

NOTES TO DECISIONS

ANALYSIS

Transacting business in Ohio

Transacting business in Ohio

Kentucky resident transacted business in Ohio where, although the vehicle was located in Kentucky and picked up and paid for there, the negotiations and dealings for its sale were primarily in Ohio. There were sufficient contacts with Ohio to satisfy due process. Muzzin v. Brooks, 168 Ohio App. 3d 231, 2006 Ohio 3844, 859 N.E.2d 584, 2006 Ohio App. LEXIS 3811 (2006).

RULE 44. Proof of official record

(A) **Authentication.**

(1) **Domestic.** An official record, or an entry therein, kept within a state or within the United States or within a territory or other jurisdiction of the United States, when admissible for any purpose, may be evidenced by an official publication thereof or by a copy attested by the officer having the legal custody of the record, or by his deputy, and accompanied by a certificate that such officer has the custody. The certificate may be made by a judge of a court of record in which the record is kept or may be made by any public officer having a seal of office and having official duties in the political subdivision in which the record is kept, authenticated by the seal of his office.

(2) **Foreign.** A foreign official record, or an entry therein, when admissible for any purpose, may be evidenced by an official publication thereof; or a copy thereof, attested by a person authorized to make the attestation, and accompanied by a final certification as to the genuineness of the signature and official position (a) of the attesting person or (b) of any foreign official whose certificate of genuineness of signature and official position relates to the attestation or is in a chain of certificates of genuineness of signature and official position relating to the attestation. A final certification may be made by a secretary of embassy or legation, consul general, consul, vice consul, or consular agent of the United States, or a diplomatic or consular official of the foreign country assigned or accredited to the United States. If reasonable opportunity has been given to all parties to investigate the authenticity and accuracy of the documents, the court may, for good cause shown, (a) admit an attested copy without final certification or (b) permit the foreign official record to be evidenced by an attested summary with or without a final certification.

(B) **Lack of record.** A written statement that after diligent search no record or entry of a specified tenor is found to exist in the records designated by the statement, authenticated as provided in subdivision (A)(1) of this rule in the case of a domestic record, or complying with the requirements of subdivision (A)(2) of this rule for a summary in the case of a foreign record, is admissible as evidence that the records contain no such record or entry.

(C) **Other proof.** This rule does not prevent the

proof of official records or of entry or lack of entry therein by any other method authorized by law.

NOTES TO DECISIONS

ANALYSIS

Public records

Public records

Where a city employee "certified" the authenticity of ordinances attached to referendum petitions and it was undisputed that the documents attached to those petitions were in fact true and accurate copies of the ordinances, such was sufficient under RC § 731.32, as the statute did not required a "certified copy" of the ordinance to be signed by the city clerk of council as the official custodian of the applicable records; although Ohio R. Civ. P. 44 and Ohio R. Evid. 901(B) set out requirements for establishing the authenticity of public records, such was applicable to litigation, pursuant to Ohio R. Civ. P. 1(A), and as they were not specifically referenced in Ohio's election law statutes, they were not the only required method pursuant to RC § 731.32. Rankin v. Underwood, — Ohio App. 3d —, 2006 Ohio 1237, — N.E. 2d —, 2006 Ohio App. LEXIS 1098 (Mar. 17, 2006).

RULE 44.1. Judicial notice of certain law; determination of foreign law

(A) Judicial notice of certain law.

(1) Judicial notice shall be taken of the rules of the supreme court of this state and of the decisional, constitutional, and public statutory law of this state.

(2) A party who intends to rely on a municipal ordinance, a local rule of court, or an administrative regulation within this state shall give notice in his pleading or other reasonable written notice. The court in taking judicial notice of a municipal ordinance, a local rule of court, or an administrative regulation within this state may inform itself in such manner as it deems proper, and may call upon counsel to aid in obtaining such information. The court's determination shall be treated as a ruling on a question of law and shall be made by the court and not the jury. A court may, however, take judicial notice of its own rules or of a municipal ordinance within the territorial jurisdiction of the court without advance notice in the pleading of a party or other written notice.

(3) A party who intends to rely on the decisional, constitutional, public statutory law, rules of court, municipal ordinances, or administrative regulations of any other state, territory, and jurisdiction of the United States shall give notice in his pleading or other reasonable notice. The court in taking judicial notice of the decisional, constitutional, public statutory law, rules of court, municipal ordinances, or administrative regulations of any other state, territory, and jurisdiction of the United States may inform itself in such manner as it deems proper, and may call upon counsel to aid in obtaining such information. The court's determination shall be treated as a ruling on a question of law, and shall be made by the court and not the jury.

(B) **Determination of foreign law.** A party who intends to rely on the law of a foreign country shall give notice in his pleadings or other reasonable written notice. The court in determining the law of a foreign country may consider any relevant material or source, including testimony, whether or not submitted by a party. The court's determination shall be treated as a ruling on a question of law and shall be made by the court and not the jury.

NOTES TO DECISIONS

ANALYSIS

Reliance on foreign law

Reliance on foreign law

Trial court erred, in determining the date the parties were married, when it declined to take notice of the Hindu Marriage Act, as requested by the wife: Verma v. Verma, 179 Ohio App. 3d 637, 2008 Ohio 6244, 903 N.E.2d 343, 2008 Ohio App. LEXIS 5218 (2008).

RULE 45. Subpoena

(A) Form; Issuance; Notice.

(1) Every subpoena shall do all of the following:

(a) state the name of the court from which it is issued, the title of the action, and the case number;

(b) command each person to whom it is directed, at a time and place specified in the subpoena, to:

(i) attend and give testimony at a trial, hearing, or deposition;

(ii) produce documents, electronically stored information, or tangible things at a trial, hearing, or deposition;

(iii) produce and permit inspection and copying of any designated documents or electronically stored information that are in the possession, custody, or control of the person;

(iv) produce and permit inspection and copying, testing, or sampling of any tangible things that are in the possession, custody, or control of the person; or

(v) permit entry upon designated land or other property that is in the possession or control of the person for the purposes described in Civ. R. 34(A)(3).

(c) set forth the text of divisions (C) and (D) of this rule.

A command to produce and permit inspection may be joined with a command to attend and give testimony, or may be issued separately. A subpoena may specify the form or forms in which electronically stored information is to be produced, but may not require the production of the same information in more than one form.

A subpoena may not be used to obtain the attendance of a party or the production of documents by a party in discovery. Rather, a party's attendance at a deposition may be obtained only by notice under Civ. R. 30, and documents or electronically stored information may be obtained from a party in discovery only pursuant to Civ. R. 34.

(2) The clerk shall issue a subpoena, signed, but otherwise in blank, to a party requesting it, who shall complete it before service. An attorney who has filed an appearance on behalf of a party in an action may also sign and issue a subpoena on behalf of the court in which the action is pending.

(3) A party on whose behalf a subpoena is issued under division (A)(1)(b)(ii), (iii), (iv), or (v) of this rule shall serve prompt written notice, including a copy of the subpoena, on all other parties as provided in Civ. R. 5. If the issuing attorney modifies a subpoena issued under division (A)(1)(b)(ii), (iii), (iv), or (v) of this rule in any way, the issuing attorney shall give prompt written notice of the modification, including a copy of the subpoena as modified, to all other parties.

(B) **Service.** A subpoena may be served by a sheriff, bailiff, coroner, clerk of court, constable, or a deputy of any, by an attorney at law, or by any other person designated by order of court who is not a party and is not less than eighteen years of age. Service of a subpoena upon a person named therein shall be made by delivering a copy of the subpoena to the person, by reading it to him or her in person, by leaving it at the person's usual place of residence, or by placing a sealed envelope containing the subpoena in the United States mail as certified or express mail return receipt requested with instructions to the delivering postal authority to show to whom delivered, date of delivery and address where delivered, and by tendering to the person upon demand the fees for one day's attendance and the mileage allowed by law. The person responsible for serving the subpoena shall file a return of the subpoena with the clerk. When the subpoena is served by mail delivery, the person filing the return shall attach the signed receipt to the return. If the witness being subpoenaed resides outside the county in which the court is located, the fees for one day's attendance and mileage shall be tendered without demand. The return may be forwarded through the postal service or otherwise.

(C) **Protection of persons subject to subpoenas**
.

(1) A party or an attorney responsible for the issuance and service of a subpoena shall take reasonable steps to avoid imposing undue burden or expense on a person subject to that subpoena.

(2)(a) A person commanded to produce under divisions (A)(1)(b)(ii), (iii), (iv), or (v) of this rule need not appear in person at the place of production or inspection unless commanded to attend and give testimony at a deposition, hearing, or trial.

(b) Subject to division (D)(2) of this rule, a person commanded to produce under divisions (A)(1)(b)(ii), (iii), (iv), or (v) of this rule may, within fourteen days after service of the subpoena or before the time specified for compliance if such time is less than fourteen days after service, serve upon the party or attorney designated in the subpoena written objections to production. If objection is made, the party serving the subpoena shall not be entitled to production except pursuant to an order of the court by which the subpoena was issued. If objection has been made, the party serving the subpoena, upon notice to the person commanded to produce, may move at any time for an order to compel the production. An order to compel production shall protect any person who is not a party or an officer of a party from significant expense resulting from the production commanded.

(3) On timely motion, the court from which the subpoena was issued shall quash or modify the subpoena, or order appearance or production only under specified conditions, if the subpoena does any of the following:

(a) Fails to allow reasonable time to comply;

(b) Requires disclosure of privileged or otherwise protected matter and no exception or waiver applies;

(c) Requires disclosure of a fact known or opinion held by an expert not retained or specially employed by any party in anticipation of litigation or preparation for trial as described by Civ.R. 26(B)(4), if the fact or opinion does not describe specific events or occurrences in dispute and results from study by that expert that was not made at the request of any party;

(d) Subjects a person to undue burden.

(4) Before filing a motion pursuant to division (C)(3)(d) of this rule, a person resisting discovery under this rule shall attempt to resolve any claim of undue burden through discussions with the issuing attorney. A motion filed pursuant to division (C)(3)(d) of this rule shall be supported by an affidavit of the subpoenaed person or a certificate of that person's attorney of the efforts made to resolve any claim of undue burden.

(5) If a motion is made under division (C)(3)(c) or (C)(3)(d) of this rule, the court shall quash or modify the subpoena unless the party in whose behalf the subpoena is issued shows a substantial need for the testimony or material that cannot be otherwise met without undue hardship and assures that the person to whom the subpoena is addressed will be reasonably compensated.

(D) **Duties in responding to subpoena.**

(1) A person responding to a subpoena to produce documents shall, at the person's option, produce them as they are kept in the usual course of business or organized and labeled to correspond with the categories in the subpoena. A person producing documents or electronically stored information pursuant to a subpoena for them shall permit their inspection and copying by all parties present at the time and place set in the subpoena for inspection and copying.

(2) If a request does not specify the form or forms for producing electronically stored information, a person responding to a subpoena may produce the information in a form or forms in which the information is ordinarily maintained if that form is reasonably useable, or in any form that is reasonably useable. Unless ordered by the court or agreed to by the person subpoenaed, a person responding to a subpoena need not produce the same electronically stored information in more than one form.

(3) A person need not provide discovery of electronically stored information when the production imposes undue burden or expense. On motion to compel discovery or for a protective order, the person from whom electronically stored information is sought must show that the information is not reasonably accessible because of undue burden or expense. If a showing of undue burden or expense is made, the court may nonetheless order production of electronically stored information if the requesting party shows good cause.

The court shall consider the factors in Civ. R. 26(B)(4) when determining if good cause exists. In ordering production of electronically stored information, the court may specify the format, extent, timing, allocation of expenses and other conditions for the discovery of the electronically stored information.

(4) When information subject to a subpoena is withheld on a claim that it is privileged or subject to protection as trial preparation materials, the claim shall be made expressly and shall be supported by a description of the nature of the documents, communications, or things not produced that is sufficient to enable the demanding party to contest the claim.

(5) If information is produced in response to a subpoena that is subject to a claim of privilege or of protection as trial-preparation material, the person making the claim may notify any party that received the information of the claim and the basis for it. After being notified, a receiving party must promptly return, sequester, or destroy the specified information and any copies within the party's possession, custody or control. A party may not use or disclose the information until the claim is resolved. A receiving party may promptly present the information to the court under seal for a determination of the claim of privilege or of protection as trial-preparation material. If the receiving party disclosed the information before being notified, it must take reasonable steps to retrieve it. The person who produced the information must preserve the information until the claim is resolved.

(E) **Sanctions.** Failure by any person without adequate excuse to obey a subpoena served upon that person may be deemed a contempt of the court from which the subpoena issued. A subpoenaed person or that person's attorney who frivolously resists discovery under this rule may be required by the court to pay the reasonable expenses, including reasonable attorney's fees, of the party seeking the discovery. The court from which a subpoena was issued may impose upon a party or attorney in breach of the duty imposed by division (C)(1) of this rule an appropriate sanction, which may include, but is not limited to, lost earnings and reasonable attorney's fees.

(F) **Privileges.** Nothing in this rule shall be construed to authorize a party to obtain information protected by any privilege recognized by law, or to authorize any person to disclose such information.

History: Amended, eff 7-1-71; 7-1-72; 7-1-93; 7-1-94; 7-1-05; 7-1-08.

NOTES TO DECISIONS

Analysis

Discretion of court
Motion to quash subpoena
Privileged documents
— Trade secrets
Service of subpoena
Subpoena
Witness fees

Discretion of court

Trial court abused its discretion in denying the motion to quash and for a protective order. The court failed to consider whether the plaintiff had a substantial need for the discovery and failed to provide any safeguards to protect trade secrets and confidential information: Lambda Research v. Jacobs, 170 Ohio App. 3d 750, 2007 Ohio 309, 869 N.E.2d 39, 2007 Ohio App. LEXIS 280 (2007).

Motion to quash subpoena

Trial court abused its discretion under Ohio R. Civ. P. 26(C) and 45(C) when it denied a former customer's motions to quash subpoenas and for a protective order with respect to requested documents that the customer claimed contained proprietary information and trade secrets, as there was no indication that the trial court considered whether the requesting party, a former supplier, had a substantial need for the discovery. Further, the trial court failed to provide any safeguards to protect the customer's trade secrets and confidential information. Lambda Research v. Jacobs, 170 Ohio App. 3d 750, 2007 Ohio 309, 869 N.E.2d 39, 2007 Ohio App. LEXIS 280 (2007).

Only the physicians who had been subpoenaed had standing to file motions to quash the subpoenas under Ohio R. Civ. P. 45(C). A trial court erred when it considered and ruled on the motions to quash the subpoenas filed by a doctor and a health system who were named defendants in a medical malpractice case. Abels v. Ruf, — Ohio App. 3d —, 2006 Ohio 3813, — N.E. 2d —, 2006 Ohio App. LEXIS 3788 (July 26, 2006).

Privileged documents

When a physician sued a medical practice for not offering the physician a partnership, and the physician subpoenaed hospitals' records to counter the practice's claim that the physician was not treated differently from other physicians, it was error not to quash the physician's subpoenas for peer-review reports because (1) such reports were privileged under RC § 2305.252 as the physician sought to show the physician's performance compared to that of other physicians employed by the practice, so the reports concerned a subject of review by the peer review committee, within the statute's ambit, and (2) it would be unduly burdensome, under Ohio R. Civ. P. 45(C)(3)(d) to place the onus on the nonparty hospitals to provide discovery that was either privileged or available elsewhere. Wright v. Perioperative Medical Consultants, — Ohio App. 3d —, 2007 Ohio 3090, — N.E. 2d —, 2007 Ohio App. LEXIS 2838 (June 22, 2007).

When a physician sued a medical practice for not offering the physician a partnership, and the physician subpoenaed hospitals' records to counter the practice's claim that the physician was not treated differently from other physicians, it was error not to quash the physician's subpoenas for incident reports because such reports were privileged under RC § 2305.253(A), and if the privilege did not apply because the physician's complaint sounded in contract, production of the records would still be unduly burdensome, under Ohio R. Civ. P. 45(C)(3)(d). Wright v. Perioperative Medical Consultants, — Ohio App. 3d —, 2007 Ohio 3090, — N.E. 2d —, 2007 Ohio App. LEXIS 2838 (June 22, 2007).

— Trade secrets

Trial court did not abuse its discretion under Ohio R. Civ. P. 26(C)(7), 34(C), and 45(C)(3)(b) in denying a product user's motion to compel disclosure of a nonparty manufacturer's formulae for polyethylene tubing in the user's products liability action, as the formulae were clearly trade secrets pursuant to RC § 1333.61(D) and the user did not show such a compelling need for the disclosure that it outweighed the manufacturer's interests in maintaining confidentiality of the information. It was noted that one of the opposing parties in the action was the manufacturer's direct competitor, which would have had access to that confidential information, and the user's expert only opined that the disclosure would have been "helpful" in his determination as to why the tubing had failed, which was not sufficiently compelling to require the requested disclosure. Splater v. Thermal Ease Hydronic Sys., Inc., 169 Ohio App. 3d 514, 2006 Ohio 5452, 863 N.E.2d 1060, 2006 Ohio App. LEXIS 5438 (2006).

When a franchisee subpoenaed a competitor's financial information, and, in response to the competitor's claim that the subpoenaed information qualified as trade secrets, under RC § 1333.61(D), the franchisee did not deny this claim but said it could discover the information nonetheless, the competitor was not required, in response, to address the six-factor definition of a trade secret, so it was an abuse of discretion for a trial court to order the production of information in response to the subpoena without giving the competitor a chance to address these factors and without conducting an in camera review of the documents. GZK, Inc. v. Schumaker, 168 Ohio App. 3d 106, 2006 Ohio 3744, 858 N.E.2d 867, 2006 Ohio App. LEXIS 3696 (2006).

Service of subpoena

It was error for a trial court to enforce a subpoena served by mail because the subpoena was actually served by a mail carrier, and not by the attorney who placed the subpoena in the mail, and, under Ohio R. Civ. P. 45(B), a mail carrier was not authorized to serve subpoenas. GZK, Inc. v. Schumaker, 168 Ohio App. 3d 106, 2006 Ohio 3744, 858 N.E.2d 867, 2006 Ohio App. LEXIS 3696 (2006).

Attorney did not deliver a subpoena to a person, within the meaning of Ohio R. Civ. P. 45(B), by placing it in the mail, but, rather, the term "delivering" in Rule 45(B) contemplated an attorney or another individual who fits within one of the categories set forth in the first sentence of the Rule actually presenting the subpoena in person, and delivery of a subpoena by an attorney and delivery by a mail carrier, who was not an authorized server, were not the same thing. If a subpoena could be served merely by placing it in the mail, the recipient would have no way of knowing whether the person who did so was an authorized server under the first sentence of Ohio R. Civ. P. 45. GZK, Inc. v. Schumaker, 168 Ohio App. 3d 106, 2006 Ohio 3744, 858 N.E.2d 867, 2006 Ohio App. LEXIS 3696 (2006).

Mail service of a subpoena was accomplished by a mail carrier delivering a copy of the subpoena to the person to be served, but a mail carrier was not authorized to do so, unless he or she happened to be a sheriff, bailiff, coroner, clerk of court, constable, or a deputy of any, an attorney at law, or any other person designated by order of court who was not a party and was not less than eighteen years of age. GZK, Inc. v. Schumaker, 168 Ohio App. 3d 106, 2006 Ohio 3744, 858 N.E.2d 867, 2006 Ohio App. LEXIS 3696 (2006).

Subpoena

Although the trial court erred in striking the neighbor's testimony (because a copy of the subpoena was not required to be provided to the other party under Ohio R. Civ. P. 45(A)(1)(b)(i)), the error was harmless because the testimony did not negate the wife's testimony concerning the incident, and thus, no substantial right of the husband was affected since the trial court was correct in entering the civil protection order. The testimony merely gave an overall impression of the husband's general demeanor when dealing with the neighbor, together with a statement about the wife's mental state sometime after the incident had occurred. Cauwenbergh v. Cauwenbergh, — Ohio App. 3d —, 2007 Ohio 1070, — N.E. 2d —, 2007 Ohio App. LEXIS 1011 (Mar. 9, 2007).

Witness fees

Where a witness was subpoenaed to testify for a party but he was not compensated as an expert, the trial court did not err in excusing him from appearing, pursuant to Ohio R. Civ. P. 45(C)(3)(c), (d), and (C)(5). Although it was error not to have allowed the party to testify as to what the expert had told him because the rules of evidence were relaxed in the small claims court action pursuant to Ohio R. Evid. 101(C)(8), as

the party failed to proffer what his testimony would have been under Ohio R. Evid. 103(A)(2), the error was deemed waived for purposes of appeal. Melcher v. Ryan, — Ohio App. 3d —, 2006 Ohio 4609, — N.E. 2d —, 2006 Ohio App. LEXIS 4565 (Aug. 31, 2006).

Portion of Ohio R. Civ. P. 45(B) stating that if a witness being subpoenaed resided outside the county in which the court was located, the fees for one day's attendance and mileage were to be tendered without demand contemplated the subpoenaed witness being required to travel for an "appearance" at some type of proceeding. GZK, Inc. v. Schumaker, 168 Ohio App. 3d 106, 2006 Ohio 3744, 858 N.E.2d 867, 2006 Ohio App. LEXIS 3696 (2006).

As a husband in a divorce action subpoenaed the wife's psychologist on short notice, which required her to rearrange her professional schedule, the imposition of fees incurred by the psychologist on the husband might have been reasonable if the trial court had determined that the ill-timed subpoena created an undue burden or expense on the psychologist pursuant to Ohio R. Civ. P. 45(C)(1) and (E). As a portion of the subpoenaed records were quashed due to the lack of adequate time to gather them, it was unclear what basis the fees were imposed on the husband, and a remand for determination thereof was necessary in the circumstances. Panico v. Panico, — Ohio App. 3d —, 2006 Ohio 6650, — N.E. 2d —, 2006 Ohio App. LEXIS 6502 (Dec. 14, 2006).

RULE 46.   Exceptions unnecessary

An exception at any stage or step of the case or matter is unnecessary to lay a foundation for review whenever a matter has been called to the attention of the court by objection, motion, or otherwise and the court has ruled thereon.

History: Amended, eff 7-1-75.

NOTES TO DECISIONS

ANALYSIS

Conditions of bail

———————

Conditions of bail

Judge's motion to dismiss a prohibition action by a chief public defender (CPD) for a county was granted where the action sought to enjoin the judge's imposition of anger management counseling as a condition of pretrial bail under Ohio R. Crim. P. 46(B) for certain indigent defendants who were charged with domestic violence offenses, as the CPD lacked standing to assert such a claim and the public action exception to the standing doctrine was inapplicable. No claim was stated, as any error in imposing such a condition would not have deprived the trial court of jurisdiction over the criminal cases because such error was procedural in nature. Lager v. Plough, — Ohio App. 3d —, 2006 Ohio 2772, — N.E. 2d —, 2006 Ohio App. LEXIS 2621 (June 2, 2006).

RULE 47.   Jurors

(A) **Brief introduction of case.** To assist prospective jurors in understanding the general nature of the case, the court, in consultation with the parties, may give jurors a brief introduction to the case. The brief introduction may include a general description of the legal claims and defenses of the parties.

(B) **Examination of prospective jurors.** Any person called as a prospective juror for the trial of any cause shall be examined under oath or upon affirmation as to the prospective juror's qualifications. The court may permit the parties or their attorneys to conduct the examination of the prospective jurors or may itself conduct the examination. In the latter event, the court shall permit the parties or their attorneys to supplement the examination by further inquiry. Nothing in this rule shall limit the court's discretion to allow the examination of all prospective jurors in the array or, in the alternative, to permit individual examination of each prospective juror seated on a panel, prior to any challenges for cause or peremptory challenges.

(C) **Challenges to prospective jurors.** In addition to challenges for cause provided by law, each party peremptorily may challenge three prospective jurors. If the interests of multiple litigants are essentially the same, "each party" shall mean "each side."

Peremptory challenges shall be exercised alternately, with the first challenge exercised by the plaintiff. The failure of a party to exercise a peremptory challenge constitutes a waiver of that challenge, but does not constitute a waiver of any subsequent challenge. However, if all parties or sides, alternately and in sequence, fail to exercise a peremptory challenge, the joint failure constitutes a waiver of all peremptory challenges.

A prospective juror peremptorily challenged by either party shall be excused.

Nothing in this rule shall limit the court's discretion to allow challenges to be made outside the hearing of prospective jurors.

(D) **Alternate jurors.** The court may direct that no more than four jurors in addition to the regular jury be called and impaneled to sit as alternate jurors. Alternate jurors in the order in which they are called shall replace jurors who, prior to the time the jury retires to consider its verdict, become or are found to be unable or disqualified to perform their duties. Alternate jurors shall be drawn in the same manner, shall have the same qualifications, shall be subject to the same examination and challenges, shall take the same oath, and shall have the same functions, powers, facilities, and privileges as the regular jurors. An alternate juror who does not replace a regular juror shall be discharged after the jury retires to consider its verdict. Each party is entitled to one peremptory challenge in addition to those otherwise allowed by law if one or two alternate jurors are to be impaneled, and two peremptory challenges if three or four alternate jurors are to be impaneled. The additional peremptory challenges may be used against an alternate juror only, and the other peremptory challenges allowed shall not be used against an alternate juror.

(E) **Taking of notes by jurors.** The court, after providing appropriate cautionary instructions, may permit jurors who wish to do so to take notes during a trial. If the court permits the taking of notes, notes taken by a juror may be carried into deliberations by that juror. The court shall require that all juror notes be collected and destroyed promptly after the jury renders a verdict.

(F) **Juror questions to witnesses.** The court may permit jurors to propose questions for the court to ask of the witnesses. If the court permits jurors to propose questions, the court shall use procedures that minimize the risk of prejudice, including all of the following:

(1) Require jurors to propose any questions to the court in writing;

(2) Retain a copy of each proposed question for the record;

(3) Instruct the jurors that they shall not display or discuss a proposed question with other jurors;

(4) Before reading a question to a witness, provide counsel with an opportunity to object to each question on the record and outside the hearing of the jury;

(5) Read the question, either as proposed or re-phrased, to the witness;

(6) Permit counsel to reexamine the witness regarding a matter addressed by a juror question;

(7) If a question proposed by a juror is not asked, instruct the jurors that they should not draw any adverse inference from the court's refusal to ask any question proposed by a juror.

History: Amended, eff 7-1-71; 7-1-72; 7-1-75; 7-1-05; 7-1-06; 7-1-09.

NOTES TO DECISIONS

ANALYSIS

Peremptory challenges
Voir dire

Peremptory challenges

Trial court did not err in refusing to remove a juror for cause, based upon the possibility that she had a previous adversarial relationship with counsel for an executrix of a deceased patient's estate in the patient's medical malpractice action, as there was no showing under RC §§ 2313.42 and 2313.43 that the juror was partial because she indicated that she did not recall ever seeing counsel previously. The issue had not been waived under Ohio R. Civ. P. 47(C), as the executrix had exhausted all of her peremptory challenges. Iglodi v. Tolentino, — Ohio App. 3d —, 2007 Ohio 1982, — N.E. 2d —, 2007 Ohio App. LEXIS 1832 (Apr. 26, 2007).

Voir dire

Trial court did not abuse its discretion by imposing a time limit on voir dire. The time limitations on counsel were equally enforced, and the trial court even allowed appellant's counsel to exceed the time limitation imposed by almost 15 minutes. Dedmon v. Mack, — Ohio App. 3d —, 2006 Ohio 2113, — N.E. 2d —, 2006 Ohio App. LEXIS 1952 (Apr. 28, 2006).

RULE 48. Juries: majority verdict; stipulation of number of jurors

In all civil actions, a jury shall render a verdict upon the concurrence of three-fourths or more of their number. The verdict shall be in writing and signed by each of the jurors concurring therein. All jurors shall then return to court where the judge shall cause the verdict to be read and inquiry made to determine if the verdict is that of three-fourths or more of the jurors. Upon request of either party, the jury shall be polled by asking each juror if the verdict is that of the juror; if more than one-fourth of the jurors answer in the negative, or if the verdict in substance is defective, the jurors must be sent out again for further deliberation. If three-fourths or more of the jurors answer affirmatively, the verdict is complete and the jury shall be discharged from the case. If the verdict is defective in form only, with the assent of the jurors and before their discharge, the court may correct it.

The parties may stipulate that the jury shall consist of any number less than the maximum number provided by Rule 38(B). For the purpose of rendering a verdict, whenever three-fourths of the jury does not consist of an integral number, the next higher number shall be construed to represent three-fourths of the jury. For juries with less than four members, the verdict must be unanimous.

History: Amended, eff 7-1-71; 7-1-72.

NOTES TO DECISIONS

ANALYSIS

Deciding liability and damages
Defective verdicts
Inconsistencies

Deciding liability and damages
Pursuant to Ohio R. Civ. P. 48 and Ohio Const. art. I, § 5, the jurors fully complied with their duty, in that at least three-fourths of them found that a towing company had violated a bailment regarding an owner's vehicle, that the company had committed a conversion, that it was liable for punitive damages, and that it should pay for the owner's attorney fees. There was nothing to show that some jurors determined the company's liability for one claim and that different jurors then decided the compensatory damages for that claim. Williams v. Mike Kaeser Towing, — Ohio App. 3d —, 2006 Ohio 6976, — N.E. 2d —, 2006 Ohio App. LEXIS 6946 (Dec. 29, 2006).

Defective verdicts
Trial court correctly granted a new trial, pursuant to Ohio R. Civ. P. 59(A), on the basis of a defective verdict form. After the jury was dismissed, the trial court discovered that the jurors failed to sign their names on the lines next to their seat assignments on the verdict form and instead had written "nominal damages," in violation of Ohio R. Civ. P. 48. Rohr v. Gustin, — Ohio App. 3d —, 2006 Ohio 3043, — N.E. 2d —, 2006 Ohio App. LEXIS 2922 (June 16, 2006).

Inconsistencies
There was no inconsistency between the final interrogatory responses and the final verdict. The trial court's reconciliation instructions cleared up the jury's misconceptions without attempting to impose the court's will on the jurors: Segedy v. Cardiothoracic & Vascular Surgery of Akron, Inc., 182 Ohio App. 3d 768, 2009 Ohio 2460, 915 N.E.2d 361, 2009 Ohio App. LEXIS 2067 (2009).

RULE 49.   Verdicts; interrogatories

(A) **General verdict.** A general verdict, by which the jury finds generally in favor of the prevailing party, shall be used.

(B) **General verdict accompanied by answer to interrogatories.** The court shall submit written interrogatories to the jury, together with appropriate forms for a general verdict, upon request of any party prior to the commencement of argument. Counsel shall submit the proposed interrogatories to the court and to opposing counsel at such time. The court shall inform counsel of its proposed action upon the requests prior to their arguments to the jury, but the interrogatories shall be submitted to the jury in the form that the court approves. The interrogatories may be directed to one or more determinative issues whether issues of fact or mixed issues of fact and law.

The court shall give such explanation or instruction as may be necessary to enable the jury both to make answers to the interrogatories and to render a general verdict, and the court shall direct the jury both to make written answers and to render a general verdict.

When the general verdict and the answers are consistent, the appropriate judgment upon the verdict and answers shall be entered pursuant to Rule 58. When one or more of the answers is inconsistent with the general verdict, judgment may be entered pursuant to Rule 58 in accordance with the answers, notwithstanding the general verdict, or the court may return the jury for further consideration of its answers and verdict or may order a new trial.

(C) **Special verdicts abolished.** Special verdicts shall not be used.

History: Amended, eff 7-1-80.

NOTES TO DECISIONS

ANALYSIS

Answers to interrogatories
Harmless error
Inconsistency between verdict and interrogatories
Interrogatories
Remedies
Verdict form

Answers to interrogatories
Jury's failure to answer some of the interrogatories constitutes a mistrial and necessitates a new trial, regardless of whether there is a timely motion for a new trial. A judgment that leaves issues unresolved and contemplates that further action must be taken is not a final appealable order, and procedendo will issue to compel a court to retry the unresolved claims: State ex rel. Bd. of State Teachers Ret. Sys. v. Davis, 113 Ohio St. 3d 410, 2007 Ohio 2205, 865 N.E.2d 1289, 2007 Ohio LEXIS 1264 (2007).

Harmless error
Although jury interrogatories in an adverse possession and quiet title action could have been interpreted as being inconsistent, where no objection was made pursuant to Ohio R. Civ. P. 49(B), the matter was reviewed under a plain error standard, and no such error was found in the jury verdict in favor of the property owners and against appellants. Once adverse possession of the owners had been established pursuant to RC § 2305.04, they no longer had to show that they continued to act adversely to a titled owner's interests for purposes of a quiet title claim, nor that they adversely possessed the property for 21 years immediately prior to filing the quiet title claim, but rather, only that they maintained their possessory interest. Heider v. Unknown Heirs, — Ohio App. 3d —, 2006 Ohio 122, — N.E. 2d —, 2006 Ohio App. LEXIS 95 (Jan. 13, 2006).

Inconsistency between verdict and interrogatories
There was no inconsistency between the final interrogatory responses and the final verdict. The trial court's reconciliation instructions cleared up the jury's misconceptions without attempting to impose the court's will on the jurors: Segedy v. Cardiothoracic & Vascular Surgery of Akron, Inc., 182 Ohio App. 3d 768, 2009 Ohio 2460, 915 N.E.2d 361, 2009 Ohio App. LEXIS 2067 (2009).

Trial court did not err when it returned a matter to the jury for further deliberations pursuant to Ohio R. Civ. P. 49(B) after the jury failed to award actual damages to used vehicle purchasers against a vehicle dealership, despite finding the dealership liable for fraud in the general verdict, as the general verdict was inconsistent with the interrogatory on actual damages; the jury had assessed punitive damages against the dealership, and the trial court judge informed the jury before returning the matter to them that punitive damages required an award of compensatory damages. Anousheh v. Planet Ford, — Ohio App. 3d —, 2007 Ohio 4543, — N.E. 2d —, 2007 Ohio App. LEXIS 4092 (Aug. 31, 2007).

Interrogatories

Trial court did not commit plain error under Ohio R. Civ. P. 49(B) when it dismissed the jury after reading the jury's answers to the interrogatories into the record, but without affording the parties any opportunity to review the jury's answers for inconsistencies. The doctor had an affirmative duty to ask to see the interrogatory answers before the trial court dismissed the jury and the doctor's own arguments revealed that at least some of the inconsistencies were readily apparent to his counsel upon a quick inspection of the completed interrogatory forms. Lewis v. Nease, — Ohio App. 3d —, 2006 Ohio 4362, — N.E. 2d —, 2006 Ohio App. LEXIS 4274 (Aug. 21, 2006).

If a court does not specifically invite the parties to view the jury's answers to the interrogatories or state their objections to those answers upon the record, counsel has an affirmative duty to speak up and request the opportunity to do so. Lewis v. Nease, — Ohio App. 3d —, 2006 Ohio 4362, — N.E. 2d —, 2006 Ohio App. LEXIS 4274 (Aug. 21, 2006).

Trial court did not abuse its discretion in limiting the proposed interrogatories pursuant to Ohio R. Civ. P. 49(B) submitted to a jury in a product liability action involving a medical device used for neurosurgery, as there was no objection to the interrogatory that was submitted; the interrogatories which were not submitted involved negligent misrepresentation, rather than the theory of negligence for which the product manufacturer and its representative had been found liable. Zappola v. Leibinger, — Ohio App. 3d —, 2006 Ohio 2207, — N.E. 2d —, 2006 Ohio App. LEXIS 2058 (May 4, 2006).

Remedies

Trial court abused its discretion in modifying the amount of the patient's judgment in its effort to reconcile the inconsistencies in the jury's answers to the interrogatories because it did not give the patient the opportunity to consent to the trial court's reduction of the jury's damage award. Lewis v. Nease, — Ohio App. 3d —, 2006 Ohio 4362, — N.E. 2d —, 2006 Ohio App. LEXIS 4274 (Aug. 21, 2006).

Verdict form

When competing theories of liability are advanced against separate defendants, separate verdict forms should be used. Prymas v. Kassai, 168 Ohio App. 3d 123, 2006 Ohio 3726, 858 N.E.2d 1209, 2006 Ohio App. LEXIS 3691 (2006).

RULE 50. Motion for a directed verdict and for judgment notwithstanding the verdict

(A) **Motion for directed verdict.**

(1) **When made.** A motion for a directed verdict may be made on the opening statement of the opponent, at the close of the opponent's evidence or at the close of all the evidence.

(2) **When not granted.** A party who moves for a directed verdict at the close of the evidence offered by an opponent may offer evidence in the event that the motion is not granted, without having reserved the right so to do and to the same extent as if the motion

had not been made. A motion for a directed verdict which is not granted is not a waiver of trial by jury even though all parties to the action have moved for directed verdicts.

(3) **Grounds.** A motion for a directed verdict shall state the specific grounds therefore.

(4) **When granted on the evidence.** When a motion for a directed verdict has been properly made, and the trial court, after construing the evidence most strongly in favor of the party against whom the motion is directed, finds that upon any determinative issue reasonable minds could come to but one conclusion upon the evidence submitted and that conclusion is adverse to such party, the court shall sustain the motion and direct a verdict for the moving party as to that issue.

(5) **Jury assent unnecessary.** The order of the court granting a motion for a directed verdict is effective without any assent of the jury.

(B) **Motion for judgment notwithstanding the verdict.** Whether or not a motion to direct a verdict has been made or overruled and not later than fourteen days after entry of judgment, a party may move to have the verdict and any judgment entered thereon set aside and to have judgment entered in accordance with his motion; or if a verdict was not returned, such party, within fourteen days after the jury has been discharged, may move for judgment in accordance with his motion. A motion for a new trial may be joined with this motion, or a new trial may be prayed for in the alternative. If a verdict was returned, the court may allow the judgment to stand or may reopen the judgment. If the judgment is reopened, the court shall either order a new trial or direct the entry of judgment, but no judgment shall be rendered by the court on the ground that the verdict is against the weight of the evidence. If no verdict was returned the court may direct the entry of judgment or may order a new trial.

(C) **Conditional rulings on motion for judgment notwithstanding verdict.**

(1) If the motion for judgment notwithstanding the verdict, provided for in subdivision (B) of this rule, is granted, the court shall also rule on the motion for a new trial, if any, by determining whether it should be granted if the judgment is thereafter vacated or reversed. If the motion for a new trial is thus conditionally granted, the order thereon does not affect the finality of the judgment. In case the motion for a new trial has been conditionally granted and the judgment is reversed on appeal, the new trial shall proceed unless the appellate court has otherwise ordered. In case the motion for a new trial has been conditionally denied, the appellee on appeal may assert error in that denial; and if the judgment is reversed on appeal, subsequent proceedings shall be in accordance with the order of the appellate court.

(2) The party whose verdict has been set aside on motion for judgment notwithstanding the verdict may serve a motion for a new trial pursuant to Rule 59 not later than fourteen days after entry of the judgment notwithstanding the verdict.

(D) **Denial of motion for judgment notwithstanding verdict.** If the motion for judgment notwithstanding the verdict is denied, the party who prevailed on that motion may, as appellee, assert grounds entitling him to a new trial in the event the appellate court concludes that the trial court erred in denying the motion for judgment notwithstanding the verdict. If the appellate court reverses the judgment, nothing in this rule precludes it from determining that the appellee is entitled to a new trial, or from directing the trial court to determine whether a new trial shall be granted.

(E) **Statement of basis of decision.** When in a jury trial a court directs a verdict or grants judgment without or contrary to the verdict of the jury, the court shall state the basis for its decision in writing prior to or simultaneous with the entry of judgment. Such statement may be dictated into the record or included in the entry of judgment.

NOTES TO DECISIONS

ANALYSIS

Appeal
Applicability
Directed verdict in bench trial
Directed verdict proper
Dismissal
Illustrative cases
Interrogatories
Judgment notwithstanding the verdict
Motion to dismiss
Record
Remittitur
Test for directed verdict or judgment n.o.v.

Appeal

Although a former employer that was sued in a discrimination and retaliation action by a former employee sought a directed verdict at the close of the employee's evidence, where it failed to renew its motion at the close of all of the evidence, it did not preserve any alleged error in the denial of its motion for appellate review. Hollingsworth v. Time Warner Cable, — Ohio App. 3d —, 2006 Ohio 4903, — N.E. 2d —, 2006 Ohio App. LEXIS 4833 (Sept. 22, 2006).

Appeal by an insured from a directed verdict pursuant to Ohio R. Civ. P. 50 for an insurer on her declaratory judgment claim, seeking a determination that she was entitled to underinsured motorist coverage, was dismissed due to lack of a final appealable order under RC § 2505.02, as no declaration of rights was made, no correlation was drawn between the reason that the insured was not entitled to coverage and the terms of her policy, and the order was too vague to satisfy Rule 50. Thomas v. Nationwide Mut. Ins. Co., — Ohio App. 3d —, 2006 Ohio 4487, — N.E. 2d —, 2006 Ohio App. LEXIS 4399 (Aug. 31, 2006).

Where a trial court entered a judgment while motions under Ohio R. Civ. P. 50(B) and 59 were pending, and the entry postponed the question of court costs, the judgment entry was not a final appealable order and the postponement meant that the entry did not "determine the action" for purposes of RC § 2505.02(B)(1). There was no final appealable order for purposes of invoking the jurisdiction of the appellate court, and the inclusion of certification language under Ohio R. Civ. P. 54(B) did not remedy that defect. Wells Fargo Fin. Leasing v. Gilliland, — Ohio App. 3d —, 2006 Ohio 2756, — N.E. 2d —, 2006 Ohio App. LEXIS 2576 (May 22, 2006).

Trial court's dismissal of appellee's claims against appellant was a granting of a directed verdict under Ohio R. Civ. P. 50, not a dismissal under Ohio R. Civ. P. 41(B)(2) because a jury had been empaneled at the time that the trial court entered its dismissal, and Ohio R. Civ. P. 41(B)(2) applies only to dismissals in non-jury actions. As a result, the order dismissing the complaint was a final, appealable order, and appellee's challenge to the propriety of the order after a trial was held on appellant's counterclaims that had been later reinstated was dismissed as untimely. Nelson Jewellery Arts Co. v. Fein Designs Co., — Ohio App. 3d —, 2006 Ohio 2276, — N.E. 2d —, 2006 Ohio App. LEXIS 2120 (May 10, 2006).

Applicability

As a motion for a directed verdict pursuant to Ohio R. Civ. P. 50 only lay in a jury trial and not in a bench trial, the proper standard of review from a denial of such a request in a bench trial was whether the trial court judgment was against the manifest weight of the evidence. Bradford v. B & P Wrecking Co., — Ohio App. 3d —, 2007 Ohio 1732, — N.E. 2d —, 2007 Ohio App. LEXIS 1599 (Apr. 13, 2007).

Directed verdict in bench trial

When a trial court grants a "directed verdict" in a bench trial, an appellate court must first determine whether evidence of substantial, probative value supports each element of a plaintiff's claims. If the plaintiff has presented such evidence and the trial court nevertheless granted a "directed verdict" without weighing the evidence and determining the credibility of the witnesses, then an appellate court cannot treat the directed verdict as a CivR 41(B)(2) involuntary dismissal. The appellate court must remand so the trial court can fulfill its role as trier of fact: Jarupan v. Hanna, 173 Ohio App. 3d 284, 2007 Ohio 5081, 878 N.E.2d 66, 2007 Ohio App. LEXIS 4498 (2007).

Directed verdict proper

No error was found in granting a directed verdict on the intentional infliction of emotional distress claim because the record failed to demonstrate that the student suffered extreme emotional distress. The psychologist's testimony described the student's condition as mild in her functioning and severity of symptoms, meaning that the impact of her condition on her ability to function was mild and the severity of her symptoms was mild, and the fact that the psychologist described the student's mild symptoms as chronic did not render those symptoms severe. Weir v. Krystie's, — Ohio App. 3d —, 2007 Ohio 5910, — N.E. 2d —, 2007 Ohio App. LEXIS 5212 (Nov. 2, 2007).

Dismissal

Because the standard for a directed verdict under Ohio R. Civ. P. 50(A) was much more rigorous than the standard for dismissal under Ohio R. Civ. P. 41(B)(2), the trial court's dismissal of the complaint under the directed verdict standard satisfied the standard for a Rule 41 dismissal and thus, there was no error. Whitestone Co. v. Stittsworth, — Ohio App. 3d —, 2007 Ohio 233, — N.E. 2d —, 2007 Ohio App. LEXIS 216 (Jan. 23, 2007).

When, in a bench trial of a suit for breach of contract, a trial court granted one party's motion for a directed verdict, under Ohio R. Civ. P. 50(A), the motion was properly reviewed, on appeal, as one for involuntary dismissal, under Ohio R. Civ. P. 41(B)(2), because a motion for a directed verdict did not apply in a non-jury trial. U.S. Constr. Corp. v. Harbor Bay Estates, — Ohio App. 3d —, 2007 Ohio 3823, — N.E. 2d —, 2007 Ohio App. LEXIS 3496 (July 27, 2007).

Illustrative cases

Store's motion for a directed verdict and for judgment notwithstanding the verdict, filed after a jury found in favor of a customer on her claim for spoliation of evidence, was properly denied because the evidence showed that the store, through its employee, willfully destroyed video surveillance containing necessary evidence for customer in her assault and battery, malicious prosecution, and false imprisonment case against the store, hindering the customer's ability to show what had happened during an incident where she was accused of shoplifting. Abbott v. Marshalls of Ma, Inc., — Ohio App. 3d —, 2007 Ohio 1146, — N.E. 2d —, 2007 Ohio App. LEXIS 1056 (Mar. 15, 2007).

When, in a workers' compensation appeal, it was determined that an aggravation condition an employee asserted had not been considered administratively, it would have been error for the trial court hearing the appeal to render any adjudication on the merits of that condition, by directed verdict or otherwise, as the trial court lacked jurisdiction to decide it, so it was not error, under Ohio R. Civ. P. 50(A)(4), for the trial court to deny the employer's motion for a directed verdict as to that condition. Coffey v. Dolgencorp, Inc., — Ohio App. 3d —, 2007 Ohio 2274, — N.E. 2d —, 2007 Ohio App. LEXIS 2112 (May 14, 2007).

When a consumer sued a vehicle dealer under the Magnuson-Moss Warranty Act, 15 U.S.C.S. § 2301 et seq., for breach of the implied warranty of merchantability, the dealer was not entitled to a directed verdict, under Ohio R. Civ. P. 50(A), because the consumer showed that the truck the consumer bought from the dealer was unfit for the ordinary purposes for which a vehicle was used, under RC § 1302.27(B)(3), because of a significant oil leak and because of numerous problems with the vehicle before the dealer sold the vehicle. Urso v. Compact Cars, — Ohio App. 3d —, 2007 Ohio 4375, — N.E. 2d —, 2007 Ohio App. LEXIS 3946 (Aug. 24, 2007).

When a deputy sheriff sued a children's services board and the board's social worker for an investigation the worker performed of the deputy's relationship with a minor, at the request of a hospital, a directed verdict, under Ohio R. Civ. P. 50(A), was properly granted to the worker because (1) the worker's investigation was performed within the scope of the worker's employment by a political subdivision, and (2) there was no evidence of the worker's malice, intent to harm the deputy, bad faith, wanton misconduct, or recklessness, so the worker was immune from any liability, under RC § 2744.03(A)(6). Thornton v. Summit County, — Ohio App. 3d —, 2007 Ohio 4657, — N.E. 2d —, 2007 Ohio App. LEXIS 4190 (Sept. 12, 2007).

When a deputy sheriff sued a children's services board and the board's social worker for an investigation the worker performed of the deputy's relationship with a minor, at the request of a hospital, a directed verdict, under Ohio R. Civ. P. 50(A), was properly granted to the worker and the board as to the deputy's claim under 42 U.S.C.S. § 1983 because (1) the deputy did not identify any constitutional or federally protected right that might have been violated, and (2) it was not shown that the deputy suffered any employment injury or was otherwise harmed. Thornton v. Summit County, — Ohio App. 3d —, 2007 Ohio 4657, — N.E. 2d —, 2007 Ohio App. LEXIS 4190 (Sept. 12, 2007).

Officer could not be held liable for false arrest because, while there was a factual dispute as to whether plaintiff did anything wrong on the night in question, the information before the officer at the time of the arrest, to the effect that a barmaid at a bar had asked plaintiff to leave and that he had refused, would cause a reasonable person to believe that plaintiff was continuing to criminally trespass in violation of Columbus, Ohio, City Code 2311.21(A)(4) and provided probable cause for plaintiff's arrest, thereby rendering the arrest lawful. Hinkle v. City of Columbus, — Ohio App. 3d —, 2006 Ohio 1522, — N.E. 2d —, 2006 Ohio App. LEXIS 1393 (Mar. 30, 2006).

Trial court did not err in granting a motion for a directed verdict filed by a doctor and a hospital immediately after it granted the executor's motion to amend the pleadings to conform to the evidence to assert a claim for lack of informed consent because the executor failed to provide testimony to establish the standard of care required of the doctor, in that no expert was provided to establish what a reasonable doctor under similar circumstances would have told the executor's decedent in obtaining her consent to the procedure performed. Further, when the executor made his motion to amend, he and appellees had both rested their cases. Therefore, appellees' motion for a directed verdict was appropriately timed, and based on the evidence that had been presented at trial, the trial court properly granted a directed verdict. Dedmon v. Mack, — Ohio App. 3d —, 2006 Ohio 2113, — N.E. 2d —, 2006 Ohio App. LEXIS 1952 (Apr. 28, 2006).

In a suit brought by a client seeking to recover for damages sustained to her home while it was in the care of a realtor, the realtor's motion for a directed verdict on the ground that the client failed to present expert testimony that the costs of repairing the client's home were reasonable and necessary was properly denied. Expert testimony was not required under Ohio R. Evid. 702(A) because jurors could be presumed to understand what defects made a property uninhabitable or otherwise diminished the owner's enjoyment and use of it, and the jury could reasonably infer from the client's testimony and that of a plumber and a representative of the construction company, properly submitted under Ohio R. Evid. 701, that the repairs to her house were necessary to restore the property to its prior condition. Reynolds v. Bauer, — Ohio App. 3d —, 2006 Ohio 2912, — N.E. 2d —, 2006 Ohio App. LEXIS 2730 (June 9, 2006).

Verdict for defendant in plaintiff's suit arising out of a car accident was not against the manifest weight of evidence, and therefore, plaintiff's motion for judgment notwithstanding the verdict or, in the alternative, for a new trial was properly denied. The jury was not required to ignore defendant's testimony as the testimony of plaintiff's expert did not conclusively show that plaintiff's damage was inconsistent with defendant's theory of the accident; thus, the physical facts rule did not apply. Turner v. Chapa, — Ohio App. 3d —, 2006 Ohio 3175, — N.E. 2d —, 2006 Ohio App. LEXIS 3072 (June 23, 2006).

When an insurance agent sued an insurer, after the insurer terminated the agent for violating a contractual requirement that the agent was to place all business with the insurer, the insurer was properly granted a directed verdict, under Ohio R. Civ. P. 50(A)(4), as to the agent's claim of tortious interference with business relations, based on the insurer's employees terminating the agent's computer access and assigning his clients to other agents, because the agent was properly terminated, so the insurer's employees were permitted to take the actions they did. Chuparkoff v. Farmers Ins. of Columbus, — Ohio App. 3d —, 2006 Ohio 3281, — N.E. 2d —, 2006 Ohio App. LEXIS 3198 (June 28, 2006).

When an insurance agent sued an insurer, after the insurer terminated the agent for violating a contractual requirement that the agent was to place all business with the insurer, the insurer was properly granted a directed verdict, under Ohio R. Civ. P. 50(A)(4), as to the agent's claim of conversion, based on the insurer exercising dominion over the agent's customers and business, because the agent was properly terminated, so the insurer acted within its contractual rights when it reallocated the agent's customers. Chuparkoff v. Farmers Ins. of Columbus, — Ohio App. 3d —, 2006 Ohio 3281, — N.E. 2d —, 2006 Ohio App. LEXIS 3198 (June 28, 2006).

When an insurance agent sued an insurer, after the insurer terminated the agent for violating a contractual requirement that the agent was to place all business with the insurer, the insurer was properly granted a directed verdict, under Ohio R. Civ. P. 50(A)(4), as to the agent's claim of unjust enrichment because unjust enrichment was not available where there was an express contract covering the same subject, as there was here. Chuparkoff v. Farmers Ins. of Columbus, — Ohio App. 3d —, 2006 Ohio 3281, — N.E. 2d —, 2006 Ohio App. LEXIS 3198 (June 28, 2006).

When an owner sued a contractor for breach of contract for refusing to execute a contract after the owner accepted the contractor's bid, it was error to grant the contractor's directed verdict motion, under Ohio R. Civ. P. 50(A)(4), because (1) RC § 153,12(A), while requiring the owner's execution of a contract, which had to be written, did not, under these facts, bar the owner from entering into an oral contract with the contractor and later memorializing it, and (2) a contract was a mere formality, given the information that was provided to the contractor in the bidding process, so a contract was formed upon the owner's notification to the contractor of its acceptance of the contractor's bid. White Hat Mgmt. v. Ohio Farmers Ins. Co., 167 Ohio App. 3d 663, 2006 Ohio 3280, 856 N.E. 2d 991, 2006 Ohio App. LEXIS 3211 (June 28, 2006).

When a worker alleged that he was injured due to a knee strain in the course of his employment, but his claim for workers' compensation was denied, so he appealed that denial, the administrator of the Bureau of Workers' Compensation was not entitled to a directed verdict, under Ohio R. Civ. P. 50(A), due to the worker's failure to produce expert testimony linking his injury to his job-related accident, because the worker submitted medical reports on the injury's etiology, the worker and his wife testified that the affected area of the worker's leg was swollen subsequent to the accident, and the worker testified his knee was warm to the touch and exhibited a purple discoloration after the initial injury, and this testimony, with the medical reports, sufficiently showed the injury was accompanied by readily observable, external, evidence, so the facts surrounding the worker's injury were within the knowledge and experience of an average individual. Chilson v. Conrad, — Ohio App. 3d —, 2006 Ohio 3423, — N.E. 2d —, 2006 Ohio App. LEXIS 3347 (June 30, 2006).

When investors sued a broker and his employer because the broker sold securities in the investors' non-discretionary accounts without their consent, the broker and employer were not entitled to a directed verdict, under Ohio R. Civ. P. 50(A)(4), on the theory that the investors ratified the broker's acts by failing to subsequently object within the time periods provided in their contract with the employer because, while the investors' accounts were non-discretionary, the broker's unauthorized sale raised the level of fiduciary duty he owed the investors to that owed by the broker of a discretionary account, including disclosing his unauthorized sale to the investors, which was not done, so, because this was never disclosed, ratification could not be found because the investors did not know all the material facts they were entitled to know. Burns v. Prudential Securities, Inc., 167 Ohio App. 3d 809, 2006 Ohio 3550, 857 N.E. 2d 621, 2006 Ohio App. LEXIS 3500 (July 11, 2006).

Trial court properly granted a directed verdict to a party organizer on a claim of recklessness advanced by the parents of a minor son who fell on the ice while racing a friend at a party planned by the organizer because the evidence did not support a claim of recklessness. While a sign at the ice rink prohibited racing, that rule was generally relaxed during private parties, there was no evidence that anyone on duty thought that the activities were unsafe, and the evidence showed that the organizer took certain precautions when she initiated the race, separating the more skilled skaters from those who were less skilled. Santho v. BSA, 168 Ohio App. 3d 27, 2006 Ohio 3656, 857 N.E. 2d 1255, 2006 Ohio App. LEXIS 3606 (July 18, 2006).

In a suit by debtors against a lender, a trial court properly granted the lender a directed verdict, under Ohio R. Civ. P. 50(A)(4), as to the debtors' unjust enrichment claim because the claim was based on the lender's retention of loan proceeds pending the completion of certain repairs to property that was

the subject of the loan, and alleged the lender collected interest on these retained proceeds and re-loaned them, but a provision allowing the retention was a part of the loan contract to which the debtors agreed, the proceeds were placed in escrow, and the note provided that interest was due on the entire amount of the loan for its life. Lotfi-Fard v. First Fed. of Lakewood, — Ohio App. 3d —, 2006 Ohio 3727, — N.E. 2d —, 2006 Ohio App. LEXIS 3686 (July 20, 2006).

In a suit by debtors against a lender, a trial court properly granted the lender a directed verdict, under Ohio R. Civ. P. 50(A)(4), as to the debtors' breach of contract claim because the claim was based on the lender's retention of loan proceeds pending the completion of certain repairs to property that was the subject of the loan, and this provision was a part of the loan contract to which the debtors agreed. Lotfi-Fard v. First Fed. of Lakewood, — Ohio App. 3d —, 2006 Ohio 3727, — N.E. 2d —, 2006 Ohio App. LEXIS 3686 (July 20, 2006).

In a suit by debtors against a lender, a trial court properly granted the lender a directed verdict, under Ohio R. Civ. P. 50(A)(4), as to the debtors' fraud claim because the claim was based on the lender's retention of loan proceeds pending the completion of certain repairs to property that was the subject of the loan and the lender's collection of interest on these retained proceeds, but the fact that the proceeds were retained was not concealed, and the note provided that interest was due on the entire amount of the loan for its life. Lotfi-Fard v. First Fed. of Lakewood, — Ohio App. 3d —, 2006 Ohio 3727, — N.E. 2d —, 2006 Ohio App. LEXIS 3686 (July 20, 2006).

Issue of fact was presented as to whether a client's legal malpractice suit was brought within the limitations period of RC § 2305.11(A), and thus, the motion for a directed verdict filed by an attorney and a law firm was properly denied. While the client expressed her dissatisfaction with the representation provided her and contacted a second law firm to discuss her concerns about her case, the evidence did not reveal any affirmative actions by either party that were patently inconsistent with or that expressly terminated attorney-client relationship before the client signed an agreement retaining the second law firm. Steindler v. Meyers, — Ohio App. 3d —, 2006 Ohio 4097, — N.E. 2d —, 2006 Ohio App. LEXIS 4067 (Aug. 10, 2006).

Motion for a directed verdict filed in a client's legal malpractice action arguing that the client had waived her claim by her settlements reached in the underlying dissolution case was properly denied because the client was able to demonstrate that she suffered financial loss as a result of the failure of the law firm and her attorney to clarify and enforce the various settlements reached throughout the course of the dissolution. Steindler v. Meyers, — Ohio App. 3d —, 2006 Ohio 4097, — N.E. 2d —, 2006 Ohio App. LEXIS 4067 (Aug. 10, 2006).

In a pedestrian's suit alleging that a city breached its duty under RC §§ 723.01 and 2744.02(B)(3) and its common-law duty to insure that a public street was in repair and free from nuisances, there was competent evidence upon which reasonable minds could reach different conclusions about whether the city had constructive notice of the defects on the street, in that the pedestrian and her daughter testified that, during the months preceding the accident, they had seen city trucks on the street working to patch a section of the road, and photographs revealed that the street was in significant disrepair; thus, the city's motion for a directed verdict under Ohio R. Civ. P. 50(A) was properly denied. While the city's evidence showed that the potholes were less than two inches deep, therefore giving rise to a presumption that the defect was trivial as a matter of law, the pedestrian presented evidence of attendant circumstances that could have allowed the jury to conclude that the defect was substantial in light of the circumstances, in that the evidence showed that there were no sidewalks for the pedestrian to use, that the road was narrowly constructed, and that the pedestrian was also forced to watch for oncoming traffic as she stepped out to enter the street. Shepherd v. City of Cincinnati, 168 Ohio App. 3d 444, 2006 Ohio 4286, 860 N.E. 2d 808, 2006 Ohio App. LEXIS 4208 (Aug. 18, 2006).

Trial court did not err in overruling a property owner's motion for a directed verdict in the neighbors' action to quiet title to a small parcel of property, claiming that they obtained title to the property through adverse possession because the neighbors, who had lived on the parcel for less than the 21-year period required to establish a claim of adverse possession, presented the testimony of two of their predecessors in interest, to the effect that the first predecessor, upon buying the property more than 21 years before the neighbors filed their suit, erected a fence next to the existing fence on the parcel; that they treated the parcel as part of their property; that their children played on the parcel; and that they maintained it. The predecessors did not indicate an understanding that they used the parcel under authority of the easement found in the deed and permitting the parcel to be used for "driveway purposes." Enderle v. Zettler, — Ohio App. 3d —, 2006 Ohio 4326, — N.E. 2d —, 2006 Ohio App. LEXIS 4256 (Aug. 21, 2006).

Employee failed to show that the employer knew that an injury to the operator of its power press was substantially certain to occur because the evidence established that the employee's accident was the only such accident ever to take place running the type of job on the press, that the employee was unaware of any other employee sustaining any injury while operating the press, that no employee had complained that the press was dangerous, that the employee was instructed in the operation of the press, and that the employee had violated the established safety procedure when he reached into the moving machine. Even if a guard should have been in place, the failure to provide the guard did not constitute substantial certainty, and as a result, the trial court properly granted a directed verdict to the employer on the employee's workplace intentional tort claim. Reising v. Broshco Fabricated Prods., — Ohio App. 3d —, 2006 Ohio 4449, — N.E. 2d —, 2006 Ohio App. LEXIS 4376 (Aug. 25, 2006).

In a Federal Employers' Liability Act suit, the employee's motion for judgment notwithstanding the verdict was properly denied because reasonable minds could form different conclusions as to whether the employee met his burden of proof. While the employee's evidence tended to show that he sustained a knee injury when certain equipment malfunctioned on him, the employer pointed out to the jury that the employee was the only witness to the injury and argued that the injuries could be explained as being the result of the employee's gout or weight. Staerker v. CSX Transp., Inc., — Ohio App. 3d —, 2006 Ohio 4803, — N.E. 2d —, 2006 Ohio App. LEXIS 4707 (Sept. 15, 2006).

When an insured was sued in a personal injury case, and his insurer provided counsel to represent him under a reservation of rights, but the insurer also intervened in the personal injury case and sought a declaration that it did not have to represent the insured, counsel provided by the insurer had no duty to represent the insured in opposition to the insurer's declaratory judgment complaint, so counsel's failure to do so, when the insured sued counsel for legal malpractice, counsel was entitled to a directed verdict, under Ohio R. Civ. P. 50(A)(4). Patitucci v. McNeal Schick Archibald & Biro, — Ohio App. 3d —, 2006 Ohio 5727, — N.E. 2d —, 2006 Ohio App. LEXIS 5728 (Nov. 2, 2006).

When a jury found against a gas company that alleged the operation of a landfill on property crossed by its pipeline caused it to have to move the pipeline, the company was not entitled to judgment notwithstanding the verdict because the jury could have reasonably found that the landfill operators did not interfere with the company's pipeline easement because dumping was occurring on the property when the company acquired the easement, and it could have found that the Environmental Protection Agency required the company to move its pipeline. Columbia Gas of Ohio, Inc. v. R.S.V. Inc., — Ohio App. 3d —, 2006 Ohio 7064, — N.E. 2d —, 2006 Ohio App. LEXIS 6987 (Dec. 29, 2006).

Interrogatories

Jury's failure to answer some of the interrogatories constitutes a mistrial and necessitates a new trial, regardless of whether there is a timely motion for a new trial. A judgment that leaves issues unresolved and contemplates that further action must be taken is not a final appealable order, and procedendo will issue to compel a court to retry the unresolved claims: State ex rel. Bd. of State Teachers Ret. Sys. v. Davis, 113 Ohio St. 3d 410, 2007 Ohio 2205, 865 N.E.2d 1289, 2007 Ohio LEXIS 1264 (2007).

Judgment notwithstanding the verdict

Motion for judgment notwithstanding the verdict is not the proper mechanism for challenging the excessiveness of a jury's verdict: Desai v. Franklin, 177 Ohio App. 3d 679, 2008 Ohio 3957, 895 N.E.2d 875, 2008 Ohio App. LEXIS 3335 (2008).

Trial court properly rejected the driver's motion for judgment notwithstanding the verdict because any issue of the truck driver's liability was not properly before the jury and therefore the jury did not and could not reach the issue. There was no determination that the truck driver was a person liable in tort and such a determination was necessary to entitle the driver to a setoff. Kane v. O'Day, — Ohio App. 3d —, 2007 Ohio 702, — N.E. 2d —, 2007 Ohio App. LEXIS 638 (Feb. 21, 2007).

Trial court properly denied a law firm's motions for a directed verdict and judgment notwithstanding the verdict after entering a jury award in favor of law clients in their legal malpractice action, as they met their standard of proof under Vahila of showing "some evidence of the merits" with respect to causation and damages. Envtl. Network Corp. v. Goodman Weiss Miller, L.L.P., — Ohio App. 3d —, 2007 Ohio 831, — N.E.2d —, 2007 Ohio App. LEXIS 760 (Mar. 1, 2007).

Trial court erred by granting the judgment notwithstanding the verdict motion, under Ohio R. Civ. P. 50(B), and reducing the total legal malpractice judgment from $382,000.00 to $100,000.00 because it limited consideration of damages to the collectability of damages in the underlying case against the tortfeasor, which was an improper "case within a case" analysis. The trial court's duty was to examine whether the verdict was supported by "substantial evidence," not whether the verdict was collectible and the fact that the jury did not enhance the award with any other damages that may have related to the malpractice committed, did not enable the trial court to step in and reduce the jury verdict due to considerations of collectability of the verdict. Paterek v. Petersen & Ibold, — Ohio App. 3d —, 2006 Ohio 4179, — N.E. 2d —, 2006 Ohio App. LEXIS 4127 (Aug. 11, 2006).

After a trial court had granted partial summary judgment to a real estate purchaser on its anticipatory breach of contract claim against the seller, and a visiting judge held a trial on damages only and thereafter granted judgment notwithstanding the verdict pursuant to Ohio R. Civ. P. 50(A)(4) to the seller upon finding that the purchaser had failed to show that it was ready, willing, and able to purchase the property, such was error; liability had already been determined in favor of the purchaser by the prior summary judgment ruling, the parties had proceeded in the trial as if the matter was only an issue of damages, and accordingly, the purchaser was not required to show such proof. Allegro Realty Advisors, Ltd. v. Orion Assocs. Ltd., — Ohio App. 3d —, 2006 Ohio 4588, — N.E. 2d —, 2006 Ohio App. LEXIS 4531 (Sept. 7, 2006).

Motion to dismiss

When a party's motion to dismiss argued that the evidence was insufficient to allow the opposing party's claims to be sent to the jury for its consideration, the motion actually sought a directed verdict, under Ohio R. Civ. P. 50(A), and it was not error for a presiding magistrate to consider the motion as one for a directed verdict. Sain v. Estate of Haas, — Ohio App. 3d —, 2007 Ohio 1705, — N.E. 2d —, 2007 Ohio App. LEXIS 1548 (Apr. 10, 2007).

Record

When an alleged insured claimed an insurer issued him a title insurance policy and then denied its existence, and the trial court granted a directed verdict to the insurer, under Ohio R. Civ. P. 50(A), the alleged insured could not demonstrate the trial court's alleged error because he did not submit a record of the trial court's proceedings, under Ohio R. App. P. 9(A), so the appellate court could not review the evidence before the trial court and had to presume the regularity of the trial court's proceedings. Clair v. First American Title Ins., — Ohio App. 3d —, 2007 Ohio 1681, — N.E. 2d —, 2007 Ohio App. LEXIS 1537 (Apr. 11, 2007).

Remittitur

Trial court's partial remittitur of an award of back pay to an employee in her discrimination action against an employer was proper where she had found employment by starting a house cleaning business, but it was determined that she had not made a serious investment in it and had treated it as part-time employment, and accordingly, the trial court's denial of the employer's motions for new trial under Ohio R. Civ. P. 59 or for judgment notwithstanding the verdict under Ohio R. Civ. P. 50 was proper. Hollingsworth v. Time Warner Cable, — Ohio App. 3d —, 2006 Ohio 4903, — N.E. 2d —, 2006 Ohio App. LEXIS 4833 (Sept. 22, 2006).

Test for directed verdict or judgment n.o.v.

In a bench trial, a trial court erred in entering a "directed verdict" under Ohio R. Civ. P. 50(A)(4) for a contractor in an owner's breach of contract action, as she provided evidence on each element of the claims with respect to the breaches of two contracts and the damages that she incurred thereby, and as such, the trial court could only have denied her claim if it weighed the evidence or judged the credibility of it and determined that the owner's testimony and exhibits was not believable; however, that was done under an involuntary dismissal standard pursuant to Ohio R. Civ. P. 41(B)(2), which should have been the proper procedural vehicle used by the trial court, such that its improper standard of review resulted in an erroneous determination. Jarupan v. Hanna, 173 Ohio App. 3d 284, 2007 Ohio 5081, 878 N.E.2d 66, 2007 Ohio App. LEXIS 4498 (2007).

RULE 51. Instructions to the jury; objection

(A) **Instructions; error; record.** At the close of the evidence or at such earlier time during the trial as the court reasonably directs, any party may file written requests that the court instruct the jury on the law as set forth in the requests. Copies shall be furnished to all other parties at the time of making the requests. The court shall inform counsel of its proposed action on the requests prior to counsel's arguments to the jury and shall give the jury complete instructions after the arguments are completed. The court also may give some or all of its instructions to the jury prior to counsel's arguments. The court shall reduce its final instructions to writing or make an audio, electronic, or other recording of those instructions, provide at least one written copy or recording of those instructions to

the jury for use during deliberations, and preserve those instructions for the record.

On appeal, a party may not assign as error the giving or the failure to give any instruction unless the party objects before the jury retires to consider its verdict, stating specifically the matter objected to and the grounds of the objection. Opportunity shall be given to make the objection out of the hearing of the jury.

(B) **Cautionary instructions.** At the commencement and during the course of the trial, the court may give the jury cautionary and other instructions of law relating to trial procedure, credibility and weight of the evidence, and the duty and function of the jury and may acquaint the jury generally with the nature of the case.

History: Amended, eff 7-1-72; 7-1-75; 7-1-92; 7-1-05.

NOTES TO DECISIONS

ANALYSIS

Failure to give an instruction

Jury instructions may have misled the jury into believing that the manufacturer could escape liability if the jury found that the dealership or the previous dealer had caused the damage, regardless of when the damage occurred and thus, the jury could have believed the buyer's scenario, but improperly rendered a verdict in favor of the manufacturer. The requested jury instruction would have informed the jury that in a Lemon Law situation, the defense of abuse, neglect, or modification was only valid as to damages caused by persons other than the manufacturer or the manufacturer's authorized dealer. Dressler v. Daimler Chrysler Corp., — Ohio App. 3d —, 2006 Ohio 4448, — N.E. 2d —, 2006 Ohio App. LEXIS 4378 (Aug. 25, 2006).

Jury instructions

Considering the totality of the jury charge and the fact that the jury never even had to consider the proximate cause issue, the intermittent use of "the" instead of "a" did not affect the children's substantial rights. The court did say "a proximate cause" multiple times and further explained that there can be more than one proximate cause and, furthermore, the jury found no breach of the standard of care, which in turn failed to necessitate an analysis of proximate cause. Hanni v. Tofil, — Ohio App. 3d —, 2006 Ohio 1284, — N.E. 2d —, 2006 Ohio App. LEXIS 1176 (Mar. 16, 2006).

Objection to jury instruction

Trial court did not err in failing to give jury instructions on comparative negligence, pursuant to RC § 2315.19(B), because Ohio R. Civ. P. 51, which required that an objection be made prior to appealing an issue, superseded RC § 2315.19(B), which mandated a jury instruction on comparative negligence. Plaintiffs did not object when the instruction was not given. Kukla v. Field Energy Servs., — Ohio App. 3d —, 2006 Ohio 3114, — N.E. 2d —, 2006 Ohio App. LEXIS 2996 (June 21, 2006).

— Timely objections

Parties' objections to the jury charge were timely under the circumstances. The trial court included instructions on its own initiative and did not give the parties an opportunity to object until after the court had instructed the jury: Peffer v. Cleveland Clinic Found., 177 Ohio App. 3d 403, 2008 Ohio 3688, 894 N.E.2d 1273, 2008 Ohio App. LEXIS 3091 (2008).

— Waiver

Trial court's award of rescission and damages to manufactured home purchasers in their action against a general contractor/retailer (GC/R) of the home upon finding that the GC/R breached the parties' contract and was negligent, which actions proximately caused damage to the purchasers, was proper, as the jury also found that the GC/R had breached implied warranties and committed unfair, deceptive, and unconscionable acts under RC § 1345.02(A) of the Ohio Consumer Sales Practices Act. As the trial court instructed the jury about the possible remedies that it could award without objection by the GC/R, it could not assign an error on appeal regarding the jury instructions pursuant to Ohio R. Civ. P. 51(A). Drenning v. Blue Ribbon Homes, — Ohio App. 3d —, 2007 Ohio 1323, — N.E. 2d —, 2007 Ohio App. LEXIS 1230 (Mar. 23, 2007).

Trial court's award of rescission and damages to manufactured home purchasers in their action against a general contractor/retailer (GC/R) of the home upon finding that the GC/R breached the parties' contract and was negligent, which actions proximately caused damage to the purchasers, was proper, as the jury also found that the GC/R had breached implied warranties and committed unfair, deceptive, and unconscionable acts under RC § 1345.02(A) of the Ohio Consumer Sales Practices Act. As the trial court instructed the jury about the possible remedies that it could award without objection by the GC/R, it could not assign an error on appeal regarding the jury instructions pursuant to Ohio R. Civ. P. 51(A). Drenning v. Blue Ribbon Homes, — Ohio App. 3d —, 2007 Ohio 1323, — N.E. 2d —, 2007 Ohio App. LEXIS 1230 (Mar. 23, 2007).

As children of a deceased patient failed to object during trial to a jury instruction on the issue of foreseeability in their medical malpractice action, they waived the right to object to the instruction on appeal, pursuant to Ohio R. Civ. P. 51(A). Joiner v. Simon, — Ohio App. 3d —, 2007 Ohio 425, — N.E. 2d —, 2007 Ohio App. LEXIS 372 (Feb. 2, 2007).

While an operator raised the issue of a curative jury instruction in a motion in limine, arguing that the trial court erred in allowing appellees to introduce evidence of collateral sources, he failed to object to the jury instruction when given the opportunity during the course of trial, and thus, pursuant to Ohio R. Civ. P. 51(A), the operator waived the right to raise the issue on appeal. Chehi v. Keifer, — Ohio App. 3d —, 2006 Ohio 5904, — N.E. 2d —, 2006 Ohio App. LEXIS 5869 (Nov. 9, 2006).

Where appellants failed to object to jury instructions in property owners' adverse possession and quiet title action, pursuant to Ohio R. Civ. P. 51(A), the error raised on appeal with respect to the instructions was reviewed under the plain error standard. No error existed where the trial court failed to instruct the jury that appellants were the equitable title holders of the disputed property, as neither party held legal title to the land and the jury had sufficient evidence before it to understand that the disputed property arose from a gap in a title description that was meant to be included in appellants' predecessors' title. Heider v. Unknown Heirs, — Ohio App. 3d —, 2006 Ohio 122, — N.E. 2d —, 2006 Ohio App. LEXIS 95 (Jan. 13, 2006).

Since appellant failed to object to a trial court's instruction to the jury, to the effect that, the jury's verdict should be for appellee if the jury found that appellant had failed to prove that appellee's negligence proximately caused appellant's in-

juries, pursuant to Ohio R. Civ. P. 51(A), appellant waived all but plain error with respect to the jury instruction. The trial court's instruction was a correct statement of Ohio negligence law. McBride v. Quebe, — Ohio App. 3d —, 2006 Ohio 5128, — N.E. 2d —, 2006 Ohio App. LEXIS 5055 (Sept. 29, 2006).

Plain error rule

When applicants for membership in an all-male club claimed gender discrimination, and the jury awarded them punitive damages without awarding them compensatory or nominal damages, requiring that the punitive damages award be stricken, the applicants did not show, under Ohio R. Civ. P. 51(A), that the trial court's failure to instruct the jury on when it could award punitive damages was plain error, as the applicants did not object to the trial court's failure to so instruct, because it could not be said that but for the failure to give this instruction the jury would not have awarded punitive damages and/or would have awarded compensatory or nominal damages, allowing the punitive damages award to stand. Wilson v. United Fellowship Club, — Ohio App. 3d —, 2007 Ohio 2089, — N.E. 2d —, 2007 Ohio App. LEXIS 1949 (May 2, 2007).

Preservation for review

Since a jury instruction on the issue of patient contributory negligence that was proffered by a radiologist and her employer was reduced to writing, was tendered to the court reporter at the trial court's direction, and was available for review in the exhibits for the appeal, Ohio R. Civ. P. 51(A) did not act as a bar to the appellate court's consideration of the proffered instruction. Viox v. Weinberg, — Ohio App. 3d —, 2006 Ohio 5075, — N.E. 2d —, 2006 Ohio App. LEXIS 5010 (Sept. 29, 2006).

Unsupported by pleadings or evidence

As the issue of fiduciary duty did not appear in the pleadings in a multi-tort action, and there was no motion made during the trial to amend the pleadings in order to conform them to the evidence pursuant to Ohio R. Civ. P. 15(B), the trial court did not abuse its discretion in declining to instruct the jury on the issue of fiduciary duty. Domer v. Joan, — Ohio App. 3d —, 2007 Ohio 6877, — N.E. 2d —, 2007 Ohio App. LEXIS 6032 (Dec. 14, 2007).

RULE 52. Findings by the court

When questions of fact are tried by the court without a jury, judgment may be general for the prevailing party unless one of the parties in writing requests otherwise before the entry of judgment pursuant to Civ.R. 58, or not later than seven days after the party filing the request has been given notice of the court's announcement of its decision, whichever is later, in which case, the court shall state in writing the conclusions of fact found separately from the conclusions of law.

When a request for findings of fact and conclusions of law is made, the court, in its discretion, may require any or all of the parties to submit proposed findings of fact and conclusions of law; however, only those findings of fact and conclusions of law made by the court shall form part of the record.

Findings of fact and conclusions of law required by this rule and by Rule 41(B)(2) are unnecessary upon all other motions including those pursuant to Rule 12, Rule 55 and Rule 56.

An opinion or memorandum of decision filed in the action prior to judgment entry and containing findings of fact and conclusions of law stated separately shall be sufficient to satisfy the requirements of this rule and Rule 41(B)(2).

History: Amended, eff 7-1-71; 7-1-89.

NOTES TO DECISIONS

ANALYSIS

Appeal
Applicability
Attorney fees
Custody modification
Findings of fact and conclusions of law
Harmless error
No duty to make factual findings
Specific findings
Summary judgment
Timeliness

Appeal

Where an appellate court vacated portions of a trial court judgment in parties' dissolution action that contained legal or factual errors, issues regarding the trial court's denial of the husband's motion for a new trial under Ohio R. Civ. P. 59 or the trial court's adoption of the wife's counsel's proposed findings of fact and conclusions of law pursuant to Ohio R. Civ. P. 52 without modification were deemed moot for purposes of appellate review under Ohio R. App. P. 12(A)(1)(c), as the vacated portions of the judgment related to those issues. Janosek v. Janosek, — Ohio App. 3d —, 2007 Ohio 68, — N.E. 2d —, 2007 Ohio App. LEXIS 59 (Jan. 11, 2007).

Where parents involved in a dependency proceeding for one of their children did not request that the trial court include findings of fact and conclusions of law in the judgment entries pursuant to Ohio R. Civ. P. 52, their claim on appeal that the trial judge relied improperly on challenged evidentiary rulings in making his decision was not cognizable. In re E. R., — Ohio App. 3d —, 2006 Ohio 4816, — N.E. 2d —, 2006 Ohio App. LEXIS 4745 (Sept. 18, 2006).

Applicability

It was well established that it was not error for a trial court to adopt, verbatim, a party's proposed findings of fact and conclusions of law based upon a theory that might differ from that of another party, so it was certainly not error for the trial court to prepare its own findings of fact and conclusions of law based upon its adoption based on the evidence presented at trial of a particular theory or argument although it was not the theory or argument a party might have asserted, as long as there was a basis in law and fact for the trial court's finding, and, in such case, error could only be found when the findings of fact and/or conclusions of law were against the manifest weight of the evidence. MacDowell v. Decarlo, — Ohio App. 3d —, 2007 Ohio 249, — N.E. 2d —, 2007 Ohio App. LEXIS 235 (Jan. 24, 2007).

Purpose of Ohio R. Civ. P. 52 was to aid an appellate court in reviewing the record and determining the validity of the basis of the trial court's judgment, and, in light of its purpose, while there was no precise rule regarding compliance with Rule 52, a trial court's findings and conclusions had to articulate an adequate basis upon which a party could mount a challenge to, and the appellate court could make a determination as to the propriety of, resolved disputed issues of fact and the trial court's application of the law. MacDowell v. Decarlo, — Ohio App. 3d —, 2007 Ohio 249, — N.E. 2d —, 2007 Ohio App. LEXIS 235 (Jan. 24, 2007).

Attorney fees

Although a trial court did not provide requested findings of fact and conclusions of law pursuant to Ohio R. Civ. P. 52 with respect to its decision to grant a party attorney's fees, it provided specific reasons supporting the award, which was sufficient to comply with Rule 52. Savage v. Cody-Zeigler,

Inc., — Ohio App. 3d —, 2006 Ohio 2760, — N.E. 2d —, 2006 Ohio App. LEXIS 2601 (May 25, 2006).

Custody modification

Although a magistrate found that a change of circumstances had occurred pursuant to RC § 3109.04(E), after considering the relevant best interest factors under § 3109.04(F)(1) and (2), it was determined that a modification of the shared parenting plan that was incorporated into the parties' dissolution decree was not warranted in the circumstances, which determination was properly adopted by the trial court; the trial court expressly considered each of the best interest factors under § 3109.04(F), but where the former husband had failed to file a motion under Ohio R. Civ. P. 52, the court was not required to explicitly reiterate its findings with regard to those factors. Hodson v. Hodson, — Ohio App. 3d —, 2007 Ohio 4419, — N.E. 2d —, 2007 Ohio App. LEXIS 3987 (Aug. 29, 2007).

Findings of fact and conclusions of law

Trial court did not abuse its discretion by denying a father's motion to modify the parties' prior allocation of parental rights and responsibilities. The father failed to request that the trial court make findings of fact and conclusions of law under Ohio R. Civ. P. 52, so the court reviewed the record and presumed both that the trial court applied the law correctly and that there was some evidence in the record to support the trial court's judgment. McClead v. McClead, — Ohio App. 3d —, 2007 Ohio 4624, — N.E. 2d —, 2007 Ohio App. LEXIS 4163 (Sept. 5, 2007).

When a trial court made findings of fact and conclusions of law in support of the trial court's determinations that a mother's child was dependent and to grant the child's custody to the child's father, those findings and conclusions were insufficient and were prejudicial error because an appellate court could not clearly distinguish the basis for the trial court's dependency and custody determinations because the trial court neglected to cite which evidence the court considered in making these determinations, and the trial court failed to link its findings to applicable statutes. In re J.M., — Ohio App. 3d —, 2007 Ohio 4219, — N.E. 2d —, 2007 Ohio App. LEXIS 3816 (Aug. 20, 2007).

Because the trial court was ruling on motions for judgment on the pleadings, brought pursuant to Ohio R. Civ. P. 12(C), the trial court had no duty to make findings of fact and conclusions of law. Bradigan v. Strongsville City Schs., — Ohio App. 3d —, 2007 Ohio 2773, — N.E. 2d —, 2007 Ohio App. LEXIS 2571 (June 7, 2007).

Findings of fact and conclusions of law under Ohio R. Civ. P. 52 were unnecessary in regard to the husband's motion for contempt against the wife after their divorce. Yarchak v. Yarchak, — Ohio App. 3d —, 2007 Ohio 2619, — N.E. 2d —, 2007 Ohio App. LEXIS 2435 (May 29, 2007).

Trial court did not abuse its discretion where it ordered a husband to pay the existing mortgages on real property, based upon a determination that he had engaged in misconduct in transferring the property to relatives and in taking out a line of credit on the marital home and then dissipating the funds, as the trial court carefully considered the relevant factors under RC § 3105.171(F). The trial court complied with the requirement under § 3105.171(G) and Ohio R. Civ. P. 52 to make findings of fact to support its decision for purposes of appellate review, as the decision was replete with detailed findings to support the trial court's division of the parties' property. Hamad v. Hamad, — Ohio App. 3d —, 2007 Ohio 2239, — N.E. 2d —, 2007 Ohio App. LEXIS 2069 (May 10, 2007).

In divorce proceedings, a trial court did not err under Ohio R. Civ. P. 52 in adopting a former husband's proposed findings of fact and conclusions of law; the trial court did not abdicate its responsibility to review the testimony and documentary evidence and reach its own conclusions because the findings were manifestly shaped by the trial court's interlocutory pronouncements and ultimate judgment during the course of the trial. An v. Manson, — Ohio App. 3d —, 2006 Ohio 6733, — N.E. 2d —, 2006 Ohio App. LEXIS 6632 (Dec. 19, 2006).

In denying defendant's petition for post-conviction relief from convictions for robbery, escape, and other offenses under RC § 2953.21(A)(1), a trial court did not err in adopting the State's proposed findings of fact and conclusions of law because such a practice was not prohibited under Ohio R. Civ. P. 52 and there was no evidence that the petition was not reviewed and considered in its entirety; therefore, defendant demonstrated no prejudice. State v. Thomas, — Ohio App. 3d —, 2006 Ohio 6588, — N.E. 2d —, 2006 Ohio App. LEXIS 6494 (Dec. 14, 2006).

In light of the father's failure to request the trial court to issue separate findings of fact and conclusions of law, the trial court did not err in failing to do so. Williams v. Mabra, — Ohio App. 3d —, 2006 Ohio 5845, — N.E. 2d —, 2006 Ohio App. LEXIS 5798 (Nov. 6, 2006).

Trial court's adoption of findings of fact and conclusions of law proposed by anesthesiologists in an action by a terminated anesthesiologist from the parties' practice was proper under Ohio R. Civ. P. 52, as they articulated an adequate basis upon which the appellate court could make a determination regarding the issues raised on appeal. Mulchin v. Zzz Anesthesia, Inc., — Ohio App. 3d —, 2006 Ohio 5773, — N.E. 2d —, 2006 Ohio App. LEXIS 5757 (Nov. 3, 2006).

When a mother did not seek findings of fact or conclusions of law, under Ohio R. Civ. P. 52, when a trial court appointed the father of her children as their residential parent, the regularity of the trial court's proceedings had to be presumed, and, as some evidence supported the trial court's decision, because the mother's learning disability kept her from helping the children with their homework and an improvement in the children's posture and self-confidence could be attributed to the father without expert testimony, the father's appointment was not an abuse of discretion, under the factors in RC § 3109.04(F)(1)(a) through (j). Siefker v. Siefker, — Ohio App. 3d —, 2006 Ohio 5154, — N.E. 2d —, 2006 Ohio App. LEXIS 5057 (Oct. 2, 2006).

When an alleged mentally ill person claimed a magistrate's decision that, under RC § 5122.01(B)(3) and (B)(4), she was a danger to herself and could not provide for her basic needs due to mental illness was against the manifest weight of the evidence because the magistrate's decision did not specifically state which evidence supported the respective decisions, the magistrate did not have to state the evidence he relied on, absent a request for findings of fact and conclusions of law, under Ohio R. Civ. P. 52, unless such findings and conclusions were otherwise required by law or an order of reference, under Ohio R. Civ. P. 53. In re L.G., — Ohio App. 3d —, 2006 Ohio 5043, — N.E. 2d —, 2006 Ohio App. LEXIS 5182 (Sept. 28, 2006).

Where the trial court issued a modification of a preliminary injunction requiring the union to remove windbreaker structures erected for striking union members, the trial court was not required by Ohio R. Civ. P. 52 to state its reasons for ordering the removal of the windbreaker, as a motion to modify an injunction fell into an exception to the findings of fact and conclusions of law requirement. Ormet Aluminum Mill Prods. Corp. v. USW, — Ohio App. 3d —, 2006 Ohio 3782, — N.E. 2d —, 2006 Ohio App. LEXIS 3736 (July 20, 2006).

Because an attorney failed to request findings of fact and conclusions of law pursuant to Ohio R. Civ. P. 52, he was not permitted to complain on appeal as to a lack of specificity as to which charges and services were deemed unnecessary or unreasonable by the trial court in the attorney's suit against a client seeking payment of fees. Lehmkuhl v. Vermillion, — Ohio App. 3d —, 2006 Ohio 3701, — N.E. 2d —, 2006 Ohio App. LEXIS 3622 (July 19, 2006).

In awarding spousal support to the wife and in dividing the parties' assets pursuant to RC §§ 3105.18 and 3105.171(F), the trial court did not have to address each factor in its judgment, although it had to consider each factor and it had to classify property as either marital or separate and then award each spouse his or her separate property; sufficient reasons were given by the trial court with respect to the spousal support award to the wife, but there were no conclusions made regarding the parties' retention of separate assets, which required a remand for findings of fact and conclusions of law pursuant to Ohio R. Civ. P. 52. Cangemi v. Cangemi, — Ohio App. 3d —, 2006 Ohio 2879, — N.E. 2d —, 2006 Ohio App. LEXIS 2780 (June 8, 2006).

Trial court was not required to issue findings of fact and conclusions of law pursuant to Ohio R. Civ. P. 52 relating to its decision to grant a bank the right to intervene in a pending action pursuant to Ohio R. Civ. P. 24(A)(2), as the determination was based on mainly legal issues and no "trial" took place in making the decision thereon. The fact that the request for findings and conclusions was not complied with did not impair the ability to appeal another ruling in the matter, nor did it toll the time for appealing under Ohio R. App. P. 4(B)(2). Savage v. Cody-Zeigler, Inc., — Ohio App. 3d —, 2006 Ohio 2760, — N.E. 2d —, 2006 Ohio App. LEXIS 2601 (May 25, 2006).

Where plaintiff failed to provide proposed findings of fact and conclusions of law after he moved the court to make them pursuant to Ohio R. Civ. P. 52, the trial court did not err in adopting defendant's proposed findings and conclusions of law without change, as plaintiff did not object in any way to defendant's filing and the adoption thereof, without more, did not demonstrate an abuse of discretion by the trial court. Neubauer v. Ohio Remcon, Inc., — Ohio App. 3d —, 2006 Ohio 1481, — N.E. 2d —, 2006 Ohio App. LEXIS 1335 (Mar. 28, 2006).

In a child custody dispute, it was not error for a trial court to adopt some findings of fact proposed by one of the parties. Smith v. Quigg, — Ohio App. 3d —, 2006 Ohio 1494, — N.E. 2d —, 2006 Ohio App. LEXIS 1371 (Mar. 22, 2006).

Trial court's finding of a police officer's income from his operation of a construction business was affirmed as a union agreed to rely on submitted briefs and could not complain of the trial court's reliance on the calculations set forth in a township's brief. The union did not request findings of fact under Ohio R. Civ. P. 52 and there was some evidence supporting the trial court's finding, so the finding had to be affirmed. Board of Trustees of Miami Twp. v. FOP, Ohio Labor Council, Inc., — Ohio App. 3d —, 2006 Ohio 150, — N.E. 2d —, 2006 Ohio App. LEXIS 118 (Jan. 17, 2006).

Harmless error

Defendant was not eligible for judicial release after serving 5 years of his 19-year sentence, so the trial court erred in informing defendant that he was; however, while the sentence resulted from a plea agreement, defendant's agreement to the plea was not conditional on his eligibility for judicial release, and, thus, the trial court's misstatement was a harmless error pursuant to Ohio R. Crim. P. 52(A). State v. Woody, — Ohio App. 3d —, 2006 Ohio 1624, — N.E. 2d —, 2006 Ohio App. LEXIS 1529 (Mar. 24, 2006).

No duty to make factual findings

In a suit claiming that a decedent's ex-husband unduly influenced her to transfer certain assets to him, in which it was claimed that the decedent had a fiduciary relationship with the ex-husband, the trial court was not required to make findings addressing arguments which assumed that a fiduciary relationship existed because it did not find that such a relationship was demonstrated, so its findings were sufficient to allow appellate review of the trial court's resolution of factual disputes and its

conclusions of law. MacDowell v. Decarlo, — Ohio App. 3d
—, 2007 Ohio 249, — N.E. 2d —, 2007 Ohio App. LEXIS 235
(Jan. 24, 2007).

Trial court did not abuse its discretion in its decision on a
former husband's request for modification of his child support
obligation, as it impliedly adopted a magistrate's findings of
fact and it made its own findings with respect to the needs and
standard of living of the children and the parents, pursuant to
RC § 3119.04(B). As the wife did not request findings
pursuant to Ohio R. Civ. P. 52, the trial court was not required
to make them. Guertin v. Guertin, — Ohio App. 3d —, 2007
Ohio 2008, — N.E. 2d —, 2007 Ohio App. LEXIS 1785 (Apr.
26, 2007).

As a trial court's judgment entry that sustained a wife's
motion to enforce a contempt sentence against her husband
was a final appealable order pursuant to RC § 2505.02, and
findings of fact and conclusions of law under Ohio R. Civ. P. 52
were not required from the trial court, the time for filing an
appeal was not tolled pending such findings and conclusions
pursuant to Ohio R. App. P. 4(A). Where the husband failed to
file a timely appeal from the trial court judgment, he waived
his right to assert any errors related to the contempt enforcement proceeding. Hamad v. Hamad, — Ohio App. 3d —,
2007 Ohio 2239, — N.E. 2d —, 2007 Ohio App. LEXIS 2069
(May 10, 2007).

When, in a child support case, a father did not request that
the trial court enter written findings of fact and conclusions of
law, it had no duty to issue such findings and conclusions, and
its failure to do so was not reversible error. Combs v. Walsh, —
Ohio App. 3d —, 2006 Ohio 7026, — N.E. 2d —, 2006 Ohio
App. LEXIS 7022 (Dec. 28, 2006).

As a former guardian for an adjudicated incompetent failed
to request findings of fact and conclusions of law from a
magistrate's decision, pursuant to Ohio R. Civ. P. 52, an
argument on appeal with respect to the lack thereof lacked
merit. In re Norwood, — Ohio App. 3d —, 2006 Ohio 4504,
— N.E. 2d —, 2006 Ohio App. LEXIS 4404 (Aug. 31, 2006).

Specific findings

Trial court did not err in denying a mother's request for
specific findings of fact and conclusions of law pursuant to
Ohio R. Civ. P. 52 in its decision that denied her request for
a child support guideline deviation under RC §§ 3119.22 and
3119.23, as the trial court's decision was thorough and
well-reasoned and it was not required to make specific
findings as to why it denied the deviation request. Logan v.
Gregrow, — Ohio App. 3d —, 2007 Ohio 4585, — N.E. 2d —,
2007 Ohio App. LEXIS 4122 (Sept. 4, 2007).

Summary judgment

Trial court did not err in denying a property owner's request
for findings of fact and conclusions of law pursuant to Ohio R.
Civ. P. 52, as the trial court had resolved the pending litigation
by a grant of summary judgment under Ohio R. Civ. P. 56, to
which Ohio R. Civ. P. 52 was inapplicable. Joyce v. Godale, —
Ohio App. 3d —, 2007 Ohio 473, — N.E. 2d —, 2007 Ohio
App. LEXIS 421 (Feb. 2, 2007).

Trial court did not err when it did not set forth findings of
fact and conclusions of law in granting a property owner's
motion for summary judgment because, pursuant to Ohio R.
Civ. P. 52, findings of fact and conclusions of law were not
necessary when a trial court rules on a party's motion for
summary judgment. Burdette v. Stevens, — Ohio App. 3d —,
2007 Ohio 4604, — N.E. 2d —, 2007 Ohio App. LEXIS 4140
(Aug. 30, 2007).

Timeliness

When, in a permanent custody proceeding, a magistrate
denied a mother's motion to rehear an agency's motion for
temporary custody of her children, she did not timely seek
findings of fact and conclusions of law regarding that decision,
under Ohio R. Civ. P. 52 and 53(D)(3)(a)(ii), because she did

not seek them within seven days after her motion was denied.
In re G.N., 170 Ohio App. 3d 76, 2007 Ohio 126, 866 N.E.2d
32, 2007 Ohio App. LEXIS 104 (2007).

Appellant failed to file a timely motion requesting findings
of fact and conclusions of law following the magistrate's
decision denying her motion for a rehearing: In re G.N., 170
Ohio App. 3d 76, 2007 Ohio 126, 866 N.E.2d 32, 2007 Ohio
App. LEXIS 104 (2007).

Probate court erred in denying a successor in interest to a
fidelity bond issuer's request for a findings of fact and
conclusions of law, pursuant to Ohio R. Civ. P. 52, upon the
probate court's finding that the request was untimely, as the
request was made within the seven-day period from when the
successor received notice of the probate court's judgment, and
the decision of the magistrate, upon which the probate court's
decision was based, was not a trigger of the time period
because the magistrate could not file a "judgment" under Ohio
R. Civ. P. 53. The probate court could not withhold the filing
of the request until a resolution of the filing fee was made, as
there was no such requirement regarding the fee prior to
allowing a filing under Montgomery County, Ohio, Ct. C.P.
Prob. Div. R. 58.1. In re Estate of Bishop, 165 Ohio App. 3d
761, 2006 Ohio 1252, 848 N.E. 2d 567, 2006 Ohio App.
LEXIS 1148 (Mar. 17, 2006).

Although a trial court erred in accepting a party's late filing
of proposed findings of fact and conclusions of law where no
request for an extension of time was made pursuant to Ohio R.
Civ. P. 6(B)(2), the late filing did not cause prejudice, as only
the findings and conclusions made by the court became part of
the record and accordingly, pursuant to Ohio R. Civ. P. 52, the
parties' proposed findings and conclusions did not even
comprise part of the record. The findings of fact and conclusions of law were supported by competent, credible evidence
and were not contrary to law. Kimbler v. Kimbler, — Ohio
App. 3d —, 2006 Ohio 2695, — N.E. 2d —, 2006 Ohio App.
LEXIS 2516 (May 23, 2006).

RULE 53.   Magistrates

(A) **Appointment.** A court of record may appoint
one or more magistrates who shall be attorneys at law
admitted to practice in Ohio.

(B) **Compensation.** The compensation of magistrates shall be fixed by the court, and no part of the
compensation shall be taxed as costs under Civ. R.
54(D).

(C) **Authority.**

(1) **Scope.** To assist courts of record and pursuant
to reference under Civ. R. 53(D)(1), magistrates are
authorized, subject to the terms of the relevant reference, to do any of the following:

(a) Determine any motion in any case;

(b) Conduct the trial of any case that will not be tried
to a jury;

(c) Upon unanimous written consent of the parties,
preside over the trial of any case that will be tried to a
jury;

(d) Conduct proceedings upon application for the
issuance of a temporary protection order as authorized
by law;

(e) Exercise any other authority specifically vested in
magistrates by statute and consistent with this rule.

(2) **Regulation of proceedings.** In performing the
responsibilities described in Civ. R. 53(C)(1), magistrates are authorized, subject to the terms of the
relevant reference, to regulate all proceedings as if by

the court and to do everything necessary for the efficient performance of those responsibilities, including but not limited to, the following:

(a) Issuing subpoenas for the attendance of witnesses and the production of evidence;

(b) Ruling upon the admissibility of evidence;

(c) Putting witnesses under oath and examining them;

(d) Calling the parties to the action and examining them under oath;

(e) When necessary to obtain the presence of an alleged contemnor in cases involving direct or indirect contempt of court, issuing an attachment for the alleged contemnor and setting the type, amount, and any conditions of bail pursuant to Crim. R. 46;

(f) Imposing, subject to Civ. R. 53(D)(8), appropriate sanctions for civil or criminal contempt committed in the presence of the magistrate.

(D) Proceedings in Matters Referred to Magistrates.

(1) **Reference by court of record.**

(a) **Purpose and method.** A court of record may, for one or more of the purposes described in Civ. R. 53(C)(1), refer a particular case or matter or a category of cases or matters to a magistrate by a specific or general order of reference or by rule.

(b) **Limitation.** A court of record may limit a reference by specifying or limiting the magistrate's powers, including but not limited to, directing the magistrate to determine only particular issues, directing the magistrate to perform particular responsibilities, directing the magistrate to receive and report evidence only, fixing the time and place for beginning and closing any hearings, or fixing the time for filing any magistrate's decision on the matter or matters referred.

(2) **Magistrate's order; motion to set aside magistrate's order.**

(a) **Magistrate's order.**

(i) **Nature of order.** Subject to the terms of the relevant reference, a magistrate may enter orders without judicial approval if necessary to regulate the proceedings and if not dispositive of a claim or defense of a party.

(ii) **Form, filing, and service of magistrate's order.** A magistrate's order shall be in writing, identified as a magistrate's order in the caption, signed by the magistrate, filed with the clerk, and served by the clerk on all parties or their attorneys.

(b) **Motion to set aside magistrate's order.** Any party may file a motion with the court to set aside a magistrate's order. The motion shall state the moving party's reasons with particularity and shall be filed not later than ten days after the magistrate's order is filed. The pendency of a motion to set aside does not stay the effectiveness of the magistrate's order, though the magistrate or the court may by order stay the effectiveness of a magistrate's order.

(3) **Magistrate's decision; objections to magistrate's decision.**

(a) **Magistrate's decision.**

(i) **When required.** Subject to the terms of the relevant reference, a magistrate shall prepare a magistrate's decision respecting any matter referred under Civ. R. 53(D)(1).

(ii) **Findings of fact and conclusions of law.** Subject to the terms of the relevant reference, a magistrate's decision may be general unless findings of fact and conclusions of law are timely requested by a party or otherwise required by law. A request for findings of fact and conclusions of law shall be made before the entry of a magistrate's decision or within seven days after the filing of a magistrate's decision. If a request for findings of fact and conclusions of law is timely made, the magistrate may require any or all of the parties to submit proposed findings of fact and conclusions of law.

(iii) **Form; filing, and service of magistrate's decision.** A magistrate's decision shall be in writing, identified as a magistrate's decision in the caption, signed by the magistrate, filed with the clerk, and served by the clerk on all parties or their attorneys no later than three days after the decision is filed. A magistrate's decision shall indicate conspicuously that a party shall not assign as error on appeal the court's adoption of any factual finding or legal conclusion, whether or not specifically designated as a finding of fact or conclusion of law under Civ. R. 53(D)(3)(a)(ii), unless the party timely and specifically objects to that factual finding or legal conclusion as required by Civ. R. 53(D)(3)(b).

(b) **Objections to magistrate's decision.**

(i) **Time for filing.** A party may file written objections to a magistrate's decision within fourteen days of the filing of the decision, whether or not the court has adopted the decision during that fourteen-day period as permitted by Civ. R. 53(D)(4)(e)(i). If any party timely files objections, any other party may also file objections not later than ten days after the first objections are filed. If a party makes a timely request for findings of fact and conclusions of law, the time for filing objections begins to run when the magistrate files a decision that includes findings of fact and conclusions of law.

(ii) **Specificity of objection.** An objection to a magistrate's decision shall be specific and state with particularity all grounds for objection.

(iii) **Objection to magistrate's factual finding; transcript or affidavit.** An objection to a factual finding, whether or not specifically designated as a finding of fact under Civ. R. 53(D)(3)(a)(ii), shall be supported by a transcript of all the evidence submitted to the magistrate relevant to that finding or an affidavit of that evidence if a transcript is not available. With leave of court, alternative technology or manner of reviewing the relevant evidence may be considered. The objecting party shall file the transcript or affidavit with the court within thirty days after filing objections unless the court extends the time in writing for preparation of the transcript or other good cause. If a party files timely objections prior to the date on which a transcript is prepared, the party may seek leave of court to supplement the objections.

(iv) **Waiver of right to assign adoption by court**

as error on appeal. Except for a claim of plain error, a party shall not assign as error on appeal the court's adoption of any factual finding or legal conclusion, whether or not specifically designated as a finding of fact or conclusion of law under Civ. R. 53(D)(3)(a)(ii), unless the party has objected to that finding or conclusion as required by Civ. R. 53(D)(3)(b).

(4) **Action of court on magistrate's decision and on any objections to magistrate's decision; entry of judgment or interim order by court.**

(a) **Action of court required.** A magistrate's decision is not effective unless adopted by the court.

(b) **Action on magistrate's decision.** Whether or not objections are timely filed, a court may adopt or reject a magistrate's decision in whole or in part, with or without modification. A court may hear a previously-referred matter, take additional evidence, or return a matter to a magistrate.

(c) **If no objections are filed.** If no timely objections are filed, the court may adopt a magistrate's decision, unless it determines that there is an error of law or other defect evident on the face of the magistrate's decision.

(d) **Action on objections.** If one or more objections to a magistrate's decision are timely filed, the court shall rule on those objections. In ruling on objections, the court shall undertake an independent review as to the objected matters to ascertain that the magistrate has properly determined the factual issues and appropriately applied the law. Before so ruling, the court may hear additional evidence but may refuse to do so unless the objecting party demonstrates that the party could not, with reasonable diligence, have produced that evidence for consideration by the magistrate.

(e) **Entry of judgment or interim order by court**. A court that adopts, rejects, or modifies a magistrate's decision shall also enter a judgment or interim order.

(i) **Judgment.** The court may enter a judgment either during the fourteen days permitted by Civ. R. 53(D)(3)(b)(i) for the filing of objections to a magistrate's decision or after the fourteen days have expired. If the court enters a judgment during the fourteen days permitted by Civ. R. 53(D)(3)(b)(i) for the filing of objections to the magistrate's decision shall operate as an automatic stay of execution of the judgment until the court disposes of those objections and vacates, modifies, or adheres to the judgment previously entered.

(ii) **Interim order.** The court may enter an interim order on the basis of a magistrate's decision without waiting for or ruling on timely objections by the parties where immediate relief is justified. The timely filing of objections does not stay the execution of an interim order, but an interim order shall not extend more than twenty-eight days from the date of entry, subject to extension by the court in increments of twenty-eight additional days for good cause shown. An interim order shall comply with Civ. R. 54(A), be journalized pursuant to Civ. R. 58(A), and be served pursuant to Civ. R. 58(B).

(5) **Extension of time.** For good cause shown, the court shall allow a reasonable extension of time for a party to file a motion to set aside a magistrate's order or file objections to a magistrate's decision. "Good cause" includes, but is not limited to, a failure by the clerk to timely serve the party seeking the extension with the magistrate's order or decision.

(6) **Disqualification of a magistrate.** Disqualification of a magistrate for bias or other cause is within the discretion of the court and may be sought by motion filed with the court.

(7) **Recording of proceedings before a magistrate.** Except as otherwise provided by law, all proceedings before a magistrate shall be recorded in accordance with procedures established by the court.

(8) **Contempt in the presence of a magistrate.**

(a) **Contempt order.** Contempt sanctions under Civ. R. 53(C)(2)(f) may be imposed only by a written order that recites the facts and certifies that the magistrate saw or heard the conduct constituting contempt.

(b) **Filing and provision of copies of contempt order.** A contempt order shall be filed and copies provided forthwith by the clerk to the appropriate judge of the court and to the subject of the order.

(c) **Review of contempt order by court; bail.** The subject of a contempt order may by motion obtain immediate review by a judge. A judge or the magistrate entering the contempt order may set bail pending judicial review of the order.

History: Amended, eff 7-1-75; 7-1-85; 7-1-92; 7-1-93; 7-1-95; 7-1-96; 7-1-98; 7-1-03; 7-1-06.

NOTES TO DECISIONS

ANALYSIS

Additional evidence
Adoption of magistrate's decision
Affidavit
Appeal
— Abuse of discretion
—— Standing of minor child
Applicability
Authority of magistrate
Child support
Clarification
De novo review
Disposition of objections
Disqualification
Failure to consider transcript
Failure to provide transcript
Final appealable order
Findings
Harmless error
Hearing
Independent review
Interim orders
Jurisdiction
Magistrate's decision
— Service
Modification
Objections
— Failure to object
— Opportunity to register objections
— Overruling objections

Additional evidence

Ohio R. Civ. P. 53(D)(4)(b), allowing a trial court reviewing a magistrate's decision to hear additional evidence, mirrors the provisions of Ohio R. Civ. P. 60(B)(2) and is not meant to cover situations where the evidence is created pursuant to the court's own discretionary powers, via its magistrate. In re Adkins, — Ohio App. 3d —, 2007 Ohio 4629, — N.E. 2d —, 2007 Ohio App. LEXIS 4170 (Sept. 7, 2007).

When a trial court heard objections to a magistrate's recommendation that a temporary guardianship of a child be terminated, the trial court was not required to admit a psychological evaluation of the child which the magistrate had ordered because nothing in Ohio R. Civ. P. 53(D)(4)(b) or (d) required a trial court ruling on objections to a magistrate's recommendation to accept further evidence, and the matter was within the court's discretion. In re Adkins, — Ohio App. 3d —, 2007 Ohio 4629, — N.E. 2d —, 2007 Ohio App. LEXIS 4170 (Sept. 7, 2007).

Adoption of magistrate's decision

Trial court erred by holding a bench trial of a matter that had already been reduced to judgment without first having disposed of pending, timely objections to the Magistrate's decision that had been adopted as the judgment of the trial court: O'Bryan v. K & H Co. Lakeshore Apts., 181 Ohio App. 3d 741, 2009 Ohio 1417, 910 N.E.2d 1071, 2009 Ohio App. LEXIS 1221 (2009).

Trial court erred by adopting the magistrate's decision without affording the appellant a reasonable time to file the transcript of the proceedings before the magistrate: Black v. Brewer, 178 Ohio App. 3d 113, 2008 Ohio 4365, 897 N.E.2d 163, 2008 Ohio App. LEXIS 3687 (2008).

In a dispute between lessors and lessees regarding a lease allowing the lessees to maintain a communication tower on the lessors' land, it was not an abuse of discretion to adopt a magistrate's decision, under Ohio R. Civ. P. 53(E)(4), finding that the lessees did not exercise their option to renew the lease, as (1) a letter the lessees sent to the lessors purportedly exercising the option was sent after the lease expired, and (2) a conversation before the lease expired between a lessee and a lessor, in which the lessee purportedly exercised the option, was not shown to bind either the other lessee or the other lessor involved to any renewal. Berry v. Firis, — Ohio App. 3d —, 2006 Ohio 4924, — N.E. 2d —, 2006 Ohio App. LEXIS 4897 (Sept. 25, 2006).

Even in the face of objections, a trial court was not required to conduct an independent review of the facts and make its own factual determination when adopting a magistrate's decision, so there existed no requirement that the trial court conduct a de novo review of the magistrate's decision simply because the magistrate received conflicting evidence, as such a requirement would abrogate the role of a magistrate in a majority of cases. Berry v. Firis, — Ohio App. 3d —, 2006 Ohio 4924, — N.E. 2d —, 2006 Ohio App. LEXIS 4897 (Sept. 25, 2006).

In a dispute between lessors and lessees regarding a lease allowing the lessees to maintain a communications tower on the lessors' land, and a subsequent agreement that the lessors would pay the lessees a portion of the income the lessors received from a lease with a third party allowing the maintenance of a communications tower on the same land, it was not an abuse of discretion to adopt a magistrate's decision, under Ohio R. Civ. P. 53(E)(4), finding (1) a lessor credibly testified that the agreement to pay the lessees part of the income from the other lease expired when the lessees' lease expired, and (2) a lessee's testimony that the lessors agreed to pay the lessees part of the income from the second lease 17 years after any renewed lease would expire was not credible. Berry v. Firis, — Ohio App. 3d —, 2006 Ohio 4924, — N.E. 2d —, 2006 Ohio App. LEXIS 4897 (Sept. 25, 2006).

Trial court's adoption of a magistrate's decision which granted parties a divorce did not merge the wife's claim of assault against the husband into that divorce judgment pursuant to Ohio R. Civ. P. 53(E)(3)(d) and (E)(4)(a), as the trial court's failure or refusal to consider the tort claim was not a "final disposition of the claim" and further, the wife had not been provided an opportunity to exercise her right to trial by jury of the assault claim, pursuant to Ohio R. Civ. P. 38(A). Reimund v. Hanna, — Ohio App. 3d —, 2006 Ohio 6848, — N.E. 2d —, 2006 Ohio App. LEXIS 6762 (Dec. 26, 2006).

Affidavit

Trial court's modification of a magistrate's decision when, due to an error, no transcript had been created reflecting the contents of the proceeding before the magistrate was not an abuse of discretion because the trial court complied with Ohio R. Civ. P. 53(E)(3)(c) by having the parties file with the trial court affidavits of the evidence presented to the magistrate. Trucks, Inc. v. Valley Ford Truck Sales, — Ohio App. 3d —, 2006 Ohio 1609, — N.E. 2d —, 2006 Ohio App. LEXIS 1498 (Mar. 30, 2006).

Because the client failed to provide a valid statement of the evidence from the evidentiary hearing, under Ohio R. Civ. P. 53(E)(c)(3), the magistrate's decision could only be reviewed to determine if his legal conclusions were consistent with his factual findings; although the client attempted to comply with the requirements of Ohio R. Civ. P. 53(E)(c)(3), by submitting an affidavit regarding the evidence that had been presented at the hearing, the client only provided the evidence that supported his arguments. Accordingly, the trial court did not err in adopting the magistrate's decision regarding the "fee" claim, for a legal consultation, as the magistrate's findings of fact supported the application of the doctrine of quantum meruit. Bodor v. Fontanella, — Ohio App. 3d —, 2006 Ohio 3883, — N.E. 2d —, 2006 Ohio App. LEXIS 3841 (July 28, 2006).

Appeal

Where a putative father did not file an objection to a magistrate's decision in his action, seeking to establish a parent-child relationship, he waived that error for purposes of appeal pursuant to Ohio R. Civ. P. 53(E)(3)(d). E.B. v. T.J., — Ohio App. 3d —, 2006 Ohio 441, — N.E. 2d —, 2006 Ohio App. LEXIS 383 (Feb. 2, 2006).

Where service of a probate court judgment, adopting a magistrate's decision to remove a guardian of an incompetent from her position, was not made on the guardian within the three-day period of entering the judgment, the guardian had 30 days to file her notice of appeal from when she was served, pursuant to Ohio R. App. P. 4(A). Where the notice of appeal was filed beyond the 30-day period, and the guardian's failure to file timely objections to the magistrate's decision resulted in the automatic stay provisions of Ohio R. Civ. P. 53(E)(4) of the magistrate's decision not being triggered, the appellate court lacked jurisdiction to review the matter on appeal. In re Riccardi, — Ohio App. 3d —, 2006 Ohio 24, — N.E. 2d —, 2006 Ohio App. LEXIS 13 (Jan. 6, 2006).

— Abuse of discretion

Trial court abused its discretion when it upheld a former wife's objections pursuant to a magistrate's decision under Ohio R. Civ. P. 53 and it included a cash draw from the former husband's business in the calculation of his income for purposes of his spousal support modification request under RC § 3105.18(E), as the draw was only based on conjecture and not on a proper basis to determine that it should have been included in the husband's income. Accordingly, a determination of the spousal support arrears was also erroneous because it was unclear how the cash draw was calculated into the trial court's determination of that issue. Burkart v. Burkart, — Ohio App. 3d —, 2007 Ohio 3992, — N.E. 2d —, 2007 Ohio App. LEXIS 3576 (Aug. 2, 2007).

Although neither party filed objections as required by Ohio R. Civ. P. 53(E)(4)(a) to the commencement date for additional spousal support or the refinancing of the marital home, although objections to other aspects of the magistrate's order were filed, such was an abuse of discretion by the trial court when it adopted the date of the magistrate's decision as the instructive date, as the time for refinancing had already passed by the time that objections were overruled and the magistrate's order was adopted, and as to support, the wife had not engaged in delay tactics; similarly, it was an abuse of discretion to state in the trial court order that the child support order was in effect and to require the husband to attend monthly anger management counseling without indicating the effective date. Yasinow v. Yasinow, — Ohio App. 3d —, 2006 Ohio 1355, — N.E. 2d —, 2006 Ohio App. LEXIS 1237 (Mar. 23, 2006).

In reviewing an appeal from a trial court's order adopting a magistrate's decision under Ohio R. Civ. P. 53(E)(4), an appellate court had to determine whether the trial court abused its discretion in adopting the decision, and any claim of trial court error had to be based on the actions of the trial court, not on the magistrate's findings or proposed decision. Berry v. Firis, — Ohio App. 3d —, 2006 Ohio 4924, — N.E. 2d —, 2006 Ohio App. LEXIS 4897 (Sept. 25, 2006).

In a supplier's suit against the alleged guarantor of debtors' obligation to the supplier, it was not an abuse of discretion, under Ohio R. Civ. P. 53(E)(4), for a trial court to adopt a magistrate's finding that the guarantor did not sign a contract guaranteeing the debtors' obligation because, under Ohio R. Evid. 901(B)(3), the magistrate could compare the disputed signature with known examples of the guarantor's handwriting without further testimony and determine whether the signatures were made by the same person. Medina Drywall Supply v. Procom Stucco Sys., — Ohio App. 3d —, 2006 Ohio 5062, — N.E. 2d —, 2006 Ohio App. LEXIS 4985 (Sept. 29, 2006).

—— Standing of minor child

Minor child does not have an independent legal right, separate and apart from the child's parents, to commence or maintain an action requesting a court to modify its prior custody decree and grant shared custody. Thus the child lacked standing to maintain objections to the magistrate's decision after the parent withdrew his own objections to the decision: Hanna v. Hanna, 177 Ohio App. 3d 233, 2008 Ohio 3523, 894 N.E.2d 355, 2008 Ohio App. LEXIS 2970 (2008).

Applicability

Version of Ohio R. Civ. P. 53 that became effective after the July 1, 2006 amendments applied pursuant to Ohio R. Civ. P. 86(CC) to a former husband's matter involving his request for modification of parental rights and child support, as there was no reason to believe that application of the amended version of Rule 53 was not feasible or would work an injustice on the husband's matter; further, the husband's objections to a magistrate's decision were filed after the effective date of the

amendment, such that the trial court was obligated to conduct an independent review of the magistrate's decision. Davidson v. Davidson, — Ohio App. 3d —, 2007 Ohio 6919, — N.E. 2d —, 2007 Ohio App. LEXIS 6071 (Dec. 13, 2007).

Authority of magistrate

As a husband in a divorce proceeding was given the opportunity to present his arguments to a magistrate who heard the matter pursuant to Ohio R. Civ. P. 53, and he was also able to file objections to the magistrate's decision with the trial court, and the trial court then conducted a de novo review of the magistrate's decision in compliance with the civil rules and with Ohio law, there was no error in having the property and support hearings conducted before the magistrate instead of before the trial court pursuant to Ohio R. Civ. P. 75 and Ohio Const art. IV, § 1. Metz v. Metz, — Ohio App. 3d —, 2007 Ohio 549, — N.E. 2d —, 2007 Ohio App. LEXIS 507 (Feb. 9, 2007).

Child support

When a father did not file objections, pursuant to Ohio R. Civ. P. 53(D)(3)(b)(iv), to a magistrate's decision adopting the decision of an administrative hearing officer increasing the father's child support obligation, the father's appeal of a trial court's judgment adopting the magistrate's decision could nonetheless be considered because it was apparent that the trial court committed plain error when the trial court did not recognize that the administrative hearing officer improperly exercised judicial authority when the hearing officer did not apply the correct statute, RC § 3119.89, in reviewing the father's child support obligation, even though the hearing officer said this statute was applied, because it was apparent from the hearing officer's decision that, instead, RC § 3119.64 was improperly applied, denying the father the process mandated by RC § 3119.89. Hilton v. Hilton, — Ohio App. 3d —, 2007 Ohio 5195, — N.E. 2d —, 2007 Ohio App. LEXIS 4610 (Oct. 1, 2007).

Trial court did not abuse its discretion in ordering the father, without a hearing, to pay the $86,327.74 arrearage in three monthly installments, payable quarterly because, at no time, did the father provide the trial court with any evidence of his changed financial circumstances as was permitted by Civ. R. 53(E)(4)(b). Also, the father's financial status and activities had been analyzed thoroughly; he was more than capable of paying the arrearage as ordered at the time of the trial and if his circumstances changed so as to make it financially impossible for him to comply, it was likely due to the lifestyle that he was living, which lifestyle was established at trial. Collette v. Baxter, — Ohio App. 3d —, 2006 Ohio 6555, — N.E. 2d —, 2006 Ohio App. LEXIS 6474 (Dec. 13, 2006).

Clarification

It was not error, under Ohio R. Civ. P. 53(E)(4), to grant clarification of a magistrate's decision in a case dealing with, inter alia, child support, because a magistrate's decision was always interlocutory until it was adopted as a final judgment by a trial court, so a trial court was free to modify, reconsider or clarify the decision. Frey v. Frey, — Ohio App. 3d —, 2007 Ohio 2991, — N.E. 2d —, 2007 Ohio App. LEXIS 2747 (June 18, 2007).

It was not error, under Ohio R. Civ. P. 53(E)(4), to grant clarification of a magistrate's decision in a case dealing with, inter alia, child support, because the decision did not address a child support issue a mother had raised, so it was not final under Ohio R. Civ. P. 54(B), because it did not dispose of all issues. Frey v. Frey, — Ohio App. 3d —, 2007 Ohio 2991, — N.E. 2d —, 2007 Ohio App. LEXIS 2747 (June 18, 2007).

De novo review

Trial court did not err in finding that a magistrate abused her discretion in a custody case when the mother had not argued that issue in her objections. While a trial court is not required, under Ohio R. Civ. P. 53(E)(4), to conduct a de novo review of a magistrate's decision, it is not prohibited from exercising its discretion and conducting such a review. Love v. Love, — Ohio App. 3d —, 2006 Ohio 3559, — N.E. 2d —, 2006 Ohio App. LEXIS 3506 (July 12, 2006).

Disposition of objections

Fact that a neighbor's objections to the entry of a default judgment in a dog bite case had been misfiled in the clerk of the court's criminal traffic division qualified as a reason for relief from the judgment under CivR 60(B)(5). Consideration of objections to a magistrate's decision was mandatory under CivR 53, and as the trial court was not even aware that the objections had been filed, the requirements of Rule 53 were not fulfilled. Zwahlen v. Brown, — Ohio App. 3d —, 2008 Ohio 151, — N.E. 2d —, 2008 Ohio App. LEXIS 129 (Jan. 18, 2008).

Disqualification

There were no cognizable grounds under Ohio Code Jud. Conduct Canon 3 under which the trial court would have been required to disqualify the magistrate to heard a mother's legal custody matter, and thus, the trial court did not abuse its discretion by overruling the mother's objections on the basis that the magistrate had been exposed to circumstances which may have required him to be a witness in a potential criminal case against her. The grounds for disqualification in Ohio Code Jud. Conduct Canon 3 are limited to those situations in which a magistrate would be a material witness to the proceeding being heard before him, rather than a separate criminal proceeding which may result from incidents which happen to occur within the courtroom. In re Memic, — Ohio App. 3d —, 2006 Ohio 6346, — N.E. 2d —, 2006 Ohio App. LEXIS 6302 (Dec. 1, 2006).

Failure to consider transcript

Since a trial court failed to consider a property owner's timely-filed transcript of a hearing before a magistrate, it could not sufficiently rule, pursuant to Ohio R. Civ. P. 53(D)(4)(d), on the owner's fact-based objections to the decision; thus, the court remanded the case to the trial court so that it could have the opportunity to consider whether the evidence supported the magistrate's factual findings. Morgan v. Charvat, — Ohio App. 3d —, 2007 Ohio 5927, — N.E. 2d —, 2007 Ohio App. LEXIS 5194 (Nov. 6, 2007).

Failure to provide transcript

Since a wife failed to provide a transcript to support her objections to a magistrate's decision issued in a divorce action, as required by Ohio R. Civ. P. 53(D)(3)(b)(iii), the wife waived the right to challenge the factual findings made by the trial court. Ordean v. Ordean, — Ohio App. 3d —, 2007 Ohio 3979, — N.E. 2d —, 2007 Ohio App. LEXIS 3598 (Aug. 6, 2007).

Magistrate's factual findings were considered established as the insurer, who appealed the trial court's decision adopting the magistrate's decision, failed to file with the trial court a transcript of the evidence from the magistrate's hearing or an affidavit in place of the transcript; thus, the trial court's factual findings could not be attacked on appeal. The insurer could not circumvent the transcript requirement of Ohio R. Civ. P. 53(D)(3)(b)(iii) by filing an Ohio R. App. P. 9(C) statement of the evidence. Vidalis v. Medical Mut. of Ohio, — Ohio App. 3d —, 2007 Ohio 4656, — N.E. 2d —, 2007 Ohio App. LEXIS 4186 (Sept. 12, 2007).

As an attorney who sought recovery of fees for services rendered in a collection matter and in a guardianship proceeding for an elderly ward objected to a magistrate's decision regarding the reasonable value of his services, but he failed to provide a transcript as required by Ohio R. Civ. P. 53(D)(3)(h)(iii), only the application of the law to the facts was reviewable. In re Bess, — Ohio App. 3d —, 2007 Ohio 5032, — N.E. 2d —, 2007 Ohio App. LEXIS 4456 (Sept. 26, 2007).

Since a father failed to provide a transcript to the trial court to support his objections to a magistrate's decision, as required by Ohio R. Civ. P. 53(D)(3)(b)(iii), he waived the right to challenge the factual findings of the trial court. Though the father attempted to challenge the conclusions of law, the resolution of the father's objections necessarily involved a factual analysis of the evidence presented at the hearing before the magistrate; therefore, Ohio R. Civ. P. 53(D)(3)(b)(iii) required a transcript or affidavit. Colo. v. Ledesma, — Ohio App. 3d —, 2007 Ohio 3975, — N.E. 2d —, 2007 Ohio App. LEXIS 3594 (Aug. 6, 2007).

Trial court did not err in adopting a magistrate's decision in favor of a landlord because the tenant did not file a transcript with the trial court along with his objections to the magistrate's decision. Thus, without a transcript or exhibits, the appellate court had to presume that the evidence supported the magistrate's findings. Blaser v. McNulty, — Ohio App. 3d —, 2007 Ohio 3320, — N.E. 2d —, 2007 Ohio App. LEXIS 3046 (June 28, 2007).

Where a former husband failed to file a transcript of the proceedings before a magistrate in post-divorce proceedings, as required by Ohio R. Civ. P. 53(D)(3)(b), his objection to the magistrate's decision was not properly made and his appeal of the magistrate's factual findings was deemed waived; the regularity of the trial court proceedings was presumed. Dinunzio v. Dinunzio, — Ohio App. 3d —, 2007 Ohio 2578, — N.E. 2d —, 2007 Ohio App. LEXIS 2397 (May 25, 2007).

Because a transcript was not filed with the car seller's objections to the magistrate's report granting judgment in favor of the car buyer, factual issues objected to were waived for appeal. Midcap v. Rayners Auto, — Ohio App. 3d —, 2007 Ohio 2182, — N.E. 2d —, 2007 Ohio App. LEXIS 2046 (May 7, 2007).

As a lessee failed to file a transcript of the proceedings pursuant to former Ohio R. Civ. P. 53(E)(3)(c) before a magistrate who heard the parties' breach of contract claims when he objected to the magistrate's decision, the trial court had to accept the magistrate's factual findings, as did the appellate court which could only review whether the trial court properly applied the law to the magistrate's findings of fact. The resolution of whether the parties had the requisite intent to form the contract, whether the lessee should have been held liable for breach thereof, whether the lessor repudiated the contract, and which party actually breached the contract were factual determinations made by the magistrate, and there was no showing that the trial court incorrectly applied the law to those facts. Farmers Mkt. Drive-in Shopping Ctrs. v. Magana, — Ohio App. 3d —, 2007 Ohio 2653, — N.E. 2d —, 2007 Ohio App. LEXIS 2450 (May 31, 2007).

Father's claim on appeal that a magistrate's decision to increase his child support obligation was against the manifest weight of the evidence failed, as he had failed to provide a transcript when he objected to the magistrate's findings pursuant to Ohio R. Civ. P. 53(D)(3)(b)(iii); the findings by the magistrate, which were adopted by the trial court, were presumed correct on appeal. Maynard v. Landon, — Ohio App. 3d —, 2007 Ohio 2813, — N.E. 2d —, 2007 Ohio App. LEXIS 2599 (May 29, 2007).

As former wife failed to carry her burden of filing transcripts from all four hearings a magistrate held on the division of property in a dissolution of marriage proceeding, the trial court did not abuse its discretion when it overruled the wife's objections to the magistrate's division of the property without making an independent review of the evidence. Stricker v. Stricker, — Ohio App. 3d —, 2007 Ohio 3309, — N.E. 2d —, 2007 Ohio App. LEXIS 3040 (June 29, 2007).

Trial court did not err in summarily overruling a tenant's objections to a magistrate's decision because, at time that the tenant filed his objections, the tenant did not request that a transcript of the proceedings before the magistrate be prepared, as required by Ohio R. Civ. P. 53(D)(3)(b)(iii), nor did the tenant seek leave to supplement his objections when the transcript became available. While the tenant submitted on appeal a transcript of the evidentiary hearing held before the magistrate for the appellate court's review, the appellate court was precluded from reviewing any exhibits that were accepted into evidence because only the transcript would indicate which exhibits were accepted into evidence. Blaser v. Mc-Nulty, — Ohio App. 3d —, 2007 Ohio 3320, — N.E. 2d —, 2007 Ohio App. LEXIS 3046 (June 28, 2007).

Although a wife filed objections pursuant to Ohio R. Civ. P. 53 to a magistrate's determinations regarding property and support in the husband's divorce action, as a written objection was not provided to the trial court and leave of court was not obtained pursuant to Rule 53(D)(3)(b)(iii) for an alternative means of the record, the court on appeal could only review the magistrate's findings to determine whether they were sufficient to support the conclusions of law. Dennis v. Dennis, — Ohio App. 3d —, 2007 Ohio 6758, — N.E. 2d —, 2007 Ohio App. LEXIS 5929 (Dec. 17, 2007).

Since appellant failed to file with the trial court a transcript of the hearing or an affidavit in support of her objections to a magistrate's decision, as required by Ohio R. Civ. P. 53(E)(3)(c), there was no proper evidentiary ground for the trial court to rule on the fact-specific objections. Estate of Stambolia, — Ohio App. 3d —, 2006 Ohio 4314, — N.E. 2d —, 2006 Ohio App. LEXIS 4238 (Aug. 18, 2006).

In a car owner's suit to recover for damages sustained to his car due to the defective condition of a landowner's parking lot, the trial court erred when, on reviewing the magistrate's decision finding that the landowner was 70 percent negligent and that the car owner's wife, who was driving the car at the time of the damage, was 30 percent negligent, it reallocated the comparative negligence of the parties and modified the award. Contributory negligence was a factual determination, and there was no evidence that the trial court reviewed the transcript or conducted a de novo proceeding. Merkel v. Chamoun, — Ohio App. 3d —, 2006 Ohio 5367, — N.E. 2d —, 2006 Ohio App. LEXIS 5379 (Oct. 13, 2006).

When a magistrate recommended that judgment be entered against a boyfriend on his former girlfriend's counterclaim, the boyfriend did not properly object to this recommendation because, under Ohio R. Civ. P. 53(D)(3)(b)(iii), he did not file a transcript of the proceedings before the magistrate with the trial court, so his claim that the girlfriend did not serve him with her counterclaim until the day of trial could not be considered because (1) there was nothing properly in the record showing that the boyfriend raised a lack of personal jurisdiction to enter judgment against him on the counterclaim, (2) nothing showed that a continuance of the trial was due to the boyfriend's objection to late service of the counterclaim, and (3) if the continuance was due to late service, this showed the boyfriend had notice of the counterclaim on the date on which the trial was originally scheduled, and there was no showing that he sought additional time to prepare a defense to the counterclaim. Harris v. Mapp, — Ohio App. 3d —, 2006 Ohio 5515, — N.E. 2d —, 2006 Ohio App. LEXIS 5500 (Oct. 24, 2006).

When a transcript of proceedings before a magistrate was not filed with the trial court which entered judgment, an appellate court's review was limited to whether the trial court correctly applied the law to the facts set forth in the magistrate's decision. Harris v. Mapp, — Ohio App. 3d —, 2006 Ohio 5515, — N.E. 2d —, 2006 Ohio App. LEXIS 5500 (Oct. 24, 2006).

When a wife appealed a trial court's adoption of a magistrate's decision granting a husband credit against his child support obligation for tuition he paid for the parties' children, the husband's argument, under Ohio R. Civ. P. 53(E)(3)(c), that the wife was barred from claiming factual error because she did not file a transcript of the hearing before the magistrate with the trial court was not well taken because the

husband filed the transcript, so it was before the trial court when it entered judgment, and any error was harmless. Berthelot v. Berthelot, — Ohio App. 3d —, 2006 Ohio 1317, — N.E. 2d —, 2006 Ohio App. LEXIS 1194 (Mar. 22, 2006).

Since the errors which seven of a husband's eight assignments of error involved each implicated a finding of fact that the magistrate made and since the common pleas court did not have a transcript of the evidence before the magistrate relevant to these findings and conclusions of law, the common pleas court could properly reject the husband's objections to the magistrate's decision as it did. Further, pursuant to Ohio R. Civ. P. 53(E)(3)(c) and (d), the husband had waived the error in the common pleas court's rulings he presented in those assignments of error. Daniel v. Daniel, — Ohio App. 3d —, 2006 Ohio 411, — N.E. 2d —, 2006 Ohio App. LEXIS 351 (Jan. 27, 2006).

Trial court erred in failing to review a condominium association's objections to a magistrate's decision in an action by a condominium owner, wherein the magistrate concluded that the association was entitled to only some of the fees and fines that it had sought payment of in its counterclaim, as the failure of the association to have provided a transcript was not an impediment to review of issues involving questions of law pursuant to Ohio R. Civ. P. 53(E)(3); as to those objections that involved questions of fact, such as noise violations, review was properly declined by the trial court. Hagans v. Habitat Condo. Owners Ass'n, 166 Ohio App. 3d 508, 2006 Ohio 1970, 851 N.E. 2d 544, 2006 Ohio App. LEXIS 1801 (Apr. 21, 2006).

Where a law firm objected to a magistrate's decision on grounds of manifest weight of the evidence and credibility, but it failed to file a transcript from the magistrate's proceeding, as required by Ohio R. Civ. P. 53(E)(3)(c), the reviewing court presumed the regularity of the proceedings and accordingly, the decision required affirmance. Harris v. Dwight-Killian, 166 Ohio App. 3d 786, 2006 Ohio 2347, 853 N.E. 2d 364, 2006 Ohio App. LEXIS 2225 (May 12, 2006).

Although a former husband raised objections to a magistrate's decision in his application for reallocation of parental rights and responsibilities between himself and his former wife regarding their minor children, the husband failed to provide the requisite transcript pursuant to Ohio R. Civ. P. 53(E)(3)(c). The appellate court's review of the trial court's decisions was limited to whether the trial court abused its discretion in adopting the magistrate's report, and the trial court's review without the transcript was limited to determining whether those findings were sufficient to support the conclusions of law reached by the magistrate. Weisberg v. Sampson, — Ohio App. 3d —, 2006 Ohio 3646, — N.E. 2d —, 2006 Ohio App. LEXIS 3569 (July 14, 2006).

Maternal grandmother's claim that extensions of her temporary guardianship over her grandchildren changed the guardianship to a permanent one, such that the good cause standard for termination under RC § 2111.46 was inapplicable, could not be properly reviewed, as the termination decision had been heard by a magistrate and the grandmother had failed to include a copy of the transcript from those proceedings, as required by Ohio R. Civ. P. 53. Whether the interval between the father's consent to the initial guardianship and his attempt to terminate it could have been deemed a surrender of his right to preferential treatment could not be shown by the grandmother and the trial court's decision had to be deemed correct. In re Clowtis, — Ohio App. 3d —, 2006 Ohio 6868, — N.E. 2d —, 2006 Ohio App. LEXIS 6811 (Dec. 22, 2006).

Maternal grandmother's claim that extensions of her temporary guardianship over her grandchildren changed the guardianship to a permanent one, such that the good cause standard for termination under RC § 2111.46 was inapplicable, could not be properly reviewed, as the termination decision had been heard by a magistrate and the grandmother had failed to include a copy of the transcript from those proceedings, as required by Ohio R. Civ. P. 53. Whether the interval between the father's consent to the initial guardianship and his attempt to terminate it could have been deemed a surrender of his right to preferential treatment could not be shown by the grandmother and the trial court's decision had to be deemed correct. In re Clowtis, — Ohio App. 3d —, 2006 Ohio 6868, — N.E. 2d —, 2006 Ohio App. LEXIS 6811 (Dec. 22, 2006).

Where an awning customer's objections to a magistrate's determination that the awning company was not negligent in the installation of awnings over the customer's office window and door were based on facts that were not included in the magistrate's decision, and the customer had failed to provide a transcript of those proceedings in the trial court for review with his objections, as required by former Ohio R. Civ. P. 53(E)(3)(c), the trial court's adoption of the magistrate's decision was not deemed an abuse of discretion; based on just the facts described in the magistrate's decision, the magistrate reached a reasonable conclusion that the company was not negligent. Boswell v. Wheeling Canvas Prods., — Ohio App. 3d —, 2006 Ohio 7051, — N.E. 2d —, 2006 Ohio App. LEXIS 6978 (Dec. 22, 2006).

Since appellants, the dominant owners of an estate, failed to provide the trial court with a transcript of the hearing before the magistrate, they were precluded from challenging on appeal the trial court's adoption of any of the magistrate's findings of fact. While the dominant owners provided a transcript of the hearing before the magistrate with the record on appeal, the court could not consider the transcript. Colace v. Wander, — Ohio App. 3d —, 2006 Ohio 7094, — N.E. 2d —, 2006 Ohio App. LEXIS 7015 (Dec. 26, 2006).

Husband's assignments of error in his appeal from a finding of contempt, contending that the trial court erred when it found that payment was possible and erred when it imposed an impracticable purge, were fact based and could not be reviewed by the court because they had been waived by the husband's failure to file a transcript with the trial court when filing his objections to the magistrate's report, as required by Ohio R. Civ. P. 53(E)(3)(d). Habig v. Habig, — Ohio App. 3d —, 2006 Ohio 7103, — N.E. 2d —, 2006 Ohio App. LEXIS 7053 (Nov. 30, 2006).

Final appealable order

Trial court's judgment adopting a magistrate's decision denying a debtor's motion to vacate a default judgment against the debtor was final and appealable, under RC § 2505.02 because the debtor's untimely objections to the magistrate's decision did not trigger the tolling provisions of Ohio R. App. P. 4(B)(2), nor did the objections effectuate an Ohio R. Civ. P. 53(D)(4)(e)(i) stay of execution. OSI Funding Corp. v. Huth, — Ohio App. 3d —, — N.E. 2d —, 2007 Ohio App. LEXIS 4654 (Sept. 28, 2007).

License holder's appeal from the trial court's denial of her motion to vacate an Administrative License Suspension notification form completed by a magistrate was dismissed because the court lacked jurisdiction under Ohio Const. art. IV, § 3(B)(2) as there was no final appealable order under RC § 2505.02(B)(1) due to the fact that the trial court had never adopted the magistrate's decision, as required by former Ohio R. Civ. P. 53(E)(4)(a). State v. Makoroff, — Ohio App. 3d —, 2007 Ohio 4348, — N.E. 2d —, 2007 Ohio App. LEXIS 3897 (Aug. 27, 2007).

License holder's appeal from a trial court's order overruling his objections to a magistrate's decision was dismissed because the trial court failed both to adopt the magistrate's decision and to enter judgment stating the relief to be afforded. Pursuant to Ohio R. Civ. P. 53, the magistrate's decision remained an interlocutory order, and there was no final appealable order under RC § 2505.02(B)(1), depriving the court of jurisdiction pursuant to Ohio Const. art. IV, § 3(B)(2).

Robinson v. Bureau of Motor Vehicles, — Ohio App. 3d —, 2007 Ohio 1162, — N.E. 2d —, 2007 Ohio App. LEXIS 1087 (Mar. 15, 2007).

License holder's appeal from a trial court's order overruling his objections to a magistrate's decision was dismissed because the trial court failed both to adopt the magistrate's decision and to enter judgment stating the relief to be afforded. Pursuant to Ohio R. Civ. P. 53, the magistrate's decision remained an interlocutory order, and there was no final appealable order under RC § 2505.02(B)(1), depriving the court of jurisdiction pursuant to Ohio Const. art. IV, § 3(B)(2). Robinson v. Bureau of Motor Vehicles, — Ohio App. 3d —, 2007 Ohio 1162, — N.E. 2d —, 2007 Ohio App. LEXIS 1087 (Mar. 15, 2007).

As no appeal was taken from a trial court's decision on objections to a magistrate's determination under Ohio R. Civ. P. 53(4)(b) of a former husband's child support obligation, based on the wife's request for an upward modification pursuant to RC § 3119.79(A), the decision was final and the wife's subsequent request for an upward modification of child support should have been denied as barred by res judicata. The second modification request by the wife was based on the same issues as were raised by her in her objections to the prior magistrate's decision, and as there were no changed circumstances alleged and no appeal taken from the prior order, it barred further adjudication on the merits as to those same issues. Kean v. Kean, — Ohio App. 3d —, 2006 Ohio 3222, — N.E. 2d —, 2006 Ohio App. LEXIS 3141 (June 23, 2006).

Since a trial court failed both to adopt the magistrate's decision and to enter judgment stating the relief afforded under Ohio R. Civ. P. 53(E)(4), the trial court's order denying appellant's objections to the magistrate's decision was not a final appealable order pursuant to RC § 2505.02(B)(1) and Ohio R. Civ. P. 54(B); thus, the court lacked jurisdiction under Ohio Const. art. IV, § 3(B)(2) to rule on appellant's challenge to the decision. Ingledue v. Premier Siding & Roofing, Inc., — Ohio App. 3d —, 2006 Ohio 2698, — N.E. 2d —, 2006 Ohio App. LEXIS 2543 (May 30, 2006).

Although the preprinted form sheet attached to the magistrate's decision was signed by the trial judge, it was not checked to indicate whether the decision was expressly accepted, modified, or rejected, as required by Ohio R. Civ. P. 53(E)(4)(a). Accordingly, the decision was not a final appealable order. State v. Dickerson, — Ohio App. 3d —, 2006 Ohio 2082, — N.E. 2d —, 2006 Ohio App. LEXIS 1934 (Apr. 27, 2006).

Where a trial court overruled a former wife's objections to a magistrate's decision, pursuant to Ohio R. Civ. P. 53, but the trial court failed to separately set forth its own judgment, there was no final appealable order pursuant to Ohio R. Civ. P. 54 and RC § 2505.02(B)(1). As the appellate court lacked jurisdiction pursuant to Ohio Const. art. IV, § 3(B)(2) and RC § 2501.02, dismissal of the appeal was mandated. Burns v. Morgan, 165 Ohio App. 3d 694, 2006 Ohio 1213, 847 N.E. 2d 1288, 2006 Ohio App. LEXIS 1087 (Mar. 13, 2006).

When a wife appealed a trial court's adoption of a magistrate's decision granting a husband credit against his child support obligation for tuition he paid for the parties' children, Ohio R. Civ. P. 53(E)(4) was satisfied, and the trial court's judgment was final and appealable because, after the parties' filed objections, the trial court issued an order overruling the parties' objections, granted the wife's motion to modify child support, claimed it evaluated income considerations and deviation factors, and calculated the amount of child support that was due. Berthelot v. Berthelot, — Ohio App. 3d —, 2006 Ohio 1317, — N.E. 2d —, 2006 Ohio App. LEXIS 1194 (Mar. 22, 2006).

Findings

When, in a permanent custody proceeding, a magistrate denied a mother's motion to rehear an agency's motion for temporary custody of her children, she did not timely seek findings of fact and conclusions of law regarding that decision, under Ohio R. Civ. P. 52 and 53(D)(3)(a)(ii), because she did not seek them within seven days after her motion was denied. In re G.N., 170 Ohio App. 3d 76, 2007 Ohio 126, 866 N.E.2d 32, 2007 Ohio App. LEXIS 104 (2007).

Appellant failed to file a timely motion requesting findings of fact and conclusions of law following the magistrate's decision denying her motion for a rehearing: In re G.N., 170 Ohio App. 3d 76, 2007 Ohio 126, 866 N.E.2d 32, 2007 Ohio App. LEXIS 104 (2007).

Magistrate's decision that awarded the amount for a printer/fax/copier bought by a former city finance director that remained in the possession of the city but did not specifically deny the director's claim for accrued vacation pay was proper under Ohio R. Civ. P. 53(D)(3)(a)(ii) because the decision could be general unless findings of fact and conclusions of law were timely requested by a party or otherwise required by law, which did not occur in the instant case. Condron v. City of Willoughby Hills, — Ohio App. 3d —, 2007 Ohio 5208, — N.E. 2d —, 2007 Ohio App. LEXIS 4609 (Sept. 28, 2007).

Trial court did not err when it independently assessed the evidence, including witness credibility, and made its own factual determinations regarding a spousal support modification; the trial court simply disagreed with some of the magistrate's factual findings. The trial court was obligated to independently review the evidence and to substitute its judgment for that of the magistrate if it disagreed with the magistrate's decision. Sweeney v. Sweeney, — Ohio App. 3d —, 2006 Ohio 6988, — N.E. 2d —, 2006 Ohio App. LEXIS 6952 (Dec. 29, 2006).

When an alleged mentally ill person claimed a magistrate's decision that, under RC § 5122.01(B)(3) and (B)(4), she was a danger to herself and could not provide for her basic needs due to mental illness was against the manifest weight of the evidence because the magistrate's decision did not specifically state which evidence supported the respective decisions, the magistrate did not have to state the evidence he relied on, absent a request for findings of fact and conclusions of law, under Ohio R. Civ. P. 52, unless such findings and conclusions were otherwise required by law or an order of reference, under Ohio R. Civ. P. 53. In re L.G., — Ohio App. 3d —, 2006 Ohio 5043, — N.E. 2d —, 2006 Ohio App. LEXIS 5182 (Sept. 28, 2006).

Although a probate court ruled properly that certain objections by a decedent's children to the factual findings of a magistrate with respect to their motion to remove the co-executors of the estate were more properly reviewed in another proceeding involving the inventory of the estate, as the objections raised issues regarding questionable transactions of estate assets, such was a modification of the magistrate's decision under Ohio R. Civ. P. 53(E)(4)(b) without an adoption of the findings therein. As the probate court did not adopt or use the findings to make its determination, the findings of fact made by the magistrate were a nullity. In re Estate of Knowlton, — Ohio App. 3d —, 2006 Ohio 4905, — N.E. 2d —, 2006 Ohio App. LEXIS 4835 (Sept. 22, 2006).

Pursuant to Ohio R. Civ. P. 53(D)(4)(b), a trial court properly adopted a magistrate's decision that found that a commercial lease was valid and enforceable, and that the tenants had defaulted in their payment obligations, as the evidence supported the magistrate's findings; the tenants' claim that they had vacated the rental premises due to security concerns was not deemed credible, as they were aware of the neighborhood when they rented the premises and they did not assert such a claim until months after their default in payments, and further, attempts at settlement did not waive the landlords' right to seek enforcement of the lease terms. Yoder v. Hurst, — Ohio App. 3d —, 2007 Ohio 4861, — N.E. 2d —, 2007 Ohio App. LEXIS 4310 (Sept. 20, 2007).

As an employee did not challenge a magistrate's findings of fact in her mandamus action, pursuant to Ohio R. Civ. P. 53(D)(3)(b)(iv), any such claim of error was waived on appeal except for plain error. State ex rel. Taylor v. Industrial Comm'n of Ohio, — Ohio App. 3d —, 2006 Ohio 4781, — N.E. 2d —, 2006 Ohio App. LEXIS 4664 (Sept. 14, 2006).

In her relief motion, the mother raised issues of excusable neglect under Ohio R. Civ. P. 60(B)(1) and fraud under Ohio R. Civ. P. 60(B)(3), respectively, which were factual issues upon which the magistrate was required, under Ohio R. Civ. P. 53(E)(2), to make findings of fact and conclusions of law. It was anomalous, therefore, for the trial court to require a transcript of proceedings to challenge findings of fact and conclusions of law where none were furnished in the magistrate's decision. Stone v. Stone, — Ohio App. 3d —, 2006 Ohio 3420, — N.E. 2d —, 2006 Ohio App. LEXIS 3350 (June 30, 2006).

Probate court erred in denying a successor in interest to a fidelity bond issuer's request for a findings of fact and conclusions of law, pursuant to Ohio R. Civ. P. 52, upon the probate court's finding that the request was untimely, as the request was made within the seven-day period from when the successor received notice of the probate court's judgment, and the decision of the magistrate, upon which the probate court's decision was based, was not a trigger of the time period because the magistrate could not file a "judgment" under Ohio R. Civ. P. 53. The probate court could not withhold the filing of the request until a resolution of the filing fee was made, as there was no such requirement regarding the fee prior to allowing a filing under Montgomery County, Ohio, Ct. C.P. Prob. Div. R. 58.1. In re Estate of Bishop, 165 Ohio App. 3d 761, 2006 Ohio 1252, 848 N.E. 2d 567, 2006 Ohio App. LEXIS 1148 (Mar. 17, 2006).

Harmless error

Although a magistrate, and then the trial court, misstated that a party's objection to the opposing party's expert witness was sustained rather than overruled, such was harmless error as the expert was deemed not qualified to provide an expert opinion on the valuation of the parties' business and accordingly, there was no abuse of discretion pursuant to Ohio R. Civ. P. 53(E)(3). Stumpff v. Harris, — Ohio App. 3d —, 2006 Ohio 4796, — N.E. 2d —, 2006 Ohio App. LEXIS 4691 (Sept. 15, 2006).

Hearing

Trial court did not abuse its discretion in not holding a hearing on a former husband's objections to a magistrate's decision on his request for a change in custody, as the use of the word "may" in Ohio R. Civ. P. 53(3)(a) and (4)(b) indicated that the trial court had the right to hold a hearing if it chose to do so, but not that it had an obligation to hold a hearing. The trial court's determination that no additional evidence existed for consideration was supported by the record. Livermore v. Livermore, 2006 Ohio 485, 2006 Ohio App. LEXIS 405 (2006). .

In a child custody dispute, it was not error for part of the proceedings to be conducted before a magistrate and for the remainder of the proceedings to be conducted before the trial court judge, as Ohio R. Civ. P. 53 allowed the trial court to refer part of a case to a magistrate. Smith v. Quigg, — Ohio App. 3d —, 2006 Ohio 1494, — N.E. 2d —, 2006 Ohio App. LEXIS 1371 (Mar. 22, 2006).

When a husband sought relief from a trial court's order modifying his child support obligation, he did not show he was entitled to an evidentiary hearing on his motion because he alleged that fraud or mistake was committed in the preparation of his child support worksheet because Ohio R. Civ. P. 53 did not support his claim that an allegation of mistake or fraud entitled him to a hearing. Sterling v. Sterling, — Ohio App. 3d —, 2006 Ohio 5437, — N.E. 2d —, 2006 Ohio App. LEXIS 5430 (Oct. 19, 2006).

When a husband sought relief from a trial court's order modifying his child support obligation, he was not entitled to an evidentiary hearing because, while he filed objections to the magistrate's decision alleging fraud, he neglected to include a transcript or affidavit of the modification hearing, which violated Ohio R. Civ. P. 53(D)(3)(a)(iii). Sterling v. Sterling, — Ohio App. 3d —, 2006 Ohio 5437, — N.E. 2d —, 2006 Ohio App. LEXIS 5430 (Oct. 19, 2006).

Independent review

Based on the substantial differences in the trial court judge's review with the opinion of the magistrate who heard the parties' dissolution matter, the trial court sufficiently addressed the objections made by the husband to the magistrate's decision and it conducted an independent review, as required by Ohio R. Civ. P. 53 and case law. Wayland v. Wayland, — Ohio App. 3d —, 2007 Ohio 1149, — N.E. 2d —, 2007 Ohio App. LEXIS 1073 (Mar. 1, 2007).

Based on the substantial differences in the trial court judge's review with the opinion of the magistrate who heard the parties' dissolution matter, the trial court sufficiently addressed the objections made by the husband to the magistrate's decision and it conducted an independent review, as required by Ohio R. Civ. P. 53 and case law. Wayland v. Wayland, — Ohio App. 3d —, 2007 Ohio 1149, — N.E. 2d —, 2007 Ohio App. LEXIS 1073 (Mar. 1, 2007).

Husband did not show a trial court did not conduct an independent review of a magistrate's decision, as required by Ohio R. Civ. P. 53(D)(4)(b), in the husband's divorce case because (1) the trial court issued a 12-page judgment entry overruling the husband's objections, (2) the trial court's analysis cited to case law and directly to evidence in the record, (3) the court sustained the husband's objection to allowing the husband's counsel to withdraw, (4) the court partially granted the husband's objection to a decision finding the wife was entitled to a divorce on grounds of gross neglect of duty and referred to those parts of the record supporting a finding that she was entitled to a divorce on grounds of extreme cruelty, (5) considered and rejected the husband's objections to the division of property, after recalculating the award based on the magistrate's findings, (6) rejected the husband's claim that he did not stipulate to dividing tax refunds by citing to the record, (7) rejected his claim that the magistrate's personal property division was prejudiced by noting the property's value was determined by an independent appraiser, and (8) noted both parties removed personal property from the marital residence and that the husband's proposal for dividing personal property was cumbersome and impractical. Doody v. Doody, — Ohio App. 3d —, 2007 Ohio 2567, — N.E. 2d —, 2007 Ohio App. LEXIS 2387 (May 25, 2007).

In a landlord's action for a breach of lease, the trial court did not abuse its discretion in adopting a magistrate's decisions under Ohio R. Civ. P. 53 because the record indicated that the trial court undertook an independent review of the magistrate's findings and decisions awarding a judgment to the landlord before overruling a tenant's objections. Homestead Real Estate LLC v. Shampay, — Ohio App. 3d —, 2007 Ohio 3202, — N.E. 2d —, 2007 Ohio App. LEXIS 2952 (June 22, 2007).

Trial court properly independently reviewed a magistrate's decision, under Ohio R. Civ. P. 53, reducing a father's child support obligation because the trial court modified that decision and properly considered the father's bonuses, which the magistrate failed to consider. Bradach v. Bradach, — Ohio App. 3d —, 2007 Ohio 3417, — N.E. 2d —, 2007 Ohio App. LEXIS 3163 (July 5, 2007).

Evidence demonstrated that the trial court took the necessary time to conduct an independent analysis of the magistrate's decision. Moreover, the husband failed to offer any evidence that the trial court did not conduct an independent

analysis; he simply stated that the trial court erred when it denied his request for continuance, permitted hearsay evidence, and asked leading questions. Abriani v. Abriani, — Ohio App. 3d —, 2007 Ohio 3534, — N.E. 2d —, 2007 Ohio App. LEXIS 3249 (July 12, 2007).

As both an employee and the Industrial Commission of Ohio filed objections to a decision of a magistrate in the employee's writ of mandamus action, pursuant to Ohio R. Civ. P. 53(D)(4)(d) the court was obligated to independently review the matters to which the parties objected to determine whether the magistrate's determination regarding the factual issues and application of the law was proper. State ex rel. Perry v. Indus. Comm'n of Ohio, — Ohio App. 3d —, 2007 Ohio 4687, — N.E. 2d —, 2007 Ohio App. LEXIS 4222 (Sept. 13, 2007).

Former husband failed to meet his burden of rebutting the presumption of regularity regarding the trial court's independent review of a magistrate's decision pursuant to Ohio R. Civ. P. 53(D)(4)(d) in a post-divorce modification matter, as his claim that the trial court's language almost exactly mapped the language of the magistrate's decision did not show that there was a lack of such independent review. Davidson v. Davidson, — Ohio App. 3d —, 2007 Ohio 6919, — N.E. 2d —, 2007 Ohio App. LEXIS 6071 (Dec. 13, 2007).

In a child custody matter, a mother did not affirmatively demonstrate, under either Ohio R. Juv. P. 40 or Ohio R. Civ. P. 53, that a trial court did not independently review a magistrate's recommendations, because the absence of language in the trial court's judgment that it had conducted such an independent review was insufficient to make this showing. In re Taylor G., — Ohio App. 3d —, 2006 Ohio 1992, — N.E. 2d —, 2006 Ohio App. LEXIS 1824 (Apr. 21, 2006).

Interim orders

While a trial court entered an interim order immediately enforcing a magistrate's decision granting custody of the parties' child to the father and did not extend it for an additional twenty eight days according to the procedure set forth in Ohio R. Civ. P. 53(E)(4)(c) but, instead, allowed the child to remain with the father beyond the expiration of the twenty-eight day period, finally entering its final order granting the father custody of the child six months later, the court refused to hold that the trial court's delay and failure to comply with the time requirements of Ohio R. Civ. P. 53(E)(4)(c) was an abuse of discretion since the delay was attributed to the mother's failure to ensure that a transcript was made a part of the record, Dexter v. Dexter, — Ohio App. 3d —, 2007 Ohio 2568, — N.E. 2d —, 2007 Ohio App. LEXIS 2388 (May 25, 2007).

Jurisdiction

As the sole issue referred to a magistrate in an action to determine who was a member of a limited liability company was plaintiffs' motion for a preliminary injunction, the trial court retained jurisdiction to decide all other issues and it properly resolved competing summary judgment motions as to other issues; accordingly, Ohio R. Civ. P. 53(E)(4)(b) did not apply and did not impede the trial court's ruling. Matthews v. D'Amore, — Ohio App. 3d —, 2006 Ohio 5745, — N.E. 2d —, 2006 Ohio App. LEXIS 5704 (Nov. 2, 2006).

Trial court had subject-matter jurisdiction over an assault claim by a wife against her husband in her divorce action, pursuant to RC § 2305.01, and the magistrate who heard the divorce matter had authority to hear the assault claim under Hancock County, Ohio, Ct. C.P. Dom. Rel. Div. R. 2.06(A) and Ohio R. Civ. P. 53(C)(1)(b). The fact that the assault claim had to be separated and tried independently of the divorce claim did not render it void ab initio. Reimund v. Hanna, — Ohio App. 3d —, 2006 Ohio 6848, — N.E. 2d —, 2006 Ohio App. LEXIS 6762 (Dec. 26, 2006).

Magistrate's decision

Under former Ohio R. Civ. P. 53(D)(3)(a)(iii), which was in effect at the time that a magistrate filed an Administrative License Suspension notification form, the magistrate was required only to prepare, sign, and file the decision. Under that version of the rule, therefore, the fact that the form was not identified as a "magistrate's decision" did not necessarily disqualify it from being one. State v. Makoroff, — Ohio App. 3d —, 2007 Ohio 4348, — N.E. 2d —, 2007 Ohio App. LEXIS 3897 (Aug. 27, 2007).

Pursuant to Ohio R. Civ. P. 53(E), the magistrate should have prepared and filed a decision for the trial court to review prior to the trial court entering a final judgment, thus allowing plaintiffs to file timely objections for the trial court to review and then enter its final judgment. Failing to follow Ohio R. Civ. P. 53 resulted in prejudicial error to plaintiffs. Ford v. Gooden, — Ohio App. 3d —, 2006 Ohio 1907, — N.E. 2d —, 2006 Ohio App. LEXIS 1753 (Apr. 19, 2006).

Appeal from a final judgment entered by a trial court in a spousal support matter was remanded to the trial court for the magistrate who heard the matter to issue her decision and allow parties to file objections because the magistrate never issued a decision, and thus, the parties were precluded from filing objections to the magistrate's decision. Davis v. Davis, — Ohio App. 3d —, 2006 Ohio 3384, — N.E. 2d —, 2006 Ohio App. LEXIS 3302 (June 29, 2006).

— Service

Proper service of notice of a magistrate's decision includes service on a party's attorney of record in accordance with CivR 5(B) unless the court expressly orders otherwise: Roberts v. Skaggs, 176 Ohio App. 3d 251, 2008 Ohio 1954, 891 N.E.2d 827, 2008 Ohio App. LEXIS 1674 (2008).

Modification

Trial court's adoption of a magistrate's grant of a civil protection order to a wife and her two children against her husband, with a modification to impose the order for a duration of five years rather than the magistrate's recommendation of three years, was not an abuse of discretion pursuant to RC § 2903.214(E)(2)(a) and Ohio R. Civ. P. 53(D)(4), as the wife had testified that the children were afraid of the husband, that his own mother had moved away and not told him where she was, and that he had engaged in incidents of harassment, vandalism, and attempts to gain entry into her home. Jenkins v. Jenkins, — Ohio App. 3d —, 2007 Ohio 422, — N.E. 2d —, 2007 Ohio App. LEXIS 367 (Feb. 1, 2007).

Trial court acted within its authority, based upon its full and independent judgment of a referred matter from a magistrate pursuant to Ohio R. Civ. P. 53(E)(4)(b), where it did not fully agree with a decision of the magistrate that did not expressly resolve the issue of a former wife's contempt for failure to appear at a child support contempt hearing, and as such, the trial court "modified" the magistrate's decision by resolving that issue. Sansom v. Sansom, — Ohio App. 3d —, 2006 Ohio 3909, — N.E. 2d —, 2006 Ohio App. LEXIS 3869 (Aug. 1, 2006).

Objections

Trial court erred in finding that a party had been required to file objections in response to the magistrate's decision on liability when the decision clearly left unresolved other disputed issues related to transfer of the annuity. Requiring objections to decisions that are interlocutory in nature does not promote judicial efficiency, and the absence of an objection at that juncture did not divest the trial court of subject matter jurisdiction to consider objections once all the issues had been resolved: Underhill v. Underhill, 181 Ohio App. 3d 298, 2009 Ohio 907, 908 N.E.2d 1009, 2009 Ohio App. LEXIS 753 (2009).

When a party did not timely object to a magistrate's decisions within 14 days, as required by Ohio R. Civ. P.

53(D)(3)(b), its appeal was considered nonetheless because those decisions did not "conspicuously indicate" that a party could not assign as error on appeal the trial court's adoption of any factual finding or legal conclusion unless the party timely and specifically objected to the finding or conclusion, as required by Ohio R. Civ. P. 53(D)(3)(a)(iii). D.A.N. Joint Venture III v. Armstrong, — Ohio App. 3d —, 2007 Ohio 898, — N.E. 2d —, 2007 Ohio App. LEXIS 805 (Mar. 2, 2007).

Since a husband failed to file objections to a magistrate's decision in a divorce action, he waived all but plain error pursuant to Ohio R. Civ. P. 53(D)(3)(b)(iv). There was no plain error in the magistrate's decision finding that the husband had the ability to give informed consent at the time when stipulations were entered in the case despite the fact that he was on prescription medications at the time because the husband did not file objections or provide an Ohio R. Civ. P. 53 record of the proceedings, and thus, the court could not question the magistrate's finding. Nitschke v. Nitschke, — Ohio App. 3d —, 2007 Ohio 1550, — N.E. 2d —, 2007 Ohio App. LEXIS 1416 (Mar. 30, 2007).

Trial court properly adopted a magistrate's decision in favor of a repairman in a repairman's suit to recover from a car owner the amount that the owner owed for repairs performed to the owner's car. Since the owner failed to file written objections to the magistrate's decision or findings of fact pursuant to Ohio R. Civ. P. 53(E)(3)(d), the owner was precluded from assigning as error on appeal the trial court's adoption of any finding of fact or conclusion of law. Montgomery v. Owensby, — Ohio App. 3d —, 2007 Ohio 1340, — N.E. 2d —, 2007 Ohio App. LEXIS 1219 (Mar. 23, 2007).

Trial court properly adopted a magistrate's decision in favor of a repairman in a repairman's suit to recover from a car owner the amount that the owner owed for repairs performed to the owner's car. Since the owner failed to file written objections to the magistrate's decision or findings of fact pursuant to Ohio R. Civ. P. 53(E)(3)(d), the owner was precluded from assigning as error on appeal the trial court's adoption of any finding of fact or conclusion of law. Montgomery v. Owensby, — Ohio App. 3d —, 2007 Ohio 1340, — N.E. 2d —, 2007 Ohio App. LEXIS 1219 (Mar. 23, 2007).

As a magistrate never held an evidentiary hearing on a father's contempt motion, instead ruling on the motion after an ex parte communication with a guardian ad litem (GAL), there was no transcript of proceedings and no evidence from which the father's counsel could submit an affidavit of evidence. The affidavit filed by the father's counsel, which explained what had transpired before the magistrate and contained the averment that counsel thought the magistrate intended hold an evidentiary hearing after speaking with the GAL, was an appropriate method of bringing the father's objections to the magistrate's ruling before the trial. In re Gruber, — Ohio App. 3d —, 2007 Ohio 3188, — N.E. 2d —, 2007 Ohio App. LEXIS 2929 (June 22, 2007).

Referee's decision granting summary judgment to a contractor in its claim to recover damages arising from a state university's withholding of final payment of a construction contract price was proper, and the university's objections to the decision under Ohio R. Civ. P. 53 were overruled. Contrary to the university's contention, the referee based his analysis on the contract terms and on the deposition testimony of the university's project manager, and the referee's decision was consistent with the argument presented by both parties. Certek, Inc. v. Ohio State Univ., — Ohio Misc. 2d —, 2007 Ohio 5418, — N.E. 2d —, 2007 Ohio Misc. LEXIS 388 (Sept. 17, 2007).

Referee's decision granting summary judgment to a contractor in its claim to recover damages arising from a state university's withholding of final payment of a construction contract price was proper, and the university's objections to the decision under Ohio R. Civ. P. 53 were overruled, because the evidence showed that the university made changes to the cost of the contract without negotiating those changes with the contractor, in violation of the terms of the contract. Certek, Inc. v. Ohio State Univ., — Ohio Misc. 2d —, 2007 Ohio 5418, — N.E. 2d —, 2007 Ohio Misc. LEXIS 388 (Sept. 17, 2007).

Because the mother did not comply with the specificity requirements of Ohio R. Civ. P. 53(D)(3)(b)(ii) or Summit County, Ohio, Ct. C.P. Dom. Rel. Div. R.12.03(B), her objection to the standard visitation order, the child support calculations, and the tax exemption had no factual or legal support. Stanley v. Stanley, — Ohio App. 3d —, 2007 Ohio 2740, — N.E. 2d —, 2007 Ohio App. LEXIS 2528 (June 6, 2007).

Plain error doctrine was inapplicable in a divorce action, wherein the trial court had adopted a decision of the magistrate who heard the matter, as the husband had timely and specifically objected to the magistrate's findings of fact and conclusions of law with respect to property division issues, as required by Ohio R. Civ. P. 53(D)(3)(b). Phillips v. Phillips, — Ohio App. 3d —, 2007 Ohio 3368, — N.E. 2d —, 2007 Ohio App. LEXIS 3116 (June 29, 2007).

In an appeal by neighbors of a zoning board of appeals' grant of a zoning variance to landowners, the neighbors could not complain that the neighbors were not allowed to supplement the neighbors' objections to a magistrate's decision, under Ohio R. Civ. P. 53(D)(3)(b)(iii), because, other than an initial "reservation" of the right to supplement the neighbors' objections, the neighbors filed nothing indicating an intent to supplement the neighbors' objections between the time a transcript of the proceedings before the magistrate was filed and the time the trial court entered judgment adopting the magistrate's decision, and the trial court was not required to ascertain whether the neighbors were going to supplement the neighbors' objections before entering judgment. Malone v. Bd. of Zoning Appeals of Xenia Twp., — Ohio App. 3d —, 2007 Ohio 3812, — N.E. 2d —, 2007 Ohio App. LEXIS 3468 (July 27, 2007).

Juvenile court properly adopted a magistrate's decision to vacate an award of temporary custody to maternal relatives of a child, and to dismiss their action that sought custody of her, as North Carolina was the more appropriate forum pursuant to RC § 3127.15(A) of the Uniform Child Custody Jurisdiction Enforcement Act, RC § 3127.01 et seq. under the plain error standard of review where no objections were filed to the magistrate's decision pursuant to Ohio R. Civ. P. 53(D)(3)(b)(iv). Both parents resided in North Carolina, they were granted a divorce in North Carolina, a custody action was pending in North Carolina, and the biological father lacked the funds to hire an attorney in Ohio and was financially unable to travel to and from Ohio for litigation. In re Craig, — Ohio App. 3d —, 2007 Ohio 3843, — N.E. 2d —, 2007 Ohio App. LEXIS 3494 (July 27, 2007).

In a contract dispute between a homeowner and a contractor, a trial court's review of the contractor's objection to a magistrate's decision was limited, under Ohio R. Civ. P. 53(D)(4)(c), to whether there was an error of law or other defect on the face of the magistrate's decision, and appellate review of the trial court's adoption of the magistrate's decision was limited to determining whether, in adopting the decision, the trial court failed to correct an obvious error of law or other such defect in the decision because the contractor's objection was not sufficiently specific, as required by Ohio R. Civ. P. 53(D)(3)(b)(ii). Burkett v. Cook, — Ohio App. 3d —, 2007 Ohio 4652, — N.E. 2d —, 2007 Ohio App. LEXIS 4188 (Sept. 12, 2007).

Mother did not waive her right to argue on appeal a trial court's error with respect to the imposition of a shared parenting plan because the waiver provisions of Ohio R. Civ. P. 53(E)(3) apply to issues of fact or law the magistrate decision, not to those that were decided by the trial court itself. Kayrouz v. Kayrouz, — Ohio App. 3d —, 2006 Ohio 149, — N.E. 2d —, 2006 Ohio App. LEXIS 121 (Jan. 17, 2006).

Where the seller argued that the trial court failed to consider additional evidence and damages pursuant to Ohio R. Civ. P. 53(E)(4)(b) in a case in which the trial court ruled on a magistrate's opinion, the argument failed. The trial court did not refuse to consider the seller's cross-objections that contained new evidence regarding additional expenses incurred by the seller, rather the trial court specifically indicated that the seller filed a limited objection to the magistrate's decision, which the trial court overruled, in addition to overruling the company's objections. Bennington v. Austin Square, Inc., — Ohio App. 3d —, 2006 Ohio 75, — N.E. 2d —, 2006 Ohio App. LEXIS 61 (Jan. 9, 2006).

Although a guardian of an incompetent did not receive a copy of a probate court judgment, adopting a magistrate's decision to remove her from that position, until after the expiration of the 14-day period within which to file objections, pursuant to Ohio R. Civ. P. 53, the probate court did not abuse its discretion in denying her motion for leave to file late objections, pursuant to Ohio R. Civ. P. 6(B), as there was no excusable neglect on the part of the guardian where she waited another 19 days after receiving the judgment before filing her motion for leave. In re Riccardi, — Ohio App. 3d —, 2006 Ohio 24, — N.E. 2d —, 2006 Ohio App. LEXIS 13 (Jan. 6, 2006).

In a divorce, the husband's May 25, 2005, objection to the magistrate's April 28, 2005, decision was untimely since it was not filed within 14 days of the magistrate's decision pursuant to Ohio R. Civ. P. 53. Havel v. Havel, — Ohio App. 3d —, 2006 Ohio 1692, — N.E. 2d —, 2006 Ohio App. LEXIS 1547 (Mar. 31, 2006).

Father's objections to a magistrate's decision on post-decree parenting and child support motions were conclusory statements which contained no factual or legal support, and thus failed to comply with the specificity requirements of Ohio R. Civ. P. 53(E)(3)(b); as such, the father waived his alleged errors on appeal. Young v. Young, — Ohio App. 3d —, 2006 Ohio 2274, — N.E. 2d —, 2006 Ohio App. LEXIS 2126 (May 10, 2006).

Husband's objections to a magistrate's order were timely filed, under Ohio R. Civ. P. 53(C)(3)(b), because the tenth day after the order was journalized was a Sunday, so, under Ohio R. Civ. P. 6(A), he had an additional day to file them, and he filed them on the following Monday. Rinkel v. Rinkel, — Ohio App. 3d —, 2006 Ohio 2560, — N.E. 2d —, 2006 Ohio App. LEXIS 2407 (May 24, 2006).

By failing to timely object to the magistrate's decision, the husband was prohibited from challenging the trial court's adoption of the findings, pursuant to Ohio R. Civ. P. 53(E)(3)(d). Planin v. Planin, — Ohio App. 3d —, 2006 Ohio 2933, — N.E. 2d —, 2006 Ohio App. LEXIS 2819 (June 9, 2006).

Relative of a child waived her argument that the trial court erred in failing to place the child with her prior to the final adjudication of custody because the relative failed to properly raise the issue in her objections to the magistrate's decision. The only reference to the issue in the relative's objections concerned the agency's bad faith; however, the relative's reference to this issue in her objections did not comply with the specificity requirements of Ohio R. Civ. P. 53. In re A.V., — Ohio App. 3d —, 2006 Ohio 3149, — N.E. 2d —, 2006 Ohio App. LEXIS 3021 (June 22, 2006).

Trial court did not err in overruling the objections filed by a relative of a child to a magistrate's report that concerned the magistrate's curtailment of the relative's cross-examination of the child's foster mother, who was competing for custody of the child, as to the religious practices of the mother and her husband on the basis of relevancy. The mother's objections were merely conclusory statements and were without factual or legal support; thus, the objections did not comply with Ohio

R. Civ. P. 53(E). In re A.V., — Ohio App. 3d —, 2006 Ohio 3149, — N.E. 2d —, 2006 Ohio App. LEXIS 3021 (June 22, 2006).

When a consumer sued a company and its sole proprietor, and the proprietor claimed, on appeal of the trial court's ruling entering the company's default, that the proprietor's pro se answer was a sufficient response on behalf of the company, this issue could not be raised on appeal because the proprietor did not, under Ohio R. Civ. P. 53(E)(3)(d), raise it in an objection to a magistrate's findings and conclusions, which the trial court adopted. Vilardo v. Sheets, — Ohio App. 3d —, 2006 Ohio 3473, — N.E. 2d —, 2006 Ohio App. LEXIS 3415 (July 3, 2006).

When a requester of public records, under RC § 149.43, sought review of a magistrate's decision finding it committed frivolous conduct, under RC § 2323.51, and awarding attorney's fees against it, its objections to the magistrate's decision were sufficiently specific, under Ohio R. Civ. P. 53(D)(3)(b)(ii), because they did not have to state the numbers of the findings of fact or conclusions of law to which an objection was stated, as long as it was reasonably discernible which findings and conclusions were objected to, and, in this case, these findings and conclusions were discernible. Shihab & Assocs. Co. v. Ohio DOT, 168 Ohio App. 3d 405, 2006 Ohio 4456, 860 N.E.2d 155, 2006 Ohio App. LEXIS 4371 (2006).

When a requester of public records sought review of an award of attorney's fees against it for engaging in frivolous conduct, under RC § 2323.51, because differing interpretations were reasonable based on the evidence, and because the requester's objections were sufficiently specific, under Ohio R. Civ. P. 53(D)(3)(b)(ii), a trial court had to conduct an independent review of the record, including the transcript filed with the objections, and rule upon the requester's objections before an appellate court could properly determine the merits of the requester's assignments of error. Shihab & Assocs. Co. v. Ohio DOT, 168 Ohio App. 3d 405, 2006 Ohio 4456, 860 N.E.2d 155, 2006 Ohio App. LEXIS 4371 (2006).

Objections to the magistrate's decision were sufficiently specific and stated with sufficient particularity to meet the requirements of former CivR 53(E)93)(b). Shihab & Assocs. Co. v. Ohio DOT, 168 Ohio App. 3d 405, 2006 Ohio 4456, 860 N.E.2d 155, 2006 Ohio App. LEXIS 4371 (2006).

As a husband did not specifically object to a magistrate's findings regarding the value of certain property in the parties' divorce proceeding, but instead he generally objected to the decision to credit the wife's evidence regarding the value of personal property over the husband's evidence, his general objections were insufficient for purposes of Ohio R. Civ. P. 53(E) to preserve any error on that issue for appeal. Dunn v. Dunn, — Ohio App. 3d —, 2006 Ohio 4649, — N.E. 2d —, 2006 Ohio App. LEXIS 4551 (Sept. 8, 2006).

There was no abuse of discretion in the trial court's refusal to grant the father's motion for leave when the reason given for the late objections was due to a problem with the calendar program in the attorney's office; it was entirely within the trial court's discretion to determine whether a calendar problem was "excusable neglect." The trial court found that filing the objections one day late was not excusable and amending the proof of service did not correct the fact that it was originally filed late. Hale v. Hale, — Ohio App. 3d —, 2006 Ohio 5164, — N.E. 2d —, 2006 Ohio App. LEXIS 5123 (Sept. 29, 2006).

Where a former husband failed to file an objection to the magistrate's limitation of evidence in modification of spousal support proceedings, and his objections did not proffer the need for additional evidence as was contemplated by Ohio R. Civ. P. 53(E)(4)(b), such issue was waived under Rule 53(E)(3)(d). Carroll v. Carroll, — Ohio App. 3d —, 2006 Ohio 5531, — N.E. 2d —, 2006 Ohio App. LEXIS 5511 (Oct. 16, 2006).

As a father's objections to a magistrate's decision involving the date that child support was to commence were clearly untimely under Ohio R. Juv. P. 40(E)(3)(a) and Ohio R. Civ. P. 53(E)(3), warranting dismissal thereof by the juvenile court, and the father he did not seek to enlarge the time within which to file objections pursuant to Ohio R. Juv. P. 18(B) and Ohio R. Civ. P. 6(B), his time to appeal was not extended by the objections. His failure to appeal within 30 days of the juvenile court's adoption of the magistrate's decision did not preserve his merit issue for appellate review under Ohio R. App. P. 4(A). In re D.K.K., — Ohio App. 3d —, 2006 Ohio 5576, — N.E. 2d —, 2006 Ohio App. LEXIS 5590 (Oct. 20, 2006).

Former wife failed to preserve for review the trial court's adoption of a magistrate's decision, denying her request for reimbursement of payments to have been made by her former husband under the parties' separation agreement that was incorporated into their divorce decree, as she failed to file objections to the magistrate's decision despite substantial compliance with the notice requirements pursuant to Ohio R. Civ. P. 53(E)(3); there was no plain error. McBroom v. Loveridge, — Ohio App. 3d —, 2006 Ohio 5908, — N.E. 2d —, 2006 Ohio App. LEXIS 5861 (Nov. 9, 2006).

There was no plain error in a decision by a magistrate to continue a parental rights termination proceeding on a second-day of a hearing, although a mother's guardian ad litem was not available on that day, as a substitute attorney was sent who duly represented the mother and further, there was overwhelming evidence that it was in the child's best interest for the county agency's request for permanent court commitment to be granted; the plain error standard was applied due to the mother's failure to have filed a proper objection to the magistrate's ruling, as required by Ohio R. Civ. P. 53(D)(3)(b)(iv). In re J.J., — Ohio App. 3d —, 2006 Ohio 6151, — N.E. 2d —, 2006 Ohio App. LEXIS 6101 (Nov. 21, 2006).

Father's motion for change of custody was properly granted since the mother's letter sent to the trial court after the magistrate recommended that the father's motion be granted did not state her objections to the magistrate's findings or conclusions with specificity as required by Ohio R. Civ. P. 53(E)(3)(b); rather, the mother did not even raise the main issue that the mother argued in her appellate brief, which was whether the trial court erred in determining that the mother's affair caused a change of circumstances sufficient to warrant a change of custody. Further, the trial court's best interest findings involved questions of fact, and since the mother failed to support her objections to those findings with a transcript of the custody hearing, the court had to accept the magistrate's findings as true. In re Harman, — Ohio App. 3d —, 2006 Ohio 2257, — N.E. 2d —, 2006 Ohio App. LEXIS 2102 (May 3, 2006).

Because the mother failed to file any objections to the magistrate's decision, she waived her appellate rights to challenge the issues regarding the order of supervised visitation. Issues of manifest weight of the evidence, abuse of discretion in construction of the facts, and the contents of the in camera interview had to have been initially raised to the trial court in objections, under Ohio R. Civ. P. 53(E)(3)(d). Mlinarcik v. Mlinarcik, — Ohio App. 3d —, 2006 Ohio 1287, — N.E. 2d —, 2006 Ohio App. LEXIS 1180 (Mar. 17, 2006).

— Failure to object

Since the owner of a charter bus company failed to object, in his objections to a magistrate's decision, to the magistrate's characterization of the owner's business as a "common carrier," as required by Ohio R. Civ. P. 53(D)(3)(b), the owner, pursuant to Ohio R. Civ. P. 53(D)(3)(b)(iv), waived any right to assign this as error on appeal. Sutton v. Crawford, — Ohio App. 3d —, 2007 Ohio 4444, — N.E. 2d —, 2007 Ohio App. LEXIS 3997 (Aug. 30, 2007).

Trial court did not abuse its discretion under RC § 3105.171 in adopting a magistrate's determination regarding valuation of parties' personal property in their divorce action, as the magistrate had relied on the opinion of an expert whose testimony was supported by competent and credible evidence with respect to her valuation opinion. Any such error was not preserved for review pursuant to Ohio R. Civ. P. 53 where the husband failed to object to the magistrate's determination on that issue. Phillips v. Phillips, — Ohio App. 3d —, 2007 Ohio 3368, — N.E. 2d —, 2007 Ohio App. LEXIS 3116 (June 29, 2007).

Since a mother failed to file objections to a magistrate's decision denying the mother's motion for the termination of an order granting legal custody of the mother's children to the children's maternal grandmother, she was precluded under Ohio R. Civ. P. 53(E)(3)(d) from assigning as error on appeal the trial court's adoption of magistrate's findings of fact or conclusions of law. Although the court reviewed the decision for plain error, no plain error was found. In re J.M.B, 2007 Ohio 3876, 2007 Ohio App. LEXIS 3516 (2007).

When, in a divorce proceeding, a husband did not object to certain findings made by a magistrate, he could not, under Ohio R. Civ. P. 53(E)(3)(d), raise those matters in his appeal of the trial court's decision. Varner v. Varner, — Ohio App. 3d —, 2007 Ohio 675, — N.E. 2d —, 2007 Ohio App. LEXIS 619 (Feb. 20, 2007).

Landlord's issues regarding the merits of the case could not be addressed because the landlord failed to timely file any objections to the magistrate's decision within 14 days of the decision, as required by former Ohio R. Civ. P. 53(E)(3). Tidwell v. Quaglieri, — Ohio App. 3d —, 2007 Ohio 569, — N.E. 2d —, 2007 Ohio App. LEXIS 530 (Feb. 9, 2007).

Because the father did not specifically object to the magistrate's decision denying his motion to dismiss (the mother's motion for modification of custody), he failed to preserve the issue for appellate review, pursuant to former Ohio R. Civ. P. 53(E)(3)(b). Jones v. Jones, — Ohio App. 3d —, 2007 Ohio 4255, — N.E. 2d —, 2007 Ohio App. LEXIS 3934 (Aug. 14, 2007).

Trial court did not err in using March 7, the date of the second trial set for the parties' divorce action, as the termination date of the parties' marriage instead of the date of separation. The magistrate determined that the parties attempted to reconcile and continued to maintain intertwined assets, and in the absence of objections or a record of the proceedings, the court had to accept the magistrate's factual findings. Nitschke v. Nitschke, — Ohio App. 3d —, 2007 Ohio 1550, — N.E. 2d —, 2007 Ohio App. LEXIS 1416 (Mar. 30, 2007).

Mother waived her arguments advanced in support of her contention that the trial court erred in adopting a magistrate's decision in a custody case because the mother failed to raise the arguments as objections to the magistrate's decision, as required by Ohio R. Civ. P. 53(D)(3)(b)(iv). Bowers v. Bowers, — Ohio App. 3d —, 2007 Ohio 1739, — N.E. 2d —, 2007 Ohio App. LEXIS 1586 (Apr. 13, 2007).

Because the trial court gave the prisoner adequate notice of the requirements in Civ. R. 53 in its judgment entry in favor of the corrections department, including the need to file objections, the prisoner was not relieved from compliance. Judicial notice was taken that he received the judgment entry since he filed his notice of appeal seven days later. Watley v. Department of Rehabilitation & Correction, — Ohio App. 3d —, 2007 Ohio 1841, — N.E. 2d —, 2007 Ohio App. LEXIS 1666 (Apr. 19, 2007).

After a trial court adopted a magistrate's decision that determined the amount of child support arrearages due from a former husband to the former wife, the doctrine of res judicata barred the trial court's vacatur thereof and a remand for further consideration, as no appeal was taken from the judgment, no motion for relief from judgment was made, and no objections were filed under Ohio R. Civ. P. 53; accordingly, relitigation of the child support arrearage issue by the magis-

trate was error. Campbell v. Campbell, — Ohio App. 3d —, 2007 Ohio 2175, — N.E. 2d —, 2007 Ohio App. LEXIS 2028 (May 3, 2007).

As mortgagors failed to object to a magistrate's decision pursuant to Ohio R. Civ. P. 53(D)(3)(b)(iv), they waived any alleged error with respect to her determination that a foreclosure judgment was warranted against the mortgagors. C&W Asset Acquistion, LLC v. Forster, — Ohio App. 3d —, 2007 Ohio 2081, — N.E. 2d —, 2007 Ohio App. LEXIS 1942 (Apr. 30, 2007).

Where a magistrate determined that a former wife was in contempt of court for failing to repay her former husband for his share of a loan to her mother, the wife should have filed objections to that decision rather than seek relief from judgment after the trial court approved and adopted the magistrate's determination. Such use of a motion under Ohio R. Civ. P. 60(B) was not permitted, and further, there was no plain error under Ohio R. Civ. P. 53(D)(3)(b) where the magistrate's determination was properly based on the parties' divorce decree. Brennan v. Brennan, — Ohio App. 3d —, 2007 Ohio 2097, — N.E. 2d —, 2007 Ohio App. LEXIS 1953 (Apr. 27, 2007).

When a husband sought to have a wife held in contempt for violating the parties' shared parenting plan, and the wife sought to have one of the parties' children testify at the contempt hearing, while it was arbitrary for a magistrate to exclude the child's testimony, the wife did not proffer the evidence the child would offer, as required by Ohio R. Evid. 103(A)(2), nor did the wife object to the exclusion, as required by Ohio R. Civ. P. 53(D)(3)(a)(iv) to preserve the issue for appeal, so the issue was waived. Carver v. Halley, — Ohio App. 3d —, 2007 Ohio 2351, — N.E. 2d —, 2007 Ohio App. LEXIS 2188 (May 11, 2007).

Where a father whose paternity and child support obligations were established by a magistrate failed to file objections to that decision, and he failed to file objections to a magistrate's later decision to deny his motion under Ohio R. Civ. P. 60(B) to vacate the earlier judgment, he waived his right to appeal under Ohio R. Civ. P. 53(D)(3)(b). As the father failed to provide the appellate court with a trial court transcript, as required by Ohio R. App. P. 9(B), there was nothing to review and the appellate court had to presume the validity of the trial court proceedings. T.S. v. W.D., — Ohio App. 3d —, 2007 Ohio 3795, — N.E. 2d —, 2007 Ohio App. LEXIS 3454 (July 26, 2007).

As a former husband objected to the coverture fraction used by a magistrate in the magistrate's decision, finding that a retirement bonus was a retirement benefit which the former wife was entitled to a share of, but he did not object to the determination of the bonus being a retirement benefit or the wife's entitlement thereto, he could not assert such errors on appeal, as he waived his right to do so by his failure to object, as required by Ohio R. Civ. P. 53(E)(3). Koeller v. Koeller, — Ohio App. 3d —, 2007 Ohio 2998, — N.E. 2d —, 2007 Ohio App. LEXIS 2749 (June 18, 2007).

Trial court's adoption of a magistrate's decision to affirm the denial of property owners' request for height and area variances by a city board of zoning appeals was supported by the evidence pursuant to RC § 2506.04, as some of the findings of the magistrate which were not objected to pursuant to Ohio R. Civ. P. 53(E)(3)(d) were deemed waived for purposes of appeal, and the magistrate relied on the proper sections of the city codified ordinances and the factors construed in judicial precedents in determining that the variance requests were not appropriate. Stovall v. City of Streetsboro, — Ohio App. 3d —, 2007 Ohio 3381, — N.E. 2d —, 2007 Ohio App. LEXIS 3101 (June 29, 2007).

As a legal client failed to object to a magistrate's finding, which was adopted by a trial court, that the client had instructed his attorneys in a personal injury action not to pay certain medical bills, any error asserted on appeal was judged under a plain error standard of review pursuant to Ohio R. Civ. P. 53(D)(3)(b)(iv). There was no plain error in the attorneys' failure to pay those bills, as they acted as instructed after the personal injury action was settled. Ealy v. Switala, — Ohio App. 3d —, 2007 Ohio 3438, — N.E. 2d —, 2007 Ohio App. LEXIS 3146 (June 29, 2007).

Although the magistrate fulfilled its obligation under Ohio R. Civ. P. 53 and provided the requisite notice to the parties, the daughter failed to file any objections to the magistrate's decision, which denied her motion for relief from judgment. Ohio R. Civ. P. 53 provided the daughter with the mechanism to raise her arguments before the trial court, but she failed to utilize that method by failing to file objections to the magistrate's decision, and she did not allege plain error or the existence of a defect on the face of the magistrate's decision. In re Sheares, — Ohio App. 3d —, 2007 Ohio 3624, — N.E. 2d —, 2007 Ohio App. LEXIS 3318 (July 17, 2007).

Since a wife did not object to the fact that a magistrate found her in default for failing to appear at the divorce hearing, the appellate court was bound to review the assignment of error to this effect presented on appeal under the plain error standard. Plain error did not occur when the magistrate found the wife "in default for appearance" because the magistrate did not enter a default judgment, as prohibited in a divorce action by Ohio R. Civ. P. 75(F), but, instead, considered the evidence presented and issued his decision accordingly. Ordean v. Ordean, — Ohio App. 3d —, 2007 Ohio 3979, — N.E. 2d —, 2007 Ohio App. LEXIS 3598 (Aug. 6, 2007).

Since a wife did not object to the fact that a magistrate proceeded with a divorce matter as an uncontested divorce hearing, the court was bound to review the assignment of error presented by the wife on appeal under the plain error standard. Plain error did not occur when the magistrate proceeded with the divorce action in the absence of the wife because the wife received proper notice prior to the hearing yet failed to appear at the hearing without providing any excuse. Ordean v. Ordean, — Ohio App. 3d —, 2007 Ohio 3979, — N.E. 2d —, 2007 Ohio App. LEXIS 3598 (Aug. 6, 2007).

As a mother failed to object to a magistrate's use of RC § 3119.04 in determining that a father's child support obligation that was originally made under former RC § 3113.215 was to be reduced, she waived any objection thereto pursuant to Ohio R. Civ. P. 53(D)(3)(a)(ii) for purposes of appeal; further, there was no plain error in the magistrate's use of RC § 3119.04. Kassicieh v. Mascotti, — Ohio App. 3d —, 2007 Ohio 5079, — N.E. 2d —, 2007 Ohio App. LEXIS 4494 (Sept. 27, 2007).

Mother's complaint that, in custody proceedings before a magistrate, the magistrate did not consider a child's autism was not sustained because, when the mother filed objections to the magistrate's decision, the mother did not raise this objection, so, under Ohio R. Civ. P. 53(D)(3)(b)(iv), due to the mother's failure to raise the objection or provide a proper evidentiary record to support the objection, the mother waived this alleged error. Selby v. Selby, — Ohio App. 3d —, 2007 Ohio 6700, — N.E. 2d —, 2007 Ohio App. LEXIS 5857 (Dec. 14, 2007).

Where a husband in a divorce action failed to file timely objections pursuant to Ohio R. Civ. P. 53(3)(d) to a magistrate's temporary financial orders, the husband waived the ability to claim on appeal that the orders were vague and ambiguous. Goe v. Goe, — Ohio App. 3d —, 2007 Ohio 6767, — N.E. 2d —, 2007 Ohio App. LEXIS 5937 (Dec. 17, 2007).

Widower's objections to a magistrate's decision regarding his request for an accounting and his supplement to exceptions to a partial inventory were not timely filed, pursuant to Ohio R. Civ. P. 53(E)(3)(a), because they were not filed within 14 days of the entry of the magistrate's decision, and the date of the probate court's entry adopting the magistrate's decision

was irrelevant for purposes of determining whether the objections were timely filed. In re Estate of Jaric, — Ohio App. 3d —, 2006 Ohio 7066, — N.E. 2d —, 2006 Ohio App. LEXIS 6979 (Dec. 28, 2006).

Where a father in a custody dispute failed to object to the trial court's ruling that the child's two sets of grandparents who were involved in a custody determination of the father's minor child could submit proposed findings of fact and conclusions of law, but that the father could not submit them, he waived any error for purposes of appeal; however, the record indicated that the father vigorously advanced his position throughout the litigation and the trial court thoroughly understood all parties' positions. Smith v. Quigg, — Ohio App. 3d —, 2006 Ohio 1495, — N.E. 2d —, 2006 Ohio App. LEXIS 1368 (Mar. 22, 2006).

Magistrate's temporary orders required that the father pay the mortgage on both parcels of property, but did not specify that he would receive credit for those payments. Because the father never moved to set aside that order and he never moved to modify that order, he waived any argument regarding whether he should receive credit for the mortgage payments on those properties made while the divorce was pending. Spier v. Spier, — Ohio App. 3d —, 2006 Ohio 1289, — N.E. 2d —, 2006 Ohio App. LEXIS 1181 (Mar. 7, 2006).

In a divorce, when a wife did not timely object to a magistrate's recommendations, under Ohio R. Civ. P. 53(E)(3)(a), or timely seek an extension, the trial court lacked jurisdiction to consider her objections and a finding that the husband was in contempt was erroneous, but, as no penalty was ordered, and the trial court, pursuant to its own jurisdiction, ordered the return of the property at issue, the error was harmless. Bawa v. Bawa, — Ohio App. 3d —, 2006 Ohio 2522, — N.E. 2d —, 2006 Ohio App. LEXIS 2399 (May 18, 2006).

Appellant failed to object to the magistrate's findings of fact which were attached and incorporated into the magistrate's decision, and, consequently, pursuant to Ohio R. Civ. P. 53(E)(3)(d), appellant waived any error in the trial court's adoption of the magistrate's decision by failing to object to the magistrate's findings. Santee v. Mansell, — Ohio App. 3d —, 2006 Ohio 2980, — N.E. 2d —, 2006 Ohio App. LEXIS 2860 (June 14, 2006).

Pursuant to Ohio R. Civ. P. 53, appellant waived all but plain error in the trial court's decision finding him in contempt of court, awarding attorney fees to appellee, and holding that appellant was a vexatious litigator because appellant failed to file with the trial court objections to the magistrate's decision. Since appellant failed to file any transcripts and failed to provide a statement of the evidence or an agreed statement of the case under Ohio R. App. P. 9(D), the court was prevented from effectively the assignments of error as it related to the contempt finding and the award of attorney fees by his failure to timely object to the magistrate's decision for plain error; thus, the court presumed the validity of the judgment as to those two decisions. Gevedon v. Gevedon, 167 Ohio App. 3d 450, 2006 Ohio 3195, 855 N.E. 2d 548, 2006 Ohio App. LEXIS 3087 (June 23, 2006).

Where a mother failed to file objections to a magistrate's decision regarding a shared parenting plan in a timely manner pursuant to Ohio R. Civ. P. 53(E)(3)(a) and (d), such issues were not reviewable on appeal. Waclawski v. Waclawski, — Ohio App. 3d —, 2006 Ohio 3213, — N.E. 2d —, 2006 Ohio App. LEXIS 3125 (June 23, 2006).

Husband's objection to a magistrate's decision, which basically asserted that guardian ad litem fees were attorney fees which were dischargeable in bankruptcy, did not preserve, for appellate review, under Ohio R. Civ. P. 53(E)(3)(d), an objection to the magistrate's decision finding him in contempt for not providing the wife with insurance documents required by the divorce decree, and there was no plain error because he had still not provided the documents years after he was ordered to. Carter v. Carter, — Ohio App. 3d —, 2006 Ohio 1206, — N.E. 2d —, 2006 Ohio App. LEXIS 1078 (Mar. 16, 2006).

Wife was barred from arguing on appeal that a trial court erred in adopting a magistrate's decision on the ground that the magistrate's valuation of household goods was erroneous because the wife did not specifically argue this in her objections to the magistrate's decision, as required by Ohio R. Civ. P. 53(E)(3)(b). While the argument was made in supplemental memorandum, the memorandum was untimely, and the wife did not obtain leave of court to file the untimely objections. Beasley v. Beasley, — Ohio App. 3d —, 2006 Ohio 5000, — N.E. 2d —, 2006 Ohio App. LEXIS 4940 (Sept. 25, 2006).

In making a property distribution award in the parties' divorce proceeding, the magistrate's decision to use the date that the parties began living together based on their antenuptial agreement rather than the date of the marriage,was not challengeable on appeal where the wife did not object to that determination pursuant to Ohio R. Civ. P. 53(E)(3)(d). Henley v. Henley, — Ohio App. 3d —, 2006 Ohio 3336, — N.E. 2d —, 2006 Ohio App. LEXIS 3263 (June 30, 2006).

Since appellant failed to file objections to a magistrate's decision concluding that appellee was entitled to a stalking civil protection order (SCPO) against appellant, she was precluded from challenging on appeal the trial court's entry adopting the magistrate's decision. Even if the issue were properly before the court, there was competent, credible evidence to support the trial court's issuance of the SCPO since the evidence showed that the boyfriend observed appellant appear at appellee's residence uninvited and that, on several different occasions, appellant threatened appellee and her children with physical harm. Dickson v. Ball, — Ohio App. 3d —, 2006 Ohio 3436, — N.E. 2d —, 2006 Ohio App. LEXIS 3358 (June 30, 2006).

When a putative father who had acknowledged his paternity of a child sought relief from a resulting judgment of paternity, after genetic testing showed a zero percent chance that he was the child's father, he could not claim, on appeal of the denial of his motion for relief, that the trial court should have considered granting him relief under Ohio R. Civ. P. 60(B) because he did not raise this in his motion for relief or in objections to a magistrate's decision. Vah v. Mahan, — Ohio App. 3d —, 2006 Ohio 3476, — N.E. 2d —, 2006 Ohio App. LEXIS 3432 (June 30, 2006).

When a putative father who had acknowledged his paternity of a child sought relief from a resulting judgment of paternity, after genetic testing showed a zero percent chance that he was the child's father, he could not claim, on appeal of the denial of his motion for relief, that the trial court should have considered granting him relief under its continuing jurisdiction in RC § 3111.16 because (1) he did not raise this in his motion for relief or in objections to a magistrate's decision, as required by Ohio R. Civ. P. 53(E)(3)(b) and (d), and (2) the more general RC § 3111.16 was not inconsistent with the more specific RC § 3119.962, pursuant to which the father sought relief and pursuant to which his request was denied. Vah v. Mahan, — Ohio App. 3d —, 2006 Ohio 3476, — N.E. 2d —, 2006 Ohio App. LEXIS 3432 (June 30, 2006).

Where a wife raised assorted constitutional claims in her motion for relief from a divorce judgment pursuant to Ohio R. Civ. P. 60(B), but she failed to raise them in her objections to the decision of the magistrate who considered her motion and recommended denial thereof, which was adopted by the trial court, those issues were not preserved for review pursuant to Ohio R. Civ. P. 53(E)(3)(d). Wilson v. Wilson, — Ohio App. 3d —, 2006 Ohio 4261, — N.E. 2d —, 2006 Ohio App. LEXIS 4187 (Aug. 17, 2006).

When a husband appealed a trial court's judgment adopting a magistrate's decision finding him in contempt, the fact that the trial court adopted the magistrate's decision on the same day it was issued did not prevent the husband from filing objections to the magistrate's decision with the trial court, and his failure to do so, pursuant to Ohio R. Civ. P. 53(D)(3)(b), barred the appellate court from considering his assignments of error. Diment v. Diment, — Ohio App. 3d —, 2006 Ohio 5295, — N.E. 2d —, 2006 Ohio App. LEXIS 5281 (Oct. 6, 2006).

When a husband appealed the trial court's judgment adopting a magistrate's decision finding him in contempt, the appellate court could not consider his assignments of error because he did not comply with Ohio R. Civ. P. 53(D)(3)(b) by filing objections to the magistrate's decision with the trial court, so he could not raise factual issues on appeal, and no plain error was evident. Diment v. Diment, — Ohio App. 3d —, 2006 Ohio 5295, — N.E. 2d —, 2006 Ohio App. LEXIS 5281 (Oct. 6, 2006).

Trial court's adoption of a magistrate's decision to appoint a receiver on behalf of judgment creditors in order to collect default judgments obtained against a judgment debtor was presumed proper due to the lack of a transcript or other alternative statement that reflected the proceedings held before the magistrate pursuant to the debtor's duty under Ohio R. App. P. 9(B). The claims raised on appeal by the debtor were not raised as objections to the magistrate's decision, as required by Ohio R. Civ. P. 53(E)(3)(d), and accordingly, they were waived for purposes of appeal. Mahoning Nat'l Bank v. Wilhelm, — Ohio App. 3d —, 2006 Ohio 6132, — N.E. 2d —, 2006 Ohio App. LEXIS 6104 (Nov. 15, 2006).

Pursuant to Ohio R. Juv. P. 40(D)(3)(a) and Ohio R. Civ. P. 53(D)(3)(b), where a juvenile was adjudicated as delinquent and was thereafter found guilty of committing probation violations, which decisions were adopted by the trial court from a magistrate's determinations, and the juvenile failed to file objections to the magistrate's decision with respect to the failure of the magistrate to appoint a guardian ad litem for him and to determine whether the juvenile's waiver of the right to counsel was voluntary, intelligent, or knowing, he waived any challenge on those issues on appeal except as to possible plain error. In re J-M, — Ohio App. 3d —, — N.E. 2d —, 2006 Ohio App. LEXIS 6131 (Nov. 22, 2006).

Where a father and son did not object to any factual findings by a magistrate, and specifically did not object to the finding under Ohio R. Civ. P. 12(B) that their action arising from a dog bite suffered by the son was precluded by principles of res judicata, the procedural irregularities were deemed waived pursuant to Ohio R. Civ. P. 53(D)(3)(b)(iv), as there was no plain error. A motion to dismiss under Ohio R. Civ. P. 12(B) based on res judicata was improper, as such was an affirmative defense which was to be have been pleaded under Ohio R. Civ. P. 8(C) and was properly disposed of by conversion of the dismissal motion to one for summary judgment under Ohio R. Civ. P. 56. Montecalvo v. American Family Ins. Co., — Ohio App. 3d —, 2006 Ohio 6881, — N.E. 2d —, 2006 Ohio App. LEXIS 6793 (Dec. 22, 2006).

Where a grandmother who was a temporary guardian for her grandchildren's estates and persons failed to object to a magistrate's decision to terminate the guardianship in its totality rather than separately over the children's estates and persons, pursuant to former Ohio R. Civ. P. 53(E)(3)(d), there was no plain error. In re Clowtis, — Ohio App. 3d —, 2006 Ohio 6868, — N.E. 2d —, 2006 Ohio App. LEXIS 6811 (Dec. 22, 2006).

Where a grandmother who was a temporary guardian for her grandchildren's estates and persons failed to object to a magistrate's decision to terminate the guardianship in its totality rather than separately over the children's estates and persons, pursuant to former Ohio R. Civ. P. 53(E)(3)(d), there was no plain error. In re Clowtis, — Ohio App. 3d —, 2006 Ohio 6868, — N.E. 2d —, 2006 Ohio App. LEXIS 6811 (Dec. 22, 2006).

Where a former wife failed to contest the trial court's adoption of a magistrate's decision to terminate the parties' shared parenting plan over their daughter, pursuant to RC § 3109.04(E)(2)(c), as she did not file any objections to the magistrate's decision, the wife waived her arguments contesting that portion of the decision on appeal pursuant to Ohio R. Civ. P. 53(D)(3)(b)(iv). Hamby v. Hamby, — Ohio App. 3d —, 2006 Ohio 6905, — N.E. 2d —, 2006 Ohio App. LEXIS 6825 (Dec. 27, 2006).

In divorce proceedings, a former wife waived her objection to the allocation of post-separation credit card debt by failing to move to modify or to set aside a magistrate's temporary order requiring each party to pay individual debts under Ohio R. Civ. P. 53(C)(3)(a) because, although she moved to modify the temporary order pursuant to Ohio R. Civ. P. 75(N)(2), her request was limited to modification of temporary child support. Galloway v. Khan, — Ohio App. 3d —, 2006 Ohio 6637, — N.E. 2d —, 2006 Ohio App. LEXIS 6463 (Dec. 12, 2006).

When a homeowner claimed a township's storm sewer system caused his basement to flood, and a magistrate recommended that judgment be entered against the township, the township did not adequately preserve the record of the proceedings before the magistrate, under Ohio R. Civ. P. 53(E), because it did not offer into evidence a diagram which was drawn by several witnesses, on which the magistrate relied in rendering a decision, and, had it sought to offer additional evidence after it filed objections to the magistrate's decision, the trial court could have refused to consider such evidence, under Ohio R. Civ. P. 53(E)(4)(b), because the township conceded that the evidence was before the magistrate and was simply not preserved. Sturgis v. E. Union Township, — Ohio App. 3d —, 2006 Ohio 4309, — N.E. 2d —, 2006 Ohio App. LEXIS 4249 (Aug. 21, 2006).

— Opportunity to register objections

As a magistrate failed to include in his decisions the necessary language under former Ohio R. Civ. P. 53(E) (now at Rule 53(D)) regarding the need for the parties to file objections to his decision, his findings of fact, and his conclusions of law in order to preserve the issues for later review, an automobile manufacturer suffered prejudicial error where a jury verdict was entered against it. Ulrich v. Mercedes-benz United States, — Ohio App. 3d —, 2007 Ohio 5034, — N.E. 2d —, 2007 Ohio App. LEXIS 4450 (Sept. 26, 2007).

— Overruling objections

Trial court properly overruled objections to a magistrate's decision pursuant to Ohio R. Civ. P. 53(E)(4) and adopted the determination that a former employee's solicitation of clients from his former employer, based on memorized client lists and information about them, was a trade secret in violation of RC § 1333.61(D). Although the employee did not take any physical document with him, the client list was clearly a trade secret because the employer used adequate measures to protect the client information from its competitors and the public had no readily available means to acquire it. Al Minor & Assocs. v. Martin, — Ohio App. 3d —, 2006 Ohio 5948, — N.E. 2d —, 2006 Ohio App. LEXIS 5881 (Nov. 9, 2006).

— Specificity requirement

An administrative hearing officer properly increased a father's child support obligation because the officer used a standard reference to impute income to the father, under RC § 3119.01(C)(11), by determining what the father should have been earning in the father's stated occupation of carpet layer, and this determination was not modified on appeal because, inter alia, the father did not specifically object, as required by Ohio R. Civ. P. 53(D)(3)(b)(iv), to a magistrate's determination accepting the use of the standard reference. Mortine v. Slagle, — Ohio App. 3d —, — N.E. 2d —, 2007 Ohio App. LEXIS 4510 (Sept. 21, 2007).

When, in a child support case, a father alleged that a trial court's failure to appoint counsel for the father violated the father's due process rights, the father's claim could not be considered on appeal of the trial court's adoption of a magistrate's decision because the father did not raise this claim at the trial court level, so the father did not comply with the requirement of Ohio R. Civ. P. 53(D)(3)(b)(ii) to state an objection to a magistrate's decision with specificity. Bamba v. Derkson, — Ohio App. 3d —, 2007 Ohio 5192, — N.E. 2d —, 2007 Ohio App. LEXIS 4577 (Oct. 1, 2007).

— Support for objections

Although the grandparents' arguments challenged the magistrate's proceedings, neither of their two motions to set aside the entries of the magistrate was accompanied by a transcript of the evidence relevant to their claims, nor did they explain why a transcript was not available so that an affidavit of that evidence could be presented. Their reliance on two personal affidavits which were attached to their motion and response was misplaced because the affidavits failed to satisfy the requirements of the Ohio Rules of Civil Procedure and the Juvenile Rules for the support of challenges to the factual findings of a magistrate. In re I. S., — Ohio App. 3d —, 2007 Ohio 47, — N.E. 2d —, 2007 Ohio App. LEXIS 42 (Jan. 10, 2007).

Party who objects to the decision of a magistrate has the obligation to provide a transcript of the proceedings, or an affidavit if a transcript is not available, under Ohio R. Civ. P. 53(E)(3)(c), and the Rule does not provide the objecting party with an option to file either a transcript or an affidavit, as an affidavit may be employed only where a transcript of the proceedings is not available, and a transcript is not unavailable merely because the original stenographic notes have not been transcribed or because a party elects not to order a transcript of the proceedings. Sain v. Estate of Haas, — Ohio App. 3d —, 2007 Ohio 1705, — N.E. 2d —, 2007 Ohio App. LEXIS 1548 (Apr. 10, 2007).

When an attorney sued a former client for fees and sued her daughter for persuading her mother to fire the attorney, the attorney's arguments which involved a consideration of the evidence could not be considered because he did not file a transcript of the trial proceedings before a magistrate or a reason why a transcript was not available, under Ohio R. Civ. P. 53(E)(3)(c), and he could not file an affidavit without showing the unavailability of a transcript. Sain v. Estate of Haas, — Ohio App. 3d —, 2007 Ohio 1705, — N.E. 2d —, 2007 Ohio App. LEXIS 1548 (Apr. 10, 2007).

Trial court was not required to request a transcript of proceedings before a magistrate involving a former wife's objections to the husband's request for modification of his child support obligation, as the wife objected to the magistrate's decision and accordingly, she had the duty to provide the transcript pursuant to Ohio R. Civ. P. 53(E)(3)(b). Guertin v. Guertin, — Ohio App. 3d —, 2007 Ohio 2008, — N.E. 2d —, 2007 Ohio App. LEXIS 1785 (Apr. 26, 2007).

When a developer sought review of the decision of a magistrate, it was not necessary, under Ohio R. Civ. P. 53(E)(3)(c) (now Ohio R. Civ. P. 53(D)(3)(b)(iii)), for the developer to submit a transcript of the proceedings before the magistrate, or an affidavit stating that a transcript was unavailable, to the reviewing trial court because the case was decided on competing summary judgment motions, so there was no evidence to transcribe that was not already in the court's file, which was automatically part of the record, and, when the trial court adopted the magistrate's ruling, the developer could further appeal. Frederick v. Cocca Dev., — Ohio App. 3d —, 2006 Ohio 7273, — N.E. 2d —, 2006 Ohio App. LEXIS 7076 (May 11, 2006).

When review of the decision of a magistrate is sought, an affidavit that a transcript is not available is not required where there was no hearing from which a transcript could be generated, such as when the matter is decided on motions for summary judgment, and this is especially obvious considering that an evidentiary hearing is not even permitted on summary judgment decisions. Frederick v. Cocca Dev., — Ohio App. 3d —, 2006 Ohio 7273, — N.E. 2d —, 2006 Ohio App. LEXIS 7076 (May 11, 2006).

— Waiver

Tenant who appealed a trial court's adoption of a magistrate's decision, awarding damages to a landlord based on money due to him after crediting the tenant for his work performed on the landlord's rental properties, failed to properly object and file a transcript pursuant to Ohio R. Civ. P. 53(D)(3)(b)(iii) and (v), and accordingly, his manifest weight of the evidence argument was deemed waived. Cooper v. Cain, — Ohio App. 3d —, 2007 Ohio 4889, — N.E. 2d —, 2007 Ohio App. LEXIS 4368 (Sept. 21, 2007).

When a debtor did not timely object to a magistrate's decision denying the debtor's motion to vacate a default judgment against the debtor, the debtor did not waive the debtor's right to appeal a trial court's judgment adopting the magistrate's decision because the magistrate's decision was facially defective in that the decision did not contain language required by Ohio R. Civ. P. 53(D)(3)(a)(iii) stating that an objection to the magistrate's decision was waived on appeal if the objection was not specifically and timely raised, so a trial court erred in adopting the decision. OSI Funding Corp. v. Huth, — Ohio App. 3d —, — N.E. 2d —, 2007 Ohio App. LEXIS 4654 (Sept. 28, 2007).

As a magistrate in a child custody and support modification proceeding had determined that the father could provide health insurance coverage for the child for a stated sum, and the mother thereafter asserted objections to the magistrate's decision but she did not raise an objection with respect to the health insurance issue, that matter was deemed waived under Ohio R. Civ. P. 53(D)(3)(b)(iv) for purposes of appeal. In re Smith, — Ohio App. 3d —, 2007 Ohio 893, — N.E. 2d —, 2007 Ohio App. LEXIS 812 (Mar. 2, 2007).

As a magistrate in a child custody and support modification proceeding had determined that the father could provide health insurance coverage for the child for a stated sum, and the mother thereafter asserted objections to the magistrate's decision but she did not raise an objection with respect to the health insurance issue, that matter was deemed waived under Ohio R. Civ. P. 53(D)(3)(b)(iv) for purposes of appeal. In re Smith, — Ohio App. 3d —, 2007 Ohio 893, — N.E. 2d —, 2007 Ohio App. LEXIS 812 (Mar. 2, 2007).

In a mother's appeal from a decision adopting a magistrate's decision granting a father's motion to reallocate parental rights and responsibilities, the mother failed to raise several evidentiary issues in her objection to the magistrate's decision; her assignments of error on appeal raising those issues were therefore waived for purposes of appeal under Ohio R. Civ. P. 53(D)(3)(b)(iv). Stephens v. Bertin, — Ohio App. 3d —, 2006 Ohio 6401, — N.E. 2d —, 2006 Ohio App. LEXIS 6358 (Dec. 4, 2006).

Mother waived her arguments regarding an adjustment in child support because at no time did she object to the magistrate's report and recommendations. She did not make the claim that any decision by the trial court constituted plain error, nor were the decisions found to be plain error. Doerfler v. Doerfler, — Ohio App. 3d —, 2006 Ohio 6960, — N.E. 2d —, 2006 Ohio App. LEXIS 6925 (Dec. 29, 2006).

Where the mother failed to file objections from the April 4, 2005, magistrate's decision before the trial court's April 25, 2005, judgment adopting the magistrate's decision, the mother waived any error on appeal, as the mother did not file objections within 14 days as required by Ohio R. Civ. P. 53(E)(3)(b), and the mother also improperly failed to file or obtain a transcript of the trial proceedings as required by Ohio

R. Civ. P. 53(E)(3)(c). O'Brien v. O'Brien, 167 Ohio App. 3d 584, 2006 Ohio 1729, 856 N.E. 2d 274, 2006 Ohio App. LEXIS 1588 (Apr. 6, 2006).

Where no objections were filed to a magistrate's decision after a jury trial and to his decision denying post-trial motions, pursuant to Ohio R. Civ. P. 53(E)(3)(d), any errors thereon were waived for purposes of appeal absent plain error, of which there were none found. O'Connor v. Trans World Servs., — Ohio App. 3d —, 2006 Ohio 2747, — N.E. 2d —, 2006 Ohio App. LEXIS 2571 (June 1, 2006).

Appellant waived appellate review of trial court's decision when she: (1) failed to file timely objections to the magistrate's decision, (2) failed to file a direct appeal of the trial court's entry adopting that decision, (3) failed to file a direct appeal of the trial court's entry overruling appellant's untimely objections to the magistrate's decision, and (4) failed to comply with Ohio R. Civ. P. 53(E)(3)(c) and Franklin County, Ohio, Ct. C.P. R. 75.11 when she did not support her objections to the decision with a transcript. Even if the appeal was timely, the court observed that appellant's brief failed to comply with Ohio R. App. P. 16(A)(3) and (7), in that it was unintelligible and consisted of incoherent arguments interspersed with references to irrelevant legal authority. In re Neff, — Ohio App. 3d —, 2006 Ohio 4460, — N.E. 2d —, 2006 Ohio App. LEXIS 4375 (Aug. 29, 2006).

When a widower did not timely file objections to a magistrate's decision regarding his request for an accounting and his supplement to exceptions to a partial inventory, pursuant to Ohio R. Civ. P. 53(E)(3)(a), the objections were waived for purposes of appeal, pursuant to RC § 53(E)(3)(d). In re Estate of Jaric, — Ohio App. 3d —, 2006 Ohio 7066, — N.E. 2d —, 2006 Ohio App. LEXIS 6979 (Dec. 28, 2006).

Order of reference

There was no error in a trial court's reference of a summary judgment motion to a magistrate, as such was clearly authorized by Ohio R. Civ. P. 53(C)(1)(a) and the trial court made a proper order of reference on that issue. Myles v. Johnson, — Ohio App. 3d —, 2007 Ohio 2963, — N.E. 2d —, 2007 Ohio App. LEXIS 2724 (June 15, 2007).

Record

Where a mother filed objections to a magistrate's determination regarding a shared parenting plan as to the parties' son, but she failed to file a complete transcript for purposes of reviewing the fact-based claims that she raised, pursuant to Ohio R. Civ. P. 53(E)(3)(c) and Ohio R. App. P. 9(B), the trial court and the appellate court had to accept the magistrate's findings of fact as proper in the circumstances; accordingly, the mother's objections were properly dismissed. Waclawski v. Waclawski, — Ohio App. 3d —, 2006 Ohio 3213, — N.E. 2d —, 2006 Ohio App. LEXIS 3125 (June 23, 2006).

As a tenant and guarantor who appealed a trial court's adoption of a magistrate's decision in an action regarding the rights and obligations of the parties and the landlord with respect to a commercial lease did not include the full transcript from the proceedings before the magistrate, pursuant to Ohio R. Civ. P. 53(E)(3)(c), the trial court was required to accept the magistrate's findings of fact and examine only the legal conclusions based on those facts, and the appellate court's standard of review was whether the trial court abused its discretion in adopting that decision. Below Clearance LLC v. Refugee Rd., Ltd., — Ohio App. 3d —, 2006 Ohio 6562, — N.E. 2d —, 2006 Ohio App. LEXIS 6487 (Nov. 30, 2006).

Recusal of magistrate

Where the magistrate recused herself during a hearing, after conducting prior hearings in the case, the trial court erred by taking over the hearing and continuing it without the parties' agreement: Place v. Seibert, 173 Ohio App. 3d 653, 880 NE2d 100, 2007 Ohio App LEXIS 3942 (2007).

Referred issue

After a trial court adopted a magistrate's decision in a commercial lease dispute, it properly recommitted the matter to the magistrate pursuant to Ohio R. Civ. P. 53(D)(4)(b) for a hearing to determine damages, prejudgment interest, and attorneys' fees. Yoder v. Hurst, — Ohio App. 3d —, 2007 Ohio 4861, — N.E. 2d —, 2007 Ohio App. LEXIS 4310 (Sept. 20, 2007).

Rejecting findings

Trial court did not abuse its discretion under Ohio R. Civ. P. 53(E)(4)(b) in reversing a decision by a magistrate who found that property owners had paid a builder for its construction of a patio and porch on their residence, as it was within the trial court's province to assess the weight and credibility of the evidence. There was an absence of documentary evidence to support a finding that payment to the builder had been made. W. R. Martin, Inc. v. Zukowski, — Ohio App. 3d —, 2006 Ohio 6866, — N.E. 2d —, 2006 Ohio App. LEXIS 6785 (Dec. 22, 2006).

Res judicata

Trial court's adoption of a magistrate's decision that ordered a former husband to pay child support was a modification of the child support provision which was expressly authorized in the parties' separation agreement, which was previously incorporated into their divorce decree; the trial court order satisfied Ohio R. Civ. P. 53 and was a final appealable order, and as the issue regarding child support could have been previously raised by the husband in a prior appeal, it was barred from review by res judicata. Weisberg v. Sampson, — Ohio App. 3d —, 2006 Ohio 3646, — N.E. 2d —, 2006 Ohio App. LEXIS 3569 (July 14, 2006).

Review of magistrate's trial

While appellant included a compact disc of the Ohio R. Civ. P. 60(B) hearing in the trial court record, she did not file a transcript of the evidence nor did she submit an affidavit of evidence as required by Ohio R. Civ. P. 53(E)(3). Thus, the trial court properly limited its decision to whether the magistrate erred as a matter of law. Leibold v. Hiddens, — Ohio App. 3d —, 2007 Ohio 2972, — N.E. 2d —, 2007 Ohio App. LEXIS 2732 (June 8, 2007).

Trial court did not abuse its discretion by refusing to either modify a magistrate's report or hold a re-hearing pursuant to Ohio R. Civ. P. 53(e)(4)(b) in a foreclosure action involving allegations by the mortgagors of fraud and corrupt activity, as the magistrate's hearing was very lengthy, the mortgagors were allowed to proffer evidence in certain instances, and the trial court carefully reviewed the transcripts from the magistrate proceedings. Harajli Mgmt. & Inv. v. A&M Inv. Strategies, 167 Ohio App. 3d 546, 2006 Ohio 3052, 855 N.E. 2d 1262, 2006 Ohio App. LEXIS 2927 (June 16, 2006).

Father did not allege that his newly proffered evidence in a civil protective order case could not have been produced before the magistrate through reasonable diligence, and thus, the mandatory provision of Ohio R. Civ. P. 53(E)(4)(b) was not at issue. The father was unable to show prejudice from the denial of his motion for an in camera interview with the parties' son. Dunfee v. Dunfee, — Ohio App. 3d —, 2006 Ohio 2971, — N.E. 2d —, 2006 Ohio App. LEXIS 2877 (June 14, 2006).

Review of referee's report

Cutting and pasting of a magistrate's decision into a judgment entry does not show mere rubber-stamping, especially when the court also sets forth its standard of review: Ramos v. Khawli, 181 Ohio App. 3d 176, 2009 Ohio 798, 908 N.E.2d 495, 2009 Ohio App. LEXIS 661 (2009).

Scope of review

Former wife's due process rights under Ohion Const. art. I, § 16 were violated where she was not provided with notice of the hearing date or of the modified hearing date for a modification of the former husband's visitation pursuant to RC § 3109.051(D); although she failed to object under Ohio R. Civ. P. 53(D)(3)(b)(iv) to the magistrate's determination, which awarded the husband significant visitation, the wife had the right to appeal because she was not raising the impropriety of any finding or conclusion, but instead, she asserted that the hearing should not have taken place at all without her knowledge. Hoppel v. Hoppel, — Ohio App. 3d —, 2007 Ohio 5246, — N.E. 2d —, 2007 Ohio App. LEXIS 4638 (Sept. 24, 2007).

Standard of review

When an assignee sought review of a trial court's decision adopting a magistrate's summary determination imposing penalties against the assignee under the Fair Debt Collection Practices Act, 15 U.S.C.S. § 1692 et seq. and the Ohio Consumer Sales Practices Act, RC § 1345.01 et seq., de novo review, rather than abuse of discretion review was applied because Ohio R. Civ. P. 53 did not mandate abuse of discretion review, and an appellate court's de novo review of summary judgment should not be able to be circumvented by referral of a matter to a magistrate, as this would allow for the termination of potentially meritorious claims under the extremely deferential abuse of discretion standard. D.A.N. Joint Venture III v. Armstrong, — Ohio App. 3d —, 2007 Ohio 898, — N.E. 2d —, 2007 Ohio App. LEXIS 805 (Mar. 2, 2007).

When an assignee sought review of a trial court's decision adopting a magistrate's summary determination imposing penalties against the assignee under the Fair Debt Collection Practices Act, 15 U.S.C.S. § 1692 et seq. and the Ohio Consumer Sales Practices Act, RC § 1345.01 et seq., de novo review, rather than abuse of discretion review was applied because Ohio R. Civ. P. 53 did not mandate abuse of discretion review, and an appellate court's de novo review of summary judgment should not be able to be circumvented by referral of a matter to a magistrate, as this would allow for the termination of potentially meritorious claims under the extremely deferential abuse of discretion standard. D.A.N. Joint Venture III v. Armstrong, — Ohio App. 3d —, 2007 Ohio 898, — N.E. 2d —, 2007 Ohio App. LEXIS 805 (Mar. 2, 2007).

Time for filing objections

Where a court closed early due to Election Day, which was the last day under CivR 53(D)(2)(b)(i) for landlords to file objections to a magistrate's decision in a dispute with tenants, the time for filing the objections was extended to the next succeeding day under CivR 6(A), such that an attempt to file the objections at that time should have been accepted as timely. Sharla v. Yates, — Ohio App. 3d —, 2008 Ohio 616, — N.E. 2d —, 2008 Ohio App. LEXIS 534 (Feb. 15, 2008).

When, in a child support case, a father alleged that a trial court's failure to appoint counsel for the father was improperly based on the retroactive application of an amendment to RC § 2151.352, the father's claim could not be considered on appeal of the trial court's adoption of a magistrate's decision because, while the father specifically objected to a magistrate's retroactive application of the amendment, the father did not do so timely, as required by Ohio R. Civ. P. 53(D)(3)(b)(i). Bamba v. Derkson, — Ohio App. 3d —, 2007 Ohio 5192, — N.E. 2d —, 2007 Ohio App. LEXIS 4577 (Oct. 1, 2007).

When, in a child support case, a father alleged that a trial court had no jurisdiction because RC § 3115.06(A) was not complied with, this argument could not be considered because, while the father raised the argument in the father's brief in support of the father's objections to a magistrate's decision, the objections were not filed within the time limit required by Ohio R. Civ. P. 53(D)(3)(b)(i), so the father waived the right to argue this issue on appeal. Bamba v. Derkson, — Ohio App. 3d —, 2007 Ohio 5192, — N.E. 2d —, 2007 Ohio App. LEXIS 4577 (Oct. 1, 2007).

Trial court did not err in denying property owners' objections to a magistrate's decision on the ground that the objections were untimely under Ohio R. Civ. P. 53(E)(3)(a)(i). The refiled objections, which were not filed until after the magistrate had corrected errors raised by the owners' original objections, raised issues that could have been raised in the owners' original objections but were not, and they were merely an attempt for a second chance to argue new objections. Ingledue v. Premier Siding & Roofing, Inc., — Ohio App. 3d —, 2006 Ohio 5977, — N.E. 2d —, 2006 Ohio App. LEXIS 5918 (Nov. 9, 2006).

— Extension of time

Trial court did not err in denying the landlord an extension of time to object to the magistrate's decision as it appropriately chose to serve the landlord by ordinary mail, even though he claimed to have been out of the country, and did not err in finding that his motion to extend time to filed objections to be untimely. Tidwell v. Quaglieri, — Ohio App. 3d —, 2007 Ohio 569, — N.E. 2d —, 2007 Ohio App. LEXIS 530 (Feb. 9, 2007).

There was no error in denying the husband's motion for an extension of time to file objections to the magistrate's decision because the 14-day period for filing objections, pursuant to Ohio R. Civ. P. 53(E)(3)(a), had already passed by the time the husband filed the motion. He did not explain why it was necessary for him to receive a physical copy of the decision before deciding to request additional time to file objections or why it was necessary for him to request additional time pro se, when he had retained counsel in Ohio. Planin v. Planin, — Ohio App. 3d —, 2006 Ohio 2933, — N.E. 2d —, 2006 Ohio App. LEXIS 2819 (June 9, 2006).

— Three-day mail rule

Mail rule did not apply to the time for filing objections to a magistrate's decision because the event that triggered the period for filing objections was not the service of the decision, as provided in Ohio R. Civ. P. 6(E), but the "filing" of the magistrate's decision, so the three-day mail rule did not extend the time for filing objections to a magistrate's decision. In re Estate of Jaric, — Ohio App. 3d —, 2006 Ohio 7066, — N.E. 2d —, 2006 Ohio App. LEXIS 6979 (Dec. 28, 2006).

Transcript

Trial court abused its discretion by weighing the credibility of evidence and testimony which it was never provided. The trial court did not have a transcript of the proceedings before the magistrate, and there was no demonstration that a transcript was unavailable. The affidavit provided by a party was insufficient: State Farm Mut. Auto. Ins. Co. v. Fox, 182 Ohio App. 3d 17, 2009 Ohio 1965, 911 N.E.2d 339, 2009 Ohio App. LEXIS 1644 (2009).

Trial court's denial of a former wife's motion to unseal the in camera interview between a magistrate and the parties' youngest child pursuant to RC § 3109.04(B)(1) with respect to the wife's post-decree request to modify the parental rights and responsibilities in order to designate her as the residential parent of that child was proper, as the purpose behind § 3109.04(B)(1) mandated that the confidentiality in the magistrate and child's discussion be maintained in order to foster free and uninhibited communication. The disclosure of the transcript upon court order was permitted in certain circumstances, the filing of the sealed transcript satisfied Montgomery County, Ohio, Ct. C.P. R. 4.31, and it was sufficient for purposes of a trial court's review of objections to the magistrate's decision under Ohio R. Civ. P. 53(D)(3)(b)(ii). Chapman v. Chapman, — Ohio App. 3d —, 2007 Ohio 2968, — N.E. 2d —, 2007 Ohio App. LEXIS 2728 (June 15, 2007).

When review is sought of a magistrate's decision, a transcript is necessary to attack factual findings, under Ohio R. Civ. P. 53(D)(3)(b)(iii), but, despite the fact that a transcript was not filed, a trial court can and must still assess whether the

magistrate's factual findings support his or her conclusions of law, and, absent a transcript, the trial court has absolutely no way of knowing what evidence was presented, so it is limited to accepting the factfinder's determination of fact based on the evidence and may only review for errors in applying these facts to the relevant law. Hipple v. Hipple, — Ohio App. 3d —, 2007 Ohio 4524, — N.E. 2d —, 2007 Ohio App. LEXIS 4045 (Aug. 29, 2007).

When a husband objecting to a magistrate's decision did not file a transcript of the proceedings before the magistrate in the trial court, as required by Ohio R. Civ. P. 53(D)(3)(iii), and the trial court adopted the magistrate's decision, an appellate court could not consider a transcript of the magistrate's proceedings because the appellate court's review had to be based on the record that was before the trial court, under Ohio R. App. P. 12(A)(1)(b). Hipple v. Hipple, — Ohio App. 3d —, 2007 Ohio 4524, — N.E. 2d —, 2007 Ohio App. LEXIS 4045 (Aug. 29, 2007).

There was no evidence that the trial court did not consider the evidence such that its decision on the father's objections to the magistrate's decision was improper because any testimony relevant to the two issues presented by the mother discussed in the November portion of the transcript was thoroughly discussed in the April portion of the transcript as well and nothing presented during the November hearing changed or contradicted the facts as presented during the April portion of the hearing. Rather, the transcripts indicated that any information as to those two issues described in the November transcript was duplicated and, in fact, expounded upon in the April transcript. Hueber v. Hueber, — Ohio App. 3d —, 2007 Ohio 913, — N.E. 2d —, 2007 Ohio App. LEXIS 822 (Mar. 5, 2007).

When a husband objecting to a magistrate's decision did not file a transcript of the proceedings before the magistrate in the trial court, as required by Ohio R. Civ. P. 53(D)(3)(iii), and the trial court adopted the magistrate's decision, the husband could not object to any factual determinations concerning the issues on appeal because no transcript was properly presented from which the trial or appellate courts could analyze the magistrate's factual findings. Hipple v. Hipple, — Ohio App. 3d —, 2007 Ohio 4524, — N.E. 2d —, 2007 Ohio App. LEXIS 4045 (Aug. 29, 2007).

It was an abuse of discretion for a trial court to sustain objections to a magistrate's decision denying an agency's motion for permanent custody of children because the record did not reflect that the trial court conducted an independent review of the magistrate's decision, as required by Ohio R. Civ. P. 53(D)(4)(b) and Ohio R. Juv. P. 40(D)(4)(b), because no transcript of the proceedings held before the magistrate was filed by the trial court, as required by Ohio R. Civ. P. 53(D)(3)(b)(iii) and Ohio R. Juv. P. 40(D)(3)(b)(iii). Children, — Ohio App. 3d —, 2007 Ohio 5123, — N.E. 2d —, 2007 Ohio App. LEXIS 4516 (Sept. 28, 2007).

In an inmate's negligence suit against a correctional facility, a magistrate's recommendation of judgment for the inmate was adopted because (1) the facility did not provide a full transcript of testimony before the magistrate relevant to the facility's objections, as required by Ohio R. Civ. P. 53(D)(3)(b)(iii), and (2) the transcript the facility provided did not support the facility's objections. Case v. Grafton Corr. Inst., — Ohio Misc. 2d —, 2007 Ohio 4140, — N.E. 2d —, 2007 Ohio Misc. LEXIS 275 (July 18, 2007).

Because the mother challenged the magistrate's legal conclusion that the parties' third child was unemancipated, and thus, challenged the application of the law to the facts, no transcript was necessary. Berthelot v. Berthelot, — Ohio App. 3d —, 2007 Ohio 3884, — N.E. 2d —, 2007 Ohio App. LEXIS 3526 (Aug. 1, 2007).

Denial of the mother's objections to the denial of the name change applications was not error. Because the mother failed to file a transcript of the magistrate's hearing in support of her objections, as required by Ohio R. Civ. P. 53(E)(3)(c), there was no proper evidentiary basis for the trial court to rule on those objections. In re Change of Name of Frenchko-Nagy, — Ohio App. 3d —, 2006 Ohio 3427, — N.E.2d —, 2006 Ohio App. LEXIS 3362 (June 30, 2006).

Trial court abused its discretion in overruling a business purchaser's objections to a magistrate's decision with respect to a dispute between the purchaser and seller regarding monies owed as a result of the transaction and accompanying agreements, as issues of fact and evidence were raised and the trial court should have waited for the trial transcript under Ohio R. Civ. P. 53(E)(3)(c) before ruling on the objections. Gruger v. Diversified Air Systems, Inc., — Ohio App. 3d —, 2006 Ohio 3568, — N.E. 2d —, 2006 Ohio App. LEXIS 3516 (July 7, 2006).

As a wife failed to include a transcript of a proceeding before a magistrate when she filed objections to the magistrate's decision, pursuant to Ohio R. Civ. P. 53(E)(3)(c), and she also failed to request an extension for the filing thereof prior to the hearing date on her objections in her divorce action, the trial court properly overruled her objections. Her motion to vacate the judgment pursuant to Ohio R. Civ. P. 60(B) was also properly denied where she was clearly on notice of the importance of the transcript having been filed, yet she still had not filed it or sought an extension of time to file it prior to that motion. Ludlow v. Ludlow, — Ohio App. 3d —, 2006 Ohio 6864, — N.E. 2d —, 2006 Ohio App. LEXIS 6778 (Dec. 22, 2006).

As a car purchaser who filed objections to a magistrate's decision failed to include a copy of the transcript from the magistrate's proceedings, as required by Ohio R. Civ. P. 53(E)(3)(c), review of his fact-based objections could not be had by the trial court and it only reviewed objections based in law; similarly, on review of the trial court's adoption of the magistrate's decision, the same issues were again not reviewable because they had not been before the trial court. Long v. Northern Illinois Classic Auto, — Ohio App. 3d —, 2006 Ohio 6907, — N.E. 2d —, 2006 Ohio App. LEXIS 6822 (Dec. 27, 2006).

As a car purchaser who filed objections to a magistrate's decision failed to include a copy of the transcript from the magistrate's proceedings, as required by Ohio R. Civ. P. 53(E)(3)(c), review of his fact-based objections could not be had by the trial court and it only reviewed objections based in law; similarly, on review of the trial court's adoption of the magistrate's decision, the same issues were again not reviewable because they had not been before the trial court. Long v. Northern Illinois Classic Auto, — Ohio App. 3d —, 2006 Ohio 6907, — N.E. 2d —, 2006 Ohio App. LEXIS 6822 (Dec. 27, 2006).

In a divorce heard before a magistrate, where the husband argued that the trial court abused its discretion in accepting the judgment entry of divorce submitted by the wife because it did not reflect the in-court agreement of the parties and where the husband did not file with the trial court a transcript with the husband's objections to the magistrate's decision, thus depriving the trial court with an opportunity to examine the testimony from the magistrate's hearing, this violated the Ohio R. Civ. P. 53(E)(3)(c) transcript requirement; the appellate court agreed with the trial court, which found, after reviewing the magistrate's decision pursuant to Ohio R. Civ. P. 53(E)(4)(a), no error of law or other defect on the face of the decision. Havel v. Havel, — Ohio App. 3d —, 2006 Ohio 1692, — N.E. 2d —, 2006 Ohio App. LEXIS 1547 (Mar. 31, 2006).

Apartment building owner's failure to provide the trial court with a transcript of the magistrate trial, as required by Ohio R. Civ. P. 53(E)(3)(c), precluded it from challenging the decision or judgment as being against the manifest weight of the evidence. GMS Mgmt. Co. v. Coulter, — Ohio App. 3d —, 2006 Ohio 1263, — N.E. 2d —, 2006 Ohio App. LEXIS 1152 (Mar. 17, 2006).

TITLE VII
JUDGMENT

RULE 54. Judgments; costs

(A) **Definition; form.** "Judgment" as used in these rules includes a decree and any order from which an appeal lies as provided in section 2505.02 of the Revised Code. A judgment shall not contain a recital of pleadings, the magistrate's decision in a referred matter, or the record of prior proceedings.

(B) **Judgment upon multiple claims or involving multiple parties.** When more than one claim for relief is presented in an action whether as a claim, counterclaim, cross-claim, or third-party claim, and whether arising out of the same or separate transactions, or when multiple parties are involved, the court may enter final judgment as to one or more but fewer than all of the claims or parties only upon an express determination that there is no just reason for delay. In the absence of a determination that there is no just reason for delay, any order or other form of decision, however designated, which adjudicates fewer than all the claims or the rights and liabilities of fewer than all the parties, shall not terminate the action as to any of the claims or parties, and the order or other form of decision is subject to revision at any time before the entry of judgment adjudicating all the claims and the rights and liabilities of all the parties.

(C) **Demand for judgment.** A judgment by default shall not be different in kind from or exceed in amount that prayed for in the demand for judgment. Except as to a party against whom a judgment is entered by default, every final judgment shall grant the relief to which the party in whose favor it is rendered is entitled, even if the party has not demanded the relief in the pleadings.

(D) **Costs.** Except when express provision therefore is made either in a statute or in these rules, costs shall be allowed to the prevailing party unless the court otherwise directs.

History: Amended, eff 7-1-89; 7-1-92; 7-1-94; 7-1-96.

NOTES TO DECISIONS

Analysis

Generally
Amendment to conform to evidence
Applicability
Arbitration
Attorney fees
Certification
Consolidated cases
Costs
— Cost of deposition
— Cost of expert witness
— Costs of videotape depositions
— Denial
— Prevailing party
Declaratory judgment
Dismissal
Failure to dispose of all claims
Failure to dispose of counterclaim
Final appealable order
— Fewer than all claims decided

Generally

Costs may be taxed under Civil Rule 54(D) in actions decided on summary judgment. If deposition costs are recoverable pursuant to RC § 2301.21, a court clerk need only receive a billing from the prevailing party to compute costs; the civil rules do not specifically require that a motion be filed to recover costs. The better practice, however, is to request the taxing of costs by motion. RC § 2303.21 provides authority to award transcript costs: Boomershine v. Lifetime Capital, Inc., 182 Ohio App. 3d 495, 913 N.E.2d 520, 2009 Ohio App. LEXIS 2320 (2009).

Amendment to conform to evidence

Where plaintiff orally moved to amend the pleadings to conform to the evidence at trial and defendant did not object, the judgment entry was not a final appealable order where it did not address the issues raised by the asserted amendment: North Shore Auto Fin., Inc. v. Block, 176 Ohio App. 3d 205, 2008 Ohio 1708, 891 N.E.2d 793, 2008 Ohio App. LEXIS 1466 (2008).

Applicability

As a lessor's breach of contract action against one of two lessees was not formally commenced within the one-year time period for obtaining service under Ohio R. Civ. P. 3(A) and 4(E), as the lessor was unable to serve her, and a judgment was entered in favor of the lessor with respect to all other claims between the lessor and the other lessee who was properly served, the entry thereof was a final judgment pursuant to RC § 2505.02(B)(1) for purposes of appellate review. As there were no unresolved claims, the requirement of Ohio R. Civ. P. 54(B) was inapposite. Farmers Mkt. Drive-in Shopping Ctrs. v. Magana, — Ohio App. 3d —, 2007 Ohio 2653, — N.E. 2d —, 2007 Ohio App. LEXIS 2450 (May 31, 2007).

Trial court judgment which dismissed a corrections officer's motion to vacate an adverse arbitration award was a final appealable order pursuant to RC § 2505.02, which judgment provided subject matter jurisdiction to the appellate court to review the officer's appeal of that ruling, as the dismissal of the motion due to lack of standing was an implied denial of the officer's motion to vacate the award. As a complete determination of all matters was had, there was no need for the language under Ohio R. Civ. P. 54(B). Koehring v. Ohio State Dep't of Rehabilitation & Correction, — Ohio App. 3d —, 2007 Ohio 2652, — N.E. 2d —, 2007 Ohio App. LEXIS 2463 (May 31, 2007).

Where the trial court entered judgments in favor of a real property purchaser in his action, alleging breach of a real estate contract arising from the sellers' failure to have delivered a deed to him, but the trial court never disposed of the purchaser's requests for punitive damages and prejudgment interest as part of his damages award, there were no final appealable orders under RC § 2505.02(B) and accordingly, the appellate court lacked jurisdiction to review the matter pursuant to Ohio Const. art. IV, § 3(B)(2); as only one claim for breach of contract was involved, Ohio R. Civ. P. 54(B) was inapplicable. Adkins v. Bratcher, — Ohio App. 3d —, 2007 Ohio 3587, — N.E. 2d —, 2007 Ohio App. LEXIS 3286 (July 10, 2007).

Arbitration

Trial court's denial of a nursing home's motion to compel arbitration pursuant to RC § 2711.02 was a final appealable order for purposes of RC § 2505.02 and Ohio Const. art. IV, § 3(B)(2), such that an appeal therefrom was reviewable on the merits; there was no requirement that the trial court order contain the "no just reason for delay" language of Ohio R. Civ. P. 54(b). Barnes v. Andover Village Ret. Cmty., — Ohio App. 3d —, 2007 Ohio 4112, — N.E. 2d —, 2007 Ohio App. LEXIS 3728 (Aug. 10, 2007).

Attorney fees

When attorney fees are requested in the original pleadings, an order that does not dispose of the attorney fee claim and does not include, pursuant to CivR 54(B), an express determination that there is no just reason for delay, is not a final, appealable order: IBEW, Local Union No. 8 v. Vaughn Indus., L.L.C., 116 Ohio St. 3d 335, 2007 Ohio 6439, 879 N.E.2d 187, 2007 Ohio LEXIS 3051 (2007).

Certification

Where multiple defendants remained in a personal representative's asbestos action after a manufacturer was granted summary judgment and there was no certification under Ohio R. Civ. P. 54(B), the order was not a final appealable one and the appellate court lacked jurisdiction to review the appeal on the merits pursuant to RC § 2505.02(B)(1) and Ohio Const. art. IV, § 3(B)(2). Polanco v. Asbestos Corp., — Ohio App. 3d —, 2007 Ohio 5488, — N.E. 2d —, 2007 Ohio App. LEXIS 4821 (Oct. 15, 2007).

Where a trial court adopted a magistrate's decision that granted summary judgment to a bank in a foreclosure action, but there was no certification language as required by Ohio R. Civ. P. 54(B) and there were other outstanding issues for which a ruling had been reserved, the appellate court lacked jurisdiction over an appeal from the summary judgment, as there was no final appealable order; dismissal of the appeal was mandated. Charter One Bank v. Tutin, — Ohio App. 3d —, 2006 Ohio 1361, — N.E. 2d —, 2006 Ohio App. LEXIS 1235 (Mar. 23, 2006).

Consolidated cases

Requirements of CivR 54(B) were not satisfied where the operational effect of consolidating two foreclosure cases was to join different lienholders who obtained their interests at different times and under different circumstances, and the CivR 60(B) entry granted relief in only one case: Milton Banking Co. v. Dulaney, 182 Ohio App. 3d 634, 2009 Ohio 1939, 914 N.E.2d 433, 2009 Ohio App. LEXIS 1617 (2009).

Costs

In an employee's successful intentional tort suit against his employer, in which the trial court neither awarded the employee costs, under Ohio R. Civ. P. 54(D), as the prevailing party nor "otherwise directed" him to bear all or part of his own costs, and the record did not reflect any consideration by the trial court of the employee's motion for costs, the trial court abused its discretion because it failed to address the matter of costs, so the trial court was directed to award the employee his costs. Maynard v. Eaton Corp., — Ohio App. 3d —, 2007 Ohio 1906, — N.E. 2d —, 2007 Ohio App. LEXIS 1742 (Apr. 23, 2007).

There was no abuse of discretion in a trial court's award of only some of the costs requested by a terminated employee in her action against her former employer and others, arising from alleged retaliation, defamation, and discrimination, as costs were assessed to the employer and others pursuant to Ohio R. Civ. P. 54(D) on the claims that the employee prevailed on. Although she asserted that she was entitled to other costs which were not awarded to her, she failed to cite to any statute that provided for the payment of each particular fee or expense. Lynch v. Studebaker, — Ohio App. 3d —, 2007 Ohio 4014, — N.E. 2d —, 2007 Ohio App. LEXIS 3651 (Aug. 9, 2007).

Trial court did not abuse its discretion when it ordered a husband to pay, pursuant to Ohio R. Civ. P. 54(D), court reporter fees and the fees remaining for an expert witness, as the reporter was hired because the hearing in the parties' divorce matter was held outside of court business hours due to the schedule of the husband's attorney; the husband originally hired the expert to testify, and although he later chose not to use him because he was dissatisfied with his opinion, the costs related to the husband's own cross-examination of the expert. Sadowski v. Sadowski, — Ohio App. 3d —, 2007 Ohio 5061, — N.E. 2d —, 2007 Ohio App. LEXIS 4478 (Sept. 27, 2007).

In a divorce, the wife was entitled to an award of her witness fee costs, under Ohio R. Civ. P. 54(D), because she was the prevailing party. Dinunzio v. Dinunzio, — Ohio App. 3d —, 2006 Ohio 3888, — N.E. 2d —, 2006 Ohio App. LEXIS 3863 (July 28, 2006).

Decision to award or to decline to award costs was a matter within the discretion of a trial court and, absent an abuse of discretion, would not be reversed on appeal; the trial court had to examine the expenses within the context of each case and determine which expenses were taxable, bearing in mind that Ohio R. Civ. P. 54(D) was not to be construed as a "tax all" provision. Holmes County Bd. of Comm'rs v. McDowell, — Ohio App. 3d —, 2006 Ohio 5017, — N.E. 2d —, 2006 Ohio App. LEXIS 4972 (Sept. 27, 2006).

Language of Civ. R. 54(D) granted a trial court discretion to order a prevailing party to bear all or part of his or her own costs but did not empower the court to award costs to a non-prevailing party. Holmes County Bd. of Comm'rs v. McDowell, — Ohio App. 3d —, 2006 Ohio 5017, — N.E. 2d —, 2006 Ohio App. LEXIS 4972 (Sept. 27, 2006).

Costs were generally defined as the statutory fees to which officers, witnesses, jurors and others were entitled for their services in an action and which were authorized to be taxed and included in a judgment. Holmes County Bd. of Comm'rs v. McDowell, — Ohio App. 3d —, 2006 Ohio 5017, — N.E. 2d —, 2006 Ohio App. LEXIS 4972 (Sept. 27, 2006).

Trial court did not abuse its discretion by imposing on appellants, pursuant to Ohio R. Civ. P. 54(D), the costs of service by publication on non-appearing codefendants. Ohio R. Civ. P. 54(D) vests a trial court with discretion to award costs to the prevailing party. Heider v. Heirs, Devisees, & Personal Representatives of Francis Bernot, — Ohio App. 3d —, 2006 Ohio 5111, — N.E. 2d —, 2006 Ohio App. LEXIS 5027 (Sept. 29, 2006).

Based on Ohio R. Civ. P. 54(D) and RC § 2335.28, a trial court did not abuse its discretion in imposing payment of court costs, including juror fees and costs for a court stenographer, on house purchasers after a jury verdict was rendered for the sellers, as a trial court evaluated the parties during the trial, and it informed them of the expenses associated with a jury trial before the matter proceeded. Jarratt v. Dickinson, — Ohio App. 3d —, 2006 Ohio 462, — N.E. 2d —, 2006 Ohio App. LEXIS 396 (Feb. 2, 2006).

Trial court's award of costs to a motorist in his personal injury action, arising from a vehicular collision, was proper under Ohio R. Civ. P. 54(D), as the requisite costs associated with the videotaped deposition of an expert witness were awarded pursuant to Ohio Superintendence R. 13(D), there was no authority to award costs for a court reporter, subpoena expenses, or filing fees pursuant to RC § 2303.20, and costs for medical records were properly not included. Wingfield v. Howe, — Ohio App. 3d —, 2006 Ohio 276, — N.E. 2d —, 2006 Ohio App. LEXIS 245 (Jan. 26, 2006).

— Cost of deposition

Where the trial court included expert witness fees and court report deposition fees as costs under Ohio R. Civ. P. 54(D), those fees were improperly awarded as costs to the wife, as expert witness fees did not constitute costs, and RC § 2319.27 did not provide for taxation of costs of the services of a court reporter at a deposition. Atkinson v. T.A.R.T.A., — Ohio App. 3d —, 2006 Ohio 1638, — N.E. 2d —, 2006 Ohio App. LEXIS 1518 (Mar. 31, 2006).

— Cost of expert witness

When county commissioners filed a quiet title action against landowners regarding a certain strip of land adjacent to the owners' property, it was error to award the costs of the preparation of a judicial title report against the landowners, under Ohio R. Civ. P. 54(D) or RC § 2317.27, because this award related to fees incurred in the preparation of an expert opinion, rather than attorney fees, even though the opinion was prepared by an attorney, and expert witness fees could not be awarded as costs. Holmes County Bd. of Comm'rs v. McDowell, — Ohio App. 3d —, 2006 Ohio 5017, — N.E. 2d —, 2006 Ohio App. LEXIS 4972 (Sept. 27, 2006).

— Costs of videotape depositions

Driver who was awarded a judgment in his favor, arising from a motor vehicle accident with a motorist, was not entitled to costs for a court reporter's services to attend the deposition of the driver's medical expert pursuant to RC §§ 2319.27 and 2303.21, although the expense of procuring the transcript of the expert's videotaped deposition was possibly recoverable under RC § 2303.21; although the reasonable expenses of recording the testimony on a videotape and playing it at trial were possibly recoverable under Ohio Superintendence Ct. R. 13(D)(2), the cost of the videotape itself was not a recoverable cost under Ohio R. Civ. P. 54(D). Naples v. Kinczel, — Ohio App. 3d —, 2007 Ohio 4851, — N.E. 2d —, 2007 Ohio App. LEXIS 4332 (Sept. 20, 2007).

Trial court properly awarded costs under Ohio R. Civ. P. 54(D) to the wife for the videotaped depositions of the wife's physician and fellow real estate broker that were used as evidence at trial; under Lucas County, Ohio, Ct. C.P. Supp. R. 13(D), the trial court was permitted to assess as costs the expense of recording the videotape and playing it at trial, but it could not order the wife to pay the price of the videotape itself as a cost. Atkinson v. T.A.R.T.A., — Ohio App. 3d —, 2006 Ohio 1638, — N.E. 2d —, 2006 Ohio App. LEXIS 1518 (Mar. 31, 2006).

Trial court did not err in awarding as costs pursuant to Ohio R. Civ. P. 54(D) to the wife the expense of filing a transcript of a videotaped deposition, as the local rules required the filing of a transcript of a videotaped deposition, therefore making it a taxable cost under RC § 2303.21. Atkinson v. T.A.R.T.A., — Ohio App. 3d —, 2006 Ohio 1638, — N.E. 2d —, 2006 Ohio App. LEXIS 1518 (Mar. 31, 2006).

— Denial

Copying and mounting expenses, medical record expenses, and exhibit fees were not costs that were recoverable under Ohio R. Civ. P. 54(D) in an action by a driver against a motorist, arising from a motor vehicle accident, wherein the driver was awarded a jury verdict for monetary damages. Naples v. Kinczel, — Ohio App. 3d —, 2007 Ohio 4851, — N.E. 2d —, 2007 Ohio App. LEXIS 4332 (Sept. 20, 2007).

Trial court's denial of a driver's motion to tax litigation expenses as costs pursuant to Ohio R. Civ. P. 54(D) was not reviewable where it failed to provide reasons for the denial and the basis thereof could not be discerned from the record. Naples v. Kinczel, — Ohio App. 3d —, 2007 Ohio 4851, — N.E. 2d —, 2007 Ohio App. LEXIS 4332 (Sept. 20, 2007).

Writ of mandamus alleging that respondents violated the Ohio Public Records Act was dismissed as moot because relator had now received from respondents the documents originally requested. The court refused to assess costs against relator as respondents were not the prevailing party simply because the action was dismissed as moot; instead, under Ohio R. Civ. P. 54(D), the court had the discretion to make either party bear the costs. State Ex Rel. Mitchell v. Evans, — Ohio App. 3d —, 2007 Ohio 5055, — N.E. 2d —, 2007 Ohio App. LEXIS 4438 (Sept. 19, 2007).

— Prevailing party

There was no abuse of discretion in the award of costs to the condominium association board and individual board members because the trial court dismissed the majority of the condominium owner's claims, while finding in her favor on only one claim; therefore, the owner did not prevail as to a substantial part of her litigation. Kleemann v. Carriage Trace, — Ohio App. 3d —, 2007 Ohio 4209, — N.E. 2d —, 2007 Ohio App. LEXIS 3804 (Aug. 17, 2007).

Since a father prevailed on his motion to change custody, the trial court did not abuse its discretion in assessing the costs of the action to the mother as the losing party. Welly v. Hartsel, — Ohio App. 3d —, 2006 Ohio 1413, — N.E. 2d —, 2006 Ohio App. LEXIS 1306 (Mar. 27, 2006).

Declaratory judgment

While an insurer's appeal of a trial court's order determining, in the insurer's declaratory judgment action, that the insurer's right of subrogation had been extinguished and that it owed its insureds underinsured motorists coverage to the extent that damages could be proven was not subject to dismissal on the ground that it did not contain the "no just reason for delay" language of Ohio R. Civ. P. 54(B) since the there remained no claims pending against the insurer, the order was not a final appealable order since the issue of the extent of damages remained. Layman v. Welch, — Ohio App. 3d —, 2006 Ohio 1157, — N.E. 2d —, 2006 Ohio App. LEXIS 1060 (Mar. 13, 2006).

Dismissal

In a legal malpractice action, the first former client's motion for reconsideration of an involuntary dismissal of the action with prejudice could not be considered as invoking Ohio R. Civ. P. 54(B) to request a "revision" of a judgment as to fewer than all the claims or parties as the dismissal disposed of all the claims and parties. McGee v. Lynch, — Ohio App. 3d —, 2007 Ohio 3954, — N.E. 2d —, 2007 Ohio App. LEXIS 3619 (Aug. 3, 2007).

Dismissal with prejudice constituted a final appealable order where it left a party with no pending claims, thereby denying the party the right to redress injury and determined the action in favor of the opposing party. CivR 54(B) certification was not required where the court's action effectively resolved the only remaining claims: Sunkin v. Collision Pro, Inc., 174 Ohio App. 3d 56, 2007 Ohio 6046, 880 N.E.2d 947, 2007 Ohio App. LEXIS 5323 (2007).

Failure to dispose of all claims

Appeal from a trial court's judgment in favor of appellee on appellant's third party claim was dismissed because the court lacked jurisdiction under Ohio Const. art. IV, § 3(B)(2) to hear the appeal. Though the trial court resolved all the issues in the third party claim, and thus, met the requirements of RC § 2505.02, claims were still pending in appellee's suit, and the trial court's failure to include "no just reason for delay" language did not comport with Ohio R. Civ. P. 54(B). Thomas v. Harmon, — Ohio App. 3d —, 2007 Ohio 5374, — N.E. 2d —, 2007 Ohio App. LEXIS 4725 (Oct. 02, 2007).

Order that disposed of fewer than all of the claims in an action, and contained an Ohio R. Civ. P. 54(B) determination that there was no just reason for delay, was appealable if the claim or claims disposed of were entirely disposed of and either the disposed of claim(s) were factually separate and independent from the remaining claim(s), or, if the claims were not factually separate and independent, the legal theo-

ries presented in the disposed of claim(s) required proof of substantially different facts and/or provided for different relief from the remaining claim(s). Todd Dev. Co. v. Morgan, — Ohio App. 3d —, 2006 Ohio 4825, — N.E. 2d —, 2006 Ohio App. LEXIS 4752 (Sept. 18, 2006).

When developers sought a declaratory judgment that certain restrictive covenants did not apply to lots they purchased and owners of other lots in the subdivision filed a counterclaim asserting the developers' violations of restrictive covenants, a trial court's grant of the owners' summary judgment motion as to some claims was appealable, under RC § 2505.02 and Ohio R. Civ. P. 54(B), despite some factual overlap between claims adjudicated and claims pending, because there was a substantial difference in the proof required as to the pending and adjudicated claims and as to the relief requested, and the trial court entered the certification required by Rule 54(B). Todd Dev. Co. v. Morgan, — Ohio App. 3d —, 2006 Ohio 4825, — N.E. 2d —, 2006 Ohio App. LEXIS 4752 (Sept. 18, 2006).

Failure to dispose of counterclaim

Because a trial court's judgment entry did not address an owner's counterclaim, and did not make a specific determination there was no just reason for delay pursuant to Ohio R. Civ. P. 54(B), the judgment entry was not a final appealable order despite the fact that there was but one consistent disposition of the counterclaim in light of the findings relative to the claims of the complaint. Wallick v. Lent, — Ohio App. 3d —, 2006 Ohio 5224, — N.E. 2d —, 2006 Ohio App. LEXIS 5200 (Sept. 25, 2006).

Final appealable order

Trial court's decision was appealable, and CivR 54(B) did not apply, where it dismissed the only claim brought by the plaintiffs and offered the plaintiffs an opportunity to amend the complaint to state a claim that they did not wish to assert: Venture Props. of Boardman, Inc. v. Boardman Steel, Inc., 177 Ohio App. 3d 572, 2008 Ohio 3088, 895 N.E.2d 569, 2008 Ohio App. LEXIS 2601 (2008).

When a creditor sued two debtors on separate loan agreements, and the trial court granted a default judgment against one of the debtors, despite having granted that debtor's motion for leave to move or plead, and the creditor and this debtor jointly moved to vacate the default judgment, but the trial court refused to rule on the motion because the other debtor filed a suggestion of bankruptcy, an appellate court dismissed the first debtor's appeal from both the default judgment and the refusal to vacate the default judgment because these were not final, appealable orders, as the default judgment did not dispose of all claims and parties, and the trial court did not find, under Ohio R. Civ. P. 54(B), that there was no just reason for delay, and a ruling on a motion to vacate a judgment that was not final was also not final. Stephens v. Deighan, — Ohio App. 3d —, 2007 Ohio 5030, — N.E. 2d —, 2007 Ohio App. LEXIS 4446 (Sept. 26, 2007).

Judgment entries of a trial court that interpreted provisions in a commercial lease and denied a motion for a new trial were not final appealable orders under RC § 2505.02(B)(1) and (2), such that the appellate court lacked jurisdiction pursuant to Ohio Const. art. IV, § 3(B)(2) to review them; the entries did not affect the parties' substantial rights, did not determine the action, did not fully adjudicate the claims, and the certification language of Ohio R. Civ. P. 54(B) was lacking. Epic Props. v. Osu, — Ohio App. 3d —, 2007 Ohio 5021, — N.E. 2d —, 2007 Ohio App. LEXIS 4468 (Sept. 25, 2007).

Although a trial court's adoption of a magistrate's decision to deny a city's motion to intervene pursuant to Ohio R. Civ. P. 24(A)(2) in an adminstrative appeal by a union from a decision of the State Employment Relations Board affected a substantial right of the city, effectively determined the action as to it, and prevented a judgment for it for purposes of being a "final order" under RC § 2505.02(B)(1), (2), or (4), as the trial court failed to include the language of Ohio R. Civ. P. 54(B) and the substantive claims of the parties remained outstanding, the appellate court lacked jurisdiction over the appealed order pursuant to Ohio Const. art. IV, § 3(B)(2). Queen City Lodge No. 69 v. State Empl. Rels. Bd., — Ohio App. 3d —, 2007 Ohio 170, — N.E. 2d —, 2007 Ohio App. LEXIS 173 (Jan. 19, 2007).

When an alleged injured party sued a city and its police officer for personal injuries, and the city asserted a counterclaim against the alleged injured party, the trial court's judgment granting summary judgment to the city and officer on the alleged injured party's claims was not a final appealable order, under RC § 2505.02, because the counterclaim remained outstanding, and the trial court's judgment entry contained no finding, under Ohio R. Civ. P. 54(B), that there was no just reason for delay, so the judgment entry's statement that it was "final" was immaterial, and an appellate court had no jurisdiction, under Ohio Const. art. IV, § 3(B)(2), to consider an appeal. Vandyke v. City of Columbus, — Ohio App. 3d —, 2007 Ohio 2088, — N.E. 2d —, 2007 Ohio App. LEXIS 1939 (May 1, 2007).

To be final and appealable, an order that adjudicates one or more but fewer than all claims or the rights and liabilities of fewer than all the parties must meet the finality requirements of RC § 2505.02 and must properly contain the lower court's certification pursuant to Ohio R. Civ. P. 54(B), and RC § 2505.02 defines a final order as, inter alia, an order that affects a substantial right in an action that in effect determines the action and prevents a judgment, under RC § 2505.02(B)(1). Vandyke v. City of Columbus, — Ohio App. 3d —, 2007 Ohio 2088, — N.E. 2d —, 2007 Ohio App. LEXIS 1939 (May 1, 2007).

Appellant sister could not appeal an order of partition because the order did not constitute a final appealable order under RC § 2505.02(B)(1) as there were outstanding counterclaims for an accounting by both appellant and defendant sister; the order did not contain the language that "there is no just reason for delay" under Ohio R. Civ. P. 54(B). Ellis v. Iesulauro, — Ohio App. 3d —, 2007 Ohio 3153, — N.E. 2d —, 2007 Ohio App. LEXIS 2936 (June 25, 2007).

Insurer's appeal from trial court's order denying its motion for summary judgment was dismissed because the court lacked jurisdiction to review the order as the order did not determine the action or prevent a judgment and, thus, was not a final appealable order under RC § 2505.02. While the order contained the "no just reason for delay" language of Ohio R. Civ. P. 54(B), it was not a final appealable order. The mere incantation of the required language did not turn an otherwise non-final order into a final appealable order. Brewer v. Doe, — Ohio App. 3d —, 2007 Ohio 3528, — N.E. 2d —, 2007 Ohio App. LEXIS 3252 (July 12, 2007).

In a foreclosure action where the state attorney general, on behalf of the State had filed a cross-claim, a judgment entry granting summary judgment to a second mortgagee did not required Ohio R. Civ. P. 54 to make it a final appealable order because the summary judgment resolved all the issues raised in the cross-claim. Firstmerit Mortg. Co. v. Beers, — Ohio App. 3d —, 2007 Ohio 4253, — N.E. 2d —, 2007 Ohio App. LEXIS 3925 (Aug. 13, 2007).

Appellees' motion to dismiss the appeal filed by appellant was granted because the judgment entry denying appellant's motion to reconsider a prior entry ordering appellant to cease and desist from the practice of taking company funds to pay his legal fees was not a final appealable order under RC § 2505.02(B)(1), in that it only addressed on claim in a multi-claim complaint, and the trial court indicated that it planned to revisit the issue at a later date. The inclusion of Ohio R. Civ. P. 54(B) language in the judgment entry denying the motion to reconsider did not transform that entry into a

final and appealable order. Miller v. Miller, — Ohio App. 3d —, 2007 Ohio 5212, — N.E. 2d —, 2007 Ohio App. LEXIS 4587 (Sept. 28, 2007).

There was no appellate jurisdiction to decide the indemnification issue because the August 9, 2004 judgment entry was not a final, appealable order. Several claims and cross-claims remained unresolved, and the trial court did not certify the entry pursuant to Ohio R. Civ. P. 54(B). Grieshop v. Hoyng, — Ohio App. 3d —, 2007 Ohio 2861, — N.E. 2d —, 2007 Ohio App. LEXIS 2619 (June 11, 2007).

Appeal from a trial court's order dismissing appellant's motion to quiet title and finding in favor of one appellee was dismissed because there were still claims pending in the trial court, and the judgment entry that was appealed from did not contain any Ohio R. Civ. P. 54(B) language; thus, there was no final appealable order. Kessler v. Tuus, — Ohio App. 3d —, 2007 Ohio 3019, — N.E. 2d —, 2007 Ohio App. LEXIS 2773 (June 15, 2007).

As discussions by members of a city board of zoning appeals concerning the Duncan factors in property owners' requests for area and height variances were not part of the board's findings of fact and they were not part of the oral announcement of the board's decision, pursuant to Ohio R. Civ. P. 54(B) they were not subject to objection; as the owners failed to object to that discussion at the board hearing, they waived the right to appeal any errors thereon. Stovall v. City of Streetsboro, — Ohio App. 3d —, 2007 Ohio 3381, — N.E. 2d —, 2007 Ohio App. LEXIS 3101 (June 29, 2007).

Trial court order which vacated a prior order that stayed disbursement of child support money pending further order of the court and directed a child support enforcement agency to disburse the money to a child's mother was a final order under RC § 2505.02 and Ohio R. Civ. P. 54(B), as it satisifed the requirements thereof. The trial court retained the ability to modify that decision based on its continuing jurisdiction under RC § 3111.16. Spencer v. Gatten, — Ohio App. 3d —, 2007 Ohio 4071, — N.E. 2d —, 2007 Ohio App. LEXIS 3684 (Aug. 9, 2007).

Trial court orders that stayed an employee's sexual harassment action against her employer and a supervisor and that compelled arbitration pursuant to RC § 2711.02(C) were final but they were not appealable under RC § 2505.02 and Ohio Const. art. IV, § 3, as a claim against another supervisor was unresolved and the "no just reason for delay" language from Ohio R. Civ. P. 54(B) was lacking. Redmond v. Big Sandy Furniture, Inc., — Ohio App. 3d —, 2007 Ohio 1024, — N.E. 2d —, 2007 Ohio App. LEXIS 953 (Mar. 5, 2007).

Trial court's denial of defendants' motion for judgment on the pleadings pursuant to Ohio R. Civ. P. 12(C) was not a final appealable order, and absent the required language of Ohio R. Civ. P. 54(B), the order was interlocutory in nature, such that the issues raised therein could be further addressed by a trial court. The failure to appeal the denial of that motion did not have any res judicata or collateral estoppel effect for purposes of defendants' later summary judgment motion. Myles v. Johnson, — Ohio App. 3d —, 2007 Ohio 2963, — N.E. 2d —, 2007 Ohio App. LEXIS 2724 (June 15, 2007).

Denial of inmates' request for a preliminary and permanent injunction pursuant to Ohio R. Civ. P. 65, and for a temporary restraining order in their class action that challenged the parole procedure applicable to them was not a final appealable order where the requirements of RC § 2505.02(B)(4)(a) but not of § 2505.02(B)(4)(b) were met with respect to the provisional remedies, the necessary language of Ohio R. Civ. P. 54(B) was lacking, and an adequate remedy by appeal at the conclusion of all of the proceedings existed. Ankrom v. Hageman, — Ohio App. 3d —, 2007 Ohio 5092, — N.E. 2d —, 2007 Ohio App. LEXIS 4496 (Sept. 27, 2007).

When an alleged injured party and the party's spouse sought uninsured motorist/underinsured motorist coverage from the alleged injured party's employer's insurer, and the trial court granted summary judgment in favor of the alleged injured party, this judgment became final and appealable when the trial court included language from Ohio R. Civ. P. 54(B) that there was no just reason to delay an appeal because (1) the judgment effectively terminated the alleged injured party's claim against the insurer, (2) the judgment was entered in a special proceeding, and (3) the judgment affected the substantial rights of both the alleged injured party and the insurer, so it was error for the trial court to grant the insurer's motion to vacate that judgment in the belief that the judgment was not final, and, when the trial court subsequently entered summary judgment in favor of the alleged injured party, again, an appellate court had no jurisdiction to consider that appeal because the insurer's appeal of the judgment which actually disposed of the alleged injured party's claim against the insurer had been dismissed, pursuant to the insurer's motion. Walburn v. Dunlap, — Ohio App. 3d —, 2007 Ohio 5398, — N.E. 2d —, 2007 Ohio App. LEXIS 4756 (Oct. 2, 2007).

Where a trial court overruled a former wife's objections to a magistrate's decision, pursuant to Ohio R. Civ. P. 53, but the trial court failed to separately set forth its own judgment, there was no final appealable order pursuant to Ohio R. Civ. P. 54 and RC § 2505.02(B)(1). As the appellate court lacked jurisdiction pursuant to Ohio Const. art. IV, § 3(B)(2) and RC § 2501.02, dismissal of the appeal was mandated. Burns v. Morgan, 165 Ohio App. 3d 694, 2006 Ohio 1213, 847 N.E. 2d 1288, 2006 Ohio App. LEXIS 1087 (Mar. 13, 2006).

When, in a zoning case, a trial court ordered a board of county commissioners to rezone certain land within 60 days, the board did not comply, and the land's owners sought further relief, under RC § 2721.09, the trial court's judgment denying further relief and granting the board additional time within which to rezone the land affected a substantial right and occurred in a special proceeding, so it was final and appealable, under RC § 2505.02(B), because the owners' claims for damages and attorney fees were not then before the trial court, so it was not required to make a finding pursuant to Ohio R. Civ. P. 54(B), and the owners' failure to appeal the order caused it to be res judicata. Clarke v. Board of County Comm'rs of Warren County, — Ohio App. 3d —, 2006 Ohio 1271, — N.E. 2d —, 2006 Ohio App. LEXIS 1161 (Mar. 20, 2006).

Where a tenant filed a declaratory judgment action, seeking an interpretation of a percentage rent provision in the parties' lease, and the landlord counterclaimed for rent due, the trial court's directive that the percentage rent was to be based on commissions of liquor and lottery sales and that the rent due to the landlord was to be recalculated was not a final appealable order under Ohio R. Civ. P. 54(B); as the "no just reason for delay" language was missing and all of the claims between the parties were not adjudicated, the court dismissed the appeal. Mapletown Foods, Inc. v. Mid-America Mgmt. Corp., — Ohio App. 3d —, 2006 Ohio 2218, — N.E. 2d —, 2006 Ohio App. LEXIS 2065 (May 4, 2006).

When a property owner sued the builders of an adjacent hotel for damaging his land and trespass, the trial court's pretrial order that any damages the owner was found entitled to would be measured by the diminution in the value of the owner's land, rather than the cost of restoring it, this was not a final appealable order, under RC § 2505.02 and Ohio R. Civ. P. 54(B), regarding which an appellate court could properly assert jurisdiction, under Ohio Const. art. IV, § 3(B)(2), because neither liability for the damage nor the existence of any damage had been found. Interstate Props. v. Prasanna, Inc., — Ohio App. 3d —, 2006 Ohio 2686, — N.E. 2d —, 2006 Ohio App. LEXIS 2521 (May 31, 2006).

When more than one claim was presented in an action, a court could enter final judgment as to one or more, but fewer than all of the claims only if it expressly determined that "there is no just reason for delay," under Ohio R. Civ. P. 54(B), and, absent such a determination, any order which presumed

to adjudicate fewer than all the claims did not terminate any of the claims, and therefore, was not a final, appealable order. so, with regard to the phrase "there is no just reason for delay," these seven words were mandatory, and, as delineated, this language was not a meaningless litany, but mandatory, so its omission was fatal not only to the order's finality, but also to the appellate court's jurisdiction; absent such certification by the trial court, the action remained interlocutory. Spano Bros. Constr. Co. v. Adolph Johnson & Son Co., — Ohio App. 3d —, 2006 Ohio 4083, — N.E. 2d —, 2006 Ohio App. LEXIS 4039 (Aug. 9, 2006).

When a construction company sued a corporation for breach of contract, a prompt payment statute violation, and unjust enrichment, and was granted summary judgment and damages on its breach of contract claim, but it was not found that there was no just reason to delay an appeal, under Ohio R. Civ. P. 54(B), nor were the other claims properly voluntarily dismissed, under Ohio R. Civ. P. 41(A) by a notice of dismissal, stipulation, or journalized court order, those claims remained pending and an appellate court had no jurisdiction, under Ohio R. App. P. 12(A)(1)(a), or RC § 2505.02, to hear an appeal of the breach of contract judgment. Spano Bros. Constr. Co. v. Adolph Johnson & Son Co., — Ohio App. 3d —, 2006 Ohio 4083, — N.E. 2d —, 2006 Ohio App. LEXIS 4039 (Aug. 9, 2006).

When an employee sued her employer, a hospital, and supervisory employees for disability discrimination and wrongful discharge, and related claims, and the trial court denied the hospital's and supervisors' summary judgment motion asserting immunity, the trial court's judgment could not be reviewed, under Ohio Const. art. IV, § 3(B)(2) or RC § 2505.02, because the trial court did not include language in Ohio R. Civ. P. 54(B) in its denial, except that the denial of summary judgment as to the employee's disability discrimination claim against the supervisors was a matter of law, so, under RC § 2744.02(C), the judgment could be reviewed. Hall v. Mem'l Hosp., — Ohio App. 3d —, 2006 Ohio 4552, — N.E.2d —, 2006 Ohio App. LEXIS 4515 (Sept. 5, 2006).

Denial of summary judgment to an insurance agency in an insurer's indemnification claim regarding payments made over the original policy limits was proper despite an earlier grant of summary judgment to the agency on the insurer's declaratory judgment claim regarding the actual policy limits and its coverage obligations, as the law of the case doctrine did not preclude a review of the facts where the first summary judgment order was not final and accordingly, it was subject to revision at any time before the entry of a judgment that adjudicated all of the claims and rights and liabilities of the parties, pursuant to Ohio R. Civ. P. 54(B). Progressive Preferred Ins. Co. v. Hammerlein Helton Ins., — Ohio App. 3d —, 2006 Ohio 4601, — N.E. 2d —, 2006 Ohio App. LEXIS 4546 (Sept. 8, 2006).

As a probate court did not finally determine who the heirs of a decedent were in a declaratory judgment action, based on the magistrate's determination that the residue of a decedent's estate and the remainder of her trust were to be distributed to her heirs as if she died intestate, there was no final order under Ohio R. Civ. P. 54(B), and res judicata did not preclude further review of the issue of who was an heir of the decedent. Sangrik v. Radey, — Ohio App. 3d —, 2006 Ohio 5579, — N.E. 2d —, 2006 Ohio App. LEXIS 5573 (Oct. 26, 2006).

Trial court's order denying a labor union's motion for summary judgment did not affect a substantial right, and thus, was not an appealable order, because it did not decide anything except that the issues would be decided at trial. Since the order denying summary judgment did not fit into any of the RC § 2505.02 categories, the trial court's Ohio R. Civ. P. 54(B) determination that there is no just reason for delay did not magically transform it into an appealable order. Ibew,

Local Union No. 8 v. Vaughn Indus., — Ohio App. 3d —, 2006 Ohio 475, — N.E. 2d —, 2006 Ohio App. LEXIS 416 (Feb. 2, 2006).

Where a trial court entered a judgment on a jury verdict in appellee's premises liability action, which found the premises owner liable and awarded her damages, but it left unresolved her motion for prejudgment interest pursuant to RC § 1343.03(C), such was a non-final order that was not appealable under RC § 2505.02, despite language that there was "no just cause for delay" pursuant to Ohio R. Civ. P. 54(B), as the interest was another element of the damage award and courts did not favor piecemeal litigation. The Court of Appeals of Ohio, Sixth Appellate District, Lucas County followed the McKee line of cases in adopting this line of reasoning, which resulted in the dismissal of the owner's appeal and the court's certification of the issue pursuant to Ohio Const. art. IV, § 3(B)(4) due to the noted conflict with decisions from the Fifth, Eighth, and Eleventh Appellate Districts. Miller v. First Int'l Fid. & Trust Bldg., 165 Ohio App. 3d 281, 2006 Ohio 187, 846 N.E. 2d 87, 2006 Ohio App. LEXIS 152 (Jan. 17, 2006).

When, in a union's suit against a city and the city's civil service commission, on behalf of a union member, a trial court found that a writ of mandamus should be issued requiring that the member be appointed to a certain civil service position, and directed the union's counsel to prepare a writ, which did not occur, the order contemplated further action, so it was not final, under RC § 2505.02 or Ohio R. Civ. P. 54(B), and it could be reconsidered. State ex rel. Int'l Ass'n of Firefighters, Local 381 v. City of Findlay, — Ohio App. 3d —, 2006 Ohio 1774, — N.E. 2d —, 2006 Ohio App. LEXIS 1654 (Apr. 10, 2006).

Trial court's judgment awarding declaratory judgment to appellee was not a final appealable order under RC § 2505.02 because the declaratory judgment claim was asserted within the context of an ordinary civil action for breach of contract, and the judgment determined only the issue of liability under the agreement between the parties but did not determine the issue of damages. Since the judgment was not final, the fact that the trial court used Ohio R. Civ. P. 54(B) language in its judgment entry was irrelevant. State v. McMarty, — Ohio App. 3d —, 2006 Ohio 2019, — N.E. 2d —, 2006 Ohio App. LEXIS 1843 (Apr. 21, 2006).

Orders from which appellant and appellee filed an appeal and a cross-appeal were not final appealable orders under Ohio R. Civ. P. 54(B) and RC § 2505.02(B) since the jury's verdict in favor of appellant on its breach of contract counterclaim was against an intervenor, to whom appellee had assigned its interests in its breach of contract and unjust enrichment claims, not appellee, against which appellant's breach of contract claim was filed, and thus, appellee's liabilities had not been adjudicated. As a result, the appeal was dismissed since, pursuant to Ohio Const. art. IV, § 3(B)(2), the appellate court lacked jurisdiction . Nelson Jewellery Arts Co. v. Fein Designs Co., — Ohio App. 3d —, 2006 Ohio 2276, — N.E. 2d —, 2006 Ohio App. LEXIS 2120 (May 10, 2006).

Orders entered by a trial court in a multi-party foreclosure action involving counterclaims and cross-claims, which struck certain pleadings and addressed a motion for a default judgment, were not final appealable orders under RC § 2505.02, as they lacked the necessary language under Ohio R. Civ. P. 54(B); accordingly, claims asserted on appeal were not reviewable. Miles Landing Homeowners Ass'n v. Bikkani, — Ohio App. 3d —, 2006 Ohio 3328, — N.E. 2d —, 2006 Ohio App. LEXIS 3244 (June 29, 2006).

Appeal from a trial court's order granting summary judgment to appellee was dismissed. The order was not a final appealable order under RC § 2505.02(B) because other claims were still pending against appellee's co-defendant and because the order did not contain Ohio R. Civ. P. 54(B)

language. Whelan v. Vanderwist of Cincinnati, Inc., — Ohio App. 3d —, 2006 Ohio 6690, — N.E. 2d —, 2006 Ohio App. LEXIS 6568 (Dec. 15, 2006).

Where a trial court dismissed all claims for injunctive relief by property owners against a neighboring property owner in a multi-count action, the trial court used the language of Ohio R. Civ. P. 54(B), and it appeared that the property owners could be immediately harmed by the judgment because the neighboring property owner was poised to clear a path on land that was disputed, the judgment qualified as a final appealable order pursuant to RC § 2505.02(B)(1) and (4). Thompson v. Smith, — Ohio App. 3d —, 2006 Ohio 7270, — N.E. 2d —, 2006 Ohio App. LEXIS 7075 (May 24, 2006).

Summary judgment against fewer than all defendants, which order stated "this is a final order as against these Defendants only that shall not be delayed," did not substantially comply with Ohio R. Civ. P. 54(B), and thus the summary judgment was not a final, appealable order; an appeal from the order was dismissed. Monitor Transporation Servs. v. Tri Port Transporation, — Ohio App. 3d —, 2006 Ohio 2689, — N.E. 2d —, 2006 Ohio App. LEXIS 2520 (May 31, 2006).

Where a trial court entered a judgment while motions under Ohio R. Civ. P. 50(B) were pending, and the entry postponed the question of court costs, the judgment entry was not a final appealable order and the postponement meant that the entry did not "determine the action" for purposes of RC § 2505.02(B)(1). There was no final appealable order for purposes of invoking the jurisdiction of the appellate court, and the inclusion of certification language under Ohio R. Civ. P. 54(B) did not remedy that defect. Wells Fargo Fin. Leasing v. Gilliland, — Ohio App. 3d —, 2006 Ohio 2756, — N.E. 2d —, 2006 Ohio App. LEXIS 2576 (May 22, 2006).

As an attempt to voluntarily dismiss one count of a multi-count complaint pursuant to Ohio R. Civ. P. 41(A) was a nullity because dismissal had to be of the entire complaint under that Rule, the claim was still pending and absent the "no just reason for delay" language of Ohio R. Civ. P. 54(B), the appellate court lacked jurisdiction to decide an appeal because there was no final appealable order pursuant to Rule 54(B) and RC § 2505.02. Savage v. Cody-Zeigler, Inc., — Ohio App. 3d —, 2006 Ohio 2760, — N.E. 2d —, 2006 Ohio App. LEXIS 2601 (May 25, 2006).

Ohio R. Civ. P. 54(B) language and certification was not necessary for purposes of making a denial of an insurer's motion to intervene, pursuant to Ohio R. Civ. P. 24(A)(2), a final appealable order pursuant to RC § 2505.02(B), as the language of Ohio R. Civ. P. 54(B) connoted that claims or rights and liabilities of parties was involved, and the insurer was clearly not a party if it had to seek intervention to participate in the action. It was not included in the pleadings pursuant to Ohio R. Civ. P. 10(A), wherein a patient of the insured, a doctor, filed a civil tort action arising from the doctor's inappropriate conduct during a gynecological examination, and the insurer's intent in seeking intervention was to secure a specific, rather than general, verdict in order to deny the coverage to the doctor, which was provided under a reservation of rights. Filippi v. Ahmed, — Ohio App. 3d —, 2006 Ohio 4368, — N.E. 2d —, 2006 Ohio App. LEXIS 4290 (Aug. 24, 2006).

As judgment entries in parties' action involving their property rights did not resolve all of the pending issues between them and there was no language indicating that there was no just cause for delay pursuant to Ohio R. Civ. P. 54(B), there was no final appealable order and appeals taken therefrom required dismissal. Longo v. Longo, — Ohio App. 3d —, 2006 Ohio 4943, — N.E. 2d —, 2006 Ohio App. LEXIS 4869 (Sept. 22, 2006).

Trial court's order which granted summary judgment as to an insurance obligation only, but denied summary judgment on other breach of contract claims, was not a final appealable order pursuant to Civ. R. 54(B); further, the trial court did not finally determine damages on the one breach of contract theory as to which it found liability. Penske Truck Leasing v. TCI Ins., — Ohio App. 3d —, 2006 Ohio 5256, — N.E. 2d —, 2006 Ohio App. LEXIS 5214 (Oct. 5, 2006).

In circumstances in which attorney fees were requested in the original pleadings, a judgment that adjudicated all issues except the attorney fee issue was not final absent a Civ. R. 54(B) certification; because a trial court had not ruled on an LLC's motion for attorney fees, its summary judgment in a prevailing wage claim was not final and appealable. IBEW, Local Union No. 8 v. Vaughn Indus., — Ohio App. 3d —, 2006 Ohio 5280, — N.E. 2d —, 2006 Ohio App. LEXIS 5265 (Sept. 25, 2006).

While the parties represented that their settlement agreement disposed of all the issues, the trial court continued the matter for final hearing and formal determination of the existence and continuance of an alleged nuisance; the trial court did not conduct a final hearing on the matter, and thus the order appealed from was not final. State ex rel. Spies v. Lent, — Ohio App. 3d —, 2006 Ohio 5315, — N.E. 2d —, 2006 Ohio App. LEXIS 5287 (Oct. 4, 2006).

Trial court's entry of a cognovit judgment was not a final appealable order in consolidated actions, as unresolved claims were still pending, and accordingly, relief under Ohio R. Civ. P. 60(B) could not be obtained because the judgment was interlocutory rather than final. Although the trial court used language from Ohio R. Civ. P. 54(B), the requirements of RC § 2505.02(B) were not met and an appeal taken from the trial court's denial of the motion for relief from judgment required dismissal. Gilligan v. Robinson, — Ohio App. 3d —, 2006 Ohio 4619, — N.E. 2d —, 2006 Ohio App. LEXIS 5305 (Aug. 31, 2006).

Trial court's grant of summary judgment to a judgment creditor in its action to foreclose on a judgment debtor's real property was not a final appealable order, despite the "no just reason for delay" language of Ohio R. Civ. P. 54(B), as the priorities of all interests in the real property had not been determined; accordingly, a mortgagee was not precluded from relitigating the issue of its lien priority. Wells Fargo Fin. Leasing v. Rinard, — Ohio App. 3d —, 2006 Ohio 5544, — N.E. 2d —, 2006 Ohio App. LEXIS 5541 (Oct. 19, 2006).

Where a trial court granted summary judgment to an insurer in its declaratory judgment action, wherein the trial court determined that it had no obligation to provide coverage to an insured for an underlying action based on the claims asserted in the underlying original complaint, such was not in compliance with Ohio R. Civ. P. 56(C) because an amended complaint that asserted additional claims had been filed and the trial court had an obligation to review all pleadings. The trial court's order was a partial summary judgment, in that all claims were not resolved, but as the necessary language under Ohio R. Civ. P. 54(B) was not included, the grant of partial summary judgment was not a final appealable order pursuant to RC § 2505.02, and the insured's appeal taken therefrom required dismissal. Westfield Ins. Co. v. Towne Inv. II, — Ohio App. 3d —, 2006 Ohio 5830, — N.E. 2d —, 2006 Ohio App. LEXIS 5764 (Nov. 3, 2006).

Trial court's order that found that collateral estoppel was inapplicable to bar a village's attempt to recover expenses incurred in cleaning up an owner's property through a foreclosure action was not a final and appealable order because it would not have prevented a judgment in the owner's third-party action, seeking release from the expense assessment or indemnification thereon. Where the trial court dismissed the owner's third-party action based on the owner's failure to meet his burden of proof and it included the necessary Ohio R. Civ. P. 54(B) language, the order was final and appealable under RC § 2505.02 and the appellate court had jurisdiction under Ohio Const. art. IV, § 3(B)(2) to review it. Treasurer v. Ludwig, — Ohio App. 3d —, 2006 Ohio 6486, — N.E. 2d —, 2006 Ohio App. LEXIS 6430 (Dec. 11, 2006).

While the trial court established paternity and ordered past and current child support, it did not adjudicate all of the support issues raised in the mother's complaint; the issue of past medical expenses remained unresolved. Therefore, the judgment entry was not a final, appealable order under RC § 2505.02(B)(2). Post v. Caycedo, — Ohio App. 3d —, 2006 Ohio 6750, — N.E. 2d —, 2006 Ohio App. LEXIS 6662 (Dec. 20, 2006).

Since a trial court failed both to adopt the magistrate's decision and to enter judgment stating the relief afforded under Ohio R. Civ. P. 53(E)(4), the trial court's order denying appellant's objections to the magistrate's decision was not a final appealable order pursuant to RC § 2505.02(B)(1) and Ohio R. Civ. P. 54(B); thus, the court lacked jurisdiction under Ohio Const. art. IV, § 3(B)(2) to rule on appellant's challenge to the decision. Ingledue v. Premier Siding & Roofing, Inc., — Ohio App. 3d —, 2006 Ohio 2698, — N.E. 2d —, 2006 Ohio App. LEXIS 2543 (May 30, 2006).

Note maker's appeal was dismissed for lack of a final appealable order since all of the maker's assignments of error related to the trial court's original judgment, which was not a final judgment in that it adjudicated fewer than all of the claims and the rights and liabilities of fewer than all of the parties and it failed to include an express determination that there was no just reason for delay, rather than the judgment granting his motion for relief from judgment. Irion v. Incomm Electronics, — Ohio App. 3d —, 2006 Ohio 362, — N.E. 2d —, 2006 Ohio App. LEXIS 297 (Jan. 24, 2006).

While a trial court erroneously granted a note maker's Ohio R. Civ. P. 60(B)(5) motion for the express purpose of extending his time to file an appeal from the trial court's judgment against him, the error was harmless because the judgment that the maker sought to avoid was not a final order under Ohio R. Civ. P. 54(B), in that it adjudicated fewer than all of the claims and the rights and liabilities of fewer than all of the parties, and it failed to include an express determination that there was no just reason for delay. Irion v. Incomm Electronics, — Ohio App. 3d —, 2006 Ohio 362, — N.E. 2d —, 2006 Ohio App. LEXIS 297 (Jan. 24, 2006).

Pursuant to Ohio Const. art. IV, § 3(B)(2), an appellate court's jurisdiction was limited to review of final judgments of lower courts; an appellate court lacked jurisdiction to review a trial court order which merely adopted and approved a magistrate's decision since, without a statement of relief, the trial court's entry did not create a final appealable order. Long v. Northern Illinois Classic Auto, — Ohio App. 3d —, 2006 Ohio 2279, — N.E. 2d —, 2006 Ohio App. LEXIS 2125 (May 10, 2006).

Trial court's order entering a decree of divorce did not constitute a final appealable order under RC § 2505.02 since the issue of custody of the parties' children was not fully and finally determined, as required by Ohio R. Civ. P. 75(F). Further, the trial court's subsequent judgment entry granting the father's "motion for a new trial" was not a final appealable order since the trial court had issued no "judgment," within the meaning of Ohio R. Civ. P. 54(A), from which the husband could file his new trial motion. Salisbury v. Salisbury, — Ohio App. 3d —, 2006 Ohio 3543, — N.E. 2d —, 2006 Ohio App. LEXIS 3493 (July 7, 2006).

— Fewer than all claims decided

When a plaintiff has asserted multiple claims against one defendant, and some of those claims have been ruled upon but not converted into a final order through CivR 54(B), the plaintiff may not create a final order by voluntarily dismissing pursuant to CivR 41(A) the remaining claims against the same defendant: Pattison v. W.W. Grainger, Inc., 120 Ohio St. 3d 142, 2008 Ohio 5276, 897 N.E.2d 126, 2008 Ohio LEXIS 2785 (2008).

Trial court's order granting the city summary judgment for the city on the home owners' claim was not a final appealable order because it neither adjudicated all the clams nor the rights and liabilities of all the parties and did not include a determination that there was no just reason for delay, as required by Civ. R. 54(B). Although the owners had sought a declaratory judgment with respect to the establishment of an equalization board to hear their written protests and objections, the trial court failed to declare whether the city was required to establish an equalization board, and the trial court did not adjudicate the owners' claims against the county auditor and treasurer. Abram v. City of Avon Lake, — Ohio App. 3d —, 2007 Ohio 5476, — N.E. 2d —, 2007 Ohio App. LEXIS 4813 (Oct. 15, 2007).

Corporations' appeal was dismissed for lack of a final appealable order under RC § 2505.02 because the first and second judgment entries that the corporations were appealing were both interlocutory, and the third judgment entry did not dispose of the punitive damages issue and did not contain any Ohio R. Civ. P. 54(B) language; thus, there were still claims pending in the trial court. Koski v. Babies R Us, — Ohio App. 3d —, 2007 Ohio 6730, — N.E. 2d —, 2007 Ohio App. LEXIS 5885 (Dec. 14, 2007).

— **Motions for reconsideration**

Trial court's February 25, 2005, order in which it awarded compensatory damages to appellants was a final judgment pursuant to Ohio R. Civ. P. 54, 58; thus, the trial court's amended judgment that reduced appellants' damages award by $10,000 was a nullity because a motion for reconsideration of a final judgment was a nullity. Squires v. Luckey Farmers, Inc., — Ohio App. 3d —, 2006 Ohio 1640, — N.E. 2d —, 2006 Ohio App. LEXIS 1512 (Mar. 31, 2006).

— **No just reason for delay**

When a wife sought, and was granted, an accounting of her former husband's payment to her of half of his pension benefits, pursuant to a divorce decree, and the trial court, in the same order, held she was not entitled to share in cost of living adjustments to the husband's pension, this was not a final appealable order, under RC § 2505.02(B)(1), despite the trial court's inclusion of Ohio R. Civ. P. 54(B) language to the contrary, because the parties could not determine their rights and obligations from it, and the order did not contain a statement of the relief being afforded to the parties, nor did it terminate the controversy submitted to the court, so an appellate court had no jurisdiction to consider an appeal from the order. Guziak v. Guziak, — Ohio App. 3d —, 2007 Ohio 514, — N.E. 2d —, 2007 Ohio App. LEXIS 454 (Feb. 7, 2007).

Since the trial court had not found that there was "no just reason for delay" in its original judgment entry, pursuant to Ohio R. Civ. P. 54(B), the entry was subject to revision at any time. The trial court was not required to give a reason for any subsequent revision. Choby v. Aylsworth, — Ohio App. 3d —, 2007 Ohio 3375, — N.E. 2d —, 2007 Ohio App. LEXIS 3091 (June 29, 2007).

Because the trial court's entry denying the insurer's motion to intervene did not include the required Ohio R. Civ. P. 54(B) language of no just reason for delay, and because the victim's claims were still pending as of the date of the entry, the trial court's order was not final and appealable at that time. The insurer's initial appeal did not vest the appellate court with jurisdiction, and the trial court was not divested of its jurisdiction to try the case. Davis v. Border, 170 Ohio App. 3d 758, 2007 Ohio 692, 869 N.E.2d 46, 2007 Ohio App. LEXIS 613 (2007).

Ohio R. Civ. P. 54(B) certification of no just reason to delay an appeal is not necessary to appeal provisional remedies under RC § 2505.02(B)(4). MD Acquisition v. Myers, — Ohio App. 3d —, 2007 Ohio 3521, — N.E. 2d —, 2007 Ohio App. LEXIS 3227 (July 10, 2007).

When, in a lawsuit filed by a corporation against the corporation's executive, the corporation was ordered to advance the executive's legal expenses to the executive, pursuant to corporate by-laws, the trial court's refusal to include a certification, under Ohio R. Civ. P. 54(B), that there was no just reason to delay an appeal did not determine whether the order was final and appealable because an otherwise appealable order granting a provisional remedy was not rendered unappealable by the absence of such a certification. MD Acquisition v. Myers, — Ohio App. 3d —, 2007 Ohio 3521, — N.E. 2d —, 2007 Ohio App. LEXIS 3227 (July 10, 2007).

Trial court should not have included the "no just reason for delay" language in its order entered after finding in favor of a construction company on its claim for money owed to it by a property owner but before resolving the owner's counterclaim because: (1) nothing in the record suggested that the certification served sound judicial administration, in that less effort could be expended by resolving the company's claim and the owner's counterclaim simultaneously; and (2) the claim and counterclaims all focused on the very same facts, legal issues, and circumstances as the original claim. The court struck the Ohio R. Civ. P. 54(B) finding and held that the trial court's judgment was neither final nor appealable; therefore, the court lacked jurisdiction under Ohio Const. art. IV, § 3 and RC § 2501.02 to conduct a review. Portco, Inc. v. Eye Specialists, Inc., 173 Ohio App. 3d 108, 2007 Ohio 4403, 877 N.E.2d 709, 2007 Ohio App. LEXIS 3964 (2007).

Although the trial court's order affected a substantial right, entered in a special proceeding, which satisfied the definition of a final order in RC § 2505.02(B)(2), because the trial court had not yet entered a judgment on the rights and liabilities that the insurer's claim for relief against the insured involved, the judgment that the trial court entered on the insurer's claim for attorney's fees (based on frivolous conduct by the insurer) remained subject to revision, and therefore was not final and appealable since the trial court did not certify that there was no just reason for delay, as required by Ohio R. Civ. P. 54(B). State Auto Mut. Ins. Co. v. Tatone, — Ohio App. 3d —, 2007 Ohio 4726, — N.E. 2d —, 2007 Ohio App. LEXIS 4239 (Sept. 14, 2007).

In a mother-in-law's suit to recover a sum from a son-in-law, in which judgment was entered against the son-in-law under a resulting trust theory, the judgment was final and appealable, under RC § 2505.02(B)(1), because the issue before the trial court was whether the son-in-law was under a duty to pay the mother-in-law a sum, and the judgment disposed of all issues by finding the son-in-law was obligated, under a resulting trust theory, to pay that sum, so the complaint's stated contract claim was converted into a resulting trust claim, making resolution of the contract claim unnecessary, and making language under Ohio R. Civ. P. 54(B) that there was no just reason for delay unnecessary. Ila Woodward v. Kleese, — Ohio App. 3d —, 2007 Ohio 5218, — N.E. 2d —, 2007 Ohio App. LEXIS 4585 (Sept. 28, 2007).

Appeal from a trial court's order granting appellee's motion for partial summary judgment and stating that there was "no cause for delay" was dismissed because the language used by the trial court showed that it did not make the essential determination required by Ohio R. Civ. P. 54(B) that there was no "just" reason for delay. As a result, the order was not a final, appealable order, and pursuant to Ohio Const. art. IV, § 3(B)(2), the court did not have jurisdiction to review it. Bankers Trust Co. v. Tutin, — Ohio App. 3d —, 2006 Ohio 1178, — N.E. 2d —, 2006 Ohio App. LEXIS 1065 (Mar. 15, 2006).

Since appellants' claim against another defendant was still pending and since the trial court did not expressly determine, pursuant to Ohio R. Civ. P. 54(B), that there was no just reason for delay in its entry granting summary judgment to appellee, the entry of summary judgment in favor of appellee was not a final judgment, and their appeal was dismissed. Turner v.

C.G.R., Inc., — Ohio App. 3d —, 2006 Ohio 1580, — N.E. 2d —, 2006 Ohio App. LEXIS 1483 (Mar. 31, 2006).

Because a surviving spouse's claims against a decedent's children arising from the decedent's alleged violation of a domestic relations temporary restraining order in the decedent's changing of the beneficiaries in a life insurance policy and in transferring two autos to one of the children were so intertwined, the trial court erred in including Ohio R. Civ. P. 54(B) language in its order granting summary judgment to the children on the auto claims but denying summary judgment on the insurance claims, and the appellate court lacked jurisdiction to consider the surviving spouse's appeal of that order. Dodrill v. Prudential Ins. Co., — Ohio App. 3d —, 2006 Ohio 3674, — N.E. 2d —, 2006 Ohio App. LEXIS 3611 (July 13, 2006).

When a trial court entered a foreclosure decree, it was not required to state, under Ohio R. Civ. P. 54(B), that there was no just reason for delay because, at the time of foreclosure, asset interests were addressed, so this language would have been superfluous, and the fact that a party was later allowed to intervene was irrelevant. Keybank Nat'l Ass'n v. Estate of Wright, — Ohio App. 3d —, 2006 Ohio 4643, — N.E. 2d —, 2006 Ohio App. LEXIS 4564 (Sept. 1, 2006).

— Preliminary injunction

Preliminary injunction, which contained a conclusion of law that the continued presence of the owners' boat upon a boat yard owner's premises was a willful and wanton continuing trespass and a nuisance, was not final for purposes of RC § 2505.02 because the boat owners had the ability to appeal the ruling after a final judgment, and, thus, the issues of trespass and willful conduct were not res judicata; the court's use of Ohio R. Civ. P. 54(B) language was of no consequence as certification language could not convert a non-final order into a final order. Sailing, Inc. v. Pavarini, — Ohio App. 3d —, 2007 Ohio 6844, — N.E. 2d —, 2007 Ohio App. LEXIS 5992 (Dec. 20, 2007).

Finding of no just reason for delay

Trial court's CivR 54(B) finding of "no just reason for delay" may be struck by an appellate court, and an appeal dismissed, where judicial economy and justice are better served by resolving claims together: Portco, Inc. v. Eye Specialists, Inc., 173 Ohio App. 3d 108, 2007 Ohio 4403, 877 N.E.2d 709, 2007 Ohio App. LEXIS 3964 (2007).

Insurance matters

Order that declares that an insured is entitled to coverage but does not address damages is not a final order as defined in RC § 2505.02(B)(2), because the order does not affect a substantial right even though made in a special proceeding: Walburn v. Dunlap, 121 Ohio St. 3d 373, 2009 Ohio 1221, 904 N.E.2d 863, 2009 Ohio LEXIS 714 (2009).

Interlocutory order

Trial court did not err in granting an employer's motion for summary judgment dismissing an employee's employer intentional tort claim nine months after orally denying the employer's summary judgment motion because the trial court neither journalized its interlocutory decision nor certified it under Ohio R. Civ. P. 54(B); thus, the trial court was free to revise its oral decision at any time. Moore v. Ohio Valley Coal Co., — Ohio App. 3d —, 2007 Ohio 1123, — N.E. 2d —, 2007 Ohio App. LEXIS 1040 (Mar. 7, 2007).

Trial court did not err in granting an employer's motion for summary judgment dismissing an employee's employer intentional tort claim nine months after orally denying the employer's summary judgment motion because the trial court neither journalized its interlocutory decision nor certified it under Ohio R. Civ. P. 54(B); thus, the trial court was free to revise its oral decision at any time. Moore v. Ohio Valley Coal Co., — Ohio App. 3d —, 2007 Ohio 1123, — N.E. 2d —, 2007 Ohio App. LEXIS 1040 (Mar. 7, 2007).

When, in a legal malpractice case, a trial court granted a motion to strike certain claims in a client's complaint, its ruling was an interlocutory order and was not immediately appealable because an interlocutory order was subject to revision by the trial court at any time prior to the entry of a final judgment, under Ohio R. Civ. P. 54(B), and, once a final judgment was entered, all interlocutory orders merged into that final judgment and became appealable, but, when the action was voluntarily dismissed without prejudice, any interlocutory orders were dissolved and were not appealable. Marc Glassman, Inc. v. Fagan, — Ohio App. 3d —, 2006 Ohio 5577, — N.E. 2d —, 2006 Ohio App. LEXIS 5569 (Oct. 26, 2006).

Ruling on a motion to strike was an interlocutory order and was not immediately appealable, as an interlocutory order was subject to revision by the trial court at any time prior to the entering of a final judgment in the case, under Ohio R. Civ. P. 54(B), and, once a final judgment was entered, all interlocutory orders were merged into the final judgment of the court and became appealable, but, when an entire action was voluntarily dismissed without prejudice, any interlocutory orders made by the trial court were dissolved and were not appealable. Marc Glassman, Inc. v. Fagan, — Ohio App. 3d —, 2006 Ohio 5577, — N.E. 2d —, 2006 Ohio App. LEXIS 5569 (Oct. 26, 2006).

Multiple parties

Although RC § 2744.02(C) provides that an order that denies a political subdivision the benefit of an alleged immunity is a final order, it is not an appealable order absent compliance with CivR 54(B) in a case involving multiple claims or parties: Swint v. Auld, 178 Ohio App. 3d 531, 2008 Ohio 5381, 898 N.E.2d 1044, 2008 Ohio App. LEXIS 4524 (2008).

In suit brought against property owner and John Doe defendants, since the one year period for service on the John Doe defendants, specified in Ohio R. Civ. P. 3(A), had not expired before the trial court entered judgment for the owner and since the entry granting summary judgment to the owner did not include Ohio R. Civ. P. 54(B) language, the trial court's order was not an appealable order. Mosley v. 131 Foods, Inc., — Ohio App. 3d —, 2006 Ohio 5719, — N.E. 2d —, 2006 Ohio App. LEXIS 5732 (Nov. 2, 2006).

Proceedings in aid of execution

There was a final appealable order pursuant to RC § 2505.02 and CivR 54(B) where the trial court issued an order establishing the creditors' priority for payment and fully adjudicated one creditor's application for relief under RC § 2333.21: Olive Branch Holdings v. Smith, 181 Ohio App. 3d 479, 2009 Ohio 1105, 909 N.E.2d 671, 2009 Ohio App. LEXIS 859 (2009).

Punitive damages

Pursuant to Ohio R. Civ. P. 54(C), appellant failed to show that damages awarded to a patrolman in his multi-tort action against her were excessive, as the mere fact that the amount awarded for punitive damages exceeded the patrolman's demand did not compel a finding of excessiveness; the trial court properly denied appellant's motion for relief from judgment under Ohio R. Civ. P. 60(B)(5). Earl v. Nelson, — Ohio App. 3d —, 2006 Ohio 3341, — N.E. 2d —, 2006 Ohio App. LEXIS 3270 (June 30, 2006).

Reconsideration

Trial court had the authority to clarify in its March 2005 judgment entry which method of payment should be used to divide the husband's retirement account to effectuate the divorce decree; since the wife's motion for relief from judgment was premature, it was treated as a motion for reconsideration under Ohio R. Civ. P. 54(B). Given that the divorce decree was an interlocutory order which the trial court could revise or clarify at any time, the issues of whether the wife timely filed her motion, whether the language in the divorce decree was ambiguous, and whether the trial court reserved jurisdiction to modify the final divorce decree were irrelevant. Forman v. Forman, — Ohio App. 3d —, 2007 Ohio 4938, — N.E. 2d —, 2007 Ohio App. LEXIS 4618 (Sept. 24, 2007).

Relief claim in pleadings

Where property owners asserted three claims against the adjacent property owners (APOs), arising from the APOs' excavation of their property to construct a road to the lake in front of their home and their installation of concrete blocks to help prevent erosion at the beachfront, but their claim for relief sought one demand for compensatory damages, the trial court's award of damages in one amount fulfilled the trial court's duty under Ohio R. Civ. P. 54(C), as there was no indication in the complaint that they were seeking an itemized judgment entry that would separately detail each claim for relief. Parker v. Hegler, — Ohio App. 3d —, 2006 Ohio 6495, — N.E. 2d —, 2006 Ohio App. LEXIS 6419 (Dec. 8, 2006).

Although a credit card assignee did not seek interest in its claim for relief in an action against a credit card holder, wherein it sought recovery of the sum due under an account, the trial court's award of the amount due plus interest was not error under Ohio R. Civ. P. 54(C), as the assignee was entitled to the relief it was due even if such relief was not specifically requested in the pleadings. Great Seneca Fin. v. Felty, 170 Ohio App. 3d 737, 2006 Ohio 6618, 869 N.E.2d 30, 2006 Ohio App. LEXIS 6547 (2006).

Summary judgment

Order granting partial summary judgment to a trust company and an investment company could not be reviewed by an appellate court. Because the case involved multiple claims and multiple parties, Ohio R. Civ. P. 54(B) was applicable, and the order did not contain the requisite Rule 54(B) language because the trial court recognized that an issue of lien priority between the trust company and a bank had not yet been resolved. Bankers Trust Co. v. Tutin, — Ohio App. 3d —, 2008 Ohio 551, — N.E. 2d —, 2008 Ohio App. LEXIS 471 (Feb. 13, 2008).

Although a trial court's grant of summary judgment to one driver in an action by vehicle passengers against three drivers, arising from a three-car collision, did not resolve all of the pending claims in the action, upon the trial court's grant of default judgments against the other two drivers, the summary judgment ruling became a final appealable order pursuant to RC § 2505.02. The summary judgment ruling lacked the requisite language that there was no just cause for delay under Ohio R. Civ. P. 54(B). Goldney v. Byrd, — Ohio App. 3d —, 2007 Ohio 1985, — N.E. 2d —, 2007 Ohio App. LEXIS 1828 (Apr. 26, 2007).

When a property owner sued the builders of an adjacent hotel for damaging his land and trespass, the trial court's finding that there was a genuine issue of material fact as to whether the builders were liable for trespass was not a final appealable order, under RC § 2505.02 and Ohio R. Civ. P. 54(B), regarding which an appellate court could properly assert jurisdiction, under Ohio Const. art. IV, § 3(B)(2), because the denial of the builders' summary judgment motion on this basis did not determine the action or prevent a judgment. Interstate Props. v. Prasanna, Inc., — Ohio App. 3d —, 2006 Ohio 2686, — N.E. 2d —, 2006 Ohio App. LEXIS 2521 (May 31, 2006).

Where the trial court granted summary judgment to a hospital and others on four of six counts in former patients' complaint arising from the mishandling of fetal tissue, and it included the "no just cause of delay" language of Ohio R. Civ. P. 54(B), that order was final and appealable pursuant to Rule 54(B) and RC § 2505.02, as the four claims ruled upon required proof of different facts and provided for different relief from the two remaining claims although the four claims were not factually separate and independent from the remain-

ing claims. Walker v. Firelands Community Hosp., — Ohio App. 3d —, 2006 Ohio 2930, — N.E. 2d —, 2006 Ohio App. LEXIS 2805 (June 9, 2006).

Trial court's denial of summary judgment as to two of six counts in a complaint was not a final appealable order from which a cross-appeal could have been taken, even with the "no just cause of delay" language of Ohio R. Civ. P. 54(B); accordingly, the cross-appeal required dismissal. Walker v. Firelands Community Hosp., — Ohio App. 3d —, 2006 Ohio 2930, — N.E. 2d —, 2006 Ohio App. LEXIS 2805 (June 9, 2006).

Trial court's denial of summary judgment to a school district board of education was not a final appealable order pursuant to RC § 2505.02 and Ohio R. Civ. P. 54(B), as the denial was based on factual issues regarding the merits of the claim. Although the board claimed that it was entitled to appeal the order because the trial court denied its summary judgment motion on the question of its immunity under RC § 2744.02(C), the decision dealt with the fact-related legal issues underlying the claim, which was not a final appealable order within the meaning of § 2744.02(C). Alden v. Kovar, — Ohio App. 3d —, 2006 Ohio 3400, — N.E. 2d —, 2006 Ohio App. LEXIS 3372 (June 30, 2006).

Appellants' second suit against a manufacturer was improperly dismissed on the basis of res judicata because, although the trial court had granted summary judgment to the manufacturer in the first suit, the order was not a final appealable order under RC § 2505.02 as claims remained pending against other defendants and the order did not contain Ohio R. Civ. P. 54(B) language. Appellants' subsequent Ohio R. Civ. P. 41(A) dismissal of the entire case dissolved all interlocutory orders, including the order granting summary judgment. Hutchinson v. Beazer East, Inc., — Ohio App. 3d —, 2006 Ohio 6761, — N.E. 2d —, 2006 Ohio App. LEXIS 6672 (Dec. 21, 2006).

Trial court's denial of a decedent's son's motion for summary judgment in a claim asserted against him by the decedent's estate beneficiaries of unjust enrichment was not a final appealable order under RC § 2505.02, despite the use of the language under Ohio R. Civ. P. 54(B). The appellate court lacked jurisdiction over the issue pursuant to Ohio Const. art. IV, § 3(B)(2), and dismissal of that aspect of the appeal was granted. Schlegel v. Gindlesberger, — Ohio App. 3d —, 2006 Ohio 6916, — N.E. 2d —, 2006 Ohio App. LEXIS 6813 (Dec. 26, 2006).

RULE 55. Default

(A) Entry of judgment. When a party against whom a judgment for affirmative relief is sought has failed to plead or otherwise defend as provided by these rules, the party entitled to a judgment by default shall apply in writing or orally to the court therefore; but no judgment by default shall be entered against a minor or an incompetent person unless represented in the action by a guardian or other such representative who has appeared therein. If the party against whom judgment by default is sought has appeared in the action, he (or, if appearing by representative, his representative) shall be served with written notice of the application for judgment at least seven days prior to the hearing on such application. If, in order to enable the court to enter judgment or to carry it into effect, it is necessary to take an account or to determine the amount of damages or to establish the truth of any averment by evidence or to make an investigation of any other matter, the court may conduct such hearings or order such references as it deems necessary and proper and shall when applicable accord a right of trial by jury to the parties.

(B) **Setting aside default judgment.** If a judgment by default has been entered, the court may set it aside in accordance with Rule 60(B).

(C) **Plaintiffs, counterclaimants, cross-claimants.** The provisions of this rule apply whether the party entitled to the judgment by default is a plaintiff, a third-party plaintiff or a party who has pleaded a cross-claim or counterclaim. In all cases a judgment by default is subject to the limitations of Rule 54(C).

(D) **Judgment against this state.** No judgment by default shall be entered against this state, a political subdivision, or officer in his representative capacity or agency of either unless the claimant establishes his claim or right to relief by evidence satisfactory to the court.

History: Amended, eff 7-1-71.

NOTES TO DECISIONS

Analysis

Generally
Appeals
Appearance
Application for default judgment
Damages
Default judgment improper
Default judgment improperly denied
Default judgment improperly granted
Default judgment properly granted
Excusable neglect
Failure to file an answer
Failure to hold required hearing
Foreclosure
Hearing on damages necessary
Hearings
Inmates
Motion for relief from default judgment
Motion to set aside default judgment
Notice
Notice of application for default judgment
Relief from default judgment
Service and default
Small claims
Uncontested divorce
Vacating default judgment
Workers' compensation

Generally

As mortgagors filed a counterclaim that incorporated the allegations of their answer to the mortgagee's foreclosure action, and they sought relief thereon, despite the fact that the trial court failed to rule on the mortgagee's motion for a more definite statement pursuant to Ohio R. Civ. P. 12(E), such constituted activity by the mortgagee to "otherwise defend" on the claim under Ohio R. Civ. P. 55, such that the mortgagors' motion for a default judgment was properly denied. Lasalle Nat'l Bank v. Ingle, — Ohio App. 3d —, 2007 Ohio 77, — N.E. 2d —, 2007 Ohio App. LEXIS 71 (Jan. 11, 2007).

Because defendants contested the allegations in the mother's complaint in their answer and defended by filing two motions for summary judgment, defendants' were clearly not in default, and the mother's motion for default judgment was

appropriately denied. Nadra v. Mbah, — Ohio App. 3d —, 2007 Ohio 501, — N.E. 2d —, 2007 Ohio App. LEXIS 448 (Feb. 6, 2007).

In a foreclosure action, when a creditor sought to recover on both a secured and an unsecured loan, and the debtors filed a counterclaim related to the unsecured loan, and the trial court's judgment in favor of the creditor for all amounts sought was reversed, but it was unclear, from the trial court, due, in part, to a change of judges, whether a previous stay remained in effect, it was not error for the trial court to deny the debtors' motion for a default judgment as to their counterclaim, or to deny the debtors' motion to strike the creditor's untimely answer to the counterclaim. Ohio Farm Bur. Fedn., Inc. v. Amos, — Ohio App. 3d —, — N.E. 2d —, 2006 Ohio App. LEXIS 1408 (Mar. 29, 2006).

Trial court did not err by failing to abide by Summit County, Ohio, Ct. C.P. R. 7.14(A) as the 14-day waiting period was inapplicable in cases where a default judgment was appropriate and the party in default had not entered an appearance in the case at the time of the filing of the motion for default judgment. Preferred Capital, Inc. v. Wheaton Trenching, Inc., — Ohio App. 3d —, 2006 Ohio 1554, — N.E. 2d —, 2006 Ohio App. LEXIS 1486 (Mar. 31, 2006).

Although the time for answering plaintiff's amended complaint had not run when plaintiff filed his motion for default judgment, the trial court did not err in rendering default judgment against defendants because plaintiff's motion was based upon defendants' failure to comply with various discovery orders, in accordance with Ohio R. Civ. P. 37(B)(2)(c), not on defendants' failure to file a timely answer under Ohio R. Civ. P. 55(A). Sparks v. Gray's Used Tractors, — Ohio App. 3d —, 2006 Ohio 2658, — N.E. 2d —, 2006 Ohio App. LEXIS 2489 (May 19, 2006).

Trial court did not err in denying debtors' motion for default judgment on their counterclaim against a creditor because, while the creditor did not respond within the time permitted by the Ohio Rules of Civil Procedure, it was within the trial court's discretion to grant the creditor leave to plead and to denying the debtors' motion for default judgment upon a finding that the creditor had shown excusable neglect for its delay, in that the creditor's counsel inadvertently failed to timely reply to the counterclaim due to a death in counsel's immediate family that required counsel's presence out-of-state for an extended period of time. Under Ohio R. Civ. P. 6(B)(2), the trial court had the discretion to allow for an extension of time to file a late pleading upon the showing of excusable neglect. Bank v. Damsel, — Ohio App. 3d —, 2006 Ohio 4071, — N.E. 2d —, 2006 Ohio App. LEXIS 3991 (Aug. 8, 2006).

Trial court did not err in denying defendant's motion for default judgment since the motion was filed prior to expiration of the time for appellee to answer. Smith v. Ramsey, — Ohio App. 3d —, 2006 Ohio 4859, — N.E. 2d —, 2006 Ohio App. LEXIS 4775 (Sept. 8, 2006).

Trial court's denial of a contractor's motion for contempt and for a default judgment against a home owner in his breach of contract action, wherein the contractor alleged that the owner had failed to comply with the trial court's order requiring her to disclose her insurance coverage within a set period of time, was not an abuse of discretion, as a review of the record indicated that there was no such mandate by the trial court. Jones v. Dillard, — Ohio App. 3d —, 2006 Ohio 6417, — N.E. 2d —, 2006 Ohio App. LEXIS 6370 (Dec. 7, 2006).

Appeals

When a default judgment was improperly entered against alleged promisors, because they had answered the complaint filed against them, and they then sought relief from that judgment, under Ohio R. Civ. P. 60(B)(5), while Rule 60(B)(5) was not generally a substitute for a timely appeal, and the promisors were entitled to relief due to the trial court's misapplication of Ohio R. Civ. P. 55(A), rather than under Ohio R. Civ. P. 60(B)(5), the promisors could raise their arguments about the misapplication of Ohio R. Civ. P. 55(A) in their appeal of the trial court's denial of their motion for relief from judgment because the trial court's record indicated conflicting addresses for the promisors to which notice of the entry of their default was sent, and due process required that they be allowed to raise these arguments in this manner. Skinner v. Leyland, 167 Ohio App. 3d 226, 2006 Ohio 3186, 854 N.E. 2d 573, 2006 Ohio App. LEXIS 3069 (June 23, 2006).

Appearance

When alleged promisors answered a complaint filed against them but did not appear for trial, and the trial court erroneously entered their default, under Ohio R. Civ. P. 55(A), rather than holding an ex parte trial, the trial court's denial of the promisors' motion to vacate the judgment was an abuse of discretion. Skinner v. Leyland, 167 Ohio App. 3d 226, 2006 Ohio 3186, 854 N.E. 2d 573, 2006 Ohio App. LEXIS 3069 (June 23, 2006).

When a consumer sued a company and its sole proprietor, and the proprietor filed an answer, pro se, under Ohio R. Civ. P. 12(A), the trial court properly granted the consumer's motion for the company's default judgment, under Ohio R. Civ. P. 55(A), because the proprietor's answer was an insufficient response for the company as the company had to be represented by counsel. Vilardo v. Sheets, — Ohio App. 3d —, 2006 Ohio 3473, — N.E. 2d —, 2006 Ohio App. LEXIS 3415 (July 3, 2006).

Denial of a medical practice's motion for relief from judgment pursuant to Ohio R. Civ. P. 60(B) was proper where it never appeared in an action asserted against it by a patient, and accordingly, it was not entitled to notice under Ohio R. Civ. P. 55(A) prior to entry of a default judgment against it in the patient's medical malpractice action; private communications did not constitute an "appearance" for purposes of requiring notice under Rule 55(A). Bright v. Family Med. Found., Inc., — Ohio App. 3d —, 2006 Ohio 5037, — N.E.2d —, 2006 Ohio App. LEXIS 4947 (Sept. 28, 2006).

Since appellee "appeared in the action," under Ohio R. Civ. P. 55(A), by writing a letter to appellant's attorney disputing claims in appellant's complaint, he was entitled to notice and a hearing prior to the entry of default judgment against him even though he had never filed any documents with the trial court. The trial court's failure to follow these notification procedures constituted a ground for relief under Ohio R. Civ. P. 60(B)(5); thus, appellee's Ohio R. Civ. P. 60(B) motion was properly granted. Johnson v. Romeo, — Ohio App. 3d —, 2006 Ohio 7073, — N.E. 2d —, 2006 Ohio App. LEXIS 7003 (Dec. 14, 2006).

Trial court abuse its discretion in denying the employee's Ohio R. Civ. P. 60(B) motion for relief from judgment because he was entitled to relief on the grounds of excusable neglect. He claimed that he was the wrong party, which was a meritorious defense; he attempted to contact the buyer's attorney many times without success, which showed an intent to "appear" for purposes of Ohio R. Civ. P. 55; and the relief motion was filed within a reasonable time as it was only two months after service of the complaint. Rocha v. Salsbury, — Ohio App. 3d —, 2006 Ohio 2615, — N.E. 2d —, 2006 Ohio App. LEXIS 2448 (May 26, 2006).

Defendant can "appear in an action," within the meaning of Ohio R. Civ. P. 55, by clearly expressing to the opposing party an intention and purpose to defend the suit, regardless of whether a formal filing is made. Johnson v. Romeo, — Ohio App. 3d —, 2006 Ohio 7073, — N.E. 2d —, 2006 Ohio App. LEXIS 7003 (Dec. 14, 2006).

Application for default judgment

When an Ohio client sued, in Ohio, a Rhode Island law firm, which represented him in a lawsuit in Rhode Island, and the law firm did not file an answer to the client's complaint, but did enter a special appearance to contest jurisdiction, the client was not entitled to have the trial court enter a default judgment against the law firm when he did not move for such a judgment or provide the law firm with notice of an intention to seek default judgment, to which the law firm was entitled, under Ohio R. Civ. P. 55(A), by virtue of its special appearance. Gerber v. Blish & Cavanagh, — Ohio App. 3d —, 2006 Ohio 2252, — N.E. 2d —, 2006 Ohio App. LEXIS 2097 (May 8, 2006).

Damages

Even though a party defaults and admits the allegations of the complaint, a plaintiff must still establish his damages. Social security records were not properly authenticated, and were not admissible merely because they looked like official agency documents. However, the amount of loan proceeds appropriated by the defendant and the conversion of the life insurance policies were properly established: Reinbolt v. Kern, 183 Ohio App. 3d 287, 2009 Ohio 3492, 916 N.E.2d 1100, 2009 Ohio App. LEXIS 3027 (2009).

Trial court's denial of a medical practice's motion to vacate a default judgment pursuant to Ohio R. Civ. P. 60(B) was proper where, upon finding that the practice was in default of a patient's action, alleging inter alia, medical malpractice and negligent infliction of emotional distress, a hearing was held before a magistrate on the issue of damages; the damages awarded under Ohio R. Civ. P. 55(A) were not deemed excessive in the circumstances, as the patient had been injected with an HIV-contaminated drug which affected her state of mind, her ability to parent her son, and her employment possibilities. Bright v. Family Med. Found., Inc., — Ohio App. 3d —, 2006 Ohio 5037, — N.E.2d —, 2006 Ohio App. LEXIS 4947 (Sept. 28, 2006).

Trial court did not abuse its discretion in disallowing the claimed contractual rate of prejudgment interest (23 percent) on the assigned retail installment contract and instead awarding the company the post-judgment rate of interest of five percent in the default judgment award, under Civ. R. 55. The stipulated interest rate was just under usury and the finance company stood to benefit far more from the breach of the contract than from its performance. Mercury Fin. Co. v. Smith, — Ohio App. 3d —, 2006 Ohio 5730, — N.E. 2d —, 2006 Ohio App. LEXIS 5726 (Nov. 2, 2006).

Default judgment improper

Trial court did not err in overruling the applicant's motion for default judgment due to the Sheriff's failure to file a record with the trial court because the Sheriff was not under any obligation to file the confidential concealed handgun license records until the trial court ordered him to do so. In re Notice of Denial of Appeal of Billy J. Watson v. Licking County, — Ohio App. 3d —, 2007 Ohio 4856, — N.E. 2d —, 2007 Ohio App. LEXIS 4319 (Sept. 19, 2007).

Trial court abused its discretion in granting judgment to an employee in her action under RC § 4123.512(D), as the employer's counsel's failure to appear at a pretrial conference could not have resulted in a default judgment under Ohio R. Civ. P. 7(A) and 55(A) because the employee did not offer evidence in an ex parte hearing to support her claims and further, the employer had filed an answer; the judgment could not have been based on a dismissal under Ohio R. Civ. P. 41(B) as a sanction, as the employer was never notified that such a sanction could be imposed if it failed to appear and further, counsel's 15-minute delay due to long elevator lines did not warrant such a harsh sanction in the circumstances. Baur v. Co-Ax Tech., — Ohio App. 3d —, 2007 Ohio 3910, — N.E. 2d —, 2007 Ohio App. LEXIS 3565 (Aug. 2, 2007).

Since a prisoner's complaint alleging a defamation claim did not state a claim for which relief could be granted, the trial court did not err in denying the prisoner's motion for default judgment. Whiteside v. Williams, — Ohio App. 3d —, 2007 Ohio 1100, — N.E. 2d —, 2007 Ohio App. LEXIS 1017 (Mar. 12, 2007).

Trial court erred in granting an employer's oral request for a default judgment, made on the day of the trial, as an employee's counsel was not afforded sufficient time to show good cause as to his failure to answer a counterclaim within 28 days of the service of the counterclaim and why leave to plead was appropriate. Absent seven days' written notice, the employee's ability to show cause under Ohio R. Civ. P. 55(A) was emasculated. Shikner v. Solutions, — Ohio App. 3d —, 2006 Ohio 127, — N.E. 2d —, 2006 Ohio App. LEXIS 104 (Jan. 13, 2006).

Court erred in entering a default judgment against a guarantor when she failed to appear at a status conference since there was no local rule authorizing the action taken, no judgment entry providing for default judgment had been issued, and no opportunity to respond was provided. Thus, the trial court should have granted guarantor's Ohio R. Civ. P. 60(B) motion for relief from the default judgment. Creative Capital Leasing v. Baker, — Ohio App. 3d —, 2006 Ohio 4444, — N.E. 2d —, 2006 Ohio App. LEXIS 4386 (Aug. 28, 2006).

Default judgment improperly denied

Trial court abused its discretion when it denied the bank's motion for a default judgment. Because the debtor did not answer the complaint, the bank was entitled to pursue a default judgment. MBNA Am. Bank, N.A. v. Canfora, — Ohio App. 3d —, 2007 Ohio 4137, — N.E. 2d —, 2007 Ohio App. LEXIS 3754 (Aug. 15, 2007).

Trial court erred in denying a creditor's motion for default judgment under Ohio R. Civ. P. 55 filed after the debtor failed to respond to the creditor's complaint for monies owed on credit card account. The debtor's failure to deny the creditor's averment in the complaint that he owed $ 4,317.58 on his account constituted an admission of the allegations under Ohio R. Civ. P. 8(D). Discover Bank v. Hicks, — Ohio App. 3d —, 2007 Ohio 4448, — N.E. 2d —, 2007 Ohio App. LEXIS 4185 (Aug. 22, 2007).

In homeowners' claims against mortgage brokers and the brokers' principal for violations of the Mortgage Broker Act, RC § 1322.01 et seq., and civil conspiracy, a trial court improperly denied the homeowners' motion for a default judgment against one broker because the broker did not answer the complaint served on the broker, and, under Ohio R. Civ. P. 8(D), the allegations against the broker should have been construed as admitted. Roark v. Rydell, 174 Ohio App. 3d 186, 2007 Ohio 6873, 881 N.E. 2d 333, 2007 Ohio App. LEXIS 6043 (Dec. 21, 2007).

Trial court abused its discretion by ignoring an attorney's failure to comply with the Ohio Rules of Civil Procedure, effectively overruling the client's motion for a default judgment, and entertaining the attorney's motion for summary judgment as the attorney did not file a request for an extension of time to answer a client's legal malpractice complaint under Ohio R. Civ. P. 6(B)(1) and filed his answer one week after the client filed a motion for default judgment, but did not file a motion showing excusable neglect and requesting leave of court to file his untimely answer. Rowe v. Stillpass, — Ohio App. 3d —, 2006 Ohio 3789, — N.E. 2d —, 2006 Ohio App. LEXIS 3748 (July 13, 2006).

Trial court erred by denying a consumer's Ohio R. Civ. P. 55(A) motion for default judgment since defendants did not file a responsive pleading denying the allegations in the complaint; thus, the trial court, under Ohio R. Civ. P. 8(D) must have construed the allegations in the complaint as admitted and was compelled to conclude that there was no contest in the case. Burdge v. On Guard Sec. Servs., Inc., —

Ohio App. 3d —, 2006 Ohio 2092, — N.E. 2d —, 2006 Ohio App. LEXIS 1940 (Apr. 28, 2006).

Default judgment improperly granted

When alleged promisors answered a complaint filed against them but did not appear for trial, it was reversible error to enter their default, under Ohio R. Civ. P. 55(A), because they had not failed to plead or otherwise defend, and the trial court should have held an ex parte trial at which the promisors' opponents would be required to demonstrate that they were entitled to judgment. Skinner v. Leyland, 167 Ohio App. 3d 226, 2006 Ohio 3186, 854 N.E. 2d 573, 2006 Ohio App. LEXIS 3069 (June 23, 2006).

When alleged promisors answered a complaint filed against them but did not appear for trial, and the trial court erroneously entered their default, under Ohio R. Civ. P. 55(A), rather than holding an ex parte trial, this violated due process and rendered the default judgment void. Skinner v. Leyland, 167 Ohio App. 3d 226, 2006 Ohio 3186, 854 N.E. 2d 573, 2006 Ohio App. LEXIS 3069 (June 23, 2006).

Default judgment properly granted

In a legal malpractice case, it was not error for a trial court to enter an attorney's default judgment, under Ohio R. Civ. P. 55(A), without waiting 14 days after the clients who brought suit filed the clients' second motion for default judgment because neither the attorney nor the attorney's representative had appeared in the action, so the attorney was not entitled to notice of the clients' application for default judgment, and a local rule providing the time within which a response to a motion had to be filed did not apply. Hover v. O'Hara, — Ohio App. 3d —, 2007 Ohio 3614, — N.E. 2d —, 2007 Ohio App. LEXIS 3308 (July 16, 2007).

Trial court did not err in entering default judgment in favor of appellee corporation pursuant to Ohio R. Civ. P. 55 because (1) in circumstances involving a pending action in a sister state, Ohio courts could maintain the action in Ohio, (2) a document in which a forum selection clause appeared was an application, not a binding contract, and (3) appellant corporation was not prejudiced when the trial court conducted a particular hearing because appellant was on notice and given an opportunity to defend. Stradiot Specialty, Inc. v. Am. Calendar Co., Inc., — Ohio App. 3d —, 2007 Ohio 3364, — N.E. 2d —, 2007 Ohio App. LEXIS 3087 (June 29, 2007).

Excusable neglect

Trial court properly granted a default judgment pursuant to Ohio R. Civ. P. 55(A) to business purchasers in their action against the business seller, as the seller had failed to file a timely answer and counterclaim to the purchasers' amended complaint and he failed to show excusable neglect pursuant to Ohio R. Civ. P. 6(B)(2) for the untimely filing for purposes of his motion to file the answer and counterclaim instanter. As the seller also failed to show excusable neglect for the lack of reasonable diligence in filing the answer in a timely manner, as well as a meritorious defense to the complaint, his motion to vacate under Ohio R. Civ. P. 60(B) was properly denied. Ear v. Phnom Penh Rest., — Ohio App. 3d —, 2007 Ohio 3069, — N.E. 2d —, 2007 Ohio App. LEXIS 2811 (June 21, 2007).

Trial court did not abuse its discretion under Ohio R. Civ. P. 55(B) and 60(B)(1) when it denied a law client's motion for relief from a default judgment that had been entered against it on a law firm's complaint, seeking recovery for services rendered, as the client did not show that the failure to answer the firm's complaint was excusable neglect. Although the client asserted that a temporary employee of another company that shared office space with the client had mishandled the complaint upon signing for it by certified mail, the president of the client had admitted that he may have learned of the receipt of the complaint or been shown a copy of it, such that there was no excuse for having failed to answer in the circumstances. Benesch, Friedlander, Coplan & Arnoff v. City

Concrete, LLC, — Ohio App. 3d —, 2007 Ohio 3331, — N.E. 2d —, 2007 Ohio App. LEXIS 3126 (June 21, 2007).

Failure to file an answer

Even assuming, arguendo, that the dentist was not on notice that the trial court had ruled on his motion to quash until he received the motion for default judgment, the trial court did not err in denying his motion for leave; it acted within its discretion in finding that the dentist's belated explanation did not constitute excusable neglect. The facts as set forth in the dentist's affidavit would have been known to him at the time that he initially sought leave and he could have informed the trial court, at that first opportunity, of the reason for missing the deadline, which he failed to do, resulting in further delay which was within his control to prevent. R.J. Donovan Co. v. Sohi, — Ohio App. 3d —, 2007 Ohio 3620, — N.E. 2d —, 2007 Ohio App. LEXIS 3316 (July 17, 2007).

Failure to hold required hearing

In an assignee's suit against a debtor on a credit card account, it was error for a trial court to grant the assignee's motion for default judgment because, when the debtor filed a motion for leave to file an answer out of time, the debtor's motion was an appearance in the case which required the trial court to provide the debtor with seven days' notice and a hearing on the assignee's motion, pursuant to Ohio R. Civ. P. 55(A), and the trial court failed to provide the debtor with such notice and hearing. Columbia Credit Servs., Inc. v. Ruetschle, — Ohio App. 3d —, 2007 Ohio 4332, — N.E. 2d —, 2007 Ohio App. LEXIS 3870 (Aug. 24, 2007).

Since appellee presented evidence that he had contacted the insurer after being served with the insurer's complaint and that he had communicated to the insurer that he was disputing the merits of the claim, the trial court properly determined that appellee had appeared in the action, despite the fact that he never filed an answer, and, pursuant to Ohio R. Civ. P. 55, was entitled to a hearing on the insurer's motion for a default judgment; thus, appellee's Ohio R. Civ. P. 60(B) motion was properly granted. Allstate Ins. Co. v. Hunt, — Ohio App. 3d —, 2006 Ohio 238, — N.E. 2d —, 2006 Ohio App. LEXIS 194 (Jan. 13, 2006).

Foreclosure

Ultimate assignee of a second mortgage on the property did not establish that it was entitled to relief pursuant to CivR 55(B) and 60(B) where the various assignments were "inexplicably" not recorded and it did not receive notice of the foreclosure action. Fifth Third Bank v. NCS Mortg. Lending Co., 168 Ohio App. 3d 413, 2006 Ohio 571, 860 N.E.2d 785, 2006 Ohio App. LEXIS 518 (2006).

Hearing on damages necessary

As a default judgment was properly granted against a driver upon her failure to file an answer in a timely manner, pursuant to Ohio R. Civ. P. 55, a damages-only hearing on a motorist's complaint, seeking recovery for injuries sustained in a vehicle accident between the parties, was proper and there was no need to submit evidence on the issue of causation. By failing to answer the complaint, the allegations therein were deemed admitted pursuant to Ohio R. Civ. P. 8(D), leaving only the issue of damages as a triable matter. Sokol v. Spigiel, — Ohio App. 3d —, 2006 Ohio 4408, — N.E. 2d —, 2006 Ohio App. LEXIS 4345 (Aug. 28, 2006).

Hearings

Trial court did not err by failing to hold an evidentiary hearing on a law client's motion for relief from a default judgment that was entered against it and in favor of a law firm pursuant to Ohio R. Civ. P. 55(B) and 60(B)(1), as there was no dispute about the facts regarding the handling of the complaint when it was served on the client by certified mail, such that no hearing was required. The motion to vacate the default judgment had been based on excusable neglect due to the mishandling of the complaint by the employee upon whom it was served by certified mail. Benesch, Friedlander, Coplan & Arnoff v. City Concrete, LLC, — Ohio App. 3d —, 2007 Ohio 3331, — N.E. 2d —, 2007 Ohio App. LEXIS 3126 (June 21, 2007).

Trial court did not abuse its discretion in awarding default judgment under Ohio R. Civ. P. 55(A) against a contractor and determining damages without first conducting a hearing. Since the contractor did not enter an appearance prior to the scheduled hearing date and failed to appear at the scheduled hearing, he was not entitled to notice of the default proceedings. Turnbull v. Arthur, — Ohio App. 3d —, 2006 Ohio 1669, — N.E. 2d —, 2006 Ohio App. LEXIS 1569 (Mar. 31, 2006).

Inmates

Where an inmate entered an appearance in the action via pro se filings, the court could not grant a default judgment without complying with the notice and hearing requirements: Young v. Hobbs, 182 Ohio App. 3d 649, 2009 Ohio 3181, 914 N.E.2d 444, 2009 Ohio App. LEXIS 2784 (2009).

Motion for relief from default judgment

Trial court properly granted a property seller's motion pursuant to Ohio R. Civ. P. 55(B) and 60(B) to set aside a default judgment that was granted in favor of a property owner, as the seller had not been given the requisite time to respond pursuant to Lucas County, Ohio, Ct. C.P. Gen. Div. R. 5.04(D), she was not served with a copy of the motion, and she asserted that the parties had signed a settlement agreement with a release of all claims. Chiaverini, Inc. v. Little, — Ohio App. 3d —, 2007 Ohio 3683, — N.E. 2d —, 2007 Ohio App. LEXIS 3392 (July 20, 2007).

When a merchant sued a consumer on account, and the merchant's complaint did not specifically name the consumer, but the consumer did not appear after being served with process, the consumer was not entitled to relief, under Ohio R. Civ. P. 60(B), from the default judgment entered against him, because he did not show fraud, misrepresentation, mistake, or any other reason justifying relief from the judgment because he had the opportunity to appear in the trial court and raise his arguments, but he chose not to do so. River City Tire & Serv. Ctr. v. Erb, — Ohio App. 3d —, 2006 Ohio 6700, — N.E. 2d —, 2006 Ohio App. LEXIS 6598 (Dec. 12, 2006).

Motion to set aside default judgment

When an insurer filed a declaratory judgment action seeking a declaration that it was not obligated to indemnify its insureds due to an alleged injured party's suit against them, and a default judgment was entered in the insurer's favor, after which the alleged injured party moved to set aside that default, and subsequently moved to intervene, it was not error for the trial court to grant the motion to set aside the default judgment, even though it was technically filed by a non-party, because the trial court's order implicitly granting the motion to set the judgment aside also allowed the alleged injured party to intervene. State Farm Mut. Ins. Cos. v. Young, — Ohio App. 3d —, 2006 Ohio 3812, — N.E. 2d —, 2006 Ohio App. LEXIS 3784 (July 26, 2006).

Notice

Guarantors established that they were entitled to relief under Ohio R. Civ. P. 60(B)(5) from a default judgment entered against them since the trial court improperly entered the default judgment against them without providing them with the seven-day notice mandated by Ohio R. Civ. P. 55(A) for parties who had entered an appearance in the action. The guarantors' attorney filed a notice of appearance in the action after the motion for default judgment was filed but before the trial court entered the default judgment against the guarantors, and this constituted an "appearance" for purposes of Ohio R. Civ. P. 55(A). Meglan, Meglan & Co. v. Bostic, —

Ohio App. 3d —, 2006 Ohio 2270, — N.E. 2d —, 2006 Ohio App. LEXIS 2107 (May 9, 2006).

Employee's failure to contest damages after a default judgment was entered against him on a counterclaim was irrelevant to the issue of the lack of proper notice of a motion for default judgment as the default judgment effectively admitted the averments of the counterclaim and precluded the employee from asserting any affirmative defense that would have been considered an avoidance of the counterclaim. The prejudice resulting from the lack of notice lies in the admission of the counterclaim averments and preclusion of an affirmative defense, not the issue of damages. Shikner v. Solutions, — Ohio App. 3d —, 2006 Ohio 127, — N.E. 2d —, 2006 Ohio App. LEXIS 104 (Jan. 13, 2006).

Trial court did not abuse its discretion in denying a law client's motion to vacate a default judgment pursuant to Ohio R. Civ. P. 60(B)(1), where her claim of excusable neglect based on her alleged failure to have received sufficient notice of the default hearing lacked merit; rather, the client was served with the law firm's motion for default judgment, she received two letters, one via certified mail and one via regular mail, notifying her of the hearing, and there was sufficient and timely notice pursuant to Ohio R. Civ. P. 55(A). Rotatori v. Signer, — Ohio App. 3d —, 2006 Ohio 1354, — N.E. 2d —, 2006 Ohio App. LEXIS 1240 (Mar. 23, 2006).

As Ohio R. Civ. P. 55(A) only applied to a party who had appeared in an action, and a mortgage seller failed to appear where it only disputed the allegations of the mortgage buyer's claim in a letter directly to the buyer rather than in a responsive court pleading. Even if the letter had been deemed an appearance in the trial court proceeding, the failure to receive the requisite notice prior to entry of a default judgment was merely voidable and not void, and as the issue was not raised in the seller's motion for relief from default judgment under Ohio R. Civ. P. 60(B), it was waived for purposes of appeal. National City Mortgage Co. v. Johnson & Associates Financial Services, Inc., — Ohio App. 3d —, — N.E. 2d —, 2006 Ohio App. LEXIS 2216 (May 12, 2006).

Notice of application for default judgment

Once a party or the party's representative has appeared in a case as a matter of record in any manner, the notice and hearing required by Ohio R. Civ. P. 55(A) must be given that party before default judgment can be properly granted against the party, and even where a defendant's filings are subsequent to a plaintiff's motion for default, the defendant is deemed to have made an appearance and is entitled to the notice and hearing required under Rule 55(A). Columbia Credit Servs., Inc. v. Ruetschle, — Ohio App. 3d —, 2007 Ohio 4332, — N.E. 2d —, 2007 Ohio App. LEXIS 3870 (Aug. 24, 2007).

Trial court properly denied an insurer's motion under Ohio R. Civ. P. 60(B)(3) for relief from a default judgment, as there was no fraud, misrepresentation, or misconduct by a movant's counsel's failure to notify the insurer's counsel that a default judgment was forthcoming where the insurer had not appeared in the action pursuant to Ohio R. Civ. P. 5(A) and 55(A). Linquist v. Allstate, — Ohio App. 3d —, 2007 Ohio 4587, — N.E. 2d —, 2007 Ohio App. LEXIS 4121 (Aug. 27, 2007).

When counsel for a party did not appear at a scheduling conference at which he was ordered to appear after the trial court purportedly vacated its order granting counsel's motion to dismiss, under Ohio R. Civ. P. 12(B)(6), it was egregious error for the trial court to enter a default judgment against counsel's client because (1) the time within which counsel had to file an answer, under Ohio R. Civ. P. 12(A)(2), had not expired, (2), under Ohio R. Civ. P. 55(A), counsel's opponent had to apply to the court for default judgment, which he did not, and, (3) under Rule 55(A), counsel had to receive written notice of an application for default judgment at least seven days prior to a hearing on the application, which he did not.

Bowersmith v. UPS, 166 Ohio App. 3d 22, 2006 Ohio 1417, 848 N.E. 2d 919, 2006 Ohio App. LEXIS 1297 (Mar. 27, 2006).

Default judgment entered against a customer in a creditor's action on an open account was not void for lack of due process on the ground that the customer did not receive seven days' notice of the motion for default pursuant to Ohio R. Civ. P. 55(A) because the customer did not appear in the action until after the motion for default judgment was filed. A party who has not appeared prior to the filing of a motion for default judgment is not entitled to seven days' notice pursuant to Ohio R. Civ. P. 55(A). Carter-Jones Lumber Co. v. Willard, — Ohio App. 3d —, 2006 Ohio 6629, — N.E. 2d —, 2006 Ohio App. LEXIS 6551 (Dec. 15, 2006).

Relief from default judgment

Trial court erred in granting defendant's motion for a new trial pursuant to Ohio R. Civ. P. 59 because the trial court's grant of default judgment did not contain sufficient indicia of trial, in that neither counsel nor parties were at the non-oral hearing on the default judgment, and the issue of default was ancillary to the primary issue between the parties. Tipton v. Goodnight, — Ohio App. 3d —, 2006 Ohio 113, — N.E. 2d —, 2006 Ohio App. LEXIS 93 (Jan. 10, 2006).

Trial court properly allowed a mortgagee bank, as a post-judgment intervenor, to seek relief pursuant to Ohio R. Civ. P. 60(B)(5) in order to set aside a default judgment entered under Ohio R. Civ. P. 55 against a bankruptcy trustee by a mortgagor with respect to a dispute as to the mortgagor's dower interests in real property that the mortgagee was foreclosing upon, as the mortgagee had standing, the bankruptcy trustee was a cross-defendant, the motion to set aside the default judgment was made within one month after the judgment was obtained, and the trustee was not served at a valid address. The mortgagor met all three necessary elements to show it was entitled to relief from the default judgment. Standard Fed. Bank v. Staff, 168 Ohio App. 3d 14, 2006 Ohio 3601, 857 N.E. 2d 1245, 2006 Ohio App. LEXIS 3544 (July 14, 2006).

Service and default

When it was alleged that a default judgment was improperly entered against an excavating company because the company was never served with process, the company did not have to satisfy the requirements of Ohio R. Civ. P. 60(B) because a lack of service deprived the trial court of jurisdiction to consider the complaint, so that any judgment entered on that complaint was void ab initio. Tractor Serv. & Supply v. Excavating, — Ohio App. 3d —, 2007 Ohio 5255, — N.E. 2d —, 2007 Ohio App. LEXIS 4643 (Sept. 19, 2007).

When an attempt to serve an excavating company by certified mail was returned unclaimed, service by ordinary mail, under Ohio R. Civ. P. 4.6(D), was presumed complete when it was mailed, but an affidavit filed on behalf of the company alleging that service of process was never received required an oral hearing to determine if sufficient competent, credible evidence of nonservice existed, to show that a default judgment against the company was void ab initio, due to a lack of service and resulting lack of jurisdiction. Tractor Serv. & Supply v. Excavating, — Ohio App. 3d —, 2007 Ohio 5255, — N.E. 2d —, 2007 Ohio App. LEXIS 4643 (Sept. 19, 2007).

Small claims

Ohio R. Civ. P. 55(A), by its nature, was inapplicable to small claims matters, and Ohio Summit County Mun. Ct. R. 36 provided a quick, inexpensive means of resolving disputes, while Ohio R. Civ. P. 55(A) was more complex, requiring consideration of whether the party against whom default judgment was sought had appeared in the action, and if so, the party had to be served with written notice of the application for judgment at least seven days prior to the hearing on such application. Miller v. McStay, — Ohio App. 3d —, 2007 Ohio 369, — N.E. 2d —, 2007 Ohio App. LEXIS 335 (Jan. 31, 2007).

When, in a former tenant's suit in small claims court for return of a security deposit, the landlord did not appear at a mandatory mediation hearing, despite receiving notice that default judgment could be entered against him if he did not appear, Ohio Summit County Mun. Ct. R. 36 authorized the trial court to enter default judgment against the landlord, even though Ohio R. Civ. P. 55(A) did not apply to small claims proceedings. Miller v. McStay, — Ohio App. 3d —, 2007 Ohio 369, — N.E. 2d —, 2007 Ohio App. LEXIS 335 (Jan. 31, 2007).

Uncontested divorce

In adopting a magistrate's decision that precluded a mother from offering evidence on custody issues under Stark County, Ohio, Ct. C.P. Dom. Rel. Div. R. 13.01 because of her failure to answer the father's divorce complaint, a trial court did not improperly grant a default judgment under Ohio R. Civ. P. 55 which could not be granted in a domestic relations case under Ohio R. Civ. P. 75(F); the father never moved for a default judgment, no default judgment was granted, the matter was properly treated as an uncontested divorce, and it was not treated as an ex parte trial since the mother appeared at trial, testified, and was given the opportunity to cross-examine the father. Whited v. Whited, — Ohio App. 3d —, 2006 Ohio 5551, — N.E. 2d —, 2006 Ohio App. LEXIS 5546 (Oct. 16, 2006).

Vacating default judgment

Dismissal of an adult daughter's complaint, seeking to collect child support arrearage from her parents, was proper by a trial court where it lacked jurisdiction over the action because there was already an action pending in the juvenile court regarding the same issue, and the juvenile court had continuing and exclusive jurisdiction under RC §§ 2151.23(A)(11) and 3105.011. As the trial court lacked jurisdiction, it was proper for it to have vacated a default judgment entered earlier against the father and in favor of the daughter, pursuant to Ohio R. Civ. P. 55 and 60. Madewell v. Powell, — Ohio App. 3d —, 2006 Ohio 7046, — N.E. 2d —, 2006 Ohio App. LEXIS 7043 (Dec. 28, 2006).

Workers' compensation

When an employer sought judicial review of an Industrial Commission decision in a workers' compensation case, pursuant to RC § 4123.512, and the employee did not file a petition within 30 days of the employer's notice of appeal, as required by RC § 4123.512(D), it was error for a trial court to enter the employee's default, under Ohio R. Civ. P. 55, because Rule 55 did not apply to these proceedings because the employee was not a party against whom a judgment for affirmative relief was sought. Klepinger v. Alterra Healthcare Corp., — Ohio App. 3d —, 2007 Ohio 3811, — N.E. 2d —, 2007 Ohio App. LEXIS 3463 (July 27, 2007).

RULE 56.   Summary judgment

(A) **For party seeking affirmative relief.** A party seeking to recover upon a claim, counterclaim, or cross-claim or to obtain a declaratory judgment may move with or without supporting affidavits for a summary judgment in the party's favor as to all or any part of the claim, counterclaim, cross-claim, or declaratory judgment action. A party may move for summary judgment at any time after the expiration of the time permitted under these rules for a responsive motion for pleading by the adverse party, or after service of a motion for summary judgment by the adverse party. If the action has been set for pretrial or trial, a motion for summary judgment may be made only with leave of court.

(B) **For defending party.** A party against whom a claim, counterclaim, or cross-claim is asserted or a declaratory judgment is sought may, at any time, move with or without supporting affidavits for a summary judgment in the party's favor as to all or any part of the claim, counterclaim, cross-claim, or declaratory judgment action. If the action has been set for pretrial or trial, a motion for summary judgment may be made only with leave of court.

(C) **Motion and proceedings.** The motion shall be served at least fourteen days before the time fixed for hearing. The adverse party prior to the day of hearing may serve and file opposing affidavits. Summary judgment shall be rendered forthwith if the pleadings, depositions, answers to interrogatories, written admissions, affidavits, transcripts of evidence, and written stipulations of fact, if any, timely filed in the action, show that there is no genuine issue as to any material fact and that the moving party is entitled to judgment as a matter of law. No evidence or stipulation may be considered except as stated in this rule. A summary judgment shall not be rendered unless it appears from the evidence or stipulation, and only from the evidence or stipulation, that reasonable minds can come to but one conclusion and that conclusion is adverse to the party against whom the motion for summary judgment is made, that party being entitled to have the evidence or stipulation construed most strongly in the party's favor. A summary judgment, interlocutory in character, may be rendered on the issue of liability alone although there is a genuine issue as to the amount of damages.

(D) **Case not fully adjudicated upon motion.** If on motion under this rule summary judgment is not rendered upon the whole case or for all the relief asked and a trial is necessary, the court in deciding the motion, shall examine the evidence or stipulation properly before it, and shall if practicable, ascertain what material facts exist without controversy and what material facts are actually and in good faith controverted. The court shall thereupon make an order on its journal specifying the facts that are without controversy, including the extent to which the amount of damages or other relief is not in controversy, and directing such further proceedings in the action as are just. Upon the trial of the action the facts so specified shall be deemed established and the trial shall be conducted accordingly.

(E) **Form of affidavits; further testimony; defense required.** Supporting and opposing affidavits shall be made on personal knowledge, shall set forth such facts as would be admissible in evidence, and shall show affirmatively that the affiant is competent to testify to the matters stated in the affidavit. Sworn or certified copies of all papers or parts of papers referred to in an affidavit shall be attached to or served with the affidavit. The court may permit affidavits to be supplemented or opposed by depositions or by further affidavits. When a motion for summary judgment is made and supported as provided in this rule, an adverse party may not rest upon the mere allegations or denials of the party's pleadings, but the party's response, by affidavit or as otherwise provided in this rule, must set forth specific facts showing that there is a genuine issue for trial. If the party does not so respond, summary judgment, if appropriate, shall be entered against the party.

(F) **When affidavits unavailable.** Should it appear from the affidavits of a party opposing the motion for summary judgment that the party cannot for sufficient reasons stated present by affidavit facts essential to justify the party's opposition, the court may refuse the application for judgment or may order a continuance to permit affidavits to be obtained or discovery to be had or may make such other order as is just.

(G) **Affidavits made in bad faith.** Should it appear to the satisfaction of the court at any time that any of the affidavits presented pursuant to this rule are presented in bad faith or solely for the purpose of delay, the court shall forthwith order the party employing them to pay to the other party the amount of the reasonable expenses which the filing of the affidavits caused the other party to incur, including reasonable attorney's fees, and any offending party or attorney may be adjudged guilty of contempt.

History: Amended, eff 7-1-76; 7-1-97; 7-1-99.

NOTES TO DECISIONS

ANALYSIS

Affidavits
— Contradicting prior testimony
— Experts
— Personal knowledge
Affirmative defenses
Briefs and memoranda of law
Burden of proof
Continuance
Continuance to conduct discovery
— Failure to rule on CivR 56(F) motion
Conversion of motion to dismiss
Court of claims
Criminal matters
Denial, generally
Depositions
Dismissal without prejudice
Evidence
— Authentication
— Construing evidence
— Court's duty to consider all materials
— Expert
— Nonconforming evidence
Failure to respond to motion
Findings
Grounds for summary judgment
Harmless error
Hearing
Judgment on pleadings
Leave of court
Motion to supplement
Notice and opportunity to respond
Partial summary judgment
Party not requesting summary judgment
Reconsideration
Small claims court
Successive motions
Time for filing or responding to motion

Affidavits

Affidavit submitted by plaintiff's counsel did not satisfy the personal knowledge requirement of CivR 56(E). A motel's incident report could be considered an exception to the hearsay rule, but would have to be properly incorporated into an affidavit by a person with knowledge of the circumstances surrounding the preparation of the report: Ray v. Ramada Inn North, 171 Ohio App. 3d 1, 2007 Ohio 1341, 869 N.E.2d 95, 2007 Ohio App. LEXIS 1220 (2007).

In a business invitee's suit to recover for injuries she sustained when she walked off of a lighted path on an owner's property and fell into a ravine, the affidavits of the invitee's friends, to the effect that they heard a security guard state that the invitee was not the first to fall into the ravine and that she would not be the last, were insufficient to establish a genuine issue of material fact as the affidavits did not provide the names of the employees who allegedly made the statements, the names of other guests who allegedly fell in that area, the dates or the time of day of the purported falls, the number of purported falls, or any circumstances surrounding the alleged falls. Further, even if there were falls at the same spot, that did nothing to lessen the duty of the invitee to recognize and protect herself against the darkness. Rezac v. Cuyahoga Falls Concerts, Inc., — Ohio App. 3d —, 2007 Ohio 703, — N.E. 2d —, 2007 Ohio App. LEXIS 639 (Feb. 21, 2007).

As nephew stated in his deposition that he learned in the spring of 1998 that his aunt would not go through with an oral contract for the purchase of land, his affidavit averring he did not learn of that decision until 1999 did not create a genuine issue of fact that could defeat his aunt's motion for summary judgment based on the statute of limitations in RC § 2305.07. Harris v. Harris, — Ohio App. 3d —, 2007 Ohio 4385, — N.E. 2d —, 2007 Ohio App. LEXIS 3955 (Aug. 24, 2007).

Though a business invitee, in support of his memorandum in opposition to a property owner's motion for summary judgment, filed an affidavit averring that he looked at the water through which he was walking before he slipped and fell on algae under the water but could not see the algae due to the discoloration of the water from the lights and sunlight, the affidavit had to be disregarded because the statements in the affidavit contradicted the invitee's statements in his earlier deposition that he was not paying attention to the water as he was walking through it. Sherlock v. Shelly Co., — Ohio App. 3d —, 2007 Ohio 4522, — N.E. 2d —, 2007 Ohio App. LEXIS 4061 (Sept. 4, 2007).

In light of the Ohio Supreme Court's opinion in Byrd v. Smith, 110 Ohio St. 3d 24, 2006 Ohio 3455, 850 N.E.2d 47, 2006 Ohio LEXIS 2153, to the extent prior decisions from the Court of Appeals of Ohio, Ninth Judicial District, appear to hold that a nonmoving party may never defeat a properly supported motion for summary judgment with a "self-serving" affidavit, they are overruled. Stone v. Cazeau, — Ohio App. 3d —, 2007 Ohio 6213, — N.E. 2d —, 2007 Ohio App. LEXIS 5465 (Nov. 26, 2007).

Opposing affidavit was not absolutely necessary in response to a summary judgment motion. Filipovic v. Dash, — Ohio App. 3d —, 2006 Ohio 2809, — N.E. 2d —, 2006 Ohio App. LEXIS 2629 (May 22, 2006).

Vehicle manufacturer, as a lender under a retail installment contract with a vehicle owner, failed to meet its burden of proof under Ohio R. Civ. P. 56 in its motion for summary judgment with respect to its action seeking recovery of a deficiency judgment on the amount due after the vehicle was repossessed, as the documents offered in support of the summary judgment motion were not within Rule 56(E) and were improperly considered by the trial court where they were not incorporated by reference into an affidavit that was based on personal knowledge pursuant to Rule 56(F); as the lender failed to meet its burden under RC § 1317.16(B) of showing that the vehicle disposition was done in a commercially reasonable manner, that the notice of sale was properly published, and that the notice of sale was sent to the owner, summary judgment should have been denied. Daimler Chrysler Servs. North America v. Lennington, — Ohio App. 3d —, 2006 Ohio 1546, — N.E. 2d —, 2006 Ohio App. LEXIS 1445 (Mar. 31, 2006).

In ruling on a rental car company's motion for summary judgment, the trial court properly relied on the affidavit of the company's claims manager, who averred that the rental agreement attached to his affidavit was a true copy of the agreement entered into between the renter and the company, because, under Ohio R. Civ. P. 56, the affidavit was used to authenticate the rental agreement. Lane v. McFarland, — Ohio App. 3d —, 2006 Ohio 3681, — N.E. 2d —, 2006 Ohio App. LEXIS 3634 (July 20, 2006).

In a pedestrian's suit to recover for injuries that he sustained when he was struck by a recreational vehicle (RV), which was being pushed by a tow truck and being operated by an operator, while the operator stated in a second affidavit that he did not know that the RV's brakes did not work and that he did not put the RV in neutral, the facts averred in the second affidavit could not create an issue of fact because the statements in the second affidavit contradicted the statements in the operator's first affidavit, and the operator failed to give an explanation for this contradiction. Chehi v. Keifer, — Ohio App. 3d —, 2006 Ohio 5904, — N.E. 2d —, 2006 Ohio App. LEXIS 5869 (Nov. 9, 2006).

In property owners' trespass suit against a utility company, the trial court properly denied the company's motion for summary judgment on the basis of the existence of an easement by prescription because the claim relied solely on an affidavit, which was not filed until two years after the issue had been decided. The inclusion of this affidavit in a separate motion for summary judgment made almost two years after the issue of prescriptive easement had been decided failed to meet either the evidentiary or time requirements of Ohio R. Civ. P. 56(C). Ranallo v. First Energy Corp., — Ohio App. 3d —, 2006 Ohio 6105, — N.E. 2d —, 2006 Ohio App. LEXIS 6028 (Nov. 17, 2006).

Summary judgment under Ohio R. Civ. P. 56(C) was improperly granted to driver of car in suit brought by passenger in car one to recover for injuries sustained when car two struck car one as it made turn across traffic. Trial court had insufficient information to determine whether allegations in affidavit to effect that insurance agent had said that driver was speeding were hearsay and, if so, whether exceptions applied, in that the driver of car two failed to meet his burden of demonstrating that the statement should be stricken; thus, an issue of material fact existed, and summary judgment was improper. Luke v. Tonner, — Ohio App. 3d —, 2006 Ohio 6120, — N.E. 2d —, 2006 Ohio App. LEXIS 6093 (Nov. 17, 2006).

Suit alleging that a property owner was liable for a child's injuries occurring when the child built a bike ramp out of a barrel and plywood found on the owner's land was properly dismissed on summary judgment because the attractive nuisance doctrine did not apply as a barrel and plywood did not involve unreasonable risk of serious bodily injury, and the child knew of the danger involved in jumping his bicycle. The child's attempt to contradict his deposition testimony that he knew of the danger of jumping his bike over a ramp by submitting a contradictory subsequent affidavit was insufficient to create a genuine issue of material fact. McDaniels v. Sovereign Homes, — Ohio App. 3d —, 2006 Ohio 6149, — N.E. 2d —, 2006 Ohio App. LEXIS 6112 (Nov. 21, 2006).

— Contradicting prior testimony

While an ex-husband's affidavit somewhat contradicted his deposition testimony and could not be used to create a genuine issue of material fact in response to a motion for summary judgment, the affidavit of another witness, a non-party to the action, created a genuine issue of material fact and could be used to defeat the motion for summary judgment. Walker v. Bunch, — Ohio App. 3d —, 2006 Ohio 4680, — N.E. 2d —, 2006 Ohio App. LEXIS 4603 (Sept. 5, 2006).

— Experts

Employer's motion for summary judgment should have been denied where it merely stated that the claimant could not prove his case after the exclusion of the testimony of his expert witness. The employee had no duty to offer "the opinion testimony of any other expert witness" absent the employer's pointing to any materials listed in CivR 56(C): Brown v. Mabe, 170 Ohio App. 3d 13, 2007 Ohio 90, 865 N.E.2d 934, 2007 Ohio App. LEXIS 96 (2007).

— Personal knowledge

While an employee asserted that the trial court wrongly relied on two individuals' depositions submitted by the employer in the employee's employer intentional tort claim, alleging that neither of the two individuals actually worked at the plant where the accident occurred, the individuals attested that they were making their affidavit based on their personal knowledge. This was sufficient to meet the requirement of Ohio R. Civ. P. 56(E); thus, the court refused to disregard the individuals' affidavits. Schaad v. Valley Proteins, Inc., — Ohio App. 3d —, 2006 Ohio 5273, — N.E. 2d —, 2006 Ohio App. LEXIS 5253 (July 28, 2006).

Affirmative defenses

Plaintiff or counterclaimant moving for summary judgment does not bear the initial burden of addressing the nonmoving party's affirmative defenses: Todd Dev. Co. v. Morgan, 116 Ohio St. 3d 461, 2008 Ohio 87, 880 N.E.2d 88, 2008 Ohio LEXIS 20 (2007).

Briefs and memoranda of law

Appellant failed to demonstrate how he was prejudiced by a trial court's failure to provide notice of the deadline to file a brief in opposition to appellee's summary judgment motion before ruling on the motion as appellant, who had been given three months to respond to appellee's motion, had filed a brief in opposition to the motion, which the trial court considered in deciding the motion. Moreover, Summit County, Ohio, Ct. C.P. R. 7.14(C)(1) requires that a non-moving party must file its brief in opposition to summary judgment within fourteen days of service of the motion; thus, the trial court was not required to notify the parties of the deadlines for submitting briefs since the local rule provided sufficient notice of the submission deadlines. Marino v. Oriana House, Inc., — Ohio App. 3d —, 2007 Ohio 1823, — N.E. 2d —, 2007 Ohio App. LEXIS 1664 (Apr. 18, 2007).

In property owners' trespass suit, summary judgment was improperly granted to a utility company on ground that the company had a license coupled with an interest to maintain utility poles on the owners' property because the only issue raised and argued in the trial court was whether the company, by virtue of an easement, was entitled to erect utility poles on the owners' property. While the issue was raised in the company's reply brief to the owners' brief in opposition, reply briefs are limited to matters in rebuttal, and a party may not raise new issues for the first time in such a brief. Ranallo v. First Energy Corp., — Ohio App. 3d —, 2006 Ohio 6105, — N.E. 2d —, 2006 Ohio App. LEXIS 6028 (Nov. 17, 2006).

Burden of proof

Neighbor's argument that a property owner failed to meet its burden as the moving party on a motion for summary judgment because it omitted citation to legal authority in its summary judgment motion was rejected. Ohio R. Civ. P. 56 does not mandate the use of legal citations. Harvest Land Co-op, Inc. v. Sandlin, — Ohio App. 3d —, 2006 Ohio 4207, — N.E. 2d —, 2006 Ohio App. LEXIS 4140 (Aug. 14, 2006).

Continuance

Trial court did not abuse its discretion by denying the motion for a continuance by the former member of the single's corporation to pursue further discovery, in order to develop his opposition to the summary judgment motion, because he did not file an affidavit in support of his motion for a continuance stating the reasons justifying an extension, as required by Ohio R. Civ. P. 56(F). There had to be a factual basis stated and reasons given why the member could not present facts essential to his opposition to the motion. Sherman v. Glass City Singles, — Ohio App. 3d —, 2007 Ohio 5997, — N.E. 2d —, 2007 Ohio App. LEXIS 5241 (Nov. 9, 2007).

Continuance to conduct discovery

As the appellant failed to support her request for additional time under CivR 56(F), as required by that rule, the court could not abuse its discretion in denying the request: Ramos v. Khawli, 181 Ohio App. 3d 176, 2009 Ohio 798, 908 N.E.2d 495, 2009 Ohio App. LEXIS 661 (2009).

Trial court abused its discretion by denying the motion under CivR 56(F) where the party seeking discovery had not succeeded in obtaining discovery under its prior motions: Scaccia v. Dayton Newspapers, Inc., 170 Ohio App. 3d 471, 2007 Ohio 869, 867 N.E.2d 874, 2007 Ohio App. LEXIS 770 (2007).

Under Ohio R. Civ. P. 56(F), a party who seeks a continuance for further discovery is not required to specify what facts he hopes to discover, especially where the facts are in the control of the party moving for summary judgment, but a trial court must be convinced that there is a likelihood of discovering some such facts, and lack of diligence in pursuing discovery by the party moving under Rule 56(F) militates against grant of a delay, but generally the trial court should exercise its discretion in favor of a party seeking further time for discovery under Rule 56(F). Drake Constr. Co. v. Kemper House Mentor, Inc., 170 Ohio App. 3d 19, 2007 Ohio 120, 865 N.E.2d 938, 2007 Ohio App. LEXIS 99 (2007).

In a consumer's "lemon law" suit against a vehicle manufacturer, under RC § 1345.71 et seq., it was not an abuse of discretion for a trial court to hold that the manufacturer's second Ohio R. Civ. P. 56(F) motion was untimely because that motion was filed after a response deadline proposed in the manufacturer's first Rule 56(F) motion, even though the second motion was timely under the trial court's original scheduling order, and the manufacturer had reasonable and constructive notice that the deadline the manufacturer had proposed in the manufacturer's first motion was adopted. Evans v. Mazda Motors of Am., — Ohio App. 3d —, 2007 Ohio 4622, — N.E. 2d —, 2007 Ohio App. LEXIS 4164 (2007).

Even though various motions for summary judgment were pending before the trial court, the joint motion for continuance filed by plaintiff and defendants did not request a delay in the trial court's resolution of those motions; that is, although the parties requested an extension of the discovery cutoff, they did not move, pursuant to Ohio R. Civ. P. 56(F), for a delay in the trial court's consideration of the summary judgment motions pending further discovery. Thus, the trial court did not err in ruling on the motions without granting a continuance. Scott v. Hertz Corp., — Ohio App. 3d —, 2006 Ohio 4982, — N.E. 2d —, 2006 Ohio App. LEXIS 4924 (Sept. 26, 2006).

Trial court did not abuse its discretion in permitting an ex-husband to file his motion for summary judgment out of rule. The ex-wife had not shown that she was prejudiced by the trial court's decision; instead, the docket indicated that the ex-wife was allowed time to respond to the motion for summary judgment and that she did not ask for any additional time. Sumser-Armstrong v. Armstrong, — Ohio App. 3d —, 2006 Ohio 1924, — N.E. 2d —, 2006 Ohio App. LEXIS 1764 (Apr. 17, 2006).

Since a policyholder did not seek a continuance, pursuant to Ohio R. Civ. P. 56(F), to allow him to conduct further discovery, he could not complain that the trial court should have granted additional discovery before deciding defendants' motions for summary judgment. MacConnell v. Safeco Prop., — Ohio App. 3d —, 2006 Ohio 2910, — N.E. 2d —, 2006 Ohio App. LEXIS 2735 (June 9, 2006).

Trial court did not err in refusing to grant appellant a continuance to conduct further discovery before she responded to a father's motion for summary judgment because, while appellant pointed out the issues about which she hoped to gather additional evidence, she did not explain why no steps had been taken to gather such evidence within the time that had already elapsed. Shirdon v. Houston, — Ohio App. 3d —, 2006 Ohio 4521, — N.E. 2d —, 2006 Ohio App. LEXIS 4447 (Sept. 1, 2006).

In a medical malpractice action, a trial court did not abuse its discretion under Ohio R. Civ. P. 6(B) in denying a patient's motion for an extension of time to pursue further discovery in opposition to summary judgment motions filed by a hospital and other defendants because the patient did not explain why discovery involved in the hospital's appeal from a discovery order was necessary in order to formulate his opposition and, in fact, he did not need such discovery; in addition, he failed to provide an affidavit in support of his motion as required by Ohio R. Civ. P. 56(F). Cook v. Toledo Hosp., — Ohio App. 3d —, 2006 Ohio 5278, — N.E. 2d —, 2006 Ohio App. LEXIS 5266 (Oct. 6, 2006).

When an inmate sued correctional officials for an alleged denial of recreation time and sought a stay on the officials' summary judgment motion until his discovery materials were returned to him, his request was properly considered an Ohio R. Civ. P. 56(F) motion for an extension of time to respond to the summary judgment motion, and, because it was not supported by an affidavit, as required by the Rule, the trial court properly ruled on the summary judgment motion without ruling on the motion for an extension, and the lack of an affidavit barred further review. Watley v. Coval, — Ohio App. 3d —, 2006 Ohio 5694, — N.E. 2d —, 2006 Ohio App. LEXIS 5689 (Oct. 31, 2006).

Patient's second Ohio R. Civ. P. 56(F) motion for extension of time to respond to motions for summary judgment filed by a doctor and a surgery center in the patient's medical malpractice suit was properly denied because the patient failed to explain why she needed the doctor's deposition to respond to the undisputed argument that the patient's complaint was untimely. She also provided no explanation as to why her second Ohio R. Civ. P. 56(F) motion was not filed until two months after her responses to the motions for summary judgment were due. Porter v. Ettinger, — Ohio App. 3d —, 2006 Ohio 6842, — N.E. 2d —, 2006 Ohio App. LEXIS 6747 (Dec. 22, 2006).

Contention that a trial court erred in granting summary judgment to appellees since appellants were not given adequate time to conduct discovery was rejected. Given the fact that seven months elapsed before one appellee was dismissed from the case and more than one year elapsed before judgment was granted in favor of the remaining appellees, and given the absence of a proper Ohio R. Civ. P. 56(F) request for more time to conduct depositions, the trial court did not abuse its discretion in the discovery process when ruling on the motions. State Farm Mut. Auto. Ins. Co. v. King, — Ohio App. 3d —, 2006 Ohio 336, — N.E. 2d —, 2006 Ohio App. LEXIS 315 (Jan. 30, 2006).

When a consumer sued a company and its sole proprietor, and the proprietor did not respond to the consumer's request for admissions, under Ohio R. Civ. P. 36(A), resulting in summary judgment being entered against the proprietor, the proprietor could not assert that this summary judgment was error, under Ohio R. Civ. P. 56(F), because the proprietor needed more time to pursue discovery, as the proprietor did not submit an affidavit detailing his reasons justifying an extension of time. Vilardo v. Sheets, — Ohio App. 3d —, 2006 Ohio 3473, — N.E. 2d —, 2006 Ohio App. LEXIS 3415 (July 3, 2006).

Party needing evidence to oppose a motion for summary judgment, but who failed to seek relief under Ohio R. Civ. P. 56(F) in the trial court, did not preserve his rights under the rules for purposes of appeal. Jackson v. Walker, — Ohio App. 3d —, 2006 Ohio 4351, — N.E. 2d —, 2006 Ohio App. LEXIS 4270 (Aug. 23, 2006).

— Failure to rule on CivR 56(F) motion

By never ruling on the motion seeking further time for discovery under CivR 56(F), the court denied it. This implicit denial resulted in substantial injustice to the party seeking a delay: Drake Constr. Co. v. Kemper House Mentor, Inc., 170 Ohio App. 3d 19, 2007 Ohio 120, 865 N.E.2d 938, 2007 Ohio App. LEXIS 99 (2007).

Conversion of motion to dismiss

Employer's contention that a trial court properly considered matters outside the pleadings in ruling on the employer's motion to dismiss was rejected as there was no evidence that the trial court provided notice to the parties that it intended to convert the employer's motion to dismiss into a motion for summary judgment. Goss v. Kmart Corp., — Ohio App. 3d —, 2007 Ohio 3200, — N.E. 2d —, 2007 Ohio App. LEXIS 2923 (June 22, 2007).

Court rejected plaintiff's contention that a trial court improperly converted an attorney's motion for summary judgment into a motion to dismiss without notice of conversion under Ohio R. Civ. P. 12(B). When a motion for summary judgment is converted into a motion to dismiss, notice of conversion does not have to be given. Sat Adlaka v. Giannini, — Ohio App. 3d —, 2006 Ohio 4611, — N.E. 2d —, 2006 Ohio App. LEXIS 4574 (Sept. 1, 2006).

Ohio R. Civ. P. 12(B)(6) motion based on res judicata as procedurally inappropriate as the prior civil actions did not appear in the complaint, and the procedural course required was to convert the motion to a summary judgment motion; the trial court's ruling on the Ohio R. Civ. P. 12(B)(6) motion obviated the need for an answer, so the trial court did not err in failing to grant the buyer's motion for default judgment. Suarez Corp. Indus. v. Biern, — Ohio App. 3d —, 2006 Ohio 1510, — N.E. 2d —, 2006 Ohio App. LEXIS 1410 (Mar. 27, 2006).

Court of claims

Because the plaintiff did not raise a declaratory judgment or RC § 2743.03(A)(2) argument in his motion for summary judgment, the court of appeals erred by granting summary judgment on grounds not specified in the motion. The exception under RC § 2743.03(A)(2) concerning actions in which the "sole relief" sought is a declaratory judgment, injunctive relief, or other equitable relief did not apply where the plaintiff also sought monetary damages: State ex rel. Sawicki v. Court of Common Pleas of Lucas Cty., 121 Ohio St. 3d 507, 2009 Ohio 1523, 905 N.E.2d 1192, 2009 Ohio LEXIS 897 (2009).

Criminal matters

As defendant inmate's request for post-conviction relief pursuant to RC § 2953.21 was civil in nature, the State of Ohio appropriately could request summary judgment under Ohio R. Civ. P. 56(C); the Ohio Rules of Civil Procedure governed postconviction proceedings. State v. Qualls, — Ohio App. 3d —, 2007 Ohio 3938, — N.E. 2d —, 2007 Ohio App. LEXIS 3579 (June 14, 2007).

Denial, generally

Trial court's ruling denying the defendants' motion for summary judgment was premature where it was not clear that the court considered the substance of the motion and the supporting materials filed with it before denying the motion: Hollins v. Shaffer, 182 Ohio App. 3d 282, 2009 Ohio 2136, 912 N.E.2d 637, 2009 Ohio App. LEXIS 1832 (2009).

Depositions

As a deposition of a driver-insured was not actually filed in the trial court, it was not proper summary judgment evidence pursuant to Ohio R. Civ. P. 56(C) in an action by the insureds against their insurer, seeking underinsured motorist coverage. However, where neither party objected on the record to the consideration of the deposition in the summary judgment proceeding, the trial court properly exercised its discretion to consider the nonconforming evidence. Whanger v. Grange Mut. Cas. Co., — Ohio App. 3d —, 2007 Ohio 3187, — N.E. 2d —, 2007 Ohio App. LEXIS 2966 (June 21, 2007).

Party's deposition taken in another case could properly be considered as just as good as an affidavit for purposes of summary judgment: Hastings Mut. Ins. v. Halatek, 174 Ohio App. 3d 252, 2007 Ohio 6923, 881 N.E. 2d 897, 2007 Ohio App. LEXIS 6070 (Dec. 11, 2007).

Trial court properly considered a party's deposition that was taken in another matter for purposes of determining whether there was a genuine issue of material fact to preclude summary judgment in a separate declaratory judgment action, as pursuant to Ohio R. Civ. P. 32(A) and 56(C), the deposition was just as good as an affidavit, which was permissible; the deposition was based on personal knowledge, the deponent was available to testify at trial, and it was only used for summary judgment purposes. Hastings Mut. Ins. v. Halatek, 174 Ohio App. 3d 252, 2007 Ohio 6923, 881 N.E. 2d 897, 2007 Ohio App. LEXIS 6070 (Dec. 11, 2007).

Depositions submitted by a property owner in support of its motion for summary judgment were not filed with the trial court, pursuant to Ohio R. Civ. P. 32(A) and, thus, could not be considered. Moore v. Tall Timbers Banquet & Conf. Ctr., — Ohio App. 3d —, 2006 Ohio 3249, — N.E. 2d —, 2006 Ohio App. LEXIS 3135 (June 22, 2006).

Trial court did not err in relying upon plaintiff's deposition testimony in rendering its decision even though defendant failed to file or otherwise authenticate the transcript prior to or at the time of the filing of defendant's motion for summary judgment because plaintiff failed to object to the unfiled deposition testimony and used the same testimony in her brief in opposition and her brief on appeal. Shreves v. Meridia Health Sys., — Ohio App. 3d —, 2006 Ohio 5724, — N.E. 2d —, 2006 Ohio App. LEXIS 5729 (Nov. 2, 2006).

Dismissal without prejudice

Trial court's grant of summary judgment was based on a procedural matter and was not an adjudication on the merits where it was based on a foreign corporation's noncompliance with RC § 1703.29. Thus the dismissal should have been without prejudice: Nat'l Crime Reporting, Inc. v. McCord & Akamine, LLP, 177 Ohio App. 3d 551, 2008 Ohio 3950, 895 N.E.2d 255, 2008 Ohio App. LEXIS 3314 (2008).

Evidence

Trial court erred in granting summary judgment to the mortgagee in a foreclosure action brought against mortgagors as a condition precedent to the acceleration clause was a notice of default, and the mortgagors' affidavit established that they did not receive the notice of default. While the mortgagee attached a demand letter to the reply, there was no affidavit accompanying the document to authenticate or verify it under Ohio R. Civ. P. 56(E). The trial court should not have considered it when it rendered its decision. Wells Fargo Bank, N.A. v. Shalvey, — Ohio App. 3d —, 2007 Ohio 3928, — N.E. 2d —, 2007 Ohio App. LEXIS 3535 (July 26, 2007).

Trial court erred in granting summary judgment to a franchisor after converting the franchisor's Ohio R. Civ. P. 12(B)(6) motion to an Ohio R. Civ. P. 56(C) motion for summary judgment without notice to the parties of the conversion. Since none of the evidentiary materials was supported or opposed by affidavits made on personal knowledge, as required by Ohio R. Civ. P. 56(E), the trial court, pursuant to Ohio R. Civ. P. 56(C), could not consider the evidence before it and, thus, erred when it granted summary judgment to the franchisor. Ihenacho v. Coverall of S. Ohio, 173 Ohio App. 3d 13, 2007 Ohio 4206, 877 N.E.2d 351, 2007 Ohio App. LEXIS 3801 (2007).

In a medical malpractice action, when a doctor moved for summary judgment, alleging that the suing patient's identified expert was an ophthalmologist who was not qualified to give an opinion about whether the doctor's acts as a general surgeon met the applicable standard of care, the motion was only supported by the trial court's pretrial order giving the patient until a date certain to identify lay and expert witnesses, so the motion was not supported by an affidavit or other evidentiary quality material listed in Ohio R. Civ. P. 56(C), and it was error to grant the motion. Young v. Spangler, — Ohio App. 3d —, 2006 Ohio 401, — N.E. 2d —, 2006 Ohio App. LEXIS 343 (Jan. 30, 2006).

In a defamation case between insurance agencies, a summary judgment was not properly supported, under Ohio R. Civ. P. 56(C), because the movant only attached a reported judicial decision, and this was not the type of evidentiary material listed in Rule 56(C) which could be used to support a summary judgment motion. Carl Ralston Ins. Agency v. Kenneth A. Boldt Ins. Agency, — Ohio App. 3d —, 2006 Ohio 3916, — N.E. 2d —, 2006 Ohio App. LEXIS 3880 (Aug. 2, 2006).

There was no requirement in Ohio R. Civ. P. 56 that a moving party support its motion for summary judgment with any affirmative evidence, i.e., affidavits or similar materials produced by the movant, and, instead, it bore only the initial burden of informing the trial court of the basis for the motion, and identifying those portions of the record that demonstrated the absence of a genuine issue of material fact on the essential element(s) of the nonmoving party's claims. Jackson v. Walker, — Ohio App. 3d —, 2006 Ohio 4351, — N.E. 2d —, 2006 Ohio App. LEXIS 4270 (Aug. 23, 2006).

— Authentication

Since an investigative report generated after a workplace injury was never authenticated, it should not have been considered by the trial court in ruling on a motion for summary judgment. Switka v. City of Youngstown, — Ohio App. 3d —, 2006 Ohio 4617, — N.E. 2d —, 2006 Ohio App. LEXIS 4575 (Sept. 1, 2006).

— Construing evidence

Trial court erred by granting summary judgment where it determined issues of witness credibility and weighed conflicting evidence of record: Stewart v. Urig, 176 Ohio App. 3d 658, 2008 Ohio 3215, 893 N.E.2d 245, 2008 Ohio App. LEXIS 2741 (2008).

Employee's argument that a trial court failed to construe the evidence in his favor when ruling on an employer's motion for summary judgment filed in the employee's intentional tort action was rejected because there was no evidence to support the employee's assertion. Instead, the trial court twice expressly stated that summary judgment motions required a court to construe the evidence most strongly in favor of the non-moving party, and it also stated that, in ruling on the employer's motion, it had construed the facts most strongly in favor of the employee. Vance v. Akers Packaging Serv., — Ohio App. 3d —, 2006 Ohio 7032, — N.E. 2d —, 2006 Ohio App. LEXIS 7025 (Dec. 28, 2006).

Summary judgment was error because the trial court effectively weighed the evidence and credibility of the employee's allegations and enforced its own factual conclusion regarding the evidence. The trial court assessed the factual circumstances that occurred subsequent to the incident in question, in order to determine that the employee's submission to the manager's demands had been voluntary. The employee produced sufficient probative evidence to establish a genuine dispute over material facts in her quid pro quo sexual harassment case. Scarvelli v. Melmont Holding Co., — Ohio App. 3d —, 2006 Ohio 4019, — N.E. 2d —, 2006 Ohio App. LEXIS 3986 (Aug. 7, 2006).

— Court's duty to consider all materials

Where a trial court granted summary judgment to an insurer in its declaratory judgment action, wherein the trial court determined that it had no obligation to provide coverage to an insured for an underlying action based on the claims asserted in the underlying original complaint, such was not in compliance with Ohio R. Civ. P. 56(C) because an amended complaint that asserted additional claims had been filed and the trial court had an obligation to review all pleadings. The trial court's order was a partial summary judgment, in that all claims were not resolved, but as the necessary language under Ohio R. Civ. P. 54(B) was not included, the grant of partial summary judgment was not a final appealable order pursuant to RC § 2505.02, and the insured's appeal taken therefrom required dismissal. Westfield Ins. Co. v. Towne Inv. II, — Ohio App. 3d —, 2006 Ohio 5830, — N.E. 2d —, 2006 Ohio App. LEXIS 5764 (Nov. 3, 2006).

— Expert

In an administrator's wrongful death suit, the trial court improperly held that the administrator was not allowed to rely on expert testimony offered by another party in opposition to appellees' motion for summary judgment. The administrator did not necessarily need to rely on an expert for purposes of summary judgment who would also be his expert at trial especially in light of the fact that, at the time that the motion for summary judgment was filed, no trial date had been set, and the administrator presumably had several additional months to obtain experts for trial if the expert was truly unwilling to testify for him. Roberts v. Frasier, — Ohio App. 3d —, 2006 Ohio 312, — N.E. 2d —, 2006 Ohio App. LEXIS 263 (Jan. 20, 2006).

— Nonconforming evidence

As a trial court held an evidentiary hearing on competing summary judgment motions and it granted summary judgment to various defendants based upon the oral testimony of a witness at that hearing, such was error, as the trial court was not permitted to rely on such new testimony in making its summary judgment disposition. Transcribed testimony was admissible in the event a subsequent summary judgment proceeding was held. Ohio Civ. Rights Comm'n v. Triangle Inv. Co., — Ohio App. 3d —, 2007 Ohio 2937, — N.E. 2d —, 2007 Ohio App. LEXIS 2688 (June 14, 2007).

Even if a trial court had given proper notice of its intention to convert an employer's motion to dismiss into a motion for summary judgment, it relied on evidence not permitted by Ohio R. Civ. P. 56 in granting summary judgment in favor of the employer. Since the employer's motion to dismiss its former employee's disability discrimination claim was predicated on the fact that a valid collective bargaining agreement (CBA) was in effect, that the CBA covered the employee, and that the application of the CBA operated to preclude the employee's claims, the trial court's reliance on the CBA, which was simply attached to the motion to dismiss and was not properly authenticated by incorporation by reference in a properly framed affidavit pursuant to Ohio R. Civ. P. 56(E), despite the fact that it held a hearing on the employer's motion, was reversible error. Goss v. Kmart Corp., — Ohio App. 3d —, 2007 Ohio 3200, — N.E. 2d —, 2007 Ohio App. LEXIS 2923 (June 22, 2007).

Although final judgments attached to a warden's motion for summary judgment in an inmate's habeas corpus action, which were intended to support the warden's claim that the inmate had not served the maximum term of his sentences and that he was accordingly not entitled to immediate release by habeas corpus, were not properly certified or accompanied by a proper affidavit pursuant to Ohio R. Civ. P. 56(C), they were properly considered where the inmate did not object thereto. Some of the factual assertions in the inmate's motion were consistent with the contents of the copy of the final judgment in one of the inmate's criminal proceedings, and there were no defects found in the judgments which made the authenticity thereof questionable. Robinson v. Gansheimer, — Ohio App. 3d —, 2007 Ohio 3845, — N.E. 2d —, 2007 Ohio App. LEXIS 3481 (July 27, 2007).

Common pleas court properly rejected a claim form and recorded statement attached to appellant's memorandum in response to a hotel's summary judgment motion since neither the claim form nor the recorded statement indicated who prepared the report or statement; appellant's attorney, who submitted an affidavit stating that the documents were "true copies" of the form and statement, did not submit an affidavit stating that he had conducted the audio interview of appellant; and the documents were not properly qualified under Ohio R. Evid. 803(6) as they were not incorporated into an affidavit by a person with knowledge of the circumstances surrounding the preparation of the report. Ray v. Ramada Inn North, 171 Ohio App. 3d 1, 2007 Ohio 1341, 869 N.E.2d 95, 2007 Ohio App. LEXIS 1220 (2007).

Trial court did not abuse its discretion in not considering nonconforming evidence pursuant to Ohio R. Civ. P. 56(C) offered by a police dispatcher and her husband in their action against a city and a police chief, as despite no objection having been filed to the lack of certification on the depositions sought to be considered, the tial court was not obligated to consider the evidence. Armaly v. City of Wapakoneta, — Ohio App. 3d —, 2006 Ohio 3629, — N.E. 2d —, 2006 Ohio App. LEXIS 3562 (July 17, 2006).

While a passenger contended that her expert was unable to fully inspect a rental company's vehicle that had been involved in an accident because the company's expert performed a destructive examination of the vehicle, her expert's contention that the vehicle could not be inspected was set forth in a report that had neither been notarized nor incorporated by reference in an affidavit and, thus, could not be considered. Scott v. Hertz Corp., — Ohio App. 3d —, 2006 Ohio 4982, — N.E. 2d —, 2006 Ohio App. LEXIS 4924 (Sept. 26, 2006).

In a defamation case between insurance agencies, when an opponent of a summary judgment motion attached a trial court's docket sheet, referring to another trial court case, to its memorandum in opposition, this did not require the trial court to consider the other case because the opponent did not file an affidavit, under Ohio R. Civ. P. 56(E), referring to pleadings in that case with sworn or certified copies of the pleadings. Carl Ralston Ins. Agency v. Kenneth A. Boldt Ins. Agency, — Ohio App. 3d —, 2006 Ohio 3916, — N.E. 2d —, 2006 Ohio App. LEXIS 3880 (Aug. 2, 2006).

Failure to respond to motion

Summary judgment was properly granted to the State of Ohio, Crime Victims Reparation Fund, on its claims for reimbursement of reparations paid to victims of a perpetrator's criminal acts because the Fund demonstrated the absence of a genuine issue of fact, and the perpetrator failed to respond with materials setting forth facts showing the existence of a genuine issue of fact, as required by Ohio R. Civ. P. 56(E). The fact that the perpetrator was a pro se litigant did not require that he be treated any differently than a member

of the bar. State v. Pryor, — Ohio App. 3d —, 2007 Ohio 4275, — N.E. 2d —, 2007 Ohio App. LEXIS 3935 (Aug. 21, 2007).

Even though a patron never filed a brief in opposition to appellees' motion for summary judgment, the trial court did not err in ruling on appellees' motion after giving the parties the appropriate time in which to file response briefs. The patron never gave any indication of an intent to file a response to the motion for summary judgment and never requested a simple extension of time. Collins v. Marc Glassman, Inc., — Ohio App. 3d —, 2006 Ohio 3493, — N.E. 2d —, 2006 Ohio App. LEXIS 3454 (July 6, 2006).

Findings

Trial court did not err when it did not set forth findings of fact and conclusions of law in granting a property owner's motion for summary judgment because, pursuant to Ohio R. Civ. P. 52, findings of fact and conclusions of law were not necessary when a trial court rules on a party's motion for summary judgment. Burdette v. Stevens, — Ohio App. 3d —, 2007 Ohio 4604, — N.E. 2d —, 2007 Ohio App. LEXIS 4140 (Aug. 30, 2007).

Since issues raised by appellant in his motion for summary judgment, to the effect that the company had not timely responded to appellant's requests for admissions and that those admissions established appellant's case and disproved the company's counterclaim, did not require the type of fact-finding in which a jury normally engaged, the issues were not rendered moot by the subsequent trial. Grenga v. K.D. Mach., Inc., — Ohio App. 3d —, 2007 Ohio 6911, — N.E. 2d —, 2007 Ohio App. LEXIS 6058 (Nov. 28, 2007).

Grounds for summary judgment

It is reversible error to award summary judgment on grounds not specified in the motion for summary judgment. A passing allusion to a contested element is not sufficient to delineate it with specificity as the basis for a motion for summary judgment: Patterson v. Ahmed, 176 Ohio App. 3d 596, 2008 Ohio 362, 893 N.E.2d 198, 2008 Ohio App. LEXIS 329 (2008).

In a dispute over the sale of a business, a trial court erred in granting summary judgment to the business buyers on a ground that was not raised or argued by them in their motion for summary judgment pursuant to Ohio R. Civ. P. 56(C). The fact that the issue was discussed in a pre-trial proceeding was not sufficient because the sellers did not have an opportunity to address the issue, as they would have if it had been properly raised in the motion papers, and the ruling by the trial court was reversible error. KRK, Inc. v. Crone, — Ohio App. 3d —, 2006 Ohio 4415, — N.E. 2d —, 2006 Ohio App. LEXIS 4340 (Aug. 28, 2006).

Harmless error

Trial court did not abuse its discretion under Ohio R. Civ. P. 56(C) and (E) in denying a decedent's second wife's motion to strike exhibits attached to the decedent's sister's reply brief in a summary judgment proceeding with respect to who was entitled to the decedent's life insurance proceeds, as the life insurance policy was properly considered as part of the pleading because it was attached to the initial complaint. The separation agreement between the decedent and his second wife was not properly authenticated pursuant to Rule 56(C), but the trial court did not base its decision on any term thereof and it did not reference that document in its decision, and any error was harmless because the trial court's decision was wholly based on applicability of a controlling statute. Nationwide Life Ins. Co. v. Kallberg, — Ohio App. 3d —, 2007 Ohio 2041, — N.E. 2d —, 2007 Ohio App. LEXIS 1930 (Apr. 30, 2007).

Hearing

Trial court did not err in ruling on appellant's motion for summary judgment without providing notice of a hearing because a trial court is not required by rule to even set a hearing. Marino v. Oriana House, Inc., — Ohio App. 3d —, 2007 Ohio 1823, — N.E. 2d —, 2007 Ohio App. LEXIS 1664 (Apr. 18, 2007).

Ohio R. Civ. P. 56(C) and the local practice rules for the Summit County, Ohio, Court of Common Pleas did not require that a trial court hold a hearing on a motion for summary judgment, as Summit County, Ohio, Ct. C.P. R. 7.14(B) provided that a trial court, in its sole discretion, could grant an oral argument on any motion, and Summit County, Ohio, Ct. C.P. R. 7.14(C)(1) set out the time frame in which a party opposing a motion for summary judgment could file a brief in opposition, as well as the time in which the movant could file a reply brief in support of the motion. Elite Designer Homes, Inc. v. Landmark, — Ohio App. 3d —, 2006 Ohio 4079, — N.E. 2d —, 2006 Ohio App. LEXIS 4041 (Aug. 9, 2006).

Trial court's denial of a lessee's request to reschedule a hearing on a lessor's motion for summary judgment was not an abuse of discretion. While the lessee averred that he did not have access to his files since he was incarcerated, the lessee had access to his files for more than two months after the motion for summary judgment was filed in order to allow him to formulate a response to the motion before he was incarcerated. Polaris Ventures IV v. Silverman, — Ohio App. 3d —, 2006 Ohio 4138, — N.E. 2d —, 2006 Ohio App. LEXIS 4081 (Aug. 9, 2006).

Judgment on pleadings

Trial court erred by converting the CivR 12(B)(6) motion into a motion for summary judgment and then granting that motion without notice to the parties of the conversion. None of the materials submitted was supported or opposed by affidavits made on personal knowledge as required by CivR 56(E): Ihenacho v. Coverall of S. Ohio, 173 Ohio App. 3d 13, 2007 Ohio 4206, 877 N.E.2d 351, 2007 Ohio App. LEXIS 3801 (2007).

Leave of court

Trial court did not abuse its discretion in granting a sheriff leave, pursuant to Ohio R. Civ. P. 56(B), to file a motion for summary judgment after the case had been set for trial. Graham v. Allen County Sheriff's Office, — Ohio App. 3d —, 2006 Ohio 4183, — N.E. 2d —, 2006 Ohio App. LEXIS 4098 (Aug. 14, 2006).

In a workers' compensation claimant's appeal from the Industrial Commission of Ohio's denial of his workers' compensation claim, the employer's motion to supplement its answer so as to allege, as an affirmative defense, that the claimant, since the time that the appeal was filed, had executed a settlement agreement covering the claims at issue in the appeal was properly granted. The employer followed the appropriate procedure in raising its affirmative defenses, and since the supplemental answer raised an affirmative defense that could bar the claims, the trial court did not abuse its discretion in allowing the employer to file its motion for summary judgment even though the motion was not made until after the case was set for pretrial. Zestos v. Powertrain Div., GMC, — Ohio App. 3d —, 2006 Ohio 4545, — N.E. 2d —, 2006 Ohio App. LEXIS 4511 (Sept. 5, 2006).

Motion to supplement

Trial court abused its discretion in overruling the laborer's motion to supplement his brief in opposition to motions for summary judgment filed against him with the affidavit of a safety expert on the ground that the laborer had been unable to obtain the expert's sworn statement at the time that his response was due and that no new claims were being added because the trial court had stated that discovery was to continue expeditiously, the laborer had apprised the opposing party that he was reserving the right to call an additional expert, and no prejudice had been shown especially since the case had not yet been set for trial. Ross v. William E. Platten

Contr. Co., — Ohio App. 3d —, 2007 Ohio 5733, — N.E. 2d —, 2007 Ohio App. LEXIS 5017 (Oct. 25, 2007).

Notice and opportunity to respond

Contrary to a patient's contention, there was no conflict between Ohio R. Civ. P. 56(C) and Miami County, Ohio, Ct. C.P. R. 3.04, which sets the date for hearing on a summary judgment motion as twenty days after the motion is filed, because the local rule gave the patient notice of the date after which a summary judgment motion would be decided as well as the deadline for a response to such motion, which is consistent with Ohio R. Civ. P. 56(C). Since the patient failed to oppose the motion for summary judgment prior to the hearing date set in Miami County, Ohio, Ct. C.P. R. 3.04, the trial court properly granted summary judgment after the twenty days expired. Davis v. Valley, — Ohio App. 3d —, 2007 Ohio 1332, — N.E. 2d —, 2007 Ohio App. LEXIS 1227 (Mar. 23, 2007).

Since summary judgment in favor of appellee was an interlocutory order subject to revision, the trial court was in a position to comply with the requirement that it give the non-moving party notice of the date on or after a motion for summary judgment would be submitted for decision by vacating the summary judgment in favor of appellee and providing appellants the requisite notice. Pursuant to Ohio R. Civ. P. 56(C), the notice had to allow appellants at least 14 days before the submission date to respond. Turner v. C.G.R., Inc., — Ohio App. 3d —, 2006 Ohio 1580, — N.E. 2d —, 2006 Ohio App. LEXIS 1483 (Mar. 31, 2006).

Trial court abused its discretion by denying a landlord's motion to vacate an order awarding summary judgment to a tenant and dismissing the landlord's counterclaim following the landlord's absence from the initial pretrial conference because the oversight of the landlord's counsel in noting an incorrect time for the pretrial conference did not exhibit a deliberate act of ignoring a judicial directive such as constituted excusable neglect, the landlord asserted a meritorious defense, and filed the motion in a timely manner. The trial court also erred in granting the tenant's oral motion for summary judgment because the landlord never had a chance to respond and in dismissing the counterclaim because the trial court failed to give the landlord the notice required by Ohio R. Civ. P. 41(B)(1) prior to dismissal of the counterclaim. Maddox v. Ward, — Ohio App. 3d —, 2006 Ohio 4099, — N.E. 2d —, 2006 Ohio App. LEXIS 4073 (Aug. 10, 2006).

Trial court did not have to notify parties of the date of consideration of a motion for summary judgment or the deadlines for submitting briefs and Ohio R. Civ. P. 56 materials if a local rule of court provided sufficient notice of the hearing date or submission deadlines. Elite Designer Homes, Inc. v. Landmark, — Ohio App. 3d —, 2006 Ohio 4079, — N.E. 2d —, 2006 Ohio App. LEXIS 4041 (Aug. 9, 2006).

Partial summary judgment

Trial court did not err in issuing a nunc pro tunc order granting summary judgment to a former employee on all of the former employer's claims against the employee because nothing had been provided to refute the trial court's note that a clerical error occurred, and in any event, the trial court's actions did not prejudice either party, in that, following the initial ruling awarding partial summary judgment to the employee, the trial court retained jurisdiction over the remaining claim and would have been permitted to reconsider the employee's motion for summary judgment as to that claim. Facility Servs. & Sys. v. Vaiden, — Ohio App. 3d —, 2006 Ohio 2895, — N.E. 2d —, 2006 Ohio App. LEXIS 2789 (June 8, 2006).

Party not requesting summary judgment

CivR 56 does not permit a trial court to grant summary judgment to a party that has not requested it: S. Cohn & Son

Co. v. Kinstle, 174 Ohio App. 3d 81, 2007 Ohio 6237, 880 N.E.2d 965, 2007 Ohio App. LEXIS 5495 (2007).

Reconsideration

Trial court did not err in granting an employer's motion for summary judgment dismissing an employee's employer intentional tort claim nine months after orally denying the employer's summary judgment motion because the trial court neither journalized its interlocutory decision nor certified it under Ohio R. Civ. P. 54(B); thus, the trial court was free to revise its oral decision at any time. Moore v. Ohio Valley Coal Co., — Ohio App. 3d —, 2007 Ohio 1123, — N.E. 2d —, 2007 Ohio App. LEXIS 1040 (Mar. 7, 2007).

Small claims court

Motions for summary judgment are permissible in small claims actions: Norwalk MK, Inc. v. McCormick, 170 Ohio App. 3d 147, 2006 Ohio 4640, 866 N.E.2d 516, 2006 Ohio App. LEXIS 4560 (2006).

Successive motions

Unlike Ohio R. Civ. P. 12, which requires all applicable defenses to be consolidated in a single motion, Ohio R. Civ. P. 56 contains no such provision. Ohio R. Civ. P. 12(G)-(H). The Court of Appeals of Ohio, Third Appellate District, Allen County is aware of no rule that prohibits a party from filing a subsequent motion for summary judgment. Graham v. Allen County Sheriff's Office, — Ohio App. 3d —, 2006 Ohio 4183, — N.E. 2d —, 2006 Ohio App. LEXIS 4098 (Aug. 14, 2006).

Time for filing or responding to motion

Where a motion for summary judgment was filed after the court's deadline for such motions, leave of court was required. Where the court allowed the motion to be filed instanter and denied the motion to strike, the court should have given the nonmoving party an opportunity to respond prior to granting the motion: Cheap Escape Co. v. Tri-State Constr., LLC, 173 Ohio App. 3d 683, 2007 Ohio 6185, 880 N.E.2d 122, 2007 Ohio App. LEXIS 5425 (2007).

RULE 57.   Declaratory judgments

The procedure for obtaining a declaratory judgment pursuant to Sections 2721.01 to 2721.15, inclusive, of the Revised Code, shall be in accordance with these rules. The existence of another adequate remedy does not preclude a judgment for declaratory relief in cases where it is appropriate. The court may advance on the trial list the hearing of an action for a declaratory judgment.

NOTES TO DECISIONS

ANALYSIS

Declaratory judgment proper
Immunity

Declaratory judgment proper

Trial court's declaratory judgment holding that a City had a right to temporarily use a sewer was affirmed as there was no language in a sewer agreement with a property owner prohibiting the City from temporarily using the sewer to service properties until another sewer line was completed and the City was the absolute owner of the sewer. Pingue v. City of Delaware, — Ohio App. 3d —, 2006 Ohio 3796, — N.E. 2d —, 2006 Ohio App. LEXIS 3768 (July 21, 2006).

Trial court erred in granting a City's motion for judgment on the pleadings as the residents stated a constitutional claim for a declaratory judgment where they alleged that: (1) the City's actions violated the Home Rule Amendment, Ohio Const. art. XVIII, § 3, and the Due Process Clause of the Fourteenth Amendment, (2) the ordinance and the installation of cross-walks, ramps, and stop signs were unreasonably dangerous, arbitrary, capricious, and bore no relation to the health, safety, morals or general welfare of the public, (3) the configuration of the intersection resulted in a limited sight distance for drivers, (4) a driver only narrowly missed striking children using the crosswalk, and (5) two traffic engineers reviewed the intersection and determined that its configuration was dangerous. Parker v. City of Upper Arlington, — Ohio App. 3d —, 2006 Ohio 1649, — N.E. 2d —, 2006 Ohio App. LEXIS 1431 (Mar. 31, 2006).

Immunity

Trial court properly granted a judgment on the pleadings as to the residents' claim for declaratory relief seeking monetary damages for public nuisance as: (1) the residents alleged that they were damaged when the City passed an ordinance and constructed a dangerous and unnecessary traffic pattern, (2) when the City allegedly incurred liability, it was performing a governmental function, the regulation of traffic, (3) as the City was performing a governmental function, it was immune, and (4) the RC § 2744.02(B)(3) exception was inapplicable as the placement of stop signs, painted crosswalks, and sidewalk ramps did not serve to "block up" the intersection or to present an "obstacle or impediment to passing" through on either road. Parker v. City of Upper Arlington, — Ohio App. 3d —, 2006 Ohio 1649, — N.E. 2d —, 2006 Ohio App. LEXIS 1431 (Mar. 31, 2006).

RULE 58.   Entry of judgment

(A) **Preparation; entry; effect.** Subject to the provisions of Rule 54(B), upon a general verdict of a jury, upon a decision announced, or upon the determination of a periodic payment plan, the court shall promptly cause the judgment to be prepared and, the court having signed it, the clerk shall thereupon enter it upon the journal. A judgment is effective only when entered by the clerk upon the journal.

(B) **Notice of filing.** When the court signs a judgment, the court shall endorse thereon a direction to the clerk to serve upon all parties not in default for failure to appear notice of the judgment and its date of entry upon the journal. Within three days of entering the judgment upon the journal, the clerk shall serve the parties in a manner prescribed by Civ. R. 5(B) and note the service in the appearance docket. Upon serving the notice and notation of the service in the appearance docket, the service is complete. The failure of the clerk to serve notice does not affect the validity of the judgment or the running of the time for appeal except as provided in App. R. 4(A).

(C) **Costs.** Entry of the judgment shall not be delayed for the taxing of costs.

History: Amended, eff 7-1-71; 7-1-89.

NOTES TO DECISIONS

ANALYSIS

Appeals
Entry of judgment
Notice
Notice of judgment
Reconsideration
Service
Timeliness
Tolling

Appeals

Litigant's appeal was dismissed because (1) the litigant's notice of appeal was filed 31 days after the judgment entry the litigant sought to appeal, (2) the litigant did not allege the trial court clerk failed to comply with Ohio R. Civ. P. 58(B), (3) the litigant did not comply with Ohio R. App. P. 3(A) by filing a notice of appeal with the appellate court, and (4) the litigant failed to attach the judgment entry being appealed to the litigant's notice of appeal. In re Devin Krafft, — Ohio App. 3d —, 2007 Ohio 5377, — N.E. 2d —, 2007 Ohio App. LEXIS 4731 (Oct. 5, 2007).

When a litigant filed a notice of appeal 46 days after the judgment appealed from was issued and did not allege a failure by the trial court clerk to comply with Civ. R. 58(B), an appellate court had no jurisdiction to consider the appeal and dismissed the appeal, sua sponte. Mills v. Mills, — Ohio App. 3d —, 2007 Ohio 3714, — N.E. 2d —, 2007 Ohio App. LEXIS 3393 (July 20, 2007).

Dismissal of a tenant's appeal from a default judgment entered against her and from the denial of her motion under Ohio R. Civ. P. 60(B) for relief from that judgment was not warranted where the clerk failed to show service in the docket, as required by Ohio R. Civ. P. 58(B), such that the appeal from the original judgment was deemed timely. Frampton v. Mike & Betty Sekula, — Ohio App. 3d —, 2007 Ohio 5039, — N.E. 2d —, 2007 Ohio App. LEXIS 4461 (Sept. 20, 2007).

Appeal from a trial court's judgment was dismissed because appellant had neither filed her notice of appeal within thirty days of service of the notice of the judgment, as required by Ohio R. App. P. 4(A), nor had she alleged, pursuant to Ohio 11th Dist. Ct. App. R. 3(D)(2), that the trial court had failed to comply with Ohio R. Civ. P. 58(B). A.K.A. Alphonso Dion Godfrey, — Ohio App. 3d —, 2007 Ohio 5501, — N.E. 2d —, 2007 Ohio App. LEXIS 4820 (Oct. 15, 2007).

Defendant inmate could not seek to file a delayed appeal pursuant to Ohio R. App. P. 5(A) from a trial court determination on his post-conviction relief (PCR) petition, as such was specifically unavailable from PCR determinations; as he failed to comply with the time requirement of Ohio R. App. P. 4(A) and he failed to allege a trial court clerk's lack of compliance with Ohio R. Civ. P. 58(B) for purposes of Ohio Eleventh Dist. Ct. App. R. 3(D)(2), the appeal was untimely and the time could not be enlarged by the appellate court under Ohio R. App. P. 14(B). Ohio v. Johnson, — Ohio App. 3d —, 2007 Ohio 5500, — N.E. 2d —, 2007 Ohio App. LEXIS 4832 (Oct. 15, 2007).

Court sua sponte dismissed an appeal from a trial court's judgment because appellant had not filed the notice of appeal within thirty days of the judgment, as required by Ohio R. App. P. 4(A), and he had not submitted an affidavit under Ohio 11th Dist. Ct. App. R. 3(D)(2) that there was a failure by the trial court clerk to comply with Ohio R. Civ. P. 58(B). Pursuant to Ohio R. App. P. 14(B), the time requirement for filing a notice of appeal was jurisdictional and could not be enlarged by an appellate court. De Leon Lomaz v. Gibel, — Ohio App. 3d —, 2007 Ohio 5908, — N.E. 2d —, 2007 Ohio App. LEXIS 5210 (Nov. 2, 2007).

As appellant's notice of appeal was filed 44 days after entry of a trial court judgment of dismissal of his complaint, the notice of appeal was untimely under Ohio R. App. P. 4(A). Appellant failed to allege that the trial court clerk did not comply with Ohio R. Civ. P. 58(B), as required by Ohio 11th Dist. Ct. App. R. 3(D)(2), which resulted in a lack of jurisdiction in the appellate court, and the appeal was dismissed. Sterling v. Ashtabula County, — Ohio App. 3d —, 2006 Ohio 4421, — N.E. 2d —, 2006 Ohio App. LEXIS 4338 (Aug. 25, 2006).

Entry of judgment

In an action on an account by a creditor bank against a debtor, the trial court erred in denying the debtor's motion under Ohio R. Civ. P. 12(E) for a more definite statement due to the creditor's failure to have attached a copy of the account pursuant to Ohio R. Civ. P. 10(D), and as the debtor was entitled to await that decision prior to responding to the creditor's request for admissions pursuant to Ohio R. Civ. P. 36(A), which decision was not properly served and filed as required by Ohio R. Civ. P. 58(B), the trial court erred in relying on the debtor's failure to respond to the discovery requests as support for the creditor's summary judgment motion under Ohio R. Civ. P. 56(C). As the creditor's motion to file summary judgment instanter was granted and the debtor was not thereafter given proper notice and time to file his response to the summary judgment motion, the trial court erred in granting summary judgment to the creditor four days later. Capital One Bank v. Toney, — Ohio App. 3d —, 2007 Ohio 1571, — N.E. 2d —, 2007 Ohio App. LEXIS 1443 (Mar. 28, 2007).

As the jury awarded a terminated employee punitive damages but it failed to fill in the verdict form to award compensatory damages for claims of retaliation and defamation against her employer and board members of the employer, the trial court did not err in sending the matter back to the jury for it to clarify the blank entries for compensatory damages; the trial court did not have to enter the appropriate judgment upon the verdict pursuant to Ohio R. Civ. P. 58 in that instance, as it instead gave the jury an opportunity to conform its verdict to its intention and it provided appropriate curative instructions. Lynch v. Studebaker, — Ohio App. 3d —, 2007 Ohio 4014, — N.E. 2d —, 2007 Ohio App. LEXIS 3651 (Aug. 9, 2007).

Trial court did not abuse its discretion in denying a former husband's motion for relief from judgment pursuant to Ohio R. Civ. P. 60(B)(1) and (5) from a division of property order (DPO) that was entered by the trial court, as he failed to show operative facts that constituted a meritorious defense to the DPO, and the fact that he had not been served with the DPO was not grounds to grant the Rule 60(B) motion; his right to appeal from that order did not start to run under Ohio R. App. P. 4(A) and Ohio R. Civ. P. 58(B) until such service occurred, but such was not grounds to grant relief from the order. Bevan v. Bevan, — Ohio App. 3d —, 2006 Ohio 1306, — N.E. 2d —, 2006 Ohio App. LEXIS 1203 (Mar. 22, 2006).

Notice

As a trial court record indicated that within three days of entry of the trial court's summary judgment ruling in favor of an employee, the clerk of the trial court served the notice of final judgment on the counsel for the parties in a manner provided by Ohio R. Civ. P. 5 and the service was recorded in the court's docket, the requirements of Ohio R. Civ. P. 58(B) were met and due process under Ohio Const. art. I, § 16 was satisfied, such that the clerk was deemed to have issued proper service of the notice even if the employer's counsel did not actually receive it. There was no abuse of discretion in the trial court's denial of the employer's motion under Ohio R. Civ. P. 60(B)(5) for relief from judgment based on lack of service, as it did not meet the first prong of the GTE test because it sought to reargue issues raised and decided in the summary judgment motion, such that there was no showing of a meritorious defense if relief from judgment was granted. Leonard v. Consulting, — Ohio App. 3d —, 2007 Ohio 1846, — N.E. 2d —, 2007 Ohio App. LEXIS 1671 (Apr. 19, 2007).

City's motion to dismiss an individual's appeal was denied as, despite the notation on the appearance docket that the clerk served the individual with notice of the judgment by mail on November 22, 2005, the envelope that the clerk mailed to the individual's counsel containing the final appealable order was mailed on November 28, 2005. Service of the final judgment was not made until November 28, 2005, as service was complete upon mailing under Ohio R. Civ. P. 5(B), and the notice of appeal, which was filed on December 23,

2005, was timely filed under Ohio R. App. P. 4(A). Muranyi v. City of Oregon, — Ohio App. 3d —, 2006 Ohio 203, — N.E. 2d —, 2006 Ohio App. LEXIS 172 (Jan. 23, 2006).

When a homeowner did not appeal a trial court's forfeiture order or order to disburse funds derived from the sale of her home, and subsequently moved the trial court to vacate its order under Ohio R. Civ. P. 60(B), which the trial court denied, her appeal of that denial was insufficient because she did not explain how the facts justified reversing that order, and her claim that she was deprived of due process because she was not given notice of the final order to disburse the funds, under Ohio R. Civ. P. 58(B), depriving her of due process, was insufficient because she did not state which Ohio R. Civ. P. 60(B) ground applied, nor did she show that the trial court's denial of her motion was an abuse of discretion. State v. Young, — Ohio App. 3d —, 2006 Ohio 4304, — N.E. 2d —, 2006 Ohio App. LEXIS 4248 (Aug. 21, 2006).

Although the trial court made three orders regarding denial of a bail bond company's motion for remittitur of a bond pursuant to RC § 2937.39, the first two never directed that the clerk of the court was to serve notice of the order on the bond company and accordingly, the failure to file an appeal within 30 days of those orders did not render the notice of appeal filed within 30 days of the third order, which did contain such a direction pursuant to Ohio R. Civ. P. 58(B), untimely under Ohio R. App. P. 4(A). Based on the nature of a bond remittitur denial case, which is more civil in nature with respect to the bond company, the Ohio Court of Appeals for the Seventh Appellate District, Jefferson County, holds that a trial court should direct the clerk of courts to serve copies of the judgments on the bond company or, in other words, to follow the dictates of Ohio R. Civ. P. 58(B). State v. Smith, — Ohio App. 3d —, 2006 Ohio 4614, — N.E. 2d —, 2006 Ohio App. LEXIS 4572 (Sept. 1, 2006).

In a biological mother's appeal from the denial of her motion to vacate a final order for the adoption of her biological child 10 months earlier, her claim that she did not receive notice of the entry of the final order of adoption did not affect its validity under Ohio R. Civ. P. 58(B); as a party, she had a duty to keep apprised of the progress of the case on the docket, and she signed an acknowledgement of natural parent form in which she acknowledged that she was giving up the right to receive notice of the entry of the final order and therefore would not know specifically when her rights of appeal would expire. In re J.H., — Ohio App. 3d —, 2006 Ohio 5957, — N.E. 2d —, 2006 Ohio App. LEXIS 5927 (Nov. 13, 2006).

Notice of judgment

Although a judgment and decree of foreclosure were not void due to a failure by a court clerk to serve the property owner therewith pursuant to CivR 58(B), the owner was still entitled to the notice under Rule 58(B) prior to the sale of the property; accordingly, the trial court's confirmation of the sale of the property prior to the owner having received the proper notice was error. Jpmorgan Chase Bank, N.A. v. Brown, — Ohio App. 3d —, 2008 Ohio 200, — N.E. 2d —, 2008 Ohio App. LEXIS 179 (Jan. 11, 2008).

Inmate's mandamus action under RC § 2731.04, seeking to compel a court clerk to serve a denial of the inmate's Ohio R. Civ. P. 60(B) motion in an underlying matter on the inmate, lacked merit, as the clerk had complied with Ohio R. Civ. P. 58(B) when the clerk served notice of the denial on the inmate at the address of record; further, the inmate failed to show that there was no adequate remedy at law, as the inmate could have sought relief from the alleged improper service under Ohio R. Civ. P. 60(B)(5). State Ex Rel. Halder, — Ohio App. 3d —, 2007 Ohio 5938, — N.E. 2d —, 2007 Ohio App. LEXIS 5231 (Nov. 2, 2007).

Reconsideration

Trial court's February 25, 2005, order in which it awarded compensatory damages to appellants was a final judgment pursuant to Ohio R. Civ. P. 54, 58; thus, the trial court's amended judgment that reduced appellants' damages award by $10,000 was a nullity because a motion for reconsideration of a final judgment was a nullity. Squires v. Luckey Farmers, Inc., — Ohio App. 3d —, 2006 Ohio 1640, — N.E. 2d —, 2006 Ohio App. LEXIS 1512 (Mar. 31, 2006).

Service

When a trial court granted summary judgment in favor of a school sued by a student, and the clerk did not serve notice of that judgment entry on the student, as required by Ohio R. Civ. P. 58(B), and the student did not learn of the judgment until more than 30 days after it was entered, the student did not need to file a motion for relief from that judgment, under Ohio R. Civ. P. 60(B), to be able to timely appeal it, pursuant to Ohio R. App. P. 4(A), because the student's time for appealing did not begin running until the student had notice of the judgment. Frazier v. Cincinnati Sch. of Med. Massage, — Ohio App. 3d —, 2007 Ohio 2390, — N.E. 2d —, 2007 Ohio App. LEXIS 2256 (May 18, 2007).

Ohio R. Civ. P. 60(B) motion is an adequate remedy at law to request an additional 30 days to perfect an appeal when a party claims not to have received notice of the judgment the party seeks to appeal, but pursuit of a Rule 60(B) motion is a futile and unnecessary act when the clerk of court has not even served a party with notice of a judgment as required by Ohio R. Civ. P. 58(B). Frazier v. Cincinnati Sch. of Med. Massage, — Ohio App. 3d —, 2007 Ohio 2390, — N.E. 2d —, 2007 Ohio App. LEXIS 2256 (May 18, 2007).

Appellate court proceeded to the merits of a mother's appeal from a decision granting a father's motion to reallocate parental rights and responsibilities in spite of the father's claim that the notice of appeal was untimely under Ohio R. App. P. 4 because it was filed 31 days after the judgment entry under appeal; the trial court's docket sheet did not reflect when or how the judgment entry was served upon the parties pursuant to Ohio R. Civ. P. 58(B). Stephens v. Bertin, — Ohio App. 3d —, 2006 Ohio 6401, — N.E. 2d —, 2006 Ohio App. LEXIS 6358 (Dec. 4, 2006).

Timeliness

Where a notation in a trial court's appearance docket did not comply with the requirements of Ohio R. Civ. P. 58(B) with respect to indicating the method of service of the appealed order on the parties by the court clerk, pursuant to Ohio R. Civ. P. 5(B), the time to file a notice of appeal had not yet begun to run pursuant to Ohio R. App. P. 4(A); accordingly, a motion by appellee to dismiss the appeal as untimely was denied. Carter-Jones Lumber Co. v. Willard, — Ohio App. 3d —, 2006 Ohio 1980, — N.E. 2d —, 2006 Ohio App. LEXIS 1822 (Apr. 17, 2006).

Tolling

Because post-conviction proceedings were civil in nature, App. R. 5(A) was not available to seek leave from the denial of a post-conviction action where the time for an appeal as of right as provided in App. R. 4 had passed; however, because the clerk did not serve a copy of the judgment denying appellant's petition for post-conviction relief on appellant in the manner prescribed in Civ. R. 58(B), appellant's notice of appeal filed in the trial court was timely. State v. Williams, — Ohio App. 3d —, 2006 Ohio 5415, — N.E. 2d —, 2006 Ohio App. LEXIS 5406 (Oct. 17, 2006).

RULE 59. New trials

(A) **Grounds.** A new trial may be granted to all or any of the parties and on all or part of the issues upon any of the following grounds:

(1) Irregularity in the proceedings of the court, jury, magistrate, or prevailing party, or any order of the court or magistrate, or abuse of discretion, by which an aggrieved party was prevented from having a fair trial;

(2) Misconduct of the jury or prevailing party;

(3) Accident or surprise which ordinary prudence could not have guarded against;

(4) Excessive or inadequate damages, appearing to have been given under the influence of passion or prejudice;

(5) Error in the amount of recovery, whether too large or too small, when the action is upon a contract or for the injury or detention of property;

(6) The judgment is not sustained by the weight of the evidence; however, only one new trial may be granted on the weight of the evidence in the same case;

(7) The judgment is contrary to law;

(8) Newly discovered evidence, material for the party applying, which with reasonable diligence he could not have discovered and produced at trial;

(9) Error of law occurring at the trial and brought to the attention of the trial court by the party making the application.

In addition to the above grounds, a new trial may also be granted in the sound discretion of the court for good cause shown.

When a new trial is granted, the court shall specify in writing the grounds upon which such new trial is granted.

On a motion for a new trial in an action tried without a jury, the court may open the judgment if one has been entered, take additional testimony, amend findings of fact and conclusions of law or make new findings and conclusions, and enter a new judgment.

(B) **Time for motion.** A motion for a new trial shall be served not later than fourteen days after the entry of judgment.

(C) **Time for serving affidavits.** When a motion for a new trial is based upon affidavits they shall be served with the motion. The opposing party has fourteen days after such service within which to serve opposing affidavits, which period may be extended for an additional period not exceeding twenty-one days either by the court for good cause shown or by the parties by written stipulation. The court may permit supplemental and reply affidavits.

(D) **On initiative of court.** Not later than fourteen days after entry of judgment the court of its own initiative may order a new trial for any reason for which it might have granted a new trial on motion of a party.

The court may also grant a motion for a new trial, timely served by a party, for a reason not stated in the party's motion. In such case the court shall give the parties notice and an opportunity to be heard on the matter. The court shall specify the grounds for new trial in the order.

History: Amended, eff 7-1-96.

NOTES TO DECISIONS

ANALYSIS

Basis for new trial generally

When a printer sued newspapers on a past due account and moved for a new trial as to the trial court's refusal to award the printer damages for lost profits, after a bench trial, the printer's motion was properly denied because, when the printer cited Ohio R. Civ. P. 59(A)(9) as the basis for the printer's motion, the printer cited to a paragraph regarding bench trials which was not part of Rule 59(A)(9) and was not a separate reason to grant a new trial, as the paragraph was merely intended to provide a trial court with remedial options upon granting a new trial if the original trial was to the court. Marysville v. Del. Gazette Co., — Ohio App. 3d —, 2007 Ohio 4365, — N.E. 2d —, 2007 Ohio App. LEXIS 3943 (Aug. 27, 2007).

Trial court erred when it ordered a new trial because the jury verdict was supported by substantial competent, credible evidence and the flaws cited by the trial court in making its determination did not support the order of a new trial. While the remarks by counsel may have been questionable, they were not so outrageous as to warrant a new trial; much of the evidence was not rebutted; and there was no challenge on appeal to the jury's finding of liability. McLeod v. Mt. Sinai Med. Ctr., 166 Ohio App. 3d 647, 2006 Ohio 2206, 852 N.E. 2d 1235, 2006 Ohio App. LEXIS 2059 (May 4, 2006).

Trial court failed to meet the specificity requirement of Ohio R. Civ. P. 59(A) where it granted new trial motions to both parties in competing negligence claims, arising from a vehicle accident that caused injury to the passenger and the driver, as the trial court's indication that the motions were "well-taken" and that "good cause was shown" was not sufficient. Jacobs v. McAllister, — Ohio App. 3d —, 2006 Ohio 123, — N.E. 2d —, 2006 Ohio App. LEXIS 94 (Jan. 13, 2006).

Trial court's sua sponte grant of a new trial to an employer in an action by an employee was unreasonable where the new trial was granted on the basis of "fairness," which was not within the "good cause shown" provisions of Ohio R. Civ. P. 59(D) to support the grant of a new trial, rendering the judgment after the new trial void; the employer had claimed that its answer was mailed to the trial court prior to the trial date, at which time it had failed to appear and testimony was taken from the employee in support of his claim. Derden v. Sylvester Material Co., — Ohio App. 3d —, 2006 Ohio 5467, — N.E. 2d —, 2006 Ohio App. LEXIS 5465 (Oct. 20, 2006).

Court must state reasons for new trial

Trial court's order granting an accident victim a new trial where a jury awarded $500 in damages after the victim presented $67,000 in out-of-pocket expenses related to her injuries, could not be sustained as it failed to comply with the Antal standard. The order set out the evidence presented by the parties but did not contain any rationale or analysis of how any irregularity in the "damages only" trial might have contributed to the verdict. Marquez v. Jackson, — Ohio App. 3d —, 2007 Ohio 3299, — N.E. 2d —, 2007 Ohio App. LEXIS 3058 (June 29, 2007).

Trial court's journal entry supporting its order for a new trial pursuant to Ohio R. Civ. P. 59(A), which merely said that plaintiff presented medical bills of $66,721, then quoted Ohio R. Civ. P. 59(A)(6) and the appellate standard of review, was insufficient. The trial court did not discuss any of the evidence produced by either party at the trial seeking damages arising from a traffic accident, nor did it state that the jury erred in concluding that only $500 of plaintiff's damages was attributable to the driver's negligence. Marquez v. Jackson, — Ohio App. 3d —, 2006 Ohio 2043, — N.E. 2d —, 2006 Ohio App. LEXIS 1882 (Apr. 26, 2006).

Damages excessive

Where competent, credible evidence exists to support the trial court's finding of an excessive verdict given under passion or prejudice or misconduct of counsel, the order granting a new trial is not an abuse of discretion and should remain undisturbed: Harris v. Mt. Sinai Med. Ctr., 116 Ohio St. 3d 139, 2007 Ohio 5587, 876 N.E.2d 1201, 2007 Ohio LEXIS 2585 (2007).

There was no error in overruling the manufacturer's motion for a new trial court or remittitur because, in light of the evidence presented, and in spite of any inappropriate behavior by the attorney of the decedent's widow, the jury's verdict was not excessive. The wife testified about the family's financial situation before and after decedent's death due to a defective dump truck bed and thus, the record did not support the manufacturer's argument there was no evidence of loss of support. Sandra K. Ronske v. Heil, — Ohio App. 3d —, 2007 Ohio 5417, — N.E. 2d —, 2007 Ohio App. LEXIS 4763 (Oct. 9, 2007).

Trial court did not err in denying a construction company's motions for judgment notwithstanding the verdict, for remittitur, or for a new trial pursuant to Ohio R. Civ. P. 50 and 59, as the evidence supported a jury's determination of damages to property owners who had contracted with the company to have their home remodeled, as the company had failed in its obligation under RC § 1345.09 of the Ohio Consumer Sales Practices Act, RC ch. 1345, to advise the owners of their right to an estimate and it failed to provide a written form as required with respect to an estimate. The owners had paid an amount to the company that greatly exceeded the amount originally agreed by the parties as the maximum cost for the project. Hudson-Wobbecke Enterprises v. Burwell, — Ohio App. 3d —, 2007 Ohio 1728, — N.E. 2d —, 2007 Ohio App. LEXIS 1892 (Apr. 12, 2007).

Although denial of the driver's motion for a new trial was not error, the trial court did err by awarding excessive damages because, at the time of trial, the victim had accrued only $ 82,760.97 in medical bills; thus, since those medical bills were the only expenses presented to the jury, it was inappropriate for the jury to extend its award beyond those expenses. In light of the additional damage award (the jury awarded $ 100,000 for past medical expenses), the proper course of action for the trial court was to reduce the damage award to the victim by $ 17,239.03, in order to appropriately reflect the damages she submitted to the jury. Krider v. Gayle H. Price, — Ohio App. 3d —, 2007 Ohio 5233, — N.E. 2d —, 2007 Ohio App. LEXIS 4634 (Sept. 28, 2007).

Damages inadequate

Where the jury awarded a general verdict exceeding the plaintiff's medical bills, the appellate court could presume that the excess was to compensate the plaintiff for pain and suffering and that the jury did not fail to make an award for pain and suffering: Frazier v. Swierkos, 183 Ohio App. 3d 77, 2009 Ohio 3353, 915 N.E.2d 724, 2009 Ohio App. LEXIS 2869 (2009).

Where a party was entitled to recover at least nominal damages, the portion of the verdict awarding no damages was inconsistent with the finding of liability for breach of contract and against the manifest weight of the evidence: Meyer v. Chieffo, 180 Ohio App. 3d 78, 2008 Ohio 6603, 904 N.E.2d 560, 2008 Ohio App. LEXIS 5506 (2008).

Plaintiff was not entitled to a new trial in a case where the jury awarded nothing for his alleged injuries in a motor vehicle accident. His credibility was undermined, and his prior workers' compensation and social security claims cast doubt on the cause of his conditions: Sims v. Dibler, 172 Ohio App. 3d 486, 2007 Ohio 3035, 875 N.E.2d 965, 2007 Ohio App. LEXIS 2879 (2007).

Where a trial court's award of damages to a home owner in her negligent construction action was improper, as the trial court relied on the fair market value approach, the restoration cost approach, and a reproduction cost approach in making its damage calculation, the owner's new trial motion under Ohio R. Civ. P. 59(A) had merit; as the matter was tried in a bench trial, a remand for a new trial was not mandated because the trial court could take additional evidence or amend its findings of fact and conclusions of law. Stackhouse v. Logangate Prop. Mgmt., — Ohio App. 3d —, 2007 Ohio 3171, — N.E. 2d —, 2007 Ohio App. LEXIS 2962 (June 21, 2007).

In a negligence case arising from an automobile accident in which a motorist admitted negligence but contested proximate cause, and a jury awarded an alleged injured party zero damages, it was not an abuse of discretion for a trial court to grant the alleged injured party's motion for a new trial, despite evidence that the alleged injured party repeatedly modified the alleged injured party's medical records and did not call the author of those records to testify, because there was some competent medical testimony at trial that the alleged injured party sustained some soft tissue injury as a result of the accident. Gorney v. Naus, — Ohio App. 3d —, 2007 Ohio 2827, — N.E. 2d —, 2007 Ohio App. LEXIS 2645 (June 8, 2007).

Plaintiff was entitled to a new trial pursuant to CivR 59(A)(5) where defense counsel admitted liability and that some damages should be awarded, but the jury found zero damages: Zerkle v. Kendall, 172 Ohio App. 3d 468, 2007 Ohio 3432, 875 N.E.2d 652, 2007 Ohio App. LEXIS 3144 (2007).

Trial court properly granted plaintiff's motion for a new trial under CivR 59(A)(6). In light of testimony that plaintiff suffered headaches, neck, shoulder, and arm pain after her car accident with defendant and that she saw a doctor because of the pain, there was no evidence upon which the jury could have awarded plaintiff's medical bills but not have awarded damages for the non-economic damages suffered in the time period after the accident with defendant and the second accident in which she was involved four months later. Yock v. Kovalyk, — Ohio App. 3d —, 2007 Ohio 6259, — N.E. 2d —, 2007 Ohio App. LEXIS 5501 (Nov. 26, 2007).

When, in a personal injury case in which a motorist stipulated to her negligence, the jury awarded the alleged injured party zero damages, it was not an abuse of discretion for the trial court to deny the alleged injured party's motion for a new trial, under Ohio R. Civ. P. 59(A)(6), because, inter alia, (1) an expert opined that the force of the accident could not have caused the alleged injured party's shoulder injury, (2) neither of two methods which could have caused the injury, according to medical testimony, was present in the accident, and (3) the alleged injured party's job duties required him to engage in activities which could have caused the injury. Brown v. Mariano, — Ohio App. 3d —, 2006 Ohio 6671, — N.E. 2d —, 2006 Ohio App. LEXIS 6601 (Dec. 18, 2006).

When, in a personal injury case in which a motorist stipulated to her negligence, the jury awarded the alleged injured party zero damages, it was not an abuse of discretion for the trial court to deny the alleged injured party's motion for a new trial, under Ohio R. Civ. P. 59(A)(6), because, inter alia, the motorist's evidence that the alleged injured party did not require treatment for a neck injury after the accident rebutted any presumption of injury created by the alleged injured party's medical bills. Brown v. Mariano, — Ohio App. 3d —, 2006 Ohio 6671, — N.E. 2d —, 2006 Ohio App. LEXIS 6601 (Dec. 18, 2006).

When, in a personal injury case in which a motorist stipulated to her negligence, the jury awarded the alleged injured party zero damages, it was not an abuse of discretion for the trial court to deny the alleged injured party's motion for a new trial, under Ohio R. Civ. P. 59(A)(6), because, inter alia, the alleged injured party's testimony that he did not feel the accident's impact supported an expert opinion that he could not have been hurt in the accident. Brown v. Mariano, — Ohio App. 3d —, 2006 Ohio 6671, — N.E. 2d —, 2006 Ohio App. LEXIS 6601 (Dec. 18, 2006).

When, in a personal injury case in which a motorist stipulated to her negligence, the jury awarded the alleged injured party zero damages, it was not an abuse of discretion for the trial court to deny the alleged injured party's motion for a new trial, under Ohio R. Civ. P. 59(A)(6), because, inter alia, the alleged injured party's medical evidence did not show that he was treated for such an injury after the accident, and he admitted that any neck pain disappeared a few days after the accident. Brown v. Mariano, — Ohio App. 3d —, 2006 Ohio 6671, — N.E. 2d —, 2006 Ohio App. LEXIS 6601 (Dec. 18, 2006).

When, in a personal injury case in which a motorist stipulated to her negligence, the jury awarded the alleged injured party zero damages, it was not an abuse of discretion for the trial court to deny the alleged injured party's motion for a new trial, under Ohio R. Civ. P. 59(A)(6), because, inter alia, the motorist's stipulation that her negligence resulted in some injury was not a stipulation that it resulted in some compensable injury. Brown v. Mariano, — Ohio App. 3d —, 2006 Ohio 6671, — N.E. 2d —, 2006 Ohio App. LEXIS 6601 (Dec. 18, 2006).

When, in a personal injury case in which a motorist stipulated to her negligence, the jury awarded the alleged injured party zero damages, it was not an abuse of discretion for the trial court to deny the alleged injured party's motion for a new trial, under Ohio R. Civ. P. 59(A)(6), because, inter alia, medical evidence did not indicate any objective signs of a back injury after the accident, so the jury could find that any such injury was caused by a source other than the accident. Brown v. Mariano, — Ohio App. 3d —, 2006 Ohio 6671, — N.E. 2d —, 2006 Ohio App. LEXIS 6601 (Dec. 18, 2006).

When an alleged injured party claimed that the damages he was awarded in a personal injury case were inadequate, under Ohio R. Civ. P. 59(A)(4), because they only compensated him for two missed days of work and he had missed additional days due to medical appointments and nausea and continued to suffer constant headaches, he did not show that the jury's verdict was so inadequate as to shock the conscience because (1) there was no medical evidence in the appellate record showing that any work he missed was due to the accident, (2) his supervisor's testimony that he missed additional days of work was not causally linked to the accident, and (3) he admitted that he had been in a previous accident which also caused him pain, so it was not shown that the jury's verdict was the result of passion or prejudice. Rinehart v. Brown, — Ohio App. 3d —, 2006 Ohio 1912, — N.E. 2d —, 2006 Ohio App. LEXIS 1766 (Apr. 17, 2006).

Where an injured driver provided undisputed evidence that he would continue to suffer pain as a result of a vehicle accident, the jury's express decision not to award him damages for future pain and suffering was against the manifest weight of the evidence, and the trial court abused its discretion in denying the motion under Ohio R. Civ. P. 59(A)(6) of the driver and his wife for a new trial on that issue; pursuant to Ohio R. App. P. 12(D), the court could grant a new trial on that issue alone. White v. Bennett, — Ohio App. 3d —, 2006 Ohio 3600, — N.E. 2d —, 2006 Ohio App. LEXIS 3541 (July 14, 2006).

Denial of the victim's motion for a new trial, under Civ. R. 59(A), on the issue of damages was an abuse of discretion because, given that the victim's and the driver's experts agreed that the accident caused some injury to the victim's knee, hip, and back and that it involved a vehicle hitting a pedestrian without a vehicle around him to absorb some of the impact, the accident was not minor and an emergency room visit was warranted. Because the victim's emergency room bills totaled $1,951, and the driver was found to be 70 percent negligent, the jury's award of $ 500 in damages was inadequate and against the manifest weight of the evidence. Hook v. Brinker, — Ohio App. 3d —, 2006 Ohio 5583, — N.E. 2d —, 2006 Ohio App. LEXIS 5589 (Oct. 20, 2006).

Trial court did not abuse its discretion when it granted the motion for a new trial and determined that the jury's verdict was inadequate, was contrary to applicable legal rules, and was against the manifest weight of the evidence. Because the victim presented claims for medical bills and lost wages greatly in excess of the verdict in addition to the testimony of his pain and suffering, the jury's verdict of $1,126 was illogical, particularly in light of the fact that the driver did not challenge the medical charges. Kiley v. Romaniak, — Ohio App. 3d —, 2006 Ohio 5602, — N.E. 2d —, 2006 Ohio App. LEXIS 5626 (Oct. 26, 2006).

Default judgment

Trial court erred in granting defendant's motion for a new trial pursuant to Ohio R. Civ. P. 59 because the trial court's grant of default judgment did not contain sufficient indicia of trial, in that neither counsel nor parties were at the non-oral hearing on the default judgment, and the issue of default was ancillary to the primary issue between the parties. Tipton v. Goodnight, — Ohio App. 3d —, 2006 Ohio 113, — N.E. 2d —, 2006 Ohio App. LEXIS 93 (Jan. 10, 2006).

Denial of motion for new trial

Trial court did not abuse its discretion in denying a real property seller's motion for a new trial after a jury returned a verdict in favor of the purchasers on their breach of contract claim, arising from the seller's repudiation of their option to purchase her land, as there was some competent, credible evidence from which the jury could have found that the 30-day limit to close on the transaction was not of the essence, especially given the seller's conduct in continuing to negotiate and pursue the matter with the purchasers after that period had expired. Pohle v. Lord, — Ohio App. 3d —, 2007 Ohio 55, — N.E. 2d —, 2007 Ohio App. LEXIS 50 (Jan. 8, 2007).

Where an appellate court vacated portions of a trial court judgment in parties' dissolution action that contained legal or factual errors, issues regarding the trial court's denial of the husband's motion for a new trial under Ohio R. Civ. P. 59 or the trial court's adoption of the wife's counsel's proposed findings of fact and conclusions of law pursuant to Ohio R. Civ. P. 52 without modification were deemed moot for purposes of appellate review under Ohio R. App. P. 12(A)(1)(c), as the vacated portions of the judgment related to those issues. Janosek v. Janosek, — Ohio App. 3d —, 2007 Ohio 68, — N.E. 2d —, 2007 Ohio App. LEXIS 59 (Jan. 11, 2007).

Trial court did not abuse its discretion in overruling the motion of a doctor and a medical practice for a new trial in a patient's medical malpractice and negligent infliction of emotional distress action, arising from a misdiagnosed pregnancy and a subsequent procedure performed on the patient which threatened the health of the baby, as the jury verdict in favor of the patient was not against the manifest weight of the evidence, the damages awarded were not excessive, and they were not shown to have been influenced by passion and prejudice; the doctor had performed a procedure on the patient as if she had a "blighted ovum" without conducting further tests to determine if she was pregnant or not, and her actual pregnancy was later confirmed, causing the patient much anxiety and other psychological difficulties from her fear for her baby's health. Strasel v. Seven Hills Ob-Gyn Assocs., 170 Ohio App. 3d 98, 2007 Ohio 171, 866 N.E.2d 48, 2007 Ohio App. LEXIS 172 (2007).

Trial court's denial of a new trial motion pursuant to Ohio R. Civ. 59(A) by children of a deceased patient in their medical malpractice action was not an abuse of discretion, as they failed to show that the jury verdict in favor of the cardiologists and their medical practice was based on false testimony from one of the cardiologists. The cardiologist had indicated that he had read another doctor's typewritten angiogram report before performing a cardiac procedure, although that report had not been typed until after the patient's death following the procedure, but the jury could have reasonably concluded that the cardiologist was mistaken on that point, as he had indicated that he had discussed the matter with the other doctor and had seen the angiogram film firsthand. Joiner v. Simon, — Ohio App. 3d —, 2007 Ohio 425, — N.E. 2d —, 2007 Ohio App. LEXIS 372 (Feb. 2, 2007).

Trial court's denial of an employer's motion for a new trial, based on its claim that an employee's counsel made improper remarks during closing argument in her sexual harassment action, was proper, as the remarks which indicated that the employer's witnesses were lying and that trial counsel for the employer was suborning perjury were not sufficiently egregious to require the trial court to have interjected sua sponte, as there was no objection to the remarks by either party. The remarks were tied to the testimony of the witnesses and were within the bounds of acceptable argument. Edwards v. Ohio Inst. of Cardiac Care, — Ohio App. 3d —, 2007 Ohio 1333, — N.E. 2d —, 2007 Ohio App. LEXIS 1214 (Mar. 23, 2007).

Trial court's denial of an employer's motion for a new trial, based on its claim that an employee's counsel made improper remarks during closing argument in her sexual harassment action, was proper, as the remarks which indicated that the employer's witnesses were lying and that trial counsel for the employer was suborning perjury were not sufficiently egregious to require the trial court to have interjected sua sponte, as there was no objection to the remarks by either party. The remarks were tied to the testimony of the witnesses and were within the bounds of acceptable argument. Edwards v. Ohio Inst. of Cardiac Care, — Ohio App. 3d —, 2007 Ohio 1333, — N.E. 2d —, 2007 Ohio App. LEXIS 1214 (Mar. 23, 2007).

Trial court properly denied a surgeon's motion for a new trial and his motion for remittitur of a jury verdict, awarding damages for pain and suffering to a patient in her medical malpractice action, as the award was supported by the evidence and was not a product of passion or prejudice. Wynn v. Gilbert, — Ohio App. 3d —, 2007 Ohio 2798, — N.E. 2d —, 2007 Ohio App. LEXIS 2596 (June 8, 2007).

Motion for a new trial was properly denied because any error on the bailiff's part due to his communication with the jury foreperson was harmless error. Although the bailiff should not have communicated with the foreperson, as prohibited by RC § 2315.04, the conversation did not deal with any facts crucial to the ultimate issue. Myers v. Street, — Ohio App. 3d —, 2007 Ohio 2811, — N.E. 2d —, 2007 Ohio App. LEXIS 2600 (June 5, 2007).

Trial court did not abuse its discretion when it denied a motorist's new trial motion pursuant to Ohio R. Civ. P. 59(A)

in his personal injury action against a driver, arising from a motor vehicle collision which was admittedly the driver's fault, as there were credibility issues regarding the motorist's extensive prior back injuries, such that the jury verdict finding that the accident did not proximately cause the back injuries was not a manifest injustice; the record revealed that the motorist and his expert witnesses were extensively rebutted by their own testimony, and that the motorist's history of back troubles was extensive and ongoing prior to the accident, which was a rear-end collision while the vehicles were traveling very slowly. Sims v. Dibler, 172 Ohio App. 3d 486, 2007 Ohio 3035, 875 N.E.2d 965, 2007 Ohio App. LEXIS 2879 (2007).

Trial court properly overruled a motorist's new trial motion pursuant to Ohio R. Civ. P. 59 after the jury returned a verdict in favor of a driver in the motorist's personal injury action that arose from a motor vehicle accident that was admittedly caused by the driver, as the issue of proximate cause regarding the motorist's spinal injuries was decided against him based on the fact that he had experienced prior back injuries, had undergone back surgery, and had filed social security and workers' compensation claims for those injuries. The admission of the workers' compensation claim information was proper, as it was directly relevant to the issue at trial pursuant to Ohio R. Evid. 402 and 403(A), the motorist actually raised it first in depositions and at trial such that although he had moved to exclude it by a motion in limine, he waived that evidentiary issue where he did not wait and then object to such evidence at trial, and accordingly he could not fault the trial court for allowing the driver's counsel to cross-examine on that issue pursuant to the allowable scope under Ohio R. Evid. 611(B). Sims v. Dibler, 172 Ohio App. 3d 486, 2007 Ohio 3035, 875 N.E.2d 965, 2007 Ohio App. LEXIS 2879 (2007).

Although a developer's motion for a new trial should have been denied due to lack of timeliness under Ohio R. Civ. P. 59(D), it was lacking in meritorious grounds, as there was competent credible evidence to find that the developer had filled in a ravine on a real properly lot with organic material and had covered it over to appear that the lot was suitable for building, such that the finding that it engaged in fraudulent concealment of a latent defect on the lot was proper. Stackhouse v. Logangate Prop. Mgmt., — Ohio App. 3d —, 2007 Ohio 3171, — N.E. 2d —, 2007 Ohio App. LEXIS 2962 (June 21, 2007).

Trial court's denial of a printing plant's motion for a new trial pursuant to Ohio R. Civ. P. 59(A)(7) and (9) was not an abuse of discretion, as neither section applied to the trial court's denial of an award of lost profits to the plant in its action against publishing companies, as such damages were denied where the evidence was deemed too speculative; Rule 59(A)(7) applied when a judgment was contrary to law and Rule 59(A)(9) applied when the trial court's actions at trial constituted an error of law. Marysville Newspapers, Inc. v. Del. Gazette Co., — Ohio App. 3d —, 2007 Ohio 3838, — N.E. 2d —, 2007 Ohio App. LEXIS 3485 (July 30, 2007).

Trial court did not err in denying a restaurant owner's motion for a new trial, seeking a new trial on his tort claims on the ground that the trial court denied the onwer a jury trial because, though counsel admitted that he knew that Lucas County, Ohio, Ct. C.P. R. 5.07(F) required him to pay the jury deposit by noon on the Friday before trial, he did not make the payment until 3:40 p.m. on that day. In light of evidence that the trial judge's criminal bailiff saw counsel for the owner getting his shoes shined at the courthouse at noon on Friday, the trial judge did not abuse his discretion in disbelieving counsel's explanation for the delay and in denying the owner a jury trial. Skiadas v. Finkbeiner, — Ohio App. 3d —, 2007 Ohio 3956, — N.E. 2d —, 2007 Ohio App. LEXIS 3608 (Aug. 3, 2007).

As a motorist failed to file the record from a trial court proceeding pursuant to Ohio R. App. P. 9(B) in her negligence action, arising from a vehicle collision, the court presumed that the trial court's denial of her motions for a new trial, a directed verdict, and a judgment notwithstanding the verdict pursuant to Ohio R. Civ. P. 59 and 50, based on the alleged inadequacy of the damages awarded to her, were proper and were supported by competent, credible evidence. Hoskins v. Simones, — Ohio App. 3d —, 2007 Ohio 4084, — N.E. 2d —, 2007 Ohio App. LEXIS 3669 (Aug. 3, 2007).

Trial court did not abuse its discretion when it denied a property owner's new trial motion under Ohio R. Civ. P. 59 after the trial court denied his administrative appeal from a decision by a township board of trustees, finding that the owner had to pay one-half of the cost of a partition fence along a boundary line, as he failed to appear at the trial court hearing and he accordingly did not apprise the trial court that an appraisal report was lacking from the record; accordingly, he could not seek a new trial based on an inadequate record. Dunn v. Reed, — Ohio App. 3d —, 2007 Ohio 4075, — N.E. 2d —, 2007 Ohio App. LEXIS 3670 (Aug. 2, 2007).

Trial court did not abuse its discretion under Ohio R. Civ. P. 59(A)(1) and (3) when it denied a patient's new trial motion after a jury entered a unanimous verdict in favor of a doctor in the patient's medical malpractice action, as an inconsistency in the doctor's testimony at his deposition and at trial was not objected to by the patient and was the subject of a jury instruction; although the doctor failed to apprise the patient of the change in his opinion with respect to the inconsistencies of his testimony, as required by Ohio R. Civ. P. 26(E), the patient was not prejudiced by the change in his testimony, as the statements did not involve the critical issue in the case. Garbers v. Rachwal, — Ohio App. 3d —, 2007 Ohio 4903, — N.E. 2d —, 2007 Ohio App. LEXIS 4361 (Sept. 21, 2007).

In a malpractice case it could not be said that the trial court abused its discretion in denying a patient's motion for a new trial based upon the weight of the evidence. There were many reasonable conclusions that could be drawn from the evidence presented; the jury could have determined that an infection caused bone disintegration and thus the failure of fixation in the patient's leg. Duponty v. Kasamias, — Ohio App. 3d —, — N.E. 2d —, 2007 Ohio App. LEXIS 4441 (Sept. 19, 2007).

Trial court did not err by denying the administratrix's motion for a new trial in the medical malpractice action because it was not found that references to God improperly swayed the jury, and as such they fell far short of plain error. A review of the transcript made it clear that both the surgeon's counsel and a medical witness meant that, because the surgeon was not negligent, the decedent's passing was not a result of any negligence, and therefore natural or "an act of God." Ponder v. Kamienski, — Ohio App. 3d —, 2007 Ohio 5035, — N.E. 2d —, 2007 Ohio App. LEXIS 4453 (Sept. 26, 2007).

Appellant driver was not entitled to a new trial in her personal injury action in which appellee driver admitted negligence, but a jury, finding no proximate cause, returned a verdict in favor of appellee. Appellant failed to establish proximate cause where the record showed that (1) immediately after an accident, appellant told the police that she was not injured; (2) when appellant saw her doctor two days later, she equivocated that her back pain might have been caused by standing too long rather than by the accident; (3) a follow-up MRI showed no acute injury; and (4) appellant's own doctor stated that based on her history of back problems, there were numerous issues that could be causing appellant's lower back pain. Kas v. Silverman, — Ohio App. 3d —, 2007 Ohio 6889, — N.E. 2d —, 2007 Ohio App. LEXIS 6000 (Dec. 21, 2007).

Although home owners combined assignments of error with respect to their appeal of a denial of their new trial motion, the appellate court chose to review the claims on the merits rather than to disregard the joined arguments pursuant to

Ohio R. App. P. 12(A)(2). The denial by the trial court of the new trial motion was not an abuse of discretion under Ohio R. Civ. P. 59(A)(6), as there was competent and credible evidence that supported the trial court's determination in the personal injury action. Griffiths v. Airko, — Ohio App. 3d —, 2006 Ohio 3152, — N.E. 2d —, 2006 Ohio App. LEXIS 3045 (June 22, 2006).

Trial court did not err in denying a motorist's post-trial motions for judgment notwithstanding the verdict or for a new trial, pursuant to Ohio R. Civ. P. 50(B) and 59, as there was competent credible evidence upon which reasonable minds could have reached different conclusions with repsect to the issue of damages in the motorist's personal injury action arising from a vehicle collision. Wingfield v. Howe, — Ohio App. 3d —, 2006 Ohio 276, — N.E. 2d —, 2006 Ohio App. LEXIS 245 (Jan. 26, 2006).

Trial court's denial of a vehicle occupant's new trial motion under Ohio R. Civ. P. 59(A)(4), (6), and (7), arising out of a personal injury action due to a vehicle collision where a minimal damage award representing her medical expenses was entered, was proper where the evidence regarding whether her injuries were a result of the particular collision or any combination of several other collisions in which she was involved, some of which were part of the same lawsuit, was disputed, the issues of evidence weight and witness credibility were within the province of the jury, there was no showing that the verdict was the result of passion or prejudice, and it was not against the manifest weight of the evidence due to the vigorous defense evidence that was presented. Welch v. Ameritech Credit Corp., — Ohio App. 3d —, 2006 Ohio 2528, — N.E. 2d —, 2006 Ohio App. LEXIS 2384 (May 23, 2006).

Trial court's denial of a property owner's new trial motions under Ohio R. Civ. P. 59(A) was not an abuse of discretion, as his procedural claims regarding his right to a jury trial and his right to have obtained new counsel lacked merit, and the trial court's compensation award was adequate; the trial court had properly permitted the owner to testify as to his property's fair market value, but the appraisals were not admissible where the experts who prepared them did not testify, pursuant to Ohio R. Evid. 801(C) and 802, and testimony by the owner as to other appropriation awards was properly excluded, as the price paid in a "forced" sale of comparable property was not competent evidence to establish fair market value. Proctor v. Hall, — Ohio App. 3d —, 2006 Ohio 2228, — N.E. 2d —, 2006 Ohio App. LEXIS 2072 (Apr. 27, 2006).

When a worker alleged that he was injured due to a knee strain in the course of his employment, but his claim for workers' compensation was denied, so he appealed that denial, and a jury returned a verdict in favor of the worker, the administrator of the Bureau of Workers' Compensation was not entitled to a new trial, under Ohio R. Civ. P. 59(A)(6), due to the worker's failure to produce expert testimony linking his injury to his job-related accident, because the worker submitted medical reports on the injury's etiology, the worker and his wife testified that the affected area of the worker's leg was swollen subsequent to the accident, and the worker testified his knee was warm to the touch and exhibited a purple discoloration after the initial injury, and this testimony, with the medical reports, sufficiently showed the injury was accompanied by readily observable, external, evidence, so the facts surrounding the worker's injury were within the knowledge and experience of an average individual. Chilson v. Conrad, — Ohio App. 3d —, 2006 Ohio 3423, — N.E. 2d —, 2006 Ohio App. LEXIS 3347 (June 30, 2006).

Where each of the errors asserted on appeal by an executrix of a deceased patient in her negligence action against a doctor and others were deemed to lack merit, the trial court's denial of her new trial motion under Ohio R. Civ. P. 59(A) based on cumulative error lacked merit. Frost v. Snitzer, — Ohio App. 3d —, 2006 Ohio 3882, — N.E. 2d —, 2006 Ohio App. LEXIS 3864 (July 28, 2006).

Trial court did not err in denying a motion by an executrix of a deceased patient for a new trial pursuant to Ohio R. Civ. P. 59(A) in her negligence action against a doctor and others, as the trial judge's comment regarding the veracity of the doctor's office manager did not skew the proceedings or prejudice the jury, the comment was inadvertent and did not indicate an endorsement of the witness's general credibility, the jury was presumed to have followed the judge's curative instruction on that issue, and as there was no objection to the instruction or motion for a mistrial, the plain error standard of review was applicable to the matter. Frost v. Snitzer, — Ohio App. 3d —, 2006 Ohio 3882, — N.E. 2d —, 2006 Ohio App. LEXIS 3864 (July 28, 2006).

Trial court's denial of an automobile dealer's new trial motion was not an abuse of discretion, as the admission of testimony of an expert for car owners was proper and helpful to explain terms ordinarily not known to a lay juror, the evidence supported the finding that the dealer engaged in fraud in a transaction with the owners, and the award of punitive damages was not excessive in the circumstances. The dealer had agreed to give the owners a new vehicle at no cost in exchange for the "lemon" that they had purchased, and thereafter forced them to sign new loan papers at a higher interest rate in order to keep the traded vehicle. Smith v. GMC, 168 Ohio App. 3d 336, 2006 Ohio 4283, 859 N.E.2d 1035, 2006 Ohio App. LEXIS 4197 (2006).

Language contained in a charitable remainder unitrust which indicated that the trustee had the power to retain, without liability for loss or depreciation, the trust property did not clearly indicate the intention to abrogate the duty to diversify pursuant to RC § 1339.52(C), and accordingly, after a jury verdict was rendered for a trust settlor and a successor trustee in a breach of fiduciary duty action against a former trustee, the former trustee's motion for judgment notwithstanding the verdict pursuant to Ohio R. Civ. P. 50(A)(4), or alternatively, for a new trial under Ohio R. Civ. P. 59, was properly denied. One of the stated purposes of the trust was to diversify the heavy concentration in one particular stock held in trust. Fifth Third Bank v. Firstar Bank, N.A., — Ohio App. 3d —, 2006 Ohio 4506, — N.E. 2d —, 2006 Ohio App. LEXIS 4456 (Sept. 1, 2006).

There was no abuse of discretion in a trial court's denial of an insurer's motion for a new trial pursuant to Ohio R. Civ. P. 59(A)(9) in an action by insureds, arising from their involvement in a vehicle collision, as the admission of expert testimony pursuant to Ohio R. Evid. 702 from doctors who treated one of the insureds was not prejudicial error where they were not required to testify in terms of reasonable medical probability because they had not been asked whether the insured's depression or medical condition was proximately caused by the pain she experienced or by the accident itself. Butler v. Minton, — Ohio App. 3d —, 2006 Ohio 4800, — N.E. 2d —, 2006 Ohio App. LEXIS 4710 (Sept. 15, 2006).

Trial court did not abuse its discretion in submitting the issue of punitive damages to the jury in an employee's claim of pregnancy discrimination under the Pregnancy Discrimination Act, 42 U.S.C.S. § 2000e(k), and the denial of its judgment notwithstanding the verdict motion under Ohio R. Civ. P. 50 was also proper, as there was sufficient evidence that the employer had acted with "malice" or "reckless indifference" to the employee's federally protected rights and that it had not exhibited a good faith attempt to comply with Title VII where it ignored its own anti-discriminatory policies when it terminated her from employment; denial of the new trial motion under Ohio R. Civ. P. 59 was also proper, as there was no indication that the jury award was either excessive, the result of passion or prejudice, or against the manifest weight of the evidence. Hollingsworth v. Time Warner Cable, — Ohio App. 3d —, 2006 Ohio 4903, — N.E. 2d —, 2006 Ohio App. LEXIS 4833 (Sept. 22, 2006).

Trial court's denial of a former employer's motions for judgment notwithstanding the verdict pursuant to Ohio R. Civ. P. 50 and for a new trial pursuant to Ohio R. Civ. P. 59 was proper where a jury had rendered a verdict in favor of a former employee in her pregnancy discrimination action under the Pregnancy Discrimination Act, 42 U.S.C.S. § 2000e(k), as the employer's nondiscriminatory reasons for terminating the employee based on her alleged poor job performance were sufficiently rebutted by the employee's evidence that she was singled out for disciplinary purposes, she had not caused the amount of errors charged against her, and that the employer had engaged in intentional discrimination against her; accordingly, she satisfied her burden of showing that the employer's reasons for her termination was pretextual, and the denial of the motions with respect to her claims of discrimination under the Family and Medical Leave Act and for retaliation was also proper. Hollingsworth v. Time Warner Cable, — Ohio App. 3d —, 2006 Ohio 4903, — N.E. 2d —, 2006 Ohio App. LEXIS 4833 (Sept. 22, 2006).

Trial court's decision that denied a former employer's motions for judgment notwithstanding the verdict pursuant to Ohio R. Civ. P. 50, for remittitur, and for a new trial under Ohio R. Civ. P. 59 was proper on the issue of liquidated damages in the employee's claim under the Family and Medical Leave Act, as the jury could have found that the employer terminated the employee for taking intermittent leave under the Act, and that the employer failed to prove that it acted in good faith and with reasonable grounds for believing that it had not violated the Act. Hollingsworth v. Time Warner Cable, — Ohio App. 3d —, 2006 Ohio 4903, — N.E. 2d —, 2006 Ohio App. LEXIS 4833 (Sept. 22, 2006).

Workers' compensation claimant's motion for a new trial of the claimant's workers' compensation claim was properly denied because evidence that the claimant's expert witness was not familiar with many of the claimant's medical records, that the claimant had incurred a similar, non-work-related injury four months earlier, and that the claimant waited 18 months to seek treatment for his work injury and failed to file a claim for his neck injury until more than two and one-half years after he sustained it supported the jury's verdict. Porach v. Spincycle, — Ohio App. 3d —, 2006 Ohio 5004, — N.E. 2d —, 2006 Ohio App. LEXIS 4954 (Sept. 28, 2006).

Patient's motion for a new trial was properly denied under Ohio R. Civ. P. 59 after a jury found that a physician and his employer were not liable to her for medical negligence because the verdict was not against the manifest weight of the evidence. Reasonable minds could have differed as to whether the physician upheld the standard of care by telling the patient that an ovarian cyst discovered in 1999 was probably benign, and the jury could have found that he properly discharged his duty to inform her of the need for follow-up care. Gerke v. Norwalk Clinic, Inc., — Ohio App. 3d —, 2006 Ohio 5621, — N.E. 2d —, 2006 Ohio App. LEXIS 5605 (Oct. 27, 2006).

Although a trial court did not set forth the basis for its decision to deny a new trial motion pursuant to Ohio R. Civ. P. 59(A), no such reasoning was required unless the motion was granted. There was cause to believe that the decision was based on anything other than the trial court judge's review of the evidence and her memory thereof as presiding judge at trial, which was sufficient Turner v. Nationwide Ins. Co., — Ohio App. 3d —, 2006 Ohio 6063, — N.E. 2d —, 2006 Ohio App. LEXIS 6041 (Nov. 20, 2006).

In a contractor's action against a city and others, seeking various relief including lost profits for the city's having awarded an expansion and renovation project to a competing contractor due to the contractor's failure to meet the required percentage of small business enterprise participation for purposes of its bid, pursuant to Cincinnati, Ohio, Mun. Code 321-37, where the classification was deemed facially unconstitutional, the trial court erred in granting a directed verdict pursuant to Ohio R. Civ. P. 50(A)(4) and in denying its new trial motion under Ohio R. Civ. P. 59 with respect to its claim for lost profits. The contractor was entitled to seek the lost profits under its claim pursuant to 42 U.S.C.S. § 1983. Cleveland Constr., Inc. v. City of Cincinnati, — Ohio App. 3d —, 2006 Ohio 6452, — N.E. 2d —, 2006 Ohio App. LEXIS 6410 (Dec. 8, 2006).

Trial court did not abuse its discretion in overruling the landlords' motion for a new trial or for judgment notwithstanding the verdict because the tenant presented evidence that she was injured by contaminated well water. Spidel v. Ross, — Ohio App. 3d —, 2006 Ohio 6718, — N.E. 2d —, 2006 Ohio App. LEXIS 6652 (Dec. 18, 2006).

Trial court erred when it overruled property owners' motions for judgment notwithstanding the verdict pursuant to Ohio R. Civ. P. 50(B) or alternatively, for a new trial pursuant to Ohio R. Civ. P. 59(A), with respect to their claim that a builder had violated the Ohio Consumer Sales Practices Act, RC § 1345.01 et seq., with respect to the builder's construction of their home, as the evidence clearly demonstrated that the builder had committed various violations during his construction of the home; denial of those motions with respect to the builder's unjust enrichment claim was proper, as the written contract did not bar the builder's claim. Ward v. Geiger, — Ohio App. 3d —, 2006 Ohio 6853, — N.E. 2d —, 2006 Ohio App. LEXIS 6768 (Dec. 26, 2006).

When a jury found against a gas company that alleged the operation of a landfill on property crossed by its pipeline caused it to have to move the pipeline, it was not an abuse of discretion to deny the company's motion for a new trial because the trial court could have reasonably found that there was credible evidence upon which the jury could have arrived at its verdict because the jury could have found the company's easement was breached the day it was signed and the landfill operators were not responsible for the pipeline's relocation. Columbia Gas of Ohio, Inc. v. R.S.V. Inc., — Ohio App. 3d —, 2006 Ohio 7064, — N.E. 2d —, 2006 Ohio App. LEXIS 6987 (Dec. 29, 2006).

Trial court did not err in failing to grant the motion for a new trial filed by the dominant owners of an estate, seeking a new trial on the ground that, before filing objections to magistrate's decision, the servient owner was permitted to review the notes of the magistrate, depriving the dominant owners of a fair trial. There was no evidence that such communication denied the dominant owners a fair trial because, while the trial court did not sustain the dominant owners' objections, it did not sustain the servient owner's objections either. Colace v. Wander, — Ohio App. 3d —, 2006 Ohio 7094, — N.E. 2d —, 2006 Ohio App. LEXIS 7015 (Dec. 26, 2006).

Evidence

Trial court did not abuse its discretion in overruling the motion for a new trial because the jury's verdict was supported by the evidence. The record contained evidence that eroded the credibility of the victim's witnesses including that the victim was involved in at least three prior motor vehicle accidents in which she suffered similar symptoms and she failed to fully disclose those past accidents, injuries, and/or symptoms to her treating physicians prior to their forming opinions. Because the doctors based their causation opinions upon an incomplete medical history, the jury could reasonably have discounted their opinions. Roscoe-Herbert v. Fabian, — Ohio App. 3d —, 2007 Ohio 3263, — N.E. 2d —, 2007 Ohio App. LEXIS 3009 (June 28, 2007).

Although the admission of medical bills incurred by an injured car occupant created the presumption that the charges and fees therein were reasonable pursuant to RC § 2317.421, there was no presumption that the bills were necessitated by a car accident caused by a vehicle driver and as such, there was no automatic right to a new trial under Ohio R. Civ. P. 59(A) after a jury returned a verdict in favor of the occupant and his wife for zero damages in their personal injury action. Turner v. Nationwide Ins. Co., — Ohio App. 3d —, 2006 Ohio 6063, — N.E. 2d —, 2006 Ohio App. LEXIS 6041 (Nov. 20, 2006).

— Manifest weight of the evidence

There was no error in granting a new trial under Ohio R. Civ. P. 59(A)(6) or in finding that the jury's award was insufficient to compensate the insureds for their injuries and thus, against the manifest weight of the evidence. Because the insureds' experts agreed that the victim's present pain was a result of the accident and the defense experts could not rule it out as a possible source of the pain, the evidence clearly supported the conclusion that the victim should receive some compensation for her injuries. Longo v. Nationwide Insurance Co., — Ohio App. 3d —, 2007 Ohio 1126, — N.E. 2d —, 2007 Ohio App. LEXIS 1053 (Feb. 20, 2007).

There was no error in granting a new trial under Ohio R. Civ. P. 59(A)(6) or in finding that the jury's award was insufficient to compensate the insureds for their injuries and thus, against the manifest weight of the evidence. Because the insureds' experts agreed that the victim's present pain was a result of the accident and the defense experts could not rule it out as a possible source of the pain, the evidence clearly supported the conclusion that the victim should receive some compensation for her injuries. Longo v. Nationwide Insurance Co., — Ohio App. 3d —, 2007 Ohio 1126, — N.E. 2d —, 2007 Ohio App. LEXIS 1053 (Feb. 20, 2007).

Evidence was consistent with a jury determination that neither party established negligence in their claim and counterclaim alleging that the other's negligence caused a single-car accident as neither party presented persuasive evidence of negligence against the other party. As a result, the trial court's conclusion that the verdict was against the manifest weight of the evidence and granting a new trial under Ohio R. Civ. P. 59 was arbitrary and unreasonable. Jacobs v. McAllister, — Ohio App. 3d —, 2007 Ohio 2032, — N.E. 2d —, 2007 Ohio App. LEXIS 1840 (Apr. 27, 2007).

Trial court did not abuse its discretion in granting a husband and a wife a new trial under Ohio R. Civ. P. 59(A)(6) after the jury returned a verdict denying them compensatory damages arising out of a car accident. The testimony of the treating doctor that he treated the husband and the wife for injuries related to accident was undisputed, and the trial court was in a better position than the appellate court to determine the credibility of witnesses. Palmer v. Hopkins, — Ohio App. 3d —, 2007 Ohio 3026, — N.E. 2d —, 2007 Ohio App. LEXIS 2780 (June 15, 2007).

Denial of the driver's motion for a new trial was not error because the trial court's judgment awarding damages for the driver's negligence was supported by the weight of the evidence; the medical records created immediately following the accident referred to injuries to the victim's knees and the victim's general physician detailed in a patient history that the victim suffered from injury of the neck, shoulder, and knee after having been hit by a car, which emphasized that the genesis of the victim's injuries was the accident. Also, the victim's orthopedic surgeon testified to a reasonable medical probability that the victim would not have suffered the debilitating injuries, medical treatments, and surgical treatments if the automobile accident had not happened. Krider v. Gayle H. Price, — Ohio App. 3d —, 2007 Ohio 5233, — N.E. 2d —, 2007 Ohio App. LEXIS 4634 (Sept. 28, 2007).

Summary judgment was properly granted and there was no error in denying the manufacturer's motion for a new trial because the jury's verdict in favor of the wife of the decedent in the wrongful death product liability case was supported by the manifest weight of the evidence. Although the manufacturer spent considerable time at trial demonstrating that the decedent knew that he should never place himself under the dump bed unless it was properly braced (certainly, the general danger that anyone beneath the dump bed would be injured if it fell was open and obvious), a reasonable jury could have found that the danger posed by the exposed and unguarded spool valve was not open and obvious. Sandra K. Ronske v. Heil, — Ohio App. 3d —, 2007 Ohio 5417, — N.E. 2d —, 2007 Ohio App. LEXIS 4763 (Oct. 9, 2007).

While a trial court incorrectly concluded that appellant had already appealed from the trial court's judgment and, thus, denied appellant's motion for a new trial, the denial of the motion was still proper because there was no support for appellant's claim that the trial court's judgment was against the manifest weight of the evidence. The facts clearly showed that the company against whom appellant brought suit was entitled to recover on the contractual price for performing work for appellant as the company performed its end of the contract, and any problem with the product produced by the company was actually the fault of appellant, not the company. Grenga v. K.D. Mach., Inc., — Ohio App. 3d —, 2007 Ohio 6911, — N.E. 2d —, 2007 Ohio App. LEXIS 6058 (Nov. 28, 2007).

In a patient's suit to recover for injuries sustained when she fell while at a hospital, a new trial was properly granted to the patient under Ohio R. Civ. P. 59(A)(6) because the jury's verdict for the hospital was against the manifest weight of the evidence. The nurses were aware of their duty toward the patient, who was in a highly confused state, was at a high risk for falling, and had hallucinated for the previous several days, and they failed to take steps to prevent the patient's fall, including failing to regularly check on the patient while she was sleeping. McLaughlin v. Firelands Community Hosp., — Ohio App. 3d —, 2006 Ohio 1984, — N.E. 2d —, 2006 Ohio App. LEXIS 1815 (Apr. 21, 2006).

Ohio Court of Appeals, Tenth Appellate District, Franklin County disagrees with the Ohio courts who hold that a damage award for medical expenses in a personal injury action, without an award for pain and suffering, is against the manifest weight of the evidence, as there are circumstances, such as when the evidence is controverted, where such an award is not against the manifest weight of the evidence. There was no error in a trial court's denial of a new trial motion under Ohio R. Civ. P. 59(A)(6) on the grounds that the damage award was against the manifest weight of the evidence because evidence as to which of multiple vehicle collisions a vehicle occupant's injuries were attributable to was disputed. Welch v. Ameritech Credit Corp., — Ohio App. 3d —, 2006 Ohio 2528, — N.E. 2d —, 2006 Ohio App. LEXIS 2384 (May 23, 2006).

Verdict for defendant in plaintiff's suit arising out of a car accident was not against the manifest weight of evidence, and therefore, plaintiff's motion for judgment notwithstanding the verdict or, in the alternative, for a new trial was properly denied. The jury was not required to ignore defendant's testimony as the testimony of plaintiff's expert did not conclusively show that plaintiff's damage was inconsistent with defendant's theory of the accident; thus, the physical facts rule did not apply. Turner v. Chapa, — Ohio App. 3d —, 2006 Ohio 3175, — N.E. 2d —, 2006 Ohio App. LEXIS 3072 (June 23, 2006).

Trial court did not abuse its discretion in denying defendants' motion for a new trial, under Ohio R. Civ. P. 59, because the husband's case-in-chief clearly contained competent, credible evidence and supported the theory that the doctor fell below the standard of care of an emergency room physician. The trial court properly concluded that a new trial based on a manifest weight analysis was not appropriate. Defendants' theory of non-liability, regarding the thrombus that had developed in the decedent, did not trump the standard-of-care theory of liability advanced by the husband. Reihard v. Trumbull Cardiovascular Care, Inc., — Ohio App. 3d —, 2006 Ohio 4312, — N.E. 2d —, 2006 Ohio App. LEXIS 4239 (Aug. 18, 2006).

In appellant's personal injury suit alleging that she sustained injuries as the result of a car accident involving appellant and appellee, the jury's verdict for appellee was not against the manifest weight of the evidence, and the common pleas court did not err in overruling appellant's motion for a new trial. The expert's opinion that the accident proximately caused appellant's muscle spasm and headaches was clearly inconsistent with the expert's own medical records showing that, for years, he had treated appellant for migraines, neck pain, and back pain, and that before the accident he had diagnosed appellant with cervical, thoracic, lumbar sprain 19 times within a five-year period before the accident. McBride v. Quebe, — Ohio App. 3d —, 2006 Ohio 5128, — N.E. 2d —, 2006 Ohio App. LEXIS 5055 (Sept. 29, 2006).

Trial court abused its discretion when it denied a new trial motion under Ohio R. Civ. P. 59(A)(6) by a vehicle occupant and her husband after a jury in their negligence action against a decedent's estate returned a verdict in the decedent's favor, as liability on the part of the decedent had been determined, decedent's counsel had acknowledged that the occupant's detailed physical injuries were a proximate result of the accident, and there was sufficient support in the record to find that at least some of the emotional injuries that the occupant suffered after the accident, including post-traumatic stress disorder and severe depession, were a proximate result of the accident. The jury's verdict which awarded no damages to the occupant and her husband was against the manifest weight of the evidence. Luther v. Estate of Skrinjar, — Ohio App. 3d —, 2006 Ohio 7117, — N.E. 2d —, 2006 Ohio App. LEXIS 7063 (Dec. 29, 2006).

— **Medical malpractice cases**

Trial court did not abuse its discretion in denying motions for a new trial pursuant to Ohio R. Civ. P. 59 or for a judgment notwithstanding the verdict pursuant to Ohio R. Civ. P. 50 after a jury entered a verdict in favor of cardiologists and their medical practice in a medical malpractice action based in part on informed consent on behalf of their deceased mother who was a patient of the cardiologists, as reasonable minds could have differed as to whether the cardiologists failed to disclose the material risks of angioplasty to the patient, and the "standard" consent form used was not shown to be improper. Joiner v. Simon, — Ohio App. 3d —, 2007 Ohio 425, — N.E. 2d —, 2007 Ohio App. LEXIS 372 (Feb. 2, 2007).

Competent, credible evidence supported a jury verdict in favor of cardiologists and their medical practice in a medical malpractice action by children of a deceased patient and there was no showing that certain testimony was offered in surprise, such that the children's motions for judgment notwithstanding the verdict or for a new trial pursuant to Ohio R. Civ. P. 50 and 59 were properly denied. Joiner v. Simon, — Ohio App. 3d —, 2007 Ohio 425, — N.E. 2d —, 2007 Ohio App. LEXIS 372 (Feb. 2, 2007).

Substantial evidence supported appellees' contention that the doctor did not puncture or injure the decedent's brain during the sinus surgery since the doctor testified that he did not puncture the brain, that the hole found in the decedent's sinus had already existed when surgery began, and that the pathology report would have referenced brain tissue being found during surgery if he had picked up brain tissue upon puncturing the brain during the surgery. Appellees' evidence competently and credibly refuted the administrator's claim that the doctor punctured the decedent's brain; thus, the administrator's motions for judgment notwithstanding the verdict under Ohio R. Civ. P. 50(B) and for a new trial under Ohio R. Civ. P. 59(A)(6) were properly denied. Further, substantial evidence supported appellees' contention that the doctor did not deviate from the requisite standard of care by operating on the decedent despite concerns of pneumonia. Expert testimony supported the finding that the doctor made the right decision to proceed with surgery since the reason for the surgery, a lesion in the decedent's sinus, demanded immediate medical attention. The record supported the credibility and weight of the doctor's claim about the urgency of the surgery. Duffer v. Powell, — Ohio App. 3d —, 2006 Ohio 2613, — N.E. 2d —, 2006 Ohio App. LEXIS 2428 (May 25, 2006).

Substantial evidence supported the contention of a doctor and a medical office that the doctor did not deviate from the requisite standard of care by operating on the administrator's decedent despite concerns of pneumonia since expert testimony supported the finding that the doctor made the right decision to proceed with surgery since the reason for the surgery, a lesion in the decedent's sinus, demanded immediate medical attention. The record supported the credibility and weight of the doctor's claim about the urgency of the surgery; thus, the administrator's motions for judgment notwithstanding the verdict under Ohio R. Civ. P. 50(B) and for a new trial under Ohio R. Civ. P. 59(A)(6) were properly denied. Duffer v. Powell, — Ohio App. 3d —, 2006 Ohio 2613, — N.E. 2d —, 2006 Ohio App. LEXIS 2428 (May 25, 2006).

Because the trial court did not abuse its discretion in permitting the patient's medical expert to testify, the trial court did not abuse its discretion in denying the doctor's motion for a new trial for reasons based upon the trial court's decision to admit the expert's testimony. Lewis v. Nease, — Ohio App. 3d —, 2006 Ohio 4362, — N.E. 2d —, 2006 Ohio App. LEXIS 4274 (Aug. 21, 2006).

— Newly discovered evidence

When, in a personal injury trial, an alleged injured party denied having ever filed a workers' compensation claim for a neck injury, but opposing counsel produced a document showing that a person with the alleged injured party's name had filed such a claim, and the jury returned a verdict against the alleged injured party, it was not an abuse of discretion, under Ohio R. Civ. P. 59(A)(8), for a trial court to deny the alleged injured party's motion for a new trial, based on evidence that the person who filed the workers' compensation claim was not the alleged injured party, because (1) the alleged injured party's claim that the jury "punished" the alleged injured party because of the mistaken impeachment document was too speculative to reverse the trial court's judgment, as the jury also reached a zero verdict regarding the alleged injured party's co-plaintiff, and (2) while the erroneous document might have caused jurors to infer that the alleged injured party had a pre-existing condition or to doubt the alleged injured party's credibility, it was undisputed that the alleged injured party had a prior workers' compensation claim, contrary to the alleged injured party's deposition testimony. Sabo v. Wahl, — Ohio App. 3d —, 2007 Ohio 5296, — N.E. 2d —, 2007 Ohio App. LEXIS 4657 (Sept. 28, 2007).

Mother's motion for a new trial of a permanent custody matter on the ground of newly discovered evidence in the form of a letter from one of the mother's daughters stating that she loved her family was properly denied. The mother never requested an in camera interview of the children during the proceeding, and the letter was consistent with the guardian ad litem's testimony that the daughter did not want to go home as the daughter never stated in the letter that she wanted to return to the mother. Children, — Ohio App. 3d —, 2007 Ohio 6828, — N.E. 2d —, 2007 Ohio App. LEXIS 6024 (Dec. 17, 2007).

Trial court did not err in denying a motion for a new trial based on newly discovered evidence, filed by a radiologist and her employer, because the motion was filed nearly two months after the entry of judgment on the jury's verdict. The radiologist and her employer had a remedy available under Ohio R. Civ. P. 60(B)(2) but failed to avail themselves of it. Viox v. Weinberg, — Ohio App. 3d —, 2006 Ohio 5075, — N.E. 2d —, 2006 Ohio App. LEXIS 5010 (Sept. 29, 2006).

Trial court did not abuse its discretion by denying the Ohio R. Civ. P. 59(A)(8) motion for a new trial because the apartment building owner failed to present any evidence which demonstrated that the alleged newly discovered evidence could not have been discovered prior to trial via the exercise of due diligence since the evidence (checks made out to one of the managers to show payment) was produced from the owner's own business records. Also, the alleged newly discovered evidence failed to establish that the outcome of the trial would have probably changed. GMS Mgmt. Co. v. Coulter, — Ohio App. 3d —, 2006 Ohio 1263, — N.E. 2d —, 2006 Ohio App. LEXIS 1152 (Mar. 17, 2006).

In a personal injury action filed by a wife and her family against a driver, a misrepresentation by the driver's expert neurologist as to his status in a professional organization did not constitute newly discovered evidence requiring a new trial under Ohio R. Civ. P. 59(A)(8) because the misrepresentation was presented to the jury in the first trial, it was unlikely that the jury's verdict was based solely on the neurologist's credentials given the extensive other evidence supporting the verdict, the information could have been discovered with due diligence before the trial, the expert's true status was not material to the issues, and the wife and her family sought to present the new evidence in a new trial for the impermissible purpose of impeaching or contradicting the neurologist's prior testimony. Wood v. Gutierrez, — Ohio App. 3d —, 2006 Ohio 5384, — N.E. 2d —, 2006 Ohio App. LEXIS 5380 (Oct. 16, 2006).

Final judgment

Trial court's order entering a decree of divorce did not constitute a final appealable order under RC § 2505.02 since the issue of custody of the parties' children was not fully and finally determined, as required by Ohio R. Civ. P. 75(F). Further, the trial court's subsequent judgment entry granting the father's "motion for a new trial" was not a final appealable order since the trial court had issued no "judgment," within the meaning of Ohio R. Civ. P. 54(A), from which the husband could file his new trial motion. Salisbury v. Salisbury, — Ohio App. 3d —, 2006 Ohio 3543, — N.E. 2d —, 2006 Ohio App. LEXIS 3493 (July 7, 2006).

Irregularity in proceedings

There was nothing in the record to establish that a trial judge's actions in obtaining the consent of counsel and entering the jury room during deliberations to replace incomplete interrogatory forms with complete forms prevented either party from having a fair trial; thus, the judgment granting a new trial, pursuant to Ohio R. Civ. P. 59, based upon irregularity in the proceedings was arbitrary and unreasonable. Jacobs v. McAllister, — Ohio App. 3d —, 2007 Ohio 2032, — N.E. 2d —, 2007 Ohio App. LEXIS 1840 (Apr. 27, 2007).

In a legal malpractice case, an attorney did not show that the attorney was entitled to a new trial, under Ohio R. Civ. P. 59(A)(1) or (9), due to the trial court's alleged error in granting a motion to find the attorney in default, error in failing to relieve the attorney of the default judgment, and error in placing limits on the damages trial which did not let the attorney introduce evidence as to negligence because it was not shown that the trial court erred in any of these respects. Hover v. O'Hara, — Ohio App. 3d —, 2007 Ohio 3614, — N.E. 2d —, 2007 Ohio App. LEXIS 3308 (July 16, 2007).

— Defective verdict form

Trial court correctly granted a new trial, pursuant to Ohio R. Civ. P. 59(A), on the basis of a defective verdict form. After the jury was dismissed, the trial court discovered that the jurors failed to sign their names on the lines next to their seat assignments on the verdict form and instead had written "nominal damages," in violation of Ohio R. Civ. P. 48. Rohr v.

Gustin, — Ohio App. 3d —, 2006 Ohio 3043, — N.E. 2d —, 2006 Ohio App. LEXIS 2922 (June 16, 2006).

Jury instructions

When applicants for membership in an all-male club claimed gender discrimination, the applicants did not show that the trial court's instruction on what constituted a place of public accommodation was erroneous because it was, in part, a quote from the definition of place of public accommodation in RC § 4112.01, so it was a correct statement of Ohio law, and the applicants did not cite any Ohio law which supported the applicants' proposed instruction on this subject, so it was not an abuse of discretion to deny them a new trial on these grounds. Wilson v. United Fellowship Club, — Ohio App. 3d —, 2007 Ohio 2089, — N.E. 2d —, 2007 Ohio App. LEXIS 1949 (May 2, 2007).

Jury misconduct

Trial court abused its discretion by failing to grant the new trial motion because juror misconduct occurred by a juror's failure to disclose an incident regarding his son's experience at the hospital emergency room at issue in the case. Because at no time during the entire trial did the juror reveal that he had taken his son to the emergency room, yet he relayed that information to an attorney moments after the trial ended, his conduct revealed that his failure to disclose his son's experience with the emergency room was a failure to honestly answer a yes or no question on voir dire; the administrator was prejudiced because an impartial jury was not seated. Grundy v. Dhillon, — Ohio App. 3d —, 2007 Ohio 2693, — N.E. 2d —, 2007 Ohio App. LEXIS 2495 (June 1, 2007).

Since three allegations of juror misconduct were allegedly made during jury deliberations and were not brought before the trial court from an outside source, they violated the aliunde evidence rule under Ohio R. Evid. 606(B) and could not be considered in support of a motion for a new trial. Dedmon v. Mack, — Ohio App. 3d —, 2006 Ohio 2113, — N.E. 2d —, 2006 Ohio App. LEXIS 1952 (Apr. 28, 2006).

Although a juror in a medical malpractice suit admitted that she was a current patient of the hospital against which suit was brought, the trial court properly denied the executor's motion for a new trial on the ground of juror misconduct since, contrary to the executor's contention, there was no evidence that the trial court and counsel agreed that any current patient of the hospital would be dismissed for cause. Further, while the executor also alleged that another juror made a statement to his fellow jurors prior to deliberation that they should not be at trial because doctors were allowed to make mistakes, the executor failed to offer any corroboration for this allegation. Dedmon v. Mack, — Ohio App. 3d —, 2006 Ohio 2113, — N.E. 2d —, 2006 Ohio App. LEXIS 1952 (Apr. 28, 2006).

Loss of support

Although it might ordinarily follow that a surviving spouse experiences a loss of support when her husband dies while employed, a jury may reach a contrary conclusion in a particular case: Lehrner v. Safeco Insurance/American States Ins. Co., 171 Ohio App. 3d 570, 2007 Ohio 795, 872 N.E.2d 295, 2007 Ohio App. LEXIS 727 (2007).

Misconduct of counsel

Defense counsel's comments, while zealous, were not so outrageous or heinous as to improperly prejudice or inflame the jury. Thus the trial court abused its discretion by ordering a new trial on the basis of misconduct by counsel: Redlin v. Rath, 171 Ohio App. 3d 717, 2007 Ohio 2540, 872 N.E.2d 997, 2007 Ohio App. LEXIS 2356 (2007).

There was no error in denying the manufacturer's motion for a new trial based on attorney misconduct because the manufacturer's counsel chose to rehabilitate the witness rather than lodging an objection, seeking a curative instruction from the trial court, or moving for mistrial; the trial court permitted the manufacturer to call a witness not on its original witness list in order to confirm the challenged portion of the witness's testimony, which was what the manufacturer had requested. Regarding the "from the grave" final argument, the manufacturer did not object and the trial court had sua sponte intervened to ensure the jury was not misled; although the argument was calculated to appeal to the jury's emotions, there was testimony elicited at trial, to which the manufacturer did not object, which supported the closing argument. Sandra K. Ronske v. Heil, — Ohio App. 3d —, 2007 Ohio 5417, — N.E. 2d —, 2007 Ohio App. LEXIS 4763 (Oct. 9, 2007).

Trial court properly denied plaintiff's motion for a new trial in which plaintiff argued that she had been prejudiced by improper remarks made by defense counsel during closing arguments. Plaintiff failed to object when defense counsel made the remarks, and while the remarks were inappropriate, they did not rise to the level of abusive conduct that required the trial court to sua sponte take action to correct the prejudicial effect of the remarks. Messenger v. Timko, — Ohio App. 3d —, 2007 Ohio 6914, — N.E. 2d —, 2007 Ohio App. LEXIS 6062 (Nov. 29, 2007).

Verdict for the doctor was reversed because there was a substantial likelihood that the jury was misled and that the verdict was influenced by defense counsel's improper and inflammatory remarks in the medical malpractice case; defense counsel sought to arouse the jury's passion and prejudice by repeatedly making improper remarks about the husband, his counsel, and their expert witnesses. Moreover, defense counsel's comments to the jury to consider only whether the doctor had done his best were extremely pervasive and prejudicial to the husband's case and misled the jury away from considering the proper legal standard, the care of a reasonably prudent physician, to only considering whether the doctor personally did his best. Thamann v. Bartish, 167 Ohio App. 3d 620, 2006 Ohio 3346, 856 N.E.2d 301, 2006 Ohio App. LEXIS 3258 (June 30, 2006).

Motion for new trial

There was no error in denying the neighbor's motion for a new trial because she failed to establish any of the circumstances set forth in Ohio R. Civ. P. 59. Rather, the neighbor sought another opportunity to present evidence through live testimony that she was not allowed to present through affidavits; the trial court gave the neighbor the opportunity to present witness testimony at trial, but she chose not to do so. Shirley v. Kruse, — Ohio App. 3d —, 2007 Ohio 193, — N.E. 2d —, 2007 Ohio App. LEXIS 168 (Jan. 19, 2007).

In a former employee's suit against a former employer for overtime pay, in which the jury found in favor of the employer, the trial court properly denied the employee's motion for a new trial because she waived any objections to a witness's testimony by not stating an objection when the witness testified, and the trial court did not fail to maintain control of the proceedings. Choate v. Tranet, Inc., — Ohio App. 3d —, 2006 Ohio 4565, — N.E. 2d —, 2006 Ohio App. LEXIS 4497 (Sept. 5, 2006).

When tenants who were allowed by a landowner to live on the owner's property rent free sued the owner for unjust enrichment after the owner required them to leave the property, claiming they contributed substantially to renovating the home in which they lived, and a jury found against them, it was not error for the trial court to deny their motion for a new trial because both the tenants and the owner contributed to the home's renovation, and the jury could reasonably find that the owner was entitled to retain the benefits she conferred on the home, especially in light of the fact that the tenants were allowed to live there rent free for 27 years, and received various other free services from the owner, even though the owner admitted that her contributions to the home were a gift to the tenants. Baier v. Holden, — Ohio App. 3d —, 2006 Ohio 2053, — N.E. 2d —, 2006 Ohio App. LEXIS 1876 (Apr. 24, 2006).

New trial granted following defense verdict

In plaintiffs' personal injury suit, their motion for judgment notwithstanding the verdict or, in the alternative, a new trial under Ohio R. Civ. P. 59, filed after the jury returned a defense verdict, should have been granted because, while the parties disagreed as to the extent of the injured plaintiff's injuries, defendant admitted negligence, and there was a certain amount of uncontroverted evidence that the injured plaintiff suffered some damages as a proximate result of defendant's negligence. Defendant did not dispute that the injured plaintiff required medical attention as a result of the accident, including an ambulance trip to the emergency room, and one of defendant's experts actually concluded that the injured plaintiff suffered back injures as a result of the accident. Bryan-Wollman v. Domonko, 167 Ohio App. 3d 261, 2006 Ohio 2318, 854 N.E. 2d 1108, 2006 Ohio App. LEXIS 2182 (May 11, 2006).

New trial on damages

Trial court abused its discretion in failing to order a new trial because the evidence, combined with the jury's question (asking if they could they compensate the victim for a portion of his medical expenses if they found for the driver), revealed that the jury lost its way when it failed to award the victim any compensation for his uncontested emergency treatment and transport on the day of the accident; liability was admitted and there was undisputed evidence of some resulting damage. A reasonably prudent person in an accident of significant force would have sought emergency treatment, and the driver did not challenge the emergency treatment. Hoschar v. Welton, — Ohio App. 3d —, 2007 Ohio 7196, — N.E. 2d —, 2007 Ohio App. LEXIS 6317 (Dec. 28, 2007).

Passion or prejudice

Trial court abused its discretion in denying a new trial on the ground that the jury awarded excessive or inadequate damages, appearing to have been given under the influence of passion or prejudice, because defense counsel's comments were not so egregious as to inflame the jury or to prejudice the car accident victim. Given the evidence, defense counsel could have drawn a reasonable inference that the car accident victim suffered from a prior condition and had a motive of secondary gain. Roscoe-Herbert v. Fabian, — Ohio App. 3d —, 2007 Ohio 3263, — N.E. 2d —, 2007 Ohio App. LEXIS 3009 (June 28, 2007).

Trial court's denial of a former employer's new trial motion was proper, as comments by counsel during closing were not so inflammatory or disparaging that they would likely have inflamed the jury with passion and prejudice in a discrimination action by a former employee. Hollingsworth v. Time Warner Cable, — Ohio App. 3d —, 2006 Ohio 4903, — N.E. 2d —, 2006 Ohio App. LEXIS 4833 (Sept. 22, 2006).

Perjury

Losing party seeking a new trial on the grounds of a witness' perjury had to establish that false testimony occurred and that it was probable an adverse verdict was based on this false testimony. Ward-Sugar v. Collins, — Ohio App. 3d —, 2006 Ohio 5589, — N.E. 2d —, 2006 Ohio App. LEXIS 5567 (Oct. 26, 2006).

In a personal injury suit arising from an automobile accident in which the jury found in favor of a motorist sued by an alleged injured party, the alleged injured party was not entitled to a new trial, under Ohio R. Civ. P. 59(A)(2), due to the motorist's alleged perjury when he testified there was no damage to the alleged injured party's vehicle, because, even if the motorist testified falsely, the alleged injured party did not show that the jury's verdict was based on this false testimony because the alleged injured party's testimony that the accident caused her to suffer from carpal tunnel syndrome was not credible. Ward-Sugar v. Collins, — Ohio App. 3d —, 2006 Ohio 5589, — N.E. 2d —, 2006 Ohio App. LEXIS 5567 (Oct. 26, 2006).

Remedy improper

In a real estate dispute in which a trial court ordered rescission of a real estate contract, the sellers were entitled to a new trial, under Ohio R. Civ. P. 59(A)(6) or (7) on the theory that rescission was an improper remedy because it did not restore the parties to the parties' prior positions. Bell v. Turner, — Ohio App. 3d —, 2007 Ohio 3054, — N.E. 2d —, 2007 Ohio App. LEXIS 2792 (June 13, 2007).

Remittitur

Trial court's partial remittitur of an award of back pay to an employee in her discrimination action against an employer was proper where she had found employment by starting a housecleaning business, but it was determined that she had not made a serious investment in it and had treated it as part-time employment, and accordingly, the trial court's denial of the employer's motions for new trial under Ohio R. Civ. P. 59 or for judgment notwithstanding the verdict under Ohio R. Civ. P. 50 was proper. Hollingsworth v. Time Warner Cable, — Ohio App. 3d —, 2006 Ohio 4903, — N.E. 2d —, 2006 Ohio App. LEXIS 4833 (Sept. 22, 2006).

Sua sponte order

Notice and a hearing are not required when a trial court sua sponte order a new trial pursuant to CivR 59(D): Redlin v. Rath, 171 Ohio App. 3d 717, 2007 Ohio 2540, 872 N.E.2d 997, 2007 Ohio App. LEXIS 2356 (2007).

Summary judgment

Trial court properly denied a father's motion for a new trial pursuant to Ohio R. Civ. P. 59(A)(1) after the trial court granted summary judgment to the mother of his child and others in an action by the father, alleging that false charges were filed against him concerning his alleged interference with his child's visitation, as the motion for a new trial was not applicable to a judgment entry that granted a summary judgment because it was a hearing on a motion. Kuzniak v. Midkiff, — Ohio App. 3d —, 2006 Ohio 6133, — N.E. 2d —, 2006 Ohio App. LEXIS 6110 (Nov. 15, 2006).

Transcript

As an insurance agency and an agent filed a new trial motion pursuant to Ohio R. Civ. P. 59 upon a judgment being entered in favor of a home owner in her negligence action against them, but they failed to meet their burden of filing the transcript from the trial court proceedings, the denial of the motion was not an abuse of discretion; they had the burden of providing evidence to support their new trial request. Schroeder v. Roger Foos Ins. Agency, — Ohio App. 3d —, 2007 Ohio 5990, — N.E. 2d —, 2007 Ohio App. LEXIS 5248 (Nov. 9, 2007).

Trial court conduct

In a close case which depended on the credibility of the witnesses, the trial court's improper and prejudicial questions and comments warranted a new trial: Harper v. Roberts, 173 Ohio App. 3d 560, 2007 Ohio 5726, 879 N.E.2d 264, 2007 Ohio App. LEXIS 5013 (2007).

Trial court did not abuse its discretion by imposing a time limit on voir dire. The time limitations on counsel were equally enforced, and the trial court even allowed appellant's counsel to exceed the time limitation imposed by almost 15 minutes. Dedmon v. Mack, — Ohio App. 3d —, 2006 Ohio 2113, — N.E. 2d —, 2006 Ohio App. LEXIS 1952 (Apr. 28, 2006).

RULE 60. Relief from judgment or order

(A) **Clerical mistakes.** Clerical mistakes in judgments, orders or other parts of the record and errors therein arising from oversight or omission may be corrected by the court at any time on its own initiative or on the motion of any party and after such notice, if any, as the court orders. During the pendency of an appeal, such mistakes may be so corrected before the appeal is docketed in the appellate court, and thereafter while the appeal is pending may be so corrected with leave of the appellate court.

(B) **Mistakes; inadvertence; excusable neglect; newly discovered evidence; fraud; etc.** On motion and upon such terms as are just, the court may relieve a party or his legal representative from a final judgment, order or proceeding for the following reasons: (1) mistake, inadvertence, surprise or excusable neglect; (2) newly discovered evidence which by due diligence could not have been discovered in time to move for a new trial under Rule 59(B); (3) fraud (whether heretofore denominated intrinsic or extrinsic), misrepresentation or other misconduct of an adverse party; (4) the judgment has been satisfied, released or discharged, or a prior judgment upon which it is based has been reversed or otherwise vacated, or it is no longer equitable that the judgment should have prospective application; or (5) any other reason justifying relief from the judgment. The motion shall be made within a reasonable time, and for reasons (1), (2) and (3) not more than one year after the judgment, order or proceeding was entered or taken. A motion under this subdivision (B) does not affect the finality of a judgment or suspend its operation.

The procedure for obtaining any relief from a judgment shall be by motion as prescribed in these rules.

NOTES TO DECISIONS

ANALYSIS

Abuse of discretion
Abuse of trial court's discretion
Administrative Appeals
Adoption decree
Appeal
Attorney general
Attorney's misconduct or negligence
— Ineffective assistance of counsel
Burden of proof
Change in circumstances
Child support order
Clerical mistake
Cognovit judgment
Collateral estoppel
Consent judgments
Correcting errors
Criminal matters
Damages
Default judgment
Delay
Discovery orders
Dissolution decree
Divorce decree
Domestic relations orders
Equity
Excusable neglect
Extraordinary circumstances
Failure to answer
Failure to attend hearing
Failure to produce evidence

Final appealable order
Final judgment
Findings
Foreclosure
Forfeiture judgments
Fraud and misrepresentation
— Fraud upon the court
Grounds for relief from judgment
—— Incompetence
Hearing
Jurisdiction
Law of the case
Mandamus
Meritorious defense
Mistake
Mootness
Motion for reconsideration
Motion for relief from judgment
Motion properly denied
Motion to vacate judgment
Newly discovered evidence
Not a substitute for appeal
Notice
Nunc pro tunc orders
Objections to magistrate's report
Paternity
Personal jurisdiction
Pro se litigants
Prohibition
Relief from default
Res judicata
Service
Settlement
Summary judgment
Tax matters
Timeliness
Transcripts
Vacating portion of decree
Void judgments
Voluntary dismissal
Waiver

Abuse of discretion

Trial court erred by denying the motion for relief from judgment without an evidentiary hearing because the motion for relief from the denial of the mortgage company's first motion for relief (from the voluntary dismissal of the second foreclosure action) set forth operative facts arguably demonstrating entitlement to relief. The second and third foreclosure actions involved the same claims, arising from the same mortgage and note, and requested the same relief; the defendant was the same in both actions, and the named plaintiffs were in privity, as the result of the assignment of the mortgage and note from the bank to the company; and after the third foreclosure action was ordered dismissed, the basis for the trial court's denial of the first Civ. R. 60(B) motion was eradicated and thus, the scenario fit within Ohio R. Civ. P. 60(B)(4) and arguably provided a basis for relief from judgment. Chase Manhattan Bank v. Jenkins, — Ohio App. 3d —, 2007 Ohio 3622, — N.E. 2d —, 2007 Ohio App. LEXIS 3314 (July 17, 2007).

Trial court abused its discretion in denying the landlord relief from judgment under Ohio R. Civ. P. 60(B)(1); because the landlord alleged a meritorious defense and made an attempt to participate in the legal proceedings, and the amount at issue was in excess of $ 69,000.00, doubt should have been resolved in favor of relief so that the case could have been decided on its merits. At the very least, the landlord's affidavit testimony raised some question as to whether his failure to act was due to inadvertence and his misunderstanding of the pleadings did not rise to the level of a complete disregard for the judicial system. Wilson v. Lee, 172 Ohio App. 3d 791, 2007 Ohio 4542, 876 N.E.2d 1312, 2007 Ohio App. LEXIS 4091 (2007).

Trial court abused its discretion by granting the guardian's Ohio R. Civ. P. 60(B) motion for relief because it was an improper attempt at an appeal and was based upon a determination that the order for a new trial was incorrect on the merits. The opinion and order granting relief was completely void of any citation to extraordinary circumstances justifying the granting of relief. McLeod v. Mt. Sinai Med. Ctr., 166 Ohio App. 3d 647, 2006 Ohio 2206, 852 N.E. 2d 1235, 2006 Ohio App. LEXIS 2059 (May 4, 2006).

Denial of the mother's Ohio R. Civ. P. 60(B) motion for relief from judgment was an abuse of discretion because the mother had correctly asserted that her prior motion to modify parental rights had never been considered; had the trial court adjudicated her motion, the inequity of her paying child support for a child in her care and custody could have been rectified. Thus, her relief motion was timely filed and presented a meritorious claim on a legal issue that should have been considered by the trial court. Stone v. Stone, — Ohio App. 3d —, 2006 Ohio 3420, — N.E. 2d —, 2006 Ohio App. LEXIS 3350 (June 30, 2006).

Trial court's denial of defendant's motion for relief from judgment pursuant to Ohio R. Civ. P. 60(B)(5) was an abuse of discretion, as defendant never received service of the complaint or other court documents, wherein a security service company was suing for unpaid services to a mini-mart, there was no evidence that defendant ever had any interest, ownership or otherwise, in the mini-mart, and his motion within two years from the judgment was considered timely in the circumstances. Guardian Alarm Co. v. Mahmoud, 166 Ohio App. 3d 51, 2006 Ohio 1227, 849 N.E. 2d 58, 2006 Ohio App. LEXIS 1099 (Mar. 17, 2006).

Abuse of trial court's discretion

Trial court abused its discretion when it converted the State's motion to vacate into a motion for relief from judgment, and then denied the State's motion to vacate the expungement order as untimely without considering whether the State could be entitled to relief from judgment under Ohio R. Civ. P. 60(B)(5). The motion was filed within a reasonable time and defendant had not listed a previous conviction on his application, which made him ineligible for expungement. In re Bowers, — Ohio App. 3d —, 2007 Ohio 5969, — N.E. 2d —, 2007 Ohio App. LEXIS 5232 (Nov. 8, 2007).

Administrative Appeals

Pursuant to the language of RC § 4112.06(F), a motion for relief from judgment under Ohio R. Civ. P. 60(B) could not be taken from an administrative appeal, as the language of the statute only provided for further appellate review. Housing Advocates, Inc. v. American Fire & Cas. Co., — Ohio App. 3d —, 2006 Ohio 4880, — N.E. 2d —, 2006 Ohio App. LEXIS 4807 (Aug. 31, 2006).

Adoption decree

Denial of a biological mother's motion to vacate a final order for the adoption of her biological child under Ohio R. Civ. P. 60(B) on the ground that no assessor met with her before the adoption as required by RC § 3107.082 was not an abuse of discretion. A deviation from the requirements of § 3107.082 was not necessarily fatal to a natural parent's consent if a strict interpretation would result in an unjust or unreasonable result and consent was given knowingly and voluntarily, the transcript supported the trial court's determination that the mother's consent was given knowingly and voluntarily, and it could reasonably have found that vacating the adoption order would have been unreasonable because it

was contrary to the child's best interests. In re J.H., — Ohio App. 3d —, 2006 Ohio 5957, — N.E. 2d —, 2006 Ohio App. LEXIS 5927 (Nov. 13, 2006).

Denial of a biological mother's motion to vacate a final order for the adoption of her biological child under Ohio R. Civ. P. 60(B) on the ground that the adoptive parents fraudulently misrepresented to her and to the child's natural father that they were merely consenting to a guardianship was not an abuse of discretion. The mother's claim was supported only by her own self-serving affidavit, while the colloquy between the mother and the trial judge suggested that she knowingly and voluntarily consented to the adoption. In re J.H., — Ohio App. 3d —, 2006 Ohio 5957, — N.E. 2d —, 2006 Ohio App. LEXIS 5927 (Nov. 13, 2006).

Appeal

Where a judgment has been reversed and remanded, relief from the original judgment pursuant to CivR 60(B) is not available: In re G.N., 176 Ohio App. 3d 236, 2008 Ohio 1796, 891 N.E.2d 816, 2008 Ohio App. LEXIS 1539 (2008).

Trial court did not err by failing to grant a land purchaser's motion under Ohio R. Civ. P. 60(B) for relief from a foreclosure judgment granted in favor of a bank, as the purchaser's appeal from the foreclosure judgment divested the trial court of jurisdiction to consider the subsequently filed Rule 60(B) motion; however, after the appeal was determined, the trial court would regain jurisdiction. Liberty Sav. Bank v. Jones, — Ohio App. 3d —, 2007 Ohio 198, — N.E. 2d —, 2007 Ohio App. LEXIS 189 (Jan. 19, 2007).

As a trial court did not journalize its denial of an electrical customer's motion under Ohio R. Civ. P. 60(B) to vacate a default judgment obtained against her, there was no final order under RC § 2505.02 for purposes of appellate review; the appellate court accordingly lacked jurisdiction to review the matter. Ohio Edison Co. v. Williams, — Ohio App. 3d —, 2007 Ohio 5028, — N.E. 2d —, 2007 Ohio App. LEXIS 4449 (Sept. 26, 2007).

Dismissal of a tenant's appeal from a default judgment entered against her and from the denial of her motion under Ohio R. Civ. P. 60(B) for relief from that judgment was not warranted where the clerk failed to show service in the docket, as required by Ohio R. Civ. P. 58(B), such that the appeal from the original judgment was deemed timely. Frampton v. Mike & Betty Sekula, — Ohio App. 3d —, 2007 Ohio 5039, — N.E. 2d —, 2007 Ohio App. LEXIS 4461 (Sept. 20, 2007).

As a vexatious litigator's appeal from a trial court's denial of his motion for relief from a foreclosure judgment pursuant to Ohio R. Civ. P. 60(B)(4) was not accompanied by the necessary application for leave to proceed in the appellate court pursuant to RC § 2323.52(D)(3) and (F)(2), the 30-day time period for filing the appeal under Ohio R. App. P. 3(A) and 4(A) was not tolled; that 30-day period was jurisdictional and accordingly, the court lacked jurisdiction over the matter. Huntington Nat'l Bank v. Lomaz, — Ohio App. 3d —, 2006 Ohio 3880, — N.E. 2d —, 2006 Ohio App. LEXIS 3843 (July 28, 2006).

Father's pending appeals from the denial of his motion for relief from judgment pursuant to Ohio R. Civ. P. 60(B) with respect to denial of his motion for a nunc pro tunc order to reflect what was allegedly agreed to between the parents of a minor child regarding custody and visitation, and from the dismissal of his declaratory judgment action that was also related to the parties' agreement on those issues, divested the trial court of further jurisdiction, as the orders therein were final and appealable under RC § 2505.02, and as the father had no adequate remedy at law if the trial court proceeded to hold a hearing on the father's objections to the mother's notice of her intent to relocate, the father's request for a writ of prohibition to preclude further proceedings by the trial court in the custody matter was granted. State ex rel. Lemerand v.

Woessner, — Ohio App. 3d —, 2006 Ohio 4916, — N.E. 2d —, 2006 Ohio App. LEXIS 4840 (Sept. 22, 2006).

Appellant's claims against appellee were validly reinstated because, while the trial court's order reinstating the claims did not reference appellant's motion for relief from judgment, appellant's Ohio R. Civ. P. 60(B) motion was pending prior to the order, and an Ohio R. Civ. P. 60(B) motion for relief from judgment is a proper post-judgment motion. Nelson Jewellery Arts Co. v. Fein Designs Co., — Ohio App. 3d —, 2006 Ohio 2276, — N.E. 2d —, 2006 Ohio App. LEXIS 2120 (May 10, 2006).

While a lessee contended that the trial court erred in failing to grant him relief under Ohio R. Civ. P. 60(B), the lessee's Ohio R. Civ. P. 60(B) motion had not been ruled upon by the trial court. His assignment of error in this respect was premature. A pending appeal from a final judgment divests a common pleas court of jurisdiction to consider a subsequently-filed Ohio R. Civ. P. 60(B) motion. Following the disposition of an appeal under such circumstances, the common pleas court regains jurisdiction to determine the Ohio R. Civ. P. 60(B) motion. Polaris Ventures IV v. Silverman, — Ohio App. 3d —, 2006 Ohio 4138, — N.E. 2d —, 2006 Ohio App. LEXIS 4081 (Aug. 9, 2006).

As a tenant failed to appeal from a trial court's denials of his motions for relief from judgment under Ohio R. Civ. P. 60(B) in an eviction matter by a housing authority, he lost his right to appeal therefrom under Ohio R. App. P. 4(A); further, an appeal from any of the successor motions would have been barred by res judicata, as they were based on the same facts and same grounds that could have been raised, or were raised, in the prior motions. Cuyahoga Metro. Hous. Auth. v. Rhoades, — Ohio App. 3d —, 2006 Ohio 4896, — N.E. 2d —, 2006 Ohio App. LEXIS 4819 (Sept. 21, 2006).

Denial of a father's motion for relief from judgment pursuant to Ohio R. Civ. P. 60(A) by a trial court in his multi-tort action against the mother of his child and others, wherein the father asserted that false charges that he interfered with his child's visitation were filed against him, was not reviewable on appeal, as the appellate court could not review the correctness of the trial court's original underlying judgment. Kuzniak v. Midkiff, — Ohio App. 3d —, 2006 Ohio 6133, — N.E. 2d —, 2006 Ohio App. LEXIS 6110 (Nov. 15, 2006).

When a trial court did not rule, on a limited remand, on appellants' Ohio R. Civ. P. 60(B) motion to vacate a cognovit judgment, appellants' proper course of action was file for a writ of procedendo rather than to raise an assignment of error on appeal of the judgment; even if the trial court had ruled, a separate notice of appeal had to be filed. Cherol v. Sieben Invs., — Ohio App. 3d —, 2006 Ohio 7048, — N.E. 2d —, 2006 Ohio App. LEXIS 6973 (Dec. 22, 2006).

Attorney general

Attorney general has common law standing as chief law officer of the state to act in the public interest and bring a prohibition action to compel a judge to vacate entries granting relief from judgment to a defendant on grounds that had already been rejected on appeal: State ex rel. Cordray v. Marshall, 123 Ohio St. 3d 229, 2009 Ohio 4986, 915 N.E.2d 633, 2009 Ohio LEXIS 2690 (2009).

Attorney's misconduct or negligence

In a legal malpractice action, if the first former client's motion for reconsideration of an involuntary dismissal of the action with prejudice could be considered a motion for relief from judgment under Ohio R. Civ. P. 60(B), it was insufficient to grant the relief requested as the age (90), inter alia, of the first client's counsel could not excuse the first client's failure to file a complaint that complied with Ohio R. Civ. P. 8(A) requirements or to comply with court-ordered deadlines. McGee v. Lynch, — Ohio App. 3d —, 2007 Ohio 3954, — N.E. 2d —, 2007 Ohio App. LEXIS 3619 (Aug. 3, 2007).

— Ineffective assistance of counsel

Trial court properly denied a husband's motion for relief from judgment pursuant to Ohio R. Civ. P. 60(B)(1) and (5), wherein a permanent civil protection order had been granted to his wife against him, as his claim that his counsel did not represent him effectively did not constitute "excusable" neglect under Rule 60(B)(1), and Rule 60(B)(5) did not apply where other provisions within the rule were applicable. Chapman v. Chapman, — Ohio App. 3d —, 2006 Ohio 2328, — N.E. 2d —, 2006 Ohio App. LEXIS 2169 (May 5, 2006).

Burden of proof

Grant of a worker's motion under CivR 60(B)(1) for relief from judgment with respect to a second voluntary dismissal that the worker had filed pursuant to CivR 41(A)(1)(a) in an action involving a workers' compensation claim dispute was an abuse of discretion where the worker failed to show entitlement to relief; the worker made a unilateral allegation that the second filing was "in error," but there were no facts or evidence in the record to determine the reasonableness thereof. Smith v. Laidlaw Transp., Inc., — Ohio App. 3d —, 2008 Ohio 1642, — N.E. 2d —, 2008 Ohio App. LEXIS 1409 (Apr. 4, 2008).

Facsimile recipient who established his claim under the Telephone Consumer Protection Act, 47 U.S.C.S. § 227, based on his receipt of four unsolicited facsimile advertisements, but who was not awarded damages due to his lack of proof, failed to meet his burden of proof for purposes of his motion for relief from judgment under Ohio R. Civ. P. 60(B)(1) and (5), as he should have properly appealed the trial court's adverse damage determination. Mokrytzky v. Job Shop Network, — Ohio App. 3d —, 2007 Ohio 2232, — N.E. 2d —, 2007 Ohio App. LEXIS 2089 (May 10, 2007).

Change in circumstances

Mortgage company's failure to appeal the denial of its first motion for relief from judgment did not bar its subsequent motion, given the subsequent events that provided the basis for the motion under Ohio R. Civ. P. 60(B)(4). At the time that the trial court denied the first motion for relief from judgment, the court had already rejected the debtor's argument that the two-dismissal rule barred the third foreclosure action; thus, the company's claims remained pending in the third foreclosure action. Chase Manhattan Bank v. Jenkins, — Ohio App. 3d —, 2007 Ohio 3622, — N.E. 2d —, 2007 Ohio App. LEXIS 3314 (July 17, 2007).

Child support order

When a father said a calculation of the father's past due child support was erroneous, the father's motion to vacate a judgment based on that calculation was properly denied because (1) it was considered under Ohio R. Civ. P. 60(B)(1) because mistake was alleged and because the father could not rely on Ohio R. Civ. P. 60(B)(5), since another provision of Ohio R. Civ. P. 60(B) applied, (2) the motion was untimely because it was not filed within one year of judgment it sought to vacate, and (3) when asked, the father's counsel stated that counsel had no evidence that the records calculating past due child support, which the trial court inspected in camera and found accurate, were erroneous. Donna G. v. Dean S., — Ohio App. 3d —, 2007 Ohio 2667, — N.E.2d —, 2007 Ohio App. LEXIS 2487 (June 1, 2007).

When a father said a calculation of the father's past due child support was erroneous, the father's motion to vacate a judgment based on that calculation was properly denied because (1) the motion was untimely, under Ohio R. Civ. P. 60(B)(1), and (2) the father submitted no evidentiary material showing the father did not have notice of the judgment in time to file a timely motion for relief from it. Donna G. v. Dean S., — Ohio App. 3d —, 2007 Ohio 2667, — N.E.2d —, 2007 Ohio App. LEXIS 2487 (June 1, 2007).

Mother's motion for relief from a divorce decree containing a significant deviation from the child support guidelines was properly denied because the mother invited any error relating to support, in that the mother was a signatory to the separation agreement and knew that the agreement, with its voluntary deviation from the support guidelines, would be incorporated into the divorce decree. Since there was no basis for granting relief from judgment, the trial court did not err in refusing to hold a hearing on the mother's motion. Grubb v. Grubb, — Ohio App. 3d —, 2006 Ohio 6760, — N.E. 2d —, 2006 Ohio App. LEXIS 6683 (Dec. 21, 2006).

Clerical mistake

Appellate court's review was limited to the issue raised in a motion under Ohio R. Civ. P. 60(A) by judgment debtors, seeking to correct the date that interest was to accrue, such that the judgment creditor's claim that the trial court erred in denying her motion for prejudgment interest was not reviewable as it was not timely asserted under Ohio R. App. P. 4(A). The creditor had not appealed or sought relief from that determination, and the trial court's decision under Ohio R. Civ. P. 60(A) was for the sole purpose of making a clerical correction to the interest date. Brush v. Hassertt, — Ohio App. 3d —, 2007 Ohio 2419, — N.E. 2d —, 2007 Ohio App. LEXIS 2235 (May 18, 2007).

Trial court's sua sponte amendment of a civil protection order issued to protect a mother from the mother's child's father was not an abuse of discretion because, under Ohio R. Civ. P. 60(A), the amendment corrected clerical error when it added the parties' child as a person to be protected by the order because (1) the mother's petition for a civil protection order named the child as a party for whom protection was necessary, (2) the child was named as a protected individual in the court's temporary ex parte order, and (3) in issuing its decision denying the father's motion to set aside the order, the trial court found the child needed to be protected. Ashburn v. Roth, — Ohio App. 3d —, 2007 Ohio 2995, — N.E. 2d —, 2007 Ohio App. LEXIS 2751 (June 18, 2007).

When a vehicle dealer appealed the decision of the Ohio Motor Vehicle Dealers' Board to revoke the dealer's used motor vehicle dealer's license, the dealer's claim that the Board did not timely certify the administrative record to the tral court was not sustained because the evidence showed that the Board submitted a complete administrative record to the trial court, verified the court's receipt of the record, and notified the dealer's counsel of that certification, all within the required 30-day period, and the trial court's failure to time-stamp that record within that period was due solely to clerical error, as defined in Ohio R. Civ. P. 60(A). Kroehle v. Bmv, — Ohio App. 3d —, 2007 Ohio 5204, — N.E. 2d —, 2007 Ohio App. LEXIS 4584 (Sept. 28, 2007).

Trial court abused its discretion in denying a motion for relief from judgment pursuant to Ohio R. Civ. P. 60(B) in order to correct a clerical error with respect to the trial court's entry of a jury verdict, as the trial court indicated that the verdict was entered in favor of plaintiffs, and it indicated the apportionment of negligence as to each defendant with respect to the cross-claims, but it failed to indicate the jury resolution of the cross-claims in its judgment. Zappola v. Leibinger, — Ohio App. 3d —, 2006 Ohio 3592, — N.E. 2d —, 2006 Ohio App. LEXIS 3537 (July 13, 2006).

Cognovit judgment

Where a company president filed a motion for relief from judgment under Ohio R. Civ. P. 60(B) in a timely manner and the president asserted a meritorious defense to a cognovit judgment by asserting that the underlying promissory note was signed in the president's corporate capacity only and not in the president's personal capacity, the trial court's grant of the motion was not an abuse of discretion. Ohio Carpenters'

Fringe Benefit Fund v. Krulak, — Ohio App. 3d —, 2008 Ohio 220, — N.E. 2d —, 2008 Ohio App. LEXIS 203 (Jan. 24, 2008).

Guarantor did not meet his burden of alleging the existence of operative facts supporting his defenses to a cognovit guaranty that was allegedly signed on his behalf where the signer indicated that the document was executed based on fraudulent inducement, but there was no evidence that the signer did not have the guarantor's authorization to enter into such a document; accordingly, there was no abuse of discretion in the trial court's denial of the guarantor's motion under Ohio R. Civ. P. 60(B)(5) to vacate the cognovit judgment. World Tire Corp. v. Webb, — Ohio App. 3d —, 2007 Ohio 5135, — N.E. 2d —, 2007 Ohio App. LEXIS 4517 (Sept. 27, 2007).

Trial court's grant of an equipment lessee's motion for relief from judgment pursuant to Ohio R. Civ. P. 60(B)(4) with respect to damages only was proper as to a cognovit judgment obtained against the lessee by a successor lessor assignee (SLA) where the lessee filed the motion in a timely manner and he offered a meritorious defense of the SLA's violation of the doctrine of avoidable consequences; although the motion was not filed for a year, it was timely where it was substantially related to the SLA's inaction in attempting to minimize or mitigate its damages, which formed the basis of the meritorious defense and the reason that the damage issue of the judgment required vacatur. Wells Fargo Fin. Leasing v. Pero, — Ohio App. 3d —, 2006 Ohio 1459, — N.E. 2d —, 2006 Ohio App. LEXIS 1293 (Mar. 24, 2006).

Trial court did not abuse its discretion in denying a refrigerated trailer lessee's motion for relief from judgment pursuant to Ohio R. Civ. P. 60(B) after a cognovit judgment was entered against it for failure to pay the amount due on the lease to the lessor, as the motion for relief was untimely where it was not brought for more than a year after judgment was entered, for which the lessee had received notice. The lessee's claim that it was involved in settlement negotiations was not sufficient where there was no evidence that the settlement negotiations were continued once the breach of lease agreement was commenced and until a time just prior to when execution was sought over the lessee's property. Star Leasing Co. v. Central States Distribution, — Ohio App. 3d —, 2006 Ohio 3509, — N.E. 2d —, 2006 Ohio App. LEXIS 3406 (July 6, 2006).

Trial court erred in denying a judgment debtor's motion pursuant to Ohio R. Civ. P. 60(B) to vacate a cognovit judgment entered against her based on amounts due under a promissory note, as the note was for a loan to purchase a family residence, which was a consumer loan under RC § 2323.13(E). The trial court lacked subject matter jurisdiction to enter a cognovit judgment, and the defense of laches was inapplicable to a lack of subject matter jurisdiction. Solomon v. Vizurraga, — Ohio App. 3d —, 2006 Ohio 3841, — N.E. 2d —, 2006 Ohio App. LEXIS 3816 (July 27, 2006).

When a debtor sought relief from a judgment entered against him based on his guaranty of his companies' cognovit note, under Ohio R. Civ. P. 60(B), he did not show that he had a meritorious defense when he claimed the bank which obtained the judgment breached agreements with him by seizing trust fund accounts, causing his companies' demise, because he waived all defenses other than payment or performance and did not allege those defenses and the defense he alleged did not go to the integrity and validity of the creation of the debt or note, the state of the underlying debt at the time of confession of judgment, or the procedure utilized in the confession of judgment on the note. First Merit Bank, N.A. v. Nebs Fin. Servs., — Ohio App. 3d —, 2006 Ohio 5260, — N.E. 2d —, 2006 Ohio App. LEXIS 5217 (Oct. 5, 2006).

When a debtor sought relief from a judgment entered against him based on his guaranty of his companies' cognovit note, under Ohio R. Civ. P. 60(B), claimed the bank which obtained the judgment breached agreements with him by seizing trust fund accounts, causing his companies' demise, this was a thinly-veiled counterclaim or set-off claim, which were unavailable defenses to a cognovit judgment, and which he expressly waived in his guaranty. First Merit Bank, N.A. v. Nebs Fin. Servs., — Ohio App. 3d —, 2006 Ohio 5260, — N.E. 2d —, 2006 Ohio App. LEXIS 5217 (Oct. 5, 2006).

Trial court abused its discretion in denying guarantors' motion under Ohio R. Civ. P. 60(B) for relief from a cognovit judgment entered against them where they filed their motion for relief within 30 days of the judgment having been entered in favor of the creditor and they established a meritorious defense. The guarantors attacked the validity and the amount of the judgment against them by claiming, in part, that they paid for fuel that was not delivered, they were not provided with the right brand of fuel, the best price was not secured for the fuel as promised by the creditor, and the creditor had withheld credits for imaging support that had been provided for in the contract. Lykins Oil Co. v. Pritchard, — Ohio App. 3d —, 2006 Ohio 5262, — N.E. 2d —, 2006 Ohio App. LEXIS 5248 (Oct. 6, 2006).

Trial court did not err in denying a guarantor's motion for relief from judgment pursuant to Ohio R. Civ. P. 60(B) with respect to a cognovit note, as the guarantor's assertions of breach of contract or breach of fiduciary duty by the mortgagee were not valid defenses to justify such relief. Ohio Carpenters' Pension Fund v. La Centre, — Ohio App. 3d —, 2006 Ohio 2214, — N.E. 2d —, 2006 Ohio App. LEXIS 2060 (May 4, 2006).

Trial court's denial of a debtor's motion for relief from a cognovit judgment, pursuant to Ohio R. Civ. P. 60(B), was proper where the debtor's claims of oral misrepresentations by the bank were not wholly extrinsic to signed loan documents and accordingly, she was unable to establish a meritorious defense due to the Statute of Frauds under RC § 1335.02. Fifth Third Bank v. Labate, — Ohio App. 3d —, 2006 Ohio 4239, — N.E. 2d —, 2006 Ohio App. LEXIS 4168 (Aug. 14, 2006).

Collateral estoppel

When a physician's partner paid the physician a judgment entered against the partner, collateral estoppel barred the partner from seeking relief from that judgment, under Ohio R. Civ. P. 60(B), because the parties' dispute was presented to a jury, and the partner was aware of the possibility that the physician would not apply the partner's payment of the judgment to a bank loan on which both of them remained liable. Lowrey v. Degenova, — Ohio App. 3d —, 2006 Ohio 2835, — N.E. 2d —, 2006 Ohio App. LEXIS 2656 (June 6, 2006).

Consent judgments

Landowner was not entitled to relief from a consent judgment requiring the landowner to clean up the landowner's property, under Ohio R. Civ. P. 60(B), over four years after the judgment was entered, because the landowner, while making diligent efforts to comply with the judgment, did not satisfy all of the judgment's provisions, and a village's failure to enforce the judgment for four years did not relieve the landowner of the landowner's obligation to comply with the judgment. Rock Creek v. Shinkle, — Ohio App. 3d —, 2007 Ohio 4769, — N.E. 2d —, 2007 Ohio App. LEXIS 4251 (Sept. 14, 2007).

Correcting errors

Alleged error in computing attorneys fees that that a party asked the court to correct was substantive, not clerical, and could not be corrected pursuant to CivR 60(A): Blust v. Lamar Adver. of Mobile, Inc., 183 Ohio App. 3d 478, 2009 Ohio 3947, 917 N.E.2d 373, 2009 Ohio App. LEXIS 3370 (2009).

Trial court's nunc pro tunc correction of a mathematical error in its judgment was proper, as such was within the authority of the trial court pursuant to Ohio R. Civ. P. 60(A). Nothing was added in the nunc pro tunc order that was not decided by the trial court, as the original order indicated that the amount of interest was actually the amount that was meant to be the full amount of the damages. Drenning v. Blue Ribbon Homes, — Ohio App. 3d —, 2007 Ohio 1323, — N.E. 2d —, 2007 Ohio App. LEXIS 1230 (Mar. 23, 2007).

Trial court's nunc pro tunc correction of a mathematical error in its judgment was proper, as such was within the authority of the trial court pursuant to Ohio R. Civ. P. 60(A). Nothing was added in the nunc pro tunc order that was not decided by the trial court, as the original order indicated that the amount of interest was actually the amount that was meant to be the full amount of the damages. Drenning v. Blue Ribbon Homes, — Ohio App. 3d —, 2007 Ohio 1323, — N.E. 2d —, 2007 Ohio App. LEXIS 1230 (Mar. 23, 2007).

Trial court erred in granting the emergency order, pursuant to Ohio R. Civ. P. 60(A), because the commercial tenants failed to ask for leave from the appellate court to correct a mistake in the permanent injunction order regarding the landlord's duty to sign the development application. The emergency order was vacated. Outback/Buckeye II v. Grandchildren's Trust, — Ohio App. 3d —, 2007 Ohio 577, — N.E. 2d —, 2007 Ohio App. LEXIS 535 (Feb. 9, 2007).

Trial court properly adopted a magistrate's decision to grant a husband's request for relief from the parties' divorce judgment pursuant to Ohio R. Civ. P. 60(A) where the separation agreement which was incorporated into their divorce judgment misidentified an account held by the wife which was to have been divided between the parties, with the majority thereof going to the husband. As the error was not a substantive one but instead, a blunder in execution, a correction to identify the account intended was needed. Binder v. Binder, — Ohio App. 3d —, 2007 Ohio 4038, — N.E. 2d —, 2007 Ohio App. LEXIS 3673 (Aug. 9, 2007).

Criminal matters

Regardless of the caption, a motion is a petition for postconviction relief if the defendant files the motion after the defendant's direct appeal, claims a denial of a constitutional right, seeks to render a final judgment void, and asks the trial court to vacate the judgment and sentence. CrimR 35 governs the procedure for postconviction relief and, because a criminal rule exists, CrimR 57(B) does not apply. Thus CivR 60(B) cannot be used to circumvent the time limits under RC § 2953.21: State v. Fulk, 172 Ohio App. 3d 635, 2007 Ohio 3141, 876 N.E.2d 983, 2007 Ohio App. LEXIS 2888 (2007).

Defendant's Ohio R. Civ. P. 60(B)(5) motion to vacate was not the proper method of asserting constitutional errors in sentencing because a petition for post-conviction relief under RC § 2953.21 was the exclusive remedy by which defendant could have brought a collateral challenge to his sentence. Accordingly, since there existed an applicable rule of criminal procedure, defendant could not assert an Ohio R. Civ. P. 60(B)(5) challenge via Ohio R. Crim. P. 57(B). State v. Randlett, — Ohio App. 3d —, 2007 Ohio 3546, — N.E. 2d —, 2007 Ohio App. LEXIS 3243 (July 12, 2007).

Trial court's failure to consider defendant's challenge under Ohio R. Civ. P. 60(B)(4) was not prejudicial because defendant was not entitled to relief; since defendant's direct appeals were final before Foster was decided, the holdings contained therein did not retroactively apply to defendant. Also, a remand for resentencing would not have benefited defendant because he would then be subjected to the trial court's "full discretion" to impose more than minimum and consecutive sentences within the statutory range with no need to make any findings to support its decision. State v. Randlett, — Ohio App. 3d —, 2007 Ohio 3546, — N.E. 2d —, 2007 Ohio App. LEXIS 3243 (July 12, 2007).

As Ohio R. Crim. P. 35 governed criminal procedure for post-conviction relief petitions, an inmate could not seek to vacate his sentence by moving under Ohio R. Civ. P. 60(B)(5) and Ohio R. Crim. P. 57(B). As his petition was not timely filed under RC § 2953.21(A)(2) and he was not within either of the exceptions to timeliness under RC § 2953.23(A)(1) and (2), the trial court properly denied his request for relief. State v. Brenton, — Ohio App. 3d —, 2007 Ohio 901, — N.E. 2d —, 2007 Ohio App. LEXIS 789 (Mar. 5, 2007).

Inmate's failure to have filed a direct appeal pursuant to Ohio R. App. P. 4(A) from his convictions and sentences constituted a waiver of his right to seek review of issues involving the voluntariness and knowing aspect of his plea, and from his sentence. His motion for relief from judgment under Ohio R. Civ. P. 60(B) was clearly inapplicable, and he could not seek relief under Ohio R. Crim. P. 57(B) where there was a proper procedure prescribed by the rules, and that procedure was through the appellate process. State v. Hagler, — Ohio App. 3d —, 2007 Ohio 433, — N.E. 2d —, 2007 Ohio App. LEXIS 385 (Feb. 2, 2007).

As Ohio R. Crim. P. 35 governed criminal procedure for post-conviction relief petitions, an inmate could not seek to vacate his sentence by moving under Ohio R. Civ. P. 60(B)(5) and Ohio R. Crim. P. 57(B). As his petition was not timely filed under RC § 2953.21(A)(2) and he was not within either of the exceptions to timeliness under RC § 2953.23(A)(1) and (2), the trial court properly denied his request for relief. State v. Brenton, — Ohio App. 3d —, 2007 Ohio 901, — N.E. 2d —, 2007 Ohio App. LEXIS 789 (Mar. 5, 2007).

Although the appellate court accepted defendant's statement of facts and issues as correct and could have reversed the trial court judgment if it was supported by defendant's brief pursuant to Ohio R. App. P. 18(C), based on the fact that the State failed to file a brief in defendant's matter, defendant's claim lacked substantive merit. His motion to vacate judgment pursuant to Ohio R. Civ. P. 60(B) had been properly denied because it was made in an untimely manner, and his claim that sentencing was unconstitutional lacked merit, as Blakely and Foster did not apply to his case because it was final on direct review. State v. Cottrill, — Ohio App. 3d —, 2007 Ohio 2006, — N.E. 2d —, 2007 Ohio App. LEXIS 1783 (Apr. 26, 2007).

As Ohio R. Crim. P. 35 governed the procedures for post-conviction petitions, defendant's reliance on Ohio R. Civ. P. 60(B)(5) and Ohio R. Crim. P. 57(B) for sentencing relief was error; as the request for sentencing relief was untimely under RC § 2953.21(A)(2) and it was not within either of the exceptions to timeliness under RC § 2953.23(A)(1) and (2), the trial court lacked jurisdiction to grant the requested relief and to resentence defendant. State v. Fulk, 172 Ohio App. 3d 635, 2007 Ohio 3141, 876 N.E.2d 983, 2007 Ohio App. LEXIS 2888 (2007).

Defendant's Ohio R. Civ. P. 60(B) motion for relief from his criminal sentence had to be treated as a petition for post-conviction relief, pursuant to RC § 2953.21. Because he did not timely file his petition for post-conviction relief, his argument based upon Blakely, which dealt with judicial factfinding during sentencing, was unpersuasive since that sentencing issue was not raised on direct review; Blakely did not apply retroactively. State v. Wagner, — Ohio App. 3d —, 2007 Ohio 3629, — N.E. 2d —, 2007 Ohio App. LEXIS 3328 (July 9, 2007).

Although the State of Ohio, as appellee, failed to file a responsive brief in defendant's appeal from the trial court's denial of his motion to vacate his sentence, pursuant to Ohio R. App. P. 18(C) the judgment of the trial court was not reversed because that action was not reasonably supported by defendant's brief. Defendant had not directly appealed his convictions and sentences, he did not file a post-conviction petition, and his motion under Ohio R. Civ. P. 60(B) was improperly filed and it also lacked merit, as Foster, Blakely, and Apprendi only applied retroactively to cases pending on direct review or which were not yet final, which made them inapplicable to defendant's matter. State v. McDowell, —

Ohio App. 3d —, 2007 Ohio 3728, — N.E. 2d —, 2007 Ohio App. LEXIS 3413 (July 23, 2007).

Motion for relief from judgment under Ohio R. Civ. P. 60(B) cannot be used as a substitute for an untimely petition for post-conviction relief. The reason is that the same analysis used to find that a petition for post-conviction relief is untimely also applies to the third element of the GTE test for a motion for relief from judgment. State v. Hatton, — Ohio App. 3d —, 2007 Ohio 3725, — N.E. 2d —, 2007 Ohio App. LEXIS 3417 (July 19, 2007).

Although the trial court should have ruled on defendant's Ohio R. Civ. P. 60(B)(5) motion, instead of converting it to a petition for post-conviction relief, defendant did not establish that he filed his motion for relief within a reasonable time. State v. Hatton, — Ohio App. 3d —, 2007 Ohio 3725, — N.E. 2d —, 2007 Ohio App. LEXIS 3417 (July 19, 2007).

Inmate's Ohio R. Civ. P. 60(B) motion that (1) was filed after the time for his direct appeal had passed, (2) claimed a denial of constitutional rights, (3) sought to render a judgment void, and (4) requested a vacation of the judgment and sentence entered on his pleas of guilty to two cocaine trafficking charges, was in reality a motion for post-conviction relief that could not circumvent the procedure for filing motions for post-conviction relief set forth in Ohio R. Crim. P. 35. State v. Frenzel, — Ohio App. 3d —, 2007 Ohio 4487, — N.E. 2d —, 2007 Ohio App. LEXIS 4051 (Sept. 4, 2007).

If defendant's motion alleging that defendant's sentence should be vacated because defendant's constitutional rights were violated when the trial court used defective verdict forms in defendant's murder trial was properly considered as a motion for relief from judgment under Ohio R. Civ. P. 60(B), the motion was properly denied because defendant did not explain how defendant met any of the requisites for relief under Rule 60(B), but, instead, defendant apparently intended to use the motion as a substitute for an appeal, which was an improper use of the motion. State v. Rippey, — Ohio App. 3d —, 2007 Ohio 4521, — N.E. 2d —, 2007 Ohio App. LEXIS 4067 (Sept. 4, 2007).

Trial court's denial of defendant inmate's motion under Ohio R. Civ. P. 60(B) for relief from a judgment that imposed various jointly recommended terms of imprisonment on him in his criminal matter was proper, as defendant made no showing for purposes of the GTE requirements of Rule 60(B), and as a post-conviction relief petition, the motion was untimely under RC § 2953.21(A)(2) and no exceptions to timeliness applied under RC § 2953.23; moreover, issues relating to Foster and Blakely did not apply to jointly recommended sentences, and claims that sentences under those precedents violated defendant's ex post facto rights and rights to due process under Ohio Const. art. I, § 10 were unavailing. State v. Felder, — Ohio App. 3d —, 2007 Ohio 4595, — N.E. 2d —, 2007 Ohio App. LEXIS 4132 (Sept. 6, 2007).

As defendant inmate could have sought appellate review of the alleged sentencing error under Blakely and Foster, his petition under Ohio R. Civ. P. 60(B) and Ohio R. Crim. P. 57(B) to vacate the sentence was properly denied, as a motion under Ohio R. Civ. P. 60(B) was not a substitute for appeal. Ohio v. Dunn, — Ohio App. 3d —, 2007 Ohio 4890, — N.E. 2d —, 2007 Ohio App. LEXIS 4365 (Sept. 21, 2007).

Because Ohio R. Crim. P. 32.1 contained the specific, proper procedure to withdraw a guilty plea, to the extent that defendant relied upon Ohio R. Civ. P. 60(B) to withdraw her plea, that reliance was misplaced. City of Jackson v. Friley, — Ohio App. 3d —, 2007 Ohio 6755, — N.E. 2d —, 2007 Ohio App. LEXIS 5912 (Dec. 14, 2007).

Defendant's motion claiming that defendant's maximum, consecutive sentences were erroneously imposed in violation of Foster and Blakely was properly summarily denied because (1) defendant was sentenced after the Blakely decision was issued but defendant did not preserve a Blakely objection by raising such an objection when defendant was sentenced, and

(2) defendant's Ohio R. Civ. P. 60(B) motion was not the appropriate vehicle for raising alleged sentencing error. State v. Hill, — Ohio App. 3d —, 2007 Ohio 6763, — N.E. 2d —, 2007 Ohio App. LEXIS 5942 (Dec. 17, 2007).

Denial of defendant's Ohio R. Civ. P. 60(B) motion to vacate a void judgment was appropriate regardless of whether it was considered a Rule 60(B) motion or a petition for postconviction relief. Defendant failed to explain how he met the requirements for relief under Rule 60(B), and with regard to postconviction relief, his claim was untimely and was subject to res judicata denial as the claim that defendant's sentence was void due to an irregularity in the verdict form could have been raised at the time of trial or on direct appeal. State v. Santiago, — Ohio App. 3d —, 2007 Ohio 6863, — N.E. 2d —, 2007 Ohio App. LEXIS 6009 (Dec. 20, 2007).

If defendant was deprived of the right to file timely objections to the magistrate's decision because neither he nor his counsel received that decision until more than 14 days after it was filed, defendant could have moved to vacate his conviction and sentence for that reason pursuant to Ohio R. Crim. P. 57(B) and Ohio R. Civ. P. 60(B)(1). However, the one-year provision of Ohio R. Civ. P. 60(B) would have applied, and more than one year had passed since the trial court entered its judgment; defendant's appeal did not toll the time. State v. Gilreath, 174 Ohio App. 3d 327, 2007 Ohio 6899, 882 N.E. 2d 22, 2007 Ohio App. LEXIS 6057 (Dec. 21, 2007).

As a criminal defendant's conviction was affirmed on appeal, based on the determination that his claims regarding allegedly erroneous jury instructions lacked merit, the criminal trial court judge lacked jurisdiction to rule on defendant's motion for relief from judgment based on the same instructional defects, pursuant to Ohio R. Crim. P. 57(B) and Ohio R. Civ. P. 60(B), as the law of the case precluded such further adjudication of the issues which had been determined by a higher court. The Ohio Attorney General's writ of prohibition was granted to require the judge to vacate that ruling. State ex rel. Petro v. Marshall, — Ohio App. 3d —, 2006 Ohio 5357, — N.E. 2d —, 2006 Ohio App. LEXIS 5327 (Oct. 10, 2006).

With respect to the inmate's motion to vacate or set aside his convictions pursuant to Ohio R. Civ. P. 60(B), the trial court properly found that the motion was an untimely petition for post conviction relief under RC § 2953.21 and the motion was properly denied as out of rule. The trial court could not entertain the untimely motion, under RC § 2953.23, since the inmate failed to show that he was unavoidably prevented from discovering the facts upon which he relied, and he could have raised the Brady issues on appeal. The doctrine of res judicata also barred his petition since he could have raised the issues in his direct appeal. State v. Graham, — Ohio App. 3d —, 2006 Ohio 352, — N.E. 2d —, 2006 Ohio App. LEXIS 313 (Jan. 30, 2006).

Appellant's Ohio R. Civ. P. 60(B) motion to have his sentence vacated was properly dismissed because the motion was limited to the issue raised in appellant's previous petition for post-conviction relief under RC § 2953.21, challenging his trial by an anonymous jury, since that was the only issue raised in original post-conviction petition. Further, appellant could not prevail in his post-conviction challenge to his sentence on Apprendi-Blakely grounds because retroactive application of the holdings in Blakely, Apprendi, and State v. Foster was limited to cases on direct review. State v. Brack, — Ohio App. 3d —, 2006 Ohio 3783, — N.E. 2d —, 2006 Ohio App. LEXIS 3724 (July 19, 2006).

Juvenile court's summary dismissal of a juvenile's postconviction relief petition pursuant to RC § 2953.21, without waiting for the juvenile to reply to the State's answer, was not error, and there was also no error in the juvenile's court's denial of the juvenile's motion for relief from judgment pursuant to Ohio R. Civ. P. 60(B)(5), as dismissal without the opportunity to file any supplemental or responsive pleading

was not error where the petition failed to set forth any substantive ground upon which relief could be granted. Butler County, Ohio, Ct. C.P. Gen. Div. R. 3.06(d) did not apply because the pleading by the State in response to the juvenile's petition did not qualify as a motion. In re J.B., — Ohio App. 3d —, 2006 Ohio 2715, — N.E. 2d —, 2006 Ohio App. LEXIS 2552 (May 30, 2006).

Defendant could not rely on Ohio R. Civ. P . 60(B) to challenge his sentence as his conviction and sentence arose out of a criminal proceeding, in which Rule 60(B) had no application; relief was instead available in a motion for post-conviction relief filed pursuant to RC § 2953.21, but not when the claim involved was barred by res judicata. State v. Muhleka, — Ohio App. 3d —, 2006 Ohio 1603, — N.E. —, 2006 Ohio App. LEXIS 1456 (Mar. 31, 2006).

Although a criminal court was entitled to rely on civil rules where there was no applicable criminal rule pursuant to Ohio R. Crim. P. 57(B), a trial court's determination that an inmate's motion for relief from judgment under Ohio R. Civ. P. 60(B) was actually a petition for post-conviction relief under RC § 2953.21 was proper, as it was filed after a direct appeal and sought vacation of his sentence on the basis that his constitutional rights were violated; as it was untimely filed without justification, it was properly dismissed. State v. Schlee, — Ohio App. 3d —, 2006 Ohio 3208, — N.E. 2d —, 2006 Ohio App. LEXIS 3116 (June 23, 2006).

Ohio Court of Appeals for the Eleventh Appellate District, Lake County, holds that Ohio R. Civ. P. 60 can be applied in criminal cases under certain circumstances, such as when there is no applicable criminal rule to address the specific issue pursuant to Ohio R. Crim. P. 57(B). State v. Schlee, — Ohio App. 3d —, 2006 Ohio 3208, — N.E. 2d —, 2006 Ohio App. LEXIS 3116 (June 23, 2006).

Damages

Trial court's denial of a medical practice's motion to vacate a default judgment pursuant to Ohio R. Civ. P. 60(B) was proper where, upon finding that the practice was in default of a patient's action, alleging inter alia, medical malpractice and negligent infliction of emotional distress, a hearing was held before a magistrate on the issue of damages; the damages awarded under Ohio R. Civ. P. 55(A) were not deemed excessive in the circumstances, as the patient had been injected with an HIV-contaminated drug which affected her state of mind, her ability to parent her son, and her employment possibilities. Bright v. Family Med. Found., Inc., — Ohio App. 3d —, 2006 Ohio 5037, — N.E.2d —, 2006 Ohio App. LEXIS 4947 (Sept. 28, 2006).

Default judgment

CivR 60(B) motion, filed by individuals connected with a home inspection company with regard to a default judgment entered in an action arising out of a home inspection was properly denied as personal service of the complaint against the individuals provided sufficient notice of the action, a letter sent to the trial court by one of the individuals was not a responsive pleading, and a claimed meritorious defense was unsupported. Arbogast v. Werley, — Ohio App. 3d —, 2008 Ohio 1555, — N.E. 2d —, 2008 Ohio App. LEXIS 1340 (Mar. 31, 2008).

Trial court properly granted a property seller's motion pursuant to Ohio R. Civ. P. 55(B) and 60(B) to set aside a default judgment that was granted in favor of a property owner, as the seller had not been given the requisite time to respond pursuant to Lucas County, Ohio, Ct. C.P. Gen. Div. R. 5.04(D), she was not served with a copy of the motion, and she asserted that the parties had signed a settlement agreement with a release of all claims. Chiaverini, Inc. v. Little, — Ohio App. 3d —, 2007 Ohio 3683, — N.E. 2d —, 2007 Ohio App. LEXIS 3392 (July 20, 2007).

When an insurer voluntarily dismissed and refiled its complaint, and the party it sued did not answer the refiled complaint, causing the insurer to move for the party's default, which was granted, it was not error to grant relief from that default judgment because the insurer was aware, from the proceedings prior to the voluntary dismissal, of the meritorious defense of the party it sued, and that meritorious defense was sufficiently stated in the answer which the party sought leave to file out of rule, even though it was not stated in the party's motion for relief from the default judgment. American Select Ins. Co. v. Riggs, — Ohio App. 3d —, 2007 Ohio 1808, — N.E. 2d —, 2007 Ohio App. LEXIS 1632 (Apr. 17, 2007).

Trial court did not abuse its discretion when it granted customers' motion under Ohio R. Civ. P. 60(B) for relief from a default judgment entered against them by a window and door company in its non-payment action, as the customers had no notice that the trial court might enter a default judgment as a potential sanction pursuant to Ohio R. Civ. P. 37(B) for their discovery non-compliance and no hearing was held on the issue of damages; although the docket incorrectly reflected that the default was entered due to lack of answer, such did not change the outcome of the matter where the right result was reached for the wrong reason. Gunton Corp. v. Architectural Concepts, — Ohio App. 3d —, 2007 Ohio 6805, — N.E. 2d —, 2007 Ohio App. LEXIS 5970 (Dec. 20, 2007).

Trial court properly allowed a mortgagee bank, as a post-judgment intervenor, to seek relief pursuant to Ohio R. Civ. P. 60(B)(5) in order to set aside a default judgment entered under Ohio R. Civ. P. 55 against a bankruptcy trustee by a mortgagor with respect to a dispute as to the mortgagor's dower interests in real property that the mortgagee was foreclosing upon, as the mortgagee had standing, the bankruptcy trustee was a cross-defendant, the motion to set aside the default judgment was made within one month after the judgment was obtained, and the trustee was not served at a valid address. The mortgagor met all three necessary elements to show it was entitled to relief from the default judgment. Standard Fed. Bank v. Staff, 168 Ohio App. 3d 14, 2006 Ohio 3601, 857 N.E. 2d 1245, 2006 Ohio App. LEXIS 3544 (July 14, 2006).

Since appellee presented evidence that he had contacted the insurer after being served with the insurer's complaint and that he had communicated to the insurer that he was disputing the merits of the claim, the trial court properly determined that appellee had appeared in the action, despite the fact that he never filed an answer, and, pursuant to Ohio R. Civ. P. 55, was entitled to a hearing on the insurer's motion for a default judgment; thus, appellee's Ohio R. Civ. P. 60(B) motion was properly granted. Allstate Ins. Co. v. Hunt, — Ohio App. 3d —, 2006 Ohio 238, — N.E. 2d —, 2006 Ohio App. LEXIS 194 (Jan. 13, 2006).

Trial court did not err in dismissing appellant's motion to vacate a default judgment under Ohio R. Civ. P. 60(B). Appellant failed to set forth in her motion any of the requirements of Ohio R. Civ. P. 60(B) and failed to present any affidavit quality evidence to establish any prong of Ohio R. Civ. P. 60(B)(1)-(5) or to show that she had a meritorious defense; thus, the motion was factually incomplete and did not set forth a legitimate basis for granting relief. Citibank, N.A. v. Stein, — Ohio App. 3d —, 2006 Ohio 2674, — N.E. 2d —, 2006 Ohio App. LEXIS 2506 (May 22, 2006).

When an insurer filed a declaratory judgment action seeking a declaration that it was not obligated to indemnify its insureds due to an alleged injured party's suit against them, and a default judgment was entered in the insurer's favor, after which the alleged injured party moved to set aside that default, under Ohio R. Civ. P. 60(B), and subsequently moved to intervene, it was not error for the trial court to grant the motion to set aside the default judgment, even though it was technically filed by a non-party, because the trial court's order implicitly granting the motion to set the judgment aside also allowed the alleged injured party to intervene. State Farm

Mut. Ins. Cos. v. Young, — Ohio App. 3d —, 2006 Ohio 3812, — N.E. 2d —, 2006 Ohio App. LEXIS 3784 (July 26, 2006).

Trial court improperly acted sua sponte to vacate a default judgment entered against a customer in a creditor's action on an open account because pursuant to Toledo, Ohio, Mun. Ct. R. 29(H), a default judgment could be vacated only in accordance with Ohio R. Civ. P. 60. No motion was filed under Rule 60 and there was no substantial compliance with Ohio R. Civ. P. 60(B) because when the customer filed a notice of appearance and request for an extension after the application for a default judgment was filed, the customer offered no argument or evidence in support of either his failure to appear and timely respond to the complaint or his request for a continuance, and therefore did not even substantially comply with the requirements of Rule 60(B). Carter-Jones Lumber Co. v. Willard, — Ohio App. 3d —, 2006 Ohio 6629, — N.E. 2d —, 2006 Ohio App. LEXIS 6551 (Dec. 15, 2006).

When a merchant sued a consumer on account, and the merchant's complaint did not specifically name the consumer, but the consumer did not appear after being properly served with process, the consumer was not entitled to relief, under Ohio R. Civ. P. 60(B), from the default judgment entered against him, because he did not show fraud, misrepresentation, mistake, or any other reason justifying relief from the judgment because he had the opportunity to appear in the trial court and raise his arguments, but he chose not to do so. River City Tire & Serv. Ctr. v. Erb, — Ohio App. 3d —, 2006 Ohio 6700, — N.E. 2d —, 2006 Ohio App. LEXIS 6598 (Dec. 12, 2006).

Delay

Given the unexplained four-year delay, the trial court was within its discretion to deny the State relief from judgment under Ohio R. Civ. P. 60(B) due to the untimeliness of the motion. The motion sought to have the order expunging defendant's criminal record, pursuant to RC § 2953.32, vacated because defendant was ineligible due to the fact that she had not been a first time offender. State v. Smith, — Ohio App. 3d —, 2007 Ohio 2873, — N.E. 2d —, 2007 Ohio App. LEXIS 2659 (June 12, 2007).

Where a mother's motion to vacate a prior court decision awarding custody of her child to legal custodians was treated as a motion for relief from judgment under Ohio R. Civ. P. 60(B), and she failed to show why she waited almost two years from the time of the prior decision to file her motion, and further, she had failed to file objections thereto and she did not appeal it in a timely manner, she failed to satisfy the reasonable time requirement under the third prong of the Rule 60(B) test. As the mother did not offer any justification for the delay in filing her motion to vacate the custody determination, there was no abuse of discretion in the trial court's denial of her motion. In re H.B., — Ohio App. 3d —, 2006 Ohio 2124, — N.E. 2d —, 2006 Ohio App. LEXIS 1969 (Apr. 28, 2006).

Where appellant claimed that he was unable to answer an action by a condominium owners association because he could not afford counsel, and his motion to vacate a judgment entered against him was filed just five days short of the one-year mark due to the same inability to find affordable representation, the trial court properly adopted a magistrate's decision to deny his motion under Ohio R. Civ. P. 60(B) to vacate the default judgment entered against him, as he failed to show a meritorious defense and he did not seek relief within a reasonable time. Bonnieville Towers Condo. Owners Ass'n v. Andrews, — Ohio App. 3d —, 2006 Ohio 2219, — N.E. 2d —, 2006 Ohio App. LEXIS 2063 (May 4, 2006).

Debtors' Ohio R. Civ. P. 60(B) motion to vacate a cognovit judgment against them was properly denied because the debtors waited nearly six months to file their motion and failed to give any reason for the delay. While the debtors contended that they were never served with copies of the notices of the judgment, the creditor's motion to intervene in a separate foreclosure action would have notified the debtors of the cognovit judgment. Federal Nat'l Mortg. Assoc. v. Goldstein, — Ohio App. 3d —, 2006 Ohio 6769, — N.E. 2d —, 2006 Ohio App. LEXIS 6677 (Dec. 21, 2006).

Discovery orders

As a trial court dismissed an employee's action against his employer due to his failure to produce various tax returns and other tax documents, as previously ordered by the trial court, the denial of the employee's motion for relief from judgment pursuant to Ohio R. Civ. P. 60(B)(1) and (5) was not an abuse of discretion, as the employee could have sought procedural devices throughout the litigation to protect the confidentiality of his documents, rather than having simply failed to produce the required documentation. Shikner v. S&P Solutions, — Ohio App. 3d —, 2007 Ohio 86, — N.E. 2d —, 2007 Ohio App. LEXIS 73 (Jan. 11, 2007).

Because the buyer failed to set forth operative facts justifying relief under Ohio R. Civ. P. 60(B), the trial court did not abuse its discretion by denying the motion for relief from judgment without a hearing. This was not a case where a party discovered post-judgment that the opposing party failed to produce material discovery, the buyer not only knew during the pendency of the proceedings that the seller had not produced all the requested discovery, he obtained a court order compelling the seller to produce that information. Rather than seek an extension of his briefing deadline to enforce his right to discovery as defined by the court's order granting his motion to compel, the buyer filed his brief in opposition to summary judgment and, by doing so, he forfeited the right to claim that the seller engaged in misconduct that left him at a disadvantage in responding to the motion for summary judgment. Pearlman v. Sukenik, — Ohio App. 3d —, 2007 Ohio 542, — N.E. 2d —, 2007 Ohio App. LEXIS 484 (Feb. 8, 2007).

As a note debtor failed to comply with a note holder's discovery request for the production of documents, a trial court's entry of a default judgment in favor of the holder pursuant to Ohio R. Civ. P. 37 as a discovery sanction was warranted, and as the debtor failed to establish any meritorious defense or claim if relief under Ohio R. Civ. P. 60(B) was granted, and the debtor also failed to show entitlement to relief thereunder, denial of the debtor's motion for relief from the default judgment was not an abuse of discretion; the debtor had failed to respond timely to the discovery request, had not responded to two additional letter requests for the discovery, and the debtor also failed to comply with a trial court order that set a date for the response to the discovery. Paparodis v. Snively, — Ohio App. 3d —, 2007 Ohio 6910, — N.E. 2d —, 2007 Ohio App. LEXIS 6064 (Dec. 12, 2007).

When, in response to an order compelling the production of evidence, in a negligence case, a nursing home sought relief, under Ohio R. Civ. P. 60(B)(1), and claimed that the material it was ordered to produce could be privileged, under RC § 2305.24 et seq., it was not an abuse of discretion for the trial court to find that a change in counsel handling the case did not show excusable neglect, and the nursing home did not present a meritorious defense because it did not show (1) it had a peer review committee, (2) that those sought to be deposed were members of such a committee, (3) that a peer review committee reviewed the subject matter of the case, (4) that any information ordered produced was presented to a peer review committee, or (5) that information ordered produced was used to assess the quality of care or for a disciplinary action. Smith v. Manor Care of Canton, Inc., — Ohio App. 3d —, 2006 Ohio 1182, — N.E. 2d —, 2006 Ohio App. LEXIS 1076 (Mar. 13, 2006).

Dissolution decree

Trial court did not abuse its discretion by denying the wife's Ohio R. Civ. P. 60(B) motion for relief from the decree of

dissolution because she chose to sit on her rights and failed to take any action to insure her own interests and equity did not demand that the judgment be set aside since the wife did not make even a cursory examination of the assets or debts and the husband took no actions to prevent her from doing so. There was no mutual mistake and the wife failed to demonstrate the existence of any fraud, misrepresentation, or misconduct in connection with the separation agreement as the husband did not misrepresent the amount of his pension. In re McLoughlin, — Ohio App. 3d —, 2006 Ohio 1530, — N.E. 2d —, 2006 Ohio App. LEXIS 1403 (Mar. 30, 2006).

There was no error in denying the wife's motion for relief from the marriage dissolution because she did not establish a basis for relief, nor did she make a convincing case for a meritorious defense if granted relief. Regarding her claims of mistake, excusable neglect, fraud, and duress, the evidence revealed that the husband was barely literate, the wife handled their financial affairs, both sides executed waiver of counsel, and the wife admitted that she wanted to extricate herself from the marriage as quickly as possible. Her desire to speed the proceedings along did not transform inexcusable neglect into excusable neglect. Wine v. Wine, — Ohio App. 3d —, 2006 Ohio 6995, — N.E. 2d —, 2006 Ohio App. LEXIS 6948 (Dec. 20, 2006).

Divorce decree

When a QDRO is inconsistent with a divorce decree, a trial court lacks jurisdiction to issue it, and it is void. A provision in a QDRO that the wife would forfeit her half of the husband's retirement benefits was unenforceable where there was no such provision in the separation agreement incorporated into the decree: Bagley v. Bagley, 181 Ohio App. 3d 141, 2009 Ohio 688, 908 N.E.2d 469, 2009 Ohio App. LEXIS 567 (2009).

Husband's Ohio R. Civ. P. 60(B) motion for relief from a divorce decree was properly denied because (1) the only provision of Rule 60(B) which could apply was the provision in Ohio R. Civ. P. 60(B)(4) about the prospective application of a judgment not being equitable, because the one-year limitation applicable to Ohio R. Civ. P. 60(B)(1), (2) and (3) had passed, the remainder of Ohio R. Civ. P. 60(B)(4) did not apply, and no other reason justifying relief was shown, under Ohio R. Civ. P. 60(B)(5), and (2) the husband's motion did not show the decree was no longer equitable because it only said more money would be paid from the husband's pension to the husband's former wife, and the motion mentioned no other adverse impact. Brown v. Brown, — Ohio App. 3d —, 2007 Ohio 4183, — N.E. 2d —, 2007 Ohio App. LEXIS 3764 (Aug. 16, 2007).

When a husband and wife continued to jointly own certain real property after their divorce, and the husband then sought its partition, it was not error for the trial court to decline to grant the wife's motion for a stay pending a ruling on her motion, in the divorce court, under Ohio R. Civ. P. 60(B), for relief from the divorce decree granting joint ownership, because she did not seek relief from this judgment for three years after the divorce was granted and several months after the husband filed for partition, and nothing showed whether or not the wife was likely to succeed on the merits in the divorce court. Stone v. Stone, — Ohio App. 3d —, 2006 Ohio 1996, — N.E. 2d —, 2006 Ohio App. LEXIS 1861 (Apr. 24, 2006).

There was no error in denying the Ohio R. Civ. P. 60(B) motion to vacate the divorce decree as the wife failed to meet her burden of proving that she was incapable of understanding the nature of the proceedings going on around her, especially when she actively participated in her divorce in open court. The trial court found that the wife's claim of incapacity and incompetence lacked credibility since it had specifically asked the wife whether she was under any emotional condition or whether the divorce was so overwhelming that it stopped her from thinking clearly and she responded in the negative. Miller v. Miller, — Ohio App. 3d —, 2006 Ohio 1288, — N.E. 2d —, 2006 Ohio App. LEXIS 1186 (Mar. 7, 2006).

When a husband sought relief, under Ohio R. Civ. P. 60(B)(5), from a divorce decree and a judgment distributing the proceeds of the parties' marital home, both of which he had agreed to, alleging that his wife had obtained credit cards in his name without his knowledge, and he was not aware of this until she pled not guilty by reason of insanity to resulting criminal charges, after the judgments from which he sought relief had been entered, his admission that he was aware that fraudulent credit charges were being made against his name and that he "strongly suspected" that the wife was responsible showed that he should have requested a hearing on her alleged violation of a preliminary injunction barring either party from incurring debt in the other's name, but, instead, he agreed to the judgments from which he sought relief to which he was not entitled. Pappas v. Pappas, — Ohio App. 3d —, 2006 Ohio 1403, — N.E. 2d —, 2006 Ohio App. LEXIS 1264 (Mar. 24, 2006).

Trial court did not abuse its discretion in overruling a former wife's motion under Ohio R. Civ. P. 60(B) to vacate a judgment entry of divorce on the ground that the incorporated parenting agreement was not the agreement of the parties; nothing in the record indicated that the wife was subjected to threats, harassment, or duress, the proximity of witnesses prepared to testify for the former husband and against the wife did not amount to undue influence, and the trial court properly found that the wife's alleged misunderstanding, lack of clear thinking, and sense of pressure while negotiating the agreement did not constitute mistake or inadvertence as contemplated in Rule 60(B). Hardesty v. Hardesty, — Ohio App. 3d —, 2006 Ohio 5648, — N.E. 2d —, 2006 Ohio App. LEXIS 5646 (Oct. 27, 2006).

There was no abuse of discretion by the trial court in ruling on the Ohio R. Civ. P. 60(B) motion because, although the husband suggested that he was entitled to start the whole divorce case over and have a new hearing on the issues, no such relief was requested, nor would it have been warranted by the death of his prior counsel, after the hearing. The husband had moved for relief from judgment with a supporting affidavit that stated that there were grievous errors in the magistrate's decision which would have been addressed by timely objection and timely appeal and by allowing him to file objections, the trial court corrected any prejudice to the husband that resulted from the untimely death of his former counsel. Rezack v. Rezack, — Ohio App. 3d —, 2006 Ohio 4471, — N.E. 2d —, 2006 Ohio App. LEXIS 4389 (Aug. 30, 2006).

When a husband sought relief, under Ohio R. Civ. P. 60(B)(5), from a divorce decree and a judgment distributing the proceeds of the parties' marital home, both of which he had agreed to, alleging that his wife had obtained credit cards in his name without his knowledge, and he was not aware of this until she pled not guilty by reason of insanity to resulting criminal charges, after the judgments from which he sought relief had been entered, an affidavit from the wife's divorce counsel stating that the parties' credit card debt had been thoroughly discussed in pre-decree negotiations showed operative facts that the husband had sufficient knowledge at the time of the decree and the subsequent order distributing proceeds from which to include this in negotiations about the wife's alimony, so he was not entitled to relief from these judgments. Pappas v. Pappas, — Ohio App. 3d —, 2006 Ohio 1403, — N.E. 2d —, 2006 Ohio App. LEXIS 1264 (Mar. 24, 2006).

When a husband sought relief, under Ohio R. Civ. P. 60(B)(5), from a divorce decree and a judgment distributing the proceeds of the parties' marital home, both of which he had agreed to, alleging that his wife had obtained credit cards in his name without his knowledge, it appeared that the facts alleged more properly fit under Ohio R. Civ. P. 60(B)(2) or (3), and it was improper to seek relief under Ohio R. Civ. P. 60(B)(5) when another provision of Ohio R. Civ. P. 60(B) applied, but the husband could not meet the one-year time limit under Ohio R. Civ. P. 60(B)(2) and (3). Pappas v. Pappas, — Ohio App. 3d —, 2006 Ohio 1403, — N.E. 2d —, 2006 Ohio App. LEXIS 1264 (Mar. 24, 2006).

Wife's Ohio R. Civ. P. 60(B) motion was properly denied as there was no mutual mistake since the parties had agreed that the market value of their condominium was $530,000 for the purpose of determining the wife's share of the value for their divorce and the subsequent $615,000 appraisal did not demonstrate that the parties were mistaken in their opinion. There was no evidence that the husband learned of the higher $615,000 appraised value until after the final decree had been granted and the wife was represented by an attorney and could have acted to protect her interests by obtaining a more competent appraisal. Wourms v. Wourms, 166 Ohio App. 3d 519, 2006 Ohio 1968, 851 N.E. 2d 553, 2006 Ohio App. LEXIS 1800 (Apr. 21, 2006).

Trial court did not abuse its discretion in denying a former wife's motion to either enforce the provisions of the parties' divorce judgment with respect to the division of the 401(K) profit-sharing plan, or alternatively, to vacate the judgment pursuant to Ohio R. Civ. P. 60(B), as the provision of the divorce judgment that divided that asset, which included three sub-accounts that held the parties' retirement accounts, was not "clear and unambiguous," and the trial court was empowered within its inherent authority to clarify the prior order as to the distribution intent regarding that asset. Rubin v. Rubin, — Ohio App. 3d —, 2006 Ohio 2383, — N.E. 2d —, 2006 Ohio App. LEXIS 2260 (May 12, 2006).

Wife's claim that she did not know of her husband's pension until shortly before she filed her post-decree motion to divide the pension raised a basis for relief from judgment under Ohio R. Civ. P. 60(B)(2) for newly discovered evidence; however, a party was not allowed to circumvent the one year limitation by seeking to vacate a judgment under Ohio R. Civ. P. 60(B)(5) when the grounds was duplicative of a ground subject to the time limitation. A trial court did not err in finding that it lacked jurisdiction to divide the husband's pension where the parties' original separation agreement was silent as to the pension, the wife's motion to divide the pension was filed 16 years after the original divorce decree, and the record revealed no reason why the wife, or her counsel, could not have discovered the pension at the time of the original proceeding. Stetler v. Stetler, — Ohio App. 3d —, 2006 Ohio 2663, — N.E. 2d —, 2006 Ohio App. LEXIS 2504 (May 30, 2006).

Where a magistrate determined that a husband and wife consented to the settlement agreement that was read onto the record and that supported their divorce decree, the wife's subsequent request for relief from judgment pursuant to Ohio R. Civ. P. 60(B) with respect to the divorce decree and a Qualified Domestic Relations Order was summarily denied, as she failed to show that there was newly discovered evidence which could not have been discovered at the time of the divorce decree for purposes of vacatur under Rule 60(B)(2). The wife's dissatisfaction with her counsel's performance did not amount to mistake or inadvertence for purposes of Rule 60(B)(1), and her attempt to relitigate issues that could have been directly appealed was improper. Laatsch v. Laatsch, — Ohio App. 3d —, 2006 Ohio 2923, — N.E. 2d —, 2006 Ohio App. LEXIS 2802 (June 9, 2006).

Trial court properly denied a husband's motion to vacate judgment due to alleged misrepresentation pursuant to Ohio R. Civ. P. 60(B)(3) in the parties' divorce action where there was no evidence that the wife misrepresented the value of her IRA or attempted to obscure the actual value of the account for purposes of the allocation of the retirement assets. Mamula v. Mamula, — Ohio App. 3d —, 2006 Ohio 4176, — N.E. 2d —, 2006 Ohio App. LEXIS 4131 (Aug. 11, 2006).

Wife's motion for relief from judgment under Ohio R. Civ. P. 60(B) was not a substitute for a direct appeal from a divorce judgment, and she could not claim in the motion that the trial court's distribution of the parties' property was inequitable, as such should have been properly raised in an appeal from the divorce judgment. Wilson v. Wilson, — Ohio App. 3d —, 2006 Ohio 4261, — N.E. 2d —, 2006 Ohio App. LEXIS 4187 (Aug. 17, 2006).

While a trial court cannot modify its property division, the parties themselves are free to modify the division by agreement. Where a party authorized her attorney to bind her to the agreed amended QDRO, her assertion that she misunderstood the agreed entry did not provide a basis for the court to vacate the agreed entry. The party failed to utilize the mechanism provided by CivR 60(B) concerning an alleged mistake. McGee v. McGee, 168 Ohio App. 3d 512, 2006 Ohio 4417, 860 N.E.2d 1054, 2006 Ohio App. LEXIS 4343 (2006).

Trial court did not abuse its discretion in overruling a former wife's motion under Ohio R. Civ. P. 60(B) to vacate a judgment entry of divorce because of the former husband's failure to disclose a pension; both parties worked at the same employer, both parties had pensions with that employer which they both failed to disclose, the proceeding was a contested divorce rather than a dissolution with an integral element of mutuality, and the evidence indicated that the wife was aware of the existence of the husband's pension. Hardesty v. Hardesty, — Ohio App. 3d —, 2006 Ohio 5648, — N.E. 2d —, 2006 Ohio App. LEXIS 5646 (Oct. 27, 2006).

Domestic relations orders

Pursuant to the parties' settlement agreement in their divorce action and under RC § 3105.171(I), a Qualified Domestic Relations Order properly included the former husband's early retirement supplement and his basic pension benefits, and the valuation date was set at the date of the divorce judgment. As the Order indicated that the wife was entitled to share in any post-retirement increase, which was inconsistent with the language of the parties' divorce decree, vacatur of the Order pursuant to the husband's motion under Ohio R. Civ. P. 60 was proper. Hale v. Hale, — Ohio App. 3d —, 2007 Ohio 867, — N.E. 2d —, 2007 Ohio App. LEXIS 774 (Mar. 2, 2007).

Pursuant to the parties' settlement agreement in their divorce action and under RC § 3105.171(I), a Qualified Domestic Relations Order properly included the former husband's early retirement supplement and his basic pension benefits, and the valuation date was set at the date of the divorce judgment. As the Order indicated that the wife was entitled to share in any post-retirement increase, which was inconsistent with the language of the parties' divorce decree, vacatur of the Order pursuant to the husband's motion under Ohio R. Civ. P. 60 was proper. Hale v. Hale, — Ohio App. 3d —, 2007 Ohio 867, — N.E. 2d —, 2007 Ohio App. LEXIS 774 (Mar. 2, 2007).

As a temporary agreed order between divorcing parties, wherein the husband was obligated to pay a home equity loan, was merged into the parties' final divorce decree and there was no indication in the decree that the husband was still obligated to make such loan payments, the trial court did not err in denying the wife's motion under Ohio R. Civ. P. 60(B)(5) to clarify the decree for purposes of recoupment of the loan payments that she had made post-divorce; further, the wife failed to appeal in a timely manner under Ohio R. App. P. 4(A) from the final divorce decree and she did not raise the issue regarding the loan payments until approximately six years and eight months after the divorce decree was entered. Kovacic v. Kovacic, — Ohio App. 3d —, 2007 Ohio 5956, — N.E. 2d —, 2007 Ohio App. LEXIS 5226 (Nov. 8, 2007).

Magistrate properly rejected a husband's request for relief from judgment pursuant to Ohio R. Civ. P. 60(B)(4), where he had been ordered to pay child support for a child over which he doubted paternity, although it was determined that he in fact was the father, as the husband should have taken steps sooner than 13 years after the parties' divorce on the matter if he had doubts as to his paternity; the motion was not filed within a reasonable time, which was an independent basis for denial of the motion. White v. Jacques, — Ohio App. 3d —, 2006 Ohio 464, — N.E. 2d —, 2006 Ohio App. LEXIS 424 (Feb. 3, 2006).

Trial court did not abuse its discretion in denying a former husband's motion for relief from judgment pursuant to Ohio R. Civ. P. 60(B)(1) and (5) from a division of property order (DPO) that was entered by the trial court, as he failed to show operative facts that constituted a meritorious defense to the DPO, and the fact that he had not been served with the DPO was not grounds to grant the Rule 60(B) motion; his right to appeal from that order did not start to run under Ohio R. App. P. 4(A) and Ohio R. Civ. P. 58(B) until such service occurred, but such was not grounds to grant relief from the order. Bevan v. Bevan, — Ohio App. 3d —, 2006 Ohio 1306, — N.E. 2d —, 2006 Ohio App. LEXIS 1203 (Mar. 22, 2006).

Trial court's denial of a husband's motion for relief from judgment pursuant to Ohio R. Civ. P. 60(B)(4), arising from the granting to the wife of a permanent civil protection order, was proper where the fact that custody of one of the parties' children was modified did not change the need for the civil protection order, as that had been based on threats from the husband to the wife and not on his conduct towards the children. Chapman v. Chapman, — Ohio App. 3d —, 2006 Ohio 2328, — N.E. 2d —, 2006 Ohio App. LEXIS 2169 (May 5, 2006).

Equity

Trial court properly denied guarantors' motion under Ohio R. Civ. P. 60(B) to vacate a default judgment obtained against them and their business by a supply seller, as the guarantors were unjustly enriched by the goods acquired from the seller, and a limit to their liability would have been inequitable; accordingly, the judgment entered against them for monies due on their business account was proper. Seal Master Industries, Inc. v. Bay Area Seal Coating & Stripping, — Ohio App. 3d —, 2006 Ohio 3610, — N.E. 2d —, 2006 Ohio App. LEXIS 3547 (July 14, 2006).

When a mortgagee claimed it was equitably entitled to relief from a summary judgment, under Ohio R. Civ. P. 60(B)(4), it was not an abuse of discretion for a trial court to decline to hear the claim because Ohio R. Civ. P. 60(B)(4) did not apply, as, under that provision, circumstances justifying relief had to occur subsequent to the entry of the judgment, and the circumstances which the mortgagee said justified relief were that the summary judgment movant was unjustly enriched when summary judgment was granted and she was found not responsible for loan proceeds she used to pay off her property, but the alleged unjust enrichment occurred before or at the same time as the judgment. National City Home Loan Servs. v. Gillette, — Ohio App. 3d —, 2006 Ohio 2881, — N.E. 2d —, 2006 Ohio App. LEXIS 2716 (June 2, 2006).

When a mortgagee claimed it was equitably entitled to relief from a summary judgment, under Ohio R. Civ. P. 60(B)(5), it was not an abuse of discretion for a trial court to decline to hear the claim because even assuming that the mortgagee's claim that the summary judgment movant's affidavit was false was true and that judgment in her favor inflicted an injustice on the mortgagee, the mortgagee could have presented that injustice by taking timely steps to present its evidence in response to the motion, so the public policy supporting the finality of judgments outweighed any injustice. National City Home Loan Servs. v. Gillette, — Ohio App. 3d —, 2006 Ohio 2881, — N.E. 2d —, 2006 Ohio App. LEXIS 2716 (June 2, 2006).

Excusable neglect

Trial court did not abuse its discretion in granting a temporary employment agency's motion under Ohio R. Civ. P. 60(B)(1) for relief from a default judgment against it where it showed excusable neglect, a meritorious defense, and that the motion was timely filed. An employee for the agency testified that despite having followed the normal procedures for lawsuits, the complaint was not answered, the claim against the agency lacked merit in law, and the motion was timely. Heard v. Dubose, — Ohio App. 3d —, 2007 Ohio 551, — N.E. 2d —, 2007 Ohio App. LEXIS 510 (Feb. 9, 2007).

Landlord was not entitled to relief from judgment under Ohio R. Civ. P. 60(B) because the trial court did not abuse its discretion in finding that the landlord's actions, in failing to object to the magistrate's decision because he was out of the country and could not receive his mail, were inexcusable neglect. The landlord was aware that he was a party to a pending litigation and that a final judgment was scheduled to be rendered and it was his responsibility to make arrangements for mail addressed to him to ultimately be delivered to him. Tidwell v. Quaglieri, — Ohio App. 3d —, 2007 Ohio 569, — N.E. 2d —, 2007 Ohio App. LEXIS 530 (Feb. 9, 2007).

Even though a defendant has promptly notified an insurance company of the filing of a lawsuit, his neglect in failing to independently determine whether an answer has been filed on his behalf may well change from "excusable" to "inexcusable" upon the passage of time, without regard to the one year provision regulating the timeliness of a motion for relief from a default judgment. Federico v. Langham, — Ohio App. 3d —, 2007 Ohio 2168, — N.E. 2d —, 2007 Ohio App. LEXIS 2015 (May 4, 2007).

When a motorist who was sued by an alleged injured party notified the motorist's insurer of the complaint, but the insurer did not file an answer, and a default judgment was entered against the motorist, the motorist did not show excusable neglect, under Ohio R. Civ. P. 60(B)(1), because (1) more than 100 days elapsed between the answer due date and the date of the default judgment motion, (2) the motorist had a duty to ensure that the insurer had filed an answer, particularly when the motorist was notified that the alleged injured party was seeking a default judgment against the motorist, which notified the motorist that the insurer had not taken proper measures to defend him, and (3) the insurer's neglect was attributable to the motorist. Federico v. Langham, — Ohio App. 3d —, 2007 Ohio 2168, — N.E. 2d —, 2007 Ohio App. LEXIS 2015 (May 4, 2007).

Husband demonstrated that he was entitled to relief from a judgment entered in a divorce action on the ground of excusable neglect under Ohio R. Civ. P. 60(B)(1) because it was readily apparent that everyone in the courtroom at the divorce trial was aware that the husband, who had already been convicted of crimes in which the wife was a victim, was in a state prison when he failed to attend the divorce trial and that the husband had not received the notice of hearing sent to the county jail. The husband's whereabouts could have been readily ascertained by a simple search of the Department of Rehabilitation and Corrections website. Dottore v. Feathers, — Ohio App. 3d —, 2007 Ohio 2435, — N.E. 2d —, 2007 Ohio App. LEXIS 2266 (May 18, 2007).

Car lessee was not entitled to relief from a judgment of the trial court, which dismissed her third-party complaint for failure to prosecute, as her claim under Ohio R. Civ. P. 60(B)(1) that her lawyer was engaged in other matters did not constitute excusable neglect and further, final judgment was entered against her at an earlier time. First Merit Bank v. Crouse, — Ohio App. 3d —, 2007 Ohio 2440, — N.E. 2d —, 2007 Ohio App. LEXIS 2278 (May 21, 2007).

Trial court properly granted a default judgment pursuant to Ohio R. Civ. P. 55(A) to business purchasers in their action against the business seller, as the seller had failed to file a timely answer and counterclaim to the purchasers' amended complaint and he failed to show excusable neglect pursuant to Ohio R. Civ. P. 6(B)(2) for the untimely filing for purposes of his motion to file the answer and counterclaim instanter. As the seller also failed to show excusable neglect for the lack of reasonable diligence in filing the answer in a timely manner, as well as a meritorious defense to the complaint, his motion to vacate under Ohio R. Civ. P. 60(B) was properly denied. Ear v. Phnom Penh Rest., — Ohio App. 3d —, 2007 Ohio 3069, — N.E. 2d —, 2007 Ohio App. LEXIS 2811 (June 21, 2007).

Trial court did not abuse its discretion under Ohio R. Civ. P. 55(B) and 60(B)(1) when it denied a law client's motion for relief from a default judgment that had been entered against it on a law firm's complaint, seeking recovery for services rendered, as the client did not show that the failure to answer the firm's complaint was excusable neglect. Although the client asserted that a temporary employee of another company that shared office space with the client had mishandled the complaint upon signing for it by certified mail, the president of the client had admitted that he may have learned of the receipt of the complaint or been shown a copy of it, such that there was no excuse for having failed to answer in the circumstances. Benesch, Friedlander, Coplan & Arnoff v. City Concrete, LLC, — Ohio App. 3d —, 2007 Ohio 3331, — N.E. 2d —, 2007 Ohio App. LEXIS 3126 (June 21, 2007).

When a default judgment was entered against an attorney in a legal malpractice suit, the attorney's counsel's brain surgery did not show excusable neglect, under Ohio R. Civ. P. 60(B)(1), for failing to timely file an answer because the attorney was aware of the time limits for filing an answer but did nothing while awaiting counsel's recovery. Hover v. O'Hara, — Ohio App. 3d —, 2007 Ohio 3614, — N.E. 2d —, 2007 Ohio App. LEXIS 3308 (July 16, 2007).

As credit card holders failed to show excusable neglect for purposes of their motion under Ohio R. Civ. P. 60(B)(1), seeking relief from a trial court's adoption of an arbitration report that recommended judgment in favor of the credit card issuer's assignee, their motion lacked merit. Their claim that their attorney failed to familiarize himself with the local rules did not constitute excusable neglect. Cavalry Invs., LLC v. Dzilinski, — Ohio App. 3d —, 2007 Ohio 3767, — N.E. 2d —, 2007 Ohio App. LEXIS 3435 (July 26, 2007).

Ohio R. Civ. P. 60(B) motion to set aside judgments of dismissal entered against appellant was properly denied. Appellant's claim that his failure to respond to appellees' motions to dismiss was the result of excusable neglect was without merit because, though appellant's counsel was a sole practitioner and was bombarded with multiple motions at one time, he should have filed a motion for extension of time to respond to the dismissal motions. Peoples v. Lang, — Ohio App. 3d —, 2007 Ohio 4249, — N.E. 2d —, 2007 Ohio App. LEXIS 3923 (Aug. 13, 2007).

Trial court did not abuse its discretion in denying an insurer's motion under Ohio R. Civ. P. 60(B)(1) for relief from a default judgment where the failure to answer the complaint that was served upon it was inexcusable neglect; the insurer failed to provide sufficient evidence that it had a procedure in place at its branch offices to deal with legal process, such that the insurer's claim that the employee upon whom the complaint was served failed to forward it to the corporate office lacked merit. Linquist v. Allstate, — Ohio App. 3d —, 2007 Ohio 4587, — N.E. 2d —, 2007 Ohio App. LEXIS 4121 (Aug. 27, 2007).

When an insured sought relief, under Ohio R. Civ. P. 60(B)(5), from the insured's alleged inadvertent dismissal of a party, due to excusable neglect, the insured was not entitled to such relief because the insured did not show that any neglect was excusable since the insured's counsel presumably read the insured's notice of dismissal before filing the notice. Len-ran, Inc. v. Erie Ins. Group, — Ohio App. 3d —, 2007 Ohio 4763, — N.E. 2d —, 2007 Ohio App. LEXIS 4250 (Sept. 14, 2007).

When an insured sought relief, under Ohio R. Civ. P. 60(B)(5), from the insured's alleged inadvertent dismissal of a party, due to excusable neglect, the insured was not entitled to such relief because excusable neglect was a ground for relief under Ohio R. Civ. P. 60(B)(1), so the insured could not use excusable neglect as a ground for relief under Ohio R. Civ. P. 60(B)(5). Len-ran, Inc. v. Erie Ins. Group, — Ohio App. 3d —, 2007 Ohio 4763, — N.E. 2d —, 2007 Ohio App. LEXIS 4250 (Sept. 14, 2007).

Trial court did not abuse its discretion when it granted an advertising company's motion for relief from a default judgment pursuant to Ohio R. Civ. P. 60(B), as it moved for that relief within 30 days of the entry of the default judgment, it asserted several meritorious defenses to the advertising customer's breach of contract and fraud action, and it provided reasons why the company did not defend the case that amounted to "excusable neglect." Beauty Max Llc v. Wbuy Tv, — Ohio App. 3d —, 2007 Ohio 4831, — N.E. 2d —, 2007 Ohio App. LEXIS 4322 (Sept. 20, 2007).

Debtor's Ohio R. Civ. P. 60(B)(1) motion for relief from default judgment was improperly granted as the motion was not timely filed, in that it was not filed within one year after the default judgment was entered against him. Moreover, the debtor could not rely on his lack of legal training to excuse his failure to file an answer to the creditor's complaint on the ground of excusable neglect. First Resolution Inv. Corp. v. Coffey, — Ohio App. 3d —, 2007 Ohio 6827, — N.E. 2d —, 2007 Ohio App. LEXIS 6011 (Dec. 19, 2007).

Store had established excusable neglect for its failure to file a response to a customer's personal injury complaint by evidence that the store had established a procedure that was to be followed upon service of a complaint and that the procedure was inadvertently not followed. Chirico v. Home Depot, — Ohio App. 3d —, 2006 Ohio 291, — N.E. 2d —, 2006 Ohio App. LEXIS 228 (Jan. 26, 2006).

Trial court abused its discretion by denying a landlord's motion to vacate an order awarding summary judgment to a tenant and dismissing the landlord's counterclaim following the landlord's absence from the initial pretrial conference because the oversight of the landlord's counsel in noting an incorrect time for the pretrial conference did not exhibit a deliberate act of ignoring a judicial directive such as constituted excusable neglect, the landlord asserted a meritorious defense, and filed the motion in a timely manner. Maddox v. Ward, — Ohio App. 3d —, 2006 Ohio 4099, — N.E. 2d —, 2006 Ohio App. LEXIS 4073 (Aug. 10, 2006).

Company's Ohio R. Civ. P. 60(B) motion was properly granted because the affidavit of the company's receiver supported a finding that the company was experiencing some type of organizational crisis when the proceedings were first begun, thereby justifying its failure to timely respond to plaintiffs' complaint. The trial court was permitted to consider that the company's receivership condition contributed to its failure to make an appearance. Garcia v. Denne Indus., — Ohio App. 3d —, 2006 Ohio 107, — N.E. 2d —, 2006 Ohio App. LEXIS 83 (Jan. 12, 2006).

Trial court abuse its discretion in denying the employee's Ohio R. Civ. P. 60(B) motion for relief from judgment because he was entitled to relief on the grounds of excusable neglect. He claimed that he was the wrong party, which was a meritorious defense; he attempted to contact the buyer's attorney many times without success, which showed an intent to "appear" for purposes of Ohio R. Civ. P. 55; and the relief motion was filed within a reasonable time as it was only two months after service of the complaint. Rocha v. Salsbury, — Ohio App. 3d —, 2006 Ohio 2615, — N.E. 2d —, 2006 Ohio App. LEXIS 2448 (May 26, 2006).

When it was undisputed that a complaint filed against a restaurant was served on it in its business name at its business address, the fact that the individual who signed a certified mail receipt for the complaint was not authorized to do so, was fired two weeks later, and did not forward the complaint to the proper person did not show that the restaurant's neglect in losing the complaint within its business premises was excusable, under Ohio R. Civ. P. 60(B)(1). Kemer v. Glass, — Ohio App. 3d —, 2006 Ohio 2979, — N.E. 2d —, 2006 Ohio App. LEXIS 2865 (June 14, 2006).

Defendant's Ohio R. Civ. P. 60(B) motion for relief from default judgment was properly denied because defendant failed to set forth with sufficient specificity the circumstances that prevented her from filing timely answer; thus, defendant failed to establish excusable neglect. While defendant was traveling when the complaint was mailed, she did not set forth specific dates and did not aver why the person who was collecting her mail did not sort through it earlier. National City Bank v. Calvey, — Ohio App. 3d —, 2006 Ohio 3101, — N.E. 2d —, 2006 Ohio App. LEXIS 2966 (June 20, 2006).

When a mother sought relief from a judgment granting sole custody of her children to their father, after she did not appear at a hearing, it was not an abuse of discretion to grant her relief under Ohio R. Civ. P. 60(B)(1), due to excusable neglect, because she showed that her failure to appear was not due to a total disregard of the judicial system, as she had attended numerous other hearings in the case and a related case, and her claim that she became confused about the hearing date due to her busy schedule was credible. Anderson-Harber v. Harber, — Ohio App. 3d —, 2006 Ohio 3106, — N.E. 2d —, 2006 Ohio App. LEXIS 3098 (June 20, 2006).

Trial court did not err in denying the appraiser's Ohio R. Civ. P. 60(B) motion because she failed to sufficiently support a motion under Ohio R. Civ. P. 60(B)(1) for mistake, inadvertence, surprise, or excusable neglect. She merely stated that she did not answer the complaint because of other professional obligations and oversight. Because any possible delay in the receipt of the complaint did not explain her delay in filing her reply and because her general, unspecified medical problems did not form a basis for excusable neglect, the appraiser failed to show that one of the circumstances rendering relief under Ohio R. Civ. P. 60(B)(1)-(5) existed. Mortgage Lenders Network USA v. Riggins, — Ohio App. 3d —, 2006 Ohio 3292, — N.E. 2d —, 2006 Ohio App. LEXIS 3210 (June 28, 2006).

Home owner's Ohio R. Civ. P. 60(B) motion to set aside a default judgment was properly denied because the owner failed to demonstrate excusable neglect or inadvertence when he appeared to defend the action against him at the wrong place and on the wrong date. The owner acknowledged that he received notice and complaint in which the correct date and place for the hearing was clearly stated and admitted that he largely disregarded it because he thought that the allegations in the complaint were false. Hicks v. Walcher, — Ohio App. 3d —, 2006 Ohio 3382, — N.E. 2d —, 2006 Ohio App. LEXIS 3300 (June 30, 2006).

Trial court properly denied a former boyfriend's motion for relief from judgment pursuant to Ohio R. Civ. P. 60(B)(1) and (5), seeking to vacate a settlement agreement entered into after mediation with his former girlfriend regarding the disposition of their jointly-acquired real property, as his neglect in seeking legal assistance was not excusable, he was not entitled to standards other than those applicable to litigants represented by counsel, and his change of heart after entering the settlement agreement and having it filed with the court did not support the request to vacate it. Szabo v. Lepore, — Ohio App. 3d —, 2006 Ohio 3569, — N.E. 2d —, 2006 Ohio App. LEXIS 3517 (July 5, 2006).

Appellee demonstrated excusable neglect under Ohio R. Civ. P. 60(B) justifying relief from a default judgment entered against her. Appellee's failure to appear at trial was not a complete disregard for the judicial system especially when she failed to appear because she assumed that appellant's motion for a continuance, filed the day before trial but served on her 10 days earlier, would be granted and, thus, appeared instead for jury duty in a different courtroom. State Auto Ins. Co. v. Colclough, — Ohio App. 3d —, 2006 Ohio 3654, — N.E. 2d —, 2006 Ohio App. LEXIS 3599 (July 14, 2006).

Trial court abused its discretion in denying a mechanical company's motion for relief from judgment pursuant to Ohio R. Civ. P. 60(B) where it claimed that an attorney who contacted the trial court on the company's behalf represented that the trial court had agreed to provide the company an additional few weeks to secure counsel in order to pursue settlement possibilities. The trial court had entered judgment for builders when the company had not obtained counsel to represent it by a date set by the trial court after its attorney's motion to withdraw shortly prior to the date set for trial had been granted. Seitz Builders, Inc. v. Kaplan Mech. Corp., — Ohio App. 3d —, 2006 Ohio 3965, — N.E. 2d —, 2006 Ohio App. LEXIS 3911 (Aug. 3, 2006).

Customer's Ohio R. Civ. P. 60(B) motion was properly denied since the customer failed to establish excusable neglect, in that she had over two months to retain counsel before the hearing on a motion to dismiss her suit but failed to do so. Further, while the customer alleged that she had sustained a brain injury and, as a result, was impeded in her ability to abide by time limitations, the customer's appearances at two hearings indicated that she had retained the ability to function and respond to time demands and that her injury was not responsible for her delay. Newman v. The Farmacy Natural & Specialty Foods, — Ohio App. 3d —, 2006 Ohio 4633, — N.E. 2d —, 2006 Ohio App. LEXIS 4549 (Aug. 31, 2006).

Customer's Ohio R. Civ. P. 60(B) motion was properly denied since the customer's motion was not timely filed. Because the customer had been given two chances to retain new counsel and had more than a year in which to do so, the trial court did not err in concluding that the customer's unsuccessful attempts to secure counsel justified the customer's 14-month delay in filing the Ohio R. Civ. P. 60(B) motion. Newman v. The Farmacy Natural & Specialty Foods, — Ohio App. 3d —, 2006 Ohio 4633, — N.E. 2d —, 2006 Ohio App. LEXIS 4549 (Aug. 31, 2006).

Trial court's denial of a medical practice's motion for relief from judgment pursuant to Ohio R. Civ. P. 60(B) was proper where excusable neglect was not shown, as pursuant to case law at the time that a patient's complaint, asserting medical malpractice and other claims, was filed against it, the fact that the patient had sued the practice by a fictitious name was not fatal to the claim; pursuant to RC § 1329.10(C), a suit against a party by only its fictitious name was permissible, and the practice erred in failing to answer the complaint. Bright v. Family Med. Found., Inc., — Ohio App. 3d —, 2006 Ohio 5037, — N.E.2d —, 2006 Ohio App. LEXIS 4947 (Sept. 28, 2006).

Trial court did not abuse its discretion in granting a passenger's motion for relief from judgment pursuant to Ohio R. Civ. P. 60(B) after a judgment was rendered in favor of a driver's insurer in its declaratory judgment action, wherein it was determined that the insurer had no duty to provide coverage or defense to its insured, the driver, or indemnity to the passenger, based on the driver's failure to cooperate, as the passenger showed that he had a meritorious defense because he was entitled to coverage for his injuries sustained in an accident caused by the driver, he was entitled to relief due to excusable neglect under Rule 60(B)(1), and he moved within two months, which was reasonable; the absence of affidavits did not preclude relief from judgment, based on the requirements for factual assertions under Hamilton County, Ohio, Ct. C.P. R. 14. Pfeiffer v. State Auto. Mut. Ins. Co., — Ohio App. 3d —, 2006 Ohio 5074, — N.E. 2d —, 2006 Ohio App. LEXIS 5009 (Sept. 29, 2006).

After a patient's medical malpractice complaint was dismissed for failure to file an affidavit of merit along with her complaint, the patient's motion for relief from judgment on the ground of excusable neglect under Civ. R. 60(B) was

properly granted because the evidence showed that the patient's attorney had diligently researched whether an affidavit of merit was required in filing a medical malpractice complaint but had missed the new version of Civ. R. 10, which required such an affidavit but had become effective only 27 days before patient's complaint was filed. The attorney had tried to be in compliance with the relevant law instead of choosing to be willfully ignorant of whether he was in compliance. Banfield v. Brodell, — Ohio App. 3d —, 2006 Ohio 5267, — N.E. 2d —, 2006 Ohio App. LEXIS 5262 (Sept. 27, 2006).

Food stores that asserted that they were entitled to vacatur of a default judgment entered against them on the basis of excusable neglect failed to warrant relief where no details were offered to support that claim for purposes of a reconsideration motion, as one count of the complaint by the food supplier was still pending when the default was entered as to the other claims and accordingly, the order of default was interlocutory. Even if the motion was deemed one that was appropriate under Ohio R. Civ. P. 60(B) for final orders, there was no abuse of discretion in the trial court's denial thereof where the required proof by the stores was not shown for purposes of relief. Tusco Grocers v. Rulli Family Foods, — Ohio App. 3d —, 2006 Ohio 6665, — N.E. 2d —, 2006 Ohio App. LEXIS 6564 (Dec. 11, 2006).

When a trial court entered summary judgment in favor of the Ohio Supreme Court's Client Security Fund, in its suit against a former attorney for funds it had paid to his former client, the attorney sufficiently showed he was surprised by the judgment because his numerous filings indicated that he would have defended himself against the Fund's summary judgment motion had he been aware of it, so he was entitled to relief from the judgment, under Ohio R. Civ. P. 60(B)(1). State v. Potts, — Ohio App. 3d —, 2006 Ohio 7057, — N.E. 2d —, 2006 Ohio App. LEXIS 6989 (Dec. 28, 2006).

When a mortgagee claimed its failure to respond to a landowner's summary judgment motion was due to excusable neglect, under Ohio R. Civ. P. 60(B)(1), it was not an abuse of discretion for the trial court to decline to hear this claim because (1) it did not allege that its failure to respond was due to any extenuating circumstances, but, instead, simply relied on its claim that it did not exhibit dilatory conduct in the proceedings leading up to the motion, and (2) it did not state some operative facts to assist the trial court in finding if its neglect was excusable. National City Home Loan Servs. v. Gillette, — Ohio App. 3d —, 2006 Ohio 2881, — N.E. 2d —, 2006 Ohio App. LEXIS 2716 (June 2, 2006).

Extraordinary circumstances

Landowner was not entitled to relief from a consent judgment requiring the landowner to clean up the landowner's property, under Ohio R. Civ. P. 60(B)(5), over four years after the judgment was entered, because the landowner did not show that extraordinary circumstances existed which warranted relieving the owner of the owner's obligations under the judgment, as the owner stated no factual grounds for relief or right to relief. Rock Creek v. Shinkle, — Ohio App. 3d —, 2007 Ohio 4769, — N.E. 2d —, 2007 Ohio App. LEXIS 4251 (Sept. 14, 2007).

Example of substantial grounds justifying relief from a judgment under Ohio R. Civ. P. 60B(B)(5) was court errors and omissions affecting a party's ability to pursue a cause of action, as justice abhorred the loss of causes of action by pure technicalities. Dunn v. Marthers, — Ohio App. 3d —, 2006 Ohio 4923, — N.E. 2d —, 2006 Ohio App. LEXIS 4890 (Sept. 25, 2006).

When, in a personal injury case, a trial court granted an insurer's dismissal motion, and, at the same time, dismissed a motorist who had been sued, the alleged injured party who filed the suit was entitled to relief from the judgment dismissing the motorist, under Ohio R. Civ. P. 60(B)(5), because the alleged injured party had no notice that dismissal of the motorist was contemplated, the motorist conceded that the alleged injured party's complaint stated a claim against the motorist, and the motorist's dismissal was due to a technical error, all creating extraordinary circumstances which warranted the application of Rule 60(B)(5). Dunn v. Marthers, — Ohio App. 3d —, 2006 Ohio 4923, — N.E. 2d —, 2006 Ohio App. LEXIS 4890 (Sept. 25, 2006).

Failure to answer

Trial court did not abuse its discretion under Ohio R. Civ. P. 60(B) when it denied mortgagors' motion to vacate a summary judgment that was granted without opposition to a mortgagee in his foreclosure action, as the mortgagors' failure to have filed their opposition by the scheduled date was not shown to have been caused by excusable neglect under Rule 60(B)(1), and they offered no additional operative facts that would have allowed them to seek relief under the "catchall" provision of Rule 60(B)(5). As they did not request an evidentiary hearing and did not offer any meritorious reason to have one, the faiure to hold such a hearing was not error. Jones v. Gayhart, — Ohio App. 3d —, 2007 Ohio 3584, — N.E. 2d —, 2007 Ohio App. LEXIS 3292 (July 13, 2007).

Under the test used to determine whether a particular defendant's actions in relying on his or her notification of his or her insurance carrier was "excusable neglect," the factors considered were (1) whether the defendant promptly notified the insurance carrier regarding the complaint, (2) the lapse of time between the date the answer was due and the date a default judgment against the defendant was entered, (3) the amount of the default judgment, and (4) the degree of the defendant's legal experience. Federico v. Langham, — Ohio App. 3d —, 2007 Ohio 2168, — N.E. 2d —, 2007 Ohio App. LEXIS 2015 (May 4, 2007).

Trial court erred in granting plaintiffs Ohio R. Civ. P. 60(B) relief from summary judgment where they failed to respond to the owners' summary judgment motion. Erie County, Ohio, Ct. C.P. R. 4.01, which governed the time limitations for summary judgment related filings, provided sufficient notice of the deadlines for filing memoranda and evidence with regard to summary judgment, plaintiffs had no legitimate reason for failing to respond to the owners' summary judgment motion after the depositions they sought to take had been taken, and, pursuant to interpretation of the interplay between Ohio R. Civ. P. 56(C) and local civil procedure rules, the trial court had discretion under Erie County, Ohio, Ct. C.P. R. 4.01 in determining whether to grant the owners oral argument, and it determined that a hearing was not necessary. Tuttle v. Cafaro Co., — Ohio App. 3d —, 2006 Ohio 1641, — N.E. 2d —, 2006 Ohio App. LEXIS 1528 (Mar. 31, 2006).

Failure to attend hearing

Trial court did not abuse its discretion in denying an insurer's motion under Ohio R. Civ. P. 60(B)(1) for relief from judgment, arising from the insurer's counsel's failure to appear at the third pretrial hearing on a car owner's property damage claim, as the insurer only asserted that counsel made an honest mistake in failing to appear at that time; however, the insurer failed to meet the other requirements in order to show its right to relief from the default judgment, such as the existence of a meritorious defense or sufficient grounds to warrant relief. Grabowski v. Allstate Ins. Co., — Ohio App. 3d —, 2007 Ohio 2765, — N.E. 2d —, 2007 Ohio App. LEXIS 2558 (June 7, 2007).

When a bank did not appear at a hearing on its garnishment of a debtor's bank account, pursuant to RC § 2716.13(C)(2), and the trial court found the account was exempt from garnishment and assessed costs against the bank as a sanction for its failure to appear, it was not entitled to relief from this judgment because it had filed a release of the garnishment before the hearing because it was still obligated to attend the hearing, and the trial court's records did not indicate the release was filed, so its failure to appear was not excusable neglect, under Ohio R. Civ. P. 60(B)(1), nor was there "any other reason" to grant the bank relief. MBNA America Bank v. Speegle, — Ohio App. 3d —, 2006 Ohio 3817, — N.E. 2d —, 2006 Ohio App. LEXIS 3786 (July 26, 2006).

When a mother sought relief from a judgment granting sole custody of her children to their father, after she did not appear at a hearing, it was not an abuse of discretion to grant her relief because, even if she did not show excusable neglect, under Ohio R. Civ. P. 60(B)(1), relief had also been granted in the interest of justice, pursuant to Ohio R. Civ. P. 60(B)(5), and no error was assigned to this, so she showed she was entitled to relief under this provision. Anderson-Harber v. Harber, — Ohio App. 3d —, 2006 Ohio 3106, — N.E. 2d —, 2006 Ohio App. LEXIS 3098 (June 20, 2006).

Failure to produce evidence

Appellant's motion for relief from judgment pursuant to Ohio R. Civ. P. 60(B) was properly denied by the trial court, as her speculation as to what evidence she would have offered in defense of tort claims filed against her lacked merit where she failed to offer any reason for her failure to present such evidence. Her claim that she had relied on her attorney, who then withdrew on the eve of trial, also lacked merit because she had notice for a long time prior to trial that her attorney, who has defending her based on representation through her homeowner's policy, might not be able to continue representation due to an issue as to whether coverage applied. Earl v. Nelson, — Ohio App. 3d —, 2006 Ohio 3341, — N.E. 2d —, 2006 Ohio App. LEXIS 3270 (June 30, 2006).

Final appealable order

When a trial court, after granting a default judgment against appellee Illinois corporation, but before finding damages, granted the Illinois corporation's Ohio R. Civ. P. 60(B) motion for relief from that judgment, appellant Ohio corporation's appeal of that order was dismissed because the trial court's judgment was not a final appealable order, as damages had not yet been decided. Arrow Mach. Co. v. Rapid Rigging, — Ohio App. 3d —, 2008 Ohio 526, — N.E. 2d —, 2008 Ohio App. LEXIS 443 (Feb. 8, 2008).

Final judgment

When a landlord sued tenants for possession, back rent, damages to the leased premises, and punitive damages and attorney fees, and an insurer intervened to assert a subrogation claim to any recovery by the landlord, which it later voluntarily dismissed, the landlord was not entitled to a hearing on its motion for relief from a judgment, under Ohio R. Civ. P. 60(B), because the order from which it sought relief was not a final order, due to the pendency of the insurer's subrogation claim. Love Props., Inc. v. Kyles, — Ohio App. 3d —, 2007 Ohio 1966, — N.E. 2d —, 2007 Ohio App. LEXIS 1772 (Apr. 23, 2007).

As an order appealed from vacated an earlier judgment pursuant to Ohio R. Civ. P. 60 that had been granted by the trial court, the appellate court had jurisdiction over the appeal pursuant to RC § 2505.02(B)(3). First Merit Bank v. Crouse, — Ohio App. 3d —, 2007 Ohio 2440, — N.E. 2d —, 2007 Ohio App. LEXIS 2278 (May 21, 2007).

License holder's appeal from the trial court's denial of her Ohio R. Civ. P. 60(A) motion to vacate an Administrative License Suspension notification form completed by a magistrate was dismissed because the court lacked jurisdiction under Ohio Const. art. IV, § 3(B)(2) as there was no final appealable order under RC § 2505.02(B)(1) due to the fact that the trial court had never adopted the magistrate's decision, as required by former Ohio R. Civ. P. 53(E)(4)(a). State v. Makoroff, — Ohio App. 3d —, 2007 Ohio 4348, — N.E. 2d —, 2007 Ohio App. LEXIS 3897 (Aug. 27, 2007).

Lessees' appeal from a trial court's judgment denying their Ohio R. Civ. P. 60(B) motion for relief from judgment was dismissed for lack of a final order. Since the trial court's Ohio R. Civ. P. 41(B) dismissal of the lessees' counterclaim was without prejudice, it was not a final order and, thus, was not final adjudication subject to the relief provided in Ohio R. Civ. P. 60(B). Ebbets Partners, Ltd. v. Day, 171 Ohio App. 3d 20, 2007 Ohio 1667, 869 N.E.2d 110, 2007 Ohio App. LEXIS 1531 (2007).

When landowners sued the landowners' neighbors for part of the cost of repairing a common driveway, and the neighbors asserted a cross claim for indemnification against the contractor which performed the repairs, and obtained a default judgment against the contractor, it was no error for a trial court to deny the neighbors' indemnification claim in spite of the default judgment and in spite of the contractor's failure to seek relief from that judgment, under Ohio R. Civ. P. 60(B), because the contractor did not have to seek Rule 60(B) relief, as the default judgment was interlocutory because the landowners' claim against the neighbors was still pending when the default judgment was entered, so the trial court was free to vacate it without granting relief under Rule 60(B). Brush v. Hassertt, — Ohio App. 3d —, 2007 Ohio 2978, — N.E. 2d —, 2007 Ohio App. LEXIS 2742 (June 8, 2007).

Trial court's affirmance of a magistrate's decision to grant a motion under Ohio R. Civ. P. 60(B) for relief from a judgment was a final appealable order under RC § 2505.02(B)(3). Summit Gardens Ass'n v. Lemongelli, — Ohio App. 3d —, 2007 Ohio 6720, — N.E. 2d —, 2007 Ohio App. LEXIS 5891 (Dec. 14, 2007).

As a trial court had not ruled on a minor child's mother's objections to a magistrate's decision, which had granted legal custody of the child to the maternal aunt and uncle, the decision was not a final order and a motion to vacate under Ohio R. Civ. P. 60(B) was not proper. The trial court had jurisdiction to vacate, modify, or adopt the magistrate's decision pursuant to the mother's pending objections under Ohio R. Juv. P. 40. In re Murphy, — Ohio App. 3d —, 2006 Ohio 5527, — N.E. 2d —, 2006 Ohio App. LEXIS 5518 (Oct. 17, 2006).

Probate court's grant of a default judgment to a testator's sons and ex-wife in their will contest was not a final appealable order under RC § 2505.02 because the parties could not determine their rights and obligations therefrom, there was no disposition as to the validity of the will, and no relief was granted. An appeal could not be taken from that order, and motions for reconsideration and for relief from judgment under Ohio R. Civ. P. 60(B) were not properly taken from that order, as such motions only were appropriate from a final judgment or order. Viets v. Viets, — Ohio App. 3d —, 2006 Ohio 5818, — N.E. 2d —, 2006 Ohio App. LEXIS 5772 (Nov. 6, 2006).

When a wife obtained an agreed temporary support order requiring her husband to pay half of certain specified household expenses, and then sought judgment under that order when the husband did not pay his obligations, the dismissal of his motion, under Ohio R. Civ. P. 60(B)(4), for relief from the order, was not an abuse of discretion because Ohio R. Civ. P. 60(B) only provided for relief from final orders, and a temporary support order was, by definition, not final. Ronyak-Bogert v. Bogert, — Ohio App. 3d —, 2006 Ohio 1168, — N.E. 2d —, 2006 Ohio App. LEXIS 1058 (Mar. 14, 2006).

Where a trial court did not actually order forfeiture of a bond or order a surety to pay the bond to the court, the trial court's later denial of the surety's Ohio R. Civ. P. 60(B) motion to vacate a bond forfeiture failed to fall into any of the RC § 2505.02(B) categories and did not create a final judgment where none previously existed. There was no final order from which to appeal. A letter from the court clerk to the surety, stating that the bond had been forfeited and that payment of the bond amount was due on a date certain, was not signed by the judge and thus was not a court order. State v. Hein, —

Ohio App. 3d —, 2006 Ohio 2850, — N.E. 2d —, 2006 Ohio App. LEXIS 2680 (June 7, 2006).

Bond company's appeal from a trial court's denial of the company's motion to vacate a bond forfeiture order was dismissed for lack of a final appealable order under RC § 2505.02. Since there was no forfeiture order in the record, no relief from judgment could lie under Ohio R. Civ. P. 60(B); thus, the trial court's denial of the Ohio R. Civ. P. 60(B) motion was not a final appealable order, and the court lacked jurisdiction under Ohio Const. art. IV, § 3(B)(2) to entertain the appeal. State ex rel. Elyria v. Lantz, — Ohio App. 3d —, 2006 Ohio 3115, — N.E. 2d —, 2006 Ohio App. LEXIS 3004 (June 21, 2006).

Trial court's entry of a cognovit judgment was not a final appealable order in consolidated actions, as unresolved claims were still pending, and accordingly, relief under Ohio R. Civ. P. 60(B) could not be obtained because the judgment was interlocutory rather than final. Although the trial court used language from Ohio R. Civ. P. 54(B), the requirements of RC § 2505.02(B) were not met and an appeal taken from the trial court's denial of the motion for relief from judgment required dismissal. Gilligan v. Robinson, — Ohio App. 3d —, 2006 Ohio 4619, — N.E. 2d —, 2006 Ohio App. LEXIS 5305 (Aug. 31, 2006).

While a trial court erroneously granted a note maker's Ohio R. Civ. P. 60(B)(5) motion for the express purpose of extending his time to file an appeal from the trial court's judgment against him, the error was harmless because the judgment that the maker sought to avoid was not a final order under Ohio R. Civ. P. 54(B), in that it adjudicated fewer than all of the claims and the rights and liabilities of fewer than all of the parties, and it failed to include an express determination that there was no just reason for delay. Irion v. Incomm Electronics, — Ohio App. 3d —, 2006 Ohio 362, — N.E. 2d —, 2006 Ohio App. LEXIS 297 (Jan. 24, 2006).

Findings

Trial court made adequate findings when it denied a motion for relief from judgment, under Ohio R. Civ. P. 60(B), despite its entry which only stated that the motion was not well taken under the circumstances, because, at the hearing on the motion, it stated that the movant did not have a meritorious defense, immediately after which it said it was going to deny the motion. Fitzwater v. Woodruff, — Ohio App. 3d —, 2006 Ohio 7040, — N.E. 2d —, 2006 Ohio App. LEXIS 7027 (Dec. 28, 2006).

Foreclosure

Ultimate assignee of a second mortgage on the property did not establish that it was entitled to relief pursuant to CivR 55(B) and 60(B) where the various assignments were "inexplicably" not recorded and it did not receive notice of the foreclosure action. Fifth Third Bank v. NCS Mortg. Lending Co., 168 Ohio App. 3d 413, 2006 Ohio 571, 860 N.E.2d 785, 2006 Ohio App. LEXIS 518 (2006).

Trial court's denial of a mortgagor's motion to vacate an order confirming a foreclosure sale and authorizing distribution of the proceeds, pursuant to Ohio R. Civ. P. 60(B), was proper where the mortgagor failed to show that he had made payments in full of the amount due; he failed to sufficiently show that the "bill" he created and submitted to the mortgagee was subject to the United Nations Convention on International Bills of Exchange and International Promissory Notes or that the document had any validity as an "international bill of exchange." Bank of New York v. Markos, — Ohio App. 3d —, 2006 Ohio 2073, — N.E. 2d —, 2006 Ohio App. LEXIS 1906 (Apr. 27, 2006).

In a foreclosure action, a mortgagor's two motions for relief from a default judgment taken against her by the mortgagee were properly denied where she failed to assert any of the grounds enumerated under Ohio R. Civ. P. 60(B) to support her claim for relief, and she failed to show that she had a meritorious defense to the foreclosure action, which was based on her default in payments. American Bus. Mortg. Servs. v. Barclay, — Ohio App. 3d —, 2006 Ohio 2532, — N.E. 2d —, 2006 Ohio App. LEXIS 2390 (May 23, 2006).

Trial court erred when it granted the homeowners' motion to vacate the default judgment pursuant to Ohio R. Civ. P. 60(B) because, although the homeowners argued that the creditor did not comply with Ohio R. Civ. P. 10(D) when it failed to attach a copy of the promissory note to its original complaint for foreclosure, the creditor provided the reason for the omission of the document and thus, reliance on Ohio R. Civ. P. 10(D) as a basis for vacation of the default judgment was misplaced. More importantly, the homeowners did not provide an adequate reason for their failure to file an answer to the complaint, with which there had been properly served. They provided no reason as to why they chose not to file a responsive pleading and their failure to file an answer was inexcusable, within the contemplation of Ohio R. Civ. P. 60(B). Associates First Capital Corp. v. Crane, — Ohio App. 3d —, 2006 Ohio 4145, — N.E. 2d —, 2006 Ohio App. LEXIS 4101 (Aug. 11, 2006).

Finance company did not show, under Ohio R. Civ. P. 60(B), that it was entitled to relief from a judgment of foreclosure because (1) it did not prove a written assignment of a prior lienholder's interest in the subject property to it, contrary to the statute of frauds, RC § 1335.04, and (2) if the affidavit of its custodian of records claiming such an interest was a sufficient writing, there was no evidence that the company ever recorded its interest, as required by RC § 5301.23(A). Keybank Nat'l Ass'n v. Estate of Wright, — Ohio App. 3d —, 2006 Ohio 4643, — N.E. 2d —, 2006 Ohio App. LEXIS 4564 (Sept. 1, 2006).

Forfeiture judgments

Since the trial court did not abuse its discretion in denying the State's motion for relief from judgment, the State was required to return the vehicle and the $67,487 to the accused. The State neither challenged the accused's motion for return of the property nor appealed that order; it failed to assert any basis for entitlement to relief, the vehicle was not contraband per se; and the State offered no evidence, untainted by the illegal search, to show that the vehicle or the cash were used in commission of a crime. State v. Loza-Gonzalez, — Ohio App. 3d —, 2007 Ohio 1044, — N.E. 2d —, 2007 Ohio App. LEXIS 970 (Mar. 9, 2007).

When a homeowner did not appeal a trial court's forfeiture order or order to disburse funds derived from the sale of her home, and subsequently moved the trial court to vacate its order under Ohio R. Civ. P. 60(B), which the trial court denied, her appeal of that denial was insufficient because she did not explain how the facts justified reversing that order, and her claim that she was deprived of due process because she was not given notice of the final order to disburse the funds, under Ohio R. Civ. P. 58(B), depriving her of due process, was insufficient because she did not state which Ohio R. Civ. P. 60(B) ground applied, nor did she show that the trial court's denial of her motion was an abuse of discretion. State v. Young, — Ohio App. 3d —, 2006 Ohio 4304, — N.E. 2d —, 2006 Ohio App. LEXIS 4248 (Aug. 21, 2006).

Fraud and misrepresentation

Car lessee was not entitled to relief from a judgment of the trial court, which dismissed her third-party complaint for failure to prosecute, wherein she claimed that her signature had been forged on an agreement regarding a car lease, as such was not the type of fraud contemplated by Ohio R. Civ. P. 60(B)(3); rather, fraud under that rule covered fraud or misconduct material to obtaining the judgment. First Merit Bank v. Crouse, — Ohio App. 3d —, 2007 Ohio 2440, — N.E. 2d —, 2007 Ohio App. LEXIS 2278 (May 21, 2007).

Trial court properly denied a motion under Ohio R. Civ. P. 60(B) to reinstate a matter after appellees had entered into a settlement agreement which provided that they would pay a set sum to appellants within 10 days but then failed to make the payment in a timely manner, as there was no showing by appellants of a fraudulent intent by appellees. The fact that the payment was not made in a timely manner was not sufficient to justify vacating the judgment. Morris-Walden v. Moore, — Ohio App. 3d —, 2007 Ohio 262, — N.E. 2d —, 2007 Ohio App. LEXIS 255 (Jan. 25, 2007).

Homeowner's motion to vacate a judgment of foreclosure in favor of a homeowners' association did not show the homeowner was entitled to relief under Ohio R. Civ. P. 60(B)(3) because the homeowner did not support the homeowner's conclusory allegations that various counsel and witnesses committed perjury and knowingly made false statements to the court with specific facts ascertainable from the record. Miles Landing Homeowners Ass'n v. Harris, — Ohio App. 3d —, 2007 Ohio 3411, — N.E. 2d —, 2007 Ohio App. LEXIS 3165 (July 5, 2007).

When an insurer filed a declaratory judgment action seeking a declaration that it was not obligated to indemnify its insureds due to an alleged injured party's suit against them, and a default judgment was entered in the insurer's favor, after which the alleged injured party moved to set aside that default, and subsequently moved to intervene, it was not error for the trial court to implicitly grant the motion to set aside the default judgment by granting the alleged injured party's motion to intervene because the alleged injured party claimed the insurer misrepresented facts regarding whether the insurance policy was void, placing the matter under Ohio R. Civ. P. 60(B)(3), regarding misrepresentation of an adverse party, and the alleged injured party stated a meritorious defense by claiming the alleged misrepresentations on which the trial court relied in finding the policy void did not occur. State Farm Mut. Ins. Cos. v. Young, — Ohio App. 3d —, 2006 Ohio 3812, — N.E. 2d —, 2006 Ohio App. LEXIS 3784 (July 26, 2006).

When a physician's partner paid the physician a judgment entered against the partner, he could not then seek relief from that judgment, under Ohio R. Civ. P. 60(B), without showing the physician's fraud intervened, and, as the physician's failure to pay a bank loan on which both of them remained liable was not fraudulent, because he did not deceive the partner about his future intentions, but, rather, the partner knew of the possibility that the physician would not make loan payments and failed to take steps to prevent it, the partner was not entitled to relief from the judgment. Lowrey v. Degenova, — Ohio App. 3d —, 2006 Ohio 2835, — N.E. 2d —, 2006 Ohio App. LEXIS 2656 (June 6, 2006).

Trial court properly determined that a former boyfriend failed to show that his former girlfriend's counsel engaged in misrepresentation for purposes of the boyfriend's motion under Ohio R. Civ. P. 60(B)(3) for relief from a settlement agreement entered into following court-ordered mediation, as he failed to show operative facts in a form that met evidentiary standards to support his claim. The boyfriend had alleged that the girlfriend's counsel had informed him that because the parties had lived together, she had rights as a "life partner" in the real property that they jointly acquired. Szabo v. Lepore, — Ohio App. 3d —, 2006 Ohio 3569, — N.E. 2d —, 2006 Ohio App. LEXIS 3517 (July 5, 2006).

When a mortgagee claimed it was entitled to relief from a summary judgment, under Ohio R. Civ. P. 60(B)(3), because the movant's affidavit, claiming there was no intent that the movant's land would secure a mortgage, was fraudulent, because the value of another parcel which secured the mortgage was grossly inadequate, the mortgagee's claim strongly suggested that there had been a mistake in the mortgage, but it did not contradict the movant's claim that the mistake was unilateral, so it was not an abuse of discretion for a trial court to decline to hear the claim, and, more importantly, the facts the mortgagee relied on to support its claim were within its knowledge when the movant sought summary judgment, so it could not show it was taken by surprise when false testimony was given. National City Home Loan Servs. v. Gillette, — Ohio App. 3d —, 2006 Ohio 2881, — N.E. 2d —, 2006 Ohio App. LEXIS 2716 (June 2, 2006).

— Fraud upon the court

Trial court did not abuse its discretion when it found that appellees had not committed any fraud as contemplated by Ohio R. Civ. P. 60(B)(3), nor was there a suggestion in the record that an officer of the court involved in the instant proceedings committed a fraud upon the court or attempted to "defile the court" in any way. There was simply nothing in the record upon which to conclude that any fraudulent conduct or misrepresentations were made that would justify sustaining appellant's motion for relief from judgment pursuant to Ohio R. Civ. P. 60(B)(3). Leibold v. Hiddens, — Ohio App. 3d —, 2007 Ohio 2972, — N.E. 2d —, 2007 Ohio App. LEXIS 2732 (June 8, 2007).

In a personal injury action filed by a wife and her family against a driver, no fraud on the court requiring a new trial occurred under Ohio R. Civ. P. 60(B)(3) when the driver's expert neurologist misrepresented his status in a professional organization because, by its plain terms, Rule 60(B)(3) applied only when an adverse party, not an adverse witness, testified falsely. Wood v. Gutierrez, — Ohio App. 3d —, 2006 Ohio 5384, — N.E. 2d —, 2006 Ohio App. LEXIS 5380 (Oct. 16, 2006).

Wife and her family were not entitled to a new trial in their personal injury action against a driver for fraud on the court under Ohio R. Civ. P. 60(B)(3) on the ground that the driver's expert neurologist misrepresented his status in a professional organization because they did not show that, if not for the misrepresentation, the result of the trial would have been different or that they were prejudicially surprised. Extensive medical records and the testimony of other experts, including the wife's own expert, supported the result, and the wife and her family learned about the neurologist's misrepresentation before he testified and cross-examined him extensively about it. Wood v. Gutierrez, — Ohio App. 3d —, 2006 Ohio 5384, — N.E. 2d —, 2006 Ohio App. LEXIS 5380 (Oct. 16, 2006).

Grounds for relief from judgment

When an insurer voluntarily dismissed and refiled its complaint, and the party it sued did not answer the refiled complaint, causing the insurer to move for the party's default, which was granted, it was not error for a trial court to grant the party sued relief from that default judgment, under Ohio R. Civ. P. 60(B)(5), rather than under Ohio R. Civ. P. 60(B)(1), based on inadvertence, because the inadvertence was that of the trial court, rather than a party, when it granted the motion for default judgment without being aware that the party sued had moved for leave to file an answer out of rule and had filed a memorandum opposing the motion for default judgment, due to a delay in those documents appearing in the court's records. American Select Ins. Co. v. Riggs, — Ohio App. 3d —, 2007 Ohio 1808, — N.E. 2d —, 2007 Ohio App. LEXIS 1632 (Apr. 17, 2007).

Where a car lessee who was involved in a dispute with a car dealership and a lender on her car lease filed a motion, seeking relief from the trial court's judgment which dismissed her third-party complaint for failure to prosecute, and she asserted grounds under Ohio R. Civ. P. 60(B)(1) and (3), the trial court erred in granting the relief from judgment on other grounds under Rule 60(B)(5), as such amounted to a sua sponte action by the trial court and it lacked that authority. Such a ruling did not afford the dealership due process under Ohio Const. art. I, § 16, in that it did not provide it with an ample opportunity to respond to the unasserted grounds for relief, and it violated the requirement of Ohio R. Civ. P. 7(B)(1) of setting out the grounds for a motion with particu-

larity. First Merit Bank v. Crouse, — Ohio App. 3d —, 2007 Ohio 2440, — N.E. 2d —, 2007 Ohio App. LEXIS 2278 (May 21, 2007).

Trial court properly overruled an ex-husband's Civ. R. 60(B)(3) motion to vacate a divorce judgment based on his ex-wife's concealment of a large disability payment from her insurance company; the record established that the ex-husband was aware of the ex-wife's disability payments but never inquired as to the size of the payments. Miller v. Miller, — Ohio App. 3d —, 2007 Ohio 4401, — N.E. 2d —, 2007 Ohio App. LEXIS 3966 (Aug. 27, 2007).

Appellant's motion for relief from judgment under Ohio R. Civ. P. 60(B) was properly denied because it did not set forth any meritorious claim, and appellant failed to set forth any basis to support a finding that one of the five enumerated reasons set out in Ohio R. Civ. P. 60(B) would support relief from judgment. Riser v. Wade, — Ohio App. 3d —, 2006 Ohio 3552, — N.E. 2d —, 2006 Ohio App. LEXIS 3503 (July 11, 2006).

Appellant's Ohio R. Civ. P. 60(B) motion for relief from default judgment was properly denied because the affidavit filed in support of the motion relied on third-hand information, and nothing provided to the trial court was sufficient to indicate the reasons that appellant did not timely respond to the suit against it. As a result, appellant failed to allege operative facts warranting relief from judgment requiring an evidentiary hearing. State ex rel. Ferrero v. Industrial Prop. Mgmt., Inc., — Ohio App. 3d —, 2006 Ohio 6568, — N.E. 2d —, 2006 Ohio App. LEXIS 6478 (Dec. 4, 2006).

Where a husband's grounds for relief from judgment were embraced within Ohio R. Civ. P. 60(B)(1), (3), and (4) with respect to his claim that it was not equitable for him to pay child support for a child that he did not believe was his, there was no available basis for relief under Rule 60(B)(5), as that only applied when a more specific provision was inapplicable. White v. Jacques, — Ohio App. 3d —, 2006 Ohio 464, — N.E. 2d —, 2006 Ohio App. LEXIS 424 (Feb. 3, 2006).

—— Incompetence

Based on an individual's incompetence, a trial court's grant of a motion for relief from judgment pursuant to Ohio R. Civ. P. 60(B)(5) was not an abuse of discretion, as a meritorious defense was offered to claims asserted by a tenant, the motion was made in a timely manner given the individual's incompetence, and there were grounds that supported the relief due to the incompetence; although the motion was filed approximately 18 months after the entry of a default judgment, it was timely where the individual was incompetent and the individual's attorney had been removed and thereafter disbarred, such that the attorney's failure to notify the court of the individual's incompetency under Ohio R. Civ. P. 25(E) was not attributed to the individual. Summit Gardens Ass'n v. Lemongelli, — Ohio App. 3d —, 2007 Ohio 6720, — N.E. 2d —, 2007 Ohio App. LEXIS 5891 (Dec. 14, 2007).

Hearing

As appellants failed to allege operative facts that would have supported their motion for relief from judgment under Ohio R. Civ. P. 60(B), the trial court did not err in summarily denying the motion without holding a hearing. Morris-Walden v. Moore, — Ohio App. 3d —, 2007 Ohio 262, — N.E. 2d —, 2007 Ohio App. LEXIS 255 (Jan. 25, 2007).

Trial court did not err by failing to hold a hearing on a debtor's motion for relief from judgment since the debtor failed to explain why he was entitled to relief under Ohio R. Civ. P. 60(B) or why he needed a hearing. Cavalry Portfolio Servs. v. Terrell, — Ohio App. 3d —, 2007 Ohio 1331, — N.E. 2d —, 2007 Ohio App. LEXIS 1215 (Mar. 23, 2007).

Trial court did not err by failing to hold a hearing on a debtor's motion for relief from judgment since the debtor failed to explain why he was entitled to relief under Ohio R. Civ. P. 60(B) or why he needed a hearing. Cavalry Portfolio

Servs. v. Terrell, — Ohio App. 3d —, 2007 Ohio 1331, — N.E. 2d —, 2007 Ohio App. LEXIS 1215 (Mar. 23, 2007).

Trial court erred in denying a former wife's motion under Ohio R. Civ. P. 60(B) for relief from a dissolution decree without holding an evidentiary hearing to determine if her unchallenged allegations regarding her claim that she lacked competence to have entered a separation agreement and addendum which were incorporated into the parties' divorce decree met the necessary proof requirements for relief. The wife and former husband each submitted affidavits that contradicted each other with respect to the wife's knowledge of the husband's sale of his businesses and her participation therein during their marriage, such that the wife raised sufficient allegations of operative facts that could have supported a meritorious defense and which required an evidentiary hearing to resolve. Wright-Long v. Long, — Ohio App. 3d —, — N.E. 2d —, 2007 Ohio App. LEXIS 2601 (May 31, 2007).

Person filing a motion for relief from judgment under Ohio R. Civ. P. 60(B) was not automatically entitled to a hearing on the motion because, to be entitled to a hearing on a motion for relief from judgment, a movant had to do more than make bare allegations that he was entitled to relief, and where the movant's motion and accompanying materials failed to provide the operative facts to support relief under Rule 60(B), a trial court could refuse to grant a hearing and summarily dismiss the motion for relief from judgment. JMA N. Coast Prop. Mgmt. v. Sutera, — Ohio App. 3d —, 2007 Ohio 3071, — N.E. 2d —, 2007 Ohio App. LEXIS 2806 (June 21, 2007).

When a default judgment was entered against an attorney in a legal malpractice suit, a trial court was not required to hold a hearing on the attorney's Ohio R. Civ. P. 60(B) motion for relief from that judgment because the attorney did not ask for a hearing. Hover v. O'Hara, — Ohio App. 3d —, 2007 Ohio 3614, — N.E. 2d —, 2007 Ohio App. LEXIS 3308 (July 16, 2007).

Where credit card holders did not set forth operative facts that justified their request for relief under Ohio R. Civ. P. 60(B), the trial court did not abuse its discretion in failing to hold an evidentiary hearing prior to denying the motion. Cavalry Invs., LLC v. Dzilinski, — Ohio App. 3d —, 2007 Ohio 3767, — N.E. 2d —, 2007 Ohio App. LEXIS 3435 (July 26, 2007).

When a husband sought relief from a divorce decree, no evidentiary hearing was required on the husband's motion because the alleged fact that the husband would have to pay more money to the husband's former wife than the husband originally planned did not warrant a hearing. Brown v. Brown, — Ohio App. 3d —, 2007 Ohio 4183, — N.E. 2d —, 2007 Ohio App. LEXIS 3764 (Aug. 16, 2007).

Trial court did not err by failing to hold an evidentiary hearing on a law client's motion for relief from a default judgment that was entered against it and in favor of a law firm pursuant to Ohio R. Civ. P. 55(B) and 60(B)(1), as there was no dispute about the facts regarding the handling of the complaint when it was served on the client by certified mail, such that no hearing was required. The motion to vacate the default judgment had been based on excusable neglect due to the mishandling of the complaint by the employee upon whom it was served by certified mail. Benesch, Friedlander, Coplan & Arnoff v. City Concrete, LLC, — Ohio App. 3d —, 2007 Ohio 3331, — N.E. 2d —, 2007 Ohio App. LEXIS 3126 (June 21, 2007).

Where it was determined that a guarantor's motion for relief from judgment pursuant to Ohio R. Civ. P. 60(B) failed to show that he had a meritorious defense to a judgment obtained on a cognovit note due to non-payment, he was not entitled to an evidentiary hearing. Ohio Carpenters' Pension Fund v. La Centre, — Ohio App. 3d —, 2006 Ohio 2214, — N.E. 2d —, 2006 Ohio App. LEXIS 2060 (May 4, 2006).

When a debtor sought relief from a judgment entered against him based on his guaranty of his companies' cognovit note, under Ohio R. Civ. P. 60(B), he did not show he had a meritorious defense to the judgment, so he was not entitled to an evidentiary hearing. First Merit Bank, N.A. v. Nebs Fin. Servs., — Ohio App. 3d —, 2006 Ohio 5260, — N.E. 2d —, 2006 Ohio App. LEXIS 5217 (Oct. 5, 2006).

When a husband sought relief from a trial court's order modifying his child support obligation, he did not show the trial court had to hold an evidentiary hearing on his motion, based on his claim of excusable neglect, under Ohio R. Civ. P. 60(B)(1), because he became confused about the date of the modification hearing, as he did not show his confusion constituted excusable neglect, so he did not allege operative facts entitling him to relief, and, as a result, the trial court did not have to hold an evidentiary hearing. Sterling v. Sterling, — Ohio App. 3d —, 2006 Ohio 5437, — N.E. 2d —, 2006 Ohio App. LEXIS 5430 (Oct. 19, 2006).

Trial court did not err in denying a customer's motion for leave to conduct discover and in failing to hold an evidentiary hearing on the store's Ohio R. Civ. P. 60(B) motion for relief from a default judgment entered against it because the store sufficiently set forth evidence establishing the requirements of the GTE test; thus, an evidentiary hearing on the issue was not necessary. Chirico v. Home Depot, — Ohio App. 3d —, 2006 Ohio 291, — N.E. 2d —, 2006 Ohio App. LEXIS 228 (Jan. 26, 2006).

Where the mother and brother sought relief from the default judgment more than six years after the default judgment was entered, the trial court was not required to hold a hearing on the Ohio R. Civ. P. 60(B) motion for relief from judgment, as the mother and brother, who presented no explanation for the delay, presented no operative facts or evidentiary quality affidavits to demonstrate that relief was warranted. Brode v. Brode, — Ohio App. 3d —, 2006 Ohio 143, — N.E. 2d —, 2006 Ohio App. LEXIS 112 (Jan. 6, 2006).

Since appellant failed to submit material containing operative facts with his Ohio R. Civ. P. 60(B) motion, the trial court did not abuse its discretion in failing to hold a hearing before denying the motion. Estate of Mallory, — Ohio App. 3d —, 2006 Ohio 1265, — N.E. 2d —, 2006 Ohio App. LEXIS 1151 (Mar. 17, 2006).

Since note makers alleged a meritorious defense to a cognovit judgment entered against them, the trial court abused its discretion in ultimately denied their Ohio R. Civ. P. 60(B) motion without an evidentiary hearing. Simmons Capital Advisors, Ltd. v. Kendall Group, — Ohio App. 3d —, 2006 Ohio 2272, — N.E. 2d —, 2006 Ohio App. LEXIS 2106 (May 9, 2006).

If a movant filed a motion for relief from judgment and it contained allegations of operative facts which would warrant relief under Ohio R. Civ. P. 60(B), a trial court was to grant a hearing to take evidence and verify these facts before it ruled on the motion, and the converse was equally true, so a trial court abused its discretion in denying a hearing where grounds for relief from judgment were sufficiently alleged and were supported with evidence which warranted relief from judgment. In re Estate of Perez, — Ohio App. 3d —, 2006 Ohio 2841, — N.E. 2d —, 2006 Ohio App. LEXIS 2665 (June 5, 2006).

It was error for a trial court to deny a son's motion for relief from judgments entered in a probate case without a hearing, under Ohio R. Civ. P. 60(B), because the son's affidavit attached to his motion for relief from judgment provided the trial court with information of evidentiary quality showing that (1) the son never lived at the address at which notice was mailed to him, (2) a party knew the identity of the son's wife, and (3) the son's address and telephone number were listed in the local telephone book, under his wife's name, providing operative facts supporting the son's meritorious defense. In re

Estate of Perez, — Ohio App. 3d —, 2006 Ohio 2841, — N.E. 2d —, 2006 Ohio App. LEXIS 2665 (June 5, 2006).

When a son moved for relief from judgments entered in a probate case, under Ohio R. Civ. P. 60(B), the fact that a statutory beneficiary's notice, pursuant to Ohio Superintendence Ct. R. 70(B), differed from service of process, under Ohio R. Civ. P. 4, went to the merits of the son's motion for relief from judgment rather than whether the trial court should have held an evidentiary hearing on the son's motion. In re Estate of Perez, — Ohio App. 3d —, 2006 Ohio 2841, — N.E. 2d —, 2006 Ohio App. LEXIS 2665 (June 5, 2006).

Neither Ohio R. Civ. P. 60(B) nor the case law pertaining to this Rule indicated that a party moving for relief from a judgment had to specifically request a hearing, as the case law indicated that, where the motion and supporting evidence contained sufficient allegations of operative facts supporting a meritorious defense to a judgment, a trial court had to assign the matter for evidentiary hearing. In re Estate of Perez, — Ohio App. 3d —, 2006 Ohio 2841, — N.E. 2d —, 2006 Ohio App. LEXIS 2665 (June 5, 2006).

Trial court did not abuse its discretion under Ohio R. Civ. P. 60(B) in failing to hold a hearing prior to overruling a husband's motion for relief from the trial court's divorce decree, as he failed to present operative facts which would have warranted relief from the equitable distribution aspect of the decree. Mamula v. Mamula, — Ohio App. 3d —, 2006 Ohio 4176, — N.E. 2d —, 2006 Ohio App. LEXIS 4131 (Aug. 11, 2006).

Trial court's failure to conduct an evidentiary hearing before denying a corporation's Civ. R. 60(B) motion for relief from a judgment by confession against it on a note was error in circumstances in which the corporation provided the affidavit of its president, who was the person who allegedly signed the note, asserting that the note was forged, and provided an expert's opinion that the president did not sign the note. Firstmerit Bank v. Reliable Auto Body Co., — Ohio App. 3d —, 2006 Ohio 5056, — N.E. 2d —, 2006 Ohio App. LEXIS 4986 (Sept. 29, 2006).

Trial court's summary denial of a loan officer's motion to vacate a judgment against him pursuant to Ohio R. Civ. P. 60(B) was an abuse of discretion where no hearing was held despite the officer's having rebutted the presumption of effective service on him pursuant to Ohio R. Civ. P. 4.1 and 4.6. An issue was created as to whether service had been attempted at the proper business address for the loan officer, and where such issue was raised, it was reversible error to fail to hold a hearing in order to resolve the issue as to effective service. Money Tree Loan Co. v. Williams, 169 Ohio App. 3d 336, 2006 Ohio 5568, 862 N.E.2d 885, 2006 Ohio App. LEXIS 5553 (2006).

Trial court did not err in failing to hold an evidentiary hearing on a former wife's motion under Ohio R. Civ. P. 60(B) to vacate a judgment entry of divorce because of the former husband's failure to disclose a pension; the parties stipulated that the motion could be decided on the briefs without the necessity for a hearing, and in certain circumstances it was appropriate for courts to rule on motions under Rule 60(B) based on the written materials in lieu of an oral evidentiary hearing. Hardesty v. Hardesty, — Ohio App. 3d —, 2006 Ohio 5648, — N.E. 2d —, 2006 Ohio App. LEXIS 5646 (Oct. 27, 2006).

Trial court did not err by not holding a hearing prior to denying the attorney's motion for relief from judgment under Ohio R. Civ. P. 60(B) because the attorney failed to allege any operative facts to support his motion; thus, a hearing was not required. Cooley v. Sherman, — Ohio App. 3d —, 2006 Ohio 6065, — N.E. 2d —, 2006 Ohio App. LEXIS 6051 (Nov. 20, 2006).

Jurisdiction

Trial court properly ruled on an advertising company's motion under Ohio R. Civ. P. 60(B) for relief from judgment, as the matter had been previously appealed and the court of appeals had remanded the case pursuant to Ohio Eighth Dist. Ct. App. R. 4(A) for the limited purpose of the trial court's determination of the pending Rule 60(B) motion. Beauty Max Llc v. Wbuy Tv, — Ohio App. 3d —, 2007 Ohio 4831, — N.E. 2d —, 2007 Ohio App. LEXIS 4322 (Sept. 20, 2007).

Trial court did not retain jurisdiction to entertain a motion for relief from judgment after it had dismissed the movants' counterclaim without prejudice for want of prosecution under CivR 41(B)(1). Because the dismissal was without prejudice, it was not a final appealable order: Ebbets Partners, Ltd. v. Day, 171 Ohio App. 3d 20, 2007 Ohio 1667, 869 N.E.2d 110, 2007 Ohio App. LEXIS 1531 (2007).

Trial court erred in granting a wife's motion for relief from judgment, pursuant to Ohio R. Civ. P. 60(B), with respect to a divorce decree obtained by the husband, as the decree itself was an in rem judgment because the marital status was a res that followed the domiciles of the parties, and the husband was domiciled in Ohio at the time of his action; although the trial court had not secured sufficient service over the wife, who resided in Germany, the in rem judgment was proper under RC § 3105.17 and within the trial court's authority. Collins v. Collins, 165 Ohio App. 3d 71, 2006 Ohio 181, 844 N.E. 2d 910, 2006 Ohio App. LEXIS 159 (Jan. 20, 2006).

Trial court did not err in denying the Ohio R. Civ. P. 60(B) motion because, while the decedent's will stated that the decedent was "presently residing" in another county, residence is not synonymous with domicile, and pursuant to RC § 2107.11(A), it is the decedent's domicile at the time of her death that is important. Further, in the application to probate the will, the decedent's domicile was listed as the county where the will was applied to probate, and all of the decedent's next of kin, including appellant, signed waivers agreeing that the facts in the application were correct. Estate of Mallory, — Ohio App. 3d —, 2006 Ohio 1265, — N.E. 2d —, 2006 Ohio App. LEXIS 1151 (Mar. 17, 2006).

When a physician's partner paid the physician a judgment entered against the partner, he could not then seek relief from that judgment, under Ohio R. Civ. P. 60(B), without showing the judgment was absolutely void due to the trial court's lack of jurisdiction or that the physician's fraud intervened, and, as he could show neither, it was error for a trial court to grant his motion for relief. Lowrey v. Degenova, — Ohio App. 3d —, 2006 Ohio 2835, — N.E. 2d —, 2006 Ohio App. LEXIS 2656 (June 6, 2006).

Trial court lacked jurisdiction to grant relief from judgment under Ohio R. Civ. P. 60(B), as a notice of appeal from the judgment had already been filed from the judgment and accordingly, the jurisdiction of the trial court was transferred to the appellate court. Forg v. Gammarino, — Ohio App. 3d —, 2006 Ohio 6977, — N.E. 2d —, 2006 Ohio App. LEXIS 6934 (Dec. 29, 2006).

Trial court properly denied a nurse's motion for relief from default judgment, pursuant to Ohio R. Civ. P. 60(B), in her action against a physician arising from his alleged tortious conduct against her, as an action by the nurse was also pending in the Ohio Court of Claims and a personal immunity determination under RC §§ 2743.02(F) and 9.86 regarding the physician had not yet been made. The Court of Claims still retained jurisdiction over the physician and as the trial court lacked jurisdiction the nurse failed to present a meritorious defense to support the relief from judgment motion. Peachock v. Momen, — Ohio App. 3d —, 2006 Ohio 6439, — N.E. 2d —, 2006 Ohio App. LEXIS 6392 (Dec. 7, 2006).

Law of the case

Where a trial court denied a law client's motion for relief from a judgment that settled his legal malpractice action, and the client's appeal therefrom was dismissed sua sponte as untimely, such constituted the law of the case, and the client could not thereafter seek relief from the denial decision pursuant to Ohio R. Civ. P. 60(B); his claims in that second motion should have been raised in the direct appeal, and the motion for relief from judgment could not be used to substitute for an appeal. Tihansky v. Weston, — Ohio App. 3d —, 2006 Ohio 1359, — N.E. 2d —, 2006 Ohio App. LEXIS 1236 (Mar. 23, 2006).

Mandamus

As a board of county commissioners complied with the statutory requirements of RC §§ 305.25 and 307.561, which made a potentially void settlement agreement into a valid contract between parties who were disputing zoning resolutions directed at landfill operation and licensing, a trial court's declaratory judgment thereon was not void. Relief from that judgment could have been obtained by a direct appeal or through a motion under Ohio R. Civ. P. 60(B), such that there was no right to a writ of mandamus pursuant to RC § 2731.04 or to a writ of prohibition, as there was an adequate remedy at law and the trial court clearly had jurisdiction over the matter. State ex rel. Sautter v. Grey, — Ohio App. 3d —, 2007 Ohio 1831, — N.E. 2d —, 2007 Ohio App. LEXIS 1673 (Apr. 18, 2007).

Meritorious defense

Relief under Ohio R. Civ. P. 60(B) from a magistrate's judgment adopting an "agreed judgment entry" purportedly entered between a mother and a father in a child support matter was properly granted to the mother as the mother presented a meritorious defense. There was no indication that parties reached the agreement stated in the judgment entry as the mother never signed the entry, she did not appear at the hearing where it was adopted, and she informed the trial court that she had told the magistrate that there were "too many strings attached" to the agreement and that she never signed it. In re Adair, — Ohio App. 3d —, 2007 Ohio 409, — N.E. 2d —, 2007 Ohio App. LEXIS 357 (Feb. 1, 2007).

Trial court properly concluded that a patient could not demonstrate, in his Ohio R. Civ. P. 60(B) motion for relief from a summary judgment entered against him, that he had a meritorious claim for relief because the statute of limitations had run on his claim against a medical center center. The patient's complaint asserted a "medical claim" against the center, as defined in RC § 2305.11(D)(3) (2002); thus, the one year statute of limitations in RC § 2305.113(A) applied, and the trial court properly denied the patient's Ohio R. Civ. P. 60(B) motion. Davis v. Valley, — Ohio App. 3d —, 2007 Ohio 1332, — N.E. 2d —, 2007 Ohio App. LEXIS 1227 (Mar. 23, 2007).

Trial court properly concluded that a patient could not demonstrate, in his Ohio R. Civ. P. 60(B) motion for relief from a summary judgment entered against him, that he had a meritorious claim for relief because the statute of limitations had run on his claim against a medical center center. The patient's complaint asserted a "medical claim" against the center, as defined in RC § 2305.11(D)(3) (2002); thus, the one year statute of limitations in RC § 2305.113(A) applied, and the trial court properly denied the patient's Ohio R. Civ. P. 60(B) motion. Davis v. Valley, — Ohio App. 3d —, 2007 Ohio 1332, — N.E. 2d —, 2007 Ohio App. LEXIS 1227 (Mar. 23, 2007).

Trial court did not abuse its discretion when it denied a motion under Ohio R. Civ. P. 60(B) by property owners after their property was foreclosed upon by a county treasurer due to their delinquency in paying their property taxes, as their claim that if they had received notice of the foreclosure sale, they would have paid off the taxes due did not constitute a meritorious defense. Kest v. Leasor, — Ohio App. 3d —, 2007 Ohio 1871, — N.E. 2d —, 2007 Ohio App. LEXIS 1705 (Apr. 20, 2007).

It was error for a trial court to find that a motorist, against whom a default judgment was entered in a personal injury suit, did not demonstrate that the motorist had a meritorious defense, for purposes of relief from the judgment under Ohio R. Civ. P. 60(B), when the motorist alleged that the accident from which the lawsuit arose was caused by the fault of the alleged injured party who sued the motorist, because the motorist did not have to show the motorist would ultimately prevail on the defense alleged, but only that the defense was meritorious. Federico v. Langham, — Ohio App. 3d —, 2007 Ohio 2168, — N.E. 2d —, 2007 Ohio App. LEXIS 2015 (May 4, 2007).

In his motion for relief from judgment entered against him in a divorce action, a husband alleged a meritorious defense, asserting that the trial court improperly distributed his personal injury settlement to the wife. Personal property settlements were generally characterized as separate property, and the trial court's judgment entry did not provide any reasoning explaining why the trial court deviated from this general rule. Dottore v. Feathers, — Ohio App. 3d —, 2007 Ohio 2435, — N.E. 2d —, 2007 Ohio App. LEXIS 2266 (May 18, 2007).

Ohio R. Civ. P. 60(B) motion was properly denied because appellant was legally bound by the terms of the consent agreement which she voluntarily entered into. She did not demonstrate any factual basis upon which the consent agreement should have been vacated. The record clearly demonstrated that appellant entered into the agreement in order to have the civil stalking protection order vacate and thus, the trial court did not err in adopting the magistrate's conclusions of law regarding appellant's failure to demonstrate a meritorious defense. Leibold v. Hiddens, — Ohio App. 3d —, 2007 Ohio 2972, — N.E. 2d —, 2007 Ohio App. LEXIS 2732 (June 8, 2007).

Trial court properly granted relief from a judgment against a business employee in an action by a lessor against the employee, the business as lessee, and others, arising from nonpayment of rental under the lease and damage to fixtures on the rental premises, as the employee met the GTE requirements for purposes of Ohio R. Civ. P. 60(B)(5). He asserted a meritorious defense where he showed that he did not have an ownership interest in the business, he had not received notice of summary judgment proceedings and related judgment entries, and his motion to vacate the judgment against him within eight months was deemed a reasonable time. Kostoglou v. D&A Trucking & Excavating, — Ohio App. 3d —, 2007 Ohio 3399, — N.E. 2d —, 2007 Ohio App. LEXIS 3155 (June 25, 2007).

Trial court did not abuse its discretion in denying an insurer's motion under Ohio R. Civ. P. 60(B) for relief from a default judgment where it failed to assert that it had a meritorious defense other than that if a default judgment in an underlying matter against its insured was vacated, then the insurer's potential liability would be extinguished. Linquist v. Allstate, — Ohio App. 3d —, 2007 Ohio 4587, — N.E. 2d —, 2007 Ohio App. LEXIS 4121 (Aug. 27, 2007).

Trial court's denial of a tenant's motion under Ohio R. Civ. P. 60(B) for relief from a default judgment entered against her and in favor of a landlord in the landlord's action, seeking recovery of unpaid rent, was an abuse of discretion, as the tenant presented a meritorious defense where she indicated that she was not the tenant, and her motion was filed in a timely manner; there was statutory authority under RC § 1925.14 to vacate the small claims court judgment where the circumstances warranted that relief. Frampton v. Mike & Betty Sekula, — Ohio App. 3d —, 2007 Ohio 5039, — N.E. 2d —, 2007 Ohio App. LEXIS 4461 (Sept. 20, 2007).

Ohio R. Civ. P. 60(B) motion for relief from judgment filed by a minor and his parents was properly denied because they did not offer any meritorious defenses or claims to a property owners' motion for summary judgment, granted by the trial court. Instead, the minor and his parents only argued that matter should be reopened because they filed a dismissal in the wrong court. Meyer v. Geyman, — Ohio App. 3d —, 2007 Ohio 5474, — N.E. 2d —, 2007 Ohio App. LEXIS 4801 (Oct. 12, 2007).

Store presented a meritorious defense to a customer's personal injury suit, in that it submitted the affidavit of the store's manager to the effect that the accident that was reported by the customer on the date in question related to an injury to the customer's thumb, not an injury to his foot as the customer alleged in his complaint. Chirico v. Home Depot, — Ohio App. 3d —, 2006 Ohio 291, — N.E. 2d —, 2006 Ohio App. LEXIS 228 (Jan. 26, 2006).

Debtors failed to show that they had a meritorious claim or defense to a deficiency judgment entered against them. While they alleged that they tendered payments on the note in question to the creditor to make the account current but that the creditor refused the payments, the debtors provided no documentation or evidence in support of their motion. French v. Gruber, — Ohio App. 3d —, 2006 Ohio 1167, — N.E. 2d —, 2006 Ohio App. LEXIS 1057 (Mar. 14, 2006).

Trial court properly denied defendant's motion for relief from a default judgment as a renter lacked a meritorious defense in light of the fact that all of its jurisdictional arguments regarding a commercial agreement had been rejected in prior appeals concerning identical agreements and in light of the doctrine of stare decisis. Preferred Capital, Inc. v. Wheaton Trenching, Inc., — Ohio App. 3d —, 2006 Ohio 1554, — N.E. 2d —, 2006 Ohio App. LEXIS 1486 (Mar. 31, 2006).

Note makers' motion under Ohio R. Civ. P. 60(B) for relief from a cognovit judgment was improperly summarily denied on the ground that the note makers failed to present a meritorious defense. Payment was not the only meritorious defense available to the makers since the terms of the note allowed the makers to contest the amount owed on the note. The makers, who challenged the amount due on the note, alleged a meritorious defense. Simmons Capital Advisors, Ltd. v. Kendall Group, — Ohio App. 3d —, 2006 Ohio 2272, — N.E. 2d —, 2006 Ohio App. LEXIS 2106 (May 9, 2006).

Guarantors presented evidence sufficient to establish that they had a meritorious defense to an action brought by a law firm to recover on a debt that the guarantors allegedly agreed to pay, in that the affidavit and testimony of one of the guarantors established that neither he nor the other guarantor told the firm that they would pay the debtor's debt. Meglan, Meglan & Co. v. Bostic, — Ohio App. 3d —, 2006 Ohio 2270, — N.E. 2d —, 2006 Ohio App. LEXIS 2107 (May 9, 2006).

While a father's arguments that he was denied the right to counsel in a case alleging that his children were abused, and that the trial court improperly admitted hearsay evidence, may have formed basis for an appeal, they did not establish a meritorious defense, and the denial of the father's Ohio R. Civ. P. 60(B) motion for relief from judgment was proper; further, the father did not produce any "extraordinary circumstances" in this case to warrant the use of Ohio R. Civ. P. 60(B)(5). In re Yates, — Ohio App. 3d —, 2006 Ohio 2761, — N.E. 2d —, 2006 Ohio App. LEXIS 2602 (May 26, 2006).

When a father stipulated that he was in contempt of a child support order and that he owed certain arrearages, after which he learned that the mother of his child filed a motion to waive those arrearages, causing him to seek relief, under Ohio R. Civ. P. 60(B), from a judgment which was based on his prior stipulation, he was not entitled to relief because he could not demonstrate that he had a meritorious defense, as was required, because the trial court had denied the mother's motion, and that denial was not timely appealed. Jones v. Jones, — Ohio App. 3d —, 2006 Ohio 3136, — N.E. 2d —, 2006 Ohio App. LEXIS 2994 (June 14, 2006).

When a mother sought relief from a judgment granting sole custody of her children to their father, after she did not appear at a hearing, it was not an abuse of discretion to grant her relief because she submitted sufficient evidence to show she had a meritorious defense, under the factors the trial court had to consider in deciding if an award of the children's custody was in their best interest, under RC § 3109.04(F)(1), as she submitted affidavits supporting her willingness and ability to care for the children, a letter indicating her initiative in finding mental health care for one child, and her affidavit stating that separating the children from her other child negatively impacted all the children. Anderson-Harber v. Harber, — Ohio App. 3d —, 2006 Ohio 3106, — N.E. 2d —, 2006 Ohio App. LEXIS 3098 (June 20, 2006).

Trial court properly overruled a patron's motion for relief from judgment pursuant to Ohio R. Civ. P. 60(B) because the patron did not advance a meritorious claim to show that summary judgment in favor of appellees was inappropriate, in that she never set forth specific operative facts showing that her fall on a property owner's property was the result of an unnatural accumulation of snow and ice and that the raised pavement that she allegedly tripped on was more than a minor imperfection in the parking lot. Additionally, the patron did not establish that her failure to file a response to the summary judgment motion was the result of excusable neglect. Collins v. Marc Glassman, Inc., — Ohio App. 3d —, 2006 Ohio 3493, — N.E. 2d —, 2006 Ohio App. LEXIS 3454 (July 6, 2006).

Trial court's denial of guarantors' motion for relief from a default judgment pursuant to Ohio R. Civ. P. 60(B)(5) was not an abuse of discretion, as the service on them by ordinary mail was reasonably calculated to give them notice in the circumstances, and their failure to have obtained notice was due to their decision to ignore the mail. A claim of medical hardship also lacked merit, as the guarantor continued to operate the business, after surgery he regularly checked his mail, and he was notified by his postal carrier when the mailbox at his business was full. Seal Master Industries, Inc. v. Bay Area Seal Coating & Stripping, — Ohio App. 3d —, 2006 Ohio 3610, — N.E. 2d —, 2006 Ohio App. LEXIS 3547 (July 14, 2006).

Trial court did not abuse its discretion in denying guarantors' request for vacatur of a default judgment pursuant to Ohio R. Civ. P. 60(B), as they failed to assert a meritorious defense where credit extensions which were the subject of the default judgment were clearly covered by the guarantee, as it was continuing in nature, and there was no specification to the speculative claim that the account under which money was allegedly owed may not have been accurate. Seal Master Industries, Inc. v. Bay Area Seal Coating & Stripping, — Ohio App. 3d —, 2006 Ohio 3610, — N.E. 2d —, 2006 Ohio App. LEXIS 3547 (July 14, 2006).

In appellant's suit to recover for money paid to its insured for damage allegedly caused by appellee to the insured's property, appellee demonstrated a meritorious defense to at least a portion of the damages claimed due by appellant, and thus, appellee's motion for relief from judgment was properly granted. The evidence showed that appellant was seeking to recover from appellee an amount in excess of the amount paid by it to its insured. State Auto Ins. Co. v. Colclough, — Ohio App. 3d —, 2006 Ohio 3654, — N.E. 2d —, 2006 Ohio App. LEXIS 3599 (July 14, 2006).

Ohio R. Civ. P. 60(B)(5) motion to vacate a judgment entered against appellant in a breach of contract action was properly denied. Since the court had previously held that appellant had breached the parties' contract by its conduct, the issue raised by appellant as to whether the parties ever terminated their agreement was irrelevant to whether a breach of that contract had occurred at an earlier time; thus, appellant had failed to raise a meritorious defense. Bench Signs Unlimited v. Stark Area Regional Transit Auth., — Ohio App. 3d —, 2006 Ohio 6556, — N.E. 2d —, 2006 Ohio App. LEXIS 6475 (Dec. 13, 2006).

When a trial court entered summary judgment in favor of the Ohio Supreme Court's Client Security Fund, when it sued a former attorney for funds it had paid to his former client, the attorney showed that he might have a meritorious defense to the judgment when he alleged that he was not notified of the client's claim against the Fund and that the claim was improperly paid, because, while the Fund did not have to notify the attorney of the client's claim, under Ohio Sup. Ct. R. Gov't Bar VIII, the attorney had to be able to defend himself in the Fund's collection case against him, and, if he could prove the client's claim was improperly paid, this would constitute a defense to the collection case, so he was entitled to relief from the judgment. State v. Potts, — Ohio App. 3d —, 2006 Ohio 7057, — N.E. 2d —, 2006 Ohio App. LEXIS 6989 (Dec. 28, 2006).

When a lessee sued a lessor for failure to deliver the title to a leased tractor-trailer, pursuant to a purchase agreement, and the lessor successfully counterclaimed for the lessee's failure to maintain the tractor-trailer, pursuant to the parties' lease, the lessee did not show he was entitled to relief from the judgment on the counterclaim due to the fact that the lessor's attorney had previously represented the lessee, because he did not show how this prevented him from raising a meritorious defense to the counterclaim, and it was clear from the lease that he had a duty to maintain the tractor-trailer, but he did not claim that he had properly maintained it or that he was somehow relieved of that duty. Fitzwater v. Woodruff, — Ohio App. 3d —, 2006 Ohio 7040, — N.E. 2d —, 2006 Ohio App. LEXIS 7027 (Dec. 28, 2006).

Mistake

Trial court erred by sua sponte vacating a final order under RC § 2505.02 that dissolved a receivership almost a year after dissolving the receivership because, by sua sponte vacating its earlier dissolution of the receivership, the trial court substantively altered its final order dissolving the receivership. The trial court's alteration of its entry did not constitute a correction of a clerical error as contemplated under Ohio R. Civ. P. 60(A). Moreover, since no party moved for relief under Ohio R. Civ. P. 60(B), the trial court lacked jurisdiction to vacate its order vacating the receivership. Lakhi v. Healthcare Choices & Consultants, LLC, — Ohio App. 3d —, 2007 Ohio 4127, — N.E. 2d —, 2007 Ohio App. LEXIS 3747 (Aug. 14, 2007).

Trial court's decision to deny a mother's Ohio R. Civ. P. 60(B) motion was within its sound discretion because, though the mother contended that she was misled by a notarized statement she signed and attached to a dissolution petition, to the effect that the mother would have a chance in one year to regain custody of the parties' child if both parties agreed and if it was in the best interest of the parties' child, and that she thought that she would automatically receive custody one year after the dissolution, the agreement clearly stated that it was not an automatic change of custody. Moreover, even had the mother known that the change of custody was not automatic, she was not in a position, at the time of the final hearing, to care for the child. Kier v. Kier, — Ohio App. 3d —, 2007 Ohio 4190, — N.E. 2d —, 2007 Ohio App. LEXIS 3780 (July 27, 2007).

Trial court's decision to overrule a motion under Ohio R. Civ. P. 60(B)(1) and (5), seeking relief from a judgment entered in favor of a merchandise seller in its claim for recovery of sums due from a contracting company and its president as personal guarantor, was not an abuse of discretion, as the assertion that counsel failed to apprise the trial court during summary judgment proceedings that the authenticity of the president's signature on the guarantee had been disputed in the initial pleadings was not within "mistake" under Rule 60(B)(1). Ohio Cat v. N. Valley Contrs., — Ohio App. 3d —, 2007 Ohio 5050, — N.E. 2d —, 2007 Ohio App. LEXIS 4463 (Sept. 24, 2007).

Homeowner's motion to vacate a judgment of foreclosure in favor of a homeowners' association did not show the homeowner was entitled to relief under Ohio R. Civ. P. 60(B)(1) because the homeowner said the homeowner did not know why the homeowner's attorney did not oppose the association's summary judgment motion. Miles Landing Homeowners Ass'n v. Harris, — Ohio App. 3d —, 2007 Ohio 3411, — N.E. 2d —, 2007 Ohio App. LEXIS 3165 (July 5, 2007).

When an insurer voluntarily dismissed and refiled its complaint, and the party it sued did not answer the refiled complaint, causing the insurer to move for the party's default, which was granted, the party sued adequately showed both excusable neglect and mistake allowing relief from the default judgment, under Ohio R. Civ. P. 60(B)(1), because the party's neglect or mistake was not in failing to file an answer but, instead, in her failure to contact her attorney because she believed her attorney would receive the refiled complaint and take necessary action. American Select Ins. Co. v. Riggs, — Ohio App. 3d —, 2007 Ohio 1808, — N.E. 2d —, 2007 Ohio App. LEXIS 1632 (Apr. 17, 2007).

Debtors failed to establish a basis for relief from a deficiency judgment under one of the five grounds in Ohio R. Civ. P. 60(B). They were time-barred from seeking relief under Ohio R. Civ. P. 60(B)(1) because their motion was filed more than one year after the judgment entry from which they were seeking relief, and they were not entitled to relief under the catch-all provision of Ohio R. Civ. P. 60(B)(5) because the record reflected that the debtors were represented by counsel who asserted some of the same defenses that the debtors claimed that they were unable to assert. French v. Gruber, — Ohio App. 3d —, 2006 Ohio 1167, — N.E. 2d —, 2006 Ohio App. LEXIS 1057 (Mar. 14, 2006).

Trial court did not err in granting the wife's Ohio R. Civ. P. 60(B) motion with respect to the issue of adjustment of support arrearages in the settlement agreement as the omission of that language was a result of mistake or inadvertence by the wife's counsel. Clearly, the parties intended the adjustment to be part of the judgment entry. Bodnar v. Bodnar, — Ohio App. 3d —, 2006 Ohio 3300, — N.E. 2d —, 2006 Ohio App. LEXIS 3214 (June 23, 2006).

Ohio R. Civ. P. 60(A) was not appropriate because the use of the mother's former name in the caption of the motion to modify support was not an error by the trial court and it could not be said to have been inadvertent or a mistake on the father's part. The father failed to show that his omission of her new last name was not deliberate; he did not claim that her remarriage three years prior to his initial motion to modify was unknown to him and it was referenced within the motion. Pulice v. Collins, — Ohio App. 3d —, 2006 Ohio 3950, — N.E. 2d —, 2006 Ohio App. LEXIS 3903 (Aug. 3, 2006).

Trial court's summary denial of a husband's motion to vacate judgment pursuant to Ohio R. Civ. P. 60(B)(1) was not an abuse of discretion, as there was no evidence of a mutual mistake of a material fact in the parties' divorce decree with respect to the division of the parties' retirement assets. There was no indication that the parties expected the trial court to apply an adjustment to the values of the retirement assets due to alleged loans and withdrawals on the accounts. Mamula v. Mamula, — Ohio App. 3d —, 2006 Ohio 4176, — N.E. 2d —, 2006 Ohio App. LEXIS 4131 (Aug. 11, 2006).

As a former husband and wife, through their counsel, agreed to an amended qualified domestic relations order arising from the property distribution in their divorce proceeding pursuant to RC § 3105.171, wherein the husband was entitled to 50 percent of the wife's pension in her retirement plan after a determination by the wife's employer that it could not calculate her premarital portion of the pension due to bookkeeping errors, the trial court erred in sua sponte vacating the amended order upon the wife's assertion that she misread it and had not intended to give up her premarital portion of the plan. The trial court had jurisdiction to enter the amended order, and as the order was voidable but not void, the trial court lacked jurisdiction to vacate the order without a motion under Ohio R. Civ. P. 60(B), which the wife failed to do. McGee v. McGee, 168 Ohio App. 3d 512, 2006 Ohio 4417, 860 N.E.2d 1054, 2006 Ohio App. LEXIS 4343 (2006).

Mootness

Where an appellate court held that a trial court's adoption of a divorce decree was an abuse of discretion because there were issues of dispute regarding the terms of the settlement agreement upon which the decree was based, such that an evidentiary hearing should have been held, the husband's additional claim on appeal that the trial court's denial of his motion for relief from judgment pursuant to Ohio R. Civ. P. 60(B) was error was rendered moot pursuant to Ohio R. App. P. 12(A)(1)(c). Hornung v. Hornung, — Ohio App. 3d —, 2007 Ohio 3222, — N.E. 2d —, 2007 Ohio App. LEXIS 2844 (June 21, 2007).

As landlords failed to seek a stay order pending their appeal of a trial court judgment that was rendered in favor of a tenant for damages, and they did not post a supersedeas bond, the tenant's satisfaction of the judgment through garnishment proceedings rendered the landlords' appeal moot. The trial court was without jurisdiction to thereafter grant relief from the judgment pursuant to Ohio R. Civ. P. 60(B). Wiest v. Wiegele, — Ohio App. 3d —, 2006 Ohio 5348, — N.E. 2d —, 2006 Ohio App. LEXIS 5322 (Oct. 13, 2006).

Where a magistrate issued a decision on a civil protection order litigant's (CPOL) motion under Ohio R. Civ. P. 60(B) in an underlying domestic relations matter, which was the relief requested in the CPOL's mandamus action pursuant to RC § 2731.04, the mandamus action was subject to dismissal because the issue requested therein was moot. Review of the propriety of the decision on the Ohio R. Civ. P. 60(B) motion was not proper in the mandamus action, as an adequate remedy existed through a direct appeal from that ruling. State ex rel. Feathers v. Badger, — Ohio App. 3d —, 2007 Ohio 3195, — N.E. 2d —, 2007 Ohio App. LEXIS 2931 (June 22, 2007).

Motion for reconsideration

Where a house seller failed to appeal from a trial court's grant of a stay of litigation pending arbitration pursuant to RC § 2711.02(B), and instead he sought relief from the stay order pursuant to Ohio R. Civ. P. 60(B), which motion was denied, the seller's appeal from that order lacked merit because it was untimely and procedurally improper. The motion under Rule 60(B) did not state any grounds and accordingly, it was deemed an attempt at reconsideration of the stay order which was a nullity, and the time to appeal from the stay order had already run pursuant to Ohio R. App. P. 4(A), such that the appeal was untimely. Schmidt v. Bankers Title & Escrow Agency, — Ohio App. 3d —, 2007 Ohio 3924, — N.E. 2d —, 2007 Ohio App. LEXIS 3569 (Aug. 2, 2007).

Trial court's denial of an insurer's motion for reconsideration under Ohio R. Civ. P. 60(B) was not an abuse of discretion where it sought to have a trial court consider a deposition of a decedent's fiance for the purpose of showing that the decedent was not a "relative" under her parents' automobile insurance policy with respect to a coverage dispute, as the insurer did not seek the trial court's permission for the untimely filing of the deposition testimony with respect to resolving summary judgment motions. Lager v. Miller-Gonzalez, — Ohio App. 3d —, 2007 Ohio 4094, — N.E. 2d —, 2007 Ohio App. LEXIS 3713 (Aug. 10, 2007).

Trial court did not err in denying the father's motion to reconsider because there was no provision for a motion to reconsider in the Ohio Rules of Civil Procedure and thus, it was a nullity. There was also no indication that the original trial judge construed the motion as a motion to vacate pursuant to RC § 60(B). Because his motion to reconsider concerned substantive, contested factual issues and potentially complex legal arguments, the only proper vehicle for the correction of those perceived errors was a direct appeal. Perez

v. Angell, — Ohio App. 3d —, 2007 Ohio 4519, — N.E. 2d —, 2007 Ohio App. LEXIS 3759 (Aug. 9, 2007).

Trial court had the authority to clarify in its March 2005 judgment entry which method of payment should be used to divide the husband's retirement account to effectuate the divorce decree; since the wife's motion for relief from judgment was premature, it was treated as a motion for reconsideration under Ohio R. Civ. P. 54(B). Given that the divorce decree was an interlocutory order which the trial court could revise or clarify at any time, the issues of whether the wife timely filed her motion, whether the language in the divorce decree was ambiguous, and whether the trial court reserved jurisdiction to modify the final divorce decree were irrelevant. Forman v. Forman, — Ohio App. 3d —, 2007 Ohio 4938, — N.E. 2d —, 2007 Ohio App. LEXIS 4618 (Sept. 24, 2007).

Trial court erred in construing appellee's motion for reconsideration as an Ohio R. Civ. P. 60(B) motion because appellee neither asked the trial court to "vacate" its judgment nor set forth any ground cognizable under any provision of Ohio R. Civ. P. 60(B); instead, appellee clearly argued the merits of the damages award, an argument that was appropriate for a direct appeal. Squires v. Luckey Farmers, Inc., — Ohio App. 3d —, 2006 Ohio 1640, — N.E. 2d —, 2006 Ohio App. LEXIS 1512 (Mar. 31, 2006).

Although a trial court failed to rule on a party's motion seeking relief under Ohio R. Civ. P. 60(B)(5) and/or reconsideration of the trial court's judgment that allowed a party to intervene, such did not preclude the ability to appeal an order of the trial court, as the intervention motion was not a final appealable order and accordingly, the post-trial motion was properly construed as a motion for reconsideration; the failure to rule on a reconsideration motion was deemd a decision to overrule it. Savage v. Cody-Zeigler, Inc., — Ohio App. 3d —, 2006 Ohio 2760, — N.E. 2d —, 2006 Ohio App. LEXIS 2601 (May 25, 2006).

Motion for relief from judgment

As a legal client's motion for relief from judgment under Ohio R. Civ. P. 60(B) did not address or challenge the trial court's final judgment, which granted the attorney's motion to dismiss the client's multi-claim action, but instead, the motion sought to extend the client's time to appeal, the motion was improper and it was properly denied without a hearing. As grounds for relief from judgment under Rule 60(B), the client had asserted that his notice of appeal was not timely due to interruptions in the prison mailing system. Wilmore v. Bruner, — Ohio App. 3d —, 2006 Ohio 3361, — N.E. 2d —, 2006 Ohio App. LEXIS 3283 (June 29, 2006).

Motion properly denied

Inmate's mandamus action under RC § 2731.04, seeking to compel a court clerk to serve a denial of the inmate's Ohio R. Civ. P. 60(B) motion in an underlying matter on the inmate, lacked merit, as the clerk had complied with Ohio R. Civ. P. 58(B) when the clerk served notice of the denial on the inmate at the address of record; further, the inmate failed to show that there was no adequate remedy at law, as the inmate could have sought relief from the alleged improper service under Ohio R. Civ. P. 60(B)(5). State Ex Rel. Halder, — Ohio App. 3d —, 2007 Ohio 5938, — N.E. 2d —, 2007 Ohio App. LEXIS 5231 (Nov. 2, 2007).

Trial court's denial of a taxpayer's motion under Ohio R. Civ. P. 60(B) for vacatur of a judgment that was entered pursuant to RC § 5747.13(C), based upon a personal income tax assessment against him, was proper because the taxpayer's claim that the matter was within the Fair Debt and Collection Practices Act, 15 U.S.C.S. § 1692g(b), lacked merit; the personal income tax obligation was not a consumer debt within the coverage of the Act. State v. Diefenbaugh, — Ohio App. 3d —, 2007 Ohio 5996, — N.E. 2d —, 2007 Ohio App. LEXIS 5240 (Nov. 9, 2007).

Motion to vacate judgment

While the mother's attempted use of Ohio R. Civ. P. 60(B) to vacate the trial court's void judgment was technically incorrect, the trial court erred by not treating the Ohio R. Civ. P. 60(B) motion as a common law motion to vacate or set aside the trial court's judgment based on a lack of personal jurisdiction. Beachler v. Beachler, — Ohio App. 3d —, 2007 Ohio 1220, — N.E. 2d —, 2007 Ohio App. LEXIS 1151 (Mar. 19, 2007).

Newly discovered evidence

Trial court did not err in overruling a husband's motion to vacate a divorce decree in order to consider the tax ramifications resulting from the liquidation of a certain account in the parties' divorce proceeding, as the account was in the husband's name and accordingly, he possessed standing to pursue any action against the account holder. The husband did not allege operative facts to support a claim of newly discovered evidence in existence at the time of the divorce trial that he was ignorant of for purposes of Ohio R. Civ. P. 60(B)(2) and (5). Dunham v. Dunham, — Ohio App. 3d —, 2007 Ohio 1167, — N.E. 2d —, 2007 Ohio App. LEXIS 1066 (Mar. 15, 2007).

Trial court did not err in overruling a husband's motion to vacate a divorce decree in order to consider the tax ramifications resulting from the liquidation of a certain account in the parties' divorce proceeding, as the account was in the husband's name and accordingly, he possessed standing to pursue any action against the account holder. The husband did not allege operative facts to support a claim of newly discovered evidence in existence at the time of the divorce trial that he was ignorant of for purposes of Ohio R. Civ. P. 60(B)(2) and (5). Dunham v. Dunham, — Ohio App. 3d —, 2007 Ohio 1167, — N.E. 2d —, 2007 Ohio App. LEXIS 1066 (Mar. 15, 2007).

Where relief was sought from the issuance of a civil stalking protection order rather than a judgment following a new trial, appellant's motion and memorandum made no effort to demonstrate how its contents was "newly discovered evidence," or, if so, why it could not with due diligence had been earlier discovered. Examination of the Ohio R. Civ. P. 60 (B) motion, memorandum, and exhibits strongly suggested that none of it was newly discovered evidence. Leibold v. Hiddens, — Ohio App. 3d —, 2007 Ohio 2972, — N.E. 2d —, 2007 Ohio App. LEXIS 2732 (June 8, 2007).

Homeowner's motion to vacate a judgment of foreclosure in favor of a homeowners' association did not show the homeowner was entitled to relief under Ohio R. Civ. P. 60(B)(2) because the homeowner did not identify any newly discovered evidence or support the proposition that the evidence could not have been discovered before summary judgment in favor of the association was granted. Miles Landing Homeowners Ass'n v. Harris, — Ohio App. 3d —, 2007 Ohio 3411, — N.E. 2d —, 2007 Ohio App. LEXIS 3165 (July 5, 2007).

When a church was sued on a mortgage the church granted in favor of a financial services company to secure a trust indenture agreement, and summary judgment was issued against the church, the church's motion under Ohio R. Civ. P. 60(B)(2) for relief from that judgment due to newly discovered evidence was properly denied because the newly discovered evidence the church wanted to raise consisted of a judicial decision in another state holding an associate of the company liable for selling unregistered church bonds, and an investigation of the associate for this activity, and it had been previously determined in this case that the bonds this church issued did not have to be registered. First Fin. Servs. v. Cross Tabernacle Deliverance Church, — Ohio App. 3d —, 2007 Ohio 4274, — N.E. 2d —, 2007 Ohio App. LEXIS 3937 (Aug. 21, 2007).

Trial court properly overruled appellant's motion, pursuant to Ohio R. Civ. P. 60(B)(2) for relief from judgment on the basis of newly discovered evidence filed after a stalking civil protection order was issued against her because the alleged "newly discovered evidence" was just an attempt to impeach appellee's credibility and did not constitute newly discovered evidence. Dickson v. Ball, — Ohio App. 3d —, 2006 Ohio 3436, — N.E. 2d —, 2006 Ohio App. LEXIS 3358 (June 30, 2006).

Not a substitute for appeal

When a trial court granted summary judgment in favor of a school sued by a student, and the clerk did not serve notice of that judgment entry on the student, as required by Ohio R. Civ. P. 58(B), and the student did not learn of the judgment until more than 30 days after it was entered, the student did not need to file a motion for relief from that judgment, under Ohio R. Civ. P. 60(B), to be able to timely appeal it, pursuant to Ohio R. App. P. 4(A), because the student's time for appealing did not begin running until the student had notice of the judgment. Frazier v. Cincinnati Sch. of Med. Massage, — Ohio App. 3d —, 2007 Ohio 2390, — N.E. 2d —, 2007 Ohio App. LEXIS 2256 (May 18, 2007).

Denial of a husband's Ohio R. Civ. P. 60(B) motion for relief from judgment was proper, as the husband was inappropriately attempting to use Ohio R. Civ. P. 60(B)(2) and (B)(4) to re-litigate and negate the trial court's findings of fact and conclusions of law regarding educational loans and spousal support. The evidence at trial consistently showed that either the husband or his children had been making payments on the loans, and that the husband, not the wife, was a guarantor on the loans; thus, the loans were not a marital debt, and this fact had not changed. Biro v. Biro, — Ohio App. 3d —, 2007 Ohio 3191, — N.E. 2d —, 2007 Ohio App. LEXIS 2922 (June 22, 2007).

As a juvenile court decision pursuant to Ohio R. Civ. P. 60(B) that vacated a prior judgment was a final appealable order pursuant to RC § 2505.02(B)(3), an appeal had to be taken within 30 days thereof pursuant to Ohio R. App. P. 4(A) in order to be reviewed as timely. As a mother did not file a timely appeal from the vacatur of the juvenile court's judgment that had closed a pending matter regarding an agency's temporary custody over her children, her appeal from that order was not reviewable. In re L.S., — Ohio App. 3d —, 2007 Ohio 1583, — N.E. 2d —, 2007 Ohio App. LEXIS 1455 (Apr. 4, 2007).

When an attorney who represented a client in a wrongful imprisonment claim before a court of common pleas and the Ohio Court of Claims sued the client for attorney's fees and received a default judgment, the client could not base his Ohio R. Civ. P. 60(B) motion to vacate the default judgment on the fact that the trial court awarded the attorney the fees he requested without a hearing because that issue could have been raised in a direct appeal from the default judgment, but it was not as no such appeal was filed. Watkins v. Williams, — Ohio App. 3d —, 2007 Ohio 513, — N.E. 2d —, 2007 Ohio App. LEXIS 460 (Feb. 7, 2007).

When an attorney who represented a client in a wrongful imprisonment claim before a court of common pleas and the Ohio Court of Claims sued the client for attorney's fees and received a default judgment, the client could not base his Ohio R. Civ. P. 60(B) motion to vacate the default judgment on claims the trial court considered and overruled before granting a default judgment because those claims could have been raised on a direct appeal from the default judgment, but no such appeal was filed, and a Rule 60(B) was not a substitute for an appeal. Watkins v. Williams, — Ohio App. 3d —, 2007 Ohio 513, — N.E. 2d —, 2007 Ohio App. LEXIS 460 (Feb. 7, 2007).

Since, instead of appealing a trial court's grant of summary judgment to a mortgagee in its foreclosure action, the mortgagor filed an Ohio R. Civ. P. 60(B) motion to vacate the judgment, the mortgagor's appeal, which raised errors related to validity of the judgment for foreclosure, was not timely under Ohio R. App. P. 4(A), and the court could not address the merits of the original judgment. Citimortgage, Inc. v. Clardy, — Ohio App. 3d —, 2007 Ohio 2940, — N.E. 2d —, 2007 Ohio App. LEXIS 2692 (June 14, 2007).

Trial court did not abuse its discretion in finding that the mother's motion to vacate the judgment finding that her child was dependent was not filed within a reasonable time and, in addition, she failed to demonstrate that she was entitled to relief under any of the grounds set forth in Ohio R. Civ. P. 60(B). The mother's motion was nothing more than a challenge to the legal correctness of the trial court's original adjudication of dependency, which should have been raised on appeal, but the mother failed to do so. In re S.J., — Ohio App. 3d —, 2006 Ohio 6381, — N.E. 2d —, 2006 Ohio App. LEXIS 6335 (Dec. 6, 2006).

As a husband in a divorce litigation matter did not appeal from an order by the trial court which denied his motion for relief from judgment pursuant to Ohio R. Civ. P. 60(b), based on the husband's claim that the failure to return the divorce matter to the docket of a judge whom the matter had been before previously deprived the trial court of subject matter and personal jurisdiction, he waived the right to raise it as a potential error on appeal pursuant to Ohio R. App. P. 4(A); further, pursuant to Cuyahoga County, Ohio, Ct. C.P. Dom. Rel. Div. R. 2(A)(2), reassignment was not required. Rahawangi v. Alsamman, — Ohio App. 3d —, 2006 Ohio 3163, — N.E. 2d —, 2006 Ohio App. LEXIS 3034 (June 22, 2006).

If debtors were seeking relief from a trial court's judgment entry confirming the sale of their property, they should have asserted those allegations in a timely appeal pursuant to Ohio R. App. P. 4(A), not via a motion for relief from judgment under Ohio R. Civ. P. 60(B) filed 23 months after the sale of their property. A motion pursuant to Ohio R. Civ. P. 60(B) is not a substitute for a timely appeal, and thus, the debtors had run out of time in which to challenge the judgment entry confirming the sale. French v. Gruber, — Ohio App. 3d —, 2006 Ohio 1167, — N.E. 2d —, 2006 Ohio App. LEXIS 1057 (Mar. 14, 2006).

Similar to a motion for relief from judgment under Ohio R. Civ. P. 60(B), a motion for modification of child support cannot be used as a substitute for an appeal. Kean v. Kean, — Ohio App. 3d —, 2006 Ohio 3222, — N.E. 2d —, 2006 Ohio App. LEXIS 3141 (June 23, 2006).

When a trial court entered summary judgment in favor of the Ohio Supreme Court's Client Security Fund, in its suit against a former attorney for funds it had paid to his former client, the attorney's motion for relief from that judgment was not a substitute for an appeal because he alleged that he never received a copy of the Fund's summary judgment motion, so he was not arguing the merits of the case, and the issue he raised was appropriate for an Ohio R. Civ. P. 60(B) motion for relief from the judgment. State v. Potts, — Ohio App. 3d —, 2006 Ohio 7057, — N.E. 2d —, 2006 Ohio App. LEXIS 6989 (Dec. 28, 2006).

Seller's motion for relief from judgment was properly denied because the seller did not assert any viable grounds for the motion. The seller's assertion of mistake under Ohio R. Civ. P. 60(B)(1), in that summary judgment had been granted, and surprise, in that the trial court denied his motion for an extension of time to respond to the motion, could have been raised on direct appeal from the summary judgment. Fairbanks Capital Corp. v. Richards, — Ohio App. 3d —, 2006 Ohio 102, — N.E. 2d —, 2006 Ohio App. LEXIS 72 (Jan. 12, 2006).

When a husband appealed the denial of his motion for relief from a judgment, under Ohio R. Civ. P. 60(B)(1), he could not also argue issues regarding the judgment from which he sought relief because he should have raised those issues in a properly filed appeal from that judgment, under the strictures of Ohio R. App. P. 4. Williams v. Williams, — Ohio App. 3d —, 2006 Ohio 2566, — N.E. 2d —, 2006 Ohio App. LEXIS 2420 (May 18, 2006).

Since appellant failed to file an appeal within 30 days of the trial court's entry of a default judgment, as required by Ohio R. App. P. 4(A), she had not properly perfected for appeal her assignment of error challenging the trial court's denial of her motion to dismiss for lack of subject matter jurisdiction. The appeal, which was filed only after the trial court denied appellant's motion for relief from the default judgment, was untimely since an Ohio R. Civ. P. 60(B) motion is not a substitute for appeal. Citibank, N.A. v. Stein, — Ohio App. 3d —, 2006 Ohio 2674, — N.E. 2d —, 2006 Ohio App. LEXIS 2506 (May 22, 2006).

When a bank did not appear at a hearing on its garnishment of a debtor's bank account, pursuant to RC § 2716.13(C)(2), and the trial court found the account was exempt from garnishment and assessed costs against the bank as a sanction for its failure to appear, and then denied its motion for relief from this judgment, it could not appeal the judgment when it appealed the denial of its motion for relief because the time within which to perfect an appeal of that judgment, under Ohio R. App. P. 4(A), had expired, and the motion for relief did not extend the time within which to appeal. MBNA America Bank v. Speegle, — Ohio App. 3d —, 2006 Ohio 3817, — N.E. 2d —, 2006 Ohio App. LEXIS 3786 (July 26, 2006).

When defendant did not timely appeal a trial court's denial of his petition to vacate his sentence, resulting in the dismissal of that appeal, he could not use a motion for relief from that denial, under Ohio R. Civ. P. 60(B), as a substitute for his failure to timely appeal. State v. Keister, — Ohio App. 3d —, 2006 Ohio 4440, — N.E. 2d —, 2006 Ohio App. LEXIS 4366 (Aug. 28, 2006).

Trial court did not abuse its discretion in overruling a husband's motion for relief from judgment pursuant to Ohio R. Civ. P. 60(B), and his claim on appeal that the divorce decree was not an equitable division of marital assets and violated RC § 3105.171(C)(1) was beyond the scope of appellate review of the relief motion, which only raised issues regarding the division of the husband's 401(K) plan. The motion under Ohio R. Civ. P. 60(B) was not a substitute for a timely perfected appeal. Mamula v. Mamula, — Ohio App. 3d —, 2006 Ohio 4176, — N.E. 2d —, 2006 Ohio App. LEXIS 4131 (Aug. 11, 2006).

Appellant's Ohio R. Civ. P. 60(B) motion for relief from judgment was properly denied. Appellant's motion raised alleged errors that were apparent from the record, and thus, these errors could have been alleged on direct appeal. Further, appellant had wholly failed to assert a meritorious claim or defense in his Ohio R. Civ. P. 60(B) motion. Mitchell v. Haynes, — Ohio App. 3d —, 2006 Ohio 4607, — N.E. 2d —, 2006 Ohio App. LEXIS 4580 (Aug. 30, 2006).

Filing an Ohio R. Civ. P. 60(B) motion could neither substitute for a timely appeal nor extend the time for perfecting an appeal from the original judgment, and, where a motion to vacate was based entirely upon issues that could have been raised on direct appeal, a trial court did not abuse its discretion when it denied the motion to vacate. Schutte v. Akron Pub. Schs. Bd. of Educ., — Ohio App. 3d —, 2006 Ohio 4726, — N.E. 2d —, 2006 Ohio App. LEXIS 4647 (Sept. 13, 2006).

When an employee settled his employment dispute with a school district and a trial court issued an order enforcing that settlement agreement, the employee could not wait four and one-half months after that order was issued to move to vacate it, under Ohio R. Civ. P. 60(B), because Rule 60(B) was not a substitute for a timely appeal, and he could have appealed the order as soon as he believed it did not contain a provision to which the parties agreed. Schutte v. Akron Pub. Schs. Bd. of

Educ., — Ohio App. 3d —, 2006 Ohio 4726, — N.E. 2d —, 2006 Ohio App. LEXIS 4647 (Sept. 13, 2006).

Attorney's motion, pursuant to Ohio R. Civ. P. 60(B), to vacate a judgment against him was properly denied because the attorney's motion merely reiterated his arguments regarding his perceived impropriety of a magistrate's decision. These arguments should have been brought through the filing of a timely appeal and not raised in an Ohio R. Civ. P. 60(B) motion. Cooley v. Sherman, — Ohio App. 3d —, 2006 Ohio 6065, — N.E. 2d —, 2006 Ohio App. LEXIS 6051 (Nov. 20, 2006).

Notice

Trial court abused its discretion when it dismissed the case without prejudice without first providing notice pursuant to CivR 41(B)(1). Thus the plaintiff was entitled to relief pursuant to CivR 60(B)(5): Montgomery v. Tenneco Auto. Operating, Inc., 183 Ohio App. 3d 164, 2009 Ohio 3394, 916 N.E.2d 530, 2009 Ohio App. LEXIS 2925 (2009).

Trial court properly denied an insurer's motion under Ohio R. Civ. P. 60(B)(3) for relief from a default judgment, as there was no fraud, misrepresentation, or misconduct by a movant's counsel's failure to notify the insurer's counsel that a default judgment was forthcoming where the insurer had not appeared in the action pursuant to Ohio R. Civ. P. 5(A) and 55(A). Linquist v. Allstate, — Ohio App. 3d —, 2007 Ohio 4587, — N.E. 2d —, 2007 Ohio App. LEXIS 4121 (Aug. 27, 2007).

Where an injured motorist appealed from a trial court's grant of summary judgment to a former car owner in the motorist's negligent entrustment action, arising from injuries he sustained in a car accident caused by a driver of the former owner's car, but on appeal the motorist asserted that the trial court erred in denying his later motion under Ohio R. Civ. P. 60(B)(1) for relief from judgment, the appeal lacked merit, as the court had no jurisdiction to review such an assignment of error; the motorist had not filed a separate notice of appeal from the denial of his Rule 60(B)(1) motion. Yerkey v. Reichenbach, — Ohio App. 3d —, 2007 Ohio 2757, — N.E. 2d —, 2007 Ohio App. LEXIS 2548 (June 1, 2007).

Ohio R. Civ. P. 60(B) motion is an adequate remedy at law to request an additional 30 days to perfect an appeal when a party claims not to have received notice of the judgment the party seeks to appeal, but pursuit of a Rule 60(B) motion is a futile and unnecessary act when the clerk of court has not even served a party with notice of a judgment as required by Ohio R. Civ. P. 58(B). Frazier v. Cincinnati Sch. of Med. Massage, — Ohio App. 3d —, 2007 Ohio 2390, — N.E. 2d —, 2007 Ohio App. LEXIS 2256 (May 18, 2007).

Trial court did not abuse its discretion in denying a law client's motion to vacate a default judgment pursuant to Ohio R. Civ. P. 60(B)(1), where her claim of excusable neglect based on her alleged failure to have received sufficient notice of the default hearing lacked merit; rather, the client was served with the law firm's motion for default judgment, she received two letters, one via certified mail and one via regular mail, notifying her of the hearing, and there was sufficient and timely notice pursuant to Ohio R. Civ. P. 55(A). Rotatori v. Signer, — Ohio App. 3d —, 2006 Ohio 1354, — N.E. 2d —, 2006 Ohio App. LEXIS 1240 (Mar. 23, 2006).

As Ohio R. Civ. P. 55(A) only applied to a party who had appeared in an action, and a mortgage seller failed to appear where it only disputed the allegations of the mortgage buyer's claim in a letter directly to the buyer rather than in a responsive court pleading. Even if the letter had been deemed an appearance in the trial court proceeding, the failure to receive the requisite notice prior to entry of a default judgment was merely voidable and not void, and as the issue was not raised in the seller's motion for relief from default judgment under Ohio R. Civ. P. 60(B), it was waived for purposes of appeal. National City Mortgage Co. v. Johnson &

Associates Financial Services, Inc., — Ohio App. 3d —, — N.E. 2d —, 2006 Ohio App. LEXIS 2216 (May 12, 2006).

It was not an abuse of discretion for the trial court to grant the husband's Ohio R. Civ. P. 60(B) motion for relief from judgment because the motion fulfilled each of the requirements; it presented a meritorious claim, as well as a reason upon which relief could be granted, in asserting that he had not received a seven-day notice, pursuant to Ohio R. Civ. P. 6(D). It was also made within a reasonable time and the trial court held a hearing to verify operative facts set forth in the motion prior to ruling on the motion. Murphy v. Murphy, — Ohio App. 3d —, 2006 Ohio 4876, — N.E. 2d —, 2006 Ohio App. LEXIS 4791 (Sept. 1, 2006).

Denial of a medical practice's motion for relief from judgment pursuant to Ohio R. Civ. P. 60(B) was proper where it never appeared in an action asserted against it by a patient, and accordingly, it was not entitled to notice under Ohio R. Civ. P. 55(A) prior to entry of a default judgment against it in the patient's medical malpractice action; private communications did not constitute an "appearance" for purposes of requiring notice under Rule 55(A). Bright v. Family Med. Found., Inc., — Ohio App. 3d —, 2006 Ohio 5037, — N.E.2d —, 2006 Ohio App. LEXIS 4947 (Sept. 28, 2006).

Guarantors established that they were entitled to relief under Ohio R. Civ. P. 60(B)(5) from a default judgment entered against them since the trial court improperly entered the default judgment against them without providing them with the seven-day notice mandated by Ohio R. Civ. P. 55(A) for parties who had entered an appearance in the action. The guarantors' attorney filed a notice of appearance in the action after the motion for default judgment was filed but before the trial court entered the default judgment against the guarantors, and this constituted an "appearance" for purposes of Ohio R. Civ. P. 55(A). Meglan, Meglan & Co. v. Bostic, — Ohio App. 3d —, 2006 Ohio 2270, — N.E. 2d —, 2006 Ohio App. LEXIS 2107 (May 9, 2006).

When a judgment debtor did not apply a judgment creditor's contributions toward a disability insurance policy to the policy, causing the creditor to have no disability insurance when he became disabled, and the creditor obtained a default judgment against the debtor, and then filed a supplemental proceeding against the debtor's insurer, after the debtor's motion for relief from the default judgment was denied, the fact that this motion was denied did not mean that the insurer was not prejudiced by the creditor's late notice to it of the creditor's claim, which was given after the time to appeal the default judgment against the debtor had expired, because the term "meritorious defense," under Ohio R. Civ. P. 60(B), was not synonymous with a successful defense, which the insurer could potentially have raised had it received timely notice. Sesko v. Hutchins Caw, Inc., — Ohio App. 3d —, 2006 Ohio 5434, — N.E. 2d —, 2006 Ohio App. LEXIS 5433 (Oct. 19, 2006).

Nunc pro tunc orders

It was an abuse of discretion for a trial court to deny a wife's Ohio R. Civ. P. 60(B)(5) motion for relief from the trial court's nunc pro tunc order awarding a life insurance policy she jointly owned with the husband to the husband alone because the order was an improper nunc pro tunc order as it did not merely correct a clerical error but addressed a matter not previously specifically addressed by the parties, and it attempted to modify the parties' contract to divide their marital property, contrary to RC § 3105.171(I). Smith v. Smith, — Ohio App. 3d —, 2007 Ohio 1089, — N.E. 2d —, 2007 Ohio App. LEXIS 1244 (Mar. 12, 2007).

It was an abuse of discretion for a trial court to deny a wife's Ohio R. Civ. P. 60(B)(5) motion for relief from the trial court's nunc pro tunc order awarding a life insurance policy she jointly owned with the husband to the husband alone because the order was an improper nunc pro tunc order as it did not merely correct a clerical error but addressed a matter not previously specifically addressed by the parties, and it attempted to modify the parties' contract to divide their marital property, contrary to RC § 3105.171(I). Smith v. Smith, — Ohio App. 3d —, 2007 Ohio 1089, — N.E. 2d —, 2007 Ohio App. LEXIS 1244 (Mar. 12, 2007).

As a trial court was best situated to know whether its initial award of interest from a particular date was a deliberate choice or whether it resulted from a clerical mistake or oversight, its issuance of a nunc pro tunc order to change the date of interest in order to reflect accrual from the time that judgment was entered was not an abuse of discretion under Ohio R. Civ. P. 60(A). Brush v. Hassertt, — Ohio App. 3d —, 2007 Ohio 2419, — N.E. 2d —, 2007 Ohio App. LEXIS 2235 (May 18, 2007).

Because the father failed under Ohio R. Civ. P. 75(J) to perfect service of his motion on the mother, the trial court did not err when it vacated the nunc pro tunc entry changing her name in the caption under Ohio R. Civ. P. 60(A). It was undisputed that the mother did not receive a copy of the motion for nunc pro tunc order to change the caption. Pulice v. Collins, — Ohio App. 3d —, 2006 Ohio 3950, — N.E. 2d —, 2006 Ohio App. LEXIS 3903 (Aug. 3, 2006).

Objections to magistrate's report

Where a magistrate determined that a former wife was in contempt of court for failing to repay her former husband for his share of a loan to her mother, the wife should have filed objections to that decision rather than seek relief from judgment after the trial court approved and adopted the magistrate's determination. Such use of a motion under Ohio R. Civ. P. 60(B) was not permitted, and further, there was no plain error under Ohio R. Civ. P. 53(D)(3)(b) where the magistrate's determination was properly based on the parties' divorce decree. Brennan v. Brennan, — Ohio App. 3d —, 2007 Ohio 2097, — N.E. 2d —, 2007 Ohio App. LEXIS 1953 (Apr. 27, 2007).

Where a wife raised assorted constitutional claims in her motion for relief from a divorce judgment pursuant to Ohio R. Civ. P. 60(B), but she failed to raise them in her objections to the decision of the magistrate who considered her motion and recommended denial thereof, which was adopted by the trial court, those issues were not preserved for review pursuant to Ohio R. Civ. P. 53(E)(3)(d). Wilson v. Wilson, — Ohio App. 3d —, 2006 Ohio 4261, — N.E. 2d —, 2006 Ohio App. LEXIS 4187 (Aug. 17, 2006).

Paternity

Where a father whose paternity and child support obligations were established by a magistrate failed to file objections to that decision, and he failed to file objections to a magistrate's later decision to deny his motion under Ohio R. Civ. P. 60(B) to vacate the earlier judgment, he waived his right to appeal under Ohio R. Civ. P. 53(D)(3)(b). As the father failed to provide the appellate court with a trial court transcript, as required by Ohio R. App. P. 9(B), there was nothing to review and the appellate court had to presume the validity of the trial court proceedings. T.S. v. W.D., — Ohio App. 3d —, 2007 Ohio 3795, — N.E. 2d —, 2007 Ohio App. LEXIS 3454 (July 26, 2007).

When a putative father who had acknowledged his paternity of a child sought relief from a resulting judgment of paternity, after genetic testing showed a zero percent chance that he was the child's father, he could not claim, on appeal of the denial of his motion for relief, that the trial court should have considered granting him relief under Ohio R. Civ. P. 60(B) because he did not raise this in his motion for relief or in objections to a magistrate's decision. Vah v. Mahan, — Ohio App. 3d —, 2006 Ohio 3476, — N.E. 2d —, 2006 Ohio App. LEXIS 3432 (June 30, 2006).

Language of RC § 3119.962 plainly and unambiguously required that before a trial court could grant relief from a parentage determination or child support order, a genetic test relied upon had to have been administered no later than six months prior to the filing of the motion for relief from judgment. Hardy v. Wilson, — Ohio App. 3d —, 2006 Ohio 4532, — N.E. 2d —, 2006 Ohio App. LEXIS 4501 (Sept. 5, 2006).

When a putative father sought relief, pursuant to RC § 3119.962 and Ohio R. Civ. P. 60(B), from a judgment finding his paternity and ordering him to pay child support, his motion did not comply with the statute because the genetic test results filed with it, finding a zero percent likelihood of his paternity, were from genetic testing performed more than six months before the motion was filed, so, when a trial court granted him relief on this basis, it improperly created an exception to the statute which the legislature did not contemplate. Hardy v. Wilson, — Ohio App. 3d —, 2006 Ohio 4532, — N.E. 2d —, 2006 Ohio App. LEXIS 4501 (Sept. 5, 2006).

When a putative father sought relief, pursuant to RC § 3119.962 and Ohio R. Civ. P. 60(B), from a judgment finding his paternity and ordering him to pay child support, if a recertification of the results of genetic testing performed more than six months before the motion was filed, and an affidavit from the laboratory's director attesting to the validity of the testing, brought the test results into compliance with RC § 3119.962(A)(1)(a), the motion still did not comply with the statute because the recertification occurred after the motion was filed and the statute explicitly required testing to have been administered before filing a motion for relief. Hardy v. Wilson, — Ohio App. 3d —, 2006 Ohio 4532, — N.E. 2d —, 2006 Ohio App. LEXIS 4501 (Sept. 5, 2006).

Personal jurisdiction

In a law firm's suit against a former client for past due fees, in which the trial court had entered a default judgment against the client, the trial court properly vacated that default judgment pursuant to the client's letter to the court because that letter alleged that the client was never served with process, so the letter contested the trial court's jurisdiction over the client, and, as a result, the requirements of Ohio R. Civ. P. 60(B) did not apply to the letter, so the letter did not have to allege a meritorious defense or be timely filed. Bringman v. Smith, — Ohio App. 3d —, 2007 Ohio 4684, — N.E. 2d —, 2007 Ohio App. LEXIS 4214 (Sept. 12, 2007).

Trial court's grant of a wife's motion for relief from judgment, pursuant to Ohio R. Civ. P. 60(B), with respect to the prior grant of a divorce to the husband, including provisions as to spousal support and property division pursuant to RC §§ 3105.18 and 3105.171, was proper with respect to the property and support determinations, as the wife, who was a German citizen and still resided in Germany, was not properly served with the divorce complaint pursuant to the provisions of the Hague Convention. As those service provisions had to be complied with pursuant to the supremacy principles under U.S. Const. art. VI, the service was insufficient under Ohio R. Civ. P. 4.5(A) in order to give the trial court jurisdiction over the wife, and as such, the financial awards could not be made because the trial court lacked jurisdiction. Collins v. Collins, 165 Ohio App. 3d 71, 2006 Ohio 181, 844 N.E. 2d 910, 2006 Ohio App. LEXIS 159 (Jan. 20, 2006).

Trial court erred in not holding a hearing on the driver's Civ. R. 60(B) motion to vacate judgment for lack of personal jurisdiction. He presented operative facts warranting relief when he presented uncontroverted, sworn statements alleging that he did not receive the summons and complaint, rebutting the presumption of proper service. Miller v. Booth, — Ohio App. 3d —, 2006 Ohio 5679, — N.E. 2d —, 2006 Ohio App. LEXIS 5668 (Oct. 26, 2006).

Pro se litigants

When an insurer voluntarily dismissed and refiled its complaint, and the party it sued did not answer the refiled complaint, causing the insurer to move for the party's default, which was granted, after which the trial court granted relief from that default judgment, it was not reversible error for the trial court to state that laymen were not expected to have an intricate knowledge of the Rules of Civil Procedure because it was not shown that the trial court would have made a different decision had the neglect or mistake it found been made by an attorney, and it only said that laymen were not required to have an "intricate" knowledge of the Rules, rather than stating they were not expected to have any knowledge of them. American Select Ins. Co. v. Riggs, — Ohio App. 3d —, 2007 Ohio 1808, — N.E. 2d —, 2007 Ohio App. LEXIS 1632 (Apr. 17, 2007).

Prohibition

Where a domestic relations court magistrate clearly had authority pursuant to RC § 3113.31 over a civil protection order (CPO) sought by a former wife, and the former husband was served with the temporary CPO, such that personal jurisdiction was obtained over him with respect to the matter, his request for a writ of prohibition, seeking a determination that the CPO was unenforceable due to his lack of notice of the time for a final hearing on it, lacked merit. There was no showing of a patent and unambiguous lack of jurisdiction on the part of the magistrate, and the husband had adequate remedies at law through seeking relief from judgment under Ohio R. Civ. P. 60(B) and through appeal. State ex rel. Feathers v. Hayes, — Ohio App. 3d —, 2007 Ohio 3852, — N.E. 2d —, 2007 Ohio App. LEXIS 3490 (July 27, 2007).

Relief from default

Trial court did not abuse its discretion in setting aside a default judgment entered in a dog bite case two years after the judgment was entered where (1) the neighbor against whom the action was brought had a defense to the case in that she asserted she had no knowledge of the dog being kept at her home; (2) the fact that the neighbor's objections to the entry of the default by a magistrate were misfiled so that the trial court never saw them qualified as a reason for relief under CivR 60(B)(5); and (3) the delay in filing the motion for relief was reasonable because the neighbor heard nothing more about the case, she believed that the objections she filed had resolved the case, and the neighbor was unaware that a judgment had been entered until the alleged dog bit victim filed a foreclosure action to satisfy the judgment. Zwahlen v. Brown, — Ohio App. 3d —, 2008 Ohio 151, — N.E. 2d —, 2008 Ohio App. LEXIS 129 (Jan. 18, 2008).

Res judicata

In an action involving a civil stalking protection order (CSPO), res judicata barred defendant's third motion for relief from judgment under Ohio R. Civ. P. 60(B) because all the exhibits were either capable of being produced at the original hearing on the CSPO or were included in the prior Ohio R. Civ. P. 60(B) motion. Hangen v. McCaleb, — Ohio App. 3d —, 2007 Ohio 3160, — N.E. 2d —, 2007 Ohio App. LEXIS 2911 (June 22, 2007).

Tenant's arguments in his Ohio R. Civ. P. 60(B) motion that a landlord committed a fraud on the trial court by presenting a fraudulent copy of the lease at issue between the parties and that the landlord lied to the trial court about when the lease became effective were issues that were raised at trial and that could have been raised on appeal. Thus, the issues were barred by res judicata, and Ohio R. Civ. P. 60(B) relief was not proper. Boardman Canfield Ctr., Inc. v. Dr. David Baer, — Ohio App. 3d —, 2007 Ohio 2609, — N.E. 2d —, 2007 Ohio App. LEXIS 2436 (May 23, 2007).

Trial court erred in refusing to consider the mortgage company's motion for relief from judgment (from the voluntary dismissal of the second foreclosure action) based on its conclusion that the issues raised therein were not wholly distinguishable from the issues raised in the company's first motion for relief from judgment. Because the trial court did not address the merits of the first motion, res judicata did not preclude consideration of the arguments raised therein. Chase Manhattan Bank v. Jenkins, — Ohio App. 3d —, 2007 Ohio 3622, — N.E. 2d —, 2007 Ohio App. LEXIS 3314 (July 17, 2007).

Great-grandson's request for a declaration implicated issues of fact and law different from those which the probate court determined when it vacated the joint stipulation of parentage pursuant to Ohio R. Civ. P. 60(B). Therefore, the prior ruling created no bar pursuant to the doctrine of res judicata with respect to the issues of fact or law that the great-grandson's motion presented. Bank One Trust Co. N.A. v. Reynolds, — Ohio App. 3d —, 2007 Ohio 4197, — N.E. 2d —, 2007 Ohio App. LEXIS 3794 (Aug. 17, 2007).

Where a vehicle owner's initial motion to vacate a default judgment entered against him, pursuant to Ohio R. Civ. P. 60(B), was denied, and his second motion to vacate the default judgment raised the same issues, the trial court did not abuse its discretion in denying the second motion based on principles of res judicata. Turner v. Headbangers Inc., — Ohio App. 3d —, 2006 Ohio 2211, — N.E. 2d —, 2006 Ohio App. LEXIS 2052 (May 4, 2006).

Trial court did not abuse its discretion under Ohio R. Civ. P. 60(B)(5) in overruling a husband's motion for relief from the parties' divorce judgment, which also granted ancillary relief, as he failed to allege new grounds that entitled him to relief and accordingly, as the issues raised either could have been decided or already were decided in a prior appeal from that judgment, the matter was res judicata. He failed to set forth a meritorious claim and failed to show that he had a right to relief under Rule 60(B). Eyre v. Eyre, — Ohio App. 3d —, 2006 Ohio 6492, — N.E. 2d —, 2006 Ohio App. LEXIS 6416 (Dec. 8, 2006).

Service

Trial court's denial of a telephone book customer's motion to set aside a default judgment pursuant to Ohio R. Civ. P. 60(B) was proper, as service was made of the telephone book service's complaint by certified mail which was signed by an officer of the customer, the motion to vacate the default judgment was made 20 months after the complaint was received, which was not reasonable in the circumstances, and there was no meritorious defense where the customer's claim that it had no contract for advertising services was contradicted by copies of the advertising agreements between the parties. Cincinnati Bell Directory, Inc. v. Midwest Distribs., — Ohio App. 3d —, 2006 Ohio 2225, — N.E. 2d —, 2006 Ohio App. LEXIS 2048 (May 5, 2006).

As a trial court record indicated that within three days of entry of the trial court's summary judgment ruling in favor of an employee, the clerk of the trial court served the notice of final judgment on the counsel for the parties in a manner provided by Ohio R. Civ. P. 5 and the service was recorded in the court's docket, the requirements of Ohio R. Civ. P. 58(B) were met and due process under Ohio Const. art. I, § 16 was satisfied, such that the clerk was deemed to have issued proper service of the notice even if the employer's counsel did not actually receive it. There was no abuse of discretion in the trial court's denial of the employer's motion under Ohio R. Civ. P. 60(B)(5) for relief from judgment based on lack of service, as it did not meet the first prong of the GTE test because it sought to reargue issues raised and decided in the summary judgment motion, such that there was no showing of a meritorious defense if relief from judgment was granted. Leonard v. Consulting, — Ohio App. 3d —, 2007 Ohio 1846, — N.E. 2d —, 2007 Ohio App. LEXIS 1671 (Apr. 19, 2007).

Trial court did not err in denying a property owner's motion to set aside a default judgment pursuant to Ohio R. Civ. P. 60(B) in a tax foreclosure action, as multiple certified mail attempts came back, but the two that were marked as "unclaimed" led to service by ordinary mail at those addresses, one of which was not returned; pursuant to Ohio R. Civ. P. 4.6(D), the presumption that service was accomplished was not overcome, as the owner did not present any evidence that he did not actually receive service or notice of the complaint. Kapszukiewicz v. Samuel, — Ohio App. 3d —, 2007 Ohio 2152, — N.E. 2d —, 2007 Ohio App. LEXIS 1996 (May 4, 2007).

Judgment entered against children of judgment debtors was not void ab initio for lack of personal service on them, as the complaint was sent by certified mail to their permanent addresses and it was accepted by their grandmother, who was over the age of 16 years and was competent. Service was properly made under Ohio R. Civ. P. 4.1(A) and 4.2(A), and the trial court did not err in denying the children's motion for relief from judgment under Ohio R. Civ. P. 60(B). Tube City, Inc. v. Halishak, — Ohio App. 3d —, 2007 Ohio 2118, — N.E. 2d —, 2007 Ohio App. LEXIS 1976 (May 3, 2007).

Trial court's grant of an apartment complex's motion for relief from a default judgment under Ohio R. Civ. P. 60(B)(5) was proper where the complex asserted sufficient operative facts to support its potentially meritorious defense of lack of proper service. The large amount of damages awarded were partially based on an invalid loss of consortium claim, as the mother of the visitor was not added as a party-plaintiff and the amended complaint was not against the correctly named complex. Watts v. Forest Ridge Apts. & Town Homes, — Ohio App. 3d —, 2007 Ohio 1176, — N.E. 2d —, 2007 Ohio App. LEXIS 1091 (Mar. 16, 2007).

Trial court's grant of an apartment complex's motion for relief from a default judgment under Ohio R. Civ. P. 60(B)(5) was proper where the complex asserted sufficient operative facts to support its potentially meritorious defense of lack of proper service. The large amount of damages awarded were partially based on an invalid loss of consortium claim, as the mother of the visitor was not added as a party-plaintiff and the amended complaint was not against the correctly named complex. Watts v. Forest Ridge Apts. & Town Homes, — Ohio App. 3d —, 2007 Ohio 1176, — N.E. 2d —, 2007 Ohio App. LEXIS 1091 (Mar. 16, 2007).

When it was alleged that a default judgment was improperly entered against an excavating company because the company was never served with process, the company did not have to satisfy the requirements of Ohio R. Civ. P. 60(B) because a lack of service deprived the trial court of jurisdiction to consider the complaint, so that any judgment entered on that complaint was void ab initio. Tractor Serv. & Supply v. Excavating, — Ohio App. 3d —, 2007 Ohio 5255, — N.E. 2d —, 2007 Ohio App. LEXIS 4643 (Sept. 19, 2007).

It was not an abuse of discretion for a trial court to grant a motion to vacate a summary judgment because (1) the motion to vacate presented a meritorious defense given service problems with the summary judgment motion, (2) the party seeking summary judgment appeared to be entitled to relief under Ohio R. Civ. P. 60(B)(1) due to mistake or excusable neglect in not timely responding to the summary judgment motion, and (3) the motion to vacate was filed within one year after the summary judgment was entered. Crown Prop. Consultants v. USI Storage, — Ohio App. 3d —, 2007 Ohio 4736, — N.E. 2d —, 2007 Ohio App. LEXIS 4246 (Sept. 17, 2007).

Trial court's grant of individual debtors' motion under Ohio R. Civ. P. 60(B)(5) to vacate a default judgment obtained against them by a creditor, based on their claim that they were not properly served by certified mail at their business address pursuant to Ohio R. Civ. P. 4.1(1), was error where the creditor was not given an opportunity to respond to the motion and an evidentiary hearing was not held for the trial court's factual determination regarding whether the debtors had a physical presence at the business address for purposes of finding that their due process rights under Ohio Const. art.

I, § 16 were not violated by such service. Carter-Jones Lumber Co. v. Meyers, — Ohio App. 3d —, 2006 Ohio 5380, — N.E. 2d —, 2006 Ohio App. LEXIS 5336 (Oct. 13, 2006).

Trial court's denial of a motion by a business and guarantors, seeking either relief from a default judgment or to vacate the default judgment, pursuant to Ohio R. Civ. P. 60(B), was proper where the seller who obtained the default judgment had originally pursued service through certified mail, which was returned "unclaimed," and thereafter, service by ordinary mail was authorized, which was not returned to the court; further, the guarantors had another business only one mile away, they had the same postal carrier for both businesses who informed them when their business mailbox was full, they received utility bills and customer payments at the mailbox, and the circumstances indicated that the service by ordinary mail was reasonably calculated to reach them pursuant to Ohio R. Civ. P. 4.6(D). Seal Master Industries, Inc. v. Bay Area Seal Coating & Stripping, — Ohio App. 3d —, 2006 Ohio 3610, — N.E. 2d —, 2006 Ohio App. LEXIS 3547 (July 14, 2006).

Motion under Ohio R. Civ. P. 60(B) for relief from default judgment was properly denied. Since the record did not indicate that the complaint sent to appellant by regular mail was returned, a presumption arose under Ohio R. Civ. P. 4.6(D) that service was properly completed, and appellant failed to rebut the presumption, presenting no evidence before the trial court to support his assertion that he never received the complaint. Erie Ins. v. Williams, — Ohio App. 3d —, 2006 Ohio 6754, — N.E. 2d —, 2006 Ohio App. LEXIS 6661 (Dec. 20, 2006).

Denial of the driver's Ohio R. Civ. P. 60(B) motion to vacate the default judgment was proper because he failed to set forth a meritorious defense; the docket reflected that regular mail service was issued to the driver in response to the unclaimed certified mail service and that service was "deemed complete." Further, the driver's assertions did not refute the presumption of proper service that arose after the victim followed the procedure outlined in Ohio R. Civ. P. 4.6(D) because the driver presented no affidavit, deposition testimony, stipulations, or other evidence that would have demonstrated that service was improper. Harless v. Sprague, — Ohio App. 3d —, 2006 Ohio 4472, — N.E. 2d —, 2006 Ohio App. LEXIS 4391 (Aug. 30, 2006).

Trial court errs in summarily overruling a defendant's motion to set aside a judgment for lack of service, when the defendant submits a sworn statement that he or she did not receive service of process, without affording the defendant a hearing: Money Tree Loan Co. v. Williams, 169 Ohio App. 3d 336, 2006 Ohio 5568, 862 N.E.2d 885, 2006 Ohio App. LEXIS 5553 (2006).

Ohio law clearly provides that a judgment rendered without personal jurisdiction over a defendant is void ab initio rather than voidable, so a judgment rendered without proper service is a nullity and is void, and the authority to vacate a void judgment, thus, is not derived from Ohio R. Civ. P. 60(B), but rather constitutes an inherent power possessed by Ohio courts. Wayne Homes v. Demand, — Ohio App. 3d —, 2006 Ohio 2843, — N.E. 2d —, 2006 Ohio App. LEXIS 2660 (June 5, 2006).

Trial court did not err in denying the motion to vacate the default judgment for want of service in Germany because the trial court file contained the returned addressee signature card with the driver's name signed and the transcript of the hearing on the driver's motion contained no testimony by her or other evidence as to the veracity of her apparent signature. She waived her right to appeal reliance on the Hague Convention or any other international agreements regarding service of legal documents as she did not invoke them in the trial court. Linquist v. Drossel, — Ohio App. 3d —, 2006 Ohio 5712, — N.E. 2d —, 2006 Ohio App. LEXIS 5698 (Oct. 30, 2006).

Settlement

CivR 60(B)(3) did not apply where the plaintiffs were suing for damages for the alleged fraud, rather than looking to rescind the settlement agreement: Berry v. Javitch, Block & Rathbone, L.L.P., 182 Ohio App. 3d 795, 2009 Ohio 3067, 915 N.E.2d 382, 2009 Ohio App. LEXIS 2632 (2009).

Opponent did not show the opponent was entitled to relief from a judgment against the opponent, under Ohio R. Civ. P. 60(B), by claiming the parties had reached a settlement "in principle," because the opponent did not present a final settlement signed by all parties. JMA N. Coast Prop. Mgmt. v. Sutera, — Ohio App. 3d —, 2007 Ohio 3071, — N.E. 2d —, 2007 Ohio App. LEXIS 2806 (June 21, 2007).

Appellate court could not construe a motion to enforce a settlement as a motion for relief from judgment under Ohio R. Civ. P. 60(B), and a judgment entry by a trial court that enforced the settlement was void ab initio because the trial court lost jurisdiction to enforce the settlement when it entered an order dismissing a breach of contract action with prejudice and without any further reservation of jurisdiction. Nova Info. Sys. v. Current Directions, 2007 Ohio 4373, 2007 Ohio App. LEXIS 4014 (Aug. 24, 2007).

When, in a probate case, a widow said she was entitled to relief from a settlement agreement under the standard set forth in Ohio R. Civ. P. 60(B), the appellate court declined to apply that standard because the widow did not move for relief from the judgment adoptiing the settlement, nor did she file any written motion to set it aside. Estate of Stamm, — Ohio App. 3d —, 2006 Ohio 5176, — N.E. 2d —, 2006 Ohio App. LEXIS 5160 (Sept. 29, 2006).

Summary judgment

Debtor's Ohio R. Civ. P. 60(B) motion for relief from summary judgment entered against him in a creditor's suit on a credit card obligation was properly granted because the debtor's counsel represented that he never received a copy of the summary judgment motion. He proffered a meritorious defense, in that the debtor averred that he applied for the credit card in a corporate capacity; and the motion was timely made. National Check Bur., Inc. v. Johnson, — Ohio App. 3d —, 2007 Ohio 1053, — N.E. 2d —, 2007 Ohio App. LEXIS 962 (Mar. 9, 2007).

Trial court properly denied a debtor's Ohio R. Civ. P. 60(B) motion for relief from summary judgment entered in favor of an assignee of a creditor because the debtor failed to demonstrate that he was entitled to relief under one of the grounds in Ohio R. Civ. P. 60(B)(1)-(5). The debtor was not entitled to relief due to the creditor's alleged failure to acknowledge the existence of a settlement agreement between the creditor and the debtor as there was no evidence in the record before the trial court supporting the existence of such an agreement. Cavalry Portfolio Servs. v. Terrell, — Ohio App. 3d —, 2007 Ohio 1331, — N.E. 2d —, 2007 Ohio App. LEXIS 1215 (Mar. 23, 2007).

Trial court properly denied a debtor's Ohio R. Civ. P. 60(B) motion for relief from summary judgment entered in favor of an assignee of a creditor because the debtor failed to demonstrate that he was entitled to relief under one of the grounds in Ohio R. Civ. P. 60(B)(1)-(5). The debtor was not entitled to relief due to the creditor's alleged failure to acknowledge the existence of a settlement agreement between the creditor and the debtor as there was no evidence in the record before the trial court supporting the existence of such an agreement. Cavalry Portfolio Servs. v. Terrell, — Ohio App. 3d —, 2007 Ohio 1331, — N.E. 2d —, 2007 Ohio App. LEXIS 1215 (Mar. 23, 2007).

Trial court properly overruled clients' motion for reconsideration or relief from the trial court's decision granting summary judgment to an attorney in the attorney's suit to recover legal fees owed to him by the clients because the clients did not submit any evidence with their motion to

support their claims. Koblentz & Koblentz v. Ferrante, — Ohio App. 3d —, 2006 Ohio 1740, — N.E. 2d —, 2006 Ohio App. LEXIS 1600 (Apr. 6, 2006).

Tax matters

Denial by a trial court of a taxpayer's motion under Ohio R. Civ. P. 60(B) for relief from a judgment lien that was filed against him as a corporate president for unpaid corporate sales taxes pursuant to RC § 5739.13 was proper, as the trial court lacked authority to vacate the judgment based on RC § 5703.38. The trial court could not take action that would suspend or stay the Ohio Department of Taxation's determination regarding the assessment against the taxpayer, although it was noted that if collection measures were instituted, the taxpayer could then assert affirmative defenses. State Dep't of Taxation v. Kroeger, — Ohio App. 3d —, 2007 Ohio 2859, — N.E. 2d —, 2005 Ohio App. LEXIS 6398 (June 8, 2005).

Timeliness

Trial court abused its discretion by finding that the movant met its burden as to timeliness under CivR 60(B)(1) or (5): JP Morgan Chase Bank v. Wells Fargo Fin. Leasing, Inc., 180 Ohio App. 3d 1, 2008 Ohio 6354, 903 N.E.2d 1249, 2008 Ohio App. LEXIS 5299 (2008).

When the administrator of a decedent's estate moved to vacate an order approving the settlement of the decedent's guardianship estate over a year after the order was entered, the motion was not untimely because the administrator did not seek relief due to fraud, under RC § 2109.35(A), but sought relief on other grounds, under RC § 2109.35(B), by (1) expressly moving under § 2109.35(B), (2) alleging an inherent conflict of interest because the guardian was also the executor of the decedent's estate, and (3) alleging the guardian's conduct violated his fiduciary duty to manage the estate for his ward's best interest, under RC § 2111.14(B), and that the guardian named himself beneficiary of certain annuities while acting as guardian. In re Atkinson, — Ohio App. 3d —, 2007 Ohio 765, — N.E. 2d —, 2007 Ohio App. LEXIS 711 (Feb. 26, 2007).

Trial court's finding that the husband's motion for relief from judgment was not pursued within a reasonable time was not error because his delay was inexcusable. By ignoring the vexatious litigator issue in the case from at least June 2004 until late February 2005, the husband was not entitled to relief from judgment. Also, the trial court's findings that the husband's motion was not timely, but that the wife's motion was timely, did not violate equal protection principles because the husband had legal training and was a former member of the Ohio Bar Association. Scotland Yard Condo. Ass'n v. Spencer, — Ohio App. 3d —, 2007 Ohio 1239, — N.E. 2d —, 2007 Ohio App. LEXIS 1166 (Mar. 20, 2007).

Trial court's finding that the husband's motion for relief from judgment was not pursued within a reasonable time was not error because his delay was inexcusable. By ignoring the vexatious litigator issue in the case from at least June 2004 until late February 2005, the husband was not entitled to relief from judgment. Also, the trial court's findings that the husband's motion was not timely, but that the wife's motion was timely, did not violate equal protection principles because the husband had legal training and was a former member of the Ohio Bar Association. Scotland Yard Condo. Ass'n v. Spencer, — Ohio App. 3d —, 2007 Ohio 1239, — N.E. 2d —, 2007 Ohio App. LEXIS 1166 (Mar. 20, 2007).

Trial court did not abuse its discretion in denying a husband's motion for relief from judgment under Ohio R. Civ. P. 60(B) with respect to the equitable distribution of his military pension between himself and his wife, as his motion under Rule 60(B)(1) and (3) was untimely where it was not filed within one year; as to the grounds under Rule 60(B)(5), the husband failed to meet his burden of showing that the motion was filed within a "reasonable time," as he was aware of a problem with the pension and the payments thereunder for a period of years prior to the time that he made his motion, and further, the distribution was based on an agreement between the parties that had been adopted by the trial court at the time of the divorce, such that the husband could have raised an issue at that time if he was dissatisfied for any reason with the distribution. Rotroff v. Rotroff, — Ohio App. 3d —, 2007 Ohio 2391, — N.E. 2d —, 2007 Ohio App. LEXIS 2249 (May 18, 2007).

Ohio R. Civ. P. 60(B) motion for relief from a judgment entered in a divorce action while the husband was in prison was timely filed since, although it was filed three months after the judgment, it was filed once the husband learned of the judgment entered in a divorce action. Dottore v. Feathers, — Ohio App. 3d —, 2007 Ohio 2435, — N.E. 2d —, 2007 Ohio App. LEXIS 2266 (May 18, 2007).

Although the mortgage company filed its motion for relief from judgment nearly 16 months after the trial court denied its first Ohio R. Civ. P. 60(B) motion (for relief from the voluntary dismissal of the second foreclosure action), it did so within two months after reversal of the trial court's judgment in the third foreclosure action. Because the mortgage company filed its motion within two months after the reversal, it appropriately alleged facts regarding the timeliness of its second motion for relief from judgment. Chase Manhattan Bank v. Jenkins, — Ohio App. 3d —, 2007 Ohio 3622, — N.E. 2d —, 2007 Ohio App. LEXIS 3314 (July 17, 2007).

When a church was sued on a mortgage the church granted to secure a trust indenture agreement, and summary judgment was issued against the church, the church's motion under Ohio R. Civ. P. 60(B)(2) for relief from that judgment due to newly discovered evidence was not timely, even though the motion was filed within one year of the judgment, because the church did not explain why the church did not file the motion in a more timely manner. First Fin. Servs. v. Cross Tabernacle Deliverance Church, — Ohio App. 3d —, 2007 Ohio 4274, — N.E. 2d —, 2007 Ohio App. LEXIS 3937 (Aug. 21, 2007).

When an insured sought relief, under Ohio R. Civ. P. 60(B)(5), from the insured's alleged inadvertent dismissal of a party, due to excusable neglect, the insured was not entitled to such relief because the insured's motion was not filed within a reasonable time as the 14 months between the insured's notice of dismissal and the insured's motion was unreasonable since, due to numerous intervening events in the litigation, the insured knew or should have known of the effect of the insured's notice long before the insured filed the insured's motion. Len-ran, Inc. v. Erie Ins. Group, — Ohio App. 3d —, 2007 Ohio 4763, — N.E. 2d —, 2007 Ohio App. LEXIS 4250 (Sept. 14, 2007).

When an insured sought relief, under Ohio R. Civ. P. 60(B), from the insured's alleged inadvertent dismissal of a party, the insured was not entitled to such relief for inadvertence, under Ohio R. Civ. P. 60(B)(1), because the insured's motion was filed more than one year after the insured filed a notice of dismissal which dismissed the party in question, and the requirement that a motion seeking relief under Rule 60(B)(1) be filed within one year of the act from which relief was sought was absolute. Len-ran, Inc. v. Erie Ins. Group, — Ohio App. 3d —, 2007 Ohio 4763, — N.E. 2d —, 2007 Ohio App. LEXIS 4250 (Sept. 14, 2007).

Requirement in Ohio R. Civ. P. 60(B) that a motion for relief from judgment "shall be made within a reasonable time" applies to all of the five grounds for vacation, so a party has the possible right to bring a motion to vacate the judgment on the grounds of, for example, newly discovered evidence up to one year after entry of judgment, but the motion is also subject to the "reasonable time" provision. Village of Lakemore v. SN Servicing Corp., — Ohio App. 3d —, 2007 Ohio 4650, — N.E. 2d —, 2007 Ohio App. LEXIS 4187 (Sept. 12, 2007).

When a property owner sought relief from a default judgment against the owner, under Ohio R. Civ. P. 60(B)(1),

(4) and (5), the owner was not entitled to relief, even though the owner's motion for relief was filed within one year of the default judgment, because the requirement in Ohio R. Civ. P. 60(B) that a motion for relief from judgment be filed within a reasonable time applied to all grounds for relief in the Rule so that, even if a motion seeking relief under Ohio R. Civ. P. 60(B)(1) was filed within one year of the judgment from which relief was sought, the movant still had to demonstrate that the motion was filed within a reasonable time, and, when the owner did not explain why it was reasonable for the owner's motion to have been filed six months after the default judgment, the owner did not satisfy this requirement. Village of Lakemore v. SN Servicing Corp., — Ohio App. 3d —, 2007 Ohio 4650, — N.E. 2d —, 2007 Ohio App. LEXIS 4187 (Sept. 12, 2007).

Ohio R. Civ. P. 60(B) requires all motions for relief from judgment to be filed within a reasonable time, so motions based on Ohio R. Civ. P. 60(B)(1), (2), and (3) not only must be filed within a reasonable time, but under no circumstances may be filed more than a year after the judgment from which relief is sought. Village of Lakemore v. SN Servicing Corp., — Ohio App. 3d —, 2007 Ohio 4650, — N.E. 2d —, 2007 Ohio App. LEXIS 4187 (Sept. 12, 2007).

When a motorist, against whom a default judgment was entered in a personal injury suit, sought relief from that judgment, under Ohio R. Civ. P. 60(B), slightly more than one month after the default judment entry was filed, this was reasonable for purposes of obtaining such relief. Federico v. Langham, — Ohio App. 3d —, 2007 Ohio 2168, — N.E. 2d —, 2007 Ohio App. LEXIS 2015 (May 4, 2007).

Ohio R. Civ. P. 60(B) sets forth a two-part standard for the timely filing of a motion for relief from judgment, so, while a movant may have up to one year from the date of a judgment to file a motion to vacate, the movant is also bound by the "reasonable time" provision, and, thus, a motion may be filed within one year under Rule 60(B), but still may not be considered within a "reasonable time," as it is the movant's burden of proof to present factual material that, on its face, establishes the timeliness or justifies delays in filing the motion to vacate, and, in order to sustain this burden, the movant must present allegations of operative facts to demonstrate that the movant is filing the movant's motion within a reasonable period of time, and, in the absence of any explanation for a delay in filing a Rule 60(B) motion, the movant has failed to meet the movant's burden to establish timeliness of the movant's motion, and the motion to vacate should be denied. EMC Mortgage Corp. v. Pratt, — Ohio App. 3d —, 2007 Ohio 4669, — N.E. 2d —, 2007 Ohio App. LEXIS 4201 (Sept. 11, 2007).

When, in a foreclosure case, the buyers of the foreclosed property moved, under Ohio R. Civ. P. 60(B), to vacate an order confirming the sale to the buyers, which held the buyers liable for taxes on the property, the buyers' motion was not filed within a reasonable time because the motion was filed almost six months after the order clearly requiring the buyers to pay the taxes was entered, and the buyers offered no explanation for the buyers' delay in filing the motion to try to show that the delay was reasonable. EMC Mortgage Corp. v. Pratt, — Ohio App. 3d —, 2007 Ohio 4669, — N.E. 2d —, 2007 Ohio App. LEXIS 4201 (Sept. 11, 2007).

When a homeowner sought relief from a judgment of foreclosure, the homeowner's delay in seeking relief was unreasonable because the homeowner's motion was filed approximately eleven months after the judgment was entered, three weeks after the homeowner was given notice of the proposed sale of the foreclosed premises, and ten days before a court-ordered sale, after the homeowner did not respond to a homeowners' association's summary judgment motion or object to or appeal the judgment of foreclosure. Miles

Landing Homeowners Ass'n v. Harris, — Ohio App. 3d —, 2007 Ohio 3411, — N.E. 2d —, 2007 Ohio App. LEXIS 3165 (July 5, 2007).

Former wife's motion under Civ. R. 60(B) for relief from the parties' divorce decree, based on the fact that her husband's pension was not equitably divided, was untimely for purposes of Rule 60(B)(1) and (2) where it was brought more than 22 years after the decree was entered, and she did not show that the untimeliness was reasonable in the circumstances for purposes of Rule 60(B)(5); she did not show that she had a meritorious claim or that she was entitled to relief, as her allegations were refuted by the former husband's testimony that the trial court had considered the pension issue and had found that his pension was "synonymous" with the wife's similar pension. Yancey v. Yancey, — Ohio App. 3d —, 2007 Ohio 5045, — N.E. 2d —, 2007 Ohio App. LEXIS 4444 (Sept. 19, 2007).

When a taxpayer sought relief, pursuant to Ohio R. Civ. P. 60(B)(3), from a judgment against him approximately 30 months after the judgment was entered, his motion was clearly filed after the one year time limit applied to motions under Rule 60(B)(3), and his motion was not timely under any other provision of Ohio R. Civ. P. 60(B) because he was warned at a debtor's examination, held approximately 18 months before he filed his motion, that he might wish to consider retaining counsel and/or filing such a motion, so his motion was not filed within a reasonable time. State Dep't of Taxation v. Freeman, — Ohio App. 3d —, 2006 Ohio 2372, — N.E. 2d —, 2006 Ohio App. LEXIS 2265 (May 15, 2006).

Ohio R. Civ. P. 60(B) motion for relief from default judgment entered was properly denied. While the motion was filed within one year of judgment, it was not filed within a reasonable time as appellant failed to acknowledge the entry of default judgment until eight months later despite having received the complaint, the order granting default judgment, and several cost bills after the entry of judgment. James Remodeling & Bldg., Inc. v. Rhines, — Ohio App. 3d —, 2006 Ohio 6962, — N.E. 2d —, 2006 Ohio App. LEXIS 6918 (Dec. 29, 2006).

When a default judgment was entered against a mortgagee, and it did not seek relief from the judgment for almost 10 months after judgment was filed, despite (1) notice of the default judgment hearing, at which it did not appear, (2) a bill from the clerk's office taxing costs, (3) personal service of an order granting a mortgagor's motion in aid of execution and a notice to appear for a debtor's examination almost six months after judgment was entered, at which it did not appear, and (4) the mortgagor's efforts to resolve the matter short of litigation over several years, to which it did not respond, it was unnecessary to determine if its motion for relief from judgment, under Ohio R. Civ. P. 60(B), stated a meritorious defense or if it might be entitled to relief under Ohio R. Civ. P. 60(B)(1) through (5), because its motion seeking relief was not timely, so the trial court did not abuse its discretion in denying the motion. Flores v. Beneficial Mortg. Co., — Ohio App. 3d —, 2006 Ohio 393, — N.E. 2d —, 2006 Ohio App. LEXIS 332 (Feb. 1, 2006).

Debtors motion for relief from a deficiency judgment entered against them was not filed within a reasonable time. The motion was filed 23 months after their property sold and 21 months after the deficiency judgment was entered. French v. Gruber, — Ohio App. 3d —, 2006 Ohio 1167, — N.E. 2d —, 2006 Ohio App. LEXIS 1057 (Mar. 14, 2006).

It was the burden of proof of a movant to vacate a judgment, under Ohio R. Civ. P. 60(B), to present factual material that on its face established the timeliness or justified delays in filing the motion to vacate, and, in order to sustain this burden, good legal practice dictated that the movant present allegations of operative facts to demonstrate that he was filing his motion within a reasonable period of time, but, in the absence of any explanation for a delay in filing a Rule 60(B) motion, the movant failed to meet his burden of establishing the timeliness of his motion and the motion to vacate was to be denied. Dunn v. Marthers, — Ohio App. 3d —, 2006 Ohio 4923, — N.E. 2d —, 2006 Ohio App. LEXIS 4890 (Sept. 25, 2006).

When a mortgagee claimed it was entitled to relief from a summary judgment, under Ohio R. Civ. P. 60(B), even if it had submitted necessary operative facts, it was not an abuse of discretion for a trial court to decline to hear the claim because the motion was not timely, as the mortgagee possessed the facts on which it relied for ten months before it filed its motion, and it did not explain its delay. National City Home Loan Servs. v. Gillette, — Ohio App. 3d —, 2006 Ohio 2881, — N.E. 2d —, 2006 Ohio App. LEXIS 2716 (June 2, 2006).

Father's Ohio R. Civ. P. 60(B) relief motion was properly denied as it was untimely since he filed it more than 16 years after the trial court issued its decision regarding child support. Further, he did not demonstrate that he had a meritorious claim to pursue should relief from judgment be granted and his claims were barred by the doctrine of res judicata since the exact argument had been made and rejected previously. Danforth v. Danforth, — Ohio App. 3d —, 2006 Ohio 2890, — N.E. 2d —, 2006 Ohio App. LEXIS 2785 (June 8, 2006).

Parents' allegations of fraud underlying an agreed custody entry involved Ohio R. Civ. P. 60(B)(3), but a motion for relief from judgment based on that provision was required to have been filed within one year from the date of judgment; because the parents' motion was filed three years after judgment, the trial court properly denied it as untimely. In re Weller, — Ohio App. 3d —, 2006 Ohio 3015, — N.E. 2d —, 2006 Ohio App. LEXIS 2880 (June 15, 2006).

Trial court's finding that the lessee's Ohio R. Civ. P. 60(B) motion for relief from judgment more than a year after judgment was entered was not timely filed was not an abuse of discretion. The settlement negotiations did not establish a reasonable delay in initiating the motion for relief and, even if the lessee's contention as to when it first received notice of the judgment were accepted, the sixth-month delay in filing the motion for relief was unreasonable. Star Leasing Co. v. Central States Distribution, — Ohio App. 3d —, 2006 Ohio 3314, — N.E. 2d —, 2006 Ohio App. LEXIS 3232 (June 29, 2006).

Trial court erred in granting a note maker's Ohio R. Civ. P. 60(B) motion to vacate a judgment by confession entered against it on a cognovit note because the maker filed its motion seven months after judgment was entered, and it failed to provide the trial court with any explanation or factual support for why its seven month delay in filing the motion to vacate was "reasonable." Waldman Fin. v. Digital Color Imaging, Inc., — Ohio App. 3d —, 2006 Ohio 4077, — N.E. 2d —, 2006 Ohio App. LEXIS 4040 (Aug. 9, 2006).

When, in a personal injury case, a trial court granted an insurer's dismissal motion, and, at the same time, dismissed a motorist who had been sued, the alleged injured party who filed the suit sought relief from the judgment dismissing the motorist within a reasonable time because he stated that he did not learn of the court's error until he met with an attorney almost a year after the judgment was entered, after which he promptly sought relief. Dunn v. Marthers, — Ohio App. 3d —, 2006 Ohio 4923, — N.E. 2d —, 2006 Ohio App. LEXIS 4890 (Sept. 25, 2006).

When, in a personal injury case, a trial court granted an insurer's dismissal motion, and, at the same time, dismissed a motorist who had been sued, the trial court's subsequent order changing the dismissal of the motorist from a dismissal with prejudice to a dismissal without prejudice was void, but the fact that the pro se alleged injured party who brought the suit and sought relief from the motorist's dismissal relied on this void judgment to establish the timeliness of his motion for relief from the trial court's original judgment did not show the motion was not timely filed, because the alleged injured party stated other justifications for his delay in seeking relief. Dunn v. Marthers, — Ohio App. 3d —, 2006 Ohio 4923, — N.E. 2d —, 2006 Ohio App. LEXIS 4890 (Sept. 25, 2006).

When a trial court entered summary judgment in favor of the Ohio Supreme Court's Client Security Fund, in its suit against a former attorney for funds it had paid to his former client, the attorney timely filed a motion for relief from that judgment because his motion was filed 21 days after the summary judgment was entered. State v. Potts, — Ohio App. 3d —, 2006 Ohio 7057, — N.E. 2d —, 2006 Ohio App. LEXIS 6989 (Dec. 28, 2006).

Claims of the mother and brother seeking, under Ohio R. Civ. P. 60(B)(1), (3), (5), relief from the default judgment entered in favor of the owner in the quiet title action were untimely, as the Ohio R. Civ. P. 60(B)(1), (3) claims were not filed within one year of the default, and the Ohio R. Civ. P. 60(B)(5) claim failed because no explanation was given as to why the motion for relief from judgment was filed more than six years after the default judgment. Brode v. Brode, — Ohio App. 3d —, 2006 Ohio 143, — N.E. 2d —, 2006 Ohio App. LEXIS 112 (Jan. 6, 2006).

When a husband sought relief from a trial court's order under Ohio R. Civ. P. 60(B)(1), Ohio R. Civ. P. 6(E) did not extend the one-year period within which he was required to file his motion because Ohio R. Civ. P. 60(B) did not trigger the running of this one-year limitation period with a service of notice requirement. Williams v. Williams, — Ohio App. 3d —, 2006 Ohio 2566, — N.E. 2d —, 2006 Ohio App. LEXIS 2420 (May 18, 2006).

Transcripts

While appellant included a compact disc of the Ohio R. Civ. P. 60(B) hearing in the trial court record, she did not file a transcript of the evidence nor did she submit an affidavit of evidence as required by Ohio R. Civ. P. 53(E)(3). Thus, the trial court properly limited its decision to whether the magistrate erred as a matter of law. Leibold v. Hiddens, — Ohio App. 3d —, 2007 Ohio 2972, — N.E. 2d —, 2007 Ohio App. LEXIS 2732 (June 8, 2007).

In her relief motion, the mother raised issues of excusable neglect under Ohio R. Civ. P. 60(B)(1) and fraud under Ohio R. Civ. P. 60(B)(3), respectively, which were factual issues upon which the magistrate was required, under Ohio R. Civ. P. 53(E)(2), to make findings of fact and conclusions of law. It was anomalous, therefore, for the trial court to require a transcript of proceedings to challenge findings of fact and conclusions of law where none were furnished in the magistrate's decision. Stone v. Stone, — Ohio App. 3d —, 2006 Ohio 3420, — N.E. 2d —, 2006 Ohio App. LEXIS 3350 (June 30, 2006).

As a wife failed to include a transcript of a proceeding before a magistrate when she filed objections to the magistrate's decision, pursuant to Ohio R. Civ. P. 53(E)(3)(c), and she also failed to request an extension for the filing thereof prior to the hearing date on her objections in her divorce action, the trial court properly overruled her objections. Her motion to vacate the judgment pursuant to Ohio R. Civ. P. 60(B) was also properly denied where she was clearly on notice of the importance of the transcript having been filed, yet she still had not filed it or sought an extension of time to file it prior to that motion. Ludlow v. Ludlow, — Ohio App. 3d —, 2006 Ohio 6864, — N.E. 2d —, 2006 Ohio App. LEXIS 6778 (Dec. 22, 2006).

Vacating portion of decree

Entire settlement agreement did not need to be vacated because there was not a lack of meeting of the minds at the time that the agreement was reached since the mistake occurred during the drafting of the judgment entry. The trial court did not change the terms of the agreement by granting the wife's Ohio R. Civ. P. 60(B) motion; the original agreement as hashed out between the parties was restored. Bodnar v. Bodnar, — Ohio App. 3d —, 2006 Ohio 3300, — N.E. 2d —, 2006 Ohio App. LEXIS 3214 (June 23, 2006).

Void judgments

Debtor's Ohio R. Civ. P. 60(B) motion to vacate a void judgment entered against her in a foreclosure action was properly denied because the debtor was unable to show that she had a meritorious defense or that she was entitled to relief under one of the grounds set forth in Ohio R. Civ. P. 60(B), in that the "vapor money" theory and the "legal tender" argument advanced by the debtor had previously been rejected. Wells Fargo Bank, NA v. Ward, — Ohio App. 3d —, 2006 Ohio 6744, — N.E. 2d —, 2006 Ohio App. LEXIS 6647 (Dec. 19, 2006).

Voluntary dismissal

As an employee, through his counsel, filed a voluntary dismissal pursuant to Ohio R. Civ. P. 41(A)(1) of his personal injury action against his employer, which dismissal did not indicate that a refiling was required within one year, the trial court did not err in denying the employee's later motion for relief from the dismissal judgment pursuant to Ohio R. Civ. P. 60(B), as the voluntary dismissal was not a final order within Rule 60, such that the trial court lacked jurisdiction to grant relief from it. The employee had refiled his action within one year but it was during a bankruptcy of the employer, such that any litigation was stayed, and the stay was lifted prior to the termination of the limitations period. Lowenborg v. Oglebay Norton Co., — Ohio App. 3d —, 2007 Ohio 3408, — N.E. 2d —, 2007 Ohio App. LEXIS 3177 (July 5, 2007).

Waiver

Trial court did not abuse its discretion in denying a motion to vacate a void judgment under Ohio R. Civ. P. 60(B) by a promissory note debtor in a bank's foreclosure action, wherein the debtor claimed that the bank was not the real party in interest pursuant to Ohio R. Civ. P. 17; the real party in interest claim was not raised within a "reasonable time," such that it was deemed waived, and the debtor failed to show any evidence to support that claim or to support his request for relief from judgment based on the necessary showing required under Ohio R. Civ. P. 60(B). Washington Mutual Bank v. Novak, — Ohio App. 3d —, 2007 Ohio 996, — N.E. 2d —, 2007 Ohio App. LEXIS 990 (Mar. 8, 2007).

RULE 61. Harmless error

No error in either the admission or the exclusion of evidence and no error or defect in any ruling or order or in anything done or omitted by the court or by any of the parties is ground for granting a new trial or for setting aside a verdict or for vacating, modifying or otherwise disturbing a judgment or order, unless refusal to take such action appears to the court inconsistent with substantial justice. The court at every stage of the proceeding must disregard any error or defect in the proceeding which does not affect the substantial rights of the parties.

NOTES TO DECISIONS

ANALYSIS

Evidentiary rulings
Harmless error
Nunc pro tunc entry
Policies and procedures
Probate
Small claims litigation
Substantial rights

Evidentiary rulings

Although a trial court's exclusion of medical records pursuant to Ohio R. Evid. 803(4) was proper as to physician statements regarding a father's diagnosis where no physicians testified in a contempt proceeding against the father due to his failure to pay child support, exclusion of the father's statements concerning his symptoms reported to the physician was error; however, the error was harmless under Ohio R. Civ. P. 61 where the father testified as to his symptoms, such that he was not prejudiced by the exclusion. Jones v. Jones, — Ohio App. 3d —, 2007 Ohio 5492, — N.E. 2d —, 2007 Ohio App. LEXIS 4827 (Oct. 15, 2007).

Secretary was not prejudiced by the trial court's refusal to order the president's wife to provide an answer regarding a conversation with her husband about an E-mail because the president acknowledged that he had access to the secretary's e-mail account, had on one occasion read an e-mail from the secretary to his wife, and had talked to his wife about that e-mail. Thus, because compelling an answer to the question would have simply provided additional evidence of something that the president had already acknowledged, any error was harmless. Olson v. Holland Computers, — Ohio App. 3d —, 2007 Ohio 4727, — N.E. 2d —, 2007 Ohio App. LEXIS 4265 (Sept. 17, 2007).

Although the trial court erred in striking the neighbor's testimony (because a copy of the subpoena was not required to be provided to the other party under Ohio R. Civ. P. 45(A)(1)(b)(i)), the error was harmless because the testimony did not negate the wife's testimony concerning the incident, and thus, no substantial right of the husband was affected since the trial court was correct in entering the civil protection order. The testimony merely gave an overall impression of the husband's general demeanor when dealing with the neighbor, together with a statement about the wife's mental state sometime after the incident had occurred. Cauwenbergh v. Cauwenbergh, — Ohio App. 3d —, 2007 Ohio 1070, — N.E. 2d —, 2007 Ohio App. LEXIS 1011 (Mar. 9, 2007).

Trial court's partial grant of a motion in limine by medical professionals and entities in a patient's medical malpractice and informed consent action, whereby it excluded the hospital manual and regulations with respect to the policies regarding supervision of anesthesia students, was not harmless error under Ohio R. Civ. P. 61 where the evidence was relevant and admissible under Ohio R. Evid. 401 to determine the standard of care required, and such evidence would not have been prejudicial or confusing to the jury under Ohio R. Evid. 403(A). The alleged malpractice occurred due to the actions of a student nurse who performed anesthesia procedures without first having identified herself to the patient and who was not supervised by an anesthesiologist at the time, as required in the hospital's manual and regulations, and only two standards of care had been introduced in the case, such that the issue would not have been confusing for the jury to hear. Luettke v. St. Vincent Mercy Med. Ctr., — Ohio App. 3d —, 2006 Ohio 3872, — N.E. 2d —, 2006 Ohio App. LEXIS 3828 (July 28, 2006).

In a suit by debtors against a lender, when a trial court refused to admit evidence of a suit against the debtors, the debtors could not show they were prejudiced because this evidence went to damages, but the debtors did not show they were entitled to receive damages as to any of the claims they asserted, so, under Ohio R. Civ. P. 61, they did not show they were prejudiced. Lotfi-Fard v. First Fed. of Lakewood, — Ohio App. 3d —, 2006 Ohio 3727, — N.E. 2d —, 2006 Ohio App. LEXIS 3686 (July 20, 2006).

Harmless error

Trial court's having taken judicial notice of a docket in a prior action was harmless error under Ohio R. Civ. P. 61 in an action by a first mortgagee, seeking summary judgment on its foreclosure claim against mortgagors, as it considered an affidavit submitted by the mortgagors regarding a purported settlement agreement previously reached between the parties, which contained simply a legal conclusion or opinion absent the admissible hearsay. JP Morgan Chase Bank v. Murdock, — Ohio App. 3d —, 2007 Ohio 751, — N.E. 2d —, 2007 Ohio App. LEXIS 688 (Feb. 23, 2007).

Any potential error by the trial court in its instructions, wherein it advised the jury about the "clear and convincing" evidence standard within the circumstantial evidence jury instruction, did not cause confusion, so it was harmless error under Ohio R. Civ. P. 61. Domer v. Joan, — Ohio App. 3d —, 2007 Ohio 6877, — N.E. 2d —, 2007 Ohio App. LEXIS 6032 (Dec. 14, 2007).

Husband's claim that the trial court abused its discretion in not ordering the wife to pay child support to the State of Ohio while their son was incarcerated at a juvenile correction center, pursuant to RC § 3119.07(C), lacked merit where he failed to show that he was prejudiced by her failure to pay such support. Such an order would not have impacted the husband's child support obligation which was imposed by a magistrate and adopted by the trial court in the parties' divorce, and as such, it was harmless error that was to be disregarded pursuant to Ohio R. Civ. P. 61 and RC § 2309.59. Dunn v. Dunn, — Ohio App. 3d —, 2006 Ohio 4649, — N.E. 2d —, 2006 Ohio App. LEXIS 4551 (Sept. 8, 2006).

Trial court's reliance on the version of RC § 1705.04(A), rather than the version in effect at the time that the parties signed and filed articles of organization and an original appointment of agent with respect to a limited liability company on May 7, 1998, was harmless under Ohio R. Civ. P. 61 because two statutory versions only had minor variations between them. The disputed issue was who was a member of the company, whch was determined under RC § 1705.01(G) and (H). Matthews v. D'Amore, — Ohio App. 3d —, 2006 Ohio 5745, — N.E. 2d —, 2006 Ohio App. LEXIS 5704 (Nov. 2, 2006).

Although a father was entitled to appointment of counsel in a civil proceeding pursuant to due process under Ohio Const. art. I, § 16 where a trial court ordered him to show cause as to why he should not have been held in contempt for possibly authoring a derogatory letter to the judge, where the judge later determined that the father was not in contempt and the order to show cause was dropped, no prejudice to the father was shown; accordingly, any error was harmless. Kuzniak v. Midkiff, — Ohio App. 3d —, 2006 Ohio 6133, — N.E. 2d —, 2006 Ohio App. LEXIS 6110 (Nov. 15, 2006).

As a trial court entered an order confirming an execution sale pursuant to RC § 2329.13(B)(4), which was an implicit finding that there was no prejudice to either party, and debtors who sought to have that sale vacated also failed to show that they had suffered any prejudice, any lack of notice to them as to the sale was harmless error under Ohio R. Civ. P. 61. Bank One, N.A. v. DWT Realty, Inc., — Ohio App. 3d —, 2006 Ohio 7271, — N.E. 2d —, 2006 Ohio App. LEXIS 7072 (May 23, 2006).

Nunc pro tunc entry

Because the trial court had already granted appellee's summary judgment motion in its entirety, which included damages in the amount of $12,408.70, the nunc pro tunc entry entered after the appeal was filed was superfluous and affected no substantial right of the tenants and was thus, harmless. Trala v. Turney, — Ohio App. 3d —, 2006 Ohio 6999, — N.E. 2d —, 2006 Ohio App. LEXIS 6913 (Dec. 29, 2006).

Policies and procedures

Trial court abused its discretion by denying an administratrix's motion to compel production of documents regarding a clinic's internal policies and procedures regarding acquiring items from an outside hospital's pathology department in a case in which the administratrix claimed that the clinic was negligent in failing to properly review outside pathology slides before surgery. Lostracco v. Cleveland Clinic Found., — Ohio App. 3d —, 2006 Ohio 3694, — N.E. 2d —, 2006 Ohio App. LEXIS 3640 (July 20, 2006).

Probate

Daughter failed to introduced sufficient evidence showing that the son unduly influenced the father when the will was executed and none of the evidentiary issues which she raised appeared to address her failure of proof on that point. Thus, any error in those rulings did not affect her substantial rights and the errors were harmless. Theis v. Stanko, — Ohio App. 3d —, 2007 Ohio 1127, — N.E. 2d —, 2007 Ohio App. LEXIS 1049 (Mar. 2, 2007).

Daughter failed to introduced sufficient evidence showing that the son unduly influenced the father when the will was executed and none of the evidentiary issues which she raised appeared to address her failure of proof on that point. Thus, any error in those rulings did not affect her substantial rights and the errors were harmless. Theis v. Stanko, — Ohio App. 3d —, 2007 Ohio 1127, — N.E. 2d —, 2007 Ohio App. LEXIS 1049 (Mar. 2, 2007).

Small claims litigation

When an automobile dealer sued a consumer in small claims court for failing to honor an agreement to make a down payment on a vehicle, and, on remand, the trial court reviewed the transcripts and exhibits of the initial trial in considering the dealer's summary judgment motion, thereby treating the motion as a post-trial brief, while this was procedural error, it was harmless under the circumstances, and was treated simply as a ruling enforcing the contract between the parties. Norwalk MK, Inc. v. McCormick, 170 Ohio App. 3d 147, 2006 Ohio 4640, 866 N.E.2d 516, 2006 Ohio App. LEXIS 4560 (2006).

Substantial rights

When homeowners said a developer negligently misrepresented to them that a home they wanted to build would fit on two lots he proposed to sell them, but a trial court properly found that there was no evidence that the developer made an affirmative false statement to the homeowners, it was unnecessary to consider whether the evidence supported the homeowners' claim that they justifiably relied on the developer's misrepresentations because any decision on this alleged error would not impact the trial court's judgment against the owners, under Ohio R. Civ. P. 61. Brothers v. Morrone-O'Keefe Dev. Co., — Ohio App. 3d —, 2007 Ohio 1942, — N.E. 2d —, 2007 Ohio App. LEXIS 1762 (Apr. 24, 2007).

When homeowners said a developer negligently misrepresented to them that a home they wanted to build would fit on two lots he proposed to sell them, but a trial court properly found that there was no evidence that the developer made an affirmative false statement to the homeowners, it was unnecessary to consider whether the trial court erred in finding they did not justifiably rely on the developer's statements because any decision on this alleged error would not impact the trial court's judgment against the owners, under Ohio R. Civ. P. 61. Brothers v. Morrone-O'Keefe Dev. Co., — Ohio App. 3d —, 2007 Ohio 1942, — N.E. 2d —, 2007 Ohio App. LEXIS 1762 (Apr. 24, 2007).

In a workers' compensation case, the trial court's abuse of discretion in allowing a physician's testimony affected a substantial right of a former employee. The physician's testimony that the former employee's surgery "had nothing to do with" the former employee's 1984 injuries and that lumbar disc disease was not related to one episode, if believed by the jury, invalidated the former employee's entire case. Hickle v. Hayes-Albion Corp., — Ohio App. 3d —, 2007 Ohio 4236, — N.E. 2d —, 2007 Ohio App. LEXIS 3889 (Aug. 20, 2007).

In a mother-in-law's suit to recover a sum from a son-in-law, a magistrate's failure to explicitly acknowledge, in the magistrate's decision, the son-in-law's admitted exhibits did not prejudice the son-in-law's substantial rights, and any error was harmless, because several of the exhibits were in the record, and it was evident from the magistrate's decision that the exhibits were considered. Ila Woodward v. Kleese, — Ohio App. 3d —, 2007 Ohio 5218, — N.E. 2d —, 2007 Ohio App. LEXIS 4585 (Sept. 28, 2007).

When a trial court did not comply with the court's local rules by granting a motion to compel discovery four days after the motion was filed, there was no abuse of discretion because the trial court could choose to deviate from the court's local rules, and the court's order merely required a party to provide the discovery the party was already required to provide under Ohio R. Civ. P. 26. Flatt v. Atwood, — Ohio App. 3d —, 2007 Ohio 5387, — N.E. 2d —, 2007 Ohio App. LEXIS 4735 (Oct. 9, 2007).

Trial court's error of staying child visitation proceedings until resolution of the matter did not affect the substantial rights of the parties in this case; it did not stop the father from asserting custody, visitation, or any other rights, and therefore was harmless error. In re N.A.E., — Ohio App. 3d —, 2006 Ohio 5395, — N.E. 2d —, 2006 Ohio App. LEXIS 5391 (Oct. 13, 2006).

When a decedent's estate's beneficiary, who was also the estate's attorney, moved for the removal of her sisters as co-executrices of the estate, withdrew that motion, and then filed a second, similar, motion, the trial court's reliance, when granting the second motion, on claims made in the first motion did not affect the sisters' substantial rights, as it relied on the constant flow of contentious motions, objections and oppositions to find acrimony between the parties, justifying the sisters' removal, so any error by the trial court was harmless. In re Estate of Howard, — Ohio App. 3d —, 2006 Ohio 2176, — N.E. 2d —, 2006 Ohio App. LEXIS 2026 (May 3, 2006).

RULE 62.   Stay of proceedings to enforce a judgment

(A) **Stay on motion for new trial or for judgment.** In its discretion and on such conditions for the security of the adverse party as are proper, the court may stay the execution of any judgment or stay any proceedings to enforce judgment pending the disposition of a motion for a new trial, or of a motion for relief from a judgment or order made pursuant to Rule 60, or of a motion for judgment notwithstanding the verdict made pursuant to Rule 50.

(B) **Stay upon appeal.** When an appeal is taken the appellant may obtain a stay of execution of a judgment or any proceedings to enforce a judgment by giving an adequate supersedeas bond. The bond may be given at or after the time of filing the notice of appeal. The stay is effective when the supersedeas bond is approved by the court.

(C) **Stay in favor of the government.** When an appeal is taken by this state or political subdivision, or administrative agency of either, or by any officer thereof acting in his representative capacity and the operation or enforcement of the judgment is stayed, no bond, obligation or other security shall be required from the appellant.

(D) **Power of appellate court not limited.** The provisions in this rule do not limit any power of an appellate court or of a judge or justice thereof to stay proceedings during the pendency of an appeal or to suspend, modify, restore, or grant an injunction during the pendency of an appeal or to make any order appropriate to preserve the status quo or the effectiveness of the judgment subsequently to be entered.

(E) **Stay of judgment as to multiple claims or multiple parties.** When a court has ordered a final judgment under the conditions stated in Rule 54(B), the court may stay enforcement of that judgment until the entering of a subsequent judgment or judgments and may prescribe such conditions as are necessary to secure the benefit thereof to the party in whose favor the judgment is entered.

NOTES TO DECISIONS

ANALYSIS

Bond
Denial of stay

Bond
When a husband appealed from a trial court's denial of the husband's motion for relief from a judgment awarding the net proceeds of the sale of certain marital property to the wife, the husband's appeal was dismissed because, when the husband did not post a supersedeas bond as required by Ohio R. Civ. P. 62(B) and the trial court's order, the wife's motion to release the sale proceeds, which had been deposited with the court, to the wife was granted, so no live controversy remained before the appellate court, since the issue of the overall division of the parties' marital property had not been presented to the appellate court, causing the husband's appeal to be moot. Tereletsky v. Tereletsky, — Ohio App. 3d —, 2007 Ohio 4132, — N.E. 2d —, 2007 Ohio App. LEXIS 3753 (Aug. 15, 2007).

Denial of stay
Trial court's denial of a guarantor's motion to stay execution of a cognovit judgment pending appeal was not an abuse of discretion under Ohio R. Civ. P. 62(B) and RC § 2505.09, as the guarantor's claim that posting the supersedeas bond would pose a financial hardship to his family did not provide an adequate basis to exclude or reduce the bond requirement. Ohio Carpenters' Pension Fund v. La Centre, — Ohio App. 3d —, 2006 Ohio 2214, — N.E. 2d —, 2006 Ohio App. LEXIS 2060 (May 4, 2006).

RULE 63. Disability of a judge

(A) **During trial.** If for any reason the judge before whom a jury trial has been commenced is unable to proceed with the trial, another judge, designated by the administrative judge, or in the case of a single-judge division by the chief justice of the supreme court, may proceed with and finish the trial upon certifying in the record that he has familiarized himself with the record of the trial; but if such other judge is satisfied that he cannot adequately familiarize himself with the record, he may in his discretion grant a new trial.

(B) **[After verdict or findings.]** If for any reason the judge before whom an action has been tried is unable to perform the duties to be performed by the court after a verdict is returned or findings of fact and conclusions of law are filed, another judge designated by the administrative judge, or in the case of a single-judge division by the Chief Justice of the Supreme Court, may perform those duties; but if such other judge is satisfied that he cannot perform those duties, he may in his discretion grant a new trial.

History: Amended, eff 7-1-72; 7-1-73; 7-1-94.

NOTES TO DECISIONS

ANALYSIS

Applicability
Judgment on transcript
Successor judge

Applicability
Reference to Ohio R. Civ. P. 63 to determine the propriety of a trial judge's action in taking over a hearing after a magistrate judge recused herself was improper because Ohio R. Civ. P. 63 was not applicable to hearings conducted before magistrates. Place v. Seibert, 173 Ohio App. 3d 653, 880 NE2d 100, 2007 Ohio App LEXIS 3942 (2007).

Judgment on transcript
There was nothing infirm with the successor judge in the case at bar finalizing the case, even though he did not hear the matter at trial: Myers v. Wild Wilderness Raceway, L.L.C., 181 Ohio App. 3d 221, 2009 Ohio 874, 908 N.E.2d 950, 2009 Ohio App. LEXIS 728 (2009).

Successor judge
Because the decision to classify defendant as a sexual predator was never journalized, there was no final appealable order and, on remand, nothing precluded the successor judge from carrying out its duty to journalize that decision on remand. Although the trial court retained jurisdiction to journalize defendant's sexual predator classification made by the original trial judge, the State's cross-appeal had to be dismissed because procedendo, not appeal, was the proper remedy for the State. State v. Ronan, — Ohio App. 3d —, 2007 Ohio 168, — N.E. 2d —, 2007 Ohio App. LEXIS 142 (Jan. 18, 2007).

TITLE VIII
PROVISIONAL AND FINAL REMEDIES

RULE 64. Seizure of person or property

At the commencement of and during the course of an action, all remedies providing for seizure of person or property for the purpose of securing satisfaction of the judgment ultimately to be entered in the action are available under the circumstances and in the manner provided by law. The remedies thus available include arrest, attachment, garnishment, replevin, sequestration, and other corresponding or equivalent remedies, however designated and regardless of whether the remedy is ancillary to an action or must be obtained by independent action.

NOTES TO DECISIONS

ANALYSIS

Clearance of post-judgment motions
Clearance before garnishment

Clearance of post-judgment motions
There was no statutory requirement that a bank submit its post-judgment motions for a garnishment order for "clearance" before filing, and a trial court's order, prohibiting any further action by a bank in the case and any action in any other case without prior approval by the trial court, was an abuse of discretion. MBNA America Bank v. Bailey, — Ohio App. 3d —, 2006 Ohio 1550, — N.E. 2d —, 2006 Ohio App. LEXIS 1436 (Mar. 31, 2006).

Clearance before garnishment

There was no statutory requirement that a bank submit its post-judgment motions for a garnishment order for "clearance" before filing, and a trial court's order, prohibiting any further action by a bank in the case and any action in any other case without prior approval by the trial court, was an abuse of discretion. MBNA America Bank v. Bailey, — Ohio App. 3d —, 2006 Ohio 1550, — N.E. 2d —, 2006 Ohio App. LEXIS 1436 (Mar. 31, 2006).

RULE 65. Injunctions

(A) **Temporary restraining order; notice; hearing; duration.** A temporary restraining order may be granted without written or oral notice to the adverse party or his attorney only if (1) it clearly appears from specific facts shown by affidavit or by the verified complaint that immediate and irreparable injury, loss or damage will result to the applicant before the adverse party or his attorney can be heard in opposition, and (2) the applicant's attorney certifies to the court in writing the efforts, if any, which have been made to give notice and the reasons supporting his claim that notice should not be required. The verification of such affidavit or verified complaint shall be upon the affiant's own knowledge, information or belief; and so far as upon information and belief, shall state that he believes this information to be true. Every temporary restraining order granted without notice shall be filed forthwith in the clerk's office; shall define the injury and state why it is irreparable and why the order was granted without notice; and shall expire by its terms within such time after entry, not to exceed fourteen days, as the court fixes, unless within the time so fixed the order, for good cause shown, is extended for one like period or unless the party against whom the order is directed consents that it may be extended for a longer period. The reasons for the extension shall be set forth in the order of extension. In case a temporary restraining order is granted without notice, the motion for a preliminary injunction shall be set down for hearing at the earliest possible time and takes precedence over all matters except older matters of the same character. When the motion comes on for hearing the party who obtained the temporary restraining order shall proceed with the application for a preliminary injunction and, if he does not do so, the court shall dissolve the temporary restraining order. On two days' notice to the party who obtained the temporary restraining order without notice or on such shorter notice to that party as the court may prescribe, the adverse party may appear and move its dissolution or modification, and in that event the court shall proceed to hear and determine such motion as expeditiously as the ends of justice require.

(B) **Preliminary injunction.**

(1) Notice. No preliminary injunction shall be issued without reasonable notice to the adverse party. The application for preliminary injunction may be included in the complaint or may be made by motion.

(2) Consolidation of hearing with trial on merits. Before or after the commencement of the hearing of an application for a preliminary injunction, the court may order the trial of the action on the merits to be advanced and consolidated with the hearing of the application. Even when this consolidation is not ordered, any evidence received upon an application for a preliminary injunction which would be admissible upon the trial on the merits becomes part of the record on the trial and need not be repeated upon the trial. This subdivision (B)(2) shall be so construed and applied as to save to the parties any rights they may have to trial by jury.

(C) **Security.** No temporary restraining order or preliminary injunction is operative until the party obtaining it gives a bond executed by sufficient surety, approved by the clerk of the court granting the order or injunction, in an amount fixed by the court or judge allowing it, to secure to the party enjoined the damages he may sustain, if it is finally decided that the order or injunction should not have been granted.

The party obtaining the order or injunction may deposit, in lieu of such bond, with the clerk of the court granting the order or injunction, currency, cashier's check, certified check or negotiable government bonds in the amount fixed by the court.

Before judgment, upon reasonable notice to the party who obtained an injunction, a party enjoined may move the court for additional security. If the original security is found to be insufficient, the court may vacate the injunction unless, in reasonable time, sufficient security is provided.

No security shall be required of this state or political subdivision, or agency of either, or of any officer thereof acting in his representative capacity.

A surety upon a bond or undertaking under this rule submits himself to the jurisdiction of the court and irrevocably appoints the clerk of the court as his agent upon whom any papers affecting his liability on the bond or undertaking may be served. His liability as well as the liability of the party obtaining the order or injunction may be enforced by the court without jury on motion without the necessity for an independent action. The motion and such notice of the motion as the court prescribes may be served on the clerk of the curt who shall forthwith mail copies to the persons giving the security if their addresses are known.

(D) **Form and scope of restraining order or injunction.** Every order granting an injunction and every restraining order shall set forth the reasons for its issuance; shall be specific in terms; shall describe in reasonable detail, and not by reference to the complaint or other document, the act or acts sought to be restrained; and is binding upon the parties to the action, their officers, agents, servants, employees, attorneys and those persons in active concert or participation with them who receive actual notice of the order whether by personal service or otherwise.

(E) **Service of temporary restraining orders and injunctions.** Restraining orders which are granted ex parte shall be served in the manner provided for service of process under Rule 4 through Rule 4.3 and Rule 4.6, or in a manner directed by order of the court. If the restraining order is granted upon a pleading or motion accompanying a pleading the order may be served with the process and pleading. When service is made pursuant to Rule 4 through Rule 4.3 and Rule 4.6, the sheriff or the person designated by order of the court shall forthwith make his return.

Restraining orders or injunctions which are granted with notice may be served in the manner provided under Rule 4 through Rule 4.3 and Rule 4.6, in the manner provided in Rule 5 or in the manner designated by order of the court. When service is made pursuant to Rule 4 through Rule 4.3 and Rule 4.6, the sheriff or the person designated by order of the court shall forthwith make his return.

NOTES TO DECISIONS

ANALYSIS

Adequate remedy at law
Appeal
Bond
Consolidation
Effect on nonparties
Employee noncompetition agreement
Harmless error
Hearings
Irreparable harm
Jurisdiction
Lack of harm to third parties
Nuisances
Preliminary injunction
— Denial
Public interest

Adequate remedy at law

Neighbors seeking to enforce a restrictive covenant in property owners' deed, which restricted the height of boat shelters, were entitled to injunctive relief because the owners' boat shelter was substantially taller than what was allowed by the restrictive covenant, as well as being taller than any other boat shelter on the channel on which the parties lived, so it diminished a uniform and aesthetically pleasing neighborhood, and the neighbors had no adequate remedy at law and suffered sufficient harm to warrant injunctive relief. Baker v. Adams, — Ohio App. 3d —, 2006 Ohio 3232, — N.E. 2d —, 2006 Ohio App. LEXIS 3127 (June 26, 2006).

Appeal

Denial of inmates' request for a preliminary and permanent injunction pursuant to Ohio R. Civ. P. 65, and for a temporary restraining order in their class action that challenged the parole procedure applicable to them was not a final appealable order where the requirements of RC § 2505.02(B)(4)(a) but not of § 2505.02(B)(4)(b) were met with respect to the provisional remedies, the necessary language of Ohio R. Civ. P. 54(B) was lacking, and an adequate remedy by appeal at the conclusion of all of the proceedings existed. Ankrom v. Hageman, — Ohio App. 3d —, 2007 Ohio 5092, — N.E. 2d —, 2007 Ohio App. LEXIS 4496 (Sept. 27, 2007).

Trial court's denial of home buyers' request for a preliminary injunction pursuant to Ohio R. Civ. P. 65(B) was not a final appealable order pursuant to RC § 2505.02, as it sought rescission of a home purchase agreement and the denial thereof did not prevent meaningful relief. The issue of rescission was determined by the trial court after a jury award on damages was rendered, and that decision was a final and appealable order. Zappitelli v. Miller, — Ohio App. 3d —, 2006 Ohio 279, — N.E. 2d —, 2006 Ohio App. LEXIS 239 (Jan. 26, 2006).

Bond

Trial court's failure to include any indication as to a bond, or even a waiver thereof, in the journalized entry of a preliminary injunction (PI) rendered the PI inoperative for failing to comply with the express provisions of Ohio R. Civ. P. 65(B). The trial court erred in holding a property resident in contempt for his violation of the terms of the PI, which required that he not display protest signs on his property. Skiles v. Bellevue Hosp., — Ohio App. 3d —, 2006 Ohio 5361, — N.E. 2d —, 2006 Ohio App. LEXIS 5332 (Oct. 13, 2006).

Consolidation

As a trial court consolidated a ferryboat service provider's requests for a preliminary and permanent injunction pursuant to Ohio R. Civ. P. 65(B)(2) with respect to the leasing of dock space from a marina owner and it granted the provider a permanent injunction to allow it to maintain the dock space for the remainder of the particular boating season, such was a determination on the merits, such that the provider was collaterally estopped in another related action from relitigating the issue of whether it had a binding written agreement to lease the dock space after the boating season had ended. Island Express Boat Lines, Ltd. v. Put-in-bay Boat Line Co., — Ohio App. 3d —, 2007 Ohio 1041, — N.E. 2d —, 2007 Ohio App. LEXIS 977 (Mar. 9, 2007).

Under Ohio R. Civ. P. 65, a trial court has discretionary power to advance a trial on its merits and consolidate the trial with a hearing on a preliminary injunction to prevent two hearings and save time and expense for the court and parties, under Ohio R. Civ. P. 65(B)(2), but it is generally improper to dispose of a case on the merits following a hearing for a preliminary injunction without consolidating that hearing with a trial on the merits or otherwise giving notice to counsel that the merits would be considered, so, before consolidation, the parties should normally receive clear and unambiguous notice of the court's intent to consolidate the trial and the hearing either before the hearing commences or at a time which will still afford the parties a full opportunity to present their respective cases. Ohio Serv. Group, Inc. v. Integrated & Open Systems, LLC, — Ohio App. 3d —, 2006 Ohio 6738, — N.E. 2d —, 2006 Ohio App. LEXIS 6633 (Dec. 19, 2006).

When a trial court denied an affiliate's preliminary injunction motion, after hearing, but allowed discovery as to the affiliate's motion to enforce an agreed judgment, and then denied the motion to enforce the judgment without further hearing, the court deprived the affiliate of the procedural due process protections of Ohio Const. art. I, § 16 because the court gave no notice that it intended to consolidate a hearing on the merits of the motion to enforce the judgment with the preliminary injunction hearing. Ohio Serv. Group, Inc. v. Integrated & Open Systems, LLC, — Ohio App. 3d —, 2006 Ohio 6738, — N.E. 2d —, 2006 Ohio App. LEXIS 6633 (Dec. 19, 2006).

Ohio R. Civ. P. 65(B) simply does not permit an advancement and consolidation of a trial on the merits at a preliminary injunction hearing without an order of the trial court, as the purpose of the order is obviously to notify both parties so that they can prepare their respective cases accordingly as there are fundamental differences between a trial on the merits and a hearing for a preliminary injunction, since a preliminary injunction is a provisional remedy and requires that the plaintiff demonstrate that he is entitled to the relief demanded, i.e., the preliminary injunction, and that such relief consists of some act that during the litigation would produce irreparable injury to the plaintiff, and the plaintiff must also show a substantial likelihood of success on the merits, whether the issuance of a preliminary injunction would cause substantial harm to others, and whether the public interest would be served by issuing a preliminary injunction, but an action on the merits involves very few, if any, of the aforementioned issues. Ohio Serv. Group, Inc. v. Integrated & Open Systems, LLC, — Ohio App. 3d —, 2006 Ohio 6738, — N.E. 2d —, 2006 Ohio App. LEXIS 6633 (Dec. 19, 2006).

Effect on nonparties

Non-parties could be bound by an injunction to ensure that defendants did not nullify a decree by carrying out prohibited acts through aiders and abettors, even though the aiders and abettors were not parties to the original proceeding, but those persons had to have actual notice of the injunction in order to be bound by it. Columbus Homes Ltd. v. S.A.R. Constr. Co., — Ohio App. 3d —, 2007 Ohio 1702, — N.E. 2d —, 2007 Ohio App. LEXIS 1549 (Apr. 10, 2007).

Employee noncompetition agreement

Employee noncompete agreement was reasonable and enforceable via a preliminary injunction. Enforcement would not impose an undue burden on the former employees. Confidential information need not meet the stringent requirements of a trade secret to be the subject of a valid nondisclosure agreement: Life Line Screening of Am., Ltd. v. Calger, 145 Ohio Misc. 2d 6, 2006 Ohio 7322, 2006 Ohio Misc. LEXIS 384 (2007).

Harmless error

Although the preliminary injunction order was quite specific in informing the commercial landlord of what acts were restrained, the trial court should not have referred to other documents when it issued the permanent injunction order. The order was also somewhat broad, in terms of restraining the landlord from interfering with any business relationships, however, because the parties were well aware of what acts were being restrained, there would have been no confusion about the terms of the permanent injunction and the landlord was not prejudiced; therefore, the error was harmless. Outback/Buckeye II v. Grandchildren's Trust, — Ohio App. 3d —, 2007 Ohio 577, — N.E. 2d —, 2007 Ohio App. LEXIS 535 (Feb. 9, 2007).

Hearings

As a temporary restraining order pursuant to Ohio R. Civ. P. 65(A) was not granted to inmates, a hearing was not required for purposes of a preliminary injunction request; further, as the inmates never requested a hearing on the restraing order or injunction, the trial court did not err in failing to hold one. Ridenour v. Wilkinson, — Ohio App. 3d —, 2007 Ohio 5965, — N.E. 2d —, 2007 Ohio App. LEXIS 5238 (Nov. 8, 2007).

Irreparable harm

Trial court did not abuse its discretion in granting an injunction to a former employer against its former employee and the employee's retail fireworks store, as the store was in violation of the employee's non-compete clause because it was within the radius of the geographic prohibition which caused irreparable harm to the employer, and enforcement of the agreement was in the public interest. A second store of the employee was not within the prohibited zone, as the fireworks of the employer were sold in a chain store rather than a temporary fireworks stand, such that different geographical provisions applied. Alan v. Andrews, — Ohio App. 3d —, 2007 Ohio 2608, — N.E. 2d —, 2007 Ohio App. LEXIS 2437 (May 22, 2007).

In a suit claiming that an employee formed his own company, which competed with his employer, while still working for the employer, it was an abuse of discretion to grant a preliminary injunction in favor of the employer, under Ohio R. Civ. P. 65(B), because the employer offered no evidence, including evidence that it would be irreparably harmed if the injunction was not granted. King's Welding & Fabricating v. King, — Ohio App. 3d —, 2006 Ohio 5231, — N.E. 2d —, 2006 Ohio App. LEXIS 5207 (Sept. 27, 2006).

Trial court erred in employing an actual harm standard, instead of a threat of harm standard, as the basis for denying a motion for a preliminary injunction by an employer seeking to enforce a covenant not to compete: Convergys Corp. v. Tackman, 169 Ohio App. 3d 665, 2006 Ohio 6616, 864 N.E.2d 145, 2006 Ohio App. LEXIS 6544 (2006).

Jurisdiction

Because the trial court imposed a permanent injunction incorporating the terms of the agreed preliminary injunction in its order granting partial summary judgment, and entered a final judgment resolving the remaining claims, the trial court erred when it concluded that it lacked subject matter jurisdiction to enforce the terms of the agreed preliminary injunction. The trial court had continuing jurisdiction under Ohio R. Civ. P. 65(C). Hosta v. Chrysler, 172 Ohio App. 3d 654, 2007 Ohio 4205, 876 N.E.2d 998, 2007 Ohio App. LEXIS 3803 (2007).

Lack of harm to third parties

In a suit claiming that an employee formed his own company, which competed with his employer, while still working for the employer, it was an abuse of discretion to grant a preliminary injunction in favor of the employer, under Ohio R. Civ. P. 65(B), because the employer offered no evidence, including evidence that no third parties would be unjustifiably harmed if the injunction was granted, while the employee asserted that the customers of his company would be harmed. King's Welding & Fabricating v. King, — Ohio App. 3d —, 2006 Ohio 5231, — N.E. 2d —, 2006 Ohio App. LEXIS 5207 (Sept. 27, 2006).

Nuisances

Expert testimony was not required to establish that commercial operation of a raceway severely impacted surrounding property owners due to noise, dust, and bright lights. The injunction was properly tailored to protect the interests of those owners. An award of damages does not inevitably follow the finding of a nuisance: Myers v. Wild Wilderness Raceway, L.L.C., 181 Ohio App. 3d 221, 2009 Ohio 874, 908 N.E.2d 950, 2009 Ohio App. LEXIS 728 (2009).

Preliminary injunction

Where the trial court adopted the terms of the agreed preliminary injunction as a remedy for the plaintiffs on the merits of their claim, the order in effect granted a permanent injunction that would terminate when the shareholders' meeting was held. The trial court's imposition of a permanent injunction without a hearing, based on its grant of summary judgment in plaintiffs' favor, was permissible: Hosta v. Chrysler, 172 Ohio App. 3d 654, 2007 Ohio 4205, 876 N.E.2d 998, 2007 Ohio App. LEXIS 3803 (2007).

Public interest and the former employer's proof by clear and convincing evidence of a strong or substantial likelihood of success on its claim against former employees for intentional interference with a business relationship warranted granting of a preliminary injunction: Brakefire, Inc. v. Overbeck, 144 Ohio Misc. 2d 35, 2007 Ohio 6464, 878 N.E.2d 84, 2007 Ohio Misc. LEXIS 487 (2007).

If a trial court imposed an injunction based on trade secrets, that injunction was not necessarily permanent, as once a trade secret was no longer secret, any injunction imposed had to be terminated, under RC § 1333.62, and an injunction had to generally terminate when a former trade secret became either known to good faith competitors, or was obtained by them because of the lawful availability of products that could be reverse engineered to reveal such trade secrets, subject to any additional period of restraint necessary to negate lead time acquired by the misappropriator, so it followed logically then that no injunction was to be imposed if the trade secret was no longer secret at the time the moving party sought the injunction. Jacono v. Invacare Corp., — Ohio App. 3d —, 2006 Ohio 1596, — N.E. 2d —, 2006 Ohio App. LEXIS 1501 (Mar. 30, 2006).

Under Ohio law, even the threat of harm was a sufficient basis on which a court could grant injunctive relief, as courts found that an actual threat of harm existed when an employee possessed knowledge of an employer's trade secrets and began working in a position that caused her to compete directly with the former employer or the product line that the employee formerly supported, and this was similar to the inevitable-disclosure rule, which reasoned that a threat of harm warranting injunctive relief could be shown by facts establishing that an employee with detailed and comprehensive knowledge of the former employer's trade secrets and confidential information now worked for a competitor of the former employer in a position that was substantially similar to the position held during the former employment, but any harm or threat of harm was not irreparable if money damages could serve as an adequate remedy. Jacono v. Invacare Corp., — Ohio App. 3d —, 2006 Ohio 1596, — N.E. 2d —, 2006 Ohio App. LEXIS 1501 (Mar. 30, 2006).

Preliminary injunction complied with CivR 65(D) and did not constitute an undue restraint of freedom of speech; it merely sought to preserve the status quo in a case where a party was allegedly about to breach a confidentiality provision in a settlement agreement entered into in an earlier action. Aultcare v. Roach, — Ohio App. 3d —, 2007 Ohio 5686, — N.E. 2d —, 2007 Ohio App. LEXIS 4995 (Oct. 22, 2007).

Trial court's grant of a preliminary injunction pursuant to Ohio R. Civ. P. 65(B) to a former employer in order to preclude a former employee from operating a competing business was proper, as the elements were shown by clear and convincing evidence, which was the proper standard for determining such a request for relief; the employee was in violation of a noncompetition clause where he started a competing business, hired other former employees, and did work for the employer's former customers, and there was a sufficient showing that the employer had a substantial likelihood of succeeding on the merits, the employer would suffer irreparable injury to an extent if the business were allowed to continue, no third parties would be unjustifiably harmed, and the public interest warranted granting such relief. Mike McGarry & Sons v. Gross, — Ohio App. 3d —, 2006 Ohio 1759, — N.E. 2d —, 2006 Ohio App. LEXIS 1620 (Apr. 6, 2006).

— Denial

Trial court's denial of an employer's motion for a preliminary injunction against a former employee to enforce the terms of a noncompete agreement was improper because the trial court applied the wrong legal standard. The employer was not required to demonstrate that it had suffered actual harm as a result of the employee's possession of confidential information; rather, a threat of harm is a sufficient basis on which to grant injunctive relief. Convergys Corp. v. Tackman, 169 Ohio App. 3d 665, 2006 Ohio 6616, 864 N.E.2d 145, 2006 Ohio App. LEXIS 6544 (2006).

Public interest

In a suit claiming that an employee formed his own company, which competed with his employer, while still working for the employer, when the trial court granted a preliminary injunction in favor of the employer, under Ohio R. Civ. P. 65(B), even though the employer did not present any evidence, the trial court could have found, as to the element of whether the injunction was in the public interest, that it was necessary to punish the employee for starting his own company while receiving a paycheck from the employer. King's Welding & Fabricating v. King, — Ohio App. 3d —, 2006 Ohio 5231, — N.E. 2d —, 2006 Ohio App. LEXIS 5207 (Sept. 27, 2006).

RULE 66.   Receivers

An action wherein a receiver has been appointed shall not be dismissed except by order of the court. Receiverships shall be administered in the manner provided by law and as provided by rules of court.

RULE 67.   [Reserved]

RULE 68.   Offer of judgment

An offer of judgment by any party, if refused by an opposite party, may not be filed with the court by the offering party for purposes of a proceeding to determine costs.

This rule shall not be construed as limiting voluntary offers of settlement made by any party.

RULE 69.   Execution

Process to enforce a judgment for the payment of money shall be a writ of execution, unless the court directs otherwise. The procedure on execution, in proceedings supplementary to and in aid of a judgment, and in proceedings on and in aid of execution shall be as provided by law. In aid of the judgment or execution, the judgment creditor or his successor in interest when that interest appears of record, may also obtain discovery from any person, including the judgment debtor, in the manner provided in these rules.

RULE 70.   Judgment for specific acts; vesting title

If a judgment directs a party to execute a conveyance of land, to transfer title or possession of personal property, to deliver deeds or other documents, or to perform any other specific act, and the party fails to comply within the time specified, the court may, where necessary, direct the act to be done at the cost of the disobedient party by some other person appointed by the court, and the act when so done has like effect as if done by the party. On application of the party entitled to performance, the clerk shall issue a writ of attachment against the property of the disobedient party to compel obedience to the judgment. The court may also in proper cases adjudge the party in contempt. If real or personal property is within this state, the court in lieu of directing a conveyance thereof may enter a judgment divesting the title of any party and vesting it in others, and such judgment has the effect of a conveyance executed in due form of law. When any order or judgment is for the delivery of possession, the party in whose favor it is entered is entitled to a writ of execution upon application to the clerk.

NOTES TO DECISIONS

ANALYSIS

Authority of court

Authority of court

By its order of transfer, the trial court was merely enforcing its judgment entry awarding the asset of the home to wife, and the order was not a modification of the divorce decree. In the event wife failed to refinance, the husband would have had the opportunity to exercise his right to refinance, tender the wife's equity, and seek a quit-claim deed from the wife or order of transfer of wife's interest in the marital home and thus, the issue of refinancing was not relevant to the appeal. Pursuant to Ohio R. Civ. P. 70, the trial court was authorized to order a transfer of the property to the wife to carry out the provisions of its earlier divorce decree and, pursuant to RC § 3105.011, it had broad discretion to enforce its own orders. Dvorak v. Dvorak, — Ohio App. 3d —, 2006 Ohio 6875, — N.E. 2d —, 2006 Ohio App. LEXIS 6796 (Dec. 22, 2006).

RULE 71. Process in behalf of and against persons not parties

When an order is made in favor of a person who is not a party to the action, he may enforce obedience to the order by the same process as if he were a party; and, when obedience to an order may be lawfully enforced against a person who is not a party, he is liable to the same process for enforcing obedience to the order as if he were a party.

RULE 72. [Reserved]

TITLE IX
PROBATE, JUVENILE, AND DOMESTIC RELATIONS PROCEEDINGS

RULE 73. Probate division of the court of common pleas

(A) **Applicability.** These Rules of Civil Procedure shall apply to proceedings in the probate division of the court of common pleas as indicated in this rule. Additionally, all of the Rules of Civil Procedure, though not specifically mentioned in this rule, shall apply except to the extent that by their nature they would be clearly inapplicable.

(B) **Venue.** Civ. R. 3(B) shall not apply to proceedings in the probate division of the court of common pleas, which shall be venued as provided by law. Proceedings under Chapters 2101. through 2131. of the Revised Code, which may be venued in the general division or the probate division of the court of common pleas, shall be venued in the probate division of the appropriate court of common pleas.

Proceedings that are improperly venued shall be transferred to a proper venue provided by law and division (B) of this rule, and the court may assess costs, including reasonable attorney fees, to the time of transfer against the party who commenced the action in an improper venue.

(C) **Service of summons.** Civ. R. 4 through 4.6 shall apply in any proceeding in the probate division of the court of common pleas requiring service of summons.

(D) **Service and filing of pleadings and papers subsequent to original pleading.** In proceedings requiring service of summons, Civ. R. 5 shall apply to the service and filing of pleadings and papers subsequent to the original pleading.

(E) **Service of notice.** In any proceeding where any type of notice other than service of summons is required by law or deemed necessary by the court, and the statute providing for notice neither directs nor authorizes the court to direct the manner of its service, notice shall be given in writing and may be served by or on behalf of any interested party without court intervention by one of the following methods:

(1) By delivering a copy to the person to be served;

(2) By leaving a copy at the usual place of residence of the person to be served;

(3) By certified or express mail, addressed to the person to be served at the person's usual place of residence with instructions to forward, return receipt requested, with instructions to the delivering postal employee to show to whom delivered, date of delivery, and address where delivered, provided that the certified or express mail envelope is not returned with an endorsement showing failure of delivery;

(4) By ordinary mail after a certified or express mail envelope is returned with an endorsement showing that it was refused;

(5) By ordinary mail after a certified or express mail envelope is returned with an endorsement showing that it was unclaimed, provided that the ordinary mail envelope is not returned by the postal authorities with an endorsement showing failure of delivery;

(6) By publication once each week for three consecutive weeks in some newspaper of general circulation in the county when the name, usual place of residence, or existence of the person to be served is unknown and cannot with reasonable diligence be ascertained; provided that before publication may be utilized, the person giving notice shall file an affidavit which states that the name, usual place of residence, or existence of the person to be served is unknown and cannot with reasonable diligence be ascertained;

(7) By other method as the court may direct.

Civ. R. 4.2 shall apply in determining who may be served and how particular persons or entities must be served.

(F) **Proof of service of notice; when service of notice complete.** When service is made through the court, proof of service of notice shall be in the same manner as proof of service of summons.

When service is made without court intervention, proof of service of notice shall be made by affidavit. When service is made by certified or express mail, the certified or express mail return receipt which shows delivery shall be attached to the affidavit. When service is made by ordinary mail, the prior returned certified or express mail envelope which shows that the mail was refused or unclaimed shall be attached to the affidavit.

Service of notice by ordinary mail shall be complete when the fact of mailing is entered of record except as stated in division (E)(5) of this rule. Service by publication shall be complete at the date of the last publication.

(G) **Waiver of service of notice.** Civ. R. 4(D) shall apply in determining who may waive service of notice.

(H) **Forms used in probate practice.** Forms used in proceedings in the probate division of the courts of common pleas shall be those prescribed in the rule applicable to standard probate forms in the Rules of Superintendence. Forms not prescribed in such rule may be used as permitted in that rule.

Blank forms reproduced for use in probate practice for any filing to which the rule applicable to specifications for printing probate forms of the Rules of Superintendence applies shall conform to the specifications set forth in that rule.

No pleading, application, acknowledgment, certification, account, report, statement, allegation, or other matter filed in the probate division of the courts of common pleas shall be required to be executed under oath, and it is sufficient if it is made upon the signature alone of the person making it.

(I) **Notice of filing of judgments.** Civ. R. 58(B) shall apply to all judgments entered in the probate division of the court of common pleas in any action or proceeding in which any party other than a plaintiff, applicant, or movant has filed a responsive pleading or exceptions. Notice of the judgment shall be given to each plaintiff, applicant, or movant, to each party filing a responsive pleading or exceptions, and to other parties as the court directs.

(J) **Filing with the court defined.** The filing of documents with the court, as required by these rules, shall be made by filing them with the probate judge as the ex officio clerk of the court. A court may provide, by local rules adopted pursuant to the Rules of Superintendence, for the filing of documents by electronic means. If the court adopts such local rules, they shall include all of the following:

(1) Any signature on electronically transmitted documents shall be considered that of the attorney or party it purports to be for all purposes. If it is established that the documents were transmitted without authority, the court shall order the filing stricken.

(2) A provision shall specify the days and hours during which electronically transmitted documents will be received by the court, and a provision shall specify when documents received electronically will be considered to have been filed.

(3) Any document filed electronically that requires a filing fee may be rejected by the clerk of court unless the filer has complied with the mechanism established by the court for the payment of filing fees.

History: Amended, eff 7-1-71; 7-1-75; 7-1-77; 7-1-80; 7-1-96; 7-1-97; 7-1-01.

NOTES TO DECISIONS

ANALYSIS

Applicability
Attorneys' fees

Applicability

CivR 73(B) was not applicable where the action to foreclose the mortgage was not one of the proceedings under RC Chapters 2101 through 2131. United States Bank, N.A. v. Webb, 139 Ohio Misc. 2d 54, 2006 Ohio 5462, 860 N.E.2d 161, 2006 Ohio Misc. LEXIS 211 (2006).

Attorneys' fees

Probate court did not abuse its discretion in refusing to impose attorney's fees under Ohio R. Civ. P. 73(B) on a daughter for filing her mother's guardianship application in an improper venue. Although it was ultimately determined that the mother's physical presence in the county where the daughter selected venue did not have the degree of permanence necessary to make her a resident or to have legal settlement there, the daughter's argument for venue was not baseless because the mother was living in that county and had bank accounts and personal items there. In re Estate of Lilley, — Ohio App. 3d —, 2006 Ohio 5510, — N.E. 2d —, 2006 Ohio App. LEXIS 5491 (Oct. 23, 2006).

Son was properly ordered to reimburse his mother's estate for attorney's fees he incurred while contesting the venue of a guardianship proceeding filed by his sister under Ohio R. Civ. P. 73(B); although the son's action was successful in that venue in the proceeding was ultimately transferred, he provided no authority supporting his assertion that his use of guardianship funds for the attorney's fees was proper or that the fees were anything but his personal obligation. In re Estate of Lilley, — Ohio App. 3d —, 2006 Ohio 5510, — N.E. 2d —, 2006 Ohio App. LEXIS 5491 (Oct. 23, 2006).

RULE 74. Juvenile proceedings [Abrogated]

History: Abrogated, eff 7-1-77.

RULE 75. Divorce, annulment, and legal separation actions

(A) **Applicability.** The Rules of Civil Procedure shall apply in actions for divorce, annulment, legal separation, and related proceedings, with the modifications or exceptions set forth in this rule.

(B) **Joinder of parties.** Civ.R. 14, 19, 19.1, and 24 shall not apply in divorce, annulment, or legal separation actions, however:

(1) A person or corporation having possession of, control of, or claiming an interest in property, whether real, personal, or mixed, out of which a party seeks a division of marital property, a distributive award, or an award of spousal support or other support, may be made a party defendant;

(2) When it is essential to protect the interests of a child, the court may join the child of the parties as a party defendant and appoint a guardian ad litem and legal counsel, if necessary, for the child and tax the costs;

(3) When child support is ordered, the court, on its own motion or that of an interested person, after notice to the party ordered to pay child support and to his or her employer, may make the employer a party defendant.

(C) **Trial by court or magistrate.** In proceedings under this rule there shall be no right to trial by jury. All issues may be heard either by the court or by a magistrate as the court, on the request of any party or on its own motion, may direct. Civ. R. 53 shall apply to all cases or issues directed to be heard by a magistrate.

(D) **Investigation.** On the filing of a complaint for divorce, annulment, or legal separation, where minor children are involved, or on the filing of a motion for the modification of a decree allocating parental rights and responsibilities for the care of children, the court may cause an investigation to be made as to the character, family relations, past conduct, earning ability, and financial worth of the parties to the action. The report of the investigation shall be made available to either party or their counsel of record upon written request not less than seven days before trial. The report shall be signed by the investigator and the investigator shall be subject to cross-examination by either party concerning the contents of the report. The court may tax as costs all or any part of the expenses for each investigation.

(E) **Subpoena where custody involved.** In any case involving the allocation of parental rights and responsibilities for the care of children, the court, on its own motion, may cite a party to the action from any point within the state to appear in court and testify.

(F) **Judgment.** The provisions of Civ. R. 55 shall not apply in actions for divorce, annulment, legal separation, or civil protection orders. For purposes of Civ. R. 54(B), the court shall not enter final judgment as to a claim for divorce, dissolution of marriage, annulment, or legal separation unless one of the following applies:

(1) The judgment also divides the property of the parties, determines the appropriateness of an order of spousal support, and, where applicable, either allocates parental rights and responsibilities, including payment of child support, between the parties or orders shared parenting of minor children;

(2) Issues of property division, spousal support, and allocation of parental rights and responsibilities or shared parenting have been finally determined in orders, previously entered by the court, that are incorporated into the judgment;

(3) The court includes in the judgment the express determination required by Civ. R. 54(B) and a final determination that either of the following applies:

(a) The court lacks jurisdiction to determine such issues;

(b) In a legal separation action, the division of the property of the parties would be inappropriate at that time.

(G) **Civil protection order.** A claim for a civil protection order based upon an allegation of domestic violence shall be a separate claim from a claim for divorce, dissolution of marriage, annulment, or legal separation.

(H) **Relief pending appeal.** A motion to modify, pending appeal, either a decree allocating parental rights and responsibilities for the care of children, or a spousal or other support order, shall be made to the trial court in the first instance, whether made before or after a notice of appeal is filed. The trial court may grant relief upon terms as to bond or otherwise as it considers proper for the security of the rights of the adverse party and in the best interests of the children involved. Civ. R. 62(B) does not apply to orders allocating parental rights and responsibilities for the care of children or a spousal or other support order. An order entered upon motion under this rule may be vacated or modified by the appellate court. The appellate court has authority to enter like orders pending appeal, but an application to the appellate court for relief shall disclose what has occurred in the trial court regarding the relief.

(I) **Temporary restraining orders.**

(1) Restraining order: exclusion. The provisions of Civ. R. 65(A) shall not apply in divorce, annulment, or legal separation actions.

(2) Restraining order: grounds, procedure. When it is made to appear to the court by affidavit of a party sworn to absolutely that a party is about to dispose of or encumber property, or any part thereof of property, so as to defeat another party in obtaining an equitable division of marital property, a distributive award, or spousal or other support, or that a party to the action or a child of any party is about to suffer physical abuse, annoyance, or bodily injury by the other party, the court may allow a temporary restraining order, with or without bond, to prevent that action. A temporary restraining order may be issued without notice and shall remain in force during the pendency of the action unless the court or magistrate otherwise orders.

(J) **Continuing jurisdiction.** The continuing jurisdiction of the court shall be invoked by motion filed in the original action, notice of which shall be served in the manner provided for the service of process under Civ. R. 4 to 4.6. When the continuing jurisdiction of the court is invoked pursuant to this division, the discovery procedures set forth in Civ. R. 26 to 37 shall apply.

(K) **Hearing.** No action for divorce, annulment, or legal separation may be heard and decided until the expiration of forty-two days after the service of process or twenty-eight days after the last publication of notice of the complaint, and no action for divorce, annulment, or legal separation shall be heard and decided earlier than twenty-eight days after the service of a counterclaim, which under this rule may be designated a cross-complaint, unless the plaintiff files a written waiver of the twenty-eight day period.

(L) **Notice of trial.** In all cases where there is no counsel of record for the adverse party, the court shall give the adverse party notice of the trial upon the merits. The notice shall be made by regular mail to the party's last known address, and shall be mailed at least seven days prior to the commencement of trial.

(M) **Testimony.** Judgment for divorce, annulment, or legal separation shall not be granted upon the testimony or admission of a party not supported by other credible evidence. No admission shall be received that the court has reason to believe was obtained by fraud, connivance, coercion, or other improper means. The parties, notwithstanding their marital relations, shall be competent to testify in the proceeding to the same extent as other witnesses.

(N) **Allowance of spousal support, child support, and custody pendente lite.**

(1) When requested in the complaint, answer, or counterclaim, or by motion served with the pleading, upon satisfactory proof by affidavit duly filed with the clerk of the court, the court or magistrate, without oral hearing and for good cause shown, may grant spousal support pendente lite to either of the parties for the party's sustenance and expenses during the suit and may make a temporary order regarding the support, maintenance, and allocation of parental rights and responsibilities for the care of children of the marriage, whether natural or adopted, during the pendency of the action for divorce, annulment, or legal separation.

(2) Counter affidavits may be filed by the other party within fourteen days from the service of the complaint, answer, counterclaim, or motion, all affidavits to be used by the court or magistrate in making a temporary spousal support order, child support order, and order

allocating parental rights and responsibilities for the care of children. Upon request, in writing, after any temporary spousal support, child support, or order allocating parental rights and responsibilities for the care of children is journalized, the court shall grant the party so requesting an oral hearing within twenty-eight days to modify the temporary order. A request for oral hearing shall not suspend or delay the commencement of spousal support or other support payments previously ordered or change the allocation of parental rights and responsibilities until the order is modified by journal entry after the oral hearing.

(O) **Delay of decree.** When a party who is entitled to a decree of divorce or annulment is ordered to pay spousal support or child support for a child not in his or her custody, or to deliver a child to the party to whom parental rights and responsibilities for the care of the child are allocated, the court may delay entering a decree for divorce or annulment until the party, to the satisfaction of the court, secures the payment of the spousal support or the child support for the child, or delivers custody of the child to the party to whom parental rights and responsibilities are allocated.

History: Amended, eff 7-1-71; 7-1-72; 7-1-77; 7-1-78; 7-1-91; 7-1-96; 7-1-97; 7-1-98; 7-1-01.

NOTES TO DECISIONS

ANALYSIS

Appeals
Appointment of guardian ad litem
Default judgment in divorce
Evidence in divorce proceeding
Fees
Final appealable order
Intervention in divorce case
Joinder
Jurisdiction
— Continuing jurisdiction
Magistrate
Modifying visitation agreement
Notice
Restraining orders
Sanctions
Service
Temporary orders
Temporary support
— Modification
Time limitations

Appeals

Divorce decree that provides for the issuance of a qualified domestic relations order ("QDRO") is a final, appealable order, even before the QDRO is issued: Wilson v. Wilson, 116 Ohio St. 3d 268, 2007 Ohio 6056, 878 N.E.2d 16, 2007 Ohio LEXIS 2875.

Appointment of guardian ad litem

Where a guardian ad litem was appointed in a custody case and an appeal was filed by the paternal grandparents challenging an award of custody after the paternal grandparents were found to be unsuitable for custody purposes, the trial court did not abuse its discretion under Ohio R. Civ. P. 75(B)(2) in reappointing the guardian ad litem for appellate purposes. Smith v. Quigg, — Ohio App. 3d —, 2006 Ohio 1670, — N.E. 2d —, 2006 Ohio App. LEXIS 1566 (Mar. 27, 2006).

Default judgment in divorce

Since a wife did not object to the fact that a magistrate found her in default for failing to appear at the divorce hearing, the appellate court was bound to review the assignment of error to this effect presented on appeal under the plain error standard. Plain error did not occur when the magistrate found the wife "in default for appearance" because the magistrate did not enter a default judgment, as prohibited in a divorce action by Ohio R. Civ. P. 75(F), but, instead, considered the evidence presented and issued his decision accordingly. Ordean v. Ordean, — Ohio App. 3d —, 2007 Ohio 3979, — N.E. 2d —, 2007 Ohio App. LEXIS 3598 (Aug. 6, 2007).

In adopting a magistrate's decision that precluded a mother from offering evidence on custody issues under Stark County, Ohio, Ct. C.P. Dom. Rel. Div. R. 13.01 because of her failure to answer the father's divorce complaint, a trial court did not improperly grant a default judgment under Ohio R. Civ. P. 55 which could not be granted in a domestic relations case under Ohio R. Civ. P. 75(F); the father never moved for a default judgment, no default judgment was granted, the matter was properly treated as an uncontested divorce, and it was not treated as an ex parte trial since the mother appeared at trial, testified, and was given the opportunity to cross-examine the father. Whited v. Whited, — Ohio App. 3d —, 2006 Ohio 5551, — N.E. 2d —, 2006 Ohio App. LEXIS 5546 (Oct. 16, 2006).

Evidence in divorce proceeding

Trial court committed reversible error when it concluded that, since the mother had not filed an answer, she could not contest any of the issues in the divorce, including the issue of which parent should be named the residential parent; the mother was not permitted to present any evidence or argument concerning the best interests of the children, and the trial court had no evidence before it on the subject, beyond the father's bare assertion of his desire to be named the residential parent. The fact that the mother had not filed an answer did not prevent her from contesting one or more issues in the divorce because the pre-trial conference alerted the trial court to the fact that it was a contested case, despite the fact that the mother had not answered the complaint. Rue v. Rue, — Ohio App. 3d —, 2006 Ohio 5131, — N.E. 2d —, 2006 Ohio App. LEXIS 5092 (Sept. 29, 2006).

Fees

There was no error in ordering the mother to pay a portion of the fees incurred by the guardian ad litem. Because the mother's motion for legal custody was the precipitating event requiring the appointment of a guardian ad litem, the mother could not claim that it was inequitable for the trial court to order her to pay a portion of the fees incurred. In re Aiello, — Ohio App. 3d —, 2007 Ohio 492, — N.E. 2d —, 2007 Ohio App. LEXIS 438 (Feb. 5, 2007).

Although the guardian ad litem (GAL) was entitled to the fees owed to him, it was possible that a portion of the amount owed represented an amount incurred while he attempted to collect his original fee. That would have constituted collection fees, which was a civil debt, rather than child support, and could have affected the contempt holding and the status of the mother's bankruptcy proceeding. In re Thomas, — Ohio App. 3d —, 2006 Ohio 3324, — N.E. 2d —, 2006 Ohio App. LEXIS 3237 (June 29, 2006).

Trial court erred when it failed to hold a mandatory hearing on the guardian ad litem fees, as required by Cuyahoga County, Ohio, CT. C.P. Dom. Rel. Div. R. 35(E). Rausch v. Rausch, — Ohio App. 3d —, 2006 Ohio 3847, — N.E. 2d —, 2006 Ohio App. LEXIS 3810 (July 27, 2006).

Final appealable order

Because a trial court's entry expressly terminated a prior child support order, designating the father as the obligor, based upon the court's award of custody to him, the judgment entry did not fully determine the divorce proceeding, and was not a final appealable order. Atkinson v. Atkinson, 167 Ohio App. 3d 704, 2006 Ohio 3676, 856 N.E. 2d 1023, 2006 Ohio App. LEXIS 3610 (July 13, 2006).

Trial court's order entering a decree of divorce did not constitute a final appealable order under RC § 2505.02 since the issue of custody of the parties' children was not fully and finally determined, as required by Ohio R. Civ. P. 75(F). Salisbury v. Salisbury, — Ohio App. 3d —, 2006 Ohio 3543, — N.E. 2d —, 2006 Ohio App. LEXIS 3493 (July 7, 2006).

Intervention in divorce case

Denial of a motion by the mother of a former wife to intervene in a dissolution of marriage proceeding so that she could assert her interest in certain marital assets that were awarded to the former husband, was proper as the mother's attempt to intervene came after the evidence had been submitted at the property trial and after the magistrate had issued a decision on the division of household goods and furnishings. The mother should have known that she might have had an interest in the goods and furnishings, but she failed to promptly assert that alleged interest. Stricker v. Stricker, — Ohio App. 3d —, 2007 Ohio 3309, — N.E. 2d —, 2007 Ohio App. LEXIS 3040 (June 29, 2007).

Joinder

Because CivR 75(B)(2) and RC § 3109.04 address joinder of a child in divorce custody action and appointment of counsel for the child, reliance on permanent custody case law and juvenile court statutes is not warranted: Wilburn v. Wilburn, 169 Ohio App. 3d 415, 2006 Ohio 5820, 863 N.E.2d 204, 2006 Ohio App. LEXIS 5777 (2006).

Jurisdiction

Juvenile court erred in modifying a father's child support pursuant to RC §§ 3105.21, 3109.05 because service on the mother had to be by personal service pursuant to CivR 4.1(A) where the father requested personal service; the residential service effected was inadequate for notice because the mother had moved from the residence. Any failure by the mother to notify the juvenile court promptly of any change in her address could not justify ineffective service of process when the juvenile court's continuing jurisdiction was invoked, because those service requirements were rooted in the mother's constitutional due process right to notice and an opportunity to be heard. In re Alexander-segar, — Ohio App. 3d —, 2008 Ohio 1580, — N.E. 2d —, 2008 Ohio App. LEXIS 1325 (Mar. 28, 2008).

Trial court had authority to order the release of funds in a bank account under a husband's new wife's name, as a temporary restraining order had been issued on that account and the bank had subsequently entered an appearance for purposes of jurisdiction necessary to enjoin the bank from disbursing the funds. The new wife's motion to dissolve the restraining order during the pendency of the dissolution proceedings between the husband and his former wife constituted a waiver of service under Ohio R. Civ. P. 75(I). Glassman v. Offenberg, — Ohio App. 3d —, 2006 Ohio 3837, — N.E. 2d —, 2006 Ohio App. LEXIS 3801 (July 27, 2006).

As a trial court issued an order "concerning the allocation of a former married couple's parental rights and responsibilities" where its determination that a Texas court's decree as to custody and visitation issues regarding the parties' minor child was made without proper jurisdiction, and as the wife had no forum to turn to for help in gaining access to her child, the appellate court granted her motion for immediate visitation pursuant to Ohio R. Civ. P. 75(H) by vacating the trial court's decision to deny her motion for parenting time; however, the court noted that the trial court was in the best position to allocate parental rights and responsibilities, and it directed the parties to apply to that forum for appropriate relief. Ronny T.

v. Phillip T., — Ohio App. 3d —, 2006 Ohio 5103, — N.E. 2d —, 2006 Ohio App. LEXIS 5029 (Sept. 28, 2006).

— Continuing jurisdiction

When a former husband did not obey a trial court's order to name the former husband's former wife as a 50 percent beneficiary of the husband's post-death retirement benefits, and, instead, named the former husband's current wife as the husband's survivor, while a trial court did not have jurisdiction to modify the terms of the original divorce decree, because the trial court did not reserve such jurisdiction, the trial court could issue a remedial order upon holding the former husband in contempt because, under Ohio R. 75(J), the trial court had continuing jurisdiction to enforce the trial court's prior orders. Leslie v. Johnston, — Ohio App. 3d —, 2007 Ohio 2901, — N.E. 2d —, 2007 Ohio App. LEXIS 2670 (June 8, 2007).

Trial court properly concluded that a father had failed to invoke the continuing jurisdiction of the trial court pursuant to Ohio R. Civ. P. 75(J) on the father's motion or modification and/or termination of child support where, while the father requested service of his motions by certified mail upon the Lake County Child Support Enforcement Agency and Ohio Child Support Payment Central, neither of which was currently a party to the action, there was no evidence that the father perfected or even attempted service upon the opposing party, the mother. Corrao v. Corrao, — Ohio App. 3d —, 2006 Ohio 1686, — N.E. 2d —, 2006 Ohio App. LEXIS 1545 (Mar. 31, 2006).

Magistrate

As a husband in a divorce proceeding was given the opportunity to present his arguments to a magistrate who heard the matter pursuant to Ohio R. Civ. P. 53, and he was also able to file objections to the magistrate's decision with the trial court, and the trial court then conducted a de novo review of the magistrate's decision in compliance with the civil rules and with Ohio law, there was no error in having the property and support hearings conducted before the magistrate instead of before the trial court pursuant to Ohio R. Civ. P. 75 and Ohio Const art. IV, § 1. Metz v. Metz, — Ohio App. 3d —, 2007 Ohio 549, — N.E. 2d —, 2007 Ohio App. LEXIS 507 (Feb. 9, 2007).

Modifying visitation agreement

Trial court erred in finding the mother in contempt for failing to comply with the modified visitation order because modifying the civil protection order was error; RC § 3113.31 did not vest any authority in the trial court to modify the terms of the allocation of parental rights and responsibilities under the civil protection order. Even if the trial court had intended to modify the order under Ohio R. Civ. P. 75(N), its failure to hold a hearing violated the civil rule, and the modification order would have been void. Signer v. Signer, — Ohio App. 3d —, 2006 Ohio 3580, — N.E. 2d —, 2006 Ohio App. LEXIS 3531 (July 13, 2006).

Notice

Although the portion of a motion filed by the Allen County Child Support Enforcement Agency for the distribution of a forfeited appearance bond posted by a father did not require any additional notice to the father since the distribution was not a new action but, rather, the conclusion of the prior action, the portion of the motion requesting that the trial court order the father to post a bond securing future child support payments was a new request not covered by the prior appearance bond and one for which the father should have received notice under Ohio R. Civ. P. 75(J). As nothing showed that the father received notice of the motion, the judgment granting that portion of the motion was improper. Stuber v. Stuber, — Ohio App. 3d —, 2007 Ohio 3981, — N.E. 2d —, 2007 Ohio App. LEXIS 3600 (Aug. 6, 2007).

Because there was no evidence that the wife received notice of the divorce hearing as required by Ohio R. Civ. P. 75(L), the trial court committed reversible error by entering judgment against her. The wife was unrepresented by Ohio counsel at the time of the hearing and there was no evidence that the magistrate's notice of the hearing was mailed to her. Jensen v. Lillian, — Ohio App. 3d —, 2007 Ohio 894, — N.E. 2d —, 2007 Ohio App. LEXIS 806 (Mar. 2, 2007).

There was no abuse of discretion in a trial court's adoption of a magistrate's recommendation to deny a wife's motion for relief from a divorce judgment, pursuant to Ohio R. Civ. P. 60(B)(1) and (5), as her claim that she was not given notice of the final divorce hearing as required by Ohio R. Civ. P. 75(L) lacked merit where the record indicated that she at least had constructive notice due to the fact that she admitted that she was aware that there was a hearing set for an hour later on the same date regarding her petition for a domestic violence civil protection order; further, there was an entry on the trial court's docket, which constituted reasonable, constructive notice of the trial date. Wilson v. Wilson, — Ohio App. 3d —, 2006 Ohio 4261, — N.E. 2d —, 2006 Ohio App. LEXIS 4187 (Aug. 17, 2006).

There was no abuse of discretion in a trial court's adoption of a magistrate's recommendation to deny a wife's motion for relief from a divorce judgment, pursuant to Ohio R. Civ. P. 60(B)(1) and (5), as her claim that she was not given notice of the final divorce hearing as required by Ohio R. Civ. P. 75(L) lacked merit where the record indicated that she at least had constructive notice due to the fact that she admitted that she was aware that there was a hearing set for an hour later on the same date regarding her petition for a domestic violence civil protection order. There was an entry on the trial court's docket, which constituted reasonable, constructive notice of the trial date. Wilson v. Wilson, — Ohio App. 3d —, 2006 Ohio 4261, — N.E. 2d —, 2006 Ohio App. LEXIS 4187 (Aug. 17, 2006).

Restraining orders

Trial court erred in issuing a temporary restraining order (TRO) against a former husband and his attorneys who represented him in an unrelated federal civil lawsuit, as the restraint was for purposes of protecting potential settlement proceeds or a judgment in that action from dissipation due to the husband's arrearage in his child support obligation. However, no judgment or settlement had yet been reached, and no affidavits as required by Ohio R. Civ. P. 75(B)(1) were filed for purposes of supporting the issuance of the TRO. Ransom v. Ransom, — Ohio App. 3d —, 2007 Ohio 457, — N.E. 2d —, 2007 Ohio App. LEXIS 411 (Feb. 5, 2007).

Sanctions

Although an attorney for a county child support enforcement agency erred under Ohio R. Civ. P. 75(B)(1) and (I)(2) in filing motions to join a former husband's attorneys who represented him in a federal civil lawsuit into the support arrearage action, and to have restraining orders issued against the attorneys and the husband, as the motions were filed in good faith and there was no willful violation of Ohio R. Civ. P. 11 shown, the trial court did not abuse its discretion in denying a request by one of the attorneys for imposition of sanctions under Rule 11 against the attorney for the agency. Ransom v. Ransom, — Ohio App. 3d —, 2007 Ohio 457, — N.E. 2d —, 2007 Ohio App. LEXIS 411 (Feb. 5, 2007).

Service

Because the father failed under Ohio R. Civ. P. 75(J) to perfect service of his motion on the mother, the trial court did not err when it vacated the nunc pro tunc entry changing her name in the caption under Ohio R. Civ. P. 60(A). It was undisputed that the mother did not receive a copy of the motion for nunc pro tunc order to change the caption. Pulice v. Collins, — Ohio App. 3d —, 2006 Ohio 3950, — N.E. 2d —, 2006 Ohio App. LEXIS 3903 (Aug. 3, 2006).

Temporary orders

Magistrate's temporary orders required that the father pay the mortgage on both parcels of property, but did not specify that he would receive credit for those payments. Because the father never moved to set aside that order and he never moved to modify that order, he waived any argument regarding whether he should receive credit for the mortgage payments on those properties made while the divorce was pending. Spier v. Spier, — Ohio App. 3d —, 2006 Ohio 1289, — N.E. 2d —, 2006 Ohio App. LEXIS 1181 (Mar. 7, 2006).

Temporary support

When a husband objected to a trial court's order requiring the husband to pay temporary spousal support, the husband did not show a magistrate violated Ohio R. Civ. P. 75(N)(2) by not holding a hearing on the objections within 28 days because the motion for temporary spousal support was filed seven days before trial, at which the issues relevant to temporary support were discussed. Doody v. Doody, — Ohio App. 3d —, 2007 Ohio 2567, — N.E. 2d —, 2007 Ohio App. LEXIS 2387 (May 25, 2007).

Trial court erred when it ordered a modification retroactive to its previous temporary order of child support. The final divorce decree essentially created an obligation on the husband to pay an additional sum of money, after the fact, and then penalized him for not having paid it. Ostmann v. Ostmann, 168 Ohio App. 3d 59, 2006 Ohio 3617, 858 N.E.2d 831, 2006 Ohio App. LEXIS 3578 (2006).

Trial court did not abuse its discretion where it characterized as "support" the temporary spousal support arrearage that the wife had failed to pay to the husband with respect to unpaid mortgage payments, as that support order was reasonable under the circumstances at the time it was made, based on the financial situations of the parties and pursuant to RC § 3105.18(B) and Ohio R. Civ. P. 75(N)(1), and accordingly, it was a non-dischargeable debt under the wife's bankruptcy pursuant to 11 U.S.C.S. § 523(a)(5). House v. House, — Ohio App. 3d —, 2006 Ohio 2776, — N.E. 2d —, 2006 Ohio App. LEXIS 2616 (June 2, 2006).

Merger doctrine did not operate to extinguish any arrearages claims arising from temporary alimony orders, under Ohio R. Civ. P. 75(N), until there was a final judgment of divorce, as it was the conclusive nature of the final judgment entry that triggered the merger doctrine, and, until there had been a final judgment entry of divorce, there remained the possibility for the preservation of arrearages. Blais v. Blais, — Ohio App. 3d —, 2006 Ohio 4662, — N.E. 2d —, 2006 Ohio App. LEXIS 4586 (Sept. 8, 2006).

When, under Ohio R. Civ. P. 75(N), a husband was ordered to pay temporary alimony, and the trial court subsequently found his arrearages regarding that obligation, the wife did not have to preserve the arrearages found in the final decree of divorce because that final decree was entered after the arrearages were found, so the husband was properly held liable for those arrearages. Blais v. Blais, — Ohio App. 3d —, 2006 Ohio 4662, — N.E. 2d —, 2006 Ohio App. LEXIS 4586 (Sept. 8, 2006).

Once a trial court entered final judgment in a divorce action or alimony action it could not reinstate its order for temporary alimony pending the litigation because the trial court had no authority to make such an order, as the theory of merger precluded a retroactive ruling on temporary support orders after a final judgment entry, and it was well established that an order for temporary alimony pending litigation was merged into the final judgment in a divorce and any temporary order and arrearages incident thereto was terminated when final judgment was entered. In other words, the final judgment encompassed all that had passed before it, including temporary orders. Blais v. Blais, — Ohio App. 3d —, 2006 Ohio 4662, — N.E. 2d —, 2006 Ohio App. LEXIS 4586 (Sept. 8, 2006).

— **Modification**

Trial court did not err in ordering the husband to pay a set amount of temporary spousal support and in not modifying it retroactively pursuant to Ohio R. Civ. P. 75(N), as the husband failed to prove that the amount which he was ordered to pay exceeded the amount permitted by law pursuant to RC § 3121.033 and 15 U.S.C.S. § 1673; as the husband did not present proof that his current net pay was the maximum he could have received and that the amount ordered for support exceeded the statutory limit of 60 percent of that amount, his claim failed. Lentz v. Lentz, — Ohio App. 3d —, 2006 Ohio 3168, — N.E. 2d —, 2006 Ohio App. LEXIS 3217 (June 22, 2006).

Time limitations

Trial court erred in granting a wife's complaint for divorce less than 42 days after the complaint was served on the husband because the language of Ohio R. Civ. P. 75(K) is mandatory and requires a 42-day waiting period before a complaint for divorce is granted. This waiting period cannot be waived. Clark v. Clark, — Ohio App. 3d —, 2006 Ohio 2902, — N.E. 2d —, 2006 Ohio App. LEXIS 2724 (June 9, 2006).

RULE 76. Time for perfecting appeal stayed [Abrogated]

RULE 77. [Reserved]

RULE 78. [Reserved]

RULE 79. [Reserved]

RULE 80. [Reserved]

RULE 81. References to Ohio Revised Code

A reference in these rules to a section of the Revised Code shall mean the section as amended from time to time including the enactment of additional sections the numbers of which are subsequent to the section referred to in the rules.

TITLE X
GENERAL PROVISIONS

RULE 82. Jurisdiction unaffected

These rules shall not be construed to extend or limit the jurisdiction of the courts of this state.

RULE 83. Local rules of practice

(A) A court may adopt local rules of practice which shall not be inconsistent with these rules or with other rules promulgated by the Supreme Court and shall file its local rules of practice with the Clerk of the Supreme Court.

(B) Local rules of practice shall be adopted only after the court gives appropriate notice and an opportunity for comment. If a court determines that there is an immediate need for a rule, it may adopt the rule

without prior notice and opportunity for comment, but promptly shall afford notice and opportunity for comment.

History: Amended, eff 7-1-94; 7-1-00.

NOTES TO DECISIONS
ANALYSIS

Substantial disregard for local court rules

Substantial disregard for local court rules

When a trial court did not comply with the court's local rules by granting a motion to compel discovery four days after the motion was filed, there was no abuse of discretion because the trial court could choose to deviate from the court's local rules, and the court's order merely required a party to provide the discovery the party was already required to provide under Ohio R. Civ. P. 26, so the party's substantial rights were not affected. Flatt v. Atwood, — Ohio App. 3d —, 2007 Ohio 5387, — N.E. 2d —, 2007 Ohio App. LEXIS 4735 (Oct. 9, 2007).

RULE 84. Forms

The forms contained in the Appendix of Forms which the supreme court from time to time may approve are sufficient under these rules and are intended to indicate the simplicity and brevity of statement which these rules contemplate.

RULE 85. Title

These rules shall be known as the Ohio Rules of Civil Procedure and may be cited as "Civil Rules" or "Civ. R. ____."

History: Amended, eff 7-1-71.

RULE 86. Effective date

(A) **Effective date of rules.** These rules shall take effect on the first day of July, 1970. They govern all proceedings in actions brought after they take effect and also all further proceedings in actions then pending, except to the extent that in the opinion of the court their application in a particular action pending when the rules take effect would not be feasible or would work injustice, in which event the former procedure applies.

(B) **Effective date of amendments.** The amendments submitted by the Supreme Court to the General Assembly on January 15, 1971, on April 14, 1971, and on April 30, 1971, shall take effect on the first day of July, 1971. They govern all proceedings in actions brought after they take effect and also all further proceedings in actions then pending, except to the extent that in the opinion of the court their application in a particular action pending when the rules take effect would not be feasible or would work injustice, in which event the former procedure applies.

(C) **Effective date of amendments.** The amendments submitted by the Supreme Court to the General Assembly on January 15, 1972, and on May 1, 1972, shall take effect on the first day of July, 1972. They govern all proceedings in actions brought after they take effect and also all further proceedings in actions then pending, except to the extent that their application in a particular action pending when the rules take effect would not be feasible or would work injustice, in which event the former procedure applies.

(D) **Effective date of amendments.** The amendments submitted by the Supreme Court to the General Assembly on January 12, 1973, shall take effect on the first day of July, 1973. They govern all proceedings in actions brought after they take effect and also all further proceedings in actions then pending, except to the extent that their application in a particular action pending when the amendments take effect would not be feasible or would work injustice, in which event the former procedure applies.

(E) **Effective date of amendments.** The amendments submitted by the Supreme Court to the General Assembly on January 10, 1975 and on April 29, 1975, shall take effect on July 1, 1975. They govern all proceedings in actions brought after they take effect and also all further proceedings in actions then pending, except to the extent that their application in a particular action pending when the amendments take effect would not be feasible or would work injustice, in which event the former procedure applies.

(F) **Effective date of amendments.** The amendments submitted by the Supreme Court to the General Assembly on January 9, 1976 shall take effect on July shall take effect on the first day of July, 1972. They govern all proceedings in actions brought after they take effect and also all further proceedings in actions then pending, except to the extent that their application in a particular action pending when the rules take effect would not be feasible or would work injustice, in which event the former procedure applies.

(G) **Effective date of amendments.** The amendments submitted by the Supreme Court to the General Assembly on January 12, 1978, and on April 28, 1978, shall take effect on July 1, 1978. They govern all proceedings in actions brought after they take effect and also all further proceedings in actions then pending, except to the extent that their application in a particular action pending when the amendments take effect would not be feasible or would work injustice, in which event the former procedure applies.

(H) **Effective date of amendments.** The amendments submitted by the Supreme Court to the General Assembly on January 14, 1980 shall take effect on July 1, 1980. They govern all proceedings in actions brought after they take effect and also all further proceedings in actions then pending, except to the extent that their application in a particular action pending when the amendments take effect would not be feasible or would work injustice, in which event the former procedure applies.

(I) **Effective date of amendments.** The amendments submitted by the Supreme Court to the General Assembly on January 12, 1983 shall take effect on July 1, 1983. They govern all proceedings in actions brought after they take effect and also all further proceedings in actions then pending, except to the extent that their application in a particular action pending when the

amendments take effect would not be feasible or would work injustice, in which event the former procedure applies.

(J) **Effective date of amendments.** The amendments submitted by the Supreme Court to the General Assembly on January 12, 1984 shall take effect on July 1, 1984. They govern all proceedings in actions brought after they take effect and also all further proceedings in actions then pending, except to the extent that their application in a particular action pending when the amendments take effect would not be feasible or would work injustice, in which event the former procedure applies.

(K) **Effective date of amendments.** The amendments submitted by the Supreme Court to the General Assembly on December 24, 1984 and January 8, 1985 shall take effect on July 1, 1985. They govern all proceedings in actions brought after they take effect and also all further proceedings in actions then pending, except to the extent that their application in a particular action pending when the amendments take effect would not be feasible or would work injustice, in which event the former procedure applies.

(L) **Effective date of amendments.** The amendments submitted by the Supreme Court to the General Assembly on January 9, 1986 shall take effect on July 1, 1986. They govern all proceedings in actions brought after they take effect and also all further proceedings in actions then pending, except to the extent that their application in a particular action pending when the amendments take effect would not be feasible or would work injustice, in which event the former procedure applies.

(M) **Effective date of amendments.** The amendments submitted by the Supreme Court to the General Assembly on January 14, 1988 shall take effect on July 1, 1988. They govern all proceedings in actions brought after they take effect and also all further proceedings in actions then pending, except to the extent that their application in a particular action pending when the amendments take effect would not be feasible or would work injustice, in which event the former procedure applies.

(N) **Effective date of amendments.** The amendments submitted by the Supreme Court to the General Assembly on January 6, 1989 shall take effect on July 1, 1989. They govern all proceedings in actions brought after they take effect and also all further proceedings in actions then pending, except to the extent that their application in a particular action pending when the amendments take effect would not be feasible or would work injustice, in which event the former procedure applies.

(O) **Effective date of amendments.** The amendments submitted by the Supreme Court to the General Assembly on January 10, 1991 and further revised and submitted on April 29, 1991, shall take effect on July 1, 1991. They govern all proceedings in actions brought after they take effect and also all further proceedings in actions then pending, except to the extent that their application in a particular action pending when the amendments take effect would not be feasible or would work injustice, in which event the former procedure applies.

(P) **Effective date of amendments.** The amendments filed by the Supreme Court with the General Assembly on January 14, 1992 and further revised and filed on April 30, 1992, shall take effect on July 1, 1992. They govern all proceedings in actions brought after they take effect and also all further proceedings in actions then pending, except to the extent that their application in a particular action pending when the amendments take effect would not be feasible or would work injustice, in which event the former procedure applies.

(Q) **Effective date of amendments.** The amendments submitted by the Supreme Court to the General Assembly on January 8, 1993 and further revised and filed on April 30, 1993 shall take effect on July 1, 1993. They govern all proceedings in actions brought after they take effect and also all further proceedings in actions then pending, except to the extent that their application in a particular action pending when the amendments take effect would not be feasible or would work injustice, in which event the former procedure applies.

(R) **Effective date of amendments.** The amendments submitted by the Supreme Court to the General Assembly on January 14, 1994 shall take effect on July 1, 1994. They govern all proceedings in actions brought after they take effect and also all further proceedings in actions then pending, except to the extent that their application in a particular action pending when the amendments take effect would not be feasible or would work injustice, in which event the former procedure applies.

(S) **Effective date of amendments.** The amendments to Rules 11 and 53 filed by the Supreme Court with the General Assembly on January 11, 1995 and refiled on April 25, 1995 shall take effect on July 1, 1995. They govern all proceedings in actions brought after they take effect and also all further proceedings in actions then pending, except to the extent that their application in a particular action pending when the amendments take effect would not be feasible or would work injustice, in which event the former procedure applies.

(T) **Effective date of amendments.** The amendments to Rules 4.2, 19.1, 53, 54, 59, 73, and 75 filed by the Supreme Court with the General Assembly on January 5, 1996 and refiled on April 26, 1996 shall take effect on July 1, 1996. They govern all proceedings in actions brought after they take effect and also all further proceedings in actions then pending, except to the extent that their application in a particular action pending when the amendments take effect would not be feasible or would work injustice, in which event the former procedure applies.

(U) **Effective date of amendments.** The amendments to Rules 4.1, 4.2, 4.3, 4.5, 4.6, 30, 56, 73, and 75 filed by the Supreme Court with the General Assembly on January 10, 1997 and refiled on April 24, 1997 shall take effect on July 1, 1997. They govern all proceedings in actions brought after they take effect and also all further proceedings in actions then pending, except to the extent that their application in a particular action

pending when the amendments take effect would not be feasible or would work injustice, in which event the former procedure applies.

(V) **Effective date of amendments.** The amendments to Rules 3, 53, and 75 filed by the Supreme Court with the General Assembly on January 15, 1998 and further revised and refiled on April 30, 1998, shall take effect on July 1, 1998. They govern all proceedings in actions brought after they take effect and also all further proceedings in actions then pending, except to the extent that their application in a particular action pending when the amendments take effect would not be feasible or would work injustice, in which event the former procedure applies.

(W) **Effective date of amendments.** The amendments to Rules 24, 33, and 56 filed by the Supreme Court with the General Assembly on January 13, 1999 shall take effect on July 1, 1999. They govern all proceedings in actions brought after they take effect and also all further proceedings in actions then pending, except to the extent that their application in a particular action pending when the amendments take effect would not be feasible or would work injustice, in which event the former procedure applies.

(X) **Effective date of amendments.** The amendments to Civil Rule 83 filed by the Supreme Court with the General Assembly on January 13, 2000 and refiled on April 27, 2000 shall take effect on July 1, 2000. They govern all proceedings in actions brought after they take effect and also all further proceedings in actions then pending, except to the extent that their application in a particular action pending when the amendments take effect would not be feasible or would work injustice, in which event the former procedure applies.

(Y) **Effective date of amendments.** The amendments to Civil Rules 5, 11, 28, 41, 73, and 75 filed by the Supreme Court with the General Assembly on January 12, 2001, and revised and refiled on April 26, 2001, shall take effect on July 1, 2001. They govern all proceedings in actions brought after they take effect and also all further proceedings in actions then pending, except to the extent that their application in a particular action pending when the amendments take effect would not be feasible or would work injustice, in which event the former procedure applies.

(Z) **Effective date of amendments.** The amendments to Civil Rule 53 filed by the Supreme Court with the General Assembly on January 9, 2003 and refiled on April 28, 2003, shall take effect on July 1, 2003. They govern all proceedings in actions brought after they take effect and also all further proceedings in actions then pending, except to the extent that their application in a particular action pending when the amendments take effect would not be feasible or would work injustice, in which event the former procedure applies.

(AA) **Effective date of amendments.** The amendments to Civil Rule 33 and 36 filed by the Supreme Court with the General Assembly on January 7, 2004 and refiled on April 28, 2004 shall take effect on July 1, 2004. They govern all proceedings in actions brought after they take effect and also all further proceedings in actions then pending, except to the extent that their application in a particular action pending when the amendments take effect would not be feasible or would work injustice, in which event the former procedure applies.

(BB) **Effective date of amendments.** The amendments to Civil Rules 3, 10, 34, 36, 42, 45, 47, and 51 filed by the Supreme Court with the General Assembly on January 14, 2005 and revised and refiled on April 20, 2005 shall take effect on July 1, 2005. They govern all proceedings in actions brought after they take effect and also all further proceedings in actions then pending, except to the extent that their application in a particular action pending when the amendments take effect would not be feasible or would work injustice, in which event the former procedure applies.

(CC) **Effective date of amendments.** The amendments to Civil Rules 30, 47, and 53 filed by the Supreme Court with the General Assembly on January 12, 2006 shall take effect on July 1, 2006. They govern all proceedings in actions brought after they take effect and also all further proceedings in actions then pending, except to the extent that their application in a particular action pending when the amendments take effect would not be feasible or would work injustice, in which event the former procedure applies.

(DD) **Effective date of amendments.** The amendments to Civil Rule 10 filed by the Supreme Court with the General Assembly on January 11, 2007 and refiled April 30, 2007 shall take effect on July 1, 2007. They govern all proceedings in actions brought after they take effect and also all further proceedings in actions then pending, except to the extent that their application in a particular action pending when the

amendments take effect would not be feasible or would work injustice, in which event the former procedure applies.

(EE) **Effective date of amendments.** The amendments to Civil Rules 4, 16, 26, 33, 34, 36, 37, and 45 filed by the Supreme Court with the General Assembly on January 14, 2008 and refiled on April 28, 2008 shall take effect on July 1, 2008. They govern all proceedings in actions brought after they take effect and also all further proceedings in actions then pending, except to the extent that their application in a particular action pending when the amendments take effect would not be feasible or would work injustice, in which event the former procedure applies.

(FF) **Effective date of amendments.** The amendments to Civil Rules 4.2, 33, 36 and 47 filed by the Supreme Court with the General Assembly on January 14, 2009 and revised and refiled on April 30, 2009 shall take effect on July 1, 2009. They govern all proceedings in actions brought after they take effect and also all further proceedings in actions then pending, except to the extent that their application in a particular action pending when the amendments take effect would not be feasible or would work injustice, in which event the former procedure applies.

History: Amended, eff 7-1-71; 7-1-72; 7-1-73; 7-1-75; 7-1-76; 7-1-78; 7-1-80; 7-1-83; 7-1-84; 7-1-85; 7-1-86; 7-1-88; 7-1-89; 7-1-91; 7-1-92; 7-1-93; 7-1-94; 7-1-95; 7-1-96; 7-1-97; 7-1-98; 7-1-99; 7-1-00; 7-1-01; 7-1-03; 7-1-04; 7-1-05; 7-1-06; 7-1-07; 7-1-08; 7-1-09.

APPENDIX OF OFFICIAL FORMS

(See Rule 84)

Introductory Statement

The forms which follow are intended for illustration only. They are limited in number inasmuch as no attempt is made to furnish a manual of forms.

The forms are expressly declared by Rule 84 to be sufficient under the rules. Departures from the forms shall not void papers which are otherwise sufficient, and the forms may be varied when necessary to meet the facts of a particular case.

Where appropriate, the forms assume that the action has been brought in the Court of Common Pleas, Franklin County, Ohio.

FORM 1. CAPTION AND SUMMONS

COURT OF COMMON PLEAS
FRANKLIN COUNTY, OHIO

A.B.   )
221 E. West Street   )
Columbus, Ohio 43215   )
    Plaintiff   )   No. _____
         v.   )   SUMMONS
C.D.   )
122 W. East Street   )
Columbus, Ohio 43214   )
    Defendant   )

To the following named defendants:

Name _____   Address _____

_____   _____

_____   _____

_____   _____

_____   _____

You have been named defendant(s) in a complaint filed in _____ County
Court of Common Pleas, _____County Court House, _____ Ohio 43215, by

Name _____   Address _____

_____   _____

_____   _____

_____   _____

_____   _____

_____   _____

plaintiff(s). A copy of the complaint is attached hereto. The name and address of the plaintiff's
attorney is _____

_____

You are hereby summoned and required to serve upon the plaintiff's attorney, or upon the plaintiff, if he has no attorney of record, a copy of an answer to the complaint within twenty-eight days after service of this summons on you, exclusive of the day of service. Your answer must be filed with the Court within three days after the service of a copy of the answer on the plaintiff's attorney.

If you fail to appear and defend, judgment by default will be rendered against you for the relief demanded in the complaint.

Clerk, Court of Common Pleas,
_____County, Ohio

Date: _____   By_____
                                      Deputy

Note

The caption above designates the particular paper as a "SUMMONS." The particular pleading or paper should contain an appropriate designation, thus: "COMPLAINT," "ANSWER," etc. A more specific designation in a caption is also appropriate, thus: "MOTION TO INTERVENE AS A DEFENDANT."

* *

INSTRUCTIONS FOR PERSONAL OR RESIDENCE SERVICE

To:_____

You are instructed to make personal--residence [cross out one] service upon defendant(s)

_____
(name)

at _____
(address for service if different from body of summons).

_____

Special instructions for server:_____

_____

_____

* *

RETURN OF SERVICE OF SUMMONS
(PERSONAL)

Fees	
Service	$_____
Mileage	$_____
Copy	$_____
Docket	$_____
Return	$_____
Total	$_____

I received this summons on _____, 20____, at _____ o'clock, __.m., and made personal service of it upon _____ by locating him -- them (cross out one) and tendering a copy of the summons and accompanying documents, on _____, 20 ___.

_____

Sheriff -- Bailiff -- Process Server

By _____

Deputy

* *

RETURN OF SERVICE OF SUMMONS
(RESIDENCE)

	Fees
Service	$
Mileage	$
Copy	$
Docket	$
Return	$
Total	$

I received this summons on _____, 20____, at _____ o'clock, ___.m., and made residence service of it upon _____by leaving it at his -- their (cross out one) usual place of residence with _____, a person of suitable age and discretion then residing therein, a copy of the summons, a copy of the complaint and accompanying documents, on _____, 20 ___.

_____
Sheriff -- Bailiff -- Process Server
By _____
Deputy

* *

RETURN OF SERVICE OF SUMMONS
(FAILURE OF SERVICE)

	Fees
Service	$_____
Mileage	$_____
Copy	$_____
Docket	$_____
Return	$_____
Total	$_____

I received this summons on _____, 20___, at _____ o'clock, __.m., with instructions to make personal -- residence (cross out one) service upon _____ and I was unable to serve a copy of the summons upon him-- them (cross out one) for the following reasons:

_____

_____

_____

Date: _____

Sheriff -- Bailiff -- Process Server

By _____

Deputy

* *

Note

Returns shall be made pursuant to Rule 4 through Rule 4.6 and pertinent sections of the Ohio Revised Code which are not in conflict with the Rules of Civil Procedure and which establish particular duties for the serving officer, i.e., Sections 311.08, 311.17 and 2335.31, Revised Code.

[Effective: July 1, 1970.]

FORM 2. COMPLAINT ON A PROMISSORY NOTE

COURT OF COMMON PLEAS
FRANKLIN COUNTY, OHIO

A.B., Plaintiff	)	
(address)	)	
v.	)	No._____
C.D., Defendant	)	
(address)	)	COMPLAINT

    1. Defendant on or about _____, 20___, executed and delivered to plaintiff a promissory note, a copy of which is hereto attached as Exhibit A.

    2. Defendant owes to plaintiff the amount of said note and interest.

    Wherefore plaintiff demands judgment against defendant for the sum of _____dollars, interest, and costs.

_____
(Attorney for Plaintiff)

_____
(Address)

_____

Note

    1. The pleader should follow the form above if he has possession of a copy of the note. The pleader should attach a copy of the note to the pleading. See Rule 10(D).

    2. Under the rules free joinder of claims is permitted. See Rule 8(E) and Rule 18. Consequently the claims set forth in each and all of the following forms may be joined with this complaint or with each other. Ordinarily each claim should be stated in a separate division of the complaint, and the divisions should be designated as counts successively numbered (i.e., COUNT ONE, COUNT TWO, etc.). See Rule 10(B). In particular the rules permit alternative and inconsistent pleading. See Rule 8(E)(2).

    3. The attorney must sign the pleading. See Rule 11. The pleading need not be verified. See Rule 11.

    [Effective: July 1, 1970.]

FORM 2A. COMPLAINT ON A PROMISSORY NOTE
(REASON FOR OMISSION OF COPY STATED)

1. Defendant on or about_____, 20____, executed and delivered to plaintiff a promissory note

[in the following words and figures: (here set out the note verbatim)]

or

[whereby defendant promised to pay plaintiff or order on_____, 20 _____, the sum of _____ dollars with interest thereon at the rate of _____ percent per annum].

2. Plaintiff is unable to attach a copy of the said note because (here set out the reason for failure to attach the note).

3. Defendant owes to plaintiff the amount of said note and interest.

Wherefore (etc. as in Form 2).

Note

1. The pleader states why, under Rule 10(D), he is unable to attach a copy of the note.

2. If pleader can set forth the note verbatim from information at hand, he may do so.

3. Or pleader may plead the legal effect of the note, he being unable to attach a copy of the note.

4. This type form may be used in other situations whenever pleader is required to attach a copy of an instrument, but a copy of the instrument is not available to him.

[Effective: July 1, 1970.]

FORM 3. COMPLAINT ON AN ACCOUNT

Defendant owes plaintiff _____ dollars according to the account hereto annexed as Exhibit A.

Wherefore (etc. as in Form 2).

[Effective: July 1, 1970.]

FORM 4. COMPLAINT FOR GOODS SOLD AND DELIVERED

Defendant owes plaintiff _____ dollars for goods sold and delivered by plaintiff to defendant between_____, 20_____, and_____, 20_____.

Wherefore (etc. as in Form 2).

Note

This form may be used where the action is for an agreed price or for the reasonable value of the goods.

[Effective: July 1, 1970.]

FORM 5. COMPLAINT FOR MONEY LENT

Defendant owes plaintiff _____ dollars for money lent by plaintiff to defendant on_____, 20____.

Wherefore (etc. as in Form 2).

[Effective: July 1, 1970.]

FORM 6. COMPLAINT FOR MONEY PAID BY MISTAKE

Defendant owes plaintiff _____ dollars for money paid by plaintiff to defendant by mistake on_____, 20____, under the following circumstances: [here state the circumstances with particularity--see Rule 9(B)].

Wherefore (etc. as in Form 2).

[Effective: July 1, 1970.]

FORM 7. COMPLAINT FOR MONEY HAD AND RECEIVED

Defendant owes plaintiff _____ dollars for money had and received from one G.H. on_____, 20_____, to be paid by defendant to plaintiff.

Wherefore (etc. as in Form 2).

[Effective: July 1, 1970.]

FORM 8. COMPLAINT FOR NEGLIGENCE

1.   On_____, 20_____, in a public highway called _____Street in_____, Ohio, defendant negligently drove a motor vehicle against plaintiff who was then crossing said highway.

2.   As a result plaintiff was thrown down and had his leg broken and was otherwise injured, was prevented from transacting his business, suffered great pain of body and mind, and incurred expenses for medical attention and hospitalization in the sum of one thousand dollars.

Wherefore plaintiff demands judgment against defendant in the sum of _____ dollars and costs.

Note

Since contributory negligence is an affirmative defense, the complaint need contain no allegation of due care of plaintiff.

[Effective: July 1, 1970.]

FORM 9. COMPLAINT FOR NEGLIGENCE WHERE PLAINTIFF IS UNABLE TO DETERMINE DEFINITELY WHETHER THE PERSON RESPONSIBLE IS C.D. OR E.F. OR WHETHER BOTH ARE RESPONSIBLE AND WHERE HIS EVIDENCE MAY JUSTIFY A FINDING OF WILFULNESS OR OF RECKLESSNESS OR OF NEGLIGENCE

A.B., Plaintiff	)	
(address)	)	No. _____
	)	
v.	)	
	)	
C.D. and E.F., Defendants	)	COMPLAINT
(addresses)	)	

1. On ___, 19_, in a public highway called ____Street in ___, Ohio, defendant C.D. or defendant E.F., or both defendants C.D. and E.F. wilfully or recklessly or negligently drove or caused to be driven a motor vehicle against plaintiff who was then crossing said highway.

2. As a result plaintiff was thrown down and had his leg broken and was otherwise injured, was prevented from transacting his business, suffered great pain of body and mind, and incurred expenses for medical attention and hospitalization in the sum of one thousand dollars.

Wherefore plaintiff demands judgment against C.D. or against E.F. or against both in the sum of _____ dollars and costs.

[Effective: July 1, 1970.]

FORM 10. COMPLAINT FOR CONVERSION

On or about ___, 19_, defendant converted to his own use ten bonds of the ___ Company (here insert brief identification as by number and issue) of the value of ___dollars, the property of plaintiff.

Wherefore plaintiff demands judgment against defendant in the sum of ___ dollars, interest, and costs.

[Effective: July 1, 1970.]

FORM 11. COMPLAINT FOR SPECIFIC PERFORMANCE OF CONTRACT TO CONVEY LAND

1. On our about ____, 19_, plaintiff and defendant entered into an agreement in writing a copy of which is hereto annexed as Exhibit A.

2. In accord with the provisions of said agreement plaintiff tendered to defendant the purchase price and requested a conveyance of the land, but defendant refused to accept the tender and refused to make the conveyance.

3. Plaintiff now offers to pay the purchase price.

Wherefore plaintiff demands (1) that defendant be required specifically to perform said agreement, (2) damages in the sum of one thousand dollars, and (3) that if specific performance is not granted plaintiff have judgment against defendant in the sum of ____ dollars.

Note

The demand for relief seeks specific performance as well as ancillary damages resulting from the delay. In addition the demand for relief seeks damages in a certain sum if the court finds it impossible to grant specific performance as where, in the interim, defendant has conveyed the property to a purchaser for value without notice.

[Effective: July 1, 1970.]

FORM 12. COMPLAINT ON CLAIM FOR DEBT
AND TO SET ASIDE FRAUDULENT CONVEYANCE UNDER RULE 18(B)

A.B., Plaintiff   )
(address)   )   No. _____
)
      v.   )
)
C.D. and E.F., Defendants   ) COMPLAINT
(addresses)   )

    1. Defendant C.D. on or about ___ executed and delivered to plaintiff a promissory note, a copy of which is hereto annexed as Exhibit A.

    2. Defendant C.D. owes to plaintiff the amount of said note and interest.

    3. Defendant C.D. on or about ___ conveyed all his property, real and personal [or specify and describe] to defendant E.F. for the purpose of defrauding plaintiff and hindering and delaying the collection of the indebtedness evidenced by the note above referred to.

    Wherefore plaintiff demands:

    (1) That plaintiff have judgment against defendant C.D. for ___ dollars and interest; (2) that the aforesaid conveyance to defendant E.F. be declared void and the judgment herein be declared a lien on said property; (3) that plaintiff have judgment against the defendants for costs.

    [Effective: July 1, 1970.]

FORM 13. COMPLAINT FOR INTERPLEADER AND DECLARATORY RELIEF

1. On or about ___, 19_, plaintiff issued to G.H. a policy of life insurance, a copy of which is attached as Exhibit A, whereby plaintiff promised to pay to K.L. as beneficiary the sum of ___ dollars upon the death of G.H. The policy required the payment by G.H. of a stipulated premium on ___, 19_, and annually thereafter as a condition precedent to its continuance in force.

2. No part of the premium due ___, 19_, was ever paid and the policy ceased to have any force or effect on ___, 19_.

3. Thereafter, on ___, 19_, G.H. and K.L. died as the result of a collision between a locomotive and the automobile in which G.H. and K.L. were riding.

4. Defendant C.D. is the duly appointed and acting executor of the will of G.H.; defendant E.F. is the duly appointed and acting executor of the will of K.L.; defendant X.Y. claims to have been duly designated as beneficiary of said policy in place of K.L.

5. Each of defendants, C.D., E.F., and X.Y. is claiming that the abovementioned policy was in full force and effect at the time of the death of G.H.; each of them is claiming to be the only person entitled to receive payment of the amount of the policy and has made demand for payment thereof.

6. By reason of these conflicting claims of the defendants, plaintiff is in great doubt as to which defendant is entitled to be paid the amount of the policy, if it was in force at the death of G.H.

Wherefore plaintiff demands that the court adjudge:

(1) That none of the defendants is entitled to recover from plaintiff the amount of said policy or any part thereof.

(2) That each of the defendants be restrained from instituting any action against plaintiff for the recovery of the amount of said policy or any part thereof.

(3) That, if the court shall determine that said policy was in force at the death of G.H., the defendants be required to interplead and settle between themselves their rights to the money due under said policy, and that plaintiff be discharged from all liability in the premises except to the person whom the court shall adjudge entitled to the amount of said policy.

(4) That plaintiff recover its costs.

[Effective: July 1, 1970.]

FORM 14. MOTION TO DISMISS, PRESENTING DEFENSES OF FAILURE TO STATE A CLAIM, OF LACK OF SERVICE OF PROCESS, AND OF LACK OF JURISDICTION UNDER RULE 12(B)

COURT OF COMMON PLEAS
FRANKLIN COUNTY, OHIO

A.B., Plaintiff	)	
(address)	)	No. _____
	)	
v.	)	
	)	
C.D. Corporation, Defendant	)	MOTION TO DISMISS
(address)	)	

The defendant moves the court as follows:

1. To dismiss the action because the complaint fails to state a claim against defendant upon which relief can be granted.

2. To dismiss the action or in lieu thereof to quash the return of service of summons on the grounds (a) that the defendant is a corporation organized under the laws of Delaware and was not and is not subject to service of process within this state, and (b) that the defendant has not been properly served with process in this action, all of which more clearly appears in the affidavits of M.N. and X.Y. hereto attached as Exhibit A and Exhibit B, respectively.

3. To dismiss the action on the ground that the court lacks jurisdiction because [here state the reasons why the court lacks jurisdiction].

_____
(Attorney for Defendant)

_____
(Address)

_____

SERVICE OF COPY

A copy hereof was served upon X.Y., attorney for plaintiff, by mailing it to him on June 1, 19 [or set forth other method of service upon X.Y.].

_____
(Attorney for Defendant)

Note

1. The form gives various examples of defenses which may be raised by motion under Rule 12(B).

2. Whether the motion should be accompanied by a notice of hearing on the motion or whether the motion should be accompanied by a memorandum brief depends upon the rules of a particular local court. See Rule 7(B) and the rules of the local court regarding motion practice.

3. All papers after the original pleading required to be served upon an opposite party shall have endorsed thereon, when filed with the court, a statement setting forth the date and method of service. See Rule 5.

[Effective: July 1, 1970; amended effective July 1, 1971.]

FORM 15. ANSWER PRESENTING DEFENSES UNDER RULE 12(B)

A.B., Plaintiff	)
(address)	) No. _____
	)
v.	)
	)
C.D. and E.F., Defendants	) ANSWER, COUNTERCLAIM,
(addresses)	) AND CROSS-CLAIM

FIRST DEFENSE

The complaint fails to state a claim against defendant C.D. upon which relief can be granted.

SECOND DEFENSE

If defendant C.D. is indebted to plaintiff for the goods mentioned in the complaint, he is indebted to him jointly with G.H. G.H. is alive, is a resident of this state, is subject to the jurisdiction of this court and can be made a party but has not been made one.

THIRD DEFENSE

Defendant C.D. admits the allegation contained in paragraphs 1 and 4 of the complaint; alleges that he is without knowledge or information sufficient to form a belief as to the truth of the allegations contained in paragraph 2 of the complaint; and denies each and every other allegation contained in the complaint.

FOURTH DEFENSE

The right of action set forth in the complaint did not accrue within ___ years next before the commencement of this action.

COUNTERCLAIM

[Here set forth any claim as a counterclaim in the manner in which a claim is pleaded in a complaint.]

CROSS-CLAIM AGAINST DEFENDANT M.N.

[Here set forth the claim constituting a cross-claim against defendant M.N. in the manner in which a claim is pleaded in a complaint.]

_____
(Attorney for Defendant, C.D.)

_____
(Address)

_____

(Service of Copy as in Form 14)

Note

1. The above form contains examples of certain defenses provided for in Rule 12(B). The first defense challenges the legal sufficiency of the complaint. It is a substitute for a motion to dismiss; that is, under former practice the issue raised by the first defense would have been raised by demurrer, and under present practice the same issue might have been raised by motion at the option of the defendant. See Rule 12(B).

2. The second defense embodies the old plea in abatement. The decision thereon, however, may, for example, well provide under Rule 19(A) or Rule 21 for the citing in of the party rather than an abatement of the action.

3. The third defense is an answer on the merits.

4. The fourth defense is one of the affirmative defenses provided for in Rule 8(C).

5. The answer also includes a counterclaim and a cross-claim. See Rule 12(B).

[Effective: July 1, 1970.]

FORM 16. SUMMONS AGAINST THIRD-PARTY DEFENDANT

COURT OF COMMON PLEAS
FRANKLIN COUNTY, OHIO

A.B., Plaintiff   )
(address)   )
       v.   )
C.D., Defendant and Third-Party   )   No. _____
Plaintiff   )
(address)   )   SUMMONS
       v.   )
E.F., Third-Party Defendant   )
(address)   )

To the above-named Third-Party Defendant:

    You are hereby summoned and required to serve upon ___, plaintiff's attorney whose address is ___ and upon ___, who is attorney for C.D., defendant and third-party plaintiff, and whose address is ___, an answer to the third-party complaint which is herewith served upon you within twenty-eight days after the service of this summons upon you exclusive of the day of service. If you fail to do so, judgment by default will be taken against you for the relief demanded in the third-party complaint. There is also served upon you herewith a copy of the complaint of the plaintiff which you may but are not required to answer. Your answer to the third-party complaint and your answer to the plaintiff's complaint must also be filed with the court.

                                            _____

                                            (Clerk of Court)

                                            By _____ Deputy

Clerk

Dated _____

Note

    It may be necessary, depending upon when the third-party complaint is served, to seek leave of court by motion to bring in a third-party defendant. See Rule 14(A).

    [Effective: July 1, 1970.]

FORM 16A. COMPLAINT AGAINST THIRD-PARTY DEFENDANT

COURT OF COMMON PLEAS
FRANKLIN COUNTY, OHIO

A.B., Plaintiff	)
(address)	)
v.	)
C.D., Defendant and Third-Party	) No. _____
Plaintiff	)
(address)	) THIRD-PARTY COMPLAINT
v.	)
E.F., Third-Party Defendant	)
(address)	)

1. Plaintiff A.B. has filed against defendant C.D. a complaint, a copy of which is hereto attached as Exhibit A.

2. [Here state the grounds upon which C.D. is entitled to recover from E.F., all or part of what A.B. may recover from C.D. The statement should be framed as in an original complaint.]

Wherefore C.D. demands judgment against third-party defendant E.F. for all sums [make appropriate change where C.D. is entitled to only partial recovery over against E.F.] that may be adjudged against defendant C.D. in favor of plaintiff A.B.

_____
(Attorney for C.D.,
Third-Party Plaintiff)

_____
(Address)

_____

Note

It is necessary to comply with Rule 5 regarding service of third-party papers on plaintiff.

[Effective: July 1, 1970.]

FORM 17. MOTION TO INTERVENE AS A DEFENDANT UNDER RULE 24

COURT OF COMMON PLEAS
FRANKLIN COUNTY, OHIO

A.B., Plaintiff	)
(address)	) No. ___
v.	)
C.D., Defendant	) MOTION TO INTERVENE
(address)	) AS A DEFENDANT
E.F., Applicant for Intervention	)
(address)	)

     E.F. moves for leave to intervene as a defendant in this action in order to assert the defenses set forth in his proposed answer, of which a copy is hereto attached, on the ground that [here insert the appropriate grounds of intervention].

_____

(Attorney for E.F.,
Applicant for Intervention)

_____

(Address)

(Adopted eff. 7-1-70)

Note (Amended Effective July 1, 1999)

    It is necessary that a motion to intervene be accompanied by a pleading as required in Civ.R. 24(C). It is also necessary to comply with Civ.R. 5 regarding service of the motion on the parties to the action.

FORM 18. JUDGMENT ON JURY VERDICT

COURT OF COMMON PLEAS
FRANKLIN COUNTY OHIO

A.B., Plaintiff	)	
(address)	)	No. _____
v.	)	
C.D., Defendant	)	JUDGMENT
(address)	)	

      This action came on for trial before the Court and a jury, and the issues having been duly tried and the jury having duly rendered its verdict,

      It is ordered and adjudged [that the plaintiff A.B. recover of the defendant C.D. the sum of ___, with interest thereon at the rate of ___ percent as provided by law, and his costs of action.]

      [that the plaintiff take nothing, that the action be dismissed on the merits, and that the defendant C.D. recover of the plaintiff A.B. his costs of action.]

      Dated at ___, Ohio, this ___ day of ___ , 19_

                           _____
                           Judge, Court of Common Pleas

Journalized this ___ day of ___, 19_

_____
Clerk of Court

By _____ Deputy Clerk

Note

      This form is illustrative of the judgment to be entered upon the general verdict of a jury. It deals with the cases where there is a general jury verdict awarding the plaintiff money damages or finding for the defendant, but is adaptable to other situations of jury verdict.

      [Effective: July 1, 1970.]

FORM 19. JUDGMENT ON DECISION BY THE COURT

COURT OF COMMON PLEAS
FRANKLIN COUNTY, OHIO

A.B., Plaintiff) (address)) v.) C.D., Defendant) (address))	No. _____ JUDGMENT

This action came on for [trial] [hearing] before the Court, and the issues having been duly [tried] [heard] and a decision having been duly rendered,

It is ordered and adjudged [that the plaintiff A.B. recover of the defendant C.D. the sum of ___, with interest thereon at the rate of ___ percent as provided by law, and his costs of action.]

[that the plaintiff take nothing, that the action be dismissed on the merits, and that the defendant C.D. recover of the plaintiff A.B. his costs of action.]

Dated at ___, Ohio, this ___ day of ___, 19_

_____
Judge, Court of Common Pleas

Journalized this ___ day of ___, 19_

_____
Clerk of Court

By _____ Deputy Clerk

Note

This form is illustrative of the judgment to be entered upon a decision of the court. It deals with the cases of decisions by the court awarding a party only money damages or costs, but is adaptable to other decisions by the court.

[Effective: July 1, 1970.]

FORM 20. COMPLAINT FOR DIVORCE, ALIMONY
AND CUSTODY OF CHILDREN

COURT OF COMMON PLEAS
FRANKLIN COUNTY, OHIO

A.B., Plaintiff   )
(address)   )   No. _____
          v.   )
C.D., Defendant   )   COMPLAINT
(address)   )

    1. Plaintiff has been a resident of Ohio for at least six months immediately preceding the filing of this complaint.

    2. Plaintiff and defendant were married at ____, in the state of ____, on the ____ day of ____ , 19_, and there are [no] ____ children, the issue of such marriage [whose names and ages are, respectively (stating them, and as to who has custody)].

    3. Plaintiff says that defendant [here set forth one or more of the statutory grounds for divorce as provided for by law].

    Wherefore, plaintiff demands that she [he] be granted a divorce from defendant and awarded custody of their minor children; that she [he] be granted reasonable alimony and support for their minor children; [that she be restored to her former name of ____]; and for her costs herein, including a reasonable sum for her expenses and attorney's fees in this action, and for such other relief as shall be proper and necessary.

_____
(Attorney for Plaintiff)

_____
(Address)

_____

[Effective: July 1, 1970.]

UNIFORM DOMESTIC RELATIONS FORMS

(See Rule 84)

Form
1. Affidavit of Income and Expenses
2. Affidavit of Property.
3. Parenting Proceeding Affidavit (RC § 3127.23(A))
4. Health Insurance Affidavit
5. Motion and Affidavit or Counter Affidavit for Temporary Orders Without Oral Hearing

COURT OF COMMON PLEAS
_____ COUNTY, OHIO

_____
Plaintiff/Petitioner

v./and

_____
Defendant/Petitioner

Case No.   _____

Judge   _____

Magistrate   _____

Instructions: Check local court rules to determine when this form must be filed.
This affidavit is used to make complete disclosure of income, expenses and money owed. It is used to determine child and spousal support amounts. Do not leave any category blank. Write "none" where appropriate. If you do not know exact figures for any item, give your best estimate, and put "EST." **If you need more space, add additional pages.**

AFFIDAVIT OF INCOME AND EXPENSES

Affidavit of _____
(Print Your Name)

Date of marriage _____ Date of separation _____

SECTION I - INCOME

	Husband	**Wife**
Employed	☐ Yes ☐ No	☐ Yes ☐ No
Employer	_____	_____
Payroll address	_____	_____
Payroll city, state, zip	_____	_____
Scheduled paychecks per year	☐ 12 ☐ 24 ☐ 26 ☐ 52	☐ 12 ☐ 24 ☐ 26 ☐ 52

A.   YEARLY INCOME, OVERTIME, COMMISSIONS AND BONUSES FOR PAST THREE YEARS

	Husband		**Wife**
Base yearly income	$ _____ 3 years ago	20 ____	$ _____
	$ _____ 2 years ago	20 ____	$ _____
	$ _____ Last year	20 ____	$ _____
Yearly overtime, commissions and/or bonuses	$ _____ 3 years ago	20 ____	$ _____
	$ _____ 2 years ago	20 ____	$ _____
	$ _____ Last year	20 ____	$ _____

Supreme Court of Ohio
Uniform Domestic Relations Form – Affidavit 1
Affidavit of Income and Expenses
Approved under Ohio Civil Rule 84
Effective Date: July 1, 2010

Page 1 of 7

B.   COMPUTATION OF CURRENT INCOME

	Husband	**Wife**
Base yearly income	$ _____	$ _____
Average yearly overtime, commissions and/or bonuses over last 3 years (from part A)	$ _____	$ _____
Unemployment compensation	$ _____	$ _____

Disability benefits

☐ Workers' Compensation

☐ Social Security

☐ Other: _____	$ _____	$ _____

Retirement benefits

☐ Social Security

☐ Other: _____	$ _____	$ _____
Spousal support received	$ _____	$ _____

Interest and dividend income (source)

_____

_____	$ _____	$ _____

Other income (type and source)

_____

_____	$ _____	$ _____
TOTAL YEARLY INCOME	$ _____	$ _____
Supplemental Security Income (SSI) or public assistance	$ _____	$ _____
Court-ordered child support that you receive for minor and/or dependent child(ren) not of the marriage or relationship	$ _____	$ _____

Supreme Court of Ohio
Uniform Domestic Relations Form – Affidavit 1
Affidavit of Income and Expenses
Approved under Ohio Civil Rule 84
Effective Date: July 1, 2010

Page 2 of 7

SECTION II – CHILDREN AND HOUSEHOLD RESIDENTS

Minor and/or dependent child(ren) who are adopted or born of this marriage or relationship:

Name	Date of birth	Living with
_____	_____	_____
_____	_____	_____
_____	_____	_____
_____	_____	_____

In addition to the above children there is/are in your household:

_____ adult(s)

_____ other minor and/or dependent child(ren).

SECTION III – EXPENSES

List monthly expenses below for your present household.

A.   <u>MONTHLY HOUSING EXPENSES</u>

Rent or first mortgage (including taxes and insurance)	$ _____
Real estate taxes (if not included above)	$ _____
Real estate/homeowner's insurance (if not included above)	$ _____
Second mortgage/equity line of credit	$ _____
Utilities	
o Electric	$ _____
o Gas, fuel oil, propane	$ _____
o Water and sewer	$ _____
o Telephone	$ _____
o Trash collection	$ _____
o Cable/satellite television	$ _____
Cleaning, maintenance, repair	$ _____
Lawn service, snow removal	$ _____
Other: _____	$ _____
_____	$ _____
TOTAL MONTHLY :	$ _____

Supreme Court of Ohio
Uniform Domestic Relations Form – Affidavit 1
Affidavit of Income and Expenses
Approved under Ohio Civil Rule 84
Effective Date: July 1, 2010

Page 3 of 7

B.   OTHER MONTHLY LIVING EXPENSES

Food

    o   Groceries (including food, paper, cleaning products, toiletries, other) $ _____

    o   Restaurant $ _____

Transportation

    o   Vehicle loans, leases $ _____

    o   Vehicle maintenance (oil, repair, license) $ _____

    o   Gasoline $ _____

    o   Parking, public transportation $ _____

Clothing

    o   Clothes (other than children's) $ _____

    o   Dry cleaning, laundry $ _____

Personal grooming

    o   Hair, nail care $ _____

    o   Other _____ $ _____

Cell phone $ _____

Internet (if not included elsewhere) $ _____

Other _____ $ _____

                                              TOTAL MONTHLY $ _____

C.   MONTHLY CHILD-RELATED EXPENSES
     (for children of the marriage or relationship)

Work/education-related child care $ _____

Other child care $ _____

Unusual parenting time travel $ _____

Special and unusual needs of child(ren) (not included elsewhere) $ _____

Clothing $ _____

School supplies $ _____

Child(ren)'s allowances $ _____

Extracurricular activities, lessons $ _____

School lunches $ _____

Other _____ $ _____

                                              TOTAL MONTHLY $ _____

Supreme Court of Ohio
Uniform Domestic Relations Form – Affidavit 1
Affidavit of Income and Expenses
Approved under Ohio Civil Rule 84
Effective Date: July 1, 2010

Page 4 of 7

D.   INSURANCE PREMIUMS

Life	$	
Auto	$	
Health	$	
Disability	$	
Renters/personal property (if not included in part A above)	$	
Other _____	$	
TOTAL MONTHLY	$	

E.   MONTHLY EDUCATION EXPENSES

Tuition		
o Self	$	
o Child(ren)	$	
Books, fees, other	$	
College loan repayment	$	
Other _____	$	
	$	
TOTAL MONTHLY:	$	

F.   MONTHLY HEALTH CARE EXPENSES
(not covered by insurance)

Physicians	$	
Dentists	$	
Optometrists/opticians	$	
Prescriptions	$	
Other	$	
_____	$	
TOTAL MONTHLY:	$	

G.   MISCELLANEOUS MONTHLY EXPENSES

Extraordinary obligations for other minor/handicapped child(ren) (not stepchildren)	$	
Child support for children who were not born of this marriage or relationship and were not adopted of this marriage	$	
Spousal support paid to former spouse(s)	$	
Subscriptions, books	$	
Entertainment	$	

Supreme Court of Ohio
Uniform Domestic Relations Form – Affidavit 1
Affidavit of Income and Expenses
Approved under Ohio Civil Rule 84
Effective Date: July 1, 2010

Page 5 of 7

Charitable contributions	$ _____
Memberships (associations, clubs)	$ _____
Travel, vacations	$ _____
Pets	$ _____
Gifts	$ _____
Bankruptcy payments	$ _____
Attorney fees	$ _____
Required deductions from wages (excluding taxes, Social Security and Medicare) (type)	$ _____
Additional taxes paid (not deducted from wages) (type) _____	$ _____
Other _____	$ _____
_____	$ _____
TOTAL MONTHLY:	$ _____

H.   **MONTHLY INSTALLMENT PAYMENTS**
       (Do not repeat expenses already listed.)
       Examples: car, credit card, rent-to-own, cash advance payments

To whom paid	Purpose	Balance due	Monthly payment
_____	_____	$ _____	$ _____
_____	_____	$ _____	$ _____
_____	_____	$ _____	$ _____
_____	_____	$ _____	$ _____
_____	_____	$ _____	$ _____
_____	_____	$ _____	$ _____
_____	_____	$ _____	$ _____
_____	_____	$ _____	$ _____
_____	_____	$ _____	$ _____
_____	_____	$ _____	$ _____
_____	_____	$ _____	$ _____
_____	_____	$ _____	$ _____
_____	_____	$ _____	$ _____
_____	_____	$ _____	$ _____
		TOTAL MONTHLY:	$ _____

GRAND TOTAL MONTHLY EXPENSES (Sum of A through H):　$ _____

OATH
[Do not sign until notary is present.]

I, (print name) _____ , swear or affirm that I have read
this document and, to the best of my knowledge and belief, the facts and information stated in this
document are true, accurate and complete. I understand that if I do not tell the truth, I may be subject
to penalties for perjury.

_____
Your signature

Sworn before me and signed in my presence this ____ day of _____ , _____ .

_____
Notary Public
My commission expires:

Supreme Court of Ohio
Uniform Domestic Relations Form – Affidavit 1
Affidavit of Income and Expenses
Approved under Ohio Civil Rule 84
Effective Date: July 1, 2010

Page 7 of 7

COURT OF COMMON PLEAS

_____ **COUNTY, OHIO**

_____	Case No. _____
Plaintiff/Petitioner	Judge _____
v./and	Magistrate _____
_____	
Respondent/Petitioner	

Instructions: Check local court rules to determine when this form must be filed.
List ALL OF YOUR PROPERTY AND DEBTS, the property and debts of your spouse, and any joint property or debts. Do not leave any category blank. For each item, if none, put "NONE." If you do not know exact figures for any item, give your best estimate, and put "EST." **If more space is needed, add additional pages.**

AFFIDAVIT OF PROPERTY

Affidavit of _____
(Print Your Name)

I. REAL ESTATE INTERESTS

Address	Present Fair Market Value	Titled To	Mortgage Balance	Equity (as of date)
1. _____ _____	$ _____	☐ Husband ☐ Wife ☐ Both	$ _____	$ _____ _____
2. _____ _____	$ _____	☐ Husband ☐ Wife ☐ Both	$ _____	$ _____ _____

TOTAL SECTION I: REAL ESTATE INTERESTS $ _____

Supreme Court of Ohio
Uniform Domestic Relations Form – Affidavit 2
Affidavit of Property
Approved under Ohio Civil Rule 84
Effective Date: July 1, 2010

Page 1 of 7

II. OTHER ASSETS

Category	Description (list who has possession)	Titled To	Value/Date of Value
A. Vehicles and Other Certificate of Title Property	(Include model and year of automobiles, trucks, motorcycles, boats, motors, motor homes, etc.)		
1. _____	_____	☐ Husband ☐ Wife ☐ Both	$ _____
2. _____	_____	☐ Husband ☐ Wife ☐ Both	$ _____
3. _____	_____	☐ Husband ☐ Wife ☐ Both	$ _____
4. _____	_____	☐ Husband ☐ Wife ☐ Both	$ _____
5. _____	_____	☐ Husband ☐ Wife ☐ Both	$ _____
6. _____	_____	☐ Husband ☐ Wife ☐ Both	$ _____
B. Financial Accounts	(Include checking, savings, CDs, POD accounts, money market accounts, etc.)		
1. _____	_____	☐ Husband ☐ Wife ☐ Both	$ _____
2. _____	_____	☐ Husband ☐ Wife ☐ Both	$ _____
3. _____	_____	☐ Husband ☐ Wife ☐ Both	$ _____
4. _____	_____	☐ Husband ☐ Wife ☐ Both	$ _____

Supreme Court of Ohio
Uniform Domestic Relations Form – Affidavit 2
Affidavit of Property
Approved under Ohio Civil Rule 84
Effective Date: July 1, 2010

Page 2 of 7

Category	Description (List who has possession)	Titled To	Value/Date of Value

C. Pensions & Retirement plans — (Include profit-sharing, IRAs, 401k plans, etc.; Describe each type of plan)

1. _____   _____   ☐ Husband ☐ Wife ☐ Both $ _____

2. _____   _____   ☐ Husband ☐ Wife ☐ Both $ _____

3. _____   _____   ☐ Husband ☐ Wife ☐ Both $ _____

4. _____   _____   ☐ Husband ☐ Wife ☐ Both $ _____

D. Publicly Held Stocks, Bonds, Securities & Mutual Funds

1. _____   _____   ☐ Husband ☐ Wife ☐ Both $ _____

2. _____   _____   ☐ Husband ☐ Wife ☐ Both $ _____

3. _____   _____   ☐ Husband ☐ Wife ☐ Both $ _____

4. _____   _____   ☐ Husband ☐ Wife ☐ Both $ _____

Category	Description (List who has possession)	Titled To	Value/Date of Value

E. Closely Held Stocks & Other Business Interests and Name of Company — (Type of ownership and number)

1. _____   _____   ☐ Husband ☐ Wife ☐ Both $ _____

2. _____   _____   ☐ Husband ☐ Wife ☐ Both $ _____

Supreme Court of Ohio
Uniform Domestic Relations Form – Affidavit 2
Affidavit of Property
Approved under Ohio Civil Rule 84
Effective Date: July 1, 2010

Page 3 of 7

F. Life Insurance Type   (Any cash value or loans)   (Insured party
(Term/Whole Life)   & value upon death)

1. _____   _____   ☐ Husband $ _____
              ☐ Wife
              ☐ Both
_____   _____   _____

2. _____   _____   ☐ Husband $ _____
              ☐ Wife
              ☐ Both
_____   _____   _____

3. _____   _____   ☐ Husband $ _____
              ☐ Wife
              ☐ Both
_____   _____   _____

4. _____   _____   ☐ Husband $ _____
              ☐ Wife
              ☐ Both
_____   _____   _____

<u>Category</u>	<u>Description</u>	<u>Who Has Possession</u>	<u>Value/Date of Value</u>

**G. Furniture
& Appliances**

(Estimate value of those in your possession, and value of those in your spouse's possession)

1. _____   _____   ☐ Husband $ _____
              ☐ Wife
              ☐ Both

2. _____   _____   ☐ Husband $ _____
              ☐ Wife
              ☐ Both

3. _____   _____   ☐ Husband $ _____
              ☐ Wife
              ☐ Both

4. _____   _____   ☐ Husband $ _____
              ☐ Wife
              ☐ Both

H. Safe Deposit Box   (Give location and describe contents)   <u>Titled To</u>

1. _____   _____   ☐ Husband $ _____
              ☐ Wife
              ☐ Both

2. _____   _____   ☐ Husband $ _____
              ☐ Wife
              ☐ Both

Supreme Court of Ohio
Uniform Domestic Relations Form – Affidavit 2
Affidavit of Property
Approved under Ohio Civil Rule 84
Effective Date: July 1, 2010

Page 4 of 7

I. Transfer of Assets

Explanation: List the name and address of any person (other than creditors listed on your Affidavit) who has received money or property from you exceeding $300 in value in the past 12 months and the reason for each transfer.

1. _____ _____ ☐ Husband ☐ Wife ☐ Both $ _____

2. _____ _____ ☐ Husband ☐ Wife ☐ Both $ _____

3. _____ _____ ☐ Husband ☐ Wife ☐ Both $ _____

4. _____ _____ ☐ Husband ☐ Wife ☐ Both $ _____

Category	Description (Also list who has possession)	Titled To	Value/Date of Value

J. All Other Assets Not Listed Above

Explanation: List any item you have not listed above that is considered an asset.

1. _____ _____ ☐ Husband ☐ Wife ☐ Both $ _____

2. _____ _____ ☐ Husband ☐ Wife ☐ Both $ _____

TOTAL SECTION II: OTHER ASSETS $ _____

III. SEPARATE PROPERTY CLAIMS: Pre-marital assets, gifts to one spouse only, inheritances

If you are making any claims in any of the categories below, explain the nature and amount of your claim. **This includes, but is not limited to, inheritances, property owned before marriage, and any pre-marital agreements.**

Category (Pre-marital Gift, Inheritance, etc., acquired after separation)	Description	Why do you claim this as a separate property?	Present Fair Market Value
1. _____	_____	_____	$ _____
2. _____	_____	_____	$ _____
3. _____	_____	_____	$ _____
4. _____	_____	_____	$ _____
5. _____	_____	_____	$ _____

TOTAL SECTION III: SEPARATE PROPERTY CLAIMS $ _____

IV. DEBT

List ALL OF YOUR DEBTS, the debts of your spouse, and any joint debts. Do not leave any category blank. For each item, if none, put "NONE." If you don't know exact figures for any item, give your best estimate, and put "EST." **If more space is needed to explain, please attach an additional page with the explanation and identify which question you are answering.**

Type	Name of Creditor/Purpose of Debt	Account Name	Name(s) on Account	Total Debt Due	Monthly Payment

A. Secured Debt (Mortgages, Car, etc.)

1. ___ ___ ___ ☐ Husband ☐ Wife ☐ Joint $___ $___
2. ___ ___ ___ ☐ Husband ☐ Wife ☐ Joint $___ $___
3. ___ ___ ___ ☐ Husband ☐ Wife ☐ Joint $___ $___
4. ___ ___ ___ ☐ Husband ☐ Wife ☐ Joint $___ $___
5. ___ ___ ___ ☐ Husband ☐ Wife ☐ Joint $___ $___

B. Unsecured Debt, including credit cards

1. ___ ___ ___ ☐ Husband ☐ Wife ☐ Joint $___ $___
2. ___ ___ ___ ☐ Husband ☐ Wife ☐ Joint $___ $___
3. ___ ___ ___ ☐ Husband ☐ Wife ☐ Joint $___ $___
4. ___ ___ ___ ☐ Husband ☐ Wife ☐ Joint $___ $___
5. ___ ___ ___ ☐ Husband ☐ Wife ☐ Joint $___ $___

TOTAL SECTION IV: DEBT $___

Supreme Court of Ohio
Uniform Domestic Relations Form – Affidavit 2
Affidavit of Property
Approved under Ohio Civil Rule 84
Effective Date: July 1, 2010

Page 6 of 7

V. BANKRUPTCY

Filed by: Wife, Husband, Both	Date of Filing: Case Number	Date of Discharge or Relief from Stay	Type of Case (Ch. 7, 11, 12, 13)	Current Monthly Payments
1. ☐ Husband ☐ Wife ☐ Both	_____			
	_____	_____	_____	$ _____
2. ☐ Husband ☐ Wife ☐ Both	_____			
	_____	_____	_____	$ _____

TOTAL SECTION V: BANKRUPTCY $ _____

OATH

[Do Not Sign Until Notary is Present]

I, (print name) _____ **swear or affirm that I have read**
this document and, to the best of my knowledge and belief, the facts and information stated in this
document are true, accurate and complete. I understand that if I do not tell the truth, I may be subject to
penalties for perjury.

_____
Your signature

Sworn before me and signed in my presence this _____ day of _____ , _____ .

_____
Notary Public
My Commission Expires:

_____

COURT OF COMMON PLEAS

_____ **COUNTY, OHIO**

_____	Case No. _____
Plaintiff/Petitioner	Judge _____
v./and	Magistrate _____
_____	
Defendant/Petitioner/Respondent	

Instructions: Check local court rules to determine when this form must be filed.
By law, an affidavit must be filed and served with the first pleading filed by each party in every parenting (custody/visitation) proceeding in this Court, including Dissolutions, Divorces and Domestic Violence Petitions. Each party has a continuing duty while this case is pending to inform the Court of any parenting proceeding concerning the child(ren) in any other court in this or any other state. **If more space is needed, add additional pages.**

PARENTING PROCEEDING AFFIDAVIT (R.C. 3127.23(A))

Affidavit of _____
(Print Your Name)

Check and complete ALL THAT APPLY:

1. ☐   I request that the court not disclose my current address or that of the child(ren). My address is confidential pursuant to R.C. 3127.23(D) and should be placed under seal to protect the health, safety, or liberty of myself and/or the child(ren).

2. ☐   Minor child(ren) are subject to this case as follows:

Insert the information requested below for all minor or dependent children of this marriage. You must list the residences for all places where the children have lived for the last **FIVE** years.

a.	Child's Name: _____	Place of Birth: _____
	Date of Birth: _____	Sex: ☐ Male ☐ Female

Period of Residence			Check if Confidential	Person(s) With Whom Child Lived (name & address)	Relationship
_____	to	present	☐ Address Confidential?	_____	_____
_____	to	_____	☐ Address Confidential?	_____	_____
_____	to	_____	☐ Address Confidential?	_____	_____
_____	to	_____	☐ Address Confidential?	_____	_____

Supreme Court of Ohio
Uniform Domestic Relations Form – Affidavit 3
Parenting Proceeding Affidavit
Approved under Ohio Civil Rule 84
Effective Date: July 1, 2010

b.   Child's Name: _____   **Place of Birth:** _____

Date of Birth: _____   **Sex:** ☐ Male ☐ Female

☐ Check this box if the information requested below would be the same as in subsection 2a and skip to the next question.

Period of Residence		Check if Confidential	Person(s) With Whom Child Lived (name & address)	Relationship
_____ to	present	☐ Address Confidential?	_____	_____
_____ to _____		☐ Address Confidential?	_____	_____
_____ to _____		☐ Address Confidential?	_____	_____
_____ to _____		☐ Address Confidential?	_____	_____

c.   Child's Name: _____   **Place of Birth:** _____

Date of Birth: _____   **Sex:** ☐ Male ☐ Female

☐ Check this box if the information requested below would be the same as in subsection 2a and skip to the next question.

Period of Residence		Check if Confidential	Person(s) With Whom Child Lived (name & address)	Relationship
_____ to	present	☐ Address Confidential?	_____	_____
_____ to _____		☐ Address Confidential?	_____	_____
_____ to _____		☐ Address Confidential?	_____	_____
_____ to _____		☐ Address Confidential?	_____	_____

IF MORE SPACE IS NEEDED FOR ADDITIONAL CHILDREN, ATTACH A SEPARATE PAGE AND CHECK THIS BOX ☐.

3.   **Participation in custody case(s): (Check only one box.)**

☐   I **HAVE NOT** participated as a party, witness, or in any capacity in any other case, in this or any other state, concerning the custody of, or visitation (parenting time), with any child subject to this case.

☐   I **HAVE** participated as a party, witness, or in any capacity in any other case, in this or any other state, concerning the custody of, or visitation (parenting time), with any child subject to this case. For each case in which you participated, give the following information:

Supreme Court of Ohio
Uniform Domestic Relations Form – Affidavit 3
Parenting Proceeding Affidavit
Approved under Ohio Civil Rule 84
Effective Date: July 1, 2010

Page 2 of 4

a. Name of each child: _____ _____

_____ _____ _____

b. Type of case: _____

c. Court and State: _____

d. Date and court order or judgment (if any): _____

_____

IF MORE SPACE IS NEEDED FOR ADDITIONAL CUSTODY CASES, ATTACH A SEPARATE PAGE AND CHECK THIS BOX ☐.

4. **Information about other civil case(s) that could affect this case: (Check only one box.)**

☐ **I HAVE NO INFORMATION** about any other civil cases that could affect the current case, including any cases relating to custody, domestic violence or protection orders, dependency, neglect or abuse allegations or adoptions concerning any child subject to this case.

☐ **I HAVE THE FOLLOWING INFORMATION** concerning other civil cases that could affect the current case, including any cases relating to custody, domestic violence or protection orders, dependency, neglect or abuse allegations or adoptions concerning a child subject to this case. Do not repeat cases already listed in Paragraph 3. Explain:

a. Name of each child: _____ _____

_____ _____ _____

b. Type of case: _____

c. Court and State: _____

d. Date and court order or judgment (if any): _____

_____

IF MORE SPACE IS NEEDED FOR ADDITIONAL CASES, ATTACH A SEPARATE PAGE AND CHECK THIS BOX ☐.

5. **Information about criminal case(s):**
List all of the criminal convictions, including guilty pleas, for you and the members of your household for the following offenses: any criminal offense involving acts that resulted in a child being abused or neglected; any domestic violence offense that is a violation of R.C. 2919.25; any sexually oriented offense as defined in R.C. 2950.01; and any offense involving a victim who was a family or household member at the time of the offense and caused physical harm to the victim during the commission of the offense.

Name	Case Number	Court/State/County	Convicted of What Crime?

IF MORE SPACE IS NEEDED FOR ADDITIONAL CASES, ATTACH A SEPARATE PAGE AND CHECK THIS BOX ☐.

Supreme Court of Ohio
Uniform Domestic Relations Form – Affidavit 3
Parenting Proceeding Affidavit
Approved under Ohio Civil Rule 84
Effective Date: July 1, 2010

Page 3 of 4

6. **Persons not a party to this case who have physical custody or claim to have custody or visitation rights to children subject to this case: (Check only one box.)**

    ☐ **I DO NOT KNOW OF ANY PERSON(S)** not a party to this case who has physical custody or claims to have custody or visitation rights with respect to any child subject to this case.

    ☐ **I KNOW THAT THE FOLLOWING NAMED PERSON(S)** not a party to this case has/have physical custody or claim(s) to have custody or visitation rights with respect to any child subject to this case.

    a.   Name/Address of Person _____
    ☐ Has physical custody   ☐ Claims custody rights   ☐ Claims visitation rights
    Name of each child: _____   _____   _____

    _____   _____   _____

    b.   Name/Address of Person _____
    ☐ Has physical custody   ☐ Claims custody rights   ☐ Claims visitation rights
    Name of each child: _____   _____   _____

    _____   _____   _____

    c.   Name/Address of Person _____
    ☐ Has physical custody   ☐ Claims custody rights   ☐ Claims visitation rights
    Name of each child: _____   _____   _____

    _____   _____   _____

OATH

[Do Not Sign Until Notary is Present]

I, (print name) _____ , swear or affirm that I have read this document and, to the best of my knowledge and belief, the facts and information stated in this document are true, accurate and complete. I understand that if I do not tell the truth, I may be subject to penalties for perjury.

_____
Your signature

Sworn before me and signed in my presence this ____ day of _____ , _____ .

_____
Notary Public

My Commission Expires:

_____

Supreme Court of Ohio
Uniform Domestic Relations Form – Affidavit 3
Parenting Proceeding Affidavit
Approved under Ohio Civil Rule 84
Effective Date: July 1, 2010

COURT OF COMMON PLEAS
_____ COUNTY, OHIO

_____   Case No. _____

Plaintiff/Petitioner   Judge _____

v./and

                                           Magistrate _____

_____

Defendant/Petitioner

> **Instructions:** Check local court rules to determine when this form must be filed.
> This affidavit is used to disclose health insurance coverage that is available for children. It is also used to determine child support. It must be filed if there are minor children of the relationship. **If more space is needed, add additional pages.**

HEALTH INSURANCE AFFIDAVIT

Affidavit of _____
(Print Your Name)

	Mother	**Father**
Are your child(ren) currently enrolled in a low-income government-assisted health care program (Healthy Start/Medicaid)?	☐ Yes ☐ No	☐ Yes ☐ No
Are you enrolled in an individual (non-group or COBRA) health insurance plan?	☐ Yes ☐ No	☐ Yes ☐ No
Are you enrolled in a health insurance plan through a group (employer or other organization)?	☐ Yes ☐ No	☐ Yes ☐ No
If you are not enrolled, do you have health insurance available through a group (employer or other organization)?	☐ Yes ☐ No	☐ Yes ☐ No
Does the available insurance cover primary care services within 30 miles of the child(ren)'s home?	☐ Yes ☐ No	☐ Yes ☐ No

Supreme Court of Ohio
Uniform Domestic Relations Form – Affidavit 4
Health Insurance Affidavit
Approved under Ohio Civil Rule 84
Effective Date: July 1, 2010

Page 1 of 2

	Mother	**Father**
Under the available insurance, what would be the annual premium for a plan covering you and the child(ren) of this relationship (not including a spouse)?	$ _____	$ _____
Under the available insurance, what would be the annual premium for a plan covering you alone (not including children or spouse)?	$ _____	$ _____

If you are enrolled in a health insurance plan through a group (employer or other organization) or individual insurance plan, which of the following people is/are covered:

	Mother	Father
Yourself?	☐ Yes ☐ No	☐ Yes ☐ No
Your spouse?	☐ Yes ☐ No	☐ Yes ☐ No
Minor child(ren) of this relationship?	☐ Yes ☐ No Number _____	☐ Yes ☐ No Number _____
Other individuals?	☐ Yes ☐ No Number _____	☐ Yes ☐ No Number _____
Name of group (employer or organization) that provides health insurance	_____	_____
Address	_____ _____	_____ _____
Phone number	_____	_____

OATH

[Do not sign until notary is present.]

I, (print name) _____ , swear or affirm that I have read this document and, to the best of my knowledge and belief, the facts and information stated in this document are true, accurate and complete. I understand that if I do not tell the truth, I may be subject to penalties for perjury.

_____
Your signature

Sworn before me and signed in my presence this _____ day of _____ , _____ .

_____
Notary Public
My commission expires:

_____

Supreme Court of Ohio
Uniform Domestic Relations Form – Affidavit 4
Health Insurance Affidavit
Approved under Ohio Civil Rule 84
Effective Date: July 1, 2010

COURT OF COMMON PLEAS

_____ COUNTY, OHIO

_____   Case No.   _____

Plaintiff   Judge   _____

               v.   Magistrate _____

_____

Defendant

Instructions: Check local court rules to determine when this form must be filed.
This form is used to request temporary orders in your divorce or legal separation case. After a party serves a Motion and Affidavit, the other party has 14 days to file a Counter Affidavit and serve it on the party who filed the motion. **If more space is needed, add additional pages.**

MOTION AND AFFIDAVIT OR COUNTER AFFIDAVIT
FOR TEMPORARY ORDERS
WITHOUT ORAL HEARING

Check one box below to show whether you are filing a (1) Motion and Affidavit or (2) Counter Affidavit.

☐   **(1) Motion and Affidavit**

(Print Your Name)   _____ files this Motion and Affidavit under Rule 75(N) of the Ohio Rules of Civil Procedure to request the temporary orders checked here.

Check only those that apply.   _____   Residential parenting rights (custody)

                                    _____   Parenting time (visitation)

                                    _____   Child support

                                    _____   Spousal support (alimony)

                                    _____   Payment of debts and/or expenses

THE OTHER PARTY HAS 14 DAYS FROM THE DATE ON WHICH THIS MOTION IS SERVED TO FILE A COUNTER AFFIDAVIT AND SERVE IT UPON THE PARTY WHO FILED THE MOTION. (See below.)

☐   **(2) Counter Affidavit**

(Print Your Name)   _____ files this Counter Affidavit in response to a Motion and Affidavit.

Supreme Court of Ohio
Uniform Domestic Relations Form – Affidavit 5
Motion and Affidavit or Counter Affidavit for Temporary Orders
    Without Oral Hearing
Approved under Ohio Civil Rule 84
Effective Date: July 1, 2010   Page 1 of 4

Complete the following information, whether filing Motion and Affidavit or Counter Affidavit. Check all that apply.

1. ☐ My spouse and I are living separately.

        Date of separation is   _____ .

    ☐ My spouse and I are living together.

    ☐ We have no minor children. (Skip to number 5.)

    ☐ There are minor child(ren) who are adopted or born of this marriage.
       (List children here.)

Name	Date of birth	Living with
_____	_____	_____
_____	_____	_____
_____	_____	_____
_____	_____	_____

    ☐ In addition to the above children there is/are in my household:

           _____ adult(s)

           _____ other minor and/or dependent child(ren).

2. My child(ren) attend(s) school in:

    ☐ Father's school district

    ☐ Mother's school district

    ☐ Open enrollment

    ☐ Other (Explain.) _____ .

    ☐ All children do not attend school in the same district. (Explain.)

_____

3. ☐ I request to be named the temporary residential parent and legal custodian of the child(ren).

    (Specify child(ren) if request is not for all children.) _____

    ☐ I do not object to my spouse being named the temporary residential parent of the child(ren).

    ☐ I request the following parenting time order:

        ☐ The Court's standard parenting order (See county's local rules of court.)

        ☐ A specific parenting time order as follows:

_____

_____

Supreme Court of Ohio
Uniform Domestic Relations Form – Affidavit 5
Motion and Affidavit or Counter Affidavit for Temporary Orders
   Without Oral Hearing
Approved under Ohio Civil Rule 84
Effective Date: July 1, 2010   Page 2 of 4

☐   I have reached an agreement regarding parenting time with my spouse as follows:

_____

_____

☐   I request that my spouse's parenting time (visitation) be supervised. (Explain--supervised parenting time order will NOT be granted if the reasons are not explained.)

_____

_____

Name of an appropriate supervisor   _____

4.   ☐   A court or agency has made a child support order concerning the child(ren).

Name of Court/Agency   _____

Date of Order   _____

SETS No.   _____

5.   I request the Court to order my spouse to pay:

☐ $ _____ child support per month

☐ $ _____ spousal support per month

☐ $ _____ attorney fees, expert fees, court costs

☐   The following debts and/or expenses:

_____

_____

☐   Other

_____

6.   ☐   I am willing to attend mediation.

☐   I am not willing to attend mediation.

☐   I request the following court services. (See local rules of court for available services.)

_____

_____

State specific reasons why court services are required.

_____

_____

Supreme Court of Ohio
Uniform Domestic Relations Form – Affidavit 5
Motion and Affidavit or Counter Affidavit for Temporary Orders
    Without Oral Hearing
Approved under Ohio Civil Rule 84
Effective Date: July 1, 2010   Page 3 of 4

OATH

[Do not sign until notary is present.]

I, (print name) _____ , swear or affirm that I have read
this document and, to the best of my knowledge and belief, the facts and information stated in this
document are true, accurate and complete. I understand that if I do not tell the truth, I may be subject to
penalties for perjury.

_____
Your signature

Sworn before me and signed in my presence this _____ day of _____ , _____ .

_____
Notary Public
My commission expires:

NOTICE OF HEARING
(Check with local court for scheduling procedure.)

You are hereby given notice that this motion for temporary orders will be heard upon affidavits only, and
without oral testimony, before Judge/Magistrate _____ ,
Hearing Room _____ , at _____ a.m./p.m. on _____ , 20 _____ , at
_____ , _____ floor .

CERTIFICATE OF SERVICE

Check the boxes that apply.

I delivered a copy of my: ☐ Motion and Affidavit or ☐ Counter Affidavit

On: (Date) _____ , 20 _____

To: (Print name of other party's attorney or, if there is no attorney, print name of the party.)

_____

At: (Print address or fax number.)

_____ .

By: ☐   U.S. Mail
      ☐   Fax
      ☐   Messenger
      ☐   Clerk of courts (if address is unknown)

_____
Your signature

Supreme Court of Ohio
Uniform Domestic Relations Form – Affidavit 5
Motion and Affidavit or Counter Affidavit for Temporary Orders
   Without Oral Hearing
Approved under Ohio Civil Rule 84
Effective Date: July 1, 2010

Page 4 of 4

TIME TABLE UNDER THE CIVIL RULES

A. GENERAL PROVISIONS

1. Computation of Time
2. Extension of Time
3. Expiration of Term
4. Time for Service of a Motion
5. Additional Time if Service by Mail
6. Time for Filing Papers After Service

B. COMMENCEMENT OF THE ACTION AND SERVICE OF PROCESS

1. Commencement of the Action
2. Statute of Limitations
3. Issuance of Original Summons
4. Issuance of Separate or Additional Summons
5. Return of Personal or Residence Service
6. Notification by Clerk if Service Fails
7. Amendment of Process
8. Time Limit for Service

C. PLEADINGS AND MOTIONS

1. Removal to Federal Court
2. Answer to Complaint
3. Answer to Cross-Claim
4. Reply to Counterclaim
5. Reply Ordered by Court
6. Time for Pleading Altered by Service of Motion
7. Motion for Definite Statement
8. Motion to Strike
9. Motions Presenting Defenses to Pleadings
10. Motion for Judgment on the Pleadings
11. Motion for Summary Judgment
12. Counterclaim
13. Cross-Claim
14. Third-Party Complaint
15. Answer, Counterclaim or Cross-Claim to Third-Party Complaint
16. Amended Pleadings
17. Response to Amended Pleadings
18. Supplemental Pleadings
19. Motion to Drop or Add Parties
20. Intervention
21. Suggestion of Death or Incompetency
22. Substitution of Parties in Event of Death or Incompetency
23. Demand for Jury Trial
24. Injunctions
25. Divorce, Annulment, and Legal Separation Actions

D. DISCOVERY

1. Perpetuation of Testimony
2. Oral Depositions
3. Depositions Upon Written Questions
4. Notice of Filing of a Deposition
5. Motion to Suppress Deposition
6. Interrogatories
7. Production of Documents and Entry Upon Land
8. Physical and Mental Examinations
9. Requests for Admission
10. Sequence and Timing of Discovery
11. Supplementation of Responses

E. TRIAL

1. Written Interrogatories to Jury
2. Motion for Directed Verdict
3. Motion for Judgment Notwithstanding the Verdict
4. Instructions to the Jury
5. Trial to the Court
6. Magistrates

F. DISMISSALS AND JUDGMENTS

1. Voluntary Dismissal
2. Dismissal by Stipulation
3. Dismissal by Order of Court
4. Involuntary Dismissal
5. Amendment of Demand for Money Damages
6. Default Judgment
7. Entry of Judgment
8. Motion for New Trial
9. Clerical Mistakes in Judgment
10. Motion for Relief From Judgment
11. Time for Perfecting Appeal

A. GENERAL PROVISIONS

1. Computation of Time.

In computing any period of time prescribed or allowed by the Civil Rules, by the local rules of any court, by order of court, or by any applicable statute, the day of the act, event or default from which the designated period of time begins to run shall not be included. The last day of the period so computed shall be included, unless it is a Saturday, a Sunday, or a legal holiday, in which event the period runs until the end of the next day which is not a Saturday, a Sunday, or a legal holiday. When the period of time prescribed or allowed is less than seven days, intermediate Saturdays, Sundays, and legal holidays shall be excluded in the computation. When a public office in which an act, required by law, rule, or order of court, is to be performed is closed to the public for the entire day which constitutes the last day for doing such an act, or before its usual closing time on such day, then such act may be performed on the next succeeding day which is not a Saturday, a Sunday, or a legal holiday.[1]

For example, if the day of the order is Wednesday, and the time permitted is fourteen days, the last day for performing the act shall be Wednesday two weeks hence unless that day is a legal holiday in which case the day after, Thursday, is the final day. If the day of the order is Wednesday and the time permitted is five days, the final day is the following Wednesday as the intermediate Saturday and Sunday are excluded. If a legal holiday intervenes, that day is also excluded.

When a public office in which an act, required by law, rule, or order of the court, is to be performed is closed to the public for the entire day which constitutes the last day for doing such an act, or before its usual closing time on such day, then such act may be performed on the next succeeding day which is not a Saturday, a Sunday, or a legal holiday.[2]

2. Extension of Time.

Under no circumstances may time be extended for serving a motion for judgment notwithstanding a verdict, a motion for a new trial, or a motion for relief from a judgment. Otherwise the court for cause shown may at any time in its discretion with or without motion or notice order the time enlarged if request therefore is made before the expiration of the period originally prescribed or as extended by a previous order. However if the specified time for performing the act has expired, the court may permit the act to be done only upon motion where the failure to act was the result of excusable neglect.[3]

3. Expiration of Term.

The period of time provided for the doing of any act or the taking of any proceeding is not affected or limited by the continued existence or expiration of a term of court.[4] In other words, if fourteen days is provided for taking action, there is always fourteen days as computed under Civil Rule 6(A) regardless of the term of court.

4. Time for Service of a Motion.

A written motion, other than one which may be heard ex parte, and notice of the hearing thereof shall be served not later than seven days before the time fixed for the hearing, unless a different time is fixed by the Civil Rules or by order of the court.[5] The affidavits supporting the motion shall be served with the motion and opposing affidavits may be served not later than one day before the hearing unless the court permits them to be served at some other time.

5. Additional Time if Service by Mail.

Three days are added to the time prescribed for doing an act or taking a proceeding if the service of the notice or paper pertaining to the matter is served by mail.[6] The reason for the additional time is that the time is calculated from the date of mailing and three days are allowed for delivery. This added time does not apply to service of original summons as the answer time is figured from receipt of the summons rather than the mailing thereof.

6. Time for Filing Papers After Service.

All papers, after the complaint, required to be served upon a party shall be filed with the court within three days after service.[7]

Discovery papers shall not be filed unless on order of the court or for use as evidence or for consideration of a motion in the proceeding.[8]

Time for filing by electronic means may be provided for by local rule of court.[9]

B. COMMENCEMENT OF THE ACTION AND SERVICE OF PROCESS

1. Commencement of the Action.

An action is not commenced unless service is obtained within one year from filing of the complaint.[10]

2. Statute of Limitations.

The Civil Rules do not affect the statute of limitations. Applicable statutes should be checked to determine the time permitted for bringing the particular action involved.

3. Issuance of Original Summons.

Upon the filing of a complaint the clerk shall forthwith issue a summons for service upon each defendant.[11]

4. Issuance of Separate or Additional Summons

Upon request of the plaintiff separate or additional summons shall issue at any time against any defendant.[12]

5. Return of Personal or Residence Service.

The person serving process is required to serve the process within twenty-eight days or to make return to the clerk indicating the reasons for failure to make service.[13] Failure to make service within the twenty-eight day period does not affect the validity of service.

6. Notification by Clerk if Service Fails.

The clerk is required to notify, by mail, forthwith the attorney or party, if no attorney of record, at whose instance process was issued.[14]

7. Amendment of Process.

The court may at any time allow the amendment of any process or proof of service thereof, unless the amendment would cause material prejudice to the party against whom process was issued.[15]

8. Time Limit for Service.

If a service of the summons and complaint is not made upon a defendant within six months after the filing of the complaint and the party on whose behalf such service was required cannot show good cause why such service was not made within that period, the action shall be dismissed as to that defendant without prejudice upon the court's own initiative with notice to such party or upon motion. This division shall not apply to out-of-state service pursuant to Rule 4.3 or to service in a foreign country pursuant to Rule 4.5.[16]

C. PLEADINGS AND MOTIONS

1. Removal to Federal Court.

Notice of removal must be filed within 30 days after receipt of the initial pleading setting forth a claim on which removal is based, or within 30 days after the service of the summons if the initial pleading has then been filed in the court and is not required to be served on the defendant, whichever period is shorter. It is further provided that if the cause stated by the initial pleading is not removable, the petition for removal may be filed within 30 days after receipt by the defendant, through service or otherwise, a copy of the motion or pleading from which it may first be ascertained that the case is one which is or has become removable.[17]

2. Answer to Complaint.

The answer must be served within twenty-eight days after service of the summons and complaint upon the defendant; if service is by publication, the answer must be served within twenty-eight days after the completion of service by publication.[18]

3. Answer to Cross-Claim.

The answer must be served within twenty-eight days after service of the cross-claim.[19]

4. Reply to Counterclaim.

The reply must be served within twenty-eight days after service of the pleading containing the counterclaim.[20]

5. Reply Ordered by Court.

The reply must be served within twenty-eight days after service of the order, unless the order otherwise directs.[21]

6. Time for Pleading Altered by Service of Motion.

The time for responses to a pleading are altered by service of a motion. If the court denies a motion, a responsive pleading, delayed because of service of the motion, shall be served within fourteen days after notice of the court's action unless a different time is fixed by order of the court. If the court grants the motion, the responsive pleading, delayed because of service of the motion, shall be served within fourteen days after service of the pleading which complies with the court order.[22]

7. Motion for Definite Statement.

This motion must be served within the period permitted for a responsive pleading which cannot be framed without further information. If the motion is granted, the pleading must be amended within fourteen days after notice of the order.[23]

8. Motion to Strike.

This motion must be made before responding to a pleading within the time permitted therefore or within twenty-eight days after the pleading to which it is directed is served if no responsive pleading is permitted.[24]

9. Motions Presenting Defenses to Pleadings.

If presented by motion, defenses described in Civil Rule 12(B) must be served within the time permitted for a responsive pleading and they must be served before a pleading is served.[25]

10. Motion for Judgment on the Pleadings.

A motion for judgment on the pleadings must be served after the pleadings are closed but within such time as to not delay the trial.[26]

11. Motion for Summary Judgment.

This motion may be served by the party seeking affirmative relief at any time after the expiration of the time permitted for a responsive motion or pleading by the adverse party or after service of a motion for summary judgment by the adverse party. The defending party may move for summary judgment at any time. If the action has been set for pretrial or trial, a motion for summary judgment may be made only with leave of court.[27]

The motion for summary judgment must be served at least fourteen days before hearing.[28]

12. Counterclaim.

Any counterclaim may be asserted within the time permitted for pleading and thereafter with leave of court by amendment.[29]

13. Cross-Claim.

A cross-claim must be served within the time permitted for pleading.[30]

14. Third-Party Complaint.

The defending party may serve a third-party complaint without leave of court not later than fourteen days after service of his answer. Otherwise leave of court is required.[31]

15. Answer, Counterclaim or Cross-Claim to Third-Party Complaint.

Responses to a third-party complaint shall be served within twenty-eight days after service of the third-party complaint.[32]

16. Amended Pleadings.

A party may amend a pleading without leave at any time before a responsive pleading is served or, if no responsive pleading is permitted and the action has not been placed upon the trial calendar, within twenty-eight days after it is served. Thereafter leave of court is required.[33]

17. Response to Amended Pleadings.

A party shall plead in response to an amended pleading within the time remaining for response to the original pleading or within fourteen days after service of the amended pleading, whichever is longer, unless the court otherwise orders.[34]

18. Supplemental Pleadings.

Supplemental pleadings may be served with leave of court upon motion served at any time.[35]

19. Motion to Drop or Add Parties.

Parties may be dropped or added at any time upon motion of a party with leave of court or on the court's own initiative.[36]

20. Intervention.

A motion to intervene either of right or permissively must be timely served.[37]

21. Suggestion of Death or Incompetency.

The attorney of record of the party is required to suggest such fact on the record and serve notice on all other parties within fourteen days after acquiring actual knowledge thereof.[38]

22. Substitution of Parties in Event of Death or Incompetency.

Where substitution is required, a motion for substitution must be served not later than ninety days after suggestion is made upon the record.[39]

23. Demand for Jury Trial.

A jury demand must be made in writing not later than fourteen days after service of the last pleading directed to the issue.[40]

24. Injunctions.

A temporary restraining order, except in domestic relations court, expires within fourteen days unless extended for one like period.[41]

25. Divorce, Annulment, and Legal Separation Actions.

No action may be heard and decided until forty-two days after the service of process or twenty-eight days after the last publication. Such action may not be heard and decided until twenty-eight days after service of a counterclaim unless a written waiver is filed.[42]

Notice of trial must be mailed to the adverse party who has no counsel of record at least seven days prior to the commencement.[43]

Upon written request not less than seven days before trial, the investigator's report shall be made available.[44]

Affidavits may be filed with a pleading or motion for spousal support, child support, maintenance, and allocation of parental rights and responsibilities pendente lite. The other party may file counter affidavits within fourteen days from service. If temporary orders are made on affidavits, upon request the court shall grant a party an oral hearing within twenty-eight days.[45]

D. DISCOVERY

1. Perpetuation of Testimony.

Service of notice with a copy of the petition must be made upon the expected adverse parties at least twenty-eight days before the date of hearing unless the court prescribes shorter notice.[46]

2. Oral Depositions.

After commencement of the action, any party may take the testimony of any person upon reasonable notice in writing to every other party to the action.[47]

A transcribed deposition must be signed by the witness within thirty days from submission of the deposition to the witness to review and sign the deposition unless the deposition is taken within thirty days of a trial or hearing, in which case the witness has seven days to review and sign the deposition, or within less than seven days of a trial or hearing, in which case the court may establish a deadline for the witness to review and sign the deposition.[48]

3. Deposition Upon Written Questions.

Notice and written questions may be served at any time after commencement of the action by any party thereto. Within twenty-one days thereafter, cross questions may be served. Redirect questions may be served within fourteen days after service of the cross questions and recross questions within fourteen days after service of the cross questions.[49]

4. Notice of Filing of a Deposition.

The party requesting the filing is required to give notice of its filing to all other parties.[50] The deposition must be filed at least one day before the trial or hearing if it is to be presented as evidence unless the court permits a later filing.[51]

5. Motion to Suppress Deposition.

A motion to suppress the deposition or some part thereof must be made with reasonable promptness after the defect is ascertained.[52]

6. Interrogatories.

Interrogatories may be served upon the plaintiff after commencement of the action and upon any other party with or after service of the summons and complaint upon that party.[53] Answers and objections to interrogatories must be served within a period designated by the party submitting the interrogatories, not less than twenty-eight days after service unless the court allows a shorter or longer time.[54]

7. Production of Documents and Entry Upon Land.

A request therefore may be served upon the plaintiff after commencement of the action and upon any other party with or after service of the summons and complaint upon that party. A reasonable time, not less than twenty-eight days after service, shall be specified in the request. The other party has twenty-eight days to serve a response unless the court specifies a different time.[55]

8. Physical and Mental Examinations.

A motion for submission to such examination may be served upon the person to be examined and all parties at any time after commencement of the action.[56]

9. Requests for Admission.

Any party may serve a request at any time after commencement of the action. The request must designate a time for response of not less than twenty-eight days after service. Answers or objections must be served within the specified time unless the court orders a different time.[57]

10. Sequence and Timing of Discovery.

Unless the court orders otherwise, methods of discovery may be used simultaneously or in any sequence.[58]

11. Supplementation of Responses.

A party is required to supplement responses seasonably when required to supplement.[59]

E. TRIAL

1. Written Interrogatories to Jury.

Any party who wishes to submit written interrogatories to the jury must submit a request to the court prior to the commencement of the argument. Copies of the proposed interrogatories must be submitted at that time.[60]

2. Motion for Directed Verdict.

A motion for a directed verdict may be made on the opening statement of the opponent, at the close of the opponent's evidence or at the close of all the evidence.[61]

3. Motion for Judgment Notwithstanding the Verdict.

A motion for judgment notwithstanding the verdict must be made not later than fourteen days after entry of judgment. If a verdict was not returned, a motion for judgment must be served within fourteen days after the jury has been discharged.[62] The time for making this motion cannot be extended.[63] If the motion or a motion for a directed verdict is granted, the court is required to state the basis for its decision prior to or simultaneous with the entry of judgment.[64]

4. Instructions to the Jury.

Complete instructions except cautionary instructions must be given after the arguments are completed. The court also may give some or all of its instructions prior to arguments. Written requests for instructions must be filed at the close of the evidence or at such earlier time during the trial as the court directs.[65]

5. Trial to the Court.

The court may render judgment generally for the prevailing party unless one of the parties in writing requests otherwise before the entry of judgment, or not later than seven days after the party filing the request has been given notice of the court's announcement of its decision, whichever is later.[66]

6. Magistrates.

Subject to the terms of the relevant reference, a magistrate may enter orders without judicial approval if necessary to regulate the proceedings and if not dispositive of a claim or defense of a party. Any party may file, not later than ten days after the magistrate's order is filed, a motion with the court to set an order, stating the party's reasons with particularity. The pendency of a motion to set aside does not stay the effectiveness of the magistrate's order unless the magistrate or the court grants a stay.[67]

Within fourteen days of the filing of a proposed decision, a party may file written objections to the proposed decision. If any party timely files objections, any other party may also file objections not later than ten days after the first objections are filed. If a party makes a request for findings of fact and conclusions of law under Civ. R. 52, the time for filing objections begins to run only when the magistrate files a proposed decision including findings of fact and conclusions of law. Objections to a magistrate's decision must be specific and state with particularity all grounds for objection.[68]

Objections to factual findings must be supported by a transcript of all the evidence submitted to the magistrate relevant to that finding or an affidavit of that evidence if a transcript is not available. The objecting party must file the transcript or affidavit with the court within thirty days after filing objections unless the court extends the time in writing. A party may with leave of court supplement objections filed prior to the date on which the transcript is prepared.[69]

F. DISMISSALS AND JUDGMENTS

1. Voluntary Dismissal.

The plaintiff may voluntarily dismiss an action without leave at any time before commencement of the trial by filing a notice of dismissal.[70]

2. Dismissal by Stipulation.

The plaintiff may dismiss at any time without leave by filing a stipulation of dismissal signed by all parties who have appeared in the action.[71]

3. Dismissal by Order of Court.

An action may be dismissed upon motion of plaintiff at any time upon approval of court upon such terms and conditions as the court deems proper.[72]

4. Involuntary Dismissal.

The defendant may move for dismissal or the court upon notice may dismiss at any time for failure to prosecute or to comply with the Civil Rules or an order of court.[73] The defendant may move for dismissal at the conclusion of plaintiff's evidence in a non-jury action.[74]

5. Amendment of Demand for Money Damages.

The provision that demand for judgment for money must be amended not later than seven days before the commencement of the trial has been deleted.[75]

6. Default Judgment.

Notice of application for judgment must be served upon a defaulting party who has previously appeared in the action at least seven days before the hearing on the application.[76]

7. Entry of Judgment.

Within three days of entering the judgment upon the journal, the clerk shall serve the parties in a manner prescribed by Civ. R. 5(B) and note the service in the appearance docket. Upon serving the notice and notation of the service in the appearance docket, the service is complete. The failure of the clerk to serve notice does not affect the validity of the judgment or the running of the time for appeal except as provided in App. R. 4(A).

76a. Civil Rule 58(B).

The court shall promptly cause the judgment to be prepared and entered after a jury verdict or decision of the court unless it is a partial disposition only.[77]

If trial is to the court, a general verdict may be rendered immediately unless a party in writing requests otherwise before the entry of judgment, or not later than seven days after the party filing the request has been given notice of the court's announcement of its decision, whichever is later, in which case, the court shall state in writing the conclusions of fact found separately from the conclusions of law.[78]

8. Motion for New Trial.

A motion for a new trial must be served not later than fourteen days after the entry of judgment.[79] The court may grant a new trial on its own initiative not later than fourteen days after entry of judgment.[80] These time periods are mandatory and may not be extended.[81]

9. Clerical Mistakes in Judgment.

Clerical mistakes may be corrected at any time by the court on its own initiative or on the motion of any party.[82]

10. Motion for Relief From Judgment.

A motion for relief from judgment must be made within a reasonable time and not to exceed one year if based upon mistake, inadvertence, surprise or excusable neglect, newly discovered evidence, or fraud.[83]

The one-year period is mandatory and may not be extended.[84]

11. Time for Perfecting Appeal.

The time for perfecting an appeal ordinarily runs from the date of the judgment entry. However, if a motion for judgment notwithstanding the verdict or motion for new trial is properly served, the time permitted for appeal begins to run when the order disposing of the motion is entered.[85]

1. Civil Rule 6(A).
2. *Id.*
3. Civil Rule 6(B).
4. Civil Rule 6(C).
5. Civil Rule 6(D).
6. Civil Rule 6(E).
7. Civil Rule 5(D).
8. *Id.*
9. Civil Rule 5(E) and 73(J).
10. Civil Rule 3(A).
11. Civil Rule 4(A).
12. *Id.*
13. Civil Rule 4.1(B) and 4.1(C).
14. Civil Rule 4.1(A), 4.1(B), and 4.1(C).
15. Civil Rule 4.6(B).
16. Civil Rule 4(E).
17. 28 U.S.C. Sec. 1446 (b).
18. Civil Rule 12(A)(1).
19. Civil Rule 12(A)(2).
20. *Id.*
21. *Id.*
22. *Id.*
23. Civil Rule 12(E).
24. Civil Rule 12(F).
25. Civil Rule 12(B).
26. Civil Rule 12(C).
27. Civil Rule 56(A) and (B).
28. Civil Rule 56(C).
29. Civil Rule 13.
30. Civil Rule 13(G).
31. Civil Rule 14(A).
32. Civil Rule 12(A); Civil Rule 14(A).
33. Civil Rule 15(A).
34. *Id.*
35. Civil Rule 15(E).
36. Civil Rule 21.
37. Civil Rule 24.
38. Civil Rule 25(E).
39. Civil Rule 25(A).
40. Civil Rule 38(B).
41. Civil Rule 65(A).
42. Civil Rule 75(K).
43. Civil Rule 75(L).
44. Civil Rule 75(D).
45. Civil Rule 75(N).
46. Civil Rule 27(A)(2).
47. Civil Rule 30(A) and (B)(1).
48. Civil Rule 30(E).
49. Civil Rule 31.
50. Civil Rule 30(F)(3) and 31(C).
51. Civil Rule 32(A).
52. Civil Rule 32(D)(4).
53. Civil Rule 33(A).
54. *Id.*
55. Civil Rule 34(B).
56. Civil Rule 35.
57. Civil Rule 36(A).
58. Civil Rule 26(D).
59. Civil Rule 26(E).
60. Civil Rule 49(B).
61. Civil Rule 50(A)(1).
62. Civil Rule 50(B).
63. Civil Rule 6(B).
64. Civil Rule 50(E).
65. Civil Rule 51(A) and (B).
66. Civil Rule 52.
67. Civil Rule 53(D)(2)(a)(i), (b), (b).
68. Civil Rule 53(D)(3)(b)(i), (ii).
69. Civil Rule 53(D)(3)(b)(iii).
70. Civil Rule 41(A)(1).
71. *Id.*
72. Civil Rule 41(A)(2).
73. Civil Rule 41(B)(1).
74. Civil Rule 41(B)(2).
75. Civil Rule 54(C), effective 7-1-94.
76. Civil Rule 55(A).
77. Civil Rule 58.
78. Civil Rule 52.
79. Civil Rule 59(B).
80. Civil Rule 59(D).
81. Civil Rule 6(B).
82. Civil Rule 60(A).
83. Civil Rule 60(B).
84. Civil Rule 6(B).
85. Appellate Rule 4(A) and (B)(2).

Index to Ohio Rules of Civil Procedure

OHIO RULES OF CRIMINAL PROCEDURE

APPENDIX OF FORMS

RULE 1. Scope of Rules: Applicability; Construction; Exceptions

(A) **Applicability.** These rules prescribe the procedure to be followed in all courts of this state in the exercise of criminal jurisdiction, with the exceptions stated in division (C) of this rule.

(B) **Purpose and construction.** These rules are intended to provide for the just determination of every criminal proceeding. They shall be construed and applied to secure the fair, impartial, speedy, and sure administration of justice, simplicity in procedure, and the elimination of unjustifiable expense and delay.

(C) **Exceptions.** These rules, to the extent that specific procedure is provided by other rules of the Supreme Court or to the extent that they would by their nature be clearly inapplicable, shall not apply to procedure (1) upon appeal to review any judgment, order or ruling, (2) upon extradition and rendition of fugitives, (3) in cases covered by the Uniform Traffic Rules, (4) upon the application and enforcement of peace bonds, (5) in juvenile proceedings against a child as defined in Rule 2(D) of the Rules of Juvenile Procedure, (6) upon forfeiture of property for violation of a statute of this state, or (7) upon the collection of fines and penalties. Where any statute or rule provides for procedure by a general or specific reference to the statutes governing procedure in criminal actions, the procedure shall be in accordance with these rules.

History: Amended, eff 7-1-75; 7-1-96.

NOTES TO DECISIONS

ANALYSIS

Applicability
Juvenile proceedings

───────────

Applicability

Inmate's declaratory judgment action against a county prosecutor pursuant to RC § 2721.03, seeking withdrawal of his guilty plea, required dismissal other than for failure to comply with pleading requirements, as relief from the plea could only be obtained from the trial court pursuant to Ohio R. Crim. P. 32.1 and as such, the prosecutor had no authority to provide such relief and was not a proper party; further, the criminal rules did not apply in the civil context of the declaratory judgment, pursuant to Ohio R. Crim. P. 1(A). Hall v. Watkins, — Ohio App. 3d —, 2007 Ohio 209, — N.E. 2d —, 2007 Ohio App. LEXIS 196 (Jan. 19, 2007).

Trial court properly denied defendant's motion for leave to file a motion for new trial pursuant to Ohio R. Crim. P. 33(B), as he did not meet his burden of establishing by clear and convincing proof that he was unavoidably prevented from filing his motion within the statutory time limits. Although Rule 33(B) was silent regarding a time limit for filing the motion, reliance on Ohio R. Crim. P. 1(B) and 57(B) indicated that defendant's knowledge of various individuals' evidence years prior to the making of his motion was an unreasonable delay, for which no explanation was offered. State v. Berry, — Ohio App. 3d —, 2007 Ohio 2244, — N.E. 2d —, 2007 Ohio App. LEXIS 2083 (May 10, 2007).

Juvenile proceedings

Motion for acquittal under Ohio R. Crim. P. 29 was allowed in a juvenile delinquency proceeding, as it was arguably within the extended scope of Ohio R. Crim. P. 1(C) since no specific procedure for an analogous motion was found in the Ohio Rules of Juvenile Procedure. In re A.K., — Ohio App. 3d —, 2007 Ohio 2095, — N.E. 2d —, 2007 Ohio App. LEXIS 1951 (Apr. 27, 2007).

RULE 2.   Definitions

As used in these rules:

(A) "Felony" means an offense defined by law as a felony.

(B) "Misdemeanor" means an offense defined by law as a misdemeanor.

(C) "Serious offense" means any felony, and any misdemeanor for which the penalty prescribed by law includes confinement for more than six months.

(D) "Petty offense" means a misdemeanor other than a serious offense.

(E) "Judge" means judge of the court of common pleas, juvenile court, municipal court, or county court, or the mayor or mayor's court magistrate of a municipal corporation having a mayor's court.

(F) "Magistrate" means any person appointed by a court pursuant to Crim. R. 19. "Magistrate" does not include an official included within the definition of magistrate contained in section 2931.01 of the Revised Code, or a mayor's court magistrate appointed pursuant to section 1905.05 of the Revised Code.

(G) "Prosecuting attorney" means the attorney general of this state, the prosecuting attorney of a county, the law director, city solicitor, or other officer who prosecutes a criminal case on behalf of the state or a city, village, township, or other political subdivision, and the assistant or assistants of any of them. As used in Crim. R. 6, "prosecuting attorney" means the attorney general of this state, the prosecuting attorney of a county, and the assistant or assistants of either of them.

(H) "State" means this state, a county, city, village, township, other political subdivision, or any other entity of this state that may prosecute a criminal action.

(I) "Clerk of court" means the duly elected or appointed clerk of any court of record or the deputy clerk, and the mayor or mayor's court magistrate of a municipal corporation having a mayor's court.

(J) "Law enforcement officer" means a sheriff, deputy sheriff, constable, municipal police officer, marshal, deputy marshal, or state highway patrolman, and also means any officer, agent, or employee of the state or any of its agencies, instrumentalities, or political subdivisions, upon whom, by statute, the authority to arrest violators is conferred, when the officer, agent, or employee is acting within the limits of statutory authority. The definition of "law enforcement officer" con-

tained in this rule shall not be construed to limit, modify, or expand any statutory definition, to the extent the statutory definition applies to matters not covered by the Rules of Criminal Procedure.

History: Amended, eff 7-1-76; 7-1-90.

NOTES TO DECISIONS

Analysis

Petty offenses
Serious offense

Petty offenses

When defendant was charged with driving under suspension, this charge was a petty offense, under Ohio R. Crim. P. 2(D), because it carried a maximum fine of $1,000 and the possibility of up to six months in jail, so he had to demand a jury trial in writing or waive his right to such a trial. City of Macedonia v. Ewing, — Ohio App. 3d —, 2007 Ohio 2194, — N.E. 2d —, 2007 Ohio App. LEXIS 2055 (May 9, 2007).

Domestic violence in violation of RC § 2919.25(A) is a first degree misdemeanor subject to a sentence of 180 days, under RC §§ 2919.25(D)(1)(2) and 2929.24(A)(1), so it is a petty offense, under Ohio R. Crim. P. 2(D). State v. Jones, — Ohio App. 3d —, 2006 Ohio 3636, — N.E. 2d —, 2006 Ohio App. LEXIS 3586 (July 13, 2006).

Where the maximum penalty for defendant's conviction of a first degree misdemeanor was 180 days pursuant to RC § 2929.24(A)(1), it was presumed to be a petty offense and further, petty offenses had been defined as those involving a maximum sentence of six months or less pursuant to Ohio R. Crim. P. 2(C) and (D). The right to a jury trial under U.S. Const. amend. VI did not apply to the offense. State v. Brooks, — Ohio App. 3d —, 2006 Ohio 4610, — N.E. 2d —, 2006 Ohio App. LEXIS 4569 (Sept. 1, 2006).

Serious offense

In defendant's trial for two aggravated robberies, in which he stated the desire to represent himself, his written waiver of counsel was required, under Ohio R. Crim. P. 44(C), because the offenses were considered to be serious crimes, under Ohio R. Crim. P. 2(C), given a potential prison sentence of more than six months, but the trial court's failure to obtain a written waiver was harmless error because defendant was properly advised, under Ohio R. Crim. P. 44(A), of the matters required for a knowing and intelligent waiver. State v. Andrews, — Ohio App. 3d —, 2006 Ohio 3764, — N.E. 2d —, 2006 Ohio App. LEXIS 3706 (July 24, 2006).

Where defendant was charged with carrying a concealed weapon, having a weapon while under a disability, and tampering with evidence, which were "serious offenses" pursuant to Ohio R. Crim. P. 2(C), and the trial court asked him at every stage of the proceedings whether he would obtain counsel or seek appointed counsel, defendant's decision to proceed pro se was not deemed knowingly, voluntarily, or intelligently made pursuant to Ohio R. Crim. P. 44, as the trial court failed to determine whether defendant understood the nature of the charges and the penalties or possible defenses, and it failed to make any of the determinations deemed essential under Martin. State v. Stubbs, — Ohio App. 3d —, 2006 Ohio 3858, — N.E. 2d —, 2006 Ohio App. LEXIS 3799 (July 28, 2006).

RULE 3.   Complaint

The complaint is a written statement of the essential facts constituting the offense charged. It shall also state the numerical designation of the applicable statute or ordinance. It shall be made upon oath before any person authorized by law to administer oaths.

NOTES TO DECISIONS

ANALYSIS

Generally
Citizen complaint form
Complaint

Generally

Trial court erred in convicting the defendant upon his no contest plea where the complaint did not set forth the elements of the offense, the essential facts constituting the offense, or the name of the offense, and stated only the numerical designation of the code section allegedly violated: State v. Hoerig, 181 Ohio App. 3d 86, 2009 Ohio 541, 907 N.E.2d 1238, 2009 Ohio App. LEXIS 457 (2009).

Citizen complaint form

Defendant did not file a "complaint," for purposes of RC § 2921.15 and CrimR 3, by completing a citizen complaint form for use by the police department's office of professional standards: Cleveland v. Lester, 143 Ohio Misc. 2d 39, 2007 Ohio 5375, 876 N.E.2d 1318, 2007 Ohio Misc. LEXIS 445 (2007).

Complaint

Although defendant was charged in a complaint, pursuant to Ohio R. Crim. P. 3 with disorderly conduct, in violation of RC § 2917.11(B)(1), for causing alarm when he attempted to climb out of an apartment window, there was no plain error under Ohio R. Crim. P. 52 when the prosecution proceeded on a completely different theory of defendant's disorderly conduct towards investigating officers, as defendant's counsel did not object, there was no argument or showing of reliance or surprise, and there was no indication that the defense was hindered. State v. Barnes, — Ohio App. 3d —, 2006 Ohio 1748, — N.E. 2d —, 2006 Ohio App. LEXIS 1617 (Apr. 7, 2006).

Defendant was not prejudicially misled by the trial court due to charging documents that were void, lacking elements, or failed to give him proper notice of the allegations he was charged with because it was clear that the charging documents did fully apprise defendant of the specific numerical code section of the charges against him and that sufficient notice as to each of the charges. Also, defendant entered a no contest plea as to the charges after the facts surrounding his charges were read into the record at the hearing and the trial court recited in open court each of the charges and specifically provided the proper language of the statute, the numerical code section of the charges, and the possible sentence for each charge. State v. Terry, — Ohio App. 3d —, 2006 Ohio 4320, — N.E. 2d —, 2006 Ohio App. LEXIS 4235 (Aug. 21, 2006).

RULE 4.   Warrant or Summons; Arrest

(A) Issuance.

(1) Upon complaint. If it appears from the complaint, or from an affidavit or affidavits filed with the complaint, that there is probable cause to believe that an offense has been committed, and that the defendant has committed it, a warrant for the arrest of the defendant, or a summons in lieu of a warrant, shall be issued by a judge, magistrate, clerk of court, or officer of the court designated by the judge, to any law enforcement officer authorized by law to execute or serve it.

The finding of probable cause may be based upon hearsay in whole or in part, provided there is a substantial basis for believing the source of the hearsay to be credible and for believing that there is a factual basis for the information furnished. Before ruling on a request for a warrant, the issuing authority may require the complainant to appear personally and may examine under oath the complainant and any witnesses. The testimony shall be admissible at a hearing on a motion to suppress, if it was taken down by a court reporter or recording equipment.

The issuing authority shall issue a summons instead of a warrant upon the request of the prosecuting attorney, or when issuance of a summons appears reasonably calculated to ensure the defendant's appearance.

(2) By law enforcement officer with warrant. In misdemeanor cases where a warrant has been issued to a law enforcement officer, the officer, unless the issuing authority includes a prohibition against it in the warrant, may issue a summons in lieu of executing the warrant by arrest, when issuance of a summons appears reasonably calculated to ensure the defendant's appearance. The officer issuing the summons shall note on the warrant and the return that the warrant was executed by issuing summons, and shall also note the time and place the defendant shall appear. No alias warrant shall be issued unless the defendant fails to appear in response to the summons, or unless subsequent to the issuance of summons it appears improbable that the defendant will appear in response to the summons.

(3) By law enforcement officer without a warrant. In misdemeanor cases where a law enforcement officer is empowered to arrest without a warrant, the officer may issue a summons in lieu of making an arrest, when issuance of a summons appears reasonably calculated to assure the defendant's appearance. The officer issuing the summons shall file, or cause to be filed, a complaint describing the offense. No warrant shall be issued unless the defendant fails to appear in response to the summons, or unless subsequent to the issuance of summons it appears improbable that the defendant will appear in response to the summons.

(B) Multiple issuance; sanction. More than one warrant or summons may issue on the same complaint. If the defendant fails to appear in response to summons, a warrant or alias warrant shall issue.

(C) Warrant and summons: form.

(1) Warrant. The warrant shall contain the name of the defendant or, if that is unknown, any name or description by which the defendant can be identified with reasonable certainty, a description of the offense charged in the complaint, whether the warrant is being issued before the defendant has appeared or was scheduled to appear, and the numerical designation of the applicable statute or ordinance. A copy of the complaint shall be attached to the warrant.

(a) If the warrant is issued after the defendant has made an initial appearance or has failed to appear at an initial appearance, the warrant shall command that the defendant be arrested and either of the following:

(i) That the defendant shall be required to post a sum of cash or secured bail bond with the condition that the defendant appear before the issuing court at a time and date certain;

(ii) That the defendant shall be held without bail until brought before the issuing court without unnecessary delay.

(b) If the warrant is issued before the defendant has appeared or is scheduled to appear, the warrant shall so indicate and the bail provisions of Crim. R. 46 shall apply.

(2) **Summons.** The summons shall be in the same form as the warrant, except that it shall not command that the defendant be arrested, but shall order the defendant to appear at a stated time and place and inform the defendant that he or she may be arrested if he or she fails to appear at the time and place stated in the summons. A copy of the complaint shall be attached to the summons, except where an officer issues summons in lieu of making an arrest without a warrant, or where an officer issues summons after arrest without a warrant.

(D) **Warrant or summons: execution or service; return.**

(1) **By whom.** Warrants shall be executed and summons served by any officer authorized by law.

(2) **Territorial limits.** Warrants may be executed or summons may be served at any place within this state.

(3) **Manner.** Except as provided in division (A)(2) of this rule, warrants shall be executed by the arrest of the defendant. The officer need not have the warrant in the officer's possession at the time of the arrest. In such case, the officer shall inform the defendant of the offense charged and of the fact that the warrant has been issued. A copy of the warrant shall be given to the defendant as soon as possible.

Summons may be served upon a defendant by delivering a copy to the defendant personally, or by leaving it at the defendant's usual place of residence with some person of suitable age and discretion then residing therein, or, except when the summons is issued in lieu of executing a warrant by arrest, by mailing it to the defendant's last known address by certified mail with a return receipt requested. When service of summons is made by certified mail it shall be served by the clerk in the manner prescribed by Civil Rule 4.1(1). A summons to a corporation shall be served in the manner provided for service upon corporations in Civil Rules 4 through 4.2 and 4.6(A) and (B), except that the waiver provisions of Civil Rule 4(D) shall not apply. Summons issued under division (A)(2) of this rule in lieu of executing a warrant by arrest shall be served by personal or residence service. Summons issued under division (A)(3) of this rule in lieu of arrest and summons issued after arrest under division (F) of this rule shall be served by personal service only.

(4) **Return.** The officer executing a warrant shall make return of the warrant to the issuing court before whom the defendant is brought pursuant to Crim. R. 5. At the request of the prosecuting attorney, any unexecuted warrant shall be returned to the issuing court and cancelled by a judge of that court.

When the copy of the summons has been served, the person serving summons shall endorse that fact on the summons and return it to the clerk, who shall make the appropriate entry on the appearance docket.

When the person serving summons is unable to serve a copy of the summons within twenty-eight days of the date of issuance, the person serving summons shall endorse that fact and the reasons for the failure of service on the summons and return the summons and copies to the clerk, who shall make the appropriate entry on the appearance docket.

At the request of the prosecuting attorney, made while the complaint is pending, a warrant returned unexecuted and not cancelled, or a summons returned unserved, or a copy of either, may be delivered by the court to an authorized officer for execution or service.

(E) **Arrest.**

(1) **Arrest upon warrant.**

(a) Where a person is arrested upon a warrant that states it was issued before a scheduled initial appearance, or the warrant is silent as to when it was issued, the judicial officer before whom the person is brought shall apply Crim. R. 46.

(b) Where a person is arrested upon a warrant that states it was issued after an initial appearance or the failure to appear at an initial appearance and the arrest occurs either in the county from which the warrant issued or in an adjoining county, the arresting officer shall, except as provided in division (F) of this rule, where the warrant provides for the posting of bail, permit the arrested person to post a sum of cash or secured bail bond as contained in the warrant with the requirement that the arrested person appear before the warrant issuing court at a time and date certain, or bring the arrested person without unnecessary delay before the court that issued the warrant.

(c) Where a person is arrested upon a warrant that states it was issued after an initial appearance or the failure to appear at an initial appearance and the arrest occurs in any county other than the county from which the warrant was issued or in an adjoining county, the following sequence of procedures shall be followed:

(i) Where the warrant provides for the posting of bail, the arrested person shall be permitted to post a sum of cash or secured bail bond as contained in the warrant with the requirement that the arrested person appear before the warrant issuing court at a time and date certain.

(ii) The arrested person may in writing waive the procedures in division (E)(1)(c)(iii) of this rule after having been informed in writing and orally by a law enforcement officer of those procedures, and consenting to being removed to the warrant issuing court without further delay. This waiver shall contain a representation by a law enforcement officer that the waiver was read to the arrested person and that the arrested person signed the waiver in the officer's presence.

(iii) Where the warrant is silent as to the posting of bail, requires that the arrested person be held without bail, the arrested person chooses not to post bail, or the arrested person chooses not to waive the procedures contained in division (E)(1) of this rule, the arrested person shall, except as provided in division (F) of this rule, be brought without unnecessary delay before a court of record therein, having jurisdiction over such an offense, and the arrested person shall not be removed from that county until the arrested person has been given a reasonable opportunity to consult with an attorney, or individual of the arrested person's choice, and to post bail to be determined by the judge or magistrate of that court not inconsistent with the directions of the issuing court as contained in the warrant or after consultation with the issuing court. If the warrant is silent as to the posting of bail or holding the arrested person without bail, the court may permit the arrested person to post bail, hold the arrested person without bail, or consult with the warrant issuing court on the issue of bail.

(d) If the arrested person is not released, the arrested person shall then be removed from the county and brought before the court issuing the warrant, without unnecessary delay. If the arrested person is released, the release shall be on condition that the arrested person appear in the issuing court at a time and date certain.

(2) **Arrest without warrant.** Where a person is arrested without a warrant the arresting officer shall, except as provided in division (F), bring the arrested person without unnecessary delay before a court having jurisdiction of the offense, and shall file or cause to be filed a complaint describing the offense for which the person was arrested. Thereafter the court shall proceed in accordance with Crim. R. 5.

(F) **Release after arrest.** In misdemeanor cases where a person has been arrested with or without a warrant, the arresting officer, the officer in charge of the detention facility to which the person is brought or the superior of either officer, without unnecessary delay, may release the arrested person by issuing a summons when issuance of a summons appears reasonably calculated to assure the person's appearance. The officer issuing such summons shall note on the summons the time and place the person must appear and, if the person was arrested without a warrant, shall file or cause to be filed a complaint describing the offense. No warrant or alias warrant shall be issued unless the person fails to appear in response to the summons.

History: Amended, eff 7-1-75; 7-1-90; 7-1-98.

NOTES TO DECISIONS

ANALYSIS

Arrest pursuant to warrant
Complaint
Good faith exception
Service of summons

Arrest pursuant to warrant

Because the second arrest warrant was properly returned to the court and because defendant properly waived her right to have an attorney, her Sixth Amendment rights were not violated. The first warrant was not returned to the court, however, another warrant for aggravated murder was issued and executed and that warrant was properly returned to the court on that same day. There was no evidence to indicate that, even if the first warrant had been returned on March 22, defendant would have been arraigned and had counsel assigned on March 23. State v. Barnes, — Ohio App. 3d —, 2007 Ohio 4019, — N.E. 2d —, 2007 Ohio App. LEXIS 3654 (Aug. 9, 2007).

Complaint

When a village filed a complaint under Ohio R. Crim. P. 4 naming "John Does" as defendants and requesting a hearing

to determine if the village had probable cause to believe a crime was committed when defendant disclosed village employees' social security numbers to non-village-council-members, the trial court's issuance of an order to charge defendant with a crime, under Ohio R. Crim. P. 4(A)(1), did not bar the trial court from presiding over defendant's trial, because Ohio law recognized that judges who issued arrest warrants and presided at preliminary hearings were not barred from presiding over a defendant's trial, even though they had already found the existence of probable cause. Village of Sabina v. Kress, — Ohio App. 3d —, 2007 Ohio 1224, — N.E. 2d —, 2007 Ohio App. LEXIS 1149 (Mar. 19, 2007).

Good faith exception

There is no rational distinction between search warrants and arrest warrants for Fourth Amendment purposes: both warrants will issue only upon probable cause. Hence, the good faith exception applies equally to arrest warrants obtained pursuant to Ohio R. Crim. P. 4 and RC § 2935.08. State v. Palinkas, — Ohio App. 3d —, 2006 Ohio 2083, — N.E. 2d —, 2006 Ohio App. LEXIS 1931 (Apr. 27, 2006).

Service of summons

Defendant's counsel was not ineffective for failing to move for dismissal on speedy trial grounds because defendant's failure to claim a summons issued by certified mail to an address that he furnished was, at the least, delay occasioned by his own neglect and thus, the time was properly excluded from the speedy trial time, pursuant to RC § 2945.72. Also, because defendant was charged with a felony and the summons was issued pursuant to Ohio R. Crim. P. 9, certified mail was an appropriate means of service and personal service was not mandated. State v. Gums, — Ohio App. 3d —, 2006 Ohio 3159, — N.E. 2d —, 2006 Ohio App. LEXIS 3036 (June 22, 2006).

Where an arrest pursuant to a warrant is made in any county other than the county from which the warrant issued or an adjoining county, CrimR 4(E)(1) mandates that the individual who is the subject of the warrant be taken forthwith by the arresting officer before a court of record in the county of arrest, and that the individual not be removed from the county of arrest until he has been given an opportunity to consult with an attorney, or another person of his choice, and to post bail: OAG No. 94-029 (1994).

If an arrest pursuant to a warrant is made in any county other than the county from which the warrant issued or an adjoining county, the individual who is arrested may not waive the jurisdiction of the arresting county's court as provided by CrimR 4(E)(1) and immediately consent, in writing, to be delivered into the custody of the law enforcement officials of the county that issued the arrest warrant: OAG No. 94-029 (1994).

RULE 4.1.   Optional Procedure in Minor Misdemeanor Cases

(A) **Procedure in minor misdemeanor cases.** Notwithstanding Rule 3, Rule 5(A), Rule 10, Rule 11(A), Rule 11(E), Rule 22, Rule 43(A), and Rule 44, a court may establish the following procedure for all or particular minor misdemeanors other than offenses covered by the Uniform Traffic Rules.

(B) **Definition of minor misdemeanor.** A minor misdemeanor is an offense for which the potential penalty does not exceed a fine of one hundred fifty dollars. With respect to offenses committed prior to January 1, 2004, a minor misdemeanor is an offense for which the potential penalty does not exceed a fine of one hundred dollars.

(C) **Form of citation.** In minor misdemeanor cases

a law enforcement officer may issue a citation. The citation shall: contain the name and address of the defendant; describe the offense charged; give the numerical designation of the applicable statute or ordinance; state the name of the law enforcement officer who issued the citation; and order the defendant to appear at a stated time and place.

The citation shall inform the defendant that, in lieu of appearing at the time and place stated, he may, within that stated time, appear personally at the office of the clerk of court and upon signing a plea of guilty and a waiver of trial pay a stated fine and stated costs, if any. The citation shall inform the defendant that, in lieu of appearing at the time and place stated, he may, within a stated time, sign the guilty plea and waiver of trial provision of the citation, and mail the citation and a check or money order for the total amount of the fine and costs to the violations bureau. The citation shall inform the defendant that he may be arrested if he fails to appear either at the clerk's office or at the time and place stated in the citation.

(D) **Duty of law enforcement officer.** A law enforcement officer who issues a citation shall complete and sign the citation form, serve a copy of the completed form upon the defendant and, without unnecessary delay, swear to and file the original with the court.

(E) **Fine schedule.** The court shall establish a fine schedule which shall list the fine for each minor misdemeanor, and state the court costs. The fine schedule shall be prominently posted in the place where violation fines are paid.

(F) **Procedure upon failure to appear.** When a defendant fails to appear, the court may issue a supplemental citation, or a summons or warrant under Rule 4. Supplemental citations shall be in the form prescribed by subdivision (C), but shall be issued and signed by the clerk and served in the same manner as a summons under Rule 4.

(G) **Procedure where defendant does not enter a waiver.** Where a defendant appears but does not sign a guilty plea and waiver of trial, the court shall proceed in accordance with Rule 5.

History: Amended, eff 7-1-78; 7-1-04.

NOTES TO DECISIONS

Analysis

Contents of citation

Contents of citation
Defendant's claim that a trial court had no jurisdiction over defendant because the complaint against defendant was not properly signed or sworn by a law enforcement officer, under Ohio R. Crim. P. 4.1(D), had no merit because an officer stated under penalty of perjury and falsification that the officer had read the complaint and that it was true. State v. Gatto, — Ohio App. 3d —, 2007 Ohio 4609, — N.E. 2d —, 2007 Ohio App. LEXIS 4154 (Sept. 7, 2007).

RULE 5. Initial Appearance, Preliminary Hearing

(A) **Procedure upon initial appearance.** When a defendant first appears before a judge or magistrate, the judge or magistrate shall permit the accused or his counsel to read the complaint or a copy thereof, and shall inform the defendant:

(1) Of the nature of the charge against him;

(2) That he has a right to counsel and the right to a reasonable continuance in the proceedings to secure counsel, and, pursuant to Crim. R. 44, the right to have counsel assigned without cost to himself if he is unable to employ counsel;

(3) That he need make no statement and any statement made may be used against him;

(4) Of his right to a preliminary hearing in a felony case, when his initial appearance is not pursuant to indictment;

(5) Of his right, where appropriate, to jury trial and the necessity to make demand therefore in petty offense cases.

In addition, if the defendant has not been admitted to bail for a bailable offense, the judge or magistrate shall admit the defendant to bail as provided in these rules.

In felony cases the defendant shall not be called upon to plead either at the initial appearance or at a preliminary hearing.

In misdemeanor cases the defendant may be called upon to plead at the initial appearance. Where the defendant enters a plea the procedure established by Crim. R. 10 and Crim. R. 11 applies.

(B) **Preliminary hearing in felony cases; procedure.**

(1) In felony cases a defendant is entitled to a preliminary hearing unless waived in writing. If the defendant waives preliminary hearing, the judge or magistrate shall forthwith order the defendant bound over to the court of common pleas. If the defendant does not waive the preliminary hearing, the judge or magistrate shall schedule a preliminary hearing within a reasonable time, but in any event not later than ten consecutive days following arrest or service of summons if the defendant is in custody and not later than fifteen consecutive days following arrest or service of summons if he is not in custody. The preliminary hearing shall not be held, however, if the defendant is indicted. With the consent of the defendant and upon a showing of good cause, taking into account the public interest in the prompt disposition of criminal cases, time limits specified in this division may be extended. In the absence of such consent by the defendant, time limits may be extended only as required by law, or upon a showing that extraordinary circumstances exist and that delay is indispensable to the interests of justice.

(2) At the preliminary hearing the prosecuting attorney may state orally the case for the state, and shall then proceed to examine witnesses and introduce exhibits for the state. The defendant and the judge or magistrate have full right of cross-examination, and the defendant has the right of inspection of exhibits prior to their introduction. The hearing shall be conducted under the rules of evidence prevailing in criminal trial generally.

(3) At the conclusion of the presentation of the state's case, defendant may move for discharge for failure of proof, and may offer evidence on his own

behalf. If the defendant is not represented by counsel, the court shall advise him, prior to the offering of evidence on behalf of the defendant:

(a) That any such evidence, if unfavorable to him in any particular, may be used against him at later trial.

(b) That he may make a statement, not under oath, regarding the charge, for the purpose of explaining the facts in evidence.

(c) That he may refuse to make any statement, and such refusal may not be used against him at trial.

(d) That any statement he makes may be used against him at trial.

(4) Upon conclusion of all the evidence and the statement, if any, of the accused, the court shall do one of the following:

(a) Find that there is probable cause to believe the crime alleged or another felony has been committed and that the defendant committed it, and bind the defendant over to the court of common pleas of the county or any other county in which venue appears.

(b) Find that there is probable cause to believe that a misdemeanor was committed and that the defendant committed it, and retain the case for trial or order the defendant to appear for trial before an appropriate court.

(c) Order the accused discharged.

(5) Any finding requiring the accused to stand trial on any charge shall be based solely on the presence of substantial credible evidence thereof. No appeal shall lie from such decision and the discharge of defendant shall not be a bar to further prosecution.

(6) In any case in which the defendant is ordered to appear for trial for any offense other than the one charged the court shall cause a complaint charging such offense to be filed.

(7) Upon the conclusion of the hearing and finding, the court or the clerk of such court, shall, within seven days, complete all notations of appearance, motions, pleas, and findings on the criminal docket of the court, and shall transmit a transcript of the appearance docket entries, together with a copy of the original complaint and affidavits, if any, filed with the complaint, the journal or docket entry of reason for changes in the charge, if any, together with the order setting bail and the bail including any bail deposit, if any, filed, to the clerk of the court in which defendant is to appear. Such transcript shall contain an itemized account of the costs accrued.

History: Amended, eff 7-1-75; 7-1-76; 7-1-82; 7-1-90.

NOTES TO DECISIONS

Analysis

Explanation of rights
Habeas corpus
Initial appearance
Initial appearance generally
Invalid proceeding
Jury trial right
Subsequent indictment

Explanation of rights

CrimR 5, CrimR 10, and TrafR 8 were violated where the defendant's rights were not explained at the arraignment on the traffic offenses. A video explanation of rights played for the benefit of all defendants did not suffice: State v. Donkers, 170 Ohio App. 3d 509, 2007 Ohio 1557, 867 N.E.2d 903, 2007 Ohio App. LEXIS 1424 (2007).

Habeas corpus

Habeas corpus relief was denied to defendant where his claim that he did not have a preliminary hearing pursuant to Ohio R. Crim. P. 5 lacked merit, as his indictment by the grand jury rendered any defects in the preliminary hearing moot. His claim that his speedy trial rights under RC § 2945.71 were violated was not cognizable in habeas corpus. Clarke v. McFaul, — Ohio App. 3d —, 2007 Ohio 1592, — N.E. 2d —, 2007 Ohio App. LEXIS 1457 (Apr. 3, 2007).

Defendant's petition for habeas corpus was procedurally defective where it was improperly captioned and it was not verified, as required by RC § 2725.04, there was no certified statement from the prison cashier pursuant to RC § 2969.25(C), and affidavits as to the details of the claims or as to the prior actions or appeals pursuant to § 2969.25 and Ohio Eighth Dist. Ct. App. R. 45(B)(1)(a) were not attached. As defendant had been indicted pursuant to a grand jury, any defect pursuant to a lack of a preliminary hearing pursuant to Ohio R. Crim. P. 5 was rendered moot. State v. Addison, — Ohio App. 3d —, 2007 Ohio 1978, — N.E. 2d —, 2007 Ohio App. LEXIS 1833 (Apr. 24, 2007).

Initial appearance

When it was alleged that defendant was advised of her rights, as required by Ohio R. Crim. P. 5 and 10 and Ohio Traf. R. 8, by means of a mass video advisement, this was insufficient because (1) the contents of the advisement were not shown, (2) it was not demonstrated that defendant saw the advisement, and (3) even if the advisement covered the required rights and it was shown that defendant saw it, an individualized finding that she understood those rights was still required, and such a finding was absent. State v. Donkers, 170 Ohio App. 3d 509, 2007 Ohio 1557, 867 N.E.2d 903, 2007 Ohio App. LEXIS 1424 (2007).

Initial appearance generally

Because defendant was charged with first degree misdemeanor assault, she was entitled to a jury trial pursuant to RC § 2945.17; because the trial court failed to inform defendant of her right to a jury trial at her initial appearance, the trial court did not comply with Ohio R. Crim. P. 5(A), and the entire proceeding against defendant was invalid. State v. Bates, — Ohio App. 3d —, 2006 Ohio 3777, — N.E. 2d —, 2006 Ohio App. LEXIS 3730 (July 21, 2006).

Invalid proceeding

Entire proceeding against defendant on an ordinance violation was invalid because the trial court failed to advise defendant of his rights or to ensure that defendant fully understood his rights and was intelligently relinquishing his right to counsel. The trial court simply inquired if defendant wanted to proceed before a magistrate or a judge and whether he had counsel that would appear. City of Middletown v. McIntosh, — Ohio App. 3d —, 2007 Ohio 3348, — N.E. 2d —, 2007 Ohio App. LEXIS 3122 (July 2, 2007).

Jury trial right

Defendant's claim that his jury trial right under U.S. Const. amend. VI was violated where a charge against him of child endangerment, in violation of RC § 2919.22, which was deemed a "petty offense" pursuant to RC § 2919.24(A)(1) and Ohio R. Crim. P. 2, was tried in a bench trial, lacked merit, as the appellate court presumed the regularity of the trial court proceedings pursuant to Ohio R. App. P. 9(B) where there was no record to support defendant's claim that he was never informed by the trial court, as required under Ohio R. Crim. P. 5(A)(5), of the need to make a jury trial demand pursuant to Ohio R. Crim. P. 23(A) and RC § 1901.24(B); defendant's claim that he made an oral demand was not proved by a record and further, such would not have satisfied the requirements for the demand, as it had to be in writing. State v. Miyamoto, — Ohio App. 3d —, 2006 Ohio 1776, — N.E. 2d —, 2006 Ohio App. LEXIS 1648 (Apr. 10, 2006).

Subsequent indictment

Inmate's petition for a writ of habeas corpus pursuant to RC § 2725.01 et seq. was denied because the inmate was not entitled to a preliminary hearing pursuant to Ohio R. Crim. P. 5(B) where an indictment had been returned; the inmate's petition included a copy of the indictment underlying the conviction. State ex rel. Pena v. Konteh, — Ohio App. 3d —, 2007 Ohio 3955, — N.E. 2d —, 2007 Ohio App. LEXIS 3612 (Aug. 1, 2007).

RULE 6.   The Grand Jury

(A) **Summoning grand juries.** The judge of the court of common pleas for each county, or the administrative judge of the general division in a multi-judge court of common pleas or a judge designated by him, shall order one or more grand juries to be summoned at such times as the public interest requires. The grand jury shall consist of nine members, including the foreman, plus not more than five alternates.

(B) **Objections to grand jury and to grand jurors.**

(1) **Challenges.** The prosecuting attorney, or the attorney for a defendant who has been held to answer in the court of common pleas, may challenge the array of jurors or an individual juror on the ground that the grand jury or individual juror was not selected, drawn, or summoned in accordance with the statutes of this state. Challenges shall be made before the administration of the oath to the jurors and shall be tried by the court.

(2) **Motion to dismiss.** A motion to dismiss the indictment may be based on objections to the array or on the lack of legal qualification of an individual juror, if not previously determined upon challenge. An indictment shall not be dismissed on the ground that one or more members of the grand jury were not legally qualified, if it appears from the record kept pursuant to subdivision (C) that seven or more jurors, after deducting the number not legally qualified, concurred in finding the indictment.

(C) **Foreman and deputy foreman.** The court may appoint any qualified elector or one of the jurors to be foreman and one of the jurors to be deputy foreman. The foreman shall have power to administer oaths and affirmations and shall sign all indictments. He or another juror designated by him shall keep a record of the number of jurors concurring in the finding of every indictment and shall upon the return of the indictment file the record with the clerk of court, but the record shall not be made public except on order of the court. During the absence or disqualification of the foreman, the deputy foreman shall act as foreman.

(D) **Who may be present.** The prosecuting attorney, the witness under examination, interpreters when needed and, for the purpose of taking the evidence, a stenographer or operator of a recording device may be present while the grand jury is in session, but no person other than the jurors may be present while the grand jury is deliberating or voting.

(E) **Secrecy of proceedings and disclosure.** De-liberations of the grand jury and the vote of any grand juror shall not be disclosed. Disclosure of other matters occurring before the grand jury may be made to the prosecuting attorney for use in the performance of his duties. A grand juror, prosecuting attorney, interpreter, stenographer, operator of a recording device, or typist who transcribes recorded testimony, may disclose matters occurring before the grand jury, other than the deliberations of a grand jury or the vote of a grand juror, but may disclose such matters only when so directed by the court preliminary to or in connection with a judicial proceeding, or when permitted by the court at the request of the defendant upon a showing that grounds may exist for a motion to dismiss the indictment because of matters occurring before the grand jury. No grand juror, officer of the court, or other person shall disclose that an indictment has been found against a person before such indictment is filed and the case docketed. The court may direct that an indictment shall be kept secret until the defendant is in custody or has been released pursuant to Rule 46. In that event the clerk shall seal the indictment, the indictment shall not be docketed by name until after the apprehension of the accused, and no person shall disclose the finding of the indictment except when necessary for the issuance of a warrant or summons. No obligation of secrecy may be imposed upon any person except in accordance with this rule.

(F) **Finding and return of indictment.** An indictment may be found only upon the concurrence of seven or more jurors. When so found the foreman or deputy foreman shall sign the indictment as foreman or deputy foreman. The indictment shall be returned by the foreman or deputy foreman to a judge of the court of common pleas and filed with the clerk who shall endorse thereon the date of filing and enter each case upon the appearance and trial dockets. If the defendant is in custody or has been released pursuant to Rule 46 and seven jurors do not concur in finding an indictment, the foreman shall so report to the court forthwith.

(G) **Discharge and excuse.** A grand jury shall serve until discharged by the court. A grand jury may serve for four months, but the court upon a showing of good cause by the prosecuting attorney may order a grand jury to serve more than four months but not more than nine months. The tenure and powers of a grand jury are not affected by the beginning or expiration of a term of court. At any time for cause shown the court may excuse a juror either temporarily or permanently, and in the latter event the court may impanel another eligible person in place of the juror excused.

(H) **Alternate grand jurors.** The court may order that not more than five grand jurors, in addition to the regular grand jury, be called, impanelled and sit as alternate grand jurors. Alternate grand jurors, in the order in which they are called, shall replace grand jurors who, prior to the time the grand jury votes on an indictment, are found to be unable or disqualified to perform their duties. Alternate grand jurors shall be drawn in the same manner, shall have the same qualifications, shall be subjected to the same examination and challenges, shall take the same oath, and shall have the same functions, powers, facilities, and privileges as the regular grand jurors. Alternate grand jurors may sit with the regular grand jury, but shall not be present when the grand jury deliberates and votes.

NOTES TO DECISIONS

ANALYSIS

Disclosure
Disclosure of testimony
Habeas corpus
Indictment sufficient
Jurisdiction of court of common pleas
Public records law
Required Signatures

Disclosure

Trial court did not abuse its discretion in denying access to the grand jury transcripts because defendant merely speculated that the testimony could have contained material evidence, or could have aided his cross-examination by revealing contradictions. Defendant did not demonstrate a particularized need for disclosure of the grand jury testimony, and he did not show grounds for a motion to dismiss the indictment based upon matters occurring before the grand jury. State v. Howard, — Ohio App. 3d —, 2007 Ohio 3669, — N.E. 2d —, 2007 Ohio App. LEXIS 3339 (July 13, 2007).

Disclosure of testimony

Showing of a particularized need for the release of grand jury testimony cannot be established on the basis of speculative pretrial allegations of potentially inconsistent testimony. Grand jury transcripts cannot be used by an accused for ascertaining the prosecution's evidence for the purpose of trial preparation; it is a discovery device only for purposes of impeachment upon cross-examination: State v. Godfrey, 181 Ohio App. 3d 75, 2009 Ohio 547, 907 N.E.2d 1230, 2009 Ohio App. LEXIS 443 (2009).

Impeachment through material inconsistencies may be a proper basis for disclosure of grand jury testimony, but that purpose alone is not sufficient. A claim that a witness' grand jury testimony may differ from trial testimony is insufficient to show a particularized need. The trial court should have conducted an in camera examination prior to granting disclosure of the child's grand jury testimony: State v. Horger, 170 Ohio App. 3d 383, 2007 Ohio 665, 867 N.E.2d 466, 2007 Ohio App. LEXIS 596 (2007).

Defendant, a public employee, showed a particularized need for grand jury testimony, under Ohio R. Crim. P. 6(E), to show that defendant's supervisor used a witness's telephone number revealed in defendant's immunized statements to the supervisor to obtain the witness's address for a prosecutor, and a trial court's error in denying defendant's request for this grand jury testimony was harmless beyond a reasonable doubt because investigators could have obtained the witness's address from other sources, since the investigators were familiar with the witness. Ohio v. Parsons, — Ohio App. 3d —, 2007 Ohio 4812, — N.E. 2d —, 2007 Ohio App. LEXIS 4295 (Sept. 13, 2007).

When defendant, a public employee, claimed that statements defendant made about the crime defendant was charged with to defendant's supervisor were improperly used in defendant's prosecution, and defendant sought a transcript of grand jury testimony to prove this claim, competent credible evidence supported a trial court's finding that defendant did not show a particularized need for this transcript, under Ohio R. Crim. P. 6(E), except as to one witness, because the State showed that the State's evidence was derived from legitimate sources wholly independent of defendant's statements. Ohio v. Parsons, — Ohio App. 3d —, 2007 Ohio 4812, — N.E. 2d —, 2007 Ohio App. LEXIS 4295 (Sept. 13, 2007).

Trial court order that denied an inmate's post-trial motion for excerpts of grand jury testimony pursuant to Ohio R. Crim. P. 6(E) did not affect a substantial right in the action and determine the action and prevent a judgment, as Rule 6(E) only applied to requests prior to or during a trial, and there was no pending matter when the inmate made his request; there was no final appealable order under RC § 2505.02(B) and accordingly, dismissal of the inmate's appeal from the trial court's order was mandated. State v. Parks, — Ohio App. 3d —, 2006 Ohio 4604, — N.E. 2d —, 2006 Ohio App. LEXIS 4566 (Aug. 30, 2006).

Where defendant did not show a particularized need for grand jury testimony, pursuant to Ohio R. Crim. P. 6(E), the trial court did not abuse its discretion in refusing to disclose it. State v. Davis, — Ohio App. 3d —, 2006 Ohio 1958, — N.E. 2d —, 2006 Ohio App. LEXIS 1787 (Apr. 19, 2006).

Although a trial court denied defendant's motion for disclosure of grand jury transcripts pursuant to Ohio R. Crim. P. 6(E), as the dismissal of two charges against defendant were reversed on appeal and the matter was remanded for further review of whether defendant's plea agreement was breached under principles of contract law, the court noted that it was possible that if such a breach occurred, defendant would be entitled to the disclosure by showing the particularized need and evidence that he made statements to officers regarding offenses that were charged against him. State v. Dillon, — Ohio App. 3d —, 2006 Ohio 4931, — N.E. 2d —, 2006 Ohio App. LEXIS 4867 (Sept. 22, 2006).

Trial court's denial of defendant's request for production of grand jury testimony was not an abuse of discretion, as his "particularized need" for disclosure was nothing more than a fishing expedition where he opined that the the victim had been pressured into making a complaint that supported the second indictment against him. State v. Kelly, — Ohio App. 3d —, 2006 Ohio 5902, — N.E. 2d —, 2006 Ohio App. LEXIS 5862 (Nov. 9, 2006).

Habeas corpus

Defendant's habeas corpus petition under RC § 2725.04 was dismissed where he failed to state cognizable claims arising under Ohio R. Crim. P. 6 and 7, as he only made unsupported conclusions regarding the denial of his rights under Ohio R. Crim. P. 6 and further, a motion to dismiss was the appropriate remedy for those rights. As to Ohio R. Crim. P. 7, once defendant was indicted by the grand jury, he could no longer waive the indictment and further, habeas corpus relief was not available to challenge the validity or sufficiency of an indictment. Clarke v. McFaul, — Ohio App. 3d —, 2007 Ohio 1592, — N.E. 2d —, 2007 Ohio App. LEXIS 1457 (Apr. 3, 2007).

Indictment sufficient

Grand jury foreperson's signature on the last page of a five-count indictment, each count of which was printed on a separate page, was sufficient under Ohio R. Crim. P. 6 and 7, as the last page listed the five statutes involved in the multi-count indictment and it included, in addition to the signature, the notation "True Bill" and a certification by the clerk of courts. State v. Koval, — Ohio App. 3d —, 2006 Ohio 5377, — N.E. 2d —, 2006 Ohio App. LEXIS 5340 (Oct. 16, 2006).

Jurisdiction of court of common pleas

Trial court did not abuse its discretion under Ohio R. Crim. P. 6(E) when it denied an inmate's motion for production of grand jury testimony, arising from his criminal matter wherein he had been convicted of murder with specifications, as there was no criminal matter pending before the trial court and accordingly, it had no authority or jurisdiction to grant such a motion. The inmate had failed to show a particularized need for such production that outweighed the need for secrecy, as his assertions in support of disclosure were vague and speculative. State v. Russell, — Ohio App. 3d —, 2006 Ohio 5945, — N.E. 2d —, 2006 Ohio App. LEXIS 5882 (Nov. 9, 2006).

Public records law

Trial court's denial of an inmate's request under the Ohio Public Records Act, RC § 149.43, for disclosure of grand jury minutes was not an abuse of discretion, as the inmate did not meet his burden of showing a particularized need for the disclosure under Ohio R. Crim. P. 6(E) where he claimed that they were necessary to establish that the prosecutor had withheld evidence and had misinformed the grand jury. State v. Gibson, — Ohio App. 3d —, 2007 Ohio 4547, — N.E. 2d —, 2007 Ohio App. LEXIS 4088 (Aug. 31, 2007).

Required Signatures

Inmate's indictment was not defective for a lack of certification by a foreman or deputy foreman of a grand jury, as required by Ohio R. Crim. P. 6(C) and (F), because the grand jury foreman's signature was placed conspicuously below the indictment's charges. Ohio v. Wilson, — Ohio App. 3d —, 2007 Ohio 4885, — N.E. 2d —, 2007 Ohio App. LEXIS 4369 (Sept. 21, 2007).

RULE 7. The Indictment and the Information

(A) **Use of indictment or information.** A felony that may be punished by death or life imprisonment shall be prosecuted by indictment. All other felonies shall be prosecuted by indictment, except that after a defendant has been advised by the court of the nature of the charge against the defendant and of the defendant's right to indictment, the defendant may waive that right in writing and in open court.

Where an indictment is waived, the offense may be prosecuted by information, unless an indictment is filed within fourteen days after the date of waiver. If an information or indictment is not filed within fourteen days after the date of waiver, the defendant shall be discharged and the complaint dismissed. This division shall not prevent subsequent prosecution by information or indictment for the same offense.

A misdemeanor may be prosecuted by indictment or information in the court of common pleas, or by complaint in the juvenile court, as defined in the Rules of Juvenile Procedure, and in courts inferior to the court of common pleas. An information may be filed without leave of court.

(B) **Nature and contents.** The indictment shall be signed, in accordance with Crim. R. 6 (C) and (F) and contain a statement that the defendant has committed a public offense specified in the indictment. The information shall be signed by the prosecuting attorney or in the name of the prosecuting attorney by an assistant prosecuting attorney and shall contain a statement that the defendant has committed a public offense specified in the information. The statement may be made in ordinary and concise language without technical averments or allegations not essential to be proved. The statement may be in the words of the applicable section of the statute, provided the words of that statute charge an offense, or in words sufficient to give the defendant notice of all the elements of the offense with which the defendant is charged. It may be alleged in a single count that the means by which the defendant committed the offense are unknown or that the defendant committed it by one or more specified

means. Each count of the indictment or information shall state the numerical designation of the statute that the defendant is alleged to have violated. Error in the numerical designation or omission of the numerical designation shall not be ground for dismissal of the indictment or information, or for reversal of a conviction, if the error or omission did not prejudicially mislead the defendant.

(C) **Surplusage.** The court on motion of the defendant or the prosecuting attorney may strike surplusage from the indictment or information.

(D) **Amendment of indictment, information, or complaint.** The court may at any time before, during, or after a trial amend the indictment, information, complaint, or bill of particulars, in respect to any defect, imperfection, or omission in form or substance, or of any variance with the evidence, provided no change is made in the name or identity of the crime charged. If any amendment is made to the substance of the indictment, information, or complaint, or to cure a variance between the indictment, information, or complaint and the proof, the defendant is entitled to a discharge of the jury on the defendant's motion, if a jury has been impanelled, and to a reasonable continuance, unless it clearly appears from the whole proceedings that the defendant has not been misled or prejudiced by the defect or variance in respect to which the amendment is made, or that the defendant's rights will be fully protected by proceeding with the trial, or by a postponement thereof to a later day with the same or another jury. Where a jury is discharged under this division, jeopardy shall not attach to the offense charged in the amended indictment, information, or complaint. No action of the court in refusing a continuance or postponement under this division is reviewable except after motion to grant a new trial therefore is refused by the trial court, and no appeal based upon such action of the court shall be sustained nor reversal had unless, from consideration of the whole proceedings, the reviewing court finds that a failure of justice resulted.

(E) **Bill of particulars.** When the defendant makes a written request within twenty-one days after arraignment but not later than seven days before trial, or upon court order, the prosecuting attorney shall furnish the defendant with a bill of particulars setting up specifically the nature of the offense charge and of the conduct of the defendant alleged to constitute the offense. A bill of particulars may be amended at any time subject to such conditions as justice requires.

History: Amended, eff 7-1-93; 7-1-00.

NOTES TO DECISIONS

ANALYSIS

Culpable mental states
Double jeopardy
Due process
Guilty plea
Indictment
Indictment sufficient
Lesser included offenses
Notice
Plain error
Prejudice
Right to appeal
Service of indictment
Specific dates
Sufficiency of indictment
—— Plain error
Timeliness
Traffic citation
Waiver
Wrong offense charged

Amendment

Amendment of an indictment for intimidation of witnesses was not permissible under CrimR 7(D) where the amendment elevated the offenses from misdemeanors to felonies: State v. Fairbanks, 172 Ohio App. 3d 766, 2007 Ohio 4117, 876 N.E.2d 1293, 2007 Ohio App. LEXIS 3737 (2007).

Where the trial court orally stated that it was amending the bill of information but failed to journalize the amendment, the amendment was not effective: State v. Maisch, 173 Ohio App. 3d 724, 2007 Ohio 6230, 880 N.E.2d 153, 2007 Ohio App. LEXIS 5493 (2007).

Where the State orally amended the indictment against defendant to assert a charge of kidnapping in violation of RC § 2905.01(A)(2) instead of the original charge of § 2905.01(A)(3), such amendment was proper under Ohio R. Crim. P. 7(D), as it was made pursuant to the terms of a plea agreement that defendant voluntarily entered into, defendant was apprised of the details and contents of the amended charge in open court and he assented thereto, and he did not show that he was prejudiced by the change. It was also noted that the amendment to the charge did not change the name or identity of the crime charged. State v. Freeman, — Ohio App. 3d —, 2006 Ohio 492, — N.E. 2d —, 2006 Ohio App. LEXIS 403 (2006).

Because the 11-year-old victim testified that defendant touched her vagina with his hand, the trial court did not abuse its discretion by allowing the amendment of the indictment, under Ohio R. Crim. P. 7(D), from cunnilingus to digital vaginal penetration. Absent prejudice, defendant was not entitled to a continuance or a discharge of the jury and he failed to request a discharge of the jury or a continuance but, instead, chose to proceed with the trial and thus, he waived any alleged error relating to the trial court's failure to discharge the jury or to grant a continuance. State v. Martin, — Ohio App. 3d —, 2006 Ohio 2749, — N.E. 2d —, 2006 Ohio App. LEXIS 2564 (June 1, 2006).

Because there was no change in the amended indictment to the substance of the crime charged, it only changed the name of one of the victims, defendant was not entitled to a continuance or to have the matter resubmitted to the Grand Jury. Despite defendant's protestations to the contrary, he should not have been surprised or prejudiced by the amendment, since the pre-trial discovery produced to him reflected the identity of the victims. State v. Henley, — Ohio App. 3d —, 2006 Ohio 2728, — N.E. 2d —, 2006 Ohio App. LEXIS 2590 (June 1, 2006).

Defendant's rights under Ohio Const. art. I, § 10 were not violated where a trial court allowed an amendment to the indictment against defendant pursuant to Ohio R. Crim. P. 7(D) in order to add the name of a victim without resubmission to the grand jury, as it did not change the nature or identity of the crime charged, and defendant was already aware of the facts and circumstances of the proof to be offered at trial regarding the offense of felonious assault, in violation of RC § 2903.11. State v. Thompson, — Ohio App. 3d —, 2006 Ohio 3162, — N.E. 2d —, 2006 Ohio App. LEXIS 3039 (June 22, 2006).

Defendant failed to demonstrate that the trial court erred in amending the complaint or that the amendment prejudiced his defense because the amendment clarified that the charge of resisting arrest arose out of defendant's actions inside the gas station at the time he was informed of his arrest for obstructing official business rather than out of his subsequent actions in resisting police efforts to place him in the police cruiser. Thus, it changed neither the name nor the identity of the charged offense and defendant was not misled or prejudiced by the amendment. State v. Kates, 169 Ohio App. 3d 766, 2006 Ohio 6779, 865 N.E.2d 66, 2006 Ohio App. LEXIS 6699 (2006).

Coupling defendant's trial strategy with the vagueness of his objection and his failure to move to discharge the jury or to continue the case, defendant failed to demonstrate either that the trial court abused its discretion in amending the complaint or that the amendment prejudiced his defense: State v. Kates, 169 Ohio App. 3d 766, 2006 Ohio 6779, 865 N.E.2d 66, 2006 Ohio App. LEXIS 6699 (2006).

Amendment changing date

Trial court did not err by permitting the State to amend the indictment with respect to the dates, nor did defendant show any prejudice from the indictment. By failing to object to the amendment of counts 1, 2, and 5, defendant waived any error on appeal. State v. Pickett, — Ohio App. 3d —, 2007 Ohio 3899, — N.E. 2d —, 2007 Ohio App. LEXIS 3552 (Aug. 2, 2007).

Amendment of indictment

mendment of the indictment to change the charge to a violation of RC § 2923.13(A)(3) to a violation of RC § 2923.13(A)(2) was properly allowed where the amendment only changed the category of the grounds for the disability and cured the variance between the facts behind the disability and the category of the disability: State v. Craft, 181 Ohio App. 3d 150, 2009 Ohio 675, 908 N.E.2d 476, 2009 Ohio App. LEXIS 553 (2009).

CrimR 7(D) does not permit the amendment of an indictment when the amendment changes the penalty or degree of the charged offense; amending the indictment to change the penalty or degree changes the identity of the offense: State v. Davis, 121 Ohio St. 3d 239, 2008 Ohio 4537, 903 N.E.2d 609, 2008 Ohio LEXIS 2525 (2008).

City's amendment of charges in an indictment, changing the charge from criminal trespass to disorderly conduct, on the day of trial violated Ohio R. Crim. P. 7(D). Disorderly conduct under RC § 2917.11(A)(5), is not a lesser included offense of criminal trespass; thus, the amendment of the charges changed the identity of the offense in violation of Ohio R. Crim. P. 7(D). State v. Barnick, — Ohio App. 3d —, 2007 Ohio 397, — N.E. 2d —, 2007 Ohio App. LEXIS 344 (Feb. 1, 2007).

Trial court properly allowed an amendment to one charge in an indictment against defendant pursuant to Ohio R. Crim. P. 7(D), wherein the word "felony" was substituted for the erroneous word "aggravated," as the amendment did not alter the name or identity of the crime charged of conspiracy to commit trafficking and possession of drugs, in violation of RC § 2923.01(A), and further, defendant did not show that he was misled or prejudiced by the amendment. The amendment allowed the charge to properly conform with RC § 2923.01(A). State v. Cabrales, — Ohio App. 3d —, 2007 Ohio 857, — N.E. 2d —, 2007 Ohio App. LEXIS 767 (Mar. 2, 2007).

Where an indictment against defendant reflected the elements of resisting arrest as a second degree misdemeanor, in violation of RC § 2921.33(A), it was conceded that the charge was proper, the evidence introduced at trial corresponded to the elements of the charged offense, and the jury was instructed on that offense, even though the indictment indicted mistakenly that the charge was a misdemeanor of the first degree, the judge's statement that he would amend the charge so that it was correct was the functional equivalent to an oral order or journal entry pursuant to Ohio R. Crim. P. 7(D), such that the indictment was deemed amended. State v. Coughlin, — Ohio App. 3d —, 2007 Ohio 897, — N.E. 2d —, 2007 Ohio App. LEXIS 803 (Mar. 2, 2007).

Trial court committed plain error by permitting the State to amend the indictment under Ohio R. Crim. P. 7(D) because the increase in the severity of the offense of aggravated drug trafficking, pursuant to RC § 2925.03(A)(1), from a fourth-degree felony to a second-degree felony changed the identity of the offense due to the lack of notice to defendant and the violation of his right of presentment of the charges to the grand jury. State v. Davis, — Ohio App. 3d —, 2007 Ohio 2249, — N.E. 2d —, 2007 Ohio App. LEXIS 2084 (Apr. 27, 2007).

Trial court did not err by permitting the State to amend the indictments because defendant pled guilty to the amended indictments without objecting to the amendments and the amendments in both cases were in accordance with Ohio R. Crim. P. 7(D). The trial court addressed the amendments at the plea hearing, and defendant indicated that he understood the changes; defendant affirmatively stated that he was entering his plea of his own free will. State v. Ashipa, — Ohio App. 3d —, 2007 Ohio 2245, — N.E. 2d —, 2007 Ohio App. LEXIS 2098 (May 11, 2007).

During a bench trial on charges of wrongful entrustment of a motor vehicle under RC § 4511.203(A)(4), a trial court improperly permitted amendment of the complaint under Ohio R. Crim. P. 7(D) to include additional charges under RC § 4511.203(A)(1) and (2) because § 4511.203(A)(4) focussed on the physical condition of the driver while § 4511.203(A)(1) and (2) addressed proof of a person's legal driving status. Because all the offenses were first-degree misdemeanors, the latter could not be lesser-included offenses of the former. State v. Pignaloso, — Ohio App. 3d —, 2007 Ohio 3194, — N.E. 2d —, 2007 Ohio App. LEXIS 2944 (June 22, 2007).

Since escape was listed in the original indictment and the language used in that indictment referenced escape by name and by the elements needed to commit the offense, the amendment of the statutory section was not a change to the identity of the crime charged. The amendment was merely correcting a typographical error that listed the incorrect statute for escape as RC § 2921.31 instead of RC § 2921.34. Moreover, defendant explicitly consented to the amendment and, as such, he could not complain of the alleged error. State v. Beckett, — Ohio App. 3d —, 2007 Ohio 3175, — N.E. 2d —, 2007 Ohio App. LEXIS 2963 (June 21, 2007).

While the charged offense required the State to prove that defendant aided or abetted "another person," the identity of the person was not an essential element of the charge. Amending the indictment and removing the names of some of the individuals that defendant aided or abetted did not change the charge alleged in the indictment. Also, defendant was not prejudiced by the amendment to the indictment because he was free to subpoena the witnesses himself and to argue that the individuals committed the act themselves; he was not forced to defend against new allegations; and he was not prevented from presenting his defense. State v. Howard, — Ohio App. 3d —, 2007 Ohio 3669, — N.E. 2d —, 2007 Ohio App. LEXIS 3339 (July 13, 2007).

Trial court might have prejudiced defendant's right to present his defense and his due process rights under Ohio Const. art. I, § 10 by granting the State's motion to amend the indictment pursuant to Ohio R. Crim. P. 7(D) with respect to the time period during which defendant allegedly committed the offense of escape, in violation of RC § 2921.34(A)(1). The time period was greatly expanded and upon review of appellate counsel's Anders brief on that issue, an arguable issue of merit was presented which warranted appointment of new counsel to argue that issue further on appeal. State v. Wilkinson, — Ohio App. 3d —, 2007 Ohio 3692, — N.E. 2d —, 2007 Ohio App. LEXIS 3359 (July 20, 2007).

Trial court erred in granting the State's request to amend an indictment against defendant under Ohio R. Crim. P. 7(D), such that the original charge found by the grand jury of misdemeanor intimidation of a witness, in violation of RC § 2921.04(A), was changed to a felony charge under § 2921.04(B); the change was unlawful because it involved the identity of the crime, in violation of the grand jury requirement of Ohio Const. art. I, § 10, as the essential element of "force or unlawful threat of force" was not included in the grand jury's original charge. State v. Fairbanks, 172 Ohio App. 3d 766, 2007 Ohio 4117, 876 N.E.2d 1293, 2007 Ohio App. LEXIS 3737 (2007).

Defendant suffered no prejudice by the amendment of the invoice numbers (work invoices that defendant had submitted for payment on work he had not performed) on the indictment because they did not change the name or identity of the offense but, rather, corrected two typographical errors. State v. Alexander, — Ohio App. 3d —, 2007 Ohio 4177, — N.E. 2d —, 2007 Ohio App. LEXIS 3767 (Aug. 16, 2007).

Trial court did not err by allowing the State to amend the indictments (to reflect that defendant was a complicitor rather than the principal and that the underlying felony for the murder was aggravated robbery rather than felonious assault) because, although defendant had a right to request that the jury be discharged or a continuance since the substance of the indictment was changed by the amendments, he made no such request. Even if he had requested the discharge of the jury or a continuance, it would not have been error to deny the request because defendant would not have been able to prove that he was misled or prejudiced by the amendments. State v. McGlothin, — Ohio App. 3d —, 2007 Ohio 4707, — N.E. 2d —, 2007 Ohio App. LEXIS 4227 (Sept. 14, 2007).

Trial court did not abuse its discretion when it allowed the State to amend the indictment to state the victim's name. Also, the amendment did not prejudice defendant's defense because defendant knew who "Jane Doe" was prior to his indictment. State v. Valenzona, — Ohio App. 3d —, 2007 Ohio 6892, — N.E. 2d —, 2007 Ohio App. LEXIS 6002 (Dec. 20, 2007).

When trial evidence was insufficient to support an indictment's claim that defendant vaginally raped his victim, but it was sufficient to show he digitally penetrated her, it was proper to allow the trial court to consider a post-trial amendment of the indictment, under Ohio R. Crim. P. 7(D), because both acts were forms of sexual conduct barred by RC § 2907.02(A)(1)(b), as defined in RC § 2907.01(A), so the trial court only had to consider if such an amendment would mislead or prejudice defendant. State v. Abdullah, — Ohio App. 3d —, 2006 Ohio 5412, — N.E. 2d —, 2006 Ohio App. LEXIS 5404 (Oct. 17, 2006).

Trial court did not abuse its discretion in allowing the State to amend the indictment against defendant, pursuant to Ohio R. Crim. P. 7(D), to amend the name of one of the stores where a criminal incident occurred, as there was no omission from the original indictment of one of the vital elements that identified the crime; rather, the State's amendment conformed the indictment to the evidence. State v. Bennett, — Ohio App. 3d —, 2006 Ohio 5530, — N.E. 2d —, 2006 Ohio App. LEXIS 5510 (Oct. 18, 2006).

Trial court's grant of a motion by the State to broaden by one month the time period in an indictment against defendant during which he allegedly committed acts of sexual misconduct against a minor victim was proper pursuant to Ohio R. Crim. P. 7(D), as there was no change to the name or identity of the offense, additional allowance was made when a minor sexual offense victim was involved, the amendment did not mislead defendant or prejudice him in any way, and his grand jury right under Ohio Const. art. I, § 10 was not violated. State v. Henderson, — Ohio App. 3d —, 2006 Ohio 5567, — N.E. 2d —, 2006 Ohio App. LEXIS 5554 (Oct. 26, 2006).

Absent prejudice, defendant was not entitled to a continuance, because the amended indictment added statutory language to correct an omission of an element of the crime charged (disorderly conduct) but did not change the name or identity of the crime charged. The identity of the offense before and after the amendments did not change; defendant was still charged with persistent disorderly conduct, in violation of RC § 2917.11(A)(2). State v. Cunningham, — Ohio App. 3d —, 2006 Ohio 6373, — N.E. 2d —, 2006 Ohio App. LEXIS 6328 (Dec. 5, 2006).

There was no error in allowing the amended indictment because it did not alter the essential terms of the original indictment and it did not reflect an increased range of dates or the addition of a new date. At all times, defendant was aware that the grand jury had indicted him on allegations of rape beginning with a series of on-going events from January 1, 1996 through October 31, 2002. The alteration of the time periods did not condemn the indictment process as the grand jury issued a true bill on the exact same charges and range of dates as the amended indictment. State v. Gau, — Ohio App. 3d —, 2006 Ohio 6531, — N.E. 2d —, 2006 Ohio App. LEXIS 6424 (Dec. 8, 2006).

State's motion to amend an indictment charging defendant with burglary and other crimes was properly granted under Ohio R. Crim. P. 7(D) because a change from an allegation that defendant violated RC § 2911.12(A)(1) to an allegation that he violated RC § 2911.12(A)(2) did not alter the name or identity of the crime charged. An amendment that merely changed the violation from one subpart of a statute to another did not change the name or identity of the crime. State v. Bell, — Ohio App. 3d —, 2006 Ohio 6560, — N.E. 2d —, 2006 Ohio App. LEXIS 6485 (Dec. 4, 2006).

Trial court did not err in allowing the State to amend the indictment against defendant with respect to rape charges involving a minor victim after the State had rested its case, as pursuant to Ohio R. Crim. P. 7(D), the amendment did not change the characteristics of the offenses except as to an alteration of the timeframe involved, and there was no material prejudice to defendant by allowing such amendment. State v. Boyer, — Ohio App. 3d —, 2006 Ohio 6992, — N.E. 2d —, 2006 Ohio App. LEXIS 6954 (Dec. 29, 2006).

— Generally

Trial court properly allowed the State to amend a charge of kidnapping, in violation of RC § 2905.01(A)(2) and (3), in an indictment against defendant pursuant to Ohio R. Crim. P. 7(D), as the amendment merely changed the method of kidnapping, but it did not change the identity or nature of the offense charged. State v. Smith, — Ohio App. 3d —, 2007 Ohio 6772, — N.E. 2d —, 2007 Ohio App. LEXIS 5939 (Dec. 18, 2007).

Amendment of indictment information or complaint

Indictments were sufficient because the date of the crime was not an essential element of any of defendant's offenses and specific dates were narrowed down as the minor victims testified and the State amended the indictments accordingly. Defendant made no plausible argument as to why general time frames, as opposed to specific dates, deprived him of any constitutional rights and there was no error in amending the indictments because adding more specificity to the offense dates did not alter the substance of the crime charged. State v. Ali, — Ohio App. 3d —, 2007 Ohio 3776, — N.E. 2d —, 2007 Ohio App. LEXIS 3436 (July 26, 2007).

— Generally

Trial court's grant of the State's request to amend the indictment against defendant pursuant to Ohio R. Crim. P. 7(D) in order to correct the date of the offense was proper, as the amended indictment did not seek to alter the name or identity of the crime charged, it did not add new language to the indictment, and it did not add any additional elements that the State was required to prove. State v. Bevins, — Ohio App. 3d —, 2006 Ohio 5455, — N.E. 2d —, 2006 Ohio App. LEXIS 5453 (Oct. 20, 2006).

There was no evidence that the trial court abused its discretion when it permitted the indictment to be amended or that the amendment to the indictment prejudiced his defense. Since defendant went to trial on only 12, and not 13 counts, and since the superseding indictment neither created a new charge nor changed the name or identity of the offense, the trial court merely amended the original charge and thus, there was no speedy trial violation as defendant waived his speedy trial right to count one. State v. Dudukovich, — Ohio App. 3d —, 2006 Ohio 1309, — N.E. 2d —, 2006 Ohio App. LEXIS 1201 (Mar. 22, 2006).

— Changing date

Trial court could properly enlarge the dates in the indictment, pursuant to CrimR 7(D), because the defendant's failure to report to his parole officer, which was the basis of the alleged breaking of detention in violation of RC § 2921.34(A)(1), was a continuing, recurring offense and a pattern of conduct spanning every day until the defendant was apprehended. However, the court erred by amending the indictment to include dates after the filing of the indictment: State v. Wilkinson, 178 Ohio App. 3d 99, 2008 Ohio 4400, 896 N.E.2d 1027, 2008 Ohio App. LEXIS 3697 (2008).

Trial court did not err in allowing the State to amend an indictment against defendant pursuant to Ohio R. Crim. P. 7(D) in order to correct a typographical error in the date of the alleged criminal incident to reflect the correct year, as such did not violate defendant's due process rights under Ohio Const. art. I, § 10, and the date of the offense was not an essential element of the offense; there was no showing that defendant was prejudiced due to the typographical error in the date, nor was it shown that a failure of justice resulted from the amendment of the indictment. State v. Ray, — Ohio App. 3d —, 2007 Ohio 6836, — N.E. 2d —, 2007 Ohio App. LEXIS 5975 (Dec. 20, 2007).

— Guilty plea

Amendment of an indictment for breaking and entering to receiving stolen property constituted plain error where the defendant's guilty plea to the latter offense did not contain a waiver of the right to a grand jury indictment: State v. Rohrbaugh, 178 Ohio App. 3d 211, 2008 Ohio 4781, 897 N.E.2d 238, 2008 Ohio App. LEXIS 4020 (2008).

As defendant was prosecuted by indictment and the indictment was then amended pursuant to a plea agreement, there was no issue regarding defendant's waiver of the rights contained in Ohio R. Crim. P. 7(A); as defendant voluntarily participated in the amendment of the charges, including one from aggravated murder to kidnapping, which he then entered guilty pleas to, he could not assert on appeal that there were any errors under Rule 7(D) associated with the amendments. State v. Williams, — Ohio App. 3d —, 2007 Ohio 5073, — N.E. 2d —, 2007 Ohio App. LEXIS 4475 (Sept. 27, 2007).

Bill of information

Defendant's conviction for two counts of aggravated vehicular homicide, in violation of RC § 2903.06(A)(2)(a), was based on a void bill of information, as the information did not properly charge defendant with any offense pursuant to Ohio R. Crim. P. 7(B). It failed to charge him with vehicular manslaughter under RC § 2903.06(A)(4) due to the State's failure to charge a predicate offense, as "reckless operation of a motor vehicle" was under a collection of statutes pursuant to RC §§ 4511.20 and 4511.203 and did not refer to a singular offense, and the information did not charge him with aggravated vehicular homicide under RC § 2903.06(A)(2)(a) because the information charged defendant with "reckless operation of a motor vehicle," which was not synonymous with the required element of "recklessness." State v. Reinhart, — Ohio App. 3d —, 2007 Ohio 2284, — N.E. 2d —, 2007 Ohio App. LEXIS 2120 (May 14, 2007).

Bill of particulars

Bill of particulars adequately notified defendant that the jury could be instructed on complicity, even though the charge was drawn in terms of the principal offense of aggravated burglary. The bill of particulars identified defendant and his friend as the individuals who kicked the door in and assaulted the victim. State v. Templeton, — Ohio App. 3d —, 2007 Ohio 1148, — N.E. 2d —, 2007 Ohio App. LEXIS 1074 (Mar. 14, 2007).

Although the bill of particulars in defendant's criminal matter indicated that her conduct was as a principal and at trial she was cast as an aider and abettor, the denial of her motion for a mistrial was proper pursuant to RC § 2923.03 and Ohio R. Crim. P. 7(D), as such a change in the role attributed to defendant did not constitute a reversible error; any remedy for such a change would have been by amendment to the bill of particulars and moreover, defendant failed to show any prejudice. State v. White, — Ohio App. 3d —, 2007 Ohio 3217, — N.E. 2d —, 2007 Ohio App. LEXIS 2849 (June 21, 2007).

Culpable mental states

Failure of an indictment charging a violation of RC § 2907.323 to include the element of recklessness was harmless error beyond a reasonable doubt where the defendant had notice that recklessness was an element of the offense, the jury was properly charged on that element, and the state argued at trial that defendant's conduct was reckless: State v. Hurst, 181 Ohio App. 3d 454, 2009 Ohio 983, 909 N.E.2d 653, 2009 Ohio App. LEXIS 946 (2009).

Double jeopardy

Where a trial court granted defendant a continuance of a trial date upon the State's amendment of charges pursuant to CrimR 7(D) after the jury had already been selected and sworn, and the original jurors could not be reseated on the continued date due to unavailability of some of the jurors, such constituted a "manifest necessity" that allowed a retrial without violating double jeopardy principles. State v. Bentley, — Ohio App. 3d —, 2008 Ohio 195, — N.E. 2d —, 2008 Ohio App. LEXIS 166 (Jan. 11, 2008).

Due process

Notice requirement of Ohio R. Crim. P. 7 was not met at the time that the City amended its charges against defendant because defendant demonstrated that the notation on the City's file (noting an amendment in the charge) was never journalized in the court's docket; nor was defendant ever served with an amended complaint notifying him of the change in the disorderly conduct charge. City of Brooklyn v. Fouche, — Ohio App. 3d —, 2006 Ohio 169, — N.E. 2d —, 2006 Ohio App. LEXIS 151 (Jan. 19, 2006).

Guilty plea

Guilty plea waives any defect in an indictment occasioned by a failure to allege a culpable mental state: State v. Lawrence, 180 Ohio App. 3d 468, 2009 Ohio 33, 905 N.E.2d 1268, 2009 Ohio App. LEXIS 21 (2009).

Where defendant entered into a plea agreement which required his entry of a guilty plea to a new amended drug count in exchange for an agreed sentence, he waived his ability to challenge the amended indictment under Ohio R.

Crim. P. 7(D). State v. Spurling, — Ohio App. 3d —, 2007 Ohio 858, — N.E. 2d —, 2007 Ohio App. LEXIS 766 (Mar. 2, 2007).

Indictment

Defendant's habeas corpus petition under RC § 2725.04 was dismissed where he failed to state cognizable claims arising under Ohio R. Crim. P. 6 and 7, as he only made unsupported conclusions regarding the denial of his rights under Ohio R. Crim. P. 6 and further, a motion to dismiss was the appropriate remedy for those rights. As to Ohio R. Crim. P. 7, once defendant was indicted by the grand jury, he could no longer waive the indictment and further, habeas corpus relief was not available to challenge the validity or sufficiency of an indictment. Clarke v. McFaul, — Ohio App. 3d —, 2007 Ohio 1592, — N.E. 2d —, 2007 Ohio App. LEXIS 1457 (Apr. 3, 2007).

There was insufficient evidence for one of the counts of gross sexual imposition, under RC § 2907.05(A)(4), because the State's evidence at trial simply did not correspond to the specific allegation contained in the indictment since there was no evidence that the victim was still under the age of 13 for the second count. The indictment put defendant on notice that she had to defend against two counts of using "breast cups" on the victim before she reached 13 years of age; thus, because the State identified a particular device and a particular time frame as integral parts of the indictment, defendant could not be convicted of another offense that involved other activities or other devices. State v. Bowers, — Ohio App. 3d —, 2007 Ohio 3986, — N.E. 2d —, 2007 Ohio App. LEXIS 3596 (May 23, 2007).

Indictment sufficient

Given the nature of the offenses (rape of a minor) and the testimony offered, the indictment was not insufficient as to dates. At trial, the victim testified that the rapes occurred after she turned 14 and continued up until prior to her 17th birthday and she stated that during this time period, it occurred almost on a weekly basis. State v. Haschenburger, — Ohio App. 3d —, 2007 Ohio 1562, — N.E. 2d —, 2007 Ohio App. LEXIS 1446 (Mar. 27, 2007).

Indictment on counts one and two was not insufficient nor was it constitutionally defective because the indictment did not fail to set forth essential facts showing the element of deception for theft by deception. The indictment stated that defendant did, with purpose to deprive the owner, knowingly obtain or exert control over the property by deception, the value being $5,000 or more. State v. Untied, — Ohio App. 3d —, 2007 Ohio 1804, — N.E. 2d —, 2007 Ohio App. LEXIS 1643 (Apr. 12, 2007).

Indictment was not insufficient nor did the trial court err by denying defendant's motion for a more specific bill of particulars because the victim was a child and the available details of each offense were limited. The State supplied defendant with the information that it had through discovery. The time ranges included in the indictment for each offense allowed the trial court to associate particular charges with particular incidents to which the victim testified at trial. State v. Russell, — Ohio App. 3d —, 2007 Ohio 2108, — N.E. 2d —, 2007 Ohio App. LEXIS 1962 (May 3, 2007).

Where defendant was charged with aggravated burglary, in violation of RC § 2911.11(A)(2), the trial court did not abuse its discretion when it overruled defendant's dismissal motion based on his assertion that the indictment merely recited the language of the statute and did not specify the intended crime that defendant was going to commit upon entry into the occupied structure, as such did not make the indictment defective on its face. Defendant was sufficiently appraised of the charge against him where he was supplied with information in a bill of particulars which indicated the date, time, location, and defendant's conduct pursuant to Ohio R. Crim. P. 7(E), such that defendant's due process rights under Ohio

Const. art. I, § 10 were not violated. State v. Morris, — Ohio App. 3d —, 2007 Ohio 3591, — N.E. 2d —, 2007 Ohio App. LEXIS 3298 (July 13, 2007).

Trial court had subject matter jurisdiction to convict defendant and did not err when it found defendant guilty of both assaults, fifth-degree felonies, under RC § 2903.13(C)(2)(a), because the indictment gave adequate notice when it referenced the degree of the offense; the State used language within the indictment that comported with Ohio R. Crim. P. 7(B) and RC § 2945.75(A)(1). In addition, the State provided defendant with a bill of particulars that notified him of the enhancement element in more detail and the trial court gave an instruction to the jury regarding the enhancement element. State v. Fields, — Ohio App. 3d —, 2007 Ohio 4191, — N.E. 2d —, 2007 Ohio App. LEXIS 3779 (Aug. 13, 2007).

Indictment was sufficient because it used the exact language of the statute, quoted the statutory section, and specified when defendant committed the acts. Although the indictment did not state the particular facts upon which the indictment was based, the statutory elements were all present; defendant was able to obtain the factual basis from the bill of particulars and the State's prosecutorial file. Ohio v. Sessler, — Ohio App. 3d —, 2007 Ohio 4931, — N.E. 2d —, 2007 Ohio App. LEXIS 4631 (Sept. 24, 2007).

Indictment charging defendant with felony murder was not defective because it did not specify the underlying felony, because such a specification was not required, and the crime was properly stated in the words of the applicable statute, pursuant to Ohio R. Crim. P. 7(B). State v. Hunter, — Ohio App. 3d —, 2006 Ohio 20, — N.E. 2d —, 2006 Ohio App. LEXIS 9 (Jan. 5, 2006).

There was no plain error under Ohio R. Crim. P. 52 in the trial court's denial of defendant's motion to dismiss an indictment against him, charging him with multiple counts of sexual battery against a victim that he was in a relationship of "in loco parentis" with, as the indictment sufficiently advised defendant of that relationship pursuant to Ohio R. Crim. P. 7(B) and was not deficient. Defendant waived any argument with respect to alleged defects in the charging instrument except as to plain error where he failed to challenge the sufficiency thereof prior to trial pursuant to Ohio R. Crim. P. 12(C)(2). State v. Funk, — Ohio App. 3d —, 2006 Ohio 2068, — N.E. 2d —, 2006 Ohio App. LEXIS 1916 (Apr. 27, 2006).

Under the plain error standard of review pursuant to Ohio R. Crim. P. 52(B) due to defendant's failure to object, the indictments charging defendant with a variety of sexual offenses were sufficient and provided notice of all of the essential elements of the offenses charged against him, pursuant to Ohio R. Crim. P. 7(B) and RC § 2941.03. Defendant was provided with a bill of particulars which further specified the details of the crimes charged against him, and to which defendant again failed to file any objection as to the sufficiency thereof. State v. Carnes, — Ohio App. 3d —, 2006 Ohio 2134, — N.E. 2d —, 2006 Ohio App. LEXIS 1974 (May 1, 2006).

Grand jury foreperson's signature on the last page of a five-count indictment, each count of which was printed on a separate page, was sufficient under Ohio R. Crim. P. 6 and 7, as the last page listed the five statutes involved in the multi-count indictment and it included, in addition to the signature, the notation "True Bill" and a certification by the clerk of courts. State v. Koval, — Ohio App. 3d —, 2006 Ohio 5377, — N.E. 2d —, 2006 Ohio App. LEXIS 5340 (Oct. 16, 2006).

Charges against defendant of pandering of obscenity involving a minor, in violation of RC § 2907.321(A)(2) and (5), were stated with sufficiency in the indictment against him pursuant to Ohio R. Crim. P. 7(B) where the words of the statutory section were alleged in each count. The specific file name of the computer program where the images were allegedly stored was not required in the indictment, and any error was

waived by defendant's failure to object in the trial court. State v. Gillingham, — Ohio App. 3d —, 2006 Ohio 5758, — N.E. 2d —, 2006 Ohio App. LEXIS 5738 (Oct. 27, 2006).

Lesser included offenses

Because theft is a lesser included offense of robbery, an indictment for robbery necessarily includes all the elements of all lesser included offenses, together with any of the special, statutory findings dictated by the evidence produced in the case. When an indictment charges a defendant with robbery, the defendant may be convicted of theft as a lesser included offense of robbery, and the degree of the offense will depend on the special finding of the value of the property stolen: State v. Smith, 121 Ohio St. 3d 409, 2009 Ohio 787, 905 N.E.2d 151, 2009 Ohio LEXIS 549 (2009).

Notice

Indictment gave defendant sufficient notice because the indictment clearly tracked the language of both RC § 2911.11(A)(1), setting forth the elements of aggravated burglary, and RC § 2911.12(A)(1), setting forth the elements of the lesser included offense burglary. State v. Cloud, — Ohio App. 3d —, 2007 Ohio 4241, — N.E. 2d —, 2007 Ohio App. LEXIS 3931 (Aug. 14, 2007).

Plain error

Plain error analysis, rather that structural error analysis, normally applies to defective indictment cases. Defendant's failure to object to the use of conjunctive language in some counts of the indictment waived all but plain error as to whether those counts were improperly duplicitous: State v. Robertson, 180 Ohio App. 3d 365, 2008 Ohio 6909, 905 N.E.2d 678, 2008 Ohio App. LEXIS 5775 (2008).

Prejudice

Because the jury found defendant guilty of both aggravated robbery and aggravated burglary, no prejudice resulted from the indictment for felony murder not containing the essential elements of aggravated robbery and aggravated burglary. State v. Torres, — Ohio App. 3d —, 2006 Ohio 3696, — N.E. 2d —, 2006 Ohio App. LEXIS 3641 (July 20, 2006).

Right to appeal

Trial court's amendment of the indictment, reducing the receiving stolen property charge under RC § 2913.51 to a misdemeanor, was not appealable under RC § 2945.67(A), which gave the State the right to appeal the dismissal of an indictment; no part of the indictment was dismissed, and the trial court, under Ohio R. Crim. P. 7, did not change the nature or charge of the indictment. State v. Gordon, — Ohio App. 3d —, 2006 Ohio 1732, — N.E. 2d —, 2006 Ohio App. LEXIS 1590 (Apr. 6, 2006).

Service of indictment

Trial court did not err in failing to hold a hearing on defendant's objection to service of his indictment because, since defendant filed an untimely objection, he waived any objection to service of his indictment, under Ohio R. Crim. P. 12(H). Also, his arraignment was conducted in compliance with the time requirements of RC § 2941.49 because the indictment was issued and the Return of Executed Warrant form completed by the arresting officer provided that defendant had received a copy of both the indictment and the warrant on the indictment. State v. Kirk, — Ohio App. 3d —, 2007 Ohio 1228, — N.E. 2d —, 2007 Ohio App. LEXIS 1138 (Mar. 19, 2007).

Specific dates

There was no error in the trial court's decision concerning defendant's motion to compel the State to plead more specifically because specific dates and times were not elements of the offenses for which defendant was charged (rape, sexual battery, and pandering sexually oriented matter involving a minor). There was no evidence indicating that the State possessed specific dates or times the abuse occurred, or that specific dates were ascertainable, given the pervasive nature of the conduct alleged. Also, defendant failed to demonstrate prejudiced because his defense centered upon his denial that the acts in question ever occurred, regardless of when the acts were alleged to have occurred. State v. Rogers, — Ohio App. 3d —, 2007 Ohio 1890, — N.E. 2d —, 2007 Ohio App. LEXIS 1745 (Apr. 23, 2007).

Sufficiency of indictment

Failure to include the culpable mental state of recklessness, pursuant to RC § 2901.21(B), in the indictment charging defendant with illegal use of a minor in nudity-oriented material, in violation of RC § 2907.323(A)(1), rendered the indictment invalid. Thus, the trial court lacked subject matter jurisdiction to try defendant on that charge. State v. Smith, — Ohio App. 3d —, 2007 Ohio 502, — N.E. 2d —, 2007 Ohio App. LEXIS 423 (Jan. 29, 2007).

Indictment charging inmate with rape and gross sexual imposition was sufficient because the indictment stated the offenses in the explicit language used within the applicable statutes, RC §§ 2907.02(A)(1)(b) and 2907.05(A)(4), so the indictment included all the essential elements necessary to inform the inmate of the specific conduct that gave rise to the charges against the inmate. Ohio v. Wilson, — Ohio App. 3d —, 2007 Ohio 4885, — N.E. 2d —, 2007 Ohio App. LEXIS 4369 (Sept. 21, 2007).

Defendant's waiver extended to his superseding indictment because defendant was fully aware of the charged offenses when he executed a waiver of his right to a speedy trial; defendant, himself, in his speedy trial waiver specifically identified the statutory subsection, RC § 2907.02(B), which made his charged offense punishable by life imprisonment. The State only issued the superseding indictment to add statutorily mandated language; the superseding indictment was issued to add statutorily mandated language; and the original indictment twice referred to the fact that defendant was facing life imprisonment and cited RC § 2907.02(B) twice. State v. Clark, — Ohio App. 3d —, 2006 Ohio 1155, — N.E. 2d —, 2006 Ohio App. LEXIS 1059 (Mar. 8, 2006).

Indictment sufficiently charged defendant with the "knowingly" element of aggravated robbery, under Ohio R. Crim. P. 7(B), as (1) the indictment charged defendant with attempting or committing a theft offense, as defined in RC § 2913.01, and (2) RC § 2913.01(K)(1) defined a theft offense as including a violation of RC § 2913.02, which contained the element of knowingly. State v. McCoy, — Ohio App. 3d —, 2006 Ohio 56, — N.E. 2d —, 2006 Ohio App. LEXIS 37 (Jan. 5, 2006).

Indictment was not deficient because RC § 2925.05(A) provided that the purpose of providing money was to violate RC § 2925.04 or for the purpose of selling or offering to sell a controlled substance. RC § 2925.04 prohibited the engaging in any part of the production of a controlled substance, and production was inclusive of distribution. State v. Wilson, — Ohio App. 3d —, 2006 Ohio 1672, — N.E. 2d —, 2006 Ohio App. LEXIS 1561 (Mar. 31, 2006).

Inmate did not show that his counsel rendered ineffective assistance in violation of U.S. Const. amend. VI and Ohio Const. art. I, § 10 where counsel failed to object to a criminal indictment against him, as it was sufficient pursuant to Ohio R. Crim. P. 7 where it adequately recited the language of RC §§ 2905.01 and 2923.02 regarding the attempted kidnapping charge. State v. Flora, — Ohio App. 3d —, 2006 Ohio 5732, — N.E. 2d —, 2006 Ohio App. LEXIS 5730 (Nov. 2, 2006).

—— Plain error

In most defective indictment cases in which the indictment fails to include an essential element of the charge, plain error analysis, pursuant to CrimR 52(B), will be the proper analysis to apply. The syllabus in State v. Colon, 118 Ohio St. 3d 26, 2008 Ohio 1624, 885 N.E.2d 917, 2008 Ohio LEXIS 874, is confined to the facts in that case: State v. Colon, 119 Ohio St. 3d 204, 2008 Ohio 3749, 893 N.E.2d 169, 2008 Ohio LEXIS 1979 (2008).

Timeliness

Ohio R. Crim. P. 7(A) was inapplicable to defendant's matter with respect to the fact that an information or indictment was not filed within 14 days, as there was no waiver of an indictment by defendant. State v. Mincy, — Ohio App. 3d —, 2007 Ohio 1316, — N.E. 2d —, 2007 Ohio App. LEXIS 1212 (Mar. 23, 2007).

Traffic citation

As a complaint charging defendant with a violation of RC § 4511.19(A)(1) met the requirements of Ohio Traf. R. 3 because it advised defendant of the offense with which she was charged in a manner that she could reasonably understand, especially given the fact that the ticket contained the language set forth in RC § 4511.19(A)(1)(a), there was no error in the trial court's denial of defendant's dismissal motion, based on her claim that § 4511.19(A)(1) was not a sufficient charge because there was no penalty associated with it. The trial court's grant of defendant's motion to amend the ticket pursuant to Ohio R. Crim. P. 7(D) to reflect that she was charged with § 4511.19(A)(1)(a) was not error. State v. Valdez, — Ohio App. 3d —, 2006 Ohio 3298, — N.E. 2d —, 2006 Ohio App. LEXIS 3215 (June 28, 2006).

Waiver

When defendant was initially charged with and advised regarding, a violation of RC § 2921.02(A), but signed a waiver of indictment and a guilty plea regarding a violation of RC § 2921.02(C), defendant did not show that the trial court violated RC § 2941.021 or CrimR 7(A), because (1) defendant was aware of the nature of the charges, (2) the two charges subjected defendant to the same penalty, (3) both charges were applicable to the facts, and (4) defendant did not show that defendant received a harsher sentence due to pleading guilty to a violation of RC § 2921.02(C), rather than a violation of RC § 2921.02(A). State v. Susany, — Ohio App. 3d —, 2008 Ohio 1543, — N.E. 2d —, 2008 Ohio App. LEXIS 1355 (Mar. 20, 2008).

Trial court did not err by refusing to dismiss the felonious assault charge after the State moved to amend the charge just before trial because the trial court offered defendant the remedy allowed by rule. That defendant elected not to accept a continuance, constituted an express waiver of any error implicated therein. State v. Benton, — Ohio App. 3d —, 2007 Ohio 3945, — N.E. 2d —, 2007 Ohio App. LEXIS 3625 (Aug. 3, 2007).

Wrong offense charged

Trial court committed plain error because count two of the indictment to which defendant entered a plea of no contest failed to charge a valid statutory offense; the indictment charged defendant with possessing a particular controlled substance, crack cocaine, that was not only different from the controlled substance that he actually possessed, powder cocaine, but in a gross amount that did not constitute an offense under RC § 2925.11(C)(4)(b). The evidence, including the testimony of the trooper at the suppression hearing, unequivocally demonstrated that the cocaine that defendant possessed was in fact powder cocaine, not crack cocaine. Ohio v. Yslas, — Ohio App. 3d —, 2007 Ohio 5646, — N.E. 2d —, 2007 Ohio App. LEXIS 4964 (Oct. 19, 2007).

RULE 8. Joinder of Offenses and Defendants

(A) **Joinder of offenses.** Two or more offenses may be charged in the same indictment, information or complaint in a separate count for each offense if the offenses charged, whether felonies or misdemeanors or both, are of the same or similar character, or are based on the same act or transaction, or are based on two or more acts or transactions connected together or constituting parts of a common scheme or plan, or are part of a course of criminal conduct.

(B) **Joinder of defendants.** Two or more defendants may be charged in the same indictment, information or complaint if they are alleged to have participated in the same act or transaction or in the same series of acts or transactions constituting an offense or offenses, or in the same course of criminal conduct. Such defendants may be charged in one or more counts together or separately, and all of the defendants need not be charged in each count.

NOTES TO DECISIONS

ANALYSIS

Discretion of the court
Ineffective assistance of counsel
—Failure to move to sever charges
Joinder
Joinder of defendants
Joinder of offenses
Motion for severance
Severance of offenses

Discretion of the court

Trial court did not abuse its discretion under Ohio R. Crim. P. 8(A) and 14 when it denied defendant's motion for relief from prejudicial joinder of two drug-related offenses which arose from incidents that occurred several months apart, as his defense to the possession of drugs charge implicated him in other drug-related criminal activity, which was admissible under Ohio R. Evid. 404(B). Ohio v. Anzures, — Ohio App. 3d —, 2007 Ohio 4817, — N.E. 2d —, 2007 Ohio App. LEXIS 4342 (Sept. 18, 2007).

Ineffective assistance of counsel

Defendant failed to demonstrate ineffective assistance of counsel because it was entirely reasonable that defense counsel believed that the evidence regarding the confusion over the co-defendant's identity and a defense that defendant was just in the wrong place at the wrong time would have resulted in acquittal. Further, trial counsel could have anticipated prior to trial that the evidence of drug dealing would have been elicited from the co-defendant or defendant and sought a separate trial but, it appeared to have been co-defendant's and defendant's trial tactic to paint the prosecution witnesses as drug users and to show that they had been wrongly accused because they had wanted to get the co-defendant and defendant out of the neighborhood. State v. Quinn, — Ohio App. 3d —, 2007 Ohio 878, — N.E. 2d —, 2007 Ohio App. LEXIS 787 (Mar. 2, 2007).

—Failure to move to sever charges

In a prosecution for possession of methamphetamine and possession of anhydrous ammonia, defense counsel's failure to move, under Ohio R. Crim. P. 14, to sever the charges against defendant, which had been joined, under Ohio R. Crim. P. 8(A), was not ineffective assistance of counsel because defendant could not show his rights were prejudiced by joining the offenses, as the evidence of each crime, which occurred on different dates, was simple and direct. State v. Rollins, — Ohio App. 3d —, 2006 Ohio 1879, — N.E. 2d —, 2006 Ohio App. LEXIS 1726 (Apr. 17, 2006).

Joinder

Evidence of a bicycle used in the commission of an abduction offense would have been admissible in the trial on the kidnapping, rape, and robbery charges against defendant, involving the same bicycle but a different victim, time, and place, as probative evidence of the identity of the perpetrator under Ohio R. Evid. 404(B), and the evidence used to prove the abduction count was sufficiently simple and direct that it was not an abuse of discretion to join the counts for purposes of trial. State v. Brown, — Ohio App. 3d —, 2006 Ohio 42, — N.E. 2d —, 2006 Ohio App. LEXIS 45 (Jan. 6, 2006).

Joinder of defendants

Joinder of the four defendants for trial was proper because they acted in concert and participated in the same criminal enterprise, the same series of acts and transactions, and the same course of criminal conduct and the various offenses charged, which were identical for each defendant, were the result of defendants' participation in a common scheme or plan, and the same course of criminal conduct. Defendant's motion for a separate trial was not based upon the same grounds and concerns being raised and argued for the first time on appeal and, for that reason alone, the trial court did not abuse its discretion in denying defendant's motion for a separate trial. State v. Patterson, — Ohio App. 3d —, 2007 Ohio 29, — N.E. 2d —, 2007 Ohio App. LEXIS 22 (Jan. 5, 2007).

Where defendant failed to object to the joinder of her criminal trial with that of one of her co-defendants, pursuant to Ohio R. Crim. P. 8, as she did not file a motion to sever the case at any stage of the proceedings pursuant to Ohio R. Crim. P. 14, any objection to such joinder was waived for purposes of appeal. There was no plain error under Ohio R. Crim. P. 52, as she failed to show that she was prejudiced from the joinder where there was no evidence that the jury was influenced thereby. State v. Harris-Powers, — Ohio App. 3d —, 2007 Ohio 389, — N.E. 2d —, 2007 Ohio App. LEXIS 349 (Feb. 1, 2007).

Trial court's decision to try two co-defendants jointly pursuant to Ohio R. Crim. P. 8(B) was not an abuse of discretion, as defendant had failed to properly preserve his claim of misjoinder pursuant to Ohio R. Crim. P. 14 where he did not renew the motion at the close of the State's case or at the conclusion of all of the evidence, and further, he failed to provide the trial court with any information as to factors against joinder in his severance hearing. State v. Holbert, — Ohio App. 3d —, 2007 Ohio 986, — N.E. 2d —, 2007 Ohio App. LEXIS 916 (Mar. 8, 2007).

Defendant's claim that her trial counsel was ineffective in violation of her rights under U.S. Const. amend. VI and Ohio Const. art. I, § 10 by not seeking to have separate trials of defendant and her co-defendant pursuant to RC § 2945.13 and Ohio R. Crim. P. 14 lacked merit, as joinder of defendants under Ohio R. Crim. P. 8(B) was favored and no reason was shown for severance, such that counsel was not required to perform a futile act. Defendant's claim that she had a defense that was "antagonistic" to that of her co-defendant did not show prejudice, as she did not present a defense and further, her codefendant could have asserted the right to remain silent. State v. Henderson, — Ohio App. 3d —, 2007 Ohio 2372, — N.E. 2d —, 2007 Ohio App. LEXIS 2212 (May 17, 2007).

Joinder of offenses

Defendant failed to demonstrate that his rights were prejudiced by the joinder and denial of his motion to sever because the evidence presented would have been admissible in separate trials if the charges had been severed. Although he was correct that the State could not have introduced the evidence to show that defendant had a propensity to commit the crimes, the evidence was admissible, under Evid. R. 404 and RC § 2945.59, to show defendant's motive or intent, an element of the crime charged (attempted rape and robbery), which defendant placed at issue. State v. Hill, — Ohio App. 3d —, 2007 Ohio 56, — N.E. 2d —, 2007 Ohio App. LEXIS 51 (Jan. 5, 2007).

Defendant was properly charged with two separate counts each of gross sexual imposition and kidnapping where his 10-year-old victim alleged two separate but similar incidents that occurred during two trips by her to defendant's bedroom under the guise of looking for defendant's cat, such that joinder of the offenses pursuant to Ohio R. Crim. P. 8(A) was proper. State v. Djuric, — Ohio App. 3d —, 2007 Ohio 413, — N.E. 2d —, 2007 Ohio App. LEXIS 362 (Feb. 1, 2007).

Charges against defendant arising from two incidents were properly tried together, under Ohio R. Crim. P. 13(A) and 8(A), and this did not violate Ohio R. Crim. P. 14, because (1), in one incident, it was alleged that defendant had committed a murder, and, in the other incident, the weapon allegedly used to commit that murder was recovered from the vehicle defendant had been driving, so, under Ohio R. Evid. 404(B), evidence of one incident would have been admissible in a separate trial of the other incident, and (2) the evidence related to the two incidents was simple and direct so that a jury would not become confused by presenting such evidence at one trial. State v. Nelms, — Ohio App. 3d —, 2007 Ohio 4664, — N.E. 2d —, 2007 Ohio App. LEXIS 4205 (Sept. 11, 2007).

Trial court's joinder under Ohio R. Crim. P. 8(A) of multiple robbery offenses and its denial of defendant's request to sever each offense from the other under Ohio R. Crim. P. 14 was not an abuse of discretion, as each of the victims identified defendant as the robber, he used the same characteristics in each robbery of wearing costumes and disguises and making smart existing remarks, and the facts were straightforward and uncomplicated; the robberies all had a common thread, such that they could have been brought in a single indictment or information pursuant to Ohio R. Crim. P. 13. State v. Starks, — Ohio App. 3d —, 2007 Ohio 4897, — N.E. 2d —, 2007 Ohio App. LEXIS 4364 (Sept. 21, 2007).

Trial court did not abuse its discretion under Ohio R. Crim. P. 8 and 13 in failing to join an indictment that charged defendant with escape for failing to report to his parole officer with an indictment that arose out of defendant's failure to heed a police car's siren to pull over, as the charges in each indictment bore no relation to one another, and they were not based on a common scheme or plan. Ohio v. Anderson, — Ohio App. 3d —, 2007 Ohio 5326, — N.E. 2d —, 2007 Ohio App. LEXIS 4692 (Oct. 4, 2007).

Similarity in the offenses alleged involving both victims justified the joinder of the offenses at trial under the criteria set forth in Ohio R. Crim. P. 8; in both cases, defendant convinced the victims that he could help them avoid foreclosure by a system of payments, and in both cases he collected the money, but the money was never paid towards the mortgages. Because defendant did not present any factual basis upon which to conclude that there would be prejudice, he did not affirmatively demonstrate that his right to a fair trial was compromised. State v. Webb, 173 Ohio App. 3d 547, 2007 Ohio 5670, 879 N.E.2d 254, 2007 Ohio App. LEXIS 4991 (2007).

Joinder was warranted where both offenses involved the defendant's use of his position at a foreclosure prevention company to steal funds from homeowners involved in the foreclosure process: State v. Webb, 173 Ohio App. 3d 547, 2007 Ohio 5670, 879 N.E.2d 254, 2007 Ohio App. LEXIS 4991 (2007).

Defendant failed to show how the results of the trial would have been different had the different drug offenses been tried separately. The jury found defendant not guilty on one count, which demonstrated that the jury was able to separate its analysis of the individual charges and impartially decide each count. State v. Reuschling, — Ohio App. 3d —, 2007 Ohio 6726, — N.E. 2d —, 2007 Ohio App. LEXIS 5895 (Dec. 14, 2007).

Defendant suffered no prejudice by the joinder of the escape charge because, although the evidence of the escape charge was simple and distinct from the rape, kidnapping, and bribery charges, it was part of a course of criminal conduct. Defendant committed the crimes against the victim, tried to bribe her not to go to the police, and then left town. State v. Spruce, — Ohio App. 3d —, 2006 Ohio 1730, — N.E. 2d —, 2006 Ohio App. LEXIS 1594 (Apr. 6, 2006).

Defendant was not prejudiced by the joinder of offenses because both theft offenses were of the same character and constituted parts of a common plan; both theft offenses occurred on the university campus, were closely committed in place and time, and had the same modus operandi--a woman starting a conversation with the victims while using a jacket to conceal a theft. The offenses were related by time, day, location, and common scheme and, even if the charges had been separated, evidence of one offense would still have been admissible in the trial of the other, under Ohio R. Evid. 404(B). State v. Brotherton, — Ohio App. 3d —, 2006 Ohio 1747, — N.E. 2d —, 2006 Ohio App. LEXIS 1622 (Apr. 7, 2006).

Trial court did not err in joining the two indictments for trial, under Ohio R. Crim. P. 8(A) and 13; because the evidence of the second robbery would have been admissible at a separate trial of the first robbery, no prejudice stemmed from the jury's consideration of evidence relating to both robberies in reaching their verdicts. Moreover, the evidence of both robberies was simple and direct, and neither crime was so complex that the jury would have had difficulty separating the proof required for each offense. State v. Tipton, — Ohio App. 3d —, 2006 Ohio 2066, — N.E. 2d —, 2006 Ohio App. LEXIS 1911 (Apr. 27, 2006).

Joinder, under Ohio R. Crim. P. 8(A) and 13, was proper since the incidents were based on the same course of conduct in that the charges in all three cases alleged a course of consistent drug-related activity on housing authority property. Defendant failed to demonstrate any prejudice by the joinder since the evidence in each case was simple and direct, involving easily distinguishable fact patterns. State v. Gilbert, — Ohio App. 3d —, 2006 Ohio 3595, — N.E. 2d —, 2006 Ohio App. LEXIS 3533 (July 13, 2006).

Trial court's denial of defendant's motion to sever offenses under Ohio R. Crim. P. 14 was not an abuse of discretion, as joinder under Ohio R. Crim. P. 8(A) was proper where the offenses of pandering and sexual battery involved minors and all of the offenses occurred at defendant's residence, the evidence was not deemed confusing or difficult for the jurors to separate, and the trial court determined that the jury could segregate the evidence involving sexual contact from the evidence involving possession of pornographic pictures of minors. State v. Purkhiser, — Ohio App. 3d —, 2006 Ohio 4014, — N.E. 2d —, 2006 Ohio App. LEXIS 3969 (Aug. 4, 2006).

In a drug prosecution, the joinder of two indictments, under Ohio R. Crim. P. 8, did not prejudice defendant because they were all evidence of defendant's modus operandi, so, had the offenses been tried separately, the evidence would have been admissible at the separate trials, so defendant was not prejudiced when the offenses were joined in one trial, nor was he entitled to have the offenses severed, under Ohio R. Crim. P. 14. State v. Bundy, — Ohio App. 3d —, 2006 Ohio 4062, — N.E. 2d —, 2006 Ohio App. LEXIS 4021 (Aug. 8, 2006).

Trial court did not abuse its discretion in denying defendant's motion under Ohio R. Crim. P. 8(A) and 14 to sever four counts of rape against him, arising from two separate incidents with different victims, as joinder of the claims was appropriate to show a "common scheme or plan" because defendant's conduct was the same in both instances, whereby he lured the victims with drugs, took them to an abandoned building, and threatened them. As the victims did not know each other, the similarity of their versions of events undermined defendant's claim that the sexual acts were consensual and that the victims' testimony was not credible. State v. Boyd, — Ohio App. 3d —, 2006 Ohio 4132, — N.E. 2d —, 2006 Ohio App. LEXIS 4076 (Aug. 11, 2006).

Evidence from two criminal incidents which formed the basis of multiple charges against defendant was of the same or similar character where both were crimes against women involving kidnapping and aggravated robbery, and both incidents shared a common or similar scheme or plan and accordingly, the trial court did not abuse its discretion in joining the offenses for trial under Ohio R. Crim. P. 8(A). There was no showing that joinder was prejudicial, as the evidence of one incident could have been admitted in the other incident's trial under Ohio R. Evid. 404(B) to show defendant's identity or plan, the the likelihood of confusion was minimal. State v. Lininger, — Ohio App. 3d —, 2006 Ohio 4136, — N.E. 2d —, 2006 Ohio App. LEXIS 4085 (Aug. 11, 2006).

Motion for severance

Trial court's denial of defendant's initial motion to sever a felony domestic violence charge, in violation of RC § 2919.25, from other charges against him, based on his claim that evidence of his prior domestic violence convictions would be prejudicial to him pursuant to Ohio R. Crim. P. 8(A) and 14 in his criminal matter on multiple charges, was not reviewable on appeal, as defendant failed to renew the motion at the end of the State's case or at the end of the trial. He waived the right to assert an error in the trial court's ruling for purposes of appeal. State v. Feathers, — Ohio App. 3d —, 2007 Ohio 3024, — N.E. 2d —, 2007 Ohio App. LEXIS 2778 (June 15, 2007).

Trial court did not abuse its discretion by denying defendant's motion to sever his offenses because the evidence of both the 2004 break-in and the 2005 home-invasion could just as easily have been introduced in two trials and the underlying facts were "simple and direct." Additionally, because the victims in the home invasion both affirmatively identified defendant as one of the men involved in the 2005 home-invasion, but that identification was subject to some degree of doubt, introduction of defendant's DNA from a year earlier was relevant to show that defendant knew the funeral home (the location of the home invasion), may have previously robbed it, and might have chosen to again break-in and vandalize the facility. State v. Hairston, — Ohio App. 3d —, 2007 Ohio 3880, — N.E. 2d —, 2007 Ohio App. LEXIS 3519 (July 27, 2007).

Even if defendant had preserved his right to appeal from the trial court's refusal to sever, defendant was not prejudiced by the joinder; because, at the time that the motion to sever was ruled upon, it was unknown whether defendant would testify or admit to engaging in sexual conduct with the victims, other acts testimony would have been admissible under Ohio R. Evid. 404(B) to demonstrate modus operandi and to prove identity. The similarities between the two cases were sufficient to support the trial court's conclusion that the evidence of one crime would have been admissible at the trial of the other even if the counts were severed. State v. Elijah, — Ohio App. 3d —, 2006 Ohio 2635, — N.E. 2d —, 2006 Ohio App. LEXIS 2471 (May 19, 2006).

In defendant's trial for two aggravated robberies, in which he moved for severance, under Ohio R. Crim. P. 14, while it was error for the trial court not to rule on the motion, the error was harmless because, under Ohio R. Evid. 404(B), evidence of one of the robberies would have been admissible at a separate trial of the other robbery to prove modus operandi, given the similarity between the two crimes, intent and plan, and identity, so joinder of the offenses, under Ohio R. Crim. P. 8(A), was proper. State v. Andrews, — Ohio App. 3d —, 2006 Ohio 3764, — N.E. 2d —, 2006 Ohio App. LEXIS 3706 (July 24, 2006).

Trial court did not err in denying defendant's motion to sever charges in the original indictment charging him with illegal manufacture of drugs, illegal assembly or possession of chemicals for the manufacture of drugs, and illegal use or possession of drug paraphernalia from the charges in a supplemental indictment charging him with an additional count of illegal manufacture of drugs and illegal assembly or possession of chemicals for the manufacture of drugs. Joinder of the offenses was permitted under Ohio R. Crim. P. 8(A) since the two indictments related to the same crime and involved the same charges and the same chemicals. State v. Morgan, — Ohio App. 3d —, 2006 Ohio 3921, — N.E. 2d —, 2006 Ohio App. LEXIS 3878 (Aug. 2, 2006).

Trial court did not abuse its discretion in overruling defendant's motion to sever because the jury was not likely to be improperly influenced by evidence of defendant's earlier conviction or more likely to believe him guilty of the assault charge against him in the instant matter. The simple and direct nature of the witnesses' testimony regarding each offense negated defendant's assertion of prejudice. State v. Bates, — Ohio App. 3d —, 2006 Ohio 4146, — N.E. 2d —, 2006 Ohio App. LEXIS 4163 (Aug. 11, 2006).

In defendant's trial for multiple counts of aggravated robbery, aggravated burglary, kidnapping, felonious assault, and impersonating a police officer growing out of two separate incidents, denial of his motion to sever the charges related to the first incident from those concerning the second incident did not violate Crim. R. 8(A) or improperly circumvent Ohio R. Evid. 404(b) by prejudicing defendant; simple and direct evidence supported each of the 13 counts, the incidents occurred two days apart in the same neighborhood and were of a similar character, the evidence was sufficient to sustain each verdict, and the State did not need the evidence of one case to prove the other. State v. Wilson, — Ohio App. 3d —, 2006 Ohio 5253, — N.E. 2d —, 2006 Ohio App. LEXIS 5212 (Oct. 5, 2006).

Severance of offenses

Trial counsel was not ineffective for not moving to sever the counts because the case involved very "simple and distinct" evidence and was not confusing; each victim testified about separate offenses and provided sufficient evidence of each offense charged, the victims were all cousins and were acquainted with defendant as an older family friend and neighbor of their grandparents, and the offenses occurred in the same general time frame and occurred in the same general location. Moreover, there was sufficient evidence to convict defendant of each charge relating to each victim without necessitating the evidence from one case to prove the other. State v. Eads, — Ohio App. 3d —, 2007 Ohio 539, — N.E. 2d —, 2007 Ohio App. LEXIS 488 (Feb. 8, 2007).

Trial court did not abuse its discretion by overruling defendant's motion to sever because the finding was supported by credible evidence and was consistent with the expectations of Ohio R. Crim. P. 8. The events involved as to all of the counts took place within a period of nine hours, some of which occurred while defendant was in the jail, and all of the events involved defendant and his live-in girlfriend. State v. Cohen, — Ohio App. 3d —, 2007 Ohio 4546, — N.E. 2d —, 2007 Ohio App. LEXIS 4085 (Aug. 31, 2007).

Pursuant to Ohio R. Crim. P. 8(A) and 14, there was no undue prejudice caused by the joinder of two counts in defendant's criminal trial, as each of the counts required the State to prove that defendant had or used a firearm and the evidence was so strong against defendant that there was no reasonable possibility that, even if the counts were severed, they would have led to anything other than guilty verdicts; accordingly, defendant's claim that his counsel was ineffective in violation of U.S. Const. amend. VI and Ohio Const. art. I, § 10 for failing to seek severance lacked merit where he could not show that the outcome of the trial would have been otherwise. Ohio v. Riffle, — Ohio App. 3d —, 2007 Ohio 5299, — N.E. 2d —, 2007 Ohio App. LEXIS 4656 (Sept. 28, 2007).

Where a trial court granted the State's motion to join charges in two indictments that arose from separate criminal incidents and the offenses met the "simple and distinct" test pursuant to Ohio R. Crim. P. 8(A), there was no error in the trial court's refusal to sever the offenses. State v. Allen, — Ohio App. 3d —, 2006 Ohio 2338, — N.E. 2d —, 2006 Ohio App. LEXIS 2206 (May 12, 2006).

RULE 9. Warrant or Summons Upon Indictment or Information

(A) **Issuance.** Upon the request of the prosecuting attorney the clerk shall forthwith issue a warrant for each defendant named in the indictment or in the information. The clerk shall issue a summons instead of a warrant where the defendant has been released pursuant to Rule 46 and is indicted for the same offense for which he was bound over pursuant to Rule 5. In addition, the clerk shall issue a summons instead of a warrant upon the request of the prosecuting attorney or by direction of the court.

Upon like request or direction, the clerk shall issue more than one warrant or summons for the same defendant. He shall deliver the warrant or summons to any officer authorized by law to execute or serve it. If a defendant fails to appear in response to summons, a warrant shall issue.

(B) **Form of warrant and summons.**

(1) **Warrant.** The form of the warrant shall be as provided in Rule 4(C)(1) except that it shall be signed by the court or clerk. It shall describe the offense charged in the indictment or information. A copy of the indictment or information shall be attached to the warrant which shall command that the defendant be arrested and brought before the court issuing the warrant without unnecessary delay.

(2) **Summons.** The summons shall be in the same form as the warrant, except that it shall not command that the defendant be arrested, but shall order the defendant to appear before the court at a stated time and place and inform him that he may be arrested if he fails to appear at the time and place stated in the summons. A copy of the indictment or information shall be attached to the summons.

(C) **Execution or service; return.**

(1) **Execution or service.** Warrants shall be executed or summons served as provided in Rule 4(D) and the arrested person shall be treated in accordance with Rule 4(E)(1).

(2) **Return.** The officer executing a warrant shall make return thereof to the court.

When the person serving summons is unable to serve a copy of the summons within twenty-eight days of the date of issuance, he shall endorse that fact and the reasons therefore on the summons and return the summons and copies to the clerk, who shall make the appropriate entry on the appearance docket.

At the request of the prosecuting attorney made at any time while the indictment or information is pending, a warrant returned unexecuted and not cancelled, or a summons returned unserved, or a copy thereof, may be delivered by the clerk to the sheriff or other authorized person for execution or service.

History: Amended, eff 7-1-75.

NOTES TO DECISIONS

ANALYSIS

Certified mail

Certified mail

Defendant's counsel was not ineffective for failing to move for dismissal on speedy trial grounds because defendant's failure to claim a summons issued by certified mail to an address that he furnished was, at the least, delay occasioned by his own neglect and thus, the time was properly excluded from the speedy trial time, pursuant to RC § 2945.72. Also, because defendant was charged with a felony and the summons was issued pursuant to Ohio R. Crim. P. 9, certified mail was an appropriate means of service and personal service was not mandated. State v. Gums, — Ohio App. 3d —, 2006 Ohio 3159, — N.E. 2d —, 2006 Ohio App. LEXIS 3036 (June 22, 2006).

RULE 10. Arraignment

(A) **Arraignment procedure.** Arraignment shall be conducted in open court, and shall consist of reading the indictment, information or complaint to the defendant, or stating to the defendant the substance of the charge, and calling on the defendant to plead thereto. The defendant may in open court waive the reading of the indictment, information, or complaint. The defendant shall be given a copy of the indictment, information, or complaint, or shall acknowledge receipt thereof, before being called upon to plead.

(B) **Presence of defendant.**

(1) The defendant must be present, except that the court, with the written consent of the defendant and the approval of the prosecuting attorney, may permit arraignment without the presence of the defendant, if a plea of not guilty is entered.

(2) In a felony or misdemeanor arraignment or a felony initial appearance, a court may permit the presence and participation of a defendant by remote contemporaneous video provided the use of video complies with the requirements set out in Rule 43(A)(2) of these rules. This division shall not apply to any other felony proceeding.

(C) **Explanation of rights.** When a defendant not represented by counsel is brought before a court and called upon to plead, the judge or magistrate shall cause the defendant to be informed and shall determine that the defendant understands all of the following:

(1) The defendant has a right to retain counsel even if the defendant intends to plead guilty, and has a right to a reasonable continuance in the proceedings to secure counsel.

(2) The defendant has a right to counsel, and the right to a reasonable continuance in the proceeding to secure counsel, and, pursuant to Crim. R. 44, the right to have counsel assigned without cost if the defendant is unable to employ counsel.

(3) The defendant has a right to bail, if the offense is bailable.

(4) The defendant need make no statement at any point in the proceeding, but any statement made can and may be used against the defendant.

(D) **Joint arraignment.** If there are multiple defendants to be arraigned, the judge or magistrate may by general announcement advise them of their rights as prescribed in this rule.

History: Amended, eff 7/1/08.

NOTES TO DECISIONS

ANALYSIS

Explanation of rights
Unrepresented defendants

Explanation of rights

CrimR 5, CrimR 10, and TrafR 8 were violated where the defendant's rights were not explained at the arraignment on the traffic offenses. A video explanation of rights played for the benefit of all defendants did not suffice: State v. Donkers, 170 Ohio App. 3d 509, 2007 Ohio 1557, 867 N.E.2d 903, 2007 Ohio App. LEXIS 1424 (2007).

Unrepresented defendants

Entire proceeding against defendant on an ordinance violation was invalid because the trial court failed to advise defendant of his rights or to ensure that defendant fully understood his rights and was intelligently relinquishing his right to counsel. The trial court simply inquired if defendant wanted to proceed before a magistrate or a judge and whether he had counsel that would appear. City of Middletown v. McIntosh, — Ohio App. 3d —, 2007 Ohio 3348, — N.E. 2d —, 2007 Ohio App. LEXIS 3122 (July 2, 2007).

Failure to re-advise defendant of his right to counsel after a superseding indictment was issued charging him with ethnic intimidation and aggravated menacing did not violate his rights because the trial court strictly complied with Crim. R. 10(C) after his first indictment. The record showed that defendant knowingly and voluntarily waived his right after the first recitation of his rights under Rule 10(C), the record of the original colloquy and of the motions he filed pro se thereafter demonstrated his clear and deliberate intent to manage his own defense, and the record showed that he understood and appreciated his right to obtain an attorney if he so desired. State v. Bristow, — Ohio App. 3d —, 2006 Ohio 6493, — N.E. 2d —, 2006 Ohio App. LEXIS 6415 (Dec. 8, 2006).

RULE 11.   Pleas, Rights Upon Plea

(A) **Pleas.** A defendant may plead not guilty, not guilty by reason of insanity, guilty or, with the consent of the court, no contest. A plea of not guilty by reason of insanity shall be made in writing by either the defendant or the defendant's attorney. All other pleas may be made orally. The pleas of not guilty and not guilty by reason of insanity may be joined. If a defendant refuses to plead, the court shall enter a plea of not guilty on behalf of the defendant.

(B) **Effect of guilty or no contest pleas.** With reference to the offense or offenses to which the plea is entered:

(1) The plea of guilty is a complete admission of the defendant's guilt.

(2) The plea of no contest is not an admission of defendant's guilt, but is an admission of the truth of the facts alleged in the indictment, information, or complaint, and the plea or admission shall not be used against the defendant in any subsequent civil or criminal proceeding.

(3) When a plea of guilty or no contest is accepted pursuant to this rule, the court, except as provided in divisions (C)(3) and (4) of this rule, shall proceed with sentencing under Crim. R. 32.

(C) **Pleas of guilty and no contest in felony cases.**

(1) Where in a felony case the defendant is unrepresented by counsel the court shall not accept a plea of guilty or no contest unless the defendant, after being readvised that he or she has the right to be represented by retained counsel, or pursuant to Crim. R. 44 by appointed counsel, waives this right.

(2) In felony cases the court may refuse to accept a plea of guilty or a plea of no contest, and shall not accept a plea of guilty or no contest without first addressing the defendant personally and doing all of the following:

(a) Determining that the defendant is making the plea voluntarily, with understanding of the nature of the charges and of the maximum penalty involved, and, if applicable, that the defendant is not eligible for probation or for the imposition of community control sanctions at the sentencing hearing.

(b) Informing the defendant of and determining that the defendant understands the effect of the plea of guilty or no contest, and that the court, upon acceptance of the plea, may proceed with judgment and sentence.

(c) Informing the defendant and determining that the defendant understands that by the plea the defendant is waiving the rights to jury trial, to confront witnesses against him or her, to have compulsory process for obtaining witnesses in the defendant's favor, and to require the state to prove the defendant's guilt beyond a reasonable doubt at a trial at which the defendant cannot be compelled to testify against himself or herself.

(3) With respect to aggravated murder committed on and after January 1, 1974, the defendant shall plead separately to the charge and to each specification, if any. A plea of guilty or no contest to the charge waives the defendant's right to a jury trial, and before accepting a plea of guilty or no contest the court shall so advise the defendant and determine that the defendant understands the consequences of the plea.

If the indictment contains no specification, and a plea of guilty or no contest to the charge is accepted, the court shall impose the sentence provided by law.

If the indictment contains one or more specifications, and a plea of guilty or no contest to the charge is accepted, the court may dismiss the specifications and impose sentence accordingly, in the interests of justice.

If the indictment contains one or more specifications that are not dismissed upon acceptance of a plea of guilty or no contest to the charge, or if pleas of guilty or no contest to both the charge and one or more specifications are accepted, a court composed of three judges shall: (a) determine whether the offense was aggravated murder or a lesser offense; and (b) if the offense is determined to have been a lesser offense, impose sentence accordingly; or (c) if the offense is determined to have been aggravated murder, proceed as provided by law to determine the presence or absence of the specified aggravating circumstances and of mitigating circumstances, and impose sentence accordingly.

(4) With respect to all other cases the court need not take testimony upon a plea of guilty or no contest.

(D) **Misdemeanor cases involving serious offenses.** In misdemeanor cases involving serious offenses the court may refuse to accept a plea of guilty or no contest, and shall not accept such plea without first addressing the defendant personally and informing the defendant of the effect of the pleas of guilty, no contest, and not guilty and determining that the defendant is making the plea voluntarily. Where the defendant is unrepresented by counsel the court shall not accept a plea of guilty or no contest unless the defendant, after being readvised that he or she has the right to be represented by retained counsel, or pursuant to Crim. R. 44 by appointed counsel, waives this right.

(E) **Misdemeanor cases involving petty offenses.** In misdemeanor cases involving petty offenses the court may refuse to accept a plea of guilty or no contest, and shall not accept such plea without first informing the defendant of the effect of the pleas of guilty, no contest, and not guilty.

The counsel provisions of Crim. R. 44(B) and (C) apply to division (E) of this rule.

(F) **Negotiated plea in felony cases.** When, in felony cases, a negotiated plea of guilty or no contest to one or more offenses charged or to one or more other or lesser offenses is offered, the underlying agreement upon which the plea is based shall be stated on the record in open court.

(G) **Refusal of court to accept plea.** If the court refuses to accept a plea of guilty or no contest, the court shall enter a plea of not guilty on behalf of the defendant. In such cases neither plea shall be admissible in evidence nor be the subject of comment by the prosecuting attorney or court.

(H) **Defense of insanity.** The defense of not guilty by reason of insanity must be pleaded at the time of arraignment, except that the court for good cause shown shall permit such a plea to be entered at any time before trial.

History: Amended, eff 7-1-76; 7-1-80; 7-1-98.

NOTES TO DECISIONS

ANALYSIS

Abuse of discretion
Acceptance of guilty plea
Aggravated murder
Allied offenses
Allocution sufficient
Appeal
Applicability
Blanket policy against no contest pleas
Civil proceedings
Colloquy
Competency of defendant
Complaint, deficiencies in
Complete admission of guilt
Compliance
Compliance with criminal rule

Consecutive terms of imprisonment
Constitutional rights generally
Defect in indictment
Denial of plea
Dismissal, reduction of charges after plea
Driving under influence
Due process
Duty of trial court
Effect of subsequent change in law
Explanation of circumstances
Failure to inform defendant
Guilty or no contest plea generally
— Confrontation rights
— Eligibility for judicial release
— Factual issues
Guilty or no contest pleas generally
Guilty plea
— Acceptance of court
Guilty pleas
Guilty pleas generally
Illiteracy
Indictment, defects in
Ineffective assistance of counsel
— Guilty plea
—Sentencing
Informing of post-release control
Interpreters
Jury waiver, coercion
Mandatory prison term
Maximum penalties
No contest plea
No contest pleas
No contest pleas generally
— Explanation of circumstances
Petty offenses
Plea bargaining
— Claim of innocence
Plea requirements
Post-release control
Postrelease control
Prejudice
Recording of proceedings
Robbery
Strict compliance
Substantial compliance
Sufficiency of allocution
Traffic cases
Understatement of penalty
Voluntariness
Waiver
Withdrawal of guilty plea

Abuse of discretion

Trial court erred by failing to either forewarn defendant of the potential for prison at the plea hearing or to give him the opportunity to withdraw his guilty plea at the sentencing hearing because defendant had a reasonable expectation that he would get community control sanctions and he did not breach any part of the agreement that he knowingly entered into with the State. Thus, the trial court abused its discretion when it did not impose community control sanctions, or allow defendant to vacate his plea. State v. Dunbar, — Ohio App. 3d —, 2007 Ohio 3261, — N.E. 2d —, 2007 Ohio App. LEXIS 3025 (June 28, 2007).

Acceptance of guilty plea

It was not error for a trial court to accept defendant's guilty pleas to sexual battery and gross sexual imposition because the record indicated that the trial court conducted a full plea colloquy with defendant, advising him of the consequences of his plea and his potential sentence, as well as of the fact that it was likely to accept the jointly recommended sentence, and defendant did not indicate any confusion at any point in the proceedings, so his claim that he did not understand them had no merit. State v. Hawkins, — Ohio App. 3d —, 2006 Ohio 7038, — N.E. 2d —, 2006 Ohio App. LEXIS 7026 (Dec. 28, 2006).

Aggravated murder

When a three-judge panel accepted defendant's guilty plea to aggravated murder, it did not satisfy the requirements of Ohio R. Crim. P. 11(C)(3) or RC § 2945.06 because (1) no witnesses testified about the facts of the aggravated murder, nor were any exhibits offered, except four photographs, (2) the prosecutor's recitations about the facts of the murder were not evidence sufficient to satisfy Ohio R. Crim. P. 11(C)(3) or RC § 2945.06, (3) guilt was imposed without deliberation among the members of the panel, raising questions about whether the finding of guilt was unanimous, and (4) a journal entry finding defendant guilty was absent. State v. Kelley, — Ohio App. 3d —, 2006 Ohio 5432, — N.E. 2d —, 2006 Ohio App. LEXIS 5426 (Oct. 19, 2006).

Allied offenses

Because the trial court erred when it concluded that the offenses of kidnapping and gross sexual imposition were not allied offenses of similar import under RC § 2941.25(A), defendant did not voluntarily, knowingly, and intelligently enter his guilty plea to gross sexual imposition; the trial court's error affected defendant's substantial rights. The plea agreement did not resolve the allied offense issue and did not include an agreed or recommended sentence; until the allied offense issue was resolved, defendant could not have subjectively understood the implications of his plea. State v. Taylor, — Ohio App. 3d —, 2008 Ohio 484, — N.E. 2d —, 2008 Ohio App. LEXIS 429 (Feb. 4, 2008).

Allocution sufficient

Court rejected defendant's contention that his guilty plea was not knowing, intelligent, and voluntary because the trial court failed to advise defendant that he had a right to counsel at trial and that he had a right to cross-examine witnesses. A thorough review of the transcript revealed that the trial court informed defendant that he had a right to cross-examine witnesses, and since defendant was already represented by counsel at trial, the trial court was not required under Ohio R. Crim. P. 11(C)(1) to inform defendant of his right to counsel at trial; thus, the trial court did not err in denying defendant's Ohio R. Crim. P. 32.1 motion to withdraw his guilty plea. State v. Hitchcock, — Ohio App. 3d —, 2007 Ohio 5059, — N.E. 2d —, 2007 Ohio App. LEXIS 4474 (Sept. 27, 2007).

Appeal

Defendant's claim that his jointly recommended sentence based on a plea agreement was due to his counsel's ineffective assistance in violation of U.S. Const. amend. VI and Ohio Const. art. I, § 10 lacked merit, as such a sentence was not appealable under RC § 2953.08(D) except upon showing that it was based on a plea that was not intelligently, knowingly, or voluntarily entered. As the trial court properly advised defendant pursuant to Ohio R. Crim. P. 11(C), defendant was properly informed of the sentencing range he faced if he did not enter the plea, and his counsel engaged in a tactical decision in negotiating the plea which was for a much lower sentence than the maximum defendant faced, defendant's claim failed. State v. Smith, — Ohio App. 3d —, 2007 Ohio 1626, — N.E. 2d —, 2007 Ohio App. LEXIS 1478 (Apr. 9, 2007).

When an appellate court reviews a plea submitted by a defendant, its focus is whether the dictates of Ohio R. Crim. P. 11 have been followed; defendant's appeal from a guilty plea was frivolous where the record showed, inter alia, that the trial court informed defendant of his constitutional rights, as required by Ohio R. Crim. P. 11(C)(2)(c), informed defendant that by entering a guilty plea, he was waiving those rights, and explained the consequences of entering a guilty plea. State v. Hamilton, — Ohio App. 3d —, 2006 Ohio 2255, — N.E. 2d —, 2006 Ohio App. LEXIS 2100 (May 5, 2006).

Defendant did not meet her burden to show manifest injustice in order to support her post-sentence motion to withdraw her guilty plea pursuant to Ohio R. Crim. P. 32.1 where she failed to attach of a copy of the transcript from the plea hearing pursuant to Ohio R. App. P. 9(B). The regularity of the proceedings was presumed, and defendant's claim that she was not properly advised under Ohio R. Crim. P. 11(D) prior to entering her pro se plea of guilty was deemed to lack merit. City of Parma v. Taylor, — Ohio App. 3d —, 2006 Ohio 3973, — N.E. 2d —, 2006 Ohio App. LEXIS 3947 (Aug. 3, 2006).

Applicability

As Ohio R. Crim. P. 11(C)(2) was inapplicable to defendant's community control violation proceeding and the record supported a determination that the trial court complied with Ohio R. Crim. P. 32.3(A), the revocation of defendant's community control sanction due to violations thereof was proper; there was nothing in the record to suggest that defendant did not understand the consequences of her no contest plea. State v. Alexander, — Ohio App. 3d —, — N.E. 2d —, 2007 Ohio App. LEXIS 4807 (Oct. 12, 2007).

Blanket policy against no contest pleas

Trial court abused its discretion when it refused to accept defendant's Alford plea because it gave no reason for refusing to accept the tendered plea other than a blanket policy of not accepting pleas from people that did not think that they did anything wrong. The trial court's refusal to accept defendant's plea was a refusal to exercise its discretion. Reversal was warranted because the failure to accept the tendered plea prejudiced defendant insofar as his stated reason for attempting to enter a plea to a lesser offense was to avoid the harsher consequences that a jury's guilty verdicts might bring. State v. Raymond, — Ohio App. 3d —, 2006 Ohio 3259, — N.E. 2d —, 2006 Ohio App. LEXIS 3181 (June 27, 2006).

Civil proceedings

In a case where the conviction was not made relevant by statute, CrimR 11(B)(2) and EvidR 410 prohibited introduction of a party's convictions following no contest pleas to arson and insurance fraud: Elevators Mut. Ins. Co. v. J. Patrick O'Flaherty's, Inc., 180 Ohio App. 3d 315, 2008 Ohio 6946, 905 N.E.2d 259, 2008 Ohio App. LEXIS 5839 (2008).

Colloquy

Defendant's post-sentence motion to withdraw defendant's guilty plea, which alleged defendant's counsel manipulated defendant into pleading guilty, was properly denied because the record reflected that, (1) after a lengthy hearing on defendant's motion to suppress, defendant withdrew the motion and pled guilty in response to the State's offer to dismiss two other felonious-assault charges, (2) before accepting defendant's pleas, the trial court twice personally addressed defendant and told defendant of the consequences of defendant's pleas, under Ohio R. Crim. P. 11(C), (3) defendant, at that time, told the trial court defendant was satisfied with counsel's efforts, and (4) while there was no sentencing agreement, defendant received the sentence the State recommended at the plea hearing. State v. Henderson, — Ohio App. 3d —, — N.E. 2d —, 2007 Ohio App. LEXIS 4512 (Sept. 28, 2007).

Trial court erred in failing to inform defendant during his plea colloquy on charges including three counts of possession of drugs that defendant was not eligible for probation, community control, or judicial release and, thus, failed to comply with Ohio R. Crim. P. 11(C)(2)(a). Ohio v. Mayle, —

Ohio App. 3d —, 2007 Ohio 5298, — N.E. 2d —, 2007 Ohio App. LEXIS 4653 (Sept. 25, 2007).

CrimR 11(C)(2)(c) does not require a trial court to advise a defendant that each element of an offense must be proven beyond a reasonable doubt. The rule also does not contain a requirement that a defendant must be advised that a decision not to testify cannot be used against the defendant or commented on: State v. Eckles, 173 Ohio App. 3d 606, 2007 Ohio 6220, 879 N.E.2d 829, 2007 Ohio App. LEXIS 5452 (2007).

Strict compliance standard applies to a trial court's duty, under CrimR11(C), to explain the constitutional rights the defendant is waiving with the plea. The trial court did not inform the defendant of his rights to compel witnesses to testify in his favor and to have the state prove the elements of the offense beyond a reasonable doubt: State v. Rowbotham, 173 Ohio App. 3d 642, 2007 Ohio 6227, 879 N.E.2d 856, 2007 Ohio App. LEXIS 5453 (2007).

Under the totality of the circumstances, the trial court substantially complied with Ohio R. Crim. P. 11(C) when it accepted defendant's plea because, while the trial court did not tell him that he was giving up his right to a trial and everything that goes with it, it also separately enumerated the rights being waived early in the colloquy before acceptance of the plea. There was no evidence to suggest that defendant did not understand what he was being asked and his responses indicated that he understood the rights he was waiving, as enumerated by the trial court; thus, defendant suffered no prejudice. State v. Reynolds, — Ohio App. 3d —, 2007 Ohio 6903, — N.E. 2d —, 2007 Ohio App. LEXIS 6052 (Dec. 21, 2007).

Trial court properly complied with Ohio R. Crim. P. 11(C) during a colloquy with defendant, such that there was strict compliance with informing defendant about the constitutional rights that were being waived, substantial compliance with respect to informing defendant about non-constitutional rights that were waived, and it was clear that despite defendant's mental illness, the guilty plea that defendant entered was voluntarily and intelligently made. State v. Long, — Ohio App. 3d —, 2007 Ohio 6921, — N.E. 2d —, 2007 Ohio App. LEXIS 6072 (Dec. 18, 2007).

Defendant failed to show that the trial court did not provide a sufficient colloquy pursuant to Ohio R. Crim. P. 11(C) prior to accepting his pleas of no contest to multiple sexual offenses, as there was an explanation of the facts and potential penalties facing defendant, and his plea was deemed to have been entered freely, intelligently, and voluntarily. The prosecutor had indicated what potential maximum sentence accompanied each charge, and there was no requirement that the trial court advise defendant of the aggregate term that he faced. State v. Hanning, — Ohio App. 3d —, 2006 Ohio 460, — N.E. 2d —, 2006 Ohio App. LEXIS 395 (Feb. 2, 2006).

Where defendant entered into a plea agreement and in conducting the guilty plea colloquy pursuant to Ohio R. Crim. P. 11, the trial court mistakenly advised defendant of the sentencing possibilities that he faced for a fifth-degree felony, although his conviction for receiving stolen property in violation of RC § 2913.51 was a fourth-degree felony, the plea required vacatur and a remand was necessitated for purposes of a new plea and a new sentence. State v. Lumpkin, — Ohio App. 3d —, 2006 Ohio 1334, — N.E. 2d —, 2006 Ohio App. LEXIS 1228 (Mar. 23, 2006).

Denial of defendant's motion to withdraw his guilty plea was improper to the extent that it was based on defendant's failure to file a written motion with the court as a written motion was filed with the court and such motions did not have to be written; however, the denial of the motion was proper as: (1) the trial court gave defendant an ample opportunity to argue why he wanted to withdraw his plea and questioned him about his admissions to the crimes, despite his assertion that he had not committed any crime, (2) it was presumed that the

trial court complied with Ohio R. Crim. P. 11(C)(2)(a) as no record of the plea hearing was filed, and (3) defendant was eligible for community control sanctions as he pleaded guilty to fourth-degree felonies. State v. Beckwith, — Ohio App. 3d —, 2006 Ohio 1571, — N.E. 2d —, 2006 Ohio App. LEXIS 1471 (Mar. 30, 2006).

When defendant pled guilty to violations of RC §§ 4510.16(A), 4510.11(A), and 4510.21(A), the Ohio Traffic Rules applied to the acceptance of his plea, requiring the trial court to comply with Ohio Traf. R. 10(D) by informing him of the information in Ohio Traf. R. 10(B), regarding the effect of his plea, and, as the trial court complied with these requirements, the plea was knowing, intelligent, and voluntary because no constitutional informational requirement applied to accepting his plea, nor did the trial court have to engage defendant in an Ohio R. Crim. P. 11(C) colloquy before accepting the plea. State v. Brackens, — Ohio App. 3d —, 2006 Ohio 2143, — N.E. 2d —, 2006 Ohio App. LEXIS 1981 (May 1, 2006).

Although a trial court's failure to notify defendant pursuant to RC § 2950.03(A)(2) at sentencing of his registration and reporting requirements under RC § 2950.04 upon being convicted of sexually oriented offenses did not affect defendant's duty to report, as it arose by operation of law upon his guilty plea and conviction of the offenses, the trial court's failure to have informed defendant of such registration and reporting requirements prior to acceptance of his plea under Ohio R. Crim. P. 11 may have caused prejudice to defendant, as he may have proceeded differently if he had been so informed. Accordingly, the matter was reversed and remanded for the proper notification of defendant, at which time he could seek to vacate his plea if that was the course he chose to follow. State v. Freeman, — Ohio App. 3d —, 2006 Ohio 2583, — N.E. 2d —, 2006 Ohio App. LEXIS 2459 (May 25, 2006).

Underlying purpose, from a defendant's perspective, of Ohio R. Crim. P. 11(C) is to convey to the defendant certain information so that he can make a voluntary and intelligent decision whether to plead guilty. State v. Daugherty, — Ohio App. 3d —, 2006 Ohio 2684, — N.E. 2d —, 2006 Ohio App. LEXIS 2518 (May 31, 2006).

Although defendant cited to Ohio R. Crim. P. 11 in his appeal that raised an issue as to the plea he entered to reckless operation, in violation of RC § 4511.20, as Ohio R. Crim. P. 11(E) and Ohio Traf. R. 10(D) were identical in all parts that were relevant to the issues raised, the court reviewed the claim of error under a violation of Rule 10(D), which was the applicable section for the charge involved. State v. Powell, — Ohio App. 3d —, 2006 Ohio 3477, — N.E. 2d —, 2006 Ohio App. LEXIS 3422 (June 27, 2006).

Competency of defendant

Trial court was not in error when it accepted the guilty plea because, although defendant asserted that he had no memory of the crime that he committed, his memory loss did not prevent him from entering a valid guilty plea. It was clear from the record that defendant was competent to enter a valid plea because there was no indication that defendant was unable to consult with his attorney, or that he did not have a rational or factual understanding of the proceedings against him. State v. Leonard, — Ohio App. 3d —, 2006 Ohio 1943, — N.E. 2d —, 2006 Ohio App. LEXIS 1793 (Apr. 20, 2006).

Defendant's pleas to a forgery charge and to a subsequent charge of committing community control violations were knowingly entered pursuant to Ohio R. Crim. P. 11, although he made isolated comments that he was confused, as a review of the entire proceedings indicated that he knowingly entered the pleas and waived his constitutional rights, and there was no evidence to show that he was incompetent to stand trial. Despite counsel's knowledge that defendant suffered from depression and bipolar disorder, as his pleas were knowingly entered and there was no indication of incompetency, there was no cause to have sought an incompetency hearing under RC § 2945.37 and counsel was not ineffective under U.S. Const. amend. VI in failing to do so. State v. Jones, — Ohio App. 3d —, 2006 Ohio 2339, — N.E. 2d —, 2006 Ohio App. LEXIS 2204 (May 12, 2006).

Complaint, deficiencies in

Trial court erred in convicting the defendant upon his no contest plea where the complaint did not set forth the elements of the offense, the essential facts constituting the offense, or the name of the offense, and stated only the numerical designation of the code section allegedly violated: State v. Hoerig, 181 Ohio App. 3d 86, 2009 Ohio 541, 907 N.E.2d 1238, 2009 Ohio App. LEXIS 457 (2009).

Complete admission of guilt

Because defendant pled guilty to the attempted rape of his daughter, which was a complete admission of his guilt under Ohio R. Crim. P. 11(B)(1), the State was not required to present any evidence of defendant's guilt. Thus, his conviction, being predicated upon his guilty plea, could not have been against the manifest weight of the evidence. State v. Hall, — Ohio App. 3d —, 2007 Ohio 4203, — N.E. 2d —, 2007 Ohio App. LEXIS 3786 (Aug. 17, 2007).

Compliance

Trial court did not err in imposing on defendant a four-year prison sentence upon his conviction for cocaine possession. The trial court complied with Crim. R. 11 before accepting defendant's guilty plea and clearly informed defendant that he could be sentenced to up to 10 years in prison, and there was no evidence that the trial court promised to sentence defendant only to three years in prison. State v. Walker, — Ohio App. 3d —, 2006 Ohio 5197, — N.E. 2d —, 2006 Ohio App. LEXIS 5119 (Oct. 2, 2006).

Nothing in the record indicated that defendant did not fully understand the consequences of a guilty plea. The trial court complied with Crim. R. 11(C)(2)'s requirements by informing defendant of his rights and his potential sentence and defendant's responses proved that he had full knowledge of the consequences of a guilty plea. State v. Pakulniewicz, — Ohio App. 3d —, 2006 Ohio 5654, — N.E. 2d —, 2006 Ohio App. LEXIS 5655 (Oct. 27, 2006).

Defendant's guilty pleas to domestic violence and failure to appear were made knowingly, intelligently, and voluntarily because defendant acknowledged, in signed plea agreements, that he could receive prison terms of between three and 10 years for aggravated burglary and between six and 18 months for failure to appear. The trial court satisfied the requirements of Ohio R. Crim. P. 11 because it was only required to determine if defendant understood the maximum penalty involved; it was not required to apprise defendant of the possibility of consecutive sentences. State v. Green, — Ohio App. 3d —, 2006 Ohio 6695, — N.E. 2d —, 2006 Ohio App. LEXIS 6593 (Dec. 15, 2006).

Compliance with criminal rule

Defendant's conviction and sentence were reversed where his counsel indicated that defendant wished to enter a no contest plea but there was no indication in the trial court record that defendant ever actually entered the plea, the trial court never made the required finding that defendant was "guilty," and there was no explanation to defendant of the effects of the plea, as required by Ohio R. Crim. P. 11(E). State v. Meese, — Ohio App. 3d —, 2007 Ohio 742, — N.E. 2d —, 2007 Ohio App. LEXIS 668 (Feb. 16, 2007).

Although at defendant's change of plea hearing, a prosecutor omitted the element of venue with respect to charges against defendant of third and fourth degree felonies of burglary and attempted burglary, as venue was included in the indictment which defendant indicated that he received and understood, the acceptance of defendant's no contest plea by the trial court was proper under Ohio R. Crim. P. 11; there was nothing in the record to show that defendant was prejudiced, confused, or misled by the omission of that element in the prosecutor's statement of facts. State v. Elliott, — Ohio App. 3d —, 2007 Ohio 4503, — N.E. 2d —, 2007 Ohio App. LEXIS 4053 (Aug. 30, 2007).

Defendant's guilty plea was not knowing, intelligent, or voluntary because defendant did not admit the facts making up the offenses, but the trial court did not explore that further; the issue of defendant's competency to understand the proceedings and charges against him was not properly resolved; defendant was promised the right to withdraw his guilty plea but never given the opportunity to do so; and he entered the guilty plea primarily based upon assurances made by the trial court that that he would receive the minimum six-year sentence. State v. Schreiber, — Ohio App. 3d —, 2007 Ohio 6030, — N.E. 2d —, 2007 Ohio App. LEXIS 5316 (Nov. 13, 2007).

Although the trial court did not indicate specifically that defendant was waiving his right to a "jury" trial when it engaged in a colloquy with him regarding his guilty plea, it adequately informed defendant of such right, as well as his constitutional and non-constitutional rights where a meaningful discussion was had as to defendant's rights and what he was waiving by entering the plea, such that his plea was knowingly, intelligently, and voluntarily entered, and there was strict compliance with Ohio R. Crim. P. 11(C)(2)(c) for purposes of constitutional issues, and substantial compliance for purposes of the nonconstitutional issues. State v. Gibson, — Ohio App. 3d —, 2006 Ohio 4182, — N.E. 2d —, 2006 Ohio App. LEXIS 4118 (Aug. 11, 2006).

After defendant's guilty plea was sealed by the trial court upon its grant of defendant's motion for intervention in lieu of conviction, thereafter when defendant was found to have failed to comply with the conditions of the intervention, the stay of the criminal proceedings was lifted and the plea was properly accepted pursuant to Ohio R. Crim. P. 11 for purposes of defendant's conviction; there was no violation of Rule 11. State v. White, — Ohio App. 3d —, 2006 Ohio 4746, — N.E. 2d —, 2006 Ohio App. LEXIS 4660 (Sept. 12, 2006).

Trial court fully complied with both the constitutional and non-constitutional provisions of Crim. R. 11 before accepting defendant's guilty plea. The trial court informed defendant of his right against self-incrimination in a reasonably intelligible manner which did not convey to defendant that if he elected to testify, such testimony would have been meaningless. There was no indication that the remark engendered any confusion or misunderstanding; and defendant's counsel stated on the record that he had explained defendant's rights to him. State v. Delgado, — Ohio App. 3d —, 2006 Ohio 5928, — N.E. 2d —, 2006 Ohio App. LEXIS 5848 (Nov. 9, 2006).

Consecutive terms of imprisonment

Where a trial court incorrectly advised defendant during his no contest plea hearing under Ohio R. Crim. P. 11(C)(2) that a concurrent sentence was an option for sentencing upon his conviction for escape, in violation of RC § 2921.34, when in fact that advice was erroneous and prejudicial to defendant because he was subject to a mandatory consecutive prison term under RC § 2929.14(E)(2), his plea was invalid. Defendant was serving other prison terms when he committed his escape, such that he was subject to the consecutive prison term for that crime. State v. Hayes, — Ohio App. 3d —, 2007 Ohio 2837, — N.E. 2d —, 2007 Ohio App. LEXIS 2631 (June 8, 2007).

Trial court's allocution to defendant was sufficient, he indicated that he understood the implication of his guilty plea, and there was substantial compliance with Ohio R. Crim. P. 11(C)(2), such that defendant's plea was deemed voluntary, intelligent, and knowing. The fact that the trial court did not apprise him specifically that he could be sentenced to consecutive terms of imprisonment did not change the validity of the plea. State v. Jackson, — Ohio App. 3d —, 2006 Ohio 3165, — N.E. 2d —, 2006 Ohio App. LEXIS 3044 (June 22, 2006).

Constitutional rights generally

Trial court properly advised defendant pursuant to Ohio R. Crim. P. 11(C)(2) prior to defendant's acceptance of a plea agreement, such that the guilty plea was deemed voluntarily, knowingly, and intelligently entered and defendant's due process rights were not violated; defendant was not deprived of the right to counsel under the Sixth Amendment, nor was defendant deprived of effective assistance of counsel, as defendant failed to show prejudice and the trial court had appointed new counsel for defendant upon defendant's acceptance of the plea agreement for the specific purpose of reviewing the terms thereof. Ohio v. Pippin, — Ohio App. 3d —, 2007 Ohio 5974, — N.E. 2d —, 2007 Ohio App. LEXIS 5275 (Nov. 9, 2007).

Defect in indictment

Guilty plea waives any defect in an indictment occasioned by a failure to allege a culpable mental state: State v. Lawrence, 180 Ohio App. 3d 468, 2009 Ohio 33, 905 N.E.2d 1268, 2009 Ohio App. LEXIS 21 (2009).

Denial of plea

There was no abuse of discretion in the trial court's decision to reject the negotiated plea to a lesser charge on the day of trial. The trial court was not required to accept a plea at that time and it stated its reasons for rejecting the plea bargain. State v. Rust, — Ohio App. 3d —, 2007 Ohio 50, — N.E. 2d —, 2007 Ohio App. LEXIS 40 (Jan. 10, 2007).

Dismissal, reduction of charges after plea

Trial court committed plain error under Ohio R. Crim. P. 52(B) when it accepted defendant's no contest plea pursuant to Ohio R. Crim. P. 11(A) and (C) to an indicted charge of felony theft, and then it held an evidentiary hearing on the value of the property that was stolen based on defendant's challenge thereto, whereupon it convicted defendant of a lesser included offense of misdemeanor theft; once defendant entered the no contest plea, that constituted an admission of the facts in the indictment, including the value of the property stolen, such that the court's hearing and conviction on a lesser included offense was void and jeopardy did not attach. State v. Zilka, — Ohio App. 3d —, 2007 Ohio 6206, — N.E. 2d —, 2007 Ohio App. LEXIS 5462 (Nov. 26, 2007).

Trial court acted in excess of its authority under CrimR 11 when it accepted defendant's guilty plea to indicted charges and then upon an ex parte review of the facts underlying the indicted charges, based upon the trial court's review of a presentence investigation report, it reduced and/or dismissed the charges sua sponte State v. Lange, — Ohio App. 3d —, 2007 Ohio 6211, — N.E. 2d —, 2007 Ohio App. LEXIS 5469 (Nov. 26, 2007).

Driving under influence

Before accepting a guilty plea on a 20-year look-back specification, a trial court is required to instruct on the maximum penalty for the specification: State v. Eckles, 173 Ohio App. 3d 606, 2007 Ohio 6220, 879 N.E.2d 829, 2007 Ohio App. LEXIS 5452 (2007).

Due process

Acceptance of a guilty plea violates due process where: (1) the defendant pleads to an offense which is not a lesser included offense of the charged crime; (2) there is a failure to explain the additional elements of the offense to which the defendant will plead: and (3) under the facts of the indictment, the defendant could not have committed nor been convicted of the offense: State v. Jones, 181 Ohio App. 3d 47, 2009 Ohio 483, 907 N.E.2d 1209, 2009 Ohio App. LEXIS 405 (2009).

Duty of trial court

Although a trial judge asked an inmate questions to ensure that the judge understood the terms of the plea agreement and to ensure that the inmate was knowingly and voluntarily entering his no contest plea, there was nothing in the judge's comments during the plea negotiations that intimidated the inmate into accepting the plea agreement, such that the voluntariness of the plea was not negated for purposes of Ohio R. Crim. P. 11 or in violation of the inmate's rights under U.S. Const. amend. V and Ohio Const. art. I, § 10. State v. Smith, — Ohio App. 3d —, 2006 Ohio 1482, — N.E. 2d —, 2006 Ohio App. LEXIS 1352 (Mar. 21, 2006).

When defendant pled no contest to receiving stolen property, the trial court strictly complied with its obligation to advise him that he could not be required to testify, and nothing in Ohio R. Crim. P. 11 specifically required the trial court to advise him that he had the right to testify, but it was clear from the record that defendant had been previously advised of a right to testify, so he did not demonstrate error. State v. Ip, — Ohio App. 3d —, 2006 Ohio 2303, — N.E. 2d —, 2006 Ohio App. LEXIS 2161 (May 11, 2006).

When defendant, after pleading guilty to the first degree misdemeanor of domestic violence, under RC § 2919.25(A), moved to withdraw his plea, it was error for a trial court to deny the motion because the trial court did not comply with Ohio R. Crim. P. 11(B) and (E) when it accepted the plea because, while it went to great lengths to explain certain constitutional rights defendant waived by pleading guilty, it did not inform him of the effect of his plea because it did not tell him that a guilty plea was a complete admission of guilt. State v. Jones, — Ohio App. 3d —, 2006 Ohio 3636, — N.E. 2d —, 2006 Ohio App. LEXIS 3586 (July 13, 2006).

When defendant said her guilty pleas were not knowingly, intelligently or voluntarily entered, the record did not support her claim because it showed the trial court, pursuant to Ohio R. Crim. P. 11(C)(2)(a), personally addressed her about her pleas, explained the maximum penalty. told her she was not eligible for judicial release until she served her mandatory term, inquired extensively of her understanding of the proceedings, her rights and the effect of pleading guilty. State v. Weaks, — Ohio App. 3d —, 2006 Ohio 5150, — N.E. 2d —, 2006 Ohio App. LEXIS 5101 (Oct. 2, 2006).

Effect of subsequent change in law

Defendant's guilty plea was not rendered involuntary and unknowing once he was subject to resentencing under State v. Foster. The trial court complied with Ohio R. Crim. P. 11(C), and defendant could not show that he would not have otherwise pled guilty had he known about the change in law brought forth by Foster. State v. Lochett, — Ohio App. 3d —, 2007 Ohio 308, — N.E. 2d —, 2007 Ohio App. LEXIS 285 (Jan. 26, 2007).

While RC § 2953.08(D) does not preclude a court from reviewing the validity of a defendant's guilty plea leading to an agreed sentence, defendant had not shown that his plea was involuntary as the record showed that the trial court complied with Ohio R. Crim. P. 11(C). The changes State v. Foster made in Ohio's sentencing scheme did not affect whether a plea was voluntary. State v. Canady, — Ohio App. 3d —, 2007 Ohio 313, — N.E. 2d —, 2007 Ohio App. LEXIS 286 (Jan. 26, 2007).

Explanation of circumstances

No testimony was required prior to accepting defendant's no contest plea under Ohio R. Crim. P. 11(C)(4) to abusing harmful intoxicants as the instant case was a felony case because defendant had prior drug abuse convictions. State v. Reynolds, — Ohio App. 3d —, 2007 Ohio 6902, — N.E. 2d —, 2007 Ohio App. LEXIS 6050 (Dec. 21, 2007).

Failure to inform defendant

Guilty plea entered after a colloquy in which the judge gives incorrect information regarding a defendant's legal status after release from incarceration renders the plea unknowing, unintelligent, and involuntary: State v. Clark, 119 Ohio St. 3d 239, 2008 Ohio 3748, 893 N.E.2d 462, 2008 Ohio LEXIS 1977 (2008).

Trial court abused its discretion when it did not impose community control sanctions, or allow defendant to vacate his plea because, although the trial court advised defendant of the potential sentencing range for abduction, it did not state that it could impose prison, rather than community control, to which defendant had agreed; nor did it inform defendant that in order to comply with his part of the bargain, he had to do anything but stay away from the victim. Moreover, when the trial court decided to deviate from the plea agreement, it should have clearly advised defendant of its intentions, and allowed him to reconsider his plea. State v. Dunbar, — Ohio App. 3d —, 2007 Ohio 1693, — N.E. 2d —, 2007 Ohio App. LEXIS 1557 (Apr. 12, 2007).

Where a trial court informed defendant at a guilty plea hearing that he could be imprisoned for up to "one half of the original sentence" upon violating post-release control sanctions, but the sentence was not imposed at that time, the notification was inadequate for purposes of RC § 2943.032(E) because defendant was not aware of the maximum penalty involved for purposes of Ohio R. Crim. P. 11(C)(2)(a); the guilty plea was not voluntarily and knowingly entered. State v. Poston, — Ohio App. 3d —, 2007 Ohio 3936, — N.E. 2d —, 2007 Ohio App. LEXIS 3539 (May 14, 2007).

As a trial court and prosecutor repeatedly referred to a charge as aggravated trafficking in drugs, in violation of RC § 2925.03(A)(1), which was a misstatement because the actual charge was aggravated possession of drugs, in violation of RC § 2925.11(A), and the trial court did not properly advise defendant pursuant to its duty under Ohio R. Crim. P. 11(C)(2) of the nature of the charge, defendant's plea was not voluntarily, intelligently, and knowingly entered under a plain error standard of review pursuant to Ohio R. Crim. P. 52(B), which violated his due process rights under Ohio Const. art. I, § 10. State v. Davis, — Ohio App. 3d —, 2007 Ohio 3944, — N.E. 2d —, 2007 Ohio App. LEXIS 3583 (July 26, 2007).

Although it was presumed that defense counsel explained the nature of the charges to defendant, a juvenile, prior to his entry of a guilty plea to multiple offenses, the trial court erred with it informed defendant that he was waiving the right to have the State prove each element of each charge against him, as it did not mention that each element had to be proven beyond a reasonable doubt, which standard of proof was a constitutional right; as strict compliance was required for a constitutional right waiver under Ohio R. Crim. P. 11(C)(2)(c), which was not satisfied, defendant's plea was not deemed knowingly and intelligently entered and his motion to withdraw the plea under Ohio R. Crim. P. 32.1 should have been granted. State v. Roman, — Ohio App. 3d —, 2007 Ohio 5243, — N.E. 2d —, 2007 Ohio App. LEXIS 4641 (Sept. 26, 2007).

Trial court erred in denying defendant's motion to vacate his guilty pleas because, at the time of the pleas, the trial court failed to inform defendant that his pleas were complete admissions, as required by Ohio Traf. R. 10(B). Moreover, defendant proceeded without counsel and was not informed of a mandatory license suspension. State v. Neff, — Ohio App. 3d —, 2006 Ohio 6608, — N.E. 2d —, 2006 Ohio App. LEXIS 6520 (Dec. 8, 2006).

Guilty or no contest plea generally

Although substantial compliance with CrimR 11(C)(2) was all that was required, a trial court failed to even substantially comply with the rule. While the trial court made an extensive inquiry into defendant's waiver of his constitutional rights and thoroughly explained other matters, the trial court did not explain or even mention the effect of a no contest plea. State v. Lamb, — Ohio App. 3d —, 2008 Ohio 1569, — N.E. 2d —, 2008 Ohio App. LEXIS 1374 (Mar. 31, 2008).

For purposes of penalty enhancement in later convictions under RC § 4511.19, when the defendant presents a prima facie showing that prior convictions were unconstitutional because they were uncounseled and resulted in confinement, the burden shifts to the state to prove that the right to counsel was properly waived. Waiver of counsel must be made on the record in open court, and in cases involving serious offenses where the penalty includes confinement for more than six months, the waiver must also be in writing and filed with the court: State v. Brooke, 113 Ohio St. 3d 199, 2007 Ohio 1533, 863 N.E.2d 1024, 2007 Ohio LEXIS 852 (2007).

Defendant's guilty pleas were rendered invalid because the trial court's failure to strictly comply with the requirement of informing defendant of his constitutional right to compulsory process was a substantial error and constituted a manifest miscarriage of justice. The trial court only advised him that he had the right to call witnesses to appear and testify, which implied that defendant could only proffer witnesses that he could obtain himself; it did not use the term "compulsory process," or instruct defendant that witnesses could be forced, compelled, subpoenaed, summoned, or otherwise required to appear. State v. Day, — Ohio App. 3d —, 2007 Ohio 4052, — N.E. 2d —, 2007 Ohio App. LEXIS 3707 (Aug. 9, 2007).

Defendant's guilty plea was voluntarily, intelligently, and knowingly entered where it was conceded that the trial court strictly complied with Ohio R. Crim. P. 11(C)(2) with respect to defendant's constitutional rights, and the record supported the determination that the trial court substantially complied with Rule 11(C)(2) with respect to defendant's non-constitutional rights, as counsel indicated that the nature of the charges, the elements of the offenses, and the effects of the plea were discussed with defendant; further, as defendant did not assert innocence with respect to the charges and defendant clearly understood the rights being waived by entry of the plea, it was presumed that defendant completely admitted guilt to the charges and the trial court's failure to so inform was not prejudicial. State v. Bell, — Ohio App. 3d —, 2007 Ohio 6924, — N.E. 2d —, 2007 Ohio App. LEXIS 6067 (Dec. 11, 2007).

Under a plain error analysis, it was determined that defendant's plea was voluntarily, knowingly, and intelligently made as defendant clearly indicated to the trial court that he understood his rights. The plea hearing transcript demonstrated that, despite defendant's impaired intellectual functioning and depression, he understood his rights, the consequences of the plea, and that he voluntarily, knowingly and intelligently wished to waive his rights and pled guilty. State v. Edwards, — Ohio App. 3d —, 2006 Ohio 2315, — N.E. 2d —, 2006 Ohio App. LEXIS 2178 (May 11, 2006).

Where defendant pleaded guilty to multiple counts of rape which he had committed against a six-year-old victim, the trial court did not err in choosing not to accept the recommended sentence of the prosecutor, to which the victim had indicated her consent, as the trial court was not bound by such a recommendation and the facts alone made it clear why the trial court felt justified in deviating from the recommended term of imprisonment. State v. Gant, — Ohio App. 3d —, 2006 Ohio 1469, — N.E. 2d —, 2006 Ohio App. LEXIS 1345 (Mar. 22, 2006).

Trial court substantially complied with the requirements of Ohio R. Crim. P. 11 when it accepted defendant's guilty plea, even though it did not advise defendant, pursuant to Ohio R. Crim. P. 11(C)(2)(b), that the court could immediately proceed to judgment and sentence upon accepting defendant's plea, because defendant knew that his case would be referred for a presentence investigation, which it was, after which he was sentenced, so defendant did not show he was prejudiced by the lack of literal compliance with Rule 11(C)(2)(b). State

v. Woods, — Ohio App. 3d —, 2006 Ohio 2325, — N.E. 2d —, 2006 Ohio App. LEXIS 2152 (May 5, 2006).

Defendant was sufficiently informed of the maximum potential sentence for each sexual battery offense. While an explicit explanation of the potential for consecutive sentences might have been preferable, it was not required by either the Unite States or Ohio Constitution or by Ohio R. Crim. P. 11(C). State v. Shie, — Ohio App. 3d —, 2006 Ohio 2314, — N.E. 2d —, 2006 Ohio App. LEXIS 2181 (May 11, 2006).

Defendant's plea was voluntary and intelligent because the trial court did engage in the requisite dialogue with defendant and complied with the strictures of Ohio R. Crim. P. 11(C) before accepting his guilty plea. Although the trial court failed to mention the possibility of the fact that the state sentences could be served concurrently to the federally imposed sentence, there was also no evidence to show that either the state court or the federal court contemplated concurrent sentences. State v. Davis, — Ohio App. 3d —, 2006 Ohio 2350, — N.E. 2d —, 2006 Ohio App. LEXIS 2224 (May 12, 2006).

When defendant, who pled guilty to three counts of rape, claimed the witnesses against her were not competent to testify, due to their ages, under Ohio R. Evid. 601, at the times of the crimes, thereby compromising defendant's right to confrontation, the issue was waived by defendant's guilty plea, because, under Ohio R. Crim. P. 11(B)(1), that plea was a complete admission of her guilt, so defendant was not entitled to a reversal of her convictions on this basis. State v. Bene, — Ohio App. 3d —, 2006 Ohio 3628, — N.E. 2d —, 2006 Ohio App. LEXIS 3579 (July 17, 2006).

Because defendant failed to include a transcript of the plea hearings in the record on appeal, regularity was presumed, and therefore, compliance with Ohio R. Crim. P. 11(C) requirements was presumed in the proceedings below. State v. Vinson, — Ohio App. 3d —, 2006 Ohio 3971, — N.E. 2d —, 2006 Ohio App. LEXIS 3954 (Aug. 3, 2006).

— Confrontation rights

Defendant's due process rights under Ohio Const. art. I, § 10 were not violated by her inability to confront her probation officer in a revocation of her community control, as she entered a no contest plea to a charge that she violated the community control, such that she admitted the facts alleged in the complaint and waived certain due process rights pursuant to Ohio R. Crim. P. 11(B)(2). State v. Alexander, — Ohio App. 3d —, — N.E. 2d —, 2007 Ohio App. LEXIS 4807 (Oct. 12, 2007).

— Eligibility for judicial release

Defendant's guilty plea was not knowing or intelligent, under Ohio R. Crim. P. 11(C)(2)(a), because, when defendant entered the plea, the trial court essentially informed defendant that defendant would be eligible for judicial release, under RC § 2929.20, but, because the court subsequently sentenced defendant to more than ten years in prison, defendant was ineligible for judicial release. State v. Trainer, — Ohio App. 3d —, 2007 Ohio 6698, — N.E. 2d —, 2007 Ohio App. LEXIS 5882 (Dec. 14, 2007).

— Factual issues

As defendant entered a no contest plea pursuant to Ohio R. Crim. P. 11(B)(2) to two drug-related offenses, the prosecution did not need to produce evidence to support the charges, such that defendant's claim that the State failed to show that money seized from him was contraband lacked merit for purposes of his conviction for possession of criminal tools, in violation of RC § 2923.24; as the sentences imposed were within the allowable range for fifth degree felonies and were based on consideration of the factors under RC § 2929.11, they were proper. State v. Harrell, — Ohio App. 3d —, 2007 Ohio 5322, — N.E. 2d —, 2007 Ohio App. LEXIS 4665 (Oct. 4, 2007).

Guilty or no contest pleas generally

The defendant never actually tendered the no contest plea. To effectuate the tendering of a no contest plea, the defendant must do so by either signing a writing reflecting an express plea, or orally, either by saying, affirmatively, that he is pleading no contest or by responding affirmatively to the trial court's question, "Are you pleading no contest?": State v. Singleton, 169 Ohio App. 3d 585, 2006 Ohio 6314, 863 N.E.2d 1114, 2006 Ohio App. LEXIS 6283 (2006).

Guilty plea

Defendant's counsel was not ineffective in violation of U.S. Const. amend. VI and Ohio Const. art. I, § 10 in negotiating a plea agreement, whereby defendant entered a guilty plea to possession of crack cocaine as a third-degree felony as an amended charge in place of a trafficking charge and another charge was dismissed, although defendant had only possessed 1.35 grams of crack cocaine, which was a fourth-degree felony under RC § 2925.11(C)(4)(b), as there was a full colloquy under Ohio R. Crim. P. 11, an agreed sentence of a term much less than what defendant faced from the original charges was imposed, and defendant knowingly and intelligently agreed to enter the plea. State v. Spurling, — Ohio App. 3d —, 2007 Ohio 858, — N.E. 2d —, 2007 Ohio App. LEXIS 766 (Mar. 2, 2007).

RC § 2907.02(B), pursuant to which defendant was sentenced to life in prison without parole after pleading guilty to rape, in violation of RC § 2907.02(A)(1)(b), was not unconstitutional as applied to defendant because, when defendant pled guilty, defendant admitted, pursuant to Ohio R. Crim. P. 11(B)(1), that the victim was less than ten years of age and that, during the commission of the rape, defendant caused serious physical harm to the victim, authorizing the trial court to impose defendant's sentence without engaging in impermissible judicial fact-finding. State v. Hardie, — Ohio App. 3d —, 2007 Ohio 2755, — N.E. 2d —, 2007 Ohio App. LEXIS 2535 (May 31, 2007).

Acceptance of defendant's guilty plea to trafficking in crack cocaine did not violate Ohio R. Crim. P. 11(C)(2), as defendant stated that defendant understood that defendant was giving up defendant's constitutional rights by entering defendant's plea, consulted with defendant's attorney repeatedly during the plea hearing, and did not express any concerns about proceeding with defendant's counsel. There was no evidence that defendant was under the influence of drugs or medication at the time. State v. Brown, — Ohio App. 3d —, 2007 Ohio 6675, — N.E. 2d —, 2007 Ohio App. LEXIS 5850 (Dec. 14, 2007).

Trial court, by stating that defendant had a right to subpoena witnesses, clearly informed defendant at the time of his plea of his right to compulsory process. Moreover, it did not appear that defendant was confused by the terminology because he stated on the record that he understood when the trial court explained that he had a right to subpoena and call witnesses. State v. Parks, — Ohio App. 3d —, 2006 Ohio 1352, — N.E. 2d —, 2006 Ohio App. LEXIS 1242 (Mar. 23, 2006).

Even if defendant's claim that his convictions for voluntary manslaughter and felonious assault, in violation of RC §§ 2903.03 and 2903.11, were allied offenses pursuant to RC § 2941.25 was proper, the fact that he was sentenced under a plea agreement to those charges was not error that invalidated the plea, as it was already determined that the plea was entered by defendant voluntarily, knowingly, and intelligently pursuant to Ohio R. Crim. P. 11. An allied offense determination hearing under Kent was not required because the sentence entered was part of an agreed sentence under the plea bargain and accordingly, there was no double jeopardy violation under U.S. Const. amend. V and Ohio Const. art. I, § 10. State v. Jackson, — Ohio App. 3d —, 2006 Ohio 3165, — N.E. 2d —, 2006 Ohio App. LEXIS 3044 (June 22, 2006).

Defendant's plea was voluntary because it was clear from the record that the trial court satisfied Ohio R. Crim. P. 11 and that defendant was advised, not only by the trial court of the possible sanctions for the offenses, but that counsel advised him as well and defendant's counsel explained the consequences of the plea bargain to his client. The record also reflected that defendant was advised that post-release control was also a part of his sentence, both at the plea hearing and through the corresponding journal entry. State v. Garrett, — Ohio App. 3d —, 2006 Ohio 3836, — N.E. 2d —, 2006 Ohio App. LEXIS 3806 (July 27, 2006).

Defendant's plea was knowingly, intelligently, and voluntarily made as the trial court substantially complied with the requirements of Ohio R. Crim. P. 11(C). Defendant's affirmative responses regarding the sexual offender classification demonstrated his understanding that he would be subject to such classification. The trial court not only informed him that it was required to hold a sexual offender hearing, but also informed him of the registration requirements, the duration of the registration requirements, the penalties for failing to register, and that the facts of his crime may be posted on the sheriff's web page. State v. Tackett, — Ohio App. 3d —, 2006 Ohio 3953, — N.E. 2d —, 2006 Ohio App. LEXIS 3902 (Aug. 3, 2006).

Trial court did not err in accepting defendant's Alford plea to charges of, inter alia, rape in violation of RC § 2907.02(A)(1)(b), arising from crimes committed against defendant's wife's five-year-old niece, as a typographical error in the indictment regarding the age of the victim did not prejudice defendant and as the issue was pointed out prior to defendant's entry of his plea, his claim that the plea was not knowing, voluntary, or based on consideration lacked merit. State v. Gonzalez, — Ohio App. 3d —, 2006 Ohio 6458, — N.E. 2d —, 2006 Ohio App. LEXIS 6402 (Dec. 8, 2006).

— Acceptance of court

Since defendant knowingly and voluntarily pled guilty, the trial court properly accepted and entered his pleas because defendant's statement that he had no choice but to take the plea did not assert his innocence to the charge of attempted murder. Absent an assertion of innocence, the trial court did not err when it accepted defendant's guilty pleas because it complied with Ohio R. Crim. P. 11 and determined that defendant entered his guilty pleas voluntarily, with an understanding of the nature of the charges against him, the maximum penalties involved, and the rights he was waiving by pleading guilty. State v. Darks, — Ohio App. 3d —, 2006 Ohio 3144, — N.E. 2d —, 2006 Ohio App. LEXIS 3022 (June 22, 2006).

Guilty pleas

Defendant's appeal of his conviction for municipal code violations of an ex parte temporary protection order failed; defendant's guilty plea to the charge constituted a complete admission of defendant's guilt and provided the necessary proof of the elements of the crime sufficient to support defendant's conviction. City of Mason v. Lawhorn, — Ohio App. 3d —, 2007 Ohio 2289, — N.E. 2d —, 2007 Ohio App. LEXIS 2156 (May 14, 2007).

Trial court erred, pursuant to Ohio R. Crim. P. 11(C)(2), when it advised defendant that the maximum sentence for a felony of the fourth degree was eight months in prison when the maximum possible sentence was eighteen months in prison. As a result, defendant's plea was not knowingly, intelligently, or voluntarily entered into. State v. Howard, — Ohio App. 3d —, 2007 Ohio 2771, — N.E. 2d —, 2007 Ohio App. LEXIS 2577 (June 7, 2007).

Defendant's pleas were voluntarily entered because the trial court substantially complied with its duties under Ohio R. Crim. P. 11, and the totality of circumstances indicated that defendant subjectively understood that his guilty pleas were a complete admission of his guilt as to those offenses. Defendant did protest that the police lied, but that apparently referred to the search warrant affidavit and did not refer to the events which occurred when the search was conducted. State v. Neely, — Ohio App. 3d —, 2007 Ohio 2965, — N.E. 2d —, 2007 Ohio App. LEXIS 2725 (June 15, 2007).

Defendant's guilty pleas were knowingly, voluntarily, and intelligently made because his unsubstantiated claims that he was coerced by the trial court were not sufficient to overcome the evidence in the hearing transcript. The trial court complied with all the requirements of Ohio R. Crim. P. 11, and showed great patience and diligence in explaining the sexually oriented offender classification to him and it gave him ample opportunity to change his mind and not plead guilty. State v. Burton, — Ohio App. 3d —, 2006 Ohio 391, — N.E. 2d —, 2006 Ohio App. LEXIS 336 (Feb. 1, 2006).

When defendant claimed a manifest injustice justified the post-sentence withdrawal of his guilty pleas because his heroin addiction rendered him unable to understand the sentencing proceedings, the record of his plea hearings did not support this claim as the trial court asked him if he was under the influence of anything that would affect his understanding of the proceedings, and he replied that he was not. State v. Plemons, — Ohio App. 3d —, 2006 Ohio 1608, — N.E. 2d —, 2006 Ohio App. LEXIS 1454 (Mar. 31, 2006).

Trial court complied with the requirements of Ohio R. Crim. P. 11(C) and due process in accepting defendant's guilty pleas because the fact that defendant provided simple "yes" or "no" responses to the trial court's questions regarding his rights did not render the dialogue as non-meaningful since the responses were not equivocal. Although the trial court did not stop after each constitutional right and ask whether defendant understood that right, it clearly explained defendant's constitutional rights in a manner "reasonably intelligible" to him. State v. Sahr, — Ohio App. 3d —, 2006 Ohio 3260, — N.E. 2d —, 2006 Ohio App. LEXIS 3178 (June 27, 2006).

Guilty pleas generally

As a trial court properly informed defendant of the rights that he was waiving by entering a guilty plea, there was "substantial compliance" with the requirements of Ohio R. Crim. P. 11(C), such that defendant's claim that his plea was not knowingly and voluntarily entered because he was not properly advised of all of the rights that he was waiving lacked merit. There was no requirement that the trial court inform defendant that he had the right to testify at trial or that he had the right to assert self-defense. State v. Exline, — Ohio App. 3d —, 2007 Ohio 272, — N.E. 2d —, 2007 Ohio App. LEXIS 258 (Jan. 25, 2007).

There was nothing to suggest that defendant's plea was not knowingly, voluntarily, and intelligently made because the trial court did not promise that defendant would be sentenced to the minimum term, but merely stated that the minimum term was the starting point. Further, the totality of the circumstances indicated that defendant understood the nature of the charges against him as the record demonstrated that, after the trial judge reviewed the charges with defendant, he stated that he understood the charges. State v. Halloman-Cross, — Ohio App. 3d —, 2007 Ohio 290, — N.E. 2d —, 2007 Ohio App. LEXIS 274 (Jan. 25, 2007).

Defendant failed to show that his counsel provided ineffective assistance in violation of U.S. Const. amend. VI and Ohio Const. art. I, § 10 with respect to counsel's advice for defendant to enter a guilty plea to various charges, as his claim that some of the offenses were allied offenses of similar import lacked merit under RC § 2941.25, and there was no duty by the prosecution under Ohio R. Crim. P. 11 to recite facts at the plea hearing that established various elements of the pleaded offenses. State v. Shields, — Ohio App. 3d —, 2007 Ohio 462, — N.E. 2d —, 2007 Ohio App. LEXIS 422 (Feb. 5, 2007).

Defendant failed to show that his counsel provided ineffective assistance in violation of U.S. Const. amend. VI and Ohio Const. art. I, § 10 where counsel did not advise defendant to withdraw his guilty plea pursuant to Ohio R. Crim. P. 32.1 after he had committed further criminal acts while out on bond, such that the trial court was not going to impose the agreed upon sentences pursuant to the plea agreement, as the trial court had fully complied with Ohio R. Crim. P. 11 in accepting defendant's guilty plea, there was no showing of a probability of success on the withdrawal motion, and even if withdrawal was allowed, the overwhelming evidence against defendant would have resulted in his conviction. State v. Gordon, — Ohio App. 3d —, 2007 Ohio 1177, — N.E. 2d —, 2007 Ohio App. LEXIS 1089 (Mar. 16, 2007).

Because the trial court substantially complied with the nonconstitutional requirements of Ohio R. Crim. P. 11 and strictly complied with its constitutional mandates, the plea was made knowingly, intelligently, and voluntarily. Since Ohio R. Crim. P. 11 did not require the trial court to inform defendant of the possible defenses to the charge or of the dangers and disadvantages of representing himself, those issues were waived and defendant failed to demonstrate that he suffered any prejudice by the trial court's failure to advise him as to any possible defenses or as to the dangers and disadvantages of representing himself. State v. Goddard, — Ohio App. 3d —, 2007 Ohio 1229, — N.E. 2d —, 2007 Ohio App. LEXIS 1142 (Mar. 19, 2007).

While a trial court erred in informing defendant that the maximum possible sentence for his conviction for operating a vehicle under the influence of alcohol was 32 months, as the maximum possible sentence was 30 months, defendant was not prejudiced by the error since defendant had not even argued that he would not have entered a guilty plea had the trial court properly informed him of the shorter sentence. State v. Gourley, — Ohio App. 3d —, 2007 Ohio 1221, — N.E. 2d —, 2007 Ohio App. LEXIS 1150 (Mar. 19, 2007).

Defendant's plea to trafficking in cocaine was entered knowingly, intelligently, and voluntarily because there was nothing in the record to suggest that defendant was misinformed, or otherwise operating under a misconception concerning the status of the pending, unresolved issue the constitutionality of RC § 2929.14(D)(3)(b), which involved enhanced sentences, when he entered the plea. State v. Harrington, — Ohio App. 3d —, 2007 Ohio 1335, — N.E. 2d —, 2007 Ohio App. LEXIS 1218 (Mar. 23, 2007).

Trial court did not err in accepting defendant's Alford plea because it was clear that his motive in entering a plea was to procure a lesser sentence or because he feared the consequences of a jury trial. The State's recitation of the facts contained all of the necessary elements to prove the crime of felonious assault; it stated that defendant shot the victim in her apartment and that she sustained injuries. State v. Al-Jumailee, — Ohio App. 3d —, 2007 Ohio 2061, — N.E. 2d —, 2007 Ohio App. LEXIS 1920 (Apr. 27, 2007).

Defendant's guilty plea to operating a vehicle while under the influence of alcohol and/or drugs (DUI) under RC § 4511.19(A)(1) was not knowing, voluntary, or intelligent because the trial court erroneously indicated that the maximum possible penalty under RC § 4511.99(A)(4)(a) was 18, not 30, months based on a specification that within the six years preceding the indictment defendant had been convicted of three prior DUI offenses and, thus, violated Ohio R. Crim. P. 11(C)(2)(a). State v. Carney, — Ohio App. 3d —, 2007 Ohio 3180, — N.E. 2d —, 2007 Ohio App. LEXIS 2954 (June 21, 2007).

Defendant's claim that the trial court failed to advise him that it was not bound to adhere to a joint sentencing recommendation lacked merit, as the record supported a finding that the trial court had advised defendant of that fact on multiple occasions pursuant to Ohio R. Crim. P. 11(B)(1). Defendant's guilty plea was knowingly, voluntarily, and intel-

ligently entered. State v. Wilson, — Ohio App. 3d —, 2007 Ohio 3571, — N.E. 2d —, 2007 Ohio App. LEXIS 3280 (July 13, 2007).

Defendant's guilty pleas were invalid because the trial court failed to comply with Ohio R. Crim. P. 11(C)(2) when it accepted defendant's guilty pleas in the underlying criminal cases. The record revealed that the trial court did not, in any manner, refer to the privilege against self-incrimination in its colloquy with defendant and thus, the trial court did not strictly comply with the requirements of Ohio R. Crim. P. 11(C)(2) as to a constitutional right listed therein. State v. Reece, — Ohio App. 3d —, 2006 Ohio 4073, — N.E. 2d —, 2006 Ohio App. LEXIS 3992 (Aug. 8, 2006).

Trial court's failure to inform defendant that it could order him to serve any of the sentences imposed consecutively, rather than concurrently, was not a violation of Ohio R. Crim. P. 11(C)(2), and did not render the plea involuntary. Further, the trial court informed him of the potential penalties for the fourth degree felony charges. State v. Slagle, — Ohio App. 3d —, 2006 Ohio 4101, — N.E. 2d —, 2006 Ohio App. LEXIS 4070 (Aug. 10, 2006).

Where a trial court failed to inform defendant of the maximum post-release sentence that could have been imposed upon her entry of a guilty plea, as required by RC § 2943.032 and Ohio R. Crim. P. 11, her plea was not knowingly entered, and her motion to withdraw the plea pursuant to Ohio R. Crim. P. 32.1 should have been granted. State v. Smith, — Ohio App. 3d —, 2006 Ohio 4271, — N.E. 2d —, 2006 Ohio App. LEXIS 4184 (Aug. 17, 2006).

Defendant was properly informed that the "disability" on a weapons charge against him was that he was a "fugitive from justice" due to the fact that he was wanted on drug charges, such that there was substantial compliance with the requirements of Ohio R. Crim. P. 11 for purposes of his guilty plea to assorted charges, including having a weapon while under disability, in violation of RC § 2923.13. State v. Longworth, — Ohio App. 3d —, 2006 Ohio 4280, — N.E. 2d —, 2006 Ohio App. LEXIS 4192 (Aug. 18, 2006).

Trial court complied with Ohio R. Crim. P. 11(C) in all respects and defendant's plea was voluntarily entered where the colloquy was sufficient and discussed all of the rights that were specified within Rule 11(C). Before accepting defendant's guilty plea, the trial court was not required to inform him that he was waiving the right to contest the denial of his motion to suppress, as that was not one of those specifically enumerated rights within the rule. State v. Jones, — Ohio App. 3d —, 2006 Ohio 4284, — N.E. 2d —, 2006 Ohio App. LEXIS 4210 (Aug. 18, 2006).

Trial court substantially complied with the requirement of Ohio R. Crim. P. 11(C)(2)(a) that defendant, who pled guilty, had to understand the nature of the charges against him, when it listed the charges and described the maximum penalty for each charge and then asked the prosecutor to recite the facts of the case, even though it did not specifically ask defendant if he understood the charges against him because it could be assumed from the circumstances that he understood the nature of the charges. State v. Goens, — Ohio App. 3d —, 2006 Ohio 4324, — N.E. 2d —, 2006 Ohio App. LEXIS 4250 (Aug. 21, 2006).

As defendant responded to the trial court's inquiry during a plea colloquy with unequivocal affirmative answers, the trial court had no further duty to inquire as to whether defendant understood his rights. State v. Payne, — Ohio App. 3d —, 2006 Ohio 4624, — N.E. 2d —, 2006 Ohio App. LEXIS 4450 (Aug. 31, 2006).

Because the purpose of informing a defendant about post-release control as part of his sentence was to notify him of the maximum sentence to which he could be exposed, and because defendant was adequately so notified, the trial court did not err by including the words "up to" in describing post-release control to defendant at his plea hearing. State v.

Simmons, — Ohio App. 3d —, 2006 Ohio 4751, — N.E. 2d —, 2006 Ohio App. LEXIS 4681 (Sept. 14, 2006).

Trial court fulfilled the requirements of Ohio R. Crim. P. 11 concerning defendant's right to compulsory process when it asked if he understood that he had the right to subpoena witnesses to appear and testify on his behalf. State v. Simmons, — Ohio App. 3d —, 2006 Ohio 4751, — N.E. 2d —, 2006 Ohio App. LEXIS 4681 (Sept. 14, 2006).

Defendant's counsel was not ineffective under U.S. Const. amend. VI and Ohio Const. art. I, § 10 in allowing defendant to enter guilty pleas to two counts of aggravated robbery without the prosecution having recited facts to show that a BB gun that defendant used was a deadly weapon, as the prosecution was not obligated to do so pursuant to Ohio R. Crim. P. 11. State v. Gooden, — Ohio App. 3d —, 2006 Ohio 5387, — N.E. 2d —, 2006 Ohio App. LEXIS 5378 (Oct. 16, 2006).

State was not required to recite facts at defendant's plea hearing to establish the elements of defendant's aggravated robbery, in violation of RC § 2911.01(A)(1), as such was not required by Ohio R. Crim. P. 11, and further, by his guilty plea, defendant admitted his guilt the charge; accordingly, defendant could not challenge his factual guilt on appeal. State v. Gooden, — Ohio App. 3d —, 2006 Ohio 5387, — N.E. 2d —, 2006 Ohio App. LEXIS 5378 (Oct. 16, 2006).

Trial court's dialogue with defendant at the plea hearing accomplished the goal of making certain that defendant was knowingly, voluntarily, and intelligently pleading to the charge despite defendant's later claim that his diabetes interfered with his ability to understand the plea. The trial court asked defendant if he was under the influence of any substance or medication that would make it difficult for him to understand the proceedings, and defendant answered in the negative. Thereafter, the trial court asked defendant, among other things, if he understood that a plea of guilty would foreclose a trial and the rights lost when a trial does not occur, including the right to subpoena witnesses on his behalf, the right to cross-examine witnesses, and the right not to testify, and at no point did it appear as if defendant did not fully understand the purpose and result of the proceedings. State v. Anderson, — Ohio App. 3d —, 2006 Ohio 5440, — N.E. 2d —, 2006 Ohio App. LEXIS 5422 (Oct. 19, 2006).

Where defendant entered a guilty plea under Ohio R. Crim. P. 11(B)(1) to two counts of robbery, in violation of RC § 2911.02(A)(2), such plea constituted a waiver of his right to challenge the weight and sufficiency of the evidence on appeal. State v. Patterson, — Ohio App. 3d —, 2006 Ohio 5627, — N.E. 2d —, 2006 Ohio App. LEXIS 5622 (Oct. 17, 2006).

Defendant knowingly, intelligently, and voluntarily entered his guilty plea because, at the plea hearing, the trial court conducted a thorough colloquy to ensure that defendant was aware of the nature of the charges and the effects of his plea. With each count, the court explained the charge and described the possible sentence it carried including any applicable fine and the court specifically stated that the sentence for each charge could be imposed consecutively or concurrently. State v. Payne, — Ohio App. 3d —, 2006 Ohio 6539, — N.E. 2d —, 2006 Ohio App. LEXIS 6452 (Dec. 11, 2006).

Trial court did not err by accepting defendant's guilty plea to vehicular homicide and failure to stop after an accident because his plea was knowingly, voluntarily, and intelligently made. Defendant could not demonstrate a prejudicial effect from the disputed quantity of beers consumed by him throughout the day at issue since he admitted to consuming alcohol and pled guilty to the charges against him. State v. Azbill, — Ohio App. 3d —, 2006 Ohio 6886, — N.E. 2d —, 2006 Ohio App. LEXIS 6787 (Dec. 22, 2006).

Trial court did not err by not informing defendant before accepting his guilty plea that his sentences could be served consecutively. There is no specific requirement in Ohio R. Crim. P. 11 that an explanation be made that any sentences as given could run consecutively or concurrently. State v. Jasper, — Ohio App. 3d —, 2006 Ohio 7025, — N.E. 2d —, 2006 Ohio App. LEXIS 7041 (Dec. 28, 2006).

Illiteracy

When defendant pled guilty to a charge of rape, the fact that he could not read did not render his plea involuntary because the trial court fully complied with Ohio R. Crim. P. 11(C)(2) by advising defendant of the charges against him, the possible penalties, the various rights he could assert at trial, and the possible penalties for violating post-release control, and defendant affirmed that he understood each one of the matters that were explained to him. State v. Daugherty, — Ohio App. 3d —, 2006 Ohio 2684, — N.E. 2d —, 2006 Ohio App. LEXIS 2518 (May 31, 2006).

Indictment, defects in

Defendant's guilty plea waived the alleged defects in the indictment, including a failure to allege a culpable mental state: State v. Morgan, 181 Ohio App. 3d 747, 2009 Ohio 1370, 910 N.E.2d 1075, 2009 Ohio App. LEXIS 1148 (2009).

Ineffective assistance of counsel

Defendant did not suffer ineffective assistance of counsel by counsel's failure to ascertain whether defendant was able to enter a valid guilty plea in light of his past mental and physical history because there were no objective indicators that defendant's ability to reason or act under his own volition was compromised; thus, counsel could reasonably infer that he was in full possession of his mental and physical faculties. Moreover, defendant could not demonstrate prejudice, in that the trial court's Ohio R. Crim. P. 11 colloquy was sufficient to ensure that defendant's plea was made knowingly, voluntarily, and intelligently. State v. Greenleaf, — Ohio App. 3d —, 2006 Ohio 4317, — N.E. 2d —, 2006 Ohio App. LEXIS 4241 (Aug. 18, 2006).

As the trial court during an inmate's plea colloquy pursuant to Ohio R. Crim. P. 11 informed him of the potential sentences that he faced upon entering a guilty plea to various charges, and the plea form that the inmate signed plainly indicated that mandatory prison terms were required pursuant to RC § 2929.13(F) and that the inmate was not eligible for, inter alia, judicial release, his claim in his post-conviction relief petition under RC § 2953.21 that his counsel was ineffective for misinforming him that he was in fact eligible for judicial release after a period of time was denied, as the misinformation that counsel admittedly imparted did not cause the inmate prejudice. Based on the circumstances, there was no showing that the inmate would not have entered the plea but for the misrepresentation regarding the judicial release. State v. Cline, — Ohio App. 3d —, 2006 Ohio 4782, — N.E. 2d —, 2006 Ohio App. LEXIS 4666 (Sept. 14, 2006).

— Guilty plea

Defendant's guilty plea was voluntarily made; the record was devoid of any evidentiary materials concerning trial counsel's alleged failure to advise defendant concerning allied offenses. Because there was no evidence that defendant would not have pled guilty if his attorney had discussed the effect of allied offenses of similar import, he was not prejudiced from any alleged deficient conduct on the part of his counsel. State v. Gotel, — Ohio App. 3d —, 2007 Ohio 888, — N.E. 2d —, 2007 Ohio App. LEXIS 809 (Mar. 2, 2007).

Defense counsel was not ineffective because, at the plea hearing, the trial court specifically explained the individual sentences and their consecutive nature, and informed defendant of the aggregate sentence; defendant was given the opportunity to respond and object, but he declined to do so. Thus, defendant did not have a reasonable belief that he would receive concurrent, rather than consecutive, sentences. State v. McKim, — Ohio App. 3d —, 2007 Ohio 6876, — N.E. 2d —, 2007 Ohio App. LEXIS 6030 (Dec. 20, 2007).

—Sentencing

As defendant was properly advised pursuant to Ohio R. Crim. P. 11 at the plea hearing of the maximum sentence that could be imposed upon him if he entered a guilty plea and he indicated that he understood, his plea was deemed knowingly, voluntarily, and intelligently entered, such that his counsel was not ineffective in violation of U.S. Const. amend. VI and Ohio Const. art. I, § 10 for failing to advise him of the possible sentence that could have been imposed. Any such errors were waived by entry of the guilty plea where defendant did not show that there was an error in the proceeding that prevented him from entering a knowing and voluntary plea. State v. Salce, — Ohio App. 3d —, 2007 Ohio 3687, — N.E. 2d —, 2007 Ohio App. LEXIS 3390 (July 20, 2007).

Informing of post-release control

Since the trial court never informed defendant of the length of the term of his mandatory post-release control, the trial court failed to substantially comply with Ohio R. Crim. P. 11(C)(2)(a) and RC § 2943.032(E). Thus, the order finding defendant guilty had to be vacated. State v. Morgan, — Ohio App. 3d —, 2007 Ohio 71, — N.E. 2d —, 2007 Ohio App. LEXIS 67 (Jan. 11, 2007).

Although a trial court, in an Ohio R. Crim. P. 11 colloquy, overstated the length of the new sentence that could be imposed under RC § 2943.032 if defendant violated the provisions of his post-release control, reversal of his burglary conviction was not warranted as defendant would have entered his guilty plea even if he had known the correct length of additional sentence. Ohio v. Young, — Ohio App. 3d —, 2007 Ohio 5232, — N.E. 2d —, 2007 Ohio App. LEXIS 4633 (Sept. 28, 2007).

Interpreters

There was no evidence to support defendant's claim that a trial court's plea colloquy was inadequate due to the interpreter's translation, as there was nothing in the record to show that defendant did not understand the interpreter's translations or that they were inadequate, and defendant had expressly approved the translator's expertise on the record. State v. Lopez, — Ohio App. 3d —, 2007 Ohio 202, — N.E. 2d —, 2007 Ohio App. LEXIS 190 (Jan. 19, 2007).

There was no evidence in the record that defendant did not enter his plea knowingly, intelligently, or voluntarily or that he would not have entered his plea if the trial court had appointed an interpreter because, at no time during the trial court's explanation of defendant's rights pursuant to Ohio R. Crim. P. 11, did defendant indicate confusion or uncertainty about the proceedings. Defendant stated on the record that he understood English and he could have expressed confusion at any time but, instead, the colloquy between the trial court and defendant at the plea hearing illustrated that the trial court thoroughly advised him, in accordance with Ohio R. Crim. P. 11(C), and that he did understand, as he affirmatively answered each question posed by the trial court without requesting an explanation. State v. Mota, — Ohio App. 3d —, 2006 Ohio 3800, — N.E. 2d —, 2006 Ohio App. LEXIS 3779 (July 21, 2006).

Jury waiver, coercion

Trial court cannot threaten jail time on one case, but offer to suspend that time if the defendant waives a jury and pleads no contest in another case: City of Cincinnati v. Smith, 180 Ohio App. 3d 587, 2009 Ohio 143, 906 N.E.2d 497, 2009 Ohio App. LEXIS 171 (2009).

Mandatory prison term

When a defendant who is subject to a mandatory prison sentence enters a plea of guilty or no contest, CrimR 11(C)(20(a) requires the court, before accepting the plea, to determine that the defendant understands that the mandatory sentence renders the defendant ineligible for community control sanctions. The pleas were invalid where the court failed to correct errors in the plea form: Daniel v. McKinney, 181 Ohio App. 3d 1, 2009 Ohio 690, 907 N.E.2d 787, 2009 Ohio App. LEXIS 563 (2009).

Maximum penalties

Defendant's motion to withdraw his no contest pleas was erroneously denied because the trial court did not substantially comply with Ohio R. Crim. P. 11(C)(2)(a) when it accepted those pleas because, while it informed defendant that the counts he did not contest contained firearm specifications, it did not tell him that those specifications carried mandatory one- and three-year prison terms, so defendant was not advised of the maximum sentence applicable to the counts he did not contest. State v. Douglas, — Ohio App. 3d —, 2007 Ohio 714, — N.E. 2d —, 2007 Ohio App. LEXIS 650 (Feb. 22, 2007).

Because defendant was not subject to post-release control, since he pled guilty to aggravated murder, the trial judge's erroneous statements regarding post-release control made at the sentencing hearing had no bearing on the validity of defendant's plea, and because the "maximum penalty" that could be imposed on defendant was imprisonment for life, the trial court was under no duty to explain the circumstances of parole and it substantially complied with Ohio R. Crim. P. 11(C)(2)(a)'s requirement to explain the maximum penalty. Further, there was no evidence to suggest defendant's belief that he would be subject to post-release control, assuming he would be released after 28 years, induced him to enter his plea of guilty. State v. Clark, — Ohio App. 3d —, 2007 Ohio 1780, — N.E. 2d —, 2007 Ohio App. LEXIS 1619 (Apr. 13, 2007).

Defendant showed that he suffered a prejudicial effect under Ohio R. Crim. P. 52(A) due to the trial court's failure to substantially comply with Ohio R. Crim. P. 11(C), in that the trial court did not inform defendant that by entering a guilty plea to two charges, he potentially faced a lifetime driver's license suspension under RC § 4510.02. Accordingly, the plea was not knowingly and voluntarily entered and it required vacatur. State v. Greene, — Ohio App. 3d —, 2006 Ohio 480, — N.E. 2d —, 2006 Ohio App. LEXIS 408 (2006).

Defendant did not adequately support his claim that he pled guilty because his trial counsel advised him that he would receive a lighter sentence than the one he received because his statements to this effect were insufficient, absent concrete evidence that he was improperly induced to plead guilty. State v. Sarkozy, — Ohio App. 3d —, 2006 Ohio 3977, — N.E. 2d —, 2006 Ohio App. LEXIS 3956 (Aug. 3, 2006).

Trial court substantially complied with the requirement under Ohio R. Crim. P. 11(C)(2)(a) to inform defendant of the maximum penalty he faced by entering a guilty plea where defendant was aware that he faced a term of life imprisonment, and the trial court's misstatement as to the possibility of post-release control did not render the plea involuntary, as it did not change the maximum penalty faced and it was not prejudicial to defendant where he did not show that but for the misstatements, he would not have entered the plea. State v. Baker, — Ohio App. 3d —, 2006 Ohio 4902, — N.E. 2d —, 2006 Ohio App. LEXIS 4830 (Sept. 22, 2006).

From the context of defendant's plea colloquy, it was clear he faced a mandatory 10-year sentence, pursuant to RC § 2929.14(D)(3)(a), for being a major drug offender, so he was properly advised, under Ohio R. Crim. P. 11(C). State v. Coleman, — Ohio App. 3d —, 2006 Ohio 5363, — N.E. 2d —, 2006 Ohio App. LEXIS 5345 (Oct. 16, 2006).

No contest plea

Defendant's conviction for failing to verify his residence as required by RC § 2950.06(F) was appropriate based on the fact that 1) defendant pled no contest to the charge; 2) defendant was properly advised by the trial court of the consequences of a no contest plea, and 3) by making the plea, defendant admitted to the facts alleged by the State in the charging document; under those circumstances, the trial court was required to make a guilty finding against defendant for failure as a sex offender to verify his residence. State v. Campos, — Ohio App. 3d —, 2007 Ohio 3316, — N.E. 2d —, 2007 Ohio App. LEXIS 3066 (June 29, 2007).

Trial court complied with Ohio R. Crim. P. 11 when it accepted defendant's plea because, prior to entering his no-contest pleas, defendant signed a written form in which he acknowledged that he had received an explanation and understood that his no-contest pleas were an admission of the facts in the criminal complaints but were not an admission of guilt, and that such pleas could not be used against him in any future civil or criminal proceedings. He also specifically acknowledged that he understood that by entering his no-contest pleas he was not fighting the allegations in the complaint. State v. Wallace, — Ohio App. 3d —, 2007 Ohio 3451, — N.E. 2d —, 2007 Ohio App. LEXIS 3199 (July 6, 2007).

Trial court is not required to have before it a statement of the particular conduct constituting the alleged offense when it accepts a plea of no contest to a felony charge. However, if the prosecutor presents a statement of facts and those facts positively contradict the felony charged by negating an essential element to commission of the offense alleged, the court cannot make a finding of guilty on the basis of the charges alleged in the indictment. State v. Cooper, 168 Ohio App. 3d 378, 2006 Ohio 4004, 860 N.E.2d 135, 2006 Ohio App. LEXIS 3922 (2006).

No contest pleas

Defendant's entry of a no contest plea pursuant to Ohio R. Crim. P. 11(B)(2) to a charge of theft by deception, in violation of RC § 2913.02(A)(2), based on her having stopped payment on post-dated checks that she had provided to a lender under a payday loan agreement, precluded her from asserting on appeal that the conviction was erroneous due to an alleged lack of proof that she had acted deceptively. Her plea constituted an admission to the allegations contained in the charging instrument. State v. Widener, — Ohio App. 3d —, 2007 Ohio 429, — N.E. 2d —, 2007 Ohio App. LEXIS 381 (Feb. 2, 2007).

Although the trial court did not inform defendant of his right to confront adverse witnesses, it had no obligation to do so. Because the language of Ohio Traf. R. 10(C) and Ohio R. Crim. P. 11(D) was the same, the trial court was not required to inform defendant of the specific rights he was waiving by entering a no-contest plea. State v. Dobbins, — Ohio App. 3d —, 2007 Ohio 1665, — N.E. 2d —, 2007 Ohio App. LEXIS 1527 (Apr. 6, 2007).

Record supported the conclusion that defendant's no contest plea was knowing, voluntary, and intelligent because the record contained a sufficient basis for the trial court to have made the determinations of defendant's understanding required by Ohio R. Crim. P. 11(C)(2), in spite of defendant's limited intelligence. The trial court elicited defendant's plea of no contest to each of the charges and specifications, found that he understood the waivers of his rights, the nature of the offenses, the maximum penalties that could be imposed, that he was not eligible for community control or judicial release, and that he might be required to pay a fine and restitution and it found that he understood the effects of his pleas, that the pleas were made voluntarily, and that there was a factual basis for the pleas. State v. Wilson, — Ohio App. 3d —, 2006 Ohio 269, — N.E. 2d —, 2006 Ohio App. LEXIS 219 (Jan. 13, 2006).

When defendant pled no contest to charges of drug trafficking and possession of criminal tools, he admitted that the indictment charging him with these crimes sufficiently stated them, under Ohio R. Crim. P. 11(B)(2), so the trial court was required to find him guilty of these offenses. State v. Simms, — Ohio App. 3d —, 2006 Ohio 22, — N.E. 2d —, 2006 Ohio App. LEXIS 10 (Jan. 5, 2006).

Trial court complied with Ohio R. Crim. P. 11 because, at the plea hearing, the trial court judge orally conducted a plea colloquy with defendant which addressed defendant's constitutional rights, the effect on his parole conditions, the possible sanctions and maximum sentence, the court proceeding with judgment and sentencing, and defendant's voluntariness in making the no contest plea. Additionally, defendant completed and executed a written plea colloquy and the trial court also inquired with defendant to ensure that he understood the contents of the written plea colloquy. State v. Smith, — Ohio App. 3d —, 2006 Ohio 4419, — N.E. 2d —, 2006 Ohio App. LEXIS 4339 (Aug. 28, 2006).

Where the trial court explained to defendant that the one-year and three-year firearm specifications for underlying felonies would merge at sentencing, but it did not tell him that all of the firearm specifications would be merged, there was no misrepresentation by the trial court pursuant to Ohio R. Crim. P. 11(C)(2), and based on the record, defendant's no contest plea was knowingly and voluntarily entered. State v. McCrimon, — Ohio App. 3d —, 2006 Ohio 5722, — N.E. 2d —, 2006 Ohio App. LEXIS 5713 (Nov. 2, 2006).

There was no error in the trial court's admission of defendant's no contest plea pursuant to Ohio R. Crim. P. 11(B)(2) during his sexual predator hearing, as the sexual predator hearing was not a proceeding that was "subsequent" to his conviction and accordingly, the trial court was not barred under Rule 11(B)(2) from using the plea. There was no evidence that the trial court actually relied on the plea, and further, there was evidence from a police officer that established the facts which gave rise to the conviction. State v. Troutman, — Ohio App. 3d —, 2006 Ohio 6066, — N.E. 2d —, 2006 Ohio App. LEXIS 6050 (Nov. 20, 2006).

Defendant's no contest plea, in a prosecution for aggravated vehicular assault, under RC § 2903.08(A)(1)(a), was not knowing, intelligent, or voluntary, as required by Ohio R. Crim. P. 11(C)(2), because he was led to believe that he would receive judicial release after serving one year in prison, and this was instrumental in inducing his plea, but judicial release was a matter separate from the sentence imposed. State v. Baker, 170 Ohio App. 3d 331, 2006 Ohio 7085, 867 N.E.2d 426, 2006 Ohio App. LEXIS 7013 (2006).

Plea of no contest has the effect of admitting all facts, but denying guilt as to those admissions; since defendant pled no contest to charges, and since evidentiary issues involved in a trial court's denial of defendant's motion in limine were never presented at a trial, the denial of defendant's motion in limine was not preserved for appellate review. State v. Sanchez, — Ohio App. 3d —, 2006 Ohio 2141, — N.E. 2d —, 2006 Ohio App. LEXIS 1979 (May 1, 2006).

Where it was clear from the trial court's plea colloquy pursuant to Ohio R. Crim. P. 11(C)(2)(a) that defendant understood the nature of the charges against him, his plea of no contest was deemed voluntary; the trial court was not required to elicit a recitation of the facts of the offense pursuant to RC § 2937.07, as defendant was entering a plea to a felony offense rather than to a misdemeanor. State v. Kruger, — Ohio App. 3d —, 2006 Ohio 2361, — N.E. 2d —, 2006 Ohio App. LEXIS 2211 (May 12, 2006).

No contest pleas generally

Trial court substantially complied with the requirements of Ohio R. Crim. P. 11(C)(2)(b) and, thus, did not err when it accepted defendant's guilty plea because a review of the totality of the circumstances revealed that defendant subjectively understood the implications of his pleas and the rights that he was waiving. The trial court also did not err in considering at the plea hearing the prosecutor's statement as to the facts constituting the offense of burglary because the prosecutor's statement indicating that police followed footprints from a burglarized home to a location where stolen property was located and defendant was found hiding did not positively contradict the elements of burglary. State v. Rohda, — Ohio App. 3d —, 2006 Ohio 6463, — N.E. 2d —, 2006 Ohio App. LEXIS 6398 (Dec. 8, 2006).

— Explanation of circumstances

Record did not reflect that defendant's no contest pleas to forcible rape, under RC § 2907.02, and gross sexual imposition, under RC § 2907.05, were knowing and voluntary, under Ohio R. Crim. P. 11(C), because the trial court incorrectly informed defendant that defendant "could" be classified as a habitual sexual offender or a sexual predator, when, in fact, defendant's classification as an aggravated sexually oriented offender was mandatory, based on the convictions resulting from defendant's pleas, and it was not shown that defendant would have entered defendant's pleas had defendant been told defendant's classification was mandatory. Ohio v. Oldham, — Ohio App. 3d —, 2007 Ohio 5184, — N.E. 2d —, 2007 Ohio App. LEXIS 4569 (Sept. 28, 2007).

Petty offenses

In accepting a plea to a misdemeanor involving a petty offense, a trial court is required to inform the defendant only of the effect of the specific plea being entered. To satisfy the requirement of informing a defendant of the effect of a plea, a trial court must inform the defendant of the appropriate language under CrimR 11(B): State v. Jones, 116 Ohio St. 3d 211, 2007 Ohio 6093, 877 N.E.2d 677, 2007 Ohio LEXIS 2885 (2007).

Requirement that a trial judge personally address a defendant to insure the voluntariness of a plea and that the defendant understands the rights being waived are not included in the language of Ohio R. Crim. P. 11(E), which controls acceptance of pleas in petty offense cases. State v. Howard, — Ohio App. 3d —, 2007 Ohio 2048, — N.E. 2d —, 2007 Ohio App. LEXIS 1907 (Apr. 30, 2007).

Plea bargaining

Defendant's guilty plea was vacated where the state and defendant's parole officer stated that they would not seek jail time and the trial court ambiguously indicated that it would abide by the plea agreement, but a different judge presided over sentencing and imposed a prison term: State v. Asberry, 173 Ohio App. 3d 443, 2007 Ohio 5436, 878 N.E.2d 1082, 2007 Ohio App. LEXIS 4783 (2007).

Defendant's claim that he was subject to racial and gender discrimination by the trial court's application of RC § 2929.11 and Ohio R. Crim. P. 11 with respect to the plea deal that he was offered compared to that of the white female who was also charged with the same offenses as defendant lacked merit, as defendant had a lengthy history of drug offenses and of violating community control sanctions, whereas the female was a first-time offender. State v. Bulger, — Ohio App. 3d —, 2006 Ohio 3046, — N.E. 2d —, 2006 Ohio App. LEXIS 2928 (June 16, 2006).

Because defendant entered his guilty plea voluntarily, intelligently, and knowingly, and without any suggestion of anticipated leniency, the disagreement at sentencing between defendant's two counsel about a plea agreement that could not be produced, was never performed upon, and may not have even related to the case under discussion, was simply not enough to establish the terms of an agreement under Ohio R. Crim. P. 11(F) or to show a potential breach by the prosecution. Therefore, a remand to discuss it further was not appropriate or necessary. State v. Speakman, — Ohio App. 3d —, 2006 Ohio 6378, — N.E. 2d —, 2006 Ohio App. LEXIS 6330 (Dec. 5, 2006).

Defendant's no contest plea was not knowing, intelligent, and voluntary where the court led him to believe that it would impose sentence in accord with the state's recommendation, but then imposed a harsher sentence: State v. Baker, 170 Ohio App. 3d 331, 2006 Ohio 7085, 867 N.E.2d 426, 2006 Ohio App. LEXIS 7013 (2006).

— Claim of innocence

Trial court failed to comply with the constitutional standards for accepting defendant's Alford plea because the State did not proffer the evidence which it intended to present to prove defendant's guilt under the indictment; instead, the State merely referred to the words of the indictment. There was no evidence from which the trial court could find that defendant had rationally calculated his decision to plead guilty. Ohio v. Dunnier, — Ohio App. 3d —, 2007 Ohio 4891, — N.E. 2d —, 2007 Ohio App. LEXIS 4373 (Sept. 21, 2007).

Plea requirements

Trial court did not err by accepting defendant's Alford plea because, at the plea hearing, defendant not only admitted the factual basis of the charges but acknowledged that these facts constituted a criminal offense and that, by admitting them, she would be found guilty of the crime. Thus, pursuant to Ohio R. Crim. P. 11(C)(2), defendant understood that she was completely admitting her guilt by entering an Alford plea. State v. Anderson, — Ohio App. 3d —, 2006 Ohio 5167, — N.E. 2d —, 2006 Ohio App. LEXIS 5107 (Sept. 29, 2006).

While defendant contended that the trial court failed to advise him of his right to testify in violation of Ohio R. Crim. P. 11, the right to testify was not specifically enumerated in Ohio R. Crim. P. 11. Since the trial court specifically advised defendant that he had the right to remain silent and the right not to testify at trial, the trial court strictly complied with the requirements of Ohio R. Crim. P. 11. State v. Anderson, — Ohio App. 3d —, 2006 Ohio 5431, — N.E. 2d —, 2006 Ohio App. LEXIS 5424 (Oct. 19, 2006).

Post-release control

Defendant's plea was not knowingly, voluntarily, and intelligently made because the trial court failed to advise defendant regarding post-release control; there was no specific reference to post-release control anywhere in the record. Without an adequate explanation of post-release control from the trial court, defendant could not have fully understood the consequences of his plea, as required by Ohio R. Crim. P. 11(C). State v. Cortez, — Ohio App. 3d —, 2007 Ohio 261, — N.E. 2d —, 2007 Ohio App. LEXIS 259 (Jan. 25, 2007).

As the trial court properly advised defendant under Ohio R. Crim. P. 11 during his plea hearing, it answered defendant's questions regarding why he was being prosecuted by both federal and state authorities for possession of a firearm, and it informed him that he was subject to post-release control pursuant to RC § 2943.032, there was no showing that defendant's plea was not knowingly and voluntarily entered. State v. Hall, — Ohio App. 3d —, 2007 Ohio 414, — N.E. 2d —, 2007 Ohio App. LEXIS 353 (Feb. 1, 2007).

Although a trial court misinformed defendant that he could face a period of post-release control upon his conviction of aggravated trafficking in drugs, as such period was mandatory pursuant to RC § 2967.28(B)(1), the trial court substantially complied with the requirements of Ohio R. Crim. P. 11(C)(2)(a). Defendant's claim that his plea was not knowingly, voluntarily, and intelligently entered due to such misinformation lacked merit. State v. Fuller, — Ohio App. 3d —, 2007 Ohio 1020, — N.E. 2d —, 2007 Ohio App. LEXIS 960 (Mar. 9, 2007).

Trial court's failure to inform defendant of the length of his post-release control, which carried a mandatory five-year term, was contrary to the requirement of RC § 2943.032(E) and rendered the plea colloquy conducted upon defendant's guilty plea insufficient as the trial court did not substantially comply with Ohio R. Crim. P. 11's requirement that every defendant be made aware of the maximum possible sentence. State v. Bingham, — Ohio App. 3d —, 2007 Ohio 1161, — N.E. 2d —, 2007 Ohio App. LEXIS 1088 (Mar. 15, 2007).

Although a trial court judge voluntarily advised defendant of the consequences of his not guilty plea with respect to the potential terms of incarceration he faced by entering a plea that was offered by the State or by going to trial, the judge was not obligated to inform defendant of the post-release control possibility. The protections of Ohio R. Crim. P. 11(C) were not afforded to a defendant who entered a not guilty plea and accordingly, defendant's plea of not guilty was knowingly and intelligently entered. State v. Reed, — Ohio App. 3d —, 2007 Ohio 3106, — N.E. 2d —, 2007 Ohio App. LEXIS 2871 (June 22, 2007).

Trial court substantially complied with Ohio R. Crim. P. 11(C)(2)(a) in accepting defendant's no contest plea, even though the trial court's plea colloquy did not state that post-release control, under RC § 2967.28(B), was mandatory, because defendant's written plea agreement stated that post-release control was mandatory, so defendant had actual notice of the mandatory nature of post-release control. State v. Reed, — Ohio App. 3d —, 2007 Ohio 4087, — N.E. 2d —, 2007 Ohio App. LEXIS 3711 (Aug. 10, 2007).

Trial court "substantially complied" with Ohio R. Crim. P. 11(C)(2)(a) where defendant was apprised in the waiver form when he entered his guilty plea that he was subject to a mandatory three-year term of post-release control pursuant to RC § 2967.28(B)(2); although the trial court mistakenly had informed defendant during the oral allocution that he was subject to a discretionary post-release control term, there was no need to vacate the plea, as defendant indicated that he was aware of the penalties he faced, he indicated that he had discussed the terms of the waiver form with his counsel, and he never indicated that he would not have entered the plea if he had been correctly informed at the plea hearing that the post-release control was mandatory. State v. Whitesell, — Ohio App. 3d —, 2006 Ohio 1781, — N.E. 2d —, 2006 Ohio App. LEXIS 1641 (Apr. 10, 2006).

Defendant's pleas were not knowingly, intelligently, and voluntarily made because the trial court failed to comply with Ohio R. Crim. P. 11(C)(2)(a) by failing to advise him that he was subject to a mandatory five-year period of post-release control, RC § 2967.28(B)(1). Although the trial court correctly advised defendant of the five-year period, it failed to advise him that it was mandatory and thus, the trial court inadvertently understated the sentence that he would receive by pleading guilty. State v. Holloway, — Ohio App. 3d —, 2006 Ohio 2591, — N.E. 2d —, 2006 Ohio App. LEXIS 2441 (May 25, 2006).

Trial court was in full compliance with the mandates of RC § 2943.032(E) when it addressed the issue of post release control. Although defendant argued that the trial court's use of the words "up to" in reference to the possible length of post release control was improper, the use of that phrase was entirely appropriate and, in accordance with RC § 2943.032(E), defendant was informed in a reasonably thorough manner that upon his release he would be subject to mandatory post release control that could span a period of time up to five years. State v. Shorter, — Ohio App. 3d —, 2006 Ohio 2882, — N.E. 2d —, 2006 Ohio App. LEXIS 2783 (June 8, 2006).

As defendant was not fully apprised by the trial court during the plea hearing of the maximum post-release sentence that could have been imposed against him when he changed his plea from not guilty to guilty, his plea was not knowingly and voluntarily entered as required by Ohio R. Crim. P. 11(C)(2)(a), and RC §§ 2943.032(E) and 2967.28, requiring vacatur of the plea. State v. McCollins, — Ohio App. 3d —, 2006 Ohio 4886, — N.E. 2d —, 2006 Ohio App. LEXIS 4801 (Sept. 21, 2006).

As defendant was subject to a mandatory three-year term of post-release control pursuant to RC §§ 2929.19(B)(3)(c) and 2967.28(B), and the trial court failed to advise him of the correct term of post-release control that would be imposed upon his guilty plea, there was no substantial compliance with Ohio R. Crim. P. 11(C)(2)(a) and RC § 2943.032, requiring vacatur of the plea. State v. Brusiter, — Ohio App. 3d —, 2006 Ohio 6444, — N.E. 2d —, 2006 Ohio App. LEXIS 6396 (Dec. 7, 2006).

Postrelease control
In order to comply with RC § 2943.032 and CrimR 11(C)(2)(a), at the plea hearing the trial court must personally advise the defendant concerning postreleasecontrol. State v. Conrad, — Ohio App. 3d —, 2007 Ohio 5717, — N.E. 2d —, 2007 Ohio App. LEXIS 5021 (Oct. 25, 2007).

Prejudice
Defendant was not entitled to a reversal of his conviction even though a trial court failed to substantially comply with the requirements of CrimR 11(C)(2) by explaining to defendant the effect of a no contest plea. Defendant failed to establish prejudice as defendant failed to show that he would not have entered the no contest plea if he had been aware of the fact that the plea admitted the facts alleged against defendant by the state. State v. Lamb, — Ohio App. 3d —, 2008 Ohio 1569, — N.E. 2d —, 2008 Ohio App. LEXIS 1374 (Mar. 31, 2008).

Recording of proceedings
Where the parties placed a plea agreement on the record in chambers in the presence of the parties and the judge, the parties were aware of the agreement, and the inmate signed a written petition to enter his no contest plea that specifically set forth the terms of the plea agreement, the technical violation of Ohio R. Crim. P. 11(F) by not putting the plea agreement on the record in open court did not require prejudice; further, no prejudice as a result of the violation was shown. State v. Smith, — Ohio App. 3d —, 2006 Ohio 1482, — N.E. 2d —, 2006 Ohio App. LEXIS 1352 (Mar. 21, 2006).

Robbery
When defendant, upon pleading guilty to robbery, under RC § 2911.02(A)(3), admitted he ran up behind an elderly victim, snatched her purse and ran, and admitted it was possible she fell, this satisfied the "force" element of robbery, as the victim was exposed to potential harm, so the trial court substantially complied with Ohio R. Crim. P. 11(C) in accepting defendant's guilty plea, and defendant entered that plea knowingly, intelligently, and voluntarily, as he was fully informed of the nature of the charges. State v. Heidelburg, — Ohio App. 3d —, 2006 Ohio 474, — N.E. 2d —, 2006 Ohio App. LEXIS 413 (Feb. 3, 2006).

Trial court was not required to determine whether attempted theft by threat was a lesser included offense of robbery, in violation of RC § 2911.02(A)(3), as defendant's entry of a guilty plea to the robbery charge pursuant to Ohio R. Crim. P. 11(B)(1) constituted a complete admission that he was guilty of robbery. State v. Johnson, — Ohio App. 3d —, 2006 Ohio 4934, — N.E. 2d —, 2006 Ohio App. LEXIS 4866 (Sept. 22, 2006).

Strict compliance
Defendant's conviction based on his plea was vacated; the trial court did not strictly comply with the constitutional requirements of Ohio R. Crim. P. 11(C)(2)(c) when it accepted defendant's guilty plea to attempted felonious assault because it failed to inform defendant of his right to have his guilt determined under a beyond a reasonable doubt standard. The right to have the State prove guilt beyond a reasonable doubt was a constitutionally-protected right of a criminal defendant. State v. Veney, — Ohio App. 3d —, 2007 Ohio 1295, — N.E. 2d —, 2007 Ohio App. LEXIS 1179 (Mar. 22, 2007).

Substantial compliance
Although the trial court did not use the statutory language of RC § 2943.031(A) when it advised defendant of the consequences of his plea with respect to his immigration status, there was substantial compliance for purposes of the

plea colloquy under Ohio R. Crim. P. 11 where under the totality of the circumstances, defendant subjectively understood the implication of his plea and the rights that he was waiving. State v. Lopez, — Ohio App. 3d —, 2007 Ohio 202, — N.E. 2d —, 2007 Ohio App. LEXIS 190 (Jan. 19, 2007).

Where a trial court substantially complied with the requirements of Ohio R. Crim. P. 11(C)(2), and defendant failed to show that he was prejudiced by his counsel's erroneous representation about defendant's eligibility for judicial release, there was no showing of manifest injustice under Ohio R. Crim. P. 32.1 to support defendant's post-sentence request to withdraw his guilty plea. State v. Aleshire, — Ohio App. 3d —, 2007 Ohio 4446, — N.E. 2d —, 2007 Ohio App. LEXIS 4010 (Aug. 29, 2007).

Trial court substantially complied with Ohio R. Crim. P. 11(C) in accepting defendant's plea. Defendant was, in fact, advised of his right to confront witnesses and of his mandatory five-year term of post-release control, and of the effect his pleas would have on his rights, by the trial court. The signed plea agreement demonstrated that defendant knew that he would be subject to a mandatory term of post-release control of up to five years and that a five-year term of post-release control was required pursuant to RC § 2967.28(B)(1). State v. Bublitz, — Ohio App. 3d —, 2007 Ohio 5029, — N.E. 2d —, 2007 Ohio App. LEXIS 4457 (Sept. 26, 2007).

Trial court did substantially comply with Ohio R. Crim. P. 11(C)(2) prior to accepting defendant's guilty plea because, although the trial court initially misinformed defendant regarding his eligibility for probation, defendant was subjectively aware that he was not eligible. Defendant demonstrated a subjective understanding of the consequences of his plea and the rights he was waiving, through his acknowledgement that a waiver of his right to a presentence investigation report would preclude probation as a sentencing option. Ohio v. Fink, — Ohio App. 3d —, 2007 Ohio 5220, — N.E. 2d —, 2007 Ohio App. LEXIS 4581 (Sept. 28, 2007).

When a trial court did not advise defendant that defendant's guilty plea was a complete admission of guilt, pursuant to Ohio R. Crim. P. 11(C)(2)(b), defendant's guilty plea was not rendered involuntary because the trial court strictly complied with the requirement to advise defendant of defendant's federal constitutional rights, and the trial court substantially complied with the requirement to advise defendant of defendant's remaining rights, including advising defendant of the effect of defendant's guilty plea, because defendant signed a plea form stating the effect of defendant's plea, and both the State and the trial court went over the facts supporting the charges, which defendant acknowledged to be true, so, under the totality of the circumstances, defendant subjectively understood the implications of defendant's pleas and the rights defendant waived. Ohio v. Vanover, — Ohio App. 3d —, 2007 Ohio 1057, — N.E. 2d —, 2007 Ohio App. LEXIS 4748 (Mar. 9, 2007).

Although the trial court's statements concerning withdrawal of a guilty plea were not wholly accurate representations of the law, the trial court substantially complied with the mandates of CrimR 11 when it accepted defendant's guilty plea, and no prejudice resulted from the inclusion of the additional admonition by the trial court that a guilty plea would not be easily withdrawn. State v. Moore, — Ohio App. 3d —, 2007 Ohio 6018, — N.E. 2d —, 2007 Ohio App. LEXIS 5300 (Nov. 13, 2007).

Trial court substantially complied with the requirements of Ohio R. Crim. P. 11(C)(2)(a) and (b) in conducting a colloquy with defendant prior to accepting his guilty plea to a lesser charge of burglary than that which he was originally charged, as defendant understood the nature of the charge based on the totality of the circumstances, despite the fact that the trial court did not discuss the elements of the charge or specifically ask defendant if he understood the nature thereof; defendant heard the prosecutor recite the facts of the case and no

objection was made, and he stated that he reviewed the facts and law of his case with his counsel. State v. Frazier, — Ohio App. 3d —, 2006 Ohio 1475, — N.E. 2d —, 2006 Ohio App. LEXIS 1340 (Mar. 28, 2006).

Trial court substantially complied with the requirements of Ohio R. Crim. P. 11(C)(2), as the record showed that defendant subjectively understood the implications of his plea and the rights that he waived by entering the plea, that the plea was entered voluntarily, knowingly, and intelligently, and that defendant possessed the requisite capacity to waive his rights and enter the plea. State v. Johnson, — Ohio App. 3d —, 2006 Ohio 4934, — N.E. 2d —, 2006 Ohio App. LEXIS 4866 (Sept. 22, 2006).

Defendant entered his guilty plea knowingly, intelligently, and voluntarily because the trial court was in substantial compliance with Crim. R. 11(C)(2)(a) and it was clear from the record that defendant entered the pleas with an understanding of the charges, the implications of his pleas, and the rights that he was waiving. Defendant was not prejudiced by the trial court's alleged failure to expressly inform him that he was waiving his constitutional rights by pleading guilty. State v. Myler, — Ohio App. 3d —, 2006 Ohio 5607, — N.E. 2d —, 2006 Ohio App. LEXIS 5628 (Oct. 26, 2006).

Sufficiency of allocution

As a trial court complied with Ohio R. Crim. P. 11(C) by ascertaining each requirement listed therein and in Boykin, defendant's Alford plea was deemed voluntarily entered and constituted a waiver of his right to appeal his claim that his counsel was ineffective for failing to call eyewitnesses to testify at his suppression hearing. Other claims relating to the trial court's denial of his suppression motion were also deemed waived. State v. Leasure, — Ohio App. 3d —, 2007 Ohio 100, — N.E. 2d —, 2007 Ohio App. LEXIS 92 (Jan. 12, 2007).

Totality of the circumstances revealed that defendant was fully aware of the effect of his Alford plea. The trial judge complied with Ohio R. Crim. P. 11(C), and although defendant contended that the judge's explanation of an Alford plea confused defendant, the judge explained the plea to defendant, and defendant, whose counsel was present, indicated that he understood. State v. Johnson, — Ohio App. 3d —, 2007 Ohio 781, — N.E. 2d —, 2007 Ohio App. LEXIS 698 (Feb. 23, 2007).

Defendant's plea was knowingly, intelligently, and voluntarily entered. He was presumed competent to stand trial, under RC § 2945.37(G), and the record showed that he understood the nature of the proceedings and was advised by counsel from the outset. The trial court meticulously performed its duties in conformity with Ohio R. Crim. P. 11 and defendant expressed himself well on the record and engaged in a number of relevant and meaningful discussions with the trial court. State v. Dombrowsky, — Ohio App. 3d —, 2007 Ohio 1194, — N.E. 2d —, 2007 Ohio App. LEXIS 1125 (Mar. 16, 2007).

Trial court did not err in accepting defendant's guilty pleas because Ohio R. Crim. P. 11 did not require defendant to provide sworn testimony when he pled guilty. The trial court ascertained that defendant was satisfied with his counsel's representation and that defendant was not under the influence of drugs or alcohol at the time that he entered his pleas. State v. Springs, — Ohio App. 3d —, 2007 Ohio 1343, — N.E. 2d —, 2007 Ohio App. LEXIS 1223 (Mar. 23, 2007).

Defendant's pleas were knowing, intelligent, and voluntary because the trial court fully complied with all of the requirements of Ohio R. Crim. P. 11(C)(2) before accepting defendant's guilty pleas. Although when defendant was initially asked by the trial court if the charges as explained by the prosecutor were true, defendant responded "no," after further discussion, defendant recanted that statement and twice reaffirmed that he understood the charges against him and that they were true. State v. Randle, — Ohio App. 3d —, 2007 Ohio 2967, — N.E. 2d —, 2007 Ohio App. LEXIS 2727 (June 15, 2007).

As defendant raised a claim in a prior appeal with respect to his post-sentence motion to withdraw his guilty plea, which was deemed to have lacked merit because he was found to have been fully advised pursuant to Ohio R. Crim. P. 11 that the maximum sentence that he could face was the death penalty, his later appeal from the trial court's denial of his successive motion to withdraw his guilty plea pursuant to Ohio R. Crim. P. 32.1 was barred by the doctrine of res judicata. State v. Lankford, — Ohio App. 3d —, 2007 Ohio 3330, — N.E. 2d —, 2007 Ohio App. LEXIS 3120 (June 12, 2007).

Trial court did not abuse its discretion when it denied defendant's pre-sentence motion to withdraw his guilty plea pursuant to Ohio R. Crim. P. 32.1, as he waited until halfway through the sentencing hearing to make his motion, defendant had entered his plea knowingly, voluntarily, and intelligently after a sufficient colloquy under Ohio R. Crim. P. 11, defendant indicated that he was satisfied with his counsel's representation, a comprehensive hearing was held on defendant's withdrawal motion, and it did not appear that defendant had a meritorious defense. Defendant simply changed his mind about his plea, which was not a sufficient justification to withdraw it. State v. Johnson, — Ohio App. 3d —, 2007 Ohio 3405, — N.E. 2d —, 2007 Ohio App. LEXIS 3157 (June 26, 2007).

Defendant's argument that the trial court failed to ensure that defendant fully understood the nature of the charges against defendant was without merit. The trial court followed a statement by defense counsel by asking defendant whether defendant had any questions regarding defendant's case or the hearing, to which defendant replied that defendant did not. State v. Divens, — Ohio App. 3d —, 2007 Ohio 3923, — N.E. 2d —, 2007 Ohio App. LEXIS 3568 (Aug. 2, 2007).

Trial court's colloquy complied with the requirements of Ohio R. Crim. P. 11(C) when it accepted defendant's plea; defendant expressed himself clearly on the record and engaged in meaningful discussions with the trial court. The trial court engaged the defendant in an active colloquy, receiving appropriate answers of "yes sir" and "no sir," when determining whether defendant's no contest plea was knowingly and voluntarily entered. State v. Wilder, — Ohio App. 3d —, 2007 Ohio 4186, — N.E. 2d —, 2007 Ohio App. LEXIS 3793 (Aug. 17, 2007).

Trial court did not err in failing to specifically inquire into whether defendant had any "mental diagnoses" or whether he was on medications for the same prior to accepting his guilty plea because the record reflected that defendant was in no way mentally or physically compromised during the hearing, he stated that he understood his plea, and he immediately admitted his guilt. The record demonstrated that defendant was informed of his constitutional rights during the guilty plea hearing, and his guilty plea represented a knowing and voluntary forfeiture of his rights. State v. Greenleaf, — Ohio App. 3d —, 2006 Ohio 4317, — N.E. 2d —, 2006 Ohio App. LEXIS 4241 (Aug. 18, 2006).

As defendant's ability to obtain post-conviction review was not a constitutional right under Ohio R. Crim. P. 11(C)(2)(c), defendant had to show that the trial court's alleged misrepresentation regarding his ability to raise his claim of lack of speedy trial in such a proceeding caused him prejudice in order to invalidate the plea. As there was nothing in the record to show that the trial court's statement that he could raise the issue in post-conviction review, although it would not be successful in all likelihood, was relied upon by defendant in entering his guilty plea, he failed to meet his burden. State v. Payne, — Ohio App. 3d —, 2006 Ohio 4624, — N.E. 2d —, 2006 Ohio App. LEXIS 4450 (Aug. 31, 2006).

Ohio Court of Appeals, First Appellate District, Hamilton County, holds that before accepting a plea of guilty or no contest under Crim. R. 11(E), a trial court need not inform an offender of the offender's constitutional rights that are being waived, of the amount of restitution that could be assessed against him, or of the various community-control sanctions, including electronic monitoring, that might be imposed; accordingly, the trial court provided a sufficient allocution prior to accepting defendant's pleas where it fully complied with Rule 11(E) by informing her of the effect of her pleas, and the maximum penalty and fine that could be imposed on each offense. State v. Anderson, — Ohio App. 3d —, 2006 Ohio 4602, — N.E. 2d —, 2006 Ohio App. LEXIS 4544 (Sept. 8, 2006).

As defendant pled guilty to attempted possession of drugs, in violation of RC §§ 2923.02 and 2925.11, pursuant to RC § 2923.02(E) he was to be punished according to the next lower range from the possession charge, which in defendant's matter was a felony of the third degree. As imposition of a mandatory fine was required for a felony-three drug possession, pursuant to RC §§ 2925.11(E)(1)(a) and 2929.18(B)(1), defendant's claim that the mandatory fine was inapplicable due to the attempt nature of the conviction lacked merit, and the record indicated that the trial court adequately informed defendant as to the fine pursuant to Ohio R. Crim. P. 11. State v. Miller, — Ohio App. 3d —, 2006 Ohio 4894, — N.E. 2d —, 2006 Ohio App. LEXIS 4817 (Sept. 21, 2006).

Defendant's negotiated plea of guilty was deemed knowingly and voluntarily made pursuant to the requirements of Ohio R. Crim. P. 11(C) where the trial court informed him of the constitutional and non-constitutional rights that he was waiving, the nature of the charges against him, and the possible penalties that he faced. Although the trial court was not required to inform defendant of the affirmative defenses because they were not elements of a charge, the trial court did indicate to defendant that by entry of the plea, he was giving up the right to assert self-defense, which defendant indicated that he understood. State v. Black, — Ohio App. 3d —, 2006 Ohio 5720, — N.E. 2d —, 2006 Ohio App. LEXIS 5712 (Nov. 2, 2006).

Appellate counsel was not ineffective in violation of U.S. Const. amend. VI and Ohio Const. art. I, § 10 in failing to raise on defendant's direct appeal that his plea agreement was not properly followed by the trial court judge, as the judge had specifically indicated to defendant that he was not bound to follow the recommendation for sentencing, defendant was apprised sufficiently under Ohio R. Crim. P. 11(C) and he indicated that he understood and still wished to plead guilty, and the record indicated that defendant's plea was knowingly, intelligently, and voluntarily entered; accordingly, there was no cause to grant defendant's application to reopen his appeal pursuant to Ohio R. App. P. 26(B)(5). State v. Parks, — Ohio App. 3d —, 2006 Ohio 7269, — N.E. 2d —, 2006 Ohio App. LEXIS 7074 (May 23, 2006).

Traffic cases

Since the trial court improperly informed defendant that RC § 4549.08 was a strict liability offense and that, as a result, her defense that she was operating someone else's car and did not know that the temporary tags had been altered had no merit, defendant's subsequent no contest plea was not knowingly and intelligently tendered. Moreover, the trial court failed to comply with Ohio Traf. R. 10(D) by informing defendant of the effect of her no contest plea. State v. Howard, — Ohio App. 3d —, 2007 Ohio 6591, — N.E. 2d —, 2007 Ohio App. LEXIS 5761 (Dec. 7, 2007).

Where defendant entered guilty pleas to various traffic offenses, pursuant to Ohio Traf. R. 10(D), the allocution was governed by Ohio R. Crim. P. 2(D) and 11(E), and was sufficient in the circumstances where defendant was advised of his right to an attorney, to a trial by a judge or jury, as to the State's evidentiary burden, his rights to cross-examine witnesses and compulsory process, his right against self-incrimination, and the maximum penalties that could be imposed; as defendant entered guilty pleas, he waived alleged errors as to the denial of his request for counsel to withdraw and for a continuance. State v. MacConnell, — Ohio App. 3d —, 2006 Ohio 1973, — N.E. 2d —, 2006 Ohio App. LEXIS 1802 (Apr. 21, 2006).

Understatement of penalty

When defendant pled guilty to operation while under the influence of alcohol, the trial court's understatement of the maximum penalty defendant faced did not render defendant's guilty plea involuntary, under CrimR 11(C)(2)(a), because (1) nothing showed defendant would not have pled guilty had defendant been aware of the true maximum penalty, and (2) the sentence defendant actually received did not exceed the penalty stated by the court. State v. Bailey, — Ohio App. 3d —, 2007 Ohio 6160, — N.E. 2d —, 2007 Ohio App. LEXIS 5392 (Nov. 16, 2007).

Voluntariness

Defendant's contention that he was coerced and deceived by trial counsel into signing a guilty plea document was rejected. The trial court personally addressed defendant, and defendant gave no indication that he had been coerced or deceived by his attorney at any time. State v. Canady, — Ohio App. 3d —, 2007 Ohio 313, — N.E. 2d —, 2007 Ohio App. LEXIS 286 (Jan. 26, 2007).

Record fell short of establishing that defendant's guilty plea was entered other than knowingly and voluntarily because there was no reason to suppose that the trial court knew, or had reason to know, that defendant's negative response to the question whether he had any prior convictions was incorrect; that fact came out only later, at the sentencing hearing, as a result of the pre-sentence investigation report ordered by the trial court after it accepted defendant's plea. Without knowledge of that discrepancy, the trial court would have had no reason to believe, at the time that it accepted defendant's plea, that his plea was tendered other than knowingly and voluntarily. State v. Hall, — Ohio App. 3d —, 2007 Ohio 4203, — N.E. 2d —, 2007 Ohio App. LEXIS 3786 (Aug. 17, 2007).

Court rejected defendant's argument that his plea was not knowingly, intelligently, or voluntarily made on the ground that he suffered from mental illness and was unaware of what was transpiring when he entered his plea as defendant's written plea of guilty showed that defendant was advised of his rights and that defendant agreed to waive them, and a review of the transcript showed that the trial court engaged in the requisite Ohio R. Crim. P. 11 colloquy and that defendant understood the nature of the charges against him. There was no evidence that the trial court or defendant's counsel should have had any doubts about defendant's competency at the time that his plea was entered. State v. Boyce, — Ohio App. 3d —, 2007 Ohio 4379, — N.E. 2d —, 2007 Ohio App. LEXIS 3945 (Aug. 24, 2007).

Where defendant entered his no contest plea to two charges in reliance on the trial court's promise to place him into a group home rather than to impose imprisonment on him, defendant's entry of the plea was later deemed not voluntarily made where the trial court did impose terms of imprisonment on him; such constituted a violation of defendant's due process rights under U.S. Const. amend. XIV, as well as reversible error. State v. Elias, — Ohio App. 3d —, 2007 Ohio 5444, — N.E. 2d —, 2007 Ohio App. LEXIS 4781 (Oct. 11, 2007).

Defendant's guilty plea was vacated because the trial judge's use of the word "however," immediately following the judge's statement that there was a presumption of incarceration, to inform defendant that the State would not seek jail time was misleading; instead, the trial court should have forewarned defendant that the sentencing judge was not bound by the State's position against incarceration and could impose a prison term. Further, the judge who sentenced defendant was different from the judge who accepted the plea, and the record did not indicate that the sentencing judge was aware of the plea colloquy and the State's position regarding jail time. State v. Asberry, 173 Ohio App. 3d 443, 2007 Ohio 5436, 878 N.E.2d 1082, 2007 Ohio App. LEXIS 4783 (2007).

Waiver

Defendant's entry of an Alford plea pursuant to Ohio R. Crim. P. 11 to various charges constituted a waiver of his right to assert on appeal that the trial court's denial of his suppression motion was error due to the alleged unlawfulness of the searches and seizures; further, as the convictions were based on the plea and not on the evidence seized, any error in the trial court's ruling was harmless under Ohio R. Crim. P. 52. State v. Montgomery, — Ohio App. 3d —, 2007 Ohio 440, — N.E. 2d —, 2007 Ohio App. LEXIS 389 (Feb. 2, 2007).

As defendant was represented by counsel when he entered into a plea agreement with the State, he entered guilty pleas to multiple offenses which were accepted by the trial court pursuant to Ohio R. Crim. P. 11, and his plea was voluntarily, knowingly, and intelligently entered, his claim on appeal that it was an abuse of discretion for the trial court to have denied his request for a continuance in order to secure new counsel and that such denial violated his constitutional right to counsel under U.S. Const. amend. V, VI, and Ohio Const. art. I, § 10 was deemed waived. State v. Sage, — Ohio App. 3d —, 2007 Ohio 442, — N.E. 2d —, 2007 Ohio App. LEXIS 390 (Feb. 2, 2007).

Defendant's claim that his counsel provided ineffective assistance in violation of U.S. Const. amend. VI and Ohio Const. art. I, § 10 by failing to object to an allegedly defective indictment lacked merit, as defendant's entry of a guilty plea constituted a waiver of any such error pursuant to Ohio R. Crim. P. 12(C)(2) and 11(B)(1). State v. Carrico, — Ohio App. 3d —, 2007 Ohio 559, — N.E. 2d —, 2007 Ohio App. LEXIS 517 (Feb. 5, 2007).

In entering his guilty plea, defendant waived any claims that his conviction was not supported by sufficient evidence or was against the manifest weight of the evidence. State v. Flowers, — Ohio App. 3d —, 2006 Ohio 1426, — N.E. 2d —, 2006 Ohio App. LEXIS 1295 (Mar. 24, 2006).

Defendant's claim that the trial court's denial of his motion to suppress evidence was error lacked merit, as defendant was represented by competent counsel when he entered a guilty plea and accordingly, he waived any nonjurisdictional defects such as the suppression issue for purposes of appeal. State v. Bulger, — Ohio App. 3d —, 2006 Ohio 3046, — N.E. 2d —, 2006 Ohio App. LEXIS 2928 (June 16, 2006).

Because defendant did not claim that his guilty plea was involuntary, unknowing, or unintelligently given or challenge any jurisdictional defect, he could not argue that his confession was coerced, that the trial court erred in overruling his motion to suppress, or that he received constitutionally ineffective assistance from trial counsel. State v. Storms, — Ohio App. 3d —, 2006 Ohio 3547, — N.E. 2d —, 2006 Ohio App. LEXIS 3499 (June 26, 2006).

Defendant's conviction upon his guilty plea to a charge of possession of crack cocaine was affirmed. On appeal from his conviction, defendant challenged only the trial court's decision overruling his motion to dismiss for lack of a speedy trial; however, by pleading guilty, defendant waived his right to challenge his conviction on speedy trial grounds. State v. Rogers, — Ohio App. 3d —, 2006 Ohio 3651, — N.E. 2d —, 2006 Ohio App. LEXIS 3598 (July 14, 2006).

Defendant's guilty plea precluded his challenge to venue. State v. Teel, — Ohio App. 3d —, 2006 Ohio 5281, — N.E. 2d —, 2006 Ohio App. LEXIS 5264 (Oct. 6, 2006).

As commission of an aggravated robbery in violation of RC § 2911.01(A)(1) and commission of theft by threat in violation of RC § 2913.02(A)(4) could each be done without committing the other offense, the crimes were not allied offenses of similar import under RC § 2941.25, and accordingly, there was no plain error under Ohio R. Crim. P. 52(B) in the trial court's conviction of defendant for both offenses. As defendant had entered his guilty plea to the offenses under Ohio R. Crim. P. 11(B)(1) and he had failed to raise an argument regarding whether they were allied offenses at the trial court level, the plain error standard of review was employed. State v. Gooden, — Ohio App. 3d —, 2006 Ohio 5387, — N.E. 2d —, 2006 Ohio App. LEXIS 5378 (Oct. 16, 2006).

Withdrawal of guilty plea

Defendant's Ohio R. Crim. P. 32.1 motion to withdraw his guilty plea was properly denied as defendant was represented by competent counsel, he was afforded a full hearing under Ohio R. Crim. P. 11 before entering his guilty plea, and he was afforded a full hearing on his motion to withdraw his guilty plea. Though defendant claimed that he was not guilty of the offenses charged in the indictment, he had not factually substantiated his claim. State v. Jordon, — Ohio App. 3d —, 2007 Ohio 6795, — N.E. 2d —, 2007 Ohio App. LEXIS 5952 (Dec. 14, 2007).

Trial court did not abuse its discretion in denying defendant's motion to withdraw his guilty plea as defendant was represented by a highly experienced criminal defense attorney with forty years of experience, the trial court afforded defendant a full hearing on his motion, defendant was afforded a complete Ohio R. Crim. P. 11 hearing prior to entering his plea, defendant fully understood the nature of the charges that he was facing and the potential penalties, and defendant had no real defense to the charges in light of his confession to the rape and sexual battery of his foster son and the results of the DNA testing corroborating the foster son's allegations. State v. Thomas, — Ohio App. 3d —, 2007 Ohio 6908, — N.E. 2d —, 2007 Ohio App. LEXIS 6048 (Dec. 21, 2007).

RULE 12. Pleadings and Motions Before Trial: Defenses and Objections

(A) **Pleadings and motions.** Pleadings in criminal proceedings shall be the complaint, and the indictment or information, and the pleas of not guilty, not guilty by reason of insanity, guilty, and no contest. All other pleas, demurrers, and motions to quash, are abolished. Defenses and objections raised before trial which heretofore could have been raised by one or more of them shall be raised only by motion to dismiss or to grant appropriate relief, as provided in these rules.

(B) **Filing with the court defined.** The filing of documents with the court, as required by these rules, shall be made by filing them with the clerk of court, except that the judge may permit the documents to be filed with the judge, in which event the judge shall note the filing date on the documents and transmit them to the clerk. A court may provide, by local rules adopted pursuant to the Rules of Superintendence, for the filing of documents by electronic means. If the court adopts such local rules, they shall include all of the following:

(1) the complaint, if permitted by local rules to be filed electronically, shall comply with Crim. R. 3.

(2) any signature on electronically transmitted documents shall be considered that of the attorney or party it purports to be for all purposes. If it is established that the documents were transmitted without authority, the court shall order the filing stricken.

(3) a provision shall specify the days and hours during which electronically transmitted documents will

be received by the court, and a provision shall specify when documents received electronically will be considered to have been filed.

(4) any document filed electronically that requires a filing fee may be rejected by the clerk of court unless the filer has complied with the mechanism established by the court for the payment of filing fees.

(C) **Pretrial motions.** Prior to trial, any party may raise by motion any defense, objection, evidentiary issue, or request that is capable of determination without the trial of the general issue. The following must be raised before trial:

(1) Defenses and objections based on defects in the institution of the prosecution;

(2) Defenses and objections based on defects in the indictment, information, or complaint (other than failure to show jurisdiction in the court or to charge an offense, which objections shall be noticed by the court at any time during the pendency of the proceeding);

(3) Motions to suppress evidence, including but not limited to statements and identification testimony, on the ground that it was illegally obtained. Such motions shall be filed in the trial court only.

(4) Requests for discovery under Crim. R. 16;

(5) Requests for severance of charges or defendants under Crim. R. 14.

(D) **Motion date.** All pretrial motions except as provided in Crim. R. 7(E) and 16(F) shall be made within thirty-five days after arraignment or seven days before trial, whichever is earlier. The court in the interest of justice may extend the time for making pretrial motions.

(E) **Notice by the prosecuting attorney of the intention to use evidence.**

(1) At the discretion of the prosecuting attorney. At the arraignment or as soon thereafter as is practicable, the prosecuting attorney may give notice to the defendant of the prosecuting attorney's intention to use specified evidence at trial, in order to afford the defendant an opportunity to raise objections to such evidence prior to trial under division (C)(3) of this rule.

(2) At the request of the defendant. At the arraignment or as soon thereafter as is practicable, the defendant, in order to raise objections prior to trial under division (C)(3) of this rule, may request notice of the prosecuting attorney's intention to use evidence in chief at trial, which evidence the defendant is entitled to discover under Crim. R. 16.

(F) **Ruling on motion.** The court may adjudicate a motion based upon briefs, affidavits, the proffer of testimony and exhibits, a hearing, or other appropriate means.

A motion made pursuant to divisions (C)(1) to (C)(5) of this rule shall be determined before trial. Any other motion made pursuant to division (C) of this rule shall be determined before trial whenever possible. Where the court defers ruling on any motion made by the prosecuting attorney before trial and makes a ruling adverse to the prosecuting attorney after the commencement of trial, and the ruling is appealed pursuant to law with the certification required by division (K) of this rule, the court shall stay the proceedings without discharging the jury or dismissing the charges.

Where factual issues are involved in determining a motion, the court shall state its essential findings on the record.

(G) **Return of tangible evidence.** Where a motion to suppress tangible evidence is granted, the court upon request of the defendant shall order the property returned to the defendant if the defendant is entitled to possession of the property. The order shall be stayed pending appeal by the state pursuant to division (K) of this rule.

(H) **Effect of failure to raise defenses or objections.** Failure by the defendant to raise defenses or objections or to make requests that must be made prior to trial, at the time set by the court pursuant to division (D) of this rule, or prior to any extension of time made by the court, shall constitute waiver of the defenses or objections, but the court for good cause shown may grant relief from the waiver.

(I) **Effect of plea of no contest.** The plea of no contest does not preclude a defendant from asserting upon appeal that the trial court prejudicially erred in ruling on a pretrial motion, including a pretrial motion to suppress evidence.

(J) **Effect of determination.** If the court grants a motion to dismiss based on a defect in the institution of the prosecution or in the indictment, information, or complaint, it may also order that the defendant be held in custody or that the defendant's bail be continued for a specified time not exceeding fourteen days, pending the filing of a new indictment, information, or complaint. Nothing in this rule shall affect any statute relating to periods of limitations. Nothing in this rule shall affect the state's right to appeal an adverse ruling on a motion under divisions (C)(1) or (2) of this rule, when the motion raises issues that were formerly raised pursuant to a motion to quash, a plea in abatement, a demurrer, or a motion in arrest of judgment.

(K) When the state takes an appeal as provided by law from an order suppressing or excluding evidence, or from an order directing pretrial disclosure of evidence, the prosecuting attorney shall certify that both of the following apply:

(1) the appeal is not taken for the purpose of delay;

(2) the ruling on the motion or motions has rendered the state's proof with respect to the pending charge so weak in its entirety that any reasonable possibility of effective prosecution has been destroyed, or the pretrial disclosure of evidence ordered by the court will have one of the effects enumerated in Crim. R. 16(D).

The appeal from an order suppressing or excluding evidence shall not be allowed unless the notice of appeal and the certification by the prosecuting attorney are filed with the clerk of the trial court within seven days after the date of the entry of the judgment or order granting the motion. Any appeal taken under this rule shall be prosecuted diligently.

If the defendant previously has not been released, the defendant shall, except in capital cases, be released from custody on the defendant's own recognizance pending appeal when the prosecuting attorney files the notice of appeal and certification.

This appeal shall take precedence over all other appeals.

If an appeal from an order suppressing or excluding evidence pursuant to this division results in an affirmance of the trial court, the state shall be barred from prosecuting the defendant for the same offense or offenses except upon a showing of newly discovered evidence that the state could not, with reasonable diligence, have discovered before filing of the notice of appeal.

History: Amended, eff 7-1-75; 7-1-80; 7-1-95; 7-1-98; 7-1-01; 7-1-10.

NOTES TO DECISIONS

ANALYSIS

Appeal
Appeal by state
Collateral estoppel
Confrontation rights
Consent to search coerced
Denial of motion to suppress
Dismissal of indictment
Evidence
Evidentiary hearing
Findings of fact
Guilty plea
Indictment
Ineffective assistance of counsel
Investigatory stop
Motion in limine
Motion to dismiss hearing
Motion to suppress
— Confessions, statements
—Miranda warnings
— Search of student
— Speedy trial rights
Motion to suppress properly denied
No contest plea
Omission of element in indictment
Probable cause
Reopening of hearing
Rules of evidence
Suppression improperly denied
Suppression improperly granted
Suppression properly denied
Suppression properly granted
Waiver of error
Waiver of objections
Waiver of right to appeal

Appeal

Defendant's assignment of error relating to a trial court's decision on his motion to suppress had been waived because no ruling on the motion was found in the record. The trial court never adopted the magistrate's findings and recommendations, in which the magistrate recommended that the motion be denied, and as a result, pursuant to Ohio R. Crim. P. 19(E)(3)(a), the magistrate's findings and recommendations were not final, compelling the conclusion that the motion was pending at the time of defendant's plea. If the trial court did not issue a ruling, defendant had waived his objection by pleading no contest before obtaining a ruling on the motion, and if the trial court did rule on the motion, defendant had not provided the court with a record of that ruling, which was his duty. State v. Romandetti, — Ohio App. 3d —, 2007 Ohio 363, — N.E. 2d —, 2007 Ohio App. LEXIS 325 (Jan. 31, 2007).

Appeal by state

Because the State was entitled as a matter of right under RC § 2945.67 to appeal the granting of defendant's motion to suppress, it was not required to make a motion for leave to appeal under Ohio R. App. P. 5(C) but was required to file its notice of appeal in seven days under Ohio R. Crim. P. 12(K); therefore, the State's notice of appeal was untimely as it was not filed within seven days. State v. Coffman, — Ohio App. 3d —, 2007 Ohio 3384, — N.E. 2d —, 2007 Ohio App. LEXIS 3084 (June 29, 2007).

Because the trial court immediately dismissed the charges arising from the stop after granting the motion to suppress, the trial court erred by not allowing the State an opportunity to appeal the granting of the motion to suppress, pursuant to Ohio R. Crim. P. 12(K), prior to dismissing the case. However, the error was harmless because the State could not proceed with the prosecution of the charges without the evidence from the stop. State v. Bressler, 167 Ohio App. 3d 772, 2006 Ohio 3632, 857 N.E. 2d 177, 2006 Ohio App. LEXIS 3558 (July 17, 2006).

State's appeal from a trial court's order granting defendant's motion to suppress was dismissed because the State failed to file the certification required by Ohio R. Crim. P. 12(K), and thus, the court lacked jurisdiction to consider the State's appeal. The certification was a valid, mandatory procedural requirement under Ohio Const. art. IV, § 5(B). State v. Crockett, — Ohio App. 3d —, 2006 Ohio 4040, — N.E. 2d —, 2006 Ohio App. LEXIS 3981 (Aug. 4, 2006).

Collateral estoppel

Defendant's second motion to suppress was not barred by collateral estoppel as: (1) the State of Ohio (State) was not a party to the proceedings in Georgia in which defendant filed a first motion to suppress, (2) there was not mutuality of the parties, (3) without mutuality of the parties, the Georgia adjudication of defendant as a probation violator could not be asserted against the State, and (4) the Georgia ruling was not a final appealable order. State v. Boulis, — Ohio App. 3d —, 2006 Ohio 3693, — N.E. 2d —, 2006 Ohio App. LEXIS 3629 (July 20, 2006).

Confrontation rights

Federal and state confrontation clauses apply to OVI suppression hearings. Granville v. Graziano, 139 Ohio Misc. 2d 29, 2006 Ohio 3551, 858 N.E.2d 879, 2006 Ohio Misc. LEXIS 191 (2006).

Consent to search coerced

Denial of the motion to suppress was error because defendant's consent to search (the cocaine packets in his shoe) was coerced, rather than freely and voluntarily given. Defendant was unlawfully arrested for the minor misdemeanor offense of possession of 12 grams of marijuana, because none of the RC § 2935.26 exceptions to allow a misdemeanor arrest applied, and the detective implied that if any contraband on defendant's person were disclosed at the scene, rather than at the jail, there would be no additional charges. State v. Melvin, — Ohio App. 3d —, 2007 Ohio 3779, — N.E. 2d —, 2007 Ohio App. LEXIS 3441 (July 26, 2007).

Denial of motion to suppress

Defendant's rights under U.S. Const. amend. IV were not implicated, and thus, defendant's motion to suppress evidence of the purported stop of defendant was properly denied, because the encounter between a police officer and defendant was consensual in nature. The officer did not effectuate a stop of defendant; rather, the officer approached defendant who was sitting in his parked vehicle with the engine running at a restaurant open to the public. State v. Kaercher, — Ohio App. 3d —, 2006 Ohio 31, — N.E. 2d —, 2006 Ohio App. LEXIS 19 (Jan. 5, 2006).

Trial court did not err in finding that defendant's motion to dismiss, for suppression, and in limine lacked the specificity

necessary to put the State on notice of the specific alleged deficiencies in the field sobriety and breathalyzer tests administered to defendant, as he provided a "laundry list" of allegations to support his claim that the tests were not performed in strict compliance with the law, but he provided no factual basis to support the allegations. The suppression motion under Ohio R. Crim. P. 12 was not sufficiently particular pursuant to Ohio R. Crim. P. 47. State v. Stoner, — Ohio App. 3d —, 2006 Ohio 2122, — N.E. 2d —, 2006 Ohio App. LEXIS 1955 (Apr. 28, 2006).

Trial court committed constitutional error in refusing to continue the suppression hearing in light of the defense attorney's absence and ruling on defendant's motion while he was effectively unrepresented. The suppression hearing was a "critical stage" of the prosecution, defendant was confronted by his adversary and the system, the process was adversarial in nature, and it was clear from the record that defendant did not waive his right to counsel at the hearing. City of Medina v. Pfaff, — Ohio App. 3d —, 2007 Ohio 2675, — N.E. 2d —, 2007 Ohio App. LEXIS 2498 (June 4, 2007).

Dismissal of indictment

Trial court did not err when it dismissed the charges for pandering obscenity against defendant because, due to circumstances beyond his or the trial court's control, defendant was denied the assistance of an expert witness and, without the services of an expert witness, there was no way to provide defendant a fair trial. The expert, a computer image analyst, testified that, upon the advice of counsel and due to the threat of additional federal prosecution, he could not possess another copy of a compact disc containing the allegedly illegal images, he could not conduct a proper investigation of any websites from which the images might have allegedly originated, and he could not use his expertise to create potential exhibits for defendant's trial. Not only was defendant denied the expert services of the expert, he was denied the expert services of all potential experts. State v. Brady, — Ohio App. 3d —, 2007 Ohio 1779, — N.E. 2d —, 2007 Ohio App. LEXIS 1622 (Apr. 13, 2007).

It was premature for the trial court to grant defendant's Crim. R. 12 motion to dismiss based on stipulated facts regarding the blood alcohol test and thus, the trial court's consideration of the motion to dismiss was an improper exercise of judicial authority. The motion went beyond the face of the indictment and did not challenge the sufficiency of the indictment as far as charging the proper offenses or the constitutionality of the offense charged. State v. Serban, — Ohio App. 3d —, 2007 Ohio 3634, — N.E. 2d —, 2007 Ohio App. LEXIS 3324 (July 16, 2007).

Because defendant did not establish actual prejudice, the trial court properly denied defendant's motion to dismiss for pre-indictment delay; defendant failed to explain how "re-preparing and re-strategizing" caused him actual, substantial prejudice. He also failed to demonstrate how his alibi witnesses would have testified differently with a shorter delay or how their testimony would have changed the outcome of the trial; nor did he clarify how the testimony of his missing alibi witnesses would have been exculpatory in nature. State v. Dennis, — Ohio App. 3d —, 2006 Ohio 5777, — N.E. 2d —, 2006 Ohio App. LEXIS 4764 (Sept. 19, 2006).

Defendant's motion, pursuant to Ohio R. Crim. P. 12(C), to dismiss a weapons charge filed against defendant was improperly granted because the trial court's consideration of the alleged facts of the case went beyond merely considering the face of the indictment and constituted an inappropriate analysis to undertake on a motion to dismiss an indictment. State v. Ethridge, — Ohio App. 3d —, 2006 Ohio 6768, — N.E. 2d —, 2006 Ohio App. LEXIS 6668 (Dec. 21, 2006).

Evidence

Motion to suppress was properly denied because the photographic array was not unduly suggestive since defendant was depicted along with five other men, all approximately the same age, with the same skin tone and hair. The witness identified defendant within seconds, she was subject to cross-examination by defendant, and the jury could weigh the circumstances surrounding her identification. State v. Blakely, — Ohio App. 3d —, 2006 Ohio 185, — N.E. 2d —, 2006 Ohio App. LEXIS 154 (Jan. 20, 2006).

Because the rules of evidence did not strictly apply at the suppression hearing, the trial court did not err in allowing the detective to testify about what the informant had told him. State v. Simmons, — Ohio App. 3d —, 2006 Ohio 4751, — N.E. 2d —, 2006 Ohio App. LEXIS 4681 (Sept. 14, 2006).

Evidentiary hearing

In defendant's prosecution, inter alia, for aggravated vehicular homicide, RC § 2903.06(A)(1)(a) and (A)(2), the State was improperly prohibited from presenting blood test results on the ground that it destroyed defendant's blood sample in bad faith as the trial court failed to hold a requested evidentiary hearing, Ohio R. Crim. P. 12(F), on the issue. State v. Thompson, — Ohio App. 3d —, 2006 Ohio 6798, — N.E. 2d —, 2006 Ohio App. LEXIS 6714 (Dec. 19, 2006).

Findings of fact

Since the record did not indicate that defendant ever requested the trial court to issue findings of fact in ruling on the State's motion to deny bail, the trial court had no duty under Ohio R. Crim. P. 12(F) to issue such findings of fact. Even so, the record clearly delineated the evidence that was before the trial court when it made its determination to deny defendant bail. State v. Sands, — Ohio App. 3d —, 2007 Ohio 35, — N.E. 2d —, 2007 Ohio App. LEXIS 27 (Jan. 5, 2007).

While the record was devoid of the trial court's findings of facts in connection with its denial of defendant's motion to suppress, defendant did not ask the trial court for findings of fact relating to the motion to suppress. Further, the record was sufficient to allow a full review of defendant's claim on appeal regarding the motion to suppress as the transcript from the hearing provided the court with a sufficient basis to determine whether the trial court's decision was supported by competent, credible evidence. State v. Hahn, — Ohio App. 3d —, 2007 Ohio 557, — N.E. 2d —, 2007 Ohio App. LEXIS 515 (Feb. 7, 2007).

Judgment granting defendant's motion to suppress evidence of crack cocaine found during a search of him was vacated because conflicting evidence existed as to whether the officers searched defendant before or after they arrested him, and the trial court's failure to make a finding on when the search occurred, as required by Ohio R. Crim. P. 12(E), precluded the court from properly reviewing the suppression order. State v. Groce, — Ohio App. 3d —, 2007 Ohio 2874, — N.E. 2d —, 2007 Ohio App. LEXIS 2664 (June 12, 2007).

Common pleas court erred by failing to make findings on the issue of whether officers and defendant engaged in a consensual encounter when the officers approached defendant on the street corner because findings of fact under Ohio R. Crim. P. 12(F) were crucial to resolution of issue. Facially, the evidence tended to suggest a consensual encounter since the arresting officer's testimony that he simply approached defendant and asked him what was going on allowed the finding that defendant had every opportunity to walk away from the police officers. State v. Ogletree, — Ohio App. 3d —, 2006 Ohio 448, — N.E. 2d —, 2006 Ohio App. LEXIS 385 (Feb. 2, 2006).

Trial court erred in failing to make sufficient factual findings on a motion to suppress regarding whether a police cruiser videotape and other conflicting testimony showed that a police officer had probable cause under U.S. Const. amend. IV to believe that defendant had committed a traffic violation by failing to stay in a marked lane while driving, thereby rendering the officer's stop of defendant's vehicle proper. The case was remanded for the trial court to determine if the officer had probable cause to believe that defendant violated a statute or an ordinance. State v. Korman, — Ohio App. 3d —, 2006 Ohio 1795, — N.E. 2d —, 2006 Ohio App. LEXIS 1640 (Apr. 7, 2006).

Guilty plea

By pleading guilty, defendant waived any error in the proceedings that did not implicate the validity of the guilty plea. Defendant's conviction did not depend upon any of the evidence that was the subject of his motion to suppress, resting instead upon his guilty plea, so any error in the disposition of his motion to suppress was harmless. State v. Montgomery, — Ohio App. 3d —, 2007 Ohio 439, — N.E. 2d —, 2007 Ohio App. LEXIS 388 (Feb. 2, 2007).

Since defendant entered a plea of guilty, he waived the right to challenge on appeal the trial court's denial of his motion to suppress. State v. Thomas, — Ohio App. 3d —, 2007 Ohio 6908, — N.E. 2d —, 2007 Ohio App. LEXIS 6048 (Dec. 21, 2007).

Indictment

In most defective indictment cases in which the indictment fails to include an essential element of the charge, plain error analysis, pursuant to CrimR 52(B), will be the proper analysis to apply. The syllabus in State v. Colon, 118 Ohio St. 3d 26, 2008 Ohio 1624, 885 N.E.2d 917, 2008 Ohio LEXIS 874, is confined to the facts in that case: State v. Colon, 119 Ohio St. 3d 204, 2008 Ohio 3749, 893 N.E.2d 169, 2008 Ohio LEXIS 1979 (2008).

Plain error analysis, rather that structural error analysis, normally applies to defective indictment cases. Defendant's failure to object to the use of conjunctive language in some counts of the indictment waived all but plain error as to whether those counts were improperly duplicitous: State v. Robertson, 180 Ohio App. 3d 365, 2008 Ohio 6909, 905 N.E.2d 678, 2008 Ohio App. LEXIS 5775 (2008).

Defendant's failure to object to an indictment, charging him with rape, gross sexual imposition, and kidnapping, on the ground that it joined two distinct offenses in a single count constituted a waiver of his objection under Ohio R. Crim. P. 12(H). State v. Thrasher, — Ohio App. 3d —, 2006 Ohio 1260, — N.E. 2d —, 2006 Ohio App. LEXIS 1134 (Mar. 17, 2006).

Because defendant did not object to any alleged defect in the indictment prior to pleading guilty, as required by RC § 2941.29 and Ohio R. Crim. P. 12(C)(2), defendant waived his right to object to any defect in the indictment. However, the indictment did contain a force specification, which would have served only to enhance his possible sentence; because force was not required to convict defendant of rape in violation of RC § 2907.02(A)(1)(b), the indictment was not defective. Ohio v. Jenkins, — Ohio App. 3d —, 2007 Ohio 4770, — N.E. 2d —, 2007 Ohio App. LEXIS 4263 (Sept. 14, 2007).

Ineffective assistance of counsel

Because defendant could not establish that there was a basis to suppress the evidence obtained as a result of the traffic stop, he could not demonstrate that defense counsel was deficient for failing to pursue the suppression motion. Defense counsel did file a motion to suppress, specifically arguing that the initial stop of defendant for his alleged violation of the traffic ordinance violated his constitutional rights, the fact that he later withdrew the motion was evidence of a tactical decision. State v. Taylor, — Ohio App. 3d —, 2008 Ohio 482, — N.E. 2d —, 2008 Ohio App. LEXIS 426 (Feb. 4, 2008).

Investigatory stop

Trial court properly denied defendant's motion to suppress because the officers had reasonable grounds to stop defendant under the totality of the circumstances. One officer testified that he had observed defendant engaging in various hand to hand (drug-like) transactions four days earlier but, when the officer attempted to question defendant about the suspected drug activity that day, defendant fled and was not seen again by the officer until four days later; at that point, the officer saw defendant approaching a stopped vehicle in the same high crime/drug area and defendant again fled when police tried to question him. State v. Lane, — Ohio App. 3d —, 2007 Ohio 5948, — N.E. 2d —, 2007 Ohio App. LEXIS 5255 (Nov. 8, 2007).

Though a K-9 unit did not arrive until 15 minutes after a traffic stop was initiated, in contrast to the seven to nine minutes a typical stop took, the length of the detention was permissible in light of the fact that additional facts were encountered during the initial stop that gave rise to a reasonable suspicion of criminal activity. Specifically, the officer observed more than eight air fresheners in various locations of the vehicle, the driver appeared very nervous, neither passenger would meet the officer's gaze, and the driver relayed conflicting stories about the identification of the passengers; thus, defendant's motion to suppress evidence discovered during the dog sniff of the car was properly denied. State v. Henry, — Ohio App. 3d —, 2007 Ohio 6732, — N.E. 2d —, 2007 Ohio App. LEXIS 5904 (Dec. 14, 2007).

Police officer had both probable cause and a reasonable suspicion to stop defendant's car as the officer had been called to the location by another officer who had seen defendant driving erratically, and the officer himself saw defendant's car twice cross over edge line, once by more than a foot, which constituted a violation of Ohio's marked lanes statute, RC § 4511.33(A). Thus, the officer's stop of the vehicle was proper, and defendant's motion to suppress evidence of her intoxication obtained pursuant to the stop was properly denied. State v. McEldowney, — Ohio App. 3d —, 2007 Ohio 6690, — N.E. 2d —, 2007 Ohio App. LEXIS 5906 (Dec. 14, 2007).

Motion in limine

Trial court erred in granting the motion in limine without stating its essential findings as required because, after denying the motion in limine, the trial court stated that it was granting the motion because the contested statements did not rise to the level of excited utterances. Although Ohio R. Crim. P. 12 allowed the trial court to rule on a motion without a full hearing, the trial court abused its discretion because it reversed its prior ruling without allowing the State to proceed with its evidence. State v. Steele, — Ohio App. 3d —, 2007 Ohio 395, — N.E. 2d —, 2007 Ohio App. LEXIS 347 (Feb. 1, 2007).

Motion to dismiss hearing

CrimR 12 permits a court to consider evidence beyond the face of an indictment when ruling on a pretrial motion to dismiss the indictment if the matter is capable of determination without trial of the general issue: State v. Brady, 119 Ohio St. 3d 375, 2008 Ohio 4493, 894 N.E.2d 671, 2008 Ohio LEXIS 2312 (2008).

Crim.R. 12(F) governs pretrial motions and permits a trial court to rule on the motion upon briefs, affidavits, the proffer of testimony and exhibits, a hearing, or other appropriate means, but does not require the court to hold an evidentiary or oral hearing. Where defendant's motion to dismiss contained nothing to suggest that an evidentiary hearing would aid the court in ruling upon the motion, the trial court did not deprive defendant of his due process rights in ruling on the motion without a hearing. State v. Perry, — Ohio App. 3d —, 2006 Ohio 220, — N.E. 2d —, 2006 Ohio App. LEXIS 179 (Jan. 20, 2006).

Motion to suppress

Defendant's motion to suppress was properly denied because (1) it was not timely filed, under Ohio R. Crim. P. 12(D), because it was filed 49 days after defendant's arraignment, (2) defendant did not attempt to explain the untimely filing until he moved for reconsideration of its denial, (3) defendant did

not timely move for leave to file the motion out of rule, (4) his claim that he only realized he needed to move to suppress after viewing a videotape of his arrest was insufficient because most issues raised in the motion could have been raised without the videotape, and (5) the reasons he gave for being unable to view the videotape sooner, which were being unaware of the tape until pretrial, needing prosecutor approval, and counsel's schedule, did not establish that it was in the best interest of justice to allow an untimely filing, as he had five days from learning of the tape's existence to timely file his motion or move for leave to file out of rule. State v. Pelsozy, — Ohio App. 3d —, 2007 Ohio 148, — N.E. 2d —, 2007 Ohio App. LEXIS 136 (Jan. 17, 2007).

Contrary to the State's contention, the record reflected that the State had sufficient notice of the grounds that the trial court considered in deciding defendant's motion to suppress and had an adequate opportunity to address those grounds but failed to do so. Since the State was given sufficient notice and ample opportunity to defend, no manifest miscarriage of justice resulted from the trial court's decision to address the issue of whether the search warrant affidavit contained a material knowing, intentional or reckless falsity, and the trial court did not commit plain error under Ohio R. Crim. P. 52(B) in this regard. State v. Ralston, — Ohio App. 3d —, 2007 Ohio 177, — N.E. 2d —, 2007 Ohio App. LEXIS 175 (Jan. 11, 2007).

Because all of defendant's statements were properly admissible, trial counsel did not err in not filing a futile motion to suppress the statements; since defendant's statement was not made in the context of a custodial interrogation, it was admissible; a police officer testified that upon arresting defendant after the victim identified him, the police immediately advised him of his Miranda rights, but did not ask him any questions. Defendant then volunteered his statement that he had offered the victim 50 cents to braid his hair and thus, because the statement was not made in response to police questioning nor compelled by the police in any manner, it was properly admissible. State v. Anderson, — Ohio App. 3d —, 2007 Ohio 821, — N.E. 2d —, 2007 Ohio App. LEXIS 763 (Mar. 1, 2007).

Trial court's decision to deny defendant's motion to suppress the cold-stand identification was supported by sufficient, competent evidence because the victims had an opportunity to view the suspect, the assault occurred in a well-lit area, and they were in close proximity to the assailant. Also, the male victim provided a sufficient description of his assailant prior to the cold-stand identification as a tall, black man with a smudge nose. State v. Jackson, — Ohio App. 3d —, 2007 Ohio 1598, — N.E. 2d —, 2007 Ohio App. LEXIS 1473 (Apr. 5, 2007).

Trial court did not abuse its discretion in concluding that there were no constitutional defects in the identification testimony and in refusing to suppress it. The victim's inability or unwillingness to make an identification based on the photo array did not discredit his in-court identification of defendant, and there was no other basis to conclude that his in-court identification was unreliable. State v. Brown, — Ohio App. 3d —, 2007 Ohio 2098, — N.E. 2d —, 2007 Ohio App. LEXIS 1954 (Apr. 27, 2007).

Pursuant to Ohio R. Crim. P. 12(C)(3), a motion to suppress evidence on the ground that it was illegally obtained must be raised before trial, and Ohio R. Crim. P. 12(H) provides that a defendant's failure to raise defenses or objections or make requests that must be made prior to trial, at the time set by the court, shall constitute waiver of the defenses or objections, but the court for good cause shown may grant relief from the waiver, and Ohio R. Crim. P. 47 provides that a motion shall state with particularity the grounds upon which it is made and shall set forth the relief or order sought and shall be supported by a memorandum containing citations of authority, and may also be supported by an affidavit, so pursuant to the Criminal Rules, a defendant bears the initial burden of providing the

State with adequate notice of the grounds for challenging the admissibility of evidence he seeks to suppress. State v. Ellis, — Ohio App. 3d —, 2007 Ohio 2177, — N.E. 2d —, 2007 Ohio App. LEXIS 2023 (May 2, 2007).

Defendant's motion to suppress and motion in limine were properly denied as untimely under Ohio R. Crim. P. 12(D). Pursuant to Ohio R. Crim. P. 12(D), the motions should have been filed within 35 days after arraignment but were not filed until more than two months after arraignment. State v. Bartram, — Ohio App. 3d —, 2006 Ohio 3505, — N.E. 2d —, 2006 Ohio App. LEXIS 3410 (June 30, 2006).

It was not error for a trial court to deny defendant's motion to suppress without a hearing because (1) the motion was not filed within the time limits required by Ohio R. Crim. P. 12(D), (2) defendant did not offer any explanation, in the trial court or on appeal, for her untimely filing, and (3) defendant's ability to file the motion was not hindered, as she was provided discovery before the deadline for filing the motion. State v. Lisle, — Ohio App. 3d —, 2006 Ohio 3877, — N.E. 2d —, 2006 Ohio App. LEXIS 3851 (July 31, 2006).

When defendant filed a motion to suppress three days before trial, the motion was treated as a motion in limine because the motion did not comply with the requirements for timely filing, under Ohio R. Crim. P. 12(D), leave to file out of rule was not sought or granted, and no time limitations applied to a motion in limine. State v. Baker, 170 Ohio App. 3d 331, 2006 Ohio 7085, 867 N.E.2d 426, 2006 Ohio App. LEXIS 7013 (2006).

— Confessions, statements

Trial court did not err in denying defendant's motion to suppress because defendant's statements to the police were knowing and voluntary. The arresting officer testified that he notified defendant of his rights concurrent with his arrest, and that defendant acknowledged that he understood those rights; during the booking process, defendant was twice read his rights from two separate Miranda cards, there was no evidence that defendant ever requested an attorney at any point and his demeanor was described as cooperative and pleasant; and there was no evidence that any promises were made of a reduced charge or sentence, only that defendant's cooperation would be noted to the prosecutor. State v. Garner, 2007 Ohio 5914, 2007 Ohio App. LEXIS 5204 (Nov. 2, 2007).

Trial court did not err when it denied defendant's motion to suppress his statement to the police because, insofar as the trial court may have determined that all discussion occurred subsequent to defendant's waiver of his rights, such determination was supported by competent, credible evidence. Alternatively, insofar as the trial court may have credited defendant's version of events, i.e., that during fingerprinting, he asked the detective why he had been arrested, then told him that he did not rape or rob anyone, such statement was not made in response to police questioning, and was not compelled by the police in any manner. State v. Priest, — Ohio App. 3d —, 2007 Ohio 5958, — N.E. 2d —, 2007 Ohio App. LEXIS 5225 (Nov. 8, 2007).

Trial court erred by suppressing defendant's statement, made immediately after he was notified that the police officers had found a gun in the car, as the fruit of the search because defendant's voluntary statement made after he was properly under arrest was were not subject to suppression. State v. Bragg, — Ohio App. 3d —, 2007 Ohio 5993, — N.E. 2d —, 2007 Ohio App. LEXIS 5242 (Nov. 9, 2007).

—Miranda warnings

Court rejected defendant's contention that, since he did not speak to the police until approximately 3:00 a.m., he was too tired to comprehend what he was doing, and thus, the waiver of his Miranda rights signed prior to giving his statement to police was not knowingly, voluntarily, and intelligently given. There was no evidence that defendant was confused or did not

understand the rights he was waiving as the evidence showed that the officer read defendant his Miranda rights while defendant followed along on a Miranda waiver form and that, at no time did defendant indicate that he did not understand his rights, that he wanted to talk to an attorney, or that he wanted to stop the interview; thus, defendant's motion to suppress the statement he provided was properly denied. State v. Henry, — Ohio App. 3d —, 2007 Ohio 6732, — N.E. 2d —, 2007 Ohio App. LEXIS 5904 (Dec. 14, 2007).

— Search of student

Trial court's decision to overrule a student's motion to suppress was not against the manifest weight of the evidence; the search by a school principal, in which the principal emptied the contents of the student's purse, including a zippered pocket which contained a hand written note about a murder plan involving a fellow student, was not excessively intrusive in light of the age of the student and the nature of the threats, i.e. murder. The principal's decision was suitably based on the principal's common sense, duty to students and staff, and experience in light of the circumstances. In re Garn, — Ohio App. 3d —, 2007 Ohio 6765, — N.E. 2d —, 2007 Ohio App. LEXIS 5941 (Dec. 13, 2007).

— Speedy trial rights

When a misdemeanor charge is voluntarily dismissed, the speedy trial time that elapsed with respect to the dismissed charge must be added to the speedy trial time that elapsed with respect to a subsequent misdemeanor charge when the new charge arises from the same set of circumstances, unless the subsequent charge was based on new and additional facts that the state did not have knowledge of when the dismissed charge was filed. The trial court abused its discretion when it denied without a hearing the defendant's motion to dismiss based on speedy trial rights: State v. Dillon, 181 Ohio App. 3d 69, 2009 Ohio 530, 907 N.E.2d 1226, 2009 Ohio App. LEXIS 452 (2009).

Motion to suppress properly denied

Trial court did not err in denying defendant's motion to suppress evidence because search of defendant, which revealed crack cocaine, was justified; police officers had a reasonable, articulable suspicion of criminal activity that justified a brief investigatory stop and information obtained by the officers gave them probable cause to arrest defendant. State v. Palmer, — Ohio App. 3d —, 2007 Ohio 6694, — N.E. 2d —, 2007 Ohio App. LEXIS 5876 (Dec. 14, 2007).

No contest plea

Defendant's motion to dismiss the indictments was properly denied because any error regarding his right to possess digital images that appeared to be minors engaged in sexual conduct where the images are not actual minors was waived when defendant pled no contest. Although defendant claimed that he could not determine whether the images depicted actual children, the State was prepared to offer the expert testimony of a computer forensic examiner. State v. Mansfield, — Ohio App. 3d —, 2007 Ohio 333, — N.E. 2d —, 2007 Ohio App. LEXIS 293 (Jan. 29, 2007).

Trial court's ruling as to the admissibility of the proposed expert's testimony was not a proper subject for a pretrial motion within the meaning of Ohio R. Crim. P. 12(B) and, therefore, was not saved for review on appeal by Ohio R. Crim. P. 12(I) after defendant pled no contest. State v. Mansfield, — Ohio App. 3d —, 2007 Ohio 333, — N.E. 2d —, 2007 Ohio App. LEXIS 293 (Jan. 29, 2007).

When defendant pled no contest to domestic violence after defendant's motion to dismiss on speedy trial grounds was denied, defendant was not barred from raising defendant's speedy trial argument on appeal because, under Ohio R. Crim. P. 12(I), a no contest plea did not preclude a defendant from asserting on appeal that a trial court prejudicially erred in ruling on a pretrial motion. State v. Walker, — Ohio App. 3d —, 2007 Ohio 4666, — N.E. 2d —, 2007 Ohio App. LEXIS 4208 (Sept. 11, 2007).

By his plea of no contest, which permitted the trial court to determine defendant's guilt or innocence from the facts in the indictment that he admitted were true, defendant waived his right to assign error to the trial court's decision overruling his motion to disclose a confidential informant's identity. State v. Evans, — Ohio App. 3d —, 2007 Ohio 6587, — N.E. 2d —, 2007 Ohio App. LEXIS 5760 (Dec. 7, 2007).

Defendant's no-contest plea was premised upon a plea bargain that included the erroneous belief by defense counsel, the prosecutor, and the trial court that he would be able to preserve his appellate rights to contest the pretrial evidentiary decisions made by the trial court and that the issue regarding the admissibility of evidence would be decided on appeal by the appellate court. Accordingly, since the full plea bargain agreement could not be effected, the no-contest plea had to be vacated and the matter was remanded for further proceedings. State v. Brock, — Ohio App. 3d —, 2006 Ohio 6681, — N.E. 2d —, 2006 Ohio App. LEXIS 6588 (Dec. 18, 2006).

Omission of element in indictment

Defendant's contention that the failure of an indictment, charging him with child endangering, in violation of RC § 2919.22, to contain the required mental state of recklessness rendered the indictment defective and could not give the trial court subject matter jurisdiction was rejected because defendant did not raise such a challenge to the indictment in the trial court, as required by Ohio R. Crim. P. 12 and RC § 2941.29, and the failure to object to an indictment on the grounds that it did not state an offense did not deprive the trial court of subject matter jurisdiction. The failure of the indictment to contain the element of recklessness was not plain error under Ohio R. Crim. P. 52(B) as the indictment referred to the statute, thus apprising defendant of the charged offense, and as the evidence adduced at trial was clearly sufficient to show that defendant, in fact, acted recklessly. State v. Batich, — Ohio App. 3d —, 2007 Ohio 2305, — N.E. 2d —, 2007 Ohio App. LEXIS 2127 (May 11, 2007).

Probable cause

Motion to suppress was properly denied because, even excluding the information to which defendant objected (a past conviction belonging to someone else and that he was a Jamaican male) from the affidavit, there was sufficient probable cause under the totality of the circumstances to support the issuance of a warrant. Defendant's additional claim that the affidavit contained material omissions was unavailing because the presence of the itinerary and a box from a flower shop did not negate the probability that defendant was using the residence as a marijuana "stash-house" for repackaging and resale as alleged by the informant; even if those facts had been included, they would not have overcome the other information in the affidavit that corroborated the informant's allegations and established a fair probability that marijuana would be found in the residence. State v. Frazer, — Ohio App. 3d —, 2007 Ohio 5954, — N.E. 2d —, 2007 Ohio App. LEXIS 5221 (Nov. 8, 2007).

Reopening of hearing

Because the trial court did not consider a videotape that was supplied after denial of defendant's suppression motion, and twice denied a motion to reopen the suppression hearing, the trial court's factual findings were incomplete. Failure to consider the new evidence denied defendant a full and fair opportunity to present defendant's case on the validity of a seizure of marijuana following a traffic stop. State v. Lashuay, — Ohio App. 3d —, 2007 Ohio 6365, — N.E. 2d —, 2007 Ohio App. LEXIS 5578 (Nov. 30, 2007).

Rules of evidence

Rules of Evidence do not apply to suppression hearings: State v. Boczar, 113 Ohio St. 3d 148, 2007 Ohio 1251, 863 N.E.2d 155, 2007 Ohio LEXIS 800 (2007).

Suppression improperly denied

Suppression of evidence of guns found in defendant's house in a case under one of the beds should have been granted because, though the officer had the consent of defendant's wife to search defendant's house for an individual named in an arrest warrant, the officer testified that no human body could fit in the case found under the bed; thus, the officer did not have authorization to open and search the case. State v. Giamarco, — Ohio App. 3d —, 2007 Ohio 6794, — N.E. 2d —, 2007 Ohio App. LEXIS 5950 (Dec. 3, 2007).

Suppression improperly granted

Trial court erred by granting defendant's motion to suppress because the police officers acted within Fourth Amendment bounds when they searched the SUV's passenger compartment. Because the officers' articulable suspicion that the SUV contained a handgun (a person told them that a gun was pointed at him from the SUV) justified a protective sweep of the passenger compartment, they were also justified in searching compartments in the passenger compartment where a handgun could have been placed or hidden. State v. Bragg, — Ohio App. 3d —, 2007 Ohio 5993, — N.E. 2d —, 2007 Ohio App. LEXIS 5242 (Nov. 9, 2007).

Suppression properly denied

Trial court did not err in denying defendant's motion to suppress statements obtained during an interrogation before Miranda warnings had been given because the evidence presented at the hearing supported a finding that defendant was not subjected to a custodial interrogation, in that a reasonable man in defendant's position would have believed he was free to leave. Defendant voluntarily accompanied the detectives to the police station in the back of an unlocked, unmarked car with no protective cage between the front and back seats; he was left alone in an open room before the interview and had access to his cell phone; probable cause did not exist for an arrest; he left with his girlfriend following the interview; defendant was not formally arrested before the interview; and he was never restrained to a degree equivalent to formal arrest. Ohio v. Luke, — Ohio App. 3d —, 2007 Ohio 5906, — N.E. 2d —, 2007 Ohio App. LEXIS 5213 (Nov. 5, 2007).

Defendant's motion to suppress drug evidence was properly denied, as competent, credible evidence showed that evidence was discovered following a consensual encounter and consensual search under the Fourth Amendment. Defendant was not restrained by a detective, and there was no indication that defendant was impeded from continuing on defendant's way. State v. Cobbs, — Ohio App. 3d —, 2007 Ohio 5950, — N.E. 2d —, 2007 Ohio App. LEXIS 5215 (Nov. 8, 2007).

Evidence did not support defendant's claim that the voice identification made by defendant was impermissibly suggestive and that the placement of defendant in an adjacent interview room was done for the purpose of aiding the victim in identifying defendant. The evidence suggested that defendant spontaneously yelled to an officer as the officer left the interview room at a time when the door to the victim's interview room also happened to be open, and the officers could not have reasonably anticipated this confluence of events; thus, defendant's motion to suppress the victim's voice identification of him was properly denied. Ohio v. Cullins, — Ohio App. 3d —, 2007 Ohio 5978, — N.E. 2d —, 2007 Ohio App. LEXIS 5269 (Nov. 9, 2007).

Trial court did not err in denying defendant's motion to suppress on the ground that the affidavit offered in support of his arrest warrant contained false information, and that, if this information had been excluded, there would have been insufficient information to establish probable cause. The false statement was made after the victim's car keys had been recovered from defendant and after the victim had identified defendant's voice as that of one of the perpetrators of the aggravated robbery; thus, the alleged false statement did not justify the suppression of the voice identification evidence or the car keys. Ohio v. Cullins, — Ohio App. 3d —, 2007 Ohio 5978, — N.E. 2d —, 2007 Ohio App. LEXIS 5269 (Nov. 9, 2007).

Police officer's observations of the vehicle in which defendant was a passenger, along with the furtive movements of its occupants when they saw him, ducking down as the police cruiser drove by, and the odor of marijuana coming from inside the car, gave the officer reasonable suspicion of criminal activity and allowed the officer to detain defendant for investigation. As a result, defendant's Ohio R. Crim. P. 12(C)(3) motion to suppress evidence obtained during the officer's encounter with defendant was properly denied. State v. Dunson, — Ohio App. 3d —, 2007 Ohio 6681, — N.E. 2d —, 2007 Ohio App. LEXIS 5851 (Dec. 14, 2007).

Defendant's history of violence toward police officers, coupled with his having slumped down toward the floor of his vehicle when defendant saw the police officer approach the vehicle on foot, gave the officer reasonable and articulable suspicion that defendant could be armed and dangerous, sufficient to authorize a weapons pat-down of defendant. State v. Dunson, — Ohio App. 3d —, 2007 Ohio 6681, — N.E. 2d —, 2007 Ohio App. LEXIS 5851 (Dec. 14, 2007).

Police officer had probable cause to believe that a plastic baggie he felt inside defendant's pocket contained illegal drugs as he could smell marijuana coming from inside the vehicle where defendant had been seated when the officer arrived, defendant was a person known for engaging in drug activity, defendant had acted furtively when the officer drove by the car in which defendant was a passenger, defendant moved violently away when the officer patted the pocket where the baggie was located during a weapons pat-down, and the officer had knowledge that baggies were often used by people who carried drugs to conceal the drugs. As a result, defendant's Ohio R. Crim. P. 12(C)(3) motion to suppress evidence of the drugs retrieved from his pants pocket was properly denied. State v. Dunson, — Ohio App. 3d —, 2007 Ohio 6681, — N.E. 2d —, 2007 Ohio App. LEXIS 5851 (Dec. 14, 2007).

Length of the detention of the occupants of a vehicle stopped for several traffic violations was proper under the Fourth Amendment as the police officer who stopped the vehicle was unable to verify the owner of the vehicle, the driver did not appear to have a valid license, the officer received conflicting information as to the duration of the occupants' trip, and the entire detention lasted less than half an hour from the time of the stop until the drug dog indicated a positive sniff on the vehicle; thus, defendant's motion to suppress evidence found during the detention was properly denied. State v. Ramsey, — Ohio App. 3d —, 2007 Ohio 6687, — N.E. 2d —, 2007 Ohio App. LEXIS 5863 (Dec. 17, 2007).

Since there were specific and articulable facts supporting the initial traffic stop of the vehicle in which defendant was a passenger, in that the officer witnessed several traffic violations, defendant's motion to suppress evidence found during the stop of the vehicle was properly denied. State v. Ramsey, — Ohio App. 3d —, 2007 Ohio 6687, — N.E. 2d —, 2007 Ohio App. LEXIS 5863 (Dec. 17, 2007).

Suppression of evidence of guns found in the closet of defendant's house was properly denied because the officer had the consent of defendant's wife to search defendant's house for an individual named in an arrest warrant, and since the individual could have been hiding in the closet, the officer was permitted to look in the closet for the individual. The officer properly removed the guns found in the closet for his protection and for the protection of the children who were sleeping in the bedroom until he could find out who owned the guns. State v. Giamarco, — Ohio App. 3d —, 2007 Ohio 6794, — N.E. 2d —, 2007 Ohio App. LEXIS 5950 (Dec. 3, 2007).

Totality of the circumstances, viewed through the eyes of a reasonable police officer, provided a police detective with reasonable suspicion of criminal activity under Fourth Amendment to justify an investigative stop of defendant as the detective, who had extensive experience in the investigation of drug crime, saw defendant's codefendant make a short phone call, drive to a nearby location, and approach defendant's vehicle for a quick hand-to-hand exchange. Since a second detective, upon approaching defendant's vehicle, saw cocaine in plain view in defendant's car, he had probable cause to arrest defendant and to seize the cocaine; thus, defendant's motion to suppress evidence of the cocaine seized was properly denied. State v. Hayes, — Ohio App. 3d —, 2007 Ohio 6901, — N.E. 2d —, 2007 Ohio App. LEXIS 6051 (Dec. 21, 2007).

Suppression properly granted

Detective's seizure of a crack pipe during a pat-down search of defendant did not comport with the Fourth Amendment because the detective did not immediately identify the two-inch long object with the diameter of a pencil as contraband during the search; instead, the detective stated that, though he had a hunch that the object was a crack pipe, he was not sure what it was. As a result, defendant's motion to suppress was properly granted. State v. Daugherty, — Ohio App. 3d —, 2007 Ohio 6822, — N.E. 2d —, 2007 Ohio App. LEXIS 5961 (Dec. 20, 2007).

Waiver of error

Since defendant failed to file, pursuant to Ohio R. Crim. P. 12, a motion to suppress evidence that, before receiving his Miranda rights, he acknowledged to police his phone call to the victim and that he promised police that he would not bother the victim anymore, defendant waived all but plain error in the admission of that evidence. There was ample evidence that defendant made the threatening phone call; thus, it could not be shown that, but for the error in admitting the evidence of defendant's statements to police, the outcome of the trial would have been different. State v. Nelson, — Ohio App. 3d —, 2007 Ohio 3162, — N.E. 2d —, 2007 Ohio App. LEXIS 2907 (June 22, 2007).

Waiver of objections

Trial court did not err in failing to hold a hearing on defendant's objection to service of his indictment because, since defendant filed an untimely objection, he waived any objection to service of his indictment, under Ohio R. Crim. P. 12(H). Also, his arraignment was conducted in compliance with the time requirements of RC § 2941.49 because the indictment was issued and the Return of Executed Warrant form completed by the arresting officer provided that defendant had received a copy of both the indictment and the warrant on the indictment. State v. Kirk, — Ohio App. 3d —, 2007 Ohio 1228, — N.E. 2d —, 2007 Ohio App. LEXIS 1138 (Mar. 19, 2007).

Defendant's challenge to blood test results on the issue of substantial compliance with statutory and regulatory requirements had been waived on appeal since his motion to suppress did not seek suppression on that basis. State v. Jackson, — Ohio App. 3d —, 2006 Ohio 4453, — N.E. 2d —, 2006 Ohio App. LEXIS 4379 (Aug. 28, 2006).

Waiver of right to appeal

If defendant believed that he was erroneously indicted, he certainly failed to raise it to the trial court at any time, thus waiving the right to appeal, and no error was discernible in either the indictment or in the subsequent evidence going to the charges in that indictment. While the medical expert did testify that the child presented with evidence of old brain injury, on the date in question the child showed evidence of new injury, injury that ultimately proved to be permanent and serious; it was undisputed that defendant was alerted in the indictment of all the elements of his offense. State v. Bailey, — Ohio App. 3d —, 2007 Ohio 4995, — N.E. 2d —, 2007 Ohio App. LEXIS 4389 (Sept. 20, 2007).

Because defendant did not claim that his guilty plea was involuntary, unknowing, or unintelligently given or challenge any jurisdictional defect, he could not argue that his confession was coerced, that the trial court erred in overruling his motion to suppress, or that he received constitutionally ineffective assistance from trial counsel. State v. Storms, — Ohio App. 3d —, 2006 Ohio 3547, — N.E. 2d —, 2006 Ohio App. LEXIS 3499 (June 26, 2006).

RULE 12.1.   Notice of Alibi

Whenever a defendant in a criminal case proposes to offer testimony to establish an alibi on his behalf, he shall, not less than seven days before trial, file and serve upon the prosecuting attorney a notice in writing of his intention to claim alibi. The notice shall include specific information as to the place at which the defendant claims to have been at the time of the alleged offense. If the defendant fails to file such written notice, the court may exclude evidence offered by the defendant for the purpose of proving such alibi, unless the court determines that in the interest of justice such evidence should be admitted.

NOTES TO DECISIONS

ANALYSIS

Alibi evidence not permitted
Jury instructions
Preservation for appeal
Specificity

Alibi evidence not permitted
Defendant was not deprived of his right to a fair trial when the trial court did not allow him to present alibi testimony since defendant did not file a notice of alibi required by Ohio R. Crim. P. 12.1. Defendant's only alibi testimony would have been that he was at work, and since he stated so twice during his trial, he did not suffer prejudice from the trial court's decision. State v. Brasty, — Ohio App. 3d —, 2006 Ohio 3752, — N.E. 2d —, 2006 Ohio App. LEXIS 3734 (July 24, 2006).

Jury instructions
Where defendant filed a timely notice of alibi pursuant to Ohio R. Crim. P. 12.1, and he thereafter filed an amended notice in order to provide additional specificity in response to the State's motion to strike the defense, the trial court was required to give the jury an instruction on the defense of alibi, pursuant to RC § 2945.11, as defendant provided evidence to support the defense; where it failed to do so, such was reversible error. State v. Walton, — Ohio App. 3d —, 2006 Ohio 1974, — N.E. 2d —, 2006 Ohio App. LEXIS 1798 (Apr. 21, 2006).

Preservation for appeal
Trial court did not abuse its discretion in granting the State's motion to exclude the alibi evidence, which was essentially a motion in limine. Defendant waived his right to appeal the issue. In order to preserve the alibi issue for appeal, defendant had to go to trial and raise the alibi issue, however, prior to the trial, defendant pled no contest to the bill of information. State v. Scales, — Ohio App. 3d —, 2007 Ohio 3840, — N.E. 2d —, 2007 Ohio App. LEXIS 3483 (July 30, 2007).

Specificity
Trial court did not abuse its discretion by excluding defendant's alibi testimony because, in defendant's notice of alibi, defendant stated that he was at a location other than the locations of the various alleged offenses but did not state a specific location and/or address, as required by Ohio R. Crim. P. 12.1. During the hearing on the State's motion to exclude the alibi evidence, defendant again failed to provide any specific information regarding his location at the time the offenses were committed. State v. Taylor, — Ohio App. 3d —, 2006 Ohio 2041, — N.E. 2d —, 2006 Ohio App. LEXIS 1874 (Apr. 26, 2006).

RULE 13.   Trial Together of Indictments or Informations or Complaints

The court may order two or more indictments or informations or both to be tried together, if the offenses or the defendants could have been joined in a single indictment or information. The procedure shall be the same as if the prosecution were under such single indictment or information.

The court may order two or more complaints to be tried together, if the offenses or the defendants could have been joined in a single complaint. The procedure shall be the same as if the prosecution were under such single complaint.

NOTES TO DECISIONS

ANALYSIS

Joinder
Prejudice to defendant

Joinder
Joinder of the offenses of gross sexual imposition was favored where they involved different granddaughters of the defendant, even though the offenses against the alleged victims were separated by seven to nine years. The defendant was not prejudiced by the fact that evidence concerning the offenses would be introduced at the same trial where the evidence concerning each offense was so simple and distinct that a jury could not be confused: State v. Barnes, 149 Ohio Misc. 2d 1, 2008 Ohio 5609, 2008 Ohio Misc. LEXIS 278 (2008).

Charges against defendant arising from two incidents were properly tried together, under Ohio R. Crim. P. 13(A) and 8(A), and this did not violate Ohio R. Crim. P. 14, because (1), in one incident, it was alleged that defendant had committed a murder, and, in the other incident, the weapon allegedly used to commit that murder was recovered from the vehicle defendant had been driving, so, under Ohio R. Evid. 404(B), evidence of one incident would have been admissible in a separate trial of the other incident, and (2) the evidence related to the two incidents was simple and direct so that a jury would not become confused by presenting such evidence at one trial. State v. Nelms, — Ohio App. 3d —, 2007 Ohio 4664, — N.E. 2d —, 2007 Ohio App. LEXIS 4205 (Sept. 11, 2007).

Trial court's joinder under Ohio R. Crim. P. 8(A) of multiple robbery offenses and its denial of defendant's request to sever each offense from the other under Ohio R. Crim. P. 14 was not an abuse of discretion, as each of the victims identified defendant as the robber, he used the same characteristics in each robbery of wearing costumes and disguises and making smart existing remarks, and the facts were straightforward and uncomplicated; the robberies all had a common thread, such that they could have been brought in a single indictment or information pursuant to Ohio R. Crim. P. 13. State v. Starks,

— Ohio App. 3d —, 2007 Ohio 4897, — N.E. 2d —, 2007 Ohio App. LEXIS 4364 (Sept. 21, 2007).

Trial court did not abuse its discretion under Ohio R. Crim. P. 8 and 13 in failing to join an indictment that charged defendant with escape for failing to report to his parole officer with an indictment that arose out of defendant's failure to heed a police car's siren to pull over, as the charges in each indictment bore no relation to one another, and they were not based on a common scheme or plan. Ohio v. Anderson, — Ohio App. 3d —, 2007 Ohio 5326, — N.E. 2d —, 2007 Ohio App. LEXIS 4692 (Oct. 4, 2007).

Trial court did not err in joining the two indictments for trial, under Ohio R. Crim. P. 8(A) and 13; because the evidence of the second robbery would have been admissible at a separate trial of the first robbery, no prejudice stemmed from the jury's consideration of evidence relating to both robberies in reaching their verdicts. Moreover, the evidence of both robberies was simple and direct, and neither crime was so complex that the jury would have had difficulty separating the proof required for each offense. State v. Tipton, — Ohio App. 3d —, 2006 Ohio 2066, — N.E. 2d —, 2006 Ohio App. LEXIS 1911 (Apr. 27, 2006).

Trial court's denial of defendant's motion to sever his criminal trial from that of his co-defendant pursuant to Ohio R. Crim. P. 13 and 14 was not an abuse of discretion where there was no evidence of "prejudicial surprise," no showing that the jury was unable to separate the testimony with regard to each co-defendant, and joinder furthered the interests of judicial efficiency because the charges against each defendant arose out of a single incident. State v. Galloway, — Ohio App. 3d —, 2006 Ohio 3051, — N.E. 2d —, 2006 Ohio App. LEXIS 2930 (June 16, 2006).

Joinder, under Ohio R. Crim. P. 8(A) and 13, was proper since the incidents were based on the same course of conduct in that the charges in all three cases alleged a course of consistent drug-related activity on housing authority property. Defendant failed to demonstrate any prejudice by the joinder since the evidence in each case was simple and direct, involving easily distinguishable fact patterns. State v. Gilbert, — Ohio App. 3d —, 2006 Ohio 3595, — N.E. 2d —, 2006 Ohio App. LEXIS 3533 (July 13, 2006).

Joinder of a charge of gross sexual imposition, in violation of RC § 2907.05(A)(4), with other charges was proper under Ohio R. Crim. P. 13 and 14, as evidence of pornographic video images involving children, which formed the basis of charges of pandering obscenity involving a minor, in violation of RC § 2907.321(A)(2) and (5), was admissible under Ohio R. Evid. 404(B) and RC § 2945.59 to prove that defendant's motive was sexual gratification based on sexual contact pursuant to RC § 2907.01(B). State v. Gillingham, — Ohio App. 3d —, 2006 Ohio 5758, — N.E. 2d —, 2006 Ohio App. LEXIS 5738 (Oct. 27, 2006).

Prejudice to defendant

Defendant was not prejudiced by the joinder under Crim. R. 13 because the evidence of each crime was simple and distinct. The facts supporting the robbery offenses were direct and uncomplicated because defendant aided and abetted the armed robbery of a store by taking money out of the cash register and fleeing and, for having a weapon-under-disability, defendant possessed a weapon while under indictment for aggravated robbery. Further, the State did not present any evidence or argument connecting the crimes the jury was instructed twice to consider separate counts separately. State v. Bailey, — Ohio App. 3d —, 2007 Ohio 2014, — N.E. 2d —, 2007 Ohio App. LEXIS 1886 (Apr. 27, 2007).

RULE 14. Relief from Prejudicial Joinder

If it appears that a defendant or the state is prejudiced by a joinder of offenses or of defendants in an indictment, information, or complaint, or by such joinder for trial together of indictments, informations or complaints, the court shall order an election or separate trial of counts, grant a severance of defendants, or provide such other relief as justice requires. In ruling on a motion by a defendant for severance, the court shall order the prosecuting attorney to deliver to the court for inspection pursuant to Rule 16(B)(1)(a) any statements or confessions made by the defendants which the state intends to introduce in evidence at the trial.

When two or more persons are jointly indicted for a capital offense, each of such persons shall be tried separately, unless the court orders the defendants to be tried jointly, upon application by the prosecuting attorney or one or more of the defendants, and for good cause shown.

NOTES TO DECISIONS

ANALYSIS

Appeal
Final order
Improper joinder
Ineffective assistance
Joinder
Motion for severance
No prejudice from joinder
Prejudice to defendant
Request for separate trials
Severance
Waiver

Appeal

Although defendant filed a motion for severance of a murder charge from a felonious assault charge, which the trial court denied, where he failed to renew the motion at the end of the State's evidence or at the end of the evidence in the case, the matter was not preserved for review on appeal. State v. Markovanovich, — Ohio App. 3d —, 2007 Ohio 5676, — N.E. 2d —, 2007 Ohio App. LEXIS 5000 (Oct. 24, 2007).

Final order

Although a trial court denied defendant's motion under Ohio R. Crim. P. 14 for relief from prejudicial joinder on the record but it failed to journalize the ruling, the order was a final appealable one under RC § 2505.02, as the trial proceeded on both counts and guilty verdicts were rendered thereon. Ohio v. Anzures, — Ohio App. 3d —, 2007 Ohio 4817, — N.E. 2d —, 2007 Ohio App. LEXIS 4342 (Sept. 18, 2007).

Improper joinder

Although a trial court erred in denying defendant's motion to sever his criminal trial from his co-defendant's pursuant to Ohio R. Crim. P. 14 because they presented mutually antagonistic defenses by blaming the other for the victim's death, the error was harmless under Ohio R. Crim. P. 52 where defendant was not prejudiced by the admission of a videotaped statement of his co-defendant, as the evidence of defendant's guilt was overwhelming; the co-defendant did not take the stand, such that defendant's confrontation rights under U.S. Const. amend. VI were violated by the admission of the co-defendant's statement that accused defendant of committing the crime, as he had no opportunity to cross-examine the co-defendant. State v. Love, — Ohio App. 3d —, 2006 Ohio 1762, — N.E. 2d —, 2006 Ohio App. LEXIS 1619 (Mar. 27, 2006).

Ineffective assistance

Defendant failed to demonstrate ineffective assistance of counsel because it was entirely reasonable that defense counsel believed that the evidence regarding the confusion over the co-defendant's identity and a defense that defendant was just in the wrong place at the wrong time would have resulted in acquittal. Further, trial counsel could have anticipated prior to trial that the evidence of drug dealing would have been elicited from the co-defendant or defendant and sought a separate trial but, it appeared to have been co-defendant's and defendant's trial tactic to paint the prosecution witnesses as drug users and to show that they had been wrongly accused because they had wanted to get the co-defendant and defendant out of the neighborhood. State v. Quinn, — Ohio App. 3d —, 2007 Ohio 878, — N.E. 2d —, 2007 Ohio App. LEXIS 787 (Mar. 2, 2007).

Joinder

Joinder of the four defendants for trial was proper because they acted in concert and participated in the same criminal enterprise, the same series of acts and transactions, and the same course of criminal conduct and the various offenses charged, which were identical for each defendant, were the result of defendants' participation in a common scheme or plan, and the same course of criminal conduct. Defendant's motion for a separate trial was not based upon the same grounds and concerns being raised and argued for the first time on appeal and, for that reason alone, the trial court did not abuse its discretion in denying defendant's motion for a separate trial. State v. Patterson, — Ohio App. 3d —, 2007 Ohio 29, — N.E. 2d —, 2007 Ohio App. LEXIS 22 (Jan. 5, 2007).

Trial court's denial of defendant's motion to sever his criminal trial from that of his co-defendant pursuant to Ohio R. Crim. P. 13 and 14 was not an abuse of discretion where there was no evidence of "prejudicial surprise," no showing that the jury was unable to separate the testimony with regard to each co-defendant, and joinder furthered the interests of judicial efficiency because the charges against each defendant arose out of a single incident. State v. Galloway, — Ohio App. 3d —, 2006 Ohio 3051, — N.E. 2d —, 2006 Ohio App. LEXIS 2930 (June 16, 2006).

Trial court's denial of defendant's motion to sever offenses under Ohio R. Crim. P. 14 was not an abuse of discretion, as joinder under Ohio R. Crim. P. 8(A) was proper where the offenses of pandering and sexual battery involved minors and all of the offenses occurred at defendant's residence, the evidence was not deemed confusing or difficult for the jurors to separate, and the trial court determined that the jury could segregate the evidence involving sexual contact from the evidence involving possession of pornographic pictures of minors. State v. Purkhiser, — Ohio App. 3d —, 2006 Ohio 4014, — N.E. 2d —, 2006 Ohio App. LEXIS 3969 (Aug. 4, 2006).

Motion for severance

Trial court did not abuse its discretion by denying defendant's motion to sever his offenses because the evidence of both the 2004 break-in and the 2005 home-invasion could just as easily have been introduced in two trials and the underlying facts were "simple and direct." Additionally, because the victims in the home invasion both affirmatively identified defendant as one of the men involved in the 2005 home-invasion, but that identification was subject to some degree of doubt, introduction of defendant's DNA from a year earlier was relevant to show that defendant knew the funeral home (the location of the home invasion), may have previously robbed it, and might have chosen to again break-in and vandalize the facility. State v. Hairston, — Ohio App. 3d —, 2007 Ohio 3880, — N.E. 2d —, 2007 Ohio App. LEXIS 3519 (July 27, 2007).

Trial court did not abuse its discretion by overruling defendant's motion to sever because the finding was supported by credible evidence and was consistent with the expectations of Ohio R. Crim. P. 8. The events involved as to all of the counts took place within a period of nine hours, some of which occurred while defendant was in the jail, and all of the events involved defendant and his live-in girlfriend. State v. Cohen, — Ohio App. 3d —, 2007 Ohio 4546, — N.E. 2d —, 2007 Ohio App. LEXIS 4085 (Aug. 31, 2007).

Trial court did not abuse its discretion in denying defendant's motion under Ohio R. Crim. P. 14 to sever a misdemeanor charge of child endangerment from more serious crimes in her criminal trial, as the "other acts" evidence regarding defendant's alleged neglect of her children would have been admissible in a separate trial on the other charges, including murder, pursuant to the admissibility rule of Ohio R. Evid. 404(B) as a means to establish defendant's motive for having committed the serious crimes. Defendant could not show that she was prejudiced by the denial of her severance request. State v. Roseborough, — Ohio App. 3d —, 2006 Ohio 2254, — N.E. 2d —, 2006 Ohio App. LEXIS 2101 (May 5, 2006).

Trial court did not abuse its discretion in denying defendant's motion to sever offenses in his criminal trial pursuant to Ohio R. Crim. P. 14, as the fact that identification evidence by way of defendant's drug possession was offered into evidence in his aggravated robbery trial before the jury was proper for purposes of the identification pursuant to Ohio R. Evid. 404(B). As identification was important to the case, evidence that supported the identifications made by the eyewitnesses was admissible. State v. Marinello, — Ohio App. 3d —, 2006 Ohio 282, — N.E. 2d —, 2006 Ohio App. LEXIS 255 (Jan. 26, 2006).

Even if defendant had preserved his right to appeal from the trial court's refusal to sever, defendant was not prejudiced by the joinder; because, at the time that the motion to sever was ruled upon, it was unknown whether defendant would testify or admit to engaging in sexual conduct with the victims, other acts testimony would have been admissible under Ohio R. Evid. 404(B) to demonstrate modus operandi and to prove identity. The similarities between the two cases were sufficient to support the trial court's conclusion that the evidence of one crime would have been admissible at the trial of the other even if the counts were severed. State v. Elijah, — Ohio App. 3d —, 2006 Ohio 2635, — N.E. 2d —, 2006 Ohio App. LEXIS 2471 (May 19, 2006).

In defendant's trial for two aggravated robberies, in which he moved for severance, under Ohio R. Crim. P. 14, while it was error for the trial court not to rule on the motion, the error was harmless because, under Ohio R. Evid. 404(B), evidence of one of the robberies would have been admissible at a separate trial of the other robbery to prove modus operandi, given the similarity between the two crimes, intent and plan, and identity, so joinder of the offenses, under Ohio R. Crim. P. 8(A), was proper. State v. Andrews, — Ohio App. 3d —, 2006 Ohio 3764, — N.E. 2d —, 2006 Ohio App. LEXIS 3706 (July 24, 2006).

No prejudice from joinder

Joinder of the offenses of gross sexual imposition was favored where they involved different granddaughters of the defendant, even though the offenses against the alleged victims were separated by seven to nine years. The defendant was not prejudiced by the fact that evidence concerning the offenses would be introduced at the same trial where the evidence concerning each offense was so simple and distinct that a jury could not be confused: State v. Barnes, 149 Ohio Misc. 2d 1, 2008 Ohio 5609, 2008 Ohio Misc. LEXIS 278 (2008).

Defendant failed to demonstrate that his rights were prejudiced by the joinder and denial of his motion to sever because the evidence presented would have been admissible in separate trials if the charges had been severed. Although he was correct that the State could not have introduced the evidence to show that defendant had a propensity to commit the crimes, the evidence was admissible, under Evid. R. 404 and RC § 2945.59, to show defendant's motive or intent, an element of the crime charged (attempted rape and robbery), which defendant placed at issue. State v. Hill, — Ohio App. 3d —, 2007 Ohio 56, — N.E. 2d —, 2007 Ohio App. LEXIS 51 (Jan. 5, 2007).

Where defendant failed to object to the joinder of her criminal trial with that of one of her co-defendants, pursuant to Ohio R. Crim. P. 8, as she did not file a motion to sever the case at any stage of the proceedings pursuant to Ohio R. Crim. P. 14, any objection to such joinder was waived for purposes of appeal. There was no plain error under Ohio R. Crim. P. 52, as she failed to show that she was prejudiced from the joinder where there was no evidence that the jury was influenced thereby. State v. Harris-Powers, — Ohio App. 3d —, 2007 Ohio 389, — N.E. 2d —, 2007 Ohio App. LEXIS 349 (Feb. 1, 2007).

Trial counsel was not ineffective for not moving to sever the counts because the case involved very "simple and distinct" evidence and was not confusing; each victim testified about separate offenses and provided sufficient evidence of each offense charged, the victims were all cousins and were acquainted with defendant as an older family friend and neighbor of their grandparents, and the offenses occurred in the same general time frame and occurred in the same general location. Moreover, there was sufficient evidence to convict defendant of each charge relating to each victim without necessitating the evidence from one case to prove the other. State v. Eads, — Ohio App. 3d —, 2007 Ohio 539, — N.E. 2d —, 2007 Ohio App. LEXIS 488 (Feb. 8, 2007).

Trial court's decision to try two co-defendants jointly pursuant to Ohio R. Crim. P. 8(B) was not an abuse of discretion, as defendant had failed to properly preserve his claim of misjoinder pursuant to Ohio R. Crim. P. 14 where he did not renew the motion at the close of the State's case or at the conclusion of all of the evidence, and further, he failed to provide the trial court with any information as to factors against joinder in his severance hearing. State v. Holbert, — Ohio App. 3d —, 2007 Ohio 986, — N.E. 2d —, 2007 Ohio App. LEXIS 916 (Mar. 8, 2007).

Defendant's claim that her trial counsel was ineffective in violation of her rights under U.S. Const. amend. VI and Ohio Const. art. I, § 10 by not seeking to have separate trials of defendant and her co-defendant pursuant to RC § 2945.13 and Ohio R. Crim. P. 14 lacked merit, as joinder of defendants under Ohio R. Crim. P. 8(B) was favored and no reason was shown for severance, such that counsel was not required to perform a futile act. Defendant's claim that she had a defense that was "antagonistic" to that of her co-defendant did not show prejudice, as she did not present a defense and further, her codefendant could have asserted the right to remain silent. State v. Henderson, — Ohio App. 3d —, 2007 Ohio 2372, — N.E. 2d —, 2007 Ohio App. LEXIS 2212 (May 17, 2007).

Counsel was not ineffective for failing to request that the trial be severed because the evidence of the codefendant having brandished a firearm and making threats to the victim was, for the most part, cumulative of other evidence already introduced since many witnesses testified that tensions had been rising between defendant and the codefendant on one side and friends of the victim. The fact that the codefendant had brandished a firearm and/or threatened the victim did not add much to the State's overall evidence. State v. Robinson, — Ohio App. 3d —, 2007 Ohio 3501, — N.E. 2d —, 2007 Ohio App. LEXIS 3224 (July 5, 2007).

Charges against defendant arising from two incidents were properly tried together, under Ohio R. Crim. P. 13(A) and 8(A), and this did not violate Ohio R. Crim. P. 14, because (1), in one incident, it was alleged that defendant had committed a murder, and, in the other incident, the weapon allegedly used to commit that murder was recovered from the vehicle defendant had been driving, so, under Ohio R. Evid. 404(B), evidence of one incident would have been admissible in a separate trial of the other incident, and (2) the evidence related to the two incidents was simple and direct so that a jury would not become confused by presenting such evidence at one trial. State v. Nelms, — Ohio App. 3d —, 2007 Ohio 4664, — N.E. 2d —, 2007 Ohio App. LEXIS 4205 (Sept. 11, 2007).

Trial court did not abuse its discretion under Ohio R. Crim. P. 8(A) and 14 when it denied defendant's motion for relief from prejudicial joinder of two drug-related offenses which arose from incidents that occurred several months apart, as his defense to the possession of drugs charge implicated him in other drug-related criminal activity, which was admissible under Ohio R. Evid. 404(B). Ohio v. Anzures, — Ohio App. 3d —, 2007 Ohio 4817, — N.E. 2d —, 2007 Ohio App. LEXIS 4342 (Sept. 18, 2007).

Trial court's joinder under Ohio R. Crim. P. 8(A) of multiple robbery offenses and its denial of defendant's request to sever each offense from the other under Ohio R. Crim. P. 14 was not an abuse of discretion, as each of the victims identified defendant as the robber, he used the same characteristics in each robbery of wearing costumes and disguises and making smart existing remarks, and the facts were straightforward and uncomplicated; the robberies all had a common thread, such that they could have been brought in a single indictment or information pursuant to Ohio R. Crim. P. 13. State v. Starks, — Ohio App. 3d —, 2007 Ohio 4897, — N.E. 2d —, 2007 Ohio App. LEXIS 4364 (Sept. 21, 2007).

Defendant failed to show how the results of the trial would have been different had the different drug offenses been tried separately. The jury found defendant not guilty on one count, which demonstrated that the jury was able to separate its analysis of the individual charges and impartially decide each count. State v. Reuschling, — Ohio App. 3d —, 2007 Ohio 6726, — N.E. 2d —, 2007 Ohio App. LEXIS 5895 (Dec. 14, 2007).

In a drug prosecution, the joinder of two indictments, under Ohio R. Crim. P. 8, did not prejudice defendant because they were all evidence of defendant's modus operandi, so, had the offenses been tried separately, the evidence would have been admissible at the separate trials, so defendant was not prejudiced when the offenses were joined in one trial, nor was he entitled to have the offenses severed, under Ohio R. Crim. P. 14. State v. Bundy, — Ohio App. 3d —, 2006 Ohio 4062, — N.E. 2d —, 2006 Ohio App. LEXIS 4021 (Aug. 8, 2006).

Trial court did not abuse its discretion in denying defendant's motion under Ohio R. Crim. P. 8(A) and 14 to sever four counts of rape against him, arising from two separate incidents with different victims, as joinder of the claims was appropriate to show a "common scheme or plan" because defendant's conduct was the same in both instances, whereby he lured the victims with drugs, took them to an abandoned building, and threatened them. As the victims did not know each other, the similarity of their versions of events undermined defendant's claim that the sexual acts were consensual and that the victims' testimony was not credible. State v. Boyd, — Ohio App. 3d —, 2006 Ohio 4132, — N.E. 2d —, 2006 Ohio App. LEXIS 4076 (Aug. 11, 2006).

Trial court did not abuse its discretion in overruling defendant's motion to sever because the jury was not likely to be improperly influenced by evidence of defendant's earlier conviction or more likely to believe him guilty of the assault charge against him in the instant matter. The simple and direct nature of the witnesses' testimony regarding each offense negated defendant's assertion of prejudice. State v.

Bates, — Ohio App. 3d —, 2006 Ohio 4146, — N.E. 2d —, 2006 Ohio App. LEXIS 4163 (Aug. 11, 2006).

Even though the crimes defendant was charged with committing on two different dates were similar and involved the same victim, he was not prejudiced by their joinder because the evidence of each crime was simple and distinct, and the jury's verdict acquitting him of some crimes showed it appreciated the differences in the evidence. State v. Johnson, — Ohio App. 3d —, 2006 Ohio 4540, — N.E. 2d —, 2006 Ohio App. LEXIS 4505 (Sept. 1, 2006).

Joinder of a charge of gross sexual imposition, in violation of RC § 2907.05(A)(4), with other charges was proper under Ohio R. Crim. P. 13 and 14, as evidence of pornographic video images involving children, which formed the basis of charges of pandering obscenity involving a minor, in violation of RC § 2907.321(A)(2) and (5), was admissible under Ohio R. Evid. 404(B) and RC § 2945.59 to prove that defendant's motive was sexual gratification based on sexual contact pursuant to RC § 2907.01(B). State v. Gillingham, — Ohio App. 3d —, 2006 Ohio 5758, — N.E. 2d —, 2006 Ohio App. LEXIS 5738 (Oct. 27, 2006).

There was no plain error under Ohio R. Crim. P. 52 in the trial court's denial of defendant's motion pursuant to Ohio R. Crim. P. 14 to sever two counts against him of having a weapon while under a disability, in violation of RC § 2923.13(A), as the State showed that the evidence of each offense was simple and direct and it was unlikely that the jury would be confused on the issues. State v. Reid, — Ohio App. 3d —, 2006 Ohio 6450, — N.E. 2d —, 2006 Ohio App. LEXIS 6405 (Dec. 8, 2006).

Trial court did not commit plain by failing to sever the cases against defendant because any allegation of prejudice was negated by the State under the "joinder" test since all of the evidence relied upon by the State was simple and direct. The State relied upon straightforward circumstantial evidence in an attempt to meet its burden on the breaking and entering counts and, for the remaining counts, the State relied upon the testimony of the victim, the documentary evidence, and the medical records and photographs of the injuries, which supported her account. State v. Sadler, — Ohio App. 3d —, 2006 Ohio 6910, — N.E. 2d —, 2006 Ohio App. LEXIS 6820 (Dec. 27, 2006).

Prejudice to defendant
Defendant was not prejudiced by the joinder under Crim. R. 13 because the evidence of each crime was simple and distinct. The facts supporting the robbery offenses were direct and uncomplicated because defendant aided and abetted the armed robbery of a store by taking money out of the cash register and fleeing and, for having a weapon-under-disability, defendant possessed a weapon while under indictment for aggravated robbery. Further, the State did not present any evidence or argument connecting the crimes the jury was instructed twice to consider separate counts separately. State v. Bailey, — Ohio App. 3d —, 2007 Ohio 2014, — N.E. 2d —, 2007 Ohio App. LEXIS 1886 (Apr. 27, 2007).

Defendant suffered no prejudice by the joinder of the escape charge because, although the evidence of the escape charge was simple and distinct from the rape, kidnapping, and bribery charges, it was part of a course of criminal conduct. Defendant committed the crimes against the victim, tried to bribe her not to go to the police, and then left town. State v. Spruce, — Ohio App. 3d —, 2006 Ohio 1730, — N.E. 2d —, 2006 Ohio App. LEXIS 1594 (Apr. 6, 2006).

Defendant was not prejudiced by the joinder of offenses because both theft offenses were of the same character and constituted parts of a common plan; both theft offenses occurred on the university campus, were closely committed in place and time, and had the same modus operandi--a woman starting a conversation with the victims while using a jacket to conceal a theft. The offenses were related by time, day,

location, and common scheme and, even if the charges had been separated, evidence of one offense would still have been admissible in the trial of the other, under Ohio R. Evid. 404(B). State v. Brotherton, — Ohio App. 3d —, 2006 Ohio 1747, — N.E. 2d —, 2006 Ohio App. LEXIS 1622 (Apr. 7, 2006).

Trial court did not err in joining the two indictments for trial, under Ohio R. Crim. P. 8(A) and 13; because the evidence of the second robbery would have been admissible at a separate trial of the first robbery, no prejudice stemmed from the jury's consideration of evidence relating to both robberies in reaching their verdicts. Moreover, the evidence of both robberies was simple and direct, and neither crime was so complex that the jury would have had difficulty separating the proof required for each offense. State v. Tipton, — Ohio App. 3d —, 2006 Ohio 2066, — N.E. 2d —, 2006 Ohio App. LEXIS 1911 (Apr. 27, 2006).

Joinder, under Ohio R. Crim. P. 8(A) and 13, was proper since the incidents were based on the same course of conduct in that the charges in all three cases alleged a course of consistent drug-related activity on housing authority property. Defendant failed to demonstrate any prejudice by the joinder since the evidence in each case was simple and direct, involving easily distinguishable fact patterns. State v. Gilbert, — Ohio App. 3d —, 2006 Ohio 3595, — N.E. 2d —, 2006 Ohio App. LEXIS 3533 (July 13, 2006).

Request for separate trials
No abuse of discretion on the part of the trial court in denying defendant's motion for a separate trial had been demonstrated because the evidence did not constitute "other acts" prohibited by Evid. R. 404(B) that was erroneously admitted against defendant because the trial court improperly refused to grant her motion for a separate trial. Evidence of conduct constituting a theft offense by any of the defendants from a store in the mall, in furtherance of their common criminal enterprise, was admissible against all of the defendants and such evidence presented a question for the jury as to whether any particular defendant participated in or aided and abetted any particular theft offense. State v. Patterson, — Ohio App. 3d —, 2007 Ohio 29, — N.E. 2d —, 2007 Ohio App. LEXIS 22 (Jan. 5, 2007).

Severance
Counsel was not ineffective for failing to request that the trial be severed based on the bribery evidence since that evidence was rebuttal evidence which was not made known to counsel prior to trial. Counsel could not reasonably have been expected to anticipate that the State would bring evidence that one codefendant attempted to bribe witnesses when he was not given any advance warning of such evidence prior to trial. State v. Carter, — Ohio App. 3d —, 2007 Ohio 3502, — N.E. 2d —, 2007 Ohio App. LEXIS 3223 (June 29, 2007).

Pursuant to Ohio R. Crim. P. 8(A) and 14, there was no undue prejudice caused by the joinder of two counts in defendant's criminal trial, as each of the counts required the State to prove that defendant had or used a firearm and the evidence was so strong against defendant that there was no reasonable possibility that, even if the counts were severed, they would have led to anything other than guilty verdicts; accordingly, defendant's claim that his counsel was ineffective in violation of U.S. Const. amend. VI and Ohio Const. art. I, § 10 for failing to seek severance lacked merit where he could not show that the outcome of the trial would have been otherwise. Ohio v. Riffle, — Ohio App. 3d —, 2007 Ohio 5299, — N.E. 2d —, 2007 Ohio App. LEXIS 4656 (Sept. 28, 2007).

Waiver
Trial court's denial of defendant's initial motion to sever a felony domestic violence charge, in violation of RC § 2919.25, from other charges against him, based on his claim that evidence of his prior domestic violence convictions would be

prejudicial to him pursuant to Ohio R. Crim. P. 8(A) and 14 in his criminal matter on multiple charges, was not reviewable on appeal, as defendant failed to renew the motion at the end of the State's case or at the end of the trial. He waived the right to assert an error in the trial court's ruling for purposes of appeal. State v. Feathers, — Ohio App. 3d —, 2007 Ohio 3024, — N.E. 2d —, 2007 Ohio App. LEXIS 2778 (June 15, 2007).

RULE 15.   Deposition

(A) **When taken.** If it appears probable that a prospective witness will be unable to attend or will be prevented from attending a trial or hearing, and if it further appears that his testimony is material and that it is necessary to take his deposition in order to prevent a failure of justice, the court at any time after the filing of an indictment, information, or complaint shall upon motion of the defense attorney or the prosecuting attorney and notice to all the parties, order that his testimony be taken by deposition and that any designated books, papers, documents or tangible objects, not privileged, be produced at the same time and place.

If a witness is committed for failure to give bail or to appear to testify at a trial or hearing, the court on written motion of the witness and notice to the parties, may direct that his deposition be taken. After the deposition is completed, the court may discharge the witness.

(B) **Notice of taking.** The party at whose instance a deposition is to be taken shall give to every other party reasonable written notice of the time and place for taking the deposition. The notice shall state the name and address of each person to be examined. On motion of a party upon whom the notice is served, the court for cause shown may extend or shorten the time or fix the place of deposition.

(C) **Attendance of defendant.** The defendant shall have the right to attend the deposition. If he is confined the person having custody of the defendant shall be ordered by the court to take him to the deposition. The defendant may waive his right to attend the deposition, provided he does so in writing and in open court, is represented by counsel, and is fully advised of his right to attend by the court at a recorded proceeding.

(D) **Counsel.** Where a defendant is without counsel the court shall advise him of his right to counsel and assign counsel to represent him unless the defendant waives counsel or is able to obtain counsel. If it appears that a defendant at whose instance a deposition is to be taken cannot bear the expense thereof, the court may direct that all deposition expenses, including but not limited to travel and subsistence of the defendant's attorney for attendance at such examination together with a reasonable attorney fee, in addition to the compensation allowed for defending the defendant, and the expenses of the prosecuting attorney in the taking of such deposition, shall be paid out of public funds upon the certificate of the court making such order. Waiver of counsel shall be as prescribed in Rule 44(C).

(E) **How taken.** Depositions shall be taken in the manner provided in civil cases. The prosecution and defense shall have the right, as at trial, to full examination of witnesses. A deposition taken under this rule shall be filed in the court in which the action is pending.

(F) **Use.** At the trial or upon any hearing, a part or all of a deposition, so far as otherwise admissible under the rules of evidence, may be used if it appears: that the witness is dead; or, that the witness is out of the state, unless it appears that the absence of the witness was procured by the party offering the deposition; or that the witness is unable to attend or testify because of sickness or infirmity; or that the party offering the deposition has been unable to procure the attendance of the witness by subpoena. Any deposition may also be used by any party for the purpose of refreshing the recollection, or contradicting or impeaching the testimony of the deponent as a witness. If only a part of a deposition is offered in evidence by a party, any party may offer other parts.

(G) **Objections to admissibility.** Objections to receiving in evidence a deposition or a part thereof shall be made as provided in civil actions.

NOTES TO DECISIONS

ANALYSIS

Admissibility
Deposition of victim
Due diligence
Impeachment evidence
Videotaped deposition

Admissibility

As CrimR 15(A) requires a showing that a prospective witness is unavailable or prevented from attending trial, the court did not abuse its discretion by denying the request for a deposition to be used at trial: State v. Weaver, 178 Ohio App. 3d 504, 2008 Ohio 5022, 898 N.E.2d 1023, 2008 Ohio App. LEXIS 4242 (2008).

Defendant failed to show that the trial court's denial of his request to admit a statement in a police summary from a witness who died unexpectedly prior to trial was reversible error, as there was no support for a determination that defendant had intended to depose the witness, such that the fact that the State untimely disclosed her identity did not result in his inability to have preserved her testimony pursuant to Ohio R. Crim. P. 15. The police summary was hearsay and the witness could not testify at trial due to her early demise, and there was no due process violation under Ohio Const. art. I, § 10 pursuant to Brady, as there were multiple other witnesses who testified that defendant wielded a knife during a fight that resulted in the stabbing death of the victim, and accordingly, it was not shown that the outcome of the trial would have been different if such evidence would have been admitted. State v. Hillyer, — Ohio App. 3d —, 2006 Ohio 4621, — N.E. 2d —, 2006 Ohio App. LEXIS 4453 (Aug. 31, 2006).

Deposition of victim

Deposition testimony of the victim, preserved pursuant to Crim. R. 15, satisfied the requirements of the confrontation clause of the Sixth Amendment because the victim was unavailable at trial (he had died from Lou Gehrig's disease), and because defendant had an opportunity, and in fact, did cross-examine the victim during the deposition. The victim was capable of giving basic affirmative or negative responses to leading questions at his deposition and there was no mention that the victim was confused, was too tired to answer counsel's questions, or was unwilling to continue with the cross-examination for any reason. State v. Irwin, — Ohio App. 3d —, 2007 Ohio 4996, — N.E. 2d —, 2007 Ohio App. LEXIS 4391 (Sept. 19, 2007).

Due diligence

Trial court's grant of a continuance to the State was not a "reasonable continuance" under RC § 2945.72(H), in that the State failed to use due diligence to ensure the attendance of the victim; thus, defendant's right to a speedy trial was denied. The State could have followed the procedure set forth in RC § 2939.27 allowing for a material witness to be summoned from another state via a certificate issued by the judge of the court where the prosecution was pending or could have taken the victim's testimony by deposition pursuant to Ohio R. Crim. P. 15(A). State v. Angus, — Ohio App. 3d —, 2006 Ohio 4971, — N.E. 2d —, 2006 Ohio App. LEXIS 4911 (Sept. 19, 2006).

Impeachment evidence

Where the trial court initially announced that it was suppressing an alleged, inculpatory statement to an officer as a sanction for the state's failure to properly disclose it and directed the prosecution to tell its witnesses not to make any reference to the statement, the court committed prejudicial error by allowing use of the statement to impeach the defendant on cross-examination: State v. Brooks, 176 Ohio App. 3d 210, 2008 Ohio 1726, 891 N.E.2d 797, 2008 Ohio App. LEXIS 1472 (2008).

Videotaped deposition

Trial court did not err in permitting the jury to view the videotaped deposition of the officer's deposition because the officer was scheduled to be out of town on the trial date and his testimony was material to the case. The Confrontation Clause was not violated because defendant and counsel were present and participated in the deposition and cross-examined the officer extensively, and it was properly authenticated because the record contained a written transcription of the officer's deposition, filed with the trial court, with a certification from the court reporter that the officer was duly sworn and the typed transcript was true and correct. State v. Hill, — Ohio App. 3d —, 2007 Ohio 56, — N.E. 2d —, 2007 Ohio App. LEXIS 51 (Jan. 5, 2007).

With respect to the unavailability of one of the victims, defendant's adopted son, due to his deployment to Iraq, defendant failed to demonstrate prejudice because he was able to depose the son prior to trial. The jury was permitted to view a videotape of the testimony during defendant's trial, which was within the allowances of Ohio R. Crim. P. 15. State v. Rogers, — Ohio App. 3d —, 2007 Ohio 1890, — N.E. 2d —, 2007 Ohio App. LEXIS 1745 (Apr. 23, 2007).

RULE 16.   Discovery and Inspection

(A) **Purpose, Scope and Reciprocity.** This rule is to provide all parties in a criminal case with the information necessary for a full and fair adjudication of the facts, to protect the integrity of the justice system and the rights of defendants, and to protect the well-being of witnesses, victims, and society at large. All duties and remedies are subject to a standard of due diligence, apply to the defense and the prosecution equally, and are intended to be reciprocal. Once discovery is initiated by demand of the defendant, all parties have a continuing duty to supplement their disclosures.

(B) **Discovery: Right to Copy or Photograph.** Upon receipt of a written demand for discovery by the defendant, and except as provided in division (C), (D), (E), (F), or (J) of this rule, the prosecuting attorney shall provide copies or photographs, or permit counsel for the defendant to copy or photograph, the following items related to the particular case indictment, information, or complaint, and which are material to the preparation of a defense, or are intended for use by the prosecuting attorney as evidence at the trial, or were obtained from or belong to the defendant, within the possession of, or reasonably available to the state, subject to the provisions of this rule:

(1) Any written or recorded statement by the defendant or a co-defendant, including police summaries of such statements, and including grand jury testimony by either the defendant or co-defendant;

(2) Criminal records of the defendant, a co-defendant, and the record of prior convictions that could be admissible under Rule 609 of the Ohio Rules of Evidence of a witness in the state's case-in-chief, or that it reasonably anticipates calling as a witness in rebuttal;

(3) Subject to divisions (D)(4) and (E) of this rule, all laboratory or hospital reports, books, papers, documents, photographs, tangible objects, buildings, or places;

(4) Subject to division (D)(4) and (E) of this rule, results of physical or mental examinations, experiments or scientific tests;

(5) Any evidence favorable to the defendant and material to guilt or punishment;

(6) All reports from peace officers, the Ohio State Highway Patrol, and federal law enforcement agents, provided however, that a document prepared by a person other than the witness testifying will not be considered to be the witness's prior statement for purposes of the cross examination of that particular witness under the Rules of Evidence unless explicitly adopted by the witness;

(7) Any written or recorded statement by a witness in the state's case-in-chief, or that it reasonably anticipates calling as a witness in rebuttal.

(C) **Prosecuting Attorney's Designation of "Counsel Only" Materials.** The prosecuting attorney may designate any material subject to disclosure under this rule as "counsel only" by stamping a prominent notice on each page or thing so designated. "Counsel only" material also includes materials ordered disclosed under division (F) of this rule. Except as otherwise provided, "counsel only" material may not be shown to the defendant or any other person, but may be disclosed only to defense counsel, or the agents or employees of defense counsel, and may not otherwise be reproduced, copied or disseminated in any way. Defense counsel may orally communicate the content of the "counsel only" material to the defendant.

(D) **Prosecuting Attorney's Certification of Nondisclosure.** If the prosecuting attorney does not disclose materials or portions of materials under this rule, the prosecuting attorney shall certify to the court that the prosecuting attorney is not disclosing material or portions of material otherwise subject to disclosure under this rule for one or more of the following reasons:

(1) The prosecuting attorney has reasonable, articulable grounds to believe that disclosure will compromise the safety of a witness, victim, or third party, or subject them to intimidation or coercion;

(2) The prosecuting attorney has reasonable, articulable grounds to believe that disclosure will subject a witness, victim, or third party to a substantial risk of serious economic harm;

(3) Disclosure will compromise an ongoing criminal investigation or a confidential law enforcement technique or investigation regardless of whether that investigation involves the pending case or the defendant;

(4) The statement is of a child victim of sexually oriented offense under the age of thirteen;

(5) The interests of justice require non-disclosure.

Reasonable, articulable grounds may include, but are not limited to, the nature of the case, the specific course of conduct of one or more parties, threats or prior instances of witness tampering or intimidation, whether or not those instances resulted in criminal charges, whether the defendant is pro se, and any other relevant information.

The prosecuting attorney's certification shall identify the nondisclosed material.

(E) **Right of Inspection in Cases of Sexual Assault.**

(1) In cases of sexual assault, defense counsel, or the agents or employees of defense counsel, shall have the right to inspect photographs, results of physical or mental examinations, or hospital reports, related to the indictment, information, or complaint as described in section (B)(3) or (B)(4) of this rule. Hospital records not related to the information, indictment, or complaint are not subject to inspection or disclosure. Upon motion by defendant, copies of the photographs, results of physical or mental examinations, or hospital reports, shall be provided to defendant's expert under seal and under protection from unauthorized dissemination pursuant to protective order.

(2) In cases involving a victim of a sexually oriented offense less than thirteen years of age, the court, for good cause shown, may order the child's statement be provided, under seal and pursuant to protective order from unauthorized dissemination, to defense counsel and the defendant's expert. Notwithstanding any provision to the contrary, counsel for the defendant shall be permitted to discuss the content of the statement with the expert.

(F) **Review of Prosecuting Attorney's Certification of Non-Disclosure.** Upon motion of the defendant, the trial court shall review the prosecuting attorney's decision of nondisclosure or designation of "counsel only" material for abuse of discretion during an *in camera* hearing conducted seven days prior to trial, with counsel participating.

(1) Upon a finding of an abuse of discretion by the prosecuting attorney, the trial court may order disclosure, grant a continuance, or other appropriate relief.

(2) Upon a finding by the trial court of an abuse of discretion by the prosecuting attorney, the prosecuting attorney may file an interlocutory appeal pursuant to division (K) of Rule 12 of the Rules of Criminal Procedure.

(3) Unless, for good cause shown, the court orders otherwise, any material disclosed by court order under this section shall be deemed to be "counsel only" material, whether or not it is marked as such.

(4) Notwithstanding the provisions of (E)(2), in the case of a statement by a victim of a sexually oriented offense less than thirteen years of age, where the trial court finds no abuse of discretion, and the prosecuting attorney has not certified for nondisclosure under (D)(1) or (D)(2) of this rule, or has filed for nondisclosure under (D)(1) or (D)(2) of this rule and the court has found an abuse of discretion in doing so, the prosecuting attorney shall permit defense counsel, or the agents or employees of defense counsel to inspect the statement at that time.

(5) If the court finds no abuse of discretion by the prosecuting attorney, a copy of any discoverable material that was not disclosed before trial shall be provided to the defendant no later than commencement of trial. If the court continues the trial after the disclosure, the testimony of any witness shall be perpetuated on motion of the state subject to further cross-examination for good cause shown.

(G) **Perpetuation of Testimony.** Where a court has ordered disclosure of material certified by the prosecuting attorney under division (F) of this rule, the prosecuting attorney may move the court to perpetuate the testimony of relevant witnesses in a hearing before the court, in which hearing the defendant shall have the right of cross-examination. A record of the witness's testimony shall be made and shall be admissible at trial as part of the state's case in chief, in the event the witness has become unavailable through no fault of the state.

(H) **Discovery: Right to Copy or Photograph.** If the defendant serves a written demand for discovery or any other pleading seeking disclosure of evidence on the prosecuting attorney, a reciprocal duty of disclosure by the defendant arises without further demand by the state. The defendant shall provide copies or photographs, or permit the prosecuting attorney to copy or photograph, the following items related to the particular case indictment, information or complaint, and which are material to the innocence or alibi of the defendant, or are intended for use by the defense as evidence at the trial, or were obtained from or belong to the victim, within the possession of, or reasonably available to the defendant, except as provided in division (J) of this rule:

(1) All laboratory or hospital reports, books, papers, documents, photographs, tangible objects, buildings or places;

(2) Results of physical or mental examinations, experiments or scientific tests;

(3) Any evidence that tends to negate the guilt of the defendant, or is material to punishment, or tends to support an alibi. However, nothing in this rule shall be construed to require the defendant to disclose information that would tend to incriminate that defendant;

(4) All investigative reports, except as provided in division (J) of this rule;

(5) Any written or recorded statement by a witness in the defendant's case-in-chief, or any witness that it reasonably anticipates calling as a witness in surrebuttal.

(I) **Witness List.** Each party shall provide to opposing counsel a written witness list, including names and addresses of any witness it intends to call in its case-in-chief, or reasonably anticipates calling in rebuttal or surrebuttal. The content of the witness list may not be commented upon or disclosed to the jury by opposing counsel, but during argument, the presence or absence of the witness may be commented upon.

(J) **Information Not Subject to Disclosure.** The following items are not subject to disclosure under this rule:

(1) Materials subject to the work product protection. Work product includes, but is not limited to, reports, memoranda, or other internal documents made by the prosecuting attorney or defense counsel, or their agents in connection with the investigation or prosecution or defense of the case;

(2) Transcripts of grand jury testimony, other than transcripts of the testimony of a defendant or co-defendant. Such transcripts are governed by Crim. R. 6;

(3) Materials that by law are subject to privilege, or confidentiality, or are otherwise prohibited from disclosure.

(K) **Expert Witnesses; Reports.** An expert witness for either side shall prepare a written report summarizing the expert witness's testimony, findings, analysis, conclusions, or opinion, and shall include a summary of the expert's qualifications. The written report and summary of qualifications shall be subject to disclosure under this rule no later than twenty-one days prior to trial, which period may be modified by the court for good cause shown, which does not prejudice any other party. Failure to disclose the written report to opposing counsel shall preclude the expert's testimony at trial.

(L) **Regulation of discovery.**

(1) The trial court may make orders regulating discovery not inconsistent with this rule. If at any time during the course of the proceedings it is brought to the attention of the court that a party has failed to comply with this rule or with an order issued pursuant to this rule, the court may order such party to permit the discovery or inspection, grant a continuance, or prohibit the party from introducing in evidence the material not disclosed, or it may make such other order as it deems just under the circumstances.

(2) The trial court specifically may regulate the time, place, and manner of a *pro se* defendant's access to any discoverable material not to exceed the scope of this rule.

(3) In cases in which the attorney-client relationship is terminated prior to trial for any reason, any material that is designated "counsel only", or limited in dissemination by protective order, must be returned to the state. Any work product derived from said material shall not be provided to the defendant.

(M) **Time of motions.** A defendant shall make his demand for discovery within twenty-one days after arraignment or seven days before the date of trial, whichever is earlier, or at such reasonable time later as the court may permit. A party's motion to compel compliance with this rule shall be made no later than seven days prior to trial, or three days after the opposing party provides discovery, whichever is later. The motion shall include all relief sought under this

rule. A subsequent motion may be made only upon showing of cause why such motion would be in the interest of justice.

History: Amended, eff 7-1-10.

NOTES TO DECISIONS

ANALYSIS

Abuse of discretion
Applicability
Child protection agency's records
Co-defendant's statements
Confidential informant
Confrontation rights
Court's discretion to impose sanctions
Cross-examination
Curative instruction
Defendant's oral statements to officer
Defendant's statements to undercover agent
Delayed disclosure of state witness
Demand for discovery
Disclosure by defendant
Disclosure of evidence
Disclosure of testimony
Disclosure of victim's statements
Disclosure of victim's statements to police
Disclosure of witness
Discovery
Discovery violations
Discretion of trial court
Dismissal for failure to comply
Dismissal of charges
Due process
—Access to interviews with victim
—Access to medical records
Excluding defense witness
Exclusion of witness
Exculpatory evidence
Failure to disclose
Failure to disclose defendant's statement
Failure to disclose
Failure to timely disclose expert
Identification evidence
Identity of confidential informant
In camera inspection
In camera inspection of statement
Ineffective assistance of counsel
—Failure to review evidence
—Identification of witnesses
Mistrial
Motion to compel discovery
Officer's notes
Open file discovery
Photographic evidence
Police reports
—Not discoverable
Police reports generally
Prohibition
Prosecutorial misconduct
Rebuttal witness
Rebuttal witnesses
Reports of examination and tests
Restrictions
Sanctions
Speedy trial tolling
State's failure to disclose
Tapes of telephone conversations
Testimony of undisclosed witness
Transcript of computer records
Transcript of conversation

Victim's medical examination
Victim's mother's counseling records
Waiver
Witness list

Abuse of discretion

Defendant was deprived of his due process right to a fair trial by the prosecutor's failure to provide defense counsel evidence of a prior inconsistent statement made by the alleged sexual assault victim, evidence that was exculpatory and material to guilt or punishment. There was a Brady violation because the victim's statement was not disclosed by the prosecution, it was favorable to defendant, and it was material since it could have produced a different outcome and the prior inconsistent statement could have been used to impeach the victim's testimony, under Ohio R. Evid. 613, had it been disclosed to defense counsel. State v. Scheidel, — Ohio App. 3d —, 2006 Ohio 195, 844 N.E. 2d 1248, 2006 Ohio App. LEXIS 166 (Jan. 20, 2006).

Trial court committed an abuse of discretion in failing to hold an in camera inspection of a lead detective's arrest and narrative reports in defendant's criminal matter, as there was no ability to determine if there were inconsistencies between the reports and the detective's testimony for purposes of allowing defense counsel to use the reports for cross-examination, which was error under Ohio R. Crim. P. 16(B)(1)(g). State v. Spraggins, — Ohio App. 3d —, 2006 Ohio 5739, — N.E. 2d —, 2006 Ohio App. LEXIS 5722 (Nov. 2, 2006).

Applicability

Despite a prosecuting attorney's claim that records contained in his file on behalf of a county board of elections were not information subject to discovery in a criminal action which was pending against the board employees pursuant to Ohio R. Crim. P. 16(B), and that the records were not subject to release as "public records" under RC § 149.43 because they were specifically exempt as trial preparation records under § 149.43(A)(4), they were deemed subject to release to the employees with respect to files pertaining to a general election and a recount, as the prosecutor held the records in his capacity as legal counsel for the board of elections, which had authorized release of the records to the employees. As the employees met the necessary showing for their mandamus action under RC § 2731.04, in that they had no adequate legal remedy and they showed their entitlement to the records, the prosecuting attorney was ordered to turn over the requested records to them. State ex rel. Dreamer v. Mason, — Ohio App. 3d —, 2007 Ohio 271, — N.E. 2d —, 2007 Ohio App. LEXIS 249 (Jan. 25, 2007).

Court rejected defendant's contention that the trial court's failure to preserve the written statement of an eyewitness to an assault for purposes of appeal because it contained inconsistent statements ran afoul of Ohio R. Crim. P. 16. Defendant's reliance on Ohio R. Crim. P. 16 was misplaced since defendant's attorney was able to review the eyewitness's entire statement for any inconsistencies; therefore, the trial court was not required to preserve the written statement for appellate review. State v. Barnes, — Ohio App. 3d —, 2006 Ohio 5239, — N.E. 2d —, 2006 Ohio App. LEXIS 5233 (Oct. 5, 2006).

Child protection agency's records

When defendant was prosecuted for rape and unlawful sexual conduct with a minor, and he sought to discover an agency's file regarding the victim, he was not entitled, under Ohio R. Crim. P. 16(B)(2), to (1) a case worker's notes concerning what was said and done, (2) a report detailing interviews with the victim at the police department, and (3) the report of the initial police officer because internal documents made by a prosecuting attorney or his agents in connection with the investigation of a case were not discov-

erable, and this Rule excluded statements made by witnesses to an investigatory agent, and these documents contained no statements by defendant or his co-defendant, no documents material to the preparation of a defense, no prior record of defendant, no reports of examinations or tests, and no evidence favorable to defendant. State v. Donnal, — Ohio App. 3d —, 2007 Ohio 1632, — N.E. 2d —, 2007 Ohio App. LEXIS 1488 (Apr. 9, 2007).

Co-defendant's statements

When defendant was prosecuted for rape and unlawful sexual conduct with a minor, and he sought to discover an agency's file regarding the victim, a suicide note written by the victim's father, who was a co-defendant, was relevant because it related to the victim's alleged abuse, so, pursuant to Ohio R. Crim. P. 16(B)(1)(a)(i), it should have been disclosed. State v. Donnal, — Ohio App. 3d —, 2007 Ohio 1632, — N.E. 2d —, 2007 Ohio App. LEXIS 1488 (Apr. 9, 2007).

Confidential informant

There was no error in the trial court's decision to permit the State to withhold the identity of a confidential informant in defendant's drug trafficking trial, which resulted from defendant's sales of drugs to the confidential informant on two occasions, as the State had filed a discovery compliance statement pursuant to Ohio R. Crim. P. 16 which indicated that it had not disclosed the informant's name due to concerns of physical or substantial economic harm or coercion. State v. Melton, — Ohio App. 3d —, 2007 Ohio 1154, — N.E. 2d —, 2007 Ohio App. LEXIS 1062 (Mar. 14, 2007).

Confrontation rights

Defendant's confrontation rights under U.S. Const. amend. VI and Ohio Const. art. I, § 10 were not violated by the trial court's grant of a protective order to the State pursuant to Ohio R. Crim. P. 16(B)(1)(e), allowing the State not to disclose the names and addresses of two witnesses, as the State showed that the witnesses had an undue risk of harm if their identities were revealed to the defense prior to trial and further, they each testified at trial and were subject to cross-examination, such that defendant was not prejudiced with respect to his ability to defend himself. Defendant had put the word out on the street that he was looking for those two witnesses, he had an extensive and violent criminal history, he was heavily involved in the drug trade, and when he was apprehended he had guns and knives in his possession. State v. McCree, — Ohio App. 3d —, 2007 Ohio 268, — N.E. 2d —, 2007 Ohio App. LEXIS 252 (Jan. 25, 2007).

Court's discretion to impose sanctions

Trial court did not abuse its discretion in simply delaying the testimony of one of the State's witnesses when the State inadvertently omitted the witness's name from the State's witness list since the trial court gave defendant the opportunity for a continuance, which defendant failed to request. There was no evidence of prejudice because defendant's vigorous cross-examination of the witness established that defendant had adequate time to prepare. State v. Brown, — Ohio App. 3d —, 2006 Ohio 129, — N.E. 2d —, 2006 Ohio App. LEXIS 107 (Jan. 13, 2006).

Cross-examination

As a trial cout properly conducted an in camera inspection of a victim's statement pursuant to Ohio R. Crim. P. 16(B)(1)(g) and determined that there were two areas of inconsistencies, which it allowed defendant's counsel to cross-examine the victim on, counsel was not unlawfully prohibited from cross-examining the victim. State v. Quinones, — Ohio App. 3d —, 2007 Ohio 70, — N.E. 2d —, 2007 Ohio App. LEXIS 57 (Jan. 11, 2007).

Curative instruction

Trial court reasonably decided that a curative instruction, rather than a mistrial, was the proper remedy for an inadvertent discovery violation: State v. Person, 174 Ohio App. 3d 287, 2007 Ohio 6869, 881 N.E. 2d 924, 2007 Ohio App. LEXIS 6039 (Dec. 21, 2007).

Defendant's oral statements to officer

Where defendant and a co-defendant gave oral statements to a police detective, which the trial court instructed the State to provide to defendants' counsel, but no such statements were disclosed until testimony during the second day of trial, there was no abuse of discretion under Ohio R. Crim. P. 16(E)(3) in the trial court's admission of the detective's testimony as to the statements made to him, as defense counsel were both aware that the statements had been made, they were given an opportunity prior to trial to question the detective about the statements, and there was no evidence of a willful discovery violation or that the outcome would have been different if the evidence was excluded. State v. Washington, — Ohio App. 3d —, 2006 Ohio 3001, — N.E. 2d —, 2006 Ohio App. LEXIS 2896 (June 15, 2006).

Defendant's statements to undercover agent

Defendant did not show that a prosecutor violated his discovery obligations, under Ohio R. Crim. P. 16(B)(1)(a)(i), by not disclosing an undercover agent's recording of a drug transaction with defendant because the record revealed that the prosecutor made the existence of the recording known over two weeks before trial, the prosecutor was not obligated to provide defense counsel with a copy of it, and nothing showed defense counsel was not given an opportunity to listen to the recording or to copy it. State v. Wood, — Ohio App. 3d —, 2006 Ohio 3781, — N.E. 2d —, 2006 Ohio App. LEXIS 3732 (July 24, 2006).

Delayed disclosure of state witness

Where the State disclosed the names of witnesses it expected to call at trial four days before defendant's criminal trial, and the trial court gave defense counsel time to interview each of the disputed witnesses prior to their taking the stand, the trial court did not abuse its discretion under the circumstances by allowing the witnesses to testify. There was no discovery violation under Ohio R. Crim. P. 16(E)(3) where the State had originally complied with defendant's discovery request and then updated the request as more names became available. State v. Taylor, — Ohio App. 3d —, 2006 Ohio 3019, — N.E. 2d —, 2006 Ohio App. LEXIS 2890 (June 15, 2006).

Demand for discovery

When defendant filed a "praecipe for demand of official oaths and bonds" after he was convicted and sentenced, he did not comply with Ohio R. Crim. P. 47 because it was unclear to whom the motion was addressed and what information and relief he sought, nor, to the extent his motion sought discovery, did he comply with Ohio R. Crim. P. 16(F) because such a motion had to be filed within 21 days after arraignment or seven days before trial, whichever was earlier, rather than after conviction and sentencing. State v. Dallas, — Ohio App. 3d —, 2007 Ohio 1214, — N.E. 2d —, 2007 Ohio App. LEXIS 1144 (Mar. 19, 2007).

Disclosure by defendant

Although the trial court erred in requiring defendant to provide discovery to the State under Ohio R. Crim. P. 16(C) because defendant had not made any discovery requests under Rule 16(B)(1)(c), (d), or (e), where defendant failed to assert that he suffered prejudice as a result thereof, pursuant to Ohio R. App. P. 12(D) there was no cause to reverse the trial court decision. State v. Glick, — Ohio App. 3d —, 2007 Ohio 4104, — N.E. 2d —, 2007 Ohio App. LEXIS 3735 (Aug. 13, 2007).

Disclosure of evidence

There was no error in the trial court's denial of defendant's dismissal motion, as the record supported the determination that the State had complied with defendant's discovery re-

quests pursuant to Ohio R. Crim. P. 16 and under Brady by providing defendant with all of the medical records that it had in its possession relating to the child victim. As an extended period of time passed between defendant's discovery request and his attempt to follow it up with a dismissal motion the week before trial was to commence, it could have been reasonably concluded that defendant was engaged in a delay tactic. State v. Wood, — Ohio App. 3d —, 2007 Ohio 1027, — N.E. 2d —, 2007 Ohio App. LEXIS 954 (Mar. 9, 2007).

When defendant was prosecuted for rape and unlawful sexual conduct with a minor, and he asserted that he was entitled to discover various records about his victim, he could not discover the victim's school records, the file of a county department of job and family services, a sheriff's department files, the files of the Ohio Department of Job and Family Services, health department records, or a hospital file on the victim's sister to the extent those records contained no information relevant to the case, under Ohio R. Evid. 401, because they contained neither information concerning the alleged offenses nor information which could potentially be of consequence to the action. State v. Donnal, — Ohio App. 3d —, 2007 Ohio 1632, — N.E. 2d —, 2007 Ohio App. LEXIS 1488 (Apr. 9, 2007).

State did not fail to provide discovery information required under Ohio R. Crim. P. 16(B)(1)(d) because, while the victim was being treated at the hospital for a drug overdose, she disclosed that she had been raped four months previously. Because the State presented no medical evidence pertaining to the rape, the State did not violate Ohio R. Crim. P. 16(B)(1)(d). State v. Brown, — Ohio App. 3d —, 2006 Ohio 2573, — N.E. 2d —, 2006 Ohio App. LEXIS 2425 (May 25, 2006).

There was no unfair prejudice to defendant and no abuse of discretion in the trial court's admitting the testimony regarding the camouflage bandana because there was no evidence that the State willfully withheld the bandana. The prosecutor represented that the State provided the defense with everything the prosecution had in discovery, and defendant did not argue that the State deliberately violated Ohio R. Crim. P. 16. Even if defendant had been aware of the bandana, and DNA testing had been performed, the presence of any DNA other than defendant's, or the absence of his DNA, would not have been exculpatory because the victim testified that defendant wore a blue bandana. State v. Bates, — Ohio App. 3d —, 2006 Ohio 4146, — N.E. 2d —, 2006 Ohio App. LEXIS 4163 (Aug. 11, 2006).

When, in an aggravated murder case, the prosecution did not disclose that one of its witnesses took a polygraph, this did not violate its disclosure obligations, under Ohio R. Crim. P. 16, because witness polygraphs were not discoverable. State v. Hairston, — Ohio App. 3d —, 2006 Ohio 4925, — N.E. 2d —, 2006 Ohio App. LEXIS 4886 (Sept. 25, 2006).

Disclosure of testimony

When defendant complained, in his prosecution for gross sexual imposition, that it was error to allow a social worker to testify as an expert, if he did not waive any error by failing to object, he could not claim that the testimony was erroneous because the witness did not submit a report prior to trial, under Lorain County, Ohio, Ct. C.P. R. 14.1, because Ohio R. Crim. P. 16 governed discovery in criminal cases, and any contrary provision in a local rule was of no effect. State v. Rivera, — Ohio App. 3d —, 2007 Ohio 2156, — N.E. 2d —, 2007 Ohio App. LEXIS 2030 (May 7, 2007).

Disclosure of victim's statements

Trial court erred when it declined to allow defendant's attorney to review two out of three statements made by the victim of his alleged criminal conduct, as well as one statement of another witness, but it failed to preserve those statements for appellate review pursuant to Ohio R. Crim. P.

16(B)(1)(g). State v. Bullock, — Ohio App. 3d —, 2007 Ohio 4846, — N.E. 2d —, 2007 Ohio App. LEXIS 4335 (Sept. 20, 2007).

When, in a rape case, a transcript of the victim's police interview, which contained the victim's prior inconsistent statements, was not disclosed to the defense until trial, Ohio R. Crim. P. 16(B)()(f) was not violated because the trial court conducted an in camera hearing on the transcript, found the statements were inconsistent, and the defense was allowed to cross-examine the victim about any inconsistency, so the evidence was not material as it did not undermine confidence in the jury's verdict. State v. Chaney, — Ohio App. 3d —, 2006 Ohio 5288, — N.E. 2d —, 2006 Ohio App. LEXIS 5273 (Oct. 10, 2006).

When, in a rape case, a report of the victim's therapist, on which the State relied at sentencing, was not disclosed to the defense, this was not a violation of Ohio R. Crim. P. 16(B)(1)(f) because defendant did not show that the report was material, as parts of the report read into the record at sentencing were damaging to defendant, so confidence in the jury's verdict was not undermined. State v. Chaney, — Ohio App. 3d —, 2006 Ohio 5288, — N.E. 2d —, 2006 Ohio App. LEXIS 5273 (Oct. 10, 2006).

Disclosure of victim's statements to police

Trial court's denial of defendant's motion under Ohio R. Crim. P. 16(B)(1)(a) and (g), seeking disclosure of a police report that contained "statements" of an alleged victim of multiple sexual offenses committed by defendant, and the prosecution's failure to disclose that information, which was Brady material, violated defendant's right to a fair trial under the due process clause of U.S. Const. amend. XIV; the police report contained notes from a detective who interviewed the victim, wherein there were "inconsistent statements" with the victim's trial testimony that could have been used to impeach his version of events and could have resulted in a different trial outcome due to the materiality thereof. State v. Carroll, — Ohio App. 3d —, 2007 Ohio 5313, — N.E. 2d —, 2007 Ohio App. LEXIS 4680 (Sept. 28, 2007).

Disclosure of witness

Trial court did not err in permitting the testimony of the complained of witnesses, who were disclosed seven days before trial, because it afforded defense counsel the opportunity to talk to the State's witness prior to trial in that the veterinary report signed by both witnesses was referenced and made available. Defendant had her own expert veterinarian, who testified as to the cause of death of the dogs and the condition of the dogs in contradiction to the State's witnesses. State v. Martin, — Ohio App. 3d —, — N.E. 2d —, 2007 Ohio App. LEXIS 4339 (Sept. 17, 2007).

As the trial court granted defendant's motion for a witness protection order in part and granted his motion to reactivate discovery pursuant to Ohio R. Crim. P. 16, wherein defendant was advised that the trial court would have to know the identity of his witnesses to protect them, and that their identity would have to be revealed when the matter was tried, there was no abuse of discretion in the trial court's ruling - it acted within its discretion in making its ruling. State v. Anderson, — Ohio App. 3d —, 2007 Ohio 5068, — N.E. 2d —, 2007 Ohio App. LEXIS 4477 (Sept. 27, 2007).

Since it appeared that the State did not intend to willfully surprise defendant when it failed to place one witness's name on the witness list until four days before trial, in that defense counsel was aware of the existence of this eyewitness and his potential testimony through the police report given to counsel by the State, and since the trial court attempted to cure any prejudice caused by the witness testifying by allowing defense counsel an opportunity to interview the witness and prepare for as long as necessary prior to him testifying, the trial court did not abuse its discretion by allowing the witness to testify.

State v. McLeod, — Ohio App. 3d —, 2006 Ohio 7076, — N.E. 2d —, 2006 Ohio App. LEXIS 7004 (Dec. 19, 2006).

Discovery

In a murder prosecution, it was not error for the trial court to decline to require the State to give defendant the tape-recorded statements of witnesses police interviewed, under Ohio R. Crim. P. 16(B)(2) or 16(B)(1)(g), because none of these witnesses testified and their statements were not inconsistent with any previous statements they made, nor were the statements exculpatory, under Ohio R. Crim. P. 16(B)(1)(f). State v. Jenkins, — Ohio App. 3d —, 2006 Ohio 2546, — N.E. 2d —, 2006 Ohio App. LEXIS 2405 (May 12, 2006).

Defendant's claim that his brother's testimony should have been excluded in defendant's criminal trial lacked merit, as defendant's claim that his brother's testimony was "unreliable" dealt with the weight of the evidence and did not warrant exclusion under Ohio R. Evid. 403(A), which dealt with other issues entirely. As there was no indication that any written summary of the brother's statement existed, there was no reason to exclude the statement under Ohio R. Crim. P. 16(B)(1)(a)(ii). State v. Bennett, — Ohio App. 3d —, 2006 Ohio 2757, — N.E. 2d —, 2006 Ohio App. LEXIS 2592 (May 22, 2006).

Discovery violations

Trial court did not abuse its discretion when it refused to either exclude the State's fingerprint evidence or grant the continuance requested by defendant as a sanction for the State's failure to comply with defendant's discovery request. Defendant did not demonstrate that foreknowledge of the fingerprint analysis report would have benefited him in preparing his defense, since he claimed that it was reasonable to find his fingerprints on a plate since he lived in the apartment, and a more timely request could have been made rather than on the day of trial. State v. Mabry, — Ohio App. 3d —, 2007 Ohio 1895, — N.E. 2d —, 2007 Ohio App. LEXIS 1723 (Apr. 20, 2007).

Defendant did not establish that he prejudiced by the trial court's failure to grant a continuance because he had not alleged that the State's failure to respond to his request for discovery was a willful violation of Crim. R. 16 and there was no evidence to indicate that the result of trial would have been different. The trial court conducted numerous pretrials where defendant had the opportunity to examine witnesses and the evidence prior to trial and the State supplied a copy of the police report to defense counsel before trial commenced. State v. Woods, — Ohio App. 3d —, 2007 Ohio 2229, — N.E. 2d —, 2007 Ohio App. LEXIS 2095 (May 10, 2007).

Although the State failed to comply with Ohio R. Crim. P. 16(B)(1), since the knowledge of the detective regarding the videotape of defendant's stop for operating a vehicle while under the influence of alcohol had to be imputed to the State for discovery purposes, such imputed knowledge was not sufficient to constitute a willful violation of the discovery rules. Defendant was not prevented from requesting a continuance to review the tape and obtain an expert and he was not prejudiced by the introduction into evidence of the videotape. State v. Clark, — Ohio App. 3d —, 2007 Ohio 3777, — N.E. 2d —, 2007 Ohio App. LEXIS 3442 (July 26, 2007).

Discretion of trial court

Even if defendant did not receive an actual photograph of a knife that was allegedly seized from the crime scene, there was ample reference to the seized knife within the sheriff's department's report, there was no evidence that the State failed to disclose the existence of the knife, and no evidence that any alleged failure to do so was willful; accordingly, there was no abuse of discretion in the trial court's admission of the knife into evidence. State v. Larger, — Ohio App. 3d —, 2007 Ohio 201, — N.E. 2d —, 2007 Ohio App. LEXIS 192 (Jan. 19, 2007).

Dismissal for failure to comply

Trial court erred by dismissing the complaint with prejudice, based on the state's failure to provide discovery. The prosecutor's motion for a brief continuance so that defense counsel could prepare should have been granted: State v. Johnson, 169 Ohio App. 3d 552, 2006 Ohio 6227, 863 N.E.2d 1088, 2006 Ohio App. LEXIS 6196 (2006).

Dismissal of charges

When defendant was charged with carrying an unregistered handgun, under Cleveland, Ohio, Codified Ordinance § 674.02, it was not error for a trial court to dismiss these charges, under Ohio R. Crim. P. 16(E), because it was shown that defendant had a permit for his handgun which, under Cleveland, Ohio, Codified Ordinance § 674.06, created an exemption from the registration requirement, because he was not a city resident, and it was further shown that arresting officers seized this permit from defendant and this exculpatory information was only disclosed after defendant's repeated requests and a specific instruction by the trial court. City of Cleveland v. Stoutemire, — Ohio App. 3d —, 2007 Ohio 721, — N.E. 2d —, 2007 Ohio App. LEXIS 657 (Feb. 22, 2007).

Trial court's dismissal of charges against defendant due to the State's discovery misconduct in failing to turn over a complete copy of a videotape from a police cruiser to defendant was an abuse of discretion under Ohio R. Crim. P. 16(E)(3) where the State's failure was not willful or intentional because it was unaware that it had not also been provided with a full and complete copy of the tape; however, upon the State's realization of the incompleteness of the tape, its failure to supplement discovery under Rule 16(D) supported a sanction, although under the totality of the circumstances, dismissal was not warranted. State v. Siemer, — Ohio App. 3d —, 2007 Ohio 4600, — N.E. 2d —, 2007 Ohio App. LEXIS 4142 (Sept. 7, 2007).

Trial court abused its discretion when it dismissed the case with prejudice, under the authority of Ohio R. Crim. P. 16(E)(3), because there was no indication that the State's failure to abide by the discovery request and order of the trial court was done willfully or was motivated by bad faith. At the compliance hearing, the State claimed, that despite its best efforts, it was unable to produce the pivotal rent receipt. The trial court's decision to dismiss the indictment went beyond the least severe sanction consistent with the purpose of the rules of discovery. State v. Warfield, — Ohio App. 3d —, 2006 Ohio 96, — N.E. 2d —, 2006 Ohio App. LEXIS 76 (Jan. 12, 2006).

Trial court's grant of defendant's dismissal motion of criminal charges against him due to the State's alleged failure to have preserved evidence was reversible error pursuant to Ohio R. Crim. P. 16(E)(3), as imposition of a discovery sanction without providing the State an opportunity to respond and without an adequate inquiry into the circumstances surrounding the conduct was improper. State v. Palivoda, — Ohio App. 3d —, 2006 Ohio 6494, — N.E. 2d —, 2006 Ohio App. LEXIS 6421 (Dec. 8, 2006).

Due process

Defendant was not denied due process under Ohio Const. art. I, § 10 by the prosecutor's failure to disclose evidence pursuant to Ohio R. Crim. P. 16(B)(1)(f) which was obtained from an interview with the co-defendant, as some of the information obtained was not material to defendant's guilt, and the value of another statement obtained for purposes of impeaching one of the victims of defendant's burglaries was not apparent until trial. Defendant's counsel was not ineffective in violation of U.S. Const. amend. VI in failing to request a continuance or a mistrial in response to the allegedly withheld information, as there was no showing that either such motion was warranted or what purpose would have been served if they were granted. State v. Frock, — Ohio App. 3d —, 2006 Ohio 1254, — N.E. 2d —, 2006 Ohio App. LEXIS 1141 (Mar. 17, 2006).

—Access to interviews with victim

Defendant failed to show that his due process rights under Ohio Const. art. I, § 10 were violated by the State's failure under Ohio R. Crim. P. 16 to disclose DVDs of interviews between the child victim of defendant's sexual offenses and experts, as defendant did not show that the DVDs were favorable to defendant's case and material to his guilt or punishment. Defendant had the written reports and was given additional leeway in questioning on cross-examination for purposes of demonstrating inconsistencies, and the trial court had reviewed the DVDs and the reports and found no inconsistencies of a material nature. State v. Thomas, — Ohio App. 3d —, 2007 Ohio 3466, — N.E. 2d —, 2007 Ohio App. LEXIS 3197 (July 6, 2007).

—Access to medical records

Defendant failed to show that his due process rights under Ohio Const. art. I, § 10 were violated by the State's failure under Ohio R. Crim. P. 16 to have provided him with certain medical records of the victim of his sexual offenses, as he did not show that the alleged medical records were favorable to him and material to his guilt, that they were still in existence, or that there was a reasonable probability that the outcome of the trial court was undermined. State v. Thomas, — Ohio App. 3d —, 2007 Ohio 3466, — N.E. 2d —, 2007 Ohio App. LEXIS 3197 (July 6, 2007).

Excluding defense witness

In a prosecution for unlawful sexual conduct with a minor it was not an abuse of discretion for a trial court to exclude witnesses for both the prosecution and the defense, pursuant to Ohio R. Crim. P. 16(E)(3), because (1) they were disclosed shortly before trial, (2) the trial court inquired into the late disclosures before excluding the witnesses, and (3) exclusion of the defense witness, who purportedly would have testified that he overheard the victim tell her mother that she was not sure if defendant's sexual conduct with her occurred, did not deprive defendant of his right to present a defense, as most of the witness' testimony would have been hearsay. State v. Kelly, — Ohio App. 3d —, 2007 Ohio 124, — N.E. 2d —, 2007 Ohio App. LEXIS 110 (Jan. 16, 2007).

Trial court did balance the State's interest against defendant's Sixth Amendment right to present a defense, as required, before precluding testimony from defendant's mother as a sanction for the discovery violation of failing to list the witness for the prosecution. The trial court noted that the request to continue in order to obtain the mother's testimony was made at the "eleventh hour;" that seventeen witnesses had been subpoenaed, and were prepared to go forward; that defendant had another alibi witness, his grandmother; and that the case against defendant had been pending for six months prior to trial, and that it was somewhat incredible that his own mother had only recalled her testimony, and contacted his counsel, days prior to trial. State v. Cochran, — Ohio App. 3d —, 2007 Ohio 345, — N.E. 2d —, 2007 Ohio App. LEXIS 291 (Jan. 26, 2007).

Trial court did not err in precluding defendant's wife from testifying in defendant's criminal action, as he had failed to provide her name to the State pursuant to Ohio R. Crim. P. 16 prior to trial, and she was present in the courtroom during the presentation of the State's case. There was clearly a possibility of prejudice to the State if she had been allowed to testify under those circumstances. State v. Carey, — Ohio App. 3d —, 2007 Ohio 3073, — N.E. 2d —, 2007 Ohio App. LEXIS 2812 (June 21, 2007).

Exclusion of witness

Pursuant to an analysis under Ohio R. Crim. P. 16 for failure of the State to have disclosed a police officer as a witness until just a few days prior to the scheduled trial date, the trial court's denial of defendant's request to exclude the witness from testifying at trial was proper, as there was no showing by defendant that foreknowledge of the witness would have assisted him in preparing his defense, that the State willfully failed to disclose the witness's identity, or that defendant was prejudiced by the lack of disclosure. It was noted that the police report had been disclosed and it contained the name of the witness. State v. Standen, — Ohio App. 3d —, 2006 Ohio 3344, — N.E. 2d —, 2006 Ohio App. LEXIS 3275 (June 30, 2006).

Exculpatory evidence

State did not violate CrimR 16(B)(1)(f) because the witness's identification testimony was not favorable to defendant; the state complied with CrimR 16(B)(1)(e) by providing defendant with the witness's name and address as a potential witness. Defendant failed to identify anything the state violated by failing to disclose the fact that the witness would identify defendant as having been present at the scene of the shooting. State v. Hayes, — Ohio App. 3d —, 2008 Ohio 16, — N.E. 2d —, 2008 Ohio App. LEXIS 8 (Jan. 4, 2008).

Trial court did not abuse its discretion in overruling defendant's motion for exculpatory evidence because Ohio's rape-shield law, RC § 2907.02(D), prohibited the disclosure of any extrinsic evidence related to past sexual abuse of the victim. The evidence sought by defendant was for the limited purpose of establishing an alternative source of knowledge of sexual functions, in other words, the evidence was sought for impeachment purposes, and that did not come within the exceptions of Ohio's rape-shield statute. State v. Murphy, — Ohio App. 3d —, 2007 Ohio 2068, — N.E. 2d —, 2007 Ohio App. LEXIS 1933 (Apr. 30, 2007).

There was no Brady violation because the alleged inconsistencies in the statements by the five-month-old victim's mother were about issues tangential to the merits of the State's case against defendant and were thus immaterial. The mere possibility that the defense may have used them in an attempt to affect the mother's credibility was not enough to undermine the confidence of defendant's convictions. State v. Hardley, — Ohio App. 3d —, 2007 Ohio 3530, — N.E. 2d —, 2007 Ohio App. LEXIS 3251 (July 12, 2007).

The burden of proving that destroyed evidence was materially exculpatory remains on the defendant where the evidence is destroyed prior to the initiation of criminal proceedings. The rule in State v. Forest only shifts the burden onto the State after a specific discovery request has been made, because that request puts the State on notice that the defendant may have considered the evidence relevant to his defense. State v. Geeslin, — Ohio App. 3d —, 2006 Ohio 1261, — N.E. 2d —, 2006 Ohio App. LEXIS 1162 (Mar. 20, 2006).

Prosecution did not violate Brady by failing to discover or disclose the information as defendant did not demonstrate that the evidence in question, the addresses of the people present at the time of the incident, was material. Because defendant did not provide any indication of the substance of the putative witnesses' testimony, other than to say that they were disinterested, it could not be said that that the disclosure of the putative witnesses' addresses would have resulted in a different outcome at trial. State v. Cunningham, — Ohio App. 3d —, 2006 Ohio 6373, — N.E. 2d —, 2006 Ohio App. LEXIS 6328 (Dec. 5, 2006).

Failure to disclose

Prosecutor did not commit discovery misconduct under Ohio R. Crim. P. 16(B)(1)(e) when he failed to disclose the name of the victim's friend prior to trial, although she was called as a witness, as the friend was unknown to the

prosecutor until defendant provided information regarding her name and role in the incident during the trial; further, the prosecutor had not acted intentionally in failing to disclose evidence and defendant was not prejudiced thereby. State v. West, — Ohio App. 3d —, — N.E. 2d —, 2007 Ohio App. LEXIS 4637 (Sept. 24, 2007).

Failure to disclose defendant's statement

Although a trial court should not have allowed a police officer to testify about a statement that defendant made which the State had failed to disclose in discovery pursuant to Ohio R. Crim. P. 16(B)(1)(a)(ii), such misconduct did not warrant a mistrial, as the trial court gave the jury a curative instruction and directed them to strike and disregard that statement, and defendant was not prejudiced by the admission thereof. State v. Matthews, — Ohio App. 3d —, — N.E. 2d —, 2007 Ohio App. LEXIS 4349 (Sept. 21, 2007).

Although the State failed to disclose a statement that defendant made pursuant to Ohio R. Crim. P. 16(B)(1)(a)(ii) to arresting officers, denying that boots which were tracked from a crime scene to where defendant was found were his, there was no abuse of discretion in the introduction thereof because defendant suffered no prejudice based on the overwhelming evidence against him; the verdict would not have been altered irrespective of whether testimony of defendant's prior statement was admitted or not. State v. Lopez, — Ohio App. 3d —, 2007 Ohio 5473, — N.E. 2d —, 2007 Ohio App. LEXIS 4802 (Oct. 1?, 2007).

In defendant's prosecution for, inter alia, felonious assault, while the State should have produced a statement made by defendant to police when he was arrested, the court found that the failure to disclose was inadvertent and that defendant would have been prejudiced if the jury were permitted to consider the statement; rather than granting a mistrial, the trial court properly gave a curative instruction as a remedy under Ohio R. Crim. P. 16(E). State v. Person, 174 Ohio App. 3d 287, 2007 Ohio 6869, 881 N.E. 2d 924, 2007 Ohio App. LEXIS 6039 (Dec. 21, 2007).

Although the State failed to reduce defendant's statements to writing in the form of a summary and provide it to the defense, as required by Ohio R. Crim. P. 16(B)(1)(a)(ii), the retrial was not barred by double jeopardy because the State did not act with intent to "goad" defendant into asking for a mistrial. The declaration of a mistrial neither impaired defendant's chances for acquittal nor inured to the benefit of the prosecution; the undisclosed statements of defendant tended to incriminate him; and defendant commenced the second trial with the advantage of having already heard the testimony of several of the State's witnesses. State v. Serafini, — Ohio App. 3d —, 2006 Ohio 1187, — N.E. 2d —, 2006 Ohio App. LEXIS 1071 (Mar. 13, 2006).

State committed a discovery violation, in that, although there was nothing in the record suggesting that the State was aware of defendant's nondisclosed statement, the knowledge of the detective, who testified during defendant's prosecution for drug possession that defendant had stated that he had used a crack pipe found near defendant to smoke crack, was imputed to the State, and thus, the State was under the obligation to disclose the statement to defendant. However, the admission of the statement did not constitute reversible error because there was no indication that the prosecution willfully failed to disclose the statement; the disclosure of the information would not have aided defendant's defense, in that he was not prevented from calling other witnesses that were present in the room on the night in question; and defendant was not prejudiced by the admission of the statements, in that there was sufficient circumstantial evidence to convict defendant including evidence that defendant was found sitting at a table with a crack pipe directly in front of him, that the residue in the pipe tested positive for cocaine, and that defendant had been smoking crack for four months and had an addiction.

State v. Muszynec, — Ohio App. 3d —, 2006 Ohio 5444, — N.E. 2d —, 2006 Ohio App. LEXIS 5434 (Oct. 19, 2006).

Failure to disclose

Trial court properly dismissed defendant's indictment as a sanction for the State's discovery violation as an order granting a new trial was law of the case, Ohio R. Crim. P. 33(D) and RC § 2945.82 governed the manner in which the new trial was to be conducted, and the trial court possessed all authority to reopen discovery or to entertain any pretrial motions available at law. The State violated Ohio R. Crim. P. 16(B)(1)(f) in willfully withholding exculpatory material from defendant and defendant's prejudice could not be cured by a new trial as almost 20 years had elapsed, eight witnesses for the defense were deceased, 16 witnesses had unknown addresses, and to present the witnesses' prior testimony would have been useless as none of the witnesses had been questioned about the exculpatory evidence. State v. Larkins, — Ohio App. 3d —, 2006 Ohio 90, — N.E. 2d —, 2006 Ohio App. LEXIS 80 (Jan. 12, 2006).

Failure to timely disclose expert

Because defendant conceded that the State's failure to timely disclose an expert as a witness was not willful, there was no indication that knowledge of the witness's identity would have aided in the defense or that defendant was prejudiced by not knowing her identity before trial, defendant did not show that he was unfairly surprised by the testimony, and defense counsel declined the trial court's offer for an overnight continuance in order to prepare questioning on the witness's testing methodology, the trial court did not abuse its discretion in permitting the testimony of the expert. State v. Horton, — Ohio App. 3d —, 2006 Ohio 3736, — N.E. 2d —, 2006 Ohio App. LEXIS 3680 (July 20, 2006).

Identification evidence

During defendant's trial for aggravated robbery and other crimes, the State did not violate Crim. R. 16(B)(1)(f) in failing to disclose that a victim had made two out-of-court photo identifications of defendant because the identifications were not favorable to defendant or material to his guilt or punishment; the State did not rely on the identifications at trial, and the victim's in-court identification of defendant was cumulative to other in-court identifications and testimony. State v. Wilson, — Ohio App. 3d —, 2006 Ohio 5253, — N.E. 2d —, 2006 Ohio App. LEXIS 5212 (Oct. 5, 2006).

During defendant's trial for aggravated robbery and other crimes, even if the State's failure to disclose that a victim made two out-of-court identifications of defendant violated Crim. R. 16(B)(1)(f), the trial court's denial of defendant's motion to strike the victim's testimony was not an abuse of discretion. Prior knowledge of the identifications would not have benefited defendant in preparing his defense, the State's withholding of the information was not willful because the victim did not make the first identification until the day of a hearing on defendant's motion to suppress photo identifications, defendant was not unfairly prejudiced by the out-of-court identifications because the victim positively identified him at trial, and the victim's in-court identification was cumulative to other witnesses' identifications. State v. Wilson, — Ohio App. 3d —, 2006 Ohio 5253, — N.E. 2d —, 2006 Ohio App. LEXIS 5212 (Oct. 5, 2006).

Identity of confidential informant

State was properly ordered to reveal the identity of a confidential informant to defendant because the informant had told the trial judge that the landlord of the apartment where a large quantity of drugs were found, in connection with which defendant's charges of drug trafficking and drug possession arose, had told him the location of hidden marijuana, offering to pay him $10,000 to retrieve the marijuana. This information could be helpful to defendant in defending against the charge of possession since the landlord's knowl-

edge of the specific location of the hidden marijuana could be interpreted as tending to show that the landlord was the person who actually possessed the marijuana. State v. Perez, — Ohio App. 3d —, 2006 Ohio 1262, — N.E. 2d —, 2006 Ohio App. LEXIS 1159 (Mar. 20, 2006).

In camera inspection

Trial court did not abuse its discretion when it granted defendant, after an in camera inspection, access to some but not all of the agency records regarding possible abuse by the victim of her children because the unreleased records did not contain information that was either material to defendant's defense or otherwise favorable to defendant. That included inconsistent statements or other information that defendant could have used to impeach the victim's daughter. State v. Moore, — Ohio App. 3d —, 2007 Ohio 3600, — N.E. 2d —, 2007 Ohio App. LEXIS 3306 (July 16, 2007).

Because the police officer's report was an investigative report and not a witness statement, Ohio R. Crim. P. 16(B)(1)(g) was not applicable and an in camera review of the report was not required. State v. Priest, — Ohio App. 3d —, 2007 Ohio 5958, — N.E. 2d —, 2007 Ohio App. LEXIS 5225 (Nov. 8, 2007).

In camera inspection of statement

Trial court gave defense counsel an opportunity to inspect the statements of all witnesses who had given written out-of-court statements and defense counsel reviewed the statements and then stated that he declined their use for cross-examination. Having given defense counsel an opportunity to review the statements in their entirety, there was no requirement that the trial court preserve the statements in the record. State v. Walker, — Ohio App. 3d —, 2007 Ohio 3772, — N.E. 2d —, 2007 Ohio App. LEXIS 3437 (July 26, 2007).

Defendant did not show his counsel provided ineffective assistance by not properly asserting Ohio R. Crim. P. 16(B)(1)(g), regarding receiving a prosecution witness's prior inconsistent statements for cross-examination purposes, because counsel did assert this Rule, even though he did not formally participate in the trial court's examination of the statements, and received the statements to use in cross examination. State v. Grimes, — Ohio App. 3d —, 2006 Ohio 2144, — N.E. 2d —, 2006 Ohio App. LEXIS 1983 (May 1, 2006).

When defendant sought an in camera inspection of parts of police reports which were not disclosed to him, under Ohio R. Crim. P. 16(B)(1)(g), no such inspection was required because these parts of the reports were not discoverable, as they recited matters beyond a witness's personal observations and were privileged, under Ohio R. Crim. P. 16(B)(2). State v. Villa, — Ohio App. 3d —, 2006 Ohio 4529, — N.E. 2d —, 2006 Ohio App. LEXIS 4522 (Sept. 5, 2006).

When defendant alleged a testifying officer's police report contained statements inconsistent with his testimony, and the trial court conducted an in camera inspection of the report, pursuant to Ohio R. Crim. P. 16(B)(1)(g), defendant was not entitled to a copy of the report because the trial court found that it did not contain inconsistent statements, nor was the trial court's failure to make the report part of the appellate record reversible error, as defendant did not ask that it be preserved or object to a failure to preserve it, and he did not show that he was prejudiced. State v. Doyle, — Ohio App. 3d —, 2006 Ohio 5373, — N.E. 2d —, 2006 Ohio App. LEXIS 5346 (Oct. 16, 2006).

Ineffective assistance of counsel

Defendant's right to effective assistance of counsel under U.S. Const. amend. VI and Ohio Const. amend. I, § 10 was not violated by his counsel's alleged failure to comply with the reciprocal discovery rule, whereupon defendant's failure to have disclosed a coat that he was wearing on the night of a criminal attack resulted in the trial court's exclusion of the coat from trial pursuant to Ohio R. Crim. P. 16(C)(1)(a) and (E)(3), as there was no showing that the results of the trial would have been different even if trial counsel had complied with the discovery rule; the jury did not believe that defendant had acted in self-defense and accordingly, whether the jacket which allegedly had blood all over it was introduced for purposes of showing that defendant was being attacked or not, the evidence did not support a finding that defendant was provoked to the point of warranting his use of deadly force against the victim. State v. Briggs, — Ohio App. 3d —, 2006 Ohio 5144, — N.E. 2d —, 2006 Ohio App. LEXIS 5108 (Oct. 2, 2006).

As a photograph was properly admitted by the State in defendant's criminal trial, pursuant to Ohio R. Crim. P. 16(E)(3), defendant's counsel did not provide ineffective assistance in violation of defendant's rights under U.S. Const. amend. VI and Ohio Const. art. I, § 10 by failing to object thereto. There was no showing that the State's failure to disclose the photograph was a willful violation of Ohio R. Crim. P. 16, there was no showing how foreknowledge of the non-disclosed photograph would have benefited defendant, and there was no prejudicial effect on defendant by admission, as it was a true representation of defendant's appearance at the time of the criminal incident. State v. Blacker, — Ohio App. 3d —, 2006 Ohio 5214, — N.E. 2d —, 2006 Ohio App. LEXIS 5170 (Oct. 2, 2006).

—Failure to review evidence

Defendant's counsel was not ineffective under U.S. Const. amend. VI in failing to review a tape of a witness's statement given to prosecutors while the witness was in jail on unrelated charges pursuant to Ohio R. Crim. P. 16, as the outcome of the trial could not have been affected because the trial court judge had listened to it and determined that nothing could have been used for purposes of cross-examination, as there were no significant discrepancies between the witness's statements thereon and his trial testimony. State v. Swann, 171 Ohio App. 3d 304, 2007 Ohio 2010, 870 N.E.2d 754, 2007 Ohio App. LEXIS 1780 (2007).

—Identification of witnesses

In a prosecution for unlawful sexual conduct with a minor in which defendant's proposed witness was excluded, under Ohio R. Crim. P. 16(E)(3), because the witness was not revealed until a few days before trial, counsel did not provide ineffective assistance by not revealing the witness because counsel did not know about the witness until shortly before revealing the witness. State v. Kelly, — Ohio App. 3d —, 2007 Ohio 124, — N.E. 2d —, 2007 Ohio App. LEXIS 110 (Jan. 16, 2007).

Mistrial

In a case where defendant contended that the State failed to disclose a DNA report and cell phone records, the severe remedy of a mistrial was not required. There was no abuse of discretion in the trial court's remedy concerning the phone records, as the trial court gave defense counsel an entire evening to review the phone records, and the court gave defense counsel a recess to review the DNA report; following the recess, counsel stated that counsel was not seeking a sanction against the State. State v. Gibson, — Ohio App. 3d —, 2007 Ohio 3345, — N.E. 2d —, 2007 Ohio App. LEXIS 3076 (July 2, 2007).

Denial of defendant's motion for a mistrial was proper because the State provided the defense witness's statement to defendant before the witness was called to testify and, while defendant could have requested a recess or a continuance in order to confer with the witness prior to his taking the stand, defendant did not do so but chose instead to move for a mistrial. Further, the witness's testimony did not differ from his statement; in both his statement to the police and at trial, the witness identified his other friend as the assailant, rather than defendant. State v. Schenker, — Ohio App. 3d —, 2007 Ohio 3732, — N.E. 2d —, 2007 Ohio App. LEXIS 3415 (July 19, 2007).

Trial court did not abuse its discretion in denying the motion for a mistrial based on the State's failure to disclose defendant's statements to intake personnel, in violation of Ohio R. Crim. P. 16, because the State had already adduced evidence that defendant had been belligerent after her arrest and thus, to the extent that the challenged statements tended to demonstrate that defendant had been drunk and belligerent, they were cumulative to other evidence. Given the strength of the State's case, the challenged statements could not be said to have changed the outcome of the trial since as already described, the State presented compelling evidence that she had been intoxicated and that her intoxication had led to the victims' deaths. In the context of the entire proceedings, her belligerence toward the intake person was inconsequential. State v. Weir, — Ohio App. 3d —, 2006 Ohio 4127, — N.E. 2d —, 2006 Ohio App. LEXIS 4053 (Aug. 11, 2006).

Motion to compel discovery

There was no error in the trial court's denial of defendant's motion to compel discovery in a timely fashion because the record indicated that the State provided defendant with the requested discovery several months prior to trial. Defendant did not file his motion to compel regarding the discovery at issue until the day before the victim was scheduled to be deposed, and only then requested that discovery be complete well in advance to the date of the victim's deposition. State v. Rogers, — Ohio App. 3d —, 2007 Ohio 1890, — N.E. 2d —, 2007 Ohio App. LEXIS 1745 (Apr. 23, 2007).

Officer's notes

Trial court properly declined to review in an in camera inspection the reporting officer's notes regarding the victim's allegations, under Ohio R. Crim. P. 16(B)(1)(g), because it was not a statement by the victim, but rather the reporting officer's interpretations and interpolations. State v. Valenzona, — Ohio App. 3d —, 2007 Ohio 6892, — N.E. 2d —, 2007 Ohio App. LEXIS 6002 (Dec. 20, 2007).

Open file discovery

Ohio R. Crim. P. 16(B)(1)(b) requires a prosecutor to "furnish" defendant a copy of her prior criminal record, and this section (along with the witness list section) does not mention that the State can merely permit the defendant to inspect and copy, as Ohio R. Crim. P. 16(B)(1)(a), (c) and (d) allow, so use of the word "furnish" places an affirmative duty on the prosecutor to produce and hand over, rather than allowing reliance on open file discovery. State v. Donkers, 170 Ohio App. 3d 509, 2007 Ohio 1557, 867 N.E.2d 903, 2007 Ohio App. LEXIS 1424 (2007).

Although a witness statement from a civil deposition would not have been disclosed to the State pursuant to Ohio R. Crim. P. 16, where both parties agreed to an open discovery management plan pursuant to Montgomery County, Ohio, Ct. C.P. R. 3.03(I)(D)(2)(f), defendant was obligated to disclose that information to the State and where he did not disclose it, the trial court did not err in excluding the evidence. Although the statement was intended to be used by defendant to show that another individual who was riding in defendant's car at the time that it went off a road had indicated that he was driving at the time, the statement was admitted through testimony of another witness who heard it. State v. Flanigan, — Ohio App. 3d —, 2007 Ohio 3158, — N.E. 2d —, 2007 Ohio App. LEXIS 2909 (June 22, 2007).

Photographic evidence

Defendant's claim that prosecutorial misconduct resulted from the failure to have disclosed photographs of the damage to motor vehicles prior to trial lacked merit, as his own counsel objected to the photographs and the objection was sustained, such that the photographs were not used at trial. Moreover, the photographs were made available to defendant prior to trial pursuant to Ohio R. Crim. P. 16, but as they were not actually used in evidence, they had no impact on the trial. State v. Nottingham, — Ohio App. 3d —, 2007 Ohio 3040, — N.E. 2d —, 2007 Ohio App. LEXIS 2878 (June 13, 2007).

In defendant's prosecution for raping his daughter and pandering obscenity involving a minor, in which videos defendant took of his encounters with his daughter were provided to the defense, photographs captured from those videos were discreet, discoverable, evidence which the State was obligated to provide to the defense, under Ohio R. Crim. P. 16(B), even though it had provided the videos, but its failure to do so was not willful, as it only learned of the photographs immediately before a witness testified about them, and defendant's failure to seek a continuance showed that he was not prejudiced by the late production of this evidence. State v. Heilman, — Ohio App. 3d —, 2006 Ohio 1680, — N.E. 2d —, 2006 Ohio App. LEXIS 1538 (Mar. 31, 2006).

Defendant was not prejudiced by the State's failure to provide the complete file names for the child pornography images because the State's failure to provide the complete file names was not deliberate, the State learned of the difference between the exhibit and the images from defendant's expert at trial, foreknowledge of the difference would not have benefited defendant in the preparation of his case, the trial court found defendant not guilty of the counts that were based on the four images. State v. Taylor, — Ohio App. 3d —, 2006 Ohio 6813, — N.E. 2d —, 2006 Ohio App. LEXIS 6748 (Dec. 22, 2006).

Police reports

When defendant was prosecuted for rape and unlawful sexual conduct with a minor, and he sought to discover an agency's file regarding the victim, police reports in that file which were not signed by witnesses were statements under Ohio R. Crim. P. 16(B)(1)(g) which merely stated what officers remembered a witness stating, and they were not discoverable under Ohio R. Crim. P. 16(B)(1) because they contained no information which was either material to the preparation of a defense or favorable to defendant. State v. Donnal, — Ohio App. 3d —, 2007 Ohio 1632, — N.E. 2d —, 2007 Ohio App. LEXIS 1488 (Apr. 9, 2007).

Trial court did not err when it overruled defendant's motion for a new trial because, other than his bare assertion, defendant failed to provide any evidence that the police department incident report was not included in the State's discovery materials. More importantly, defendant did not even attempt to provide any evidence that clearly and convincingly demonstrated that he was prevented from or otherwise unable to procure the incident report within 120 days of his guilty verdict. State v. Greenwood, — Ohio App. 3d —, 2007 Ohio 4202, — N.E. 2d —, 2007 Ohio App. LEXIS 3787 (Aug. 17, 2007).

—Not discoverable

Summary denial of an untimely post-conviction relief petition was proper where, while the petition alleged that defense counsel was ineffective for failing to discover a police report containing inconsistent dates and times relating to the rape charges, police reports were not discoverable under Ohio R. Crim. P. 16(B)(2) and so counsel's failure to obtain the police report was not deficient. State v. Bluford, — Ohio App. 3d —, 2006 Ohio 2217, — N.E. 2d —, 2006 Ohio App. LEXIS 2057 (May 4, 2006).

Police reports generally

Due process was not violated by the State's failure to disclose a police report during defendant's trial for robbery and other crimes because defendant did not show that the police report was material to his guilt or his punishment. The report was not discoverable as inconsistent with the victim's trial testimony under Ohio R. Crim. P. 16(B)(1)(g) because information in the report that the victim refused medical treatment did not indicate that she sustained no injury when defendant attacked her, and any distinction between injury necessitating medical treatment and the level of injury necessary to sustain his conviction for second-degree robbery under RC § 2911.02(A)(2) was irrelevant because no showing of serious injury was required. State v. Thomas, — Ohio App. 3d —, 2006 Ohio 6588, — N.E. 2d —, 2006 Ohio App. LEXIS 6494 (Dec. 14, 2006).

Prohibition

Court did not address a county prosecutor's jurisdictional claim that a common pleas court judge abused her discretion in issuing a pretrial discovery order under Ohio R. Crim. P. 16 compelling the prosecutor to provide all police reports and witness statements to criminal defense counsel because the court's duty in writ of prohibition cases was limited to determining whether jurisdiction was patently and unambiguously lacking. State Ex Rel. Mason v. Burnside, 117 Ohio St. 3d 1, 2007 Ohio 6754, 881 N.E. 2d 224, 2007 Ohio LEXIS 3332 (Dec. 20, 2007).

Prosecutorial misconduct

Defendant, who was convicted of, inter alia, operating a vehicle under the influence of alcohol, did not show defendant was entitled to a new trial under Ohio R. Crim. P. 33(A)(6) due to the prosecutor's failure to disclose, under Ohio R. Crim. P. 16(B)(1)(c), certain tangible evidence in the prosecutor's possession, including keys to the involved vehicle, ignition, and an empty beer keg, because defendant did not object to admission of the evidence at trial, waiving all but plain error, under Ohio R. Crim. P. 52(B), and there was no plain error because (1) it was not shown that the prosecutor's failure to disclose was willful, and (2) defendant did not show that defendant was prejudiced. State v. Cummings, — Ohio App. 3d —, 2007 Ohio 4970, — N.E. 2d —, 2007 Ohio App. LEXIS 4386 (Sept. 24, 2007).

When defendant, who was convicted of, inter alia, operating a vehicle under the influence of alcohol, alleged the prosecutor violated Ohio R. Crim. P. 16(B)(1)(f) by not informing defendant that the vehicle involved in the crime had been destroyed, this claim was not sustained because the language of Rule 16(B)(1)(f) created a prosecutorial duty that was coextensive with the duty created under Brady, so, once it was determined that no Brady violation occurred, because no exculpatory evidence was concealed, no violation of Rule 16(B)(1)(f) could be found. State v. Cummings, — Ohio App. 3d —, 2007 Ohio 4970, — N.E. 2d —, 2007 Ohio App. LEXIS 4386 (Sept. 24, 2007).

There was no Brady violation and thus, no prosecutorial misconduct because defendant failed to prove that the prosecutor failed to disclose evidence upon request, pursuant to Ohio R. Crim. P. 16 (B)(1)(f), because the prosecutor did disclose the evidence two days before trial, five days after the request was made. State v. Duffy, — Ohio App. 3d —, 2006 Ohio 2724, — N.E. 2d —, 2006 Ohio App. LEXIS 2578 (June 1, 2006).

Trial court did not abuse its discretion in denying defendant's motion for a mistrial based on alleged misconduct by the prosecution during her trial on charges for driving under the influence because the fact that the prosecutor made reference to "divided attention skills tests" did not lead to a conclusion that the trial court abused its discretion in denying the motion for mistrial. Further, because the alleged exculpatory material was presented during trial, and defendant's counsel first referenced the station videotape and the booking photograph during his cross-examination of the police officer, defense counsel had actual knowledge of the items at issue and the element of surprise was totally absent and thus, there existed no Brady violation requiring a new trial. State v. Albanese, — Ohio App. 3d —, 2006 Ohio 4819, — N.E. 2d —, 2006 Ohio App. LEXIS 4724 (Sept. 15, 2006).

Rebuttal witness

Trial court did not abuse its discretion when it allowed the State to recall a defense witness pursuant to Evid. R. 611 and Crim. R. 16 where it discovered new evidence that contradicted her testimony regarding having worked for defendant until a particular period of time. Although she had not been listed as a witness for the State, the rebuttal testimony was proper where the State could not have known earlier that it would find evidence to contradict her testimony. State v. Burneson, — Ohio App. 3d —, 2007 Ohio 4037, — N.E. 2d —, 2007 Ohio App. LEXIS 3675 (Aug. 9, 2007).

State did not violate Ohio R. Crim. P. 16 when it failed to disclose that it intended to call a scoring official at a youth athletic event to testify as a rebuttal witness in defendant's criminal trial, as defendant had been informed that the official would be called to testify at trial and she did, in fact, testify in the State's case-in-chief. The State was not required to provide more detail regarding her testimony than that she was going to testify at trial. City of Urbana v. Locke, — Ohio App. 3d —, 2006 Ohio 6606, — N.E. 2d —, 2006 Ohio App. LEXIS 6518 (Dec. 8, 2006).

Rebuttal witnesses

In a marijuana trafficking prosecution, a prosecutor did not violate Ohio R. Crim. P. 16(B)(1)(e) by calling, as a rebuttal witness, the supervisor of an undercover agent involved in the case to testify that the agent had not tested positive for drugs, even though the supervisor had not been listed as a possible witness, because (1) the prosecutor could not reasonably anticipate that defendant would contest the agent's claim that, when the agent was interacting with defendant, the agent simulated the smoking of a marijuana cigarette, making testing showing that the agent did not test positive for marijuana relevant, and (2) the supervisor's testimony would not likely have been admissible in the prosecutor's case-in-chief, under Ohio R. Evid. 608(A)(2), because the agent's credibility had not been challenged. State v. Wood, — Ohio App. 3d —, 2006 Ohio 3781, — N.E. 2d —, 2006 Ohio App. LEXIS 3732 (July 24, 2006).

Reports of examination and tests

There was no error in ruling that there was no written report to provide to defendant and that, therefore, there was no violation of Ohio R. Crim. P. 16(B)(1)(d). The evidence revealed that there was no written report or opinion by the State's medical expert, as he testified from the medical reports in his possession; defendant had the medical records the expert relied upon during his testimony. State v. Marshall, — Ohio App. 3d —, 2007 Ohio 1686, — N.E. 2d —, 2007 Ohio App. LEXIS 1538 (Apr. 3, 2007).

There was no violation by the prosecutor of Ohio R. Crim. P. 16(B)(1)(d), as it made doctor reports regarding a victim's physical condition available to defendant, and the fact that the doctor's testimony varied from the written report he submitted during discovery was due to the doctor's examination of photographs two weeks after the report was submitted, which indicated new information to him; further, defendant's counsel had access to the same photographs prior to trial. State v. West, — Ohio App. 3d —, — N.E. 2d —, 2007 Ohio App. LEXIS 4637 (Sept. 24, 2007).

When, in a drug prosecution, the State did not provide the defense with a report analyzing drugs upon which certain charges were based, the State violated the State's discovery obligations, and it was error to deny defendant a requested continuance, under Ohio R. Crim. P. 16(E)(3), because (1) foreknowledge of the report would have assisted defendant, (2) defendant's entrapment defense did not render the report irrelevant, (3) the report was critical, and (4) defendant's inability to meaningfully contest the report was prejudicial. Ohio v. Bowshier, — Ohio App. 3d —, 2007 Ohio 5364, — N.E. 2d —, 2007 Ohio App. LEXIS 4730 (Oct. 5, 2007).

Restrictions

Restrictions by the trial court on defendant's discovery and inspection of the images on his computer, which was seized by the State with respect to criminal charges arising from his pornographic images of children thereon, were within the trial court's discretion pursuant to Ohio R. Crim. P. 16(B)(1)(c) and (E). Defendant failed to make a particularized showing that the restrictions were not appropriate, and they had been imposed to protect the images of the children that were contained therein. State v. Gillingham, — Ohio App. 3d —, 2006 Ohio 5758, — N.E. 2d —, 2006 Ohio App. LEXIS 5738 (Oct. 27, 2006).

Sanctions

Trial court did not abuse its discretion when it excluded one of the state's witnesses and three of its four documents. The state had more than three months to respond to the discovery request and motion to compel, and the sanction was reasonably related to the noncompliant conduct: State v. Jones, 183 Ohio App. 3d 189, 2009 Ohio 2381, 916 N.E.2d 828, 2009 Ohio App. LEXIS 2009 (2009).

Where the state was unreasonably prejudiced in its ability to secure an expert to evaluate and respond to the proposed expert testimony, the court did not abuse its discretion by excluding the testimony of a defense expert as a sanction for the defendant's failure to make timely disclosure: State v. Weaver, 178 Ohio App. 3d 504, 2008 Ohio 5022, 898 N.E.2d 1023, 2008 Ohio App. LEXIS 4242 (2008).

Trial court's grant of additional time during trial for defendant and his counsel to review medical records that had not been previously disclosed by the prosecution was a proper cure for the discovery violation pursuant to Ohio R. Crim. P. 16(E)(3), and as defendant failed to indicate that he was prejudiced, there was no abuse of discretion by the trial court. State v. Bennett, — Ohio App. 3d —, 2006 Ohio 2757, — N.E. 2d —, 2006 Ohio App. LEXIS 2592 (May 22, 2006).

Where the trial court never determined whether the State failed to comply with defendant's discovery request pursuant to Ohio R. Crim. P. 16(B)(1)(g) for production of statements of two witnesses for the State, the trial court did not err in denying defendant's motion for sanctions, including a mistrial or exclusion of the witness testimony, pursuant to Rule 16(E)(3), as the sanctions allowed therein were only trigged upon a determination that there was a failure to comply. It was noted that the State had indicated that it did not believe that such statements were in fact in existence, and there was no cause to grant a new trial or mistrial pursuant to Ohio R. Crim. P. 33(E)(3), as defendant failed to show that he was prejudiced. State v. Scott, — Ohio App. 3d —, 2006 Ohio 3527, — N.E. 2d —, 2006 Ohio App. LEXIS 3479 (June 29, 2006).

Speedy trial tolling

Failure of a criminal defendant to respond within a reasonable time to a prosecution request for reciprocal discovery constitutes neglect that tolls the running of speedy-trial time pursuant to RC § 2945.72(D). The tolling of statutory speedy-trial time based on a defendant's neglect in failing to respond within a reasonable time to a prosecution request for discovery is not dependent upon the filing of a motion to compel discovery by the prosecution. A trial court shall determine the date by which a defendant should reasonably have responded to a reciprocal discovery request based on the totality of facts and circumstances of the case, including the time established for response by local rule, if applicable. State v. Palmer, 112 Ohio St. 3d 457, 2007 Ohio 374, 860 N.E.2d 1011, 2007 Ohio LEXIS 327 (2007).

State's failure to disclose

State did not fail to comply with its discovery requirements since it had no advance knowledge that the witness was the person making the call to the victim at the time of the incident and defendant did not show that the State was under any further obligation to investigate, nor did he show any intentional acts on the part of the State. There was also nothing in the record reflecting that the State intentionally failed to disclose the witness because the prosecutor indicated, and the trial court noted, that the State did not learn of the witness's identity until the day of trial, at which time it promptly notified the defense that it intended to call the witness. State v. Adams, — Ohio App. 3d —, 2006 Ohio 1761, — N.E. 2d —, 2006 Ohio App. LEXIS 1625 (Mar. 31, 2006).

Trial court's decision to exclude a letter written by the victim of defendant's inappropriate sexual conduct in defendant's criminal trial due to the State's failure to have disclosed it to defendant, pursuant to Ohio R. Crim. P. 16(E)(3), and thereafter the decision to allow some testimony that the victim wrote a letter about the incident and that this was the method that the victim chose to divulge the information to her mother, was not error, as defendant did not seek a continuance to address the admission for the limited purpose, the contents of the letter were never admitted, and the outcome of the trial would not clearly have been otherwise. State v. Carnes, — Ohio App. 3d —, 2006 Ohio 2134, — N.E. 2d —, 2006 Ohio App. LEXIS 1974 (May 1, 2006).

Tapes of telephone conversations

Since defendant did not object based on lack of discovery, and he never informed the trial court that the State did not comply with the discovery request for a second copy of the CDs (of recorded telephone conversations), the trial court did not have a duty to inquire about whether the State had provided the requested discovery. The State's discovery compliance filed with the trial court on indicated that the State did in fact comply with the requested discovery. State v. Jones, — Ohio App. 3d —, 2006 Ohio 5147, — N.E. 2d —, 2006 Ohio App. LEXIS 5111 (Oct. 2, 2006).

Testimony of undisclosed witness

Trial court's decision to allow the State to present an undisclosed witness as a rebuttal witness did not qualify as an abuse of discretion or, otherwise, as reversible error because defendant introduced new evidence in that he indicated that a former employee of the dairy, picked him up in the delivery truck and asked him to help move furniture in Indiana; the State introduced the employee's testimony to rebut defendant's contention. The State could not have reasonably anticipated that defendant's counsel would ask the delivery truck's owner whether he had employed someone named Larry and that defendant would indicate that a man named Larry had asked him to go to Indiana in the stolen delivery truck. State v. Mossburg, — Ohio App. 3d —, 2007 Ohio 3343, — N.E. 2d —, 2007 Ohio App. LEXIS 3070 (July 2, 2007).

Trial court did not abuse its discretion when it admitted the testimony of a State witness who was not disclosed to defendant, as there was no showing that the prosecutor willfully violated Ohio R. Crim. P. 16, any foreknowledge that such witness was going to testify would not have assisted defendant in the preparation of his defense as the witness's testimony was cumulative to that of his wife's, and there was no showing that the admission of the testimony caused prejudice to defendant. State v. Hamilton, — Ohio App. 3d —, 2006 Ohio 1949, — N.E. 2d —, 2006 Ohio App. LEXIS 1789 (Apr. 20, 2006).

Transcript of computer records

Pursuant to a CrimR 16(B)(1)(c) discovery request, when a prosecutor has provided a written transcript that purports to accurately reflect data stored on a computer hard drive, a court may not order an examination of the computer hard drive unless the defense makes a prima facie showing that the state has provided false, incomplete, adulterated, or spoliated evidence: State v. Rivas, 121 Ohio St. 3d 469, 2009 Ohio 1354, 905 N.E.2d 618, 2009 Ohio LEXIS 861 (2009).

Transcript of conversation

Where there is direct evidence of a conversation allegedly constituting the crime with which a defendant is charged, the right to a fair trial includes the right of the defendant to some reasonable means of verifying that a purported transcript of the conversation, prepared from the direct evidence by the adverse party, is accurate and complete. The trial court had an obligation to conduct an in camera review of the accuracy of the copied records. Forcing a litigant to rely on an adverse party's representation that a transcript from a hard drive is accurate is inconsistent with due process when the accuracy can be directly verified: State v. Rivas, 172 Ohio App. 3d 473, 2007 Ohio 3593, 875 N.E.2d 655, 2007 Ohio App. LEXIS 3299 (2007).

Victim's medical examination

When defendant was prosecuted for rape and unlawful sexual conduct with a minor, a medical report concerning a sexual abuse examination of the victim was discoverable pursuant to Ohio R. Crim. P. 16(B)(1)(d). State v. Donnal, — Ohio App. 3d —, 2007 Ohio 1632, — N.E. 2d —, 2007 Ohio App. LEXIS 1488 (Apr. 9, 2007).

Victim's mother's counseling records

When defendant was prosecuted for rape and unlawful sexual conduct with a minor, records of the victim's mother's counseling were not discoverable, under Ohio R. Crim. P. 16, because they contained no statements by any witnesses, made only a passing mention of the victim's sexual abuse, did not refer to defendant, his trial, or his alleged acts, so they could not possibly have any effect on the defense strategy and were not favorable to the defense. State v. Donnal, — Ohio App. 3d —, 2007 Ohio 1632, — N.E. 2d —, 2007 Ohio App. LEXIS 1488 (Apr. 9, 2007).

Waiver

Since defendant did not object to a paramedic's testimony during trial, he had failed to preserve the issue regarding the denial of his motion in limine seeking to exclude the paramedic's testimony as a Ohio R. Crim. P. 16 sanction for the prosecution's failure to provide discovery of the paramedic's name in connection with defendant's demand for discovery. City of Columbus v. Thevenin, — Ohio App. 3d —, 2006 Ohio 4714, — N.E. 2d —, 2006 Ohio App. LEXIS 4626 (Sept. 12, 2006).

Witness list

State complied with Ohio R. Crim. P. 16(B)(I)(e), (D), and Montgomery County, Ohio, Ct. C.P. R. 3.03(III)(A) with respect to disclosure of witnesses to be called at trial, and with respect to the continuing duty to disclose, and as defendant did not show that the State attempted to hinder his trial preparation, his claim that he was denied a fair trial lacked merit. The State filed a written witness list and then it supplemented it with one additional name. State v. Johnson, — Ohio App. 3d —, 2007 Ohio 437, — N.E. 2d —, 2007 Ohio App. LEXIS 374 (Feb. 2, 2007).

RULE 17.   Subpoena

(A) **For attendance of witnesses; form; issuance** . Every subpoena issued by the clerk shall be under the seal of the court, shall state the name of the court and the title of the action, and shall command each person to whom it is directed to attend and give testimony at a time and place therein specified. The clerk shall issue a subpoena, or a subpoena for the production of documentary evidence, signed and sealed but otherwise in blank, to a party requesting it, who shall fill it in and file a copy thereof with the clerk before service.

(B) **Defendants unable to pay.** The court shall order at any time that a subpoena be issued for service on a named witness upon an *ex parte* application of a defendant upon a satisfactory showing that the presence of the witness is necessary to an adequate defense and that the defendant is financially unable to pay the witness fees required by subdivision (D). If the court orders the subpoena to be issued the costs incurred by the process and the fees of the witness so subpoenaed shall be taxed as costs.

(C) **For production of documentary evidence.** A subpoena may also command the person to whom it is directed to produce the books, papers, documents or other objects designated therein; but the court, upon motion made promptly and in any event made at or before the time specified in the subpoena for compliance therewith, may quash or modify the subpoena if compliance would be unreasonable or oppressive. The court may direct that the books, papers, documents or other objects designated in the subpoena be produced before the court at a time prior to the trial or prior to the time they are offered in evidence, and may, upon their production, permit them or portions thereof to be inspected by the parties or their attorneys.

(D) **Service.** A subpoena may be served by a sheriff, bailiff, coroner, clerk of court, constable, marshal, or a deputy of any, by a municipal or township policeman, by an attorney at law or by any person designated by order of the court who is not a party and is not less than eighteen years of age. Service of a subpoena upon a person named therein shall be made by delivering a copy thereof to such person or by reading it to him in person or by leaving it at his usual place of residence, and by tendering to him upon demand the fees for one day's attendance and the mileage allowed by law. The person serving the subpoena shall file a return thereof with the clerk. If the witness being subpoenaed resides outside the county in which the court is located, the fees for one day's attendance and mileage shall be tendered without demand. The return may be forwarded through the postal service, or otherwise.

(E) **Subpoena for taking depositions; place of examination.** When the attendance of a witness before an official authorized to take depositions is required, the subpoena shall be issued by such person and shall command the person to whom it is directed to attend and give testimony at a time and place specified therein. The subpoena may command the person to whom it is directed to produce designated books, papers, documents, or tangible objects which constitute or contain evidence relating to any of the matters within the scope of the examination permitted by Rule 16.

A person whose deposition is to be taken may be required to attend an examination in the county wherein he resides or is employed or transacts his business in person, or at such other convenient place as is fixed by an order of court.

(F) **Subpoena for a hearing or trial.** At the request of any party, subpoenas for attendance at a hearing or trial shall be issued by the clerk of the court in which the hearing or trial is held. A subpoena requiring the attendance of a witness at a hearing or trial may be served at any place within this state.

(G) **Contempt.** Failure by any person without adequate excuse to obey a subpoena served upon him may be deemed a contempt of the court or officer issuing the subpoena.

NOTES TO DECISIONS

Analysis

Compulsory process, right to
Grounds for quashing subpoena
Mandamus
Service of subpoena

Compulsory process, right to

Defendant was entitled to a new trial where the court violated his right to compulsory process by refusing to enforce a subpoena: State v. Moesle, 181 Ohio App. 3d 696, 2009 Ohio 1326, 910 N.E.2d 531, 2009 Ohio App. LEXIS 1142 (2009).

Grounds for quashing subpoena

Trial court did not err in quashing the subpoena where the defendant failed to make any plausible showing that the testimony sought from the mayor concerning the crime situation would have been both material and favorable to the defense. State v. Smith, 168 Ohio App. 3d 141, 2006 Ohio 3720, 858 N.E.2d 1222, 2006 Ohio App. LEXIS 3669 (2006).

Mandamus

Criminal defendant was not entitled to mandamus because if an assistant county prosecutor failed to appear pursuant to a defense subpoena duces tecum, the criminal defendant had an adequate remedy at law; the criminal defendant could file a motion for contempt pursuant to Ohio R. Crim. P. 17(g). State ex rel. Brady v. Russo, — Ohio App. 3d —, 2007 Ohio 3277, — N.E. 2d —, 2007 Ohio App. LEXIS 3033 (June 22, 2007).

Service of subpoena

Because defendant was able to serve the siblings of one of the victims, and he determined that they were not needed to testify, he was not prejudiced by the trial court's prior ruling that those children had not been served. Also, the trial court reasonably concluded that enforcement of the subpoena for the other children, who were possible witnesses, was unreasonable because the children were out-of-state with their mother and there was no evidence that the family had avoided being served or had left Ohio to avoid testifying. State v. Mullins, — Ohio App. 3d —, 2007 Ohio 1051, — N.E. 2d —, 2007 Ohio App. LEXIS 969 (Mar. 9, 2007).

RULE 17.1. Pretrial Conference

At any time after the filing of an indictment, information or complaint the court may, upon its own motion or the motion of any party, order one or more conferences to consider such matters as will promote a fair and expeditious trial. At the conclusion of a conference the court shall prepare and file a memorandum of the matters agreed upon. No admissions made by the defendant or defendant's counsel at the conference shall be used against the defendant unless the admissions are reduced to writing and signed by the defendant and defendant's counsel. The court shall not conduct pretrial conferences in any case in which a term of imprisonment is a possible penalty unless the defendant is represented by counsel or counsel has been waived pursuant to Crim. R. 44. In any case in which the defendant is not represented by counsel, any pretrial conference shall be conducted in open court and shall be recorded as provided in Crim. R. 22.

History: Amended, eff 7-1-00.

NOTES TO DECISIONS

ANALYSIS

Pretrial conference

Pretrial conference

Defendant's pretrial conference was improper, under Ohio R. Crim. P. 17.1, because she was not represented by counsel, and the record did not indicate that the pretrial conference was conducted in open court and recorded, nor was there any indication that defendant waived her right to counsel. State v. Donkers, 170 Ohio App. 3d 509, 2007 Ohio 1557, 867 N.E.2d 903, 2007 Ohio App. LEXIS 1424 (2007).

RULE 18.   Venue and Change of Venue

(A) **General venue provision.** The venue of a criminal case shall be as provided by law.

(B) **Change of venue; procedure upon change of venue.** Upon the motion of any party or upon its own motion the court may transfer an action to any court having jurisdiction of the subject matter outside the county in which trial would otherwise be held, when it appears that a fair and impartial trial cannot be held in the court in which the action is pending.

(1) **Time of motion.** A motion under this rule shall be made within thirty-five days after arraignment or seven days before trial, whichever is earlier, or at such reasonable time later as the court may permit.

(2) **Clerk's obligations upon change of venue.** Where a change of venue is ordered the clerk of the court in which the cause is pending shall make copies of all of the papers in the action which, with the original complaint, indictment, or information, he shall transmit to the clerk of the court to which the action is sent for trial, and the trial and all subsequent proceedings shall be conducted as if the action had originated in the latter court.

(3) **Additional counsel for prosecuting attorney**. The prosecuting attorney of the political subdivision in which the action originated shall take charge of and try the case. The court to which the action is sent may on application appoint one or more attorneys to assist the prosecuting attorney in the trial, and allow the appointed attorneys reasonable compensation.

(4) **Appearance of defendant, witnesses.** Where a change of venue is ordered and the defendant is in custody, a warrant shall be issued by the clerk of the court in which the action originated, directed to the person having custody of the defendant commanding him to bring the defendant to the jail of the county to which the action is transferred, there to be kept until discharged. If the defendant on the date of the order changing venue is not in custody, the court in the order changing venue shall continue the conditions of release and direct the defendant to appear in the court to which the venue is changed. The court shall recognize the witnesses to appear before the court in which the accused is to be tried.

(5) **Expenses.** The reasonable expenses of the prosecuting attorney incurred in consequence of a change of venue, compensation of counsel appointed pursuant to Rule 44, the fees of the clerk of the court to which the venue is changed, the sheriff or bailiff, and of the jury shall be allowed and paid out of the treasury of the political subdivision in which the action originated.

NOTES TO DECISIONS

ANALYSIS

Denial of change of venue
Pretrial publicity
Proof of venue
Proper venue

Denial of change of venue

Trial court's denial of defendant's motion for a change of venue pursuant to Ohio R. Crim. P. 18(B) was not an abuse of discretion, although all of the jurors indicated that they had heard of the murder case involving a student from a well-known high school, as they all also indicated upon questioning that they could render a fair and impartial verdict. State v. Reid, — Ohio App. 3d —, 2006 Ohio 6450, — N.E. 2d —, 2006 Ohio App. LEXIS 6405 (Dec. 8, 2006).

Pretrial publicity

Denial of a change of venue was not an abuse of discretion where several jurors indicated an awareness of pretrial publicity, but there was no evidence that any juror was influenced by the publicity or had formed an opinion based on it: State v. Gabriel, 170 Ohio App. 3d 393, 2007 Ohio 794, 867 N.E.2d 474, 2007 Ohio App. LEXIS 721 (2007).

There was no error in denying defendant's motion to change venue because the pretrial publicity did not prevent defendant from receiving a fair trial. Because defendant did not show that any of the people who ultimately served on the jury were exposed to publicity concerning his prior conviction, defendant was not prejudiced by that publicity. State v. Goff, — Ohio App. 3d —, 2007 Ohio 2735, — N.E. 2d —, 2007 Ohio App. LEXIS 2526 (June 6, 2007).

There was no plain error regarding venue due to pretrial coverage because defendant did not file a motion for a change of venue and all of the jurors impaneled who were aware in some way of the media coverage in the case indicated that they could proceed impartially. Defendant raised no other evidence to show actual prejudice on the part of any juror; as such, no bias or prejudice was found. State v. Bailey, — Ohio App. 3d —, 2007 Ohio 4995, — N.E. 2d —, 2007 Ohio App. LEXIS 4389 (Sept. 20, 2007).

Proof of venue

Testimony showing that an offense occurred at a particular street address, standing alone, is generally insufficient to prove venue, since such addresses often are not "sufficiently unique" to permit the conclusion that the address is located in a particular city or county. Consequently, the trial court could not take judicial notice pursuant to Ohio R. Evid. 201(B)(1) that the crime for which defendant was charged occurred in the proper city and county of Ohio, simply on the basis that the evidence showed that the offense took place at the specific address because it was not generally known within the trial court's jurisdiction that that specific address was in the specific city and county of Ohio. State v. Lahmann, — Ohio App. 3d —, 2007 Ohio 1795, — N.E. 2d —, 2007 Ohio App. LEXIS 1651 (Apr. 16, 2007).

Proper venue

Trial court did not abuse its discretion in overruling the motion to change venue because, although several of the jurors indicated an awareness of the pretrial publicity, there was no evidence that any of the jurors were influenced by that publicity or had formed any opinions based on that publicity. State v. Gabriel, — Ohio App. 3d —, 2007 Ohio 794, — N.E. 2d —, 2007 Ohio App. LEXIS 721 (Feb. 23, 2007).

RULE 19.   Magistrates

(A) **Appointment.** A court other than a mayor's court may appoint one or more magistrates who shall be attorneys at law admitted to practice in Ohio.

(B) **Compensation.** The compensation of magistrates shall be fixed by the court, and no part of the compensation shall be taxed as costs.

(C) **Authority.**

(1) **Scope.** To assist courts of record and pursuant to reference under Crim. R. 19(D)(1), magistrates are authorized, subject to the terms of the relevant reference, to do any of the following:

(a) Conduct initial appearances and preliminary hearings pursuant to Crim. R. 5.

(b) Conduct arraignments pursuant to Crim. R. 10.

(c) Receive pleas, in accordance with Crim R. 11, only as follows:

(ii) In felony and misdemeanor cases, accept and enter not guilty pleas.

(ii) In misdemeanor cases, accept and enter guilty and no contest pleas, determine guilt or innocence, receive statements in explanation and in mitigation of sentence, and recommend a penalty to be imposed. If imprisonment is a possible penalty for the offense charged, the matter may be referred only with the unanimous consent of the parties, in writing or on the record in open court.

(d) Conduct pretrial conferences pursuant to Crim. R. 17.1.

(e) Conduct proceedings to establish bail pursuant to Crim. R. 46.

(f) Hear and decide the following motions:

(i) Any pretrial or post-judgment motion in any misdemeanor case for which imprisonment is not a possible penalty.

(ii) Upon the unanimous consent of the parties in writing or on the record in open court, any pretrial or post-judgment motion in any misdemeanor case for which imprisonment is a possibility.

(g) Conduct proceedings upon application for the issuance of a temporary protection order as authorized by law.

(h) Conduct the trial of any misdemeanor case that will not be tried to a jury. If the offense charged is an offense for which imprisonment is a possible penalty, the matter may be referred only with unanimous consent of the parties in writing or on the record in open court.

(i) Exercise any other authority specifically vested in magistrates by statute and consistent with this rule.

(2) **Regulation of proceedings.** In performing the responsibilities described in Crim. R. 19(C)(1), magistrates are authorized, subject to the terms of the relevant reference, to regulate all proceedings as if by the court and to do everything necessary for the efficient performance of those responsibilities, including but not limited to, the following:

(a) Issuing subpoenas for the attendance of witnesses and the production of evidence;

(b) Ruling upon the admissibility of evidence in misdemeanor cases in accordance with division (C)(1)(f) of this rule;

(c) Putting witnesses under oath and examining them;

(d) When necessary to obtain the presence of an alleged contemnor in cases involving direct or indirect contempt of court, issuing attachment for the alleged contemnor and setting the type, amount, and any conditions of bail pursuant to Crim. R. 46;

(e) Imposing, subject to Crim. R. 19(D)(8), appropriate sanctions for civil or criminal contempt committed in the presence of the magistrate.

(D) **Proceedings in Matters Referred to Magistrates**

(1) **Reference by court of record.**

(a) **Purpose and method.** A court of record may, for one or more of the purposes described in Crim. R. 19(C)(1), refer a particular case or matter of a category of cases or matters to a magistrate by a specific or general order of reference or by a rule.

(b) **Limitation.** A court of record may limit a reference by specifying or limiting the magistrate's powers, including, but not limited to, directing the magistrate to determine only particular issues, directing the magistrate to perform particular responsibilities, directing the magistrate to receive and report evidence only, fixing the time and place for beginning and closing any hearings, or fixing the time for filing any magistrate's decision on the matter or matters referred.

(2) **Magistrate's order; motion to set aside magistrate's order.**

(a) **Magistrate's order.**

(i) **Nature of order.** Subject to the terms of the relevant reference, a magistrate may enter pretrial orders without judicial approval if necessary to regulate the proceedings and if not dispositive of a claim or defense of a party.

(ii) **Form, filing, and service of magistrate's order.** A magistrate's order shall be in writing, identified as a magistrate's order in the caption, signed by the magistrate, filed with the clerk, and served by the clerk on all parties or their attorneys.

(b) **Motion to set aside magistrate's order.** Any party may file a motion with the court to set aside a magistrate's order. The motion shall state the moving party's reasons with particularity and shall be filed not later than ten days after the magistrate's order is filed. The pendency of a motion to set aside does not stay the effectiveness of the magistrate's order, though the magistrate or the court may by order stay the effectiveness of a magistrate's order.

(3) **Magistrate's decision; objections to magistrate's decision.**

(a) **Magistrate's decision.**

(i) **When required.** Subject to the terms of the relevant reference, a magistrate shall prepare a magistrate's decision respecting any matter referred under Crim. R. 19(D)(1).

(ii) **Findings of fact and conclusions of law.** Subject to the terms of the relevant reference, a magistrate's decision may be general unless findings of fact and conclusions of law are timely requested by a party or otherwise required by law. A request for findings of fact and conclusions of law shall be made before the entry of a magistrate's decision or within seven days after the filing of a magistrate's decision. If a request for findings of fact and conclusions of law is timely made, the magistrate may require any or all of the parties to submit proposed findings of fact and conclusions of law.

(iii) **Form; filing; and service of magistrate's decision.** A magistrate's decision shall be in writing, identified as a magistrate's decision in the caption, signed by the magistrate, filed with the clerk, and served by the clerk on all parties or their attorneys no later than three days after the decision is filed. A magistrate's decision shall indicate conspicuously that a party shall not assign as error on appeal the court's adoption of any factual finding or legal conclusion, whether or not specifically designated as a finding of fact or conclusion of law under Crim. R.19(D)(3)(a)(ii), unless the party timely and specifically objects to that factual finding or legal conclusion as required by Crim. R.19(D)(3)(b).

(b) **Objections to magistrate's decision.**

(i) **Time for filing.** A party may file written objections to a magistrate's decision within fourteen days of the filing of the decision, whether or not the court has adopted the decision during that fourteen-day period as permitted by Crim. R. 19(D)(4)(e)(i). If any party timely files objections, any other party may also file objections not later than ten days after the first objections are filed. If a party makes a timely request for findings of fact and conclusions of law, the time for filing objections begins to run when the magistrate files a decision that includes findings of fact and conclusions of law.

(ii) **Specificity of objection.** An objection to a magistrate's decision shall be specific and state with particularity all grounds for objection.

(iii) **Objection to magistrate's factual finding; transcript or affidavit.** An objection to a factual finding, whether or not specifically designated as a finding of fact under Crim. R. 19(D)(3)(a)(ii), shall be supported by a transcript of all the evidence submitted to the magistrate relevant to that finding or an affidavit of that evidence if a transcript is not available. With leave of court, alternative technology or manner of reviewing the relevant evidence may be considered. The objecting party shall file the transcript or affidavit with the court within thirty days after filing objections unless the court extends the time in writing for preparation of the transcript or other good cause. If a party files timely objections prior to the date on which a transcript is prepared, the party may seek leave of court to supplement the objections.

(iv) **Waiver of right to assign adoption by court as error on appeal.** Except for a claim of plain error, a party shall not assign on appeal the court's adoption of any factual finding or legal conclusion, whether or not specifically designated as a finding of fact or conclusion of law under Crim. R. 19(D)(3)(a)(ii), unless the party has objected to that finding or conclusion as required by Crim. R. 19(D)(3)(b).

(4) **Action of court on magistrate's decision and on any objection to magistrate's decision; entry of judgment or interim order by court.**

(a) **Action of court required.** A magistrate's decision is not effective unless adopted by the court.

(b) **Action on magistrate's decision.** Whether or not objections are timely filed, a court may adopt or reject a magistrate's decision in whole or in part, with or without modification. A court may hear a previously-referred matter, take additional evidence, or return a matter to a magistrate. No sentence recommended by a magistrate shall be enforced until the court has entered judgment.

(c) **If no objections are filed.** If no timely objections are filed, the court may adopt a magistrate's decision, unless it determines that there is an error of law or other defect evident on the face of the magistrate's decision.

(d) **Action on objections.** If one or more objections to a magistrate's decision are timely filed, the court shall rule on those objections. In ruling on objections, the court shall undertake an independent review as to the objected matters to ascertain that the magistrate has properly determined the factual issues and appropriately applied the law. Before so ruling, the court may hear additional evidence but may refuse to do so unless the objecting party demonstrates that the party could not, with reasonable diligence, have produced that evidence for consideration by the magistrate.

(e) **Entry of Judgment or interim order by court.** A court that adopts, rejects, or modifies a magistrate's decision shall also enter a judgment or interim order.

(i) **Judgment.** The court may enter a judgment either during the fourteen days permitted by Crim. R. 19(D)(3)(b)(i) for the filing of objections to a magistrate's decision or after the fourteen days have expired. If the court enters a judgment during the fourteen days permitted by Crim. R. 19(D)(3)(b)(i) for the filing of objections to the magistrate's decision shall operate as an automatic stay of execution of the judgment until the court disposes of those objections and vacates, modifies, or adheres to the judgment previously entered.

(ii) **Interim order.** The court may enter an interim order on the basis of a magistrate's decision without waiting for or ruling on timely objections by the parties where immediate relief is justified. The timely filing of objections does not stay the execution of an interim order, but an interim order shall not extend more than twenty-eight days from the date of entry, subject to extension by the court in increments of twenty-eight additional days for good cause shown. An interim order shall comply with Civ. R. 54(A), be journalized pursuant to Civ. R. 58(A), and be served pursuant to Civ. R. 58(B).

(5) **Extension of time.** For good cause shown, the court shall allow a reasonable extension of time for a party to file a motion to set aside a magistrate's order or file objections to a magistrate's decision. "Good cause" includes, but is not limited to, a failure by the clerk to timely serve the party seeking the extension with the magistrate's order or decision.

(6) **Disqualification of a magistrate.** Disqualification of a magistrate for bias or other cause is within the discretion of the court and may be sought by motion filed with the court.

(7) **Recording of proceedings before a**

magistrate. Except as otherwise provided by law, all proceedings before a magistrate shall be recorded in accordance with procedures established by the court.

(8) **Contempt in the presence of a magistrate.**

(a) **Contempt Order.** Contempt sanctions under Crim. R. 19 (C)(2)(e) may be imposed only by a written order that recites the facts and certifies that the magistrate saw or heard the conduct constituting contempt.

(b) **Filing and provision of copies of contempt order.** A contempt order shall be filed and copies provided forthwith by the clerk to the appropriate judge of the court and to the subject of the order.

(c) **Review of contempt order by court; bail.** The subject of a contempt order may by motion obtain immediate review by a judge. A judge or the magistrate entering the contempt order may set bail pending judicial review of the order.

History: Effective 7-1-90; amended, eff 7-1-95; 7-1-00; 7-1-06.

NOTES TO DECISIONS

ANALYSIS

Adoption of magistrate's decision
Appeal
Applicability
Failure to file objections
Magistrate's failure to file decision
Presence of defendant
Preservation for appellate review

Adoption of magistrate's decision

Defendant's appeal from a magistrate's decision finding him guilty of speeding was dismissed. Because the trial court did not properly adopt the magistrate's decision, pursuant to Ohio R. Crim. P. 19(E)(3)(a) and Ohio Traf. R. 14(C), there was no final order for defendant to appeal; thus, defendant's appeal was not properly before the court. State v. Dixon, — Ohio App. 3d —, 2006 Ohio 4932, — N.E. 2d —, 2006 Ohio App. LEXIS 4861 (Sept. 22, 2006).

Appeal

When a magistrate who found defendant guilty of speeding did not file a written decision, as required by Ohio R. Crim. P. 19(E)(1), this did not deprive a trial court of jurisdiction to find defendant guilty and sentence him, despite the procedural error which left defendant without a magistrate's decision to object to, and the trial court's judgment was a final appealable order, under RC § 2505.02, because it affected a substantial right in an action and, in effect, determined the action. State v. Litreal, 170 Ohio App. 3d 670, 2006 Ohio 5416, 868 N.E.2d 1018, 2006 Ohio App. LEXIS 5410 (2006).

Trial court's finding of guilty was a final appealable order, despite the defendant's failure to file objections to the magistrate's decision, where the magistrate never filed a written decision: State v. Litreal, 170 Ohio App. 3d 670, 2006 Ohio 5416, 868 N.E.2d 1018, 2006 Ohio App. LEXIS 5410 (2006).

Applicability

Court rejected a license holder's contention that a trial court incorrectly denied her motion to vacate an Administrative License Suspension (ALS) notification form completed by a magistrate on the ground that the magistrate's decision was not identified as a "magistrate's decision" in its caption, as required by Ohio R. Crim. P. 29(D)(3)(a)(iii). The current version of Ohio R. Crim. P. 19, upn which the holder relied,

did not become effective until eight days after the magistrate filed the form, and even so an appeal of an ALS was a civil proceeding, and thus, Ohio R. Crim. P. 19 did not apply to the ALS appeal. State v. Makoroff, — Ohio App. 3d —, 2007 Ohio 4348, — N.E. 2d —, 2007 Ohio App. LEXIS 3897 (Aug. 27, 2007).

Failure to file objections

If defendant was deprived of the right to file timely objections to the magistrate's decision because neither he nor his counsel received that decision until more than 14 days after it was filed, defendant could have moved to vacate his conviction and sentence for that reason pursuant to Ohio R. Crim. P. 57(B) and Ohio R. Civ. P. 60(B)(1). However, the one-year provision of Ohio R. Civ. P. 60(B) would have applied, and more than one year had passed since the trial court entered its judgment; defendant's appeal did not toll the time. State v. Gilreath, 174 Ohio App. 3d 327, 2007 Ohio 6899, 882 N.E. 2d 22, 2007 Ohio App. LEXIS 6057 (Dec. 21, 2007).

Since defendant failed to file objections to a magistrate's decision finding him guilty of speeding, as required by Ohio R. Crim. P. 19(E)(2)(b), he waived all but plain error. Upon reviewing the record, the court found no plain error. State v. Palmer, — Ohio App. 3d —, 2006 Ohio 2712, — N.E. 2d —, 2006 Ohio App. LEXIS 2555 (May 30, 2006).

Magistrate's failure to file decision

Trial court's judgment entered on a magistrate's decision finding defendant guilty of operating a vehicle under the influence of alcohol was improper because there was no evidence of a journalized magistrate's decision, as required by Ohio R. Crim. P. 19. Defendant was never provided the opportunity to file objections to the magistrate's decision, and she suffered prejudice as a result. State v. Romans, — Ohio App. 3d —, 2007 Ohio 1215, — N.E. 2d —, 2007 Ohio App. LEXIS 1145 (Mar. 19, 2007).

Presence of defendant

Trial court may adopt a sentence the magistrate recommended without the defendant then being present before the court. However, consistent with the purposes of CrimR 43(A) and the requirements of due process, in that event the defendant must have been present before the magistrate when the magistrate pronounced the sentence recommended to the court: State v. Gilreath, 174 Ohio App. 3d 327, 2007 Ohio 6899, 882 N.E. 2d 22, 2007 Ohio App. LEXIS 6057 (Dec. 21, 2007).

Trial court erred when it imposed the sentence because defendant was not present. The magistrate did not pronounce a recommended sentence when defendant was before him, but instead pronounced a recommended sentence in a written decision that was filed and adopted by the trial court the same day. State v. Gilreath, 174 Ohio App. 3d 327, 2007 Ohio 6899, 882 N.E. 2d 22, 2007 Ohio App. LEXIS 6057 (Dec. 21, 2007).

Preservation for appellate review

Defendant's assignment of error relating to a trial court's decision on his motion to suppress had been waived because no ruling on the motion was found in the record. The trial court never adopted the magistrate's findings and recommendations, in which the magistrate recommended that the motion be denied, and as a result, pursuant to Ohio R. Crim. P. 19(E)(3)(a), the magistrate's findings and recommendations were not final, compelling the conclusion that the motion was pending at the time of defendant's plea. If the trial court did not issue a ruling, defendant had waived his objection by pleading no contest before obtaining a ruling on the motion, and if the trial court did rule on the motion, defendant had not provided the court with a record of that ruling, which was his duty. State v. Romandetti, — Ohio App. 3d —, 2007 Ohio 363, — N.E. 2d —, 2007 Ohio App. LEXIS 325 (Jan. 31, 2007).

Where defendant did not object to a police officer's testimony at a hearing before a magistrate, but he filed timely objections to the magistrate's decision that included objections to the officer's testimony, the matter was preserved for appellate review pursuant to Ohio R. Crim. P. 19(E)(2)(B). City of Cleveland Hts. v. Reid, — Ohio App. 3d —, 2006 Ohio 170, — N.E. 2d —, 2006 Ohio App. LEXIS 163 (Jan. 19, 2006).

RULE 20.   Reserved.

RULE 21.   Transfer From Common Pleas Court for Trial

(A) **When permitted.** Where an indictment or information charging only misdemeanors is filed in the court of common pleas, such court may retain the case for trial or the administrative judge may, within fourteen days after the indictment or information is filed with the clerk of the court of common pleas, transfer it to the court from which the bindover to the grand jury was made or to the court of record of the jurisdiction in which venue appears.

(B) **Proceedings on transfer.** When a transfer is ordered, the clerk of the court of common pleas, within three days, shall transmit to the clerk of the court to which the case is transferred, certified copies of the indictment, information, and all other papers in the case, and any bail taken, and the prosecution shall continue in that court.

History: Amended, eff 7-1-04.

RULE 22.   Recording of Proceedings

In serious offense cases all proceedings shall be recorded.

In petty offense cases all waivers of counsel required by Rule 44(B) shall be recorded, and if requested by any party all proceedings shall be recorded.

Proceedings may be recorded in shorthand, or stenotype, or by any other adequate mechanical, electronic or video recording device.

NOTES TO DECISIONS

ANALYSIS

Capital cases
Petty offense cases
Prejudice
Sidebar conferences
Transcript for appeal
Waiver of counsel

Capital cases

Proceedings in which a deliberating juror is dismissed in a capital case, and an alternate juror is seated, must be recorded. Under former CrimR 24(G)(2), a juror cannot be replaced by an alternate juror during deliberations in a capital case: State v. Clinkscale, 122 Ohio St. 3d 351, 2009 Ohio 2746, 911 N.E.2d 862, 2009 Ohio LEXIS 1736 (2009).

Petty offense cases

Trial court did not have the authority to impose a jail sentence after finding defendant guilty of failing to constrain or confine her dogs, under RC § 955.22(C), because she never waived her right to appointed counsel in a knowing, intelligent, and voluntary manner. Although the underlying offense was a "petty" misdemeanor, and Ohio R. Crim. P.

44(B) was applicable, defendant did not have the benefit of counsel at trial; the trial court never tried to have the necessary dialog with defendant during the proceeding; and the transcript showed that defendant did not seek to waive her right to have an attorney appointed for her and, in fact, she expressly asked for the appointment of counsel. State v. Mogul, — Ohio App. 3d —, 2006 Ohio 1873, — N.E. 2d —, 2006 Ohio App. LEXIS 1728 (Apr. 14, 2006).

Prejudice

Despite defendant's assertion that he was severely prejudiced by the trial court's failure to record all sidebar conferences, he presented no evidence to demonstrate that he was prejudiced in any way by that error. Defendant was allowed to proffer anything he wished in order to preserve the matter for purposes of appeal. State v. Barton, — Ohio App. 3d —, 2007 Ohio 1099, — N.E. 2d —, 2007 Ohio App. LEXIS 1020 (Mar. 12, 2007).

Sidebar conferences

While several sidebar conferences were not recorded, any alleged error in that regard was rendered moot by virtue of defendant's supplementation of the record pursuant to Ohio R. App. P. 9(C). Defendant filed a statement of evidence setting forth the substances of the sidebar conferences and thus, any alleged error on the part of the trial court in failing to record the sidebar conferences was rendered moot. State v. Schenker, — Ohio App. 3d —, 2007 Ohio 3732, — N.E. 2d —, 2007 Ohio App. LEXIS 3415 (July 19, 2007).

Transcript for appeal

Although, as originally transcribed, the proceedings were not recorded in such a way as to enable defendant to file an adequate transcript, because an amended transcript had been filed, pursuant to Ohio R. App. P. 9, defendant was not prejudiced by any inadequacies in the transcript. The amended transcript was found to be in compliance with the order of remand. Further, defendant was not prejudiced by the filing of an amended transcript pursuant to Ohio R. App. P. 9(B) instead of a statement of the evidence pursuant to Ohio R. App. P. 9(C) because defendant and his counsel were given ample opportunity to review the original transcript, as filed, and to make corrections and/or objections to the amended transcript. State v. Beltowski, — Ohio App. 3d —, 2007 Ohio 3372, — N.E. 2d —, 2007 Ohio App. LEXIS 3090 (June 29, 2007).

When defendant's motion to an appellate court to correct the record, under Ohio R. App. P. 9(E), due to numerous gaps in the original trial transcript, was granted, defendant could not claim it was an abuse of discretion for the trial court to have recorded defendant's trial by means of a tape recorder because the electronic recording of the trial was specifically authorized by Ohio R. Crim. P. 22. Ohio v. Liddy, — Ohio App. 3d —, 2007 Ohio 5225, — N.E. 2d —, 2007 Ohio App. LEXIS 4597 (Sept. 28, 2007).

Requirements in Ohio R. App. P. 9 and Ohio R. Crim. P. 22 of a complete transcript of a criminal trial does not mean that the transcript must be perfect for appellate review, so an adequate transcript does not mean a perfect transcript. Ohio v. Liddy, — Ohio App. 3d —, 2007 Ohio 5225, — N.E. 2d —, 2007 Ohio App. LEXIS 4597 (Sept. 28, 2007).

Waiver of counsel

Trial court record did not contain sufficient information to establish that defendant's waiver of counsel pursuant to Ohio R. Crim. P. 22 and 44 was knowingly and intelligently made for purposes of his constitutional right under U.S. Const. amend. VI and Ohio Const. art. I, § 10, as defendant had filed a pro se motion to have his appointed attorney disqualified and to represent himself, his attorney had sought withdrawal, and the trial court's judgment indicated that a hearing was held but there was no transcript of those proceedings in the record. Accordingly, it was unclear whether defendant's waiver of the right to counsel was knowingly and intelligently made. State v. Melton, — Ohio App. 3d —, 2007 Ohio 1154, — N.E. 2d —, 2007 Ohio App. LEXIS 1062 (Mar. 14, 2007).

Defendant did not knowingly and voluntarily waive his right to counsel because the trial court never informed him on the record of the inherent dangers of proceeding pro se and never warned him that if he did not retain counsel he would be forced to proceed pro se; thus, waiver could not be inferred. Given that defendant possibly believed that he had retained counsel, the trial court should have continued the trial and warned him that if he did not show up with an attorney at the next trial date, it would construe that as a waiver of the right to counsel and he would have to proceed pro se. State v. Koons, — Ohio App. 3d —, 2007 Ohio 4985, — N.E. 2d —, 2007 Ohio App. LEXIS 4451 (Sept. 25, 2007).

Defendant's Sixth Amendment right to counsel was violated where there was no record to indicate that he waived that right, and a presumption of regularity as to the trial court proceedings in the absence of a record, pursuant to Ohio R. App. P. 9(B), was not made in such an instance; accordingly, where there was no showing that defendant knowingly and intelligently waived his right to counsel, pursuant to Ohio R. Crim. P. 22 and 44(B), a sentence of imprisonment could not be imposed against him, although other sentencing terms were proper. State v. Miyamoto, — Ohio App. 3d —, 2006 Ohio 1776, — N.E. 2d —, 2006 Ohio App. LEXIS 1648 (Apr. 10, 2006).

As there was no showing by the State that defendant had waived his right to counsel pursuant to Ohio R. Crim. P. 44(C) and 22 where he was charged with, inter alia, driving under the influence of alcohol, in violation of RC § 4511.19(G)(1)(b), which was a petty offense as defined in Ohio R. Crim. P. 2(D), it was presumed that defendant did not knowingly and intelligently waive his right to counsel; accordingly, imposition of a jail term on defendant was error which required vacatur. State v. West, — Ohio App. 3d —, 2006 Ohio 5834, — N.E. 2d —, 2006 Ohio App. LEXIS 5762 (Nov. 6, 2006).

RULE 23. Trial by Jury or by the Court

(A) **Trial by jury.** In serious offense cases the defendant before commencement of the trial may knowingly, intelligently and voluntarily waive in writing his right to trial by jury. Such waiver may also be made during trial with the approval of the court and the consent of the prosecuting attorney. In petty offense cases, where there is a right of jury trial, the defendant shall be tried by the court unless he demands a jury trial. Such demand must be in writing and filed with the clerk of court not less than ten days prior to the date set for trial, or on or before the third day following receipt of notice of the date set for trial, whichever is later. Failure to demand a jury trial as provided in this subdivision is a complete waiver of the right thereto.

(B) **Number of jurors.** In felony cases juries shall consist of twelve.

In misdemeanor cases juries shall consist of eight.

If a defendant is charged with a felony and with a misdemeanor or, if a felony and a misdemeanor involving different defendants are joined for trial, the jury shall consist of twelve.

(C) **Trial without a jury.** In a case tried without a jury the court shall make a general finding.

History: Amended, eff 7-1-80.

NOTES TO DECISIONS

Analysis

Continuance
Failure to demand jury trial
Filing of jury demand, time limitations
Jury waiver
Number of jurors
Right not waived

Continuance

Trial court did not err in denying a father's request, pursuant to Ohio R. Juv. P. 23, for a second continuance of a permanent custody hearing in order to allow him time to participate in case planning services and comply with the newly stated goals for him because, while the father's reason for requesting the second continuance in order to demonstrate his willingness and ability to provide a home for the child was a legitimate reason, his actions of choosing not to establish paternity, visit, or receive services for over seven months were dilatory. The father's delay in taking these basic, necessary steps toward reunification with the child demonstrated a lack of commitment and an unwillingness to provide a permanent home. In re Nevaeh J., — Ohio App. 3d —, 2006 Ohio 6628, — N.E. 2d —, 2006 Ohio App. LEXIS 6539 (Dec. 15, 2006).

Failure to demand jury trial

When defendant was convicted of driving under suspension, he was not improperly denied a jury trial because the charge against him was a petty offense, which meant, under Ohio R. Crim. P. 23(A), that he had to demand a jury trial in writing, and the appellate record contained no such demand, and his failure to demand a jury trial was a complete waiver of his right to such a trial. City of Macedonia v. Ewing, — Ohio App. 3d —, 2007 Ohio 2194, — N.E. 2d —, 2007 Ohio App. LEXIS 2055 (May 9, 2007).

Defendant's claim that his jury trial right under U.S. Const. amend. VI was violated where a charge against him of child endangerment, in violation of RC § 2919.22, which was deemed a "petty offense" pursuant to RC § 2919.24(A)(1) and Ohio R. Crim. P. 2, was tried in a bench trial, lacked merit, as the appellate court presumed the regularity of the trial court proceedings pursuant to Ohio R. App. P. 9(B) where there was no record to support defendant's claim that he was never informed by the trial court, as required under Ohio R. Crim. P. 5(A)(5), of the need to make a jury trial demand pursuant to Ohio R. Crim. P. 23(A) and RC § 1901.24(B); defendant's claim that he made an oral demand was not proved by a record and further, such would not have satisfied the requirements for the demand, as it had to be in writing. State v. Miyamoto, — Ohio App. 3d —, 2006 Ohio 1776, — N.E. 2d —, 2006 Ohio App. LEXIS 1648 (Apr. 10, 2006).

There was no showing that defendant's counsel provided ineffective assistance in violation of defendant's rights under U.S. Const. amend. VI and Ohio Const. art. I, § 10 by his failure to have filed a written demand for a jury trial in defendant's criminal trial on a charge of having physical control of a vehicle while under the influence of alcohol, in violation of RC § 4511.194(B), which was a misdemeanor of the first degree and a petty offense under Ohio R. Crim. P. 2(C)-(D), as the only evidence in the record supported counsel's claim that defendant failed to inform him that he wanted a jury trial until the time for filing a writte jury demand under Ohio R. Crim. P. 23(A) had passed. State v. Short, — Ohio App. 3d —, 2006 Ohio 6611, — N.E. 2d —, 2006 Ohio App. LEXIS 6523 (Dec. 8, 2006).

Filing of jury demand, time limitations

Although the trial court purportedly denied defendant's jury trial demand on the grounds that he had been charged with a minor misdemeanor and was not entitled to a jury, when in fact he was charged with a first degree misdemeanor, there was no error because defendant filed his demand out of rule pursuant to Ohio R. Crim. P. 23(A), such that it was properly denied. Woodmere v. Di Fiore, — Ohio App. 3d —, 2007 Ohio 5327, — N.E. 2d —, 2007 Ohio App. LEXIS 4691 (Oct. 4, 2007).

Jury waiver

Waiver of the right to a trial by jury must not only be made in writing, signed by the defendant, and filed as a part of the record, but must also be made in open court. To satisfy the "in open court" requirement in RC § 2945.05, there must be some evidence in the record that the defendant while in the courtroom and in the presence of counsel, if any, acknowledged the jury waiver to the trial court: State v. Lomax, 114 Ohio St. 3d 350, 2007 Ohio 4277, 872 N.E.2d 279, 2007 Ohio LEXIS 2164 (2007).

Where defendant signed a written jury trial waiver which was filed and docketed pursuant to Ohio R. Crim. P. 23(A) and RC § 2945.05, she signed a written guilty plea, and the trial court conducted a colloquy under Ohio R. Crim. P. 11 and determined that defendant understood what she had signed and that she had voluntarily, intelligently, and knowingly entered the plea, her claim that her Sixth Amendment jury trial waiver was not sufficient was not supported by the evidence. State v. Barnett, — Ohio App. 3d —, 2007 Ohio 4599, — N.E. 2d —, 2007 Ohio App. LEXIS 4145 (Sept. 7, 2007).

Although defendant had a right under Ohio R. Crim. P. 23(A) and RC § 2945.05 to waive his jury trial right in his criminal matter, where there was only a brief mention of that waiver prior to opening statements for purposes of being "on the record" and defendant had signed a jury waiver form, there was not sufficient compliance and defendant's conviction after a bench trial required reversal; the Ohio Court of Appeals for the First Appellate District, Hamilton County holds that a jury waiver has to be made in "open court," which means orally and on the record, and that a colloquy is necessary to ensure that the waiver of a defendant's constitutional jury trial right under Ohio Const. art. I, § 10 is knowingly, voluntarily, and intelligently made. State v. Lomax, 166 Ohio App. 3d 555, 2006 Ohio 1373, 852 N.E. 2d 205, 2006 Ohio App. LEXIS 1248 (Mar. 24, 2006).

Requirements of RC § 2945.05 had been satisfied, and thus, the trial court had jurisdiction to conduct a bench trial on a charge of having a weapon while under disability, because the record reflected that defendant signed a jury waiver form with regard to the charge at issue, and the journal entry reflected that the waiver was filed the same day. State v. Howard, — Ohio App. 3d —, 2006 Ohio 2060, — N.E. 2d —, 2006 Ohio App. LEXIS 1889 (Apr. 27, 2006).

Where defendant executed a jury trial waiver which was found to have been entered knowingly, intelligently, and voluntarily, and on that same day, a bench trial was commenced regarding criminal charges against defendant, the waiver was valid pursuant to RC § 2945.05 and Ohio R. Crim. P. 23(A); although the waiver and order was filed on the day of trial and not memorialized by entry until five days later, there was no requirement that the jury waiver had to be filed prior to the start of a trial in order to be valid. State v. Soto, — Ohio App. 3d —, 2006 Ohio 2319, — N.E. 2d —, 2006 Ohio App. LEXIS 2175 (May 11, 2006).

Defendant's waiver of his jury trial right under Ohio R. Crim. P. 23(A) and RC § 2945.05 was valid with respect to a forfeiture of funds that were seized at the time of his arrest on multiple drug-related charges, as his plea agreement was deemed valid and that included the forfeiture issue; defendant was fully apprised of the terms of the plea agreement and accepted those terms. State v. Rankin, — Ohio App. 3d —, 2006 Ohio 2571, — N.E. 2d —, 2006 Ohio App. LEXIS 2423 (May 25, 2006).

Trial court had jurisdiction to conduct a bench trial because the requirements of RC § 2945.05 had been satisfied since the record reflected that defendant had executed two separate jury waiver forms. Thus, pursuant to Ohio R. Crim. P. 23(A), defendant knowingly, intelligently, and voluntarily waived his right to trial by jury. State v. Gums, — Ohio App. 3d —, 2006 Ohio 3159, — N.E. 2d —, 2006 Ohio App. LEXIS 3036 (June 22, 2006).

Trial court had jurisdiction under R.C. § 2931.03 to find defendant guilty of having a weapon while under a disability because defendant failed to show that his jury waiver was not voluntarily, knowingly, and intelligently made, pursuant to Ohio R. Crim. P. 23(A) and R.C. § 2945.05. Since the record contained defendant's written waiver, which was properly executed, the written waiver was presumptively voluntary, knowing, and intelligent. State v. Daniel, — Ohio App. 3d —, 2006 Ohio 4627, — N.E. 2d —, 2006 Ohio App. LEXIS 4482 (Aug. 31, 2006).

Number of jurors

Trial court did not err in using an eight-person jury panel in defendant's criminal matter involving traffic violations and driving under the influence charges, as that amount of jurors was provided by Ohio R. Crim. P. 23(B) and there was no violation of Ohio Const. art. I, § 5. State v. West, — Ohio App. 3d —, 2006 Ohio 5834, — N.E. 2d —, 2006 Ohio App. LEXIS 5762 (Nov. 6, 2006).

Right not waived

Trial court erred by conducting a bench trial because a written jury waiver was never filed with the clerk of courts or made a part of the record. Because defendant was charged with a first-degree misdemeanor for assault, punishable by a maximum of six months in prison, defendant had a right to be tried by a jury, pursuant to Ohio R. Crim. P. 23(A). City of Zanesville v. Maxwell, — Ohio App. 3d —, 2007 Ohio 2624, — N.E. 2d —, 2007 Ohio App. LEXIS 2445 (May 24, 2007).

Although defendant indicated that he would waive a jury as to the charge of having a weapon while under disability, no waiver was executed as required by Ohio R. Crim. P. 23(A) and RC § 2945.05. State v. Priest, — Ohio App. 3d —, 2007 Ohio 5958, — N.E. 2d —, 2007 Ohio App. LEXIS 5225 (Nov. 8, 2007).

RULE 24. Trial Jurors

(A) **Brief introduction of case.** To assist prospective jurors in understanding the general nature of the case, the court, in consultation with the parties, may give jurors a brief introduction to the case.

(B) **Examination of prospective jurors.** Any person called as a prospective juror for the trial of any cause shall be examined under oath or upon affirmation as to the prospective juror's qualifications. The court may permit the attorney for the defendant, or the defendant if appearing *pro se*, and the attorney for the state to conduct the examination of the prospective jurors or may itself conduct the examination. In the latter event, the court shall permit the state and defense to supplement the examination by further inquiry. Nothing in this rule shall limit the court's discretion, with timely notice to the parties at anytime prior to trial, to allow the examination of all prospective jurors in the array or, in the alternative, to permit individual examination or each prospective juror seated on a panel, prior to any challenges for cause or peremptory challenges.

(C) **Challenge for cause.** A person called as a juror may be challenged for the following causes:

(1) That the juror has been convicted of a crime which by law renders the juror disqualified to serve on a jury.

(2) That the juror is a chronic alcoholic, or drug dependent person.

(3) That the juror was a member of the grand jury that found the indictment in the case.

(4) That the juror served on a petit jury drawn in the same cause against the same defendant, and the petit jury was discharged after hearing the evidence or rendering a verdict on the evidence that was set aside.

(5) That the juror served as a juror in a civil case brought against the defendant for the same act.

(6) That the juror has an action pending between him or her and the State of Ohio or the defendant.

(7) That the juror or the juror's spouse is a party to another action then pending in any court in which an attorney in the cause then on trial is an attorney, either for or against the juror.

(8) That the juror has been subpoenaed in good faith as a witness in the case.

(9) That the juror is possessed of a state of mind evincing enmity or bias toward the defendant or the state; but no person summoned as a juror shall be disqualified by reason of a previously formed or expressed opinion with reference to the guilt or innocence of the accused, if the court is satisfied, from the examination of the juror or from other evidence, that the juror will render an impartial verdict according to the law and the evidence submitted to the jury at the trial.

(10) That the juror is related by consanguinity or affinity within the fifth degree to the person alleged to be injured or attempted to be injured by the offense charged, or to the person on whose complaint the prosecution was instituted; or to the defendant.

(11) That the juror is the person alleged to be injured or attempted to be injured by the offense charged, or the person on whose complaint the prosecution was instituted, or the defendant.

(12) That the juror is the employer or employee, or the spouse, parent, son, or daughter of the employer or employee, or the counselor, agent, or attorney, of any person included in division (B)(11) of this rule.

(13) That English is not the juror's native language, and the juror's knowledge of English is insufficient to permit the juror to understand the facts and the law in the case.

(14) That the juror is otherwise unsuitable for any other cause to serve as a juror.

The validity of each challenge listed in division (B) of this rule shall be determined by the court.

(D) **Peremptory challenges.** In addition to challenges provided in division (C) of this rule, if there is one defendant, each party peremptorily may challenge three prospective jurors in misdemeanor cases, four prospective jurors in felony cases other than capital cases, and six prospective jurors in capital cases. If there is more than one defendant, each defendant peremptorily may challenge the same number of prospective jurors as if the defendant was the sole defendant.

In any case where there are multiple defendants, the prosecuting attorney peremptorily may challenge a number of prospective jurors equal to the total peremptory challenges allowed all defendants. In case of the consolidation of any indictments, informations, or complaints for trial, the consolidated cases shall be considered, for purposes of exercising peremptory challenges, as though the defendants or offenses had been joined in the same indictment, information, or complaint.

(E) **Manner of exercising peremptory challenges.** Peremptory challenges shall be exercised alternately, with the first challenge exercised by the state. The failure of a party to exercise a peremptory challenge constitutes a waiver of that challenge, but does not constitute a waiver of any subsequent challenge. However, if all parties, alternately and in sequence, fail to exercise a peremptory challenge, the joint failure constitutes a waiver of all peremptory challenges.

A prospective juror peremptorily challenged by either party shall be excused.

Nothing in this rule shall limit the court's discretion to allow challenges under this division or division (D) of this rule to be made outside the hearing of prospective jurors.

(F) **Challenge to array.** The prosecuting attorney or the attorney for the defendant may challenge the array of petit jurors on the ground that it was not selected, drawn or summoned in accordance with law. A challenge to the array shall be made before the examination of the jurors pursuant to division (A) of this rule and shall be tried by the court.

No array of petit jurors shall be set aside, nor shall any verdict in any case be set aside because the jury commissioners have returned such jury or any juror in any informal or irregular manner, if in the opinion of the court the irregularity is unimportant and insufficient to vitiate the return.

(G) **Alternate jurors.**

(1) **Non-capital cases.** The court may direct that not more than six jurors in addition to the regular jury be called and impaneled to sit as alternate jurors. Alternate jurors in the order in which they are called shall replace jurors who, prior to the time the jury retires to consider its verdict, become or are found to be unable or disqualified to perform their duties. Alternate jurors shall be drawn in the same manner, have the same qualifications, be subject to the same examination and challenges, take the same oath, and have the same functions, powers, facilities, and privileges as the regular jurors. The court may retain alternate jurors after the jury retires to deliberate. The court must ensure that a retained alternate does not discuss the case with anyone until that alternate replaces a juror or is discharged. If an alternate replaces a juror after deliberations have begun, the court must instruct the jury to begin its deliberations anew. Each party is entitled to one peremptory challenge in addition to those otherwise allowed if one or two alternate jurors are to be impaneled, two peremptory challenges if three or four alternate jurors are to be impaneled, and three peremptory challenges if five or six alterna-

tive jurors are to be impaneled. The additional peremptory challenges may be used against an alternate juror only, and the other peremptory challenges allowed by this rule may not be used against an alternate juror.

(2) **Capital cases.** The procedure designated in division (G)(1) of this rule shall be the same in capital cases, except that any alternate juror shall continue to serve if more than one deliberation is required. If an alternate juror replaces a regular juror after a guilty verdict, the court shall instruct the alternate juror that the juror is bound by that verdict.

(H) **Control of juries.**

(1) **Before submission of case to jury.** Before submission of a case to the jury, the court, upon its own motion or the motion of a party, may restrict the separation of jurors or may sequester the jury.

(2) **After submission of case to jury.**

(a) **Misdemeanor cases.** After submission of a misdemeanor case to the jury, the court, after giving cautionary instructions, may permit the separation of jurors.

(b) **Non-capital felony cases.** After submission of a non-capital felony case to the jury, the court, after giving cautionary instructions, may permit the separation of jurors during any period of court adjournment or may require the jury to remain under the supervision of an officer of the court.

(c) **Capital cases.** After submission of a capital case to the jury, the jury shall remain under the supervision of an officer of the court until a verdict is rendered or the jury is discharged by the court.

(3) **Separation in emergency.** Where the jury is sequestered or after a capital case is submitted to the jury, the court may, in an emergency and upon giving cautionary instructions, allow temporary separation of jurors.

(4) **Duties of supervising officer.** Where jurors are required to remain under the supervision of an officer of the court, the court shall make arrangements for their care, maintenance and comfort.

When the jury is in the care of an officer of the court and until the jury is discharged by the court, the officer may inquire whether the jury has reached a verdict, but shall not:

(a) Communicate any matter concerning jury conduct to anyone except the judge or;

(b) Communicate with the jurors or permit communications with jurors, except as allowed by court order.

(I) **Taking of notes by jurors.** The court, after providing appropriate cautionary instructions, may permit jurors who wish to do so to take notes during a trial. If the court permits the taking of notes, notes taken by a juror may be carried into deliberations by that juror. The court shall require that all juror notes be collected and destroyed promptly after the jury renders a verdict.

(J) **Juror questions to witnesses.** The court may permit jurors to propose questions for the court to ask of the witnesses. If the court permits jurors to propose questions, the court shall use procedures that minimize the risk of prejudice, including all of the following:

(1) Require jurors to propose any questions to the court in writing;

(2) Retain a copy of each proposed question for the record;

(3) Instruct the jurors that they shall not display or discuss a proposed question with other jurors;

(4) Before reading a question to a witness, provide counsel with an opportunity to object to each question on the record and outside the hearing of the jury;

(5) Read the question, either as proposed or rephrased, to the witness;

(6) Permit counsel to reexamine the witness regarding a matter addressed by a juror question;

(7) If a question proposed by a juror is not asked, instruct the jurors that they should not draw any adverse inference from the court's refusal to ask any question proposed by a juror.

History: Amended, eff 7-1-75; 7-1-02; 7-1-05; 7-1-06; 7-1-08; 7-1-09.

NOTES TO DECISIONS

ANALYSIS

Alternate jurors
Capital cases
Challenge for cause
Dismissal for cause
Dismissal of juror sua sponte
Ineffective assistance
Peremptory challenges
— Discrimination
Removal of juror

Alternate jurors

Proceedings in which a deliberating juror is dismissed in a capital case, and an alternate juror is seated, must be recorded. Under former CrimR 24(G)(2), a juror cannot be replaced by an alternate juror during deliberations in a capital case: State v. Clinkscale, 122 Ohio St. 3d 351, 2009 Ohio 2746, 911 N.E.2d 862, 2009 Ohio LEXIS 1736 (2009).

Trial court erred in allowing an alternate juror to be present during deliberations. However, the error was harmless where there was no evidence that the alternate juror participated in any way during deliberations and the court gave the appropriate instructions: State v. Downour, 182 Ohio App. 3d 12, 2009 Ohio 1812, 911 N.E.2d 336, 2009 Ohio App. LEXIS 1585 (2009).

Trial court did not abuse its discretion in allowing jurors and alternate jurors to question witnesses in defendant's criminal trial, as the procedure to allow jurors to question witnesses was approved by the Ohio Supreme Court, and as alternate jurors had the same qualifications as regular jurors pursuant to Ohio R. Crim. P. 24(G)(1), there was no reason to disallow their questioning as well. State v. Berry, — Ohio App. 3d —, 2007 Ohio 278, — N.E. 2d —, 2007 Ohio App. LEXIS 263 (Jan. 25, 2007).

Trial court did not err by removing a juror for cause (bias) and replacing her with an alternate prior to the time the jury retired for deliberations. The trial court noted that the juror undeniably found the term "black" offensive enough to raise the issue with the court, that she was not calm during the discussion of the issue, and that it would put the attorneys in a terrible position to try to do their jobs. State v. Smith, — Ohio App. 3d —, 2007 Ohio 1680, — N.E. 2d —, 2007 Ohio App. LEXIS 1535 (Apr. 11, 2007).

Where the jurors retired to deliberate, which they did for one hour before the end of the day break, and upon returning the next day, one of the jurors was discharged because she claimed that she was fearful for her life and could not render a fair verdict, the replacement of the discharged juror with an alternate juror was not error under Ohio R. Crim. P. 24(G)(1), as the deliberations had not been ongoing for a great length of time, the jury was clearly instructed to begin deliberating again, and there was no showing by defendant that the outcome of the trial would have been different or that he suffered prejudice. State v. Felder, — Ohio App. 3d —, 2006 Ohio 5332, — N.E. 2d —, 2006 Ohio App. LEXIS 5311 (Oct. 12, 2006).

Trial court erred in not removing a juror who indicated that he had a social relationship with one of the victims involved in defendant's crime spree, pursuant to Ohio R. Crim. P. 24(F), as that juror's guarantee that he would "probably" not return to the victim's bar, and that he would "do the oath," was not of the necessary strength to show that the juror was not prejudiced by his relationship. State v. Strowder, — Ohio App. 3d —, 2006 Ohio 442, — N.E. 2d —, 2006 Ohio App. LEXIS 380 (Feb. 2, 2006).

RC § 2313.37 and Ohio R. Crim. P. 24(G)(1) required alternate jurors to be discharged once a case was submitted to the jury for deliberations, so it was clearly an error to not discharge the alternates and instead require them to sit in on the deliberations, but not participate, but, in capital cases, alternate jurors were not to be discharged until after the jury retired to deliberate regarding the penalty phase, under Ohio R. Crim. P. 24(G)(2), so an alternate juror could not be present nor participate in the deliberations for the guilt phase, and instead, the trial court had to retain the alternate jurors and continue to instruct them with the same rules and admonitions until such time as they were discharged. State v. Hairston, — Ohio App. 3d —, 2006 Ohio 4925, — N.E. 2d —, 2006 Ohio App. LEXIS 4886 (Sept. 25, 2006).

Capital cases

Although the trial court erred when it answered a jury question without first consulting counsel for defendant and the state, the error was harmless. Given the short period of time the jury had been deliberating, the court's response to the question, "What would require declaration of a hung jury?" of, "Many more hours of deliberation" was reasonable and not inherently coercive. When the jury asked, apparently in response to the reservations of one juror, whether a finding of guilty could be based on one witness's testimony, the court correctly responded that the testimony of any witness is sufficient, if believed, to prove any fact. Trial court's replacement of a deliberating juror with an alternate juror in a capital case, contrary to CrimR 24(G)(2), did not constitute plain error: State v. Clinkscale, 177 Ohio App. 3d 294, 2008 Ohio 1677, 894 N.E.2d 700, 2008 Ohio App. LEXIS 1439 (2008).

Challenge for cause

Trial court abused its discretion in denying the defendant's challenge for cause as it related to a hearing-impaired juror: State v. Speer, 180 Ohio App. 3d 230, 2008 Ohio 6947, 904 N.E.2d 956, 2008 Ohio App. LEXIS 5833 (2008).

Trial court properly denied defense counsel's request to remove a juror for cause in defendant's criminal trial, as the juror clearly indicated that he could be fair and impartial with respect to testimony regarding fingerprints found at the scene; there was no cause to remove him under Ohio R. Crim. P. 24(C)(9) and (14), RC §§ 2313.42(J), and 2313.43, as he indicated that he assumed defendant was innocent, that he could maintain the presumption of innocence until the conclusion of the evidence, and that he could listen to the evidence and judge it fairly. State v. Phillips, — Ohio App. 3d —, 2007 Ohio 2150, — N.E. 2d —, 2007 Ohio App. LEXIS 2005 (May 4, 2007).

Trial court did not abuse its discretion when it denied defendant's request to dismiss a deputy sheriff for cause during jury selection. The deputy told the trial court that the county sheriff's office had not been the investigating agency in the case, that the deputy could fairly assess the investigating officer's credibility, and that the deputy could follow the court's instructions. State v. Farr, — Ohio App. 3d —, 2007 Ohio 3136, — N.E. 2d —, 2007 Ohio App. LEXIS 2900 (June 25, 2007).

Where a prospective juror indicated that she was not "perfectly happy" to be there because she was a school secretary and it was a busy time just prior to the school opening, the trial court's denial of defendant's challenge of that juror for cause was not an abuse of discretion, as such did not constitute a valid challenge for cause under Ohio R. Crim. P. 24(C). State v. Wilson, — Ohio App. 3d —, 2007 Ohio 4564, — N.E. 2d —, 2007 Ohio App. LEXIS 4089 (Aug. 31, 2007).

There was no error under RC §§ 2313.42(J) and 2313.43, and under Ohio R. Crim. P. 24(C), by the trial court's excusing a prospective juror for cause where the juror indicated that she had previously worked as a victim/witness advocate, was the victim of a sex offense, and had been robbed twice at gunpoint. The juror had also indicated that she was not sure if she would be able to serve on the jury and be unbiased, and that she would tend to favor the defendant. State v. Hinson, — Ohio App. 3d —, 2006 Ohio 3831, — N.E. 2d —, 2006 Ohio App. LEXIS 3803 (July 27, 2006).

There was no error in the trial court's refusal to excuse two prospective jurors for cause pursuant to Ohio R. Crim. P. 24(C)(9), and there was no violation of defendant's Sixth Amendment right by the trial court's action therein, as one juror was removed by a peremptory challenge and the other juror did not even hear the case. Although the jurors initially expressed some doubt, they both thereafter indicated that they could be fair and impartial. State v. Bell, — Ohio App. 3d —, 2006 Ohio 6592, — N.E. 2d —, 2006 Ohio App. LEXIS 6531 (Dec. 14, 2006).

Dismissal for cause

Trial court did not abuse its discretion in dismissing a prospective juror for cause where there was a lack of cooperation with the jury selection process by the prospective juror, and dismissal was within the trial court's discretion pursuant to Ohio R. Crim. P. 24(B). State v. Woods, — Ohio App. 3d —, 2006 Ohio 1342, — N.E. 2d —, 2006 Ohio App. LEXIS 1218 (Mar. 23, 2006).

Dismissal of juror sua sponte

Trial court did not commit plain error by failing to, sua sponte, remove a juror whose daughters knew the victim and her sister because, when the juror was asked if his familiarity would affect his judgment, he unequivocally stated that it would not. Thus, the trial court had no basis to remove the juror from the panel. Ohio v. Danny W. Thompson, — Ohio App. 3d —, 2007 Ohio 5419, — N.E. 2d —, 2007 Ohio App. LEXIS 4762 (Oct. 4, 2007).

When a trial court dismissed jurors sua sponte, under Ohio R. Crim. P. 24, without explicitly stating its reasons for doing so, defendant was not prejudiced because the reasons for the trial court's actions were apparent from the record. State v. Wood, — Ohio App. 3d —, 2006 Ohio 3781, — N.E. 2d —, 2006 Ohio App. LEXIS 3732 (July 24, 2006).

Ineffective assistance

Defendant's counsel's failure to exercise a peremptory challenge to remove a juror pursuant to Ohio R. Crim. P. 24(B) was a tactical decision, as the fact that the juror had previously been a prosecuting attorney who currently did defense work, and the fact that he knew both the prosecutor and defendant's counsel, did not indicate bias where he stated that he could remain impartial. There was no ineffectiveness of counsel shown in violation of U.S. Const. amend. VI and Ohio Const. art. I, § 10. State v. Lee, — Ohio App. 3d —, 2007 Ohio 288, — N.E. 2d —, 2007 Ohio App. LEXIS 273 (Jan. 25, 2007).

Peremptory challenges

Defense counsel was not ineffective for failing to raise a Batson challenge where there was no pattern of strikes against

African-American jurors and no evidence of a discriminatory motive of the state: State v. Cicerchi, 182 Ohio App. 3d 753, 2009 Ohio 2249, 915 N.E.2d 350, 2009 Ohio App. LEXIS 1923 (2009).

Prosecutor did not present a race-neutral reason for exercising a peremptory challenge against an African-American prospective jury where he merely speculated or assumed that she had been involved in a protest by African-Americans concerning another case, without making the required effort to find out whether the juror was, in fact, involved: State v. Manns, 169 Ohio App. 3d 687, 2006 Ohio 5802, 864 N.E.2d 657, 2006 Ohio App. LEXIS 5749 (2006).

— Discrimination
State provided two race-neutral reasons for the peremptory challenge of the only black potential juror: State v. Franklin, 178 Ohio App. 3d 460, 2008 Ohio 4811, 898 N.E.2d 990, 2008 Ohio App. LEXIS 4046 (2008).

Defendant did not establish that the state's peremptory challenges of two African-American prospective jurors violated Batson: State v. Frazier, 115 Ohio St. 3d 139, 2007 Ohio 5048, 873 N.E.2d 1263, 2007 Ohio LEXIS 2519 (2007).

Removal of juror
Trial court's removal of a juror and replacement of that juror with an alternate where he merely speculated or assumed that under RC § 2945.29 and Ohio R. Crim. P. 24(F)(1) because the juror was observed speaking to a prospective witness, and this was sufficient, in and of itself, to support the trial court's decision. Ohio v. Mitchell, — Ohio App. 3d —, 2007 Ohio 5519, — N.E. 2d —, 2007 Ohio App. LEXIS 4852 (Oct. 9, 2007).

RULE 25.   Disability of a Judge

(A) **During trial.** If for any reason the judge before whom a jury trial has commenced is unable to proceed with the trial, another judge designated by the administrative judge, or, in the case of a single-judge division, by the Chief Justice of the Supreme Court of Ohio, may proceed with and finish the trial, upon certifying in the record that he has familiarized himself with the record of the trial. If such other judge is satisfied that he cannot adequately familiarize himself with the record, he may in his discretion grant a new trial.

(B) **After verdict or finding of guilt.** If for any reason the judge before whom the defendant has been tried is unable to perform the duties of the court after a verdict or finding of guilt, another judge designated by the administrative judge, or, in the case of a single-judge division, by the Chief Justice of the Supreme Court of Ohio, may perform those duties. If such other judge is satisfied that he cannot perform those duties because he did not preside at the trial, he may in his discretion grant a new trial.

NOTES TO DECISIONS
ANALYSIS
Trial transcript and record

Trial transcript and record
Successor judge did not err in granting a new trial under Ohio R. Crim. P. 25(B), after the trial judge recused himself after the verdict but before sentencing, without first reviewing the trial transcript and the record as Ohio R. Crim. P. 25(B) does not require a judge to review the transcript or record

before finding that the judge cannot perform the post-verdict duties. State v. Rhoads, — Ohio App. 3d —, 2007 Ohio 3890, — N.E. 2d —, 2007 Ohio App. LEXIS 3527 (May 21, 2007).

RULE 26.   Substitution of Photographs for Physical Evidence

Physical property, other than contraband, as defined by statute, under the control of a Prosecuting Attorney for use as evidence in a hearing or trial should be returned to the owner at the earliest possible time. To facilitate the early return of such property, where appropriate, and by court order, photographs, as defined in Evid. R. 1001(2), may be taken of the property and introduced as evidence in the hearing or trial. The admission of such photographs is subject to the relevancy requirements of Evid. R. 401, Evid. R. 402, Evid. R. 403, the authentication requirements of Evid. R. 901, and the best evidence requirements of Evid. R. 1002.

History: Effective, 7-1-81.

RULE 27.   Proof of Official Record; Judicial Notice: Determination of Foreign Law

The proof of official records provisions of Civil Rule 44, and the judicial notice and determination of foreign law provisions of Civil Rule 44.1 apply in criminal cases.

RULE 28.   Reserved.

RULE 29.   Motion for Acquittal

(A) **Motion for judgment of acquittal.** The court on motion of a defendant or on its own motion, after the evidence on either side is closed, shall order the entry of a judgment of acquittal of one or more offenses charged in the indictment, information, or complaint, if the evidence is insufficient to sustain a conviction of such offense or offenses. The court may not reserve ruling on a motion for judgment of acquittal made at the close of the state's case.

(B) **Reservation of decision on motion.** If a motion for a judgment of acquittal is made at the close of all the evidence, the court may reserve decision on the motion, submit the case to the jury and decide the motion either before the jury returns a verdict, or after it returns a verdict of guilty, or after it is discharged without having returned a verdict.

(C) **Motion after verdict or discharge of jury.** If a jury returns a verdict of guilty or is discharged without having returned a verdict, a motion for judgment of acquittal may be made or renewed within fourteen days after the jury is discharged or within such further time as the court may fix during the fourteen day period. If a verdict of guilty is returned, the court may on such motion set aside the verdict and enter judgment of acquittal. If no verdict is returned, the court may enter judgment of acquittal. It shall not be a prerequisite to the making of such motion that a similar motion has been made prior to the submission of the case to the jury.

NOTES TO DECISIONS

ANALYSIS

Appeal
Appeal by state
Applicability
Bench trials
Denial of acquittal
Denial of motion moot
Failure to preserve
Ineffective assistance of counsel
Motion improperly denied
Motion properly denied
Preservation for review
Procedure
Properly preserved
Reopening of state's case
Sexual arousal
Sufficiency of evidence
Timeliness
Venue
Waiver
Waiver of right to appeal

Appeal

Although defendant did not file a motion for acquittal pursuant to Ohio R. Crim. P. 29(A) during his criminal trial, his right to raise the issue of the sufficiency of the evidence on appeal was not waived thereby, as he preserved his right to object to any alleged insufficiency when he entered a plea of not guilty. A conviction based on insufficient evidence would violate due process, such that it would almost always be plain error in any event and accordingly, could be raised on appeal. State v. Cooper, 170 Ohio App. 3d 418, 2007 Ohio 1186, 867 N.E.2d 493, 2007 Ohio App. LEXIS 1115 (2007).

Although defendant's counsel failed to renew an acquittal motion pursuant to Ohio R. Crim. P. 29 at the close of defendant's case, defendant did not waive his right to argue the sufficiency of the evidence on appeal, as he argued that his conviction was against the manifest weight of the evidence. A determination of whether the conviction was supported by the weight of the evidence necessarily rested on the existence of sufficient evidence. State v. Pesec, — Ohio App. 3d —, 2007 Ohio 3846, — N.E. 2d —, 2007 Ohio App. LEXIS 3487 (July 27, 2007).

Trial court's denial of defendant's acquittal motion pursuant to Ohio R. Crim. P. 29 was not properly reviewable by an appellate court because defendant's brief did not comply with the requirements of Ohio R. App. P. 16(A)(7) and Ohio 9th Dist. Ct. App. R. 7(B)(7) where there was no citation to any authority that supported defendant's position, and his contentions did not constitute an argument; accordingly, affirmance of the trial court's decision was proper under Ohio R. App. P. 12(A)(2). State v. Stelzer, — Ohio App. 3d —, 2006 Ohio 6912, — N.E. 2d —, 2006 Ohio App. LEXIS 6818 (Dec. 27, 2006).

Appeal by state

As a verdict of acquittal granted by the trial court under Ohio R. Crim. P. 29(C) was a final verdict within the meaning of RC § 2945.67(A), the State was specifically statutorily barred from appealing directly from the acquittal decision in defendant's matter; the State could have sought leave to appeal the ruling under Ohio R. App. P. 5(C), but it failed to follow that procedure. State v. Selinka, — Ohio App. 3d —, 2007 Ohio 5435, — N.E. 2d —, 2007 Ohio App. LEXIS 4779 (Oct. 11, 2007).

State's appeal of the grant of defendant's motion for acquittal was dismissed sua sponte because a judgment of acquittal was not appealable by the State as a matter of right or by leave of court under RC § 2945.67, and the State was statutorily prohibited from appealing the final verdict without putting defendant in double jeopardy. State v. Hoffstetter, — Ohio App. 3d —, 2007 Ohio 6727, — N.E. 2d —, 2007 Ohio App. LEXIS 5893 (Dec. 14, 2007).

State was barred from appealing the grant of an acquittal motion under Ohio R. Crim. P. 29, as it represented a "final verdict" and the situation was not one of those enumerated for purposes of allowing an appeal by the State as of right under RC § 2945.67(A). State v. Rivers, — Ohio App. 3d —, 2006 Ohio 3949, — N.E. 2d —, 2006 Ohio App. LEXIS 3905 (Aug. 3, 2006).

Applicability

Motion for acquittal under Ohio R. Crim. P. 29 was allowed in a juvenile delinquency proceeding, as it was arguably within the extended scope of Ohio R. Crim. P. 1(C) since no specific procedure for an analogous motion was found in the Ohio Rules of Juvenile Procedure. In re A.K., — Ohio App. 3d —, 2007 Ohio 2095, — N.E. 2d —, 2007 Ohio App. LEXIS 1951 (Apr. 27, 2007).

Bench trials

Trial court did not err in not granting defendant's motion for acquittal because Ohio R. Crim. P. 29 has no application in a bench trial. State v. Massie, — Ohio App. 3d —, 2006 Ohio 1515, — N.E. 2d —, 2006 Ohio App. LEXIS 1407 (Mar. 29, 2006).

Denial of acquittal

Trial court's denial of defendant's acquittal motion pursuant to Ohio R. Crim. P. 29(A) was proper, as the weight and sufficiency of the evidence supported defendant's convictions for having a weapon while under a disability, in violation of RC § 2923.13(A)(3), and murder as a lesser included offense, in violation of RC § 2903.02(A); there was witness testimony and physical evidence to support the determination that defendant had driven a particular vehicle, had a verbal confrontation with the victim, and then defendant fatally shot the victim before driving away, and further, defendant admitted to a prior conviction for purposes of satisfying the disability element of the weapons offense. State v. Hooks, — Ohio App. 3d —, 2007 Ohio 5944, — N.E. 2d —, 2007 Ohio App. LEXIS 5257 (Nov. 8, 2007).

Denial of motion moot

Defendant's argument that the trial court erred in denying his Ohio R. Crim. P. 29 motion, seeking the dismissal of a charge of felonious assault was moot since defendant was found not guilty of felonious assault. State v. Powers, — Ohio App. 3d —, 2007 Ohio 4420, — N.E. 2d —, 2007 Ohio App. LEXIS 3985 (Aug. 29, 2007).

Failure to preserve

When defendant asserted that the evidence was insufficient to support his conviction under RC § 2921.34(A)(1), his claim was not preserved because the record did not indicate that he moved for a judgment of acquittal at the close of all the evidence, under Ohio R. Crim. P. 29, even though the trial court directed him to make his post-evidence motions at side bar, because he could have submitted a statement pursuant to Ohio R. App. P. 9(C) indicating that such a motion was made, but he did not. State v. McCuller, — Ohio App. 3d —, 2007 Ohio 348, — N.E. 2d —, 2007 Ohio App. LEXIS 312 (Jan. 29, 2007).

Since defendant failed to move for an Ohio R. Crim. P. 29(A) judgment of acquittal, she waived all but plain error regarding her contention that her conviction for assault on a peace officer was not supported by sufficient evidence. State v. Dixon, — Ohio App. 3d —, 2007 Ohio 2989, — N.E. 2d —, 2007 Ohio App. LEXIS 2745 (June 18, 2007).

Defendant failed to preserve his argument that the trial court erred in denying his motion to dismiss the indictment because his motion to dismiss went beyond the face of indictment, and thus, he could present his challenge only as a motion for acquittal at the close of the State's case under Ohio R. Crim. P. 29(A). His failure to do so precluded appellate review of the issue. State v. Roman, — Ohio App. 3d —, 2007 Ohio 4341, — N.E. 2d —, 2007 Ohio App. LEXIS 3896 (Aug. 27, 2007).

When defendant was charged with underage consumption of alcohol, evidence that his parents were present at the home at which defendant consumed alcohol, even though they were asleep in a different room, established, as a matter of law, the statutory defense in RC § 4301.69(E)(1), under which an underage person could consume alcohol when accompanied by a parent, because the parents did not have to supervise defendant while he consumed alcohol, and the evidence showed that defendant's parents were exercising their right to allow their son to drink in their home, so plain error was shown, under Ohio R. Crim. P. 52(B), despite defendant's failure to renew his motion for a judgment of acquittal, under Ohio R. Crim. P. 29(A), after presenting evidence. State v. Pelfrey, 167 Ohio App. 3d 388, 2006 Ohio 1416, 855 N.E. 2d 501, 2006 Ohio App. LEXIS 1309 (Mar. 27, 2006).

Since defendant failed to renew his motion for acquittal at the close of all the evidence, pursuant to Ohio R. Crim. P. 29(A), he waived his challenge to the trial court's denial of his motion for acquittal. State v. Joziuk, — Ohio App. 3d —, 2006 Ohio 5421, — N.E. 2d —, 2006 Ohio App. LEXIS 5418 (Oct. 18, 2006).

Ineffective assistance of counsel

Where the evidence was found to have been sufficient to support defendant's convictions, her claim that her counsel was ineffective in violation of U.S. Const. amend. VI for failing to file a motion for acquittal under Ohio R. Crim. P. 29 lacked merit. State v. Davidson, — Ohio App. 3d —, 2006 Ohio 1458, — N.E. 2d —, 2006 Ohio App. LEXIS 1291 (Mar. 24, 2006).

Because an Ohio R. Crim. P. 29 motion had virtually no chance of success, defense counsel did not perform deficiently in failing to file that motion. State v. Horton, — Ohio App. 3d —, 2006 Ohio 3736, — N.E. 2d —, 2006 Ohio App. LEXIS 3680 (July 20, 2006).

Motion improperly denied

In defendant's prosecution for wrongful entrustment of a motor vehicle, in violation of Bedford, Ohio, Municipal Ordinance 335.05(A)(2), which was the counterpart of RC § 4507.33, the fact that defendant posted bond for her son-in-law six years earlier when the son-in-law was charged with driving with a suspended license did not constitute evidence proving that defendant "knew," within the meaning of RC § 2901.22(B), or had reasonable cause to know that the son-in-law had a suspended license six years later when he drove defendant's vehicle; thus, defendant's Ohio R. Crim. P. 29(A) motion for judgment of acquittal should have been granted. City of Bedford v. Davis, — Ohio App. 3d —, 2007 Ohio 5949, — N.E. 2d —, 2007 Ohio App. LEXIS 5253 (Nov. 8, 2007).

Defendant's motion for acquittal, filed in her prosecution for wrongful entrustment of a motor vehicle, in violation of Bedford, Ohio, Municipal Ordinance 335.05(A)(2), which was the counterpart of RC § 4507.33, should have been granted because the city failed to present any evidence that defendant permitted her son-in-law to drive her car and that defendant "knew," within the meaning of RC § 2901.22(B) or had reasonable cause to know that her son-in-law's license was suspended. The fact that defendant knew at the police station, after her son-in-law had been arrested in her car and her car was impounded, that her son-in-law had driven her car did not prove that defendant permitted him to drive it; thus, defendant's Ohio R. Crim. P. 29(A) motion for judgment of acquittal

should have been granted. City of Bedford v. Davis, — Ohio App. 3d —, 2007 Ohio 5949, — N.E. 2d —, 2007 Ohio App. LEXIS 5253 (Nov. 8, 2007).

Motion properly denied

Though defendant contended that his conviction for driving under suspension was not supported by sufficient evidence because the State failed to introduce the LEADS report into evidence until after defendant made an Ohio R. Crim. P. 29 motion, defendant failed to include, pursuant to Ohio R. App. P. 9, the portion of the transcript related to any discussions on the admission of the LEADS report had at the end of the case, and the evidence of record showed that the officer had discovered that defendant's driver's license was under suspension. Thus, defendant's motion for acquittal under Ohio R. Crim. P. 29(A) was properly denied. Ohio v. Evans, — Ohio App. 3d —, 2007 Ohio 5934, — N.E. 2d —, 2007 Ohio App. LEXIS 5199 (Nov. 7, 2007).

Defendant's conviction for failure to comply was supported by evidence that defendant drove away from the officer during a traffic stop and that defendant caused substantial risk of harm to person and property, within the meaning of RC § 2901.01(A)(5) and (6), when he passed traffic on the berm and when he went into the median on the highway as he tried to elude the officer; thus, the trial court properly denied defendant's Ohio R. Crim. P. 29 motion for acquittal. Ohio v. Evans, — Ohio App. 3d —, 2007 Ohio 5934, — N.E. 2d —, 2007 Ohio App. LEXIS 5199 (Nov. 7, 2007).

Trial court did not err by denying defendant's Ohio R. Crim. P. 29 motion for acquittal, as the State submitted sufficient evidence, including a victim's testimony and defendant's child's out-of-court statements, to establish that contact involving defendant's child was for the purpose of sexually arousing defendant (RC § 2907.01). State v. D.H., 2007 Ohio 5970, 2007 Ohio App. LEXIS 5236 (Nov. 8, 2007).

Trial court did not err in denying defendant's motion for a judgment of acquittal, as the State made a prima facie case that defendant altered defendant's Social Security card. There was testimony from a Social Security employee that the number on the card defendant presented was not defendant's and, in fact, belonged to someone living in Alabama; additionally, a license examiner testified that defendant both presented the altered card and signed an application form, attesting that the Social Security number belonged to defendant. State v. Dixon, — Ohio App. 3d —, 2007 Ohio 6882, — N.E. 2d —, 2007 Ohio App. LEXIS 5999 (Dec. 21, 2007).

Preservation for review

While defendant failed to renew his Ohio R. Crim. P. 29 motion at the close of his defense, the court was permitted to consider whether defendant's conviction was based upon sufficient evidence because defendant also argued that his conviction was against the manifest weight of the evidence, the determination of which necessarily rested on the existence of sufficient evidence. City of Chardon v. Patterson, — Ohio App. 3d —, 2007 Ohio 1769, — N.E. 2d —, 2007 Ohio App. LEXIS 1627 (Apr. 13, 2007).

Procedure

Although a defendant was generally required to seek acquittal both after the close of the State's case and at the close of all evidence, as defendant did not put forth any evidence in his criminal jury trial, his initial motion made after the State's case was presented met the procedural requirements. State v. Coughlin, — Ohio App. 3d —, 2007 Ohio 897, — N.E. 2d —, 2007 Ohio App. LEXIS 803 (Mar. 2, 2007).

Properly preserved

Since defendant pled not guilty before being tried to the bench, it was not necessary for him to renew his motion for acquittal at the close of all the evidence; therefore, defendant did not waive the issue of the sufficiency of the evidence to support his conviction for assault. State v. Artemus, — Ohio App. 3d —, 2007 Ohio 864, — N.E. 2d —, 2007 Ohio App. LEXIS 772 (Mar. 2, 2007).

Reopening of state's case

During a trial on charges of trafficking in marijuana and possession of marijuana, the trial court did not abuse its discretion in allowing the State to reopen its case after defendant filed his motion for acquittal in order to allow a sergeant to testify that the total weight of all the marijuana found was in excess of 20,000 grams because testimony as to the weight of the marijuana was already present for the trier of fact to consider after the sergeant testified the first time, and the subsequent testimony showed merely the basis for determining the average derived from the total weight of all the bricks found. State v. Mathis, — Ohio App. 3d —, 2007 Ohio 2345, — N.E. 2d —, 2007 Ohio App. LEXIS 2206 (May 16, 2007).

It was not an abuse of discretion for the trial court to allow the State to reopen its case to present evidence on an element of the charged offense after defendant moved for a judgment of acquittal, under Ohio R. Crim. P. 29(A), in a prosecution for receiving stolen property, under RC § 2913.51(A), because the new evidence the State presented, to show defendant's knowledge that the property he possessed was stolen, was in the State's possession at the beginning of its case, and the State only inadvertently failed to present it, and it was in the interest of justice to allow the trier of fact to hear all relevant evidence. State v. Nerren, — Ohio App. 3d —, 2006 Ohio 2855, — N.E. 2d —, 2006 Ohio App. LEXIS 2672 (June 7, 2006).

Sexual arousal

Trial court did not err by denying defendant's Ohio R. Crim. P. 29 motion for acquittal, as the State submitted sufficient evidence, including a victim's testimony and defendant's child's out-of-court statements, to establish that contact involving defendant's child was for the purpose of sexually arousing defendant (RC § 2907.01). State v. D.H., 2007 Ohio 5970, 2007 Ohio App. LEXIS 5236 (Nov. 8, 2007).

Sufficiency of evidence

Lack of an arraignment cannot be used as a basis to find that the evidence presented by the state on the material elements of the charge was insufficient for purposes of CrimR 29: State v. Bickel, 178 Ohio App. 3d 535, 899 N.E.2d 154, 2008 Ohio App. LEXIS 4837 (2008).

Although defendant did not file a motion for acquittal pursuant to Ohio R. Crim. P. 29(A), he was not deemed to have waived his right to appeal the sufficiency of the evidence against him, as a conviction based on insufficient evidence would almost always amount to plain error and a not guilty plea preserved the issue for review. Defendant's conviction of domestic violence, in violation of RC § 2919.25(F), was supported by sufficient evidence where the victim stated that she had been together with defendant on and off for the prior eight years, she had lived with him on the day of the offense and afterwards, and they were married prior to trial. State v. Brown, — Ohio App. 3d —, 2007 Ohio 2005, — N.E. 2d —, 2007 Ohio App. LEXIS 1782 (Apr. 26, 2007).

Timeliness

Trial court properly overruled defendant's motion for a judgment of acquittal because the motion was untimely, in that it was filed more than 14 days after the jury was discharged. State v. Wilder, — Ohio App. 3d —, 2006 Ohio 1975, — N.E. 2d —, 2006 Ohio App. LEXIS 1803 (Apr. 21, 2006).

Venue

Defendant's counsel's failure to move for acquittal pursuant to Ohio R. Crim. P. 29 due to an alleged lack of venue was not ineffective assistance, as the State's evidence was sufficient to establish venue; although counsel had argued about the venue issue and then failed to raise it in either of the arguments under Rule 29, there was no prejudice to defendant and the outcome of the trial would not have been different. State v. Skinner, — Ohio App. 3d —, 2007 Ohio 6793, — N.E. 2d —, 2007 Ohio App. LEXIS 5948 (Dec. 14, 2007).

Waiver

Court rejected the State's contention that defendant waived any error as to both weight and sufficiency of the evidence on the ground that defendant failed to move for acquittal at the end of the State's case and at the close of all testimony pursuant to Ohio R. Crim. P. 29. The three cases cited by the State in support of its argument all related to challenges to the sufficiency of the evidence, and defendant argued only that his conviction was against the manifest weight of the evidence. State v. Bertram, — Ohio App. 3d —, 2007 Ohio 3107, — N.E. 2d —, 2007 Ohio App. LEXIS 2864 (June 22, 2007).

Since defendant did not move for acquittal at close of the evidence, he waived his right to challenge on sufficiency grounds his convictions for felonious assault and robbery. Even so, the victim's testimony that defendant pulled her hair and punched her in the face several times and that he refused to allow her to leave his locked car until the victim gave him money, the investigating officer's testimony, and the victim's medical records constituted sufficient evidence to convict. State v. McCloud, — Ohio App. 3d —, 2006 Ohio 5317, — N.E. 2d —, 2006 Ohio App. LEXIS 5288 (Oct. 10, 2006).

Defendant waived any claim that his convictions for aggravated trespassing and intimidation of a witness were not supported by sufficient evidence because he did not move for acquittal, under Ohio R. Crim. P. 29. State v. Blausey, — Ohio App. 3d —, 2006 Ohio 5536, — N.E. 2d —, 2006 Ohio App. LEXIS 5513 (Oct. 24, 2006).

Waiver of right to appeal

Defendant waived his challenge to the sufficiency of the evidence to convict him of assault and criminal damaging or endangering because he moved for acquittal in the trial court only as to the felonious assault charge against him. If an Ohio R. Crim. P. 29 motion for acquittal is not made by a defendant, he waives all arguments regarding sufficiency on appeal. State v. Campbell, — Ohio App. 3d —, 2006 Ohio 4977, — N.E. 2d —, 2006 Ohio App. LEXIS 4930 (Sept. 27, 2006).

RULE 30. Instructions

(A) **Instructions; error; record.** At the close of the evidence or at such earlier time during the trial as the court reasonably directs, any party may file written requests that the court instruct the jury on the law as set forth in the requests. Copies shall be furnished to all other parties at the time of making the requests. The court shall inform counsel of its proposed action on the requests prior to counsel's arguments to the jury and shall give the jury complete instructions after the arguments are completed. The court also may give some or all of its instructions to the jury prior to counsel's arguments. The court shall reduce its final instructions to writing or make an audio, electronic, or other recording of those instructions, provide at least one written copy or recording of those instructions to the jury for use during deliberations, and preserve those instructions for the record.

On appeal, a party may not assign as error the giving or the failure to give any instructions unless the party objects before the jury retires to consider its verdict, stating specifically the matter objected to and the grounds of the objection. Opportunity shall be given to make the objection out of the hearing of the jury.

(B) **Cautionary instructions.** At the commencement and during the course of the trial, the court may give the jury cautionary and other instructions of law relating to trial procedure, credibility and weight of the evidence, and the duty and function of the jury and may acquaint the jury generally with the nature of the case.

History: Amended, eff 7-1-75; 7-1-82; 7-1-92; 7-1-05.

NOTES TO DECISIONS

ANALYSIS

Abandonment as defense
Accident as defense
Accomplice testimony
Alibi
Alternative counts
Burden of proof
Causation and natural consequences
Cautionary instructions
Complicity
Credibility
Culpable mental states
Drug offenses, generally
Elements of offense
Entrapment
Failure to object to instructions
Failure to object to jury instruction
Flight
Force
Inferior degree offense
Insanity
Instruction of aggravated assault
Intoxication as defense
Jury deadlock
Jury instruction
Jury request during deliberations
Lesser included offense
Lesser included offenses
Limiting instruction
Objections
Plain error rule
Purpose, instruction on
Request for instruction
Self-defense
Unanimity
Written instructions

Abandonment as defense

Trial court did not err in instructing the jury on renunciation (abandonment of any criminal purpose) because under the attempt statute, RC § 2923.02, the affirmative defense of abandonment required a complete and voluntary renunciation of the criminal purpose. There had been no "complete and voluntary renunciation" of a criminal purpose because the abandonment of the criminal activity was undertaken under fear of imminent detection or apprehension. State v. McGhee, — Ohio App. 3d —, 2007 Ohio 6527, — N.E. 2d —, 2007 Ohio App. LEXIS 5696 (Dec. 7, 2007).

Accident as defense

There was no abuse of discretion in the trial court's decision not to instruct the jury regarding accident because the State presented overwhelming evidence that the victim's death was not an accident. The State presented expert testimony that the shotgun required multiple actions to be discharged and that the shotgun could not have "accidentally" discharged. Further, the State presented evidence that the bullet traveled from the back to the front of the victim's body and that it was physically improbable that the victim had been holding onto the gun when it discharged given the length of the gun and the length of her arm. State v. Elwell, — Ohio App. 3d —, — N.E. 2d —, 2007 Ohio 3122, 2007 Ohio App. LEXIS 2935 (June 25, 2007).

Defendant failed to show that a plain error under Ohio R. Crim. P. 52(B) affected his substantial rights where his counsel chose to pursue a negligent homicide defense rather than a defense of an accident in defendant's murder trial, and accordingly, defense counsel did not request an instruction on accident, nor was one given, under Ohio R. Crim. P. 30(A). The theory of an accident was contradicted by an instruction that the homicide occurred negligently, as the trial court did instruct the jury pursuant to defense counsel's request on that defense theory. State v. James, — Ohio App. 3d —, 2006 Ohio 271, — N.E. 2d —, 2006 Ohio App. LEXIS 240 (Jan. 23, 2006).

Accomplice testimony

Trial court admonished the jury on three separate occasions that it had to view the testimony of defendant's alleged accomplices with great caution and suspicion. Viewing the jury charge as a whole, that was all that was required regarding accomplice testimony. State v. Cochran, — Ohio App. 3d —, 2007 Ohio 345, — N.E. 2d —, 2007 Ohio App. LEXIS 291 (Jan. 26, 2007).

Alibi

Because the alibi witness's testimony did not support defendant's alibi, the trial court did not err in failing to give the jury an alibi instruction. The alibi witness's testimony highlighted the fact that he was not with defendant during the time of the robbery because he stated that he left defendant around midnight and, according to the testimony of the three eyewitnesses, the robbery occurred sometime between midnight and 2:00 a.m. State v. Nicholson, — Ohio App. 3d —, 2006 Ohio 1569, — N.E. 2d —, 2006 Ohio App. LEXIS 1466 (Mar. 30, 2006).

Alternative counts

Trial court did not err in failing to give a jury instruction on alternative counts as the two crimes, unlawful sexual conduct with a minor, under RC § 2907.04, and rape, under RC § 2907.02(A)(2), were separate criminal offenses, not alternatively charged counts of the same crime. The two offenses were not allied offenses of similar import because rape required proof of force or threat of force, but age was not a factor, and unlawful sexual conduct with a minor did not require force but required proof of sexual conduct with another who was between 13 and 16 years of age, or was reckless in that regard. State v. Dinkins, — Ohio App. 3d —, 2007 Ohio 1917, — N.E. 2d —, 2007 Ohio App. LEXIS 1728 (Apr. 23, 2007).

Burden of proof

Defendant's motion for a new trial was properly denied. There was no prejudice to defendant from the jury instruction because the instruction as given placed the entire burden of proof on the State, noting that it was beyond a reasonable doubt, and no burden was placed upon defendant. State v. Williams, — Ohio App. 3d —, 2007 Ohio 4845, — N.E. 2d —, 2007 Ohio App. LEXIS 4329 (Sept. 20, 2007).

Causation and natural consequences

Jury instruction on causation and natural consequences did not lower the mens rea requirement because the trial court gave the instruction in connection with a charge of felonious assault; the instruction did not contain references to presumptions, intent, or a reasonably prudent person; and the instruction did not constitute prejudicial error with respect to the jury instructions as a whole. Read in its full context, the jury instruction merely informed the jury that despite the existence of multiple causes for the victim's injuries, defendant was responsible for the natural consequences of his actions and the multiple causes were not a defense; thus, the jury instruction did not make an impermissible factual finding. State v. Nichols, — Ohio App. 3d —, 2006 Ohio 2934, — N.E. 2d —, 2006 Ohio App. LEXIS 2820 (June 9, 2006).

Cautionary instructions

Trial court properly instructed the jury on the essential elements of the charge of domestic violence. Also, the comments by the trial court were viewed to be cautionary instructions and the trial court did not error when it gave them after instructing the jury on the elements of the offense. Nor was there error in giving the cautionary instructions after arguments were completed, rather than at the commencement and during the course of the trial. State v. Wojtkiewicz, — Ohio App. 3d —, 2006 Ohio 6094, — N.E. 2d —, 2006 Ohio App. LEXIS 6030 (Nov. 17, 2006).

Complicity

Complicity instruction was proper because the evidence demonstrated that defendant rented, controlled, and had sole responsibility for the apartment wherein the trafficking and manufacturing of crack cocaine took place. Even if, for the sake of argument, defendant's role in those activities was nothing more than allowing them to occur in her apartment, she still could have been found guilty of complicity. State v. Kidd, — Ohio App. 3d —, 2007 Ohio 4113, — N.E. 2d —, 2007 Ohio App. LEXIS 3727 (Aug. 10, 2007).

Since it was determined that defendant's convictions for the principal offenses (involving drugs) were supported by sufficient evidence and not against the manifest weight of the evidence, the trial court did not abuse its discretion by also providing a complicity jury instruction. Ohio v. Darrin G. Sweeney, — Ohio App. 3d —, 2007 Ohio 5223, — N.E. 2d —, 2007 Ohio App. LEXIS 4604 (Sept. 28, 2007).

Trial court did not abuse its discretion by providing the jury with an instruction relating to complicity, pursuant to RC § 2923.03(F), because there was ample evidence presented at trial which established that defendant acted as the principal offender and engaged in complicity during the assaults. State v. Nichols, — Ohio App. 3d —, 2006 Ohio 2934, — N.E. 2d —, 2006 Ohio App. LEXIS 2820 (June 9, 2006).

Defendant failed to establish that he received ineffective assistance of counsel because it was clearly not error for defense counsel to fail to object to an instruction on complicity, as set forth in RC § 2923.03(F). The evidence established that defendant drove another man to a supermarket for the purpose of stealing merchandise, that he waited outside for the stolen items to be brought out, and that he helped load some of the stolen merchandise into the car; thus, because there was abundant evidence to show that defendant aided and abetted the man, the complicity instruction was entirely proper. State v. Demecs, — Ohio App. 3d —, 2006 Ohio 3802, — N.E. 2d —, 2006 Ohio App. LEXIS 3777 (July 21, 2006).

Credibility

General instruction on credibility was appropriate because the informant's testimony was corroborated by the audio tape of the transaction, the detectives' observations before the transaction, and the search after the arrest. State v. Oko, — Ohio App. 3d —, 2007 Ohio 538, — N.E. 2d —, 2007 Ohio App. LEXIS 490 (Feb. 8, 2007).

Culpable mental states

Although the trial court erred by refusing to give defendant's requested jury instruction on recklessly, as defined by RC § 2901.22(C), because its instruction on the harm element was incomplete, the error was harmless under Ohio R. Crim. P. 52(A). The evidence demonstrated that defendant's acts in committing aggravated robbery were done at least recklessly. State v. Renicker, — Ohio App. 3d —, 2008 Ohio 288, — N.E. 2d —, 2008 Ohio App. LEXIS 250 (Jan. 22, 2008).

Drug offenses, generally

When defendant was prosecuted for drug possession, under RC § 2925.11, because a crack pipe containing cocaine residue was found in defendant's car, it was not an abuse of discretion, under Ohio R. Crim. P. 30(A), for the trial court to deny defendant's request to instruct the jury on possession of drug paraphernalia, under RC § 2925.14(C), because the latter crime was not a lesser included offense of the former, nor were the crimes allied offenses of similar import. State v. Broughton, — Ohio App. 3d —, 2007 Ohio 5067, — N.E. 2d —, 2007 Ohio App. LEXIS 4472 (Sept. 27, 2007).

Elements of offense

Because the record did not demonstrate that the jury unanimously agreed upon the identity of the underlying offense of aggravated burglary that defendant had a purpose to commit, a manifest injustice occurred and plain error existed. The trial court did not specify any particular underlying criminal offense and there was no explanation or suggestion as to what crime could have constituted the underlying criminal offense that would prove the "purpose to commit any criminal offense" element of aggravated burglary. State v. Gardner, — Ohio App. 3d —, 2007 Ohio 182, — N.E. 2d —, 2007 Ohio App. LEXIS 163 (Jan. 19, 2007).

Record failed to demonstrate that the jury ever found beyond a reasonable doubt that anybody was "present or likely to be present" as to the charge of complicity to burglary, under RC § 2911.12(A)(2), because the trial court failed to properly instruct the jury on that element of burglary, which amounted to plain error. However, there was sufficient evidence to support a conviction under RC § 2911.12(A)(3), which did not contain the element of "present or likely to be present." State v. Recker, — Ohio App. 3d —, 2007 Ohio 216, — N.E. 2d —, 2007 Ohio App. LEXIS 209 (Jan. 22, 2007).

Trial court's instruction regarding burglary properly contained a definition of the term "occupied structure" and thus, the trial court did not fail to instruct on an element of the offense. Further, the trial court's definition of "occupied structure" was sufficient because, for the purpose of burglary, a garage attached to a house was obviously a "portion" of that house and thus, of an "occupied structure." State v. Cochran, — Ohio App. 3d —, 2007 Ohio 345, — N.E. 2d —, 2007 Ohio App. LEXIS 291 (Jan. 26, 2007).

Trial court did not abuse its discretion in overruling defendant's request for a mistrial because trial counsel failed to call the error (inadvertently omitting the definition of knowingly in the jury instructions) to the trial court's attention at a time when the error could have been corrected or avoided altogether, and the error of which he complained was minor and promptly corrected. Further, the trial court did not commit any error in issuing a Howard charge to the jury because the jury was unable to reach a consensus. State v. Barton, — Ohio App. 3d —, 2007 Ohio 1099, — N.E. 2d —, 2007 Ohio App. LEXIS 1020 (Mar. 12, 2007).

Although the word "purposely" should have been defined in the jury instruction, the failure to define it did not per se constitute plain error; it would only have constituted plain error if it could have been determined that had "purposely" been defined the jury would not have found defendant guilty of attempted murder. However, since the testimony established that defendant shot defendant multiple times and stated, "Die, Bitch" while he was shooting her, even if "purposely" had been defined, defendant would still have been convicted of attempted murder. State v. Jones, — Ohio App. 3d —, 2007 Ohio 3183, — N.E. 2d —, 2007 Ohio App. LEXIS 2961 (June 21, 2007).

There was no plain error in the jury instructions because the trial court's instruction was a proper statement of the law since it contemplated that the State had to prove each element, including the mens rea of the crime, in order for the jury to properly return a guilty verdict. Also, the order of the trial court's usage of the words guilty and not guilty was not outcome determinative in the case and the jury was instructed that it could not consider the fact that defendant did not testify. State v. Guidry, — Ohio App. 3d —, 2007 Ohio 4422, — N.E. 2d —, 2007 Ohio App. LEXIS 3983 (Aug. 20, 2007).

Taken as a whole, the trial court's instructions effectively advised the jury on the charged offenses, including assault on a peace officer; referring to the assault victim as "officer" and providing his badge number was not error because there was no dispute that he was an officer and that his badge number was 2449. Also, since the trial court previously defined the term "knowingly" for the jury in its instructions, it was not necessary for the trial court to re-read the definition of that term repeatedly throughout the instructions. State v. Lane, — Ohio App. 3d —, 2007 Ohio 5948, — N.E. 2d —, 2007 Ohio App. LEXIS 5255 (Nov. 8, 2007).

Even if the trial court had included the language that defendant had to be a person confined in a detention facility, for harassment by an inmate under RC § 2921.38, the outcome of the trial would not have been otherwise because there was ample evidence that defendant was confined to a detention facility at the time of the offense. Not only did the testimony of the two deputies, and the videotape establish defendant's confinement, defendant admitted to his confinement during his testimony. State v. Markin, — Ohio App. 3d —, 2006 Ohio 1534, — N.E. 2d —, 2006 Ohio App. LEXIS 1397 (Mar. 30, 2006).

Trial court did not err in failing to give an instruction on knowing assault that caused physical harm. Defendant's intent was not the focus of a criminal act that involved the mental state of "knowingly." Instead, the focus was on whether defendant's conduct would probably have caused a certain result or would probably have been of a certain nature, under RC § 2901.22(B). State v. Blanton, — Ohio App. 3d —, 2006 Ohio 1785, — N.E. 2d —, 2006 Ohio App. LEXIS 1652 (Apr. 10, 2006).

Trial court properly instructed the jury that the "bulk amount" of Oxycodone was defined as six unit dosages of 80 milligram doses and the arresting officer specifically testified as to the bulk amount of Oxycodone in 80 milligram tablets. Laboratory testing revealed that the substance seized from defendant was Oxycontin consisting of 49 green round marked tablets, approximately 13.42 grams, and the trial court took judicial notice that Oxycodone was a Schedule II controlled substance. State v. Fisher, — Ohio App. 3d —, 2006 Ohio 2201, — N.E. 2d —, 2006 Ohio App. LEXIS 2038 (May 3, 2006).

There was no error in the jury instruction because the trial court followed Ohio law when it instructed the jury on constructive possession and the two police officers testified that defendant admitted the crack was his. It was reasonable for a juror to conclude that as the driver of the car, defendant had access to, or exercised the ability to control, the crack in the center armrest of the car. State v. Burrell, — Ohio App. 3d —, 2006 Ohio 2593, — N.E. 2d —, 2006 Ohio App. LEXIS 2446 (May 25, 2006).

Jury instruction given by the trial court gave the essence of the definition of "force," as provided by RC § 2901.01(A). The use of the word "effort" in addition to the normal definitional terms was not error since the instruction correctly conveyed the concept of force necessary to commit burglary, under RC § 2911.12. State v. New, — Ohio App. 3d —, 2006 Ohio 2965, — N.E. 2d —, 2006 Ohio App. LEXIS 2851 (June 13, 2006).

Trial court did not err in instructing the jury because nowhere in the jury instructions did the trial court substitute "knowingly" for "purposefully;" rather, the trial court's instructions mirrored the language contained in RC § 2913.48(A) (workers' compensation fraud). The trial court charged the jury that it had to find that defendant acted "with purpose to defraud," and it only included the definition of "knowingly" in

the instructions because the statutory definition of "defraud" included that word, pursuant to RC § 2913.01(B). State v. Dillon, — Ohio App. 3d —, 2006 Ohio 3312, — N.E. 2d —, 2006 Ohio App. LEXIS 3229 (June 29, 2006).

Entrapment

There was no abuse of discretion by the trial judge for failing to give a jury instruction on entrapment because defendant's testimony at trial was not evidence of entrapment. His defense was based on the claims that he did not know that the furniture was stolen and that the money laundering was legitimate. Also, the police detective merely provided several opportunities for defendant to engage in criminal activity and he readily acquiesced. State v. Strunk, — Ohio App. 3d —, 2007 Ohio 683, — N.E. 2d —, 2007 Ohio App. LEXIS 609 (Feb. 20, 2007).

In a drug prosecution, the trial court should have granted defendant's request for an instruction on entrapment as to a possession charge because the evidence showed police proposed an exchange of money and cocaine for marijuana before defendant first met with an undercover officer, and the instruction was given as to a trafficking charge based on the same drugs. Ohio v. Bowshier, — Ohio App. 3d —, 2007 Ohio 5364, — N.E. 2d —, 2007 Ohio App. LEXIS 4730 (Oct. 5, 2007).

Failure to object to instructions

Although defendant failed to object under Ohio R. Crim. P. 30 to the trial court's failure to instruct the jury that his burden of proving self-defense pursuant to RC § 2905.01(A) was by a preponderance of the evidence, there was plain error under Ohio R. Crim. P. 52(B) where such error constituted a manifest miscarriage of justice. As the jury was instructed that the State's burden of proof on the substantive offenses was beyond a reasonable doubt, the logical result was that the jury might have believed that such burden of proof was equally applicable to the affirmative defense, which was a fundamental error. State v. Cooper, 170 Ohio App. 3d 418, 2007 Ohio 1186, 867 N.E.2d 493, 2007 Ohio App. LEXIS 1115 (2007).

There was no plain error under Ohio R. Crim. P. 52(B) by the trial court's jury instructions on a charge against defendant of corrupting a juvenile with drugs, in violation of RC § 2925.02(A)(4)(c) as it properly set forth the definitions of induce, which was an alternative to cause, and it properly explained complicity with respect to a juvenile's aiding and abetting in the drug offense committed by defendant. The plain error standard of review was used due to defendant's failure to have objected to the jury instruction pursuant to Ohio R. Crim. P. 30. State v. Simmons, — Ohio App. 3d —, 2007 Ohio 1570, — N.E. 2d —, 2007 Ohio App. LEXIS 1442 (Mar. 28, 2007).

Based on defendant's failure to submit proposed jury instructions and his failure under Ohio R. Crim. P. 30(A) to object to the jury instructions given by the trial court regarding the issue of complicity, the plain error standard of review pursuant to Ohio R. Crim. P. 52(B) was applicable in defendant's appeal, wherein he raised the alleged error in the trial court's instructions. When the instructions were read as a whole, there was no finding that but for the alleged error in the complicity instruction, the outcome of defendant's trial on drug offenses would clearly have been different, such that there was no plain error. State v. Bridge, — Ohio App. 3d —, 2007 Ohio 1764, — N.E. 2d —, 2007 Ohio App. LEXIS 1607 (Apr. 16, 2007).

In a prosecution for failure to comply with an order or signal of a police officer, under RC § 2921.331(B), when the State objected to the instructions and verdict form because they did not ask the jury to find a factor enhancing the charge from a misdemeanor to a felony, and the trial court overruled the objection, defendant waived any error because the State did not actually seek a change in the instructions and defendant did not raise a specific objection to the trial court's ruling, as required by Ohio R. Crim. P. 30(A). State v. Wilson, — Ohio App. 3d —, 2006 Ohio 6930, — N.E. 2d —, 2006 Ohio App. LEXIS 6836 (Dec. 28, 2006).

There was no plain error under Ohio R. Crim. P. 52 in the trial court's instruction to the jury regarding defendant's testimony, as defendant failed to object thereto and accordingly, any error other than plain error was waived pursuant to Ohio R. Crim. P. 30(A). The evidence did not indicate that the verdict would have been different absent the challenged portion of the jury instructions. State v. Lawwill, — Ohio App. 3d —, 2007 Ohio 2627, — N.E. 2d —, 2007 Ohio App. LEXIS 2457 (May 31, 2007).

Failure to object to jury instruction

Trial court's jury instruction was adequate where the instruction served its purpose of informing the jurors that a foreperson's role was simply to maintain order, not to persuade jurors to vote one way or another; as defendant failed to object to the instruction pursuant to Ohio R. Crim. P. 30(A) and there was no showing that but for the instruction, the outcome of the trial would have been different, defendant did not meet his burden of showing error. State v. Gay, — Ohio App. 3d —, 2007 Ohio 2420, — N.E. 2d —, 2007 Ohio App. LEXIS 2236 (May 18, 2007).

Since defendant did not object to the jury instructions given by the trial court on the ground that the trial court did not specifically instruct the jury that it had to agree on one theory or the other advanced by the City in defendant's prosecution for operating a vehicle while under the influence of alcohol and specifically state the matter to which he objected, as required by Ohio R. Crim. P. 30, he had waived all challenges except plain error. The trial court's unanimity instruction, instructing the jury that all eight members had to agree upon a verdict and had to sign the verdict form, was sufficient, defendant could not establish that the jury's result would have been different, and defendant could not show that his right to a fair trial under Ohio Const. art. I, § 10 had been violated. City of Akron v. Stalnaker, — Ohio App. 3d —, 2007 Ohio 6789, — N.E. 2d —, 2007 Ohio App. LEXIS 5953 (Dec. 19, 2007).

Where defendant did not request that the court read the jury instructions in their entirety, nor did he object to the failure to do so at the conclusion of the reading of the jury instructions, there was no plain error with the instructions given to the jury pursuant to Ohio R. Crim. P. 30(A), as they were given a written copy of the jury instructions at the conclusion of the closing arguments, the court reminded the jury of all of the instructions that had been previously read, and no prejudice was shown to defendant. State v. Galluzzo, — Ohio App. 3d —, 2006 Ohio 309, — N.E. 2d —, 2006 Ohio App. LEXIS 271 (Jan. 20, 2006).

There was no plain error pursuant to Ohio R. Crim. P. 52(B) by the trial court's jury instruction on a charge of aggravated burglary against defendant, in violation of RC § 2911.11(A)(2), as the trial court properly instructed the jury that the underlying offense that defendant had the purpose to commit was theft when defendant trespassed into the victim's apartment. The plain error standard of review was employed due to defendant's failure to object to the jury instruction pursuant to Ohio R. Crim. P. 30(A). State v. Parrish, — Ohio App. 3d —, 2006 Ohio 4161, — N.E. 2d —, 2006 Ohio App. LEXIS 4094 (Aug. 11, 2006).

Where defendant failed to object at trial to various jury instructions, he waived all but plain error for purposes of his appeal, pursuant to Ohio R. Crim. P. 52, wherein he asserted that the prosecutor committed misconduct. There was no misconduct where the jury instructions provided to the jury were proper and the jury was presumed to have followed them, and it was incumbent upon defendant to have timely objected to jury instructions that he felt prejudiced him pursuant to Ohio R. Crim. P. 30(A), as the prosecutor had no

such duty. State v. Justice, — Ohio App. 3d —, 2006 Ohio 5965, — N.E. 2d —, 2006 Ohio App. LEXIS 5911 (Nov. 9, 2006).

Flight

There was ample evidence to support the trial court's decision to give the jury an instruction on flight because testimony was adduced at trial that defendant fled after the shooting and a warrant was issued for his arrest. Defendant testified that he left the scene after the shooting and threw the gun into a lake and that the only thing that crossed his mind was to run; he did not turn himself in until three days after the shooting. State v. French, — Ohio App. 3d —, 2007 Ohio 4400, — N.E. 2d —, 2007 Ohio App. LEXIS 3968 (Aug. 27, 2007).

There was no error in giving a jury instruction on flight because there were two incidents of flight. First, during the investigation of the shooting, defendant vehicle and someone matching his description immediately left upon seeing the Sheriff's deputies and, second, witnesses testified that defendant called them from locations outside of the state of Ohio. State v. Huber, — Ohio App. 3d —, 2006 Ohio 2600, — N.E. 2d —, 2006 Ohio App. LEXIS 2451 (May 22, 2006).

Although there was weak support for a trial court's flight instruction to the jury over defendant's counsel's objection pursuant to Ohio R. Crim. P. 30, where that support was based for the most part on testimony from defendant's probation officer which had been deemed an abuse of discretion to admit, an argument on appeal regarding the instruction was sustained as part of the cumulative error found from the admission of the officer's testimony as well as testimony from another alleged victim of a prior attack by defendant. State v. Anderson, — Ohio App. 3d —, 2006 Ohio 4618, — N.E. 2d —, 2006 Ohio App. LEXIS 4581 (Sept. 1, 2006).

Force

Trial court properly instructed the jury regarding the use of force for the rape charge and the instruction comported with the definition of force in RC § 2901.01(A). Defendant's imposing size and age difference (all of the victims were under the age of 13), along with his position as an older family friend to all three victims supported the jury instruction given. State v. Eads, — Ohio App. 3d —, 2007 Ohio 539, — N.E. 2d —, 2007 Ohio App. LEXIS 488 (Feb. 8, 2007).

There was no plain error in the psychological force jury instruction because, since the rape victim was 14 years old, the question was whether her will was overcome by fear or duress. Also, no plain error resulted from the position of authority instruction because, given defendant's close interaction with the family and the way they treated defendant, the evidence supported a position of authority finding and thus, the instruction was warranted. The instruction properly left the jury free to determine whether or not defendant held a position of authority. State v. Haschenburger, — Ohio App. 3d —, 2007 Ohio 1562, — N.E. 2d —, 2007 Ohio App. LEXIS 1446 (Mar. 27, 2007).

Jury instruction was accurate regarding force or threat of force for rape, under RC § 2907.02(A)(2) because the instruction did not allow the jury to convict based merely upon the victim's subjective state of mind. Rather, before a threat of force could have been inferred, the instruction required the jury to find beyond a reasonable doubt that defendant acted to overcome the victim's will by fear or duress. State v. Rupp, — Ohio App. 3d —, 2007 Ohio 1561, — N.E. 2d —, 2007 Ohio App. LEXIS 1449 (Mar. 27, 2007).

Inferior degree offense

Having determined in its discretion to give an instruction on aggravated assault, the trial court was obliged to give a correct one. The trial court erroneously defined aggravated assault as being a lesser included offense of felonious assault, instead of being an offense of an inferior degree, and it implied to the jury that aggravated assault could only be considered if defendant was not found guilty of felonious assault. Ohio v. Michael W. Nichols, — Ohio App. 3d —, 2007 Ohio 5219, — N.E. 2d —, 2007 Ohio App. LEXIS 4594 (Sept. 28, 2007).

Insanity

Trial court committed plain error when it gave jury instructions on the defense of insanity because the initial and latter instructions given were in clear conflict with each other, and the conflict was never resolved. Because the clearly conflicting instructions made it impossible for the jury to properly consider the affirmative defense of insanity, defendant's substantial right to present a viable affirmative defense to voluntary manslaughter was undermined. State v. Thomas, — Ohio App. 3d —, 2007 Ohio 1344, — N.E. 2d —, 2007 Ohio App. LEXIS 1224 (Mar. 23, 2007).

Instruction of aggravated assault

Trial court's instruction did not constitute plain error because, although the trial court initially incorrectly advised the jury that they could consider the charge of aggravated assault only if they found defendant not guilty of felonious assault, it did later correctly advise the jury. Defendant was not prejudiced by the trial court's initial misstatement of law because the jury found him guilty of aggravated assault, not felonious assault. State v. Courtney, — Ohio App. 3d —, 2006 Ohio 4264, — N.E. 2d —, 2006 Ohio App. LEXIS 4178 (Aug. 17, 2006).

Intoxication as defense

Trial court did not err in failing to instruct the jury on blackout because the evidence did not support defendant's claim that he was in a blackout when he made the threatening statements to the police officer. The mere fact that defendant was intoxicated, standing by itself, would not have been sufficient to provide a defense to the charge of intimidation, under RC § 2921.03(A). Defendant's condition would have to have risen to the level of unconsciousness before the blackout defense would have been available but the taped statements demonstrated that defendant had a great deal of interaction with the police officers and that he was not in such a state of unconsciousness that he could not have known what he was saying. State v. McClaskey, — Ohio App. 3d —, 2006 Ohio 6646, — N.E. 2d —, 2006 Ohio App. LEXIS 6509 (Dec. 14, 2006).

Jury deadlock

Trial court's final statement (wherein it asked the jury to please return to the verdict room and continue to deliberate) was not part of the jury charge because it was merely a concluding remark to release the jury so that they could go and follow the Howard charge and the "verdict impossible" charge. In order to follow such charges, the jury had to retire to the jury room to jointly consider the new instructions and to discuss in private whether further deliberations would be useful; they could not be expected to conduct some kind of public vote from the jury box as to whether they in fact could not reach a verdict. State v. Smith, — Ohio App. 3d —, 2007 Ohio 3182, — N.E. 2d —, 2007 Ohio App. LEXIS 2981 (June 21, 2007).

In cases where a jury communicates that it may be deadlocked, the Howard charge is not an absolute mandate, but a suggestion. If a court deviates from the Howard language, it must ensure that the charge satisfies the concerns of the Howard opinion: State v. Clifton, 172 Ohio App. 3d 86, 2007 Ohio 3392, 872 N.E.2d 1310, 2007 Ohio App. LEXIS 3130 (2007).

Trial court used its discretion to determine that the jury was deadlocked and that it was time to provide them with the Howard instruction based on a message relayed to it from the jury asking what they should do if they could not come to a unanimous decision. Because, despite initial reservations,

defendant agreed that the court should give the jury the Howard instruction, defendant waived his right to raise the issue on appeal. State v. Witcher, — Ohio App. 3d —, 2007 Ohio 3960, — N.E. 2d —, 2007 Ohio App. LEXIS 3609 (Aug. 3, 2007).

Trial court was not required upon the first sign of difficulty in the jury's deliberations to give a Howard instruction and the court's instruction to the jury was not coercive. The court instructed the jury to "seek to reach verdicts," "take a break from deliberations," and "resume with the hope you can reach a verdict; " the jurors were polled after their verdict was announced and each juror indicated that the verdict reflected their vote. State v. Parker, — Ohio App. 3d —, 2006 Ohio 3684, — N.E. 2d —, 2006 Ohio App. LEXIS 3642 (July 20, 2006).

Jury instruction

There was no plain error in the trial court's omission of the Souel instruction to the jury regarding the polygraph examiner because the trial court gave a thorough instruction regarding expert testimony. The distinction between affirmative evidence of guilt and evidence which said that defendant was lying when he claimed that he did not rape the victim was a very fine distinction in the mind of an average person; the distinction was so fine that it could not be said that the jury's verdict would have been different had the charge required by Souel been given. State v. Madison, — Ohio App. 3d —, 2007 Ohio 3547, — N.E. 2d —, 2007 Ohio App. LEXIS 3244 (July 12, 2007).

Because the corpus delicti of the crime of receiving stolen property was sufficiently established, a jury instruction on an uncorroborated admission was not required; independent evidence was presented to establish that tools had been stolen and that defendant had disposed of those tools. Thus, because the State's case did not rest on defendant's unsigned statement alone, but included independent evidence establishing the crime of receiving stolen property, no instruction was required. State v. Chambers, — Ohio App. 3d —, 2007 Ohio 4732, — N.E. 2d —, 2007 Ohio App. LEXIS 4273 (Sept. 17, 2007).

Jury request during deliberations

Although the trial court erred when it answered a jury question without first consulting counsel for defendant and the state, the error was harmless. Given the short period of time the jury had been deliberating, the court's response to the question, "What would require declaration of a hung jury?" of, "Many more hours of deliberation" was reasonable and not inherently coercive. When the jury asked, apparently in response to the reservations of one juror, whether a finding of guilty could be based on one witness's testimony, the court correctly responded that the testimony of any witness is sufficient, if believed, to prove any fact. Trial court's replacement of a deliberating juror with an alternate juror in a capital case, contrary to CrimR 24(G)(2), did not constitute plain error: State v. Clinkscale, 177 Ohio App. 3d 294, 2008 Ohio 1677, 894 N.E.2d 700, 2008 Ohio App. LEXIS 1439 (2008).

There was no error in the jury instructions given in answer to questions from the jury during deliberations because the instructions on "other causes" and "intervening causes" were correct statements of the law as applicable to the case. The "cause" of the victim's death was a jury question, and the additional instructions to the jury merely clarified that defendant would be criminally responsible for his acts even if other "causes" came into play. State v. Filchock, 166 Ohio App. 3d 611, 2006 Ohio 2242, 852 N.E.2d 759, 2006 Ohio App. LEXIS 2096 (May 5, 2006).

Lesser included offense

Trial court's refusal to give an instruction on reckless homicide as a lesser-included offense of murder was not unreasonable or arbitrary because defendant could not demonstrate that the evidence supported both an acquittal on the crime charged (murder) and a conviction on the lesser-included offense (reckless homicide). The State presented ample evidence that defendant intentionally murdered the victim and that defendant had admitted to two officers that he had killed the victim; defendant did not deny the admissions. State v. Elwell, — Ohio App. 3d —, — N.E. 2d —, 2007 Ohio 3122, 2007 Ohio App. LEXIS 2935 (June 25, 2007).

Trial court properly declined to give a jury instruction on voluntary manslaughter as a lesser-included offense of murder because defendant set forth no evidence or testimony to demonstrate that he killed the victim while under the influence of a sudden passion or fit of rage. Rather, defendant specifically testified that he did not know how it ended up happening and surmised that the gun may have "accidentally" discharged. State v. Elwell, — Ohio App. 3d —, — N.E. 2d —, 2007 Ohio 3122, 2007 Ohio App. LEXIS 2935 (June 25, 2007).

Trial court did not commit plain error by failing to instruct on aiding escape because aiding escape was not a lesser included offense of escape since escape could have been committed without the crime of aiding escape being committed. However, even if it had been determined that it was a lesser included offense, defendant did not show that the outcome of the trial would have been different had the instruction been given because the uncontroverted facts showed that defendant was in custody at the time of the escape; he was handcuffed to a hitching post so that he could smoke; another prisoner was handcuffed to defendant so that he could also smoke; defendant slipped his hand out of the handcuff attached to the hitching post and he and the other prisoner took off; and the other prisoner testified that it was defendant who slipped the cuff off. State v. Beckett, — Ohio App. 3d —, 2007 Ohio 3175, — N.E. 2d —, 2007 Ohio App. LEXIS 2963 (June 21, 2007).

Trial court did not err when it failed to instruct the jury on the offense of voluntary manslaughter because the facts did not reasonably support both an acquittal on the charged crime of murder and a conviction for voluntary manslaughter. The facts did not demonstrate a "sudden fit of passion" or a "sudden fit of rage." The case did not involve a typical voluntary manslaughter situation because: defendant and his codefendant had been angry with the victim for over a month; on the night of the victim's death, defendant and the codefendant were acting in such a way as to make a friend of the victim believe that something bad would happen; defendant and the codefendant then went to the victim's residence, armed, to wait for him to arrive; and when the victim arrived, they shot and killed him. State v. Robinson, — Ohio App. 3d —, 2007 Ohio 3501, — N.E. 2d —, 2007 Ohio App. LEXIS 3224 (July 5, 2007).

Trial court did not err by failing to instruct the jury as to theft as a lesser included offense because a reasonable jury would not have acquitted defendant of robbery. The uncontroverted evidence indicated that defendant threatened the victims by stating that he was going to "pop" them, which provided a sufficient basis for the jury to find that defendant threatened to inflict physical harm. In addition, defendant's hands were concealed in a bundled sweatshirt that he was carrying and thus, the victims believed that defendant could have been concealing a gun and testified to feeling threatened and scared that defendant was going to shoot them. State v. Thomas, — Ohio App. 3d —, 2007 Ohio 3522, — N.E. 2d —, 2007 Ohio App. LEXIS 3254 (July 12, 2007).

Trial court did not err in failing to instruct the jury on the lesser included offense of assault, under RC § 2903.13(B). Based on the victim's testimony and the nature of her injuries, the evidence did not support an acquittal on the offense of felonious assault, under RC § 2903.11(A)(1), and a conviction

on the offense of assault. State v. Burks, — Ohio App. 3d —, 2007 Ohio 3562, — N.E. 2d —, 2007 Ohio App. LEXIS 3270 (July 13, 2007).

Trial court's decision not to give a jury instruction on the lesser included offense of aggravated assault was not an abuse of discretion because the evidence would not have supported a conviction for the lesser offense because there was no serious provocation. While defendant argued that he was provoked by the thought of his girlfriend having sex and using drugs with the victim (whom he knew was his girlfriend's drug supplier), that was not found to be a serious provocation that would have aroused defendant to use deadly force; he calculatingly entered his girlfriend's home and attacked the victim. State v. Douglas, — Ohio App. 3d —, 2007 Ohio 2625, — N.E. 2d —, 2007 Ohio App. LEXIS 2455 (May 31, 2007).

Because defendant did not deny having a sexual encounter with the victim, but instead claimed it was consensual, a lesser included instruction on gross sexual imposition was not warranted; the jury could not reasonably have disbelieved the victim's testimony concerning the sexual conduct and at the same time reasonably believe her testimony on a contrary theory of mere "sexual contact." The victim testified that defendant was engaging in cunnilingus (while she was passed out), which fell within the statutory definition of "sexual conduct," and the DNA evidence corroborated that aspect of the victim's testimony. State v. Gholston, — Ohio App. 3d —, 2007 Ohio 4053, — N.E. 2d —, 2007 Ohio App. LEXIS 3700 (Aug. 9, 2007).

Jury instruction on criminal damaging was not warranted because the evidence did not support both an acquittal on the offense of complicity to vandalism and a conviction on criminal damaging; the evidence demonstrated that defendant participated in a plan with the others to break into the school, he was present during the entire incident, and actively engaged in conduct that resulted in the destruction of school property. Because the events of that evening resulted in approximately $ 15,000 in damages to the school, under a complicity theory, no reasonable jury could have found that defendant's conduct resulted in less than $ 500. State v. Baltzer, — Ohio App. 3d —, 2007 Ohio 6719, — N.E. 2d —, 2007 Ohio App. LEXIS 5881 (Nov. 28, 2007).

Lesser included offenses

Jury instruction on the lesser included offense of third degree burglary was required for one of the burglary counts because there was no evidence that there was any likelihood, from the victim's known schedule or intentions, that anyone would have been present when the burglary occurred. Thus, a jury could have reasonably found against the State on one element of second degree burglary, and still have found against defendant for third degree burglary. State v. Cochran, — Ohio App. 3d —, 2007 Ohio 345, — N.E. 2d —, 2007 Ohio App. LEXIS 291 (Jan. 26, 2007).

No jury instruction on negligent assault was required because there was no actual harm caused and thus, it was not a lesser included offense of felonious assault. There was sufficient evidence to establish that defendant knowingly attempted to cause harm to the victim. State v. Robinson, — Ohio App. 3d —, 2007 Ohio 354, — N.E. 2d —, 2007 Ohio App. LEXIS 311 (Jan. 29, 2007).

Trial court did not err in refusing to allow an instruction on the lesser-included offense of voluntary manslaughter because there was no indication in the evidence presented at trial that the murder victim did anything to provoke defendant. State v. Jones, — Ohio App. 3d —, 2007 Ohio 1301, — N.E. 2d —, 2007 Ohio App. LEXIS 1194 (Mar. 22, 2007).

Defendant was not entitled to a jury instruction on negligent homicide because that offense was not a lesser included offense of murder, under RC § 2903.02, or reckless homicide, under RC § 2903.041, the offense for which he was convicted. Negligent homicide, under RC § 2903.05, required the additional element of negligently causing a death by means of a deadly weapon. State v. Smith, — Ohio App. 3d —, 2007 Ohio 2969, — N.E. 2d —, 2007 Ohio App. LEXIS 2729 (June 15, 2007).

Trial court did not abuse its discretion by denying the requested inferior-degree offense jury instruction as the evidence did not reasonably support an acquittal on the charged offense of murder and a conviction for voluntary manslaughter because the trial court could reasonably have concluded that no reasonable jury would have failed to find that sufficient time had passed between the incident with the car and the shooting to allow defendant to calm down. The fact that defendant walked over to the victim, who, after the first shot fell to the ground, and proceeded to stand over him and shoot him multiple times, was consistent with defendant having acted deliberately, and was inconsistent with his having acted with sudden passion in shooting the victim. State v. Davis, — Ohio App. 3d —, 2007 Ohio 6680, — N.E. 2d —, 2007 Ohio App. LEXIS 5852 (Dec. 14, 2007).

Trial court did not abuse its discretion by refusing to instruct the jury on the lesser included offense of aggravated assault because, although defendant admitted that he pushed the victim so that he could get out of the house, he consistently denied harming her in any manner. Thus, if the jury were to believe that defendant did nothing wrong and never harmed the victim, it would have been impossible to convict him of aggravated assault. State v. Powell, — Ohio App. 3d —, 2006 Ohio 1778, — N.E. 2d —, 2006 Ohio App. LEXIS 1644 (Apr. 10, 2006).

Limiting instruction

Defendant was not unduly prejudiced by the admission of evidence of charges in a subsequent indictment that arose from the same criminal incident as the charges in the original indictment, as the second set of charges relating to defendant's possession of a victim's identification and checks were offered to prove his identity as the perpetrator of a robbery and assault on the victim, pursuant to Ohio R. Evid. 404(B). Although a limiting instruction was not given on that or on the fact that one of the subsequent charges involved defendant's possession of weapons while under disability, as defendant's counsel failed to object pursuant to Ohio R. Crim. P. 30(A) and the evidence of defendant's guilt was overwhelming, the error was harmless under Ohio R. Crim. P. 52. State v. Johnson, — Ohio App. 3d —, 2007 Ohio 437, — N.E. 2d —, 2007 Ohio App. LEXIS 374 (Feb. 2, 2007).

Trial court did not commit plain error because it gave a limiting instruction on any hearsay admitted in defendant's tape recorded with a detective. Defense counsel expressed satisfaction with the instruction and any potential prejudice was mitigated by the fact the challenged evidence was duplicative of testimony presented by the victim's internal audit manager and defendant's accomplice. State v. Alexander, — Ohio App. 3d —, 2007 Ohio 4177, — N.E. 2d —, 2007 Ohio App. LEXIS 3767 (Aug. 16, 2007).

Because defendant failed to request a limiting instruction with regard to the testimony, wherein the victim was permitted to read part of her online diary into the record, including references to defendant's other bad acts, the trial court's failure to give a limiting instruction at that time could not be assigned as error on appeal. State v. Travis, — Ohio App. 3d —, 2007 Ohio 6683, — N.E. 2d —, 2007 Ohio App. LEXIS 5859 (Dec. 17, 2007).

Admission of the witness's prior inconsistent statement did not constitute plain error because, even assuming that the witness's prior inconsistent statement was improperly admitted as substantive evidence of defendant's guilt, and that a limiting instruction should have been given, there was overwhelming evidence of defendant's guilt. The testimony showed that defendant, who was driving a truck, pursued the victim who was trying to evade him, that there were guns and ammo in the truck, and that, in a signed sworn statement to the police, defendant admitted that he told the witness (a passenger) to fire the gun at the van. State v. Rose, — Ohio App. 3d —, 2006 Ohio 397, — N.E. 2d —, 2006 Ohio App. LEXIS 337 (Jan. 30, 2006).

Trial court did not err in failing to give a limiting instruction to the jury because it was not clear that the observers of defendant in the hallway were jurors or potential jurors or that they saw defendant in handcuffs. As such, defendant failed to demonstrate prejudice and failed to object to the omission of the limiting instruction. State v. Elijah, — Ohio App. 3d —, 2006 Ohio 2635, — N.E. 2d —, 2006 Ohio App. LEXIS 2471 (May 19, 2006).

Trial court did not commit plain error by instructing the jury when it stated that the jury could only consider defendant's previous juvenile adjudication to judge whether his specific testimony was credible. Although the jury was not specifically instructed to not consider his prior juvenile adjudication as evidence that he acted in conformity with the adjudication, the jury was instructed that it could consider the evidence for only one reason: to determine the credibility of defendant's testimony. State v. Edwards, — Ohio App. 3d —, 2006 Ohio 6987, — N.E. 2d —, 2006 Ohio App. LEXIS 6944 (Dec. 29, 2006).

Objections

Defendant's objection to the trial court's affirmative defense instruction preserved the issue for appellate review pursuant to Ohio R. Crim. P. 30, as defendant had proffered instructions that set up no affirmative defense and he then objected to the trial court's failure to give his requested instruction. He also stated that he intended for his objection to the trial court's affirmative defense instruction to be sufficient for purposes of Rule 30. State v. Nucklos, 171 Ohio App. 3d 38, 2007 Ohio 1025, 869 N.E.2d 674, 2007 Ohio App. LEXIS 958 (2007).

There was no plain error under Ohio R. Crim. P. 52(B) in the trial court's jury instructions on a charge against defendant of failing to appear, as his counsel did not object to the jury instructions as required by Ohio R. Crim. P. 30(A), and defendant had admitted to the charge. There could be no showing that the outcome of the trial would clearly have been different but for the error. State v. Nichols, — Ohio App. 3d —, 2007 Ohio 3257, — N.E. 2d —, 2007 Ohio App. LEXIS 2999 (June 25, 2007).

Where defendant's co-defendant, who was his alleged accomplice in a criminal incident, did not actually testify at trial but instead, his previously recorded police interview was played for the jury as part of the State's case against the co-defendant, there was no accomplice testimony that required the accomplice instruction pursuant to RC § 2923.03(D); as defendant failed to object to the lack of such an instruction, the matter was reviewed under a plain error standard pursuant to Ohio R. Crim. P. 30(A) and 52(B). State v. Love, — Ohio App. 3d —, 2006 Ohio 1762, — N.E. 2d —, 2006 Ohio App. LEXIS 1619 (Mar. 27, 2006).

Plain error rule

Where defendant failed to request jury instructions on lesser included offenses in his criminal trial, he waived all but plain error pursuant to Ohio R. Crim. P. 30(A); there was no plain error found under Ohio R. Crim. P. 52(B) where no manifest miscarriage of justice was shown, as such failure to request those instructions could have been a strategic decision to present the jury with an all-or-nothing proposition in the hope of an acquittal. State v. Herrera, — Ohio App. 3d —, 2006 Ohio 3053, — N.E. 2d —, 2006 Ohio App. LEXIS 2931 (June 16, 2006).

Where defendant's conviction for tampering with a coin machine, in violation RC § 2911.32, was supported by both direct and circumstantial evidence that he used a wire that was in his pocket with the intent to remove money from the machine, it could not be said that had the trial court instructed the jury on the lesser included offense of attempt, the result necessarily would have been otherwise. The alleged error in failing to give the instruction was evaluated under the plain error standard due to defendant's failure to have requested such an instruction during trial, pursuant to Ohio R. Crim. P. 30 and 52. State v. Cook, — Ohio App. 3d —, 2006 Ohio 3443, — N.E. 2d —, 2006 Ohio App. LEXIS 3393 (June 30, 2006).

Purpose, instruction on

Defendant's trial counsel was ineffective as she failed to object to the trial court's erroneous jury instruction concerning the necessary mental state for the offense of complicity to breaking and entering; the initial instruction improperly indicated that the mens rea element was "knowingly" rather than "purposely." Whether defendant acted with the necessary culpable mental state to support a conviction for the offense of complicity to breaking and entering was a central issue at trial and there was a reasonable probability that, had counsel sought a proper instruction, the result of the trial would have been different. State v. Baltzer, — Ohio App. 3d —, 2007 Ohio 6719, — N.E. 2d —, 2007 Ohio App. LEXIS 5881 (Nov. 28, 2007).

Request for instruction

Trial court did not err in denying defendant's request because he did not properly request an instruction regarding his failure to testify. He did not file proposed jury instructions prior to trial, and his counsel did not subsequently request the special jury instruction in writing, as required by Ohio R. Crim. P. 30. State v. Mullins, — Ohio App. 3d —, 2007 Ohio 1051, — N.E. 2d —, 2007 Ohio App. LEXIS 969 (Mar. 9, 2007).

Trial court did give the jury an instruction on the elements for the offense of operating a vehicle while under the influence of alcohol or a drug of abuse and the law was clearly and fairly expressed. Although the jury instruction given by the trial court differed from the instruction requested by the defense, the trial court was not required to give the jury instruction in the exact language requested by defendant. Ohio v. Adams, — Ohio App. 3d —, 2007 Ohio 4932, — N.E. 2d —, 2007 Ohio App. LEXIS 4621 (Sept. 24, 2007).

Self-defense

There was no abuse of discretion in the trial court's decision not to instruct the jury on self-defense because defendant could have avoided any confrontation with the victim by remaining in his house and seeking police protection but, instead, defendant chose to leave his house and confront the victim in his front yard, while wielding an aluminum bat. Also, the victim's act of brushing the back of defendant's shirt did not justify defendant's response of deadly force, and defendant failed to demonstrate that he was in imminent danger of death or great bodily harm when he struck the victim with the bat. State v. Rust, — Ohio App. 3d —, 2007 Ohio 50, — N.E. 2d —, 2007 Ohio App. LEXIS 40 (Jan. 10, 2007).

Trial court's jury charge was a plain, distinct, and unambiguous statement of the law as applicable to the actual issues in the case, including the issue of self-defense, as posited by the evidence and pleadings. The trial court's jury instruction did not mislead the jury in a matter materially affecting defendant's substantial rights. State v. Calderon, — Ohio App. 3d —, 2007 Ohio 377, — N.E. 2d —, 2007 Ohio App. LEXIS 322 (Jan. 30, 2007).

Because the record did not support defendant's self-defense assertion, the trial court did not err in failing to give a jury instruction on self-defense. Also, an accident defense jury instruction would not have affected the outcome of defendant's case, and the trial court did not commit plain error by failing to provide an accident defense jury instruction because the trial court defined for the jury the "purposely" mental element, noting that to do an act purposely was to do it intentionally and not accidentally. State v. Johnson, — Ohio App. 3d —, 2007 Ohio 2792, — N.E. 2d —, 2007 Ohio App. LEXIS 2544 (June 7, 2007).

Although the trial court's jury instruction was error since it did not include that defendant did not have a duty to retreat (because it was defendant's house and he cohabited with the victim, his son), it was harmless error, not plain error. By convicting defendant of involuntary manslaughter rather than murder, the jury believed that he was under "sudden passion" or a "sudden fit of rage" and not in fear for his life at the time of the shooting; thus, the outcome would not have been different had a different instruction on self-defense been given. State v. Huff, — Ohio App. 3d —, 2007 Ohio 3360, — N.E. 2d —, 2007 Ohio App. LEXIS 3082 (June 29, 2007).

Trial court did not commit plain error when it refused to instruct the jury on self-defense because defendant did not present sufficient evidence to establish that he did not create the situation; although defendant and others asserted that the victim, a bouncer, and the other bouncer started the fight, the portion of the video that captured the initial confrontation established otherwise. The video showed that defendant physically charged into the bar through the bouncers, who blocked the front door. State v. Castle, — Ohio App. 3d —, 2007 Ohio 3599, — N.E. 2d —, 2007 Ohio App. LEXIS 3304 (July 16, 2007).

Trial court did not abuse its discretion by denying the requested jury instruction on self-defense because defendant did not prove that he acted in self-defense; defendant did not attempt to retreat from any danger. The evidence showed that defendant had easy access to his vehicle, and that he actually was partially in his car at the time that he turned around and started shooting and that, after the initial shots knocked two of the victims to the ground, defendant walked up to them and continued to shoot them multiple times, which belied his claim that he was in reasonable fear of imminent danger. State v. Davis, — Ohio App. 3d —, 2007 Ohio 6680, — N.E. 2d —, 2007 Ohio App. LEXIS 5852 (Dec. 14, 2007).

Since defense counsel did not object pursuant to Ohio R. Crim. P. 30(A) to a trial court's refusal to instruct the jury on self-defense in defendant's domestic violence prosecution under RC § 2919.25(A), the court reviewed defendant's challenge on appeal to the trial court's failure to give such an instruction under a plain error analysis pursuant to Ohio R. Crim. P. 52(B). The facts of the case supported a defense of reasonable parental discipline as opposed to a self-defense instruction since the victim's mother, who was involved in the altercation and who gave testimony favorable to defendant, refuted in her testimony the claim that defendant was acting in self-defense, specifically stating that the case did not involve self-defense, and since defendant did not state that he was threatened with physical harm by the victim. State v. Craft, — Ohio App. 3d —, 2006 Ohio 4236, — N.E. 2d —, 2006 Ohio App. LEXIS 4165 (Aug. 11, 2006).

Given the evidence regarding the circumstances of the fight in question in the instant case, it was plain error for the trial court to require defendant to prove that he believed he was about to be killed or suffer great bodily harm in order to defend himself against the complaining witness when he allegedly came back at defendant after head-butting him. In light of the fact that the question of defendant's guilt turned on which version of events the jury believed--defendant's or the victim's--it could not be said that the outcome of the trial was not substantially affected by the trial court's erroneous self-defense instruction. State v. Durham, — Ohio App. 3d —, 2006 Ohio 5015, — N.E. 2d —, 2006 Ohio App. LEXIS 4952 (Sept. 28, 2006).

Because the record did not support defendant's self-defense assertion, the trial court did not err in failing to give a jury instruction on self-defense. Also, an accident defense jury instruction would not have affected the outcome of defendant's case, and the trial court did not commit plain error by failing to provide an accident defense jury instruction because the trial court defined for the jury the "purposely" mental element, noting that to do an act purposely was to do it intentionally and not accidentally. State v. Johnson, — Ohio App. 3d —, 2007 Ohio 2595, — N.E. 2d —, 2007 Ohio App. LEXIS 2404 (May 29, 2007).

Unanimity

Based on the evidence presented, the jury could have reasonably concluded that defendant had committed gross sexual imposition as it could not be concluded that, had a more specific instruction on unanimity been given, the outcome of the trial would have been different. The victim's testimony in support of the gross sexual imposition count consisted of testimony that defendant, her stepfather, "put his private area on her private area" and pressed up against the victim; while the activity allegedly occurred several times over a five year period, the activity was not divisible into more than one conceptual grouping and thus, concern about a "patchwork" verdict was not present. State v. Huber, — Ohio App. 3d —, 2006 Ohio 3514, — N.E. 2d —, 2006 Ohio App. LEXIS 3476 (July 7, 2006).

Trial court did not commit plain error because it could not be concluded that, had a more specific instruction on unanimity been given, the outcome of the trial of the rape charges clearly would have been different. The victim's testimony recounted at least three instances of rape and, although defendant was convicted of only two counts, it could not clearly be determined that the jury was not unanimous as to what specific activity constituted each of the two rapes of which he was found guilty. State v. Herron, — Ohio App. 3d —, 2006 Ohio 4400, — N.E. 2d —, 2006 Ohio App. LEXIS 4324 (Aug. 25, 2006).

Written instructions

Trial court did not commit plain error by failing to give all of the instructions to the jury in writing because, had the written instructions been provided to the jury, the outcome of the trial would not have clearly been different. Also, the complicity instruction was entirely proper since there was an abundance of evidence that defendant aided and abetted the principal in the theft and thus, did not constitute error, at all. State v. Demecs, — Ohio App. 3d —, 2006 Ohio 3802, — N.E. 2d —, 2006 Ohio App. LEXIS 3777 (July 21, 2006).

RULE 31.   Verdict

(A) **Return.** The verdict shall be unanimous. It shall be in writing, signed by all jurors concurring therein, and returned by the jury to the judge in open court.

(B) **Several defendants.** If there are two or more defendants the jury at any time during its deliberations may return a verdict or verdicts with respect to a defendant or defendants as to whom it has agreed. If the jury cannot agree with respect to all, the defendant or defendants as to whom it does not agree may be tried again.

(C) **Conviction of lesser offense.** The defendant may be found not guilty of the offense charged but guilty of an attempt to commit it if such an attempt is an offense at law. When the indictment, information, or complaint charges an offense including degrees, or if lesser offenses are included within the offense charged, the defendant may be found not guilty of the degree charged but guilty of an inferior degree thereof, or of a lesser included offense.

(D) **Poll of jury.** When a verdict is returned and before it is accepted the jury shall be polled at the request of any party or upon the court's own motion. If upon the poll there is not unanimous concurrence, the jury may be directed to retire for further deliberation or may be discharged.

NOTES TO DECISIONS

ANALYSIS

Poll of jury
Unanimous verdict

Poll of jury

Trial court did not commit error by accepting the jury's guilty verdict because the colloquy between the trial court and one juror during a polling of the jury revealed no "then-existing doubt" as to the juror's verdict. Although the record revealed some initial confusion as to what the juror's initial response meant, when the trial court sought clarification as to whether the verdict of guilty was hers, the juror unequivocally responded that it was. State v. Garner, 2007 Ohio 5914, 2007 Ohio App. LEXIS 5204 (Nov. 2, 2007).

Unanimous verdict

Although CrimR 31(A) requires jury unanimity on each element of a crime, jurors need not agree to a single way by which an element is satisfied. Ohio's burglary statutes proscribe a single crime that may be carried out in more than one manner or method. Thus a defendant is not deprived of a unanimous verdict simply because the jury was not required to agree unanimously as to the nature of the crime the defendant intended to commit at the time of the unlawful entry: State v. Gardner, 118 Ohio St. 3d 420, 2008 Ohio 2787, 889 N.E.2d 995, 2008 Ohio LEXIS 1619 (2008).

As the trial court failed to instruct the jury as to any underlying offense that defendant may have had the purpose to commit for purposes of a charge against him of aggravated burglary, in violation of RC § 2911.11(A), his due process rights under Ohio Const. art. I, § 10 were violated because the jury could not find every fact necessary to constitute the crime charged beyond a reasonable doubt, as they were not instructed on every essential element of the charged offense. The jury was required to have unanimously found a particular underlying offense for purposes of that charge pursuant to Ohio R. Crim. P. 31(A), and no such instruction was provided to them on that requirement. State v. Justice, — Ohio App. 3d —, 2006 Ohio 5965, — N.E. 2d —, 2006 Ohio App. LEXIS 5911 (Nov. 9, 2006).

RULE 32.   Sentence

(A) **Imposition of sentence.** Sentence shall be imposed without unnecessary delay. Pending sentence, the court may commit the defendant or continue or alter the bail. At the time of imposing sentence, the court shall do all of the following:

(1) Afford counsel an opportunity to speak on behalf of the defendant and address the defendant personally and ask if he or she wishes to make a statement in his or her own behalf or present any information in mitigation of punishment.

(2) Afford the prosecuting attorney an opportunity to speak;

(3) Afford the victim the rights provided by law;

(4) In serious offenses, state its statutory findings and give reasons supporting those findings, if appropriate.

(B) **Notification of right to appeal.**

(1) After imposing sentence in a serious offense that has gone to trial, the court shall advise the defendant that the defendant has a right to appeal the conviction.

(2) After imposing sentence in a serious offense, the court shall advise the defendant of the defendant's right, where applicable, to appeal or to seek leave to appeal the sentence imposed.

(3) If a right to appeal or a right to seek leave to appeal applies under division (B)(1) or (B)(2) of this rule, the court shall also advise the defendant of all of the following:

(a) That if the defendant is unable to pay the cost of an appeal, the defendant has the right to appeal without payment;

(b) That if the defendant is unable to obtain counsel for an appeal, counsel will be appointed without cost;

(c) That if the defendant is unable to pay the costs of documents necessary to an appeal, the documents will be provided without cost;

(d) That the defendant has a right to have a notice of appeal timely filed on his or her behalf.

Upon defendant's request, the court shall forthwith appoint counsel for appeal.

(C) **Judgment.** A judgment of conviction shall set forth the plea, the verdict, or findings, upon which each conviction is based, and the sentence. Multiple judgments of conviction may be addressed in one judgment entry. If the defendant is found not guilty or for any other reason is entitled to be discharged, the court shall render judgment accordingly. The judge shall sign the judgment and the clerk shall enter it on the journal. A judgment is effective only when entered on the journal by the clerk.

History: Amended, eff 7-1-92; 7-1-98; 7-1-04; 7-1-09.

NOTES TO DECISIONS

ANALYSIS

Allocution
Appealable orders
Continuance
Defense witnesses
Delay in sentencing
Double jeopardy
Execution of sentence
Final appealable order
Final judgment
Habeas corpus
Judgment entry
— Mandamus or procedendo to compel entry
Resentencing
Right for allocution
Right to appeal
Sentencing

Allocution

Trial court failed to comply with Ohio R. Crim. P. 32(A)(1) because defendant was not given an opportunity to address the trial court until after the trial court imposed its sentence. The error was neither invited nor harmless. State v. Mikolaj, — Ohio App. 3d —, 2007 Ohio 1563, — N.E. 2d —, 2007 Ohio App. LEXIS 1447 (Mar. 29, 2007).

Trial court's exchange with defendant at defendant's sentencing, when the trial court permitted defendant to speak, pursuant to Ohio R. Crim. P. 32(A), did not show that the trial court acted as a prosecutor or that defendant's privilege against self-incrimination was violated because defendant did not show that the State compelled defendant to testify against

defendant's will. State v. Blackmon, — Ohio App. 3d —, 2007 Ohio 3068, — N.E. 2d —, 2007 Ohio App. LEXIS 2808 (June 21, 2007).

Defendant had ample opportunity to address the information produced by the State at his sentencing hearing and considered by the trial court, and there was no violation of Ohio R. Crim. P. 32(A)(1) where the trial court asked defendant whether the State's recitation of the facts at the plea hearing was correct, defendant was given time to review the victim impact statements, and defendant and counsel were allowed to speak in mitigation. The trial court's denial of defendant's request for a continuance for the purpose of a presentence investigation was not an abuse of discretion in the circumstances. State v. Smith, — Ohio App. 3d —, 2007 Ohio 3129, — N.E. 2d —, 2007 Ohio App. LEXIS 2885 (June 25, 2007).

Inmate's application for a writ of mandamus seeking to compel the judge to grant him his right of allocution was dismissed because the inmate's unsupported conclusions were not considered admitted and were not sufficient to withstand the motion to dismiss. Further, mandamus was not the proper legal remedy to correct errors and procedural irregularities and the inmate had adequate remedies at law through appeal and postconviction relief for review of his claimed errors. State ex rel. Clark v. Krichbaum, — Ohio App. 3d —, 2007 Ohio 3185, — N.E. 2d —, 2007 Ohio App. LEXIS 2967 (June 20, 2007).

Trial court committed reversible error when it failed to ask defendant if he wished to make a statement on his own behalf prior to the imposition of sentence pursuant to Ohio R. Crim. P. 32(A)(1). The trial court had only asked defendant's counsel if he wished to make a statement on defendant's behalf, which was not sufficient. State v. Nelson, 172 Ohio App. 3d 419, 2007 Ohio 3459, 875 N.E.2d 137, 2007 Ohio App. LEXIS 3183 (2007).

Trial court's failure to provide the defendant with an opportunity to personally address the court and make a statement on his behalf before sentence was imposed constituted reversible error: State v. Nelson, 172 Ohio App. 3d 419, 2007 Ohio 3459, 875 N.E.2d 137, 2007 Ohio App. LEXIS 3183 (2007).

While the record revealed that the trial court addressed counsel for defendant, it committed reversible error by failing to afford defendant an opportunity to speak on his own behalf at sentencing, pursuant to Ohio R. Crim. P. 32(A)(1). State v. Devaughns, — Ohio App. 3d —, 2007 Ohio 3455, — N.E. 2d —, 2007 Ohio App. LEXIS 3187 (July 6, 2007).

When, upon re-sentencing defendant, a trial court did not use the exact words of Ohio R. Crim. P. 32 to advise defendant of defendant's right to allocution, there was no error because the trial court gave both defendant and defendant's counsel the opportunity to make a statement, so the trial court adhered to the standard imposed by Ohio R. Crim. P. 32(A)(1) because defendant was asked personally if defendant wanted to speak on defendant's behalf before sentencing. State v. Massey, — Ohio App. 3d —, 2007 Ohio 3637, — N.E. 2d —, 2007 Ohio App. LEXIS 3322 (July 16, 2007).

Trial court did not abuse its discretion by failing to allow defendant's relatives to testify on his behalf at sentencing. In context of the hearing, the trial court's alleged insistence of a "guarantee" of defendant's behavior from his family was rhetorical. Defense counsel indicated uncertainty regarding whether defendant's family could testify to any issue not already before the trial court, either through their letters, or his own speech in mitigation. State v. Anderson, 172 Ohio App. 3d 603, 2007 Ohio 3849, 876 N.E.2d 632, 2007 Ohio App. LEXIS 3493 (2007).

Although defendant had a right of "allocution" pursuant to Ohio R. Crim. P. 32(A) and RC § 2929.19(A)(1), which allowed him to make a statement in his own behalf and to present any information in mitigation of punishment at a sentencing hearing, he did not have a right to present witnesses on his behalf to provide mitigation testimony. State v. Lowe, — Ohio App. 3d —, 2007 Ohio 4039, — N.E. 2d —, 2007 Ohio App. LEXIS 3677 (Aug. 9, 2007).

When a trial court used improper language toward defense counsel because counsel attempted to discuss the merits of defendant's motion to suppress at defendant's change-of-plea hearing, at which defendant pled no contest, this did not establish that the trial court violated Ohio R. Crim. P. 32(A)(1) because the record reflected that defendant and defense counsel were allowed to make statements in mitigation of punishment both at defendant's change-of-plea hearing and at sentencing. State v. Urban, — Ohio App. 3d —, 2007 Ohio 4237, — N.E. 2d —, 2007 Ohio App. LEXIS 3884 (Aug. 20, 2007).

Trial court's discussion with defendant and her counsel at sentencing fulfilled the requirements of RC § 2929.19(A)(1) and Ohio R. Crim. P. 32 because defendant's counsel informed the trial court that defendant was not an active participant in the offenses and that the amount of cocaine involved was relatively small. He also stated that defendant had a drug problem, but had never had the opportunity for rehabilitation, and that she had six minor children; defendant declined to say anything. State v. Franklin, — Ohio App. 3d —, 2007 Ohio 4649, — N.E. 2d —, 2007 Ohio App. LEXIS 4184 (Sept. 10, 2007).

Defendant's sentence was reversed because, when defendant was resentenced, the trial court did not, as required by Ohio R. Crim. P. 32(A), personally address defendant and ask defendant if defendant wished to speak, and this error was not invited when defense counsel referred the trial court to a prior sentencing in the same case, held a year earlier, at which defendant spoke, because this did not induce the trial court into believing that the trial court was not required to observe the absolute requirements of Rule 32(A). State v. Joshua Steven Banks, — Ohio App. 3d —, 2007 Ohio 4968, — N.E. 2d —, 2007 Ohio App. LEXIS 4437 (Sept. 24, 2007).

Where a trial court gave defendant's counsel the opportunity to speak on behalf of defendant during his sentencing, and the trial court also addressed defendant personally, defendant was afforded his right of allocution under Ohio R. Crim. P. 32(A)(1); although the opportunity to address the court was during the initial plea hearing, it was after defendant was found guilty and the matter then proceeded to sentencing, which was rescheduled based on defendant's request in order to resolve certain outstanding issues. State v. Robles, — Ohio App. 3d —, 2007 Ohio 5241, — N.E. 2d —, 2007 Ohio App. LEXIS 4635 (Sept. 28, 2007).

Trial court did not deny defendant the right to allocution by interrupting and terminating defendant's allocution because defendant's allocution turned to matters unrelated to mitigation in violation of CrimR 32(A); defendant's statement of allocution totaled 12 transcript pages. State v. Copeland, — Ohio App. 3d —, 2007 Ohio 6168, — N.E. 2d —, 2007 Ohio App. LEXIS 5402 (Nov. 19, 2007).

Defendant's right to allocution, under Ohio R. Crim. P. 32(A)(1), was not violated because, at his sentencing, the trial court specifically invited him to speak, and the fact that the record did not indicate any response from defendant to that invitation was not evidence that his right to allocution was violated. State v. Mosley, — Ohio App. 3d —, 2006 Ohio 3102, — N.E. 2d —, 2006 Ohio App. LEXIS 2969 (June 20, 2006).

While a defendant could waive the right of allocution, Ohio R. Crim. P. 32(A)(1) imposed an affirmative duty on a trial court to speak directly to the defendant on the record and inquire whether he or she wished to exercise that right or waive it. State v. Cowen, 167 Ohio App. 3d 233, 2006 Ohio 3191, 854 N.E. 2d 579, 2006 Ohio App. LEXIS 3080 (June 23, 2006).

Trial court complied with the duties set forth in Ohio R. Crim. P. 32(A)(1) because defendant declined to make any

statement at the appropriate time; instead, when the court had fulfilled its duty and was ready to proceed to sentence, defendant sought to deflect the court with an extraneous matter. The court's decision to forestall him did not constitute a violation of his rights. State v. Storey, — Ohio App. 3d —, 2006 Ohio 3498, — N.E. 2d —, 2006 Ohio App. LEXIS 3441 (July 6, 2006).

While defendant made a statement before the trial court found him guilty, the trial court never gave him an opportunity to speak after the State gave a statement of facts and a sentence recommendation; hence, the trial court did not comply with Ohio R. Crim. P. 32(A)(1), and the error was not harmless. State v. Leeth, — Ohio App. 3d —, 2006 Ohio 3575, — N.E. 2d —, 2006 Ohio App. LEXIS 3511 (July 7, 2006).

Where defendant made an unsworn statement to the sentencing court and his counsel presented ample evidence in mitigation of punishment, the fact that the trial court did not technically provide him with an opportunity for an allocution pursuant to Ohio R. Crim. P. 32(A) was harmless. Although the three-judge panel considered the victim-impact statement after the mitigation phase, but prior to sentencing, defendant had waived any error thereon. State v. Harmon, — Ohio App. 3d —, 2006 Ohio 4642, — N.E. 2d —, 2006 Ohio App. LEXIS 4563 (Sept. 1, 2006).

Defendant's right to allocution at his sentencing, under Ohio R. Crim. P. 32(A)(1), was not violated because the trial court, after hearing comments from defense counsel, addressed defendant and specifically asked him if he wanted to say anything, at which time defendant spoke. State v. Shelton, — Ohio App. 3d —, 2006 Ohio 6895, — N.E. 2d —, 2006 Ohio App. LEXIS 6803 (Dec. 26, 2006).

Appealable orders

Judgment of conviction is a final appealable order under RC § 2505.02 when it sets forth (1) the guilty plea, the jury verdict, or the finding of the court upon which the conviction is based; (2) the sentence; (3) the signature of the judge; and (4) entry on the journal by the clerk of court: State v. Baker, 119 Ohio St. 3d 197, 2008 Ohio 3330, 893 N.E.2d 163, 2008 Ohio LEXIS 1774 (2008).

Court lacked jurisdiction to entertain defendant's appeal from a trial court's judgment convicting him of five of the six offenses with which he was charged because the judgment entry only disposed of five of the six charges. Pursuant to Ohio R. Crim. P. 32(C), a trial court had to dispose of each and every charge prosecuted against a defendant, and the failure to do so rendered the trial court's order merely interlocutory. State v. Johnson, — Ohio App. 3d —, 2007 Ohio 1003, — N.E. 2d —, 2007 Ohio App. LEXIS 910 (Mar. 1, 2007).

Court of appeals had no jurisdiction to consider defendant's appeal of the imposition of a definite period of post-release control, under Ohio Const. art. IV, § 3(B)(2), because the trial court's judgment entry was not a final appealable order because it did not comply with Ohio R. Crim. P. 32(C). State v. Bashlor, — Ohio App. 3d —, 2007 Ohio 2039, — N.E. 2d —, 2007 Ohio App. LEXIS 1926 (Apr. 30, 2007).

Appellate court had no jurisdiction, under Ohio Const. art. IV, § 3(B)(2), to consider defendant's appeal of his sentence for importuning and attempted sexual conduct with a minor because the trial court's sentencing entry was not final and appealable as it did not comply with Ohio R. Crim. P. 32(C), because it did not contain a finding that defendant was guilty of the crimes he pled guilty to, even though it noted that he pled guilty and otherwise complied with Rule 32(C) by including the sentence, the judge's signature, and the clerk's time stamp, indicating the entry was properly journalized. State v. Hultz, — Ohio App. 3d —, 2007 Ohio 2040, — N.E. 2d —, 2007 Ohio App. LEXIS 1928 (Apr. 30, 2007).

Judgment entry resentencing defendant to a definite term of post-release control, under RC § 2929.191, did not comply with Ohio R. Crim. P. 32(C), because (1) it did not refer to a plea to the charges for which defendant was sentenced, (2) it did not state a finding of guilt, and (3) it did not state defendant's complete sentence, as it only said he had already been sentenced and then imposed a five-year term of post-release control, so it was not a final appealable order, and an appellate court had no jurisdiction to consider defendant's appeal from it, under Ohio Const. art. IV, § 3(B)(2). State v. Nevedale, — Ohio App. 3d —, 2007 Ohio 2042, — N.E. 2d —, 2007 Ohio App. LEXIS 1929 (Apr. 30, 2007).

Appellate court lacked subject matter jurisdiction to consider defendant's appeal of his conviction for aggravated robbery and theft as neither an original jugment of conviction journal entry nor the nunc pro tunc entry meant to correct the first entry complied with Ohio R. Crim. P. 32(C). The first entry did not identify the jury's guilty verdict, and the nunc pro tunc entry lacked defendant's not guilty plea and sentence. State v. Vargas, — Ohio App. 3d —, 2007 Ohio 2264, — N.E. 2d —, 2007 Ohio App. LEXIS 2149 (May 14, 2007).

As the trial court's grant of defendant's motion in limine, excluding statements of his child victim, rendered the State's case so weak as to preclude effective prosecution, the trial court decision was treated as a ruling on a motion to suppress which was a final order that was properly appealed pursuant to Ohio R. Crim. P. 12(K) because it was timely filed under Ohio R. App. P. 4(D) and Ohio R. Crim. P. 32(C) and properly certified by the prosecutor; the State did not waive its right to appeal by electing to proceed to trial, as after the motion was ruled upon and the jury was impaneled, the prosecution sought reconsideration, which was denied, and then the State was granted leave to appeal. State v. Redfearn, — Ohio App. 3d —, 2007 Ohio 4108, — N.E. 2d —, 2007 Ohio App. LEXIS 3736 (Aug. 13, 2007).

Journal entry that does not dispose of a court's rulings as to each charge renders the order merely interlocutory and not appealable. Ohio v. Moore, — Ohio App. 3d —, 2007 Ohio 4941, — N.E. 2d —, 2007 Ohio App. LEXIS 4627 (Sept. 24, 2007).

As a trial court imposed a sentence of community control upon defendant's conviction of five counts each of nonsupport of dependents, in violation of RC § 2919.21(A)(2) and (b), but it failed to specify which count or counts the sentence applied to, the journal entry of sentence violated Ohio R. Crim. P. 32(C); accordingly, there was no final journal entry for purposes of appeal under RC § 2505.02 and the appellate court lacked jurisdiction under Ohio Const. art. IV, § 3(B)(2) to review the merits. Ohio v. Goldsberry, — Ohio App. 3d —, 2007 Ohio 5493, — N.E. 2d —, 2007 Ohio App. LEXIS 4833 (Oct. 15, 2007).

Where defendant was found guilty of criminal charges but a sentence had not been rendered by the trial court, there was no judgment of conviction under Ohio R. Crim. P. 32(C) and no "judgment or final order" under RC § 2953.02 for appellate purposes; further, the judgment entry did not contain the sentence, the trial judge's signature, or a time stamp indicating the filing of the judgment with the clerk and accordingly, the criteria for a final judgment were not met and the appeal required dismissal. Division of Waterworks v. Ardale, — Ohio App. 3d —, 2006 Ohio 1464, — N.E. 2d —, 2006 Ohio App. LEXIS 1334 (Mar. 24, 2006).

Trial court's judgment entry that found defendant guilty of RC § 2950.06, which was an offense that he was not charged with in the indictment, and which did not dispose of the offense charged in the indictment of failure to register a change of address under RC § 2950.05, but which imposed a sentence, did not comply with the requirements of Ohio R. Crim. P. 32(C), and was not a final appealable order, such that the appellate court lacked subject matter jurisdiction over the trial court's judgment under Ohio Const. art. IV, § 3(B)(2); accordingly, defendant's appeal was dismissed. State v. Frazier, — Ohio App. 3d —, 2006 Ohio 3334, — N.E. 2d —, 2006 Ohio App. LEXIS 3265 (June 30, 2006).

When defendant pled guilty to two counts of deception to obtain a dangerous drug but was not convicted of those offenses, pursuant to the granting of his motion for treatment in lieu of conviction, and, subsequently, in proceedings on whether he violated the terms of his supervision, he was convicted of drug possession and appropriately sentenced, he could not appeal that conviction or sentence because the trial court did not, pursuant to Ohio R. Crim. P. 32(C), dispose of every charge pending against him, so his conviction and sentence were interlocutory, and an appellate court had no jurisdiction to consider them because the conviction and sentence were not final, under RC § 2505.02. State v. Hoelscher, — Ohio App. 3d —, 2006 Ohio 3531, — N.E. 2d —, 2006 Ohio App. LEXIS 3483 (July 10, 2006).

As a judge who presided over defendant's criminal proceedings, wherein defendant entered a guilty plea and was convicted and sentenced, did not sign the judgment of conviction and sentencing order pursuant to Ohio R. Crim. P. 32(C), there was no final appealable order. The signature on the judgment was virtually illegible but it was clearly not that of the presiding judge. State v. Anderson, — Ohio App. 3d —, 2006 Ohio 3905, — N.E. 2d —, 2006 Ohio App. LEXIS 3874 (July 27, 2006).

As a trial court judgment in defendant's criminal matter failed to set forth the verdict reflecting that defendant was convicted of tampering with evidence and forgery, as required by Ohio R. Crim. P. 32(C), there was no final appealable order and defendant's appeal required dismissal because the appellate court was without jurisdiction under Ohio Const. art. IV, § 3(B)(2) to review the merits of the appeal. State v. Sandlin, — Ohio App. 3d —, 2006 Ohio 5021, — N.E. 2d —, 2006 Ohio App. LEXIS 5172 (Sept. 25, 2006).

Continuance

Trial court did not abuse its discretion when it denied defendant's motion to continue his sentencing to allow his mother to be present and testify on his behalf because the court complied with Ohio R. Crim. R. 32(A)(1) when it allowed defendant and his counsel make statements, and it gave defense counsel an opportunity to proffer the mother's testimony, but counsel declined. State v. Payne, — Ohio App. 3d —, 2007 Ohio 1553, — N.E. 2d —, 2007 Ohio App. LEXIS 1420 (Apr. 2, 2007).

Defense witnesses

Neither RC § 2947.06 nor CrimR 32(A) requires a trial court to hear from defense witnesses before imposing sentence: State v. Anderson, 172 Ohio App. 3d 603, 2007 Ohio 3849, 876 N.E.2d 632, 2007 Ohio App. LEXIS 3493 (2007).

Delay in sentencing

Unreasonable delay between a plea and sentencing, which cannot be attributed to the defendant, will invalidate that sentence. The remedy for an unreasonable delay in sentencing is vacation of the sentence, not a resentencing hearing: State v. Owens, 181 Ohio App. 3d 725, 2009 Ohio 1508, 910 N.E.2d 1059, 2009 Ohio App. LEXIS 1302 (2009).

Double jeopardy

Upon a trial court's journalization of a finding that defendant was not guilty of violating a notice of building code violations, the trial court was obligated to enter a judgment of acquittal and discharge him pursuant to Ohio R. Crim. P. 32(C) and pursuant to the Double Jeopardy Clause of U.S. Const. amend. V and Ohio Const. art. I, § 10; it could not attempt to vacate that finding and reinstate a prior oral finding of guilt that was never journalized. City of Cleveland Heights v. Difrancesco, — Ohio App. 3d —, 2007 Ohio 4680, — N.E. 2d —, 2007 Ohio App. LEXIS 4216 (Sept. 13, 2007).

Execution of sentence

Defendant did not show that a 16-month delay between the imposition and execution of defendant's prison sentence entitled defendant to have defendant's sentence vacated because defendant did not show that defendant's right to due process was violated by the delay as the delay resulted when defendant failed to appear for execution of defendant's sentence following the affirmance of defendant's convictions and sentence and because defendant did not obey the trial court's order to respond to the State's motion to dismiss defendant's post-conviction relief petition on res judicata grounds, once defendant's appeal was disposed of. State v. Lovell, — Ohio App. 3d —, 2007 Ohio 4352, — N.E. 2d —, 2007 Ohio App. LEXIS 3911 (Aug. 27, 2007).

Final appealable order

Defendant's appeal from a trial court's judgment entry finding him guilty on four of seven counts of cruelty to animals was dismissed because the judgment entry that defendant appealed did not address the other three counts of cruelty to animals. The entry did not comport with Ohio R. Crim. P. 32(C) and was an interlocutory entry, not a final order, thereby depriving the court of jurisdiction, pursuant to Ohio Const. art. IV, § 3, to consider the appeal. State v. Nichols, — Ohio App. 3d —, 2007 Ohio 1933, — N.E. 2d —, 2007 Ohio App. LEXIS 1739 (Apr. 16, 2007).

Appellate court lacked subject matter jurisdiction to consider defendant's appeal of a 13 year prison sentence on several charges; while the entry of judgment indicated that defendant had pled guilty to the charges, it did not include a finding of guilt by the trial court, and without that finding, the entry of judgment was not yet final and appealable. State v. O'Neal, — Ohio App. 3d —, 2007 Ohio 2266, — N.E. 2d —, 2007 Ohio App. LEXIS 2145 (May 14, 2007).

Courts have interpreted the requirements of Ohio R. Crim. P. 32(C) as imposing a mandatory duty on a trial court to deal with each and every charge prosecuted against a defendant, and the failure of a trial court to comply rendered the judgment of the trial court substantively deficient under Rule 32(C), and such a deficient journal entry was not a final, appealable order. State v. Goodwin, — Ohio App. 3d —, 2007 Ohio 2343, — N.E. 2d —, 2007 Ohio App. LEXIS 2203 (May 16, 2007).

Journal entry that did not include a finding defendant was guilty and stated that defendant pled guilty on rape, gross sexual imposition, and kidnapping charges, when in fact, defendant plead no contest to the charges, did not satisfy the requirements of Ohio R. Crim. P. 32(C), and thus, the journal entry did not constitute a final and appealable order. State v. Dobrski, — Ohio App. 3d —, 2007 Ohio 3121, — N.E. 2d —, 2007 Ohio App. LEXIS 2917 (June 25, 2007).

Pursuant to Ohio Const. art. IV, § 3(B)(2), the appellate court was without jurisdiction to consider the merits of defendant's appeal because the trial court's judgment entry was not a final appealable order where it did not satisfy Ohio R. Crim. P. 32(C)' s requirement that the judgment of conviction set forth the plea, the verdict or findings, and the sentence. State v. Salupo, — Ohio App. 3d —, 2007 Ohio 3303, — N.E. 2d —, 2007 Ohio App. LEXIS 3057 (June 29, 2007).

Because the trial court did not enter a finding of guilt in its September 15, 2006 judgment of conviction, that entry was neither final nor appealable. Although the July 17, 2006 entry did include a finding of guilt, it was insufficient to cure the defect in the September 15, 2006 entry. The July 17, 2006 entry set forth a finding of guilt, but did not include a sentence, and the September 15, 2006 entry set forth a sentence, but did not include a finding of guilt; and thus, neither judgment entry complied with Ohio R. Crim. P. 32(C). State v. Fitzpatrick, — Ohio App. 3d —, 2007 Ohio 3985, — N.E. 2d —, 2007 Ohio App. LEXIS 3586 (May 29, 2007).

As a trial court, upon finding defendant guilty of failing to abate public nuisances as ordered by a city building inspector, imposed sentences of suspended monetary and imprisonment conditions, it lacked authority under Toledo, Ohio, Mun. Code 1726.99, as well as jurisdiction, to additionally order that the properties were to be demolished and to impose additional sentencing orders upon the failure to do so because the original sentences were final judgments under Ohio R. Crim. P. 32(C) and Ohio R. App. P. 4(C), such that reconsideration was not permitted as to the additional sentencing orders; further, as defendant did not originally appeal from the imposition of community control on him, which had not been stayed, he could not later challenge that aspect of his sentence pursuant to Ohio Const. art. IV, § 3(B)(2), Ohio R. Crim. P. 32(B)(1), and Ohio R. App. P. 4(A). City of Toledo v. Samuel, — Ohio App. 3d —, 2007 Ohio 5303, — N.E. 2d —, 2007 Ohio App. LEXIS 4669 (Sept. 28, 2007).

When defendant pled guilty to felonious assault and domestic violence, among other crimes, but the trial court erroneously declined to impose sentence on the felonious assault charge, resulting in a reversal and imposition of a felonious assault sentence, an appellate court had no jurisdiction, under Ohio Const. art. IV, § 3(B)(2), to consider the State's appeal of the felonious assault sentence because the judgment entry imposing that sentence did not comply with Ohio R. Crim. P. 32(C), as the entry did not dispose of all charges against defendant in a single judgment entry, since the entry only addressed the felonious assault charge, so the entry was not a final appealable order, under RC § 2505.02. Ohio v. Sammy Carey Ford, — Ohio App. 3d —, 2007 Ohio 5935, — N.E. 2d —, 2007 Ohio App. LEXIS 5198 (Nov. 7, 2007).

Trial court's ruling imposing a sentence on defendant was not a final appealable order because the trial court only imposed sentence on one of the two charges upon which defendant was found guilty, and Ohio R. Crim. P. 32(C) imposes a duty to set forth the sentence for each charge prosecuted. While the trial court stated that it suspended the sentence on the other count, it could not do so since the sentence had not yet been imposed. State v. Brown, — Ohio App. 3d —, 2006 Ohio 152, — N.E. 2d —, 2006 Ohio App. LEXIS 128 (Jan. 12, 2006).

Because the journal entry ordering defendant to pay court costs for a third-degree felony (violating the registered sex offender notice of change of address requirement, under RC § 2950.05) did not satisfy Ohio R. Crim. P. 32(C) by setting forth the plea and the sentence, it was not a final appealable order. State v. Earley, — Ohio App. 3d —, 2006 Ohio 4466, — N.E. 2d —, 2006 Ohio App. LEXIS 4393 (Aug. 30, 2006).

Motion for reconsideration was denied because it failed to call attention to an obvious error in the prior decision or to raise an issue that was not properly considered in the first instance; the purported judgment entry did not constitute a final judgment from which an appeal could be taken. While the notations on the file jacket contained some of the material required by Ohio R. Crim. P. 32(B), it was deficient in other respects, and the evidence was undisputed that the notation, while apparently file stamped, was never properly journalized by the clerk. State v. French, — Ohio App. 3d —, 2006 Ohio 7115, — N.E. 2d —, 2006 Ohio App. LEXIS 7062 (Dec. 14, 2006).

Final judgment

Since a trial court's judgment entry sentencing defendant to six months in prison became final under Ohio R. Crim. P. 32(C) when it was entered on the journal and since the entry did not provide that defendant would face a more severe sentence if he did not turn himself in, the trial court was not permitted to revisit the final judgment and increase defendant's sentence after he failed to turn himself in. State v. Eungard, — Ohio App. 3d —, 2007 Ohio 4677, — N.E. 2d —, 2007 Ohio App. LEXIS 4220 (Sept. 13, 2007).

Trial court's judgment was not final under Ohio Const. art. IV, § 3 and RC § 2505.02 because, although the State brought three charges against defendant, the trial court dismissed one charge, imposed a sentence for the aggravated-burglary charge, but imposed no sentence on the domestic violence charge. Thus, the judgment below did not impose a sentence for both of the two charges, as required by Ohio R. Crim. P. 32(C). State v. Phillis, — Ohio App. 3d —, 2007 Ohio 6893, — N.E. 2d —, 2007 Ohio App. LEXIS 6034 (Dec. 18, 2007).

Habeas corpus

Habeas corpus is not a proper action to raise a claimed violation of CrimR 32(C): Dunn v. Smith, 119 Ohio St. 3d 364, 2008 Ohio 4565, 894 N.E.2d 312, 2008 Ohio LEXIS 2532 (2008).

Judgment entry

Appeal from a judgment in a criminal case was dismissed because the judgment entry failed to comply with Ohio R. Crim. P. 32(C), in that it lacked a proper record of the verdict. The specification in the judgment entry form that defendant had been found guilty of the charges for which he was ultimately sentenced was not sufficient to satisfy the requirement in Ohio R. Crim. P. 32(C) that the judgment entry set forth the jury's verdict. The court lacked jurisdiction to hear the appeal under Ohio Const. art. IV, § 3(B)(2). State v. Taylor, — Ohio App. 3d —, 2007 Ohio 2038, — N.E. 2d —, 2007 Ohio App. LEXIS 1927 (Apr. 30, 2007).

Defendant's appeal from a judgment in a criminal case was dismissed for lack of a final appealable order because the judgment entry failed to comply with Ohio R. Crim. P. 32(C), in that it lacked a finding of guilt. The trial court's specification in judgment entry that defendant had "previously been convicted" of the offenses at issue was not a finding of guilt as required by Ohio R. Crim. P. 32(C); thus, the court lacked jurisdiction under Ohio Const. art. IV, § 3(B)(2) to consider the appeal. State v. Combs, — Ohio App. 3d —, 2007 Ohio 2155, — N.E. 2d —, 2007 Ohio App. LEXIS 2032 (May 7, 2007).

Defendant's appeal from a judgment in a criminal case was dismissed for lack of a final appealable order because the judgment entry failed to comply with Ohio R. Crim. P. 32(C), in that it lacked a finding of guilt. The specification in the judgment entry that defendant "has been convicted of rape" was not a finding of guilt as required by Ohio R. Crim. P. 32(C); thus, the court lacked jurisdiction to hear the appeal pursuant to Ohio Const. art. IV, § 3(B)(2). State v. Reese, — Ohio App. 3d —, 2007 Ohio 2267, — N.E. 2d —, 2007 Ohio App. LEXIS 2147 (May 14, 2007).

When it was alleged that defendants' penalties for driving while intoxicated should be enhanced due to defendants' prior convictions, those prior convictions which did not indicate that a defendant's guilt was found could not be used to enhance that defendant's penalty because Ohio R. Crim. P. 32(C) required such a finding, and a lack thereof rendered those judgments invalid. State v. Hill, — Ohio App. 3d —, 2007 Ohio 2832, — N.E. 2d —, 2007 Ohio App. LEXIS 2647 (June 8, 2007).

When it was alleged that defendants' penalties for driving while intoxicated should be enhanced due to defendants' prior convictions, those prior convictions which did not indicate on their faces that the convictions had been journalized could be used to enhance the penalties because, (1) while Ohio R. Crim. P. 32(C) required that judgments be journalized to be effective, nothing required that journalization be noted in another place, and (2) defendants stipulated that the courts which issued those judgments kept the courts' journals in computer records and that these judgments were entered on those records, so it was unnecessary for the State to prove journalization. State v. Hill, — Ohio App. 3d —, 2007 Ohio 2832, — N.E. 2d —, 2007 Ohio App. LEXIS 2647 (June 8, 2007).

Defendant timely filed an appeal under Ohio R. App. P. 3(A) and 4(A) because the original judgment entry on March 2, 2006, which defendant sought to appeal from was not time stamped and, thus, not an effective final judgment under Ohio R. Crim. P. 32(C); once a second judgment entry with a time stamp was filed on October 12, defendant timely filed his appeal within 30 days. Ohio v. Charlton, — Ohio App. 3d —, 2007 Ohio 5202, — N.E. 2d —, 2007 Ohio App. LEXIS 4599 (Sept. 28, 2007).

Because RC § 2929.15 did not require that a sentencing court impose only a single term of community control for multiple violations, a sentencing journal entry that indicated that defendant pled guilty on five charges but imposed only one three-year community control sanction with no statement as to which count or counts it applied to, did not comport with the formalities of Ohio R. Crim. P. 32(C), which required sentencing courts to deal with each and every charge against defendant. Ohio v. Moore, — Ohio App. 3d —, 2007 Ohio 4941, — N.E. 2d —, 2007 Ohio App. LEXIS 4627 (Sept. 24, 2007).

Trial court's journal entry during defendant's bench trial, which indicated that defendant committed a fourth degree felony for carrying a concealed weapon under RC § 2923.12 with a simple notation of "F4," was proper under Ohio R. Crim. P. 32(C); as there was no jury, the trial court's judgment did not have to comply with RC § 2945.75. State v. Sims, — Ohio App. 3d —, 2007 Ohio 6821, — N.E. 2d —, 2007 Ohio App. LEXIS 5968 (Dec. 20, 2007).

Relator, a criminal defendant, was not entitled to a writ of mandamus and/or procedendo to compel the entry of a valid final judgment pursuant to Ohio R. Crim. P. 32(C) in his criminal case because the common pleas court had been divested of jurisdiction to take such action as relator's conviction and sentence had been previously affirmed on direct appeal. State Ex Rel. Agosto, — Ohio App. 3d —, 2007 Ohio 6806, — N.E. 2d —, 2007 Ohio App. LEXIS 5976 (Dec. 19, 2007).

As defendant received a copy of a judgment that indicated that it was filed on June 9, 2006 and journalized on June 13, 2006, although the court appearance docket indicated that the judgment was both filed and journalized on June 9, 2006, defendant was deemed to have timely appealed under Ohio R. App. P. 4(A) and Ohio R. Crim. P. 32(C) by filing his notice of appeal on July 11, 2006, as he had no way of knowing that his copy of the judgment might have been inaccurate regarding the date of judgment entry. The court clerk was not required to journalize a judgment the day that it was filed, and the judgment herein was within the time constraints for entry under Ohio Superintendence R. 7. State v. Ulis, — Ohio App. 3d —, 2006 Ohio 3987, — N.E. 2d —, 2006 Ohio App. LEXIS 3962 (Aug. 2, 2006).

Where the docket noted that the three-judge panel imposed costs on defendant but there was no journalized judgment entry indicating that the court actually imposed such costs, there was no effective decision to that effect pursuant to Ohio R. Crim. P. 32(B). In such an instance, a remand for imposition of mandatory costs pursuant to RC § 2947.23 and for consideration of defendant's ability to pay other non-mandatory costs pursuant to RC § 2929.18 was required. State v. Harmon, — Ohio App. 3d —, 2006 Ohio 4642, — N.E. 2d —, 2006 Ohio App. LEXIS 4563 (Sept. 1, 2006).

Trial court's dismissal of two counts in an indictment that were based on defendant's prior convictions for driving under the influence of alcohol (DUI), in violation of RC § 4511.19, was proper where the prior convictions were not journalized as required by Ohio R. Crim. P. 32(C) and accordingly, there could be no proof of the specifications under RC § 4511.19(G)(1)(d) pursuant to RC § 2945.75(B). As the prior convictions enhanced the degree of the DUI offenses charged against defendant, they were essential elements of that offense which the State would have been required to prove beyond a reasonable doubt. State v. Finney, — Ohio App. 3d —, 2006 Ohio 5770, — N.E. 2d —, 2006 Ohio App. LEXIS 5755 (Nov. 3, 2006).

— Mandamus or procedendo to compel entry

Writs of mandamus and procedendo may issue to compel a court to comply with CrimR 32(C) and issue a sentencing entry that constitutes a final appealable order: State ex rel. Culgan v. Medina County Court of Common Pleas, 119 Ohio St. 3d 535, 2008 Ohio 4609, 895 N.E.2d 805, 2008 Ohio LEXIS 2540 (2008).

Resentencing

Defendant's notification of post-release control in resentencing did not equate to an increase in his overall sentence because the purpose of the resentencing was to give defendant notice of a condition that already existed at the time of his original sentence; defendant's right to allocution was not affected as the right to allocution only applied during the time of sentencing and the very purpose of allocution was to mitigate the punishment. Although defendant was entitled, pursuant to RC § 2929.191(C), to have a right to speak at the hearing, defendant's right to speak did not affect the length of the post-release control that had to be applied and thus, the trial court's failure to allow defendant to speak was harmless error at best. State v. Barnes, — Ohio App. 3d —, 2007 Ohio 3362, — N.E. 2d —, 2007 Ohio App. LEXIS 3088 (June 29, 2007).

Right for allocution

Defendant's sentence imposed upon his conviction for attempted sexual misconduct was vacated because the trial court did not personally address defendant and ask him for a statement prior to sentencing but, instead, proceeded directly to sentencing following statements from the victim and her family. This violated defendant's right of allocution under Ohio R. Crim. P. 32(A). S/O, City of Garfield Hts v. J.P., — Ohio App. 3d —, 2006 Ohio 4590, — N.E. 2d —, 2006 Ohio App. LEXIS 4529 (Sept. 7, 2006).

Right to appeal

Defendant did not show his guilty plea was not knowing or intelligent because the trial court did not advise him when he pled guilty of his right to appeal, because, under Ohio R. Crim. P. 32(B)(2), the trial court did not have to advise him of this right until he was sentenced. State v. Atkinson, — Ohio App. 3d —, 2006 Ohio 5806, — N.E. 2d —, 2006 Ohio App. LEXIS 5783 (Nov. 6, 2006).

Sentencing

Defendant's rights at sentencing under Ohio R. Crim. P. 32 were not violated where his attorney spoke, defendant spoke, he was allowed to address every count that he was charged with, and further, his father was afforded the opportunity to speak on defendant's behalf. State v. Bulger, — Ohio App. 3d —, 2006 Ohio 3046, — N.E. 2d —, 2006 Ohio App. LEXIS 2928 (June 16, 2006).

Trial court erred in refusing to impose sentence on each of defendant's convictions because the trial court was obligated to impose a sentence on each of defendant's convictions. State v. Ford, — Ohio App. 3d —, 2006 Ohio 6961, — N.E. 2d —, 2006 Ohio App. LEXIS 6917 (Dec. 29, 2006).

RULE 32.1.   Withdrawal of Guilty Plea

A motion to withdraw a plea of guilty or no contest may be made only before sentence is imposed; but to correct manifest injustice the court after sentence may set aside the judgment of conviction and permit the defendant to withdraw his or her plea.

History: Amended, eff 7-1-98.

NOTES TO DECISIONS

ANALYSIS

Abuse of discretion
Appeal
Claim of innocence
Coercion
Competency
Competency of defendant
Consideration of motion
Counsel's conflict of interest
Counsel's erroneous advice about sentence
Denial of motion
Denial of motion to withdraw guilty plea
Denial of motion to withdraw plea
Deportation consequences
Discovery violation
Duty of the court
Erroneous advice about sentence
Failure to advise alien defendant
Guilty plea
Guilty plea coerced by counsel
Harsher sentence than expected
Health of defendant at time of plea
Hearing
Immigration status
Ineffective assistance
Ineffective assistance of counsel
—Guilty plea
—Insufficient evidence
—Sentencing
Ineffective assistsance
Jurisdiction of trial court
Knowing and intelligent
Mandamus
Manifest injustice
Medications
Mistake as to sentencing options
Mistake concerning sentencing
Motion after sentencing
Motion to withdraw guilty plea
Motion to withdraw plea
Motion to withdraw plea properly denied
No contest plea
Plea withdrawal
Post-conviction relief
Presentence motion to withdraw plea
Procedure
Reply to state's memorandum
Res judicata
Res judicata
Review
Right to counsel
Rules of civil procedure
Sentencing
Timeliness
Transcript
Void sentence
Withdrawal not warranted
Withdrawal of guilty plea
Withdrawal warranted

Abuse of discretion

Trial court abused its discretion when it failed to conduct a hearing regarding defendant's motion under Ohio R. Crim. P. 32.1 to withdraw his guilty plea, as his claim that he was pressured into entering the plea and that he did not want to do so established a prima facie showing of merit, such that a hearing was warranted to determine the voluntariness of the plea. State v. McDaniel, — Ohio App. 3d —, 2007 Ohio 5441, — N.E. 2d —, 2007 Ohio App. LEXIS 4770 (Oct. 11, 2007).

Trial court abused its discretion by failing to consider the defendant's presentence motion to withdraw his no contest plea to a charge of nonsupport where the defendant raised the defense of inability to pay the amount of support ordered. State v. Tull, 168 Ohio App. 3d 54, 2006 Ohio 3365, 858 N.E.2d 828, 2006 Ohio App. LEXIS 3257 (2006).

Appeal

Defendant's appeal challenging the purported denial of his motion to withdraw his guilty plea was dismissed because defendant filed his notice of appeal before filing the motion to withdraw, thus divesting the trial court of jurisdiction to consider the motion to withdraw. Further, since the trial court never ruled on the motion, it was premature for the appellate court to do so. State v. Morgan, — Ohio App. 3d —, 2007 Ohio 398, — N.E. 2d —, 2007 Ohio App. LEXIS 343 (Feb. 1, 2007).

Four factors were considered when a defendant sought to withdraw a guilty plea: (1) did the trial court follow Ohio R. Crim. P. 11 and ensure defendant understood defendant's rights and voluntarily waived those rights by pleading guilty; (2) was defendant represented by highly competent counsel; (3) was defendant given a hearing wherein defendant could assert all arguments supporting defendant's motion to withdraw the plea; and (4) did the trial court give careful consideration to the merits of defendant's motion. State v. Haney, — Ohio App. 3d —, 2007 Ohio 3712, — N.E. 2d —, 2007 Ohio App. LEXIS 3394 (July 20, 2007).

Defendant's challenge on appeal to a trial court's denial of her Ohio R. Crim. P. 32.1 motion to withdraw her no contest pleas was not properly before the court because defendant had not filed an appeal from the trial court's denial of her motion to withdraw within thirty days of the denial, as required by Ohio R. App. P. 4(A). State v. Summers, — Ohio App. 3d —, 2007 Ohio 4576, — N.E. 2d —, 2007 Ohio App. LEXIS 4114 (Aug. 31, 2007).

Because defendant entered his guilty plea as part of a plea bargain, he waived all appealable errors, unless such errors precluded a knowing and voluntary plea, and a trial court did not err in denying defendant's Ohio R. Crim. P. 32.1 motion to withdraw his guilty plea; a hearing on the motion was not required since defendant had already been sentenced. State v. Wilkey, — Ohio App. 3d —, 2006 Ohio 3276, — N.E. 2d —, 2006 Ohio App. LEXIS 3189 (June 19, 2006).

Defendant did not meet her burden to show manifest injustice in order to support her post-sentence motion to withdraw her guilty plea pursuant to Ohio R. Crim. P. 32.1 where she failed to attach of a copy of the transcript from the plea hearing pursuant to Ohio R. App. P. 9(B). The regularity of the proceedings was presumed, and defendant's claim that she was not properly advised under Ohio R. Crim. P. 11(D) prior to entering her pro se plea of guilty was deemed to lack merit. City of Parma v. Taylor, — Ohio App. 3d —, 2006 Ohio 3973, — N.E. 2d —, 2006 Ohio App. LEXIS 3947 (Aug. 3, 2006).

When defendant sought to appeal the trial court's denial of his oral motion at sentencing to withdraw his guilty plea, the fact that the entry appealed was the trial court's sentencing entry did not deprive the appellate court of jurisdiction because there was no separate entry denying the motion to withdraw the plea. State v. Eversole, — Ohio App. 3d —, 2006 Ohio 3988, — N.E. 2d —, 2006 Ohio App. LEXIS 3958 (Aug. 4, 2006).

Claim of innocence

Trial court abused its discretion in overruling defendant's pre-sentence motion under Ohio R. Crim. P. 32.1 to withdraw his guilty plea, as defendant claimed that he had entered the plea to end the matter and because of financial hardship although he did not believe that he was guilty of the charged offense, his counsel had acquired evidence to support his claim of innocence, and defendant further asserted that he had been mistaken that the guilty plea to the felony offense would not hamper his prospects for a career in the educational field, as his further questioning on that issue after he entered his plea convinced him that he might be unable to get certain teaching jobs if he had a felony conviction. The trial court erred in focusing almost exclusively on the voluntary, knowing, and intelligent factor of the plea pursuant to Ohio R. Crim. P. 11 in determining to overrule the withdrawal motion, as in the circumstances, he should have been restored to his constitutional right under U.S. Const. amend. VI and Ohio Const. art. I, § 10 to put the State to its proof at trial under RC § 2901.05 on the charged offenses. State v. Sykes, — Ohio App. 3d —, 2007 Ohio 3086, — N.E. 2d —, 2007 Ohio App. LEXIS 2841 (June 22, 2007).

Defendant's claims that she was pressured by her attorneys to plead guilty and that she was in fact innocent were not sufficient to require the court to permit withdrawal of her plea: State v. Holin, 174 Ohio App. 3d 1, 2007 Ohio 6255, 880 N.E.2d 515, 2007 Ohio App. LEXIS 5487 (2007).

Coercion

Defendant's contention that the trial court was coercive in making unfavorable rulings during her hearing on her motion to withdraw her no contest plea was rejected. Making rulings is the duty of the trial court, and whether they are favorable to a defendant or not bears absolutely no relation to whether said defendant feels coerced to plead. State v. Brown, — Ohio App. 3d —, 2007 Ohio 2885, — N.E. 2d —, 2007 Ohio App. LEXIS 2683 (June 13, 2007).

Competency

When defendant pled guilty, the transcript of his plea hearing did not demonstrate that his plea was not knowing or voluntary, as, inter alia, he denied that any medication he was taking had an adverse effect on his ability to understand the proceedings, he appeared to be lucid when he addressed the trial court, and, even if he was mentally ill, the transcript did not show he was incompetent to plead guilty, under RC § 2945.37(G), so it was not an abuse of discretion to deny his motion to withdraw his plea. State v. Humphrey, — Ohio App. 3d —, 2006 Ohio 1630, — N.E. 2d —, 2006 Ohio App. LEXIS 1516 (Mar. 31, 2006).

Competency of defendant

Denial of defendant's request to withdraw his guilty plea was not error because the transcript indicated that defendant had the ability to consult with his lawyer with a reasonable degree of understanding and also had a rational and factual understanding of the proceedings against him, thus fulfilling the competency requirements. Although a psychiatric evaluation several months after the plea determined that defendant was mentally incompetent at the time of the evaluation, his actions during the hearing indicated otherwise. State v. Martinez, — Ohio App. 3d —, 2006 Ohio 1331, — N.E. 2d —, 2006 Ohio App. LEXIS 1222 (Mar. 23, 2006).

Consideration of motion

When defendant, who pled guilty to domestic violence, attempted, at sentencing, to withdraw his guilty plea, because his victim was not his spouse, the trial court properly gave his motion full consideration when it inquired about his relationship to the victim, and, upon being told the victim was the mother of defendant's child, found there was no legal basis for defendant's motion, under RC § 2919.25(F)(1)(b). State v. Woods, — Ohio App. 3d —, 2006 Ohio 2325, — N.E. 2d —, 2006 Ohio App. LEXIS 2152 (May 5, 2006).

When, after defendant's sentence was reversed and his case was remanded for resentencing, the trial court granted his motion to withdraw his prior guilty plea and the State then moved to reconsider that decision, the trial court had no authority to consider either defendant's motion or the State's motion because its authority was limited to the appellate court's mandate, which directed defendant's resentencing. The trial court's error was harmless, under Ohio R. Crim. P. 52(B), because it did not violate defendant's substantial rights, which were limited to the right to be resentenced, as he was eventually resentenced. State v. Roper, — Ohio App. 3d —, 2006 Ohio 3661, — N.E. 2d —, 2006 Ohio App. LEXIS 3613 (July 19, 2006).

In reviewing a trial court's decision regarding a motion to withdraw a plea, a non-exhaustive list of factors to weigh included: (1) whether the prosecution would be prejudiced if the plea was vacated; (2) whether the accused was represented by highly competent counsel; (3) whether the accused was given a full Ohio R. Crim. P. 11 hearing; (4) whether a full hearing was held on the motion; (5) whether the trial court gave full and fair consideration to the motion; (6) whether the motion was made within a reasonable time; (7) whether the motion set forth specific reasons for the withdrawal; (8) whether the accused understood the nature of the charges and possible penalties; and (9) whether the accused was perhaps not guilty or had a complete defense to the crime, and a change of heart or mistaken belief about pleading guilty was not a reasonable basis that required a trial court to permit a defendant to withdraw his guilty plea. State v. Eversole, — Ohio App. 3d —, 2006 Ohio 3988, — N.E. 2d —, 2006 Ohio App. LEXIS 3958 (Aug. 4, 2006).

Counsel's conflict of interest

Defendant's claim that his counsel also represented defendant's co-defendant without telling defendant did not require the trial court to allow defendant to withdraw his guilty plea because (1) the alleged undisclosed dual representation had no bearing on whether the trial court complied with Ohio R. Crim. P. 11(C) in accepting defendant's plea or whether that plea was knowing and voluntary, and (2) defendant did not show that any actual conflict arising from the dual representation caused his counsel's representation to be inadequate. State v. Clark, — Ohio App. 3d —, 2007 Ohio 713, — N.E. 2d —, 2007 Ohio App. LEXIS 649 (Feb. 22, 2007).

Denial of defendant's motion to withdraw his no contest pleas was proper because, although defendant claimed that his plea was not knowing and intelligent due to allegedly tainted advice from his attorney, he failed to establish any connection between the asserted conflict of interest and any effect it had on his attorney's advice or his decision to plead. Defendant was required to establish an actual conflict of interest during the attorney's representation in order to withdraw his guilty plea; the "dual representation" reflected in the facts simply did not amount to a conflict of interest which would have permitted defendant to withdraw his guilty plea because both defendant and his father had a common interest in attacking the credibility of prosecution witnesses. State v. Osborne, — Ohio App. 3d —, 2007 Ohio 1794, — N.E. 2d —, 2007 Ohio App. LEXIS 1652 (Apr. 16, 2007).

Counsel's erroneous advice about sentence

Trial court did not abuse its discretion by finding that defendant failed to demonstrate that any manifest injustice would occur if he were not allowed to withdraw his guilty plea, pursuant to Ohio R. Crim. P. 32.1. Defendant failed to show that, but for counsel's alleged errors, he would not have entered his guilty plea because it was apparent that defendant pled guilty after having been correctly informed of the sentence he could receive. State v. Pruitt, — Ohio App. 3d —, 2006 Ohio 4106, — N.E. 2d —, 2006 Ohio App. LEXIS 4066 (Aug. 10, 2006).

Denial of motion

Trial court's denial of defendant's post-sentence motion to withdraw his guilty plea pursuant to Ohio R. Crim. P. 32.1 was proper without holding an evidentiary hearing, as defendant's claim that his counsel had promised him that he would receive probation if he entered a guilty plea was totally contradicted by the record, including the trial court's explanation of the potential sentences that defendant faced as well as defendant's own statements. State v. Okogie, — Ohio App. 3d —, 2006 Ohio 1247, — N.E. 2d —, 2006 Ohio App. LEXIS 1094 (Mar. 16, 2006).

There was no abuse of discretion in a trial court's denial of defendant's post-sentence motion to withdraw his guilty plea pursuant to Ohio R. Crim. P. 32.1, as he failed to show evidence that his plea was induced by assertions of the trial court and counsel that he could raise the issue of lack of a speedy trial on appeal, and his attached documentation supported the determination that he understood the rights he waived under Ohio R. Crim. P. 11 and the reasoning for the denial of his speedy trial claim; further, he did not explain the five-year delay between his plea and his request to withdraw it. State v. McKinney, — Ohio App. 3d —, 2006 Ohio 5364, — N.E. 2d —, 2006 Ohio App. LEXIS 5344 (Oct. 16, 2006).

Based on a trial court's full compliance with Ohio R. Crim. P. 11(C) in accepting defendant's guilty pleas to a variety of offenses, the denial of his motion to withdraw his pleas pursuant to Ohio R. Crim. P. 32.1, was proper. The record clearly indicated that defendant had entered his pleas voluntarily and with an understanding of the nature of the charges, as he was fully aware of the exact sentence that would be imposed based upon a plea agreement. State v. Griffin, — Ohio App. 3d —, 2006 Ohio 6660, — N.E. 2d —, 2006 Ohio App. LEXIS 6557 (Dec. 15, 2006).

Denial of motion to withdraw guilty plea

Although it was unclear what status defendant had after he initially entered a guilty plea, was sentenced, and on appeal his sentence was vacated under Foster and the matter was remanded for resentencing, there was no basis for defendant's withdrawal of his plea pursuant to Ohio R. Crim. P. 32.1 in any event, as he did not set forth any grounds to show a basis for withdrawal of the plea or to show that a manifest injustice warranted withdrawal. State v. Rose, — Ohio App. 3d —, 2007 Ohio 1627, — N.E. 2d —, 2007 Ohio App. LEXIS 1480 (Apr. 9, 2007).

Trial court properly denied defendant's post-sentence motions under Ohio R. Crim. P. 32.1 to withdraw his guilty pleas in two separate matters, as his pleas were voluntarily and knowingly entered, the trial court had complied with Ohio R. Crim. P. 11 at the plea hearing, and defendant had previously raised his claims of prosecutorial misconduct and ineffectiveness of counsel and they were found to be lacking in merit. Defendant failed in his burden of showing that there was a manifest injustice that required withdrawal of the pleas. State v. Wheeler, — Ohio App. 3d —, 2007 Ohio 3226, — N.E. 2d —, 2007 Ohio App. LEXIS 2980 (June 26, 2007).

Where a trial court substantially complied with the requirements of Ohio R. Crim. P. 11(C)(2), and defendant failed to show that he was prejudiced by his counsel's erroneous representation about defendant's eligibility for judicial release, there was no showing of manifest injustice under Ohio R. Crim. P. 32.1 to support defendant's post-sentence request to withdraw his guilty plea. State v. Aleshire, — Ohio App. 3d —, 2007 Ohio 4446, — N.E. 2d —, 2007 Ohio App. LEXIS 4010 (Aug. 29, 2007).

Trial court did not abuse its discretion when it denied defendant's post-sentence motion to withdraw his guilty plea to charges that included conspiracy to commit aggravated murder as the denial of the motion did not work a manifest injustice; the plea colloquy established that defendant understood that he could not seek judicial release until he had served at least five years of his nine year sentence, even if counsel failed to advise defendant regarding Alford pleas, such a plea would not have resulted in a different sentence, the evidence did not show undue influence regarding the plea by the attorney or defendant's family, and defendant's statement to the plea court that he was ashamed of his actions belied his claim that he was innocent of the charges. Ohio v. Vogelsong, — Ohio App. 3d —, 2007 Ohio 4935, — N.E. 2d —, 2007 Ohio App. LEXIS 4617 (Sept. 24, 2007).

Although defendant entered his guilty plea after his criminal trial had been ongoing for seven days before a single judge of the trial court, rather than a three-judge panel as directed by Ohio R. Crim. P. 11(C)(3) and RC § 2945.06, such did not constitute "manifest injustice" that warranted granting defendant's motion to withdraw his guilty plea, pursuant to Ohio R. Crim. P. 32.1, although the claims were all barred by res judicata in any event, as the motion was made 11 years after defendant was convicted, the death penalty specifications were dismissed as nolle prosequi by the State in exchange for defendant's guilty pleas to certain charges, and he did not face the possibility of a death sentence when he entered his plea; the fact that there were alleged omissions in the written plea agreement did not require reversal where the colloquy indicated clearly that defendant intended to plead guilty to the charges for which he was convicted and sentenced, and that his plea was knowingly and voluntarily entered. State v. Thomson, — Ohio App. 3d —, 2006 Ohio 1224, — N.E. 2d —, 2006 Ohio App. LEXIS 1104 (Mar. 17, 2006).

Defendant's motion to withdraw his guilty plea was properly denied because (1) defendant had a complete Ohio R. Crim. P. 11 plea hearing at which he was advised of the charges against him, the penalty he faced due to those charges, and the rights he waived by pleading guilty, (2) the record showed he understood those advisements, (3) he expressed satisfaction with his legal representation, (4) the trial court fully and fairly considered defendant's motion to withdraw his plea at the sentencing hearing, giving defendant an opportunity to explain the basis of the motion, (5) defendant offered no defense to the crime other than a general statement that he was not guilty, and (6) he admitted, when he pled guilty, the truth of the prosecutor's statements of fact, which showed he aided and abetted another in committing a crime. State v. Moore, — Ohio App. 3d —, 2006 Ohio 6353, — N.E. 2d —, 2006 Ohio App. LEXIS 6314 (Dec. 4, 2006).

Defendant's motion to withdraw his guilty plea to rape and other offenses was properly denied under Ohio R. Crim. P. 32.1 because he was fully advised during the plea hearing of the penalties he would face in pleading guilty, his claim that the plea did not accurately reflect his level of culpability was essentially a claim of change of heart, which was not a sufficient basis for a plea withdrawal, and no evidence supported his claim that he was pressured or coerced into entering the plea. State v. Vaughn, — Ohio App. 3d —, 2006 Ohio 6577, — N.E. 2d —, 2006 Ohio App. LEXIS 6497 (Dec. 14, 2006).

Trial court did not abuse its discretion in denying defendant's motion to withdraw his guilty plea. Because the subsequent change in law that Foster made regarding sentencing did not alone invalidate defendant's guilty plea, defendant failed to present a legitimate and reasonable basis to withdraw his guilty plea. State v. Harper, — Ohio App. 3d —, 2007 Ohio 2590, — N.E. 2d —, 2007 Ohio App. LEXIS 2400 (May 29, 2007).

In review of a trial court's denial of defendant's motion under Ohio R. Crim. P. 32.1 to withdraw his guilty plea, the court noted that the State's case would have been prejudiced by withdrawal, defendant understood the nature of the charges and the potential penalties he faced, his counsel was not ineffective, he was given full hearing prior to entering his guilty plea under Ohio R. Crim. P. 11, and he was also given a full and complete hearing on his withdrawal request; the reasons asserted for withdrawal lacked merit. State v. Phillips, — Ohio App. 3d —, 2007 Ohio 2671, — N.E. 2d —, 2007 Ohio App. LEXIS 2483 (June 1, 2007).

Because all four elements set forth in State v. Peterseim, 68 Ohio App.2d 211, 428 N.E.2d 863, 1980 Ohio App. LEXIS

9665 (1980), were satisfied, the trial court did not abuse its discretion in denying defendant's motion to withdraw defendant's guilty plea, Ohio R. Crim. P. 32.1. There was no evidence that counsel was incompetent or ineffective, as during the plea colloquy defendant told the trial court that defendant was satisfied with the attorney who had assisted defendant in preparing for trial and in entering the plea, and the record showed that the trial court gave full and fair consideration to defendant's motion. State v. Pierce, — Ohio App. 3d —, 2007 Ohio 3416, — N.E. 2d —, 2007 Ohio App. LEXIS 3161 (July 5, 2007).

Denial of motion to withdraw plea

Although defendant indicated to the trial court prior to sentencing that he wished to withdraw his guilty plea, upon being questioned by the trial court about it, defendant was clear that he wished to withdraw his request to withdraw his plea; accordingly, the trial court did not err in failing to grant a motion that was no longer before it. State v. Lopez, — Ohio App. 3d —, 2007 Ohio 202, — N.E. 2d —, 2007 Ohio App. LEXIS 190 (Jan. 19, 2007).

Ohio R. Crim. P. 32.1 motion to withdraw a no contest plea was properly denied because, while defendant contended that he did not understand the specifics of judicial release, the record showed that the trial court painstakingly described how judicial release would work. State v. Wallen, — Ohio App. 3d —, 2007 Ohio 2129, — N.E. 2d —, 2007 Ohio App. LEXIS 1985 (May 4, 2007).

Denials of defendant's oral motion to withdraw defendant's guilty plea at the beginning of defendant's sentencing hearing and defendant's written post-sentence motion to withdraw the plea did not abuse discretion because (1) the trial court fully complied with Crim. R. 11 when accepting defendant's plea and defendant voluntarily waived defendant's rights, (2) defendant did not allege defendant's counsel was incompetent, nor was there any evidence of incompetence, (3) defendant had a full hearing on defendant's motions to withdraw, and (4) the trial court carefully considered defendant's motions, because it appeared that defendant changed heart after the trial court saw a video of defendant's police chase, but this was an insufficient basis for withdrawing defendant's plea. State v. Haney, — Ohio App. 3d —, 2007 Ohio 3712, — N.E. 2d —, 2007 Ohio App. LEXIS 3394 (July 20, 2007).

Trial court's denial of defendant's motions under Ohio R. Crim. P. 32.1 to withdraw his guilty pleas in two matters was not an abuse of discretion, as the trial court's case files established that defendant was afforded an explanation of his rights under Ohio R. Crim. P. 11, that he validly waived those rights, and that defendant had created the lapse of more than 19 years from the time of the pleas to the time of sentencing due to his having left the State of Ohio in the interim. Ohio v. Deavers, — Ohio App. 3d —, 2007 Ohio 5464, — N.E. 2d —, 2007 Ohio App. LEXIS 4794 (Oct. 1, 2007).

Trial court's denial of defendant's pre-sentence motion to withdraw his guilty plea was not an abuse of discretion, as the trial court carefully considered the relevant factors relating to such a motion and it found that there was no reason to grant the motion, as the only circumstance that had changed was defendant's change of heart, which did not justify a change of plea; defendant understood the nature of the charges and the potential sentences prior to accepting the plea. State v. Gant, — Ohio App. 3d —, 2006 Ohio 1469, — N.E. 2d —, 2006 Ohio App. LEXIS 1345 (Mar. 22, 2006).

Where a trial court transcript from defendant's plea allocution pursuant to Ohio R. Crim. P. 11 indicated that defendant understood the nature of the crimes to which he was pleading guilty, that he was advised of the potential penalties, and that he was informed of the rights he was surrendering by entering the plea, there was no evidence that his counsel rendered ineffective assistance in violation of defendant's Sixth Amendment rights by pressuring him to plead guilty; the plea was knowingly, voluntarily, and intelligently entered, and the trial court's denial of his post-sentence motion to withdraw the plea pursuant to Ohio R. Crim. P. 32.1 was proper without an evidentiary hearing. State v. Finkbine, — Ohio App. 3d —, 2006 Ohio 1788, — N.E. 2d —, 2006 Ohio App. LEXIS 1649 (Apr. 10, 2006).

Trial court did not abuse its discretion in denying defendant's pre-sentence motion to withdraw his Alford plea pursuant to Ohio R. Crim. P. 32.1, as defendant breached the plea agreement when he failed to appear for sentencing, withdrawal of the plea would have unfairly prejudiced the State, and defendant was fully informed during the colloquy under Ohio R. Crim. P. 11 prior to entering the plea. State v. Walker, — Ohio App. 3d —, 2006 Ohio 2929, — N.E. 2d —, 2006 Ohio App. LEXIS 2811 (June 9, 2006).

There was no error in the denial of defendant's motion to withdraw his plea as counsel was not ineffective; since the trial court fully complied with the requirements of Ohio R. Civ. P. 11, no evidence was presented that the plea was not knowingly, intelligently, and voluntarily entered. Counsel negotiated a plea agreement which reduced the potential sentence from a maximum of eight years for a second degree felony to a maximum of 18 months for a fourth degree felony. State v. Zamora, — Ohio App. 3d —, 2006 Ohio 3393, — N.E. 2d —, 2006 Ohio App. LEXIS 3308 (July 3, 2006).

Trial court did not err in overruling defendant's motion to withdraw his guilty plea. The record showed that defendant was represented by two competent attorneys, that the trial court conducted a full hearing under Ohio R. Crim. P. 11 before defendant entered his plea, that the trial court conducted a hearing on defendant's motion to withdraw his plea, and that the trial court fully considered the motion to withdraw. State v. Haywood, — Ohio App. 3d —, 2006 Ohio 6445, — N.E. 2d —, 2006 Ohio App. LEXIS 6394 (Dec. 7, 2006).

Deportation consequences

Trial court's denial of defendant's request for leave to withdraw his guilty plea pursuant to Ohio R. Crim. P. 32.1 was not an abuse of discretion, as the fact that defendant's counsel misadvised him as to the consequences of the guilty plea on defendant's possibility of being deported was not ineffectiveness in violation of U.S. Const. amend. VI and Ohio Const. art. I, § 10 because the duty to notify defendant of the consequences of the plea under RC § 2943.031(A) belonged to the trial court and not to counsel, and defendant did not show that the outcome would have been different if he had not entered the plea. The trial court properly advised defendant on two occasions as to the deportation possibility under § 2943.031(A) after counsel's erroneous advice, and defendant indicated that he understood. State v. Sok, — Ohio App. 3d —, 2007 Ohio 729, — N.E. 2d —, 2007 Ohio App. LEXIS 665 (Feb. 23, 2007).

Defendant's presentence motion under Ohio R. Crim. P. 32.1 to withdraw his Alford plea was properly denied. While defendant asserted that his plea was entered under the misapprehension that he was a United States citizen, the trial court had cautioned defendant of the fact that, if he were not citizen, he could be deported as a result of his plea, and a suggestion that defendant was unaware that immigration sanctions were a consequence of a guilty plea was belied by defendant's own affirmation in the executed guilty plea form and by the record of proceedings at the guilty plea hearing. State v. Vazquez, — Ohio App. 3d —, 2006 Ohio 4074, — N.E.2d —, 2006 Ohio App. LEXIS 4017 (Aug. 8, 2006).

Discovery violation

When defendant said documents showing he had made payments to his victim before trial impacted his decision to plead guilty, and the State's failure to provide them to him was a discovery violation which caused his plea not to be knowing, intelligent or voluntary, he did not establish a legitimate basis for withdrawing his plea, nor did he show prejudice, so his pre-sentence motion to withdraw his plea was properly denied. State v. Carswell, — Ohio App. 3d —, 2006 Ohio 5210, — N.E. 2d —, 2006 Ohio App. LEXIS 5177 (Oct. 4, 2006).

Duty of the court

When defendant pled guilty to attempted murder with specifications, aggravated robbery, and kidnapping, the fact that the trial court did not advise him about post-release control did not compel that the plea be vacated, under Ohio R. Crim. P. 11(C), because the trial court substantially complied with the requirements of Rule 11(C), as it directly addressed defendant, went to great lengths to ensure his plea was voluntary, that he was informed of the maximum penalty, that he was advised of and understood the effect of his plea, and that he knew of his right to a jury trial, and it was clear defendant subjectively understood his plea's implications and the rights he waived. State v. Sarkozy, — Ohio App. 3d —, 2006 Ohio 3977, — N.E. 2d —, 2006 Ohio App. LEXIS 3956 (Aug. 3, 2006).

Erroneous advice about sentence

Defendant did not adequately support his claim that he pled guilty because his trial counsel advised him that he would receive a lighter sentence than the one he received because his statements to this effect were insufficient, absent concrete evidence that he was improperly induced to plead guilty. State v. Sarkozy, — Ohio App. 3d —, 2006 Ohio 3977, — N.E. 2d —, 2006 Ohio App. LEXIS 3956 (Aug. 3, 2006).

Failure to advise alien defendant

As defendant's entry of a no contest plea resulted in his participation in a domestic violence diversion program and the subsequent dismissal of the criminal charge against him, the trial court thereafter properly exercised its discretion in denying defendant's motion under RC § 2943.031(D) and Ohio R. Crim. P. 32.1 to withdraw the plea and to vacate the dismissal of the charge, as the dismissal of the charge rendered the plea null and void and there was no longer a case in existence. Defendant had properly made a showing that he was not a United States citizen, that deportation proceedings had been commenced against him, and that he suffered a prejudicial effect from the trial court's failure to have properly advised him under RC § 2943.031(A). City of Willoughby Hills v. Qasim, — Ohio App. 3d —, 2007 Ohio 2860, — N.E. 2d —, 2007 Ohio App. LEXIS 2618 (June 8, 2007).

Guilty plea

Denial of defendant's motion to withdraw the guilty plea was not error because defendant's self-serving declarations that he entered his guilty plea unintelligently because he was under the impression that his jury would be made up of six persons, instead of eight, was insufficient to demonstrate that his plea was entered in violation of Ohio R. Crim. P. 11. He signed a jury waiver that stated three times that a jury would be comprised of eight persons. State v. Kerns, — Ohio App. 3d —, 2006 Ohio 6435, — N.E. 2d —, 2006 Ohio App. LEXIS 6360 (Dec. 7, 2006).

Guilty plea coerced by counsel

Defendant did not show he was entitled to withdraw his guilty plea, based on his claim that counsel coerced him to plead guilty, because the record demonstrated that defendant told the trial court he had discussed his case with counsel, had enough time to discuss the case, and that no one coerced him to plead guilty, so he did not show he suffered a manifest injustice allowing him to withdraw his plea, nor was the trial court required to hold a hearing on the motion, as defendant's allegations were unsupported. State v. Atkinson, — Ohio App. 3d —, 2006 Ohio 4656, — N.E. 2d —, 2006 Ohio App. LEXIS 4591 (Sept. 11, 2006).

Harsher sentence than expected

Defendant's Ohio R. Crim. P. 32.1 motion to withdraw his guilty pleas was properly overruled. While defendant claimed that he agreed to plead guilty because he understood that he would receive a ten-month sentence, the record showed that the common pleas court clearly informed defendant at the plea hearing that it did not have to impose the recommended ten-month sentence. State v. Summers, — Ohio App. 3d —, 2007 Ohio 3168, — N.E. 2d —, 2007 Ohio App. LEXIS 2895 (June 22, 2007).

Defendant was not entitled to withdraw his no contest plea under Ohio R. Crim. P. 32.1 to possession of drugs because while defendant claimed that he believed that the charge was a misdemeanor and thus he would only be sentenced to time served, the trial court and the State referred to the charge as a felony in the fifth degree during the plea colloquy and defendant acknowledged that he understood that the charge was a felony with a penalty of six months to twelve months in prison. State v. Williamson, — Ohio App. 3d —, 2007 Ohio 6812, — N.E. 2d —, 2007 Ohio App. LEXIS 5979 (Dec. 20, 2007).

Trial court did not abuse its discretion when it denied defendant's oral motion to withdraw his guilty plea to domestic violence because defendant's wish to withdraw his guilty plea could only be characterized as a change of heart, and defendant failed to demonstrate a reasonable basis for requesting to withdraw his plea. When asked why he entered a plea of guilty, defendant indicated that he believed he might receive a sentence of time served and probation. State v. Dafforn, — Ohio App. 3d —, 2006 Ohio 7035, — N.E. 2d —, 2006 Ohio App. LEXIS 7030 (Dec. 28, 2006).

Health of defendant at time of plea

Trial court properly denied defendant's motion to withdraw his guilty plea under circumstances in which, although defendant claimed that his diabetes interfered with his ability to understand the plea, the trial court's questions at the plea hearing and defendant's responses showed that defendant knowingly, voluntarily, and intelligently waived his rights. Defendant told the trial court that he was voluntarily pleading guilty, and that he understood the maximum authorized prison terms for the offense, and further, defendant signed a guilty plea form wherein he indicated that he understood the maximum terms for the offense and affirmed that he was voluntarily pleading guilty. There was no indication that defendant did not understand or was not aware of his actions, that his medication or his diabetes were enough to render his plea invalid, or that he was either physically or mentally impaired during the plea hearing. State v. Anderson, — Ohio App. 3d —, 2006 Ohio 5440, — N.E. 2d —, 2006 Ohio App. LEXIS 5422 (Oct. 19, 2006).

Hearing

Since it was clear from the record that a denial of defendant's motion to withdraw his no contest plea was warranted, the common pleas court did not err in failing to hold a hearing on defendant's motion. State v. Booker, — Ohio App. 3d —, 2007 Ohio 430, — N.E. 2d —, 2007 Ohio App. LEXIS 378 (Feb. 2, 2007).

Trial court erred in failing to provide defendant a hearing on his Ohio R. Crim. P. 32.1 motion to withdraw his guilty plea because its failure to provide a hearing made it impossible to review the denial of the motion. There was no transcript of the sentencing proceedings, and the trial court's sentencing entry indicated neither that it had complied with Ohio R. Crim. P. 11 in obtaining defendant's plea nor that it was satisfied that defendant's plea was knowingly, intelligently, and voluntarily entered into with full knowledge of its consequences. State v. Veneroni, — Ohio App. 3d —, 2007 Ohio 444, — N.E. 2d —, 2007 Ohio App. LEXIS 383 (Feb. 2, 2007).

Trial court abused its discretion in overruling defendant's motion to withdraw his guilty plea without first conducting a hearing because defendant was entitled to a hearing to establish the truth of the ineffective assistance of counsel allegations asserted in his motion to withdraw. If defendant was denied an opportunity to present a self-defense claim at trial because of his trial counsel's erroneous advice that defendant was not entitled to assert that defense, the trial court would be obligated to permit withdrawal of defendant's guilty plea because counsel's deficient performance created a manifest injustice by impairing the knowing, intelligent, and voluntary character of defendant's plea. State v. Turner, 171 Ohio App. 3d 82, 2007 Ohio 1346, 869 N.E.2d 708, 2007 Ohio App. LEXIS 1240 (2007).

Defendant's Ohio R. Crim. P. 32.1 motion to withdraw his guilty pleas was properly overruled. Contrary to defendant's contention, the trial court gave defendant a full and fair hearing on his motion, and the trial court's failure to give a particularized explanation as to why it denied defendant's motion did not render the hearing unfair as the trial court was not required to give an explanation. State v. Summers, — Ohio App. 3d —, 2007 Ohio 3168, — N.E. 2d —, 2007 Ohio App. LEXIS 2895 (June 22, 2007).

Trial court was not required to hold a hearing on defendant's post-sentence motion to withdraw his guilty plea because, even if the court accepted the facts alleged by defendant as true, the trial court would not have been required to withdraw the guilty plea. State v. Bell, — Ohio App. 3d —, 2007 Ohio 3276, — N.E. 2d —, 2007 Ohio App. LEXIS 3031 (June 28, 2007).

Trial court's failure to hold an evidentiary hearing on defendant's motion to withdraw his guilty plea pursuant to Ohio R. Crim. P. 32.1 was not an abuse of discretion, as all of his claims were barred by res judicata, and even if such doctrine had been found inapplicable, the claims would have still failed on the merits where they did not rise to the level of manifest injustice. State v. Thomson, — Ohio App. 3d —, 2006 Ohio 1224, — N.E. 2d —, 2006 Ohio App. LEXIS 1104 (Mar. 17, 2006).

Defendant was not entitled to a hearing on his post-sentence motion to withdraw his guilty plea, filed 17 months after he pled guilty, because he showed no substantive grounds for relief, and many of his claims were barred by res judicata. State v. McGuire, — Ohio App. 3d —, 2006 Ohio 1330, — N.E. 2d —, 2006 Ohio App. LEXIS 1227 (Mar. 23, 2006).

Defendant's claim of ineffective assistance of counsel, in conjunction with his failure to file a transcript of his guilty plea hearing, did not mandate a hearing on his post-sentence motion to withdraw his guilty plea. Because a transcript of the guilty plea hearing was not available, it could not be determined whether defendant fully understood the sentencing consequences of his guilty plea, or what effect the alleged misinformation would have had on his guilty plea. State v. Mack, — Ohio App. 3d —, 2006 Ohio 1694, — N.E. 2d —, 2006 Ohio App. LEXIS 1550 (Mar. 31, 2006).

Trial court did not err in denying defendant's presentence motion under Ohio R. Crim. P. 32.1 to withdraw his guilty plea. Contrary to defendant's contention, he was afforded a hearing on his oral motion, in that the trial court allowed defendant to explain his reasons for wishing to withdraw his plea, and there was no indication that the trial court did not fully consider defendant's motion. State v. Heidelburg, — Ohio App. 3d —, 2006 Ohio 1979, — N.E. 2d —, 2006 Ohio App. LEXIS 1825 (Apr. 21, 2006).

Trial court did not abuse its discretion in failing to hold a hearing on an inmate's motion to withdraw his guilty plea, as he sought modification of his sentences, which was relief that was not afforded under Ohio R. Crim. P. 32.1. State v. Peoples, — Ohio App. 3d —, 2006 Ohio 2614, — N.E. 2d —, 2006 Ohio App. LEXIS 2439 (May 26, 2006).

Trial court erred in failing to hold an evidentiary hearing on defendant's motion to withdraw his guilty plea pursuant to

Ohio R. Crim. P. 32.1 based on alleged ineffective assistance of counsel in violation of U.S. Const. amend. VI and Ohio Const. art. I, § 10 where defendant asserted that his counsel failed to obtain the lab reports which indicated that less than five grams of crack cocaine was recovered, and that if he had known of that information prior to entering his guilty plea, he would not have entered it to charges of trafficking in crack cocaine in an amount exceeding five grams but les than 10 grams. Based on defendant's allegations, his plea could have been found to have been entered without knowledge and not voluntarily, and accordingly, a hearing was required. State v. Kidd, 168 Ohio App. 3d 382, 2006 Ohio 4008, 860 N.E.2d 138, 2006 Ohio App. LEXIS 3936 (2006).

When defendant orally moved at sentencing to withdraw his guilty plea, it could not be said that the trial court denied him a hearing on his motion as the trial court gave him an opportunity to make the motion and to explain his reasons for believing that he should be allowed to withdraw his plea, and he did not seek a continuance or other accomodation for preparation. State v. Eversole, — Ohio App. 3d —, 2006 Ohio 3988, — N.E. 2d —, 2006 Ohio App. LEXIS 3958 (Aug. 4, 2006).

Trial court did not err in failing to conduct a hearing on defendant's pro se motion to withdraw his guilty plea because defendant's motion was an attempt to operate as co-counsel on his own case and, thus, engage in a prohibited "hybrid-representation." The motion was not properly before the trial court, and the trial court was not required to hold a hearing on the matter. Even so, the trial court did not err in overruling the motion to withdraw because defendant was represented by highly competent counsel, he was afforded a full Ohio R. Crim. P. 11 hearing, he was given an opportunity to be heard and inform the trial court of the basis for his Ohio R. Crim. P. 32.1 motion, and the record showed that the trial court gave the necessary consideration to his motion. State v. Greenleaf, — Ohio App. 3d —, 2006 Ohio 4317, — N.E. 2d —, 2006 Ohio App. LEXIS 4241 (Aug. 18, 2006).

Evidentiary hearing was not required on every post-sentence motion to withdraw a plea, as the movant had to establish a reasonable likelihood that withdrawal of his plea was necessary to correct a manifest injustice before a trial court had to hold a hearing on his motion. State v. Youngblood, — Ohio App. 3d —, 2006 Ohio 4390, — N.E. 2d —, 2006 Ohio App. LEXIS 4316 (Aug. 25, 2006).

Evidentiary hearing on a post-sentence motion to withdraw a guilty plea was not required if the record indicated that the movant was not entitled to relief and the movant had failed to submit evidentiary documents sufficient to demonstrate a manifest injustice. State v. Atkinson, — Ohio App. 3d —, 2006 Ohio 4656, — N.E. 2d —, 2006 Ohio App. LEXIS 4591 (Sept. 11, 2006).

Trial court erred in denying defendant's pre-sentence motion, pursuant to Ohio R. Crim. P. 32.1, to withdraw his guilty plea because the trial court denied the motion prior to asking defendant if he wished to say or explain the reasons for the motion. State v. Clarke, — Ohio App. 3d —, 2006 Ohio 4993, — N.E. 2d —, 2006 Ohio App. LEXIS 4939 (Sept. 27, 2006).

Although a court has the discretion to grant or deny an Ohio R. Crim. P. 32.1 motion, it must afford the defendant the due-process right of a hearing. State v. Spurling, — Ohio App. 3d —, 2006 Ohio 5595, — N.E. 2d —, 2006 Ohio App. LEXIS 5618 (Oct. 27, 2006).

Trial court properly declined to hold an evidentiary hearing on defendant's motion to withdraw his guilty plea because the motion was based on the purely legal question of whether it was error to impose a non-minimum sentence in light of Foster, so it raised no factual issue requiring an evidentiary hearing. State v. Grier, — Ohio App. 3d —, 2007 Ohio 2597, — N.E. 2d —, 2007 Ohio App. LEXIS 2419 (May 25, 2007).

Immigration status

Where defendant's counsel represented to the trial court that he had advised defendant, who was an immigrant, that his guilty plea could result in consequences including deportation, but it was unclear that counsel advised defendant on the issues of exclusion from admission into the United States and denial of naturalization, and further, the trial court had failed to give a verbatim advisement under RC § 2943.031(A), there was no "substantial compliance" similar to that allowed under Ohio R. Crim. P. 11(C)(2)(a), such that the trial court abused its discretion in denying defendant's motion under Ohio R. Crim. P. 32.1 for withdrawal of the plea without holding a hearing thereon for purposes of RC § 2943.031(D). State v. Ouch, — Ohio App. 3d —, 2006 Ohio 6949, — N.E. 2d —, 2006 Ohio App. LEXIS 6873 (Dec. 28, 2006).

Ineffective assistance

Although the trial court erred in applying the doctrine of res judicata as a basis for denying defendant's Ohio R. Crim. P. 32.1 motion, the error was harmless because defendant failed to show that he suffered any prejudice due to his counsel's failure to file a motion to suppress. The transcript failed to show that defendant invoked his right to counsel or that he made statements that affected his plea in any way. State v. Cochran, — Ohio App. 3d —, 2007 Ohio 4545, — N.E. 2d —, 2007 Ohio App. LEXIS 4090 (Aug. 31, 2007).

Because defendant was not prejudiced by defense counsel's representation, defendant failed to meet the burden of proving a manifest injustice resulting from the trial court's denial of his post-sentence motion to withdraw his guilty plea, under Ohio R. Crim. P. 32.1. Defense counsel testified at the withdrawal hearing that the recommendation made by Adult Court Services was not a plea agreement; that the notation regarding a 10-year sentence was a suggestion to the trial court and not a recommendation; and that the judge never promised that defendant would receive a certain sentence. State v. Millette, — Ohio App. 3d —, 2006 Ohio 2099, — N.E. 2d —, 2006 Ohio App. LEXIS 1923 (Apr. 27, 2006).

Ineffective assistance of counsel

Defendant's Ohio R. Crim. P. 32.1 motion to withdraw his guilty plea was properly denied without a hearing. Since, under RC § 2923.03(F), a defendant can be convicted of complicity to commit burglary even where the indictment charged him with only the principal offense, defense counsel's advice to this effect was proper and did not constitute ineffective assistance of counsel, rendering defendants plea unknowing and involuntary. State v. Allison, — Ohio App. 3d —, 2007 Ohio 789, — N.E. 2d —, 2007 Ohio App. LEXIS 706 (Feb. 22, 2007).

While matters outside the record that allegedly corrupted a defendant's choice to enter a guilty plea so as to render that plea less than knowing and voluntary, such as ineffective assistance of counsel, are proper grounds for post-conviction relief pursuant to RC § 2953.21 and removes a claim from the type of extraordinary circumstances that demonstrate the manifest injustice required for Ohio R. Crim. P. 32.1 relief, the court concluded that it would not be appropriate to follow this rule to preclude defendant's attempt to obtain relief under Ohio R. Crim. P. 32.1 since defendant had submitted a letter that his trial counsel had sent to him which may have misled defendant and dissuaded him from timely seeking RC § 2953.21 or Ohio R. Crim. P. 32.1 relief. State v. Turner, 171 Ohio App. 3d 82, 2007 Ohio 1346, 869 N.E.2d 708, 2007 Ohio App. LEXIS 1240 (2007).

Ineffective assistance of counsel is a proper basis for seeking postsentence withdrawal of a guilty plea. Defendant was entitled to a hearing on his claim that counsel erroneously advised him that he could not claim self-defense because he was engaged in criminal activity, attempting to buy drugs, at the time: State v. Turner, 171 Ohio App. 3d 82, 2007 Ohio 1346, 869 N.E.2d 708, 2007 Ohio App. LEXIS 1240 (2007).

Trial court did not err when it denied defendant's motion to withdraw his plea because defendant failed to show that a manifest injustice occurred. Because counsel's assessment that defendant should take the good plea deal rather than risking everything on a "toss-up" motion to suppress (based on mistaken identity) was reasonable, his performance did not fall below an objective standard of reasonable representation. Ohio v. Brown, — Ohio App. 3d —, 2007 Ohio 5002, — N.E. 2d —, 2007 Ohio App. LEXIS 4462 (Sept. 21, 2007).

Defendant's claim that he was deprived of the effective assistance of counsel by his trial counsel's refusal to allow him to withdraw his guilty plea at a sentencing hearing failed because he could not show that the trial court would have allowed him to withdraw his plea prior to sentencing based on his belief that the trial court guaranteed him a 10-day sentence. Defendant could not show that counsel's deficiency prejudiced his defense. Defendant also could not demonstrate that he was prejudiced by the failure of his counsel to seek withdrawal of his guilty plea based on the contention that his ex-wife's involvement in the presentence investigation process affected the trial court's sentencing decision since the record supported the trial court's finding that any information provided by the ex-wife did not impact the contents of the report and, therefore, did not influence the trial court's decision to impose a more severe sentence than was initially discussed. State v. Glass, — Ohio App. 3d —, 2006 Ohio 229, — N.E. 2d —, 2006 Ohio App. LEXIS 184 (Jan. 24, 2006).

Trial court erred in failing to hold an evidentiary hearing on appellant's motion to withdraw his guilty pleas where he alleged ineffective assistance of counsel in that counsel failed to inform him that lab tests revealed a lesser amount of cocaine than indicated in the guilty pleas. State v. Kidd, 168 Ohio App. 3d 382, 2006 Ohio 4008, 860 N.E.2d 138, 2006 Ohio App. LEXIS 3936 (2006).

Defendant's post-sentence motion to withdraw his guilty plea pursuant to Ohio R. Crim. P. 32.1 was properly denied where defendant's claim that his counsel provided ineffective assistance during the plea hearing because defendant was unaware of the evidence against him was contradicted by defendant's statements at the sentencing hearing; further, his claim that he received ineffective assistance of counsel in violation of his rights under U.S. Const. amend. VI and Ohio Const. art. I, § 10 was barred by res judicata where defendant had previously raised in his post-conviction relief petition. State v. Kimbrough, — Ohio App. 3d —, 2006 Ohio 4907, — N.E. 2d —, 2006 Ohio App. LEXIS 4831 (Sept. 22, 2006).

Denial of defendant's motion to withdraw his guilty plea was not error because defendant failed to establish that he received ineffective assistance of counsel with respect to his guilty plea since his contentions that his counsel was ill prepared and failed to inform him of the correct number of jurors was uncorroborated. Defendant presented no evidence that he ever attempted to contact his attorney during his period of incarceration, or that he informed her of any potential witnesses to be subpoenaed, and defendant signed a jury waiver that stated three times that a jury would be comprised of eight persons. State v. Kerns, — Ohio App. 3d —, 2006 Ohio 6435, — N.E. 2d —, 2006 Ohio App. LEXIS 6360 (Dec. 7, 2006).

Defendant's motion to withdraw his guilty plea to one count of rape in violation of RC § 2907.02(A)(2) and gross sexual imposition on the ground of ineffective assistance of counsel was properly denied because defendant had previously received a definitive DNA test and defendant received a penalty of only nine years when he faced a possible life sentence on the original charges, which included three counts of rape. State v. Gibson, — Ohio App. 3d —, 2006 Ohio 6820, — N.E. 2d —, 2006 Ohio App. LEXIS 6743 (Dec. 22, 2006).

—Guilty plea

Defendant failed to show that his counsel provided ineffective assistance in violation of U.S. Const. amend. VI and Ohio Const. art. I, § 10 where counsel did not advise defendant to withdraw his guilty plea pursuant to Ohio R. Crim. P. 32.1 after he had committed further criminal acts while out on bond, such that the trial court was not going to impose the agreed upon sentences pursuant to the plea agreement, as the trial court had fully complied with Ohio R. Crim. P. 11 in accepting defendant's guilty plea, there was no showing of a probability of success on the withdrawal motion, and even if withdrawal was allowed, the overwhelming evidence against defendant would have resulted in his conviction. State v. Gordon, — Ohio App. 3d —, 2007 Ohio 1177, — N.E. 2d —, 2007 Ohio App. LEXIS 1089 (Mar. 16, 2007).

Trial court's refusal to hold a hearing on defendant's post-sentence motion under Ohio R. Crim. P. 32.1 to withdraw his guilty pleas was not an abuse of discretion in the circumstances, as defendant did not show a "manifest injustice" where his claim that his counsel provided ineffective assistance in violation of U.S. Const. amend. VI and Ohio Const. art. I, § 10 lacked merit; counsel had advised defendant to accept one of two plea agreements offered by the State based on counsel's professional opinion as to the potential sentence that would be imposed, which advice might have been erroneous in hindsight, but there were no misrepresentations and defendant freely accepted the advice. State v. Williams, — Ohio App. 3d —, 2007 Ohio 5073, — N.E. 2d —, 2007 Ohio App. LEXIS 4475 (Sept. 27, 2007).

Trial court properly denied defendant's post-sentence motion to withdraw his guilty plea to a drug abuse charge. Defense counsel's failure to mention in a motion to suppress evidence that the drugs seized from defendant's car were found in a search conducted two days after a consent search in which a K-9 unit alerted to drugs in the car, did not constitute ineffective assistance of counsel because there was but one legal search, albeit one that was conducted at two separate times. State v. Ali, — Ohio App. 3d —, 2007 Ohio 6845, — N.E. 2d —, 2007 Ohio App. LEXIS 5986 (Dec. 20, 2007).

Trial court properly denied defendant's post-sentence motion to withdraw his guilty plea to a drug abuse charge. Defense counsel's misstatement in a motion to suppress evidence that defendant had been "chased" by the police prior to a search when in fact defendant had not been chased, did not constitute ineffective assistance as it could not be said that removal of the word "chased" from the motion would have resulted in defendant deciding not to plead guilty to the charge. State v. Ali, — Ohio App. 3d —, 2007 Ohio 6845, — N.E. 2d —, 2007 Ohio App. LEXIS 5986 (Dec. 20, 2007).

—Insufficient evidence

Defendant's motion to withdraw his plea was properly denied because defendant's assertion that his counsel's alleged deficient performance resulted in him making an involuntary guilty plea was not supported by the record. It was apparent that defendant was primarily motivated by a desire to get out of jail as quickly as possible and that he was willing to plead guilty to effectuate that end; there was nothing in the record to suggest that the representation offered by defense counsel was deficient in such a way that would have required vacation of defendant's knowing and voluntary guilty plea. State v. Walker, — Ohio App. 3d —, 2007 Ohio 4195, — N.E. 2d —, 2007 Ohio App. LEXIS 3797 (Aug. 17, 2007).

—Sentencing

Trial counsel did not err by failing to file a post-sentence motion to withdraw defendant's guilty plea because defendant did not demonstrate that a manifest injustice had occurred and therefore failed to establish grounds for relief under Ohio R. Crim. P. 32.1. Moreover, defendant did not presented any evidence to support his allegations that trial counsel was ineffective. State v. Looney, — Ohio App. 3d —, 2007 Ohio 1848, — N.E. 2d —, 2007 Ohio App. LEXIS 1689 (Apr. 19, 2007).

Ineffective assistsance

Where defendant used his key to enter his employer's premises after hours and he also entered into other employees' offices, he exceeded his right of entry, and his counsel's advice for him to plead guilty to the charge of breaking and entering in violation of RC § 2911.13 was not contrary to law and was not ineffective assistance in violation of U.S. Const. amend. VI and Ohio Const. art. I, § 10. As defendant failed to show ineffective assistance and it was clear that his post-sentence motion pursuant to Ohio R. Crim. P. 32.1 to withdraw his plea on that ground lacked merit, the trial court's denial of the motion without holding an evidentiary hearing was not an abuse of discretion. State v. Welty, — Ohio App. 3d —, 2006 Ohio 5257, — N.E. 2d —, 2006 Ohio App. LEXIS 5215 (Oct. 5, 2006).

Jurisdiction of trial court

Ohio R. Crim. P. 32.1 does not vest jurisdiction in a trial court to maintain and determine a motion to withdraw a guilty plea subsequent to an appeal and an affirmance by an appellate court, because, while Rule 32.1 apparently enlarges the power of the trial court over its judgments without respect to the running of the court term, it does not confer upon the trial court the power to vacate a judgment which has been affirmed by the appellate court, for this action would affect the decision of the reviewing court, which is not within the power of the trial court to do. State v. Sanchez, — Ohio App. 3d —, 2007 Ohio 218, — N.E. 2d —, 2007 Ohio App. LEXIS 210 (Jan. 22, 2007).

Because defendant's convictions had been affirmed on appeal, including the trial court's denial of his motion to withdraw his plea, the trial court had no jurisdiction to permit defendant to withdraw his plea thereafter. The original judgment of conviction and sentencing order was valid and final, and was affirmed on appeal, as was the trial court's order overruling defendant's motion to withdraw his plea and thus, the trial court lacked jurisdiction to vacate, amend, or modify the 1995 judgment. State v. Vild, — Ohio App. 3d —, 2007 Ohio 987, — N.E. 2d —, 2007 Ohio App. LEXIS 918 (Mar. 8, 2007).

Trial court did not have jurisdiction to entertain defendant's motion to withdraw his plea because the convictions had already been affirmed on appeal. State v. Shie, — Ohio App. 3d —, 2007 Ohio 3773, — N.E. 2d —, 2007 Ohio App. LEXIS 3431 (July 26, 2007).

Ohio R. Crim. P. 32.1 does not vest jurisdiction in a trial court to maintain and determine a motion to withdraw a guilty plea subsequent to an appeal and an affirmance by an appellate court because, while Rule 32.1 apparently enlarges the power of the trial court over its judgments without respect to the running of the court term, it does not confer upon the trial court the power to vacate a judgment which has been affirmed by the appellate court, for this action would affect the decision of the reviewing court, which is not within the power of the trial court to do, so after the direct appeal of a judgment is decided, the trial court has no jurisdiction to consider a defendant's Rule 32.1 motion to withdraw his guilty plea, and the appropriate action for the trial court is to dismiss the motion. State v. Herbert, — Ohio App. 3d —, 2007 Ohio 4496, — N.E. 2d —, 2007 Ohio App. LEXIS 4069 (Sept. 4, 2007).

Where defendant's convictions were affirmed on direct appeal, but the sentences imposed by the trial court were vacated and the matter was remanded for resentencing pursuant to Foster, the trial court erred in considering defendant's motion to withdraw the guilty pleas pursuant to Ohio R. Crim. P. 32.1; the trial court lacked jurisdiction on remand for the purpose of resentencing to revisit the issue of

the plea. State v. Moviel, — Ohio App. 3d —, 2007 Ohio 5947, — N.E. 2d —, 2007 Ohio App. LEXIS 5283 (Nov. 8, 2007).

By filing a notice of appeal while his motion to withdraw his plea was pending in the trial court, defendant divested that court of jurisdiction to consider his motion. Thus, there was no appellate jurisdiction to consider the trial court's judgment denying the motion. State v. Dudas, — Ohio App. 3d —, 2007 Ohio 6739, — N.E. 2d —, 2007 Ohio App. LEXIS 5896 (Dec. 14, 2007).

Where defendant's sentence had been reversed on appeal two times and remanded for resentencing, the trial court had no jurisdiction to thereafter entertain defendant's motion to withdraw his guilty plea prior to resentencing, as the court had affirmed his convictions and hence, his guilty plea. As the issue of juidicial release was part of the plea hearing initially, it could have been raised on direct appeal and the matter was barred by res judicata. State v. Craddock, — Ohio App. 3d —, 2006 Ohio 5915, — N.E. 2d —, 2006 Ohio App. LEXIS 5874 (Nov. 9, 2006).

Knowing and intelligent

Trial court did not abuse its discretion in denying defendant's Ohio R. Crim. P. 32.1 motion to withdraw his guilty pleas because the trial court substantially complied with the mandates in Ohio R. Crim. P. 11 and defendant entered a counseled plea with knowledge of the mandatory period of postrelease control. The trial court specifically advised defendant at least once during the plea hearing of the mandatory nature and length of his postrelease control and several times that there was postrelease control. State v. Imburgia, — Ohio App. 3d —, 2007 Ohio 390, — N.E. 2d —, 2007 Ohio App. LEXIS 348 (Feb. 1, 2007).

Defendant's Ohio R. Crim. P. 32.1 motion to withdraw his guilty pleas was properly overruled. Defendant's contention that his pleas were not knowing since he was taking methadone when he entered them was belied by defendant's statements during the plea hearing that he had not had any drugs in the past seven days. State v. Summers, — Ohio App. 3d —, 2007 Ohio 3168, — N.E. 2d —, 2007 Ohio App. LEXIS 2895 (June 22, 2007).

Although it was presumed that defense counsel explained the nature of the charges to defendant, a juvenile, prior to his entry of a guilty plea to multiple offenses, the trial court erred with it informed defendant that he was waiving the right to have the State prove each element of each charge against him, as it did not mention that each element had to be proven beyond a reasonable doubt, which standard of proof was a constitutional right; as strict compliance was required for a constitutional right waiver under Ohio R. Crim. P. 11(C)(2)(c), which was not satisfied, defendant's plea was not deemed knowingly and intelligently entered and his motion to withdraw the plea under Ohio R. Crim. P. 32.1 should have been granted. State v. Roman, — Ohio App. 3d —, 2007 Ohio 5243, — N.E. 2d —, 2007 Ohio App. LEXIS 4641 (Sept. 26, 2007).

Denial of the motion to withdraw his plea was proper because defendant's guilty plea was knowingly, intelligently, and voluntarily made. The trial court did not commit plain error by failing to provide an adequate explanation of postrelease control because defendant was never sentenced to postrelease control; rather, he was sentenced to one year of community control, which he completed six years earlier. State v. Ellington, — Ohio App. 3d —, 2007 Ohio 5959, — N.E. 2d —, 2007 Ohio App. LEXIS 5218 (Nov. 8, 2007).

Trial court did not abuse its discretion by denying defendant's Ohio R. Crim. P. 32.1 motion to withdraw his guilty plea because the transcript from the Ohio R. Crim. P. 11 colloquy showed that he knew what he was doing when he entered his guilty plea and that the plea was voluntary, since he indicated that he agreed with the plea on two separate occasions. In addition, the fact that he waited nearly a full year to file his motion to withdraw his guilty plea deflated his argument that his guilty plea was not knowingly, intelligently, and voluntarily entered and he defendant did not meet his burden of demonstrating that a manifest injustice occurred. State v. Perri, — Ohio App. 3d —, 2006 Ohio 5185, — N.E. 2d —, 2006 Ohio App. LEXIS 5127 (Sept. 29, 2006).

Defendant did not show the trial court's failure to advise him that he was not eligible for probation rendered his guilty plea involuntary or unintelligent because it was clear that the mandatory nature of defendant's sentence was conveyed to him, and he acknowledged on the record that he would receive a prison sentence. State v. Atkinson, — Ohio App. 3d —, 2006 Ohio 5806, — N.E. 2d —, 2006 Ohio App. LEXIS 5783 (Nov. 6, 2006).

Defendant's self-serving claims in his post-sentence motion to withdraw his guilty plea that his trial counsel's ineffective assistance kept his plea from being knowing and voluntary did not rebut the record which showed he said he had sufficient time to discuss his case with counsel and that he raised no concerns about counsel's representation at either his change of plea hearing or at his sentencing, so he showed no manifest injustice and was not entitled to an evidentiary hearing on his motion. State v. Atkinson, — Ohio App. 3d —, 2006 Ohio 5806, — N.E. 2d —, 2006 Ohio App. LEXIS 5783 (Nov. 6, 2006).

Mandamus

Inmate's action for a writ of mandamus to compel a criminal court judge in the inmate's underlying criminal matter to adhere to a plea agreement regarding a period of post-release control lacked merit, as the inmate failed to meet his burden of showing that he was entitled to relief in mandamus pursuant to RC § 2731.04. The inmate had an adequate remedy at law through appeal or a motion to withdraw his guilty plea pursuant to Ohio R. Crim. P. 32.1. Mauer v. Cuyahoga Co. Court of Common Pleas, — Ohio App. 3d —, 2007 Ohio 3641, — N.E. 2d —, 2007 Ohio App. LEXIS 3348 (July 18, 2007).

Manifest injustice

Since the sentence, consisting of consecutive prison terms, imposed on defendant was one that defendant could have received either before or after State v. Foster, defendant could not demonstrate manifest injustice allowing him to withdraw his guilty plea under Ohio R. Crim. P. 32.1. State v. Brito, — Ohio App. 3d —, 2007 Ohio 1311, — N.E. 2d —, 2007 Ohio App. LEXIS 1204 (Mar. 22, 2007).

Defendant's assertion that changes to the guidelines for granting parole, made after defendant entered a guilty plea to two rape charges, violated the ex post facto clause of U.S. Const. art. I, § 10, and that Ohio had provided no meaningful review for adverse parole determinations of the Ohio Adult Parole Authority, did not constitute the manifest injustice necessary to support a withdrawal of the guilty plea; even if defendant's claims were valid, they did not implicate the validity of defendant's guilty plea. State v. Ferguson, — Ohio App. 3d —, 2007 Ohio 2352, — N.E. 2d —, 2007 Ohio App. LEXIS 2189 (May 11, 2007).

Inmate failed to demonstrate the manifest injustice required by Ohio R. Crim. P. 32.1 for the withdrawal of his 1997 guilty pleas to two counts of attempted murder; the inmate shot people he knew and if tried, a sentence of 23 years or even 26 years was possible as opposed to the 18 year sentence that was imposed as a result of the guilty pleas. State v. Williams, — Ohio App. 3d —, 2007 Ohio 4411, — N.E. 2d —, 2007 Ohio App. LEXIS 3973 (Aug. 28, 2007).

Defendant failed to present evidence that his counsel rendered ineffective assistance or that he was convicted of offenses far more severe than he actually committed and, although the trial court made findings under RC § 2929.14(B) and (C) (found later to be unconstitutional), defendant received the sentence that he and the State had presented to the trial court as a negotiated agreed sentence, years before Blakely and Foster were decided. Accordingly, defendant did not suffer a manifest injustice in his sentencing; there was also no reason why defendant could not have raised his counsel's alleged ineffectiveness in a timely petition for postconviction relief. State v. Cochran, — Ohio App. 3d —, 2007 Ohio 4545, — N.E. 2d —, 2007 Ohio App. LEXIS 4090 (Aug. 31, 2007).

Defendant did not show the manifest injustice necessary to withdraw, pursuant to Ohio R. Crim. P. 32.1, his guilty plea to rape because any modification to the opinion of the State's expert witness, who had previously suggested that the victim had been vaginally penetrated, was irrelevant as defendant had pleaded guilty to alleged anal rape. Ohio v. Shupp, — Ohio App. 3d —, 2007 Ohio 4896, — N.E. 2d —, 2007 Ohio App. LEXIS 4367 (Sept. 21, 2007).

When defendant moved to withdraw his guilty plea over two years after he pled guilty and was sentenced, claiming he received ineffective assistance of counsel, he did not meet his burden of proving he suffered a manifest injustice because he provided no references to the record or evidence showing that counsel's performance was deficient, nor did he show that he was prejudiced by counsel's performance. State v. Mitchell, — Ohio App. 3d —, 2006 Ohio 64, — N.E. 2d —, 2006 Ohio App. LEXIS 49 (Jan. 5, 2006).

As an inmate had prior opportunities to challenge the amendment of the indictment against him, as well as the trial court's determination that he knowingly and voluntarily entered his no contest plea to the charge, his motion to withdraw his plea based on a challenge to the indictment was barred by res judicata where the inmate did not show that application of that doctrine would be unjust; further, even if the doctrine was found inapplicable, there was no manifest injustice which would have warranted granting his post-sentence motion to withdraw his plea, as the inmate had acknowledged that he understood the nature of the charges, that his plea was entered freely and voluntarily, and that he was aware of the charge he was entering the plea to. State v. Smith, — Ohio App. 3d —, 2006 Ohio 1482, — N.E. 2d —, 2006 Ohio App. LEXIS 1352 (Mar. 21, 2006).

Denial of defendant's Ohio R. Crim. P. 32.1 post-sentence motion to withdraw his guilty plea was not error because there was no manifest injustice. The record was silent as to the nature of any supposed conflict between defendant and his attorney; the trial court specifically found that counsel's performance had been satisfactory; when defendant entered his plea, he made no mention that he was dissatisfied with his counsel's representation; defendant was appropriately sentenced to separate prison terms; and defendant did not receive a maximum sentence even though the prosecutor recommended that the trial court impose maximum terms. State v. Woods, — Ohio App. 3d —, 2006 Ohio 2368, — N.E. 2d —, 2006 Ohio App. LEXIS 2262 (May 15, 2006).

Inmate failed to show that the withdrawal of his guilty pleas pursuant to Ohio R. Crim. P. 32.1 was necessary to correct a manifest injustice, as the holding in Foster invalidated portions of RC § 2929.14(B) and (C) with respect to sentencing length, and would have opened the inmate up to longer potential prison terms on the charges under which he pleaded guilty as well as to other charges that were dismissed. His claim that his counsel was ineffective in advising him to accept the aggregate prison term offered lacked merit. State v. Peoples, — Ohio App. 3d —, 2006 Ohio 2614, — N.E. 2d —, 2006 Ohio App. LEXIS 2439 (May 26, 2006).

Trial court did not abuse its discretion when it denied defendant's motion to "correct illegal sentence imposed" because, when construed as an Ohio R. Crim. P. 32.1 motion to withdraw his guilty pleas, the motion did not address a manifest injustice. State v. Hall, — Ohio App. 3d —, 2006 Ohio 2742, — N.E. 2d —, 2006 Ohio App. LEXIS 2575 (June 1, 2006).

Defendant's motion to withdraw her guilty plea pursuant to Ohio R. Crim. P. 32.1 was properly denied, as new case law which she relied on for purposes of showing a manifest injustice did not exist at the time of the dismissal of her direct appeal, which was made before the motion to withdraw was made, and accordingly, defendant was not entitled to the benefit of the new case law. State v. Rhodes, — Ohio App. 3d —, 2006 Ohio 3996, — N.E. 2d —, 2006 Ohio App. LEXIS 3927 (Aug. 4, 2006).

Trial court misinformed defendant that it could include his parole violation into the sentence imposed on defendant's guilty plea and terminate the parole violation matter, which was not possible under RC § 2929.141, as that was only applicable to post-release control violations involving "releasees" under RC § 2967.01(J) rather than "parolees" under § 2967.01(I). As defendant clearly was concerned about the parole violation and would not have pleaded guilty absent the trial court's promise, which it could not keep, a manifest injustice occurred which warranted withdrawal of the plea under Ohio R. Crim. P. 32.1. State v. Ricks, — Ohio App. 3d —, 2006 Ohio 4268, — N.E. 2d —, 2006 Ohio App. LEXIS 4183 (Aug. 17, 2006).

Defendant's post-sentence motion to withdraw his guilty plea to felonious assault did not demonstrate the existence of the required manifest injustice as (1) his plea was knowing, intelligent, and voluntary, (2) there was no showing of a substantial violation of counsel's duties to defendant, (3) defendant's self-serving affidavit did not rebut the record showing that his plea was voluntary, and (4) the affidavit of defendant's victim questioning whether defendant committed the crime was unreliable, in light of defendant's guilty plea. State v. Youngblood, — Ohio App. 3d —, 2006 Ohio 4390, — N.E. 2d —, 2006 Ohio App. LEXIS 4316 (Aug. 25, 2006).

Since defendant had not filed a transcript of the guilty plea hearing, the court on appeal had no way of knowing whether the guilty plea was knowingly and voluntarily entered; thus, the court could not conclude that the trial court should have permitted withdrawal of the guilty plea on the basis of a manifest injustice resulting from the alleged ineffective assistance rendered by defense counsel. Pursuant to Ohio R. App. P. 9(B), it is an appellant's duty to ensure that the portions of the record necessary for appellate review are filed with the appellate court. State v. Smith, — Ohio App. 3d —, 2006 Ohio 5478, — N.E. 2d —, 2006 Ohio App. LEXIS 5484 (Oct. 23, 2006).

Trial court did not abuse its discretion in overruling defendant's post-sentence motion to withdraw his guilty plea pursuant to Ohio R. Crim. P. 32.1, as the plea was deemed to have been entered voluntarily, knowingly, and intelligently, the trial court engaged in a sufficient colloquy with defendant pursuant to Ohio R. Crim. P. 11(C) prior to accepting his plea, there was no undue involvement by the trial court in the plea bargaining, and there was no requirement that the trial court inform defendant about judicial release prior to his entering his plea. There was no showing that had he been so informed, he would not have entered the plea, and there was also no evidence that counsel provided poor and threatening advice as to the plea, or that a manifest injustice had occurred which required withdrawal of the plea. State v. Simmons, — Ohio App. 3d —, 2006 Ohio 5760, — N.E. 2d —, 2006 Ohio App. LEXIS 5746 (Nov. 3, 2006).

Trial court's denial of defendant's motion to withdraw his no contest and guilty pleas pursuant to Ohio R. Crim. P. 32.1 was proper in the circumstances, as the trial court had sufficiently advised defendant pursuant to its duty under Ohio R. Crim. P. 11, defendant's counsel was competent in advising defendant to accept the plea and there was accordingly no violation of defendant's rights under U.S. Const. amend. VI and Ohio Const. art. I, § 10, and defendant's claim at the withdrawal hearing that he was innocent was deemed to lack credibility. Defendant failed to show manifest injustice to support withdrawal, as it was determined that he merely "had a change of heart." State v. Hall, — Ohio App. 3d —, 2006 Ohio 6116, — N.E. 2d —, 2006 Ohio App. LEXIS 6087 (Nov. 17, 2006).

Because defendant pled guilty to each element of the offense of failure to appear, and additionally admitted to knowingly committing the offense, he failed to demonstrate a manifest injustice as required by Ohio R. Crim. P. 32.1 to withdraw his guilty plea. Although the term "recklessness" did not appear in the indictment, defendant entered a plea to a sufficient culpable mental state. State v. Meadows, — Ohio App. 3d —, 2006 Ohio 6183, — N.E. 2d —, 2006 Ohio App. LEXIS 6141 (Nov. 22, 2006).

Defendant failed to establish that withdrawal of the plea, under Crim. R. 32.1, was necessary to correct manifest injustice. Although defendant stated that he had told his attorney that pleading guilty would be a complete and utter lie, his self-serving declarations or affidavits were insufficient to demonstrate manifest injustice. Defendant could have pled guilty even though he was innocent to avoid the risk of trial and that did not invalidate the plea. State v. Kerns, — Ohio App. 3d —, 2006 Ohio 6435, — N.E. 2d —, 2006 Ohio App. LEXIS 6360 (Dec. 7, 2006).

Trial court did not abuse its discretion when it held that defendant failed to establish a "manifest injustice" within the meaning of Ohio R. Crim. P. 32.1 and dismissed defendant's motion to withdraw his guilty plea because the record did not indicate that he was unaware of the charges or the consequences of his plea. The transcript of the change-of-plea hearing indicated that the trial court repeatedly informed defendant of his rights and of the possible penalties associated with the charges at issue and that after engaging in a dialogue with the trial court, defendant chose to waive his rights and plead guilty. State v. Leugers, — Ohio App. 3d —, 2006 Ohio 6928, — N.E. 2d —, 2006 Ohio App. LEXIS 6832 (Dec. 28, 2006).

Medications

Defendant was not entitled to withdraw his guilty plea after he was sentenced and 17 months after he entered his plea because he was taking medication at the time he pled guilty because this, alone, did not show he was incompetent to plead guilty, and, when he was asked if he was under the influence of anything that would affect his thinking, he responded that he was not. State v. McGuire, — Ohio App. 3d —, 2006 Ohio 1330, — N.E. 2d —, 2006 Ohio App. LEXIS 1227 (Mar. 23, 2006).

Mistake as to sentencing options

Trial court abused its discretion by denying a presentence motion to withdraw a guilty plea where, at the time of the plea colloquy, the defendant, defense counsel, the court, and probably the prosecutor thought that a community-based treatment sentencing option was available, but the defendant then discovered that it was not an available option: State v. Murphy, 176 Ohio App. 3d 345, 2008 Ohio 2382, 891 N.E.2d 1255, 2008 Ohio App. LEXIS 2027 (2008).

Mistake concerning sentencing

Plea agreement was subject to rescission where the prosecution, the defendant, and the trial court were all under the mistaken impression that the defendant would be eligible for judicial release after serving four years, rather than the mandated five years: State v. Johnson, 182 Ohio App. 3d 628, 2009 Ohio 1871, 914 N.E.2d 429, 2009 Ohio App. LEXIS 1575 (2009).

Motion after sentencing

Even though defendant invoked Ohio R. Crim. P. 32.1 in support of his oral motion to withdraw his guilty plea, he did not expressly seek to withdraw his plea and go to trial. Rather, he argued that his sentence should be modified; Ohio R. Crim. P. 32.1 did not afford such relief. State v. Ashipa, — Ohio App. 3d —, 2007 Ohio 2245, — N.E. 2d —, 2007 Ohio App. LEXIS 2098 (May 11, 2007).

Defendant's Ohio R. Crim. P. 32.1 motion to vacate her guilty plea was properly overruled without a hearing because the affidavits submitted by defendant, to the effect that her attorney failed to adequately prepare himself for her case, were not supported by the record. Defendant's claim that her attorney failed to interview witnesses was without merit since there was no showing what information would have been gleaned from these witnesses who did not observe the admitted criminal conduct, and her claim that her attorney did not make himself available to discuss the case with defendant was not supported by any showing of prejudice. State v. Hoffman, — Ohio App. 3d —, 2006 Ohio 6119, — N.E. 2d —, 2006 Ohio App. LEXIS 6059 (Nov. 17, 2006).

Motion to withdraw guilty plea

Since the record did not show that defendant ever filed a motion to withdraw his guilty plea under Ohio R. Crim. P. 32.1, defendant was unable to prove the error assigned on appeal to the effect that the trial court erred in denying his motion to withdraw. Instead, the record showed that the trial court invited defendant to file a motion to withdraw but that defendant never did so. State v. Carter, — Ohio App. 3d —, 2007 Ohio 20, — N.E. 2d —, 2007 Ohio App. LEXIS 14 (Jan. 5, 2007).

As defendant's claims in support of his pre-sentence motion to withdraw his guilty plea pursuant to Ohio R. Crim. P. 32.1 were mostly based on his change of heart, such was an insufficient basis to grant the requested relief; further, the State would have been prejudiced due to the reluctance of a witness to testify, the request was untimely, defendant did not establish his innocence or a valid defense to the charges against him, he failed to show that he did not understand the nature of the jointly recommended sentence, and defendant's counsel adequately advised him prior to the plea pursuant to his rights under U.S. Const. amend. VI and Ohio Const. art. I, § 10. State v. Johnston, — Ohio App. 3d —, 2007 Ohio 4620, — N.E. 2d —, 2007 Ohio App. LEXIS 4160 (Aug. 28, 2007).

Defendant's pre-sentence motion to withdraw his guilty plea was properly denied because nothing in the transcript of the hearing at which he pled guilty showed he did not knowingly, intelligently, and voluntarily plead guilty, and the trial court did not abuse its discretion when it was not persuaded by his argument that he pled guilty because he felt pressured and did not want to serve 180 days in jail. State v. Nickel, — Ohio App. 3d —, 2006 Ohio 2202, — N.E. 2d —, 2006 Ohio App. LEXIS 2039 (May 2, 2006).

Denial of defendant's motion to withdraw his guilty plea was improper to the extent that it was based on defendant's failure to file a written motion with the court as a written motion was filed with the court and such motions did not have to be written; however, the denial of the motion was proper as: (1) the trial court gave defendant an ample opportunity to argue why he wanted to withdraw his plea and questioned him about his admissions to the crimes, despite his assertion that he had not committed any crime, (2) it was presumed that the trial court complied with Ohio R. Crim. P. 11(C)(2)(a) as no record of the plea hearing was filed, and (3) defendant was eligible for community control sanctions. State v. Beckwith, — Ohio App. 3d —, 2006 Ohio 1571, — N.E. 2d —, 2006 Ohio App. LEXIS 1471 (Mar. 30, 2006).

Defendant's motion to withdraw his no contest plea, filed after sentencing, was properly denied without a hearing where the motion failed to establish that allowing the plea to stand was a clear or openly unjust result. While defendant alleged that he was fatigued and in pain at the hearing, he did not contend that he was incompetent, the transcript reflected that the trial court notified defendant of the specific offense and potential sentence, and defendant did not specifically assert particular rights that the trial court failed to address and how the trial court erred in this regard, or acknowledge that the trial court was not required to do so. State v. Richardson, —

Ohio App. 3d —, 2006 Ohio 386, — N.E. 2d —, 2006 Ohio App. LEXIS 328 (Jan. 24, 2006).

There was no abuse of discretion in the denial of defendant's Ohio R. Crim. P. 32.1 motion to withdraw his guilty plea to felonious assault because the trial court held a full hearing and afforded defendant an opportunity to be heard on his motion and, the fact that the court said it would consider the motion prior to sentencing reflected the trial court's understanding of the motion's procedural priority and was not a predisposition to deny the motion. The plea hearing adequately established that defendant knowingly, intelligently, and voluntarily entered his plea. State v. Phipps, — Ohio App. 3d —, 2006 Ohio 99, — N.E. 2d —, 2006 Ohio App. LEXIS 71 (Jan. 12, 2006).

Defendant's motion to withdraw his guilty plea was properly denied because defendant did not demonstrate that he suffered prejudice as the result of counsel's failure to advise him with regard to a United States Supreme Court ruling finding a portion of the Child Pornography Prevention Act unconstitutional. Defendant could not demonstrate prejudice suffered as a result of counsel's performance because the court had already held that RC § 2907.322(A) was not unconstitutional, in that it prohibited only pornography produced by use of real children. State v. Jackson, — Ohio App. 3d —, 2006 Ohio 1922, — N.E. 2d —, 2006 Ohio App. LEXIS 1762 (Apr. 17, 2006).

Where a trial court failed to inform defendant of the maximum post-release sentence that could have been imposed upon her entry of a guilty plea, as required by RC § 2943.032 and Ohio R. Crim. P. 11, her plea was not knowingly entered, and her motion to withdraw the plea pursuant to Ohio R. Crim. P. 32.1 should have been granted. State v. Smith, — Ohio App. 3d —, 2006 Ohio 4271, — N.E. 2d —, 2006 Ohio App. LEXIS 4184 (Aug. 17, 2006).

Motion to withdraw plea

When defendant filed a post-sentence motion to withdraw his guilty plea approximately 17 months after he entered it, the motion was properly denied because no manifest injustice was shown, because defendant was properly advised of his rights, the effect of a guilty plea, the possible penalties, and the possiblity of post-release control when he pled guilty, so the trial court sufficiently complied with Ohio R. Crim. P. 11. State v. McGuire, — Ohio App. 3d —, 2006 Ohio 1330, — N.E. 2d —, 2006 Ohio App. LEXIS 1227 (Mar. 23, 2006).

Motion to withdraw plea properly denied

Denial of defendant's Crim. R. 32.1 motion to withdraw his plea two years after his conviction was proper as there was no manifest injustice. Because defendant testified at the motion hearing, the trial court was in the best position to determine whether he was sufficiently proficient in the language to understand the proceedings and Ohio R. Crim. P. 11 did not apply to traffic cases. State v. Dzodzomenyo, — Ohio App. 3d —, 2007 Ohio 22, — N.E. 2d —, 2007 Ohio App. LEXIS 13 (Jan. 5, 2007).

Defendant's pre-sentence Ohio R. Crim. P. 32.1 motion to withdraw guilty plea was properly overruled because defendant did not present sufficient evidence from which the trial court could conclude that he was innocent or that he had a complete defense to charges. The trial court gave full and fair consideration to the motion to withdraw and considered all appropriate factors, including the fact that defendant had an extensive Ohio R. Crim. P. 11 plea hearing in which he stated that his plea was voluntary and without reservation. State v. Thomas, — Ohio App. 3d —, 2007 Ohio 443, — N.E. 2d —, 2007 Ohio App. LEXIS 382 (Feb. 2, 2007).

Defendant's presentence motion to withdraw his guilty plea was properly denied because defendant was afforded a complete Ohio R. Crim. P. 11 hearing before entering his plea, and the record showed that he understood his rights. Moreover, the "newly discovered evidence" proffered by defendant in his motion to withdraw was readily available to defendant before entering his plea. State v. Gabbard, — Ohio App. 3d —, 2007 Ohio 461, — N.E. 2d —, 2007 Ohio App. LEXIS 410 (Feb. 5, 2007).

As a trial court conducted a hearing on defendant's presentence motion to withdraw his guilty plea pursuant to Ohio R. Crim. P. 32.1, at which it was determined that defendant was given a full Ohio R. Crim. P. 11 colloquy, he affirmatively waived his constitutional rights knowingly and intelligently by entering his guilty plea, he indicated that he understood the charge against him, and he also indicated that he had entered into an agreed sentence of imprisonment, there was no abuse of discretion in the trial court's denial of the withdrawal motion. The trial court had fully and fairly considered the withdrawal motion. State v. Spurling, — Ohio App. 3d —, 2007 Ohio 858, — N.E. 2d —, 2007 Ohio App. LEXIS 766 (Mar. 2, 2007).

Trial court properly denied defendant's motion to withdraw his guilty plea because his agreed-upon sentence was not subject to appellate review since it was within the authorized range. Both defendant and the State agreed that, in exchange for his cooperation, defendant would not receive a sentence exceeding 16 years total. Also, the trial court complied with Ohio R. Crim. P. 11(C) because defendant entered his plea with full knowledge of the possible sentence; he stated his understanding of the agreement's 16 year cap on his total sentence, stated his awareness that the trial court was free to deviate from the recommendation, and stated that he entered the plea in his own best interest. State v. Allen, — Ohio App. 3d —, 2007 Ohio 1521, — N.E. 2d —, 2007 Ohio App. LEXIS 1408 (Mar. 30, 2007).

There was no abuse of discretion in the trial court's denial of defendant's motion to withdraw his guilty pleas because the trial court held an extensive hearing on the motion and defendant was represented by competent counsel because defendant was given a complete and impartial hearing, full and fair consideration to his plea withdrawal request, and every opportunity to establish his argument for withdrawing his pleas. The trial court was permitted to question witnesses, pursuant to Ohio R. Evid. 614(B), and, although some questions asked by the trial court could have been viewed as direct, they did not indicate any clear predisposition on the part of the trial court to deny defendant's motion. State v. Torres, — Ohio App. 3d —, 2007 Ohio 1602, — N.E. 2d —, 2007 Ohio App. LEXIS 1467 (Apr. 5, 2007).

Trial court properly overruled defendant's motion to withdraw his guilty plea to a charge of domestic violence without holding a hearing because there was no support in the record for the affidavit of defendant's wife, to the effect that defendant never hit her. At his sentencing hearing, defendant stated that he needed to go to jail because he knew that what he did was wrong, and the presentence investigation report included substantial evidence that the wife had been assaulted by the husband. State v. Spencer, — Ohio App. 3d —, 2007 Ohio 2140, — N.E. 2d —, 2007 Ohio App. LEXIS 1995 (May 4, 2007).

Defendant's Ohio R. Crim. P. 32.1 motion to withdraw her no contest plea was properly denied as defendant did not show that she suffered a manifest injustice, in that she was provided with effective assistance and full hearings on both her plea and her motion to withdraw. Moreover, the record did not support defendant's claim that she was coerced to enter into a joint plea agreement that was conditional on acceptance by defendant's co-defendant, defendant's son as defendant was the primary beneficiary of the plea and, thus, had much more personal incentive to accept the plea than did her son. State v. Brown, — Ohio App. 3d —, 2007 Ohio 2885, — N.E. 2d —, 2007 Ohio App. LEXIS 2683 (June 13, 2007).

Trial court did not err in denying defendant's post-sentence motion to withdraw his guilty plea since, despite defendant's contention on appeal that the trial court was aware that he was not satisfied with his trial counsel, the record indicated that, during the plea colloquy, defendant told the trial court that he was satisfied with his counsel. Even if the trial court was aware of defendant's dissatisfaction with his counsel, it was within the trial court's discretion to deny defendant's request for a continuance of his trial in order to obtain new counsel in light of the fact that the trial of the matter was continued at defendant's request on six separate occasions. The trial court could have justifiably presumed that defendant was merely attempting to delay the proceedings when he requested a continuance to obtain new counsel. State v. Bell, — Ohio App. 3d —, 2007 Ohio 3276, — N.E. 2d —, 2007 Ohio App. LEXIS 3031 (June 28, 2007).

Trial court did not err in denying defendant's post-sentence motion to withdraw his guilty plea on the ground that defendant never admitted his guilt. Since defendant never asserted his innocence at the time of his plea, the court presumed that he understood that he was admitting to his guilt. State v. Bell, — Ohio App. 3d —, 2007 Ohio 3276, — N.E. 2d —, 2007 Ohio App. LEXIS 3031 (June 28, 2007).

Decision to deny defendant's motion to withdraw defendant's guilty plea was not an abuse of discretion. The realization that defendant faced significantly more prison time because he had committed new crimes while awaiting sentencing did not justify allowing the withdrawal. State v. Harris, — Ohio App. 3d —, 2007 Ohio 3308, — N.E. 2d —, 2007 Ohio App. LEXIS 3041 (June 29, 2007).

Trial court did not err in denying defendant's motion to withdraw his guilty plea as the record reflected that the trial court conducted a hearing on the motion; that defendant was represented by competent counsel, different from the attorney who represented him at the plea hearing; that the trial court fully considered his reasons for filing the motion to withdraw; and that there was nothing in the record supporting defendant's claim that he was under substantial duress when he entered his plea State v. Gonzales, — Ohio App. 3d —, 2007 Ohio 3565, — N.E. 2d —, 2007 Ohio App. LEXIS 3273 (July 13, 2007).

Trial court satisfied all four factors prior to denying defendant's motion to withdraw his plea: defendant acknowledged that he was satisfied with his attorney; defendant was afforded a full hearing pursuant to Ohio R. Crim. P. 11; the trial court took sufficient testimony from defendant on his motion to withdraw; and the trial court gave full and fair consideration to defendant's request to withdraw his plea. Resentencing under Foster did not provide adequate cause to grant defendant's withdrawal motion because, despite his assertion that he may have relied on law that was no longer in effect, defendant never offered anything specific that he relied on in proffering his original plea that would be different if the ruling in Foster were applied. State v. Stokes, — Ohio App. 3d —, 2007 Ohio 5063, — N.E. 2d —, 2007 Ohio App. LEXIS 4479 (Sept. 27, 2007).

Defendant's post-sentence motion to withdraw defendant's guilty plea, which alleged defendant's counsel manipulated defendant into pleading guilty, was properly denied because the record reflected that, (1) after a lengthy hearing on defendant's motion to suppress, defendant withdrew the motion and pled guilty in response to the State's offer to dismiss two other felonious-assault charges, (2) before accepting defendant's pleas, the trial court twice personally addressed defendant and told defendant of the consequences of defendant's pleas, under Ohio R. Crim. P. 11(C), (3) defendant, at that time, told the trial court defendant was satisfied with counsel's efforts, and (4) while there was no sentencing agreement, defendant received the sentence the State recommended at the plea hearing. State v. Henderson, — Ohio App. 3d —, — N.E. 2d —, 2007 Ohio App. LEXIS 4512 (Sept. 28, 2007).

Although a trial court did not fully explain the effects of entering a no contest plea to defendant, it substantially complied with Ohio R. Crim. P. 11(E) by explaining to her the charge against her, the potential sentence that she faced, and the rights that she had, such that there was no abuse of discretion in the trial court's decision to overrule her post-sentence motion to withdraw the plea pursuant to Ohio R. Crim. P. 32.1; defendant failed to show that a manifest injustice would occur if she was not permitted to withdraw the plea. Ohio v. Haught, — Ohio App. 3d —, 2007 Ohio 5736, — N.E. 2d —, 2007 Ohio App. LEXIS 5036 (Oct. 23, 2007).

Trial court did not abuse its discretion when it denied defendant's guilty plea withdrawal motion because defendant did not provide a reasonable and legitimate basis for his plea withdrawal motion because, although defendant pled guilty without having received any guarantees as to the sentence that the trial court would impose, he later asked to withdraw his guilty pleas at the sentencing hearing upon learning about the sentence that the trial court was about to impose. Further, the trial court gave full and fair consideration to defendant's plea withdrawal motion, and conducted an adequate hearing on the motion when it gave defendant an opportunity to explain his reasons for the plea withdrawal motion. Ohio v. Hairston, — Ohio App. 3d —, 2007 Ohio 5928, — N.E. 2d —, 2007 Ohio App. LEXIS 5190 (Nov. 6, 2007).

Defendant's Ohio R. Crim. P. 32.1 motion to withdraw his guilty plea was properly denied as defendant was represented by competent counsel, he was afforded a full hearing under Ohio R. Crim. P. 11 before entering his guilty plea, and he was afforded a full hearing on his motion to withdraw his guilty plea. Though defendant claimed that he was not guilty of the offenses charged in the indictment, he had not factually substantiated his claim. State v. Jordon, — Ohio App. 3d —, 2007 Ohio 6795, — N.E. 2d —, 2007 Ohio App. LEXIS 5952 (Dec. 14, 2007).

Trial court did not err by finding that defendant failed to articulate a reasonable and legitimate basis to withdraw his guilty plea to child endangering because the trial court was in the best position to determine the credibility of defendant's claims regarding his understanding of the meaning of the Alford plea he entered, as well as his claims of undue coercion by his counsel and the prosecutor. The record established that the trial court had before it sufficient information to determine that defendant's decision to plead guilty notwithstanding his assertion of innocence was a rational decision, and was therefore made knowingly, voluntarily, and intelligently. State v. Kirigiti, — Ohio App. 3d —, 2007 Ohio 6852, — N.E. 2d —, 2007 Ohio App. LEXIS 6028 (Dec. 20, 2007).

Trial court did not abuse its discretion in denying defendant's motion to withdraw his guilty plea as defendant was represented by a highly experienced criminal defense attorney with forty years of experience, the trial court afforded defendant a full hearing on his motion, defendant was afforded a complete Ohio R. Crim. P. 11 hearing prior to entering his plea, defendant fully understood the nature of the charges that he was facing and the potential penalties, and defendant had no real defense to the charges in light of his confession to the rape and sexual battery of his foster son and the results of the DNA testing corroborating the foster son's allegations. State v. Thomas, — Ohio App. 3d —, 2007 Ohio 6908, — N.E. 2d —, 2007 Ohio App. LEXIS 6048 (Dec. 21, 2007).

Trial court did not abuse its discretion when it denied defendant's pre-sentence motion to withdraw his guilty plea where a majority of the nine factors used in considering such motions weighed against granting the motion. Only three factors, lack of prejudice to the State, the timing of defendant's telling counsel he wanted to withdraw his plea, and defendant's assertion of actual innocence, weighed in favor of granting the motion. State v. Peterson, — Ohio App. 3d —, 2007 Ohio 6917, — N.E. 2d —, 2007 Ohio App. LEXIS 6068 (Dec. 3, 2007).

Trial court did not abuse its discretion when it denied defendant's motion to withdraw his guilty plea as it held an impartial hearing to determine whether defendant had a legitimate basis for withdrawing his plea and engaged in an extensive colloquy to ensure that defendant was making his plea voluntarily, knowingly, and intelligently. In light of the evidence that could have been presented against him, the plea agreement appeared to be wisely negotiated by his attorneys, as it included a dismissal of the attempted murder and rape charges and a reduction in the drug charge, as well as an agreement from the state that it would recommend a sentence of only six years in prison. State v. Breeden, — Ohio App. 3d —, 2006 Ohio 98, — N.E. 2d —, 2006 Ohio App. LEXIS 69 (Jan. 12, 2006).

Trial court properly denied defendant's presentence motion to withdraw his guilty plea to a charge of murder because the evidence showed that defendant clearly understood what he was doing when he entered his plea and that the real reason for seeking withdrawal was that defendant had a change of heart about serving a possible life sentence. This was insufficient to justify withdrawal. State v. Strodes, — Ohio App. 3d —, 2006 Ohio 2335, — N.E. 2d —, 2006 Ohio App. LEXIS 2146 (May 5, 2006).

Defendant's presentence motion under Ohio R. Crim. P. 32.1 to withdraw his guilty plea was properly denied. While there did not appear to be any prejudice to the State and while the motion was timely filed, the record showed that defendant was represented by competent counsel at all times prior to the entry of his guilty plea, that the trial court conducted an extensive hearing both at the Ohio R. Crim. P. 11 hearing and at the hearing on the motion to withdraw, and that it was unlikely that defendant had any defense to the charges. State v. Ramsey, — Ohio App. 3d —, 2006 Ohio 2795, — N.E. 2d —, 2006 Ohio App. LEXIS 2610 (June 5, 2006).

Trial court did not abuse its discretion when it denied defendant's presentence Ohio R. Crim. P. 32.1 motion to withdraw his plea because defendant did not point to any persuasive evidence that his former counsel failed to adequately represent him and the trial court conducted a thorough colloquy under Ohio R. Crim. P. 11 and informed him of all of the rights he waived by pleading guilty. Also, defendant's alibi defense was questionable at best, it was found that the evidence presented a "serious probability" that a jury would have found him guilty, and he did, in fact, admit his guilt when he opted to change his plea. State v. Schmidt, — Ohio App. 3d —, 2006 Ohio 2948, — N.E. 2d —, 2006 Ohio App. LEXIS 2815 (June 12, 2006).

Defendant's displeasure with the media coverage and ensuing regret concerning his guilty plea was not a legitimate basis for granting his motion to withdraw his plea under Ohio R. Crim. P. 32.1; the trial court did not abuse its discretion in denying defendant's motion to withdraw his guilty plea. State v. D.D., — Ohio App. 3d —, 2006 Ohio 3180, — N.E. 2d —, 2006 Ohio App. LEXIS 3071 (June 23, 2006).

Trial court's denial of defendant's plea withdrawal motion was not an abuse of discretion, as there was no legitimate reason offered why defendant did not produce the allegedly new evidence in support of his defense sooner, the new evidence did not change his theory of defense, and he was deemed to lack credibility and to have engaged in a pattern of delay tactics throughout the course of the proceedings. He had originally indicated that his theft by deception of two elderly persons was due to mismanagement of his business because he was preoccupied by his father's illness, and his withdrawal motion was based on information from his accountant regarding the same theory without specifying any individual who was responsible for the misconduct of the accounts. State v. Webb, — Ohio App. 3d —, 2006 Ohio 3512, — N.E. 2d —, 2006 Ohio App. LEXIS 3472 (July 7, 2006).

Denial of defendant's post-sentence Ohio R. Crim. P. 32.1 motion to withdraw his guilty pleas to two counts of felony tampering with records was proper because the trial court did not substantially violate Ohio R. Crim. P. 11 by not going over every possible ramification of the guilty pleas. Defendant could not establish prejudice because the revocation of his notary public license was prescribed by RC § 147.03, not imposed by the sentencing court. State v. Absher, — Ohio App. 3d —, 2006 Ohio 3717, — N.E. 2d —, 2006 Ohio App. LEXIS 3651 (July 20, 2006).

Where the trial court provided a full plea hearing under Ohio R. Crim. P. 11, defendant was represented by highly competent counsel at the time, and he was given a complete and impartial hearing on his presentence motion to withdraw his plea pursuant to Ohio R. Crim. P. 32.1, the trial court's denial of his motion was not an abuse of discretion. The Court of Appeals of Ohio, Eighth Appellate District, Cuyahoga County notes that it would also include consideration of the genuineness of the withdrawal motion in a circumstance where the plea was entered at the time that the case was called for trial, the parties were fully prepared to go forward, and the witnesses were present. State v. Montgomery, — Ohio App. 3d —, 2006 Ohio 3850, — N.E. 2d —, 2006 Ohio App. LEXIS 3817 (July 27, 2006).

Denial of defendant's motion to withdraw his no contest plea was not error because it could not be said that the trial court abused its discretion in finding that defendant had failed to articulate a reasonable and legitimate basis for withdrawal of his no contest plea. The trial court provided defendant with a full hearing during which it considered each of his reasons for withdrawing his plea. It was believed that defendant merely had a change of heart and he did not provide the trial court with any evidence to support his claims of innocence or establish a meritorious defense. State v. Smith, — Ohio App. 3d —, 2006 Ohio 4419, — N.E. 2d —, 2006 Ohio App. LEXIS 4339 (Aug. 28, 2006).

When defendant's pre-sentence motion to withdraw his guilty plea erroneously cited the manifest injustice standard, instead of the applicable abuse of discretion standard, and the trial court's order denying the motion also cited the incorrect manifest injustice standard, defendant could not complain of this error on appeal because this was invited error, and he did not show that the trial court's application of this standard prejudiced him. State v. Carswell, — Ohio App. 3d —, 2006 Ohio 5210, — N.E. 2d —, 2006 Ohio App. LEXIS 5177 (Oct. 4, 2006).

Trial court did not abuse its discretion in refusing to allow defendant to withdraw his plea because defendant failed to articulate a valid reason for the withdrawal and he admitted that he was content with the plea. Even if trial counsel's performance was ineffective, defendant admitted that he was happy with the plea agreement. Further, the record supported the trial court's ultimate conclusion that faced with a definite imprisonment term and an additional prison term beyond that as a result of the guilty verdict from another criminal case, defendant had a change of heart and attempted to withdraw the original plea. State v. Kimble, — Ohio App. 3d —, 2006 Ohio 6096, — N.E. 2d —, 2006 Ohio App. LEXIS 6034 (Nov. 17, 2006).

Trial court did not err in denying defendant's presentence Ohio R. Crim. P. 32.1 motion to withdraw his guilty plea to a charge of aggravated robbery and rape. The trial court complied with Ohio R. Crim. P. 11 when defendant entered his plea, conducted a full hearing on the Ohio R. Crim. P. 32.1 motion, and gave consideration to the motion to withdraw, ultimately rejecting defendant's contention that the victim was forced to prosecute defendant. State v. Seay, — Ohio App. 3d —, 2006 Ohio 6454, — N.E. 2d —, 2006 Ohio App. LEXIS 6408 (Dec. 8, 2006).

Trial court applied the correct legal standard and did not abuse its discretion by not allowing defendant to withdraw his guilty plea. In view of his open admission of guilt at the plea hearing, it appeared that he suffered a change of heart only after he realized that he could be sentenced to more than a year and thus, his motion to withdraw essentially amounted to

a desire for a shorter prison term rather than to assert his innocence. State v. Payne, — Ohio App. 3d —, 2006 Ohio 6539, — N.E. 2d —, 2006 Ohio App. LEXIS 6452 (Dec. 11, 2006).

Trial court did not abuse its discretion in denying defendant's motion to withdraw his guilty plea because defendant told the trial court that he did not want to go to trial and that he had understood what he was doing when he pled guilty. It was clear that the trial court took into consideration the fact that trial had commenced, a jury was empaneled, and opening statements were completed when defendant decided to accept the plea and the record demonstrated that the trial court complied with the mandates of Ohio R. Crim. P. 11(C) for the plea and with Ohio R. Crim. P. 32.1 for the motion to withdraw. State v. Larry, — Ohio App. 3d —, 2006 Ohio 6578, — N.E. 2d —, 2006 Ohio App. LEXIS 6491 (Dec. 14, 2006).

Defendant's presentence Ohio R. Crim. P. 32.1 motion to withdraw his guilty plea was properly denied because the record showed that the State would be prejudiced if it were required to prepare for trial again as eight months had elapsed before defendant moved to withdraw his plea. The trial court gave full and fair consideration to defendant's motion and simply rejected defendant's claim that his guilty plea was not voluntary, noting that defendant was represented by counsel, that he received an extensive Ohio R. Crim. P. 11 inquiry, and that he understood the nature of the charges and possible sentencing. State v. Urbina, — Ohio App. 3d —, 2006 Ohio 6921, — N.E. 2d —, 2006 Ohio App. LEXIS 6844 (Dec. 28, 2006).

Trial court did not abuse its discretion when it denied defendant's motion to withdraw his plea prior to issuing his sentence because, although defendant argued that he would not have entered a guilty plea had the information that the victim was the owner of the vehicle been available, the information was not actually relevant to the charges levied against him. The information was not available at the preliminary hearing because it was not a necessary part of the investigation. State v. Henry, — Ohio App. 3d —, 2006 Ohio 6942, — N.E. 2d —, 2006 Ohio App. LEXIS 6847 (Dec. 20, 2006).

Trial court did not abuse its discretion in denying defendant a hearing on the post-sentence motion to withdraw his guilty plea, under Crim. R. 32.1, because, aside from defendant's self-serving affidavit, there was nothing in the record to demonstrate that defendant's trial counsel was deficient, nor evidence of a reasonable probability that, but for trial counsel's errors, he would not have pled guilty. There was a nearly four-year delay in filing the motion to withdraw the plea, and defendant only offered an explanation that he discovered the basis for the motion a few months earlier. State v. Heath, — Ohio App. 3d —, 2006 Ohio 7045, — N.E. 2d —, 2006 Ohio App. LEXIS 7032 (Dec. 28, 2006).

Defendant's motion to withdraw his guilty plea or modify his sentence was properly denied because it was based solely on the application of Foster to his non-minimum sentence imposed pursuant to unconstitutional judicial fact-finding formerly required by RC § 2929.14(B) and defendant's case was neither on direct appeal nor pending in a trial court when Foster and Blakely, upon which Foster was based, were decided, so those decisions did not apply to the case. State v. Grier, — Ohio App. 3d —, 2007 Ohio 2597, — N.E. 2d —, 2007 Ohio App. LEXIS 2419 (May 25, 2007).

No contest plea

Defendant's motion to withdraw his no contest pleas was erroneously denied because the trial court did not substantially comply with Ohio R. Crim. P. 11(C)(2)(a) when it accepted those pleas because, while it informed defendant that the counts he did not contest contained firearm specifications, it did not tell him that those specifications carried mandatory one- and three-year prison terms, so defendant was not advised of the maximum sentence applicable to the counts he did not contest. State v. Douglas, — Ohio App. 3d —, 2007 Ohio 714, — N.E. 2d —, 2007 Ohio App. LEXIS 650 (Feb. 22, 2007).

Plea withdrawal

Trial court erred when it did not allow any evidence during the hearing on defendant's plea withdrawal concerning possible defenses to the charges because, although the trial court had substantial discretion in deciding the scope of the evidence it would allow at the hearing on the motion, some inquiry concerning whether defendant had a substantial defense to the charge should have been allowed. State v. Fugate, — Ohio App. 3d —, 2007 Ohio 26, — N.E. 2d —, 2007 Ohio App. LEXIS 20 (Jan. 5, 2007).

Trial court erred when it applied the post-sentence standard in determining whether to grant defendant's presentence motion to withdraw his plea because, not only was the motion literally made before sentencing, the reasons for applying a stricter standard did not apply since defendant was not changing his plea because he was unhappy with his sentence. Defendant still did not know exactly what his sentence was going to be and he learned nothing new about his sentence after his plea was tendered. State v. Fugate, — Ohio App. 3d —, 2007 Ohio 26, — N.E. 2d —, 2007 Ohio App. LEXIS 20 (Jan. 5, 2007).

Post-conviction relief

Trial court incorrectly treated defendant's Ohio R. Crim. P. 32.1 motion as a petition for post-conviction relief under RC § 2953.21 on the authority of the Ohio Supreme Court's decision in State v. Reynolds. Since defendant's motion was specifically filed pursuant to Ohio R. Crim. P. 32.1, the trial court erred in analyzing it as a petition for post-conviction relief. State v. Spencer, — Ohio App. 3d —, 2007 Ohio 2140, — N.E. 2d —, 2007 Ohio App. LEXIS 1995 (May 4, 2007).

When defendant claimed a manifest injustice justified the post-sentence withdrawal of his guilty pleas because (1) his heroin addiction rendered him unable to understand the sentencing proceedings, and (2) counsel ineffectively did not advise the trial court of this and falsely promised defendant he would receive a lighter sentence, defendant did not show a manifest injustice because these claims could have been raised in a petition for postconviction relief, but defendant filed no such petition and the time within which to file one, under RC § 2953.21, had expired. State v. Plemons, — Ohio App. 3d —, 2006 Ohio 1608, — N.E. 2d —, 2006 Ohio App. LEXIS 1454 (Mar. 31, 2006).

Presentence motion to withdraw plea

As defendant received competent assistance of counsel when he entered his guilty plea, he had a full hearing before the trial court prior to entry of his plea, and his reasons for seeking withdrawal of the plea were not deemed reasonable or legitimate, the trial court did not abuse its discretion in denying his pre-sentence withdrawal request. Defendant had claimed that his plea was involuntary and not knowingly entered due to his concerns for his family and his alcoholism. State v. Scarbro, — Ohio App. 3d —, 2007 Ohio 582, — N.E. 2d —, 2007 Ohio App. LEXIS 547 (Feb. 12, 2007).

Defendant's bare assertion that he had uncovered new information failed to make the threshold showing required for withdrawal of a no contest plea prior to sentencing: State v. Webb, 173 Ohio App. 3d 547, 2007 Ohio 5670, 879 N.E.2d 254, 2007 Ohio App. LEXIS 4991 (2007).

Procedure

Inmate's declaratory judgment action against a county prosecutor pursuant to RC § 2721.03, seeking withdrawal of his guilty plea, required dismissal other than for failure to comply with pleading requirements, as relief from the plea could only be obtained from the trial court pursuant to Ohio R. Crim. P. 32.1 and as such, the prosecutor had no authority

to provide such relief and was not a proper party. The criminal rules did not apply in the civil context of the declaratory judgment, pursuant to Ohio R. Crim. P. 1(A). Hall v. Watkins, — Ohio App. 3d —, 2007 Ohio 209, — N.E. 2d —, 2007 Ohio App. LEXIS 196 (Jan. 19, 2007).

Trial court did not abuse its discretion in not allowing an inmate to file a response to the State's opposition to his motion to withdraw his guilty plea pursuant to Ohio R. Crim. P. 32.1, as Ohio R. Civ. P. 12(A)(2) only applied to responses and motions in civil proceedings, and Hamilton County, Ohio, Ct. C.P. R. 14(B) did not implicate constitutional rights for purposes of showing a manifest injustice in his post-sentencing motion. State v. Peoples, — Ohio App. 3d —, 2006 Ohio 2614, — N.E. 2d —, 2006 Ohio App. LEXIS 2439 (May 26, 2006).

Reply to state's memorandum

Trial court erred when it overruled the motion to withdraw the guilty pleas before the defendant could reply to the state's opposing memorandum: State v. Akemon, 173 Ohio App. 3d 709, 2007 Ohio 6217, 880 N.E.2d 143, 2007 Ohio App. LEXIS 5500 (2007).

Res judicata

Defendant's argument that the trial court erred by denying her motion to withdraw her plea was barred by doctrine of res judicata; defendant's allegation of ineffective assistance of counsel should have been raised on direct appeal because each of the alleged failings of her counsel was known to her at the time of her conviction. To the extent that any of the evidence was outside the record, it was in existence, known to defendant, and was available for use had she chosen to file a direct appeal. City of Jackson v. Friley, — Ohio App. 3d —, 2007 Ohio 6755, — N.E. 2d —, 2007 Ohio App. LEXIS 5912 (Dec. 14, 2007).

Res judicata

Defendant's third post-sentence motion pursuant to Ohio R. Crim. P. 32.1 to withdraw defendant's 1995 guilty plea to rape was barred by res judicata because neither of defendant's two prior motions raised the issue of a breach of the plea agreement by initiating sex offender proceedings under RC § 2950.09 in 1997. Such proceedings did not violate the prohibition against retroactive laws under the Ohio Constitution. State v. Vernon, — Ohio App. 3d —, 2007 Ohio 3376, — N.E. 2d —, 2007 Ohio App. LEXIS 3092 (June 29, 2007).

As defendant raised a claim in a prior appeal with respect to his post-sentence motion to withdraw his guilty plea, which was deemed to have lacked merit because he was found to have been fully advised pursuant to Ohio R. Crim. P. 11 that the maximum sentence that he could face was the death penalty, his later appeal from the trial court's denial of his successive motion to withdraw his guilty plea pursuant to Ohio R. Crim. P. 32.1 was barred by the doctrine of res judicata. State v. Lankford, — Ohio App. 3d —, 2007 Ohio 3330, — N.E. 2d —, 2007 Ohio App. LEXIS 3120 (June 12, 2007).

When defendant pled guilty to various crimes and defendant's conviction pursuant to that plea was affirmed, even if a trial court had jurisdiction to consider defendant's subsequent motion to withdraw defendant's plea, the motion was barred by the doctrine of res judicata because the matters raised in the motion could have been raised on defendant's direct appeal of defendant's conviction, but they were not. State v. Herbert, — Ohio App. 3d —, 2007 Ohio 4496, — N.E. 2d —, 2007 Ohio App. LEXIS 4069 (Sept. 4, 2007).

When, after defendant pled no contest, he appealed the sentence imposed and that sentence was vacated and his case was remanded for resentencing, res judicata barred the trial court's consideration, on remand, of defendant's motion to withdraw his no contest plea because he could have raised that motion when his case was first before the trial court, or on appeal from those proceedings, but he did not. State v.

Sanchez, — Ohio App. 3d —, 2007 Ohio 218, — N.E. 2d —, 2007 Ohio App. LEXIS 210 (Jan. 22, 2007).

Trial court erred in granting defendant's Crim. R. 32.1 motion to withdraw her plea; because the issue of disproportionate sentencing could have been raised on direct appeal, res judicata barred defendant from relying upon such a theory to withdraw her plea. Even if it had not been barred by res judicata, because defendant did not identify a similarly situated defendant, she could not rely upon the sentence of a single other individual, one who was arguably distinct for the purposes of sentencing, to support her claim of a manifest injustice. State v. Ruby, — Ohio App. 3d —, 2007 Ohio 244, — N.E. 2d —, 2007 Ohio App. LEXIS 227 (Jan. 24, 2007).

Defendant's argument that his post-sentence Ohio R. Crim. P. 32.1 motion to withdraw his plea should have been granted since he received ineffective assistance of counsel was barred by the doctrine of res judicata because the issue and argument made by defendant were identical to the issue and argument made in his pre-sentence motion. State v. Mack, — Ohio App. 3d —, 2006 Ohio 1694, — N.E. 2d —, 2006 Ohio App. LEXIS 1550 (Mar. 31, 2006).

Defendant had his opportunity to address the issue of what he was promised to induce his plea when he challenged the original sentence, and the trial court rectified the situation and cured any manifest injustice by giving him probation; defendant was not allowed to later complain that he misunderstood the charge, since res judicata barred his objection. State v. Allen, — Ohio App. 3d —, 2006 Ohio 3164, — N.E. 2d —, 2006 Ohio App. LEXIS 3031 (June 22, 2006).

Denial of defendant's post sentence Ohio R. Crim. P. 32.1 motion to withdraw his guilty plea was proper; his claims were barred by doctrine of res judicata since he raised the same issues in the trial court, the trial court addressed them multiple times, and defendant could have raised them on appeal. There was also no exception to res judicata applicable since defendant submitted no evidence from outside the record, or any evidence at all, to support his motion. State v. Brown, 167 Ohio App. 3d 239, 2006 Ohio 3266, 854 N.E. 2d 583, 2006 Ohio App. LEXIS 3179 (June 27, 2006).

As defendant's second post-sentence motion to withdraw his guilty pleas pursuant to Ohio R. Crim. P. 32.1 raised multiple issues that could have been previously raised at the trial court level, in his direct appeal, or in his prior post-sentence motion to withdraw the pleas, the claims were barred by res judicata. State v. Stevens, — Ohio App. 3d —, 2006 Ohio 5358, — N.E. 2d —, 2006 Ohio App. LEXIS 5331 (Oct. 13, 2006).

Although Blakely was decided after defendant's sentence was imposed, that holding was based on Apprendi, which was decided prior to defendant's sentence and accordingly, defendant could have raised a challenge to the unconstitutionality of his maximum and consecutive sentences pursuant to U.S. Const. amend. VI and Ohio Const. art. I, § 10 in his prior direct appeal of his sentence; accordingly, his motion to withdraw his guilty plea pursuant to Ohio R. Crim. P. 32.1 was properly denied on grounds of res judicata. State v. Waters, — Ohio App. 3d —, 2006 Ohio 5528, — N.E. 2d —, 2006 Ohio App. LEXIS 5519 (Oct. 24, 2006).

Defendant's post-appeal motion to withdraw his guilty plea to failure to appear was barred by the doctrine of res judicata. Because defendant challenged his sentence on direct appeal, but did not challenge the entry of his plea for failure to appear, he was barred from raising issues regarding that plea. State v. Green, — Ohio App. 3d —, 2006 Ohio 6695, — N.E. 2d —, 2006 Ohio App. LEXIS 6593 (Dec. 15, 2006).

Review

There were no arguable flaws in a trial court's reasoning employed in denying defendant's motion to withdraw his guilty plea. The trial court analyzed the standard that should be applied to a presentence motion to withdraw a guilty plea

and found that defendant was represented by highly-competent counsel, that he received a full hearing under Ohio R. Crim. P. 11, and that defendant was afforded a full hearing on his motion to withdraw. State v. Dawkins, — Ohio App. 3d —, 2006 Ohio 307, — N.E. 2d —, 2006 Ohio App. LEXIS 264 (Jan. 20, 2006).

It was not an abuse of discretion to deny defendant's post-sentence motion to withdraw his guilty plea filed after a prison sentence was imposed following a finding that he violated the community control imposed after he pled guilty because defendant did not provide a transcript of the hearing at which he pled guilty, under Ohio R. App. P. 9(B), so the regularity of that hearing was presumed. State v. Seeley, — Ohio App. 3d —, 2006 Ohio 2376, — N.E. 2d —, 2006 Ohio App. LEXIS 2272 (May 15, 2006).

Right to counsel

Trial court engaged in the proper analysis of defendant's Ohio R. Crim. P. 32.1 motion to withdraw his plea, and since it required no hearing, the trial court's decision to deny defendant's request for counsel was not an abuse of its discretion. Although he was entitled to appointed counsel to represent him at a hearing on a motion to withdraw a plea, if the motion had been made prior to sentencing, however, because he filed his motion to withdraw six years after his conviction and sentence, he no longer had a right to counsel. State v. Meadows, — Ohio App. 3d —, 2006 Ohio 2622, — N.E. 2d —, 2006 Ohio App. LEXIS 2450 (May 26, 2006).

Rules of civil procedure

Because Ohio R. Crim. P. 32.1 contained the specific, proper procedure to withdraw a guilty plea, to the extent that defendant relied upon Ohio R. Civ. P. 60(B) to withdraw her plea, that reliance was misplaced. City of Jackson v. Friley, — Ohio App. 3d —, 2007 Ohio 6755, — N.E. 2d —, 2007 Ohio App. LEXIS 5912 (Dec. 14, 2007).

Sentencing

Trial court abused its discretion when it did not impose community control sanctions, or allow defendant to vacate his plea because, although the trial court advised defendant of the potential sentencing range for abduction, it did not state that it could impose prison, rather than community control, to which defendant had agreed; nor did it inform defendant that in order to comply with his part of the bargain, he had to do anything but stay away from the victim. Moreover, when the trial court decided to deviate from the plea agreement, it should have clearly advised defendant of its intentions, and allowed him to reconsider his plea. State v. Dunbar, — Ohio App. 3d —, 2007 Ohio 1693, — N.E. 2d —, 2007 Ohio App. LEXIS 1557 (Apr. 12, 2007).

Trial court's judgment denying defendant's motion to withdraw defendant's guilty plea pursuant to Ohio R. Crim. P. 32.1 was affirmed. Contrary to defendant's assertions that defendant was misled and/or uninformed regarding sentencing discretion, the record showed that defendant reviewed every term of the plea agreement and assented to it. State v. Jones, — Ohio App. 3d —, 2007 Ohio 4090, — N.E. 2d —, 2007 Ohio App. LEXIS 3709 (Aug. 10, 2007).

Trial court did not abuse its discretion in denying defendant's motion to withdraw his plea because defendant signed a written plea agreement, which stated that sentence would be argued and that the State would agree to judicial release after six months of incarceration. The State argued for consecutive sentences at the original sentencing hearing; the trial court imposed consecutive sentences at the sentencing hearing; and the judgment entry stated that consecutive sentences were imposed. State v. Findley, — Ohio App. 3d —, 2007 Ohio 6706, — N.E. 2d —, 2007 Ohio App. LEXIS 5879 (Dec. 17, 2007).

When the allegations of defendant's post-sentence motion to withdraw his guilty plea were aimed at the sentence imposed following a finding that he violated the community control imposed after he pled guilty, it was not an abuse of discretion to deny the motion because a post-sentence motion to withdraw a guilty plea was used to attack a manifest injustice under Ohio R. Crim. P. 11, dealing with defendant's plea being knowing, voluntary and intelligent, and nothing stated in either the motion or on appeal claimed the initial plea was unknowing or involuntary. State v. Seeley, — Ohio App. 3d —, 2006 Ohio 2376, — N.E. 2d —, 2006 Ohio App. LEXIS 2272 (May 15, 2006).

There was no error in denying defendant's Ohio R. Crim. P. 32.1 motion to correct his sentence after his guilty plea. Because there was no statutory authority granting a trial court the power to lessen a sentence after execution, the trial court did not have the authority to consider defendant's motion and properly denied it. State v. Savage, — Ohio App. 3d —, 2006 Ohio 3419, — N.E. 2d —, 2006 Ohio App. LEXIS 3369 (June 30, 2006).

Defendant's guilty pleas to domestic violence and failure to appear were made knowingly, intelligently, and voluntarily because defendant acknowledged, in signed plea agreements, that he could receive prison terms of between three and 10 years for aggravated burglary and between six and 18 months for failure to appear. The trial court satisfied the requirements of Ohio R. Crim. P. 11 because it was only required to determine if defendant understood the maximum penalty involved; it was not required to apprise defendant of the possibility of consecutive sentences. State v. Green, — Ohio App. 3d —, 2006 Ohio 6695, — N.E. 2d —, 2006 Ohio App. LEXIS 6593 (Dec. 15, 2006).

Timeliness

Although the trial court should not have treated defendant's motion as a motion for post-conviction relief under RC § 2953.21 since his motion was clearly captioned as a request to withdraw his guilty plea under Ohio R. Crim. P. 32.1, the error was harmless since the trial court also addressed the merits of the motion. Defendant filed the motion over six years after sentence was imposed, which was an undue delay and factored against granting the motion. State v. Meadows, — Ohio App. 3d —, 2006 Ohio 6183, — N.E. 2d —, 2006 Ohio App. LEXIS 6141 (Nov. 22, 2006).

Defendant's Ohio R. Crim. P. 32.1 motion to withdraw his plea of no contest to two counts of aggravated murder was properly overruled because defendant waited almost 20 years after his plea to file his motion to withdraw his plea and because the evidence that he presented in support of his motion had been available for just as long; thus, no manifest injustice had occurred. State v. Alexander, — Ohio App. 3d —, 2006 Ohio 7049, — N.E. 2d —, 2006 Ohio App. LEXIS 6982 (Dec. 22, 2006).

Transcript

Trial court properly denied defendant's motion for a transcript of his plea hearing at the State's expense in support of his motion to withdraw his plea, pursuant to Ohio R. Crim. P. 32.1, as he was not entitled to the paid-for transcript where his conviction was no longer subject to appellate review. State v. McKinney, — Ohio App. 3d —, 2006 Ohio 5364, — N.E. 2d —, 2006 Ohio App. LEXIS 5344 (Oct. 16, 2006).

Void sentence

Motion to withdraw a plea of guilty or no contest made by a defendant who has been given a void sentence must be considered as a presentence motion under CrimR 32.1: State v. Boswell, 121 Ohio St. 3d 575, 2009 Ohio 1577, 906 N.E.2d 422, 2009 Ohio LEXIS 899 (2009).

Withdrawal not warranted

Common pleas court did not err in overruling defendant's presentence motion to withdraw his no contest plea. While defendant contended that withdrawal should be permitted because a detective he wished to call was precluded from

testifying due to his relationship with the prosecutor, this was not case; instead, the transcript showed that the detective's testimony was excluded because it was based on inadmissible hearsay. State v. Booker, — Ohio App. 3d —, 2007 Ohio 430, — N.E. 2d —, 2007 Ohio App. LEXIS 378 (Feb. 2, 2007).

Factors to be considered when determining a pre-sentence motion to withdraw a guilty plea included: (1) whether the prosecution would be prejudiced if the plea was vacated; (2) whether the accused was represented by highly competent counsel; (3) whether the accused was given a full Ohio R. Crim. P. 11 hearing; (4) whether a full hearing was held on the motion; (5) whether the trial court gave full and fair consideration to the motion; (6) whether the motion was made within a reasonable time; (7) whether the motion set forth specific reasons for the withdrawal; (8) whether the accused understood the nature of the charges and possible penalties; and (9) whether the accused was perhaps not guilty or had a complete defense to the crime. State v. Mace, — Ohio App. 3d —, 2007 Ohio 1113, — N.E. 2d —, 2007 Ohio App. LEXIS 1038 (Mar. 6, 2007).

Trial court did not abuse its discretion in denying the motion to withdraw the no contest pleas, entered more than four years earlier, because the trial court's presumption of prejudice to the State and potential for stale evidence, combined with the fact that defendant had a full Ohio R. Crim. P. 11 hearing (including his satisfaction with his attorney) were relevant considerations in denying the motion to withdraw. Further, although the trial court's hearing on the motion to withdraw was brief, it was clear that the motion was without merit and that defendant failed to establish any conflict of interest which would have justified the withdrawal of his pleas. State v. Osborne, — Ohio App. 3d —, 2007 Ohio 1794, — N.E. 2d —, 2007 Ohio App. LEXIS 1652 (Apr. 16, 2007).

While a common pleas court erred in concluding that the stricter standard imposed by Ohio R. Crim. P. 32.1 for the granting of post-sentence motions to withdraw a plea should apply, defendant waived all but plain error in this regard because he never objected to this finding. There was no plain error, in that the common pleas court expressly found that it would not grant the motion even applying the more liberal standard reserved for pre-sentence motions to withdraw a plea as defendant's motion was based on a mere change of heart, which was an insufficient basis for granting a motion to withdraw a plea. State v. Wallen, — Ohio App. 3d —, 2007 Ohio 2129, — N.E. 2d —, 2007 Ohio App. LEXIS 1985 (May 4, 2007).

Trial court did not abuse its discretion when it denied defendant's pre-sentence motion to withdraw his guilty plea pursuant to Ohio R. Crim. P. 32.1, as he waited until halfway through the sentencing hearing to make his motion, defendant had entered his plea knowingly, voluntarily, and intelligently after a sufficient colloquy under Ohio R. Crim. P. 11, defendant indicated that he was satisfied with his counsel's representation, a comprehensive hearing was held on defendant's withdrawal motion, and it did not appear that defendant had a meritorious defense. Defendant simply changed his mind about his plea, which was not a sufficient justification to withdraw it. State v. Johnson, — Ohio App. 3d —, 2007 Ohio 3405, — N.E. 2d —, 2007 Ohio App. LEXIS 3157 (June 26, 2007).

Trial court did not abuse its discretion in denying defendant's pre-sentence motion to withdraw his guilty plea pursuant to Ohio R. Crim. P. 32.1, as it concluded that he was engaging in gamesmanship because he asserted no reason to allow withdrawal, his rights had been carefully explained at a plea hearing under Ohio R. Crim. P. 11, such that it was determined that his guilty plea was voluntarily, intelligently, and knowingly entered, and his attorneys were very experienced and diligently pursued various defenses on defendant's behalf. State v. Lowe, — Ohio App. 3d —, 2007 Ohio 4039, — N.E. 2d —, 2007 Ohio App. LEXIS 3677 (Aug. 9, 2007).

Court rejected defendant's contention that his guilty plea was grounded on inaccurate information provided by a jailhouse informant as defendant failed to demonstrate that the information provided by the jailhouse informant was inaccurate; thus, the trial court did not err in denying defendant's Ohio R. Crim. P. 32.1 motion to withdraw his guilty plea. State v. Hitchcock, — Ohio App. 3d —, 2007 Ohio 5059, — N.E. 2d —, 2007 Ohio App. LEXIS 4474 (Sept. 27, 2007).

Court rejected defendant's contention that his guilty plea was not knowing, intelligent, and voluntary because the trial court failed to advise defendant that he had a right to counsel at trial and that he had a right to cross-examine witnesses. A thorough review of the transcript revealed that the trial court informed defendant that he had a right to cross-examine witnesses, and since defendant was already represented by counsel at trial, the trial court was not required under Ohio R. Crim. P. 11(C)(1) to inform defendant of his right to counsel at trial; thus, the trial court did not err in denying defendant's Ohio R. Crim. P. 32.1 motion to withdraw his guilty plea. State v. Hitchcock, — Ohio App. 3d —, 2007 Ohio 5059, — N.E. 2d —, 2007 Ohio App. LEXIS 4474 (Sept. 27, 2007).

Denial of defendant's post-sentence motion under Crim. R. 32.1 to withdraw his guilty plea was not an abuse of discretion, as there was no support for defendant's claim regarding the certainty of federal charges being filed against him; rather, such charges were always considered just a possibility, and there was no breach of the plea agreement. Ohio v. Makupson, — Ohio App. 3d —, 2007 Ohio 5329, — N.E. 2d —, 2007 Ohio App. LEXIS 4693 (Oct. 4, 2007).

Trial court properly denied defendant's pre-sentence motion under Ohio R. Crim. P. 32.1 to withdraw his guilty pleas, as the trial court had provided sufficient information to defendant under Ohio R. Crim. P. 11(C)(2) as to his rights and those that he was waiving, defendant's pleas were knowingly, intelligently, and voluntarily entered as a result of a plea agreement, and his request to withdraw was deemed a mere change of heart. Ohio v. Minkner, — Ohio App. 3d —, 2007 Ohio 5574, — N.E. 2d —, 2007 Ohio App. LEXIS 4892 (Oct. 12, 2007).

Trial court did not abuse its discretion in overruling defendant's Ohio R. Crim. P. 32.1 motion to withdraw his plea because, although defendant's motion was submitted prior to resentencing, and thus, it was as if he had not been sentenced, RC § 2907.322, the statute to which defendant pled guilty for pandering sexually oriented material involving a minor, remained constitutional. Because the argument that defendant used in support of his motion to withdraw was premised upon a holding which was overruled by the Ohio Supreme Court, defendant's motion failed to assert a reasonable and legitimate basis for withdrawal of his guilty pleas. Ohio v. Ziefle, — Ohio App. 3d —, 2007 Ohio 5621, — N.E. 2d —, 2007 Ohio App. LEXIS 4941 (Oct. 19, 2007).

Trial court did not err in denying defendant's presentencing motion to withdraw his plea because it reasonably concluded that defendant's bare assertion that he had uncovered new information that proved his innocence failed to make the threshold showing of a reasonable and legitimate basis for the withdrawal. State v. Webb, 173 Ohio App. 3d 547, 2007 Ohio 5670, 879 N.E.2d 254, 2007 Ohio App. LEXIS 4991 (2007).

Trial court did not abuse its discretion in denying defendant's withdrawal motion, under Ohio R. Crim. P. 32.1, because, in view of the fact that the trial court set the date for sentencing at the conclusion of the hearing, defendant could not claim that he did not know sentencing would soon follow. Also, discordant relations with his first attorney did not alone render his plea involuntary; defendant did not maintain his innocence or present a viable defense; and defendant's withdrawal motion essentially amounted to a desire to evade prison rather than to assert his innocence. State v. Ward, —

Ohio App. 3d —, 2006 Ohio 1662, — N.E. 2d —, 2006 Ohio App. LEXIS 1568 (Apr. 3, 2006).

Defendant's Ohio R. Crim. P. 32.1 post-sentence motion to vacate his no contest plea was properly denied as the record was clear that defendant was fully advised of his constitutional rights, including his right to counsel, and that he voluntarily, knowingly and intelligently waived his rights, including his right to an attorney. City of Euclid v. Gage-Vaughn, — Ohio App. 3d —, 2006 Ohio 1941, — N.E. 2d —, 2006 Ohio App. LEXIS 1778 (Apr. 20, 2006).

Trial court did not err in denying defendant's Ohio R. Crim. P. 32.1 motion to withdraw her guilty plea to murder, under RC § 2903.02(A), because, since defendant confessed to the murder of her mother, there was ample justification to counsel defendant to plea to murder in exchange for dropping the remaining charges. The trial court conducted a thorough colloquy pursuant to Ohio R. Crim. P. 11 when it accepted the guilty plea; and defendant was permitted to verbally address the court and explain her reasons for wanting to withdraw her plea but her stated reasons for seeking to withdraw her plea were unpersuasive. There was strong evidence that defendant was in fact guilty and lacked a complete defense to the charge. State v. Orta, — Ohio App. 3d —, 2006 Ohio 1995, — N.E. 2d —, 2006 Ohio App. LEXIS 1866 (Apr. 24, 2006).

When defendant pled guilty to a charge of rape, his motion to withdraw that plea, before he was sentenced, was properly denied because (1) he was represented by competent counsel and did not allege that he was not, (2) he received a full hearing when he pled guilty at which the trial court fully complied with the requirements of Ohio R. Civ. P. 11(C)(2), and (3) he received a full hearing on his motion to withdraw his plea, but he did not provide a reasonable and legitimate reason for withdrawing his plea, despite his claim that he was innocent of the crime, because the only witness who testified on his behalf in this regard, who first said the victim admitted setting defendant up, admitted that defendant paid him to lie, and then the witness asserted his privilege against self-incrimination. State v. Daugherty, — Ohio App. 3d —, 2006 Ohio 2684, — N.E. 2d —, 2006 Ohio App. LEXIS 2518 (May 31, 2006).

Defendant's claim that his trial counsel was ineffective in advising him to plea guilty to voyeurism, in violation of RC § 2907.08(C) and (D)(1), because he had erased the videotape of two minors in the shower prior to watching it and accordingly, he could not have been convicted of the crimes, lacked merit because the crime was committed when he invaded the minors' privacy and videotaped them, whether he viewed the tape or not; accordingly, his motion to withdraw his guilty pleas pursuant to Ohio R. Crim. P. 32.1 was properly summarily denied without a hearing, as there was no manifest injustice. State v. Larimer, — Ohio App. 3d —, 2006 Ohio 3252, — N.E. 2d —, 2006 Ohio App. LEXIS 3144 (June 14, 2006).

Where defendant's arguments to support his post-sentence motion to withdraw his guilty plea pursuant to Ohio R. Crim. P. 32.1 could have and should have been raised in a direct appeal, and he failed to show any "manifest injustice," the trial court's denial of the motion was summarily affirmed on appeal. The court determined that defendant was attempting to use the motion to substitute for an appeal, which was impermissible. State v. Dawson, — Ohio App. 3d —, 2006 Ohio 3503, — N.E. 2d —, 2006 Ohio App. LEXIS 3450 (July 6, 2006).

Trial court did not abuse its discretion in denying defendant's motion to withdraw his plea because nothing in the record suggested that defendant's decision to seek to withdraw his plea was anything more than a change of heart, most likely brought on by his realization that, as a result of the recommendation in the pre-sentence investigation report, he was not going to be sentenced to community control sanctions, but to incarceration in prison. There was no error in finding that defendant's testimony that he did not understand the significance of the language used in the colloquy was not credible as the pressure that led him to plead guilty was the fear of losing the case. State v. Lellock, — Ohio App. 3d —, 2006 Ohio 4515, — N.E. 2d —, 2006 Ohio App. LEXIS 4462 (Sept. 1, 2006).

Trial court did not abuse its discretion in determining that defendant's reason to withdraw her plea was not reasonable nor legitimate because defendant's basis for withdrawing her plea focused on inadmissible evidence, a polygraph examination. Rather, the record revealed that defendant sought to withdraw her plea because she had changed her mind. State v. Apple-Wright, — Ohio App. 3d —, 2006 Ohio 5805, — N.E. 2d —, 2006 Ohio App. LEXIS 5784 (Nov. 6, 2006).

Trial court did not err in overruling defendant's Crim. R. 32.1 motion as a majority of the Fish factors weighed against allowing defendant to withdraw his guilty plea. The State would have been prejudiced since the two alleged victims were reluctant witnesses, defendant was afforded the representation of three different, competent counsel, the trial court gave full and fair consideration to the motion, and it was clear that defendant understood the nature of the charges and potential sentences as reflected by his signature on the detailed Ohio R. Crim. P. 11 plea agreement. State v. Banks, — Ohio App. 3d —, 2006 Ohio 5836, — N.E. 2d —, 2006 Ohio App. LEXIS 5800 (Oct. 31, 2006).

Withdrawal of guilty plea

Trial court did not abuse its discretion in denying defendant's pre-sentence motions under Ohio R. Crim. P. 32.1 to withdraw his guilty pleas to various charges, as the trial court found that defendant was properly advised, he understood his rights, his plea was entered on the record, he had conferred with his counsel regarding his potential defenses, and the State was prejudiced by the time lapse that occurred when defendant fled the State. There was no showing that defendant's counsel was not competent in his representation of defendant pursuant to defendant's rights under U.S. Const. amend. VI and Ohio Const. art. I, § 10, as he negotiated the plea deal and investigated the potential witnesses, and a statement that the victim was shot in the head rather than the chest was not incompetence. State v. Carpenter, — Ohio App. 3d —, 2007 Ohio 3798, — N.E. 2d —, 2007 Ohio App. LEXIS 3456 (July 20, 2007).

Defendant's post-sentence motion to withdraw his guilty plea was properly denied because defendant failed to establish a manifest injustice, in that, while the trial court noted that it was inclined, prior to the sentencing hearing, to impose 10 days of work release, the trial court never promised such a sentence. Further, even assuming that the record supported defendant's assertion that there was an agreement with the trial court whereby defendant's ex-wife would have no involvement in the preparation of the presentence investigation (PSI), the record supported the trial court's finding that the PSI was totally unaffected by any actions of the ex-wife. State v. Glass, — Ohio App. 3d —, 2006 Ohio 229, — N.E. 2d —, 2006 Ohio App. LEXIS 184 (Jan. 24, 2006).

Defendant's presentence Ohio R. Crim. P. 32.1 motion to withdraw his guilty plea was properly denied because defendant failed to offer any evidentiary basis for his claim of innocence, and thus, the motion was based merely on defendant's change of heart. The record showed that defense counsel was highly competent, that defendant was given a full Ohio R. Crim. P. 11 hearing prior to entering his guilty plea, that he was provided with an impartial hearing on the motion to withdraw, and that the trial court fully and fairly considered his motion to withdraw his plea. State v. Scott, — Ohio App. 3d —, 2006 Ohio 3875, — N.E. 2d —, 2006 Ohio App. LEXIS 3827 (July 28, 2006).

Withdrawal warranted

Given the substance of the witnesses' unrebutted testimony and its potential to exculpate defendant, the trial court abused its discretion when it denied the motion to withdraw the plea. The witnesses' testimony coupled with defendant's continued denials of harming the baby were significant enough to constitute a reasonable and legitimate basis for defendant's desire to withdraw his plea. There was no evidence to indicate any reason why either witness would fabricate a story in support of defendant to implicate the injured child's mother. State v. Wheeland, — Ohio App. 3d —, 2007 Ohio 1213, — N.E. 2d —, 2007 Ohio App. LEXIS 1137 (Mar. 19, 2007).

Under the circumstances, especially given a legitimate argument that defendant was not guilty and the admitted fact that he was lapsing into periods of being incomprehensible, the trial court should have allowed defendant to withdraw his guilty plea prior to sentencing. The events at the time of the plea and soon thereafter raised serious questions about defendant's clarity of mind and the incomprehensible document he filed pro se 11 days later raised serious questions about his mental health and sobriety. State v. Sellers, — Ohio App. 3d —, 2007 Ohio 4523, — N.E. 2d —, 2007 Ohio App. LEXIS 4057 (Sept. 4, 2007).

Defendant's presentence Ohio R. Crim. P. 32.1 motion to withdraw his guilty plea should have been granted. Defendant could not be convicted of escape, arising out of his violation of post-release control, because he was not under a valid form of detention when the charge arose, in that post-release control was improperly imposed on him because there was no provision for post-release control in his original sentencing entry. State v. North, — Ohio App. 3d —, — N.E. 2d —, 2007 Ohio App. LEXIS 4755 (Oct. 9, 2007).

Trial court erred by denying defendant's presentence motions to withdraw his no contest plea to injuring animals because the motions were based upon newly discovered evidence, which was material to the issue of defendant's guilt. The uncontested evidence established that defendant was not given expert reports that suggested that he may not have caused the extensive injuries to the dog at the time that he entered his no contest plea and, instead of granting the motions, the trial court engaged in a weighing of inadmissible evidence and concluded that defendant was, in fact, guilty. State v. Lausin, — Ohio App. 3d —, 2006 Ohio 5649, — N.E. 2d —, 2006 Ohio App. LEXIS 5648 (Oct. 27, 2006).

Trial court erred in denying defendant's motion to vacate his guilty pleas because, at the time of the pleas, the trial court failed to inform defendant that his pleas were complete admissions, as required by Ohio Traf. R. 10(B). Moreover, defendant proceeded without counsel and was not informed of a mandatory license suspension. State v. Neff, — Ohio App. 3d —, 2006 Ohio 6608, — N.E. 2d —, 2006 Ohio App. LEXIS 6520 (Dec. 8, 2006).

RULE 32.2. Presentence Investigation

In felony cases the court shall, and in misdemeanor cases the court may, order a presentence investigation and report before imposing community control sanctions or granting probation.

History: Amended, eff 7-1-76; 7-1-98.

NOTES TO DECISIONS

ANALYSIS

Credit for pretrial confinement and detention
Ineligibility for probation
Plea agreement
Presentence investigation
Probation violation
Review by defense counsel

Credit for pretrial confinement and detention

Trial court did not err in failing to award jail time credit in each of defendant's concurrent sentences of imprisonment, as based on judicial precedent and Ohio R. Crim. P. 32.2(D) and RC § 2967.191, duplicate pretrial detention credit was not intended by the legislature. Defendant's claim that such failure constituted a violation of his equal protection rights under U.S. Const. amend. XIV lacked merit where there was no evidence and no allegations of purposeful or intentional discrimination. State v. Fugate, — Ohio App. 3d —, 2006 Ohio 5748, — N.E. 2d —, 2006 Ohio App. LEXIS 5706 (Nov. 2, 2006).

Ineligibility for probation

Trial court did not abuse its discretion by failing to grant a continuance for a presentence investigation because defendant was not eligible for probation. Ohio v. Furr, — Ohio App. 3d —, 2007 Ohio 5548, — N.E. 2d —, 2007 Ohio App. LEXIS 4881 (Oct. 16, 2007).

Plea agreement

Where defendant entered into a plea agreement and the trial court immediately sentenced him pursuant to defendant's request after acceptance of his plea, there was no requirement that the trial court order a presentence report pursuant to RC § 2951.03 or Ohio R. Crim. P. 32.2(A). A sentence imposed upon a plea agreement was not subject to review pursuant to RC § 2953.08(D). State v. McIntire, — Ohio App. 3d —, 2006 Ohio 2118, — N.E. 2d —, 2006 Ohio App. LEXIS 1957 (Apr. 28, 2006).

Presentence investigation

Trial court's imposition of a maximum term of imprisonment on defendant was proper where defendant failed to rebut the presumption that the trial court considered the factors under RC § 2929.12(C) in making its sentencing determination. There was no presentence investigation report required pursuant to Ohio R. Crim. P. 32.2, as defendant was sentenced to a term of incarceration rather than to community control sanctions or to probation. State v. Exline, — Ohio App. 3d —, 2007 Ohio 272, — N.E. 2d —, 2007 Ohio App. LEXIS 258 (Jan. 25, 2007).

As defendant was sentenced to a prison term, there was no requirement that a presentence investigation report be ordered; pursuant to Ohio R. Crim. P. 32.2, such report was only mandated when the court imposed community control sanctions or probation. State v. Alvarez, — Ohio App. 3d —, 2007 Ohio 3114, — N.E. 2d —, 2007 Ohio App. LEXIS 2870 (June 22, 2007).

As defendant was subject to a mandatory prison term for firearm specifications, and the trial court did not consider placing him on probation or community control sanctions for the underlying offenses as evideced by its imposition of maximum, consecutive sentences, Ohio R. Crim. P. 32.2 did not apply and the trial court was not required to order a presentence investigation. Such an investigation was only applicable where either community control sanctions or probation were at issue. State v. Smith, — Ohio App. 3d —, 2007 Ohio 3129, — N.E. 2d —, 2007 Ohio App. LEXIS 2885 (June 25, 2007).

Trial court's failure to order a mental health evaluation along with a presentence investigation report was not error where community control sanctions were not imposed, pursuant to Ohio R. Crim. P. 32.2; further, there was no indication that defendant was not competent to enter his guilty pleas pursuant to RC § 2945.37(G), as he indicated that although he took medication for a mental condition, there was nothing that affected his ability to understand the plea. State v. Johnson, — Ohio App. 3d —, 2006 Ohio 4934, — N.E. 2d —, 2006 Ohio App. LEXIS 4866 (Sept. 22, 2006).

Probation violation

Defendant's due process rights under U.S. Const. amend. XIV and Ohio Const. art. I, § 10 were not violated where his community control was revoked upon his conviction of an uncounseled first-degree misdemeanor theft, as the original term of imprisonment was imposed upon him; accordingly, there was no violation of Ohio R. Crim. P. 44(B) and 32.2(C). State v. Isles, — Ohio App. 3d —, 2006 Ohio 6567, — N.E. 2d —, 2006 Ohio App. LEXIS 6477 (Dec. 11, 2006).

Review by defense counsel

Pursuant to Ohio R. Crim. P. 32.2 and RC § 2951.03(B)(1) and (2), defendant was not denied the opportunity to challenge his presentence investigation report where the record indicated that a copy of the report was made available for him and his counsel to review and he indicated, in response to questioning by the trial court, that the report contained no factual inaccuracies. State v. Salce, — Ohio App. 3d —, 2007 Ohio 3687, — N.E. 2d —, 2007 Ohio App. LEXIS 3390 (July 20, 2007).

RULE 32.3.   Revocation of Community Release

(A) **Hearing.** The court shall not impose a prison term for violation of the conditions of a community control sanction or revoke probation except after a hearing at which the defendant shall be present and apprised of the grounds on which action is proposed. The defendant may be admitted to bail pending hearing.

(B) **Counsel.** The defendant shall have the right to be represented by retained counsel and shall be so advised. Where a defendant convicted of a serious offense is unable to obtain counsel, counsel shall be assigned to represent the defendant, unless the defendant after being fully advised of his or her right to assigned counsel, knowingly, intelligently, and voluntarily waives the right to counsel. Where a defendant convicted of a petty offense is unable to obtain counsel, the court may assign counsel to represent the defendant.

(C) **Confinement in petty offense cases.** If confinement after conviction was precluded by Crim. R. 44(B), revocation of probation shall not result in confinement.

If confinement after conviction was not precluded by Crim. R. 44(B), revocation of probation shall not result in confinement unless, at the revocation hearing, there is compliance with Crim. R. 44(B).

(D) **Waiver of counsel.** Waiver of counsel shall be as prescribed in Crim. R. 44(C).

History: Amended, eff 7-1-98.

NOTES TO DECISIONS

ANALYSIS

Notice of hearing
Revocation hearing
Right to confront witnesses
Right to counsel

Notice of hearing

Trial court violated defendant's due process right to receive notice of her alleged probation violation and hearing by failing to provide the requisite notice under CrimR 32.3(A). The record reflected no evidence that defendant received notice that a probation revocation proceeding was pending against her or that such a hearing was to be held; the record also did not show that the trial court notified defendant that the preliminary hearing regarding her pending felony of permitting child abuse would also constitute her probation revocation hearing. State v. Hutchins, — Ohio App. 3d —, 2007 Ohio 6020, — N.E. 2d —, 2007 Ohio App. LEXIS 5296 (Nov. 13, 2007).

Revocation hearing

Trial court complied with Ohio R. Crim. P. 32.3 before revoking defendant's community control as defendant was given the opportunity for a hearing at which he was present and represented by counsel. Defendant did not have to be afforded the full panoply of rights given a defendant in a criminal proceeding at a community control revocation hearing. State v. Bond, — Ohio App. 3d —, 2006 Ohio 470, — N.E. 2d —, 2006 Ohio App. LEXIS 421 (Feb. 3, 2006).

Defendant's failure to perform his community service could only have been characterized as indirect contempt, and a trial court erred where it failed to properly charge defendant with indirect contempt, but, rather, the procedure more resembled a proceeding in direct contempt, which was not appropriate given nature of defendant's dereliction. State v. Daugherty, 165 Ohio App. 3d 115, 2006 Ohio 240, 844 N.E. 2d 1236, 2006 Ohio App. LEXIS 197 (Jan. 13, 2006).

As Ohio R. Crim. P. 11(C)(2) was inapplicable to defendant's community control violation proceeding and the record supported a determination that the trial court complied with Ohio R. Crim. P. 32.3(A), the revocation of defendant's community control sanction due to violations thereof was proper; there was nothing in the record to suggest that defendant did not understand the consequences of her no contest plea. State v. Alexander, — Ohio App. 3d —, — N.E. 2d —, 2007 Ohio App. LEXIS 4807 (Oct. 12, 2007).

Right to confront witnesses

Defendant had the right to cross-examine witnesses during two probable cause hearings on probation violations filed against him after his misdemeanor conviction, but a statement that he made to the court during the probable cause hearings constituted a waiver of that right. State v. Cogar, — Ohio App. 3d —, 2006 Ohio 5218, — N.E. 2d —, 2006 Ohio App. LEXIS 5194 (Sept. 29, 2006).

Right to counsel

Trial court's judgment revoking defendant's community control was reversed because (1) defendant was unrepresented at the community control revocation hearing, (2) the trial court did not advise defendant that defendant had the right to be represented by retained counsel, under Ohio R. Crim. P. 32.3(B), (3) the trial court did not inquire into defendant's ability to retain counsel, and (4) there was no evidence that defendant had waived counsel. Ohio v. Roger W. Lemley, — Ohio App. 3d —, 2007 Ohio 5257, — N.E. 2d —, 2007 Ohio App. LEXIS 4646 (Sept. 28, 2007).

Failure to appoint counsel for defendant or to allow him to have counsel of his choice did not violate his right to counsel under Ohio R. Crim. P. 32.3 on two probable cause hearings on probation violations filed against him to which Ohio R. Crim. P. 44(B) applied because he had been convicted of misdemeanor assault. The right to counsel did not attach until the dispositional hearing because the probable cause hearings were not the final determination of the probation violations, and defendant was represented by counsel during his dispositional hearing. State v. Cogar, — Ohio App. 3d —, 2006 Ohio 5218, — N.E. 2d —, 2006 Ohio App. LEXIS 5194 (Sept. 29, 2006).

RULE 33. New Trial

(A) **Grounds.** A new trial may be granted on motion of the defendant for any of the following causes affecting materially his substantial rights:

(1) Irregularity in the proceedings, or in any order or ruling of the court, or abuse of discretion by the court, because of which the defendant was prevented from having a fair trial;

(2) Misconduct of the jury, prosecuting attorney, or the witnesses for the state;

(3) Accident or surprise which ordinary prudence could not have guarded against;

(4) That the verdict is not sustained by sufficient evidence or is contrary to law. If the evidence shows the defendant is not guilty of the degree of crime for which he was convicted, but guilty of a lesser degree thereof, or of a lesser crime included therein, the court may modify the verdict or finding accordingly, without granting or ordering a new trial, and shall pass sentence on such verdict or finding as modified;

(5) Error of law occurring at the trial;

(6) When new evidence material to the defense is discovered, which the defendant could not with reasonable diligence have discovered and produced at the trial. When a motion for a new trial is made upon the ground of newly discovered evidence, the defendant must produce at the hearing on the motion, in support thereof, the affidavits of the witnesses by whom such evidence is expected to be given, and if time is required by the defendant to procure such affidavits, the court may postpone the hearing of the motion for such length of time as is reasonable under all the circumstances of the case. The prosecuting attorney may produce affidavits or other evidence to impeach the affidavits of such witnesses.

(B) **Motion for new trial; form, time.** Application for a new trial shall be made by motion which, except for the cause of newly discovered evidence, shall be filed within fourteen days after the verdict was rendered, or the decision of the court where a trial by jury has been waived, unless it is made to appear by clear and convincing proof that the defendant was unavoidably prevented from filing his motion for a new trial, in which case the motion shall be filed within seven days from the order of the court finding that the defendant was unavoidably prevented from filing such motion within the time provided herein.

Motions for new trial on account of newly discovered evidence shall be filed within one hundred twenty days after the day upon which the verdict was rendered, or the decision of the court where trial by jury has been waived. If it is made to appear by clear and convincing proof that the defendant was unavoidably prevented from the discovery of the evidence upon which he must rely, such motion shall be filed within seven days from an order of the court finding that he was unavoidably prevented from discovering the evidence within the one hundred twenty day period.

(C) **Affidavits required.** The causes enumerated in subsection (A)(2) and (3) must be sustained by affidavit showing their truth, and may be controverted by affidavit.

(D) **Procedure when new trial granted.** When a new trial is granted by the trial court, or when a new trial is awarded on appeal, the accused shall stand trial upon the charge or charges of which he was convicted.

(E) **Invalid grounds for new trial.** No motion for

a new trial shall be granted or verdict set aside, nor shall any judgment of conviction be reversed in any court because of:

(1) An inaccuracy or imperfection in the indictment, information, or complaint, provided that the charge is sufficient to fairly and reasonably inform the defendant of all the essential elements of the charge against him.

(2) A variance between the allegations and the proof thereof, unless the defendant is misled or prejudiced thereby;

(3) The admission or rejection of any evidence offered against or for the defendant, unless the defendant was or may have been prejudiced thereby;

(4) A misdirection of the jury, unless the defendant was or may have been prejudiced thereby;

(5) Any other cause, unless it affirmatively appears from the record that the defendant was prejudiced thereby or was prevented from having a fair trial.

(F) **Motion for new trial not a condition for appellate review.** A motion for a new trial is not a prerequisite to obtain appellate review.

NOTES TO DECISIONS

ANALYSIS

Abuse of discretion
Affidavits
Appeal
Appeal by state
Appealable orders
Appointment of expert
Brady violation
Denial of motion for new trial
Disclosure by prosecutor
Due process
Failure to disclose information
Handcuffs
Ineffective assistance of counsel
Jurisdiction
Juror misconduct
Jury instructions
Jury issues generally
Lesser included offenses
Misconduct by prosecutor
Mistrial
Motion denied
Motion for new trial
New trial
Newly discovered evidence
— Motion denied
Procedure
Recantation by victim
Recantation by witness
Sufficiency of evidence
Time limit
Untimely motion
Variance from indictment, etc.
Verdict against weight of evidence
Verdict modification
Waiver of jury trial

Abuse of discretion

When a trial court approved defendant's request to retain a forensic expert, reserving ruling regarding the amount of payment because no specific expert was named nor was a fee schedule provided, it was not an abuse of discretion entitling defendant to a new trial, under Ohio R. Crim. P. 33(A)(1), for the trial court to decline to release funds for this purpose because he did not retain the approved expert, and the evidence did not weigh heaviliy in his favor, nor was there any indication that a different result would have been reached had he pursued and retained the approved expert. State v. Williams, — Ohio App. 3d —, 2007 Ohio 212, — N.E. 2d —, 2007 Ohio App. LEXIS 211 (Jan. 19, 2007).

Affidavits

When defendant filed a "Motion for Summary Judgment ew Trial/Modify Sentence," based on newly discovered evidence, it was not an abuse of discretion to deny the motion if it was considered as a motion for new trial because it was not supported by affidavits from witnesses stating what the new evidence was, as required by Ohio R. Crim. P. 33(A)(6), as defendant merely relied on case law decided since his conviction and sentence became final, and he was actually seeking to correct his sentence based on the premise that his constitutional rights had been violated. State v. Abbott, — Ohio App. 3d —, 2006 Ohio 2398, — N.E. 2d —, 2006 Ohio App. LEXIS 2269 (May 15, 2006).

Appeal

Defendant's appeal was premature because the journal entry required by Ohio R. Crim. P. 32(C) sentencing defendant after his conviction of inciting to violence under RC § 2917.01(A) was not in the record on appeal; the record also did not reflect that the trial court had ruled on defendant's Ohio R. Crim. P. 33 motion for new trial and, thus, the time for appeal had not begun to run under Ohio R. App. P. 4(B)(3). State v. Turner, — Ohio App. 3d —, 2007 Ohio 3264, — N.E. 2d —, 2007 Ohio App. LEXIS 3015 (June 28, 2007).

Appeal by state

Because the state did not file a brief in opposition to defendant's motion for leave to file a motion for a new trial and/or file any objections to the trial court's order granting leave, the state forfeited any argument as to the propriety of the trial court's determination that defendant was entitled to move for a new trial based on newly discovered evidence. State v. Covender, — Ohio App. 3d —, 2008 Ohio 1453, — N.E. 2d —, 2008 Ohio App. LEXIS 1281 (Mar. 31, 2008).

State's motion for leave to file an appeal, under RC § 2945.67(A) was denied because the trial court had jurisdiction to hear defendant's motion for a new trial under Ohio R. Crim. P. 33(A)(6) based on newly discovered evidence and it did not err in finding that the forensic pathologist's changed testimony created a strong probability of a different outcome. The forensic pathologist's prior testimony that some of the victim's knife wounds were healing for an hour before his death was very strong evidence that the killer waited an hour to kill him and thus, absent such evidence, it was not unreasonable, arbitrary, or unconscionable for the trial court to determine that a different outcome was a strong probability. State v. Burke, — Ohio App. 3d —, 2006 Ohio 4597, — N.E. 2d —, 2006 Ohio App. LEXIS 4540 (Sept. 7, 2006).

Appealable orders

Defendant's appeal was premature because the journal entry required by Ohio R. Crim. P. 32(C) sentencing defendant after his conviction of inciting to violence under RC § 2917.01(A) was not in the record on appeal. The record also did not reflect that the trial court had ruled on defendant's Ohio R. Crim. P. 33 motion for new trial and, thus, the time for appeal had not begun to run under Ohio R. App. P. 4(B)(3). State v. Turner, — Ohio App. 3d —, 2007 Ohio 3264, — N.E. 2d —, 2007 Ohio App. LEXIS 3015 (June 28, 2007).

Appointment of expert

Trial court erred by denying defendant's motion for a new trial because the trial court erred by failing to appoint an eyewitness-identification expert. The State's case was based primarily on one person's identification of defendant as the robber, and that person was under the stress of having been accosted at gunpoint. Under such circumstances, eyewitness identification could be untrustworthy and the State produced no fingerprint or other physical evidence tying defendant to the crime. State v. Sargent, — Ohio App. 3d —, 2006 Ohio 6823, — N.E. 2d —, 2006 Ohio App. LEXIS 6736 (Dec. 22, 2006).

Brady violation

Determination that defendant was not entitled to a new trial on a murder charge was correct because the jury was presumed to have followed the curative instruction given by the trial court after an investigator made an isolated comment about defendant's arrest on another unrelated charge and also because the exculpatory evidence defendant argued was not disclosed to him had either not been disclosed to the prosecution either or it was properly determined that the evidence was not exculpatory. State v. Babos, — Ohio App. 3d —, 2007 Ohio 2393, — N.E. 2d —, 2007 Ohio App. LEXIS 2253 (May 18, 2007).

Defendant's due process rights under Ohio Const. art. I, § 10 were not violated by the prosecutor's decision to only introduce some of the photographs taken from defendant's criminal conduct and from the victim's apartment, as there was no showing by defendant that the photographs which were not introduced by the prosecutor at trial were favorable to defendant or that the result of the trial would have been different. The trial court's denial of defendant's new trial motion pursuant to Ohio R. Crim. P. 33 on the asserted basis of a Brady violation due to the failure to admit all of the photographs was proper. State v. Bevins, — Ohio App. 3d —, 2006 Ohio 6974, — N.E. 2d —, 2006 Ohio App. LEXIS 6936 (Dec. 29, 2006).

County court properly denied defendant's motion, pursuant to Ohio R. Crim. P. 33, for a new trial on a criminal charge of domestic violence because the submission offered by defendant in support of his motion fell short of establishing a violation of Brady v. Maryland, in that defendant's allegations that the State failed to disclose evidence of the complaining witness's prior convictions were laced with speculation. Defendant merely alleged that his wife "may" have been convicted of passing bad checks and that there "may" have been a warrant for her arrest. State v. Tietge, — Ohio App. 3d —, 2006 Ohio 236, — N.E. 2d —, 2006 Ohio App. LEXIS 200 (Jan. 13, 2006).

Denial of motion for new trial

There was no abuse of discretion in a trial court's denial of defendant's new trial motion, as his alleged new evidence from an eyewitness to the criminal incident for which defendant was convicted was not deemed reliable, as the statements of the eyewitness conflicted with a taped statement that he had given to police with respect to the investigation of a different crime. As the requirements of Petro were not satisfied, a new trial was not warranted. State v. Bell, — Ohio App. 3d —, 2007 Ohio 310, — N.E. 2d —, 2007 Ohio App. LEXIS 282 (Jan. 26, 2007).

Defendant's motion for a new trial pursuant to Ohio R. Crim. P. 33(A)(3) and (6) was properly denied by a trial court where an individual indicated that he was actually the co-defendant who had walked on the city bus behind defendant, had carried an allegedly toy gun that had terrorized the passengers and the bus driver, and that the named co-defendant was not involved in the incident. The statement that the gun was a toy was self-serving, and there was no reasonable likelihood that the "newly discovered evidence" as to the identity of the co-defendant would have changed the outcome of the trial with respect to defendant's convictions. State v. Mincy, — Ohio App. 3d —, 2007 Ohio 1316, — N.E. 2d —, 2007 Ohio App. LEXIS 1212 (Mar. 23, 2007).

Defendant's motions for a new trial were properly overruled. The fact that defendant might have had a witness who could have corroborated his testimony did not affect the sufficiency of the evidence the State presented at trial and the existence of uncalled witnesses did not establish that defendant's convictions were contrary to law. Also, defendant failed to demonstrate how defense counsel's failure to request separate trial dates for the two cases against him fit within the grounds for a new trial provided by Ohio R. Crim. P. 33(A)(4) or (A)(6). City of Beavercreek v. Levalley, — Ohio App. 3d —, 2007 Ohio 2105, — N.E. 2d —, 2007 Ohio App. LEXIS 1960 (Apr. 27, 2007).

Trial court's denial of defendant's motion for a new trial under Ohio R. Crim. P. 33(E) was not an abuse of discretion, as the fact that defendant's original counsel did not raise the defense of "diminished capacity" was not an inexcusable "omission" where that defense was not recognized in Ohio. Defendant had undergone an independent psychological evaluation at the beginning of the proceedings, whereupon it was determined that he was sane at the time that he committed the criminal act and he was competent to stand trial. State v. Thomas, — Ohio App. 3d —, 2006 Ohio 280, — N.E. 2d —, 2006 Ohio App. LEXIS 253 (Jan. 26, 2006).

Defendant failed to demonstrate sufficient grounds to warrant the granting of a new trial because the trial court made an extensive record following defendant's motion for a mistrial on the subject of the preparation and assembly of the photo arrays by the police. The confusion, if any, regarding photo arrays appeared to have been caused by defense counsel's review of the discovery materials and his misreading of them; the record made by the trial court adequately addressed the fact that there was no irregularity in the proceedings caused by this procedure. State v. Barringer, — Ohio App. 3d —, 2006 Ohio 2649, — N.E. 2d —, 2006 Ohio App. LEXIS 2497 (May 26, 2006).

Trial court did not err when it denied defendant's motion for a new trial because the evidence she cited as the basis for her motion for new trial was provided to her prior to trial and thus, could not be the basis for granting a motion for new trial based on newly discovered evidence. Further, because it had been determined that the prosecutor did not commit misconduct, the prosecutor's conduct in providing the challenged evidence two days prior to the commencement of trial also did not support defendant's motion for new trial. State v. Duffy, — Ohio App. 3d —, 2006 Ohio 2724, — N.E. 2d —, 2006 Ohio App. LEXIS 2578 (June 1, 2006).

Trial court did not abuse its discretion in denying defendant's new trial motion pursuant to Ohio R. Crim. P. 33(A)(6), based on his claim that he was unaware that a scoring official at a youth athletic event would testify as a rebuttal witness until after another witness had testified, which violated Ohio R. Crim. P. 16, and that defendant had discovered new evidence that would have impeached the rebuttal witness's testimony, as the trial court could have concluded that defendant could have discovered the evidence that the rebuttal witness was biased against another witness before the trial, and it could have further determined that the new evidence would not have changed the result of his disorderly conduct trial, based on other witnesses' versions of events. City of Urbana v. Locke, — Ohio App. 3d —, 2006 Ohio 6606, — N.E. 2d —, 2006 Ohio App. LEXIS 6518 (Dec. 8, 2006).

Disclosure by prosecutor

Trial court did not err when it overruled defendant's motion for a new trial because, other than his bare assertion, defendant failed to provide any evidence that the police department incident report was not included in the State's discovery materials. More importantly, defendant did not even attempt to provide any evidence that clearly and convincingly demonstrated that he was prevented from or otherwise unable to procure the incident report within 120 days of his guilty verdict. State v. Greenwood, — Ohio App. 3d —, 2007 Ohio 4202, — N.E. 2d —, 2007 Ohio App. LEXIS 3787 (Aug. 17, 2007).

Due process

Due process considerations arising from an appearance of unfairness required reversal of a conviction under RC § 2903.21 where the trial court entered a guilty verdict and then five minutes later recused himself from sentencing the defendant: State v. Ludt, 180 Ohio App. 3d 672, 2009 Ohio 416, 906 N.E.2d 1182, 2009 Ohio App. LEXIS 342 (2009).

Failure to disclose information

Where the trial court never determined whether the State failed to comply with defendant's discovery request pursuant to Ohio R. Crim. P. 16(B)(1)(g) for production of statements of two witnesses for the State, the trial court did not err in denying defendant's motion for sanctions, including a mistrial or exclusion of the witness testimony, pursuant to Rule 16(E)(3), as the sanctions allowed therein were only trigged upon a determination that there was a failure to comply; it was noted that the State had indicated that it did not believe that such statements were in fact in existence, and there was no cause to grant a new trial or mistrial pursuant to Ohio R. Crim. P. 33(E)(3), as defendant failed to show that he was prejudiced. State v. Scott, — Ohio App. 3d —, 2006 Ohio 3527, — N.E. 2d —, 2006 Ohio App. LEXIS 3479 (June 29, 2006).

Handcuffs

Trial court's denial of defendant's motion for a mistrial was not error where two jurors inadvertently saw defendant in shackles and handcuffs, as they were both questioned about the incident and indicated that their fairness and impartiality was not in jeopardy; their view of defendant was brief, it was outside of the courtroom, and no prejudice was shown that would have impaired defendant's right to a fair trial. State v. Johnson, — Ohio App. 3d —, 2006 Ohio 5195, — N.E. 2d —, 2006 Ohio App. LEXIS 5120 (Oct. 2, 2006).

Ineffective assistance of counsel

Defendant failed to show that his counsel was ineffective, in violation of his rights under U.S. Const. amend. VI and Ohio Const. art. I, § 10, in failing to request a jury trial in defendant's criminal matter, as counsel testified that she discussed the options with defendant and recommended that he have a jury trial but that he opted to have a bench trial instead, and further, defendant was well-educated and it was reasonable to conclude that he was aware of his jury trial right; accordingly, the denial of his new trial motion under Ohio R. Crim. P. 33 based on his counsel's alleged ineffectiveness in that regard was proper. City of E. Cleveland v. Arnett, — Ohio App. 3d —, 2007 Ohio 5075, — N.E. 2d —, 2007 Ohio App. LEXIS 4480 (Sept. 27, 2007).

Defense counsel was not ineffective for failing to seek new trial on three affirmed convictions after several other convictions were vacated; defendant failed to support his claim that the jury was possibly swayed to convict defendant by cumulative effect of the multiple charges, the evidence supported affirmed convictions, and the law of the case doctrine prevented counsel from seeking new trial. State v. Kelly, — Ohio App. 3d —, 2007 Ohio 6838, — N.E. 2d —, 2007 Ohio App. LEXIS 5980 (Dec. 20, 2007).

There was no error in denying defendant's Ohio R. Crim. P. 33(A)(1) and (5) motion for a new trial or in the determination that there was no ineffective assistance of counsel because the trial court found that the attorney did properly advise defendant of the deportation consequences of a domestic violence conviction. Although defendant declined the plea bargain and did not testify at trial, she exercised her rights to a trial before an impartial finder of fact. State v. Lei, — Ohio App. 3d —, 2006 Ohio 2608, — N.E. 2d —, 2006 Ohio App. LEXIS 2434 (May 25, 2006).

Jurisdiction

Because defendant's appeal was pending when the trial court ruled on his motion for a new trial, the trial court had no jurisdiction to rule on the motion. Accordingly, the trial court erred not only in denying the motion, but in subsequently denying the motion to vacate its ruling on the motion for a new trial. State v. Abboud, — Ohio App. 3d —, 2006 Ohio 6587, — N.E. 2d —, 2006 Ohio App. LEXIS 6492 (Dec. 14, 2006).

Juror misconduct

Trial court did not abuse its discretion in denying defendant's new trial motion under Ohio R. Crim. P. 33 based on juror misconduct, as the fact that one juror failed to disclose, upon convoluted and confusing questioning during voir dire, that one of her brothers had shot another brother, did not result in an impartial trial in violation of defendant's Ohio Const. art. I, § 10 rights. As her sentiments arising from that family incident could have made her more aligned with either party, and there was extensive questioning, none of which supported a determination that the juror was biased or that she was unable to weigh the evidence without partiality. State v. Jeffers, — Ohio App. 3d —, 2007 Ohio 3213, — N.E. 2d —, 2007 Ohio App. LEXIS 2830 (June 21, 2007).

Court refused to consider whether a juror's failure to list her family on the juror questionnaire constituted misconduct and warranted a new trial under Ohio R. Crim. P. 33(A)(2) because defendant failed to bring this omission to the trial court's attention during the jury selection process and, thus, waived his right to raise that issue on appeal. State v. Coleman, — Ohio App. 3d —, 2006 Ohio 3200, — N.E. 2d —, 2006 Ohio App. LEXIS 3093 (June 20, 2006).

Trial court did not abuse its discretion in overruling defendant's motion for a new trial on the ground of juror misconduct. While a juror's affidavit was submitted averring that she overheard another juror stating that criminals like defendant were taking up her time, the juror's actions did not reach the point of becoming misconduct since it occurred after the evidence had been presented, and even so, the conduct did not materially affect defendant's substantial rights. State v. Jordan, — Ohio App. 3d —, 2006 Ohio 3425, — N.E. 2d —, 2006 Ohio App. LEXIS 3360 (June 30, 2006).

Defendant was not entitled to a new trial because it was not shown that his jury was exposed to or influenced by any improper statements by third parties. State v. Turner, 168 Ohio App. 3d 176, 2006 Ohio 3786, 858 N.E. 2d 1249, 2006 Ohio App. LEXIS 3723 (July 21, 2006).

Defendant's self-serving affidavit claiming juror misconduct did not entitle him to a new trial because the affidavit claimed a juror knew two defense witnesses but did not assert that defendant had personal knowledge that the juror knew these witnesses, only asserting he had "knowledge" of the facts alleged in his affidavit, and the testimony of these witnesses had a limited impact on the trial, as it was not about the transaction leading to the marijuana trafficking charge against defendant. State v. Wood, — Ohio App. 3d —, 2006 Ohio 3781, — N.E. 2d —, 2006 Ohio App. LEXIS 3732 (July 24, 2006).

Jury instructions

Defendant's motion for a new trial was properly denied. There was no prejudice to defendant from the jury instruction because the instruction as given placed the entire burden of proof on the State, noting that it was beyond a reasonable doubt, and no burden was placed upon defendant. State v. Williams, — Ohio App. 3d —, 2007 Ohio 4845, — N.E. 2d —, 2007 Ohio App. LEXIS 4329 (Sept. 20, 2007).

Jury issues generally

There was no error in refusing to grant a new trial because defendant, during trial, expressly waived any objection to the juror on the basis of the overheard conversation. With respect to whether the juror was one of defendant's drug customers, even if that were true, it was information uniquely in the possession of defendant during voir dire and at trial; thus, that defendant sought to exploit the information after conviction was invited error. State v. Benton, — Ohio App. 3d —, 2007 Ohio 3945, — N.E. 2d —, 2007 Ohio App. LEXIS 3625 (Aug. 3, 2007).

Lesser included offenses

Although there was sufficient evidence to support the six counts of vaginal rape, as well as the six counts of rape by cunnilingus, and the six counts of gross sexual imposition, because the prosecution failed to present any evidence that defendant digitally penetrated the 12-year-old victim's vagina, the evidence was insufficient to support the six charges of rape by digital vaginal penetration and the verdict was modified to convictions for gross sexual imposition, as lesser offenses. The victim testified that defendant repeatedly and at least once during each year of the indictment (1) put his penis in her vagina; (2) touched her vagina with his hand or penis; (3) put his tongue on her vagina; and (4) touched her breasts with his hands. State v. Frazier, — Ohio App. 3d —, 2007 Ohio 11, — N.E. 2d —, 2007 Ohio App. LEXIS 6 (Jan. 4, 2007).

State failed to prove that anyone was present or likely to be present during the burglary as the victim worked the 11:00 p.m. to 7:00 a.m. shift, and the burglary, which occurred at 4:00 a.m., occurred near the middle of the victim's shift, not when she would typically be at home. A reasonable jury could not find that someone was objectively "likely to be present" at the home when the burglary occurred. Although the State did not satisfy its burden under RC § 2911.12(A)(2), the evidence supported a conviction under § 2911.12(A)(3), and thus, pursuant to Ohio R. Crim. P. 33(A)(4), the court entered a judgment of conviction on the lesser included offense of third-degree burglary. State v. Miller, — Ohio App. 3d —, 2007 Ohio 2361, — N.E. 2d —, 2007 Ohio App. LEXIS 2196 (May 11, 2007).

Misconduct by prosecutor

Trial court's denial of defendant's motion for new trial under Ohio R. Crim. P. 33(A)(2) was proper where it did not appear that the prosecutor withheld any of the documentation that defendant alleged was not produced for him as there was evidence that the State disclosed what information it had. There was no reasonable likelihood that the material, even if utilized by defendant at trial, would have affected the guilty verdict against him, as the subject evidence would not have undermined confidence in the verdict. State v. Peters, — Ohio App. 3d —, 2007 Ohio 1285, — N.E. 2d —, 2007 Ohio App. LEXIS 1181 (Mar. 22, 2007).

Trial court did not abuse its discretion when it denied defendant's motion for a new trial because there was no prosecutorial misconduct. Because the defense at trial rested on the claim that the detectives had fabricated the statement given to the detective, the prosecutor had attempted to refute that claim in closing argument; regardless, the prosecutor's isolated remark was not so prejudicial as to deprive defendant of a fair trial. State v. Chambers, — Ohio App. 3d —, 2007 Ohio 4732, — N.E. 2d —, 2007 Ohio App. LEXIS 4273 (Sept. 17, 2007).

Defendant, who was convicted of, inter alia, operating a vehicle under the influence of alcohol, did not show defendant was entitled to a new trial under Ohio R. Crim. P. 33(A)(2) due to the prosecutor not informing defendant that the vehicle involved in the crime had been destroyed because defendant did not clearly articulate how the destruction of the vehicle would have rebutted any of the State's evidence, and defendant's speculation that, had defendant known the vehicle was destroyed, defendant would have been able to argue that defendant was denied the opportunity to introduce evidence to rebut the State's evidence or impeach the State's witnesses, did not show how the destruction of the vehicle was

in any way exculpatory, so there was no Brady violation which might have entitled defendant to a new trial. State v. Cummings, — Ohio App. 3d —, 2007 Ohio 4970, — N.E. 2d —, 2007 Ohio App. LEXIS 4386 (Sept. 24, 2007).

Defendant was not entitled to a new trial regarding defendant's prosecution for pandering obscenity involving a minor, under RC § 2907.321(A)(5), based on a claim, under Ohio R. Crim. P. 33(A)(2), that the State did not disclose a document indicating that defendant's internet account was closed because defendant admitted that the information was given to defendant's attorney, so the information was not withheld. Ohio v. King, — Ohio App. 3d —, 2007 Ohio 5297, — N.E. 2d —, 2007 Ohio App. LEXIS 4658 (Sept. 28, 2007).

Statements in a prosecutor's closing argument beginning with "I don't know about you, but if it were me," "I don't believe," "I was quite confused," and "I do know that" were not prosecutorial misconduct entitling defendant to a new trial as such misconduct justified reversal only when it was expressed in such a manner as to permit a jury to infer that the opinion was based on the prosecutor's knowledge of facts outside the record. State v. Wilson, — Ohio App. 3d —, 2006 Ohio 1333, — N.E. 2d —, 2006 Ohio App. LEXIS 1223 (Mar. 23, 2006).

In a prosecution for forgery, Medicaid fraud, and theft, the denial of defendant's motion, under Ohio R. Crim. P. 33(B), for a new trial, claiming, inter alia, that the prosecution, in its memorandum in opposition to the motion, mischaracterized the testimony of an expert witness which was excluded after it was given, was not an abuse of discretion because, if the prosecutor mischaracterized the testimony, it was given in open court, and the trial court could form its own, independent, characterization, so defendant was not prejudiced. State v. Breckenridge, — Ohio App. 3d —, 2006 Ohio 5038, — N.E. 2d —, 2006 Ohio App. LEXIS 5175 (Sept. 28, 2006).

Trial court erred by denying defendant's motion for a new trial because the prosecutor's remarks on defendant's pre-arrest silence were both improper and prejudicial. The prosecutor also impermissibly suggested to the jury that defendant was required to prove his innocence when he told the jury that the defense could have given an alternative version of events. State v. Sargent, — Ohio App. 3d —, 2006 Ohio 6823, — N.E. 2d —, 2006 Ohio App. LEXIS 6736 (Dec. 22, 2006).

Defendant was entitled to a new trial on the basis of prosecutorial misconduct during closing argument where the prosecutor's remarks on the defendant's pre-arrest silence were improper and prejudicial, and another remark impermissibly suggested that the defendant was required to prove his innocence: State v. Sargent, 169 Ohio App. 3d 679, 2006 Ohio 6823, 864 N.E.2d 155, 2006 Ohio App. LEXIS 6736 (2006).

Mistrial

Prosecution's persistent questioning of the mother about other crimes committed by defendant, including asking her about an assault on a police officer charge after being told three times that she could not recall other "criminal situations," clearly deprived defendant of a fair trial. The evidence of other crimes that the prosecutor introduced, none of which was substantiated by documents establishing that other crimes were committed, was offered to demonstrate defendant's bad character and not to prove that he committed the instant offense; the error should have been rectified by granting defendant's motion for a mistrial. State v. Brown, — Ohio App. 3d —, 2007 Ohio 464, — N.E. 2d —, 2007 Ohio App. LEXIS 420 (Feb. 2, 2007).

Trial court did not abuse its discretion in overruling defendant's request for a mistrial because trial counsel failed to call the error (inadvertently omitting the definition of knowingly in the jury instructions) to the trial court's attention at a time when the error could have been corrected or avoided altogether, and the error of which he complained was minor and promptly corrected. Further, the trial court did not commit any error in issuing a Howard charge to the jury because the jury was unable to reach a consensus. State v. Barton, — Ohio App. 3d —, 2007 Ohio 1099, — N.E. 2d —, 2007 Ohio App. LEXIS 1020 (Mar. 12, 2007).

Trial court did not err in refusing to grant a mistrial because the witness merely noted an offer to take, not the actual administration of a polygraph examination. The trial court gave a proper curative instruction it specifically inquired whether the jurors could abide by its order; there was no reason to presume that the jury failed to follow the trial court's admonition. State v. Charley, — Ohio App. 3d —, 2007 Ohio 1108, — N.E. 2d —, 2007 Ohio App. LEXIS 1029 (Mar. 6, 2007).

Trial court did not abuse its discretion when it overruled defendant's motion for a mistrial because defendant did not prove that any member of the jury was biased as a result of one juror's safety concerns. The juror told the judge that he could decide the case based on the facts presented at trial and the juror's concerns would have made him more likely to find defendant not guilty, rather than guilty, since he was afraid of retaliation. Also, the trial court did not abuse its discretion by not questioning each juror, especially in the absence of a request to do so by the defense. State v. Carter, — Ohio App. 3d —, 2007 Ohio 3502, — N.E. 2d —, 2007 Ohio App. LEXIS 3223 (June 29, 2007).

Trial court's decision not to grant a mistrial was not so unreasonable that it amounted to an abuse of discretion because the trial court's actions were reasonably aimed at ensuring that the jury would not consider the facts brought up by one juror (who realized that he knew a witness and became concerned about retaliation) would not be considered during deliberations. Accordingly, the trial court did not abuse its discretion by not questioning each juror, especially in the absence of a request to do so by the defense. State v. Robinson, — Ohio App. 3d —, 2007 Ohio 3501, — N.E. 2d —, 2007 Ohio App. LEXIS 3224 (July 5, 2007).

Trial court did not abuse its discretion when it denied defendant's motion for a mistrial because a mistrial was not warranted since the police sergeant merely made a vague, isolated remark concerning defendant decision to consult counsel. The trial court sustained defense counsel's objection and instructed the jury to disregard the remark and nothing in the record indicated that the prosecution intentionally elicited the remark; that the remark equated silence with guilt; or that the remark harmed defendant in any way. State v. Castle, — Ohio App. 3d —, 2007 Ohio 3599, — N.E. 2d —, 2007 Ohio App. LEXIS 3304 (July 16, 2007).

Trial court did not err when it denied defendant's motion for a new trial because the record did not support defendant's argument that a mistrial was warranted. Nothing in the record indicated that the jurors learned about the bomb threat or the substance of the investigation, nor did anything exist in the record that established that the bomb threat prejudiced defendant in any way. State v. Moore, — Ohio App. 3d —, 2007 Ohio 3600, — N.E. 2d —, 2007 Ohio App. LEXIS 3306 (July 16, 2007).

Trial court did not abuse its discretion by refusing to grant a mistrial because the trial court went to great lengths to ensure that the jury panel was not tainted, despite the actions of defendant and his co-defendants. Evidence showed that they called out to the jurors to see them in their shackles and chains. Once the incident came to the court's attention, the judge questioned every member of the jury panel, actually excused two members, and instructed the remaining jurors that they must not consider any evidence from "outside" the courtroom. State v. Hairston, — Ohio App. 3d —, 2007 Ohio 3707, — N.E. 2d —, 2007 Ohio App. LEXIS 3387 (June 4, 2007).

Denial of defendant's motion for a mistrial was proper because the State provided the defense witness's statement to defendant before the witness was called to testify and, while defendant could have requested a recess or a continuance in order to confer with the witness prior to his taking the stand, defendant did not do so but chose instead to move for a mistrial. Further, the witness's testimony did not differ from his statement; in both his statement to the police and at trial, the witness identified his other friend as the assailant, rather than defendant. State v. Schenker, — Ohio App. 3d —, 2007 Ohio 3732, — N.E. 2d —, 2007 Ohio App. LEXIS 3415 (July 19, 2007).

Trial court erred by failing to grant a mistrial because the comments by the prosecutor could have been read as an impermissible inference of guilt regarding defendant's decision not to testify. Despite the trial judge's stern admonitions, the prosecutor continuously referenced defendant's decision to take the Fifth Amendment on certain matters and thus, defendant's rights were adversely affected and he was denied a fair trial. His conviction and sentence were vacated and a new trial was ordered. State v. Beebe, — Ohio App. 3d —, 2007 Ohio 3746, — N.E. 2d —, 2007 Ohio App. LEXIS 3422 (July 18, 2007).

Trial court did not err by refusing to grant a mistrial because the brief, inadvertent sighting of defendant in restraints was not prejudicial; as the jurors were leaving for lunch, two jurors observed defendant in restraints because defendant and his codefendants began to yell and to make gestures to draw attention to themselves. Once the incident came to the trial court's attention, the judge questioned every member of the jury panel and actually excused two members, and it instructed the remaining jurors not to consider any evidence from "outside" the courtroom. State v. Hairston, — Ohio App. 3d —, 2007 Ohio 3880, — N.E. 2d —, 2007 Ohio App. LEXIS 3519 (July 27, 2007).

There was no abuse of discretion in the trial court's decision to overrule defendant's pre-trial motion for mistrial because defendant did not establish actual bias or prejudice; none of the potential jurors were empaneled to sit on the final jury and defendant cited nothing in the record to demonstrate that the remarks biased or prejudiced the empaneled jurors other than the fact that the remarks occurred. Also, the remarks were not so egregious as to presume to prejudice because, although the incident at the funeral home resulted in media coverage, reading a newspaper article or viewing a television report did not necessarily require a determination that a prospective juror could not be fair and impartial. State v. Hairston, — Ohio App. 3d —, 2007 Ohio 3880, — N.E. 2d —, 2007 Ohio App. LEXIS 3519 (July 27, 2007).

Trial court did not err in refusing to declare a mistrial because the police officer's comments about aliases and/or street names did not rise to the level necessary that would have adversely affected defendant's substantial rights and cause him to receive an unfair trial. It could not be inferred that because defendant allegedly had an alias, he must have had a criminal record. State v. Braun, — Ohio App. 3d —, 2007 Ohio 4578, — N.E. 2d —, 2007 Ohio App. LEXIS 4128 (Sept. 6, 2007).

Trial court did not abuse its discretion when it refused to declare a mistrial because defendant did not demonstrate juror misconduct; the juror came forward with the information, without having discussed it with fellow jurors, and the juror was not even certain that the witness was the same person whom she had known. There was no evidence that the juror had concealed her potential knowledge about the witness during voir dire and the trial court was in the best position to weigh the juror's credibility when she stated that she could remain fair and impartial. State v. McGlothin, — Ohio App. 3d —, 2007 Ohio 4707, — N.E. 2d —, 2007 Ohio App. LEXIS 4227 (Sept. 14, 2007).

Denial of the motion for a mistrial was not error because defendant's substantial rights were not violated and a fair trial was possible; the State elicited certain testimony to show when and how defendant was taken into custody and why the federal agent did not seize the money. Because the testimony did not leave the jury with any idea that defendant was involved in other crimes (all the jury knew was that he was arrested, he had money on him, and that money was returned to his girlfriend), the testimony did not warrant a mistrial. State v. Ervin, — Ohio App. 3d —, 2007 Ohio 5942, — N.E. 2d —, 2007 Ohio App. LEXIS 5224 (Nov. 8, 2007).

Trial court did not abuse its discretion in denying defendant's motion for a mistrial based on alleged misconduct by the prosecution during her trial on charges for driving under the influence because the fact that the prosecutor made reference to "divided attention skills tests" did not lead to a conclusion that the trial court abused its discretion in denying the motion for mistrial. Further, because the alleged exculpatory material was presented during trial, and defendant's counsel first referenced the station videotape and the booking photograph during his cross-examination of the police officer, defense counsel had actual knowledge of the items at issue and the element of surprise was totally absent and thus, there existed no Brady violation requiring a new trial. State v. Albanese, — Ohio App. 3d —, 2006 Ohio 4819, — N.E. 2d —, 2006 Ohio App. LEXIS 4724 (Sept. 15, 2006).

There was no error in denying defendant's motion for a mistrial because the learned and veteran trial judge did exactly what the law required: he voir dired the jury, to determine prejudice (which could have been caused by a prospective juror's negative feelings toward defendant based on knowing him previously) and, finding none, he continued empanelling the petit jury. Defendant pointed to nothing in the record indicating that the jury panel was dishonest with the trial court, and thus, failed to meet his burden of showing the jury was not fair and impartial. State v. Bekesz, — Ohio App. 3d —, 2007 Ohio 2573, — N.E. 2d —, 2007 Ohio App. LEXIS 2393 (May 25, 2007).

Motion denied

Defendant was not entitled to a new trial pursuant to Ohio R. Crim. P. 33(A) following his conviction for aggravated murder because defendant's claim that the State failed to disclose that one of its witnesses was a probation violator had been made both on direct appeal and in a petition for postconviction relief and, thus, was res judicata. State v. Thompson, — Ohio App. 3d —, 2007 Ohio 6818, — N.E. 2d —, 2007 Ohio App. LEXIS 5960 (Dec. 20, 2007).

Defendant's claim that his motion for leave for a delayed application pursuant to Ohio R. Crim. P. 33(B)(6) was unavoidably delayed due to the newly discovered evidence pursuant to the Ohio Supreme Court's holding in Comer did not establish that the three-year delay from the time that his criminal verdict was rendered until he brought his application was reasonable, as Comer was decided when his prior appeal from his conviction was pending; as he failed to offer an explanation to explain the delay, the motion for leave was not filed within a reasonable amount of time. State v. Griffith, — Ohio App. 3d —, 2006 Ohio 2935, — N.E. 2d —, 2006 Ohio App. LEXIS 2817 (June 9, 2006).

Defendant's motion for a new trial, alleging that jurors in her murder trial were misled and confused by the jury instructions, was properly denied because defendant had not alleged that any evidence aliunde existed that would impeach the jury's verdict, and thus, the juror statements submitted by defendant could not be considered under Ohio R. Evid. 606(B). State v. Franklin, — Ohio App. 3d —, 2006 Ohio 4569, — N.E. 2d —, 2006 Ohio App. LEXIS 4524 (Sept. 6, 2006).

Trial court did not err in refusing to grant defendant a new trial on the basis of all the errors that allegedly permeated his original trial. Defendant only recited arguments made earlier in his brief regarding the trial court's alleged bias, the trial court's refusal to allow him to impeach a witness with evidence of the witness' prior arrest, and the fact that the trial court permitted another witness to testify despite the fact that the State had not listed the witness as a witness until four days before trial; and since the court had already concluded that those assignments of error were meritless, the trial court did not abuse its discretion for failing to grant a new trial based on those same arguments. State v. McLeod, — Ohio App. 3d —, 2006 Ohio 7076, — N.E. 2d —, 2006 Ohio App. LEXIS 7004 (Dec. 19, 2006).

Motion for new trial

In defendant's motion for leave to file a new trial motion pursuant to Ohio R. Crim. P. 33, his claims under 28 U.S.C.S. § 1915 of the Prisoner Litigation Reform Act of 1996 were not subject to review, as defendant's motion was brought in an Ohio state court which was not within the coverage under § 1915 of a "court of the United States." State v. Berry, — Ohio App. 3d —, 2007 Ohio 2244, — N.E. 2d —, 2007 Ohio App. LEXIS 2083 (May 10, 2007).

Trial court did not err by denying defendant's motion for a new trial because defendant had intended to open the door to the victim's prior convictions, which had been excluded from being introduced into evidence before trial when the trial court granted the state's motion in limine. Also, the State did not put the victim's character into evidence because the victim's longtime friend did not give an opinion as to the victim's reputation during her testimony; also, any knowledge on the part of the friend as to the character of the victim was not the same as defendant's knowledge of the victim's character. Ohio v. Horace K. Vinson, — Ohio App. 3d —, 2007 Ohio 5199, — N.E. 2d —, 2007 Ohio App. LEXIS 4608 (Sept. 28, 2007).

Trial court did not abuse its discretion in denying the inmate's Ohio R. Crim. P. 33 motions for a new trial alleging newly discovered evidence. The inmate, whose motions were filed outside the Ohio R. Crim. P. 33(B) 120-day limitations period for such motions, did not file a motion for leave to file the late motions. State v. Morgan, — Ohio App. 3d —, 2006 Ohio 145, — N.E. 2d —, 2006 Ohio App. LEXIS 122 (Jan. 17, 2006).

Trial court's denial of defendant's motion for leave to file a motion for a new trial before the State responded to the motion and without giving defendant notice of its intention to deny it was proper because there was no requirement in Ohio R. Crim. P. 33 that the State respond to the motion, and unlike the case of a sua sponte dismissal of an action, the denial of a motion does not require prior notice. State v. Muff, — Ohio App. 3d —, 2006 Ohio 57, — N.E. 2d —, 2006 Ohio App. LEXIS 40 (Jan. 6, 2006).

New trial

Defendant's motion for a new trial pursuant to Crim. R. 33(A)(6) does not give a trial court authority to convict the defendant of a lesser included offense based on newly discovered evidence. Where the new evidence meets the required factors, the remedy is a new trial. State v. Burke, — Ohio App. 3d —, 2007 Ohio 1810, — N.E. 2d —, 2007 Ohio App. LEXIS 1640 (Apr. 17, 2007).

Trial court properly dismissed defendant's indictment as a sanction for the State's discovery violation as an order granting a new trial was law of the case, Ohio R. Crim. P. 33(D) and RC § 2945.82 governed the manner in which the new trial was to be conducted, and the trial court possessed all authority to reopen discovery or to entertain any pretrial motions available at law. The State violated Ohio R. Crim. P. 16(B)(1)(f) in willfully withholding exculpatory material from defendant and defendant's prejudice could not be cured by a new trial as almost 20 years had elapsed, eight witnesses for the defense were deceased, 16 witnesses had unknown addresses, and to present the witnesses' prior testimony would have been useless as none of the witnesses had been questioned about the exculpatory evidence. State v. Larkins, — Ohio App. 3d —, 2006 Ohio 90, — N.E. 2d —, 2006 Ohio App. LEXIS 80 (Jan. 12, 2006).

Trial court's ruling denying defendant's motion in limine to exclude "other acts" evidence was not an irregularity or error of law sufficient to warrant a new trial. Evidence of a prior burglary was proper in defendant's trial for a later burglary under circumstances in which a white van was driven in both burglaries, in both burglaries, the co-defendant waited in the car as a lookout while defendant broke into the rear or side door of the house, in both burglaries, defendant moved in and out of house quickly stealing objects that were quickly and easily removed, and the burglaries took place within 15 minutes of each other. State v. Blazo, — Ohio App. 3d —, 2006 Ohio 5418, — N.E. 2d —, 2006 Ohio App. LEXIS 5416 (Oct. 18, 2006).

Newly discovered evidence

There was no error in denying the new trial motion because the codefendant's statement at the sentencing hearing that he had shot the victim did not constitute "newly discovered evidence" since his willingness to take the blame for defendant could have been known to defendant at any time, as they were friends both before and during the proceedings. Also, the codefendant's statement contradicted the testimony and evidence presented at trial, which was overwhelming that defendant was aware of what was happening, that he was a participant in the incident, and most importantly that he was not an innocent bystander. State v. Scott, — Ohio App. 3d —, 2007 Ohio 528, — N.E. 2d —, 2007 Ohio App. LEXIS 479 (Feb. 8, 2007).

There was no abuse of discretion in denying defendant's motion for a new trial because the witness's affidavit was wholly inconsistent with the facts of the murder and contradicted by the overwhelming evidence of defendant's guilt presented at trial. She claimed that she was with the victim minutes before he was shot and that he was shot inside his car, while the witnesses at trial testified that the victim had been alone and he was shot outside of his car. Accordingly, defendant's "newly discovered evidence" would not have affected his trial result. State v. Taylor, — Ohio App. 3d —, 2007 Ohio 825, — N.E. 2d —, 2007 Ohio App. LEXIS 753 (Mar. 1, 2007).

Trial court did not abuse its discretion in denying the motion for a new trial based on newly discovered evidence because defendant failed to show that the result of his trial would have been different if a new trial had been granted. Although defendant presented evidence that the State's key witness knew that defendant was innocent, the witness stated that he lied to other inmates to avoid being labeled a snitch. The witness's trial testimony was corroborated by other evidence that strongly pointed to defendant's guilt, including a 911 tape and the testimony of several police officers who testified that the burglary which resulted in the rape and murder of defendant's wife appeared to have been staged. State v. Barton, — Ohio App. 3d —, 2007 Ohio 1099, — N.E. 2d —, 2007 Ohio App. LEXIS 1020 (Mar. 12, 2007).

Defendant was entitled at least to a hearing on his motion for leave to file for a new trial based on newly discovered evidence where the minor victim had allegedly recanted her testimony at the trial: State v. McConnell, 170 Ohio App. 3d 800, 2007 Ohio 1181, 869 N.E.2d 77, 2007 Ohio App. LEXIS 1114 (2007).

Trial court's denial of defendant's successive new trial motion pursuant to Ohio R. Crim. P. 33(A)(6) was proper with respect to his convictions for sexual offenses, arising from his alleged conduct regarding his minor daughter, as the asserted newly discovered evidence either failed to disclose a strong probability that it would change the outcome in the event of a new trial, was cumulative of other evidence disclosed to the defense and/or presented to the jury at trial, or merely

contradicted other evidence. State v. Peters, — Ohio App. 3d —, 2007 Ohio 1285, — N.E. 2d —, 2007 Ohio App. LEXIS 1181 (Mar. 22, 2007).

In defendant's prosecution for, inter alia, burglary under RC § 2911.12(A)(3), defendant was not entitled to a new trial under Ohio R. Crim. P. 33(A)(6) on the basis of newly discovered evidence as defendant failed to sufficiently establish that a defense witness's "surprise testimony" could not have been discovered before trial or that it did not merely impeach or contradict former evidence. State v. Urbina, — Ohio App. 3d —, 2007 Ohio 3131, — N.E. 2d —, 2007 Ohio App. LEXIS 2901 (June 25, 2007).

Trial court's denial of defendant's motion to file a delayed motion for a new trial pursuant to Ohio R. Crim. P. 33(A)(6) and RC § 2945.80 was not an abuse of discretion where testimony regarding other similar criminal conduct that defendant had engaged in was deemed properly admitted pursuant to Ohio R. Evid. 404(B) in defendant's prior direct appeal, there was no mention in the trial testimony that such conduct resulted in convictions, and defendant did not raise the issue in a timely manner. The other similar criminal conduct had resulted in convictions which were thereafter reversed and the charges were either dismissed or resulted in an acquittal upon retrial. State v. Elersic, — Ohio App. 3d —, 2007 Ohio 3371, — N.E. 2d —, 2007 Ohio App. LEXIS 3103 (June 29, 2007).

Trial court did not abuse its discretion in denying defendant's motion for a new trial because defendant did not demonstrate that his work schedule for the summer of 2003 (which defendant argued could impeach the victim's testimony by showing that defendant was at work when the alleged acts of abuse occurred) could not have been discovered before trial. The trial court also properly found that the newly discovered evidence did not disclose a strong probability that it would change the result of defendant's conviction if a new trial was granted. State v. Henson, — Ohio App. 3d —, 2007 Ohio 3567, — N.E. 2d —, 2007 Ohio App. LEXIS 3274 (July 13, 2007).

Defendant's motion for a new trial based on newly discovered evidence was properly denied because any testimony offered by the new witness at a new trial would merely be utilized to contradict the witnesses, which did not warrant a new trial. The evidence did not show that three witnesses fabricated their story claiming that defendant had a gun because one witness testified that she did not see a gun and the statements that the three witnesses gave to the police at the time of the incident were substantially the same as their respective trial testimony. State v. Zwelling, — Ohio App. 3d —, 2007 Ohio 3691, — N.E. 2d —, 2007 Ohio App. LEXIS 3365 (July 16, 2007).

Trial court did not abuse its discretion when it denied defendant's motion for a new trial because the trial court was unable to determine if the juror (who defendant claimed did not like him) even participated in the grand jury deliberations or voting; the trial court also reviewed appellant's affidavit and found the evidence lacking. Further, the trial court correctly analyzed the cell phone records and determined that the records were not newly discovered evidence and the evidence was of low probative value and would not likely have changed the result in the case. State v. Cloud, — Ohio App. 3d —, 2007 Ohio 4241, — N.E. 2d —, 2007 Ohio App. LEXIS 3931 (Aug. 14, 2007).

Trial court did not err in denying defendant's motion for a new trial under Ohio R. Crim. P. 33(A)(6) because the evidence offered in the affidavit of a trial witness who chose not to incriminate himself at that time was not newly discovered. The defense attorneys knew about the testimony, which was why they called him to testify at trial, and thus, defendant was unable to show that the evidence had been discovered since the trial. State v. McGlothin, — Ohio App. 3d —, 2007 Ohio 4707, — N.E. 2d —, 2007 Ohio App. LEXIS 4227 (Sept. 14, 2007).

Trial court did not err in denying defendant's motion for a new trial on the ground of newly discovered evidence, which was the fact that the alleged driver of a vehicle that had failed to stop upon an officer's order had been located and had indicated his willingness to testify that he was the one driving the car, because defendant did not exercise due diligence in attempting to discover this evidence prior to trial as defendant made no attempt to subpoena the alleged driver prior to trial and did not request a continuance prior to trial to secure the alleged driver's testimony. City of Columbus v. Stargell, — Ohio App. 3d —, 2007 Ohio 5004, — N.E. 2d —, 2007 Ohio App. LEXIS 4918 (Sept. 25, 2007).

Trial court did not err when it denied defendant's motions for leave to file a delayed motion for new trial and/or motion for a new trial because the motions did not meet the requirements of Ohio R. Crim. P. 33(A)(6), and defendant failed to establish that the new evidence created a strong probability of a different result if the motions were granted. Given that defendant's motion was supported only by his affidavit, which was largely based upon hearsay and unverified documents, the trial court could have reasonably determined that the evidence submitted did not create a strong probability that it would change the result if a new trial were granted. State v. Holmes, — Ohio App. 3d —, 2006 Ohio 1310, — N.E. 2d —, 2006 Ohio App. LEXIS 1204 (Mar. 22, 2006).

Trial court did not abuse its discretion under Ohio R. Crim. P. 33(B) by denying defendant leave to file a delayed motion for new trial because defendant offered no new evidence. The fact that the eyewitness had recanted his identification of defendant was not new evidence because the eyewitness had done so at trial, and the only "new" aspect to the motion, the eyewitness's motivation for recanting, was irrelevant. State v. Houston, — Ohio App. 3d —, 2006 Ohio 1599, — N.E. 2d —, 2006 Ohio App. LEXIS 1480 (Mar. 30, 2006).

Trial court did not abuse its discretion in denying defendant's motion for a new trial based on newly discovered evidence, under Ohio R. Crim. P. 33(A)(6), because the trial court properly found the documentary evidence attached to defendant's motion to be collateral and cumulative. Defendant's witness, his girlfriend, had already testified at trial that she did not attend school on the date identified in the victim's testimony and documentation in that regard was available prior to trial. State v. Ruhlman, — Ohio App. 3d —, 2006 Ohio 2137, — N.E. 2d —, 2006 Ohio App. LEXIS 1976 (May 1, 2006).

Denial of defendant's Ohio R. Crim. P. 33(A)(6) motion for a new trial was not error because, even if the evidence in dispute had been discovered after the trial, the evidence did not disclose a strong probability of a different result. The fact that defendant was acquitted on two counts of rape and that he testified at trial regarding the events did not create a strong probability of a different result, especially given the prosecution's presentation of two video taped interviews in which defendant confessed to hitting the victim, raping her, and stealing money from her purse, as well as numerous photographs of the victim's bruises. In re Hill, — Ohio App. 3d —, 2006 Ohio 2504, — N.E. 2d —, 2006 Ohio App. LEXIS 2381 (May 22, 2006).

Defendant, convicted of aggravated murder and related crimes, did not show, in his motion for a new trial pursuant to Ohio R. Crim. P. 33(B), that, by clear and convincing evidence, he was unavoidably prevented from discovering alleged new evidence, despite due diligence, because he only said could not get witnesses' affidavits until they were signed and sent to him, and he had confessed to his part in the crime and had not previously asserted an alibi, as his new trial motion did. State v. Martin, — Ohio App. 3d —, 2006 Ohio 4582, — N.E. 2d —, 2006 Ohio App. LEXIS 4534 (Sept. 7, 2006).

Trial court did not err when it denied defendant's motion for a new trial, under Ohio R. Crim. P. 33(A)(6), because the evidence that a woman had been in possession of defendant's cell phone during the relevant time period when the victim had been contacted by text messages in violation of a civil protection order against defendant could have been discovered before trial in the exercise of due diligence. Since defendant did not claim that the woman had his cell phone without permission or consent, defendant should have known that the woman had his cell phone. State v. McCaleb, — Ohio App. 3d —, 2006 Ohio 4652, — N.E. 2d —, 2006 Ohio App. LEXIS 4554 (Sept. 8, 2006).

— Motion denied

Denial of defendant's motion for a new trial was not an abuse of discretion because defendant relied upon recanted testimony given by his fiance, the mother of the baby who was killed, that he asked her to provide so that he could escape his sentence and defendant went so far as to craft the confession that the fiance sent to defendant's attorney. Thus, based on the various statements made by the fiance and defendant, it was not an abuse of discretion for the trial court to find that her confession, as set forth in her letter to the attorney, was not credible or true; in light of the lack of credibility of the newly discovered evidence advanced by defendant, there was no probability that the new evidence would have changed the outcome of the case if a new trial had been granted. State v. Guidry, — Ohio App. 3d —, 2007 Ohio 4422, — N.E. 2d —, 2007 Ohio App. LEXIS 3983 (Aug. 20, 2007).

Trial court did not err in overruling defendant's Ohio R. Crim. P. 33(A)(6) motion for a new trial, filed after defendant was convicted of felonious assault, because the confession of defendant's companion that he was the one who fired the gun, not defendant, did not warrant a new trial as defendant had failed to establish that, with due diligence, he could not have discovered and produced at trial evidence of his companion's alleged guilt. Ohio v. Henderson, — Ohio App. 3d —, 2007 Ohio 5982, — N.E. 2d —, 2007 Ohio App. LEXIS 5266 (Nov. 9, 2007).

Trial court did not err in overruling defendant's Ohio R. Crim. P. 33(A)(6) motion for a new trial because, though the victim's roommate sought to recant her testimony, given in defendant's prosecution for felonious assault, that defendant shot the victim, there was not a strong probability that the witness's recantation would change the result if a new trial were granted as the victim did not identify a shooter in her recantation but stated merely that she did not see who shot the victim. Ohio v. Henderson, — Ohio App. 3d —, 2007 Ohio 5982, — N.E. 2d —, 2007 Ohio App. LEXIS 5266 (Nov. 9, 2007).

Procedure

There was no jurisdiction for review as there was no final order since the trial court did not rule on defendant's motion for a new trial, under Ohio R. Crim. P. 33, and, even if the original motion had been tacitly overruled, the "supplement" to the original motion to dismiss certainly revived the substance of the first motion. The trial court's failure to rule on the supplemental motion meant that the time in which to appeal under Ohio R. App. P. 4(B)(3) did not begin to run, which rendered the notice of appeal premature. City of Cleveland v. Kline, — Ohio App. 3d —, 2006 Ohio 2087, — N.E. 2d —, 2006 Ohio App. LEXIS 1929 (Apr. 27, 2006).

Recantation by victim

Trial court abused its discretion in ordering a new trial based on newly discovered evidence because the victim's testimony at the hearing did not recant her trial testimony; her testimony was not based on personal knowledge, as required by EvidR 602, but instead was based on "feelings" and "beliefs;" and she had no memory of the years during which the abuse took place. Accordingly, there was no evidence properly before the trial court that would have given the trial court the reasonable belief that the victim's trial testimony was false. State v. Covender, — Ohio App. 3d —, 2008 Ohio 1453, — N.E. 2d —, 2008 Ohio App. LEXIS 1281 (Mar. 31, 2008).

At a minimum, the affidavit attached to defendant's motion for leave to move for a new trial based on newly discovered evidence, under Crim. R. 33, entitled him to a hearing on whether he was unavoidably prevented from discovering his daughter's alleged recantation within 120 days of the jury's verdict. The alleged admission that nothing had happened between the child and her father was sufficiently specific and the trial court's finding that the affidavit was controverted by medical evidence of a small, anal fissure went to the merits of defendant's right to a new trial rather than the threshold issue of whether he was unavoidably prevented from discovering the evidence upon which he relied. State v. McConnell, 170 Ohio App. 3d 800, 2007 Ohio 1181, 869 N.E.2d 77, 2007 Ohio App. LEXIS 1114 (2007).

Recantation by witness

Victim's affidavit partially recanting her testimony at the trial was not sufficient to establish, by clear and convincing evidence, that the court should have granted a delayed motion for a new trial: State v. Parker, 178 Ohio App. 3d 574, 899 N.E.2d 183, 2008 Ohio App. LEXIS 4355 (2008).

Defendant was entitled to a new trial on all counts, both counts of aggravated murder and the aggravated robbery charge, because the forensic pathologist's recanted testimony affected not only the prior calculation and design element of aggravated murder, but also defendant's credibility generally, to the point of corroborating some of defendant's version of the events the night that the victim was murdered. A reasonable juror could have concluded that the State's "evidence" both failed to demonstrate that defendant "purposely" killed the victim and failed to establish that defendant was involved in the stabbing; had the jury heard the two forensic pathologists testify that the fence may have caused some of the wounds, the jury could far more easily have believed defendant's testimony and determined that only the friend stabbed and robbed the victim. State v. Burke, — Ohio App. 3d —, 2007 Ohio 1810, — N.E. 2d —, 2007 Ohio App. LEXIS 1640 (Apr. 17, 2007).

Sufficiency of evidence

As the evidence against defendant supported his convictions for a variety of sexual offenses, arising from actions he engaged in upon his minor daughter, his motion for a new trial under Ohio R. Crim. P. 33(A)(4) was properly denied; the sexual abuse engaged in by defendant and his wife upon the child was supported by medical evidence and counselor's statements, as well as the child's own testimony. State v. Peters, — Ohio App. 3d —, 2007 Ohio 1285, — N.E. 2d —, 2007 Ohio App. LEXIS 1181 (Mar. 22, 2007).

It was reasonable for a juror to have found that defendant stole the vehicle himself, was with the driver when the vehicle was stolen, or at least knew that the vehicle was stolen when he got into it and/or sometime before he ran from the police, which was enough to convict him of receiving stolen property and was sufficient evidence for a denial of his motion for a new trial. A police officer testified that the driver's side window of the car was broken out, glass was on the seat in plain view, and the bottom part of the ignition was clearly and obviously broken and the keyhole was damaged. State v. Johnson, — Ohio App. 3d —, 2007 Ohio 4133, — N.E. 2d —, 2007 Ohio App. LEXIS 3755 (Aug. 15, 2007).

Defendant's conviction for attempted rape, under RC § 2907.02(A)(1)(b), was not against the manifest weight of the evidence, because the testimony of the 11-year-old victim was clear and significantly detailed and she testified to acts committed against her despite the fact that her accusations resulted in her removal from her home and placement in foster care. Also, there was no error in denying defendant's motion for a new trial under Ohio R. Crim. P. 33(A)(4) because there was sufficient evidence of defendant's guilt based on the victim's testimony in which she clearly testified to two separate occurrences in which defendant forcibly removed her pants, digitally penetrated her vagina, and attempted to engage in sexual intercourse with her. State v. Ruhlman, — Ohio App. 3d —, 2006 Ohio 2137, — N.E. 2d —, 2006 Ohio App. LEXIS 1976 (May 1, 2006).

Defendant's conviction for felonious assault, in violation of RC § 2903.11(A)(2) and (D), was supported by sufficient evidence and was not against the manifest weight of the evidence, and thus, the trial court properly denied defendant's motion for a new trial, because defendant could not establish that he acted in self-defense under RC § 2901.05, in that the evidence did not show that defendant had a genuine belief that he was in imminent danger of death or great bodily harm when he shot the victim. Defendant's own statements established that he had his gun in plain sight when the victim came running toward him. While the evidence showed that the victim appeared to want to fight with defendant, none of the evidence showed that the victim made any threats to defendant or that defendant believed that the victim had a weapon. State v. Jordan, — Ohio App. 3d —, 2006 Ohio 3425, — N.E. 2d —, 2006 Ohio App. LEXIS 3360 (June 30, 2006).

Time limit

Defendant's motion for a new trial pursuant to Ohio R. Crim. P. 33(A)(4) was properly granted where, although the motion was filed outside of the 14-day time period for filing motions for new trial, the trial court found by clear and convincing evidence that defendant was unavoidably prevented from filing the motion within the 14-day period because he was involved in potential presentence plea negotiations with the State and two co-defendants, and his counsel believed that filing the motion would prejudice the ongoing negotiations; there were permissible grounds for granting a new trial other than newly discovered evidence, and the trial court's finding that defendant's aggravated robbery conviction was not supported by sufficient evidence was a proper basis to grant the motion. State v. Bialec, — Ohio App. 3d —, 2006 Ohio 1585, — N.E. 2d —, 2006 Ohio App. LEXIS 1504 (Mar. 30, 2006).

After his conviction for drug offenses, defendant's motion for a new trial, filed seven days after the verdict was rendered, was improperly overruled as untimely because, under Ohio Const. art. IV, § 5(B), the 14-day limit imposed by Crim. R. 33(B) for filing a motion for a new trial was purely procedural and superseded the three-day limit for such motions in R.C. § 2945.80. State v. Ray, — Ohio App. 3d —, 2006 Ohio 5640, — N.E. 2d —, 2006 Ohio App. LEXIS 5643 (Oct. 30, 2006).

Under Ohio Const. art. IV, § 5(B), the 14-day limit imposed by Crim. R. 33(B) for filing a motion for a new trial is purely procedural and supersedes the three-day limit for filing such motions in R.C. § 2945.80. State v. Ray, — Ohio App. 3d —, 2006 Ohio 5640, — N.E. 2d —, 2006 Ohio App. LEXIS 5643 (Oct. 30, 2006).

Untimely motion

Trial court properly denied defendant's motion for leave to file a motion for new trial pursuant to Ohio R. Crim. P. 33(B), as he did not meet his burden of establishing by clear and convincing proof that he was unavoidably prevented from filing his motion within the statutory time limits. Although Rule 33(B) was silent regarding a time limit for filing the motion, reliance on Ohio R. Crim. P. 1(B) and 57(B) indicated that defendant's knowledge of various individuals' evidence years prior to the making of his motion was an unreasonable delay, for which no explanation was offered. State v. Berry, — Ohio App. 3d —, 2007 Ohio 2244, — N.E. 2d —, 2007 Ohio App. LEXIS 2083 (May 10, 2007).

Trial court did not abuse its discretion in overruling defendant's motion for a new trial because defendant did not demonstrate by clear and convincing evidence that he was unavoidably detained from filing his motion for new trial within the time parameters set forth by Ohio R. Crim. P. 33(B). State v. Hudgins, — Ohio App. 3d —, 2007 Ohio 3361, — N.E. 2d —, 2007 Ohio App. LEXIS 3083 (June 25, 2007).

Defendant was not entitled to a new trial pursuant to Ohio R. Crim. P. 33(B) in his prosecution for aggravated murder and aggravated robbery because a witness's recantation affidavit had been filed three years before defendant filed his motion for new trial; thus, the motion, which did not explain the delay, was untimely. State v. Willis, — Ohio App. 3d —, 2007 Ohio 3959, — N.E. 2d —, 2007 Ohio App. LEXIS 3604 (Aug. 3, 2007).

Trial court's finding that defendant failed to prove by clear and convincingly evidence that he was unavoidably prevented from discovering the alleged newly discovered evidence in sufficient time to file a timely motion for a new trial, pursuant to Ohio R. Crim. P. 33(A)(6), was supported by sufficient evidence, was not an abuse of discretion, and was a sufficient, independent basis for its decision to overrule his motion. Although defendant attached an affidavit from an investigator, it provided no specific information, it merely provided conclusions that the affidavits of two witnesses contained inadmissible information and that two other people were unavailable for trial; the two witnesses were known to defendant, since they testified in his defense at trial and the investigator's affidavit fell far short of establishing that a one person could not, with reasonable diligence, have been located before trial, and did not even assert that the other person could not be located before trial. Ohio v. Anthony K. Bolling, — Ohio App. 3d —, 2007 Ohio 5976, — N.E. 2d —, 2007 Ohio App. LEXIS 5271 (Nov. 9, 2007).

Trial court did not abuse its discretion in finding that the inmate's motion for a new trial was untimely as it was clearly filed beyond the 120 days allowed under Ohio R. Crim. P. 33(B). It was filed 16 months after his convictions and sentences were affirmed on appeal. State v. Graham, — Ohio App. 3d —, 2006 Ohio 352, — N.E. 2d —, 2006 Ohio App. LEXIS 313 (Jan. 30, 2006).

In addition to being barred by res judicata, defendant's motion for new trial was untimely where the motion was filed over eight years after his trial; while defendant argued that he was unavoidably prevented from the discovery of the information in support of his claim because the affiant who offered evidence of juror bias lived outside of Ohio and only recently returned, this assertion was completely contradicted by defendant's first motion for a new trial filed eight years earlier, which was accompanied by an affidavit from the same witness setting forth the same evidence defendant later claimed he was unavoidably prevented from discovering. State v. Amato, — Ohio App. 3d —, 2006 Ohio 1789, — N.E. 2d —, 2006 Ohio App. LEXIS 1632 (Apr. 7, 2006).

Trial court's summary denial of defendant's motion for leave to file a motion for a new trial under Ohio R. Crim. P. 33 or alternatively, to file a petition for post-conviction relief under RC §§ 2953.21 and 2953.23, was not an abuse of discretion where the motion was untimely under either the rule or the statute, and there was a lack of compliance with the necessary showing. Defendant did not show that he was unavoidably prevented from the discovery of evidence under Ohio R. Crim. P. 33 or that he had an adequate excuse for noncompliance pursuant to RC § 2953.23. State v. Holly, — Ohio App. 3d —, 2006 Ohio 3845, — N.E. 2d —, 2006 Ohio App. LEXIS 3812 (July 27, 2006).

Variance from indictment, etc.

It was not improper for the State to both proceed against defendant as a principal offender and to seek an instruction of aiding and abetting because Ohio R. Crim. P. 33(E)(2) provided that a variance between the allegations and the evidence at a criminal trial was not reversible error unless

defendant could show defendant was prejudiced or misled, and defendant was unable to make such a showing. State v. Walton, — Ohio App. 3d —, 2007 Ohio 5070, — N.E. 2d —, 2007 Ohio App. LEXIS 4476 (Sept. 27, 2007).

Verdict against weight of evidence

As defendant committed a burglary between 1:00 and 1:30 p.m. and the victim testified that it was her routine practice to return home from work every day around 2:00 p.m., the State failed to establish the presence or likely presence of someone other than an accomplice in the residence for purposes of defendant's conviction of burglary, in violation of RC § 2911.12(A)(2). As the proof was sufficient to find defendant guilty of having committed the lesser included offense under § 2911.12(A)(3), the court had authority under Ohio R. Crim. P. 33(A)(4) to modify the verdict of conviction to reflect that defendant was guilty of the lesser included offense. State v. Frock, — Ohio App. 3d —, 2006 Ohio 1254, — N.E. 2d —, 2006 Ohio App. LEXIS 1141 (Mar. 17, 2006).

Verdict modification

Trial court erred in entering a judgment of conviction for burglary as a second-degree felony because the evidence adduced at trial was not sufficient to support the finding that any person other than an accomplice of the offender was present or likely to be present as was required in RC § 2911.12(A)(2). Rather, since the evidence established that the victims were out of town on vacation, the evidence was sufficient for a third-degree burglary conviction, a lesser-included offense, under RC § 2911.12(A)(3); pursuant to Ohio R. Crim. P. 33(A)(4), the verdict was modified. State v. Brown, — Ohio App. 3d —, 2006 Ohio 2307, — N.E. 2d —, 2006 Ohio App. LEXIS 2156 (May 11, 2006).

Waiver of jury trial

Trial court did not abuse its discretion in denying defendant's new trial motion, as defendant's claim that a jury trial waiver in defendant's criminal matter was not knowingly and intelligently made was not deemed credible in the circumstances; defendant had claimed that prior trial counsel had misinformed defendant regarding the jury trial right. State v. Tapplar, — Ohio App. 3d —, 2007 Ohio 6868, — N.E. 2d —, 2007 Ohio App. LEXIS 6037 (Dec. 21, 2007).

RULE 34.   Arrest of Judgment

The court on motion of the defendant shall arrest judgment if the indictment, information, or complaint does not charge an offense or if the court was without jurisdiction of the offense charged. The motion shall be made within fourteen days after verdict, or finding of guilty, or after plea of guilty or no contest, or within such further time as the court may fix during the fourteen day period.

When the judgment is arrested, the defendant shall be discharged, and his position with respect to the prosecution is as if the indictment, information, or complaint had not been returned or filed.

NOTES TO DECISIONS

ANALYSIS

Motion denied
Time limitations

Motion denied

Trial court's decision to overrule defendant's motion for arrest of judgment, pursuant to Ohio R. Crim. P. 34, was proper where defendant's claim that the indictment that charged him with abduction, in violation of RC § 2905.02(A)(2), was defective lacked merit; although the indictment did not specify that the mens rea for the crime was "knowingly," it identified the name of the crime and the statutory cite, which included the element of "knowingly" as the applicable mens rea and accordingly made the indictment sufficient. State v. Proctor, — Ohio App. 3d —, 2006 Ohio 6876, — N.E. 2d —, 2006 Ohio App. LEXIS 6795 (Dec. 22, 2006).

Time limitations

Defendant's motion to arrest judgment under Ohio R. Crim. P. 34 was properly denied because it was not filed within 14 days of the verdict but, instead, was filed almost two years after defendant's conviction. Further, Ohio R. Crim. P. 34 is not applicable following resentencing when a defendant's guilt is no longer at issue. State v. Langley, — Ohio App. 3d —, 2006 Ohio 3871, — N.E. 2d —, 2006 Ohio App. LEXIS 3830 (July 28, 2006).

RULE 35.   Post-Conviction Petition

(A) A petition for post-conviction relief pursuant to section 2953.21 of the Revised Code shall contain a case history, statement of facts, and separately identified grounds for relief. Each ground for relief shall not exceed three pages in length. (See recommended Form XV in Appendix of Forms.) A petition may be accompanied by an attachment of exhibits or other supporting materials. A trial court may extend the page limits provided in this rule, request further briefing on any ground for relief presented, or direct the petitioner to file a supplemental petition in the recommended form.

(B) The clerk of court immediately shall send a copy of the petition to the prosecuting attorney. Upon order of the trial court, the clerk of court shall duplicate all or any part of the record that the trial court requires.

(C) The trial court shall file its ruling upon a petition for post-conviction relief, including findings of fact and conclusions of law if required by law, not later than one hundred eighty days after the petition is filed.

History: Effective 7-1-97.

NOTES TO DECISIONS

ANALYSIS

Generally
Post-conviction relief
Practice and procedure
Procedure

Generally

Regardless of the caption, a motion is a petition for postconviction relief if the defendant files the motion after the defendant's direct appeal, claims a denial of a constitutional right, seeks to render a final judgment void, and asks the trial court to vacate the judgment and sentence. CrimR 35 governs the procedure for postconviction relief and, because a criminal rule exists, CrimR 57(B) does not apply. Thus CivR 60(B) cannot be used to circumvent the time limits under RC § 2953.21: State v. Fulk, 172 Ohio App. 3d 635, 2007 Ohio 3141, 876 N.E.2d 983, 2007 Ohio App. LEXIS 2888 (2007).

Post-conviction relief

Defendant's Ohio R. Civ. P. 60(B)(5) motion to vacate was not the proper method of asserting constitutional errors in sentencing because a petition for post-conviction relief under RC § 2953.21 was the exclusive remedy by which defendant could have brought a collateral challenge to his sentence. Accordingly, since there existed an applicable rule of criminal procedure, defendant could not assert an Ohio R. Civ. P.

60(B)(5) challenge via Ohio R. Crim. P. 57(B). State v. Randlett, — Ohio App. 3d —, 2007 Ohio 3546, — N.E. 2d —, 2007 Ohio App. LEXIS 3243 (July 12, 2007).

Practice and procedure

As Ohio R. Crim. P. 35 governed the procedures for post-conviction petitions, defendant's reliance on Ohio R. Civ. P. 60(B)(5) and Ohio R. Crim. P. 57(B) for sentencing relief was error. As the request for sentencing relief was untimely under RC § 2953.21(A)(2) and it was not within either of the exceptions to timeliness under RC § 2953.23(A)(1) and (2), the trial court lacked jurisdiction to grant the requested relief and to resentence defendant. State v. Fulk, 172 Ohio App. 3d 635, 2007 Ohio 3141, 876 N.E.2d 983, 2007 Ohio App. LEXIS 2888 (2007).

Procedure

As Ohio R. Crim. P. 35 governed criminal procedure for post-conviction relief petitions, an inmate could not seek to vacate his sentence by moving under Ohio R. Civ. P. 60(B)(5) and Ohio R. Crim. P. 57(B). As his petition was not timely filed under RC § 2953.21(A)(2) and he was not within either of the exceptions to timeliness under RC § 2953.23(A)(1) and (2), the trial court properly denied his request for relief. State v. Brenton, — Ohio App. 3d —, 2007 Ohio 901, — N.E. 2d —, 2007 Ohio App. LEXIS 789 (Mar. 5, 2007).

Inmate's Ohio R. Civ. P. 60(B) motion that (1) was filed after the time for his direct appeal had passed, (2) claimed a denial of constitutional rights, (3) sought to render a judgment void, and (4) requested a vacation of the judgment and sentence entered on his pleas of guilty to two cocaine trafficking charges, was in reality a motion for post-conviction relief that could not circumvent the procedure for filing motions for post-conviction relief set forth in Ohio R. Crim. P. 35. State v. Frenzel, — Ohio App. 3d —, 2007 Ohio 4487, — N.E. 2d —, 2007 Ohio App. LEXIS 4051 (Sept. 4, 2007).

RULE 36.   Clerical Mistakes

Clerical mistakes in judgments, orders, or other parts of the record, and errors in the record arising from oversight or omission, may be corrected by the court at any time.

NOTES TO DECISIONS

ANALYSIS

Applicability
Correction for clerical mistake
Correction improper
Final appealable order

Applicability

Defendant's motion for re-sentencing, which was made after his time to file a direct appeal had run, was properly considered a petition for post-conviction relief pursuant to RC § 2953.21, and as it was filed in an untimely manner and the exceptions to timelieness under RC § 2953.23 were inapplicable, dismissal was proper. The trial court no longer had jurisdiction over the matter, as there was neither a void judgment nor a clerical error to correct pursuant to Ohio R. Crim. P. 36. State v. Coleman, — Ohio App. 3d —, 2007 Ohio 4235, — N.E. 2d —, 2007 Ohio App. LEXIS 3891 (Aug. 20, 2007).

Where a trial court correctly informed defendant at sentencing that he was subject to a mandatory three-year term of post-release control pursuant to RC § 2967.28(B)(2), but the sentencing entry indicated that defendant faced "up to a maximum of three years" of post-release control, vacatur of the sentence was not mandated in the circumstances, as there was no violation of RC § 2929.19(B)(3); rather, the sentencing entry required a correction pursuant to Ohio R. Crim. P. 36 to indicate the mandatory nature of the post-release control term. State v. Whitesell, — Ohio App. 3d —, 2006 Ohio 1781, — N.E. 2d —, 2006 Ohio App. LEXIS 1641 (Apr. 10, 2006).

Where the trial court correctly found defendant guilty of driving under the influence of alcohol, but it indicated that she was convicted of RC § 4511.19(A)(1)(a-e), the conviction was affirmed and the matter was remanded to the trial court for correction of the clerical error in the judgment, pursuant to Ohio R. Crim. P. 36, in order to reflect that defendant was convicted of RC § 4511.19(A)(1)(a). State v. Valdez, — Ohio App. 3d —, 2006 Ohio 3298, — N.E. 2d —, 2006 Ohio App. LEXIS 3215 (June 28, 2006).

Correction for clerical mistake

Trial court abused its discretion when it dismissed an indictment against defendant with prejudice pursuant to Ohio R. Crim. P. 48(B) without making the requisite findings that defendant was denied a constitutional or statutory right; further, the trial court lacked jurisdiction thereafter to enter a nunc pro tunc judgment to indicate that the dismissal was without prejudice, as the State of Ohio had already appealed the prior dismissal order, which divested the trial court of jurisdiction, and further, the nunc pro tunc judgment was improper where it was not entered to correct a clerical order pursuant to Ohio R. Crim. P. 36(A). State v. Walton, — Ohio App. 3d —, 2006 Ohio 4771, — N.E. 2d —, 2006 Ohio App. LEXIS 4721 (Sept. 14, 2006).

Trial court erred when it declined to grant defendant's motion to the extent of its challenge to the jail-time-credit calculation and to enter judgment, nunc pro tunc to the date of the judgment of conviction, correcting his jail-time credit to reflect his 203 days of prior confinement. Because the trial court's failure to afford defendant 203 days of jail-time credit was the consequence of a mistake of fact, the trial court's miscalculation was subject to correction pursuant to Crim. R. 36. State v. Weaver, — Ohio App. 3d —, 2006 Ohio 5072, — N.E. 2d —, 2006 Ohio App. LEXIS 5007 (Sept. 29, 2006).

Where a trial court's sentencing entry contained a clerical error, correction thereof was permitted under Ohio R. Crim. P. 36 and by the appellate court's direction to correct the misstatement pursuant to Ohio R. App. P. 9(E). State v. Simmons, — Ohio App. 3d —, 2006 Ohio 5760, — N.E. 2d —, 2006 Ohio App. LEXIS 5746 (Nov. 3, 2006).

When a trial court corrected its sentencing entry which had stated that, under RC § 2929.13(F), prison was not mandatory for defendant's rape conviction, replacing it with an entry providing that prison was mandatory, it was unnecessary to remand the entry for the purpose of clarifying that prison was not also mandatory for defendant's felonious assault conviction, because the trial court's statement that prison was mandatory for the rape conviction was a correct statement of the law, and the entry did not state that prison was mandatory for felonious assault or that both of defendant's prison terms were mandatory. State v. Gibson, — Ohio App. 3d —, 2006 Ohio 6899, — N.E. 2d —, 2006 Ohio App. LEXIS 6808 (Dec. 26, 2006).

Trial court had the authority under Ohio R. Crim. P. 36 to correct its clerical error in specifying that the driving while under the influence of alcohol or drugs (DUI) offense to which defendant pled guilty was a fifth-degree felony by issuing a nunc pro tunc entry providing that the DUI offense was a fourth-degree felony. It was clear that the trial court intended to enter the conviction as a fourth-degree felony and just made clerical error as it consistently advised defendant during his plea colloquy that he was pleading to DUI as a fourth-degree felony. State v. Legner, — Ohio App. 3d —, 2007 Ohio 2600, — N.E. 2d —, 2007 Ohio App. LEXIS 2422 (May 25, 2007).

Correction improper

Trial court's attempt to rectify its judgment entry dismissing defendant's criminal prosecution on speedy trial grounds by the issuance of a nunc pro tunc journal entry was improper. The trial court lacked jurisdiction to issue such an entry since the nunc pro tunc entry was filed after the State had already filed its notice of appeal, and the entry did not merely correct a clerical mistake, as permitted by Ohio R. Crim. P. 36, but indicated what the trial court should have decided. State v. Peek, — Ohio App. 3d —, 2007 Ohio 2674, — N.E. 2d —, 2007 Ohio App. LEXIS 2499 (June 4, 2007).

Final appealable order

Because the trial court did not comply with Ohio R. Crim. P. 32(C) in taking defendant's plea, the judgment entry was not a final appealable order. The trial court was required to make a present finding of guilt in order to comply with Ohio R. Crim. P. 32(C); it was also not sufficient for the trial court to note only that it accepted defendant's plea. State v. Williams, — Ohio App. 3d —, 2007 Ohio 1897, — N.E. 2d —, 2007 Ohio App. LEXIS 1750 (Apr. 23, 2007).

RULE 37. Reserved.

RULE 38. Reserved.

RULE 39. Reserved.

RULE 40. Reserved.

RULE 41. Search and Seizure

(A) **Authority to issue warrant.** A search warrant authorized by this rule may be issued by a judge of a court of record to search and seize property located within the court's territorial jurisdiction, upon the request of a prosecuting attorney or a law enforcement officer.

(B) **Property which may be seized with a warrant.** A warrant may be issued under this rule to search for and seize any: (1) evidence of the commission of a criminal offense; or (2) contraband, the fruits of crime, or things otherwise criminally possessed; or (3) weapons or other things by means of which a crime has been committed or reasonably appears about to be committed.

(C) **Issuance and contents.**

(1) A warrant shall issue on either an affidavit or affidavits sworn to before a judge of a court of record or an affidavit or affidavits communicated to the judge by reliable electronic means establishing the grounds for issuing the warrant. The affidavit shall name or describe the person to be searched or particularly describe the place to be searched, name or describe the property to be searched for and seized, state substantially the offense in relation thereto, and state the factual basis for the affiant's belief that such property is there located. If the affidavit is provided by reliable electronic means, the applicant communicating the affidavit shall be placed under oath and shall swear to or affirm the affidavit communicated.

(2) If the judge is satisfied that probable cause for the search exists, the judge shall issue a warrant identifying the property and naming or describing the person or place to be searched. The warrant may be issued to the requesting prosecuting attorney or other law enforcement officer through reliable electronic

means. The finding of probable cause may be based upon hearsay in whole or in part, provided there is a substantial basis for believing the source of the hearsay to be credible and for believing that there is a factual basis for the information furnished. Before ruling on a request for a warrant, the judge may require the affiant to appear personally, and may examine under oath the affiant and any witnesses the affiant may produce. Such testimony shall be admissible at a hearing on a motion to suppress if taken down by a court reporter or recording equipment, transcribed, and made part of the affidavit. The warrant shall be directed to a law enforcement officer. It shall command the officer to search, within three days, the person or place named for the property specified. The warrant shall be served in the daytime, unless the issuing court, by appropriate provision in the warrant, and for reasonable cause shown, authorizes its execution at times other than daytime. The warrant shall designate a judge to whom it shall be returned.

(D) **Execution and return with inventory.** The officer taking property under the warrant shall give to the person from whom or from whose premises the property was taken a copy of the warrant and a receipt for the property taken, or shall leave the copy and receipt at the place from which the property was taken. The return shall be made promptly and shall be accompanied by a written inventory of any property taken. The inventory shall be made in the presence of the applicant for the warrant and the person from whose possession or premises the property was taken, if they are present, or in the presence of at least one credible person other than the applicant for the warrant or the person from whose possession or premises the property was taken, and shall be verified by the officer. The judge shall upon request deliver a copy of the inventory to the person from whom or from whose premises the property was taken and to the applicant for the warrant. Property seized under a warrant shall be kept for use as evidence by the court which issued the warrant or by the law enforcement agency which executed the warrant.

(E) **Return of papers to clerk.** The judge before whom the warrant is returned shall attach to the warrant a copy of the return, inventory, and all other papers in connection therewith and shall file them with the clerk.

(F) **Definition of property and daytime.** The term "property" is used in this rule to include documents, books, papers and any other tangible objects. The term "daytime" is used in this rule to mean the hours from 7:00 a.m. to 8:00 p.m.

History: Amended, eff 7-1-10.

NOTES TO DECISIONS

ANALYSIS

Affidavit
— Generally
Good faith exception
Hearsay statements
Informants, generally
Probable cause
Signature requirements

Suppression

Affidavit

Under the totality of the circumstances, the affidavit which served as the basis for the search warrant provided a substantial basis for the issuing judge to conclude that there was a fair probability that marihuana, drug paraphernalia, documents, monies, weapons etc. would be found at that location: State v. Craft, 181 Ohio App. 3d 150, 2009 Ohio 675, 908 N.E.2d 476, 2009 Ohio App. LEXIS 553 (2009).

Even under the totality of the circumstances standard, an affidavit in support of a search warrant must contain some indicia of the veracity of the informant or the reliability of the information material to the probability of evidence of crime; the events observed in surveillance were too neutral in nature to corroborate the informants' tips. The good faith exception applied where the surveillance provided an objectively reasonable basis for the sheriff's department to conclude that probable cause existed for the search. Exclusionary rule does not apply in all instances where the knock and announce rule is violated: State v. Nunez, 180 Ohio App. 3d 189, 2008 Ohio 6806, 904 N.E.2d 924, 2008 Ohio App. LEXIS 5680 (2008).

Affidavit for a warrant to search the defendant's home for drugs was deficient where it contained no statements providing indicia of either the veracity of the informants or the basis of their knowledge. The good faith exception did not apply where a trained officer should have known that the affidavit was deficient. Officers possessed sufficient reasonable suspicion to investigate the defendant and his vehicle where an informant who had worked with the police for 12 years told them that the defendant would be dealing drugs and provided a specific location and time and a description of the vehicle: State v. Williams, 173 Ohio App. 3d 119, 2007 Ohio 4472, 877 N.E.2d 717, 2007 Ohio App. LEXIS 4038 (2007).

— Generally

Language of RC § 2933.51 et seq. supports application of those statutes only to ongoing seizures of "real time" communications, not to the seizure of a computer in order to retrieve stored information. Officer's omission in the affidavit for the search warrant of discrepancies in the statements of the alleged minor victims and of previous false allegations of sexual abuse by a victim did not invalidate the warrant: State v. Bell, 142 Ohio Misc. 2d 72, 2007 Ohio 2629, 870 N.E.2d 1256, 2007 Ohio Misc. LEXIS 283 (2007).

Good faith exception

Ohio Court of Appeals, Fifth Appellate District, Delaware County holds that a trial court may go beyond the four corners of an affidavit submitted in support of a search warrant subsequently found to be invalid and consider unrecorded oral testimony to determine whether the police officer executing the search warrant did so in good faith reliance upon the magistrate's having found probable cause to issue it. In looking at all of the circumstances, including the evidence enumerated in Ohio R. Crim. P. 41(C), a police detective was deemed aware of a drug dog's reliability when it corroborated an informant's tip regarding drugs in defendant's vehicle by alerting to the vehicle, such that the detective executed a warrant on the vehicle in good faith as an exception to the exclusionary rule under U.S. Const. amends. IV and XIV and Ohio Const. art. I, §§ 10 and 14, and suppression of drugs seized was not required. State v. Berry, — Ohio App. 3d —, 2007 Ohio 4122, — N.E. 2d —, 2007 Ohio App. LEXIS 3742 (Aug. 6, 2007).

When a search warrant affidavit did not identify the sources of its factual statements, the issuing judge was deprived of the ability to evaluate their reliability, under Ohio R. Crim. P. 41(C), but officers executing the warrant issued in reliance on that affidavit did so in good faith and acted in objectively reasonable reliance on the warrant as the information in the affidavit had been supplied to the affiant by another officer so, from the officers' standpoint, their reliance on the warrant was objectively reasonable, as there was no suggestion that the affiant falsified or recklessly disregarded the truth of the information supplied or that the issuing judge abandoned his judicial role. State v. Landis, — Ohio App. 3d —, 2006 Ohio 3538, — N.E. 2d —, 2006 Ohio App. LEXIS 3482 (July 10, 2006).

Hearsay statements

Defendant's motion to suppress was properly sustained because the judge issuing the search warrant did not have a substantial basis for concluding that probable cause existed, in that the affidavit in support of the warrant was based entirely on hearsay since the affiant had no personal knowledge of the alleged drug transaction, and the affidavit provided no information regarding the reliability or credibility of the confidential informant, as required by Ohio R. Crim. P. 41(C). State v. Goins, — Ohio App. 3d —, 2006 Ohio 74, — N.E. 2d —, 2006 Ohio App. LEXIS 59 (Jan. 6, 2006).

Basis of knowledge and the veracity of a person supplying hearsay information were circumstances that had to be considered in determining the value of the information and whether probable cause to issue a search warrant existed, and, as indicated in Ohio R. Crim. P. 41(C), hearsay information was relevant to the determination of probable cause so long as the affiant presented the magistrate with the affiant's basis of knowledge and some underlying circumstances supporting the affiant's belief that the source of the information was credible. State v. Landis, — Ohio App. 3d —, 2006 Ohio 3538, — N.E. 2d —, 2006 Ohio App. LEXIS 3482 (July 10, 2006).

Pursuant to Ohio R. Crim. P. 41(C), hearsay is permissible in determining probable cause if the court has reason to believe the source of the hearsay is credible and that there is a factual basis for the information furnished. The trial court knew that the drug agents on the scene conducted the controlled buy and observed the informant entering and exiting defendant's apartment and, as the source of the hearsay concerning the controlled purchase was a law enforcement official, there was reason to believe that he was credible. State v. Norris, — Ohio App. 3d —, 2006 Ohio 4022, — N.E. 2d —, 2006 Ohio App. LEXIS 3988 (Aug. 7, 2006).

Informants, generally

Trial court did not err in overruling defendant's Ohio R. Crim. P. 12(C)(3) motion to suppress because probable cause for the search warrant was shown where there was a fair probability that evidence of criminal activity would be found in the place to be searched; the reliability of information from two different confidential informants was corroborated by a detective. State v. Lane, — Ohio App. 3d —, 2008 Ohio 1605, — N.E. 2d —, 2008 Ohio App. LEXIS 1393 (Mar. 28, 2008).

Trial court was not required to believe the informant's testimony that an officer asked her to enter the defendant's residence to search for drugs: State v. Willis, 169 Ohio App. 3d 364, 2006 Ohio 5754, 862 N.E.2d 906, 2006 Ohio App. LEXIS 5739 (2006).

Probable cause

Trial court did not err in denying defendant's motion to suppress because the affidavit of the special agent involved in the case provided the judge with probable cause to issue a search warrant, in that the affidavit indicated that the county narcotics agency received complaints from a concerned citizen regarding extremely high volume short-term and long-term traffic at the condominium where defendant lived and outlined how two controlled drug buys were made by the confidential informant from defendant. While the informant hid drugs in his pocket after meeting with defendant during the second drug buy, this conduct occurred at or after the probable cause evidential basis had been completed for the request of a search warrant, and, thus, did not invalidate the existence of probable cause. State v. James, — Ohio App. 3d —, 2006 Ohio 4543, — N.E. 2d —, 2006 Ohio App. LEXIS 4488 (Sept. 1, 2006).

Officer's affidavit issued in support of a search warrant was legally sufficient under the totality of the circumstances. Anonymous tips of methamphetamine sales, the officer's knowledge of defendant's past drug activity, and a confidential informant who gave information on drug activity in progress were circumstances sufficient to uphold the validity of affidavit even though the officer did not state in his affidavit the reasons why the confidential informant could be considered to be reliable; thus, defendant's motion to suppress evidence obtained pursuant to the search warrant was properly denied. State v. Smith, — Ohio App. 3d —, 2006 Ohio 5186, — N.E. 2d —, 2006 Ohio App. LEXIS 5140 (Sept. 29, 2006).

Defendant's motion to suppress the evidence was properly overruled because the search warrant was valid. The totality of the facts and circumstances of the plain view observations of drugs and weapons of the initial officers on the scene (responding to a call that armed men were in defendant's home and were shooting) which were set forth in the detective's averments in his affidavit for the search warrant constituted sufficient probable cause to search defendant's home. State v. Newell, — Ohio App. 3d —, 2006 Ohio 5980, — N.E. 2d —, 2006 Ohio App. LEXIS 5903 (Nov. 9, 2006).

Signature requirements

Search warrant is void ab initio if it is not signed by a judge prior to the search, and any evidence seized pursuant to the warrant must be suppressed. Defense counsel provides ineffective assistance by failing to challenge a warrant on that basis. State v. Carpenter, — Ohio App. 3d —, 2007 Ohio 5790, — N.E. 2d —, 2007 Ohio App. LEXIS 5086 (Oct. 29, 2007).

Suppression

Based on the statutory requisites under R.C. §§ 2933.22(A), 2933.21(A), 1901.02, and Crim. R. 41 for issuance of a search warrant in defendant's matter involving the obtaining of DNA evidence from his person, a trial court committed violations when it issued the search warrant beyond its jurisdiction, but suppression was not mandated where no constitutional violation under Ohio Const. art. I, § 14 occurred. The execution of the warrant by police officers outside of their jurisdictional limits did not require suppression where there was no constitutional violation of defendant's rights to be free from unreasonable search and seizure. State v. Bowman, — Ohio App. 3d —, 2006 Ohio 6146, — N.E. 2d —, 2006 Ohio App. LEXIS 6094 (Nov. 21, 2006).

RULE 42. Reserved.

RULE 43. Presence of the Defendant

(A) Defendant's presence.

(1) Except as provided in Rule 10 of these rules and division (A)(2) of this rule, the defendant must be physically present at every stage of the criminal proceeding and trial, including the impaneling of the jury, the return of the verdict, and the imposition of sentence, except as otherwise provided by these rules. In all prosecutions, the defendant's voluntary absence after the trial has been commenced in the defendant's presence shall not prevent continuing the trial to and including the verdict. A corporation may appear by counsel for all purposes.

(2) Notwithstanding the provisions of division (A)(1) of this rule, in misdemeanor cases or in felony cases where a waiver has been obtained in accordance with division (A)(3) of this rule, the court may permit the

presence and participation of a defendant by remote contemporaneous video for any proceeding if all of the following apply:

(a) The court gives appropriate notice to all the parties;

(b) The video arrangements allow the defendant to hear and see the proceeding;

(c) The video arrangements allow the defendant to speak, and to be seen and heard by the court and all parties;

(d) The court makes provision to allow for private communication between the defendant and counsel. The court shall inform the defendant on the record how to, at any time, communicate privately with counsel. Counsel shall be afforded the opportunity to speak to defendant privately and in person. Counsel shall be permitted to appear with defendant at the remote location if requested.

(e) The proceeding may involve sworn testimony that is subject to cross examination, if counsel is present, participates and consents.

(3) The defendant may waive, in writing or on the record, the defendant's right to be physically present under these rules with leave of court.

(B) **Defendant excluded because of disruptive conduct.** Where a defendant's conduct in the courtroom is so disruptive that the hearing or trial cannot reasonably be conducted with the defendant's continued physical presence, the hearing or trial may proceed in the defendant's absence or by remote contemporaneous video, and judgment and sentence may be pronounced as if the defendant were present. Where the court determines that it may be essential to the preservation of the constitutional rights of the defendant, it may take such steps as are required for the communication of the courtroom proceedings to the defendant.

History: Amended, eff. 07/01/08.

NOTES TO DECISIONS

ANALYSIS

Corporations
Defendant's right to be present
Disruptive conduct
Harmless error
Jury view
Magistrate's recommended sentence
Presence of defendant
Right to be present
Sentencing
Voluntary absence

Corporations

RC § 2941.47 did not apply where a corporation was charged by a complaint, not an indictment or information. CrimR 43 does not allow a court clerk to enter a plea on the defendant's behalf or allow for a trial in absentia of a corporate defendant when the defendant has never appeared in the case: City of Cleveland v. Wash. Mut. Bank, 179 Ohio App. 3d 692, 2008 Ohio 6956, 903 N.E.2d 384, 2008 Ohio App. LEXIS 5827 (2008).

Defendant's right to be present

Defendant's right to be present at various aspects of his criminal trial under Ohio Const. art. I, § 10 and Ohio R.

Crim. P. 43(A) was not violated by various in-chambers conferences that occurred outside of his presence, as they were either attended by his counsel, who was competent to handle the issues raised, the presence was waived either expressly or implicitly, or defendant did not show prejudice by his absence from a particular conference. State v. Frazier, 115 Ohio St. 3d 139, 2007 Ohio 5048, 873 N.E.2d 1263, 2007 Ohio LEXIS 2519 (2007).

Trial court's refusal to play the videotape during trial was neither a constitutional error, nor a prejudicial one; because it merely corroborated the testimony extrapolated at trial, the videotape was not a critical portion of the State's case or an item that would have assured defendant's acquittal. Defendant's entire trial was open to the public and it was not cloaked in secrecy so as to offend the underlying principles of Sixth Amendment; defendant did not show that the refusal to play at least portions of the videotape deprived her of a fair trial and amounted to constitutional or prejudicial error. State v. Dovala, — Ohio App. 3d —, 2007 Ohio 4914, — N.E. 2d —, 2007 Ohio App. LEXIS 4377 (Sept. 24, 2007).

Although an inmate was prejudiced by his counsel's waiver of the inmate's presence for the discussions of the jury questions, as the inmate had a right to be present pursuant to Ohio R. Crim. P. 43, there was no indication that the proceedings would have gone differently if the inmate had been present and there was also no showing that the inmate was prejudiced by his counsel's conduct; there was no showing that counsel was ineffective under U.S. Const. amend. VI and Ohio Const. art. I, § 10. State v. Flora, — Ohio App. 3d —, 2006 Ohio 5732, — N.E. 2d —, 2006 Ohio App. LEXIS 5730 (Nov. 2, 2006).

Disruptive conduct

Defendant's due process rights under Ohio Const. art. I, § 10 were not violated where he was removed from the courtroom following his disruptive conduct of flipping over the defense table, as he was allowed to watch the rest of the trial, which only consisted of part of the closing arguments, on a monitor and the jury was properly instructed not to make its decision based on his courtroom conduct. There was no violation of defendant's right to be present during the trial pursuant to Ohio R. Crim. P. 43(A). State v. Greathouse, — Ohio App. 3d —, 2007 Ohio 2136, — N.E. 2d —, 2007 Ohio App. LEXIS 1991 (May 4, 2007).

Defendant's rights to due process and confrontation of witnesses pursuant to U.S. Const. amend. VI and Ohio Const. art. I, § 10 were not violated where defendant voluntarily chose to remain outside of the courtroom for a part of his trial pursuant to Ohio R. Crim. P. 43, and to thereafter attend the trial in restraints, as he had displayed violent outbursts and disruptive behavior which he attributed to an undisclosed medical condition, and the trial court carefully explained defendant's rights and provided options to him in order to ensure a fair trial; when he appeared in the courtroom, towels and cloths were used to cover the nature of the restraint chair and the restraints from the view of the jury. State v. Murphy, 173 Ohio App. 3d 221, 2007 Ohio 4535, 877 N.E.2d 1034, 2007 Ohio App. LEXIS 4101 (2007).

Defendant's rights were not violated where he voluntarily chose to be excluded from the courtroom during part of the trial rather than be restrained and the court did not abuse its discretion by restraining the defendant after his violent outburst: State v. Murphy, 173 Ohio App. 3d 221, 2007 Ohio 4535, 877 N.E.2d 1034, 2007 Ohio App. LEXIS 4101 (2007).

When a trial court held a hearing, after defendant appealed defendant's convictions, to correct the record, pursuant to the granting of defendant's motion to the appellate court, the trial court was authorized, under Ohio R. Crim. P. 43(B), to remove defendant from that hearing because defendant constantly interrupted the trial judge, refused to answer the judge's questions, refused to explain or support defendant's objections, tried to bait and provoke the judge, and, in general, was argumentative during the hearing. Ohio v. Liddy, — Ohio App. 3d —, 2007 Ohio 5225, — N.E. 2d —, 2007 Ohio App. LEXIS 4597 (Sept. 28, 2007).

When defendant verbally confronted a prosecution witness, during his trial, was warned that continuing this behavior would result in his removal from the courtroom, and he requested that he be removed, it was no error, under Ohio R. Crim. P. 43(A), to remove him from the courtroom, as he waived his presence by asking to be removed, particularly when he would not promise to conform his behavior to courtroom decorum. State v. Kilgore, — Ohio App. 3d —, 2006 Ohio 2139, — N.E. 2d —, 2006 Ohio App. LEXIS 1978 (May 1, 2006).

Harmless error

Although it was error for a trial court bailiff to have responded to a jury question during their deliberations outside of the presence of defendant and her counsel, in violation of defendant's right under Ohio R. Crim. P. 43, such was harmless error pursuant to Ohio R. Crim. P. 52 where the judge himself did not speak to the jury and the communication was not at all prejudicial to defendant, as the bailiff's communication did not supplement the instructions that the jury had been already given, nor was an explanation of the charge given. State v. Manns, 169 Ohio App. 3d 687, 2006 Ohio 5802, 864 N.E.2d 657, 2006 Ohio App. LEXIS 5749 (2006).

Defendant's rights under Ohio Const. art. I, § 10 and Ohio R. Crim. P. 43(A) were not violated by his absence from a discussion regarding the questioning of a juror as to her familiarity with the investigating detective in the case, as defendant's counsel was present at the time, the hearing was conducted on the record, and defendant's interests were more than adequately protected; defendant's presence would have made little contribution to the hearing. State v. Lawwill, — Ohio App. 3d —, 2007 Ohio 2627, — N.E. 2d —, 2007 Ohio App. LEXIS 2457 (May 31, 2007).

Jury view

Trial court did not deny defendant the right to be at the jury view because it merely conditioned the exercise of that right by requiring that defendant wear leg restraints if he decided to attend the jury view; since the trial court could have denied defendant any ability to attend the jury view without violating due process, conditioning his ability to so attend also does not violate due process. Also, defendant could not show that he was materially prejudiced by his absence from the jury view because his counsel was present and there was no indication in the record that anything improper occurred at the jury view. State v. Loveless, — Ohio App. 3d —, 2007 Ohio 1560, — N.E. 2d —, 2007 Ohio App. LEXIS 1453 (Mar. 26, 2007).

Magistrate's recommended sentence

Trial court may adopt a sentence the magistrate recommended without the defendant then being present before the court. However, consistent with the purposes of CrimR 43(A) and the requirements of due process, in that event the defendant must have been present before the magistrate when the magistrate pronounced the sentence recommended to the court: State v. Gilreath, 174 Ohio App. 3d 327, 2007 Ohio 6899, 882 N.E. 2d 22, 2007 Ohio App. LEXIS 6057 (Dec. 21, 2007).

Trial court erred when it imposed the sentence because defendant was not present. The magistrate did not pronounce a recommended sentence when defendant was before him, but instead pronounced a recommended sentence in a written decision that was filed and adopted by the trial court the same day. State v. Gilreath, 174 Ohio App. 3d 327, 2007 Ohio 6899, 882 N.E. 2d 22, 2007 Ohio App. LEXIS 6057 (Dec. 21, 2007).

Presence of defendant

Trial court erred when it sentenced defendant without informing him of the specific sentence imposed for each individual count for which the jury found him guilty and the trial court erred in imposing court costs outside defendant's presence. Ohio R. Crim. P. 43(A) required the physical presence of defendant during sentencing and the trial court could not abrogate his right of allocution by imposing sentence in his absence. State v. Tripplett, — Ohio App. 3d —, 2007 Ohio 75, — N.E. 2d —, 2007 Ohio App. LEXIS 68 (Jan. 11, 2007).

Defendant failed to establish reversible error regarding a jury question to the court which he and his counsel were allegedly not present for, as it was presumed in the absence of a showing to the contrary that defendant and his counsel were in fact present for purposes of Ohio Const. art. I, § 10 and Ohio R. Crim. P. 43(A). Although the record was silent concerning any objection by defendant's counsel, defendant could have utilized a statement under Ohio R. App. P. 9 to supplement the record, and further, no prejudice was shown even if the absence were proved. State v. Simmons, — Ohio App. 3d —, 2007 Ohio 1570, — N.E. 2d —, 2007 Ohio App. LEXIS 1442 (Mar. 28, 2007).

When defendant was removed from the courtroom, during his criminal trial, after he requested his removal, after being told that continuing his disruptive behavior would require removal, the better procedure would have been to communicate the trial proceedings to him, but Ohio R. Crim. P. 43(B) imposed no mandatory duty to do so, and, as defendant did not object to a failure to communicate the proceedings to him, he gave the trial court no chance to correct this issue. State v. Kilgore, — Ohio App. 3d —, 2006 Ohio 2139, — N.E. 2d —, 2006 Ohio App. LEXIS 1978 (May 1, 2006).

When defendant was removed from the courtroom, during his criminal trial, after he requested his removal, after being told that continuing his disruptive behavior would require removal, it was not error to allow witnesses to use a photo array to identify him, rather than returning him to the courtroom for an identification. State v. Kilgore, — Ohio App. 3d —, 2006 Ohio 2139, — N.E. 2d —, 2006 Ohio App. LEXIS 1978 (May 1, 2006).

Pursuant to Ohio R. Crim. P. 43(A), it was error for a trial court to amend defendant's sentence outside his presence. State v. Haymon, — Ohio App. 3d —, 2006 Ohio 3296, — N.E. 2d —, 2006 Ohio App. LEXIS 3196 (June 28, 2006).

Although the trial court erred in communicating with the jurors through a bailiff and outside the presence of the defendant and defense counsel, that error was harmless beyond a reasonable doubt: State v. Manns, 169 Ohio App. 3d 687, 2006 Ohio 5802, 864 N.E.2d 657, 2006 Ohio App. LEXIS 5749 (2006).

Right to be present

Although the trial court corrected an error in sentencing in its judgment entries thereon, such correction did not cure the error, as defendant's right to be present at every critical stage of the proceedings pursuant to Ohio Const. art. I, § 10 and Ohio R. Crim. P. 43(A) encompassed the right to be present during the imposition of the sentence. State v. Nichols, — Ohio App. 3d —, 2007 Ohio 3257, — N.E. 2d —, 2007 Ohio App. LEXIS 2999 (June 25, 2007).

Sentencing

Trial court erred by including additional sanctions in its sentencing entry that were not imposed at the sentencing hearing. State v. Clark, — Ohio App. 3d —, 2007 Ohio 1780, — N.E. 2d —, 2007 Ohio App. LEXIS 1619 (Apr. 13, 2007).

Trial court's sentencing entry was ambiguous and unclear where the trial judge indicated to defendant that it had imposed the aggregate term that he had agreed to, but in actuality the total term imposed exceeded the recommended sentence that was submitted as part of a negotiated plea agreement; defendant had a right to know the sentence that was imposed on him at the sentencing hearing pursuant to Ohio R. Crim. P. 43, and it was unclear whether the trial court had intended to deviate from the agreed term or not. State v. Barker, — Ohio App. 3d —, 2007 Ohio 1915, — N.E. 2d —, 2007 Ohio App. LEXIS 1722 (Apr. 23, 2007).

Ohio R. Crim. P. 43(A) requires that a criminal defendant be present for sentencing, so, when a sentence pronounced in open court is subsequently modified and a judgment entry reflects the modification, the modification must have been made in the defendant's presence. State v. Mullens, — Ohio App. 3d —, 2007 Ohio 2893, — N.E. 2d —, 2007 Ohio App. LEXIS 2676 (June 13, 2007).

When defendant said the trial court violated Ohio R. Crim. P. 43(A) because his sentence imposed in a judgment entry differed from that imposed at a sentencing hearing because the jail-time credit awarded at the sentencing hearing was only applied to one case, when it shold have been applied to two cases, because it was clear from reviewing the transcript of the sentencing hearing that the jail-time credit was applied to both cases, and this was consistent with the trial court's subsequent judgment entry. State v. Aliane, — Ohio App. 3d —, 2006 Ohio 228, — N.E. 2d —, 2006 Ohio App. LEXIS 188 (Jan. 24, 2006).

There was no statutory requirement under RC § 4511.19(G)(3) that required a trial court to conduct a separate hearing on the issue of the availability of jail space before making a finding under § 4511.19(G)(3), although it had to conduct a hearing in the same manner required when a sentence was modified under Ohio R. Crim. P. 43(A). State v. Beatty, — Ohio App. 3d —, 2006 Ohio 4904, — N.E. 2d —, 2006 Ohio App. LEXIS 4834 (Sept. 22, 2006).

Since the downward modification of defendant's sentence was not made in defendant's presence but was, instead, made after the sentencing hearing, the trial court's judgment entry of sentence was void. Although defendant benefited from the shorter term, pursuant to Crim. R. 43, any modification of a sentence had to be made in the defendant's presence. State v. Zelinko, — Ohio App. 3d —, 2006 Ohio 5106, — N.E. 2d —, 2006 Ohio App. LEXIS 5034 (Sept. 29, 2006).

When a magistrate took the disposition of a juvenile delinquency case under advisement, after conducting adjudicatory and dispositional hearings, and then issued a sentencing decision without holding a hearing, Ohio R. Juv. P. 34 provided the procedure for dispositional hearings in juvenile delinquency cases and did not require the juvenile to be present for sentencing, so the Ohio R. Crim. P. 43 requirement that the defendant be present for the imposition of sentence did not apply. In re Gibson, — Ohio App. 3d —, 2006 Ohio 5145, — N.E. 2d —, 2006 Ohio App. LEXIS 5109 (Oct. 2, 2006).

Because the trial court's judgment entry pronounced consecutive sentences on certain counts even though the trial court made no such indications in defendant's presence during the sentencing hearing, defendant was entitled to be present at a new sentencing hearing in regards to such sentencing matters. State v. Jordan, — Ohio App. 3d —, 2006 Ohio 5208, — N.E. 2d —, 2006 Ohio App. LEXIS 5165 (Oct. 3, 2006).

Where defendant was convicted of multiple offenses and concurrent terms of imprisonment were imposed, the reversal of his conviction for aggravated burglary and the vacatur of that sentence did not change the aggregate length of the term imposed, and a remand for correction of the sentence did not require defendant's presence under Ohio Const. art. I, § 10 and Ohio R. Crim. P. 43, as nothing new was imposed and no hearing was held. State v. Howard, — Ohio App. 3d —, 2006 Ohio 6412, — N.E. 2d —, 2006 Ohio App. LEXIS 6374 (Dec. 7, 2006).

Voluntary absence

Trial court did not err when it allowed defendant's criminal trial to proceed in defendant's absence pursuant to Ohio R. Crim. P. 43(A), as defendant was present in the morning for jury selection and counsels' opening statements, but she failed to return after the lunch break without explanation and the trial court denied her counsel's request for a continuance; a presumption arose that defendant's absence from the courtroom was voluntary, which defendant failed to offer evidence to show otherwise until she appeared two weeks later at her sentencing hearing and indicated that she had gone to the hospital because she was suffering from extreme anxiety. State v. Timiko Banks, — Ohio App. 3d —, 2007 Ohio 5311, — N.E. 2d —, 2007 Ohio App. LEXIS 4676 (Sept. 28, 2007).

As it was determined that defendant's failure to appear on the second day of his criminal trial without an explanation to either the trial court or his counsel was a voluntary absence from court and a waiver of his right to be present pursuant to Ohio R. Crim. P. 43, his counsel's objection to the trial court's proceeding in defendant's absence or counsel's request for a continuance would have been futile. Accordingly, counsel's failure to have objected or requested a continuance did not constitute ineffective assistance of counsel in violation of defendant's rights under U.S. Const. amend. XIV and Ohio Const. art. I, § 10. State v. Hicks, — Ohio App. 3d —, 2006 Ohio 6662, — N.E. 2d —, 2006 Ohio App. LEXIS 6562 (Dec. 15, 2006).

RULE 44. Assignment of Counsel

(A) **Counsel in serious offenses.** Where a defendant charged with a serious offense is unable to obtain counsel, counsel shall be assigned to represent him at every stage of the proceedings from his initial appearance before a court through appeal as of right, unless the defendant, after being fully advised of his right to assigned counsel, knowingly, intelligently, and voluntarily waives his right to counsel.

(B) **Counsel in petty offenses.** Where a defendant charged with a petty offense is unable to obtain counsel, the court may assign counsel to represent him. When a defendant charged with a petty offense is unable to obtain counsel, no sentence of confinement may be imposed upon him, unless after being fully advised by the court, he knowingly, intelligently, and voluntarily waives assignment of counsel.

(C) **Waiver of counsel.** Waiver of counsel shall be in open court and the advice and waiver shall be recorded as provided in Rule 22. In addition, in serious offense cases the waiver shall be in writing.

(D) **Assignment procedure.** The determination of whether a defendant is able or unable to obtain counsel shall be made in a recorded proceeding in open court.

NOTES TO DECISIONS

ANALYSIS

Determination of ability to obtain counsel
Effective assistance
Failure to advise defendant of rights
Ineffective assistance
Petty offenses
Probation violation
Replacement of counsel
Self-representation
Waiver of counsel
Waiver of right to counsel

Determination of ability to obtain counsel

Reversal of the convictions was required where the trial court failed to inquire fully into the circumstances impinging on the defendant's claimed inability to obtain counsel and his consequent need for assistance in employing counsel or for the assistance of appointed counsel: State v. Williams, 173 Ohio App. 3d 556, 2007 Ohio 5672, 879 N.E.2d 261, 2007 Ohio App. LEXIS 4983 (2007).

Defendant was denied his right to counsel because the trial court failed to inquire fully into the circumstances impinging upon defendant's claimed inability to obtain counsel and his consequent need for assistance in employing counsel or for the assistance of court-appointed counsel. The trial court merely proceeded to inform defendant that he had to write on a form that he waived his right to counsel because he could not afford one or however he wanted to word it; that comment by the trial court did not suffice to demonstrate that defendant was knowingly and intelligently waiving his right to be represented by counsel. State v. Williams, 173 Ohio App. 3d 556, 2007 Ohio 5672, 879 N.E.2d 261, 2007 Ohio App. LEXIS 4983 (2007).

Effective assistance

Defendant was not denied the effective assistance of counsel during his trial for felonious assault and related offenses when his trial counsel did not file a motion to suppress the victim's identification of him in a photographic display provided by a police officer. Defendant's counsel was not ineffective for failing to challenge the procedure because the officer did not engage in any suggestive behavior before the victim identified defendant's picture. State v. Cleaver, — Ohio App. 3d —, 2006 Ohio 5962, — N.E. 2d —, 2006 Ohio App. LEXIS 5913 (Nov. 9, 2006).

Failure to advise defendant of rights

Although the trial court satisfied Ohio R. Crim. P. 22, since defendant's petty offenses (misdemeanor drug possession and possession of drug paraphernalia) did not require a waiver in writing, the trial court failed to make an adequate determination that defendant sufficiently understood the possible consequences of waiving counsel, as required by Ohio R. Crim. P. 44. Review of the record demonstrated an absence of any explanation of the right to counsel or an affirmative waiver of the right on the record by defendant; the trial court did not engage in any dialogue with defendant at any stage prior to trial or at trial of the nature of the charged offenses, the range of possible punishment for the crimes as charged, possible defenses, or the dangers of self-representation. State v. Mays, — Ohio App. 3d —, — N.E. 2d —, 2007 Ohio App. LEXIS 4857 (Oct. 15, 2007).

Where defendant was charged with carrying a concealed weapon, having a weapon while under a disability, and tampering with evidence, which were "serious offenses" pursuant to Ohio R. Crim. P. 2(C), and the trial court asked him at every stage of the proceedings whether he would obtain counsel or seek appointed counsel, defendant's decision to proceed pro se was not deemed knowingly, voluntarily, or intelligently made pursuant to Ohio R. Crim. P. 44, as the trial court failed to determine whether defendant understood the nature of the charges and the penalties or possible defenses, and it failed to make any of the determinations deemed essential under Martin. State v. Stubbs, — Ohio App. 3d —, 2006 Ohio 3858, — N.E. 2d —, 2006 Ohio App. LEXIS 3799 (July 28, 2006).

Ineffective assistance

During defendant's trial for receiving stolen property, his counsel did not render ineffective assistance by failing to object to the admission of evidence that was determined on defendant's appeal from his conviction to be admissible. State v. Ewing, — Ohio App. 3d —, 2006 Ohio 5523, — N.E. 2d —, 2006 Ohio App. LEXIS 5503 (Oct. 24, 2006).

Reversal of defendant's aggravated robbery conviction and sentence was not required even if the performance of his trial counsel was deficient for failing to request a continuance when a defense witness did not appear at the hearing on his motion to suppress his statements to police because the record showed no resulting prejudice to defendant; it did not appear that the witness in question was present when defendant made the challenged statement, and no proffer was made to indicate what the witness's testimony was expected to be or how it would have demonstrated the involuntariness of defendant's statement. State v. Peck, — Ohio App. 3d —, 2006 Ohio 5796, — N.E. 2d —, 2006 Ohio App. LEXIS 5752 (Nov. 3, 2006).

Petty offenses

Trial court did not have the authority to impose a jail sentence after finding defendant guilty of failing to constrain or confine her dogs, under RC § 955.22(C), because she never waived her right to appointed counsel in a knowing, intelligent, and voluntary manner. Although the underlying offense was a "petty" misdemeanor, and Ohio R. Crim. P. 44(B) was applicable, defendant did not have the benefit of counsel at trial; the trial court never tried to have the necessary dialog with defendant during the proceeding; and the transcript showed that defendant did not seek to waive her right to have an attorney appointed for her and, in fact, she expressly asked for the appointment of counsel. State v. Mogul, — Ohio App. 3d —, 2006 Ohio 1873, — N.E. 2d —, 2006 Ohio App. LEXIS 1728 (Apr. 14, 2006).

Trial court did not have the authority to impose a jail sentence after finding defendant guilty of failing to confine his dogs, under RC § 955.22(C), because he did not waive his right to appointed counsel in a knowing, intelligent, and voluntary manner. Although the offense was a "petty" misdemeanor and Ohio R. Crim. P. 44(B) was applicable, the trial court never tried to have the necessary dialog with defendant during the proceeding; not only did defendant did not seek to waive his right to have an attorney appointed, he expressly asked for the appointment of counsel. State v. Mogul, — Ohio App. 3d —, 2006 Ohio 1878, — N.E. 2d —, 2006 Ohio App. LEXIS 1732 (Apr. 14, 2006).

Failure to appoint counsel for defendant or to allow him to have counsel of his choice did not violate his right to counsel under Ohio R. Crim. P. 32.3 on two probable cause hearings on probation violations filed against him to which Ohio R. Crim. P. 44(B) applied because he had been convicted of misdemeanor assault. The right to counsel did not attach until the dispositional hearing because the probable cause hearings were not the final determination of the probation violations, and defendant was represented by counsel during his dispositional hearing. State v. Cogar, — Ohio App. 3d —, 2006 Ohio 5218, — N.E. 2d —, 2006 Ohio App. LEXIS 5194 (Sept. 29, 2006).

Probation violation

Defendant's due process rights under U.S. Const. amend. XIV and Ohio Const. art. I, § 10 were not violated where his community control was revoked upon his conviction of an uncounseled first-degree misdemeanor theft, as the original term of imprisonment was imposed upon him; accordingly, there was no violation of Ohio R. Crim. P. 44(B) and 32.2(C). State v. Isles, — Ohio App. 3d —, 2006 Ohio 6567, — N.E. 2d —, 2006 Ohio App. LEXIS 6477 (Dec. 11, 2006).

Replacement of counsel

Trial court did not abuse its discretion by denying either defendant's motion for new counsel or his counsel's motion to withdraw because defendant's protests stemmed from his erroneous belief that his speedy trial right had been violated and had nothing to do with the merits of the case. Likewise, nothing in the record indicated that appointed counsel was unprepared to represent defendant at his trial or that defendant was prejudiced in any way by the trial court's refusal to appoint new counsel. State v. Kirk, — Ohio App. 3d —, 2007 Ohio 1228, — N.E. 2d —, 2007 Ohio App. LEXIS 1138 (Mar. 19, 2007).

Trial counsel's failure to file frivolous motions did not show a complete breakdown of communication between client and counsel and there was no evidence suggesting such a breakdown. Accordingly, the trial court did not abuse its discretion when it denied defendant's request to substitute trial counsel. State v. Loveless, — Ohio App. 3d —, 2007 Ohio 1560, — N.E. 2d —, 2007 Ohio App. LEXIS 1453 (Mar. 26, 2007).

Trial court did not deny defendant counsel because the record did not show that there was a complete breakdown in the attorney-client relationship between defendant and his counsel. Furthermore, given that defendant requested that counsel be removed as counsel and new counsel be appointed on the day of trial after the case had been pending for over a year supported the trial court's decision to deny new counsel; likewise, so did the number of attorneys that defendant had gone through and the fact that the record showed that the were effectively representing defendant. State v. Beckett, — Ohio App. 3d —, 2007 Ohio 3175, — N.E. 2d —, 2007 Ohio App. LEXIS 2963 (June 21, 2007).

There was no abuse of discretion in refusing to allow counsel to withdraw, or to appoint new counsel, because defense counsel did not tell the trial court that he could not represent defendant because he was afraid for his life or that the attorney/client relationship was so broken that he could not represent defendant. Defendant's "pretrial panic" about whether his attorney had done enough to prepare for trial was not sufficient to demonstrate such a breakdown in the attorney/client relationship. Defense counsel worked diligently on defendant's behalf before and during trial and he moved to withdraw only upon defendant's insistence that he do so, not because he was unwilling to represent defendant. State v. Walker, — Ohio App. 3d —, 2007 Ohio 3772, — N.E. 2d —, 2007 Ohio App. LEXIS 3437 (July 26, 2007).

Trial court did not err in failing to grant defendant's motion to terminate his counsel because defendant did not ask for a continuance in order to retain counsel until the day before trial and because defendant's counsel clearly provided competent representation. Defendant was acquitted on one charge of unlawful sexual conduct with a minor. State v. Gaskins, — Ohio App. 3d —, 2007 Ohio 4103, — N.E. 2d —, 2007 Ohio App. LEXIS 3739 (Aug. 13, 2007).

Trial court did not abuse its discretion in denying either of defendant's requests for new counsel. In the first instance, defendant merely stated, without elaboration, that he did not feel "comfortable" with his counsel. In the second instance, he gave no reason at all for wanting alternate counsel; he merely stated--six months after his arraignment, and just minutes before trial--that his family would (at some unspecified point in the future) retain private counsel. State v. Diaz, — Ohio App. 3d —, 2007 Ohio 4480, — N.E. 2d —, 2007 Ohio App. LEXIS 4037 (Aug. 31, 2007).

Self-representation

While the trial court cautioned defendant against self representation, it did not adequately explain the nature of the charges, the statutory offenses included within them, the range of allowable punishments, possible defenses, mitigation, or other facts essential to a broad understanding of the whole matter. Thus, defendant was not made aware of the dangers and disadvantages of self-representation and the trial court failed to substantially comply with Ohio R. Crim. P. 44(A) by failing to make a sufficient inquiry to determine whether defendant fully understood and intelligently relinquished his right to counsel. State v. Smith, — Ohio App. 3d —, 2007 Ohio 51, — N.E. 2d —, 2007 Ohio App. LEXIS 37 (Jan. 10, 2007).

Trial court sufficiently complied with CrimR 44 where the defendant chose to represent himself by questioning a witness and making a closing statement after the state and defense counsel rested. State v. Johnson, 112 Ohio St. 3d 210, 2006 Ohio 6404, 858 N.E.2d 1144, 2006 Ohio LEXIS 3410 (2006).

Where defendant's second appointed counsel sought withdrawal several days prior to the set date for trial, which the trial court allowed but then appointed counsel as defendant's legal advisor, and on the day of trial, the trial court summarily stated that defendant had discharged his legal advisor, sought a continuance which the trial court denied, and was representing himself, the dictates of Ohio R. Crim. P. 44(C) were not satisfied, as the trial court was required to inquire into defendant's alleged desire to represent himself and to fully inform him of the consequences of such a decision. While there were allegations that defendant was aware of his rights and made a conscious choice, such decision was not reflected on the record, and the court on review had to indulge in every reasonable presumption against the waiver of defendant's fundamental constitutional right to counsel pursuant to U.S. Const. amend. VI. City of Dayton v. Ealy, — Ohio App. 3d —, 2006 Ohio 308, — N.E. 2d —, 2006 Ohio App. LEXIS 267 (Jan. 20, 2006).

Trial court substantially complied with its duty to ensure that defendant knowingly, intelligently, and voluntarily waived his right to counsel and chose to represent himself in his criminal matter, pursuant to Ohio R. Crim. P. 44(A) and (C), as well as pursuant to defendant's constitutional right under U.S. Const. amend. VI, as it informed defendant of his rights, what he was waiving, the possible charges and sentences that he faced, and defendant indicated that he understood. Although a written waiver of the right to counsel was not executed, such was harmless error. State v. Bowman, — Ohio App. 3d —, 2006 Ohio 6146, — N.E. 2d —, 2006 Ohio App. LEXIS 6094 (Nov. 21, 2006).

Waiver of counsel

Trial court committed prejudicial error, in violation of CrimR 44(B), by imposing confinement upon the offender where he was not represented by counsel and did not knowingly, intelligently, and voluntarily waive the assignment of counsel: State v. Thompson, 180 Ohio App. 3d 714, 2009 Ohio 185, 907 N.E.2d 329, 2009 Ohio App. LEXIS 167 (2009).

Where the trial court failed at the resentencing hearing to comply with the requirements of CrimR 44 concerning waiver of counsel, the cause was remanded for another resentencing hearing: State v. Webb, 177 Ohio App. 3d 289, 2008 Ohio 3719, 894 N.E.2d 396, 2008 Ohio App. LEXIS 3131 (2008).

Waiver of counsel must be made on the record in open court, and in cases involving serious offenses where the penalty includes confinement for more than six months, the waiver must also be in writing and filed with the court: State v. Brooke, 113 Ohio St. 3d 199, 2007 Ohio 1533, 863 N.E.2d 1024, 2007 Ohio LEXIS 852 (2007).

Trial court record did not contain sufficient information to establish that defendant's waiver of counsel pursuant to Ohio R. Crim. P. 22 and 44 was knowingly and intelligently made for purposes of his constitutional right under U.S. Const. amend. VI and Ohio Const. art. I, § 10, as defendant had filed a pro se motion to have his appointed attorney disqualified and to represent himself, his attorney had sought withdrawal, and the trial court's judgment indicated that a hearing was held but there was no transcript of those proceedings in the record. Accordingly, it was unclear whether defendant's waiver of the right to counsel was knowingly and intelligently made. State v. Melton, — Ohio App. 3d —, 2007 Ohio 1154, — N.E. 2d —, 2007 Ohio App. LEXIS 1062 (Mar. 14, 2007).

Defendant voluntarily, knowingly and intelligently elected to defend himself; the trial court went to extraordinary measures to insure that defendant's constitutional rights were protected. After being offered, and refusing, legal representation by three different court-appointed attorneys, defendant elected to represent himself with the assistance of another court-appointed attorney; although the trial court thoroughly advised defendant of the perils of representing himself, throughout the proceeding, defendant vehemently asserted that he had the right to represent himself and that he did not want to be represented by appointed counsel. State v. Turner, — Ohio App. 3d —, 2007 Ohio 5732, — N.E. 2d —, 2007 Ohio App. LEXIS 5014 (Oct. 25, 2007).

In defendant's trial for two aggravated robberies, in which he stated the desire to represent himself, his written waiver of counsel was required, under Ohio R. Crim. P. 44(C), because the offenses were considered to be serious crimes, under Ohio R. Crim. P. 2(C), given a potential prison sentence of more than six months, but the trial court's failure to obtain a written waiver was harmless error because defendant was properly advised, under Ohio R. Crim. P. 44(A), of the matters required for a knowing and intelligent waiver. State v. Andrews, — Ohio App. 3d —, 2006 Ohio 3764, — N.E. 2d —, 2006 Ohio App. LEXIS 3706 (July 24, 2006).

Although a defendant did not himself have to have the skill and experience of a lawyer in order to competently and intelligently choose self-representation, he had to be made aware of the dangers and disadvantages of self-representation, so that the record would establish that he knew what he was doing and his choice was made with eyes open. State v. Doyle, — Ohio App. 3d —, 2006 Ohio 5373, — N.E. 2d —, 2006 Ohio App. LEXIS 5346 (Oct. 16, 2006).

As there was no showing by the State that defendant had waived his right to counsel pursuant to Ohio R. Crim. P. 44(C) and 22 where he was charged with, inter alia, driving under the influence of alcohol, in violation of RC § 4511.19(G)(1)(b), which was a petty offense as defined in Ohio R. Crim. P. 2(D), it was presumed that defendant did not knowingly and intelligently waive his right to counsel; accordingly, imposition of a jail term on defendant was error which required vacatur. State v. West, — Ohio App. 3d —, 2006 Ohio 5834, — N.E. 2d —, 2006 Ohio App. LEXIS 5762 (Nov. 6, 2006).

Waiver of right to counsel

Defendant voluntarily, knowingly, and intelligently waived his right to counsel because the trial court adequately covered the issues of possible defenses and circumstances in mitigation given defendant's statement that he had a strategy prepared and informed defendant of the charges against him and the possible sentences. Defendant indicated that he understood. Also, defendant's strategy was partially effective because the jury returned verdicts of not guilty on the aggravated robbery and felonious assault charges. State v. Smith, — Ohio App. 3d —, 2007 Ohio 738, — N.E. 2d —, 2007 Ohio App. LEXIS 672 (Feb. 20, 2007).

Trial court erred by failing to substantially comply with the requirements of Ohio R. Crim. P. 44; because the driving under the influence charge qualified as a "serious offense" under Ohio R. Crim. P. 2(C), the trial court failed to make an adequate determination that defendant sufficiently understood the possible consequences of declining counsel. The trial court never clearly ascertained whether defendant actually wanted to waive his right to counsel, the record contained no discussion about the ramifications of waiving the right to counsel, and the record contained no written waiver of defendant's right to counsel. State v. Dobbins, — Ohio App. 3d —, 2007 Ohio 1665, — N.E. 2d —, 2007 Ohio App. LEXIS 1527 (Apr. 6, 2007).

Trial court's inquiry to determine that defendant knowingly, intelligently, and voluntarily waived his right to counsel pursuant to U.S. Const. amend. VI and Ohio Const. art. I, § 10 was sufficient where defendant did not display any confusion about what he wanted or what self-representation

meant and he was deemed competent, such that there was substantial compliance with Ohio R. Crim. P. 44. Although the trial court erred when it failed to obtain a written waiver of counsel pursuant to Rule 44(C), such failure was harmless error under Ohio R. Crim. P. 52. State v. Julian, — Ohio App. 3d —, 2007 Ohio 3568, — N.E. 2d —, 2007 Ohio App. LEXIS 3277 (July 13, 2007).

Defendant did not knowingly and voluntarily waive his right to counsel because the trial court never informed him on the record of the inherent dangers of proceeding pro se and never warned him that if he did not retain counsel he would be forced to proceed pro se; thus, waiver could not be inferred. Given that defendant possibly believed that he had retained counsel, the trial court should have continued the trial and warned him that if he did not show up with an attorney at the next trial date, it would construe that as a waiver of the right to counsel and he would have to proceed pro se. State v. Koons, — Ohio App. 3d —, 2007 Ohio 4985, — N.E. 2d —, 2007 Ohio App. LEXIS 4451 (Sept. 25, 2007).

Trial court erred when it enhanced defendant's penalty based on prior OVI convictions because the record contained no evidence that the prior waivers of defendant's right to counsel were made on the record in open court, nor were they shown through the trial court's colloquy with defendant to have been knowingly and voluntarily made. Additionally, the waiver forms did not indicate that defendant was asked if he understood everything, or that the trial court was satisfied that defendant did, and that he wished to waive his right to counsel; neither waiver form was signed by the trial court. State v. Thompson, — Ohio App. 3d —, 2007 Ohio 6098, — N.E. 2d —, 2007 Ohio App. LEXIS 5381 (Nov. 8, 2007).

Defendant's Sixth Amendment right to counsel was violated where there was no record to indicate that he waived that right, and a presumption of regularity as to the trial court proceedings in the absence of a record, pursuant to Ohio R. App. P. 9(B), was not made in such an instance; accordingly, where there was no showing that defendant knowingly and intelligently waived his right to counsel, pursuant to Ohio R. Crim. P. 22 and 44(B), a sentence of imprisonment could not be imposed against him, although other sentencing terms were proper. State v. Miyamoto, — Ohio App. 3d —, 2006 Ohio 1776, — N.E. 2d —, 2006 Ohio App. LEXIS 1648 (Apr. 10, 2006).

Where defendant was not provided with a sufficient discussion by the trial court regarding his waiver of the right to counsel pursuant to Ohio R. Crim. P. 44(C) because the trial court did not advise him of the range of sentences that the charges against him carried, the possible defenses or mitigation that he could assert, and the dangers and disadvantages of self-representation, his waiver of the right to counsel under U.S. Const. amend. VI and Ohio Const. art. I, § 10 was not deemed voluntary, intelligent, and knowing. State v. Petaway, — Ohio App. 3d —, 2006 Ohio 2941, — N.E. 2d —, 2006 Ohio App. LEXIS 2814 (June 12, 2006).

Trial court did not make a sufficient inquiry to determine whether defendant fully understood and intelligently relinquished his right to counsel and therefore, his waiver of his right to counsel was invalid as he did not knowingly and intelligently waive his right to counsel, pursuant to Ohio R. Crim. P. 44. At no time did the trial court explain or discuss with him the nature of the charges, the statutory offenses included within them, the range of allowable punishments, possible defenses to the charges, possible mitigating circumstances, or other facts essential to a broad understanding of the whole matter. Defendant was not given adequate warnings about the seriousness of the trial, the possible results it could have for his liberty and life, and the dangers and disadvantages of self-representation and the waiver was not put in writing when it was accepted, but was executed by defendant only after the prejudicial effects of his self-representation had occurred. State v. Youngblood, — Ohio App. 3d —, 2006 Ohio 3853, — N.E. 2d —, 2006 Ohio App. LEXIS 3794 (July 28, 2006).

Defendant's right to counsel was violated because the trial court did not engage in any dialog with him regarding the nature of the charged offense, the range of possible punishments, possible defenses, or any other matters that would apprise him of the difficulties in attempting to represent himself throughout a criminal case. Because defendant was convicted of a petty offense without the benefit of counsel and without executing a valid waiver of counsel, his sentence had to be vacated even though the assault conviction itself was affirmed. McCrory v. State, — Ohio App. 3d —, 2006 Ohio 6348, — N.E. 2d —, 2006 Ohio App. LEXIS 6301 (Dec. 1, 2006).

RULE 45.   Time

(A) **Time: computation.** In computing any period of time prescribed or allowed by these rules, by the local rules of any court, by order of court, or by any applicable statute, the date of the act or event from which the designated period of time begins to run shall not be included. The last day of the period so computed shall be included, unless it is a Saturday, Sunday, or legal holiday, in which event the period runs until the end of the next day which is not Saturday, Sunday, or legal holiday. When the period of time prescribed or allowed is less than seven days, intermediate Saturdays, Sundays, and legal holidays shall be excluded in computation.

(B) **Time: enlargement.** When an act is required or allowed to be performed at or within a specified time, the court for cause shown may at any time in its discretion (1) with or without motion or notice, order the period enlarged if application therefore is made before expiration of the period originally prescribed or as extended by a previous order; or (2) upon motion permit the act to be done after expiration of the specified period, if the failure to act on time was the result of excusable neglect or would result in injustice to the defendant. The court may not extend the time for taking any action under Rule 23, Rule 29, Rule 33, and Rule 34 except to the extent and under the conditions stated in them.

(C) **Time: unaffected by expiration of term.** The period of time provided for the doing of any act or the taking of any proceeding is not affected or limited by the expiration of a term of court. The expiration of a term of court in no way affects the power of a court to do any act in a criminal proceeding.

(D) **Time: for motions; affidavits.** A written motion, other than one which may be heard *ex parte*, and notice of the hearing thereof, shall be served not later than seven days before the time specified for the hearing unless a different period is fixed by rule or order of the court. For cause shown such an order may be made on ex parte application. When a motion is supported by affidavit, the affidavit shall be served with the motion. Opposing affidavits may be served not less than one day before the hearing, unless the court permits them to be served at a later time.

(E) **Time: additional time after service by mail** . Whenever a party has the right or is required to do an act within a prescribed period after the service of a notice or other paper upon him, and the notice or other paper is served upon him by mail, three days shall be added to the prescribed period. This subdivision does not apply to responses to service of summons under Rule 4 and Rule 9.

NOTES TO DECISIONS

ANALYSIS

Speedy trial

Speedy trial

A trial court erred in dismissing criminal charges against defendant due to a speedy trial violation under R.C. §§ 2945.71(C)(2) and 2945.73(B), as the trial court should not have counted Saturday and Sunday prior to trial pursuant to Crim. R. 45(A) and the motion to dismiss was made on the 270th day. State v. Johnson, — Ohio App. 3d —, 2006 Ohio 4650, — N.E. 2d —, 2006 Ohio App. LEXIS 4553 (Sept. 8, 2006).

RULE 46.   Bail

(A) **Types and amounts of bail.** Any person who is entitled to release shall be released upon one or more of the following types of bail in the amount set by the court:

(1) The personal recognizance of the accused or an unsecured bail bond;

(2) A bail bond secured by the deposit of ten percent of the amount of the bond in cash. Ninety percent of the deposit shall be returned upon compliance with all conditions of the bond;

(3) A surety bond, a bond secured by real estate or securities as allowed by law, or the deposit of cash, at the option of the defendant.

(B) **Conditions of bail.** The court may impose any of the following conditions of bail:

(1) Place the person in the custody of a designated person or organization agreeing to supervise the person;

(2) Place restrictions on the travel, association, or place of abode of the person during the period of release;

(3) Place the person under a house arrest, electronic monitoring, or work release program;

(4) Regulate or prohibit the person's contact with the victim;

(5) Regulate the person's contact with witnesses or others associated with the case upon proof of the likelihood that the person will threaten, harass, cause injury, or seek to intimidate those persons;

(6) Require a person who is charged with an offense that is alcohol or drug related, and who appears to need treatment, to attend treatment while on bail;

(7) Any other constitutional condition considered reasonably necessary to ensure appearance or public safety.

(C) **Factors.** In determining the types, amounts, and conditions of bail, the court shall consider all relevant information, including but not limited to:

(1) The nature and circumstances of the crime charged, and specifically whether the defendant used or had access to a weapon;

(2) The weight of the evidence against the defendant;

(3) The confirmation of the defendant's identity;

(4) The defendant's family ties, employment, financial resources, character, mental condition, length of residence in the community, jurisdiction of residence, record of convictions, record of appearance at court proceedings or of flight to avoid prosecution;

(5) Whether the defendant is on probation, a community control sanction, parole, post-release control, bail, or under a court protection order.

(D) Appearance pursuant to summons. When summons has been issued and the defendant has appeared pursuant to the summons, absent good cause, a recognizance bond shall be the preferred type of bail.

(E) Amendments. A court, at any time, may order additional or different types, amounts, or conditions of bail.

(F) Information need not be admissible. Information stated in or offered in connection with any order entered pursuant to this rule need not conform to the rules pertaining to the admissibility of evidence in a court of law. Statements or admissions of the defendant made at a bail proceeding shall not be received as substantive evidence in the trial of the case.

(G) Bond schedule. Each court shall establish a bail bond schedule covering all misdemeanors including traffic offenses, either specifically, by type, by potential penalty, or by some other reasonable method of classification. The court also may include requirements for release in consideration of divisions (B) and (C)(5) of this rule. Each municipal or county court shall, by rule, establish a method whereby a person may make bail by use of a credit card. No credit card transaction shall be permitted when a service charge is made against the court or clerk unless allowed by law.

(H) Continuation of bonds. Unless otherwise ordered by the court pursuant to division (E) of this rule, or if application is made by the surety for discharge, the same bond shall continue until the return of a verdict or the acceptance of a guilty plea. In the discretion of the court, the same bond may also continue pending sentence or disposition of the case on review. Any provision of a bond or similar instrument that is contrary to this rule is void.

(I) Failure to appear; breach of conditions. Any person who fails to appear before any court as required is subject to the punishment provided by the law, and any bail given for the person's release may be forfeited. If there is a breach of condition of bail, the court may amend the bail.

(J) Justification of sureties. Every surety, except a corporate surety licensed as provided by law, shall justify by affidavit, and may be required to describe in the affidavit, the property that the surety proposes as security and the encumbrances on it, the number and amount of other bonds and undertakings for bail entered into by the surety and remaining undischarged, and all of the surety's other liabilities. The surety shall provide other evidence of financial responsibility as the court or clerk may require. No bail bond shall be approved unless the surety or sureties appear, in the opinion of the court or clerk, to be financially responsible in at least the amount of the bond. No licensed attorney at law shall be a surety.

History: Amended, eff 7-1-90; 7-1-94; 7-1-98; 7-1-06.

NOTES TO DECISIONS

ANALYSIS

Amount of bail
Appeal
Bond
Factors considered
Increase in bail amount
Reinstatement of forfeited bond
Revocation of bail
Surety bonds

Amount of bail

Defendant's claim that her rights under Ohio Const. art. IV, §§ 5(B) and 9, as well as under Ohio R. Crim. P. 46 not to have excessive bail applied were violated by the trial court's imposition of the amount of bail against her was deemed moot where she raised the issue after conviction. State v. Albardis Towns, — Ohio App. 3d —, 2007 Ohio 529, — N.E. 2d —, 2007 Ohio App. LEXIS 481 (Feb. 8, 2007).

Prisoner's petition for a writ of habeas corpus was dismissed because the prisoner had improperly captioned his petition by failing to identify the parties as petitioner or respondent and by failing to include the address of the sheriff, as required by Ohio R. Civ. P. 10(A); he had not verified his petition, as required by RC § 2725.04; he had failed to support his petition with a sworn affidavit specifying the details of the claim, as required by Ohio 8th Dist. Ct. App. R. 45(B)(1)(a); and he had failed to file an affidavit describing each civil action or appeal of a civil action that had been docketed in the previous five years, as required by RC § 2969.25(A). Notwithstanding the procedural defects, the prisoner had failed to substantively demonstrate that his bail was excessive as he did not address the factors as enumerated within Ohio R. Crim. P. 46(A). State v. Thomas, — Ohio App. 3d —, 2007 Ohio 1692, — N.E. 2d —, 2007 Ohio App. LEXIS 1555 (Apr. 10, 2007).

Appeal

Where a trial court entered an order that forfeited a bail bond due to defendant's having escaped from the jurisdiction during a lunch break in his criminal trial, such was not a final appealable order pursuant to Ohio R. Crim. P. 46(I). The trial court was acting with its power to declare the bond forfeited, and any appeal therefrom would have accordingly lacked merit. State v. Smith, — Ohio App. 3d —, 2006 Ohio 4614, — N.E. 2d —, 2006 Ohio App. LEXIS 4572 (Sept. 1, 2006).

Bond

Under Ohio R. Crim. P. 46(A)(2), a criminal defendant is given the benefit of not having to cover 90 percent of the full amount of bond set by the trial court. To this extent, the bond requirement of Ohio R. Crim. P. 46(A)(2) cannot be characterized as a "cash only" bond in the same respect as the bonds in the Smith v. Leis and State ex rel. Jones v. Hendon cases. State ex rel. Williams v. Fankhauser, — Ohio App. 3d —, 2006 Ohio 1170, — N.E. 2d —, 2006 Ohio App. LEXIS 1054 (Mar. 14, 2006).

Factors considered

Defendant was not entitled to a writ of habeas corpus based on defendant's claim that excessive bail ($100,000 with no 10 percent) was imposed because considering the factors in RC § 2937.23(A)(3) and Ohio R. Crim. P. 46, defendant was charged with serious offenses, including gang activity and aggravated burglary, making him a risk to public safety under Ohio Const. art. I, § 9, and defendant's only ties to the community were his parents, making him a flight risk. Garcia v. Wasylyshyn, 2007 Ohio 3951, 2007 Ohio App. LEXIS 3623 (2007).

Increase in bail amount

Ohio R. Crim. P. 46(H) indicated that, subject to a trial judge's sound discretion, the same bond should continue until the return of a verdict or the acceptance of a guilty plea, and, if there was no showing of any changed circumstances of the accused or his surrounding, the bond as set should continue. State ex rel. Sellers v. McFaul, — Ohio App. 3d —, 2006 Ohio 1936, — N.E. 2d —, 2006 Ohio App. LEXIS 1781 (Apr. 18, 2006).

Reinstatement of forfeited bond

Trial court erred in reinstating a forfeited recognizance bond as there was no statutory procedure to do so; once the bond was forfeited under RC § 2937.36 and Ohio R. Crim. P. 46, if the trial court found that any part of that bond should be remitted, it had to use the statutory procedure for remission under RC 2937.39. State v. Hancock, — Ohio App. 3d —, 2006 Ohio 1594, — N.E. 2d —, 2006 Ohio App. LEXIS 1470 (Mar. 31, 2006).

Revocation of bail

Petition for habeas corpus pursuant to Ohio Const. art. I, § 9 was granted because the trial court abused its discretion in revoking petitioner's recognizance bond. Pursuant to Ohio R. Crim. P. 46, there was no evidence of any changed circumstances that would warrant the alteration of petitioner's bond. Leu v. Telb, — Ohio App. 3d —, 2007 Ohio 3317, — N.E. 2d —, 2007 Ohio App. LEXIS 3063 (June 29, 2007).

When a trial court continued defendant's bond until defendant appeared to begin serving defendant's sentence, and defendant did not so appear, the trial court could properly forfeit and revoke the bond, under RC § 2937.35, because Ohio R. Crim. P. 46 allowed the trial court to continue the bond in this manner, as defendant's jail sentence did not commence until defendant reported to begin serving the sentence, giving the court continuing jurisdiction, and the purpose of the bond was to ensure defendant's appearance at all stages of the criminal proceedings. City of E. Liverpool v. Stith, — Ohio App. 3d —, 2007 Ohio 4637, — N.E. 2d —, 2007 Ohio App. LEXIS 4180 (Sept. 5, 2007).

Surety bonds

Subsequent and additional $25,000 bond did not relieve the bail bondsman of his obligations on the $5,000 bond he previously posted, an obligation which continued until the proceedings terminated, whether or not the additional $25,000 bond was also forfeited. State v. Johnson, — Ohio App. 3d —, 2006 Ohio 417, — N.E. 2d —, 2006 Ohio App. LEXIS 352 (Jan. 27, 2006).

Where a bond had been forfeited, once defendant was in custody, the trial court had to provide for a new bond; even if there had been a procedure to reinstate a forfeited bond, the trial court should not have reinstated the surety bond without giving the surety notice and opportunity to be heard. State v. Hancock, — Ohio App. 3d —, 2006 Ohio 1594, — N.E. 2d —, 2006 Ohio App. LEXIS 1470 (Mar. 31, 2006).

RULE 47. Motions

An application to the court for an order shall be by motion. A motion, other than one made during trial or hearing, shall be in writing unless the court permits it to be made orally. It shall state with particularity the grounds upon which it is made and shall set forth the relief or order sought. It shall be supported by a memorandum containing citations of authority, and may also be supported by an affidavit.

To expedite its business, the court may make provision by rule or order for the submission and determi-nation of motions without oral hearing upon brief written statements of reasons in support and opposition.

NOTES TO DECISIONS

ANALYSIS

Contents of motion
Determination without oral hearing
Motion to suppress
Post-conviction relief

Contents of motion

When defendant filed a "praecipe for demand of official oaths and bonds" after he was convicted and sentenced, he did not comply with Ohio R. Crim. P. 47 because it was unclear to whom the motion was addressed and what information and relief he sought, nor, to the extent his motion sought discovery, did he comply with Ohio R. Crim. P. 16(F) because such a motion had to be filed within 21 days after arraignment or seven days before trial, whichever was earlier, rather than after conviction and sentencing. State v. Dallas, — Ohio App. 3d —, 2007 Ohio 1214, — N.E. 2d —, 2007 Ohio App. LEXIS 1144 (Mar. 19, 2007).

Determination without oral hearing

Trial court committed reversible error when it granted defendant's motion to dismiss criminal charges against him due to the State's alleged failure to preserve evidence within 24 hours of the motion having been made and without giving the State an opportunity to respond in an oral hearing or by submitted opposition. Although a hearing was not required for disposition of a dismissal motion, both Crim. R. 12(F) and 47 required that both parties be given an opportunity to submit their positions to the court prior to a ruling having been made. State v. Palivoda, — Ohio App. 3d —, 2006 Ohio 6494, — N.E. 2d —, 2006 Ohio App. LEXIS 6421 (Dec. 8, 2006).

Motion to suppress

Trial court erred when it denied defendant an evidentiary hearing on the motion to suppress because defendant was not required to demonstrate a specific defect in the blood alcohol machine. His motion was sufficiently particular to satisfy CrimR 47 because the state and the trial court were put on notice of the issues that defendant intended to raise; the burden then shifted to the state to show that it substantially complied with OAC 3701-53-04. State v. Conley, — Ohio App. 3d —, 2008 Ohio 609, — N.E. 2d —, 2008 Ohio App. LEXIS 531 (Feb. 15, 2008).

Court rejected defendant's attempt to attack the propriety of a pat-down search conducted by police officers after they stopped defendant because defendant did not give fair notice that the pat-down search was at issue, as required by Ohio R. Crim. P. 47, as he did not raise the issue until the end of his closing argument at the suppression hearing. State v. Robinson, — Ohio App. 3d —, 2007 Ohio 850, — N.E. 2d —, 2007 Ohio App. LEXIS 741 (Feb. 26, 2007).

Since defendant raised only one issue in his motion to suppress, the appellate court could not consider the multiple other issues raised by defendant on appeal. Pursuant to Ohio R. Crim. P. 47, a motion had to state with particularity the grounds upon which it was made, and a failure to adequately raise the basis of his challenge constitutes a waiver of that issue on appeal. State v. McDaniel, — Ohio App. 3d —, 2007 Ohio 1227, — N.E. 2d —, 2007 Ohio App. LEXIS 1141 (Mar. 19, 2007).

Trial court did not err in finding that defendant's motion to dismiss, for suppression, and in limine lacked the specificity necessary to put the State on notice of the specific alleged deficiencies in the field sobriety and breathalyzer tests administered to defendant, as he provided a "laundry list" of allegations to support his claim that the tests were not performed in strict compliance with the law, but he provided no factual basis to support the allegations. The suppression motion under Ohio R. Crim. P. 12 was not sufficiently particular pursuant to Ohio R. Crim. P. 47. State v. Stoner, — Ohio App. 3d —, 2006 Ohio 2122, — N.E. 2d —, 2006 Ohio App. LEXIS 1955 (Apr. 28, 2006).

Ohio R. Crim. P. 47 operated to require that the prosecution be given notice of the specific legal and factual grounds upon which the validity of a search and seizure was challenged, so, to suppress evidence obtained pursuant to a warrantless search or seizure, a defendant had to (1) demonstrate the lack of a warrant, and (2) raise the grounds upon which the validity of the search or seizure was challenged in such a manner as to give the prosecutor notice of the basis for the challenge. State v. Landis, — Ohio App. 3d —, 2006 Ohio 3538, — N.E. 2d —, 2006 Ohio App. LEXIS 3482 (July 10, 2006).

In defendant's prosecution for driving while intoxicated and with a prohibited level of alcohol, his motion to suppress the results of chemical breath tests for alleged failure to establish substantial compliance with the required testing procedures was sufficiently specific to meet the requirements of Ohio R. Crim. P. 47 and to put the State on notice of the issues; the transcript indicated that the State acknowledged that the suppression motion was very specific. State v. Wetherill, — Ohio App. 3d —, 2006 Ohio 5687, — N.E. 2d —, 2006 Ohio App. LEXIS 5686 (Oct. 18, 2006).

Post-conviction relief

Inmate's reliance on Ohio R. Crim. P. 47 and 57 for his motion to vacate and/or correct his sentence was misplaced, as those rules did not specifically authorize the filing of such a motion, and as the inmate's request for relief was based on his claim that his constitutional rights were violated, RC §§ 2953.21 and 2953.23(A) were necessarily applicable. State v. Foti, — Ohio App. 3d —, 2007 Ohio 887, — N.E. 2d —, 2007 Ohio App. LEXIS 808 (Mar. 2, 2007).

Defendant inmate's motion to vacate and correct his sentence under Ohio R. Crim. P. 47 was properly summarily denied, as it was an untimely petition for postconviction relief under RC § 2953.21(A)(2), it was not within the exception to timeliness under RC § 2953.23, and even if it was timely, the sentencing issues under Blakely and Foster that were raised therein would have been barred by res judicata; further, there was no authority under Ohio R. Crim. P. 47 to seek the requested relief. State v. Payne, — Ohio App. 3d —, 2007 Ohio 4594, — N.E. 2d —, 2007 Ohio App. LEXIS 4135 (Sept. 6, 2007).

RULE 48. Dismissal

(A) **Dismissal by the state.** The state may by leave of court and in open court file an entry of dismissal of an indictment, information, or complaint and the prosecution shall thereupon terminate.

(B) **Dismissal by the court.** If the court over objection of the state dismisses an indictment, information, or complaint, it shall state on the record its findings of fact and reasons for the dismissal.

NOTES TO DECISIONS

ANALYSIS

Dismissal
Dismissal by court
Dismissal with prejudice
Findings and reasons

Dismissal

Trial court did not abuse its discretion by dismissing the domestic violence charges against defendant under Ohio R. Crim. P. 48 because the State violated an express and unambiguous trial court order to have witnesses present at the specified time for trial; when the trial court called the matter to trial, the State did not have any witnesses present. State v. Congrove, — Ohio App. 3d —, 2007 Ohio 3323, — N.E. 2d —, 2007 Ohio App. LEXIS 3048 (June 29, 2007).

Dismissal by court

When a jury convicted defendant of two counts in an indictment but could not agree as to another count, which was dismissed without prejudice, defendant could not appeal the counts defendant was convicted of because there was not a final appealable order, under RC § 2505.02, until the other count was disposed of by a dismissal with prejudice, under Ohio R. Crim. P. 48(A), or retrial. State v. Cole, — Ohio App. 3d —, 2007 Ohio 3076, — N.E. 2d —, 2007 Ohio App. LEXIS 2816 (June 21, 2007).

Dismissal with prejudice

Where defendant filed a motion to dismiss a criminal charge against him on speedy trial grounds, which motion was orally granted by the trial court but never reduced to writing, and thereafter, the State sought leave of court to dismiss the charge with prejudice pursuant to Ohio R. Crim. P. 48(A), it could not later appeal the dismissal by claiming that the trial court erred on the speedy trial issue; the claim by the State that the trial court should not have granted its request for leave to dismiss the charge was invited or induced by the State and accordingly, it lacked merit. State v. Wrage, — Ohio App. 3d —, 2006 Ohio 3526, — N.E. 2d —, 2006 Ohio App. LEXIS 3478 (June 28, 2006).

Trial court abused its discretion when it dismissed an indictment against defendant with prejudice pursuant to Ohio R. Crim. P. 48(B) without making the requisite findings that defendant was denied a constitutional or statutory right. The trial court lacked jurisdiction thereafter to enter a nunc pro tunc judgment to indicate that the dismissal was without prejudice, as the State of Ohio had already appealed the prior dismissal order, which divested the trial court of jurisdiction, and further, the nunc pro tunc judgment was improper where it was not entered to correct a clerical order pursuant to Ohio R. Crim. P. 36(A). State v. Walton, — Ohio App. 3d —, 2006 Ohio 4771, — N.E. 2d —, 2006 Ohio App. LEXIS 4721 (Sept. 14, 2006).

Findings and reasons

When a trial court dismissed charges of carrying an unregistered handgun, under Cleveland, Ohio, Codified Ordinance § 674.02, because the city did not disclose the concealed weapons permit that arresting officers seized from defendant until after defendant made repeated requests for the information, pursuant to Ohio R. Crim. P. 16, and the trial court specifically directed that it be disclosed, the trial court's failure to provide findings and reasons for the dismissal, as required by Ohio R. Crim. P. 48, was harmless because the court's reasons were apparent from a transcript of the proceedings. City of Cleveland v. Stoutemire, — Ohio App. 3d —, 2007 Ohio 721, — N.E. 2d —, 2007 Ohio App. LEXIS 657 (Feb. 22, 2007).

Where defendant filed a motion for dismissal of criminal charges against him, which was granted by the trial court, the requirement of findings of fact and reasons for the dismissal in the trial court's order under Ohio R. Crim. P. 48 was not applicable, as that rule contemplated a trial court's sua sponte dismissal rather than one entered at the request of a party. State v. Palivoda, — Ohio App. 3d —, 2006 Ohio 6494, — N.E. 2d —, 2006 Ohio App. LEXIS 6421 (Dec. 8, 2006).

There was no abuse of discretion in the trial court's denial of defendant's dismissal motion with respect to the lack of specific dates in the indictment, charging him with, inter alia, gross sexual imposition involving a victim under the age of 13 years, in violation of RC § 2907.05, as defendant entered a general denial to all counts in the indictment, which did not warrant specific dates for purposes of his defense, the dates were not an element of the offense, and dates were not required in the case of a child victim. The prosecution did establish that the offenses were committed within the time frame alleged, and as the trial court denied dismissal, there was no requirement that findings of fact and reasons pursuant to Ohio R. Crim. P. 48(B) be provided. State v. Lawwill, — Ohio App. 3d —, 2007 Ohio 2627, — N.E. 2d —, 2007 Ohio App. LEXIS 2457 (May 31, 2007).

RULE 49.   Service and Filing of Papers

(A) **Service: when required.** Written notices, requests for discovery, designation of record on appeal, written motions other than those heard ex parte, and similar papers, shall be served upon each of the parties.

(B) **Service: how made.** Whenever under these rules or by court order service is required or permitted to be made upon a party represented by an attorney, the service shall be made upon the attorney unless service upon the party himself is ordered by the court. Service upon the attorney or upon the party shall be made in the manner provided in Civil Rule 5(B).

(C) **Filing.** All papers required to be served upon a party shall be filed simultaneously with or immediately after service. Papers filed with the court shall not be considered until proof of service is endorsed thereon or separately filed. The proof of service shall state the date and the manner of service and shall be signed and filed in the manner provided in Civil Rule 5(D).

NOTES TO DECISIONS

ANALYSIS

Service

Service

Trial court properly denied an inmate's motion to strike responses and motions by the State from the record in the inmate's postconviction relief request, as the State properly served the inmate's attorney, as directed and required by Ohio R. Crim. P. 49(B), and thereafter the inmate was served directly pursuant to the court's directive. State v. Schlee, — Ohio App. 3d —, 2006 Ohio 3208, — N.E. 2d —, 2006 Ohio App. LEXIS 3116 (June 23, 2006).

RULE 50.   Calendars

Criminal cases shall be given precedence over civil matters and proceedings.

RULE 51.   Exceptions Unnecessary

An exception, at any stage or step of the case or matter, is unnecessary to lay a foundation for review, whenever a matter has been called to the attention of the court by objection, motion, or otherwise, and the court has ruled thereon.

RULE 52.   Harmless Error and Plain Error

(A) **Harmless error.** Any error, defect, irregularity, or variance which does not affect substantial rights shall be disregarded.

(B) **Plain error.** Plain errors or defects affecting substantial rights may be noticed although they were not brought to the attention of the court.

NOTES TO DECISIONS

ANALYSIS

Allied offenses
Amendment of indictment
Cumulative errors
Erroneous sentencing
Failure to object
Failure to object to jury instruction
Failure to object to testimony
Guilty plea
Indictment, defects in
Ineffective assistance
Intervention in lieu of conviction
Jury instructions
Lesser included offenses
Misconduct by prosecutor
Motion for acquittal
Motion to suppress
No contest plea
No plain error
Opportunity to present defense
Other act testimony
Photographs
Plain error
Plain error analysis
Plain error, generally
Post-release control
Prior convictions
Prosecutor's comments
Prosecutorial misconduct
Right to remain silent
Self-defense
Sentence
Sentencing
Speedy trial
Venue
Verdict forms
Withdrawal of guilty plea

Allied offenses

As defendant inmate had previously raised the claim on direct appeal that a trial court erred in failing to merge convictions for aggravated robbery and kidnapping for purposes of sentencing because they were allied offenses of similar import under RC § 2941.25(A), which claim was rejected, defendant's subsequent request for an evidentiary hearing on that same issue was barred by res judicata; there was no plain error under Ohio R. Crim. P. 52(B) by the trial court's sentencing decision in the circumstances. State v. Marshall, — Ohio App. 3d —, 2007 Ohio 6830, — N.E. 2d —, 2007 Ohio App. LEXIS 5958 (Dec. 20, 2007).

Amendment of indictment

Amendment of an indictment for breaking and entering to receiving stolen property constituted plan error where the defendant's guilty plea to the latter offense did not contain a waiver of the right to a grand jury indictment: State v. Rohrbaugh, 178 Ohio App. 3d 211, 2008 Ohio 4781, 897 N.E.2d 238, 2008 Ohio App. LEXIS 4020 (2008).

Cumulative errors

Where a trial court abused its discretion by allowing the admission of testimony from an alleged prior victim of defendant's attack and from defendant's probation officer, such cumulative errors prejudiced defendant pursuant to Ohio R. Crim. P. 52(A) and Ohio R. Evid. 103(A), as despite other substantial evidence against defendant in the murder trial, it was clear that his counsel's trial strategy was seriously altered or abandoned when the trial court allowed such testimony, as it had been restricted or precluded in a prior trial that ended in a mistrial. As the testimony was extensive, largely irrelevant, and highly prejudicial, it appeared that defendant would have presented his defense differently if the testimony were not admitted, and further, that the outcome of the matter would have been different as well. State v. Anderson, — Ohio App. 3d —, 2006 Ohio 4618, — N.E. 2d —, 2006 Ohio App. LEXIS 4581 (Sept. 1, 2006).

Erroneous sentencing

It was plain error, under Ohio R. Crim. P. 52(B), for a trial court not to grant defendant jail-time credit, under RC § 2967.191 and OAC 5120-2-04(B), because defendant was jailed when defendant could not post a bond which was increased due to a crime allegedly committed in another state and another crime allegedly committed in Ohio, but those other crimes were not pending when defendant was jailed, nor could defendant have been jailed in Ohio for a crime committed in another state, and this error prejudiced defendant because it affected the outcome of defendant's total sentence, as the fact that defendant received the credit in another case in which defendant received a five-year sentence did not alleviate the error because the resulting reduction in the five-year term did not reduce defendant's total prison time for both cases due to defendant's concurrent 16-year prison term in the instant case. Ohio v. Miller, — Ohio App. 3d —, 2007 Ohio 5931, — N.E. 2d —, 2007 Ohio App. LEXIS 5197 (Nov. 2, 2007).

Failure to object

Defendant's failure to object to the City's failure to properly authenticate under Ohio R. Evid. 901 a 911 tape at trial, used to establish that one of the City's witnesses called 911 immediately after seeing a car crash, waived all but plain error for appeal. Since the City presented other admissible evidence that contradicted the testimony of defendant's witness that a female, not defendant, was driving the car at the time of the accident, the jury could have convicted defendant solely on the testimony of the City's witnesses without the unauthenticated 911 tape. City of Akron v. Stalnaker, — Ohio App. 3d —, 2007 Ohio 6789, — N.E. 2d —, 2007 Ohio App. LEXIS 5953 (Dec. 19, 2007).

Defendant failed to preserve for appeal his argument that the trial court's failure to notify counsel that two jurors were sleeping during the presentation of evidence violated his right to a fair and impartial jury as he failed to object and state his dissatisfaction with the way that the trial court handled the sleeping jurors and failed to request that the trial court remedy the alleged juror misconduct. Moreover, defendant had provided no evidence of prejudice to support a finding of plain error under Ohio R. Crim. P. 52(B) as there was no evidence that the two jurors missed large or critical portions of the trial. State v. Terry, — Ohio App. 3d —, 2007 Ohio 6790, — N.E. 2d —, 2007 Ohio App. LEXIS 5956 (Dec. 19, 2007).

Where defendant did not object to a trial judge's comments to a jury during voir dire, any issue that could have been raised on appeal with respect to those comments was deemed waived, and there was no plain error under Ohio R. Crim. P. 52(B) where there was no finding that the outcome of the trial clearly would have gone the other way but for the alleged error. State v. Woods, — Ohio App. 3d —, 2006 Ohio 1342, — N.E. 2d —, 2006 Ohio App. LEXIS 1218 (Mar. 23, 2006).

Failure to object to jury instruction

Although defendant failed to object under Ohio R. Crim. P. 30 to the trial court's failure to instruct the jury that his burden of proving self-defense pursuant to RC § 2905.01(A) was by a preponderance of the evidence, there was plain error under Ohio R. Crim. P. 52(B) where such error constituted a manifest miscarriage of justice. As the jury was instructed that the State's burden of proof on the substantive offenses was beyond a reasonable doubt, the logical result was that the jury might have believed that such burden of proof was equally applicable to the affirmative defense, which was a fundamental error. State v. Cooper, 170 Ohio App. 3d 418, 2007 Ohio 1186, 867 N.E.2d 493, 2007 Ohio App. LEXIS 1115 (2007).

Since defendant did not object to the jury instructions given by the trial court on the ground that the trial court did not specifically instruct the jury that it had to agree on one theory or the other advanced by the City in defendant's prosecution for operating a vehicle while under the influence of alcohol and specifically state the matter to which he objected, as required by Ohio R. Crim. P. 30, he had waived all challenges except plain error. The trial court's unanimity instruction, instructing the jury that all eight members had to agree upon a verdict and had to sign the verdict form, was sufficient, defendant could not establish that the jury's result would have been different, and defendant could not show that his right to a fair trial under Ohio Const. art. I, § 10 had been violated. City of Akron v. Stalnaker, — Ohio App. 3d —, 2007 Ohio 6789, — N.E. 2d —, 2007 Ohio App. LEXIS 5953 (Dec. 19, 2007).

Failure to object to testimony

Trial court did not commit plain error under Ohio R. Crim. P. 52(B) where it did not give the jury instructions to disregard testimony that defendant claimed was "highly prejudicial," as he failed to object during the trial, such that the trial court had no duty to give curative instructions; moreover, the testimony regarding defendant's prior conduct of alcohol abuse and spousal abuse was admissible under Ohio R. Evid. 404(B) where defendant claimed that he was not a violent person and that it was not his intention to hurt his wife. State v. Wilson, — Ohio App. 3d —, 2007 Ohio 4564, — N.E. 2d —, 2007 Ohio App. LEXIS 4089 (Aug. 31, 2007).

Guilty plea

Defendant's entry of an Alford plea pursuant to Ohio R. Crim. P. 11 to various charges constituted a waiver of his right to assert on appeal that the trial court's denial of his suppression motion was error due to the alleged unlawfulness of the searches and seizures; further, as the convictions were based on the plea and not on the evidence seized, any error in the trial court's ruling was harmless under Ohio R. Crim. P. 52. State v. Montgomery, — Ohio App. 3d —, 2007 Ohio 440, — N.E. 2d —, 2007 Ohio App. LEXIS 389 (Feb. 2, 2007).

As a trial court and prosecutor repeatedly referred to a charge as aggravated trafficking in drugs, in violation of RC § 2925.03(A)(1), which was a misstatement because the actual charge was aggravated possession of drugs, in violation of RC § 2925.11(A), and the trial court did not properly advise defendant pursuant to its duty under Ohio R. Crim. P. 11(C)(2) of the nature of the charge, defendant's plea was not voluntarily, intelligently, and knowingly entered under a plain error standard of review pursuant to Ohio R. Crim. P. 52(B), which violated his due process rights under Ohio Const. art. I, § 10. State v. Davis, — Ohio App. 3d —, 2007 Ohio 3944, — N.E. 2d —, 2007 Ohio App. LEXIS 3583 (July 26, 2007).

Indictment, defects in

Failure of an indictment charging a violation of RC § 2907.323 to include the element of recklessness was harmless error beyond a reasonable doubt where the defendant had notice that recklessness was an element of the offense, the jury was properly charged on that element, and the state argued at trial that defendant's conduct was reckless: State v. Hurst, 181 Ohio App. 3d 454, 2009 Ohio 983, 909 N.E.2d 653, 2009 Ohio App. LEXIS 946 (2009).

Ineffective assistance

Under the plain error standard of review pursuant to Ohio R. Crim. P. 52, there was no ineffectiveness of counsel pursuant to U.S. Const. amend. VI and Ohio Const. art. I, § 10 by counsel's failure to seek a mistrial due to comments made by prospective jurors, some of whom were selected to sit on the jury panel, as the comments were not so inflammatory as to require a mistrial, either upon a request by counsel or by the trial court sua sponte. There was no showing that the failure of defendant's counsel to have requested a mistrial prejudiced his defense. State v. Harrington, — Ohio App. 3d —, 2006 Ohio 4388, — N.E. 2d —, 2006 Ohio App. LEXIS 4285 (Aug. 14, 2006).

Intervention in lieu of conviction

Abuse of discretion in denying a motion under RC § 2951.041 without a hearing is harmless error that an appellate court is charged by CrimR 52(A) to disregard because a defendant could have suffered no prejudice to a legal right enforced and protected by law as a result: State v. Rice, 180 Ohio App. 3d 599, 2009 Ohio 162, 906 N.E.2d 506, 2009 Ohio App. LEXIS 129 (2009).

Jury instructions

There was no plain error under Ohio R. Crim. P. 52(B) in a trial court's jury instructions during defendant's criminal trial with respect to the credibility of witnesses, as the trial court properly instructed the jury that no inferences would be drawn from the decision of defendant not to testify; any improper emphasis in an instruction regarding defendant's lack of testimony was corrected thereby. State v. Thompson, — Ohio App. 3d —, 2007 Ohio 6839, — N.E. 2d —, 2007 Ohio App. LEXIS 6023 (Dec. 14, 2007).

There was no plain error under Ohio R. Crim. P. 52(B) in a trial court's jury instruction regarding the State's burden of proving each element of an offense against defendant beyond a reasonable doubt in order to find defendant guilty, as such was a correct statement of law; the instruction that if the State failed to prove each and every element of the offense beyond a reasonable doubt then the jury would find defendant not guilty did not confuse the jury or constitute an error. State v. Thompson, — Ohio App. 3d —, 2007 Ohio 6839, — N.E. 2d —, 2007 Ohio App. LEXIS 6023 (Dec. 14, 2007).

There was no plain error under Ohio R. Crim. P. 52(B) in a trial court's jury instruction concerning the offense of illegal use of food stamps, as the trial court only had to summarize and paraphrase the relevant sections of the Food Stamp Act; defendant failed to show how the definition of the offense was confusing to the jury or that there was any authority to support defendant's claim that the language used in that instruction was inadequate. State v. Thompson, — Ohio App. 3d —, 2007 Ohio 6839, — N.E. 2d —, 2007 Ohio App. LEXIS 6023 (Dec. 14, 2007).

In a juvenile delinquency proceeding, it was not plain error, under Ohio R. Crim. P. 52(B), not to instruct the jury on self-defense because appellant admitted that he fired a weapon because he saw that a group of individuals was attempting to harm his associate, so he was not defending himself. State v. D.H., — Ohio App. 3d —, 2006 Ohio 6953, — N.E. 2d —, 2006 Ohio App. LEXIS 6862 (Dec. 28, 2006).

Lesser included offenses

Trial court did not commit plain error under Ohio R. Crim. P. 52(B) in failing to instruct the jury on the lesser-included offense of involuntary manslaughter. The transcript showed that defense counsel's failure to request such an instruction was the result of a deliberate, tactical decision of counsel, thus exercising defendant's right to waive a lesser-included instruction. State v. Riley, — Ohio App. 3d —, 2007 Ohio 4409, — N.E. 2d —, 2007 Ohio App. LEXIS 3980 (Aug. 28, 2007).

While a trial court improperly gave an acquittal-first instruction to the jury when it instructed the jury that it had to first find defendant not guilty of assault before considering whether he was guilty of the lesser-included offense of disorderly conduct, the error was harmless since the evidence did not reasonably permit an acquittal on the offense of assault and a conviction on the offense of disorderly conduct. Chillicothe v. Ramey, — Ohio App. 3d —, 2006 Ohio 3548, — N.E. 2d —, 2006 Ohio App. LEXIS 3497 (June 23, 2006).

Misconduct by prosecutor

Under the plain error standard of review due to defendant's failure to have objected to the prosecutor's remarks at trial, no prosecutorial misconduct was found, as there was no indication that a manifest miscarriage of justice occurred that clearly affected the outcome of defendant's trial. State v. Alvarez, — Ohio App. 3d —, 2007 Ohio 3114, — N.E. 2d —, 2007 Ohio App. LEXIS 2870 (June 22, 2007).

Motion for acquittal

Since defendant failed to move for an Ohio R. Crim. P. 29(A) judgment of acquittal, she waived all but plain error regarding her contention that her conviction for assault on a peace officer was not supported by sufficient evidence. State v. Dixon, — Ohio App. 3d —, 2007 Ohio 2989, — N.E. 2d —, 2007 Ohio App. LEXIS 2745 (June 18, 2007).

Motion to suppress

Contrary to the State's contention, the record reflected that the State had sufficient notice of the grounds that the trial court considered in deciding defendant's motion to suppress and had an adequate opportunity to address those grounds but failed to do so. Since the State was given sufficient notice and ample opportunity to defend, no manifest miscarriage of justice resulted from the trial court's decision to address the issue of whether the search warrant affidavit contained a material knowing, intentional or reckless falsity, and the trial court did not commit plain error under Ohio R. Crim. P. 52(B) in this regard. State v. Ralston, — Ohio App. 3d —, 2007 Ohio 177, — N.E. 2d —, 2007 Ohio App. LEXIS 175 (Jan. 11, 2007).

No contest plea

There was no plain error under Ohio R. Crim. P. 52(B) by the trial court's having found defendant guilty after he entered a no contest plea to felony drug charges, as the trial court was not required to provide an explanation of the facts and circumstances involved in defendant's arrest and bill of information where the offenses involved were felonies; defendant's due process rights under U.S. Const. amend. V and Ohio Const. art. I, § 10 were not violated. State v. Peoples, — Ohio App. 3d —, 2006 Ohio 4162, — N.E. 2d —, 2006 Ohio App. LEXIS 4095 (Aug. 11, 2006).

No plain error

Trial court did not commit plain error under Ohio R. Crim. P. 52(B) in advising the prospective jurors during voir dire of their sentencing options, as it used the term "consider" in connection with the jurors' potential choice of life-sentence options, but it never suggested that they might be required to vote for a death sentence. State v. Frazier, 115 Ohio St. 3d 139, 2007 Ohio 5048, 873 N.E.2d 1263, 2007 Ohio LEXIS 2519 (2007).

Where defendant's counsel only made a general objection to the trial court's admission of a statement that defendant made to police at the time of his arrest, which the State had agreed during a suppression hearing would not be admitted at trial, such was not error under Ohio R. Evid. 103(A)(1) because a properly specific objection was not made to preserve any error for review. Under Ohio R. Crim. P. 52, the statement did not undermine confidence in the outcome of the trial and did not create such prejudice as to constitute plain error. State v. Smith, — Ohio App. 3d —, 2006 Ohio 4163, — N.E. 2d —, 2006 Ohio App. LEXIS 4096 (Aug. 11, 2006).

Opportunity to present defense

Trial court violated due process and committed plain error by finding the defendant guilty of the charged offense without offering him an opportunity to present a defense: State v. Litreal, 170 Ohio App. 3d 670, 2006 Ohio 5416, 868 N.E.2d 1018, 2006 Ohio App. LEXIS 5410 (2006).

Other act testimony

There was no error in admitting the testimony during cross-examination that defendant had tried to induce his son into robbing the witness because any error in the admission of the evidence was invited error, as the statement was made in response to a question by the defense attorney. Also, there was no plain error in admitting evidence of defendant's regular drug use because even if the statements had not been admitted, the result of the trial would not have changed. State v. McGlothin, — Ohio App. 3d —, 2007 Ohio 4707, — N.E. 2d —, 2007 Ohio App. LEXIS 4227 (Sept. 14, 2007).

Photographs

There was no plain error in admitting the photographs because, in addition to demonstrating the cause of the victim's death, the photos were relevant and helped to prove defendant's intent, as well as the lack of accident or mistake. The photos further illustrated the testimony of the detectives who described the crime scene and the coroner and paramedic who described the wounds and injuries sustained by the victim and gave the jury an appreciation of the nature and circumstances of the crimes. State v. Wharton, — Ohio App. 3d —, 2007 Ohio 1817, — N.E. 2d —, 2007 Ohio App. LEXIS 1660 (Apr. 18, 2007).

Trial court abused its discretion where it admitted photographs of a victim's deceased body that not only showed the effects of defendant's attack on her, which aspect of the photographs was admittedly probative, but it also showed the reflection of her scalp that was performed during her autopsy, which aspect was gruesome and prejudicial. Although the prejudicial aspect of the photographs outweighed the probative value pursuant to Ohio R. Evid. 403(A) and 611(A), there was no plain error under Ohio R. Crim. P. 52 by the admission thereof, as the results of the trial would not have been different without the admission of the photographs. State v. Warner, — Ohio App. 3d —, 2007 Ohio 3016, — N.E. 2d —, 2007 Ohio App. LEXIS 2770 (June 15, 2007).

Plain error

Although a juvenile failed to object to a magistrate's determination in his delinquency matter, as required by Ohio R. Juv. P. 40(D)(3)(b)(i), the exception to waiver under Rule 40(D)(4) applied, as the magistrate committed prejudicial, plain error under Ohio R. Crim. P. 52 when she failed to personally address the juvenile to ascertain that he voluntarily, knowingly, and intelligently waived his rights as required by Ohio R. Juv. P. 29(D). The magistrate's reliance on counsel's statement that he had explained the waiver of rights to the juvenile was improper, as was reliance on the juvenile's written waiver form, such that there was no substantial compliance with Rule 29(D). In re Tabler, — Ohio App. 3d —, 2007 Ohio 411, — N.E. 2d —, 2007 Ohio App. LEXIS 366 (Jan. 29, 2007).

Because Ohio R. Crim. P. 7(D) flatly prohibited amendments changing the identity of a charge, the amendment was unlawful and thus, the trial court erred by permitting the State to amend the indictment. Because of its constitutional nature, the error was one that merited applying the plain error doctrine and defendant did not need to demonstrate that he suffered any prejudice as a result of the forbidden amendment. State v. Davis, — Ohio App. 3d —, 2007 Ohio 2249, — N.E. 2d —, 2007 Ohio App. LEXIS 2084 (Apr. 27, 2007).

Plain error analysis

In most defective indictment cases in which the indictment fails to include an essential element of the charge, plain error analysis, pursuant to CrimR 52(B), will be the proper analysis to apply. The syllabus in State v. Colon, 118 Ohio St. 3d 26, 2008 Ohio 1624, 885 N.E.2d 917, 2008 Ohio LEXIS 874, is confined to the facts in that case: State v. Colon, 119 Ohio St. 3d 204, 2008 Ohio 3749, 893 N.E.2d 169, 2008 Ohio LEXIS 1979 (2008).

Although the trial court committed structural error in failing to provide defendant an opportunity to make a closing argument on the fleeing charge, and the record established no express, voluntary, or intentional relinquishment of such a closing argument, applying the plain error doctrine because defense counsel failed to object to such error at trial, it was not plain error that needed to be recognized given the evidence supporting the conviction. State v. Garrard, 170 Ohio App. 3d 487, 2007 Ohio 1244, 867 N.E.2d 887, 2007 Ohio App. LEXIS 1158 (2007).

Although the trial court committed structural error in failing to provide defendant an opportunity to make a closing argument on the fleeing charge, and the record established no express, voluntary, or intentional relinquishment of such a closing argument, applying the plain error doctrine because defense counsel failed to object to such error at trial, it was not plain error that needed to be recognized given the evidence supporting the conviction. State v. Garrard, 170 Ohio App. 3d 487, 2007 Ohio 1244, 867 N.E.2d 887, 2007 Ohio App. LEXIS 1158 (2007).

When defendant's counsel did not object to the courtroom being closed for closing arguments at defendant's trial, this alleged infringement on defendant's right to a public trial could be reviewed for plain error, under Ohio R. Crim. P. 52(B), as the right was not waived but was merely forfeited. State v. Hairston, — Ohio App. 3d —, 2006 Ohio 4925, — N.E. 2d —, 2006 Ohio App. LEXIS 4886 (Sept. 25, 2006).

When defendant's counsel withdrew his objection to the presence of alternate jurors at the jury's deliberation, this waived any error, so the issue could not be reviewed for plain error on appeal. State v. Hairston, — Ohio App. 3d —, 2006 Ohio 4925, — N.E. 2d —, 2006 Ohio App. LEXIS 4886 (Sept. 25, 2006).

There was no plain error under Ohio R. Crim. P. 52 in the trial court's admission of opinion testimony by a police detective that he believed defendant was guilty, although those statements were inadmissible under Ohio R. Evid. 701 because they were not based on the detective's own perceptions and the statements were subjective expressions of his opinion that did not explain or help the jurors to understand his testimony, as the evidence of defendant's guilt was overwhelming; the plain error standard of review was employed due to defendant's failure to have objected to the testimony at trial. State v. Edwards, — Ohio App. 3d —, 2006 Ohio 5596, — N.E. 2d —, 2006 Ohio App. LEXIS 5619 (Oct. 27, 2006).

Plain error, generally

Trial court's failure to provide the defendant an opportunity for closing argument in a non-jury trial constituted plain error. Reversal was not required, however, where there was no manifest miscarriage of justice: State v. Garrard, 170 Ohio App. 3d 487, 2007 Ohio 1244, 867 N.E.2d 887, 2007 Ohio App. LEXIS 1158 (2007).

Trial court committed plain error in denying defendant's motion to dismiss as defendant's constitutional right to a speedy trial was violated where: (1) there was a 19-month delay between defendant's arrest and trial, (2) 25 continuances were granted, most at the request of defendant's counsel, (3) defendant did not sign a waiver of his right to a speedy trial, (4) defendant repeatedly asserted his right to a speedy trial, orally and in a pro se motion, and (5) defendant was in custody during the entire 19-month period; the cumulative effect of the delays warranted the remedy of dismissal required by RC § 2945.73. State v. Wells, — Ohio App. 3d —, 2006 Ohio 87, — N.E. 2d —, 2006 Ohio App. LEXIS 70 (Jan. 12, 2006).

Trial court did not commit plain error in failing to instruct the jury as to defendant's alibi as the alibi evidence did not pertain to the date of the alleged incident. State v. Moser, — Ohio App. 3d —, 2006 Ohio 165, — N.E. 2d —, 2006 Ohio App. LEXIS 133 (Jan. 19, 2006).

Post-release control

Trial court's failure to inform defendant about postrelease control during the plea hearing, as required by RC § 2943.032(E), constituted plain error under Ohio R. Crim. P. 52(A). State v. Conrad, — Ohio App. 3d —, 2007 Ohio 5717, — N.E. 2d —, 2007 Ohio App. LEXIS 5021 (Oct. 25, 2007).

Prior convictions

Defendant failed to show that his counsel was ineffective in violation of U.S. Const. amend. VI and Ohio Const. art. I, § 10 for agreeing to a stipulation, wherein the jury was informed of the specific nature of defendant's prior offenses and the judgment entry was admitted into evidence rather than being simply informed that defendant had been convicted of prior offenses that constituted "offenses of violence" under RC § 2901.01(A)(9) for purposes of his conviction for having a weapon while under a disability, in violation of RC § 2923.13(A)(2), as any error was harmless under Ohio R. Crim. P. 52(A); without admission of that evidence, there was sufficient evidence to support defendant's conviction for the weapon offense, such that there was no reasonable possibility that defendant would not have been found guilty. Ohio v. Riffle, — Ohio App. 3d —, 2007 Ohio 5299, — N.E. 2d —, 2007 Ohio App. LEXIS 4656 (Sept. 28, 2007).

During defendant's trial for receiving stolen property under RC § 2913.51, whether evidence regarding his prior convictions and sentences was properly admitted was reviewed for plain error under Ohio R. Crim. P. 52(B) because his counsel did not object. Allowing the State to inquire about sentences for the prior crimes was not plain error because it was within the trial court's broad discretion to limit cross-examination on prior crimes when the convictions were admitted solely to impeach general credibility. State v. Ewing, — Ohio App. 3d —, 2006 Ohio 5523, — N.E. 2d —, 2006 Ohio App. LEXIS 5503 (Oct. 24, 2006).

Prosecutor's comments

Although a prosecutor's comment that defendant's testimony was a recent fabrication was a Doyle violation, as the prosecutor asserted that defendant had not previously revealed that his sexual conduct with a victim was allegedly consensual, the error was harmless where the evidence of defendant's guilt was overwhelming when standing alone. State v. Jaradat, — Ohio App. 3d —, 2007 Ohio 1971, — N.E. 2d —, 2007 Ohio App. LEXIS 1823 (Apr. 26, 2007).

There was no plain error under Ohio R. Crim. P. 52(B) by the prosecutor's remarks during closing argument in defendant's criminal trial on drug-related charges, as they constituted fair commentary on the evidence and not an improper attempt to personally vouch for the credibility of the witnesses; as defendant had failed to object during trial to the prosecutor's remarks, the plain error standard of review was applicable. Ohio v. Roberts, — Ohio App. 3d —, 2007 Ohio 4882, — N.E. 2d —, 2007 Ohio App. LEXIS 4345 (Sept. 21, 2007).

Prosecutorial misconduct

Prosecutor did not commit plain error under Ohio R. Crim. P. 52(B) with respect to various remarks made during closing argument, to which defendant's counsel failed to object, as most of the comments were based on evidence that the jury had heard during the trial and there was no prejudice shown to defendant by any of the comments. Comments that identified the victim running from his attacker in a videotape and discussing the lack of any ballistic evidence were not related by the prosecutor to defendant, a comment that the victim was in pain after the shooting did not prejudice defendant, and a comment regarding the victim was in response to an attack on the victim's credibility. State v.

Richardson, — Ohio App. 3d —, 2007 Ohio 204, — N.E. 2d —, 2007 Ohio App. LEXIS 187 (Jan. 19, 2007).

There was no plain error under Ohio R. Crim. P. 52(B) by comments made by the prosecutor in defendant's trial, as his statements indicated that the jury was to consider the testimony of the witnesses in rendering a decision, there was no vouching for the credibility of the State's witnesses by his comments when he merely commented on what the evidence showed and what reasonable inferences could have been drawn from it, and he only commented on the credibility of defendant's witnesses based on their in-court testimony; the prosecutor stayed within the wide latitude that he was given to comment on the evidence. State v. Ferko, — Ohio App. 3d —, 2007 Ohio 1588, — N.E. 2d —, 2007 Ohio App. LEXIS 1464 (Apr. 5, 2007).

Right to remain silent

There was no plain error under Ohio R. Crim. P. 52(B) by the prosecutor's questioning of detectives as to defendant's oral statement regarding a criminal incident for which he was on trial, and the reason for the lack of a written statement memorializing his oral statement, as defendant waived his Miranda rights and gave an oral statement to police, and then he exercised his right to remain silent when the detectives told him that his oral statement was going to be put in writing; accordingly, there was no Doyle violation. State v. Smith, — Ohio App. 3d —, 2006 Ohio 3156, — N.E. 2d —, 2006 Ohio App. LEXIS 3032 (June 22, 2006).

If testimony admitted at defendant's trial erroneously showed that he had invoked his right to remain silent, the error was harmless, under Ohio R. Crim. P. 52(A), because the evidence of his guilt was overwhelming, so there was no reasonably probability that the testimony contributed to his convictions, and the extent of the comments was not pervasive, nor did the State stress an inference of guilt to the jury in closing argument or otherwise try to capitalize on defendant's silence. State v. Anderson, — Ohio App. 3d —, 2006 Ohio 5048, — N.E. 2d —, 2006 Ohio App. LEXIS 4995 (Sept. 29, 2006).

It was plain error, under Ohio R. Crim. P. 52(B), to admit a detective's testimony that defendant did not discuss the allegations against defendant with the detective until after indictments against defendant and an arrest warrant for defendant had been issued because this subverted the policy behind the privilege against self-incrimination and the other evidence against defendant was not overwhelming, as it relied entirely on the testimony of the victims, which was conflicting, so it could not be said that the result of defendant's trial would not have been different had the detective's testimony not been admitted. State v. Estepp, — Ohio App. 3d —, 2007 Ohio 2596, — N.E. 2d —, 2007 Ohio App. LEXIS 2418 (May 25, 2007).

Defendant's due process rights under Ohio Const. art. I, § 10 and U.S. Const. amend. V were not violated where the prosecutor attempted to impeach defendant by commenting on defendant's post-arrest silence, as there was no evidence that Miranda warnings were given to defendant in order to trigger the constitutional protection that if defendant chose to remain silent, such silence would not be used against him. Defendant took the witness stand in his own defense which opened his testimony up to impeachment, and there was no harmless error pursuant to Ohio R. Crim. P. 52 in the circumstances. State v. Exum, — Ohio App. 3d —, 2007 Ohio 2648, — N.E. 2d —, 2007 Ohio App. LEXIS 2446 (May 31, 2007).

Self-defense

Trial court's failure to instruct the jury that the defendant had the burden of proving self-defense by a preponderance of the evidence constituted plain error: State v. Cooper, 170 Ohio App. 3d 418, 2007 Ohio 1186, 867 N.E.2d 493, 2007 Ohio App. LEXIS 1115 (2007).

Sentence

Ohio R. Crim. P. 52(B) motion was not recognized under the Ohio Rules of Criminal Procedure to challenge a criminal sentence. State v. Frazier, — Ohio App. 3d —, 2007 Ohio 1851, — N.E. 2d —, 2007 Ohio App. LEXIS 1691 (Apr. 19, 2007).

Sentencing

Lack of an objection in the trial court forfeits a Blakely issue for purposes of appeal when the sentencing occurred after the announcement of Blakely. Thus, the constitutional error involved in a Blakely violation case is not structural and should ordinarily be analyzed pursuant to a plain error analysis. State v. Payne, 114 Ohio St. 3d 502, 2007 Ohio 4642, 873 N.E.2d 306, 2007 Ohio LEXIS 2222 (2007).

Because Blakely was announced prior to defendant's plea and sentence, and because the error was not structural, in failing to make a Blakely objection, defendant forfeited the issue for appellate purposes. There was no plain error since defendant failed to establish that he was prejudiced by the judicial fact-finding requirements; if defendant were to be resentenced, nothing in the record would hinder the trial court from considering the same factors it previously had been required to consider and imposing the same sentence or even a more stringent one. State v. Payne, 114 Ohio St. 3d 502, 2007 Ohio 4642, 873 N.E.2d 306, 2007 Ohio LEXIS 2222 (2007).

Because defendant was sentenced before Foster was decided, his sentence was voidable. However, since defendant did not object to the constitutionality of his sentence at the sentencing hearing, he forfeited the issue for appellate purposes and thus, the trial court was confined to a plain error analysis. State v. Baccus, — Ohio App. 3d —, 2007 Ohio 5991, — N.E. 2d —, 2007 Ohio App. LEXIS 5251 (Nov. 9, 2007).

When sentencing occurs after Blakely v. Washington (2004), 542 US 296, 124 Sct 2531, 159 Led2d 403, 2004 U.S. LEXIS 4573, failure to object to the sentence as violating Blakely forfeits the issue on appeal: State v. Payne, 114 Ohio St. 3d 502, 2007 Ohio 4642, 873 N.E.2d 306, 2007 Ohio LEXIS 2222 (2007).

Speedy trial

Defendant could not argue, for the first time on appeal, that his right to a speedy trial, under RC § 2945.71, was violated because this deprived the State of the ability to demonstrate that the statute was tolled, so the plain error doctrine, under Ohio R. Crim. P. 52(B), did not apply, even if a statutory violation appeared on the face of the record. State v. Turner, 168 Ohio App. 3d 176, 2006 Ohio 3786, 858 N.E. 2d 1249, 2006 Ohio App. LEXIS 3723 (July 21, 2006).

Venue

There was no plain error under Ohio R. Crim. P. 52(B) in the court's denial of defendant's motion on appeal to take judicial notice of the fact that the victim's apartment where some of the alleged menacing occurred that he was convicted of was not within the trial court's venue, as other acts of menacing were in locations that were within the trial court's venue; the matter was reviewed under a plain error standard because defendant had not raised the issue on the trial court level. State v. Harshaw, — Ohio App. 3d —, 2006 Ohio 3907, — N.E. 2d —, 2006 Ohio App. LEXIS 3873 (Aug. 1, 2006).

Verdict forms

There was no plain error under Ohio R. Crim. P. 52(B) where a single verdict form was used in defendant's criminal trial, although defendant was tried for two separate charges, as the jury was sufficiently instructed that it had to make a determination of guilt on each count individually and the single verdict form was divided into two sections so that a decision could be made as to each count; further, defendant failed to object to the jury instructions that detailed the verdict form, such that any error was deemed waived. State v.

Thompson, — Ohio App. 3d —, 2007 Ohio 6839, — N.E. 2d —, 2007 Ohio App. LEXIS 6023 (Dec. 14, 2007).

Withdrawal of guilty plea

While a common pleas court erred in concluding that the stricter standard imposed by Ohio R. Crim. P. 32.1 for the granting of post-sentence motions to withdraw a plea should apply, defendant waived all but plain error in this regard because he never objected to this finding. There was no plain error, in that the common pleas court expressly found that it would not grant the motion even applying the more liberal standard reserved for pre-sentence motions to withdraw a plea as defendant's motion was based on a mere change of heart, which was an insufficient basis for granting a motion to withdraw a plea. State v. Wallen, — Ohio App. 3d —, 2007 Ohio 2129, — N.E. 2d —, 2007 Ohio App. LEXIS 1985 (May 4, 2007).

Denial of the motion to withdraw his plea was proper because defendant's guilty plea was knowingly, intelligently, and voluntarily made. The trial court did not commit plain error by failing to provide an adequate explanation of postrelease control because defendant was never sentenced to postrelease control; rather, he was sentenced to one year of community control, which he completed six years earlier. State v. Ellington, — Ohio App. 3d —, 2007 Ohio 5959, — N.E. 2d —, 2007 Ohio App. LEXIS 5218 (Nov. 8, 2007).

Defendant showed that he suffered a prejudicial effect under Ohio R. Crim. P. 52(A) due to the trial court's failure to substantially comply with Ohio R. Crim. P. 11(C), in that the trial court did not inform defendant that by entering a guilty plea to two charges, he potentially faced a lifetime driver's license suspension under RC § 4510.02. Accordingly, the plea was not knowingly and voluntarily entered and it required vacatur. State v. Greene, — Ohio App. 3d —, 2006 Ohio 480, — N.E. 2d —, 2006 Ohio App. LEXIS 408 (2006).

RULE 53. Reserved.

RULE 54. Amendment of Incorporated Civil Rules

An amendment to or rescission of any provision of the Ohio Rules of Civil Procedure which has been incorporated by reference in these rules, shall, without the necessity of further action, be incorporated by reference in these rules unless the amendment or rescission specifies otherwise, effective on the effective date of the amendment or rescission.

RULE 55. Records

(A) **Criminal appearance docket.** The clerk shall keep a criminal appearance docket. Upon the commencement of a criminal action the clerk shall assign each action a number. This number shall be placed on the first page, and every continuation page, of the appearance docket which concerns the particular action. In addition this number and the names of the parties shall be placed on the case file and every paper filed in the action.

At the time the action is commenced the clerk shall enter in the appearance docket the names, except as provided in Rule 6(E), of the parties in full, the names of counsel and index the action by the name of each defendant. Thereafter the clerk shall chronologically note in the appearance docket all: process issued and returns, pleas and motions, papers filed in the action, orders, verdicts and judgments. The notations shall be brief but shall show the date of filing and the substance of each order, verdict and judgment.

An action is commenced for purposes of this rule by the earlier of, (a) the filing of a complaint, uniform traffic ticket, citation, indictment, or information with the clerk, or (b) the receipt by the clerk of the court of common pleas of a bind over order under Rule 5(B)(4)(a).

(B) **Files.** All papers filed in a case shall be filed in a separate file folder and on or after July 1, 1986 shall not exceed 8 inches x 11 inches in size and without backing or cover.

(C) **Other books and records.** The clerk shall keep such other books and records as required by law and as the supreme court or other court may from time to time require.

(D) **Applicability to courts not of record.** In courts not of record the notations required by subdivision (A) shall be placed on a separate sheet or card kept in the file folder.

History: Amended, eff 7-1-85.

RULE 56.   Reserved.

RULE 57.   Rule of court; procedure not otherwise specified

(A) **Rule of court.**

(1) The expression "rule of court" as used in these rules means a rule promulgated by the Supreme Court or a rule concerning local practice adopted by another court that is not inconsistent with the rules promulgated by the Supreme Court and is filed with the Supreme Court.

(2) Local rules shall be adopted only after the court gives appropriate notice and an opportunity for comment. If the court determines that there is an immediate need for a rule, the court may adopt the rule without prior notice and opportunity for comment, but promptly shall afford notice and opportunity for comment.

(B) **Procedure not otherwise specified.** If no procedure is specifically prescribed by rule, the court may proceed in any lawful manner not inconsistent with these rules of criminal procedure, and shall look to the rules of civil procedure and to the applicable law if no rule of criminal procedure exists.

History: Amended, eff 7-1-94.

NOTES TO DECISIONS

ANALYSIS

Appeal
Applicability
Civil rules
Post-conviction relief
Vacation of judgment

Appeal

Inmate's failure to have filed a direct appeal pursuant to Ohio R. App. P. 4(A) from his convictions and sentences constituted a waiver of his right to seek review of issues involving the voluntariness and knowing aspect of his plea, and from his sentence. His motion for relief from judgment under Ohio R. Civ. P. 60(B) was clearly inapplicable, and he could not seek relief under Ohio R. Crim. P. 57(B) where

there was a proper procedure prescribed by the rules, and that procedure was through the appellate process. State v. Hagler, — Ohio App. 3d —, 2007 Ohio 433, — N.E. 2d —, 2007 Ohio App. LEXIS 385 (Feb. 2, 2007).

Applicability

Trial court properly denied defendant's motion for leave to file a motion for new trial pursuant to Ohio R. Crim. P. 33(B), as he did not meet his burden of establishing by clear and convincing proof that he was unavoidably prevented from filing his motion within the statutory time limits. Although Rule 33(B) was silent regarding a time limit for filing the motion, reliance on Ohio R. Crim. P. 1(B) and 57(B) indicated that defendant's knowledge of various individuals' evidence years prior to the making of his motion was an unreasonable delay, for which no explanation was offered. State v. Berry, — Ohio App. 3d —, 2007 Ohio 2244, — N.E. 2d —, 2007 Ohio App. LEXIS 2083 (May 10, 2007).

Civil rules

As Ohio R. Crim. P. 35 governed the procedures for post-conviction petitions, defendant's reliance on Ohio R. Civ. P. 60(B)(5) and Ohio R. Crim. P. 57(B) for sentencing relief was error. As the request for sentencing relief was untimely under RC § 2953.21(A)(2) and it was not within either of the exceptions to timeliness under RC § 2953.23(A)(1) and (2), the trial court lacked jurisdiction to grant the requested relief and to resentence defendant. State v. Fulk, 172 Ohio App. 3d 635, 2007 Ohio 3141, 876 N.E.2d 983, 2007 Ohio App. LEXIS 2888 (2007).

Motion by the attorney for the beneficiaries of the restitution acted as a motion to intervene because neither the attorney nor the beneficiaries of the estate of one of the victims were actual parties to defendant's underlying criminal case. The attorney did not provide any case law or other authority to support his presumed ability to intervene in the case to request that the trial court determine the outstanding restitution balance (the attorney also did not comply with Ohio R. Civ. P. 24(C) as he did not serve a copy of his motion on the county prosecutor's office); the attorney and the beneficiaries should not have been permitted to request that the trial court continue restitution payments and determine the balance of restitution due as their interests were adequately represented by existing parties. Ohio v. Dillon, — Ohio App. 3d —, 2007 Ohio 4934, — N.E. 2d —, 2007 Ohio App. LEXIS 4619 (Sept. 24, 2007).

Ohio Court of Appeals for the Eleventh Appellate District, Lake County, holds that Ohio R. Civ. P. 60 can be applied in criminal cases under certain circumstances, such as when there is no applicable criminal rule to address the specific issue pursuant to Ohio R. Crim. P. 57(B). State v. Schlee, — Ohio App. 3d —, 2006 Ohio 3208, — N.E. 2d —, 2006 Ohio App. LEXIS 3116 (June 23, 2006).

Post-conviction relief

Inmate's reliance on Ohio R. Crim. P. 47 and 57 for his motion to vacate and/or correct his sentence was misplaced, as those rules did not specifically authorize the filing of such a motion, and as the inmate's request for relief was based on his claim that his constitutional rights were violated, RC §§ 2953.21 and 2953.23(A) were necessarily applicable. State v. Foti, — Ohio App. 3d —, 2007 Ohio 887, — N.E. 2d —, 2007 Ohio App. LEXIS 808 (Mar. 2, 2007).

Vacation of judgment

Attorney general has common law standing as chief law officer of the state to act in the public interest and bring a prohibition action to compel a judge to vacate entries granting relief from judgment to a defendant on grounds that had already been rejected on appeal: State ex rel. Cordray v. Marshall, 123 Ohio St. 3d 229, 2009 Ohio 4986, 915 N.E.2d 633, 2009 Ohio LEXIS 2690 (2009).

As Ohio R. Crim. P. 35 governed criminal procedure for post-conviction relief petitions, an inmate could not seek to vacate his sentence by moving under Ohio R. Civ. P. 60(B)(5) and Ohio R. Crim. P. 57(B). As his petition was not timely filed under RC § 2953.21(A)(2) and he was not within either of the exceptions to timeliness under RC § 2953.23(A)(1) and (2), the trial court properly denied his request for relief. State v. Brenton, — Ohio App. 3d —, 2007 Ohio 901, — N.E. 2d —, 2007 Ohio App. LEXIS 789 (Mar. 5, 2007).

Regardless of the caption, a motion is a petition for postconviction relief if the defendant files the motion after the defendant's direct appeal, claims a denial of a constitutional right, seeks to render a final judgment void, and asks the trial court to vacate the judgment and sentence. CrimR 35 governs the procedure for postconviction relief and, because a criminal rule exists, CrimR 57(B) does not apply. Thus CivR 60(B) cannot be used to circumvent the time limits under RC § 2953.21: State v. Fulk, 172 Ohio App. 3d 635, 2007 Ohio 3141, 876 N.E.2d 983, 2007 Ohio App. LEXIS 2888 (2007).

Defendant's Ohio R. Civ. P. 60(B)(5) motion to vacate was not the proper method of asserting constitutional errors in sentencing because a petition for post-conviction relief under RC § 2953.21 was the exclusive remedy by which defendant could have brought a collateral challenge to his sentence. Accordingly, since there existed an applicable rule of criminal procedure, defendant could not assert an Ohio R. Civ. P. 60(B)(5) challenge via Ohio R. Crim. P. 57(B). State v. Randlett, — Ohio App. 3d —, 2007 Ohio 3546, — N.E. 2d —, 2007 Ohio App. LEXIS 3243 (July 12, 2007).

If defendant was deprived of the right to file timely objections to the magistrate's decision because neither he nor his counsel received that decision until more than 14 days after it was filed, defendant could have moved to vacate his conviction and sentence for that reason pursuant to Ohio R. Crim. P. 57(B) and Ohio R. Civ. P. 60(B)(1). However, the one-year provision of Ohio R. Civ. P. 60(B) would have applied, and more than one year had passed since the trial court entered its judgment; defendant's appeal did not toll the time. State v. Gilreath, 174 Ohio App. 3d 327, 2007 Ohio 6899, 882 N.E. 2d 22, 2007 Ohio App. LEXIS 6057 (Dec. 21, 2007).

RULE 58. Forms

The forms contained in the Appendix of Forms which the supreme court from time to time may approve are illustrative and not mandatory.

RULE 59. Effective date

(A) **Effective date of rules.** These rules shall take effect on July 1, 1973, except for rules or portions of rules for which a later date is specified, which shall take effect on such later date. They govern all proceedings in actions brought after they take effect, and also all further proceedings in actions then pending, except to the extent that their application in a particular action pending when the rules take effect would not be feasible or would work injustice, in which event the former procedure applies.

(B) **Effective date of amendments.** The amendments submitted by the Supreme Court to the general assembly on January 10, 1975, shall take effect on July 1, 1975. They govern all proceedings in actions brought after they take effect and also all further proceedings in actions then pending, except to the extent that their application in a particular action pending when the amendments take effect would not be feasible or would work injustice, in which event the former procedure applies.

(C) **Effective date of amendments.** The amendments submitted by the Supreme Court to the general assembly on January 9, 1976 shall take effect on July 1, 1976. They govern all proceedings in actions brought after they take effect and also all further proceedings in actions then pending, except to the extent that their application in a particular action pending when the amendments take effect would not be feasible or would work injustice, in which event the former procedure applies.

(D) **Effective date of amendments.** The amendments submitted by the Supreme Court to the general assembly on January 12, 1978, and on April 28, 1978, shall take effect on July 1, 1978. They govern all proceedings in actions brought after they take effect and also all further proceedings in actions then pending, except to the extent that their application in a particular action pending when the amendments take effect would not be feasible or would work injustice, in which event the former procedure applies.

(E) **Effective date of amendments.** The amendments submitted by the Supreme Court to the general assembly on January 14, 1980, shall take effect on July 1, 1980. They govern all proceedings in actions brought after they take effect and also all further proceedings in actions then pending, except to the extent that their application in a particular action pending when the amendments take effect would not be feasible or would work injustice, in which event the former procedure applies.

(F) **Effective date of amendments.** The amendments submitted by the Supreme Court to the general assembly on January 14, 1981, and on April 29, 1981, shall take effect on July 1, 1981. They govern all proceedings in actions brought after they take effect and also all further proceedings in actions then pending, except to the extent that their application in a particular action pending when the amendments take effect would not be feasible or would work injustice, in which event the former procedure applies.

(G) **Effective date of amendments.** The amendments submitted by the Supreme Court to the general assembly on January 14, 1982 shall take effect on July 1, 1982. They govern all proceedings in actions brought after they take effect and also all further proceedings in actions then pending, except to the extent that their application in a particular action pending when the amendments take effect would not be feasible or would work injustice, in which event the former procedure applies.

(H) **Effective date of amendments.** The amendments submitted by the Supreme Court to the general assembly on December 24, 1984 and January 8, 1985 shall take effect on July 1, 1985. They govern all proceedings in actions brought after they take effect and also all further proceedings in actions then pending, except to the extent that their application in a particular action pending when the amendments take effect would not be feasible or would work injustice, in which event the former procedure applies.

(I) **Effective date of amendments.** The amendments submitted by the Supreme Court to the General Assembly on January 12, 1990 and further revised and submitted on April 16, 1990, shall take effect on July 1, 1990. They govern all proceedings in actions brought after they take effect and also all further proceedings in actions then pending, except to the extent that their application in a particular action pending when the amendments take effect would not be feasible or would work injustice, in which event the former procedure applies.

(J) **Effective date of amendments.** The amendments filed by the Supreme Court with the General Assembly on January 14, 1992 and further revised and filed on April 30, 1992, shall take effect on July 1, 1992. They govern all proceedings in actions brought after they take effect and also all further proceedings in actions then pending, except to the extent that their application in a particular action pending when the amendments take effect would not be feasible or would work injustice, in which event the former procedure applies.

(K) **Effective date of amendments.** The amendments submitted by the Supreme Court to the General Assembly on January 8, 1993 and further filed on April 30, 1993 shall take effect on July 1, 1993. They govern all proceedings in actions brought after they take effect and also all further proceedings in actions then pending, except to the extent that their application in a particular action pending when the amendments take effect would not be feasible or would work injustice, in which event the former procedure applies.

(L) **Effective date of amendments.** The amendments submitted by the Supreme Court to the General Assembly on January 14, 1994 shall take effect on July 1, 1994. They govern all proceedings in actions brought after they take effect and also all further proceedings in actions then pending, except to the extent that their application in a particular action pending when the amendments take effect would not be feasible or would work injustice, in which event the former procedure applies.

(M) **Effective date of amendments.** The amendments to rules 12 and 19 filed by the Supreme Court with the General Assembly on January 11, 1995 and refiled on April 25, 1995 shall take effect on July 1, 1995. They govern all proceedings in actions brought after they take effect and also all further proceedings in actions then pending, except to the extent that their application in a particular action pending when the amendments take effect would not be feasible or would work injustice, in which event the former procedure applies.

(N) **Effective date of amendments.** The amendments to Rule 1 filed by the Supreme Court with the General Assembly on January 5, 1996 and refiled on April 26, 1996 shall take effect on July 1, 1996. They govern all proceedings in actions brought after they take effect and also all further proceedings in actions then pending, except to the extent that their application in a particular action pending when the amendments take effect would not be feasible or would work injustice, in which event the former procedure applies.

(O) **Effective date of amendments.** The amendments to Rule 35 filed by the Supreme Court with the

General Assembly on January 10, 1997 and refiled on April 24, 1997 shall take effect on July 1, 1997. They govern all proceedings in actions brought after they take effect and also all further proceedings in actions then pending, except to the extent that their application in a particular action pending when the amendments take effect would not be feasible or would work injustice, in which event the former procedure applies.

(P) **Effective date of amendments.** The amendments to Rules 4, 11, 12, 32, 32.1, 32.2, 32.3, and 46 filed by the Supreme Court with the General Assembly on January 15, 1998 and further revised and refiled on April 30, 1998 shall take effect on July 1, 1998. They govern all proceedings in actions brought after they take effect and also all further proceedings in actions then pending, except to the extent that their application in a particular action pending when the amendments take effect would not be feasible or would work injustice, in which event the former procedure applies.

(Q) **Effective date of amendments.** The amendments to Criminal Rules 7, 17.1, and 19 filed by the Supreme Court with the General Assembly on January 13, 2000 and refiled on April 27, 2000 shall take effect on July 1, 2000. They govern all proceedings in actions brought after they take effect and also all further proceedings in actions then pending, except to the extent that their application in a particular action pending when the amendments take effect would not be feasible or would work injustice, in which event the former procedure applies.

(R) **Effective date of amendments.** The amendments to Criminal Rule 12 filed by the Supreme Court with the General Assembly on January 12, 2001, and refiled on April 26, 2001, shall take effect on July 1, 2001. They govern all proceedings in actions brought after they take effect and also all further proceedings in actions then pending, except to the extent that their application in a particular action pending when the amendments take effect would not be feasible or would work injustice, in which event the former procedure applies.

(S) **Effective date of amendments.** The amendments to Criminal Rule 24 filed by the Supreme Court with the General Assembly on January 11, 2002, and refiled on April 18, 2002, shall take effect on July 1, 2002. They govern all proceedings in actions brought after they take effect and also all further proceedings in actions then pending, except to the extent that their application in a particular action pending when the amendments take effect would not be feasible or would work injustice, in which event the former procedure applies.

(T) **Effective date of amendments.** The amendments to Criminal Rules 4.1, 21, and 32, filed by the Supreme Court with the General Assembly on January 7, 2004 and refiled on April 28, 2004 shall take effect on July 1, 2004. They govern all proceedings in actions brought after they take effect and also all further proceedings in actions then pending, except to the extent that their application in a particular action pending when the amendments take effect would not be feasible or would work injustice, in which event the former procedure applies.

(U) **Effective date of amendments.** The amendments to Criminal Rules 24 and 30 filed by the Supreme Court with the General Assembly on Jan. 14, 2005 and revised and refiled on April 20, 2005 shall take effect on July 1, 2005. They govern all proceedings in actions brought after they take effect and also all further proceedings in actions then pending, except to the extent that their application in a particular action pending when the amendments take effect would not be feasible or would work injustice, in which event the former procedure applies.

(V) **Effective date of amendments.** The amendments to Criminal Rules 19, 24, and 46 filed by the Supreme Court with the General Assembly on January 12, 2006 shall take effect on July 1, 2006. They govern all proceedings in actions brought after they take effect and also all further proceedings in actions then pending, except to the extent that their application in a particular action pending when the amendments take effect would not be feasible or would work injustice, in which event the former procedure applies.

(W) **Effective date of amendments.** The amendments to Criminal Rules 10, 24, and 43 filed by the Supreme Court with the General Assembly on January 14, 2008 and refiled on April 28, 2008 shall take effect on July 1, 2008. They govern all proceedings in actions brought after they take effect and also all further proceedings in actions then pending, except to the extent that their application in a particular action pending when the amendments take effect would not be feasible or would work injustice, in which event the former procedure applies.

(X) **Effective date of amendments.** The amendments to Criminal Rules 24 and 32 filed by the Supreme Court with the General Assembly on January 14, 2009 and refiled on April 30, 2009 shall take effect on July 1, 2009. They govern all proceedings in actions brought after they take effect and also all further proceedings in actions then pending, except to the extent that their application in a particular action pending when the amendments take effect would not be feasible or would work injustice, in which event the former procedure applies.

(Y) **Effective date of amendments.** The amendments to Criminal Rules 12, 16 and 41 filed by the Supreme Court with the General Assembly on January 14, 2010 and revised and refiled on April 28, 2010 shall take effect on July 1, 2010. They govern all proceedings in actions brought after they take effect and also all further proceedings in actions then pending, except to the extent that their application in a particular action pending when the amendments take effect would not be feasible or would work injustice, in which event the former procedure applies.

History: Amended, eff 7-1-75; 7-1-76; 7-1-78; 7-1-80; 7-1-81; 7-1-82; 7-1-85; 7-1-90; 7-1-92; 7-1-93; 7-1-94; 7-1-95; 7-1-96; 7-1-97; 7-1-98; 7-1-00; 7-1-01; 7-1-02; 7-1-04; 7-1-05; 7-1-06; 7-1-08; 7-1-09; 7-1-10.

RULE 60. Title

These rules shall be known as the Ohio Rules of Criminal Procedure and may be cited as "Criminal Rules" or "Crim. R. ____."

APPENDIX OF FORMS

(See Crim. R. 58)

The forms which follow are intended for illustration only. They are limited in number, their being no attempt to furnish a complete manual of forms.

Although the forms are for illustrative purposes, they have been drafted to conform to the policies expressed in the Criminal Rules.

In the illustrations, the Franklin County Court of Common Pleas and the Franklin County Municipal Court identifications have each been used with the forms to show the adjustments required at the two levels of adjudication.

FORM I

FRANKLIN COUNTY MUNICIPAL COURT
FRANKLIN COUNTY, OHIO

State of Ohio)
/City of Columbus/)
)   NO._____
v.)
)   COMPLAINT
_____)
name)   (Rule 4)
)
_____)
address)

Complainant being duly sworn states that _____ C.D.
_____ defendant
at _____ , County, Ohio on or about _____ ,
          place
19_____ , _____
          state the essential facts
_____
_____

in violation of _____
          state the numerical designation of the applicable statute or ordinance

A.B. _____
Complainant

Sworn to and subscribed before me by _____ on
_____ , 19 _____

_____
/ Judge / Clerk / Deputy Clerk /
Franklin County Municipal Court

or

_____
Notary Public,
My Commission expires _____ , 19 _____
/ Franklin County / State of Ohio /

445

FORM II

FRANKLIN COUNTY MUNICIPAL COURT
FRANKLIN COUNTY, OHIO

State of Ohio   )

/City of Columbus/   )   NO._____

)

      v.   )   **COMPLAINT BY**

)   **PROSECUTING ATTORNEY**

_____)   **UPON AFFIDAVIT**

name   )

)   (Rule 4)

_____)

address   )

Complainant prosecuting attorney being duly sworn states that _____
_____ name of affiant

has filed an affidavit, a copy of which is attached hereto, stating that _____

_____ C.D. _____ at _____, County, Ohio on or
                                  place

about _____, 19 _____, _____
                            state the essential facts

_____

Upon this affidavit complainant states that _____ C.D. _____ on or
                                 defendant

about the above date and at the above place did violate _____
                              state the numerical designation

_____ .

of the applicable statute or ordinance

                          A.B. _____
                          Complainant, Title

Sworn to and subscribed before me by _____ **A.B.** _____

on _____, 19 _____.

                          _____

                          / Judge / Clerk / Deputy Clerk /
                          Franklin County Municipal Court

                                  or

                          _____

                          Notary Public,
                          My Commission expires _____, 19 _____
                          / Franklin County / State of Ohio /

FORM III

/ FRANKLIN COUNTY MUNICIPAL COURT /
/ COURT OF COMMON PLEAS /
FRANKLIN COUNTY, OHIO

State of Ohio   )
/City of Columbus/   )
)   NO._____
        v.   )
)   **DIRECTION TO ISSUE SUMMONS**
_____   )
name   )   (Rules 4 and 9)
)
)
_____   )
address   )

TO_____
        / Clerk / Deputy Clerk /

Issue summons to an appropriate officer and direct him to make / personal service /
residence service / certified mail service / upon _____C.D._____ at / the address
                                                            defendant
stated in the caption of this direction./ _____

_____/
            fill in address if different from caption

Special instructions for server:_____

_____

_____

                                    _____
                                    / Judge / Officer Designated by Judge(s) /
                                    Franklin County Municipal Court

                                                    or

                                    _____
                                    Judge
                                    Court of Common Pleas
                                    Franklin County, Ohio

FORM IV

FRANKLIN COUNTY MUNICIPAL COURT
FRANKLIN COUNTY, OHIO

State of Ohio   )
/City of Columbus/   )
)   NO._____
   v.   )
)   CLERK'S MEMORANDUM
_____)   OF DETERMINATION TO ISSUE
name   )   SUMMONS UPON COMPLAINT
)
)   (Rule 4)
_____)
address   )

It appearing that summons will reasonably assure the appearance of _____C.D._____
                                                         defendant

summons shall issue:

/ to an appropriate officer and such officer shall be directed to make / personal service / residence service /.

/ by certified mail /

Service shall be at / the address stated in the caption of this notice / _____
_____
                fill in address if different from caption

Special instructions for server: _____
_____
_____

                            _____
                            / Clerk / Deputy Clerk /
                            Franklin County Municipal Court

FORM V

FRANKLIN COUNTY MUNICIPAL COURT
FRANKLIN COUNTY, OHIO

State of Ohio	)
/City of Columbus/	) NO._____
	)
v.	) PROSECUTING ATTORNEY'S
_____	) REQUEST FOR ISSUANCE OF
name	) SUMMONS UPON COMPLAINT
	)
_____	) (Rule 4)
address	)

TO_____
/ Clerk / Deputy Clerk /

A complaint has been filed against _____ C.D._____
defendant

Issue summons to an appropriate officer and direct him to make / personal service / residence service / certified mail service / upon defendant at / the address stated in the caption of this request. / _____
_____/
fill in address if different from caption

Special instructions for server: _____
_____
_____

_____
Prosecuting Attorney, Title

FORM VI

/ FRANKLIN COUNTY MUNICIPAL COURT /
/ COURT OF COMMON PLEAS /
FRANKLIN COUNTY, OHIO

State of Ohio   )   NO._____
/City of Columbus/   )
)
      v.   )   SUMMONS UPON / COMPLAINT /
)   INDICTMENT / INFORMATION /
_____)
name   )
)
)
_____)   (Rules 4 and 9)
address   )
)

TO _____ C.D. _____
                               defendant

A / complaint / indictment / information /, a copy of which is attached hereto, has been filed in the / Franklin County Municipal Court, 120 West Gay Street, Columbus, Ohio 43215, / Franklin County Court of Common Pleas, 410 South High Street, Columbus, Ohio 43215, / charging that you: _____
                                      describe the offense

_____
    and state the numerical designation of the applicable statute or ordinance

_____ .

You are hereby summoned and ordered to appear at _____
_____, / Franklin County Municipal Court, 120 West Gay
time, day, date, room

Street, Columbus, Ohio 43215. / Franklin County Court of Common Pleas, 410 South High Street, Columbus, Ohio 43215. /

If you fail to appear at the time and place stated above you may be arrested.

                           _____
                           / Judge / Officer Designated by Judge(s) /
                           / Clerk / Deputy Clerk /
                           Franklin County Municipal Court

                                    (or)

                           _____
                           / Judge / Clerk / Deputy Clerk /
                           Court of Common Pleas
                           Franklin County, Ohio

NOTICE TO DEFENDANT: For information regarding your duty to appear call

_____
fill in phone number(s)

CLERK'S INSTRUCTIONS TO SERVING OFFICER
FOR PERSONAL OR RESIDENCE SERVICE

TO _____
        officer other than clerk authorized to serve summons

Make / personal service / residence service / upon _____
                                                              defendant

at / the address stated in the caption of the summons. / _____

_____/
            fill in address for service if different from caption of summons

Special instructions for server: _____

_____

_____

_____
                / Clerk / Deputy Clerk /

• • • • • • • • • •

CLERK'S INSTRUCTIONS FOR
CERTIFIED MAIL SERVICE

TO _____
                            clerk

Make certified mail service upon _____
                                            defendant

at / the address stated in the caption of the summons. / _____

_____/
            fill in address for service if different from caption of summons

Special instructions for server: _____

_____

_____ .

_____
                / Clerk / Deputy Clerk /

RECEIPT OF SUMMONS BY
SERVING AUTHORITY

First Receipt

Received this summons on _____, 19 _____,
at _____ o'clock ____m.

_____
Officer

By _____
Title

Subsequent Receipt

Received this summons on _____, 19 _____,
at _____ o'clock ____m.

_____
Officer

By _____
Title

RETURN OF SERVICE OF SUMMONS
(PERSONAL)

```
+--------------------------+
|          Fees            |
|  Mileage $ ____          |
|             ____         |
|             ____         |
|             ____         |
|             ____         |
|  Total $ ____            |
+--------------------------+
```

I received this summons on _____, 19 ____,
at _____ o'clock, ____.m., and made personal
service of it upon _____
                              fill in name
by locating / him/her / and tendering a copy of the
summons, a copy of the / complaint / indictment
/ information / and accompanying documents, on
_____, 19 ____.

_____
Serving Officer, Title

Date return made: _____, 19 ____

• • • • • • • • • •

RETURN OF SERVICE OF SUMMONS
(RESIDENCE)

```
+--------------------------+
|          Fees            |
|  Mileage $ ____          |
|             ____         |
|             ____         |
|             ____         |
|             ____         |
|  Total $ ____            |
+--------------------------+
```

I received this summons on _____, 19 ____,
at _____ o'clock, ____.m., and made residence
service of it upon _____
                              fill in name
by leaving, at / his/her / usual place of residence with
_____ a person of suitable
         fill in name
age and discretion then residing therein, a copy of
the summons, a copy of the / complaint / indictment
/ information / and accompanying documents, on
_____, 19 ____ .

_____
Serving Officer, Title

Date return made: _____, 19 ____

RETURN OF SERVICE OF SUMMONS
(FAILURE OF SERVICE)

Fees

Mileage $ ____

____

____

____

____

Total $ ____

I received this summons on _____, 19 _____,
at _____ o'clock, ____.m., with instructions to
make / personal service / residence service / upon

_____
fill in name

and I was unable to serve a copy of the summons upon
/ him/her / for the following reasons: _____

_____

_____

_____

_____

Serving Officer, Title

Date return made: _____, 19 _____

• • • • • • • • •

RETURN OF SERVICE OF SUMMONS
(FAILURE OF SERVICE)

Fees

Mileage $ ____

____

____

____

____

Total $ ____

I received this summons on _____, 19 _____,
at _____ o'clock, ____.m., with instructions to
make / personal service / residence service / upon

_____
fill in name

and I was unable to serve a copy of the summons upon
/ him/her / for the following reasons: _____

_____

_____

_____

Serving Officer, Title

Date return made: _____, 19 _____

FORM VII

FRANKLIN COUNTY MUNICIPAL COURT
FRANKLIN COUNTY, OHIO

State of Ohio   )
/City of Columbus/   )
) NO._____

     v.   )

_____) **WARRANT ON COMPLAINT**
name   )

_____)   (Rule 4)
address   )

TO _____
              officer authorized to execute a warrant

A complaint, a copy of which is attached hereto, has been filed in this court charging _____

_____
describe the offense and state the numerical designation of the applicable statute or ordinance

_____

You are ordered to arrest _____ C.D. _____ and bring / him/her / before
                            defendant
this court without unnecessary delay.

You / may / may not / issue summons in lieu of arrest under Rule 4(A)(2) or issue
summons after arrest under Rule 4(F) because _____
                        state specific reasons if issuance of summons

_____
    restricted

Special instructions to executing officer: _____

_____

_____

                          _____
                / Judge / Officer Designated by Judge(s) /
                   / Clerk / Deputy Clerk /
                Franklin County Municipal Court

SUMMONS ENDORSEMENT

See NOTE: Use only in appropriate case

This warrant was executed / by arrest and / by issuing the following summons:

TO _____ C.D. _____
defendant

You are hereby summoned and ordered to appear at _____
time, day, date, room

Franklin County Municipal Court, 120 West Gay Street, Columbus, Ohio 43215.

If you fail to appear at the time and place stated above you may be arrested.

_____
Issuing Officer, Title
See Rule 4(A)(2), Rule 4(F) and Return
Forms

NOTICE TO DEFENDANT: For information regarding your duty to appear call _____

_____
fill in telephone number(s)

· · · · · · · · · ·

RECEIPT OF WARRANT BY EXECUTING AUTHORITY

First Receipt

Received this warrant on _____ , 19 _____, at _____ o'clock _____.m.

_____
Officer
By _____
Title

Subsequent Receipt

Received this / alias / warrant on _____ , 19 _____, at _____ o'clock _____.m.

_____
Officer
By _____
Title

RETURN OF EXECUTED WARRANT

Fees

Mileage $ ____

____

____

____

Total $ ____

1. <u>Execution By Arrest</u>

I received this warrant on _____, 19 ____,
at _____ o'clock ____.m. On _____, 19 ____,
I arrested _____ and gave / him/
her / a copy of this warrant with complaint attached
and brought / him/her / to _____
state the place

_____
Arresting Officer, Title

Fees

Mileage $ ____

____

____

____

____

Total $ ____

**2. <u>Execution By Issuance Of Summons Under Rule
4(A)(2) By Executing Officer</u>**

I received this warrant on _____, 19 ____, at
_____ o'clock ____.m. On _____, 19 ____, I
executed this warrant by issuing _____ C.D. _____
a summons by / personal service / residence service /
which ordered / him/her / to appear at _____
time, day, date
_____, Franklin County Municipal Court,
room

120 West Gay Street, Columbus, Ohio, 43215. The summons was endorsed upon the warrant and accompanied by a copy of the complaint.

_____
Arresting Officer, Title

Fees

Mileage $ ____

____

____

____

____

Total $ ____

3. Execution By Arrest And Issuance Of Summons Under Rule 4(F) By Arresting Officer

I received this warrant on _____, 19 ____, at _____ o'clock ____.m. On _____, 19 ____, I arrested _____C.D._____ and after arrest I issued _____C.D._____ a summons by personal service which ordered / him/her / to appear at _____ , Franklin County Municipal Court, 120 West Gay Street, Columbus, Ohio, 43215. The summons was endorsed upon the warrant and accompanied by a copy of the complaint.

_____

Arresting-Issuing Officer, Title

4. Execution By Arrest And Issuance Of Summons Under Rule 4(F) By Superior Of Arresting Officer

On _____ , 19 ___, _____C.D._____ was arrested by _____
                    name of arresting officer
and I issued _____C.D._____ a summons by personal service which ordered / him/ her / to appear at _____
              time, day, date, room
Franklin County Municipal Court, 120 West Gay Street, Columbus, Ohio 43215. The summons was endorsed upon the warrant and accompanied by a copy of the complaint.

_____

Arresting-Issuing Officer, Title

RETURN OF UNEXECUTED WARRANT

Fees

Mileage $ ____

____

____

____

____

Total $ ____

I received this warrant on _____, 19 _____, at _____ o'clock, _____.m. On _____, 19 _____, I attempted to execute this warrant but was unable to to so because _____

state specific reason or reasons and

additional information regarding defendant's whereabouts

_____

_____
Executing Officer, Title

RETURN OF UNEXECUTED WARRANT

Fees

Mileage $ ____

____

____

____

____

Total $ ____

I received this warrant on _____, 19 _____, at _____ o'clock, _____.m. On _____, 19 _____, I attempted to execute this warrant but was unable to to so because _____

state specific reason or reasons and

additional information regarding defendant's whereabouts

_____

_____
Executing Officer, Title

FORM VIII

COURT OF COMMON PLEAS
FRANKLIN COUNTY, OHIO

State of Ohio   )
)   NO._____

   v.   )
)   CLERK'S MEMORANDUM OF
_____)   DETERMINATION TO ISSUE
name   )   SUMMONS UPON INDICTMENT
)
_____)   (Rule 9)
address   )

It appearing that defendant _____ was released pursuant to
                                      name

Rule 46 by the _____ on the same offense for which / he/she
                  bind-over court
/ was indicted in this court, summons shall issue: / to an appropriate officer and such officer shall be
directed to make / personal service / residence service /.

/ by certified mail service /

Service shall be at / the address stated in the caption of this notice / _____

_____
            fill in address if different from caption
Special instructions for server: _____

_____

_____

_____
/ Clerk / Deputy Clerk /
Court of Common Pleas
Franklin County, Ohio

FORM IX

**COURT OF COMMON PLEAS
FRANKLIN COUNTY, OHIO**

State of Ohio   )
)   NO._____
        v.   )
)   PROSECUTING ATTORNEY'S
_____   )   REQUEST FOR ISSUANCE OF
            name   )   SUMMONS UPON/INDICTMENT
)   /INFORMATION/
_____   )   (Rule 9)
          address   )
)
)

TO _____
                    / Clerk / Deputy Clerk /

_____C.D._____ has been named a defendant in an / indictment re-
                defendant
turned by the grand jury / information filed by the prosecuting attorney. / Issue summons
to an appropriate officer and direct him to make / personal service / residence service /
certified mail service / upon defendant at / the address stated in the caption of this request./_____
              fill in address if different from caption

Special instructions for server: _____
_____
_____

                              _____
                              Prosecuting Attorney, Title

FORM X

COURT OF COMMON PLEAS
FRANKLIN COUNTY, OHIO

State of Ohio   )
)   NO._____

    v.   )
)   PROSECUTING ATTORNEY'S
_____)   REQUEST FOR ISSUANCE OF
name   )   WARRANT UPON
_____)   /INDICTMENT/INFORMATION/
address   )
)   (Rule 9)

TO: _____
               / Clerk / Deputy Clerk /

_____ C.D. _____ has been named a defendant in an / indictment re-
            defendant
turned by the grand jury / information filed by the prosecuting attorney./

Issue a warrant to an appropriate officer and direct him to execute it upon _____
_____ C.D. _____ / at the address stated in the caption of this request./
            defendant
_____ /
         fill in address if different from caption

Special instructions for executing officer: _____
_____
_____

_____
Prosecuting Attorney, Title

FORM XI

COURT OF COMMON PLEAS
FRANKLIN COUNTY, OHIO

State of Ohio   )

)

     v.   )   NO. _____

)

_____)   WARRANT UPON/INDICTMENT/

name   )   INFORMATION/

)

_____)   (Rule 9)

address   )

)

TO _____
        officer authorized to execute warrant

An / indictment / information /, a copy of which is attached hereto has been filed in the Franklin County Court of Common Pleas, 410 South High Street, Columbus, Ohio 43215, charging _____ C.D. _____ with: _____
                     defendant

_____
    describe the offense and state the numerical designation of the applicable statute

You are ordered to arrest _____ C.D. _____ and bring him before this
                        defendant
court without unnecessary delay.

Special instructions to executing officer: _____

_____

_____

_____
/ Judge / Clerk / Deputy Clerk /
Court of Common Pleas
Franklin County, Ohio

RECEIPT OF WARRANT
BY EXECUTING AUTHORITY

First Receipt

Received this warrant on _____ , 19 _____, at _____ o'clock _____.m.

_____
Officer

By _____
Title

Subsequent Receipt

Received this warrant on _____ , 19 _____, at _____ o'clock _____.m.

_____
Officer

By _____
Title

• • • • • • • • • •

RETURN OF EXECUTED WARRANT

Fees
Mileage $ _____
_____
_____
_____
_____
Total $ _____

I received this warrant on _____ , 19 ____, at _____ o'clock _____.m. On _____ , 19 ____, I arrested _____ , gave / him/her a copy of this warrant with / indictment / information / attached and brought / him/her / to _____
state the place

_____

_____
Arresting Officer, Title

RETURN OF UNEXECUTED WARRANT

Fees

Mileage $ ____

____

____

____

____

Total $ ____

I received this warrant on _____, 19 ____,

at _____ o'clock, ____.m. On _____, 19 ____,

I attempted to execute this warrant but was unable to

do so because _____

                 state specific reason or reasons and

_____

      additional information regarding defendant's

_____

                     whereabouts

_____

_____

Executing Officer, Title

• • • • • • • • • •

RETURN OF UNEXECUTED WARRANT

Fees

Mileage $ ____

____

____

____

____

Total $ ____

I received this warrant on _____, 19 ____,

at _____ o'clock, ____.m. On _____, 19 ____,

I attempted to execute this warrant but was unable to

do so because _____

                 state specific reason or reasons and

_____

      additional information regarding defendant's

_____

                     whereabouts

_____

_____

Executing Officer, Title

FORM XII

FRANKLIN COUNTY MUNICIPAL COURT
FRANKLIN COUNTY, OHIO

State of Ohio)	SUMMONS NO. _____
/City of Columbus/)	
)	CASE NO._____
v.)	
)	SUMMONS IN LIEU OF ARREST
_____)	WITHOUT WARRANT, AND
name of defendant)	COMPLAINT UPON SUCH
_____)	SUMMONS
address)	
_____)	(Rule 4 (A) (3))
age)	

TO DEFENDANT:

SUMMONS

In lieu of immediate arrest upon a misdemeanor you are summoned and ordered to appear / at _____
                              time, day, date, room
Franklin County Municipal Court, 120 West Gay Street, Columbus, Ohio 43215. / before the Franklin County Juvenile Court, 50 East Mound Street, Columbus, Ohio 43215 at the time and place ordered by that court. / If you fail to appear at this time and place you may be arrested.

This summons served personally on the defendant on _____ , 19 _____

COMPLAINT

On _____ , 19_____ , at _____

_____
                              place

you _____
            describe the offense charged and state the numerical

_____
            designation of the applicable statute or ordinance

_____

_____

_____

                              _____
                              Signature of Issuing-Charging
                              Law Enforcement Officer

Being duly sworn the issuing-charging law enforcement officer states that he has read the above complaint and that it is true.

_____
Issuing-Charging Law Enforcement Officer

Sworn to and subscribed before me by _____

on _____, 19_____.

_____
/ Judge / Clerk / Deputy Clerk
Franklin County Municipal Court

or

_____
Notary Public
My Commission Expires _____, 19_____.
/ Franklin County / State of Ohio /

NOTICE TO DEFENDANT: The officer is not required to swear to the complaint upon your copy of the summons and complaint. He swears to the complaint on the copy he files with the court. You may obtain a copy of the sworn complaint before hearing time. You will be given a copy of the sworn complaint before or at the hearing. For information regarding your duty to appear call _____
fill in telephone number(s)

NOTICE TO DEFENDANT UNDER EIGHTEEN YEARS OF AGE: You must appear before the Franklin County Juvenile Court, 50 East Mound Street, Columbus, Ohio 43215, at the time and place determined by that Court. The Juvenile Court will notify you when and where to appear. This Summons and Complaint will be filed with the Juvenile Court. The Complaint may be used as a juvenile complaint. You may obtain a copy of the sworn complaint from the Juvenile Court before the Juvenile Court hearing. You will be given a copy of the sworn complaint before or at the Juvenile Court hearing. For information regarding your duty to appear at Juvenile Court call _____
fill in telephone number(s)

FORM XIII

FRANKLIN COUNTY MUNICIPAL COURT
FRANKLIN COUNTY, OHIO

State of Ohio
/City of Columbus/   )   SUMMONS NO. _____

)
     v.   )   CASE NO. _____

)
_____)   SUMMONS AFTER ARREST
name of defendant   )   WITHOUT WARRANT, AND
)   COMPLAINT UPON EACH SUCH
_____)   SUMMONS
address   )
)   (Rule 4 (F))
_____)
age   )

TO DEFENDANT:

SUMMONS

In lieu of continued custody upon a misdemeanor you are summoned and ordered to appear / at _____
                            time, day, date, room

Franklin County Municipal Court, 120 West Gay Street, Columbus, Ohio 43215. / before the Franklin County Juvenile Court, 50 East Mound Street, Columbus, Ohio 43215 at the time and place ordered by that court. / If you fail to appear at this time and place you may be rearrested.

This summons served personally on the defendant on _____ , 19 _____.

COMPLAINT

On _____ , 19 _____ , at _____
                                        place

_____

you _____
      describe the offense charged and state the numerical

      designation of the applicable statute or ordinance

_____

_____

_____

                          _____
                           Signature of Issuing-Charging
                           Law Enforcement Officer

Being duly sworn the issuing-charging law enforcement officer states that he has read the above complaint and that it is true.

_____
Issuing-Charging Law Enforcement Officer

Sworn to and subscribed before me by _____

on _____, 19_____.

_____
/ Judge / Clerk / Deputy Clerk
Franklin County Municipal Court

or

_____
Notary Public
My Commission Expires _____, 19_____.
/ Franklin County / State of Ohio /

NOTICE TO DEFENDANT: The officer is not required to swear to the complaint upon your copy of the summons and complaint. He swears to the complaint on the copy he files with the court. You may obtain a copy of the sworn complaint before hearing time. You will be given a copy of the sworn complaint before or at the hearing. For information regarding your duty to appear call _____
fill in telephone number(s)

NOTICE TO DEFENDANT UNDER EIGHTEEN YEARS OF AGE: You must appear before the Franklin County Juvenile Court, 50 East Mound Street, Columbus, Ohio 43215, at the time and place determined by that Court. The Juvenile Court will notify you when and where to appear. This Summons and Complaint will be filed with the Juvenile Court. The Complaint may be used as a juvenile complaint. You may obtain a copy of the sworn complaint from the Juvenile Court before the Juvenile Court hearing. You will be given a copy of the sworn complaint before or at the Juvenile Court hearing. For information regarding your duty to appear at Juvenile Court call _____
fill in telephone number(s)

FORM XIV

FRANKLIN COUNTY MUNICIPAL COURT
FRANKLIN COUNTY, OHIO

State of Ohio
/City of Columbus/

Citation No. _____

Case No. _____

v.

MINOR MISDEMEANOR CITATION

_____
name of defendant

(Rule 4.1)

_____
address

_____
age

TO DEFENDANT:

On _____ , 19_____ , at _____
    date   place

_____

You _____
              describe the offense charged and state the

_____
       numerical designation of the applicable statute or ordinance

_____

_____

_____

_____

You are ordered to appear at _____
                           time, day, date, room

Franklin County Municipal Court, 120 West Gay Street, Columbus, Ohio 43215,/ before the Franklin County Juvenile Court, 50 East Mound Street, Columbus, Ohio 43215, at the time and place ordered by that court. /

If you wish to contest this matter you must appear at the above time and place. In lieu of appearing at the above time and place you may, within the time stated above, appear personally at 120 West Gay Street, Columbus, Ohio 43215, Room 120, sign the guilty plea and waiver of trial which appear in this form, and pay a fine of $ _____ and court costs of $ _____ .

If you fail to appear at the time and place stated above you may be arrested.

This citation was served personally on the defendant.

_____
Signature of Issuing Law Enforcement
Officer

Being duly sworn the issuing law enforcement officer states that he has read the citation and that it is true.

_____
Issuing Officer

Sworn to and subscribed before me by _____
on _____, 19_____ .

_____
/ Judge / Clerk / Deputy Clerk /

or

_____
Notary Public,
My Commission expires _____, 19_____
Franklin County / State of Ohio /

NOTICE TO DEFENDANT: The officer is not required to swear to your copy of the citation and complaint. He swears to citation in the copy he files with the court. You may obtain a copy of the sworn citation before hearing time. You will be given a copy of the sworn citation before or at the hearing. For information regarding your duty to appear call

_____
fill in telephone number(s)

NOTICE TO DEFENDANT UNDER EIGHTEEN YEARS OF AGE: The appearance, guilty plea, waiver and payment provisions of this form do not apply to you. You must appear before the Franklin County Juvenile Court, 50 East Mound Street, Columbus, Ohio 43215, at the time and place determined by that Court. The Juvenile Court will notify you when and where to appear. This citation will be filed with the Juvenile Court. The citation may be used as a juvenile complaint. You may obtain a copy of the sworn citation from the Juvenile Court before the Juvenile Court hearing. You will be given a copy of the sworn citation before or at the Juvenile Court hearing. For information regarding your duty to appear at Juvenile Court call _____

_____

fill in telephone number(s)

GUILTY PLEA, WAIVER OF TRIAL, PAYMENT OF FINE AND COSTS

I, the undersigned defendant, do hereby enter my written plea of guilty to the offense charged in this citation. I realize that by signing this guilty plea I admit my guilt of the offense charged and waive my right to contest the offense in a trial before the court. I plead guilty to the offense charged in the citation.

FINE   _____   _____

                                         Signature of Defendant

COST   _____   _____

                                         address

TOTAL   _____   _____

                                         Signature And Title Of Person Taking Guilty
                                         Plea, Waiver And Payment

RECEIPT NO. _____

FORM XV

UNIFORM PETITION FORM

IN THE COURT OF COMMON PLEAS
_____ COUNTY, OHIO

CASE NOS.: _____
_____
JUDGE: _____

STATE OF OHIO
        Plaintiff-Respondent

-vs-   **POST-CONVICTION PETITION**
_____

        Defendant-Petitioner

I. CASE HISTORY

TRIAL:

Charge (include specifications)   Disposition
_____   _____
_____   _____

Date Sentenced: _____
Name of Attorney: _____
Was this conviction the result of a (circle one):   **Guilty Plea**   **No Contest Plea**   **Trial**
If the conviction resulted in a trial, what was the length of the trial?
_____

Appeal to Court of Appeals
Number or citation _____
Disposition _____
Name of Attorney _____

Appeal to Supreme Court of Ohio
Number or citation _____
Disposition _____
Name of Attorney _____

HAS A POST-CONVICTION PETITION BEEN FILED BEFORE IN THIS CASE?
      YES   NO

   If YES, attach a copy of the Petition and the Judgment Entry showing how it was disposed.

IF THIS IS NOT THE FIRST POST-CONVICTION PETITION, OR IT IS FILED OUTSIDE THE TIME LIMITS PROVIDED BY LAW, STATE THE REASONS WHY THE COURT SHOULD CONSIDER THIS PETITION: _____

_____

_____

_____

_____

OTHER RELEVANT CASE HISTORY: _____

II. STATEMENT OF FACTS

III. GROUNDS FOR RELIEF

(each ground not to exceed three pages)

Ground for relief 1: _____

_____

_____

_____

_____

Attached exhibit numbers which support ground for relief:

_____

_____

Legal authority (constitutional provisions, statutes, cases, rules, etc.) in support of ground for relief: _____

_____

_____

_____

_____
(name)

Index to Ohio Rules of Criminal Procedure

OHIO RULES OF APPELLATE PROCEDURE

TITLE I
APPLICABILITY OF RULES

RULE 1. Scope of rules

(A) These rules govern procedure in appeals to courts of appeals from the trial courts of record in Ohio.

(B) Procedure in appeals to courts of appeals from the board of tax appeals shall be as provided by law, except that App. R. 13 to 33 shall be applicable to those appeals.

(C) Procedures in appeals to courts of appeals from juvenile courts pursuant to section 2505.073 of the Revised Code shall be as provided by that section, except that these rules govern to the extent that the rules do not conflict with that section.

History: Amended, eff 7-1-94.

RULE 2. Law and fact appeals abolished

Appeals on questions of law and fact are abolished.

TITLE II
APPEALS FROM JUDGMENTS AND ORDERS OF COURT OF RECORD

RULE 3. Appeal as of right—how taken

(A) **Filing the notice of appeal.** An appeal as of right shall be taken by filing a notice of appeal with the clerk of the trial court within the time allowed by Rule 4. Failure of an appellant to take any step other than the timely filing of a notice of appeal does not affect the validity of the appeal, but is ground only for such action as the court of appeals deems appropriate, which may include dismissal of the appeal. Appeals by leave of court shall be taken in the manner prescribed by Rule 5.

(B) **Joint or consolidated appeals.** If two or more persons are entitled to appeal from a judgment or order of a trial court and their interests are such as to make joinder practicable, they may file a joint notice of appeal, or may join in appeal after filing separate timely notices of appeal, and they may thereafter proceed on appeal as a single appellant. Appeals may be consolidated by order of the court of appeals upon its own motion or upon motion of a party, or by stipulation of the parties to the several appeals.

(C) **Cross appeal.**

(1) Cross appeal required. A person who intends to defend a judgment or order against an appeal taken by an appellant and who also seeks to change the judgment or order or, in the event the judgment or order

may be reversed or modified, an interlocutory ruling merged into the judgment or order, shall file a notice of cross appeal within the time allowed by App.R. 4.

(2) Cross appeal not required. A person who intends to defend a judgment or order appealed by an appellant on a ground other than that relied on by the trial court but who does not seek to change the judgment or order is not required to file a notice of cross appeal.

(D) **Content of the notice of appeal.** The notice of appeal shall specify the party or parties taking the appeal; shall designate the judgment, order or part thereof appealed from; and shall name the court to which the appeal is taken. The title of the case shall be the same as in the trial court with the designation of the appellant added, as appropriate. Form 1 in Appendix of Forms is a suggested form of a notice of appeal.

(E) **Service of the notice of appeal.** The clerk of the trial court shall serve notice of the filing of a notice of appeal and, where required by local rule, a docketing statement, by mailing, or by facsimile transmission, a copy to counsel of record of each party other than the appellant, or, if a party is not represented by counsel, to the party at the party's last known address. The clerk shall mail or otherwise forward a copy of the notice of appeal and of the docket entries, together with a copy of all filings by appellant pursuant to App.R. 9(B), to the clerk of the court of appeals named in the notice. The clerk shall note on each copy served the date on which the notice of appeal was filed. Failure of the clerk to serve notice shall not affect the validity of the appeal. Service shall be sufficient notwithstanding the death of a party or a party's counsel. The clerk shall note in the docket the names of the parties served, the date served, and the means of service.

(F) **Amendment of the notice of appeal.** The court of appeals within its discretion and upon such terms as are just may allow the amendment of a timely filed notice of appeal.

(G) **Docketing statement.** If a court of appeals has adopted an accelerated calendar by local rule pursuant to Rule 11.1, a docketing statement shall be filed with the clerk of the trial court with the notice of appeal. (See Form 2, Appendix of Forms.)

The purpose of the docketing statement is to determine whether an appeal will be assigned to the accelerated or the regular calendar.

A case may be assigned to the accelerated calendar if any of the following apply:

(1) No transcript is required (e.g. summary judgment or judgment on the pleadings);

(2) The length of the transcript is such that its preparation time will not be a source of delay;

(3) An agreed statement is submitted in lieu of the record;

(4) The record was made in an administrative hearing and filed with the trial court;

(5) All parties to the appeal approve an assignment of the appeal to the accelerated calendar; or

(6) The case has been designated by local rule for the accelerated calendar.

The court of appeals by local rule may assign a case to the accelerated calendar at any stage of the proceeding. The court of appeals may provide by local rule for an oral hearing before a full panel in order to assist it in determining whether the appeal should be assigned to the accelerated calendar.

Upon motion of appellant or appellee for a procedural order pursuant to App.R. 15(B) filed within seven days after the notice of appeal is filed with the clerk of the trial court, a case may be removed for good cause from the accelerated calendar and assigned to the regular calendar. Demonstration of a unique issue of law which will be of substantial precedential value in the determination of similar cases will ordinarily be good cause for transfer to the regular calendar.

History: Amended, eff 7-1-72; 7-1-77; 7-1-82; 7-1-91; 7-1-92; 7-1-94.

NOTES TO DECISIONS

ANALYSIS

Appellate review limited
Conditional assignments of error
Cross appeals
Cross-assignments of error
Filing
— Requirements
Final judgment
Identification of judgment
Identification of judgment appealed from
Jurisdiction
Jurisdictional defects
— Notice of appeal
Notice of appeal
Procedural requirements
Right to file appeal
Timeliness of appeal

Appellate review limited

As defendant's notice of appeal pursuant to Ohio R. app. P. 3(D) indicated that he sought review of the trial court's termination entry following imposition of sentence, his claim that he informed his trial counsel about his inability to pay a mandatory fine at the time of sentencing, and that the affidavit of indigency was filed subsequently thereto, was outside of the appellate record and not within the scope of review. State v. Howard, — Ohio App. 3d —, 2007 Ohio 3582, — N.E. 2d —, 2007 Ohio App. LEXIS 3290 (July 13, 2007).

Conditional assignments of error

Since the court found that the trial court properly granted summary judgment to an employer on an employee's employer intentional tort claim, there was no need to address the employer's conditional assignment of error. While RC § 2505.22 and Ohio R. App. P. 3(C) allowed an appellee who had not filed a notice of appeal to assign error to the trial court's action, these errors could only be used for the limited purpose of preventing the reversal of the judgment under review. The court's decision affirming the trial court's judgment rendered consideration of the employer's assignment of error unnecessary. Hostein v. Ohio Valley Vulcanizing, Inc., — Ohio App. 3d —, 2007 Ohio 3329, — N.E. 2d —, 2007 Ohio App. LEXIS 3127 (June 18, 2007).

Cross appeals

As a cross-appellant attempted to raise an assignment of error which sought to change the trial court's ruling but it failed to file a cross-notice of appeal pursuant to Ohio R. App. P. 3(C), the court did not address the assignment asserted. Automated Solutions Corp. v. Paragon Data Sys., 167 Ohio App. 3d 685, 2006 Ohio 3492, 856 N.E. 2d 1008, 2006 Ohio App. LEXIS 3446 (July 6, 2006).

As the requirement of informed consent in RC § 2317.54(A) was not met due to the failure of the patient's informed consent form regarding a hernia procedure and the administration of anesthesia to indicate the name of the anesthesiologist who was responsible for that aspect of the medical procedure, as well as the lack of any indication of the name of the student nurse anesthetist who performed the procedure, an erroneous trial court judgment in favor of medical professionals in the patient's medical malpractice action would not have been upheld on the alternative informed consent claim pursuant to a cross-appeal by the professionals pursuant to Ohio R. App. P. 3(C)(2). Luettke v. St. Vincent Mercy Med. Ctr., — Ohio App. 3d —, 2006 Ohio 3872, — N.E. 2d —, 2006 Ohio App. LEXIS 3828 (July 28, 2006).

As a city filed an assignment of error for purposes of a cross-appeal in a civil matter, but it failed to file a notice of cross-appeal pursuant to Ohio R. App. P. 3(C), the assignment of error asserted could not be used to modify or reverse the judgment of the trial court, but instead, could only be used to protect the judgment of the trial court from reversal pursuant to RC § 2505.22. Jackson v. City of Columbus, — Ohio App. 3d —, 2006 Ohio 5209, — N.E. 2d —, 2006 Ohio App. LEXIS 5166 (Oct. 3, 2006).

In a putative Ohio resident's appeal from the dismissal of his action for a partnership accounting against an out-of-state resident for lack of jurisdiction and improper venue, cross-assignments of error filed by the out-of-state resident were moot as a result of the appellate court's affirmance of the dismissal of the action. The cross-assignments of error were not properly before the appellate court under Ohio R. App. P. 3(C) because the out-of-state resident had filed no cross appeal. Stoughton v. Ryan, — Ohio App. 3d —, 2006 Ohio 5277, — N.E. 2d —, 2006 Ohio App. LEXIS 5250 (Oct. 2, 2006).

Court rejected the request advanced by the Ohio Civil Rights Commission that the court dismiss the attorney general as a party to a mandamus action dismissed by the trial court because, by making such a request, the Commission was essentially seeking to change the order from which the appeal had been taken, and consequently, pursuant to Ohio R. App. P. 3(C)(1), the Commission needed to file a cross appeal in order to accomplish that objective. State ex rel. American Legion Post 25 v. Ohio Civ. Rights Comm'n, — Ohio App. 3d —, 2006 Ohio 5509, — N.E. 2d —, 2006 Ohio App. LEXIS 5492 (Oct. 23, 2006).

Oil and natural gas exploration companies' failure to file a notice of cross appeal from a judgment that was entered in their favor, although the trial court had upheld a determination that the companies were not entitled to a claimed exemption under 17 C.F.R. § 230.506 because they engaged in general solicitation and general advertising, did not result in that holding becoming the law of the case, as under Ohio R. App. P. 3(C)(2), the companies did not seek to defend the judgment on a ground other than that relied upon by the trial court. Blue Flame Energy Corp. v. Ohio Dep't of Commerce, 171 Ohio App. 3d 514, 2006 Ohio 6892, 871 N.E.2d 1227, 2006 Ohio App. LEXIS 6809 (2006).

Cross-assignments of error

Although a city presented and briefed an assignment of error in a matter appealed by a city police chief involving a claim of defamation, which had been resolved by a grant of summary judgment in favor of the city, as the city did not file a notice of cross-appeal under Ohio R. App. P. 3(C), the proposed assignment of error was only considered for the purpose of preventing a reversal of the appealed judgment, and not as its own assertion of an error. Jackson v. City of Columbus, — Ohio App. 3d —, 2006 Ohio 5089, — N.E. 2d —, 2006 Ohio App. LEXIS 5019 (Sept. 29, 2006).

Filing

Defendant failed to comply with Ohio R. App. P. 3(A) where he filed his notice of appeal from an underlying criminal matter with the clerk of the common pleas court, rather than with the clerk of the county court where his matter was heard. State v. Charlton, — Ohio App. 3d —, 2006 Ohio 3642, — N.E. 2d —, 2006 Ohio App. LEXIS 3568 (July 14, 2006).

— Requirements

Litigant's appeal was dismissed because (1) the litigant's notice of appeal was filed 31 days after the judgment entry the litigant sought to appeal, (2) the litigant did not allege the trial court clerk failed to comply with Ohio R. Civ. P. 58(B), (3) the litigant did not comply with Ohio R. App. P. 3(A) by filing a notice of appeal with the appellate court, and (4) the litigant failed to attach the judgment entry being appealed to the litigant's notice of appeal. In re Devin Krafft, — Ohio App. 3d —, 2007 Ohio 5377, — N.E. 2d —, 2007 Ohio App. LEXIS 4731 (Oct. 5, 2007).

Final judgment

In a supplier's suit against the manufacturer of products the supplier distributed, alleging defective products, the manufacturer could appeal the denial of its summary judgment motion, despite the fact that a prior appeal had been taken in the case, because that denial could not have been raised in the prior appeal, as it was an interlocutory order and final judgment had not yet been entered, so the denial did not merge into the judgment appealed previously, under Ohio R. App. P. 3(C)(1), and, now that a final judgment had been entered, the denial was appealable, under RC § 2505.02. Norcold, Inc. v. Gateway Supply Co., — Ohio App. 3d —, 2006 Ohio 6919, — N.E. 2d —, 2006 Ohio App. LEXIS 6827 (Dec. 28, 2006).

Identification of judgment

Where an employer's notice of appeal from a trial court's default judgment in favor of an employee in her workers' compensation action pursuant to RC § 4123.512(D) only designated the order that granted judgment to the employee, the court on appeal could only consider issues arising therefrom pursuant to Ohio R. App. P. 3(C). Baur v. Co-Ax Tech., — Ohio App. 3d —, 2007 Ohio 3910, — N.E. 2d —, 2007 Ohio App. LEXIS 3565 (Aug. 2, 2007).

Appellate court lacked jurisdiction to review errors asserted in judgments or orders by the trial court in a foreclosure proceeding which were not designated in home owners' notice of appeal pursuant to Ohio R. App. P. 3(D). Miles Landing Homeowners Ass'n v. Bikkani, — Ohio App. 3d —, 2006 Ohio 3328, — N.E. 2d —, 2006 Ohio App. LEXIS 3244 (June 29, 2006).

Identification of judgment appealed from

As a juvenile defendant failed to designate a particular judgment of conviction as to domestic violence in his notice of appeal, pursuant to Ohio R. App. P. 3(D), the appellate court declined to review his assignments of error relating thereto. In re P.M., — Ohio App. 3d —, 2006 Ohio 5917, — N.E. 2d —, 2006 Ohio App. LEXIS 5873 (Nov. 9, 2006).

When, in a personal injury action, an alleged injured party filed a timely notice of appeal to which one of the trial court's orders being appealed was attached, but other orders being appealed were not attached, the appellate court had discretion, under Ohio R. App. P. 3(D), to consider all the orders of which review was sought, and considered all orders in the interest of determining the case on its merits. Armbruster v. Hampton, — Ohio App. 3d —, 2006 Ohio 4530, — N.E. 2d —, 2006 Ohio App. LEXIS 4518 (Sept. 5, 2006).

Jurisdiction

When a father filed notices of appeal, pursuant to RC § 2505.04 and Ohio R. App. P. 3(A), regarding trial court orders finding the father's children to be dependent, those notices deprived the trial court of jurisdiction to hold a dispositional hearing regarding the children because such a hearing was inconsistent with the appellate court's jurisdiction, even though the orders finding the children dependent were not final and appealable, so the trial court's dispositional orders regarding the children were void ab initio, and, absent valid dispositional orders, an appellate court had no jurisdiction to consider them. In re Miller, — Ohio App. 3d —, 2007 Ohio 4238, — N.E. 2d —, 2007 Ohio App. LEXIS 3882 (Aug. 20, 2007).

As a vexatious litigator's appeal from a trial court's denial of his motion for relief from a foreclosure judgment pursuant to Ohio R. Civ. P. 60(B)(4) was not accompanied by the necessary application for leave to proceed in the appellate court pursuant to RC § 2323.52(D)(3) and (F)(2), the 30-day time period for filing the appeal under Ohio R. App. P. 3(A) and 4(A) was not tolled; that 30-day period was jurisdictional and accordingly, the court lacked jurisdiction over the matter. Huntington Nat'l Bank v. Lomaz, — Ohio App. 3d —, 2006 Ohio 3880, — N.E. 2d —, 2006 Ohio App. LEXIS 3843 (July 28, 2006).

Jurisdictional defects

Court lacked jurisdiction to consider whether a trial court erred in accepting defendant's guilty plea to a charge of gross abuse of a corpse because the charge arose in a separate case from the conspiracy charge, which was properly before the court, and defendant had not filed either a timely notice of appeal under Ohio R. App. P. 4(A) or a motion for leave to file a delayed appeal under Ohio R. App. P. 5(A). State v. Cremeens, — Ohio App. 3d —, 2006 Ohio 7092, — N.E. 2d —, 2006 Ohio App. LEXIS 7014 (Nov. 13, 2006).

— Notice of appeal

In plaintiffs' appeal from a decision granting an insurer's motion for summary judgment on its claim that it was entitled to set off amounts received from a medical malpractice settlement against its uninsured/underinsured motorist (UM/UIM) coverage in a negligence and wrongful death action arising out of the death of plaintiffs' decedent in an automobile accident, plaintiffs' motion to strike the insurer's claim that an other owned vehicle exclusion in the policy precluded UM/UIM coverage on the ground that the claim was not raised in a cross-appeal was denied. Pursuant to Ohio R. App. P. 3(C)(2), the insurer was not required to file a notice of cross-appeal because it was merely attempting to defend the trial court's judgment on a ground other than that relied upon by the trial court. Gray v. Grange Mut. Cas. Co., — Ohio App. 3d —, 2006 Ohio 6370, — N.E. 2d —, 2006 Ohio App. LEXIS 6329 (Dec. 5, 2006).

Notice of appeal

Court of appeals had discretion to overlook the defect in a timely filed notice of appeal which referred only to the magistrate's decision, rather than the trial court's adoption of the that decision. No prejudice resulted from the deficiency: Roberts v. Skaggs, 176 Ohio App. 3d 251, 2008 Ohio 1954, 891 N.E.2d 827, 2008 Ohio App. LEXIS 1674 (2008).

Where a trial court first determined that a city's summary judgment motion was moot, and after former property owners appealed another ruling in the case that granted summary judgment to a current property owner and such appeal also included the determination regarding the city, the matter was remanded and the city was granted summary judgment, such was not reviewable where the new order was not included in a notice of appeal pursuant to Ohio R. App. P. 3, 4(A), 5, and 16(A). Pursuant to its discretion to impose sanctions, the court found that declining to review the assignments of error related to the summary judgment for the city was proper, as it had no notice that such decision was the subject of appeal. MDM

Realty, Ltd. v. Progress Properties. So., LP, — Ohio App. 3d —, 2007 Ohio 3668, — N.E. 2d —, 2007 Ohio App. LEXIS 3375 (July 19, 2007).

Ohio R. App. P. 3(A) provided that failure of an appellant to take any step other than the timely filing of a notice of appeal did not affect the validity of the appeal, but was ground only for such action as the court of appeals deemed appropriate, which might include dismissal of the appeal, and, pursuant to Rule 3(A), the only jurisdictional requirement for the filing of a valid appeal was the timely filing of a notice of appeal, so, when presented with other defects in the notice of appeal, a court of appeals was vested with discretion to determine whether sanctions, including dismissal, were warranted, and its decision would not be overturned absent an abuse of discretion. Armbruster v. Hampton, — Ohio App. 3d —, 2006 Ohio 4530, — N.E. 2d —, 2006 Ohio App. LEXIS 4518 (Sept. 5, 2006).

Since defendant did not designate an order which vacated an earlier assignment of his case to the mental health docket in his notice of appeal, the appellate court lacked jurisdiction to consider this claim. State v. Doing, — Ohio App. 3d —, 2006 Ohio 5252, — N.E. 2d —, 2006 Ohio App. LEXIS 5227 (Oct. 5, 2006).

Where defendant filed his notice of appeal after the denial by the trial court of his post-sentence motion to withdraw his guilty plea but he did not specifically refer to that decision, noting only that the appeal was from the judgment of conviction and sentences imposed, he did not comply with Ohio R. App. P. 3(D). As the notice of appeal provided adequate notice to the State of the issues that defendant was appealing, including the trial court's decision to overrule that motion, the omission in the notice of appeal was not a jurisdictional defect and therefore, it was reviewable. State v. Simmons, — Ohio App. 3d —, 2006 Ohio 5760, — N.E. 2d —, 2006 Ohio App. LEXIS 5746 (Nov. 3, 2006).

Since a father's notice of appeal did not reference the father's other two children involved in the legal custody case but, instead, attached a copy of the trial court's judgment issuing an order of disposition only for one of the father's sons, the scope of the appeal was limited to the judgment entry relating to the son. In re Anthony C., — Ohio App. 3d —, 2006 Ohio 6812, — N.E. 2d —, 2006 Ohio App. LEXIS 6725 (Dec. 20, 2006).

Procedural requirements

Defendant filed an appeal from the wrong trial court judgment and, thus, his appeal challenging the trial court's denial of his motion to suppress filed in a second, unrelated case was dismissed. Defendant's notice of appeal did not refer to the second case, the record transmitted was the record in first case, and the docketing statement did not reference suppression issue; thus, defendant's appeal failed to comply with Ohio R. App. P. 3(D), Ohio R. App. P. 9(B), and Ohio R. App. P. 10(A). State v. Bleehash, — Ohio App. 3d —, 2006 Ohio 4580, — N.E. 2d —, 2006 Ohio App. LEXIS 4526 (Aug. 31, 2006).

Right to file appeal

Although the Ohio Constitution does not expressly provide for a "right" to appeal, Ohio Const. art. IV, § 3(B)(1)(f) does provide for the establishment of an appellate court system, and RC § 2505.03 further provides that every final order, judgment, or decree of a court and, when provided by law, the final order of any administrative officer, agency, board, department, tribunal, commission, or other instrumentality, may be reviewed unless otherwise provided by law, and Ohio R. App. P. 3(A) makes every litigant entitled to an appeal as of right by filing a notice of appeal within the time allowed by Ohio R. App. P. 4. State v. Firouzmandi, — Ohio App. 3d —, 2006 Ohio 5823, — N.E. 2d —, 2006 Ohio App. LEXIS 5802 (Nov. 3, 2006).

Timeliness of appeal

As defendant failed to file his notice of appeal pursuant to Ohio R. App. P. 3 and 4(A) in a timely manner from the trial court's denial of his initial request for jail time credit with respect to the time period where he was electronically monitored under house arrest, the court of appeals lacked jurisdiction under Ohio Const. art. IV, § 3(B)(2) and RC § 2501.02 to review the asserted error. Although defendant filed a second motion for jail time credit, that was deemed a motion for reconsideration and was therefore a nullity, and further, the matter was barred by res judicata where an appeal was not taken from the first denial of his request for relief. State v. Ward, — Ohio App. 3d —, 2007 Ohio 302, — N.E. 2d —, 2007 Ohio App. LEXIS 284 (Jan. 25, 2007).

Appellate court was foreclosed from addressing the merits of defendant's contention that the trial court abused its discretion in denying defendant's motion for a continuance in order to retain new counsel because defendant did not timely take issue with or appeal the trial court's decision to deny defendant's request, as required by Ohio R. App. P. 3(A) and Ohio R. App. P. 4(A). State v. Bell, — Ohio App. 3d —, 2007 Ohio 3276, — N.E. 2d —, 2007 Ohio App. LEXIS 3031 (June 28, 2007).

Appellate court could not consider defendant's appeal of a trial court's denial of defendant's motion to correct or modify defendant's sentence, in which defendant argued that breaking and entering and vandalism were allied offenses of similar import, barring the consecutive sentences defendant received, because any appeal of that issue had to be brought, under Ohio R. App. P. 4, by filing a timely notice of appeal required by Ohio R. App. 3 within 30 days of defendant's original community control sentence in which the trial court made it clear that it did not consider these offenses to be allied offenses of similar import, rather than within 30 days of the denial of defendant's motion, after defendant's community control was revoked and defendant was sentenced to prison. State v. Staats, — Ohio App. 3d —, 2007 Ohio 3638, — N.E. 2d —, 2007 Ohio App. LEXIS 3320 (July 16, 2007).

Defendant timely filed an appeal under Ohio R. App. P. 3(A) and 4(A) because the original judgment entry on March 2, 2006, which defendant sought to appeal from was not time stamped and, thus, not an effective final judgment under Ohio R. Crim. P. 32(C); once a second judgment entry with a time stamp was filed on October 12, defendant timely filed his appeal within 30 days. Ohio v. Charlton, — Ohio App. 3d —, 2007 Ohio 5202, — N.E. 2d —, 2007 Ohio App. LEXIS 4599 (Sept. 28, 2007).

Surety's appeal from trial court's nunc pro tunc order dismissing surety's motion to vacate order forfeiting bond was dismissed because the appeal was untimely under Ohio R. App. P. 3(A) and 4(A), in that it was not filed within 30 days of the date of the entry of the judgment from which the appeal was filed. The trial court's nunc pro tunc order merely clarified the initial entry, and thus, it related back to the time of the filing of the initial entry and did not extend the time for appeal. State v. Perry, — Ohio App. 3d —, 2006 Ohio 5320, — N.E. 2d —, 2006 Ohio App. LEXIS 5316 (Oct. 12, 2006).

RULE 4.   Appeal as of right—when taken

(A) **Time for appeal.** A party shall file the notice of appeal required by App.R. 3 within thirty days of the later of entry of the judgment or order appealed or, in a civil case, service of the notice of judgment and its entry if service is not made on the party within the three day period in Rule 58(B) of the Ohio Rules of Civil Procedure.

(B) **Exceptions.** The following are exceptions to the appeal time period in division (A) of this rule:

(1) Multiple or cross appeals. If a notice of appeal is timely filed by a party, another party may file a notice of appeal within the appeal time period otherwise prescribed by this rule or within ten days of the filing of the first notice of appeal.

(2) **Civil or juvenile post-judgment motion** In a civil case or juvenile proceeding, if a party files a timely motion for judgment under Civ. R. 50(B), a new trial under Civ. R. 59(B), vacating or modifying a judgment by an objection to a magistrate's decision under Civ. R 53(D)(4)(e)(i) or (ii) or Rule 40(D)(4)(e)(i) or (ii) of the Ohio Rules of Juvenile Procedure, or findings of fact and conclusions of law under Civ. R. 52, the time for filing a notice of appeal begins to run as to all parties when the order disposing of the motion is entered.

(3) Criminal post-judgment motion. In a criminal case, if a party timely files a motion for arrest of judgment or a new trial for a reason other than newly discovered evidence, the time for filing a notice of appeal begins to run when the order denying the motion is entered. A motion for a new trial on the ground of newly discovered evidence made within the time for filing a motion for a new trial on other grounds extends the time for filing a notice of appeal from a judgment of conviction in the same manner as a motion on other grounds. If made after the expiration of the time for filing a motion on other grounds, the motion on the ground of newly discovered evidence does not extend the time for filing a notice of appeal.

(4) Appeal by prosecution. In an appeal by the prosecution under Crim.R. 12(K) or Juv.R. 22(F), the prosecution shall file a notice of appeal within seven days of entry of the judgment or order appealed.

(5) Partial final judgment or order. If an appeal is permitted from a judgment or order entered in a case in which the trial court has not disposed of all claims as to all parties, other than a judgment or order entered under Civ.R. 54(B), a party may file a notice of appeal within thirty days of entry of the judgment or order appealed or the judgment or order that disposes of the remaining claims. Division (A) of this rule applies to a judgment or order entered under Civ.R. 54(B).

(C) **Premature notice of appeal.** A notice of appeal filed after the announcement of a decision, order, or sentence but before entry of the judgment or order that begins the running of the appeal time period is treated as filed immediately after the entry.

(D) **Definition of "entry" or "entered".** As used in this rule, "entry" or "entered" means when a judgment or order is entered under Civ.R. 58(A) or Crim.R. 32(C).

History: Amended, eff 7-1-72; 7-1-85; 7-1-89; 7-1-92; 7-1-96; 7-1-02; 7-1-09.

NOTES TO DECISIONS

ANALYSIS

Appeal requirements

Where a trial court first determined that a city's summary judgment motion was moot, and after former property owners appealed another ruling in the case that granted summary judgment to a current property owner and such appeal also included the determination regarding the city, the matter was remanded and the city was granted summary judgment, such was not reviewable where the new order was not included in a notice of appeal pursuant to Ohio R. App. P. 3, 4(A), 5, and 16(A). Pursuant to its discretion to impose sanctions, the court found that declining to review the assignments of error related to the summary judgment for the city was proper, as it had no notice that such decision was the subject of appeal. MDM Realty, Ltd. v. Progress Properties. So., LP, — Ohio App. 3d —, 2007 Ohio 3668, — N.E. 2d —, 2007 Ohio App. LEXIS 3375 (July 19, 2007).

Appeal untimely

As a mother's appeal from a juvenile court judgment that had found her in direct contempt and had awarded temporary custody of her child to a county agency was not filed within the 30-day limit under Ohio R. App. P. 4(A), her appeal of that issue was untimely and the court lacked jurisdiction to review the merits of the claim. In re Smith, — Ohio App. 3d —, 2007 Ohio 893, — N.E. 2d —, 2007 Ohio App. LEXIS 812 (Mar. 2, 2007).

As a juvenile court decision pursuant to Ohio R. Civ. P. 60(B) that vacated a prior judgment was a final appealable order pursuant to RC § 2505.02(B)(3), an appeal had to be taken within 30 days thereof pursuant to Ohio R. App. P. 4(A) in order to be reviewed as timely. As a mother did not file a timely appeal from the vacatur of the juvenile court's judgment that had closed a pending matter regarding an agency's temporary custody over her children, her appeal from that order was not reviewable. In re L.S., — Ohio App. 3d —, 2007 Ohio 1583, — N.E. 2d —, 2007 Ohio App. LEXIS 1455 (Apr. 4, 2007).

Defendant's appeal of a trial court's denial of defendant's motion to reconsider the trial court's denial of defendant's "Motion for Permission to file a Supplemental to the Motion to Amend the Appeal in R.C. 2950" was dismissed because defendant did not timely appeal the denial of defendant's original motion, and defendant's motion to reconsider was a nullity which did not extend the time within which to appeal the denial of the original motion. State v. Call, — Ohio App. 3d —, 2007 Ohio 4199, — N.E. 2d —, 2007 Ohio App. LEXIS 3795 (Aug. 17, 2007).

Litigant's appeal was dismissed because (1) the litigant's notice of appeal was filed 31 days after the judgment entry the litigant sought to appeal, (2) the litigant did not allege the trial court clerk failed to comply with Ohio R. Civ. P. 58(B), (3) the litigant did not comply with Ohio R. App. P. 3(A) by filing a notice of appeal with the appellate court, and (4) the litigant failed to attach the judgment entry being appealed to the litigant's notice of appeal. In re Devin Krafft, — Ohio App. 3d —, 2007 Ohio 5377, — N.E. 2d —, 2007 Ohio App. LEXIS 4731 (Oct. 5, 2007).

As a temporary agreed order between divorcing parties, wherein the husband was obligated to pay a home equity loan, was merged into the parties' final divorce decree and there was no indication in the decree that the husband was still obligated to make such loan payments, the trial court did not err in denying the wife's motion under Ohio R. Civ. P. 60(B)(5) to clarify the decree for purposes of recoupment of the loan payments that she had made post-divorce; further, the wife failed to appeal in a timely manner under Ohio R. App. P. 4(A) from the final divorce decree and she did not raise the issue regarding the loan payments until approximately six years and eight months after the divorce decree was entered. Kovacic v. Kovacic, — Ohio App. 3d —, 2007 Ohio 5956, — N.E. 2d —, 2007 Ohio App. LEXIS 5226 (Nov. 8, 2007).

Court lacked jurisdiction over defendant's appeal of a trial court's denial of his motion to reconsider its original denial of his motions for postconviction relief because defendant should have appealed from the trial court's original denial of the motions by filing notice of appeal within 30 days of the original denial. When defendant filed a motion to reconsider instead, the court lost jurisdiction pursuant to Ohio R. App. P. 4. State v. Bennett, — Ohio App. 3d —, 2006 Ohio 2812, — N.E. 2d —, 2006 Ohio App. LEXIS 2627 (May 31, 2006).

Although a husband's claim on appeal that the trial court lacked personal jurisdiction over him was not reviewable due to the failure to file a timely appeal pursuant to Ohio R. App. P. 4(A), where he filed an answer, numerous motions, and attended hearings, he clearly submitted to the jurisdiction of the court and waived any defect. Rahawangi v. Alsamman, — Ohio App. 3d —, 2006 Ohio 3163, — N.E. 2d —, 2006 Ohio App. LEXIS 3034 (June 22, 2006).

Where defendant's motion for a delayed appeal pursuant to Ohio R. App. P. 5(A) was filed more than four and a half years after the trial court's judgment entry and he failed to provide reasons for his lack of timeliness under Ohio R. App. P. 4(A), his motion was overruled and the appeal was dismissed; the reasons asserted by defendant went to the merits of the appeal but did not explain his failure to timely appeal, and the lengthy delay in making the motion showed a lack of diligence by defendant in attempting to protect his own rights. State v. Constant, — Ohio App. 3d —, 2006 Ohio 3224, — N.E. 2d —, 2006 Ohio App. LEXIS 3145 (June 23, 2006).

As appellant's notice of appeal was filed 44 days after entry of a trial court judgment of dismissal of his complaint, the notice of appeal was untimely under Ohio R. App. P. 4(A). Appellant failed to allege that the trial court clerk did not comply with Ohio R. Civ. P. 58(B), as required by Ohio 11th Dist. Ct. App. R. 3(D)(2), which resulted in a lack of jurisdiction in the appellate court, and the appeal was dismissed. Sterling v. Ashtabula County, — Ohio App. 3d —, 2006 Ohio 4421, — N.E. 2d —, 2006 Ohio App. LEXIS 4338 (Aug. 25, 2006).

Although a trial court erred in suspending mandatory fines against defendant without his having filed an affidavit of indigency, as required by RC §§ 2925.11 and 2925.14, such did not create a void sentence, as there was no finding of an attempt to disregard statutory requirements. Any challenge to the procedural error should have been made in a direct appeal within the time limits provided by Ohio R. App. P. 4(A), and the State's motion more than eight years later to reinstate the fines and for a writ of execution for costs was denied, as the court lacked jurisdiction over the matter. State v. Deloach, — Ohio App. 3d —, 2006 Ohio 4409, — N.E. 2d —, 2006 Ohio App. LEXIS 4346 (Aug. 28, 2006).

As a tenant failed to appeal from a trial court's denials of his motions for relief from judgment under Ohio R. Civ. P. 60(B) in an eviction matter by a housing authority, he lost his right to appeal therefrom under Ohio R. App. P. 4(A); further, an appeal from any of the successor motions would have been barred by res judicata, as they were based on the same facts and same grounds that could have been raised, or were raised, in the prior motions. Cuyahoga Metro. Hous. Auth. v. Rhoades, — Ohio App. 3d —, 2006 Ohio 4896, — N.E. 2d —, 2006 Ohio App. LEXIS 4819 (Sept. 21, 2006).

In a biological mother's appeal from the denial of her motion to vacate a final order for the adoption of her biological child 10 months earlier, her claim that no assessor met with her as required by RC § 3107.082 and to certain other procedures related to the adoption was not addressed. The challenge pertained to the adoption decree, not to the denial of her motion to vacate, and she had filed no appeal from the decree within the 30-day limit of Ohio R. App. P. 4(A). In re J.H., — Ohio App. 3d —, 2006 Ohio 5957, — N.E. 2d —, 2006 Ohio App. LEXIS 5927 (Nov. 13, 2006).

Appealability of orders

Trial court did not abuse its discretion in denying a former husband's motion for relief from judgment pursuant to Ohio R. Civ. P. 60(B)(1) and (5) from a division of property order (DPO) that was entered by the trial court, as he failed to show operative facts that constituted a meritorious defense to the DPO, and the fact that he had not been served with the DPO was not grounds to grant the Rule 60(B) motion; his right to appeal from that order did not start to run under Ohio R. App. P. 4(A) and Ohio R. Civ. P. 58(B) until such service occurred, but such was not grounds to grant relief from the order. Bevan v. Bevan, — Ohio App. 3d —, 2006 Ohio 1306, — N.E. 2d —, 2006 Ohio App. LEXIS 1203 (Mar. 22, 2006).

Although the Ohio Constitution does not expressly provide for a "right" to appeal, Ohio Const. art. IV, § 3(B)(1)(f) does provide for the establishment of an appellate court system, and RC § 2505.03 further provides that every final order, judgment, or decree of a court and, when provided by law, the final order of any administrative officer, agency, board, department, tribunal, commission, or other instrumentality, may be reviewed unless otherwise provided by law, and Ohio R. App. P. 3(A) makes every litigant entitled to an appeal as of right by filing a notice of appeal within the time allowed by Ohio R. App. P. 4. State v. Firouzmandi, — Ohio App. 3d —, 2006 Ohio 5823, — N.E. 2d —, 2006 Ohio App. LEXIS 5802 (Nov. 3, 2006).

Appeals in criminal cases

As the trial court's grant of defendant's motion in limine, excluding statements of his child victim, rendered the State's case so weak as to preclude effective prosecution, the trial court decision was treated as a ruling on a motion to suppress which was a final order that was properly appealed pursuant to Ohio R. Crim. P. 12(K) because it was timely filed under Ohio R. App. P. 4(D) and Ohio R. Crim. P. 32(C) and properly certified by the prosecutor; the State did not waive its right to appeal by electing to proceed to trial, as after the motion was ruled upon and the jury was impaneled, the prosecution sought reconsideration, which was denied, and then the State was granted leave to appeal. State v. Redfearn, — Ohio App. 3d —, 2007 Ohio 4108, — N.E. 2d —, 2007 Ohio App. LEXIS 3736 (Aug. 13, 2007).

As a trial court, upon finding defendant guilty of failing to abate public nuisances as ordered by a city building inspector, imposed sentences of suspended monetary and imprisonment conditions, it lacked authority under Toledo, Ohio, Mun. Code 1726.99, as well as jurisdiction, to additionally order that the properties were to be demolished and to impose additional sentencing orders upon the failure to do so because the original sentences were final judgments under Ohio R. Crim. P. 32(C) and Ohio R. App. P. 4(C), such that reconsideration was not permitted as to the additional sentencing orders; further, as defendant did not originally appeal from the imposition of community control on him, which had not been stayed, he could not later challenge that aspect of his sentence pursuant to Ohio Const. art. IV, § 3(B)(2), Ohio R. Crim. P. 32(B)(1), and Ohio R. App. P. 4(A). City of Toledo v. Samuel, — Ohio App. 3d —, 2007 Ohio 5303, — N.E. 2d —, 2007 Ohio App. LEXIS 4669 (Sept. 28, 2007).

Defendant inmate could not seek to file a delayed appeal pursuant to Ohio R. App. P. 5(A) from a trial court determination on his post-conviction relief (PCR) petition, as such was specifically unavailable from PCR determinations; as he failed to comply with the time requirement of Ohio R. App. P. 4(A) and he failed to allege a trial court clerk's lack of compliance with Ohio R. Civ. P. 58(B) for purposes of Ohio Eleventh Dist. Ct. App. R. 3(D)(2), the appeal was untimely and the time could not be enlarged by the appellate court under Ohio R. App. P. 14(B). Ohio v. Johnson, — Ohio App. 3d —, 2007 Ohio 5500, — N.E. 2d —, 2007 Ohio App. LEXIS 4832 (Oct. 15, 2007).

Appellate review limited

Trial court did not have the authority to reconsider its final judgment regarding issues of child custody, child support, and visitation because (1) the Ohio Rules of Civil Procedure did not provide for motions for reconsideration in the trial court and motions for reconsideration were considered a nullity, (2) the only issue remaining was a determination of which six weeks a mother would have her children during the summer, which was an ancillary issue that did not affect a substantial right, as her right to visitation had already been determined, and (3) the parties did not timely appeal, under Ohio R. App. P. 4(A), the judgment the trial court modified, so the trial court's order purporting to reconsider these issues was a nullity, and an appeal from it did not vest an appellate court with jurisdiction. Barnhisel v. Barnhisel, — Ohio App. 3d —, 2007 Ohio 446, — N.E. 2d —, 2007 Ohio App. LEXIS 395 (Feb. 2, 2007).

As a husband in a divorce litigation matter did not appeal from an order by the trial court which denied his motion for relief from judgment pursuant to Ohio R. Civ. P. 60(b), based on the husband's claim that the failure to return the divorce matter to the docket of a judge whom the matter had been before previously deprived the trial court of subject matter and personal jurisdiction, he waived the right to raise it as a potential error on appeal pursuant to Ohio R. App. P. 4(A); further, pursuant to Cuyahoga County, Ohio, Ct. C.P. Dom. Rel. Div. R. 2(A)(2), reassignment was not required. Rahawangi v. Alsamman, — Ohio App. 3d —, 2006 Ohio 3163, — N.E. 2d —, 2006 Ohio App. LEXIS 3034 (June 22, 2006).

Bar to appeal

When defendant, who was ordered to register as a sex offender, did not appeal that judgment, under Ohio R. App. P. 4(A), but, subsequent to the time limit specified in Rule 4(A), moved the trial court to remove the registration requirement, arguing that it violated the Full Faith and Credit Clause, U.S. Const. art. IV, § 1, res judicata barred this argument because it could have been raised on the direct appeal that was not pursued. State v. Hobbs, — Ohio App. 3d —, 2006 Ohio 3121, — N.E. 2d —, 2006 Ohio App. LEXIS 2986 (June 15, 2006).

As a vexatious litigator's appeal from a trial court's denial of his motion for relief from a foreclosure judgment pursuant to Ohio R. Civ. P. 60(B)(4) was not accompanied by the necessary application for leave to proceed in the appellate court pursuant to RC § 2323.52(D)(3) and (F)(2), the 30-day time period for filing the appeal under Ohio R. App. P. 3(A) and 4(A) was not tolled; that 30-day period was jurisdictional and accordingly, the court lacked jurisdiction over the matter. Huntington Nat'l Bank v. Lomaz, — Ohio App. 3d —, 2006 Ohio 3880, — N.E. 2d —, 2006 Ohio App. LEXIS 3843 (July 28, 2006).

Final appealable orders

Etna zoning regulations clearly provide that a letter giving notice of a decision of the board of zoning appeals is not the final appealable order, but rather, the approval and signing of the minutes triggers the running of the time for appeal. Appellant did not establish any basis that would provide standing to bring an appeal from the decision of the board: Guttentag v. Etna Twp. Bd. of Zoning Appeals, 177 Ohio App. 3d 53, 2008 Ohio 2642, 893 N.E.2d 890, 2008 Ohio App. LEXIS 2232 (2008).

Trial court's judgment adopting a magistrate's decision denying a debtor's motion to vacate a default judgment against the debtor was final and appealable, under RC § 2505.02 because the debtor's untimely objections to the magistrate's decision did not trigger the tolling provisions of Ohio R. App. P. 4(B)(2), nor did the objections effectuate an Ohio R. Civ. P. 53(D)(4)(e)(i) stay of execution. OSI Funding Corp. v. Huth, — Ohio App. 3d —, — N.E. 2d —, 2007 Ohio App. LEXIS 4654 (Sept. 28, 2007).

Defendant's appeal from a trial court's ruling finding him guilty of aggravated robbery and kidnapping was dismissed because the appeal was premature under RC § 2505.02 and Ohio R. App. P. 4(B), in that the appeal was filed before the trial court entered its judgment in the case; thus, pursuant to Ohio Const. art. IV, § 3(B)(2), the court was without jurisdiction to rule on the merits of the appeal. State v. Evans, — Ohio App. 3d —, 2006 Ohio 6933, — N.E. 2d —, 2006 Ohio App. LEXIS 6839 (Dec. 28, 2006).

Motion for reconsideration was denied because it failed to call attention to an obvious error in the prior decision or to raise an issue that was not properly considered in the first instance; the purported judgment entry did not constitute a final judgment from which an appeal could be taken. While the notations on the file jacket contained some of the material required by Ohio R. Crim. P. 32(B), it was deficient in other respects, and the evidence was undisputed that the notation, while apparently file stamped, was never properly journalized by the clerk. State v. French, — Ohio App. 3d —, 2006 Ohio 7115, — N.E. 2d —, 2006 Ohio App. LEXIS 7062 (Dec. 14, 2006).

Even if a school district board of education's appeal from a trial court order that consolidated two actions was filed in a timely manner under Ohio R. App. P. 4(A) rather than more than two years after the order was issued by the trial court, such an order was not a final, appealable order under RC § 2505.02. Such an order could not be appealed until the trial court resolved the case and accordingly, the appeal required dismissal. Alden v. Kovar, — Ohio App. 3d —, 2006 Ohio 3400, — N.E. 2d —, 2006 Ohio App. LEXIS 3372 (June 30, 2006).

Trial court was not required to issue findings of fact and conclusions of law pursuant to Ohio R. Civ. P. 52 relating to its decision to grant a bank the right to intervene in a pending action pursuant to Ohio R. Civ. P. 24(A)(2), as the determination was based on mainly legal issues and no "trial" took place in making the decision thereon. The fact that the request for findings and conclusions was not complied with did not impair the ability to appeal another ruling in the matter, nor did it toll the time for appealing under Ohio R. App. P. 4(B)(2). Savage v. Cody-Zeigler, Inc., — Ohio App. 3d —, 2006 Ohio 2760, — N.E. 2d —, 2006 Ohio App. LEXIS 2601 (May 25, 2006).

Guardians

Guardian ad litem appointed by a probate court for purposes of a guardianship proceeding has standing to appeal on the ward's behalf from a final judgment appointing a guardian for the ward. However, appointment of a guardian ad litem does not necessarily divest the ward or prospective ward of the right to appear and act on his or her behalf against the claims of an adverse party that affect the interests of the ward that are at issue: In re Guardianship of Richardson, 172 Ohio App. 3d 410, 2007 Ohio 3462, 875 N.E.2d 129, 2007 Ohio App. LEXIS 3182 (2007).

Judgment entries

Appellate court proceeded to the merits of a mother's appeal from a decision granting a father's motion to reallocate parental rights and responsibilities in spite of the father's claim that the notice of appeal was untimely under Ohio R. App. P. 4 because it was filed 31 days after the judgment entry under appeal; the trial court's docket sheet did not reflect when or how the judgment entry was served upon the parties pursuant to Ohio R. Civ. P. 58(B). Stephens v. Bertin, — Ohio App. 3d —, 2006 Ohio 6401, — N.E. 2d —, 2006 Ohio App. LEXIS 6358 (Dec. 4, 2006).

Jurisdiction

Appellate court could not consider defendant's appeal of a trial court's denial of defendant's motion to correct or modify defendant's sentence, in which defendant argued that breaking and entering and vandalism were allied offenses of similar import, barring the consecutive sentences defendant received, because any appeal of that issue had to be brought, under Ohio R. App. P. 4, by filing a timely notice of appeal required by Ohio R. App. 3 within 30 days of defendant's original community control sentence in which the trial court made it clear that it did not consider these offenses to be allied offenses of similar import, rather than within 30 days of the denial of defendant's motion, after defendant's community control was revoked and defendant was sentenced to prison. State v. Staats, — Ohio App. 3d —, 2007 Ohio 3638, — N.E. 2d —, 2007 Ohio App. LEXIS 3320 (July 16, 2007).

When a Maryland court issued an order granting a father custody of his children less than 30 days after an Ohio court, which had previously granted custody of the children to their mother, waived jurisdiction, the Maryland court's order was issued when a custody proceeding was still pending in Ohio, contrary to the Parental Kidnapping Prevention Act, 28 U.S.C.S. § 1738A, and Md. Code Ann., Fam. Law § 9.5-206, because, under Ohio R. App. P. 4(A), the mother had 30 days to appeal the Ohio court's waiver of jurisdiction. Snowberger v. Wesley, — Ohio App. 3d —, 2006 Ohio 3343, — N.E. 2d —, 2006 Ohio App. LEXIS 3262 (June 30, 2006).

Notice of appeal

Appeal of a trial court's judgment granting appellee's petition for a civil stalking protection order was dismissed because it was untimely under Ohio R. App. P. 4(A). Since the judgment granting the petition was a final appealable order, appellant's subsequent motion for reconsideration was a nullity, and the motion did not extend the time for filing the notice of appeal. Koehler v. Deluzia, — Ohio App. 3d —, 2007 Ohio 2167, — N.E. 2d —, 2007 Ohio App. LEXIS 2014 (May 4, 2007).

Party

Guardian's motion to dismiss an appeal filed by her ward and the ward's adult child was denied because the fact that a guardian was appointed for the ward did not deprive the ward of the status as a "party" to the guardianship proceeding as the ward's present interest in the litigation and the fact that she was prejudiced by the order appealed from were beyond dispute. Moreover, as a next of kin who was entitled by RC § 2111.04(B)(2)(b) to notice of the guardianship application, the child had an interest in the proceeding concerning her mother that conferred on the child the status of a "party" for purposes of Ohio R. App. P. 4(A); thus, the child also did not lack standing to appeal. In re Guardianship of Richardson, 172 Ohio App. 3d 410, 2007 Ohio 3462, 875 N.E.2d 129, 2007 Ohio App. LEXIS 3182 (2007).

As a driver's insurer was not held liable in an action arising from the death of a passenger of an automobile that was involved in a collision with the driver's truck, it was not a proper "party" under Ohio R. App. P. 4(A) and accordingly, it had no standing to appeal from the judgment that required the driver to pay prejudgment interest on the jury verdict. Conway v. Dravenstott, — Ohio App. 3d —, 2007 Ohio 4933, — N.E. 2d —, 2007 Ohio App. LEXIS 4630 (Sept. 24, 2007).

Post conviction petition

Court of Appeals of Ohio, First Appellate District, Hamilton County holds that RC §§ 2953.21 and 2953.23 plainly afford a post-conviction defendant who has timely filed an appeal by right under Ohio R. App. P. 4, who has been granted a delayed appeal under Ohio R. App. P. 5(A), or whose appeal has been reopened pursuant to Ohio R. App. P. 26(B) 180 days from the date on which the trial transcript is filed in his appeal to file his collateral challenge to the judgment of conviction. The phrase "direct appeal of the judgment of conviction," as used in the statutes, is undefined and does not expressly apply or exclude any type of appeal from its operation pursuant to statutory interpretation principles under RC § 1.47(B) and (C). State v. Fuller, — Ohio App. 3d —, 2007 Ohio 2018, — N.E. 2d —, 2007 Ohio App. LEXIS 1885 (Apr. 27, 2007).

Premature appeal

Premature notice of appeal under AppR 4(C) does not divest the trial court of jurisdiction to proceed because the appeal has not yet been perfected: State ex rel. Everhart v. McIntosh, 115 Ohio St. 3d 195, 2007 Ohio 4798, 874 N.E.2d 516, 2007 Ohio LEXIS 2209 (2007).

Premature notice of appeal

Defendant's appeal was premature because the journal entry required by Ohio R. Crim. P. 32(C) sentencing defendant after his conviction of inciting to violence under RC § 2917.01(A) was not in the record on appeal; the record also did not reflect that the trial court had ruled on defendant's Ohio R. Crim. P. 33 motion for new trial and, thus, the time for appeal had not begun to run under Ohio R. App. P. 4(B)(3). State v. Turner, — Ohio App. 3d —, 2007 Ohio 3264, — N.E. 2d —, 2007 Ohio App. LEXIS 3015 (June 28, 2007).

Although an appraiser filed his notice of appeal prematurely, as it was taken from the trial court's adoption of a magistrate's decision in favor of the appraisal customer and the appraiser had requested that findings of fact and conclusions of law be made, the court treated the notice as if it had been filed immediately after approval and confirmation of the magistrate's findings and conclusions, pursuant to Ohio R. App. P. 4(C). Lynch v. Richards, — Ohio App. 3d —, 2007 Ohio 3532, — N.E. 2d —, 2007 Ohio App. LEXIS 3250 (July 12, 2007).

Premature notice of appeal filed before pending issues of attorney fees and prejudgment interest were resolved was acceptable, under Ohio R. App. P. 4(C), to vest an appellate court with jurisdiction over appellant's claims. Carter v. Bernard, — Ohio App. 3d —, 2006 Ohio 7058, — N.E. 2d —, 2006 Ohio App. LEXIS 6986 (Dec. 28, 2006).

Although debtors filed a premature notice of appeal in a sale of goods execution action pursuant to RC § 2329.13(B), the notice was deemed to have been filed in a timely manner pursuant to Ohio R. App. P. 4(C) after the trial court entered an order confirming the sale of the goods; accordingly, the appeal was from a final appealable order pursuant to RC § 2505.02. Bank One, N.A. v. DWT Realty, Inc., — Ohio App. 3d —, 2006 Ohio 7271, — N.E. 2d —, 2006 Ohio App. LEXIS 7072 (May 23, 2006).

Standing

Although a city had no standing under Ohio R. App. P. 4(A) to appeal from a judgment in the trial court that was in favor of a union in the union's administrative appeal of a decision by the State Employment Relations Board, as the trial court had adopted a magistrate's decision to deny the city's motion to intervene in the trial court proceedings, and the Board could not assert as error on appeal that the trial court had improp-

erly denied intervention to the city, as it was not "aggrieved" by that decision, the city could seek to intervene on the appellate level pursuant to Ohio R. Civ. P. 24 and 1(C); the city could not be substituted for the Board on appeal pursuant to Ohio R. App. P. 29(B), as such substitution was not "necessary." Queen City Lodge No. 69 v. State Empl. Rels. Bd., — Ohio App. 3d —, 2007 Ohio 170, — N.E. 2d —, 2007 Ohio App. LEXIS 173 (Jan. 19, 2007).

Time for appeal

Inmate's failure to have filed a direct appeal pursuant to Ohio R. App. P. 4(A) from his convictions and sentences constituted a waiver of his right to seek review of issues involving the voluntariness and knowing aspect of his plea, and from his sentence. His motion for relief from judgment under Ohio R. Civ. P. 60(B) was clearly inapplicable, and he could not seek relief under Ohio R. Crim. P. 57(B) where there was a proper procedure prescribed by the rules, and that procedure was through the appellate process. State v. Hagler, — Ohio App. 3d —, 2007 Ohio 433, — N.E. 2d —, 2007 Ohio App. LEXIS 385 (Feb. 2, 2007).

As a trial court's judgment entry that sustained a wife's motion to enforce a contempt sentence against her husband was a final appealable order pursuant to RC § 2505.02, and findings of fact and conclusions of law under Ohio R. Civ. P. 52 were not required from the trial court, the time for filing an appeal was not tolled pending such findings and conclusions pursuant to Ohio R. App. P. 4(A). Where the husband failed to file a timely appeal from the trial court judgment, he waived his right to assert any errors related to the contempt enforcement proceeding. Hamad v. Hamad, — Ohio App. 3d —, 2007 Ohio 2239, — N.E. 2d —, 2007 Ohio App. LEXIS 2069 (May 10, 2007).

When a trial court granted summary judgment in favor of a school sued by a student, and the clerk did not serve notice of that judgment entry on the student, as required by Ohio R. Civ. P. 58(B), and the student did not learn of the judgment until more than 30 days after it was entered, the student did not need to file a motion for relief from that judgment, under Ohio R. Civ. P. 60(B), to be able to timely appeal it, pursuant to Ohio R. App. P. 4(A), because the student's time for appealing did not begin running until the student had notice of the judgment. Frazier v. Cincinnati Sch. of Med. Massage, — Ohio App. 3d —, 2007 Ohio 2390, — N.E. 2d —, 2007 Ohio App. LEXIS 2256 (May 18, 2007).

Where a house seller failed to appeal from a trial court's grant of a stay of litigation pending arbitration pursuant to RC § 2711.02(B), and instead he sought relief from the stay order pursuant to Ohio R. Civ. P. 60(B), which motion was denied, the seller's appeal from that order lacked merit because it was untimely and procedurally improper. The motion under Rule 60(B) did not state any grounds and accordingly, it was deemed an attempt at reconsideration of the stay order which was a nullity, and the time to appeal from the stay order had already run pursuant to Ohio R. App. P. 4(A), such that the appeal was untimely. Schmidt v. Bankers Title & Escrow Agency, — Ohio App. 3d —, 2007 Ohio 3924, — N.E. 2d —, 2007 Ohio App. LEXIS 3569 (Aug. 2, 2007).

Where a notation in a trial court's appearance docket did not comply with the requirements of Ohio R. Civ. P. 58(B) with respect to indicating the method of service of the appealed order on the parties by the court clerk, pursuant to Ohio R. Civ. P. 5(B), the time to file a notice of appeal had not yet begun to run pursuant to Ohio R. App. P. 4(A); accordingly, a motion by appellee to dismiss the appeal as untimely was denied. Carter-Jones Lumber Co. v. Willard, — Ohio App. 3d —, 2006 Ohio 1980, — N.E. 2d —, 2006 Ohio App. LEXIS 1822 (Apr. 17, 2006).

As defendant received a copy of a judgment that indicated that it was filed on June 9, 2006 and journalized on June 13, 2006, although the court appearance docket indicated that the judgment was both filed and journalized on June 9, 2006, defendant was deemed to have timely appealed under Ohio R. App. P. 4(A) and Ohio R. Crim. P. 32(C) by filing his notice of appeal on July 11, 2006, as he had no way of knowing that his copy of the judgment might have been inaccurate regarding the date of judgment entry. The court clerk was not required to journalize a judgment the day that it was filed, and the judgment herein was within the time constraints for entry under Ohio Superintendence R. 7. State v. Ulis, — Ohio App. 3d —, 2006 Ohio 3987, — N.E. 2d —, 2006 Ohio App. LEXIS 3962 (Aug. 2, 2006).

Because the Ohio Rules of Civil Procedure did not provide for a motions for reconsideration, such a motion was a nullity, a judgment entered on a motion for reconsideration was a nullity, and there was no appeal from such a judgment; further, a motion for reconsideration was not included in the exceptions to App. R. 4(A). An appeal was thus untimely despite appellant's motion for reconsideration filed after entry of the judgment. Kelly v. Fitzgerald, — Ohio App. 3d —, 2006 Ohio 5405, — N.E. 2d —, 2006 Ohio App. LEXIS 5399 (Oct. 16, 2006).

Because post-conviction proceedings were civil in nature, App. R. 5(A) was not available to seek leave from the denial of a post-conviction action where the time for an appeal as of right as provided in App. R. 4 had passed; however, because the clerk did not serve a copy of the judgment denying appellant's petition for post-conviction relief on appellant in the manner prescribed in Civ. R. 58(B), appellant's notice of appeal filed in the trial court was timely. State v. Williams, — Ohio App. 3d —, 2006 Ohio 5415, — N.E. 2d —, 2006 Ohio App. LEXIS 5406 (Oct. 17, 2006).

As the trial court's reimposition of maximum and consecutive terms of imprisonment pursuant to RC § 2929.14(C) and (E)(4) following a finding that defendant violated the conditions of his judicial release was the only sentence of imprisonment that could be imposed pursuant to RC § 2929.20(I), such reimposition was not erroneous. The reimposed sentence was not subject to a Foster challenge as being violative of defendant's jury trial rights under U.S. Const. amend. VI and Ohio Const. art. I, § 10, as the term of judicial release had merely suspended the original sentence and as the sentence was not challenged within 30 days of the original sentencing entry pursuant to the time limitations of Ohio R. App. P. 4(A), the challenge was untimely. State v. Smith, — Ohio App. 3d —, 2006 Ohio 5972, — N.E. 2d —, 2006 Ohio App. LEXIS 5910 (Nov. 13, 2006).

Time for filing notice of appeal

Appellate court did not have jurisdiction to consider defendant's appeal from a trial court's order denying his motion to vacate the trial court's prior order requiring him to pay court costs because this issue had to be raised at or on appeal from sentencing, and defendant did not raise it within 30 days of the entry of his sentence, as required by Ohio R. App. P. 4(A), so the issue was not preserved, and it was considered waived and res judicata. State v. Dye, — Ohio App. 3d —, 2007 Ohio 1965, — N.E. 2d —, 2007 Ohio App. LEXIS 1774 (Apr. 23, 2007).

When a landowner was sanctioned for failing to comply with a settlement of a prior motion to hold the owner in contempt for not complying with an earlier settlement of the owner's alleged zoning violations, the owner could not complain that a trial court's order memorializing the second settlement did not accurately reflect the settlement because the owner did not timely appeal the order, under Ohio R. App. P. 4(A), when the owner had the opportunity to do so. Ray v. Bd. of Union Twp. Trs., — Ohio App. 3d —, — N.E. 2d —, 2007 Ohio 3001, 2007 Ohio App. LEXIS 2753 (June 18, 2007).

When a litigant filed a notice of appeal 46 days after the judgment appealed from was issued and did not allege a

failure by the trial court clerk to comply with Civ. R. 58(B), an appellate court had no jurisdiction to consider the appeal and dismissed the appeal, sua sponte. Mills v. Mills, — Ohio App. 3d —, 2007 Ohio 3714, — N.E. 2d —, 2007 Ohio App. LEXIS 3393 (July 20, 2007).

When, in a permanent custody proceeding, a trial court denied the motion of the child's paternal grandparents to intervene, that denial was a final appealable order, under RC § 2505.03, because the order involved a "special proceeding," and the order affected a substantial right, but, when the grandparents did not appeal the order within 30 days, as required by Ohio R. App. P. 4, an appellate court had no jurisdiction, under Ohio Const. art. IV, § 3(B)(2), to review the denial. In re C.G., — Ohio App. 3d —, 2007 Ohio 4361, — N.E. 2d —, 2007 Ohio App. LEXIS 3913 (Aug. 27, 2007).

In a permanent custody proceeding, a mother's claim that the trial court did not comply with Ohio R. Juv. P. 29(D) when the court accepted the mother's admission to a dependency complaint could not be considered because the trial court's order adjudicating the mother's child a dependent child, based, in part, on the mother's admission, became final upon the entry of a dispositional order, but the mother did not appeal the order of adjudication within 30 days, as required by Ohio R. App. P. 4. In re C.G., — Ohio App. 3d —, 2007 Ohio 4361, — N.E. 2d —, 2007 Ohio App. LEXIS 3913 (Aug. 27, 2007).

In a suit by debtors against a lender, the trial court's denial of the debtors' motion for class certification was a final appealable order, under RC § 2505.02(B)(5), so, when the debtors did not appeal that denial within 30 days, as required by Ohio R. App. P. 4(A), they waived appellate review of the issue. Lotfi-Fard v. First Fed. of Lakewood, — Ohio App. 3d —, 2006 Ohio 3727, — N.E. 2d —, 2006 Ohio App. LEXIS 3686 (July 20, 2006).

When a bank did not appear at a hearing on its garnishment of a debtor's bank account, pursuant to RC § 2716.13(C)(2), and the trial court found the account was exempt from garnishment and assessed costs against the bank as a sanction for its failure to appear, and then denied its motion for relief from this judgment, it could not appeal the judgment when it appealed the denial of its motion for relief because the time within which to perfect an appeal of that judgment, under Ohio R. App. P. 4(A), had expired, and the motion for relief did not extend the time within which to appeal. MBNA America Bank v. Speegle, — Ohio App. 3d —, 2006 Ohio 3817, — N.E. 2d —, 2006 Ohio App. LEXIS 3786 (July 26, 2006).

Magistrate's judgment entry, which recommended that defendant be found guilty of the charges upon his no contest plea, and which was signed by defendant, was a final appealable order; defendant's later pleading seeking clarification or reconsideration as to imposition of the sentence, which stated that defendant did not object to the sentence itself, did not toll 30-day period for filing a notice of appeal, and thus, pursuant to Ohio R. App. P. 4(A), defendant's appeal was untimely. State v. Hasseman, — Ohio App. 3d —, 2006 Ohio 1465, — N.E. 2d —, 2006 Ohio App. LEXIS 1349 (Mar. 23, 2006).

Time for filing of notice of appeal

Defendant's appeal of defendant's sentence was timely, under Ohio R. App. P. 4(A), because the time for filing an appeal ran from an order in which the trial court declined to impose a fine, rather than from a prior order in which the trial court left the issue of a fine open. State v. Shamaly, — Ohio App. 3d —, 2007 Ohio 3409, — N.E. 2d —, 2007 Ohio App. LEXIS 3174 (July 5, 2007).

As a trial court failed to appoint appellate counsel for defendant after he indicated at his resentencing hearing that he intended to file an appeal until after the deadline for filing his notice of appeal had passed under Ohio R. App. P. 4(A), the trial court effectively denied defendant's right to counsel under U.S. Const. amend. VI and Ohio Const. art. I, § 10; the trial court's denial of defendant's postconviction relief petition pursuant to RC § 2953.21, wherein defendant sought to have the trial court judgment vacated and then reentered in order to give him time to file an appeal, was also error. State v. Lynch, — Ohio App. 3d —, 2007 Ohio 4678, — N.E. 2d —, 2007 Ohio App. LEXIS 4221 (Sept. 13, 2007).

When defendant was sentenced to prison for two crimes, then granted judicial release and placed on community control, and then sentenced for violating community control, the sentences defendant received were a re-imposition of defendant's original sentences, so defendant could not appeal any alleged error in the imposition of the original sentences because, under Ohio R. App. P. 4, the time within which to do so had expired. State v. Broughton, — Ohio App. 3d —, 2007 Ohio 5312, — N.E. 2d —, 2007 Ohio App. LEXIS 4675 (Sept. 28, 2007).

Time limitations

As an inmate failed to file a direct appeal from his conviction and sentence pursuant to Ohio R. App. P. 4(A), his petition for post-conviction relief was not within the time limitations or exceptions of RC §§ 2953.21(A)(2) and 2953.23(A), and Foster was not applicable to the inmate's matter because it was not pending on direct appeal, the trial court lacked jurisdiction to consider the issues raised. Resentencing under Foster was error and reinstatement of the original sentencing order was mandated in the circumstances. State v. Courtney, — Ohio App. 3d —, 2007 Ohio 1165, — N.E. 2d —, 2007 Ohio App. LEXIS 1112 (Mar. 12, 2007).

Appeals filed by appellants were dismissed because appellants had not complied with the thirty-day rule set forth in Ohio R. App. P. 4(A) for filing their notices of appeal and had not alleged in an affidavit that there was a failure by the trial court clerk to comply with Ohio R. Civ. P. 58(B), as required by Ohio 11th Dist. Ct. App. R. 3(D)(2), In re Clowtis, — Ohio App. 3d —, 2007 Ohio 1543, — N.E. 2d —, 2007 Ohio App. LEXIS 1414 (Mar. 30, 2007).

Motion for a transcript of proceedings relative to defendant's plea, conviction, and sentence at state expense to file in defendant's criminal appeal was properly denied because defendant had not filed a timely appeal of his criminal conviction and sentence pursuant to Ohio R. App. P. 4(A) and had not filed a motion for a delayed appeal under Ohio R. App. P. 5; thus, he was not entitled to the transcript. State v. Crawford, — Ohio App. 3d —, 2007 Ohio 2263, — N.E. 2d —, 2007 Ohio App. LEXIS 2109 (May 11, 2007).

Appellate court's review was limited to the issue raised in a motion under Ohio R. Civ. P. 60(A) by judgment debtors, seeking to correct the date that interest was to accrue, such that the judgment creditor's claim that the trial court erred in denying her motion for prejudgment interest was not reviewable as it was not timely asserted under Ohio R. App. P. 4(A). The creditor had not appealed or sought relief from that determination, and the trial court's decision under Ohio R. Civ. P. 60(A) was for the sole purpose of making a clerical correction to the interest date. Brush v. Hassertt, — Ohio App. 3d —, 2007 Ohio 2419, — N.E. 2d —, 2007 Ohio App. LEXIS 2235 (May 18, 2007).

Where a trial court entered a default judgment in favor of a car owner in his property damage claim against an insurer, and the insurer did not file its direct appeal therefrom within the allotted time period pursuant to Ohio R. App. P. 4(A), any issues arising from the default judgment were not within the court's jurisdiction for review purposes due to the untimely filing. Grabowski v. Allstate Ins. Co., — Ohio App. 3d —, 2007 Ohio 2765, — N.E. 2d —, 2007 Ohio App. LEXIS 2558 (June 7, 2007).

Litigant's appeal of an opponent's Ohio R. Civ. P. 41(A)(1)(a) voluntary dismissal had to be filed within 30 days of the date the dismissal was filed, rather than within 30 days

of the trial court's approval of the dismissal because the dismissal was self-executing, and the trial court's approval was an unnecessary nullity. Stern v. Stern, — Ohio App. 3d —, 2007 Ohio 3473, — N.E. 2d —, 2007 Ohio App. LEXIS 3202 (July 6, 2007).

Appeal from a trial court's order noting that "it is so ordered," filed after appellee submitted notice of voluntary dismissal under Ohio R. Civ. P. 41(A)(1)(a), was dismissed as untimely because a notice of voluntary dismissal under Ohio R. Civ. P. 41(A)(1)(a) was self-executing, and as a result, the time for filing the notice of appeal began to run from the time that appellee filed the notice of voluntary dismissal, not when the trial court made the notation. Since appellant had not complied with the thirty-day rule in App. R. 4(A) nor had it alleged that there was a failure by the trial court clerk to comply with Ohio R. Civ. P. 58(B), as specified in Ohio 11th Dist. Ct. App. R. 3(D)(2), the appeal was untimely. Thorton v. Montville Plastics & Rubber, — Ohio App. 3d —, 2007 Ohio 3475, — N.E. 2d —, 2007 Ohio App. LEXIS 3204 (July 6, 2007).

Court sua sponte dismissed an appeal from a trial court's judgment because appellant had not filed the notice of appeal within thirty days of the judgment, as required by App. R. 4(A), and she had not submitted an affidavit under Ohio 11th Dist. Ct. App. R. 3(D)(2) that there was a failure by the trial court clerk to comply with Civ. R. 58(B). Hitchcock v. Johnson, — Ohio App. 3d —, 2007 Ohio 4222, — N.E. 2d —, 2007 Ohio App. LEXIS 3818 (Aug. 17, 2007).

Defendant's challenge on appeal to a trial court's denial of her Ohio R. Crim. P. 32.1 motion to withdraw her no contest pleas was not properly before the court because defendant had not filed an appeal from the trial court's denial of her motion to withdraw within thirty days of the denial, as required by Ohio R. App. P. 4(A). State v. Summers, — Ohio App. 3d —, 2007 Ohio 4576, — N.E. 2d —, 2007 Ohio App. LEXIS 4114 (Aug. 31, 2007).

Appeal from a trial court's judgment was dismissed because appellant had neither filed her notice of appeal within thirty days of service of the notice of the judgment, as required by Ohio R. App. P. 4(A), nor had she alleged, pursuant to Ohio 11th Dist. Ct. App. R. 3(D)(2), that the trial court had failed to comply with Ohio R. Civ. P. 58(B). A.K.A. Alphonso Dion Godfrey, — Ohio App. 3d —, 2007 Ohio 5501, — N.E. 2d —, 2007 Ohio App. LEXIS 4820 (Oct. 15, 2007).

Court sua sponte dismissed an appeal from a trial court's judgment because appellant had not filed the notice of appeal within thirty days of the judgment, as required by Ohio R. App. P. 4(A), and he had not submitted an affidavit under Ohio 11th Dist. Ct. App. R. 3(D)(2) that there was a failure by the trial court clerk to comply with Ohio R. Civ. P. 58(B). Pursuant to Ohio R. App. P. 14(B), the time requirement for filing a notice of appeal was jurisdictional and could not be enlarged by an appellate court. De Leon Lomaz v. Gibel, — Ohio App. 3d —, 2007 Ohio 5908, — N.E. 2d —, 2007 Ohio App. LEXIS 5210 (Nov. 2, 2007).

If debtors were seeking relief from a trial court's judgment entry confirming the sale of their property, they should have asserted those allegations in a timely appeal pursuant to Ohio R. App. P. 4(A), not via a motion for relief from judgment under Ohio R. Civ. P. 60(B) filed 23 months after the sale of their property. The debtors had run out of time in which to challenge the judgment entry confirming the sale. French v. Gruber, — Ohio App. 3d —, 2006 Ohio 1167, — N.E. 2d —, 2006 Ohio App. LEXIS 1057 (Mar. 14, 2006).

When a husband appealed the denial of his motion for relief from a judgment, under Ohio R. Civ. P. 60(B)(1), he could not also argue issues regarding the judgment from which he sought relief because he should have raised those issues in a properly filed appeal from that judgment, under the strictures of Ohio R. App. P. 4. Williams v. Williams, — Ohio App. 3d —, 2006 Ohio 2566, — N.E. 2d —, 2006 Ohio App. LEXIS 2420 (May 18, 2006).

When summary judgment was granted in favor of a party sued by a landowner in a trespass action, and the landowner did not file a notice of appeal within 30 days of that judgment, the landowner's subsequent attempt to appeal it had to be dismissed because she did not comply with the 30-day time limit in Ohio R. App. P. 4(A). K Transp., — Ohio App. 3d —, 2006 Ohio 5426, — N.E. 2d —, 2006 Ohio App. LEXIS 5411 (Oct. 18, 2006).

As a father's objections to a magistrate's decision involving the date that child support was to commence were clearly untimely under Ohio R. Juv. P. 40(E)(3)(a) and Ohio R. Civ. P. 53(E)(3), warranting dismissal thereof by the juvenile court, and the father he did not seek to enlarge the time within which to file objections pursuant to Ohio R. Juv. P. 18(B) and Ohio R. Civ. P. 6(B), his time to appeal was not extended by the objections. His failure to appeal within 30 days of the juvenile court's adoption of the magistrate's decision did not preserve his merit issue for appellate review under Ohio R. App. P. 4(A). In re D.K.K., — Ohio App. 3d —, 2006 Ohio 5576, — N.E. 2d —, 2006 Ohio App. LEXIS 5590 (Oct. 20, 2006).

Administrator's appeal from a trial court's judgment was dismissed because the notice of appeal was filed over fifteen months after the judgment had been issued. Since the administrator had neither complied with the thirty-day time limitation for filing a notice of appeal found in App. R. 4(A) and had not alleged, pursuant to Ohio 11th Dist. Ct. App. R. 3(D)(2), that there was a failure by the trial court clerk to comply with Ohio R. Civ. P. 58(B), the court was without jurisdiction to consider the appeal. Dasch v. Lake Hosp. System, Inc., — Ohio App. 3d —, 2006 Ohio 6691, — N.E. 2d —, 2006 Ohio App. LEXIS 6587 (Dec. 15, 2006).

Court lacked jurisdiction to consider whether a trial court erred in accepting defendant's guilty plea to a charge of gross abuse of a corpse because the charge arose in a separate case from the conspiracy charge, which was properly before the court, and defendant had not filed either a timely notice of appeal under Ohio R. App. P. 4(A) or a motion for leave to file a delayed appeal under Ohio R. App. P. 5(A). State v. Cremeens, — Ohio App. 3d —, 2006 Ohio 7092, — N.E. 2d —, 2006 Ohio App. LEXIS 7014 (Nov. 13, 2006).

Timeliness

Defendant's appeal from a judgment denying her motion for reconsideration was dismissed because the appeal was untimely under Ohio R. App. P. 4(A) as it was not filed within thirty days of the judgment. State v. Cornwell, — Ohio App. 3d —, 2007 Ohio 1068, — N.E. 2d —, 2007 Ohio App. LEXIS 1002 (Mar. 9, 2007).

As the State appealed a judgment of the trial court that granted defendant's dismissal motion pursuant to Ohio R. Crim. P. 12(C), and the notice of appeal was filed within 14 days of the journal entry of that decision, the notice of appeal was timely pursuant to Ohio R. App. P. 4(A). State v. Lee, — Ohio App. 3d —, 2007 Ohio 5952, — N.E. 2d —, 2007 Ohio App. LEXIS 5220 (Nov. 8, 2007).

Since appellant failed to file an appeal within 30 days of the trial court's entry of a default judgment, as required by Ohio R. App. P. 4(A), she had not properly perfected for appeal her assignment of error challenging the trial court's denial of her motion to dismiss for lack of subject matter jurisdiction. The appeal, which was filed only after the trial court denied appellant's motion for relief from the default judgment, was untimely since an Ohio R. Civ. P. 60(B) motion is not a substitute for appeal. Citibank, N.A. v. Stein, — Ohio App. 3d —, 2006 Ohio 2674, — N.E. 2d —, 2006 Ohio App. LEXIS 2506 (May 22, 2006).

Attorney's appeal from a trial court's judgment in favor of a client was timely filed pursuant to Ohio R. App. P. 4(A) since, under Ohio R. App. P. 4(A), a notice of appeal filed after the announcement of a decision but before entry of the judgment that begins the running of the appeal time period is treated as filed immediately after the entry. Taylor v. Oglesby, — Ohio App. 3d —, 2006 Ohio 1225, — N.E. 2d —, 2006 Ohio App. LEXIS 1140 (Mar. 17, 2006).

Although the trial court made three orders regarding denial of a bail bond company's motion for remittitur of a bond pursuant to RC § 2937.39, the first two never directed that the clerk of the court was to serve notice of the order on the bond company and accordingly, the failure to file an appeal within 30 days of those orders did not render the notice of appeal filed within 30 days of the third order, which did contain such a direction pursuant to Ohio R. Civ. P. 58(B), untimely under Ohio R. App. P. 4(A). Based on the nature of a bond remittitur denial case, which is more civil in nature with respect to the bond company, the Ohio Court of Appeals for the Seventh Appellate District, Jefferson County, holds that a trial court should direct the inmate's failure to serve copies of the judgments on the bond company or, in other words, to follow the dictates of Ohio R. Civ. P. 58(B). State v. Smith, — Ohio App. 3d —, 2006 Ohio 4614, — N.E. 2d —, 2006 Ohio App. LEXIS 4572 (Sept. 1, 2006).

While an inmate's notice of appeal filed after the post-conviction court denied the inmate's petition for postconviction relief was filed more than 30 days after the judgment entry, the docket did not clearly indicate when service of the judgment entry was made on the inmate; thus, the court found that it had jurisdiction under Ohio R. App. P. 4. State v. Cobb, — Ohio App. 3d —, 2006 Ohio 4700, — N.E. 2d —, 2006 Ohio App. LEXIS 4629 (Sept. 11, 2006).

Timeliness of appeal

As defendant failed to file his notice of appeal pursuant to Ohio R. App. P. 3 and 4(A) in a timely manner from the trial court's denial of his initial request for jail time credit with respect to the time period where he was electronically monitored under house arrest, the court of appeals lacked jurisdiction under Ohio Const. art. IV, § 3(B)(2) and RC § 2501.02 to review the asserted error. Although defendant filed a second motion for jail time credit, that was deemed a motion for reconsideration and was therefore a nullity, and further, the matter was barred by res judicata where an appeal was not taken from the first denial of his request for relief. State v. Ward, — Ohio App. 3d —, 2007 Ohio 302, — N.E. 2d —, 2007 Ohio App. LEXIS 284 (Jan. 25, 2007).

Since defendant failed to file a timely notice of appeal, under Ohio R. App. P. 4(A), of his original sentence of community control, did not seek to file delayed appeal of that sentence, did not file a direct appeal of the subsequent four-year prison sentence imposed upon his violation of community control, and since his motion to file a delayed appeal of the four-year prison sentence was denied, the court was without jurisdiction, and res judicata prevented the court from reviewing the merits of defendant's appeal of his sentence. State v. Seeley, — Ohio App. 3d —, 2007 Ohio 1538, — N.E. 2d —, 2007 Ohio App. LEXIS 1426 (Apr. 2, 2007).

Defendant's appeal from a trial court's denial of his motion to vacate court costs was dismissed because a sentencing entry is a final appealable order as to costs, and defendant failed to file notice of appeal from the imposition of court costs within 30 days after the sentencing entry, as required by Ohio R. App. P. 4(A). Thus, defendant's appeal was untimely, and the court lacked jurisdiction to consider defendant's assignments of error. State v. Vogt, — Ohio App. 3d —, 2007 Ohio 1576, — N.E. 2d —, 2007 Ohio App. LEXIS 1430 (Mar. 26, 2007).

Since, instead of appealing a trial court's grant of summary judgment to a mortgagee in its foreclosure action, the mortgagor filed an Ohio R. Civ. P. 60(B) motion to vacate the judgment, the mortgagor's appeal, which raised errors related to validity of the judgment for foreclosure, was not timely under Ohio R. App. P. 4(A), and the court could not address the merits of the original judgment. Citimortgage, Inc. v. Clardy, — Ohio App. 3d —, 2007 Ohio 2940, — N.E. 2d —, 2007 Ohio App. LEXIS 2692 (June 14, 2007).

Employee's appeal from a grant of summary judgment on his age discrimination claim was dismissed as untimely. When the employee voluntarily dismissed his other claim under Ohio R. Civ. P. 41(A)(1)(a), he converted the non-final summary judgment into a final order, and since the dismissal became effective upon filing, the notice of appeal, filed more than 30 days later, was untimely under Ohio R. App. P. 4(A). Pattison v. Grainger, — Ohio App. 3d —, 2007 Ohio 3081, — N.E. 2d —, 2007 Ohio App. LEXIS 2860 (June 21, 2007).

Appellate court was foreclosed from addressing the merits of defendant's contention that the trial court abused its discretion in denying defendant's motion for a continuance in order to retain new counsel because defendant did not timely take issue with or appeal the trial court's decision to deny defendant's request, as required by Ohio R. App. P. 3(A) and Ohio R. App. P. 4(A). State v. Bell, — Ohio App. 3d —, 2007 Ohio 3276, — N.E. 2d —, 2007 Ohio App. LEXIS 3031 (June 28, 2007).

When a dispositional order was entered against defendant juvenile following an adjudication of his delinquency due to having committed felony rape, such was a final appealable order under RC § 2505.02, and the time to file an appeal therefrom under Ohio R. App. P. 4(A) began to run from the issuance of that order; defendant's appeal was thus untimely, and an appellate court lacked jurisdiction to review assigned errors. In re Magers, — Ohio App. 3d —, 2007 Ohio 5136, — N.E. 2d —, 2007 Ohio App. LEXIS 4518 (Sept. 21, 2007).

Defendant timely filed an appeal under Ohio R. App. P. 3(A) and 4(A) because the original judgment entry on March 2, 2006, which defendant sought to appeal from was not time stamped and, thus, not an effective final judgment under Ohio R. Crim. P. 32(C); once a second judgment entry with a time stamp was filed on October 12, defendant timely filed his appeal within 30 days. Ohio v. Charlton, — Ohio App. 3d —, 2007 Ohio 5202, — N.E. 2d —, 2007 Ohio App. LEXIS 4599 (Sept. 28, 2007).

Surety's appeal from trial court's nunc pro tunc order dismissing surety's motion to vacate order forfeiting bond was dismissed because the appeal was untimely under Ohio R. App. P. 3(A) and 4(A), in that it was not filed within 30 days of the date of the entry of the judgment from which the appeal was filed. The trial court's nunc pro tunc order merely clarified the initial entry, and thus, it related back to the time of the filing of the initial entry and did not extend the time for appeal. State v. Perry, — Ohio App. 3d —, 2006 Ohio 5320, — N.E. 2d —, 2006 Ohio App. LEXIS 5316 (Oct. 12, 2006).

While defendant, a juvenile, was entitled to a right of appeal, that right to appeal expired when both defendant and defense counsel failed to file a notice of appeal within the time required by Ohio R. App. P. 4(A). Therefore, there was no jurisdiction to entertain an appeal as of right from the conviction and sentence below. In re Gerken, — Ohio App. 3d —, 2006 Ohio 6720, — N.E. 2d —, 2006 Ohio App. LEXIS 6653 (Dec. 18, 2006).

RULE 5. Appeals by leave of court

(A) Motion by defendant for delayed appeal.

(1) After the expiration of the thirty day period provided by App. R. 4(A) for the filing of a notice of appeal as of right, an appeal may be taken by a defendant with leave of the court to which the appeal is taken in the following classes of cases:

(a) Criminal proceedings;

(b) Delinquency proceedings; and

(c) Serious youthful offender proceedings.

(2) A motion for leave to appeal shall be filed with the court of appeals and shall set forth the reasons for the failure of the appellant to perfect an appeal as of right. Concurrently with the filing of the motion, the movant shall file with the clerk of the trial court a notice of appeal in the form prescribed by App. R. 3 and shall file a copy of the notice of the appeal in the court of appeals. The movant also shall furnish an additional copy of the notice of appeal and a copy of the motion for leave to appeal to the clerk of the court of appeals who shall serve the notice of appeal and the motions upon the prosecuting attorney.

(B) Motion to reopen appellate proceedings. If a federal court grants a conditional writ of habeas corpus upon a claim that a defendant's constitutional rights were violated during state appellate proceedings terminated by a final judgment, a motion filed by the defendant or on behalf of the state to reopen the appellate proceedings may be granted by leave of the court of appeals that entered the judgment. The motion shall be filed with the clerk of the court of appeals within forty-five days after the conditional writ is granted. A certified copy of the conditional writ and any supporting opinion shall be filed with the motion. The clerk shall serve a copy of a defendant's motion on the prosecuting attorney.

(C) Motion by prosecution for leave to appeal. When leave is sought by the prosecution from the court of appeals to appeal a judgment or order of the trial court, a motion for leave to appeal shall be filed with the court of appeals within thirty days from the entry of the judgment and order sought to be appealed and shall set forth the errors that the movant claims occurred in the proceedings of the trial court. The motion shall be accompanied by affidavits, or by the parts of the record upon which the movant relies, to show the probability that the errors claimed did in fact occur, and by a brief or memorandum of law in support of the movant's claims. Concurrently with the filing of the motion, the movant shall file with the clerk of the trial court a notice of appeal in the form prescribed by App. R. 3 and file a copy of the notice of appeal in the court of appeals. The movant also shall furnish a copy of the motion and a copy of the notice of appeal to the clerk of the court of appeals who shall serve the notice of appeal and a copy of the motion for leave to appeal upon the attorney for the defendant who, within thirty days from the filing of the motion, may file affidavits, parts of the record, and brief or memorandum of law to refute the claims of the movant.

(D) Motion by defendant for leave to appeal consecutive sentences pursuant to R.C. 2953.08(C).

(1) When leave is sought from the court of appeals for leave to appeal consecutive sentences pursuant to R.C. 2953.08(C), a motion for leave to appeal shall be filed with the court of appeals within thirty days from the entry of the judgment and order sought to be appealed and shall set forth the reason why the consecutive sentences exceed the maximum prison term allowed. The motion shall be accompanied by a copy of

the judgment and order stating the sentences imposed and stating the offense of which movant was found guilty or to which movant pled guilty. Concurrently with the filing of the motion, the movant shall file with the clerk of the trial court a notice of appeal in the form prescribed by App.R. 3 and file a copy of the notice of appeal in the court of appeals. The movant also shall furnish a copy of the notice of appeal and a copy of the motion to the clerk of the court of appeals who shall serve the notice of appeal and the motion upon the prosecuting attorney.

(2) **Leave to appeal consecutive sentences incorporated into appeal as of right.** When a criminal defendant has filed a notice of appeal pursuant to App. R. 4, the defendant may elect to incorporate in defendant's initial appellate brief an assignment of error pursuant to R.C. 2953.08(C), and the assignment of error shall be deemed to constitute a timely motion for leave to appeal pursuant to R.C. 2953.08(C).

(E) **Determination of the motion.** Except when required by the court the motion shall be determined by the court of appeals on the documents filed without formal hearing or oral argument.

(F) **Order and procedure following determination.** Upon determination of the motion, the court shall journalize its order and the order shall be filed with the clerk of the court of appeals, who shall certify a copy of the order and mail or otherwise forward the copy to the clerk of the trial court. If the motion for leave to appeal is overruled, except as to motions for leave to appeal filed by the prosecution, the clerk of the trial court shall collect the costs pertaining to the motion, in both the court of appeals and the trial court, from the movant. If the motion is sustained and leave to appeal is granted, the further procedure shall be the same as for appeals as of right in criminal cases, except as otherwise specifically provided in these rules.

History: Amended, eff 7-1-88; 7-1-92; 7-1-94; 7-1-96; 7-1-03.

NOTES TO DECISIONS

ANALYSIS

Appeal as of right

Because the State was entitled as a matter of right under RC § 2945.67 to appeal the granting of defendant's motion to suppress, it was not required to make a motion for leave to appeal under Ohio R. App. P. 5(C) but was required to file its notice of appeal in seven days under Ohio R. Crim. P. 12(K); therefore, the State's notice of appeal was untimely as it was not filed within seven days. State v. Coffman, — Ohio App. 3d —, 2007 Ohio 3384, — N.E. 2d —, 2007 Ohio App. LEXIS 3084 (June 29, 2007).

Applicability

Defendant inmate could not seek to file a delayed appeal pursuant to Ohio R. App. P. 5(A) from a trial court determi-

nation on his post-conviction relief (PCR) petition, as such was specifically unavailable from PCR determinations; as he failed to comply with the time requirement of Ohio R. App. P. 4(A) and he failed to allege a trial court clerk's lack of compliance with Ohio R. Civ. P. 58(B) for purposes of Ohio Eleventh Dist. Ct. App. R. 3(D)(2), the appeal was untimely and the time could not be enlarged by the appellate court under Ohio R. App. P. 14(B). Ohio v. Johnson, — Ohio App. 3d —, 2007 Ohio 5500, — N.E. 2d —, 2007 Ohio App. LEXIS 4832 (Oct. 15, 2007).

Because post-conviction proceedings were civil in nature, App. R. 5(A) was not available to seek leave from the denial of a post-conviction action where the time for an appeal as of right as provided in App. R. 4 had passed; however, because the clerk did not serve a copy of the judgment denying appellant's petition for post-conviction relief on appellant in the manner prescribed in Civ. R. 58(B), appellant's notice of appeal filed in the trial court was timely. State v. Williams, — Ohio App. 3d —, 2006 Ohio 5415, — N.E. 2d —, 2006 Ohio App. LEXIS 5406 (Oct. 17, 2006).

Delayed appeal

Delayed appeal granted pursuant to AppR 5(A) is substantively and procedurally the same as a timely filed direct appeal: State v. Silsby, 119 Ohio St. 3d 370, 2008 Ohio 3834, 894 N.E.2d 667, 2008 Ohio LEXIS 1987 (2008).

When a trial court ruled that an inmate's sentences for a probation violation and for an underlying crime were to be served consecutively, and the inmate sought a writ of mandamus, mandamus was inappropriate because he had an adequate legal remedy by way of an appeal, and the lack of a timely appeal did not deprive him of this legal remedy because, under Ohio R. App. P. 5(A). he could have sought leave to file a delayed appeal. State ex rel. Duffy v. Pittman, — Ohio App. 3d —, 2007 Ohio 346, — N.E. 2d —, 2007 Ohio App. LEXIS 307 (Jan. 26, 2007).

Court of Appeals of Ohio, First Appellate District, Hamilton County holds that RC §§ 2953.21 and 2953.23 plainly afford a post-conviction defendant who has timely filed an appeal by right under Ohio R. App. P. 4, who has been granted a delayed appeal under Ohio R. App. P. 5(A), or whose appeal has been reopened pursuant to Ohio R. App. P. 26(B) 180 days from the date on which the trial transcript is filed in his appeal to file his collateral challenge to the judgment of conviction; the phrase "direct appeal of the judgment of conviction," as used in the statutes, is undefined and does not expressly apply or exclude any type of appeal from its operation pursuant to statutory interpretation principles under RC § 1.47(B) and (C). State v. Fuller, — Ohio App. 3d —, 2007 Ohio 2018, — N.E. 2d —, 2007 Ohio App. LEXIS 1885 (Apr. 27, 2007).

Filing of notice of appeal

Where a trial court first determined that a city's summary judgment motion was moot, and after former property owners appealed another ruling in the case that granted summary judgment to a current property owner and such appeal also included the determination regarding the city, the matter was remanded and the city was granted summary judgment, such was not reviewable where the new order was not included in a notice of appeal pursuant to Ohio R. App. P. 3, 4(A), 5, and 16(A). Pursuant to its discretion to impose sanctions, the court found that declining to review the assignments of error related to the summary judgment for the city was proper, as it had no notice that such decision was the subject of appeal. MDM Realty, Ltd. v. Progress Properties. So., LP, — Ohio App. 3d —, 2007 Ohio 3668, — N.E. 2d —, 2007 Ohio App. LEXIS 3375 (July 19, 2007).

Leave to appeal

As the State of Ohio properly complied with Ohio R. App. P. 5(C) when it sought leave to appeal from a trial court decision, finding defendant not guilty of a charged offense due to the trial court's determination that the statute under which he was charged was inapplicable to the allegedly criminal conduct, the appellate court had discretion under RC § 2945.67(A) to exercise its authority and review the matter. State v. Bouman, — Ohio App. 3d —, 2007 Ohio 824, — N.E. 2d —, 2007 Ohio App. LEXIS 761 (Mar. 1, 2007).

State's appeal from the trial court's sua sponte removal of defendant from post-release control was dismissed. Because there was no basis for appeal as a matter of right by the State under RC § 2945.67(A) and RC § 2953.08(B), and because the State did not in the alternative seek leave to appeal pursuant to RC § 2945.67(A) and Ohio R. App. P. 5(C), there was no appellate jurisdiction to address the merits of the State's argument. State v. Crawford, — Ohio App. 3d —, 2007 Ohio 3516, — N.E. 2d —, 2007 Ohio App. LEXIS 3225 (July 5, 2007).

Pursuant to the applicable version of Ohio R. App. P. R. 5, in recognition of the leave of court requirements of RC § 2945.67(A), the State was required to file an Ohio R. App. P. R. 5(C) motion for leave to appeal to initiate its appeal from the juvenile case. Because the State failed to obtain leave to appeal, there was no jurisdiction to entertain its appeal. In re T.A., — Ohio App. 3d —, 2007 Ohio 4417, — N.E. 2d —, 2007 Ohio App. LEXIS 3978 (Aug. 28, 2007).

As a verdict of acquittal granted by the trial court under Ohio R. Crim. P. 29(C) was a final verdict within the meaning of RC § 2945.67(A), the State was specifically statutorily barred from appealing directly from the acquittal decision in defendant's matter; the State could have sought leave to appeal the ruling under Ohio R. App. P. 5(C), but it failed to follow that procedure. State v. Selinka, — Ohio App. 3d —, 2007 Ohio 5435, — N.E. 2d —, 2007 Ohio App. LEXIS 4779 (Oct. 11, 2007).

Motion by defendant for delayed appeal

As defendant waited over one and one-half years from the time that she was convicted and sentenced until she filed her motion for leave to file a delayed appeal, and she claimed that she was not timely in perfecting her appeal because she was unaware that she could file an appeal from convictions based on her guilty plea, she did not meet the requirements of Ohio R. App. P. 5(A); her motion was denied and her appeal was dismissed. State v. Brakefield, — Ohio App. 3d —, 2007 Ohio 776, — N.E. 2d —, 2007 Ohio App. LEXIS 691 (Feb. 23, 2007).

Motion for a transcript of proceedings relative to defendant's plea, conviction, and sentence at state expense to file in defendant's criminal appeal was properly denied because defendant had not filed a timely appeal of his criminal conviction and sentence pursuant to Ohio R. App. P. 4(A) and had not filed a motion for a delayed appeal under Ohio R. App. P. 5; thus, he was not entitled to the transcript. State v. Crawford, — Ohio App. 3d —, 2007 Ohio 2263, — N.E. 2d —, 2007 Ohio App. LEXIS 2109 (May 11, 2007).

Although defendant, a juvenile, was not necessarily entitled under Ohio R. Juv. P. 34(J) to advisement of his right to appeal in a juvenile delinquency matter after he admitted to the charge alleged in the complaint, he satisfied the requirements for filing a delayed notice of appeal under Ohio R. App. P. 5(A)(2) where he filed a motion that explained the reasons for the failure to appeal, he filed a notice of appeal, and he filed an affidavit of good cause. In re A.S., — Ohio App. 3d —, 2007 Ohio 3434, — N.E. 2d —, 2007 Ohio App. LEXIS 3142 (June 29, 2007).

Defendant failed to support his motion for a delayed appeal where he provided no legitimate explanation for why he did not submit his motion for leave within a reasonable time after the end of the period to file a timely appeal; defendant's basic

ignorance of the law justified only a short delay, and did not justify his 22-month delay in seeking a late appeal. State v. Coulter, — Ohio App. 3d —, 2006 Ohio 1462, — N.E. 2d —, 2006 Ohio App. LEXIS 1333 (Mar. 24, 2006).

Where defendant's motion for delayed appeal pursuant to Ohio R. App. P. 5(A) was not filed for more than two years from the time of her judgment of conviction and sentence, her claim that she was afraid that if she acted while still under court control, a suspended sentence would be imposed was not an adequate justification for the delay. The two-year lapse indicated a lack of diligence on defendant's part to protect her rights, and as the requirements of Rule 5(A) were not met, the appeal was dismissed. State v. Benton, — Ohio App. 3d —, 2006 Ohio 2152, — N.E. 2d —, 2006 Ohio App. LEXIS 2013 (Apr. 28, 2006).

Where defendant's motion for a delayed appeal pursuant to Ohio R. App. P. 5(A) was filed more than four and a half years after the trial court's judgment entry and he failed to provide reasons for his lack of timeliness under Ohio R. App. P. 4(A), his motion was overruled and the appeal was dismissed; the reasons asserted by defendant went to the merits of the appeal but did not explain his failure to timely appeal, and the lengthy delay in making the motion showed a lack of diligence by defendant in attempting to protect his own rights. State v. Constant, — Ohio App. 3d —, 2006 Ohio 3224, — N.E. 2d —, 2006 Ohio App. LEXIS 3145 (June 23, 2006).

Defendant's motion under App. R. 5 for leave to file a delayed appeal from a judgment of conviction entered five months earlier was denied because, while defendant alleged that his trial counsel had represented to him that he would file an appeal, defendant failed to explain why he waited so long after receiving the docket statement and learning that no appeal had been filed to file his motion. State v. Jackson, — Ohio App. 3d —, 2006 Ohio 4787, — N.E. 2d —, 2006 Ohio App. LEXIS 4668 (Sept. 14, 2006).

Defendant's motion for leave to file a delayed appeal under Ohio R. App. P. 5(A) from a trial court's denial of his motion for judicial release was overruled, and the appeal was dismissed, because there is no right to judicial release. The denial of the motion for judicial release cannot affect a "substantial right," as defined in RC § 2505.02(A)(1). State v. Goss, — Ohio App. 3d —, 2006 Ohio 6693, — N.E. 2d —, 2006 Ohio App. LEXIS 6586 (Dec. 15, 2006).

Motion by prosecution for leave to appeal

State's motion for leave to file an appeal, under RC § 2945.67(A) was denied because the trial court had jurisdiction to hear defendant's motion for a new trial under Ohio R. Crim. P. 33(A)(6) based on newly discovered evidence and it did not err in finding that the forensic pathologist's changed testimony created a strong probability of a different outcome. The forensic pathologist's prior testimony that some of the victim's knife wounds were healing for an hour before his death was very strong evidence that the killer waited an hour to kill him and thus, absent such evidence, it was not unreasonable, arbitrary, or unconscionable for the trial court to determine that a different outcome was a strong probability. State v. Burke, — Ohio App. 3d —, 2006 Ohio 4597, — N.E. 2d —, 2006 Ohio App. LEXIS 4540 (Sept. 7, 2006).

Timeliness of appeal

Court lacked jurisdiction to consider whether a trial court erred in accepting defendant's guilty plea to a charge of gross abuse of a corpse because the charge arose in a separate case from the conspiracy charge, which was properly before the court, and defendant had not filed either a timely notice of appeal under Ohio R. App. P. 4(A) or a motion for leave to file a delayed appeal under Ohio R. App. P. 5(A). State v.

Cremeens, — Ohio App. 3d —, 2006 Ohio 7092, — N.E. 2d —, 2006 Ohio App. LEXIS 7014 (Nov. 13, 2006).

RULE 6. Concurrent jurisdiction in criminal actions

(A) Whenever a trial court and an appellate court are exercising concurrent jurisdiction to review a judgment of conviction, and the trial court files a written determination that grounds exist for granting a petition for post-conviction relief, the trial court shall notify the parties and the appellate court of that determination. On such notification, or pursuant to a party's motion in the court of appeals, the appellate court may remand the case to the trial court.

(B) When an appellate court reverses, vacates, or modifies a judgment of conviction on direct appeal, the trial court may dismiss a petition for post-conviction relief to the extent that it is moot. The petition shall be reinstated pursuant to motion if the appellate court's judgment on direct appeal is reversed, vacated, or modified in such a manner that the petition is no longer moot.

(C) Whenever a trial court's grant of post-conviction relief is reversed, vacated, or modified in such a manner that the direct appeal is no longer moot, the direct appeal shall be reinstated pursuant to the statute. Upon knowledge that a statutory reinstatement of the appeal has occurred, the court of appeals shall enter an order journalizing the reinstatement and providing for resumption of the appellate process.

(D) Whenever a direct appeal is pending concurrently with a petition for post-conviction relief or a review of the petition in any court, each party shall include, in any brief, memorandum, or motion filed, a list of case numbers of all actions and appeals, and the court in which they are pending, regarding the same judgment of conviction.

History: Effective 7-1-97.

RULE 7. Stay or injunction pending appeal — civil and juvenile actions

(A) **Stay must ordinarily be sought in the first instance in trial court; motion for stay in court of appeals.** Application for a stay of the judgment or order of a trial court pending appeal, or for the determination of the amount of and the approval of a supersedeas bond, must ordinarily be made in the first instance in the trial court. A motion for such relief or for an order suspending, modifying, restoring or granting an injunction during the pendency of an appeal may be made to the court of appeals or to a judge thereof, but, except in cases of injunction pending appeal, the motion shall show that application to the trial court for the relief sought is not practicable, or that the trial court has, by journal entry, denied an application, or failed to afford the relief which the applicant requested. The motion shall also show the reasons for the relief requested and the facts relied upon, and if the facts are subject to dispute the motion shall be supported by affidavits or other sworn statements or copies thereof. With the motion shall be filed such parts of the record as are relevant and as are reasonably available at the time the motion is filed. Reasonable notice of the motion and the intention to apply to the court shall be given by the movant to all parties. The motion shall be filed with the clerk of the court of appeals and normally will be considered by at least two judges of the court, but in exceptional cases where the attendance of two judges of the court would be impracticable due to the requirements of time, the application may be made to and considered by a single judge of the court on reasonable notice to the adverse party, provided, however, that when an injunction is appealed from it shall be suspended only by order of at least two of the judges of the court of appeals, on reasonable notice to the adverse party.

(B) **Stay may be conditioned upon giving of bond; proceedings against sureties.** Relief available in the court of appeals under this rule may be conditioned upon the filing of a bond or other appropriate security in the trial court. If security is given in the form of a bond or stipulation or other undertaking with one or more sureties, each surety submits himself or herself to the jurisdiction of the trial court and irrevocably appoints the clerk of the trial court as the surety's agent upon whom any process affecting the surety's liability on the bond or undertaking may be served. Subject to the limits of its monetary jurisdiction, this liability may be enforced on motion in the trial court without the necessity of an independent action. The motion and such notice of the motion as the trial court prescribes may be served on the clerk of the trial court, who shall forthwith mail copies to the sureties if their addresses are known.

(C) **Stay in juvenile actions.** No order, judgment, or decree of a juvenile court, concerning a dependent, neglected, unruly, or delinquent child, shall be stayed upon appeal, unless suitable provision is made for the maintenance, care, and custody of the dependent, neglected, unruly, or delinquent child pending the appeal.

History: Amended, eff 7-1-73; 7-1-01.

NOTES TO DECISIONS

ANALYSIS

Applicability
Time for execution of bond

Applicability

Family business and its owner's "original" action which was commenced by a motion seeking emergency relief, including injunctive relief and appointment of a receiver over the business to avoid the liquidation of the business assets, was not properly commenced where no complaint or petition was filed, and the court of appeals lacked jurisdiction where an extraordinary writ of the type encompassed by Ohio Const. art. IV, § 3(B)(1) was not sought. As there was no proper action pending before the court, appointment of a receiver could not be had under RC § 2735.01, and Ohio R. App. P. 7 was inapplicable where an appeal had not been commenced. Lakeland Bolt & Nut Co. v. Grdina, — Ohio App. 3d —, 2007 Ohio 2908, — N.E. 2d —, 2007 Ohio App. LEXIS 2709 (June 13, 2007).

Time for execution of bond

Although the arbitration confirmation case was pending before the state high court, the trial court, under RC § 2505.20 and Ohio R. App. P. 7(B), properly ordered the surety to pay on the supersedeas bond, as those provisions established that the stay ended when the intermediate appellate court affirmed the final judgment. Northern Ohio Sewer Contrs., Inc. v. Bradley Dev. Co., — Ohio App. 3d —, 2006 Ohio 1741, — N.E. 2d —, 2006 Ohio App. LEXIS 1599 (Apr. 6, 2006).

RULE 8.   Bail and suspension of execution of sentence in criminal cases

(A) **Discretionary right of court to release pending appeal.** The discretionary right of the trial court or the court of appeals to admit a defendant in a criminal action to bail and to suspend the execution of his sentence during the pendency of his appeal is as prescribed by law.

(B) **Release on bail and suspension of execution of sentence pending appeal from a judgment of conviction.** Application for release on bail and for suspension of execution of sentence after a judgment of conviction shall be made in the first instance in the trial court. Thereafter, if such application is denied, a motion for bail and suspension of execution of sentence pending review may be made to the court of appeals or to two judges thereof. The motion shall be determined promptly upon such papers, affidavits, and portions of the record as the parties shall present and after reasonable notice to the appellee.

History: Amended, eff 7-1-75.

RULE 9.   The record on appeal

(A) **Composition of the record on appeal.** The original papers and exhibits thereto filed in the trial court, the transcript of proceedings, if any, including exhibits, and a certified copy of the docket and journal entries prepared by the clerk of the trial court shall constitute the record on appeal in all cases. A videotape recording of the proceedings constitutes the transcript of proceedings other than hereinafter provided, and, for purposes of filing, need not be transcribed into written form. Proceedings recorded by means other than videotape must be transcribed into written form. When the written form is certified by the reporter in accordance with App. R. 9(B), such written form shall then constitute the transcript of proceedings. When the transcript of proceedings is in the videotape medium, counsel shall type or print those portions of such transcript necessary for the court to determine the questions presented, certify their accuracy, and append such copy of the portions of the transcripts to their briefs.

In all capital cases the trial proceedings shall include a written transcript of the record made during the trial by stenographic means.

(B) **The transcript of proceedings; duty of appellant to order; notice to appellee if partial transcript is ordered.** At the time of filing the notice of appeal the appellant, in writing, shall order from the reporter a complete transcript or a transcript of the parts of the proceedings not already on file as the appellant considers necessary for inclusion in the record and file a copy of the order with the clerk. The reporter is the person appointed by the court to transcribe the proceedings for the trial court whether by stenographic, phonogramic, or photographic means, by the use of audio electronic recording devices, or by the use of video recording systems. If there is no officially appointed reporter, App.R. 9(C) or 9(D) may be utilized. If the appellant intends to urge on appeal that a finding or conclusion is unsupported by the evidence or is contrary to the weight of the evidence, the appellant shall include in the record a transcript of all evidence relevant to the findings or conclusion.

Unless the entire transcript is to be included, the appellant, with the notice of appeal, shall file with the clerk of the trial court and serve on the appellee a description of the parts of the transcript that the appellant intends to include in the record, a statement that no transcript is necessary, or a statement that a statement pursuant to either App.R. 9(C) or 9(D) will be submitted, and a statement of the assignments of error the appellant intends to present on the appeal. If the appellee considers a transcript of other parts of the proceedings necessary, the appellee, within ten days after the service of the statement of the appellant, shall file and serve on the appellant a designation of additional parts to be included. The clerk of the trial court shall forward a copy of this designation to the clerk of the court of appeals.

If the appellant refuses or fails, within ten days after service on the appellant of appellee's designation, to order the additional parts, the appellee, within five days thereafter, shall either order the parts in writing from the reporter or apply to the court of appeals for an order requiring the appellant to do so. At the time of ordering, the party ordering the transcript shall arrange for the payment to the reporter of the cost of the transcript.

A transcript prepared by a reporter under this rule shall be in the following form:

(1) The transcript shall include a front and back cover; the front cover shall bear the title and number of the case and the name of the court in which the proceedings occurred;

(2) The transcript shall be firmly bound on the left side;

(3) The first page inside the front cover shall set forth the nature of the proceedings, the date or dates of the proceedings, and the judge or judges who presided;

(4) The transcript shall be prepared on white paper eight and one-half inches by eleven inches in size with the lines of each page numbered and the pages sequentially numbered;

(5) An index of witnesses shall be included in the front of the transcript and shall contain page and line references to direct, cross, re-direct, and re-cross examination;

(6) An index to exhibits, whether admitted or rejected, briefly identifying each exhibit, shall be included following the index to witnesses reflecting the page and line references where the exhibit was identified and offered into evidence, was admitted or rejected, and if any objection was interposed;

(7) Exhibits such as papers, maps, photographs, and similar items that were admitted shall be firmly attached, either directly or in an envelope to the inside rear cover, except as to exhibits whose size or bulk

makes attachment impractical; documentary exhibits offered at trial whose admission was denied shall be included in a separate envelope with a notation that they were not admitted and also attached to the inside rear cover unless attachment is impractical;

(8) No volume of a transcript shall exceed two hundred and fifty pages in length, except it may be enlarged to three hundred pages, if necessary, to complete a part of the voir dire, opening statements, closing arguments, or jury instructions; when it is necessary to prepare more than one volume, each volume shall contain the number and name of the case and be sequentially numbered, and the separate volumes shall be approximately equal in length.

The reporter shall certify the transcript as correct, whether in written or videotape form, and state whether it is a complete or partial transcript, and, if partial, indicate the parts included and the parts excluded.

If the proceedings were recorded in part by videotape and in part by other media, the appellant shall order the respective parts from the proper reporter. The record is complete for the purposes of appeal when the last part of the record is filed with the clerk of the trial court.

(C) **Statement of the evidence or proceedings when no report was made or when the transcript is unavailable.** If no report of the evidence or proceedings at a hearing or trial was made, or if a transcript is unavailable, the appellant may prepare a statement of the evidence or proceedings from the best available means, including the appellant's recollection. The statement shall be served on the appellee no later than twenty days prior to the time for transmission of the record pursuant to App.R. 10, who may serve objections or propose amendments to the statement within ten days after service. The statement and any objections or proposed amendments shall be forthwith submitted to the trial court for settlement and approval. The trial court shall act prior to the time for transmission of the record pursuant to App.R. 10, and, as settled and approved, the statement shall be included by the clerk of the trial court in the record on appeal.

(D) **Agreed statement as the record on appeal.** In lieu of the record on appeal as defined in division (A) of this rule, the parties, no later than ten days prior to the time for transmission of the record pursuant to App.R. 10, may prepare and sign a statement of the case showing how the issues presented by the appeal arose and were decided in the trial court and setting forth only so many of the facts averred and proved or sought to be proved as are essential to a decision of the issues presented. If the statement conforms to the truth, it, together with additions as the trial court may consider necessary to present fully the issues raised by the appeal, shall be approved by the trial court prior to the time for transmission of the record pursuant to App.R. 10 and shall then be certified to the court of appeals as the record on appeal and transmitted to the court of appeals by the clerk of the trial court within the time provided by App.R. 10.

(E) **Correction or modification of the record.** If any difference arises as to whether the record truly discloses what occurred in the trial court, the difference shall be submitted to and settled by that court and the record made to conform to the truth. If anything material to either party is omitted from the record by error or accident or is misstated therein, the parties by stipulation, or the trial court, either before or after the record is transmitted to the court of appeals, or the court of appeals, on proper suggestion or of its own initiative, may direct that omission or misstatement be corrected, and if necessary that a supplemental record be certified and transmitted. All other questions as to the form and content of the record shall be presented to the court of appeals.

History: Amended, eff 7-1-77; 7-1-78; 7-1-88; 7-1-92.

NOTES TO DECISIONS

Analysis

Absence of record
— Presumption of validity
— Request for continuance
Absence of transcript
Appeal
Appeals
Appellant's duty to provide record
Burden of appellant
Burden to furnish record
Capital cases
Correction
Correction of record
Defects in record
Duty to provide transcript
Errors
Evidence never filed with trial court
Failure to file portions of transcript
Failure to file pre-sentence report
Failure to provide transcript
Indigents
Jury instructions
Jury interrogatories
Mandamus
Preservation of arguments for appeal
Presumption of regularity
Record
Record on appeal
Statement in lieu of transcript
Statement of evidence
Transcript
Transcript requirements
Videotape
— Written transcript
Videotape transcript

Absence of record

As appellant failed to file a transcript from the trial court proceedings or an acceptable alternative, as required by Ohio R. App. P. 9, a presumption of correctness with respect to the trial court's determinations regarding a motion to dismiss and a general verdict against appellant's counterclaim arose, requiring an affirmance of the trial court's decisions. Williams v. Vahila, — Ohio App. 3d —, 2007 Ohio 730, — N.E. 2d —, 2007 Ohio App. LEXIS 681 (Feb. 5, 2007).

As defendant failed to provide the appellate court with a transcript from the bench trial in his criminal matter on a charge of speeding, in violation of Wellington, Ohio, Codified Ordinance 333.03, the court could not review the assigned errors on appeal; it had to presume the regularity of the trial court proceedings and affirm the decision thereof. Village of Wellington v. Kohut, — Ohio App. 3d —, 2007 Ohio 766, — N.E. 2d —, 2007 Ohio App. LEXIS 714 (Feb. 26, 2007).

Because defendant was charged with a petty offense under RC § 4511.19(A)(1)(a), his right to a jury trial was not absolute; defendant could not claim that he was not advised at arraignment of the need for a jury trial demand because he failed to provide a complete record of the arraignment as required by Ohio R. App. P. 9(B). State v. Zaken, — Ohio App. 3d —, 2007 Ohio 2306, — N.E. 2d —, 2007 Ohio App. LEXIS 2128 (May 11, 2007).

When, in a breach of contract action, a contractor claimed a trial court erred by not awarding the contractor damages based on a stipulation of fact presented to the trial court, no error was demonstrated because the contractor did not submit any stipulations for the appellate court's review, and, without such stipulations, the appellate court had to presume that the trial court correctly applied the law to the facts. J.L. Wilson Co. v. Ca-Mill Holdings, — Ohio App. 3d —, 2007 Ohio 2916, — N.E. 2d —, 2007 Ohio App. LEXIS 2695 (June 14, 2007).

In an appeal from an order modifying custody and terminating a shared parenting plan, the father did not have a constitutional right to transcripts at the State's expense because the case did not concern the permanent termination of the father's parental rights. Without a transcript of the proceedings pursuant to Ohio R. App. P. 9(B), the appellate court had nothing upon which to pass and had no choice but to presume the validity of the trial court proceedings. Murray v. Murray, — Ohio App. 3d —, 2007 Ohio 3301, — N.E. 2d —, 2007 Ohio App. LEXIS 3060 (June 29, 2007).

Husband's appellate complaints about various orders entered by a trial court in the husband's divorce could not be considered by the appellate court because the husband did not satisfy the husband's obligation, under Ohio R. App. P. 9, to provide the appellate court with an adequate record because the husband did not provide a transcript of the final hearing held in the case, so the regularity of the trial court's proceedings had to be presumed. Moinuddin v. Moinuddin, — Ohio App. 3d —, 2007 Ohio 4165, — N.E. 2d —, 2007 Ohio App. LEXIS 3772 (Aug. 16, 2007).

As a driver and his wife who appealed from a jury verdict in favor of a motorist in their personal injury and loss of consortium action, arising from a motor vehicle accident, failed to provide the complete trial court proceedings in their appeal, pursuant to Ohio R. App. P. 9(B) the correctness of the trial court proceedings was presumed. Gau v. Mottice, — Ohio App. 3d —, 2007 Ohio 4529, — N.E. 2d —, 2007 Ohio App. LEXIS 4103 (Sept. 5, 2007).

Where defendant appealed the trial court's order of restitution pursuant to RC § 2929.19(b)(6), but he failed to include the presentence investigation report as part of the appellate record, as required by Ohio R. App. P. 9, the court presumed that the trial court had relied on that report and that the trial court's factual findings were valid with respect to the imposition thereof. State v. Myers, — Ohio App. 3d —, 2006 Ohio 5958, — N.E. 2d —, 2006 Ohio App. LEXIS 5924 (Nov. 13, 2006).

Because tenants failed to include a transcript or agreed statement of the relevant record through which they might have demonstrated their alleged errors, an appellate court had nothing to pass upon and thus, had no choice but to presume the validity of the trial court's conclusions which found against the tenants in their counterclaim against the owner of a rental unit. Epling Estates v. Cunningham, — Ohio App. 3d —, 2006 Ohio 1457, — N.E. 2d —, 2006 Ohio App. LEXIS 1331 (Mar. 24, 2006).

Absent a transcript of the hearing or a statement of the evidence, an appellate court presumed the validity of a trial court's order; where neither party requested a court reporter at the hearing on a father's motions in a custody dispute, there was no transcript, and where the father did not file an Ohio R.

App. P. 9(C) statement of the evidence, the trial court's judgment finding that it had jurisdiction was presumed valid. Buzard v. Triplett, — Ohio App. 3d —, 2006 Ohio 1478, — N.E. 2d —, 2006 Ohio App. LEXIS 1343 (Mar. 28, 2006).

Where a hearing took place on the probate court's jurisdiction over guardianship applications but the transcript was not attached to the record on appeal, the appellate court presumed the regularity of the probate court proceedings, pursuant to Ohio R. App. P. 9(B). In re Campbell, — Ohio App. 3d —, 2006 Ohio 1764, — N.E. 2d —, 2006 Ohio App. LEXIS 1614 (Mar. 31, 2006).

Defendant's claim that his jury trial right under U.S. Const. amend. VI was violated where a charge against him of child endangerment, in violation of RC § 2919.22, which was deemed a "petty offense" pursuant to RC § 2919.24(A)(1) and Ohio R. Crim. P. 2, was tried in a bench trial, lacked merit, as the appellate court presumed the regularity of the trial court proceedings pursuant to Ohio R. App. P. 9(B) where there was no record to support defendant's claim that he was never informed by the trial court, as required under Ohio R. Crim. P. 5(A)(5), of the need to make a jury trial demand pursuant to Ohio R. Crim. P. 23(A) and RC § 1901.24(B); defendant's claim that he made an oral demand was not proved by a record and further, such would not have satisfied the requirements for the demand, as it had to be in writing. State v. Miyamoto, — Ohio App. 3d —, 2006 Ohio 1776, — N.E. 2d —, 2006 Ohio App. LEXIS 1648 (Apr. 10, 2006).

Where a recruiting agency failed to provide a full transcript of the trial court proceedings on appeal, its claim that the judgment was against the manifest weight of the evidence could not be sustained because without an adequate record, the court presumed the regularity of the trial court proceedings pursuant to Ohio R. App. P. 9(B). Www.headhunting-.com, LLC v. Logicalis, Inc., — Ohio App. 3d —, 2006 Ohio 2619, — N.E. 2d —, 2006 Ohio App. LEXIS 2438 (May 26, 2006).

When a husband complained that a trial court, in appointing his former wife as the residential custodian of the parties' children, relied on the reports of a guardian ad litem and a Family Court Services Representative, he did not meet his burden, under Ohio R. App. P. 9(B), to include these reports in the appellate record, so the regularity of the trial court's proceedings concerning them had to be presumed. Saluppo v. Saluppo, — Ohio App. 3d —, 2006 Ohio 2694, — N.E. 2d —, 2006 Ohio App. LEXIS 2544 (May 31, 2006).

Maternal step-grandfather who appealed the denial of his request for visitation with his granddaughter failed to meet his burden of providing a transcript of a hearing or a statement of evidence for review purposes under Ohio R. App. P. 9(C); accordingly, the appellate court presumed the validity of the trial court's actions and affirmed its decision. In re Sadie Elizabeth S., — Ohio App. 3d —, 2006 Ohio 2928, — N.E. 2d —, 2006 Ohio App. LEXIS 2800 (June 9, 2006).

Defendant did not meet her burden to show manifest injustice in order to support her post-sentence motion to withdraw her guilty plea pursuant to Ohio R. Crim. P. 32.1 where she failed to attach of a copy of the transcript from the plea hearing pursuant to Ohio R. App. P. 9(B). The regularity of the proceedings was presumed, and defendant's claim that she was not properly advised under Ohio R. Crim. P. 11(D) prior to entering her pro se plea of guilty was deemed to lack merit. City of Parma v. Taylor, — Ohio App. 3d —, 2006 Ohio 3973, — N.E. 2d —, 2006 Ohio App. LEXIS 3947 (Aug. 3, 2006).

Where a landlord appealed a judgment from a trial court in his eviction action, wherein he was awarded damages for back rent due from the tenant but not damages for alleged property damage, but he failed to file the complete transcript as required by Ohio R. App. P. 9(B), the appellate court presumed the regularity of the trial court proceedings and affirmed the factual findings made therein. Tillimon v. Kalbfliesh, — Ohio App. 3d —, 2006 Ohio 4806, — N.E. 2d —, 2006 Ohio App. LEXIS 4705 (Sept. 15, 2006).

As a trial court made findings of fact and conclusions of law regarding frivolous conduct by a law client and her attorney under RC § 2323.51 in their filing of a legal malpractice action against multiple attorneys listed on a letterhead, who in fact were not partners in a law firm but instead were attorneys engaged in an office-sharing arrangement, there was no abuse of discretion in the trial court's award on remand of attorney fees as sanctions for the frivolous conduct, as the findings and conclusions regarding the conduct that warranted sanctions were not reversed. The reversal was for the purpose of determining the appropriate amount of fees to award only, based on an error on the face of the trial court opinion, as there was no transcript of the trial court proceedings for the appellate court's review pursuant to Ohio R. App. P. 9(B) and accordingly, it had affirmed the findings and conclusions by presuming the regularity of the trial court proceedings. Soler v. Evans, — Ohio App. 3d —, 2006 Ohio 5402, — N.E. 2d —, 2006 Ohio App. LEXIS 5304 (Oct. 12, 2006).

Where defendant failed to produce the record on appeal, as was his duty pursuant to Ohio R. App. P. 9(B), the appellate court presumed the regularity of the trial court proceedings and it affirmed rulings with respect to evidence and credibility determinations. State v. West, — Ohio App. 3d —, 2006 Ohio 5834, — N.E. 2d —, 2006 Ohio App. LEXIS 5762 (Nov. 6, 2006).

— Presumption of validity

When a corporation said it was error for a trial court to find that a shareholder was a dissenting shareholder, under RC § 1701.85, the corporation's claim could not be sustained because the corporation did not present the appellate court with a transcript of the hearing after which the trial court's finding was implicitly made, nor did the corporation present an Ohio R. App. P. 9 substitute for a transcript, so the regularity of the trial court's proceedings had to be presumed, and it had to further be presumed that the corporation received proper notice of this hearing. Callos Prof'l Empl. v. Greco, — Ohio App. 3d —, 2007 Ohio 4983, — N.E. 2d —, 2007 Ohio App. LEXIS 4405 (Sept. 17, 2007).

— Request for continuance

Where there was nothing in the trial court record, either in a transcript or a substitute statement of the record under Ohio R. App. P. 9(C) and (D), to confirm a property owner's assertions that he had requested a continuance upon his counsel's request to withdraw just days before a scheduled trial date, the trial court's claim that the owner had in fact not requested a continuance but instead had accepted his counsel's request to withdraw and indicated that he would represent himself was presumed to be valid. The owner's claim that he was denied a fair trial because he had to represent himself lacked merit, as the trial court had determined that counsel could withdraw without prejudicing the owner pursuant to Ohio Code Prof. Resp. DR 2-110(A)(1) and (2). Proctor v. Hall, — Ohio App. 3d —, 2006 Ohio 2228, — N.E. 2d —, 2006 Ohio App. LEXIS 2072 (Apr. 27, 2006).

Absence of transcript

Dismissal of an appeal under Ohio R. App. P. 11(C) by property owners with respect to various rulings made by a trial court regarding a dispute with a pole barn user that was situated on the owners' property was denied, although the owners had ordered a transcript pursuant to Ohio R. App. P. 9(B) but they had not requested that it be prepared for inclusion in the record that was transmitted by the clerk of court pursuant to Ohio R. App. P. 10(B). The transcript was only applicable to one of four assignments of error, and that assignment would be evaluated to determine the necessity of the transcript with respect to the review thereof. Camp-Out,

Inc. v. Adkins, — Ohio App. 3d —, 2007 Ohio 447, — N.E. 2d —, 2007 Ohio App. LEXIS 398 (Jan. 29, 2007).

Court disregarded a wife's assignments of error presented in her appeal from trial court's judgment and presumed the validity of the proceedings below because the wife failed to include page references to the places in the record where the errors involved in the assignments occurred, as required by Ohio R. App. P. 16(A)(3); she did not argue the assignments of error separately in her brief; and she did not provide transcripts of the hearings cited in her reply brief, as required by Ohio R. App. P. 9. Thus, the court disregarded the wife's assignments of error, as it was permitted to do under Ohio R. App. P. 12(A)(2) and presumed the validity of the trial court's proceedings. Dunina v. Stemple, — Ohio App. 3d —, 2007 Ohio 4719, — N.E. 2d —, 2007 Ohio App. LEXIS 4228 (Sept. 14, 2007).

When defendant, who appealed the denial of his motion to suppress, did not meet his burden, under Ohio R. App. P. 9(B), to submit a transcript of his suppression hearing, the appellate court had nothing to consider and had to presume the regularity of that hearing and affirm the trial court's decision. State v. Kearns, — Ohio App. 3d —, 2006 Ohio 5811, — N.E. 2d —, 2006 Ohio App. LEXIS 5781 (Nov. 6, 2006).

Since plaintiff failed to file a copy of the transcript to support his assignments of error, all of which asserted propositions based on evidence introduced at trial, the court, pursuant to Ohio R. App. P. 9(B), had to presume regularity in the proceedings on any finding of fact made by the trial court; thus, plaintiff was unable to demonstrate the claimed errors. Additionally, plaintiff had failed to affirmatively establish error on appeal because, in each of his assignments of error, he asserted arguments unsupported by any legal authority or any specific portion of the record, as required by Ohio R. App. P. 16(A), and thus, pursuant to Ohio R. App. P. 12(A)(2), the court overruled the assignments of error. Calabrese v. Zmijewski, — Ohio App. 3d —, 2006 Ohio 2322, — N.E. 2d —, 2006 Ohio App. LEXIS 2179 (May 11, 2006).

Trial court did not abuse its discretion in affirming administrative appeals that found that a county children services agency negotiated with adoptive parents in good faith and that offers made with respect to the financial needs of three special needs children that the parents had adopted were reasonable and sufficient, as there was no showing that consideration was not properly given under OAC 5101:2-47-43(A), 5101:2-47-38(B), and 5101:2-47-42(A). As the parents failed to provide a transcript or statement under Ohio R. App. P. 9(B), they did not meet their burden of providing sufficient proof to establish their challenges to the affirmance. J.S. v. Dept. of Job & Family Servs., — Ohio App. 3d —, — N.E. 2d —, 2006 Ohio App. LEXIS 2427 (May 25, 2006).

Since a husband, in his appeal from a trial court's order granting a civil protection order to the husband's former wife, failed to provide the appellate court with a transcript of the trial court's proceedings, as required by Ohio R. App. P. 9(B), the court presumed the regularity of the trial court's proceedings and judgment and affirmed the judgment. Gibson v. Gibson, — Ohio App. 3d —, 2006 Ohio 2880, — N.E. 2d —, 2006 Ohio App. LEXIS 2715 (June 2, 2006).

Where the union raised arguments concerning findings and factors that it alleged that the trial court failed to consider in modifying preliminary injunctions relating to a strike, the appellate court had to presume the regularity of the trial court's proceedings due to the union's failure to file an appellate transcript as required by Ohio R. App. P. 10(A) or a transcript substitute pursuant to Ohio R. App. P. 9(C). Ormet Aluminum Mill Prods. Corp. v. USW, — Ohio App. 3d —, 2006 Ohio 3782, — N.E. 2d —, 2006 Ohio App. LEXIS 3736 (July 20, 2006).

Lack of the transcript required by Ohio R. App. P. 9(A) precluded the appellate court from determining whether the common pleas court made a finding regarding defendant's amenability to community control. State v. Caver, — Ohio App. 3d —, 2006 Ohio 4278, — N.E. 2d —, 2006 Ohio App. LEXIS 4195 (Aug. 18, 2006).

While defendant failed to file the transcript required by Ohio R. App. P. 9(A), the court was not precluded from reviewing defendant's sentences and remanding the case for resentencing. If the trial court made findings to support defendant's more than minimum and consecutive sentences, it violated State v. Foster through its judicial fact-finding; however, if it failed to make findings, resentencing still would be required under State v. Mathis. State v. Caver, — Ohio App. 3d —, 2006 Ohio 4278, — N.E. 2d —, 2006 Ohio App. LEXIS 4195 (Aug. 18, 2006).

Defendant had not met his burden of showing that he received ineffective assistance of counsel. Defendant failed to meet his burden under Ohio R. App. P. 9(B) of providing a transcript of the hearing at which he entered his guilty plea; thus, the court had no way of knowing whether any statements were made in court that would have given defendant notice of his attorney's joint representation of defendant and his co-defendant and whether defendant consented to it. State v. Smith, — Ohio App. 3d —, 2006 Ohio 5478, — N.E. 2d —, 2006 Ohio App. LEXIS 5484 (Oct. 23, 2006).

Appeal

Defendant's claim that his trial counsel's advice to plead guilty to charges of illegal use of a minor in nudity-oriented material, in violation of RC § 2907.323(A)(1), was ineffective assistance lacked merit, as defendant relied solely on the videotape that he made of his live-in girlfriend's 11-year-old daughter for support of this argument, but as that tape was not admitted into evidence in the trial and did not constitute a part of the trial court record pursuant to Ohio R. App. P. 9(A), the court could not consider it on appeal; the facts properly before the trial court supported the advice given to defendant regarding entry of a plea. State v. Robinson, — Ohio App. 3d —, 2006 Ohio 1217, — N.E. 2d —, 2006 Ohio App. LEXIS 1103 (Mar. 17, 2006).

Appeals

Where an assignment of error on appeal from a trial court's dismissal with prejudice of an action raised evidence outside the record, it was not reviewed because the appellate court could only rely on the record on appeal pursuant to Ohio R. App. P. 9(A). Garnett v. Nationwide Prop. Ins., — Ohio App. 3d —, 2007 Ohio 2774, — N.E. 2d —, 2007 Ohio App. LEXIS 2574 (June 7, 2007).

Appellant's duty to provide record

As a civil protection order (CPO) applicant failed to provide a record or statement pursuant to Ohio R. App. P. 9(C) and (D) on appeal of a trial court decision which granted the CPO subject's motion to dismiss it, claims by the applicant that dismissal was improper and that it was against the manifest weight of the evidence under RC § 3113.31 were not review-able. Eble v. Emery, — Ohio App. 3d —, 2007 Ohio 4857, — N.E. 2d —, 2007 Ohio App. LEXIS 4312 (Sept. 20, 2007).

In defendant's appeal from his convictions for OVI and related offenses, his assignment of error pertaining to the jury's screening of a dashboard videotape could not be reviewed because defendant did not meet his burden to properly preserve the record. After his proposed agreed statement of the record was rejected, defendant did not develop an agreed statement of the record or schedule a hearing so that the trial court could assist the parties in settling any disputed facts, and the affidavit submitted by his counsel did not meet the requirements of Ohio R. App. P. 9(C). State v. Dunn, — Ohio App. 3d —, 2006 Ohio 6550, — N.E. 2d —, 2006 Ohio App. LEXIS 6459 (Dec. 7, 2006).

There was no prejudice to defendant found by the trial court's exclusion of his wife's testimony due to the fact that the wife remained in the courtroom despite a sequestration order pursuant to Ohio R. Evid. 615, as defendant failed to provide a transcript of the videotaped proceeding pursuant to his duty under Ohio R. App. P. 9(A) which indicated that part of the trial, and he also failed to make a proffer of the testimony that the wife would have given pursuant to Ohio R. Evid. 103(A)(2); as defendant did not show that he was prejudiced by the evidentiary ruling and the matter did not relate to the offenses for which he was convicted, it was disregarded as harmless error under Ohio R. Crim. P. 52. Ohio v. Shropshire, — Ohio App. 3d —, 2007 Ohio 5185, — N.E. 2d —, 2007 Ohio App. LEXIS 4567 (Sept. 28, 2007).

Burden of appellant

As a city prosecutor's claim on appeal that he was present in court on the scheduled trial date and ready to proceed at that time was not supported by anything in the record, he failed to meet his burden on appeal pursuant to Ohio R. App. P. 9(B), 16(A)(7), and Ohio Ninth Dist. Ct. App. R. 5(A) and 7(B)(7) of supporting his assignment of error through citations to legal authority and facts in the record and accordingly, the court presumed the regularity of the trial court proceedings. The trial court had dismissed the criminal matter that was pending against defendant for want of prosecution, which was in part based on the city's failure to appear for trial. City of Lorain v. Hodges, — Ohio App. 3d —, 2007 Ohio 456, — N.E. 2d —, 2007 Ohio App. LEXIS 406 (Feb. 5, 2007).

On appeal of a judgment in favor of a contractor, a home owner failed to meet the burden under Ohio R. App. P. 9, 12(A)(2), and 16(A)(7), as the owner failed to cite to the place in the record upon which the assignment of error was based, and there was no citation to legal authority in support of the assignment of error. Prater v. Dashkovsky, — Ohio App. 3d —, 2007 Ohio 6785, — N.E. 2d —, 2007 Ohio App. LEXIS 5919 (Dec. 18, 2007).

Burden to furnish record

Trial judge did not err in acknowledging the jury's hard work on the case after they returned their penalty-phase verdict but before the trial court imposed sentence, as no prejudice was shown from the conversation, defendant failed to attempt to reconstruct what the trial court discussed with the jury for purposes of showing prejudice pursuant to Ohio R. App. P. 9(B) and (E), and the trial court was presumed to consider only relevant, material, and competent evidence. State v. Frazier, 115 Ohio St. 3d 139, 2007 Ohio 5048, 873 N.E.2d 1263, 2007 Ohio LEXIS 2519 (2007).

Although there were portions of a transcript from a juvenile's parole-violation hearing that were not transcribable due to the juvenile's "inaudible" responses, pursuant to Ohio R. Juv. P. 37(A) there was no violation of the right to a recorded proceeding, as the transcript that was recorded was sufficient to show that the juvenile had waived his right to have counsel represent him in a knowing, voluntary, and intelligent manner. The juvenile failed in his burden to supplement the record with a statement pursuant to Ohio R. App. P. 9(C) where he failed to file such a statement. In re Andrew, — Ohio App. 3d —, 2007 Ohio 1021, — N.E. 2d —, 2007 Ohio App. LEXIS 927 (Mar. 9, 2007).

Where the record on appeal was unclear due to defendant's failure to provide a bond or a clerk's office form, as required by Ohio R. App. P. 9(B) and 10(A), it was unclear exactly who posted the bond that was used to pay fines assessed against defendant, as the appellate court's review was limited to the record presented before it pursuant to Ohio R. App. P. 9 and 12(A)(1)(b). The appellate court could not review defendant's assignment of error regarding a taking of his property with respect to the bail money, as the regularity of the trial court proceedings was presumed. State v. Ahmed, — Ohio App. 3d —, 2007 Ohio 2639, — N.E. 2d —, 2007 Ohio App. LEXIS 2478 (May 31, 2007).

As an appraiser failed to answer a complaint by an appraisal customer in a small claims action, he could not thereafter raise an issue on appeal regarding the failure to have included his partner as a necessary party to the litigation pursuant to Cleveland, Ohio, Mun. Ct. R. Prac. & P. 13.01. As he failed to provide a transcript of the proceedings pursuant to Ohio R. App. P. 9(B), there was no ability to review the claim that he never received the customer's money. Lynch v. Richards, — Ohio App. 3d —, 2007 Ohio 3532, — N.E. 2d —, 2007 Ohio App. LEXIS 3250 (July 12, 2007).

Property purchaser who appealed a foreclosure judgment in consolidated trial court cases only filed a single notice of appeal, rather than one in each case pursuant to Ohio Third Dist. Ct. App. R. 6(A), and accordingly, only documents from that one case were included in the record, which was inadequate under App. R. 9(A) and 11(C) and required dismissal of the appeal under Ohio Third Dist. Ct. App. R. 15. Lasalle Nat'l Bank v. Cline, — Ohio App. 3d —, 2006 Ohio 5152, — N.E. 2d —, 2006 Ohio App. LEXIS 5104 (Oct. 2, 2006).

Although defendant was not entitled to court-appointed counsel on minor misdemeanor charges for which he did not face jail time, he was still entitled to be advised of his right to counsel under U.S. Const. amend. VI and Ohio Const. art. I, § 10, and to make a knowing, intelligent, and voluntary waiver thereof. As there was no indication in the record of such advice and waiver, the error was prejudicial to defendant, and the State's claim that there was in fact such advisement and waiver in another portion of the proceedings was not reviewable where the State should have supplemented defendant's record pursuant to Ohio R. App. P. 9(B) in order to provide that necessary portion of the record for the court's review. State v. Shreve, — Ohio App. 3d —, 2006 Ohio 5080, — N.E. 2d —, 2006 Ohio App. LEXIS 4963 (Sept. 27, 2006).

As adoptive parents failed to provide a transcript or statement under Ohio R. App. P. 9, a reviewing court could not properly determine whether their claim that a hearing officer did not properly develop the "fullest possible record" and state the issues under OAC 5101:6-6-02(C)(6) and (10) had merit. Although the hearing officer did not calculate the actual costs of the children's daily living expenses for purposes of the parents' request for additional funds, it was ultimately determined that the county children services agency had made appropriate offers "to meet the needs of each child." J.S. v. Dept. of Job & Family Servs., — Ohio App. 3d —, — N.E. 2d —, 2006 Ohio App. LEXIS 2427 (May 25, 2006).

When the owners of a business sued a company for negligently installing an oil-interceptor system at the business because, in doing so, it crushed a drain line running from the owners' property, they could not complain, on appeal, that the trial court considered a videotape made by their expert when he excavated the system because they did not include the videotape in the appellate record, so they did not meet their obligation to provide the appellate court with a record demonstrating the error they complained of. Loukinas v. Roto-Rooter Servs. Co., 167 Ohio App. 3d 559, 2006 Ohio 3172, 855 N.E. 2d 1272, 2006 Ohio App. LEXIS 3081 (June 23, 2006).

Where a mother filed objections to a magistrate's determination regarding a shared parenting plan as to the parties' son, but she failed to file a complete transcript for purposes of reviewing the fact-based claims that she raised, pursuant to Ohio R. Civ. P. 53(E)(3)(c) and Ohio R. App. P. 9(B), the trial court and the appellate court had to accept the magistrate's findings of fact as proper in the circumstances; accordingly, the mother's objections were properly dismissed. Waclawski v. Waclawski, — Ohio App. 3d —, 2006 Ohio 3213, — N.E. 2d —, 2006 Ohio App. LEXIS 3125 (June 23, 2006).

Court presumed the regularity of the trial court proceedings in adopting a decision by a magistrate to deny a former husband's request to reallocate parental rights and responsibilities between himself and his former wife regarding their two minor children, although he showed a change of circumstances by his daughter's desire to live with him, as the magistrate's reliance on the guardian ad litem's recommendation that the children should not be separated and that the parties' son wished to remain with the wife for purposes of a best interest analysis under RC § 3109.04(F)(1) was not reviewable where the husband failed to include the guardian ad litem report in the record on appeal, as required by Ohio R. App. P. 9. Weisberg v. Sampson, — Ohio App. 3d —, 2006 Ohio 3646, — N.E. 2d —, 2006 Ohio App. LEXIS 3569 (July 14, 2006).

Capital cases

Proceedings in which a deliberating juror is dismissed in a capital case, and an alternate juror is seated, must be recorded. Under former CrimR 24(G)(2), a juror could not be replaced by an alternate juror during deliberations in a capital case: State v. Clinkscale, 122 Ohio St. 3d 351, 2009 Ohio 2746, 911 N.E.2d 862, 2009 Ohio LEXIS 1736 (2009).

Correction

Where a trial court's sentencing entry contained a clerical error, correction thereof was permitted under Ohio R. Crim. P. 36 and by the appellate court's direction to correct the misstatement pursuant to Ohio R. App. P. 9(E). State v. Simmons, — Ohio App. 3d —, 2006 Ohio 5760, — N.E. 2d —, 2006 Ohio App. LEXIS 5746 (Nov. 3, 2006).

Correction of record

When a litigant sought a writ of mandamus to compel a trial court clerk to submit certain documents the litigant had filed in the litigant's divorce case, which were stricken, with the record in the litigant's divorce appeal, the litigant's complaint was dismissed because the litigant had an adequate remedy at law, under Ohio R. App. P. 9(E), pursuant to which the litigant could seek to correct or modify the trial court record. State ex rel. Maury v. Martin, — Ohio App. 3d —, 2007 Ohio 2708, — N.E. 2d —, 2007 Ohio App. LEXIS 2510 (June 1, 2007).

When defendant's motion to an appellate court to correct the record, under Ohio R. App. P. 9(E), due to numerous gaps in the original trial transcript, was granted and, pursuant to the appellate court's order, the trial court certified a supplemental transcript, after holding a hearing at which counsel for the State, defendant, and defendant himself were present, defendant could not claim that gaps in the original transcript prejudiced defendant or violated defendant's due process rights because (1) a supplemental transcript was certified, and (2) the invited error doctrine barred defendant from complaining that the trial court acted pursuant to the appellate court's order which granted defendant's motion. Ohio v. Liddy, — Ohio App. 3d —, 2007 Ohio 5225, — N.E. 2d —, 2007 Ohio App. LEXIS 4597 (Sept. 28, 2007).

Where a note from a juror to a judge and then back to the juror was found in defendant's criminal file, but it did not appear in the record on appeal, and pursuant to a request, the trial court judge indicated that he did not recall the issue and that in his recollection, the note was not part of defendant's matter, the trial court fulfilled its duty under Ohio R. App. P. 9(E). There was no abuse of discretion found in the trial court's determination of the record, and further, even if the note was deemed part of the record, it did not address any legal issues or fact in controversy and was not substantive, such that defendant's claim that there was an improper ex parte communication lacked merit. State v. Cook, — Ohio App. 3d —, 2006 Ohio 3443, — N.E. 2d —, 2006 Ohio App. LEXIS 3393 (June 30, 2006).

Appellate record did not reflect that a trial court properly adjudicated the children who were the subject of a motion for permanent custody to be abused, neglected or dependent, despite a nunc pro tunc order of adjudication, because (1) the order only mentioned one of the children, and (2) it could not be found that the nunc pro tunc order reflected an action actually taken at an adjudicatory hearing, as was required for such an order, because no transcript of the adjudicatory hearing was furnished to the appellate court, so the trial court had no authority, under RC § 2151.353(A), to make any order of disposition regarding the children, including a grant of their permanent custody. In re Ronald H., — Ohio App. 3d —, 2006 Ohio 4693, — N.E. 2d —, 2006 Ohio App. LEXIS 4638 (Sept. 11, 2006).

Defendant's counsel's attempt to move for an Ohio R. App. P. 9(E) correction of the record with respect to a particular objection to the admission of a prescription pill bottle was irrelevant, as there were objections made whenever the warning label on the bottle was mentioned, but there was no specific assigment of error as to the admission of the bottle itself into admission. State v. Taylor, — Ohio App. 3d —, 2006 Ohio 6559, — N.E. 2d —, 2006 Ohio App. LEXIS 6483 (Dec. 7, 2006).

Defects in record

Although, as originally transcribed, the proceedings were not recorded in such a way as to enable defendant to file an adequate transcript, because an amended transcript had been filed, pursuant to Ohio R. App. P. 9, defendant was not prejudiced by any inadequacies in the transcript. The amended transcript was found to be in compliance with the order of remand. Further, defendant was not prejudiced by the filing of an amended transcript pursuant to Ohio R. App. P. 9(B) instead of a statement of the evidence pursuant to Ohio R. App. P. 9(C) because defendant and his counsel were given ample opportunity to review the original transcript, as filed, and to make corrections and/or objections to the amended transcript. State v. Beltowski, — Ohio App. 3d —, 2007 Ohio 3372, — N.E. 2d —, 2007 Ohio App. LEXIS 3090 (June 29, 2007).

Duty to provide transcript

In a law firm's suit against a former client for past due fees, in which the trial court had entered a default judgment against the client, the trial court's judgment vacating that default judgment, based on the client's letter to the court stating that the client was not served with process, was not disturbed on appeal because, while it was presumed, under Ohio R. Civ. P. 4.6(D), that service was proper, since process was sent to the client by ordinary mail and not returned, the firm did not file a transcript of the hearing at which the trial court decided to vacate the judgment, so the appellate court had to presume that the hearing was properly conducted and affirm the trial court's decision. Bringman v. Smith, — Ohio App. 3d —, 2007 Ohio 4684, — N.E. 2d —, 2007 Ohio App. LEXIS 4214 (Sept. 12, 2007).

Where an employee raised evidentiary rulings at the trial court level in her assignments of error but she failed to attach a trial court transcript or other statement to reflect the proceedings therein, as required by Ohio R. App. P. 9(B), (C), and (D), she did not provide anything for the court to review with respect to the errors asserted and the court was required to presume the regularity of the trial court proceedings; the trial court proceedings were necessary to determine what evidence was admitted and what was excluded, what context the evidence was sought for and whether it was relevant in the circumstances, and whether the employee had attempted to introduce it. Wilmington v. Kent State Univ., — Ohio App. 3d —, 2006 Ohio 3218, — N.E. 2d —, 2006 Ohio App. LEXIS 3132 (June 23, 2006).

Errors

Defendant failed to establish reversible error regarding a jury question to the court which he and his counsel allegedly not present for, as it was presumed in the absence of a showing to the contrary that defendant and his counsel were in fact present for purposes of Ohio Const. art. I, § 10 and

Ohio R. Crim. P. 43(A). Although the record was silent concerning any objection by defendant's counsel, defendant could have utilized a statement under Ohio R. App. P. 9 to supplement the record, and further, no prejudice was shown even if the absence were proved. State v. Simmons, — Ohio App. 3d —, 2007 Ohio 1570, — N.E. 2d —, 2007 Ohio App. LEXIS 1442 (Mar. 28, 2007).

Evidence never filed with trial court

Former city finance director's claim for accrued vacation time was denied because Willoughby Hills, Ohio, Ordinance No. 2002-02 provided that city employees, such as the director, who resigned would not be entitled to vacation pay; information that another employee took his remaining vacation time after his effective resignation could not be considered on appeal under Ohio R. App. P. 12(A)(1)(b) as that information was not before the trial court or the magistrate prior to the final judgment and, thus, was not part of the record on appeal under Ohio R. App. P. 9(A). Condron v. City of Willoughby Hills, — Ohio App. 3d —, 2007 Ohio 5208, — N.E. 2d —, 2007 Ohio App. LEXIS 4609 (Sept. 28, 2007).

While appellant filed an affidavit on appeal from a trial court's denial of his motion for relief from default judgment swearing that he did not receive service, the court could not consider it under Ohio R. App. P. 9(A) as the affidavit was never filed with the trial court. Erie Ins. v. Williams, — Ohio App. 3d —, 2006 Ohio 6754, — N.E. 2d —, 2006 Ohio App. LEXIS 6661 (Dec. 20, 2006).

Failure to file portions of transcript

Since defendant failed to file a presentence investigation report in his appeal from a trial court's classification of him as a habitual sexual offender, the court had to presume, pursuant to Ohio R. App. P. 9(B) and Ohio 9th Dist. Ct. App. R. 5(A), that defendant's juvenile adjudication for rape was accompanied by defendant's classification as juvenile offender, which was sufficient to satisfy the requirements of RC § 2950.01(B)(2). State v. Barnes, — Ohio App. 3d —, 2007 Ohio 2460, — N.E. 2d —, 2007 Ohio App. LEXIS 2280 (May 21, 2007).

In a divorce, a husband did not support the husband's claim that no settlement agreement was reached between the parties because the husband did not provide a transcript or Ohio R. App. P. 9(C) statement of the evidence from the hearing at which it was apparent that the parties' agreement was approved, and at which it was conceded that the husband testified that he understood and agreed to be bound by the agreement's terms. Montgomery v. Montgomery, — Ohio App. 3d —, 2007 Ohio 2787, — N.E. 2d —, 2007 Ohio App. LEXIS 2539 (June 7, 2007).

Since defendant did not provide the court with a transcript of the final charge to the jury but, instead, presented the written jury instructions prepared by the trial court as an appendix to his appellate brief, the court had no way of knowing whether the written copy was a verbatim recitation of the instructions the jury actually received at the conclusion of defendant's trial. Absent the transcript required by Ohio R. App. P. 9, the court was unable to review the jury instructions in context. State v. Tapp, — Ohio App. 3d —, 2007 Ohio 2959, — N.E. 2d —, 2007 Ohio App. LEXIS 2713 (June 14, 2007).

Appellate court was unable to review several assignments of error asserted by the wife in an appeal from a trial court's judgment in a divorce proceeding. Since the parties, for purposes of the final hearing, had stipulated that the trial court take judicial notice of all actions and hearings prior to the final hearing and specifically included all evidence and exhibits presented at those hearings, the court had only the transcript for the final hearing. The court was unable to review the merits of the wife's assignments of error relating to single factors of the trial court's decisions on custody and the division of marital debt because the court did not have a complete record of all prior hearings, as required by Ohio R. App. P. 9.

Eastwood v. Eastwood, — Ohio App. 3d —, 2007 Ohio 3096, — N.E. 2d —, 2007 Ohio App. LEXIS 2833 (June 15, 2007).

Though defendant contended that his conviction for driving under suspension was not supported by sufficient evidence because the State failed to introduce the LEADS report into evidence until after defendant made an Ohio R. Crim. P. 29 motion, defendant failed to include, pursuant to Ohio R. App. P. 9, the portion of the transcript related to any discussions on the admission of the LEADS report had at the end of the case, and the evidence of record showed that the officer had discovered that defendant's driver's license was under suspension. Thus, defendant's motion for acquittal under Ohio R. Crim. P. 29(A) was properly denied. Ohio v. Evans, — Ohio App. 3d —, 2007 Ohio 5934, — N.E. 2d —, 2007 Ohio App. LEXIS 5199 (Nov. 7, 2007).

Although a father's record on appeal in his parental rights termination proceeding did not contain a transcript for certain hearing dates and there was no statement of the evidence or agreed statement pursuant to Ohio R. App. P. 9(C) and (D), the transcript that was provided formed an adequate basis for the court's review of the father's assignments of error and accordingly, the court addressed them pursuant to Rule 9(B). In re Shifflet, — Ohio App. 3d —, 2006 Ohio 3576, — N.E. 2d —, 2006 Ohio App. LEXIS 3521 (July 10, 2006).

Failure to file pre-sentence report

When defendant appealed his sentence, but did not include the report of the pre-sentence investigation the trial court ordered, the record was incomplete, and the appellate court had to presume the regularity of the trial court's proceedings and affirm defendant's sentence. State v. Turner, — Ohio App. 3d —, 2007 Ohio 1961, — N.E. 2d —, 2007 Ohio App. LEXIS 1769 (Apr. 23, 2007).

Failure to provide transcript

Since, in an insured's appeal from a trial court's judgment in favor of an insurer, the insured failed to file transcript of proceedings or a suitable substitute under Ohio R. App. P. 9(C) or (D), the court was unable to determine whether the trial court's judgment was against the manifest weight of the evidence; instead, it had to presume the regularity of the proceedings, and it affirmed the trial court's judgment. West v. Allstate Ins. Co., — Ohio App. 3d —, 2007 Ohio 76, — N.E. 2d —, 2007 Ohio App. LEXIS 60 (Jan. 11, 2007).

As defendant failed to file a transcript from the trial court proceedings for purposes of his appeal, as required by Ohio R. App. P. 9, his claim that his counsel provided ineffective assistance in violation of U.S. Const. amend. VI and Ohio Const. art. I, § 10 by failing to file an appeal as allegedly promised lacked merit. There was nothing to show that counsel made such a promise and without a transcript to support the assertion, the court presumed the regularity of the trial court proceedings and affirmed. State v. Carrico, — Ohio App. 3d —, 2007 Ohio 559, — N.E. 2d —, 2007 Ohio App. LEXIS 517 (Feb. 5, 2007).

Since the record before the appellate court contained neither a transcript of the hearing before the trial court nor some acceptable alternative under Ohio R. App. P. 9, the court's review of a trial court's custody decision was confined only to those matters that were contained in the record before the court. Schilling v. Ball, — Ohio App. 3d —, 2007 Ohio 889, — N.E. 2d —, 2007 Ohio App. LEXIS 794 (Mar. 2, 2007).

Since defendant failed to provide a transcript of her plea hearing, as required by Ohio R. App. P. 9, the court was unable to determine whether the trial court complied with RC § 2937.07, which required an explanation of the circumstances of the offense before the trial court could make a finding of guilty on the basis of a no contest plea. State v. Bugaj, — Ohio App. 3d —, 2007 Ohio 964, — N.E. 2d —, 2007 Ohio App. LEXIS 902 (Feb. 14, 2007).

When an alleged insured claimed an insurer issued him a title insurance policy and then denied its existence, and the trial court granted a directed verdict to the insurer, under Ohio R. Civ. P. 50(A), the alleged insured could not demonstrate the trial court's alleged error because he did not submit a record of the trial court's proceedings, under Ohio R. App. P. 9(A), so the appellate court could not review the evidence before the trial court and had to presume the regularity of the trial court's proceedings. Clair v. First American Title Ins., — Ohio App. 3d —, 2007 Ohio 1681, — N.E. 2d —, 2007 Ohio App. LEXIS 1537 (Apr. 11, 2007).

Since defendant failed to file a transcript of the suppression hearing, as required by Ohio R. App. P. 9(A), the appellate court could only review the trial court's determination overruling defendant's motion to suppress as a matter of law. State v. Barton, — Ohio App. 3d —, 2007 Ohio 2348, — N.E. 2d —, 2007 Ohio App. LEXIS 2185 (May 11, 2007).

When a father appealed a trial court's judgment entry overruling the father's objections to a magistrate's finding by clear and convincing evidence that the father's child was abused and dependent, the father did not satisfy the father's burden, under Ohio R. App. P. 9(B), to file a transcript of the trial court's proceedings, so the appellate court presumed the regularity of those proceedings and affirmed the trial court's judgment. In re J.W., — Ohio App. 3d —, 2007 Ohio 2598, — N.E. 2d —, 2007 Ohio App. LEXIS 2420 (May 25, 2007).

Although a trial court's decision to allow a county coroner to testify that a doctor was not negligent in treating a patient who later died and that the doctor performed his examination and assessment of the patient according to the relevant standards of care was arguably erroneous, an appellate court had to presume the regularity of the trial court's rulings on evidence pursuant to Ohio R. Evid. 103(A) where the complete transcript of the trial testimony was not provided by the patient's estate executor pursuant to her duty under Ohio R. App. P. 9(B) in her wrongful death action; due to the incomplete transcript, the court could not determine whether or not the coroner's testimony affected a substantial right of the executor and warranted reversal. Frazier v. Pruitt, — Ohio App. 3d —, 2007 Ohio 3256, — N.E. 2d —, 2007 Ohio App. LEXIS 3002 (June 22, 2007).

Since a company failed to file a transcript or an appropriate substitute, as required by Ohio R. App. P. 10(A) and Ohio R. App. P. 9(C), in its appeal from a trial court's decision granting a preliminary injunction to a customer, the court could not determine whether the customer's testimony helped to demonstrate that he was entitled to injunctive relief. Davis v. Domestic Linen Supply Co., — Ohio App. 3d —, 2007 Ohio 3498, — N.E. 2d —, 2007 Ohio App. LEXIS 3219 (June 28, 2007).

Even if defendant had filed with the appellate court the transcript from his resentencing hearing, as was his duty under Ohio R. App. P. 9(B), defendant could not show that his sentences violated due process as defendant had notice of the sentencing ranges at the time he committed the offenses, and his sentences were within the statutory ranges for the offenses to which he pled guilty. State v. Shields, — Ohio App. 3d —, 2007 Ohio 3535, — N.E. 2d —, 2007 Ohio App. LEXIS 3245 (July 12, 2007).

As defendant failed to include the transcript from a resentencing hearing in the record on appeal, as required by Ohio R. App. P. 9(B), the appellate court presumed that the trial court merely used its discretion to impose the identical sentences of imprisonment that had been previously entered; accordingly, no due process violation under Ohio Const. art. I, § 10 was found. State v. Evans, — Ohio App. 3d —, 2007 Ohio 3580, — N.E. 2d —, 2007 Ohio App. LEXIS 3297 (July 13, 2007).

Defendant juvenile did not meet her burden, under Ohio R. App. P. 9(B), and supply a transcript of the proceedings from her original admission and the original delinquency disposition. Nor were transcripts provided from the 2005 adjudication for defendant's first violation of a prior court order charge. In re Burt, — Ohio App. 3d —, 2007 Ohio 4034, — N.E. 2d —, 2007 Ohio App. LEXIS 3649 (Aug. 6, 2007).

When a father found in contempt for failing to pay child support alleged, on appeal, that the trial court should have granted the father's counsel's motion to withdraw, that claim was not sustained because (1) the father, on appeal, gave no reasons why the trial court should have granted the request, nor did the father state what the good cause, under Ohio R. Juv. P. 4(F), for granting it might have been, as the father merely said the record reflected irreconcilable differences, and (2) the father did not provide a transcript or transcript substitute, under Ohio R. App. P. 9, from which such reasons might have been discerned. Midkiff v. Kuzniak, — Ohio App. 3d —, 2007 Ohio 5936, — N.E. 2d —, 2007 Ohio App. LEXIS 5201 (Nov. 2, 2007).

Defendant's more than minimum prison sentences were reversed because, although defendant failed to provide typed or printed portions of transcripts of proceedings, as required by Ohio R. App. P. 9(A), necessary to review whether the trial court's findings supported the imposition of the more than minimum sentences, defendant's sentences were imposed under a statute that had been declared unconstitutional by the Ohio Supreme Court in State v. Foster. State v. Arrellano, — Ohio App. 3d —, 2006 Ohio 5961, — N.E. 2d —, 2006 Ohio App. LEXIS 5915 (Nov. 9, 2006).

When defendant claimed the trial court did not comply with the terms of his plea agreement, the terms of which were stated on the record at his plea hearing, pursuant to Ohio R. Crim. P. 11(F), but he did not include a transcript of this hearing as part of the record on appeal, as he only requested a transcript of the sentencing hearing, the appellate court had nothing to consider on appeal, under Ohio R. App. P. 9, and had no choice but to affirm, and defendant's submission of an uncertified copy of the plea hearing transcript as an attachment to his brief was improper, and the transcript was stricken. State v. Robinson, — Ohio App. 3d —, 2006 Ohio 2283, — N.E. 2d —, 2006 Ohio App. LEXIS 2122 (May 10, 2006).

It was not an abuse of discretion to deny defendant's post-sentence motion to withdraw his guilty plea filed after a prison sentence was imposed following a finding that he violated the community control imposed after he pled guilty because defendant did not provide a transcript of the hearing at which he pled guilty, under Ohio R. App. P. 9(B), so the regularity of that hearing was presumed. State v. Seeley, — Ohio App. 3d —, 2006 Ohio 2376, — N.E. 2d —, 2006 Ohio App. LEXIS 2272 (May 15, 2006).

Defendant's claim that his trial counsel was ineffective in violation of his Sixth Amendment rights because counsel filed defendant's guilty plea prior to the date that defendant instructed him to do so lacked merit, as defendant filed no affidavit or transcript, pursuant to his burden under Ohio R. App. P. 9, in order to support his claim that he had instructed his counsel to wait until a particular date to file the plea in order for defendant to seek dismissal of the charges against him on speedy trial grounds pursuant to RC § 2945.73(B). Defendant's attempted tactic to file his guilty plea beyond the speedy trial time period in order to then seek dismissal of the charges was an improper act which would have tolled the speedy trial time period under RC § 2945.72(D), and there was no prejudice suffered by defendant from his counsel's earlier filing of the plea, as the filing at any date constituted a waiver of defendant's right to a trial and hence, right to a speedy trial. State v. Short, — Ohio App. 3d —, 2006 Ohio 2914, — N.E. 2d —, 2006 Ohio App. LEXIS 2731 (June 9, 2006).

Defendant filed an appeal from the wrong trial court judgment and, thus, his appeal challenging the trial court's denial of his motion to suppress filed in a second, unrelated case was dismissed. Defendant's notice of appeal did not refer to the second case, the record transmitted was the record in first case, and the docketing statement did not reference suppression issue; thus, defendant's appeal failed to comply with Ohio R. App. P. 3(D), Ohio R. App. P. 9(B), and Ohio R. App. P. 10(A). State v. Bleehash, — Ohio App. 3d —, 2006 Ohio 4580, — N.E. 2d —, 2006 Ohio App. LEXIS 4526 (Aug. 31, 2006).

In a consumer's appeal of the judgment entered against her in a credit corporation's suit for violation of a vehicle lease, when she turned in the vehicle before the lease expired, the correctness of the trial court's proceedings had to be presumed because the consumer did not file a transcript of those proceedings, and, despite the consumer's claim that no transcript was required because the issues on appeal were matters of law, a transcript was required because, while the consumer cited various statutes in her appellate arguments, those statutes had to be applied to the underlying facts to determine the merits of the consumer's appeal. Toyota Motor Credit Corp. v. Delaine, — Ohio App. 3d —, 2006 Ohio 4681, — N.E. 2d —, 2006 Ohio App. LEXIS 4606 (Sept. 8, 2006).

Indigents

Transcript was unavailable for purposes of Ohio R. App. P. 9(C) to an indigent party unable to bear the cost of providing a transcript; relator had the right to use an Ohio R. App. P. 9(C) statement because of his indigence. State ex rel. Madorsky v. Buchanan, — Ohio App. 3d —, 2006 Ohio 3682, — N.E. 2d —, 2006 Ohio App. LEXIS 3637 (July 17, 2006).

Jury instructions

Since a jury instruction on the issue of patient contributory negligence that was proffered by a radiologist and her employer was reduced to writing, was tendered to the court reporter at the trial court's direction, and was available for review in the exhibits for the appeal, Ohio R. Civ. P. 51(A) did not act as a bar to the appellate court's consideration of the proffered instruction. Viox v. Weinberg, — Ohio App. 3d —, 2006 Ohio 5075, — N.E. 2d —, 2006 Ohio App. LEXIS 5010 (Sept. 29, 2006).

Jury interrogatories

In a negligence case in which the jury did not answer interrogatories on proximate cause or comparative negligence, as it found no negligence, an appellate court had to presume that it was properly instructed as to the use of interrogatories, and that the interrogatories were proper, because neither the jury instructions nor the interrogatories were included in the appellate record, under Ohio R. App. P. 9(B). Capital v. I-X Center Park Corp., — Ohio App. 3d —, 2006 Ohio 4881, — N.E. 2d —, 2006 Ohio App. LEXIS 4805 (Sept. 21, 2006).

Mandamus

Motion under AppR 9(E) constitutes an adequate means by which a party to a civil appeal can obtain correction of the trial record so that it accurately depicts the nature of all proceedings at the trial level. Thus mandamus was not an available remedy: State ex rel. Amon v. Bernard, 180 Ohio App. 3d 707, 2009 Ohio 405, 906 N.E.2d 1208, 2009 Ohio App. LEXIS 375 (2009).

Preservation of arguments for appeal

In an action by a condominium unit owner against assorted condominium entities and individuals, alleging that the owner never received notice of a motorcycle ban that was imposed and which resulted in his being fined for having a motorcycle on the premises, there was no violation of his due process rights under Ohio Const. art. I, § 16 regarding notice of the ban, as he was deemed to have been given constructive notice through correspondence sent to all unit owners and discussions with owners at a unit owners meeting. As the owner did not claim in the trial court that he had not received an agenda regarding the meeting, such circumstances could not be considered on appeal pursuant to Ohio R. App. P. 9. Tallis v. Woodrun Place Unit Owners' Ass'n, — Ohio App. 3d —, 2006 Ohio 3267, — N.E. 2d —, 2006 Ohio App. LEXIS 3180 (June 27, 2006).

Presumption of regularity

Where a sewer contractor that appealed a judgment in favor of a limited partner of Ohio Utility Protection Services provided a statement of evidence and the partner's objections to an appellate court, although proper filing was with the trial court under Ohio R. App. P. 9(C), the statement was stricken; the contractor failed to properly filed the statement or provide any other form of record, such that the appellate court had to affirm the trial court based on a presumption of regularity. Eastern Natural Gas Co. v. A.P. O'Horo Co., — Ohio App. 3d —, 2007 Ohio 342, — N.E. 2d —, 2007 Ohio App. LEXIS 305 (Jan. 26, 2007).

Since debtors failed to comply with Ohio R. App. P. 9(B) by filing with the appellate the court transcript of the trial court's hearing where the trial court rejected a magistrate's findings, the court was unable to resolve the debtors' assignment of error on appeal, challenging the trial court's action. Since the trial court's action comported with Ohio R. Civ. P. 53(D)(4)(b), the court had to presume the validity of the trial court's proceedings. Leasecomm Corp. v. Dull, — Ohio App. 3d —, 2007 Ohio 454, — N.E. 2d —, 2007 Ohio App. LEXIS 405 (Feb. 5, 2007).

Where real property title holders did not indicate that they were going to provide an appellate court with a complete or partial transcript under Ohio R. App. P. 9(B), a statement of the evidence or proceedings under Rule 9(C), or an agreed statement of the case under Rule 9(D), and there was no transcript of the proceedings upon agreement of the parties, the appellate court could not review their claim that the magistrate's findings of fact and conclusions of law were against the manifest weight of the evidence; the court had to presume the regularity of the probate court proceedings and affirm. Hardy v. Fell, — Ohio App. 3d —, 2007 Ohio 1287, — N.E. 2d —, 2007 Ohio App. LEXIS 1182 (Mar. 22, 2007).

Where it was unclear exactly which portions of a builder's deposition were read into the trial court record in an action between the general contractor/retailer of a manufactured home and the purchasers thereof, the contractor failed in its burden of providing a record on appeal pursuant to Ohio R. App. P. 9(B) and 10(A), such that the appellate court had to presume the regularity of the trial court proceedings with respect to the contractor's assignment of error on appeal regarding admission of the deposition testimony. Drenning v. Blue Ribbon Homes, — Ohio App. 3d —, 2007 Ohio 1323, — N.E. 2d —, 2007 Ohio App. LEXIS 1230 (Mar. 23, 2007).

As a patient who filed a breach of contract action against a doctor for his having retained a portion of her surgical procedure fee due to her late cancellation failed to provide a record for purposes of appeal pursuant to Ohio R. App. P. 9(B) or (C), the appellate court presumed the regularity of the trial court proceedings. Accordingly, the patient's claim that the doctor had committed fraud or intentional misrepresentation by requesting her credit card information for a rescheduled date when in fact her credit card was charged for the cancelled appointment, which was resolved in favor of the doctor by the trial court, was affirmed on appeal. Groedel v. Arsham, — Ohio App. 3d —, 2007 Ohio 1715, — N.E. 2d —, 2007 Ohio App. LEXIS 1565 (Apr. 12, 2007).

Twelve-month sentence imposed upon defendant's conviction for permitting drug abuse under RC § 2925.13(B) was not invalid on ground that defendant's co-defendants received lesser sentences because there was nothing in record to show that difference in defendant's sentence from those of co-defendants was result of anything other than individualized factors that were applied to her. Since defendant did not make the co-defendants' sentencing hearings part of the record,

pursuant to Ohio R. App. P. 9(B), the court had no choice but to presume the validity of the trial court's proceedings and affirm. State v. Wickham, — Ohio App. 3d —, 2007 Ohio 1754, — N.E. 2d —, 2007 Ohio App. LEXIS 1624 (Apr. 10, 2007).

When defendant claimed that his conviction for driving under suspension was against the manifest weight of the evidence, his claim could not be considered because he only provided a partial transcript of the proceedings before the trial court and did not supplement that transcript with a statement under either Ohio R. App. P. 9(C) or 9(D), so the regularity of the trial court's proceedings had to be presumed because the partial transcript did not contain all of the evidence relevant to this assignment of error. City of Macedonia v. Ewing, — Ohio App. 3d —, 2007 Ohio 2194, — N.E. 2d —, 2007 Ohio App. LEXIS 2055 (May 9, 2007).

Since a patron provided an appellate court with only a partial transcript of the trial in his negligence action against a restaurant, the court was unable to evaluate whether the jury verdict in favor of the restaurant was against the manifest weight of the evidence. Thus, the court presumed the validity of the trial court's proceedings and affirmed the judgment. Bohrer v. Bakers Square Restaurant, — Ohio App. 3d —, 2007 Ohio 2223, — N.E. 2d —, 2007 Ohio App. LEXIS 2075 (May 10, 2007).

As trial counsel and the trial court adequately advised defendant of the consequences of his plea, it was deemed knowingly and voluntarily entered pursuant to Ohio R. Crim. P. 11, as there was no obligation for counsel to have predicted the issuance of the Foster decision and to have advised defendant of the possible consequences thereof when the guilty plea was entered pre-Foster, such that counsel was not shown to have rendered ineffective assistance in violation of U.S. Const. amend. VI and Ohio Const. art. I, § 10. As the record on appeal did not include the transcript of the guilty plea hearing, the regularity and correctness of that proceeding was presumed pursuant to Ohio R. App. P. 9(B). State v. Lloyd, — Ohio App. 3d —, 2007 Ohio 3013, — N.E. 2d —, 2007 Ohio App. LEXIS 2767 (June 15, 2007).

Although defendant claimed on appeal that his counsel was ineffective for failing to have obtained cell phone records, where the cell phone records were not part of the record on appeal, the appellate court had no information as to what they would have contained and defendant could not show that he was prejudiced by counsel's failure to have obtained them. As the cell phone records were not included, the court presumed the regularity of the trial court proceedings under Ohio R. App. P. 9(B). State v. Feathers, — Ohio App. 3d —, 2007 Ohio 3024, — N.E. 2d —, 2007 Ohio App. LEXIS 2778 (June 15, 2007).

Since, in defendant's appeal, no complete transcript of either the suppression hearing or the trial on a charge of operating a vehicle while under the influence of alcohol was provided, the appellate court was unable to review the facts underlying defendant's stop and arrest in context and, pursuant to Ohio R. App. P. 9(B), had to presume the validity of the trial court's proceedings. State v. Hartman, — Ohio App. 3d —, 2007 Ohio 3051, — N.E. 2d —, 2007 Ohio App. LEXIS 2794 (June 18, 2007).

Trial court did not commit error under RC § 2506.03 in reviewing a city employee's appeal of an administrative decision when it considered the administrative record supplied by the city, and in holding a hearing for the presentation of additional evidence, as there was no indication that the employee or his counsel objected to unsworn testimony by witnesses, such that any issue thereon was waived. Even if it was error to have considered the administrative record, the taking of additional evidence could not have been plain error, although without a transcript of the hearing where additional evidence was taken, the regularity of the proceedings was presumed pursuant to Ohio R. App. P. 9(A). Shields v. City of

Englewood, 172 Ohio App. 3d 620, 2007 Ohio 3165, 876 N.E.2d 972, 2007 Ohio App. LEXIS 2905 (2007).

Trial court did not violate defendant's due process rights under U.S. Const. amend. XIV in refusing either to suppress evidence or to dismiss defendant's criminal case based on the State's alleged failure to disclose or preserve exculpatory evidence, consisting of a surveillance videotape taken of a parking lot where the criminal incident occurred, as it was uncertain where such a tape even existed and if so, it was made by a private entity that had no connection with the police department or the prosecutor and defendant had as much opportunity as the prosecution to have secured the tape. As defendant failed to comply with Ohio R. App. P. 9(A), the trial court's finding as to the absence of evidence that the prosecution or the police had control of the surveillance system was presumed correct. State v. Grigley, — Ohio App. 3d —, 2007 Ohio 3159, — N.E. 2d —, 2007 Ohio App. LEXIS 2908 (June 22, 2007).

In a deceased patient's estate executor's wrongful death action that was resolved by a jury verdict in favor of the medical individual and entities sued, her claim on appeal that the trial court erred in providing the jury with an instruction regarding the coroner's opinion pursuant to the precedent of Vargo and under RC § 313.19 was not reviewable, as she failed to provide a transcript of the jury instructions that were read to the jury pursuant to Ohio R. App. P. 9(B); accordingly, the court presumed the regularity of the trial court proceedings. Frazier v. Pruitt, — Ohio App. 3d —, 2007 Ohio 3256, — N.E. 2d —, 2007 Ohio App. LEXIS 3002 (June 22, 2007).

Because defendant juvenile's Ohio R. App. P. 9(C) statement was silent on whether an investigating police officer was questioned as to whether any citations were issued to any of the other drivers involved in a three-car collision, the court had to presume the regularity of the trial court's proceedings and affirm defendant's conviction for failing to keep an assured clear distance. In re S.G., — Ohio App. 3d —, 2007 Ohio 3271, — N.E. 2d —, 2007 Ohio App. LEXIS 3030 (June 28, 2007).

Although a county dog warden failed to file a brief in defendant's appeal from a finding that he had failed to have his dog vaccinated against rabies, as required by Ohio Health Dept. Reg. 221.11(b), defendant failed to support his asserted errors under Ohio R. App. P. 18(C) where he failed to file a record of the trial court proceedings, as required by Ohio R. App. P. 9. The regularity of the trial court proceedings was presumed and it was determined that defendant failed to show proof of a valid defense to the charge, such as that the dog was less than three months old or that defendant had owned it for less than 30 days. Stark County Dog Dep't v. Robinson, — Ohio App. 3d —, — N.E. 2d —, 2007 Ohio 3394, 2007 Ohio App. LEXIS 3131 (July 2, 2007).

Where defendant failed to provide a transcript of the voir dire proceedings, as required by Ohio R. App. P. 9(B), the court presumed the regularity of the trial court's decision to deny defendant's motion for a change of venue due to alleged pretrial publicity that would deny him a fair trial; the trial court was presumed to have ruled appropriately. State v. Dewitt, — Ohio App. 3d —, 2007 Ohio 3437, — N.E. 2d —, 2007 Ohio App. LEXIS 3143 (June 29, 2007).

As defendant waived his right to counsel in criminal trial court proceedings, and he failed to provide the appellate court with a record of the trial court proceedings with respect to his pro se request on appeal for psychological help rather than jail time, the regularity of the trial court proceedings was presumed. State v. Morrison, — Ohio App. 3d —, 2007 Ohio 3458, — N.E. 2d —, 2007 Ohio App. LEXIS 3185 (July 6, 2007).

Because defendant did not provide a complete transcript of the suppression hearing, the validity of the trial court's findings was presumed. Defendant appended copies of nine pages of testimony from an unidentified officer from the

motion to suppress hearing, but did not certify the accuracy of the portions of the transcript as required by App. R. 9(A); no transcript concerning the stop of defendant, statements made by defendant to the officer, if any, other observations made by the officer concerning his assessment of defendant's impairment or other field sobriety testing were provided by either party. State v. Auld, — Ohio App. 3d —, 2007 Ohio 3508, — N.E. 2d —, 2007 Ohio App. LEXIS 3215 (July 9, 2007).

Defendant failed to show that his counsel was ineffective in violation of U.S. Const. amend. VI and Ohio Const. art. I, § 10 for failing to investigate the possibility of entering a plea of not guilty by reason of insanity, as there was no evidence to support such a claim pursuant to RC § 2901.04(A)(14), and further, defendant failed to show deficient performance and prejudice. Defendant had not included the plea hearing transcript in the record on appeal pursuant to Ohio R. App. P. 9(B) for purposes of review, such that the regularity of the proceedings therein were presumed. State v. Martinez, — Ohio App. 3d —, 2007 Ohio 3575, — N.E. 2d —, 2007 Ohio App. LEXIS 3266 (July 13, 2007).

Where a personal guarantor appealed a damage award against her on a credit card charge intermediary's breach of contract action, and she failed in her duty under Ohio R. App. P. 9(B) to provide the appellate court with a transcript from the trial court proceedings, the court was unable to review her assignments of error regarding the propriety of a particular exhibit and the appropriateness of the damages awarded; the appellate court had to presume the regularity of the trial court proceedings. Nat'l Debit Corp. v. Trump Travel, — Ohio App. 3d —, 2007 Ohio 3740, — N.E. 2d —, 2007 Ohio App. LEXIS 3407 (July 24, 2007).

Where a father whose paternity and child support obligations were established by a magistrate failed to file objections to that decision, and he failed to file objections to a magistrate's later decision to deny his motion under Ohio R. Civ. P. 60(B) to vacate the earlier judgment, he waived his right to appeal under Ohio R. Civ. P. 53(D)(3)(b). As the father failed to provide the appellate court with a trial court transcript, as required by Ohio R. App. P. 9(B), there was nothing to review and the appellate court had to presume the validity of the trial court proceedings. T.S. v. W.D., — Ohio App. 3d —, 2007 Ohio 3795, — N.E. 2d —, 2007 Ohio App. LEXIS 3454 (July 26, 2007).

As a motorist failed to file the record from a trial court proceeding pursuant to Ohio R. App. P. 9(B) in her negligence action, arising from a vehicle collision, the court presumed that the trial court's denial of her motions for a new trial, a directed verdict, and a judgment notwithstanding the verdict pursuant to Ohio R. Civ. P. 59 and 50, based on the alleged inadequacy of the damages awarded to her, were proper and were supported by competent, credible evidence. Hoskins v. Simones, — Ohio App. 3d —, 2007 Ohio 4084, — N.E. 2d —, 2007 Ohio App. LEXIS 3669 (Aug. 3, 2007).

As a wife's appeal of a trial court's determination of her husband's income for purposes of its calculation of child support did not include a complete record, as was the wife's obligation under Ohio R. App. P. 9(B), the appellate court presumed the regularity of the trial court proceedings and affirmed the trial court decision. Garner v. Garner, — Ohio App. 3d —, 2006 Ohio 5109, — N.E. 2d —, 2006 Ohio App. LEXIS 5030 (Sept. 29, 2006).

Since appellant filed only a partial transcript of the proceedings before the trial court and did not comply with the requirements in Ohio R. App. P. 9(B) for filing only a partial transcript of the proceedings, the appellate court presumed the validity of the trial court proceedings and affirmed the trial court's judgment. Conley v. Smith, — Ohio App. 3d —, 2006 Ohio 1498, — N.E. 2d —, 2006 Ohio App. LEXIS 1369 (Mar. 27, 2006).

Where a tenant appealed a decision of a trial court which adopted a magistrate's determination that she had breached a lease and that the landlord was entitled to a money judgment, but the tenant failed to provide a copy of the trial court record, she did not meet her burden under Ohio R. App. P. 9(B) and the trial court presumed the validity of the trial court proceedings; accordingly, there was no basis to support her issue on appeal that the findings and judgment of the trial court were not supported by the evidence. Rinehart v. Hauck, — Ohio App. 3d —, 2006 Ohio 1719, — N.E. 2d —, 2006 Ohio App. LEXIS 1581 (Apr. 4, 2006).

While the record did not reflect which state's law the trial court applied in a passenger's negligence suit against the driver of a motorized personal watercraft arising out of an accident occurring in Kentucky, since the transcript of the bench conference was not available and since, under Ohio R. App. P. 9, it was the appellant's duty to provide a transcript or to supplement the record, the court presumed that the trial court properly applied Kentucky substantive law. Scanlon v. Pfaller, — Ohio App. 3d —, 2006 Ohio 2022, — N.E. 2d —, 2006 Ohio App. LEXIS 1854 (Apr. 24, 2006).

Where a car repair business owner or president appealed the denial of his motion for summary judgment in an action by a car owner, but the car repair business owner or president failed to provide the transcript of the hearing for purposes of appellate review, he failed to meet his burden under Ohio R. App. P. 9(B) and the appellate court presumed the regularity of the trial court proceedings. Pickett v. Pro Car Assocs., — Ohio App. 3d —, 2006 Ohio 3342, — N.E. 2d —, 2006 Ohio App. LEXIS 3266 (June 30, 2006).

Although defendant failed to submit a written transcript of a suppression hearing, as required by Ohio R. App. P. 9, the appellate court acted within its discretion in deciding to address the merits of the appeal based on the videotape medium of the transcript that was submitted, rather than declining to view it and instead, presuming the regularity of the proceedings below. State v. Collins, — Ohio App. 3d —, 2006 Ohio 4155, — N.E. 2d —, 2006 Ohio App. LEXIS 4089 (Aug. 11, 2006).

As defendant failed to provide a transcript under Ohio R. App. P. 9 for appellate review of his expungement hearing, wherein the trial court denied the request, the appellate court presumed the regularity of the trial court proceedings. However, consideration of the factors set forth under RC § 2953.32(C) by the trial court was not necessary in reaching its determination, as defendant was ineligible where he was not a first offender and had committed second-degree felonies. State v. Stislow, — Ohio App. 3d —, 2006 Ohio 4168, — N.E. 2d —, 2006 Ohio App. LEXIS 4113 (Aug. 11, 2006).

Defendant's claim that she was not afforded due process, in violation of Ohio Const. art. I, § 10, in a proceeding where a trial court found her guilty of having violated a city property maintenace code lacked merit, as there was no showing that evidence obtained from an allegedly illegal search warrant was relied upon by the trial court in making its finding of guilt, and as defendant failed to attach a transcript of the trial court proceedings or a statement of the evidence pursuant to Ohio R. App. P. 9(C), the court presumed the regularity of the proceedings with respect to claims that she did not have an opportunity to be heard or that the evidence was not sufficient. City of Whitehall v. Ruckman, — Ohio App. 3d —, 2006 Ohio 4717, — N.E. 2d —, 2006 Ohio App. LEXIS 4622 (Sept. 12, 2006).

As defendant failed to file the trial court transcript as part of the record on appeal pursuant to his duty under Ohio R. App. P. 9(B), the court presumed the regularity of the trial court proceedings. Defendant's assignments of error relating to evidentiary issues and the manifest weight of the evidence from his criminal matter were overruled. State v. Rupert, — Ohio App. 3d —, 2006 Ohio 5816, — N.E. 2d —, 2006 Ohio App. LEXIS 5789 (Nov. 6, 2006).

Where defendant's plea agreement indicated that the State would not oppose judicial release upon stated conditions, but that the trial court was not bound thereto, the denial of defendant's judicial release request pursuant to RC § 2929.20 was not error because it did not violate the terms of the plea agreement. The regularity of the plea proceedings were presumed on appeal where defendant had failed to include the plea hearing transcript in the appellate record pursuant to Ohio R. App. P. 9(B). State v. Carter, — Ohio App. 3d —, 2006 Ohio 5822, — N.E. 2d —, 2006 Ohio App. LEXIS 5801 (Oct. 30, 2006).

As a property owner failed to provide a transcript excerpt pursuant to her obligation under Ohio R. App. P. 9(B) and 10(A) to support her claim that the trial court had deferred her counsel's re-direct examination, and instead, the trial court's denial of her new trial motion indicated that it had denied her re-direct examination, the court had nothing to review on appeal and accordingly, it presumed the regularity of the trial court proceedings. Jarupan v. Hanna, 173 Ohio App. 3d 284, 2007 Ohio 5081, 878 N.E.2d 66, 2007 Ohio App. LEXIS 4498 (2007).

As a husband failed to provide a transcript pursuant to Ohio R. App. P. 9 for purposes of his challenge on appeal to the trial court's division of marital property and debt in the parties' divorce action, the regularity of the trial court proceedings and decisions was presumed. Blackstone v. Blackstone, — Ohio App. 3d —, 2007 Ohio 5138, — N.E. 2d —, 2007 Ohio App. LEXIS 4511 (Sept. 27, 2007).

Record

Where defendant's claim in her trial on a charge of driving with a suspended license was that she believed that the court which suspended her license had allowed her "driving to work privileges," but those prior court records were excluded from the trial, there was nothing for the appellate court to review after defendant appealed her conviction, as she failed to include the proffered records in the record on appeal pursuant to her obligation under Ohio R. App. P. 9(B). Accordingly, she failed to show prejudice by the exclusion of the evidence, but conversely, even if such evidence had been reviewable, it would not have prevented the conviction, but only acted to possibly mitigate the sentence imposed. State v. Lammers, — Ohio App. 3d —, 2006 Ohio 2125, — N.E. 2d —, 2006 Ohio App. LEXIS 1970 (Apr. 28, 2006).

Pursuant to Ohio R. Civ. P. 53, appellant waived all but plain error in the trial court's decision finding him in contempt of court, awarding attorney fees to appellee, and holding that appellant was a vexatious litigator because appellant failed to file with the trial court objections to the magistrate's decision. Since appellant failed to file any transcripts and failed to provide a statement of the evidence or an agreed statement of the case under Ohio R. App. P. 9(D), the court was prevented from effectively the assignments of error as it related to the contempt finding and the award of attorney fees by his failure to timely object to the magistrate's decision for plain error; thus, the court presumed the validity of the judgment as to those two decisions. Gevedon v. Gevedon, 167 Ohio App. 3d 450, 2006 Ohio 3195, 855 N.E. 2d 548, 2006 Ohio App. LEXIS 3087 (June 23, 2006).

Trial court based its decision regarding a child's custody and care on the recommendation of the guardian ad litem (GAL); yet, the record was void of any documentation regarding the GAL's recommendations. Thus, since the father, who was the appellant, failed to sustain his burden on appeal under Ohio R. App. P. 16(A)(7) and Ohio 9th Dist. Ct. App. R. 7(B)(7) of supplying those portions of the record which demonstrated the error on appeal and under Ohio R. App. P. 9(B) and Ohio 9th Dist. Ct. App. R. 5(A) of ensuring that the record necessary to determine the appeal is before the appellate court, the court presumed that the record before the trial court, which included the GAL's recommendation, supported the trial court's decisions. Love v. Love, — Ohio App. 3d —, 2006 Ohio 3559, — N.E. 2d —, 2006 Ohio App. LEXIS 3506 (July 12, 2006).

Former husband's claims on appeal were not supported by an adequate record pursuant to his duty under Ohio R. App. P. 9(B) and accordingly, there was no basis for the review of his assertions that a continuance of a custody modification hearing had been granted to his counsel and that an order entered therein was ex parte by his former wife due to her failure to have provided notice of the proposed order to him. Solovyov v. Solovyov, — Ohio App. 3d —, 2006 Ohio 6406, — N.E. 2d —, 2006 Ohio App. LEXIS 6450 (Dec. 7, 2006).

Record on appeal

When a patient sought a writ of prohibition in the court of appeals to bar a trial judge from proceeding in a medical malpractice case because the patient had appealed the trial court's denial of the patient's motion for a protective order, the supreme court could take judicial notice of the fact that the court of appeals had dismissed the patient's appeal, in deciding whether dismissal of the patient's prohibition claim was proper, even though the dismissal of the patient's appeal was not part of the record in the prohibition case, because the supreme court had plenary authority in extraordinary actions to consider an appeal as if the case had been filed in the supreme court originally, and the parties agreed that the court of appeals did, in fact, dismiss the patient's appeal from the trial court's denial of the patient's motion. State ex rel. Everhart v. McIntosh, 115 Ohio St. 3d 195, 2007 Ohio 4798, 874 N.E.2d 516, 2007 Ohio LEXIS 2209 (2007).

Mortgagee's two prior foreclosure actions against a mortgagor, which it voluntarily dismissed pursuant to Ohio R. Civ. P. 41(A)(1), did not bar it from bringing a third foreclosure action against the mortgagor, as the two-dismissal rule and res judicata were inapplicable because the third foreclosure action listed a default date that was subsequent to the second action's dismissal and accordingly, covered different months and stated a new claim. As the mortgagor had failed to attach the prior two complaints to his summary judgment motion, the appellate court could not consider them pursuant to Ohio R. App. P. 9(A) in order to determine if the third action stated a new claim, although they were included in the mortgagor's brief on appeal. United States Bank Nat'l Ass'n v. Gullotta, — Ohio App. 3d —, 2007 Ohio 2085, — N.E. 2d —, 2007 Ohio App. LEXIS 1935 (Apr. 30, 2007).

Court could not consider a pension evaluation report attached to a wife's brief on appeal in the parties' divorce proceedings, which report calculated the value of the husband's military retirement benefits with cost of living adjustments, as the wife never included the report as part of the trial court record of proceedings pursuant to Ohio R. App. P. 9. Hornung v. Hornung, — Ohio App. 3d —, 2007 Ohio 3222, — N.E. 2d —, 2007 Ohio App. LEXIS 2844 (June 21, 2007).

While several sidebar conferences were not recorded, any alleged error in that regard was rendered moot by virtue of defendant's supplementation of the record pursuant to Ohio R. App. P. 9(C). Defendant filed a statement of evidence setting forth the substances of the sidebar conferences and thus, any alleged error on the part of the trial court in failing to record the sidebar conferences was rendered moot. State v. Schenker, — Ohio App. 3d —, 2007 Ohio 3732, — N.E. 2d —, 2007 Ohio App. LEXIS 3415 (July 19, 2007).

Defendant's Sixth Amendment right to counsel was violated where there was no record to indicate that he waived that right, and a presumption of regularity as to the trial court proceedings in the absence of a record, pursuant to Ohio R. App. P. 9(B), was not made in such an instance; accordingly, where there was no showing that defendant knowingly and intelligently waived his right to counsel, pursuant to Ohio R. Crim. P. 22 and 44(B), a sentence of imprisonment could not be imposed against him, although other sentencing terms

were proper. State v. Miyamoto, — Ohio App. 3d —, 2006 Ohio 1776, — N.E. 2d —, 2006 Ohio App. LEXIS 1648 (Apr. 10, 2006).

Trial court's division of property and debt constituted reversible error because neither the reconciliation of statement of evidence, pursuant to Ohio R. App. P. 9(C), nor the trial court's judgment entry indicated that the trial court considered the factors enumerated in RC § 3105.171. Further, there was no statement of any specific evidence nor any factual findings regarding the values of any marital or separate property or debt in either the reconciliation of statement of evidence or the judgment entry. Phillips v. Phillips, — Ohio App. 3d —, 2006 Ohio 2098, — N.E. 2d —, 2006 Ohio App. LEXIS 1925 (Apr. 24, 2007).

Where defendant was not attempting to supplement the record on appeal pursuant to Ohio R. App. P. 9(C) from her criminal convictions with affidavits because the affidavits were attachments to defendant's motion to withdraw her plea and as such, were part of the trial court record, the State's motion to strike them was denied. State v. Summers, — Ohio App. 3d —, 2006 Ohio 3199, — N.E. 2d —, 2006 Ohio App. LEXIS 3085 (June 23, 2006).

Statement in lieu of transcript

Court rejected a wife's contention that a record of the in camera hearing of her children conducted by the trial court in a custody case, pursuant to RC § 3109.04(B)(2)(c), should have been made because the wife never requested a record, as required by Licking County, Ohio, Ct. C.P. Dom. Rel. Div. R. 32.1. While the wife alleged that the husband made such a request, the wife, upon realizing that there was no record of the in camera interview, was under obligation to attempt to supplement the record with an Ohio R. App. P. 9(C) statement, which could have been filed under seal. Since the wife failed to do so, the wife was estopped from arguing any error with respect to the lack of a transcript of the interview. Eastwood v. Eastwood, — Ohio App. 3d —, 2007 Ohio 3096, — N.E. 2d —, 2007 Ohio App. LEXIS 2833 (June 15, 2007).

Trial court's denial of a mother's request for a deviation from child support guidelines was not an abuse of discretion where the denial was based on a consideration of statutory factors under RC §§ 3119.22 and 3119.23, including that the mother already received credit for child care and for another child's support, that there was a disparity of income between the parties, and that she shared the living expenses with her boyfriend; as she did not supply the transcript or a statement under Ohio R. App. P. 9(C) for purposes of her claim that there was no evidence that she shared expenses with her boyfriend, the regularity of the trial court proceedings was presumed. Logan v. Gregrow, — Ohio App. 3d —, 2007 Ohio 4585, — N.E. 2d —, 2007 Ohio App. LEXIS 4122 (Sept. 4, 2007).

Magistrate's factual findings were considered established as the insurer, who appealed the trial court's decision adopting the magistrate's decision, failed to file with the trial court a transcript of the evidence from the magistrate's hearing or an affidavit in place of the transcript; thus, the trial court's factual findings could not be attacked on appeal. The insurer could not circumvent the transcript requirement of Ohio R. Civ. P. 53(D)(3)(b)(iii) by filing an Ohio R. App. P. 9(C) statement of the evidence. Vidalis v. Medical Mut. of Ohio, — Ohio App. 3d —, 2007 Ohio 4656, — N.E. 2d —, 2007 Ohio App. LEXIS 4186 (Sept. 12, 2007).

In an appeal from defendant's conviction for criminal damaging,though the trial court's statement of evidence in lieu of a transcript, under Ohio R. App. P. 9(C), conflicted in many respects with trial counsel's recollection of the evidence as the trial court's statement recalled that the State's witnesses all testified that the victim's door was damaged when defendant threw a chair at it, the court had to accept trial court's statement. Based on the trial court's statement of the evidence, the court could not find that the judgment was against the manifest weight of the evidence. State v. Cobb, — Ohio App. 3d —, 2007 Ohio 4718, — N.E. 2d —, 2007 Ohio App. LEXIS 4229 (Sept. 14, 2007).

When child custody proceedings before a magistrate were inadvertently not recorded, a mother did not show that the mother was deprived of the mother's right to a fair appeal because (1) the mother waived any error caused by the lack of a transcript by not using the procedural methods available to correct the record by providing a statement of the evidence, pursuant to Ohio R. App. P. 9(C), and (2) the mother did not object to the Rule 9(C) statement of the evidence provided by the trial court. Selby v. Selby, — Ohio App. 3d —, 2007 Ohio 6700, — N.E. 2d —, 2007 Ohio App. LEXIS 5857 (Dec. 14, 2007).

Where a juvenile court failed to comply with the recording requirement pursuant to Ohio R. Juv. P. 37(A) in a juvenile's delinquency proceeding, and the juvenile was unable to prepare an Ohio R. App. P. 9(C) statement for appellate purposes because he could not reach his prior counsel, the lack of clarity as to whether the juvenile was adjudicated as delinquent for a felony-level offense in order to determine if he was eligible for commitment to the Ohio Department of Youth Services required a remand for a new adjudication hearing. In re G.W., — Ohio App. 3d —, 2006 Ohio 5327, — N.E. 2d —, 2006 Ohio App. LEXIS 5320 (Oct. 12, 2006).

Statement of evidence

Where the trial court refused to comply with multiple remand orders to settle and approve a statement of evidence, the defendant was deprived of his constitutional right to appeal the conviction. The matter was remanded for the limited purpose of vacating the conviction and entering a judgment of acquittal: City of Aurora v. Belinger, 180 Ohio App. 3d 178, 2008 Ohio 6772, 904 N.E.2d 916, 2008 Ohio App. LEXIS 5669 (2008).

Although a juvenile court erred under Ohio R. Juv. P. 37(A) in failing to record an amenability hearing, wherein it relinquished jurisdiction over a juvenile defendant with respect to a criminal charge against him in favor of the general trial court, such was harmless error where a statement of evidence under Ohio R. App. P. 9(C) was deemed adequate to determine the question of whether the relinquishment of jurisdiction by the juvenile court was proper. State v. Lucas, — Ohio App. 3d —, 2007 Ohio 188, — N.E. 2d —, 2007 Ohio App. LEXIS 178 (Jan. 19, 2007).

When defendant asserted that the evidence was insufficient to support his conviction under RC § 2921.34(A)(1), his claim was not preserved because the record did not indicate that he moved for a judgment of acquittal at the close of all the evidence, under Ohio R. Crim. P. 29, even though the trial court directed him to make his post-evidence motions at side bar, because he could have submitted a statement pursuant to Ohio R. App. P. 9(C) indicating that such a motion was made, but he did not. State v. McCuller, — Ohio App. 3d —, 2007 Ohio 348, — N.E. 2d —, 2007 Ohio App. LEXIS 312 (Jan. 29, 2007).

Transcript

Following the trial court's denial of the prisoner's motion to be provided with a transcript at the state's expense, the prisoner did not assemble or provide an alternate record, such as the one described in Ohio R. App. P. 9(D). Thus, as to the errors he assigned, the validity of the proceedings below was presumed. Watley v. Department of Rehabilitation & Correction, — Ohio App. 3d —, 2007 Ohio 1841, — N.E. 2d —, 2007 Ohio App. LEXIS 1666 (Apr. 19, 2007).

Since neither an arresting officer or plaintiff provided a complete transcript of all the evidence before the trial court and since the disposition of both assignments of error alleged by both the officer and plaintiff on appeal required a review of more than a partial transcript, the court ordered the record in the case supplemented. Hinkle v. City of Columbus, — Ohio App. 3d —, 2006 Ohio 1522, — N.E. 2d —, 2006 Ohio App. LEXIS 1393 (Mar. 30, 2006).

Partial transcript an alleged injured party submitted to the appellate court did not support his claims that the trial court's jury instructions erred or that the trial court failed to consider a medical exhibit because he did not order a transcript of the jury instructions or of the medical testimony which was allegedly not considered, so, under Ohio R. App. P. 9(B), the appellate court had no alternative but to presume the regularity of the trial court's proceedings. Rinehart v. Brown, — Ohio App. 3d —, 2006 Ohio 1912, — N.E. 2d —, 2006 Ohio App. LEXIS 1766 (Apr. 17, 2006).

Because defendant failed to provide a transcript as required, regularity of the proceedings below was presumed. Since defendant's appeal challenged his sentence and the plea hearing, transcripts of the sentencing hearing and plea hearing were necessary. State v. Boylen, — Ohio App. 3d —, 2006 Ohio 5685, — N.E. 2d —, 2006 Ohio App. LEXIS 5672 (Oct. 23, 2006).

Defendant's contention that the presence of 232 "inaudible" sections of the transcripts rendered the criminal proceedings incapable of review was rejected because, while defendant submitted a motion seeking to correct the record pursuant to Ohio R. App. P. 9(E), defendant failed to demonstrate that effective review was precluded by any of the inaudible portions of the record. Village of Kirtland Hills v. Deir, — Ohio App. 3d —, 2006 Ohio 6536, — N.E. 2d —, 2006 Ohio App. LEXIS 6458 (Dec. 8, 2006).

Transcript requirements

Requirements in Ohio R. App. P. 9 and Ohio R. Crim. P. 22 of a complete transcript of a criminal trial does not mean that the transcript must be perfect for appellate review, so an adequate transcript does not mean a perfect transcript. Ohio v. Liddy, — Ohio App. 3d —, 2007 Ohio 5225, — N.E. 2d —, 2007 Ohio App. LEXIS 4597 (Sept. 28, 2007).

When a court reporter was unable to certify that a transcript of a damages hearing was correct, pursuant to Ohio R. App. P. 9(B), the transcript was stricken because the Rule required that the transcript be so certified, and, as a result, the correctness of the damages hearing was presumed. Flatt v. Atwood, — Ohio App. 3d —, 2007 Ohio 5387, — N.E. 2d —, 2007 Ohio App. LEXIS 4735 (Oct. 9, 2007).

Correspondence attached to the affidavit reveals that what the client failed to obtain from the court reporter were portions of the trial transcript containing jokes that the judge had allegedly told during trial. Even if the jokes were told, however, the client's inability to obtain a transcript excerpt containing them did not constitute grounds for reversal, particularly where he failed to utilize Ohio R. App. P. 9(C), which provided a remedy when a transcript was unavailable. Nunn v. Cornyn, — Ohio App. 3d —, 2007 Ohio 5894, — N.E. 2d —, 2007 Ohio App. LEXIS 5185 (Nov. 5, 2007).

Former husband who sought an evidentiary hearing to enforce a settlement agreement which modified the parties' shared parenting plan regarding their child, and which the former wife refused to sign due to a dispute that arose regarding child support calculations, was excused from the requirement of filing a transcript of the hearing or alternatively, from including a statement pursuant to Ohio R. App. P. 9(C) upon his appeal of the trial court's entry of a modified plan, as there was no evidence that a hearing was ever held on the matter. Michelle M. S. v. Eduardo H. T., — Ohio App. 3d —, 2006 Ohio 2119, — N.E. 2d —, 2006 Ohio App. LEXIS 1956 (Apr. 28, 2006).

Videotape

When a customer appealing a judgment in favor of a contractor presented the appellate court with a videotape of the trial court's proceedings but did not print or type those parts of this video transcript necessary for the appellate court to address the questions presented, certify their accuracy, and append them to her brief, her failure to comply with this mandatory provision of Ohio R. App. P. 9(A) was a failure to demonstrate claimed error, and the lack of a proper transcript allowed the appellate court to presume that the trial court's proceedings were valid and to affirm its judgment. Ruckman v. Hovatter, — Ohio App. 3d —, 2007 Ohio 920, — N.E. 2d —, 2007 Ohio App. LEXIS 879 (Mar. 2, 2007).

Defendant's claim on appeal that defendant's sentence was contrary to law could not be reviewed because defendant did not provide a proper transcript as defendant only provided a videotape of defendant's sentencing hearing and did not provide a written transcript of those proceedings, so defendant did not meet defendant's burden to provide a transcript for appellate review. State v. Scott, — Ohio App. 3d —, 2007 Ohio 3815, — N.E. 2d —, 2007 Ohio App. LEXIS 3466 (July 27, 2007).

— Written transcript

When defendant, who appealed his municipal court convictions, submitted a videotape of his trial, but did not append printed or typewritten portions of the videotape regarding his assignments of error to his initial brief, as required by Ohio R. App. P. 9(A), he did not comply with the mandates of Ohio R. App. P. 9, and the appellate court had to presume the regularity of his trial and affirm his convictions. State v. Kearns, — Ohio App. 3d —, 2006 Ohio 5811, — N.E. 2d —, 2006 Ohio App. LEXIS 5781 (Nov. 6, 2006).

Videotape transcript

AppR 9(A) provides that when the transcript of proceedings is in the videotape medium, counsel shall type or print those portions of the transcript necessary for the court to determine the questions presented, certify their accuracy, and append such copy of the portions of the transcript to their briefs. Without a transcript, the appellate court must presume the regularity of the trial court's proceedings: Shields v. City of Englewood, 172 Ohio App. 3d 620, 2007 Ohio 3165, 876 N.E.2d 972, 2007 Ohio App. LEXIS 2905 (2007).

RULE 10. Transmission of the record

(A) **Time for transmission; duty of appellant.** The record on appeal, including the transcript and exhibits necessary for the determination of the appeal, shall be transmitted to the clerk of the court of appeals when the record is complete for the purposes of appeal, or when forty days, which is reduced to twenty days for an accelerated calendar case, have elapsed after the filing of the notice of appeal and no order extending time has been granted under subdivision (C). After filing the notice of appeal the appellant shall comply with the provisions of Rule 9(B) and shall take any other action necessary to enable the clerk to assemble and transmit the record. If more than one appeal is taken, each appellant shall comply with the provisions of Rule 9(B) and this subdivision, and a single record shall be transmitted when forty days have elapsed after the filing of the final notice of appeal.

(B) **Duty of clerk to transmit the record.** The clerk of the trial court shall prepare the certified copy of the docket and journal entries, assemble the original papers, (or in the instance of an agreed statement of the case pursuant to Rule 9(D), the agreed statement of the case), and transmit the record upon appeal to the clerk of the court of appeals within the time stated in subdivision (A). The clerk of the trial court shall number the documents comprising the record and shall transmit with the record a list of the documents

correspondingly numbered and identified with reasonable definiteness. Documents of unusual bulk or weight and physical exhibits other than documents shall not be transmitted by the clerk unless he is directed to do so by a party or by the clerk of the court of appeals. A party must make advance arrangements with the clerks for the transportation and receipt of exhibits of unusual bulk or weight.

Transmission of the record is effected when the clerk of the trial court mails or otherwise forwards the record to the clerk of the court of appeals. The clerk of the trial court shall indicate, by endorsement on the face of the record or otherwise, the date upon which it is transmitted to the court of appeals and shall note the transmission on the appearance docket.

The record shall be deemed to be complete for the purposes of appeal under the following circumstances:

(1) When the transcript of proceedings is filed with the clerk of the trial court.

(2) When a statement of the evidence or proceedings, pursuant to Rule 9(C), is settled and approved by the trial court, and filed with the clerk of the trial court.

(3) When an agreed statement in lieu of the record, pursuant to Rule 9(D), is approved by the trial court, and filed with the clerk of the trial court.

(4) Where appellant, pursuant to Rule 9(B), designates that no part of the transcript of proceedings is to be included in the record or that no transcript is necessary for appeal, after the expiration of ten days following service of such designation upon appellee, unless appellee has within such time filed a designation of additional parts of the transcript to be included in the record.

(5) When forty days have elapsed after filing of the last notice of appeal, and there is no extension of time for transmission of the record.

(6) When twenty days have elapsed after filing of the last notice of appeal, in an accelerated calendar case and there is no extension of time for transmission of the record.

(7) Where the appellant fails to file either the docketing statement or the statement required by AppR 9(B), ten days after filing the notice of appeal.

(C) **Extension of time for transmission of the record; reduction of time.** Except as may be provided by local rule adopted by the court of appeals pursuant to Rule 30, the trial court for cause shown set forth in the order may extend the time for transmitting the record. The clerk shall certify the order of extension to the court of appeals. A request for extension to the trial court and a ruling by the trial court must be made within the time originally prescribed or within an extension previously granted. If the trial court is without authority to grant the relief sought, by operation of this rule or local rule, or has denied a request therefore, the court of appeals may on motion for cause shown extend the time for transmitting the record or may permit the record to be transmitted and filed after the expiration of the time allowed or fixed. If a request for an extension of time for transmitting the record has been previously denied, the motion shall set forth the denial and shall state the reasons therefore, if any were given. The court of appeals may require the record to be transmitted and the appeal to be docketed at any time within the time otherwise fixed or allowed therefore.

(D) **Retention of the record in the trial court by order of the court.** If the record or any part thereof is required in the trial court for use there pending the appeal, the trial court may make an order to that effect, and the clerk of the trial court shall retain the record or parts thereof subject to the request of the court of appeals, and shall transmit a copy of the order and of the docket and journal entries together with such parts of the original record as the trial court shall allow and copies of such parts as the parties may designate.

(E) **Stipulation of parties that parts of the record be retained in the trial court.** The parties may agree by written stipulation filed in the trial court that designated parts of the record shall be retained in the trial court unless thereafter the court of appeals shall order or any party shall request their transmittal. The parts thus designated shall nevertheless be a part of the record on appeal for all purposes.

(F) **Record for preliminary hearing in the court of appeals.** If prior to the time the record is transmitted a party desires to make in the court of appeals a motion for dismissal, for release, for a stay pending appeal, for additional security on the bond on appeal or on a supersedeas bond, or for any intermediate order, the clerk of the trial court at the request of any party shall transmit to the court of appeals such parts of the original record as any party shall designate.

(G) **Transmission of the record when leave to appeal obtained.** In all cases where leave to appeal must first be obtained all time limits for the preparation and transmission of the record hereinbefore set forth shall run from the filing of the journal entry of the court of appeals granting such leave rather than from the filing of the notice of appeal.

History: Amended, eff 7-1-72; 7-1-73; 7-1-75; 7-1-76; 7-1-77; 7-1-82.

NOTES TO DECISIONS

Analysis

Absence of transcript
Record on appeal
Transcript

Absence of transcript

Dismissal of an appeal under Ohio R. App. P. 11(C) by property owners with respect to various rulings made by a trial court regarding a dispute with a pole barn user that was situated on the owners' property was denied, although the owners had ordered a transcript pursuant to Ohio R. App. P. 9(B) but they had not requested that it be prepared for inclusion in the record that was transmitted by the clerk of court pursuant to Ohio R. App. P. 10(B). The transcript was only applicable to one of four assignments of error, and that assignment would be evaluated to determine the necessity of the transcript with respect to the review thereof. Camp-Out, Inc. v. Adkins, — Ohio App. 3d —, 2007 Ohio 447, — N.E. 2d —, 2007 Ohio App. LEXIS 398 (Jan. 29, 2007).

Since a company failed to file a transcript or an appropriate substitute, as required by Ohio R. App. P. 10(A) and Ohio R. App. P. 9(C), in its appeal from a trial court's decision granting a preliminary injunction to a customer, the court could not determine whether the customer's testimony helped to demonstrate that he was entitled to injunctive relief. Davis v. Domestic Linen Supply Co., — Ohio App. 3d —, 2007 Ohio 3498, — N.E. 2d —, 2007 Ohio App. LEXIS 3219 (June 28, 2007).

As a property owner failed to provide a transcript excerpt pursuant to her obligation under Ohio R. App. P. 9(B) and 10(A) to support her claim that the trial court had deferred her counsel's re-direct examination, and instead, the trial court's denial of her new trial motion indicated that it had denied her re-direct examination, the court had nothing to review on appeal and accordingly, it presumed the regularity of the trial court proceedings. Jarupan v. Hanna, 173 Ohio App. 3d 284, 2007 Ohio 5081, 878 N.E.2d 66, 2007 Ohio App. LEXIS 4498 (2007).

Where the union raised arguments concerning findings and factors that it alleged that the trial court failed to consider in modifying preliminary injunctions relating to a strike, the appellate court had to presume the regularity of the trial court's proceedings due to the union's failure to file an appellate transcript as required by Ohio R. App. P. 10(A) or a transcript substitute pursuant to Ohio R. App. P. 9(C). Ormet Aluminum Mill Prods. Corp. v. USW, — Ohio App. 3d —, 2006 Ohio 3782, — N.E. 2d —, 2006 Ohio App. LEXIS 3736 (July 20, 2006).

Record on appeal

Where it was unclear exactly which portions of a builder's deposition were read into the trial court record in an action between the general contractor/retailer of a manufactured home and the purchasers thereof, the contractor failed in its burden of providing a record on appeal pursuant to Ohio R. App. P. 9(B) and 10(A), such that the appellate court had to presume the regularity of the trial court proceedings with respect to the contractor's assignment of error on appeal regarding admission of the deposition testimony. Drenning v. Blue Ribbon Homes, — Ohio App. 3d —, 2007 Ohio 1323, — N.E. 2d —, 2007 Ohio App. LEXIS 1230 (Mar. 23, 2007).

Where the record on appeal was unclear due to defendant's failure to provide a bond or a clerk's office form, as required by Ohio R. App. P. 9(B) and 10(A), it was unclear exactly who posted the bond that was used to pay fines assessed against defendant, as the appellate court's review was limited to the record presented before it pursuant to Ohio R. App. P. 9 and 12(A)(1)(b). The appellate court could not review defendant's assignment of error regarding a taking of his property with respect to the bail money, as the regularity of the trial court proceedings was presumed. State v. Ahmed, — Ohio App. 3d —, 2007 Ohio 2639, — N.E. 2d —, 2007 Ohio App. LEXIS 2478 (May 31, 2007).

When defendant appealed his aggravated robbery and kidnapping sentences, he did not provide the appellate court with the information the trial court relied on in making its sentencing determination, so he did not meet his duty, under Ohio R. App. P. 10(A) and Ohio Ninth Dist. Ct. App. R. 5(A) to provide the appellate court with all parts of the record necessary to his appeal because he did not provide the victim impact statement or a psychological report the trial court said it relied on, so regularity in the trial court's proceedings had to be presumed. State v. Sawyer, — Ohio App. 3d —, 2006 Ohio 4308, — N.E. 2d —, 2006 Ohio App. LEXIS 4244 (Aug. 21, 2006).

Defendant filed an appeal from the wrong trial court judgment and, thus, his appeal challenging the trial court's denial of his motion to suppress filed in a second, unrelated case was dismissed. Defendant's notice of appeal did not refer to the second case, the record transmitted was the record in first case, and the docketing statement did not reference suppression issue; thus, defendant's appeal failed to comply with Ohio R. App. P. 3(D), Ohio R. App. P. 9(B), and Ohio R.

App. P. 10(A). State v. Bleehash, — Ohio App. 3d —, 2006 Ohio 4580, — N.E. 2d —, 2006 Ohio App. LEXIS 4526 (Aug. 31, 2006).

Transcript

Defendant's counsel was not ineffective in violation of U.S. Const. amend. VI and Ohio Const. art. I, § 10 by failing to point out inconsistencies in the victim's testimony between the preliminary hearing and the trial, as the inconsistencies were minor and would not have changed the outcome of the proceeding; further, the transcript of the preliminary hearing was not properly before the court for revview, as defendant failed to transmit that part of the record within 40 days of the filing of his notice of appeal pursuant to Ohio R. App. P. 10(A). State v. Adams, — Ohio App. 3d —, 2007 Ohio 2583, — N.E. 2d —, 2007 Ohio App. LEXIS 2430 (May 29, 2007).

RULE 11.   Docketing the appeal; filing of the record

(A) **Docketing the appeal.** Upon receiving a copy of the notice of appeal, as provided in App. R. 3(D) and App. R. 5, the clerk of the court of appeals shall enter the appeal upon the docket. An appeal shall be docketed under the title given to the action in the trial court, with the appellant identified as such, but if the title does not contain the name of the appellant, the appellant's name, identified as appellant, shall be added parenthetically to the title.

(B) **Filing of the record.** Upon receipt of the record, the clerk shall file the record, and shall immediately give notice to all parties of the date on which the record was filed. When a trial court is exercising concurrent jurisdiction to review a judgment of conviction pursuant to a petition for post-conviction relief, the clerk shall either make a duplicate record and send it to the clerk of the trial court or arrange for each court to have access to the original record.

(C) **Dismissal for failure of appellant to cause timely transmission of record.** If the appellant fails to cause timely transmission of the record, any appellee may file a motion in the court of appeals to dismiss the appeal. The motion shall be supported by a certificate of the clerk of the trial court showing the date and substance of the judgment or order from which the appeal was taken, the date on which the notice of appeal was filed, the expiration date of any order extending the time for transmitting the record, and by proof of service. The appellant may respond within ten days of such service.

(D) **Leave to appeal.** In all cases where leave to appeal must first be obtained the docketing of the appeal by the clerk of the court of appeals upon receiving a copy of the notice of appeal filed in the trial court shall be deemed conditional and subject to such leave being granted.

History: Amended, eff 7-1-75; 7-1-97.

NOTES TO DECISIONS

ANALYSIS

Burden to furnish record
Dismissal

Burden to furnish record

Property purchaser who appealed a foreclosure judgment in consolidated trial court cases only filed a single notice of appeal, rather than one in each case pursuant to Ohio Third

Dist. Ct. App. R. 6(A), and accordingly, only documents from that one case were included in the record, which was inadequate under App. R. 9(A) and 11(C) and required dismissal of the appeal under Ohio Third Dist. Ct. App. R. 15. Lasalle Nat'l Bank v. Cline, — Ohio App. 3d —, 2006 Ohio 5152, — N.E. 2d —, 2006 Ohio App. LEXIS 5104 (Oct. 2, 2006).

Dismissal

Dismissal of an appeal under Ohio R. App. P. 11(C) by property owners with respect to various rulings made by a trial court regarding a dispute with a pole barn user that was situated on the owners' property was denied, although the owners had ordered a transcript pursuant to Ohio R. App. P. 9(B) but they had not requested that it be prepared for inclusion in the record that was transmitted by the clerk of court pursuant to Ohio R. App. P. 10(B). The transcript was only applicable to one of four assignments of error, and that assignment would be evaluated to determine the necessity of the transcript with respect to the review thereof. Camp-Out, Inc. v. Adkins, — Ohio App. 3d —, 2007 Ohio 447, — N.E. 2d —, 2007 Ohio App. LEXIS 398 (Jan. 29, 2007).

RULE 11.1.   Accelerated calendar

(A) **Applicability.** If a court of appeals has adopted an accelerated calendar by local rule, cases designated by its rule shall be placed on an accelerated calendar. The Ohio Rules of Appellate Procedure shall apply with the modifications or exceptions set forth in this rule.

The accelerated calendar is designated to provide a means to eliminate delay and unnecessary expense in effecting a just decision on appeal by the recognition that some cases do not require as extensive or time consuming procedure as others.

(B) **Record.** The record on appeal, including the transcripts and the exhibits necessary for the determination of the appeal, shall be transmitted to the clerk of the court of appeals as provided by AppR 10.

(C) **Briefs.** Briefs shall be in the form specified by AppR 16. Appellant shall serve and file his brief within fifteen days after the date on which the record is filed. The appellee shall serve and file his brief within fifteen days after service of the brief of the appellant. Reply briefs shall not be filed unless ordered by the court.

(D) **Oral argument.** Oral argument will apply as provided by AppR 21. If oral argument is waived, the case will be submitted to the court for disposition upon filing of appellee's brief.

(E) **Determination and judgment on appeal.** The appeal will be determined as provided by AppR 11.1. It shall be sufficient compliance with AppR 12(A) for the statement of the reason for the court's decision as to each error to be in brief and conclusionary form.

The decision may be by judgment entry in which case it will not be published in any form. (See Form 3, Appendix of Forms.)

History: Effective, 7-1-82.

NOTES TO DECISIONS

ANALYSIS

Applicability

Applicability

Pursuant to an appeal on the accelerated calendar, the court noted that it would render a decision in compliance with Ohio

R. App. P. 11.1(E), which allowed that a statement of the reason for the court's decision on appeal as to each error raised could be in brief and conclusionary form. Parrot v. A.R.E., Inc., — Ohio App. 3d —, 2006 Ohio 4527, — N.E. 2d —, 2006 Ohio App. LEXIS 4458 (Aug. 28, 2006).

RULE 11.2. Expedited Appeals

(A) **Applicability.** Appeals in actions described in this rule shall be expedited and given calendar priority over all other cases, including criminal and administrative appeals. The Ohio Rules of Appellate Procedure shall apply with the modifications or exceptions set forth in this rule.

(B) **Abortion-related appeals from juvenile courts.**

(1) **Applicability.** App. R. 11.2(B) shall govern appeals pursuant to sections 2151.85, 2505.073, and 2919.121 of the Revised Code.

(2) **General rule of expedition.** If an appellant files her notice of appeal on the same day as the dismissal of her complaint or petition by the juvenile court, the entire court process, including the juvenile court hearing, appeal, and decision, shall be completed in sixteen calendar days from the time the original complaint or petition was filed.

(3) **Processing appeal.**

(a) Immediately after the notice of appeal has been filed by the appellant, the clerk of the juvenile court shall notify the court of appeals. Within four days after the notice of appeal is filed in juvenile court, the clerk of the juvenile court shall deliver a copy of the notice of appeal and the record, except page two of the complaint or petition, to the clerk of the court of appeals who immediately shall place the appeal on the docket of the court of appeals.

(b) Record of all testimony and other oral proceedings in actions pursuant to sections 2151.85 or 2919.121 of the Revised Code may be made by audio recording. If the testimony is on audio tape and a transcript cannot be prepared timely, the court of appeals shall accept the audio tape as the transcript in this case without prior transcription. The juvenile court shall ensure that the court of appeals has the necessary equipment to listen to the audio tape.

(c) The appellant under division (B) of this rule shall file her brief within four days after the appeal is docketed. Unless waived, the oral argument shall be within five days after docketing. Oral arguments must be closed to the public and exclude all persons except the appellant, her attorney, her guardian *ad litem*, and essential court personnel.

(d) Under division (B) of this rule, "days" means calendar days and includes any intervening Saturday, Sunday, or legal holiday. To provide full effect to the expedition provision of the statute, if the last day on which a judgment is required to be entered falls on a Saturday, Sunday, or legal holiday, the computation of days shall not be extended and judgment shall be made either on the last business day before the Saturday, Sunday, or legal holiday, or on the Saturday, Sunday, or legal holiday.

(4) **Confidentiality.** All proceedings in appeals governed by App. R. 11.2(B) shall be conducted in a manner that will preserve the anonymity of the appellant. Except as set forth in App. R. 11.2(B)(7), all papers and records that pertain to the appeal shall be kept confidential.

(5) **Judgment entry.** The court shall enter judgment immediately after conclusion of oral argument or, if oral argument is waived, within five days after the appeal is docketed.

(6) **Release of records.** The public is entitled to secure all of the following from the records pertaining to appeals governed by App. R. 11.2(B):

(a) The docket number;

(b) The name of the judge;

(c) The judgment entry and, if appropriate, a properly redacted opinion.

Opinions shall set forth the reasoning in support of the decision in a way that does not directly or indirectly compromise the anonymity of the appellant. Opinions written in compliance with this requirement shall be considered public records available upon request. If, in the judgment of the court, it is impossible to release an opinion without compromising the anonymity of the appellant, the entry that journalizes the outcome of the case shall include a specific finding that no opinion can be written without disclosing the identity of the appellant. Such finding shall be a matter of public record. It is the obligation of the court to remove any and all information in its opinion that would directly or indirectly disclose the identity of the appellant.

(7) **Notice and hearing before release of opinion.** After an opinion is written and before it is available for release to the public, the appellant must be notified and be given the option to appear and argue at a hearing if she believes the opinion may disclose her identity. Notice may be provided by including the following language in the opinion:

If appellant believes that this opinion may disclose her identity, appellant has the right to appear and argue at a hearing before this court. Appellant may perfect this right to a hearing by filing a motion for a hearing within fourteen days of the date of this opinion.

The clerk is instructed that this opinion is not to be made available for release until either of the following:

(a) Twenty-one days have passed since the date of the opinion and appellant has not filed a motion;

(b) If appellant has filed a motion, after this court has ruled on the motion.

Notice shall be provided by mailing a copy of the opinion to the attorney for the appellant or, if she is not represented, to the address provided by appellant for receipt of notice.

(8) **Form 25-A.** Upon request of the appellant or her attorney, the clerk shall verify on Form 25-A, as provided in the Rules of Superintendence, the date the appeal was docketed and whether a judgment has been entered within five days of that date. The completed form shall include the case number from the juvenile court and the court of appeals, and shall be filed and included as part of the record. A date-stamped copy shall be provided to the appellant or her attorney.

(C) **Adoption and parental rights appeals.**

(1) **Applicability.** Appeals from orders granting or denying adoption of a minor child or from orders granting or denying termination of parental rights shall be given priority over all cases except those governed by App. R. 11.2(B).

(2) **Record.** Preparation of the record, including the transcripts and exhibits necessary for determination of the appeal, shall be given priority over the preparation and transmission of the records in all cases other than those governed by App. R. 11.2(B).

(3) **Briefs.** Extensions of time for filing briefs shall not be granted except in the most unusual circumstances and only for the most compelling reasons in the interest of justice.

(4) **Oral argument.** After briefs have been filed, the case shall be considered submitted for immediate decision unless oral argument is requested or ordered. Any oral argument shall be heard within thirty days after the briefs have been filed.

(5) **Entry of judgment.** The court shall enter judgment within thirty days of submission of the briefs, or of the oral argument, whichever is later, unless compelling reasons in the interest of justice require a longer time.

(D) **Dependent, abused, neglected, unruly, or delinquent child appeals.** Appeals concerning a dependent, abused, neglected, unruly, or delinquent child shall be expedited and given calendar priority over all cases other than those governed by App. R. 11.2(B) and (C).

History: Effective 7-1-00; 7-1-01.

RULE 12. Determination and judgment on appeal

(A) **Determination.**

(1) On an undismissed appeal from a trial court, a court of appeals shall do all of the following:

(a) Review and affirm, modify, or reverse the judgment or final order appealed;

(b) Determine the appeal on its merits on the assignments of error set forth in the briefs under App.R. 16, the record on appeal under App.R. 9, and, unless waived, the oral argument under App.R. 21;

(c) Unless an assignment of error is made moot by a ruling on another assignment of error, decide each assignment of error and give reasons in writing for its decision.

(2) The court may disregard an assignment of error presented for review if the party raising it fails to identify in the record the error on which the assignment of error is based or fails to argue the assignment separately in the brief, as required under App.R. 16(A).

(B) **Judgment as a matter of law.** When the court of appeals determines that the trial court committed no error prejudicial to the appellant in any of the particulars assigned and argued in appellant's brief and that the appellee is entitled to have the judgment or final order of the trial court affirmed as a matter of law, the court of appeals shall enter judgment accordingly. When the court of appeals determines that the trial court committed error prejudicial to the appellant and

that the appellant is entitled to have judgment or final order rendered in his favor as a matter of law, the court of appeals shall reverse the judgment or final order of the trial court and render the judgment or final order that the trial court should have rendered, or remand the cause to the court with instructions to render such judgment or final order. In all other cases where the court of appeals determines that the judgment or final order of the trial court should be modified as a matter of law it shall enter its judgment accordingly.

(C) **Judgment in civil action or proceeding when sole prejudicial error found is that judgment of trial court is against the manifest weight of the evidence.** In any civil action or proceeding which was tried to the trial court without the intervention of a jury, and when upon appeal a majority of the judges hearing the appeal find that the judgment or final order rendered by the trial court is against the manifest weight of the evidence and do not find any other prejudicial error of the trial court in any of the particulars assigned and argued in the appellant's brief, and do not find that the appellee is entitled to judgment or final order as a matter of law, the court of appeals shall reverse the judgment or final order of the trial court and either weigh the evidence in the record and render the judgment or final order that the trial court should have rendered on that evidence or remand the case to the trial court for further proceedings; provided further that a judgment shall be reversed only once on the manifest weight of the evidence.

(D) **All other cases.** In all other cases where the court of appeals finds error prejudicial to the appellant, the judgment or final order of the trial court shall be reversed and the cause shall be remanded to the trial court for further proceedings.

History: Amended, eff 7-1-73; 7-1-92.

NOTES TO DECISIONS

ANALYSIS

Absence of record
Absence of transcript
Appeal
Appellant required to set forth argument
Assignment of error
— Brief requirements
— Lack of briefing
Briefs
Consideration of errors
Consideration of issues
Court's duty to decide assignments
Dispositive assignments of error
Failure to cite to authority
Failure to cite to record
Failure to make argument
Failure to support
Final judgment
Judgment
Jurisdiction
Limited remand
Modification
Moot issues
Power to modify judgment
Power to render judgment
Power to reverse judgment

Prejudicial error not found
Record on appeal
Remand to trial court
Reversal of judgment
Right to disregard errors
— Discretionary right
Sentencing
Weighing of evidence

Absence of record

Because tenants failed to include a transcript or agreed statement of the relevant record through which they might have demonstrated their alleged errors, an appellate court had nothing to pass upon and thus, had no choice but to presume the validity of the trial court's conclusions which found against the tenants in their counterclaim against the owner of a rental unit. Epling Estates v. Cunningham, — Ohio App. 3d —, 2006 Ohio 1457, — N.E. 2d —, 2006 Ohio App. LEXIS 1331 (Mar. 24, 2006).

Absence of transcript

When a husband objecting to a magistrate's decision did not file a transcript of the proceedings before the magistrate in the trial court, as required by Ohio R. Civ. P. 53(D)(3)(iii), and the trial court adopted the magistrate's decision, an appellate court could not consider a transcript of the magistrate's proceedings because the appellate court's review had to be based on the record that was before the trial court, under Ohio R. App. P. 12(A)(1)(b). Hipple v. Hipple, — Ohio App. 3d —, 2007 Ohio 4524, — N.E. 2d —, 2007 Ohio App. LEXIS 4045 (Aug. 29, 2007).

State agency employee failed in her duty under Ohio R. App. P. 16 when she did not set forth assignments of error for purposes of her challenge on appeal to a judgment in favor of a state agency in her disability discrimination action. She also failed to provide a transcript of the trial court proceedings in the record, such that the appellate court was required to presume the regularity of the trial court proceedings and affirm the trial court decision pursuant to Ohio R. App. P. 12. Lee v. Ohio Dep't of Jobs & Family Servs., — Ohio App. 3d —, — N.E. 2d —, 2006 Ohio App. LEXIS 6504 (Dec. 14, 2006).

Appeal

While defendant appealed her consecutive sentences, she did not appeal the non-minimum prison terms imposed for the three felonies; an appellate court was allowed only to modify or vacate a sentence that was appealed by a defendant and was not allowed to modify or vacate the entire multiple-offense sentence based upon an appealed error in the sentence for a single offense. State v. Johnson, — Ohio App. 3d —, 2006 Ohio 1896, — N.E. 2d —, 2006 Ohio App. LEXIS 1746 (Apr. 17, 2006).

Appellant required to set forth argument

Where a next of kin to an incompetent and a guardian applicant appealed a probate court's rejection of part of a magistrate's decision that found the applicant was not a suitable appointee, but the appeal did not separately argue the issue of the alleged error and there were no citations to the authorities, statutes, and parts of the record that were relied upon, pursuant to Ohio R. App. P. 16(A)(7) and 12(A)(2) the court declined to review the asserted error. In re Guardianship of Blair, — Ohio App. 3d —, — N.E. 2d —, 2007 Ohio 3335, 2007 Ohio App. LEXIS 3124 (June 11, 2007).

Since a mother failed to specifically argue how counsel's performance in a permanent custody proceeding in failing to request the alternative disposition of a planned permanent living arrangement and in failing to request independent counsel for the mother's children fell below an objective standard of reasonableness and also failed to establish that the result would have been different but for the alleged deficiencies of counsel, the court, pursuant to Ohio R. App. P. 16(A)(7) and Ohio R. App. P. 12(A)(2), did not need to further address the mother's assertion that she was deprived of the effective assistance of counsel in this respect. In re A.T., — Ohio App. 3d —, 2006 Ohio 3919, — N.E. 2d —, 2006 Ohio App. LEXIS 3883 (Aug. 2, 2006).

Assignment of error

Although defendant combined the argument for two of his assignments of error on appeal, which was improper, the appellate court chose to review the assignments in the interests of justice although it had the option of disregarding them due to the failure to separately argue the issues pursuant to Ohio R. App. P. 12(A)(2). State v. Marcinko, — Ohio App. 3d —, 2007 Ohio 1166, — N.E. 2d —, 2007 Ohio App. LEXIS 1113 (Mar. 2, 2007).

Since appellant failed to provide the appellate court with a meaningful argument in support of his contention that genuine issues of fact remained, thereby precluding summary judgment, appellant failed to satisfy his burden on appeal under Ohio R. App. P. 16(A)(7) and Ohio 9th Dist. Ct. App. R. 7(B)(7). Thus, pursuant to Ohio R. App. P. 12(A)(2) and Ohio 9th Dist. Ct. App. R. 7(F), the court disregarded appellant's argument. Marino v. Oriana House, Inc., — Ohio App. 3d —, 2007 Ohio 1823, — N.E. 2d —, 2007 Ohio App. LEXIS 1664 (Apr. 18, 2007).

As the six assignments of error in a brief by children of judgment debtors were not separately argued, they did not comply with the requirement of Ohio R. App. P. 16(A) and the court could have chosen to disregard its review of them pursuant to Ohio R. App. P. 12(A)(2). The court could also have chosen to review the assignments of error on the merits in the interest of justice, which it did. Tube City, Inc. v. Halishak, — Ohio App. 3d —, 2007 Ohio 2118, — N.E. 2d —, 2007 Ohio App. LEXIS 1976 (May 3, 2007).

Although township trustees who appealed a trial court's grant of summary judgment against them failed to identify the relevant portions of the record from which their appealed errors were based, as required by Ohio R. App. P. 12(A)(2) and Ohio Ninth Dist. Ct. App. R. 7(F), and they also did not support their argument with citations to legal authority and facts in the record as required by Ohio R. App. P. 16(A)(7) and Ohio Ninth Dist. Ct. App. R. 7(B)(7), the court chose to review the issues on the merits rather than disregard them, as it had a right to do in that situation. Brunswick Hills Twp. v. City of Cleveland, — Ohio App. 3d —, 2007 Ohio 2560, — N.E. 2d —, 2007 Ohio App. LEXIS 2382 (May 29, 2007).

Pursuant to Ohio R. App. P. 12(A)(2) and 16(A)(7), the court declined to address defendant's cruel and unusual punishment argument on appeal, as he failed to address it in his brief. State v. Sutton, — Ohio App. 3d —, 2007 Ohio 3792, — N.E. 2d —, 2007 Ohio App. LEXIS 3455 (July 26, 2007).

Since appellant presented only one argument in support of its two assignments of error, in contravention of Ohio R. App. P. 16(A)(7), the appellate court would have been in its discretion under Ohio R. App. P. 12(A)(2) simply to disregard appellant's assignments of error and summarily affirm the trial court; however, in the interest of justice, the court chose to review appellant's arguments. Keffer v. Cent. Mut. Ins. Co., — Ohio App. 3d —, 2007 Ohio 3984, — N.E. 2d —, 2007 Ohio App. LEXIS 3587 (May 17, 2007).

Pursuant to Ohio R. App. P. 12(A)(2), the court rejected a father's assignment of error which was contained in the table of contents of his merit brief but which was neither recited nor argued in the body of his merit brief. In re R.N.L.O., — Ohio App. 3d —, 2007 Ohio 4215, — N.E. 2d —, 2007 Ohio App. LEXIS 3817 (Aug. 20, 2007).

Court disregarded a wife's assignments of error presented in her appeal from trial court's judgment and presumed the validity of the proceedings below because the wife failed to include page references to the places in the record where the errors involved in the assignments occurred, as required by Ohio R. App. P. 16(A)(3); she did not argue the assignments of error separately in her brief; and she did not provide transcripts of the hearings cited in her reply brief, as required by Ohio R. App. P. 9. Thus, the court disregarded the wife's assignments of error, as it was permitted to do under Ohio R. App. P. 12(A)(2) and presumed the validity of the trial court's proceedings. Dunina v. Stemple, — Ohio App. 3d —, 2007 Ohio 4719, — N.E. 2d —, 2007 Ohio App. LEXIS 4228 (Sept. 14, 2007).

Defendant's argument on appeal that State v. Foster effectively raised the maximum penalty from the maximum authorized by the facts established by a plea of guilty or a jury verdict to the statutory maximum, in violation of ex post facto principles, was not specifically raised in an assignment of error set forth in the briefs, as required by Ohio R. App. P. 12(A)(1)(b) and Ohio R. App. P. 16. Since the trial court had yet to resentence defendant, any argument as to the terms or propriety of his new sentence was premature. State v. White, — Ohio App. 3d —, 2006 Ohio 4226, — N.E. 2d —, 2006 Ohio App. LEXIS 4149 (Aug. 15, 2006).

While an insurer set forth two assignments of error at the commencement of its brief, it failed to argue them separately, as required by Ohio R. App. P. 16(A); thus, the court treated the insurer's argument as one and indivisible, pursuant to Ohio R. App. P. 12(A)(2). Nationwide Mut. Ins. Co. v. Godwin, — Ohio App. 3d —, 2006 Ohio 4167, — N.E. 2d —, 2006 Ohio App. LEXIS 4114 (Aug. 11, 2006).

While an appellate court could, under Ohio R. App. P. 12(A)(2), disregard an assignment of error if the party raising it did not identify in the record the error on which the assignment was based or did not argue the assignment separately in the brief, the Rule did not require the appellate court to disregard the assignment, as fairness and justice were best served when a court disposed of a case on the merits. Berthelot v. Berthelot, — Ohio App. 3d —, 2006 Ohio 1317, — N.E. 2d —, 2006 Ohio App. LEXIS 1194 (Mar. 22, 2006).

Where a credit card holder appealed a grant of summary judgment to the credit card issuer in its breach of contract action against him, but the holder's "assignments of error" were not separately argued in his brief as required by Ohio R. App. P. 12(A)(2) and 16(A)(7), the appellate court disregarded them. Discover Fin. Servs. v. Belmont, — Ohio App. 3d —, 2006 Ohio 1539, — N.E. 2d —, 2006 Ohio App. LEXIS 1418 (Mar. 30, 2006).

Since plaintiff failed to file a copy of the transcript to support his assignments of error, all of which asserted propositions based on evidence introduced at trial, the court, pursuant to Ohio R. App. P. 9(B), had to presume regularity in the proceedings on any finding of fact made by the trial court; thus, plaintiff was unable to demonstrate the claimed errors. Additionally, plaintiff had failed to affirmatively establish error on appeal because, in each of his assignments of error, he asserted arguments unsupported by any legal authority or any specific portion of the record, as required by Ohio R. App. P. 16(A), and thus, pursuant to Ohio R. App. P. 12(A)(2), the court overruled the assignments of error. Calabrese v. Zmijewski, — Ohio App. 3d —, 2006 Ohio 2322, — N.E. 2d —, 2006 Ohio App. LEXIS 2179 (May 11, 2006).

Although defendant's appellate brief advanced a single, joint argument for multiple assignments of error, which was not permitted under Ohio R. App. P. 16(A)(7) and could have led to the court's disregard of those assignments pursuant to Ohio R. App. P. 12(A)(2), the court chose to review them in the interests of justice. State v. Bennett, — Ohio App. 3d —, 2006 Ohio 2757, — N.E. 2d —, 2006 Ohio App. LEXIS 2592 (May 22, 2006).

In an appeal from a grant of summary judgment for a former employer in an employee's action, alleging claims of wrongful discharge and retaliatory discharge, the employee's failure to provide any arguments regarding the wrongful discharge claim resulted in a lack of review on that issue pursuant to Ohio R. App. P. 12(A)(2) and 16(A)(7). Prox v. Cleveland Steel Container Corp., — Ohio App. 3d —, 2006 Ohio 2770, — N.E. 2d —, 2006 Ohio App. LEXIS 2619 (June 2, 2006).

Although home owners combined assignments of error with respect to their appeal of a denial of their new trial motion, the appellate court chose to review the claims on the merits rather than to disregard the joined arguments pursuant to Ohio R. App. P. 12(A)(2). The denial by the trial court of the new trial motion was not an abuse of discretion under Ohio R. Civ. P. 59(A)(6), as there was competent and credible evidence that supported the trial court's determination in the personal injury action. Griffiths v. Airko, — Ohio App. 3d —, 2006 Ohio 3152, — N.E. 2d —, 2006 Ohio App. LEXIS 3045 (June 22, 2006).

Where an appellate court clerk stamped one notice of appeal and brief filed by an inmate, raising the issue of the trial court's denial of his request for appointed counsel, as "filed," and the clerk mistakenly filed the other notice of appeal and brief filed by the inmate from the trial court's denial of his plea withdrawal request as "copy," the appellate court's disregard of the inmate's claim on the withdrawal issue upon determining that it was not argued pursuant to Ohio R. App. P. 12 and 16 was an "obvious error"; as the court did not review the brief relating to the plea withdrawal request due to the clerk's clerical mistake, the inmate's application for reconsideration pursuant to Ohio R. App. P. 26 was granted on the limited issue of arguments relating to the plea withdrawal request. State v. Meadows, — Ohio App. 3d —, 2006 Ohio 3375, — N.E. 2d —, 2006 Ohio App. LEXIS 3304 (June 29, 2006).

Where an insurer failed to present any arguments to support an issue that it raised on appeal in a declaratory judgment action regarding its duty to provide a defense and to indemnify its insured from an employer intentional tort claim, the appellate court disregarded the assignment of error pursuant to Ohio R. App. P. 12(A)(2) and 16(A)(7). Cincinnati Ins. Co. v. Schwerha, — Ohio App. 3d —, 2006 Ohio 3521, — N.E. 2d —, 2006 Ohio App. LEXIS 3440 (June 28, 2006).

Although a workers' compensation claimant contended on appeal that a particular statute violated her equal protection and due process rights, but her argument only addressed equal protection issues, the appellate court did not conduct a due process analysis pursuant to Ohio R. App. P. 12(A)(2) and 16(A). Ireland v. Southern Ohio Correctional Facility, — Ohio App. 3d —, 2006 Ohio 3519, — N.E. 2d —, 2006 Ohio App. LEXIS 3470 (June 22, 2006).

Where an employee failed to cite to any legal authority or to parts of the record which she relied upon to support her argument on appeal that a trial court's dismissal of her intentional infliction of emotional distress claim, arising from her alleged constructive discharge from employment, was error, pursuant to Ohio R. App. P. 12(A)(2) and 16(A) the court disregarded the assigned error for purposes of appellate review. Simmons-Means v. Cuyahoga County Dep't of Justice Affairs, — Ohio App. 3d —, 2006 Ohio 4123, — N.E.2d —, 2006 Ohio App. LEXIS 4057 (Aug. 10, 2006).

Real property owners who appealed a judgment of foreclosure in favor of a county treasurer failed to comply with Ohio R. App. P. 12(A) and 16(A) where they did not identify assignments of error for the appellate court to review, and their appellate brief was largely a recitation of incomplete thoughts and citations; the court only addressed three general arguments raised in the brief, but it refused to scour the record. Callison v. Huelsman, 168 Ohio App. 3d 471, 2006 Ohio 4395, 860 N.E. 2d 829, 2006 Ohio App. LEXIS 4322 (Aug. 25, 2006).

Where a trial court found that an inmate failed to satisfy the first prong of RC § 2953.23(A)(1)(a) for purposes of review of his untimely petition for post-conviction relief, it did not need to review the remaining arguments regarding satisfaction of the second prong under § 2953.23(A)(1)(b); as the inmate had to satisfy both prongs in order to have his untimely petition reviewed, his failure to satisfy the first prong rendered any further arguments moot, and the court declined to review anything further pursuant to Ohio R. App. P. 12(A)(1)(c). State v. Barney, — Ohio App. 3d —, 2006 Ohio 4676, — N.E. 2d —, 2006 Ohio App. LEXIS 4594 (Sept. 6, 2006).

Where a property owner appealed from a grant of summary judgment to other property owners in a dispute over ownership of a piece of land, and one of the assignments of error asserted in her appeal was not separately argued in her brief, the court disregarded it pursuant to Ohio R. App. P. 12 and 16(A)(7). King v. Hazen, — Ohio App. 3d —, 2006 Ohio 4823, — N.E. 2d —, 2006 Ohio App. LEXIS 4735 (Sept. 15, 2006).

Where defendant claimed that his statutory speedy trial right under RC § 2945.71(C)(2) was violated, although he conceded that his filing of various motions tolled the time period pursuant to RC § 2945.72(E) such that he was brought to trial in a timely manner, his claim that the State's "machinations" in the indictment and charging process caused a delay that was unjustified and unreasonable was not properly reviewable under Ohio R. App. P. 12(A)(2), as defendant did not separately argue or cite to legal authority regarding the claim of an alleged irregularity or abuse of the grand jury process, which was a markedly different legal argument; accordingly, the court declined to review that claim. State v. Kelly, — Ohio App. 3d —, 2006 Ohio 4879, — N.E. 2d —, 2006 Ohio App. LEXIS 4800 (Sept. 21, 2006).

Although defendant only assigned as error that her conviction was against the manifest weight of the evidence, she asserted in her argument thereunder that the evidence was insufficient to support the conviction, and although the court was not required to address that latter claim pursuant to Ohio R. App. P. 12(A)(2), it chose to review both claims of error. State v. Varence-Parks, — Ohio App. 3d —, 2006 Ohio 5034, — N.E. 2d —, 2006 Ohio App. LEXIS 4968 (Sept. 28, 2006).

Since a mother failed to offer any explanation, analysis, or citations to the record or to specific Ohio cases or statutes in support of her assertions that the trial court's decision awarding legal custody of the mother's two sons to the sons' paternal grandparents was against the manifest weight of the evidence, the mother's brief failed to comply with Ohio R. App. P. 16(A)(7). Thus, pursuant to Ohio R. App. P. 12(A)(2), the court declined to address the mother's assignment of error due to the mother's failure to brief the assigned error. In re C.S., — Ohio App. 3d —, 2006 Ohio 5198, — N.E. 2d —, 2006 Ohio App. LEXIS 5117 (Oct. 2, 2006).

Since defendant did not designate an order which vacated an earlier assignment of his case to the mental health docket in his notice of appeal, the appellate court lacked jurisdiction to consider this claim. State v. Doing, — Ohio App. 3d —, 2006 Ohio 5252, — N.E. 2d —, 2006 Ohio App. LEXIS 5227 (Oct. 5, 2006).

Since defendant failed to point the court to any specific evidence in the record to support his contention that his conviction was against the manifest weight of the evidence, he failed to satisfy his burden under Ohio R. App. P. 16(A)(7) of affirmatively demonstrating error on appeal; thus, the court, pursuant to Ohio R. App. P. 12(A)(2), disregarded defendant's argument and found that his assignment of error was without merit. State v. Joziuk, — Ohio App. 3d —, 2006 Ohio 5421, — N.E. 2d —, 2006 Ohio App. LEXIS 5418 (Oct. 18, 2006).

Since a father failed to brief two assignments of error challenging a trial court's custody decision, as required by Ohio R. App. P. 16(A)(7), the appellate court declined to address those assignments of error pursuant to Ohio R. App. P. 12(A)(2). In re T.G., — Ohio App. 3d —, 2006 Ohio 5504, — N.E. 2d —, 2006 Ohio App. LEXIS 5489 (Oct. 23, 2006).

Where an appealing member of a limited liability company failed to comply with Ohio R. App. P. 12(A)(2) and 16(A)(7), the appellate court chose to disregard the assignment of error raised. All Star Land Title Agency, Inc. v. Surewin Inv., — Ohio App. 3d —, 2006 Ohio 5729, — N.E. 2d —, 2006 Ohio App. LEXIS 5727 (Nov. 2, 2006).

As defendant's appeal from various rulings by the trial court on his motions both before and during trial did not comply with the brief requirements of Ohio R. App. P. 12 and 16(A)(7) and it did not constitute an Anders brief, the court chose to disregard the assignment of error relating thereto. Defendant's argument had not cited any authority, had indicated that his counsel had determined that the trial court rulings were correct, and had simply asked the court to "carefully review the record" to determine if he had been denied a fair trial. State v. Moyar, — Ohio App. 3d —, 2006 Ohio 5974, — N.E. 2d —, 2006 Ohio App. LEXIS 5914 (Nov. 13, 2006).

After an appellate court determined that summary judgment was properly granted to apartment building owners and a city in an action filed by developers contesting the city's right under a utility easement to reroute sewer connections through lines on the developers' land, remaining assignments of error raised by the developers were rendered moot and the court declined to address them under Ohio R. App. P. 12(A)(1)(c). Carter v. City of Orrville, — Ohio App. 3d —, 2006 Ohio 6476, — N.E. 2d —, 2006 Ohio App. LEXIS 6455 (Dec. 11, 2006).

Although property owners appealed a finding that they were in contempt and the imposition of monetary sanctions and fines due to their failure to remove items from their property that constituted a nuisance, where they failed to separately assign as error the numerous arguments set out in their brief, pursuant to Ohio R. App. P. 12 and 16, review thereof was declined. Board of Trustees Thorn Twp. v. Dillow, — Ohio App. 3d —, 2006 Ohio 6888, — N.E. 2d —, 2006 Ohio App. LEXIS 6780 (Dec. 20, 2006).

Although a property owner did not properly set forth his assignment of error in his brief on appeal, pursuant to Ohio R. App. P. 16(A)(3) and 12(A), as he asserted that the trial court wrongfully granted summary judgment to a builder when in fact the trial court had deemed that motion moot because it had granted the builder's dismissal motion, the court reviewed the owner's argument in the interest of justice. The owner had set forth an argument to support a claimed error relating to the trial court's dismissal of his claim. Carlton v. Alar Dev. Co., — Ohio App. 3d —, 2006 Ohio 6877, — N.E. 2d —, 2006 Ohio App. LEXIS 6797 (Dec. 22, 2006).

Employee failed to meet her burden on appeal pursuant to Ohio R. App. P. 12(A)(2), 16(A)(7), and Ohio 9th Dist. Ct. App. R. 7(A)(7) and (F) where she failed to cite in her brief to any portions of the record to support her claim that the trial court's grant of summary judgment to the employer on her age discrimination claim was error. Although her brief cited to the record in her statement of facts, that structure did not comport with the appellate rules, and as she failed to demonstrate error on appeal, the court disregarded the assignment of error. Urda v. Buckingham, Doolittle, & Burroughs, — Ohio App. 3d —, 2006 Ohio 6915, — N.E. 2d —, 2006 Ohio App. LEXIS 6816 (Dec. 27, 2006).

Court, pursuant to Ohio R. App. P. 12(A), rejected certain arguments contained in appellant's brief on appeal because. while the issues were stated in the argument section of the brief, appellant did not reference the assignments of error to which these issues related, in contravention of Ohio R. App. P. 16(A)(4). In re A.V., — Ohio App. 3d —, 2006 Ohio 3149, — N.E. 2d —, 2006 Ohio App. LEXIS 3021 (June 22, 2006).

Where defendant did not present any specific argument with respect to his claim on appeal that the trial court erred in failing to suppress certain statements that he made to the police, the court disregarded those arguments on appeal pursuant to Ohio R. App. P. 12(A)(2) and 16(A)(7). State v. Haney, — Ohio App. 3d —, 2006 Ohio 3899, — N.E. 2d —, 2006 Ohio App. LEXIS 3855 (July 31, 2006).

Pro se note debtor who appealed the grant of a default judgment in favor of the note holder was required to comply with the appellate rules for purposes of filing the brief pursuant to Ohio R. App. P. 16(A)(7) and 12(A)(2); the court found four central themes to the purported assignments of error on appeal which it reviewed. Paparodis v. Snively, — Ohio App. 3d —, 2007 Ohio 6910, — N.E. 2d —, 2007 Ohio App. LEXIS 6064 (Dec. 12, 2007).

— Brief requirements

As an electrical customer failed to comply with the brief and record requirements of Ohio R. App. P. 16 and Ohio Ninth Dist. Ct. App. R. 7(B)(7) with respect to her appeal of a garnishment order, the appellate court acted within its authority in disregarding her assignments of error pursuant to Ohio R. App. P. 12(A) and 16(A)(7). Ohio Edison Co. v. Williams, — Ohio App. 3d —, 2007 Ohio 5028, — N.E. 2d —, 2007 Ohio App. LEXIS 4449 (Sept. 26, 2007).

Court disregarded various issues raised by property owners on appeal from a decision of the Ohio Reclamation Commission, approving a mining permit, where the owners failed to cite to a part of the record that established prejudice to them under Ohio R. App. P. 16(A)(6), they failed to provide citations to legal authority to supprt their arguments under Rule 16(A)(7), they cited issues for the first time in their reply brief under Rule 16(C), and they failed to raise certain issues in the administrative level proceeding, such that they were waived for purposes of judicial review; the court acted within its authority in disregarding the improperly raised issues pursuant to Ohio R. App. P. 12(A)(2). Spires v. Div. of Mineral Res. Mgmt., — Ohio App. 3d —, 2007 Ohio 5038, — N.E. 2d —, 2007 Ohio App. LEXIS 4458 (Sept. 24, 2007).

Although an assignment of error raised on appeal on defendant's behalf regarding his resentencing contained two separate arguments, in derogation of the requirements of Ohio R. App. P. 12(A)(1)(b) and 16(A)(7), the court acted within its discretion and pursuant to the interest of justice when it considered the arguments presented, as only "one" assignment of error was presented in the case and it was easily decided. State v. Nicholson, — Ohio App. 3d —, 2007 Ohio 5429, — N.E. 2d —, 2007 Ohio App. LEXIS 4773 (Oct. 11, 2007).

— Lack of briefing

On appeal of a judgment in favor of a contractor, a home owner failed to meet the burden under Ohio R. App. P. 9, 12(A)(2), and 16(A)(7), as the owner failed to cite to the place in the record upon which the assignment of error was based, and there was no citation to legal authority in support of the assignment of error. Prater v. Dashkovsky, — Ohio App. 3d —, 2007 Ohio 6785, — N.E. 2d —, 2007 Ohio App. LEXIS 5919 (Dec. 18, 2007).

Briefs

Although the assignments of error raised by a husband in his appeal from a trial court's adoption of a magistrate's grant of a civil protection order to his wife were not a "model of clarity," as it was possible for the appellate court to determine what the husband claimed as error, it could review the assignments of error pursuant to Ohio R. App. P. 12(A)(2). Jenkins v. Jenkins, — Ohio App. 3d —, 2007 Ohio 422, — N.E. 2d —, 2007 Ohio App. LEXIS 367 (Feb. 1, 2007).

Where an investor's appeal of the trial court's denial of his new trial motion merely quoted the applicable procedural rule and then stated in a conclusory fashion that the trial court's judgment was contrary to law without citing to any authority or to the record, as required by Ohio R. App. P. 12(A)(2) and 16(A)(7) and Ohio Ninth Dist. Ct. App. R. 7(A)(7) and (F), he did not meet his burden of demonstrating error. Macken v.

KDR Holdings, — Ohio App. 3d —, 2007 Ohio 4106, — N.E. 2d —, 2007 Ohio App. LEXIS 3733 (Aug. 13, 2007).

Consideration of errors

When a landlord sued tenants for possession, back rent, damages to the leased premises, and punitive damages and attorney fees, and an insurer intervened to assert a subrogation claim to any recovery by the landlord, which it later voluntarily dismissed, the landlord could not, on appeal, vicariously allege omissions in the trial court's order which were actually detrimental to the insurer because it did not demonstrate prejudice to its own position warranting reversal, under Ohio R. App. P. 12(D). Love Props., Inc. v. Kyles, — Ohio App. 3d —, 2007 Ohio 1966, — N.E. 2d —, 2007 Ohio App. LEXIS 1772 (Apr. 23, 2007).

Where a patient only identified portions of a record as error in his appeal from a judgment against him in his medical malpractice action, pursuant to Ohio R. App. P. 12(A)(2) the court limited its review to only those portions of the record cited in the appellate brief. Nead v. Brown County Gen. Hosp., — Ohio App. 3d —, 2007 Ohio 2443, — N.E. 2d —, 2007 Ohio App. LEXIS 2259 (May 21, 2007).

Trial court's determinations in favor of remaining anesthesiologists and a medical practice in claims by a terminated anesthesiologist of breach of fiduciary duties, breach of an oral contract/promissory estoppel, and breach of contractual duties, arising from his ouster from the parties' joint medical practice, were not against the manifest weight of the evidence and were accordingly affirmed pursuant to Ohio R. App. P. 12(C) where the evidence did not support a finding of any breach on the part of the remaining anesthesiologists. Even assuming arguendo that breaches could have been shown, the issue of whether the terminated anesthesiologist suffered damages was disputed, such that deference was given to the trial court's determination. Mulchin v. Zzz Anesthesia, Inc., — Ohio App. 3d —, 2006 Ohio 5773, — N.E. 2d —, 2006 Ohio App. LEXIS 5757 (Nov. 3, 2006).

Consideration of issues

As defendant only challenged the sufficiency of the evidence with respect to one of two offenses that he was convicted of, the appellate court only addressed defendant's assertion of error with respect to that one offense pursuant to Ohio R. App. P. 12(A)(2) and 16(A)(7). State v. Johnson, — Ohio App. 3d —, 2007 Ohio 2385, — N.E. 2d —, 2007 Ohio App. LEXIS 2216 (May 17, 2007).

Court declined to review an assignment of error raised on appeal by a current property owner pursuant to Ohio R. App. P. 12(B) with respect to the trial court's denial of its request for leave to amend its answer, as such did not need to be considered where the former property owners appeal was not successful. MDM Realty, Ltd. v. Progress Properties. So., LP, — Ohio App. 3d —, 2007 Ohio 3668, — N.E. 2d —, 2007 Ohio App. LEXIS 3375 (July 19, 2007).

Court's duty to decide assignments

AppR 12(A)(1)(c) requires an appellate court to decide each assignment of error and give written reasons for its decision unless the assignment of error is made moot by a ruling on another assignment of error. State v. Evans, 113 Ohio St. 3d 100, 2007 Ohio 861, 863 N.E.2d 113, 2007 Ohio LEXIS 506 (2007).

AppR 12(A)(1)(c) requires an appellate court to decide each assignment of error and give written reasons for its decision unless the assignment of error is made moot by a ruling on another assignment of error: State v. Evans, 113 Ohio St. 3d 100, 2007 Ohio 861, 863 N.E.2d 113, 2007 Ohio LEXIS 506 (2007).

Dispositive assignments of error

Where the appellate court already determined that the trial court's determination that a contract between a waterproofing company and homeowners was not procedurally unconscionable, there was no need for it to review the assignment of error regarding substantive unconscionability, as both types had to be found in order for the contractual provision to have been deemed unconscionable; accordingly, the second assignment of error was not reviewed pursuant to Ohio R. App. P. 12(A)(1)(c). Ball v. Ohio State Home Servs., — Ohio App. 3d —, 2006 Ohio 4464, — N.E. 2d —, 2006 Ohio App. LEXIS 4396 (Aug. 30, 2006).

As an appellate court's disposition of one error raised on appeal required a reversal of a trial court judgment and a remand for a new trial, it declined to review any further errors asserted on appeal pursuant to Ohio R. App. P. 12(A)(1)(c). Newport Harbor Ass'n, Inc. v. Dicello, — Ohio App. 3d —, 2006 Ohio 4493, — N.E. 2d —, 2006 Ohio App. LEXIS 4414 (Aug. 31, 2006).

Failure to cite to authority

As a building owner who appealed an administrative decision regarding her violations of the housing code failed to cite to case law in making her argument on appeal, as required by Ohio R. App. P. 16(A)(7), the court had grounds to disregard the assigned error pursuant to Ohio R. App. P. 12(A)(2); the court indicated that despite its ability to disregard, the result was the same because the assigned error lacked merit. Spires v. Board of Bldgs. Stds. & Bldg. Appeals, — Ohio App. 3d —, 2007 Ohio 391, — N.E. 2d —, 2007 Ohio App. LEXIS 351 (Feb. 1, 2007).

Although defendant raised numerous errors on appeal in his claim that he was denied a fair trial based on cumulative errors, where he failed to cite case law to support many of the errors, they were not addressed on appeal pursuant to Ohio R. App. P. 12(A)(2) and 16(A)(7). State v. Djuric, — Ohio App. 3d —, 2007 Ohio 413, — N.E. 2d —, 2007 Ohio App. LEXIS 362 (Feb. 1, 2007).

In an appeal from a trial court's decision in a permanent custody case, while the mother had failed to cite any legal authority in support of her assignment of error, as required by Ohio R. App. P. 16(A)(7), thereby giving the court the right under Ohio R. App. P. 12(A)(2) to disregard the assignment of error, the court, in the interest of justice, addressed the merits of the appeal. In re R.L., — Ohio App. 3d —, 2007 Ohio 3553, — N.E. 2d —, 2007 Ohio App. LEXIS 3238 (July 12, 2007).

Although an appellate court had a right to disregard assignments of error pursuant to Ohio R. App. P. 12(A)(2) where defendant failed to cite to legal authority in support thereof pursuant to Ohio R. App. P. 16(A)(7), it acted within its authority in choosing to undertake an independent review of the assignments. Ohio v. Anderson, — Ohio App. 3d —, 2007 Ohio 5326, — N.E. 2d —, 2007 Ohio App. LEXIS 4692 (Oct. 4, 2007).

Where property owners did not cite to any legal authority in a variety of their arguments on appeal from a village's determination that they had committed nuisances by violating municipal ordinances, pursuant to Ohio R. App. P. 12(A)(2) and 16(A)(7) the court chose to disregard those unsupported arguments. Village of Ottawa Hills v. Abdollah, — Ohio App. 3d —, 2006 Ohio 2618, — N.E. 2d —, 2006 Ohio App. LEXIS 2461 (May 26, 2006).

Defendants' assignment of error on appeal from their felonious assault convictions that the verdict was improper in that the defense did not identify the real culprits and that defendants were in proximity to the victim was disregarded pursuant to Ohio R. App. P. 12(A)(2) because defendants failed to cite to any legal authority in support of the argument as required by Ohio R. App. P. 16(A)(7); if an argument existed that could support the assignment of error, it was not the appellate court's duty to root it out. State v. Armstrong, — Ohio App. 3d —, 2006 Ohio 5447, — N.E. 2d —, 2006 Ohio App. LEXIS 5437 (Oct. 19, 2006).

Trial court's denial of defendant's acquittal motion pursuant to Ohio R. Crim. P. 29 was not properly reviewable by an appellate court because defendant's brief did not comply with the requirements of Ohio R. App. P. 16(A)(7) and Ohio 9th Dist. Ct. App. R. 7(B)(7) where there was no citation to any authority that supported defendant's position, and his contentions did not constitute an argument; accordingly, affirmance of the trial court's decision was proper under Ohio R. App. P. 12(A)(2). State v. Stelzer, — Ohio App. 3d —, 2006 Ohio 6912, — N.E. 2d —, 2006 Ohio App. LEXIS 6818 (Dec. 27, 2006).

Failure to cite to record

Though a husband alleged that the trial court, in denying his motion for reduction of child support, ignored evidence of the wife's extravagant spending, the husband failed to point to portions of the record regarding the wife's spending or standard of living. Since the husband had the burden on appeal, the court had the authority under Ohio R. App. P. 12(A)(2), 7(F), Summit County, Ohio, App. R. 7(F), and Ohio R. App. P. 16(A)(7) to disregard assignments of error that were not supported by the relevant portions of the record from which the errors were based. Maguire v. Maguire, — Ohio App. 3d —, 2007 Ohio 4531, — N.E. 2d —, 2007 Ohio App. LEXIS 4104 (Sept. 5, 2007).

Failure to make argument

While the appellate court, pursuant to Ohio R. App. P. 12(A)(2) could choose to disregard any assignment of error that the father had failed to separately argue, as required by Ohio R. App. P. 16(A)(7), the court chose to review the father's assignments of error because courts strive to decide appeals on their merits instead of on technicalities. In re Gallion, — Ohio App. 3d —, 2006 Ohio 3204, — N.E. 2d —, 2006 Ohio App. LEXIS 3095 (June 12, 2006).

Where appellant failed to make the necessary arguments in her brief to support her claim that punitive damages awarded to a patrolman in his assorted tort claims against appellant were excessive, the appellate court was not required under Ohio R. App. P. 12(A)(2) to address the argument. Earl v. Nelson, — Ohio App. 3d —, 2006 Ohio 3341, — N.E. 2d —, 2006 Ohio App. LEXIS 3270 (June 30, 2006).

Defendant's speedy trial rights under RC § 2945.71(C)(2) were not violated, as various tolling provisions under RC § 2945.72(E) applied to extend the time within which he was to be brought to trial. Defendant's claim that the State's "machinations" in the indictment and charging process constituted an unreasonable and unjustified delay in bringing him to trial was not separately argued and there was no citation to legal authority for support, as required by Ohio R. App. P. 12(A)(2), and accordingly, the court chose to disregard that claim. State v. Kelly, — Ohio App. 3d —, 2006 Ohio 5902, — N.E. 2d —, 2006 Ohio App. LEXIS 5862 (Nov. 9, 2006).

Where the State of Ohio only appealed the trial court's grant of an inmate's petition for habeas corpus but it did not seek reversal of the trial court's denial of its extradition motion, only the assignment of error relating to the habeas petition was addressed on appeal pursuant to Ohio R. App. P. 12(A)(1)(b). Kinzey v. Steyer, — Ohio App. 3d —, 2006 Ohio 5971, — N.E. 2d —, 2006 Ohio App. LEXIS 5909 (Nov. 13, 2006).

Failure to support

When defendant claimed his sentence was an abuse of discretion but offered no argument or legal authority to support his claim, an appellate court could properly disregard the claim, under Ohio R. App. P. 12(A)(2). State v. Sheets, — Ohio App. 3d —, 2007 Ohio 1799, — N.E. 2d —, 2007 Ohio App. LEXIS 1648 (Apr. 16, 2007).

Where condominium residents failed to cite to portions of the record or their affidavits to support their claim on appeal pursuant to Ohio R. App. P. 12(A) that genuine issues of material fact remained after a trial court granted summary judgment against them, their claims lacked merit. Tonti v. East

Bank Condos., Llc, — Ohio App. 3d —, 2007 Ohio 6779, — N.E. 2d —, 2007 Ohio App. LEXIS 5931 (Dec. 18, 2007).

Since defendant's contentions, asserted on appeal from her conviction for reckless operation, that she was not given discovery and that certain evidence should have been admitted while other evidence should have been suppressed were not supported by evidence contained in the record but were based on speculation and unsupported allegations, the court declined to address the remainder of defendant's arguments pursuant to Ohio R. App. P. 12 and Ohio R. App. P. 16. City of Whitehall v. Ruckman, — Ohio App. 3d —, 2007 Ohio 6780, — N.E. 2d —, 2007 Ohio App. LEXIS 5932 (Dec. 18, 2007).

Final judgment

When a trial court only found that a judgment debtor did not show good cause why the Bureau of Workers' Compensation's judgment against him should not be revived, this was not a final appealable order, under Ohio R. App. P. 12(A)(1)(a) or RC § 2505.02, because it did not award judgment for one party against another, nor could the parties determine their rights and obligations from this judgment, without referring to other judgments, so the debtor's appeal of this judgment was dismissed for lack of appellate court jurisdiction. State Bur. of Workers Compensation v. Testa, — Ohio App. 3d —, 2006 Ohio 2179, — N.E. 2d —, 2006 Ohio App. LEXIS 2027 (May 3, 2006).

Summary judgment against fewer than all defendants, which order stated "this is a final order as against these Defendants only that shall not be delayed," did not substantially comply with Ohio R. Civ. P. 54(B), and thus the summary judgment was not a final, appealable order; an appeal from the order was dismissed. Monitor Transporation Servs. v. Tri Port Transporation, — Ohio App. 3d —, 2006 Ohio 2689, — N.E. 2d —, 2006 Ohio App. LEXIS 2520 (May 31, 2006).

As a trial court's order which granted an employer's motion to enforce the parties' settlement agreement, arising out of a dispute over an appealed decision from the Industrial Commission which disallowed several of the employee's conditions in her workers' compensation claim, was indefinite with respect to directions to the parties and it did not notify the parties or courts of the parties' rights and obligations, it was not a final appealable order for purposes of RC § 2505.02, and the court lacked jurisdiction to review it and make a disposition thereon pursuant to Ohio R. App. P. 12(A)(1)(a). Landis v. Associated Materials, — Ohio App. 3d —, 2006 Ohio 5060, — N.E. 2d —, 2006 Ohio App. LEXIS 4991 (Sept. 29, 2006).

Judgment

Although there was sufficient evidence to support the six counts of vaginal rape, as well as the six counts of rape by cunnilingus, and the six counts of gross sexual imposition, because the prosecution failed to present any evidence that defendant digitally penetrated the 12-year-old victim's vagina, the evidence was insufficient to support the six charges of rape by digital vaginal penetration and the verdict was modified to convictions for gross sexual imposition, as lesser offenses. The victim testified that defendant repeatedly and at least once during each year of the indictment (1) put his penis in her vagina; (2) touched her vagina with his hand or penis; (3) put his tongue on her vagina; and (4) touched her breasts with his hands. State v. Frazier, — Ohio App. 3d —, 2007 Ohio 11, — N.E. 2d —, 2007 Ohio App. LEXIS 6 (Jan. 4, 2007).

Pursuant to Ohio R. App. P. 12(B), the trial court's judgment of conviction and sentence were corrected to indicate that the trial court dismissed the three charges of intimidation of a crime victim or witness, and the accompanying firearm specifications. State v. Johnson, — Ohio App. 3d —, 2007 Ohio 2792, — N.E. 2d —, 2007 Ohio App. LEXIS 2544 (June 7, 2007).

Jurisdiction

When a construction company sued a corporation for breach of contract, a prompt payment statute violation, and unjust enrichment, and was granted summary judgment and damages on its breach of contract claim, but it was not found that there was no just reason to delay an appeal, under Ohio R. Civ. P. 54(B), nor were the other claims properly voluntarily dismissed, under Ohio R. Civ. P. 41(A) by a notice of dismissal, stipulation, or journalized court order, those claims remained pending and an appellate court had no jurisdiction, under Ohio R. App. P. 12(A)(1)(a), or RC § 2505.02, to hear an appeal of the breach of contract judgment. Spano Bros. Constr. Co. v. Adolph Johnson & Son Co., — Ohio App. 3d —, 2006 Ohio 4083, — N.E. 2d —, 2006 Ohio App. LEXIS 4039 (Aug. 9, 2006).

Limited remand

Jury award of damages to a home owner upon finding that a guest had negligently disposed of her smoking materials and was responsible for a fire that caused damages to the home was against the manifest weight of the evidence where the damage evidence was uncontroverted and was for an amount more than double that awarded by the jury; pursuant to the court's authority under Ohio R. App. P. 12(D), it could order a retrial just on the issue of damages. Morelli v. Walker, — Ohio App. 3d —, 2007 Ohio 4832, — N.E. 2d —, 2007 Ohio App. LEXIS 4327 (Sept. 20, 2007).

Where an injured driver provided undisputed evidence that he would continue to suffer pain as a result of a vehicle accident, the jury's express decision not to award him damages for future pain and suffering was against the manifest weight of the evidence, and the trial court abused its discretion in denying the motion under Ohio R. Civ. P. 59(A)(6) of the driver and his wife for a new trial on that issue; pursuant to Ohio R. App. P. 12(D), the court could grant a new trial on that issue alone. White v. Bennett, — Ohio App. 3d —, 2006 Ohio 3600, — N.E. 2d —, 2006 Ohio App. LEXIS 3541 (July 14, 2006).

Modification

Trial court erred in ordering that defendant's sentence be served consecutively under RC § 2929.14(E) with any future sentence that might be imposed for defendant's parole violation because a court could not order that a sentence run consecutively with a future sentence. Since the trial court's order was improper, the court, acting pursuant to its authority in Ohio R. App. P. 12(B), modified the judgment entry so as to delete the provision ordering the sentence to be served consecutively to any time imposed for the parole violation. State v. Biegaj, — Ohio App. 3d —, 2007 Ohio 5992, — N.E. 2d —, 2007 Ohio App. LEXIS 5249 (Nov. 9, 2007).

Temporary spousal support order pursuant to RC § 3105.18 and Ohio R. Civ. P. 75(N)(1) that was reduced to a judgment in the parties' divorce decree based on the arrearages owed by the wife was assessed interest at an improper rate, requiring modification on appeal pursuant to Ohio R. App. P. 12(A)(1)(a); pursuant to RC § 1343.03(A), interest was to be determined pursuant to RC § 5703.47, which yielded a different rate than that which was imposed by the trial court. House v. House, — Ohio App. 3d —, 2006 Ohio 2776, — N.E. 2d —, 2006 Ohio App. LEXIS 2616 (June 2, 2006).

Moot issues

Where an appellate court vacated portions of a trial court judgment in parties' dissolution action that contained legal or factual errors, issues regarding the trial court's denial of the husband's motion for a new trial under Ohio R. Civ. P. 59 or the trial court's adoption of the wife's counsel's proposed findings of fact and conclusions of law pursuant to Ohio R. Civ. P. 52 without modification were deemed moot for purposes of appellate review under Ohio R. App. P.

12(A)(1)(c), as the vacated portions of the judgment related to those issues. Janosek v. Janosek, — Ohio App. 3d —, 2007 Ohio 68, — N.E. 2d —, 2007 Ohio App. LEXIS 59 (Jan. 11, 2007).

As an appellate court determined that the trial court properly denied an inmate's motions that sought sentencing relief, which were treated as petitions for post-conviction relief under RC § 2953.21, due to timeliness issues, the trial court's alternative ground for denial of the petitions based on grounds of res judicata was not reviewed because it was deemed moot under Ohio R. App. P. 12(A)(1)(c). State v. Williams, — Ohio App. 3d —, 2007 Ohio 1015, — N.E. 2d —, 2007 Ohio App. LEXIS 907 (Mar. 8, 2007).

Where an appellate court affirmed a jury verdict in favor of doctors in a medical malpractice action, consideration of one doctor's cross-assignments of error would not have afforded him relief, such that the court chose to disregard it as moot under Ohio R. App. P. 12(A)(1)(c). Iglodi v. Tolentino, — Ohio App. 3d —, 2007 Ohio 1982, — N.E. 2d —, 2007 Ohio App. LEXIS 1832 (Apr. 26, 2007).

Where an appellate court's disposition of an assignment of error rendered a second assignment of error moot, the court did not have to reach the merits of that challenge pursuant to Ohio R. App. P. 12(A)(1)(c). State v. Fuller, — Ohio App. 3d —, 2007 Ohio 2018, — N.E. 2d —, 2007 Ohio App. LEXIS 1885 (Apr. 27, 2007).

Where an appellate court held that a trial court's adoption of a divorce decree was an abuse of discretion because there were issues of dispute regarding the terms of the settlement agreement upon which the decree was based, such that an evidentiary hearing should have been held, the husband's additional claim on appeal that the trial court's denial of his motion for relief from judgment pursuant to Ohio R. Civ. P. 60(B) was error was rendered moot pursuant to Ohio R. App. P. 12(A)(1)(c). Hornung v. Hornung, — Ohio App. 3d —, 2007 Ohio 3222, — N.E. 2d —, 2007 Ohio App. LEXIS 2844 (June 21, 2007).

Where defendant's assignment of error on appeal regarding his convictions resulted in a vacatur thereof, his assignments of error that related to sentencing issues were rendered moot and were disregarded pursuant to Ohio R. App. P. 12(A)(1)(c). State v. Poston, — Ohio App. 3d —, 2007 Ohio 3936, — N.E. 2d —, 2007 Ohio App. LEXIS 3539 (May 14, 2007).

Based on an appellate court's determination that a trial court's declaratory judgment was void ab initio, requiring dismissal of the action, any other assignments of error that were asserted were deemed moot pursuant to Ohio R. App. P. 12(A)(1)(c). Young v. Wells, — Ohio App. 3d —, 2007 Ohio 4568, — N.E. 2d —, 2007 Ohio App. LEXIS 4094 (Aug. 28, 2007).

Defendant's sentence was vacated as it was imposed under RC § 2929.14(B), which later was found to be unconstitutional and was severed. As defendant's sentence was based on an unconstitutional statute, it was void. Defendant's remaining claim of error in his sentencing was moot under Ohio R. App. P. 12(A)(1)(c). State v. Gay, — Ohio App. 3d —, 2006 Ohio 3683, — N.E. 2d —, 2006 Ohio App. LEXIS 3638 (July 20, 2006).

Where an appellate court's disposition of one of two assignments of error raised by a putative father in a paternity action determined that the trial court had committed reversible error which necessitated a remand for further proceedings, the remaining assignment of error was deemed moot and the issues asserted therein were not addressed on appeal pursuant to Ohio R. App. P. 12(A)(1)(c). Kennedy v. Oliver, — Ohio App. 3d —, 2006 Ohio 5814, — N.E. 2d —, 2006 Ohio App. LEXIS 5780 (Nov. 6, 2006).

As the appellate court found that an insured's and insurance broker's assignments of error on appeal lacked merit with respect to the trial court's grant of partial summary judgment and summary judgment to insurers, resolving issues of insur-ance coverage for the insured's property damage occasioned by a tornado, it was unnecessary to consider the insurers' cross-assignments of error. They were disregarded as moot pursuant to Ohio R. App. P. 12(A)(1)(c). Cooper Farms, Inc. v. Brown & Brown of Ohio, Inc., — Ohio App. 3d —, 2006 Ohio 5982, — N.E. 2d —, 2006 Ohio App. LEXIS 5921 (Nov. 13, 2006).

As a sentencing error required vacatur of the sentence imposed on defendant by the trial court and a remand for resentencing, defendant's second assignment of error which also raised a sentencing issue was rendered moot and accordingly, it was disregarded for purposes of appeal under Ohio R. App. P. 12(A)(1)(c). State v. Doyle, — Ohio App. 3d —, 2006 Ohio 5211, — N.E. 2d —, 2006 Ohio App. LEXIS 5167 (Sept. 25, 2006).

Power to modify judgment

Juvenile court's transfer of all issues between parents to a New York court was error, wherein the father had sought modification of the allocation of parental rights and responsibilities and of child support, as both parties did not consent to the transfer of the child support issue to the New York court pursuant to RC § 3115.07(A). Pursuant to the appellate court's authority under Ohio R. App. P. 12(A)(1)(a), it ordered modification of the juvenile court judgment to reflect that the child support issue was to remain within the exclusive jurisdiction of the Ohio juvenile court pending the consent by both parties to the transfer thereof. In re A.M., — Ohio App. 3d —, 2007 Ohio 2234, — N.E. 2d —, 2007 Ohio App. LEXIS 2093 (May 10, 2007).

Trial court's award of punitive damages pursuant to RC § 2315.21 in three times the amount awarded as compensatory damages was deemed excessive in an action by an insured against an insurance agency and the agency owner, as an award of double the compensatory damages was adequate to accomplish the twin aims of punishment and deterrence. Pursuant to Ohio R. App. P. 12(B), the appellate court modified the trial court judgment to reflect the new punitive damage award. Winner Trucking, Inc. v. Victor L. Dowers & Associates, — Ohio App. 3d —, 2007 Ohio 3447, — N.E. 2d —, 2007 Ohio App. LEXIS 3178 (June 29, 2007).

Power to render judgment

As the evidence was not sufficient to support defendant's conviction for possession of marijuana, in violation of RC § 2925.11(A), but it was sufficient to find that he had attempted to knowingly possess the marijuana, the court on appeal acted within its authority under Ohio R. App. P. 12(B) when it directed an acquittal on remand for his possession conviction, and a conviction for attempted possession, in violation of RC § 2923.02. State v. Bettis, — Ohio App. 3d —, 2007 Ohio 1724, — N.E. 2d —, 2007 Ohio App. LEXIS 1560 (Apr. 13, 2007).

Trial court erred in granting summary judgment to an insurer on its subrogation claim against orchard owners on theories that they were liable for an employee's motor vehicle accident under either negligent entrustment or respondeat superior, as the evidence did not support liability under either theory because the employee had used a vehicle owned by the orchard without authority where it was not a work-related purpose and it was not during working hours; as there was no evidence to support the insurer's claim, pursuant to its authority under Ohio R. App. P. 12(B), summary judgment could be entered for the owners where it was deemed appropriate. Nationwide Mut. Ins. Co. v. Cano, — Ohio App. 3d —, 2007 Ohio 5354, — N.E. 2d —, 2007 Ohio App. LEXIS 4718 (Oct. 5, 2007).

Evidence was insufficient to prove that defendant acted with the purpose to "deprive" owners of a van within the meaning of RC § 2913.01(C)(1) since the evidence tended to show that defendant was returning to the party with the van when the accident occurred, and thus, the State failed to prove that defendant intended to withhold the owners' van permanently so as to constitute the offense of theft of a motor vehicle under RC § 2913.02(A)(1). Since the evidence showed that defendant was guilty of the lesser-included offense of unauthorized use of a motor vehicle, the court modified the conviction, as it was authorized to do under Ohio R. App. P. 12(B), and remanded the case with instructions to the trial court to enter a conviction on the lesser-included offense. State v. Davis, — Ohio App. 3d —, 2006 Ohio 4599, — N.E. 2d —, 2006 Ohio App. LEXIS 4545 (Sept. 8, 2006).

Power to reverse judgment

As a judge's note to a pro se defendant regarding the admissibility of a polygraph test was less than clear, wherein defendant claimed that he would not have incurred the expense of undergoing such a test if he was aware that the results were inadmissible in the absence of a stipulation, the appellate court exercised its authority under Ohio Const. art. IV, § 3(B)(2) and Ohio R. App. P. 12(B) to modify the criminal conviction against defendant by reversing the fine imposed on him. State v. Erwin, — Ohio App. 3d —, 2007 Ohio 1741, — N.E. 2d —, 2007 Ohio App. LEXIS 1596 (Apr. 13, 2007).

Prejudicial error not found

Since a trial court's judgment granting appellee's request for annulment was mere surplusage in light of the trial court's other determinations that the parties' purported marriage was void ab initio and that the parties had no common law marriage, the court was not required to reverse the trial court's judgment in this respect as appellant could not show any error that was prejudicial to her pursuant to Ohio R. App. P. 12(D). Tabler v. Tabler, — Ohio App. 3d —, 2007 Ohio 1579, — N.E. 2d —, 2007 Ohio App. LEXIS 1433 (Mar. 26, 2007).

Although the trial court erred in requiring defendant to provide discovery to the State under Ohio R. Crim. P. 16(C) because defendant had not made any discovery requests under Rule 16(B)(1)(c), (d), or (e), where defendant failed to assert that he suffered prejudice as a result thereof, pursuant to Ohio R. App. P. 12(D) there was no cause to reverse the trial court decision. State v. Glick, — Ohio App. 3d —, 2007 Ohio 4104, — N.E. 2d —, 2007 Ohio App. LEXIS 3735 (Aug. 13, 2007).

Record on appeal

As defendant's claim on appeal that the jury's verdict was against the manifest weight of the evidence was not identified in the record, as required by Ohio R. App. P. 12(A)(2), and he failed to set forth an argument that met the requirements of Ohio R. App. P. 16(A)(7), the assignment of error was not reviewable. Defendant only offered a comprehensive statement of the law relating to review of arguments on the issue of manifest weight of the evidence, but he failed to state exactly what evidence he relied on that made the law applicable to his case. State v. Harris, — Ohio App. 3d —, 2007 Ohio 526, — N.E. 2d —, 2007 Ohio App. LEXIS 482 (Feb. 8, 2007).

Where the record on appeal was unclear due to defendant's failure to provide a bond or a clerk's office form, as required by Ohio R. App. P. 9(B) and 10(A), it was unclear exactly who posted the bond that was used to pay fines assessed against defendant, as the appellate court's review was limited to the record presented before it pursuant to Ohio R. App. P. 9 and 12(A)(1)(b). The appellate court could not review defendant's assignment of error regarding a taking of his property with respect to the bail money, as the regularity of the trial court proceedings was presumed. State v. Ahmed, — Ohio App. 3d —, 2007 Ohio 2639, — N.E. 2d —, 2007 Ohio App. LEXIS 2478 (May 31, 2007).

Defendant's assignments of error on appeal regarding sufficiency of the evidence and denial of his speedy trial rights were not properly supported by legal authority and were not

referenced in the record, as required by Ohio R. App. P. 12(A)(2), 16(A)(7), and Ohio Ninth Dist. Ct. App. R. 7(A)(7) and (F), such that they were not reviewable. State v. Mastice, — Ohio App. 3d —, 2007 Ohio 4107, — N.E. 2d —, 2007 Ohio App. LEXIS 3732 (Aug. 13, 2007).

Former city finance director's claim for accrued vacation time was denied because Willoughby Hills, Ohio, Ordinance No. 2002-02 provided that city employees, such as the director, who resigned would not be entitled to vacation pay; information that another employee took his remaining vacation time after his effective resignation could not be considered on appeal under Ohio R. App. P. 12(A)(1)(b) as that information was not before the trial court or the magistrate prior to the final judgment and, thus, was not part of the record on appeal under Ohio R. App. P. 9(A). Condron v. City of Willoughby Hills, — Ohio App. 3d —, 2007 Ohio 5208, — N.E. 2d —, 2007 Ohio App. LEXIS 4609 (Sept. 28, 2007).

Since a detective's affidavit filed in support of a search warrant was not included in the "record on appeal," as defined in Ohio R. App. P. 9, and since the affidavit was essential to determining the validity of the trial court's judgment denying defendant's motion to suppress, defendant could not meet his burden of showing error on appeal. Pursuant to Ohio R. App. P. 12, the court could not consider the affidavit when it was only attached to defendant's brief but was not made part of the trial court record. State v. Freeman, — Ohio App. 3d —, 2006 Ohio 5020, — N.E. 2d —, 2006 Ohio App. LEXIS 5181 (Sept. 18, 2006).

Remand to trial court

When, in a permanent custody case, a trial court erroneously used the time between filing and hearing the permanent custody motion to find the subject children were in the custody of a chidren's services agency for more than 12 of the last 22 months, under RC § 2515.414(B)(1)(d), requiring a remand, a new evidentiary hearing was not required on remand because the record from the prior hearing allowed the trial court to find, under RC § 2151.414(B)(1), that the children could not be returned to either parent within a reasonable time. In re Arnold, — Ohio App. 3d —, 2006 Ohio 2794, — N.E. 2d —, 2006 Ohio App. LEXIS 2608 (June 5, 2006).

Reversal of judgment

Appellant's motion to vacate court costs was improperly denied because the trial court waived appellant's requirement to pay court costs at the time of sentencing due to appellant's indigence, and there was no indication that appellant's circumstances had changed since the sentencing hearing. Pursuant to Ohio R. App. P. 12(B), the court granted appellant's motion to vacate court costs and barred the collection efforts of the clerk of courts against appellant for payment of court costs. Even though RC § 2947.23 requires a judge to assess costs against all convicted criminal defendants, waiver of costs is permitted if a defendant is indigent. State v. Mamontov, — Ohio App. 3d —, 2007 Ohio 1863, — N.E. 2d —, 2007 Ohio App. LEXIS 1702 (Apr. 20, 2007).

Right to disregard errors

Although a father who appealed a probate court's denial of his request to remove the guardian for his mentally disabled son failed to support his assignments of error with argument, legal authority, or citation to the relevant portions of the record, such that the court could have chosen to disregard the non-complying assignments of error pursuant to Ohio R. App. P. 12(A)(2) and 16(A), the court reviewed the issues raised on the merits in the interests of justice. In re Constable, — Ohio App. 3d —, 2007 Ohio 3346, — N.E. 2d —, 2007 Ohio App. LEXIS 3105 (July 2, 2007).

Pursuant to Ohio R. App. P. 12(A) and 16(A)(7), an appellate court disregarded various assignments of error raised by defendant in his appeal from his conviction, as he failed to specifically cite to the record to support his arguments. State v. Anderson, — Ohio App. 3d —, 2007 Ohio 5068, — N.E. 2d —, 2007 Ohio App. LEXIS 4477 (Sept. 27, 2007).

Where inmates raised an issue on appeal but they failed to identify the specific portions of the record upon which their claim of error was based, the court had authority to decline to address the assignment of error under Ohio R. App. P. 12(A)(2). Ridenour v. Wilkinson, — Ohio App. 3d —, 2007 Ohio 5965, — N.E. 2d —, 2007 Ohio App. LEXIS 5238 (Nov. 8, 2007).

When members of an administrative board elected by a faction of a church, who sought a declaratory judgment that they were the church's proper administrative board, did not articulate an applicable standard of review, cite to any legal authority in support of their claims, or develop their arguments sufficiently to support their claim that the trial court abused its discretion by ratifying an illegal election or that a subsequently elected board in any way abused the election process, their failure to meet their burden under Ohio R. App. P. 16(A)(7) or Ohio Ninth Dist. Ct. App. R. 7(B)(7) allowed the appellate court to disregard their assignment of error, under Ohio R. App. P. 12(A)(2). St. Nikola Macedonian Orthodox Church v. Zoran, — Ohio App. 3d —, 2006 Ohio 2561, — N.E. 2d —, 2006 Ohio App. LEXIS 2409 (May 24, 2006).

Appellate court declined to review errors asserted on appeal by home owners after a judgment of foreclosure was granted to a homeowners association, as their argument on appeal was unclear pursuant to Ohio R. App. P. 12(A)(2) and 16(A)despite repeated readings and the brief failed to mention a motion which was apparently referenced therein and denied by the trial court. Miles Landing Homeowners Ass'n v. Bikkani, — Ohio App. 3d —, 2006 Ohio 3328, — N.E. 2d —, 2006 Ohio App. LEXIS 3244 (June 29, 2006).

— Discretionary right

Husband's assignments of error on appeal from a trial court decree of divorce were not disregarded pursuant to Ohio R. App. P. 12(A)(2), although he failed to properly cite to the record in his brief, as required by Ohio R. App. P. 16(A)(3) and (D), as he indicated that the references to the wife's testimony in the last two hours of the trial transcript were where the assigned errors related to. Jack H. Parker v. Susanne Kohl Parker, — Ohio App. 3d —, 2007 Ohio 4895, — N.E. 2d —, 2007 Ohio App. LEXIS 4366 (Sept. 21, 2007).

Sentencing

Although a trial court had orally amended a charge against defendant to accurately reflect that it was to be a second degree misdemeanor of resisting arrest, in violation of R.C. § 2921.33(A), rather than a first degree misdemeanor, where the sentencing entry indicated that the sentence imposed was based on the first degree offense and the sentencing range of six months' imprisonment exceeded the maximum period of confinement available, the sentence imposed was contrary to law; however, as it was a sentence that was concurrent to another sentence of equal length, such that defendant suffered no prejudice, pursuant to Ohio R. App. P. 12(B) the court modified the sentencing entry to accurately reflect the correct conviction and the proper term of imprisonment thereon. State v. Coughlin, — Ohio App. 3d —, 2007 Ohio 897, — N.E. 2d —, 2007 Ohio App. LEXIS 803 (Mar. 2, 2007).

Pursuant to RC § 2953.08(G) and Ohio R. App. P. 12(B) and in the interests of justice, the appellate court modified the imposition of a term of imprisonment on defendant for one of the drug trafficking charges to which he entered a guilty plea. State v. Gibson, — Ohio App. 3d —, 2006 Ohio 4171, — N.E. 2d —, 2006 Ohio App. LEXIS 4132 (Aug. 11, 2006).

Weighing of evidence

After a trial court adopted a magistrate's decision that found that a property transfer was fraudulent and the matter was reversed on appeal and remanded for further determinations pursuant to Ohio R. App. P. 12(C), the appeal from the decision on remand could not be reviewed on manifest weight of the evidence grounds, as the prior reversal on those grounds precluded a second reversal for manifest weight of the evidence; however, a sufficiency of the evidence review could be had. Gevedon v. Ivey, — Ohio App. 3d —, 2007 Ohio 2970, — N.E. 2d —, 2007 Ohio App. LEXIS 2730 (June 15, 2007).

TITLE III
GENERAL PROVISIONS

RULE 13. Filing and service

(A) **Filing.** Documents required or permitted to be filed in a court of appeals shall be filed with the clerk. Filing may be accomplished by mail addressed to the clerk, but filing shall not be timely unless the documents are received by the clerk within the time fixed for filing, except that briefs shall be deemed filed on the day of mailing. If a motion requests relief which may be granted by a single judge, the judge may permit the motion to be filed with the judge, in which event the judge shall note the filing date on the motion and transmit it to the clerk. A court may provide, by local rules adopted pursuant to the Rules of Superintendence, for the filing of documents by electronic means. If the court adopts such local rules, they shall include all of the following:

(1) Any signature on electronically transmitted documents shall be considered that of the attorney or party it purports to be for all purposes. If it is established that the documents were transmitted without authority, the court shall order the filing stricken.

(2) A provision shall specify the days and hours during which electronically transmitted documents will be received by the court, and a provision shall specify when documents received electronically will be considered to have been filed.

(3) Any document filed electronically that requires a filing fee may be rejected by the clerk of court unless the filer has complied with the mechanism established by the court for the payment of filing fees.

(B) **Service of all documents required.** Copies of all documents filed by any party and not required by these rules to be served by the clerk shall, at or before the time of filing, be served by a party or person acting for the party on all other parties to the appeal. Service on a party represented by counsel shall be made on counsel.

(C) **Manner of service.** Service may be personal or by mail. Personal service includes delivery of the copy to a clerk or other responsible person at the office of counsel. Service by mail is complete on mailing.

(D) **Proof of service.** Documents presented for filing shall contain an acknowledgment of service by the person served or proof of service in the form of a statement of the date and manner of service and of the names of the persons served, certified by the person who made service. Documents filed with the court shall not be considered until proof of service is endorsed on the documents or separately filed.

History: Amended, eff 7-1-01.

NOTES TO DECISIONS

ANALYSIS

Procedure

Procedure

When appellant's brief indicated that the sole method it used to serve its brief and notice of appeal was by facsimile, this violated Ohio R. App. P. 13, as did its failure to adequately identify opposing counsel upon whom service was made. Western Reserve Logistics v. Hunt Mach. & Mfg. Co., — Ohio App. 3d —, 2006 Ohio 5070, — N.E. 2d —, 2006 Ohio App. LEXIS 4980 (Sept. 29, 2006).

RULE 14. Computation and extension of time

(A) **Computation of time.** In computing any period of time prescribed or allowed by these rules, by the local rules of any court, by an order of court or by any applicable statute, the day of the act, event or default from which the designated period of time begins to run shall not be included. The last day of the period so computed shall be included, unless it is a Saturday, Sunday or a legal holiday, in which event the period runs until the end of the next day which is not a Saturday, Sunday or legal holiday. When the period of time prescribed or allowed is less than seven days, intermediate Saturdays, Sundays and legal holidays shall be excluded in the computation.

(B) **Enlargement or reduction of time.** For good cause shown, the court, upon motion, may enlarge or reduce the time prescribed by these rules or by its order for doing any act, or may permit an act to be done after the expiration of the prescribed time. The court may not enlarge or reduce the time for filing a notice of appeal or a motion to certify pursuant to App. R. 25. Enlargement of time to file an application for reconsideration or for en banc consideration pursuant to App. R. 26(A) shall not be granted except on a showing of extraordinary circumstances.

(C) **Additional time after service by mail.** Whenever a party is required or permitted to do an act within a prescribed period after service of a paper upon the party and the paper is served by mail, three days shall be added to the prescribed period.

History: Amended, eff 7-1-94; 7-1-10.

NOTES TO DECISIONS

ANALYSIS

Enlargement of time
Time requirement jurisdictional

Enlargement of time

Defendant inmate could not seek to file a delayed appeal pursuant to Ohio R. App. P. 5(A) from a trial court determination on his post-conviction relief (PCR) petition, as such was specifically unavailable from PCR determinations; as he failed to comply with the time requirement of Ohio R. App. P. 4(A) and he failed to allege a trial court clerk's lack of

compliance with Ohio R. Civ. P. 58(B) for purposes of Ohio Eleventh Dist. Ct. App. R. 3(D)(2), the appeal was untimely and the time could not be enlarged by the appellate court under Ohio R. App. P. 14(B). Ohio v. Johnson, — Ohio App. 3d —, 2007 Ohio 5500, — N.E. 2d —, 2007 Ohio App. LEXIS 4832 (Oct. 15, 2007).

Time requirement jurisdictional

Appeal from a trial court's judgment was dismissed because appellant had neither filed her notice of appeal within thirty days of service of the notice of the judgment, as required by Ohio R. App. P. 4(A), nor had she alleged, pursuant to Ohio 11th Dist. Ct. App. R. 3(D)(2), that the trial court had failed to comply with Ohio R. Civ. P. 58(B). Pursuant to Ohio R. App. P. 14, the time requirement of Ohio R. App. P. 4(A) was jurisdictional. A.K.A. Alphonso Dion Godfrey, — Ohio App. 3d —, 2007 Ohio 5501, — N.E. 2d —, 2007 Ohio App. LEXIS 4820 (Oct. 15, 2007).

Court sua sponte dismissed an appeal from a trial court's judgment because appellant had not filed the notice of appeal within thirty days of the judgment, as required by Ohio R. App. P. 4(A), and he had not submitted an affidavit under Ohio 11th Dist. Ct. App. R. 3(D)(2) that there was a failure by the trial court clerk to comply with Ohio R. Civ. P. 58(B). Pursuant to Ohio R. App. P. 14(B), the time requirement for filing a notice of appeal was jurisdictional and could not be enlarged by an appellate court. De Leon Lomaz v. Gibel, — Ohio App. 3d —, 2007 Ohio 5908, — N.E. 2d —, 2007 Ohio App. LEXIS 5210 (Nov. 2, 2007).

RULE 15. Motions

(A) **Content of motions; response; reply.** Unless another form is prescribed by these rules, an application for an order or other relief shall be made by motion with proof of service on all other parties. The motion shall contain or be accompanied by any matter required by a specific provision of these rules governing such a motion, shall state with particularity the grounds on which it is based, and shall set forth the order or relief sought. If a motion is supported by briefs, affidavits, or other papers, they shall be served and filed with the motion. Except as set forth in Rule 15(B), any party may file a response in opposition to a motion within ten days after service of the motion, and any party may file a reply in further support of a motion within seven days after service of the opposition, but motions authorized by Rule 7, Rule 8, and Rule 27 may be acted upon after reasonable notice, and the court may shorten or extend the time for a response or reply.

(B) **Determination of motions for procedural orders.** Motions for procedural orders, including any motion under Rule 14(B) may be acted upon at any time, without awaiting a response thereto. Any party adversely affected by such action may request reconsideration, vacation or modification of such action.

(C) **Power of a single judge to entertain motions.** In addition to the authority expressly conferred by these rules or by law, and unless otherwise provided by rule or law, a single judge of a court of appeals may entertain and may grant or deny any request for relief, which under these rules may properly be sought by motion, except that a single judge may not dismiss or otherwise determine an appeal or other proceeding, and except that a court of appeals may provide by order or rule that any motion or class of motions must be acted upon by the court. The action of a single judge may be reviewed by the court.

(D) **Number of copies.** Three copies of all papers relating to motions shall be filed with the original, but the court may require that additional copies be furnished.

History: Amended, eff 7-1-10.

NOTES TO DECISIONS

Analysis

Attorney fees

Attorney fees

As nothing in the Ohio Fourth District Court of Appeals Rules prohibited a neighboring property owner from filing a motion on appeal for attorney fees pursuant to Ohio R. App. P. 15 and 23, the property purchasers' motion to strike the fee request was denied. It was determined that she was entitled to a fee award on all but one of the arguments asserted on appeal by the purchasers, as they wholly lacked merit and were frivolous, but as to the one argument where the purchasers' argument on appeal was based on a contrary holding from another Ohio appellate district, such did not warrant a fee award to the neighboring property owner. Patton v. Ditmyer, — Ohio App. 3d —, 2006 Ohio 7107, — N.E. 2d —, 2006 Ohio App. LEXIS 7061 (Dec. 29, 2006).

RULE 16. Briefs

(A) **Brief of the appellant.** The appellant shall include in its brief, under the headings and in the order indicated, all of the following:

(1) A table of contents, with page references.

(2) A table of cases alphabetically arranged, statutes, and other authorities cited, with references to the pages of the brief where cited.

(3) A statement of the assignments of error presented for review, with reference to the place in the record where each error is reflected.

(4) A statement of the issues presented for review, with references to the assignments of error to which each issue relates.

(5) A statement of the case briefly describing the nature of the case, the course of proceedings, and the disposition in the court below.

(6) A statement of facts relevant to the assignments of error presented for review, with appropriate references to the record in accordance with division (D) of this rule.

(7) An argument containing the contentions of the appellant with respect to each assignment of error presented for review and the reasons in support of the contentions, with citations to the authorities, statutes, and parts of the record on which appellant relies. The argument may be preceded by a summary.

(8) A conclusion briefly stating the precise relief sought.

(B) **Brief of the appellee.** The brief of the appellee shall conform to the requirements of divisions (A)(1) to (A)(8) of this rule, except that a statement of the case or of the facts relevant to the assignments of error need not be made unless the appellee is dissatisfied with the statement of the appellant.

(C) **Reply brief.** The appellant may file a brief in reply to the brief of the appellee, and, if the appellee

has cross-appealed, the appellee may file a brief in reply to the response of the appellant to the assignments of errors presented by the cross-appeal. No further briefs may be filed except with leave of court.

(D) **References in briefs to the record.** References in the briefs to parts of the record shall be to the pages of the parts of the record involved; e.g., Answer p. 7, Motion for Judgment p. 2, Transcript p. 231. Intelligible abbreviations may be used. If reference is made to evidence, the admissibility of which is in controversy, reference shall be made to the pages of the transcript at which the evidence was identified, offered, and received or rejected.

(E) **Reproduction of statutes, rules, regulations** . If determination of the assignments of error presented requires the consideration of provisions of constitutions, statutes, ordinances, rules, or regulations, the relevant parts shall be reproduced in the brief or in an addendum at the end or may be supplied to the court in pamphlet form.

History: Amended, eff 7-1-72; 7-1-92.

NOTES TO DECISIONS

Analysis

Appellant argument
Appellant required to set forth argument
Assignment of error
— Brief requirements
Attachment to brief
Brief inadequate
Brief requirements
Citations to authorities
Consideration of errors
Error
Failure to cite to authority
Failure to cite to record
Failure to support
Procedure
—Transcript
Reply briefs

Appellant argument

Since appellant presented only one argument in support of its two assignments of error, in contravention of Ohio R. App. P. 16(A)(7), the appellate court would have been in its discretion under Ohio R. App. P. 12(A)(2) simply to disregard appellant's assignments of error and summarily affirm the trial court; however, in the interest of justice, the court chose to review appellant's arguments. Keffer v. Cent. Mut. Ins. Co., — Ohio App. 3d —, 2007 Ohio 3984, — N.E. 2d —, 2007 Ohio App. LEXIS 3587 (May 17, 2007).

Appellant required to set forth argument

As defendant reincorporated his argument on appeal relating to the sufficiency of the evidence for his drug possession conviction into his argument relating to the weight of the evidence, he failed to set forth an independent argument for the weight of the evidence assignment of error, as required by Ohio R. App. P. 16(A)(7). State v. Brown, — Ohio App. 3d —, 2007 Ohio 527, — N.E. 2d —, 2007 Ohio App. LEXIS 476 (Feb. 8, 2007).

Where a next of kin to an incompetent and a guardian applicant appealed a probate court's rejection of part of a magistrate's decision that found the applicant was not a suitable appointee, but the appeal did not separately argue the issue of the alleged error and there were no citations to the authorities, statutes, and parts of the record that were relied upon, pursuant to Ohio R. App. P. 16(A)(7) and 12(A)(2) the court declined to review the asserted error. In re Guardianship of Blair, — Ohio App. 3d —, — N.E. 2d —, 2007 Ohio 3335, 2007 Ohio App. LEXIS 3124 (June 11, 2007).

In an appeal from a grant of summary judgment for a former employer in an employee's action, alleging claims of wrongful discharge and retaliatory discharge, the employee's failure to provide any arguments regarding the wrongful discharge claim resulted in a lack of review on that issue pursuant to Ohio R. App. P. 12(A)(2) and 16(A)(7). Prox v. Cleveland Steel Container Corp., — Ohio App. 3d —, 2006 Ohio 2770, — N.E. 2d —, 2006 Ohio App. LEXIS 2619 (June 2, 2006).

Court refused to consider one of the assignments of error asserted by a father in his brief because the father presented no argument on the issue as required by Ohio R. App. P. 16(A). Newhouse v. Williams, 167 Ohio App. 3d 215, 2006 Ohio 3075, 854 N.E. 2d 565, 2006 Ohio App. LEXIS 2944 (June 19, 2006).

Defendant failed to comply with Ohio R. App. P. 16(A)(7) where his brief on appeal raised five assignments of error, but only the first two assignments had arguments made under them. State v. Powell, — Ohio App. 3d —, 2006 Ohio 3477, — N.E. 2d —, 2006 Ohio App. LEXIS 3422 (June 27, 2006).

Where an insurer failed to present any arguments to support an issue that it raised on appeal in a declaratory judgment action regarding its duty to provide a defense and to indemnify its insured from an employer intentional tort claim, the appellate court disregarded the assignment of error pursuant to Ohio R. App. P. 12(A)(2) and 16(A)(7). Cincinnati Ins. Co. v. Schwerha, — Ohio App. 3d —, 2006 Ohio 3521, — N.E. 2d —, 2006 Ohio App. LEXIS 3440 (June 28, 2006).

Since a mother failed to specifically argue how counsel's performance in a permanent custody proceeding in failing to request the alternative disposition of a planned permanent living arrangement and in failing to request independent counsel for the mother's children fell below an objective standard of reasonableness and also failed to establish that the result would have been different but for the alleged deficiencies of counsel, the court, pursuant to Ohio R. App. P. 16(A)(7) and Ohio R. App. P. 12(A)(2), did not need to further address the mother's assertion that she was deprived of the effective assistance of counsel in this respect. In re A.T., — Ohio App. 3d —, 2006 Ohio 3919, — N.E. 2d —, 2006 Ohio App. LEXIS 3883 (Aug. 2, 2006).

Husband who appealed a trial court's grant of summary judgment to his wife in her foreclosure action failed to comply with Ohio R. App. P. 16(A)(7) where he failed to discuss or justify his apparent position and he failed to assert an argument in support of his specified assignment of error; however, as the appellate court's review of summary judgment by the trial court was de novo, it independently reviewed the evidence. Welch v. Welch, — Ohio App. 3d —, 2006 Ohio 6862, — N.E. 2d —, 2006 Ohio App. LEXIS 6774 (Dec. 22, 2006).

Since appellant dominant property owners failed to set forth separate arguments for each of their assignments of error, as required by Ohio R. App. P. 16(A), the court could disregard any assignment of error not argued separately in the brief. Colace v. Wander, — Ohio App. 3d —, 2006 Ohio 7094, — N.E. 2d —, 2006 Ohio App. LEXIS 7015 (Dec. 26, 2006).

In a divorce, when a husband claimed, on appeal, that a trial court did not make findings required under RC § 3119.82, regarding the allocation of tax exemptions attributable to the parties' children, he waived this claim, under Ohio R. App. P. 16(A)(7) and Ohio Ninth Dist. Ct. App. R. 7(A)(7), because he did not affirmatively demonstrate error on appeal or substantiate his argument. Lara v. Lara, — Ohio App. 3d —, 2006 Ohio 2853, — N.E. 2d —, 2006 Ohio App. LEXIS 2675 (June 7, 2006).

Assignment of error

Although a mobile home park lessee who appealed a trial court decision failed to cite to any legal authority regarding a particular assignment of error, pursuant to her burden under Ohio R. App. P. 16(A)(7), the court chose to address the assignment of error in the interests of justice. Montgomery v. Mann, — Ohio App. 3d —, 2007 Ohio 44, — N.E. 2d —, 2007 Ohio App. LEXIS 34 (Jan. 9, 2007).

Defendant's claim, that the trial court violated his rights under certain sections of the Ohio Constitution regarding the denial of his post-conviction relief petition, failed to comply with Ohio R. App. P. 16(A)(7) because the assigned error contained no argument or analysis. State v. Edmond, — Ohio App. 3d —, 2007 Ohio 555, — N.E. 2d —, 2007 Ohio App. LEXIS 512 (Feb. 8, 2007).

As the six assignments of error in a brief by children of judgment debtors were not separately argued, they did not comply with the requirement of Ohio R. App. P. 16(A) and the court could have chosen to disregard its review of them pursuant to Ohio R. App. P. 12(A)(2). The court could also have chosen to review the assignments of error on the merits in the interest of justice, which it did. Tube City, Inc. v. Halishak, — Ohio App. 3d —, 2007 Ohio 2118, — N.E. 2d —, 2007 Ohio App. LEXIS 1976 (May 3, 2007).

Although a contractor who appealed a grant of summary judgment to a supplier did not meet his burden of affirmatively demonstrating error on appeal pursuant to Ohio R. App. P. 16(A)(7) where he failed to cite to any legal authority relative to his assignment of error, the court acted within its discretion in reviewing the claim in the interests of justice. Palmer-Donavin v. Hanna, — Ohio App. 3d —, 2007 Ohio 2242, — N.E. 2d —, 2007 Ohio App. LEXIS 2081 (May 10, 2007).

As a property owner who appealed a trial court's decision that held him in contempt and imposed sanctions against him failed to file a separate assignment of error for purposes of his brief on appeal, as required by Ohio Ninth Dist. Ct. App. R. 7(B)(7) and Ohio R. App. P. 16(A)(7), the court declined to review the asserted error. Village of Boston Hts. v. Cerny, — Ohio App. 3d —, 2007 Ohio 2886, — N.E. 2d —, 2007 Ohio App. LEXIS 2680 (June 13, 2007).

Although a tenant who appealed trial court rulings in favor of the landlord failed to present assignments of error as required by Ohio R. App. P. 16(A)(3), the court chose to review the matter on the merits in the interests of justice rather than to dismiss it, as it had a right to do. Valente v. Johnson, — Ohio App. 3d —, 2007 Ohio 2664, — N.E. 2d —, 2007 Ohio App. LEXIS 2482 (May 29, 2007).

Although an employee who appealed a trial court's grant of summary judgment to an insurer in her declaratory judgment action failed to separately set forth each statement of the three assignments of error presented for review, as required by Ohio R. App. P. 16(A)(3), the court chose to review the issues raised in the interest of justice. Hagberg v. Cincinnati Ins. Co., — Ohio App. 3d —, 2007 Ohio 2731, — N.E. 2d —, 2007 Ohio App. LEXIS 2518 (June 5, 2007).

Where a motorist appealed a jury verdict in favor of a driver in the motorist's personal injury action and he failed to provide the court on appeal with the factual details concerning an alleged evidentiary error, he failed to indicate the specific evidence that supposedly resulted in prejudice to him, and he failed to explain how the evidentiary error warranted a new trial, he defeated his assigned error based on his lack of compliance with the brief requirements of Ohio R. App. P. 16(A)(6) and (7). Sims v. Dibler, 172 Ohio App. 3d 486, 2007 Ohio 3035, 875 N.E.2d 965, 2007 Ohio App. LEXIS 2879 (2007).

Court disregarded a wife's assignments of error presented in her appeal from trial court's judgment and presumed the validity of the proceedings below because the wife failed to include page references to the places in the record where the errors involved in the assignments occurred, as required by Ohio R. App. P. 16(A)(3); she did not argue the assignments of error separately in her brief; and she did not provide transcripts of the hearings cited in her reply brief, as required by Ohio R. App. P. 9. Thus, the court disregarded the wife's assignments of error, as it was permitted to do under Ohio R. App. P. 12(A)(2) and presumed the validity of the trial court's proceedings. Dunina v. Stemple, — Ohio App. 3d —, 2007 Ohio 4719, — N.E. 2d —, 2007 Ohio App. LEXIS 4228 (Sept. 14, 2007).

Although an injured employee failed to set forth a list of assignments of error, a statement of the issues presented for review, or a statement of the case, as required by Ohio R. App. P. 16(A)(3), (4), and (5), where he set out "propositions of law" which adequately defined the issues upon which he sought review, the court chose to decide the case on the merits. Robinson v. Kokosing Constr. Co., — Ohio App. 3d —, 2006 Ohio 1532, — N.E. 2d —, 2006 Ohio App. LEXIS 1396 (Mar. 30, 2006).

Where a credit card holder appealed a grant of summary judgment to the credit card issuer in its breach of contract action against him, but the holder's "assignments of error" were not separately argued in his brief as required by Ohio R. App. P. 12(A)(2) and 16(A)(7), the appellate court disregarded them. Discover Fin. Servs. v. Belmont, — Ohio App. 3d —, 2006 Ohio 1539, — N.E. 2d —, 2006 Ohio App. LEXIS 1418 (Mar. 30, 2006).

Although defendant's appellate brief advanced a single, joint argument for multiple assignments of error, which was not permitted under Ohio R. App. P. 16(A)(7) and could have led to the court's disregard of those assignments pursuant to Ohio R. App. P. 12(A)(2), the court chose to review them in the interests of justice. State v. Bennett, — Ohio App. 3d —, 2006 Ohio 2757, — N.E. 2d —, 2006 Ohio App. LEXIS 2592 (May 22, 2006).

Where wife's argument on appeal regarding the trial court's distributive award was unclear, and she offered no evidence nor argument to support her claim that the trial court erred in finding that checking accounts contained marital funds, she failed to meet her burden on appeal pursuant to Ohio R. App. P. 16(A)(7), and the argument was not reviewable. Henley v. Henley, — Ohio App. 3d —, 2006 Ohio 3336, — N.E. 2d —, 2006 Ohio App. LEXIS 3263 (June 30, 2006).

Where an appellate court clerk stamped one notice of appeal and brief filed by an inmate, raising the issue of the trial court's denial of his request for appointed counsel, as "filed," and the clerk mistakenly filed the other notice of appeal and brief filed by the inmate from the trial court's denial of his plea withdrawal request as "copy," the appellate court's disregard of the inmate's claim on the withdrawal issue upon determining that it was not argued pursuant to Ohio R. App. P. 12 and 16 was an "obvious error"; as the court did not review the brief relating to the plea withdrawal request due to the clerk's clerical mistake, the inmate's application for reconsideration pursuant to Ohio R. App. P. 26 was granted on the limited issue of arguments relating to the plea withdrawal request. State v. Meadows, — Ohio App. 3d —, 2006 Ohio 3375, — N.E. 2d —, 2006 Ohio App. LEXIS 3304 (June 29, 2006).

Where defendant set forth assorted issues at the close of his appellate brief which were not properly raised as assigned errors pursuant to Ohio R. App. P. 16(A)(3) and (7), the issues were summarily dismissed by the appellate court for failure to comply with the appellate rules. State v. Peoples, — Ohio App. 3d —, 2006 Ohio 4162, — N.E. 2d —, 2006 Ohio App. LEXIS 4095 (Aug. 11, 2006).

Defendant's argument on appeal that State v. Foster effectively raised the maximum penalty from the maximum authorized by the facts established by a plea of guilty or a jury verdict to the statutory maximum, in violation of ex post facto principles, was not specifically raised in an assignment of error set forth in the briefs, as required by Ohio R. App. P. 12(A)(1)(b) and Ohio R. App. P. 16. Since the trial court had yet to resentence defendant, any argument as to the terms or propriety of his new sentence was premature. State v. White, — Ohio App. 3d —, 2006 Ohio 4226, — N.E. 2d —, 2006 Ohio App. LEXIS 4149 (Aug. 15, 2006).

Real property owners who appealed a judgment of foreclosure in favor of a county treasurer failed to comply with Ohio R. App. P. 12(A) and 16(A) where they did not identify assignments of error for the appellate court to review, and their appellate brief was largely a recitation of incomplete thoughts and citations. The court only addressed three general arguments raised in the brief, but it refused to scour the record. Callison v. Huelsman, 168 Ohio App. 3d 471, 2006 Ohio 4395, 860 N.E. 2d 829, 2006 Ohio App. LEXIS 4322 (Aug. 25, 2006).

Since a mother failed to offer any explanation, analysis, or citations to the record or to specific Ohio cases or statutes in support of her assertions that the trial court's decision awarding legal custody of the mother's two sons to the sons' paternal grandparents was against the manifest weight of the evidence, the mother's brief failed to comply with Ohio R. App. P. 16(A)(7). Thus, pursuant to Ohio R. App. P. 12(A)(2), the court declined to address the mother's assignment of error due to the mother's failure to brief the assigned error. In re C.S., — Ohio App. 3d —, 2006 Ohio 5198, — N.E. 2d —, 2006 Ohio App. LEXIS 5117 (Oct. 2, 2006).

Since defendant failed to point the court to any specific evidence in the record to support his contention that his conviction was against the manifest weight of the evidence, he failed to satisfy his burden under Ohio R. App. P. 16(A)(7) of affirmatively demonstrating error on appeal. The court, pursuant to Ohio R. App. P. 12(A)(2), disregarded defendant's argument and found that his assignment of error was without merit. State v. Joziuk, — Ohio App. 3d —, 2006 Ohio 5421, — N.E. 2d —, 2006 Ohio App. LEXIS 5418 (Oct. 18, 2006).

Where an appealing member of a limited liability company failed to comply with Ohio R. App. P. 12(A)(2) and 16(A)(7), the appellate court chose to disregard the assignment of error raised. All Star Land Title Agency, Inc. v. Surewin Inv., — Ohio App. 3d —, 2006 Ohio 5729, — N.E. 2d —, 2006 Ohio App. LEXIS 5727 (Nov. 2, 2006).

Where defendant failed to refer to the record in his brief to support his contentions regarding evidentiary rulings that he claimed were erroneous, the appellate court was not required to search the record to find them pursuant to Ohio R. App. P. 16(A)(7). State v. Gillingham, — Ohio App. 3d —, 2006 Ohio 5758, — N.E. 2d —, 2006 Ohio App. LEXIS 5738 (Oct. 27, 2006).

As defendant's appeal from various rulings by the trial court on his motions both before and during trial did not comply with the brief requirements of Ohio R. App. P. 12 and 16(A)(7) and it did not constitute an Anders brief, the court chose to disregard the assignment of error relating thereto. Defendant's argument had not cited any authority, had indicated that his counsel had determined that the trial court rulings were correct, and had simply asked the court to "carefully review the record" to determine if he had been denied a fair trial. State v. Moyar, — Ohio App. 3d —, 2006 Ohio 5974, — N.E. 2d —, 2006 Ohio App. LEXIS 5914 (Nov. 13, 2006).

Although property owners appealed a finding that they were in contempt and the imposition of monetary sanctions and fines due to their failure to remove items from their property that constituted a nuisance, where they failed to separately assign as error the numerous arguments set out in their brief, pursuant to Ohio R. App. P. 12 and 16, review thereof was declined. Board of Trustees Thorn Twp. v. Dillow, — Ohio App. 3d —, 2006 Ohio 6888, — N.E. 2d —, 2006 Ohio App. LEXIS 6780 (Dec. 20, 2006).

Employee failed to meet her burden on appeal pursuant to Ohio R. App. P. 12(A)(2), 16(A)(7), and Ohio 9th Dist. Ct. App. R. 7(A)(7) and (F) where she failed to cite in her brief to any portions of the record to support her claim that the trial court's grant of summary judgment to the employer on her age discrimination claim was error; although her brief cited to the record in her statement of facts, that structure did not comport with the appellate rules, and as she failed to demonstrate error on appeal, the court disregarded the assignment of error. Urda v. Buckingham, Doolittle, & Burroughs, — Ohio App. 3d —, 2006 Ohio 6915, — N.E. 2d —, 2006 Ohio App. LEXIS 6816 (Dec. 27, 2006).

Since appellant failed to provide the appellate court with a meaningful argument in support of his contention that genuine issues of fact remained, thereby precluding summary judgment, appellant failed to satisfy his burden on appeal under Ohio R. App. P. 16(A)(7) and Ohio 9th Dist. Ct. App. R. 7(B)(7). Thus, pursuant to Ohio R. App. P. 12(A)(2) and Ohio 9th Dist. Ct. App. R. 7(F), the court disregarded appellant's argument. Marino v. Oriana House, Inc., — Ohio App. 3d —, 2007 Ohio 1823, — N.E. 2d —, 2007 Ohio App. LEXIS 1664 (Apr. 18, 2007).

Where employees who appealed a trial court's grant of summary judgment to an employer on the employees' multi-count complaint failed to assign errors and to otherwise comply with Ohio R. App. P. 16 with respect to the implied breach of contract claim, the court affirmed the trial court's grant of summary judgment on that claim. Hunt v. Trumbull Community Action Program, — Ohio App. 3d —, 2006 Ohio 1698, — N.E. 2d —, 2006 Ohio App. LEXIS 1570 (Mar. 31, 2006).

When a husband claimed a trial court failed to apply unspecified local rules or conduct an evidentiary hearing regarding his motion for relief from judgment, under Ohio R. Civ. P. 60(B), but his brief only recited parts of the transcript without further discussion, he did not comply with Ohio R. App. P. 16(A)(7). Williams v. Williams, — Ohio App. 3d —, 2006 Ohio 2566, — N.E. 2d —, 2006 Ohio App. LEXIS 2420 (May 18, 2006).

Court, pursuant to Ohio R. App. P. 12(A), rejected certain arguments contained in appellant's brief on appeal because. while the issues were stated in the argument section of the brief, appellant did not reference the assignments of error to which these issues related, in contravention of Ohio R. App. P. 16(A)(4). In re A.V., — Ohio App. 3d —, 2006 Ohio 3149, — N.E. 2d —, 2006 Ohio App. LEXIS 3021 (June 22, 2006).

Where defendant did not present any specific argument with respect to his claim on appeal that the trial court erred in failing to suppress certain statements that he made to the police, the court disregarded those arguments on appeal pursuant to Ohio R. App. P. 12(A)(2) and 16(A)(7). State v. Haney, — Ohio App. 3d —, 2006 Ohio 3899, — N.E. 2d —, 2006 Ohio App. LEXIS 3855 (July 31, 2006).

While an insurer set forth two assignments of error at the commencement of its brief, it failed to argue them separately, as required by Ohio R. App. P. 16(A); thus, the court treated the insurer's argument as one and indivisible, pursuant to Ohio R. App. P. 12(A)(2). Nationwide Mut. Ins. Co. v. Godwin, — Ohio App. 3d —, 2006 Ohio 4167, — N.E. 2d —, 2006 Ohio App. LEXIS 4114 (Aug. 11, 2006).

Defendant's claim on appeal from a trial court's denial of her motion to seal her conviction was not well-taken where her brief did not contain any argument with respect to the assignment of error, as required by Ohio R. App. P. 16(A)(7). State v. Runion, — Ohio App. 3d —, 2006 Ohio 4812, — N.E. 2d —, 2006 Ohio App. LEXIS 4714 (Sept. 15, 2006).

Since a father failed to brief two assignments of error challenging a trial court's custody decision, as required by Ohio R. App. P. 16(A)(7), the appellate court declined to address those assignments of error pursuant to Ohio R. App.

P. 12(A)(2). In re T.G., — Ohio App. 3d —, 2006 Ohio 5504, — N.E. 2d —, 2006 Ohio App. LEXIS 5489 (Oct. 23, 2006).

In a dental malpractice action, the dentist's brief failed to comply with Ohio R. App. P. 16(A)(5), (7) because the statement of the case was more than 20 pages long and contained arguments that should have been presented under the corresponding assignments of error, while the argument section left out those arguments and did not include citations to the parts of the record where alleged errors occurred. In order to reach the merits of the case, the appellate court declined to disregard the assignments of error where the problem existed, but warned the dentist that there would be no reconsideration if it was perceived to have missed an argument or citation that was not specifically contained under the pertinent assignment of error. Scibelli v. Pannunzio, — Ohio App. 3d —, 2006 Ohio 5652, — N.E. 2d —, 2006 Ohio App. LEXIS 5650 (Oct. 26, 2006).

State agency employee failed in her duty under Ohio R. App. P. 16 when she did not set forth assignments of error for purposes of her challenge on appeal to a judgment in favor of a state agency in her disability discrimination action. She also failed to provide a transcript of the trial court proceedings in the record, such that the appellate court was required to presume the regularity of the trial court proceedings and affirm the trial court decision pursuant to Ohio R. App. P. 12. Lee v. Ohio Dep't of Jobs & Family Servs., — Ohio App. 3d —, — N.E. 2d —, 2006 Ohio App. LEXIS 6504 (Dec. 14, 2006).

Although defendant set out separate assignments of error in his brief on appeal from his criminal conviction and sentence, where he failed to set forth separate arguments as required by Ohio R. App. P. 16(A), the appellate court could have disregarded those assignments of error. It acted within its discretion by reviewing them. State v. Rickey, — Ohio App. 3d —, 2006 Ohio 6889, — N.E. 2d —, 2006 Ohio App. LEXIS 6779 (Dec. 21, 2006).

Although a property owner did not properly set forth his assignment of error in his brief on appeal, pursuant to Ohio R. App. P. 16(A)(3) and 12(A), as he asserted that the trial court wrongfully granted summary judgment to a builder when in fact the trial court had deemed that motion moot because it had granted the builder's dismissal motion, the court reviewed the owner's argument in the interest of justice. The owner had set forth an argument to support a claimed error relating to the trial court's dismissal of his claim. Carlton v. Alar Dev. Co., — Ohio App. 3d —, 2006 Ohio 6877, — N.E. 2d —, 2006 Ohio App. LEXIS 6797 (Dec. 22, 2006).

— Brief requirements

As an electrical customer failed to comply with the brief and record requirements of Ohio R. App. P. 16 and Ohio Ninth Dist. Ct. App. R. 7(B)(7) with respect to her appeal of a garnishment order, the appellate court acted within its authority in disregarding her assignments of error pursuant to Ohio R. App. P. 12(A) and 16(A)(7). Ohio Edison Co. v. Williams, — Ohio App. 3d —, 2007 Ohio 5028, — N.E. 2d —, 2007 Ohio App. LEXIS 4449 (Sept. 26, 2007).

Although an assignment of error raised on appeal on defendant's behalf regarding his resentencing contained two separate arguments, in derogation of the requirements of Ohio R. App. P. 12(A)(1)(b) and 16(A)(7), the court acted within its discretion and pursuant to the interest of justice when it considered the arguments presented, as only "one" assignment of error was presented in the case and it was easily decided. State v. Nicholson, — Ohio App. 3d —, 2007 Ohio 5429, — N.E. 2d —, 2007 Ohio App. LEXIS 4773 (Oct. 11, 2007).

On appeal of a judgment in favor of a contractor, a home owner failed to meet the burden under Ohio R. App. P. 9, 12(A)(2), and 16(A)(7), as the owner failed to cite to the place in the record upon which the assignment of error was based, and there was no citation to legal authority in support of the assignment of error. Prater v. Dashkovsky, — Ohio App. 3d —, 2007 Ohio 6785, — N.E. 2d —, 2007 Ohio App. LEXIS 5919 (Dec. 18, 2007).

Pro se note debtor who appealed the grant of a default judgment in favor of the note holder was required to comply with the appellate rules for purposes of filing the brief pursuant to Ohio R. App. P. 16(A)(7) and 12(A)(2); the court found four central themes to the purported assignments of error on appeal which it reviewed. Paparodis v. Snively, — Ohio App. 3d —, 2007 Ohio 6910, — N.E. 2d —, 2007 Ohio App. LEXIS 6064 (Dec. 12, 2007).

Attachment to brief

When defendant claimed that his aggravated robbery sentence was not proportionate to that imposed on similarly situated individuals, he did not adequately support this argument by attaching to his brief a portion of a newspaper article about the sentence received by another person who also robbed a gas station at knife point, as he had to support his assignments of error with citations to legal authority and facts in the record, under Ohio R. App. P. 16(A)(7) and Ohio Ninth Dist. Ct. App. R. 7(B)(7), and he did not do this. State v. Sawyer, — Ohio App. 3d —, 2006 Ohio 4308, — N.E. 2d —, 2006 Ohio App. LEXIS 4244 (Aug. 21, 2006).

Brief inadequate

Regularity of trial court's property characterization and distribution was presumed in a divorce action because the former husband's brief failed to include a transcript as required under Ohio R. App. P. 16 and, thus, the court could not determine whether the trial court factually mischaracterized the property and abused its discretion in the distribution. Estep-Baker v. Baker, — Ohio App. 3d —, 2007 Ohio 2423, — N.E. 2d —, 2007 Ohio App. LEXIS 2239 (May 10, 2007).

Because defendant failed to make any references to the record where he claimed the evidence was not sufficient and he failed to point out how the evidence presented by the State was insufficient to prove any of the elements of any of the charges he was convicted of, the issue regarding the sufficiency of defendant's convictions did not have to be considered. State v. Shelton, — Ohio App. 3d —, 2007 Ohio 3900, — N.E. 2d —, 2007 Ohio App. LEXIS 3555 (Aug. 2, 2007).

Where an investor's appeal of the trial court's denial of his new trial motion merely quoted the applicable procedural rule and then stated in a conclusory fashion that the trial court's judgment was contrary to law without citing to any authority or to the record, as required by Ohio R. App. P. 12(A)(2) and 16(A)(7) and Ohio Ninth Dist. Ct. App. R. 7(A)(7) and (F), he did not meet his burden of demonstrating error. Macken v. KDR Holdings, — Ohio App. 3d —, 2007 Ohio 4106, — N.E. 2d —, 2007 Ohio App. LEXIS 3733 (Aug. 13, 2007).

As defendant's claim that the trial court erroneously determined certain facts was not supported by substantiation of his argument on appeal, he failed to meet his burden under Ohio R. App. P. 16(A)(7) and Ohio Ninth Dist. Ct. App. R. 7(A)(6) for purposes of appeal; similarly, several other assignments of error on appeal were not supported by sufficient citation to authority for purposes of reviewability. State v. Glick, — Ohio App. 3d —, 2007 Ohio 4104, — N.E. 2d —, 2007 Ohio App. LEXIS 3735 (Aug. 13, 2007).

In tenant's appeal from a decision against her in a forcible entry and detainer action, since the tenant's allegations in her brief were not found in the record and since her arguments were not accompanied by citations to the authority on which she relied, the brief did not comply with the requirement in Ohio R. App. P. 16(A)(7). Further, since the tenant never filed a transcript of the proceedings, the court was compelled to presume the validity of the proceedings on appeal. Gunderman v. Holt, — Ohio App. 3d —, 2007 Ohio 5998, — N.E. 2d —, 2007 Ohio App. LEXIS 5252 (Nov. 9, 2007).

Since plaintiff failed to file a copy of the transcript to support his assignments of error, all of which asserted propositions based on evidence introduced at trial, the court, pursuant to Ohio R. App. P. 9(B), had to presume regularity in the proceedings on any finding of fact made by the trial court; thus, plaintiff was unable to demonstrate the claimed errors. Additionally, plaintiff had failed to affirmatively establish error on appeal because, in each of his assignments of error, he asserted arguments unsupported by any legal authority or any specific portion of the record, as required by Ohio R. App. P. 16(A), and thus, pursuant to Ohio R. App. P. 12(A)(2), the court overruled the assignments of error. Calabrese v. Zmijewski, — Ohio App. 3d —, 2006 Ohio 2322, — N.E. 2d —, 2006 Ohio App. LEXIS 2179 (May 11, 2006).

Upon consideration of the manifold, serious deficiencies in plaintiffs' appellate brief, the appellate court was not required to address any of the assignments of error contained therein. Although plaintiffs assigned numerous errors to the trial court, they failed to make necessary statements, identifications and arguments regarding those alleged errors as required by Ohio R. App. P. 16; for example, plaintiffs' brief lacked any statement of facts, whatsoever, it was void of arguments relating specific contentions. McCabe v. Ransom, — Ohio App. 3d —, 2006 Ohio 2926, — N.E. 2d —, 2006 Ohio App. LEXIS 2804 (June 9, 2006).

Plaintiffs failed to include any citation to the record as support for their assignment of error that the verdict in favor of defendants was against the manifest weight of the evidence, as required by Ohio R. App. P. 16(A)(7). Kukla v. Field Energy Servs., — Ohio App. 3d —, 2006 Ohio 3114, — N.E. 2d —, 2006 Ohio App. LEXIS 2996 (June 21, 2006).

Inmate failed to present any arguable reason why the court of claims erred in granting summary judgment for defendants. The inmate's brief was unintelligible and consisted of jumbled, unclear, and incoherent babblings interspersed with references to irrelevant legal authority, and it made no colorable effort to point out legal or factual errors in the lower court's decision. Hardy v. Belmont Correctional Inst., — Ohio App. 3d —, 2006 Ohio 3316, — N.E. 2d —, 2006 Ohio App. LEXIS 3231 (June 29, 2006).

Appellate court declined to review errors asserted on appeal by home owners after a judgment of foreclosure was granted to a homeowners association, as their argument on appeal was unclear pursuant to Ohio R. App. P. 12(A)(2) and 16(A)despite repeated readings and the brief failed to mention a motion which was apparently referenced therein and denied by the trial court. Miles Landing Homeowners Ass'n v. Bikkani, — Ohio App. 3d —, 2006 Ohio 3328, — N.E. 2d —, 2006 Ohio App. LEXIS 3244 (June 29, 2006).

Arrestee's appeal of a trial court order of dismissal was dismissed under Ohio R. App. P. 18(C) for want of prosecution where the arrestee's failure to satisfy the requirements of Ohio R. App. P. 16 and Ohio Fifth Dist. Ct. App. R. 9(A)(1) was tantamount to a failure to file a brief. Billman v. City of Canton, — Ohio App. 3d —, 2006 Ohio 3923, — N.E. 2d —, 2006 Ohio App. LEXIS 3894 (July 31, 2006).

Appellant waived appellate review of trial court's decision when she: (1) failed to file timely objections to the magistrate's decision, (2) failed to file a direct appeal of the trial court's entry adopting that decision, (3) failed to file a direct appeal of the trial court's entry overruling appellant's untimely objections to the magistrate's decision, and (4) failed to comply with Ohio R. Civ. P. 53(E)(3)(c) and Franklin County, Ohio, Ct. C.P. R. 75.11 when she did not support her objections to the decision with a transcript. Even if the appeal was timely, the court observed that appellant's brief failed to comply with Ohio R. App. P. 16(A)(3) and (7), in that it was unintelligible and consisted of incoherent arguments interspersed with references to irrelevant legal authority. In re Neff, — Ohio App. 3d —, 2006 Ohio 4460, — N.E. 2d —, 2006 Ohio App. LEXIS 4375 (Aug. 29, 2006).

Where a property owner appealed from a grant of summary judgment to other property owners in a dispute over ownership of a piece of land, and one of the assignments of error asserted in her appeal was not separately argued in her brief, the court disregarded it pursuant to Ohio R. App. P. 12 and 16(A)(7). King v. Hazen, — Ohio App. 3d —, 2006 Ohio 4823, — N.E. 2d —, 2006 Ohio App. LEXIS 4735 (Sept. 15, 2006).

Defendant's claim that his counsel was ineffective in defendant's criminal trial in violation of U.S. Const. amend. VI and Ohio Const. art. I, § 10 lacked merit where defendant failed to properly cite to the record to support his claims, in violation of Ohio R. App. P. 16(A)(7), and other general assertions were too vague to overcome the presumption of competence of his counsel. State v. Gillingham, — Ohio App. 3d —, 2006 Ohio 5758, — N.E. 2d —, 2006 Ohio App. LEXIS 5738 (Oct. 27, 2006).

Since, in his pro se document asking the court to take note of additional issues that appellate counsel did not raise in the brief filed with the court on behalf of defendant, defendant had done little more than furnish the court with a list of possible issues that could affect his conviction and had not presented the court with any arguments in support of his arguments, the brief did not comply with Ohio R. App. P. 16(A)(7), and thus, the court could not address the merits of the issues that he raised pro se in his appeal. State v. Green, — Ohio App. 3d —, 2006 Ohio 7074, — N.E. 2d —, 2006 Ohio App. LEXIS 7002 (Dec. 15, 2006).

Brief requirements

As defendant's claim on appeal that the jury's verdict was against the manifest weight of the evidence was not identified in the record, as required by Ohio R. App. P. 12(A)(2), and he failed to set forth an argument that met the requirements of Ohio R. App. P. 16(A)(7), the assignment of error was not reviewable; defendant only offered a comprehensive statement of the law relating to review of arguments on the issue of manifest weight of the evidence, but he failed to state exactly what evidence he relied on that made the law applicable to his case. State v. Harris, — Ohio App. 3d —, 2007 Ohio 526, — N.E. 2d —, 2007 Ohio App. LEXIS 482 (Feb. 8, 2007).

Although defendant claimed on appeal that the trial court improperly permitted evidence obtained following his arrest, which he contended should have been suppressed as fruits of the poisonous tree pursuant to U.S. Const. amend. IV, defendant failed to set forth in his brief exactly what evidence he felt was tainted, as required by Ohio R. App. P. 16(A)(7). The trial testimony that was admitted consisted of statements from defendant's wife, who was the victim of his domestic violence, and her mother, and the trial court had suppressed testimony from the arresting officers, such that no error was found. State v. Martindale, — Ohio App. 3d —, 2007 Ohio 3540, — N.E. 2d —, 2007 Ohio App. LEXIS 3231 (July 5, 2007).

Pursuant to Ohio R. App. P. 12(A)(2) and 16(A)(7), the court declined to address defendant's cruel and unusual punishment argument on appeal, as he failed to address it in his brief. State v. Sutton, — Ohio App. 3d —, 2007 Ohio 3792, — N.E. 2d —, 2007 Ohio App. LEXIS 3455 (July 26, 2007).

As publishing companies' brief did not contain a statement of the assignments of error and the necessary citations to authorities, statutes, and parts of the record upon which the companies relied, as required by Ohio R. App. P. 16(A)(4) and (7), as well as Ohio Third Dist. Ct. App. R. 7(A) and 11(A), the appellate court chose to disregard the assignments of error pursuant to Ohio R. App. P. 12(A)(2); the court declined to scour the record to create an appellate argument for the companies. Marysville Newspapers, Inc. v. Del. Gazette Co., — Ohio App. 3d —, 2007 Ohio 3838, — N.E. 2d —, 2007 Ohio App. LEXIS 3485 (July 30, 2007).

Though a husband alleged that the trial court, in denying his motion for reduction of child support, ignored evidence of the wife's extravagant spending, the husband failed to point to portions of the record regarding the wife's spending or standard of living. Since the husband had the burden on appeal, the court had the authority under Ohio R. App. P. 12(A)(2), 7(F), Summit County, Ohio, App. R. 7(F), and Ohio R. App. P. 16(A)(7) to disregard assignments of error that were not supported by the relevant portions of the record from which the errors were based. Maguire v. Maguire, — Ohio App. 3d —, 2007 Ohio 4531, — N.E. 2d —, 2007 Ohio App. LEXIS 4104 (Sept. 5, 2007).

Court disregarded various issues raised by property owners on appeal from a decision of the Ohio Reclamation Commission, approving a mining permit, where the owners failed to cite to a part of the record that established prejudice to them under Ohio R. App. P. 16(A)(6), they failed to provide citations to legal authority to supprt their arguments under Rule 16(A)(7), they cited issues for the first time in their reply brief under Rule 16(C), and they failed to raise certain issues in the administrative level proceeding, such that they were waived for purposes of judicial review; the court acted within its authority in disregarding the improperly raised issues pursuant to Ohio R. App. P. 12(A)(2). Spires v. Div. of Mineral Res. Mgmt., — Ohio App. 3d —, 2007 Ohio 5038, — N.E. 2d —, 2007 Ohio App. LEXIS 4458 (Sept. 24, 2007).

While the appellate court, pursuant to Ohio R. App. P. 12(A)(2) could choose to disregard any assignment of error that the father had failed to separately argue, as required by Ohio R. App. P. 16(A)(7), the court chose to review the father's assignments of error because courts strive to decide appeals on their merits instead of on technicalities. In re Gallion, — Ohio App. 3d —, 2006 Ohio 3204, — N.E. 2d —, 2006 Ohio App. LEXIS 3095 (June 12, 2006).

Court urged counsel to better observe the requirement of Ohio R. App. P. 16(A)(7) that arguments in briefs cite parts of the record on which a party relies and to follow the preferred practice of citing the docket numbers for each document assigned by the clerk. Merely referring in the argument to a motion otherwise identified in the statement of the case with reference to its filing date is inadequate and unhelpful, especially in a case in which numerous motions were filed. Robinson v. Robinson, 168 Ohio App. 3d 476, 2006 Ohio 4282, 860 N.E.2d 1027, 2006 Ohio App. LEXIS 4196 (2006).

Although a contractor who appealed a trial court dismissal of his action failed to comply with Ohio R. App. P. 16(A)(3), as his first assignment of error cited to no full journal entries, the court of appeals addressed the general assertion raised that the trial court had abused its discretion in the language used in its journal entries. Jones v. Dillard, — Ohio App. 3d —, 2006 Ohio 6417, — N.E. 2d —, 2006 Ohio App. LEXIS 6370 (Dec. 7, 2006).

Citations to authorities

When an employee was terminated and signed a release form upon his receipt of severance pay, the employer was entitled to summary judgment as to the claims the employee filed against it because the employee offered no authority, as required by Ohio R. App. P. 16(A)(7) and Ohio Ninth Dist. Ct. App. R. 7(A)(7), for the proposition that the employer owed the employee a fiduciary duty to disclose any facts material to the release. Cole v. Temple Israel, — Ohio App. 3d —, 2007 Ohio 245, — N.E.2d —, 2007 Ohio App. LEXIS 224 (Jan. 24, 2007).

When defendant claimed his trial counsel provided ineffective assistance, he did not meet his burden on appeal because he did not support his contentions with citations to appropriate authority or citations to the record below, as required by Ohio R. App. P. 16(A). State v. Dallas, — Ohio App. 3d —, 2007 Ohio 1214, — N.E. 2d —, 2007 Ohio App. LEXIS 1144 (Mar. 19, 2007).

Citations in a brief belong in footnotes. Using talking footnotes detracts from the gain in readability achieved by taking citations out of the text: M & M Metals Int'l, Inc. v. Cont'l Cas. Co., 171 Ohio App. 3d 145, 2006 Ohio 6194, 870 N.E.2d 167, 2006 Ohio App. LEXIS 6152 (2006).

Since appellant failed to cite to any legal authority relative to her assignments of error, appellant failed to meet her burden of affirmatively demonstrating error on appeal under Ohio R. App. P. 16(A)(7); thus, the court overruled the assignments of error. In re A.V., — Ohio App. 3d —, 2006 Ohio 3149, — N.E. 2d —, 2006 Ohio App. LEXIS 3021 (June 22, 2006).

Defendant trial counsel was not ineffective in violation of U.S. Const. amend. VI and Ohio Const. art. I, § 10 in failing to prevent the admission of evidence that linked him to other crimes, as counsel had objected to testimony about that topic and the witness was instructed to answer carefully to avoid such mention, and further, defendant had discussed his prior felony convictions in his own testimony, such that he opened the door to that evidence; as defendant made no specific argument and did not reference the record to support such claim, he failed to comply with Ohio R. App. P. 16(A). State v. Brocar, — Ohio App. 3d —, 2006 Ohio 5561, — N.E. 2d —, 2006 Ohio App. LEXIS 5557 (Oct. 20, 2006).

Trial court's denial of defendant's acquittal motion pursuant to Ohio R. Crim. P. 29 was not properly reviewable by an appellate court because defendant's brief did not comply with the requirements of Ohio R. App. P. 16(A)(7) and Ohio 9th Dist. Ct. App. R. 7(B)(7) where there was no citation to any authority that supported defendant's position, and his contentions did not constitute an argument. Affirmance of the trial court's decision was proper under Ohio R. App. P. 12(A)(2). State v. Stelzer, — Ohio App. 3d —, 2006 Ohio 6912, — N.E. 2d —, 2006 Ohio App. LEXIS 6818 (Dec. 27, 2006).

Consideration of errors

As defendant only challenged the sufficiency of the evidence with respect to one of two offenses that he was convicted of, the appellate court only addressed defendant's assertion of error with respect to that one offense pursuant to Ohio R. App. P. 12(A)(2) and 16(A)(7). State v. Johnson, — Ohio App. 3d —, 2007 Ohio 2385, — N.E. 2d —, 2007 Ohio App. LEXIS 2216 (May 17, 2007).

Error

Trial court based its decision regarding a child's custody and care on the recommendation of the guardian ad litem (GAL); yet, the record was void of any documentation regarding the GAL's recommendations. Thus, since the father, who was the appellant, failed to sustain his burden on appeal under Ohio R. App. P. 16(A)(7) and Ohio 9th Dist. Ct. App. R. 7(B)(7) of supplying those portions of the record which demonstrated the error on appeal and under Ohio R. App. P. 9(B) and Ohio 9th Dist. Ct. App. R. 5(A) of ensuring that the record necessary to determine the appeal is before the appellate court, the court presumed that the record before the trial court, which included the GAL's recommendation, supported the trial court's decisions. Love v. Love, — Ohio App. 3d —, 2006 Ohio 3559, — N.E. 2d —, 2006 Ohio App. LEXIS 3506 (July 12, 2006).

Failure to cite to authority

Since appellant employees failed to cite to any legal authority relative to their assignment of error on appeal, as required by Ohio R. App. P. 16(A)(7), they had not met their burden of affirmatively demonstrating error on appeal. Bauman v. Bob Evans Farms, Inc., — Ohio App. 3d —, 2007 Ohio 145, — N.E. 2d —, 2007 Ohio App. LEXIS 121 (Jan. 16, 2007).

As a building owner who appealed an administrative decision regarding her violations of the housing code failed to cite to case law in making her argument on appeal, as required by Ohio R. App. P. 16(A)(7), the court had grounds to disregard the assigned error pursuant to Ohio R. App. P. 12(A)(2); the court indicated that despite its ability to disregard, the result was the same because the assigned error lacked merit. Spires v. Board of Bldgs. Stds. & Bldg. Appeals, — Ohio App. 3d —, 2007 Ohio 391, — N.E. 2d —, 2007 Ohio App. LEXIS 351 (Feb. 1, 2007).

Although defendant raised numerous errors on appeal in his claim that he was denied a fair trial based on cumulative errors, where he failed to cite case law to support many of the errors, they were not addressed on appeal pursuant to Ohio R. App. P. 12(A)(2) and 16(A)(7). State v. Djuric, — Ohio App. 3d —, 2007 Ohio 413, — N.E. 2d —, 2007 Ohio App. LEXIS 362 (Feb. 1, 2007).

Although township trustees who appealed a trial court's grant of summary judgment against them failed to identify the relevant portions of the record from which their appealed errors were based, as required by Ohio R. App. P. 12(A)(2) and Ohio Ninth Dist. Ct. App. R. 7(F), and they also did not support their argument with citations to legal authority and facts in the record as required by Ohio R. App. P. 16(A)(7) and Ohio Ninth Dist. Ct. App. R. 7(B)(7), the court chose to review the issues on the merits rather than disregard them, as it had a right to do in that situation. Brunswick Hills Twp. v. City of Cleveland, — Ohio App. 3d —, 2007 Ohio 2560, — N.E. 2d —, 2007 Ohio App. LEXIS 2382 (May 29, 2007).

Defendant failed to meet his burden on appeal pursuant to Ohio R. App. P. 16(A)(7) with respect to a sentencing error that he raised where he did not support his argument with citations to legal authority and facts in the record. His assignment of error lacked substantive merit where the sentencing entry that was journalized was consistent with the verdict forms signed by the jurors, such that the sentences were coordinated with the convictions. State v. Fry, — Ohio App. 3d —, 2007 Ohio 3240, — N.E. 2d —, 2007 Ohio App. LEXIS 2998 (June 27, 2007).

Although a father who appealed a probate court's denial of his request to remove the guardian for his mentally disabled son failed to support his assignments of error with argument, legal authority, or citation to the relevant portions of the record, such that the court could have chosen to disregard the non-complying assignments of error pursuant to Ohio R. App. P. 12(A)(2) and 16(A), the court reviewed the issues raised on the merits in the interests of justice. In re Constable, — Ohio App. 3d —, 2007 Ohio 3346, — N.E. 2d —, 2007 Ohio App. LEXIS 3105 (July 2, 2007).

In an appeal from a trial court's decision in a permanent custody case, while the mother had failed to cite any legal authority in support of her assignment of error, as required by Ohio R. App. P. 16(A)(7), thereby giving the court the right under Ohio R. App. P. 12(A)(2) to disregard the assignment of error, the court, in the interest of justice, addressed the merits of the appeal. In re R.L., — Ohio App. 3d —, 2007 Ohio 3553, — N.E. 2d —, 2007 Ohio App. LEXIS 3238 (July 12, 2007).

Defendant's assignments of error on appeal regarding sufficiency of the evidence and denial of his speedy trial rights were not properly supported by legal authority and were not referenced in the record, as required by Ohio R. App. P. 12(A)(2), 16(A)(7), and Ohio Ninth Dist. Ct. App. R. 7(A)(1) and (F), such that they were not reviewable. State v. Mastice, — Ohio App. 3d —, 2007 Ohio 4107, — N.E. 2d —, 2007 Ohio App. LEXIS 3732 (Aug. 13, 2007).

Although an appellate court had a right to disregard assignments of error pursuant to Ohio R. App. P. 12(A)(2) where defendant failed to cite to legal authority in support thereof pursuant to Ohio R. App. P. 16(A)(7), it acted within its authority in choosing to undertake an independent review of the assignments. Ohio v. Anderson, — Ohio App. 3d —, 2007 Ohio 5326, — N.E. 2d —, 2007 Ohio App. LEXIS 4692 (Oct. 4, 2007).

Despite arguing that ten of defendant's eleven convictions were against the manifest weight of the evidence, defendant's counsel failed to list and analyze the elements of those convictions, and offered no legal authority to support any of the arguments. Accordingly, counsel's brief could only be described as woefully deficient. State v. Deitz, — Ohio App. 3d —, 2007 Ohio 2439, — N.E. 2d —, 2007 Ohio App. LEXIS 2274 (May 21, 2007).

Where property owners did not cite to any legal authority in a variety of their arguments on appeal from a village's determination that they had committed nuisances by violating municipal ordinances, pursuant to Ohio R. App. P. 12(A)(2) and 16(A)(7) the court chose to disregard those unsupported arguments. Village of Ottawa Hills v. Abdollah, — Ohio App. 3d —, 2006 Ohio 2618, — N.E. 2d —, 2006 Ohio App. LEXIS 2461 (May 26, 2006).

Where an employee failed to cite to any legal authority or to parts of the record which she relied upon to support her argument on appeal that a trial court's dismissal of her intentional infliction of emotional distress claim, arising from her alleged constructive discharge from employment, was error, pursuant to Ohio R. App. P. 12(A)(2) and 16(A) the court disregarded the assigned error for purposes of appellate review. Simmons-Means v. Cuyahoga County Dep't of Justice Affairs, — Ohio App. 3d —, 2006 Ohio 4123, — N.E.2d —, 2006 Ohio App. LEXIS 4057 (Aug. 10, 2006).

Although defendant failed to meet his burden of affirmatively demonstrating error on appeal, pursuant to Ohio R. App. P. 16(A)(7), where he failed to cite to any legal authority to support his assignment of error, the court reviewed the matter in the interests of justice. State v. Trewartha, — Ohio App. 3d —, 2006 Ohio 5040, — N.E. 2d —, 2006 Ohio App. LEXIS 5176 (Sept. 28, 2006).

Defendants' assignment of error on appeal from their felonious assault convictions that the verdict was improper in that the defense did not identify the real culprits and that defendants were in proximity to the victim was disregarded pursuant to Ohio R. App. P. 12(A)(2) because defendants failed to cite to any legal authority in support of the argument as required by Ohio R. App. P. 16(A)(7); if an argument existed that could support the assignment of error, it was not the appellate court's duty to root it out. State v. Armstrong, — Ohio App. 3d —, 2006 Ohio 5447, — N.E. 2d —, 2006 Ohio App. LEXIS 5437 (Oct. 19, 2006).

Failure to cite to record

Husband's assignments of error on appeal from a trial court decree of divorce were not disregarded pursuant to Ohio R. App. P. 12(A)(2), although he failed to properly cite to the record in his brief, as required by Ohio R. App. P. 16(A)(3) and (D), as he indicated that the references to the wife's testimony in the last two hours of the trial transcript were where the assigned errors related to. Jack H. Parker v. Susanne Kohl Parker, — Ohio App. 3d —, 2007 Ohio 4895, — N.E. 2d —, 2007 Ohio App. LEXIS 4366 (Sept. 21, 2007).

Pursuant to Ohio R. App. P. 12(A) and 16(A)(7), an appellate court disregarded various assignments of error raised by defendant in his appeal from his conviction, as he failed to specifically cite to the record to support his arguments. State v. Anderson, — Ohio App. 3d —, 2007 Ohio 5068, — N.E. 2d —, 2007 Ohio App. LEXIS 4477 (Sept. 27, 2007).

Defendant failed to support her contention that her conviction was against the manifest weight of the evidence since defendant had not cited to any portion of the record but, instead, broadly referenced that her statement of the case and facts supported her argument. Such a structure did not comport with Ohio R. App. P. 16(A)(7) and Ohio 9th Ct. App. R. 7(A)(7). State v. Franklin, — Ohio App. 3d —, 2006 Ohio 4569, — N.E. 2d —, 2006 Ohio App. LEXIS 4524 (Sept. 6, 2006).

Failure to support

As a city prosecutor's claim on appeal that he was present in court on the scheduled trial date and ready to proceed at that time was not supported by anything in the record, he failed to meet his burden on appeal pursuant to Ohio R. App. P. 9(B), 16(A)(7), and Ohio Ninth Dist. Ct. App. R. 5(A) and 7(B)(7) of supporting his assignment of error through citations to legal authority and facts in the record and accordingly, the court presumed the regularity of the trial court proceedings. The trial court had dismissed the criminal matter that was pending against defendant for want of prosecution, which was in part based on the city's failure to appear for trial. City of Lorain v. Hodges, — Ohio App. 3d —, 2007 Ohio 456, — N.E. 2d —, 2007 Ohio App. LEXIS 406 (Feb. 5, 2007).

When a city employee was laid off after he was ordered reinstated, following his firing for disciplinary reasons, his claim that the layoff was actually a job abolishment, to which different statutory procedures applied, was not considered because he did not reference where in the record he raised such an objection, as required by Ohio R. App. P. 16(A)(3). Martin v. City of Cambridge, — Ohio App. 3d —, 2007 Ohio 2172, — N.E. 2d —, 2007 Ohio App. LEXIS 2025 (May 3, 2007).

Although defendant's claim on appeal that his conviction was against the manifest weight of the evidence was not in compliance with Ohio R. App. P. 16(A)(7) where there was no argument that was supported by either the record or the law, the court found that the convictions were proper in the circumstances. State v. Smith, — Ohio App. 3d —, 2007 Ohio 3908, — N.E. 2d —, 2007 Ohio App. LEXIS 3543 (Aug. 2, 2007).

Since defendant's contentions, asserted on appeal from her conviction for reckless operation, that she was not given discovery and that certain evidence should have been admitted while other evidence should have been suppressed were not supported by evidence contained in the record but were based on speculation and unsupported allegations, the court declined to address the remainder of defendant's arguments pursuant to Ohio R. App. P. 12 and Ohio R. App. P. 16. City of Whitehall v. Ruckman, — Ohio App. 3d —, 2007 Ohio 6780, — N.E. 2d —, 2007 Ohio App. LEXIS 5932 (Dec. 18, 2007).

When an electrician who had sued a church for services performed complained of improprieties during a case management conference, the regularity of the trial court's proceedings had to be presumed by the appellate court because the electrician did not comply with Ohio R. App. P. 16(A)(7), which required him to point to specific parts of the record to show the alleged error, because the case management conference was not recorded. Bambeck v. Catholic Dioceses of Cleveland, — Ohio App. 3d —, 2006 Ohio 4883, — N.E. 2d —, 2006 Ohio App. LEXIS 4799 (Sept. 21, 2006).

When members of an administrative board elected by a faction of a church, who sought a declaratory judgment that they were the church's proper administrative board, did not articulate an applicable standard of review, cite to any legal authority in support of their claims, or develop their arguments sufficiently to support their claim that the trial court abused its discretion by ratifying an illegal election or that a subsequently elected board in any way abused the election process, their failure to meet their burden under Ohio R. App. P. 16(A)(7) or Ohio Ninth Dist. Ct. App. R. 7(A)(7) allowed the appellate court to disregard their assignment of error, under Ohio R. App. P. 12(A)(2). St. Nikola Macedonian Orthodox Church v. Zoran, — Ohio App. 3d —, 2006 Ohio 2561, — N.E. 2d —, 2006 Ohio App. LEXIS 2409 (May 24, 2006).

When a teacher sued a school district, its superintendent and other employees, and students and their parents, after he was fired due to allegations that he committed improprieties against the students, and summary judgment was granted in favor of all the parties he sued, that summary judgment was affirmed, in part, because he consistently failed to meet his burden to affirmatively demonstrate error and substantiate his arguments, as required by Ohio R. App. P. 16(A)(7) and Ohio Ninth Dist. Ct. App. R. 7(A)(7). Dennis v. Coventry Local Sch. Dist. Bd. of Educ., — Ohio App. 3d —, 2006 Ohio 2847, — N.E. 2d —, 2006 Ohio App. LEXIS 2674 (June 7, 2006).

Although a workers' compensation claimant contended on appeal that a particular statute violated her equal protection and due process rights, but her argument only addressed equal protection issues, the appellate court did not conduct a due process analysis pursuant to Ohio R. App. P. 12(A)(2) and 16(A). Ireland v. Southern Ohio Correctional Facility, — Ohio App. 3d —, 2006 Ohio 3519, — N.E. 2d —, 2006 Ohio App. LEXIS 3470 (June 22, 2006).

While defendant cited to a case that stood for the proposition that gross negligence or willful maltreatment by a treating physician was an intervening cause that would relieve a "contributing" defendant of liability for the victim's murder, defendant did not apply this law to his case. Pursuant to Ohio R. App. P. 16(A)(7) and Ohio 9th Dist. Ct. App. R. 7(A)(7), it is not the duty of the appellate court to develop arguments in support of assignments of error for an appellant. State v. Caldwell, — Ohio App. 3d —, 2006 Ohio 3560, — N.E. 2d —, 2006 Ohio App. LEXIS 3508 (July 12, 2006).

Procedure

Where a trial court first determined that a city's summary judgment motion was moot, and after former property owners appealed another ruling in the case that granted summary judgment to a current property owner and such appeal also included the determination regarding the city, the matter was remanded and the city was granted summary judgment, such was not reviewable where the new order was not included in a notice of appeal pursuant to Ohio R. App. P. 3, 4(A), 5, and 16(A). Pursuant to its discretion to impose sanctions, the court found that declining to review the assignments of error related to the summary judgment for the city was proper, as it had no notice that such decision was the subject of appeal. MDM Realty, Ltd. v. Progress Properties. So., LP, — Ohio App. 3d —, 2007 Ohio 3668, — N.E. 2d —, 2007 Ohio App. LEXIS 3375 (July 19, 2007).

—Transcript

Where defendant challenged the sufficiency of the evidence regarding criminal convictions that arose from housing violations but he failed to provide the appellate court with a complete transcript of the relevant trial court proceedings, he failed in his burden pursuant to Ohio R. App. P. 16(A)(3), and the appellate court presumed the validity of the trial court proceedings; the portions of the trial transcript provided by defendant were inadequate. City of Dayton v. Smith, — Ohio App. 3d —, 2006 Ohio 4928, — N.E. 2d —, 2006 Ohio App. LEXIS 4838 (Sept. 22, 2006).

Because tenants failed to include a transcript or agreed statement of the relevant record through which they might have demonstrated their alleged errors, an appellate court had nothing to pass upon and thus, had no choice but to presume the validity of the trial court's conclusions which found against the tenants in their counterclaim against the owner of a rental unit. Epling Estates v. Cunningham, — Ohio App. 3d —, 2006 Ohio 1457, — N.E. 2d —, 2006 Ohio App. LEXIS 1331 (Mar. 24, 2006).

Reply briefs

Creditor of a decedent's estate could not complain on appeal of fee requests made by a guardian ad litem on behalf of a minor relative of the decedent, as those matters were not raised in any briefs and as such, they were not properly presented in a reply brief pursuant to Ohio R. App. P. 16(C). The creditor lacked standing to complain about fees applied

for or allowed to others. In re Kendall, — Ohio App. 3d —, 2007 Ohio 3809, — N.E. 2d —, 2007 Ohio App. LEXIS 3474 (July 27, 2007).

RULE 17.   Brief of an amicus curiae

A brief of an amicus curiae may be filed only if accompanied by written consent of all parties, or by leave of court granted on motion or at the request of the court. The brief may be conditionally filed with the motion for leave. A motion for leave shall identify the interest of the applicant and shall state the reasons why a brief of an amicus curiae is desirable. Unless all parties otherwise consent, any amicus curiae shall file its brief within the time allowed the party whose position as to affirmance or reversal the amicus brief will support unless the court for cause shown shall grant leave for later filing, in which event it shall specify within what period an opposing party may answer. A motion of an amicus curiae to participate in the oral argument will be granted only for extraordinary reasons.

RULE 18.   Filing and service of briefs

(A) **Time for serving and filing briefs.** Except as provided in App. R. 14(C), the appellant shall serve and file the appellant's brief within twenty days after the date on which the clerk has mailed the notice required by App. R. 11(B). The appellee shall serve and file the appellee's brief within twenty days after service of the brief of the appellant. The appellant may serve and file a reply brief within ten days after service of the brief of the appellee.

(B) **Number of copies to be filed and served.** Four copies of each brief shall be filed with the clerk, unless the court by order in a particular case shall direct a different number, and one copy shall be served on counsel for each party separately represented. If the court by local rule adopted pursuant to App. R. 13 permits electronic filing of court documents, then the requirement for filing of copies with the clerk required in this division may be waived or modified by the local rule so adopted.

(C) **Consequence of failure to file briefs.** If an appellant fails to file the appellant's brief within the time provided by this rule, or within the time as extended, the court may dismiss the appeal. If an appellee fails to file the appellee's brief within the time provided by this rule, or within the time as extended, the appellee will not be heard at oral argument except by permission of the court upon a showing of good cause submitted in writing prior to argument; and in determining the appeal, the court may accept the appellant's statement of the facts and issues as correct and reverse the judgment if appellant's brief reasonably appears to sustain such action.

History: Amended, eff 7-1-82; 7-1-01.

NOTES TO DECISIONS

ANALYSIS

Presumption of correctness
Scope of review
Service

Briefs

Trial court did not abuse its discretion under RC § 3105.171(A)(6)(a)(vii) in determining that a particular residence was the wife's separate property in the parties' divorce action, as it was purchased during the pendency of the divorce with money she had received from spousal support payments after the parties had separated, and it was not even completed at the time of the divorce decree; the husband's claim on appeal that the trial court had engaged in disparate treatment based on another residence owned by the parties that was designated as marital property was not accompanied by a proper citation to the record to support the claim and accordingly, the court declined to review that issue pursuant to Ohio R. App. P. 18. Janosek v. Janosek, — Ohio App. 3d —, 2007 Ohio 68, — N.E. 2d —, 2007 Ohio App. LEXIS 59 (Jan. 11, 2007).

Although the State of Ohio, as appellee, failed to file a responsive brief in defendant's appeal from the trial court's denial of his motion to vacate his sentence, pursuant to Ohio R. App. P. 18(C) the judgment of the trial court was not reversed because that action was not reasonably supported by defendant's brief. Defendant had not directly appealed his convictions and sentences, he did not file a post-conviction petition, and his motion under Ohio R. Civ. P. 60(B) was improperly filed and it also lacked merit, as Foster, Blakely, and Apprendi only applied retroactively to cases pending on direct review or which were not yet final, which made them inapplicable to defendant's matter. State v. McDowell, — Ohio App. 3d —, 2007 Ohio 3728, — N.E. 2d —, 2007 Ohio App. LEXIS 3413 (July 23, 2007).

Although defendant's brief failed to comply with Ohio R. App. P. 19(A) and Ohio Fifth Dist. Ct. App. R. 9(B) where it asserted 33 assignments of error in a 104-page brief, the court chose not to dismiss the appeal under Ohio R. App. P. 18(C) for failure to file a brief, although the total non-compliance with the appellate rules was tantamount to failing to file any brief. The court reviewed the assignments that it could make sense of and disregarded the others. City of Mt. Vernon v. Young, — Ohio App. 3d —, 2006 Ohio 3319, — N.E. 2d —, 2006 Ohio App. LEXIS 3235 (June 28, 2006).

Failure to file brie

As a former husband failed to file a brief pursuant to Ohio R. App. P. 18(C) in an appeal by his former wife from the trial court's adoption of a magistrate's decision to award the husband significant visitation rights with the parties' child, and the errors raised by the wife were apparent from the record, she was entitled to reversal of the trial court judgment. Hoppel v. Hoppel, — Ohio App. 3d —, 2007 Ohio 5246, — N.E. 2d —, 2007 Ohio App. LEXIS 4638 (Sept. 24, 2007).

Failure to file brief

Although the appellate court accepted defendant's statement of facts and issues as correct and could have reversed the trial court judgment if it was supported by defendant's brief pursuant to Ohio R. App. P. 18(C), based on the fact that the State failed to file a brief in defendant's matter, defendant's claim lacked substantive merit. His motion to vacate judgment pursuant to Ohio R. Civ. P. 60(B) had been properly denied because it was made in an untimely manner, and his claim that sentencing was unconstitutional lacked merit, as Blakely and Foster did not apply to his case because it was final on direct review. State v. Cottrill, — Ohio App. 3d —, 2007 Ohio 2006, — N.E. 2d —, 2007 Ohio App. LEXIS 1783 (Apr. 26, 2007).

Since a daughter-in-law did not file a brief in an appeal filed by her mother-in-law and her sister-in-law, the appellate court accepted appellants' statement of the facts and issues as correct pursuant to Ohio R. App. P. 18(C) and reversed the judgment since appellants' brief and the record appeared to sustain such action. Darling v. Darling, — Ohio App. 3d —, 2007 Ohio 3151, — N.E. 2d —, 2007 Ohio App. LEXIS 2938 (June 18, 2007).

Although a county dog warden failed to file a brief in defendant's appeal from a finding that he had failed to have his dog vaccinated against rabies, as required by Ohio Health Dept. Reg. 221.11(b), defendant failed to support his asserted errors under Ohio R. App. P. 18(C) where he failed to file a record of the trial court proceedings, as required by Ohio R. App. P. 9; accordingly, the regularity of the trial court proceedings was presumed and it was determined that defendant failed to show proof of a valid defense to the charge, such as that the dog was less than three months old or that defendant had owned it for less than 30 days. Stark County Dog Dep't v. Robinson, — Ohio App. 3d —, — N.E. 2d —, 2007 Ohio 3394, 2007 Ohio App. LEXIS 3131 (July 2, 2007).

Where parents of tenants, who were sued pursuant to their lease guarantees, failed to file a brief on appeal, pursuant to Ohio R. App. P. 18(C) the court accepted the landlord's position that the trial court erred when it improperly shifted the burden of proving mitigation of damages onto the landlord in its action, based on the tenants' non-payment of rent under a residential lease; mitigation was an affirmative defense that was to have been proved by the parents. Gardens v. Fish, — Ohio App. 3d —, 2007 Ohio 4230, — N.E. 2d —, 2007 Ohio App. LEXIS 3890 (Aug. 20, 2007).

Since appellee failed to submit a brief to the court, the court elected to accept the statement of facts and issues of appellant as correct pursuant to Ohio R. App. P. 18(C). Fia v. Sipes, — Ohio App. 3d —, 2007 Ohio 4363, — N.E. 2d —, 2007 Ohio App. LEXIS 3952 (Aug. 27, 2007).

As damage awards to an insurer in its action against a negligent driver, wherein the insurer sought recovery of payments made to its insured that arose therefrom, were against the manifest weight of the evidence, and the driver failed to file a brief, pursuant to Ohio R. App. P. 18(C) a reversal of the trial court judgment was warranted because the insurer's brief reasonably supported that action; the insurer had paid the insured's medical expenses and there was uncontradicted evidence regarding his pain and suffering after the accident, and the damages awarded for the vehicle repair were less than the cost thereof. State Farm Fire & Cas. Co. v. Bowman, — Ohio App. 3d —, 2007 Ohio 4405, — N.E. 2d —, 2007 Ohio App. LEXIS 3969 (Aug. 15, 2007).

When, in a foreclosure case, a bank disputed the trial court's apparent finding that the bank had reached a settlement agreement with a mortgagor as to the rate of interest to be paid the bank after the bank was granted summary judgment, the appellate court could, under Ohio R. App. P. 18(C), accept the bank's statement of facts because the mortgagor filed no appellate brief. Wells Fargo Bank Minn. v. Schmid, — Ohio App. 3d —, 2007 Ohio 4525, — N.E. 2d —, 2007 Ohio App. LEXIS 4046 (Aug. 29, 2007).

Trial court erred in deciding to classify the marital residence of a former husband and a former wife as marital property under RC § 3105.171 and not the wife's separate property as the wife bought out her first husband's interest in the marital residence by using monies traceable to her worker's compensation awards, proceeds from the sale of her car, and a tax refund. Since the husband had not filed a brief opposing the appeal, the court, pursuant to Ohio R. App. P. 18(C), in determining the appeal accepted the wife's statement of the facts and issues as correct. Shewring v. Shewring, — Ohio App. 3d —, 2006 Ohio 3247, — N.E. 2d —, 2006 Ohio App. LEXIS 3137 (June 19, 2006).

As an appellee failed to file a brief in an appeal of a discovery sanction imposed on appellant, the appellate court was permitted to accept appellant's statement of the facts and issues as correct and reverse the judgment of the trial court if the brief reasonably appeared to sustain the action, pursuant to Ohio R. App. P. 18(C). McKowen v. United Church Homes, Inc., — Ohio App. 3d —, 2006 Ohio 6607, — N.E. 2d —, 2006 Ohio App. LEXIS 6519 (Dec. 8, 2006).

Arrestee's appeal of a trial court order of dismissal was dismissed under Ohio R. App. P. 18(C) for want of prosecution where the arrestee's failure to satisfy the requirements of Ohio R. App. P. 16 and Ohio Fifth Dist. Ct. App. R. 9(A)(1) was tantamount to a failure to file a brief. Billman v. City of Canton, — Ohio App. 3d —, 2006 Ohio 3923, — N.E. 2d —, 2006 Ohio App. LEXIS 3894 (July 31, 2006).

Where a wife appealed a trial court's grant of extended visitation to a father with his children, pursuant to RC § 3109.051, alleging that it was error to grant such visitation upon a magistrate's determination that the husband had been convicted of domestic violence and that his home was deemed inhabitable for purposes of custody, and the husband failed to file a brief in response, pursuant to Ohio R. App. P. 18(C) and the voluminous evidence referred to by the wife, the visitation order was deemed an abuse of discretion. Clinard v. Clinard, — Ohio App. 3d —, 2006 Ohio 4188, — N.E. 2d —, 2006 Ohio App. LEXIS 4099 (Aug. 14, 2006).

Where the State did not respond to defendant's appeal, the applicable standard of review allowed the appellate court to accept defendant's presentation of the facts and issues as correct, and reverse the judgment if it was reasonable to do so pursuant to Ohio R. App. P. 18(C). State v. Harmon, — Ohio App. 3d —, 2006 Ohio 4642, — N.E. 2d —, 2006 Ohio App. LEXIS 4563 (Sept. 1, 2006).

Although an employee failed to file a brief pursuant to Ohio R. App. P. 18(C) in opposition to his employer's appeal from a judgment in the employee's favor, which allowed the court to accept the employer's statement of the facts and issues as correct, the court reviewed the issues raised in the employer's brief and the record in order to adjudicate the appeal in the interest of justice. Kirby v. Elmco Trucking, Inc., — Ohio App. 3d —, 2006 Ohio 5494, — N.E. 2d —, 2006 Ohio App. LEXIS 5470 (Oct. 23, 2006).

Although the failure of appellees to have filed a brief in response to appellant's appeal of a trial court order that dismissed his matter for failure to prosecute could have resulted in a reversal if appellant's brief reasonably appeared to sustain such action under Ohio R. App. P. 18(C), the brief did not support such relief. Brown v. Weidner, — Ohio App. 3d —, 2006 Ohio 6852, — N.E. 2d —, 2006 Ohio App. LEXIS 6765 (Dec. 26, 2006).

— Presumption of correctness of appellant's brief

Despite the fact that a mother did not file a brief in response to a father's appeal of a trial court decision that found him in contempt for his failure to pay court ordered child support, pursuant to Ohio R. App. P. 18(C) the father was not entitled to a reversal of the trial court's determination, as the evidence supported the finding of contempt because the father failed to prove that he was unable to make the required child support payments; rather, his testimony indicated that he had the ability to pay the court-ordered sums, but that he chose not to do so. Jones v. Jones, — Ohio App. 3d —, 2007 Ohio 5492, — N.E. 2d —, 2007 Ohio App. LEXIS 4827 (Oct. 15, 2007).

Presumption of correctness

Although appellee failed to file an appellate brief in response to appellant's arguments on appeal, the court could not accept appellant's statements of the facts and issues as correct pursuant to Ohio R. App. P. 18(C), as appellant's brief did not describe the facts and issues which were present at trial. Williams v. Vahila, — Ohio App. 3d —, 2007 Ohio 730, — N.E. 2d —, 2007 Ohio App. LEXIS 681 (Feb. 5, 2007).

As a former wife failed to file an appellate brief in an appeal by her former husband regarding the trial court's vacatur of an amended qualified domestic relations order arising from the parties' divorce, the appellate court could accept the husband's statement of the facts and issues as correct and reverse the judgment of the trial court if the husband's brief reasonably appeared to support such action, pursuant to Ohio R. App. P. 18(C). McGee v. McGee, 168 Ohio App. 3d 512, 2006 Ohio 4417, 860 N.E.2d 1054, 2006 Ohio App. LEXIS 4343 (2006).

Scope of review

As a contractor failed to file a brief after he was awarded judgment in a property owner's action and she appealed, the owner's statement of facts and issues were accepted as correct, but the trial court judgment was reversed upon the merits rather than merely due to the contractor's lack of having filed a brief; the owner was not entitled to a per curiam reversal under Ohio R. App. P. 18(C) merely due to the fact that there was no opposing brief. Jarupan v. Hanna, 173 Ohio App. 3d 284, 2007 Ohio 5081, 878 N.E.2d 66, 2007 Ohio App. LEXIS 4498 (2007).

Where defendant's first appeal from the trial court's denial of his suppression motion was dismissed for want of prosecution pursuant to Ohio R. App. P. 18(C), his second appeal which raised the same issue was procedurally deficient because that matter was barred by res judicata and accordingly not justiciable for appeal. State v. Rhodes, — Ohio App. 3d —, 2006 Ohio 3996, — N.E. 2d —, 2006 Ohio App. LEXIS 3927 (Aug. 4, 2006).

Service

Landlord's estate's motion to dismiss an appeal for failure to comply with Ohio R. App. P. 18 was denied, as was its motion for reconsideration of a decision that denied its motion for leave to file its brief instanter, as the tenant's brief in opposition asserted that the certificate of service attached to the appellate brief established that the estate was properly served, and proper service was accordingly presumed. Estate of Tollett v. Multilnk, Inc., — Ohio App. 3d —, 2006 Ohio 5055, — N.E. 2d —, 2006 Ohio App. LEXIS 4997 (Sept. 29, 2006).

RULE 19. Form of briefs and other papers

(A) **Form of briefs.** Briefs may be typewritten or be produced by standard typographic printing or by any duplicating or copying process which produces a clear black image on white paper. Carbon copies of briefs may not be submitted without permission of the court, except in behalf of parties allowed to proceed in forma pauperis. All printed matter must appear in at least a twelve point type on opaque, unglazed paper. Briefs produced by standard typographic process shall be bound in volumes having pages 6 ⅛ by 9 ¼ inches and type matter 4 ⅙ by 7 ⅙ inches. Those produced by any other process shall be bound in volumes having pages not exceeding 8 ½ by 11 inches and type matter not exceeding 6 ½ by 9 ½ inches, with double spacing between each line of text except quoted matter which shall be single spaced. Where necessary, briefs may be of such size as required to utilize copies of pertinent documents.

Without prior leave of court, no initial brief of appellant or cross-appellant and no answer brief of appellee or cross-appellee shall exceed thirty-five pages in length, and no reply brief shall exceed fifteen pages in length, exclusive of the table of contents, table of cases, statutes and other authorities cited, and appendices, if any. A court of appeals, by local rule, may adopt shorter or longer page limitations.

The front covers of the briefs, if separately bound,

shall contain: (1) the name of the court and the number of the case; (2) the title of the case [see App. R. 11(A)]; (3) the nature of the proceeding in the court (e.g., Appeal) and the name of the court below; (4) the title of the document (e.g., Brief for Appellant); and (5) the names and addresses of counsel representing the party on whose behalf the document is filed.

(B) **Form of other papers.** Applications for reconsideration shall be produced in a manner prescribed by subdivision (A). Motions and other papers may be produced in a like manner, or they may be typewritten upon opaque, unglazed paper 8 ½ by 11 inches in size. Lines of typewritten text shall be double spaced except quoted matter which shall be single spaced. Consecutive sheets shall be attached at the left margin. Carbon copies may be used for filing and service if they are legible.

A motion or other paper addressed to the court shall contain a caption setting forth the name of the court, the title of the case, the case number and a brief descriptive title indicating the purpose of the paper.

History: Amended, eff 7-1-72; 7-1-97.

NOTES TO DECISIONS

ANALYSIS

Non-compliance

Non-compliance

Although defendant's brief failed to comply with Ohio R. App. P. 19(A) and Ohio Fifth Dist. Ct. App. R. 9(B) where it asserted 33 assignments of error in a 104-page brief, the court chose not to dismiss the appeal under Ohio R. App. P. 18(C) for failure to file a brief, although the total non-compliance with the appellate rules was tantamount to failing to file any brief; rather, the court reviewed the assignments that it could make sense of and disregarded the others. City of Mt. Vernon v. Young, — Ohio App. 3d —, 2006 Ohio 3319, — N.E. 2d —, 2006 Ohio App. LEXIS 3235 (June 28, 2006).

RULE 20.   Prehearing conference

The court may direct the attorneys for the parties to appear before the court or a judge thereof for a prehearing conference to consider the simplification of the issues and such other matters as may aid in the disposition of the proceeding by the court. The court or judge shall make an order which recites the action taken at the conference and the agreements made by the parties as to any of the matters considered and which limits the issues to those not disposed of by admissions or agreements of counsel, and such order when entered controls the subsequent course of the proceeding, unless modified to prevent manifest injustice.

RULE 21.   Oral argument

(A) **Notice of argument.** The court shall advise all parties of the time and place at which oral argument will be heard.

(B) **Time allowed for argument.** Unless otherwise ordered, each side will be allowed thirty minutes for argument. A party is not obliged to use all of the time allowed, and the court may terminate the argument whenever in its judgment further argument is unnecessary.

(C) **Order and content of argument.** The appellant is entitled to open and conclude the argument. The opening argument shall include a fair statement of the case. Counsel will not be permitted to read at length from briefs, records or authorities.

(D) **Cross and separate appeals.** A cross-appeal or separate appeal shall be argued with the initial appeal at a single argument, unless the court otherwise directs. If separate appellants support the same argument, they shall share the thirty minutes allowed to their side for argument unless pursuant to timely request the court grants additional time.

(E) **Nonappearance of parties.** If the appellee fails to appear to present argument, the court will hear argument on behalf of the appellant, if present. If the appellant fails to appear, the court may hear argument on behalf of the appellee, if his counsel is present. If neither party appears, the case will be decided on the briefs unless the court shall otherwise order.

(F) **Submission on briefs.** By agreement of the parties, a case may be submitted for decision on the briefs, but the court may direct that the case be argued.

(G) **Motions.** Oral argument will not be heard upon motions unless ordered by the court.

(H) **Authorities in briefs.** If counsel on oral argument intends to present authorities not cited in his brief, he shall, prior to oral argument, present in writing such authorities to the court and to opposing counsel.

History: Amended, eff 7-1-72; 7-1-76.

RULE 22.   Entry of judgment

(A) **Form.** All judgments shall be in the form of a judgment signed by a judge or judges of the court which shall be prepared by the court and filed with the clerk for journalization. The clerk shall enter the judgment on the journal the day it is filed. A judgment is effective only when entered by the clerk upon the journal.

(B) **Notice.** Notice of the filing of judgment and its date of entry on the journal shall be made pursuant to App. R. 30.

(C) **Filing.** The filing of a judgment by the court with the clerk for journalization constitutes entry of the judgment.

History: Amended, eff. 07-01-08.

NOTES TO DECISIONS

ANALYSIS

Time for application for reopening

Time for application for reopening

Defendant's application to reopen his appeal lacked merit procedurally where it was filed beyond the 90-day time limit and there was no showing of good cause for the delay in filing pursuant to Ohio R. App. P. 26(B)(1) and (2); the time for filing the application began to run on the date that the court affirmed the trial court judgment, wherein the volume and page number of the journalization of the judgment were indicated pursuant to Ohio R. App. P. 22 and Ohio Eighth Dist. Ct. App. R. 22. State v. Burnett, — Ohio App. 3d —, 2007 Ohio 4434, — N.E. 2d —, 2007 Ohio App. LEXIS 4003 (Aug. 24, 2007).

RULE 23. Damages for delay

If a court of appeals shall determine that an appeal is frivolous, it may require the appellant to pay reasonable expenses of the appellee including attorney fees and costs.

NOTES TO DECISIONS

ANALYSIS

Attorney fees
Fees not awarded
Frivolous appeals
Sanctions

Attorney fees

As property purchasers' appeal from a trial court judgment in favor of property sellers was frivolous except as to one argument, in that their underlying claims were based on an error in a deed that mistakenly conveyed an additional lot that the purchasers admitted that they did not intend to acquire yet they still argued against the sellers' deed reformation claims, and the purchasers' arguments on appeal similarly lacked any merit at all, the sellers' motion for attorney fees on the appellate court level was granted. The fees were not warranted on one argument put forth by the purchasers that relied on a contrary holding from another Ohio appellate district. Patton v. Ditmyer, — Ohio App. 3d —, 2006 Ohio 7107, — N.E. 2d —, 2006 Ohio App. LEXIS 7061 (Dec. 29, 2006).

Fees not awarded

As former employees presented an arguable question for review from a judgment against them in their action, seeking various payments from their employer under a breach of contract theory and also seeking attorney's fees under the Ohio Minimum Fair Wage Standards Act, RC ch. 4111, the employer's request for fees based on its claim of a frivolous appeal under Ohio R. App. P. 23 was denied. Meisler v. Toledo Sleep Disorders Center, Ltd., — Ohio App. 3d —, 2007 Ohio 1325, — N.E. 2d —, 2007 Ohio App. LEXIS 1234 (Mar. 23, 2007).

As a trial court's grant of summary judgment to a house buyer and others was reversed on an appeal by the sellers, the buyer's motion under Ohio R. App. P. 23 and RC § 2323.51(A)(2)(ii) for attorney fees on appeal due to the alleged frivolity of the sellers' appeal lacked merit; as the appeal was successful, it was clearly not frivolous. Curran v. Vincent, — Ohio App. 3d —, 2007 Ohio 3680, — N.E. 2d —, 2007 Ohio App. LEXIS 3360 (July 20, 2007).

Court did not find that consumers' appeal from a trial court's dismissal of their suit brought under the Consumer Sales Practices Act presented no reasonable question for review, and thus, it denied the company's motion, pursuant to Ohio R. App. P. 23, for attorney fees and costs. Burdge v. Children's Place Retail Stores, — Ohio App. 3d —, 2006 Ohio 4564, — N.E. 2d —, 2006 Ohio App. LEXIS 4498 (Sept. 5, 2006).

In a divorce, a wife was not entitled to an award of her reasonable expenses, including attorney fees and costs, based on a finding that a husband's appeal was frivolous because the appeal presented a reasonable question for review. Moser v. Moser, — Ohio App. 3d —, 2006 Ohio 5381, — N.E. 2d —, 2006 Ohio App. LEXIS 5341 (Oct. 16, 2006).

Frivolous appeals

Store was awarded costs and attorney fees against a store patron and his attorney pursuant to Ohio R. App. P. 23 and Ohio R. Civ. P. 11 where the action brought against the store, alleging statutory violations due to the store's receipt indicating the patron's credit card expiration date, was completely frivolous and the attorney had no good ground to support the filing of an appeal, much less the complaint. The store patron and his attorney were both aware that an actual injury was required in order to assert a statutory claim for recovery, which did not exist in the circumstances. Burdge v. Supervalu Holdings, — Ohio App. 3d —, 2007 Ohio 1318, — N.E. 2d —, 2007 Ohio App. LEXIS 1205 (Mar. 23, 2007).

In an action by a decedent's executrix against numerous parties who were involved in setting up a corporate pension trust for tax shelter purposes, attorney fees and costs under Ohio R. App. P. 23 were not awarded to an actuary for the pension plan and his employer, as the executrix presented an arguable issue for review; although she did not present sufficient evidence to prevail on appeal, her appeal was not entirely frivolous. Driftmyer v. Carlton, — Ohio App. 3d —, 2007 Ohio 2036, — N.E. 2d —, 2007 Ohio App. LEXIS 1902 (Apr. 27, 2007).

Although appellants filed an affidavit after the trial court denied their motion to stay litigation and compel arbitration and an appeal was already filed, the appellate court did not consider the affidavit nor any arguments raised in reliance thereon, as it was not part of the materials before the trial court when it made its decision; the appeal was not frivolous under Ohio R. App. P. 23 for the purpose of imposing sanctions. Eatherton v. New York Life Ins. Co., — Ohio App. 3d —, 2006 Ohio 2233, — N.E. 2d —, 2006 Ohio App. LEXIS 2070 (May 5, 2006).

Guardian ad litem's motion for an award of attorney fees under Ohio R. App. P. 23 was not warranted. Although the father's contentions were difficult to precisely ascertain, the father appeared to challenge both the trial court's finding that he engaged in frivolous conduct and the amount of the sanctions imposed. Kellogg v. Daulton, — Ohio App. 3d —, 2006 Ohio 4115, — N.E. 2d —, 2006 Ohio App. LEXIS 4044 (Aug. 10, 2006).

Where insureds who were assessed sanctions due to their having brought a frivolous lawsuit sought recovery of those sanctions under their homeowner's insurance policy, which resulted in a summary judgment as a matter of law for the insurer, their appeal from that ruling was deemed a frivolous appeal under Ohio R. App. P. 23; rather than imposing costs and fees sua sponte, the parties were given opportunities to submit documentation for the court's review. Siemientkowski v. State Auto Mut. Ins. Co., — Ohio App. 3d —, 2006 Ohio 4122, — N.E. 2d —, 2006 Ohio App. LEXIS 4072 (Aug. 10, 2006).

Defendants' motion for an award of expenses was granted because, although the arguments in the attorney's first assignment of error, while ultimately unpersuasive, presented a reasonable question for review, his second, third, fourth, and fifth assignments of error presented no reasonable questions for review since they had already been considered and rejected in previous appeals. The attorney's arguments regarding judicial bias and prejudice were not only unwarranted under existing law, but were also unsupported by the record. Cooke v. United Dairy Farmers, Inc., — Ohio App. 3d —, 2006 Ohio 4365, — N.E. 2d —, 2006 Ohio App. LEXIS 4276 (Aug. 24, 2006).

When appellant's brief was so inadequate that it did not present any argument beyond mere assertion, its appeal was frivolous, and it was appropriate to order appellant to pay, as a sanction, a portion of the opposing party's counsel fees. Western Reserve Logistics v. Hunt Mach. & Mfg. Co., — Ohio App. 3d —, 2006 Ohio 5070, — N.E. 2d —, 2006 Ohio App. LEXIS 4980 (Sept. 29, 2006).

Sanctions

Although the mother's appeal from her parental rights termination was frivolous, a sanction against her was inappropriate because, as a lay person with appointed counsel, the mother could not have been expected to evaluate complex issues of law and select issues for appellate review on her own. Rather, she was entitled to rely upon appellate counsel to prosecute the appeal on her behalf and, therefore, it was inappropriate to award sanctions against her since she acted in reliance of her appointed counsel to pursue her appeal. In re K.D., — Ohio App. 3d —, 2006 Ohio 4730, — N.E. 2d —, 2006 Ohio App. LEXIS 4650 (Sept. 13, 2006).

As an appeal of a dismissal presented a reasonable question for review on appeal, a motion for sanctions pursuant to Ohio R. App. P. 23 was denied. Madewell v. Powell, — Ohio App. 3d —, 2006 Ohio 7046, — N.E. 2d —, 2006 Ohio App. LEXIS 7043 (Dec. 28, 2006).

RULE 24.   Costs

(A) Except as otherwise provided by law or as the court may order, the party liable for costs is as follows:

(1) If an appeal is dismissed, the appellant or as agreed by the parties.

(2) If the judgment appealed is affirmed, the appellant.

(3) If the judgment appealed is reversed, the appellee.

(4) If the judgment appealed is affirmed or reversed in part or is vacated, as ordered by the court.

(B) As used in this rule, "costs" means an expense incurred in preparation of the record including the transcript of proceedings, fees allowed by law, and the fee for filing the appeal. It does not mean the expense of printing or copying a brief or an appendix.

History: Amended, eff 7-1-92.

NOTES TO DECISIONS
ANALYSIS

Costs
Costs generally

Costs

Defendant did not demonstrate why we should waive the assessment of costs pursuant to Ohio R. App. P. 24. Simply because he was found indigent for purposes of legal representation did not mean that he was indigent for purposes of paying fines or court costs. State v. Shie, — Ohio App. 3d —, 2007 Ohio 3773, — N.E. 2d —, 2007 Ohio App. LEXIS 3431 (July 26, 2007).

Costs generally

Defendant's motion to recover fees of his first appeal of his conviction after his conviction had been reversed on appeal was properly denied. Since defendant did not file for reimbursement for costs in the original appellate case in which the costs were assessed, the court could not order reimbursement under App. R. 24 in defendant's later appeal. State v. Kincer, — Ohio App. 3d —, 2007 Ohio 3352, — N.E. 2d —, 2007 Ohio App. LEXIS 3117 (July 2, 2007).

Appellate court's authority to award costs incurred on appeal pursuant to Ohio R. App. P. 24 was not the same as a motion for attorney fees under RC § 2323.51; the two requests did not constitute "two bites at the apple." Thomas v. City of Cincinnati, — Ohio App. 3d —, 2006 Ohio 3598, — N.E. 2d —, 2006 Ohio App. LEXIS 3543 (July 14, 2006).

RULE 25.   Motion to certify a conflict

(A) A motion to certify a conflict under Article IV, Section 3(B)(4) of the Ohio Constitution shall be made in writing no later than ten days after the judgment or order of the court that creates a conflict with a judgment or order of another court of appeals has been approved by the court and filed by the court with the clerk for journalization. The filing of a motion to certify a conflict does not extend the time for filing a notice of appeal in the supreme court. A motion under this rule shall specify the issue proposed for certification and shall cite the judgment or judgments alleged to be in conflict with the judgment of the court in which the motion is filed.

(B) Parties opposing the motion shall answer in writing within ten days of service of the motion. The moving party may file a reply brief within seven days after service of the answer brief in opposition. Copies of the motion, answer brief in opposition, and reply brief shall be served as prescribed for the service and filing of briefs in the initial action. Oral argument of a motion to certify a conflict shall not be permitted except at the request of the court.

(C) The court of appeals shall rule upon a motion to certify within sixty days of its filing.

History: Effective 7-1-94; 7-1-10.

NOTES TO DECISIONS
ANALYSIS

Conflict

Conflict

Trial court's denial of defendant's post-conviction relief petition did not create a conflict that could be certified to the Ohio Supreme Court by an Ohio court of appeals pursuant to Ohio P. App. R. 25 and Ohio Const. art. IV, § 3(b)(4), as such certification procedure was only authorized for conflicts between opinions of two or more courts of appeals. State v. Rivers, — Ohio App. 3d —, 2007 Ohio 2442, — N.E. 2d —, 2007 Ohio App. LEXIS 2257 (May 21, 2007).

RULE 26.   Application for reconsideration; application for en banc consideration; application for reopening

(A) **Application for reconsideration and en banc consideration.**

(1) **Reconsideration.**

(a) Application for reconsideration of any cause or motion submitted on appeal shall be made in writing before the judgment or order of the court has been approved by the court and filed by the court with the clerk for journalization or within ten days of the announcement of the court's decision, whichever is later. The filing of an application for reconsideration shall not extend the time for filing a notice of appeal in the Supreme Court unless such an extension is provided for by the Supreme Court Rules of Practice.

(b) Parties opposing the application shall answer in writing within ten days of service of the application. The party making the application may file a reply brief within seven days of service of the answer brief in opposition. Copies of the application, answer brief in opposition, and reply brief shall be served in the manner prescribed for the service and filing of briefs in the initial action. Oral argument of an application for reconsideration shall not be permitted except at the request of the court.

(c) The application for reconsideration shall be considered by the panel that issued the original decision.

(2) **En banc consideration.**

(a) Upon a determination that two or more decisions of the court on which they sit are in conflict, a majority of the court of appeals judges in an appellate district may order that an appeal or other proceeding be considered en banc. The en banc court shall consist of all full-time judges of the appellate district who have not recused themselves or otherwise been disqualified from the case. Consideration en banc is not favored and will not be ordered unless necessary to secure or maintain uniformity of decisions within the district on an issue that is dispositive in the case in which the application is filed.

(b) A party may make an application for en banc consideration. An application for en banc consideration must explain how the panel's decision conflicts with a prior panel's decision on a dispositive issue and why consideration by the court en banc is necessary to secure and maintain uniformity of the court's decisions.

(c) The rules applicable to applications for reconsideration set forth in division (A)(1) of this rule, including the timing requirements, govern applications for en banc consideration. In addition, a party may seek en banc consideration within ten days of the entry of any judgment or order of the court ruling on a timely filed application for reconsideration under division (A)(1) of this rule if an intra-district conflict first arises as a result of that judgment or order. A party filing both an application for reconsideration and an application for en banc consideration simultaneously shall do so in a single document.

(d) The decision of the en banc court shall become the decision of the court. In the event a majority of the full-time judges of the appellate district is unable to concur in a decision, the decision of the original panel shall remain the decision in the case.

(e) Other procedures governing the initiation, filing, briefing, rehearing, reconsideration, and determination of en banc proceedings may be prescribed by local rule or as otherwise ordered by the court.

(B) **Application for reopening.**

(1) A defendant in a criminal case may apply for reopening of the appeal from the judgment of conviction and sentence, based on a claim of ineffective assistance of appellate counsel. An application for reopening shall be filed in the court of appeals where the appeal was decided within ninety days from journalization of the appellate judgment unless the applicant shows good cause for filing at a later time.

(2) An application for reopening shall contain all of the following:

(a) The appellate case number in which reopening is sought and the trial court case number or numbers from which the appeal was taken;

(b) A showing of good cause for untimely filing if the application is filed more than ninety days after journalization of the appellate judgment.[;]

(c) One or more assignments of error or arguments in support of assignments of error that previously were not considered on the merits in the case by any appellate court or that were considered on an incomplete record because of appellate counsel's deficient representation;

(d) A sworn statement of the basis for the claim that appellate counsel's representation was deficient with respect to the assignments of error or arguments raised pursuant to division (B)(2)(c) of this rule and the manner in which the deficiency prejudicially affected the outcome of the appeal, which may include citations to applicable authorities and references to the record;

(e) Any parts of the record available to the applicant and all supplemental affidavits upon which the applicant relies.

(3) The applicant shall furnish an additional copy of the application to the clerk of the court of appeals who shall serve it on the attorney for the prosecution. The attorney for the prosecution, within thirty days from the filing of the application, may file and serve affidavits, parts of the record, and a memorandum of law in opposition to the application.

(4) An application for reopening and an opposing memorandum shall not exceed ten pages, exclusive of affidavits and parts of the record. Oral argument of an application for reopening shall not be permitted except at the request of the court.

(5) An application for reopening shall be granted if there is a genuine issue as to whether the applicant was deprived of the effective assistance of counsel on appeal.

(6) If the court denies the application, it shall state in the entry the reasons for denial. If the court grants the application, it shall do both of the following:

(a) Appoint counsel to represent the applicant if the applicant is indigent and not currently represented;

(b) Impose conditions, if any, necessary to preserve the status quo during pendency of the reopened appeal.

The clerk shall serve notice of journalization of the entry on the parties and, if the application is granted, on the clerk of the trial court.

(7) If the application is granted, the case shall proceed as on an initial appeal in accordance with these rules except that the court may limit its review to those assignments of error and arguments not previously considered. The time limits for preparation and transmission of the record pursuant to App. R. 9 and 10 shall run from journalization of the entry granting the application. The parties shall address in their briefs the claim that representation by prior appellate counsel was deficient and that the applicant was prejudiced by that deficiency.

(8) If the court of appeals determines that an evidentiary hearing is necessary, the evidentiary hearing may be conducted by the court or referred to a magistrate.

(9) If the court finds that the performance of appellate counsel was deficient and the applicant was prejudiced by that deficiency, the court shall vacate its prior judgment and enter the appropriate judgment. If the court does not so find, the court shall issue an order confirming its prior judgment.

(C) **[Ruling upon application for reconsideration.]** If an application for reconsideration under division (A) of this rule is filed with the court of appeals, the application shall be ruled upon within forty-five days of its filing.

History: Amended, eff 7-1-75; 7-1-93; 7-1-94; 7-1-97; 7-1-10.

NOTES TO DECISIONS

ANALYSIS

Application for reopening denied
Application to reopen
Ineffective assistance
Ineffective assistance of appellate counsel
— Failure to allege pleading insufficiency
—Sentencing
Jurisdiction
Motion for reconsideration
Reconsideration generally
Res judicata
Time limitations
Timeliness
Timeliness of application for reopening

Application for reopening denied

Defendant's application to reopen an appellate judgment pursuant to Ohio R. App. P. 26(B) was denied, as his claim that his appellate counsel was ineffective was barred by res judicata where he asserted the issues in his pro se appeal to the Ohio Supreme Court and there was no showing that application of the res judicata doctrine was unjust. There was no substantive merit to defendant's ineffectiveness claims under U.S. Const. amend. VI and Ohio Const. art. I, § 10, as counsel acted within his discretion in determining which arguments were the most fruitful for purposes of arguing them on appeal, and there was no showing that the outcome of defendant's matter would have been different if the other issues had been raised and argued. State v. Smith, — Ohio App. 3d —, 2007 Ohio 1977, — N.E. 2d —, 2007 Ohio App. LEXIS 1826 (Apr. 20, 2007).

Application to reopen appellate judgment pursuant to Ohio R. App. P. 26(B) was dismissed where there was no sworn statement of the basis for the claim that appellate counsel's representation was deficient, as required by Rule 26(B)(2)(d). State v. Block, — Ohio App. 3d —, 2007 Ohio 1979, — N.E. 2d —, 2007 Ohio App. LEXIS 1830 (Apr. 20, 2007).

Defendant's application to reopen an appellate judgment, which had affirmed his convictions, was untimely under Ohio R. App. P. 26(B)(1) where it was not filed within 90 days of the date that the judgment was journalized. Defendant failed to show good cause for his lack of timeliness pursuant to Rule 26(B)(2)(b). State v. Farrow, — Ohio App. 3d —, 2007 Ohio 1976, — N.E. 2d —, 2007 Ohio App. LEXIS 1834 (Apr. 23, 2007).

Defendant's application to reopen his appeal pursuant to Ohio R. App. P. 26 was denied where he failed to support the application with an affidavit as required by Rule 26(B)(2)(d), he failed to state what assignment of error should have been raised or was argued improperly pursuant to Rule 26(B)(2)(c), and reconsideration under Rule 26(A) was untimely and had previously been requested and denied; defendant claimed that his appellate counsel was ineffective for failing to raise various inadequacies of the prosecution. State v. Jackson, — Ohio App. 3d —, 2007 Ohio 5431, — N.E. 2d —, 2007 Ohio App. LEXIS 4772 (Oct. 9, 2007).

Defendant's application for reopening his appeal was denied as it was filed in excess of the 90-day limit of Ohio R. App. 26(B)(1) and defendant did not show good cause for filing an untimely application based on his need to file a motion for a new trial due to defendant's receipt of a witness's affidavit that stated that the witness lied under oath. The affidavit was not included in the record on appeal and defendant failed to support his claim that putative evidence that did not exist prior to the direct appeal either provided a basis for reopening or demonstrated good cause for the untimely filing of an application. State v. Clark, — Ohio App. 3d —, 2006 Ohio 3835, — N.E. 2d —, 2006 Ohio App. LEXIS 3802 (July 25, 2006).

Defendant's application for reopening an appellate court judgment pursuant to Ohio R. App. P. 26(B) was denied where the proposed assignments of error were either previously raised on appeal, or could have been raised, and accordingly, the doctrine of res judicata barred further litigation. The application was rendered moot by the reversal of the judgment and the remand to the trial court for resentencing. State v. Abboud, — Ohio App. 3d —, 2006 Ohio 4265, — N.E. 2d —, 2006 Ohio App. LEXIS 4188 (Aug. 11, 2006).

Defendant's appellate counsel did not provide ineffective assistance in violation of U.S. Const. amend. VI and Ohio Const. art. I, § 10 where he failed to argue in defendant's direct appeal that the indictment was defective, as the indictment properly charged defendant with six separate counts of rape, in violation of RC § 2907.02(A)(1)(b), the offenses met the requirements of RC § 2941.05, and they each alleged that defendant committed the offense during a different time period. As there was no reasonable probability of success if counsel had asserted such an argument on appeal, defendant's application to reopen his appeal pursuant to Ohio R. App. P. 26(B)(5) was denied. State v. Parks, — Ohio App. 3d —, 2006 Ohio 7269, — N.E. 2d —, 2006 Ohio App. LEXIS 7074 (May 23, 2006).

Appellate counsel was not ineffective in violation of U.S. Const. amend. VI and Ohio Const. art. I, § 10 in failing to raise on defendant's direct appeal that his plea agreement was not properly followed by the trial court judge, as the judge had specifically indicated to defendant that he was not bound to follow the recommendation for sentencing, defendant was apprised sufficiently under Ohio R. Crim. P. 11(C) and he indicated that he understood and still wished to plead guilty, and the record indicated that defendant's plea was knowingly, intelligently, and voluntarily entered; accordingly, there was no cause to grant defendant's application to reopen his appeal pursuant to Ohio R. App. P. 26(B)(5). State v. Parks, — Ohio App. 3d —, 2006 Ohio 7269, — N.E. 2d —, 2006 Ohio App. LEXIS 7074 (May 23, 2006).

Application to reopen

Court sua sponte struck and dismissed an application pursuant to Ohio R. App. P. 26(B) of defendant's wife to reopen an appellate judgment, which had affirmed his conviction for intimidation, as she was not a registered attorney and the fact that he had given her a durable power of attorney did not give her authority to represent him pursuant to RC § 4705.01. Her preparation of the legal papers and her management thereof constituted the unauthorized practice of law under Ohio Sup. Ct. R. Gov't Bar VII, § 4(A), which the court had an ethical duty to prohibit pursuant to Ohio Code Prof. Conduct R. 5.5(a). State v. Block, — Ohio App. 3d —, 2007 Ohio 1979, — N.E. 2d —, 2007 Ohio App. LEXIS 1830 (Apr. 20, 2007).

Court of Appeals of Ohio, First Appellate District, Hamilton County holds that RC §§ 2953.21 and 2953.23 plainly afford a post-conviction defendant who has timely filed an appeal by right under Ohio R. App. P. 4, who has been granted a delayed appeal under Ohio R. App. P. 5(A), or whose appeal has been reopened pursuant to Ohio R. App. P. 26(B) 180 days from the date on which the trial transcript is filed in his appeal to file his collateral challenge to the judgment of conviction. The phrase "direct appeal of the judgment of conviction," as used in the statutes, is undefined and does not expressly apply or exclude any type of appeal from its operation pursuant to statutory interpretation principles under RC § 1.47(B) and (C). State v. Fuller, — Ohio App. 3d —, 2007 Ohio 2018, — N.E. 2d —, 2007 Ohio App. LEXIS 1885 (Apr. 27, 2007).

Ineffective assistance

For purposes of defendant's application to reopen his appeal pursuant to Ohio R. App. P. 26(B)(5), he failed to establish that his appellate counsel rendered ineffective assistance in violation of U.S. Const. amend. VI and Ohio Const. art. I, § 10 by failing to challenge allegedly fraudulent counts of the criminal indictment against defendant and by failing to assert that there was prosecutorial misconduct, arising from the inclusion of a sexually violent predator specification against him, as that specification was bifurcated from other charges and heard by the trial court and not the jury, and further, defendant was found not guilty of the specification, such that there was no prejudice shown to defendant. State v. Hemphill, — Ohio App. 3d —, 2006 Ohio 4372, — N.E. 2d —, 2006 Ohio App. LEXIS 4294 (Aug. 23, 2006).

Defendant failed to show that his trial counsel was ineffective in violation of his rights under U.S. Const. amend. VI and Ohio Const. art. I, § 10 where counsel's decision regarding the scope of cross-examination was a matter of trial strategy and there was no showing that defendant was prejudiced. His application to reopen his appeal pursuant to Ohio R. App. P. 26(B)(5) due to his appellate counsel's failure to raise the ineffectiveness of trial counsel was denied. State v. Hemphill, — Ohio App. 3d —, 2006 Ohio 4372, — N.E. 2d —, 2006 Ohio App. LEXIS 4294 (Aug. 23, 2006).

Ineffective assistance of appellate counsel

Defendant failed to show that his appellate counsel provided ineffective assistance in violation of U.S. Const. amend. VI and Ohio Const. art. I, § 10 for purposes of his application to reopen his appeal pursuant to Ohio R. App. P. 26(B), as his counsel exercised her professional judgment in raising assignments of error regarding the trial court's evidentiary rulings that had been objected to, rather than to rulings for which there was no objection. No prejudice was shown by defendant, as the appellate court had previously overruled the evidentiary arguments that appellate counsel had raised. State v. Warren, — Ohio App. 3d —, 2007 Ohio 69, — N.E. 2d —, 2007 Ohio App. LEXIS 56 (Jan. 10, 2007).

Defendant's inmate's claim that his appellate counsel was ineffective, in violation of U.S. Const. amend. VI and Ohio Const. art. I, § 10, for failing to raise sentencing issues was reviewable pursuant to an application for reopening pursuant to Ohio R. App. P. 26(B), or on direct appeal to the Ohio Supreme Court pursuant to Ohio Const. art. IV, § 2(B)(2)(a)(iii); however, a claim in his post-conviction relief petition pursuant to RC § 2953.21 on that issue was the improper vehicle for such an argument. Ohio v. Dunn, — Ohio App. 3d —, 2007 Ohio 4890, — N.E. 2d —, 2007 Ohio App. LEXIS 4365 (Sept. 21, 2007).

— Failure to allege pleading insufficiency

As an inmate's appellate counsel was not ineffective in violation of U.S. Const. amend. VI and Ohio Const. art. I, § 10 in failing to raise, in defendant's direct appeal, that the State failed to prove that he used force or threat of force for purposes of his convictions for rape, in violation of RC § 2907.02(A)(1)(B), defendant's application to reopen his direct appeal pursuant to Ohio R. App. P. 26(B)(5) was

properly denied. Due to the fact that the victim of defendant's offenses was less than 10 years of age, the State did not have to prove that element of the offenses and defendant did not have to be informed on that issue prior to entering his guilty pleas. State v. Parks, — Ohio App. 3d —, 2006 Ohio 7269, — N.E. 2d —, 2006 Ohio App. LEXIS 7074 (May 23, 2006).

—Sentencing

As there was nothing in the trial court record of defendant's sentencing proceeding that indicated that he objected to the sentence imposed because it was allegedly not what he had agreed to during plea negotiations, his appellate counsel was not ineffective in violation of U.S. Const. amend. VI and Ohio Const. art. I, § 10 in failing to raise on appeal the claim of an involuntary and coerced plea. Defendant's application to reopen his appeal pursuant to Ohio R. App. P. 26(B) based on ineffectiveness of appellate counsel lacked merit, as the court could only review errors that had a basis in the record. State v. Moore, — Ohio App. 3d —, 2007 Ohio 2919, — N.E. 2d —, 2007 Ohio App. LEXIS 2704 (June 11, 2007).

Jurisdiction

Although a motion to reopen defendant's prior appeal pursuant to Ohio R. App. P. 26 was pending at the time that the trial court resentenced defendant pursuant to a remand order from his appeal, the trial court was not deprived of jurisdiction to issue the resentencing order; the prior appeal that ordered the resentencing was completed and closed, and the motion to reopen was not part of the original appeal but instead, was a collateral post-conviction remedy. State v. Rosado, — Ohio App. 3d —, 2007 Ohio 2782, — N.E. 2d —, 2007 Ohio App. LEXIS 2569 (June 7, 2007).

Motion for reconsideration

Ohio R. App. P. 26 provides a mechanism by which a party may prevent miscarriages of justice that could arise when an appellate court makes an obvious error or renders an unsupportable decision under the law, so, in considering an application for reconsideration, the proper standard for an appellate court's review is whether the application calls to the attention of the court an obvious error in its decision or raises an issue for its consideration that was either not considered at all or was not fully considered by it when it should have been. City of Columbus v. Peoples, — Ohio App. 3d —, 2006 Ohio 2607, — N.E. 2d —, 2006 Ohio App. LEXIS 2430 (May 25, 2006).

Reconsideration generally

There was no abuse of discretion in a trial court's denial of an award of attorney fees to a telephone customer in his action under RC § 1345.09 of the Ohio Consumer Sales Practices Act, arising from an unsolicited phone call that he received, as the admission by the telephone solicitor that the phone calls were knowingly and purposely made did not require an award of fees to the customer, but merely gave the trial court discretion to award them if it saw fit to do so; accordingly, reconsideration of the appellate court's affirmance of the trial court judgment was not warranted under Ohio R. App. P. 26. Charvat v. Ryan, — Ohio App. 3d —, 2006 Ohio 4592, — N.E. 2d —, 2006 Ohio App. LEXIS 4537 (Sept. 7, 2006).

Application for reconsideration Ohio R. App. P. 26(A) was not designed for use in instances where a party simply disagreed with the conclusions reached and the logic used by an appellate court; a motion for reconsideration was overruled where a prior appellate case cited by a former administrator failed to shed any light on the issue raised in the original opinion. In re Estate of Phelps, — Ohio App. 3d —, 2006 Ohio 1471, — N.E. 2d —, 2006 Ohio App. LEXIS 1344 (Mar. 21, 2006).

Where an appellate court clerk stamped one notice of appeal and brief filed by an inmate, raising the issue of the trial court's denial of his request for appointed counsel, as "filed," and the clerk mistakenly filed the other notice of appeal and brief filed by the inmate from the trial court's denial of his plea withdrawal request as "copy," the appellate court's disregard of the inmate's claim on the withdrawal issue upon determining that it was not argued pursuant to Ohio R. App. P. 12 and 16 was an "obvious error"; as the court did not review the brief relating to the plea withdrawal request due to the clerk's clerical mistake, the inmate's application for reconsideration pursuant to Ohio R. App. P. 26 was granted on the limited issue of arguments relating to the plea withdrawal request. State v. Meadows, — Ohio App. 3d —, 2006 Ohio 3375, — N.E. 2d —, 2006 Ohio App. LEXIS 3304 (June 29, 2006).

Res judicata

Where defendant could have sought further review to the Ohio Supreme Court with respect to his claim that his appellate counsel rendered ineffective assistance in violation of U.S. Const. amend. VI and Ohio Const. art. I, § 10, and he offered no explanation why such further review was not sought, his application to reopen his appellate judgment pursuant to Ohio R. App. P. 26(B) was denied on grounds of res judicata. There was no merit to his claim of ineffective assistance, as the decision whether to request certain records was a strategic one which did not result in ineffectiveness, and the imposition of court costs against defendant, although he was found indigent, was warranted under RC § 2947.23. State v. Melton, — Ohio App. 3d —, 2007 Ohio 849, — N.E. 2d —, 2007 Ohio App. LEXIS 745 (Feb. 27, 2007).

Application to reopen was denied regarding the repeat violent offender specification. Res judicata barred defendant's assertion that appellate counsel was ineffective for failing to argue that the trial court improperly found him guilty of the repeat violent offender specifications because the imposition of an additional penalty for a repeat violent offender specification did not require judicial factfinding and was, therefore, constitutional. Ohio v. Douglas, — Ohio App. 3d —, 2007 Ohio 5941, — N.E. 2d —, 2007 Ohio App. LEXIS 5228 (Nov. 7, 2007).

Where defendant had appealed to the Ohio Supreme Court from an appellate court judgment that affirmed his convictions and sentence imposed by the trial court, which resulted in a reversal of the appellate court judgment and a remand to the trial court for resentencing, defendant's application for reopening the appellate court judgment pursuant to Ohio R. App. P. 26(B) was moot; further, the issues were barred by res judicata where they were either raised on appeal, or could have been raised, and application of the doctrine was not unjust. State v. Bryant, — Ohio App. 3d —, 2006 Ohio 4105, — N.E. 2d —, 2006 Ohio App. LEXIS 4063 (Aug. 4, 2006).

As defendant's appeal to the Supreme Court of Ohio resulted in a dismissal thereof after the Court explicitly considered the principles of ineffective assistance of counsel, his subsequent application under Ohio R. App. P. 26(B) to reopen the judgment of the court of appeals was denied, as it was barred by res judicata. State v. Keith, — Ohio App. 3d —, 2006 Ohio 7253, — N.E. 2d —, 2006 Ohio App. LEXIS 7068 (May 12, 2006).

Time limitations

Application for reopening filed by defendant was denied because the application was filed six years after the judgment in question was rendered. Defendant's assertion that she received her paperwork late did not constitute good cause under Ohio R. App. P. 26(B)(2)(b) for the untimely filing of her application. State v. Jenkins, — Ohio App. 3d —, 2006 Ohio 4583, — N.E. 2d —, 2006 Ohio App. LEXIS 4535 (Sept. 5, 2006).

Timeliness

As defendant inmate did not file an application to reopen his appeal for 29 years following the affirmance of his conviction and sentence, and he failed to show good cause for

not filing the application within the 90-day time limit pursuant to Ohio R. App. P. 26(B)(1), the application was properly denied without review on the merits as to his claim of ineffective assistance of appellate counsel. State v. Farrow, 115 Ohio St. 3d 205, 2007 Ohio 4792, 874 N.E. 2d 526, 2007 Ohio LEXIS 2210 (Sept. 20, 2007).

Defendant's App. R. 26(B) application to reopen a court's judgment affirming his convictions was dismissed because the application, which was filed three years after the court issued its judgment, was not timely filed. Defendant's contentions that he was ignorant of the law and that he had difficulty obtaining evidence did not constitute good cause excusing the untimely filing. State v. Gaston, — Ohio App. 3d —, 2007 Ohio 155, — N.E. 2d —, 2007 Ohio App. LEXIS 147 (Jan. 17, 2007).

Timeliness of application for reopening

Defendant's application to reopen his appeal was denied pursuant to Ohio R. App. P. 26(B)(1) where he failed to show good cause for his untimely filing. His claims that his appellate counsel denied him access to the transcript, that he was unable to afford to acquire the transcript from the court reporter due to his indigency, and that the correctional institution where he was housed did not provide him with assistance did not provide sufficient good cause for the delayed filing. State v. Lawson, — Ohio App. 3d —, 2006 Ohio 3839, — N.E. 2d —, 2006 Ohio App. LEXIS 3804 (July 24, 2006).

RULE 27.   Execution, mandate

A court of appeals may remand its final decrees, judgments, or orders, in cases brought before it on appeal, to the court or agency below for specific or general execution thereof, or to the court below for further proceedings therein.

A certified copy of the judgment shall constitute the mandate. A stay of execution of the judgment mandate pending appeal may be granted upon motion, and a bond or other security may be required as a condition to the grant or continuance of the stay.

RULE 28.   Voluntary dismissal

If the parties to an appeal or other proceeding shall sign and file with the clerk of the court of appeals an agreement that the proceedings be dismissed and shall pay whatever costs are due, the court shall order the case dismissed.

An appeal may be dismissed on motion of the appellant upon such terms as may be fixed by the court.

NOTES TO DECISIONS

ANALYSIS

Effect of dismissal of appeal

Effect of dismissal of appeal

Where a former husband's timely appeal of a trial court judgment that adopted an initial decision of a magistrate regarding reallocation of parental rights and responsibilities and child support was voluntarily dismissed, presumably because the trial court was divested of jurisdiction to address the husband's subsequently filed motions to reallocate parental rights and responsibilities, the dismissal of the appeal was deemed to have been with prejudice pursuant to Ohio R. App. P. 28 and any issues raised which could have been addressed in that dismissed appeal were deemed waived and were barred from subsequent litigation under the doctrine of res judicata. Decisions regarding the children's residence with the husband's mother when they were with him due to his lack of sanitary living conditions and the issue of child support and imputation of income to the husband were barred by res judicata. Weisberg v. Sampson, — Ohio App. 3d —, 2006 Ohio 3646, — N.E. 2d —, 2006 Ohio App. LEXIS 3569 (July 14, 2006).

RULE 29.   Substitution of parties

(A) **Death of a party.** If a party dies after a notice of appeal is filed or while a proceeding is otherwise pending in the court of appeals, the personal representative of the deceased party may be substituted as a party on motion filed by the representative, or by any party, with the clerk of the court of appeals. The motion of a party shall be served upon the representative in accordance with the provisions of Rule 13. If the deceased party has no representative, any party may suggest the death on the record and proceedings shall then be had as the court of appeals may direct. If a party against whom an appeal may be taken dies after entry of a judgment or order in the trial court but before a notice of appeal is filed, an appellant may proceed as if death had not occurred. After the notice of appeal is filed substitution shall be effected in the court of appeals in accordance with this subdivision. If a party entitled to appeal shall die before filing a notice of appeal, the notice of appeal may be filed by his personal representative, or, if he has no personal representative, by his attorney of record within the time prescribed by these rules. After the notice of appeal is filed, substitution shall be effected in the court of appeals in accordance with this subdivision.

(B) **Substitution for other causes.** If substitution of a party in the court of appeals is necessary for any reason other than death, substitution shall be effected in accordance with the procedure prescribed in subdivision (A).

(C) **Public officers; death or separation from office.**

(1) When a public officer is a party to an appeal or other proceeding in the court of appeals in his official capacity and during its pendency dies, resigns or otherwise ceases to hold office, the action does not abate and his successor is automatically substituted as a party. Proceedings following the substitution shall be in the name of the substituted party, but any misnomer not affecting the substantial rights of the parties shall be disregarded. An order of substitution may be entered at any time, but the omission to enter such an order shall not affect the substitution.

(2) When a public officer is a party to an appeal or other proceeding in his official capacity, he may be described as a party by his official title rather than by name, but the court may require his name to be added.

NOTES TO DECISIONS

ANALYSIS

Necessity of substitution

Necessity of substitution
   Although a city had no standing under Ohio R. App. P. 4(A) to appeal from a judgment in the trial court that was in favor of a union in the union's administrative appeal of a decision by

the State Employment Relations Board, as the trial court had adopted a magistrate's decision to deny the city's motion to intervene in the trial court proceedings, and the Board could not assert as error on appeal that the trial court had improperly denied intervention to the city, as it was not "aggrieved" by that decision, the city could seek to intervene on the appellate level pursuant to Ohio R. Civ. P. 24 and 1(C). The city could not be substituted for the Board on appeal pursuant to Ohio R. App. P. 29(B), as such substitution was not "necessary." Queen City Lodge No. 69 v. State Empl. Rels. Bd., — Ohio App. 3d —, 2007 Ohio 170, — N.E. 2d —, 2007 Ohio App. LEXIS 173 (Jan. 19, 2007).
   When a consumer filed for bankruptcy after he appealed the dismissal of his suit against a credit union, the appeal became part of the bankruptcy estate, and the consumer did not show the estate's trustee abandoned it, under 11 U.S.C.S. § 554, so, because the trustee did not substitute into the appeal, under Ohio R. App. P. 29(B), the appellate court could dismiss it, as the consumer was no longer the real party in interest. Doucet v. Telhio Credit Union, Inc., — Ohio App. 3d —, 2006 Ohio 4342, — N.E. 2d —, 2006 Ohio App. LEXIS 4267 (Aug. 22, 2006).

RULE 30.   Duties of clerks

(A) **Notice of orders or judgments.** Immediately upon the entry of an order or judgment, the clerk shall serve by mail a notice of entry upon each party to the proceeding and shall make a note in the docket of the mailing. Service on a party represented by counsel shall be made on counsel.

(B) **Custody of records and papers.** The clerk shall have custody of the records and papers of the court. Papers transmitted as the record on appeal or review shall upon disposition of the case be returned to the court or agency from which they were received. The clerk shall preserve copies of briefs and other filings.

History: Amended, eff 7-1-72.

RULE 31.   [Reserved]

RULE 32.   [Reserved]

RULE 33.   [Reserved]

RULE 34.   Appointment of magistrates

(A) **Original actions.** Original actions in the court of appeals may be referred to a magistrate pursuant to Civ. R. 53.

(B) **Appeals.** When the court orders an evidentiary hearing in an appeal, the court may appoint a magistrate pursuant to Civ. R. 53 to conduct the hearing.

(C) **Reference to magistrates.** In any matter referred to a magistrate, all proceedings shall be governed by Civ. R. 53 and the order of reference, except that the word "judge" in Civ. R. 53 shall mean the court of appeals. An order of reference shall be signed by at least two judges of the court. Where the court has entered a general order referring a category of actions, appeals, or motions to magistrates generally, a subsequent order referring a particular action, appeal, or motion to a specific magistrate pursuant to the general order may be signed by one judge.

History: Effective 7-1-97.

RULE 35.   [Reserved]

RULE 36.   [Reserved]

RULE 37.   [Reserved]

RULE 38.   [Reserved]

RULE 39.   [Reserved]

RULE 40.   [Reserved]

RULE 41.   Rules of courts of appeals

(A) The courts of appeals may adopt rules concerning local practice in their respective courts that are not inconsistent with the rules promulgated by the Supreme Court. Local rules shall be filed with the Supreme Court.

(B) Local rules shall be adopted only after the court gives appropriate notice and an opportunity for comment. If the court determines that there is an immediate need for a rule, the court may adopt the rule without prior notice and opportunity for comment, but promptly shall afford notice and opportunity for comment.

History: Effective 7-1-94; Amended, eff 7-1-97.

RULE 42.   Title

These rules shall be known as the Ohio Rules of Appellate Procedure and may be cited as "Appellate Rules" or "App. R. ____."

History: Amended, eff 7-1-97.

RULE 43.   Effective date

(A) **Effective date of rules.** These rules shall take effect on the first day of July, 1971. They govern all proceedings in actions brought after they take effect and also all further proceedings in actions then pending, except to the extent that in the opinion of the court their application in a particular action pending when the rules take effect would not be feasible or would work injustice in which event the former procedure applies.

(B) **Effective date of amendments.** The amendments submitted by the Supreme Court to the General Assembly on January 15, 1972, shall take effect on the first day of July, 1972. They govern all proceedings in actions brought after they take effect and also all further proceedings in actions then pending, except to the extent that their application in a particular action pending when the rules take effect would not be feasible or would work injustice, in which event the former procedure applies.

(C) **Effective date of amendments.** The amendments submitted by the Supreme Court to the General Assembly on January 12, 1973, and on April 30, 1973, shall take effect on July 1, 1973. They govern all proceedings in actions brought after they take effect and also all further proceedings in actions then pending, except to the extent that their application in a particular action pending when the amendments take

effect would not be feasible or would work injustice, in which event the former procedure applies.

(D) **Effective date of amendments.** The amendments submitted by the Supreme Court to the General Assembly on January 10, 1975, and on April 29, 1975, shall take effect on July 1, 1975. They govern all proceedings in actions brought after they take effect and also all further proceedings in actions then pending, except to the extent that their application in a particular action pending when the amendments take effect would not be feasible or would work injustice, in which event the former procedure applies.

(E) **Effective date of amendments.** The amendments submitted by the Supreme Court to the General Assembly on January 9, 1976, shall take effect on July 1, 1976. They govern all proceedings in actions brought after they take effect and also all further proceedings in actions then pending, except to the extent that their application in a particular action pending when the amendments take effect would not be feasible or would work injustice, in which event the former procedure applies.

(F) **Effective date of amendments.** The amendments submitted by the Supreme Court to the General Assembly on January 12, 1978, shall take effect on July 1, 1978. They govern all proceedings in actions brought after they take effect and also all further proceedings in actions then pending, except to the extent that their application in a particular action pending when the amendments take effect would not be feasible or would work injustice, in which event the former procedure applies.

(G) **Effective date of amendments.** The amendments submitted by the Supreme Court to the General Assembly on January 14, 1982, shall take effect on July 1, 1982. They govern all proceedings in actions brought after they take effect and also all further proceedings in actions then pending, except to the extent that their application in a particular action pending when the amendments take effect would not be feasible or would work injustice, in which event the former procedure applies.

(H) **Effective date of amendments.** The amendments submitted by the Supreme Court to the General Assembly on December 24, 1984 and January 8, 1985 shall take effect on July 1, 1985. They govern all proceedings in actions brought after they take effect and also all further proceedings in actions then pending, except to the extent that their application in a particular action pending when the amendments take effect would not be feasible or would work injustice, in which event the former procedure applies.

(I) **Effective date of amendments.** The amendments submitted by the Supreme Court to the General Assembly on January 14, 1988, as amended, shall take effect on July 1, 1988. They govern all proceedings in actions brought after they take effect and also all further proceedings in actions then pending, except to the extent that their application in a particular action pending when the amendments take effect would not be feasible or would work injustice, in which event the former procedure applies.

(J) **Effective date of amendments.** The amendments submitted by the Supreme Court to the General

Assembly on January 6, 1989, shall take effect on July 1, 1989. They govern all proceedings in actions brought after they take effect and also all further proceedings in actions then pending, except to the extent that their application in a particular action pending when the amendments take effect would not be feasible or would work injustice, in which event the former procedure applies.

(K) **Effective date of amendments.** The amendments submitted by the Supreme Court to the General Assembly on January 10, 1991 shall take effect on July 1, 1991. They govern all proceedings in actions brought after they take effect and also all further proceedings in actions then pending, except to the extent that their application in a particular action pending when the amendments take effect would not be feasible or would work injustice, in which event the former procedure applies.

(L) **Effective date of amendments.** The amendments filed by the Supreme Court with the General Assembly on January 14, 1992 and further revised and filed on April 30, 1992, shall take effect on July 1, 1992. They govern all proceedings in actions brought after they take effect and also all further proceedings in actions then pending, except to the extent that their application in a particular action pending when the amendments take effect would not be feasible or would work injustice, in which event the former procedure applies.

(M) **Effective date of amendments.** The amendments submitted by the Supreme Court to the General Assembly on January 8, 1993 and further revised and filed on April 30, 1993 shall take effect on July 1, 1993. They govern all proceedings in actions brought after they take effect and also all further proceedings in actions then pending, except to the extent that their application in a particular action pending when the amendments take effect would not be feasible or would work injustice, in which event the former procedure applies.

(N) **Effective date of amendments.** The amendments submitted by the Supreme Court to the General Assembly on January 14, 1994 and further revised and filed on April 29, 1994 shall take effect on July 1, 1994. They govern all proceedings in actions brought after they take effect and also all further proceedings in actions then pending, except to the extent that their application in a particular action pending when the amendments take effect would not be feasible or would work injustice, in which event the former procedure applies.

(O) **Effective date of amendments.** The amendments to Rules 4 and 5 filed by the Supreme Court with the General Assembly on January 5, 1996 and further revised and filed on April 26, 1996 shall take effect on July 1, 1996. They govern all proceedings in actions brought after they take effect and also all further proceedings in actions then pending, except to the extent that their application in a particular action pending when the amendments take effect would not be feasible or would work injustice, in which event the former procedure applies.

(P) **Effective date of amendments.** The amendments to Rules 6, 11, 19, 26, 31, 32, 33, 34, 41, 42, and

43 filed by the Supreme Court with the General Assembly on January 10, 1997 and further revised and filed on April 24, 1997 shall take effect on July 1, 1997. They govern all proceedings in actions brought after they take effect and also all further proceedings in actions then pending, except to the extent that their application in a particular action pending when the amendments take effect would not be feasible or would work injustice, in which event the former procedure applies.

(Q) **Effective date of amendments.** The amendments to Appellate Rule 11.2 filed by the Supreme Court with the General Assembly on January 13, 2000 and refiled on April 27, 2000 shall take effect on July 1, 2000. They govern all proceedings in actions brought after they take effect and also all further proceedings in actions then pending, except to the extent that their application in a particular action pending when the amendments take effect would not be feasible or would work injustice, in which event the former procedure applies.

(R) **Effective date of amendments.** The amendments to Appellate Rules 7, 11.2, 13, and 18 filed by the Supreme Court with the General Assembly on January 12, 2001, and revised and refiled on April 26, 2001, shall take effect on July 1, 2001. They govern all proceedings in actions brought after they take effect and also all further proceedings in actions then pending, except to the extent that their application in a particular action pending when the amendments take effect would not be feasible or would work injustice, in which event the former procedure applies.

(S) **Effective date of amendments.** † The amendments to Appellate Rule 4 filed by the Supreme Court with the General Assembly on January 11, 2002, and revised and refiled on April 18, 2002 shall take effect on July 1, 2002. They govern all proceedings in actions brought after they take effect and also all further proceedings in actions then pending, except to the extent that their application in a particular action pending when the amendments take effect would not be feasible or would work injustice, in which event the former procedure applies.

(T) **Effective date of amendments.** The amendments to Appellate Rule 5 filed by the Supreme Court with the General Assembly on January 9, 2003 and refiled on April 28, 2003, shall take effect on July 1, 2003. They govern all proceedings in actions brought after they take effect and also all further proceedings in actions then pending, except to the extent that their application in a particular action pending when the amendments take effect would not be feasible or would work injustice, in which event the former procedure applies.

(U) **Effective date of amendments.** The amendments to Appellate 22 filed by the Supreme Court with the General Assembly on January 14, 2008 and refiled on April 28, 2008 shall take effect on July 1, 2008. They govern all proceedings in actions brought after they take effect and also all further proceedings in actions then pending, except to the extent that their application in a particular action pending when the amendments take effect would not be feasible or would work injustice, in which event the former procedure applies.

(V) **Effective date of amendments.** The amendments to Appellate 4 filed by the Supreme Court with the General Assembly on January 14, 2009 and refiled on April 30, 2009 shall take effect on July 1, 2009. They govern all proceedings in actions brought after they take effect and also all further proceedings in actions then pending, except to the extent that their application in a particular action pending when the amendments take effect would not be feasible or would work injustice, in which event the former procedure applies.

(W) **Effective date of amendments.** The amendments to Rules 14, 15, 25, and 26 filed by the Supreme Court with the General Assembly on January 14, 2010 and revised and refiled on April 28, 2010 shall take effect on July 1, 2010. They govern all proceedings in actions brought after they take effect and also all further proceedings in actions then pending, except to the extent that their application in a particular action pending when the amendments take effect would not be feasible or would work injustice, in which event the former procedure applies.

History: Amended, eff 7-1-72; 7-1-73; 7-1-75; 7-1-76; 7-1-78; 7-1-82; 7-1-85; 7-1-88; 7-1-89; 7-1-91; 7-1-92; 7-1-93; 7-1-94; 7-1-96; 7-1-97; 7-1-00; 7-1-01; 7-1-02; 7-1-03; 7-1-08; 7-1-09; 7-1-10.

APPENDIX OF FORMS

Introductory Statement

The form which follows is intended for illustration only.

Departure from the form shall not void papers which are otherwise sufficient, and the form may be varied when necessary to meet the facts of a particular case.

FORM 1.

NOTICE OF APPEAL TO A COURT OF APPEALS FROM A JUDGMENT OR APPEALABLE ORDER

COURT OF COMMON PLEAS
FRANKLIN COUNTY, OHIO

A. B.	:	No. _____
221 E. West Street,	:	NOTICE OF APPEAL
Columbus, Ohio 43215	:	
Plaintiff,	:	
v.	:	
C. D.,	:	
122 W. East Street,	:	
Columbus, Ohio 43214	:	
Defendant-Appellant,	:	

Notice is hereby given that C.D., defendant, hereby appeals to the Court of Appeals of Franklin County, Ohio, Tenth Appellate District (from the final judgment), from the order (describing it) entered in this action on the _____ day of _____, 19 ____.

_____
(Attorney for Defendant)

_____
(Address)

NOTE: The above form is designed for use in courts of common pleas. Appropriate changes in the designation of the court are required when the form is used for other courts.

FORM 2.

DOCKETING STATEMENT
COURT OF COMMON PLEAS
FRANKLIN COUNTY, OHIO

A. B.	:	No. CV-1981-453
221 E. West Street,	:	
Columbus, Ohio 43215	:	
Plaintiff,	:	
v.	:	
C. D.,	:	
122 W. East Street,	:	
Columbus, Ohio 43214	:	
Defendant.	:	

DOCKETING STATEMENT

(Insert one of the following statements, as applicable):

(1) No transcript is required.

(2) The approximate number of pages of transcript ordered is _____.

(3) An agreed statement will be submitted in lieu of the record.

(4) The record was made in an administrative hearing and filed with the trial court.

(5) All parties to the appeal as shown by the attached statement approve assignment of the appeal to the accelerated calendar.

(6) The case is of a category designated for the accelerated calendar by local rule. (Specify category.)

                                    _____
                                        Attorney for Appellant

                                                    (Effective 7-1-82)

FORM 3.

JUDGMENT ENTRY — ACCELERATED CALENDAR
TENTH DISTRICT COURT OF APPEALS
FRANKLIN COUNTY

A. B.	:	No. CV-1981-453
221 E. West Street,	:	
Columbus, Ohio 43215	:	
Plaintiff,	:	
v.	:	
C. D.,	:	
122 W. East Street,	:	
Columbus, Ohio 43214	:	
Defendant.	:	

JUDGMENT ENTRY

Assignment of error number one is overruled for the reason that the trial court's instruction on the burden of proof was correct. See *Jones v. State* (1980), 64 Ohio St.2d 173.

Assignment of error number two is overruled as there was sufficient evidence presented (see testimony of Smith, R 22) to support a factual finding of agency.

The judgment of the trial court is affirmed.

_____
Judge, Presiding Judge

_____
Judge

_____
Judge

(Effective 7-1-82; amended, eff 7-1-92)

Index to Ohio Rules of Appellate Procedure

OHIO RULES OF JUVENILE PROCEDURE

RULE 1. Scope of rules: applicability; construction; exceptions

(A) **Applicability.** These rules prescribe the procedure to be followed in all juvenile courts of this state in all proceedings coming within the jurisdiction of such courts, with the exceptions stated in subdivision (C).

(B) **Construction.** These rules shall be liberally interpreted and construed so as to effectuate the following purposes:

(1) to effect the just determination of every juvenile court proceeding by ensuring the parties a fair hearing and the recognition and enforcement of their constitutional and other legal rights;

(2) to secure simplicity and uniformity in procedure, fairness in administration, and the elimination of unjustifiable expense and delay;

(3) to provide for the care, protection, and mental and physical development of children subject to the jurisdiction of the juvenile court, and to protect the welfare of the community; and

(4) to protect the public interest by treating children as persons in need of supervision, care and rehabilitation.

(C) **Exceptions.** These rules shall not apply to procedure (1) Upon appeal to review any judgment, order, or ruling; (2) Upon the trial of criminal actions; (3) Upon the trial of actions for divorce, annulment, legal separation, and related proceedings; (4) In proceedings to determine parent-child relationships, provided, however that appointment of counsel shall be in accordance with Rule 4(A) of the Rules of Juvenile Procedure; (5) In the commitment of the mentally ill and mentally retarded; (6) In proceedings under section 2151.85 of the Revised Code to the extent that there is a conflict between these rules and section 2151.85 of the Revised Code.

When any statute provides for procedure by general or specific reference to the statutes governing procedure in juvenile court actions, procedure shall be in accordance with these rules.

History: Amended, eff 7-1-91; 7-1-94; 7-1-95.

RULE 2. Definitions

As used in these rules:

(A) "Abused child" has the same meaning as in section 2151.031 of the Revised Code.

(B) "Adjudicatory hearing" means a hearing to determine whether a child is a juvenile traffic offender, delinquent, unruly, abused, neglected, or dependent or otherwise within the jurisdiction of the court.

(C) "Agreement for temporary custody" means a voluntary agreement that is authorized by section 5103.15 of the Revised Code and transfers the temporary custody of a child to a public children services agency or a private child placing agency.

(D) "Child" has the same meaning as in sections 2151.011 and 2152.02 of the Revised Code.

(E) "Chronic truant" has the same meaning as in section 2151.011 of the Revised Code.

(F) "Complaint" means the legal document that sets forth the allegations that form the basis for juvenile court jurisdiction.

(G) "Court proceeding" means all action taken by a court from the earlier of (1) the time a complaint is filed and (2) the time a person first appears before an officer of a juvenile court until the court relinquishes jurisdiction over such child.

(H) "Custodian" means a person who has legal custody of a child or a public children's services agency or private child-placing agency that has permanent, temporary, or legal custody of a child.

(I) "Delinquent child" has the same meaning as in section 2152.02 of the Revised Code.

(J) "Dependent child" has the same meaning as in section 2151.04 of the Revised Code.

(K) "Detention" means the temporary care of chi'l-dren in restricted facilities pending court adjudication or disposition.

(L) "Detention hearing" means a hearing to determine whether a child shall be held in detention or shelter care prior to or pending execution of a final dispositional order.

(M) "Dispositional hearing" means a hearing to determine what action shall be taken concerning a child who is within the jurisdiction of the court.

(N) "Guardian" means a person, association, or corporation that is granted authority by a probate court pursuant to Chapter 2111 of the Revised Code to exercise parental rights over a child to the extent provided in the court's order and subject to the residual parental rights of the child's parents.

(O) "Guardian ad litem" means a person appointed to protect the interests of a party in a juvenile court proceeding.

(P) "Habitual truant" has the same meaning as in section 2151.011 of the Revised Code.

(Q) "Hearing" means any portion of a juvenile court proceeding before the court, whether summary in nature or by examination of witnesses.

(R) "Indigent person" means a person who, at the time need is determined, is unable by reason of lack of property or income to provide for full payment of legal counsel and all other necessary expenses of representation.

(S) "Juvenile court" means a division of the court of common pleas, or a juvenile court separately and independently created, that has jurisdiction under Chapters 2151 and 2152 of the Revised Code.

(T) "Juvenile judge" means a judge of a court having jurisdiction under Chapters 2151 and 2152 of the Revised Code.

(U) "Juvenile traffic offender" has the same meaning as in section 2151.021 of the Revised Code.

(V) "Legal custody" means a legal status that vests in the custodian the right to have physical care and control of the child and to determine where and with whom the child shall live, and the right and duty to protect, train, and discipline the child and provide the child with food, shelter, education, and medical care, all subject to any residual parental rights, privileges, and responsibilities. An individual granted legal custody shall exercise the rights and responsibilities personally unless otherwise authorized by any section of the Revised Code or by the court.

(W) "Mental examination" means an examination by a psychiatrist or psychologist.

(X) "Neglected child" has the same meaning as in section 2151.03 of the Revised Code.

(Y) "Party" means a child who is the subject of a juvenile court proceeding, the child's spouse, if any, the child's parent or parents, or if the parent of a child is a child, the parent of that parent, in appropriate cases, the child's custodian, guardian, or guardian ad litem, the state, and any other person specifically designated by the court.

(Z) "Permanent custody" means a legal status that vests in a public children's services agency or a private child-placing agency, all parental rights, duties, and obligations, including the right to consent to adoption, and divests the natural parents or adoptive parents of any and all parental rights, privileges, and obligations, including all residual rights and obligations.

(AA) "Permanent surrender" means the act of the parents or, if a child has only one parent, of the parent of a child, by a voluntary agreement authorized by section 5103.15 of the Revised Code, to transfer the permanent custody of the child to a public children's services agency or a private child-placing agency.

(BB) "Person" includes an individual, association, corporation, or partnership and the state or any of its political subdivisions, departments, or agencies.

(CC) "Physical examination" means an examination by a physician.

(DD) "Planned permanent living arrangement" means an order of a juvenile court pursuant to which both of the following apply:

(1) The court gives legal custody of a child to a public children's services agency or a private child-placing agency without the termination of parental rights;

(2) The order permits the agency to make an appropriate placement of the child and to enter into a written planned permanent living arrangement agreement with a foster care provider or with another person or agency with whom the child is placed.

(EE) "Private child-placing agency" means any association, as defined in section 5103.02 of the Revised Code that is certified pursuant to sections 5103.03 to 5103.05 of the Revised Code to accept temporary, permanent, or legal custody of children and place the children for either foster care or adoption.

(FF) "Public children's services agency" means a children's services board or a county department of human services that has assumed the administration of the children's services function prescribed by Chapter 5153 of the Revised Code.

(GG) "Removal action" means a statutory action filed by the superintendent of a school district for the removal of a child in an out-of-county foster home placement.

(HH) "Residence or legal settlement" means a location as defined by section 2151.06 of the Revised Code.

(II) "Residual parental rights, privileges, and responsibilities" means those rights, privileges, and responsibilities remaining with the natural parent after the transfer of legal custody of the child, including but not limited to the privilege of reasonable visitation, consent to adoption, the privilege to determine the child's religious affiliation, and the responsibility for support.

(JJ) "Rule of court" means a rule promulgated by the Supreme Court or a rule concerning local practice adopted by another court that is not inconsistent with the rules promulgated by the Supreme Court and that is filed with the Supreme Court.

(KK) "Serious youthful offender" means a child eligible for sentencing as described in sections 2152.11 and 2152.13 of the Revised Code.

(LL) "Serious youthful offender proceedings" means proceedings after a probable cause determination that a child is eligible for sentencing as described in sections 2152.11 and 2152.13 of the Revised Code. Serious youthful offender proceedings cease to be serious youthful offender proceedings once a child has been determined by the trier of fact not to be a serious youthful offender or the juvenile judge has determined not to impose a serious youthful offender disposition on a child eligible for discretionary serious youthful offender sentencing.

(MM) "Shelter care" means the temporary care of children in physically unrestricted facilities, pending court adjudication or disposition.

(NN) "Social history" means the personal and family history of a child or any other party to a juvenile proceeding and may include the prior record of the person with the juvenile court or any other court.

(OO) "Temporary custody" means legal custody of a child who is removed from the child's home, which custody may be terminated at any time at the discretion of the court or, if the legal custody is granted in an agreement for temporary custody, by the person or persons who executed the agreement.

(PP) "Unruly child" has the same meaning as in section 2151.022 of the Revised Code.

(QQ) "Ward of court" means a child over whom the court assumes continuing jurisdiction.

History: Amended, eff 7-1-94; 7-1-98; 7-1-01; 7-1-02.

NOTES TO DECISIONS

ANALYSIS

Adoption
Appeal
Counsel
Custody
Grandparents
Parentage proceedings
Party

Adoption

Mother's rights were not violated because the juvenile court could reasonably have concluded that the reasons for the mother's lack of contact with her child would be fully litigated in the probate court and that her due process rights would be protected by the adoption proceeding, as mandated by Ohio R. Juv. P. 2(II) and RC § 3107.07(A). Also, because the juvenile court's consent to the adoption was not required, both the trial court's order granting concurrent jurisdiction to the probate court and its subsequent order refusing to vacate it had no impact on the rights and obligations of the parties. In re A.H., — Ohio App. 3d —, 2006 Ohio 3285, — N.E. 2d —, 2006 Ohio App. LEXIS 3201 (June 28, 2006).

Appeal

After a trial court awarded permanent custody of two minor children to a county social service agency, the children's maternal grandmother's appeal therefrom was dismissed due to her lack of standing, as she was not a "party" to the underlying proceedings pursuant to Ohio R. Juv. P. 2(Y), she had not sought intervention in the proceedings, and she never

requested custody of the children. In re Titionna K, — Ohio App. 3d —, 2007 Ohio 1861, — N.E.2d —, 2007 Ohio App. LEXIS 1701 (Apr. 20, 2007).

Counsel

Trial court erred by failing to appoint counsel after a possible conflict became known between the child's wishes and the recommendation of the guardian ad litem during the permanent custody hearing and thus, the child was entitled to counsel pursuant to RC § 2151.352, as clarified by Ohio R. Juv. P. 4(A) and Ohio R. Juv. P. 2(Y). An attorney would have been required to provide zealous representation for his client and make every legitimate effort to secure an order allowing the child to have continued contact with her father, which the guardian ad litem could not do and remain consistent with his recommendation. In re H.R., — Ohio App. 3d —, 2006 Ohio 1595, — N.E. 2d —, 2006 Ohio App. LEXIS 1472 (Mar. 31, 2006).

In a permanent custody proceeding, a trial court did not fail to appoint counsel for the subject children when it appointed their guardian ad litem as their counsel, as this was provided for in RC § 2151.352 and Ohio R. Juv. P. 2(Y) and 4(A), and it was not claimed that the guardian ad litem's dual role resulted in a conflict of interest. In re Salsberry, — Ohio App. 3d —, 2006 Ohio 3274, — N.E. 2d —, 2006 Ohio App. LEXIS 3185 (June 19, 2006).

Trial court lacked jurisdiction under RC § 3109.04 and pursuant to the boundaries set under Ohio Const. art. IV, § 4(B) to have ordered that minor children be placed in the custody of a county agency pending a determination of parental alienation in a custody dispute between the children's parents, as there was no complaint filed in the juvenile court for such relief, as required by RC § 2151.23. The children were not "parties" to the action pursuant to Ohio R. Juv. P 2(Y) and were not entitled to counsel to represent their interests under Ohio R. Juv. P. 4(A). Curie v. Curie, — Ohio App. 3d —, 2006 Ohio 6098, — N.E. 2d —, 2006 Ohio App. LEXIS 6058 (Nov. 17, 2006).

Trial court, at a minimum, was required to interview the child, on the record, to determine if she was of sufficient maturity to benefit from separate counsel in the permanent custody proceeding, but failed to do so. There was a clear conflict because the guardian ad litem recommended to the trial court that the mother's parental rights be terminated but the agency case supervisor for the child testified at the permanent custody hearing that the child ultimately wanted to be with her mom. In re Roque, — Ohio App. 3d —, 2006 Ohio 7007, — N.E. 2d —, 2006 Ohio App. LEXIS 6961 (Dec. 29, 2006).

Custody

Trial court did not err in declining to grant change of legal custody to children's aunt and maternal grandparents pursuant to RC § 2151.415(A)(3) as the aunt had not had any contact with the children for two or three years and had no independent housing or employment, and their grandparents, who lived in New York, had also had limited contact with the children and had limited bedroom space in their residence. Moreover, the trial court expressed particular concern that these relatives expressed belief that the children should be with their mother, and pursuant to Ohio R. Juv. P. 2(Z), a trial court may properly recognize that legal custody to third parties will not provide a legal barrier to a parent's future attempted assertion of his or her residual rights concerning the child. In re Morales, — Ohio App. 3d —, 2006 Ohio 6384, — N.E. 2d —, 2006 Ohio App. LEXIS 6356 (Dec. 4, 2006).

Grandparents

Trial court does not abuse its discretion when, after a minor parent or parents involved in a custody proceeding and who were minors at the onset reach the age of majority, the court removes as parties to the action the child's grandparents, who have no independent legal interest or rights in the proceeding: In re H.W., 114 Ohio St. 3d 65, 2007 Ohio 2879, 868 N.E.2d 261, 2007 Ohio LEXIS 1573 (2007).

Trial court did not err in not joining a paternal grandmother to a parental rights termination proceeding involving the parents of 10 minor children, although the grandmother lived with the family, as she was not a necessary party pursuant to Ohio R. Juv. P. 2(Y) and RC § 2151.28(C)(1); she did not hold the title of legal custodian or guardian of any of the children, and she had actual notice of the proceedings. In re Hilyard, — Ohio App. 3d —, 2006 Ohio 1977, — N.E. 2d —, 2006 Ohio App. LEXIS 1808 (Apr. 13, 2006).

Trial court did not err in adopting a magistrate's decision to deny maternal grandparents' motion to intervene in an action commenced by their minor grandchild's biological father, seeking a determination of paternity, custody, visitation, and child support pursuant to RC § 2151.23(A)(2), as they did not establish an in loco parentis relationship with the minor child merely because they cared for the child during a period of time when the complaint was filed, and accordingly, they were not within the scope of the parties defined under Ohio R. Juv. R. 2(Y) and they did not have a right to intervene in the matter pursuant to Ohio R. Civ. P. 24(A); there was no cause to review the issue of parental unsuitability or the constitutional right of parents in the care, custody, and management of their children at that juncture of the matter. Brokaw v. Haser, — Ohio App. 3d —, 2006 Ohio 5171, — N.E. 2d —, 2006 Ohio App. LEXIS 5134 (Sept. 29, 2006).

Parentage proceedings

In a putative father's action wherein he sought to establish a parent-child relationship, it was not a trial court error to have failed to include the child as a party to the action, pursuant to RC § 3111.07(A) and Ohio R. Juv. P. 2(Y), as the father initiated the action and he failed to name the child as a party. Any error was harmless where counsel or a guardian ad litem would not have been separately appointed for the child, as there was no showing of a conflict of interest between the child and mother. E.B. v. T.J., — Ohio App. 3d —, 2006 Ohio 441, — N.E. 2d —, 2006 Ohio App. LEXIS 383 (Feb. 2, 2006).

Party

While RC § 2152.12(G), requiring notice to a juvenile's parents of a hearing to consider transferring proceedings against the juvenile from the juvenile court to the trial court's general division, did not define "parents" or indicate whether notice had to be given to both parents to satisfy due process, Ohio R. Juv. P. 2(Y) acknowledged that there were circumstances when only one parent might be involved in a juvenile proceeding by including a child's "parent or parents" as a party to the proceedings. State v. Reynolds, — Ohio App. 3d —, 2007 Ohio 4178, — N.E. 2d —, 2007 Ohio App. LEXIS 3766 (Aug. 16, 2007).

RULE 3.   Waiver of rights

A child's right to be represented by counsel at a hearing conducted pursuant to Juv. R. 30 may not be waived. Other rights of a child may be waived with the permission of the court.

History: Amended, eff 7-1-94.

NOTES TO DECISIONS

ANALYSIS

Bindover for prosecution
Waiver of counsel

Bindover for prosecution

Where there was no indication in a juvenile court bindover order that a juvenile's waiver of a probable cause and amenability hearing was knowingly, competently, and intelligently made, a later delinquency charge against him on a new criminal matter required an appropriate bindover proceeding under RC § 2152.12 and Ohio R. Juv. P. 3. The hearing on the bindover issue was a critical phase that was mandatory under RC ch. 2152 and Ohio R. Juv. P. 30. State v. Brown, — Ohio App. 3d —, 2006 Ohio 4393, — N.E. 2d —, 2006 Ohio App. LEXIS 4330 (Aug. 25, 2006).

Waiver of counsel

Trial court did not comply with Ohio R. Juv. P. 29(B)(5) for a valid waiver of counsel because it failed to inform the 12-year-old juvenile of the nature of the charges against him and the substance of the complaints, the possible dispositions which could be imposed, his right to remain silent, his right to obtain counsel at any stage of the proceedings, and his right to cross-examine witnesses and it did not adequately warn him of the dangers and disadvantages of self-representation. The juvenile's age, state of mind, emotional stability, mental capacity, and prior criminal experience indicated, at the very least, that the strictest scrutiny should have been employed in determining whether he knowingly, voluntarily, and intelligently waived his right to counsel. In re Puckett, — Ohio App. 3d —, 2007 Ohio 3927, — N.E. 2d —, 2007 Ohio App. LEXIS 3531 (Aug. 1, 2007).

RULE 4.   Assistance of counsel; guardian *ad litem*

(A) **Assistance of counsel.** Every party shall have the right to be represented by counsel and every child, parent, custodian, or other person in loco parentis the right to appointed counsel if indigent. These rights shall arise when a person becomes a party to a juvenile court proceeding. When the complaint alleges that a child is an abused child, the court must appoint an attorney to represent the interests of the child. This rule shall not be construed to provide for a right to appointed counsel in cases in which that right is not otherwise provided for by constitution or statute.

(B) **Guardian ad litem; when appointed.** The court shall appoint a guardian ad litem to protect the interests of a child or incompetent adult in a juvenile court proceeding when:

(1) The child has no parents, guardian, or legal custodian;

(2) The interests of the child and the interests of the parent may conflict;

(3) The parent is under eighteen years of age or appears to be mentally incompetent;

(4) The court believes that the parent of the child is not capable of representing the best interest of the child.

(5) Any proceeding involves allegations of abuse or neglect, voluntary surrender of permanent custody, or termination of parental rights as soon as possible after the commencement of such proceeding.

(6) There is an agreement for the voluntary surrender of temporary custody that is made in accordance with section 5103.15 of the Revised Code, and thereafter there is a request for extension of the voluntary agreement.

(7) The proceeding is a removal action.

(8) Appointment is otherwise necessary to meet the requirements of a fair hearing.

(C) Guardian ad litem as counsel.

(1) When the guardian ad litem is an attorney admitted to practice in this state, the guardian may also serve as counsel to the ward providing no conflict between the roles exist[s].

(2) If a person is serving as guardian ad litem and as attorney for a ward and either that person or the court finds a conflict between the responsibilities of the role of attorney and that of guardian ad litem, the court shall appoint another person as guardian ad litem for the ward.

(3) If a court appoints a person who is not an attorney admitted to practice in this state to be a guardian ad litem, the court may appoint an attorney admitted to practice in this state to serve as attorney for the guardian ad litem.

(D) Appearance of attorneys.
An attorney shall enter appearance by filing a written notice with the court or by appearing personally at a court hearing and informing the court of said representation.

(E) Notice to guardian ad litem.
The guardian ad litem shall be given notice of all proceedings in the same manner as notice is given to other parties to the action.

(F) Withdrawal of counsel or guardian ad litem
. An attorney or guardian ad litem may withdraw only with the consent of the court upon good cause shown.

(G) Costs.
The court may fix compensation for the services of appointed counsel and guardians ad litem, tax the same as part of the costs and assess them against the child, the child's parents, custodian, or other person in loco parentis of such child.

History: Amended, eff 7-1-76; 7-1-94; 7-1-95; 7-1-98.

NOTES TO DECISIONS

Analysis

Generally
Contempt
Guardian ad litem
Guardian ad litem as counsel
Guardian ad litem or counsel
Ineffective assistance of counsel
Right to counsel
Waiver of counsel
Withdrawal of counsel

Generally

Trial court lacked jurisdiction under RC § 3109.04 and pursuant to the boundaries set under Ohio Const. art. IV, § 4(B) to have ordered that minor children be placed in the custody of a county agency pending a determination of parental alienation in a custody dispute between the children's parents, as there was no complaint filed in the juvenile court for such relief, as required by RC § 2151.23. The children were not "parties" to the action pursuant to Ohio R. Juv. P 2(Y) and were not entitled to counsel to represent their interests under Ohio R. Juv. P. 4(A). Curie v. Curie, — Ohio App. 3d —, 2006 Ohio 6098, — N.E. 2d —, 2006 Ohio App. LEXIS 6058 (Nov. 17, 2006).

Contempt

Trial court erred when it imposed a jail sentence for contempt for failure to pay the guardian ad litem (GAL) fees, because it violated Ohio Const. art. I, § 15, which prohibited imprisonment for debt in civil actions. The GAL fees could still be collected under procedures available for the collection of civil judgments. In re Bailey, — Ohio App. 3d —, 2007 Ohio 4192, — N.E. 2d —, 2007 Ohio App. LEXIS 3799 (Aug. 17, 2007).

Guardian ad litem

Plain and unambiguous language of Ohio R. Juv. P. 4(B)(2) mandated that the possibility that a child's interests "might conflict" with the interests of a parent was sufficient for the required appointment of a guardian ad litem, but a juvenile court was in the best position to weigh the relevant facts in determining whether a potential conflict of interest existed between the parent and child, and, in the context of a delinquency proceeding, a parent's speaking out against the child's penal interest raised a colorable claim of conflict which required a "thorough inquiry" by the juvenile court to determine whether a conflict of interest existed such that the court had to appoint a guardian ad litem, and a court's failure to appoint a guardian ad litem when these mandatory provisions required such an appointment constituted reversible error. In re K.B., — Ohio App. 3d —, 2007 Ohio 396, — N.E. 2d —, 2007 Ohio App. LEXIS 346 (Feb. 1, 2007).

Absence of an objection did not preclude a reversal of a delinquency adjudication due to a juvenile court's failure to appoint a guardian ad litem when required under RC § 2151.281(A)(2) or Ohio R. Juv. P. 4(B)(2). In re K.B., — Ohio App. 3d —, 2007 Ohio 396, — N.E. 2d —, 2007 Ohio App. LEXIS 346 (Feb. 1, 2007).

When a juvenile was charged with criminal offenses for entering her mother's bedroom without permission and using the telephone, the record sufficiently demonstrated a tension between the juvenile and the mother to require a trial court, under R.C. § 2151.281(A)(2) and Ohio R. Juv. P. 4(B)(2), to inquire into the need to appoint a guardian ad litem, and the failure to do so was an abuse of discretion and reversible error. In re K.B., — Ohio App. 3d —, 2007 Ohio 396, — N.E. 2d —, 2007 Ohio App. LEXIS 346 (Feb. 1, 2007).

Juvenile court abused its discretion under RC § 2151.281(A) and Ohio R. Juv. P. 4(B) when it failed to appoint a guardian ad litem (GAL) to represent the interests of defendant, a juvenile, in delinquency proceedings, as there was a conflict of interest between the juvenile and his parents, who reported his actions to state authorities and who also testified against him in the adjudication phase of the delinquency proceeding. The fact that defendant failed to request a GAL or object to the lack of such an appointment did not preclude a reversal of the delinquency proceedings based on the juvenile court's error. In re Dennis, — Ohio App. 3d —, 2007 Ohio 2432, — N.E. 2d —, 2007 Ohio App. LEXIS 2263 (May 18, 2007).

Trial court did not abuse its discretion when it ordered that a guardian ad litem (GAL) be appointed because there remained issues pending before the trial court that required a GAL to protect the interests of the children. Several contempt motions remained pending at the time of the trial court's judgment, and the disputed issues included the allocation of parenting time; make-up parenting time; the allocation of summer time, vacation time, and holidays; and denial of parenting time. Perez v. Angell, — Ohio App. 3d —, 2007 Ohio 4519, — N.E. 2d —, 2007 Ohio App. LEXIS 3759 (Aug. 9, 2007).

Juvenile court did not abuse its discretion in maintaining the service of the guardian ad litem (GAL) because it was the parents who had requested the appointment of a GAL and who had filed numerous motions requiring the GAL to determine the bests interests of their child. They were in no position to contest the continued use of the GAL's services. Also, there was evidence that the allegations of sexual misconduct were well founded and, even if the allegations were spurious, there were numerous other circumstances supporting the conclusion that the child needed the services of a GAL to protect her interests. In re Bailey, — Ohio App. 3d —, 2007 Ohio 4192, — N.E. 2d —, 2007 Ohio App. LEXIS 3799 (Aug. 17, 2007).

Trial court failed to comply with the mandatory requirements of both RC § 2151.281(B)(1) and Ohio R. Juv. P. 4(B)(5) when it failed to appoint a guardian ad litem (GAL) to protect the child's interests because the father filed a complaint in juvenile court pursuant to RC § 2151.27(A)(1) alleging that the child was an abused, neglected, and dependent child. Although the county children services agency did not initiate the proceedings, the proceedings were, nonetheless, proceedings concerning an alleged abused or neglected child; thus, the provisions of RC § 2151.281(B)(1) and Ohio R. Juv. P. 4(B)(5) clearly applied and required the trial court to appoint a GAL to protect the child interests. In re A.G.B., 173 Ohio App. 3d 263, 2007 Ohio 4753, 878 N.E.2d 49, 2007 Ohio App. LEXIS 4287 (2007).

Trial court failed to comply with the requirements of RC § 2151.281(B)(1) and JuvR 4(B)(5), which mandate the appointment of a GAL in any proceeding concerning an alleged abused or neglected child: In re A.G.B., 173 Ohio App. 3d 263, 2007 Ohio 4753, 878 N.E.2d 49, 2007 Ohio App. LEXIS 4287 (2007).

Contrary to a mother's argument, a guardian ad litem's task in a dependency case did not involve advocating for child as his attorney where, because a conflict could have existed between the guardian ad litem's position and the child's position, a separate attorney was appointed as the child's advocate. In re Neibertt, — Ohio App. 3d —, — N.E. 2d —, 2006 Ohio App. LEXIS 1420 (Mar. 22, 2006).

There was no plain error under Ohio R. Crim. P. 52(B) by a magistrate's decision under Juv. R. 4(B)(2) and RC § 2151.281(A) not to appoint a guardian ad litem for a juvenile in his proceeding for violation of probation, although he had skipped school and his mother was charged with allowing him to commit that conduct, as he was charged with other violations besides the truancy and there appeared to be no conflict between the mother and the juvenile. In re J-M, — Ohio App. 3d —, — N.E. 2d —, 2006 Ohio App. LEXIS 6131 (Nov. 22, 2006).

There was no plain error under Ohio R. Crim. P. 52 by a juvenile court's failure to appoint a guardian pursuant to Ohio R. Juv. P. 4(B)(2) and RC § 2151.281(A)(2) for a juvenile who was the subject of delinquency proceedings, as there was no conflict of interest between the juvenile and his parents, nor was there a showing of a possibility of such conflict which would have required appointment of the guardian. In re Smith, — Ohio App. 3d —, 2006 Ohio 2788, — N.E.2d —, 2006 Ohio App. LEXIS 2625 (June 5, 2006).

Guardian ad litem as counsel

Although juvenile courts have appointed attorneys to serve as guardians ad litem with the understanding that the attorney would also serve as counsel, the better course would be for the court to expressly appoint an attorney in dual roles as guardian ad litem and as attorney for the child: In re J.W., 171 Ohio App. 3d 248, 2007 Ohio 2007, 870 N.E.2d 245, 2007 Ohio App. LEXIS 1779 (2007).

Guardian ad litem or counsel

Juvenile court did not err in failing to appoint a new guardian ad litem for the child of a custody modification battle, as the attorney who was appointed as the child's guardian ad litem was also an able legal reprentative in the juvenile court proceeding between the child's divorced parents where no conflict in serving in both capacities existed pursuant to Ohio R. Juv. P. 4(C)(1) and (2); there was no evidence that the guardian became an advocate for either party, and she acted within her authority under RC § 2151.281(I). In re Smith, — Ohio App. 3d —, 2007 Ohio 893, — N.E. 2d —, 2007 Ohio App. LEXIS 812 (Mar. 2, 2007).

Based on Ohio R. Juv. P. 4(A) and (B), as well as RC §§ 2151.281(H) and 2151.352, a trial court did not err in appointing a licensed attorney to represent 10 children in a parental rights termination proceeding as both their legal counsel and their guardian ad litem, as none of the children "repreatedly expressed a desire" to remain with the parents, and there was no apparent or actual conflict shown in the attorney's dual capacity role. In re Hilyard, — Ohio App. 3d —, 2006 Ohio 1976, — N.E. 2d —, 2006 Ohio App. LEXIS 1809 (Apr. 13, 2006).

Trial court did not err by not appointing, pursuant to Ohio R. Juv. P. 4(C)(2), a separate attorney and a separate guardian ad litem to represent a mother's child in a permanent custody proceeding because there was no evidence that a conflict existed between the attorney's performance as the children's guardian ad litem and as their attorney. In re Elder, — Ohio App. 3d —, 2006 Ohio 5889, — N.E. 2d —, 2006 Ohio App. LEXIS 5834 (Nov. 2, 2006).

Trial court did not err by not appointing, pursuant to Ohio R. Juv. P. 4(C)(2), a separate attorney and a separate guardian ad litem to represent a mother's child in a permanent custody proceeding because there was no evidence that a conflict existed between the attorney's performance as the children's guardian ad litem and as their attorney. In re Parks, — Ohio App. 3d —, 2006 Ohio 5890, — N.E. 2d —, 2006 Ohio App. LEXIS 5835 (Nov. 2, 2006).

Trial court did not err in failing to appoint separate individuals to serve as the guardian ad litem and the legal counsel for 10 children who were involved in a parental rights termination proceeding, pursuant to Ohio R. Juv. P. 4 and RC §§ 2151.353 and 2151.281(H), as there was no apparent or actual conflict shown in the appointed attorney's dual representation of the children; further, none of the children expressed a desire for custody that was adverse to the recommendation of the attorney. In re Hilyard, — Ohio App. 3d —, 2006 Ohio 1977, — N.E. 2d —, 2006 Ohio App. LEXIS 1808 (Apr. 13, 2006).

Under Ohio R. Juv. P. 4(C) and RC § 2151.281(H), the same attorney could be appointed, in a dependency proceeding, as both counsel and guardian ad litem for a child, but, when the attorney advocated a position that was adverse to the child's wishes regarding his custody, the attorney had to withdraw, under § 2151.281(H), and she had to be replaced by a new guardian ad litem. In re Butler, — Ohio App. 3d —, 2006 Ohio 4547, — N.E. 2d —, 2006 Ohio App. LEXIS 4510 (Sept. 5, 2006).

Trial court did not err in appointing the guardian ad litem (GAL) to serve in a dual capacity as GAL and as legal counsel for the children in a permanent custody proceeding instead of appointing an independent attorney to represent the children. Neither the trial court nor the parties identified a conflict with the dual representation, and the court could discern no conflict. In re B.K., — Ohio App. 3d —, 2006 Ohio 4424, — N.E. 2d —, 2006 Ohio App. LEXIS 4359 (Aug. 28, 2006).

In a permanent custody proceeding, a trial court did not fail to appoint counsel for the subject children when it appointed their guardian ad litem as their counsel, as this was provided for in RC § 2151.352 and Ohio R. Juv. P. 2(Y) and 4(A), and it was not claimed that the guardian ad litem's dual role resulted in a conflict of interest. In re Salsberry, — Ohio App. 3d —, 2006 Ohio 3274, — N.E. 2d —, 2006 Ohio App. LEXIS 3185 (June 19, 2006).

Trial court erred by failing to appoint the child's guardian ad litem to act as her attorney and did not make any determination as to whether the child possessed the competency and maturity to express her own wishes. However, the error did not require reversal because the child's wishes were evidenced by the guardian ad litem's report and witness testimony and were consistent with the guardian ad litem's recommendation. In re Kangas, — Ohio App. 3d —, 2006 Ohio 3433, — N.E. 2d —, 2006 Ohio App. LEXIS 3380 (June 30, 2006).

Ineffective assistance of counsel

Mother was represented by counsel at the permanent custody hearing although she failed to appear and trial counsel explained on the record that the mother had told him that she was moving but never gave him a forwarding address and failed to make an appointment with him as he requested. Thus, given the mother's lack of cooperation in her own defense, counsel's performance did not fall below an objective standard of reasonableness, nor did prejudice arise from his performance. In re Justin K., — Ohio App. 3d —, 2007 Ohio 4907, — N.E. 2d —, 2007 Ohio App. LEXIS 4357 (Sept. 21, 2007).

Mother was not afforded every procedural and substantive protection the law allowed in the permanent custody proceedings. The mother received ineffective assistance of counsel because court-appointed counsel completely failed to take the minimal steps necessary to allow the mother to raise the due process concerns caused by the unconscionable delay by the magistrate and the trial court and, when the magistrate issued a decision containing many questionable findings of fact, trial counsel failed to take the elementary step of challenging those factual findings via timely objections, leading the trial court to adopt those factual findings. In re Sox, — Ohio App. 3d —, 2006 Ohio 7116, — N.E. 2d —, 2006 Ohio App. LEXIS 7064 (Dec. 28, 2006).

Right to counsel

Although a juvenile court failed to appoint a separate attorney pursuant to Ohio R. Juv. P. 4(A) for a child for over one and one-half years in proceedings involving a social service agency's request for permanent court custody, there was no showing that the delay impacted the outcome of the matter. In re J.W., 171 Ohio App. 3d 248, 2007 Ohio 2007, 870 N.E.2d 245, 2007 Ohio App. LEXIS 1779 (2007).

Trial court acted reasonably in refusing to appoint an attorney for two of the children in the permanent custody proceedings because there was no evidence of a desire on the part of the children to be returned to their mother; both children were removed from the mother's home at a very young age, and had had limited, sporadic visitation with their mother thereafter. A guardian ad litem was appointed in the dual role of guardian ad litem and attorney for the children and, based on the circumstances presented, there was no basis to conclude that a conflict existed between the opinion of the guardian ad litem and the desires of the children. In re J.R., — Ohio App. 3d —, 2007 Ohio 186, — N.E. 2d —, 2007 Ohio App. LEXIS 164 (Jan. 19, 2007).

Juvenile court violated defendant juvenile's right to counsel in his delinquency proceeding pursuant to U.S. Const. amends. V, VI, and XIV, Ohio Const. art. I, § 16, RC § 2151.352, and Ohio R. Juv. P. 4 and 29 where a valid waiver of counsel was not obtained during the adjudicatory and disposition hearings and counsel was not appointed. Although defendant and his adoptive mother signed a standard form regarding his rights, the form was not accurately filled out and the court failed to review it to ascertain that defendant fully understood the rights therein. In re M.T., — Ohio App. 3d —, 2007 Ohio 2446, — N.E. 2d —, 2007 Ohio App. LEXIS 2258 (May 21, 2007).

When a trial court imposed a commitment to the Department of Youth Services on appellant, a juvenile, after having stayed it, that modification of the juvenile's disposition was reversed because the record reflected that at no point after the juvenile's initial disposition was the juvenile represented by counsel as required by Ohio R. Juv. P. 4 and RC § 2151.352, nor did the record reflect the juvenile's knowing

waiver of counsel. In re Dominique R., — Ohio App. 3d —, — N.E. 2d —, 2007 Ohio 2825, 2007 Ohio App. LEXIS 2635 (June 8, 2007).

Where a juvenile court magistrate obtained defendant juvenile's waiver of his right to counsel in a delinquency matter, wherein he was charged with truancy, and the magistrate thereafter informed the juvenile of the nature of the charges and the possible penalties, there was no compliance with Ohio R. Juv. P. 29(D), such that the waiver by the juvenile of his right to counsel was not deemed knowing and intelligent. Pursuant to RC § 2151.352, Ohio R. Juv. P. 4, 29, and 35, as well as U.S. Const. amends. V, VI, and XIV and Ohio Const. art. I, § 10 and 16, the waiver was insufficient to allow defendant to have appeared unrepresented at the adjudicatory and dispositional phases of the delinquency proceeding. In re C.K., — Ohio App. 3d —, 2007 Ohio 3234, — N.E. 2d —, 2007 Ohio App. LEXIS 2974 (June 21, 2007).

Trial court did not err when it adopted the magistrate's decision finding that the guardian ad litem's final recommendation to award permanent custody to the agency did not conflict with the child's wishes concerning her residential placement. During an in camera interview, the child still did not state a preference as to where she wanted to live; thus, without a clearly articulated preference by the child, no conflict existed between the guardian ad litem and the child warranting the appointment of independent counsel to protect the child's placement interests. In re I.M., — Ohio App. 3d —, 2007 Ohio 4614, — N.E. 2d —, 2007 Ohio App. LEXIS 4150 (Sept. 4, 2007).

As a magistrate failed to enumerate or explain defendant juvenile's rights to him, including his right to counsel, at a hearing regarding his probation violation after he had been previously adjudicated as delinquent, and she failed to find that he waived such rights prior to holding that he violated his probation, his due process rights under U.S. Const. amends. V and VI, Ohio Const. art. I, § 16, RC § 2151.352, and Ohio R. Juv. P. 4 and 35(B) were violated; although the protections and requirements of Ohio R. Juv. P. 35(B) were complied with in a prior hearing, that was a preliminary matter and no adjudication of a probation violation or a sentence were imposed at that time, such that Rule 35(B) had to be again complied with at the later hearing in order to avoid a violation of defendant's rights. In re K.E.M., — Ohio App. 3d —, 2007 Ohio 5031, — N.E. 2d —, 2007 Ohio App. LEXIS 4454 (Sept. 26, 2007).

There was no error in failing to commence the permanent custody hearing (RC § 2151.414) anew after counsel was appointed for the children, pursuant to Ohio R. Juv. P. 4 and RC § 2151.352, because the conflict between the guardian ad litem's recommendation and the children's wishes only became apparent after the hearing had commenced; the error was waived since the mother failed to object, pursuant to Ohio R. Juv. P. 40(3)(a)(i); the attorney declined the opportunity to call other witnesses who had testified at the earlier hearing, with full knowledge of what those witnesses had said, because the attorney was provided a transcript of that earlier hearing; and after the attorney was appointed to represent the children, the mother could no longer claim standing to object that the children's rights in the subsequent proceedings were violated. In re R.E., — Ohio App. 3d —, 2006 Ohio 1256, — N.E. 2d —, 2006 Ohio App. LEXIS 1145 (Mar. 17, 2006).

Under the circumstances, appointment of counsel for the children in the permanent custody proceeding was not required because the children lacked the necessary maturity to give any credible testimony to the court about their wishes with regard to custody. In re Shrider, — Ohio App. 3d —, 2006 Ohio 2792, — N.E. 2d —, 2006 Ohio App. LEXIS 2641 (June 5, 2006).

Father's contention that the trial court erred in failing to appoint counsel for his children to represent them in a permanent custody proceeding was without merit. The father waived his right to complain of the alleged error on appeal by his failure to raise the issue before the trial court, and even so, the record indicated that the trial court appointed an individual as both guardian ad litem and counsel for all three children. In re Salsberry, — Ohio App. 3d —, 2006 Ohio 3272, — N.E. 2d —, 2006 Ohio App. LEXIS 3190 (June 19, 2006).

Trial court did not err in not appointing an attorney to represent a mother's children in a permanent custody proceeding since the statements by the two older children that they loved their mother and missed her did not constitute evidence that they had an affirmative desire to live with their mother on a permanent basis that was in conflict with their guardian ad litem's recommendation that permanent custody be granted to the agency. Moreover, the second oldest son lacked maturity to understand the proceedings. In re A.T., — Ohio App. 3d —, 2006 Ohio 3919, — N.E. 2d —, 2006 Ohio App. LEXIS 3883 (Aug. 2, 2006).

In proceedings that granted a motion filed by a county children's services agency for permanent custody of a mother's three children under RC § 2151.414(B)(1), a trial court did not err in failing to appoint an attorney for each child. The appointment of separate attorneys was required only when a conflict existed between the role of guardian ad litem and that of attorney under Ohio R. Juv. P. 4(C)(2), and no evidence was presented to show that a conflict existed between the performance of the children's attorney as their appointed counsel under RC § 2151.352 and her role as their guardian ad litem. In re Parks, — Ohio App. 3d —, 2006 Ohio 5891, — N.E. 2d —, 2006 Ohio App. LEXIS 5836 (Nov. 2, 2006).

Trial court erred by failing to appoint counsel after a possible conflict became known between the child's wishes and the recommendation of the guardian ad litem during the permanent custody hearing and thus, the child was entitled to counsel pursuant to RC § 2151.352, as clarified by Ohio R. Juv. P. 4(A) and Ohio R. Juv. P. 2(Y). An attorney would have been required to provide zealous representation for his client and make every legitimate effort to secure an order allowing the child to have continued contact with her father, which the guardian ad litem could not do and remain consistent with his recommendation. In re H.R., — Ohio App. 3d —, 2006 Ohio 1595, — N.E. 2d —, 2006 Ohio App. LEXIS 1472 (Mar. 31, 2006).

Trial court, at a minimum, was required to interview the child, on the record, to determine if she was of sufficient maturity to benefit from separate counsel in the permanent custody proceeding, but failed to do so. There was a clear conflict because the guardian ad litem recommended to the trial court that the mother's parental rights be terminated but the agency case supervisor for the child testified at the permanent custody hearing that the child ultimately wanted to be with her mom. In re Roque, — Ohio App. 3d —, 2006 Ohio 7007, — N.E. 2d —, 2006 Ohio App. LEXIS 6961 (Dec. 29, 2006).

There was no merit to the mother's motion to remove the guardian ad litem (GAL) because the mother did not provide any details as to the "truly justifiable" reasons for which she alleged that the GAL should be removed. Nor did the mother point to any law supporting her contention that the vague incidents referred to amounted to a GAL failing to perform his duties. In re Thomas, — Ohio App. 3d —, 2006 Ohio 3324, — N.E. 2d —, 2006 Ohio App. LEXIS 3237 (June 29, 2006).

Mother's due process rights were not violated because she would have been entitled to the appointment of counsel during the permanent custody hearing, pursuant to RC § 2151.352 and Ohio R. Juv. P. 4, had she requested such from the trial court. The record established that she failed to appear at any of the trial court proceedings prior to the commencement of the permanent custody hearing and never filed a written request asking the trial court to appoint counsel on her behalf. In re Westfall, — Ohio App. 3d —, 2006 Ohio 6717, — N.E. 2d —, 2006 Ohio App. LEXIS 6644 (Dec. 18, 2006).

Mother's permanent surrender of parental rights was not invalid on the ground that the mother's attorney was not present when she signed the surrender because a voluntary surrender is not an adversarial proceeding, and thus, the attendance of a parent's counsel is not mandated during discussions leading to a permanent surrender of custody. Neither RC § 5103.15 nor Ohio R. Juv. P. 4(A), contemplates the right of an indigent person to have an attorney present during a private, contractual transfer of permanent custody. In re Young, — Ohio App. 3d —, 2006 Ohio 4537, — N.E. 2d —, 2006 Ohio App. LEXIS 4487 (Sept. 1, 2006).

Waiver of counsel

Appellant's purported waiver of counsel at a probation revocation hearing was not valid, under RC § 2151.352 and Ohio R. Juv. P. 4 and 35(B), because the trial court's advisement as to that right appeared to state that appellant had the right if he wanted an evidentiary hearing, but not if he wanted to admit the violation he was charged with, which was not the law. In re Lohr, — Ohio App. 3d —, 2007 Ohio 1130, — N.E. 2d —, 2007 Ohio App. LEXIS 1046 (Mar. 7, 2007).

Appellant's purported waiver of counsel at a probation revocation hearing was not valid, under RC § 2151.352 and Ohio R. Juv. P. 4 and 35(B), because the trial court's advisement as to that right appeared to state that appellant had the right if he wanted an evidentiary hearing, but not if he wanted to admit the violation he was charged with, which was not the law. In re Lohr, — Ohio App. 3d —, 2007 Ohio 1130, — N.E. 2d —, 2007 Ohio App. LEXIS 1046 (Mar. 7, 2007).

Trial court erred in failing to determine whether appellant child knowingly and voluntarily waived his right to an attorney. The trial court should have explained the elements and seriousness of the charge against him and should have determined that appellant child was not being coerced or pressured into waiving his right to counsel, addressed his parents to ensure there was no conflict of interest and that the parents also understood the proceedings. In re Mills, — Ohio App. 3d —, 2007 Ohio 924, — N.E. 2d —, 2007 Ohio App. LEXIS 882 (Mar. 5, 2007).

When a trial court did not properly accept appellant's waiver of appellant's right to counsel, it did not cure this initial deficient waiver of counsel by engaging in an additional colloquy with appellant later in the proceedings related to appellant entering an admission or denial regarding the charges against appellant. In re McDonald, — Ohio App. 3d —, 2007 Ohio 2324, — N.E. 2d —, 2007 Ohio App. LEXIS 2175 (May 10, 2007).

Appellant was improperly adjudicated to be a delinquent child because the trial court did not adequately find if appellant's waiver of appellant's right to counsel, under RC § 2151.352 and Ohio R. Juv. P. 4(A), was voluntary, knowing and intelligent, as it did not make sufficient inquiry to find if appellant fully understood and intelligently relinquished that right because, before accepting appellant's waiver of counsel, (1) it did not adequately warn appellant of the dangers and disadvantages of self-representation, (2) it should have advised appellant of the nature of the charges and the range of allowable punishments, and (3) it should have advised appellant of possible defenses to the charges and applicable mitigating circumstances. In re McDonald, — Ohio App. 3d —, 2007 Ohio 2324, — N.E. 2d —, 2007 Ohio App. LEXIS 2175 (May 10, 2007).

When a trial court did not properly accept appellant's waiver of appellant's right to counsel, at appellant's initial appearance, all subsequent proceedings, including probation revocation proceedings, were necessarily similarly tainted. In re McDonald, — Ohio App. 3d —, 2007 Ohio 2324, — N.E. 2d —, 2007 Ohio App. LEXIS 2175 (May 10, 2007).

Trial court did not comply with Ohio R. Juv. P. 29(B)(5) for a valid waiver of counsel because it failed to inform the 12-year-old juvenile of the nature of the charges against him and the substance of the complaints, the possible dispositions which could be imposed, his right to remain silent, his right to obtain counsel at any stage of the proceedings, and his right to cross-examine witnesses and it did not adequately warn him of the dangers and disadvantages of self-representation. The juvenile's age, state of mind, emotional stability, mental capacity, and prior criminal experience indicated, at the very least, that the strictest scrutiny should have been employed in determining whether he knowingly, voluntarily, and intelligently waived his right to counsel. In re Puckett, — Ohio App. 3d —, 2007 Ohio 3927, — N.E. 2d —, 2007 Ohio App. LEXIS 3531 (Aug. 1, 2007).

Juvenile's waiver of counsel was defective because the dialogue between the juvenile and the juvenile court did not thoroughly address or investigate any of the factors necessary to determine whether he knowingly, intelligently, and voluntarily waived his right to counsel. The juvenile court represented to the juvenile that counsel could only be appointed if his parents were unemployed, not based solely upon his own indigence, failed to inform him of his rights under JuvR 29(B)(5), and never explained to him how an attorney might be helpful in crafting a successful defense, or in advising him of the disadvantages of being tried with a co-defendant. In re Ramon, — Ohio App. 3d —, 2007 Ohio 5768, — N.E. 2d —, 2007 Ohio App. LEXIS 5080 (Oct. 29, 2007).

When appellant was charged with offenses in juvenile court, RC § 2151.352 did not require that counsel be appointed to represent him because the statute, as well as Ohio R. Juv. P. 4(A) and 29(B), allowed him to waive counsel, which he knowingly, intelligently, and voluntarily did. In re Spears, — Ohio App. 3d —, 2006 Ohio 1920, — N.E. 2d —, 2006 Ohio App. LEXIS 1761 (Apr. 17, 2006).

Based on a review of the record as a whole, and in consideration of the affirmations of the minor and her mother that they wished to proceed without counsel on her delinquency charge for drug possession, the requirements of Ohio R. Juv. P. 29(B) were met and the minor's waiver of counsel was voluntarily, knowingly and understandingly given. The trial court explained to the minor her right to counsel, the nature, elements, and category of the charge, her right to a trial, the possible commitment, her right to remain silent, her right to present evidence in her defense and her right to cross-examine witnesses and, as each right was explained, the minor answered that she understood the right and then the minor and her mother agreed to proceed without counsel. In re Loos, — Ohio App. 3d —, 2006 Ohio 3932, — N.E. 2d —, 2006 Ohio App. LEXIS 3891 (July 31, 2006).

Although the trial court substantially complied with Ohio R. Juv. P. 29(D) when it accepted defendant juvenile's waiver of counsel during the adjudication hearing, the trial court failed to reiterate defendant's right to counsel during disposition or allow him either to invoke or to waive his right to counsel at that stage as required by Ohio R. Juv. P. 34. In re S. J., — Ohio App. 3d —, 2006 Ohio 4467, — N.E. 2d —, 2006 Ohio App. LEXIS 4395 (Aug. 30, 2006).

As a magistrate substantially complied with the requirements of Ohio R. Juv. P. 29(B)(1) and (4), although he erroneously notified the juvenile in a probation revocation proceeding that he had a right to be represented by a lawyer if he wished and if his family could not afford a lawyer, such was not plain error under Ohio R. Crim. P. 52(B), as the magistrate carefully outlined the rights and responsibilities of the juvenile, and he made sure he understood the rights and the implications of his waiver; as the juvenile's waiver of his right to counsel was deemed knowing, voluntary, and intelligent, there was no violation of his right to counsel pursuant to RC § 2151.352 and Ohio R. Juv. P. 4. In re J-M, — Ohio App. 3d —, — N.E. 2d —, 2006 Ohio App. LEXIS 6131 (Nov. 22, 2006).

Withdrawal of counsel

When a father found in contempt for failing to pay child support alleged, on appeal, that the trial court should have granted the father's counsel's motion to withdraw, that claim was not sustained because (1) the father, on appeal, gave no reasons why the trial court should have granted the request, nor did the father state what the good cause, under Ohio R. Juv. P. 4(F), for granting it might have been, as the father merely said the record reflected irreconcilable differences, and (2) the father did not provide a transcript or transcript substitute, under Ohio R. App. P. 9, from which such reasons might have been discerned. Midkiff v. Kuzniak, — Ohio App. 3d —, 2007 Ohio 5936, — N.E. 2d —, 2007 Ohio App. LEXIS 5201 (Nov. 2, 2007).

RULE 5.   [Reserved]

RULE 6.   Taking into custody

(A) **[When.]** A child may be taken into custody:

(1) pursuant to an order of the court;

(2) pursuant to the law of arrest;

(3) by a law enforcement officer or duly authorized officer of the court when any of the following conditions exist:

(a) There are reasonable grounds to believe that the child is suffering from illness or injury and is not receiving proper care, and the child's removal is necessary to prevent immediate or threatened physical or emotional harm;

(b) There are reasonable grounds to believe that the child is in immediate danger from the child's surroundings and that the child's removal is necessary to prevent immediate or threatened physical or emotional harm;

(c) There are reasonable grounds to believe that a parent, guardian, custodian, or other household member of the child has abused or neglected another child in the household, and that the child is in danger of immediate or threatened physical or emotional harm;

(d) There are reasonable grounds to believe that the child has run away from the child's parents, guardian, or other custodian;

(e) There are reasonable grounds to believe that the conduct, conditions, or surroundings of the child are endangering the health, welfare, or safety of the child; or

(f) During the pendency of court proceedings, there are reasonable grounds to believe that the child may abscond or be removed from the jurisdiction of the court or will not be brought to the court;

(g) A juvenile judge or designated magistrate has found that there is probable cause to believe any of the conditions set forth in division (A)(3)(a), (b), or (c) of this rule are present, has found that reasonable efforts have been made to notify the child's parents, guardian ad litem or custodian that the child may be placed into shelter care, except where notification would jeopardize the physical or emotional safety of the child or result in the child's removal from the court's jurisdiction, and has ordered ex parte, by telephone or otherwise, the taking of the child into custody.

(4) By the judge or designated magistrate ex parte pending the outcome of the adjudicatory and dispositional hearing in an abuse, neglect, or dependency proceeding, where it appears to the court that the best

interest and welfare of the child require the immediate issuance of a shelter care order.

(B) **Probable cause hearing.** When a child is taken into custody pursuant to an ex parte emergency order pursuant to division (A)(3)(g) or (A)(4) of this rule, a probable cause hearing shall be held before the end of the next business day after the day on which the order is issued but not later than seventy-two hours after the issuance of the emergency order.

History: Amended, eff 7-1-94; 7-1-96.

RULE 7. Detention and shelter care

(A) **Detention: standards.** A child taken into custody shall not be placed in detention or shelter care prior to final disposition unless any of the following apply:

(1) Detention or shelter care is required:

(a) to protect the child from immediate or threatened physical or emotional harm; or

(b) to protect the person or property of others from immediate or threatened physical or emotional harm.

(2) The child may abscond or be removed from the jurisdiction of the court;

(3) The child has no parent, guardian, custodian or other person able to provide supervision and care for the child and return the child to the court when required;

(4) An order for placement of the child in detention or shelter care has been made by the court;

(5) Confinement is authorized by statute.

(B) **Priorities in placement prior to hearing.** A person taking a child into custody shall, with all reasonable speed, do either of the following:

(1) Release the child to a parent, guardian, or other custodian;

(2) Where detention or shelter care appears to be required under the standards of division (A) of this rule, bring the child to the court or deliver the child to a place of detention or shelter care designated by the court.

(C) **Initial procedure upon detention.** Any person who delivers a child to a shelter or detention facility shall give the admissions officer at the facility a signed report stating why the child was taken into custody and why the child was not released to a parent, guardian or custodian, and shall assist the admissions officer, if necessary, in notifying the parent pursuant to division (E)(3) of this rule.

(D) **Admission.** The admissions officer in a shelter or detention facility, upon receipt of a child, shall review the report submitted pursuant to division (C) of this rule, make such further investigation as is feasible and do either of the following:

(1) Release the child to the care of a parent, guardian or custodian;

(2) Where detention or shelter care is required under the standards of division (A) of this rule, admit the child to the facility or place the child in some appropriate facility.

(E) **Procedure after admission.** When a child has been admitted to detention or shelter care the admissions officer shall do all of the following:

(1) Prepare a report stating the time the child was brought to the facility and the reasons the child was admitted;

(2) Advise the child of the right to telephone parents and counsel immediately and at reasonable times thereafter and the time, place, and purpose of the detention hearing;

(3) Use reasonable diligence to contact the child's parent, guardian, or custodian and advise that person of all of the following:

(a) The place of and reasons for detention;

(b) The time the child may be visited;

(c) The time, place, and purpose of the detention hearing;

(d) The right to counsel and appointed counsel in the case of indigency.

(F) **Detention hearing.**

(1) Hearing: time; notice. When a child has been admitted to detention or shelter care, a detention hearing shall be held promptly, not later than seventy-two hours after the child is placed in detention or shelter care or the next court day, whichever is earlier, to determine whether detention or shelter care is required. Reasonable oral or written notice of the time, place, and purpose of the detention hearing shall be given to the child and to the parents, guardian, or other custodian, if that person or those persons can be found.

(2) Hearing: advisement of rights. Prior to the hearing, the court shall inform the parties of the right to counsel and to appointed counsel if indigent and the child's right to remain silent with respect to any allegation of a juvenile traffic offense, delinquency, or unruliness.

(3) Hearing procedure. The court may consider any evidence, including the reports filed by the person who brought the child to the facility and the admissions officer, without regard to formal rules of evidence. Unless it appears from the hearing that the child's detention or shelter care is required under division (A) of this rule, the court shall order the child's release to a parent, guardian, or custodian. Whenever abuse, neglect, or dependency is alleged, the court shall determine whether there are any appropriate relatives of the child who are willing to be temporary custodians and, if so, appoint an appropriate relative as the temporary custodian of the child. The court shall make a reasonable efforts determination in accordance with Juv. R. 27(B)(1).

(G) **Rehearing.** If a parent, guardian, or custodian did not receive notice of the initial hearing and did not appear or waive appearance at the hearing, the court shall rehear the matter promptly. After a child is placed in shelter care or detention care, any party and the guardian ad litem of the child may file a motion with the court requesting that the child be released from detention or shelter care. Upon the filing of the motion, the court shall hold a hearing within seventy-two hours.

(H) **Separation from adults.** No child shall be placed in or committed to any prison, jail, lockup, or any other place where the child can come in contact or communication with any adult convicted of crime, under arrest, or charged with crime.

(I) **Physical examination.** The supervisor of a

shelter or detention facility may provide for a physical examination of a child placed in the shelter or facility.

(J) **Telephone and visitation rights.** A child may telephone the child's parents and attorney immediately after being admitted to a shelter or detention facility and at reasonable times thereafter.

The child may be visited at reasonable visiting hours by the child's parents and adult members of the family, the child's pastor, and the child's teachers. The child may be visited by the child's attorney at any time.

History: Amended, eff 7-1-94; 7-1-01.

NOTES TO DECISIONS

ANALYSIS

Constitutionality
Generally

Constitutionality

Defendant juvenile's due process rights were not violated because she did not file a motion for release pursuant to Ohio R. Juv. P. 7(G) alleging that she had been held in excess of 90 days in violation of RC § 2151.354 at any time prior to entering her admission to the charge (violation of a prior court order). Also, the juvenile court notified her in writing of the conduct that was alleged to be in violation of the prior court order by the complaint, informed her of her right to a trial, and explained the possible dispositions if she were to admit the violation or be found guilty after trial. In re Burt, — Ohio App. 3d —, 2007 Ohio 4034, — N.E. 2d —, 2007 Ohio App. LEXIS 3649 (Aug. 6, 2007).

Generally

Trial court's decision granting an agency temporary custody of a mother's children, after the children had been returned to her from the agency's custody, was not against the manifest weight of the evidence because the primary concern of the shelter care hearing at which temporary custody was granted was the children's immediate safety and protection and (1) the mother, who had left the children with her husband, tested positive for marijuana and methamphetamine, and (2) her husband left the children with their father, contrary to court order. In re G.N., 170 Ohio App. 3d 76, 2007 Ohio 126, 866 N.E.2d 32, 2007 Ohio App. LEXIS 104 (2007).

RULE 8.   Filing by electronic means

A court may provide, by local rules adopted pursuant to the Rules of Superintendence, for the filing of documents by electronic means. If the court adopts such local rules, they shall include all of the following:

(A) Any signature on electronically transmitted documents shall be considered that of the attorney or party it purports to be for all purposes. If it is established that the documents were transmitted without authority, the court shall order the filing stricken.

(B) A provision shall specify the days and hours during which electronically transmitted documents will be received by the court, and a provision shall specify when documents received electronically will be considered to have been filed.

(C) Any document filed electronically that requires a filing fee may be rejected by the clerk of court unless the filer has complied with the mechanism established by the court for the payment of filing fees.

History: Effective 7-1-94; amended, eff 7-1-96; 7-1-01.

RULE 9.   Intake

(A) **Court action to be avoided.** In all appropriate cases formal action should be avoided and other community resources utilized to ameliorate situations brought to the attention of the court.

(B) **Screening; referral.** Information that a child is within the court's jurisdiction may be informally screened prior to the filing of a complaint to determine whether the filing of a complaint is in the best interest of the child and the public.

RULE 10.   Complaint

(A) **Filing.** Any person having knowledge of a child who appears to be a juvenile traffic offender, delinquent, unruly, neglected, dependent, or abused may file a complaint with respect to the child in the juvenile court of the county in which the child has a residence or legal settlement, or in which the traffic offense, delinquency, unruliness, neglect, dependency, or abuse occurred.

Persons filing complaints that a child appears to be an unruly or delinquent child for being an habitual or chronic truant and the parent, guardian, or other person having care of the child has failed to cause the child to attend school may also file the complaint in the county in which the child is supposed to attend public school.

Any person may file a complaint to have determined the custody of a child not a ward of another court of this state, and any person entitled to the custody of a child and unlawfully deprived of such custody may file a complaint requesting a writ of habeas corpus. Complaints concerning custody shall be filed in the county where the child is found or was last known to be.

Any person with standing may file a complaint for the determination of any other matter over which the juvenile court is given jurisdiction by the Revised Code. The complaint shall be filed in the county in which the child who is the subject of the complaint is found or was last known to be. In a removal action, the complaint shall be filed in the county where the foster home is located.

When a case concerning a child is transferred or certified from another court, the certification from the transferring court shall be considered the complaint. The juvenile court may order the certification supplemented upon its own motion or that of a party.

(B) **Complaint: general form.** The complaint, which may be upon information and belief, shall satisfy all of the following requirements:

(1) State in ordinary and concise language the essential facts that bring the proceeding within the jurisdiction of the court, and in juvenile traffic offense and delinquency proceedings, shall contain the numerical designation of the statute or ordinance alleged to have been violated;

(2) Contain the name and address of the parent, guardian, or custodian of the child or state that the name or address is unknown;

(3) Be made under oath.

(C) **Complaint: juvenile traffic offense.** A Uniform Traffic ticket shall be used as a complaint in juvenile traffic offense proceedings.

(D) **Complaint: permanent custody.** A complaint seeking permanent custody of a child shall state that permanent custody is sought.

(E) **Complaint: temporary custody.** A complaint seeking temporary custody of a child shall state that temporary custody is sought.

(F) **Complaint: planned permanent living arrangement.** A complaint seeking the placement of a child into a planned permanent living arrangement shall state that placement into a planned permanent living arrangement is sought.

(G) **Complaint: habeas corpus.** Where a complaint for a writ of habeas corpus involving the custody of a child is based on the existence of a lawful court order, a certified copy of the order shall be attached to the complaint.

History: Amended, eff 7-1-75; 7-1-76; 7-1-94; 7-1-98; 7-1-01; 7-1-02.

NOTES TO DECISIONS

Analysis

Child's residence
Sufficiency

Child's residence
Venue was proper for neglect and dependency hearing because the mother's residency in the county was established. The evidence showed that the mother was "habitually transient;" that she had stayed with friends in the county; and that she had her public assistance benefits transferred to the instant county. In re Zobel, — Ohio App. 3d —, 2007 Ohio 3355, — N.E. 2d —, 2007 Ohio App. LEXIS 3077 (June 27, 2007).

Sufficiency
Defendant juvenile's due process rights under U.S. Const. amend. XIV and Ohio Const. art. I, § 10 were not violated where a charge in a delinquency complaint against him based on vehicular vandalism, in violation of RC § 2909.09(B)(1), only indicated that there was damage to a car owner's windshield but defendant was thereafter ordered to make restitution to the owner under RC § 2929.28 for repair costs to other parts of the car that were damaged as well. Defendant was on notice that the State was seeking restitution beyond the windshield damages and there was no requirement of a hypertechnical application of Ohio R. Juv. P. 10(B)(1) and RC § 2151.27(A)(1) to a delinquency complaint. In re Czika, — Ohio App. 3d —, 2007 Ohio 4110, — N.E. 2d —, 2007 Ohio App. LEXIS 3724 (Aug. 10, 2007).

RULE 11.   Transfer to another county

(A) **Residence in another county; transfer optional.** If the child resides in a county of this state and the proceeding is commenced in a court of another county, that court, on its own motion or a motion of a party, may transfer the proceeding to the county of the child's residence upon the filing of the complaint or after the adjudicatory or dispositional hearing for such further proceeding as required. The court of the child's residence shall then proceed as if the original complaint had been filed in that court. Transfer may also be made if the residence of the child changes.

(B) **Proceedings in another county; transfer required.** The proceedings, other than a removal action, shall be so transferred if other proceedings involving the child are pending in the juvenile court of the county of the child's residence.

(C) **Adjudicatory hearing in county where complaint filed.** Where either the transferring or receiving court finds that the interests of justice and the convenience of the parties so require, the adjudicatory hearing shall be held in the county wherein the complaint was filed. Thereafter the proceeding may be transferred to the county of the child's residence for disposition.

(D) **Transfer of records.** Certified copies of all legal and social records pertaining to the proceeding shall accompany the transfer.

History: Amended, eff 7-1-94; 7-1-98.

NOTES TO DECISIONS

Analysis

Appeal
Jurisdiction

Appeal
Juvenile delinquency adjudication without a subsequent dispositional order did not constitute a "final order" that was subject to appeal pursuant to RC § 2501.02. A juvenile proceeding may have been transferred upon the filing of the complaint or after the adjudicatory or dispositional hearing, and the county to which the proceeding was transferred was to proceed as if the original complaint had been filed in that court. Where, after adjudication, a trial court transferred a juvenile case to a different county, where it remained pending, the order of adjudication was not subject to review. In re Williams, — Ohio App. 3d —, 2006 Ohio 2370, — N.E. 2d —, 2006 Ohio App. LEXIS 2268 (May 15, 2006).

Jurisdiction
Where a mother sought to preclude a juvenile court judge from exercising post-judgment jurisdiction over visitation and custody motions filed by the father of her child after the mother had filed her intent to relocate to North Carolina with the child, her claim that the judge no longer had jurisdiction over the matter lacked merit, as the juvenile court and the judge had general statutory authority over such issues pursuant to RC §§ 2151.23 and 2151.231. The mother also failed to show entitlement to the writ where she had an adequate remedy at law through either an appeal or a request to transfer the proceedings to North Carolina, pursuant to Ohio R. Juv. P. 11 and 39, such that dismissal of the complaint was warranted. Rivers v. Ramsey, — Ohio App. 3d —, 2006 Ohio 1744, — N.E. 2d —, 2006 Ohio App. LEXIS 1610 (Apr. 3, 2006).

RULE 12.   [Reserved]

RULE 13.   Temporary disposition; temporary orders; emergency medical and surgical treatment

(A) **Temporary disposition.** Pending hearing on a complaint, the court may make such temporary orders concerning the custody or care of a child who is the subject of the complaint as the child's interest and welfare may require.

(B) **Temporary orders.**
(1) Pending hearing on a complaint, the judge or magistrate may issue temporary orders with respect to

the relations and conduct of other persons toward a child who is the subject of the complaint as the child's interest and welfare may require.

(2) Upon the filing of an abuse, neglect, or dependency complaint, any party may by motion request that the court issue any of the following temporary orders to protect the best interest of the child:

(a) An order granting temporary custody of the child to a particular party;

(b) An order for the taking of the child into custody pending the outcome of the adjudicatory and dispositional hearings;

(c) An order granting, limiting, or eliminating visitation rights with respect to the child;

(d) An order for the payment of child support and continued maintenance of any medical, surgical, or hospital policies of insurance for the child that existed at the time of the filing of the complaint, petition, writ, or other document;

(e) An order requiring a party to vacate a residence that will be lawfully occupied by the child;

(f) An order requiring a party to attend an appropriate counseling program that is reasonably available to that party;

(g) Any other order that restrains or otherwise controls the conduct of any party which conduct would not be in the best interest of the child.

(3) The orders permitted by division (B)(2) of this rule may be granted ex parte if it appears that the best interest and welfare of the child require immediate issuance. If the court issues the requested ex parte order, the court shall hold a hearing to review the order within seventy-two hours after it is issued or before the end of the next court day after the day on which it is issued, whichever occurs first. The court shall appoint a guardian ad litem for the child prior to the hearing. The court shall give written notice of the hearing by means reasonably likely to result in the party's receiving actual notice and include all of the following:

(a) The date, time, and location of the hearing;

(b) The issues to be addressed at the hearing;

(c) A statement that every party to the hearing has a right to counsel and to court appointed counsel, if the party is indigent;

(d) The name, telephone number, and address of the person requesting the order;

(e) A copy of the order, except when it is not possible to obtain it because of the exigent circumstances in the case.

(4) The court may review any order under this rule at any time upon motion of any party for good cause shown or upon the motion of the court.

(5) If the court does not grant an ex parte order, the court shall hold a shelter care hearing on the motion within ten days after the motion is filed.

(C) **Emergency medical and surgical treatment**. Upon the certification of one or more reputable practicing physicians, the court may order such emergency medical and surgical treatment as appears to be immediately necessary for any child concerning whom a complaint has been filed.

(D) **Ex parte proceedings.** In addition to the ex parte proceeding described in division (B) of this rule, the court may proceed summarily and without notice under division (A), (B), or (C) of this rule, where it appears to the court that the interest and welfare of the child require that action be taken immediately.

(E) **Hearing; notice.** In addition to the procedures specified in division (B) of this rule and wherever possible, the court shall provide an opportunity for hearing before proceeding under division (D) of this rule. Where the court has proceeded without notice under division (D) of this rule, it shall give notice of the action it has taken to the parties and any other affected person and provide them an opportunity for a hearing concerning the continuing effects of the action.

(F) **Probable cause finding.** Upon the finding of probable cause at a shelter care hearing that a child is an abused child, the court may do any of the following:

(1) Upon motion by the court or of any party, issue reasonable protective orders with respect to the interviewing or deposition of the child;

(2) Order that the child's testimony be videotaped for preservation of the testimony for possible use in any other proceedings in the case;

(3) Set any additional conditions with respect to the child or the case involving the child that are in the best interest of the child.

(G) **Payment.** The court may order the parent, guardian, or custodian, if able, to pay for any emergency medical or surgical treatment provided pursuant to division (C) of this rule. The order of payment may be enforced by judgment, upon which execution may issue, and a failure to pay as ordered may be punished as contempt of court.

History: Amended, eff 7-1-94; 7-1-96.

NOTES TO DECISIONS

ANALYSIS

Generally

Generally

In a child custody dispute, it was not error for a trial court to grant temporary custody of the subject child to one of the parties during the course of a hearing, and the trial court's final order superceded the temporary order and corrected any error, rendering the issue moot. Smith v. Quigg, — Ohio App. 3d —, 2006 Ohio 1494, — N.E. 2d —, 2006 Ohio App. LEXIS 1371 (Mar. 22, 2006).

RULE 14. Termination, extension or modification of temporary custody orders

(A) **Termination.** Any temporary custody order issued shall terminate one year after the earlier of the date on which the complaint in the case was filed or the child was first placed into shelter care. A temporary custody order shall extend beyond a year and until the court issues another dispositional order, where any public or private agency with temporary custody, not later than thirty days prior to the earlier of the date for the termination of the custody order or the date set at the dispositional hearing for the hearing to be held pursuant to Division (A) of section 2151.415 of the Revised Code, files a motion requesting that any of the following orders of disposition be issued:

(1) An order that the child be returned home with custody to the child's parents, guardian, or custodian without any restrictions;

(2) An order for protective supervision;

(3) An order that the child be placed in the legal custody of a relative or other interested individual;

(4) An order terminating parental rights;

(5) An order for long term foster care;

(6) An order for the extension of temporary custody.

(B) **Extension.** Upon the filing of an agency's motion for the extension of temporary custody, the court shall schedule a hearing and give notice to all parties in accordance with these rules. The agency shall include in the motion an explanation of the progress on the case plan and of its expectations of reunifying the child with the child's family, or placing the child in a permanent placement, within the extension period. The court may extend the temporary custody order for a period of up to six months. Prior to the end of the extension period, the agency may request one additional extension of up to six months. The court shall grant either extension upon finding that it is in the best interest of the child, that there has been significant progress on the case plan, and that there is reasonable cause to believe that the child will be reunited with one of the child's parents or otherwise permanently placed within the period of extension. Prior to the end of either extension, the agency that received the extension shall file a motion and the court shall issue one of the orders of disposition set forth in division (A) of this rule. Upon the agency's motion or upon its own motion, the court shall conduct a hearing and issue an appropriate order of disposition.

(C) **Modification.** The court, upon its own motion or that of any party, shall conduct a hearing with notice to all parties to determine whether any order issued should be modified or terminated, or whether any other dispositional order set forth in division (A) should be issued. The court shall so modify or terminate any order in accordance with the best interest of the child.

History: Amended, eff 7-1-94.

NOTES TO DECISIONS

ANALYSIS

Discretion of court

Discretion of court

Competent, credible evidence supported the trial court's decision to place the children in the legal custody of the uncle and his wife because the trial court had discretion to make a dispositional order in the best interests of the children as it retained jurisdiction over the children. The problems that led to the original grant of temporary custody had not been resolved by the time the trial court made its dispositional order since the treatment of the children and the medical "diagnosis" of Munchausen Syndrome by Proxy and its applicability were still very much in issue. In re McCallum, — Ohio App. 3d —, 2007 Ohio 995, — N.E. 2d —, 2007 Ohio App. LEXIS 905 (Mar. 1, 2007).

RULE 15. Process: issuance, form

(A) **Summons: issuance.** After the complaint has been filed, the court shall cause the issuance of a summons directed to the child, the parents, guardian, custodian, and any other persons who appear to the court to be proper or necessary parties. The summons shall require the parties to appear before the court at the time fixed to answer the allegations of the complaint. A child alleged to be abused, neglected, or dependent shall not be summoned unless the court so directs.

(B) **Summons: form.** The summons shall contain:

(1) The name of the party or person with whom the child may be or, if unknown, any name or description by which the party or person can be identified with reasonable certainty.

(2) A summary statement of the complaint and in juvenile traffic offense and delinquency proceedings the numerical designation of the applicable statute or ordinance.

(3) A statement that any party is entitled to be represented by an attorney and that upon request the court will appoint an attorney for an indigent party entitled to appointed counsel under Juv. R. 4(A).

(4) An order to the party or person to appear at a stated time and place with a warning that the party or person may lose valuable rights or be subject to court sanction if the party or person fails to appear at the time and place stated in the summons.

(5) An order to the parent, guardian, or other person having care of a child alleged to be an unruly or delinquent child for being an habitual or chronic truant, to appear personally at the hearing and all proceedings, and an order directing the person having the physical custody or control of the child to bring the child to the hearing, with a warning that if the child fails to appear, the parent, guardian, or other person having care of the child may be subject to court sanction, including a finding of contempt.

(6) A statement that if a child is adjudicated abused, neglected, or dependent and the complaint seeks an order of permanent custody, an order of permanent custody would cause the parents, guardian, or legal custodian to be divested permanently of all parental rights and privileges.

(7) A statement that if a child is adjudicated abused, neglected, or dependent and the complaint seeks an order of temporary custody, an order of temporary custody will cause the removal of the child from the legal custody of the parents, guardian, or other custodian until the court terminates the order of temporary custody or permanently divests the parents of their parental rights.

(8) A statement that if the child is adjudicated abused, neglected, or dependent and the complaint seeks an order for a planned permanent living arrangement, an order for a planned permanent living arrangement will cause the removal of the child from the legal custody of the parent, guardian, or other custodian.

(9) A statement, in a removal action, of the specific disposition sought.

(10) The name and telephone number of the court employee designated by the court to arrange for the prompt appointment of counsel for indigent persons.

(C) **Summons: endorsement.** The court may endorse upon the summons an order directed to the parents, guardian, or other person with whom the child may be, to appear personally and bring the child to the hearing.

(D) **Warrant: issuance.** If it appears that the summons will be ineffectual or the welfare of the child requires that the child be brought forthwith to the court, a warrant may be issued against the child. A copy of the complaint shall accompany the warrant.

(E) **Warrant: form.** The warrant shall contain the name of the child or, if that is unknown, any name or description by which the child can be identified with reasonable certainty. It shall contain a summary statement of the complaint and in juvenile traffic offense and delinquency proceedings the numerical designation of the applicable statute or ordinance. A copy of the complaint shall be attached to the warrant. The warrant shall command that the child be taken into custody and be brought before the court that issued the warrant without unnecessary delay.

History: Amended, eff 7-1-94; 7-1-98; 7-1-01; 7-1-02.

NOTES TO DECISIONS

ANALYSIS

Parties

Parties

There was no error in denying the mother's motion to dismiss the stepfather, her husband, as a party in the permanent custody hearing because he was a vital part of the case; he contributed to the initiation of the agency's proceedings with his behavior, interacted with the children as a parent, and was included in the case plans and services, among other things. Several witnesses testified that the dynamics of the mother's relationship with the stepfather was an important factor in determining her ability to parent and the mother's decision to file for divorce from him a mere two weeks prior to the permanent custody hearing did not erase those facts, particularly in light of the stepfather's assertion that the divorce filing was a sham and their history of separating and reconciling. In re J.P., — Ohio App. 3d —, 2007 Ohio 1903, — N.E. 2d —, 2007 Ohio App. LEXIS 1755 (Apr. 23, 2007).

RULE 16.   Process: service

(A) **Summons: service, return.** Except as otherwise provided in these rules, summons shall be served as provided in Civil Rules 4(A), (C) and (D), 4.1, 4.2, 4.3, 4.5 and 4.6. The summons shall direct the party served to appear at a stated time and place. Where service is by certified mail, the time shall not be less than seven days after the date of mailing.

Except as otherwise provided in this rule, when the residence of a party is unknown and cannot be ascertained with reasonable diligence, service shall be made by publication. Service by publication upon a noncustodial parent is not required in delinquent child or unruly child cases when the person alleged to have legal custody of the child has been served with summons pursuant to this rule, but the court may not enter any order or judgment against any person who has not been served with process or served by publication unless that person appears. Before service by publication can be made, an affidavit of a party or party's counsel shall be filed with the court. The affidavit shall

aver that service of summons cannot be made because the residence of the person is unknown to the affiant and cannot be ascertained with reasonable diligence and shall set forth the last known address of the party to be served.

Service by publication shall be made by newspaper publication, by posting and mail, or by a combination of these methods. The court, by local rule, shall determine which method or methods of publication shall be used. If service by publication is made by newspaper publication, upon the filing of the affidavit, the clerk shall serve notice by publication in a newspaper of general circulation in the county in which the complaint is filed. If no newspaper is published in that county, then publication shall be in a newspaper published in an adjoining county. The publication shall contain the name and address of the court, the case number, the name of the first party on each side, and the name and last known address, if any, of the person or persons whose residence is unknown. The publication shall also contain a summary statement of the object of the complaint and shall notify the person to be served that the person is required to appear at the time and place stated. The time stated shall not be less than seven days after the date of publication. The publication shall be published once and service shall be complete on the date of publication.

After the publication, the publisher or the publisher's agent shall file with the court an affidavit showing the fact of publication together with a copy of the notice of publication. The affidavit and copy of the notice shall constitute proof of service.

If service by publication is made by posting and mail, upon the filing of the affidavit, the clerk shall cause service of notice to be made by posting in a conspicuous place in the courthouse in which the division of the common pleas court exercising jurisdiction over the complaint is located and in additional public places in the county that have been designated by local rule for the posting of notices pursuant to this rule. The number of additional public places to be designated shall be either two places or the number of state representative districts that are contained wholly or partly in the county in which the courthouse is located, whichever is greater. The notice shall contain the same information required to be contained in a newspaper publication. The notice shall be posted in the required locations for seven consecutive days. The clerk also shall cause the summons and accompanying pleadings to be mailed by ordinary mail, address correction requested, to the last known address of the party to be served. The clerk shall obtain a certificate of mailing from the United States Postal Service. If the clerk is notified of a corrected or forwarding address of the party to be served within the seven day period that notice is posted pursuant to this rule, the clerk shall cause the summons and accompanying pleadings to be mailed to the corrected or forwarding address. The clerk shall note the name, address, and date of each mailing in the docket.

After the seven days of posting, the clerk shall note on the docket where and when notice was posted. Service shall be complete upon the entry of posting.

(B) **Warrant: execution; return.**

(1) By whom. The warrant shall be executed by any officer authorized by law.

(2) Territorial limits. The warrant may be executed at any place within this state.

(3) Manner. The warrant shall be executed by taking the party against whom it is issued into custody. The officer is not required to have possession of the warrant at the time it is executed, but in such case the officer shall inform the party of the complaint made and the fact that the warrant has been issued. A copy of the warrant shall be given to the person named in the warrant as soon as possible.

(4) Return. The officer executing a warrant shall make return thereof to the issuing court. Unexecuted warrants shall upon request of the issuing court be returned to that court.

A warrant returned unexecuted and not cancelled or a copy thereof may, while the complaint is pending, be delivered by the court to an authorized officer for execution.

An officer executing a warrant shall take the person named therein without unnecessary delay before the court which issued the warrant.

History: Amended, eff 7-1-94; 7-1-98.

NOTES TO DECISIONS

Analysis

Permanent custody
Service by publication
Termination of parental rights
Waiver of error

Permanent custody

Children's services board exercised reasonable diligence in attempting to serve the father notice of the permanent custody proceeding because neither Ohio R. Civ. P. 4.6(D) nor the Due Process Clause required ordinary mail service when the postal authorities returned certified mail with the endorsement "Attempted Not Known" before a party attempted service by publication. The board complied with the rules by attempting to personally serve the father at one address, by attempting to serve him by certified mail at another address, and by publishing a notice in a newspaper; because the returned certified letter, endorsed "Attempted Not Known" clearly demonstrated that the father did not reside and was not known at that address, any ordinary mail addressed to him at that address could not have been reasonably calculated to give him notice and an opportunity to be heard at the permanent custody proceeding. In re Thompkins, 115 Ohio St. 3d 409, 2007 Ohio 5238, 875 N.E.2d 582, 2007 Ohio LEXIS 2523 (2007).

In a permanent custody proceeding, it was not an abuse of discretion for a trial court to deny a motion for a continuance made on behalf of a non-appearing parent because the parent had at least constructive notice of the proceedings after being properly served with notice of them pursuant to Ohio R. Juv. P. 16. In re Barnes, — Ohio App. 3d —, 2007 Ohio 3127, — N.E. 2d —, 2007 Ohio App. LEXIS 2881 (June 25, 2007).

Service by publication

RC § 2705.031(D) suggests that service in accordance with JuvR 16, rather than CivR 4.4, may be used in contempt actions in juvenile court, as long as such service comports with due process. In re I.U., — Ohio App. 3d —, 2007 Ohio 6264, — N.E. 2d —, 2007 Ohio App. LEXIS 5518 (Nov. 21, 2007).

Termination of parental rights

County children services board exercised reasonable diligence in attempting to serve the father in a proceeding to terminate parental rights. Neither CivR 4.6(D) nor the due process clause requires ordinary mail service when postal authorities return certified mail with the endorsement "attempted not known" before a party attempts service by publication: In re Thompkins, 115 Ohio St. 3d 409, 2007 Ohio 5238, 875 N.E.2d 582, 2007 Ohio LEXIS 2523 (2007).

Waiver of error

As publication on a father in a neglect and dependency proceeding regarding his children was made by publication pursuant to Ohio R. Juv. P. 16 in the county wherein the complaint was filed, and counsel appeared on behalf of the mother and father of the children and did not contest the trial court's jurisdiction, any claims on appeal regarding insufficiency of process were deemed waived. In re Hill, — Ohio App. 3d —, 2007 Ohio 1727, — N.E. 2d —, 2007 Ohio App. LEXIS 1574 (Apr. 11, 2007).

RULE 17. Subpoena

(A) **Form; issuance.**

(1) Every subpoena shall do all of the following:

(a) State the name of the court from which it is issued, the title of the action, and the case number;

(b) Command each person to whom it is directed, at a time and place specified in the subpoena, to do one or more of the following:

(i) Attend and give testimony at a trial, hearing, proceeding, or deposition;

(ii) Produce documents or tangible things at a trial, hearing, proceeding, or deposition;

(iii) Produce and permit inspection and copying of any designated documents that are in the possession, custody, or control of the person;

(iv) Produce and permit inspection and copying, testing, or sampling of any tangible things that are in the possession, custody, or control of the person.

(c) Set forth the text of divisions (D) and (E) of this rule.

A command to produce and permit inspection may be joined with a command to attend and give testimony, or may be issued separately.

(2) The clerk shall issue a subpoena, signed but otherwise in blank, to a party requesting it, who shall complete it before service. An attorney who has filed an appearance on behalf of a party in an action also may sign and issue a subpoena on behalf of the court in which the action is pending.

(3) If the issuing attorney modifies the subpoena in any way, the issuing attorney shall give prompt notice of the modifications to all other parties.

(B) **Parties unable to pay.** The court shall order at any time that a subpoena be issued for service on a named witness upon an ex parte application of a party and upon a satisfactory showing that the presence of the witness is necessary and that the party is financially unable to pay the witness fees required by division (C) of this rule. If the court orders the subpoena to be issued, the costs incurred by the process and the fees of the witness so subpoenaed shall be paid in the same manner that similar costs and fees are paid in case of a witness subpoenaed in behalf of the state in a criminal prosecution.

(C) **Service.** A subpoena may be served by a sheriff,

bailiff, coroner, clerk of court, constable, probation officer, or a deputy of any, by an attorney or the attorney's agent, or by any person designated by order of the court who is not a party and is not less than eighteen years of age. Service of a subpoena upon a person named in the subpoena shall be made by delivering a copy of the subpoena to the person, by reading it to him or her in person, or by leaving it at the person's usual place of residence, and by tendering to the person upon demand the fees for one day's attendance and the mileage allowed by the law. The person serving the subpoena shall file a return of the subpoena with the clerk. If the witness being subpoenaed resides outside the county in which the court is located, the fees for one day's attendance and mileage shall be tendered without demand. The return may be forwarded through the postal service or otherwise.

(D) **Protection of persons subject to subpoenas**

(1) A party or an attorney responsible for the issuance and service of a subpoena shall take reasonable steps to avoid imposing undue burden or expense on a person subject to that subpoena.

(2)(a) A person commanded to produce under division (A)(1)(b)(ii), (iii), or (iv) of this rule is not required to appear in person at the place of production or inspection unless commanded to attend and give testimony at a trial, hearing, proceeding, or deposition.

(b) Subject to division (E)(2) of this rule, a person commanded to produce under division (A)(1)(b)(ii), (iii), or (iv) of this rule may serve upon the party or attorney designated in the subpoena written objections to production. The objections must be served within fourteen days after service of the subpoena or before the time specified for compliance if that time is less than fourteen days after service. If objection is made, the party serving the subpoena shall not be entitled to production except pursuant to an order of the court that issued the subpoena. If objection has been made, the party serving the subpoena, upon notice to the person commanded to produce, may move at any time for an order to compel the production. An order to compel production shall protect any person who is not a party or an officer of a party from significant expense resulting from the production commanded.

(3) On timely motion, the court from which the subpoena was issued shall quash or modify the subpoena, or order appearance or production only under specified conditions, if the subpoena does any of the following:

(a) Fails to allow reasonable time to comply;

(b) Requires disclosure of privileged or otherwise protected matter and no exception or waiver applies;

(c) Requires disclosure of a fact known or opinion held by an expert not retained or specially employed by any party in anticipation of litigation or preparation for trial if the fact or opinion does not describe specific events or occurrences in dispute and results from study by that expert that was not made at the request of any party;

(d) Subjects a person to undue burden.

(4) Before filing a motion pursuant to division (D)(3)(d) of this rule, a person resisting discovery under this rule shall attempt to resolve any claim of undue burden through discussions with the issuing attorney. A motion filed pursuant to division (D)(3)(d) of this rule shall be supported by an affidavit of the subpoenaed person or a certificate of that person's attorney of the efforts made to resolve any claim of undue burden.

(5) If a motion is made under division (D)(3)(c) or (D)(3)(d) of this rule, the court shall quash or modify the subpoena unless the party in whose behalf the subpoena is issued shows a substantial need for the testimony or material that cannot be otherwise met without undue hardship and assures that the person to whom the subpoena is addressed will be reasonably compensated.

(E) **Duties in responding to subpoena.**

(1) A person responding to a subpoena to produce documents shall, at the person's option, produce the documents as they are kept in the usual course of business or organized and labeled to correspond with the categories in the subpoena. A person producing documents pursuant to a subpoena for them shall permit their inspection and copying by all parties present at the time and place set in the subpoena for inspection and copying.

(2) When information subject to a subpoena is withheld on a claim that it is privileged or subject to protection as trial preparation materials, the claim shall be made expressly and shall be supported by a description of the nature of the documents, communications, or things not produced that is sufficient to enable the demanding party to contest the claim.

(F) **Sanctions.** Failure by any person without adequate excuse to obey a subpoena served upon that person may be a contempt of the court from which the subpoena issued. A subpoenaed person or that person's attorney who frivolously resists discovery under this rule may be required by the court to pay the reasonable expenses, including reasonable attorney's fees, of the party seeking the discovery. The court from which a subpoena was issued may impose upon a party or attorney in breach of the duty imposed by division (D)(1) of this rule an appropriate sanction, that may include, but is not limited to, lost earnings and reasonable attorney's fees.

(G) **Privileges.** Nothing in this rule shall be construed to authorize a party to obtain information protected by any privilege recognized by law or to authorize any person to disclose such information.

(H) **Time.** Nothing in this rule shall be construed to expand any other time limits imposed by rule or statute. All issues concerning subpoenas shall be resolved prior to the time otherwise set for hearing or trial.

History: Amended, eff 7-1-94.

NOTES TO DECISIONS

ANALYSIS

GAL fee

GAL fee

Trial court's award of a fee to a guardian ad litem who represented three minor children of parents who were involved in a custody dispute was error, as the husband was denied his opportunity to be heard pursuant to Ohio Const.

art. I, § 16 where he was not given an opportunity to challenge her fee request through a hearing or submission of opposition. Her fee rate was excessive under Ohio R. Juv. P. 17(D)(3) and 19(D)(1) where it was not based on the rates provided by the Juvenile Division of the Court of Common Pleas and she had not applied for extraordinary fees under Ohio R. Juv. P. 17(D)(5). In re J.C., — Ohio App. 3d —, 2006 Ohio 6446, — N.E. 2d —, 2006 Ohio App. LEXIS 6395 (Dec. 7, 2006).

RULE 18. Time

(A) **Time: computation.** In computing any period of time prescribed or allowed by these rules, by the local rules of any court, by order of court, or by any applicable statute, the date of the act or event from which the designated period of time begins to run shall not be included. The last day of the period so computed shall be included, unless it is a Saturday, a Sunday, or a legal holiday, in which event the period runs until the end of the next day that is not a Saturday, a Sunday or a legal holiday. Such extension of time includes, but is not limited to, probable cause, shelter care, and detention hearings.

Except in the case of probable cause, shelter care, and detention hearings when the period of time prescribed or allowed is less than seven days, intermediate Saturdays, Sundays, and legal holidays shall be excluded in computation.

(B) **Time: enlargement.** When an act is required or allowed to be performed at or within a specified time, the court for cause shown may at any time in its discretion (1) with or without motion or notice, order the period enlarged if application therefore is made before expiration of the period originally prescribed or of that period as extended by a previous order, or (2) upon motion permit the act to be done after expiration of the specified period if the failure to act on time was the result of excusable neglect or would result in injustice to a party, but the court may not extend the time for taking any action under Rule 7(F)(1), Rule 22(F), Rule 29(A) and Rule 29(F)(2)(b), except to the extent and under the conditions stated in them.

(C) **Time: unaffected by expiration of term.** The period of time provided for the doing of any act or the taking of any proceeding is not affected or limited by the expiration of a term of court. The expiration of a term of court in no way affects the power of a court to do any act in a juvenile proceeding.

(D) **Time: for motions; affidavits.** A written motion, other than one which may be heard ex parte, and notice of the hearing thereof, shall be served not later than seven days before the time specified for the hearing unless a different period is fixed by rule or order of the court. For cause shown such an order may be made on ex parte application. When a motion is supported by affidavit, the affidavit shall be served with the motion, and opposing affidavits may be served not less than one day before the hearing unless the court permits them to be served at a later time.

(E) **Time: additional time after service by mail** . Whenever a party has the right or is required to do an act within a prescribed period after the service of a notice or other paper upon the person and the notice or other paper is served upon the person by mail, three days shall be added to the prescribed period. This division does not apply to service of summons.

History: Amended, eff 7-1-94.

NOTES TO DECISIONS

ANALYSIS

Appeal

Appeal

As a father's objections to a magistrate's decision involving the date that child support was to commence were clearly untimely under Ohio R. Juv. P. 40(E)(3)(a) and Ohio R. Civ. P. 53(E)(3), warranting dismissal thereof by the juvenile court, and the father he did not seek to enlarge the time within which to file objections pursuant to Ohio R. Juv. P. 18(B) and Ohio R. Civ. P. 6(B), his time to appeal was not extended by the objections. His failure to appeal within 30 days of the juvenile court's adoption of the magistrate's decision did not preserve his merit issue for appellate review under Ohio R. App. P. 4(A). In re D.K.K., — Ohio App. 3d —, 2006 Ohio 5576, — N.E. 2d —, 2006 Ohio App. LEXIS 5590 (Oct. 20, 2006).

RULE 19. Motions

An application to the court for an order shall be by motion. A motion other than one made during trial or hearing shall be in writing unless the court permits it to be made orally. It shall state with particularity the grounds upon which it is made and shall set forth the relief or order sought. It shall be supported by a memorandum containing citations of authority and may be supported by an affidavit.

To expedite its business, unless otherwise provided by statute or rule, the court may make provision by rule or order for the submission and determination of motions without oral hearing upon brief written statements of reasons in support and opposition.

History: Amended, eff 7-1-94.

NOTES TO DECISIONS

ANALYSIS

Generally
Dismissal
GAL fee

Generally

Juvenile court's order granting legal custody in the absence of a motion violated the mandatory statutory and procedural requirements of RC § 2151.353 and Ohio R. Juv. P. 34, and also was in direct contravention of Ohio R. Juv. P. 19, mandating that requests for relief be made by motion, Ohio R. Juv. P. 22(E), requiring that prehearing motions be filed at least seven days prior to the proceeding, Ohio R. Juv. P. 20, establishing filing and service requirements for written motions and other papers, and Ohio R. Civ. P. 5(D), imposing a proof of service requirement. In re L.R.T., 165 Ohio App. 3d 77, 2006 Ohio 207, 844 N.E. 2d 914, 2006 Ohio App. LEXIS 173 (Jan. 23, 2006).

Dismissal

There was no abuse of discretion in a trial court's dismissal of a father's motion that sought a recalculation of his child support order, as he failed to meet the motion requirements of Ohio R. Juv. P. 19; the motion was in the form of a letter, it was not served upon the parties, and it did not include any legal memorandum for the trial court. Jones v. Jones, — Ohio App. 3d —, 2007 Ohio 5492, — N.E. 2d —, 2007 Ohio App. LEXIS 4827 (Oct. 15, 2007).

GAL fee

Trial court's award of a fee to a guardian ad litem who represented three minor children of parents who were involved in a custody dispute was error, as the husband was denied his opportunity to be heard pursuant to Ohio Const. art. I, § 16 where he was not given an opportunity to challenge her fee request through a hearing or submission of opposition. Her fee rate was excessive under Ohio R. Juv. P. 17(D)(3) and 19(D)(1) where it was not based on the rates provided by the Juvenile Division of the Court of Common Pleas and she had not applied for extraordinary fees under Ohio R. Juv. P. 17(D)(5). In re J.C., — Ohio App. 3d —, 2006 Ohio 6446, — N.E. 2d —, 2006 Ohio App. LEXIS 6395 (Dec. 7, 2006).

RULE 20. Service and filing of papers when required subsequent to filing of complaint.

(A) **Service: when required.** Written notices, requests for discovery, designation of record on appeal and written motions, other than those which are heard ex parte, and similar papers shall be served upon each of the parties.

(B) **Service: how made.** Whenever under these rules or by an order of the court service is required or permitted to be made upon a party represented by an attorney, the service shall be made upon the attorney unless service is ordered by the court upon the party. Service upon the attorney or upon the party shall be made in the manner provided in Civ. R. 5(B).

(C) **Filing.** All papers required to be served upon a party shall be filed simultaneously with or immediately after service. Papers filed with the court shall not be considered until proof of service is endorsed thereon or separately filed. The proof of service shall state the date and the manner of service and shall be signed and filed in the manner provided in Civil Rule 5(D).

History: Amended, eff 7-1-94.

NOTES TO DECISIONS

ANALYSIS

Generally

Generally

Juvenile court's order granting legal custody in the absence of a motion violated the mandatory statutory and procedural requirements of RC § 2151.353 and Ohio R. Juv. P. 34, and also was in direct contravention of Ohio R. Juv. P. 19, mandating that requests for relief be made by motion, Ohio R. Juv. P. 22(E), requiring that prehearing motions be filed at least seven days prior to the proceeding, Ohio R. Juv. P. 20, establishing filing and service requirements for written motions and other papers, and Ohio R. Civ. P. 5(D), imposing a proof of service requirement. In re L.R.T., 165 Ohio App. 3d 77, 2006 Ohio 207, 844 N.E.2d 914, 2006 Ohio App. LEXIS 173 (Jan. 23, 2006).

RULE 21. Preliminary conferences

At any time after the filing of a complaint, the court upon motion of any party or upon its own motion may order one or more conferences to consider such matters as will promote a fair and expeditious proceeding.

RULE 22. Pleadings and motions; defenses and objections

(A) **Pleadings and motions.** Pleadings in juvenile proceedings shall be the complaint and the answer, if any, filed by a party. A party may move to dismiss the complaint or for other appropriate relief.

(B) **Amendment of pleadings.** Any pleading may be amended at any time prior to the adjudicatory hearing. After the commencement of the adjudicatory hearing, a pleading may be amended upon agreement of the parties or, if the interests of justice require, upon order of the court. A complaint charging an act of delinquency may not be amended unless agreed by the parties, if the proposed amendment would change the name or identity of the specific violation of law so that it would be considered a change of the crime charged if committed by an adult. Where requested, a court order shall grant a party reasonable time in which to respond to an amendment.

(C) **Answer.** No answer shall be necessary. A party may file an answer to the complaint, which, if filed, shall contain specific and concise admissions or denials of each material allegation of the complaint.

(D) **Prehearing motions.** Any defense, objection or request which is capable of determination without hearing on the allegations of the complaint may be raised before the adjudicatory hearing by motion. The following must be heard before the adjudicatory hearing, though not necessarily on a separate date:

(1) Defenses or objections based on defects in the institution of the proceeding;

(2) Defenses or objections based on defects in the complaint (other than failure to show jurisdiction in the court or to charge an offense which objections shall be noticed by the court at any time during the pendency of the proceeding);

(3) Motions to suppress evidence on the ground that it was illegally obtained;

(4) Motions for discovery;

(5) Motions to determine whether the child is eligible to receive a sentence as a serious youthful offender.

(E) **Motion time.** Except for motions filed under division (D)(5) of this rule, all prehearing motions shall be filed by the earlier of:

(1) seven days prior to the hearing, or

(2) ten days after the appearance of counsel.

Rule 22(D)(5) motions shall be filed by the later of:

(1) Twenty days after the date of the child's initial appearance in juvenile court; or

(2) Twenty days after denial of a motion to transfer.

The filing of the Rule 22(D)(5) motion shall constitute notice of intent to pursue a serious youthful offender disposition.

The court in the interest of justice may extend the time for making prehearing motions.

The court for good cause shown may permit a motion to suppress evidence under division (D)(3) of this rule to be made at the time the evidence is offered.

(F) **State's right to appeal upon granting a**

motion to suppress. In delinquency proceedings the state may take an appeal as of right from the granting of a motion to suppress evidence if, in addition to filing a notice of appeal, the prosecuting attorney certifies that (1) the appeal is not taken for the purpose of delay and (2) the granting of the motion has rendered proof available to the state so weak in its entirety that any reasonable possibility of proving the complaint's allegations has been destroyed.

Such appeal shall not be allowed unless the notice of appeal and the certification by the prosecuting attorney are filed with the clerk of the juvenile court within seven days after the date of the entry of the judgment or order granting the motion. Any appeal which may be taken under this rule shall be diligently prosecuted.

A child in detention or shelter care may be released pending this appeal when the state files the notice of appeal and certification.

This appeal shall take precedence over all other appeals.

History: Amended, eff 7-1-77; 7-1-94; 7-1-01.

NOTES TO DECISIONS

ANALYSIS

Generally
Motion to dismiss
Motion to suppress

Generally
Juvenile court's order granting legal custody in the absence of a motion violated the mandatory statutory and procedural requirements of RC § 2151.353 and Ohio R. Juv. P. 34, and also was in direct contravention of Ohio R. Juv. P. 19, mandating that requests for relief be made by motion, Ohio R. Juv. P. 22(E), requiring that prehearing motions be filed at least seven days prior to the proceeding, Ohio R. Juv. P. 20, establishing filing and service requirements for written motions and other papers, and Ohio R. Civ. P. 5(D), imposing a proof of service requirement. In re L.R.T., 165 Ohio App. 3d 77, 2006 Ohio 207, 844 N.E. 2d 914, 2006 Ohio App. LEXIS 173 (Jan. 23, 2006).

Motion to dismiss
There was no error in refusing to dismiss the case because the father waived his right to an adjudication hearing and a dispositional hearing within the applicable statutory time periods, pursuant to RC § 2151.28, and failed to file his motion to dismiss in compliance with Ohio R. Juv. P. 22(E) since he did not file his motion to dismiss until the day of the hearing. In re A.P., — Ohio App. 3d —, 2006 Ohio 2717, — N.E. 2d —, 2006 Ohio App. LEXIS 2551 (May 30, 2006).

Motion to suppress
Trial court erred when it suppressed post-Miranda statements made by defendant and presumed a coercive effect with respect to defendant's post-Miranda statements arising from inculpatory statements that defendant made before Miranda warnings were given. Instead, the trial court should have considered various factors, including whether defendant's pre-warning statements overlapped with his post-warnings statements and the degree to which the officer's questions treated the second round of questioning as continuous with the first. In re J.C., — Ohio App. 3d —, 2007 Ohio 5763, — N.E. 2d —, 2007 Ohio App. LEXIS 5055 (Oct. 26, 2007).

RULE 23.   Continuance

Continuances shall be granted only when imperative to secure fair treatment for the parties.

NOTES TO DECISIONS

ANALYSIS

Denial
Discretion of court

Denial
Denial of a mother's Ohio R. Juv. P. 23 motion for a continuance of a permanent custody hearing did not deny the mother her rights to due process under the Fourteenth Amendment and Ohio Const. art. I, § 16 as, though the mother was purportedly ill, the mother was not hospitalized on date of hearing; the mother's counsel was notified that the mother was "ill" by another person, the motion was opposed, and the mother had failed to appear at other scheduled hearings and had been unable to be located for several months. In re Jordan H., — Ohio App. 3d —, 2007 Ohio 4091, — N.E. 2d —, 2007 Ohio App. LEXIS 3708 (Aug. 10, 2007).

Mother's prior failures to appear at court hearings and the fact that she was represented by counsel compelled the conclusion that the trial court did not err in denying the mother's motions for a continuance of a permanent custody hearing under Ohio R. Juv. P. 23. In re Distafano, — Ohio App. 3d —, 2006 Ohio 4430, — N.E. 2d —, 2006 Ohio App. LEXIS 4347 (Aug. 28, 2006).

Discretion of court
In a parental rights termination matter, a juvenile court did not abuse its discretion in denying a mother's motion for a continuance of a dispositional hearing involving her child due to her claimed injury from having been hit and had coffee poured on her by the child's father, as she was represented by counsel at the hearing, she knew the importance of her attendance, and she did not assert any ineffectiveness of counsel. In re Arms, — Ohio App. 3d —, 2007 Ohio 6717, — N.E. 2d —, 2007 Ohio App. LEXIS 6329 (Dec. 17, 2007).

There was no error in failing to grant a continuance as the trial court struck an appropriate balance between the mother's right to a fair hearing and its interest in timely disposing of the case. The trial court noted that the case, a petition for permanent custody, had been pending for two and a half years and that the mother bore some fault for her attorney not being as prepared as he would have liked. In re Brown, — Ohio App. 3d —, 2006 Ohio 2863, — N.E. 2d —, 2006 Ohio App. LEXIS 2719 (May 26, 2006).

RULE 24.   Discovery

(A) Request for discovery. Upon written request, each party of whom discovery is requested shall, to the extent not privileged, produce promptly for inspection, copying, or photographing the following information, documents, and material in that party's custody, control, or possession:

(1) The names and last known addresses of each witness to the occurrence that forms the basis of the charge or defense;

(2) Copies of any written statements made by any party or witness;

(3) Transcriptions, recordings, and summaries of any oral statements of any party or witness, except the work product of counsel;

(4) Any scientific or other reports that a party intends to introduce at the hearing or that pertain to physical evidence that a party intends to introduce;

(5) Photographs and any physical evidence which a party intends to introduce at the hearing;

(6) Except in delinquency and unruly child proceedings, other evidence favorable to the requesting party and relevant to the subject matter involved in the pending action. In delinquency and unruly child proceedings, the prosecuting attorney shall disclose to respondent's counsel all evidence, known or that may become known to the prosecuting attorney, favorable to the respondent and material either to guilt or punishment.

(B) **Order granting discovery: limitations; sanctions.** If a request for discovery is refused, application may be made to the court for a written order granting the discovery. Motions for discovery shall certify that a request for discovery has been made and refused. An order granting discovery may make such discovery reciprocal for all parties to the proceeding, including the party requesting discovery. Notwithstanding the provisions of subdivision (A), the court may deny, in whole or part, or otherwise limit or set conditions on the discovery authorized by such subdivision, upon its own motion, or upon a showing by a party upon whom a request for discovery is made that granting discovery may jeopardize the safety of a party or, witness, or confidential informant, result in the production of perjured testimony or evidence, endanger the existence of physical evidence, violate a privileged communication, or impede the criminal prosecution of a minor as an adult or of an adult charged with an offense arising from the same transaction or occurrence.

(C) **Failure to comply.** If at any time during the course of the proceedings it is brought to the attention of the court that a person has failed to comply with an order issued pursuant to this rule, the court may grant a continuance, prohibit the person from introducing in evidence the material not disclosed, or enter such other order as it deems just under the circumstances.

History: Amended, eff 7-1-94.

NOTES TO DECISIONS

ANALYSIS

Generally
Motion to intervene

Generally

Because a surviving cohabiting partner agreed to a discovery order allowing the trial court to determine which of a child's records to release in a custody case, she was not allowed to complain that it was contrary to law. Nothing indicated that the trial court erred in releasing the records, and the denial of the partner's request for release of additional records pursuant to Ohio R. Juv. P. 24 was proper. In re J.W., — Ohio App. 3d —, 2006 Ohio 3753, — N.E. 2d —, 2006 Ohio App. LEXIS 3719 (July 21, 2006).

Motion to intervene

Trial court did not err in denying the motion to intervene based on its finding that the grandparents had not stood in loco parentis because they had never been in a position where they were required to make medical, dental, or other parental decisions on behalf of the children; they did not have care and control of the children before the agency's intervention existed in the absence of supervision by the mother; and the children's services agency retained temporary custody of the children, including access to medical and educational records. In re I. S., — Ohio App. 3d —, 2007 Ohio 47, — N.E. 2d —, 2007 Ohio App. LEXIS 42 (Jan. 10, 2007).

RULE 25.   Depositions

(A) Depositions in the following matters shall be governed by the Rules of Civil Procedure:

(1) Those taken in parentage actions and original actions to determine custody or the allocation of parental rights and responsibilities to which the State of Ohio is not a party;

(2) Those taken in any post-dispositional matters to which neither the State of Ohio nor any public child protective services agency is a party.

(B) Depositions shall only be taken with leave of court in delinquency, unruly, juvenile traffic offender, abuse, neglect, and dependency actions and all other juvenile court proceedings not specified in division (A). Except as provided in division (A)(2), depositions taken under this division shall only be taken to preserve testimony when it appears probable that a prospective witness will be unable to attend or will be prevented from attending a hearing, and if it further appears that the testimony is material and that it is necessary to take the deposition in order to prevent a miscarriage of justice. Depositions taken under this division shall be taken upon such terms and conditions and in such manner as the court may fix.

History: Amended, eff 7-1-09.

NOTES TO DECISIONS

ANALYSIS

Right to counsel
Sufficient evidence
Waiver of counsel

Right to counsel

Ohio Supreme Court holds that in a juvenile delinquency case, although strict compliance with Ohio R. Juv. P. 29(D) is preferred, if the trial court substantially complies with Rule 29(D) in accepting an admission by a juvenile defendant, the plea will be deemed voluntary absent a showing of prejudice by defendant or a showing that the totality of the circumstances does not support a finding of a valid waiver; such holding protects a juvenile defendant's constitutional due process right to counsel under U.S. Const. amend. XIV and Ohio Const. art. I, § 10 and 16, and provides meaningful guidelines when taken with RC § 2151.352 for determining whether the due process right to counsel has been satisfied. In re C.S., 115 Ohio St. 3d 267, 2007 Ohio 4919, 874 N.E.2d 1177, 2007 Ohio LEXIS 2234 (2007).

Sufficient evidence

Sufficient evidence supported the delinquency finding for committing aggravated vehicular homicide because a rational trier of fact could have found that the juvenile was reckless. With a posted speed limit of 35 miles per hour, the 14-year-old juvenile chose to pass another car traveling in excess of 60 miles per hour on a dark two-lane road with oncoming traffic; the risk created by that conduct was obvious: a very inexperienced driver with no driver's license or formal training, driving at night, at a speed almost twice the posted speed limit, while passing a car in a no-passing zone, was likely to cause a serious accident. In re T.S., — Ohio App. 3d —, 2007 Ohio 5085, — N.E. 2d —, 2007 Ohio App. LEXIS 4507 (Sept. 27, 2007).

Waiver of counsel

Juvenile defendant's waiver of his right to counsel pursuant to RC § 2151.352 and Ohio R. Juv. P. 29(D) in his juvenile delinquency proceeding, although his mother was present, was not deemed to have been entered knowingly or intelligently, as the sole concern of both the mother and defendant seemed to be that his placement was with his brother, who was committed to a youth facility, and although the family probably had an understanding of the juvenile legal system due to prior interactions, there was no meaningful advice provided to defendant prior to his waiver of counsel; it did not appear that the mother was in a position to render any meaningful advice to defendant, as she had not reviewed the police report and they had not spoken with each other since his arrest. In re C.S., 115 Ohio St. 3d 267, 2007 Ohio 4919, 874 N.E.2d 1177, 2007 Ohio LEXIS 2234 (2007).

RULE 26. [Reserved]

RULE 27. Hearings: general

(A) **General Provisions.** Unless otherwise stated in this rule, the juvenile court may conduct its hearings in an informal manner and may adjourn its hearings from time to time.

The court may excuse the attendance of the child at the hearing in neglect, dependency, or abuse cases.

(1) Public access to hearings. In serious youthful offender proceedings, hearings shall be open to the public. In all other proceedings, the court may exclude the general public from any hearing, but may not exclude either of the following:

(a) Persons with a direct interest in the case;

(b) Persons who demonstrate, at a hearing, a countervailing right to be present.

(2) Separation of juvenile and adult cases. Cases involving children shall be heard separate and apart from the trial of cases against adults, except for cases involving chronic or habitual truancy.

(3) Jury trials. The court shall hear and determine all cases of children without a jury, except for the adjudication of a serious youthful offender complaint, indictment, or information in which trial by jury has not been waived.

(B) **Special provisions for abuse, neglect, and dependency proceedings.**

(1) In any proceeding involving abuse, neglect, or dependency at which the court removes a child from the child's home or continues the removal of a child from the child's home, or in a proceeding where the court orders detention, the court shall determine whether the person who filed the complaint in the case and removed the child from the child's home has custody of the child or will be given custody and has made reasonable efforts to do any of the following:

(a) Prevent the removal of the child from the child's home;

(b) Eliminate the continued removal of the child from the child's home;

(c) Make it possible for the child to return home.

(2) In a proceeding involving abuse, neglect, or dependency, the examination made by the court to determine whether a child is a competent witness shall comply with all of the following:

(a) Occur in an area other than a courtroom or hearing room;

(b) Be conducted in the presence of only those individuals considered necessary by the court for the conduct of the examination or the well being of the child;

(c) Be recorded in accordance with Juv. R. 37 or Juv. R. 40. The court may allow the prosecutor, guardian ad litem, or attorney for any party to submit questions for use by the court in determining whether the child is a competent witness.

(3) In a proceeding where a child is alleged to be an abused child, the court may order that the testimony of the child be taken by deposition in the presence of a judge or a magistrate. On motion of the prosecuting attorney, guardian ad litem, or a party, or in its own discretion, the court may order that the deposition be videotaped. All or part of the deposition is admissible in evidence where all of the following apply:

(a) It is filed with the clerk;

(b) Counsel for all parties had an opportunity and similar motive at the time of the taking of the deposition to develop the testimony by direct, cross, or redirect examination;

(c) The judge or magistrate determines there is reasonable cause to believe that if the child were to testify in person at the hearing, the child would experience emotional trauma as a result of the child's participation at the hearing.

History: Amended, eff 7-1-76; 7-1-94; 7-1-96; 7-1-01.

NOTES TO DECISIONS

ANALYSIS

Access of media, public
Presence of juvenile
Testimony by child

Access of media, public

When appellant, a juvenile, moved a trial court to exclude the press, close the courtroom, order non-disclosure of information from the police to the press, and non-disclosure of personal information of the juvenile parties to appellant's trial for gross sexual imposition and unlawful restraint, it was not an abuse of discretion, under Ohio R. Juv. P. 27 and RC § 2151.35, for the trial court to deny the motion because it properly considered potential harm to appellant, the benefits of public access, and ordered a reasonable alternative when it ordered that the media could not disclose the identities of appellant or his parents and barred the use of video or photographs of appellant. In re K.J.B., — Ohio App. 3d —, 2007 Ohio 1677, — N.E. 2d —, 2007 Ohio App. LEXIS 1533 (Apr. 9, 2007).

Presence of juvenile

When a magistrate took the disposition of a juvenile delinquency case under advisement, after conducting adjudicatory and dispositional hearings, and then issued a sentencing decision without holding a hearing, Ohio R. Juv. P. 27 did not require that the juvenile who was the subject of the delinquency petition be physically present when the dispositional order was entered as the Rule only required that persons with a direct interest in a case could not be excluded from any hearing. In re Gibson, — Ohio App. 3d —, 2006 Ohio 5145, — N.E. 2d —, 2006 Ohio App. LEXIS 5109 (Oct. 2, 2006).

Testimony by child

Record supported the trial court's decision to quash the mother's subpoena of her daughter to testify at the permanent custody hearing because the trial court conducted in camera interviews of the children at mother's request and informed the mother of their statements; the mother's desire to make the daughter testify after the in camera interview would defeat its purpose. Additionally, the daughter's therapist, attorney, and guardian ad litem all stated that she was frightened to testify in front of everyone, did not wish to testify, and would be traumatized and stressed if made to do so. In re J.P., — Ohio App. 3d —, 2007 Ohio 1903, — N.E. 2d —, 2007 Ohio App. LEXIS 1755 (Apr. 23, 2007).

RULE 28. [Reserved]

RULE 29. Adjudicatory hearing

(A) **Scheduling the hearing.** The date for the adjudicatory hearing shall be set when the complaint is filed or as soon thereafter as is practicable. If the child is the subject of a complaint alleging a violation of a section of the Revised Code that may be violated by an adult and that does not request a serious youthful offender sentence, and if the child is in detention or shelter care, the hearing shall be held not later than fifteen days after the filing of the complaint. Upon a showing of good cause, the adjudicatory hearing may be continued and detention or shelter care extended.

The prosecuting attorney's filing of either a notice of intent to pursue or a statement of an interest in pursuing a serious youthful offender sentence shall constitute good cause for continuing the adjudicatory hearing date and extending detention or shelter care.

The hearing of a removal action shall be scheduled in accordance with Juv. R. 39(B).

If the complaint alleges abuse, neglect, or dependency, the hearing shall be held no later than thirty days after the complaint is filed. For good cause shown, the adjudicatory hearing may extend beyond thirty days either for an additional ten days to allow any party to obtain counsel or for a reasonable time beyond thirty days to obtain service on all parties or complete any necessary evaluations. However, the adjudicatory hearing shall be held no later than sixty days after the complaint is filed.

The failure of the court to hold an adjudicatory hearing within any time period set forth in this rule does not affect the ability of the court to issue any order otherwise provided for in statute or rule and does not provide any basis for contesting the jurisdiction of the court or the validity of any order of the court.

(B) **Advisement and findings at the commencement of the hearing.** At the beginning of the hearing, the court shall do all of the following:

(1) Ascertain whether notice requirements have been complied with and, if not, whether the affected parties waive compliance;

(2) Inform the parties of the substance of the complaint, the purpose of the hearing, and possible consequences of the hearing, including the possibility that the cause may be transferred to the appropriate

adult court under Juv. R. 30 where the complaint alleges that a child fourteen years of age or over is delinquent by conduct that would constitute a felony if committed by an adult;

(3) Inform unrepresented parties of their right to counsel and determine if those parties are waiving their right to counsel;

(4) Appoint counsel for any unrepresented party under Juv. R. 4(A) who does not waive the right to counsel;

(5) Inform any unrepresented party who waives the right to counsel of the right: to obtain counsel at any stage of the proceedings, to remain silent, to offer evidence, to cross-examine witnesses, and, upon request, to have a record of all proceedings made, at public expense if indigent.

(C) **Entry of admission or denial.** The court shall request each party against whom allegations are being made in the complaint to admit or deny the allegations. A failure or refusal to admit the allegations shall be deemed a denial, except in cases where the court consents to entry of a plea of no contest.

(D) **Initial procedure upon entry of an admission.** The court may refuse to accept an admission and shall not accept an admission without addressing the party personally and determining both of the following:

(1) The party is making the admission voluntarily with understanding of the nature of the allegations and the consequences of the admission;

(2) The party understands that by entering an admission the party is waiving the right to challenge the witnesses and evidence against the party, to remain silent, and to introduce evidence at the adjudicatory hearing.

The court may hear testimony, review documents, or make further inquiry, as it considers appropriate, or it may proceed directly to the action required by division (F) of this rule.

(E) **Initial procedure upon entry of a denial.** If a party denies the allegations, the court shall:

(1) Direct the prosecuting attorney or another attorney-at-law to assist the court by presenting evidence in support of the allegations of a complaint;

(2) Order the separation of witnesses, upon request of any party;

(3) Take all testimony under oath or affirmation in either question-answer or narrative form; and

(4) Determine the issues by proof beyond a reasonable doubt in juvenile traffic offense, delinquency, and unruly proceedings; by clear and convincing evidence in dependency, neglect, and abuse cases, and in a removal action; and by a preponderance of the evidence in all other cases.

(F) **Procedure upon determination of the issues.** Upon the determination of the issues, the court shall do one of the following:

(1) If the allegations of the complaint, indictment, or information were not proven, dismiss the complaint;

(2) If the allegations of the complaint, indictment, or information are admitted or proven, do any one of the following, unless precluded by statute:

(a) Enter an adjudication and proceed forthwith to disposition;

(b) Enter an adjudication and continue the matter for disposition for not more than six months and may make appropriate temporary orders;

(c) Postpone entry of adjudication for not more than six months;

(d) Dismiss the complaint if dismissal is in the best interest of the child and the community.

(3) Upon request make written findings of fact and conclusions of law pursuant to Civ. R. 52.

(4) Ascertain whether the child should remain or be placed in shelter care until the dispositional hearing in an abuse, neglect, or dependency proceeding. In making a shelter care determination, the court shall make written finding of facts with respect to reasonable efforts in accordance with the provisions in Juv. R. 27(B)(1) and to relative placement in accordance with Juv. R. 7(F)(3).

History: Amended, eff 7-1-76; 7-1-94; 7-1-98; 7-1-01; 7-1-04.

NOTES TO DECISIONS

Analysis

Acceptance of admissions
Admission of dependency
Admissions
Appeal
Clear and convincing evidence
Compliance
Delinquency proceedings generally
Eyewitness identification
Hearings
Jurisdiction
Probation revocation
Right to counsel
Termination of parental rights
Time limitations
Waiver of counsel
Waiver of rights

Acceptance of admissions

In a juvenile delinquency case, the preferred practice is strict compliance with JuvR 29(D). If the trial court substantially complies with JuvR 29(D) in accepting an admission by a juvenile, the plea will be deemed voluntary absent a showing of prejudice by the juvenile or a showing that the totality of the circumstances does not support a finding of a valid waiver: In re C.S., 115 Ohio St. 3d 267, 2007 Ohio 4919, 874 N.E.2d 1177, 2007 Ohio LEXIS 2234 (2007).

Juvenile court's failure to personally address a juvenile in order to determine whether he understood the nature of charges against him of delinquency arising from gross sexual imposition against his younger siblings was not substantial compliance with Ohio R. Juv. P. 29(D), such that the denial of the juvenile's motion to set aside his admissions thereto required reversal. The juvenile's affirmative response to the juvenile court's query as to whether he understood the nature of the charges against him was alone insufficient to constitute substantial compliance. In re J. T. C., — Ohio App. 3d —, 2007 Ohio 436, — N.E. 2d —, 2007 Ohio App. LEXIS 375 (Feb. 2, 2007).

Appellant, who failed to file objections to a magistrate's decision as required by Ohio R. Juv. P. 40(D)(3)(b)(iv), failed to demonstrate that the magistrate committed plain error in accepting appellant's admission in a juvenile delinquency proceeding without first informing appellant that he had the right to subpoena witnesses; instead, the magistrate substan-

tially complied with the requirements of Ohio R. Juv. P. 29(D) by informing appellant of the consequences of his plea and advising him that he was giving up the opportunity to question witnesses, to remain silent, and to call his own witnesses. Ohio R. Juv. P. 29(D) does not require a magistrate to inform an appellant of his right to subpoena witnesses. In re T.K.W., — Ohio App. 3d —, 2007 Ohio 1205, — N.E. 2d —, 2007 Ohio App. LEXIS 1026 (Mar. 13, 2007).

In a permanent custody proceeding, a mother's claim that the trial court did not comply with Ohio R. Juv. P. 29(D) when the court accepted the mother's admission to a dependency complaint could not be considered because the trial court's order adjudicating the mother's child a dependent child, based, in part, on the mother's admission, became final upon the entry of a dispositional order, but the mother did not appeal the order of adjudication within 30 days, as required by Ohio R. App. P. 4. In re C.G., — Ohio App. 3d —, 2007 Ohio 4361, — N.E. 2d —, 2007 Ohio App. LEXIS 3913 (Aug. 27, 2007).

In a permanent custody proceeding, a trial court did not comply with Ohio R. Juv. P. 29(D) when the court accepted a mother's admission to a dependency complaint because the trial court did not engage in any colloquy with the mother to determine if the mother understood the proceedings and the consequences of the mother's admission, as the court merely asked the mother if the mother's admission to the complaint was the mother's plea, so the trial court did not even substantially comply with Rule 29(D). In re C.G., — Ohio App. 3d —, 2007 Ohio 4361, — N.E. 2d —, 2007 Ohio App. LEXIS 3913 (Aug. 27, 2007).

When a mother was found to have consented to an agreement (1) granting the mother's child's father legal custody of the child, (2) granting the child's foster parents visitation with the child, and (3) continuing the mother's prior supervised visitation with the child, the magistrate who approved the agreement was not required to engage in an Ohio R. Juv. P. 29 colloquy with the mother as to the mother's consent to the agreement because neither Ohio R. Juv. P. 34 nor RC § 2151.353 required such a colloquy as to a disposition. In re S.S., — Ohio App. 3d —, 2007 Ohio 6747, — N.E. 2d —, 2007 Ohio App. LEXIS 5908 (Dec. 17, 2007).

Trial court substantially complied with the requirements of Ohio R. Juv. P. 29(D) when it accepted appellant's admission and waiver of counsel because both were made voluntarily, knowingly, and intelligently, as (1) the elements and category of each charge filed against appellant were explained to him, (2) he was informed of the possible consequences of being found delinquent or admitting to the charges, (3) he was informed that he had the right to a lawyer and that, if he could not afford a lawyer, one would be appointed for him if he qualified, (4) he was told he had the right to remain silent and the right to go to trial to present evidence in his defense, (5) he was told he had the right to cross-examine witnesses and that the State had the burden of proving beyond a reasonable doubt that he committed the offenses, (6) he said there had been no promises or threats made to coerce him into pleading guilty, (7) he was told that by entering an admission the court would proceed directly to decide what punishment he should receive, (8) he said he understood what the Department of Youth Services was and that by entering an admission he could be committed there for at least six months and as long as until his 21st birthday, (9) he said he understood all the rights he was advised of, (10) he was days short of his 14th birthday when he entered the admissions, (11) he had a previous record in juvenile court, (12) his mother was present when his rights were explained, and she concurred in his decision to waive counsel, (13) she and appellant were both informed of the right to object to the magistrate's decision, under Ohio R. Juv. P. 40, and both acknowledged receipt of the magistrate's decision and waived the right to file written objections to that decision, and (14) both appellant and his mother signed a written waiver of rights form before the plea. In re Spears, — Ohio App. 3d —, 2006 Ohio 1920, — N.E. 2d —, 2006 Ohio App. LEXIS 1761 (Apr. 17, 2006).

Juvenile did not make his admission to charges knowingly, voluntarily, and intelligently pursuant to Ohio R. Juv. P. 29(D) because the juvenile court failed to inform him, on the record, why he was required to enter new admissions and pleas under Ohio R. Crim. P. 11, based on the fact that he had been previously misinformed as to the consequences for the entry of his pleas and admissions pursuant to RC § 2152.13(D)(2). There was no indication given to the juvenile upon his second set of admissions and pleas as to why the first set were considered null and void. In re Smith, — Ohio App. 3d —, 2006 Ohio 2788, — N.E.2d —, 2006 Ohio App. LEXIS 2625 (June 5, 2006).

Defendant was improperly adjudicated a juvenile delinquent based on an admission for, inter alia, fleeing and eluding as the trial court conducted an insufficient allocution under Ohio R. Juv. P. 29(D)(2). The trial court failed to explain that defendant would be waiving his rights to challenge the witnesses and evidence against him, to remain silent, and to introduce evidence at the adjudicatory hearing. In re Higgins, — Ohio App. 3d —, 2006 Ohio 6826, — N.E. 2d —, 2006 Ohio App. LEXIS 6735 (Dec. 22, 2006).

Juvenile court properly conducted an amenability hearing to determine whether defendant, a juvenile, was amenable to the juvenile court system or whether he should be bound over to the general trial court for criminal charges, and the fact that defendant stipulated to the admission of his psychological evlauation and his family records did not constitute admissions or error by the juvenile court, pursuant to Ohio R. Juv. P. 29(D) and 30. State v. Goodwin, 166 Ohio App. 3d 709, 2006 Ohio 2311, 852 N.E. 2d 1282, 2006 Ohio App. LEXIS 2176 (May 11, 2006).

Juvenile admission under Ohio R. Juv. P. 29 was analogous to a guilty plea and a juvenile offender who entered an admission to an offense waived the right to challenge evidentiary issues on appeal, including a motion to suppress; defendant waived his right to contest the denial of his motion to suppress when he entered his plea of true to a drug possession charge. In re S.L., — Ohio App. 3d —, 2006 Ohio 1895, — N.E. 2d —, 2006 Ohio App. LEXIS 1748 (Apr. 17, 2006).

Admission of dependency

When parents entered dependency admissions as to two children, and then, years later, after a third child was born and an agency sought permanent custody of all three children, the parents filed pleas of deny, this effectively withdrew the prior admissions, where the trial court did not adjudicate the children to be dependent when the prior admissions were entered, so, once the pleas of deny were entered, the trial court could not adjudicate the children to be dependent and/or abused based on the withdrawn pleas, and, as it did not otherwise adjudicate the children, its subsequent grant of their permanent custody to an agency without an adjudication was contrary to RC ch. 2151 and Ohio R. Juv. P. 29(F) and 34. In re J.H., — Ohio App. 3d —, 2006 Ohio 3237, — N.E. 2d —, 2006 Ohio App. LEXIS 3151 (June 26, 2006).

Admissions

Defendant juvenile's admission in a delinquency proceeding was not knowingly, intelligently, and voluntarily entered where the juvenile court failed to substantially comply with the requirements of Ohio R. Juv. P. 29(D), in that it failed to engage in any meaningful exchange with defendant to ascertain whether he understood the nature of the charge against him or the rights he was waiving by admitting the charge. In re M.T., — Ohio App. 3d —, 2007 Ohio 2446, — N.E. 2d —, 2007 Ohio App. LEXIS 2258 (May 21, 2007).

Although a magistrate's explanation of the possible penalties that defendant, a juvenile, faced if he was found delinquent was slightly inaccurate, as the magistrate had indicated a possible penalty that was in fact longer than what was actually imposed, and defendant did not show that he would not have entered an admission to the charges if he had been informed accurately, no prejudice was shown; substantial compliance with Ohio R. Juv. P. 29(D) was accordingly found in the circumstances. In re L.M., — Ohio App. 3d —, 2007 Ohio 4070, — N.E. 2d —, 2007 Ohio App. LEXIS 3693 (Aug. 9, 2007).

Appeal

JuvR 29(F) requires a juvenile court to determine all of the issues and adjudicate each and every count in a multiple count complaint that is prosecuted against an accused juvenile and, where a juvenile is adjudicated delinquent on more than one count, to render disposition on each count. An entry that fails to adjudicate all of the charges is interlocutory and not a final appealable order. In re Huckleby, — Ohio App. 3d —, 2007 Ohio 6149, — N.E. 2d —, 2007 Ohio App. LEXIS 5393 (Nov. 19, 2007).

Clear and convincing evidence

Mother's contention that a trial court did not apply a clear and convincing standard of proof in the adjudication portion of a dependency proceeding, as required by RC § 2151.04(C) and Ohio R. Juv. P. 29(E)(4)was rejected. The trial court's criticism of the caseworker's handling of the case and its emphasis of the conflicting loyalties of the witnesses were compatible with application of the clear and convincing standard of proof and typified the role of the trier of fact in a contested matter. In re C.F.S., — Ohio App. 3d —, 2007 Ohio 4105, — N.E. 2d —, 2007 Ohio App. LEXIS 3730 (Aug. 13, 2007).

Trial court's finding that the children were neglected and dependent was supported by clear and convincing evidence because the girls resided in a home that was unfit for human habitation with a registered sex offender whose victim was the same age as the children. There was ample testimony that the children lacked adequate parental care and the father testified regarding the special care that one of his daughter's required as a result of her significant health problems. In re J. H., — Ohio App. 3d —, 2007 Ohio 4653, — N.E. 2d —, 2007 Ohio App. LEXIS 4192 (Sept. 12, 2007).

Weight of the evidence supported the trial court's determination that a father's minor child was an abused and dependent child pursuant to RC §§ 2151.031 and 2151.04(C), as she was a credible witness who testified that her father beat her with an extension cord and that he touched her "private parts"; although there was no physical evidence, such would have only strengthened the child's testimony but the lack of it did not require a conclusion that she was not credible where there was clear and convincing evidence to support the findings pursuant to Ohio R. Juv. P. 29(E)(4). In re A.R., — Ohio App. 3d —, 2006 Ohio 1548, — N.E. 2d —, 2006 Ohio App. LEXIS 1444 (Mar. 31, 2006).

There was sufficient evidence to allow the trial court to find by clear and convincing evidence that the elements of RC § 2151.04(D)(1) were met for a finding that the child was dependent. The mother had substance abuse problems, mental problems, and used sex offenders as caregivers and the child's three siblings had been adjudicated abused, neglected, and dependent. In re C.M., — Ohio App. 3d —, 2006 Ohio 1908, — N.E. 2d —, 2006 Ohio App. LEXIS 1752 (Apr. 19, 2006).

Clear and convincing evidence pursuant to RC § 2151.35 and Ohio R. Juv. P. 29(E)(4) supported a trial court's determination that a child was dependent pursuant to RC § 2151.04(C), as she was diagnosed with mental health issues, she had homicidal and suicidal tendencies, and had run away from home to avoid auditory hallucinations telling her to kill herself and her family. The parents' conduct adversely impacted the child and the severity of her condition, and it created a risk to her safety. In re E. R., — Ohio App. 3d —, 2006 Ohio 4816, — N.E. 2d —, 2006 Ohio App. LEXIS 4745 (Sept. 18, 2006).

Clear and convincing evidence, as required by RC § 2151.35(A)(1) and Ohio R. Juv. P. 29(E)(4), supported a trial court's decision that a child was dependent, under RC § 2151.04(B) and (C) because (1) the child's mother admitted that her mental state prevented her from adequately caring for the child, (2) she testified that the child's father was inconsistent in being willing to help her care for the child, (3) she testified the father's epilepsy caused him to "zone out" at times, (4) she accused the father of physically abusing the child but did not seek proper treatment for the child for weeks, (5) her claims of physical abuse, if true, showed the child suffered actual harm in the home and was not given appropriate treatment, and, if false, showed the mother's inability to make appropriate decisions about the child's care. In re S.J.J., — Ohio App. 3d —, 2006 Ohio 6354, — N.E. 2d —, 2006 Ohio App. LEXIS 6318 (Dec. 4, 2006).

Compliance

Juvenile court committed reversible error where it failed to follow the procedures under Ohio R. Juv. P. 29, which were mandatory, in defendant juvenile's delinquency adjudication and disposition proceeding. Although the record was not clear as to whether there was compliance with Rule 29(B)(1), the court failed to explain what the charges against defendant meant, what the possible consequences of her admissions were, and that she faced a period of mandatory confinement on one particular charge. The juvenile court provided confusing and inconsistent information about the minimum and maximum amount of time that defendant could have been held in juvenile detention, as she could only have been held until she reached the age of 21 pursuant to RC §§ 2152.02(C)(6) and 2152.16. In re Whatley, — Ohio App. 3d —, 2007 Ohio 3039, — N.E. 2d —, 2007 Ohio App. LEXIS 2877 (June 12, 2007).

Delinquency proceedings generally

Juvenile court's determination that defendant, a juvenile, was a delinquent pursuant to RC § 2151.35(A) and Ohio R. Juv. P. 29(E)(4) for committing a robbery, in violation of RC § 2911.02(A)(2), was not against the manifest weight of the evidence, as the identification of defendant as the perpetrator was supported by testimony from the victim which was deemed reliable, and there was sufficient evidence that money was taken from the victim's pocket during the criminal incident. In re Lower, — Ohio App. 3d —, 2007 Ohio 1735, — N.E. 2d —, 2007 Ohio App. LEXIS 1581 (Apr. 5, 2007).

In a delinquency proceeding, a trial judge had to find, based on the evidence produced at an adjudicatory hearing, whether the State proved delinquency beyond a reasonable doubt, under RC § 2151.35(A) and Ohio R. Juv. P. 29(E), so it was error for him to consider, in a rape trial, comments made by his wife about feminine hygiene. In re K.B., — Ohio App. 3d —, 2007 Ohio 1647, — N.E. 2d —, 2007 Ohio App. LEXIS 1501 (Apr. 9, 2007).

Although a juvenile failed to object to a magistrate's determination in his delinquency matter, as required by Ohio R. Juv. P. 40(D)(3)(b)(i), the exception to waiver under Rule 40(D)(4) applied, as the magistrate committed prejudicial, plain error under Ohio R. Crim. P. 52 when she failed to personally address the juvenile to ascertain that he voluntarily, knowingly, and intelligently waived his rights as required by Ohio R. Juv. P. 29(D). The magistrate's reliance on counsel's statement that he had explained the waiver of rights to the juvenile was improper, as was reliance on the juvenile's written waiver form, such that there was no substantial compliance with Rule 29(D). In re Tabler, — Ohio App. 3d —, 2007 Ohio 411, — N.E. 2d —, 2007 Ohio App. LEXIS 366 (Jan. 29, 2007).

Eyewitness identification

There was no plain error under Ohio R. Crim. P. 52(B), based on defendant's failure to object at trial pursuant to Ohio R. Evid. 103(A)(1), in a juvenile court's admission of a victim's identification of defendant, a juvenile, as the perpetrator of a criminal offense, as the victim indicated that he knew defendant by his face although he did not immediately know his name and the victim had an adequate amount of time to observe defendant during commission of the crime. Although the one man "show-up" identification procedure at the police station was unduly suggestive pursuant to U.S. Const. amend. V, Ohio Const. art. I, §§ 10 and 16, and Ohio R. Juv. P. 29(E)(4), it did not present a very substantial likelihood of irreparable misidentification. In re Lower, — Ohio App. 3d —, 2007 Ohio 1735, — N.E. 2d —, 2007 Ohio App. LEXIS 1581 (Apr. 5, 2007).

Hearings

When an agency filed a complaint which both alleged that a child was dependent and sought permanent custody of the child, Ohio R. Juv. P. 29 and 34 required the trial court to bifurcate proceedings as to dependency from dispositional proceedings as to permanent custody, so the trial court committed reversible error because it held one evidentiary hearing on both issues, with no clear demarcation between its considerations of each issue. In re J.H., — Ohio App. 3d —, 2006 Ohio 3237, — N.E. 2d —, 2006 Ohio App. LEXIS 3151 (June 26, 2006).

Jurisdiction

Permanent custody disposition was not void for lack of jurisdiction because the trial court complied with RC § 2151.35, Ohio R. Juv. P. 29, and Ohio R. Juv. P. 34. The agency filed a motion seeking permanent custody of two of the children as the initial disposition in an abuse, neglect, and dependency complaint, and permanent custody of the third child as a modification of a prior disposition. After the adjudication phase, the trial court found the first two children to be dependent and it then held the dispositional phase as to all three children. In re Angler, — Ohio App. 3d —, 2007 Ohio 3246, — N.E. 2d —, 2007 Ohio App. LEXIS 2986 (June 15, 2007).

Probation revocation

When, at a probation revocation hearing, appellant was informed that he waived the right to cross-examination and his right to appeal if he admitted the charge against him, but the trial court did not mention that he waived the right to present evidence and call witnesses and the right to remain silent, Ohio R. Juv. R. 29(D) was applied, and it was found that appellant did not receive the required advisement. In re Lohr, — Ohio App. 3d —, 2007 Ohio 1130, — N.E. 2d —, 2007 Ohio App. LEXIS 1046 (Mar. 7, 2007).

Right to counsel

Trial court erred in failing to determine whether appellant child knowingly and voluntarily waived his right to an attorney. The trial court should have explained the elements and seriousness of the charge against him and should have determined that appellant child was not being coerced or pressured into waiving his right to counsel, addressed his parents to ensure there was no conflict of interest and that the parents also understood the proceedings. In re Mills, — Ohio App. 3d —, 2007 Ohio 924, — N.E. 2d —, 2007 Ohio App. LEXIS 882 (Mar. 5, 2007).

Juvenile court violated defendant juvenile's right to counsel in his delinquency proceeding pursuant to U.S. Const. amends. V, VI, and XIV, Ohio Const. art. I, § 16, RC § 2151.352, and Ohio R. Juv. P. 4 and 29 where a valid waiver of counsel was not obtained during the adjudicatory and disposition hearings and counsel was not appointed. Although defendant and his adoptive mother signed a standard form regarding his rights, the form was not accurately filled out and the court failed to review it to ascertain that defendant fully understood the rights therein. In re M.T., — Ohio App. 3d —, 2007 Ohio 2446, — N.E. 2d —, 2007 Ohio App. LEXIS 2258 (May 21, 2007).

Where a juvenile court magistrate obtained defendant juvenile's waiver of his right to counsel in a delinquency matter, wherein he was charged with truancy, and the magistrate thereafter informed the juvenile of the nature of the charges and the possible penalties, there was no compliance with Ohio R. Juv. P. 29(D), such that the waiver by the juvenile of his right to counsel was not deemed knowing and intelligent. Pursuant to RC § 2151.352, Ohio R. Juv. P. 4, 29, and 35, as well as U.S. Const. amends. V, VI, and XIV and Ohio Const. art. I, § 10 and 16, the waiver was insufficient to allow defendant to have appeared unrepresented at the adjudicatory and dispositional phases of the delinquency proceeding. In re C.K., — Ohio App. 3d —, 2007 Ohio 3234, — N.E. 2d —, 2007 Ohio App. LEXIS 2974 (June 21, 2007).

Trial court's colloquy with a juvenile was insufficient under JuvR 29 to determine whether he voluntarily and intelligently waived his right to counsel because he was not specifically informed that he could obtain counsel during any stage of the parole revocation proceeding and because the court did not consider the factors under the totality of the circumstances test, such as defendant's age, intelligence, and education. In re E. H., — Ohio App. 3d —, 2007 Ohio 6263, — N.E. 2d —, 2007 Ohio App. LEXIS 5525 (Nov. 21, 2007).

When, at the arraignment of appellant, a juvenile, he responded affirmatively to a question asking if he wanted counsel, and the issue was not further discussed throughout his proceedings before the trial court, his constitutional right to counsel, also provided in RC § 2151.352 and Ohio R. Juv. P. 29(B)(3), was violated, as it could not be inferred from the record that appellant, at any time, knowingly and intelligently waived his right to counsel. In re R.B., — Ohio App. 3d —, 2006 Ohio 264, — N.E. 2d —, 2006 Ohio App. LEXIS 212 (Jan. 13, 2006).

Based on a review of the record as a whole, and in consideration of the affirmations of the minor and her mother that they wished to proceed without counsel on her delinquency charge for drug possession, the requirements of Ohio R. Juv. P. 29(B) were met and the minor's waiver of counsel was voluntarily, knowingly and understandingly given. The trial court explained to the minor her right to counsel, the nature, elements, and category of the charge, her right to a trial, the possible commitment, her right to remain silent, her right to present evidence in her defense and her right to cross-examine witnesses and, as each right was explained, the minor answered that she understood the right and then the minor and her mother agreed to proceed without counsel. In re Loos, — Ohio App. 3d —, 2006 Ohio 3932, — N.E. 2d —, 2006 Ohio App. LEXIS 3891 (July 31, 2006).

Record did not support a conclusion that defendant, a juvenile, waived his right to legal counsel, pursuant to RC § 2151.352, at either the adjudicatory hearing or the sexual offender classification hearing because defendant was never afforded the opportunity to request the assistance of legal counsel in connection with the hearing at which his admission was tendered and accepted, and he never indicated that he was waiving that right and, at the sexual classification hearing, the trial court elicited a waiver of counsel from defendant's mother, but never ascertained whether defendant, himself, was willing to waive his right to legal counsel. In re C.A.C., — Ohio App. 3d —, 2006 Ohio 4003, — N.E. 2d —, 2006 Ohio App. LEXIS 3934 (Aug. 4, 2006).

Although the trial court substantially complied with Ohio R. Juv. P. 29(D) when it accepted defendant juvenile's waiver of counsel during the adjudication hearing, the trial court failed to reiterate defendant's right to counsel during disposition or allow him either to invoke or to waive his right to counsel at

that stage as required by Ohio R. Juv. P. 34. In re S. J., — Ohio App. 3d —, 2006 Ohio 4467, — N.E. 2d —, 2006 Ohio App. LEXIS 4395 (Aug. 30, 2006).

As a magistrate substantially complied with the requirements of Ohio R. Juv. P. 29(B)(1) and (4), although he erroneously notified the juvenile in a probation revocation proceeding that he had a right to be represented by a lawyer if he wished and if his family could not afford a lawyer, such was not plain error under Ohio R. Crim. P. 52(B), as the magistrate carefully outlined the rights and responsibilities of the juvenile, and he made sure he understood the rights and the implications of his waiver; as the juvenile's waiver of his right to counsel was deemed knowing, voluntary, and intelligent, there was no violation of his right to counsel pursuant to RC § 2151.352 and Ohio R. Juv. P. 4. In re J-M, — Ohio App. 3d —, — N.E. 2d —, 2006 Ohio App. LEXIS 6131 (Nov. 22, 2006).

Termination of parental rights

Order terminating a parent's parental rights was reversed where the court did not substantially comply with JuvR 29(D) in accepting the parent's admissions: In re H.F., 176 Ohio App. 3d 106, 2008 Ohio 1627, 890 N.E.2d 341, 2008 Ohio App. LEXIS 1402 (2008).

Time limitations

Because the mother moved to dismiss the dependency complaint due to untimeliness, but never petitioned for an extraordinary writ, any failure by the trial court to complete the dispositional hearing within 90 days was waived. In re Matsko, — Ohio App. 3d —, 2007 Ohio 2060, — N.E. 2d —, 2007 Ohio App. LEXIS 1919 (Apr. 27, 2007).

Waiver of counsel

Trial court did not comply with Ohio R. Juv. P. 29(B)(5) for a valid waiver of counsel because it failed to inform the 12-year-old juvenile of the nature of the charges against him and the substance of the complaints, the possible dispositions which could be imposed, his right to remain silent, his right to obtain counsel at any stage of the proceedings, and his right to cross-examine witnesses and it did not adequately warn him of the dangers and disadvantages of self-representation. The juvenile's age, state of mind, emotional stability, mental capacity, and prior criminal experience indicated, at the very least, that the strictest scrutiny should have been employed in determining whether he knowingly, voluntarily, and intelligently waived his right to counsel. In re Puckett, — Ohio App. 3d —, 2007 Ohio 3927, — N.E. 2d —, 2007 Ohio App. LEXIS 3531 (Aug. 1, 2007).

Juvenile's waiver of counsel was defective because the dialogue between the juvenile and the juvenile court did not thoroughly address or investigate any of the factors necessary to determine whether he knowingly, intelligently, and voluntarily waived his right to counsel. The juvenile court represented to the juvenile that counsel could only be appointed if his parents were unemployed, not based solely upon his own indigence, failed to inform him of his rights under JuvR 29(B)(5), and never explained to him how an attorney might be helpful in crafting a successful defense, or in advising him of the disadvantages of being tried with a co-defendant. In re Ramon, — Ohio App. 3d —, 2007 Ohio 5768, — N.E. 2d —, 2007 Ohio App. LEXIS 5080 (Oct. 29, 2007).

When appellant was charged with offenses in juvenile court, RC § 2151.352 did not require that counsel be appointed to represent him because the statute, as well as Ohio R. Juv. P. 4(A) and 29(B), allowed him to waive counsel, which he knowingly, intelligently, and voluntarily did. In re Spears, — Ohio App. 3d —, 2006 Ohio 1920, — N.E. 2d —, 2006 Ohio App. LEXIS 1761 (Apr. 17, 2006).

Waiver of rights

Father's waiver of his parental rights regarding his daughter was deemed knowing and voluntary where the juvenile court complied with Ohio R. Juv. P. 29(D) in advising the father of the rights that he was waiving and the effect of his agreement to surrender his parental rights. There was clear and convincing evidence to support the juvenile court's determination that termination of the father's parental rights was proper and in the child's best interest pursuant to RC § 2151.414(D) and (E)(4), (13), (14), and (16). In re Isreal Y., — Ohio App. 3d —, 2007 Ohio 3685, — N.E. 2d —, 2007 Ohio App. LEXIS 3391 (July 16, 2007).

RULE 30. Relinquishment of jurisdiction for purposes of criminal prosecution

(A) **Preliminary hearing.** In any proceeding where the court considers the transfer of a case for criminal prosecution, the court shall hold a preliminary hearing to determine if there is probable cause to believe that the child committed the act alleged and that the act would be an offense if committed by an adult. The hearing may be upon motion of the court, the prosecuting attorney, or the child.

(B) **Mandatory transfer.** In any proceeding in which transfer of a case for criminal prosecution is required by statute upon a finding of probable cause, the order of transfer shall be entered upon a finding of probable cause.

(C) **Discretionary transfer.** In any proceeding in which transfer of a case for criminal prosecution is permitted, but not required, by statute, and in which probable cause is found at the preliminary hearing, the court shall continue the proceeding for full investigation. The investigation shall include a mental examination of the child by a public or private agency or by a person qualified to make the examination. When the investigation is completed, an amenability hearing shall be held to determine whether to transfer jurisdiction. The criteria for transfer shall be as provided by statute.

(D) **Notice.** Notice in writing of the time, place, and purpose of any hearing held pursuant to this rule shall be given to the state, the child's parents, guardian, or other custodian and the child's counsel at least three days prior to the hearing, unless written notice has been waived on the record.

(E) **Retention of jurisdiction.** If the court retains jurisdiction, it shall set the proceedings for hearing on the merits.

(F) **Waiver of mental examination.** The child may waive the mental examination required under division (C) of this rule. Refusal by the child to submit to a mental and physical examination or any part of the examination shall constitute a waiver of the examination.

(G) **Order of transfer.** The order of transfer shall state the reasons for transfer.

(H) **Release of child.** With respect to the transferred case, the juvenile court shall set the terms and conditions for release of the child in accordance with Crim. R. 46.

History: Amended, eff 7-1-76; 7-1-94; 7-1-97.

NOTES TO DECISIONS

ANALYSIS

Generally
Discretionary transfer

Hearings

Generally

Where there was no indication in a juvenile court bindover order that a juvenile's waiver of a probable cause and amenability hearing was knowingly, competently, and intelligently made, a later delinquency charge against him on a new criminal matter required an appropriate bindover proceeding under RC § 2152.12 and Ohio R. Juv. P. 3. The hearing on the bindover issue was a critical phase that was mandatory under RC ch. 2152 and Ohio R. Juv. P. 30. State v. Brown, — Ohio App. 3d —, 2006 Ohio 4393, — N.E. 2d —, 2006 Ohio App. LEXIS 4330 (Aug. 25, 2006).

Juvenile court did not err in finding that there were sufficient facts to establish probable cause that defendant, a juvenile, committed offenses charged against him, arising from a car-jacking incident and a subsequent attempt to escape from the police, such that the bind-over to the trial court was proper pursuant to RC § 2151.26(B) and Ohio R. Juv. P. 30; the juvenile court did not have to find that defendant was guilty of the charged offenses to support its bind-over determination. State v. Goodwin, 166 Ohio App. 3d 709, 2006 Ohio 2311, 852 N.E. 2d 1282, 2006 Ohio App. LEXIS 2176 (May 11, 2006).

Discretionary transfer

Juvenile court abused its discretion in overruling the State's motions to relinquish jurisdiction because it failed to consider whether a discretionary transfer was warranted, pursuant to RC § 2152.12(B), RC § 2152.10(B), and Ohio R. Juv. P. 30, because the juveniles met the requirements for the court to consider discretionary transfers since all five were 14 years or older at the time of the acts charged and they were all charged with acts that would be felonies if committed by an adult. The juvenile court erred in failing to make a finding as to probable cause and, if it made such a finding, it should have then proceeded with an investigation and amenability hearing pursuant to Ohio R. Juv. P. 30(C). In re Stanley, 165 Ohio App. 3d 726, 2006 Ohio 1279, 848 N.E. 2d 540, 2006 Ohio App. LEXIS 1174 (Mar. 14, 2006).

Hearings

There was no reversible error when defendant's father was not notified, under RC § 2152.12(G) and Ohio R. Juv. P. 30(D), of a hearing to consider transferring proceedings against defendant from the juvenile court to the trial court's general division because (1) it would be absurd to interpret the statute to require notice to both parents in all cases, including those in which a parent was deceased or unknown, (2) defendant could not show that defendant was prejudiced by a lack of notice to defendant's father, since defendant's mother received notice and appeared, and (3) the goal of the statute, which was to provide defendant with parental support, was satisfied by notice to and the presence of defendant's mother, so defendant's procedural due process rights were observed. State v. Reynolds, — Ohio App. 3d —, 2007 Ohio 4178, — N.E. 2d —, 2007 Ohio App. LEXIS 3766 (Aug. 16, 2007).

Juvenile court properly conducted an amenability hearing to determine whether defendant, a juvenile, was amenable to the juvenile court system or whether he should be bound over to the general trial court for criminal charges, and the fact that defendant stipulated to the admission of his psychological evlauation and his family records did not constitute admissions or error by the juvenile court, pursuant to Ohio R. Juv. P. 29(D) and 30. State v. Goodwin, 166 Ohio App. 3d 709, 2006 Ohio 2311, 852 N.E. 2d 1282, 2006 Ohio App. LEXIS 2176 (May 11, 2006).

RULE 31.   [Reserved]

RULE 32.   Social history; physical examination; mental examination; investigation involving the allocation of parental rights and responsibilities for the care of children

(A) **Social history and physical or mental examination: availability before adjudication.** The court may order and utilize a social history or physical or mental examination at any time after the filing of a complaint under any of the following circumstances:

(1) Upon the request of the party concerning whom the history or examination is to be made;

(2) Where transfer of a child for adult prosecution is an issue in the proceeding;

(3) Where a material allegation of a neglect, dependency, or abused child complaint relates to matters that a history or examination may clarify;

(4) Where a party's legal responsibility for the party's acts or the party's competence to participate in the proceedings is an issue;

(5) Where a physical or mental examination is required to determine the need for emergency medical care under Juv. R. 13; or

(6) Where authorized under Juv. R. 7(I).

(B) **Limitations on preparation and use.** Until there has been an admission or adjudication that the child who is the subject of the proceedings is a juvenile traffic offender, delinquent, unruly, neglected, dependent, or abused, no social history, physical examination or mental examination shall be ordered except as authorized under subdivision (A) and any social history, physical examination or mental examination ordered pursuant to subdivision (A) shall be utilized only for the limited purposes therein specified. The person preparing a social history or making a physical or mental examination shall not testify about the history or examination or information received in its preparation in any juvenile traffic offender, delinquency, or unruly child adjudicatory hearing, except as may be required in a hearing to determine whether a child should be transferred to an adult court for criminal prosecution.

(C) **Availability of social history or investigation report.** A reasonable time before the dispositional hearing, or any other hearing at which a social history or physical or mental examination is to be utilized, counsel shall be permitted to inspect any social history or report of a mental or physical examination. The court may, for good cause shown, deny such inspection or limit its scope to specified portions of the history or report. The court may order that the contents of the history or report, in whole or part, not be disclosed to specified persons. If inspection or disclosure is denied or limited, the court shall state its reasons for such denial or limitation to counsel.

(D) **Investigation: allocation of parental rights and responsibilities for the care of children; habeas corpus.** On the filing of a complaint for the allocation of parental rights and responsibilities for the care of children or for a writ of habeas corpus to determine the allocation of parental rights and responsibilities for the care of a child, or on the filing of a motion for change in the allocation of parental rights and responsibilities for the care of children, the court may cause an investigation to be made as to the character, health, family relations, past conduct, present living conditions, earning ability, and financial worth of the parties to the action. The report of the investigation shall be confidential, but shall be made available to the parties or their counsel upon written request not less than three days before hearing. The court may tax as costs all or any part of the expenses of each investigation.

History: Amended, eff 7-1-73; 7-1-76; 7-1-91; 7-1-94.

NOTES TO DECISIONS

Analysis

Competence to stand trial
Guardian ad litem

Competence to stand trial

Trial court erred in relying on evidence outside the record in finding the juvenile to be competent to stand trial: In re Braden, 176 Ohio App. 3d 616, 2008 Ohio 2981, 893 N.E.2d 213, 2008 Ohio App. LEXIS 2500 (2008).

It was reversible error for a trial court not to appoint an expert, under Ohio R. Juv. P. 32(A), to evaluate the competency of appellant, a juvenile, because all witnesses who were in more intense contact with appellant than the trial court supported such an evaluation, and the trial court's cursory "competency" dialogue with appellant did not mitigate against those opinions. In re Harris, — Ohio App. 3d —, 2006 Ohio 5534, — N.E. 2d —, 2006 Ohio App. LEXIS 5509 (Oct. 24, 2006).

Guardian ad litem

In a parental rights termination proceeding pursuant to RC § 2151.414, there was no error in the trial court's appointment of an agency volunteer as the children's guardian ad litem, as there was no statutory requirement that a guardian also be a licensed attorney pursuant to Ohio R. Juv. P. 32. In re D.R., — Ohio App. 3d —, 2006 Ohio 3513, — N.E. 2d —, 2006 Ohio App. LEXIS 3471 (July 7, 2006).

RULE 33.   [Reserved]

RULE 34.   Dispositional hearing

(A) **Scheduling the hearing.** Where a child has been adjudicated as an abused, neglected, or dependent child, the court shall not issue a dispositional order until after it holds a separate dispositional hearing. The dispositional hearing for an adjudicated abused, neglected, or dependent child shall be held at least one day but not more than thirty days after the adjudicatory hearing is held. The dispositional hearing may be held immediately after the adjudicatory hearing if all parties were served prior to the adjudicatory hearing with all documents required for the dispositional hearing and all parties consent to the dispositional hearing being held immediately after the adjudicatory hearing. Upon the request of any party or the guardian ad litem of the child, the court may continue a dispositional hearing for a reasonable time not to exceed the time limit set forth in this division to enable a party to obtain or consult counsel. The dispositional hearing shall not be held more than ninety days after the date on which the complaint in the case was filed. If the dispositional hearing is not held within this ninety day period of time, the court, on its own motion or the motion of any party or the guardian ad litem of the child, shall dismiss the complaint without prejudice.

In all other juvenile proceedings, the dispositional hearing shall be held pursuant to Juv. R. 29(F)(2)(a) through (d) and the ninety day requirement shall not apply. Where the dispositional hearing is to be held immediately following the adjudicatory hearing, the court, upon the request of any party, shall continue the hearing for a reasonable time to enable the party to obtain or consult counsel.

(B) **Hearing procedure.** The hearing shall be conducted in the following manner:

(1) The judge or magistrate who presided at the adjudicatory hearing shall, if possible, preside;

(2) Except as provided in division (I) of this rule, the court may admit evidence that is material and relevant, including, but not limited to, hearsay, opinion, and documentary evidence;

(3) Medical examiners and each investigator who prepared a social history shall not be cross-examined, except upon consent of all parties, for good cause shown, or as the court in its discretion may direct. Any party may offer evidence supplementing, explaining, or disputing any information contained in the social history or other reports that may be used by the court in determining disposition.

(C) **Judgment.** After the conclusion of the hearing, the court shall enter an appropriate judgment within seven days. A copy of the judgment shall be given to any party requesting a copy. In all cases where a child is placed on probation, the child shall receive a written statement of the conditions of probation. If the judgment is conditional, the order shall state the conditions. If the child is not returned to the child's home, the court shall determine the school district that shall bear the cost of the child's education and may fix an amount of support to be paid by the responsible parent or from public funds.

(D) **Dispositional orders.** Where a child is adjudicated an abused, neglected, or dependent child, the court may make any of the following orders of disposition:

(1) Place the child in protective supervision;

(2) Commit the child to the temporary custody of a public or private agency, either parent, a relative residing within or outside the state, or a probation officer for placement in a certified foster home or approved foster care;

(3) Award legal custody of the child to either parent or to any other person who, prior to the dispositional hearing, files a motion requesting legal custody;

(4) Commit the child to the permanent custody of a public or private agency, if the court determines that the child cannot be placed with one of the child's parents within a reasonable time or should not be placed with either parent and determines that the permanent commitment is in the best interest of the child;

(5) Place the child in a planned permanent living arrangement with a public or private agency if the agency requests the court for placement, if the court finds that a planned permanent living arrangement is in the best interest of the child, and if the court finds that one of the following exists:

(a) The child because of physical, mental, or psychological problems or needs is unable to function in a family-like setting;

(b) The parents of the child have significant physical, mental or psychological problems and are unable to care for the child, adoption is not in the best interest of the child and the child retains a significant and positive relationship with a parent or relative;

(c) The child is sixteen years of age or older, has been counseled, is unwilling to accept or unable to adapt to a permanent placement and is in an agency program preparing the child for independent living.

(E) **Protective supervision.** If the court issues an order for protective supervision, the court may place any reasonable restrictions upon the child, the child's parents, guardian, or any other person including, but not limited to, any of the following:

(1) Ordering a party within forty-eight hours to vacate the child's home indefinitely or for a fixed period of time;

(2) Ordering a party, parent, or custodian to prevent any particular person from having contact with the child;

(3) Issuing a restraining order to control the conduct of any party.

(F) **Case plan.** As part of its dispositional order, the court shall journalize a case plan for the child. The agency required to maintain a case plan shall file the case plan with the court prior to the child's adjudicatory hearing but not later than thirty days after the earlier of the date on which the complaint in the case was filed or the child was first placed in shelter care. The plan shall specify what additional information, if any, is necessary to complete the plan and how the information will be obtained. All parts of the case plan shall be completed by the earlier of thirty days after the adjudicatory hearing or the date of the dispositional hearing for the child. If all parties agree to the content of the case plan and the court approves it, the court shall journalize the plan as part of its dispositional order. If no agreement is reached, the court, based upon the evidence presented at the dispositional hearing and the best interest of the child, shall determine the contents of the case plan and journalize it as part of the dispositional order for the child.

(G) **Modification of temporary order.** The department of human services or any other public or private agency or any party, other than a parent whose parental rights have been terminated, may at any time file a motion requesting that the court modify or terminate any order of disposition. The court shall hold a hearing upon the motion as if the hearing were the original dispositional hearing and shall give all parties and the guardian *ad litem* notice of the hearing pursuant to these rules. The court, on its own motion and upon proper notice to all parties and any interested agency, may modify or terminate any order of disposition.

(H) **Restraining orders.** In any proceeding where a child is made a ward of the court, the court may grant a restraining order controlling the conduct of any party if the court finds that the order is necessary to control any conduct or relationship that may be detrimental or harmful to the child and tend to defeat the execution of a dispositional order.

(I) **Bifurcation; Rules of Evidence.** Hearings to determine whether temporary orders regarding custody should be modified to orders for permanent custody shall be considered dispositional hearings and need not be bifurcated. The Rules of Evidence shall apply in hearings on motions for permanent custody.

(J) **Advisement of rights after hearing.** At the conclusion of the hearing, the court shall advise the child of the child's right to record expungement and, where any part of the proceeding was contested, advise the parties of their right to appeal.

History: Amended, eff 7-1-94; 7-1-96; 7-1-02.

NOTES TO DECISIONS

ANALYSIS

Generally
Advisement
Continuance
Custody
Dependency adjudication
Evidence
Guardian ad litem's report
Hearings
Jurisdiction
Presence of juvenile
Right to appeal
Right to counsel

Generally

Since appellant entered admissions and waived the right to contest the facts relative to the admissions, and since Ohio R. Juv. P. 34 contemplates an informal dispositional hearing, appellant's arguments that he was denied his right of confrontation and contended that inadmissible evidence was presented were without merit. State v. McGrapth, — Ohio App. 3d —, 2006 Ohio 4696, — N.E. 2d —, 2006 Ohio App. LEXIS 4634 (Sept. 11, 2006).

Juvenile court's order granting legal custody in the absence of a motion violated the mandatory statutory and procedural requirements of RC § 2151.353 and Ohio R. Juv. P. 34, and also was in direct contravention of Ohio R. Juv. P. 19, mandating that requests for relief be made by motion, Ohio R. Juv. P. 22(E), requiring that prehearing motions be filed at least seven days prior to the proceeding, Ohio R. Juv. P. 20, establishing filing and service requirements for written motions and other papers, and Ohio R. Civ. P. 5(D), imposing a proof of service requirement. In re L.R.T., 165 Ohio App. 3d 77, 2006 Ohio 207, 844 N.E. 2d 914, 2006 Ohio App. LEXIS 173 (Jan. 23, 2006).

Any person who seeks an award of legal custody of a child must, in accordance with the Ohio Rules of Juvenile Procedure, file a motion, prior to the dispositional hearing, requesting such custody. In re L.R.T., 165 Ohio App. 3d 77, 2006 Ohio 207, 844 N.E. 2d 914, 2006 Ohio App. LEXIS 173 (Jan. 23, 2006).

Trial court erred as a matter of law when, in a review of a magistrate's decision granting a child's permanent custody to an agency, it overturned that decision and granted the child's legal custody to the child's great-aunt, because the great-aunt did not file a motion for the child's custody at least seven days preceding the dispositional hearing before the magistrate, pursuant to the mandatory requirements of RC § 2151.353(A)(3) and Ohio R. Juv. P. 34. In re L.R.T., 165

Ohio App. 3d 77, 2006 Ohio 207, 844 N.E. 2d 914, 2006 Ohio App. LEXIS 173 (Jan. 23, 2006).

It is inappropriate to follow the reasoning used in In re Callier, 2002 Ohio 2406, 2002 Ohio App. LEXIS 7304, with respect to compliance with the procedural requirements set forth in RC § 2151.353 and Ohio R. Juv. P. 34, regarding motions for custody, and compliance with those procedural requirements is mandatory. In re L.R.T., 165 Ohio App. 3d 77, 2006 Ohio 207, 844 N.E. 2d 914, 2006 Ohio App. LEXIS 173 (Jan. 23, 2006).

Advisement

When a mother was found to have consented to an agreement (1) granting the mother's child's father legal custody of the child, (2) granting the child's foster parents visitation with the child, and (3) continuing the mother's prior supervised visitation with the child, the magistrate who approved the agreement was not required to engage in an Ohio R. Juv. P. 29 colloquy with the mother as to the mother's consent to the agreement because neither Ohio R. Juv. P. 34 nor RC § 2151.353 required such a colloquy as to a disposition. In re S.S., — Ohio App. 3d —, 2007 Ohio 6747, — N.E. 2d —, 2007 Ohio App. LEXIS 5908 (Dec. 17, 2007).

Continuance

Under JuvR 34, the trial court should have continued the matter for at least one day, rather than proceeding directly from the adjudicatory hearing to the dispositional hearing, where counsel for the absent mother requested a continuance: In re D.H., 177 Ohio App. 3d 246, 2008 Ohio 3686, 894 N.E.2d 364, 2008 Ohio App. LEXIS 3092 (2008).

Custody

Father's dispositional hearing testimony supported a trial court's order, under RC § 2151.353(A)(2) and Ohio R. Juv. P. 34(D)(2), placing his children with their maternal grandmother, upon finding it was not in the children's best interests to place them with their mother, due to a lack of adequate housing, or to place them with their father, due to his mental instability. In re Washington, — Ohio App. 3d —, 2007 Ohio 522, — N.E. 2d —, 2007 Ohio App. LEXIS 466 (Feb. 7, 2007).

Evidence that a father had been physically violent with police when they responded to his home, that a loaded handgun was found under a recliner in the father's home five feet from where the father's child was sitting on a couch, that the father heard voices threatening him with harm, and that the father believed that he was an enemy of the state overwhelmingly supported a trial court's decision to grant temporary custody of the father's children to their maternal grandmother pursuant to RC § 2151.353(A)(2) and Ohio R. Juv. P. 34(D)(2). In re Dependent, — Ohio App. 3d —, — N.E. 2d —, 2007 Ohio App. LEXIS 467 (Feb. 7, 2007).

Dependency adjudication

When parents entered dependency admissions as to two children, and then, years later, after a third child was born and an agency sought permanent custody of all three children, the parents filed pleas of deny, this effectively withdrew the prior admissions, where the trial court did not adjudicate the children to be dependent when the prior admissions were entered, so, once the pleas of deny were entered, the trial court could not adjudicate the children to be dependent and/or abused based on the withdrawn pleas, and, as it did not otherwise adjudicate the children, its subsequent grant of their permanent custody to an agency without an adjudication was contrary to RC ch. 2151 and Ohio R. Juv. P. 29(F) and 34. In re J.H., — Ohio App. 3d —, 2006 Ohio 3237, — N.E. 2d —, 2006 Ohio App. LEXIS 3151 (June 26, 2006).

Evidence

When a child's foster parents petitioned for legal custody of the child, it was not error for the trial court to admit hearsay at the hearing conducted on that petition because Ohio R. Juv. P. 34(B)(2) allowed the admission of hearsay at this hearing, since the hearing did not concern a permanent custody petition, and Rule 34(B)(2) was a rule prescribed by the Ohio Supreme Court that constitutionally altered the general hearsay rule. In re R. R., — Ohio App. 3d —, 2007 Ohio 4808, — N.E. 2d —, 2007 Ohio App. LEXIS 4309 (Sept. 19, 2007).

While hearsay was permitted pursuant to Ohio R. Juv. P. 34(B)(2) to be presented at defendant juvenile's revocation of probation hearing, the two witnesses, his probation officer and a counselor who oversaw defendant's treatment, did not present hearsay evidence as they had personal knowledge of defendant's failure to comply with a sex offender treatment program by drawing pictures of a sexual nature and writing sexual stories. In re Justin F., — Ohio App. 3d —, 2007 Ohio 6885, — N.E. 2d —, 2007 Ohio App. LEXIS 6005 (Dec. 21, 2007).

Nothing prohibited the trial court from considering and relying upon evidence that occurred after the children's services agency filed the permanent custody request. The court could properly have considered the mother's conduct, as well as other relevant evidence, when it considered the children's best interests. In re Brown, — Ohio App. 3d —, 2006 Ohio 2863, — N.E. 2d —, 2006 Ohio App. LEXIS 2719 (May 26, 2006).

As a grandmother did not seek permanent custody of a child who was adjudicated as dependent, Ohio R. Juv. P 34(I) did not apply and the juvenile court acted within its discretion in considering hearsay testimony in making its dispositional decision. In re Brown, — Ohio App. 3d —, 2006 Ohio 3189, — N.E. 2d —, 2006 Ohio App. LEXIS 3090 (June 23, 2006).

Trial court's consideration of hearsay evidence contained in a guardian's report for purposes of making a permanent custody determination in a parental rights termination proceeding was error pursuant to Ohio R. Juv. P. 34 and RC § 2151.414(C); however, such error was deemed harmless where the consideration given to that evidence was minimal and there was an abundance of admissible evidence that supported the trial court's determination that permanent custody should be granted to a county social service agency. In re Hilyard, — Ohio App. 3d —, 2006 Ohio 1977, — N.E. 2d —, 2006 Ohio App. LEXIS 1808 (Apr. 13, 2006).

Guardian ad litem's report

Trial court erred in considering a guardian ad litem's report with respect to its determination in a parental rights termination proceeding pursuant to RC § 2151.414(C), as such was not to be considered as substantive evidence in such a decision pursuant to Ohio R. Juv. P. 34. The error was harmless where the consideration by the trial court was minimal and only as to a factor under § 2151.414(D)(2), the father was not prejudiced by the trial court's consideration, and there was ample other evidence in the record to support the trial court's permanent custody award to a county agency. In re Hilyard, — Ohio App. 3d —, 2006 Ohio 1965, — N.E. 2d —, 2006 Ohio App. LEXIS 1807 (Apr. 13, 2006).

Hearings

When an agency filed a complaint which both alleged that a child was dependent and sought permanent custody of the child, Ohio R. Juv. P. 29 and 34 required the trial court to bifurcate proceedings as to dependency from dispositional proceedings as to permanent custody, so the trial court committed reversible error because it held one evidentiary hearing on both issues, with no clear demarcation between its considerations of each issue. In re J.H., — Ohio App. 3d —, 2006 Ohio 3237, — N.E. 2d —, 2006 Ohio App. LEXIS 3151 (June 26, 2006).

Review of RC § 2151.35(B)(1) showed that it was inconsistent with Ohio R. Juv. P. 34(A) as RC § 2151.35(B)(1) allowed a trial court to hold a dispositional hearing for an adjudicated dependent child immediately after the adjudica-

tory hearing if all parties were served prior to the adjudicatory hearing with all documents required for the dispositional hearing, while Ohio R. Juv. P. 34(A) was stricter because it also required that all parties consent to the dispositional hearing being held immediately after the adjudicatory hearing, and it was well-established that in instances of procedural conflict the Ohio Rules of Juvenile Procedure, which were prepared and submitted by the Ohio Supreme Court to the legislature, controlled over inconsistent statutory provisions purporting to govern procedural matters. In re J.H., — Ohio App. 3d —, 2006 Ohio 3237, — N.E. 2d —, 2006 Ohio App. LEXIS 3151 (June 26, 2006).

Jurisdiction

Permanent custody disposition was not void for lack of jurisdiction because the trial court complied with RC § 2151.35, Ohio R. Juv. P. 29, and Ohio R. Juv. P. 34. The agency filed a motion seeking permanent custody of two of the children as the initial disposition in an abuse, neglect, and dependency complaint, and permanent custody of the third child as a modification of a prior disposition. After the adjudication phase, the trial court found the first two children to be dependent and it then held the dispositional phase as to all three children. In re Angler, — Ohio App. 3d —, 2007 Ohio 3246, — N.E. 2d —, 2007 Ohio App. LEXIS 2986 (June 15, 2007).

Presence of juvenile

When a magistrate took the disposition of a juvenile delinquency case under advisement, after conducting adjudicatory and dispositional hearings, and then issued a sentencing decision without holding a hearing, Ohio R. Juv. P. 34 provided the procedure for dispositional hearings in juvenile delinquency cases and did not require the juvenile to be present for sentencing, so the Ohio R. Crim. P. 43 requirement that the defendant be present for the imposition of sentence did not apply. In re Gibson, — Ohio App. 3d —, 2006 Ohio 5145, — N.E. 2d —, 2006 Ohio App. LEXIS 5109 (Oct. 2, 2006).

Right to appeal

Although defendant, a juvenile, was not necessarily entitled under Ohio R. Juv. P. 34(J) to advisement of his right to appeal in a juvenile delinquency matter after he admitted to the charge alleged in the complaint, he satisfied the requirements for filing a delayed notice of appeal under Ohio R. App. P. 5(A)(2) where he filed a motion that explained the reasons for the failure to appeal, he filed a notice of appeal, and he filed an affidavit of good cause. In re A.S., — Ohio App. 3d —, 2007 Ohio 3434, — N.E. 2d —, 2007 Ohio App. LEXIS 3142 (June 29, 2007).

Right to counsel

Although the trial court substantially complied with Ohio R. Juv. P. 29(D) when it accepted defendant juvenile's waiver of counsel during the adjudication hearing, the trial court failed to reiterate defendant's right to counsel during disposition or allow him either to invoke or to waive his right to counsel at that stage as required by Ohio R. Juv. P. 34. In re S. J., — Ohio App. 3d —, 2006 Ohio 4467, — N.E. 2d —, 2006 Ohio App. LEXIS 4395 (Aug. 30, 2006).

RULE 35. Proceedings after judgment

(A) **Continuing jurisdiction; invoked by motion**. The continuing jurisdiction of the court shall be invoked by motion filed in the original proceeding, notice of which shall be served in the manner provided for the service of process.

(B) **Revocation of probation.** The court shall not revoke probation except after a hearing at which the child shall be present and apprised of the grounds on which revocation is proposed. The parties shall have the right to counsel and the right to appointed counsel where entitled pursuant to Juv. R. 4(A). Probation shall not be revoked except upon a finding that the child has violated a condition of probation of which the child had, pursuant to Juv. R. 34(C), been notified.

(C) **Detention.** During the pendency of proceedings under this rule, a child may be placed in detention in accordance with the provisions of Rule 7.

History: Amended, eff 7-1-94.

NOTES TO DECISIONS

ANALYSIS

Applicability
Probation revocation
Right to counsel

Applicability

JuvR 35 governs proceedings that take place after judgment. It did not apply where the juvenile fled before the court reached a complete judgment: In re Antwon C., 182 Ohio App. 3d 237, 2009 Ohio 2567, 912 N.E.2d 182, 2009 Ohio App. LEXIS 2189 (2009).

Probation revocation

Appellant's purported waiver of counsel at a probation revocation hearing was not valid, under RC § 2151.352 and Ohio R. Juv. P. 4 and 35(B), because the trial court's advisement as to that right appeared to state that appellant had the right if he wanted an evidentiary hearing, but not if he wanted to admit the violation he was charged with, which was not the law. In re Lohr, — Ohio App. 3d —, 2007 Ohio 1130, — N.E. 2d —, 2007 Ohio App. LEXIS 1046 (Mar. 7, 2007).

As a magistrate failed to enumerate or explain defendant juvenile's rights to him, including his right to counsel, at a hearing regarding his probation violation after he had been previously adjudicated as delinquent, and she failed to find that he waived such rights prior to holding that he violated his probation, his due process rights under U.S. Const. amends. V and VI, Ohio Const. art. I, § 16, RC § 2151.352, and Ohio R. Juv. P. 4 and 35(B) were violated; although the protections and requirements of Ohio R. Juv. P. 35(B) were complied with in a prior hearing, that was a preliminary matter and no adjudication of a probation violation or a sentence were imposed at that time, such that Rule 35(B) had to be again complied with at the later hearing in order to avoid a violation of defendant's rights. In re K.E.M., — Ohio App. 3d —, 2007 Ohio 5031, — N.E. 2d —, 2007 Ohio App. LEXIS 4454 (Sept. 26, 2007).

Trial court complied with Juv. R. 35 when it revoked defendant's probation as it wrote in its judgment entry that defendant had failed to comply with the terms and conditions of the previous judgment as he had failed to comply with conditions 1 and 3 of that judgment. Nothing in the juvenile rules required the trial court to make any further findings. In re Kiser, — Ohio App. 3d —, 2006 Ohio 5970, — N.E. 2d —, 2006 Ohio App. LEXIS 5905 (Nov. 13, 2006).

When appellant received commitments to the Department of Youth Services upon her admissions to certain charges against her and, then, when she appeared before the juvenile court on new cases, which were continued, the court reimposed the previously suspended commitments, under RC § 2151.355(A)(22), without notice or any finding that she had violated a condition of probation, much less what condition, the court did not comply with the requirements of Ohio R. Juv. P. 35(B), and it committed reversible error. In re Shine, — Ohio App. 3d —, 2006 Ohio 7050, — N.E. 2d —, 2006 Ohio App. LEXIS 6977 (Dec. 20, 2006).

Magistrate complied with the requirements of Ohio R. Juv. P. 35(B) when appellant's probation was revoked and appellant was committed to the custody of the Ohio Department of Youth Services because (1) a hearing was conducted, (2) probation was revoked as a result of a motion that was filed which listed appellant's violations of appellant's probation, (3) appellant was represented by counsel, and (4) appellant admitted violating appellant's probation, and appellant admitted committing new criminal offenses. In re R.B.A., — Ohio App. 3d —, 2007 Ohio 5407, — N.E. 2d —, 2007 Ohio App. LEXIS 4741 (Oct. 9, 2007).

When a trial court imposed the suspended commitment to the Department of Youth Services of appellant, a juvenile, the court violated Ohio R. Juv. P. 35(B) and due process because the court did not give appellant notice, when appellant admitted certain offenses, that the hearing at which appellant entered this admission was, in effect, a probation revocation hearing, nor did the court give appellant notice of the condition of appellant's probation that appellant allegedly violated, and such notice was crucial to appellant's decision about whether to retain counsel. In re J. F., — Ohio App. 3d —, 2007 Ohio 5652, — N.E. 2d —, 2007 Ohio App. LEXIS 4965 (Oct. 19, 2007).

Right to counsel

Where a juvenile court magistrate obtained defendant juvenile's waiver of his right to counsel in a delinquency matter, wherein he was charged with truancy, and the magistrate thereafter informed the juvenile of the nature of the charges and the possible penalties, there was no compliance with Ohio R. Juv. P. 29(D), such that the waiver by the juvenile of his right to counsel was not deemed knowing and intelligent. Pursuant to RC § 2151.352, Ohio R. Juv. P. 4, 29, and 35, as well as U.S. Const. amends. V, VI, and XIV and Ohio Const. art. I, § 10 and 16, the waiver was insufficient to allow defendant to have appeared unrepresented at the adjudicatory and dispositional phases of the delinquency proceeding. In re C.K., — Ohio App. 3d —, 2007 Ohio 3234, — N.E. 2d —, 2007 Ohio App. LEXIS 2974 (June 21, 2007).

RULE 36. Dispositional review

(A) **Court review.** A court that issues a dispositional order in an abuse, neglect, or dependency case may review the child's placement or custody arrangement, the case plan, and the actions of the public or private agency implementing that plan at any time. A court that issues a dispositional order shall hold a review hearing one year after the earlier of the date on which the complaint in the case was filed or the child was first placed into shelter care. The court shall schedule the review hearing at the time that it holds the dispositional hearing. The court shall hold a similar review hearing no later than every twelve months after the initial review hearing until the child is adopted, returned to the child's parents, or the court otherwise terminates the child's placement or custody arrangement. A hearing pursuant to section 2151.415 of the Revised Code shall take the place of the first review hearing. The court shall schedule each subsequent review hearing at the conclusion of the review hearing immediately preceding the review hearing to be scheduled. Review hearings may be conducted by a judge or magistrate.

(B) **Citizens' review board.** The court may appoint a citizens' review board to conduct review hearings, subject to the review and approval by the court.

(C) **Agency review.** Each agency required to prepare a case plan for a child shall complete a semiannual administrative review of the case plan no later than six months after the earlier of the date on which the complaint in the case was filed or the child was first placed in shelter care. After the first administrative review, the agency shall complete semiannual administrative reviews no later than every six months. The agency shall prepare and file a written summary of the semiannual administrative review that shall include an updated case plan. If the agency, parents, guardian, or custodian of the child and guardian ad litem stipulate to the revised case plan, the plan shall be signed by all parties and filed with the written summary of the administrative review no later than seven days after the completion of the administrative review. If the court does not object to the revised case plan, it shall journalize the case plan within fourteen days after it is filed with the court. If the court does not approve of the revised case plan or if the agency, parties, guardian ad litem, and the attorney of the child do not agree to the need for changes to the case plan and to all of the proposed changes, the agency shall file its written summary and request a hearing. The court shall schedule a review hearing to be held no later than thirty days after the filing of the case plan or written summary or both, if required. The court shall give notice of the date, time, and location of the hearing to all interested parties and the guardian ad litem of the child. The court shall take one of the following actions:

(1) Approve or modify the case plan based upon the evidence presented;

(2) Return the child home with or without protective supervision and terminate temporary custody or determine which agency shall have custody;

(3) If the child is in permanent custody determine what actions would facilitate adoption;

(4) Journalize the terms of the updated case plan.

History: Effective 7-1-94; amended, eff 7-1-96.

NOTES TO DECISIONS

ANALYSIS

Applicability
Treatment programs

Applicability

Where a mother sought to vacate a prior court order that had awarded legal custody of her child to custodians, Ohio R. Juv. P. 36 and RC § 2151.417 were deemed inapplicable to the proceeding, as those dealt with modification or termination of a child custody arrangement upon a showing of a change in circumstances and a finding that such change was in the child's best interest; as no modification or termination was contemplated by the mother's motion, but rather, an examination of the circumstances at the time of the original custody award was mandated, there could have been no changed circumstances. In re H.B., — Ohio App. 3d —, 2006 Ohio 2124, — N.E. 2d —, 2006 Ohio App. LEXIS 1969 (Apr. 28, 2006).

Treatment programs

Upon a determination during reviewing hearings held pursuant to RC § 2151.417 and Ohio R. Juv. P. 36(A) that a juvenile was not benefitting from a residential treatment program that he was originally committed to upon being declared a delinquent pursuant to RC § 2151.35(A)(1) and that he was acting out, a juvenile court's placement of the

juvenile with the Department of Youth Services was not error pursuant to RC § 2151.354(5) and (6); the juvenile was not amenable to treatment or rehabilitation due to his conduct at the residential treatment facility. In re D.B., — Ohio App. 3d —, 2006 Ohio 2891, — N.E. 2d —, 2006 Ohio App. LEXIS 2738 (June 8, 2006).

RULE 37. Recording of proceedings

(A) Record of proceedings. The juvenile court shall make a record of adjudicatory and dispositional proceedings in abuse, neglect, dependent, unruly, and delinquent cases; permanent custody cases; and proceedings before magistrates. In all other proceedings governed by these rules, a record shall be made upon request of a party or upon motion of the court. The record shall be taken in shorthand, stenotype, or by any other adequate mechanical, electronic, or video recording device.

(B) Restrictions on use of recording or transcript. No public use shall be made by any person, including a party, of any juvenile court record, including the recording or a transcript of any juvenile court hearing, except in the course of an appeal or as authorized by order of the court or by statute.

History: Amended, eff 7-1-96; 7-1-01.

NOTES TO DECISIONS

ANALYSIS

Generally
Appeal
Failure to record proceedings
Harmless error
In camera interview
Transcript

Generally

Defendant juvenile's rights under due process and under JuvR 37 were not violated in a delinquency matter wherein the juvenile court judge indicated that he was taking the matter under advisement and would issue the decision later, as defendant failed to object to such procedure and any error was thereafter waived; further, although the judge announced the decision the next day and defendant was not present at the time, the evidentiary and argumentative portions of the hearing were transcribed, which was important for preserving defendant's rights. In re B.C., — Ohio App. 3d —, 2007 Ohio 6477, — N.E. 2d —, 2007 Ohio App. LEXIS 5670 (Nov. 27, 2007).

When a magistrate took the disposition of a juvenile delinquency case under advisement, after conducting adjudicatory and dispositional hearings, and then issued a sentencing decision without holding a hearing, this was not a violation of Ohio R. Juv. P. 37(A), requiring that hearings be recorded, because the decision was based on adjudicatory and dispositional hearings which were recorded, and the sentencing decision itself was not a proceeding which Rule 37(A) required to be recorded. In re Gibson, — Ohio App. 3d —, 2006 Ohio 5145, — N.E. 2d —, 2006 Ohio App. LEXIS 5109 (Oct. 2, 2006).

Appeal

Although there were portions of a transcript from a juvenile's parole-violation hearing that were not transcribable due to the juvenile's "inaudible" responses, pursuant to Ohio R. Juv. P. 37(A) there was no violation of the right to a recorded proceeding, as the transcript that was recorded was sufficient to show that the juvenile had waived his right to have counsel represent him in a knowing, voluntary, and intelligent manner. The juvenile failed in his burden to supplement the record with a statement pursuant to Ohio R. App. P. 9(C) where he failed to file such a statement. In re Andrew, — Ohio App. 3d —, 2007 Ohio 1021, — N.E. 2d —, 2007 Ohio App. LEXIS 927 (Mar. 9, 2007).

Where a juvenile court failed to comply with the recording requirement pursuant to Ohio R. Juv. P. 37(A) in a juvenile's delinquency proceeding, and the juvenile was unable to prepare an Ohio R. App. P. 9(C) statement for appellate purposes because he could not reach his prior counsel, the lack of clarity as to whether the juvenile was adjudicated as delinquent for a felony-level offense in order to determine if he was eligible for commitment to the Ohio Department of Youth Services required a remand for a new adjudication hearing. In re G.W., — Ohio App. 3d —, 2006 Ohio 5327, — N.E. 2d —, 2006 Ohio App. LEXIS 5320 (Oct. 12, 2006).

Since a trial court did not employ an adequate method of recording a change of plea hearing in a juvenile delinquency case, as required by Ohio R. Juv. P. 37, the appellate court was unable to ensure that the trial court properly complied with Ohio R. Juv. P. 29(D) and that appellant's plea was entered voluntarily, knowingly, and intelligently; thus, the trial court's judgment was reversed. In re Stoutamire, — Ohio App. 3d —, 2006 Ohio 5365, — N.E. 2d —, 2006 Ohio App. LEXIS 5374 (Oct. 13, 2006).

Failure to record proceedings

As a juvenile court failed to record hearings on three particular dates in defendant juvenile's delinquency adjudication and disposition hearings, there was a failure of compliance with the mandatory recording requirement of Ohio R. Juv. P. 37 which consituted reversible error. In re Whatley, — Ohio App. 3d —, 2007 Ohio 3039, — N.E. 2d —, 2007 Ohio App. LEXIS 2877 (June 12, 2007).

Harmless error

Although a juvenile court erred under Ohio R. Juv. P. 37(A) in failing to record an amenability hearing, wherein it relinquished jurisdiction over a juvenile defendant with respect to a criminal charge against him in favor of the general trial court, such was harmless error where a statement of evidence under Ohio R. App. P. 9(C) was deemed adequate to determine the question of whether the relinquishment of jurisdiction by the juvenile court was proper. State v. Lucas, — Ohio App. 3d —, 2007 Ohio 188, — N.E. 2d —, 2007 Ohio App. LEXIS 178 (Jan. 19, 2007).

In camera interview

When, in a dependency proceeding, a trial court interviewed the subject child in camera, the trial court's erroneous failure to make a record of that interview, pursuant to Ohio R. Juv. P. 37(A), was not reversible error because the trial court conducted a second interview of the child, which was recorded, and it appeared from a transcript of that interview that the trial court effectively questioned the child to determine the child's wishes and concerns about the allocation of parental rights and related issues, so the child's mother was not prejudiced by the court's failure to record the first interview. In re J.M., — Ohio App. 3d —, 2007 Ohio 4219, — N.E. 2d —, 2007 Ohio App. LEXIS 3816 (Aug. 20, 2007).

Transcript

Summary judgment was granted to a judge in an action by a prosecutor, seeking a writ of prohibition which was more appropriately considered as a writ of mandamus pursuant to RC § 2731.04, wherein a juvenile transcript from a bindover proceeding was sought, as the conditions under both Ohio R. Juv. P. 37(B) and Cuyahoga County, Ohio, Ct. C.P. Juv. R. 48(C)(4) were not met. The complaint was procedurally defective under Ohio Eighth Dist. Ct. App. R. 45(B)(1)(a), as it was in the form of a motion with a supportive brief rather than in the form of a complaint, and the supportive affidavit was lacking. State ex rel. Mason v. Floyd, — Ohio App. 3d —, 2007 Ohio 2368, — N.E. 2d —, 2007 Ohio App. LEXIS 2209 (May 15, 2007).

RULE 38.   Voluntary surrender of custody

(A) Temporary custody.

(1) A person with custody of a child may enter into an agreement with any public or private children services agency giving the agency temporary custody for a period of up to thirty days without the approval of the juvenile court. The agency may request the court to grant a thirty day extension of the original agreement. The court may grant the original extension if it determines the extension to be in the best interest of the child. A case plan shall be filed at the same time the request for extension is filed. At the expiration of the original thirty day extension period, the agency may request the court to grant an additional thirty day extension. The court may grant the additional extension if it determines the extension is in the child's best interest. The agency shall file an updated case plan at the same time it files the request for additional extension. At the expiration of the additional thirty day extension period, or at the expiration of the original thirty day extension period if no additional thirty day extension was requested, the agency shall either return the child to the custodian or file a complaint requesting temporary or permanent custody and a case plan.

(2) Notwithstanding division (A)(1) of this rule, the agreement may be for a period of sixty days if executed solely for the purpose of obtaining the adoption of a child less than six months of age. The agency may request the court to extend the temporary custody agreement for thirty days. A case plan shall be filed at the same time the request for extension is filed. At the expiration of the thirty day extension, the agency shall either return the child to the child's custodian or file a complaint with the court requesting temporary or permanent custody and a case plan.

(B) Permanent custody.

(1) A person with custody of a child may make an agreement with court approval surrendering the child into the permanent custody of a public children service agency or private child placing agency. A public children service agency shall request and a private child placing agency may request the juvenile court of the county in which the child had residence or legal settlement to approve the permanent surrender agreement. The court may approve the agreement if it determines it to be in the best interest of the child. The agency requesting the approval shall file a case plan at the same time it files its request for approval of the permanent surrender agreement.

(2) An agreement for the surrender of permanent custody of a child to a private service agency is not required to be approved by the court if the agreement is executed solely for the purpose of obtaining an adoption of a child who is less than six months of age on the date of the execution of the agreement.

One year after the agreement is entered and every subsequent twelve months after that date, the court shall schedule a review hearing if a final decree of adoption has not been entered for a child who is the subject of an agreement for the surrender of permanent custody.

History: Effective, 7-1-94.

RULE 39.   Out of county removal hearings

(A) **Notice of removal hearing.** Upon the filing of a removal action, the court in which the complaint is filed shall contact the court that issued the original dispositional order for information necessary for service of summons and issuance of notice of the removal hearing. The court that issued the original dispositional order shall respond within five days after receiving the request.

Summons shall issue pursuant to Juv. R. 15 and 16. Notice of the removal hearing shall be sent by first class mail, as evidenced by a certificate of mailing filed with the clerk of court, to the following, not otherwise summoned, at least five days before the hearing:

(1) The court issuing the dispositional order;

(2) The guardian ad litem for the child;

(3) Counsel for the child;

(4) The placing entity;

(5) The custodial entity;

(6) The complainant;

(7) The guardian ad litem and counsel presently representing the child in the court that issued the original dispositional order;

(8) Any other persons the court determines to be appropriate.

(B) **Removal hearing.** The removal hearing shall be held not later than thirty days after service of summons is obtained. If, after the removal hearing, the court grants relief in favor of the complainant, the court shall send written notice of such relief to the juvenile court that issued the original dispositional order.

History: Effective, 7-1-98.

NOTES TO DECISIONS

ANALYSIS

Jurisdiction

Jurisdiction

Where a mother sought to preclude a juvenile court judge from exercising post-judgment jurisdiction over visitation and custody motions filed by the father of her child after the mother had filed her intent to relocate to North Carolina with the child, her claim that the judge no longer had jurisdiction over the matter lacked merit, as the juvenile court and the judge had general statutory authority over such issues pursuant to RC §§ 2151.23 and 2151.231. The mother also failed to show entitlement to the writ where she had an adequate remedy at law through either an appeal or a request to transfer the proceedings to North Carolina, pursuant to Ohio R. Juv. P. 11 and 39, such that dismissal of the complaint was warranted. Rivers v. Ramsey, — Ohio App. 3d —, 2006 Ohio 1744, — N.E. 2d —, 2006 Ohio App. LEXIS 1610 (Apr. 3, 2006).

RULE 40.   Magistrates

(A) **Appointment.** The court may appoint one or more magistrates who shall be attorneys at law admitted to practice in Ohio. A magistrate appointed under this rule also may serve as a magistrate under Crim. R. 19. The court shall not appoint as a magistrate any person who has contemporaneous responsibility for working with, or supervising the behavior of, children who are subject to dispositional orders of the appointing court or any other juvenile court.

(B) **Compensation.** The compensation of magistrates shall be fixed by the court, and no part of the compensation shall be taxed as costs.

(C) **Authority.**

(1) *Scope.* To assist juvenile courts of record and pursuant to reference under Juv. R. 40(D)(1), magistrates are authorized, subject to the terms of the relevant reference, to do any of the following:

(a) Determine any motion in any case, except a case involving the determination of a child's status as a serious youthful offender;

(b) Conduct the trial of any case that will not be tried to a jury, except the adjudication of a case against an alleged serious youthful offender;

(c) Upon unanimous written consent of the parties, preside over the trial of any case that will be tried to a jury; except the adjudication of a case against an alleged serious youthful offender;

(d) Exercise any other authority specifically vested in magistrates by statute and consistent with this rule.

(2) *Regulation of proceedings.* In performing the responsibilities described in Juv. R. 40(C)(1), magistrates are authorized, subject to the terms of the relevant reference, to regulate all proceedings as if by the court and to do everything necessary for the efficient performance of those responsibilities, including but not limited to, the following:

(a) Issuing subpoenas for the attendance of witnesses and the production of evidence;

(b) Ruling upon the admissibility of evidence;

(c) Putting witnesses under oath and examining them;

(d) Calling the parties to the action and examining them under oath;

(e) When necessary to obtain the presence of an alleged contemnor in cases involving direct or indirect contempt of court, issuing an attachment for the alleged contemnor and setting the type, amount, and any conditions of bail pursuant to Crim. R. 46;

(f) Imposing, subject to Juv. R. 40(D)(8), appropriate sanctions for civil or criminal contempt committed in the presence of the magistrate.

(D) **Proceedings in Matters Referred to Magistrates**

(1) *Reference by court of record.*

(a) *Purpose and method.* A court may, for one or more of the purposes described in Juv. R. 40(C)(1), refer a particular case or matter or a category of cases or matters to a magistrate by a specific or general order of reference or by rule.

(b) *Limitation.* A court may limit a reference by specifying or limiting the magistrate's powers, including but not limited to, directing the magistrate to determine only particular issues, directing the magistrate to perform particular responsibilities, directing the magistrate to receive and report evidence only, fixing the time and place for beginning and closing any hearings, or fixing the time for filing any magistrate's decision on the matter or matters referred.

(2) *Magistrate's order; motion to set aside magistrate's order.*

(a) *Magistrate's order.*

(i) *Nature of order.* Subject to the terms of the relevant reference, a magistrate may enter orders without judicial approval if necessary to regulate the proceedings and if not dispositive of a claim or defense of a party.

(ii) *Form, filing, and service of magistrate's order.* A magistrate's order shall be in writing, identified as a magistrate's order in the caption, signed by the magistrate, filed with the clerk, and served on all parties or their attorneys.

(iii) *Magistrate's order include.* A magistrate's order includes any of the following:

(A) Pretrial proceedings under Civ. R. 16;

(B) Discovery proceedings under Civ. R. 26 to 37, Juv. R. 24, and Juv. R.25;

(C) Appointment of an attorney or guardian ad litem pursuant to Juv. R. 4 and Juv. R.29(B)(4);

(D) Taking a child into custody pursuant to Juv. R. 6;

(E) Detention hearings pursuant to Juv. R. 7;

(F) Temporary orders pursuant to Juv. R. 13;

(G) Extension of temporary orders pursuant to Juv. R. 14;

(H) Summons and warrants pursuant to Juv. R. 15;

(I) Preliminary conferences pursuant to Juv. R. 21;

(J) Continuances pursuant to Juv. R. 23;

(K) Deposition orders pursuant to Juv. R. 27(B)(3);

(L) Orders for social histories, physical and mental examinations pursuant to Juv. R. 32;

(M) Proceedings upon application for the issuance of a temporary protection order as authorized by law;

(N) Other orders as necessary to regulate the proceedings.

(b) *Motion to set aside magistrate's order.* Any party may file a motion with the court to set aside a magistrate's order. The motion shall state the moving party's reasons with particularity and shall be filed not later than ten days after the magistrate's order is filed. The pendency of a motion to set aside does not stay the effectiveness of the magistrate's order, though the magistrate or the court may by order stay the effectiveness of a magistrate's order.

(3) *Magistrate's decision; objections to magistrate's decision.*

(a) *Magistrate's decision.*

(i) *When required.* Subject to the terms of the relevant reference, a magistrate shall prepare a magistrate's decision respecting any matter referred under Juv. R. 40(D)(1).

(ii) *Findings of fact and conclusions of law.* Subject to the terms of the relevant reference, a magistrate's decision may be general unless findings of fact and conclusions of law are timely requested by a party or otherwise required by law. A request for findings of fact and conclusions of law shall be made before the entry of a magistrate's decision or within seven days after the filing of a magistrate's decision. If a request for findings of fact and conclusions of law is timely made, the magistrate may require any or all of the parties to submit proposed findings of fact and conclusions of law.

(iii) *Form; filing, and service of magistrate's decision.* A magistrate's decision shall be in writing, identified as a magistrate's decision in the caption, signed by the magistrate, filed with the clerk, and served on all parties or their attorneys no later than three days after the decision is filed. A magistrate's decision shall indicate conspicuously that a party shall not assign as error on appeal the court's adoption of any factual finding or legal conclusion, whether or not specifically designated as a finding of fact or conclusion of law under Juv. R. 40(D)(3)(a)(ii), unless the party timely and specifically objects to that factual finding or legal conclusion as required by Juv. R. 40(D)(3)(b).

(b) *Objections to magistrate's decision.*

(i) *Time for filing.* A party may file written objections to a magistrate's decision within fourteen days of the filing of the decision, whether or not the court has adopted the decision during that fourteen-day period as permitted by Juv. R. 40(D)(4)(e)(i). If any party timely files objections, any other party may also file objections not later than ten days after the first objections are filed. If a party makes a timely request for findings of fact and conclusions of law, the time for filing objections begins to run when the magistrate files a decision that includes findings of fact and conclusions of law.

(ii) *Specificity of objection.* An objection to a magistrate's decision shall be specific and state with particularity all grounds for objection.

(iii) Objection to magistrate's factual finding; transcript or affidavit. An objection to a factual finding, whether or not specifically designated as a finding of fact under Juv. R. 40(D)(3)(a)(ii), shall be supported by a transcript of all the evidence submitted to the magistrate relevant to that finding or an affidavit of that evidence if a transcript is not available. With leave of court, alternative technology or manner of reviewing the relevant evidence may be considered. The objecting party shall file the transcript or affidavit with the court within thirty days after filing objections unless the court extends the time in writing for preparation of the transcript or other good cause. If a party files timely objections prior to the date on which a transcript is prepared, the party may seek leave of court to supplement the objections.

(iv) *Waiver of right to assign adoption by court as error on appeal.* Except for a claim of plain error, a party shall not assign as error on appeal the court's adoption of any factual finding or legal conclusion, whether or not specifically designated as a finding of fact or conclusion of law under Juv. R. 40(D)(3)(a)(ii), unless the party has objected to that finding or conclusion as required by Juv. R. 40(D)(3)(b).

(4) *Action of court on magistrate's decision and on any objections to magistrate's decision; entry of judgment or interim order by court.*

(a) *Action of court required.* A magistrate's decision is not effective unless adopted by the court.

(b) *Action on magistrate's decision.* Whether or not objections are timely filed, a court may adopt or reject a magistrate's decision in whole or in part, with or without modification. A court may hear a previously-referred matter, take additional evidence, or return a matter to a magistrate.

(c) *If no objections are filed.* If no timely objections are filed, the court may adopt a magistrate's decision, unless it determines that there is an error of law or other defect evident on the face of the magistrate's decision.

(d) *Action on objections.* If one or more objections to a magistrate's decision are timely filed, the court shall rule on those objections. In ruling on objections, the court shall undertake an independent review as to the objected matters to ascertain that the magistrate has properly determined the factual issues and appropriately applied the law. Before so ruling, the court may hear additional evidence but may refuse to do so unless the objecting party demonstrates that the party could not, with reasonable diligence, have produced that evidence for consideration by the magistrate.

(e) *Entry of judgment or interim order by court.* A court that adopts, rejects, or modifies a magistrate's decision shall also enter a judgment or interim order.

(i) *Judgment.* The court may enter a judgment either during the fourteen days permitted by Juv. R. 40(D)(3)(b)(i) for the filing of objections to a magistrate's decision or after the fourteen days have expired. If the court enters a judgment during the fourteen days permitted by Juv. R. 40(D)(3)(b)(i) for the filing of objections, the timely filing of objections to the magistrate's decision shall operate as an automatic stay of execution of the judgment until the court disposes of those objections and vacates, modifies, or adheres to the judgment previously entered.

(ii) *Interim order.* The court may enter an interim order on the basis of a magistrate's decision without waiting for or ruling on timely objections by the parties where immediate relief is justified. The timely filing of objections does not stay the execution of an interim order, but an interim order shall not extend more than twenty-eight days from the date of entry, subject to extension by the court in increments of twenty-eight additional days for good cause shown.

(5) *Extension of time.* For good cause shown, the court shall allow a reasonable extension of time for a party to file a motion to set aside a magistrate's order or file objections to a magistrate's decision. "Good cause" includes, but is not limited to, a failure by the clerk to timely serve the party seeking the extension with the magistrate's order or decision.

(6) *Disqualification of a magistrate.* Disqualification of a magistrate for bias or other cause is within the discretion of the court and may be sought by motion filed with the court.

(7) *Recording of proceedings before a magistrate.* Except as otherwise provided by law, all proceedings before a magistrate shall be recorded in accordance with procedures established by the court.

(8) *Contempt in the presence of a magistrate.*

(a) *Contempt order.* Contempt sanctions under Juv. R. 40(C)(2)(f) may be imposed only by a written order that recites the facts and certifies that the magistrate saw or heard the conduct constituting contempt.

(b) *Filing and provision of copies of contempt order.* A contempt order shall be filed and copies provided forthwith by the clerk to the appropriate judge of the court and to the subject of the order.

(c) *Review of contempt order by court; bail.* The subject of a contempt order may by motion obtain immediate review by a judge. A judge or the magistrate entering the contempt order may set bail pending judicial review of the order.

History: Amended, eff 7-1-75; 7-1-85; 7-1-92; 7-1-95; 7-1-98; 7-1-01; 7-1-03, 7-1-06.

NOTES TO DECISIONS

Analysis

Generally
Appeal
Continuance
Error
Evidence
Interim orders
Magistrates
Objections to magistrate's findings of fact
Sentencing decision
Termination of parental rights
Time limitations
Transcript
Vacation of judgment
Void judgments
Waiver

Generally

Appellant, who failed to file objections to a magistrate's decision as required by Ohio R. Juv. P. 40(D)(3)(b)(iv), failed to demonstrate that the magistrate committed plain error in accepting appellant's admission in a juvenile delinquency proceeding without first informing appellant that he had the right to subpoena witnesses; instead, the magistrate substantially complied with the requirements of Ohio R. Juv. P. 29(D) by informing appellant of the consequences of his plea and advising him that he was giving up the opportunity to question witnesses, to remain silent, and to call his own witnesses. Ohio R. Juv. P. 29(D) does not require a magistrate to inform an appellant of his right to subpoena witnesses. In re T.K.W., — Ohio App. 3d —, 2007 Ohio 1205, — N.E. 2d —, 2007 Ohio App. LEXIS 1026 (Mar. 13, 2007).

Although a juvenile failed to object to a magistrate's determination in his delinquency matter, as required by Ohio R. Juv. P. 40(D)(3)(b)(i), the exception to waiver under Rule 40(D)(4) applied, as the magistrate committed prejudicial, plain error under Ohio R. Crim. P. 52 when she failed to personally address the juvenile to ascertain that he voluntarily, knowingly, and intelligently waived his rights as required by Ohio R. Juv. P. 29(D). The magistrate's reliance on counsel's statement that he had explained the waiver of rights to the juvenile was improper, as was reliance on the juvenile's written waiver form, such that there was no substantial compliance with Rule 29(D). In re Tabler, — Ohio App. 3d —, 2007 Ohio 411, — N.E. 2d —, 2007 Ohio App. LEXIS 366 (Jan. 29, 2007).

Even if a mother had not waived her right to challenge a decision granting legal custody of her children to their grandparents by failing to file the objections required by former Ohio R. Juv. P. 40(E)(4)(c), the record supported the grant of legal custody to the grandparents as the evidence showed that the children were doing well in the grandparents' home, that the children were attending school on a regular basis, and that the mother's progress on her case plan was slow. In re Christopher M., — Ohio App. 3d —, 2007 Ohio 1040, — N.E.2d —, 2007 Ohio App. LEXIS 975 (Mar. 9, 2007).

In a child custody matter, a mother did not affirmatively demonstrate, under either Ohio R. Juv. P. 40 or Ohio R. Civ.

P. 53, that a trial court did not independently review a magistrate's recommendations, because the absence of language in the trial court's judgment that it had conducted such an independent review was insufficient to make this showing. In re Taylor G., — Ohio App. 3d —, 2006 Ohio 1992, — N.E. 2d —, 2006 Ohio App. LEXIS 1824 (Apr. 21, 2006).

Appeal

Trial court properly adopted a magistrate's custody determination regarding parties' two children where neither party filed objections, and as the the trial court thereafter denied the mother's out-of-time objections, the waiver rule of Ohio R. Juv. P. 40(E)(3)(d) applied for purposes of her appeal, such that the custody issue was not reviewable. In re L.G., — Ohio App. 3d —, 2007 Ohio 591, — N.E. 2d —, 2007 Ohio App. LEXIS 545 (Feb. 12, 2007).

Because the father failed to file objections to the magistrate's decision which recommended granting permanent custody of his children to the agency, he waived his right to assign as error on appeal the trial court's adoption of the magistrate's decision. Although the father was required to filed objections within 14 days of the magistrate's decision, the father did not file objections despite having been advised in a written document of that right. In re Williams, — Ohio App. 3d —, 2007 Ohio 2082, — N.E. 2d —, 2007 Ohio App. LEXIS 1934 (Apr. 30, 2007).

Since a mother did not appeal from a trial court's award of permanent custody, res judicata barred the mother from challenging in her appeal from the trial court's later decision dismissing her motion for alternative disposition the trial court's award of permanent custody. Even if the mother had asserted assignments of error addressing the trial court's adoption of the magistrate's decision, the mother failed to file objections to the decision, and thus, pursuant to Ohio R. Juv. P. 40(E)(3)(d), she was precluded from assigning as error the trial court's adoption of the findings of fact and conclusions of law from that decision. In re K.B., — Ohio App. 3d —, 2006 Ohio 3104, — N.E. 2d —, 2006 Ohio App. LEXIS 2967 (June 20, 2006).

Since a mother's failure to file objections to the magistrate's decision (and attendant failure to file a transcript with the lower court) prevented the trial court from independently reviewing the error that the mother assigned on appeal, the appellate court's analysis was limited to a review of the trial court's actions in light of the facts reflected in the magistrate's decision. Hence, even though the record on appeal contained a transcript of the proceedings before the magistrate, the appellate court was precluded from considering the transcript on appeal In re Whaley, — Ohio App. 3d —, 2006 Ohio 4535, — N.E. 2d —, 2006 Ohio App. LEXIS 4512 (Sept. 1, 2006).

Father did not preserve the issue for appeal, under Ohio R. Juv. P. 40(E)(3)(d), because he failed to specifically object to the preponderance of the evidence standard which the magistrate issued to terminate his visitation rights. Instead, he objected to the result reached when applying the preponderance of evidence standard, not to the use of the standard itself. Antoine v. Lannom, — Ohio App. 3d —, 2006 Ohio 2354, — N.E. 2d —, 2006 Ohio App. LEXIS 2218 (May 10, 2006).

Since a mother failed to raise any objections to the magistrate's custody decision, as required by Ohio R. Juv. P. 40(E)(3)(d), she waived for purposes of appeal the issue of the propriety of the custody decision. In re T.G., — Ohio App. 3d —, 2006 Ohio 5504, — N.E. 2d —, 2006 Ohio App. LEXIS 5489 (Oct. 23, 2006).

Pursuant to Ohio R. Juv. P. 40(D)(3)(a) and Ohio R. Civ. P. 53(D)(3)(b), where a juvenile was adjudicated as delinquent and was thereafter found guilty of committing probation violations, which decisions were adopted by the trial court from a magistrate's determinations, and the juvenile failed to file objections to the magistrate's decision with respect to the failure of the magistrate to appoint a guardian ad litem for him

and to determine whether the juvenile's waiver of the right to counsel was voluntary, intelligent, or knowing, he waived any challenge on those issues on appeal except as to possible plain error. In re J-M, — Ohio App. 3d —, — N.E. 2d —, 2006 Ohio App. LEXIS 6131 (Nov. 22, 2006).

Continuance

When a magistrate presiding over a juvenile delinquency proceeding granted appellant juvenile's motion for acquittal after denying the State's motion for a continuance to allow a key witness to appear, and a trial court sustained the State's objection to that ruling, it was not a violation of double jeopardy to remand the matter to the magistrate for a continuation of appellant's trial because, under Ohio R. Juv. P. 40(D)(4)(a), the magistrate's decision was not effective until it was adopted by the trial court, and the trial court's decision was not an attempt to punish appellant a second time for the same crime. Brown v. State, — Ohio App. 3d —, 2006 Ohio 4791, — N.E. 2d —, 2006 Ohio App. LEXIS 4698 (Sept. 11, 2006).

Error

Because no objections were filed to the magistrate's decision, pursuant to Ohio R. Juv. P. 40(D)(3)(b)(iv), the father was precluded from directly challenging on appeal the trial court's adoption of the findings of fact and conclusions of law from the magistrate's decision. Accordingly, because there was no plain error in granting permanent custody of the children to the agency, the father's arguments were waived for appeal. In re A.J.S., — Ohio App. 3d —, 2007 Ohio 3433, — N.E. 2d —, 2007 Ohio App. LEXIS 3145 (June 29, 2007).

Evidence

There was no apparent error on the face of the magistrate's decision terminating the father's visitations rights, based on allegations that the father's live-in boyfriend had sexually abused the younger son, that the trial court ignored. The evidence which the trial court elected to credit comfortably satisfied the standard of showing extraordinary circumstances. Antoine v. Lannom, — Ohio App. 3d —, 2006 Ohio 2354, — N.E. 2d —, 2006 Ohio App. LEXIS 2218 (May 10, 2006).

Interim orders

Because the trial court never adopted the magistrate's decision, as required by former Ohio R. Juv. P. 40(E), which required the trial court to "adopt, reject, or modify" the magistrate's decision, the child support order never became a final judgment of the trial court and ceased to have any effect after the expiration of the interim order. Therefore, no material facts remained in dispute and the mother was entitled to judgment as a matter of law regarding any child support which had accrued as a result of any of the judgment entries issued after the interim order expired on February 25, 2002. State ex rel. Rangel v. Woodbury, — Ohio App. 3d —, 2007 Ohio 2151, — N.E. 2d —, 2007 Ohio App. LEXIS 1998 (May 3, 2007).

Magistrates

Although defendant, a juvenile, admitted to a misdemeanor charge of escape before a magistrate, whereupon he was adjudicated as deliquent, where the adjudication was immediately vacated due to an error in the charging complaint and defendant thereafter admitted to a felony charge of escape, whereupon he was again adjudicated delinquent, there was no double jeopardy violation under U.S. Const. amend. V. As the trial court had not accepted the first admission by defendant, pursuant to Ohio R. Juv. P. 40(D)(4) it was not effective. In re T.W., — Ohio App. 3d —, 2007 Ohio 2775, — N.E. 2d —, 2007 Ohio App. LEXIS 2578 (June 7, 2007).

Objections to magistrate's findings of fact

Trial court did not err by denying the mother's motion for leave to file supplemental objections to the child support decision because a transcript would not have aided the trial court's review of the magistrate's decision in any appreciable way. In any event, the mother could have filed an affidavit in lieu of a transcript under Ohio R. Juv. P. 40(D)(3)(a)(iii), so she had a viable alternative for supplementing her objections without a transcript. Siebert v. Tavarez, — Ohio App. 3d —, 2007 Ohio 2643, — N.E. 2d —, 2007 Ohio App. LEXIS 2472 (May 31, 2007).

Sentencing decision

When a magistrate took the disposition of a juvenile delinquency case under advisement, after conducting adjudicatory and dispositional hearings, and then issued a sentencing decision without holding a hearing, the subject juvenile did not waive his assignments of error related to the manner in which he was sentenced by not filing objections to the magistrate's decision, under Ohio R. Juv. P. 40(E)(3), because he did not contest any findings of fact or conclusions of law entered by the magistrate, but, rather, only contested the manner of his sentencing. In re Gibson, — Ohio App. 3d —, 2006 Ohio 5145, — N.E. 2d —, 2006 Ohio App. LEXIS 5109 (Oct. 2, 2006).

Termination of parental rights

There was no error in failing to commence the permanent custody hearing (RC § 2151.414) anew after counsel was appointed for the children, pursuant to Ohio R. Juv. P. 4 and RC § 2151.352, because the conflict between the guardian ad litem's recommendation and the children's wishes only became apparent after the hearing had commenced; the error was waived since the mother failed to object, pursuant to Ohio R. Juv. P. 40(3)(a)(i); the attorney declined the opportunity to call other witnesses who had testified at the earlier hearing, with full knowledge of what those witnesses had said, because the attorney was provided a transcript of that earlier hearing; and after the attorney was appointed to represent the children, the mother could no longer claim standing to object that the children's rights in the subsequent proceedings were violated. In re R.E., — Ohio App. 3d —, 2006 Ohio 1256, — N.E. 2d —, 2006 Ohio App. LEXIS 1145 (Mar. 17, 2006).

Time limitations

As a father's objections to a magistrate's decision involving the date that child support was to commence were clearly untimely under Ohio R. Juv. P. 40(E)(3)(a) and Ohio R. Civ. P. 53(E)(3), warranting dismissal thereof by the juvenile court, and the father he did not seek to enlarge the time within which to file objections pursuant to Ohio R. Juv. P. 18(B) and Ohio R. Civ. P. 6(B), his time to appeal was not extended by the objections. His failure to appeal within 30 days of the juvenile court's adoption of the magistrate's decision did not preserve his merit issue for appellate review under Ohio R. App. P. 4(A). In re D.K.K., — Ohio App. 3d —, 2006 Ohio 5576, — N.E. 2d —, 2006 Ohio App. LEXIS 5590 (Oct. 20, 2006).

Transcript

Although the grandparents' arguments challenged the magistrate's proceedings, neither of their two motions to set aside the entries of the magistrate was accompanied by a transcript of the evidence relevant to their claims, nor did they explain why a transcript was not available so that an affidavit of that evidence could be presented. Their reliance on two personal affidavits which were attached to their motion and response was misplaced because the affidavits failed to satisfy the requirements of the Ohio Rules of Civil Procedure and the Juvenile Rules for the support of challenges to the factual findings of a magistrate. In re I. S., — Ohio App. 3d —, 2007 Ohio 47, — N.E. 2d —, 2007 Ohio App. LEXIS 42 (Jan. 10, 2007).

It was an abuse of discretion for a trial court to sustain objections to a magistrate's decision denying an agency's motion for permanent custody of children because the record did not reflect that the trial court conducted an independent review of the magistrate's decision, as required by Ohio R. Civ. P. 53(D)(4)(b) and Ohio R. Juv. P. 40(D)(4)(b), because no transcript of the proceedings held before the magistrate was filed by the trial court, as required by Ohio R. Civ. P. 53(D)(3)(b)(iii) and Ohio R. Juv. P. 40(D)(3)(b)(iii). Children, — Ohio App. 3d —, 2007 Ohio 5123, — N.E. 2d —, 2007 Ohio App. LEXIS 4516 (Sept. 28, 2007).

In reviewing the decision of a magistrate granting permanent custody of a child to an agency, it was reversible error, under Ohio R. Juv. P. 40(E)(3)(b), for a trial court to overrule that decision without reviewing the entire transcript of the dispositional hearing at which that order was entered. In re L.R.T., 165 Ohio App. 3d 77, 2006 Ohio 207, 844 N.E. 2d 914, 2006 Ohio App. LEXIS 173 (Jan. 23, 2006).

Trial court properly denied objections of a father in a permanent custody proceeding to the findings and decision of a magistrate who recommended the grant of custody to the county agency, as the father failed to file a transcript with the trial court pursuant to Ohio R. Juv. P. 40(E)(3)(c); accordingly, the matter had not been properly perfected for appeal. In re Edwards, — Ohio App. 3d —, 2006 Ohio 3990, — N.E. 2d —, 2006 Ohio App. LEXIS 3919 (Aug. 3, 2006).

Vacation of judgment

As a trial court had not ruled on a minor child's mother's objections to a magistrate's decision, which had granted legal custody of the child to the maternal aunt and uncle, the decision was not a final order and a motion to vacate under Ohio R. Civ. P. 60(B) was not proper; however, the trial court had jurisdiction to vacate, modify, or adopt the magistrate's decision pursuant to the mother's pending objections under Ohio R. Juv. P. 40. In re Murphy, — Ohio App. 3d —, 2006 Ohio 5527, — N.E. 2d —, 2006 Ohio App. LEXIS 5518 (Oct. 17, 2006).

Void judgments

Trial court's decision was void because the magistrate's decision purportedly granting the mother's motion to modify custody of the child was not filed, as required by Ohio R. Juv. P. 40(D)(3)(a)(iii), and thus, had no effect at all. It did not start the time for filing objections or requesting findings of fact and conclusions of law and thus, there was nothing for the trial court to act on. In re A.R., — Ohio App. 3d —, 2007 Ohio 2910, — N.E. 2d —, 2007 Ohio App. LEXIS 2708 (June 14, 2007).

Waiver

Under Ohio R. Juv. P. 40(D)(3)(a)(iv), a claim that a decision by a magistrate is against the weight of the evidence must first be addressed to the trial court, by objection, and may not first be the subject of appeal. In re M.G., — Ohio App. 3d —, 2007 Ohio 3589, — N.E. 2d —, 2007 Ohio App. LEXIS 3294 (July 12, 2007).

Since a father failed to object to the decision of a magistrate in a permanent custody case, the father, under Ohio R. Juv. P. 40(D)(3)(a)(iv), waived all but plain error by the magistrate. A claim that a judgment is against the manifest weight of the evidence requires weighing of the evidence, involves substantial deference to the finder of fact, and does not rise to the level of plain error. In re M.G., — Ohio App. 3d —, 2007 Ohio 3589, — N.E. 2d —, 2007 Ohio App. LEXIS 3294 (July 12, 2007).

RULE 41. [Reserved]

RULE 42. Consent to marry

(A) **Application where parental consent not required.** When a minor desires to contract matrimony and has no parent, guardian, or custodian whose consent to the marriage is required by law, the minor shall file an application under oath in the county where the female resides requesting that the judge of the juvenile court give consent and approbation in the probate court for such marriage.

(B) **Contents of application.** The application required by division (A) of this rule shall contain all of the following:

(1) The name and address of the person for whom consent is sought;

(2) The age of the person for whom consent is sought;

(3) The reason why consent of a parent is not required;

(4) The name and address, if known, of the parent, where the minor alleges that parental consent is unnecessary because the parent has neglected or abandoned the child for at least one year immediately preceding the application.

(C) **Application where female pregnant or delivered of child born out of wedlock.** Where a female is pregnant or delivered of a child born out of wedlock and the parents of such child seek to marry even though one or both of them is under the minimum age prescribed by law for persons who may contract marriage, such persons shall file an application under oath in the county where the female resides requesting that the judge of the juvenile court give consent in the probate court to such marriage.

(D) **Contents of application.** The application required by subdivision (C) shall contain:

(1) The name and address of the person or persons for whom consent is sought;

(2) The age of such person;

(3) An indication of whether the female is pregnant or has already been delivered;

(4) An indication of whether or not any applicant under eighteen years of age is already a ward of the court; and

(5) Any other facts which may assist the court in determining whether to consent to such marriage.

If pregnancy is asserted, a certificate from a physician verifying pregnancy shall be attached to the application. If an illegitimate child has been delivered, the birth certificate of such child shall be attached.

The consent to the granting of the application by each parent whose consent to the marriage is required by law shall be indorsed on the application.

(E) **Investigation.** Upon receipt of an application under subdivision (C), the court shall set a date and time for hearing thereon at its earliest convenience and shall direct that an inquiry be made as to the circumstances surrounding the applicants.

(F) **Notice.** If neglect or abandonment is alleged in an application under subdivision (A) and the address of the parent is known, the court shall cause notice of the date and time of hearing to be served upon such parent.

(G) **Judgment.** If the court finds that the allegations stated in the application are true, and that the granting of the application is in the best interest of the applicants, the court shall grant the consent and shall make the applicant referred to in subdivision (C) a ward of the court.

(H) **Certified copy.** A certified copy of the judgment entry shall be transmitted to the probate court.

History: Amended, eff 7-1-80; 7-1-94.

RULE 43.   Reference to Ohio Revised Code

A reference in these rules to a section of the Revised Code shall mean the section as amended from time to time including the enactment of additional sections, the numbers of which are subsequent to the section referred to in the rules.

History: Amended, eff 7-1-94.

RULE 44.   Jurisdiction unaffected

These rules shall not be construed to extend or limit the jurisdiction of the juvenile court.

RULE 45.   Rules by juvenile courts; procedure not otherwise specified

(A) **Local rules.** The juvenile court may adopt rules concerning local practice that are not inconsistent with these rules. Local rules shall be adopted only after the court gives appropriate notice and an opportunity for comment. If the court determines that there is an immediate need for a rule, the court may adopt the rule without prior notice and opportunity for comment but promptly shall afford notice and opportunity for comment. Local rules shall be filed with the Supreme Court.

(B) **Procedure not otherwise specified.** If no procedure is specifically prescribed by these rules or local rule, the court shall proceed in any lawful manner not inconsistent with these rules or local rule.

History: Amended, eff 7-1-94.

RULE 46.   Forms

The forms contained in the Appendix of Forms which the supreme court from time to time may approve are illustrative and not mandatory.

RULE 47.   Effective Date

(A) **Effective date of rules.** These rules shall take effect on first day of July, 1972. They govern all proceedings in actions brought after they take effect and also all further proceedings in actions then pending except to the extent that their application in a particular action pending when the rules take effect would not be feasible or would work injustice, in which event the former procedure applies.

(B) **Effective date of amendments.** The amendments submitted by the Supreme Court to the General Assembly on January 12, 1973, shall take effect on the first day of July, 1973. They govern all proceedings in actions brought after they take effect and also all further proceedings in actions then pending, except to the extent that their application is a particular action pending when the amendments take effect would not be feasible or would work injustice, in which event the former procedure applies.

(C) **Effective date of amendments.** The amendments submitted by the Supreme Court to the General Assembly on January 10, 1975, and on April 29, 1975, shall take effect on July 1, 1975. They govern all proceedings in actions brought after they take effect and also all further proceedings in actions then pending, except to the extent that their application in a particular action pending when the amendments take effect would not be feasible or would work injustice, in which event the former procedure applies.

(D) **Effective date of amendments.** The amendments submitted by the Supreme Court to the General Assembly on January 9, 1976 shall take effect on July 1, 1976. They govern all proceedings in actions brought after they take effect and also all further proceedings in actions then pending, except to the extent that their application in a particular action pending when the amendments take effect would not be feasible or would work injustice, in which event the former procedure applies.

(E) **Effective date of amendments.** The amendments submitted by the Supreme Court to the General Assembly on January 14, 1980, shall take effect on July 1, 1980. They govern all proceedings in actions brought after they take effect and also all further proceedings in actions then pending, except to the extent that their application in a particular action pending when the amendments take effect would not be feasible or would work injustice, in which event the former procedure applies.

(F) **Effective date of amendments.** The amendments submitted by the Supreme Court to the General Assembly on December 24, 1984 and January 8, 1985 shall take effect on July 1, 1985. They govern all proceedings in actions brought after they take effect and also all further proceedings in actions then pending, except to the extent that their application in a particular action pending when the amendments take effect would not be feasible or would work injustice, in which event the former procedure applies.

(G) **Effective date of amendments.** The amendments submitted by the Supreme Court to the General Assembly on January 10, 1991 shall take effect on July 1, 1991. They govern all proceedings in actions brought after they take effect and also all further proceedings in actions then pending, except to the extent that their application in a particular action pending when the amendments take effect would not be feasible or would work injustice, in which event the former procedure applies.

(H) **Effective date of amendments.** The amendments filed by the Supreme Court with the General Assembly on January 14, 1992 and further filed on April 30, 1992, shall take effect on July 1, 1992. They govern all proceedings in actions brought after they take effect and also all future proceedings in actions then pending, except to the extent that their application in a particular action pending when the amendments take effect would not be feasible or would work injustice, in which event the former procedure applies.

(I) **Effective date of amendments.** The amendments filed by the Supreme Court with the General Assembly on January 14, 1994 and further revised and filed on April 29, 1994 shall take effect on July 1, 1994. They govern all proceedings in actions brought after they take effect and also all future proceedings in actions then pending, except to the extent that their application in a particular action pending when the

amendments take effect would not be feasible or would work injustice, in which event the former procedure applies.

(J) **Effective date of amendments.** The amendments to Rules 1, 4, and 40 filed by the Supreme Court with the General Assembly on January 11, 1995 and further revised and filed on April 25, 1995 shall take effect on July 1, 1995. They govern all proceedings in actions brought after they take effect and also all further proceedings in actions then pending, except to the extent that their application in a particular action pending when the amendments take effect would not be feasible or would work injustice, in which event the former procedure applies.

(K) **Effective date of amendments.** The amendments to Rules 6, 8, 13, 27, 34, 36, and 37 filed by the Supreme Court with the General Assembly on January 5, 1996 and refiled on April 26, 1996 shall take effect on July 1, 1996. They govern all proceedings in actions brought after they take effect and also all further proceedings in actions then pending, except to the extent that their application in a particular action pending when the amendments take effect would not be feasible or would work injustice, in which event the former procedure applies.

(L) **Effective date of amendments.** The amendments to Rule 30 filed by the Supreme Court with the General Assembly on January 10, 1997 and refiled on April 24, 1997 shall take effect on July 1, 1997. They govern all proceedings in actions brought after they take effect and also all further proceedings in actions then pending, except to the extent that their application in a particular action pending when the amendments take effect would not be feasible or would work injustice, in which event the former procedure applies.

(M) **Effective date of amendments.** The amendments to Rules 2, 4, 10, 11, 15, 16, 29, 39, and 40 filed by the Supreme Court with the General Assembly on January 15, 1998 and further revised and refiled on April 30, 1998 shall take effect on July 1, 1998. They govern all proceedings in actions brought after they take effect and also all further proceedings in actions then pending, except to the extent that their application in a particular action pending when the amendments take effect would not be feasible or would work injustice, in which event the former procedure applies.

(N) **Effective date of amendments.** The amendments to Juvenile Rules 2, 7, 8, 10, 15, 22, 27, 29, 37, and 40 filed by the Supreme Court with the General Assembly on January 12, 2001, and revised and refiled on April 26, 2001, shall take effect on July 1, 2001. They govern all proceedings in actions brought after they take effect and also all further proceedings in actions then pending, except to the extent that their application in a particular action pending when the amendments take effect would not be feasible or would work injustice, in which event the former procedure applies.

(O) **Effective date of amendments.** The amendments to Juvenile Rules 2, 10, 15, and 34 filed by the Supreme Court with the General Assembly on January 11, 2002, and refiled on April 18, 2002 shall take effect on July 1, 2002. They govern all proceedings in actions brought after they take effect and also all further proceedings in actions then pending, except to the extent that their application in a particular action pending when the amendments take effect would not be feasible or would work injustice, in which event the former procedure applies.

(P) **Effective date of amendments.** The amendments to Juvenile Rule 40 filed by the Supreme Court with the General Assembly on January 9, 2003 and refiled on April 28, 2003, shall take effect on July 1, 2003. They govern all proceedings in actions brought after they take effect and also all further proceedings in actions then pending, except to the extent that their application in a particular action pending when the amendments take effect would not be feasible or would work injustice, in which event the former procedure applies.

(Q) **Effective date of amendments.** The amendments to Juvenile Rule 29 filed by the Supreme Court with the General Assembly on January 7, 2004 and refiled on April 28, 2004 shall take effect on July 1, 2004. They govern all proceedings in actions brought after they take effect and also all further proceedings in actions then pending, except to the extent that their application in a particular action pending when the amendments take effect would not be feasible or would work injustice, in which event the former procedure applies.

(R) **Effective date of amendments.** The amend-

ments to Juvenile Rule 40 filed by the Supreme Court with the General Assembly on January 12, 2006 shall take effect on July 1, 2006. They govern all proceedings in actions brought after they take effect and also all further proceedings in actions then pending, except to the extent that their application in a particular action pending when the amendments take effect would not be feasible or would work injustice, in which event the former procedure applies.

(S) **Effective date of amendments.** The amendments to Juvenile Rule 25 filed by the Supreme Court with the General Assembly on January 14, 2009 and revised and refiled on April 30, 2009 shall take effect on July 1, 2009. They govern all proceedings in actions brought after they take effect and also all further proceedings in actions then pending, except to the extent that their application in a particular action pending when the amendments take effect would not be feasible or would work injustice, in which event the former procedure applies.

History: Amended, eff 7-1-73; 7-1-75; 7-1-76; 7-1-80; 7-1-85; 7-1-91; 7-1-92; 7-1-94; 7-1-95; 7-1-96; 7-1-97; 7-1-98; 7-1-01; 7-1-02; 7-1-03; 7-1-04; 7-1-06; 7-1-09.

RULE 48.   Title

These rules shall be known as Ohio Rules of Juvenile Procedure and may be cited as "Juvenile Rules" or "Juv. R.____"

Index to Ohio Rules of Juvenile Procedure

OHIO RULES OF EVIDENCE

ARTICLE I
GENERAL PROVISIONS

RULE 101. Scope of Rules: Applicability; Privileges; Exceptions

(A) **Applicability.** These rules govern proceedings in the courts of this state, subject to the exceptions stated in division (C) of this rule.

(B) **Privileges.** The rule with respect to privileges

applies at all stages of all actions, cases, and proceedings conducted under these rules.

(C) **Exceptions.** These rules (other than with respect to privileges) do not apply in the following situations:

(1) Admissibility determinations. Determinations prerequisite to rulings on the admissibility of evidence when the issue is to be determined by the court under Evid.R. 104.

(2) Grand jury. Proceedings before grand juries.

(3) Miscellaneous criminal proceedings. Proceedings for extradition or rendition of fugitives; sentencing; granting or revoking probation; proceedings with respect to community control sanctions; issuance of warrants for arrest; criminal summonses and search warrants; and proceedings with respect to release on bail or otherwise.

(4) Contempt. Contempt proceedings in which the court may act summarily.

(5) Arbitration. Proceedings for those mandatory arbitrations of civil cases authorized by the rules of superintendence and governed by local rules of court.

(6) Other rules. Proceedings in which other rules prescribed by the Supreme Court govern matters relating to evidence.

(7) Special non-adversary statutory proceedings. Special statutory proceedings of a non-adversary nature in which these rules would by nature be clearly inapplicable.

(8) Small claims division. Proceedings in the small claims division of a county or municipal court.

History: Amended, eff 7-1-90; 7-1-96; 7-1-99.

NOTES TO DECISIONS

ANALYSIS

Applicability
Community control
Exceptions
Motions to suppress
Probation hearing
Probation revocation
Sentencing hearings
Sexual classification hearings
Small claims court

Applicability

RC § 4511.19(D)(4)(b), allowing the admission, at a suppression hearing, of the results of field sobriety tests administered in substantial compliance with reliable standards, did not violate Ohio Const. art. IV, § 5(B), giving the Ohio Supreme Court the exclusive right to prescribe rules governing practice and procedure in Ohio courts, because, under Ohio R. Evid. 101(C), the Ohio Rules of Evidence did not apply to a suppression hearing, where the issue to be determined was the admissibility of evidence, under Ohio R. Evid. 104(A), and, since the Rules of Evidence did not apply in suppression hearings, RC § 4511.19(D)(4)(b) could not conflict any Rule of Evidence, including Ohio R. Evid. 702, regarding the admissibility of expert testimony, in a motion to suppress context. State v. Ladigo, — Ohio App. 3d —, 2006 Ohio 3475, — N.E. 2d —, 2006 Ohio App. LEXIS 3426 (June 27, 2006).

Trial court's determination that defendant violated his community control sanction was supported by sufficient evidence, based on testimony from a Kentucky police officer that defendant had been arrested for an incident with a 15-year-old girl and that he was in possession of pornographic material, both of which were prohibited as conditions of his sanction. The testimony was admissible because the Rules of Evidence were inapplicable to such a proceeding pursuant to Ohio R. Evid. 101(C), and a certified copy of the conviction in Kentucky was admissible pursuant to Ohio R. Evid. 902(1). State v. Kincer, — Ohio App. 3d —, 2006 Ohio 2249, — N.E. 2d —, 2006 Ohio App. LEXIS 2087 (May 8, 2006).

Community control

Trial court did not rely upon unreliable evidence or base its decision on nonexistent proof; the evidence was presented at a community control revocation hearing where the Ohio Rules of Evidence did not strictly apply. Even without the evidence concerning defendant's possession of cocaine and curfew violation, defendant signed a statement admitting his use of Xanax and that admission was sufficient to establish a violation of the condition that he not use, own, possess or have immediate control of any type of controlled substance, drug, or narcotic, except on prescription by a physician. State v. Belcher, — Ohio App. 3d —, 2007 Ohio 4256, — N.E. 2d —, 2007 Ohio App. LEXIS 3933 (Aug. 7, 2007).

Community control revocation hearings are not subjected to the rules of evidence, thus allowing for the admission of hearsay evidence, under Ohio R. Evid. 101(C)(3), since a probation revocation hearing is an informal proceeding, not a criminal trial, and the trier of fact should be able to consider any reliable and relevant evidence to determine whether the probationer has violated the conditions of his probation, but the introduction of hearsay evidence into a revocation hearing is reversible error when that evidence is the only evidence presented and is crucial to a determination of a probation violation. Ohio v. Ryan, — Ohio App. 3d —, 2007 Ohio 4743, — N.E. 2d —, 2007 Ohio App. LEXIS 4282 (Sept. 17, 2007).

During a hearing on the State's motion to revoke defendant's five-year term of community control on a felonious assault conviction because he had violated its conditions by failing to complete an inpatient drug treatment program, any error in admitting a letter from a program representative who did not testify at the hearing was harmless. The rules of evidence were inapplicable at revocation hearings under Ohio R. Evid. 101(C)(3), and defendant's due process rights to confront and cross-examine witnesses were not violated because his admissions by themselves were sufficient to prove a violation. State v. Meadows, — Ohio App. 3d —, 2006 Ohio 5887, — N.E. 2d —, 2006 Ohio App. LEXIS 5838 (Nov. 2, 2006).

Exceptions

When defendant, who pled guilty to three counts of rape, claimed inadmissible hearsay was introduced at her sentencing and that the trial court's acceptance of this evidence was plain error, because it deprived her of her right to confront the witnesses against her, her guilty plea waived her rights to confrontation and, under Ohio R. Evid. 101(C), sentencing hearings were among those certain criminal proceeidngs in which the rules of evidence, including the hearsay rule, did not apply, so the trial court could consider reliable hearsay in imposing sentence. State v. Bene, — Ohio App. 3d —, 2006 Ohio 3628, — N.E. 2d —, 2006 Ohio App. LEXIS 3579 (July 17, 2006).

Motions to suppress

Rules of Evidence do not apply to suppression hearings: State v. Boczar, 113 Ohio St. 3d 148, 2007 Ohio 1251, 863 N.E.2d 155, 2007 Ohio LEXIS 800 (2007).

Probation hearing

Trial court's finding that defendant violated his probation was supported by the evidence that he had failed to report for probation, he failed to obtain a required driver's license, and he committed other offenses, the admission of a record from the Ohio Bureau of Motor Vehicles was proper pursuant to Ohio R. Evid. 803(6) and moreover, the Ohio Rules of Evidence were inapplicable to such proceedings based on Ohio R. Evid. 101(C)(3). The sentences imposed for the revocation were within the proper range under RC §§ 2929.25(C)(2) and 2929.22. State v. Wallace, — Ohio App. 3d —, 2007 Ohio 3184, — N.E. 2d —, 2007 Ohio App. LEXIS 2968 (June 22, 2007).

Probation revocation

As the Ohio Rules of Evidence were inapplicable to defendant's community control revocation proceeding pursuant to Ohio R. Evid. 101(C)(3), there was no error in allowing a probation officer to testify as to the alleged violations of defendant's community control with respect to the probable cause hearing, although he was not the officer who prepared the motion to revoke and he had no first-hand knowledge of the alleged violations, as any violation of defendant's confrontation rights pursuant to due process under U.S. Const. amend. XIV were harmless error under Ohio R. Crim. P. 52 at that stage of the revocation proceeding. The probation officer who did prepare the motion and who had first-hand knowledge of the violations appeared and was cross-examined at the merits hearing regarding the violations. State v. Gullet, — Ohio App. 3d —, 2006 Ohio 6564, — N.E. 2d —, 2006 Ohio App. LEXIS 6482 (Nov. 13, 2006).

Trial court erred in finding that defendant committed a probation vioation by having unsupervised contact with children, as the proof of that violation was solely based on hearsay evidence and the accuser was not available for cross-examination, which was a violation of defendant's due process rights under U.S. Const. amend. XIV; however, as the Ohio Rules of Evidence were not applicable to such hearings pursuant to Ohio R. Evid. 101(C)(3) and there were other probation violations which were sufficiently shown, the revocation of his probation was not error. State v. Ohly, 166 Ohio App. 3d 808, 2006 Ohio 2353, 853 N.E. 2d 675, 2006 Ohio App. LEXIS 2221 (May 12, 2006).

Sentencing hearings

In a burglary sentencing, it was not error for a trial court to receive the testimony of a detective about the crime's impact on the victim, because the rules of evidence, including the hearsay rule, did not apply to a criminal sentencing, and there was no authority for the proposition that a trial court's findings about the impact of a crime on a victim had to be based solely on evidence from the victim, so the trial court could rely on reliable hearsay in its sentencing decision. State v. Hyland, — Ohio App. 3d —, 2006 Ohio 339, — N.E. 2d —, 2006 Ohio App. LEXIS 312 (Jan. 30, 2006).

Sexual classification hearings

Trial court did not err by admitting into evidence documents that contained hearsay at defendant's sexual predator classification hearing. Since, pursuant to Ohio R. Evid. 101(C)(3), the Ohio Rules of Evidence were not strictly applicable to a defendant's sexual classification hearing, the State was permitted to introduce into evidence the presentence investigation report to demonstrate defendant's prior convictions, the court psychiatric clinic's sexual predator evaluation to demonstrate defendant's lack of remorse for the offense, and the victim's statement. State v. Irvin, — Ohio App. 3d —, 2007 Ohio 5328, — N.E. 2d —, 2007 Ohio App. LEXIS 4663 (Oct. 4, 2007).

Small claims court

Where a witness was subpoenaed to testify for a party but he was not compensated as an expert, the trial court did not err in excusing him from appearing, pursuant to Ohio R. Civ. P. 45(C)(3)(c), (d), and (C)(5). Although it was error not to have allowed the party to testify as to what the expert had told him because the rules of evidence were relaxed in the small claims court action pursuant to Ohio R. Evid. 101(C)(8), as

the party failed to proffer what his testimony would have been under Ohio R. Evid. 103(A)(2), the error was deemed waived for purposes of appeal. Melcher v. Ryan, — Ohio App. 3d —, 2006 Ohio 4609, — N.E. 2d —, 2006 Ohio App. LEXIS 4565 (Aug. 31, 2006).

RULE 102. Purpose and Construction; Supplementary Principles

The purpose of these rules is to provide procedures for the adjudication of causes to the end that the truth may be ascertained and proceedings justly determined. The principles of the common law of Ohio shall supplement the provisions of these rules, and the rules shall be construed to state the principles of the common law of Ohio unless the rule clearly indicates that a change is intended. These rules shall not supersede substantive statutory provisions.

History: Amended, eff 7-1-96.

NOTES TO DECISIONS

ANALYSIS

Purpose of the rules

Purpose of the rules

Exclusion of the results of portable breath tests was consistent with the purpose of the Ohio Rules of Evidence, as stated in Ohio R. Evid. 102, to ascertain the truth because the results of such tests were inherently unreliable, as they measured the presence of certain chemicals in a subject's breath which were also present in non-intoxicating substances to which a subject might be exposed. State v. Shuler, 168 Ohio App. 3d 183, 2006 Ohio 4336, 858 N.E. 2d 1254, 2006 Ohio App. LEXIS 4268 (July 27, 2006).

RULE 103. Rulings on Evidence

(A) **Effect of erroneous ruling.** Error may not be predicated upon a ruling which admits or excludes evidence unless a substantial right of the party is affected, and

(1) **Objection.** In case the ruling is one admitting evidence, timely objection or motion to strike appears of record stating the specific ground of objection, if the specific ground was not apparent from the context; or

(2) **Offer of proof.** In case the ruling is one excluding evidence, the substance of the evidence was made known to the court by offer or was apparent from the context within which questions were asked. Offer of proof is not necessary if evidence is excluded during cross-examination.

(B) **Record of offer and ruling.** At the time of making the ruling, the court may add any other or further statement which shows the character of the evidence, the form in which it was offered, the objection made, and the ruling thereon. It may direct the making of an offer in question and answer form.

(C) **Hearing of jury.** In jury cases, proceedings shall be conducted, to the extent practicable, so as to prevent inadmissible evidence from being suggested to the jury by any means, such as making statements or offers of proof or asking questions in the hearing of the jury.

(D) **Plain error.** Nothing in this rule precludes

taking notice of plain errors affecting substantial rights although they were not brought to the attention of the court.

NOTES TO DECISIONS

ANALYSIS

Admission or exclusion of evidence
Cumulative errors
Error
Failure to object
Failure to object to evidence at trial
Harmless error
Necessity of proffer
Objection
Order granting or denying motion in limine
Plain error
Preservation of error
Proffer
Sentencing
Trial court ruling on admission or exclusion of evidence
Trial court's evidentiary ruling

Admission or exclusion of evidence

Trial court erred in finding that a landlord had complied with the conditions of an agreed judgment entered by a magistrate, based on testimony from an elevator inspector that the elevators were code compliant, as the agreed judgment had required more than code compliance. The elevators also had to be in good and safe working order pursuant to RC § 5321.04(A)(4) and accordingly, when the matter was remanded for determination of whether that additional standard was met, it would be an abuse of discretion if the trial court again precluded the tenants from testifying as to the condition of the elevators pursuant to Ohio R. Evid. 103(A). Community Dev. Props. Cleveland v. Griffin, — Ohio App. 3d —, 2007 Ohio 835, — N.E. 2d —, 2007 Ohio App. LEXIS 748 (Mar. 1, 2007).

Trial court properly used its broad discretion to exclude the DNA report because it appeared that the defense purposefully failed to mention the asterisked statement regarding additional unidentifiable DNA while the authoring witness was on the stand so that they could refer to the part that seemed to benefit them in closing arguments without her rebutting testimony and the defense did not have their own DNA expert mention the supposed existence of a third type of DNA. Neither the State nor the defense introduced, authenticated, or identified the report in their cases and the tactics used by the defense showed a desire to mislead or confuse the jury. State v. Charley, — Ohio App. 3d —, 2007 Ohio 1108, — N.E. 2d —, 2007 Ohio App. LEXIS 1029 (Mar. 6, 2007).

Although a trial court's decision to allow a county coroner to testify that a doctor was not negligent in treating a patient who later died and that the doctor performed his examination and assessment of the patient according to the relevant standards of care was arguably erroneous, an appellate court had to presume the regularity of the trial court's rulings on evidence pursuant to Ohio R. Evid. 103(A) where the complete transcript of the trial testimony was not provided by the patient's estate executor pursuant to her duty under Ohio R. App. P. 9(B) in her wrongful death action; due to the incomplete transcript, the court could not determine whether or not the coroner's testimony affected a substantial right of the executor and warranted reversal. Frazier v. Pruitt, — Ohio App. 3d —, 2007 Ohio 3256, — N.E. 2d —, 2007 Ohio App. LEXIS 3002 (June 22, 2007).

When a printer sued newspapers on a past due account, it was not an abuse of discretion for a trial court to admit an exhibit summarizing the newspapers' account, over the newspapers' objection, because, even if the exhibit was erroneously admitted, the newspapers did not show the court's ruling affected their substantial right because (1) other testimony had established the amount due, (2) the newspapers did not support their claim that they had only stipulated to the admission of the first page of the exhibit, and (3) the newspapers did not object at all relevant places in the record. Marysville v. Del. Gazette Co., — Ohio App. 3d —, 2007 Ohio 4365, — N.E. 2d —, 2007 Ohio App. LEXIS 3943 (Aug. 27, 2007).

Cumulative errors

Where a trial court abused its discretion by allowing the admission of testimony from an alleged prior victim of defendant's attack and from defendant's probation officer, such cumulative errors prejudiced defendant pursuant to Ohio R. Crim. P. 52(A) and Ohio R. Evid. 103(A), as despite other substantial evidence against defendant in the murder trial, it was clear that his counsel's trial strategy was seriously altered or abandoned when the trial court allowed such testimony, as it had been restricted or precluded in a prior trial that ended in a mistrial. As the testimony was extensive, largely irrelevant, and highly prejudicial, it appeared that defendant would have presented his defense differently if the testimony were not admitted, and further, that the outcome of the matter would have been different as well. State v. Anderson, — Ohio App. 3d —, 2006 Ohio 4618, — N.E. 2d —, 2006 Ohio App. LEXIS 4581 (Sept. 1, 2006).

Error

In a medical malpractice case alleging a physician's failure to diagnose and treat a decedent's colon cancer, a trial court's erroneous preclusion of non-hearsay testimony by the decedent's executrix regarding the physician's failure to prescribe a colonoscopy for the decedent affected a substantial right, under Ohio R. Evid. 103(A), and was not harmless because it left the physician's testimony that the physician had advised the decedent to have a colonoscopy unchallenged, so that the jury was left with no evidence to contradict the physician. Estate of Holman v. Kates, — Ohio App. 3d —, 2007 Ohio 3778, — N.E. 2d —, 2007 Ohio App. LEXIS 3438 (July 26, 2007).

Although a trial court erred in excluding a police report in defendant's criminal trial, as it was admissible under Ohio R. Evid. 803(8)(b) where it was offered by defendant to show alleged inconsistencies in the eyewitness testimony regarding the incident and the identification of defendant as the perpetrator, the error did not affect defendant's substantial rights under Ohio R. Evid. 103(A) because the slight inconsistencies were based on clothing worn by defendant, but there were multiple identifications of him as the shooter. State v. Tiller, — Ohio App. 3d —, 2007 Ohio 3943, — N.E. 2d —, 2007 Ohio App. LEXIS 3577 (Aug. 3, 2007).

Failure to object

In a former employee's suit against a former employer for overtime pay, when the employer's witness allegedly testified from notes from a deposition ruled inadmissible, except to impeach him, while the employee waived an objection by not timely raising one, under Ohio R. Evid. 103(A)(1), it was not plain error to allow the witness to refresh his memory, given the passage of time between the events at issue and the testimony. Choate v. Tranet, Inc., — Ohio App. 3d —, 2006 Ohio 4565, — N.E. 2d —, 2006 Ohio App. LEXIS 4497 (Sept. 5, 2006).

In an appeal in a patient's dental malpractice action, the dentist waived his assignment of error relating to comments by the patient's counsel during closing arguments about two experts who did not testify by failing to object during the trial when the dentist's experts were asked about the opinions of the experts who did not testify. Failure to object to the use of evidence when the alleged error could be remedied waived the right to address that issue on appeal under Ohio R. Evid. 103(A)(1). Scibelli v. Pannunzio, — Ohio App. 3d —, 2006 Ohio 5652, — N.E. 2d —, 2006 Ohio App. LEXIS 5650 (Oct. 26, 2006).

Failure to object to evidence at trial

There was no plain error under Ohio R. Crim. P. 52(B), based on defendant's failure to object at trial pursuant to Ohio R. Evid. 103(A)(1), in a juvenile court's admission of a victim's identification of defendant, a juvenile, as the perpetrator of a criminal offense, as the victim indicated that he knew defendant by his face although he did not immediately know his name and the victim had an adequate amount of time to observe defendant during commission of the crime. Although the one man "show-up" identification procedure at the police station was unduly suggestive pursuant to U.S. Const. amend. V, Ohio Const. art. I, §§ 10 and 16, and Ohio R. Juv. P. 29(E)(4), it did not present a very substantial likelihood of irreparable misidentification. In re Lower, — Ohio App. 3d —, 2007 Ohio 1735, — N.E. 2d —, 2007 Ohio App. LEXIS 1581 (Apr. 5, 2007).

Where an insurer's motion in limine to exclude the videotaped testimony of two treating physicians of an insured was denied by the trial court and thereafter during trial, the insurer failed to object when the videotaped testimony was offered, any error thereon was waived for purposes of appeal under Ohio R. Evid. 103(A). Butler v. Minton, — Ohio App. 3d —, 2006 Ohio 4800, — N.E. 2d —, 2006 Ohio App. LEXIS 4710 (Sept. 15, 2006).

In a former employee's suit against a former employer for overtime pay, when the employer's witness allegedly testified from notes from a deposition ruled inadmissible, except to impeach him, the employee did not timely state a specific objection, under Ohio R. Evid. 103(A)(1), so the trial court could not determine what the witness read from, and the objection was waived. Choate v. Tranet, Inc., — Ohio App. 3d —, 2006 Ohio 4565, — N.E. 2d —, 2006 Ohio App. LEXIS 4497 (Sept. 5, 2006).

During defendant's trial for two counts of nonsupport of dependents under RC § 2919.21(A)(2), defendant waived the right to challenge testimony from a former wife about his alleged sexual misconduct with a daughter under Ohio R. Evid. 103(A)(1) by failing to object to earlier cross-examination of his expert on the same subject; the trial court did not abuse its discretion in admitting the wife's testimony because the jury had already heard the same evidence before she testified. State v. Browne, — Ohio App. 3d —, 2006 Ohio 5229, — N.E. 2d —, 2006 Ohio App. LEXIS 5208 (Sept. 27, 2006).

During defendant's trial for two counts of nonsupport of dependents under RC § 2919.21(A)(2), defendant waived the right to challenge the testimony of an expert witness for the State about his alleged sexual misconduct with a daughter under Ohio R. Evid. 103(A)(1) by failing to object either to her testimony or to earlier cross-examination of his expert on the same subject. The expert did not testify directly on the subject but made passing references to the allegations while testifying about his work and psychiatric history. State v. Browne, — Ohio App. 3d —, 2006 Ohio 5229, — N.E. 2d —, 2006 Ohio App. LEXIS 5208 (Sept. 27, 2006).

Harmless error

Although it was error for a trial court to have admitted testimony from the victim of a vehicle accident in defendant's criminal action on a charge of, inter alia, aggravated vehicular assault, concerning the nature and extent of her injuries pursuant to Ohio R. Evid. 401 and 403(A), given the stipulation accepted by the State that defendant admitted to having caused the accident which caused serious physical harm to the victim, the introduction of the evidence was harmless under Ohio R. Evid. 103(A) and Ohio R. Crim. P. 52(A). There was other significant evidence indicative of defendant's guilt, and

the introduction of the victim's testimony regarding her injuries was limited by the trial court's instruction to the jury and was harmless in the circumstances. State v. Harding, — Ohio App. 3d —, 2006 Ohio 481, — N.E. 2d —, 2006 Ohio App. LEXIS 411 (2006).

Necessity of proffer

When a husband sought to have a wife held in contempt for violating the parties' shared parenting plan, and the wife sought to have one of the parties' children testify at the contempt hearing, while it was arbitrary for a magistrate to exclude the child's testimony, the wife did not proffer the evidence the child would offer, as required by Ohio R. Evid. 103(A)(2), nor did the wife object to the exclusion, as required by Ohio R. Civ. P. 53(D)(3)(a)(iv) to preserve the issue for appeal, so the issue was waived. Carver v. Halley, — Ohio App. 3d —, 2007 Ohio 2351, — N.E. 2d —, 2007 Ohio App. LEXIS 2188 (May 11, 2007).

Where a wife in a divorce action failed to proffer an expert witness's testimony, as required by Ohio R. Evid. 103(A)(2) for purposes of preserving error on appeal, the court was unable to determine whether the excluded evidence of the expert was reliable for purposes of Ohio R. Evid. 702. The magistrate who heard the matter had limited the expert's ability to testify as an expert with respect to families who were going through a divorce with one parent who made sexual allegations with regard to another parent where a child was involved, as the last training that the expert had on the related subject was approximately four years ago. Crawford v. Crawford, — Ohio App. 3d —, 2007 Ohio 3139, — N.E. 2d —, 2007 Ohio App. LEXIS 2890 (June 25, 2007).

As defendant inmate failed to proffer testimony pursuant to Ohio R. Evid. 103(A)(2) that his wife would have given in a hearing on his motion to withdraw his guilty pleas pursuant to RC § 2943.031 with respect to defendant's delay in filing the motion, the trial court's decision to deny the motion based, inter alia, on untimeliness was not subject to review. Ohio v. Balderas, — Ohio App. 3d —, 2007 Ohio 4887, — N.E. 2d —, 2007 Ohio App. LEXIS 4376 (Sept. 21, 2007).

Defendant's question to a minor sexual imposition victim's mother on direct examination if she had experienced problems in the past with the victim lying to her violated Ohio R. Evid. 608(B) because it sought extrinsic evidence to impeach the victim's credibility. Even if the question were proper, defendant did not make the substance of the evidence known to the trial court, by means of a proffer, after the State's objection was sustained, and the evidence defendant sought was not apparent from the context of his questions. Under Ohio R. Evid. 103(A)(2), defendant could not predicate error upon the ruling. State v. Smith, — Ohio App. 3d —, 2006 Ohio 45, — N.E. 2d —, 2006 Ohio App. LEXIS 44 (Jan. 6, 2006).

Trial court's exclusion of a product purchaser's exhibits in order to show that a vendor who was being sued on grounds of, inter alia, civil conspiracy had charged more than other vendors was not an error that was preserved for review on appeal pursuant to Ohio R. Evid. 103(A)(2), as the purchaser did not proffer those exhibits and the substance thereof was not apparent from the context; further, even if the excluded exhibits were admitted, such evidence would not have overcome the actual lack of evidence of the alleged conspiracy. Orbit Electronics, Inc. v. Helm Instrument Co., Inc., 167 Ohio App. 3d 301, 2006 Ohio 2317, 855 N.E. 2d 91, 2006 Ohio App. LEXIS 2172 (May 11, 2006).

Although a trial court erred in refusing to admit a juvenile's testimony as to a victim's reputation for truthfulness pursuant to Ohio R. Evid. 608(A) in the juvenile's delinquency proceeding, as he failed to proffer what his testimony would have been and he did not provide the basis for his opinion concerning the victim's reputation for truthfulness other than a conclusory statement, the issue could not be raised as error on appeal pursuant to Ohio R. Evid. 103(A). There was no ability to determine from the record whether the juvenile was prejudiced by the exclusion of the evidence. In re Shane L. F., — Ohio App. 3d —, 2006 Ohio 3876, — N.E. 2d —, 2006 Ohio App. LEXIS 3825 (July 28, 2006).

Defendant's contention that the trial court abused its discretion by refusing to permit him to present evidence, under Ohio R. Evid. 608(B), about false allegations of criminal conduct that the victim in defendant's vandalism prosecution had previously made against defendant was without merit because the mere fact that defendant was convicted of only two of the 12 charges the victim made against defendant in the past did not mean that the victim testified falsely about those accusations, and any error in the ruling was harmless because the victim's credibility was not at issue. Further, defendant never proffered what his defense witnesses would testify concerning any prior false accusations allegedly made by the victim against defendant, as required by Ohio R. Evid. 103(A)(2). State v. Mills, — Ohio App. 3d —, 2006 Ohio 4010, — N.E. 2d —, 2006 Ohio App. LEXIS 3939 (Aug. 4, 2006).

In an appropriation proceeding, Ohio Department of Transportation waived any error in the trial court's exclusion of evidence of "comparable sale" prices by failing to properly object and to properly proffer a sufficient foundation for the admissibility of the "comparable sales" price evidence, in that, without a proper objection and proffer, the court was unable to conclude that the trial court excluded the evidence. Even assuming that the trial court excluded the evidence, without a proffer the court could not conclude that it was an abuse of discretion to exclude under Ohio R. Evid. 403 evidence of sales occurring 18 months after the taking of the property. Proctor v. Dennis, — Ohio App. 3d —, 2006 Ohio 4442, — N.E. 2d —, 2006 Ohio App. LEXIS 4385 (Aug. 16, 2006).

In a workers' compensation case, when an employer appealed a trial court's judgment, based on a jury's verdict, that an injured worker was the employer's employee, the employer could not argue that the trial court erroneously excluded certain documents because the employer did not proffer them at trial or explain their contents, as required by Ohio R. Evid. 103(A)(2), so the substance of the evidence was not made known to the trial court by offer, nor was it apparent from the context within which questions were asked. Noguez v. Administrator, — Ohio App. 3d —, — N.E. 2d —, 2006 Ohio 5067, 2006 Ohio App. LEXIS 5042 (2006).

In a wrongful death suit, since the administrator, pursuant to Ohio R. Evid. 103(A)(2), did not attempt to introduce or proffer the evidence he sought to introduce through his expert's testimony on the issue of proximate cause and since he did not renew his objection during trial to the trial court's exclusion of the testimony, he waived any alleged error. Bloomfield v. Fox, — Ohio App. 3d —, 2006 Ohio 5489, — N.E. 2d —, 2006 Ohio App. LEXIS 5472 (Oct. 23, 2006).

Objection

In a child custody dispute regarding a shared parenting plan, a trial court did not abuse its discretion in admitting a report of an expert who was originally appointed by the trial court in the parties' divorce action pursuant to RC § 3109.04(C), as the mother failed to object to the admission of the written report pursuant to Ohio R. Evid. 103(A) and she failed to request in writing to view the report, and further, she took advantage of the opportunity to cross-examine the expert in regards to his report. Waclawski v. Waclawski, — Ohio App. 3d —, 2006 Ohio 3213, — N.E. 2d —, 2006 Ohio App. LEXIS 3125 (June 23, 2006).

Order granting or denying motion in limine

In a workers' compensation case, the trial court committed prejudicial error in denying a former employee's motion in limine to exclude a physician's testimony. The physician was barred under res judicata principles from testifying that the former employee's surgery had nothing to do with the former

employee's previous allowed conditions and that the former employee's lumbar disc disease could not arise from a single event, namely a 1984 fall; thus, the trial court abused its discretion in allowing the physician to testify to the contrary. Hickle v. Hayes-Albion Corp., — Ohio App. 3d —, 2007 Ohio 4236, — N.E. 2d —, 2007 Ohio App. LEXIS 3889 (Aug. 20, 2007).

Plain error

Defendant failed to raise the issue that his wife was incompetent to testify against him in his trial for operating a vehicle while under the influence of alcohol. Admitting the wife's testimony did not constitute plain error under Ohio R. Evid. 103(D) or Ohio R. Crim. P. 52(B) because the wife's testimony tended to help rather than hurt defendant (the wife claimed that defendant was agitated and suicidal but not drunk) and the evidence against defendant was overwhelming. City of Mason v. Molinari, — Ohio App. 3d —, 2007 Ohio 5395, — N.E. 2d —, 2007 Ohio App. LEXIS 4739 (Oct. 9, 2007).

Testimony from defendant's former employer as to the fact that defendant was the owner of a cell phone that had made calls prior to and after the victim's murder and within the vicinity of the crime scene was properly admitted and did not constitute plain error under Ohio R. Crim. P. 52(B) or Ohio R. Evid. 103(D) as the testimony went to identity and was permissible as such under Ohio R. Evid. 404(B), in that the testimony established that the employer, in whose name the phone was listed, was not the owner of the phone but that defendant was the owner. State v. Schumpert, — Ohio App. 3d —, 2007 Ohio 5437, — N.E. 2d —, 2007 Ohio App. LEXIS 4778 (Oct. 11, 2007).

Where defendant's counsel only made a general objection to the trial court's admission of a statement that defendant made to police at the time of his arrest, which the State had agreed during a suppression hearing would not be admitted at trial, such was not error under Ohio R. Evid. 103(A)(1) because a properly specific objection was not made to preserve any error for review. Under Ohio R. Crim. P. 52, the statement did not undermine confidence in the outcome of the trial and did not create such prejudice as to constitute plain error. State v. Smith, — Ohio App. 3d —, 2006 Ohio 4163, — N.E. 2d —, 2006 Ohio App. LEXIS 4096 (Aug. 11, 2006).

There was no plain error under Ohio R. Crim. P. 52(B) and Ohio R. Evid. 103(A)(1) by the State's admission of evidence of defendant's bad character pursuant to Ohio R. Evid. 404(A)(1), as the challenged statements were relevant to establish that two eyewitnesses had seen defendant at the crime scene, and that one of the witnesses had immediately recognized and identified defendant to her companions. The use of the pejorative term in describing defendant, while not necessarily relevant, was not outcome-determinative in light of the evidence adduced at trial. State v. Mitchell, — Ohio App. 3d —, 2006 Ohio 5073, — N.E. 2d —, 2006 Ohio App. LEXIS 5008 (Sept. 29, 2006).

Because defendant did not object to a police officer's testimony about drugs found in his home during defendant's trial for offenses related to drugs found in the bar where he worked, he was generally barred from introducing the error on appeal under Ohio R. Evid. 103(A)(1). Although the testimony was obviously unfairly prejudicial to defendant and was unnecessary for the prosecution of the case, no plain error under Ohio R. Evid. 103(D) occurred because there was substantial compelling evidence on which the jury could have based its guilty verdict, and it could not have been said that but for the inclusion of the evidence, the trial's outcome would have been otherwise. State v. Ray, — Ohio App. 3d —, 2006 Ohio 5640, — N.E. 2d —, 2006 Ohio App. LEXIS 5643 (Oct. 30, 2006).

Use of a poster to summarize telephone records during defendant's trial for engaging in a pattern of corrupt activity was reviewed for plain error under Ohio R. Evid. 103(A) because defendant did not object to the State's representation that the exhibit was being used by agreement. Any error in its use under Ohio R. Evid. 1006 did not rise to plain error because the outcome of the trial would not have been different without the evidence. State v. Welch, — Ohio App. 3d —, 2006 Ohio 6684, — N.E. 2d —, 2006 Ohio App. LEXIS 6585 (Dec. 18, 2006).

Preservation of error

In an administrator's suit against an insurer for underinsured motorist benefits, in which a trial court granted the administrator's motion to bar the insurer from introducing evidence of drug use by the administrator's decedent, the insurer adequately preserved the issue for review, under Ohio R. Evid. 103(A)(2), through the insurer's counsel's statements to the trial court concerning the purpose for which counsel sought to introduce the evidence, as well as a proffer of the decedent's medical records. Dieble v. Auto Owners Ins. Co., — Ohio App. 3d —, 2007 Ohio 3429, — N.E. 2d —, 2007 Ohio App. LEXIS 3133 (July 2, 2007).

Since an ex-husband, in his objection to his ex-wife's introduction of medical records, did not argue that the records were hearsay, the ex-husband, pursuant to Ohio R. Evid. 103(A)(1), failed to preserve for appellate review the issue of whether the records were, in fact, hearsay. Redman v. Francis, — Ohio App. 3d —, 2006 Ohio 3640, — N.E. 2d —, 2006 Ohio App. LEXIS 3566 (July 10, 2006).

Proffer

While the trial court was mistaken as to the still existing requirement of a proffer of excluded evidence, under Ohio R. Evid. 103(A)(2), no error resulted from the mistake or its refusal to permit a proffer. At the time he sought to proffer, defendant did not know what, if anything, the children would say. State v. Mullins, — Ohio App. 3d —, 2007 Ohio 1051, — N.E. 2d —, 2007 Ohio App. LEXIS 969 (Mar. 9, 2007).

As defendant did not proffer evidence regarding a writ of prohibition and a writ of mandamus, his claim that the trial court erred in his criminal trial when it denied the jury's request to be given copies of those documents was not preserved for review pursuant to Ohio R. Evid. 103(A)(2). State v. Glick, — Ohio App. 3d —, 2007 Ohio 4104, — N.E. 2d —, 2007 Ohio App. LEXIS 3735 (Aug. 13, 2007).

In proceedings to remove a son as guardian of the son's mother, when the son said the son's due process rights were violated because the trial court refused to allow the son to present the testimony of the son's brother, the son did not preserve the issue for appeal because the son did not proffer the brother's testimony, as required by Ohio R. Evid. 103(A)(2). In re Burrows, — Ohio App. 3d —, 2007 Ohio 4764, — N.E. 2d —, 2007 Ohio App. LEXIS 4261 (Sept. 14, 2007).

Where a husband in a divorce action failed to abide by the trial court's order as to when a pretrial statement disclosing information as to witnesses who would testify was to be filed, the trial court did not abuse its discretion in excluding the testimony of those witnesses, as the wife would have suffered prejudice and surprise by not having sufficient time to get witnesses who would support her claim, and there was no showing of excusable neglect in failing to have filed the statement in a timely manner. As the husband failed to proffer what evidence the witnesses would have testified to, any error in excluding them was waived pursuant to Ohio R. Evid. 103(A)(2). McCoy v. McCoy, — Ohio App. 3d —, 2006 Ohio 2363, — N.E. 2d —, 2006 Ohio App. LEXIS 2213 (May 12, 2006).

Where a witness was subpoenaed to testify for a party but he was not compensated as an expert, the trial court did not err in excusing him from appearing, pursuant to Ohio R. Civ.

P. 45(C)(3)(c), (d), and (C)(5). Although it was error not to have allowed the party to testify as to what the expert had told him because the rules of evidence were relaxed in the small claims court action pursuant to Ohio R. Evid. 101(C)(8), as the party failed to proffer what his testimony would have been under Ohio R. Evid. 103(A)(2), the error was deemed waived for purposes of appeal. Melcher v. Ryan, — Ohio App. 3d —, 2006 Ohio 4609, — N.E. 2d —, 2006 Ohio App. LEXIS 4565 (Aug. 31, 2006).

Mother waived her right to allege error in a trial court's custody determination that adopted a magistrate's decision barring the mother from presenting evidence on custody issues by failing to identify where in the record she attempted to proffer additional testimony regarding custody issues; it was incumbent upon her to offfer the evidence at trial to enable the trial court to determine its admissibility and to preserve the record for appeal under Ohio R. Evid. 103(A)(2), and by failing to make such a proffer, the mother waived any error on appeal. Whited v. Whited, — Ohio App. 3d —, 2006 Ohio 5551, — N.E. 2d —, 2006 Ohio App. LEXIS 5546 (Oct. 16, 2006).

When defendant's witness was allowed to invoke the Fifth Amendment after his testimony implicated him in a crime, defendant waived any error because he did not, as required by Evid. R. 103(A)(2), proffer the witness's expected testimony or explain its relevance to the defense. State v. Wilson, — Ohio App. 3d —, 2006 Ohio 6930, — N.E. 2d —, 2006 Ohio App. LEXIS 6836 (Dec. 28, 2006).

Sentencing

Defendant failed to demonstrate ineffective assistance of counsel because counsel's statement, while not formally presented as an objection and not made at the first opportunity to do so, nonetheless set forth the specific grounds as to why the court should not consider the victim's statement from the nolled case and afforded the trial court the opportunity to effectively identify and correct the alleged error. State v. Edwards, — Ohio App. 3d —, 2006 Ohio 2315, — N.E. 2d —, 2006 Ohio App. LEXIS 2178 (May 11, 2006).

Trial court ruling on admission or exclusion of evidence

There was no prejudice to defendant found by the trial court's exclusion of his wife's testimony due to the fact that the wife remained in the courtroom despite a sequestration order pursuant to Ohio R. Evid. 615, as defendant failed to provide a transcript of the videotaped proceeding pursuant to his duty under Ohio R. App. P. 9(A) which indicated that part of the trial, and he also failed to make a proffer of the testimony that the wife would have given pursuant to Ohio R. Evid. 103(A)(2); as defendant did not show that he was prejudiced by the evidentiary ruling and the matter did not relate to the offenses for which he was convicted, it was disregarded as harmless error under Ohio R. Crim. P. 52. Ohio v. Shropshire, — Ohio App. 3d —, 2007 Ohio 5185, — N.E. 2d —, 2007 Ohio App. LEXIS 4567 (Sept. 28, 2007).

Trial court's evidentiary ruling

Where ownership of real property was disputed, there was no abuse of discretion pursuant to Ohio R. Evid. 103 by the trial court's admission of testimony discussing the alleged ownership thereof, as the evidence was conflicting and the issue of ownership had no probative value concerning the charges against defendant, which were based on the taking of personal property without consent. Documents from a civil court proceeding regarding the alleged fraudulent nature of the conveyance were properly admitted under the public records hearsay exception pursuant to Ohio R. Evid. 803(8) and as they were not "testimonial statements," they were not subject to scrutiny under the Confrontation Clause of U.S. Const. amend. VI and Ohio Const. art. I, § 10. State v. Pesec, — Ohio App. 3d —, 2007 Ohio 3846, — N.E. 2d —, 2007 Ohio App. LEXIS 3487 (July 27, 2007).

RULE 104. Preliminary Questions

(A) **Questions of admissibility generally.** Preliminary questions concerning the qualification of a person to be a witness, the existence of a privilege, or the admissibility of evidence shall be determined by the court, subject to the provisions of subdivision (B). In making its determination it is not bound by the rules of evidence except those with respect to privileges.

(B) **Relevancy conditioned on fact.** When the relevancy of evidence depends upon the fulfillment of a condition of fact, the court shall admit it upon, or subject to, the introduction of evidence sufficient to support a finding of the fulfillment of the condition.

(C) **Hearing of jury.** Hearings on the admissibility of confessions shall in all cases be conducted out of the hearing of the jury. Hearings on other preliminary matters shall also be conducted out of the hearing of the jury when the interests of justice require.

(D) **Testimony by accused.** The accused does not, by testifying upon a preliminary matter, become subject to cross-examination as to other issues in the case.

(E) **Weight and credibility.** This rule does not limit the right of a party to introduce before the jury evidence relevant to weight or credibility.

History: Amended, eff 7-1-07.

NOTES TO DECISIONS

ANALYSIS

Abuse of discretion
Admission of evidence generally
Applicability
— Exclusion of expert testimony
—Hearing on motion to suppress evidence
Applicability of rules of evidence
Qualification as expert witness
Qualification of expert witness
Qualification of witness to testify as expert
Qualification to testify as expert
Qualifications as expert
Weight and credibility
Witness' qualifications as expert

Abuse of discretion

Trial court did not abuse its discretion under Ohio R. Evid. 104 in denying defendant's counsel full access to a victim's diary for purposes of cross-examining her, as the trial court required the State to provide defense counsel with the entries therein that discussed the way the victim felt about her stepmother or how she perceived her father, defendant, and other entries in the diary were irrelevant or immaterial to the criminal matter. Defendant's counsel was permitted to explore the dynamic of the victim's relationships on cross-examination, such that there was no due process violation under Ohio Const. art. I, § 10 and U.S. Const. amend. VI. State v. Ford, — Ohio App. 3d —, 2007 Ohio 2645, — N.E. 2d —, 2007 Ohio App. LEXIS 2473 (May 31, 2007).

Trial court did not abuse its discretion in excluding a victim's prior misdemeanor theft conviction for impeachment purposes as defendant did not suffer material prejudice from the ruling. The effects of the evidence for impeachment purposes were tenuous at best and did not rise to the level of prejudicial and the outcome of the trial most likely would not have changed, even with the admission of the evidence. State v. Gay, — Ohio App. 3d —, 2006 Ohio 3683, — N.E. 2d —, 2006 Ohio App. LEXIS 3638 (July 20, 2006).

Trial court did not abuse its discretion in excluding a police report as defendant had full access on cross-examination of all testifying police officers to establish inconsistencies in the basis of the underlying investigation. State v. Gay, — Ohio App. 3d —, 2006 Ohio 3683, — N.E. 2d —, 2006 Ohio App. LEXIS 3638 (July 20, 2006).

Admission of evidence generally

Trial court's admission of a doctor's testimony regarding her determination that a minor was the victim of sexual abuse was not an abuse of discretion under Ohio R. Evid. 104, as the doctor simply stated her diagnosis of the victim because she was a qualified physician trained in pediatrics and her opinion was based on statements made by the victim and based on physical examination; the statements fell with an exception of hearsay pursuant to Ohio R. Evid. 801(C) and 802, as they were made for purposes of diagnosis or treatment pursuant to Ohio R. Evid. 803(4). State v. Braxton, — Ohio App. 3d —, 2006 Ohio 3008, — N.E. 2d —, 2006 Ohio App. LEXIS 2885 (June 15, 2006).

Applicability

RC § 4511.19(D)(4)(b), allowing the admission, at a suppression hearing, of the results of field sobriety tests administered in substantial compliance with reliable standards, did not violate Ohio Const. art. IV, § 5(B), giving the Ohio Supreme Court the exclusive right to prescribe rules governing practice and procedure in Ohio courts, because, under Ohio R. Evid. 101(C), the Ohio Rules of Evidence did not apply to a suppression hearing, where the issue to be determined was the admissibility of evidence, under Ohio R. Evid. 104(A), and, since the Rules of Evidence did not apply in suppression hearings, RC § 4511.19(D)(4)(b) could not conflict any Rule of Evidence, including Ohio R. Evid. 702, regarding the admissibility of expert testimony, in a motion to suppress context. State v. Ladigo, — Ohio App. 3d —, 2006 Ohio 3475, — N.E. 2d —, 2006 Ohio App. LEXIS 3426 (June 27, 2006).

— Exclusion of expert testimony

Trial court properly struck expert reports pursuant to Ohio R. Evid. 104(A) that were offered by a law client in his legal malpractice action against a law firm and an attorney who represented him in an underlying personal injury action, as the reports were untimely and they did not state the bases for the conclusions reached by the experts that the client's underlying personal injury action was viable and meritorious. Jarrett v. Forbes, — Ohio App. 3d —, 2007 Ohio 5072, — N.E. 2d —, 2007 Ohio App. LEXIS 4473 (Sept. 27, 2007).

—Hearing on motion to suppress evidence

Rules of Evidence do not apply to suppression hearings: State v. Boczar, 113 Ohio St. 3d 148, 2007 Ohio 1251, 863 N.E.2d 155, 2007 Ohio LEXIS 800 (2007).

Applicability of rules of evidence

Trial court did not err in denying defendant's motion to suppress an eyewitness identification of him as the perpetrator of a home invasion based on a one-man show up, as defendant failed to show that the identification was unreliable even if it was deemed to have been impermissibly suggestive. Hearsay testimony from a police detective regarding the victim's identification of defendant was properly considered, as under Ohio R. Evid. 104(A), the trial court could rely on hearsay at suppression hearings even though such evidence was not admissible at trial. State v. Sutton, — Ohio App. 3d —, 2007 Ohio 3792, — N.E. 2d —, 2007 Ohio App. LEXIS 3455 (July 26, 2007).

Qualification as expert witness

In a parental rights termination proceeding, a juvenile court properly determined that three psychologists who were witnesses for the county agency were qualified under Ohio R. Evid. 702 and 104(A) to testify as experts on the issue of whether caged beds that the children were forced to sleep in were abusive, as the parents attempted to show that most of the children had severe behavioral and developmental problems that required putting them in cages for their own safety and the safety of the other children, and the expert testimony was helpful to the juvenile court's understanding of whether the children were abused and/or dependent. The expert testimony was useful at the disposition hearing to determine whether the children could not or should not be placed with the parents within a reasonable time pursuant to RC § 2151.414(E)(14) and (15). In re Mercy Anne G., — Ohio App. 3d —, 2007 Ohio 1197, — N.E.2d —, 2007 Ohio App. LEXIS 1132 (Mar. 14, 2007).

Trial court did not abuse its discretion when it permitted testimony from the owner of a tractor seller with respect to the repair of the type of tractor bought by a purchaser, which later malfunctioned and caused the purchaser injuries, as the owner was familiar with the recall on the tractor, he identified the relevant parts of it that were at issue, and his testimony was based on his own perceptions and was helpful to the jury pursuant to Ohio R. Evid. 701, such that it was proper lay opinion testimony. His testimony could not be considered expert testimony pursuant to Ohio R. Evid. 702 because the trial court had failed to make the threshold determination under Ohio R. Evid. 104(A) regarding the owner's qualifications to testify as an expert. Gadberry v. Eastgate Lawn & Tractor, Inc., — Ohio App. 3d —, 2007 Ohio 2849, — N.E. 2d —, 2007 Ohio App. LEXIS 2642 (June 11, 2007).

Although a trial court's threshold determination under Ohio R. Evid. 104(A) that a police officer's testimony was admissible regarding how he thought a vehicle collision occurred was an abuse of discretion, as the officer was not qualified as an expert under Ohio R. Evid. 702, such was not reversible error where there was substantial competent evidence to support the finding of defendant's guilt on the criminal charges, and but for the alleged error, the outcome of the trial would not have been different. City of Cleveland Hts. v. Reid, — Ohio App. 3d —, 2006 Ohio 170, — N.E. 2d —, 2006 Ohio App. LEXIS 163 (Jan. 19, 2006).

Qualification of expert witness

Trial court did not abuse its discretion under Ohio R. Evid. 104 when it excluded an emergency room doctor (ERD) from testifying as an expert as to the standard of care for surgeons in a medical malpractice action, as the ERD failed to demonstrate a knowledge of the standards of the school and specialty of a surgeon sufficient to enable him to give an expert opinion as to the conformity of the surgeons' conduct to the standards of surgeons under the facts of malpractice case. Nead v. Brown County Gen. Hosp., — Ohio App. 3d —, 2007 Ohio 2443, — N.E. 2d —, 2007 Ohio App. LEXIS 2259 (May 21, 2007).

In a medical malpractice suit, the trial court erred in concluding that an expert's lack of recent experience in emergency medicine made him unqualified under Ohio R. Evid. 702 to testify as to the standard of care required of the emergency room doctor against whom suit was brought because the expert presented evidence that the standard of care for the diagnosis of the decedent's condition did not vary based on whether doctor was a family physician, an emergency room physician, or a specialist. Schutte v. Mooney, 165 Ohio App. 3d 56, 2006 Ohio 44, 844 N.E. 2d 899, 2006 Ohio App. LEXIS 25 (Jan. 6, 2006).

Qualification of witness to testify as expert

Trial court did not abuse its discretion by finding that the patient's medical expert was qualified to testify as an expert regarding a nerve injury during the laparoscopic repair of an inguinal hernia because there was some evidence in the record upon which the trial court could have reasonably concluded that the expert was qualified to testify as an expert. Specifically, the expert testified that he began performing gynecologic laparoscopic surgical procedures in 1985 or 1986; that he had performed three to four such procedures a week since that time; and that in his training as a laparoscopic surgeon, he had received specific training to avoid the recognized potential for nerve injuries and to take reasonable steps to avoid such injuries. Lewis v. Nease, — Ohio App. 3d —, 2006 Ohio 4362, — N.E. 2d —, 2006 Ohio App. LEXIS 4274 (Aug. 21, 2006).

In a medical malpractice suit, the trial court did not err in permitting the patient's expert to testify as an expert witness. While the expert was not board-certified in internal medicine, this fact did not preclude him from testifying. The expert's deposition testimony showed that he was familiar with the standard of care expected of an internal medicine specialist when presented with the symptoms and the risks possessed by the patient when he presented himself to the doctor and that he was qualified to state an opinion in this regard. Trevena v. Primehealth, 171 Ohio App. 3d 501, 2006 Ohio 6535, 871 N.E.2d 1217, 2006 Ohio App. LEXIS 6461 (2006).

Qualification to testify as expert

Trial court's exclusion of defendant's expert witness pursuant to Ohio R. Evid. 104 was an abuse of discretion in his criminal trial on multiple sexual offense charges involving a child victim, as the expert's testimony was based on the alleged suggestibility of the victim and the improper interview protocols, rather than on her veracity; such exclusion was prejudicial error to defendant. State v. Ogle, — Ohio App. 3d —, 2007 Ohio 5066, — N.E. 2d —, 2007 Ohio App. LEXIS 4486 (Sept. 27, 2007).

In a suit by debtors against a lender, a trial court properly found, under Ohio R. Evid. 104(A), that the debtors' proposed expert witness was not qualified, under Ohio R. Evid. 702, because, while he was familiar with banking practices in other countries and might be qualified to testify regarding them, he had never worked as a bank regulator, bank auditor, or loan officer in the United States, so he could not testify as an expert in a case involving a loan between U.S. citizens and a federally chartered U.S. savings and loan association. Lotfi-Fard v. First Fed. of Lakewood, — Ohio App. 3d —, 2006 Ohio 3727, — N.E. 2d —, 2006 Ohio App. LEXIS 3686 (July 20, 2006).

Qualifications as expert

Trial court did not abuse its discretion under Ohio R. Evid. 104(A) in precluding a patient's expert from testifying as to the standard of care of defendant surgeons in the patient's medical malpractice action, as the expert was not qualified pursuant to Ohio R. Evid. 702(B) to testify as to the standard of care of surgeons who treated a patient that was receiving gynecological care elsewhere because the expert was not a surgeon and he was not a primary care physician. Iglodi v. Tolentino, — Ohio App. 3d —, 2007 Ohio 1982, — N.E. 2d —, 2007 Ohio App. LEXIS 1832 (Apr. 26, 2007).

Weight and credibility

Victim's first miscarriage, six months earlier, could have affected the opinion of the State's expert in defendant's trial for involuntary manslaughter and assault; although the trial court found it did not affect the expert's opinion, it was error not to let the jury determine if that was a credible deduction. However, the error was harmless because defendant could have achieved the same effect with a hypothetical question and direct evidence by his own expert, but chose not to because of the possibility of opening the door to prior bad acts, i.e., assaults. State v. Marshall, — Ohio App. 3d —, 2007 Ohio 1686, — N.E. 2d —, 2007 Ohio App. LEXIS 1538 (Apr. 3, 2007).

Witness' qualifications as expert

There was no requirement that a trial court make findings to support its determination that an expert witness' testimony was not admissible pursuant to Ohio R. Evid. 702 and 104(A) in a products liability case. It reviewed each of the conditions contained in Ohio R. Evid. 702 and then set forth its rationale in reaching its conclusion. Turker v. Ford Motor Co., — Ohio App. 3d —, 2007 Ohio 985, — N.E. 2d —, 2007 Ohio App. LEXIS 920 (Mar. 8, 2007).

RULE 105. Limited Admissibility

When evidence which is admissible as to one party or for one purpose but not admissible as to another party or for another purpose is admitted, the court, upon request of a party, shall restrict the evidence to its proper scope and instruct the jury accordingly.

NOTES TO DECISIONS

RULE 106. Remainder of or Related Writings or Recorded Statements

When a writing or recorded statement or part thereof is introduced by a party, an adverse party may require the introduction at that time of any other part or any other writing or recorded statement which is otherwise admissible and which ought in fairness to be considered contemporaneously with it.

History: Amended, eff 7-1-07.

NOTES TO DECISIONS

ANALYSIS

Doctrine of completeness

Doctrine of completeness

There was no abuse of discretion in the trial court's exclusion of the full recording from evidence because, under Ohio R. Evid. 106, defendant had the burden of showing that the additional part CD-ROM recording of the detective's interview with defendant was admissible. The entire CD-ROM was not admissible simply because the State failed to prove otherwise; and defendant made no attempt on appeal to demonstrate the admissibility of the entire recording. Also, defendant never used any portion of the recording to cross-examine the detective as the trial court authorized him to do, despite his assertion that the detective's testimony and review took his statements out of context. State v. Scott, — Ohio App. 3d —, 2006 Ohio 4016, — N.E. 2d —, 2006 Ohio App. LEXIS 3944 (Aug. 4, 2006).

ARTICLE II
JUDICIAL NOTICE

RULE 201. Judicial Notice of Adjudicative Facts

(A) **Scope of rule.** This rule governs only judicial notice of adjudicative facts; i.e., the facts of the case.

(B) **Kinds of facts.** A judicially noticed fact must be one not subject to reasonable dispute in that it is either (1) generally known within the territorial jurisdiction of the trial court or (2) capable of accurate and ready determination by resort to sources whose accuracy cannot reasonably be questioned.

(C) **When discretionary.** A court may take judicial notice, whether requested or not.

(D) **When mandatory.** A court shall take judicial notice if requested by a party and supplied with the necessary information.

(E) **Opportunity to be heard.** A party is entitled upon timely request to an opportunity to be heard as to the propriety of taking judicial notice and the tenor of the matter noticed. In the absence of prior notification, the request may be made after judicial notice has been taken.

(F) **Time of taking notice.** Judicial notice may be taken at any stage of the proceeding.

(G) **Instructing jury.** In a civil action or proceeding, the court shall instruct the jury to accept as conclusive any fact judicially noticed. In a criminal case, the court shall instruct the jury that it may, but is not required to, accept as conclusive any fact judicially noticed.

NOTES TO DECISIONS

ANALYSIS

Judicial notice
— Error
Judicial notice, when proper
Speed measuring devices

Judicial notice

Testimony showing that an offense occurred at a particular street address, standing alone, is generally insufficient to prove venue, since such addresses often are not "sufficiently unique" to permit the conclusion that the address is located in a particular city or county. Consequently, the trial court could not take judicial notice pursuant to Ohio R. Evid. 201(B)(1) that the crime for which defendant was charged occurred in the proper city and county of Ohio, simply on the basis that the evidence showed that the offense took place at the specific address because it was not generally known within the trial court's jurisdiction that that specific address was in the specific city and county of Ohio. State v. Lahmann, — Ohio App. 3d —, 2007 Ohio 1795, — N.E. 2d —, 2007 Ohio App. LEXIS 1651 (Apr. 16, 2007).

Because the trial court gave the prisoner adequate notice of the requirements in Civ. R. 53 in its judgment entry in favor of the corrections department, including the need to file objections, the prisoner was not relieved from compliance. Judicial notice was taken that he received the judgment entry since he filed his notice of appeal seven days later. Watley v. Department of Rehabilitation & Correction, — Ohio App. 3d —, 2007 Ohio 1841, — N.E. 2d —, 2007 Ohio App. LEXIS 1666 (Apr. 19, 2007).

Trial court correctly declined to take judicial notice pursuant to Ohio R. Evid. 201 of the fact that counsel for a motorist might have previously represented a physician who treated the driver in the driver's personal injury action, arising from a vehicle collision between the parties, as the alleged representation took place 26 years earlier, the driver sought treatment from the physician, and the physician only testified as a fact witness. The refusal to admit into evidence a certified copy of the journal entry from the prior matter was not error. Djukic v. Turner, — Ohio App. 3d —, 2007 Ohio 4433, — N.E. 2d —, 2007 Ohio App. LEXIS 4001 (Aug. 30, 2007).

Trial court did not abuse its discretion by taking judicial notice of the report generated by the U.S. Naval Observatory, pursuant to Ohio R. Evid. 201, because the report indicated that the sun rose on the day in question at 5:58 a.m. and, from that evidence, the jury could have drawn its own conclusions as to the reliability of the eyewitness identification of defendant. Further, in his brief, defendant failed to assert how the trial court's decision to take judicial notice of the time that the sun rose on May 28, 2004, prejudiced his defense. State v.

Johnson, — Ohio App. 3d —, 2006 Ohio 1313, — N.E. 2d —, 2006 Ohio App. LEXIS 1197 (Mar. 22, 2006).

Trial court properly took judicial notice of the National Highway Traffic Safety Administration (NHTSA) manual when it found that an officer administered three field sobriety tests in substantial compliance with the manual requirements; as the officer administered the tests in substantial compliance with the NHTSA manual, defendant's failure of all three tests, coupled with the officer's observations of defendant's pre-test conduct, gave the officer probable cause to arrest defendant for operating a motor vehicle while under the influence of alcohol. State v. Radford, — Ohio App. 3d —, 2006 Ohio 1610, — N.E. 2d —, 2006 Ohio App. LEXIS 1462 (Mar. 31, 2006).

Appellate court could take judicial notice of facts easily ascertainable from a reasonably reliable source, such as a map, as a judge could inform himself as to the facts of geography, such as the navigable character of a river, the distance between two points, or the location of a given place within the jurisdiction, by resort to public documents, maps, etc. State v. Burkhalter, — Ohio App. 3d —, 2006 Ohio 1623, — N.E. 2d —, 2006 Ohio App. LEXIS 1520 (Mar. 31, 2006).

When defendant was arrested in a jurisdiction other than the arresting officer's jurisdiction after a high-speed chase, and it was not shown at trial that the officer initiated the pursuit within his jurisdiction or saw defendant violate the law within that jurisdiction, as required by RC § 2935.03(D), the appellate court could take judicial notice by looking at a map that the officer was within his jurisdiction when he first observed defendant, and it could be inferred that defendant must have been speeding as he left the officer's jurisdiction, so it was not improper for the arresting officer to pursue and eventually arrest defendant. State v. Burkhalter, — Ohio App. 3d —, 2006 Ohio 1623, — N.E. 2d —, 2006 Ohio App. LEXIS 1520 (Mar. 31, 2006).

— Error

In a prosecution for underage consumption of alcohol, the trial court could not properly take judicial notice under Ohio R. Evid. 201(B) of the fact that wine could not leave an odor on a person for seven hours after consumption as there was caselaw tending to refute this conclusion. Since the amount of time that an odor of alcohol could remain on a person's breath was a critical issue in dispute, the State needed to rely on more than an unsubstantiated judicial presumption to establish this fact. State v. Matthews, — Ohio App. 3d —, 2007 Ohio 4999, — N.E. 2d —, 2007 Ohio App. LEXIS 4401 (Sept. 17, 2007).

Judicial notice, when proper

Trial court properly calculated liquidated damages due to a university basketball coach who was improperly terminated without "cause" by the university, as certain events that triggered incentives that were payable to the coach did not actually occur, such that a setoff was proper under RC § 2333.09 for amounts already paid to the coach under the incentive clause; as the university basketball team's records for certain years were vacated by the ruling organization due to infractions that occurred, there was no need to take judicial notice under Ohio R. Evid. 201 of the fact that the ruling organization only vacated the tournament records but not the university's championships, as they resulted in the same lack of incentive-triggering event pursuant to the contract language. O'brien v. Ohio State Univ., — Ohio App. 3d —, 2007 Ohio 4833, — N.E. 2d —, 2007 Ohio App. LEXIS 4316 (Sept. 20, 2007).

In defendant's prosecution for speeding, the trial court erred in taking judicial notice of the reliability of a laser speed-detection device because the State produced only a transcript of a prior municipal court case in which the municipal court had based a guilty finding on the result of the device. A court speaks only through its journal, and the transcript was insufficient to demonstrate that judicial notice had been taken in the prior case. State v. Polen, — Ohio App. 3d —, 2006 Ohio 5599, — N.E. 2d —, 2006 Ohio App. LEXIS 5613 (Oct. 27, 2006).

Speed measuring devices

Trial court's judicial notice of the accuracy of the reliability of a Marksman LTI 20-20 laser device for the purpose of tracking the speed of a vehicle was proper under Ohio R. Evid. 201 in defendant's criminal trial on a charge of speeding, in violation of RC § 4511.21(D)(2), as the trial court noted that it had previously considered expert testimony on the issue and found that it was appropriate. State v. McGowan, — Ohio App. 3d —, 2006 Ohio 3873, — N.E. 2d —, 2006 Ohio App. LEXIS 3824 (July 21, 2006).

Defendant's speeding conviction under RC § 4511.21(D)(1) was reversed because the State failed to introduce even the identity of the laser device used by the police officer to calculate defendant's speed. As a result, the trial court could not conclude that the reliability of this unknown machine had been recognized by other courts and could not take judicial notice of the accuracy of the device under Ohio R. Evid. 201(B). State v. Palmer, — Ohio App. 3d —, 2006 Ohio 5456, — N.E. 2d —, 2006 Ohio App. LEXIS 5454 (Oct. 20, 2006).

Trial court erred by taking judicial notice of the accuracy and reliability of the laser device used to record defendant's speed because the State did not submit evidence of what laser device the deputy used. Although the State did provide information regarding the deputy's training and qualifications to use the device, the steps he took to calibrate the device, and the procedure he used, it did not ask the deputy to identify the laser device used, nor did it submit any other evidence to specifically identify the device. State v. Freed, — Ohio App. 3d —, 2006 Ohio 6746, — N.E. 2d —, 2006 Ohio App. LEXIS 6641 (Dec. 19, 2006).

ARTICLE III
PRESUMPTIONS

RULE 301. Presumptions in General in Civil Actions and Proceedings

In all civil actions and proceedings not otherwise provided for by statute enacted by the General Assembly or by these rules, a presumption imposes on the party against whom it is directed the burden of going forward with evidence to rebut or meet the presumption, but does not shift to such party the burden of proof in the sense of the risk of non-persuasion, which remains throughout the trial upon the party on whom it was originally cast.

NOTES TO DECISIONS

ANALYSIS

Undue influence

Undue influence

Instructing the jury to presume undue influence, despite a total lack of such evidence, would have been prejudicial error: Ament v. Reassure Am. Life Ins. Co., 180 Ohio App. 3d 440, 2009 Ohio 36, 905 N.E.2d 1246, 2009 Ohio App. LEXIS 23 (2009).

RULE 302. [Reserved]

ARTICLE IV
RELEVANCY AND ITS LIMITS

RULE 401. Definition of "Relevant Evidence"

"Relevant evidence" means evidence having any tendency to make the existence of any fact that is of consequence to the determination of the action more probable or less probable than it would be without the evidence.

NOTES TO DECISIONS

ANALYSIS

Admissible evidence
Admissible evidence of similar circumstances
Admitted evidence presumed to be admissible
Battered woman syndrome
Evidence
— Sufficient
Evidence of similar incident
Harmless error
Motive
Not relevant
Opinion testimony of lay witness
Properly excluded evidence
Relevance
Relevant evidence
— Admissible
— Evidence admissible

Admissible evidence

Mere fact that defendant's parole officer testified in the rape trial was inconsequential considering the fact that the victim had already testified that defendant revealed to her that he was on parole and the reason that he was on parole. Furthermore, the parole officer's act of informing the jury that the rape allegation constituted a parole violation was not itself evidence of an other act because that very rape allegation was the offense at hand and the fact of parole was already properly admitted. State v. Rupp, — Ohio App. 3d —, 2007 Ohio 1561, — N.E. 2d —, 2007 Ohio App. LEXIS 1449 (Mar. 27, 2007).

Stories that defendant told the rape victim of his violent crimes prior to raping her were admissible as exceptions to the other acts prohibition and were not unfairly prejudicial because the evidence was not merely relevant, it was foundational evidence that bolstered the victim's claims and established defendant's preparation, intent, plan, and scheme. The relation of the stories to the victim tended to show defendant's intent to act to overcome the victim's will by fear and duress; his statements showed his intent to place the victim in a state of fear and make her fearful of rejecting him more physically or in a louder manner; and they also provided an opportunity for him to advance upon the victim without any extreme resistance. State v. Rupp, — Ohio App. 3d —, 2007 Ohio 1561, — N.E. 2d —, 2007 Ohio App. LEXIS 1449 (Mar. 27, 2007).

Although it was error for a trial court to have admitted testimony from the victim of a vehicle accident in defendant's criminal action on a charge of, inter alia, aggravated vehicular assault, concerning the nature and extent of her injuries pursuant to Ohio R. Evid. 401 and 403(A), given the stipulation accepted by the State that defendant admitted to having caused the accident which caused serious physical harm to the victim, the introduction of the evidence was harmless under Ohio R. Evid. 103(A) and Ohio R. Crim. P. 52(A). There was other significant evidence indicative of defendant's guilt, and the introduction of the victim's testimony regarding her injuries was limited by the trial court's instruction to the jury and was harmless in the circumstances. State v. Harding, — Ohio App. 3d —, 2006 Ohio 481, — N.E. 2d —, 2006 Ohio App. LEXIS 411 (2006).

Trial court properly admitted a gun clip found in defendant's home into evidence in defendant's criminal trial, as it was clearly relevant under Ohio R. Evid. 401 and 402, and the potential prejudicial effect was outweighed by the benefits of the admission under Ohio R. Evid. 403(A). The State was trying to prove that defendant shot a victim with a particular type of gun, and the gun clip was the same type and was found in defendant's home. State v. Harris, — Ohio App. 3d —, 2006 Ohio 3520, — N.E. 2d —, 2006 Ohio App. LEXIS 3439 (June 27, 2006).

In a wrongful death case, arising from a decedent's death in an automobile collision, it was not an abuse of discretion for the trial court to allow evidence that the decedent's husband was killed in the same collision, because such evidence was relevant to damages, under RC § 2125.02(A)(1) and (3)(b), nor was it unfairly prejudicial, under Ohio R. Evid. 403(A), and any error from evidence that the decedent's aunt died in the same collision was harmless as evidence the husband and aunt died in the same collsion was not unfairly prejudicial. Conway v. Dravenstott, — Ohio App. 3d —, 2006 Ohio 4840, — N.E. 2d —, 2006 Ohio App. LEXIS 4736 (Sept. 18, 2006).

Admissible evidence of similar circumstances

When an agency sought permanent custody of a mother's child, evidence that the mother's parental rights to other children had been previously terminated was relevant because RC § 2151.414(E)(11) directed the trial court to specifically consider whether the mother had had parental rights involuntarily terminated with respect to the child's sibling when determining whether permanent custody was in the child's best interest. In re P.N.M. Adjudicated Dependent, — Ohio App. 3d —, 2007 Ohio 4976, — N.E. 2d —, 2007 Ohio App. LEXIS 4432 (Sept. 17, 2007).

Admitted evidence presumed to be admissible

In defendants' nonjury trial for felonious assault, the trial court did not inappropriately rely on evidence of defendants' alleged gang activity; the presumption was applied, as usual in a bench trial, that it considered only relevant, material, and competent evidence in arriving at its judgment unless it affirmatively appeared to the contrary, and although the trial court allowed evidence of gang activity, it stated on the record that it limited its consideration of the evidence to purposes of witness credibility and did not rely on the gang evidence in determining the ultimate issue of fact or in rendering its verdict. State v. Armstrong, — Ohio App. 3d —, 2006 Ohio 5447, — N.E. 2d —, 2006 Ohio App. LEXIS 5437 (Oct. 19, 2006).

Battered woman syndrome

When a victim's credibility is challenged upon cross-examination during the state's case-in-chief, the state may introduce expert testimony regarding battered woman syndrome to aid the trier-of-fact in determining the victim's state of mind, e.g., to explain why she returned to the defendant despite his aggressions toward her. State v. Haines, 112 Ohio St. 3d 393, 2006 Ohio 6711, 860 N.E.2d 91, 2006 Ohio LEXIS 3680 (2006).

Evidence

When a wife obtained an agreed temporary support order requiring her husband to pay half of certain specified household expenses, and then sought judgment under that order when the husband did not pay his obligations, the fact that the parties were living together was properly excluded in proceedings to obtain the judgment, as that was irrelevant and inadmissible, under Ohio R. Evid. 401 and 402, as to whether the husband had satisfied his obligations under the order. Ronyak-Bogert v. Bogert, — Ohio App. 3d —, 2006 Ohio 1168, — N.E. 2d —, 2006 Ohio App. LEXIS 1058 (Mar. 14, 2006).

— Sufficient

There was no abuse of discretion in the trial court's exclusion of evidence of the alleged molestation of the nine-year-old victim and the blood in her underwear prior to her disappearance in defendant's trial for evidence tampering and gross abuse of a corpse. The evidence had little, if any, relevance, and the probative value of that evidence was substantially outweighed by the danger of unfair prejudice to the state, of confusion of the issues, and of misleading the jury. State v. Gabriel, — Ohio App. 3d —, 2007 Ohio 794, — N.E. 2d —, 2007 Ohio App. LEXIS 721 (Feb. 23, 2007).

Counsel was not ineffective for not objecting on the ground of relevancy to the admission of a transcript of a phone conversation between defendant and his brother-in-law which referenced the fact that defendant was in jail and that a polygraph test would be taken and in which defendant admitted that he had been at the victim's home during the night of the alleged rape. There was probative, relevant value in the information from defendant about his whereabouts on the evening in question, and since defendant presented his defense during the second telephone call, it was within the province of trial strategy for trial counsel not to object. State v. Canfield, — Ohio App. 3d —, 2006 Ohio 2834, — N.E. 2d —, 2006 Ohio App. LEXIS 2663 (June 5, 2006).

Evidence of similar incident

Where defendant was on trial for, inter alia, a charge of menacing by stalking, in violation of RC § 2903.211, the trial court properly allowed evidence of defendant's prior acts regarding the victim pursuant to Ohio R. Evid. 404(B) and RC § 2945.59, as such were relevant evidence pursuant to Ohio R. Evid. 401 and 402, they tended to prove defendant's state of mind which was an essential element of the offense, and the evidence was not outweighed by any prejudicial effect pursuant to Ohio R. Evid. 403. State v. Horsley, — Ohio App. 3d —, 2006 Ohio 1208, — N.E. 2d —, 2006 Ohio App. LEXIS 1080 (Mar. 16, 2006).

Harmless error

Although a state criminalist was qualified to testify as to the effects of mixing a prescription pill with alcohol, as such was within his expertise and relevant pursuant to Ohio R. Evid. 401, such testimony by a state trooper was improperly admitted because he was not qualified to provide an opinion on such evidence. The admission thereof was harmless under Ohio R. Crim. P. 52(A) because the testimony was already in evidence due to the warning label on the prescription bottle and the criminalist's testimony. State v. Taylor, — Ohio App. 3d —, 2006 Ohio 6559, — N.E. 2d —, 2006 Ohio App. LEXIS 6483 (Dec. 7, 2006).

Motive

Defendant did not receive ineffective assistance of counsel for failure to object to testimony because the testimony that the victim had been almost raped earlier in the day was relevant to a fact of consequence; during that attack, defendant accused the victim of sleeping with her man. When coupled with the statement and the link between the man and defendant, the rape accusation was relevant to a motive of retaliation. State v. Thornton, — Ohio App. 3d —, 2007 Ohio 3743, — N.E. 2d —, 2007 Ohio App. LEXIS 3425 (July 25, 2007).

Not relevant

Admission of the question and answer regarding defendant's employment was not plain error because it was not a significant factor in the guilty verdict. The question about defendant's lifestyle, the employment status of a co-defendant and of defendant's mother was of minimal or no relevance, could not have affected the trial's outcome, and therefore could not be prejudicial error. State v. Warsame, — Ohio App. 3d —, 2007 Ohio 3656, — N.E. 2d —, 2007 Ohio App. LEXIS 3334 (July 19, 2007).

Trial court's exclusion of various documents under Ohio R. Evid. 401 and 402 was not an abuse of discretion in defendant's criminal trial, as they were not deemed relevant because they dealt with an issue related to a prior escape conviction involving defendant rather than the instant escape charge that he was on trial for. State v. Anderson, — Ohio App. 3d —, 2007 Ohio 5068, — N.E. 2d —, 2007 Ohio App. LEXIS 4477 (Sept. 27, 2007).

Trial court did not abuse its discretion in its evidentiary rulings in a multi-tort action, as a granddaughter's testimony was properly excluded because her statements contained hearsay pursuant to Ohio R. Evid. 801(C) and 802 and they were not relevant to the issues being tried pursuant to Ohio R. Evid. 401. Domer v. Joan, — Ohio App. 3d —, 2007 Ohio 6877, — N.E. 2d —, 2007 Ohio App. LEXIS 6032 (Dec. 14, 2007).

When a grandmother sought custody of her grandson, over the objection of the child's parents, evidence that the child's father left the grandmother's home at age 12 was properly excluded because the trial court allowed evidence of parenting issues related to the parents and the grandmother and evidence of events occurring 26 years ago were not relevant. In the Matter of J.D., — Ohio App. 3d —, 2006 Ohio 3468, — N.E. 2d —, 2006 Ohio App. LEXIS 3419 (July 3, 2006).

Trial court erred when it allowed the jury to learn of 1993 accusations of assault and stalking of an adult complainant because defendant's direct examination did not open the door but was, instead, limited to accusations of a sexual nature involving children; thus, evidence of other, unrelated accusations held no probative value and was irrelevant. The error was prejudicial because it denied defendant the right to a fair trial in violation of his constitutional rights, in that the testimony was unrelated to the offense with which he was charged, sexual imposition on a child, and was introduced in a case in which the only evidence of defendant's guilt was the recanted testimony of a child with no attendant physical evidence. State v. Smith, — Ohio App. 3d —, 2006 Ohio 45, — N.E. 2d —, 2006 Ohio App. LEXIS 44 (Jan. 6, 2006).

Trial court abused its discretion in admitting evidence that an asbestos-containing product of a manufacturer was used at a decedent's place of employment several years after he was allegedly exposed to it, as such was not relevant evidence pursuant to Ohio R. Evid. 401 in the action by the decedent's executor, arising from the exposure of the decedent to asbestos; the only relevant evidence on that issue was what products were at the employer's place of business during the time of exposure. Barone v. GATX Corp., 167 Ohio App. 3d 744, 2006 Ohio 3221, 857 N.E. 2d 155, 2006 Ohio App. LEXIS 3146 (June 23, 2006).

Opinion testimony of lay witness

Virtually any lay witness, including a police officer, may testify as to whether an individual appears intoxicated. Such lay testimony can be crucial in prosecuting operating a vehicle while under the influence of alcohol cases and is relevant and admissible pursuant to Ohio R. Evid. 401 and 402. State v. Smith, — Ohio App. 3d —, 2007 Ohio 3182, — N.E. 2d —, 2007 Ohio App. LEXIS 2981 (June 21, 2007).

Properly excluded evidence

Sufficient evidence of the victim's intoxication was presented because, although the trial court pointed out that the legal alcohol limit was not relevant, it did not prohibit defendant from raising the issue of the victim's intoxication. The record was replete with evidence that the victim had been consuming alcohol prior to her attack and defendant's trial counsel elicited substantial testimony from the victim regarding the victim's alcohol consumption on the day of the attack. State v. Churchwell, — Ohio App. 3d —, 2007 Ohio 1600, — N.E. 2d —, 2007 Ohio App. LEXIS 1469 (Apr. 5, 2007).

When a school employee sued a television station for the station's report on the employee's actions in physically controlling students, the station's subsequent report that the employee was exonerated of any wrongdoing was properly excluded from evidence because the subsequent report was irrelevant to whether the statements the employee complained of were made with actual malice, which was the appropriate standard since the matter was of public concern. Young v. Russ, — Ohio App. 3d —, 2007 Ohio 5214, — N.E. 2d —, 2007 Ohio App. LEXIS 4591 (Sept. 28, 2007).

While the redacted portions of defendant's police interview where he stated that the victim was a crack dealer may have been self-serving hearsay, they fell outside of the purview of hearsay, since they were not being offered for the truth asserted, but rather to reflect defendant's state of mind and that he had a reasonable fear of the victim for self defense. Regardless, the statements were quite prejudicial versus their slight probative insight as to defendant's fear of the victim because there was nothing to indicate that the victim was a crack dealer, and that fact had no bearing or relation as to why defendant was fearful of the victim; also the error was harmless since the record was replete with testimony from defendant that he feared the victim because the victim made prior threats against him and was known to carry a weapon. Ohio v. Horace K. Vinson, — Ohio App. 3d —, 2007 Ohio 5199, — N.E. 2d —, 2007 Ohio App. LEXIS 4608 (Sept. 28, 2007).

In a case in which a widow alleged her husband died from mesothelioma caused, in part, by asbestos in gaskets made by a manufacturer, testimony from the manufacturer's expert about another study was properly excluded because (1) it was unknown if housekeeping measures used in that study were used when the husband worked with the manufacturer's gaskets, (2) there was no evidence of the amount of asbestos in the study's gaskets, so it was not possible to compare them to gaskets the husband was exposed to, and (3) there was no evidence that the conditions to which the study's gaskets were exposed were the same conditions to which gaskets the husband worked with were exposed, so the study could not predict the amount of asbestos the husband was exposed to. Blandford v. A Best Prods. Co., — Ohio App. 3d —, 2006 Ohio 1332, — N.E. 2d —, 2006 Ohio App. LEXIS 1226 (Mar. 23, 2006).

Trial court correctly found that the questioning of the attempted rape victim, under Ohio R. Evid. 608(B), regarding whether she had falsely accused all four of her husbands of domestic violence, was not relevant, pursuant to Ohio R. Evid. 401, because defense counsel admitted that he did not know how the victim would answer the question and, given the testimony of the various witnesses, the issue of truthfulness of what defendant actually did to the victim was not unsubstantiated. State v. Lucas, — Ohio App. 3d —, 2006 Ohio 1675, — N.E. 2d —, 2006 Ohio App. LEXIS 1563 (Mar. 29, 2006).

Trial court did not abuse its discretion in excluding the testimony regarding the decedent's refusal to submit to a medical procedure known as a fistulogram because the trial court rightly perceived the weak links in the causal chain and prevented the testimony from coming into evidence. The testimony was prejudicial, and its putative relevance in the causal chain that defendants' were hoping to construct to show that proximate cause for the decedent's death lay somewhere other than at the doctor's doorstep was tenuous, at best. Reihard v. Trumbull Cardiovascular Care, Inc., — Ohio App. 3d —, 2006 Ohio 4312, — N.E. 2d —, 2006 Ohio App. LEXIS 4239 (Aug. 18, 2006).

Evidence that a physician was allegedly negligent in treating a patient's prior ovarian cyst, discovered in 1988, was properly excluded in the patient's action against the physician and his employer for the physician's alleged medical negligence in managing a second cyst diagnosed in 1999, which the patient claimed later developed into cancer. The 1988 treatment was not admissible under Ohio R. Evid. 404(B) because it was a single occurrence which did not establish a regular or routine practice as required by Ohio R. Evid. 406, and any relevance under Ohio R. Evid. 401 was outweighed by prejudice under Ohio R. Evid. 403. Gerke v. Norwalk Clinic, Inc., — Ohio App. 3d —, 2006 Ohio 5621, — N.E. 2d —, 2006 Ohio App. LEXIS 5605 (Oct. 27, 2006).

Relevance

Evidence that the shooter had been identified by the crowd present at the scene as the boyfriend of a particular person and that jail records showed that person visited the defendant on several occasions was relevant and admissible under EvidR 401 and 403(A): State v. Nevins, 171 Ohio App. 3d 97, 2007 Ohio 1511, 869 N.E.2d 719, 2007 Ohio App. LEXIS 1379 (2007).

Question by the person who called the rape victim pretending to be defendant's parole officer asking why the victim was lying or why she did not scream, was not hearsay because none of the caller's statements to the victim were offered to prove the truth of the matter asserted. Rather, the content of the call was offered to show what triggered the victim to call the authorities and to provide context for how she finally reported her allegations; the contents of the call were not irrelevant. State v. Rupp, — Ohio App. 3d —, 2007 Ohio 1561, — N.E. 2d —, 2007 Ohio App. LEXIS 1449 (Mar. 27, 2007).

Evidence of defendant having brandished a firearm was admissible for a permissible purpose because, although no firearm matching the one used to murder the victim was ever recovered, many bullets at the scene and within the victim were recovered and numerous witnesses testified that they had seen defendant with a firearm and that the firearm matched the caliber of weapon which was used to kill the victim. Thus, the testimony established that defendant had an opportunity to murder the victim with such a weapon. The testimony could also have established intent, preparation, or plan, since defendant could arguably have been carrying the firearm in preparation for retaliation for the assault on his brother. State v. Carter, — Ohio App. 3d —, 2007 Ohio 3502, — N.E. 2d —, 2007 Ohio App. LEXIS 3223 (June 29, 2007).

Evidence of defendant having brandished a firearm was admissible for a permissible purpose because, although no firearm matching the one used to murder the victim was ever recovered, many bullets at the scene and within the victim were recovered and numerous witnesses testified that they had seen defendant with a firearm and that the firearm matched the caliber of weapon which was used to kill the victim. Thus, the testimony established that defendant had an opportunity to murder the victim with such a weapon. The testimony could also have established intent, preparation, or plan, since defendant could arguably have been carrying the firearm in preparation for retaliation for the assault on his brother. State v. Robinson, — Ohio App. 3d —, 2007 Ohio 3501, — N.E. 2d —, 2007 Ohio App. LEXIS 3224 (July 5, 2007).

When defendant was prosecuted for improperly furnishing firearms to a minor, under RC § 2923.21(A)(3), and contributing to the delinquency of a minor, under RC § 2919.24(A)(2), for giving defendant's twelve-year-old son a gun, evidence of the son's liquor bottle collection and purchase and consumption of alcohol was relevant and admissible, under Ohio R. Evid. 401 and 402, because it tended to show defendant was reckless in giving the son a gun to store in the son's bedroom. Ohio v. Slater, — Ohio App. 3d —, 2007 Ohio 3628, — N.E. 2d —, 2007 Ohio App. LEXIS 3331 (July 12, 2007).

In defendant's prosecution for raping his minor nephew, the admission of defendant's statements to police that he had undergone counseling did not violate Ohio R. Evid. 403(A) because the statements were admissions of a party opponent, under Ohio R. Evid. 801(D)(2), and the statements were relevant, under Ohio R. Evid. 401, as defendant admitted his sexual attraction to young boys, so no plain error, under Ohio R. Crim. P. 52(B), was committed, as it could not be said that defendant would not have been convicted without the statements, given the other evidence against him. State v. Palacio, — Ohio App. 3d —, 2006 Ohio 1437, — N.E. 2d —, 2006 Ohio App. LEXIS 1301 (Mar. 27, 2006).

Trial court properly admitted a videotape that was made during surveillance of a bar which showed a variety of drug transactions committed by a juvenile outside of the bar, and upon the arrival of the police, the juvenile ran inside the bar and to defendant, which supported the State's theory that defendant was involved in a drug distribution chain. The evidence was relevant under Ohio R. Evid. 401 and there was no showing that the prejudicial effect of its admission outweighed the probative value pursuant to Ohio R. Evid. 403(A). State v. Harrington, — Ohio App. 3d —, 2006 Ohio 4388, — N.E. 2d —, 2006 Ohio App. LEXIS 4285 (Aug. 14, 2006).

Defendant's substantial rights were not prejudicially affected because the prosecutor elicited relevant testimony from the arresting officer on direct examination and, on re-direct examination, although the prosecutor asked improper questions regarding the prior contact between the officer and defendant the trial court sustained timely objections to these particular interrogatories and thus, the exercise by the prosecutor did not amount to error. Further, defendant "opened the door" on cross-examination when her counsel asked the officer if he had ever seen defendant before and thus, she cannot be heard on appeal to complain about the admission of the testimony. State v. Albanese, — Ohio App. 3d —, 2006 Ohio 4819, — N.E. 2d —, 2006 Ohio App. LEXIS 4724 (Sept. 15, 2006).

Testimony in a legal custody proceeding that the mother, during a recess in the proceedings, threatened to kill a social worker and that she spat on the father's attorney was properly admitted as it was highly relevant under Ohio R. Evid. 401 for the purpose of demonstrating the mother's mental condition, which was at issue in the proceeding. In re Memic, — Ohio App. 3d —, 2006 Ohio 6346, — N.E. 2d —, 2006 Ohio App. LEXIS 6302 (Dec. 1, 2006).

In a railroad employee's action against the railroad, seeking damages due to his exposure to asbestos, silica, and diesel fumes during his work for the railroad, the trial court's admission of a videotape of a co-worker of the employee was not an abuse of discretion, as it was relevant under Ohio R. Evid. 401 because both railroad workers held the same jobs and were exposed to the same substances, the railroad had an opportunity to cross-examine the employee regarding his job relationship with his co-worker, and the evidence was not cumulative or prejudicial under Ohio R. Evid. 403 because there was nothing in the edited video shown to the jury that indicated that the co-worker was in pain or was breathing with the use of an oxygen tank. Hager v. Norfolk & Western Ry. Co., — Ohio App. 3d —, 2006 Ohio 6580, — N.E. 2d —, 2006 Ohio App. LEXIS 6489 (Dec. 14, 2006).

Relevant evidence

Although an employee's medical expert determined that the employee's "left shoulder strain and synovitis" were proximately caused by a work injury, and the administrative decision by the Ohio Bureau of Workers' Compensation had granted benefits to the employee for his "left shoulder joint effusion and tendonitis," exclusion of the medical expert's testimony by the trial court on the employer's appeal of the administrative decision was an abuse of discretion, as the expert's testimony was relevant under Ohio R. Evid. 401 and 402, and although it would have been improper to admit it at trial if the conditions were different than those upon which the administrative decision was based, it was unclear whether different conditions were stated or not. Brown v. Mabe, 170 Ohio App. 3d 13, 2007 Ohio 90, 865 N.E.2d 934, 2007 Ohio App. LEXIS 96 (2007).

Evidence that one of the officers involved in arresting defendant was absent from trial due to an injury suffered when trying to make an arrest was relevant in light of the fact that numerous officers arrested the 17 people inside defendant's house, so it was proper to give the State the opportunity to explain the absence of an arresting officer. State v. Harris, — Ohio App. 3d —, 2007 Ohio 410, — N.E. 2d —, 2007 Ohio App. LEXIS 356 (Feb. 1, 2007).

Trial court did not abuse its discretion in excluding evidence of a divorce decree between defendant and his wife, who was the victim of his criminal conduct, as there was no decree of divorce in place at the time of the acts that formed the basis of the charges against defendant; accordingly, such evidence was not deemed relevant. State v. Hardy, — Ohio App. 3d —, 2007 Ohio 1159, — N.E. 2d —, 2007 Ohio App. LEXIS 1085 (Mar. 15, 2007).

When defendant was prosecuted for rape and unlawful sexual conduct with a minor, and he asserted that he was entitled to discover various records about his victim, he could not discover the victim's school records, the file of a county department of job and family services, a sheriff's department files, the files of the Ohio Department of Job and Family Services, health department records, or a hospital file on the victim's sister to the extent those records contained no information relevant to the case, under Ohio R. Evid. 401, because they contained neither information concerning the alleged offenses nor information which could potentially be of consequence to the action. State v. Donnal, — Ohio App. 3d —, 2007 Ohio 1632, — N.E. 2d —, 2007 Ohio App. LEXIS 1488 (Apr. 9, 2007).

In a personal injury action involving an automobile accident, testimony by appellant driver's treating neurologist that appellant had made complaints on the date of the accident of sleepiness while driving was not excluded because it was relevant under Ohio R. Evid. 401 as those conditions could have potentially affected appellant's driving capabilities and was not "unfairly" prejudicial under Ohio R. Evid. 403 as appellant's counsel opened the door to the testimony by asking the neurologist about the visual complaints and the neurologist's testimony as a whole was helpful to appellant's case. Davis v. Killing, 171 Ohio App. 3d 400, 2007 Ohio 2303, 870 N.E.2d 1209, 2007 Ohio App. LEXIS 2125 (2007).

Trial court did not err in admitting evidence at defendant's criminal trial that he called his co-defendant a "snitch" when they passed by each other in a hallway, such that other inmates heard the comment, as that conduct arguably constituted an attempt to intimidate a witness and was evidence of defendant's consciousness of guilt for purposes of Ohio R. Evid. 401 and 402. State v. Exum, — Ohio App. 3d —, 2007 Ohio 2648, — N.E. 2d —, 2007 Ohio App. LEXIS 2446 (May 31, 2007).

Trial court did not abuse its discretion in allowing a patient's counsel to question a surgeon's expert on cross-examination about prior lawsuits in the patient's medical malpractice action, as the evidence was relevant pursuant to Ohio R. Evid. 401 and probative of the expert's potential bias against malpractice claimants, and the surgeon was not unfairly prejudiced by the evidence. Wynn v. Gilbert, — Ohio App. 3d —, 2007 Ohio 2798, — N.E. 2d —, 2007 Ohio App. LEXIS 2596 (June 8, 2007).

Trial court did not err in admitting the letter defendant wrote to the victim from jail as it was relevant; if the statements it contained were construed in a certain manner (defendant wrote that he was sorry that he hurt the victim), they tended to make it more probable that he physically assaulted the victim. Although the statements in the letter were not necessarily explicit confessions that he caused the victim physical injury, such did not render them inadmissible, and defendant made no argument about precisely how the letter's probative value was substantially outweighed by the danger of unfair prejudice. State v. Hunt, — Ohio App. 3d —, 2007 Ohio 3281, — N.E. 2d —, 2007 Ohio App. LEXIS 3004 (June 28, 2007).

Although defendant never opened the door to evidence of his codefendant's propensity for possessing firearms and the evidence was not relevant to the issue of defendant's guilt, the codefendant's prior possession of a firearm could potentially have shown that he had an opportunity to murder the victim with such a weapon. Thus, although it was error to allow the evidence to be introduced against defendant, the trial court did not commit plain error when it allowed the evidence to be introduced because it was highly relevant to prove the codefendant's guilt and exclusion of the evidence would not likely have affected the outcome of the case. State v. Robinson, — Ohio App. 3d —, 2007 Ohio 3501, — N.E. 2d —, 2007 Ohio App. LEXIS 3224 (July 5, 2007).

Trial court's admission of evidence that defendant was previously arrested in West Virginia in a trailer that contained a methamphetamine lab was relevant under Ohio R. Evid. 401 and 402, and it was proper for purposes of showing defendant's intent pursuant to Ohio R. Evid. 404 and RC § 2945.59(B) in a prosecution for illegal assembly or possession of chemicals for the manufacture of drugs, in violation of RC § 2925.041(A). State v. Norris, — Ohio App. 3d —, 2007 Ohio 6915, — N.E. 2d —, 2007 Ohio App. LEXIS 6066 (Dec. 11, 2007).

Trial court's partial grant of a motion in limine by medical professionals and entities in a patient's medical malpractice and informed consent action, whereby it excluded the hospital manual and regulations with respect to the policies regarding supervision of anesthesia students, was not harmless error under Ohio R. Civ. P. 61 where the evidence was relevant and admissible under Ohio R. Evid. 401 to determine the standard of care required, and such evidence would not have been prejudicial or confusing to the jury under Ohio R. Evid. 403(A). The alleged malpractice occurred due to the actions of a student nurse who performed anesthesia procedures without first having identified herself to the patient and who was not supervised by an anesthesiologist at the time, as required in the hospital's manual and regulations, and only two standards of care had been introduced in the case, such that the issue would not have been confusing for the jury to hear. Luettke v. St. Vincent Mercy Med. Ctr., — Ohio App. 3d —, 2006 Ohio 3872, — N.E. 2d —, 2006 Ohio App. LEXIS 3828 (July 28, 2006).

In a murder prosecution, when the prosecutor asked a witness if defendant had a "pot" tattoo, this was not prosecutorial misconduct because the question concerned a relevant issue, under Ohio R. Evid. 401, as a possible motive for the murder was the theft of drugs from the victim, so the answer to the question was admissible, under Ohio R. Evid. 402 and 404(B), and its probative value was not substantially outweighed by a danger of unfair prejudice, under Ohio R. Evid. 403. State v. Jenkins, — Ohio App. 3d —, 2006 Ohio 2546, — N.E. 2d —, 2006 Ohio App. LEXIS 2405 (May 12, 2006).

Evidence of procedures followed by the parents in the event of an asthma attack or request for inhaler usage by their son was relevant, pursuant to Ohio R. Evid. 401, in the wrongful death trial because the testimony went to the heart of foreseeability and consequently was a relevant factor in a determination of negligence. Spencer v. Lakeview Sch. Dist., — Ohio App. 3d —, 2006 Ohio 3429, — N.E. 2d —, 2006 Ohio App. LEXIS 3370 (June 30, 2006).

In a foreclosure action in which three lienholders sought to prove the priority of their liens, a document purporting to be a satisfaction of a lender's lien was relevant and admissible, because whether or not that lien had been satisfied was in issue, and that satisfaction tended to make whether the lien had been satisfied more or less probable. Park Nat'l Bank v. Chauvin, — Ohio App. 3d —, 2006 Ohio 5158, — N.E. 2d —, 2006 Ohio App. LEXIS 5060 (Oct. 2, 2006).

Photographs showing the murder victim's body after a shooting were properly admitted as relevant and not cumulative or prejudicial pursuant to Ohio R. Evid. 401 and 403, as each photograph showed a different aspect of the case, including the location of the body when the victim fell, the location relative to other evidence, and the wounds inflicted. State v. Reid, — Ohio App. 3d —, 2006 Ohio 6450, — N.E. 2d —, 2006 Ohio App. LEXIS 6405 (Dec. 8, 2006).

In an action by a contractor protesting the fact that its bid was not accepted for a city expansion and renovation project, the trial court did not abuse its discretion under Ohio R. Evid. 401 and 402 in ruling that testimony related to post-award enforcement by the city of a small business enterprise program with respect to the receipt and award of bids was irrelevant and inadmissible, as the contractor's complaint was predicated on the rejection of its bid and not on any post-award action. Cleveland Constr., Inc. v. City of Cincinnati, — Ohio App. 3d —, 2006 Ohio 6452, — N.E. 2d —, 2006 Ohio App. LEXIS 6410 (Dec. 8, 2006).

Prescription bottle that was seized during defendant's arrest, and which formed the basis of a charge against him, was relevant and admissible evidence under Ohio R. Evid. 401, as defendant admitted taking the pills and it was in his possession during his arrest. The references to the warning label did not constitute hearsay and were relevant. State v. Taylor, — Ohio App. 3d —, 2006 Ohio 6559, — N.E. 2d —, 2006 Ohio App. LEXIS 6483 (Dec. 7, 2006).

— Admissible

Trial court properly allowed the testimony by the police officers regarding the incidents four days prior to the day that defendant committed the instant offenses for purposes of establishing defendant's identity and the trial court's limiting instruction sufficiently instructed the jury on the purpose of that testimony. The trial court specifically denied the motion in limine on the basis that the earlier events could be probative of identity and both officers referenced the earlier incident to explain some of their reasons for stopping defendant; both indicated that they recognized defendant as someone they recognized from a prior date. State v. Lane, — Ohio App. 3d —, 2007 Ohio 5948, — N.E. 2d —, 2007 Ohio App. LEXIS 5255 (Nov. 8, 2007).

Trial court did not err by allowing a deputy to testify regarding drug evidence that he found in defendant's residence because the State's theory of the case was that defendant was reckless in shaking or dropping the child and failing to immediately call the police; to demonstrate defendant's recklessness, the State presented evidence of defendant's drug use consisting of observations by the police during the investigation, testimony of the child's mother, and defendant's own admissions. Because the deputy stated that, upon entering the residence, he detected a smell of burnt marijuana, his deputy's present sense impression testimony suggested that defendant had smoked marijuana while supervising the child. State v. Stacy, — Ohio App. 3d —, 2007 Ohio 6744, — N.E. 2d —, 2007 Ohio App. LEXIS 5911 (Dec. 17, 2007).

— Evidence admissible

In a prosecution for interference with custody, the trial court did not commit plain error under Ohio R. Crim. P. 52 in allowing a police officer to testify regarding what he thought defendant should have done under the circumstances as the officer's testimony was rendered relevant under Ohio R. Evid. 401 by the fact that it was given in a follow-up line of questioning after the defense attorney attempted to elicit testimony that defendant, when speaking with the officer after the officer had contacted defendant based on a report by the child's father that defendant had not returned the father's child to him as she had been required to do, did not have the opportunity to state that she had consent to keep the child. Moreover, the officer had previously testified that defendant had told the officer that she was not coming back with the child. State v. Sprinkle, — Ohio App. 3d —, 2007 Ohio 4967, — N.E. 2d —, 2007 Ohio App. LEXIS 4384 (Sept. 24, 2007).

RULE 402. Relevant Evidence Generally Admissible; Irrelevant Evidence Inadmissible

All relevant evidence is admissible, except as otherwise provided by the Constitution of the United States, by the Constitution of the State of Ohio, by statute enacted by the General Assembly not in conflict with a rule of the Supreme Court of Ohio, by these rules, or by other rules prescribed by the Supreme Court of Ohio. Evidence which is not relevant is not admissible.

NOTES TO DECISIONS

ANALYSIS

Admission proper
Demonstrative evidence
Evidence
— Inadmissible
Evidence of motive
Evidence of similar incident
Evidence with probative value
Hypnotically refreshed testimony
Mental health records
Not relevant
Polygraph tests
Properly excluded evidence
Relevance
Relevant admissible
Relevant evidence
— Admissible
Risk of undue confusion
Victim impact

Admission proper

Testimony did not violate other acts evidence under Ohio R. Evid. 404(B) because the testimony concerning the missing items (a gun and rent money) was given in connection with the statement to police by the victim's fiance concerning the events of the evening. Defendant was not charged with theft, and there was no evidence or argument presented that he took the items. Further, defendant testified during direct examination concerning the nature of his employment, and on cross-examination, defendant denied dubbing DVD's for income and there was no other evidence introduced to suggest that he did such a thing; the trial court did not err in overruling defendant's objections to the isolated testimony, and its probative value was not outweighed by the danger of unfair prejudice, confusion of issues, or of misleading the jury. State v. Gholston, — Ohio App. 3d —, 2007 Ohio 4053, — N.E. 2d —, 2007 Ohio App. LEXIS 3700 (Aug. 9, 2007).

Trial court properly admitted a gun clip found in defendant's home into evidence in defendant's criminal trial, as it was clearly relevant under Ohio R. Evid. 401 and 402, and the potential prejudicial effect was outweighed by the benefits of the admission under Ohio R. Evid. 403(A). The State was trying to prove that defendant shot a victim with a particular type of gun, and the gun clip was the same type and was found in defendant's home. State v. Harris, — Ohio App. 3d —, 2006 Ohio 3520, — N.E. 2d —, 2006 Ohio App. LEXIS 3439 (June 27, 2006).

Demonstrative evidence

Trial court did not abuse its discretion by permitting the State to use a handgun as demonstrative evidence because the State presented extensive testimony to establish that the handgun used as demonstrative evidence was both relevant and substantially similar to the one used in the commission of the crimes at issue; several witnesses testified regarding the actual gun and its similarity to the proffered gun. Also, the jury was given a limiting instruction regarding the handgun as demonstrative evidence. Ohio v. Rosvanis, — Ohio App. 3d —, 2007 Ohio 4943, — N.E. 2d —, 2007 Ohio App. LEXIS 4623 (Sept. 24, 2007).

Computer simulation of an injury caused by shaken baby syndrome was properly admitted because it was demonstrative of the prosecution's case of child abuse and a possible contributing factor to the child's death. A medical expert used the video simulation as a visual aid to assist the jury in understanding shaken baby syndrome. State v. Stacy, — Ohio App. 3d —, 2007 Ohio 6744, — N.E. 2d —, 2007 Ohio App. LEXIS 5911 (Dec. 17, 2007).

Evidence

When a wife obtained an agreed temporary support order requiring her husband to pay half of certain specified household expenses, and then sought judgment under that order when the husband did not pay his obligations, the fact that the parties were living together was properly excluded in proceedings to obtain the judgment, as that was irrelevant and inadmissible, under Ohio R. Evid. 401 and 402, as to whether the husband had satisfied his obligations under the order. Ronyak-Bogert v. Bogert, — Ohio App. 3d —, 2006 Ohio 1168, — N.E. 2d —, 2006 Ohio App. LEXIS 1058 (Mar. 14, 2006).

— Inadmissible

In defendant's prosecution for menacing by stalking under RC § 2903.211(A)(1), since the State does not have to prove that the defendant caused the victim actual mental distress or physical harm, defendant was properly precluded from asking the victim on cross-examination as to her prosecution for driving under the influence to establish an alternative basis for her claimed mental distress. Other possible stressors in the victim's life were irrelevant to this inquiry. State v. Bone, — Ohio App. 3d —, 2006 Ohio 3809, — N.E. 2d —, 2006 Ohio App. LEXIS 3772 (July 25, 2006).

Evidence of motive

In a murder prosecution, when the prosecutor asked a witness if defendant had a "pot" tattoo, this was not prosecutorial misconduct because the question concerned a relevant issue, under Ohio R. Evid. 401, as a possible motive for the murder was the theft of drugs from the victim, so the answer to the question was admissible, under Ohio R. Evid. 402 and 404(B), and its probative value was not substantially outweighed by a danger of unfair prejudice, under Ohio R. Evid. 403. State v. Jenkins, — Ohio App. 3d —, 2006 Ohio 2546, — N.E. 2d —, 2006 Ohio App. LEXIS 2405 (May 12, 2006).

Evidence of similar incident

Where defendant was on trial for, inter alia, a charge of menacing by stalking, in violation of RC § 2903.211, the trial court properly allowed evidence of defendant's prior acts regarding the victim pursuant to Ohio R. Evid. 404(B) and RC § 2945.59, as such were relevant evidence pursuant to Ohio R. Evid. 401 and 402, they tended to prove defendant's state of mind which was an essential element of the offense, and the evidence was not outweighed by any prejudicial effect pursuant to Ohio R. Evid. 403. State v. Horsley, — Ohio App. 3d —, 2006 Ohio 1208, — N.E. 2d —, 2006 Ohio App. LEXIS 1080 (Mar. 16, 2006).

In a drug prosecution, a confidential informant's testimony that she bought drugs from defendant on two other unspecified occasions, other than the occasions on which his criminal charges were based, and that he had a gun, was relevant and admissible, under Ohio R. Evid. 404(B), because it was proof of a common scheme or plan to sell and possess illegal drugs, and, when a charged crime was drug related, evidence of firearms was both relevant and probative. State v. Bundy, — Ohio App. 3d —, 2006 Ohio 4062, — N.E. 2d —, 2006 Ohio App. LEXIS 4021 (Aug. 8, 2006).

Evidence with probative value

When defendant was prosecuted for improperly furnishing firearms to a minor, under RC § 2923.21(A)(3), and contributing to the delinquency of a minor, under RC § 2919.24(A)(2), for giving defendant's twelve-year-old son a gun, evidence of the son's liquor bottle collection and purchase and consumption of alcohol was relevant and admissible, under Ohio R. Evid. 401 and 402, because it tended to show defendant was reckless in giving the son a gun to store in the son's bedroom. Ohio v. Slater, — Ohio App. 3d —, 2007 Ohio 3628, — N.E. 2d —, 2007 Ohio App. LEXIS 3331 (July 12, 2007).

There was no violation of Ohio R. Evid. 402 or Ohio R. Evid. 403 because the shotgun shells, rope, and handcuffs were relevant and their probative value outweighed the danger of unfair prejudice. The State connected the items to the charges in question; the charges of kidnapping, aggravated burglary, abduction, and domestic violence were crimes involving violent conduct and the use of force and they involved restraining another's liberty, causing physical harm, and threatening and/or terrorizing another. State v. Keener, — Ohio App. 3d —, 2006 Ohio 5650, — N.E. 2d —, 2006 Ohio App. LEXIS 5647 (Oct. 27, 2006).

Hypnotically refreshed testimony

Trial court did not commit plain error with respect to the hypnosis issue because the record was unclear as to whether the witness testified to facts recalled after his recollection was refreshed by hypnosis, in which case there "should" have been a pretrial hearing, or facts recalled prior to hypnosis, in which case a pretrial hearing would not have been required, As a result, it could not be said that the outcome of the proceedings clearly would have been different had the issue been raised in the trial court. State v. Barton, — Ohio App. 3d —, 2007 Ohio 1099, — N.E. 2d —, 2007 Ohio App. LEXIS 1020 (Mar. 12, 2007).

Mental health records

Trial court did not abuse its discretion in ordering defendant's institutional mental health records to be unsealed or in considering post-trial evidence regarding his Atkins claim. Because defendant's institutional mental health records could have contained relevant information and could have shed some light on whether he demonstrated limitations in two or more adaptive skills, that information should not have remained sealed; it could assist experts in making the determination of whether defendant was mentally retarded for the purpose of precluding his execution. State v. Lorraine, — Ohio App. 3d —, 2007 Ohio 6724, — N.E. 2d —, 2007 Ohio App. LEXIS 5905 (Dec. 14, 2007).

Not relevant

There was no abuse of discretion in the trial court's exclusion of the evidence from a webpage that the sexual assault victim held herself out to be 18 years or older because defendant's counsel agreed that he had no proof that defendant had ever seen the website and, more importantly, neither party disputed that the website was created after the incident in question. Thus, whether the 13-year-old victim represented herself as 18 years old after the incident occurred was not relevant because the case centered around defendant's belief regarding the victim's age at the time of the incident. State v. Gaskins, — Ohio App. 3d —, 2007 Ohio 4103, — N.E. 2d —, 2007 Ohio App. LEXIS 3739 (Aug. 13, 2007).

Trial court's exclusion of various documents under Ohio R. Evid. 401 and 402 was not an abuse of discretion in defendant's criminal trial, as they were not deemed relevant because they dealt with an issue related to a prior escape conviction involving defendant rather than the instant escape charge that he was on trial for. State v. Anderson, — Ohio App. 3d —, 2007 Ohio 5068, — N.E. 2d —, 2007 Ohio App. LEXIS 4477 (Sept. 27, 2007).

When a grandmother sought custody of her grandson, over the objection of the child's parents, evidence that the child's father left the grandmother's home at age 12 was properly excluded because the trial court allowed evidence of parenting issues related to the parents and the grandmother and evidence of events occurring 26 years ago were not relevant. In the Matter of J.D., — Ohio App. 3d —, 2006 Ohio 3468, — N.E. 2d —, 2006 Ohio App. LEXIS 3419 (July 3, 2006).

Trial court did not abuse its discretion by not permitting evidence of the police detective's unrelated case because, in the other case, the defendant had confessed to committing the crime but after an inmate confessed, that defendant recanted. Because the instant defendant claimed that he never confessed, and did not argue that the detective committed any act or procedure that was illegal or improper, the information was irrelevant. State v. Torres, — Ohio App. 3d —, 2006 Ohio 3696, — N.E. 2d —, 2006 Ohio App. LEXIS 3641 (July 20, 2006).

Trial court did not abuse its discretion in excluding the interrogation expert's testimony. Because the expert specialized in the voluntariness of a confession and defendant claimed that he never gave a confession, the expert's testimony as to whether the confession was voluntary was irrelevant. State v. Torres, — Ohio App. 3d —, 2006 Ohio 3696, — N.E. 2d —, 2006 Ohio App. LEXIS 3641 (July 20, 2006).

In an action by a contractor protesting the fact that its bid was not accepted for a city expansion and renovation project, the trial court did not abuse its discretion under Ohio R. Evid. 401 and 402 in ruling that testimony related to post-award enforcement by the city of a small business enterprise program with respect to the receipt and award of bids was irrelevant and inadmissible, as the contractor's complaint was predicated on the rejection of its bid and not on any post-award action. Cleveland Constr., Inc. v. City of Cincinnati, — Ohio App. 3d —, 2006 Ohio 6452, — N.E. 2d —, 2006 Ohio App. LEXIS 6410 (Dec. 8, 2006).

Trial court did not abuse its discretion or violate defendant's right to present a defense under U.S. Const. amend. VI and Ohio Const. art. I, § 10 in excluding testimony from a witness for defendant who allegedly was going to impeach the credibility of a narcotics officer who had testified for the prosecution, as the trial court had the discretion to determine the presentation of witnesses pursuant to Ohio R. Evid. 611, and exclusion of evidence that was not deemed relevant under Ohio R. Evid. 402 was not error. The witness's testimony was confusing, misguided, contradictory, and did not specifically relate to defendant and the underlying criminal charges against him. State v. Kimble, — Ohio App. 3d —, 2006 Ohio 6863, — N.E. 2d —, 2006 Ohio App. LEXIS 6775 (Dec. 22, 2006).

Polygraph tests

Trial court's decision to allow the testimony regarding defendant's attempt to defeat the polygraph test did not amount to an abuse of discretion because the trial court found that defense counsel's questions about whether defendant had done anything to impede the cold case investigation "opened the door" to allowing the prosecution to elicit testimony from the polygraph examiner showing that defendant had, in fact, taken steps to impede the cold case investigation by employing "counter measures" such as deep breathing techniques in an attempt to defeat the polygraph. State v. Barton, — Ohio App. 3d —, 2007 Ohio 1099, — N.E. 2d —, 2007 Ohio App. LEXIS 1020 (Mar. 12, 2007).

Properly excluded evidence

Sufficient evidence of the victim's intoxication was presented because, although the trial court pointed out that the legal alcohol limit was not relevant, it did not prohibit defendant from raising the issue of the victim's intoxication. The record was replete with evidence that the victim had been consuming alcohol prior to her attack and defendant's trial counsel elicited substantial testimony from the victim regarding the victim's alcohol consumption on the day of the attack. State v. Churchwell, — Ohio App. 3d —, 2007 Ohio 1600, — N.E. 2d —, 2007 Ohio App. LEXIS 1469 (Apr. 5, 2007).

Trial court did not abuse its discretion under Ohio R. Evid. 402 in denying defendant's request to admit a photograph in his criminal trial, wherein it showed a female occupant of the van that defendant had been riding in wearing a t-shirt that was found to contain contraband for which defendant was charged, as defendant failed to lay a foundation for the exhibit, and he failed to show how it was relevant to the case. Defendant's claim on appeal that he was prejudiced in his ability to show that the t-shirt, and hence the contraband, belonged to someone else lacked merit. State v. McCoy, — Ohio App. 3d —, 2007 Ohio 3721, — N.E. 2d —, 2007 Ohio App. LEXIS 3401 (July 23, 2007).

Trial court's exclusion of defendant's photograph showing the road where an accident occurred in defendant's criminal trial on a traffic violation was not an abuse of discretion under Ohio R. Evid. 402 and 403, as it was not taken immediately after the accident, such that the road conditions could have changed and the photograph was not relevant; the photograph was also cumulative of others that had already been admitted into evidence. State v. Dewalt, — Ohio App. 3d —, 2007 Ohio 5245, — N.E. 2d —, 2007 Ohio App. LEXIS 4640 (Sept. 25, 2007).

Relevance

Trial court's limitation on certain questions and exclusion of certain aspects of an expert's testimony in a zoning dispute was not an abuse of discretion, as the trial court admitted relevant portions of his testimony into evidence pursuant to Ohio R. Evid. 402, and excluded issues were based on the fact that his opinions were irrelevant, the questions were beyond the scope of his expertise, they were based on improper questions, or they called for legal conclusions. State ex rel. Republic Servs. of Ohio v. Bd. of Twp. Trs., — Ohio App. 3d —, 2007 Ohio 2086, — N.E. 2d —, 2007 Ohio App. LEXIS 1943 (Apr. 30, 2007).

When the robbery victim's testimony was reviewed in its entirety, it was clear that the testimony was relevant and elicited solely to support the State's position that the victim clearly remembered the night that he was robbed and that defendant was the man who robbed him. There was no relevant purpose for the testimony of the diner owner that the victim was a nice guy and never caused problems in his diner, and it was offered as victim impact evidence, however, there was no possibility that the erroneous admission of that testimony contributed to the jury's verdict. State v. Farmer, — Ohio App. 3d —, 2007 Ohio 4046, — N.E. 2d —, 2007 Ohio App. LEXIS 3679 (Aug. 9, 2007).

Trial court's admission of evidence that defendant was previously arrested in West Virginia in a trailer that contained a methamphetamine lab was relevant under Ohio R. Evid. 401 and 402, and it was proper for purposes of showing defendant's intent pursuant to Ohio R. Evid. 404 and RC § 2945.59(B) in a prosecution for illegal assembly or possession of chemicals for the manufacture of drugs, in violation of RC § 2925.041(A). State v. Norris, — Ohio App. 3d —, 2007 Ohio 6915, — N.E. 2d —, 2007 Ohio App. LEXIS 6066 (Dec. 11, 2007).

Trial court did not abuse its discretion by admitting testimony regarding defendant's interaction with the sheriff's deputy because her interaction with the deputy consisted of yelling and physical contact between the two and the testimony provided the jury with a complete description of what occurred and was evidence that defendant persisted in disorderly conduct by continuing to make unreasonable noise in the office despite being asked to leave the office. Thus, the interaction was relevant to prove that she was persistent in her disorderly conduct and the relevancy of the testimony was not substantially outweighed by its unfair prejudice. State v. Cunningham, — Ohio App. 3d —, 2006 Ohio 6373, — N.E. 2d —, 2006 Ohio App. LEXIS 6328 (Dec. 5, 2006).

Relevant admissible

Trial court did not abuse its discretion in allowing the State to present evidence of lower back injuries of a child that was being watched by defendant for purposes of his criminal trial on a charge of child endangerment, as the evidence was relevant pursuant to Ohio R. Evid. 402 and the ruling on a motion in limine with respect to certain evidence regarding the back injuries was not violated by the admission thereof; accordingly, a limiting instruction on that evidence was not required. State v. Rickey, — Ohio App. 3d —, 2006 Ohio 6889, — N.E. 2d —, 2006 Ohio App. LEXIS 6779 (Dec. 21, 2006).

Relevant evidence

Although an employee's medical expert determined that the employee's "left shoulder strain and synovitis" were proximately caused by a work injury, and the administrative decision by the Ohio Bureau of Workers' Compensation had granted benefits to the employee for his "left shoulder joint effusion and tendonitis," exclusion of the medical expert's testimony by the trial court on the employer's appeal of the administrative decision was an abuse of discretion, as the expert's testimony was relevant under Ohio R. Evid. 401 and 402, and although it would have been improper to admit it at trial if the conditions were different than those upon which the administrative decision was based, it was unclear whether different conditions were stated or not. Brown v. Mabe, 170 Ohio App. 3d 13, 2007 Ohio 90, 865 N.E.2d 934, 2007 Ohio App. LEXIS 96 (2007).

Trial court did not err in admitting evidence at defendant's criminal trial that he called his co-defendant a "snitch" when they passed by each other in a hallway, such that other inmates heard the comment, as that conduct arguably constituted an attempt to intimidate a witness and was evidence of defendant's consciousness of guilt for purposes of Ohio R. Evid. 401 and 402. State v. Exum, — Ohio App. 3d —, 2007 Ohio 2648, — N.E. 2d —, 2007 Ohio App. LEXIS 2446 (May 31, 2007).

Trial court properly overruled a motorist's new trial motion pursuant to Ohio R. Civ. P. 59 after the jury returned a verdict in favor of a driver in the motorist's personal injury action that arose from a motor vehicle accident that was admittedly caused by the driver, as the issue of proximate cause regarding the motorist's spinal injuries was decided against him based on the fact that he had experienced prior back injuries, had undergone back surgery, and had filed social security and workers' compensation claims for those injuries. The admission of the workers' compensation claim information was proper, as it was directly relevant to the issue at trial pursuant to Ohio R. Evid. 402 and 403(A), the motorist actually raised it first in depositions and at trial such that although he had moved to exclude it by a motion in limine, he waived that evidentiary issue where he did not wait and then object to such evidence at trial, and accordingly he could not fault the trial court for allowing the driver's counsel to cross-examine on that issue pursuant to the allowable scope under Ohio R. Evid. 611(B). Sims v. Dibler, 172 Ohio App. 3d 486, 2007 Ohio 3035, 875 N.E.2d 965, 2007 Ohio App. LEXIS 2879 (2007).

Virtually any lay witness, including a police officer, may testify as to whether an individual appears intoxicated. Such lay testimony can be crucial in prosecuting operating a vehicle while under the influence of alcohol cases and is relevant and admissible pursuant to Ohio R. Evid. 401 and 402. State v. Smith, — Ohio App. 3d —, 2007 Ohio 3182, — N.E. 2d —, 2007 Ohio App. LEXIS 2981 (June 21, 2007).

Trial court did not err in admitting the letter defendant wrote to the victim from jail as it was relevant; if the statements it contained were construed in a certain manner (defendant wrote that he was sorry that he hurt the victim), they tended to make it more probable that he physically assaulted the victim. Although the statements in the letter were not necessarily explicit confessions that he caused the victim physical injury, such did not render them inadmissible, and defendant made no argument about precisely how the letter's probative value was substantially outweighed by the danger of unfair prejudice. State v. Hunt, — Ohio App. 3d —, 2007 Ohio 3281, — N.E. 2d —, 2007 Ohio App. LEXIS 3004 (June 28, 2007).

In a drug prosecution, it was not prosecutorial misconduct for a prosecutor to place a quantity of marijuana, as to which defendant was not charged, on the rail of the jury box because the marijuana was involved in an alleged drug sale in which defendant was allegedly involved and was relevant to illustrate the terms of the transaction, and the State's decision to bring the marijuana into the courtroom was not prejudicial. Ohio v. Bowshier, — Ohio App. 3d —, 2007 Ohio 5364, — N.E. 2d —, 2007 Ohio App. LEXIS 4730 (Oct. 5, 2007).

Trial court did not abuse its discretion in admitting evidence regarding a former wife's lawsuit against her former employer, as it was relevant pursuant to Ohio R. Evid. 402 to show that she had been fired from her job and that she had enough funds to pay an attorney, as her claim against her former husband with respect to recoupment of loan payments that she had made was that she was in dire financial circumstances at that time; a claim that the court opinion from the employment action was not properly authenticated under Ohio R. Evid. 901 lacked merit, as the document was referred to by one party, its existence was admitted by the other party, a review of the court file indicated that such a document in fact existed, but it was not proffered into evidence. Kovacic v. Kovacic, — Ohio App. 3d —, 2007 Ohio 5956, — N.E. 2d —, 2007 Ohio App. LEXIS 5226 (Nov. 8, 2007).

Trial court did not abuse its discretion in admitting the taped statements from the victim's answering machine because the statements were relevant, they were not too remote in time from the incident, and the probative value of the evidence was not outweighed by the danger of unfair prejudice; since the statements were those of defendant, and offered against him at trial, the statements were not hearsay and were properly admissible under Ohio R. Evid. 801(D)(2). Because the messages met the requirements of Ohio R. Evid. 801(D)(2), their admission was not dependent upon one of the exceptions under Ohio R. Evid. 404(B) and, to the extent that defendant argued that the statements were precluded under Ohio R. Evid. 404(B), such evidence was relevant and admissible because it tended to prove identity. State v. Cody, — Ohio App. 3d —, 2007 Ohio 6776, — N.E. 2d —, 2007 Ohio App. LEXIS 5938 (Dec. 18, 2007).

In a product liability claim regarding an inadequate warning as to the use of a medical product in a neurosurgery procedure, a trial court did not abuse its discretion under Ohio R. Evid. 402 and 403(B) in allowing a neurosurgeon to testify as an expert on assorted issues, although portions of his testimony were cumulative because a similar expert had already testified, as he provided an additional perspective rather than simply a cumulative one. Zappola v. Leibinger, — Ohio App. 3d —, 2006 Ohio 2207, — N.E. 2d —, 2006 Ohio App. LEXIS 2058 (May 4, 2006).

In a foreclosure action in which three lienholders sought to prove the priority of their liens, a document purporting to be a satisfaction of a lender's lien was relevant and admissible, because whether or not that lien had been satisfied was in issue, and that satisfaction tended to make whether the lien had been satisfied more or less probable. Park Nat'l Bank v. Chauvin, — Ohio App. 3d —, 2006 Ohio 5158, — N.E. 2d —, 2006 Ohio App. LEXIS 5060 (Oct. 2, 2006).

— **Admissible**

Admission of the testimony of three witnesses in the property appropriation trial did not challenge or undermine the legitimacy of the judicial process. The jury's award of damages totaling $ 173,325 was amply supported by the appraiser's clearly admissible appraisal, which measured the damages to be as high as $ 275,000. City of Toledo v. Gardner, — Ohio App. 3d —, 2007 Ohio 5995, — N.E. 2d —, 2007 Ohio App. LEXIS 5244 (Nov. 9, 2007).

Trial court did not err by allowing a deputy to testify regarding drug evidence that he found in defendant's residence because the State's theory of the case was that defendant was reckless in shaking or dropping the child and failing to immediately call the police; to demonstrate defendant's recklessness, the State presented evidence of defendant's drug use consisting of observations by the police during the investigation, testimony of the child's mother, and defendant's own admissions. Because the deputy stated that, upon entering the residence, he detected a smell of burnt marijuana, his deputy's present sense impression testimony suggested that defendant had smoked marijuana while supervising the child. State v. Stacy, — Ohio App. 3d —, 2007 Ohio 6744, — N.E. 2d —, 2007 Ohio App. LEXIS 5911 (Dec. 17, 2007).

Risk of undue confusion

There was no abuse of discretion in the trial court's exclusion of the third-party perpetrator evidence on the bases of irrelevance and the potential for confusing the jury, pursuant to Ohio R. Evid. 403(A). The trial court found the evidence to be inadmissible because absolutely no nexus existed between the proffered evidence and the victim's murder and thus, clearly, the trial court did not restrictively employ an evidentiary rule categorically excluding third-party guilt evidence in violation of defendant's constitutional rights. State v. Miller, — Ohio App. 3d —, 2006 Ohio 2799, — N.E. 2d —, 2006 Ohio App. LEXIS 2628 (June 5, 2006).

Victim impact

Because the testimony regarding the victim's behavior after the rape was relevant particularly in the absence of any physical evidence of rape, and because the trial court likely found that profound changes in the victim's personality and behavior were circumstantial evidence of the rapes, they were relevant to proving the rape charges. Therefore, defense counsel had no duty to object to the testimony and defendant did not receive ineffective assistance of counsel. State v. Blackman, — Ohio App. 3d —, 2007 Ohio 4168, — N.E. 2d —, 2007 Ohio App. LEXIS 3774 (Aug. 16, 2007).

RULE 403. Exclusion of Relevant Evidence on Grounds of Prejudice, Confusion, or Undue Delay

(A) **Exclusion mandatory.** Although relevant, evidence is not admissible if its probative value is substantially outweighed by the danger of unfair prejudice, of confusion of the issues, or of misleading the jury.

(B) **Exclusion discretionary.** Although relevant, evidence may be excluded if its probative value is substantially outweighed by considerations of undue delay, or needless presentation of cumulative evidence.

History: Amended, eff 7-1-96.

NOTES TO DECISIONS

ANALYSIS

Admissibility of photographic evidence
Admissible evidence
Admissible relevant evidence
Admission
Admission proper
Applicability
Autopsy photos
Battered woman syndrome
Discretion of trial court
Drug use
Evidence
—Admissibility
— Admissible
— Prejudicial
— Rape cases
— Sufficient
— Victim impact testimony
Evidence admissible
Evidence confusing and dissimilar
Evidence of disciplinary action
Evidence of similar incident
Evidence prejudicial
Evidence unfairly prejudicial
Evidence with probative value
Experts
Harmless error
Identification evidence
Illustrative cases
Limitation of cross-examination
Limitation on evidence
Medical history
Motive
Motor vehicles sales industry
Photo array
Photographic evidence
Photographs admissible
Plain error
Prejudice outweighs probative value
Prior bad acts
Prior conviction
Probative evidence
Probative value
Probative value and prejudicial effect
Probative value of evidence
Probative value of evidence outweighs prejudicial effect
Probative value of polygraph exam
Probative value outweighed by prejudice
Probative value outweighs prejudice
Probative value outweighs prejudicial effect
Relevant evidence
Review
Substantial compliance
Unfairly prejudicial evidence
Videotape of police interview

Admissibility of photographic evidence

Trial court abused its discretion where it admitted photographs of a victim's deceased body that not only showed the effects of defendant's attack on her, which aspect of the photographs was admittedly probative, but it also showed the reflection of her scalp that was performed during her autopsy, which aspect was gruesome and prejudicial. Although the prejudicial aspect of the photographs outweighed the probative value pursuant to Ohio R. Evid. 403(A) and 611(A), there was no plain error under Ohio R. Crim. P. 52 by the admission thereof, as the results of the trial would not have been different without the admission of the photographs. State v.

Warner, — Ohio App. 3d —, 2007 Ohio 3016, — N.E. 2d —, 2007 Ohio App. LEXIS 2770 (June 15, 2007).

Trial court's exclusion of defendant's photograph showing the road where an accident occurred in defendant's criminal trial on a traffic violation was not an abuse of discretion under Ohio R. Evid. 402 and 403, as it was not taken immediately after the accident, such that the road conditions could have changed and the photograph was not relevant; the photograph was also cumulative of others that had already been admitted into evidence. State v. Dewalt, — Ohio App. 3d —, 2007 Ohio 5245, — N.E. 2d —, 2007 Ohio App. LEXIS 4640 (Sept. 25, 2007).

Trial court did not abuse its discretion under Ohio R. Evid. 403 and 611(A) in admitting photographs that showed the extent of the damage to a motorist's vehicle in the motorist's personal injury action, arising from a vehicle collision, without the aid of expert testimony, as he had testified regarding the collision and the extent of the damage, and the driver was entitled to present evidence to rebut the motorist's testimony and to show the "minimal" damage to the motorist's vehicle. Wingfield v. Howe, — Ohio App. 3d —, 2006 Ohio 276, — N.E. 2d —, 2006 Ohio App. LEXIS 245 (Jan. 26, 2006).

Although the admission of multiple photographs of the victim and the crime scene as well as the testimony of the victim's mother may have been overly repetitive or prejudicial, pursuant to Ohio R. Evid. 403 and 611(A), there was no showing that the outcome of the trial was affected under a plain error analysis pursuant to Ohio R. Crim. P. 52. State v. Love, — Ohio App. 3d —, 2006 Ohio 1762, — N.E. 2d —, 2006 Ohio App. LEXIS 1619 (Mar. 27, 2006).

Although the photographs of defendant handcuffed with drugs and money on his back had limited probative value, they were not misleading or prejudicial. The photographs were relevant because they showed the condition of the porch floor and part of the door that opens onto it, where defendant was apprehended, and how he looked on the occasion of his arrest. State v. Owings, — Ohio App. 3d —, 2006 Ohio 4281, — N.E. 2d —, 2006 Ohio App. LEXIS 4278 (Aug. 18, 2006).

There was no error in the trial court's decision to admit photographs of defendant's daughter's body after she was burned to death in an apartment fire, as there was no showing that the risk of prejudice and confusion under Ohio R. Evid. 403 outweighed the relevance thereof. The plain error standard of review under Ohio R. Crim. P. 52 was used as to those photographs for which defendant had not objected. State v. Abner, — Ohio App. 3d —, 2006 Ohio 4510, — N.E. 2d —, 2006 Ohio App. LEXIS 4523 (Sept. 1, 2006).

Admissible evidence

The officer's testimony explained the circumstances of the crime and therefore fell under the exception to the admission of other acts evidence under Ohio R. Evid. 404(B) and RC § 2945.59. The testimony regarding the place and background of the crime were blended or connected with the crime of drug possession. Because defendant denied the charges and argued that he was not in the area at the time of the incident, the officer's testimony regarding his identification of defendant was necessary. The testimony implied that defendant was in a gang, but there was no testimony that defendant was actually a member of a gang and the trial court, as the fact finder, was presumed to only consider relevant, material evidence. State v. Vason, — Ohio App. 3d —, 2007 Ohio 1599, — N.E. 2d —, 2007 Ohio App. LEXIS 1468 (Apr. 5, 2007).

Even under an abuse of discretion standard, a trial court did not err in admitting statements that defendant made before the crime as although the statements were unfavorable, they were not misleading or confusing and they arguably showed defendant's willingness to rob someone. State v. Johnson, — Ohio App. 3d —, 2006 Ohio 209, — N.E. 2d —, 2006 Ohio App. LEXIS 139 (Jan. 19, 2006).

Admissible relevant evidence

There was no error in admitting other acts evidence because the evidence established defendant's inability to accept rejection in his female relationships and it was relevant to his motive for killing the victim. The fact that the other females were still alive but the victim was dead was not the threshold or determinative issue and there was overwhelming evidence that defendant committed the murder. State v. Charley, — Ohio App. 3d —, 2007 Ohio 1108, — N.E. 2d —, 2007 Ohio App. LEXIS 1029 (Mar. 6, 2007).

Trial court abused its discretion when it disqualified an attorney and his firm from representing debtors in an action by a creditor, seeking repayment of a loan and foreclosure of the pledged collateral, as the fact that the attorney had drafted the parties' loan agreement did not necessarily require his disqualification because the proper procedure for making such a determination was not followed by the trial court. There was insufficient evidence to determine if the attorney "ought to testify," if such testimony would be admissible under Ohio R. Evid. 403(A), and if admissible, if the testimony was subject to any exceptions or would cause prejudice to the attorney's client pursuant to considerations under Ohio Code Prof. Resp. DR 5-101(B) and 5-102(A) and (B). A.B.B. Sanitec West, Inc. v. Weinsten, — Ohio App. 3d —, 2007 Ohio 2116, — N.E. 2d —, 2007 Ohio App. LEXIS 1981 (May 3, 2007).

In a forgery prosecution, in which it was alleged that defendant withdrew large sums from separate construction loan accounts of three people who contracted with him to build homes, the testimony of subcontractors that they placed liens on a victim's home because defendant had not paid them was relevant because it tended to show defendant failed to pay the subcontractors for work they did on the victim's property, and, in conjunction with testimony regarding the forging of the victim's signature on draw forms, was relevant to show defendant intended to defraud the bank, under RC §§ 2913.31(A)(3) and 2901.22(A) and (B), and the testimony did not pose unfair prejudice, confuse the issues, or mislead the jury, under Ohio R. Evid. 403(A). State v. Harpley, — Ohio App. 3d —, 2006 Ohio 2976, — N.E. 2d —, 2006 Ohio App. LEXIS 2866 (June 14, 2006).

In a wrongful death case, arising from a decedent's death in an automobile collision, it was not an abuse of discretion for the trial court to allow evidence that the decedent's husband was killed in the same collision, because such evidence was relevant to damages, under RC § 2125.02(A)(1) and (3)(b), nor was it unfairly prejudicial, under Ohio R. Evid. 403(A), and any error from evidence that the decedent's aunt died in the same collision was harmless as evidence the husband and aunt died in the same collsion was not unfairly prejudicial. Conway v. Dravenstott, — Ohio App. 3d —, 2006 Ohio 4840, — N.E. 2d —, 2006 Ohio App. LEXIS 4736 (Sept. 18, 2006).

Admission

In defendant's prosecution for raping his minor nephew, the admission of defendant's statements to police that he had undergone counseling did not violate Ohio R. Evid. 403(A) because the statements were admissions of a party opponent, under Ohio R. Evid. 801(D)(2), and the statements were relevant, under Ohio R. Evid. 401, as defendant admitted his sexual attraction to young boys, so no plain error, under Ohio R. Crim. P. 52(B), was committed, as it could not be said that defendant would not have been convicted without the statements, given the other evidence against him. State v. Palacio, — Ohio App. 3d —, 2006 Ohio 1437, — N.E. 2d —, 2006 Ohio App. LEXIS 1301 (Mar. 27, 2006).

Admission proper

When a corporation, its owner, and its employee were prosecuted for, inter alia, open dumping, because they operated a facility at which they accepted scrap tires for shredding after their permit to do so was not renewed and they were specifically ordered to cease accepting tires and to get rid of the tires they had, Ohio R. Evid. 403(A) did not bar the admission of the order directing them to receive no more tires because it was probative of their intent to commit open dumping, as it showed they knew they were not authorized to operate a tire scrap facility and that to do so violated both a court order and a statute, and nothing showed the jury was misled, as the trial court properly instructed the jury on the requirements of convicting defendants of open dumping. State v. Elyria Acquisition, Co., — Ohio App. 3d —, 2006 Ohio 1415, — N.E. 2d —, 2006 Ohio App. LEXIS 1312 (Mar. 27, 2006).

Trial court properly admitted a gun clip found in defendant's home into evidence in defendant's criminal trial, as it was clearly relevant under Ohio R. Evid. 401 and 402, and the potential prejudicial effect was outweighed by the benefits of the admission under Ohio R. Evid. 403(A). The State was trying to prove that defendant shot a victim with a particular type of gun, and the gun clip was the same type and was found in defendant's home. State v. Harris, — Ohio App. 3d —, 2006 Ohio 3520, — N.E. 2d —, 2006 Ohio App. LEXIS 3439 (June 27, 2006).

Defendant's counsel did not act in violation of U.S. Const. amend. VI and Ohio Const. art. I, § 10 when he opened the door to cross-examination of defendant and other witnesses and did not "vigorously" object to the State's cross-examination, as such was not unfair under Ohio R. Evid. 403(A), and further, defendant failed to show that but for the alleged errors by counsel, the result of the trial would have been different. Defendant's claims that many questions were speculative, repetitive, leading, or included testimony inserted by the State, lacked merit under Ohio R. Evid. 611(C), as the questions were within the trial court's discretion to allow, and many were not leading. State v. Ryan, — Ohio App. 3d —, 2006 Ohio 5120, — N.E. 2d —, 2006 Ohio App. LEXIS 5039 (Sept. 29, 2006).

Applicability

Defendant's claim that his brother's testimony should have been excluded in defendant's criminal trial lacked merit, as defendant's claim that his brother's testimony was "unreliable" dealt with the weight of the evidence and did not warrant exclusion under Ohio R. Evid. 403(A), which dealt with other issues entirely. As there was no indication that any written summary of the brother's statement existed, there was no reason to exclude the statement under Ohio R. Crim. P. 16(B)(1)(a)(ii). State v. Bennett, — Ohio App. 3d —, 2006 Ohio 2757, — N.E. 2d —, 2006 Ohio App. LEXIS 2592 (May 22, 2006).

Autopsy photos

After reviewing the relevant photographs, the appellate court concluded that the trial court did not abuse its discretion in admitting under Ohio R. Evid. 403(A) autopsy photos taken by a coroner to demonstrate the victim's cause of death. State v. Lakes, — Ohio App. 3d —, 2007 Ohio 325, — N.E. 2d —, 2007 Ohio App. LEXIS 1681 (Jan. 26, 2007).

Battered woman syndrome

When a victim's credibility is challenged upon cross-examination during the state's case-in-chief, the state may introduce expert testimony regarding battered woman syndrome to aid the trier-of-fact in determining the victim's state of mind, e.g., to explain why she returned to the defendant despite his aggressions toward her. State v. Haines, 112 Ohio St. 3d 393, 2006 Ohio 6711, 860 N.E.2d 91, 2006 Ohio LEXIS 3680 (2006).

Discretion of trial court

Sufficient evidence of the victim's intoxication was presented because, although the trial court pointed out that the legal alcohol limit was not relevant, it did not prohibit defendant from raising the issue of the victim's intoxication.

The record was replete with evidence that the victim had been consuming alcohol prior to her attack and defendant's trial counsel elicited substantial testimony from the victim regarding the victim's alcohol consumption on the day of the attack. State v. Churchwell, — Ohio App. 3d —, 2007 Ohio 1600, — N.E. 2d —, 2007 Ohio App. LEXIS 1469 (Apr. 5, 2007).

Drug use

In an administrator's suit against an insurer for underinsured motorist benefits, a trial court properly barred the insurer from introducing evidence of the administrator's decedent's drug use, under Ohio R. Evid. 403(A), because the danger of unfair prejudice substantially outweighed the probative value of such evidence, particularly because the issues of liability and causation had already been determined, and a jury was only asked to decide damages, so the insurer only sought to inflame the jury, and there was a danger that the jury would hold the decedent responsible even though that issue was not before it. Dieble v. Auto Owners Ins. Co., — Ohio App. 3d —, 2007 Ohio 3429, — N.E. 2d —, 2007 Ohio App. LEXIS 3133 (July 2, 2007).

In an attempted murder prosecution, admission of evidence of defendant's drug use did not violate Ohio R. Evid. 403, because defendant said he was in the area of the crime to buy drugs from a third individual, but a search of this individual's residence revealed nothing consistent with drug use, so the probative value of the evidence was high, as it refuted defendant's alibi, and it outweighed any danger of unfair prejudice. State v. Berrien, — Ohio App. 3d —, 2006 Ohio 4563, — N.E. 2d —, 2006 Ohio App. LEXIS 4491 (Sept. 5, 2006).

Evidence

Although it was error for a trial court to have admitted testimony from the victim of a vehicle accident in defendant's criminal action on a charge of, inter alia, aggravated vehicular assault, concerning the nature and extent of her injuries pursuant to Ohio R. Evid. 401 and 403(A), given the stipulation accepted by the State that defendant admitted to having caused the accident which caused serious physical harm to the victim, the introduction of the evidence was harmless under Ohio R. Evid. 103(A) and Ohio R. Crim. P. 52(A). There was other significant evidence indicative of defendant's guilt, and the introduction of the victim's testimony regarding her injuries was limited by the trial court's instruction to the jury and was harmless in the circumstances. State v. Harding, — Ohio App. 3d —, 2006 Ohio 481, — N.E. 2d —, 2006 Ohio App. LEXIS 411 (2006).

Significance of blood alcohol content value is beyond the comprehension of an ordinary juror, and without explanatory expert testimony, the admission of the evidence inevitably imposes unfair prejudice, confuses the issues, and misleads the jury. Thus, the trial court's admission, in a personal injury suit, of a bicyclist's BAC level without corroborating expert testimony was error. Clark v. Curnutte, — Ohio App. 3d —, 2006 Ohio 1545, — N.E. 2d —, 2006 Ohio App. LEXIS 1443 (Mar. 31, 2006).

Trial court properly admitted a videotape that was made during surveillance of a bar which showed a variety of drug transactions committed by a juvenile outside of the bar, and upon the arrival of the police, the juvenile ran inside the bar and to defendant, which supported the State's theory that defendant was involved in a drug distribution chain. The evidence was relevant under Ohio R. Evid. 401 and there was no showing that the prejudicial effect of its admission outweighed the probative value pursuant to Ohio R. Evid. 403(A). State v. Harrington, — Ohio App. 3d —, 2006 Ohio 4388, — N.E. 2d —, 2006 Ohio App. LEXIS 4285 (Aug. 14, 2006).

—Admissibility

Although defendant never opened the door to evidence of his codefendant's propensity for possessing firearms and the evidence was not relevant to the issue of defendant's guilt, the codefendant's prior possession of a firearm could potentially have shown that he had an opportunity to murder the victim with such a weapon. Thus, although it was error to allow the evidence to be introduced against defendant, the trial court did not commit plain error when it allowed the evidence to be introduced because it was highly relevant to prove the codefendant's guilt and exclusion of the evidence would not likely have affected the outcome of the case. State v. Robinson, — Ohio App. 3d —, 2007 Ohio 3501, — N.E. 2d —, 2007 Ohio App. LEXIS 3224 (July 5, 2007).

— Admissible

Trial court's denial of defendant's motion in limine with respect to certain statements by a police officer in defendant's criminal trial on multiple drug charges was not an abuse of discretion under Ohio R. Evid. 403(A), as the officer's report was not offered as evidence or used in any manner at trial, the statements made by the officer at trial were not part of the content that was sought to be precluded in the motion, and defendant did not raise on appeal the trial court's decision to overrule an objection to the officer's testimony. State v. Skinner, — Ohio App. 3d —, 2007 Ohio 6793, — N.E. 2d —, 2007 Ohio App. LEXIS 5948 (Dec. 14, 2007).

There was no error in admitting the evidence because defendant did not demonstrate that the outcome of his trial clearly would have been different but for the police detective's mention of prior contacts with police, previous court proceedings, and his use of the nicknames "Champ" and "Shawn." State v. Walker, — Ohio App. 3d —, 2006 Ohio 6488, — N.E. 2d —, 2006 Ohio App. LEXIS 6462 (Dec. 11, 2006).

— Prejudicial

In a Caucasian employee's racial discrimination suit brought against the city which employed her and her African-American supervisor, the trial court properly excluded from evidence under Ohio R. Evid. 403 a report issued by the city's Equal Employment Opportunity office because, while the statements contained in the report fell within the scope of the employment of the two representatives issuing the report and, thus, constituted an admission of a party-opponent pursuant to Ohio R. Evid. 801(D)(2)(d), the potential for unfair prejudice to the city and the supervisor and confusion of the issues before the jury substantially outweighed its probative value. The report contained lengthy discussions of and conclusions regarding claims of disparate treatment and retaliation, which were not before the jury, and it presented a substantial danger of jury confusion based on the interplay of the report's conclusion of probable cause and the jury's responsibility to independently evaluate the evidence under the trial court's instructions of law to determine whether the evidence demonstrated a violation of RC ch. 4112. Mowery v. City of Columbus, — Ohio App. 3d —, 2006 Ohio 1153, — N.E. 2d —, 2006 Ohio App. LEXIS 1051 (Mar. 14, 2006).

—- Rape cases

Trial court's exclusion of the evidence as to the victim's prior sexual assault, solely on the basis that such evidence did not fit within one of the exceptions under the rape shield statute, RC § 2907.02(D), was error because the trial court did not engage in a balancing of the state interest against the probative value of the excluded evidence and defendant's right to fair trial, nor did the trial court consider whether the relevance of the evidence was outweighed by its inflammatory character and the danger of unfair prejudice under Ohio R. Evid. 403(A). Since the prosecution highlighted the victim's ability to provide details of the sexual conduct allegedly committed by defendant, defendant was entitled to have the trial court assess whether the evidence was relevant to the theory presented, and, thus, constituted a material fact, and whether application of the rape shield statute was unconstitutional as applied to the facts. State v. N.D.C., — Ohio App. 3d —, — N.E. 2d —, 2007 Ohio App. LEXIS 4506 (Sept. 27, 2007).

— Sufficient

Evidence of defendant having brandished a firearm was admissible for a permissible purpose because, although no firearm matching the one used to murder the victim was ever recovered, many bullets at the scene and within the victim were recovered and numerous witnesses testified that they had seen defendant with a firearm and that the firearm matched the caliber of weapon which was used to kill the victim. Thus, the testimony established that defendant had an opportunity to murder the victim with such a weapon; the testimony could also have established intent, preparation, or plan, since defendant could arguably have been carrying the firearm in preparation for retaliation for the assault on his brother. State v. Carter, — Ohio App. 3d —, 2007 Ohio 3502, — N.E. 2d —, 2007 Ohio App. LEXIS 3223 (June 29, 2007).

Evidence of defendant having brandished a firearm was admissible for a permissible purpose because, although no firearm matching the one used to murder the victim was ever recovered, many bullets at the scene and within the victim were recovered and numerous witnesses testified that they had seen defendant with a firearm and that the firearm matched the caliber of weapon which was used to kill the victim. Thus, the testimony established that defendant had an opportunity to murder the victim with such a weapon; the testimony could also have established intent, preparation, or plan, since defendant could arguably have been carrying the firearm in preparation for retaliation for the assault on his brother. State v. Robinson, — Ohio App. 3d —, 2007 Ohio 3501, — N.E. 2d —, 2007 Ohio App. LEXIS 3224 (July 5, 2007).

Where defendant and the victim had a deteriorated relationship for a period of years, and upon the two arguing and the victim shoving defendant, defendant took out his single-shot gun and shot the victim twice, pausing in between shots to carefully reload the gun, there was no error in the trial court's refusal to charge defendant or instruct the jury on the crime of voluntary manslaughter, in violation of RC § 2903.03, in his criminal trial on an aggravated murder charge, as there was a sufficient cooling off period such that there could be no finding of sudden rage or passion. Excluded evidence regarding the victim's reputation for violence and defendant's knowledge thereof was not relevant or admissible under Ohio R. Evid. 403 and 404(A), and specific instances of misconduct were not admissible under Ohio R. Evid. 405. State v. Kanner, — Ohio App. 3d —, 2006 Ohio 3485, — N.E. 2d —, 2006 Ohio App. LEXIS 3428 (June 29, 2006).

Where defendant was on trial for, inter alia, engaging in a pattern of corrupt activity, in violation of RC § 2923.32(A)(2), arising from his involvement in drug distribution activities over a course of time, the State's introduction of prior acts involving shipments of drugs was relevant to establish the pattern and accordingly, it was properly admitted under Ohio R. Evid. 404(B), as the probative value thereof outweighed any possibility of prejudice pursuant to Ohio R. Evid. 403(A). State v. Koval, — Ohio App. 3d —, 2006 Ohio 5377, — N.E. 2d —, 2006 Ohio App. LEXIS 5340 (Oct. 16, 2006).

In a patient's dental malpractice action, the trial court did not abuse its discretion in failing to strike an expert's slide presentation on the ground that the slides depicted an ameloblastoma, while the patient's tumor was a myxoma. As the expert explained, the tumors looked exactly the same on x-ray and showed the same behavior, and the slides were an illustrative and relevant tool to help the jury rather than a prejudicially misleading use of a different type of tumor.

Scibelli v. Pannunzio, — Ohio App. 3d —, 2006 Ohio 5652, — N.E. 2d —, 2006 Ohio App. LEXIS 5650 (Oct. 26, 2006).

— Victim impact testimony

Although the trial court erred by admitting victim impact testimony during the guilt phase of trial, because the statements had no evidentiary/probative value concerning the question of defendant's guilt, there was no evidence that had defendant's trial counsel objected or done more to keep out the cited testimony, the outcome of defendant's trial would have been any different. State v. Milam, — Ohio App. 3d —, 2006 Ohio 4742, — N.E. 2d —, 2006 Ohio App. LEXIS 4674 (Sept. 14, 2006).

Evidence admissible

In a medical malpractice case, allowing the presentation of video of a metal plate being implanted in a cadaver arm as a demonstrative exhibit was proper. Based on the record, the demonstrative video evidence offered was not so inherently misleading to the jury that its admission was an abuse of discretion, Ohio R. Evid. 403(A). Foss v. Watson, — Ohio App. 3d —, 2007 Ohio 3861, — N.E. 2d —, 2007 Ohio App. LEXIS 3515 (July 30, 2007).

Although the trial court's admission of defendant's employer's testimony was error, as it indicated that defendant had engaged in fraudulent activity and it exceeded its foundational basis for explaining why the employer contacted the victim of defendant's allegedly criminal conduct under Ohio R. Evid. 801(C), such that the probative value was substantially outweighed by the danger of unfair prejudice, confusion, and possible misleading of the jury under Ohio R. Evid. 403(A), there was no reversible error because the trial court cautioned the jury as to the limited use of the testimony. State v. Bedell, — Ohio App. 3d —, 2006 Ohio 5746, — N.E. 2d —, 2006 Ohio App. LEXIS 5705 (Nov. 2, 2006).

Evidence confusing and dissimilar

Trial court did not abuse its discretion by relying on Ohio R. Evid. 403(A) when it excluded the psychologist's testimony in defendant's child endangering trial because, since defendant failed to meet the requirements set forth in Haines, any testimony related to battered-woman syndrome had the potential to mislead the jury and cause confusion of the issues. The psychologist's testimony went beyond merely providing a general context for defendant's behavior, and went to the very question the jury was required to determine--whether defendant had the culpable mens rea necessary for committing endangering children--and defendant did not demonstrate the required connection between the scientific research or test result and particular disputed factual issues in the case. State v. Sorah, — Ohio App. 3d —, 2007 Ohio 5898, — N.E. 2d —, 2007 Ohio App. LEXIS 5179 (Nov. 5, 2007).

Trial court did not abuse its discretion when it excluded evidence, under Ohio R. Evid. 403(A), regarding the patient's alleged emotional problems, EEOC claim, union grievance, and multi-year litigation with her former employer, a police department, because the issues raised by the hospital's proffered evidence in the medical malpractice action were totally unrelated to the burns that the patient received in 2001 during surgery and would not have assisted the jury in determining damages in the matter. McManaway v. Fairfield Med. Ctr., — Ohio App. 3d —, 2006 Ohio 1915, — N.E. 2d —, 2006 Ohio App. LEXIS 1756 (Apr. 7, 2006).

Evidence of disciplinary action

When an alleged injured party sued an employee and his employer for an assault the employee allegedly committed against the alleged injured party on the employer's premises, it was an abuse of discretion to exclude evidence of disciplinary action the employer took against the employee due to the incident, under Ohio R. Evid. 403, because the employer said the discipline was not due to any wrongdoing on the part of the employee, but, rather, was done to keep the peace in the workplace, so introduction of this evidence would not have been unduly prejudicial to the employee. Armbruster v. Hampton, — Ohio App. 3d —, 2006 Ohio 4530, — N.E. 2d —, 2006 Ohio App. LEXIS 4518 (Sept. 5, 2006).

Evidence of similar incident

Where defendant was on trial for, inter alia, a charge of menacing by stalking, in violation of RC § 2903.211, the trial court properly allowed evidence of defendant's prior acts regarding the victim pursuant to Ohio R. Evid. 404(B) and RC § 2945.59, as such were relevant evidence pursuant to Ohio R. Evid. 401 and 402, they tended to prove defendant's state of mind which was an essential element of the offense, and the evidence was not outweighed by any prejudicial effect pursuant to Ohio R. Evid. 403. State v. Horsley, — Ohio App. 3d —, 2006 Ohio 1208, — N.E. 2d —, 2006 Ohio App. LEXIS 1080 (Mar. 16, 2006).

Evidence prejudicial

In balancing the State's interests against defendant's right to confront his accuser and present evidence in his own defense, the trial court did not abuse its discretion in resolving that balance against admission of the unduly inflammatory and prejudicial evidence in accordance with Ohio R. Evid. 403(A). Defendant sought to introduce evidence of the 15-year-old victim's sexual activity with persons other than defendant in an attempt to impeach her credibility and, while the evidence had some slight relevance and probative value for that limited purpose, the key issue was whether defendant engaged in sexual conduct with the minor-victim, which was proven by seminal fluid stains on the bed sheets and DNA evidence. State v. Smiddy, — Ohio App. 3d —, 2007 Ohio 1342, — N.E. 2d —, 2007 Ohio App. LEXIS 1222 (Mar. 23, 2007).

Trial court did not err in excluding defendant's attempt to present evidence that a fellow perpetrator of a beating of a victim had two prior convictions for carrying a concealed weapon and an indictment pending against him for carrying a concealed weapon, as the other acts evidence under Ohio R. Evid. 404(B) was not sufficiently probative to allow its admission, and any probative value was outweighed by the danger of unfair prejudice pursuant to Ohio R. Evid. 403(A). The two convictions were too remote in time, and the indicted offense, although of recent vintage, had no indications of uniqueness that would help establish identity of the fellow perpetrator as the shooter of the beating victim and further, the danger of unfair prejudice was high because the guns involved in each of those situations were not the same. State v. Jeffers, — Ohio App. 3d —, 2007 Ohio 3213, — N.E. 2d —, 2007 Ohio App. LEXIS 2830 (June 21, 2007).

Evidence that a physician was allegedly negligent in treating a patient's prior ovarian cyst, discovered in 1988, was properly excluded in the patient's action against the physician and his employer for the physician's alleged medical negligence in managing a second cyst diagnosed in 1999, which the patient claimed later developed into cancer. The 1988 treatment was not admissible under Ohio R. Evid. 404(B) because it was a single occurrence which did not establish a regular or routine practice as required by Ohio R. Evid. 406, and any relevance under Ohio R. Evid. 401 was outweighed by prejudice under Ohio R. Evid. 403. Gerke v. Norwalk Clinic, Inc., — Ohio App. 3d —, 2006 Ohio 5621, — N.E. 2d —, 2006 Ohio App. LEXIS 5605 (Oct. 27, 2006).

Although the evidence of blood all over the walls in defendant's home was improperly admitted because the unfair prejudice associated with the blood evidence substantially outweighed its minimal probative value, the error was harmless because there was overwhelming evidence of defendant's guilt on the possession of cocaine charge and the jury was unable to decide on the drug trafficking charges. State v. Ogletree, — Ohio App. 3d —, 2006 Ohio 6107, — N.E. 2d —, 2006 Ohio App. LEXIS 6037 (Nov. 17, 2006).

Evidence unfairly prejudicial

Although a trial court erred in admitting a gun into evidence where the probative value was substantially outweighed by the danger of unfair prejudice pursuant to Ohio R. Evid. 403(A), as the gun was identical to the murder weapon but was not the exact murder weapon, such that it had minimal value as a physical exhibit, there was no plain error under Ohio R. Crim. P. 52, as the evidence overwhelmingly supported defendant's conviction and the admission of the evidence was accordingly not outcome-determinative. The jury was aware of the gun due to testimony from witnesses, which tempered the prejudicial impact of the admission of the actual gun. State v. Bell, — Ohio App. 3d —, 2007 Ohio 310, — N.E. 2d —, 2007 Ohio App. LEXIS 282 (Jan. 26, 2007).

Trial court abused its discretion when it allowed the State to cross-examine defendant at length about his prior convictions for the purpose of impeaching him under Ohio R. Evid. 609, as the questioning far exceeded the scope of permissible impeachment. The State not only asked general questions regarding the existence of the prior convictions, but it questioned defendant about the details of those convictions, which created a high danger of unfair prejudice and confusion of the issues under Ohio R. Evid. 403, as the questioning was an attempt by the State to show that defendant had acted in conformity with his prior bad acts. State v. Feathers, — Ohio App. 3d —, 2007 Ohio 3024, — N.E. 2d —, 2007 Ohio App. LEXIS 2778 (June 15, 2007).

Trial court abused its discretion in allowing an alleged prior female victim of defendant's attack to testify in his second criminal trial on a charge of murdering a female victim, as the evidence of the prior bad act under RC § 2945.59 and Ohio R. Evid. 404(B) was relevant to establishing identity but there were other powerful pieces of evidence to support finding that defendant was the assailant, including DNA evidence, the fact that he had scratches on his hands and arms shortly after the attack, and the fact that he had been at the victim's apartment shortly prior to the time that she was murdered, and the testimony was inordinately prejudicial and outweighed any probative value pursuant to Ohio R. Evid. 403; such testimony had been excluded pursuant to a motion in limine ruling in a prior trial and upon mention of it, a mistrial resulted, and defendant should have been able to rely on that ruling for preparation of his defense for the second trial. State v. Anderson, — Ohio App. 3d —, 2006 Ohio 4618, — N.E. 2d —, 2006 Ohio App. LEXIS 4581 (Sept. 1, 2006).

Trial court abused its discretion when it permitted the prosecutor to elicit the details of defendant's prior felonious assault charge because the probative value of the detailed circumstances surrounding defendant's prior charged crime involving his sister did not outweigh the prejudicial effect of the admission of the prior alleged crime, the details of which became the subject of nearly half of the cross-examination. Nor was the evidence properly admitted to impeach the defendant's character. State v. Durham, — Ohio App. 3d —, 2006 Ohio 5015, — N.E. 2d —, 2006 Ohio App. LEXIS 4952 (Sept. 28, 2006).

Evidence with probative value

Defendant's application to reopen his appeal was denied because admission of defendant's statements to the police was not error as the statements were not unfairly prejudicial. They were not misleading or confusing and, since they demonstrated an admission of guilt, they were extremely probative. Therefore, appellate counsel was not ineffective for failing to argue that issue in defendant's appeal. State v. Lee, — Ohio App. 3d —, 2007 Ohio 1594, — N.E. 2d —, 2007 Ohio App. LEXIS 1437 (Apr. 3, 2007).

Trial court did not abuse its discretion in allowing the State to use defendant's prior theft convictions to impeach his credibility because defendant's testimony on direct examination and cross-examination opened the door to further questioning about his prior theft convictions. Under the circumstances presented, it was appropriate for the State to impeach defendant and to test his credibility by introducing testimony regarding his prior convictions. State v. Roberson, — Ohio App. 3d —, 2007 Ohio 1981, — N.E. 2d —, 2007 Ohio App. LEXIS 1829 (Apr. 26, 2007).

Weight of the evidence supported defendant's guilty verdict for defendant guilty of domestic violence because the victim made statements immediately after the incident to her great-grandmother and the police and those statements were properly admitted as excited utterances. Although the victim recanted her initial statements at trial, the State presented evidence of a recorded telephone conversation between defendant and his mother discussing how they would get the victim to change her story. The statements by defendant's mother were allowable as admissions of a party opponent and the probative value of defendant's admissions on the tape, especially in light of the victim's recantation at trial, substantially outweighed any danger of unfair prejudice. State v. Glossip, — Ohio App. 3d —, 2007 Ohio 2066, — N.E. 2d —, 2007 Ohio App. LEXIS 1931 (Apr. 30, 2007).

Trial court properly overruled a motorist's new trial motion pursuant to Ohio R. Civ. P. 59 after the jury returned a verdict in favor of a driver in the motorist's personal injury action that arose from a motor vehicle accident that was admittedly caused by the driver, as the issue of proximate cause regarding the motorist's spinal injuries was decided against him based on the fact that he had experienced prior back injuries, had undergone back surgery, and had filed social security and workers' compensation claims for those injuries. The admission of the workers' compensation claim information was proper, as it was directly relevant to the issue at trial pursuant to Ohio R. Evid. 402 and 403(A), the motorist actually raised it first in depositions and at trial such that although he had moved to exclude it by a motion in limine, he waived that evidentiary issue where he did not wait and then object to such evidence at trial, and accordingly he could not fault the trial court for allowing the driver's counsel to cross-examine on that issue pursuant to the allowable scope under Ohio R. Evid. 611(B). Sims v. Dibler, 172 Ohio App. 3d 486, 2007 Ohio 3035, 875 N.E.2d 965, 2007 Ohio App. LEXIS 2879 (2007).

Trial court properly allowed the testimony by the police officers regarding the incidents four days prior to the day that defendant committed the instant offenses for purposes of establishing defendant's identity and the trial court's limiting instruction sufficiently instructed the jury on the purpose of that testimony. The trial court specifically denied the motion in limine on the basis that the earlier events could be probative of identity and both officers referenced the earlier incident to explain some of their reasons for stopping defendant; both indicated that they recognized defendant as someone they recognized from a prior date. State v. Lane, — Ohio App. 3d —, 2007 Ohio 5948, — N.E. 2d —, 2007 Ohio App. LEXIS 5255 (Nov. 8, 2007).

Trial court did not abuse its discretion in permitting limited testimony regarding defendant's gang membership; since the victim's' identification stemmed from his recognition of defendant as a gang member, the police officer's testimony served to buttress the victim's identification. The evidence was not more prejudicial than probative because at no time did the officer testify or imply that defendant had committed criminal activity related to his gang membership. State v. Johnson, — Ohio App. 3d —, 2006 Ohio 1313, — N.E. 2d —, 2006 Ohio App. LEXIS 1197 (Mar. 22, 2006).

Trial court did not abuse its discretion in admitting testimony of a police officer regarding his patrol routine in defendant's criminal trial on charges that she committed insurance fraud by claiming that her car was stolen and then burned pursuant to Ohio R. Evid. 403(B), as there was no showing by defendant that the testimony was irrelevant or that

the prejudicial value outweighed the probative value of the evidence. State v. Hinson, — Ohio App. 3d —, 2006 Ohio 3831, — N.E. 2d —, 2006 Ohio App. LEXIS 3803 (July 27, 2006).

Evidence that defendant drove without a license was not offered to show that he acted in conformity with his prior actions when he committed the drug offenses. The evidence was elicited in the process of refuting the witness's alibi evidence, which asserted that defendant was not at his residence at the time of one of the alleged controlled drug purchases. Thus, the admission of the evidence did not violate Ohio R. Evid. 404(B) and the probative value was not substantially outweighed by the prejudice, under Ohio R. Evid. 403. State v. Ogletree, — Ohio App. 3d —, 2006 Ohio 6107, — N.E. 2d —, 2006 Ohio App. LEXIS 6037 (Nov. 17, 2006).

Experts

Injured person was not entitled to additional financial information from a doctor who had performed an independent medical examination (IME) on the injured person, and the injured person's motion to compel disclosure of that information was properly denied, where the doctor had already provided, inter alia, the number of IMEs conducted by the doctor during a period of over six years, the price range for IMEs, the number of depositions provided by the doctor for the same period, and the charges typically associated with such depositions; additionally, the cross-examination portion of the doctor's video deposition, which was played at trial, dealt extensively with the doctor's medical-legal practice and the economic aspects thereof. Stinchcomb v. Mammone, 166 Ohio App. 3d 45, 2006 Ohio 1276, 849 N.E.2d 54, 2006 Ohio App. LEXIS 1167 (Mar. 13, 2006).

Trial court's admission of expert testimony by vehicle owners in an action against a manufacturer and dealer, arising from a purchase and trade due to the first purchased vehicle being a "lemon," was proper under Ohio R. Evid. 702(A) and was not precluded under Ohio R. Evid. 403(A), as any of the opinions that the expert made which were irrelevant to the issues were harmless error, and the majority of the expert's testimony was his analysis and interpretation of the dealer's actions, which was relevant; further, the dealer had the opportunity to discredit the expert's testimony. Smith v. GMC, 168 Ohio App. 3d 336, 2006 Ohio 4283, 859 N.E.2d 1035, 2006 Ohio App. LEXIS 4197 (2006).

Trial court did not abuse its discretion in not limiting the number of expert witnesses presented by a hospital and a health professional in a medical malpractice action against them, as the probative value substantially outweighed the other considerations under Ohio R. Evid. 403(B). Witnesses included treating physicians, who were entitled to testify regarding the proper standards of care, and other doctors who testified regarding the appropriate standard of care in the circumstances. Werden v. Children's Hosp. Med. Ctr., — Ohio App. 3d —, 2006 Ohio 4600, — N.E. 2d —, 2006 Ohio App. LEXIS 4547 (Sept. 8, 2006).

Harmless error

There was no evidence that the trial court considered any irrelevant, immaterial, or incompetent evidence in rendering its decision. The error, if any, in the admission of the evidence that defendant had been seen on other occasions carrying a gun was harmless because there was no reasonable possibility that the testimony contributed to defendant's convictions. Even without the objectionable evidence, there was ample testimony that defendant had a gun in his possession when he entered the victim's house. State v. Brown, — Ohio App. 3d —, 2007 Ohio 287, — N.E. 2d —, 2007 Ohio App. LEXIS 275 (Jan. 25, 2007).

Any violation of Ohio R. Evid. 404(B) or 403(A) that took place during defendant's trial for attempted burglary and other crimes when the testimony of an eyewitness about plans defendant had for committing other crimes and bad acts was harmless. Even if the evidence was inadmissible to show his criminal propensity, there was overwhelming other evidence of defendant's guilt. State v. Bell, — Ohio App. 3d —, 2006 Ohio 6560, — N.E. 2d —, 2006 Ohio App. LEXIS 6485 (Dec. 4, 2006).

Identification evidence

Evidence that the shooter had been identified by the crowd present at the scene as the boyfriend of a particular person and that jail records showed that person visited the defendant on several occasions was relevant and admissible under EvidR 401 and 403(A): State v. Nevins, 171 Ohio App. 3d 97, 2007 Ohio 1511, 869 N.E.2d 719, 2007 Ohio App. LEXIS 1379 (2007).

Illustrative cases

Videotape of defendant's interrogation in the back of a police car was not barred by Ohio R. Evid. 403(A) because, even though the jury could tell that defendant was in the back of a police car and, presumably, under arrest, the jury could not see that he was handcuffed, and any prejudice was outweighed by the tape's probative value because statements defendant made on the tape impeached his trial testimony that he did not commit the crime with which he was charged. State v. Muncy, — Ohio App. 3d —, 2007 Ohio 1675, — N.E. 2d —, 2007 Ohio App. LEXIS 1520 (Apr. 6, 2007).

In an appropriation proceeding, Ohio Department of Transportation waived any error in the trial court's exclusion of evidence of "comparable sale" prices by failing to properly object and to properly proffer a sufficient foundation for the admissibility of the "comparable sales" price evidence, in that, without a proper objection and proffer, the court was unable to conclude that the trial court excluded the evidence. Even assuming that the trial court excluded the evidence, without a proffer the court could not conclude that it was an abuse of discretion to exclude under Ohio R. Evid. 403 evidence of sales occurring 18 months after the taking of the property. Proctor v. Dennis, — Ohio App. 3d —, 2006 Ohio 4442, — N.E. 2d —, 2006 Ohio App. LEXIS 4385 (Aug. 16, 2006).

In a foreclosure action in which three lienholders sought to prove the priority of their liens, the admission of a document purporting to be a satisfaction of a lender's lien was not unfairly prejudicial, under Ohio R. Evid. 403(A), because the lender was able to show that it applied to a mortgage entered into prior to the mortgage upon which the lender's claim of a lien was based, so the lender was not prejudiced by its admission. Park Nat'l Bank v. Chauvin, — Ohio App. 3d —, 2006 Ohio 5158, — N.E. 2d —, 2006 Ohio App. LEXIS 5060 (Oct. 2, 2006).

Limitation of cross-examination

Trial court did not err in limiting the length of trial because the father was given great leeway by the trial court to ask questions of the witnesses. The reminders of time limitations should have been helpful in guiding the father to better organize his time and questioning but, instead, he ignored the reminders and used the available time to cover irrelevant or repetitive subject matter. Mathewson v. Mathewson, — Ohio App. 3d —, 2007 Ohio 574, — N.E. 2d —, 2007 Ohio App. LEXIS 518 (Feb. 9, 2007).

Limitation on evidence

Since plaintiffs' case-in-chief included the testimony of no less than 10 physicians, the trial court did not prejudicially abuse its discretion in limiting, as it did, plaintiffs' presentation of medical evidence, pursuant to Ohio R. Evid. 403(B). McCabe v. Ransom, — Ohio App. 3d —, 2006 Ohio 2926, — N.E. 2d —, 2006 Ohio App. LEXIS 2804 (June 9, 2006).

Medical history

In a personal injury action involving an automobile accident, testimony by appellant driver's treating neurologist that appellant had made complaints on the date of the accident of sleepiness while driving was not excluded because it was relevant under Ohio R. Evid. 401 as those conditions could have potentially affected appellant's driving capabilities and was not "unfairly" prejudicial under Ohio R. Evid. 403 as appellant's counsel opened the door to the testimony by asking the neurologist about the visual complaints and the neurologist's testimony as a whole was helpful to appellant's case. Davis v. Killing, 171 Ohio App. 3d 400, 2007 Ohio 2303, 870 N.E.2d 1209, 2007 Ohio App. LEXIS 2125 (2007).

Motive

Trial court did not err in denying defendant's motion for a mistrial based on the mention by the prosecutor during his opening statement that there was a civil judgment against defendant, a licensed physician, regarding his unlawful prescription of controlled substances, as such evidence was admissible in defendant's drug trafficking trial to show motive pursuant to Ohio R. Evid. 404(B), the probative value outweighed the prejudicial or confusing effect to the jury pursuant to Ohio R. Evid. 403, and the trial court issued cautionary instructions to the jury. Although the evidence at trial did not necessarily show that such a civil judgment was granted against defendant when the alleged offenses took place, that did not render the opening statement objectionable or worthy of supporting a mistrial. State v. Nucklos, 171 Ohio App. 3d 38, 2007 Ohio 1025, 869 N.E.2d 674, 2007 Ohio App. LEXIS 958 (2007).

In defendant's prosecution for aggravated burglary and felonious assault, the probative value of evidence that defendant sold drugs, which was relevant to motive because there was testimony that defendant was angry at the victim because the victim owed defendant money from defendant's sale of drugs to the victim, outweighed any prejudice to defendant, so Ohio R. Evid. 403(A) did not bar its admission. State v. Johnson, — Ohio App. 3d —, 2007 Ohio 2176, — N.E. 2d —, 2007 Ohio App. LEXIS 2022 (May 2, 2007).

In a murder prosecution, when the prosecutor asked a witness if defendant had a "pot" tattoo, this was not prosecutorial misconduct because the question concerned a relevant issue, under Ohio R. Evid. 401, as a possible motive for the murder was the theft of drugs from the victim, so the answer to the question was admissible, under Ohio R. Evid. 402 and 404(B), and its probative value was not substantially outweighed by a danger of unfair prejudice, under Ohio R. Evid. 403. State v. Jenkins, — Ohio App. 3d —, 2006 Ohio 2546, — N.E. 2d —, 2006 Ohio App. LEXIS 2405 (May 12, 2006).

Motor vehicles sales industry

Trial court did not abuse its discretion by allowing a witness with the appropriate knowledge of the automobile industry to testify as an expert concerning sales tactics in the industry. EvidR 403 did not preclude the testimony. Smith v. GMC, 168 Ohio App. 3d 336, 2006 Ohio 4283, 859 N.E.2d 1035, 2006 Ohio App. LEXIS 4197 (2006).

Photo array

Photo array was not unfairly prejudicial because the individuals in the photo array had almost the same haircut, were of about the same age, race, and build, and defendant was not the only one in the photo array wearing orange, all of the individuals were wearing orange. Moreover, even if admission of the photo array into evidence was error, any such error was harmless, because there was overwhelming evidence of defendant's guilt, including the fact that the victim and her boyfriend never wavered in their assertion that it was defendant who assaulted the victim. State v. Schenker, — Ohio App. 3d —, 2007 Ohio 3732, — N.E. 2d —, 2007 Ohio App. LEXIS 3415 (July 19, 2007).

Photographic evidence

Trial court did not abuse its discretion by allowing the admission of a photograph of defendant with a pistol in his pocket because the evidence was probative and defendant was not materially prejudiced by its admission. Defendant failed to establish, under Ohio R. Evid. 403(A), that the photograph was unfair, prejudicial, confusing, or misleading to the jury; the photograph showed the murder weapon, which was never recovered by the police, it showed it in the possession of defendant near the time of the incident, and it was useful to corroborate the testimony of codefendant. State v. Dossett, — Ohio App. 3d —, 2006 Ohio 3367, — N.E. 2d —, 2006 Ohio App. LEXIS 3251 (June 30, 2006).

Photographs admissible

Trial court did not err in admitting seven photographs taken of the victim's injuries the day after the assault and four photographs taken immediately after the assault because each was probative of the injuries that the victim sustained. State v. Siddell, — Ohio App. 3d —, 2007 Ohio 1875, — N.E. 2d —, 2007 Ohio App. LEXIS 1711 (Apr. 20, 2007).

Trial court properly admitted graphic photographs showing injuries of the victims of defendant's vehicular homicide, as they were admitted to corroborate the testimony of the deputy coroner as to the nature of the victims' injuries in addition to their causes of death, and the probative value under Ohio R. Evid. 403 outweighed the danger of a prejudicial effect. State v. Flanigan, — Ohio App. 3d —, 2007 Ohio 3158, — N.E. 2d —, 2007 Ohio App. LEXIS 2909 (June 22, 2007).

Admission of a photograph that depicted a small child was not error in defendant's criminal trial on drug-related charges, as the photograph depicted the location of the crack cocaine, which was a valid reason for its admission; the photograph was properly authenticated and its probative value outweighed the danger of material prejudice pursuant to Ohio R. Evid. 403. State v. Matthews, — Ohio App. 3d —, — N.E. 2d —, 2007 Ohio App. LEXIS 4349 (Sept. 21, 2007).

Trial court did not commit plain error under Ohio R. Crim. P. 52 when it admitted two photographs that showed the injuries to defendant's victim, which were caused by gunshots fired by defendant during an alleged assault between them, as the photographs were used to corroborate the testimony of the doctor and the victim regarding the wounds that he suffered from the gunshots, the probative value outweighed any unfair prejudice pursuant to Ohio R. Evid. 403, and they were not repetitive. State v. Levonyak, — Ohio App. 3d —, 2007 Ohio 5044, — N.E. 2d —, 2007 Ohio App. LEXIS 4460 (Sept. 21, 2007).

Trial court did not abuse its discretion under Ohio R. Evid. 403 and 611(A) in admitting photographs of the victim of defendant's fatal shooting, as the photographs were introduced in connection with the coroner's testimony to help explain and clarify it, and the probative value of the photographs outweighed the danger of unfair prejudice to defendant; the photographs were not so gruesome as to have produced an inflammatory reaction by the jury against defendant. State v. Levett, — Ohio App. 3d —, 2006 Ohio 2222, — N.E. 2d —, 2006 Ohio App. LEXIS 2046 (May 5, 2006).

Hospital and autopsy photographs of the victim in defendant's criminal trial were properly admitted where their probative value outweighed any prejudice due to the gruesomeness pursuant to Ohio R. Evid. 403(A), as they were relevant to explain the victim's injuries and to refute defendant's claim as to how she suffered her fatal injuries. State v. Bennett, — Ohio App. 3d —, 2006 Ohio 2757, — N.E. 2d —, 2006 Ohio App. LEXIS 2592 (May 22, 2006).

Photographs showing the murder victim's body after a shooting were properly admitted as relevant and not cumulative or prejudicial pursuant to Ohio R. Evid. 401 and 403, as each photograph showed a different aspect of the case, including the location of the body when the victim fell, the location relative to other evidence, and the wounds inflicted. State v. Reid, — Ohio App. 3d —, 2006 Ohio 6450, — N.E. 2d —, 2006 Ohio App. LEXIS 6405 (Dec. 8, 2006).

Plain error

Defendant's claim of a violation of Ohio R. Evid. 403 was evaluated under a plain error analysis as defendant objected at trial based on a violation of Ohio R. Evid. 404; the trial court did not commit plain error in admitting testimony describing statements made by defendant before the murder as the outcome would not have been different without the testimony since a passenger in the same car as defendant: (1) placed defendant inside the victim's house when shots were fired; (2) described incriminating statements defendant made upon getting back in the car; and (3) described a chain and watch that fell out of defendant's pocket, which matched a description of jewelry that was missing from the victim. State v. Johnson, — Ohio App. 3d —, 2006 Ohio 209, — N.E. 2d —, 2006 Ohio App. LEXIS 139 (Jan. 19, 2006).

Prejudice outweighs probative value

While the redacted portions of defendant's police interview where he stated that the victim was a crack dealer may have been self-serving hearsay, they fell outside of the purview of hearsay, since they were not being offered for the truth asserted, but rather to reflect defendant's state of mind and that he had a reasonable fear of the victim for self defense. Regardless, the statements were quite prejudicial versus their slight probative insight as to defendant's fear of the victim because there was nothing to indicate that the victim was a crack dealer, and that fact had no bearing or relation as to why defendant was fearful of the victim; also the error was harmless since the record was replete with testimony from defendant that he feared the victim because the victim made prior threats against him and was known to carry a weapon. Ohio v. Horace K. Vinson, — Ohio App. 3d —, 2007 Ohio 5199, — N.E. 2d —, 2007 Ohio App. LEXIS 4608 (Sept. 28, 2007).

Trial court did not abuse its discretion in excluding the testimony regarding the decedent's refusal to submit to a medical procedure known as a fistulogram because the trial court rightly perceived the weak links in the causal chain and prevented the testimony from coming into evidence. The testimony was prejudicial, and its putative relevance in the causal chain that defendants' were hoping to construct to show that proximate cause for the decedent's death lay somewhere other than at the doctor's doorstep was tenuous, at best. Reihard v. Trumbull Cardiovascular Care, Inc., — Ohio App. 3d —, 2006 Ohio 4312, — N.E. 2d —, 2006 Ohio App. LEXIS 4239 (Aug. 18, 2006).

Prior bad acts

Evidence that the defendant stole the vehicle was admissible under EvidR 404(B) to establish that he had knowledge that the vehicle was stolen in order to find him guilty of receiving stolen property. For purposes of EvidR 403(A), the probative value of the evidence outweighed any prejudicial effect its admission may have had on the jury: State v. Black, 181 Ohio App. 3d 821, 2009 Ohio 1629, 911 N.E.2d 309, 2009 Ohio App. LEXIS 1355 (2009).

Admission of other acts evidence pursuant to Ohio R. Evid. 404(B) against defendant was proper to show his intent and identity with respect to his drug offenses, as there was testimony from a confidential informant that she had traded prescription drugs for stolen credit cards with defendant, had purchased cocaine from defendant, and that he had taken over a prior drug dealer's telephone. The probative value of the statements was not outweighed by the danger of substantial prejudice pursuant to Ohio R. Evid. 403(A), and there was no requirement that a limiting instruction had to be given in the circumstances where one was not requested. State v. Simmons, — Ohio App. 3d —, 2007 Ohio 1570, — N.E. 2d —, 2007 Ohio App. LEXIS 1442 (Mar. 28, 2007).

Trial court did not abuse its discretion in admitting evidence of defendant's prior acts pursuant to Ohio R. Evid. 404(B) in having pulled up on the emergency brake while he was driving, as that was the behavioral fingerprint shared by the prior acts and the crime for which defendant was on trial, which was occasioned by the driver having pulled up on the emergency brake, causing the car to skid off the road. There were disputed issues regarding who was driving, and the evidence of the prior acts was admitted under the proof-of-identity exception to Rule 404(B), which made it more probative than prejudicial under the balancing test of Ohio R. Evid. 403(A). State v. Flanigan, — Ohio App. 3d —, 2007 Ohio 3158, — N.E. 2d —, 2007 Ohio App. LEXIS 2909 (June 22, 2007).

Although the trial court did err by allowing the State to inquire into the prior incident of domestic violence which defendant had allegedly committed against his wife (the State's inquiry did not impeach an allegation of good character; it merely amplified defendant's admission that he had a bad character trait), it was not plain error since the outcome of the trial would not have been different but for the error. Defendant's version of events lacked credibility because, although he claimed that the victim suffered her injuries before meeting him and that he did not believe that she needed medical attention so he was taking her for fast food, the victim's injuries were severe, required surgery, and altered her appearance. State v. Hohvart, — Ohio App. 3d —, 2007 Ohio 5349, — N.E. 2d —, 2007 Ohio App. LEXIS 4714 (Sept. 21, 2007).

Introduction of the testimony of defendant's stepson was not error because his trial testimony paralleled the victim's testimony, to some extent, in that both were young boys raped by defendant; defendant was in a position of authority over both victims; both boys were advised by defendant to trust him; defendant complimented both boys' bodies; and the stepson described most of the offenses as occurring at night-time, and the victim also described being raped in the middle of the night. Although the trial court failed to assess on the record whether the inflammatory or prejudicial nature of the testimony outweighed its probative value as prescribed in RC §§ 2907.02(D) and 2907.05(D), the error was harmless because the victim's testimony clearly supported the convictions. State v. Clark, — Ohio App. 3d —, 2006 Ohio 1155, — N.E. 2d —, 2006 Ohio App. LEXIS 1059 (Mar. 8, 2006).

Prior conviction

Attempt to raise a patient's prior conviction for theft by deception during cross-examination of her in her medical negligence suit was improperly excluded as unfairly prejudicial since, pursuant to Ohio R. Evid. 609(A)(3), evidence involving a prior conviction for a crime of dishonesty was automatically admissible, regardless of the punishment and without consideration of unfair prejudice under Ohio R. Evid. 403. Since credibility was a main issue in determining whether the medical assistant breached the standard of care, the trial court's erroneous exclusion of the evidence of the patient's prior criminal conviction resulted in material prejudice to the assistant, the urgent care facility, and the doctor against whom the suit was brought. Schmidt v. B.E.S. of Ohio, L.L.C., — Ohio App. 3d —, 2007 Ohio 1822, — N.E. 2d —, 2007 Ohio App. LEXIS 1661 (Apr. 18, 2007).

Trial court did not abuse its discretion in admitting evidence that defendant and his shooting victim had been co-defendants in a prior criminal matter, whereupon defendant had been sentenced to a much longer term of imprisonment than the victim, as such was probative of identification and motive of defendant for the more recent shooting incident and accordingly, it was admissible under Ohio R. Evid. 404(B). The probative value of the evidence outweighed the danger of unfair prejudice, confusion of the issues, or misleading the jury pursuant to Ohio R. Evid. 403(A). State v. Wilkins, — Ohio App. 3d —, 2007 Ohio 2962, — N.E. 2d —, 2007 Ohio App. LEXIS 2723 (June 15, 2007).

Trial court did not abuse its discretion in determining that the probative value of defendant's prior convictions substantially outweighed the prejudicial effect of such convictions because, even though the convictions had occurred 10 years and four months earlier, the convictions were relevant in assessing defendant's credibility during his testimony. Defendant acknowledged his convictions, but then claimed that the victims were lying. State v. Clark, — Ohio App. 3d —, 2006 Ohio 1155, — N.E. 2d —, 2006 Ohio App. LEXIS 1059 (Mar. 8, 2006).

It was proper to allow more extensive questioning regarding defendant's prior convictions, once defendant had incorrectly testified that he only had two past felony convictions; indeed, the receiving stolen property crime was the type of crime of dishonesty under Ohio R. Evid. 609(A)(3) which gets to the heart of a witness's credibility. The prosecutor did not improperly testify about the receiving stolen property conviction and defendant could not complain about the use of the judgment entry when his incorrect testimony necessitated the use of the entry. State v. Owings, — Ohio App. 3d —, 2006 Ohio 4281, — N.E. 2d —, 2006 Ohio App. LEXIS 4278 (Aug. 18, 2006).

Probative evidence

Stories that defendant told the rape victim of his violent crimes prior to raping her were admissible as exceptions to the other acts prohibition and were not unfairly prejudicial because the evidence was not merely relevant, it was foundational evidence that bolstered the victim's claims and established defendant's preparation, intent, plan, and scheme. The relation of the stories to the victim tended to show defendant's intent to act to overcome the victim's will by fear and duress; his statements showed his intent to place the victim in a state of fear and make her fearful of rejecting him more physically or in a louder manner; and they also provided an opportunity for him to advance upon the victim without any extreme resistance. State v. Rupp, — Ohio App. 3d —, 2007 Ohio 1561, — N.E. 2d —, 2007 Ohio App. LEXIS 1449 (Mar. 27, 2007).

Probative value

Evidence of a defense witness's nine-year-old conviction for child endangering was admissible to impeach her, under Ohio R. Evid. 609(A)(1), because her credibility was questioned when she said defendant was with her at the time of the crime, and the conviction was admissible under Ohio R. Evid. 403 because its prejudicial impact did not outweigh its probative value. State v. Williams, — Ohio App. 3d —, 2007 Ohio 212, — N.E. 2d —, 2007 Ohio App. LEXIS 211 (Jan. 19, 2007).

Trial court did not err in admitting the letter defendant wrote to the victim from jail as it was relevant; if the statements it contained were construed in a certain manner (defendant wrote that he was sorry that he hurt the victim), they tended to make it more probable that he physically assaulted the victim. Although the statements in the letter were not necessarily explicit confessions that he caused the victim physical injury, such did not render them inadmissible, and defendant made no argument about precisely how the letter's probative value was substantially outweighed by the danger of unfair prejudice. State v. Hunt, — Ohio App. 3d —, 2007 Ohio 3281, — N.E. 2d —, 2007 Ohio App. LEXIS 3004 (June 28, 2007).

Probative value and prejudicial effect

There was no abuse of discretion in the trial court's exclusion of evidence of the alleged molestation of the nine-year-old victim and the blood in her underwear prior to her disappearance in defendant's trial for evidence tampering and gross abuse of a corpse. The evidence had little, if any, relevance, and the probative value of that evidence was substantially outweighed by the danger of unfair prejudice to the state, of confusion of the issues, and of misleading the jury.

State v. Gabriel, — Ohio App. 3d —, 2007 Ohio 794, — N.E. 2d —, 2007 Ohio App. LEXIS 721 (Feb. 23, 2007).

There was no error under Ohio R. Evid. 403(A) and 702 in allowing a police detective to testify regarding his opinion as to whether defendant was involved in drug dealing, as he was a 12-year veteran of the police department, he had been involved in drug investigations for half of that time, and his testimony related to a matter beyond the knowledge or experience possessed by lay persons. His testmony was not substantially outweighed by the danger of unfair prejudice, confusion of the issues, or misleading the jury. State v. Henderson, — Ohio App. 3d —, 2007 Ohio 2372, — N.E. 2d —, 2007 Ohio App. LEXIS 2212 (May 17, 2007).

Probative value of evidence

Testimony of the minor girls was properly admitted to show that defendant engaged in a pattern of having minor girls at his house, showing them pornographic videos, and/or allowing them to drink alcohol, and acting and/or talking in a sexual manner with them. On the record, therefore, the probative value of the evidence was not substantially outweighed by the possibility of unfair prejudice. State v. Petitto, — Ohio App. 3d —, 2007 Ohio 3901, — N.E. 2d —, 2007 Ohio App. LEXIS 3554 (Aug. 2, 2007).

Probative value of evidence outweighs prejudicial effect

Trial court's admission of various exhibits by the State into evidence in his criminal trial was not error, as the probative value of the evidence, including photographs that depicted numerous injuries to the victim and clothing of the victim and her daughter which had blood stains on it, outweighed any potential prejudice that the evidence might have caused. State v. Bevins, — Ohio App. 3d —, 2006 Ohio 6974, — N.E. 2d —, 2006 Ohio App. LEXIS 6936 (Dec. 29, 2006).

Probative value of polygraph exam

Trial court's decision to allow the testimony regarding defendant's attempt to defeat the polygraph test did not amount to an abuse of discretion because the trial court found that defense counsel's questions about whether defendant had done anything to impede the cold case investigation "opened the door" to allowing the prosecution to elicit testimony from the polygraph examiner showing that defendant had, in fact, taken steps to impede the cold case investigation by employing "counter measures" such as deep breathing techniques in an attempt to defeat the polygraph. State v. Barton, — Ohio App. 3d —, 2007 Ohio 1099, — N.E. 2d —, 2007 Ohio App. LEXIS 1020 (Mar. 12, 2007).

Probative value outweighed by prejudice

Prejudicial impact that defendant complained of--that a jury might infer from the fact that he was carrying $3,549 in cash on his person, that he was currently involved in illegal activity--was, of course, precisely the reasonable inference of guilt that the jury was permitted to draw from the evidence. In other words, its prejudicial impact upon defendant was precisely the probative evidence of guilt that it represented. State v. Hancock, — Ohio App. 3d —, 2006 Ohio 5759, — N.E. 2d —, 2006 Ohio App. LEXIS 5740 (Oct. 27, 2006).

Trial court did not abuse its discretion by admitting testimony regarding defendant's interaction with the sheriff's deputy because her interaction with the deputy consisted of yelling and physical contact between the two and the testimony provided the jury with a complete description of what occurred and was evidence that defendant persisted in disorderly conduct by continuing to make unreasonable noise in the office despite being asked to leave the office. Thus, the interaction was relevant to prove that she was persistent in her disorderly conduct and the relevancy of the testimony was not substantially outweighed by its unfair prejudice. State v. Cunningham, — Ohio App. 3d —, 2006 Ohio 6373, — N.E. 2d —, 2006 Ohio App. LEXIS 6328 (Dec. 5, 2006).

Probative value outweighs prejudice

Evidence that a motorist who was involved in a disputed collision suffered from sleepiness and an eye disorder while driving was relevant and not unfairly prejudicial. The evidence was contained in a deposition of the motorist's treating physician, which was generally favorable to the motorist's case, and her counsel could have mitigated any prejudicial impact by asking her whether she suffered from an eye or sleep disturbance at the time of the collision: Davis v. Killing, 171 Ohio App. 3d 400, 2007 Ohio 2303, 870 N.E.2d 1209, 2007 Ohio App. LEXIS 2125 (2007).

Trial court did not abuse its discretion when it admitted a videotape that showed the victim of defendant's fatal stabbing alive mere hours prior to the time that the stabbing occurred, as the danger of unfair prejudice was relatively minimal because there was no audio component of the tape and only a short clip was shown; however, it was probative of the fact that the victim, defendant's wife, was alive and uninjured at the time it was taken. State v. Warner, — Ohio App. 3d —, 2007 Ohio 3016, — N.E. 2d —, 2007 Ohio App. LEXIS 2770 (June 15, 2007).

Testimony did not violate other acts evidence under Ohio R. Evid. 404(B) because the testimony concerning the missing items (a gun and rent money) was given in connection with the statement to police by the victim's fiance concerning the events of the evening. Defendant was not charged with theft, and there was no evidence or argument presented that he took the items. Further, defendant testified during direct examination concerning the nature of his employment, and on cross-examination, defendant denied dubbing DVD's for income and there was no other evidence introduced to suggest that he did such a thing; the trial court did not err in overruling defendant's objections to the isolated testimony, and its probative value was not outweighed by the danger of unfair prejudice, confusion of issues, or of misleading the jury. State v. Gholston, — Ohio App. 3d —, 2007 Ohio 4053, — N.E. 2d —, 2007 Ohio App. LEXIS 3700 (Aug. 9, 2007).

Trial court did not err by allowing a deputy to testify regarding drug evidence that he found in defendant's residence because the State's theory of the case was that defendant was reckless in shaking or dropping the child and failing to immediately call the police; to demonstrate defendant's recklessness, the State presented evidence of defendant's drug use consisting of observations by the police during the investigation, testimony of the child's mother, and defendant's own admissions. Because the deputy stated that, upon entering the residence, he detected a smell of burnt marijuana, his deputy's present sense impression testimony suggested that defendant had smoked marijuana while supervising the child. State v. Stacy, — Ohio App. 3d —, 2007 Ohio 6744, — N.E. 2d —, 2007 Ohio App. LEXIS 5911 (Dec. 17, 2007).

Trial court did not abuse its discretion in admitting the taped statements from the victim's answering machine because the statements were relevant, they were not too remote in time from the incident, and the probative value of the evidence was not outweighed by the danger of unfair prejudice; since the statements were those of defendant, and offered against him at trial, the statements were not hearsay and were properly admissible under Ohio R. Evid. 801(D)(2). Because the messages met the requirements of Ohio R. Evid. 801(D)(2), their admission was not dependent upon one of the exceptions under Ohio R. Evid. 404(B) and, to the extent that defendant argued that the statements were precluded under Ohio R. Evid. 404(B), such evidence was relevant and admissible because it tended to prove identity. State v. Cody, — Ohio App. 3d —, 2007 Ohio 6776, — N.E. 2d —, 2007 Ohio App. LEXIS 5938 (Dec. 18, 2007).

Trial court did not abuse its discretion when it admitted "other act" evidence because evidence of defendant's admission, that he stole $ 100 in cash from his employer eight days before the current burglary because his wife had a bill to pay, was introduced to show motive for the burglary, i.e., his wife's debt. Also, the trial court gave the jury a limiting instruction and, under the circumstances, the probative value of the evidence outweighed its prejudice. State v. Miller, — Ohio App. 3d —, 2007 Ohio 6909, — N.E. 2d —, 2007 Ohio App. LEXIS 6045 (Dec. 12, 2007).

Trial court did not abuse its discretion when it admitted "other act" evidence because the similarity between the other acts (other burglaries) and the charged offense, of calling the victims' homes to verify that no one was home just before committing the crimes, was so unusual as to be a "behavioral fingerprint." The behavioral fingerprint was not only the fact that someone called to make sure no one was home before burglarizing the homes, but also the fact that investigators traced all of the phone calls made on the day of each burglary to phones that defendant normally used, i.e., his cell phone or the phone where he lived; the probative value of the evidence outweighed its prejudice. State v. Miller, — Ohio App. 3d —, 2007 Ohio 6909, — N.E. 2d —, 2007 Ohio App. LEXIS 6045 (Dec. 12, 2007).

There was no violation of Ohio R. Evid. 402 or Ohio R. Evid. 403 because the shotgun shells, rope, and handcuffs were relevant and their probative value outweighed the danger of unfair prejudice. The State connected the items to the charges in question; the charges of kidnapping, aggravated burglary, abduction, and domestic violence were crimes involving violent conduct and the use of force and they involved restraining another's liberty, causing physical harm, and threatening and/or terrorizing another. State v. Keener, — Ohio App. 3d —, 2006 Ohio 5650, — N.E. 2d —, 2006 Ohio App. LEXIS 5647 (Oct. 27, 2006).

Trial court did not abuse its discretion by admitting the photograph of the victim intubated at the hospital into evidence because the probative value of the photograph was not outweighed by defendant's claimed prejudicial nature of the photograph. The photograph depicted the victim's overall condition soon after the shooting and, therefore, properly provided the jury an appreciation of the nature and circumstances of the crimes. State v. Anderson, — Ohio App. 3d —, 2006 Ohio 6152, — N.E. 2d —, 2006 Ohio App. LEXIS 6114 (Nov. 21, 2006).

Probative value outweighs prejudicial effect

Ohio R. Evid. 403(A) provides that a court must exclude relevant evidence if its probative value is substantially outweighed by the danger of unfair prejudice, confusion of the issues, or of misleading the jury, and, when determining whether the probative value of evidence is outweighed by its prejudicial effects, the evidence is viewed in a light most favorable to the proponent, maximizing its probative value and minimizing any prejudicial effect to the party opposing admission. State v. Muncy, — Ohio App. 3d —, 2007 Ohio 1675, — N.E. 2d —, 2007 Ohio App. LEXIS 1520 (Apr. 6, 2007).

Relevant evidence

In a product liability claim regarding an inadequate warning as to the use of a medical product in a neurosurgery procedure, a trial court did not abuse its discretion under Ohio R. Evid. 402 and 403(B) in allowing a neurosurgeon to testify as an expert on assorted issues, although portions of his testimony were cumulative because a similar expert had already testified, as he provided an additional perspective rather than simply a cumulative one. Zappola v. Leibinger, — Ohio App. 3d —, 2006 Ohio 2207, — N.E. 2d —, 2006 Ohio App. LEXIS 2058 (May 4, 2006).

Trial court's partial grant of a motion in limine by medical professionals and entities in a patient's medical malpractice and informed consent action, whereby it excluded the hospital manual and regulations with respect to the policies regarding supervision of anesthesia students, was not harmless error under Ohio R. Civ. P. 61 where the evidence was relevant and admissible under Ohio R. Evid. 401 to determine the standard of care required, and such evidence would not have been prejudicial or confusing to the jury under Ohio R. Evid. 403(A). The alleged malpractice occurred due to the actions of a student nurse who performed anesthesia procedures without first having identified herself to the patient and who was not supervised by an anesthesiologist at the time, as required in the hospital's manual and regulations, and only two standards of care had been introduced in the case, such that the issue would not have been confusing for the jury to hear. Luettke v. St. Vincent Mercy Med. Ctr., — Ohio App. 3d —, 2006 Ohio 3872, — N.E. 2d —, 2006 Ohio App. LEXIS 3828 (July 28, 2006).

In a railroad employee's action against the railroad, seeking damages due to his exposure to asbestos, silica, and diesel fumes during his work for the railroad, the trial court's admission of a videotape of a co-worker of the employee was not an abuse of discretion, as it was relevant under Ohio R. Evid. 401 because both railroad workers held the same jobs and were exposed to the same substances, the railroad had an opportunity to cross-examine the employee regarding his job relationship with his co-worker, and the evidence was not cumulative or prejudicial under Ohio R. Evid. 403 because there was nothing in the edited video shown to the jury that indicated that the co-worker was in pain or was breathing with the use of an oxygen tank. Hager v. Norfolk & Western Ry. Co., — Ohio App. 3d —, 2006 Ohio 6580, — N.E. 2d —, 2006 Ohio App. LEXIS 6489 (Dec. 14, 2006).

Review

Juvenile court did not commit plain error under Ohio R. Crim. P. 52, based on a failure to object under Ohio R. Evid. 103(A)(1), in admitting testimony from a police detective that at a debriefing, he suggested that the juvenile be considered a suspect in the killings of his grandmother and aunt because he had a tendency towards violent behavior after he huffed gasoline, as such testimony was not improper under Ohio R. Evid. 404(B) because it was offered to show why the State's investigation shifted its focus onto the juvenile, rather than to establish that he had a propensity to commit bad acts; further, the risk of prejudice under Ohio R. Evid. 403 was not considered where it was not raised as an objection at the juvenile court level. In re Sturm, — Ohio App. 3d —, 2006 Ohio 7101, — N.E. 2d —, 2006 Ohio App. LEXIS 7046 (Dec. 22, 2006).

Substantial compliance

Defendant's argument that RC § 4511.194 was an unconstitutional violation of separation of powers and was in conflict with Ohio R. Evid. 403(A) and Ohio R. Evid. 702(C) was rejected because the Ohio Supreme Court had previously reviewed such arguments and held that the substantial compliance standard adopted by amendment to RC § 4511.19 did not violate Ohio Const. art. IV, § 5. State v. Bay, — Ohio App. 3d —, 2007 Ohio 3727, — N.E. 2d —, 2007 Ohio App. LEXIS 3412 (July 23, 2007).

Unfairly prejudicial evidence

Exclusion of evidence pursuant to Ohio R. Evid. 403 required more than mere prejudice, as it required unfair prejudice, and unfair prejudice was that quality of evidence which might result in an improper basis for a jury decision, so evidence which aroused the jury's emotional sympathies, evoked a sense of horror, or appealed to an instinct to punish might be unfairly prejudicial, and evidence that was unfairly prejudicial appealed to the jury's emotions rather than intellect. Conway v. Dravenstott, — Ohio App. 3d —, 2006 Ohio 4840, — N.E. 2d —, 2006 Ohio App. LEXIS 4736 (Sept. 18, 2006).

Videotape of police interview

Defendant's videotaped police interviews were admissible. The interviewing officer's statements did not constitute hearsay or statements of opinion where they were not made to prove the truth of the matter asserted or to assert the officer's beliefs, but were merely interrogation techniques and were included to provide context for the defendant's statements: State v. Craycraft, 147 Ohio Misc. 2d 5, 2008 Ohio 2192, 889 N.E.2d 1100, 2008 Ohio Misc. LEXIS 130 (2008).

RULE 404. Character Evidence Not Admissible to Prove Conduct; Exceptions; Other Crimes

(A) **Character evidence generally.** Evidence of a person's character or a trait of character is not admissible for the purpose of proving action in conformity therewith on a particular occasion, subject to the following exceptions:

(1) Character of accused. Evidence of a pertinent trait of character offered by an accused, or by the prosecution to rebut the same is admissible; however, in prosecutions for rape, gross sexual imposition, and prostitution, the exceptions provided by statute enacted by the General Assembly are applicable.

(2) Character of victim. Evidence of a pertinent trait of character of the victim of the crime offered by an accused, or by the prosecution to rebut the same, or evidence of a character trait of peacefulness of the victim offered by the prosecution in a homicide case to rebut evidence that the victim was the first aggressor is admissible; however, in prosecutions for rape, gross sexual imposition, and prostitution, the exceptions provided by statute enacted by the General Assembly are applicable.

(3) Character of witness. Evidence of the character of a witness on the issue of credibility is admissible as provided in Rules 607, 608, and 609.

(B) **Other crimes, wrongs or acts.** Evidence of other crimes, wrongs, or acts is not admissible to prove the character of a person in order to show action in conformity therewith. It may, however, be admissible for other purposes, such as proof of motive, opportunity, intent, preparation, plan, knowledge, identity, or absence of mistake or accident.

History: Amended, eff 7-1-07.

NOTES TO DECISIONS

ANALYSIS

Abuse of discretion
Admissibility of character evidence
Admissibility of evidence
Admissibility of evidence of other acts
Admissibility of evidence of prior conviction
Admissibility of evidence of prior offenses
Admissibility of evidence regarding sexual acts
Admissibility of evidence to explain sequence of events
Admissibility of other acts evidence
Admissibility of prior acts of domestic violence
Admissibility of similar acts evidence
Admission of "other acts" evidence
Battered woman syndrome
Behavioral fingerprint
Character evidence
Character of accused
Character of victim
Domestic violence
Evidence
— Sufficient
Evidence admissible in sexual abuse cases
Evidence of other acts

Evidence of past offenses
Evidence of prior drug sales
Evidence properly admitted
Evidence regarding sexual acts
—Admissibility
Evidence relevant to offense
Evidence tending to show motive or intent
Failure to give limiting instruction
Harmless error
Identity
Imprisonment of defendant
Introduction of evidence of other crimes
Introduction of evidence of prior drug sales
Issues raised by defendant
Joinder of offenses
Juvenile records
Motive
Motive, intent, or purpose
Other acts
— Admissibility
Other acts evidence
—Admission for limited purpose
Other acts evidence admitted for limited purpose
Other acts generally
Other crimes admissible
Other crimes inadmissible
Other crimes, wrong or acts
Other crimes, wrongs or acts
Pattern of conduct
Plan or scheme
Prejudicial evidence
Prior bad acts admissible
Prior conviction
Prior conviction properly admitted
Prior convictions
Prior identical offense
Sequence of events
Severance of offenses
Sexual abuse cases
—Admissible evidence
Similar acts evidence
Waiver

Abuse of discretion

Trial court abused its discretion under Ohio R. Evid. 404(B) where it allowed the State to impeach a witness by admitting evidence of defendant's criminal record, as defendant had not "opened the door" by introducing positive character evidence under Rule 404(A)(1). The witness had indicated that a third person, not defendant, was a "good man," such that admission of the prior convictions was improper. State v. Feathers, — Ohio App. 3d —, 2007 Ohio 3024, — N.E. 2d —, 2007 Ohio App. LEXIS 2778 (June 15, 2007).

Admissibility of character evidence

Trial court did not err in excluding defendant's attempt to introduce evidence of his non-aggressive character pursuant to Ohio R. Evid. 404(A)(1) in his criminal trial on charges that included quite aggressive conduct towards the victim, as such evidence had already been introduced on cross-examination of two of the State's witnesses, such that the jury was cognizant of the evidence that defendant wanted to have before it regarding the type of person he was. As the evidence of defendant's guilt of the offenses in the case was overwhelming, any error in refusing to allow the admission of the character evidence was harmless under Ohio R. Crim. P. 52. State v. Alton, — Ohio App. 3d —, 2007 Ohio 2109, — N.E. 2d —, 2007 Ohio App. LEXIS 1969 (May 3, 2007).

Although defendant never opened the door to evidence of his codefendant's propensity for possessing firearms and the evidence was not relevant to the issue of defendant's guilt, the codefendant's prior possession of a firearm could potentially have shown that he had an opportunity to murder the victim with such a weapon. Thus, although it was error to allow the evidence to be introduced against defendant, the trial court did not commit plain error when it allowed the evidence to be introduced because it was highly relevant to prove the codefendant's guilt and exclusion of the evidence would not likely have affected the outcome of the case. State v. Robinson, — Ohio App. 3d —, 2007 Ohio 3501, — N.E. 2d —, 2007 Ohio App. LEXIS 3224 (July 5, 2007).

Admission of the question and answer regarding defendant's employment was not plain error because it was not a significant factor in the guilty verdict. The question about defendant's lifestyle, the employment status of a co-defendant and of defendant's mother was of minimal or no relevance, could not have affected the trial's outcome, and therefore could not be prejudicial error. State v. Warsame, — Ohio App. 3d —, 2007 Ohio 3656, — N.E. 2d —, 2007 Ohio App. LEXIS 3334 (July 19, 2007).

Admissibility of evidence

In defendant's prosecution under RC §§ 2903.11(A)(2) and 2941.145 for complicity to felonious assault with a firearm specification, based on allegations that she drove a vehicle from which her co-defendant exited to shoot at the victims, using a gun supplied by defendant, the admission of testimony that a knife was recovered in a subsequent search of defendant's car was not impermissible, under Ohio R. Evid. 404(B), because the knife was only briefly mentioned and this testimony was not used to prove defendant committed the crimes charged. State v. Myers, — Ohio App. 3d —, 2007 Ohio 915, — N.E. 2d —, 2007 Ohio App. LEXIS 817 (Mar. 5, 2007).

In defendant's criminal prosecution, the admission of testimony about her fingerprints was not impermissible "other acts" evidence, under Ohio R. Evid. 404(B), because there was no explicit reference to her prior law enforcement contacts, and an argument that such contacts were implied from the existence of defendant's prints was speculative and insufficient to show prejudice. State v. Myers, — Ohio App. 3d —, 2007 Ohio 915, — N.E. 2d —, 2007 Ohio App. LEXIS 817 (Mar. 5, 2007).

Mere police department heading of the photo array, standing alone, did not amount to "other acts" evidence under Ohio R. Evid. 404(B) nor could it have been inferred from the record that anyone noted or considered the discrepancy in rendering the verdict. Accordingly, defendant failed to show how he was prejudiced by its admission or that the failure to object to it by counsel somehow affected the outcome of his trial. State v. Jackson, — Ohio App. 3d —, 2007 Ohio 2925, — N.E. 2d —, 2007 Ohio App. LEXIS 2703 (June 14, 2007).

Because the previously excluded evidence served to prove that the weapon taken from defendant at his arrest and the weapon used in the robbery were one and the same, and defendant had elicited testimony to put that in doubt, the trial court properly allowed the evidence to come in. Additionally, because defendant himself put the identity of the gun at issue, the trial court did not err in permitting rebuttal testimony into evidence on that issue. State v. Peyton, — Ohio App. 3d —, 2006 Ohio 3951, — N.E. 2d —, 2006 Ohio App. LEXIS 3899 (Aug. 3, 2006).

Joinder of a charge of gross sexual imposition, in violation of RC § 2907.05(A)(4), with other charges was proper under Ohio R. Crim. P. 13 and 14, as evidence of pornographic video images involving children, which formed the basis of charges of pandering obscenity involving a minor, in violation of RC § 2907.321(A)(2) and (5), was admissible under Ohio R. Evid. 404(B) and RC § 2945.59 to prove that defendant's motive was sexual gratification based on sexual contact pursuant to

RC § 2907.01(B). State v. Gillingham, — Ohio App. 3d —, 2006 Ohio 5758, — N.E. 2d —, 2006 Ohio App. LEXIS 5738 (Oct. 27, 2006).

During defendant's trial for sexual battery and gross sexual imposition involving a 16-year-old victim, evidence of his prior similar conviction involving a 14-year-old victim was properly admitted under Evid. R. 404(B) to rebut his claim that the victim was lying to get back at her mother for punishing her because he had offered the same defense in the previous prosecution. The State's inquiry was limited to the details of his explanation and did not include the details of the prior offense itself. State v. Johnson, — Ohio App. 3d —, 2006 Ohio 6593, — N.E. 2d —, 2006 Ohio App. LEXIS 6538 (Dec. 14, 2006).

Admissibility of evidence of other acts

Defendant was not unduly prejudiced by the admission of evidence of charges in a subsequent indictment that arose from the same criminal incident as the charges in the original indictment, as the second set of charges relating to defendant's possession of a victim's identification and checks were offered to prove his identity as the perpetrator of a robbery and assault on the victim, pursuant to Ohio R. Evid. 404(B). Although a limiting instruction was not given on that or on the fact that one of the subsequent charges involved defendant's possession of weapons while under disability, as defendant's counsel failed to object pursuant to Ohio R. Crim. P. 30(A) and the evidence of defendant's guilt was overwhelming, the error was harmless under Ohio R. Crim. P. 52. State v. Johnson, — Ohio App. 3d —, 2007 Ohio 437, — N.E. 2d —, 2007 Ohio App. LEXIS 374 (Feb. 2, 2007).

Trial court's admission of evidence of the tumultuous and hostile marital relationship between defendant and his wife, who he was charged and convicted of murdering, was proper under Ohio R. Evid. 404(B) and RC § 2945.59, as it provided the jury with defendant's feelings towards his wife leading up to her murder and established his motive or intent to kill her. The evidence was not offered to prove defendant's character, it was presented to rebut defendant's statements to others that the shooting was only an accident, and the danger of unfair prejudice did not substantially outweigh the probative value of the evidence. State v. Benson, — Ohio App. 3d —, 2007 Ohio 830, — N.E. 2d —, 2007 Ohio App. LEXIS 765 (Mar. 1, 2007).

Trial court did not err in denying defendant's motion for a mistrial based on the mention by the prosecutor during his opening statement that there was a civil judgment against defendant, a licensed physician, regarding his unlawful prescription of controlled substances, as such evidence was admissible in defendant's drug trafficking trial to show motive pursuant to Ohio R. Evid. 404(B), the probative value outweighed the prejudicial or confusing effect to the jury pursuant to Ohio R. Evid. 403, and the trial court issued cautionary instructions to the jury. Although the evidence at trial did not necessarily show that such a civil judgment was granted against defendant when the alleged offenses took place, that did not render the opening statement objectionable or worthy of supporting a mistrial. State v. Nucklos, 171 Ohio App. 3d 38, 2007 Ohio 1025, 869 N.E.2d 674, 2007 Ohio App. LEXIS 958 (2007).

Admission of other acts evidence pursuant to Ohio R. Evid. 404(B) against defendant was proper to show his intent and identity with respect to his drug offenses, as there was testimony from a confidential informant that she had traded prescription drugs for stolen credit cards with defendant, had purchased cocaine from defendant, and that he had taken over a prior drug dealer's telephone. The probative value of the statements was not outweighed by the danger of substantial prejudice pursuant to Ohio R. Evid. 403(A), and there was no requirement that a limiting instruction had to be given in the circumstances where one was not requested. State v. Simmons, — Ohio App. 3d —, 2007 Ohio 1570, — N.E. 2d —, 2007 Ohio App. LEXIS 1442 (Mar. 28, 2007).

Defendant's claim that his counsel failed to object to prior bad acts testimony and that such was ineffective assistance in violation of U.S. Const. amend. VI and Ohio Const. art. I, § 10 lacked merit, as the admission of such evidence was deemed proper under Ohio R. Evid. 404(B), based on defendant's claim that he was not a violent person towards his wife, who was the victim of his criminal conduct. State v. Wilson, — Ohio App. 3d —, 2007 Ohio 4564, — N.E. 2d —, 2007 Ohio App. LEXIS 4089 (Aug. 31, 2007).

Trial court did not commit plain error under Ohio R. Crim. P. 52(B) where it did not give the jury instructions to disregard testimony that defendant claimed was "highly prejudicial," as he failed to object during the trial, such that the trial court had no duty to give curative instructions; moreover, the testimony regarding defendant's prior conduct of alcohol abuse and spousal abuse was admissible under Ohio R. Evid. 404(B) where defendant claimed that he was not a violent person and that it was not his intention to hurt his wife. State v. Wilson, — Ohio App. 3d —, 2007 Ohio 4564, — N.E. 2d —, 2007 Ohio App. LEXIS 4089 (Aug. 31, 2007).

When an agency sought permanent custody of a mother's child, the admission of evidence that the mother's parental rights to other children had been previously terminated was not improper, under Ohio R. Evid. 404(B), because the evidence was not offered to prove the mother's character in order to show that the mother acted in conformity therewith, but, rather, was offered to show the mother's compliance with case plans with regard to the mother's other children. In re P.N.M. Adjudicated Dependent, — Ohio App. 3d —, 2007 Ohio 4976, — N.E. 2d —, 2007 Ohio App. LEXIS 4432 (Sept. 17, 2007).

Trial court did not abuse its discretion in admitting evidence pursuant to Ohio R. Evid. 404 with respect to prior acts of defendant regarding her parenting for purposes of showing her character evidence, as the State's theory, in part, was to show that defendant committed her crimes due to her having been overwhelmed by and resentful of the task of raising three young children, and that she acted in response to those feelings in order to alleviate her situation. State v. Roseborough, — Ohio App. 3d —, 2006 Ohio 2254, — N.E. 2d —, 2006 Ohio App. LEXIS 2101 (May 5, 2006).

Trial court did not abuse its discretion in denying defendant's motion under Ohio R. Crim. P. 14 to sever a misdemeanor charge of child endangerment from more serious crimes in her criminal trial, as the "other acts" evidence regarding defendant's alleged neglect of her children would have been admissible in a separate trial on the other charges, including murder, pursuant to the admissibility rule of Ohio R. Evid. 404(B) as a means to establish defendant's motive for having committed the serious crimes. Defendant could not show that she was prejudiced by the denial of her severance request. State v. Roseborough, — Ohio App. 3d —, 2006 Ohio 2254, — N.E. 2d —, 2006 Ohio App. LEXIS 2101 (May 5, 2006).

Trial court erred when it allowed the jury to learn of 1993 accusations of assault and stalking of an adult complainant because defendant's direct examination did not open the door but was, instead, limited to accusations of a sexual nature involving children. Evidence of other, unrelated accusations held no probative value and was irrelevant. The error was prejudicial because it denied defendant the right to a fair trial in violation of his constitutional rights, in that the testimony was unrelated to the offense with which he was charged, sexual imposition on a child, and was introduced in a case in which the only evidence of defendant's guilt was the recanted testimony of a child with no attendant physical evidence. State v. Smith, — Ohio App. 3d —, 2006 Ohio 45, — N.E. 2d —, 2006 Ohio App. LEXIS 44 (Jan. 6, 2006).

Trial court's admission of prior bad acts evidence that defendant was a drug dealer and that he physically assaulted women and children was not plain error under Ohio R. Crim. P. 52(B), as the evidence fit within the exceptions to the common law rule pursuant to Ohio R. Evid. 404(B) and RC § 2945.59 relating to the motive, preparation, plan, and absence of mistake or accident. State v. Harris, — Ohio App. 3d —, 2006 Ohio 3520, — N.E. 2d —, 2006 Ohio App. LEXIS 3439 (June 27, 2006).

In defendant's prosecution for menacing by stalking under RC § 2903.211(A)(1), the trial court permissibly referred to and relied upon incidents occurring before the time period specified in the indictment because those incidents provided the context within which to determine whether defendant's conduct toward the victim constituted knowing attempts to cause her to believe that he would cause her mental distress or physical harm. State v. Bone, — Ohio App. 3d —, 2006 Ohio 3809, — N.E. 2d —, 2006 Ohio App. LEXIS 3772 (July 25, 2006).

Defendant's counsel did not provide ineffective assistance in violation of defendant's rights under U.S. Const. amend. VI and Ohio Const. art. 1, § 10 by failing to object on grounds of relevancy to the admission of evidence that defendant shot the victim's vehicle, although counsel did object to that evidence on hearsay grounds, as there was substantial evidence to support the admission of that evidence and accordingly, any objection thereto would have been meritless. The evidence that defendant used a gun to shoot at the victim's car was properly admitted under RC § 2945.59 and Ohio R. Evid. 404(B) to show the victim's subjective reasonable belief of fear, which was an element of the aggravated menacing, in violation of RC § 2903.21, which defendant was on trial for. State v. Henry, — Ohio App. 3d —, 2006 Ohio 4783, — N.E. 2d —, 2006 Ohio App. LEXIS 4657 (Sept. 14, 2006).

Evidence of a prior argument regarding defendant's alleged sale of drugs to the victim's uncle was properly admitted under Ohio R. Evid. 404(B) and RC § 2945.59 in defendant's criminal trial on a charge of aggravated menacing, in violation of RC § 2903.21, as it put defendant's threat for purposes of the menacing charge into context and provided a picture of the sequence of events leading up to the menacing act. The prior argument was "inextricably related" to the charge and it was relevant and admissible under the "scheme, plan, or system" exception to RC § 2945.59, such that the admission thereof did not lead to a conclusion that defendant's counsel provided ineffective assistance in violation of defendant's rights under U.S. Const. amend. VI and Ohio Const. art. I, § 10. State v. Henry, — Ohio App. 3d —, 2006 Ohio 4783, — N.E. 2d —, 2006 Ohio App. LEXIS 4657 (Sept. 14, 2006).

Where defendant was on trial for, inter alia, engaging in a pattern of corrupt activity, in violation of RC § 2923.32(A)(2), arising from his involvement in drug distribution activities over a course of time, the State's introduction of prior acts involving shipments of drugs was relevant to establish the pattern and accordingly, it was properly admitted under Ohio R. Evid. 404(B), as the probative value thereof outweighed any possibility of prejudice pursuant to Ohio R. Evid. 403(A). State v. Koval, — Ohio App. 3d —, 2006 Ohio 5377, — N.E. 2d —, 2006 Ohio App. LEXIS 5340 (Oct. 16, 2006).

Admission of other acts evidence regarding defendant's improper sexual conduct with a seven-year-old victim was proper under Ohio R. Evid. 404(B) and RC § 2945.59 in his trial on rape charges against the same victim, as it established that he committed similar crimes with the same victim within a period of time near to the crimes charged, and it established the element of force in the charged crimes. Although other acts evidence regarding domestic violence and "whuppings" was not admissible, there was no plain error under Ohio R. Crim. P. 52 as the evidence was relevant to the victim's state of mind and to her failed attempt to escape from defendant, and there was no showing that the outcome of the trial would have been different without the evidence. State v. Triplett, — Ohio App. 3d —, 2006 Ohio 5465, — N.E. 2d —, 2006 Ohio App. LEXIS 5464 (Oct. 20, 2006).

Evidence that a physician was allegedly negligent in treating a patient's prior ovarian cyst, discovered in 1988, was properly excluded in the patient's action against the physician and his employer for the physician's alleged medical negligence in managing a second cyst diagnosed in 1999, which the patient claimed later developed into cancer. The 1988 treatment was not admissible under Ohio R. Evid. 404(B) because it was a single occurrence which did not establish a regular or routine practice as required by Ohio R. Evid. 406, and any relevance under Ohio R. Evid. 401 was outweighed by prejudice under Ohio R. Evid. 403. Gerke v. Norwalk Clinic, Inc., — Ohio App. 3d —, 2006 Ohio 5621, — N.E. 2d —, 2006 Ohio App. LEXIS 5605 (Oct. 27, 2006).

Police officers' testimony about the sequence of events leading up to their encounter with defendant was proper as immediate background testimony because the testimony explained the setting of the case. The police were flagged down by a man who complained that a group of males were harassing or attempting to rob him, the man accompanied the police in their cruiser to look for the alleged perpetrators, and the man identified defendant; upon approaching defendant, the officers observed defendant throw a crack pipe on the ground. State v. Ogletree, — Ohio App. 3d —, 2006 Ohio 6167, — N.E. 2d —, 2006 Ohio App. LEXIS 6125 (Nov. 22, 2006).

Trial court's admission of other acts evidence that defendant allegedly robbed two men was proper under Ohio R. Evid. 404(B) and RC § 2945.59 under the plain error standard of review pursuant to Ohio R. Crim. P. 52(B), as the references to the robbery were isolated and of minor significance based on the gravity of the offenses that defendant was on trial for, and there was no showing that the admission thereof played a role in establishing defendant's character in an attempt to prove that he had committed the robbery. State v. Hannah, — Ohio App. 3d —, 2006 Ohio 6418, — N.E. 2d —, 2006 Ohio App. LEXIS 6371 (Dec. 7, 2006).

Admissibility of evidence of prior conviction

There was no error in admitting the evidence of the driver's traffic citation conviction for failure to yield because defendants, the driver and his employer, opened the door by introducing the evidence themselves. Jeavons v. Werner Enterprises, — Ohio App. 3d —, 2006 Ohio 1754, — N.E. 2d —, 2006 Ohio App. LEXIS 1626 (Apr. 7, 2006).

Under Ohio R. Evid. 609(B), evidence of a prior conviction for passing bad checks was admissible because it occurred within the past 10 years and was probative in deciding the factual issues presented in the instant case. The testimony regarding prior civil lawsuits was probative of the manager's truthfulness and therefore, was admissible to establish motive, intent, preparation and plan. Kimble Mixer Co. v. St. Vincent, — Ohio App. 3d —, 2006 Ohio 2258, — N.E. 2d —, 2006 Ohio App. LEXIS 2119 (May 2, 2006).

Under Ohio R. Evid. 608(B), the trial court did not abuse its discretion when it determined that the probative value of the manager's grand theft conviction in 1980 outweighed its prejudicial effect because the conviction was relevant since it was based upon a set of facts almost identical to those presented in the instant case. The conviction was introduced to establish that the manager was not making a mistake when he engaged in conduct contrary to the management services agreement he entered into with the manager (since in both cases he claimed that his actions were the result of misreading the contract) and the evidence established that the manager had knowledge of the various effective means to embezzle funds since he had used similar methods during his employment with a previous company. Kimble Mixer Co. v. St.

Vincent, — Ohio App. 3d —, 2006 Ohio 2258, — N.E. 2d —, 2006 Ohio App. LEXIS 2119 (May 2, 2006).

Admissibility of evidence of prior offenses

Erroneous admission of prior acts evidence pursuant to Ohio R. Evid. 404(B) and RC § 2945.59 with respect to defendant's prior convictions of weapons offenses in the same area that he was on trial for having shot a victim to death was harmless error under Ohio R. Crim. P. 52, as there was abundant evidence to support defendant's conviction, defendant testified about the prior conviction at trial pursuant to Ohio R. Evid. 609, and the impact of the erroneously admitted evidence was minimal and did not result in an outcome that would have been different had such evidence not been introduced; the fact that defendant had a gun in the prior offenses and in the offenses for which he was on trial did not establish a unique pattern or a behavioral fingerprint in order to show defendant's identity, as the prior weapons offenses were not ones of violence, the same gun was not used, and they were remote in time. Ohio v. King, — Ohio App. 3d —, 2007 Ohio 4879, — N.E. 2d —, 2007 Ohio App. LEXIS 4348 (Sept. 21, 2007).

Admissibility of evidence regarding sexual acts

Previous victim's testimony was probative as to whether defendant committed the acts for which he was indicted; the State argued that the testimony of the previous victim was introduced for the purpose of establishing identity, opportunity, intent, knowledge, and absence of mistake or accident. It could not be said that, but for the admission of the testimony the outcome of the trial would clearly have been different, and thus, the error did not rise to the high standard required for plain error. State v. Chaney, — Ohio App. 3d —, 2006 Ohio 6489, — N.E. 2d —, 2006 Ohio App. LEXIS 6417 (Dec. 11, 2006).

Introduction of the testimony of defendant's stepson was not error because his trial testimony paralleled the victim's testimony, to some extent, in that both were young boys raped by defendant; defendant was in a position of authority over both victims; both boys were advised by defendant to trust him; defendant complimented both boys' bodies; and the stepson described most of the offenses as occurring at nighttime, and the victim also described being raped in the middle of the night. Although the trial court failed to assess on the record whether the inflammatory or prejudicial nature of the testimony outweighed its probative value as prescribed in RC §§ 2907.02(D) and 2907.05(D), the error was harmless because the victim's testimony clearly supported the convictions. State v. Clark, — Ohio App. 3d —, 2006 Ohio 1155, — N.E. 2d —, 2006 Ohio App. LEXIS 1059 (Mar. 8, 2006).

Admissibility of evidence to explain sequence of events

In defendant's prosecution for involuntary manslaughter, under RC § 2903.04(A), based on defendant killing a victim in the course of a drug transaction, the admission of evidence that drugs, weapons and ammunition were found in defendant's home and that defendant was facing related criminal charges did not violate Ohio R. Evid. 404(B) because the evidence helped the jury understand the surrounding circumstances and was relevant to prove defendant's drug trafficking, which had to be proved to secure an involuntary manslaughter conviction. Ohio v. Jones, — Ohio App. 3d —, 2007 Ohio 5458, — N.E. 2d —, 2007 Ohio App. LEXIS 4810 (Oct. 12, 2007).

Admissibility of other acts evidence

Trial court did not abuse its discretion in admitting testimony of a prior rape victim in defendant's murder trial pursuant to Ohio R. Evid. 404(B) and RC § 2945.59, as it was relevant for proof of identity and method of his commission of the murder based on temporality of the crimes, the fact that defendant knew each of the victims prior to the attack, that they voluntarily let him into their homes, and his similar method of attack against them. State v. Roberts, — Ohio App. 3d —, 2007 Ohio 856, — N.E. 2d —, 2007 Ohio App. LEXIS 769 (Mar. 2, 2007).

Trial counsel's failure to object to "other acts" evidence, including evidence that, on two prior occasions, defendant had entered the victim's house without permission, did not constitute ineffective assistance of counsel as the evidence was admissible under Ohio R. Evid. 404(B) in light of the fact that the incidents went to the victim's identification of defendant. State v. Hall, — Ohio App. 3d —, 2007 Ohio 6797, — N.E. 2d —, 2007 Ohio App. LEXIS 5951 (Dec. 14, 2007).

Trial court did not abuse its discretion in overruling defendant's motion to sever because the jury was not likely to be improperly influenced by evidence of defendant's earlier conviction or more likely to believe him guilty of the assault charge against him in the instant matter. The simple and direct nature of the witnesses' testimony regarding each offense negated defendant's assertion of prejudice. State v. Bates, — Ohio App. 3d —, 2006 Ohio 4146, — N.E. 2d —, 2006 Ohio App. LEXIS 4163 (Aug. 11, 2006).

Defendant's argument concerning the introduction of prior acts were without merit because the first three acts were not introduced to prove defendant's character but to show that defendant did, in fact, commit the offense of menacing by stalking because the alleged prior acts were part of defendant's pattern of behavior. He knew that threatening the victim's family and friends, assaulting her, carrying a gun, and intimidating her employer would cause her to believe that defendant would cause her physical harm or mental distress. State v. Edwards, — Ohio App. 3d —, 2006 Ohio 5726, — N.E. 2d —, 2006 Ohio App. LEXIS 5723 (Nov. 2, 2006).

Although defendant was charged with six counts of rape, in violation of RC § 2907.02(A)(1)(b) and he claimed that there was evidence of more incidents than that, such was not error as the claim by defendant was speculative and further, the determination of whether and of what to charge against a defendant was within the prosecutor's discretion; further, any additional incidents could have been deemed relevant as prior acts under Ohio R. Evid. 404(B). State v. West, — Ohio App. 3d —, — N.E. 2d —, 2007 Ohio App. LEXIS 4637 (Sept. 24, 2007).

Admissibility of prior acts of domestic violence

Where the State charged defendant with felony domestic violence, in violation of RC § 2919.25, it met its burden of proof during direct examination of defendant's ex-wife when it questioned her regarding defendant's conviction for the prior offense, as she was the victim thereof. The subsequent testimony by the ex-wife regarding the details of defendant's prior domestic violence conviction was inadmissible under Ohio R. Evid. 404(B), and based on the nature of defendant's conduct during that incident which tended to infer that he was uncontrollable, the testimony was highly prejudicial, such that it was an abuse of the trial court's discretion to have allowed such testimony and it was also ineffectiveness of defendant's trial counsel in violation of Ohio Const. art. I, § 10 for not objecting thereto. State v. Feathers, — Ohio App. 3d —, 2007 Ohio 3024, — N.E. 2d —, 2007 Ohio App. LEXIS 2778 (June 15, 2007).

Admissibility of similar acts evidence

Due to the similarities between the string of robberies and the home-invasion for which defendant was on trial, the trial court's conclusion to allow the other acts evidence (evidence of the other robberies) to establish identity was proper, especially since two victims from the other robberies identified defendant as one of the men in their homes. In all of the cases, the perpetrators ordered the victims to remove their clothing, and tied the victims to chairs with articles of clothing. State v. Hairston, — Ohio App. 3d —, 2007 Ohio 3707, — N.E. 2d —, 2007 Ohio App. LEXIS 3387 (June 4, 2007).

Admission of "other acts" evidence

Where a department store security employee indicated that security personnel had been watching defendant for a couple of weeks prior to the incident that resulted in criminal charges against him, such was not within the prohibition of other acts testimony under Ohio R. Evid. 404(B), as it was provided for the purpose of explaining security personnel's actions in watching defendant when he entered the store. Accordingly, defendant's counsel was not ineffective in violation of U.S. Const. amend. VI and Ohio Const. art. I, § 10 in failing to object to the admission thereof. State v. Lee, — Ohio App. 3d —, 2007 Ohio 288, — N.E. 2d —, 2007 Ohio App. LEXIS 273 (Jan. 25, 2007).

Admission of other act evidence was not error because defendant opened the door to the probation officer's testimony by calling his girlfriend as a witness. It was defendant who elicited the testimony and the alibi that he had to meet with his probation officer and that his girlfriend woke him up so that he could go to that meeting. There was no mention of defendant's conviction for domestic violence, just a description of the probation officer's job, obligations, requirements, and an assessment. State v. Frazier, — Ohio App. 3d —, 2007 Ohio 1141, — N.E. 2d —, 2007 Ohio App. LEXIS 1059 (Mar. 15, 2007).

Testimony did not violate other acts evidence under Ohio R. Evid. 404(B) because the testimony concerning the missing items (a gun and rent money) was given in connection with the statement to police by the victim's fiance concerning the events of the evening. Defendant was not charged with theft, and there was no evidence or argument presented that he took the items. Further, defendant testified during direct examination concerning the nature of his employment, and on cross-examination, defendant denied dubbing DVD's for income and there was no other evidence introduced to suggest that he did such a thing; the trial court did not err in overruling defendant's objections to the isolated testimony, and its probative value was not outweighed by the danger of unfair prejudice, confusion of issues, or of misleading the jury. State v. Gholston, — Ohio App. 3d —, 2007 Ohio 4053, — N.E. 2d —, 2007 Ohio App. LEXIS 3700 (Aug. 9, 2007).

Battered woman syndrome

When a victim's credibility is challenged upon cross-examination during the state's case-in-chief, the state may introduce expert testimony regarding battered woman syndrome to aid the trier-of-fact in determining the victim's state of mind, e.g., to explain why she returned to the defendant despite his aggressions toward her. State v. Haines, 112 Ohio St. 3d 393, 2006 Ohio 6711, 860 N.E.2d 91, 2006 Ohio LEXIS 3680 (2006).

Behavioral fingerprint

Trial court did not abuse its discretion when it admitted "other act" evidence because the similarity between the other acts (other burglaries) and the charged offense, of calling the victims' homes to verify that no one was home just before committing the crimes, was so unusual as to be a "behavioral fingerprint." The behavioral fingerprint was not only the fact that someone called to make sure no one was home before burglarizing the homes, but also the fact that investigators traced all of the phone calls made on the day of each burglary to phones that defendant normally used, i.e., his cell phone or the phone where he lived; the probative value of the evidence outweighed its prejudice. State v. Miller, — Ohio App. 3d —, 2007 Ohio 6909, — N.E. 2d —, 2007 Ohio App. LEXIS 6045 (Dec. 12, 2007).

Character evidence

There was no plain error in admitting the portion of the victim's testimony in which she stated that she began seeing defendant after he got out of jail because the fact that the jury acquitted defendant on two of the charges showed that the alleged character evidence showing that defendant was previously in jail did not affect the outcome of the trial. Moreover, because the evidence of attempted murder was overwhelming, the outcome would not have been different had the evidence not been admitted. State v. Jones, — Ohio App. 3d —, 2007 Ohio 3183, — N.E. 2d —, 2007 Ohio App. LEXIS 2961 (June 21, 2007).

Trial court did not abuse its discretion by limiting defendant's counsel's examination of a witness to character evidence under Ohio R. Evid. 404(A) regarding defendant's propensity for violence or non-violence and by not allowing character evidence regarding other traits of defendant, as defendant had not yet testified so it was error to allow the witness to testify as to defendant's character for truth and veracity. State v. Herrera, — Ohio App. 3d —, 2006 Ohio 3053, — N.E. 2d —, 2006 Ohio App. LEXIS 2931 (June 16, 2006).

Trial court's admission of expert's testimony pursuant to Ohio R. Evid. 702 in an action by vehicle owners against a dealer and manufacturer, alleging that they engaged in spurious sales tactics when the owners' vehicle was a "lemon" that resulted in a replacement vehicle at a new loan cost to the owners, was proper, as the expert did not testify as to any specific instances of character evidence that should have been excluded under Ohio R. Evid. 404. Although the expert discussed nefarious sales tactics by some dealerships, he did not testify as to specific knowledge of the particular dealer's character or that it had acted in conformity with a "bad" character. Smith v. GMC, 168 Ohio App. 3d 336, 2006 Ohio 4283, 859 N.E.2d 1035, 2006 Ohio App. LEXIS 4197 (2006).

Character of accused

Trial court properly excluded testimony that a seller of commercial realty had a "habit" of defrauding purchasers. That was the sort of prejudicial evidence prohibited by EvidR 404(B): Pappas v. Ippolito, 177 Ohio App. 3d 625, 2008 Ohio 3976, 895 N.E.2d 610, 2008 Ohio App. LEXIS 3354 (2008).

Trial court abused its discretion in allowing defendant's probation officer to testify as to a multitude of probation violations that defendant committed immediately surrounding the time that a victim was murdered, for which he was on trial, as the particular violations did not relate to the murder. Such evidence was inadmissible under Ohio R. Evid. 404(B) and RC § 2945.59, as it presented an array of inadmissible character evidence that portrayed defendant as a criminal who violated basic terms of his probation and had a generally guilty state of mind, which did not go towards proving an element of the offense for which he was on trial. State v. Anderson, — Ohio App. 3d —, 2006 Ohio 4618, — N.E. 2d —, 2006 Ohio App. LEXIS 4581 (Sept. 1, 2006).

There was no plain error under Ohio R. Crim. P. 52(B) and Ohio R. Evid. 103(A)(1) by the State's admission of evidence of defendant's bad character pursuant to Ohio R. Evid. 404(A)(1), as the challenged statements were relevant to establish that two eyewitnesses had seen defendant at the crime scene, and that one of the witnesses had immediately recognized and identified defendant to her companions; the use of the pejorative term in describing defendant, while not necessarily relevant, was not outcome-determinative in light of the evidence adduced at trial. State v. Mitchell, — Ohio App. 3d —, 2006 Ohio 5073, — N.E. 2d —, 2006 Ohio App. LEXIS 5008 (Sept. 29, 2006).

Defendant's failure to object to a former wife's testimony about his personality traits during his trial for two counts of nonsupport of dependents under RC § 2919.21(A)(2) waived all but plain error, and there was no plain error in admitting the testimony under Ohio R. Evid. 404(A)(1). His personality traits were placed in issue by his defense that he had schizotypal personality disorder and therefore could not work, and the wife's testimony was properly admitted to rebut defendant's evidence about his own personality traits and the personality traits typically displayed by a person with such a disorder. State v. Browne, — Ohio App. 3d —, 2006 Ohio 5229, — N.E. 2d —, 2006 Ohio App. LEXIS 5208 (Sept. 27, 2006).

Even if the trial court had committed error in allowing character evidence of defendant or the victim, any such error was harmless because the evidence was overwhelmingly in favor of defendant's guilt since defendant has failed to establish a valid claim of self-defense; he failed to prove that he was not the initial aggressor. The evidence clearly demonstrated that upon observing the victim in his driveway, defendant went to the hall closet where he retrieved and loaded his father's gun, and, instead of locking the door and calling the police, he then proceeded to the front door and yelled at the victim, picked up a rock and threw it at the victim's jeep, and then shot and killed him. Ohio v. Horace K. Vinson, — Ohio App. 3d —, 2007 Ohio 5199, — N.E. 2d —, 2007 Ohio App. LEXIS 4608 (Sept. 28, 2007).

Character of victim

Ohio R. Evid. 405 prohibited defendant from eliciting testimony from the other witnesses on direct examination regarding their knowledge of specific instances in which the victim exhibited violent behavior towards persons other than defendant for his claim of self-defense. Furthermore, nothing in the record indicated that defendant knew about the specific instances that he sought to elicit, and he did not proffer any testimony in that regard. State v. Moore, — Ohio App. 3d —, 2007 Ohio 3600, — N.E. 2d —, 2007 Ohio App. LEXIS 3306 (July 16, 2007).

Trial court did not err by granting the State's motion in limine; because there was no evidence concerning whether the victim ever attended a "pure romance party," the purpose of her going to such party, or whether she ever bought or used any item sold at such parties, defendant failed to preserve for appeal any issue related to the victim's alleged attendance at such a party. Even if defendant had preserved the issue for appeal, the evidence that he hoped to elicit would have been protected from disclosure by the rape shield law; it could not be seen how the victim's alleged attendance at a pure romance party was evidence that the victim had a proclivity for "kinky" sex; and none of the items that defendant used to commit the rape could have been attributed to the victim. Ohio v. Archibald, — Ohio App. 3d —, 2007 Ohio 4966, — N.E. 2d —, 2007 Ohio App. LEXIS 4425 (Sept. 21, 2007).

In a prosecution for felony murder, evidence of the victim's character was erroneously admitted, under Ohio R. Evid. 404(A), because defendant did not place the victim's character in issue, but the error was harmless, given other substantial evidence of defendant's guilt. State v. Hunter, — Ohio App. 3d —, 2006 Ohio 20, — N.E. 2d —, 2006 Ohio App. LEXIS 9 (Jan. 5, 2006).

Trial court did not err by denying defendant's motion for a new trial because defendant had intended to open the door to the victim's prior convictions, which had been excluded from being introduced into evidence before trial when the trial court granted the state's motion in limine. Also, the State did not put the victim's character into evidence because the victim's longtime friend did not give an opinion as to the victim's reputation during her testimony; also, any knowledge on the part of the friend as to the character of the victim was not the same as defendant's knowledge of the victim's character. Ohio v. Horace K. Vinson, — Ohio App. 3d —, 2007 Ohio 5199, — N.E. 2d —, 2007 Ohio App. LEXIS 4608 (Sept. 28, 2007).

Domestic violence

Generally, prior bad acts by a defendant against the same victim are admissible in domestic violence cases to prove the defendant's intent: State v. Clay, 181 Ohio App. 3d 563, 2009 Ohio 1235, 910 N.E.2d 14, 2009 Ohio App. LEXIS 1061 (2009).

In defendant's prosecution for felonious assault, kidnapping and domestic violence, the victim's testimony that defendant had choked the victim on occasions prior to the incident from which the criminal charges arose was admissible, under Ohio R. Evid. 404(B), because such testimony showed defendant's scheme and intent to harm the victim, which was relevant to the domestic violence charge, under RC § 2919.25(A). State v. Smith, — Ohio App. 3d —, 2007 Ohio 5524, — N.E. 2d —, 2007 Ohio App. LEXIS 4864 (Oct. 17, 2007).

Evidence

Prosecution's persistent questioning of the mother about other crimes committed by defendant, including asking her about an assault on a police officer charge after being told three times that she could not recall other "criminal situations," clearly deprived defendant of a fair trial. The evidence of other crimes that the prosecutor introduced, none of which was substantiated by documents establishing that other crimes were committed, was offered to demonstrate defendant's bad character and not to prove that he committed the instant offense; the error should have been rectified by granting defendant's motion for a mistrial. State v. Brown, — Ohio App. 3d —, 2007 Ohio 464, — N.E. 2d —, 2007 Ohio App. LEXIS 420 (Feb. 2, 2007).

— Sufficient

Trial court did not err by prohibiting testimony regarding the prior behavior of one of the victim's when, five years earlier, she had shot at a former boyfriend, because there was no exception in Ohio R. Evid. 404(B) to allow such "bad acts" testimony to prove a "course of conduct." Although defendant was attempting to prove that the victim fired a shotgun on the night in question because she had used a shotgun some five years earlier in connection with another incident, Evid. R. 404(B) clearly prohibited such evidence, and the trial court properly prohibited defendant from questioning the victim about the incident with her former boyfriend. State v. Underdown, — Ohio App. 3d —, 2007 Ohio 1814, — N.E. 2d —, 2007 Ohio App. LEXIS 1637 (Apr. 17, 2007).

As defendant's counsel failed to object to certain testimony, an error raised on appeal regarding the admission thereof was subject to plain error review under Ohio R. Crim. P. 52. There was no plain error where the testimony was not "other acts" character evidence under Ohio R. Evid. 404(B), it was not prejudicial to defendant, and there was no showing that but for the evidence, the outcome of the trial would have been different. State v. Williams, — Ohio App. 3d —, 2007 Ohio 2699, — N.E. 2d —, 2007 Ohio App. LEXIS 2507 (June 4, 2007).

Where defendant and the victim had a deteriorated relationship for a period of years, and upon the two arguing and the victim shoving defendant, defendant took out his single-shot gun and shot the victim twice, pausing in between shots to carefully reload the gun, there was no error in the trial court's refusal to charge defendant or instruct the jury on the crime of voluntary manslaughter, in violation of RC § 2903.03, in his criminal trial on an aggravated murder charge, as there was a sufficient cooling off period such that there could be no finding of sudden rage or passion. Excluded evidence regarding the victim's reputation for violence and defendant's knowledge thereof was not relevant or admissible under Ohio R. Evid. 403 and 404(A), and specific instances of misconduct were not admissible under Ohio R. Evid. 405. State v. Kanner, — Ohio App. 3d —, 2006 Ohio 3485, — N.E. 2d —, 2006 Ohio App. LEXIS 3428 (June 29, 2006).

Evidence admissible in sexual abuse cases

Trial court did not commit plain error under Ohio R. Crim. P. 52 when it admitted testimony from the victim of defendant's sexual offenses which indicated that defendant found money at work, as such testimony did not constitute other acts testimony under Ohio R. Evid. 404(B) because it did not

allege that defendant did anything wrong. The testimony merely showed defendant's opportunity because there was other testimony that every time he brought something home for the victim, he would abuse her, and there was no showing that the outcome of the trial would have been different if such evidence had been excluded. State v. Ford, — Ohio App. 3d —, 2007 Ohio 2645, — N.E. 2d —, 2007 Ohio App. LEXIS 2473 (May 31, 2007).

Evidence of other acts

There was no error in admitting other acts evidence because neither the oblique reference to the fact that defendant had broken his arm in a bar fight nor the detective's recognition of him in the grocery store surveillance videotape resulted in a manifest miscarriage of justice in light of other evidence. The evidence did not clearly indicate that defendant had previously been involved in prior criminal activity. State v. Miller, — Ohio App. 3d —, 2007 Ohio 427, — N.E. 2d —, 2007 Ohio App. LEXIS 379 (Jan. 25, 2007).

Considering the similarities between previous robberies and a home-invasion, the trial court's conclusion to allow other acts evidence to establish identity was proper pursuant to Ohio R. Evid 404(B). This was particularly true in light of the fact that two victims identified defendant as one of the men in their homes. State v. Hairston, — Ohio App. 3d —, 2007 Ohio 4159, — N.E. 2d —, 2007 Ohio App. LEXIS 3757 (Aug. 10, 2007).

Trial court did not abuse its discretion by admitting the voicemail evidence under Ohio R. Evid. 404(B) because it was questionable whether the voicemail constituted a crime, wrong, or act within the purpose of the rule. The State offered the voicemail to identify defendant's voice and, by inference, defendant's use of an alias; nothing in the testimony could reasonably have suggested that defendant's voicemail had been improper. State v. Judd, — Ohio App. 3d —, 2007 Ohio 6811, — N.E. 2d —, 2007 Ohio App. LEXIS 5983 (Dec. 20, 2007).

Where defendant was on trial for, inter alia, a charge of menacing by stalking, in violation of RC § 2903.211, the trial court properly allowed evidence of defendant's prior acts regarding the victim pursuant to Ohio R. Evid. 404(B) and RC § 2945.59, as such were relevant evidence pursuant to Ohio R. Evid. 401 and 402, they tended to prove defendant's state of mind which was an essential element of the offense, and the evidence was not outweighed by any prejudicial effect pursuant to Ohio R. Evid. 403. State v. Horsley, — Ohio App. 3d —, 2006 Ohio 1208, — N.E. 2d —, 2006 Ohio App. LEXIS 1080 (Mar. 16, 2006).

Even if defendant had preserved his right to appeal from the trial court's refusal to sever, defendant was not prejudiced by the joinder; because, at the time that the motion to sever was ruled upon, it was unknown whether defendant would testify or admit to engaging in sexual conduct with the victims, other acts testimony would have been admissible under Ohio R. Evid. 404(B) to demonstrate modus operandi and to prove identity. The similarities between the two cases were sufficient to support the trial court's conclusion that the evidence of one crime would have been admissible at the trial of the other even if the counts were severed. State v. Elijah, — Ohio App. 3d —, 2006 Ohio 2635, — N.E. 2d —, 2006 Ohio App. LEXIS 2471 (May 19, 2006).

Evidence of past offenses

Mere fact that defendant's parole officer testified in the rape trial was inconsequential considering the fact that the victim had already testified that defendant revealed to her that he was on parole and the reason that he was on parole. Furthermore, the parole officer's act of informing the jury that the rape allegation constituted a parole violation was not itself evidence of an other act because that very rape allegation was the offense at hand and the fact of parole was already properly admitted. State v. Rupp, — Ohio App. 3d —, 2007 Ohio 1561, — N.E. 2d —, 2007 Ohio App. LEXIS 1449 (Mar. 27, 2007).

Evidence of prior drug sales

In defendant's prosecution for complicity to trafficking in cocaine, under RC §§ 2923.03(A) and 2925.03(A), and permitting drug abuse, under RC § 2925.13(A), alleging that defendant knowingly drove to a drug transaction at the instruction of her co-defendant and knew a box he placed in her car contained cocaine, the co-defendant's testimony that she had driven to ten other drug transactions at his request was not improper character evidence, under Ohio R. Evid. 404(B), because it was not used to prove she acted in conformance with this character, but it was properly used to prove the knowledge element of the crimes she was charged with. State v. Walker, — Ohio App. 3d —, 2007 Ohio 911, — N.E. 2d —, 2007 Ohio App. LEXIS 814 (Mar. 5, 2007).

Since the alleged act could not be considered "wholly independent" of the current charge against defendant, the trial court did not err in allowing the witness's testimony related to the purchase of crack cocaine from defendant. The witness's statements were highly probative in proving a course of defendant's conduct contemporaneous with and inextricably linked to the current charge; the testimony tended to show defendant's motive, opportunity, intent, preparation, plan, knowledge, and identity. Ohio v. Darrin G. Sweeney, — Ohio App. 3d —, 2007 Ohio 5223, — N.E. 2d —, 2007 Ohio App. LEXIS 4604 (Sept. 28, 2007).

Evidence properly admitted

There was no prosecutorial misconduct in the prosecutor's argument during closing, wherein he indicated that the victim of defendant's criminal conduct was raped, as the prosecutor's comments were based on the evidence; the trial court properly permitted evidence regarding rape, as it was not admitted under Ohio R. Evid. 404(B) as evidence of other crimes, wrongs, or acts, but instead, it was offered as proof of one of the underlying felonies for his felony-murder charge and as a possible motive for defendant's commission of the murder. State v. Frazier, 115 Ohio St. 3d 139, 2007 Ohio 5048, 873 N.E.2d 1263, 2007 Ohio LEXIS 2519 (2007).

No abuse of discretion on the part of the trial court in denying defendant's motion for a separate trial had been demonstrated because the evidence did not constitute "other acts" prohibited by Ohio R. Evid. 404(B) that was erroneously admitted against defendant because the trial court improperly refused to grant her motion for a separate trial. Evidence of conduct constituting a theft offense by any of the defendants from a store in the mall, in furtherance of their common criminal enterprise, was admissible against all of the defendants and such evidence presented a question for the jury as to whether any particular defendant participated in or aided and abetted any particular theft offense. State v. Patterson, — Ohio App. 3d —, 2007 Ohio 29, — N.E. 2d —, 2007 Ohio App. LEXIS 22 (Jan. 5, 2007).

The officer's testimony explained the circumstances of the crime and therefore fell under the exception to the admission of other acts evidence under Ohio R. Evid. 404(B) and RC § 2945.59. The testimony regarding the place and background of the crime were blended or connected with the crime of drug possession. Also, because defendant denied the charges and argued that he was not in the area at the time of the incident, the officer's testimony regarding his identification of defendant was necessary. The testimony implied that defendant was in a gang, but there was no testimony that defendant was actually a member of a gang and the trial court, as the fact finder, was presumed to only consider relevant, material evidence. State v. Vason, — Ohio App. 3d —, 2007 Ohio 1599, — N.E. 2d —, 2007 Ohio App. LEXIS 1468 (Apr. 5, 2007).

There was no plain error in admitting the "other act" testimony of the victim, defendant's wife, because it was apparent that the statements regarding any alleged past abuse by defendant were being used for the abduction charge, of which defendant was found not guilty. The statements were not made to show that defendant acted in conformity with the past acts, but rather were used to show why the victim acted the way she did. State v. Jones, — Ohio App. 3d —, 2007 Ohio 3183, — N.E. 2d —, 2007 Ohio App. LEXIS 2961 (June 21, 2007).

Trial court did not err by admitting other acts evidence because the evidence of the codefendant's attempts to bribe witnesses was clearly not introduced to show that he had a propensity to bribe. Instead, the bribe to the witness was offered to show that the witness had a motive to perjure herself when testifying on behalf of defendant and the codefendant. State v. Carter, — Ohio App. 3d —, 2007 Ohio 3502, — N.E. 2d —, 2007 Ohio App. LEXIS 3223 (June 29, 2007).

There was no plain error based on inadmissible other act evidence because the detective's testimony did not concern a prior crime, but concerned acts committed by defendant that were consistent with a person casing a scene. The detective's testimony that defendant was familiar with the transit stop and that he knew the route to use to get away afterwards was not used to prove defendant's propensity to commit the crime; it showed his knowledge of the area, which was specifically permissible under Ohio R. Evid. 404(B). State v. Thomas, — Ohio App. 3d —, 2007 Ohio 3522, — N.E. 2d —, 2007 Ohio App. LEXIS 3254 (July 12, 2007).

Defendant did not show that, but for the alleged instances of prosecutorial misconduct, he would not have been convicted, because the evidence supported the prosecutor's remarks calling defendant and some of the witnesses liars in that defendant's testimony differed in significant respects from that of the victim. Also, there was no reversible error in the prosecutor's questions regarding defendant's child support obligations because defendant put his character as a parent in issue, pursuant to Ohio R. Evid. 404(A)(1); thus, the prosecutor could rebut such evidence. State v. Henson, — Ohio App. 3d —, 2007 Ohio 3567, — N.E. 2d —, 2007 Ohio App. LEXIS 3274 (July 13, 2007).

Detective's testimony said nothing about any other criminal acts or burglaries by defendant; his testimony related only to daytime burglaries in general and there was nothing specific regarding defendant. That the detective's testimony about the modus operandi of daytime burglars in general happened to describe how defendant attempted to gain entry to the victim's home in the instant case did not make the testimony violative of Ohio R. Evid. 404(B). State v. Dailey, — Ohio App. 3d —, 2007 Ohio 6650, — N.E. 2d —, 2007 Ohio App. LEXIS 5836 (Dec. 13, 2007).

Prosecutor's mention of defendant's prior drug arrests during opening argument was not error, as the jury was instructed that such statements were not evidence; further, the prior drug activities were admissible under Ohio R. Evid. 404(B) to show defendant's plan, scheme, or system of ilegally trafficking drugs, and a limiting instruction thereon was properly refused by the trial court. State v. Felder, — Ohio App. 3d —, 2006 Ohio 5332, — N.E. 2d —, 2006 Ohio App. LEXIS 5311 (Oct. 12, 2006).

Ohio R. Evid. 404(B) did not exclude the victim's and her mother's testimony that the victim was harassed at school after reporting a rape to police and that she was seriously beaten by defendant's friend's girlfriend in apparent retaliation as the testimony did not concern defendant's past acts and the testimony was not to show any propensity on defendant's part to commit rape. The evidence was relevant to show that the victim faced very strong possibility of danger and harassment from reporting that she was raped, and therefore had reason to fear filing a police report. State v. Willard, — Ohio App. 3d —, 2006 Ohio 5071, — N.E. 2d —, 2006 Ohio App. LEXIS 4977 (Sept. 29, 2006).

Trial court properly admitted evidence that defendant physically abused his wife pursuant to Ohio R. Evid. 404(B) and RC § 2945.59, as such was relevant to the element of force in his criminal trial on charges of, inter alia, rape of his biological daughters, in violation of RC § 2907.02(B), as it was admissible to show that the victims' wills were overcome by fear or duress. State v. Dominic, — Ohio App. 3d —, 2006 Ohio 292, — N.E. 2d —, 2006 Ohio App. LEXIS 247 (Jan. 26, 2006).

Defendant's failure to object to a former wife's testimony about his relationship with his daughters during his trial for two counts of nonsupport of dependents under RC § 2919.21(A)(2) waived all but plain error, and there was no plain error in admitting the testimony. The testimony was not elicited to demonstrate the status of his relationship with his daughters, but as background information for the wife's testimony about defendant's personality, which was admissible as rebuttal under Ohio R. Evid. 404(A)(1). State v. Browne, — Ohio App. 3d —, 2006 Ohio 5229, — N.E. 2d —, 2006 Ohio App. LEXIS 5208 (Sept. 27, 2006).

Evidence that defendant drove without a license was not offered to show that he acted in conformity with his prior actions when he committed the drug offenses. The evidence was elicited in the process of refuting the witness's alibi evidence, which asserted that defendant was not at his residence at the time of one of the alleged controlled drug purchases. Thus, the admission of the evidence did not violate Ohio R. Evid. 404(B) and the probative value was not substantially outweighed by the prejudice, under Ohio R. Evid. 403. State v. Ogletree, — Ohio App. 3d —, 2006 Ohio 6107, — N.E. 2d —, 2006 Ohio App. LEXIS 6037 (Nov. 17, 2006).

Evidence regarding sexual acts

Trial court's admission of other acts testimony of a minor upon whom defendant allegedly committed a sexual assault was proper pursuant to RC § 2945.59 and Ohio R. Evid. 404(B) in defendant's rape trial, as the conduct and the type of victim in both instances were similar, and such evidence showed defendant's scheme, plan, motivation, and opportunity. State v. Griffin, — Ohio App. 3d —, 2007 Ohio 4431, — N.E. 2d —, 2007 Ohio App. LEXIS 3993 (Aug. 27, 2007).

—Admissibility

There was no plain error in admitting other acts evidence because it could not be found that, but for the alleged victim's statement that defendant fist raped her, he would not have been convicted of the instant offenses. State v. Goff, — Ohio App. 3d —, 2007 Ohio 2735, — N.E. 2d —, 2007 Ohio App. LEXIS 2526 (June 6, 2007).

Evidence relevant to offense

Evidence of defendant having brandished a firearm was admissible for a permissible purpose because, although no firearm matching the one used to murder the victim was ever recovered, many bullets at the scene and within the victim were recovered and numerous witnesses testified that they had seen defendant with a firearm and that the firearm matched the caliber of weapon which was used to kill the victim. Thus, the testimony established that defendant had an opportunity to murder the victim with such a weapon; the testimony could also have established intent, preparation, or plan, since defendant could arguably have been carrying the firearm in preparation for retaliation for the assault on his brother. State v. Carter, — Ohio App. 3d —, 2007 Ohio 3502, — N.E. 2d —, 2007 Ohio App. LEXIS 3223 (June 29, 2007).

Evidence of defendant having brandished a firearm was admissible for a permissible purpose because, although no firearm matching the one used to murder the victim was ever recovered, many bullets at the scene and within the victim were recovered and numerous witnesses testified that they had seen defendant with a firearm and that the firearm matched the caliber of weapon which was used to kill the victim. Thus, the testimony established that defendant had an opportunity to murder the victim with such a weapon. The testimony could also have established intent, preparation, or plan, since defendant could arguably have been carrying the firearm in preparation for retaliation for the assault on his brother. State v. Robinson, — Ohio App. 3d —, 2007 Ohio 3501, — N.E. 2d —, 2007 Ohio App. LEXIS 3224 (July 5, 2007).

Trial court properly denied defendant's motion in limine to exclude testimony regarding a phone call from his cell phone that was intercepted by police, as the conversation involved the purchase of drugs from defendant, and it was admissible under Ohio R. Evid. 404(B) in defendant's criminal trial on drug-related charges to show that defendant sold cocaine; it was also proof of intent, preparation, plan, knowledge, and absence of mistake or accident. Ohio v. Anzures, — Ohio App. 3d —, 2007 Ohio 4817, — N.E. 2d —, 2007 Ohio App. LEXIS 4342 (Sept. 18, 2007).

Trial court did not err by allowing a deputy to testify regarding drug evidence that he found in defendant's residence because the State's theory of the case was that defendant was reckless in shaking or dropping the child and failing to immediately call the police; to demonstrate defendant's recklessness, the State presented evidence of defendant's drug use consisting of observations by the police during the investigation, testimony of the child's mother, and defendant's own admissions. Because the deputy stated that, upon entering the residence, he detected a smell of burnt marijuana, his deputy's present sense impression testimony suggested that defendant had smoked marijuana while supervising the child. State v. Stacy, — Ohio App. 3d —, 2007 Ohio 6744, — N.E. 2d —, 2007 Ohio App. LEXIS 5911 (Dec. 17, 2007).

Trial court did not abuse its discretion in denying defendant's motion to sever offenses in his criminal trial pursuant to Ohio R. Crim. P. 14, as the fact that identification evidence by way of defendant's drug possession was offered into evidence in his aggravated robbery trial before the jury was proper for purposes of the identification pursuant to Ohio R. Evid. 404(B). As identification was important to the case, evidence that supported the identifications made by the eyewitnesses was admissible. State v. Marinello, — Ohio App. 3d —, 2006 Ohio 282, — N.E. 2d —, 2006 Ohio App. LEXIS 255 (Jan. 26, 2006).

Evidence tending to show motive or intent

Stories that defendant told the rape victim of his violent crimes prior to raping her were admissible as exceptions to the other acts prohibition and were not unfairly prejudicial because the evidence was not merely relevant, it was foundational evidence that bolstered the victim's claims and established defendant's preparation, intent, plan, and scheme. The relation of the stories to the victim tended to show defendant's intent to act to overcome the victim's will by fear and duress; his statements showed his intent to place the victim in a state of fear and make her fearful of rejecting him more physically or in a louder manner; and they also provided an opportunity for him to advance upon the victim without any extreme resistance. State v. Rupp, — Ohio App. 3d —, 2007 Ohio 1561, — N.E. 2d —, 2007 Ohio App. LEXIS 1449 (Mar. 27, 2007).

Trial court's admission of evidence that defendant was previously arrested in West Virginia in a trailer that contained a methamphetamine lab was relevant under Ohio R. Evid. 401 and 402, and it was proper for purposes of showing defendant's intent pursuant to Ohio R. Evid. 404 and RC § 2945.59(B) in a prosecution for illegal assembly or possession of chemicals for the manufacture of drugs, in violation of RC § 2925.041(A). State v. Norris, — Ohio App. 3d —, 2007 Ohio 6915, — N.E. 2d —, 2007 Ohio App. LEXIS 6066 (Dec. 11, 2007).

References to defendant's gang membership were background information which were necessary to give the jury the setting of the case and were permissible as an attempt to demonstrate motive, as allowed by Ohio R. Evid. 404(B), in defendant's criminal trial. State v. Smith, — Ohio App. 3d —, 2006 Ohio 3156, — N.E. 2d —, 2006 Ohio App. LEXIS 3032 (June 22, 2006).

Failure to give limiting instruction

In a sexual imposition prosecution, a trial court's failure to give a limiting instruction to the jury directing them not to consider the evidence of prior accusations of assault and stalking against defendant as evidence of proof of the crime charged constituted plain error under Ohio R. Crim. P. 52(B) because this testimony affected the substantial rights of defendant, in that the failure was highly prejudicial because the testimony was admitted in a case where the only evidence of defendant's guilt was the recanted testimony of a child with no attendant physical evidence. State v. Smith, — Ohio App. 3d —, 2006 Ohio 45, — N.E. 2d —, 2006 Ohio App. LEXIS 44 (Jan. 6, 2006).

Harmless error

There was no evidence that the trial court considered any irrelevant, immaterial, or incompetent evidence in rendering its decision. The error, if any, in the admission of the evidence that defendant had been seen on other occasions carrying a gun was harmless because there was no reasonable possibility that the testimony contributed to defendant's convictions. Even without the objectionable evidence, there was ample testimony that defendant had a gun in his possession when he entered the victim's house. State v. Brown, — Ohio App. 3d —, 2007 Ohio 287, — N.E. 2d —, 2007 Ohio App. LEXIS 275 (Jan. 25, 2007).

There was no error regarding other acts evidence because defendant was tried on one count of burglary and one count of theft and thus, any reference to his driving privileges was irrelevant to the charges and harmless error, particularly in light of the fact that the matter was tried to the bench. Even assuming that the testimony was improper under Ohio R. Evid. 404(B), there was no plain error warranting reversal because the testimony was harmless beyond a reasonable doubt; defendant's reference to a lack of driving privileges was isolated and of minor significance given the charges for which he was being tried. State v. Peterson, — Ohio App. 3d —, 2007 Ohio 543, — N.E. 2d —, 2007 Ohio App. LEXIS 483 (Feb. 8, 2007).

Although a trial court should have stricken a statement on a tape recording that defendant made to police regarding his criminal history, as it was inadmissible under Ohio R. Evid. 404, any error was harmless because the other evidence of defendant's guilt was overwhelming. State v. Patrick, — Ohio App. 3d —, 2007 Ohio 1175, — N.E. 2d —, 2007 Ohio App. LEXIS 1118 (Mar. 16, 2007).

Though character evidence consisting of testimony by defendant's brother-in-law as to defendant's character, should not have been admitted under Ohio R. Evid. 404 as it was not used for rebuttal and did not fit into any of the exceptions of Ohio R. Evid. 404(B), the error was harmless under Ohio R. Crim. P. 52(A) because the remaining evidence presented by the State constituted overwhelming proof of defendant's guilt. State v. Schumpert, — Ohio App. 3d —, 2007 Ohio 5437, — N.E. 2d —, 2007 Ohio App. LEXIS 4778 (Oct. 11, 2007).

Although evidence from defendant's statement to a police detective in which he admitted to hitting his wife on a prior occasion and using illegal drugs while living in another state was improperly admitted because the victim did not witness defendant hit his wife or use drugs, the error was harmless since the testimony regarding the prior bad acts was inconsequential and did not contribute to defendant's conviction. State v. Valenzona, — Ohio App. 3d —, 2007 Ohio 6892, — N.E. 2d —, 2007 Ohio App. LEXIS 6002 (Dec. 20, 2007).

Any violation of Ohio R. Evid. 404(B) or 403(A) that took place during defendant's trial for attempted burglary and other crimes when the testimony of an eyewitness about plans defendant had for committing other crimes and bad acts was harmless. Even if the evidence was inadmissible to show his criminal propensity, there was overwhelming other evidence of defendant's guilt. State v. Bell, — Ohio App. 3d —, 2006 Ohio 6560, — N.E. 2d —, 2006 Ohio App. LEXIS 6485 (Dec. 4, 2006).

Although a trial court erred in admitting statements made by defendant to a female booking officer as indicative of his state of mind for purposes of having committed assaults on police officers, pursuant to Ohio R. Evid. 404(B), as the statements were unrelated to his state of mind but rather were products of the fact that the officer was female, defendant was intoxicated, and the content of his statements was sexual in nature, the error was harmless under Ohio R. Crim. P. 52 because there was extensive evidence to establish defendant's guilt. Accordingly, admission of the statements would not have changed the outcome of the trial. State v. Deir, — Ohio App. 3d —, 2006 Ohio 6885, — N.E. 2d —, 2006 Ohio App. LEXIS 6786 (Dec. 22, 2006).

Identity

There was no violation of Ohio R. Evid. 404(B) because the record demonstrated that the photographs of defendant (in which he was brandishing a gun and flashing gang signs) were relevant to identification; the sole issue at trial was who committed the homicide. Some of the photographs showed defendant's unique tattoo on the right side of his face and several witnesses identified the firearm in the photographs as the same one defendant used to murder the victim. State v. Walker, — Ohio App. 3d —, 2007 Ohio 3772, — N.E. 2d —, 2007 Ohio App. LEXIS 3437 (July 26, 2007).

Testimony from defendant's former employer as to the fact that defendant was the owner of a cell phone that had made calls prior to and after the victim's murder and within the vicinity of the crime scene was properly admitted and did not constitute plain error under Ohio R. Crim. P. 52(B) as the testimony went to identity and was permissible as such under Ohio R. Evid. 404(B), in that the testimony established that the employer, in whose name the phone was listed, was not the owner of the phone but that defendant was the owner. State v. Schumpert, — Ohio App. 3d —, 2007 Ohio 5437, — N.E. 2d —, 2007 Ohio App. LEXIS 4778 (Oct. 11, 2007).

Trial court properly allowed the testimony by the police officers regarding the incidents four days prior to the day that defendant committed the instant offenses for purposes of establishing defendant's identity and the trial court's limiting instruction sufficiently instructed the jury on the purpose of that testimony. The trial court specifically denied the motion in limine on the basis that the earlier events could be probative of identity and both officers referenced the earlier incident to explain some of their reasons for stopping defendant; both indicated that they recognized defendant as someone they recognized from a prior date. State v. Lane, — Ohio App. 3d —, 2007 Ohio 5948, — N.E. 2d —, 2007 Ohio App. LEXIS 5255 (Nov. 8, 2007).

Trial court did not abuse its discretion in admitting the taped statements from the victim's answering machine because the statements were relevant, they were not too remote in time from the incident, and the probative value of the evidence was not outweighed by the danger of unfair prejudice; since the statements were those of defendant, and offered against him at trial, the statements were not hearsay and were properly admissible under Ohio R. Evid. 801(D)(2). Because the messages met the requirements of Ohio R. Evid. 801(D)(2), their admission was not dependent upon one of the exceptions under Ohio R. Evid. 404(B) and, to the extent that defendant argued that the statements were precluded under Ohio R. Evid. 404(B), such evidence was relevant and admissible because it tended to prove identity. State v. Cody, — Ohio App. 3d —, 2007 Ohio 6776, — N.E. 2d —, 2007 Ohio App. LEXIS 5938 (Dec. 18, 2007).

Imprisonment of defendant

Although a witness testified that defendant had been in the penitentiary when she was referring to her period of sobriety, such isolated reference to defendant's criminal history was not enough to support his claim that a mistrial had to be declared due to the admission of "other acts" evidence pursuant to Ohio R. Evid. 404(B), as the comment was isolated, the judge gave the jury a curative instruction to disregard the comment, and defendant did not show that he was prejudiced or that his substantial rights were affected by the admission thereof. State v. McCree, — Ohio App. 3d —, 2007 Ohio 268, — N.E. 2d —, 2007 Ohio App. LEXIS 252 (Jan. 25, 2007).

Introduction of evidence of other crimes

There was no violation of Ohio R. Evid. 404(B) because defense counsel raised the issues of defendant's prior rape convictions and a sexual predator adjudication by eliciting testimony from the victim that she had corresponded with defendant in prison and invited him to live in her home upon release. State v. McCuller, — Ohio App. 3d —, 2006 Ohio 302, — N.E. 2d —, 2006 Ohio App. LEXIS 261 (Jan. 26, 2006).

Trial court did not abuse its discretion when it prohibited defendant from cross-examining the victim of defendant's beating regarding how the victim could have afforded cocaine, as there was evidence that the victim had a prior drug conviction and the cross-examination lacked relevance under Ohio R. Evid. 404. State v. Arafat, — Ohio App. 3d —, 2006 Ohio 1722, — N.E. 2d —, 2006 Ohio App. LEXIS 1592 (Apr. 6, 2006).

Introduction of evidence of prior drug sales

There was no error in admitting prior acts evidence because the witnesses' testimony that they had purchased drugs from defendant on prior occasions was not used to show that defendant was acting in conformity with those prior acts. It was presented to show how the witnesses knew defendant and to show defendant's mode of operation, that the witnesses would purchase the drugs through an arranged meeting with defendant over the telephone. Moreover, even if the evidence was improperly admitted, it was harmless error as the evidence went towards proving the drug trafficking counts, of which defendant was acquitted. State v. Lumbus, — Ohio App. 3d —, 2007 Ohio 74, — N.E. 2d —, 2007 Ohio App. LEXIS 69 (Jan. 11, 2007).

Issues raised by defendant

Although Ohio R. Evid. 404(B) generally prohibited evidence of other bad acts, defendant, not the State, initially elicited the testimony regarding the alleged rape and the trial court did not commit prejudicial error by allowing the state to clarify such evidence when defendant "opened the door" to it. Defendant's line of questioning removed the protection afforded by Ohio R. Evid. 404(B) and any prejudice that otherwise may have accrued when the State referred to the rape allegation in questioning the victim and thus, because defendant initially elicited the prejudicial evidence, he effectively waived his right to contest its admissibility. State v. Dennis, — Ohio App. 3d —, 2006 Ohio 5777, — N.E. 2d —, 2006 Ohio App. LEXIS 4764 (Sept. 19, 2006).

Joinder of offenses

Joinder of the offenses of gross sexual imposition was favored where they involved different granddaughters of the defendant, even though the offenses against the alleged victims were separated by seven to nine years. The defendant was not prejudiced by the fact that evidence concerning the offenses would be introduced at the same trial where the evidence concerning each offense was so simple and distinct

that a jury could not be confused: State v. Barnes, 149 Ohio Misc. 2d 1, 2008 Ohio 5609, 2008 Ohio Misc. LEXIS 278 (2008).

Juvenile records

Where a defendant charged with misappropriating his grandmother's funds based his defense on a contention that he made all the purchases and transfers of funds at her request and for her benefit, EvidR 404(B) permitted the state to introduce evidence that the defendant had a juvenile conviction of misuse of the grandmother's credit cards: State v. Krueger, 176 Ohio App. 3d 95, 2008 Ohio 1566, 890 N.E.2d 332, 2008 Ohio App. LEXIS 1337 (2008).

Motive

In the criminal trial of defendant, a licensed physician, on charges involving his illegal distribution through prescriptions of controlled substances, evidence of a loaded shotgun found in his medical office was properly admitted, as it was not "extrinsic" pursuant to Ohio R. Evid. 404(B) and RC § 2945.59 because the gun was not separated by time and space from the criminal offenses that defendant was alleged to have engaged in and accordingly, Ohio R. Evid. 404(B) was not implicated; as defendant allegedly ran a cash-payment business to supply drug dealers, the gun was admissible to show his "state of mind." State v. Nucklos, 171 Ohio App. 3d 38, 2007 Ohio 1025, 869 N.E.2d 674, 2007 Ohio App. LEXIS 958 (2007).

Because the mother's testimony regarding defendant's drug use revealed defendant's possible motive to steal, her testimony was admissible under Ohio R. Evid. 404(B). There was also no error under Ohio R. Evid. 802, regarding hearsay, because it could not be determined with certainty whether the evidence was offered for the truth of the matter asserted or to show the mother's subjective belief as the basis for her reactions to defendant. State v. Parsons, — Ohio App. 3d —, 2007 Ohio 1204, — N.E. 2d —, 2007 Ohio App. LEXIS 1025 (Mar. 13, 2007).

In defendant's prosecution for aggravated burglary and felonious assault, the introduction of evidence that defendant sold drugs was not improper character evidence, under Ohio R. Evid. 404(B) and RC § 2945.59, because it was relevant to motive, as there was testimony that defendant was angry at the victim because the victim owed defendant money from defendant's sale of drugs to the victim. State v. Johnson, — Ohio App. 3d —, 2007 Ohio 2176, — N.E. 2d —, 2007 Ohio App. LEXIS 2022 (May 2, 2007).

Trial court did not abuse its discretion when it admitted "other act" evidence because evidence of defendant's admission, that he stole $ 100 in cash from his employer eight days before the current burglary because his wife had a bill to pay, was introduced to show motive for the burglary, i.e., his wife's debt. Also, the trial court gave the jury a limiting instruction and, under the circumstances, the probative value of the evidence outweighed its prejudice. State v. Miller, — Ohio App. 3d —, 2007 Ohio 6909, — N.E. 2d —, 2007 Ohio App. LEXIS 6045 (Dec. 12, 2007).

In a murder prosecution, when the prosecutor asked a witness if defendant had a "pot" tattoo, this was not prosecutorial misconduct because the question concerned a relevant issue, under Ohio R. Evid. 401, as a possible motive for the murder was the theft of drugs from the victim, so the answer to the question was admissible, under Ohio R. Evid. 402 and 404(B), and its probative value was not substantially outweighed by a danger of unfair prejudice, under Ohio R. Evid. 403. State v. Jenkins, — Ohio App. 3d —, 2006 Ohio 2546, — N.E. 2d —, 2006 Ohio App. LEXIS 2405 (May 12, 2006).

Motive, intent, or purpose

Defendant failed to demonstrate that his rights were prejudiced by the joinder and denial of his motion to sever because the evidence presented would have been admissible in separate trials if the charges had been severed. Although he was correct that the State could not have introduced the evidence to show that defendant had a propensity to commit the crimes, the evidence was admissible, under Evid. R. 404 and RC § 2945.59, to show defendant's motive or intent, an element of the crime charged (attempted rape and robbery), which defendant placed at issue. State v. Hill, — Ohio App. 3d —, 2007 Ohio 56, — N.E. 2d —, 2007 Ohio App. LEXIS 51 (Jan. 5, 2007).

Trial court did not err when it allowed testimony from a felonious assault victim that defendant, in the past, had engaged in a physical altercation with the victim and that defendant had accused his girlfriend of cheating on defendant with the victim because the testimony was admissible under Evid. R. 404(B) as it tended to prove defendant's intent or motive for shooting the victim. Further, evidence that defendant threatened and intimidated other witnesses in an attempt to keep them from testifying against him was admissible because the evidence reflected a consciousness of guilt. State v. McLeod, — Ohio App. 3d —, 2006 Ohio 7076, — N.E. 2d —, 2006 Ohio App. LEXIS 7004 (Dec. 19, 2006).

Other acts

Evidence that the defendant stole the vehicle was admissible under EvidR 404(B) to establish that he had knowledge that the vehicle was stolen in order to find him guilty of receiving stolen property. For purposes of EvidR 403(A), the probative value of the evidence outweighed any prejudicial effect its admission may have had on the jury: State v. Black, 181 Ohio App. 3d 821, 2009 Ohio 1629, 911 N.E.2d 309, 2009 Ohio App. LEXIS 1355 (2009).

Evidence of threats having been made to two State's witnesses was not inadmissible as prior acts evidence because the witnesses did not testify that defendant or his friend were responsible for the threats. The witness made clear that it was her brother who had threatened her. State v. Minor, — Ohio App. 3d —, 2007 Ohio 312, — N.E. 2d —, 2007 Ohio App. LEXIS 287 (Jan. 26, 2007).

There was no error in admitting other acts evidence because the evidence established defendant's inability to accept rejection in his female relationships and it was relevant to his motive for killing the victim. The fact that the other females were still alive but the victim was dead was not the threshold or determinative issue and there was overwhelming evidence that defendant committed the murder. State v. Charley, — Ohio App. 3d —, 2007 Ohio 1108, — N.E. 2d —, 2007 Ohio App. LEXIS 1029 (Mar. 6, 2007).

Trial court did not improperly admit other acts evidence because the detective's testimony that defendant's brother (his codefendant), standing next to defendant, possessed a small black firearm upon arrest went directly to the identity of the two brothers that victimized the victim just two days prior. Further, the brother's counsel opened the door to the line of questioning as to defendant's drug possession, to which defendant's counsel made no objection; thus, the testimony was not used to show defendant's bad character because the testimony was elicited by defense counsel for the brother, and not by the prosecution and, even if it had been error, it was not plain error because, if the jury had used the detective's testimony of drug possession as evidence of defendant's bad character, then it would have found defendant guilty of all crimes as charged, which it did not. State v. Williams, — Ohio App. 3d —, 2007 Ohio 4577, — N.E. 2d —, 2007 Ohio App. LEXIS 4127 (Sept. 6, 2007).

There was no error in admitting the testimony during cross-examination that defendant had tried to induce his son into robbing the witness because any error in the admission of the evidence was invited error, as the statement was made in response to a question by the defense attorney. Also, there was no plain error in admitting evidence of defendant's regular drug use because even if the statements had not been

admitted, the result of the trial would not have changed. State v. McGlothin, — Ohio App. 3d —, 2007 Ohio 4707, — N.E. 2d —, 2007 Ohio App. LEXIS 4227 (Sept. 14, 2007).

In a prosecution for pandering obscenity involving a minor, defendant's prior convictions for illegal use of a minor in nudity oriented material and pandering sexually oriented material involving a minor were admissible, under Ohio R. Evid. 404(B), because the identity of the sender of obscene material was in question, so the prior convictions demonstrated identity through use of a common scheme, plan or modus operandi. State v. King, — Ohio App. 3d —, 2006 Ohio 226, — N.E. 2d —, 2006 Ohio App. LEXIS 189 (Jan. 19, 2006).

There was no error in the admission of other acts evidence, under Ohio R. Evid. 404(B), because the information regarding defendant's prior arrest, his record for drug trafficking, and his coming from a dangerous family was evoked to discredit the detective's certainty as to defendant's identity as the perpetrator. State v. Jackson, — Ohio App. 3d —, 2006 Ohio 174, — N.E. 2d —, 2006 Ohio App. LEXIS 147 (Jan. 19, 2006).

Evidence of a bicycle used in the commission of an abduction offense would have been admissible in the trial on the kidnapping, rape, and robbery charges against defendant, involving the same bicycle but a different victim, time, and place, as probative evidence of the identity of the perpetrator under Ohio R. Evid. 404(B), and the evidence used to prove the abduction count was sufficiently simple and direct that it was not an abuse of discretion to join the counts for purposes of trial. State v. Brown, — Ohio App. 3d —, 2006 Ohio 42, — N.E. 2d —, 2006 Ohio App. LEXIS 45 (Jan. 6, 2006).

Trial court did not abuse its discretion when it admitted the detective's testimony under Ohio R. Evid. 404(B) for identity purposes because the other robberies testified to were admissible to prove defendant's identity as a participant in the robbery because they established a modus operandi applicable to the current robbery. Indeed, the other robberies shared common features with the current robbery: they involved a similar type of store; the perpetrators always wore the same clothing; one of the perpetrators was always armed with a knife; and the perpetrators always stole money and cigarettes and any differences between the other robberies and the current robbery did not require exclusion of the other robberies. State v. Bromagen, — Ohio App. 3d —, 2006 Ohio 4429, — N.E. 2d —, 2006 Ohio App. LEXIS 4353 (Aug. 28, 2006).

Trial court's ruling denying defendant's motion in limine to exclude "other acts" evidence was not an irregularity or error of law sufficient to warrant a new trial. Evidence of a prior burglary was proper in defendant's trial for a later burglary under circumstances in which a white van was driven in both burglaries, in both burglaries, the co-defendant waited in the car as a lookout while defendant broke into the rear or side door of the house, in both burglaries, defendant moved in and out of house quickly stealing objects that were quickly and easily removed, and the burglaries took place within 15 minutes of each other. State v. Blazo, — Ohio App. 3d —, 2006 Ohio 5418, — N.E. 2d —, 2006 Ohio App. LEXIS 5416 (Oct. 18, 2006).

Although the trial court did err by allowing the State to inquire into the prior incident of domestic violence which defendant had allegedly committed against his wife (the State's inquiry did not impeach an allegation of good character; it merely amplified defendant's admission that he had a bad character trait), it was not plain error since the outcome of the trial would not have been different but for the error. Defendant's version of events lacked credibility because, although he claimed that the victim suffered her injuries before meeting him and that he did not believe that she needed medical attention so he was taking her for fast food, the victim's injuries were severe, required surgery, and altered her appearance. State v. Hohvart, — Ohio App. 3d —, 2007 Ohio 5349, — N.E. 2d —, 2007 Ohio App. LEXIS 4714 (Sept. 21, 2007).

— Admissibility

In an attempted murder prosecution, evidence of defendant's drug use was properly admitted, under Ohio R. Evid. 404(B), because defendant said he was in the area of the crime to buy drugs from a third individual, and it was necessary to explore this alibi to reveal its inconsistencies, as the person he allegedly bought drugs from said she did not sell drugs to him. State v. Berrien, — Ohio App. 3d —, 2006 Ohio 4563, — N.E. 2d —, 2006 Ohio App. LEXIS 4491 (Sept. 5, 2006).

Other acts evidence

Evidence that the state had previously obtained a large civil judgment against the defendant was admissible under EvidR 404(B) to prove his motive for committing the crimes alleged, i.e., a need for money. Evidence that a loaded shotgun was found in the defendant-physician's office was not "extrinsic" to the alleged drug trafficking, and EvidR 404(B) was not implicated. Evidence that the defendant-physician engaged in the same wrongful conduct, concerning drug prescriptions, when he treated other patients did not demonstrate that when he treated the patients the charges in the indictment involved he acted in the knowledge that his conduct was wrongful. It merely proved prior, nonconforming conduct and was inadmissible per EvidR 404(B): State v. Nucklos, 171 Ohio App. 3d 38, 2007 Ohio 1025, 869 N.E.2d 674, 2007 Ohio App. LEXIS 958 (2007).

—Admission for limited purpose

Trial court did not abuse its discretion in admitting evidence that defendant and his shooting victim had been co-defendants in a prior criminal matter, whereupon defendant had been sentenced to a much longer term of imprisonment than the victim, as such was probative of identification and motive of defendant for the more recent shooting incident and accordingly, it was admissible under Ohio R. Evid. 404(B). The probative value of the evidence outweighed the danger of unfair prejudice, confusion of the issues, or misleading the jury pursuant to Ohio R. Evid. 403(A). State v. Wilkins, — Ohio App. 3d —, 2007 Ohio 2962, — N.E. 2d —, 2007 Ohio App. LEXIS 2723 (June 15, 2007).

Other acts evidence admitted for limited purpose

Trial court did not abuse its discretion in admitting the prior acts evidence because the evidence was properly admitted as probative for the purpose of proving plan or preparation. The limited testimony given by the witness focused on the shared, common features between what occurred to her 12 years earlier and what happened to the current victim in 2005. In both situations, defendant and his wife were babysitting, the wife was home but asleep when the abuse occurred, and defendant committed the sexual conduct both orally and with his hands. State v. Powers, — Ohio App. 3d —, 2006 Ohio 6547, — N.E. 2d —, 2006 Ohio App. LEXIS 6440 (Dec. 11, 2006).

Other acts generally

Trial court did not abuse its discretion by admission of testimony concerning defendant's arrest on another drug charge and of a search of his residence where the events in question were two weeks apart and the offense for which the defendant was being tried was included in the affidavit for the search warrant: State v. Lather, 171 Ohio App. 3d 708, 2007 Ohio 2399, 872 N.E.2d 991, 2007 Ohio App. LEXIS 2250 (2007).

Other crimes admissible

Evidence from two criminal incidents which formed the basis of multiple charges against defendant was of the same or similar character where both were crimes against women involving kidnapping and aggravated robbery, and both incidents shared a common or similar scheme or plan and accordingly, the trial court did not abuse its discretion in joining the offenses for trial under Ohio R. Crim. P. 8(A); there was no showing that joinder was prejudicial, as the evidence of one incident could have been admitted in the other incident's trial under Ohio R. Evid. 404(B) to show defendant's identity or plan, the the likelihood of confusion was minimal. State v. Lininger, — Ohio App. 3d —, 2006 Ohio 4136, — N.E. 2d —, 2006 Ohio App. LEXIS 4085 (Aug. 11, 2006).

Other crimes inadmissible

Trial court did not err in excluding defendant's attempt to present evidence that a fellow perpetrator of a beating of a victim had two prior convictions for carrying a concealed weapon and an indictment pending against him for carrying a concealed weapon, as the other acts evidence under Ohio R. Evid. 404(B) was not sufficiently probative to allow its admission, and any probative value was outweighed by the danger of unfair prejudice pursuant to Ohio R. Evid. 403(A). The two convictions were too remote in time, and the indicted offense, although of recent vintage, had no indications of uniqueness that would help establish identity of the fellow perpetrator as the shooter of the beating victim and further, the danger of unfair prejudice was high because the guns involved in each of those situations were not the same. State v. Jeffers, — Ohio App. 3d —, 2007 Ohio 3213, — N.E. 2d —, 2007 Ohio App. LEXIS 2830 (June 21, 2007).

Other crimes, wrong or acts

Trial court did not abuse its discretion when it sustained defendant's objection to testimony elicited from defendant's brother-in-law alluding to the fact that defendant had previously been in jail. State v. Schumpert, — Ohio App. 3d —, 2007 Ohio 5437, — N.E. 2d —, 2007 Ohio App. LEXIS 4778 (Oct. 11, 2007).

Other crimes, wrongs or acts

Trial court's denial of defendant's motion to file a delayed motion for a new trial pursuant to Ohio R. Crim. P. 33(A)(6) and RC § 2945.80 was not an abuse of discretion where testimony regarding other similar criminal conduct that defendant had engaged in was deemed properly admitted pursuant to Ohio R. Evid. 404(B) in defendant's prior direct appeal, there was no mention in the trial testimony that such conduct resulted in convictions, and defendant did not raise the issue in a timely manner; the other similar criminal conduct had resulted in convictions which were thereafter reversed and the charges were either dismissed or resulted in an acquittal upon retrial. State v. Elersic, — Ohio App. 3d —, 2007 Ohio 3371, — N.E. 2d —, 2007 Ohio App. LEXIS 3103 (June 29, 2007).

Testimony of various witnesses that defendant was participating in a "drug deal" when he was arrested was merely foundational information that explained why the police stopped defendant's vehicle and, thus, was not inadmissible under Ohio Evid. R. 404(B). State v. Collins, — Ohio App. 3d —, 2006 Ohio 4722, — N.E. 2d —, 2006 Ohio App. LEXIS 4644 (Sept. 13, 2006).

Evidence of defendant's actions that supported an intimidation charge, which was consolidated for trial with another charge of complicity to commit felonious assault that arose from a separate incident, was properly admitted for proof of the charge and was not other acts evidence under Ohio R. Evid. 404(B). State v. Meyers, — Ohio App. 3d —, 2006 Ohio 6125, — N.E. 2d —, 2006 Ohio App. LEXIS 6061 (Nov. 17, 2006).

In defendant's prosecution for complicity to improperly discharging a firearm at or into a habitation, testimony as to shooting incidents occurring several months earlier did not run afoul of Ohio R. Evid. 404(B). The testimony from defendant's neighbors and a police officer, to the effect that there had been similar shooting incidents several months earlier coming from the area of defendant's property resulting in at least one house in the victim's neighborhood being struck, was not offered to show that defendant acted in conformity with prior bad acts; rather, it was offered to show that defendant had previously been told about the shooting incidents and had knowledge that shootings coming from the direction of his property had hit at least one house in the victim's neighborhood, thereby showing that defendant was aware that bullets fired from his property or its vicinity could strike houses a half of a mile away. State v. Crutchfield, — Ohio App. 3d —, 2006 Ohio 6549, — N.E. 2d —, 2006 Ohio App. LEXIS 6444 (Dec. 11, 2006).

In a murder prosecution, defense counsel did not provide ineffective assistance when counsel's technical errors in playing a videotape of defendant's interview for the jury caused the jury to hear his statements about his prior arrests, incarcerations, and crimes, contrary to Ohio R. Evid. 404, because the evidence of defendant's guilt, including his confession, was overwhelming. State v. Evans, — Ohio App. 3d —, 2006 Ohio 2564, — N.E. 2d —, 2006 Ohio App. LEXIS 2416 (May 19, 2006).

Pattern of conduct

Trial court properly allowed the testimony of a detective and the alleged accomplices regarding the various crimes perpetrated because each was a discreet act, which established a pattern and thus, was fully admissible under Ohio R. Evid. 404(B). State v. Cochran, — Ohio App. 3d —, 2007 Ohio 345, — N.E. 2d —, 2007 Ohio App. LEXIS 291 (Jan. 26, 2007).

Trial court did not abuse its discretion in allowing evidence of defendant's sexual activities to be admitted because defendant's scheme was to "groom" the young girls that were under his care and control through a peculiar and unique pattern of activity until they were effectively coerced into acts of deviant sexual behavior. While some of defendant's actions--the hugs, kisses, and sitting on his lap--may have otherwise appeared innocent, when his actions were placed in context, they demonstrated a system, plan, or scheme to accomplish the crimes charged, rape and gross sexual imposition. State v. Liddle, — Ohio App. 3d —, 2007 Ohio 1820, — N.E. 2d —, 2007 Ohio App. LEXIS 1658 (Apr. 18, 2007).

In defendant's prosecution for menacing by stalking, it was no error to admit evidence on the "history of violence" element of RC § 2903.211(B)(2)(e) by admitting defendant's prior violent acts against the victim becasue these acts were inextricably related to menacing by stalking because the acts were the basis of the "engaging in a pattern of conduct" element of the crime, and the jury was instructed to use this information only in considering the menacing by stalking charge. Ohio v. Pleasant, — Ohio App. 3d —, 2007 Ohio 5643, — N.E. 2d —, 2007 Ohio App. LEXIS 4979 (Oct. 22, 2007).

Trial court did not commit reversible error when it permitted the State to elicit evidence that showed that defendant had a history of being untruthful, pursuant to Ohio R. Evid. 404(A), as defense counsel relied on the fact that defendant was a liar as a defense to the charges and to explain his varying accounts of the criminal incident. State v. Love, — Ohio App. 3d —, 2006 Ohio 1762, — N.E. 2d —, 2006 Ohio App. LEXIS 1619 (Mar. 27, 2006).

Daughter-in-law's testimony was properly admitted to show defendant's modus operandi. Her testimony described events that shared enough common features with, and were sufficiently related to, the incidents with the victim because she stated that defendant had entered her bedroom late at night, removed her clothing, and began touching her. State v. Kesler, — Ohio App. 3d —, 2006 Ohio 6340, — N.E. 2d —, 2006 Ohio App. LEXIS 6324 (Dec. 4, 2006).

Plan or scheme

Defendant was not prejudiced by the joinder of offenses because both theft offenses were of the same character and constituted parts of a common plan; both theft offenses occurred on the university campus, were closely committed in place and time, and had the same modus operandi--a woman starting a conversation with the victims while using a jacket to conceal a theft. The offenses were related by time, day, location, and common scheme and, even if the charges had been separated, evidence of one offense would still have been admissible in the trial of the other under Ohio R. Evid. 404(B). State v. Brotherton, — Ohio App. 3d —, 2006 Ohio 1747, — N.E. 2d —, 2006 Ohio App. LEXIS 1622 (Apr. 7, 2006).

In a drug prosecution, a confidential informant's testimony that she bought drugs from defendant on two other unspecified occasions, other than the occasions on which his criminal charges were based, and that he had a gun, was relevant and admissible, under Ohio R. Evid. 404(B), because it was proof of a common scheme or plan to sell and possess illegal drugs, and, when a charged crime was drug related, evidence of firearms was both relevant and probative. State v. Bundy, — Ohio App. 3d —, 2006 Ohio 4062, — N.E. 2d —, 2006 Ohio App. LEXIS 4021 (Aug. 8, 2006).

"Scheme, plan or system" evidence of a defendant's "other acts" is relevant in those situations in which the "other acts" form part of the immediate background of the alleged act which forms the foundation of the crime charged in the indictment, and identity of the perpetrator of a crime is the second factual situation in which "scheme, plan or system" evidence is admissible, as one recognized method of establishing that the accused committed the offense set forth in the indictment is to show that he has committed similar crimes within a period of time reasonably near to the offense on trial, and that a similar scheme, plan or system was utilized to commit both the offense at issue and the other crimes. State v. Miley, — Ohio App. 3d —, 2006 Ohio 4670, — N.E. 2d —, 2006 Ohio App. LEXIS 4613 (Sept. 8, 2006).

In defendant's trial for multiple sexual offenses with two minors, evidence of his prior similar misconduct was erroneously admitted, under Ohio R. Evid. 404(B) and RC § 2945.59, because the quality of the evidence was lacking as the alleged victim of defendant's conduct did not tell anyone about it when it occurred, no other witnesses testified about the misconduct, the alleged victim offered no dates, locations, details or circumstances, and the alleged victim said he smoked marijuana with defendant and the victims of the charged offenses but did not then report defendant's prior misconduct with him to authorities to save the victims from a similar experience, so using this questionable evidence to prove an element of an unrelated charge was impermissible, as there was no way defendant could respond to it. State v. Miley, — Ohio App. 3d —, 2006 Ohio 4670, — N.E. 2d —, 2006 Ohio App. LEXIS 4613 (Sept. 8, 2006).

In defendant's trial for multiple sexual offenses with two minors, evidence of his prior similar misconduct was erroneously admitted, under Ohio R. Evid. 404(B) and RC § 2945.59, because the evidence was offered to prove scheme, plan, or system, but such evidence was only admissible for this purpose if it was part of the immediate background of the charged crimes, which it was not, as it occurred over ten years earlier, or to prove identity, which was not in dispute, so it was inadmissible for that purpose. State v. Miley, — Ohio App. 3d —, 2006 Ohio 4670, — N.E. 2d —, 2006 Ohio App. LEXIS 4613 (Sept. 8, 2006).

Prejudicial evidence

Trial court abused its discretion in allowing an alleged prior female victim of defendant's attack to testify in his second criminal trial on a charge of murdering a female victim, as the evidence of the prior bad act under RC § 2945.59 and Ohio

R. Evid. 404(B) was relevant to establishing identity but there were other powerful pieces of evidence to support finding that defendant was the assailant, including DNA evidence, the fact that he had scratches on his hands and arms shortly after the attack, and the fact that he had been at the victim's apartment shortly prior to the time that she was murdered, and the testimony was inordinately prejudicial and outweighed any probative value pursuant to Ohio R. Evid. 403; such testimony had been excluded pursuant to a motion in limine ruling in a prior trial and upon mention of it, a mistrial resulted, and defendant should have been able to rely on that ruling for preparation of his defense for the second trial. State v. Anderson, — Ohio App. 3d —, 2006 Ohio 4618, — N.E. 2d —, 2006 Ohio App. LEXIS 4581 (Sept. 1, 2006).

Prior bad acts admissible

Trial court did not abuse its discretion in admitting evidence of defendant's prior acts pursuant to Ohio R. Evid. 404(B) in having pulled up on the emergency brake while he was driving, as that was the behavioral fingerprint shared by the prior acts and the crime for which defendant was on trial, which was occasioned by the driver having pulled up on the emergency brake, causing the car to skid off the road. There were disputed issues regarding who was driving, and the evidence of the prior acts was admitted under the proof-of-identity exception to Rule 404(B), which made it more probative than prejudicial under the balancing test of Ohio R. Evid. 403(A). State v. Flanigan, — Ohio App. 3d —, 2007 Ohio 3158, — N.E. 2d —, 2007 Ohio App. LEXIS 2909 (June 22, 2007).

Admission of evidence of defendant's prior criminal conduct was not error under Ohio R. Evid. 404(B) regarding whether defendant ever drove the co-defendant's car and if so, whether he might have had illegal drugs with him at the time, as it was used to show that defendant's possession of drugs was not an accident or a mistake; further, any error would have been harmless under Ohio R. Crim. P. 52 where the evidence would have supported his conviction even if the prior bad conduct was not introduced. State v. Barker, — Ohio App. 3d —, 2006 Ohio 1472, — N.E. 2d —, 2006 Ohio App. LEXIS 1347 (Mar. 27, 2006).

Trial court did not err when it denied the motion for mistrial because exclusion of the testimony, that defendant bought drugs from the victim earlier in the day, was not required under Ohio R. Evid. 404(B). The testimony merely revealed how defendant and the victim knew each other and that defendant knew where to find the victim and the jury was well aware that all of the witnesses were drug users and that the victim himself was a drug dealer. State v. Taylor, — Ohio App. 3d —, 2006 Ohio 1736, — N.E. 2d —, 2006 Ohio App. LEXIS 1596 (Apr. 6, 2006).

Trial court did not abuse its discretion by allowing the evidence. It was clear that the evidence in dispute (that defendant had spit in another officer's eye upon arrest) was not used to prove defendant's character, but rather it was used correctly under Ohio R. Evid. 404(B). The State used the testimony to show that defendant had knowledge that he was HIV positive and to show that defendant intended to transmit HIV to the police officer by spitting in his eye; both reasons for the testimony were admissible under Ohio R. Evid. 404(B). State v. Branch, — Ohio App. 3d —, 2006 Ohio 3793, — N.E. 2d —, 2006 Ohio App. LEXIS 3750 (July 21, 2006).

There was no error in admitting the testimony regarding another fight because it was not admitted to demonstrate defendant's potential propensity for violence rather, the other acts evidence was allowed, under Ohio R. Evid. 404(B), for the purpose of showing motive. The testimony showed that the two groups had confrontations in the past and it was reasonable to conclude that those issues may have been the cause of the current brawl. State v. Tran, — Ohio App. 3d —, 2006 Ohio 4463, — N.E. 2d —, 2006 Ohio App. LEXIS 4394 (Aug. 30, 2006).

Prior conviction

Evidence of the prior conviction was relevant and was not admitted in error because defendant's 1999 felony conviction for nonsupport of dependents, under RC § 2919.21(G)(1), elevated his current nonsupport conviction to a fourth-degree felony. Defendant himself testified on direct examination as to his prior criminal nonsupport conviction. State v. Fritz, — Ohio App. 3d —, 2006 Ohio 2920, — N.E. 2d —, 2006 Ohio App. LEXIS 2809 (June 9, 2006).

Trial court abused its discretion when it permitted the prosecutor to elicit the details of defendant's prior felonious assault charge because the probative value of the detailed circumstances surrounding defendant's prior charged crime involving his sister did not outweigh the prejudicial effect of the admission of the prior alleged crime, the details of which became the subject of nearly half of the cross-examination. Nor was the evidence properly admitted to impeach the defendant's character. State v. Durham, — Ohio App. 3d —, 2006 Ohio 5015, — N.E. 2d —, 2006 Ohio App. LEXIS 4952 (Sept. 28, 2006).

Prior conviction properly admitted

As there was no requirement that the prosecution produce a certified copy of a judgment entry showing defendant's prior conviction, which defendant admitted to, the admission thereof was not an abuse of discretion pursuant to Ohio R. Evid. 404(B). State v. Alvarez, — Ohio App. 3d —, 2007 Ohio 3114, — N.E. 2d —, 2007 Ohio App. LEXIS 2870 (June 22, 2007).

Trial court did not err by allowing the introduction of the evidence of defendant's prior conviction under Evid. R. 404(B) because the prior crime was used to establish defendant's knowledge. The circumstances of the prior and present crime were exactly the same. Because, in the prior case, the same co-defendant used a stolen credit card to purchase a gas cutter over the telephone, and defendant picked up the cutter, the previous theft illustrated a pattern that established that defendant had knowledge or reasonable knowledge that the cutter was fraudulently purchased. State v. Sampson, — Ohio App. 3d —, 2006 Ohio 5005, — N.E. 2d —, 2006 Ohio App. LEXIS 4951 (Sept. 28, 2006).

Prior convictions

Trial court did not abuse its discretion in denying defendant's motion for a mistrial due to testimony regarding prior acts because the detective's alleged improper statements did not prejudice defendant. The jury was told to disregard the detective's statement that defendant had been convicted of the sex offender registration offense on three prior occasions and it was presumed that the jury followed the trial court's orders. State v. Smith, — Ohio App. 3d —, 2006 Ohio 158, — N.E. 2d —, 2006 Ohio App. LEXIS 127 (Jan. 18, 2006).

Prior identical offense

Trial court did not abuse its discretion in admitting evidence of defendant's prior convictions pursuant to Ohio R. Evid. 404(B) and RC § 2945.59, as the prior convictions were based on the same conduct and same charges for which defendant was presently on trial, and the trial court was aware of the possible prejudice to defendant but found that the evidence was relevant and appropriate to the issues in the case; defendant had previously committed domestic violence against the same victim, and had started a fire, including disabling the smoke detector, in the prior incident as well as in the present charge. State v. Sines, — Ohio App. 3d —, 2006 Ohio 1956, — N.E. 2d —, 2006 Ohio App. LEXIS 1813 (Apr. 17, 2006).

Sequence of events

Juvenile court did not commit plain error under Ohio R. Crim. P. 52, based on a failure to object under Ohio R. Evid. 103(A)(1), in admitting testimony from a police detective that at a debriefing, he suggested that the juvenile be considered a suspect in the killings of his grandmother and aunt because he had a tendency towards violent behavior after he huffed gasoline, as such testimony was not improper under Ohio R. Evid. 404(B) because it was offered to show why the State's investigation shifted its focus onto the juvenile, rather than to establish that he had a propensity to commit bad acts; further, the risk of prejudice under Ohio R. Evid. 403 was not considered where it was not raised as an objection at the juvenile court level. In re Sturm, — Ohio App. 3d —, 2006 Ohio 7101, — N.E. 2d —, 2006 Ohio App. LEXIS 7046 (Dec. 22, 2006).

Severance of offenses

Trial court did not abuse its discretion by denying defendant's motion to sever his offenses because the evidence of both the 2004 break-in and the 2005 home-invasion could just as easily have been introduced in two trials and the underlying facts were "simple and direct." Additionally, because the victims in the home invasion both affirmatively identified defendant as one of the men involved in the 2005 home-invasion, but that identification was subject to some degree of doubt, introduction of defendant's DNA from a year earlier was relevant to show that defendant knew the funeral home (the location of the home invasion), may have previously robbed it, and might have chosen to again break-in and vandalize the facility. State v. Hairston, — Ohio App. 3d —, 2007 Ohio 3880, — N.E. 2d —, 2007 Ohio App. LEXIS 3519 (July 27, 2007).

Charges against defendant arising from two incidents were properly tried together, under Ohio R. Crim. P. 13(A) and 8(A), and this did not violate Ohio R. Crim. P. 14, because (1), in one incident, it was alleged that defendant had committed a murder, and, in the other incident, the weapon allegedly used to commit that murder was recovered from the vehicle defendant had been driving, so, under Ohio R. Evid. 404(B), evidence of one incident would have been admissible in a separate trial of the other incident, and (2) the evidence related to the two incidents was simple and direct so that a jury would not become confused by presenting such evidence at one trial. State v. Nelms, — Ohio App. 3d —, 2007 Ohio 4664, — N.E. 2d —, 2007 Ohio App. LEXIS 4205 (Sept. 11, 2007).

Trial court did not abuse its discretion under Ohio R. Crim. P. 8(A) and 14 when it denied defendant's motion for relief from prejudicial joinder of two drug-related offenses which arose from incidents that occurred several months apart, as his defense to the possession of drugs charge implicated him in other drug-related criminal activity, which was admissible under Ohio R. Evid. 404(B). Ohio v. Anzures, — Ohio App. 3d —, 2007 Ohio 4817, — N.E. 2d —, 2007 Ohio App. LEXIS 4342 (Sept. 18, 2007).

In defendant's trial for two aggravated robberies, in which he moved for severance, under Ohio R. Crim. P. 14, while it was error for the trial court not to rule on the motion, the error was harmless because, under Ohio R. Evid. 404(B), evidence of one of the robberies would have been admissible at a separate trial of the other robbery to prove modus operandi, given the similarity between the two crimes, intent and plan, and identity, so joinder of the offenses, under Ohio R. Crim. P. 8(A), was proper. State v. Andrews, — Ohio App. 3d —, 2006 Ohio 3764, — N.E. 2d —, 2006 Ohio App. LEXIS 3706 (July 24, 2006).

In defendant's trial for multiple counts of aggravated robbery, aggravated burglary, kidnapping, felonious assault, and impersonating a police officer growing out of two separate incidents, denial of his motion to sever the charges related to the first incident from those concerning the second incident did not violate Crim. R. 8(A) or improperly circumvent Ohio R. Evid. 404(b) by prejudicing defendant; simple and direct evidence supported each of the 13 counts, the incidents occurred two days apart in the same neighborhood and were of a similar character, the evidence was sufficient to sustain each verdict, and the State did not need the evidence of one case to prove the other. State v. Wilson, — Ohio App. 3d —, 2006 Ohio 5253, — N.E. 2d —, 2006 Ohio App. LEXIS 5212 (Oct. 5, 2006).

Sexual abuse cases

Testimony of the minor girls was properly admitted to show that defendant engaged in a pattern of having minor girls at his house, showing them pornographic videos, and/or allowing them to drink alcohol, and acting and/or talking in a sexual manner with them. On the record, therefore, the probative value of the evidence was not substantially outweighed by the possibility of unfair prejudice. State v. Petitto, — Ohio App. 3d —, 2007 Ohio 3901, — N.E. 2d —, 2007 Ohio App. LEXIS 3554 (Aug. 2, 2007).

There was no error in the admission of the testimony of the rape victim's friend because it was admissible to prove defendant's motive, plan, and scheme to commit rape against the victim. The testimony was offered to prove defendant's motive to sexually abuse a 12-year-old girl because there were similarities between the two incidents, including that the way in which defendant touched the friend's breasts over her shirt and then under her shirt was the same way in which he touched the victim's breasts; both girls' relationships with defendant first involved communication on the computer. State v. Travis, — Ohio App. 3d —, 2007 Ohio 6683, — N.E. 2d —, 2007 Ohio App. LEXIS 5859 (Dec. 17, 2007).

In defendant's prosecution for sexual offenses against his daughter, the admission of a witness's testimony that she believed defendant's relationship with his daughter was "different" and testimony that "everybody" suspected defendant behaved in a sexually inappropriate manner with his daughter, as well as testimony elicited from defendant on cross-examination about another specific instance of his own sexual activity, to which no objection was stated, was not plain error, under Ohio R. Crim. P. 52(B), as it could not be said that, but for the testimony, the result of defendant's trial would have differed, as the testimony did not speak to whether defendant sexually abused the victim, and, while the testimony was arguably character evidence contrary to Ohio R. Evid. 404(A) and RC §§ 2907.02(D) and 2907.05(D), some of it was admissible for another purpose of showing why a witness asked the victim if her father had sexually abused her, and, as defendant's trial was a bench trial, it was presumed that the trial court disregarded any improper evidence. State v. Mosley, — Ohio App. 3d —, 2006 Ohio 3102, — N.E. 2d —, 2006 Ohio App. LEXIS 2969 (June 20, 2006).

—Admissible evidence

In a prosecution for rape, gross sexual imposition, and corruption of a minor, evidence of defendant's uncharged criminal acts similar to the acts with which defendant was charged was admissible, under Ohio R. Evid. 404(B) and RC § 2945.59 because the uncharged acts were so connected to the charged acts that proof of one involved the other, and the uncharged acts showed defendant committed similar crimes against the same victim near in time to the crimes charged and used a similar system to commit both the crimes charged and the uncharged acts. State v. Frost, — Ohio App. 3d —, 2007 Ohio 3469, — N.E. 2d —, 2007 Ohio App. LEXIS 3193 (July 6, 2007).

Similar acts evidence

Trial court properly allowed evidence of the crimes in another county to establish similarities to the home invasion robbery and to establish the perpetrators' identity because, in those cases the perpetrators also ordered the victims to remove their clothing, and tied the victims to chairs with articles of clothing. A police detective testified that in her 18 years of experience, she found it was highly unusual for victims to be stripped of their clothing and to be tied to chairs with articles of their own clothing; two victims from the other county's robberies identified defendant as one of the men in their homes. State v. Hairston, — Ohio App. 3d —, 2007 Ohio 3880, — N.E. 2d —, 2007 Ohio App. LEXIS 3519 (July 27, 2007).

When, in a robbery prosecution, a co-defendant's testimony that, after committing the crime charged, he and defendant engaged in another robbery, this evidence was properly admitted, under Ohio R. Evid. 404(B) and RC § 2945.59, because it tended to show defendant's identity, plan and preparation because both crimes were committed on the same day, with the same actor, using the same weapon, and involved one man waiting in a car while the other committed the robbery. State v. Ayers, — Ohio App. 3d —, 2006 Ohio 5533, — N.E. 2d —, 2006 Ohio App. LEXIS 5508 (Oct. 17, 2006).

Waiver

Defendant's claim of a violation of Ohio R. Evid. 403 was evaluated under a plain error analysis as defendant objected at trial based on a violation of Ohio R. Evid. 404. The trial court did not commit plain error in admitting testimony describing statements made by defendant before the murder as the outcome would not have been different without the testimony since a passenger in the same car as defendant: (1) placed defendant inside the victim's house when shots were fired; (2) described incriminating statements defendant made upon getting back in the car; and (3) described a chain and watch that fell out of defendant's pocket, which matched a description of jewelry that was missing from the victim. State v. Johnson, — Ohio App. 3d —, 2006 Ohio 209, — N.E. 2d —, 2006 Ohio App. LEXIS 139 (Jan. 19, 2006).

RULE 405. Methods of Proving Character

(A) **Reputation or opinion.** In all cases in which evidence of character or a trait of character of a person is admissible, proof may be made by testimony as to reputation or by testimony in the form of an opinion. On cross-examination, inquiry is allowable into relevant specific instances of conduct.

(B) **Specific instances of conduct.** In cases in which character or a trait of character of a person is an essential element of a charge, claim, or defense, proof may also be made of specific instances of his conduct.

NOTES TO DECISIONS

Analysis

Character of victim
Cross-examination of character witnesses
Harmless error
Impeachment of character witness
Relevance
Victim's character

Character of victim

Ohio R. Evid. 405 prohibited defendant from eliciting testimony from the other witnesses on direct examination regarding their knowledge of specific instances in which the victim exhibited violent behavior towards persons other than defendant for his claim of self-defense. Furthermore, nothing in the record indicated that defendant knew about the specific instances that he sought to elicit, and he did not proffer any

testimony in that regard. State v. Moore, — Ohio App. 3d —, 2007 Ohio 3600, — N.E. 2d —, 2007 Ohio App. LEXIS 3306 (July 16, 2007).

Cross-examination of character witnesses

Prosecution was permitted during the culpability phase of the trial to rebut the testimony by defendant's mother that defendant was a follower and that because of his drug use, low intellect, and family history of crime, he had no choice but to follow the criminal path; the State attempted to show that defendant continued to break the law outside of the influence of his family members when he had his mother smuggle drugs to him in jail to sell. More importantly, however, since the trial court sustained defense counsel's objections regarding the State's question, the mother never answered whether she smuggled drugs into the county jail and the jury never heard the State's evidence concerning the recorded phone calls. State v. Ervin, — Ohio App. 3d —, 2007 Ohio 5942, — N.E. 2d —, 2007 Ohio App. LEXIS 5224 (Nov. 8, 2007).

Harmless error

Even if the trial court had committed error in allowing character evidence of defendant or the victim, any such error was harmless because the evidence was overwhelmingly in favor of defendant's guilt since defendant has failed to establish a valid claim of self-defense; he failed to prove that he was not the initial aggressor. The evidence clearly demonstrated that upon observing the victim in his driveway, defendant went to the hall closet where he retrieved and loaded his father's gun, and, instead of locking the door and calling the police, he then proceeded to the front door and yelled at the victim, picked up a rock and threw it at the victim's jeep, and then shot and killed him. Ohio v. Horace K. Vinson, — Ohio App. 3d —, 2007 Ohio 5199, — N.E. 2d —, 2007 Ohio App. LEXIS 4608 (Sept. 28, 2007).

Impeachment of character witness

Impeachment evidence did not constitute the admission of nonstatutory aggravating circumstances in the mitigation phase of defendant's trial because the crux of defense counsel's theory of mitigation was that defendant was a follower and because of his drug use, low intellect, and family history of crime, he had no choice but to follow the criminal path. The State sought to rebut that theory by demonstrating that while defendant was away from his family members and incarcerated in the county jail, he continued to sell drugs and break the law; thus, because defendant raised the issue of history, character, and background, he opened the door to all relevant evidence. State v. Ervin, — Ohio App. 3d —, 2007 Ohio 5942, — N.E. 2d —, 2007 Ohio App. LEXIS 5224 (Nov. 8, 2007).

Relevance

Where defendant and the victim had a deteriorated relationship for a period of years, and upon the two arguing and the victim shoving defendant, defendant took out his single-shot gun and shot the victim twice, pausing in between shots to carefully reload the gun, there was no error in the trial court's refusal to charge defendant or instruct the jury on the crime of voluntary manslaughter, in violation of RC § 2903.03, in his criminal trial on an aggravated murder charge, as there was a sufficient cooling off period such that there could be no finding of sudden rage or passion; excluded evidence regarding the victim's reputation for violence and defendant's knowledge thereof was not relevant or admissible under Ohio R. Evid. 403 and 404(A), and specific instances of misconduct were not admissible under Ohio R. Evid. 405. State v. Kanner, — Ohio App. 3d —, 2006 Ohio 3485, — N.E. 2d —, 2006 Ohio App. LEXIS 3428 (June 29, 2006).

Victim's character

Trial court did not err by denying defendant's motion for a new trial because defendant had intended to open the door to the victim's prior convictions, which had been excluded from being introduced into evidence before trial when the trial court granted the state's motion in limine. Also, the State did not put the victim's character into evidence because the victim's longtime friend did not give an opinion as to the victim's reputation during her testimony; also, any knowledge on the part of the friend as to the character of the victim was not the same as defendant's knowledge of the victim's character. Ohio v. Horace K. Vinson, — Ohio App. 3d —, 2007 Ohio 5199, — N.E. 2d —, 2007 Ohio App. LEXIS 4608 (Sept. 28, 2007).

RULE 406.   Habit; Routine Practice

Evidence of the habit of a person or of the routine practice of an organization, whether corroborated or not and regardless of the presence of eyewitnesses, is relevant to prove that the conduct of the person or organization on a particular occasion was in conformity with the habit or routine practice.

NOTES TO DECISIONS

ANALYSIS

Admissibility generally
Habit evidence

Admissibility generally

Trial court properly excluded testimony that a seller of commercial realty had a "habit" of defrauding purchasers. That was the sort of prejudicial evidence prohibited by EvidR 404(B): Pappas v. Ippolito, 177 Ohio App. 3d 625, 2008 Ohio 3976, 895 N.E.2d 610, 2008 Ohio App. LEXIS 3354 (2008).

Habit evidence

Because defendants never attempted to ask the trooper any of the foundational questions required to show habit, there was no objection by the landscaper (the victim of a vehicle collision) and no ruling was ever actually made by the trial court to exclude such evidence. Therefore, the trial court did not err in refusing to allow defendants to question the trooper because the trial court never actually excluded any evidence. Deskins v. Cunningham, — Ohio App. 3d —, 2006 Ohio 2003, — N.E. 2d —, 2006 Ohio App. LEXIS 1859 (Apr. 24, 2006).

Evidence that a physician was allegedly negligent in treating a patient's prior ovarian cyst, discovered in 1988, was properly excluded in the patient's action against the physician and his employer for the physician's alleged medical negligence in managing a second cyst diagnosed in 1999, which the patient claimed later developed into cancer. The 1988 treatment was not admissible under Ohio R. Evid. 404(B) because it was a single occurrence which did not establish a regular or routine practice as required by Ohio R. Evid. 406, and any relevance under Ohio R. Evid. 401 was outweighed by prejudice under Ohio R. Evid. 403. Gerke v. Norwalk Clinic, Inc., — Ohio App. 3d —, 2006 Ohio 5621, — N.E. 2d —, 2006 Ohio App. LEXIS 5605 (Oct. 27, 2006).

RULE 407.   Subsequent Remedial Measures

When, after an injury or harm allegedly caused by an event, measures are taken which, if taken previously, would have made the injury or harm less likely to occur, evidence of the subsequent measures is not admissible to prove negligence or culpable conduct in connection with the event. This rule does not require the exclusion of evidence of subsequent measures when offered for another purpose, such as proving ownership, control, or feasibility of precautionary measures, if controverted, or impeachment.

History: Amended, eff 7-1-00.

NOTES TO DECISIONS

ANALYSIS

Intentional workplace tort
Subsequent remedial measures

Intentional workplace tort

Employer's decision to replace the forklifts represented a subsequent remedial measure that the employee offered for the purpose of proving that the employer had intentionally injured him. Thus, the employee could not rely on that fact to withstand the employer's motion for a summary judgment. Hawk v. Menasha, — Ohio App. 3d —, 2008 Ohio 483, — N.E. 2d —, 2008 Ohio App. LEXIS 428 (Feb. 7, 2008).

Subsequent remedial measures

In an executrix's suit to recover for the death of her decedent caused when debris fell after a truck struck a utility pole, the executrix was not permitted to submit evidence of an e-mail sent by a utility company' manager to other supervisors in the company to show that the manager strongly advocated placing the pole under the road so as to prevent future accidents because evidence of the company's post-accident remedial measures was inadmissible under Ohio R. Evid. 407 to prove negligence or culpable conduct. Swaisgood v. Puder, — Ohio App. 3d —, 2007 Ohio 307, — N.E. 2d —, 2007 Ohio App. LEXIS 279 (Jan. 26, 2007).

In an employer intentional tort suit, the court could not consider the fact that, after the employee's accident, the employer installed a safety guard around the airlock mechanism that caused the employee's injuries because, pursuant to Ohio R. Evid. 407, evidence of subsequent remedial measures is not admissible to prove culpability in connection with an accident. Flint v. Int'l Multifoods, — Ohio App. 3d —, 2007 Ohio 679, — N.E. 2d —, 2007 Ohio App. LEXIS 623 (Feb. 20, 2007).

When a school employee sued a television station for the station's report on the employee's actions in physically controlling students, a school district's interoffice memoranda which (1) instructed the employee on the appropriate use of physical force and (2) summarized the school district's investigation of the incident were not excludable under Ohio R. Evid. 407 because they concerned the employee's use of physical force, which was a matter of consequence to the action, and the school district was not on trial. Young v. Russ, — Ohio App. 3d —, 2007 Ohio 5214, — N.E. 2d —, 2007 Ohio App. LEXIS 4591 (Sept. 28, 2007).

Although a trial court discussed a subsequent contract modification, which was inadmissible as a subsequent remedial measure under Ohio R. Evid. 407, in an ambulance patron's action against an ambulance company, asserting that the fees billed were unreasonably excessive, there was no showing that the company was prejudiced by the admission of the modification evidence. The mention of the modification appeared to help the company, as the trial court noted that due to the modification which was believed to be a good deterrent to excessive billing, the punitive damages awarded to the patron were limited. Hailey v. Medcorp, Inc., — Ohio App. 3d —, 2006 Ohio 4804, — N.E. 2d —, 2006 Ohio App. LEXIS 4706 (Sept. 15, 2006).

RULE 408.   Compromise and Offers to Compromise

Evidence of (1) furnishing or offering or promising to furnish, or (2) accepting or offering or promising to accept, a valuable consideration in compromising or attempting to compromise a claim which was disputed as to either validity or amount, is not admissible to prove liability for or invalidity of the claim or its amount. Evidence of conduct or statements made in compromise negotiations is likewise not admissible. This rule does not require the exclusion of any evidence otherwise discoverable merely because it is presented in the course of compromise negotiations. This rule also does not require exclusion when the evidence is offered for another purpose, such as proving bias or prejudice of a witness, negativing a contention of undue delay, or proving an effort to obstruct a criminal investigation or prosecution.

NOTES TO DECISIONS

ANALYSIS

Admissibility
Admissibility generally
Admissibility of settlement offer
Evidence excluded
Evidence of compromise
Scope of rule

Admissibility

When a wife sought clarification of a trial court's qualified domestic relations order regarding the distribution of her former husband's pension, it was error to exclude, under Ohio R. Evid. 408, the testimony of an expert about his discussions with the husband when the distribution of his pension was being negotiated, both about the effect of a distribution on spousal support and the husband's motives for proposing the obtaining of an insurance policy on his life, because this did not seek to impose liability for or prove the validity of a claim that the wife was entitled to half the husband's pension, as this was undisputed, but it did seek to assist the court in assessing if equitably and intentionally the pension included early retirement and/or interim supplemental benefits and why insurance on the husband's life was proposed. Hocker v. Hocker, 171 Ohio App. 3d 279, 2007 Ohio 1671, 870 N.E.2d 736, 2007 Ohio App. LEXIS 1528 (2007).

Ohio R. Evid. 408 does not require the exclusion of evidence offered to prove bias or prejudice of a witness, negative a contention of undue delay, or prove an effort to obstruct a criminal investigation or prosecution. Hocker v. Hocker, 171 Ohio App. 3d 279, 2007 Ohio 1671, 870 N.E.2d 736, 2007 Ohio App. LEXIS 1528 (2007).

Admissibility generally

Trial court has broad discretion to clarify ambiguous language in a separation agreement by considering the intent of the parties and the equities involved. Trial court abused its discretion by excluding testimony by a financial consultant hired by a party where the testimony was relevant in clarifying the terms of the settlement agreement: Hocker v. Hocker, 171 Ohio App. 3d 279, 2007 Ohio 1671, 870 N.E.2d 736, 2007 Ohio App. LEXIS 1528 (2007).

Admissibility of settlement offer

When a wife filed for divorce in one county, engaged in mediation there, and then dismissed the case and refiled it in another county, prompting her husband to seek a change of venue back to the county in which she originally filed, Ohio R. Evid. 408 did not bar the admission of statements she had made in the course of the mediation to prove in which county venue was proper because the statements were not offered to prove the validity or invalidity of her claims material to the

divorce, but, rather, proper venue. Swearingen v. Swearingen, — Ohio App. 3d —, 2007 Ohio 1241, — N.E. 2d —, 2007 Ohio App. LEXIS 1155 (Mar. 20, 2007).

Ohio R. Evid. 408 only excluded evidence of compromises and conduct or statements made in compromise negotiations when a party offered that evidence to prove or disprove liability or the amount of damages, but if a party offered such evidence for any other purpose, Rule 408 did not prohibit the introduction of that evidence. Swearingen v. Swearingen, — Ohio App. 3d —, 2007 Ohio 1241, — N.E. 2d —, 2007 Ohio App. LEXIS 1155 (Mar. 20, 2007).

Evidence excluded

Trial court did not abuse its discretion when it granted a terminated employee's motion in limine under Ohio R. Evid. 408 to exclude evidence and testimony of her offers to compromise with respect to her discrimination action against her employer and others, as there was no improper request to exclude the evidence for purposes other than liability or invalidity. Lynch v. Studebaker, — Ohio App. 3d —, 2007 Ohio 4014, — N.E. 2d —, 2007 Ohio App. LEXIS 3651 (Aug. 9, 2007).

Evidence of compromise

In a city's appropriation action involving property of an owner, there was no error in admitting evidence of settlement or compromise negotiations towards that end, as the evidence was not offered to prove liability or invalidate a claim or its amount, pursuant to Ohio R. Evid. 408, but instead, it was offered to show that the owner sought a higher recovery at the onset of the appropriation proceedings than it could ultimately prove at trial. There was no showing that introduction of such evidence prejudiced the owner. City of Toledo v. Bernard Ross Family Ltd Partnership, — Ohio App. 3d —, 2006 Ohio 117, — N.E. 2d —, 2006 Ohio App. LEXIS 90 (Jan. 13, 2006).

Evidence admitted into evidence was not improper pursuant to Ohio R. Evid. 408, although it showed that a shipper was aware of a pricing structure problem in its arrangement with a supplier, the shipper's reaction thereto, and its proposed solutions to the problem, as any perceived error in admission of the evidence was negated by the shipper's admission of evidence on its own behalf that referenced the exact same issues. Avery Dennison Corp. v. Con-Way Transp. Servs., — Ohio App. 3d —, 2006 Ohio 6106, — N.E. 2d —, 2006 Ohio App. LEXIS 6036 (Nov. 17, 2006).

Scope of rule

Trial court did not abuse its discretion in admitting evidence of a settlement between a tractor purchaser and the tractor manufacturer in the purchaser's negligence action against the manufacturer and the seller, arising from injuries he sustained when the tractor rolled backwards, as the evidence was not admitted to prove liability for or invalidity of the claim; rather, the evidence of the settlement was offered to explain why the manufacturer was not a party to the action. Gadberry v. Eastgate Lawn & Tractor, Inc., — Ohio App. 3d —, 2007 Ohio 2849, — N.E. 2d —, 2007 Ohio App. LEXIS 2642 (June 11, 2007).

There was no plain error under Ohio R. Crim. P. 52(B) by the trial court's admission of statements allegedly made during plea negotiations, as the record surrounding the giving of the statement that defendant termed a plea negotiation did not support a finding that defendant had a subjective expectation that a plea was being negotiated at the time pursuant to Ohio R. Evid. 410(A)(5). Defendant received Miranda warnings prior to giving the statement, and he specifically waived the provisions of Ohio R. Evid. 408 and 410. State v. Williams, —

Ohio App. 3d —, 2006 Ohio 1381, — N.E. 2d —, 2006 Ohio App. LEXIS 1259 (Mar. 22, 2006).

RULE 409.   Payment of Medical and Similar Expenses

Evidence of furnishing or offering or promising to pay medical, hospital, or similar expenses occasioned by an injury is not admissible to prove liability for the injury.

RULE 410.   Inadmissibility of Pleas, Offers of Pleas, and Related Statements

(A) Except as provided in division (B) of this rule, evidence of the following is not admissible in any civil or criminal proceeding against the defendant who made the plea or who was a participant personally or through counsel in the plea discussions:

(1) A plea of guilty that later was withdrawn;

(2) A plea of no contest or the equivalent plea from another jurisdiction;

(3) A plea of guilty in a violations bureau;

(4) Any statement made in the course of any proceedings under Rule 11 of the Rules of Criminal Procedure or equivalent procedure from another jurisdiction regarding the foregoing pleas;

(5) Any statement made in the course of plea discussions in which counsel for the prosecuting authority or for the defendant was a participant and that do not result in a plea of guilty or that result in a plea of guilty later withdrawn.

(B) A statement otherwise inadmissible under this rule is admissible in either of the following:

(1) Any proceeding in which another statement made in the course of the same plea or plea discussions has been introduced and the statement should, in fairness, be considered contemporaneously with it;

(2) A criminal proceeding for perjury or false statement if the statement was made by the defendant under oath, on the record, and in the presence of counsel.

History: Amended, eff 7-1-91.

NOTES TO DECISIONS

ANALYSIS

Admissibility
Admissibility of statements made during plea negotiations

———

Admissibility

In a case where the conviction was not made relevant by statute, CrimR 11(B)(2) and EvidR 410 prohibited introduction of a party's convictions following no contest pleas to arson and insurance fraud: Elevators Mut. Ins. Co. v. J. Patrick O'Flaherty's, Inc., 180 Ohio App. 3d 315, 2008 Ohio 6946, 905 N.E.2d 259, 2008 Ohio App. LEXIS 5839 (2008).

Defendant's statement given to a polygraphist, before and during plea negotiations, was subject to exclusion under Ohio R. Evid. 410; defendant may not have had a subjective expectation that defendant's counsel was preparing for a plea negotiation at the time the statement was given, but defendant definitely had such an expectation by the time the statement was presented to the prosecutor. Under the circumstances, the trial court abused its discretion by not suppressing this

statement and a related report. State v. Jeffries, — Ohio App. 3d —, 2007 Ohio 3366, — N.E. 2d —, 2007 Ohio App. LEXIS 3085 (June 29, 2007).

There was no plain error under Ohio R. Crim. P. 52(B) by the trial court's admission of statements allegedly made during plea negotiations, as the record surrounding the giving of the statement that defendant termed a plea negotiation did not support a finding that defendant had a subjective expectation that a plea was being negotiated at the time pursuant to Ohio R. Evid. 410(A)(5). Defendant received Miranda warnings prior to giving the statement, and he specifically waived the provisions of Ohio R. Evid. 408 and 410. State v. Williams, — Ohio App. 3d —, 2006 Ohio 1381, — N.E. 2d —, 2006 Ohio App. LEXIS 1259 (Mar. 22, 2006).

Admissibility of statements made during plea negotiations

Trial court did not abuse its discretion in not striking the complained of testimony, under EvidR 410(A)(5), because the discussion regarding a plea was one-sided and initiated by defendant, the police informed defendant that they were not able to negotiate any plea, a prosecutor was not involved in the discussion, and basically, no evidence other than defendant's attempt to cut a deal was admitted. State v. Foster, — Ohio App. 3d —, 2007 Ohio 6626, — N.E. 2d —, 2007 Ohio App. LEXIS 5824 (Dec. 10, 2007).

Statements that were not made in the course of plea discussions are not protected by EvidR 410, even if the statements were later provided to the state in the course of plea discussions: State v. Jeffries, 119 Ohio St. 3d 265, 2008 Ohio 3865, 893 N.E.2d 487, 2008 Ohio LEXIS 1996 (2008).

RULE 411.   Liability Insurance

Evidence that a person was or was not insured against liability is not admissible upon the issue whether the person acted negligently or otherwise wrongfully. This rule does not require the exclusion of evidence of insurance against liability when offered for another purpose, such as proof of agency, ownership or control, if controverted, or bias or prejudice of a witness.

History: Amended, eff 7-1-07.

NOTES TO DECISIONS

ANALYSIS

Evidence of existence of liability insurance
Indemnity agreement
Scope of rule

———

Evidence of existence of liability insurance

Trial court did not err by not granting a mistrial after counsel for a driver remarked during voir dire of a personal injury case that there was no insurance. The trial court offered to give a curative instruction to counteract any prejudice that might have been created from the statement, and the court could not say that the trial court's decision to give an instruction rather than declare a mistrial was an action that no conscientious judge could honestly have taken. Henson v. K. Collins Plumbing, Inc., — Ohio App. 3d —, 2006 Ohio 3090, — N.E. 2d —, 2006 Ohio App. LEXIS 2978 (June 19, 2006).

Indemnity agreement

Trial court erred by allowing the plaintiff to introduce evidence that a defendant was protected by an indemnity agreement. Prymas v. Kassai, 168 Ohio App. 3d 123, 2006 Ohio 3726, 858 N.E.2d 1209, 2006 Ohio App. LEXIS 3691 (2006).

Scope of rule

In a medical malpractice action, where the executrix of the deceased patient's estate did not introduce evidence of medical malpractice insurance, Ohio R. Evid. 411 did not apply. There was no error in the jury's having heard testimony that referenced the high cost of malpractice insurance, as any other error was deemed waived where no objection was made and any possible error had been cured by the court. Iglodi v. Tolentino, — Ohio App. 3d —, 2007 Ohio 1982, — N.E. 2d —, 2007 Ohio App. LEXIS 1832 (Apr. 26, 2007).

Ohio R. Evid. 411 did not bar the admission of evidence that an alleged injured party's insurer was reimbursed by a motorist's insurer for medical payments the alleged injured party's insurer made to the alleged injured party because this evidence was not admitted to establish liability but to establish a setoff after the jury returned its verdict. Fickes v. Kirk, — Ohio App. 3d —, 2007 Ohio 6011, — N.E. 2d —, 2007 Ohio App. LEXIS 5288 (Nov. 9, 2007).

In a property owner's suit alleging claim of trespass due to a developer's installation of a sewer line across the owner's property, the owner was improperly allowed to introduce evidence relating to the fact that the developer agreed to indemnify the neighboring landowners for any liability resulting from the sewer line because such evidence was prohibited under Ohio R. Evid. 411. Prymas v. Kassai, 168 Ohio App. 3d 123, 2006 Ohio 3726, 858 N.E.2d 1209, 2006 Ohio App. LEXIS 3691 (2006).

ARTICLE V
PRIVILEGES

RULE 501. General Rule

The privilege of a witness, person, state or political subdivision thereof shall be governed by statute enacted by the General Assembly or by principles of common law as interpreted by the courts of this state in the light of reason and experience.

NOTES TO DECISIONS

ANALYSIS

Declarant deceased
Spousal privilege

Declarant deceased

Decedent's statement to his attorney was not admissible, under Ohio R. Evid. 804(B), because (1) the entire contents of the statement were privileged, (2) the decedent did not waive his attorney-client privilege, and (3) the Ohio Rules of Evidence did not control the admissibility of privileged material, under Ohio R. Evid. 501, as the admissibility of such matters was controlled by statute and common law. Wallace v. McElwain, — Ohio App. 3d —, 2006 Ohio 5226, — N.E. 2d —, 2006 Ohio App. LEXIS 5205 (Sept. 27, 2006).

Spousal privilege

It was not error for a trial court to find that defendant's spouse could testify against him, under RC § 2945.42 and Ohio R. Evid. 501, regarding his actions when he kidnapped her, under RC § 2905.01(B)(2), and abducted her, under RC § 2905.02(A)(2), whether or not she was hurt as part of his continuous course of conduct of which his restraint of her was a part, and despite the fact that kidnapping and abduction were not specifically listed in RC § 2945.42 as offenses where an alleged victim-spouse could elect to testify in the prosecution of a defendant-spouse despite the existence of a spousal privilege, because threats of bodily harm, being a violation of

marital duty, were not privileged. State v. Purvis, — Ohio App. 3d —, 2006 Ohio 1555, — N.E. 2d —, 2006 Ohio App. LEXIS 1493 (Mar. 31, 2006).

There was no error in permitting defendant's wife to testify to the spousal communications, pursuant to RC § 2945.42, because the communications were specifically in regards to acts of rape and sexual assault against the couples' daughter. State v. Wilson, — Ohio App. 3d —, 2006 Ohio 2000, — N.E. 2d —, 2006 Ohio App. LEXIS 1860 (Apr. 24, 2006).

ARTICLE VI
WITNESSES

RULE 601. General Rule of Competency

Every person is competent to be a witness except:

(A) Those of unsound mind, and children under ten years of age, who appear incapable of receiving just impressions of the facts and transactions respecting which they are examined, or of relating them truly.

(B) A spouse testifying against the other spouse charged with a crime except when either of the following applies:

(1) A crime against the testifying spouse or a child of either spouse is charged;

(2) The testifying spouse elects to testify.

(C) An officer, while on duty for the exclusive or main purpose of enforcing traffic laws, arresting or assisting in the arrest of a person charged with a traffic violation punishable as a misdemeanor where the officer at the time of the arrest was not using a properly marked motor vehicle as defined by statute or was not wearing a legally distinctive uniform as defined by statute.

(D) A person giving expert testimony on the issue of liability in any claim asserted in any civil action against a physician, podiatrist, or hospital arising out of the diagnosis, care, or treatment of any person by a physician or podiatrist, unless the person testifying is licensed to practice medicine and surgery, osteopathic medicine and surgery, or podiatric medicine and surgery by the state medical board or by the licensing authority of any state, and unless the person devotes at least one-half of his or her professional time to the active clinical practice in his or her field of licensure, or to its instruction in an accredited school. This division shall not prohibit other medical professionals who otherwise are competent to testify under these rules from giving expert testimony on the appropriate standard of care in their own profession in any claim asserted in any civil action against a physician, podiatrist, medical professional, or hospital arising out of the diagnosis, care, or treatment of any person.

(E) As otherwise provided in these rules.

History: Amended, eff 7-1-91.

NOTES TO DECISIONS

ANALYSIS

Active clinical practice
Child witness
Children
Children under ten years of age
Competency of child to be a witness
Competency of child witness to testify

Competency of mentally challenged witness
Competency of testimony
Competency of witness to testify
Competency to testify
Expert witness
Medical expert
—— Criminal actions
Medical malpractice
Mentally challenged witness
People of unsound mind
Plaintiff's treating physician
Police officers
Spouses

Active clinical practice

Trial court's exclusion of an administratrix's expert's testimony was proper pursuant to Ohio R. Evid. 601(D) in her medical malpractice action, as the expert was not engaged in the active clinical practice of medicine at the time of the alleged negligence or at any time after the lawsuit was filed; although he still maintained his licensure to practice medicine in Ohio, he had retired long before the cause of action accrued. Berlin v. Thompson, — Ohio App. 3d —, 2007 Ohio 5700, — N.E. 2d —, 2007 Ohio App. LEXIS 5006 (Oct. 22, 2007).

Where a medical expert in a medical malpractice action testified that his professional time was spent with 40 percent on research, 25 percent seeing clinical patients, and 10 percent supervising the patient care rendered by hospital residents and fellows, the division of time satisfied the competency requirements of Ohio R. Evid. 601(D); the research was 80-90 percent clinical, and "active clinical practice" as used in Rule 601(D) was not defined in the rule, although the stated purpose of the Rule was to avoid using testimony from a physician who earned his living or spent a lot of time testifying against fellow professionals without an experiential background of his own. Werden v. Children's Hosp. Med. Ctr., — Ohio App. 3d —, 2006 Ohio 4600, — N.E. 2d —, 2006 Ohio App. LEXIS 4547 (Sept. 8, 2006).

Child witness

Although the trial court abused its discretion when it allowed the social worker to testify to everything that the nine-year-old child had told her regarding the incident regarding her mother's intoxication, the error was harmless. The child was 10 years old at the time of the dependency trial and thus, could have testified, however, the mother never attempted to call the child as a witness, or request an in-camera interview in the case in chief. In re Matsko, — Ohio App. 3d —, 2007 Ohio 2060, — N.E. 2d —, 2007 Ohio App. LEXIS 1919 (Apr. 27, 2007).

In a juvenile's criminal case, the juvenile court did not abuse its discretion in determining that a child witness who was under 10 years old and who was a victim of defendant's sexual offenses was competent to testify, pursuant to Ohio R. Evid. 601(A), as the court considered the competency factors and determined that the witness knew right from wrong and the consequences of lying. In re Moyer, — Ohio App. 3d —, 2006 Ohio 85, — N.E. 2d —, 2006 Ohio App. LEXIS 62 (Jan. 12, 2006).

Trial court did not err in finding that eight-year-old victim competent to testify, under Ohio R. Evid. 601, as she was able to recollect and communicate the specific events of the rapes in a manner sufficient to describe them accurately, demonstrate an ability to differentiate truth from falsity, and acknowledge her responsibility to be truthful. State v. Middlesworth, — Ohio App. 3d —, 2006 Ohio 12, — N.E. 2d —, 2006 Ohio App. LEXIS 3 (Jan. 4, 2006).

Children

Statements made by defendant's young daughter to others were properly admitted in his criminal trial on a murder charge where the statements were made within an hour of the incident and they qualified as excited utterances pursuant to Ohio R. Evid. 803(2) because she had seen the event and the two-year-old battered victim. The competency of the daughter was not at issue for the admission of such a statement and further, she did not testify at trial for purposes of Ohio R. Evid. 601, and as the statements made to her guardian and her neighbor were not testimonial statements, defendant's Sixth Amendment confrontation rights under Crawford were not implicated. State v. Bennett, — Ohio App. 3d —, 2006 Ohio 2757, — N.E. 2d —, 2006 Ohio App. LEXIS 2592 (May 22, 2006).

Children under ten years of age

Defendant's three rape convictions were affirmed because the four-year-old victim's statements were properly admitted in the absence of a competency hearing; the trial court did not abuse its discretion in finding that the victim's hearsay statements were made for purposes of medical diagnosis and treatment, under Ohio R. Evid. 803(4), and thus sufficiently reliable to be admitted through the testimony of a social worker and two therapists. The salient inquiry for admission of the testimony was not the child's competency, but whether her statements were made for purposes of diagnosis and treatment rather than for some other purpose. State v. Muttart, 116 Ohio St. 3d 5, 2007 Ohio 5267, 875 N.E.2d 944, 2007 Ohio LEXIS 2535 (2007).

Regardless of whether a child less than 10 years old has been determined to be competent to testify pursuant to Ohio R. Evid. 601, the child's statements may be admitted at trial as an exception to the hearsay rule under Ohio R. Evid. 803(4) if they were made for purposes of medical diagnosis or treatment. State v. Muttart, 116 Ohio St. 3d 5, 2007 Ohio 5267, 875 N.E.2d 944, 2007 Ohio LEXIS 2535 (2007).

Regardless of whether a child less than ten years old has been determined to be competent to testify pursuant to EvidR 601, the child's statements may be admitted at trial as an exception to the hearsay rule pursuant to EvidR 803(4) if they were made for purposes of medical diagnosis or treatment: State v. Muttart, 116 Ohio St. 3d 5, 2007 Ohio 5267, 875 N.E.2d 944, 2007 Ohio LEXIS 2535 (2007).

Trial court did not abuse its discretion when it allowed a young child under 10 years of age to testify, as he was sufficiently competent under Ohio R. Evid. 601(A) to corroborate incidents that the victim had testified to although he was unable to identify defendant in the courtroom; it was noted, however, that defendant's appearance had changed from when the child had last seen him. State v. West, — Ohio App. 3d —, — N.E. 2d —, 2007 Ohio App. LEXIS 4637 (Sept. 24, 2007).

Because the three-year-old victim's testimony was admissible under Ohio R. Evid. 803(4) for the purpose of medical diagnosis and treatment, it was not a condition precedent that the child be determined competent. Further, the child was competent because she had no difficulty relating the facts to the nurse and social worker, she demonstrated a mature vocabulary, and was able to easily identify body parts in explaining her attack; also, she was not called as a witness so a determination of competency was not required. State v. Goza, — Ohio App. 3d —, 2007 Ohio 6837, — N.E. 2d —, 2007 Ohio App. LEXIS 5982 (Dec. 20, 2007).

Trial court's decision to exclude the seven-year-old witness's testimony, pursuant to Ohio R. Evid. 601(A), was not an abuse of discretion because the child was unable to demonstrate that he could accurately recall events, communicate regarding them, and appreciate the necessity of being truthful. The child could recall his age and where he attended school, but was unable to name his hometown or recall past holidays within an accurate timeframe, and his answers were often contradictory. State v. Andrews, — Ohio App. 3d —, 2006 Ohio 2021, — N.E. 2d —, 2006 Ohio App. LEXIS 1850 (Apr. 24, 2006).

Trial court's finding that a seven-year-old victim-witness was competent to testify pursuant to Evid. R. 601 was proper under circumstances in which, on voir dire, the witness was able to relate the fact that she was held back to repeat the first grade and that she was in her second year in first grade, that it was wrong to tell a lie, and how many times she had talked with the prosecutor. State v. Fitch, — Ohio App. 3d —, 2006 Ohio 5406, — N.E. 2d —, 2006 Ohio App. LEXIS 5401 (Oct. 16, 2006).

Competency of child to be a witness

Trial court's decision to exclude statements by a child victim of defendant's alleged sexual conduct, which were made to a professional clinical counselor, was error where the trial court determined that although the statements might have been within the hearsay exception for medical diagnosis and treatment under Ohio R. Evid. 803(4), it could not deem them admissible because it found that the child victim was not a competent witness under Ohio R. Evid. 601; although a competency requirement existed for admission of the statements under Ohio R. Evid. 807, no such requirement existed for statements under Ohio R. Evid. 803(4) as long as the surrounding circumstances and any other factors were examined to determine that the statements were reliable. State v. Redfearn, — Ohio App. 3d —, 2007 Ohio 4108, — N.E. 2d —, 2007 Ohio App. LEXIS 3736 (Aug. 13, 2007).

Trial court did not abuse its discretion in finding that a child victim of defendant's crimes was a competent witness to testify at his criminal trial, as she was nine years old at the time of the criminal conduct, but she was 11 years old when she testified at his trial; pursuant to Ohio R. Evid. 601(A), she was presumed competent to testify and defendant did not offer proof to the contrary. State v. Johnson, — Ohio App. 3d —, 2006 Ohio 5195, — N.E. 2d —, 2006 Ohio App. LEXIS 5120 (Oct. 2, 2006).

In defendant's appeal from his adjudication as a juvenile for disseminating material harmful to juveniles under RC § 2907.31(A), his assignment of error alleging that the trial court abused its discretion in finding his five-year-old victim competent to testify was overruled; the trial court's lengthy voir dire examination of the victim adequately addressed the necessary factors to find her competent under Ohio R. Evid. 601(A). In re Z.C., — Ohio App. 3d —, 2006 Ohio 5378, — N.E. 2d —, 2006 Ohio App. LEXIS 5334 (Oct. 13, 2006).

Competency of child witness to testify

Trial court's failure to voir dire an eight-year-old child witness in defendant's criminal trial was not plain error under Ohio R. Crim. P. 52(B) where defendant failed to object to the child's testimony, as preliminary questions were asked which indicated that the child could receive just impressions of facts, relate those facts truthfully, and that he understood the importance of telling the truth, such that he was deemed competent under Ohio R. Evid. 601(B); further, there were other eyewitnesses who testified to defendant's actions. State v. Tiller, — Ohio App. 3d —, 2007 Ohio 3943, — N.E. 2d —, 2007 Ohio App. LEXIS 3577 (Aug. 3, 2007).

Although a trial court properly determined that one of the alleged child victims of defendant's sexual offenses was competent to testify under Ohio R. Evid. 601(A), as she knew right from wrong, the truth from a lie, and responded within the parameters of what was considered competent, another child witness did not appear to have that same level of understanding and accordingly, should not have been found competent; however, there was no plain error under Ohio R. Crim. P. 52(B), based on defendant's failure to object to her competency, as her testimony was not particularly helpful to the

State. State v. Conkright, — Ohio App. 3d —, 2007 Ohio 5315, — N.E. 2d —, 2007 Ohio App. LEXIS 4689 (Sept. 28, 2007).

Trial court abused its discretion in failing to conduct a more complete competency hearing, pursuant to Ohio R. Evid. 601(A), of the 12-year-old victim. Evidence in the record was replete with that the victim was in special education classes, that she had and continued to have imaginary friends, that she had at least one past diagnosis of schizophrenia, and that her ability to recollect even routine information such as the day, month, and year was severely limited. In re J.M., — Ohio App. 3d —, 2006 Ohio 1203, — N.E. 2d —, 2006 Ohio App. LEXIS 1088 (Mar. 16, 2006).

When defendant, who pled guilty to three counts of rape, claimed the witnesses against her were not competent to testify, due to their ages, under Ohio R. Evid. 601, at the times of the crimes, thereby compromising defendant's right to confrontation, the issue was waived by defendant's guilty plea, because, under Ohio R. Crim. P. 11(B)(1), that plea was a complete admission of her guilt, so defendant was not entitled to a reversal of her convictions on this basis. State v. Bene, — Ohio App. 3d —, 2006 Ohio 3628, — N.E. 2d —, 2006 Ohio App. LEXIS 3579 (July 17, 2006).

Trial court's failure to hold a competency hearing, pursuant to Ohio R. Evid. 601, did not constitute plain error. At the time of trial, the victim was 15 months shy of 10 years of age and her trial testimony did not suggest that she was incapable of receiving just impressions of facts or relating them truthfully. Additionally, defendant did not cite any of the child's trial testimony that called into question her competency to testify. State v. King, — Ohio App. 3d —, 2006 Ohio 3922, — N.E. 2d —, 2006 Ohio App. LEXIS 3875 (July 18, 2006).

In defendant's appeal from his adjudication as a juvenile for disseminating material harmful to juveniles under RC § 2907.31(A), his claim that when his five-year-old victim testified, she could not recall some events and was improperly coached by the State did not affect her competency under Ohio R. Evid. 601(A), once it had been established; such issues went, instead, to the weight of the evidence. In re Z.C., — Ohio App. 3d —, 2006 Ohio 5378, — N.E. 2d —, 2006 Ohio App. LEXIS 5334 (Oct. 13, 2006).

Trial court conducted an examination of the seven-year-old child to determine if she was able to receive just impressions of the facts and relate them truthfully and found that she clearly answered the questions posed to her during direct and cross-examination. Although defendant questioned the veracity of her testimony, including any inconsistencies, the child was a competent witness. State v. Brown, — Ohio App. 3d —, 2006 Ohio 5769, — N.E. 2d —, 2006 Ohio App. LEXIS 5759 (Nov. 3, 2006).

Competency of mentally challenged witness

Trial court properly found that the mentally challenged victim was competent to testify because a review of her testimony indicated that she was able to perceive, recall, and relate facts truthfully. Although there were clear inconsistencies between the victim's initial statements and her eventual recantation, such inconsistencies went to her credibility, and not to her competency. State v. Pflug, — Ohio App. 3d —, 2007 Ohio 2037, — N.E. 2d —, 2007 Ohio App. LEXIS 1905 (Apr. 27, 2007).

Trial court did not abuse its discretion in determining that the daughter, who was 45 years old but had been diagnosed with Down Syndrome, was incompetent to testify at trial because her answers did not demonstrate that she possessed the ability to accurately observe, recollect, or communicate what was occurring during the competency hearing portion of the trial. More often than not, her replies did not respond to the questions she was asked; rather, the daughter's responses demonstrated that her primary concern was that she be allowed to see her father. State v. Hashman, — Ohio App. 3d —, 2007 Ohio 5603, — N.E. 2d —, 2007 Ohio App. LEXIS 4934 (Oct. 22, 2007).

Competency of testimony

Trial court's admission of a social worker's testimony which contained statements made to her by a child victim of defendant's improper sexual offenses was proper under Ohio R. Evid. 803(4), as an analysis of what the social worker's function was with respect to the child indicated that the statements were made for the purposes of medical diagnosis and treatment; in such an instance, there was no need to first find that the child was competent as a witness under Ohio R. Evid. 601(A) prior to allowing admission of her statements. State v. Edinger, — Ohio App. 3d —, 2006 Ohio 1527, — N.E. 2d —, 2006 Ohio App. LEXIS 1399 (Mar. 30, 2006).

Competency of witness to testify

Trial court did not abuse its discretion in finding the victim competent to testify because, although the victim suffered from cerebral palsy and was diagnosed with having an adjustment disorder not otherwise specified, borderline intellectual functions, and symptoms of attention deficit disorder, her testimony demonstrated her ability to recite the schools that she attended and homes that she lived in. She had an understanding of truth and falsity, and indicated that she understood that an oath meant she had to tell the truth, and that bad things happen to people who don't tell the truth. State v. Hudgins, — Ohio App. 3d —, 2007 Ohio 3361, — N.E. 2d —, 2007 Ohio App. LEXIS 3083 (June 25, 2007).

Defendant did not show the elderly victim from whom she stole funds, who testified against her, was incompetent, rendering her convictions under RC § 2913.02(A)(2) against the manifest weight of the evidence because, under Ohio R. Evid. 601(A), the victim was presumed to be a competent witness, nothing in her trial testimony showed she was of unsound mind, and the weight of her testimony was for the jury to decide. State v. Harris, — Ohio App. 3d —, 2006 Ohio 1396, — N.E. 2d —, 2006 Ohio App. LEXIS 1275 (Mar. 24, 2006).

Trial court was in a position to decide whether there were any concerns regarding the victim's ability to testify as demonstrated by the fact that the trial court refused to allow the victim to testify during the morning session. There was no indication from the victim's testimony that she was experiencing any physical or mental condition that should have called into question her competency to testify. State v. Garrison, — Ohio App. 3d —, 2006 Ohio 6142, — N.E. 2d —, 2006 Ohio App. LEXIS 6096 (Nov. 21, 2006).

Competency to testify

When witnesses against defendant were under the influence of drugs at the time they observed defendant's criminal conduct, this did not render them incompetent to testify, under Ohio R. Evid. 601 and 602, because it only affected the credibility of that testimony, rather than its admissibility, so defendant's convictions of felonious assault, under RC § 2903.11(A)(1), and kidnapping, under RC § 2905.01(A)(2), based, in part, on that testimony, were supported by sufficient evidence. State v. Parker, — Ohio App. 3d —, 2007 Ohio 1512, — N.E. 2d —, 2007 Ohio App. LEXIS 1395 (Mar. 30, 2007).

Expert witness

Trial court did not abuse its discretion when it precluded the administratrix from reading the deposition because it did not include testimony sufficient to establish that the expert was licensed to practice medicine and that he devoted the appropriate amount of his professional time to active clinical practice or teaching, under Ohio R. Evid. 601(D). Further, since the administratrix dismissed the second doctor from the initial proceeding before she deposed the expert, that doctor did not have reasonable notice of the taking of the deposition,

pursuant to Ohio R. Civ. P. 32(A). Simpson v. Kuchipudi, — Ohio App. 3d —, 2006 Ohio 5163, — N.E. 2d —, 2006 Ohio App. LEXIS 5103 (Oct. 2, 2006).

Medical expert

Trial court properly deemed an expert witness for physicians who were sued in a medical malpractice action competent to testify under Ohio R. Evid. 601(D), as the witness was qualified through his active clinical practice at the time that the patient sustained his injury and at the time of the trial; although the witness had cut back on his working hours due to his own health issue, he still maintained an active practice. Nead v. Brown County Gen. Hosp., — Ohio App. 3d —, 2007 Ohio 2443, — N.E. 2d —, 2007 Ohio App. LEXIS 2259 (May 21, 2007).

—— Criminal actions

Fact that a physician's license is suspended does not preclude him from testifying as an expert witness in a criminal trial. EvidR 601(D) does not apply to criminal actions: State v. Snodgrass, 177 Ohio App. 3d 556, 2008 Ohio 4019, 895 N.E.2d 259, 2008 Ohio App. LEXIS 3399 (2008).

Medical malpractice

In a medical malpractice action where trial continuances requested by the defense and the insolvency of a defendant's carrier delay trial for such time as the plaintiff's medical expert no longer devotes one-half of his professional time to the active clinical practice of medicine, and where the medical expert is not a professional witness, a trial court has discretion to permit that witness to testify as an expert at trial: Celmer v. Rodgers, 114 Ohio St. 3d 221, 2007 Ohio 3697, 871 N.E.2d 557, 2007 Ohio LEXIS 1653 (2007).

Trial court did not abuse its discretion in admitting expert testimony of a patient's treating physician in her medical malpractice and negligent infliction of emotional distress action against a doctor and a medical practice, arising from a misdiagnosed pregnancy and subsequent procedure performed on the patient, as the expert was qualified under Ohio R. Evid. 601(D); the expert was board-certified in obstetrics and gynecology and preventative medicine, and his background indicated that he was sufficiently involved in active clinical practice and/or teaching within the meaning of Rule 601(D). Strasel v. Seven Hills Ob-Gyn Assocs., 170 Ohio App. 3d 98, 2007 Ohio 171, 866 N.E.2d 48, 2007 Ohio App. LEXIS 172 (2007).

Mentally challenged witness

There was no error in finding that the wife was competent to testify at her divorce trial, in spite of her Alzheimer's disease, because, although the wife at times struggled to communicate due to her difficulty with the English language, and at times seemed confused, she demonstrated that she was able to communicate and recollect her living apart from her husband due to her fear of him. Banez v. Banez, — Ohio App. 3d —, 2007 Ohio 4584, — N.E. 2d —, 2007 Ohio App. LEXIS 4124 (Sept. 4, 2007).

People of unsound mind

Where an adult witness was not of "unsound mind" within the meaning of EvidR 601(A), the trial court erred in placing the burden of demonstrating competency on the proponent of the witness. The error was, however, harmless beyond a reasonable doubt where the witness' expressive aphasia prevented her from accurately relating her impressions truthfully: State v. Krueger, 176 Ohio App. 3d 95, 2008 Ohio 1566, 890 N.E.2d 332, 2008 Ohio App. LEXIS 1337 (2008).

Based upon the victim's demeanor and her answers, the trial court properly overruled the motion for a mental health examination because a history of mental health problems or a history of drug abuse does not, in and of itself, render the victim incompetent to testify. The victim described herself as bipolar, for which she had been getting mental health treatment and assistance for many years; she described her mental health condition as much improved over the 14 years that she had been getting treatment; and she acknowledged a history of crack cocaine use, but denied current use of the drug. State v. Madison, — Ohio App. 3d —, 2007 Ohio 3547, — N.E. 2d —, 2007 Ohio App. LEXIS 3244 (July 12, 2007).

Plaintiff's treating physician

Plaintiff's treating physician was properly qualified to testify pursuant to EvidR 601(D): Strasel v. Seven Hills Ob-Gyn Assocs., 170 Ohio App. 3d 98, 2007 Ohio 171, 866 N.E.2d 48, 2007 Ohio App. LEXIS 172 (2007).

Police officers

Police officer who observed defendant's car driving erratically was not incompetent to testify under Ohio R. Evid. 601(C) in a hearing on defendant's motion to suppress because, although the officer was not driving a properly marked vehicle at the time of the stop, the officer did not arrest or assist in arresting defendant. Rather, the stop and arrest was conducted by another police officer. State v. Swann, — Ohio App. 3d —, 2007 Ohio 3235, — N.E. 2d —, 2007 Ohio App. LEXIS 2988 (June 27, 2007).

Plain-clothed officer was not incompetent to testimony in defendant's driving under suspension trial under Evid. R. 601(C) because, while the plain-clothed officer verified defendant's driving status, assisted in locating defendant, and initially approached defendant on the porch of a residence, the plain-clothed officer did not stop defendant in his vehicle, and a different patrolman cited defendant. State v. Lumpkin, — Ohio App. 3d —, 2006 Ohio 5353, — N.E. 2d —, 2006 Ohio App. LEXIS 5325 (Oct. 13, 2006).

As Ohio R. Evid. 601(C) only applied to traffic violations punishable as misdemeanors, a trial court's ruling that a police officer was not competent thereunder to testify regarding a driving under suspension charge against defendant did not preclude admission of his testimony with respect to a charge against defendant of carrying a concealed weapon, in violation of RC § 2923.12(A)(2). As there was sufficient evidence to support defendant's conviction of that offense, the trial court properly denied his acquittal motion under Ohio R. Crim. P. 29(C). State v. Busse, — Ohio App. 3d —, 2006 Ohio 7047, — N.E. 2d —, 2006 Ohio App. LEXIS 6971 (Dec. 27, 2006).

Spouses

Defendant was prejudiced by his trial counsel's ineffectiveness in violation of U.S. Const. amend. VI and Ohio Const. art. I, § 10 in failing to properly raise the issue of his alleged wife's competence under Ohio R. Evid. 601(B)(2) to testify against him in his criminal trial, as there was sufficient evidence regarding whether the two were married for defense counsel to have sought the competency determination; although there were many witnesses who testified for the State, the alleged wife was the only eyewitness to the murders of two individuals and without her testimony, it was questionable whether the State could have proven the prior calculation and design necessary to support the death penalty for defendant's aggravated murder conviction, in violation of RC § 2903.01. State v. Brown, 115 Ohio St. 3d 55, 2007 Ohio 4837, 873 N.E.2d 858, 2007 Ohio LEXIS 2405 (2007).

Once it has been determined that a witness is married to the defendant, the trial court must instruct the witness on spousal competency and make a finding on the record that he or she voluntarily chose to testify. Defense counsel provided ineffective assistance where they failed to request a formal decision on whether the witness and the defendant were married, and there was substantial evidence that they were in fact married: State v. Brown, 115 Ohio St. 3d 55, 2007 Ohio 4837, 873 N.E.2d 858, 2007 Ohio LEXIS 2405 (2007).

Trial court properly determined that defendant's wife, who was the victim of his criminal conduct, was a competent witness pursuant to Ohio R. Evid. 601(B) and RC § 2945.42

and that her testimony regarding a kidnapping by defendant was admissible. Defendant could not assert the privilege set forth in § 2945.42 where force was alleged pursuant to RC § 2907.02(A)(2), and where defendant was charged with kidnapping and domestic violence, in violation of RC §§ 2905.01 and 2919.25. State v. Hardy, — Ohio App. 3d —, 2007 Ohio 1159, — N.E. 2d —, 2007 Ohio App. LEXIS 1085 (Mar. 15, 2007).

Trial court did not err by allowing the testimony of defendant's estranged wife during defendant's burglary and theft trial because the testimony clearly fit within the exception in Ohio R. Evid. 601(B)(1) and the Rule did not provide protection to spouses living separate and apart. The wife testified that she moved away from defendant, that defendant did not move with her, and that she did not want to be with him anymore, all demonstrating sufficient evidence that the wife and defendant were living separate and apart at the time the crime was committed. State v. Turner, — Ohio App. 3d —, 2007 Ohio 2776, — N.E. 2d —, 2007 Ohio App. LEXIS 2575 (June 7, 2007).

Defendant failed to raise the issue that his wife was incompetent to testify against him in his trial for operating a vehicle while under the influence of alcohol. Admitting the wife's testimony did not constitute plain error under Ohio R. Evid. 103(D) or Ohio R. Crim. P. 52(B) because the wife's testimony tended to help rather than hurt defendant (the wife claimed that defendant was agitated and suicidal but not drunk) and the evidence against defendant was overwhelming. City of Mason v. Molinari, — Ohio App. 3d —, 2007 Ohio 5395, — N.E. 2d —, 2007 Ohio App. LEXIS 4739 (Oct. 9, 2007).

Because the crime was against defendant's daughter, defendant's wife was unquestionably competent to testify in the case, pursuant to Ohio R. Evid. 601(B). State v. Wilson, — Ohio App. 3d —, 2006 Ohio 2000, — N.E. 2d —, 2006 Ohio App. LEXIS 1860 (Apr. 24, 2006).

RULE 602. Lack of Personal Knowledge

A witness may not testify to a matter unless evidence is introduced sufficient to support a finding that the witness has personal knowledge of the matter. Evidence to prove personal knowledge may, but need not, consist of the witness' own testimony. This rule is subject to the provisions of Rule 703, relating to opinion testimony by expert witnesses.

History: Amended, eff 7-1-07.

NOTES TO DECISIONS

ANALYSIS

Admissibility of witness's testimony
Admissibility of witness' testimony
Personal knowledge
Testimony within personal knowledge

Admissibility of witness's testimony

Admission of the detective's testimony did not violate defendant's constitutional right against self-incrimination because the testimony concerning the missed appointments was admissible to explain the course of investigation; the detective's speculation that defendant had ample time to dispose of a weapon did not implicate defendant's Fifth Amendment right against self-incrimination. Although such testimony was arguably improper under Ohio R. Evid. 602 and 802, its admission in the instant case was harmless error. State v. Jackson, — Ohio App. 3d —, 2007 Ohio 2925, — N.E. 2d —, 2007 Ohio App. LEXIS 2703 (June 14, 2007).

Admissibility of witness' testimony

When witnesses against defendant were under the influence of drugs at the time they observed defendant's criminal conduct, this did not render them incompetent to testify, under Ohio R. Evid. 601 and 602, because it only affected the credibility of that testimony, rather than its admissibility, so defendant's convictions for felonious assault, under RC § 2903.11(A)(1), and kidnapping, under R.C. § 2905.01(A)(2), based, in part, on that testimony, were supported by sufficient evidence. State v. Parker, — Ohio App. 3d —, 2007 Ohio 1512, — N.E. 2d —, 2007 Ohio App. LEXIS 1395 (Mar. 30, 2007).

Personal knowledge

Trial court abused its discretion in ordering a new trial based on newly discovered evidence because the victim's testimony at the hearing did not recant her trial testimony; her testimony was not based on personal knowledge, as required by EvidR 602, but instead was based on "feelings" and "beliefs;" and she had no memory of the years during which the abuse took place. Accordingly, there was no evidence properly before the trial court that would have given the trial court the reasonable belief that the victim's trial testimony was false. State v. Covender, — Ohio App. 3d —, 2008 Ohio 1453, — N.E. 2d —, 2008 Ohio App. LEXIS 1281 (Mar. 31, 2008).

Defendant had the opportunity to cross-examine the witnesses and their credibility could easily have been called into question if defendant could have proved that their testimony was not based on their own personal knowledge. Furthermore, many of the witnesses based their opinions regarding the relationship between the victim and defendant and his codefendant on their personal knowledge; they did not repeat hearsay when they made the statements, but made independent observations based on what they heard. State v. Robinson, — Ohio App. 3d —, 2007 Ohio 3501, — N.E. 2d —, 2007 Ohio App. LEXIS 3224 (July 5, 2007).

Trial court did not abuse its discretion when it excluded testimony from an employee/part-owner of a business in a commercial lease dispute involving the business and the landlords, as the testimony sought to be admitted concerned conversations between another owner of the business and the landlords, however, as the part-owner did not actually hear the statements about which he intended to testify, they did not constitute admissions of a party-opponent under Ohio R. Evid. 801(D)(2); as the part-owner lacked personal knowledge, under Ohio R. Evid. 602 he could not testify thereto and further, such did not constitute hearsay within hearsay under Ohio R. Evid. 805, as each part of the combined statements did not conform to a hearsay rule exception. Yoder v. Hurst, — Ohio App. 3d —, 2007 Ohio 4861, — N.E. 2d —, 2007 Ohio App. LEXIS 4310 (Sept. 20, 2007).

In a prosecution for contributing to the delinquency of a minor, the victims could testify about their ages even though, strictly speaking, they were incapable of having personal knowledge of the facts of their births, because such testimony was subject to the scrutiny and examination of the trial court and such testimony usually had a reliable and satisfactory basis in statements of witnesses, parents, family reputation, or writings in possession of the family and preserved as records of family history. State v. Selmon, — Ohio App. 3d —, 2006 Ohio 65, — N.E. 2d —, 2006 Ohio App. LEXIS 50 (Jan. 9, 2006).

In a workers' compensation case in which a worker claimed he suffered from asbestosis as a result of his employment, the worker could testify, from his personal knowledge, about the presence of asbestos in his working environment because he testified that (1) he worked at a certain plant for most of his career, (2) he became familiar with asbestos and its applicaitons by doing research, (3) he saw professionals come into his plant to remove asbestos, (4) he saw signs in different areas of the plant indicating the presence of asbestos in pipe covering,

(5) he noticed that some pipe covering in the plant was deteriorated, and (6) he worked as a maintenance worker, sweeping up dust, including dust from pipe covering. Miller v. GMC, — Ohio App. 3d —, 2006 Ohio 5733, — N.E. 2d —, 2006 Ohio App. LEXIS 5724 (Nov. 2, 2006).

Testimony within personal knowledge

There was no abuse of discretion in the juvenile court's decision to admit the testimony of the Sheriff's deputy because his testimony was not offered by the State as an expert witness and his testimony was limited to his personal experience and information gathered in the process of investigating prior similar incidents. The deputy was subject to cross-examination regarding his experience. In re P.G., — Ohio App. 3d —, 2007 Ohio 3716, — N.E. 2d —, 2007 Ohio App. LEXIS 3399 (July 23, 2007).

RULE 603.   Oath or Affirmation

Before testifying, every witness shall be required to declare that the witness will testify truthfully, by oath or affirmation administered in a form calculated to awaken the witness' conscience and impress the witness' mind with the duty to do so.

History: Amended, eff 7-1-07.

NOTES TO DECISIONS

ANALYSIS

Oath
Prerequisite to testimony of witness

Oath

In defendant's appeal from his adjudication as a juvenile for disseminating material harmful to juveniles under RC § 2907.31(A), the requirements for administration of an oath under Ohio R. Evid. 603 were met when the trial court asked the five-year-old victim to raise her right hand, promise to tell the truth that day, and state that she would not tell a lie; no specific language was required for the oath specified in Rule 603, and the trial court's procedure adequately conformed to its requirements. In re Z.C., — Ohio App. 3d —, 2006 Ohio 5378, — N.E. 2d —, 2006 Ohio App. LEXIS 5334 (Oct. 13, 2006).

Prerequisite to testimony of witness

When a guardian ad litem testified in a dependency proceeding, the guardian ad litem had to be placed under oath, under Ohio R. Evid. 603, because, while the guardian ad litem was an attorney, the guardian ad litem was not presenting evidence as an attorney but was testifying as a witness. In re Butler, — Ohio App. 3d —, 2006 Ohio 4547, — N.E. 2d —, 2006 Ohio App. LEXIS 4510 (Sept. 5, 2006).

RULE 604.   Interpreters

An interpreter is subject to the provisions of these rules relating to qualification as an expert and the administration of an oath or affirmation to make a true translation.

History: Amended, eff 7-1-07.

NOTES TO DECISIONS

ANALYSIS

Attorney as interpreter
Qualifications
Translation adequate

Attorney as interpreter

Trial court did not abuse its discretion by failing to appoint an independent interpreter because, although defense counsel was not sworn in as an interpreter, pursuant to Ohio R. Evid. 604, counsel, who spoke fluent Spanish, was an officer of the court with all the obligations attendant thereto. Moreover, defendant did not demonstrate that his counsel was not properly qualified to translate or that he lacked veracity and, at no time, did defendant express concern that he was not able to understand counsel's explanations. State v. Mota, — Ohio App. 3d —, 2006 Ohio 3800, — N.E. 2d —, 2006 Ohio App. LEXIS 3779 (July 21, 2006).

Qualifications

Interpreter was not qualified to interpret for a defendant in court proceedings where he often guessed at the appropriate interpretation when he did not understand a word or phrase in English, often used made-up words in Spanish, and failed to abide by the proposed Ohio Canon on accuracy and completeness: City of Columbus v. Lopez-Antonio, 153 Ohio Misc. 2d 4, 2009 Ohio 4892, 914 N.E.2d 464, 2009 Ohio Misc. LEXIS 259 (2009).

Translation adequate

Trial court did not abuse its discretion when it denied defendant's motion for a mistrial because the trial court inquired into the nature of the alleged translation errors, and was informed by one interpreter that the errors were not major; the only concrete examples of errors that could be provided involved the issue of the time that the traffic stop occurred, which the trial court ruled were not sufficiently critical to the case as to constitute prejudice to defendant. Given the examples provided, it could not be concluded that the alleged translation errors were truly errors or, assuming that they were errors, that they were material errors. State v. Negash, — Ohio App. 3d —, 2007 Ohio 165, — N.E. 2d —, 2007 Ohio App. LEXIS 146 (Jan. 18, 2007).

RULE 605. Competency of Judge as Witness

The judge presiding at the trial may not testify in that trial as a witness. No objection need be made in order to preserve the point.

RULE 606. Competency of Juror as Witness

(A) **At the trial.** A member of the jury may not testify as a witness before that jury in the trial of the case in which the juror is sitting. If the juror is called so to testify, the opposing party shall be afforded an opportunity to object out of the presence of the jury.

(B) **Inquiry into validity of verdict or indictment.** Upon an inquiry into the validity of a verdict or indictment, a juror may not testify as to any matter or statement occurring during the course of the jury's deliberations or to the effect of anything upon that or any other juror's mind or emotions as influencing the juror to assent to or dissent from the verdict or indictment or concerning the juror's mental processes in connection therewith. A juror may testify on the question whether extraneous prejudicial information was improperly brought to the jury's attention or whether any outside influence was improperly brought to bear on any juror, only after some outside evidence of that act or event has been presented. However a juror may testify without the presentation of any outside evidence concerning any threat, any bribe, any attempted threat or bribe, or any improprieties of any officer of the court. A juror's affidavit or evidence of any

statement by the juror concerning a matter about which the juror would be precluded from testifying will not be received for these purposes.

History: Amended, eff 7-1-07.

NOTES TO DECISIONS

Analysis

Aliunde rule
Impeachment of verdict
Juror testimony

Aliunde rule

Since three allegations of juror misconduct were allegedly made during jury deliberations and were not brought before the trial court from an outside source, they violated the aliunde evidence rule under Ohio R. Evid. 606(B) and could not be considered in support of a motion for a new trial. Dedmon v. Mack, — Ohio App. 3d —, 2006 Ohio 2113, — N.E. 2d —, 2006 Ohio App. LEXIS 1952 (Apr. 28, 2006).

Defendant's motion for a new trial, alleging that jurors in her murder trial were misled and confused by the jury instructions, was properly denied because defendant had not alleged that any evidence aliunde existed that would impeach the jury's verdict, and thus, the juror statements submitted by defendant could not be considered under Ohio R. Evid. 606(B). State v. Franklin, — Ohio App. 3d —, 2006 Ohio 4569, — N.E. 2d —, 2006 Ohio App. LEXIS 4524 (Sept. 6, 2006).

Impeachment of verdict

Trial court did not err in refusing to hold an evidentiary hearing on the issue of the juror's potential incompetence for the purpose of impeaching the jury's verdict. Because the juror's affidavit, which was the only evidence, indicated that he suffered a nervous breakdown in 1966, and received electric shock treatments in the 1970's, or about 30 years before defendant's trial, there was no indication that the juror had been adjudicated insane or mentally incompetent at a time closely contemporaneous with defendant's trial. State v. Buelow, — Ohio App. 3d —, 2007 Ohio 131, — N.E. 2d —, 2007 Ohio App. LEXIS 122 (Jan. 12, 2007).

Juror testimony

Trial court erred by applying Ohio R. Evid. 606(B) to the juror's comments following the trial and to his testimony at the post-trial hearing. Since the comments and testimony did not concern the jury's deliberative process but, rather, concerned the issue of whether the juror failed to disclose certain information on voir dire, his testimony and comments did not violate Ohio R. Evid. 606(B). Grundy v. Dhillon, — Ohio App. 3d —, 2007 Ohio 2693, — N.E. 2d —, 2007 Ohio App. LEXIS 2495 (June 1, 2007).

Inmate's claim in his petition for post-conviction relief pursuant to RC § 2953.21 that his death sentence was unreliable due to the jury's alleged failure to understand the mitigation phase instructions lacked merit, as it was barred by res judicata where it could have been raised on direct appeal, the jury did not send any questions to the trial court after it retired to determine the penalty, as counsel failed to object to the jury instructions during trial, the matter was reviewable only for plain error, and the aliunde rule under Ohio R. Evid. 606(B) prohibited the use of a juror's testimony regarding the jury deliberations for the purpose of invalidating the jury verdict in a postconviction proceeding. State v. Tenace, — Ohio App. 3d —, 2006 Ohio 1226, — N.E. 2d —, 2006 Ohio App. LEXIS 1102 (Mar. 17, 2006).

RULE 607. Impeachment

(A) Who May Impeach. The credibility of a witness may be attacked by any party except that the credibility of a witness may be attacked by the party calling the witness by means of a prior inconsistent statement only upon a showing of surprise and affirmative damage. This exception does not apply to statements admitted pursuant to Evid. R. 801(D)(1)(a), 801(D)(2), or 803.

(B) Impeachment: reasonable basis. A questioner must have a reasonable basis for asking any question pertaining to impeachment that implies the existence of an impeaching fact.

History: Amended, eff 7-1-98.

NOTES TO DECISIONS

Analysis

Applicability
Attack of credibility of witness
Authority of trial court to call witnesses
Domestic violence
Impeachment
Impeachment of party's own witness
Impeachment of witness
Prior inconsistent statement

Applicability

EvidR 607 did not apply where the state was not impeaching its witness with a prior inconsistent statement, but instead provided the witness with her prior statement to refresh her memory, in accord with EvidR 612: State v. Counts, 170 Ohio App. 3d 339, 2007 Ohio 117, 867 N.E.2d 432, 2007 Ohio App. LEXIS 124 (2007).

Trial court did not err in permitting the State to question a victim of sexual imposition on re-direct examination with evidence of prior consistent statements concerning which she had testified in her direct testimony. The evidence the State introduced on re-direct was not inconsistent with evidence the State elicited from the victim on direct examination and was offered not to impeach her direct evidence testimony but to rehabilitate her credibility after defendant's cross-examination, and thus Ohio R. Evid. 607(A) did not apply. State v. Smith, — Ohio App. 3d —, 2006 Ohio 45, — N.E. 2d —, 2006 Ohio App. LEXIS 44 (Jan. 6, 2006).

Attack of credibility of witness

Trial court did not abuse its discretion in limiting the cross-examination of the victim. Pursuant to Evid. R. 607(B), defendant had no reasonable basis for implying, and produced no corroborating evidence or testimony, that the victim was HIV-positive; the victim, under oath, denied having AIDS. State v. Edwards, — Ohio App. 3d —, 2006 Ohio 5726, — N.E. 2d —, 2006 Ohio App. LEXIS 5723 (Nov. 2, 2006).

Authority of trial court to call witnesses

As the trial court called the victim of defendant's criminal conduct as its own witness pursuant to Ohio R. Evid. 614(A), the State was entitled to cross-examine and impeach her without a showing of surprise pursuant to Ohio R. Evid. 607(A), as Rule 607 was inapplicable where the victim was not the State's witness; she had originally accused defendant of assaulting her, but she was married to him and pregnant with his child, and she thereafter notified the trial court that she was recanting her accusation and that others were responsible for the attack. State v. Beasley, — Ohio App. 3d —, 2007 Ohio 5432, — N.E. 2d —, 2007 Ohio App. LEXIS 4774 (Oct. 11, 2007).

Domestic violence

Admission of the victim's prior, written inconsistent staTement was harmless error where the victim's statements to the officers qualified as excited utterances. The written statement was not admissible under EvidR 607(A) where the state was not surprised by the recantation at trial: State v. Clay, 181 Ohio App. 3d 563, 2009 Ohio 1235, 910 N.E.2d 14, 2009 Ohio App. LEXIS 1061 (2009).

Impeachment

Defendant failed to show that he received ineffective assistance of counsel for failure to object; evidence of defendant's 1983 rape conviction was properly admitted under Ohio R. Evid. 607, 609, and 611(B) because he did not answer truthfully when he was asked whether he had ever demanded oral sex. With regard to his prior conviction for domestic violence, the State was allowed to impeach his testimony that he got along with his wife. State v. Howard, — Ohio App. 3d —, 2007 Ohio 991, — N.E. 2d —, 2007 Ohio App. LEXIS 914 (Mar. 8, 2007).

Prosecution, in a criminal case, could use a defendant's prior inconsistent statement as rebuttal testimony to impeach the defendant's credibility, regardless of whether there was compliance with Miranda in obtaining the prior inconsistent statement, as long as the statement was voluntary. State v. Brown, — Ohio App. 3d —, 2007 Ohio 1132, — N.E. 2d —, 2007 Ohio App. LEXIS 1052 (Mar. 14, 2007).

Impeachment of party's own witness

Under the modern Ohio Rules of Evidence, the "voucher rule" no longer exists, and a party may cross-examine its own witness pursuant to Ohio R. Evid. 607(A). State v. Manzell, — Ohio App. 3d —, 2007 Ohio 4076, — N.E. 2d —, 2007 Ohio App. LEXIS 3672 (Aug. 6, 2007).

Impeachment of witness

There was no prosecutorial misconduct because, when the prosecutor asked the witness if she had been bribed in exchange for her testimony, the prosecutor then introduced the testimony of the witness's former boyfriend who stated that the witness had told him that defendant had paid her for her alibi testimony. Evidence demonstrating the attempted bribery of a witness by defendant was admissible against defendant since such an attempt was an admission of guilt. Also, the prosecutor's remarks regarding the witness's failure to appear for rebuttal to attack her credibility were not enough, on their own, to require a reversal. State v. Robinson, — Ohio App. 3d —, 2007 Ohio 3501, — N.E. 2d —, 2007 Ohio App. LEXIS 3224 (July 5, 2007).

Prior inconsistent statement

Allowing the limited questioning by the State on the victim's prior statements was not plain error because the testimony of the victim, defendant's live-in girlfriend, was disconnected and jumbled at best and clearly evasive to the State. Although she told the police at the scene that defendant had shot her, at trial she claimed not to know who shot her; on cross-examination, she admitted that someone shot her and it was either defendant or another guy. State v. Young, — Ohio App. 3d —, 2007 Ohio 1580, — N.E. 2d —, 2007 Ohio App. LEXIS 1434 (Apr. 2, 2007).

Trial court did not err in allowing the State to impeach a witness with his prior statements where the witness' trial testimony surprised the State by contradicting his grand jury testimony and his statement to police, the prior testimony involved only what the witness observed and did not involve the statements of others, and the trial court gave the jury a limiting instruction directing it to consider the witness's prior statements for impeachment purposes only. State v. Jordan, 167 Ohio App. 3d 157, 2006 Ohio 2759, 854 N.E. 2d 520, 2006 Ohio App. LEXIS 2642 (June 2, 2006).

Defendant failed to show that the trial court considered the prior inconsistent statement of his girlfriend (the grandmother of the three-year-old rape victim) to the police in determining the issues. Rather, even assuming that the testimony may have been improper in a jury trial, defendant failed to rebut the presumption that the trial judge, sitting as trier of fact, understood the applicable rules and did not consider improper evidence. State v. Copley, — Ohio App. 3d —, 2006 Ohio 2737, — N.E. 2d —, 2006 Ohio App. LEXIS 2565 (June 1, 2006).

RULE 608. Evidence of Character and Conduct of Witness

(A) **Opinion and reputation evidence of character.** The credibility of a witness may be attacked or supported by evidence in the form of opinion or reputation, but subject to these limitations: (1) the evidence may refer only to character for truthfulness or untruthfulness, and (2) evidence of truthful character is admissible only after the character of the witness for truthfulness has been attacked by opinion or reputation evidence or otherwise.

(B) **Specific instances of conduct.** Specific instances of the conduct of a witness, for the purpose of attacking or supporting the witness's character for truthfulness, other than conviction of crime as provided in Evid.R. 609, may not be proved by extrinsic evidence. They may, however, in the discretion of the court, if clearly probative of truthfulness or untruthfulness, be inquired into on cross-examination of the witness (1) concerning the witness's character for truthfulness or untruthfulness, or (2) concerning the character for truthfulness or untruthfulness of another witness as to which character the witness being cross-examined has testified.

The giving of testimony by any witness, including an accused, does not operate as a waiver of the witness's privilege against self-incrimination when examined with respect to matters that relate only to the witness's character for truthfulness.

History: Amended, eff 7-1-92.

NOTES TO DECISIONS

Analysis

Allegations of prior false rape allegations by victim
Challenging witness' credibility
Credibility
Cross-examination subjects
Evidence
— Sufficient
Evidence of conduct
Impeachment of witness' credibility
Limitation of cross-examination of victim
Limiting cross-examination of victim
Prior false accusations of rape
Reputation of witness for veracity in the community
Specific instances of conduct
Specific instances of defendant's conduct
Victim's false allegations
Videotape of police interview
Witness' character for truthfulness
Witness' prior arrest

Allegations of prior false rape allegations by victim

Defense counsel had no duty to renew an objection to the trial court's refusal to permit impeachment under Ohio R. Evid. 608(B) because the victim's testimony, read in proper context, did not contradict any earlier assertion of being raped

in Jamaica. Read in context, neither the State's question nor the victim's answer could have been fairly read as pertaining to prior allegations of rape. State v. Pickett, — Ohio App. 3d —, 2007 Ohio 3899, — N.E. 2d —, 2007 Ohio App. LEXIS 3552 (Aug. 2, 2007).

Challenging witness' credibility

In a marijuana trafficking prosecution, a prosecutor did not violate Ohio R. Crim. P. 16(B)(1)(e) by calling, as a rebuttal witness, the supervisor of an undercover agent involved in the case to testify that the agent had not tested positive for drugs, even though the supervisor had not been listed as a possible witness, because (1) the prosecutor could not reasonably anticipate that defendant would contest the agent's claim that, when the agent was interacting with defendant, the agent simulated the smoking of a marijuana cigarette, making testing showing that the agent did not test positive for marijuana relevant, and (2) the supervisor's testimony would not likely have been admissible in the prosecutor's case-in-chief, under Ohio R. Evid. 608(A)(2), because the agent's credibility had not been challenged. State v. Wood, — Ohio App. 3d —, 2006 Ohio 3781, — N.E. 2d —, 2006 Ohio App. LEXIS 3732 (July 24, 2006).

Credibility

Prosecutor's comments about a witness did not offer evidence in the form of opinion or reputation to support the witness's credibility pursuant to Ohio R. Evid. 608, but instead, merely asked the witness whether he had been in trouble before or if he had a criminal record, and why he did not help the victim of defendant's crime since the witness was a "good kid". Such was not an improper line of questioning or comment by the prosecutor that denied defendant's rights to a fair trial and due process under Ohio Const. art. I, § 10, as the questioning and responses went to the witness's role in the incident and as such, it went to his bias and credibility as a witness. State v. Richmond, — Ohio App. 3d —, 2006 Ohio 4518, — N.E. 2d —, 2006 Ohio App. LEXIS 4480 (Sept. 1, 2006).

Cross-examination subjects

In defendant's prosecution for grand theft from defendant's employer, defendant was not improperly barred from inquiring of defendant's supervisor about the supervisor's involvement in a bank robbery because (1) the supervisor was not convicted of bank robbery, so Ohio R. Evid. 609 did not apply, and (2) no probative reason to develop evidence of this charge was shown. State v. Baldwin, — Ohio App. 3d —, 2007 Ohio 3511, — N.E. 2d —, 2007 Ohio App. LEXIS 3211 (July 9, 2007).

Evidence

Defendant's question to a minor sexual imposition victim's mother on direct examination if she had experienced problems in the past with the victim lying to her violated Ohio R. Evid. 608(B) because it sought extrinsic evidence to impeach the victim's credibility. Even if the question were proper, defendant did not make the substance of the evidence known to the trial court, by means of a proffer, after the State's objection was sustained, and the evidence defendant sought was not apparent from the context of his questions; thus, under Ohio R. Evid. 103(A)(2), defendant could not predicate error upon the ruling. State v. Smith, — Ohio App. 3d —, 2006 Ohio 45, — N.E. 2d —, 2006 Ohio App. LEXIS 44 (Jan. 6, 2006).

— Sufficient

Defendant's challenge was not that he was unable to cross-examine the victim, but rather that he was unable to cross-examine the victim's mother concerning the victim's prior allegations. Such evidence was neither proper nor admissible under the law. State v. Pflug, — Ohio App. 3d —, 2007 Ohio 2037, — N.E. 2d —, 2007 Ohio App. LEXIS 1905 (Apr. 27, 2007).

Defendant's contention that the trial court abused its discretion by refusing to permit him to present evidence, under Ohio R. Evid. 608(B), about false allegations of criminal conduct that the victim in defendant's vandalism prosecution had previously made against defendant was without merit because the mere fact that defendant was convicted of only two of the 12 charges the victim made against defendant in the past did not mean that the victim testified falsely about those accusations, and any error in the ruling was harmless because the victim's credibility was not at issue. Further, defendant never proffered what his defense witnesses would testify concerning any prior false accusations allegedly made by the victim against defendant, as required by Ohio R. Evid. 103(A)(2). State v. Mills, — Ohio App. 3d —, 2006 Ohio 4010, — N.E. 2d —, 2006 Ohio App. LEXIS 3939 (Aug. 4, 2006).

Evidence of conduct

Trial court correctly found that the questioning of the attempted rape victim, under Ohio R. Evid. 608(B), regarding whether she had falsely accused all four of her husbands of domestic violence, was not relevant, pursuant to Ohio R. Evid. 401, because defense counsel admitted that he did not know how the victim would answer the question and, given the testimony of the various witnesses, the issue of truthfulness of what defendant actually did to the victim was not unsubstantiated. State v. Lucas, — Ohio App. 3d —, 2006 Ohio 1675, — N.E. 2d —, 2006 Ohio App. LEXIS 1563 (Mar. 29, 2006).

Impeachment of witness' credibility

Trial court did not abuse its discretion in not allowing defendant's counsel to impeach a witness for the State during defendant's criminal trial by questioning him about a possible drug deal on the morning that the victim was murdered, as the witness had already admitted that he had a prior drug conviction and was on probation, and pursuant to Ohio R. Evid. 608(B) and 609, there was no evidence of a drug deal on the record, such that any further questioning by counsel would have included an implication of that fact through the guise of impeachment. State v. Anderson, — Ohio App. 3d —, 2006 Ohio 4618, — N.E. 2d —, 2006 Ohio App. LEXIS 4581 (Sept. 1, 2006).

Limitation of cross-examination of victim

Trial court did not err in limiting the scope of defense counsel's cross-examination of the victim in defendant's criminal trial with respect to charges that were pending against him that allegedly tended to show the victim's bias towards the State, as the victim's character could not be attacked on cross-examination unless it was first offered on direct pursuant to Ohio R. Evid. 608. Ohio R. Evid. 609 only applied to prior convictions, not to charges that were pending. State v. Swann, 171 Ohio App. 3d 304, 2007 Ohio 2010, 870 N.E.2d 754, 2007 Ohio App. LEXIS 1780 (2007).

Limiting cross-examination of victim

In a prosecution for rape, gross sexual imposition, and corruption of a minor, defendant was not improperly barred, under Ohio R. Evid. 608(B), from inquiring into allegations that the victim had committed unrelated criminal acts because this line of questioning would not have assisted the jury in determining the victim's credibility in a case involving allegations of sexual abuse and rape, and the victim's extensive testimony gave the jury ample opportunity to assess the victim's credibility. State v. Frost, — Ohio App. 3d —, 2007 Ohio 3469, — N.E. 2d —, 2007 Ohio App. LEXIS 3193 (July 6, 2007).

Prior false accusations of rape

Trial court misconstrued the rape shield law, under RC § 2907.02(D), and failed to admit probative evidence regard-ing prior false accusations and recantations made by the victim because there was, in fact, no sexual activity between the victim and the stepbrother that she had accused. Thus, the provisions of the rape shield law were not triggered and, instead, the trial court should have considered the provisions of Ohio R. Evid. 608(B) in determining whether to admit the evidence regarding the false statements made about the stepbrother. State v. Ford, — Ohio App. 3d —, 2006 Ohio 2108, — N.E. 2d —, 2006 Ohio App. LEXIS 1948 (Apr. 28, 2006).

Trial court did not abuse its discretion by concluding that defendant's claim of fabrication was too speculative to justify an in camera hearing because defendant failed to demonstrate that the accusations previously made by the victim were totally false and unfounded. The family's failure to prosecute the Jamaican relative was not proof that the alleged sexual abuse did not occur and the fact that the victim had been in counseling since her return to the United States, suggested that she suffered some form of emotional trauma from whatever transpired in Jamaica, thus lending credence to her allegations. State v. Pickett, — Ohio App. 3d —, 2007 Ohio 3899, — N.E. 2d —, 2007 Ohio App. LEXIS 3552 (Aug. 2, 2007).

Reputation of witness for veracity in the community

In view of the witnesses' limited contacts with the community in which the victim lived, the trial court did not abuse its discretion by determining that they would not be permitted to testify about the victim's alleged reputation for being untruthful. The witnesses' contacts with the community were extremely limited, essentially consisting of knowing defendant, members of his family, and two or three other people. State v. Solomon, — Ohio App. 3d —, 2008 Ohio 553, — N.E. 2d —, 2008 Ohio App. LEXIS 473 (Feb. 13, 2008).

Specific instances of conduct

Under Ohio R. Evid. 609(B), evidence of a prior conviction for passing bad checks was admissible because it occurred within the past 10 years and was probative in deciding the factual issues presented in the instant case. The testimony regarding prior civil lawsuits was probative of the manager's truthfulness and therefore, was admissible to establish motive, intent, preparation and plan. Kimble Mixer Co. v. St. Vincent, — Ohio App. 3d —, 2006 Ohio 2258, — N.E. 2d —, 2006 Ohio App. LEXIS 2119 (May 2, 2006).

Since defendant failed to offer any substantial reason to believe that the prior allegations were false, he failed to meet his evidentiary obligation and therefore, failed to demonstrate prejudice from the trial court's refusal to allow him to cross-examine the victim regarding any alleged prior false allegations of sexual abuse, under Ohio R. Evid. 608(B). State v. Jones, — Ohio App. 3d —, 2006 Ohio 2278, — N.E. 2d —, 2006 Ohio App. LEXIS 2129 (May 10, 2006).

Specific instances of defendant's conduct

Under Ohio R. Evid. 608(B), the trial court did not abuse its discretion when it determined that the probative value of the manager's grand theft conviction in 1980 outweighed its prejudicial effect because the conviction was relevant since it was based upon a set of facts almost identical to those presented in the instant case. The conviction was introduced to establish that the manager was not making a mistake when he engaged in conduct contrary to the management services agreement he entered into with the manager (since in both cases he claimed that his actions were the result of misreading the contract) and the evidence established that the manager had knowledge of the various effective means to embezzle funds since he had used similar methods during his employment with a previous company. Kimble Mixer Co. v. St. Vincent, — Ohio App. 3d —, 2006 Ohio 2258, — N.E. 2d —, 2006 Ohio App. LEXIS 2119 (May 2, 2006).

Prosecutor's inquiry into defendant's misdemeanor convictions was not improper, under Ohio R. Evid. 609, because defendant put defendant's character in issue by saying defendant pled guilty to crimes defendant committed, and the State elicited defendant's testimony on misdemeanor convictions not to impeach defendant's credibility by showing the convictions but to show defendant was not truthful, under Ohio R. Evid. 608. Ohio v. Mitchell, — Ohio App. 3d —, 2007 Ohio 5519, — N.E. 2d —, 2007 Ohio App. LEXIS 4852 (Oct. 9, 2007).

Victim's false allegations

Under Ohio R. Evid. 608(B) and RC § 2907.02(D), it was an abuse of discretion for a trial court to deny defendant's motion to ask an alleged rape victim if she had made prior false allegations of rape because the State "opened the door" to such inquiry when it introduced evidence that the victim had previously been sexually abused by two other men, because, once this evidence was introduced, the defense had to be allowed to ask the threshold question of whether the victim had made prior false allegations, and the victim's credibility was a key aspect of the case. State v. Chaney, — Ohio App. 3d —, 2006 Ohio 5288, — N.E. 2d —, 2006 Ohio App. LEXIS 5273 (Oct. 10, 2006).

Videotape of police interview

Defendant's videotaped police interviews were admissible. The interviewing officer's statements did not constitute hearsay or statements of opinion where they were not made to prove the truth of the matter asserted or to assert the officer's beliefs, but were merely interrogation techniques and were included to provide context for the defendant's statements: State v. Craycraft, 147 Ohio Misc. 2d 5, 2008 Ohio 2192, 889 N.E.2d 1100, 2008 Ohio Misc. LEXIS 130 (2008).

Witness' character for truthfulness

Although a trial court erred in refusing to admit a juvenile's testimony as to a victim's reputation for truthfulness pursuant to Ohio R. Evid. 608(A) in the juvenile's delinquency proceeding, as he failed to proffer what his testimony would have been and he did not provide the basis for his opinion concerning the victim's reputation for truthfulness other than a conclusory statement, the issue could not be raised as error on appeal pursuant to Ohio R. Evid. 103(A). There was no ability to determine from the record whether the juvenile was prejudiced by the exclusion of the evidence. In re Shane L. F., — Ohio App. 3d —, 2006 Ohio 3876, — N.E. 2d —, 2006 Ohio App. LEXIS 3825 (July 28, 2006).

Witness' prior arrest

Trial court did not err in refusing to allow defendant's counsel to impeach a witness based on the witness' arrest record because the witness' prior arrest did not lead to a conviction and was not an arrest for a crime involving dishonesty. As a result, Ohio R. Evid. 608 and 609 barred defendant from eliciting testimony on the prior arrest. State v. McLeod, — Ohio App. 3d —, 2006 Ohio 7076, — N.E. 2d —, 2006 Ohio App. LEXIS 7004 (Dec. 19, 2006).

RULE 609. Impeachment by Evidence of Conviction of Crime

(A) **General rule.** For the purpose of attacking the credibility of a witness:

(1) Subject to Evid. R. 403, evidence that a witness other than the accused has been convicted of a crime is admissible if the crime was punishable by death or imprisonment in excess of one year pursuant to the law under which the witness was convicted.

(2) Notwithstanding Evid. R. 403(A), but subject to Evid. R. 403(B), evidence that the accused has been convicted of a crime is admissible if the crime was punishable by death or imprisonment in excess of one year pursuant to the law under which the accused was convicted and if the court determines that the probative value of the evidence outweighs the danger of unfair prejudice, of confusion of the issues, or of misleading the jury.

(3) Notwithstanding Evid. R. 403(A), but subject to Evid. R. 403(B), evidence that any witness, including an accused, has been convicted of a crime is admissible if the crime involved dishonesty or false statement, regardless of the punishment and whether based upon state or federal statute or local ordinance.

(B) **Time limit.** Evidence of a conviction under this rule is not admissible if a period of more than ten years has elapsed since the date of the conviction or of the release of the witness from the confinement, or the termination of community control sanctions, post-release control, or probation, shock probation, parole, or shock parole imposed for that conviction, whichever is the later date, unless the court determines, in the interests of justice, that the probative value of the conviction supported by specific facts and circumstances substantially outweighs its prejudicial effect. However, evidence of a conviction more than ten years old as calculated herein, is not admissible unless the proponent gives to the adverse party sufficient advance written notice of intent to use such evidence to provide the adverse party with a fair opportunity to contest the use of such evidence.

(C) **Effect of pardon, annulment, expungement, or certificate of rehabilitation.** Evidence of a conviction is not admissible under this rule if (1) the conviction has been the subject of a pardon, annulment, expungement, certificate of rehabilitation, or other equivalent procedure based on a finding of the rehabilitation of the person convicted, and that person has not been convicted of a subsequent crime which was punishable by death or imprisonment in excess of one year, or (2) the conviction has been the subject of a pardon, annulment, expungement, or other equivalent procedure based on a finding of innocence.

(D) **Juvenile adjudication.** Evidence of juvenile adjudications is not admissible except as provided by statute enacted by the General Assembly.

(E) **Pendency of appeal.** The pendency of an appeal therefrom does not render evidence of a conviction inadmissible. Evidence of the pendency of an appeal is admissible.

(F) **Methods of proof.** When evidence of a witness's conviction of a crime is admissible under this rule, the fact of the conviction may be proved only by the testimony of the witness on direct or cross-examination, or by public record shown to the witness during his or her examination. If the witness denies that he or she is the person to whom the public record refers, the court may permit the introduction of additional evidence tending to establish that the witness is or is not the person to whom the public record refers.

History: Amended, eff 7-1-91; 7-1-03.

NOTES TO DECISIONS

ANALYSIS

Admissibility of evidence of prior conviction

Admissibility of evidence of prior conviction

Trial court abused its discretion when it allowed the State to cross-examine defendant at length about his prior convictions for the purpose of impeaching him under Ohio R. Evid. 609, as the questioning far exceeded the scope of permissible impeachment. The State not only asked general questions regarding the existence of the prior convictions, but it questioned defendant about the details of those convictions, which created a high danger of unfair prejudice and confusion of the issues under Ohio R. Evid. 403, as the questioning was an attempt by the State to show that defendant had acted in conformity with his prior bad acts. State v. Feathers, — Ohio App. 3d —, 2007 Ohio 3024, — N.E. 2d —, 2007 Ohio App. LEXIS 2778 (June 15, 2007).

Admissibility of juvenile adjudications

There was no error in the admission of a juvenile's guilty plea and juvenile adjudication for complicity to trafficking in crack cocaine in defendant's criminal trial on a charge of, inter alia, corruption of a juvenile with drugs in violation of RC § 2925.02(A)(4)(c), as the conviction was not used to impeach the juvenile pursuant to Ohio R. Evid. 609(D) and RC § 2151.358(H), but rather, as substantive evidence of defendant's corruption of the minor by his involvement in the drug conduct. There was no violation of Ohio R. Evid. 803(22) where the juvenile had already admitted in his live testimony that he pled guilty to complicity to drug trafficking and then he tried to recant his statement. State v. Simmons, — Ohio App. 3d —, 2007 Ohio 1570, — N.E. 2d —, 2007 Ohio App. LEXIS 1442 (Mar. 28, 2007).

During his trial on charges of murder and aggravated murder, the trial court properly prevented defendant from confronting certain wtinesses regarding their prior juvenile adjudications because prior adjudications could not be used to impeach the credibility of a juvenile under Ohio R. Evid. 609(D) and RC § 2151.358(H); defendant did not present a plausible showing of any purpose other than to impeach the testimony of the witnesses. State v. Higgins, — Ohio App. 3d —, 2006 Ohio 5220, — N.E. 2d —, 2006 Ohio App. LEXIS 5197 (Sept. 29, 2006).

Admission of evidence of prior conviction

Trial counsel's decision to question defendant about his prior convictions was not ineffective assistance in violation of U.S. Const. amend. VI and Ohio Const. art. I, § 10, as it was a reasonable tactical decision that was intended to lessen the impact of the prior convictions on the jury, as defendant had chosen to take the witness stand and accordingly, his prior convictions were admissible under Ohio R. Evid. 609(A). State v. Ryan, — Ohio App. 3d —, 2006 Ohio 5120, — N.E. 2d —, 2006 Ohio App. LEXIS 5039 (Sept. 29, 2006).

Applicability

Trial court did not err in refusing to allow the use of a felony conviction to impeach the confidential informant because she did not testify during the trial and was not a sworn witness. Because she was not a witness, Ohio R. Evid. 609 did not apply. State v. Baker, — Ohio App. 3d —, 2007 Ohio 739, — N.E. 2d —, 2007 Ohio App. LEXIS 662 (Feb. 20, 2007).

Character trait testimony

EvidR 609 allows the state to impeach a defendant'scredibility with evidence of prior felony convictions. However, by asking the defendant whether he was a murderer and a robber, the prosecutor attempted to establish the defendant's bad character in general instead of attacking his credibility for truth and veracity as EvidR 609 intends: State v. Franklin, 178 Ohio App. 3d 460, 2008 Ohio 4811, 898 N.E.2d 990, 2008 Ohio App. LEXIS 4046 (2008).

Crime of dishonesty

Attempt to raise a patient's prior conviction for theft by deception during cross-examination of her in her medical negligence suit was improperly excluded as unfairly prejudicial since, pursuant to Ohio R. Evid. 609(A)(3), evidence involving a prior conviction for a crime of dishonesty was automatically admissible, regardless of the punishment and without consideration of unfair prejudice under Ohio R. Evid. 403. Since credibility was a main issue in determining whether the medical assistant breached the standard of care, the trial court's erroneous exclusion of the evidence of the patient's prior criminal conviction resulted in material prejudice to the assistant, the urgent care facility, and the doctor against whom the suit was brought. Schmidt v. B.E.S. of Ohio, L.L.C., — Ohio App. 3d —, 2007 Ohio 1822, — N.E. 2d —, 2007 Ohio App. LEXIS 1661 (Apr. 18, 2007).

During defendant's trial for receiving stolen property under RC § 2913.51, evidence of his prior convictions and sentences for burglary, receiving stolen property, and attempted robbery was properly admitted under Ohio R. Evid. 609(A)(3) because the convictions constituted crimes of dishonesty and were relevant and material to the issues of credibility presented at trial; the dates of the prior convictions and sentences did not trigger Ohio R. Evid. 609(B). State v. Ewing, — Ohio App. 3d —, 2006 Ohio 5523, — N.E. 2d —, 2006 Ohio App. LEXIS 5503 (Oct. 24, 2006).

Evidence of prior convictions

Defendant failed to show that he received ineffective assistance of counsel for failure to object; evidence of defendant's 1983 rape conviction was properly admitted under Ohio R. Evid. 607, 609, and 611(B) because he did not answer truthfully when he was asked whether he had ever demanded oral sex. With regard to his prior conviction for domestic violence, the State was allowed to impeach his testimony that he got along with his wife. State v. Howard, — Ohio App. 3d —, 2007 Ohio 991, — N.E. 2d —, 2007 Ohio App. LEXIS 914 (Mar. 8, 2007).

Defendant failed to establish that he received ineffective assistance of counsel for counsel having violated Ohio R. Evid. 609 by bringing up defendant's prior convictions, because it was logical to conclude that it was a strategic decision on the part of trial counsel to avoid what likely would have been a more devastating blow to defendant's credibility had his convictions been brought up first by the State on cross-examination. While the menacing conviction may not have been admissible, defendant had other convictions, both misdemeanors and felonies, that were likely admissible, but were not mentioned at all during trial. State v. Markin, — Ohio App. 3d —, 2006 Ohio 1534, — N.E. 2d —, 2006 Ohio App. LEXIS 1397 (Mar. 30, 2006).

Impeachment

Trial court did not abuse its discretion in not allowing defendant's counsel to impeach a witness for the State during defendant's criminal trial by questioning him about a possible drug deal on the morning that the victim was murdered, as the witness had already admitted that he had a prior drug conviction and was on probation, and pursuant to Ohio R. Evid. 608(B) and 609, there was no evidence of a drug deal on the record, such that any further questioning by counsel would have included an implication of that fact through the guise of impeachment. State v. Anderson, — Ohio App. 3d —, 2006 Ohio 4618, — N.E. 2d —, 2006 Ohio App. LEXIS 4581 (Sept. 1, 2006).

Impeachment of witness' credibility

Evidence of a defense witness' nine-year-old conviction for child endangering was admissible to impeach her, under Ohio R. Evid. 609(A)(1), because her credibility was questioned when she said defendant was with her at the time of the crime, and the conviction was admissible under Ohio R. Evid. 403 because its prejudicial impact did not outweigh its probative value. State v. Williams, — Ohio App. 3d —, 2007 Ohio 212, — N.E. 2d —, 2007 Ohio App. LEXIS 211 (Jan. 19, 2007).

Trial court did not err in refusing to allow defendant's counsel to impeach a witness based on the witness' arrest record because the witness' prior arrest did not lead to a conviction and was not an arrest for a crime involving dishonesty. As a result, Ohio R. Evid. 608 and 609 barred defendant from eliciting testimony on the prior arrest. State v. McLeod, — Ohio App. 3d —, 2006 Ohio 7076, — N.E. 2d —, 2006 Ohio App. LEXIS 7004 (Dec. 19, 2006).

Limitation on questioning

Trial court did not err in limiting defense counsel's cross-examination regarding the charges against the informant because the trial court permitted defense counsel to cross-examine the informant about the fact that 16 of the 18 counts against him were dismissed in exchange for his arranging the controlled buy, and that most of the counts were second-degree felonies for drug trafficking. There was no need for the jurors to hear the specifics of each count as the informant was never convicted of the dismissed charges. State v. Oko, — Ohio App. 3d —, 2007 Ohio 538, — N.E. 2d —, 2007 Ohio App. LEXIS 490 (Feb. 8, 2007).

Limits on cross-examination

In defendant's prosecution for grand theft from defendant's employer, defendant was not improperly barred from inquiring of defendant's supervisor about the supervisor's involvement in a bank robbery because (1) the supervisor was not convicted of bank robbery, so Ohio R. Evid. 609 did not apply, and (2) no probative reason to develop evidence of this charge was shown. State v. Baldwin, — Ohio App. 3d —, 2007 Ohio 3511, — N.E. 2d —, 2007 Ohio App. LEXIS 3211 (July 9, 2007).

Trial court did not err when it limited the scope of defendant's cross-examination of the eyewitness to the murder regarding a fraud conspiracy in which he was involved because the information that defense counsel was seeking was far beyond the name of the crime, the time and place of conviction, and the punishment imposed. Furthermore, there was no indication in the record that the facts of that possible prior conviction bore any relevance to defendant's credibility in the instant case. State v. Carter, — Ohio App. 3d —, 2007 Ohio 3502, — N.E. 2d —, 2007 Ohio App. LEXIS 3223 (June 29, 2007).

Trial court did not err when it limited the scope of defendant's cross-examination of the eyewitness to the murder regarding a fraud conspiracy in which he was involved because the information that defense counsel was seeking was far beyond the name of the crime, the time and place of conviction, and the punishment imposed. Furthermore, there was no indication in the record that the facts of that possible prior conviction bore any relevance to defendant's credibility

in the instant case. State v. Robinson, — Ohio App. 3d —, 2007 Ohio 3501, — N.E. 2d —, 2007 Ohio App. LEXIS 3224 (July 5, 2007).

Pending charges

Trial court did not err in limiting the scope of defense counsel's cross-examination of the victim in defendant's criminal trial with respect to charges that were pending against him that allegedly tended to show the victim's bias towards the State, as the victim's character could not be attacked on cross-examination unless it was first offered on direct pursuant to Ohio R. Evid. 608. Ohio R. Evid. 609 only applied to prior convictions, not to charges that were pending. State v. Swann, 171 Ohio App. 3d 304, 2007 Ohio 2010, 870 N.E.2d 754, 2007 Ohio App. LEXIS 1780 (2007).

Prior acts

Erroneous admission of prior acts evidence pursuant to Ohio R. Evid. 404(B) and RC § 2945.59 with respect to defendant's prior convictions of weapons offenses in the same area that he was on trial for having shot a victim to death was harmless error under Ohio R. Crim. P. 52, as there was abundant evidence to support defendant's conviction, defendant testified about the prior conviction at trial pursuant to Ohio R. Evid. 609, and the impact of the erroneously admitted evidence was minimal and did not result in an outcome that would have been different had such evidence not been introduced; the fact that defendant had a gun in the prior offenses and in the offenses for which he was on trial did not establish a unique pattern or a behavioral fingerprint in order to show defendant's identity, as the prior weapons offenses were not ones of violence, the same gun was not used, and they were remote in time. Ohio v. King, — Ohio App. 3d —, 2007 Ohio 4879, — N.E. 2d —, 2007 Ohio App. LEXIS 4348 (Sept. 21, 2007).

Prior conviction

Defendant's counsel was not ineffective in violation of U.S. Const. amend. VI and Ohio Const. art. I, § 10 in failing to object to the State's use of a 20-year old conviction for purposes of impeaching a defense witness, as whether that conviction was properly used or not under Ohio R. Evid. 609(B) was not determinative where the trial court had determined that the witness was not credible for other reasons. There was no reasonable probability that the outcome of the trial would have been different if that impeachment evidence was not admitted. State v. Adams, — Ohio App. 3d —, 2007 Ohio 3918, — N.E. 2d —, 2007 Ohio App. LEXIS 3560 (Aug. 2, 2007).

Prior convictions

Trial court did not abuse its discretion in allowing the State to use defendant's prior theft convictions to impeach his credibility because defendant's testimony on direct examination and cross-examination opened the door to further questioning about his prior theft convictions. Under the circumstances presented, it was appropriate for the State to impeach defendant and to test his credibility by introducing testimony regarding his prior convictions. State v. Roberson, — Ohio App. 3d —, 2007 Ohio 1981, — N.E. 2d —, 2007 Ohio App. LEXIS 1829 (Apr. 26, 2007).

Trial court did not err in overruling defense counsel's request to cross-examine an eyewitness by introduction of documents concerning the witness's felony conviction, pursuant to Ohio R. Evid. 609(A)(1) and (F), as counsel did not intend to introduce the conviction for purposes of impeaching the witness's credibility; rather, counsel's motive in attempting to introduce evidence of the conviction was to impeach her memory by showing that if she did not remember significant dates, she could not recall properly the incidents of the crime. State v. Love, — Ohio App. 3d —, 2006 Ohio 1762, — N.E. 2d —, 2006 Ohio App. LEXIS 1619 (Mar. 27, 2006).

Trial court's decision to permit the prosecutor to exploit defendant's prior felonious assault conviction to impeach his credibility was an abuse of discretion because the prosecutor's line of questioning was clearly designed to highlight the fact that the prior conviction was for the same crime as charged in the instant case. In a case that turned on whether the jury believed the defendant or the complaining witness, it was error to allow the prosecutor to elicit extensive details about defendant's prior conviction for the same offense. State v. Durham, — Ohio App. 3d —, 2006 Ohio 5015, — N.E. 2d —, 2006 Ohio App. LEXIS 4952 (Sept. 28, 2006).

In a prosecution for forgery, Medicaid fraud, and theft, it was not error, under Ohio R. Evid. 609(B), for a trial court to bar defense counsel from impeaching a prosecution witness with criminal convictions over ten years old because counsel was able to impeach the witness with evidence of a more recent conviction and the older convictions were not factually tied to the present case and would have had little additional probative effect to overcome their prejudicial nature, and counsel was allowed to extensively cross-examine the witness and admit numerous documents and elicit testimony about her purported bad character. State v. Breckenridge, — Ohio App. 3d —, 2006 Ohio 5038, — N.E. 2d —, 2006 Ohio App. LEXIS 5175 (Sept. 28, 2006).

Court rejected defendant's contention that the trial court erred in admitting evidence of his prior conviction for second degree murder into evidence. Since defendant presented the evidence himself, he invited the error and, thus, could not take advantage of the error that he induced the trial court to make. State v. Ransom, — Ohio App. 3d —, 2006 Ohio 6490, — N.E. 2d —, 2006 Ohio App. LEXIS 6422 (Dec. 11, 2006).

Under Ohio R. Evid. 609(B), evidence of a prior conviction for passing bad checks was admissible because it occurred within the past 10 years and was probative in deciding the factual issues presented in the instant case. The testimony regarding prior civil lawsuits was probative of the manager's truthfulness and therefore, was admissible to establish motive, intent, preparation and plan. Kimble Mixer Co. v. St. Vincent, — Ohio App. 3d —, 2006 Ohio 2258, — N.E. 2d —, 2006 Ohio App. LEXIS 2119 (May 2, 2006).

Under Ohio R. Evid. 608(B), the trial court did not abuse its discretion when it determined that the probative value of the manager's grand theft conviction in 1980 outweighed its prejudicial effect because the conviction was relevant since it was based upon a set of facts almost identical to those presented in the instant case. The conviction was introduced to establish that the manager was not making a mistake when he engaged in conduct contrary to the management services agreement he entered into with the manager (since in both cases he claimed that his actions were the result of misreading the contract) and the evidence established that the manager had knowledge of the various effective means to embezzle funds since he had used similar methods during his employment with a previous company. Kimble Mixer Co. v. St. Vincent, — Ohio App. 3d —, 2006 Ohio 2258, — N.E. 2d —, 2006 Ohio App. LEXIS 2119 (May 2, 2006).

Prior misdemeanors

Prosecutor's inquiry into defendant's misdemeanor convictions was not improper, under Ohio R. Evid. 609, because defendant put defendant's character in issue by saying defendant pled guilty to crimes defendant committed, and the State elicited defendant's testimony on misdemeanor convictions not to impeach defendant's credibility by showing the convictions but to show defendant was not truthful, under Ohio R. Evid. 608. Ohio v. Mitchell, — Ohio App. 3d —, 2007 Ohio 5519, — N.E. 2d —, 2007 Ohio App. LEXIS 4852 (Oct. 9, 2007).

Testimony as to convictions

Trial court did not abuse its discretion in determining that the probative value of defendant's prior convictions substan-tially outweighed the prejudicial effect of such convictions because, even though the convictions had occurred 10 years and four months earlier, the convictions were relevant in assessing defendant's credibility during his testimony. Defendant acknowledged his convictions, but then claimed that the victims were lying. State v. Clark, — Ohio App. 3d —, 2006 Ohio 1155, — N.E. 2d —, 2006 Ohio App. LEXIS 1059 (Mar. 8, 2006).

Testimony as to prior convictions

It was proper to allow more extensive questioning regarding defendant's prior convictions, once defendant had incorrectly testified that he only had two past felony convictions; indeed, the receiving stolen property crime was the type of crime of dishonesty under Ohio R. Evid. 609(A)(3) which gets to the heart of a witness's credibility. The prosecutor did not improperly testify about the receiving stolen property conviction and defendant could not complain about the use of the judgment entry when his incorrect testimony necessitated the use of the entry. State v. Owings, — Ohio App. 3d —, 2006 Ohio 4281, — N.E. 2d —, 2006 Ohio App. LEXIS 4278 (Aug. 18, 2006).

RULE 610. Religious Beliefs or Opinions

Evidence of the beliefs or opinions of a witness on matters of religion is not admissible for the purpose of showing that by reason of their nature the witness' credibility is impaired or enhanced.

History: Amended, eff 7-1-07.

NOTES TO DECISIONS

ANALYSIS

Use of religious affirmations to show bias

Use of religious affirmations to show bias

Trial court properly allowed the State to question a victim about her religious beliefs pursuant to Ohio R. Evid. 610, as it was not used for the purpose of proving her credibility, but rather, to show her bias towards defendant; the victim had originally indicated that defendant assaulted her but later stated that she falsely accused him and that others were responsible for the assault on her. State v. Beasley, — Ohio App. 3d —, 2007 Ohio 5432, — N.E. 2d —, 2007 Ohio App. LEXIS 4774 (Oct. 11, 2007).

RULE 611. Mode and Order of Interrogation and Presentation

(A) **Control by court.** The court shall exercise reasonable control over the mode and order of interrogating witnesses and presenting evidence so as to (1) make the interrogation and presentation effective for the ascertainment of the truth, (2) avoid needless consumption of time, and (3) protect witnesses from harassment or undue embarrassment.

(B) **Scope of cross-examination.** Cross-examination shall be permitted on all relevant matters and matters affecting credibility.

(C) **Leading questions.** Leading questions should not be used on the direct examination of a witness except as may be necessary to develop the witness' testimony. Ordinarily leading questions should be permitted on cross-examination. When a party calls a hostile witness, an adverse party, or a witness identified with an adverse party, interrogation may be by leading questions.

History: Amended, eff 7-1-07.

NOTES TO DECISIONS

ANALYSIS

Abuse of discretion
Autopsy photos
Bias
Court authority
Cross examination
— Scope
Cross-examination
Cross-examination of defendant
Discretion
Discretion of court
Juror questions
Leading questions
Limitation of cross-examination of victim
Limitation on cross-examination
Prejudice
Presentation of evidence
Rebuttal
Reopening examination of victim
Restriction of cross-examination
Restriction of cross-examination of witness
Scope of cross-examination
Scope of interrogation
Showing bias on part of expert witness
Time limitations
Witnesses

Abuse of discretion

Trial court abused its discretion when it prevented the wife from eliciting testimony about incidents of domestic violence by the husband because it was relevant to the allocation of parental rights and responsibilities regarding the children. The fact that the domestic violence was previously litigated within the confines of the case was of no moment; the hearing was not had before the judge who presided over the trial, and the wife had the right to present the evidence in the context of its effect upon the children. Barry v. Barry, — Ohio App. 3d —, 2006 Ohio 5008, — N.E. 2d —, 2006 Ohio App. LEXIS 4961 (Sept. 28, 2006).

Autopsy photos

Trial court abused its discretion where it admitted photographs of a victim's deceased body that not only showed the effects of defendant's attack on her, which aspect of the photographs was admittedly probative, but it also showed the reflection of her scalp that was performed during her autopsy, which aspect was gruesome and prejudicial. Although the prejudicial aspect of the photographs outweighed the probative value pursuant to Ohio R. Evid. 403(A) and 611(A), there was no plain error under Ohio R. Crim. P. 52 by the admission thereof, as the results of the trial would not have been different without the admission of the photographs. State v. Warner, — Ohio App. 3d —, 2007 Ohio 3016, — N.E. 2d —, 2007 Ohio App. LEXIS 2770 (June 15, 2007).

Bias

Defendant was not prejudiced by any alleged bias by the trial judge toward the State because all of the statements of which defendant complained occurred outside the hearing of the jury. Moreover, since the remarks were no more than the ordinary remarks of a trial judge attempting to expedite proceedings and protect the record, there was no impropriety. State v. Siddell, — Ohio App. 3d —, 2007 Ohio 1875, — N.E. 2d —, 2007 Ohio App. LEXIS 1711 (Apr. 20, 2007).

Court authority

When a teacher claiming racial discrimination did not list a witness on his witness list, it was not error for the trial court to bar the witness's testimony in the teacher's case in chief, and to require the teacher to call the witness on rebuttal, because, under Ohio R. Evid. 611(A), the trial court had discretion to control the mode and order of witness interrogation. Farris v. Port Clinton City Sch. Dist., — Ohio App. 3d —, 2006 Ohio 1864, — N.E. 2d —, 2006 Ohio App. LEXIS 1701 (Apr. 14, 2006).

Cross examination

Trial court properly overruled a motorist's new trial motion pursuant to Ohio R. Civ. P. 59 after the jury returned a verdict in favor of a driver in the motorist's personal injury action that arose from a motor vehicle accident that was admittedly caused by the driver, as the issue of proximate cause regarding the motorist's spinal injuries was decided against him based on the fact that he had experienced prior back injuries, had undergone back surgery, and had filed social security and workers' compensation claims for those injuries. The admission of the workers' compensation claim information was proper, as it was directly relevant to the issue at trial pursuant to Ohio R. Evid. 402 and 403(A), the motorist actually raised it first in depositions and at trial such that although he had moved to exclude it by a motion in limine, he waived that evidentiary issue where he did not wait and then object to such evidence at trial, and accordingly he could not fault the trial court for allowing the driver's counsel to cross-examine on that issue pursuant to the allowable scope under Ohio R. Evid. 611(B). Sims v. Dibler, 172 Ohio App. 3d 486, 2007 Ohio 3035, 875 N.E.2d 965, 2007 Ohio App. LEXIS 2879 (2007).

Trial court did not abuse its discretion in limiting the scope of the cross-examination of the victim by sustaining the two objections, one based on hearsay and one based on relevance. Counsel's cross-examination, when viewed in its entirety, was lengthy and thorough. State v. Burks, — Ohio App. 3d —, 2007 Ohio 3562, — N.E. 2d —, 2007 Ohio App. LEXIS 3270 (July 13, 2007).

Deposition testimony of the victim, preserved pursuant to Crim. R. 15, satisfied the requirements of the confrontation clause of the Sixth Amendment because the victim was unavailable at trial (he had died from Lou Gehrig's disease), and because defendant had an opportunity, and in fact, did cross-examine the victim during the deposition. The victim was capable of giving basic affirmative or negative responses to leading questions at his deposition and there was no mention that the victim was confused, was too tired to answer counsel's questions, or was unwilling to continue with the cross-examination for any reason. State v. Irwin, — Ohio App. 3d —, 2007 Ohio 4996, — N.E. 2d —, 2007 Ohio App. LEXIS 4391 (Sept. 19, 2007).

— Scope

Record did not support defendant's assertion that the trial court refused to permit the defense any cross-examination of the arresting officer because the transcript revealed that defense counsel cross-examined the officer at length. The prosecutor objected to the relevancy of questions defense counsel asked the officer on cross-examination, relating to compliance with the NHTSA standards and the trial court sustained the objection, indicating that the admissibility issue was already determined in the motion to suppress hearing; the trial court's limitation of cross-examination in this respect was not an abuse of discretion. State v. Albanese, — Ohio App. 3d —, 2006 Ohio 4819, — N.E. 2d —, 2006 Ohio App. LEXIS 4724 (Sept. 15, 2006).

There was no abuse of discretion by the trial court's decisions regarding the scope of cross-examination of a medical expert in a medical malpractice action, as the use of his testimony from a prior case in Michigan was used to impeach his credibility and therefore was permissible under Ohio R. Evid. 611(B). Although the trial court should not have admitted into evidence certain transcripts from the Michigan litigation, pursuant to Ohio R. Evid. 616(C), such error did not cause material prejudice within the context of the entire trial. Werden v. Children's Hosp. Med. Ctr., — Ohio App. 3d —, 2006 Ohio 4600, — N.E. 2d —, 2006 Ohio App. LEXIS 4547 (Sept. 8, 2006).

Cross-examination

In circumstances in which an administratrix in a medical malpractice wrongful death case called a doctor as if under cross-examination in her case-in-chief, pursuant to RC § 2317.07, and the doctor was then called again as a witness by a clinic in its case-in-chief, as the doctor's direct examination occurred subsequent to his cross-examination, it served as the redirect examination for the purpose of this analysis, and the trial court erred in denying further cross-examination by the administratrix. The direct examination was more extensive and covered more specific topics than the cross-examination. Lostracco v. Cleveland Clinic Found., — Ohio App. 3d —, 2006 Ohio 3694, — N.E. 2d —, 2006 Ohio App. LEXIS 3640 (July 20, 2006).

Trial court did not err in overruling the objections filed by a relative of a child to a magistrate's report that concerned the magistrate's curtailment of the relative's cross-examination of the child's foster mother, who was competing for custody of the child, as to the religious practices of the foster mother and her husband because the foster parents' religious persuasion was irrelevant because the relative still retained parental rights including the right to choose the religion in which the child would be raised. Moreover, it was clear that counsel did not possess a good faith belief that a factual predicate existed for questioning the foster mother about the level of religious observance in her household. In re A.V., — Ohio App. 3d —, 2006 Ohio 3149, — N.E. 2d —, 2006 Ohio App. LEXIS 3021 (June 22, 2006).

Defendant's counsel did not fail to adequately cross-examine an arresting officer, as the trial court record revealed that the cross-examination was vigorous and competent, the attorney repeatedly questioned the officer with respect to discrepancies between his report and his testimony, and the officer's credibility was attacked; further, cross-examination pursuant to Ohio R. Evid. 611(B) was a matter of trial strategy. State v. Tripi, — Ohio App. 3d —, 2006 Ohio 1687, — N.E. 2d —, 2006 Ohio App. LEXIS 1573 (Mar. 31, 2006).

Cross-examination of defendant

Because the doctor failed to demonstrate how the trial court's decision to permit the cross-examination of the doctor (defendant) based on his attorney's answer to the patient's complaint prejudiced him, any error in permitting that line of questioning constituted nothing more than harmless error. Despite the doctor's argument, it could not be seen how the jury's knowledge that the doctor and/or his counsel initially denied all negligence in the answer could possibly have caused the alleged inconsistencies in the jury's answers to interrogatories. Lewis v. Nease, — Ohio App. 3d —, 2006 Ohio 4362, — N.E. 2d —, 2006 Ohio App. LEXIS 4274 (Aug. 21, 2006).

Discretion

Trial court did not abuse its discretion under Ohio R. Evid. 403 and 611(A) in admitting photographs of the victim of defendant's fatal shooting, as the photographs were introduced in connection with the coroner's testimony to help explain and clarify it, and the probative value of the photographs outweighed the danger of unfair prejudice to defendant; the photographs were not so gruesome as to have produced an inflammatory reaction by the jury against defendant. State v. Levett, — Ohio App. 3d —, 2006 Ohio 2222, — N.E. 2d —, 2006 Ohio App. LEXIS 2046 (May 5, 2006).

Discretion of court

Trial court did not abuse its discretion in connection with the conduct of a will contest proceeding pursuant to Ohio R. Evid. 611, as the scope of voir dire, cross-examination, and closing argument were within the court's discretion and the trial judge was experienced. Marshall v. Scalf, — Ohio App. 3d —, 2007 Ohio 3667, — N.E. 2d —, 2007 Ohio App. LEXIS 3373 (July 19, 2007).

Trial court did not abuse its discretion under Ohio R. Evid. 611(b) when it denied defendant the opportunity to conduct recross-examination of defendant's brother in defendant's criminal trial, as the matters sought to be inquired about on recross-examination had already been explored by counsel for defendant on cross-examination; further, any error was harmless, as there was no evidence that defendant suffered prejudice or that the outcome of the trial would have been different if such recross-examination was allowed. State v. Smith, — Ohio App. 3d —, 2007 Ohio 6772, — N.E. 2d —, 2007 Ohio App. LEXIS 5939 (Dec. 18, 2007).

Trial court did not abuse its discretion in excluding the interrogation expert's testimony. Because the expert specialized in the voluntariness of a confession and defendant claimed that he never gave a confession, the expert's testimony as to whether the confession was voluntary was irrelevant. State v. Torres, — Ohio App. 3d —, 2006 Ohio 3696, — N.E. 2d —, 2006 Ohio App. LEXIS 3641 (July 20, 2006).

Since the bank teller could not see defendant's hands during the robbery, any deformity was irrelevant and thus, there was no error in denying defendant's second request to publish his hands to the jury. The trial court's decision represented the proper exercise of its authority to maintain order in the courtroom or monitor the presentation of evidence in accordance with Ohio R. Evid. 611 and was not prejudicial to defendant. State v. Tagliaferro, — Ohio App. 3d —, 2006 Ohio 1364, — N.E. 2d —, 2006 Ohio App. LEXIS 1243 (Mar. 23, 2006).

It was well within the discretion of the trial court to allow redirect examination to explore the genesis of the consent defense because the record showed that it was counsel for defendant who initiated testimony that revealed defendant's revised version of events from a denial of involvement to an unsupported claim that the sex was consensual. Permitting the State to respond by conducting redirect examination of the investigating detective on the issue of consent could not be construed as unreasonable, arbitrary, or unconscionable. State v. Bumphus, — Ohio App. 3d —, 2006 Ohio 3869, — N.E. 2d —, 2006 Ohio App. LEXIS 3834 (July 21, 2006).

Trial court did not abuse its discretion or violate defendant's right to present a defense under U.S. Const. amend. VI and Ohio Const. art. I, § 10 in excluding testimony from a witness for defendant who allegedly was going to impeach the credibility of a narcotics officer who had testified for the prosecution, as the trial court had the discretion to determine the presentation of witnesses pursuant to Ohio R. Evid. 611, and exclusion of evidence that was not deemed relevant under Ohio R. Evid. 402 was not error. The witness's testimony was confusing, misguided, contradictory, and did not specifically relate to defendant and the underlying criminal charges against him. State v. Kimble, — Ohio App. 3d —, 2006 Ohio 6863, — N.E. 2d —, 2006 Ohio App. LEXIS 6775 (Dec. 22, 2006).

Juror questions

Trial court did not err in allowing jurors to question witnesses in defendant's criminal trial, as such was within the discretion of the trial court pursuant to Ohio R. Evid. 611(A) and the trial court handled the procedure fairly; any inconsistency in the manner of questioning the witnesses was deemed harmless. State v. Myers, — Ohio App. 3d —, 2006 Ohio 1604, — N.E. 2d —, 2006 Ohio App. LEXIS 1453 (Mar. 31, 2006).

Leading questions

Trial court did not err in allowing the State to question a co-defendant who had agreed to testify against defendant by use of a leading question pursuant to Ohio R. Evid. 611(C), whereupon the co-defendant asserted his Fifth Amendment self-incrimination privilege and refused to answer or further testify, as the leading question that was asked went unanswered regarding the co-defendant's prior grand jury testimony, the jury was properly instructed to disregard the question and not to draw inferences therefrom regarding defendant's innocence or guilt, and no prejudice to defendant was shown. State v. Huggins, — Ohio App. 3d —, 2007 Ohio 1289, — N.E. 2d —, 2007 Ohio App. LEXIS 1187 (Mar. 22, 2007).

There was no abuse of discretion by the trial court in the manner in which it handled the leading questions addressed to the witness, the minor victim who was the victim of the rape and gross sexual imposition by defendant. State v. Liddle, — Ohio App. 3d —, 2007 Ohio 1820, — N.E. 2d —, 2007 Ohio App. LEXIS 1658 (Apr. 18, 2007).

In a medical malpractice action, a trial court did not abuse its discretion under Ohio R. Evid. 611(C) in allowing a patient's counsel to ask a leading question on direct examination of a friendly witness, as the testimony was not irrelevant or unfairly prejudicial to the surgeon, and there was no clear injustice that warranted appellate intervention. Wynn v. Gilbert, — Ohio App. 3d —, 2007 Ohio 2798, — N.E. 2d —, 2007 Ohio App. LEXIS 2596 (June 8, 2007).

Trial court did not err in allowing the prosecution to use leading questions pursuant to Ohio R. Evid. 611(A) and (C) when it questioned the victim of defendant's rape, in violation of RC § 2907.02, as the victim was unable to talk and he suffered from cerebral palsy, such that he could communicate in short words and phrases through an assisting device; further, questioning of a doctor who examined the victim and who collected DNA was proper where the subject was somewhat detailed and vulgar and the essential element of penetration needed to be established. Ohio v. Christopher W. Larsen, — Ohio App. 3d —, 2007 Ohio 5058, — N.E. 2d —, 2007 Ohio App. LEXIS 4470 (Sept. 24, 2007).

In a domestic violence prosecution, the State was properly allowed to question the victim on direct examination with leading questions, under Ohio R. Evid. 611(C), because the victim was an adverse witness, as the victim was married to defendant, did not want to testify against defendant, and testified that the victim wanted to reconcile with defendant. State v. Fields, — Ohio App. 3d —, 2007 Ohio 5060, — N.E. 2d —, 2007 Ohio App. LEXIS 4485 (Sept. 27, 2007).

There was no abuse of discretion in the trial court's decision to permit counsel for the education board to question the former superintendent of the school in the way that he did because, although the court did not declare him a hostile or adverse witness, counsel for the board did point out that the former director (plaintiff) intended to call the superintendent in support of his own arguments for interpreting the agreement between the board and the corporation. To the extent that counsel asked cross-examination or leading questions of the superintendent, it was apparent that he was established as having a relationship with the director and was an adverse witness. Butler County Joint Voc. Sch. Dist. Bd. of Educ. v. Andrews, — Ohio App. 3d —, 2007 Ohio 5896, — N.E. 2d —, 2007 Ohio App. LEXIS 5184 (Nov. 5, 2007).

Defendant failed to show counsel was ineffective for failing to object to the State's use of leading questions pursuant to Ohio R. Evid. 611 when it questioned a police officer in defendant's criminal trial on multiple drug charges, as such questions were mainly used to develop the officer's testimony or were inconsequential; counsel's decision not to object may have been a trial strategy not to interrupt the testimony. State v. Skinner, — Ohio App. 3d —, 2007 Ohio 6793, — N.E. 2d —, 2007 Ohio App. LEXIS 5948 (Dec. 14, 2007).

Trial court did not abuse its discretion in allowing a guardian ad litem (GAL) to ask certain leading questions in a dependency case; the GAL questioned the agency's witnesses as if on cross-examination, and to the extent that the GAL asked leading questions on direct examination, the trial court

found that the parties had competing interests. In re Neibertt, — Ohio App. 3d —, — N.E. 2d —, 2006 Ohio App. LEXIS 1420 (Mar. 22, 2006).

Trial court did not commit plain error by allowing the prosecution to ask leading questions during the direct examination of the victim and one of the investigating officers. Even assuming that some of the questions were objectionable as leading, there was no prejudice since the information elicited was already in evidence, and the questions were within the trial court's authority under Ohio R. Evid. 611(A) to exercise reasonable control over the mode of interrogation. State v. Powers, — Ohio App. 3d —, 2006 Ohio 4458, — N.E. 2d —, 2006 Ohio App. LEXIS 4372 (Aug. 29, 2006).

Ohio R. Evid. 611(C) does not strictly forbid leading questions, but states that leading questions should not be used on the direct examination of a witness except as may be necessary to develop his testimony, and this exception is broad, so it is within a trial court's discretion to allow the use of leading questions. State v. Melton, — Ohio App. 3d —, 2006 Ohio 5610, — N.E. 2d —, 2006 Ohio App. LEXIS 5625 (Oct. 26, 2006).

In a prosecution for assault on a peace officer, a question addressed to an officer who was testifying was not leading, under Ohio R. Evid. 611(C), because it was intended to elicit from the officer the amount of force that was necessary to control defendant. State v. Melton, — Ohio App. 3d —, 2006 Ohio 5610, — N.E. 2d —, 2006 Ohio App. LEXIS 5625 (Oct. 26, 2006).

There was no error in the trial court's rulings on various leading questions by the State on its direct examination of witnesses pursuant to Ohio R. Evid. 611(C), as an objection to one such question was sustained and corrective action was taken by the trial court, and another matter was based on the fact that the State was interviewing an uncooperative 17-year-old witness and it was entitled to some latitude. Although the witness had not been declared hostile, he was clearly reluctant to incriminate defendant and the questioning regarding his prior inconsistent statements was proper. State v. Meyers, — Ohio App. 3d —, 2006 Ohio 6125, — N.E. 2d —, 2006 Ohio App. LEXIS 6061 (Nov. 17, 2006).

Limitation of cross-examination of victim

Trial court did not err when it limited the scope of defendant's cross-examination of the eyewitness to the murder regarding a fraud conspiracy in which he was involved because the information that defense counsel was seeking was far beyond the name of the crime, the time and place of conviction, and the punishment imposed. Furthermore, there was no indication in the record that the facts of that possible prior conviction bore any relevance to defendant's credibility in the instant case. State v. Carter, — Ohio App. 3d —, 2007 Ohio 3502, — N.E. 2d —, 2007 Ohio App. LEXIS 3223 (June 29, 2007).

Trial court did not abuse its discretion in limiting the cross-examination of the victim. Pursuant to Evid. R. 607(B), defendant had no reasonable basis for implying, and produced no corroborating evidence or testimony, that the victim was HIV-positive; the victim, under oath, denied having AIDS. State v. Edwards, — Ohio App. 3d —, 2006 Ohio 5726, — N.E. 2d —, 2006 Ohio App. LEXIS 5723 (Nov. 2, 2006).

Limitation on cross-examination

Trial court did not abuse its discretion under Ohio R. Evid. 611 where it limited defendant's cross-examination, such that he was not permitted to have a state agent reenact events that led to his obstruction of official business charge, in violation of RC § 2921.31(A), in order for him to show that his conduct did not create a "substantial stoppage," as the reenactment could have been misleading to the jury and defendant was permitted to question the officers involved extensively about the length of time that their investigation was delayed due to his conduct; there was no constitutional violation of defendant's rights under Ohio Const. art. I, § 10. State v. Wellman, — Ohio App. 3d —, 2007 Ohio 2953, — N.E. 2d —, 2007 Ohio App. LEXIS 2720 (June 15, 2007).

Because the trial court had broad discretion in limiting the cross-examination of a witness when it had concerns about harassment, prejudice, confusion of the issues, or marginally relevant interrogation, the trial court did not abuse its discretion in disallowing defense counsel's line of questioning regarding an alleged racial epithet. Since the intended witness testimony was not obvious from the record, the record was insufficient to determine whether prejudicial error occurred. State v. Jiminez-ortiz, — Ohio App. 3d —, 2007 Ohio 5496, — N.E. 2d —, 2007 Ohio App. LEXIS 4839 (Oct. 15, 2007).

Defendant's right to confrontation under Ohio Const. art. I, § 10 was not violated; because the trial court had wide latitude in precluding repetitive interrogation and determining the relevance of a line of questioning, and because the line of questioning had been previously explored, the trial court did not err in barring certain testimony. Defense counsel did have the opportunity to question the police about whether defendants were told they were under arrest. State v. Jiminez-ortiz, — Ohio App. 3d —, 2007 Ohio 5496, — N.E. 2d —, 2007 Ohio App. LEXIS 4839 (Oct. 15, 2007).

Prejudice

Although the admission of multiple photographs of the victim and the crime scene as well as the testimony of the victim's mother may have been overly repetitive or prejudicial, pursuant to Ohio R. Evid. 403 and 611(A), there was no showing that the outcome of the trial was affected under a plain error analysis pursuant to Ohio R. Crim. P. 52. State v. Love, — Ohio App. 3d —, 2006 Ohio 1762, — N.E. 2d —, 2006 Ohio App. LEXIS 1619 (Mar. 27, 2006).

Presentation of evidence

There was no plain error under Ohio R. Evid. 611(A) by a trial court when it allowed a cardiologist to testify in narrative form in a patient's medical malpractice action, as the patient did not object initially, the form of the testimony did not negatively affect the fairness of the trial, and there was no showing that the outcome of the trial would have been different without it. Cox v. Cardiovascular Consultants, — Ohio App. 3d —, 2007 Ohio 5468, — N.E. 2d —, 2007 Ohio App. LEXIS 4793 (Oct. 9, 2007).

Although defendant's confession was offered prior to any presentation of evidence which established the existence of any charged offense, the subsequent testimony of the victim as to the alleged acts of defendant cured any error and rendered the confession admissible. Also, since the case was presented to the trial court rather than to a jury, the danger of a situation requiring a mistrial was minimal. State v. Kesler, — Ohio App. 3d —, 2006 Ohio 6340, — N.E. 2d —, 2006 Ohio App. LEXIS 6324 (Dec. 4, 2006).

Rebuttal

Defendant failed to show that he received ineffective assistance of counsel for failure to object; evidence of defendant's 1983 rape conviction was properly admitted under Ohio R. Evid. 607, 609, and 611(B) because he did not answer truthfully when he was asked whether he had ever demanded oral sex. With regard to his prior conviction for domestic violence, the State was allowed to impeach his testimony that he got along with his wife. State v. Howard, — Ohio App. 3d —, 2007 Ohio 991, — N.E. 2d —, 2007 Ohio App. LEXIS 914 (Mar. 8, 2007).

Trial court did not abuse its discretion when it allowed the State to recall a defense witness pursuant to Evid. R. 611 and Crim. R. 16 where it discovered new evidence that contradicted her testimony regarding having worked for defendant until a particular period of time. Although she had not been listed as a witness for the State, the rebuttal testimony was proper where the State could not have known earlier that it

would find evidence to contradict her testimony. State v. Burneson, — Ohio App. 3d —, 2007 Ohio 4037, — N.E. 2d —, 2007 Ohio App. LEXIS 3675 (Aug. 9, 2007).

Reopening examination of victim

Trial court did not abuse its discretion when it allowed the State to reopen its case after the State had rested and defendant had moved for on Ohio R. Crim. P. 29 judgment of acquittal because, although the State failed to present specific evidence on the value of the merchandise that defendant attempted to steal, which determined the degree of the offense of theft, the State had the evidence in its possession, prior to the presentation of any witness testimony. It was a case of mere oversight by the State which had already obtained the necessary evidence through its prior investigation of the incident and preparation for trial and there was no claim of surprise or prejudice on the part of defendant due to the nature or content of the additional testimony. State v. Roberson, — Ohio App. 3d —, 2007 Ohio 1981, — N.E. 2d —, 2007 Ohio App. LEXIS 1829 (Apr. 26, 2007).

Trial court did not abuse its discretion because the purpose for reopening was to establish where the victim was physically located at the time that she retrieved the voicemails and thus, was proper since the victim was asked originally only where she lived at the time of the voicemails and to where the calls were made. As she had not testified to that issue during the original hearing, her later testimony that she was located at the Franklin County Municipal Court at the time that she retrieved the voicemail message did not contradict and was not a change from her original testimony. State v. Stanley, — Ohio App. 3d —, 2006 Ohio 4632, — N.E. 2d —, 2006 Ohio App. LEXIS 4477 (Aug. 31, 2006).

Restriction of cross-examination

There was no error in refusing to admit the mother's decade-old diary entries, which, although attenuated in time and logic, indicated the extent of the mother's negative feelings and profound resentment toward defendant and possibly revealed a motivation to testify against him, because any error in denying defendant's cross-examination with the diary's contents was harmless since the trial court, as the trier of fact, was privy to numerous examples of how defendant's conduct over the years had negatively affected the mother's feelings toward defendant. State v. Parsons, — Ohio App. 3d —, 2007 Ohio 1204, — N.E. 2d —, 2007 Ohio App. LEXIS 1025 (Mar. 13, 2007).

Trial court did not abuse its discretion in permitting the psychological aid's testimony on cross-examination because it properly limited the testimony, which properly described the evaluation process, and did not improperly bolster the credibility of the child victim regarding the sexual abuse. The aid's conclusion was in accord with the parameters imposed by the trial court and did not improperly bolster the truthfulness of the victim. State v. Hudgins, — Ohio App. 3d —, 2007 Ohio 3361, — N.E. 2d —, 2007 Ohio App. LEXIS 3083 (June 25, 2007).

Restriction of cross-examination of witness

Trial court did not abuse its discretion by not permitting evidence of the police detective's unrelated case because, in the other case, the defendant had confessed to committing the crime but after an inmate confessed, that defendant recanted. Because the instant defendant claimed that he never confessed, and did not argue that the detective committed any act or procedure that was illegal or improper, the information was irrelevant. State v. Torres, — Ohio App. 3d —, 2006 Ohio 3696, — N.E. 2d —, 2006 Ohio App. LEXIS 3641 (July 20, 2006).

Scope of cross-examination

Trial court did not err by refusing to allow defendant to cross-examine a police officer regarding his disciplinary record for the purpose of impeachment because inquiring into the unsubstantiated charges against the officer was irrelevant to the drug trafficking and felony assault case and would have been distracting. State v. Benjamin, — Ohio App. 3d —, 2007 Ohio 84, — N.E. 2d —, 2007 Ohio App. LEXIS 78 (Jan. 11, 2007).

In balancing the State's interests against defendant's right to confront his accuser and present evidence in his own defense, the trial court did not abuse its discretion in resolving that balance against admission of the unduly inflammatory and prejudicial evidence in accordance with Ohio R. Evid. 403(A). Defendant sought to introduce evidence of the 15-year-old victim's sexual activity with persons other than defendant in an attempt to impeach her credibility and, while the evidence had some slight relevance and probative value for that limited purpose, the key issue was whether defendant engaged in sexual conduct with the minor-victim, which was proven by seminal fluid stains on the bed sheets and DNA evidence. State v. Smiddy, — Ohio App. 3d —, 2007 Ohio 1342, — N.E. 2d —, 2007 Ohio App. LEXIS 1222 (Mar. 23, 2007).

Trial court was well within its discretion to limit cross-examination on the issue of tribal friction in Somalia under the circumstances because one of the two victims displayed no knowledge of friction between different tribes in Somalia, having left the country when he was 15-years old and having no knowledge of the tribal affiliation of defendant or other witnesses. Similarly, the trial court refused some of the cross-examination of the other victim because the fighting in Somalia was too remote since the victim had arrived in the United States 15 years earlier, but the trial court did allow testimony that one victim and defendant came from different tribes. State v. Warsame, — Ohio App. 3d —, 2007 Ohio 3656, — N.E. 2d —, 2007 Ohio App. LEXIS 3334 (July 19, 2007).

In defendant's prosecution for menacing by stalking under RC § 2903.211(A)(1), since the State does not have to prove that the defendant caused the victim actual mental distress or physical harm, defendant was properly precluded from asking the victim on cross-examination as to her prosecution for driving under the influence to establish an alternative basis for her claimed mental distress. Other possible stressors in the victim's life were irrelevant to this inquiry. State v. Bone, — Ohio App. 3d —, 2006 Ohio 3809, — N.E. 2d —, 2006 Ohio App. LEXIS 3772 (July 25, 2006).

As the trial court had already allowed an employee's counsel to question the employee's former counsel regarding discussions between the employee and the former counsel as to a settlement which the employer sought enforcement of, the trial court did not abuse its discretion under Ohio R. Evid. 611(B) in limiting cross-examination of the former counsel on the issue of his alleged bias and lack of credibility. The matter was already addressed and further questioning on the issue of the employee's having filed a disciplinary complaint against the former counsel was not deemed relevant. Rogers v. Goodyear Tire & Rubber Co., — Ohio App. 3d —, 2006 Ohio 6854, — N.E. 2d —, 2006 Ohio App. LEXIS 6770 (Dec. 26, 2006).

Scope of interrogation

Trial court did not abuse its discretion by preventing defendant from questioning his daughter about a third person shooting the victim (the daughter's boyfriend) because defendant did not offer any good faith basis to suggest that the victim was shot by a third person because the third person was owed money for drugs. Defendant never indicated when he was questioned by the police after the shooting that someone else was the shooter and defendant, at trial, did not deny shooting the victim; rather, he testified that the victim was accidentally shot when he grabbed for defendant's gun. State v. French, — Ohio App. 3d —, 2007 Ohio 4400, — N.E. 2d —, 2007 Ohio App. LEXIS 3968 (Aug. 27, 2007).

Showing bias on part of expert witness

Injured person was not entitled to additional financial information from a doctor who had performed an independent medical examination (IME) on the injured person, and the injured person's motion to compel disclosure of that information was properly denied, where the doctor had already provided, inter alia, the number of IMEs conducted by the doctor during a period of over six years, the price range for IMEs, the number of depositions provided by the doctor for the same period, and the charges typically associated with such depositions; additionally, the cross-examination portion of the doctor's video deposition, which was played at trial, dealt extensively with the doctor's medical-legal practice and the economic aspects thereof. Stinchcomb v. Mammone, 166 Ohio App. 3d 45, 2006 Ohio 1276, 849 N.E. 2d 54, 2006 Ohio App. LEXIS 1167 (Mar. 13, 2006).

Time limitations

Trial court did not err in limiting the length of trial because the father was given great leeway by the trial court to ask questions of the witnesses. The reminders of time limitations should have been helpful in guiding the father to better organize his time and questioning but, instead, he ignored the reminders and used the available time to cover irrelevant or repetitive subject matter. Mathewson v. Mathewson, — Ohio App. 3d —, 2007 Ohio 574, — N.E. 2d —, 2007 Ohio App. LEXIS 518 (Feb. 9, 2007).

Witnesses

Trial court did not abuse its discretion under Ohio R. Evid. 403 and 611(A) in admitting photographs that showed the extent of the damage to a motorist's vehicle in the motorist's personal injury action, arising from a vehicle collision, without the aid of expert testimony, as he had testified regarding the collision and the extent of the damage, and the driver was entitled to present evidence to rebut the motorist's testimony and to show the "minimal" damage to the motorist's vehicle. Wingfield v. Howe, — Ohio App. 3d —, 2006 Ohio 276, — N.E. 2d —, 2006 Ohio App. LEXIS 245 (Jan. 26, 2006).

RULE 612. Writing Used to Refresh Memory

Except as otherwise provided in criminal proceedings by Rules 16(B)(1)(g) and 16(C)(1)(d) of Ohio Rules of Criminal Procedure, if a witness uses a writing to refresh memory for the purpose of testifying, either: (1) while testifying; or (2) before testifying, if the court in its discretion determines it is necessary in the interests of justice, an adverse party is entitled to have the writing produced at the hearing. The adverse party is also entitled to inspect it, to cross-examine the witness thereon, and to introduce in evidence those portions which relate to the testimony of the witness. If it is claimed that the writing contains matters not related to the subject matter of the testimony the court shall examine the writing in camera, excise any portions not so related, and order delivery of the remainder to the party entitled thereto. Any portion withheld over objections shall be preserved and made available to the appellate court in the event of an appeal. If a writing is not produced or delivered pursuant to order under this rule, the court shall make any order justice requires, except that in criminal cases when the prosecution elects not to comply, the order shall be one striking the testimony or, if the court in its discretion determines that the interests of justice so require, declaring a mistrial.

History: Amended, eff 7-1-07.

NOTES TO DECISIONS

ANALYSIS

Generally
Past recollection recorded
Writing used to refresh memory
Writing used to refresh memory of witness

Generally

EvidR 607 did not apply where the state was not impeaching its witness with a prior inconsistent statement, but instead provided the witness with her prior statement to refresh her memory, in accord with EvidR 612: State v. Counts, 170 Ohio App. 3d 339, 2007 Ohio 117, 867 N.E.2d 432, 2007 Ohio App. LEXIS 124 (2007).

Past recollection recorded

There was no error in refusing to strike the direct testimony of the case worker in the permanent custody proceeding because the record indicated that the foundation was sufficiently laid, under Ohio R. Evid. 612. Each time the witness testified about transactions memorialized in a report of activity (ROA), she testified that she needed to review the ROA to connect a particular date to a particular event, and that she indeed possessed a present recollection of the details of the event; the testimony that followed did not appear to have been read verbatim from any document. In re Baby C, — Ohio App. 3d —, 2006 Ohio 2067, — N.E. 2d —, 2006 Ohio App. LEXIS 1915 (Apr. 27, 2006).

Writing used to refresh memory

In a former employee's suit against a former employer for overtime pay, when the employer's witness allegedly testified from notes from a deposition ruled inadmissible, except to impeach him, while the employee waived an objection by not timely raising one, under Ohio R. Evid. 103(A)(1), it was not plain error to allow the witness to refresh his memory, given the passage of time between the events at issue and the testimony. Choate v. Tranet, Inc., — Ohio App. 3d —, 2006 Ohio 4565, — N.E. 2d —, 2006 Ohio App. LEXIS 4497 (Sept. 5, 2006).

Writing used to refresh memory of witness

Prosecution did not "impeach" its witness but, instead, provided the witness with her prior witness statement, which had been previously prepared, in accordance with Ohio R. Evid. 612, which specifically allowed for the use of a writing to refresh the witness's memory. State v. Counts, 170 Ohio App. 3d 339, 2007 Ohio 117, 867 N.E.2d 432, 2007 Ohio App. LEXIS 124 (2007).

RULE 613.   Impeachment by Self-Contradiction

(A) **Examining witness concerning prior statement.** In examining a witness concerning a prior statement made by the witness, whether written or not, the statement need not be shown nor its contents disclosed to the witness at that time, but on request the same shall be shown or disclosed to opposing counsel.

(B) **Extrinsic evidence of prior inconsistent statement of witness.** Extrinsic evidence of a prior inconsistent statement by a witness is admissible if both of the following apply:

(1) If the statement is offered solely for the purpose of impeaching the witness, the witness is afforded a prior opportunity to explain or deny the statement and the opposite party is afforded an opportunity to interrogate the witness on the statement or the interests of justice otherwise require;

(2) The subject matter of the statement is one of the following:

(a) A fact that is of consequence to the determination of the action other than the credibility of a witness;

(b) A fact that may be shown by extrinsic evidence under Evid. R. 608(A), 609, 616(A), 616(B) or 706;

(c) A fact that may be shown by extrinsic evidence under the common law of impeachment if not in conflict with the Rules of Evidence.

(C) **Prior inconsistent conduct.** During examination of a witness, conduct of the witness inconsistent with the witness's testimony may be shown to impeach. If offered for the sole purpose of impeaching the witness's testimony, extrinsic evidence of the prior inconsistent conduct is admissible under the same circumstances as provided for prior inconsistent statements by Evid. R. 613(B)(2).

History: Amended, eff 7-1-98.

NOTES TO DECISIONS

ANALYSIS

Admissibility of medical reports
Admission of prior inconsistent statement
Exclusion of prior statement
Extrinsic evidence of prior inconsistent statement
Harmless error
Limiting instructions
Prior inconsistent statement

Admissibility of medical reports

Trial court did not abuse its discretion in admitting medical records for purposes of impeaching a motorist's claims under Ohio R. Evid. 613(B) as to his injuries in a personal injury action, arising from a vehicular collision, as the motorist had stated that he was not in pain after a prior accident until the time of the accident upon which the litigation was based, and accordingly, the driver could impeach him by first asking if he had injured his back in a fall and upon the motorist's denial, the medical records reflecting that fall were properly admitted. Wingfield v. Howe, — Ohio App. 3d —, 2006 Ohio 276, — N.E. 2d —, 2006 Ohio App. LEXIS 245 (Jan. 26, 2006).

Admission of prior inconsistent statement

Admission of the witness's prior inconsistent statement did not constitute plain error because, even assuming that the witness's prior inconsistent statement was improperly admitted as substantive evidence of defendant's guilt, and that a limiting instruction should have been given, there was overwhelming evidence of defendant's guilt. The testimony showed that defendant, who was driving a truck, pursued the victim who was trying to evade him, that there were guns and ammo in the truck, and that, in a signed sworn statement to the police, defendant admitted that he told the witness (a passenger) to fire the gun at the van. State v. Rose, — Ohio App. 3d —, 2006 Ohio 397, — N.E. 2d —, 2006 Ohio App. LEXIS 337 (Jan. 30, 2006).

Exclusion of prior statement

Trial court did not abuse its discretion when it did not allow the cards and letters from the victim and defendant's wife into evidence. The alleged prior inconsistent statements met none of the criteria for substantive admissibility under Ohio R. Evid. 801(D)(1)(a) and were neither under oath, subject to cross-examination, nor given at a proceeding or deposition. The victim's and the wife's statements could not have been used subjectively. State v. Laboy, — Ohio App. 3d —, 2006 Ohio 5927, — N.E. 2d —, 2006 Ohio App. LEXIS 5853 (Nov. 9, 2006).

Trial court was correct in not allowing a woman, to whom the wife had allegedly admitted that she had lied on the stand, to testify because Ohio R. Evid. 613(A) did not apply since it dealt with prior inconsistent statements and defendant sought to impeach the wife through a statement she made after her testimony. Additionally, Ohio R. Evid. 613(A) did not apply because defendant was not seeking to call the wife, the person who allegedly made the statements. State v. Laboy, — Ohio App. 3d —, 2006 Ohio 5927, — N.E. 2d —, 2006 Ohio App. LEXIS 5853 (Nov. 9, 2006).

Extrinsic evidence of prior inconsistent statement

Trial court did not err in failing to apply Ohio R. Evid. 613(B) and thereby allow the proffered testimony regarding a telephone call allegedly made by defendant's friend (where he stated that he thought he shot the victim) because the record revealed that, since defense counsel did not specifically raise an Ohio R. Evid. 613(B) argument, the friend was never afforded a prior opportunity to "explain or deny" the statement in the purported telephone call, as clearly required by Ohio R. Evid. 613(B)(1). Even if trial counsel's failure to specifically raise Ohio R. Evid. 613(B) as a means of impeaching the friend constituted a violation of counsel's duty to defendant, such decision was not prejudicial based on the substantial evidence of defendant's guilt. State v. Lynch, — Ohio App. 3d —, 2006 Ohio 5630, — N.E. 2d —, 2006 Ohio App. LEXIS 5633 (Oct. 25, 2006).

Harmless error

In light of the overwhelming evidence of defendant's guilt, the trial court did not commit plain error in admitting the rebuttal testimony of the officer in order to impeach the credibility of defendant's mother. While the mother's inconsistent statements pertained to collateral matters and did not establish guilt, admission of the officer's rebuttal testimony was harmless error. State v. Hayes, — Ohio App. 3d —, 2007 Ohio 2101, — N.E. 2d —, 2007 Ohio App. LEXIS 1957 (Apr. 27, 2007).

Limiting instructions

In a domestic violence prosecution, when the victim's prior inconsistent statement was admitted, it was unnecessary to give the jury a limiting instruction, under Ohio R. Evid. 613(B), because the victim's prior statement was admitted for substantive purposes, not impeachment, and was admissible hearsay under the recorded recollection hearsay exception in Ohio R. Evid. 803(5). State v. Fields, — Ohio App. 3d —, 2007 Ohio 5060, — N.E. 2d —, 2007 Ohio App. LEXIS 4485 (Sept. 27, 2007).

Prior inconsistent statement

Defendant was deprived of his due process right to a fair trial by the prosecutor's failure to provide defense counsel evidence of a prior inconsistent statement made by the alleged sexual assault victim, evidence that was exculpatory and material to guilt or punishment. There was a Brady violation because the victim's statement was not disclosed by the prosecution, it was favorable to defendant, and it was material since it could have produced a different outcome and the prior inconsistent statement could have been used to impeach the victim's testimony, under Ohio R. Evid. 613, had it been disclosed to defense counsel. State v. Scheidel, — Ohio App. 3d —, 2006 Ohio 195, 844 N.E. 2d 1248, 2006 Ohio App. LEXIS 166 (Jan. 20, 2006).

RULE 614. Calling and Interrogation of Witnesses by Court

(A) **Calling by court.** The court may, on its own motion or at the suggestion of a party, call witnesses, and all parties are entitled to cross-examine witnesses thus called.

(B) **Interrogation by court.** The court may inter-rogate witnesses, in an impartial manner, whether called by itself or by a party.

(C) **Objections.** Objections to the calling of witnesses by the court or to interrogation by it may be made at the time or at the next available opportunity when the jury is not present.

NOTES TO DECISIONS

ANALYSIS

Authority of court to call and question witnesses
Authority of trial court to call witnesses
Comments by judge
Court calling witnesses
Court questioning
Court questioning of a witness
Impartiality required

Authority of court to call and question witnesses

Trial court did not abuse its discretion where it called a witness at the request of the state: State v. Lather, 171 Ohio App. 3d 708, 2007 Ohio 2399, 872 N.E.2d 991, 2007 Ohio App. LEXIS 2250 (2007).

Authority of trial court to call witnesses

As the trial court called the victim of defendant's criminal conduct as its own witness pursuant to Ohio R. Evid. 614(A), the State was entitled to cross-examine and impeach her without a showing of surprise pursuant to Ohio R. Evid. 607(A), as Rule 607 was inapplicable where the victim was not the State's witness; she had originally accused defendant of assaulting her, but she was married to him and pregnant with his child, and she thereafter notified the trial court that she was recanting her accusation and that others were responsible for the attack. State v. Beasley, — Ohio App. 3d —, 2007 Ohio 5432, — N.E. 2d —, 2007 Ohio App. LEXIS 4774 (Oct. 11, 2007).

Comments by judge

Although defendant did not object at the time that the judge made comments to the minor victim in defendant's criminal trial on multiple sexual offenses, his motion for a mistrial at the end of the State's case based on the judge's comments and actions was sufficient to preserve the issue for appellate review pursuant to Ohio R. Evid. 614(C). Any comments by the judge were deemed harmless error under Ohio R. Crim. P. 52(A), as the comments were borderline with respect to enhancing the victim's credibility, but a jury instruction was given which clarified the jury's duty not to consider anything done or said by the trial court as its opinion on the case. State v. Djuric, — Ohio App. 3d —, 2007 Ohio 413, — N.E. 2d —, 2007 Ohio App. LEXIS 362 (Feb. 1, 2007).

Court calling witnesses

There was nothing unreasonable, arbitrary, or unconscionable about the trial court's decision to call the victim as a court's witness, pursuant to Ohio R. Evid. 614(A), because the victim initially reported allegations of abuse to both her teacher and an investigator and then later denied those allegations. The trial court was justified in calling her as the court's witness in order to provide the prosecution an opportunity to cross-examine her about her prior inconsistent statements. State v. Pflug, — Ohio App. 3d —, 2007 Ohio 2037, — N.E. 2d —, 2007 Ohio App. LEXIS 1905 (Apr. 27, 2007).

Trial court did not abuse its discretion under Ohio R. Evid. 614(A) when it called the victim of defendant's crime as a witness in order to allow both parties to cross-examine him, as the victim had indicated that he would not testify against defendant because he feared for his family's safety, although he later indicated that he would provide testimony in exchange for time off from his prison sentence that he was currently serving; the state's hands were tied, such that it properly requested that the trial court call the witness. State v. Curry, — Ohio App. 3d —, 2007 Ohio 5721, — N.E. 2d —, 2007 Ohio App. LEXIS 5022 (Oct. 25, 2007).

Trial court's questions of the witness, pursuant to Ohio R. Evid. 614, did not constitute plain error because there was overwhelming evidence of defendant's guilt and thus, but for the alleged error, the outcome of the trial would not have been different and, a review of the transcript demonstrated no abuse of discretion or lack of impartiality by the trial court. The parties stipulated that the trial court would call the witness, pursuant to Ohio Evid. R. 614 and that both parties then would be permitted to cross-examine him, and defendant did not object. State v. Rose, — Ohio App. 3d —, 2006 Ohio 397, — N.E. 2d —, 2006 Ohio App. LEXIS 337 (Jan. 30, 2006).

Court questioning

There was no "plain error" in procedures followed by a trial court in a dispute by a tenant against his landlords following the tenant's eviction, as well as in the landlords' counterclaim against the tenant for damages, as questions asked of witnesses by the jury were not objectionable where none of the questions concerned the merits of either party's case, the trial judge's questions of a witness were authorized under Ohio R. Evid. 614(B) and were based on the tenant's having "opened the door" to the testimony that he later claimed on appeal was improper hearsay. There was nothing that precluded a trial court from dismissing the tenant's case under Ohio R. Civ. P. 50(A) while the jury was still present. Levin v. Dickerson, — Ohio App. 3d —, 2006 Ohio 1337, — N.E. 2d —, 2006 Ohio App. LEXIS 1224 (Mar. 23, 2006).

Court questioning of a witness

There was no abuse of discretion in the trial court's denial of defendant's motion to withdraw his guilty pleas because the trial court held an extensive hearing on the motion and defendant was represented by competent counsel because defendant was given a complete and impartial hearing, full and fair consideration to his plea withdrawal request, and every opportunity to establish his argument for withdrawing his pleas. The trial court was permitted to question witnesses, pursuant to Ohio R. Evid. 614(B), and, although some questions asked by the trial court could have been viewed as direct, they did not indicate any clear predisposition on the part of the trial court to deny defendant's motion. State v. Torres, — Ohio App. 3d —, 2007 Ohio 1602, — N.E. 2d —, 2007 Ohio App. LEXIS 1467 (Apr. 5, 2007).

Although a trial court was permitted to interrogate witnesses in an impartial manner during trial, questions posed to defendant about whether he received marijuana from the victim of a shooting as a present for the birth of defendant's baby were imprudent and not meant to clarify any evidence. The questions did not constitute plain error due to the overwhelming evidence against defendant. Ohio v. Qawi Payne, — Ohio App. 3d —, 2007 Ohio 3310, — N.E. 2d —, 2007 Ohio App. LEXIS 3038 (June 29, 2007).

In a close case, the trial court's comments and improper questioning of witnesses constituted prejudicial error. Harper v. Roberts, 173 Ohio App. 3d 560, 2007 Ohio 5726, 879 N.E.2d 264, 2007 Ohio App. LEXIS 5013 (2007).

In a close case which depended on the credibility of the witnesses, the trial court's improper and prejudicial questions and comments warranted a new trial: Harper v. Roberts, 173 Ohio App. 3d 560, 2007 Ohio 5726, 879 N.E.2d 264, 2007 Ohio App. LEXIS 5013 (2007).

Under a plain error standard of review, the trial court's questions of the witness did not create error that was clearly apparent on the face of the record or prejudicial to the manager because some of the questioning by the trial court was the court's attempt to clear up confusion and keep the trial moving. Although the trial court asked the manager numerous questions, prejudice was not found merely based upon the number of questions asked. Kimble Mixer Co. v. St. Vincent, — Ohio App. 3d —, 2006 Ohio 2258, — N.E. 2d —, 2006 Ohio App. LEXIS 2119 (May 2, 2006).

Trial court did allow the father to testify in narrative form and it occasionally asked questions of him to clarify his testimony. The record did not reveal that the trial court exhibited bias against either party when asking questions. Mathewson v. Mathewson, — Ohio App. 3d —, 2007 Ohio 574, — N.E. 2d —, 2007 Ohio App. LEXIS 518 (Feb. 9, 2007).

During defendant's trial for domestic violence under RC § 2919.25, the trial court did not abuse its discretion in calling his common-law wife as a court's witness under Ohio R. Evid. 614(A) when she refused to testify about physical harm at trial after previously telling police officers that defendant had struck her and had tried to strangle and suffocate her. The trial court's questions directly addressed her conflicting testimony and clarified any confusion, and both the State and the defense had ample opportunity to question her after the trial court's examination. State v. Becerra, — Ohio App. 3d —, 2006 Ohio 5245, — N.E. 2d —, 2006 Ohio App. LEXIS 5230 (Oct. 5, 2006).

When, in a robbery prosecution, the trial court, pursuant to Ohio R. Evid. 614(B), initiated interrogation of defendant's co-defendant, who testified for the State pursuant to a plea bargain, there was no evidence of an abuse of discretion or any lack of impartiality on the part of the trial court, so it was not grounds for reversal of defendant's convictions. State v. Ayers, — Ohio App. 3d —, 2006 Ohio 5533, — N.E. 2d —, 2006 Ohio App. LEXIS 5508 (Oct. 17, 2006).

During defendant's trial for OVI and related offenses, the trial court did not improperly interrogate defendant about the smell of alcohol when it asked a question about the smell of alcohol to clarify what defendant meant when he mentioned a smell of diesel fuel on his clothing. The trial court's questions were within the scope of Ohio R. Evid. 614(B), which permitted it to question a witness in an impartial manner. State v. Dunn, — Ohio App. 3d —, 2006 Ohio 6550, — N.E. 2d —, 2006 Ohio App. LEXIS 6459 (Dec. 7, 2006).

Impartiality required

Trial court's interrogation of a witness is not deemed partial for purposes of EvidR 614(B) merely because the evidence elicited during the questioning is potentially damaging to the defendant: State v. Granderson, 177 Ohio App. 3d 424, 2008 Ohio 3757, 894 N.E.2d 1290, 2008 Ohio App. LEXIS 3187 (2008).

RULE 615.   Separation and Exclusion of Witnesses

(A) Except as provided in division (B) of this rule, at the request of a party the court shall order witnesses excluded so that they cannot hear the testimony of other witnesses, and it may make the order of its own motion. An order directing the 'exclusion' or 'separation' of witnesses or the like, in general terms without specification of other or additional limitations, is effective only to require the exclusion of witnesses from the hearing during the testimony of other witnesses.

(B) This rule does not authorize exclusion of any of the following persons from the hearing:

(1) a party who is a natural person;

(2) an officer or employee of a party that is not a natural person designated as its representative by its attorney;

(3) a person whose presence is shown by a party to

be essential to the presentation of the party's cause;

(4) in a criminal proceeding, a victim of the charged offense to the extent that the victim's presence is authorized by statute enacted by the General Assembly. As used in this rule, "victim" has the same meaning as in the provisions of the Ohio Constitution providing rights for victims of crimes.

History: Amended, eff 7-1-01; 7-1-03.

NOTES TO DECISIONS

ANALYSIS

Allowing investigating officer to remain in courtroom after separation of witnesses was ordered
Officer or employee of party
Parties to a criminal action
Separation of witnesses
Violation of order of sequestration
Witness violated separation order

Allowing investigating officer to remain in courtroom after separation of witnesses was ordered

Although a police detective was listed as a possible witness by the State in its criminal prosecution of defendant, as the detective was not called to testify at trial, there was no error under Ohio R. Evid. 615 in allowing the detective to sit at the State's table during the trial despite a separation of witnesses order; further, as an officer in charge of the case, the detective could remain in court and advise counsel for the State even if he had testified pursuant to Rule 615(B)(2). Ohio v. Anderson, — Ohio App. 3d —, 2007 Ohio 5326, — N.E. 2d —, 2007 Ohio App. LEXIS 4692 (Oct. 4, 2007).

Officer or employee of party

In a permanent custody matter, the trial court did not abuse its discretion by not striking the testimony of a family services agency's case manager on the ground that she was in the courtroom after the trial court ordered a separation of witnesses. The case manager was an officer or employee of the agency and was designated as its representative by its attorney; thus, pursuant to Ohio R. Evid. 615(B)(2), she was permitted to be in the courtroom. In re Turner, — Ohio App. 3d —, 2006 Ohio 6793, — N.E. 2d —, 2006 Ohio App. LEXIS 6767 (Dec. 15, 2006).

Parties to a criminal action

Trial court did not abuse its discretion by letting defendant's wife testify simply because she heard defendant's testimony because there was no indication in the record that the State assisted in circumventing the trial court's order to separate the witnesses and defendant could have used his wife's presence during his testimony as a basis to question her credibility. There was nothing in the record showing that the State helped the wife intentionally disobey the trial court's separation order, the State could not have been sure that defendant would testify, and there was no indication that the wife could have been called in rebuttal to the testimony of any other witness, so there was no immediate reason for the wife to be excluded from hearing the rest of the testimony after she finished testifying. State v. Hohvart, — Ohio App. 3d —, 2007 Ohio 5349, — N.E. 2d —, 2007 Ohio App. LEXIS 4714 (Sept. 21, 2007).

Separation of witnesses

Trial court did not violate Ohio R. Evid. 615 by allowing two officers to remain in the courtroom during each other's testimonies, as the record did not demonstrate that defendant was prejudicially affected by the trial court's decision. There was no indication of collusion between the two officers, nor was there any evidence of outside-the-courtroom conversa-

tions that effectively tainted either officer's testimony. State v. Harrison, — Ohio App. 3d —, 2007 Ohio 2421, — N.E. 2d —, 2007 Ohio App. LEXIS 2237 (May 18, 2007).

Although a trial court imposed a separation order on the witnesses, which was understood by the parties in defendant's criminal matter, the trial court did not explicitly order that the witnesses be separated and accordingly, there was no order on the record that prevented out-of-court contact between witnesses pursuant to Ohio R. Evid. 615. Accordingly, a discussion between two witnesses during an overnight recess did not violate either the court order or Rule 615. State v. Harris, — Ohio App. 3d —, 2006 Ohio 3520, — N.E. 2d —, 2006 Ohio App. LEXIS 3439 (June 27, 2006).

Violation of order of sequestration

There was no prejudice to defendant found by the trial court's exclusion of his wife's testimony due to the fact that the wife remained in the courtroom despite a sequestration order pursuant to Ohio R. Evid. 615, as defendant failed to provide a transcript of the videotaped proceeding pursuant to his duty under Ohio R. App. P. 9(A) which indicated that part of the trial, and he also failed to make a proffer of the testimony that the wife would have given pursuant to Ohio R. Evid. 103(A)(2); as defendant did not show that he was prejudiced by the evidentiary ruling and the matter did not relate to the offenses for which he was convicted, it was disregarded as harmless error under Ohio R. Crim. P. 52. Ohio v. Shropshire, — Ohio App. 3d —, 2007 Ohio 5185, — N.E. 2d —, 2007 Ohio App. LEXIS 4567 (Sept. 28, 2007).

Absent a showing of prejudice, the plain error rule did not require reversal of a conviction where a witness may have violated a separation order: State v. Gilreath, 174 Ohio App. 3d 327, 2007 Ohio 6899, 882 N.E. 2d 22, 2007 Ohio App. LEXIS 6057 (Dec. 21, 2007).

Witness violated separation order

Although defendant requested a separation of witnesses and the trial court granted that request, the record did not reflect that the victim's grandfather did, in fact, remain in the courtroom after he was ordered to leave. Regardless, because defendant did not demonstrate how the grandfather's testimony, for whatever reason, would likely have conflicted with or failed to support his grandson's had he not heard his grandson's testimony, there was no prejudice sufficient for a finding of plain error. State v. Gilreath, 174 Ohio App. 3d 327, 2007 Ohio 6899, 882 N.E. 2d 22, 2007 Ohio App. LEXIS 6057 (Dec. 21, 2007).

There was no error in allowing an eyewitness to testify as a rebuttal witness in defendant's criminal trial, as her presence during the trial was inadvertent and she was not permitted to testify in the State's case-in-chief, she was not present when defendant and her mother testified and that was the testimony that she refuted with her own version of events, and the purposes of Ohio R. Evid. 615 were not violated by permitting such testimony. State v. Brown, — Ohio App. 3d —, 2006 Ohio 5123, — N.E. 2d —, 2006 Ohio App. LEXIS 5018 (Sept. 29, 2006).

RULE 616. Methods of Impeachment

In addition to other methods, a witness may be impeached by any of the following methods:

(A) **Bias.** Bias, prejudice, interest, or any motive to misrepresent may be shown to impeach the witness either by examination of the witness or by extrinsic evidence.

(B) **Sensory or mental defect.** A defect of capacity, ability, or opportunity to observe, remember, or relate may be shown to impeach the witness either by examination of the witness or by extrinsic evidence.

(C) **Specific contradiction.** Facts contradicting a witness's testimony may be shown for the purpose of impeaching the witness's testimony. If offered for the sole purpose of impeaching a witness's testimony, extrinsic evidence of contradiction is inadmissible unless the evidence is one of the following:

(1) Permitted by Evid. R. 608(A), 609, 613, 616(A), 616(B), or 706;

(2) Permitted by the common law of impeachment and not in conflict with the Rules of Evidence.

History: Effective 7-1-91; amended, eff 7-1-98.

NOTES TO DECISIONS

ANALYSIS

Bias
Confrontation and compulsory process
Contradiction
Fair trial tactics
Harmless error
Impeachment
Photographs
Probative evidence
— Evidence admissible to prove bias, prejudice, or motive
Scope of rule generally

Bias

There was no error in refusing to admit the mother's decade-old diary entries, which, although attenuated in time and logic, indicated the extent of the mother's negative feelings and profound resentment toward defendant and possibly revealed a motivation to testify against him, because any error in denying defendant's cross-examination with the diary's contents was harmless since the trial court, as the trier of fact, was privy to numerous examples of how defendant's conduct over the years had negatively affected the mother's feelings toward defendant. State v. Parsons, — Ohio App. 3d —, 2007 Ohio 1204, — N.E. 2d —, 2007 Ohio App. LEXIS 1025 (Mar. 13, 2007).

Cross-examination on the subject of a witness's intimidation, if any, and the witness's "motive to misrepresent" the witness's testimony, was impeachment material that defendant should have delved into in the witness's cross-examination pursuant to Ohio R. Evid. 616(A). State v. Airwyke, — Ohio App. 3d —, 2007 Ohio 3199, — N.E. 2d —, 2007 Ohio App. LEXIS 2945 (June 22, 2007).

Confrontation and compulsory process

Trial court properly determined that a children services worker's recorded summary of a rape victim's statements to her was not a prior written or recorded statement that could be relied on with any indicia of reliability, and it did not err in refusing to allow defendant to cross-examine the victim regarding statements in the summary unless they were in direct conflict with the victim's testimony. However, even if the trial court erred by limiting the scope of the cross-examination, the error was harmless because defendant elicited from the victim's own testimony on cross-examination the motive and bias he sought to introduce to the jury through the statement, as allowed by Ohio R. Evid. 616(A). Defendant's contention that he was denied his constitutional right to cross-examine adverse witnesses was without merit. State v. Montie, — Ohio App. 3d —, 2007 Ohio 2317, — N.E. 2d —, 2007 Ohio App. LEXIS 2139 (May 11, 2007).

Contradiction

State was permitted to show that defendant's girlfriend's testimony in court was different than the testimony that she gave to a detective previously pursuant to Ohio R. Evid. 616(C), such that the impeachment of that witness by specific contradiction was not error. State v. Djuric, — Ohio App. 3d —, 2007 Ohio 413, — N.E. 2d —, 2007 Ohio App. LEXIS 362 (Feb. 1, 2007).

Trial court did not abuse its discretion in permitting the police chief to testify regarding defendant's termination, because evidence regarding the date of defendant's termination was introduced to impeach the chief's testimony. The State was permitted to impeach the chief by showing a specific contradiction, pursuant to Ohio R. Evid. 616(C). State v. Travis, — Ohio App. 3d —, 2007 Ohio 6683, — N.E. 2d —, 2007 Ohio App. LEXIS 5859 (Dec. 17, 2007).

Fair trial tactics

Prosecution's questioning was proper to impeach the victim, not to discredit defendant, and therefore not an abuse of discretion, because the line of questioning regarding her sexual relationship with defendant was designed to establish a motive for the change in the victim's testimony. It was entirely appropriate for the State to pursue that line of questioning to test the victim's motive and credibility so that the jury could determine why her account of the events had changed. State v. Powers, — Ohio App. 3d —, 2007 Ohio 2738, — N.E. 2d —, 2007 Ohio App. LEXIS 2527 (June 6, 2007).

Harmless error

There was no showing that the defense was prejudiced by any alleged bias on the part of the victim, despite limitations on the ability to cross-examine him for purposes of impeachment under Ohio R. Evid. 616(A), as there were sufficient indications of the truthfulness of his trial testimony, which was consistent with his prior statements that identified defendant as the assailant immediately after the shooting. Accordingly, any such error on the limitation would have been harmless. State v. Swann, 171 Ohio App. 3d 304, 2007 Ohio 2010, 870 N.E.2d 754, 2007 Ohio App. LEXIS 1780 (2007).

Trial court did not erroneously limited the alleged victim's ability to impeach the individual because it simply noted, correctly, that the victim could not impeach the individual's credibility until he elicited some relevant testimony from her. In any event, any error involving the issue of the individual's credibility as a witness was necessarily harmless, since it could not have affected the outcome of the trial; the individual did not testify on the issue of damages, and it was a failure of proof on the issue of damages that resulted in the dismissal of the cause of action. Rieger v. Podeweltz, 2007 Ohio 5988, 2007 Ohio App. LEXIS 5264 (Nov. 9, 2007).

Impeachment

There was no abuse of discretion by the trial court's decisions regarding the scope of cross-examination of a medical expert in a medical malpractice action, as the use of his testimony from a prior case in Michigan was used to impeach his credibility and therefore was permissible under Ohio R. Evid. 611(B). Although the trial court should not have admitted into evidence certain transcripts from the Michigan litigation, pursuant to Ohio R. Evid. 616(C), such error did not cause material prejudice within the context of the entire trial. Werden v. Children's Hosp. Med. Ctr., — Ohio App. 3d —, 2006 Ohio 4600, — N.E. 2d —, 2006 Ohio App. LEXIS 4547 (Sept. 8, 2006).

Photographs

Because the officer thoroughly described the bite marks and injuries to one of the defendants to be essentially the same as what was depicted in the photographs, the trial court did not abuse its discretion in excluding the photographs. Defendants had ample opportunity to question the officers about the nature of the injuries. State v. Jiminez-ortiz, — Ohio App. 3d —, 2007 Ohio 5496, — N.E. 2d —, 2007 Ohio App. LEXIS 4839 (Oct. 15, 2007).

Probative evidence

Trial court was well within its discretion to limit cross-examination on the issue of tribal friction in Somalia under the circumstances because one of the two victims displayed no knowledge of friction between different tribes in Somalia, having left the country when he was 15-years old and having no knowledge of the tribal affiliation of defendant or other witnesses. Similarly, the trial court refused some of the cross-examination of the other victim because the fighting in Somalia was too remote since the victim had arrived in the United States 15 years earlier, but the trial court did allow testimony that one victim and defendant came from different tribes. State v. Warsame, — Ohio App. 3d —, 2007 Ohio 3656, — N.E. 2d —, 2007 Ohio App. LEXIS 3334 (July 19, 2007).

— Evidence admissible to prove bias, prejudice, or motive

Injured person was not entitled to additional financial information from a doctor who had performed an independent medical examination (IME) on the injured person, and the injured person's motion to compel disclosure of that information was properly denied, where the doctor had already provided, inter alia, the number of IMEs conducted by the doctor during a period of over six years, the price range for IMEs, the number of depositions provided by the doctor for the same period, and the charges typically associated with such depositions; additionally, the cross-examination portion of the doctor's video deposition, which was played at trial, dealt extensively with the doctor's medical-legal practice and the economic aspects thereof. Stinchcomb v. Mammone, 166 Ohio App. 3d 45, 2006 Ohio 1276, 849 N.E. 2d 54, 2006 Ohio App. LEXIS 1167 (Mar. 13, 2006).

Scope of rule generally

Trial court committed no evidentiary ruling error when it permitted defense counsel in a medical malpractice action to use a document describing time necessary for the production of a certain test result in the cross-examination of an expert for the parents of a minor patient who died while being treated, as the document was not admitted into evidence, it was not hearsay under Ohio R. Evid. 801(C), and it was properly used for impeachment purposes under Ohio R. Evid. 616(C) where the expert had testified that the time needed for test results was much shorter than indicated in the document. Werden v. Children's Hosp. Med. Ctr., — Ohio App. 3d —, 2006 Ohio 4600, — N.E. 2d —, 2006 Ohio App. LEXIS 4547 (Sept. 8, 2006).

ARTICLE VII
OPINIONS AND EXPERT TESTIMONY

RULE 701. Opinion Testimony by Lay Witnesses

If the witness is not testifying as an expert, the witness' testimony in the form of opinions or inferences is limited to those opinions or inferences which are (1) rationally based on the perception of the witness and (2) helpful to a clear understanding of the witness' testimony or the determination of a fact in issue.

History: Amended, eff 7-1-07.

NOTES TO DECISIONS

ANALYSIS

Admissibility of opinion testimony
Credibility of defendant
Lay opinion of police officer
Necessity of expert witness
Opinion testimony of lay witness
Opinion testimony of police officer
Opinions of lay witnesses
Opinions of physicians
Permissible lay opinion testimony
Police officer

Admissibility of opinion testimony

Trial court did not abuse its discretion in allowing the testimony by the homeowner regarding the improperly installed footer drains, pursuant to Ohio R. Evid. 701 as opinion testimony by a lay witness, because the homeowner had first hand knowledge of the subject of his testimony and his observations made him aware of what was needed to correct the remaining footer drain problems; and the testimony was helpful to aid the trier of fact, i.e. the court, in determining a fact at issue. Hugh v. Wills, — Ohio App. 3d —, 2006 Ohio 1282, — N.E. 2d —, 2006 Ohio App. LEXIS 1183 (Mar. 17, 2006).

Credibility of defendant

Prosecutor did not cross the line demarcated in State v. Boston by asking a police officer to testify concerning his assessment of the defendant's credibility. State v. Adrian, 168 Ohio App. 3d 300, 2006 Ohio 4143, 859 N.E.2d 1007, 2006 Ohio App. LEXIS 4088 (2006).

Lay opinion of police officer

There was no ineffectiveness of defendant's trial counsel in failing to seek suppression of the results of field sobriety tests, although there was no evidence that the administering officer substantially complied with the National Highway Traffic Safety Administration standards such that they should have been excluded in defendant's criminal matter on a charge of driving under the influence, in violation of RC § 4511.19(A)(1)(a). As the officer's observations regarding defendant's condition and his performance on the tests was admissible lay testimony under Ohio R. Evid. 701, which provided probable cause for defendant's arrest, there was no showing that defendant suffered prejudice by counsel's actions, such that the Strickland test was not met. State v. Green, — Ohio App. 3d —, 2007 Ohio 1713, — N.E. 2d —, 2007 Ohio App. LEXIS 1573 (Apr. 12, 2007).

Sufficient evidence supported the determination that defendant operated his motor vehicle while under the influence of drugs or alcohol, in violation of Middleburg Heights, Ohio, Ordinance 434.01(a)(1), where only substantial compliance was required for purposes of admitting the results of field sobriety tests pursuant to RC § 4511.19(D)(4)(b). Even if the trial court determined that there was no substantial compliance, the officer's observations of defendant's performance of the tests was admissible under Ohio R. Evid. 701 to support the determination that defendant was intoxicated when he was driving. City of Middleburg Heights v. Quinones, — Ohio App. 3d —, 2007 Ohio 3643, — N.E. 2d —, 2007 Ohio App. LEXIS 3351 (July 19, 2007).

Defendant's motion to exclude the testimony of a police officer about an automated fingerprint identification system (AFIS) was properly denied because (1) the witness did not testify as an expert, and (2) the officer's testimony about the workings of an AFIS machine was not used to determine that a palm print belonged to defendant because the officer made this determination without using the machine. State v. Keith, — Ohio App. 3d —, 2007 Ohio 4632, — N.E. 2d —, 2007 Ohio App. LEXIS 4172 (Sept. 10, 2007).

There was no error in the admission of the investigating officer's testimony pursuant to Ohio R. Evid. 701. The officer's lay testimony that the victim appeared to have "burn marks" in the photograph was based on his perceptions of her as he viewed her at the hospital that evening and was helpful in providing a clear understanding of his testimony. State v. Parker, — Ohio App. 3d —, 2006 Ohio 3684, — N.E. 2d —, 2006 Ohio App. LEXIS 3642 (July 20, 2006).

It was not permissible for police officers to testify as to the credibility of another witness, because such testimony infringed upon the role of the fact finder. State v. Haney, — Ohio App. 3d —, 2006 Ohio 4687, — N.E. 2d —, 2006 Ohio App. LEXIS 4600 (Sept. 8, 2006).

In a petty theft prosecution, it was error to allow a police officer to give an opinion as to whether a statement defendant made to the officer was an admission of guilt, because this invaded the province of the trier of fact, as it was tantamount to an opinion on whether defendant was guilty, but the error was not reversible because the trial was a bench trial in which it was presumed that the trier of fact only relied on competent evidence, and allowing the officer to state the opinion was not affirmative evidence that the trier of fact relied on incompetent evidence, so it did not rebut the presumption of regularity. State v. Haney, — Ohio App. 3d —, 2006 Ohio 4687, — N.E. 2d —, 2006 Ohio App. LEXIS 4600 (Sept. 8, 2006).

Necessity of expert witness

In a suit brought by a client seeking to recover for damages sustained to her home while it was in the care of a realtor, the realtor's motion for a directed verdict on the ground that the client failed to present expert testimony that the costs of repairing the client's home were reasonable and necessary was properly denied. Expert testimony was not required under Ohio R. Evid. 702(A) because jurors could be presumed to understand what defects made a property uninhabitable or otherwise diminished the owner's enjoyment and use of it, and the jury could reasonably infer from the client's testimony and that of a plumber and a representative of the construction company, properly submitted under Ohio R. Evid. 701, that the repairs to her house were necessary to restore the property to its prior condition. Reynolds v. Bauer, — Ohio App. 3d —, 2006 Ohio 2912, — N.E. 2d —, 2006 Ohio App. LEXIS 2730 (June 9, 2006).

Opinion testimony of lay witness

Trial court did not abuse its discretion when it permitted testimony from the owner of a tractor seller with respect to the repair of the type of tractor bought by a purchaser, which later malfunctioned and caused the purchaser injuries, as the owner was familiar with the recall on the tractor, he identified the relevant parts of it that were at issue, and his testimony was based on his own perceptions and was helpful to the jury pursuant to Ohio R. Evid. 701, such that it was proper lay opinion testimony. His testimony could not be considered expert testimony pursuant to Ohio R. Evid. 702 because the trial court had failed to make the threshold determination under Ohio R. Evid. 104(A) regarding the owner's qualifications to testify as an expert. Gadberry v. Eastgate Lawn & Tractor, Inc., — Ohio App. 3d —, 2007 Ohio 2849, — N.E. 2d —, 2007 Ohio App. LEXIS 2642 (June 11, 2007).

Trial court did not err by admitting the lab certified methamphetamine technician's testimony as to the identity of the anhydrous ammonia because he was qualified to testify as a lay witness. He testified as to his education, training, and experience in the areas of methamphetamine and anhydrous ammonia and testified that, based on the Draeger test results and the PH reading, the chemical found at the scene in the pickle jar was anhydrous ammonia. State v. Gragg, 173 Ohio App. 3d 270, 2007 Ohio 4731, 878 N.E.2d 55, 2007 Ohio App. LEXIS 4276 (2007).

Opinion testimony of police officer

Although the trial court's admission of the deputy's lay testimony regarding defendant's credibility was inappropriate and an abuse of discretion, the testimony was not unfairly prejudicial. Although the deputy's testimony was the only evidence presented by the State on the obstruction of official business charge, the deputy had already described defendant's inconsistent responses to his questioning before he stated his belief that defendant had been dishonest and that he had refused to name the female subject. The jury could have relied upon the deputy's description of defendant's inconsistencies during questioning or upon his testimony that defendant's failure to provide the female subject's name interfered with the investigation, rather than on the deputy's assessment of defendant's credibility, in convicting defendant of obstructing official business. State v. King, — Ohio App. 3d —, 2007 Ohio 335, — N.E. 2d —, 2007 Ohio App. LEXIS 306 (Jan. 29, 2007).

Trial court did not abuse its discretion in admitting expert witness testimony from a police officer pursuant to Ohio R. Evid. 702, as his testimony clearly demonstrated that he had specialized knowledge of blood interpretation with respect to defendant's criminal trial on a charge that he fatally shot a victim. The testimony was based on the officer's personal observations at the crime scene pursuant to Ohio R. Evid. 703, and the testimony was also admissible under Ohio R. Evid. 701. State v. Hopings, — Ohio App. 3d —, 2007 Ohio 450, — N.E. 2d —, 2007 Ohio App. LEXIS 397 (Feb. 2, 2007).

Trial court did not abuse its discretion when it overruled defendant's objection to testimony by a police officer regarding the lack of usable fingerprints in a bank robbery, as the testimony was based on the officer's observations throughout his many years as a police officer and a detective; however, even if his testimony was offered as an expert, he was qualified and the testimony was therefore admissible under Ohio R. Evid. 701 and 702, based on his experience and expertise in the area. State v. Starks, — Ohio App. 3d —, 2007 Ohio 4897, — N.E. 2d —, 2007 Ohio App. LEXIS 4364 (Sept. 21, 2007).

There was no plain error under Ohio R. Crim. P. 52 in the trial court's admission of opinion testimony by a police detective that he believed defendant was guilty, although those statements were inadmissible under Ohio R. Evid. 701 because they were not based on the detective's own perceptions and the statements were subjective expressions of his opinion that did not explain or help the jurors to understand his testimony, as the evidence of defendant's guilt was overwhelming; the plain error standard of review was employed due to defendant's failure to have objected to the testimony at trial. State v. Edwards, — Ohio App. 3d —, 2006 Ohio 5596, — N.E. 2d —, 2006 Ohio App. LEXIS 5619 (Oct. 27, 2006).

Testimony of a police officer, testifying pursuant to Ohio R. Evid. 701 and 702, was sufficient to support defendant's conviction for operating a vehicle while intoxicated where the officer testified that defendant continued driving for a distance of about 100 yards after the officer activated the lights on his patrol car before attempting to pull over, that the officer detected a very strong odor of alcoholic beverage coming from defendant's breath when he spoke with him, that defendant's eyes were red and bloodshot, that his speech was slurred and mumbled, that defendant was aggressive, that defendant refused to take field sobriety tests, and that he also refused to take a breath alcohol test or to submit to a physical examination. Village of Kirtland Hills v. Deir, — Ohio App. 3d —, 2006 Ohio 6536, — N.E. 2d —, 2006 Ohio App. LEXIS 6458 (Dec. 8, 2006).

Opinions of lay witnesses

In an action, inter alia, against a medical product manufacturer and its sales representative, arising from medical negligence that occurred to a patient while undergoing brain surgery with the use of the manufacturer's product, the trial court did not err in excluding expert testimony by a former sales representative pursuant to Ohio R. Evid. 701, as the witness had not been qualified as an expert, and as a lay person he could not offer opinion testimony that was not based on his own perceptions; the testimony that the witness would have given was based on his professional opinion of how a physician would react under certain circumstances, which was only appropriate if given as an expert witness. Zappola v. Leibinger, — Ohio App. 3d —, 2006 Ohio 2207, — N.E. 2d —, 2006 Ohio App. LEXIS 2058 (May 4, 2006).

Opinions of defendant's employees regarding defendant's signature on certain checks were admissible, under Ohio R. Evid. 701, because their opinions were rationally based on their perceptions given that they had worked with defendant for several years and verified that they recognized his handwriting. Their opinions were helpful to the determination of a fact in issue given that the opinions aided the trial court in determining defendant's culpability. State v. Silverman, — Ohio App. 3d —, 2006 Ohio 3826, — N.E. 2d —, 2006 Ohio App. LEXIS 3791 (July 27, 2006).

Defense counsel was not ineffective in failing to object to lay opinion testimony that defendant did not accidentally stab the victim. The witnesses' testimony was admissible under Ohio R. Evid. 701 since they were eyewitnesses to the attack and since their testimony helped the jury resolve a disputed fact: whether the stabbing was an accident. State v. Taylor, — Ohio App. 3d —, 2006 Ohio 4064, — N.E. 2d —, 2006 Ohio App. LEXIS 4031 (Aug. 8, 2006).

Opinions of physicians

In proceedings to consider the continued appointment of a daughter as guardian for her mother, it was proper to admit the opinion testimony of the mother's physician, even though the physician was not an expert in the dementia from which the mother suffered and had not seen the mother for a year, because the testimony was admitted as the opinion of a non-expert based on the physician's long term treatment of and interaction with the mother, and the trial court gave the opinion the weight it deserved as a lay person's opinion, nor did the mother show admitting the testimony materially prejudiced her. In re Binkley, — Ohio App. 3d —, 2007 Ohio 900, — N.E. 2d —, 2007 Ohio App. LEXIS 800 (Mar. 5, 2007).

Permissible lay opinion testimony

In defendant's prosecution on a charge of compelling prostitution, the 13-year-old victim's testimony that defendant's statement to her, "Fifty dollars and I'll make it worth your while," made her believe that he wanted her to have sex with him for $50 was relevant under Ohio R. Evid. 701 and 704. The statement related to money, sexual activity, and whether defendant knew what he was doing by saying it twice and then getting her reaction. State v. Williams, — Ohio App. 3d —, 2006 Ohio 3706, — N.E. 2d —, 2006 Ohio App. LEXIS 3631 (July 20, 2006).

Trial court did not abuse its discretion in allowing the victim's testimony with respect to the photographs of her because she was not testifying as an expert witness, pursuant to Ohio R. Evid. 702, rather, she testified as a lay witness, pursuant to Ohio R. Evid. 701, who had firsthand knowledge about her encounter with defendant. That testimony included her recount of defendant continually putting a gun to her head/face area and thus, she was qualified to identify herself in photographs and explain to the jury her appearance in the photographs and how that appearance came to be. The victim's testimony was rationally based on her perceptions and was helpful in providing a clear understanding of her testimony. State v. Parker, — Ohio App. 3d —, 2006 Ohio 3684, — N.E. 2d —, 2006 Ohio App. LEXIS 3642 (July 20, 2006).

Police officer

Police officer was qualified to testify as a lay witness, rather than an expert witness, where he had the proper education, training, and experience to conduct tests to identify substance as anhydrous ammonia: State v. Gragg, 173 Ohio App. 3d 270, 2007 Ohio 4731, 878 N.E.2d 55, 2007 Ohio App. LEXIS 4276 (2007).

RULE 702. Testimony by Experts

A witness may testify as an expert if all of the following apply:

(A) The witness' testimony either relates to matters beyond the knowledge or experience possessed by lay persons or dispels a misconception common among lay persons;

(B) The witness is qualified as an expert by specialized knowledge, skill, experience, training, or education regarding the subject matter of the testimony;

(C) The witness' testimony is based on reliable scientific, technical, or other specialized information. To the extent that the testimony reports the result of a procedure, test, or experiment, the testimony is reliable only if all of the following apply:

(1) The theory upon which the procedure, test, or experiment is based is objectively verifiable or is validly derived from widely accepted knowledge, facts, or principles;

(2) The design of the procedure, test, or experiment reliably implements the theory;

(3) The particular procedure, test, or experiment was conducted in a way that will yield an accurate result.

History: Amended, eff 7-1-94.

NOTES TO DECISIONS

ANALYSIS

Abuse of discretion
Admissibility of doctor's opinion
Admissibility of expert testimony
—Child sex abuse cases
Admissibility of expert testimony in child sex abuse cases
Admission of expert testimony
Allowable bases for expert opinion
Author of reference book
Battered woman syndrome
Child victim
Domestic violence
Driving under influence
Drugs expert
Exclusion of witness testimony
Expert's opinion
Expert's opinion in medical malpractice case
Expert status
Expert testimony
— Insufficient basis for opinion
Expert testimony of physician
Experts
Exposure to toxic substance
Laughter
Law enforcement officers
Limitations on testimony
Medical expert
— Criminal actions
Medical malpractice expert
Motor vehicle sales
Necessity of expert opinion
Necessity of expert testimony
Polygraph
Psychologists
Qualification as expert
Qualification of expert
Qualification of medical expert
Qualification of witness as expert

Qualifications of experts
— Doctors
— Police officers
Real estate brokers
Reliability requirement
Scientific tests
Substantial compliance

Abuse of discretion

Trial court did not abuse its discretion in determining that an electronic's expert's testimony was not admissible pursuant to Ohio R. Evid. 702(C) in a products liability case commenced by a deceased car owner and her spouse against a car manufacturer and dealership, as the scientific theory upon which the expert's opinion was based was deemed unreliable. There was a lack of evidence showing a causal connection between an electromagnetic interference and a cruise control malfunction resulting in sudden acceleration, and an absence of any verification of the validity of the theory. Turker v. Ford Motor Co., — Ohio App. 3d —, 2007 Ohio 985, — N.E. 2d —, 2007 Ohio App. LEXIS 920 (Mar. 8, 2007).

In the second trial in a patient's dental malpractice action, held because the patient's motion for a new trial had been granted after a defense verdict was rendered in the first trial, the trial court did not abuse its discretion in precluding the dentist from calling an expert witness whose testimony had been precluded as a discovery sanction in the first trial. The preclusion order did not improperly change a separate discovery order that had set a deadline for the identification of expert witnesses because that order was not final and the preclusion order did not necessarily contradict it, trial courts could exclude the presentation of expert witnesses by parties who failed to comply with pretrial orders and, under Ohio R. Civ. P. 16(7), could reasonably limit the number of expert witnesses, and the dentist showed no prejudice to the defense caused by the preclusion of the expert's testimony. Scibelli v. Pannunzio, — Ohio App. 3d —, 2006 Ohio 5652, — N.E. 2d —, 2006 Ohio App. LEXIS 5650 (Oct. 26, 2006).

Admissibility of doctor's opinion

Doctor's testimony did not relate to the rape victim's credibility; rather, the testimony established that it was the doctor's medical opinion that sometime during the victim's childhood, she was a victim of child sexual abuse and she gave no opinion of the victim's veracity. Further, the testimony fell within the hearsay exception of Ohio R. Evid. 803(4) because she stated that she was provided with the information solely for the purpose of medical treatment and diagnosis and that she worked for a children's advocacy center, not a prosecutor's or investigator's office. State v. Haschenburger, — Ohio App. 3d —, 2007 Ohio 1562, — N.E. 2d —, 2007 Ohio App. LEXIS 1446 (Mar. 27, 2007).

Admissibility of expert testimony

There was no requirement that a trial court make findings to support its determination that an expert witness' testimony was not admissible pursuant to Ohio R. Evid. 702 and 104(A) in a products liability case. It reviewed each of the conditions contained in Ohio R. Evid. 702 and then set forth its rationale in reaching its conclusion. Turker v. Ford Motor Co., — Ohio App. 3d —, 2007 Ohio 985, — N.E. 2d —, 2007 Ohio App. LEXIS 920 (Mar. 8, 2007).

When a widow sued her husband's employer for an intentional tort causing the husband's death, claiming that his exposure to chemicals in the course of his employment caused him to contract pancreatic cancer, the testimony of her proposed expert witnesses was properly excluded, under Ohio R. Evid. 702(C), because neither witness cited any studies showing a causal connection between the chemicals the husband was exposed to and pancreatic cancer. Braglin v.

Lempco Indus., — Ohio App. 3d —, 2007 Ohio 1964, — N.E. 2d —, 2007 Ohio App. LEXIS 1773 (Apr. 24, 2007).

Trial court's admission of a coroner's testimony as to the time of death of the victim was not error under Ohio R. Evid. 702(C), as the coroner indicated that he used the Hessnge method of determination, which had sufficient scientific and medical reliability. The fact that the coroner had changed his opinion as to the time of death was a credibility issue for the jury to determine. State v. Williams, — Ohio App. 3d —, 2006 Ohio 1381, — N.E. 2d —, 2006 Ohio App. LEXIS 1259 (Mar. 22, 2006).

In a product liability and medical negligence action, a trial court did not abuse its discretion in allowing neurosurgeons to testify as to what probably transpired between the operating neurosurgeon and a medical product sales representative in the operating room, as that testimony was relevant to the adequacy of the warning and information provided to the neurosurgeon and provided the jury with an opinion of what could have occurred based on the testifying neurosurgeons' professional experience. Zappola v. Leibinger, — Ohio App. 3d —, 2006 Ohio 2207, — N.E. 2d —, 2006 Ohio App. LEXIS 2058 (May 4, 2006).

Trial court did not commit plain error under Ohio R. Crim. P. 52(B) in allowing admission of expert witness testimony on the subject of DNA evidence in defendant's criminal trial, as the determination as to the reliability of the evidence was within the jury's province, and there was no obvious unreliability of the evidence that would have required the judge to preclude its admission; as defendant failed to timely object to the expert testimony as unreliable under Ohio R. Evid. 702, all but plain error was waived. State v. Harris, — Ohio App. 3d —, 2006 Ohio 3520, — N.E. 2d —, 2006 Ohio App. LEXIS 3439 (June 27, 2006).

Trial cout did not err in failing to strike an expert's testimony where it was based on reliable facts and evidence that was admissible in a negligence action arising from an accident when a truck driver's passenger side mirror hit a construction worker and her vehicle, as the expert relied in part on portions of a police report, which were an admissible public record within the hearsay exception under Ohio R. Evid. 803(8) where the portions relied on were drawn from the officer's observations of the scene. The expert was entitled to rely on the evidence, including photographs, deposition testimony, and underlying circumstances of the accident, in rendering his opinion pursuant to Ohio R. Evid. 702, 703, and 705. Wise v. Meyer, — Ohio App. 3d —, 2006 Ohio 4654, — N.E. 2d —, 2006 Ohio App. LEXIS 4556 (Sept. 8, 2006).

Although an employee's medical expert in a workers' compensation proceeding assumed in his testimony that the employee had worked for four years, when in fact the employer's human resources administrator testified that the employee worked less than two years in a particular job, such conflict did not affect the admissibility of the evidence pursuant to Ohio R. Evid. 702, but rather just the weight and credibility. The employer's motion for judgment notwithstanding the verdict or alternatively, a new trial pursuant to Ohio R. Civ. P. 50 and 59, was properly denied. Hyden v. Kroger Co., — Ohio App. 3d —, 2006 Ohio 6430, — N.E. 2d —, 2006 Ohio App. LEXIS 6367 (Dec. 7, 2006).

—Child sex abuse cases

Trial court did not abuse its discretion in permitting a nurse to testify as an expert regarding the examination and recognition of injuries and trauma to the children's' genital and vaginal areas because the nurse testified that she had received extensive training and had specialized knowledge and skills related to the examination and recognition of sexual abuse injuries, which was well beyond that possessed by lay persons. In addition, her testimony was based upon reliable procedures and information utilized within the medical field. State v.

Young, — Ohio App. 3d —, 2007 Ohio 754, — N.E. 2d —, 2007 Ohio App. LEXIS 661 (Feb. 23, 2007).

Admissibility of expert testimony in child sex abuse cases

Trial court properly allowed an expert witness to offer her opinions regarding the wide range of behavioral characteristics displayed by minor victims of sexual abuse: State v. Bell, 176 Ohio App. 3d 378, 2008 Ohio 2578, 891 N.E.2d 1280, 2008 Ohio App. LEXIS 2177 (2008).

Because the rape case constituted a credibility contest between the victim and defendant, defendant was not afforded a fair trial when the hospital's associate director testified as to the victim's veracity. Since no medical evidence existed revealing sexual abuse, the associate director's opinion that the victim was sexually abused was based solely upon the victim's statement and the admission of that testimony was not only improper, it was egregious, prejudicial, and constituted reversible error. State v. Knight, — Ohio App. 3d —, 2006 Ohio 6437, — N.E. 2d —, 2006 Ohio App. LEXIS 6388 (Dec. 7, 2006).

Admission of expert testimony

Trial court did not abuse its discretion by relying on Ohio R. Evid. 403(A) when it excluded the psychologist's testimony in defendant's child endangering trial because, since defendant failed to meet the requirements set forth in Haines, any testimony related to battered-woman syndrome had the potential to mislead the jury and cause confusion of the issues. The psychologist's testimony went beyond merely providing a general context for defendant's behavior, and went to the very question the jury was required to determine--whether defendant had the culpable mens rea necessary for committing endangering children--and defendant did not demonstrate the required connection between the scientific research or test result and particular disputed factual issues in the case. State v. Sorah, — Ohio App. 3d —, 2007 Ohio 5898, — N.E. 2d —, 2007 Ohio App. LEXIS 5179 (Nov. 5, 2007).

Trial court did not abuse its discretion under Ohio R. Evid. 702(A) in admitting expert testimony of vehicle owners' expert for purposes of rebutting the claim by an automobile dealer and manufacturer that a trade/repurchase situation involving the owners' vehicle, which turned out to be a "lemon," was not bona fide error as claimed, but instead, was a willful planned tactic meant to defraud the consumer, as many terms were used which were not familiar to an ordinary lay person. The expert was well qualified in the field, based on numerous capacities in that industry over a long period of years. Smith v. GMC, 168 Ohio App. 3d 336, 2006 Ohio 4283, 859 N.E.2d 1035, 2006 Ohio App. LEXIS 4197 (2006).

Defendant's counsel's failure to object to testimony by a dog-handler regarding accelerant-sniffing dogs and their ability to detect scents beyond what could have been detected in a laboratory was not ineffective assistance, as the dog-handler had been qualified as an expert witness under Ohio R. Evid. 702 and there was no showing that the testimony elicited prejudiced defendant. State v. Abner, — Ohio App. 3d —, 2006 Ohio 4510, — N.E. 2d —, 2006 Ohio App. LEXIS 4523 (Sept. 1, 2006).

There was no abuse of discretion in a trial court's denial of an insurer's motion for a new trial pursuant to Ohio R. Civ. P. 59(A)(9) in an action by insureds, arising from their involvement in a vehicle collision, as the admission of expert testimony pursuant to Ohio R. Evid. 702 from doctors who treated one of the insureds was not prejudicial error where they were not required to testify in terms of reasonable medical probability because they had not been asked whether the insured's depression or medical condition was proximately caused by the pain she experienced or by the accident itself. Butler v. Minton, — Ohio App. 3d —, 2006 Ohio 4800, — N.E. 2d —, 2006 Ohio App. LEXIS 4710 (Sept. 15, 2006).

Allowable bases for expert opinion

Trial court's denial of a party guest's motion for a directed verdict pursuant to Ohio R. Civ. P. 50(A)(4) in an action against her by a house owner, alleging that the guest's negligent disposal of her smoking materials caused a fire in the house, was proper, as the admission of differential diagnosis and deductive reasoning testimony by the house owner's expert with respect to the possible cause of the fire was proper under Ohio R. Evid. 702; the expert opined that the improper disposal of the cigarette material into peat moss caused a chemical reaction that started the fire, and the guest had the opportunity to present her own experts to testify as to alternative possible causes of the fire. Morelli v. Walker, — Ohio App. 3d —, 2007 Ohio 4832, — N.E. 2d —, 2007 Ohio App. LEXIS 4327 (Sept. 20, 2007).

Author of reference book

In a patient's dental malpractice action, the patient's expert witness was properly permitted to read from a treatise that he had written because he testified to his substantive opinions at trial. An expert could refer to literature as being part of the basis for an opinion because under Ohio R. Evid. 702, 703, expert testimony was inherently based upon various sources including literature. Scibelli v. Pannunzio, — Ohio App. 3d —, 2006 Ohio 5652, — N.E. 2d —, 2006 Ohio App. LEXIS 5650 (Oct. 26, 2006).

Battered woman syndrome

Expert was properly allowed to testify, in defendant's prosecution for felonious assault and abduction, regarding the battered woman syndrome because (1) sufficient evidence showed that the victim behaved like a battered woman, (2) the expert was qualified to testify about why a victim of a violent crime might change the victim's story, recant a statement to the police, or accept blame for the incident, and (3) the expert did not give an opinion about whether the victim was a battered woman, told the truth, or if defendant was a batterer or guilty of a crime. State v. Caudill, — Ohio App. 3d —, 2008 Ohio 1557, — N.E. 2d —, 2008 Ohio App. LEXIS 1342 (Mar. 31, 2008).

When a victim's credibility is challenged upon cross-examination during the state's case-in-chief, the state may introduce expert testimony regarding battered woman syndrome to aid the trier-of-fact in determining the victim's state of mind, e.g., to explain why she returned to the defendant despite his aggressions toward her. State v. Haines, 112 Ohio St. 3d 393, 2006 Ohio 6711, 860 N.E.2d 91, 2006 Ohio LEXIS 3680 (2006).

Child victim

Trial court abused its discretion when it allowed, over objection, an expert to give an opinion on whether a child was sexually abused because the only foundation for that opinion was the child's unverified allegations. It was nothing more than an opinion on the veracity of the accuser, which was inappropriate and highly prejudicial. State v. Schewirey, — Ohio App. 3d —, 2006 Ohio 7054, — N.E. 2d —, 2006 Ohio App. LEXIS 6988 (Dec. 20, 2006).

Domestic violence

Trial court did not abuse its discretion in determining that the expert on "victim dynamics" was qualified as an expert in matters involving domestic violence and the impact it had on the victims of that abuse. Her expert testimony was relevant and helpful to the jury because it involved matters beyond the jurors' knowledge or experience, and dispelled misconceptions common to lay persons; specifically, it helped the jurors to understand the victim's motives for wanting to minimize defendant's actions and to recant her prior accusations. State v. Kraus, — Ohio App. 3d —, 2007 Ohio 6027, — N.E. 2d —, 2007 Ohio App. LEXIS 5309 (Nov. 13, 2007).

Driving under influence

Placing primary reliance on an EtG test for alcohol use is inappropriate and scientifically unsupportable at this time. Serious, peer-reviewed research remains underway because the science of EtG is not fully understood. EtG testing remains at such an early stage that good science demands that no test result be given conclusive effect in legal proceedings: Johnson v. State Med. Bd., 147 Ohio Misc. 2d 121, 2008 Ohio 4376, 893 N.E.2d 565, 2008 Ohio Misc. LEXIS 209 (2008).

RC § 4511.19(D)(4)(b), which governs the admissibility of field sobriety tests, does not conflict with Ohio R. Evid. 702 and does not constitute a separation of powers violation of the state high court's authority to promulgate rules of evidence under Ohio Const. art. IV, § 5(B); expert testimony governed by Ohio R. Evid. 702 is not required as a predicate to admission of the results of a field sobriety test. State v. Cross, — Ohio App. 3d —, 2006 Ohio 1679, — N.E. 2d —, 2006 Ohio App. LEXIS 1540 (Mar. 31, 2006).

RC § 4511.19(D)(4)(b), allowing the admission, at a suppression hearing, of the results of field sobriety tests administered in substantial compliance with reliable standards, did not violate Ohio Const. art. IV, § 5(B), giving the Ohio Supreme Court the exclusive right to prescribe rules governing practice and procedure in Ohio courts, because, under Ohio R. Evid. 101(C), the Ohio Rules of Evidence did not apply to a suppression hearing, where the issue to be determined was the admissibility of evidence, under Ohio R. Evid. 104(A), and, since the Rules of Evidence did not apply in suppression hearings, RC § 4511.19(D)(4)(b) could not conflict any Rule of Evidence, including Ohio R. Evid. 702, regarding the admissibility of expert testimony, in a motion to suppress context. State v. Ladigo, — Ohio App. 3d —, 2006 Ohio 3475, — N.E. 2d —, 2006 Ohio App. LEXIS 3426 (June 27, 2006).

Testimony of a police officer, testifying pursuant to Ohio R. Evid. 701 and 702, was sufficient to support defendant's conviction for operating a vehicle while intoxicated where the officer testified that defendant continued driving for a distance of about 100 yards after the officer activated the lights on his patrol car before attempting to pull over, that the officer detected a very strong odor of alcoholic beverage coming from defendant's breath when he spoke with him, that defendant's eyes were red and bloodshot, that his speech was slurred and mumbled, that defendant was aggressive, that defendant refused to take field sobriety tests, and that he also refused to take a breath alcohol test or to submit to a physical examination. Village of Kirtland Hills v. Deir, — Ohio App. 3d —, 2006 Ohio 6536, — N.E. 2d —, 2006 Ohio App. LEXIS 6458 (Dec. 8, 2006).

Drugs expert

Trial court did not commit plain error under Ohio R. Crim. P. 52 in allowing a State's witness to testify regarding the methodology he used in testing drug paraphernalia and substances obtained from defendants' residence in their criminal matter on charges relating to having possibly operated a methamphetamine lab in their home, as the reliability of the witness's testimony was sufficient to meet the requirements of Ohio R. Evid. 702 and the Daubert standard. As there was no objection raised in the trial court regarding the testimony, the matter was judged on appeal under the plain error standard of review. State v. McDade, — Ohio App. 3d —, 2007 Ohio 749, — N.E. 2d —, 2007 Ohio App. LEXIS 685 (Feb. 23, 2007).

There was no error under Ohio R. Evid. 403(A) and 702 in allowing a police detective to testify regarding his opinion as to whether defendant was involved in drug dealing, as he was a 12-year veteran of the police department, he had been involved in drug investigations for half of that time, and his testimony related to a matter beyond the knowledge or experience possessed by lay persons. His testimony was not

substantially outweighed by the danger of unfair prejudice, confusion of the issues, or misleading the jury. State v. Henderson, — Ohio App. 3d —, 2007 Ohio 2372, — N.E. 2d —, 2007 Ohio App. LEXIS 2212 (May 17, 2007).

Exclusion of witness testimony

Where the state was unreasonably prejudiced in its ability to secure an expert to evaluate and respond to the proposed expert testimony, the court did not abuse its discretion by excluding the testimony of a defense expert as a sanction for the defendant's failure to make timely disclosure: State v. Weaver, 178 Ohio App. 3d 504, 2008 Ohio 5022, 898 N.E.2d 1023, 2008 Ohio App. LEXIS 4242 (2008).

Where a trial court excluded an expert's medical testimony pursuant to Ohio R. Evid. 702 on the issue of specific causation with respect to toxic mold claims by county employees and their spouses, alleging that there was mold in the building that they worked in, the claims failed because without establishment of both general and specific causation, a prima facie case was not shown. Terry v. Caputo, 115 Ohio St. 3d 351, 2007 Ohio 5023, 875 N.E.2d 72, 2007 Ohio LEXIS 2406 (2007).

When, in a murder prosecution, defendant wanted to introduce expert testimony from a police officer to support his self-defense claim by showing he had reason to fear the victim, the testimony was properly excluded because the jury could determine for itself whether defendant acted reasonably without the assistance of such testimony. State v. Davis, — Ohio App. 3d —, 2006 Ohio 3171, — N.E. 2d —, 2006 Ohio App. LEXIS 3082 (June 23, 2006).

Trial court's exclusion of a defense expert's testimony regarding false confessions was proper under Ohio R. Evid. 702(C), as consideration of the Daubert reliability factors indicated that defendant had not sufficiently established the reliability of the expert's opinion and of his proposed testimony; the use of the Daubert standard was appropriate, although the expert was a psychologist and not necessarily a "scientific" expert. State v. Abner, — Ohio App. 3d —, 2006 Ohio 4510, — N.E. 2d —, 2006 Ohio App. LEXIS 4523 (Sept. 1, 2006).

During defendant's trial on charges of murder and aggravated murder, a defense witness was properly not permitted to testify that he had handled and shot defendant's gun and it had a hair trigger; because whether a gun had a hair trigger was not within the common knowledge of most jurors, such testimony would have required an expert witness, the witness in question was not qualified as an expert, and defendant chose not to retain an expert to present testimony on this issue. State v. Higgins, — Ohio App. 3d —, 2006 Ohio 5220, — N.E. 2d —, 2006 Ohio App. LEXIS 5197 (Sept. 29, 2006).

Trial court did not abuse its discretion in admitting some of a police officer's testimony regarding the right of a person to act in self-defense in a civil assault and battery action between a neighbor and a dog owner who were involved in an altercation, as inadmissible prejudicial evidence that was within the auspices of expert testimony pursuant to Ohio R. Evid. 702 was excluded. Lloyd v. Rutledge, — Ohio App. 3d —, 2006 Ohio 6123, — N.E. 2d —, 2006 Ohio App. LEXIS 6066 (Nov. 17, 2006).

Expert's opinion

In a parental rights termination proceeding, a juvenile court properly determined that three psychologists who were witnesses for the county agency were qualified under Ohio R. Evid. 702 and 104(A) to testify as experts on the issue of whether caged beds that the children were forced to sleep in were abusive, as the parents attempted to show that most of the children had severe behavioral and developmental problems that required putting them in cages for their own safety and the safety of the other children, and the expert testimony was helpful to the juvenile court's understanding of whether the children were abused and/or dependent. The expert testimony was useful at the disposition hearing to determine whether the children could not or should not be placed with the parents within a reasonable time pursuant to RC § 2151.414(E)(14) and (15). In re Mercy Anne G., — Ohio App. 3d —, 2007 Ohio 1197, — N.E.2d —, 2007 Ohio App. LEXIS 1132 (Mar. 14, 2007).

Condominium residents' expert's opinion was properly excluded under Ohio R. Evid. 702 where the published noise standard with respect to the residents' complaint regarding another resident's allegedly excessive noise level was met, and the expert's personal opinion that some higher, unpublished, and unknown standard applied to the type of luxury condominium involved was lacking in any reliable scientific, technical, or other specialized basis. Tonti v. East Bank Condos., Llc, — Ohio App. 3d —, 2007 Ohio 6779, — N.E. 2d —, 2007 Ohio App. LEXIS 5931 (Dec. 18, 2007).

As a hearing examiner for the Ohio Department of Job and Family Services, in a contested hearing regarding a determination of how much a long-term care facility had to reimburse the Department for overpayments under the Ohio Medicaid program caused by the facility's officer's embezzlement over a period of years, did not find that the Department did not comply with the applicable requirements of RC § 5111.27(B)(1) through (8) for purposes of auditing procedures, a trial court's agreement with the hearing examiner's conclusion that the audits had to comply with Ohio R. Evid. 702(C) was error. St. Francis Home, Inc. v. Ohio Dep't of Job & Family Servs., — Ohio App. 3d —, 2006 Ohio 6147, — N.E. 2d —, 2006 Ohio App. LEXIS 6095 (Nov. 21, 2006).

Expert's opinion in medical malpractice case

In a medical malpractice case alleging that a child suffered a permanent brachial plexus injury after a physician delivered the child, two experts were properly allowed to testify to possible causes of the injury other than the physician's excess lateral traction because, while prospective testing of an in utero causation theory of brachial plexus injury testified to by the experts was unavailable, (1) retrospective studies reported the occurrence of brachial plexus injuries where excess lateral traction could not have been the cause, (2) prospective and objective evidence of brachial plexus injury without excess lateral traction existed even where a delivery was not complicated by shoulder dystocia, (3) the in utero alternative cause theory was supported by peer reviewed articles, (4) the role of forces other than traction as the cause of brachial plexus injuries was acknowledged in a textbook, (5) it was recognized that data suggested that a significant proportion of brachial plexus injuries were not associated with shoulder dystocia, and (6) an expert for the child admittedly could not entirely rule out endogenous forces as being the cause of the child's injuries. D'amore v. Cardwell, — Ohio App. 3d —, 2008 Ohio 1559, — N.E. 2d —, 2008 Ohio App. LEXIS 1338 (Mar. 31, 2008).

Expert status

Even if the basis for the deputy's opinion were construed as satisfying Ohio R. Evid. 702(B) (the witness was qualified as an expert), it could not be found that the State made any attempt to satisfy Ohio R. Evid. (A) (matters beyond the knowledge or experience of lay persons) and (C) (the testimony was based on scientific, technical, or other specialized information) so as to establish him as an expert. State v. King, — Ohio App. 3d —, 2007 Ohio 335, — N.E. 2d —, 2007 Ohio App. LEXIS 306 (Jan. 29, 2007).

Detective's testimony as to what he thought defendant had said on a videotape was properly admitted, as it was not given as expert opinion evidence under Ohio R. Evid. 702, but instead, it was provided in the context of the authenticity and correctness of the re-transcription of the tape that was found at defendant's home. State v. Gillingham, — Ohio App. 3d —, 2006 Ohio 5758, — N.E. 2d —, 2006 Ohio App. LEXIS 5738 (Oct. 27, 2006).

Expert testimony

It was error for the trial court to accept the testimony of the principal of the construction company with respect to an industry standard for determining the depth of poured concrete because he did not qualify as an expert, and his testimony in that regard lacked the specificity necessary to be admissible as expert testimony, pursuant to Ohio R. Evid. 702. Even apart from whether he qualified as an expert, his testimony regarding an industry standard was too general to be admissible as expert testimony. Marchese Concrete Co. v. Derubba, — Ohio App. 3d —, 2006 Ohio 330, — N.E. 2d —, 2006 Ohio App. LEXIS 283 (Jan. 27, 2006).

Significance of blood alcohol content value is beyond the comprehension of an ordinary juror, and without explanatory expert testimony, the admission of the evidence inevitably imposes unfair prejudice, confuses the issues, and misleads the jury. Thus, the trial court's admission, in a personal injury suit, of a bicyclist's BAC level without corroborating expert testimony was error. Clark v. Curnutte, — Ohio App. 3d —, 2006 Ohio 1545, — N.E. 2d —, 2006 Ohio App. LEXIS 1443 (Mar. 31, 2006).

There was no plain error in the admission of the testimony because, under Ohio R. Evid. 702(B), the veterinarian was qualified as an expert by specialized knowledge, skill, experience, training, or education to testify as to the condition of defendant's horse. Given his qualifications, the State's failure to tender him as an expert was of no consequence. State v. Dixon, — Ohio App. 3d —, 2006 Ohio 2114, — N.E. 2d —, 2006 Ohio App. LEXIS 1958 (Apr. 28, 2006).

Trial court did not abuse its discretion when it permitted the attorney to testify, on redirect, about a hypothetical concerning Person A under the management services agreement, because the attorney had already been asked, on cross-examination, to interpret certain provisions of the agreement and the testimony was not beyond the attorney's qualifications and area of expertise as an expert nor was it beyond the scope of cross-examination. Kimble Mixer Co. v. St. Vincent, — Ohio App. 3d —, 2006 Ohio 2258, — N.E. 2d —, 2006 Ohio App. LEXIS 2119 (May 2, 2006).

In defendant's prosecution for sexual imposition, the trial court erred when it allowed a psychologist to opine that she thought that the child victim was credible because an expert cannot testify as to the expert's opinion of the veracity of the statements of a child declarant. State v. Smith, — Ohio App. 3d —, 2006 Ohio 2675, — N.E. 2d —, 2006 Ohio App. LEXIS 2499 (May 26, 2006).

— Insufficient basis for opinion

Expert in forensic accounting was properly allowed to testify concerning questionable expenses charged to the company, without asserting an opinion, where he was provided insufficient documentation concerning those expenses to offer an opinion: Blair v. McDonagh, 177 Ohio App. 3d 262, 2008 Ohio 3698, 894 N.E.2d 377, 2008 Ohio App. LEXIS 3125 (2008).

Expert testimony of physician

Expert opinions were properly permitted because they were based on perceptions by each expert's examination of properly admitted evidence, including the CT scan and medical reports; two of the medical experts formed their opinions by examining the CT scan and medical records, while another personally evaluated the nine-month-old victim. State v. Stacy, — Ohio App. 3d —, 2007 Ohio 6744, — N.E. 2d —, 2007 Ohio App. LEXIS 5911 (Dec. 17, 2007).

Neurosurgeons were qualified to testify as to a causal connection between a medical product used in a neurosurgical procedure and the patient's damages as a result thereof, although they had not used the product previously, as they were trained to identify cranial injuries and their causes and they could testify as to the source of an injury. Zappola v.

Leibinger, — Ohio App. 3d —, 2006 Ohio 2207, — N.E. 2d —, 2006 Ohio App. LEXIS 2058 (May 4, 2006).

Experts

Trial court's admission of expert's testimony pursuant to Ohio R. Evid. 702 in an action by vehicle owners against a dealer and manufacturer, alleging that they engaged in spurious sales tactics when the owners' vehicle was a "lemon" that resulted in a replacement vehicle at a new loan cost to the owners, was proper, as the expert did not testify as to any specific instances of character evidence that should have been excluded under Ohio R. Evid. 404. Although the expert discussed nefarious sales tactics by some dealerships, he did not testify as to specific knowledge of the particular dealer's character or that it had acted in conformity with a "bad" character. Smith v. GMC, 168 Ohio App. 3d 336, 2006 Ohio 4283, 859 N.E.2d 1035, 2006 Ohio App. LEXIS 4197 (2006).

Exposure to toxic substance

To present a prima facie case involving an injury caused by exposure to mold or other toxic substance, a claimant must establish (1) that the toxin is capable of causing the medical condition or ailment (general causation) and (2) that the toxic substance in fact caused the claimant's medical condition (specific causation.) Establishing general causation and specific causation in cases involving exposure to mold or other toxic substances involves a scientific inquiry, and thus causation must be established by the testimony of a medical expert. Without expert testimony to establish both general causation and specific causation, a claimant cannot establish a prima facie case of exposure to mold or other toxic substance: Terry v. Caputo, 115 Ohio St. 3d 351, 2007 Ohio 5023, 875 N.E.2d 72, 2007 Ohio LEXIS 2406 (2007).

Plaintiffs needed expert medical testimony to demonstrate that the type of mold found in their home was physically harmful, thereby justifying their move and related expenses. Testimony by an industrial hygienist was too general and attenuated to be probative of an injury: Kleinholz v. Goettke, 173 Ohio App. 3d 80, 2007 Ohio 4880, 877 N.E.2d 403, 2007 Ohio App. LEXIS 4346 (2007).

Laughter

Trial court did not abuse its discretion when it refused to allow defendant to offer expert testimony regarding defendant's laughter after disembarking from a cab following the cab driver's murder, as the fact that laughter was caused by more than one state of mind was within a layperson's knowledge. State v. Rosemond, — Ohio App. 3d —, 2007 Ohio 6333, — N.E. 2d —, 2007 Ohio App. LEXIS 5570 (Nov. 30, 2007).

Law enforcement officers

Trial court did not abuse its discretion in admitting expert witness testimony from a police officer pursuant to Ohio R. Evid. 702, as his testimony clearly demonstrated that he had specialized knowledge of blood interpretation with respect to defendant's criminal trial on a charge that he fatally shot a victim. The testimony was based on the officer's personal observations at the crime scene pursuant to Ohio R. Evid. 703, and the testimony was also admissible under Ohio R. Evid. 701. State v. Hopings, — Ohio App. 3d —, 2007 Ohio 450, — N.E. 2d —, 2007 Ohio App. LEXIS 397 (Feb. 2, 2007).

Trial court did not abuse its discretion in allowing the police detective to testify about regarding the gun that defendant used in the robbery because, from the testimony, the detective was well qualified as a firearm expert by his specialized knowledge, experience, annual training, and education as a police officer/detective, pursuant to Ohio R. Evid. 702. State v. Nicholson, — Ohio App. 3d —, 2006 Ohio 1569, — N.E. 2d —, 2006 Ohio App. LEXIS 1466 (Mar. 30, 2006).

Limitations on testimony

In a patient's dental malpractice action, the trial court did not err in limiting the parameters of the testimony of an expert for the dentist as to x-rays because the dentist conceded that the witness was not an expert at reading or interpreting x-rays, and the trial court allowed the use of the x-rays for the limited purpose stated by the dentist; the dentist could not complain that the trial court limited the testimony to coincide with his stated objectives for that testimony. Scibelli v. Pannunzio, — Ohio App. 3d —, 2006 Ohio 5652, — N.E. 2d —, 2006 Ohio App. LEXIS 5650 (Oct. 26, 2006).

Medical expert

Trial court erred as a matter of law by utilizing a statute relating to medical malpractice actions, RC § 2743.43, in concluding that, due to a license suspension, the treating physician of a plaintiff in a slip and fall case could not testify as an expert witness: Ray v. Ramada Inn North, 181 Ohio App. 3d 350, 2009 Ohio 1278, 908 N.E.2d 1048, 2009 Ohio App. LEXIS 1088 (2009).

Doctor's report submitted on a workers' compensation claim was insufficient because it simply stated that the employee's tendonitis was causally connected to her prior workplace injury of six years ago. The doctor failed to set forth any principles or tests on which he relied, specific records that he reviewed in forming his opinion, or how he came to the conclusion that the employee's tendonitis was causally connected to her prior injury from six years ago. McIntyre v. Arrow International, Inc., — Ohio App. 3d —, 2007 Ohio 712, — N.E. 2d —, 2007 Ohio App. LEXIS 651 (Feb. 22, 2007).

In light of plaintiff's long history of neck and back injuries, expert testimony was required to support a claim that the motor vehicle collision at issue was the proximate cause of her present neck and back injuries: Lasley v. Nguyen, 172 Ohio App. 3d 741, 2007 Ohio 4086, 876 N.E.2d 1274, 2007 Ohio App. LEXIS 3666 (2007).

— Criminal actions

Fact that a physician's license is suspended does not preclude him from testifying as an expert witness in a criminal trial. EvidR 601(D) does not apply to criminal actions: State v. Snodgrass, 177 Ohio App. 3d 556, 2008 Ohio 4019, 895 N.E.2d 259, 2008 Ohio App. LEXIS 3399 (2008).

Medical malpractice expert

In a medical malpractice action, given a defense expert's admitted lack of training in radial nerve repair, the trial court did not act unreasonably, arbitrarily, or unconscionably in determining that the defense expert was not qualified to offer an opinion as to plaintiffs' expert's qualifications, Ohio R. Evid. 702. Foss v. Watson, — Ohio App. 3d —, 2007 Ohio 3861, — N.E. 2d —, 2007 Ohio App. LEXIS 3515 (July 30, 2007).

In a medical malpractice suit, the trial court did not err in permitting the patient's expert to testify as an expert witness. While the expert was not board-certified in internal medicine, this fact did not preclude him from testifying. The expert's deposition testimony showed that he was familiar with the standard of care expected of an internal medicine specialist when presented with the symptoms and the risks possessed by the patient when he presented himself to the doctor and that he was qualified to state an opinion in this regard. Trevena v. Primehealth, 171 Ohio App. 3d 501, 2006 Ohio 6535, 871 N.E.2d 1217, 2006 Ohio App. LEXIS 6461 (2006).

Motor vehicle sales

Trial court did not abuse its discretion by allowing a witness with the appropriate knowledge of the automobile industry to testify as an expert concerning sales tactics in the industry. EvidR 403 did not preclude the testimony. Smith v. GMC, 168 Ohio App. 3d 336, 2006 Ohio 4283, 859 N.E.2d 1035, 2006 Ohio App. LEXIS 4197 (2006).

Necessity of expert opinion

As a patient's expert would have been unable to establish the second prong of the res ipsa loquitur test relating to the determination that with the use of ordinary care, the injury would not have occurred, the trial court did not err in precluding the patient from litigating his medical malpractice claim on a theory of res ipsa loquitur. Such testimony would have been required by an expert under Ohio R. Evid. 702, as the standard of care for administering a heart catheter, and thus whether a medical professional fell below that standard of care, was not within the common knowledge of the jury. Lambert v. Metrohealth Med. Ctr., — Ohio App. 3d —, 2007 Ohio 83, — N.E. 2d —, 2007 Ohio App. LEXIS 77 (Jan. 11, 2007).

Medical malpractice suit was properly dismissed on summary judgment because the patient failed to present evidence rebutting the affidavits filed by the physicians' experts that the physicians did not depart from applicable standard of care. The patient could not rely on physician's testimony, to effect that patient's condition, which he failed to diagnose, was evident from x-rays, to create an issue of fact in light of the experts' affidavits. The patient, pursuant to Ohio Evid. R. 702 and RC § 2743.43(A), should have presented the affirmative testimony of an expert witness who was qualified to testify concerning the applicable standard of conduct. Straley v. Chand, — Ohio App. 3d —, — N.E. 2d —, 2007 Ohio App. LEXIS 2202 (May 11, 2007).

In a mother's hospital negligence suit, alleging that the hospital's failure to properly supervise her daughter, who had a medical history of seizure disorders and impaired balance, resulted in injuries to the daughter when she fell on multiple occasions while under the hospital's care, expert testimony was not required because the conduct at issue was within the common knowledge and experience of jurors. The common knowledge exception is applicable in cases involving instances of supervisory negligence, including cases, such as the one at issue, in which a patient falls and suffers an injury while left unattended. Taliaferro v. South Pointe Hosp., — Ohio App. 3d —, 2006 Ohio 1611, — N.E. 2d —, 2006 Ohio App. LEXIS 1497 (Mar. 30, 2006).

In a suit brought by a client seeking to recover for damages sustained to her home while it was in the care of a realtor, the realtor's motion for a directed verdict on the ground that the client failed to present expert testimony that the costs of repairing the client's home were reasonable and necessary was properly denied. Expert testimony was not required under Ohio R. Evid. 702(A) because jurors could be presumed to understand what defects made a property uninhabitable or otherwise diminished the owner's enjoyment and use of it, and the jury could reasonably infer from the client's testimony and that of a plumber and a representative of the construction company, properly submitted under Ohio R. Evid. 701, that the repairs to her house were necessary to restore the property to its prior condition. Reynolds v. Bauer, — Ohio App. 3d —, 2006 Ohio 2912, — N.E. 2d —, 2006 Ohio App. LEXIS 2730 (June 9, 2006).

Summary judgment was properly granted to a doctor, dismissing a patient's medical malpractice suit, because the patient failed to present expert testimony to support her claim of malpractice. The patient's claims as to a doctor's standard of care in rendering post-operative care following carpal tunnel surgeries, including treatment for a reaction to a Betadine scrub applied to her arms which allegedly caused an allergic reaction, were not so apparent as to be matters of common knowledge. George v. Arora, — Ohio App. 3d —, 2006 Ohio 3123, — N.E. 2d —, 2006 Ohio App. LEXIS 3017 (June 19, 2006).

Summary judgment was properly granted to a hospital, dismissing a patient's medical malpractice suit, because the patient failed to present expert testimony to support her claim of malpractice. The dilemma of merely sorting out the physical problems allegedly caused by the hospital due to the use of a Betadine scrub on the patient's arms from the problems allegedly caused by the post-operative treatment of the patient rendered by the doctor, who was also a defendant, was alone sufficient to place the matter outside the ordinary experience of lay jurors. George v. Arora, — Ohio App. 3d —, 2006 Ohio 3123, — N.E. 2d —, 2006 Ohio App. LEXIS 3017 (June 19, 2006).

Opinions of a longshoreman's expert on the ultimate issue of whether the employer knew certain circumstances that contributed to the longshoreman's injuries due to a falling stack of pipes that trapped his leg and resulted in amputation should have been excluded under Ohio R. Evid. 702 and 704, as they were conclusory in nature and were not necessarily helpful to the finder of fact with respect to the longshoreman's employer intentional tort claim. Other admissible evidence raised genuine issues of fact that precluded summary judgment to the employer. Talik v. Federal Marine Terminals, Inc., — Ohio App. 3d —, 2006 Ohio 3979, — N.E. 2d —, 2006 Ohio App. LEXIS 3965 (Aug. 3, 2006).

When a real estate buyer sued the seller for fraud and breach of contract, and the seller filed a third-party complaint against his real estate agent alleging, among other things, professional negligence, expert testimony was not required to support the seller's claim because a layperson could find that the agent breached a standard of care by not performing a duty which the seller delegated to him regarding the disclosure of the report of an inspection of the real estate. Carter v. Bernard, — Ohio App. 3d —, 2006 Ohio 7058, — N.E. 2d —, 2006 Ohio App. LEXIS 6986 (Dec. 28, 2006).

Necessity of expert testimony

Directed verdict under Ohio R. Civ. P. 50(A)(4) was properly granted to a doctor in a patient's medical malpractice action because the patient failed to present expert testimony on the issue of causation. Neither of the patient's experts gave an opinion that any act or omission of the doctor was the proximate cause of the patient's injury. Kester v. Brakel, — Ohio App. 3d —, 2007 Ohio 495, — N.E. 2d —, 2007 Ohio App. LEXIS 442 (Feb. 6, 2007).

Patient's medical malpractice suit was improperly dismissed on summary judgment. Since the case involved the standard of care of a therapist using common equipment and did not involve a highly technical procedure, expert testimony was not required. Krafty v. Firelands Cmty. Hosp., — Ohio App. 3d —, 2007 Ohio 5302, — N.E. 2d —, 2007 Ohio App. LEXIS 4672 (Sept. 28, 2007).

Polygraph

Given the advancements in polygraph technology, the sixth and fourteenth amendments warrant the admission of non-stipulated polygraph evidence in a situation where the trial court has independently found that the proffered polygraph is reliable under EvidR 702, the polygraphist is subject to cross-examination, and limiting instructions are given: State v. Sharma, 143 Ohio Misc. 2d 27, 2007 Ohio 5404, 875 N.E.2d 1002, 2007 Ohio Misc. LEXIS 419 (2007).

Psychologists

Trial court's decision to allow the testimony of the employee's psychologist was not arbitrary, unreasonable, or unconscionable because the testimony complied with EvidR 702(A) and (C); it related to matters beyond the common experience of laypersons and was based upon reliable information. Based upon his professional knowledge and experience, history of treatment of the employee, and review of the hospital records connected to the employee's hospitalization for an overdose of OxyContin, the psychologist concurred with the additional diagnosis by the psychiatrist and continued treating the employee in collaboration with the psychiatrist. Reneau v. Con-way Transp. Servs., — Ohio App. 3d —, 2007 Ohio 6368, — N.E. 2d —, 2007 Ohio App. LEXIS 5574 (Nov. 30, 2007).

Qualification as expert

Defendant's counsel's failure to object to the DNA testimony of an expert witness for the State was not ineffectiveness in violation of U.S. Const. amend. VI and Ohio Const. art. I, § 10, as the witness was qualified to testify as an expert pursuant to Ohio R. Evid. 702(B) although the State failed to tender him as such, as his qualifications made him a valid expert; further, it was a tactical decision of counsel not to challenge the expert's qualifications in order to avoid inviting the prosecutor to ask him questions that could have resulted in bolstering the expert's qualifications in the jury's opinion. State v. Frazier, 115 Ohio St. 3d 139, 2007 Ohio 5048, 873 N.E.2d 1263, 2007 Ohio LEXIS 2519 (2007).

Trial court did not abuse its discretion when it determined that used vehicle purchasers' experts were qualified under Ohio R. Evid. 702(B) to provide testimony in the purchasers' action against a dealership and a used vehicle owner, as they testified within their areas of expertise with respect to damages and repairs to the vehicle; their testimony with respect to a CARFAX document was properly admitted under Ohio R. Evid. 803(17), as it was a report widely used by automobile dealers. Anousheh v. Planet Ford, — Ohio App. 3d —, 2007 Ohio 4543, — N.E. 2d —, 2007 Ohio App. LEXIS 4092 (Aug. 31, 2007).

In a suit by debtors against a lender, a trial court properly found, under Ohio R. Evid. 104(A), that the debtors' proposed expert witness was not qualified, under Ohio R. Evid. 702, because, while he was familiar with banking practices in other countries and might be qualified to testify regarding them, he had never worked as a bank regulator, bank auditor, or loan officer in the United States, so he could not testify as an expert in a case involving a loan between U.S. citizens and a federally chartered U.S. savings and loan association. Lotfi-Fard v. First Fed. of Lakewood, — Ohio App. 3d —, 2006 Ohio 3727, — N.E. 2d —, 2006 Ohio App. LEXIS 3686 (July 20, 2006).

Qualification of expert

In defendant's criminal trial on a charge of, inter alia, not having tinted auto glass that conformed to the requirements of RC § 4513.241, a trial court abused its discretion in denying testimony from defendant's expert witness on the ground that the witness lacked the necessary qualifications pursuant to Ohio R. Evid. 702(B), as defendant had challenged the reliability of the window tint meter device that had been used, for which there was no Ohio authority that indicated that it was accepted as a reliable scientific device for measuring light transmittance in automobile windows. Based on the expert's background and the import of what he had planned to testify to, his testimony could have aided the trier of fact in its factfinding function, such that the expert testimony should have been allowed. State v. Bailey, — Ohio App. 3d —, 2007 Ohio 445, — N.E. 2d —, 2007 Ohio App. LEXIS 396 (Jan. 26, 2007).

Trial court abused its discretion under Ohio R. Evid. 702 when it prohibited testimony from defendant's expert regarding the effects of post traumatic stress disorder as it related to whether defendant was acting under the influence of a sudden passion or fit of rage in his trial on charges of murder and felony murder, in violation of RC § 2903.02, with an underlying predicate offense of felonious assault, in violation of RC § 2903.11, as such evidence could have supported lesser included offense instructions of voluntary manslaughter and aggravated assault, in violation of RC § 2903.03(A) and 2903.12. Defendant had been in extensive combat while in the military, he suffered from post traumatic stress disorder, and he allegedly stabbed his wife to death after she taunted him and argued with him. State v. Warner, — Ohio App. 3d —, 2007 Ohio 3016, — N.E. 2d —, 2007 Ohio App. LEXIS 2770 (June 15, 2007).

Given the relative weakness of qualifications of the iron-worker's union manager to testify in the unquestionably speculative area of predicting future business prospects, the trial court did not abuse its discretion in limiting, as it did, the manager's testimony. In an apparent effort to prove a future wage loss, the personal injury victim attempted to elicit testimony from the witness as to the future availability of construction jobs in the area over the next 10 years. McCabe v. Ransom, — Ohio App. 3d —, 2006 Ohio 2926, — N.E. 2d —, 2006 Ohio App. LEXIS 2804 (June 9, 2006).

Qualification of medical expert

Trial court did not abuse its discretion under Ohio R. Evid. 104(A) in precluding a patient's expert from testifying as to the standard of care of defendant surgeons in the patient's medical malpractice action, as the expert was not qualified pursuant to Ohio R. Evid. 702(B) to testify as to the standard of care of surgeons who treated a patient that was receiving gynecological care elsewhere because the expert was not a surgeon and he was not a primary care physician. Iglodi v. Tolentino, — Ohio App. 3d —, 2007 Ohio 1982, — N.E. 2d —, 2007 Ohio App. LEXIS 1832 (Apr. 26, 2007).

Trial court did not abuse its discretion under Ohio R. Evid. 104 when it excluded an emergency room doctor (ERD) from testifying as an expert as to the standard of care for surgeons in a medical malpractice action, as the ERD failed to demonstrate a knowledge of the standards of the school and specialty of a surgeon sufficient to enable him to give an expert opinion as to the conformity of the surgeons' conduct to the standards of surgeons under the facts of malpractice case. Nead v. Brown County Gen. Hosp., — Ohio App. 3d —, 2007 Ohio 2443, — N.E. 2d —, 2007 Ohio App. LEXIS 2259 (May 21, 2007).

Trial court abused its discretion in deeming the expert unqualified to testify as an expert regarding appellants' medical malpractice claims and in granting the motion in limine to exclude his testimony because the doctor, an internist, demonstrated that he had some degree of knowledge, skill, experience, training, or education in the field that he sought to render an expert opinion. He testified that he had treated post-operative patients after abdominal surgery and the standard of care was the same for an internist or an attending physician working in a hospital and no testimony was offered to show that such a standard was, in fact different regarding post-operative drug administration than that provided by the doctor or other internists. Smith v. Promedica Health Sys., — Ohio App. 3d —, 2007 Ohio 4189, — N.E. 2d —, 2007 Ohio App. LEXIS 3791 (Aug. 17, 2007).

Trial court did not abuse its discretion by finding that the patient's medical expert was qualified to testify as an expert regarding a nerve injury during the laparoscopic repair of an inguinal hernia because there was some evidence in the record upon which the trial court could have reasonably concluded that the expert was qualified to testify as an expert. Specifically, the expert testified that he began performing gynecologic laparoscopic surgical procedures in 1985 or 1986; that he had performed three to four such procedures a week since that time; and that in his training as a laparoscopic surgeon, he had received specific training to avoid the recognized potential for nerve injuries and to take reasonable steps to avoid such injuries. Lewis v. Nease, — Ohio App. 3d —, 2006 Ohio 4362, — N.E. 2d —, 2006 Ohio App. LEXIS 4274 (Aug. 21, 2006).

Medical expert in a medical malpractice action properly provided his opinion under Ohio R. Evid. 702, as his testimony concerned matters that were beyond the knowledge of laypersons, he possessed the specialized knowledge necessary to testify regarding symptoms and treatment of the disease that the patient died from, he specialized in that type of disease, he had published on it, and he had a medical staff position in that field. Werden v. Children's Hosp. Med. Ctr., — Ohio App. 3d —, 2006 Ohio 4600, — N.E. 2d —, 2006 Ohio App. LEXIS 4547 (Sept. 8, 2006).

Qualification of witness as expert

Trial court did not err in failing to qualify the brain injury specialist as an expert under Ohio R. Evid. 702. The specialist's experience, which consisted of case management services like coordinating benefits and assisting brain injury sufferers in retaining appropriate legal counsel, did not give him any training or experience in the medical or scientific fields so as to allow him to testify as to the medical effects that the customer suffered as a result of her head injury. Newman v. The Farmacy Natural & Specialty Foods, — Ohio App. 3d —, 2006 Ohio 4633, — N.E. 2d —, 2006 Ohio App. LEXIS 4549 (Aug. 31, 2006).

Qualifications of experts

Defense counsel was not ineffective for failing to object to the nurse's properly admitted testimony during the rape trial because, although some of her testimony was "expert" in nature, the rules enumerated in Ohio R. Evid. 702 were satisfied. The nurse's experience and education qualified her to testify as an expert in the matters at issue because her testimony was based on her training, education, and most recent literature and medical studies that had been conducted in her area. State v. Scott, — Ohio App. 3d —, 2007 Ohio 2111, — N.E. 2d —, 2007 Ohio App. LEXIS 1963 (May 3, 2007).

Although a trial court's threshold determination under Ohio R. Evid. 104(A) that a police officer's testimony was admissible regarding how he thought a vehicle collision occurred was an abuse of discretion, as the officer was not qualified as an expert under Ohio R. Evid. 702, such was not reversible error where there was substantial competent evidence to support the finding of defendant's guilt on the criminal charges, and but for the alleged error, the outcome of the trial would not have been different. City of Cleveland Hts. v. Reid, — Ohio App. 3d —, 2006 Ohio 170, — N.E. 2d —, 2006 Ohio App. LEXIS 163 (Jan. 19, 2006).

There was no error under Ohio R. Evid. 702 in admitting the testimony of the witness regarding the fact that a lack of physical evidence of sexual abuse was not abnormal because she testified that she has investigated sex abuse cases for 15 years and that she had special training in that area. Admittedly, more expertise than this would have been necessary to qualify her as a medical expert, however, based on her background and training, it could not be seen why she could not have been qualified as an expert in child sexual abuse cases had appellant raised the issue. In light of the victim's testimony regarding sexual contact with defendant, it was difficult to accept the view that the evidence deprived defendant of a fair trial. State v. King, — Ohio App. 3d —, 2006 Ohio 3922, — N.E. 2d —, 2006 Ohio App. LEXIS 3875 (July 18, 2006).

Alleged injured party did not show that a chiropractor offered an expert opinion at trial which was beyond the witness's expertise, contrary to Ohio R. Evid. 702(B), when the witness said the alleged injured party could not have been injured in a certain accident, after the witness was not allowed to offer an opinion in the field of biomechanics, because this statement was elicited from the expert by the alleged injured party on cross-examination, so the alleged injured party could not base an assignment of error on it, under the invited error doctrine. Willis v. Martin, — Ohio App. 3d —, 2006 Ohio 4846, — N.E. 2d —, 2006 Ohio App. LEXIS 4753 (Sept. 14, 2006).

— Doctors

Trial court did not abuse its discretion by allowing a physician to testify in a malpractice case even though the physician did not practice in the same specialty as the defendant-physician: Trevena v. Primehealth, 171 Ohio App. 3d 501, 2006 Ohio 6535, 871 N.E.2d 1217, 2006 Ohio App. LEXIS 6461 (2006).

— Police officers

Police officer was qualified to testify as a lay witness, rather than an expert witness, where he had the proper education, training, and experience to conduct tests to identify substance as anhydrous ammonia: State v. Gragg, 173 Ohio App. 3d 270, 2007 Ohio 4731, 878 N.E.2d 55, 2007 Ohio App. LEXIS 4276 (2007).

Trial court did not abuse its discretion when it overruled defendant's objection to testimony by a police officer regarding the lack of usable fingerprints in a bank robbery, as the testimony was based on the officer's observations throughout his many years as a police officer and a detective; however, even if his testimony was offered as an expert, he was qualified and the testimony was therefore admissible under Ohio R. Evid. 701 and 702, based on his experience and expertise in the area. State v. Starks, — Ohio App. 3d —, 2007 Ohio 4897, — N.E. 2d —, 2007 Ohio App. LEXIS 4364 (Sept. 21, 2007).

Trial court erred in allowing a state patrol trooper to testify as an expert under Ohio R. Evid. 702 regarding accident reconstruction in defendant's criminal trial on a traffic violation, as the trooper had no qualifications to testify on that issue; the error was not harmless under Ohio R. Crim. P. 52 because the trial court relied heavily on it in finding defendant guilty of the offense after a bench trial. State v. Dewalt, — Ohio App. 3d —, 2007 Ohio 5245, — N.E. 2d —, 2007 Ohio App. LEXIS 4640 (Sept. 25, 2007).

Real estate brokers

Witness who was a licensed real estate broker with over 16 years experience in commercial real estate was qualified to give his opinion as to the value of the property: Brown v. Spitzer Chevrolet Co., 181 Ohio App. 3d 642, 2009 Ohio 1196, 910 N.E.2d 490, 2009 Ohio App. LEXIS 984 (2009).

Reliability requirement

Trial court did not abuse its discretion in granting a medical center's motion in limine for the purpose of excluding the testimony of a patient's expert in the patient's medical malpractice action, although the expert was generally qualified to testify about cardiology matters, as pursuant to Ohio R. Evid. 702(C), the expert's opinion was not reliable because it was based on speculation and conjecture with regard to the acceptable standard of care, the center's having failed to meet that standard, and the causation of the injury. Lambert v. Metrohealth Med. Ctr., — Ohio App. 3d —, 2007 Ohio 83, — N.E. 2d —, 2007 Ohio App. LEXIS 77 (Jan. 11, 2007).

Where a wife in a divorce action failed to proffer an expert witness's testimony, as required by Ohio R. Evid. 103(A)(2) for purposes of preserving error on appeal, the court was unable to determine whether the excluded evidence of the expert was reliable for purposes of Ohio R. Evid. 702. The magistrate who heard the matter had limited the expert's ability to testify as an expert with respect to families who were going through a divorce with one parent who made sexual allegations with regard to another parent where a child was involved, as the last training that the expert had on the related subject was approximately four years ago. Crawford v. Crawford, — Ohio App. 3d —, 2007 Ohio 3139, — N.E. 2d —, 2007 Ohio App. LEXIS 2890 (June 25, 2007).

In a divorce matter there was no abuse of discretion in the trial court's reliance pursuant to Ohio R. Evid. 702(C) on the wife's expert's valuation of a family-owned business. The record demonstrated that the expert considered all financial data available, including the relevant financial statements (company records and tax records); learned about the company by meeting with the president; and researched the industry and economy to determine what impact it had on the business. Biro v. Biro, — Ohio App. 3d —, 2007 Ohio 3191, — N.E. 2d —, 2007 Ohio App. LEXIS 2922 (June 22, 2007).

Defendant did not challenge the principles and methodology underlying a social worker's expert opinion, but challenged the reliability and correctness of the facts the social worker relied upon when reaching the social worker's opinion. However, the focus of Ohio R. Evid. 702(C) was on the reliability of the expert's methodology. Defendant's arguments pursuant to Rule 702(C) concerning the social worker's ability to testify as an expert were meritless. State v. Jordan, — Ohio App. 3d —, 2007 Ohio 3333, — N.E. 2d —, 2007 Ohio App. LEXIS 3129 (June 22, 2007).

In an aggravated vehicular homicide prosecution, the trial court did not abuse its discretion in holding that the testimony of two patrol officers as to the speed of defendant's vehicle at the time of the accident in question was inadmissible. The trial court found that, while the officers' testimony was based on reliable scientific principles, the State failed to show that the officers' testing undertaken to determine the speed of defendant's vehicle reliably implemented the theory or that the test was conducted in a way that would yield an accurate result. State v. Hassler, — Ohio App. 3d —, 2006 Ohio 3397, — N.E. 2d —, 2006 Ohio App. LEXIS 3339 (June 29, 2006).

Trial court properly denied defendant's motion to admit the results of his portable breath test because he offered no evidence of the test's scientific reliability, as required by Ohio R. Evid. 702(C). State v. Shuler, 168 Ohio App. 3d 183, 2006 Ohio 4336, 858 N.E. 2d 1254, 2006 Ohio App. LEXIS 4268 (July 27, 2006).

Scientific tests

Expert's testimony was properly admitted where the expert explained that the methodology he employed in conducting tests that compared tool marks on the spent casings found in the victim's house to tool marks on a live round discovered in the car in which defendant was a passenger on the day of the victim's murder were essentially the same as those he normally performed in determining if two bullets were fired from the same gun; the expert's opinion was based on reliable, commonly accepted scientific principles. State v. Johnson, — Ohio App. 3d —, 2006 Ohio 209, — N.E. 2d —, 2006 Ohio App. LEXIS 139 (Jan. 19, 2006).

Denial of defendant's application for DNA testing was proper because, even if there had been sufficient biological material to perform DNA testing, the results would not have been outcome determinative under RC § 2953.74(C) since no fingerprint or hair was attributed to defendant during his trial. The testimony of the witnesses and the circumstantial evidence were sufficient to convict him even if he were excluded as the source of the hair or fingerprint; defendant had discussed killing the victim and, when stopped by the police, defendant was covered in blood and had blood and human flesh on his hunting knife. State v. Roberts, — Ohio App. 3d —, 2006 Ohio 5018, — N.E. 2d —, 2006 Ohio App. LEXIS 4964 (Sept. 27, 2006).

Substantial compliance

Defendant's argument that RC § 4511.194 was an unconstitutional violation of separation of powers and was in conflict with Ohio R. Evid. 403(A) and Ohio R. Evid. 702(C) was rejected because the Ohio Supreme Court had previously reviewed such arguments and held that the substantial compliance standard adopted by amendment to RC § 4511.19 did not violate Ohio Const. art. IV, § 5. State v. Bay, — Ohio App. 3d —, 2007 Ohio 3727, — N.E. 2d —, 2007 Ohio App. LEXIS 3412 (July 23, 2007).

RULE 703. Bases of Opinion Testimony by Experts

The facts or data in the particular case upon which an expert bases an opinion or inference may be those perceived by the expert or admitted in evidence at the hearing.

History: Amended, eff 7-1-07.

NOTES TO DECISIONS

ANALYSIS

Admissibility of expert testimony
Admissibility of expert witness' opinion
Basis for expert opinion
Basis of expert opinion
Basis of expert's opinion
Expert testimony
Facts and data upon which expert opinion is offered
Facts perceived by the expert
Medical experts
Professional literature
Relevance

Admissibility of expert testimony

Even if the State's evidence fell short of establishing the chain of custody, the record presented no prejudice to defendant because the testimony from the forensic scientists established only that defendant was in the victim's apartment at some time and defendant himself admitted that he was in the apartment and that finding his fingerprints or DNA evidence in the apartment would not have been unusual. Because the forensic witnesses were unable to ascertain when defendant's DNA or fingerprints were placed in the apartment, defendant's admission that he was there rendered nonprejudicial any error in the trial court's admitting the testimony of the forensic scientists. State v. Goodlow, — Ohio App. 3d —, 2006 Ohio 2740, — N.E. 2d —, 2006 Ohio App. LEXIS 2573 (June 1, 2006).

Admissibility of expert witness' opinion

Trial court properly overruled defendant's objection to an expert's testimony that, based on information she received from a minor sexual imposition victim, the minor's mother, and children's services, she believed that inappropriate boundaries existed in the minor's home. The expert's testimony complied with Ohio R. Evid. 703, in that the facts upon which the expert based her opinion were admitted in evidence. State v. Smith, — Ohio App. 3d —, 2006 Ohio 45, — N.E. 2d —, 2006 Ohio App. LEXIS 44 (Jan. 6, 2006).

Basis for expert opinion

House owner's expert properly testified as to his opinion regarding the cause of a fire that occurred in the owner's home, which she alleged was due to a guest's failure to dispose of her cigarette smoking materials properly, as the testimony was based upon the expert's personal observations and numerous investigations of the fire scene. Morelli v. Walker, — Ohio App. 3d —, 2007 Ohio 4832, — N.E. 2d —, 2007 Ohio App. LEXIS 4327 (Sept. 20, 2007).

Trial cout did not err in failing to strike an expert's testimony where it was based on reliable facts and evidence that was admissible in a negligence action arising from an accident when a truck driver's passenger side mirror hit a construction worker and her vehicle, as the expert relied in part on portions of a police report, which were an admissible public record within the hearsay exception under Ohio R. Evid. 803(8) where the portions relied on were drawn from the officer's observations of the scene. The expert was entitled to rely on the evidence, including photographs, deposition testimony, and underlying circumstances of the accident, in rendering his opinion pursuant to Ohio R. Evid. 702, 703, and 705. Wise v. Meyer, — Ohio App. 3d —, 2006 Ohio 4654, — N.E. 2d —, 2006 Ohio App. LEXIS 4556 (Sept. 8, 2006).

Basis of expert opinion

Trial cout did not abuse its discretion in allowing testimony from an expert for doctors in a medical malpractice action with respect to a study regarding breast cancer diagnosis timing, as the testimony was not hearsay within Ohio R. Evid.

801(C) where the expert did not quote from any portion of a study so he did not relate any oral or written assertion. As one of the investigators on the study, he testified from personal knowledge and his testimony was properly admitted under Ohio R. Evid. 703. Iglodi v. Tolentino, — Ohio App. 3d —, 2007 Ohio 1982, — N.E. 2d —, 2007 Ohio App. LEXIS 1832 (Apr. 26, 2007).

Doctor's testimony that the victim was found to be brain dead was properly admitted under Ohio R. Evid. 703 because, even though the opinion was partially based on medical reports not in evidence, the doctor had personally examined the victim in the hospital; thus, counsel was not ineffective in failing to object to the testimony. Even if the testimony had been improperly admitted, defendant could not show that she was prejudiced by defense counsel's failure to object to this testimony. State v. Taylor, — Ohio App. 3d —, 2006 Ohio 4064, — N.E. 2d —, 2006 Ohio App. LEXIS 4031 (Aug. 8, 2006).

Trial court properly allowed a railroad employee's treating physician's testimony regarding the employee's medical diagnosis in the employee's action against the railroad, based on his exposure to various substances during his employment, as the admission was proper under Ohio R. Evid. 703 because the physician's opinion was based, in part, on his years of treating the employee, and testimony by the physician based on excluded x-ray reports was excluded by the trial court. The medical diagnosis that was also contained in a hospital record was admissible as a business record. Hager v. Norfolk & Western Ry. Co., — Ohio App. 3d —, 2006 Ohio 6580, — N.E. 2d —, 2006 Ohio App. LEXIS 6489 (Dec. 14, 2006).

Basis of expert's opinion

Victim's first miscarriage, six months earlier, could have affected the opinion of the State's expert in defendant's trial for involuntary manslaughter and assault; although the trial court found it did not affect the expert's opinion, it was error not to let the jury determine if that was a credible deduction. However, the error was harmless because defendant could have achieved the same effect with a hypothetical question and direct evidence by his own expert, but chose not to because of the possibility of opening the door to prior bad acts, i.e., assaults. State v. Marshall, — Ohio App. 3d —, 2007 Ohio 1686, — N.E. 2d —, 2007 Ohio App. LEXIS 1538 (Apr. 3, 2007).

In a dependency proceeding in which it was alleged that a mother's children had been abused by members of the mother's church, a psychologist's deposition testimony was not rendered inadmissible because a caseworker had provided the psychologist with background information about the case because (1) the caseworker testified about this case history, satisfying Ohio R. Evid. 703, and (2) although the information was available to the psychologist, the psychologist did not rely on it as a basis for the psychologist's testimony, as that testimony was derived from interviews with the children. In re Miller, — Ohio App. 3d —, 2007 Ohio 2170, — N.E. 2d —, 2007 Ohio App. LEXIS 2017 (May 4, 2007).

Alleged injured party did not show, in a personal injury case, that an expert's opinion about the low-speed nature of the accident in which she said she was injured could only have been based on insurance documents because there was other evidence of this on which the expert could rely, under Ohio R. Evid. 703, including testimony admitted after the expert's testimony. Willis v. Martin, — Ohio App. 3d —, 2006 Ohio 4846, — N.E. 2d —, 2006 Ohio App. LEXIS 4753 (Sept. 14, 2006).

Ohio R. Evid. 703 does not specify that only evidence admitted at trial prior to the time an expert testifies may be used as a basis for the expert's opinion. Willis v. Martin, — Ohio App. 3d —, 2006 Ohio 4846, — N.E. 2d —, 2006 Ohio App. LEXIS 4753 (Sept. 14, 2006).

Expert testimony

Trial court's exclusion of a beneficiary's expert testimony that was for the purpose of opposing a trustee bank's motion for summary judgment in the beneficiary's claim of a breach of fiduciary duty due to the failure to have paid a principal installment from the trust in a timely manner was error, as the testimony was based on admissible evidence and should have been admitted under Ohio R. Evid. 703 and 704. Issues relating to the credibility and the weight thereof were not properly determined by summary judgment and did not affect the admissibility of the testimony. Dejaiffe v. Keybank USA Nat'l Ass'n, — Ohio App. 3d —, 2006 Ohio 2919, — N.E. 2d —, 2006 Ohio App. LEXIS 2808 (June 9, 2006).

When a real estate buyer sued the seller for fraud and breach of contract, and the seller filed a third-party complaint against his real estate agent alleging, among other things, professional negligence, expert testimony was not required to support the seller's claim because a layperson could find that the agent breached a standard of care by not performing a duty which the seller delegated to him regarding the disclosure of the report of an inspection of the real estate. Carter v. Bernard, — Ohio App. 3d —, 2006 Ohio 7058, — N.E. 2d —, 2006 Ohio App. LEXIS 6986 (Dec. 28, 2006).

Facts and data upon which expert opinion is offered

In a workers' compensation proceeding, an employee's medical expert properly based his opinion as to how much lifting the employee did on facts shown by the evidence and within the expert's personal knowledge, pursuant to Ohio R. Evid. 703, as the employee had testified how much he lifted on an hourly basis, which was the information used in the expert's testimony. As the employee's treating doctor, he had personal knowledge that he gained in the course of his treatment of the employee. Hyden v. Kroger Co., — Ohio App. 3d —, 2006 Ohio 6430, — N.E. 2d —, 2006 Ohio App. LEXIS 6367 (Dec. 7, 2006).

Facts perceived by the expert

Trial court did not abuse its discretion in admitting expert witness testimony from a police officer pursuant to Ohio R. Evid. 702, as his testimony clearly demonstrated that he had specialized knowledge of blood interpretation with respect to defendant's criminal trial on a charge that he fatally shot a victim. The testimony was based on the officer's personal observations at the crime scene pursuant to Ohio R. Evid. 703, and the testimony was also admissible under Ohio R. Evid. 701. State v. Hopings, — Ohio App. 3d —, 2007 Ohio 450, — N.E. 2d —, 2007 Ohio App. LEXIS 397 (Feb. 2, 2007).

Medical experts

Expert opinions were properly permitted because they were based on perceptions by each expert's examination of properly admitted evidence, including the CT scan and medical reports; two of the medical experts formed their opinions by examining the CT scan and medical records, while another personally evaluated the nine-month-old victim. State v. Stacy, — Ohio App. 3d —, 2007 Ohio 6744, — N.E. 2d —, 2007 Ohio App. LEXIS 5911 (Dec. 17, 2007).

Professional literature

In a patient's dental malpractice action, the patient's expert witness was properly permitted to read from a treatise that he had written because he testified to his substantive opinions at trial. An expert could refer to literature as being part of the basis for an opinion because under Ohio R. Evid. 702, 703, expert testimony was inherently based upon various sources including literature. Scibelli v. Pannunzio, — Ohio App. 3d —, 2006 Ohio 5652, — N.E. 2d —, 2006 Ohio App. LEXIS 5650 (Oct. 26, 2006).

Relevance

In a legal custody proceeding, a trial court did not err by admitting cross-examination testimony of a certified clinical nurse specialist, who had evaluated the mother, related to her opinion that her diagnosis of the mother would have changed had she known all the facts and circumstances surrounding an incident during which the mother brandished a knife in front of the father and her children or had she known that the mother had previously been under psychiatric treatment for severe depression since the facts upon which the nurse based her opinion were supported by the testimony of other witnesses during the trial. Thus, under Ohio R. Evid. 703, the nurse could base her opinion on facts admitted in evidence at the hearing. In re Memic, — Ohio App. 3d —, 2006 Ohio 6346, — N.E. 2d —, 2006 Ohio App. LEXIS 6302 (Dec. 1, 2006).

RULE 704.   Opinion on Ultimate Issue

Testimony in the form of an opinion or inference otherwise admissible is not objectionable solely because it embraces an ultimate issue to be decided by the trier of fact.

NOTES TO DECISIONS

ANALYSIS

Admissibility of expert testimony
Child abuse
Medical malpractice
Opinion which may be given by experts
Opinions on ultimate issues
Testimony not admissible
Testimony on ultimate issue

Admissibility of expert testimony

Trial court's exclusion of a beneficiary's expert testimony that was for the purpose of opposing a trustee bank's motion for summary judgment in the beneficiary's claim of a breach of fiduciary duty due to the failure to have paid a principal installment from the trust in a timely manner was error, as the testimony was based on admissible evidence and should have been admitted under Ohio R. Evid. 703 and 704. Issues relating to the credibility and the weight thereof were not properly determined by summary judgment and did not affect the admissibility of the testimony. Dejaiffe v. Keybank USA Nat'l Ass'n, — Ohio App. 3d —, 2006 Ohio 2919, — N.E. 2d —, 2006 Ohio App. LEXIS 2808 (June 9, 2006).

Child abuse

Doctor's testimony did not relate to the rape victim's credibility; rather, the testimony established that it was the doctor's medical opinion that sometime during the victim's childhood, she was a victim of child sexual abuse and she gave no opinion of the victim's veracity. Further, the testimony fell within the hearsay exception of Ohio R. Evid. 803(4) because she stated that she was provided with the information solely for the purpose of medical treatment and diagnosis and that she worked for a children's advocacy center, not a prosecutor's or investigator's office. State v. Haschenburger, — Ohio App. 3d —, 2007 Ohio 1562, — N.E. 2d —, 2007 Ohio App. LEXIS 1446 (Mar. 27, 2007).

Medical malpractice

Trial court properly allowed the medical expert to testify as to the other potential causes of the baby's injuries in the medical malpractice case because he listed four possible causes of brachial plexus injuries, other than that proposed by plaintiffs. The expert did not assert that one cause was the actual proximate cause or the more likely cause, let alone that one was the "most likely" cause, but merely espoused four other potential causes. Wasmire v. O'Dear, — Ohio App. 3d —, 2007 Ohio 736, — N.E. 2d —, 2007 Ohio App. LEXIS 674 (Feb. 20, 2007).

Opinion which may be given by experts

Defendant's counsel was not ineffective in violation of U.S. Const. amend. VI and Ohio Const. art. I, § 10 when he failed to object to a social worker's testimony that her interagency disposition was that the claim of the victim of defendant's sexual offenses was substantiated, as such testimony was admissible under Ohio R. Evid. 702 and 704 to assist the jury, and further, there was no showing that but for the admission thereof, the outcome of the trial would have been different. State v. Hall, — Ohio App. 3d —, 2007 Ohio 3531, — N.E. 2d —, 2007 Ohio App. LEXIS 3253 (July 12, 2007).

Opinions on ultimate issues

In defendant's prosecution on a charge of compelling prostitution, the 13-year-old victim's testimony that defendant's statement to her, "Fifty dollars and I'll make it worth your while," made her believe that he wanted her to have sex with him for $50 was relevant under Ohio R. Evid. 701 and 704. The statement related to money, sexual activity, and whether defendant knew what he was doing by saying it twice and then getting her reaction. State v. Williams, — Ohio App. 3d —, 2006 Ohio 3706, — N.E. 2d —, 2006 Ohio App. LEXIS 3631 (July 20, 2006).

Testimony not admissible

Because the rape case constituted a credibility contest between the victim and defendant, defendant was not afforded a fair trial when the hospital's associate director testified as to the victim's veracity. Since no medical evidence existed revealing sexual abuse, the associate director's opinion that the victim was sexually abused was based solely upon the victim's statement and the admission of that testimony was not only improper, it was egregious, prejudicial, and constituted reversible error. State v. Knight, — Ohio App. 3d —, 2006 Ohio 6437, — N.E. 2d —, 2006 Ohio App. LEXIS 6388 (Dec. 7, 2006).

Testimony on ultimate issue

Opinions of a longshoreman's expert on the ultimate issue of whether the employer knew certain circumstances that contributed to the longshoreman's injuries due to a falling stack of pipes that trapped his leg and resulted in amputation should have been excluded under Ohio R. Evid. 702 and 704, as they were conclusory in nature and were not necessarily helpful to the finder of fact with respect to the longshoreman's employer intentional tort claim. Other admissible evidence raised genuine issues of fact that precluded summary judgment to the employer. Talik v. Federal Marine Terminals, Inc., — Ohio App. 3d —, 2006 Ohio 3979, — N.E. 2d —, 2006 Ohio App. LEXIS 3965 (Aug. 3, 2006).

RULE 705.   Disclosure of Facts or Data Underlying Expert Opinion

The expert may testify in terms of opinion or inference and give the expert's reasons therefor after disclosure of the underlying facts or data. The disclosure may be in response to a hypothetical question or otherwise.

History: Amended, eff 7-1-07.

NOTES TO DECISIONS

ANALYSIS

Basis for expert opinion
Basis of expert witness' opinion
Basis of expert witness's opinion

Basis for expert opinion

Trial cout did not err in failing to strike an expert's testimony where it was based on reliable facts and evidence that was admissible in a negligence action arising from an accident when a truck driver's passenger side mirror hit a construction worker and her vehicle, as the expert relied in part on portions of a police report, which were an admissible public record within the hearsay exception under Ohio R. Evid. 803(8) where the portions relied on were drawn from the officer's observations of the scene. The expert was entitled to rely on the evidence, including photographs, deposition testimony, and underlying circumstances of the accident, in rendering his opinion pursuant to Ohio R. Evid. 702, 703, and 705. Wise v. Meyer, — Ohio App. 3d —, 2006 Ohio 4654, — N.E. 2d —, 2006 Ohio App. LEXIS 4556 (Sept. 8, 2006).

Basis of expert witness' opinion

When an alleged injured party sued an employee and his employer for an assault the employee allegedly committed against the alleged injured party on the employer's premises, it was proper to exclude the conclusory opinion of a physician about the party's pre-existing condition because the physician provided no facts or data on which his opinion was based, contrary to Ohio R. Evid. 705. Armbruster v. Hampton, — Ohio App. 3d —, 2006 Ohio 4530, — N.E. 2d —, 2006 Ohio App. LEXIS 4518 (Sept. 5, 2006).

Basis of expert witness's opinion

In a medical malpractice case, a defense expert's testimony did not violate Ohio R. Evid. 705, as the expert's statements, that swelling always and inevitably occurred with the type of fracture that the patient suffered and that a surgeon's choice to operate in the face of swelling could be approved later by the mere fact that the surgeon achieved closure of the wound, were permissible expert opinions. Duponty v. Kasamias, — Ohio App. 3d —, — N.E. 2d —, 2007 Ohio App. LEXIS 4441 (Sept. 19, 2007).

RULE 706.   Repealed.

NOTES TO DECISIONS

ANALYSIS

Learned treatise
Statements contained in medical literature

Learned treatise

There was no abuse of discretion by a trial court's decision not to allow a patient to use medical publications in his cross-examination of an expert witness for physicians who had been sued by the patient in his medical malpractice action, as he failed to adequately lay a foundation to cross-examine him on any of the publications that he later proffered pursuant to Ohio R. Evid. 706. The patient did not show how he was prejudiced by the trial court's ruling. Nead v. Brown County Gen. Hosp., — Ohio App. 3d —, 2007 Ohio 2443, — N.E. 2d —, 2007 Ohio App. LEXIS 2259 (May 21, 2007).

Statements contained in medical literature

Trial court properly sustained defendants' objections to the testimony of the doctor reading from a medical textbook. Even assuming that the doctor was declared a hostile witness, it was undisputed that he did not rely on the textbook he was questioned upon in reaching his opinion; nor was the textbook established as a reliable authority. McCabe v. Ransom, — Ohio App. 3d —, 2006 Ohio 2926, — N.E. 2d —, 2006 Ohio App. LEXIS 2804 (June 9, 2006).

ARTICLE VIII
HEARSAY

RULE 801.   Definitions

The following definitions apply under this article:

(A) **Statement.** A "statement" is (1) an oral or written assertion or (2) nonverbal conduct of a person, if it is intended by the person as an assertion.

(B) **Declarant.** A "declarant" is a person who makes a statement.

(C) **Hearsay.** "Hearsay" is a statement, other than one made by the declarant while testifying at the trial or hearing, offered in evidence to prove the truth of the matter asserted.

(D) **Statements which are not hearsay.** A statement is not hearsay if:

(1) The declarant testifies at trial or hearing and is subject to cross-examination concerning the statement, and the statement is (a) inconsistent with declarant's testimony, and was given under oath subject to cross-examination by the party against whom the statement is offered and subject to the penalty of perjury at a trial, hearing, or other proceeding, or in a deposition, or (b) consistent with declarant's testimony and is offered to rebut an express or implied charge against declarant of recent fabrication or improper influence or motive, or (c) one of identification of a person soon after perceiving the person, if the circumstances demonstrate the reliability of the prior identification.

(2) The statement is offered against a party and is (a) the party's own statement, in either an individual or a representative capacity, or (b) a statement of which the party has manifested an adoption or belief in its truth, or (c) a statement by a person authorized by the party to make a statement concerning the subject, or (d) a statement by the party's agent or servant concerning a matter within the scope of the agency or employment, made during the existence of the relationship, or (e) a statement by a co-conspirator of a party during the course and in furtherance of the conspiracy upon independent proof of the conspiracy.

History: Amended, eff 7-1-07.

NOTES TO DECISIONS

ANALYSIS

Administrative proceeding
Admission by party-opponent
Admission of a party opponent
Admission of party opponent
Admission of testimony of arresting officer
Admissions
Adoptive admission rule
Assertion
Business records
Co-conspirator's statement
Confrontation rights
Definition of statement
Diagnosis or treatment
Evidence held not hearsay
Harmless error
Hearsay
Hearsay generally
Identification evidence
Improper hearsay
Inadmissible hearsay
Invited error
Non-hearsay
Not hearsay
Plain error
Police testimony

Prejudicial error
Prejudicial error not found
Prior consistent statements
Prior identification testimony
Prior inconsistent statement
Prior statement of witness
Reversible error
Social worker's testimony
Inadmissible hearsay
Not hearsay
Prior inconsistent statement
Statement of party opponent
Statements which are not hearsay
Testimony of police officer
Testimony which explains actions
Truth of the matter asserted
Videotape of police interview

Administrative proceeding

There was no abuse of discretion in allowing a witness to read from a journal that contained hearsay evidence pursuant to Ohio R. Evid. 801(C) and 802, as such occurred in an administrative hearing before the Ohio State Board of Psychology to determine the appropriate discipline against a psychologist. The Board was not bound by the rules of evidence pursuant to OAC 4732:17-03(D)(10), and admission thereof was not arbitrary or capricious in the circumstances. Althof v. Ohio State Bd. of Psychology, — Ohio App. 3d —, 2007 Ohio 1010, — N.E. 2d —, 2007 Ohio App. LEXIS 912 (Mar. 8, 2007).

Admission by party-opponent

In a Caucasian employee's racial discrimination suit brought against the city which employed her and her African-American supervisor, the trial court properly excluded from evidence under Ohio R. Evid. 403 a report issued by the city's Equal Employment Opportunity office because, while the statements contained in the report fell within the scope of the employment of the two representatives issuing the report and, thus, constituted an admission of a party-opponent pursuant to Ohio R. Evid. 801(D)(2)(d), the potential for unfair prejudice to the city and the supervisor and confusion of the issues before the jury substantially outweighed its probative value. The report contained lengthy discussions of and conclusions regarding claims of disparate treatment and retaliation, which were not before the jury, and it presented a substantial danger of jury confusion based on the interplay of the report's conclusion of probable cause and the jury's responsibility to independently evaluate the evidence under the trial court's instructions of law to determine whether the evidence demonstrated a violation of RC ch. 4112. Mowery v. City of Columbus, — Ohio App. 3d —, 2006 Ohio 1153, — N.E. 2d —, 2006 Ohio App. LEXIS 1051 (Mar. 14, 2006).

Admission of a party opponent

Juvenile court's admission of documents regarding parents' service history and as to their own biological children was not an abuse of discretion in a parental rights proceeding regarding the parents' 11 adopted children, although some of the documents were hearsay within the definition of Ohio R. Evid. 801(C), as some of them qualified within the business records exception of Ohio R. Evid. 803(6) where they were records regularly kept by the social service agency. A therapy contract was properly admitted under the exception for an admission of a party-opponent under Ohio R. Evid. 801(D)(2). In re Mercy Anne G., — Ohio App. 3d —, 2007 Ohio 1197, — N.E.2d —, 2007 Ohio App. LEXIS 1132 (Mar. 14, 2007).

In a slip and fall suit brought against a hotel, a statement by one of the hotel's maids, to the effect that she had told the hotel about the excessive wax on the hotel's floor prior to appellant's slip and fall, was admissible under Ohio R. Evid.

801(D)(2)(d) as an admission of a party opponent made by a servant within the scope of employment during the existence of the employment. Ray v. Ramada Inn North, 171 Ohio App. 3d 1, 2007 Ohio 1341, 869 N.E.2d 95, 2007 Ohio App. LEXIS 1220 (2007).

Because the testimony by the victim's wife about the VIN (vehicle identification number) flipping was admissible under Ohio R. Evid. 801(D)(2), defense counsel did not err in failing to object to her testimony. Although the wife did not identify the source of her knowledge during direct examination, she testified during cross-examination that she learned about the VIN flipping from talking to defendant and that she had never talked to her husband about it. State v. Bach, — Ohio App. 3d —, 2007 Ohio 2130, — N.E. 2d —, 2007 Ohio App. LEXIS 1986 (May 4, 2007).

Because defendant's statements to a witness were admissible as admissions under Ohio R. Evid. 801(D)(2), there was no basis to conclude that defense counsel was ineffective by failing to object to the witness's testimony. The witness testified that defendant himself had expressed to him that he was upset about the truck and defendant had stated that he wanted his money back from the victim but that the victim would not return any of the money. State v. Bach, — Ohio App. 3d —, 2007 Ohio 2130, — N.E. 2d —, 2007 Ohio App. LEXIS 1986 (May 4, 2007).

Trial court properly admitted testimony by a witness about a telephone conversation had with an individual who called himself a name other than that of defendant, but who was allegedly defendant, as such constituted a party opponent admission pursuant to Ohio R. Evid. 801(D)(2)(a) where the voice on the other end of the phone was properly authenticated as belonging to defendant pursuant to Ohio R. Evid. 901(B)(4); the voice had the same Jamaican accent as defendant, the voice acknowledged that the victim of defendant's criminal conduct owed defendant money, and others indicated that defendant went by the name indicated during the conversation. State v. Small, — Ohio App. 3d —, 2007 Ohio 6771, — N.E. 2d —, 2007 Ohio App. LEXIS 5923 (Dec. 18, 2007).

Testimony offered by a granddaughter regarding statements made to her by her grandmother in a multi-tort action were not admissible as statements of a party-opponent under Ohio R. Evid. 801(D)(2), as the granddaughter was a witness for the grandmother and the statements supported the case-in-chief, such that they were not admissible without a showing of the grandmother's unavailability under Ohio R. Evid. 804 or a contradictory statement under Ohio R. Evid. 801(D). Domer v. Joan, — Ohio App. 3d —, 2007 Ohio 6877, — N.E. 2d —, 2007 Ohio App. LEXIS 6032 (Dec. 14, 2007).

In defendant's prosecution for raping his minor nephew, the admission of defendant's statements to police that he had undergone counseling did not violate Ohio R. Evid. 403(A) because the statements were admissions of a party opponent, under Ohio R. Evid. 801(D)(2), and the statements were relevant, under Ohio R. Evid. 401, as defendant admitted his sexual attraction to young boys, so no plain error, under Ohio R. Crim. P. 52(B), was committed, as it could not be said that defendant would not have been convicted without the statements, given the other evidence against him. State v. Palacio, — Ohio App. 3d —, 2006 Ohio 1437, — N.E. 2d —, 2006 Ohio App. LEXIS 1301 (Mar. 27, 2006).

Testimony of a supervisor in a county engineer's office, to the effect that, several days before a driver's accident involving a pothole on one of the county's roads, he had heard it mentioned several times that the potholes on the road where the driver's accident occurred were a recurring problem, was not hearsay and was admissible in the driver's suit against the county, the county engineer, and the board of commissioners. Any statement by the employee was an admission by a party opponent and, by definition, was not hearsay under Ohio R.

Evid. 801(D)(2). Kertesz v. Fulton County, — Ohio App. 3d —, 2006 Ohio 3178, — N.E. 2d —, 2006 Ohio App. LEXIS 3066 (June 23, 2006).

When defendant admitted to a police officer, after waiving his Miranda rights, that he exposed himself while sitting in his car, the officer was properly allowed to testify, in a prosecution for public indecency, under RC § 2907.09(A)(3), about defendant's statements because they were admissions of a party opponent, under Ohio R. Evid. 801(D)(2), and they were relevant to the crime for which defendant was prosecuted. State v. Bellomy, — Ohio App. 3d —, 2006 Ohio 7087, — N.E. 2d —, 2006 Ohio App. LEXIS 7017 (Dec. 29, 2006).

Admission of party opponent

Statements on the jailhouse recording were admissible because they were admissions of a party opponent and admissions by adoption of a party opponent because, not only was defendant's admission that he was on his way back to the house to get the drugs admissible, but so was the brother's question implying that defendant was referring to the drugs that the police found in the drawer. The brother's questions were admissible to give context to the statements. Defendant's silence in response to the statements made by his brother that he was in jail because of defendant's drugs amounted to an adoption of the truth of the statements. State v. Hardison, — Ohio App. 3d —, 2007 Ohio 366, — N.E. 2d —, 2007 Ohio App. LEXIS 330 (Jan. 31, 2007).

When, in defendant's conspiracy trial, a confidential informant testified that he intended to pistol-whip the victim, if necessary, and admitted that he had committed similar crimes before, counsel's failure to object to this testimony on hearsay grounds was not ineffective assistance of counsel because (1) the testimony was not hearsay, under Ohio R. Evid. 801(D)(2)(a), because it involved admissions by a party opponent, and (2) the testimony fell under Ohio R. Evid. 803(3)'s recognized exception to the hearsay rule for statements of then-existing mental condition, e.g. intent. State v. Fitzgerald, — Ohio App. 3d —, 2007 Ohio 701, — N.E. 2d —, 2007 Ohio App. LEXIS 637 (Feb. 21, 2007).

Defendants' counsel did not provide ineffective assistance in violation of U.S. Const. amend. VI and Ohio Const. art. I, § 10 when they failed to object to testimony regarding defendants' self-incriminating statements, as counsel's general hearsay objection to "anything" defendant-A had said during the testimony of a police deputy was overruled as a "statement of the defendant," which was presumably deemed an admission by a party-opponent under Ohio R. Evid. 801(D)(2). State v. McDade, — Ohio App. 3d —, 2007 Ohio 749, — N.E. 2d —, 2007 Ohio App. LEXIS 685 (Feb. 23, 2007).

Trial court did not abuse its discretion when it excluded testimony from an employee/part-owner of a business in a commercial lease dispute involving the business and the landlords, as the testimony sought to be admitted concerned conversations between another owner of the business and the landlords, however, as the part-owner did not actually hear the statements about which he intended to testify, they did not constitute admissions of a party-opponent under Ohio R. Evid. 801(D)(2); as the part-owner lacked personal knowledge, under Ohio R. Evid. 602 he could not testify thereto and further, such did not constitute hearsay within hearsay under Ohio R. Evid. 805, as each part of the combined statements did not conform to a hearsay rule exception. Yoder v. Hurst, — Ohio App. 3d —, 2007 Ohio 4861, — N.E. 2d —, 2007 Ohio App. LEXIS 4310 (Sept. 20, 2007).

In a murder prosecution, it was not error to admit defendant's prior statements against him because, under Ohio R. Evid. 801(D)(2)(a), they were not hearsay, and they were relevant to refute his account of the victim's death and his attempts to minimize his culpability, as they tended to show he harbored more animosity toward the victim than he attempted to portray in his videotaped confession and that the victim's death was not the result of a sudden, heated, lover's quarrel. State v. Evans, — Ohio App. 3d —, 2006 Ohio 2564, — N.E. 2d —, 2006 Ohio App. LEXIS 2416 (May 19, 2006).

Defendant's counsel did not provide ineffective assistance during his criminal trial, in violation of his rights under Ohio Const. art. I, § 10, by failing to object to admission of inculpatory statements made by defendant to school faculty and his peers, as such statements were not hearsay under Ohio R. Evid. 801(D)(2)(a) where they were offered against defendant as a party opponent. State v. Nutekpor, — Ohio App. 3d —, 2006 Ohio 4641, — N.E. 2d —, 2006 Ohio App. LEXIS 4582 (Sept. 1, 2006).

Invitee's slip and fall suit against hospital was properly dismissed on summary judgment because the invitee's deposition testimony concerning statements by hospital employees that people often slipped on water on the hospital's floor was not admissible as an admission of a party opponent under Ohio R. Evid. 801(D)(2)(d) and could not establish the hospital's notice of the hazard as the invitee did not identify individuals who made the statements by name or position, and she could not establish that the statements concerned a matter within the scope of the employees' authority. The invitee's self-serving assertions were insufficient under Ohio R. Civ. P. 56 to overcome a motion for summary judgment, and thus, summary judgment was properly granted to the hospital since the invitee failed to present any evidence that the hospital was responsible for the puddle of water or that it had actual or constructive knowledge of the hazard. Shreves v. Meridia Health Sys., — Ohio App. 3d —, 2006 Ohio 5724, — N.E. 2d —, 2006 Ohio App. LEXIS 5729 (Nov. 2, 2006).

Admission of testimony of arresting officer

Police officer's answer regarding what the witnesses had told him was not hearsay, but rather part of the officer's investigation. Thus, it was not offered to prove the truth of the statement made to the officer, but to show why the officer, as the testifying witness, acted in a particular manner. State v. Zwelling, — Ohio App. 3d —, 2006 Ohio 2954, — N.E. 2d —, 2006 Ohio App. LEXIS 2847 (June 5, 2006).

Admissions

Trial court did not err in admitting testimony of a doctor's officer manager in a negligence action by a deceased patient's estate administratrix, wherein the manager provided an "explanatory" statement uttered by the doctor in the course of an appointment with the deceased patient and the patient's responses thereto, as the statement by the doctor was one where he perceived, assessed, and evaluated the patient's medical condition, and it was not offered for the truth of the matter asserted. The statement was offered merely to relate what the office manager saw or heard while she was at work because an issue in the case was the fact that the possible treatment options allegedly offered to the patient and declined by him, were not noted in the patient's chart. If the statement was deemed hearsay pursuant to Ohio R. Evid. 801, then it was admissible under the present sense impression exception under Ohio R. Evid. 803(1). Frost v. Snitzer, — Ohio App. 3d —, 2006 Ohio 3882, — N.E. 2d —, 2006 Ohio App. LEXIS 3864 (July 28, 2006).

Adoptive admission rule

Hearsay to which the murder victim's father testified was not his own rendition of defendant's alleged threat but the declaration of the other woman (that the victim had been seeing) that the father repeated. Defendant was not present when the woman made the alleged declaration concerning defendant's threat to kill her and her child and thus, the adoptive admission rule, under Ohio R. Evid. 801(D)(2)(b), did not apply. State v. Evans, — Ohio App. 3d —, 2007 Ohio 4081, — N.E. 2d —, 2007 Ohio App. LEXIS 3671 (Aug. 3, 2007).

Assertion

Testimony about a victim's offer to sell his jersey or the victim's request to borrow a gun were in the form of questions, such that they were not hearsay because they were not assertions. State v. Small, — Ohio App. 3d —, 2007 Ohio 6771, — N.E. 2d —, 2007 Ohio App. LEXIS 5923 (Dec. 18, 2007).

Business records

When determining the number of days a motorist was out of the state during a limitations period, for purposes of finding the number of days the period was tolled, the motorist's bank records could not be used to make this determination because an alleged injured party attempting to defeat the application of the statute of limitations did not lay a sufficient foundation for the admission of these records under Ohio R. Evid. 803(6). Barker v. Strunk, — Ohio App. 3d —, 2007 Ohio 884, — N.E. 2d —, 2007 Ohio App. LEXIS 818 (Mar. 5, 2007).

Co-conspirator's statement

Statements made to defendant by the driver of the vehicle in which defendant was a passenger when defendant was arrested were properly admitted under Ohio R. Evid. 801(D)(2)(e) because sufficient evidence was obtained from the vehicle before the driver's statements were offered to make a prima facie showing that defendant and the driver conspired to commit illegal assembly or possession of chemicals for the manufacture of controlled substances, as significant amounts of materials used to manufacture methamphetamine were found in the vehicle. State v. Pirpich, — Ohio App. 3d —, 2007 Ohio 6745, — N.E. 2d —, 2007 Ohio App. LEXIS 5907 (Dec. 17, 2007).

In a murder prosecution, testimony about the statements of co-conspirators was properly admitted, under Ohio R. Evid. 801(D)(2)(e), even if the statements were made after the object of the conspiracy was accomplished, because the statements were made while the declarants were trying to conceal their involvement in the crime. State v. Moore, — Ohio App. 3d —, 2006 Ohio 4926, — N.E. 2d —, 2006 Ohio App. LEXIS 4884 (Sept. 25, 2006).

Confrontation rights

Admission of the search warrant and affidavit did not violate defendant's rights under the Confrontation Clause because the detective who signed the affidavit testified at trial and the hearsay statements within the affidavit were statements by a witness who testified at trial. Each were subject to cross-examination at trial, which preserved defendant's right to confront the witnesses against him. Although much of the affidavit contained impermissible hearsay which was prejudicial to defendant, the trial court did not commit plain error when it admitted the evidence because the evidence against defendant was convincing. State v. Carter, — Ohio App. 3d —, 2007 Ohio 3502, — N.E. 2d —, 2007 Ohio App. LEXIS 3223 (June 29, 2007).

Admission of the search warrant and affidavit did not violate defendant's rights under the Confrontation Clause because the detective who signed the affidavit testified at trial and the hearsay statements within the affidavit were statements by a witness who testified at trial. Each were subject to cross-examination at trial, which preserved defendant's right to confront the witnesses against him. Although much of the affidavit contained impermissible hearsay which was prejudicial to defendant, the trial court did not commit plain error when it admitted the evidence because the evidence against defendant was convincing. State v. Robinson, — Ohio App. 3d —, 2007 Ohio 3501, — N.E. 2d —, 2007 Ohio App. LEXIS 3224 (July 5, 2007).

When an alleged victim was allowed to testify that defendant's former girlfriend tried to bribe the victim not to testify, this testimony was improper under Ohio R. Evid. 801 and 802, as well as U.S. Const. amend. VI, because the statement was

offered for the truth of the matter asserted, the former girlfriend was not called as a witness, and defendant had no prior opportunity to cross-examine her regarding her statement. State v. Wilson, — Ohio App. 3d —, 2006 Ohio 1333, — N.E. 2d —, 2006 Ohio App. LEXIS 1223 (Mar. 23, 2006).

Appellant's right to confrontation was not violated, in his prosecution, as a juvenile, for gross sexual imposition, when statements made by appellant's mother upon learning of the alleged incident were admitted because the statements were not hearsay, under Ohio R. Evid. 801(C), as they were not offered for the truth of the matter asserted, so appellant's confrontation rights were not implicated. In re Sturm, — Ohio App. 3d —, 2006 Ohio 3122, — N.E. 2d —, 2006 Ohio App. LEXIS 2988 (June 16, 2006).

Definition of statement

In a murder prosecution, when a witness testified that he believed he did not cause the victim's death after speaking to his lawyer, who had spoken to the coroner, this was not hearsay, under Ohio R. Evid. 801(C), because the testimony did not contain an assertion, under Ohio R. Evid. 801(A), as the witness only stated what his belief was after his lawyer talked to the coroner. State v. Wellman, — Ohio App. 3d —, 2006 Ohio 3808, — N.E. 2d —, 2006 Ohio App. LEXIS 3774 (July 25, 2006).

Diagnosis or treatment

Trial court's admission of a doctor's testimony regarding her determination that a minor was the victim of sexual abuse was not an abuse of discretion under Ohio R. Evid. 104, as the doctor simply stated her diagnosis of the victim because she was a qualified physician trained in pediatrics and her opinion was based on statements made by the victim and based on physical examination. The statements fell with an exception of hearsay pursuant to Ohio R. Evid. 801(C) and 802, as they were made for purposes of diagnosis or treatment pursuant to Ohio R. Evid. 803(4). State v. Braxton, — Ohio App. 3d —, 2006 Ohio 3008, — N.E. 2d —, 2006 Ohio App. LEXIS 2885 (June 15, 2006).

Evidence held not hearsay

There was no plain error under Ohio R. Crim. P. 52(B), based on defendant's counsel's failure to object, to the admission of testimony from a police officer regarding statements made to him by a victim of defendant's crimes, as the victim later testified that she told police the same information, such that any error was harmless. Testimony which indicated what defendant and his accomplices said to the victim and to each other were not hearsay that required exclusion under Ohio R. Evid. 801(C) and 802, as they were not statements offered to prove the truth of the matter asserted but instead, were offered to explain the witness's activities. State v. Allen, — Ohio App. 3d —, 2006 Ohio 2338, — N.E. 2d —, 2006 Ohio App. LEXIS 2206 (May 12, 2006).

Where most of the evidence that defendant challenged on appeal under the plain error standard of review pursuant to Ohio R. Crim. P. 52(B) due to his failure to have objected at trial was not hearsay under Ohio R. Evid. 801(C) because it was not offered to prove the truth of the matter asserted, or it was properly admitted as a record kept in the regular course of business pursuant to Ohio R. Evid. 803(6), and defendant failed to show that he was prejudiced by the admission thereof, there was no plain error. State v. Payne, — Ohio App. 3d —, 2006 Ohio 3005, — N.E. 2d —, 2006 Ohio App. LEXIS 2889 (June 15, 2006).

Trial court did not abuse its discretion when it found that the humane society agent's statement that defendant had not scheduled a required follow-up visit with his veterinarian explained why she sought a warrant to seize the dogs after originally leaving them in defendant's care. The evidence was relevant to enable the jury to fully understand the case and the statement did not derive its primary value from the truth therein. State v. Angus, — Ohio App. 3d —, 2006 Ohio 4455, — N.E. 2d —, 2006 Ohio App. LEXIS 4374 (Aug. 29, 2006).

Defendant's counsel was not ineffective in failing to object to testimony from a detective regarding a witness's knowledge of a victim's statement where, during cross-examination, the matter was clarified. There was also no ineffectiveness in failing to object to evidence regarding rumors that circulated around the community as to the criminal incident committed by defendant, as another witness's testimony about the rumor was offered to explain how that witness became aware of the incident and accordingly, it was not inadmissible hearsay under Ohio R. Evid. 801(C). State v. Richmond, — Ohio App. 3d —, 2006 Ohio 4518, — N.E. 2d —, 2006 Ohio App. LEXIS 4480 (Sept. 1, 2006).

In a patient's dental malpractice action, it was not hearsay under Ohio R. Evid. 801(C) for the patient's expert to read from a treatise that he had written because the expert testified to his opinions at trial, he was subject to cross-examination, and he did not read specific statements from the treatise as substantive evidence; Ohio R. Evid. 706, pertaining to the use of statements in treatises for impeachment, did not make the expert's use of his own treatise on direct examination improper. Scibelli v. Pannunzio, — Ohio App. 3d —, 2006 Ohio 5652, — N.E. 2d —, 2006 Ohio App. LEXIS 5650 (Oct. 26, 2006).

Harmless error

As defendant admitted that he had a family relationship with the victim of his criminal conduct because he indicated that they lived together, the admission of testimony regarding the contents of his driver's license, which was hearsay under Ohio R. Evid. 801(C) and which was offered to prove that he lived at the same address as the victim, was harmless error under Ohio R. Crim. P. 52 because the outcome of the trial was not changed by the admission thereof. State v. Deer, — Ohio App. 3d —, 2007 Ohio 1866, — N.E. 2d —, 2007 Ohio App. LEXIS 1700 (Apr. 20, 2007).

In a dependency proceeding in which it was alleged that a mother's children had been abused by members of the mother's church, a caseworker's testimony about statements by one of the children was harmless and not plain error because (1) the testimony was elicited by the mother's counsel, (2) the testimony was repetitive of information obtained by a psychologist in an interview of the child, which was reported in greater detail by the psychologist, who provided transcripts of the interviews to the parties. In re Miller, — Ohio App. 3d —, 2007 Ohio 2170, — N.E. 2d —, 2007 Ohio App. LEXIS 2017 (May 4, 2007).

Evidence supported a conclusion that defendant acted purposely to cause the death of the victim, her boyfriend, when she stabbed him, and was so overwhelmingly that any error in the admission of the hearsay testimony of the victim's father, relating that defendant had threatened to kill the woman that the victim had been seeing, was harmless beyond a reasonable doubt. There was no dispute that defendant stabbed the victim in the chest with a steak knife, five to six inches deep and the stabbing occurred when defendant and the victim broke their relationship, following a loud argument between them. State v. Evans, — Ohio App. 3d —, 2007 Ohio 4081, — N.E. 2d —, 2007 Ohio App. LEXIS 3671 (Aug. 3, 2007).

While a trial court erred in admitting hearsay testimony from a police officer, a detective, and the minor victim's friend because the testimony describing what the victim told them about the alleged molestation by defendant, the victim's stepfather, were offered for the truth of the matter asserted and did not fall within the exception under Ohio R. Evid. 801(D)(1)(b), in that the witness statements were not consistent with the victim's own testimony at trial, the admission of these statements was harmless and merely cumulative since the victim testified in open court and was cross-examined on the same matters. State v. Smith, — Ohio App. 3d —, 2006 Ohio 45, — N.E. 2d —, 2006 Ohio App. LEXIS 44 (Jan. 6, 2006).

Trial court committed harmless error when it incorrectly permitted an expert witness for a medical product manufacturer to testify in a product liability and medical negligence action, as the testimony regarding the opinion of another expert who did not testify at trial was inadmissible hearsay under Ohio R. Evid. 801, but as it was cumulative, the error did not require reversal. Zappola v. Leibinger, — Ohio App. 3d —, 2006 Ohio 2207, — N.E. 2d —, 2006 Ohio App. LEXIS 2058 (May 4, 2006).

There was no plain error in the admission of testimony by a sexual offense victim and her mother regarding threats that the victim had received from members of the community, even if the testimony was construed as impermissible hearsay under Ohio R. Evid. 801(C), as any error was harmless under Ohio R. Crim. P. 52 where there was no showing that the outcome of the trial clearly would have been different. The threats went to the charged crime of intimidation, which defendant was found not guilty of having committed. State v. Jenkins, — Ohio App. 3d —, 2006 Ohio 6421, — N.E. 2d —, 2006 Ohio App. LEXIS 6373 (Dec. 7, 2006).

Although admission of a psychological report regarding interviews and evaluations of a maternal grandmother who was the temporary guardian of her grandchildren, the children, and their father was error because the psychologist did not testify at the guardianship termination proceeding, such that the report was hearsay under Ohio R. Evid. 801, such admission was harmless where there was sufficient other evidence to support the termination decision. In re Clowtis, — Ohio App. 3d —, 2006 Ohio 6868, — N.E. 2d —, 2006 Ohio App. LEXIS 6811 (Dec. 22, 2006).

Hearsay

When the owners of a business sued a company for negligently installing an oil-interceptor system at the business because, in doing so, it crushed a drain line running from the owners' property, and one of the owners testified in his deposition that an employee of the company told him that the company had crushed the line, ordinarily, deposition testimony that consituted hearsay could not be considered in determining the parties' summary judgment motions, under Ohio R. Evid. 801(C) and 802. Loukinas v. Roto-Rooter Servs. Co., 167 Ohio App. 3d 559, 2006 Ohio 3172, 855 N.E. 2d 1272, 2006 Ohio App. LEXIS 3081 (June 23, 2006).

Summary judgment under Ohio R. Civ. P. 56(C) was improperly granted to driver of car two in suit brought by passenger in car one to recover for injuries sustained when car two struck car one as it made turn across traffic. Trial court had insufficient information to determine whether allegations in affidavit to effect that insurance agent had said that driver was speeding were hearsay and, if so, whether exceptions applied, in that the driver of car two failed to meet his burden of demonstrating that the statement should be stricken; thus, an issue of material fact existed, and summary judgment was improper. Luke v. Tonner, — Ohio App. 3d —, 2006 Ohio 6120, — N.E. 2d —, 2006 Ohio App. LEXIS 6093 (Nov. 17, 2006).

Pursuant to Ohio R. Evid. 801(C) and 802, admission of testimony from a police detective, wherein he relayed statements made to him by a juvenile's mother with respect to the juvenile's conduct, as well as statements made to her by the juvenile's stepbrother, was hearsay, but as it was cumulative because the facts were already in evidence due to the juvenile's confession, the admission thereof was not so prejudicial as to be reversible error. In re Sturm, — Ohio App. 3d —, 2006 Ohio 7101, — N.E. 2d —, 2006 Ohio App. LEXIS 7046 (Dec. 22, 2006).

Trial court did not abuse its discretion in excluding testimony from a vehicle occupant that she heard someone at the scene of the vehicle accident she was involved in say that the other driver was dead, as such evidence was hearsay which was not admissible under Ohio R. Evid. 801(C) and 802. The occupant sought the introduction thereof to show the impact it had on her emotional state and her later injuries, which could have been shown without offering the exact statement, and the evidentiary ruling did not affect her substantial rights. Luther v. Estate of Skrinjar, — Ohio App. 3d —, 2006 Ohio 7117, — N.E. 2d —, 2006 Ohio App. LEXIS 7063 (Dec. 29, 2006).

Hearsay generally

Plaintiff was a business invitee of the motel where he was there at the invitation of a paying guest. There was an issue of fact as to whether the motel failed to warn the plaintiff of a dangerous condition resulting from wax on the floor. Motel employee's statement, in reaction to the plaintiff's fall, that she had almost fallen due to too much wax on the floor and had warned management did not constitute hearsay: Ray v. Ramada Inn North, 171 Ohio App. 3d 1, 2007 Ohio 1341, 869 N.E.2d 95, 2007 Ohio App. LEXIS 1220 (2007).

In a murder prosecution, when a witness testified that he believed he did not cause the victim's death after speaking to his lawyer, who had spoken to the coroner, if this testimony contained an assertion, under Ohio R. Evid. 801(A), it was not hearsay because it was not offered for the truth of the matter asserted, i.e., that the witness did not kill the victim, as it only stated why the witness believed he did not cause the victim's death. State v. Wellman, — Ohio App. 3d —, 2006 Ohio 3808, — N.E. 2d —, 2006 Ohio App. LEXIS 3774 (July 25, 2006).

Identification evidence

Identification testimony is not admissible per EvidR 801(D)(1)(c) unless the person who made the out of court identification testifies at trial and is subject to cross-examination: State v. Nevins, 171 Ohio App. 3d 97, 2007 Ohio 1511, 869 N.E.2d 719, 2007 Ohio App. LEXIS 1379 (2007).

Improper hearsay

Officer's testimony relating appellant's accomplice's inculpatory statements was inadmissible because the statements were inadmissible hearsay, under Ohio R. Evid. 801(C), because the statements were offered for the truth of the matter asserted. In re Siler, — Ohio App. 3d —, 2007 Ohio 3027, — N.E. 2d —, 2007 Ohio App. LEXIS 2781 (June 15, 2007).

Although the trial court's admission of defendant's employer's testimony was error, as it indicated that defendant had engaged in fraudulent activity and it exceeded its foundational basis for explaining why the employer contacted the victim of defendant's allegedly criminal conduct under Ohio R. Evid. 801(C), such that the probative value was substantially outweighed by the danger of unfair prejudice, confusion, and possible misleading of the jury under Ohio R. Evid. 403(A), there was no reversible error because the trial court cautioned the jury as to the limited use of the testimony. State v. Bedell, — Ohio App. 3d —, 2006 Ohio 5746, — N.E. 2d —, 2006 Ohio App. LEXIS 5705 (Nov. 2, 2006).

Inadmissible hearsay

Trial court's judgment finding defendant juvenile to be responsible for the rapes indicated that it relied upon the victim's testimony and defendant's admissions and not the inadmissible hearsay; therefore, although the trial court committed error when it allowed the detective to testify to prior statements by the victim, that error was harmless beyond a reasonable doubt. The State's contention that the detective's testimony merely explained his investigatory process was rejected, the State had no need to elicit testimony of the details of the victim's allegations, and to do so was contrary to Ohio R. Evid. 801, and there was no basis for the admission of the detective's testimony of the victim's prior statement under

Ohio R. Evid. 801(D)(1). In re J.S., — Ohio App. 3d —, 2007 Ohio 4551, — N.E. 2d —, 2007 Ohio App. LEXIS 4082 (Aug. 31, 2007).

Trial court did not abuse its discretion when it excluded a witness's oral statement in defendant's criminal trial pursuant to Ohio R. Evid. 801(C) and 802, as the statement was hearsay and accordingly, not admissible; the witness made the statement to a police detective at the scene of the crime, and at trial, defense counsel attempted to elicit that statement from a different police detective. State v. Hooks, — Ohio App. 3d —, 2007 Ohio 5944, — N.E. 2d —, 2007 Ohio App. LEXIS 5257 (Nov. 8, 2007).

Trial court did not abuse its discretion in its evidentiary rulings in a multi-tort action, as a granddaughter's testimony was properly excluded because her statements contained hearsay pursuant to Ohio R. Evid. 801(C) and 802 and they were not relevant to the issues being tried pursuant to Ohio R. Evid. 401, exclusion of the granddaughter's testimony regarding a taped conversation between herself, her grandmother, a handyman who was being sued, and another individual was not an admission of a party-opponent under Ohio R. Evid. 801(D)(2). Domer v. Joan, — Ohio App. 3d —, 2007 Ohio 6877, — N.E. 2d —, 2007 Ohio App. LEXIS 6032 (Dec. 14, 2007).

Trial court did not abuse its discretion when it excluded the testimony defendant was attempting to elicit from his brother because the out-of-court statements that the brother would have described (regarding what one of the victims had said outside of the courtroom about his inability to identify defendant) constituted inadmissible hearsay pursuant to Ohio R. Evid. 801(C). State v. Nicholson, — Ohio App. 3d —, 2006 Ohio 1569, — N.E. 2d —, 2006 Ohio App. LEXIS 1466 (Mar. 30, 2006).

Report conducted by an outside consultant employed by the county to inspect guardrails was improperly relied on by the driver as evidence of the county's failure to fulfill its statutory duties under former RC § 5591.36 and 5591.37 because the report was never authenticated by its author nor properly incorporated into the record on summary judgment and, thus, constituted inadmissible hearsay under Ohio R. Evid. 801(C). Further, compliance with Ohio Department of Transportation regulations was not required, and the county's failure to comply with the regulations could not constitute negligence; thus, summary judgment was properly granted to the county because the driver failed to present evidence that the guardrail was unfit for its intended purpose. Hamilton v. Clermont County Bd. of Comm'rs, — Ohio App. 3d —, 2006 Ohio 2024, — N.E. 2d —, 2006 Ohio App. LEXIS 1853 (Apr. 24, 2006).

In a prosecution for sexual imposition, the State should not have been able to offer the testimony of police officers as to allegations of another instance of sexual abuse made by the child victim to prove defendant's guilt in the case-in-chief for the purpose of proving the absence of mistake or accident because the testimony was hearsay, in that the victim had recanted her allegations against defendant and, thus, did not testify concerning the other act. State v. Smith, — Ohio App. 3d —, 2006 Ohio 2675, — N.E. 2d —, 2006 Ohio App. LEXIS 2499 (May 26, 2006).

At a hearing to consider a recommendation that defendant be released to a less restrictive mental health facility, pursuant to RC § 2945.401(I), a psychiatric report stating that defendant was psychotic was properly excluded as hearsay, under Ohio R. Evid. 801(C), because the author of the report was not produced. State v. Roden, — Ohio App. 3d —, 2006 Ohio 3679, — N.E. 2d —, 2006 Ohio App. LEXIS 3645 (July 20, 2006).

Trial court's admission of testimony from a witness who indicated that a victim of defendant's criminal conduct had stated that defendant was the shooter was proper as an excited utterance within Ohio R. Evid. 803(2); such statements were impermissible hearsay under Ohio R. Evid. 801(C), as they were offered for the truth of what was asserted and they were made out of court, but they were admissible within the stated exception. State v. Bell, — Ohio App. 3d —, 2006 Ohio 6592, — N.E. 2d —, 2006 Ohio App. LEXIS 6531 (Dec. 14, 2006).

Trial court properly excluded testimony by a witness regarding a statement by an alleged victim of defendant's criminal actions that indicated that he was not involved in the shooting incident, as such statement would have been offered to prove the truth of the matter asserted, namely that defendant had not fired shots, and accordingly, it was properly excluded as impermissible hearsay under Ohio R. Evid. 801(C). State v. Bell, — Ohio App. 3d —, 2006 Ohio 6592, — N.E. 2d —, 2006 Ohio App. LEXIS 6531 (Dec. 14, 2006).

Invited error

During defendant's trial for drug offenses, the invited error doctrine barred defendant from complaining that a police officer's testimony about a tip from defendant's wife that drugs were hidden in the bar where defendant worked was inadmissible hearsay because defendant's own counsel induced the trial court to allow the evidence into the record. State v. Ray, — Ohio App. 3d —, 2006 Ohio 5640, — N.E. 2d —, 2006 Ohio App. LEXIS 5643 (Oct. 30, 2006).

Non-hearsay

When the owners of a business sued a company for negligently installing an oil-interceptor system at the business because, in doing so, it crushed a drain line running from the owners' property, and one of the owners testified in his deposition that an employee of the company told him that the company had crushed the line, this testimony, which was ordinarily hearsay, could be considered in determining the parties' summary judgment motions because, under Ohio R. Evid. 801(D)(2)(d), a statement by a party's agent or servant concerning a matter within the scope of his or her agency or employment and during the existence of the relationship was not hearsay. Loukinas v. Roto-Rooter Servs. Co., 167 Ohio App. 3d 559, 2006 Ohio 3172, 855 N.E. 2d 1272, 2006 Ohio App. LEXIS 3081 (June 23, 2006).

In a negligence action by a deceased patient's executrix against a doctor, statements by the doctor's office manager and his medical assistant were not admissible as statements of a party-opponent under Ohio R. Evid. 801(D)(2), as that section explicitly applied to statements offered against a party where the statements were the party's own, and the statements of the doctor's personnel were not against his interests but merely indicated conversations and conduct that occurred in the office while the patient was being treated. The statements were admissible because they were not hearsay, as they were not offered to prove the matters asserted therein. Frost v. Snitzer, — Ohio App. 3d —, 2006 Ohio 3882, — N.E. 2d —, 2006 Ohio App. LEXIS 3864 (July 28, 2006).

In a murder prosecution, a detective's testimony that another detective received defendant's name from a third party was not inadmissible hearsay, under Ohio R. Evid. 801(C), because the testimony was not offered to prove the truth of the matter asserted. State v. Hilliard, — Ohio App. 3d —, 2006 Ohio 3918, — N.E. 2d —, 2006 Ohio App. LEXIS 3877 (Aug. 2, 2006).

Defendant's due process and confrontation rights under U.S. Const. amends. V and VI, and Ohio Const. art. I, § 10 were not implicated or violated under the plain error rule of Ohio R. Crim. P. 52(B) where the trial court admitted evidence of an anonymous tip received by police that a drug deal was going to take place at a particular location, as it was offered to explain the investigatory action of the police and it did not connect defendant to the alleged drug offense; accordingly, it was not hearsay under Ohio R. Evid. 801(C) and 802. State v. Carpenter, — Ohio App. 3d —, 2006 Ohio 4296, — N.E. 2d —, 2006 Ohio App. LEXIS 4220 (Aug. 18, 2006).

Not hearsay

In the trial for unlawful sexual conduct with a minor, because both of the statements by the witness (defendant's friend) were clearly admissible under the Ohio Rules of Evidence, trial counsel did not err by failing to object to the testimony. The statement to defendant that the victim was 15 years old was not made to prove the victim's age, since that fact had previously been established by her testimony, but rather to prove defendant's knowledge of the fact that the victim was 15 years old, or recklessness with regard to that fact; the witness's testimony with regard to defendant's reaction was undoubtedly highly relevant to the issue of his knowledge of the victim's age, or his recklessness regarding her age. State v. Romig, — Ohio App. 3d —, 2008 Ohio 525, — N.E. 2d —, 2008 Ohio App. LEXIS 445 (Feb. 8, 2008).

Defendant had the opportunity to cross-examine the witnesses and their credibility could easily have been called into question if defendant could have proved that their testimony was not based on their own personal knowledge. Furthermore, many of the witnesses based their opinions regarding the relationship between the victim and defendant and his codefendant on their personal knowledge. They did not repeat hearsay when they made the statements, but made independent observations based on what they heard. State v. Robinson, — Ohio App. 3d —, 2007 Ohio 3501, — N.E. 2d —, 2007 Ohio App. LEXIS 3224 (July 5, 2007).

Admission of testimony from a witness as to statements that she heard the victim make during a criminal incident for which defendant was on trial were not testimonial because they were casual comments between friends or acquaintances and as such, they were not within the confrontation clause pursuant to U.S. Const. amend. VI and Ohio Const. art. I, § 10. They were also not inadmissible hearsay, as one statement was deemed an excited utterance pursuant to Ohio R. Evid. 803(2) where it was made after a verbal altercation, another statement was not hearsay where it was not offered to prove the truth of the matter asserted pursuant to Ohio R. Evid. 801(C), and observations of the victim's body language and emotional state were also not hearsay. State v. McCree, — Ohio App. 3d —, 2007 Ohio 268, — N.E. 2d —, 2007 Ohio App. LEXIS 252 (Jan. 25, 2007).

Father's statements about the sexual abuse did not constitute impermissible hearsay because the testimony was not offered to prove the truth of the matter asserted, i.e., to show that the abuse occurred, but to show how the witness proceeded with the information provided by the child. In any event, the error was harmless since ample evidence existed to convict defendant, even excluding the father's testimony, because the victim testified about the abuse as well as the events leading to his disclosure to his father. State v. Mallette, — Ohio App. 3d —, 2007 Ohio 715, — N.E. 2d —, 2007 Ohio App. LEXIS 655 (Feb. 22, 2007).

Trial cout did not abuse its discretion in allowing testimony from an expert for doctors in a medical malpractice action with respect to a study regarding breast cancer diagnosis timing, as the testimony was not hearsay within Ohio R. Evid. 801(C) where the expert did not quote from any portion of a study so he did not relate any oral or written assertion. As one of the investigators on the study, he testified from personal knowledge and his testimony was properly admitted under Ohio R. Evid. 703. Iglodi v. Tolentino, — Ohio App. 3d —, 2007 Ohio 1982, — N.E. 2d —, 2007 Ohio App. LEXIS 1832 (Apr. 26, 2007).

Anonymous tip to police that drug sales were occurring at a particular location was one of the reasons why the police began an investigation that culminated in charges against defendant, such that the testimony regarding the tip was admissible, as it was not offered to prove the truth of the matter asserted, that is, that defendant was selling drugs, under Ohio R. Evid. 801(C). Accordingly, defendant failed to show that her counsel was ineffective in violation of U.S.

Const. amend. VI and Ohio Const. art. I, § 10 by failing to object to the admission thereof. State v. Henderson, — Ohio App. 3d —, 2007 Ohio 2372, — N.E. 2d —, 2007 Ohio App. LEXIS 2212 (May 17, 2007).

Defendant's counsel was not ineffective for failing to object to hearsay pursuant to Ohio R. Evid. 801(C), as the testimony raised by defendant for purposes of the assignment of error did not constitute hearsay where it was testimony by a witness about what that witness said; the fact that a witness looked away when questioned was not hearsay, and a statement by a van driver that the van did not belong to him was not offered for the truth of the matter asserted, such that it also was not hearsay. State v. Skinner, — Ohio App. 3d —, 2007 Ohio 6793, — N.E. 2d —, 2007 Ohio App. LEXIS 5948 (Dec. 14, 2007).

Statements challenged were not hearsay because they were not used to prove the truth of the matter asserted, that defendant owned the drug bags, but rather to explain the police action during investigation, namely why they searched the areas that they did. Even if the statements qualified as hearsay, the admission of the testimony was not reversible error because the statements were not necessary to sustain defendant's conviction; defendant had on his person a large amount of drugs, a weapon, ammunition, currency and a cellular phone and thus, the overwhelming circumstantial evidence supported defendant's conviction. State v. Peyton, — Ohio App. 3d —, 2006 Ohio 3735, — N.E. 2d —, 2006 Ohio App. LEXIS 3694 (July 20, 2006).

Trial court's admission of statements by a doctor's medical assistant in a negligence action by a deceased patient's executrix against the doctor was not error because the statements were not hearsay under Ohio R. Evid. 801 where they were not admitted for the truth of the matter asserted. The statements would not have fit within the hearsay exception of Ohio R. Evid. 803(2) for an excited utterance, as the assistant's statements regarding the doctor's response to the patient's death were not conclusively deemed spontaneous or excited because they were made the morning after the patient died and it was not clear when the doctor was notified of the death. Frost v. Snitzer, — Ohio App. 3d —, 2006 Ohio 3882, — N.E. 2d —, 2006 Ohio App. LEXIS 3864 (July 28, 2006).

Trial court committed no evidentiary ruling error when it permitted defense counsel in a medical malpractice action to use a document describing time necessary for the production of a certain test result in the cross-examination of an expert for the parents of a minor patient who died while being treated, as the document was not admitted into evidence, it was not hearsay under Ohio R. Evid. 801(C), and it was properly used for impeachment purposes under Ohio R. Evid. 616(C) where the expert had testified that the time needed for test results was much shorter than indicated in the document. Werden v. Children's Hosp. Med. Ctr., — Ohio App. 3d —, 2006 Ohio 4600, — N.E. 2d —, 2006 Ohio App. LEXIS 4547 (Sept. 8, 2006).

As a statement from a victim in defendant's criminal trial that the victim's uncle did not testify at the trial because he feared for his safety was not inadmissible hearsay pursuant to Ohio R. Evid. 801(C) and 802 as it was not offered for the truth of the matter asserted but merely to explain why the uncle was not questioned on the stand, defendant's counsel was not ineffective in violation of defendant's rights under U.S. Const. amend. VI and Ohio Const. art. I, § 10 in eliciting such testimony from the victim. State v. Henry, — Ohio App. 3d —, 2006 Ohio 4783, — N.E. 2d —, 2006 Ohio App. LEXIS 4657 (Sept. 14, 2006).

Trial court did not err in admitting evidence in an adjudicatory hearing during a dependency proceeding by a doctor who had treated the subject child where his statements were not admitted for the truth of the matter asserted pursuant to Ohio R. Evid. 801(C) and accordingly, they were not inadmissible hearsay. The statements were offered to show the child's perception of reality and further, they were within the hearsay

exception for statements made for purposes of medical diagnosis or treatment pursuant to Ohio R. Evid. 803(4). In re E. R., — Ohio App. 3d —, 2006 Ohio 4816, — N.E. 2d —, 2006 Ohio App. LEXIS 4745 (Sept. 18, 2006).

Victim's statement, "Stop, Mike, Stop," over the telephone was not hearsay; the challenged statement was not an assertion because it cannot be proven true or false and thus, it could not be offered to prove the truth of the matter asserted, and therefore, was not hearsay. Even if the statement had been hearsay, defendant could not demonstrate that its admission was plain error because the trial court indicated that it did not need to consider the testimony of the sister and mother. State v. West, — Ohio App. 3d —, 2006 Ohio 5095, — N.E. 2d —, 2006 Ohio App. LEXIS 5050 (Sept. 29, 2006).

Defendant's confrontation rights under U.S. Const. amend. VI and Ohio Const. art. I, § 10 were not violated by testimony from police officers regarding statements made by defendant's girlfriend, who was the victim of his crimes, where she did not testify at his criminal trial, as the statements were not offered to prove the truth of the matter asserted, they were within the testifying officer's personal knowledge, they were nontestimonial, or they were offered to explain the subsequent investigative actions of the officers, and further, the jury was properly instructed on the use of those statements for their limited purpose; they were not inadmissible hearsay under Ohio R. Evid. 801(C) and 802. State v. Chambers, — Ohio App. 3d —, 2006 Ohio 5326, — N.E. 2d —, 2006 Ohio App. LEXIS 5319 (Oct. 12, 2006).

Child's statements were properly admitted under Evid. R. 803(4) as statements made for the purpose of diagnosis and treatment because, since the child was subject to cross-examination, defendant's right to confrontation was not violated. Also, the trial court did not abuse its discretion in allowing the testimony of the psychologist because she testified regarding the child's nearly two-year course of therapy including her initial symptoms and the progress that she had made. State v. Brown, — Ohio App. 3d —, 2006 Ohio 5769, — N.E. 2d —, 2006 Ohio App. LEXIS 5759 (Nov. 3, 2006).

When an investment company sued the administrator of a decedent's estate because some of the decedent's stock the administrator had sold had previously been sold, documents the investment company received from the transfer company for the bank which had issued the stock, notifying it that the stock had previously been sold, were admissible, under Ohio R. Evid. 801(C), without the testimony of transfer company employees, for the limited purpose of showing their effect on investment company employees and their response, because the documents were not offered for the truth of the matter asserted and witnesses who testified were qualified to testify that the documents were what they purported to be and were made in the ordinary course of business to notify them of the stock's re-issuance and prior sale. Edward D. Jones & Co., L.P. v. Staley, — Ohio App. 3d —, 2006 Ohio 6122, — N.E. 2d —, 2006 Ohio App. LEXIS 6060 (Nov. 17, 2006).

Defendant failed to show that his counsel provided ineffective assistance in violation of U.S. Const. amend. VI by failing to object to testimony in defendant's criminal matter, as much of the testimony was not hearsay under Ohio R. Evid. 801(C) where it not offered to prove the truth of the matters asserted, and the failure to object was not ineffectiveness in any event because it related to isolated and stray comments. There was other admissible evidence in the record relating to the subject matter objected to in that testimony, such that there was no plain error under Ohio R. Crim. P. 52(B) in the admission of the testimony. State v. Howard, — Ohio App. 3d —, 2006 Ohio 6410, — N.E. 2d —, 2006 Ohio App. LEXIS 6372 (Dec. 7, 2006).

There was no plain error under Ohio R. Crim. P. 52(B) in a trial court's admission of testimony from a sexual offense victim's mother regarding what she had heard about her daughter, the victim, having been raped, as it did not constitute impermissible hearsay under Ohio R. Evid. 801(C) because it was not offered for the truth of the matter asserted but rather, to explain the investigation of the allegedly criminal incident. State v. Jenkins, — Ohio App. 3d —, 2006 Ohio 6421, — N.E. 2d —, 2006 Ohio App. LEXIS 6373 (Dec. 7, 2006).

Police officer's testimony was an attempt to rehabilitate the witnesses against the charges that they had fabricated the allegations of abuse. Therefore, since the children testified at trial and were subject to cross-examination, the statements were not hearsay under Ohio R. Evid. 801(D)(1)(b). State v. Schewirey, — Ohio App. 3d —, 2006 Ohio 7054, — N.E. 2d —, 2006 Ohio App. LEXIS 6988 (Dec. 20, 2006).

Plain error

When a landowner was sanctioned for failing to comply with a settlement of a prior motion to hold the owner in contempt for not complying with an earlier settlement of the owner's alleged zoning violations, the owner did not show that the admission of two affidavits was plain error for allegedly being hearsay, under Ohio R. Evid. 801(C), not within a recognized exception, rendering them inadmissible, under Ohio R. Evid. 802, because substantial other evidence showed the owner's failure to comply with the settlement. Ray v. Bd. of Union Twp. Trs., — Ohio App. 3d —, — N.E. 2d —, 2007 Ohio 3001, 2007 Ohio App. LEXIS 2753 (June 18, 2007).

Police testimony

Police officer's statement that a witness corroborated information during an investigation constituted inadmissible hearsay: State v. Platfoot, 183 Ohio App. 3d 349, 2009 Ohio 3769, 916 N.E.2d 1147, 2009 Ohio App. LEXIS 3191 (2009).

Prejudicial error

Court rejected a father's contention that, in recommending that his children could not be placed with the father within a reasonable time, the psychologist who evaluated the father in terms of his parenting capabilities relied, to the father's prejudice, on hearsay statements made by the father's girlfriend to the family services agency. The psychologist interviewed the father over a period of four days; his report was based on the clinical interviews, his observation of parent-child interaction, a review of the father's records with the agency, and the results of certain psychological tests; and the information given by the girlfriend and passed on to the psychologist was just one detail from the background information contained in the agency's file. In re Joseph C.P., — Ohio App. 3d —, 2007 Ohio 1528, — N.E.2d —, 2007 Ohio App. LEXIS 1397 (Mar. 30, 2007).

Prejudicial error not found

Even if an a victim's statements to police detective made after an aggravated burglary were hearsay under Ohio R. Evid. 801 and should have been excluded under Ohio R. Evid. 802, defendant failed to demonstrate prejudicial error arising from the admission of the statements. Defendant's cross-examination of the victim included questions concerning her conversation with the detective, and the detective's testimony, in any event, was merely cumulative of the victim's testimony offered at trial. State v. Holloman, — Ohio App. 3d —, 2007 Ohio 840, — N.E. 2d —, 2007 Ohio App. LEXIS 739 (Mar. 1, 2007).

Prior consistent statements

Trial court did not abuse its discretion when it permitted an investigator to testify on rebuttal that the murder victim's 12-year-old daughter made an out-of-court statement to him, the day after the fatal altercation, consistent with her testimony. Because defense counsel suggested on cross-examination that the victim's family prompted her to alter her account of the fatal altercation after she made the statement, the prosecution introduced the statement during its rebuttal to negate that inference; thus, the statement did not constitute

hearsay. State v. Moore, — Ohio App. 3d —, 2007 Ohio 3600, — N.E. 2d —, 2007 Ohio App. LEXIS 3306 (July 16, 2007).

Trial court did not abuse its discretion in refusing to admit the victim's prior testimony to the prosecution and the grand jury because defendant and his mother spoke in a recorded telephone conversation of influencing the victim to change her story and that recorded conversation took place prior to the victim's interview with prosecutors and her grand jury testimony. Thus, it was reasonable to infer that defendant had been successful in convincing the victim to change her story regarding the domestic violence and abduction. State v. Glossip, — Ohio App. 3d —, 2007 Ohio 2066, — N.E. 2d —, 2007 Ohio App. LEXIS 1931 (Apr. 30, 2007).

Trial court properly allowed the State to offer a witness's prior consistent statement pursuant to Ohio R. Evid. 801(D)(1)(b) where defense counsel repeatedly cross-examined the witness as to what the State had offered him in exchange for his testimony, which raised an implied charge of improper motive. State v. Townsend, — Ohio App. 3d —, 2006 Ohio 5457, — N.E. 2d —, 2006 Ohio App. LEXIS 5444 (Oct. 19, 2006).

Prior identification testimony

There was no error in allowing the detective to testify regarding the victim's prior identification because the identification did not create a "very substantial likelihood of misidentification" which would have amounted to reversible error. Further, the prior identification was reliable because the victim testified that: he owed money to the person who shot him and thus knew the assailant; his assailant hit him in the head with a pistol before shooting him in the leg; he had told the detective the street name of the person who had shot him and that person was pictured in the photo array; and he had not told the 911 operator who had shot him since the assailant was present at the time that the 911 call was placed. State v. Clements, — Ohio App. 3d —, 2007 Ohio 2617, — N.E. 2d —, 2007 Ohio App. LEXIS 2433 (May 29, 2007).

Prior inconsistent statement

Trial court did not abuse its discretion when it did not allow the cards and letters from the victim and defendant's wife into evidence. The alleged prior inconsistent statements met none of the criteria for substantive admissibility under Ohio R. Evid. 801(D)(1)(a) and were neither under oath, subject to cross-examination, nor given at a proceeding or deposition. The victim's and the wife's statements could not have been used subjectively. State v. Laboy, — Ohio App. 3d —, 2006 Ohio 5927, — N.E. 2d —, 2006 Ohio App. LEXIS 5853 (Nov. 9, 2006).

Prior statement of witness

Detective's testimony was not hearsay because the State did not use the detective's testimony for the purpose of bolstering the witness's testimony or to comment on his veracity rather, the testimony was elicited by the State in response to defense counsel's first questioning the witness about his prior statement. The witness was thoroughly cross-examined about his role in the incident and about the statement he gave to the police and the detective was also cross-examined as to the consistency between the witness's statement and testimony. The State was permitted to question the detective about the witness's prior statements. State v. Harris, — Ohio App. 3d —, 2007 Ohio 289, — N.E. 2d —, 2007 Ohio App. LEXIS 264 (Jan. 25, 2007).

Trial court erred in ruling that all prior statements by parties were inadmissible hearsay because a party's statements offered against the party were not hearsay, under Ohio R. Evid. 801(D), and each statement had to be reviewed to determine if it was an admissible statement against interest, under Ohio R. Evid. 804(B)(3). In re Butler, — Ohio App. 3d —, 2006 Ohio 4547, — N.E. 2d —, 2006 Ohio App. LEXIS 4510 (Sept. 5, 2006).

Reversible error

Where there was no showing that the jury dismissed the presumption to follow the trial court's cautionary instruction to only consider certain testimony as background and that it was not to be considered as evidence of the truth or falsity of the charge against defendant, and where no material prejudice was shown, admission of out-of-court statements was not reversible error. State v. Bedell, — Ohio App. 3d —, 2006 Ohio 5746, — N.E. 2d —, 2006 Ohio App. LEXIS 5705 (Nov. 2, 2006).

Social worker's testimony

In a prosecution for gross sexual imposition against a child victim, a social worker's testimony relating a single statement by the victim to the victim's mother identifying defendant as the perpetrator was not inadmissible hearsay, under Ohio R. Evid. 801(C), because it was not offered to prove the truth of the matter asserted and merely explained the social worker's involvement in the case. State v. Abner, — Ohio App. 3d —, 2007 Ohio 3053, — N.E. 2d —, 2007 Ohio App. LEXIS 2796 (June 18, 2007).

Inadmissible hearsay

Trial court did not abuse its discretion in excluding a document prepared by a licensed mortgage agent reflecting an accounting in an action based upon a mortgagor's default in payments, as the agent was not present to testify or authenticate the document and accordingly, it was inadmissible hearsay under Ohio R. Evid. 801(C) and 802. Urbanski v. Nuding, — Ohio App. 3d —, 2006 Ohio 467, — N.E. 2d —, 2006 Ohio App. LEXIS 423 (Feb. 3, 2006).

Not hearsay

In a prosecution for contributing to the delinquency of a minor, testimony of the victims as to their ages was not hearsay because it did not involve out-of-court statements within the definition of Ohio R. Evid. 801(C), but, rather, the victims made the statements while testifying, so defendant had the opportunity to confront them concerning the source of this information. State v. Selmon, — Ohio App. 3d —, 2006 Ohio 65, — N.E. 2d —, 2006 Ohio App. LEXIS 50 (Jan. 9, 2006).

Prior inconsistent statement

Admission of the witness's prior inconsistent statement did not constitute plain error because, even assuming that the witness's prior inconsistent statement was improperly admitted as substantive evidence of defendant's guilt, and that a limiting instruction should have been given, there was overwhelming evidence of defendant's guilt. The testimony showed that defendant, who was driving a truck, pursued the victim who was trying to evade him, that there were guns and ammo in the truck, and that, in a signed sworn statement to the police, defendant admitted that he told the witness (a passenger) to fire the gun at the van. State v. Rose, — Ohio App. 3d —, 2006 Ohio 397, — N.E. 2d —, 2006 Ohio App. LEXIS 337 (Jan. 30, 2006).

Statement of party opponent

Trial court did not commit error in failing to exclude the prison social work supervisor's testimony when he related that he had heard defendant say to the victim after he had knocked him down and kicked him that, in essence, he deserved what he got for snitching. It was not hearsay because it was a statement of a party-opponent, pursuant to Ohio R. Evid. 801(D)(2). State v. Damron, — Ohio App. 3d —, 2007 Ohio 1187, — N.E. 2d —, 2007 Ohio App. LEXIS 1116 (Mar. 13, 2007).

Even if defendant had not waived the issue by failing to object to the admission of the testimony of a witness, the trial court did not err by permitting the testimony pursuant to Evid. R. 801(D)(2), as a statement against one's own interest. The witness's testimony did not refer to defendant's acts with another victim, but rather, to the very acts charged in the indictment; he testified that defendant referred to a victim who had moved out of state, and the fact that defendant did not mention the victim's name when he made the admission to the witness weakened but did not destroy the statement's relevance to the issue of whether defendant sexually abused the victim. State v. Burton, — Ohio App. 3d —, 2007 Ohio 1660, — N.E. 2d —, 2007 Ohio App. LEXIS 1532 (Apr. 4, 2007).

Weight of the evidence supported defendant's guilty verdict for defendant guilty of domestic violence because the victim made statements immediately after the incident to her great-grandmother and the police and those statements were properly admitted as excited utterances. Although the victim recanted her initial statements at trial, the State presented evidence of a recorded telephone conversation between defendant and his mother discussing how they would get the victim to change her story. The statements by defendant's mother were allowable as admissions of a party opponent and the probative value of defendant's admissions on the tape, especially in light of the victim's recantation at trial, substantially outweighed any danger of unfair prejudice. State v. Glossip, — Ohio App. 3d —, 2007 Ohio 2066, — N.E. 2d —, 2007 Ohio App. LEXIS 1931 (Apr. 30, 2007).

Trial court did not abuse its discretion in admitting the taped statements from the victim's answering machine because the statements were relevant, they were not too remote in time from the incident, and the probative value of the evidence was not outweighed by the danger of unfair prejudice; since the statements were those of defendant, and offered against him at trial, the statements were not hearsay and were properly admissible under Ohio R. Evid. 801(D)(2). Because the messages met the requirements of Ohio R. Evid. 801(D)(2), their admission was not dependent upon one of the exceptions under Ohio R. Evid. 404(B) and, to the extent that defendant argued that the statements were precluded under Ohio R. Evid. 404(B), such evidence was relevant and admissible because it tended to prove identity. State v. Cody, — Ohio App. 3d —, 2007 Ohio 6776, — N.E. 2d —, 2007 Ohio App. LEXIS 5938 (Dec. 18, 2007).

In defendant's rape prosecution, statements made by the victim's boyfriend, who was also defendant's roommate, during his direct examination, to the effect that, after talking with defendant, it was clear that the victim did not want to have sex with him on the day in question, that defendant admitted to him that the victim said, "No," several times, and that she eventually just gave in because of his size, were properly admitted as statements of a party opponent because it was defendant's statement and was offered against him by the State. State v. Thrasher, — Ohio App. 3d —, 2006 Ohio 1260, — N.E. 2d —, 2006 Ohio App. LEXIS 1134 (Mar. 17, 2006).

Testimony that defendant offered an informant extra crack cocaine if he changed the tire on her car were those of the informant stating what defendant said to him, and two witnesses heard defendant make this statement; thus, it was properly admitted. State v. Clark, — Ohio App. 3d —, 2006 Ohio 2699, — N.E. 2d —, 2006 Ohio App. LEXIS 2536 (May 25, 2006).

Other than asserting that the micro cassette that contained the recorded interview of defendant by the detective was cumulative evidence, defendant failed to demonstrate how he was materially prejudiced by its admission because the tape was properly authenticated by the detective and was a "statement by a party opponent" pursuant to Evid. R. 801(D)(2). The contents of the tape could clearly have aided the jury in reaching a verdict and thus, the micro cassette was not cumulative in nature and the trial court did not abuse its discretion in admitting said evidence. State v. Arrone, — Ohio App. 3d —, 2006 Ohio 4144, — N.E. 2d —, 2006 Ohio App. LEXIS 4125 (Aug. 11, 2006).

Trial court erroneously ruled that defendant could testify as to out of court statements made by a victim, under Ohio R.

Evid. 801(D)(2), because, for purposes of this Rule, a victim was not a party-opponent, so her statements to defendant were inadmissible under this exception to the hearsay rule. State v. Ingram, — Ohio App. 3d —, 2006 Ohio 4559, — N.E. 2d —, 2006 Ohio App. LEXIS 4499 (Sept. 5, 2006).

When a trial court ruled that defendant could testify as to out of court statements made by a victim, under Ohio R. Evid. 801(D)(2), the State could appeal that ruling, under RC § 2945.67(A), even though defendant was either acquitted of the charges against him or a mistrial was granted, because this evidentiary ruling was capable of repetition yet evaded review. State v. Ingram, — Ohio App. 3d —, 2006 Ohio 4559, — N.E. 2d —, 2006 Ohio App. LEXIS 4499 (Sept. 5, 2006).

In a murder prosecution, when testimony about the statements of co-conspirators was admitted, an statements attributed to defendant were admissible as admissions of a party-opponent, under Ohio R. Evid. 801(D)(2)(a). State v. Moore, — Ohio App. 3d —, 2006 Ohio 4926, — N.E. 2d —, 2006 Ohio App. LEXIS 4884 (Sept. 25, 2006).

Trial court erred when it granted summary judgment as the affidavit of the victim's daughter created a genuine issue of material fact as to whether the restaurant had notice that a potential hazard existed. Striking paragraphs as hearsay was error since the statements fell within the party-opponent definition of non-hearsay, Evid. R. 801(D)(2). Cordle v. Bravo Dev., — Ohio App. 3d —, 2006 Ohio 5693, — N.E. 2d —, 2006 Ohio App. LEXIS 5692 (Oct. 31, 2006).

Statements which are not hearsay

Question by the person who called the rape victim pretending to be defendant's parole officer asking why the victim was lying or why she did not scream, was not hearsay because none of the caller's statements to the victim were offered to prove the truth of the matter asserted. Rather, the content of the call was offered to show what triggered the victim to call the authorities and to provide context for how she finally reported her allegations; the contents of the call were not irrelevant. State v. Rupp, — Ohio App. 3d —, 2007 Ohio 1561, — N.E. 2d —, 2007 Ohio App. LEXIS 1449 (Mar. 27, 2007).

When defendant's statement in furtherance of a conspiracy was offered at his trial, it was unnecessary, under Ohio R. Evid. 801(D)(2)(e), to prove the existence of a conspiracy because the statement was not hearsay, under Ohio R. Evid. 801(D)(2)(a), as it was offered against defendant, so the existence of a conspiracy was irrelevant. State v. Martin, — Ohio App. 3d —, 2006 Ohio 5263, — N.E. 2d —, 2006 Ohio App. LEXIS 5252 (Oct. 6, 2006).

Driver's statements related to a driver's intentions to purchase the truck later involved in a traffic accident from a dealer and the arrangements for that purchase, including why title was not immediately transferred, whether the driver had purchased insurance for the truck and whether he had arranged for license plates for the truck, so the dealer's testimony that the driver approached him about purchasing the vehicle, his description of the arrangements for payment, and that he saw the driver put license plates from a different vehicle on the truck were descriptions of the dealer's observations of the driver's actions, not statements by the driver, and accordingly, that testimony did not constitute hearsay. The dealer's testimony that the driver told him he had not decided what to do with the truck and that he was considering giving the truck to his son were not offered for the truth of the driver's intentions for the truck, but, rather, they were offered to explain the reasons for the dealer not transferring title to the driver immediately after he signed the sales agreement, and accordingly, those statements were also not inadmissible hearsay. Finally, although the dealer's testimony that the driver stated that he had put the truck on his insurance policy, was hearsay, it was harmless. Iker v. Estate of Jones, — Ohio App. 3d —, 2006 Ohio 5393, — N.E. 2d —, 2006 Ohio App. LEXIS 5388 (Oct. 13, 2006).

Testimony of police officer

There was no error in failing to permit the police lieutenant's statement, made to a newspaper, at trial because it was unclear why the lieutenant would have made a public statement on the matter since he had no first-hand knowledge of the incident, was not involved in the investigation, was never at the scene of the crime, never saw the victim, and never spoke to defendant. Also, the statement, since it was by a law enforcement officer, was not admissible against the prosecution as an admission of a party-opponent under Ohio R. Evid. 801(D)(2). State v. Stacy, — Ohio App. 3d —, 2007 Ohio 6744, — N.E. 2d —, 2007 Ohio App. LEXIS 5911 (Dec. 17, 2007).

Testimony which explains actions

Even if defense counsel erred in failing to object to inadmissible hearsay, any such error was harmless because the detective's testimony regarding the gun and the victim picking defendant from a photo array was admissible because the victim testified that she saw defendant take her gun and that she picked him from a photo array. The testimony of the victim's daughter was not hearsay because it was not offered for the truth of the matter asserted, but rather, was offered to explain why and how the investigation eventually led to defendant. She testified that once her mother identified defendant as the person who held a gun to her mother's head, she went to the Sheriff's office with that information. State v. Maxwell, — Ohio App. 3d —, 2007 Ohio 4027, — N.E. 2d —, 2007 Ohio App. LEXIS 3637 (Aug. 1, 2007).

Truth of the matter asserted

In defendant's prosecution under RC §§ 2903.11(A)(2) and 2941.145 for complicity to felonious assault with a firearm specification, based on allegations that she drove a vehicle from which her co-defendant exited to shoot at the victims, using a gun supplied by defendant, the admission of testimony that a child was in a car seat in the back of the victims' vehicle was not improper hearsay because the testimony was not offered for the truth of the matter asserted, as it was only a reference in describing the bullet's trajectory. State v. Myers, — Ohio App. 3d —, 2007 Ohio 915, — N.E. 2d —, 2007 Ohio App. LEXIS 817 (Mar. 5, 2007).

Where testimony by a police officer regarding what a witness told him about defendant's conduct was offered to explain the officer's investigation in a restaurant parking lot, as the witness said that criminal conduct was occurring, and it was not offered to prove the truth thereof, it was admissible because it was not hearsay under Ohio R. Evid. 801(C). State v. Deer, — Ohio App. 3d —, 2007 Ohio 1866, — N.E. 2d —, 2007 Ohio App. LEXIS 1700 (Apr. 20, 2007).

In a dependency proceeding in which it was alleged that a mother's children had been abused by members of the mother's church, a caseworker's testimony about prior experience with the children of other members of the church was not inadmissible hearsay, under Ohio R. Evid. 801(C), because it was not offered for the truth of the matter asserted, as it was merely offered to show why an agency was concerned about an anonymous report that the children had been abused by church members. In re Miller, — Ohio App. 3d —, 2007 Ohio 2170, — N.E. 2d —, 2007 Ohio App. LEXIS 2017 (May 4, 2007).

Relevant evidence indicative of the sellers' knowledge of the alleged defects in the home presented by the buyer to oppose the motion for summary judgment was not admissible either under Ohio R. Civ. P. 32, in a deposition, or under Ohio R. Civ. P. 56, as an affidavit, because any evidence (what the neighbors told the buyer) that could even remotely have been construed as creating an inference that the sellers were or should have been aware of the defects in the residence was hearsay, pursuant to Ohio R. Evid. 801, because it was offered to prove the truth of the matter asserted (knowledge of defects). Therefore, the buyer did not meet his burden of production to overcome the motion for summary judgment.

Reardon v. Hale, — Ohio App. 3d —, 2007 Ohio 4351, — N.E. 2d —, 2007 Ohio App. LEXIS 3906 (Aug. 27, 2007).

Trial court did not err by refusing to admit the victim's out-of-court statements because they were offered to prove the facts as defendant related them. Although the specific statements were not permitted, the court permitted the defense to describe the victim's conduct, tone, and demeanor and the record as a whole amply conveyed the situation, defendant's beliefs about her safety, and the events preceding the use of force. State v. Williams, — Ohio App. 3d —, 2007 Ohio 4845, — N.E. 2d —, 2007 Ohio App. LEXIS 4329 (Sept. 20, 2007).

In a suit brought by an insurer seeking reimbursement from an apartment manager for damages paid by the insurer as a result of a fire allegedly caused by the manager's negligent disposal of a cigarette, the trial court did not err in allowing an electrical repair bill to be used as evidence since it was not offered as proof of the matter asserted but was offered to show necessary electrical repair, which was already acknowledged by two other witnesses in the case. Acuity Insurance Co. v. Farmer, — Ohio App. 3d —, 2006 Ohio 1183, — N.E. 2d —, 2006 Ohio App. LEXIS 1068 (Mar. 13, 2006).

In a prosecution for obstruction of justice, an officer's testimony relating what another officer told him, to explain why he was in the area where he arrested defendant, was not hearsay, under Ohio R. Evid. 801(C), because it was not offered for the truth of the matter asserted, nor did it prejudice defendant, as the status of the felon defendant was alleged to be harboring was corroborated by the testimony of the felon's parole officer. State v. Hall, — Ohio App. 3d —, 2006 Ohio 2160, — N.E. 2d —, 2006 Ohio App. LEXIS 1987 (Apr. 26, 2006).

Trial court did not err in admitting a statement of an individual inside the house where a confidential informant completed a drug buy that "D" had the biggest pieces of crack cocaine because the statement was not hearsay under Ohio R. Evid. 801(C), in that it was not offered by the State to prove that "D" had the biggest pieces of crack cocaine. It only showed that the individual thought that "D" had the biggest pieces. Further, even if the statement were hearsay, it qualified as a present sense impression exception to the hearsay rule under Ohio R. Evid. 803(1) since the statement was made by the declarant as he was perceiving the event and was being recorded over the CI's wire. State v. Johnson, — Ohio App. 3d —, 2006 Ohio 4066, — N.E. 2d —, 2006 Ohio App. LEXIS 4033 (Aug. 7, 2006).

Because questions could not constitute hearsay as they could not prove the truth of the matter asserted, the witness's testimony relaying the question that the victim posed to defendant about getting his money back did not constitute hearsay, and the trial court did not commit error, let alone plain error, in allowing the testimony. State v. Brown, — Ohio App. 3d —, 2006 Ohio 4594, — N.E. 2d —, 2006 Ohio App. LEXIS 4541 (Sept. 7, 2006).

Videotape of police interview

Defendant's videotaped police interviews were admissible. The interviewing officer's statements did not constitute hearsay or statements of opinion where they were not made to prove the truth of the matter asserted or to assert the officer's beliefs, but were merely interrogation techniques and were included to provide context for the defendant's statements: State v. Craycraft, 147 Ohio Misc. 2d 5, 2008 Ohio 2192, 889 N.E.2d 1100, 2008 Ohio Misc. LEXIS 130 (2008).

RULE 802. Hearsay Rule

Hearsay is not admissible except as otherwise provided by the Constitution of the United States, by the Constitution of the State of Ohio, by statute enacted by the General Assembly not in conflict with a rule of the Supreme Court of Ohio, by these rules, or by other rules prescribed by the Supreme Court of Ohio.

NOTES TO DECISIONS

ANALYSIS

Administrative proceeding
Admissibility of hearsay evidence
Admission of hearsay
Admission of hearsay statements
Evidence held not admissible
Evidence properly admitted
Harmless error
Hearsay
Inadmissible hearsay
Plain error
Prejudicial error not found
What constitutes hearsay

Administrative proceeding

There was no abuse of discretion in allowing a witness to read from a journal that contained hearsay evidence pursuant to Ohio R. Evid. 801(C) and 802, as such occurred in an administrative hearing before the Ohio State Board of Psychology to determine the appropriate discipline against a psychologist. The Board was not bound by the rules of evidence pursuant to OAC 4732:17-03(D)(10), and admission thereof was not arbitrary or capricious in the circumstances. Althof v. Ohio State Bd. of Psychology, — Ohio App. 3d —, 2007 Ohio 1010, — N.E. 2d —, 2007 Ohio App. LEXIS 912 (Mar. 8, 2007).

Admissibility of hearsay evidence

Because defendant did not object to the out-of-court statement, under either hearsay or confrontation grounds, the trial court was entitled to consider the statement for whatever probative value it provided. The State was entitled to have the officer explain why he made investigation of defendant's possible involvement in the stolen vehicle and the primary value of the statement to the officer was not for the proof of the truth therein, i.e., that defendant had driven the car, but to explain why the officer went from seeking the return of the sister's car to investigating an unrelated stolen vehicle. State v. Scott, — Ohio App. 3d —, 2006 Ohio 4981, — N.E. 2d —, 2006 Ohio App. LEXIS 4923 (Sept. 26, 2006).

Admission of hearsay

Defendant showed that his counsel was ineffective in violation of defendant's Sixth Amendment rights for failing to object to testimony by the victim of defendant's shooting crime that the victim had been told previously that defendant had been hired to kill him, as such was clearly hearsay in violation of Ohio R. Evid. 802, any probative basis to explain why the victim had a gun in his car was outweighed by the prejudicial impact of the testimony, and it appeared that there was a reasonable probability that but for counsel's mistake, the result of the trial would have been different. The jury was divided and during deliberations, it only asked to see that portion of the witness's testimony regarding the hearsay prior to deciding to convict defendant. State v. Wilkins, — Ohio App. 3d —, 2007 Ohio 2962, — N.E. 2d —, 2007 Ohio App. LEXIS 2723 (June 15, 2007).

Admission of hearsay statements

Admission of the search warrant and affidavit did not violate defendant's rights under the Confrontation Clause because the detective who signed the affidavit testified at trial and the hearsay statements within the affidavit were statements by a witness who testified at trial; each were subject to cross-examination at trial, which preserved defendant's right to confront the witnesses against him. Although much of the affidavit contained impermissible hearsay which was prejudicial to defendant, the trial court did not commit plain error when it admitted the evidence because the evidence against defendant was convincing. State v. Carter, — Ohio App. 3d —, 2007 Ohio 3502, — N.E. 2d —, 2007 Ohio App. LEXIS 3223 (June 29, 2007).

Admission of the search warrant and affidavit did not violate defendant's rights under the Confrontation Clause because the detective who signed the affidavit testified at trial and the hearsay statements within the affidavit were statements by a witness who testified at tria. Each were subject to cross-examination at trial, which preserved defendant's right to confront the witnesses against him. Although much of the affidavit contained impermissible hearsay which was prejudicial to defendant, the trial court did not commit plain error when it admitted the evidence because the evidence against defendant was convincing. State v. Robinson, — Ohio App. 3d —, 2007 Ohio 3501, — N.E. 2d —, 2007 Ohio App. LEXIS 3224 (July 5, 2007).

Pursuant to Ohio R. Evid. 801(C) and 802, admission of testimony from a police detective, wherein he relayed statements made to him by a juvenile's mother with respect to the juvenile's conduct, as well as statements made to her by the juvenile's stepbrother, was hearsay, but as it was cumulative because the facts were already in evidence due to the juvenile's confession, the admission thereof was not so prejudicial as to be reversible error. In re Sturm, — Ohio App. 3d —, 2006 Ohio 7101, — N.E. 2d —, 2006 Ohio App. LEXIS 7046 (Dec. 22, 2006).

Evidence held not admissible

When a debtor's insurer paid her creditor the value of her car after a tree fell on it, and the creditor sought a deficiency judgment against her, causing her to file a third-party complaint against the city, she did not show the city was liable to her because newspaper articles and other statements she submitted in opposition to summary judgment motions filed by the creditor and the city were inadmissible hearsay, under Ohio R. Evid. 802, and she did not show, under RC § 2744.02(A) or (B)(3), or RC § 723.01, that the city was liable because she did not show that the city controlled the tree, that the tree posed a danger before the storm during which it fell, or that the city had actual or constructive notice that the tree posed a potential hazard. Consumer Portfolio Servs. v. Staples, — Ohio App. 3d —, 2007 Ohio 1531, — N.E. 2d —, 2007 Ohio App. LEXIS 1400 (Mar. 30, 2007).

Trial court did not abuse its discretion in excluding a document prepared by a licensed mortgage agent reflecting an accounting in an action based upon a mortgagor's default in payments, as the agent was not present to testify or authenticate the document and accordingly, it was inadmissible hearsay under Ohio R. Evid. 801(C) and 802. Urbanski v. Nuding, — Ohio App. 3d —, 2006 Ohio 467, — N.E. 2d —, 2006 Ohio App. LEXIS 423 (Feb. 3, 2006).

Trial court did not abuse its discretion in excluding testimony from a vehicle occupant that she heard someone at the scene of the vehicle accident she was involved in say that the other driver was dead, as such evidence was hearsay which was not admissible under Ohio R. Evid. 801(C) and 802. The occupant sought the introduction thereof to show the impact it had on her emotional state and her later injuries, which could have been shown without offering the exact statement, and the evidentiary ruling did not affect her substantial rights. Luther v. Estate of Skrinjar, — Ohio App. 3d —, 2006 Ohio 7117, — N.E. 2d —, 2006 Ohio App. LEXIS 7063 (Dec. 29, 2006).

Evidence properly admitted

Because the mother's testimony regarding defendant's drug use revealed defendant's possible motive to steal, her testimony was admissible under Ohio R. Evid. 404(B). There was also no error under Ohio R. Evid. 802, regarding hearsay,

because it could not be determined with certainty whether the evidence was offered for the truth of the matter asserted or to show the mother's subjective belief as the basis for her reactions to defendant. State v. Parsons, — Ohio App. 3d —, 2007 Ohio 1204, — N.E. 2d —, 2007 Ohio App. LEXIS 1025 (Mar. 13, 2007).

In the permanent custody proceeding, the stepfather's statement to his co-worker regarding his drinking, the statement of one of the children's counselor concerning whether the mother tried to get the child to lie about whether she was the driver of the vehicle in the fatal accident, and the statement by the psychologist were harmless errors in light of other testimony and evidence that supported the trial court's decision to award permanent custody to the children's services. Otherwise, the trial court did not abuse its discretion in admitting any of the hearsay testimony about which the mother complained because recognized exceptions to the hearsay rules permitted the admission of such testimony. In re Lambert, — Ohio App. 3d —, 2007 Ohio 2857, — N.E. 2d —, 2007 Ohio App. LEXIS 2616 (June 8, 2007).

Defendant had the opportunity to cross-examine the witnesses and their credibility could easily have been called into question if defendant could have proved that their testimony was not based on their own personal knowledge. Furthermore, many of the witnesses based their opinions regarding the relationship between the victim and defendant and his codefendant on their personal knowledge; they did not repeat hearsay when they made the statements, but made independent observations based on what they heard. State v. Robinson, — Ohio App. 3d —, 2007 Ohio 3501, — N.E. 2d —, 2007 Ohio App. LEXIS 3224 (July 5, 2007).

There was no error in admitting the testimony of the victim's mother (regarding what the victim, her daughter, told her on the telephone just after defendant, the victim's boyfriend, had raped and beaten her) under the excited utterance exception to hearsay or the examining nurse under the medical treatment and diagnosis exception. There was also no violation of the confrontation clause because, with respect to the victim's excited utterances to her mother, defendant presented no argument as to in what manner the victim could have objectively believed that those statements would have been available for use at trial later. State v. Benton, — Ohio App. 3d —, 2007 Ohio 3945, — N.E. 2d —, 2007 Ohio App. LEXIS 3625 (Aug. 3, 2007).

Even if defense counsel erred in failing to object to inadmissible hearsay, any such error was harmless because the detective's testimony regarding the gun and the victim picking defendant from a photo array was admissible because the victim testified that she saw defendant take her gun and that she picked him from a photo array. The testimony of the victim's daughter was not hearsay because it was not offered for the truth of the matter asserted, but rather, was offered to explain why and how the investigation eventually led to defendant. She testified that once her mother identified defendant as the person who held a gun to her mother's head, she went to the Sheriff's office with that information. State v. Maxwell, — Ohio App. 3d —, 2007 Ohio 4027, — N.E. 2d —, 2007 Ohio App. LEXIS 3637 (Aug. 1, 2007).

Impermissible hearsay evidence was not admitted because the State did not offer the stray remark of the police officer for purposes of proving that police were watching a house for drug activity. The remark, at best, was an unsolicited comment by the officer to explain his presence in the area and defendant was not unfairly prejudiced by its admission. State v. Lane, — Ohio App. 3d —, 2007 Ohio 5948, — N.E. 2d —, 2007 Ohio App. LEXIS 5255 (Nov. 8, 2007).

There was no plain error under Ohio R. Crim. P. 52(B), based on defendant's counsel's failure to object, to the admission of testimony from a police officer regarding statements made to him by a victim of defendant's crimes, as the victim later testified that she told police the same information, such that any error was harmless. Testimony which indicated what defendant and his accomplices said to the victim and to each other were not hearsay that required exclusion under Ohio R. Evid. 801(C) and 802, as they were not statements offered to prove the truth of the matter asserted but instead, were offered to explain the witness's activities. State v. Allen, — Ohio App. 3d —, 2006 Ohio 2338, — N.E. 2d —, 2006 Ohio App. LEXIS 2206 (May 12, 2006).

Trial court's admission of a doctor's testimony regarding her determination that a minor was the victim of sexual abuse was not an abuse of discretion under Ohio R. Evid. 104, as the doctor simply stated her diagnosis of the victim because she was a qualified physician trained in pediatrics and her opinion was based on statements made by the victim and based on physical examination. The statements fell with an exception of hearsay pursuant to Ohio R. Evid. 801(C) and 802, as they were made for purposes of diagnosis or treatment pursuant to Ohio R. Evid. 803(4). State v. Braxton, — Ohio App. 3d —, 2006 Ohio 3008, — N.E. 2d —, 2006 Ohio App. LEXIS 2885 (June 15, 2006).

Because the transcript was a "record" of the probate court's activities, it fell within the purview of Ohio R. Evid. 803(8) regarding public records, but Ohio R. Evid. 803(8) did not apply to the testimony contained within the transcript. Because each statement transcribed by the court reporter survived hearsay analysis, the trial court properly admitted into evidence from the exhibit statements by defendant and questions from the prosecutor and the judge in defendant's contempt case. State v. Silverman, — Ohio App. 3d —, 2006 Ohio 3826, — N.E. 2d —, 2006 Ohio App. LEXIS 3791 (July 27, 2006).

Defendant's due process and confrontation rights under U.S. Const. amends. V and VI, and Ohio Const. art. I, § 10 were not implicated or violated under the plain error rule of Ohio R. Crim. P. 52(B) where the trial court admitted evidence of an anonymous tip received by police that a drug deal was going to take place at a particular location, as it was offered to explain the investigatory action of the police and it did not connect defendant to the alleged drug offense; accordingly, it was not hearsay under Ohio R. Evid. 801(C) and 802. State v. Carpenter, — Ohio App. 3d —, 2006 Ohio 4296, — N.E. 2d —, 2006 Ohio App. LEXIS 4220 (Aug. 18, 2006).

Trial counsel was not ineffective for failing to object because, even if the doctor's testimony had been hearsay, an objection would not have changed the outcome of the trial since the testimony at issue was a small part of relevant, proper evidence presented by the doctor. Furthermore, since the doctor learned about the nature of the injuries while he was taking the victim's medical history, the testimony constituted a medical diagnosis exception to the hearsay rule, under Ohio R. Evid. 803(4). State v. Lewis, — Ohio App. 3d —, 2006 Ohio 4402, — N.E. 2d —, 2006 Ohio App. LEXIS 4326 (Aug. 25, 2006).

Trial court did not abuse its discretion when it found that the humane society agent's statement that defendant had not scheduled a required follow-up visit with his veterinarian explained why she sought a warrant to seize the dogs after originally leaving them in defendant's care. The evidence was relevant to enable the jury to fully understand the case and the statement did not derive its primary value from the truth therein. State v. Angus, — Ohio App. 3d —, 2006 Ohio 4455, — N.E. 2d —, 2006 Ohio App. LEXIS 4374 (Aug. 29, 2006).

As a statement from a victim in defendant's criminal trial that the victim's uncle did not testify at the trial because he feared for his safety was not inadmissible hearsay pursuant to Ohio R. Evid. 801(C) and 802 as it was not offered for the truth of the matter asserted but merely to explain why the uncle was not questioned on the stand, defendant's counsel was not ineffective in violation of defendant's rights under U.S. Const. amend. VI and Ohio Const. art. I, § 10 in eliciting

such testimony from the victim. State v. Henry, — Ohio App. 3d —, 2006 Ohio 4783, — N.E. 2d —, 2006 Ohio App. LEXIS 4657 (Sept. 14, 2006).

Harmless error

Although the testimony of the detectives was ripe with inadmissible hearsay, because the declarants testified as well, and were subjected to cross-examination, the detectives' testimony involved the normal risks attendant on hearsay. The testimony of the alleged accomplices, the various homeowners, and the purchasers of the stolen property was sufficient to overwhelm any error in admitting the detectives' testimony. State v. Cochran, — Ohio App. 3d —, 2007 Ohio 345, — N.E. 2d —, 2007 Ohio App. LEXIS 291 (Jan. 26, 2007).

Even if it was determined that the trial court erroneously admitted hearsay statements from a father's daughter pursuant to Ohio R. Evid. 802 regarding incidents that occurred while she lived in his home, there was still sufficient other evidence to support the trial court's determination that she was a dependent child pursuant to RC § 2151.04(C). The dependency determination withstood challenge under the asserted evidentiary basis. In re Myers, — Ohio App. 3d —, 2007 Ohio 1631, — N.E. 2d —, 2007 Ohio App. LEXIS 1483 (Apr. 9, 2007).

Although the trial court abused its discretion when it allowed the social worker to testify to everything that the nine-year-old child had told her regarding the incident regarding her mother's intoxication, the error was harmless. The child was 10 years old at the time of the dependency trial and thus, could have testified, however, the mother never attempted to call the child as a witness, or request an in-camera interview in the case in chief. In re Matsko, — Ohio App. 3d —, 2007 Ohio 2060, — N.E. 2d —, 2007 Ohio App. LEXIS 1919 (Apr. 27, 2007).

Admission of the detective's testimony did not violate defendant's constitutional right against self-incrimination because the testimony concerning the missed appointments was admissible to explain the course of investigation. The detective's speculation that defendant had ample time to dispose of a weapon did not implicate defendant's Fifth Amendment right against self-incrimination. Although such testimony was arguably improper under Ohio R. Evid. 602 and 802, its admission in the instant case was harmless error. State v. Jackson, — Ohio App. 3d —, 2007 Ohio 2925, — N.E. 2d —, 2007 Ohio App. LEXIS 2703 (June 14, 2007).

Evidence supported a conclusion that defendant acted purposely to cause the death of the victim, her boyfriend, when she stabbed him, and was so overwhelmingly that any error in the admission of the hearsay testimony of the victim's father, relating that defendant had threatened to kill the woman that the victim had been seeing, was harmless beyond a reasonable doubt. There was no dispute that defendant stabbed the victim in the chest with a steak knife, five to six inches deep and the stabbing occurred when defendant and the victim broke their relationship, following a loud argument between them. State v. Evans, — Ohio App. 3d —, 2007 Ohio 4081, — N.E. 2d —, 2007 Ohio App. LEXIS 3671 (Aug. 3, 2007).

Hearsay

When the owners of a business sued a company for negligently installing an oil-interceptor system at the business because, in doing so, it crushed a drain line running from the owners' property, and one of the owners testified in his deposition that an employee of the company told him that the company had crushed the line, ordinarily, deposition testimony that constituted hearsay could not be considered in determining the parties' summary judgment motions, under Ohio R. Evid. 801(C) and 802. Loukinas v. Roto-Rooter Servs. Co., 167 Ohio App. 3d 559, 2006 Ohio 3172, 855 N.E. 2d 1272, 2006 Ohio App. LEXIS 3081 (June 23, 2006).

Inadmissible hearsay

Trial court did not abuse its discretion when it excluded a witness's oral statement in defendant's criminal trial pursuant to Ohio R. Evid. 801(C) and 802, as the statement was hearsay and accordingly, not admissible; the witness made the statement to a police detective at the scene of the crime, and at trial, defense counsel attempted to elicit that statement from a different police detective. State v. Hooks, — Ohio App. 3d —, 2007 Ohio 5944, — N.E. 2d —, 2007 Ohio App. LEXIS 5257 (Nov. 8, 2007).

When an alleged victim was allowed to testify that defendant's former girlfriend tried to bribe the victim not to testify, this testimony was improper under Ohio R. Evid. 801 and 802, as well as U.S. Const. amend. VI, because the statement was offered for the truth of the matter asserted, the former girlfriend was not called as a witness, and defendant had no prior opportunity to cross-examine her regarding her statement. State v. Wilson, — Ohio App. 3d —, 2006 Ohio 1333, — N.E. 2d —, 2006 Ohio App. LEXIS 1223 (Mar. 23, 2006).

Plain error

When a landowner was sanctioned for failing to comply with a settlement of a prior motion to hold the owner in contempt for not complying with an earlier settlement of the owner's alleged zoning violations, the owner did not show that the admission of two affidavits was plain error for allegedly being hearsay, under Ohio R. Evid. 801(C), not within a recognized exception, rendering them inadmissible, under Ohio R. Evid. 802, because substantial other evidence showed the owner's failure to comply with the settlement. Ray v. Bd. of Union Twp. Trs., — Ohio App. 3d —, — N.E. 2d —, 2007 Ohio 3001, 2007 Ohio App. LEXIS 2753 (June 18, 2007).

Prejudicial error not found

Even if an a victim's statements to police detective made after an aggravated burglary were hearsay under Ohio R. Evid. 801 and should have been excluded under Ohio R. Evid. 802, defendant failed to demonstrate prejudicial error arising from the admission of the statements. Defendant's cross-examination of the victim included questions concerning her conversation with the detective, and the detective's testimony, in any event, was merely cumulative of the victim's testimony offered at trial. State v. Holloman, — Ohio App. 3d —, 2007 Ohio 840, — N.E. 2d —, 2007 Ohio App. LEXIS 739 (Mar. 1, 2007).

What constitutes hearsay

Defendant's confrontation rights under U.S. Const. amend. VI and Ohio Const. art. I, § 10 were not violated by testimony from police officers regarding statements made by defendant's girlfriend, who was the victim of his crimes, where she did not testify at his criminal trial, as the statements were not offered to prove the truth of the matter asserted, they were within the testifying officer's personal knowledge, they were nontestimonial, or they were offered to explain the subsequent investigative actions of the officers, and further, the jury was properly instructed on the use of those statements for their limited purpose; they were not inadmissible hearsay under Ohio R. Evid. 801(C) and 802. State v. Chambers, — Ohio App. 3d —, 2006 Ohio 5326, — N.E. 2d —, 2006 Ohio App. LEXIS 5319 (Oct. 12, 2006).

RULE 803. Hearsay Exceptions; Availability of Declarant Immaterial

The following are not excluded by the hearsay rule, even though the declarant is available as a witness:

(1) **Present sense impression.** A statement describing or explaining an event or condition made while the declarant was perceiving the event or condition, or immediately thereafter unless circumstances indicate lack of trustworthiness.

(2) **Excited utterance.** A statement relating to a startling event or condition made while the declarant was under the stress of excitement caused by the event or condition.

(3) **Then existing, mental, emotional, or physical condition.** A statement of the declarant's then existing state of mind, emotion, sensation, or physical condition (such as intent, plan, motive, design, mental feeling, pain, and bodily health), but not including a statement of memory or belief to prove the fact remembered or believed unless it relates to the execution, revocation, identification, or terms of declarant's will.

(4) **Statements for purposes of medical diagnosis or treatment.** Statements made for purposes of medical diagnosis or treatment and describing medical history, or past or present symptoms, pain, or sensations, or the inception or general character of the cause or external source thereof insofar as reasonably pertinent to diagnosis or treatment.

(5) **Recorded recollection.** A memorandum or record concerning a matter about which a witness once had knowledge but now has insufficient recollection to enable him to testify fully and accurately, shown by the testimony of the witness to have been made or adopted when the matter was fresh in his memory and to reflect that knowledge correctly. If admitted, the memorandum or record may be read into evidence but may not itself be received as an exhibit unless offered by an adverse party.

(6) **Records of regularly conducted activity.** A memorandum, report, record, or data compilation, in any form, of acts, events, or conditions, made at or near the time by, or from information transmitted by, a person with knowledge, if kept in the course of a regularly conducted business activity, and if it was the regular practice of that business activity to make the memorandum, report, record, or data compilation, all as shown by the testimony of the custodian or other qualified witness or as provided by Rule 901(B)(10), unless the source of information or the method or circumstances of preparation indicate lack of trustworthiness. The term "business" as used in this paragraph includes business, institution, association, profession, occupation, and calling of every kind, whether or not conducted for profit.

(7) **Absence of entry in record kept in accordance with the provisions of paragraph (6).** Evidence that a matter is not included in the memoranda, reports, records, or data compilations, in any form, kept in accordance with the provisions of paragraph (6), to prove the nonoccurrence or nonexistence of the matter, if the matter was of a kind of which a memorandum, report, record, or data compilation was regularly made and preserved, unless the sources of information or other circumstances indicate lack of trustworthiness.

(8) **Public records and reports.** Records, reports, statements, or data compilations, in any form, of public offices or agencies, setting forth (a) the activities of the office or agency, or (b) matters observed pursuant to duty imposed by law as to which matters there was a duty to report, excluding, however, in criminal cases matters observed by police officers and other law

enforcement personnel, unless offered by defendant, unless the sources of information or other circumstances indicate lack of trustworthiness.

(9) **Records of vital statistics.** Records or data compilations, in any form, of births, fetal deaths, deaths, or marriages, if the report thereof was made to a public office pursuant to requirement of law.

(10) **Absence of public record or entry.** To prove the absence of a record, report, statement, or data compilation, in any form, or the nonoccurrence or nonexistence of a matter of which a record, report, statement, or data compilation, in any form, was regularly made and preserved by a public office or agency, evidence in the form of a certification in accordance with Rule 901(B)(10) or testimony, that diligent search failed to disclose the record, report, statement, or data compilation, or entry.

(11) **Records of religious organizations.** Statements of births, marriages, divorces, deaths, legitimacy, ancestry, relationship by blood or marriage, or other similar facts of personal or family history, contained in a regularly kept record of a religious organization.

(12) **Marriage, baptismal, and similar certificates.** Statements of fact contained in a certificate that the maker performed a marriage or other ceremony or administered a sacrament, made by a clergyman, public official, or other person authorized by the rules or practices of a religious organization or by law to perform the act certified, and purporting to have been issued at the time of the act or within a reasonable time thereafter.

(13) **Family Records.** Statements of fact concerning personal or family history contained in family Bibles, genealogies, charts, engravings on rings, inscriptions on family portraits, engravings on urns, crypts, or tombstones, or the like.

(14) **Records of documents affecting an interest in property.** The record of a document purporting to establish or affect an interest in property, as proof of the content of the original recorded document and its execution and delivery by each person by whom it purports to have been executed, if the record is a record of a public office and an applicable statute authorizes the recording of documents of that kind in that office.

(15) **Statements in documents affecting an interest in property.** A statement contained in a document purporting to establish or affect an interest in property if the matter stated was relevant to the purpose of the document, unless dealings with the property since the document was made have been inconsistent with the truth of the statement or the purport of the document.

(16) **Statements in ancient documents.** Statements in a document in existence twenty years or more the authenticity of which is established.

(17) **Market reports, commercial publications.** Market quotations, tabulations, lists, directories, or other published compilations, generally used and relied upon by the public or by persons in particular occupations.

(18) **Learned Treatises.** To the extent called to the attention of an expert witness upon cross-examination or relied upon by the expert witness in direct examination, statements contained in published treatises, periodicals, or pamphlets on a subject of history, medicine, or other science or art, established as a reliable authority by the testimony or admission of the witness or by other expert testimony or by judicial notice. If admitted, the statements may be read into evidence but may not be received as exhibits.

(19) **Reputation concerning personal or family history.** Reputation among members of the declarant's family by blood, adoption, or marriage or among the declarant's associates, or in the community, concerning a person's birth, adoption, marriage, divorce, death, legitimacy, relationship by blood, adoption or marriage, ancestry, or other similar fact of the declarant's personal or family history.

(20) **Reputation concerning boundaries or general history.** Reputation in a community, arising before the controversy, as to boundaries of or customs affecting lands in the community, and reputation as to events of general history important to the community or state or nation in which located.

(21) **Reputation as to character.** Reputation of a person's character among the person's associates or in the community.

(22) **Judgment of previous conviction.** Evidence of a final judgment, entered after a trial or upon a plea of guilty (but not upon a plea of no contest or the equivalent plea from another jurisdiction), adjudging a person guilty of a crime punishable by death or imprisonment in excess of one year, to prove any fact essential to sustain the judgment, but not including, when offered by the Government in a criminal prosecution for purposes other than impeachment, judgments against persons other than the accused. The pendency of an appeal may be shown but does not affect admissibility.

(23) **Judgment as to personal, family, or general history, or boundaries.** Judgments as proof of matters of personal, family or general history, or boundaries, essential to the judgment, if the same would be provable by evidence of reputation.

History Effective: July 1, 1980; amended effective July 1, 2006; July 1, 2007.

NOTES TO DECISIONS

ANALYSIS

Admissibility of excited utterance of a child
Admission of business records
Affidavits
Assignment of account
Business records
Business records exception
Child witness
Confrontation
Diagnosis and treatment statements
Excited utterance
Failure to object
Law of the case
Market reports and commercial publications
Medical diagnosis and treatment
Medical diagnosis or treatment
Mental, emotional or physical condition
new heading
Police report
Present sense impression

Admissibility of excited utterance of a child

Defendant's gross sexual imposition conviction was not against the manifest weight of the evidence because corroboration was not required to support the child victim's testimony. The child victim immediately reported defendant's conduct to her mother in an excited state, which was admissible as an excited utterance under Ohio R. Evid. 803(2), and her mother immediately relayed that accusation to defendant, who said nothing in response. State v. Guerra, — Ohio App. 3d —, 2006 Ohio 6661, — N.E. 2d —, 2006 Ohio App. LEXIS 6559 (Dec. 15, 2006).

Admission of business records

Trial court properly denied suppression of breath test results in defendant's criminal matter on a charge of operating a motor vehicle while under the influence of alcohol, in violation of RC § 4511.19(A)(1)(H), as admission of the operator's certificate and the solution batch certificate did not violate defendant's confrontation rights pursuant to U.S. Const. amend. VI and Ohio Const. art. I, § 10. The certificates were properly admitted as business records pursuant to Ohio R. Evid. 803(6), they were deemed non-testimonial in nature, and there was no indication that they lacked trustworthiness. State v. Greene, — Ohio App. 3d —, 2006 Ohio 6084, — N.E. 2d —, 2006 Ohio App. LEXIS 6053 (Nov. 20, 2006).

Trial court properly admitted into evidence on a summary judgment motion documents that had been properly authenticated by a custodian of records pursuant to Ohio R. Evid. 901, and which were business records under Ohio R. Evid. 803(6) that were deemed reliable and trustworthy; the records properly admitted included a credit card application and credit card statements in an action by an assignee of the issuer, seeking recovery of an amount owed on the account. Great Seneca Fin. v. Felty, 170 Ohio App. 3d 737, 2006 Ohio 6618, 869 N.E.2d 30, 2006 Ohio App. LEXIS 6547 (2006).

Affidavits

Affidavit submitted by plaintiff's counsel did not satisfy the personal knowledge requirement of CivR 56(E). A motel's incident report could be considered an exception to the hearsay rule, but would have to be properly incorporated into an affidavit by a person with knowledge of the circumstances surrounding the preparation of the report: Ray v. Ramada Inn North, 171 Ohio App. 3d 1, 2007 Ohio 1341, 869 N.E.2d 95, 2007 Ohio App. LEXIS 1220 (2007).

Assignment of account

Assignee of a credit card account did not properly authenticate the assignment of the account via an accompanying affidavit. Assignee was not entitled to summary judgment where it did not provide documentation of the credits and debits that led to the starting balance on the account: Great Seneca Fin. v. Felty, 170 Ohio App. 3d 737, 2006 Ohio 6618, 869 N.E.2d 30, 2006 Ohio App. LEXIS 6547 (2006).

Business records

Transcript of the allocution of a co-participant who pled guilty and the police interview of the co-participant were not admissible under the business records or prior consistent statement exceptions: State v. Granderson, 177 Ohio App. 3d 424, 2008 Ohio 3757, 894 N.E.2d 1290, 2008 Ohio App. LEXIS 3187 (2008).

In making its determination regarding the equitable distribution of parties' property under RC § 3105.171, the trial court did not err in excluding the gift tax returns for certain business interests, despite the husband's claim that it would have furthered his claim regarding separate property, as such were not deemed competent evidence under RC § 2317.40 and Ohio R. Evid. 803(6) where the husband's expert testified that he did not produce the documents for trial, had not personally prepared them, that they were not signed by the donor, dated, or signed by the preparer, and that they appeared to have been "doctored." Janosek v. Janosek, — Ohio App. 3d —, 2007 Ohio 68, — N.E. 2d —, 2007 Ohio App. LEXIS 59 (Jan. 11, 2007).

Trial court erred in suppressing the documents regarding the qualifications of the operators to perform instrument checks and operate the BAC Datamaster (blood alcohol instrument) because the documents were business records and were non-testimonial in nature. Village of Granville v. Pumphrey, — Ohio App. 3d —, 2007 Ohio 251, — N.E. 2d —, 2007 Ohio App. LEXIS 219 (Jan. 22, 2007).

Juvenile court's admission of documents regarding parents' service history and as to their own biological children was not an abuse of discretion in a parental rights proceeding regarding the parents' 11 adopted children, although some of the documents were hearsay within the definition of Ohio R. Evid. 801(C), as some of them qualified within the business records exception of Ohio R. Evid. 803(6) where they were records regularly kept by the social service agency. A therapy contract was properly admitted under the exception for an admission of a party-opponent under Ohio R. Evid. 801(D)(2). In re Mercy Anne G., — Ohio App. 3d —, 2007 Ohio 1197, — N.E.2d —, 2007 Ohio App. LEXIS 1132 (Mar. 14, 2007).

Trial court's finding that defendant violated his probation was supported by the evidence that he had failed to report for probation, he failed to obtain a required driver's license, and he committed other offenses, the admission of a record from the Ohio Bureau of Motor Vehicles was proper pursuant to Ohio R. Evid. 803(6) and moreover, the Ohio Rules of Evidence were inapplicable to such proceedings based on Ohio R. Evid. 101(C)(3). The sentences imposed for the revocation were within the proper range under RC §§ 2929.25(C)(2) and 2929.22. State v. Wallace, — Ohio App. 3d —, 2007 Ohio 3184, — N.E. 2d —, 2007 Ohio App. LEXIS 2968 (June 22, 2007).

When an amusement park patron sued the park for negligence after the patron was stabbed by other patrons at the park, it was not improper for a trial court, when considering the park's summary judgment motion, to consider a police report, police radio log, or written witness statements, because those items were excepted from the hearsay rule because the items were covered by the business records exception in Ohio R. Evid. 803(6). Roberts v. Cedar Fair, L.P., — Ohio App. 3d —, 2007 Ohio 4187, — N.E. 2d —, 2007 Ohio App. LEXIS 3792 (Aug. 17, 2007).

Summary judgment was properly granted to a merchandise seller in its action, seeking recovery of sums due from a contracting company and its president as personal guarantor, as the supporting materials included validation of the debt by the seller's records custodian and a copy of the personal guarantee; the custodian had properly authenticated the records and documents pursuant to Ohio R. Evid. 901(B)(10) and 803(6), and as there was no assertion that a copy of the guarantee did not suffice under Ohio R. Evid. 1003, any such challenge thereto on appeal was deemed waived. Ohio Cat v. N. Valley Contrs., — Ohio App. 3d —, 2007 Ohio 5050, — N.E. 2d —, 2007 Ohio App. LEXIS 4463 (Sept. 24, 2007).

Trial court's decision to exclude the business record due to the hearsay contained within was well within the trial court's discretion since the final element of Ohio R. Evid. 803(6) regarding trustworthiness was not met. The document was excluded as evidence because the nurse could not testify as to which person specifically gave her what information. Spencer v. Lakeview Sch. Dist., — Ohio App. 3d —, 2006 Ohio 3429, — N.E. 2d —, 2006 Ohio App. LEXIS 3370 (June 30, 2006).

In a prosecution for forgery, Medicaid fraud, and theft, the denial of defendant's motion, it was not ineffective assistance for defense counsel not to object to the admission of calendar notations kept by the father of a patient for whom defendant was providing care, detailing defendant's comings and goings, because, had an objection been stated, Ohio R. Evid. 803(6) and (7) applied, and it would not have been an abuse of discretion for the trial court to find that the notations were regularly kept in the course of the father's calling of caring for his son, so the objection would have been meritless. State v. Breckenridge, — Ohio App. 3d —, 2006 Ohio 5038, — N.E. 2d —, 2006 Ohio App. LEXIS 5175 (Sept. 28, 2006).

Trial court erred in considering documents that purported to assign a credit card account from an issuer to various entities and ultimately to an assignee who brought a claim against the credit card holder, seeking recovery of sums due under the account, as the assignee did not include an affidavit or other documentation that authenticated the records pursuant to Ohio R. Evid. 901(B)(10), and it did not set forth a proper foundation for their admissibility into evidence under Ohio R. Evid. 803(6). Great Seneca Fin. v. Felty, 170 Ohio App. 3d 737, 2006 Ohio 6618, 869 N.E.2d 30, 2006 Ohio App. LEXIS 6547 (2006).

Business records exception

There was no error in permitting the testimony of the social worker regarding the removal of the child in the permanent custody proceeding because RC § 2151.35(B)(2)(b) permitted the trial court to admit any evidence that was material and relevant. Even if hearsay had been barred, under either exception to hearsay, Ohio R. Evid. 803(6) (business records) or Ohio R. Evid. 803(8) (public records), the social worker's testimony concerning statements made during the course of the agency's investigation were admissible since the contents of her file, including the statement by the cousin, had been compiled as part of the social worker's activities. In re Z.T., — Ohio App. 3d —, 2007 Ohio 827, — N.E. 2d —, 2007 Ohio App. LEXIS 759 (Mar. 1, 2007).

When determining the number of days a motorist was out of the state during a limitations period, for purposes of finding the number of days the period was tolled, the motorist's bank records could not be used to make this determination because an alleged injured party attempting to defeat the application of the statute of limitations did not lay a sufficient foundation for the admission of these records under Ohio R. Evid. 803(6). Barker v. Strunk, — Ohio App. 3d —, 2007 Ohio 884, — N.E. 2d —, 2007 Ohio App. LEXIS 818 (Mar. 5, 2007).

Trial court did not err in admitting into evidence in a permanent custody case the father's California case file, which contained references to his drug and alcohol abuse, because the evidence came under the business records exception to the general exclusion of hearsay found in Ohio R. Evid. 803(6). The custodian of records for the local California family services agency attached an affidavit to the file certifying that the documents were prepared in the ordinary course of business at or near the time of the acts, conditions, or events described, by a local social worker during her investigation of the subject child and family. In re Joseph C.P., — Ohio App. 3d —, 2007 Ohio 1528, — N.E.2d —, 2007 Ohio App. LEXIS 1397 (Mar. 30, 2007).

There was no error under Ohio R. Evid. 103(A) in a trial court's admission into evidence of an exhibit that was a summary of a printing plant's billing records for purposes of its claim for recovery under an account, as the parties had stipulated to the admission of at least the first page of the exhibit, even if the document was not admissible as a business record under Ohio R. Evid. 803(6) it was admissible under Ohio R. Evid. 1006 as a summary of the voluminous billing records, and any error in the admission was harmless because the publishing companies had admitted the amount of the unpaid bills. There was testimony that indicated that the records from which the exhibit was prepared were plentiful and that they had been retained. Marysville Newspapers, Inc. v. Del. Gazette Co., — Ohio App. 3d —, 2007 Ohio 3838, — N.E. 2d —, 2007 Ohio App. LEXIS 3485 (July 30, 2007).

Defendant's right to confrontation was not violated by a detective's testimony regarding a laboratory report verifying the operability of a gun because the report fell within the Ohio R. Evid. 803(6) business record exception to the hearsay rule. State v. Sims, — Ohio App. 3d —, 2007 Ohio 6821, — N.E. 2d —, 2007 Ohio App. LEXIS 5968 (Dec. 20, 2007).

There was sufficient evidence to support a determination that a store did not receive notification of an assignment of an invoice from a seller to an assignee, despite having exercised due diligence pursuant to former RC § 1301.01(AA) in its normal business routine of accepting and delivering faxes to the appropriate person, as the lack of such a fax was indicative of non-receipt pursuant to Ohio R. Evid. 803(7) prior to the store's payment directly to the seller of the invoice, such that the store was not liable to the assignee for payment on the invoice. Whether former RC § 1309.37(C) was implicated and whether former RC § 1301.01(Z) was applicable with respect to the circumstances did not require determination where there was no evidence of notification of the assignment for purposes of imposing liability on the store. Zenfa Labs, Inc. v. Big Lots Stores, — Ohio App. 3d —, 2006 Ohio 2069, — N.E. 2d —, 2006 Ohio App. LEXIS 1912 (Apr. 27, 2006).

Trial court's admission of testimony by an insurance fraud investigator about the contents of business records kept by the insurance company in defendant's criminal trial on insurance fraud charges was proper, as the records were within the hearsay exception of Ohio R. Evid. 803(6); the investigator was not the custodian of the records, but he was a qualified witness with knowledge thereof. State v. Hinson, — Ohio App. 3d —, 2006 Ohio 3831, — N.E. 2d —, 2006 Ohio App. LEXIS 3803 (July 27, 2006).

Child witness

Regardless of whether a child less than ten years old has been determined to be competent to testify pursuant to EvidR 601, the child's statements may be admitted at trial as an exception to the hearsay rule pursuant to EvidR 803(4) if they were made for purposes of medical diagnosis or treatment: State v. Muttart, 116 Ohio St. 3d 5, 2007 Ohio 5267, 875 N.E.2d 944, 2007 Ohio LEXIS 2535 (2007).

Confrontation

Statements made by the four-year-old victim to medical personnel regarding sexual abuse did not offend the Confrontation Clause because they were not testimonial in nature since they were not made in the context of in-court testimony or its equivalent; the victim's initial statements made to her mother and her mother's friends were deemed to be excited utterances, and the statements to a social worker and a therapist were in furtherance of medical diagnosis and treatment for the victim. The fact that the information gathered by the medical personnel was subsequently used by the State did not change the fact that the statements were not made for the State's use and the statements were admitted properly through the exception provided by the medical diagnosis and treatment exception to hearsay under Ohio R. Evid. 803(4), which specifically stated that unavailability was irrelevant to the question of admissibility. State v. Muttart, 116 Ohio St. 3d 5, 2007 Ohio 5267, 875 N.E.2d 944, 2007 Ohio LEXIS 2535 (2007).

Records of scientific tests are not "testimonial" under Crawford v. Washington (2004), 541 US 36, 124 S. Ct. 1354,

158 L. Ed. 2d 177, 2004 U.S. LEXIS 1838, 124 SCt 1354, 158 LEd2d 177. A criminal defendant's constitutional right to confrontation is not violated when a qualified expert DNA analyst testifies at trial in place of the DNA analyst who actually conducted the testing: State v. Crager, 116 Ohio St. 3d 369, 2007 Ohio 6840, 879 N.E.2d 745, 2007 Ohio LEXIS 3355 (2007).

Defendant's right to confrontation was not violated because the statements were excited utterances and non-testimonial in nature, and thus, they were properly admitted. The victim was still under the excitement of a startling event in which she personally was assaulted and the statements were intended to help apprehend the alleged perpetrator of the crime. City of Cleveland v. Colon, — Ohio App. 3d —, 2007 Ohio 269, — N.E. 2d —, 2007 Ohio App. LEXIS 254 (Jan. 25, 2007).

Diagnosis and treatment statements

There was no plain error in the admission of the social worker's testimony regarding the victim's statements made during the medical forensic interview. The hearsay exception set forth in Ohio R. Evid. 803(4) extended to the victim's statements to the social worker because the purpose of the statement was part of the initiation of medical diagnosis and treatment. State v. Vance, — Ohio App. 3d —, 2007 Ohio 4407, — N.E. 2d —, 2007 Ohio App. LEXIS 3981 (Aug. 28, 2007).

Excited utterance

dmission of the victim's prior, written inconsistent statement was harmless error where the victim's statements to the officers qualified as excited utterances. The written statement was not admissible under EvidR 607(A) where the state was not surprised by the recantation at trial: State v. Clay, 181 Ohio App. 3d 563, 2009 Ohio 1235, 910 N.E.2d 14, 2009 Ohio App. LEXIS 1061 (2009).

Trial court did not err by admitting the statements of the victim's three-year-old son as excited utterances because the child was clearly still under the stress of his mother's murder, which he may have actually witnessed, and there was no evidence that the child fabricated the statements or made them due to another's influence. Although four days had elapsed between the murder and the child's statements, the passage of time was only one factor in an excited utterance analysis. State v. McCarley, — Ohio App. 3d —, 2008 Ohio 552, — N.E. 2d —, 2008 Ohio App. LEXIS 472 (Feb. 13, 2008).

Statement of the driver (who was buying drugs from defendant) constituted an excited utterance because the driver was still under the stress of the excitement when she yelled to the officers that defendant threw the drugs at her. Her statement came within seconds of the officers approaching the truck and ordering her out of the vehicle and, even if the statement did not constitute an excited utterance, its admission was harmless error because the other drug purchaser testified to the fact that along with ordering her to hide the drugs in her pants, defendant threw the packets of heroin in the direction of the driver, causing them to hit the door and fall to the floor and thus, the admission of the statement did not alter the outcome of the trial as the witness testified to the same event. State v. Lumbus, — Ohio App. 3d —, 2007 Ohio 74, — N.E. 2d —, 2007 Ohio App. LEXIS 69 (Jan. 11, 2007).

Children's statements concerning alleged sexual abuse did not qualify as excited utterances where they were made more than two months after the alleged incident and were a product of reflective thought: State v. Butcher, 170 Ohio App. 3d 52, 2007 Ohio 118, 866 N.E.2d 13, 2007 Ohio App. LEXIS 111 (2007).

Admission of testimony from a witness as to statements that she heard the victim make during a criminal incident for which defendant was on trial were not testimonial because they were casual comments between friends or acquaintances and as such, they were not within the confrontation clause

pursuant to U.S. Const. amend. VI and Ohio Const. art. I, § 10; they were also not inadmissible hearsay, as one statement was deemed an excited utterance pursuant to Ohio R. Evid. 803(2) where it was made after a verbal altercation, another statement was not hearsay where it was not offered to prove the truth of the matter asserted pursuant to Ohio R. Evid. 801(C), and observations of the victim's body language and emotional state were also not hearsay. State v. McCree, — Ohio App. 3d —, 2007 Ohio 268, — N.E. 2d —, 2007 Ohio App. LEXIS 252 (Jan. 25, 2007).

When a store clerk approached police as they were handcuffing a defendant and said, in an excited manner, that something had just landed on the roof of his store, an officer's testimony about this statement was properly admissible under the excited utterance exception, in Ohio R. Evid. 803(2), to the hearsay rule. State v. Brooks, — Ohio App. 3d —, 2007 Ohio 506, — N.E. 2d —, 2007 Ohio App. LEXIS 462 (Feb. 7, 2007).

Weight of the evidence supported defendant's guilty verdict for defendant guilty of domestic violence because the victim made statements immediately after the incident to her great-grandmother and the police and those statements were properly admitted as excited utterances. Although the victim recanted her initial statements at trial, the State presented evidence of a recorded telephone conversation between defendant and his mother discussing how they would get the victim to change her story. The statements by defendant's mother were allowable as admissions of a party opponent and the probative value of defendant's admissions on the tape, especially in light of the victim's recantation at trial, substantially outweighed any danger of unfair prejudice. State v. Glossip, — Ohio App. 3d —, 2007 Ohio 2066, — N.E. 2d —, 2007 Ohio App. LEXIS 1931 (Apr. 30, 2007).

Trial court did not abuse its discretion by admitting the testimony of the victim's mother as an excited utterance exception to hearsay. The trial court determined that the victim was still under the stress of defendant's attack upon her when she made the statements to her mother roughly an hour later. According to the mother, the victim was hysterical and so upset that she could barely talk, but told her that she was at the police station because defendant pistol whipped her. State v. Powers, — Ohio App. 3d —, 2007 Ohio 2738, — N.E. 2d —, 2007 Ohio App. LEXIS 2527 (June 6, 2007).

Statement by defendant's sister, made during the 911 call while the victim was bleeding profusely but still alive, was unquestionably related to the startling event and thus, properly admitted as an excited utterance under Ohio R. Evid. 803(2). Even if the statement was inadmissible, any error was harmless because the evidence was cumulative; the jury could have concluded that defendant fled the scene without considering the 911 tape. State v. Harrison, — Ohio App. 3d —, 2007 Ohio 2872, — N.E. 2d —, 2007 Ohio App. LEXIS 2658 (June 12, 2007).

Woman's statements to police, to the effect that defendant had shot the victim and that defendant had a gun, were nontestimonial for Confrontation Clause purposes, and the trial court did not commit plain error under Ohio R. Crim. P. 52 in admitting them because the primary purpose of the woman's statements were to enable the police to respond to an ongoing emergency, not to establish or prove events potentially relevant to criminal prosecution. The woman's statements fell within the "excited utterance" exception to the hearsay rule under Ohio R. Evid. 803(2) as the officer testified that the woman appeared hysterical and could hardly speak when she made the statements, and the statements related to a startling event, beginning when the woman was assaulted by defendant and culminating in the woman's friend being shot and her friend's child nearly being shot. State v. Davis, — Ohio App. 3d —, 2007 Ohio 3419, — N.E. 2d —, 2007 Ohio App. LEXIS 3170 (July 5, 2007).

Defendant did not receive ineffective assistance of counsel for failure to object to testimony by a police officer because the victim's statements to the police officer were properly admitted under the excited utterance exception to hearsay. The officer testified that when she talked with the victim, approximately 30 minutes after the attack, she was crying, shaking, and she was upset; thus, the victim was clearly still under the stress of excitement stemming from an attack that occurred 30 minutes earlier. State v. Thornton, — Ohio App. 3d —, 2007 Ohio 3743, — N.E. 2d —, 2007 Ohio App. LEXIS 3425 (July 25, 2007).

There was no error in admitting the testimony of the victim's mother (regarding what the victim, her daughter, told her on the telephone just after defendant, the victim's boyfriend, had raped and beaten her) under the excited utterance exception to hearsay or the examining nurse under the medical treatment and diagnosis exception. There was also no violation of the confrontation clause because, with respect to the victim's excited utterances to her mother, defendant presented no argument as to in what manner the victim could have objectively believed that those statements would have been available for use at trial later. State v. Benton, — Ohio App. 3d —, 2007 Ohio 3945, — N.E. 2d —, 2007 Ohio App. LEXIS 3625 (Aug. 3, 2007).

Trial court properly admitted the testimony of the victim's sister under the excited utterance exception to the hearsay rule because, in permitting the complained of testimony, the trial court found that the victim was still under the influence of the event. Based upon the fact that the victim was still wounded and scared from the incident at the time of her "excited utterance" to her sister, and continued to be fearful of returning to her residence to obtain her belongings, there was no error in admitting the sister's testimony. State v. Manzell, — Ohio App. 3d —, 2007 Ohio 4076, — N.E. 2d —, 2007 Ohio App. LEXIS 3672 (Aug. 6, 2007).

In a domestic violence prosecution, the victim's statements to the police were properly admitted as excited utterances, under Ohio R. Evid. 803(2), because (1) the victim's assault was a startling event, (2) an officer testified that when the officer contacted the victim, the victim was on the floor crying and bleeding, showing the victim was still under nervous excitement when the victim made the statements, and (3) the officer testified that the victim was still upset and visibly shaken while talking with the officer. State v. Fields, — Ohio App. 3d —, 2007 Ohio 5060, — N.E. 2d —, 2007 Ohio App. LEXIS 4485 (Sept. 27, 2007).

Defendant was not deprived of the effective assistance of counsel where counsel failed to object to a mother's testimony as to statements made by her daughter as the daughter's statements fell within the excited utterance exception to the hearsay rule; the statements were made after the daughter witnessed her younger sister and defendant kissing and counsel did not fall below an objective standard of reasonable representation by failing to object to the testimony. State v. Moser, — Ohio App. 3d —, 2006 Ohio 165, — N.E. 2d —, 2006 Ohio App. LEXIS 133 (Jan. 19, 2006).

Admission, pursuant to Ohio R. Evid. 803(2), of the excited utterances of unidentified declarants, who ran out of a bar and informed police that the bouncer in the bar had a shotgun and was pointing it at people, did not violate defendant's right, as guaranteed by Ohio Const. art. I, § 10, to confront the declarants who made the statements on the ground that the State had not been required to show that the declarants were unavailable to present testimony at the trial. Excited utterances do not violate Ohio Const. art. I, § 10 because they fit the exceptional circumstances of trustworthiness for their admission without regard to the availability of the declarant as a witness. State v. Johnson, — Ohio App. 3d —, 2006 Ohio 1232, — N.E. 2d —, 2006 Ohio App. LEXIS 1109 (Mar. 17, 2006).

Trial court's admission of an apartment occupant's statement to paramedics, which was overhead by police, that defendant was ingesting alcohol and drugs which caused him to become unconscious was not an abuse of discretion, as the statement was an excited utterance under Ohio R. Evid. 803(2) because the occupant witnessed the startling event of his friend's response to the overdose. The admission did not violate the confrontation clause of U.S. Const. amend. VI, as it was not testimonial in nature. State v. Leide, — Ohio App. 3d —, 2006 Ohio 2716, — N.E. 2d —, 2006 Ohio App. LEXIS 2559 (May 30, 2006).

Statements made by defendant's young daughter to others were properly admitted in his criminal trial on a murder charge where the statements were made within an hour of the incident and they qualified as excited utterances pursuant to Ohio R. Evid. 803(2) because she had seen the event and the two-year-old battered victim. The competency of the daughter was not at issue for the admission of such a statement and further, she did not testify at trial for purposes of Ohio R. Evid. 601, and as the statements made to her guardian and her neighbor were not testimonial statements, defendant's Sixth Amendment confrontation rights under Crawford were not implicated. State v. Bennett, — Ohio App. 3d —, 2006 Ohio 2757, — N.E. 2d —, 2006 Ohio App. LEXIS 2592 (May 22, 2006).

Trial court's admission of statements by a doctor's medical assistant in a negligence action by a deceased patient's executrix against the doctor was not error because the statements were not hearsay under Ohio R. Evid. 801 where they were not admitted for the truth of the matter asserted. The statements would not have fit within the hearsay exception of Ohio R. Evid. 803(2) for an excited utterance, as the assistant's statements regarding the doctor's response to the patient's death were not conclusively deemed spontaneous or excited because they were made the morning after the patient died and it was not clear when the doctor was notified of the death. Frost v. Snitzer, — Ohio App. 3d —, 2006 Ohio 3882, — N.E. 2d —, 2006 Ohio App. LEXIS 3864 (July 28, 2006).

When defendant and his accomplices invaded the victims' home and fled before the police arrived, a statement a victim made to one of the first officers on the scene, which identified defendant, made while the victim was "hysterical," due to the events that had just transpired, was admissible as an excited utterance, under Ohio R. Evid. 803(2), and its admission, when this victim did not testify at trial, did not violate defendant's right to confrontation because the statement was non-testimonial. State v. Reardon, 168 Ohio App. 3d 386, 2006 Ohio 3984, 860 N.E.2d 141, 2006 Ohio App. LEXIS 3960 (2006).

Victim's statement was nontestimonial and did not trigger the confrontation clause where its primary purpose was to assist the officers in resolving an ongoing emergency resulting from a home invasion robbery. The statement was properly admitted as an excited utterance. State v. Reardon, 168 Ohio App. 3d 386, 2006 Ohio 3984, 860 N.E.2d 141, 2006 Ohio App. LEXIS 3960 (2006).

Exclusion of a statement by defendant's five-year-old son to a detective that the boy started an apartment fire that resulted in the death of his sister was proper, as the statement was made a few hours after the fire and was no longer an excited utterance under Ohio R. Evid. 803(2) because he was not under the stress of excitment caused by the fire when he spoke to the detective. Further, it was not a statement against interest under Ohio R. Evid. 804(B)(3) under the plain error standard of review pursuant to Ohio R. Crim. P. 52, as there was nothing to support a determination that the young child had an understanding of pecuniary or proprietary interests. State v. Abner, — Ohio App. 3d —, 2006 Ohio 4510, — N.E. 2d —, 2006 Ohio App. LEXIS 4523 (Sept. 1, 2006).

Trial court abused its discretion in excluding testimony by a witness who overheard defendant's five-year-old son say that he started a fire that killed his sister, as it should have been admitted as an excited utterance under Ohio R. Evid. 803(2) where the apartment fire qualified as an event that was startling enough to cause nervous excitement in the child, he was under the stress of excitement at the time that he made the statement, the statement related to the startling event, and the declarant personally observed at least part of the startling event; the mere possibility that the child might have been repeating what someone else said was not a sufficient reason to exclude it without actual proof of same, as that was a consideration that went to the weight of his statement, not to its admissibility, and competency to testify was not a consideration with respect to an excited utterance by a child. State v. Abner, — Ohio App. 3d —, 2006 Ohio 4510, — N.E. 2d —, 2006 Ohio App. LEXIS 4523 (Sept. 1, 2006).

Domestic violence victim's hysterical alert to a police officer who was walking by her apartment that defendant was the individual who hit her was an excited utterance under Ohio R. Evid. 803(2), as it was made in the course of an ongoing emergency since she had just been beaten by him, and the admission of the statement through the officer's testimony, as the victim refused to testify, was not a violation of defendant's confrontation rights under U.S. Const. amend. VI and Ohio Const. art. I, § 10. State v. McKenzie, — Ohio App. 3d —, 2006 Ohio 5725, — N.E. 2d —, 2006 Ohio App. LEXIS 5734 (Nov. 2, 2006).

During defendant's criminal trial, a police officer's testimony describing statements made by unidentified bystanders at the scene of a gun battle who yelled to officers that a shooting had occurred and that a car driven by defendant was involved were properly admitted under the excited utterance hearsay exception of Ohio R. Evid. 803(2). The officer's testimony showed that the bystanders were excited and yelling, and there was a sufficient evidentiary foundation to establish that the battle was an exciting event, that the bystanders made their statements immediately after the battle and before there had been time to reflect, that their statements related to the battle, and that they personally observed the matters asserted in their statements. State v. Holdbrook, — Ohio App. 3d —, 2006 Ohio 5841, — N.E. 2d —, 2006 Ohio App. LEXIS 5791 (Nov. 6, 2006).

Victim's statements, where she repeated the names of the attackers over and over as she regained consciousness after being beaten, were properly admitted as an excited utterance under Evid. R. 803(2). The victim made the statements while she was still under the stress of excitement created by that event and was a statement related to the event. State v. Garrison, — Ohio App. 3d —, 2006 Ohio 6142, — N.E. 2d —, 2006 Ohio App. LEXIS 6096 (Nov. 21, 2006).

Trial court's admission of testimony from a witness who indicated that a victim of defendant's criminal conduct had stated that defendant was the shooter was proper as an excited utterance within Ohio R. Evid. 803(2). Such statements were impermissible hearsay under Ohio R. Evid. 801(C), as they were offered for the truth of what was asserted and they were made out of court, but they were admissible within the stated exception. State v. Bell, — Ohio App. 3d —, 2006 Ohio 6592, — N.E. 2d —, 2006 Ohio App. LEXIS 6531 (Dec. 14, 2006).

Trial court did not err by admitting the victim's statements to a police officer as an excited utterance exception to hearsay, under Evid. R. 803(2), because it was not unreasonable for the trial court to conclude that the victim was still in an emotional state when she spoke to the officer shortly after reaching a safe location. There was evidence that the attack upon the victim was startling enough to produce a nervous excitement and that it was sufficient to still her reflective faculties and the evidence of the victim's behavior at the time that the officer spoke to her was sufficient to support a finding that her nervous excitement still dominated and that her statements were more

excited than reflective. State v. Albert, — Ohio App. 3d —, 2006 Ohio 6902, — N.E. 2d —, 2006 Ohio App. LEXIS 6805 (Dec. 26, 2006).

Trial court erred when it applied the excited utterance exception to hearsay, under Evid. R. 803(2), to the mother's testimony because there was evidence that the six-year-old victim was no longer under the stress of the events when she made the statements to her mother. The mother merely indicated that the victim appeared to be "confused" about what had occurred, which indicated that the victim had been reflecting on the events. Since the case essentially turned on an issue of credibility, the admission of the mother's hearsay testimony was not harmless beyond a reasonable doubt. State v. Hazlett, — Ohio App. 3d —, 2006 Ohio 6927, — N.E. 2d —, 2006 Ohio App. LEXIS 6830 (Dec. 28, 2006).

Trial court did not abuse its discretion in finding that the victim's statements to her bus driver, the school nurse, and her teacher qualified as excited utterances in exception to the hearsay rule and properly admitted their testimony because each witness testified that the victim was still upset, and appeared to have been recently crying, when she relayed the information about her injured finger. The passage of a single night was insufficient to require an assumption that the anxiety and stress of having her finger bent backwards until it broke had been calmed by the time she told her bus driver, nurse, and teacher what had happened. State v. Hunneman, — Ohio App. 3d —, 2006 Ohio 7023, — N.E. 2d —, 2006 Ohio App. LEXIS 7039 (Dec. 28, 2006).

Trial court did not err by admitting the testimony regarding a statement made by a witness about how much money she was given by defendant for her testimony under the excited utterance exception to hearsay. Because the statement was made immediately after she received the alleged bribe, an event which the trial court could reasonably have concluded would be a startling event, and the statement was related to that event and, given the immediacy between event and statement, the trial court could have reasonably concluded that the witness was under the excitement of the event when making the statement. State v. Carter, — Ohio App. 3d —, 2007 Ohio 3502, — N.E. 2d —, 2007 Ohio App. LEXIS 3223 (June 29, 2007).

Failure to object

While a trial court erred by allowing evidence of telephone records to be presented under Ohio R. Evid. 803(6) to prove that phone calls were placed by a recreational aide inside a prison to defendant's home phone number because the proper foundational testimony was not present to authenticate the records, defendant failed to object and, thus, waived all but plain error. The trial court's error did not result in plain error because there were additional submissions of evidence which demonstrated that the aide's taped phone calls were made to defendant's home phone number and that defendant was the individual speaking with the aide. State v. Brown, — Ohio App. 3d —, 2006 Ohio 129, — N.E. 2d —, 2006 Ohio App. LEXIS 107 (Jan. 13, 2006).

Law of the case

Where a trial court had admitted certain audit reports under the business records exception to the hearsay rule pursuant to Ohio R. Evid. 803(6), and in a prior appeal, the issue of the admission of those records was not raised, upon remand of the matter for a further hearing, that evidentiary ruling became the law of the case; accordingly, in a subsequent appeal, that issue could not be raised. Acuity, Inc. v. Trimat Constr., — Ohio App. 3d —, 2007 Ohio 6894, — N.E. 2d —, 2007 Ohio App. LEXIS 6040 (Dec. 18, 2007).

Market reports and commercial publications

Trial court did not abuse its discretion when it determined that used vehicle purchasers' experts were qualified under Ohio R. Evid. 702(B) to provide testimony in the purchasers' action against a dealership and a used vehicle owner, as they testified within their areas of expertise with respect to damages and repairs to the vehicle; their testimony with respect to a CARFAX document was properly admitted under Ohio R. Evid. 803(17), as it was a report widely used by automobile dealers. Anousheh v. Planet Ford, — Ohio App. 3d —, 2007 Ohio 4543, — N.E. 2d —, 2007 Ohio App. LEXIS 4092 (Aug. 31, 2007).

Medical diagnosis and treatment

Trial court's decision to exclude statements by a child victim of defendant's alleged sexual conduct, which were made to a professional clinical counselor, was error where the trial court determined that although the statements might have been within the hearsay exception for medical diagnosis and treatment under Ohio R. Evid. 803(4), it could not deem them admissible because it found that the child victim was not a competent witness under Ohio R. Evid. 601. Although a competency requirement existed for admission of the statements under Ohio R. Evid. 807, no such requirement existed for statements under Ohio R. Evid. 803(4) as long as the surrounding circumstances and any other factors were examined to determine that the statements were reliable. State v. Redfearn, — Ohio App. 3d —, 2007 Ohio 4108, — N.E. 2d —, 2007 Ohio App. LEXIS 3736 (Aug. 13, 2007).

Medical diagnosis or treatment

Unlike adults, young children may not appreciate the medical significance of an interview with a doctor. Thus, in the case of a child of tender years, the Supreme Court of Ohio has recommended that trial courts consider, through a voir dire examination of the child, the circumstances surrounding the child's making of statements to medical personnel before admitting the statements under EvidR 803(4): State v. Butcher, 170 Ohio App. 3d 52, 2007 Ohio 118, 866 N.E.2d 13, 2007 Ohio App. LEXIS 111 (2007).

Doctor's testimony did not relate to the rape victim's credibility; rather, the testimony established that it was the doctor's medical opinion that sometime during the victim's childhood, she was a victim of child sexual abuse and she gave no opinion of the victim's veracity. Further, the testimony fell within the hearsay exception of Ohio R. Evid. 803(4) because she stated that she was provided with the information solely for the purpose of medical treatment and diagnosis and that she worked for a children's advocacy center, not a prosecutor's or investigator's office. State v. Haschenburger, — Ohio App. 3d —, 2007 Ohio 1562, — N.E. 2d —, 2007 Ohio App. LEXIS 1446 (Mar. 27, 2007).

Admission of testimony from a sexual abuse investigator who was not a licensed social worker was proper, as it was within the hearsay exception of Ohio R. Evid. 803(4) with respect to statements made to her by a victim of defendant's sexual abuse, and as the victim was available and testified at trial and she was a minor, the statements were deemed "nontestimonial" for purposes of the confrontation clause of U.S. Const. amends. VI and XIV. State v. Dyer, — Ohio App. 3d —, 2007 Ohio 1704, — N.E. 2d —, 2007 Ohio App. LEXIS 1558 (Apr. 12, 2007).

In a dependency proceeding in which it was alleged that a mother's children had been abused by members of the mother's church, a psychologist's deposition testimony was properly admitted because it was based almost entirely on facts perceived by the psychologist or admitted into evidence at the hearing, consisting of the psychologist's interviews of the children, which were transcribed and provided to the parties, and the psychologist was entitled to rely on this information under the hearsay exception for medical diagnosis or treatment, under Ohio R. Evid. 803(4), and the psychologist also relied on various tests performed on the children. In re Miller, — Ohio App. 3d —, 2007 Ohio 2170, — N.E. 2d —, 2007 Ohio App. LEXIS 2017 (May 4, 2007).

Statements of the twins, victims of sexual abuse, were admissible under Ohio R. Evid. 807 as a hearsay exception for the statements of children in abuse situations and the twins' statements to a social worker were within the realm of diagnosis and treatment because the social worker's function was both to determine whether sexual abuse had been indicated and to then follow up on referring the family for appropriate care. Therefore, the statements were properly admissible pursuant to Ohio R. Evid. 803(4). In re C.C., — Ohio App. 3d —, 2007 Ohio 2226, — N.E. 2d —, 2007 Ohio App. LEXIS 2079 (May 10, 2007).

In a prosecution for gross sexual imposition against a child victim, a psychologist's testimony relating the child victim's identification of defendant as the perpetrator of abuse against the victim was properly admitted, under Ohio R. Evid. 803(4) and 807, because the victim made the statements to the psychologist for the purposes of diagnosis and treatment. State v. Abner, — Ohio App. 3d —, 2007 Ohio 3053, — N.E. 2d —, 2007 Ohio App. LEXIS 2796 (June 18, 2007).

Statement of a bystander to a paramedic following an altercation was not inherently trustworthy, and the statement was not admissible as an exception to the hearsay rule under Ohio R. Evid. 803(4). There was nothing to indicate that it was made in contemplation of medical treatment or diagnosis or treatment, even though it was made to a paramedic, and there was nothing in the statement itself that necessarily was related to diagnosis or treatment. State v. Airwyke, — Ohio App. 3d —, 2007 Ohio 3199, — N.E. 2d —, 2007 Ohio App. LEXIS 2945 (June 22, 2007).

There was no testimony in violation of Crawford or the hearsay rule because, although a doctor and a nurse testified about the victim's diagnosis and treatment, the statements were not testimonial but, rather, were for the purpose of medical diagnosis and treatment, which was excepted from the hearsay rule under Ohio R. Evid. 803(4). Additionally, the detective did not testify to the specifics of his interrogation of defendant or interview of any of the other witnesses; rather, the sum and substance of his testimony was relative to the search of defendant's house and the pornographic videos recovered therefrom. State v. Petitto, — Ohio App. 3d —, 2007 Ohio 3901, — N.E. 2d —, 2007 Ohio App. LEXIS 3554 (Aug. 2, 2007).

Although a trial court's exclusion of medical records pursuant to Ohio R. Evid. 803(4) was proper as to physician statements regarding a father's diagnosis where no physicians testified in a contempt proceeding against the father due to his failure to pay child support, exclusion of the father's statements concerning his symptoms reported to the physician was error; however, the error was harmless under Ohio R. Civ. P. 61 where the father testified as to his symptoms, such that he was not prejudiced by the exclusion. Jones v. Jones, — Ohio App. 3d —, 2007 Ohio 5492, — N.E. 2d —, 2007 Ohio App. LEXIS 4827 (Oct. 15, 2007).

Trial court did not abuse its discretion in admitting, under Ohio R. Evid. 803(4), defendant's child's out-of-court statements to a social worker. The child made statements to the social worker upon the social worker informing the child that the social worker's "job was to talk to kids about their bodies and make sure their bodies were safe" and upon the social worker telling the child that, after their discussion, the child would undergo a medical exam with medical personnel. State v. D.H., 2007 Ohio 5970, 2007 Ohio App. LEXIS 5236 (Nov. 8, 2007).

Because the three-year-old victim's statements to the social worker and the nurse were clearly for the purpose of diagnosis and treatment, they were properly admitted under Ohio R. Evid. 803(4). Regarding the nurse, the victim was seeing the nurse because of her attack; the victim did not perceive the possibility of her statements being used in a trial; and the victim spoke to the nurse believing that the nurse would help her after her terrible ordeal (attempted rape). State v. Goza,

— Ohio App. 3d —, 2007 Ohio 6837, — N.E. 2d —, 2007 Ohio App. LEXIS 5982 (Dec. 20, 2007).

Because the three-year-old victim's testimony was admissible under Ohio R. Evid. 803(4) for the purpose of medical diagnosis and treatment, it was not a condition precedent that the child be determined competent. Further, the child was competent because she had no difficulty relating the facts to the nurse and social worker, she demonstrated a mature vocabulary, and was able to easily identify body parts in explaining her attack; also, she was not called as a witness so a determination of competency was not required. State v. Goza, — Ohio App. 3d —, 2007 Ohio 6837, — N.E. 2d —, 2007 Ohio App. LEXIS 5982 (Dec. 20, 2007).

Trial court's admission of a social worker's testimony which contained statements made to her by a child victim of defendant's improper sexual offenses was proper under Ohio R. Evid. 803(4), as an analysis of what the social worker's function was with respect to the child indicated that the statements were made for the purposes of medical diagnosis and treatment; in such an instance, there was no need to first find that the child was competent as a witness under Ohio R. Evid. 601(A) prior to allowing admission of her statements. State v. Edinger, — Ohio App. 3d —, 2006 Ohio 1527, — N.E. 2d —, 2006 Ohio App. LEXIS 1399 (Mar. 30, 2006).

Trial court properly admitted testimony of a social worker who had interviewed a father's child with respect to statements that the child made, pursuant to Ohio R. Evid. 803(4), as the interview with the child was for the purpose of facilitating the medical exam; the father's general objection to such testimony did not sufficiently challenge similar testimony from other social workers, as he was required to renew his objection for that purpose during the proceeding to determine whether the children should have been adjudicated as dependent, abused, or neglected. In re A.R., — Ohio App. 3d —, 2006 Ohio 1548, — N.E. 2d —, 2006 Ohio App. LEXIS 1444 (Mar. 31, 2006).

Trial court did not abuse its discretion by admitting the social worker's statements under the medical exception to hearsay, pursuant to Ohio R. Evid. 803(4), because the 10-year-old rape victim's statements to the social worker were made for the purpose of medical diagnosis or treatment. The fact that other people, including a police detective watched the interview in real time did not change the purpose of the interview since the victim was not aware that the other people were watching the interview. State v. Martin, — Ohio App. 3d —, 2006 Ohio 2749, — N.E. 2d —, 2006 Ohio App. LEXIS 2564 (June 1, 2006).

Trial court's admission of a doctor's testimony regarding her determination that a minor was the victim of sexual abuse was not an abuse of discretion under Ohio R. Evid. 104, as the doctor simply stated her diagnosis of the victim because she was a qualified physician trained in pediatrics and her opinion was based on statements made by the victim and based on physical examination. The statements fell with an exception of hearsay pursuant to Ohio R. Evid. 801(C) and 802, as they were made for purposes of diagnosis or treatment pursuant to Ohio R. Evid. 803(4). State v. Braxton, — Ohio App. 3d —, 2006 Ohio 3008, — N.E. 2d —, 2006 Ohio App. LEXIS 2885 (June 15, 2006).

Trial court did not err in admitting the victim's medical records in defendant's trial for patient abuse because the notes were made for purposes of medical diagnosis as provided in Ohio R. Evid. 803(4). Also, both the doctor and the nurse who wrote the statements appeared and testified at defendant's trial and thus, defendant had the opportunity to cross-examine them with respect to the statements they made. State v. Grimes, — Ohio App. 3d —, 2006 Ohio 4262, — N.E. 2d —, 2006 Ohio App. LEXIS 4189 (Aug. 17, 2006).

Trial counsel was not ineffective for failing to object because, even if the doctor's testimony had been hearsay, an objection would not have changed the outcome of the trial since the testimony at issue was a small part of relevant, proper evidence presented by the doctor. Furthermore, since the doctor learned about the nature of the injuries while he was taking the victim's medical history, the testimony constituted a medical diagnosis exception to the hearsay rule, under Ohio R. Evid. 803(4). State v. Lewis, — Ohio App. 3d —, 2006 Ohio 4402, — N.E. 2d —, 2006 Ohio App. LEXIS 4326 (Aug. 25, 2006).

Trial court did not err in admitting evidence in an adjudicatory hearing during a dependency proceeding by a doctor who had treated the subject child where his statements were not admitted for the truth of the matter asserted pursuant to Ohio R. Evid. 801(C) and accordingly, they were not inadmissible hearsay. The statements were offered to show the child's perception of reality and further, they were within the hearsay exception for statements made for purposes of medical diagnosis or treatment pursuant to Ohio R. Evid. 803(4). In re E. R., — Ohio App. 3d —, 2006 Ohio 4816, — N.E. 2d —, 2006 Ohio App. LEXIS 4745 (Sept. 18, 2006).

Defendant's confrontation rights under U.S. Const. amend. VI and Ohio Const. art. I, § 10 were not violated by the admission of medical records during his criminal trial that contained the statements of a child victim to medical examiners, as such statements were not testimonial in nature, the victim was on the stand and subject to cross-examination, defendant had stipulated to the admission of the medical records, and such statements were admissible under the medical diagnosis hearsay exception pursuant to Ohio R. Evid. 803(4). State v. Johnson, — Ohio App. 3d —, 2006 Ohio 5195, — N.E. 2d —, 2006 Ohio App. LEXIS 5120 (Oct. 2, 2006).

Although a trial court erred in admitting testimony from a social worker regarding statements made to her by defendant's daughter as to defendant's actions and the molestation by defendant's boyfriend, as such was not within the medical diagnosis and treatment exception to the hearsay rule under Ohio R. Evid. 803(4) where the social worker was not involved in treating the child for the abuse that she suffered, such was harmless error under Ohio R. Crim. P. 52(A) where the statements of the child were repeated numerous times by a psychologist during the testimony at trial, and as to another statement that was not repeated, there was overwhelming evidence of the boyfriend's actions and of defendant's guilt on the charge of child endangerment. State v. Walker, — Ohio App. 3d —, 2006 Ohio 5479, — N.E. 2d —, 2006 Ohio App. LEXIS 5485 (Oct. 23, 2006).

Trial court did not violate defendant's rights under U.S. Const. amend. VI and Ohio Const. art. I, § 10 with respect to the confrontation clause when it admitted statements made by the victim of his sexual offenses, as she was in court and testified at trial, such that the Crawford analysis was inapplicable. Although some testimony from a social worker was excluded, other testimony regarding statements made to her by the victim was properly admitted under Ohio R. Evid. 803(4), as it was for the purpose of medical diagnosis and treatment. State v. Hall, — Ohio App. 3d —, 2007 Ohio 3531, — N.E. 2d —, 2007 Ohio App. LEXIS 3253 (July 12, 2007).

Mental, emotional or physical condition

When, in defendant's conspiracy trial, a confidential informant testified that he intended to pistol-whip the victim, if necessary, and admitted that he had committed similar crimes before, counsel's failure to object to this testimony on hearsay grounds was not ineffective assistance of counsel because (1) the testimony was not hearsay, under Ohio R. Evid. 801(D)(2)(a), because it involved admissions by a party opponent, and (2) the testimony fell under Ohio R. Evid. 803(3)'s recognized exception to the hearsay rule for statements of then-existing mental condition, e.g. intent. State v. Fitzgerald, — Ohio App. 3d —, 2007 Ohio 701, — N.E. 2d —, 2007 Ohio App. LEXIS 637 (Feb. 21, 2007).

new heading

Divorce record executed in India in 1961 met the requirements for authentication as an ancient document where it was in very good condition, with the signatures and thumbprint readily identifiable, and it was found among the decedent's papers where a divorce record would ordinarily be found: Kaur v. Bharmota, 182 Ohio App. 3d 696, 2009 Ohio 2344, 914 N.E.2d 1087, 2009 Ohio App. LEXIS 1985 (2009).

Police report

Although a trial court erred in excluding a police report in defendant's criminal trial, as it was admissible under Ohio R. Evid. 803(8)(b) where it was offered by defendant to show alleged inconsistencies in the eyewitness testimony regarding the incident and the identification of defendant as the perpetrator, the error did not affect defendant's substantial rights under Ohio R. Evid. 103(A) because the slight inconsistencies were based on clothing worn by defendant, but there were multiple identifications of him as the shooter. State v. Tiller, — Ohio App. 3d —, 2007 Ohio 3943, — N.E. 2d —, 2007 Ohio App. LEXIS 3577 (Aug. 3, 2007).

Although the trial court abused its discretion in failing to allow the arresting officer's police report into evidence in order to show the discrepancies between the recorded events and the officer's testimony, the error was harmless. Defense counsel was allowed to cross-examine the officer about the report and was allowed to discuss it in closing argument, and the jury was certainly made aware that the report contained no reference to any lack of headlights (the reason for the investigatory stop). State v. Williams, — Ohio App. 3d —, 2006 Ohio 6689, — N.E. 2d —, 2006 Ohio App. LEXIS 6583 (Dec. 15, 2006).

Present sense impression

Trial court did not commit error in failing to exclude the testimony because the statement overheard by the prison social work supervisor, that defendant had really stomped the victim, was admissible as a present sense exception to hearsay, under Ohio R. Evid. 803(1). The statement described the event and was made immediately after the altercation occurred and nothing in the record indicated a lack of trustworthiness. State v. Damron, — Ohio App. 3d —, 2007 Ohio 1187, — N.E. 2d —, 2007 Ohio App. LEXIS 1116 (Mar. 13, 2007).

Testimony from a witness, indicating that a victim of defendant's alleged homicidal act made statements that the victim owed money to another, feared for his life, and wanted a gun for protection, were admissible as an expression of the victim's then existing state of mind under Ohio R. Evid. 803(3); although the trial court admitted the testimony under the present sense impression exception to hearsay pursuant to Ohio R. Evid. 803(1), which was error, the testimony was nonetheless properly admitted. State v. Small, — Ohio App. 3d —, 2007 Ohio 6771, — N.E. 2d —, 2007 Ohio App. LEXIS 5923 (Dec. 18, 2007).

Trial court did not abuse its discretion in admitting the victim's statements under the present sense impression exception to the hearsay rule, under Ohio R. Evid. 803(1), because the victim's statements to her friend were not "testimonial" hearsay since the statements were not made in response to police interrogation or any other formal, structured official examination or questioning, but rather were made during a telephone call while the criminal incident itself was in progress, and that phone call had hurried and panicked overtones, much like a 911 call for help. State v. Mills, — Ohio App. 3d —, 2006 Ohio 2128, — N.E. 2d —, 2006 Ohio App. LEXIS 2010 (Apr. 28, 2006).

Trial court did not err in admitting testimony of a doctor's officer manager in a negligence action by a deceased patient's estate administratrix, wherein the manager provided an "explanatory" statement uttered by the doctor in the course of an appointment with the deceased patient and the patient's responses thereto, as the statement by the doctor was one where he perceived, assessed, and evaluated the patient's medical condition, and it was not offered for the truth of the matter asserted. The statement was offered merely to relate what the office manager saw or heard while she was at work because an issue in the case was the fact that the possible treatment options allegedly offered to the patient and declined by him were not noted in the patient's chart. If the statement was deemed hearsay pursuant to Ohio R. Evid. 801, then it was admissible under the present sense impression exception under Ohio R. Evid. 803(1). Frost v. Snitzer, — Ohio App. 3d —, 2006 Ohio 3882, — N.E. 2d —, 2006 Ohio App. LEXIS 3864 (July 28, 2006).

Trial court did not err in admitting a statement of an individual inside the house where a confidential informant completed a drug buy that "D" had the biggest pieces of crack cocaine because the statement was not hearsay under Ohio R. Evid. 801(C), in that it was not offered by the State to prove that "D" had the biggest pieces of crack cocaine. It only showed that the individual thought that "D" had the biggest pieces. Further, even if the statement were hearsay, it qualified as a present sense impression exception to the hearsay rule under Ohio R. Evid. 803(1) since the statement was made by the declarant as he was perceiving the event and was being recorded over the CI's wire. State v. Johnson, — Ohio App. 3d —, 2006 Ohio 4066, — N.E. 2d —, 2006 Ohio App. LEXIS 4033 (Aug. 7, 2006).

Previous conviction

There was no error in the admission of a juvenile's guilty plea and juvenile adjudication for complicity to trafficking in crack cocaine in defendant's criminal trial on a charge of, inter alia, corruption of a juvenile with drugs in violation of RC § 2925.02(A)(4)(c), as the conviction was not used to impeach the juvenile pursuant to Ohio R. Evid. 609(D) and RC § 2151.358(H), but rather, as substantive evidence of defendant's corruption of the minor by his involvement in the drug conduct. There was no violation of Ohio R. Evid. 803(22) where the juvenile had already admitted in his live testimony that he pled guilty to complicity to drug trafficking and then he tried to recant his statement. State v. Simmons, — Ohio App. 3d —, 2007 Ohio 1570, — N.E. 2d —, 2007 Ohio App. LEXIS 1442 (Mar. 28, 2007).

In prosecution for operating a motor vehicle while under the influence of alcohol, the trial court's decision allowing defendant's identity to be proven by testimony of the contents of information arresting officer obtained from a law enforcement automated data system printout did not violate the Confrontation Clause of U.S. Const. amend. VI and Ohio Const. art. I, § 10. The testimony was admitted for nonhearsay purposes including demonstrating the officer's process and reasoning in verifying defendant's identity. State v. Massie, — Ohio App. 3d —, 2006 Ohio 1515, — N.E. 2d —, 2006 Ohio App. LEXIS 1407 (Mar. 29, 2006).

Prior statements admissible

Transcript of the allocution of a co-participant who pled guilty and the police interview of the co-participant were not admissible under the business records or prior consistent statement exceptions: State v. Granderson, 177 Ohio App. 3d 424, 2008 Ohio 3757, 894 N.E.2d 1290, 2008 Ohio App. LEXIS 3187 (2008).

Property records

Trial court properly awarded a husband a portion of his pension plan as his separate property, as his statement of participation in his employer's pension plan was properly admitted pursuant to Ohio R. Evid. 901(A) where it was authenticated as an accurate and true document of the pension accounts and where there was testimony that the employer did not keep such records after a set period of time; further, the document was not hearsay under Ohio R. Evid.

803(A)(15). Yasinow v. Yasinow, — Ohio App. 3d —, 2006 Ohio 1355, — N.E. 2d —, 2006 Ohio App. LEXIS 1237 (Mar. 23, 2006).

Public records

Where ownership of real property was disputed, there was no abuse of discretion pursuant to Ohio R. Evid. 103 by the trial court's admission of testimony discussing the alleged ownership thereof, as the evidence was conflicting and the issue of ownership had no probative value concerning the charges against defendant, which were based on the taking of personal property without consent; documents from a civil court proceeding regarding the alleged fraudulent nature of the conveyance were properly admitted under the public records hearsay exception pursuant to Ohio R. Evid. 803(8) and as they were not "testimonial statements," they were not subject to scrutiny under the Confrontation Clause of U.S. Const. amend. VI and Ohio Const. art. I, § 10. State v. Pesec, — Ohio App. 3d —, 2007 Ohio 3846, — N.E. 2d —, 2007 Ohio App. LEXIS 3487 (July 27, 2007).

Because the transcript was a "record" of the probate court's activities, it fell within the purview of Ohio R. Evid. 803(8) regarding public records, but Ohio R. Evid. 803(8) did not apply to the testimony contained within the transcript. Because each statement transcribed by the court reporter survived hearsay analysis, the trial court properly admitted into evidence from the exhibit statements by defendant and questions from the prosecutor and the judge in defendant's contempt case. State v. Silverman, — Ohio App. 3d —, 2006 Ohio 3826, — N.E. 2d —, 2006 Ohio App. LEXIS 3791 (July 27, 2006).

Trial cout did not err in failing to strike an expert's testimony where it was based on reliable facts and evidence that was admissible in a negligence action arising from an accident when a truck driver's passenger side mirror hit a construction worker and her vehicle, as the expert relied in part on portions of a police report, which were an admissible public record within the hearsay exception under Ohio R. Evid. 803(8) where the portions relied on were drawn from the officer's observations of the scene. The expert was entitled to rely on the evidence, including photographs, deposition testimony, and underlying circumstances of the accident, in rendering his opinion pursuant to Ohio R. Evid. 702, 703, and 705. Wise v. Meyer, — Ohio App. 3d —, 2006 Ohio 4654, — N.E. 2d —, 2006 Ohio App. LEXIS 4556 (Sept. 8, 2006).

Sufficient evidence was admitted to prove defendant's prior convictions, within the last 20 years, for operating a vehicle under the influence, because, under RC § 2945.75(B) and Ohio R. Evid. 803(8), because the prior convictions were signed by a judge and sufficient evidence showed defendant's name, date of birth, and social security number were the same as those on each of the prior convictions. State v. Bolish, — Ohio App. 3d —, 2006 Ohio 5375, — N.E. 2d —, 2006 Ohio App. LEXIS 5347 (Oct. 16, 2006).

Although a probate court erroneously admitted a letter from a nursing home supervisor for a county agency with respect to a dispute over rent due by a decedent's son who had lived in the decedent's home after her death, the admission was not prejudicial error where the decedent's estate administrator testified as to the contents of the letter; although the letter was a valid public record and an official record, pursuant to Ohio R. Evid. 803(8) and RC § 2317.42, it was not properly authenticated under Ohio R. Evid. 902(2). In re Estate of Visnich, — Ohio App. 3d —, 2006 Ohio 5499, — N.E. 2d —, 2006 Ohio App. LEXIS 5477 (Oct. 23, 2006).

Public records and reports

In defendant's prosecution for receiving stolen property, the trial court properly admitted into evidence reports from the Law Enforcement Automated Data System (LEADS) as the public records hearsay exception under Ohio R. Evid. 803(8)(a) applied to the LEADS report, in that the reports contained only the routine activities of a public agency relative to the ownership of a vehicle. Moreover, the officer properly authenticated the LEADS printout in his testimony pursuant to Ohio R. Evid. 901 by his testimony as to how the system worked and the nature of the LEADS training that he obtained and his statement that the printout was identical to the report on the computer screen in his car that he used during the incident with defendant. State v. Papusha, — Ohio App. 3d —, 2007 Ohio 3966, — N.E. 2d —, 2007 Ohio App. LEXIS 3606 (Aug. 6, 2007).

Because the return of service document was admissible pursuant to the public records exception found in Ohio R. Evid. 803(8), there was no abuse of discretion in the trial court's decision to admit the hearsay evidence contained in the return of service document. The document stated that the deputy perfected service and it was signed by the deputy and included his badge number and the deputy sheriff who served the protective order was not doing so as a law enforcement officer, but was doing so in lieu of the service bailiff by order of the court. State v. Wills, — Ohio App. 3d —, 2006 Ohio 2295, — N.E. 2d —, 2006 Ohio App. LEXIS 2105 (May 9, 2006).

In a permanent custody proceeding, the trial court properly admitted the notes of the agency's caseworker under Ohio R. Evid. 803(8) because the notes reflected her observations that she had recorded as part of her duty to investigate a dependency complaint. In re Brown, — Ohio App. 3d —, 2006 Ohio 2865, — N.E. 2d —, 2006 Ohio App. LEXIS 2713 (May 26, 2006).

Trial court properly admitted the caseworker's notes, under Ohio R. Evid. 803(8), because the notes reflected the caseworker's observations that she recorded as part of her duty to investigate a neglect, abuse, or dependency complaint. The trial court explicitly recognized the limited admissibility of the caseworker's notes. In re Brown, — Ohio App. 3d —, 2006 Ohio 2863, — N.E. 2d —, 2006 Ohio App. LEXIS 2719 (May 26, 2006).

Copies of police reports which listed items from the construction site reported stolen were properly admitted, under Ohio R. Evid. 803(8), because the reports were not offered in order to demonstrate the truth of any matter "observed by police officers" and defendant testified that he had been confronted with the police reports and had confessed to taking materials listed in the reports. Moreover, any error would have been harmless since employees of the construction company also testified to the materials that were stolen from the construction site. State v. Love, — Ohio App. 3d —, 2006 Ohio 2925, — N.E. 2d —, 2006 Ohio App. LEXIS 2798 (June 9, 2006).

Trial court properly excluded a government investigative report regarding the asbestos exposure in locomotive cabs in an employee's action against the railroad, based on his exposure to asbestos and other substances, as the report was not within the public records hearsay exception of Ohio R. Evid. 803(8). There was no evidence that the statements contained in the report were an accurate reflection of the working conditions encountered by the railroad employee when he worked for the railroad, as the report was published nine years after his employment with the railroad ended. Hager v. Norfolk & Western Ry. Co., — Ohio App. 3d —, 2006 Ohio 6580, — N.E. 2d —, 2006 Ohio App. LEXIS 6489 (Dec. 14, 2006).

Recorded recollection

Trial court properly allowed a victim to read her written statement during defendant's criminal trial, as it was a recorded recollection under Ohio R. Evid. 803(5) upon which the victim had firsthand knowledge, it was made to police soon after the alleged offense, and she had insufficient memory to relate the details contained therein. Admission of the statement by the trial court upon the jury's request was error because such admission was to have been made only upon the offer of an adverse party, and further, the judge had acted outside of defendant's presence, which caused him prejudice because the jury admittedly relied on that statement in determining defendant's guilt. State v. Henson, — Ohio App. 3d —, 2007 Ohio 725, — N.E. 2d —, 2007 Ohio App. LEXIS 663 (Feb. 23, 2007).

In a domestic violence prosecution, when the victim's prior inconsistent statement was admitted, it was unnecessary to give the jury a limiting instruction, under Ohio R. Evid. 613(B), because the victim's prior statement was admitted for substantive purposes, not impeachment, and was admissible hearsay under the recorded recollection hearsay exception in Ohio R. Evid. 803(5). State v. Fields, — Ohio App. 3d —, 2007 Ohio 5060, — N.E. 2d —, 2007 Ohio App. LEXIS 4485 (Sept. 27, 2007).

In a domestic violence prosecution, the victim's prior inconsistent statement was properly admitted, under Ohio R. Evid. 803(5), because the victim signed it immediately after the victim's alleged assault, admitted the victim understood that, by signing the statement, the victim attested that the statement was truthful and accurate, and, at trial, after being given an opportunity to refresh the victim's memory with the statement, the victim's memory failed, so the victim could be asked to read the statement into the record for substantive purposes, but the statement could not be received as an exhibit. State v. Fields, — Ohio App. 3d —, 2007 Ohio 5060, — N.E. 2d —, 2007 Ohio App. LEXIS 4485 (Sept. 27, 2007).

In a domestic violence prosecution, when the victim was properly allowed to read the victim's prior inconsistent statement to the police into the record, under Ohio R. Evid. 803(5), error in allowing the statement to be received as an exhibit was harmless beyond a reasonable doubt, under Ohio R. Crim. P. 52(A), because it could not be said that the outcome of defendant's trial clearly would have been different, but for the trial court's error, as a myriad of other evidence established a basis for defendant's conviction. State v. Fields, — Ohio App. 3d —, 2007 Ohio 5060, — N.E. 2d —, 2007 Ohio App. LEXIS 4485 (Sept. 27, 2007).

There was no error in refusing to strike the direct testimony of the case worker in the permanent custody proceeding because the record indicated that the foundation was sufficiently laid, under Ohio R. Evid. 612. Each time the witness testified about transactions memorialized in a report of activity (ROA), she testified that she needed to review the ROA to connect a particular date to a particular event, and that she indeed possessed a present recollection of the details of the event; the testimony that followed did not appear to have been read verbatim from any document. In re Baby C, — Ohio App. 3d —, 2006 Ohio 2067, — N.E. 2d —, 2006 Ohio App. LEXIS 1915 (Apr. 27, 2006).

Records

There was insufficient evidence to support defendant's conviction for receiving stolen property because there was no admissible evidence as to the elements of RC § 2913.51(A). Under Ohio R. Evid. 803, the trial court erred in finding the validation sticker, and the testimony from the officers regarding the dispatcher's report that the validation sticker was stolen, admissible under the business record or public record exception since the information received from the dispatcher was clearly being offered for the truth of the statements therein: that the license validation sticker was actually stolen. State v. Wilson, — Ohio App. 3d —, 2006 Ohio 4108, — N.E. 2d —, 2006 Ohio App. LEXIS 4055 (Aug. 10, 2006).

Records of regularly conducted activity

Common pleas court properly rejected a claim form and recorded statement attached to appellant's memorandum in response to a hotel's summary judgment motion since neither the claim form nor the recorded statement indicated who prepared the report or statement. Appellant's attorney, who submitted an affidavit stating that the documents were "true copies" of the form and statement, did not submit an affidavit stating that he had conducted the audio interview of appellant; and the documents were not properly qualified under Ohio R. Evid. 803(6) as they were not incorporated into an affidavit by a person with knowledge of the circumstances surrounding the preparation of the report. Ray v. Ramada Inn North, 171 Ohio App. 3d 1, 2007 Ohio 1341, 869 N.E.2d 95, 2007 Ohio App. LEXIS 1220 (2007).

Where most of the evidence that defendant challenged on appeal under the plain error standard of review pursuant to Ohio R. Crim. P. 52(B) due to his failure to have objected at trial was not hearsay under Ohio R. Evid. 801(C) because it was not offered to prove the truth of the matter asserted, or it was properly admitted as a record kept in the regular course of business pursuant to Ohio R. Evid. 803(6), and defendant failed to show that he was prejudiced by the admission thereof, there was no plain error. State v. Payne, — Ohio App. 3d —, 2006 Ohio 3005, — N.E. 2d —, 2006 Ohio App. LEXIS 2889 (June 15, 2006).

State of mind

Court need consider EvidR 804(B)(5) only if, after an analysis of EvidR 801 and 803, objected to statements appear to be inadmissible hearsay. The decedent's statements concerning her estate plans and insurance beneficiaries were admissible under EvidR 803 as evidence of her then existing state of mind: Ament v. Reassure Am. Life Ins. Co., 180 Ohio App. 3d 440, 2009 Ohio 36, 905 N.E.2d 1246, 2009 Ohio App. LEXIS 23 (2009).

In a constructive trust and related claims action by a decedent's son against the decedent's grandson, wherein the son alleged that the decedent had intended for her farm to be divided upon her death between her son and her daughter and that her deed to the grandson during her life was for purposes of Medicaid lien avoidance and was done with the intention that the land was held by the grandson in a fiduciary capacity, the trial court's grant of summary judgment to the grandson was error. Statements in affidavits to support the son's position were admissible under Ohio R. Evid. 803(3) regarding the decedent's alleged expressed intent to give the farm to her son and daughter, although statements allegedly made by the decedent that she had gifted the farm to her grandson in order to avoid the Medicaid lien were not admissible, and statements allegedly made by the decedent were not admissible under Ohio R. Evid. 804(B)(5), as the decedent's estate was not a party to the action. McGrew v. Popham, — Ohio App. 3d —, 2007 Ohio 428, — N.E. 2d —, 2007 Ohio App. LEXIS 380 (Feb. 1, 2007).

Admission of testimony from defendant's father about a conversation that he had with an aggravated murder victim a week before his murder, to the effect that the victim wanted to turn defendant into the police to collect a reward, was proper under Ohio R. Evid. 803(3) as a statement of the victim's current intent to take future action against defendant. The statement was relevant to show defendant's motive for killing victim two. State v. Byrd, — Ohio App. 3d —, 2007 Ohio 3787, — N.E. 2d —, 2007 Ohio App. LEXIS 3447 (July 27, 2007).

Testimony from a witness, indicating that a victim of defendant's alleged homicidal act made statements that the victim owed money to another, feared for his life, and wanted a gun for protection, were admissible as an expression of the victim's then existing state of mind under Ohio R. Evid. 803(3); although the trial court admitted the testimony under the present sense impression exception to hearsay pursuant to Ohio R. Evid. 803(1), which was error, the testimony was nonetheless properly admitted. State v. Small, — Ohio App. 3d —, 2007 Ohio 6771, — N.E. 2d —, 2007 Ohio App. LEXIS 5923 (Dec. 18, 2007).

In defendant's rape prosecution, a statement made by the victim's boyfriend, who was also defendant's roommate, during his direct examination, to the effect that defendant told him that, while defendant was kissing the victim, the victim said, "No," and raised a question about her boyfriend's response to the incident was hearsay, fell under the state of mind exception to the hearsay rule because it showed the victim's state of mind regarding her feelings at the moment as well as defendant's state of mind regarding whether he knew that the encounter with the victim was not consensual. State v. Thrasher, — Ohio App. 3d —, 2006 Ohio 1260, — N.E. 2d —, 2006 Ohio App. LEXIS 1134 (Mar. 17, 2006).

Ohio R. Evid. 803(3) deemed admissible a witness's testimony that the victim indicated that he and defendant were going to fight about a situation. Through the statement, the victim revealed his "current intent to take future actions," and the State used the statement as part of its theory that defendant killed the victim during the conflict that ultimately occurred outside of the restaurant. State v. Brown, — Ohio App. 3d —, 2006 Ohio 4594, — N.E. 2d —, 2006 Ohio App. LEXIS 4541 (Sept. 7, 2006).

Because the codefendant's statement that he was angry was a statement regarding his then existing state of mind, its admission did not violate the rule against hearsay. Furthermore, the statement did not tend to incriminate defendant in the victim's death since defendant was not present to hear the statement and because the fact that the codefendant was angry that a particular person shot defendant's brother did little to prove that defendant murdered the victim. State v. Robinson, — Ohio App. 3d —, 2007 Ohio 3501, — N.E. 2d —, 2007 Ohio App. LEXIS 3224 (July 5, 2007).

Statements made for diagnosis and treatment

Child's statements were properly admitted under Evid. R. 803(4) as statements made for the purpose of diagnosis and treatment because, since the child was subject to cross-examination, defendant's right to confrontation was not violated. Also, the trial court did not abuse its discretion in allowing the testimony of the psychologist because she testified regarding the child's nearly two-year course of therapy including her initial symptoms and the progress that she had made. State v. Brown, — Ohio App. 3d —, 2006 Ohio 5769, — N.E. 2d —, 2006 Ohio App. LEXIS 5759 (Nov. 3, 2006).

Treatises

In a patient's dental malpractice action, it was not hearsay under Ohio R. Evid. 801(C) for the patient's expert to read from a treatise that he had written because the expert testified to his opinions at trial, he was subject to cross-examination, and he did not read specific statements from the treatise as substantive evidence. Ohio R. Evid. 706, pertaining to the use of statements in treatises for impeachment, did not make the expert's use of his own treatise on direct examination improper. Scibelli v. Pannunzio, — Ohio App. 3d —, 2006 Ohio 5652, — N.E. 2d —, 2006 Ohio App. LEXIS 5650 (Oct. 26, 2006).

In a patient's dental malpractice action, even if it was error to permit an expert, on redirect, to read a brief section of another author's article indicating that a tumor grew slowly after an article by that author indicating that the tumor grew quickly had been used to impeach the expert on cross-examination, no reversible prejudice resulted. The expert's testimony that such tumors could grow quickly was confirmed by the testimony of another expert, and the limited references in the article had little impact. Scibelli v. Pannunzio, — Ohio App. 3d —, 2006 Ohio 5652, — N.E. 2d —, 2006 Ohio App. LEXIS 5650 (Oct. 26, 2006).

RULE 804. Hearsay Exceptions; Declarant Unavailable

(A) **Definition of unavailability.** "Unavailability as a witness" includes any of the following situations in which the declarant:

(1) is exempted by ruling of the court on the ground of privilege from testifying concerning the subject matter of the declarant's statement;

(2) persists in refusing to testify concerning the subject matter of the declarant's statement despite an order of the court to do so;

(3) testifies to a lack of memory of the subject matter of the declarant's statement;

(4) is unable to be present or to testify at the hearing because of death or then-existing physical or mental illness or infirmity;

(5) is absent from the hearing and the proponent of the declarant's statement has been unable to procure the declarant's attendance (or in the case of a hearsay exception under division (B)(2), (3), or (4) of this rule, the declarant's attendance or testimony) by process or other reasonable means.

A declarant is not unavailable as a witness if the declarant's exemption, refusal, claim of lack of memory, inability, or absence is due to the procurement or wrongdoing of the proponent of the declarant's statement for the purpose of preventing the witness from attending or testifying.

(B) **Hearsay exceptions.** The following are not excluded by the hearsay rule if the declarant is unavailable as a witness:

(1) **Former testimony.** Testimony given as a witness at another hearing of the same or a different proceeding, or in a deposition taken in compliance with law in the course of the same or another proceeding, if the party against whom the testimony is now offered, or, in a civil action or proceeding, a predecessor in interest, had an opportunity and similar motive to develop the testimony by direct, cross, or redirect examination. Testimony given at a preliminary hearing must satisfy the right to confrontation and exhibit indicia of reliability.

(2) **Statement under belief of impending death**. In a prosecution for homicide or in a civil action or proceeding, a statement made by a declarant, while believing that his or her death was imminent, concerning the cause or circumstances of what the declarant believed to be his or her impending death.

(3) **Statement against interest.** A statement that was at the time of its making so far contrary to the declarant's pecuniary or proprietary interest, or so far tended to subject the declarant to civil or criminal liability, or to render invalid a claim by the declarant against another, that a reasonable person in the declarant's position would not have made the statement unless the declarant believed it to be true. A statement tending to expose the declarant to criminal liability, whether offered to exculpate or inculpate the accused, is not admissible unless corroborating circumstances clearly indicate the truthworthiness of the statement.

(4) **Statement against personal or family history**. A statement concerning the declarant's own birth, adoption, marriage, divorce, legitimacy, relationship by blood, adoption, or marriage, ancestry, or other similar fact of personal or family history, even though the declarant had no means of acquiring personal knowl-

edge of the matter stated; or (b) a statement concerning the foregoing matters, and death also, of another person, if the declarant was related to the other by blood, adoption, or marriage or was so intimately associated with the other's family as to be likely to have accurate information concerning the matter declared.

(5) **Statement by a deceased or incompetent person.** The statement was made by a decedent or a mentally incompetent person, where all of the following apply:

(a) the estate or personal representative of the decedent's estate or the guardian or trustee of the incompetent person is a party;

(b) the statement was made before the death or the development of the incompetency;

(c) the statement is offered to rebut testimony by an adverse party on a matter within the knowledge of the decedent or incompetent person.

(6) **Forfeiture by wrongdoing.** A statement offered against a party if the unavailability of the witness is due to the wrongdoing of the party for the purpose of preventing the witness from attending or testifying. However, a statement is not admissible under this rule unless the proponent has given to each adverse party advance written notice of an intention to introduce the statement sufficient to provide the adverse party a fair opportunity to contest the admissibility of the statement.

History: Amended, eff 7-1-81; 7-1-93; 7-1-01.

NOTES TO DECISIONS

ANALYSIS

Declarant deceased
Declarant unavailable
Dying declaration
Estate matter
Harmless error
Personal or family history
Statement against interest
— Corroborating evidence
Testimony
Testimony from hearing read into trial
Unavailability
Violation of amend VI right of confrontation
Violation of right of confrontation

Declarant deceased

Court need consider EvidR 804(B)(5) only if, after an analysis of EvidR 801 and 803, objected to statements appear to be inadmissible hearsay. The decedent's statements concerning her estate plans and insurance beneficiaries were admissible under EvidR 803 as evidence of her then existing state of mind: Ament v. Reassure Am. Life Ins. Co., 180 Ohio App. 3d 440, 2009 Ohio 36, 905 N.E.2d 1246, 2009 Ohio App. LEXIS 23 (2009).

Affidavit prepared by a person who died before he could testify at the trial was not admissible as former testimony where it did not satisfy the testimonial requirements of EvidR 804(B)(1): Kiser v. Allstate Ins. Co., 144 Ohio Misc. 2d 12, 2007 Ohio 6070, 877 N.E.2d 765, 2007 Ohio Misc. LEXIS 464 (2007).

Decedent's statement to his attorney was not admissible, under Ohio R. Evid. 804(B), because (1) the entire contents of the statement were privileged, (2) the decedent did not waive his attorney-client privilege, and (3) the Ohio Rules of

Evidence did not control the admissibility of privileged material, under Ohio R. Evid. 501, as the admissibility of such matters was controlled by statute and common law. Wallace v. McElwain, — Ohio App. 3d —, 2006 Ohio 5226, — N.E. 2d —, 2006 Ohio App. LEXIS 5205 (Sept. 27, 2006).

Declarant unavailable

Trial court did not err in admitting former testimony of a witness who was deemed unavailable at the time of defendant's third trial, as it was admitted pursuant to Ohio R. Evid. 804(B)(1) and was testimony from the prior trials. The record sufficiently established that there were good faith efforts made to locate the witness and his testimony was limited and it excluded any mention of his pretrial identification of defendant. State v. Glover, — Ohio App. 3d —, 2007 Ohio 2122, — N.E. 2d —, 2007 Ohio App. LEXIS 1982 (May 3, 2007).

Trial court properly dismissed defendant's indictment as a sanction for the State's discovery violation as an order granting a new trial was law of the case, Ohio R. Crim. P. 33(D) and RC § 2945.82 governed the manner in which the new trial was to be conducted, and the trial court possessed all authority to reopen discovery or to entertain any pretrial motions available at law. The State violated Ohio R. Crim. P. 16(B)(1)(f) in willfully withholding exculpatory material from defendant and defendant's prejudice could not be cured by a new trial as almost 20 years had elapsed, eight witnesses for the defense were deceased, 16 witnesses had unknown addresses, and to present the witnesses' prior testimony would have been useless as none of the witnesses had been questioned about the exculpatory evidence. State v. Larkins, — Ohio App. 3d —, 2006 Ohio 90, — N.E. 2d —, 2006 Ohio App. LEXIS 80 (Jan. 12, 2006).

Trial court did not abuse its discretion in declaring the victim unavailable as a witness for trial, pursuant to Ohio R. Evid. 804(A)(5), because, through legal process and other reasonable means the State was unable to locate the victim and procure her attendance at trial. State v. Mills, — Ohio App. 3d —, 2006 Ohio 2128, — N.E. 2d —, 2006 Ohio App. LEXIS 2010 (Apr. 28, 2006).

Dying declaration

Allowing the police officer's testimony regarding the victim's dying declaration, under Evid. R. 804(B)(2), did not violate defendant's right to confrontation because the dying declaration was an exception to the rule against hearsay evidence. The victim made the statements believing that his death was imminent (he died 30 minutes later) and the statements concerned the circumstances of his death. Although the statements were made to a police officer, the colloquy was not an interrogation and the victim did not make the statements in anticipation of a criminal prosecution. State v. Duncan, — Ohio App. 3d —, 2006 Ohio 5009, — N.E. 2d —, 2006 Ohio App. LEXIS 4955 (Sept. 28, 2006).

Estate matter

In a constructive trust and related claims action by a decedent's son against the decedent's grandson, wherein the son alleged that the decedent had intended for her farm to be divided upon her death between her son and her daughter and that her deed to the grandson during her life was for purposes of Medicaid lien avoidance and was done with the intention that the land was held by the grandson in a fiduciary capacity, the trial court's grant of summary judgment to the grandson was error. Statements in affidavits to support the son's position were admissible under Ohio R. Evid. 803(3) regarding the decedent's alleged expressed intent to give the farm to her son and daughter, although statements allegedly made by the decedent that she had gifted the farm to her grandson in order to avoid the Medicaid lien were not admissible, and statements allegedly made by the decedent were not admissible under Ohio R. Evid. 804(B)(5), as the decedent's estate was not a party to the action. McGrew v. Popham, — Ohio App. 3d —, 2007 Ohio 428, — N.E. 2d —, 2007 Ohio App. LEXIS 380 (Feb. 1, 2007).

Harmless error

Although Ohio R. Evid. 804(B)(1) did not apply to admit statements that defendant's client made during the contempt hearing because he actually testified at defendant's trial, the admission of statements from the client via the transcript of the contempt hearing was harmless. State v. Silverman, — Ohio App. 3d —, 2006 Ohio 3826, — N.E. 2d —, 2006 Ohio App. LEXIS 3791 (July 27, 2006).

Personal or family history

Foreign divorce record executed in 1961 was admissible pursuant to EvidR 804(B)(4) where it concerned the decedent's own divorce and was found in the decedent's papers: Kaur v. Bharmota, 182 Ohio App. 3d 696, 2009 Ohio 2344, 914 N.E.2d 1087, 2009 Ohio App. LEXIS 1985 (2009).

Statement against interest

Although the trial court should have allowed the witness to testify as to the statements made by the mother (before she died) regarding the son's investment in the bar, since they were against her pecuniary interest when she made them, the son failed to demonstrate how the error affected a substantial right. While the hearsay statement indicated that the son had invested in the bar, it did not demonstrate the existence of an oral contract for the proceeds of the bar, upon its sale, and the substantive portions of the excluded testimony were presented to the jury in other testimony. Snyder v. Snyder, 170 Ohio App. 3d 26, 2007 Ohio 122, 865 N.E.2d 944, 2007 Ohio App. LEXIS 103 (2007).

Exclusion of a declarant's statement against her pecuniary interests was error, but did not affect a substantial right: Snyder v. Snyder, 170 Ohio App. 3d 26, 2007 Ohio 122, 865 N.E.2d 944, 2007 Ohio App. LEXIS 103 (2007).

Trial court's decision to allow the witness to testify about what his brother (who committed the crime and later committed suicide) had told him about his and defendant's involvement in the staged burglary that resulted in the killing of defendant's wife was not error. The admission of the brother's statements through the witness' testimony did not violate the Confrontation Clause and was properly admitted pursuant to the hearsay exception for statements against penal interest under Ohio R. Evid. 804(B)(3). The brother's statements were non-testimonial; they possessed particularized guarantees of trustworthiness; the statements were made to his half-brother with whom he shared a close relationship; and the brother had nothing to gain from inculpating defendant in the crime. State v. Barton, — Ohio App. 3d —, 2007 Ohio 1099, — N.E. 2d —, 2007 Ohio App. LEXIS 1020 (Mar. 12, 2007).

Trial court committed an error that affected a substantial right of defendant pursuant to Ohio R. Crim. P. 52(A) where it precluded testimony concerning an alleged confession to the shooting, for which defendant was on trial, by another person due to the trial court's determination that there was insufficient corroboration for purposes of Ohio R. Evid. 804(B)(3). The evidence that another party committed the criminal conduct was crucial to defendant's constitutional right to a fair trial and as it was not speculative or remote, it should not have been excluded. State v. Swann, 171 Ohio App. 3d 304, 2007 Ohio 2010, 870 N.E.2d 754, 2007 Ohio App. LEXIS 1780 (2007).

EvidR 804(B)(3) cannot be construed in a way that denies an accused a meaningful opportunity to present a complete defense. The accused may introduce any legal evidence tending to prove that another person may have committed the crime with which the defendant is charged: State v. Swann, 171 Ohio App. 3d 304, 2007 Ohio 2010, 870 N.E.2d 754, 2007 Ohio App. LEXIS 1780 (2007).

Trial court's admission of statements allegedly made by a victim that the victim owed money and that the victim was selling drugs were proper as statements against interest under Ohio R. Evid. 804(B)(3) in defendant's criminal trial, as the statements were contrary to the victim's pecuniary or proprietary interest, the victim was unavailable because he was murdered, and corroborating circumstances indicated the trustworthiness of the statement. State v. Small, — Ohio App. 3d —, 2007 Ohio 6771, — N.E. 2d —, 2007 Ohio App. LEXIS 5923 (Dec. 18, 2007).

Trial court did not abuse its discretion in refusing to admit statements by two co-defendants that they observed the victim of their beating masturbating in the bushes outside of their apartment, as the statements were not against their interest for purposes of Ohio R. Evid. 803(4) because they would not have been subjected to civil or criminal liability; additionally, one of the co-defendants testified that she saw a pervert outside of the apartment window. State v. Arafat, — Ohio App. 3d —, 2006 Ohio 1722, — N.E. 2d —, 2006 Ohio App. LEXIS 1592 (Apr. 6, 2006).

Trial court erred in ruling that all prior statements by parties were inadmissible hearsay because a party's statements offered against the party were not hearsay, under Ohio R. Evid. 801(D), and each statement had to be reviewed to determine if it was an admissible statement against interest, under Ohio R. Evid. 804(B)(3). In re Butler, — Ohio App. 3d —, 2006 Ohio 4547, — N.E. 2d —, 2006 Ohio App. LEXIS 4510 (Sept. 5, 2006).

Exclusion of a statement by defendant's five-year-old son to a detective that the boy started an apartment fire that resulted in the death of his sister was proper, as the statement was made a few hours after the fire and was no longer an excited utterance under Ohio R. Evid. 803(2) because he was not under the stress of excitement caused by the fire when he spoke to the detective. It was not a statement against interest under Ohio R. Evid. 804(B)(3) under the plain error standard of review pursuant to Ohio R. Crim. P. 52, as there was nothing to support a determination that the young child had an understanding of pecuniary or proprietary interests. State v. Abner, — Ohio App. 3d —, 2006 Ohio 4510, — N.E. 2d —, 2006 Ohio App. LEXIS 4523 (Sept. 1, 2006).

— Corroborating evidence

Corroboration requirement of EvidR 804(B)(3) rationally serves a legitimate interest in the admission of trustworthy evidence, end therefore exclusion of a criminal defendant's proffered evidence for lack of corroboration does not deprive a defendant of the right to present a complete defense: State v. Swann, 119 Ohio St. 3d 552, 2008 Ohio 4837, 895 N.E.2d 821, 2008 Ohio LEXIS 2586 (2008).

Testimony

In a dependency proceeding in which a child was found to be dependent because the child's mother had been found to be mentally ill, it was error to admit a transcript of the probate court proceedings in which the mother was found mentally ill because the transcript was not admissible, under Ohio R. Evid. 804(B)(1), because it was not determined that the witnesses who testified in the probate court proceedings were unavailable, and this error was prejudicial because the testimony in the probate court proceedings appeared to be the basis for the trial court's dependency determination, under RC § 2151.04(B). In re J.M., — Ohio App. 3d —, 2007 Ohio 4219, — N.E. 2d —, 2007 Ohio App. LEXIS 3816 (Aug. 20, 2007).

Testimony from hearing read into trial

Trial court did not abuse its discretion in admitting the victim's preliminary hearing testimony at defendant's trial pursuant to Ohio R. Evid. 804(B)(1). Because defendant had an adequate and meaningful opportunity to test and develop the victim's former testimony under oath at the preliminary hearing, her testimony bore an indicia of trustworthiness and reliability sufficient to satisfy the confrontation clause. State v. Mills, — Ohio App. 3d —, 2006 Ohio 2128, — N.E. 2d —, 2006 Ohio App. LEXIS 2010 (Apr. 28, 2006).

Unavailability

It was error for a trial court to allow the State to use a victim's preliminary hearing testimony at defendant's trial because the State did not meet its burden of showing, under Ohio R. Evid. 804(A)(5), that the victim was unavailable for trial, as the State did not try to contact the victim at her correct address for seven months between defendant's indictment and trial, and it had that correct address in the criminal file of one of its own witnesses. State v. Reese, — Ohio App. 3d —, 2007 Ohio 1082, — N.E. 2d —, 2007 Ohio App. LEXIS 994 (Mar. 8, 2007).

Two-part test determined whether admitting hearsay testimony of an unavailable witness violated a criminal defendant's right of confrontation, and it had to be shown that the witness whose testimony was offered was unavailable and that the proffered statement bore sufficient indicia of reliability. State v. Workman, 171 Ohio App. 3d 89, 2007 Ohio 1360, 869 N.E.2d 713, 2007 Ohio App. LEXIS 1241 (2007).

Issuance of a subpoena to procure the attendance of a witness at trial alone did not constitute a sufficient effort to obtain the witness's presence, when considering if the non-appearing witness was unavailable, under Ohio R. Evid. 804(B)(1), when other reasonable methods were also available. State v. Workman, 171 Ohio App. 3d 89, 2007 Ohio 1360, 869 N.E.2d 713, 2007 Ohio App. LEXIS 1241 (2007).

First prong of the test for the admissibility of hearsay testimony of an unavailable witness was a rule of necessity which generally required a showing that the declarant was unavailable to testify, and a witness was not considered unavailable unless the prosecution had made reasonable efforts in good faith to secure his presence at trial, reflecting the preference for face-to-face confrontation which allowed demeanor to be observed and the import of the testimony to be more readily comprehended, and the proponent of the evidence had the burden of establishing that such efforts had been made, and, further, the evidence of unavailability had to be based on the personal knowledge of witnesses rather than upon hearsay not under oath, at least when unavailability had not been clearly conceded by defendant. State v. Workman, 171 Ohio App. 3d 89, 2007 Ohio 1360, 869 N.E.2d 713, 2007 Ohio App. LEXIS 1241 (2007).

Two-part test determined whether admitting hearsay testimony of an unavailable witness violated a criminal defendant's right of confrontation, and it had to be shown that the witness whose testimony was offered was unavailable and that the proffered statement bore sufficient indicia of reliability. State v. Workman, 171 Ohio App. 3d 89, 2007 Ohio 1360, 869 N.E.2d 713, 2007 Ohio App. LEXIS 1241 (2007).

State did not establish the showing of unavailability of a witness required by EvidR 804 or the confrontation clause. A single attempt to serve a subpoena on the witness did not constitute a reasonable effort to secure the witness' presence at trial: State v. Workman, 171 Ohio App. 3d 89, 2007 Ohio 1360, 869 N.E.2d 713, 2007 Ohio App. LEXIS 1241 (2007).

State sufficiently showed that it made reasonable efforts to secure the attendance of an unavailable witness where there was evidence that a subpoena was served on the witness and detectives visited the witness' home on the morning of trial and made extensive efforts to locate him: State v. Nevins, 171 Ohio App. 3d 97, 2007 Ohio 1511, 869 N.E.2d 719, 2007 Ohio App. LEXIS 1379 (2007).

Admission of the prior trial testimony of defendant's girlfriend neither violated defendant's right of confrontation nor was in error pursuant to Ohio R. Evid. 804 since she was unavailable for trial. The prosecution demonstrated a reasonable good faith effort to secure her presence as three subpoe-

nas were issued, she was spoken to by telephone, and when she did not appear, a thorough search was conducted. State v. Blakely, — Ohio App. 3d —, 2006 Ohio 185, — N.E. 2d —, 2006 Ohio App. LEXIS 154 (Jan. 20, 2006).

In a murder prosecution, the trial court properly excluded the testimony of a proffered witness that another party told her that party committed the crime because defendant did not make a reasonable effort in good faith, under Ohio R. Evid. 804(A), to show that the declarant of the statement was unavailable, as the possibility that the declarant, if produced, would assert her privilege against self-incrimination was insufficient to show the declarant was unavailable. State v. Jenkins, — Ohio App. 3d —, 2006 Ohio 2546, — N.E. 2d —, 2006 Ohio App. LEXIS 2405 (May 12, 2006).

In a murder prosecution, the trial court properly excluded the testimony of a proffered witness that another party told her that party committed the crime because defendant did not make a reasonable effort in good faith, under Ohio R. Evid. 804(A), to show that the declarant of the statement was unavailable, as counsel's statements that the declarant was in jail in another state were insufficient, and, if that were true, counsel could have attempted to utilize RC § 2939.26 or a common-law writ of habeas corpus ad testificandum to obtain the declarant's presence, or could have sought her deposition. State v. Jenkins, — Ohio App. 3d —, 2006 Ohio 2546, — N.E. 2d —, 2006 Ohio App. LEXIS 2405 (May 12, 2006).

Violation of amend VI right of confrontation

Deposition testimony of the victim, preserved pursuant to Crim. R. 15, satisfied the requirements of the confrontation clause of the Sixth Amendment because the victim was unavailable at trial (he had died from Lou Gehrig's disease), and because defendant had an opportunity, and in fact, did cross-examine the victim during the deposition. The victim was capable of giving basic affirmative or negative responses to leading questions at his deposition and there was no mention that the victim was confused, was too tired to answer counsel's questions, or was unwilling to continue with the cross-examination for any reason. State v. Irwin, — Ohio App. 3d —, 2007 Ohio 4996, — N.E. 2d —, 2007 Ohio App. LEXIS 4391 (Sept. 19, 2007).

Violation of right of confrontation

It was a violation of defendant's right to confrontation to admit a victim's preliminary hearing testimony at defendant's trial, in lieu of the victim's testimony, because (1) the State did not present testimony regarding the victim's unavailability or detailing its efforts to secure the victim's presence at trial, (2) defendant did not concede her unavailability and objected to admitting her preliminary hearing testimony, and (3) the State's single effort to subpoena the victim did not show "reasonable efforts" were made to secure the victim's attendance at trial. State v. Workman, 171 Ohio App. 3d 89, 2007 Ohio 1360, 869 N.E.2d 713, 2007 Ohio App. LEXIS 1241 (2007).

It was a violation of defendant's right to confrontation to admit a victim's preliminary hearing testimony at defendant's trial, in lieu of the victim's testimony, because (1) the State did not present testimony regarding the victim's unavailability or detailing its efforts to secure the victim's presence at trial, (2) defendant did not concede her unavailability and objected to admitting her preliminary hearing testimony, and (3) the State's single effort to subpoena the victim did not show "reasonable efforts" were made to secure the victim's attendance at trial. State v. Workman, 171 Ohio App. 3d 89, 2007 Ohio 1360, 869 N.E.2d 713, 2007 Ohio App. LEXIS 1241 (2007).

RULE 805.   Hearsay Within Hearsay

Hearsay included within hearsay is not excluded under the hearsay rule if each part of the combined statements conforms with an exception to the hearsay rule provided in these rules.

NOTES TO DECISIONS

ANALYSIS

Generally
Admissibility of double hearsay
Double hearsay, what constitutes

Generally

EvidR 805 provides that each part of a statement must conform to an exception to the hearsay rules in order for the entire statement to be admissible: State v. Butcher, 170 Ohio App. 3d 52, 2007 Ohio 118, 866 N.E.2d 13, 2007 Ohio App. LEXIS 111 (2007).

Admissibility of double hearsay

Trial court did not abuse its discretion when it excluded testimony from an employee/part-owner of a business in a commercial lease dispute involving the business and the landlords, as the testimony sought to be admitted concerned conversations between another owner of the business and the landlords, however, as the part-owner did not actually hear the statements about which he intended to testify, they did not constitute admissions of a party-opponent under Ohio R. Evid. 801(D)(2); as the part-owner lacked personal knowledge, under Ohio R. Evid. 602 he could not testify thereto and further, such did not constitute hearsay within hearsay under Ohio R. Evid. 805, as each part of the combined statements did not conform to a hearsay rule exception. Yoder v. Hurst, — Ohio App. 3d —, 2007 Ohio 4861, — N.E. 2d —, 2007 Ohio App. LEXIS 4310 (Sept. 20, 2007).

Double hearsay, what constitutes

During defendant's criminal trial, the inclusion of the words "they tell us" in a police officer's description of bystanders' statements related to a gun battle that had just occurred did not make the statements inadmissible hearsay within hearsay; read in context, the evidence indicated that the bystanders had just seen the gun battle, and the officer's testimony could not reasonably have been interpreted to mean that the bystanders themselves had been told by others that a car that later proved to be defendant's was involved in the shooting. State v. Holdbrook, — Ohio App. 3d —, 2006 Ohio 5841, — N.E. 2d —, 2006 Ohio App. LEXIS 5791 (Nov. 6, 2006).

RULE 806.   Attacking and Supporting Credibility of Declarant

(A) When a hearsay statement, or a statement defined in Evid. R. 801(D)(2), (c), (d), or (e), has been admitted in evidence, the credibility of the declarant may be attacked, and if attacked may be supported, by any evidence that would be admissible for those purposes if declarant had testified as a witness.

(B) Evidence of a statement or conduct by the declarant at any time, inconsistent with the declarant's hearsay statement, is not subject to any requirement that the declarant may have been afforded an opportunity to deny or explain.

(C) Evidence of a declarant's prior conviction is not subject to any requirement that the declarant be shown a public record.

(D) If the party against whom a hearsay statement has been admitted calls the declarant as a witness, the party is entitled to examine the declarant on the statement as if under cross-examination.

History: Amended, eff 7-1-98.

RULE 807.   Hearsay Exceptions; Child Statements in Abuse Cases

(A) An out-of-court statement made by a child who is under twelve years of age at the time of trial or hearing describing any sexual act performed by, with, or on the child or describing any act of physical violence directed against the child is not excluded as hearsay under Evid. R. 802 if all of the following apply:

(1) The court finds that the totality of the circumstances surrounding the making of the statement provides particularized guarantees of trustworthiness that make the statement at least as reliable as statements admitted pursuant to Evid. R. 803 and 804. The circumstances must establish that the child was particularly likely to be telling the truth when the statement was made and that the test of cross-examination would add little to the reliability of the statement. In making its determination of the reliability of the statement, the court shall consider all of the circumstances surrounding the making of the statement, including but not limited to spontaneity, the internal consistency of the statement, the mental state of the child, the child's motive or lack of motive to fabricate, the child's use of terminology unexpected of a child of similar age, the means by which the statement was elicited, and the lapse of time between the act and the statement. In making this determination, the court shall not consider whether there is independent proof of the sexual act or act of physical violence.

(2) The child's testimony is not reasonably obtainable by the proponent of the statement.

(3) There is independent proof of the sexual act or act of physical violence.

(4) At least ten days before the trial or hearing, a proponent of the statement has notified all other parties in writing of the content of the statement, the time and place at which the statement was made, the identity of the witness who is to testify about the statement, and the circumstances surrounding the statement that are claimed to indicate its trustworthiness.

(B) The child's testimony is "not reasonably obtainable by the proponent of the statement" under division (A)(2) of this rule only if one or more of the following apply:

(1) The child refuses to testify concerning the subject matter of the statement or claims a lack of memory of the subject matter of the statement after a person trusted by the child, in the presence of the court, urges the child to both describe the acts described by the statement and to testify.

(2) The court finds all of the following:

(a) The child is absent from the trial or hearing;

(b) The proponent of the statement has been unable to procure the child's attendance or testimony by process or other reasonable means despite a good faith effort to do so;

(c) It is probable that the proponent would be unable to procure the child's testimony or attendance if the trial or hearing were delayed for a reasonable time.

(3) The court finds both of the following:

(a) The child is unable to testify at the trial or hearing because of death or then existing physical or mental illness or infirmity;

(b) The illness or infirmity would not improve sufficiently to permit the child to testify if the trial or hearing were delayed for a reasonable time.

The proponent of the statement has not established that the child's testimony or attendance is not reasonably obtainable if the child's refusal, claim of lack of memory, inability, or absence is due to the procurement or wrongdoing of the proponent of the statement for the purpose of preventing the child from attending or testifying.

(C) The court shall make the findings required by this rule on the basis of a hearing conducted outside the presence of the jury and shall make findings of fact, on the record, as to the bases for its ruling.

History: Effective 7-1-91.

NOTES TO DECISIONS

ANALYSIS

Admissibility of child's statements
Competency determination
Statement of examining physician

Admissibility of child's statements

Statements of the twins, victims of sexual abuse, were admissible under Ohio R. Evid. 807 as a hearsay exception for the statements of children in abuse situations and the twins' statements to a social worker were within the realm of diagnosis and treatment because the social worker's function was both to determine whether sexual abuse had been indicated and to then follow up on referring the family for appropriate care. Therefore, the statements were properly admissible pursuant to Ohio R. Evid. 803(4). In re C.C., — Ohio App. 3d —, 2007 Ohio 2226, — N.E. 2d —, 2007 Ohio App. LEXIS 2079 (May 10, 2007).

Trial court's decision to exclude statements by a child victim of defendant's alleged sexual conduct, which were made to a professional clinical counselor, was error where the trial court determined that although the statements might have been within the hearsay exception for medical diagnosis and treatment under Ohio R. Evid. 803(4), it could not deem them admissible because it found that the child victim was not a competent witness under Ohio R. Evid. 601. Although a competency requirement existed for admission of the statements under Ohio R. Evid. 807, no such requirement existed for statements under Ohio R. Evid. 803(4) as long as the surrounding circumstances and any other factors were examined to determine that the statements were reliable. State v. Redfearn, — Ohio App. 3d —, 2007 Ohio 4108, — N.E. 2d —, 2007 Ohio App. LEXIS 3736 (Aug. 13, 2007).

In an action seeking a civil protection order, the trial court did not commit plain error in admitting into evidence hearsay statements of a minor child indicating that the child had been sexually abused by her father. The court reviewed the record and concluded that the statements relied upon by the trial court were not the statements contained in the Ohio R. Evid. 807 notice filed by the mother and the child, and as a result, the trial court's failure to determine the child's competency, as required by Ohio R. Evid. 807, was not plain error since the statements introduced were not admitted under Ohio R. Evid. 807. Ross v. Ross, — Ohio App. 3d —, 2006 Ohio 5274, — N.E. 2d —, 2006 Ohio App. LEXIS 5256 (Aug. 18, 2006).

Competency determination

Trial court must find that a declarant under the age of ten was competent at the time that the statement was made in order to admit that statement under EvidR 807. The alleged child-victim's death prevented the trial court from making a determination of competence: State v. Silverman, 176 Ohio App. 3d 12, 2008 Ohio 618, 889 N.E.2d 1034, 2008 Ohio App. LEXIS 532 (2008).

Statement of examining physician

In a prosecution for gross sexual imposition against a child victim, a psychologist's testimony relating the child victim's identification of defendant as the perpetrator of abuse against the victim was properly admitted, under Ohio R. Evid. 803(4) and 807, because the victim made the statements to the psychologist for the purposes of diagnosis and treatment. State v. Abner, — Ohio App. 3d —, 2007 Ohio 3053, — N.E. 2d —, 2007 Ohio App. LEXIS 2796 (June 18, 2007).

ARTICLE IX
AUTHENTICATION AND IDENTIFICATION

RULE 901. Requirement of Authentication or Identification

(A) **General provision.** The requirement of authentication or identification as a condition precedent to admissibility is satisfied by evidence sufficient to support a finding that the matter in question is what its proponent claims.

(B) **Illustrations.** By way of illustration only, and not by way of limitation, the following are examples of authentication or identification conforming with the requirements of this rule:

(1) Testimony of witness with knowledge. Testimony that a matter is what it is claimed to be.

(2) Nonexpert opinion on handwriting. Nonexpert opinion as to the genuineness of handwriting, based upon familiarity not acquired for purposes of the litigation.

(3) Comparison by trier or expert witness. Comparison by the trier of fact or by expert witness with specimens which have been authenticated.

(4) Distinctive characteristics and the like. Appearance, contents, substance, internal patterns, or other distinctive characteristics, taken in conjunction with circumstances.

(5) Voice identification. Identification of a voice, whether heard firsthand or through mechanical or electronic transmission or recording, by opinion based upon hearing the voice at any time under circumstances connecting it with the alleged speaker.

(6) Telephone conversation. Telephone conversations, by evidence that a call was made to the number assigned at the time by the telephone company to a particular person or business, if (a) in the case of a person, circumstances, including self-identification, show the person answering to be the one called, or (b) in the case of a business, the call was made to a place of business and the conversation related to business reasonably transacted over the telephone.

(7) Public records or reports. Evidence that a writing authorized by law to be recorded or filed and in fact recorded or filed in a public office, or a purported

public record, report, statement, or data compilation, in any form, is from the public office where items of this nature are kept.

(8) Ancient documents or data compilation. Evidence that a document or data compilation, in any form, (a) is in such condition as to create no suspicion concerning its authenticity, (b) was in a place where it, if authentic, would likely be, and (c) has been in existence twenty years or more at the time it is offered.

(9) Process or system. Evidence describing a process or system used to produce a result and showing that the process or system produces an accurate result.

(10) Methods provided by statute or rule. Any method of authentication or identification provided by statute enacted by the General Assembly not in conflict with a rule of the Supreme Court of Ohio by other rules prescribed by the Supreme Court.

NOTES TO DECISIONS

Analysis

Admissibility
Assignment of account
Authentication
Authentication of business records
Authentication of LEADS report
Authentication requirement
Calls to 911
Chain of custody
Default judgment
Exclusion of evidence
Handwriting
Harmless error
Phone calls
Photographic evidence
Silent witness theory
Telephone calls
Videotaped deposition
Voice identification
Witness testimony

Admissibility

Documents offered by the parties purporting to be from a court in California were not authenticated by any public office in that state. As such, they were not admissible as evidence, and should not have been considered by the trial court. Watson v. Watson, — Ohio App. 3d —, 2007 Ohio 468, — N.E. 2d —, 2007 Ohio App. LEXIS 417 (Feb. 2, 2007).

Assignment of account

Assignee of a credit card account did not properly authenticate the assignment of the account via an accompanying affidavit. Assignee was not entitled to summary judgment where it did not provide documentation of the credits and debits that led to the starting balance on the account: Great America Fin. v. Felty, 170 Ohio App. 3d 737, 2006 Ohio 6618, N.E.2d 30, 2006 Ohio App. LEXIS 6547 (2006).

Authentication

Defendant's counsel did not provide ineffective assistance in violation of U.S. Const. amend. VI and Ohio Const. art. I, when he failed to object to the admission of a photo that was properly authenticated for purposes of Ohio R. Evid. 901(A), such that any objection thereto would have been meritless. State v. Jones, — Ohio App. 3d —, 2007 Ohio 563, — N.E. —, 2007 Ohio App. LEXIS 526 (Feb. 9, 2007).

Court rejected defendant's contention that the State failed to prove that the cocaine admitted into evidence at trial was the same cocaine allegedly sold to the police officer.

Defendant not only failed to make a chain of custody objection under Ohio R. Evid. 901, he actually stipulated to the admissibility and identification of the cocaine at issue; thus, he waived his right to assert a chain of custody objection on appeal. State v. Townsend, — Ohio App. 3d —, 2007 Ohio 4421, — N.E. 2d —, 2007 Ohio App. LEXIS 3984 (Aug. 29, 2007).

Trial court did not abuse its discretion in admitting evidence regarding a former wife's lawsuit against her former employer, as it was relevant pursuant to Ohio R. Evid. 402 to show that she had been fired from her job and that she had enough funds to pay an attorney, as her claim against her former husband with respect to recoupment of loan payments that she had made was that she was in dire financial circumstances at that time; a claim that the court opinion from the employment action was not properly authenticated under Ohio R. Evid. 901 lacked merit, as the document was referred to by one party, its existence was admitted by the other party, a review of the court file indicated that such a document in fact existed, but it was not proffered into evidence. Kovacic v. Kovacic, — Ohio App. 3d —, 2007 Ohio 5956, — N.E. 2d —, 2007 Ohio App. LEXIS 5226 (Nov. 8, 2007).

Trial court properly awarded a husband a portion of his pension plan as his separate property, as his statement of participation in his employer's pension plan was properly admitted pursuant to Ohio R. Evid. 901(A) where it was authenticated as an accurate and true document of the pension accounts and where there was testimony that the employer did not keep such records after a set period of time; further, the document was not hearsay under Ohio R. Evid. 803(A)(15). Yasinow v. Yasinow, — Ohio App. 3d —, 2006 Ohio 1355, — N.E. 2d —, 2006 Ohio App. LEXIS 1237 (Mar. 23, 2006).

In a customer's suit to recover for injuries she sustained on a property owner's property, the trial court properly considered a photograph attached to the owner's motion for summary judgment because, pursuant to Ohio R. Evid. 901(B)(1) and Ohio R. Civ. P. 36(B), the photograph was properly authenticated by the customer in her answer to a request for admission. It was not required to be marked as an exhibit to have evidentiary value. Haymond v. BP America, — Ohio App. 3d —, 2006 Ohio 2732, — N.E. 2d —, 2006 Ohio App. LEXIS 2585 (June 1, 2006).

Pursuant to Ohio R. Evid. 901, an ex-wife's testimony as to her necessary medical treatment and the resulting medical bills was sufficient to support a finding that the medical bills were what the ex-wife purported them to be. Accordingly, the ex-husband's objection that the bills had not been authenticated was properly overruled. Redman v. Francis, — Ohio App. 3d —, 2006 Ohio 3640, — N.E. 2d —, 2006 Ohio App. LEXIS 3566 (July 10, 2006).

Other than asserting that the micro cassette that contained the recorded interview of defendant by the detective was cumulative evidence, defendant failed to demonstrate how he was materially prejudiced by its admission because the tape was properly authenticated by the detective and was a "statement by a party opponent" pursuant to Evid. R. 801(D)(2). The contents of the tape could clearly have aided the jury in reaching a verdict and thus, the micro cassette was not cumulative in nature and the trial court did not abuse its discretion in admitting said evidence. State v. Arrone, — Ohio App. 3d —, 2006 Ohio 4144, — N.E. 2d —, 2006 Ohio App. LEXIS 4125 (Aug. 11, 2006).

In a felonious assault prosecution, when letters defendant wrote to the victim after he was arrested were offered into evidence, the letters were sufficiently authenticated, under Ohio R. Evid. 901(A), because the testimony supported an inference that the victim could identify defendant's handwriting on the letters, as they had dated for 23 years, lived together for part of that time, and had children together, and one of the letters contained nicknames defendant customarily used for himself and for the victim, and, under Ohio R. Evid. 901(B)(2), a lay witness could testify to the authenticity of a handwritten document based on a familiarity not acquired for purposes of litigation. State v. Ramos, — Ohio App. 3d —, 2006 Ohio 4534, — N.E. 2d —, 2006 Ohio App. LEXIS 4517 (Sept. 5, 2006).

Lay witness could testify as to the authenticity of a hand-written document based upon familiarity not acquired for purposes of the litigation, under Ohio R. Evid. 901(B)(2), and a party seeking to authenticate a writing only had to offer legally sufficient evidence that the document was what that party claimed it to be, under Ohio R. Evid. 901(A). State v. Ramos, — Ohio App. 3d —, 2006 Ohio 4534, — N.E. 2d —, 2006 Ohio App. LEXIS 4517 (Sept. 5, 2006).

In a dependency proceeding pursuant to RC § 2151.04(D), the trial court's admission of a document that purported to be a copy of a judgment from another court was proper, as it was authenticated under Evid. R. 901(B)(7) for purposes of showing abuse by the mother of another sibling and that the child had been previously adjudicated dependent, and any error was harmless because the mother testified to the substance thereof. In re E. R., — Ohio App. 3d —, 2006 Ohio 4816, — N.E. 2d —, 2006 Ohio App. LEXIS 4745 (Sept. 18, 2006).

Evidence offered by the State was sufficient for purposes of authentication under Ohio R. Evid. 901(A) in defendant's criminal trial on charges of violating RC § 2907.321(A)(2) and (5) where the images on defendant's computer that were deemed obscene and depicted children being spanked were found to have been of real children. The authentication was satisfied through testimony of police witnesses and another individual involved in the criminal conduct. State v. Gillingham, — Ohio App. 3d —, 2006 Ohio 5758, — N.E. 2d —, 2006 Ohio App. LEXIS 5738 (Oct. 27, 2006).

There was no abuse of discretion in the trial court's admittance of the document showing that the marital residence was built with family funds because it was properly authenticated by the wife. She testified that the exhibit was an accurate and true document given to the parties by Barry's mother. Weisbecker v. Weisbecker, — Ohio App. 3d —, 2006 Ohio 5840, — N.E. 2d —, 2006 Ohio App. LEXIS 5794 (Nov. 6, 2006).

Although invoices admitted on behalf of a builder in his unjust enrichment claim against property owners who refused to pay for additions in the construction of their home were properly authenticated under Ohio R. Evid. 901(A), as the builder properly identified the invoices and sufficiently described them, some were improperly admitted where they did not distinguish between the cost of the additions and the cost of any overages under the contract. Ward v. Geiger, — Ohio App. 3d —, 2006 Ohio 6853, — N.E. 2d —, 2006 Ohio App. LEXIS 6768 (Dec. 26, 2006).

Authentication of business records

Summary judgment was properly granted to a merchandise seller in its action, seeking recovery of sums due from a contracting company and its president as personal guarantor, as the supporting materials included validation of the debt by the seller's records custodian and a copy of the personal guarantee; the custodian had properly authenticated the records and documents pursuant to Ohio R. Evid. 901(B)(10) and 803(6), and as there was no assertion that a copy of the guarantee did not suffice under Ohio R. Evid. 1003, any such challenge thereto on appeal was deemed waived. Ohio Cat v. N. Valley Contrs., — Ohio App. 3d —, 2007 Ohio 5050, — N.E. 2d —, 2007 Ohio App. LEXIS 4463 (Sept. 24, 2007).

Trial court properly admitted into evidence on a summary judgment motion documents that had been properly authenticated by a custodian of records pursuant to Ohio R. Evid. 901, and which were business records under Ohio R. Evid. 803(6) that were deemed reliable and trustworthy. The

records properly admitted included a credit card application and credit card statements in an action by an assignee of the issuer, seeking recovery of an amount owed on the account. Great Seneca Fin. v. Felty, 170 Ohio App. 3d 737, 2006 Ohio 6618, 869 N.E.2d 30, 2006 Ohio App. LEXIS 6547 (2006).

Authentication of LEADS report

In defendant's prosecution for receiving stolen property, the trial court properly admitted into evidence reports from the Law Enforcement Automated Data System (LEADS) as the public records hearsay exception under Ohio R. Evid. 803(8)(a) applied to the LEADS report, in that the reports contained only the routine activities of a public agency relative to the ownership of a vehicle. Moreover, the officer properly authenticated the LEADS printout in his testimony pursuant to Ohio R. Evid. 901 by his testimony as to how the system worked and the nature of the LEADS training that he obtained and his statement that the printout was identical to the report on the computer screen in his car that he used during the incident with defendant. State v. Papusha, — Ohio App. 3d —, 2007 Ohio 3966, — N.E. 2d —, 2007 Ohio App. LEXIS 3606 (Aug. 6, 2007).

Authentication requirement

Trial court properly used its broad discretion to exclude the DNA report because it appeared that the defense purposefully failed to mention the asterisked statement regarding additional unidentifiable DNA while the authoring witness was on the stand so that they could refer to the part that seemed to benefit them in closing arguments without her rebutting testimony and the defense did not have their own DNA expert mention the supposed existence of a third type of DNA. Neither the State nor the defense introduced, authenticated, or identified the report in their cases and the tactics used by the defense showed a desire to mislead or confuse the jury. State v. Charley, — Ohio App. 3d —, 2007 Ohio 1108, — N.E. 2d —, 2007 Ohio App. LEXIS 1029 (Mar. 6, 2007).

Because a township board of trustees did not call an alleged lessee or her former attorney or a witness with a generalized knowledge of the lessee's signature to authenticate a written lease between the parties under Ohio R. Evid. 901, a copy of the written lease was properly excluded from the trial in the board's action alleging a breach of the lease. Chester Twp. Bd. of Trs. v. Spellman, — Ohio App. 3d —, 2007 Ohio 5221, — N.E. 2d —, 2007 Ohio App. LEXIS 4592 (Sept. 28, 2007).

Where a city employee "certified" the authenticity of ordinances attached to referendum petitions and it was undisputed that the documents attached to those petitions were in fact true and accurate copies of the ordinances, such was sufficient under RC § 731.32, as the statute did not required a "certified copy" of the ordinance to be signed by the city clerk of council as the official custodian of the applicable records; although Ohio R. Civ. P. 44 and Ohio R. Evid. 901(B) set out requirements for establishing the authenticity of public records, such was applicable to litigation, pursuant to Ohio R. Civ. P. 1(A), and as they were not specifically referenced in Ohio's election law statutes, they were not the only required method pursuant to RC § 731.32. Rankin v. Underwood, — Ohio App. 3d —, 2006 Ohio 1237, — N.E. 2d —, 2006 Ohio App. LEXIS 1098 (Mar. 17, 2006).

Trial court erred in considering documents that purported to assign a credit card account from an issuer to various entities and ultimately to an assignee who brought a claim against the credit card holder, seeking recovery of sums due under the account, as the assignee did not include an affidavit or other documentation that authenticated the records pursuant to Ohio R. Evid. 901(B)(10), and it did not set forth a proper foundation for their admissibility into evidence under Ohio R. Evid. 803(6). Great Seneca Fin. v. Felty, 170 Ohio App. 3d 737, 2006 Ohio 6618, 869 N.E.2d 30, 2006 Ohio App. LEXIS 6547 (2006).

Calls to 911

Testimony of the police detective who obtained the tape through the chain of custody and the testimony of both the victim and defendant provided sufficient evidence from which to conclude that the evidence was what the State purported it to be, namely, 911 calls made from defendant's mother's home on the date in question. Thus, the 911 tape was sufficiently authenticated. State v. Mitchell, — Ohio App. 3d —, 2007 Ohio 1696, — N.E. 2d —, 2007 Ohio App. LEXIS 1554 (Apr. 12, 2007).

Chain of custody

Under Ohio R. Evid. 901(A), it was not plain error, under Ohio R. Crim. P. 52(B), to admit a baggy of crack cocaine and two crack pipes in defendant's prosecution for possession of crack cocaine, under RC § 2925.11(A), because an officer identified the baggy and pipes as the same ones he seized from defendant when arresting him, and a lab technician testified that the substance in the baggy was crack cocaine and that the pipes contained crack cocaine residue, even though there was a seven-day lapse between defendant's arrest and submission of the evidence to the crime lab. State v. Semedo, — Ohio App. 3d —, 2007 Ohio 1805, — N.E. 2d —, 2007 Ohio App. LEXIS 1641 (Apr. 16, 2007).

In a prosecution for felonious assault with a firearm specification, a shotgun's chain of custody was adequately shown when (1) an officer testified to the officer's collection of the gun from the crime scene, (1) the officer testified to the officer's securing and storage of the gun until it was sent to the crime lab, and (3) the officer identified it at trial, and crime lab personnel testimony was unnecessary because the gun's operability was not questioned. State v. Rigdon, — Ohio App. 3d —, 2007 Ohio 2843, — N.E. 2d —, 2007 Ohio App. LEXIS 2638 (June 11, 2007).

When appellant was prosecuted for cocaine possession, a sufficient chain of custody was shown because competent credible evidence showed the drugs seized from appellant were the same drugs analyzed by a crime lab. In re Jackson, — Ohio App. 3d —, 2007 Ohio 4955, — N.E. 2d —, 2007 Ohio App. LEXIS 4418 (Sept. 21, 2007).

Gun seized from defendant was properly admitted into evidence pursuant to Ohio R. Evid. 901 as the police officer who watched defendant being searched and marked the gun into the police property book established a sufficient chain of custody. State v. Sims, — Ohio App. 3d —, 2007 Ohio 6821, — N.E. 2d —, 2007 Ohio App. LEXIS 5968 (Dec. 20, 2007).

Absent any evidence that the stolen merchandise had been tampered with or altered after it was taken from defendant, it could not be said that the trial court erred in admitting the exhibits. The police officer and the store manager identified the items that had been stolen, which was sufficient to demonstrate that the items were the ones that had been stolen, pursuant to Ohio R. Evid. 901. State v. Rodriguez, — Ohio App. 3d —, 2006 Ohio 2121, — N.E. 2d —, 2006 Ohio App. LEXIS 1953 (Apr. 28, 2006).

When, in a prosecution for trafficking in cocaine, under RC § 2925.03(A)(1), an agent testified that alleged controlled substances offered at trial did not have the same appearance as when they were sent to a testing laboratory, this did not preclude their admission, under Ohio R. Evid. 901, because the agent testified that each substance was substantially the same after its return from the lab except for additional markings indicating chain of custody, a changed appearance for testing purposes, and being repacked into smaller bags, and he said drugs sent for testing were usually returned in an altered form, so the difference in appearance went to the weight the jury could give the exhibits, rather than to their admissibility. State v. Smith, — Ohio App. 3d —, 2006 Ohio 4684, — N.E. 2d —, 2006 Ohio App. LEXIS 4604 (Sept. 8, 2006).

Chain of custody is part of the authentication and identification requirement in Ohio R. Evid. 901, and the prosecution, in a criminal case, bears the burden of establishing a proper chain of custody, but the State has no duty to eliminate every possibility that tampering or substitution occurred, as the State must only show that it is reasonably certain that a substitution, tampering, or alteration did not occur. State v. Smith, — Ohio App. 3d —, 2006 Ohio 4684, — N.E. 2d —, 2006 Ohio App. LEXIS 4604 (Sept. 8, 2006).

Trial court committed plain error by granting the State's motion in limine and prohibiting the introduction of the surveillance videotape or any mention of it during trial, pursuant to Ohio R. Evid. 901, because the ruling went to the heart of defendant's charges and, had the trial court allowed the videotape, the outcome of the trial clearly may have been different. Any break in the chain of custody should have gone to the weight of the evidence, and not to its overall admissibility. State v. Jackim, — Ohio App. 3d —, 2006 Ohio 4756, — N.E. 2d —, 2006 Ohio App. LEXIS 4678 (Sept. 14, 2006).

While authentication of evidence was a condition precedent to its admission, the condition was satisfied when the evidence was sufficient to support a finding that the matter in question was what its proponent claimed, under Ohio R. Evid. 901(A), and the possibility of contamination went to weight, not admissibility, so a strict chain of evidence was not always necessary for the admission of physical evidence, and evidence of a process or system to produce an accurate result was sufficient to satisfy the Rule, under Ohio R. Evid. 901(B)(9). State v. Hunter, — Ohio App. 3d —, 2006 Ohio 5113, — N.E. 2d —, 2006 Ohio App. LEXIS 5028 (Sept. 29, 2006).

When defendant's rape conviction was based on a comparison, ten years after his crime, of a deoxyribonucleic acid (DNA) sample from a rape kit taken at the time of the crime to a database of such samples taken from offenders, a chain of custody, under Ohio R. Evid. 901(A), of the original rape kit was sufficiently shown through hospital business records showing the kit was used to obtain evidence from the victim, which she confirmed, and turned over to law enforcement, whose records showed a certain officer delivered the kit to a crime lab, as evidence of a process or system designed to produce an accurate result, such as hospital and law enforcement records, was sufficient to satisfy the Rule, under Ohio R. Evid. 901(B)(9). State v. Hunter, — Ohio App. 3d —, 2006 Ohio 5113, — N.E. 2d —, 2006 Ohio App. LEXIS 5028 (Sept. 29, 2006).

Default judgment

Even though a party defaults and admits the allegations of the complaint, a plaintiff must still establish his damages. Social security records were not properly authenticated, and were not admissible merely because they looked like official agency documents. However, the amount of loan proceeds appropriated by the defendant and the conversion of the life insurance policies were properly established: Reinbolt v. Kern, 183 Ohio App. 3d 287, 2009 Ohio 3492, 916 N.E.2d 1100, 2009 Ohio App. LEXIS 3027 (2009).

Exclusion of evidence

Trial court's exclusion of a letter sent to a deceased patient after her death was proper pursuant to Ohio R. Evid. 901(A) in the patient's children's medical malpractice action, as there was insufficient evidence to show that the letter was advice from the patient's treating cardiologist that her condition could have been managed by rehabilitation rather than by a surgical procedure, which resulted in her death. Exclusion due to improper authentication was proper in the circumstances. Joiner v. Simon, — Ohio App. 3d —, 2007 Ohio 425, — N.E. 2d —, 2007 Ohio App. LEXIS 372 (Feb. 2, 2007).

Handwriting

Ohio R. Evid. 901(B)(3) provided that a factfinder's comparison of a disputed item with an authenticated handwriting sample was sufficient to support a finding as to the validity of a handwriting sample, and a trier of fact could make a comparison of a known writing by a person with other writings without the assistance of an expert or a lay witness to determine whether all the writings were executed by the same person. Medina Drywall Supply v. Procom Stucco Sys., — Ohio App. 3d —, 2006 Ohio 5062, — N.E. 2d —, 2006 Ohio App. LEXIS 4985 (Sept. 29, 2006).

In a supplier's suit against the alleged guarantor of debtors' obligation to the supplier, it was not an abuse of discretion, under Ohio R. Civ. P. 53(E)(4), for a trial court to adopt a magistrate's finding that the guarantor did not sign a contract guaranteeing the debtors' obligation because, under Ohio R. Evid. 901(B)(3), the magistrate could compare the disputed signature with known examples of the guarantor's handwriting without further testimony and determine whether the signatures were made by the same person. Medina Drywall Supply v. Procom Stucco Sys., — Ohio App. 3d —, 2006 Ohio 5062, — N.E. 2d —, 2006 Ohio App. LEXIS 4985 (Sept. 29, 2006).

Harmless error

Defendant's failure to object to the City's failure to properly authenticate under Ohio R. Evid. 901 a 911 tape at trial, used to establish that one of the City's witnesses called 911 immediately after seeing a car crash, waived all but plain error for appeal. Since the City presented other admissible evidence that contradicted the testimony of defendant's witness that a female, not defendant, was driving the car at the time of the accident, the jury could have convicted defendant solely on the testimony of the City's witnesses without the unauthenticated 911 tape. City of Akron v. Stalnaker, — Ohio App. 3d —, 2007 Ohio 6789, — N.E. 2d —, 2007 Ohio App. LEXIS 5953 (Dec. 19, 2007).

Phone calls

Detective's testimony regarding his conversation with defendant arguably met the requirements of Ohio R. Evid. 901 because the detective testified that he called the telephone number for defendant appearing on his computer program; the detective spoke with defendant after his arrest and in retrospect could determine the voice to be the same, though he did not explicitly testify to the sameness. Given the broad latitude the trial court has in determining the admissibility of evidence, the trial court arguably was within its discretion in allowing the testimony under such facts because, even if the testimony were inadmissible, the record did not show the requisite prejudice since defendant, who was not under arrest, simply opted not to voluntarily speak with law enforcement when he failed to appear at police headquarters, a decision that did not carry with it the same inference of guilt associated with fleeing. State v. Kelly, — Ohio App. 3d —, 2007 Ohio 4406, — N.E. 2d —, 2007 Ohio App. LEXIS 3977 (Aug. 28, 2007).

There was no basis to find that trial counsel was ineffective because the audio tapes of defendant's telephone calls in violation of the protection order were authenticated when the victim identified them as telephone calls from defendant and identified his voice on the tapes, pursuant to Ohio R. Evid. 901(A), (B)(5) and (6); counsel could not have been ineffective in failing to object to properly authenticated and identified, non-hearsay and defendant admitted that he made the calls. Also, defendant did not support his claim that he opposed the continuances and there was no basis to conclude that, by giving professional advice as to what counsel felt was in the best interests of his client, that counsel was derelict in his performance. State v. Simms, — Ohio App. 3d —, 2006 Ohio 2960, — N.E. 2d —, 2006 Ohio App. LEXIS 2853 (June 13, 2006).

Telephonic statements made to police were properly admitted in defendant's felonious assault prosecution because they were sufficiently authenticated, under Ohio R. Evid. 901(B)(6), when defendant's victim, who was his wife, gave police her home telephone number, which was also defendant's home telephone number, they called the number and asked for defendant, and the person answering the telephone identified himself as defendant. State v. Marcum, — Ohio App. 3d —, 2006 Ohio 7068, — N.E. 2d —, 2006 Ohio App. LEXIS 6995 (Dec. 28, 2006).

Photographic evidence

In defendant's assault trial, photographs of defendant's victim's injuries were properly admitted without the testimony of the person who took the photographs because, under Ohio R. Evid. 901, such testimony was not required since the witness who testified said the witness was familiar with the victim's injuries and that the photographs accurately depicted those injuries. State v. Andric, — Ohio App. 3d —, 2007 Ohio 6701, — N.E. 2d —, 2007 Ohio App. LEXIS 5856 (Dec. 14, 2007).

Trial court correctly admitted Exhibit 21, which contained digital images of child pornography from defendant's computer, because the State adduced sufficient testimony from the computer forensic analyst and the detective to authenticate or identify the images comprising Exhibit 21 as duplicates of the images appearing on defendant's computer. State v. Taylor, — Ohio App. 3d —, 2006 Ohio 6813, — N.E. 2d —, 2006 Ohio App. LEXIS 6748 (Dec. 22, 2006).

Silent witness theory

Trial court did not err in overruling defendant's objection to the State's exhibit. Because the store manager testified with respect to the reliability of the process that produced the images and that the images represented what the State purported, that defendant robbed and bit the victim, the exhibit was properly authenticated pursuant to the silent witness theory. State v. Vonbergen, — Ohio App. 3d —, 2006 Ohio 2769, — N.E. 2d —, 2006 Ohio App. LEXIS 2606 (June 2, 2006).

Telephone calls

Trial court was within its discretion to admit the tape recording into evidence because the victim had called the telephone number for defendant's mother, when a male who identified himself as defendant answered and apologized for the assault; the victim clearly identified defendant as the primary person who assaulted him. The trial court could clearly have found that the person who had answered the telephone and was recorded was the same person who was on trial for the assault. State v. Warsame, — Ohio App. 3d —, 2007 Ohio 3656, — N.E. 2d —, 2007 Ohio App. LEXIS 3334 (July 19, 2007).

Videotaped deposition

Trial court did not err in permitting the jury to view the videotaped deposition of the officer's deposition because the officer was scheduled to be out of town on the trial date and his testimony was material to the case. The Confrontation Clause was not violated because defendant and counsel were present and participated in the deposition and cross-examined the officer extensively, and it was properly authenticated because the record contained a written transcription of the officer's deposition, filed with the trial court, with a certification from the court reporter that the officer was duly sworn and the typed transcript was true and correct. State v. Hill, — Ohio App. 3d —, 2007 Ohio 56, — N.E. 2d —, 2007 Ohio App. LEXIS 51 (Jan. 5, 2007).

Voice identification

Trial court properly admitted a tape recording of a telephone conversation between defendant and a confidential informant with respect to an anticipated drug transaction after the informant testified that he knew defendant was the other party on the telephone due to voice identification, as the recording was properly authenticated pursuant to Ohio R.

Evid. 901(B)(5). State v. Rampey, — Ohio App. 3d —, 2006 Ohio 1383, — N.E. 2d —, 2006 Ohio App. LEXIS 1256 (Mar. 20, 2006).

There was no error in admitting the tape recording of defendant talking to his girlfriend on the telephone from jail because it was sufficiently authenticated, pursuant to Ohio R. Evid. 901. The police officer testified that the voices on the tape were those of defendant and defendant's girlfriend and the officer had heard them both speak before. There were also circumstances corroborating the officer's in-court identification of the voices on the tape recording. State v. Bowshier, 167 Ohio App. 3d 87, 2006 Ohio 2822, 853 N.E. 2d 1210, 2006 Ohio App. LEXIS 2645 (June 2, 2006).

Witness testimony

Trial court did not err in admitting into evidence a "transcript" of a hearing in probate court because the probate judge properly authenticated the exhibit for purposes of admitting it into evidence, pursuant to Ohio R. Evid. 901(A), and the trial court did not abuse its discretion in concluding that the State authenticated the transcript. The judge verified that the exhibit fairly and accurately depicted what transpired at the hearing and that no substantial variances existed between the digital recording and the transcript. State v. Silverman, — Ohio App. 3d —, 2006 Ohio 3826, — N.E. 2d —, 2006 Ohio App. LEXIS 3791 (July 27, 2006).

RULE 902.   Self-Authentication

Extrinsic evidence of authenticity as a condition precedent to admissibility is not required with respect to the following:

(1) Domestic public documents under seal. A document bearing a seal purporting to be that of the United States, or of any State, district, Commonwealth, territory, or insular possession thereof, or the Panama Canal Zone, or the Trust Territory of the Pacific Islands, or of a political subdivision, department, officer, or agency thereof, and a signature purporting to be an attestation or execution.

(2) Domestic public documents not under seal. A document purporting to bear the signature in the official capacity of an officer or employee of any entity included in paragraph (1) hereof, having no seal, if a public officer having a seal and having official duties in the district or political subdivision of the officer or employee certifies under seal that the signer has the official capacity and that the signature is genuine.

(3) Foreign public documents. A document purporting to be executed or attested in the official capacity by a person authorized by the laws of a foreign country to make the execution or attestation, and accompanied by a final certification as to the genuineness of the signature and official position (a) of the executing or attesting person, or (b) of any foreign official whose certificate of genuineness of signature and official position relates to the execution or attestation or is in a chain of certificates of genuineness of signature and official position relating to the execution or attestation. A final certification may be made by a secretary of embassy or legation, consul general, consul, vice consul, or consular agent of the United States, or a diplomatic or consular official of the foreign country assigned or accredited to the United States. If reasonable opportunity has been given to all parties to investigate the authenticity and accuracy of official documents, the court may, for good cause shown, order that they be treated as presumptively authentic without final certification or permit them to be evidenced by an attested summary with or without final certification.

(4) Certified copies of public records. A copy of an official record or report or entry therein, or of a document authorized by law to be recorded or filed and actually recorded or filed in a public office, including data compilations in any form, certified as correct by the custodian or other person authorized to make the certification, by certificate complying with paragraph (1), (2), or (3) of this rule or complying with any law of a jurisdiction, state or federal, or rule prescribed by the Supreme Court of Ohio.

(5) Official publications. Books, pamphlets, or other publications purporting to be issued by public authority.

(6) Newspapers and periodicals. Printed materials purporting to be newspapers or periodicals, including notices and advertisements contained therein.

(7) Trade inscriptions and the like. Inscriptions, signs, tags, or labels purporting to have been affixed in the course of business and indicating ownership, control, or origin.

(8) Acknowledged documents. Documents accompanied by a certificate of acknowledgment executed in the manner provided by law by a notary public or other officer authorized by law to take acknowledgments.

(9) Commercial paper and related documents. Commercial paper, signatures thereon, and documents relating thereto to the extent provided by general commercial law.

(10) Presumptions created by law. Any signature, document, or other matter declared by any law of a jurisdiction, state or federal, to be presumptively or prima facie genuine or authentic.

History: Amended, eff 7-1-07.

NOTES TO DECISIONS

ANALYSIS

Admission of document into evidence
Domestic public documents
Public records
Self authenticating documents

Admission of document into evidence

Trial court's determination that defendant violated his community control sanction was supported by sufficient evidence, based on testimony from a Kentucky police officer that defendant had been arrested for an incident with a 15-year-old girl and that he was in possession of pornographic material, both of which were prohibited as conditions of his sanction. The testimony was admissible because the Rules of Evidence were inapplicable to such a proceeding pursuant to Ohio R. Evid. 101(C), and a certified copy of the conviction in Kentucky was admissible pursuant to Ohio R. Evid. 902(1). State v. Kincer, — Ohio App. 3d —, 2006 Ohio 2249, — N.E. 2d —, 2006 Ohio App. LEXIS 2087 (May 8, 2006).

Domestic public documents

Trial court did not abuse its discretion when it declined to consider a lessee's evidence of a certificate of incorporation, submitted in support of its claim in opposition to the lessor's motion for summary judgment that it could not have signed the lease in question because it was not in existence on the date that the lease was signed, because, though the certificate was a domestic public document under seal within the meaning of Ohio Evid. R. 902(1), the document was clearly a copy, and the lessee offered no evidence that the copy of the certificate it proffered was a true and correct copy, as required by Ohio R. Evid. 1005. Cong. Park Bus. Ctr., LLC v. Nitelites, Inc., — Ohio App. 3d —, 2007 Ohio 4200, — N.E. 2d —, 2007 Ohio App. LEXIS 3789 (Aug. 17, 2007).

Public records

Although a probate court erroneously admitted a letter from a nursing home supervisor for a county agency with respect to a dispute over rent due by a decedent's son who had lived in the decedent's home after her death, the admission was not prejudicial error where the decedent's estate administrator testified as to the contents of the letter. Although the letter was a valid public record and an official record, pursuant to Ohio R. Evid. 803(8) and RC § 2317.42, it was not properly authenticated under Ohio R. Evid. 902(2). In re Estate of Visnich, — Ohio App. 3d —, 2006 Ohio 5499, — N.E. 2d —, 2006 Ohio App. LEXIS 5477 (Oct. 23, 2006).

Self authenticating documents

While newspaper articles were self-authenticating pursuant to Ohio R. Evid. 902(6), they were inadmissible if offered to prove the truth of a matter asserted in an out-of-court statement because newspaper articles were generally inadmissible as evidence of the facts stated within the article because they were hearsay not within any exception. Consumer Portfolio Servs. v. Staples, — Ohio App. 3d —, 2007 Ohio 1531, — N.E. 2d —, 2007 Ohio App. LEXIS 1400 (Mar. 30, 2007).

RULE 903. Subscribing Witness' Testimony Unnecessary

The testimony of a subscribing witness is not necessary to authenticate a writing unless required by the laws of the jurisdiction whose laws govern the validity of the writing.

ARTICLE X
CONTENTS OF WRITINGS, RECORDINGS AND PHOTOGRAPHS

RULE 1001. Definitions

For purposes of this article the following definitions are applicable:

(1) **Writings and recordings.** "Writings" and "recordings" consist of letters, words, or numbers, or their equivalent, set down by handwriting, typewriting, printing, photostating, photographing, magnetic impulse, mechanical or electronic recording, or other forms of date compilation.

(2) **Photographs.** "Photographs" include still photographs, X-ray films, video tapes, and motion pictures.

(3) **Original.** An "original" of a writing or recording is the writing or recording itself or any counterpart intended to have the same effect by a person executing or issuing it. An "original" of photograph includes the negative or any print therefrom. If data are stored in a computer or similar device, any printout or other output readable by sight, shown to reflect the data accurately, is an "original."

(4) **Duplicate.** A "duplicate" is a counterpart produced by the same impression as the original, or from the same matrix, or by means of photography, including enlargements and miniatures, or by mechanical or

electronic re-recording, or by chemical reproduction, or by other equivalent techniques which accurately reproduce the original.

NOTES TO DECISIONS
ANALYSIS

Originals
Photographic evidence

Originals

Photographs that are prints from a digital program will qualify as originals under Ohio R. Evid. 1001(3). State v. Gregory, — Ohio App. 3d —, 2006 Ohio 7037, — N.E. 2d —, 2006 Ohio App. LEXIS 7028 (Dec. 28, 2006).

Photographic evidence

Trial court correctly admitted Exhibit 21, which contained digital images of child pornography from defendant's computer, because the State adduced sufficient testimony from the computer forensic analyst and the detective to authenticate or identify the images comprising Exhibit 21 as duplicates of the images appearing on defendant's computer. State v. Taylor, — Ohio App. 3d —, 2006 Ohio 6813, — N.E. 2d —, 2006 Ohio App. LEXIS 6748 (Dec. 22, 2006).

RULE 1002. Requirement of Original

To prove the content of a writing, recording, or photograph, the original writing, recording, or photograph is required, except as otherwise provided in these rules or by statute enacted by the General Assembly not in conflict with a rule of the Supreme Court of Ohio.

NOTES TO DECISIONS
ANALYSIS

Best evidence rule
Discretion of trial court
Evidence which can be admitted
Photographic evidence
Videotape

Best evidence rule

In a prosecution under RC § 2913.43, EvidR 1002 required the state to offer the actual writing into evidence because the state was attempting to prove the content of the writing: State v. Cicerchi, 182 Ohio App. 3d 753, 2009 Ohio 2249, 915 N.E.2d 350, 2009 Ohio App. LEXIS 1923 (2009).

Fact that the original reel-to-reel recording of the 911 call was interpreted by the person who transcribed the recording as saying "Phillip" rather than "Phelp" was insufficient to demonstrate that the cassette tape that was admitted into evidence should have been excluded. The trial court acted within its discretion to allow the jury to decide what was said on the cassette tape and the fact that the transcriber got the name wrong did not create a genuine question regarding the authenticity of the cassette tape at issue, nor did it render the tape's admission unfair, for purposes of Ohio R. Evid. 1003. State v. Barton, — Ohio App. 3d —, 2007 Ohio 1099, — N.E. 2d —, 2007 Ohio App. LEXIS 1020 (Mar. 12, 2007).

When a creditor sued a debtor for the balance due on a credit card account, monthly statements of the debtor's account, rather than the original charge slips the debtor signed, were properly admissible to prove the amount due, under Ohio R. Evid. 1002, because the original charge slips had been destroyed, pursuant to the creditor's business policy, so Ohio R. Evid. 1004 applied, and it was not shown that there was any reason to believe that the amounts reflected in the statements were incorrect. Discover Bank v. Brockmeier, — Ohio App. 3d —, 2007 Ohio 1552, — N.E. 2d —, 2007 Ohio App. LEXIS 1419 (Apr. 2, 2007).

Court rejected defendant's contention that the trial court erred when it admitted the testimony of a prison inspector and that of a highway patrol trooper who participated in an investigation regarding the contents of a surveillance tape of the visiting room of a correctional institution on the ground that the admission of the testimony violated the best evidence rule of Ohio R. Evid. 1002 and defendant's right to due process under Ohio Const. art. I, § 16 because the testimony strongly suggested that the video recording was negligently destroyed, and thus, the testimony was admissible under Ohio R. Evid. 1004(1). Additionally, defendant had not proven that the video recording was materially exculpatory. State v. Patterson, — Ohio App. 3d —, 2006 Ohio 4439, — N.E. 2d —, 2006 Ohio App. LEXIS 4365 (Aug. 11, 2006).

Where parties to a commercial lease disputed the authority behind a letter notifying the lessee of the lease termination, the contents of the "writing" were not in issue and accordingly, the best evidence rule under Ohio R. Evid. 1002 was not implicated. Hi-Roc Condo. Unit Owners Assoc., Inc. v. HWC Realty Inc., — Ohio App. 3d —, — N.E. 2d —, 2006 Ohio App. LEXIS 4701 (Sept. 14, 2006).

Discretion of trial court

When, in defendant's conspiracy trial, a video transcript of a recording of his conversation with a confidential informant was admitted along with the recording, this did not offend either Ohio R. Evid. 1002 or 1003 because the recording was also admitted and available to the jury in deliberations and there were numerous assurances of its reliability. State v. Fitzgerald, — Ohio App. 3d —, 2007 Ohio 701, — N.E. 2d —, 2007 Ohio App. LEXIS 637 (Feb. 21, 2007).

Evidence which can be admitted

As a photograph of a victim's living room that depicted a photograph on a television which was purportedly of defendant and the victim's grandson was not a controlling issue in defendant's criminal matter, as he had admitted that he broke into the victim's home and committed various crimes there but he asserted the affirmative defense of duress, the fact that the original photograph of defendant and the grandson was not admitted into evidence did not violate the best evidence rule under Ohio R. Evid. 1002 and 1004(4). As there was no reasonable likelihood that any such objection thereto would have changed the outcome of the trial because defendant's relationship with the grandson was a collateral matter, defendant's counsel was not ineffective in failing to raise such an objection to that evidence. State v. Winn, 173 Ohio App. 3d 202, 2007 Ohio 4327, 877 N.E.2d 1020, 2007 Ohio App. LEXIS 3875 (2007).

Photographic evidence

Admission of a photograph of a purported photograph of the defendant did not violate the best evidence rule where the depicted photograph was not closely related to a controlling issue: State v. Winn, 173 Ohio App. 3d 202, 2007 Ohio 4327, 877 N.E.2d 1020, 2007 Ohio App. LEXIS 3875 (2007).

Videotape

Trial court erred when it held that EvidR 1002 barred consideration of a DVD that was a duplicate of a videotape recording made it India, since a videotape prepared in India could not be played on recorders in this country: Verma v. Verma, 179 Ohio App. 3d 637, 2008 Ohio 6244, 903 N.E.2d 343, 2008 Ohio App. LEXIS 5218 (2008).

RULE 1003. Admissibility of Duplicates

A duplicate is admissible to the same extent as an original unless (1) a genuine question is raised as to the authenticity of the original or (2) in the circumstances it would be unfair to admit the duplicate in lieu of the original.

NOTES TO DECISIONS

ANALYSIS

Admissibility of duplicate
Tape of 911 recording
Transcript

Admissibility of duplicate

Summary judgment was properly granted to a merchandise seller in its action, seeking recovery of sums due from a contracting company and its president as personal guarantor, as the supporting materials included validation of the debt by the seller's records custodian and a copy of the personal guarantee; the custodian had properly authenticated the records and documents pursuant to Ohio R. Evid. 901(B)(10) and 803(6), and as there was no assertion that a copy of the guarantee did not suffice under Ohio R. Evid. 1003, any such challenge thereto on appeal was deemed waived. Ohio Cat v. N. Valley Contrs., — Ohio App. 3d —, 2007 Ohio 5050, — N.E. 2d —, 2007 Ohio App. LEXIS 4463 (Sept. 24, 2007).

Tape of 911 recording

Fact that the original reel-to-reel recording of the 911 call was interpreted by the person who transcribed the recording as saying "Phillip" rather than "Phelp" was insufficient to demonstrate that the cassette tape that was admitted into evidence should have been excluded. The trial court acted within its discretion to allow the jury to decide what was said on the cassette tape and the fact that the transcriber got the name wrong did not create a genuine question regarding the authenticity of the cassette tape at issue, nor did it render the tape's admission unfair, for purposes of Ohio R. Evid. 1003. State v. Barton, — Ohio App. 3d —, 2007 Ohio 1099, — N.E. 2d —, 2007 Ohio App. LEXIS 1020 (Mar. 12, 2007).

Transcript

When, in defendant's conspiracy trial, a video transcript of a recording of his conversation with a confidential informant was admitted along with the recording, this did not offend either Ohio R. Evid. 1002 or 1003 because the recording was also admitted and available to the jury in deliberations and there were numerous assurances of its reliability. State v. Fitzgerald, — Ohio App. 3d —, 2007 Ohio 701, — N.E. 2d —, 2007 Ohio App. LEXIS 637 (Feb. 21, 2007).

RULE 1004. Admissibility of Other Evidence of Contents

The original is not required, and other evidence of the contents of a writing, recording, or photograph is admissible if:

(1) **Originals lost or destroyed.** All originals are lost or have been destroyed, unless the proponent lost or destroyed them in bad faith; or

(2) **Original not obtainable.** No original can be obtained by any available judicial process or procedure; or

(3) **Original in possession of opponent.** At a time when an original was under the control of the party against whom offered, that party was put on notice, by the pleadings or otherwise, that the contents would be subject of proof at the hearing, and that party does not produce the original at the hearing; or

(4) **Collateral matters.** The writing, recording, or photograph is not closely related to a controlling issue.

History: Amended, eff July 1, 2007.

NOTES TO DECISIONS

ANALYSIS

Original not required
Photograph of photograph
Secondary evidence

Original not required

As a photograph of a victim's living room that depicted a photograph on a television which was purportedly of defendant and the victim's grandson was not a controlling issue in defendant's criminal matter, as he had admitted that he broke into the victim's home and committed various crimes there but he asserted the affirmative defense of duress, the fact that the original photograph of defendant and the grandson was not admitted into evidence did not violate the best evidence rule under Ohio R. Evid. 1002 and 1004(4). As there was no reasonable likelihood that any such objection thereto would have changed the outcome of the trial because defendant's relationship with the grandson was a collateral matter, defendant's counsel was not ineffective in failing to raise such an objection to that evidence. State v. Winn, 173 Ohio App. 3d 202, 2007 Ohio 4327, 877 N.E.2d 1020, 2007 Ohio App. LEXIS 3875 (2007).

Photograph of photograph

Admission of a photograph of a purported photograph of the defendant did not violate the best evidence rule where the depicted photograph was not closely related to a controlling issue: State v. Winn, 173 Ohio App. 3d 202, 2007 Ohio 4327, 877 N.E.2d 1020, 2007 Ohio App. LEXIS 3875 (2007).

Secondary evidence

"Best evidence rule" rests on the fact that an original writing is more reliable, complete and accurate as to its contents and meaning, but the original is not required, and other evidence of the contents of a writing is admissible if: 1) all originals are lost or have been destroyed, unless the proponent lost or destroyed them in bad faith; 2) the original is not obtainable; 3) the original is in possession of the opponent; or 4) the writing, recording, or photograph is not closely related to a controlling issue. Discover Bank v. Brockmeier, — Ohio App. 3d —, 2007 Ohio 1552, — N.E. 2d —, 2007 Ohio App. LEXIS 1419 (Apr. 2, 2007).

When a creditor sued a debtor for the balance due on a credit card account, monthly statements of the debtor's account, rather than the original charge slips the debtor signed, were properly admissible to prove the amount due, under Ohio R. Evid. 1002, because the original charge slips had been destroyed, pursuant to the creditor's business policy, so Ohio R. Evid. 1004 applied, and it was not shown that there was any reason to believe that the amounts reflected in the statements were incorrect. Discover Bank v. Brockmeier, — Ohio App. 3d —, 2007 Ohio 1552, — N.E. 2d —, 2007 Ohio App. LEXIS 1419 (Apr. 2, 2007).

Court rejected defendant's contention that the trial court erred when it admitted the testimony of a prison inspector and that of a highway patrol trooper who participated in an investigation regarding the contents of a surveillance tape of the visiting room of a correctional institution on the ground that the admission of the testimony violated the best evidence rule of Ohio R. Evid. 1002 and defendant's right to due process under Ohio Const. art. I, § 16 because the testimony strongly suggested that the video recording was negligently destroyed, and thus, the testimony was admissible under Ohio R. Evid. 1004(1). Additionally, defendant had not proven that the video recording was materially exculpatory. State v. Patter-

son, — Ohio App. 3d —, 2006 Ohio 4439, — N.E. 2d —, 2006 Ohio App. LEXIS 4365 (Aug. 11, 2006).

Although lessees failed to attach copies of restaurant leases to their complaint to support their breach of lease claims, as required by Ohio R. Civ. P. 10(D), such failure could not be the basis of a dismissal motion by defendants where they never sought a more definite statement under Ohio R. Civ. P. 12(E); further, the contents of the leases could have been proved by secondary evidence pursuant to Ohio R. Evid. 1004, and the dispute as to whether such leases ever even existed was a matter for jury resolution under Ohio R. Evid. 1008. Castle Hill Holdings v. Al Hut, Inc., — Ohio App. 3d —, 2006 Ohio 1353, — N.E. 2d —, 2006 Ohio App. LEXIS 1239 (Mar. 23, 2006).

RULE 1005.   Public Records

The contents of an official record, or of a document authorized to be recorded or filed and actually recorded or filed, including data compilations in any form if otherwise admissible, may be proved by copy, certified as correct in accordance with Rule 902, Civ. R. 44, Crim. R. 27 or testified to be correct by a witness who has compared it with the original. If a copy which complies with the foregoing cannot be obtained by the exercise of reasonable diligence, then other evidence of the contents may be given.

NOTES TO DECISIONS

RULE 1006.   Summaries

The contents of voluminous writings, recordings, or photographs which cannot conveniently be examined in court may be presented in the form of a chart, summary, or calculation. The originals, or duplicates, shall be made available for examination or copying, or both, by other parties at a reasonable time and place. The court may order that they be produced in court.

NOTES TO DECISIONS

ANALYSIS

Admissibility of summary

Admissibility of summary

When a creditor sued a debtor for the balance due on a credit card account, monthly statements of the debtor's account, rather than the original charge slips the debtor signed, were not admissible under Ohio R. Evid. 1006 because the original charge slips had been destroyed pursuant to the creditor's business policy, but the statements were admissible under Ohio R. Evid. 1004. Discover Bank v. Brockmeier, — Ohio App. 3d —, 2007 Ohio 1552, — N.E. 2d —, 2007 Ohio App. LEXIS 1419 (Apr. 2, 2007).

There was no error under Ohio R. Evid. 103(A) in a trial court's admission into evidence of an exhibit that was a summary of a printing plant's billing records for purposes of its claim for recovery under an account, as the parties had stipulated to the admission of at least the first page of the exhibit, even if the document was not admissible as a business record under Ohio R. Evid. 803(6) it was admissible under Ohio R. Evid. 1006 as a summary of the voluminous billing records, and any error in the admission was harmless because the publishing companies had admitted the amount of the unpaid bills. There was testimony that indicated that the records from which the exhibit was prepared were plentiful and that they had been retained. Marysville Newspapers, Inc.

v. Del. Gazette Co., — Ohio App. 3d —, 2007 Ohio 3838, — N.E. 2d —, 2007 Ohio App. LEXIS 3485 (July 30, 2007).

There was no error in the trial court's admission of a summary of accounts pursuant to Ohio R. Evid. 1006 in an action by a creditor against a guarantor, as the complaint put the guarantor on notice that the creditor was seeking to recover on the particular accounts, and the evidence submitted related to the accounts and was properly admissible. All-Pak, Inc. v. Snyder, — Ohio App. 3d —, 2006 Ohio 2892, — N.E. 2d —, 2006 Ohio App. LEXIS 2737 (June 8, 2006).

Trial court's admission of various items of evidence, including a spreadsheet that set forth each shipment and corresponding tariff rate discount between a shipper and a supplier, and two damage summaries, did not violate Ohio R. Evid. 1006 and 1007, as the shipper had provided the underlying documents that formed the basis of the contested ones. The calculation and spreadsheet were admissible as summaries of voluminous writings, and if the shipper wanted to contest the accuracy thereof, it could have created similar documents of its own, based on the fact that it held the original documents upon which they were created by the supplier. Avery Dennison Corp. v. Con-Way Transp. Servs., — Ohio App. 3d —, 2006 Ohio 6106, — N.E. 2d —, 2006 Ohio App. LEXIS 6036 (Nov. 17, 2006).

Use of a poster to summarize telephone records during defendant's trial for engaging in a pattern of corrupt activity was reviewed for plain error under Ohio R. Evid. 103(A) because defendant did not object to the State's representation that the exhibit was being used by agreement. Any error in its use under Ohio R. Evid. 1006 did not rise to plain error because the outcome of the trial would not have been different without the evidence. State v. Welch, — Ohio App. 3d —, 2006 Ohio 6684, — N.E. 2d —, 2006 Ohio App. LEXIS 6585 (Dec. 18, 2006).

RULE 1007. Testimony or Written Admission of Party

Contents of writings, recordings, or photographs may be proved by the testimony or deposition of the party against whom offered or by that party's written admission, without accounting for the nonproduction of the original.

History: Amended, eff July 1, 2007.

NOTES TO DECISIONS

ANALYSIS

Admissibility

Admissibility

Trial court's admission of various items of evidence, including a spreadsheet that set forth each shipment and corresponding tariff rate discount between a shipper and a supplier, and two damage summaries, did not violate Ohio R. Evid. 1006 and 1007, as the shipper had provided the underlying documents that formed the basis of the contested ones. The calculation and spreadsheet were admissible as summaries of voluminous writings, and if the shipper wanted to contest the accuracy thereof, it could have created similar documents of its own, based on the fact that it held the original documents upon which they were created by the supplier. Avery Dennison Corp. v. Con-Way Transp. Servs., — Ohio App. 3d —, 2006 Ohio 6106, — N.E. 2d —, 2006 Ohio App. LEXIS 6036 (Nov. 17, 2006).

RULE 1008. Functions of Court and Jury

When the admissibility of other evidence of contents of writings, recordings, or photographs under these rules depends upon the fulfillment of a condition of fact, the question whether the condition has been fulfilled is ordinarily for the court to determine in accordance with the provisions of Rule 104. However, when an issue is raised (a) whether the asserted writing ever existed, or (b) whether another writing, recording, or photograph produced at the trial is the original, or (c) whether other evidence of contents correctly reflects the contents, the issue is for the trier of fact to determine as in the case of other issues of fact.

NOTES TO DECISIONS

ANALYSIS

Jury issue

Jury issue

Although lessees failed to attach copies of restaurant leases to their complaint to support their breach of lease claims, as required by Ohio R. Civ. P. 10(D), such failure could not be the basis of a dismissal motion by defendants where they never sought a more definite statement under Ohio R. Civ. P. 12(E); further, the contents of the leases could have been proved by secondary evidence pursuant to Ohio R. Evid. 1004, and the dispute as to whether such leases ever even existed was a matter for jury resolution under Ohio R. Evid. 1008. Castle Hill Holdings v. Al Hut, Inc., — Ohio App. 3d —, 2006 Ohio 1353, — N.E. 2d —, 2006 Ohio App. LEXIS 1239 (Mar. 23, 2006).

ARTICLE XI
MISCELLANEOUS RULES

RULE 1101. [Reserved]

RULE 1102. Effective Date

(A) **Effective date of rules.** These rules shall take effect on the first day of July, 1980. They govern all proceedings in actions brought after they take effect and also all further proceedings in actions then pending, except to the extent that in the opinion of the court their application in a particular action pending when the rules take effect would not be feasible or would work injustice, in which event former evidentiary principles apply.

(B) **Effective date of amendments.** The amendments submitted by the Supreme Court to the General Assembly on January 14, 1981, and on April 29, 1981, shall take effect on July 1, 1981. They govern all proceedings in actions brought after they take effect and also all further proceedings in actions then pending, except to the extent that their application in a particular action pending when the amendments take effect would not be feasible or would work injustice, in which event the former procedure applies.

(C) **Effective date of amendments.** The amendments submitted by the Supreme Court to the General

Assembly on January 12, 1990, and further revised and submitted on April 16, 1990, shall take effect on July 1, 1990. They govern all proceedings in actions brought after they take effect and also further proceedings in actions then pending, except to the extent that their application in a particular action pending when the amendments take effect would not be feasible or would work injustice, in which event the former procedure applies.

(D) **Effective date of amendments.** The amendments submitted by the Supreme Court to the General Assembly on January 10, 1991 and further revised and submitted on April 29, 1991, shall take effect on July 1, 1991. They govern all proceedings in actions brought after they take effect and also all further proceedings in actions then pending, except to the extent that their application in a particular action pending when the amendments take effect would not be feasible or would work injustice, in which event the former procedure applies.

(E) **Effective date of amendments.** The amendments filed by the Supreme Court with the General Assembly on January 14, 1992 and further filed on April 30, 1992, shall take effect on July 1, 1992. They govern all proceedings in actions brought after they take effect and also all further proceedings in actions then pending, except to the extent that their application in a particular action pending when the amendments take effect would not be feasible or would work injustice, in which event the former procedure applies.

(F) **Effective date of amendments.** The amendments submitted by the Supreme Court to the General Assembly on January 8, 1993 and further filed on April 30, 1993 shall take effect on July 1, 1993. They govern all proceedings in actions brought after they take effect and also all further proceedings in actions then pending, except to the extent that their application in a particular action pending when the amendments take effect would not be feasible or would work injustice, in which event the former procedure applies.

(G) **Effective date of amendments.** The amendments submitted by the Supreme Court to the General Assembly on January 14, 1994 shall take effect on July 1, 1994. They govern all proceedings in actions brought after they take effect and also all further proceedings in actions then pending, except to the extent that their application in a particular action pending when the amendments take effect would not be feasible or would work injustice, in which event the former procedure applies.

(H) **Effective date of amendments.** The amendments to Rules 101, 102 and 403 filed by the Supreme Court with the General Assembly on January 5, 1996 and refiled on April 26, 1996 shall take effect on July 1, 1996. They govern all proceedings in actions brought after they take effect and also all further proceedings in actions then pending, except to the extent that their application in a particular action pending when the amendments take effect would not be feasible or would work injustice, in which event the former procedure applies.

(I) **Effective date of amendments.** The amendments to Rules 607, 613, 616, 706, and 806 filed by the Supreme Court with the General Assembly on January 15, 1998 and further revised and refiled on April 30, 1998 shall take effect on July 1, 1998. They govern all proceedings in actions brought after they take effect and also all further proceedings in actions then pending, except to the extent that their application in a particular action pending when the amendments take effect would not be feasible or would work injustice, in which event the former procedure applies.

(J) **Effective date of amendments.** The amendments to Rules 101 and 1102(I) filed by the Supreme Court with the General Assembly on January 13, 1999 shall take effect on July 1, 1999. They govern all proceedings in actions brought after they take effect and also all further proceedings in actions then pending, except to the extent that their application in a particular action pending when the amendments take effect would not be feasible or would work injustice, in which event the former procedure applies.

(K) **Effective date of amendments.** The amendments to Evidence Rule 407 filed by the Supreme Court with the General Assembly on January 13, 2000 and refiled on April 27, 2000 shall take effect on July 1, 2000. They govern all proceedings in actions brought after they take effect and also all further proceedings in actions then pending, except to the extent that their application in a particular action pending when the amendments take effect would not be feasible or would work injustice, in which event the former procedure applies.

(L) **Effective date of amendments.** The amendments to Evidence Rules 615 and 804 filed by the Supreme Court with the General Assembly on January 12, 2001, and refiled on April 26, 2001, shall take effect on July 1, 2001. They govern all proceedings in actions brought after they take effect and also all further proceedings in actions then pending, except to the extent that their application in a particular action pending when the amendments take effect would not be feasible or would work injustice, in which event the former procedure applies.

(M) **Effective date of amendments.** The amendments to Evidence Rules 609 and 615 filed by the Supreme Court with the General Assembly on January 9, 2003 and refiled on April 28, 2003, shall take effect on July 1, 2003. They govern all proceedings in actions brought after they take effect and also all further proceedings in actions then pending, except to the extent that their application in a particular action pending when the amendments take effect would not be feasible or would work injustice, in which event the former procedure applies.

(N) **Effective date of amendments.** The amendment to Evidence Rule 803 and the repeal of Evidence Rule 706 filed by the Supreme Court with the General Assembly on January 12, 2006 shall take effect on July 1, 2006. The amendment and repeal govern all proceedings in actions brought after they take effect and also all further proceedings in actions then pending, except to the extent that their application in a particular action pending when the amendments take effect would not be feasible or would work injustice, in which event the former procedure applies.

(O) **Effective date of amendments.** The amendments to the Rules of Evidence filed by the Supreme

Court with the General Assembly on January 11, 2007 and refiled April 30, 2007 shall take effect on July 1, 2007. They govern all proceedings in actions brought after they take effect and also all further proceedings in actions then pending, except to the extent that their application in a particular action pending when the amendments take effect would not be feasible or would work injustice, in which event the former procedure applies.

History: Amended, eff 7-1-81; 7-1-90; 7-1-91; 7-1-92; 7-1-93; 7-1-94; 7-1-96; 7-1-98; 7-1-99; 7-1-00; 7-1-01; 7-1-03; 7-1-06; 7-1-07.

RULE 1103. Title

These rules shall be known as the Ohio Rules of Evidence and may be cited as "Evidence Rules" or "Evid. R."____

Index to Ohio Rules of Evidence

A

ABSENT WITNESS.
Hearsay exceptions, EvR 804.

ABUSED CHILD.
Hearsay exceptions, EvR 807.

ACCUSED.
Character evidence to prove conduct of, admissibility of; exceptions, EvR 404.
Testimony on preliminary questions, not subject to cross-examination, EvR 104.

ACKNOWLEDGMENTS.
Documents as self-authenticating, EvR 902.

ADJUDICATIVE FACTS.
Judicial notice, EvR 201.

ADMISSIBILITY OF EVIDENCE.
Limited or restricted when; instructions to jury, EvR 105.
Plain error, EvR 103.
Preliminary questions, applicability of Rules of Evidence to determinations, EvR 101, 104.
Rulings, EvR 103.

ADMISSIONS.
Statement of party opponent as, EvR 801.

ADVERSE PARTY.
Leading questions to, EvR 611.
Writing used to refresh witness' memory, examination by, EvR 612.

AGE.
Witness, of, credibility, EvR 601.

AGENT.
Proof of agency by evidence of liability insurance, EvR 411.
Statement by, of party against whom offered, EvR 801.
  Impeaching, when, EvR 806.

ALIUNDE RULE, EvR 606.

ANCIENT DOCUMENTS.
Authentication and identification, EvR 901.
Hearsay exception, EvR 803.

ANNULMENT OF CRIME CONVICTION OF WITNESS.
Effect, EvR 609.

APPLICABILITY.
Exceptions, EvR 101, 104.
Generally, EvR 101.
Privileges, EvR 101, 104.

ARBITRATION.
Common pleas court, jurisdiction of.
  Evidence rules in, EvR 101.

ARREST.
Evidence rules not applicable to warrant, EvR 101.

AUTHENTICATION AND IDENTIFICATION.
Generally, EvR 901.
Self-authentication, EvR 902.
Subscribing witness need not testify, when, EvR 903.

B

BAIL.
Evidence rules, applicability to proceedings, EvR 101.

BAPTISMAL CERTIFICATES, HEARSAY EXCEPTION, EvR 803.

BEST EVIDENCE RULE, EvR 1002.
Duplicate as exception, EvR 1003.

BIBLE.
Family, hearsay exceptions, EvR 803.

BILLS OF LADING.
Hearsay exception, EvR 803.

BIRTHS AND DEATHS.
Birth records.
  Hearsay exceptions, EvR 803.

BRIBERY.
Juror may testify re, EvR 606.

BURDEN OF GOING FORWARD.
Presumptions in civil actions, EvR 301.

BURDEN OF PROOF.
Effect of presumptions, EvR 301.

BUSINESS RECORDS.
Admissibility, EvR 803.
Evidence, use as, EvR 803.

C

CERTIFICATES AND CERTIFICATION.
Acknowledgment, certificate of, as self-authenticating, EvR 902.
Domestic or foreign public documents, certificate of genuineness as self-authenticating, EvR 902.
Marriage, baptismal, birth or death certificates as hearsay exception, EvR 803.
Public records, certified copies of, as self-authenticating, EvR 902, 1005.
Rehabilitation certificate, effect on impeachment of witness, EvR 609.

CHARACTER, EvR 404 to 406.
Conduct, admissibility, to prove, EvR 404.
Other crimes, wrongs or acts, admissibility of, to prove, EvR 404.
Proof of, methods, EvR 405.
Reputation as to, EvR 803.
Reputation re as hearsay exception, EvR 803.
Witness' credibility attacked or supported by evidence re, EvR 404, 608.
Witnesses, EvR 608.

COMMERCIAL PAPER.
Authentication, EvR 902.

COMMERCIAL PUBLICATIONS, HEARSAY EXCEPTION, EvR 803.

COMPETENCY.
Witnesses, EvR 601 et seq.

COMPROMISE.
Admissibility of evidence, EvR 408.

M

MAGAZINES.
Self-authenticating, EvR 902.

MARRIAGE.
Certificate of.
Hearsay exceptions, EvR 803.

MEDICAL, MENTAL EXAMINATIONS.
Evidence, hearsay exception, EvR 803.

MEDICAL BILLS, STATEMENTS.
Offer to pay not admissible, EvR 409.

MEDICAL DIAGNOSIS OR TREATMENT, HEARSAY EXCEPTION, EvR 803.

MEDICAL PAYMENTS, ADMISSIBILITY OF, EvR 409.

MEMORY.
Declarant's then-existing condition, EvR 803.
Hearsay exceptions, EvR 803, 804.
Writing used to refresh witness, EvR 612.

MENTAL HEALTH, MENTAL ILLNESS.
Witnesses.
Hearsay exception when unavailable, EvR 804.

MENTAL STATE.
Hearsay exception, EvR 803.

MINORS.
Victim, testifying by deposition, videotaping or televising.
Statement not hearsay, EvR 807.
Witness, competence as, EvR 601.

MOTION PICTURES, PROOF OF CONTENTS OF, EvR 1001 to 1008.

MOTIVE.
Declarant's then-existing state of mind, EvR 803.
Evidence of other crimes, wrongs, acts to prove, EvR 404.

MUTE PERSONS.
Evidence, use of statement or, EvR 804.

N

NEGLIGENCE.
Repairs, remedial measures, admissibility, EvR 407.

NEGOTIATIONS, COMPROMISE; ADMISSIBILITY, EvR 408.

NEWSPAPERS.
Authentication, EvR 902.

NO CONTEST PLEA.
Admissibility, EvR 410.

NO CONTEST PLEAS OR OFFERS OF, ADMISSIBILITY, EvR 410.

NOTARY PUBLIC.
Notarized documents as self-authenticating, EvR 902.

O

OATH OR AFFIRMATION.
Interpreters, EvR 604.
Witnesses, EvR 603.

OBJECTIONS.
Erroneous ruling, EvR 103.
Opinion on ultimate issue, EvR 704.

OBJECTIONS—Cont'd
Witnesses.
Calling and interrogation of, EvR 614.
Judge as, EvR 605.
Juror as, EvR 606.
Writing used to refresh memory, EvR 612.

OFFER OF PROOF.
Erroneous rulings on evidence, EvR 103.

OFFER TO COMPROMISE, EvR 408.

OFFER TO PAY MEDICAL OR SIMILAR EXPENSES, EvR 409.

OFFICIAL PUBLICATIONS AS SELF-AUTHENTICATING, EvR 902.

OFFICIAL RECORD, PROOF OF, EvR 1005.

OPINIONS.
Character of witness, EvR 405, 608.
Handwriting identification by nonexpert, EvR 901.
Lay witnesses, of, EvR 701.
Religious, of witness; inadmissible re credibility, EvR 610.
Ultimate issue, on, EvR 704.
Voice identification, EvR 901.

ORGANIZATIONS.
Routine practice of, relevancy, EvR 406.

ORIGINAL DEFINED; REQUIRED, WHEN, EvR 1001 to 1008.

OTHER ACTS EVIDENCE, EvR 404.

P

PAMPHLETS.
Hearsay exception, EvR 803.

PARDONS.
Impeachment of witness.
Effect of pardon when, EvR 609.

PARTIES.
Admissions by.
Hearsay exception, EvR 801.
Impeaching, EvR 806.
Not subject to requirements re prior inconsistent statements, EvR 613.

PAST RECOLLECTION RECORDED, EvR 803.

PERIODICALS.
Hearsay exception, EvR 803.
Self-authentication, EvR 902.

PERJURY.
Impeachment of witness convicted of, EvR 609.
Inconsistent statement, hearsay exception, EvR 801.

PHOTOGRAPHS, PHOTOGRAPHY.
Discovery.
Proof, EvR 1001 to 1008.

PHOTOGRAPHS, PHOTOSTATS; PROOF OF, EvR 1001 to 1008.

PHYSICAL CONDITION.
Illness, declarant unavailable as hearsay exceptions, when, EvR 804.
Statement re declarant's then existing condition, as hearsay exception, EvR 803.

PLEADINGS.
Admissibility of, EvR 410.
Inadmissibility of, EvR 410.

OHIO TRAFFIC RULES

RULE 1. Scope of rules; applicability; authority and construction

(A) **Applicability.** These rules prescribe the procedure to be followed in all courts of this state in traffic cases and supersede the "Ohio Rules of Practice and Procedure in Traffic Cases For All Courts Inferior To Common Pleas" effective January 1, 1969, and as amended on January 4, 1971, and December 7, 1972.

(B) **Authority and construction.** These rules are promulgated pursuant to authority granted the Supreme Court by R.C. § 2935.17 and § 2937.46. They shall be construed and applied to secure the fair, impartial, speedy and sure administration of justice, simplicity and uniformity in procedure, and the elimination of unjustifiable expense and delay.

History: Effective January 1, 1975.

RULE 2. Definitions

As used in these rules:

(A) "Traffic case" means any proceeding, other than a proceeding resulting from a felony indictment, that involves one or more violations of a law, ordinance, or regulation governing the operation and use of vehicles, conduct of pedestrians in relation to vehicles, or weight, dimension, loads or equipment, or vehicles drawn or moved on highways and bridges. "Traffic case" does not include any proceeding that results in a felony indictment.

(B) "Traffic ticket" means the traffic complaint and summons described in Traffic Rule 3 and that appears in the Appendix of Forms.

(C) "Highway" includes a street or an alley.

(D) "Petty offense" means an offense for which the penalty prescribed by law includes confinement for six months or less.

(E) "Serious offense" means an offense for which the penalty prescribed by law includes confinement for more than six months.

(F) "Court" means a municipal court, county court, juvenile division of the court of common pleas, or mayor's court.

(G) "Judge" means judge of a municipal court, county court, or juvenile division of the court of common pleas, a magistrate of a municipal or county court, or a mayor or mayor's court magistrate presiding over a mayor's court.

(H) "Prosecuting attorney" means the attorney general of this state, the prosecuting attorney of a county, the law director, city solicitor, or other officer who prosecutes a criminal case on behalf of the state or a city, village, township, or other political subdivision, and the assistant or assistants of any of them.

(I) "State" means this state, a county, city, village, township, other political subdivision or any other entity of this state that may prosecute a criminal action.

(J) "Clerk of court" means the duly elected or appointed clerk of any court of record, or the deputy of any of them, and either the mayor of a municipal corporation having a mayor's court or any clerk appointed by the mayor.

History: Effective January 1, 1975; amended, eff February 1, 2002; January 1, 2006; January 1, 2010.

RULE 3. Complaint and summons; form; use

(A) **Traffic complaint and summons.** In traffic cases, the complaint and summons shall be the "Ohio Uniform Traffic Ticket" as set out in the Appendix of Forms.

(B) **Traffic complaint and summons form.** The Ohio Uniform Traffic Ticket shall consist of four sheets, padded together and bound at the top or bottom edge. Each sheet shall be four and one-fourth inches in width and nine and one-half inches in length from a perforation below the binding to the bottom edge. The first sheet shall be white and the second sheet shall be canary yellow. Where an additional copy is needed by an agency, it may be added. The first and second sheets shall be at least fifteen pound paper.

The first sheet shall be the court record.

The second sheet shall be the abstract of court record for the Bureau of Motor Vehicles as required by Section 4507.021 [4507.02.1] of the Revised Code. The second sheet may be omitted from the Ticket if the court reports violations to the Bureau by electronic or other means acceptable to the Bureau.

The third sheet shall be the defendant's copy.

The fourth sheet shall be the enforcement agency record.

A wrap-around may be added to the first sheet. The issuing authority may use the front and back of the wrap-around for any data or information it may require.

Each ticket sheet shall be perforated tab bound at the edge or end with carbon paper interleaved so that all carbon paper is securely bound to the tab and removable with it, or shall be on treated paper so that marking from the top sheet is transferred legibly to successive sheets in the group.

(C) **Use of ticket.** The Ohio Uniform Traffic Ticket shall be used in all moving traffic cases, but its use for parking and equipment violations is optional in each local jurisdiction. Any ticket properly issued by a law enforcement officer shall be accepted for filing and disposition in any court having jurisdiction over the offense alleged. An officer may include more than one alleged violation on a single ticket provided the alleged violations are numbered sequentially on the face of the ticket. An officer who completes a ticket at the scene of an alleged offense shall not be required to rewrite or type a new complaint as a condition of filing the ticket, unless the original complaint is illegible or does not state an offense. If a new complaint is executed, a copy shall be served upon defendant as soon as possible.

(D) **Issuance of tickets to enforcement agency.** The judge in a single-judge court, and the administrative judge in multi-judge courts, shall designate the issuing authority for tickets and prescribe the conditions of issuance and accountability. The issuing authority may be the clerk of the court, the violations clerk, or the enforcement agency of the municipality.

When a single enforcement agency, except the State Highway Patrol, regularly has cases in more than one court, the ticket used by the agency shall be issued through the court for adults in the most populous area in the jurisdiction of the agency. Tickets used by the State Highway Patrol shall be issued by the Superintendent of the State Highway Patrol.

(E) **Duty of law enforcement officer.**

(1) A law enforcement officer who issues a ticket shall complete and sign the ticket, serve a copy of the completed ticket on the defendant, and, without unnecessary delay, file the court copy with the court. If the issuing officer personally serves a copy of the completed ticket on the defendant, the issuing officer shall note the date of personal service on the ticket in the space provided. If the issuing officer is unable to serve a copy of the completed ticket on the defendant, the completed ticket may be served by another law enforcement officer of the law enforcement agency issuing the ticket or filed with the clerk of the court for issuance of a warrant or summons pursuant to Crim. R. 4. Tickets that solely allege one or more minor misdemeanor violations must initially be issued by summons.

(2) The officer shall notify defendant that if defendant does not appear at the time and place stated in the citation or comply with division (C) of section 2935.26 of the Revised Code, defendant's license will be cancelled, defendant will not be eligible for the reissuance of the license or the issuance of a new license for one year after cancellation, and defendant will be subject to any applicable criminal penalties.

(F) **Use of electronically produced tickets.**

(1) Local rules adopted pursuant to the Supreme Court Rules of Superintendence for the Courts of Ohio may provide for the use of a ticket that is produced by computer or other electronic means, provided that the ticket conforms in all substantive respects, including layout and content, to the "Ohio Uniform Traffic Ticket" set forth in the Appendix of Forms. The provisions of division (B) of this rule relative to the color and weight of paper and method of binding shall not be applicable to a ticket that is produced by computer or other electronic means.

(2) Local rules adopted pursuant to the Supreme Court Rules of Superintendence for the Courts of Ohio may provide for the filing of the ticket by electronic means. If a ticket is issued at the scene of an alleged offense, the local rule shall require that the issuing officer provide the defendant with a paper copy of the ticket as required by division (E) of this rule. A law enforcement officer who files a ticket electronically shall be considered to have certified the ticket and shall have the same rights, responsibilities, and liabilities as with all other tickets issued pursuant to these rules.

History: Effective January 1, 1975; amended, eff August 4, 1980; February 26, 1990; November 28, 1990; June 1, 1992; February 1, 2002; October 1, 2006; May 1, 2008; January 1, 2010.

NOTES TO DECISIONS

ANALYSIS

Generally
Amendment of ticket
Complaint
Failure to serve
Jurisdiction of municipal court
Speeding

Generally

Traffic ticket is merely a charging instrument and does not constitute evidence. The defendant could not be convicted of failure to obey a traffic control device where no evidence was presented that the device existed: State v. Kilgore, 175 Ohio App. 3d 665, 2008 Ohio 1162, 888 N.E.2d 1126, 2008 Ohio App. LEXIS 1031 (2008).

Amendment of ticket

Traffic citation was sufficient as amended to survive defendant's motion to dismiss because, although the original citation failed to charge the proper numerical statutory section, the citation was amended to reflect that defendant was charged with operating a vehicle while under the influence of alcohol under RC § 4511.19(A)(1)(a). Thus, defendant had sufficient actual notice and ample time and opportunity to prepare his defense by virtue of the language of the original ticket and the amendment to the citation was not tantamount to executing a "new complaint." State v. Alley, — Ohio App. 3d —, 2007 Ohio 4483, — N.E. 2d —, 2007 Ohio App. LEXIS 4043 (Aug. 31, 2007).

Complaint

As a complaint charging defendant with a violation of RC § 4511.19(A)(1) met the requirements of Ohio Traf. R. 3 because it advised defendant of the offense with which she was charged in a manner that she could reasonably understand, especially given the fact that the ticket contained the language set forth in RC § 4511.19(A)(1)(a), there was no error in the trial court's denial of defendant's dismissal motion, based on her claim that § 4511.19(A)(1) was not a sufficient charge because there was no penalty associated with it. The trial court's grant of defendant's motion to amend the ticket pursuant to Ohio R. Crim. P. 7(D) to reflect that she was charged with § 4511.19(A)(1)(a) was not error. State v. Valdez, — Ohio App. 3d —, 2006 Ohio 3298, — N.E. 2d —, 2006 Ohio App. LEXIS 3215 (June 28, 2006).

Failure to serve

Defendant did not raise the allegedly defective service of the traffic ticket or any lack of personal jurisdiction until mid-trial, long after he pled not guilty at his initial appearance. As such, he conferred personal jurisdiction on the trial court and thus waived the issue. State v. Smith, — Ohio App. 3d —, 2007 Ohio 3182, — N.E. 2d —, 2007 Ohio App. LEXIS 2981 (June 21, 2007).

Jurisdiction of municipal court

Where defendant was served by certified mail with a summons and citation that charged him with a violation of RC § 4511.21 and he appeared before a trial court and entered a not guilty plea without first asserting a claim that the trial court lacked personal jurisdiction over him under Ohio Traf. R. 3, the trial court thereafter properly overruled his motion to dismiss based on lack of personal jurisdiction, as that issue was deemed waived pursuant to Ohio Traf. R. 11(B). State v. Cook, — Ohio App. 3d —, 2006 Ohio 1953, — N.E. 2d —, 2006 Ohio App. LEXIS 1784 (Apr. 17, 2006).

Speeding

Citation for speeding that contains notice of both the prima facie offense and the basic facts supporting the charge includes all the necessary elements of the offense even if the citation does not also allege that the speed is unreasonable for existing conditions. The driver may rebut or negate the prima facie case with evidence that the speed was neither excessive nor unreasonable: Vill. of Bellville v. Kieffaber, 114 Ohio St. 3d 124, 2007 Ohio 3763, 870 N.E.2d 697, 2007 Ohio LEXIS 1864 (2007).

RULE 4.   Bail and security

(A) **Posting of bail; depositing of security.** The posting of bail or the depositing of security is for the purpose of securing appearance or compliance with R.C. 2935.26(C). The forfeiture of the bail or security may be a substitute for appearance in court, compliance with R.C. 2935.26(C), and payment of penalty imposed on a finding of guilt, with consent of all parties.

(B) **Bail and security procedure.** Criminal Rule 46 governs bail in traffic cases. In addition, the provisions of R.C. 2937.221 and R.C. 2935.27 apply in traffic cases.

History: Effective January 1, 1975; amended, eff August 4, 1980; January 1, 2010.

RULE 5.   Joinder of offense and defendants; consolidation for trial; relief prejudicial joinder

Criminal Rules 8, 13 and 14 govern joinder of offenses and defendants, consolidation of cases for trial and relief from prejudicial joinder in traffic cases.

History: Effective January 1, 1975.

RULE 6.   Summons, warrants: form, service and execution

(A) **Form.** The form of summons and warrants, other than the ticket, shall be as prescribed in Criminal Rule 4.

(B) **Service and execution.** Summons, other than the ticket, and warrants shall be served and executed as prescribed by Criminal Rule 4.

History: Effective January 1, 1975.

RULE 7.   Procedure upon failure to appear

(A) **Issuance of summons, warrant.** When a defendant fails to appear pursuant to a ticket issued to him, the court shall issue a supplemental summons or warrant.

If a supplemental summons is not served or a warrant is not executed within twenty-eight days of receipt by the serving officer, the court may place the case in a file of cases disposed of subject to being reopened. Where bond is forfeited, the disposition shall be reported to the Registrar of Motor Vehicles. For all other purposes, including disposition reports, the cases shall be reported as disposed of, subject to being reopened, if defendant subsequently appears or is apprehended.

(B) **Issuance of notice to nonresident.** When a nonresident of this state fails to appear pursuant to a supplemental summons or a warrant issued under division (A), the court may send by ordinary mail to defendant's address as it appears on the ticket, or the summons or warrant return, a notice ordering defendant to appear at a specified time and place.

If the defendant fails to appear or answer within twenty-eight days after the date of mailing of the notice, the court shall place the case in the file of cases disposed of subject to being reopened.

The mailing of notice in parking cases is discretionary with the court.

(C) **Effect of waiting periods and bail forfeiture.** The waiting period prescribed in division (A) does not affect forfeiture of bail.

If there is a breach of a condition of bail, the court shall declare a forfeiture of bail. Forfeiture proceedings shall be promptly enforced as provided by law.

If defendant fails to appear at the time and place specified on the citation and fails to comply with division (C) of Section 2935.26 of the Revised Code, or fails to comply with or satisfy any judgment of the court within the time allowed, the court shall declare the forfeiture of defendant's license. Thirty days after the declaration, the court shall forward a copy of the declaration to the Registrar of Motor Vehicles for cancellation in accordance with division (D) of Section 2935.27 of the Revised Code. If defendant deposits a sum of money or other security with the court, the deposit immediately shall be forfeited to the court if he fails to appear or comply with division (C) of Section 2935.26 of the Revised Code.

History: Effective January 1, 1975; amended, eff August 4, 1980; November 28, 1990.

RULE 8. Arraignment

(A) **Arraignment time.** Where practicable, every defendant shall be arraigned before contested matters are taken up. Trial may be conducted immediately following arraignment.

(B) **Arraignment procedure.** Arraignment shall be conducted in open court and shall consist of reading the complaint to the defendant, or stating to him the substance of the charge, and calling on him to plead thereto. The defendant shall be given a copy of the complaint, or shall acknowledge receipt thereof, before being called upon to plead and may in open court waive the reading of the complaint.

(C) **Presence of defendant.** The defendant must be present at the arraignment, but the court may allow the defendant to enter a not guilty plea at the clerk's office in person, by his attorney in person, or by his attorney by mail, within four days after receipt of the ticket by the defendant.

(D) **Explanation of rights.** Before calling upon a defendant to plead at arraignment the judge shall cause him to be informed and shall determine that defendant knows and understands:

(1) That he has a right to counsel and the right to a reasonable continuance in the proceedings to secure counsel, and, pursuant to Criminal Rule 44, the right to have counsel assigned without cost to himself if he is unable to employ counsel;

(2) That he has a right to bail as provided in Rule 4;

(3) That he need make no statement at any point in the proceeding; but any statement made may be used against him;

(4) That he has, where such right exists, a right to jury trial and that he must, in petty offense cases, make a demand for a jury pursuant to Criminal Rule 23;

(5) That if he is convicted a record of the conviction will be sent to the Bureau of Motor Vehicles and become a part of his driving record.

(E) **Joint arraignment.** If there are multiple defendants to be arraigned, the judge may advise, or cause them to be advised, of their rights by general announcement.

History: Effective January 1, 1975.

NOTES TO DECISIONS

ANALYSIS

Explanation of rights
Failure to advise

Explanation of rights

CrimR 5, CrimR 10, and TrafR 8 were violated where the defendant's rights were not explained at the arraignment on the traffic offenses. A video explanation of rights played for the benefit of all defendants did not suffice: State v. Donkers, 170 Ohio App. 3d 509, 2007 Ohio 1557, 867 N.E.2d 903, 2007 Ohio App. LEXIS 1424 (2007).

Failure to advise

When it was alleged that defendant was advised of her rights, as required by Ohio R. Crim. P. 5 and 10 and Ohio Traf. R. 8, by means of a mass video advisement, this was insuffi-

cient because (1) the contents of the advisement were not shown, (2) it was not demonstrated that defendant saw the advisement, and (3) even if the advisement covered the required rights and it was shown that defendant saw it, an individualized finding that she understood those rights was still required, and such a finding was absent. State v. Donkers, 170 Ohio App. 3d 509, 2007 Ohio 1557, 867 N.E.2d 903, 2007 Ohio App. LEXIS 1424 (2007).

Defendant's criminal convictions were reversed because, at two initial appearances, she was not advised of all of her rights, as required by Ohio R. Crim. P. 5 and 10 and Ohio Traf. R. 8, it was not found that she understood those rights, and there was no evidence that she was given a copy of the complaint. State v. Donkers, 170 Ohio App. 3d 509, 2007 Ohio 1557, 867 N.E.2d 903, 2007 Ohio App. LEXIS 1424 (2007).

RULE 9. Jury demand

(A) **Jury demand.** Jury demands shall be made pursuant to Criminal Rule 23.

(B) **Jury demands in mayor's court.** Where, in a mayor's court, a defendant is entitled to a jury trial and a jury demand is made pursuant to Criminal Rule 23, the mayor shall transfer the case pursuant to subdivision (C).

If a jury demand is not made pursuant to Criminal Rule 23, and the defendant waives his right to a jury trial in writing, a mayor may try the case if (1) his compensation as a judge is not directly dependent upon criminal case convictions, or (2) he is not the chief executive and administrative officer of the municipality and as such responsible for the financial condition of the municipality. Guilty and no contest pleas may be taken by any mayor, including mayors whose compensation as a judge is directly dependent upon criminal case convictions and mayors who as chief executive and administrative officer of the municipality are responsible for the financial condition of the municipality.

(C) **Transfer.** Where transfer is required, the mayor's court shall make a written order directing the defendant to appear at the transferee court, continuing the same bail, if any, and making appearance before the transferee court as a condition of bail, if any. Upon transfer, the mayor's court shall transmit to the clerk of the transferee court the ticket and all other papers in the case, and any bail taken in the case.

Upon receipt of such papers the clerk of the transferee court shall set the case for trial and shall notify the defendant by ordinary mail of his trial date.

History: Effective January 1, 1975.

RULE 10. Pleas; rights upon plea

(A) **Pleas.** A defendant may plead not guilty, guilty or, with the consent of the court, no contest. All pleas may be made orally. If a defendant refuses to plead, the court shall enter a plea of not guilty on behalf of the defendant.

(B) **Effect of guilty or no contest plea.** With reference to the offense or offenses to which the plea is entered:

(1) The plea of guilty is a complete admission of the defendant's guilt.

(2) The plea of no contest is not an admission of defendant's guilt, but is an admission of the truth of the

facts alleged in the complaint and such plea or admission shall not be used against the defendant in any subsequent civil or criminal proceeding.

(3) When a plea of guilty or no contest is accepted pursuant to this rule, the court shall proceed with sentencing under Criminal Rule 32.

(C) **Misdemeanor cases involving serious offenses.** In misdemeanor cases involving serious offenses, the court may refuse to accept a plea of guilty or no contest and shall not accept such plea without first addressing the defendant personally and informing him of the effect of the pleas of guilty, no contest, and not guilty and determining that he is making the plea voluntarily. Where the defendant is unrepresented by counsel, the court shall not accept a plea of guilty or no contest unless the defendant, after being readvised that he has a right to be represented by retained counsel, or pursuant to Criminal Rule 44 by appointed counsel, waives this right.

(D) **Misdemeanor cases involving petty offenses.** In misdemeanor cases involving petty offenses, except those processed in a traffic violations bureau, the court may refuse to accept a plea of guilty or no contest and shall not accept such pleas without first informing the defendant of the effect of the plea of guilty, no contest, and not guilty. This information may be presented by general orientation or pronouncement.

The counsel provisions of Criminal Rule 44(B), (C) and (D) apply to this subdivision.

(E) **Refusal of court to accept plea.** If the court refuses to accept a plea of guilty or no contest, the court shall enter a plea of not guilty on behalf of the defendant. In such cases neither plea shall be admissible in evidence nor be the subject of comment by the prosecuting attorney or court.

(F) **Immediate trial.** Upon written consent of defendant and the prosecuting attorney, trial may be conducted immediately after the acceptance of a plea at arraignment. If the defendant seeks a continuance, or demands a jury trial where such right exists, the court shall cause the case to be set for trial.

History: Effective January 1, 1975; amended eff. January 1, 2010.

NOTES TO DECISIONS

ANALYSIS

Colloquy
Constitutional rights
Effects of guilty plea
Failure to inform defendant
No contest plea

Colloquy

Although defendant cited to Ohio R. Crim. P. 11 in his appeal that raised an issue as to the plea he entered to reckless operation, in violation of RC § 4511.20, as Ohio R. Crim. P. 11(E) and Ohio Traf. R. 10(D) were identical in all parts that were relevant to the issues raised, the court reviewed the claim of error under a violation of Rule 10(D), which was the applicable section for the charge involved. State v. Powell, — Ohio App. 3d —, 2006 Ohio 3477, — N.E. 2d —, 2006 Ohio App. LEXIS 3422 (June 27, 2006).

Constitutional rights

Although the trial court did not inform defendant of his right to confront adverse witnesses, it had no obligation to do so. Because the language of Ohio Traf. R. 10(C) and Ohio R. Crim. P. 11(D) was the same, the trial court was not required to inform defendant of the specific rights he was waiving by entering a no-contest plea. State v. Dobbins, — Ohio App. 3d —, 2007 Ohio 1665, — N.E. 2d —, 2007 Ohio App. LEXIS 1527 (Apr. 6, 2007).

Effects of guilty plea

Where defendant entered guilty pleas to various traffic offenses, pursuant to Ohio Traf. R. 10(D), the allocution was governed by Ohio R. Crim. P. 2(D) and 11(E), and was sufficient in the circumstances where defendant was advised of his right to an attorney, to a trial by a judge or jury, as to the State's evidentiary burden, his rights to cross-examine witnesses and compulsory process, his right against self-incrimination, and the maximum penalties that could be imposed; as defendant entered guilty pleas, he waived alleged errors as to the denial of his request for counsel to withdraw and for a continuance. State v. MacConnell, — Ohio App. 3d —, 2006 Ohio 1973, — N.E. 2d —, 2006 Ohio App. LEXIS 1802 (Apr. 21, 2006).

When defendant pled guilty to violations of RC §§ 4510.16(A), 4510.11(A), and 4510.21(A), the Ohio Traffic Rules applied to the acceptance of his plea, requiring the trial court to comply with Ohio Traf. R. 10(D) by informing him of the information in Ohio Traf. R. 10(B), regarding the effect of his plea, and, as the trial court complied with these requirements, the plea was knowing, intelligent, and voluntary because no constitutional informational requirement applied to accepting his plea, nor did the trial court have to engage defendant in an Ohio R. Crim. P. 11(C) colloquy before accepting the plea. State v. Brackens, — Ohio App. 3d —, 2006 Ohio 2143, — N.E. 2d —, 2006 Ohio App. LEXIS 1981 (May 1, 2006).

Failure to inform defendant

Where a trial court failed to comply with Ohio Traf. R. 10(D) in accepting defendant's no contest plea to a reckless driving charge, his claim that his rights thereunder were violated had merit; the trial court failed to inform defendant of the effect of his no contest plea prior to its acceptance, pursuant to Rule 10(B)(2). State v. Powell, — Ohio App. 3d —, 2006 Ohio 3477, — N.E. 2d —, 2006 Ohio App. LEXIS 3422 (June 27, 2006).

While a trial court did not convey all of the information contained in Ohio Traf. R. 10(B) before accepting defendant guilty plea to a charge of driving under the influence of alcohol, defendant's plea was not invalid because of the trial court's failure to do so. There was no evidence that the trial court's failure caused defendant to enter a guilty plea that would not have otherwise been made; instead, defendant was informed that the offense was his second offense within a two-year period, and he was informed of the minimum and maximum sentences to which he could be sentenced. State v. Darden, — Ohio App. 3d —, 2006 Ohio 2908, — N.E. 2d —, 2006 Ohio App. LEXIS 2795 (June 9, 2006).

Trial court erred in denying defendant's motion to vacate his guilty pleas because, at the time of the pleas, the trial court failed to inform defendant that his pleas were complete admissions, as required by Ohio Traf. R. 10(B). Moreover, defendant proceeded without counsel and was not informed of a mandatory license suspension. State v. Neff, — Ohio App. 3d —, 2006 Ohio 6608, — N.E. 2d —, 2006 Ohio App. LEXIS 6520 (Dec. 8, 2006).

No contest plea

Trial court erred by failing to substantially comply with the requirements of Ohio R. Crim. P. 44; because the driving under the influence charge qualified as a "serious offense" under Ohio R. Crim. P. 2(C), the trial court failed to make an adequate determination that defendant sufficiently understood the possible consequences of declining counsel. The trial court never clearly ascertained whether defendant actually wanted to waive his right to counsel, the record contained no discussion about the ramifications of waiving the right to counsel, and the record contained no written waiver of defendant's right to counsel. State v. Dobbins, — Ohio App. 3d —, 2007 Ohio 1665, — N.E. 2d —, 2007 Ohio App. LEXIS 1527 (Apr. 6, 2007).

Since the trial court improperly informed defendant that RC § 4549.08 was a strict liability offense and that, as a result, her defense that she was operating someone else's car and did not know that the temporary tags had been altered had no merit, defendant's subsequent no contest plea was not knowingly and intelligently tendered. Moreover, the trial court failed to comply with Ohio Traf. R. 10(D) by informing defendant of the effect of her no contest plea. State v. Howard, — Ohio App. 3d —, 2007 Ohio 6591, — N.E. 2d —, 2007 Ohio App. LEXIS 5761 (Dec. 7, 2007).

RULE 11. Pleadings and Motions before Plea and Trial: Defenses and Objections

(A) **Pleadings and motions.** Pleadings in traffic cases shall be the complaint, the pleas of not guilty, guilty, and no contest. Defenses and objections shall be raised before plea and trial by motion to dismiss or to grant appropriate relief.

(B) **Motions before plea and trial.** Any defense, objection, or request which is capable of determination without the trial of the general issue may be raised before plea or trial by motion.

(1) The following defenses and objections must be raised before plea:

(a) Defenses and objections based on defects in the institution of the prosecution;

(b) Defenses and objections based on defects in the complaint other than failure to show jurisdiction in the court or to charge an offense, which objections shall be noticed by the court at any time during the pendency of the proceeding.

(2) The following motions and requests must be made before trial:

(a) Motions to suppress evidence, including but not limited to identification testimony, on the ground that it was illegally obtained;

(b) Requests and motions for discovery under Criminal Rule 16;

(c) Motions for severance of charges or defendants under Criminal Rule 14.

(C) **Motion date.** Pre-plea motions shall be made before or at arraignment. All pretrial motions, except as provided in Criminal Rule 16(F), shall be made within thirty-five days after arraignment or seven days before trial, whichever is earlier. The court, in the interest of justice, may extend the time for making pre-plea or pretrial motions.

(D) **Disclosure of evidence by prosecuting attorney.** At the arraignment, or as soon thereafter as is practicable, the defendant may, in order to raise objections prior to trial under subsection (B)(2), request notice of the prosecuting attorney's intention to use evidence in chief at trial, which evidence the defendant is entitled to discover under Criminal Rule 16.

(E) **Ruling on motion.** A motion made before trial, other than a motion for change of venue, shall be timely determined before trial. Where factual issues are involved in determining a motion, the court shall state its essential findings on the record.

(F) **Effect of failure to raise defenses or objections.** Failure by the defendant to raise defenses or objections or to make motions and requests which must be made prior to plea, trial, or at the time set by the court pursuant to subdivision (C), or prior to any extension thereof made by the court, shall constitute waiver thereof, but the court for good cause shown may grant relief from the waiver.

(G) **Effect of plea of no contest.** The plea of no contest does not preclude a defendant from asserting upon appeal that the trial court prejudicially erred in ruling on a pretrial motion, including a pretrial motion to suppress evidence.

(H) **Effect of determination.** If the court grants a motion to dismiss based on a defect in the institution of the prosecution or in the complaint, the court shall dismiss the case unless the prosecuting attorney can, pursuant to Criminal Rule 7(D), amend the complaint.

(I) **State's right of appeal.** The state may take an appeal in traffic cases pursuant to Criminal Rule 12(K).

History: Effective January 1, 1975; amended effective February 1, 2008.

NOTES TO DECISIONS

ANALYSIS

Jurisdiction
Waiver

Jurisdiction

Defendant did not raise the allegedly defective service of the traffic ticket or any lack of personal jurisdiction until mid-trial, long after he pled not guilty at his initial appearance. As such, he conferred personal jurisdiction on the trial court and thus waived the issue. State v. Smith, — Ohio App. 3d —, 2007 Ohio 3182, — N.E. 2d —, 2007 Ohio App. LEXIS 2981 (June 21, 2007).

Waiver

Where defendant was served by certified mail with a summons and citation that charged him with a violation of RC § 4511.21 and he appeared before a trial court and entered a not guilty plea without first asserting a claim that the trial court lacked personal jurisdiction over him under Ohio Traf. R. 3, the trial court thereafter properly overruled his motion to dismiss based on lack of personal jurisdiction, as that issue was deemed waived pursuant to Ohio Traf. R. 11(B). State v. Cook, — Ohio App. 3d —, 2006 Ohio 1953, — N.E. 2d —, 2006 Ohio App. LEXIS 1784 (Apr. 17, 2006).

RULE 12. Receipt of guilty or no contest plea

The pleas of guilty and no contest shall be received only by personal appearance of the defendant in open court, except that, the plea of guilty may be received in accordance with Rule 13 at a regularly established traffic violations bureau, or by plea in absentia presented in proper written form with leave of court, and in open court with the prosecutor participating. Pleas in absentia may be taken on charges involving operation of a motor vehicle in violation of section 4511.19 of the Revised Code or any substantially similar municipal ordinance with consent of the prosecutor. The plea in absentia shall contain a rights waiver, acknowledgement of penalties, and the defendant's signature.

The receipt of a plea contrary to the provisions of these rules is forbidden.

History: Effective January 1, 1975; amended eff. January 1, 2010.

RULE 13.   Traffic violations bureau

(A) **Establishment and operation of traffic violations bureau.** Each court shall establish a traffic violations bureau. The juvenile division of the court of common pleas may establish a violations bureau pursuant to Traffic Rule 13.1. The court shall appoint its clerk as violations clerk. If there is no clerk, the court shall appoint any appropriate person of the municipality or county in which the court sits. The violations bureau and violations clerk shall be under the direction and control of the court. Fines and costs shall be paid to, receipted by, and accounted for by the violations clerk.

The violations bureau shall accept appearance, waiver of trial, plea of guilty, and payment of fine and costs for offenses within its authority.

(B) **Authority of violations bureau.** All traffic offenses except those listed in division (B)(1) to (9) of this rule may be disposed of by a traffic violations bureau. The following traffic offenses shall not be processed by a traffic violations bureau:

(1) Indictable offenses;

(2) Operating a motor vehicle while under the influence of alcohol or any drug of abuse;

(3) Leaving the scene of an accident;

(4) Driving while under suspension or revocation of a driver's or commercial driver's license;

(5) Driving without being licensed to drive, except where the driver's or commercial driver's license had been expired for six months or less;

(6) A third moving traffic offense within a twelve-month period;

(7) Failure to stop and remain standing upon meeting or overtaking a school bus stopped on the highway for the purpose of receiving or discharging a school child;

(8) Willfully eluding or fleeing a police officer;

(9) Drag racing.

(C) **Schedule of fines.** The court shall establish and publish a schedule of fines and costs for all offenses. The schedule shall be distributed to all law enforcement agencies operating within the jurisdiction of the court and shall be prominently displayed at the place in the violations bureau where fines are paid.

(D) **Defendant's appearance, plea and waiver of trial.**

(1) At any time prior to arraignment or thereafter with leave of court, a defendant charged with an offense that can be processed by a traffic violations bureau may do either of the following:

(a) Appear in person at the traffic violations bureau, sign a plea of guilty and waiver of trial provision of the ticket, and pay the total amount of the fine and costs;

(b) Sign the guilty plea and waiver of trial provision of the ticket and mail the ticket and a check, money order, or other approved form of payment for the total amount of the fine and costs to the traffic violations bureau;

(2) A court may establish a procedure for accepting, through its traffic violations bureau, guilty pleas, waivers of trial, and payments of fines and costs by telephone or other electronic means. The form of payment accepted by telephone or other electronic means shall be approved by the bureau.

(3) Remittance of the fine and costs to the traffic violations bureau by any means other than personal appearance by the defendant at the bureau constitutes a guilty plea and waiver of trial whether or not the guilty plea and waiver of trial provision of the ticket are signed by the defendant.

(E) **Records.** All cases processed in the violations bureau shall be numbered and recorded for identification and statistical purposes. In any statistical reports required by law, the number of cases disposed of by the violations bureau shall be listed separately from those disposed of in open court.

(F) **Hours of operation; personnel.** The court shall appoint a law enforcement officer as a deputy violations bureau clerk to act as violations clerk when the violations clerk is not on duty.

History: Effective January 1, 1975; amended, eff August 4, 1980; February 26, 1990; November 1, 1994; July 1, 1997; May 3, 1999; February 1, 2002; January 1, 2010.

RULE 13.1.   Juvenile traffic violations bureau

(A) By local rule of court, the juvenile division of the court of common pleas may establish a violations bureau for juvenile traffic offenders. Except as provided in division (B) of this rule, a juvenile traffic violations bureau shall function in the same manner as a violations bureau established pursuant to Traffic Rule 13.

(B) All juvenile traffic offenses may be disposed of by a violations bureau, except as follows:

(1) An offense listed in Traffic Rule 13(B)(1) to (5) and (7) to (9);

(2) A second or subsequent moving offense;

(3) An offense that involves an accident.

History: Effective February 1, 2002.

RULE 14.   Magistrates

(A) A court may appoint one or more magistrates for the purpose of receiving pleas, determining guilt or innocence, receiving statements in explanation and in mitigation of sentence, and recommending penalty to be imposed. A magistrate shall be an attorney admitted to practice in Ohio. A magistrate shall be provided with court room accommodations resembling as nearly as possible traffic court rooms.

(B) A court may refer nonjury traffic cases to a magistrate. If the offense charged is an offense for which imprisonment is a possible penalty, the case may be referred only with the unanimous consent of the parties, in writing or on the record in open court. The consent of an alleged juvenile traffic offender or his or her parent, guardian, or custodian shall not be required.

(C) Proceedings before the magistrate shall be conducted as provided in Criminal Rule 19. A defendant's payment of a fine does not constitute a waiver of the defendant's right to file objections to the magistrate's decision.

History: Effective January 1, 1975; amended, eff September 1, 1996; February 1, 2002; October 1, 2006.

NOTES TO DECISIONS

ANALYSIS

Adoption of magistrate's decision

Adoption of magistrate's decision
Defendant's appeal from a magistrate's decision finding him guilty of speeding was dismissed. Because the trial court did not properly adopt the magistrate's decision, pursuant to Ohio R. Crim. P. 19(E)(3)(a) and Ohio Traf. R. 14(C), there was no final order for defendant to appeal; thus, defendant's appeal was not properly before the court. State v. Dixon, — Ohio App. 3d —, 2006 Ohio 4932, — N.E. 2d —, 2006 Ohio App. LEXIS 4861 (Sept. 22, 2006).

RULE 15.   [Reserved]

RULE 16.   Judicial conduct

The Code of Judicial Conduct as adopted by the Supreme Court applies to all judges and mayors.

It shall be the obligation of each mayor to conduct his court and his professional and personal relationships in accordance with the same standards as are required of judges of courts of record.

History: Effective January 1, 1975; amended, eff February 1, 2002.

RULE 17.   Traffic case scheduling

(A) **Arraignment and trial by traffic division.** Where a court sits in divisions and one division is designated as traffic court, all traffic defendants shall, where practicable, be arraigned and tried in such division.

(B) **Arraignment and trial by traffic session.** Where a court not sitting in separate divisions designates a particular session as a traffic session, traffic defendants shall, where practicable, be arraigned and tried at such session.

(C) **Single-judge courts.** In single-judge courts, traffic cases shall, where practicable, be called before nontraffic cases. Uncontested traffic cases shall be disposed of first and contested cases scheduled for later hearing.

History: Effective January 1, 1975; amended eff. January 1, 2010.

RULE 18.   Continuances

Continuances shall be granted only upon a written motion which states the grounds for the requested continuance.

When a court grants a continuance, it shall set a definite date for the hearing or trial.

History: Effective January 1, 1975.

RULE 19.   Rule of court

The expression "rule of court" as used in these rules means a rule promulgated by the Supreme Court or a rule concerning local practice adopted by another court and filed with the Supreme Court. Local rules shall be supplementary to and consistent with these rules. Each court shall publish its local rules, distribute them within its jurisdiction, and keep copies for inspection.

History: Effective January 1, 1975.

RULE 20.   Procedure not otherwise specified

If no procedure is specifically prescribed by these rules, the Rules of Criminal Procedure and the applicable law apply.

History: Effective January 1, 1975.

RULE 21.   Forms

The forms contained in the Appendix of Forms are mandatory, except that additional copies of any portions of the ticket may be made. The reverse of the enforcement agency record shall be made in the form prescribed by the issuing authority.

History: Effective January 1, 1975.

RULE 22.   [Reserved]

(Former Rule 22 entitled Review Commission was repealed effective January 1, 2006. The functions of the Review Commission were transferred to the Supreme Court Commission on the Rules of Practice and Procedure on that date.)

RULE 23.   Title

These rules shall be known as the Ohio Traffic Rules and may be cited as "Traffic Rules" or "Traf. R.____."

History: Effective January 1, 1975.

RULE 24.   Effective date

(A) **Effective date of rules.** These rules take effect on January 1, 1975. They govern all proceedings in actions brought after they take effect, and also all further proceedings in actions then pending, except to the extent that their application in a particular action pending when the rules take effect would not be feasible or would work injustice, in which event the former procedure applies.

(B) **Use of tickets conforming to prior rules.** Traffic tickets conforming to the requirements of the "Ohio Rules of Practice and Procedure in Traffic Cases For All Courts Inferior to Common Pleas" may be used after the effective date of these rules.

After the effective date of these rules, issuing authorities shall order only tickets conforming to these rules.

History: Effective January 1, 1975.

RULE 25. Effective date of amendments

(A) The amendments to these rules and the Uniform Traffic Ticket adopted by the Supreme Court of Ohio on June 17, 1980 shall take effect on August 4, 1980.

(B) The amendments to the Uniform Traffic Ticket shall take effect on September 15, 1985. The amendment to Traffic Rule 22 shall take effect on July 27, 1988.

(C) The amendment to Traffic Rule 22, adopted by the Supreme Court on December 5, 1989, shall take effect on December 5, 1989.

(D) The amendments to Traffic Rules 3, 13, and 25, and the Uniform Traffic Ticket, adopted by the Supreme Court of Ohio on February 13, 1990, shall take effect on February 26, 1990.

(E) The amendments to Traffic Rules 3 and 7, adopted by the Supreme Court of Ohio on November 20, 1990, shall take effect on November 28, 1990.

(F) The amendments to Traffic Rule 3 and to the ""Reverse of Defendant's Copy"" of the Uniform Traffic Ticket, adopted by the Supreme Court of Ohio on March 16, 1992, shall take effect on June 1, 1992.

(G) The amendments to Traffic Rule 22, adopted by the Supreme Court of Ohio on August 17, 1994, shall take effect on September 19, 1994. The amendments to Traffic Rule 13 and to the Uniform Traffic Ticket, adopted by the Supreme Court of Ohio on August 17, 1994, shall take effect on November 1, 1994.

(H) The amendments to Traffic Rule 14, adopted by the Supreme Court of Ohio on July 10, 1996, shall take effect on September 1, 1996.

(I)(1) The amendments to Traffic Rule 13, adopted by the Supreme Court of Ohio on March 31, 1997, shall take effect on July 1, 1997.

(2) The amendments to the Uniform Traffic Ticket, adopted by the Supreme Court of Ohio on March 31, 1997, shall take effect on July 1, 1997. Through June 30, 1998, jurisdictions may use tickets printed in the format that was authorized prior to July 1, 1997. All tickets ordered for use on or after July 1, 1997 and all tickets used on or after July 1, 1998 shall conform to the format of the July 1, 1997 Uniform Traffic Ticket.

(J) The amendments to Traffic Rule 13, adopted by the Supreme Court of Ohio on March 30, 1999, shall take effect on May 3, 1999.

(K) The amendments to Traffic Rules 2, 3, 13, 13.1, 14, 16, and 25, adopted by the Supreme Court of Ohio on December 11, 2001, shall take effect on February 1, 2002.

(L) The amendments to Traffic Rules 2 and 22, adopted by the Supreme Court of Ohio on October 25, 2005, shall take effect on January 1, 2006.

(M) The amendments to Traffic Rules 3, 14, and 15, adopted by the Supreme Court of Ohio on August 8, 2006, shall take effect on October 1, 2006.

(N) The amendments to Traffic Rule 11, adopted by the Supreme Court of Ohio on December 11, 2007, shall take effect on February 1, 2008.

(O) The amendments to Traffic Rule 3, adopted by the Supreme Court of Ohio on April 22, 2008 shall take effect on May 1, 2008.

(P) The amendments to Traffic Rules 2, 3, 4, 10, 12, 13, and 17 and the Uniform Traffic Ticket adopted by the Supreme Court of Ohio on September 29, 2009 shall take effect on January 1, 2010. Through June 30, 2010, jurisdictions may use tickets printed in the format that was authorized prior to January 1, 2010. All tickets ordered for use on or after July 1, 2010 and all tickets used on or after July 1, 2010 shall conform to the format of the January 1, 2010 Uniform Traffic Ticket.

Temporary Provision

Notwithstanding Traffic Rule 3, the Bowling Green Municipal Court is authorized to develop and use a modified version of the Uniform Traffic Ticket in all moving traffic cases. The modified version of the Uniform Traffic Ticket shall be used by the Bowling Green Municipal Court beginning on a date not later than three months from October 21, 1991 and its use shall terminate one year from the date on which it is first used. As used in the Ohio Traffic Rules and defined by Traffic Rule 2, ""traffic ticket"" shall include the modified version of the Uniform Traffic Ticket in all moving traffic developed and used by the Bowling Green Municipal Court pursuant to this provision.

Effective: October 21, 1991.

Temporary Provision

Notwithstanding Traffic Rule 3, the Akron Municipal Court, Berea Municipal Court, Licking County Municipal Court, Newton Falls Municipal Court, Parma Municipal Court, Brown County Court, Broadview Heights Mayor's Court, Moraine Mayor's Court, North Royalton Mayor's Court, and the Ohio Highway Patrol are authorized to use the modified version of the Uniform Traffic Ticket approved by the Supreme Court Traffic Rules Review Commission in all moving traffic cases. The modified version of the Uniform Traffic Ticket shall be used by these courts and the Highway Patrol beginning on a date no earlier than April 1, 1996. The use of the modified Uniform Traffic Ticket shall continue for a period of six months from the date on which it is first used in the individual courts or by the Highway Patrol. As used in the Ohio Traffic Rules and defined by Traffic Rule 2, "traffic ticket" shall include the modified version of the Uniform Traffic Ticket used pursuant to this provision.

Effective: April 1, 1996.

Temporary Provision

A law enforcement officer who issues an automated traffic ticket is considered to have signed the ticket, for purposes of Traffic Rule 3(E), if the issuing officer properly authorizes the appearance of his or her facsimile signature on the ticket.

For purposes of this Temporary Provision:

(A) "Automated traffic ticket" means the computerized traffic citation developed by the Office of Criminal Justice Services, Ohio Highway Patrol, and local law enforcement agencies and courts and being used on a pilot project basis by the Licking County Sheriff's Office, Newark Police Department, Heath Police Department, Licking County Municipal Court, Circleville Police Department, Pickaway County Sheriff's Office, Circleville Municipal Court, the Circleville Post of the Ohio Highway Patrol, the Newark Post of the Ohio Highway Patrol, and the General Headquarters of the Ohio Highway Patrol.

(B) "Properly authorizes" means the issuing officer uses a secure password, in the manner demonstrated to the Traffic Rules Review Commission at its December 18, 1998 meeting, that, when entered, allows an electronic version of the his or her signature to appear on the automated traffic ticket and on any printed version of that ticket.

Effective: January 12, 1999.

APPENDIX OF FORMS

(AMENDED, EFF 8-4-80; 9-15-85; 2-26-90; 6-1-92; 11-1-94; 7-1-97; 10-19-09; 1-1-10)

MULTI-COUNT UNIFORM TRAFFIC TICKET

Commission Commentary (January 1, 2010 Amendments)

On December 1, 2009, the Supreme Court of Ohio adopted a correction to the Multi-Count Uniform Traffic Ticket previously published on October 19, 2009. The correction is on the reverse side of the defendant's copy. The specific language is located under the checkbox for "Waiverable through traffic violations bureau". To comply with language adopted by the Court in Traf. R. 13(D)(1), the phrase "within seven days of the day you receive the ticket" has been replaced with "at any time prior to arraignment".

The corrected ticket is effective January 1, 2010 and mandatory July 1, 2010. Through June 30, 2010, jurisdictions may use tickets printed in the format that was authorized prior to January 1, 2010. All tickets ordered for use on or after January 1, 2010 and all tickets used on or after July 1, 2010 shall conform to the format of the January 1, 2010 Uniform Traffic Ticket.

Commission Commentary (July 1, 1997 Amendments)

The Supreme Court Traffic Rules Review Commission has developed the following Multi-Count Uniform Traffic Ticket. This ticket will significantly change the way in which traffic offenses are processed in the State of Ohio.

The Commission's comments are intended to provide an overview of the major changes, both in information and layout, to assist in understanding the new form. The Commission has worked with the input of law enforcement, judges, the Ohio Bureau of Motor Vehicles, and court personnel to solve most of the issues raised in the devising of this type of ticket. Separate comments for each side of the Multi-Count Uniform Traffic Ticket, which will be referred to as UTT.

Training, Implementation, and General Comment

Although all jurisdictions are required to use the basic UTT, some courts might not use the Face of Court Record or paper Abstract, while other might use the Face of Court Record but not the paper Abstract.

Training on the new UTT will be of great importance. Although there are a number of changes, after some relatively basic training the forms can be implemented without a significant shock in changing from the pre July 1, 1997 version of the UTT.

In the Commission's work, many issues have been raised regarding inclusion or exclusion of language, information, and what would go best in what locations. Many of the issues which may be raised as training proceeds will be primarily issues that can be resolved in training and actual use of the ticket.

Face of Court Record

The new Face of Court Record provides for the ability to write up to six separate traffic citations on one traffic ticket. The Face of Court Record is identical to the face of Defendant's copy and the Enforcement Agency Record front copy.

The Driver's Identification Information is substantially similar to the previous UTT, although certain information items, such as eye glasses and driving restrictions were deleted. Boxes are printed for officer compliance with S.B. 20, to indicate whether Financial Responsibility Proof is shown at time of the traffic stop, to provide a record for the Court System on S.B. 20 compliance.

The Citation Section consists of six separate boxes, four of which identify specific types of offenses. The two remaining boxes would be for other offenses. The Statutory Code Box provides for a check-off as to whether Ordinance, State Code, or Turnpike Rule is being cited. The Speed Section includes identification for all of the various speed measurement devices currently in use in the State of Ohio. The OMVI Section would be for the writing of one of the two potential OMVI charges, with a second OMVI charge being written in one of the other offense sections. The Driver's License Section would deal with all license-related charges, whether DUS, NOL, or restriction type offenses. The Safety Belt Section would address all belt or restraint offenses.

The Weather and Pavement information is similar to current traffic ticket forms. The UTT would not be used for the citing of non-traffic criminal charges in a traffic stop, which would be written under a separate criminal citation form. The information above the Defendant's Summons would be completed to indicate whether another complaint exists, as well as the total number of offenses being cited on the ticket for the Court to match up the total number of offenses which the officer has written. The Defendant's Summons is similar to the current Defendant's Summons.

Reverse of Court Record

The Reverse of Court Record is a significant departure from the current Reverse of Court Record, primarily so that up to six citations could be resolved on one document. The proposed Reverse of Court Record retains all of the necessary information from the current Reverse of Court Copy, but redesigns the layout to enable for information to be recorded efficiently.

The "Court Action: Orders" Section of the old ticket is replaced by the new section with bail and rescheduling information. The Bail Section enables the court to record the bail status of the Defendant, whether released without bail or bail being set, including the type of bond, and the Depositor's identification information. The Continuance Section enables space to be allotted for sufficient continuances of cases with new dates indicated, including check-off boxes for the various Failure to Appear Sanctions available under Traffic Rule 7, including License Forfeiture for Failure to Appear.

The Court Entry Section enables a court to take pleas on and dispose of up to six charges on one form. Defendant's pleas, findings and sentencing are handled vertically for each charge, as indicated (court will use "G, NG, NC" for plea and finding notations). The initial plea in each respective charge would be indicated by a "G/NG/NC" designation with a comparable finding code in the finding box. The fine would be noted and imposed for each particular offense in its appropriate box as would any jail days imposed. Any suspended costs, fines, or jail would be noted in the appropriate boxes.

Additional space is provided for limited sentencing parameters for certain mandatory OMVI issues. A 72-Hour Program box in noted. Sections include not only driver's license suspension information, but information regarding modified privileges when granted. The Court Section also provides the waiver approval so that waiver could be checked off and signed by the Judicial Official by checking the box and signing off.

The Clerk's Use Section includes all the appropriate financial information needed by the clerks, including the breaking out of local and state costs for accounting purposes. The Check Box Section provides check-off process for the waiver process and also appropriate S.B. 20 information as to the showing or failing to show of insurance proof.

The Commission acknowledges that on this page, and others, that space is at a premium. In the implementation of the UTT, fine point pens should almost certainly be used on all writing on the documents to enable all print to be read. Notwithstanding the limitations, sufficient space would be available for all necessary entries. The form in no way precludes the addition of any other forms or entries which a court may use in conjunction with the Reverse of Court Record, but this Reverse of Court Record provides a simple one-write system for a court to use, if desired.

Reverse of Defendant's Copy

The current Reverse of Defendant's Copy has been revised to not only include currently required information, but to incorporate a new warning on S.B. 20 compliance.

The language throughout the Defendant's copy is substantially similar to current language, except syntax has been changed, now referring to multiple offenses on the citation, and to also note the changes in Traffic Rule 13(B) effective November 1, 1994. It also includes the warning of License Cancellation and Forfeiture for Failure to Appear or Pay Fines. On the bottom, the clerk's receipt signature on the waiver form was eliminated, as this would be kept on the Reverse of Court Record form with receipts being separately given to the defendant.

The center of Reverse of Defendant's Copy contains a new insurance warning to place all traffic violators on notice regarding mandatory insurance showing under S.B. 20. The sections that were block lettered were done so to identify in bolder type the sanctions and warnings, to place all defendants on notice of the requirements of S.B. 20. Although the form has a blank line for filling in information as to the courts, this information could be pre-printed in the space provided to eliminate the officer having to fill in this information.

Abstract of Court Record

The Abstract of Court Record is the manual copy that is sent to the Bureau of Motor Vehicles (BMV) for the processing of necessary conviction and other information to the BMV. Many courts currently are on computer to computer information transfer to the BMV, and it may well be that all courts eventually will report electronically. This form would be used by those courts that manually report their information to the BMV.

The top two-thirds of the Abstract of Court Record is identical to the Face of Court Record with the identifying information of original charges and driver's identification information. The court code and case number identifies the court sending the Abstract. The "No FR" boxes are to identify to the BMV those situations where there has not been compliance with S.B. 20, which the clerk reports to the BMV.

The Box Section would list, vertically, for each of the offenses for which BMV requires reporting the various information items in the required BMV format, including the plea, points assessed and the BMV offense code. A Section for Reduced Offenses is also present, based upon the required reporting of reduction of OMVI and DUS offenses, regardless of disposition, to the BMV. Child Restraint convictions are included in the BMV reporting based upon current law which require escalated fines based upon prior Child Restraint convictions. The two blank boxes would be for the two charges that would come from the "other offense" boxes.

The License Information Section provides a check-off to notify the BMV of any driver's license suspension, including indication for modified driving privileges, and to indicate the charge for which the suspension was imposed. In the event of a license forfeiture, the Abstract would be accompanied by a BMV form 2528. The other information box is to provide that the clerk could send additional information. This would be dome [sic] on the reverse side of the paper Abstract by placing the information on the back side, which will be blank. The checking of this box will advise the BMV to check for additional information on the reverse side.

Reverse of Enforcement Agency Record

This is the Reverse Side of the Enforcement Agency's copy of the basic ticket. This side provides an information and tracking process for the Enforcement Agency to track court action on the case and to provide the officer with space for limited notes as to the offense at the time of citation, including identification of witnesses. The bottom of the form is to provide information location to the officer for PUCO and weight citations, so that the information may be preserved.

_____ COURT _____ COUNTY, OHIO

STATE OF OHIO _____ TICKET #_____

☐ City ☐ Village ☐ Township CASE #_____

NAME _____

STREET _____

CITY, STATE _____ ZIP_____

OPERATOR LICENSE / STATE ID# ☐ NONE*	BIRTH DATE	ISSUE DATE	STATE

CLASS	EXPIRES	ENDORSEMENT(s)/RESTRICTION(s)	SS# (last 4 digits)
		☐CDL ☐MC ☐Other_____	

SEX	HEIGHT	WEIGHT	EYES	HAIR	RACE	FINANCIAL RESPONSIBILITY PROOF?
						☐ Yes ☐ No ☐ N/A

* If no OL/State ID; **REQUIRED** documentation attached: ☐ Yes

TO DEFENDANT: COMPLAINT ON _____ 20 _____ AT _____ AM/PM, YOU

Operated/Passenger/Parked/Walked a ☐ Passenger ☐ Motorcycle ☐ Bicycle ☐ Other_____

☐Commercial DOT#_____ ☐ ≥26,001 lbs. ☐ <16 Pass. Bus ☐ ≥16 Pass. Bus ☐ Haz. Mat.

VEHICLE: YEAR _____ MAKE_____ MODEL _____

COLOR_____ LICENSE #_____ STATE _____

UPON A PUBLIC HIGHWAY, NAMELY _____

AT/NEAR _____ (M.P. ____)

IN THE _____ OF _____ IN _____

COUNTY (NO.),_____ STATE OF OHIO AND COMMITTED THE FOLLOWING OFFENSE(S).

SPEED: _____ MPH in _____ MPH zone ☐ Over limits ☐ Unsafe for conditions ☐ ACDA ☐ Radar ☐ Air ☐ VASCAR ☐ Pace ☐ Laser ☐ Stationary ☐ Moving	☐ ORC ☐ ORD ☐ T.P.
OVI: ☐ Under the influence of alcohol/drug of abuse. ☐ Prohibited blood alcohol concentration. _____ BAC ☐ Blood ☐ Breath ☐ Urine ☐ Refused Prior OVIs: # of prior OVIs Years of prior OVIs	☐ ORC ☐ ORD ☐ T.P.
DRIVER LICENSE: ☐ None ☐ Not on person ☐Revoked ☐ Suspended EXPIRED: ☐ <6 months ☐ >6 months ☐Failure to Reinstate Suspension Type: _____	☐ ORC ☐ ORD ☐ T.P.
SAFETY BELT: Failure to wear ☐ Driver ☐ Passenger ☐ Child Restraint ☐ Booster Seat	☐ ORC ☐ ORD ☐ T.P.
OTHER OFFENSE: _____	☐ ORC ☐ ORD ☐ T.P.
OTHER OFFENSE: _____	☐ ORC ☐ ORD ☐ T.P.

☐ DRIVER LICENSE HELD ☐ VEHICLE SEIZED ☐ JUVENILE OFFENDER

PAVEMENT: ☐ Dry ☐ Wet ☐ Snow ☐ Icy # of Lanes_____ ☐ **Construction Zone**

VISIBILITY: ☐ Clear ☐ Cloudy ☐ Dusk ☐ Night ☐ Dawn

WEATHER: ☐ Rain ☐ Snow ☐ Fog ☐ No Adverse

TRAFFIC: ☐ Heavy ☐ Moderate ☐ Light ☐ None

AREA: ☐ Business ☐ Rural ☐ Residential ☐ Industry ☐ School

CRASH: ☐ **Yes** ☐ No ☐ Almost Caused ☐ Non-Injury ☐ **Injury** ☐ **Fatal**

Crash Report Number:

REMARKS:

ACCOMPANYING CRIMINAL CHARGE ☐ Yes ☐ No TOTAL # OFFENSES _____

TO DEFENDANT: SUMMONS   **PERSONAL APPEARANCE REQUIRED** ☐ Yes ☐ No

You are summoned and ordered to appear on_____,20_____ at_____ AM/PM,

in_____ Court, at_____

If you fail to appear at this time and place you may be arrested or your license may be cancelled.

This summons served personally on the defendant on _____ 20_____

The issuing/charging law enforcement officer states under the penalties of perjury and falsification that he/she has read the above complaint and that it is true.

COURT CODE	UNIT	POST	DISTRICT

_____
Charging Law Enforcement Officer

Issuing Law Enforcement Officer ☐ **SAME AS ABOVE**

Issuing Officer: Verify address. If different from license address, write present address in space provided.

OHP0060 10-0060-00 (REVISION 0509) **COURT RECORD**

OSHP HP7 [B6305]

PRESENT ADDRESS · SIGNATURE X · CO. RES. · PHONE ( )

Docket #_____ Page #_____ Case #_____

Defendant's Attorney _____

Name / Address / Telephone

DATE	COURT ACTION: ORDERS
	BAIL

☐ **No Bail** - Defendant cited and released.

☐ **Bail** in the amount of $_____ set by Judge pursuant to bail schedule.

BOND AMOUNT	BOND TYPE
$_____	☐ Cash ☐ Personal ☐ 10% ☐ AAA/Insurance Bond
	☐ Unsecured ☐ Surety ☐ O.L. Held ☐ Other _____

Depositor: _____

Name / Address / Telephone

☐ Defendant released upon execution of Bail as noted:_____ See Bond forms — received by_____

CONTINUANCE Requester:_____	New DATE
CONTINUANCE Reason: _____	
☐ Defendant Failed to Appear	
☐ Order Supplemental Summons to New Date	
☐ Order Operator's License Forfeiture ☐ Bond Forfeiture	
☐ Order Warrant: Bond Amount $_____	
☐ Summons Issued Served **DATE**:	
☐ Warrant Issued Executed **DATE**:	

_____ ____/____/____
Judge/Magistrate   DATE

COURT ENTRY

Defendant present with/without Counsel. All rights pursuant to Criminal Rules 10 & 11, Traffic Rules 8 & 10 explained.

	COUNT					
	SPEED	**OVI**	**LICENSE**	**SEATBELT**		
Initial Plea						
Trial Date						
Finding						
Fine $						
Costs $						
Jailtime (Days)						
	SUSPENDED					
Fines $						
Costs $						
Jailtime (Days)						

ADDITIONAL ORDERS

☐ **If OVI conviction:** 72 hour program permitted in lieu of jail.

☐ Defendant's License is **SUSPENDED** for_____ days / month(s) / year(s),
which shall commence on_____ and end on _____

☐ Defendant is granted **Limited Driving Privileges** as follows, effective:_____

_____
_____

☐ Defendant to pay fines on **Payment Program** – see separate entry.

☐ If **WAIVERED**: ☐MET Requirements of Waiver ☐PAID Fines and Costs ☐ACCEPTED Guilty Plea(s)
☐MADE Guilty Finding(s). Imposed FINES and COSTS noted below.

_____ ____/____/____
Judge/Magistrate   DATE

FOR CLERK'S USE	COUNT					
	SPEED	**OVI**	**LICENSE**	**SEATBELT**		
Fines $						
Costs - Local $						
Costs - State $						
TOTAL $						
Receipt #(s)						

☐ If **WAIVERED**: Guilty Plea(s), Waiver(s) and Payments made: ☐ In Person ☐ By Mail
Receipt supplied to defendant: ☐ In Person ☐ Check is receipt ☐ By Mail via USPS FIRST CLASS LETTER RATE
Waiver reviewed, found to be correct and approved.   mail to defendant's present address.

☐ Financial Responsibility PROOF SHOWN

☐ NO Financial Responsibility PROOF: Clerk to notify BMV

☐ Financial Responsibility PROOF NOT APPLICABLE

_____
Clerk / Violations Clerk / Deputy Clerk

____/____/____   ____/____/____
DATE Abstract Mailed to BMV   **DATE** Mayor's Court Transfer/Notice of Appeal

COURT RECORD reverse side

_____ COURT _____ COUNTY, OHIO

STATE OF OHIO _____   TICKET #_____
       □ City   □ Village   □ Township   CASE #_____

NAME _____

STREET _____

CITY, STATE _____ ZIP_____

OPERATOR LICENSE / STATE ID#	□ None*	BIRTH DATE	ISSUE DATE	STATE

CLASS	EXPIRES	ENDORSEMENT(s)/RESTRICTION(s)	SS# (last 4 digits)
		□CDL □MC □Other_____	

SEX	HEIGHT	WEIGHT	EYES	HAIR	RACE	FINANCIAL RESPONSIBILITY PROOF?
						□ Yes □ No □ N/A

* If no OL/State ID; **REQUIRED** documentation attached: □ Yes

TO DEFENDANT: COMPLAINT ON _____, 20 ____ AT _____AM/PM, YOU
Operated/Passenger/Parked/Walked a □ Passenger □ Motorcycle □ Bicycle □ Other_____
□Commercial DOT#_____ □ ≥26,001 lbs. □ <16 Pass. Bus □ ≥16 Pass. Bus □ Haz. Mat.

VEHICLE: YEAR _____ MAKE_____ MODEL_____
COLOR_____ LICENSE #_____ STATE_____
UPON A PUBLIC HIGHWAY, NAMELY _____
AT/NEAR _____ (M.P._____)
IN THE _____ OF _____ IN _____
COUNTY (NO.),_____ STATE OF OHIO AND COMMITTED THE FOLLOWING OFFENSE(S).

SPEED: _____MPH in _____MPH zone □ Over limits □ Unsafe for conditions □ ACDA □ Radar □ Air □ VASCAR □ Pace □ Laser □ Stationary □ Moving	□ ORC □ ORD □ T.P.
OVI: □ Under the influence of alcohol/drug of abuse. □ Prohibited blood alcohol concentration. _____ BAC □ Blood □ Breath □ Urine □ Refused Prior OVIs: [# of prior OVIs] [Years of prior OVIs]	□ ORC □ ORD □ T.P.
DRIVER LICENSE: □ None □ Not on person □ Revoked □ Suspended EXPIRED: □ <6 months □ >6 months □ Failure to Reinstate Suspension Type:	□ ORC □ ORD □ T.P.
SAFETY BELT: Failure to wear □ Driver □ Passenger □ Child Restraint □ Booster Seat	□ ORC □ ORD □ T.P.
OTHER OFFENSE: _____	□ ORC □ ORD □ T.P.
OTHER OFFENSE: _____	□ ORC □ ORD □ T.P.
□ DRIVER LICENSE HELD □ VEHICLE SEIZED □ JUVENILE OFFENDER	

Court Case_____ COURT NAME _____

Case #_____ FR SHOWN □ YES □ NO FR SHOWN - BMV to process.

	Speed	OVI	License	Child Restraint		
If Bond Forfeiture, DATE FORFEITED:						
CONVICTION DATE:						
MOVING VIOLATION?	YES NO	YES NO	YES NO	NO	YES NO	YES NO
PLEA CODE						
POINTS ASSESSED						
BMV OFFENSE CODE						
IF AMENDED, OFFENSE CODE						
FATALITY						

□ License Suspended _____days/months/years Effective: _____ to _____
□ Suspension Class _____
□ MO – Limited Driving Privileges Effective: _____ to _____
  (See Separate Entry) Suspension is on Count: _____ □ FRA SUSPENSION
□ License Forfeiture — See separate BMV Form 2528
□ OL Confiscated — Date sent to BMV: _____
□ Other Information — See reverse side.

I hereby certify that the above statements are taken from the records of this Court.

_____   ___/___/___
Authorized Signature   DATE
Send completed copy to: Ohio Bureau of Motor Vehicles
        P.O. Box 16583   **ABSTRACT OF**
        Columbus, OH 43216-6583 **COURT RECORD**

(Vertical side labels: PRESENT ADDRESS | SIGNATURE X | COUNTY RESIDENCE | PHONE ( ) | FOR BMV USE)

COURT _____ COUNTY, OHIO

STATE OF OHIO _____ TICKET # _____
☐ City   ☐ Village   ☐ Township   CASE # _____

NAME _____
STREET _____
CITY, STATE _____   ZIP _____

PRESENT ADDRESS

OPERATOR LICENSE / STATE ID# ☐ NONE*	BIRTH DATE	ISSUE DATE	STATE

CLASS	EXPIRES	ENDORSEMENT(s)/RESTRICTION(s)	SS# (last 4 digits)
		☐CDL ☐MC ☐Other	

SEX	HEIGHT	WEIGHT	EYES	HAIR	RACE	FINANCIAL RESPONSIBILITY PROOF?
						☐ Yes ☐ No ☐ N/A

* If no OL/State ID; **REQUIRED** documentation attached: ☐ Yes

TO DEFENDANT: COMPLAINT ON _____, 20___ AT _____ AM/PM, YOU
Operated/Passenger/Parked/Walked a ☐ Passenger ☐ Motorcycle ☐ Bicycle ☐ Other
☐ Commercial DOT# _____ ☐ ≥26,001 lbs. ☐ <16 Pass. Bus ☐ ≥16 Pass. Bus ☐ Haz. Mat.
VEHICLE: YEAR _____ MAKE _____ MODEL _____
COLOR _____ LICENSE # _____ STATE _____
UPON A PUBLIC HIGHWAY, NAMELY _____
AT/NEAR _____ (M.P. _____)
IN THE _____ OF _____ IN _____
COUNTY (NO.), _____ STATE OF OHIO AND COMMITTED THE FOLLOWING OFFENSE(S).

SIGNATURE X

SPEED: _____ MPH in _____ MPH zone ☐ Over limits ☐ Unsafe for conditions ☐ ACDA ☐ Radar ☐ Air ☐ VASCAR ☐ Pace ☐ Laser ☐ Stationary ☐ Moving	☐ ORC ☐ ORD ☐ T.P.
OVI: ☐ Under the influence of alcohol/drug of abuse. ☐ Prohibited blood alcohol concentration. _____ BAC ☐ Blood ☐ Breath ☐ Urine ☐ Refused # of prior OVIs / Years of prior OVIs Prior OVIs:	☐ ORC ☐ ORD ☐ T.P.
DRIVER LICENSE: ☐None ☐Not on person ☐Revoked ☐Suspended EXPIRED: ☐ <6 months ☐ >6 months ☐Failure to Reinstate Suspension Type:	☐ ORC ☐ ORD ☐ T.P.
SAFETY BELT: Failure to wear ☐ Driver ☐ Passenger ☐ Child Restraint ☐ Booster Seat	☐ ORC ☐ ORD ☐ T.P.
OTHER OFFENSE:	☐ ORC ☐ ORD ☐ T.P.
OTHER OFFENSE:	☐ ORC ☐ ORD ☐ T.P.

☐ DRIVER LICENSE HELD   ☐ VEHICLE SEIZED   ☐ JUVENILE OFFENDER

PAVEMENT: ☐ Dry ☐ Wet ☐ Snow ☐ Icy # of Lanes ____ ☐ **Construction Zone**
VISIBILITY: ☐ Clear ☐ Cloudy ☐ Dusk ☐ Night ☐ Dawn
WEATHER: ☐ Rain ☐ Snow ☐ Fog ☐ No Adverse
TRAFFIC: ☐ Heavy ☐ Moderate ☐ Light ☐ None
AREA: ☐ Business ☐ Rural ☐ Residential ☐ Industry ☐ School
CRASH: ☐ **Yes** ☐ No ☐ Almost Caused ☐ Non-Injury ☐ **Injury** ☐ **Fatal**
Crash Report Number:
REMARKS:

ACCOMPANYING CRIMINAL CHARGE ☐ Yes ☐ No   TOTAL # OFFENSES _____

CO. RES.

TO DEFENDANT: SUMMONS   PERSONAL APPEARANCE REQUIRED ☐ Yes ☐ No
You are summoned and ordered to appear on _____, 20___ at _____ AM/PM,
in _____ Court, at _____
If you fail to appear at this time and place you may be arrested or your license may be cancelled.
This summons served personally on the defendant on _____, 20___
The issuing/charging law enforcement officer states under the penalties of perjury and falsification that
he/she has read the above complaint and that it is true.

PHONE ( )

Court Code	Unit	Post	District

Charging Law Enforcement Officer _____

Issuing Law Enforcement Officer _____   ☐ SAME AS ABOVE
Issuing Officer: Verify address. If different from license address, write present address in space provided.

OSHP HP7
OHP0060 10-0060-00 (REVISION 0509)   **DEFENDANT'S COPY BLUE**   [B6305]

TO DEFENDANT: Read this material carefully.

☐   **Personal Appearance Required.**
If the officer marked this block on the face of the ticket, you must appear in court. Your appearance in court is required because the offenses cannot be processed by a traffic violations bureau.

Failure to Appear and/or **Pay:**

- The posting of bail or depositing your license as bond is to secure your appearance in court or the processing of the offenses through a traffic violations bureau. It is not a payment of fines or costs.

- If you do not appear at the time and place stated in the citation or if you do not timely process this citation through a traffic violations bureau, your license will be cancelled.
- Also, a warrant may be issued for your arrest and you may be subject to additional criminal penalties.

The following offenses require court appearance and may not be processed by a traffic violations bureau:

- Any indictable offense;
- Operating a vehicle under the influence of alcohol or any drug of abuse;
- Leave scene of accident;
- Driving while under suspension or revocation of driver's or commercial driver's license;

- Driving without being licensed to drive, except where the driver's or commercial driver's license has been expired for six months or less;
- A third moving traffic offense within 12 months;
- Passing a standing school bus;
- Willfully eluding or fleeing a police officer;
- Drag racing.

☐   **Waiverable through traffic violations bureau.**
If you are charged with offenses other than those listed above, you may, within seven days after the day you received the ticket, **plead guilty** to the offenses charged and dispose of the case without court appearance by:
(1) appearing personally at the traffic violations bureau, signing the waiver printed below and paying the fines and costs or
(2) signing the waiver printed below and mailing it and a check, money order, or other approved payment for the total of the fines and costs to the traffic violations bureau at the following address:

Traffic Violations Bureau Address: _____

_____

INSURANCE WARNING

Under Ohio law you are required to show proof of financial responsibility or insurance.
If you did not do so at the time of receiving his ticket, **you must submit proof** of insurance when you appear in court on these offenses.

If you do not submit the required proof:
- your driver's license will be suspended and
- you may be subject to additional fees and insurance sanctions.

If you have any questions regarding the **proof filing**, you may call the traffic violations bureau at the telephone indicated.

For information regarding your **Duty To Appear** or the **Fines and Costs** amount(s), call:

_____

Telephone Number(s)

Contested Case; Court Appearance Required.

If you desire to **contest the offenses** or if court **appearance is required**, you must appear at the time and place stated in the summons.

Notice to Defendant under age eighteen.

You **must appear** before the Juvenile Court at the time and place determined by that Court. The Juvenile Court will notify you when and where to appear.
This ticket will be filed with the Juvenile Court and may be used as a juvenile complaint.

_____

Juvenile Court Address

_____

For information regarding your **Duty to Appear** at Juvenile Court call:

_____

Telephone Number(s)

Guilty Pleas, No Contest Pleas, Waiver of Trial, Payment of Fines and Costs

I, the undersigned defendant, do hereby enter my written pleas of guilty to the offenses charged in this ticket. I realize that by signing these guilty pleas, I admit my guilt of the offenses charged and waive my right to contest the offenses in a trial before the court or jury. Further, I realize that a record of this plea will be sent to the Ohio Bureau of Motor Vehicles. I have not been convicted of, pleaded guilty to, or forfeited bond for two or more prior moving traffic offenses within the last 12 months. I plead guilty to the offense(s) charged.

FINES $ _____   X _____
                                Defendant's Signature

COSTS $ _____   _____
                                Address

TOTAL $ _____   _____

DEFENDANT'S COPY Reverse Side

COURT _____ COUNTY, OHIO

STATE OF OHIO _____   TICKET # _____
□ City   □ Village   □ Township   CASE # _____

NAME _____

STREET _____

CITY, STATE _____ ZIP _____

OPERATOR LICENSE / STATE ID#	□ NONE*		BIRTH DATE		ISSUE DATE		STATE
CLASS	EXPIRES		ENDORSEMENT(s)/RESTRICTION(s) □ CDL □ MC □ Other		SS# (last 4 digits)		
SEX	HEIGHT	WEIGHT	EYES	HAIR	RACE	FINANCIAL RESPONSIBILITY PROOF? □ Yes □ No □ N/A	

* If no OL/State ID; **REQUIRED** documentation attached: □ Yes

TO DEFENDANT: COMPLAINT ON _____ , 20 ___ AT _____ AM/PM, YOU
Operated/Passenger/Parked/Walked a □ Passenger □ Motorcycle □ Bicycle □ Other ____
□ Commercial DOT# _____ □ ≥26,001 lbs. □ <16 Pass. Bus □ ≥16 Pass. Bus □ Haz. Mat.
VEHICLE: YEAR _____ MAKE _____ MODEL _____
COLOR _____ LICENSE # _____ STATE _____
UPON A PUBLIC HIGHWAY, NAMELY _____
AT/NEAR _____ (M.P. ____)
IN THE _____ OF _____ IN _____
COUNTY (NO.), _____ STATE OF OHIO AND COMMITTED THE FOLLOWING OFFENSE(S).

SPEED: _____ MPH in _____ MPH zone □ Over limits □ Unsafe for conditions □ ACDA □ Radar □ Air □ VASCAR □ Pace □ Laser □ Stationary □ Moving	□ ORC □ ORD □ T.P.
OVI: □ Under the influence of alcohol/drug of abuse. □ Prohibited blood alcohol concentration. _____ BAC □ Blood □ Breath □ Urine □ Refused Prior OVIs: # of prior OVIs / Years of prior OVIs	□ ORC □ ORD □ T.P.
DRIVER LICENSE: □ None □ Not on person □ Revoked □ Suspended EXPIRED: □ <6 months □ >6 months □ Failure to Reinstate Suspension Type:	□ ORC □ ORD □ T.P.
SAFETY BELT: Failure to wear □ Driver □ Passenger □ Child Restraint □ Booster Seat	□ ORC □ ORD □ T.P.
OTHER OFFENSE: _____	□ ORC □ ORD □ T.P.
OTHER OFFENSE: _____	□ ORC □ ORD □ T.P.

□ DRIVER LICENSE HELD   □ VEHICLE SEIZED   □ JUVENILE OFFENDER

PAVEMENT: □ Dry   □ Wet   □ Snow □ Icy # of Lanes ____ □ **Construction Zone**
VISIBILITY: □ Clear   □ Cloudy   □ Dusk   □ Night □ Dawn
WEATHER: □ Rain   □ Snow   □ Fog   □ No Adverse
TRAFFIC: □ Heavy   □ Moderate □ Light □ None
AREA: □ Business □ Rural   □ Residential   □ Industry   □ School
CRASH: □ **Yes**   □ No □ Almost Caused □ Non-Injury □ **Injury** □ **Fatal**
Crash Report Number:
REMARKS:

ACCOMPANYING CRIMINAL CHARGE □ Yes □ No   TOTAL # OFFENSES ____

TO DEFENDANT: SUMMONS   PERSONAL APPEARANCE REQUIRED □ Yes □ No
You are summoned and ordered to appear on _____ , 20 ___ at _____ AM/PM,
in _____ Court, at _____
If you fail to appear at this time and place you may be arrested or your license may be cancelled.
This summons served personally on the defendant on _____ 20 ___
The issuing/charging law enforcement officer states under the penalties of perjury and falsification that
he/she has read the above complaint and that it is true.

COURT CODE	UNIT	POST	DISTRICT

_____
Charging Law Enforcement Officer

_____
Issuing Law Enforcement Officer   □ **SAME AS ABOVE**
Issuing Officer: Verify address. If different from license address, write present address in space provided.

OHP0060 10-0060-00 (REVISION 0509)   **AGENCY RECORD PINK**

OSHP HP7
[B6305]

PRESENT ADDRESS

SIGNATURE X

CO. RES.

PHONE ( )

REPORT OF ACTION ON CASE

DATE OF ARREST _____ AM/PM
Month / Day / Year   Time

COURT ACTION _____

☐ GUILTY   ☐ RELEASED TO OTHER AUTHORITY

☐ NOT GUILTY   ☐ _____

OFFICER'S NOTES

A/V Record # _____

_____

_____

_____

_____

_____

_____

_____

_____

_____

_____

_____

_____

_____

_____

_____

_____

_____

_____

_____

_____

_____

_____

WITNESSES:

Name	Address	Telephone
Name	Address	Telephone

VIOLATION: _____ R.C. SECTION _____

SCALE LOCATION _____ ☐ PLATFORM   ☐ PORTABLE

AMOUNT OF OVERLOAD _____

OVERLOADED ON: ☐ Single Axle   ☐ Tandem   ☐ Inner Bridge

☐ Gross — Length if gross _____ Ft.

DOT # _____

PUCO # _____

Permit Holder or Company Name or Vehicle Owner Name _____

Street Address _____

City _____ State _____ Zip _____

NOTIFICATION OF ARREST ONLY.
NO FURTHER ACTION IS NECESSARY.

ARREST NOTIFICATION

AGENCY RECORD Reverse Side PINK

_____ COURT _____ COUNTY, OHIO

STATE OF OHIO _____   TICKET #_____
☐ City   ☐ Village   ☐ Township   CASE #_____

NAME_____

STREET_____

CITY, STATE_____ ZIP_____

OPERATOR LICENSE / STATE ID#	☐ NONE*		BIRTH DATE	ISSUE DATE	STATE
CLASS	**EXPIRES**	**ENDORSEMENT(s)/RESTRICTION(s)**		**SS#** (last 4 digits)	
		☐CDL ☐MC ☐Other_____			

SEX	HEIGHT	WEIGHT	EYES	HAIR	RACE	FINANCIAL RESPONSIBILITY PROOF?
						☐ Yes ☐ No ☐ N/A

* If no OL/State ID; **REQUIRED** documentation attached: ☐ Yes

TO DEFENDANT: COMPLAINT ON _____ 20____ AT _____ AM/PM, YOU
Operated/Passenger/Parked/Walked a   ☐ Passenger ☐ Motorcycle ☐ Bicycle ☐ Other___
☐Commercial DOT#_____ ☐ ≥26,001 lbs. ☐ <16 Pass. Bus ☐ ≥16 Pass. Bus ☐ Haz. Mat.
VEHICLE: YEAR_____ MAKE_____ MODEL_____
COLOR_____ LICENSE #_____ STATE_____
UPON A PUBLIC HIGHWAY, NAMELY_____
AT/NEAR_____ (M.P._____)
IN THE_____ OF_____ IN_____
COUNTY (NO.),_____ STATE OF OHIO AND COMMITTED THE FOLLOWING OFFENSE(S).

SPEED: _____ MPH in _____ MPH zone		☐ ORC ☐ ORD ☐ T.P.
☐ Over limits ☐ Unsafe for conditions ☐ ACDA		
☐ Radar ☐ Air ☐ VASCAR ☐ Pace ☐ Laser ☐ Stationary ☐ Moving		
OVI: ☐ Under the influence of alcohol/drug of abuse.		☐ ORC ☐ ORD ☐ T.P.
☐ Prohibited blood alcohol concentration. _____ BAC		
☐ Blood ☐ Breath ☐ Urine ☐ Refused		
# of prior OVIs Years of prior OVIs		
Prior OVIs:		
DRIVER LICENSE: ☐ None ☐ Not on person ☐ Revoked ☐ Suspended		☐ ORC ☐ ORD ☐ T.P.
EXPIRED: ☐ <6 months ☐ >6 months ☐ Failure to Reinstate		
Suspension Type:		
SAFETY BELT: Failure to wear		☐ ORC ☐ ORD ☐ T.P.
☐ Driver ☐ Passenger ☐ Child Restraint ☐ Booster Seat		
OTHER OFFENSE:_____		☐ ORC ☐ ORD ☐ T.P.
OTHER OFFENSE:_____		☐ ORC ☐ ORD ☐ T.P.

☐ DRIVER LICENSE HELD   ☐ VEHICLE SEIZED   ☐ JUVENILE OFFENDER

PAVEMENT: ☐ Dry   ☐ Wet   ☐ Snow ☐ Icy # of Lanes____ ☐ **Construction Zone**
VISIBILITY: ☐ Clear   ☐ Cloudy   ☐ Dusk ☐ Night ☐ Dawn
WEATHER: ☐ Rain   ☐ Snow   ☐ Fog ☐ No Adverse
TRAFFIC: ☐ Heavy   ☐ Moderate ☐ Light ☐ None
AREA: ☐ Business ☐ Rural   ☐ Residential   ☐ Industry   ☐ School
CRASH: ☐ **Yes**   ☐ No ☐ Almost Caused ☐ Non-Injury ☐ **Injury** ☐ **Fatal**
Crash Report Number:
REMARKS:

ACCOMPANYING CRIMINAL CHARGE   ☐ Yes   ☐ No   TOTAL # OFFENSES_____

TO DEFENDANT: SUMMONS   PERSONAL APPEARANCE REQUIRED ☐ Yes   ☐ No
You are summoned and ordered to appear on_____,20____ at_____ AM/PM,
in_____Court, at_____
If you fail to appear at this time and place you may be arrested or your license may be cancelled.
This summons served personally on the defendant on_____ 20___
The issuing/charging law enforcement officer states under the penalties of perjury and falsification that
he/she has read the above complaint and that it is true.

COURT CODE	UNIT	POST	DISTRICT

_____
Charging Law Enforcement Officer

_____   ☐ SAME AS ABOVE
Issuing Law Enforcement Officer
Issuing Officer: Verify address. If different from license address, write present address in space provided.

OSHP HP7
OHP0060 10-0060-00 (REVISION 0509)   **AGENCY RECORD 2 BUFF**   [B6305]

Side margin text: PRESENT ADDRESS   SIGNATURE X   CO. RES.   PHONE (   )

REPORT OF ACTION ON CASE

DATE OF ARREST _____ AM/PM
Month / Day / Year   Time

COURT ACTION _____

☐ GUILTY   ☐ RELEASED TO OTHER AUTHORITY

☐ NOT GUILTY   ☐ _____

OFFICER'S NOTES

Radar #   Cal. Times

Laser #   Cal. Times

A/V Record #

If juvenile, parents names:

WITNESSES:

Name	Address	Telephone
Name	Address	Telephone

VIOLATION: _____

R.C. SECTION _____

ARREST NOTIFICATION

SCALE LOCATION ☐ PLATFORM ☐ PORTABLE

AMOUNT OF OVERLOAD

OVERLOADED ON: ☐ Single Axle ☐ Tandem ☐ Inner Bridge

☐ Gross — Length if gross _____ Ft.

DOT #

PUCO #

Permit Holder or Company Name or Vehicle Owner Name

Street Address

City   State   Zip

AGENCY RECORD 2 Reverse Side BUFF

Index to Ohio Traffic Rules

RULES OF SUPERINTENDENCE FOR THE COURTS OF OHIO

PREFACE

TEMPORARY PROVISIONS

PREFACE

The foundation of our government rests upon the confidence of the people in the ability of their courts to achieve liberty and justice for all under the law. The fair, impartial, and speedy resolution of cases without unnecessary delay maintains this confidence, safeguards the rights of litigants to the just processing of their causes, and earns the trust of the public.

To secure these ends, the Supreme Court of Ohio adopts the following Rules of Superintendence for the Courts of Ohio to serve the public interest that mandates prompt disposition of all causes, at all times, in all courts of this state.

TEMPORARY PROVISIONS

(A) Notwithstanding any rule to the contrary, the Cuyahoga County Court of Common Pleas, General Division, is authorized to use electronic forms and electronic signatures as necessary to implement the pilot project outlined in the January 23, 2001 letter submitted to the Supreme Court of Ohio. This Temporary Provision applies to all forms, and the signature requirements applicable to those forms, prescribed by or pursuant to rules adopted by the Supreme Court of Ohio.

(B) For purposes of this Temporary Provision:

(1) The filing requirement of any rule shall be considered satisfied if a form containing all information required by a rule is submitted to the proper authority in an electronic format;

(2) The signature requirement of any rule shall be considered satisfied if the individual who is required by rule to affix a signature to a document properly authorizes the use of his or her electronic signature on the document.

(C) The Cuyahoga County Court of Common Pleas, General Division, shall not materially modify the electronic signature and security aspects of this project, as described in the proposal submitted to the Supreme Court of Ohio on January 23, 2001, without first notifying the Court and obtaining advance approval of the modifications.

(D) Any printed, microfilmed, or imaged copies of electronic documents shall conform to the applicable rules of the Supreme Court and maintained in accordance with the Rules of Superintendence and local records retention rules.

(E) As used in this Temporary Provision:

(1) "Rule" means any provision of the Ohio Rules of Criminal Procedure, Ohio Rules of Civil Procedure, Ohio Rules of Juvenile Procedure, Ohio Rules of Evidence, Ohio Traffic Rules, or Rules of Superintendence of the Courts of Ohio.

(2) "Properly authorizes" means the person responsible for signing a form complies with the specifications prescribed by the Cuyahoga County Court of Common Pleas, General Division, relative to the use of electronic signatures.

(F) This Temporary Provision shall remain in effect through June 30, 2003, unless modified or withdrawn by the Supreme Court of Ohio prior to that date. Effective 7-1-01.

(A) Notwithstanding any rule to the contrary, the Trumbull County Court of Common Pleas, Probate Division, is authorized to use electronic forms and electronic signatures as necessary to implement the pilot project outlined in the April 25, 2001 letter submitted to the Supreme Court of Ohio. This Temporary Provision applies to all forms, and the signature requirements applicable to those forms, prescribed by or pursuant to rules adopted by the Supreme Court of Ohio.

(B) For purposes of this Temporary Provision:

(1) The filing requirement of any rule shall be considered satisfied if a form containing all information required by a rule is submitted to the proper authority in an electronic format;

(2) The signature requirement of any rule shall be considered satisfied if the individual who is required by rule to affix a signature to a document properly authorizes the use of his or her electronic signature on the document.

(C) The Trumbull County Court of Common Pleas, Probate Division, shall not materially modify the electronic signature and security aspects of this project, as described in the proposal submitted to the Supreme Court of Ohio on April 25, 2001, without first notifying the Court and obtaining advance approval of the modifications.

(D) Any printed, microfilmed, or imaged copies of electronic documents shall conform to the applicable rules of the Supreme Court and maintained in accordance with the Rules of Superintendence and local records retention rules.

(E) As used in this Temporary Provision:

(1) "Rule" means any provision of the Ohio Rules of Criminal Procedure, Ohio Rules of Civil Procedure, Ohio Rules of Juvenile Procedure, Ohio Rules of Evidence, Ohio Traffic Rules, or Rules of Superintendence of the Courts of Ohio.

(2) "Properly authorizes" means the person responsible for signing a form complies with the specifications prescribed by the Trumbull County Court of Common Pleas, Probate Division, relative to the use of electronic signatures.

(F) This Temporary Provision shall remain in effect through June 30, 2003, unless modified or withdrawn by the Supreme Court of Ohio prior to that date.

History: Effective 7-1-01.

RULE 1. Applicability; Authority; Citation

(A) **Applicability** Except where otherwise provided, these Rules of Superintendence for the courts of Ohio are applicable to all courts of appeal, courts of common pleas, municipal courts, and county courts in this state.

(B) **Authority** These rules are promulgated pursuant to Article IV, Section 5(A)(1) of the Ohio Constitution.

(C) **Citation** These rules shall be known as the Rules of Superintendence for the Courts of Ohio and shall be cited as "Sup. R.____."

RULE 2. Definitions

As used in these rules:

(A) "Case" means a notice of appeal, petition, or complaint filed in the court of appeals and any of the following when filed in the court of common pleas, municipal court, and county court:

(1) A civil complaint, petition, or administrative appeal;

(2) A criminal indictment, complaint, or other charging instrument that charges a defendant with one or more violations of the law arising from the same act, transaction, or series of acts or transactions;

(3) A petition, complaint, or other instrument alleging that a child is delinquent, unruly, or a juvenile traffic offender based on conduct arising out of the same act, transaction, or series of acts or transactions or a petition alleging that a child is dependent, neglected, or abused;

(4) An estate, trust, guardianship, petition for adoption or other miscellaneous matter as defined in Sup. R. 50.

(B) "Court" means a court of appeals, court of common pleas, municipal court, or county court.

(C) "Division" means the general, domestic relations, juvenile, or probate division of the court of common pleas, any combination of the general, domestic relations, juvenile, or probate divisions of the court of common pleas, or the environmental or housing divisions of the municipal court.

RULE 3. Presiding Judge

(A) **Selection and term**

(1) The judges of each multi-judge court, by a majority vote of the judges of the court, shall elect a presiding judge from the judges of the court. If the judges are unable because of equal division of the vote to elect a presiding judge, the judge having the longest total service on the court shall serve as presiding judge for one term. If two or more judges have equal periods of service on the court, the presiding judge shall be determined by lot from the judges with equal periods of service. In the event of a continued failure to elect a presiding judge, the judges of the court shall rotate the position based on the order of seniority as determined by the total length of service on the court.

(2) The term of the presiding judge shall be one year beginning on the first day of January. A presiding judge may be elected to consecutive terms and may serve as administrative judge pursuant to Sup. R. 4. The presiding judge shall notify the administrative director of the Supreme Court of his or her election by the fifteenth day of January.

(3) In courts consisting of one judge, the judge shall be the presiding judge.

(B) **Powers and duties** In addition to the duties set forth in the Revised Code that do not conflict with the duties of the administrative judge set forth in Sup. R. 4, the presiding judge of the court shall do all of the following:

(1) Call and conduct an annual meeting, and other meetings as necessary, of the judges of the court for the purpose of discussing and resolving administrative problems common to all divisions of the court;

(2) Assign judges of the court on a temporary basis to serve in another division of the court as required by the business of the court.

RULE 4. Administrative Judge

(A) **Selection and term**

(1) In each court of appeals, each multi-judge municipal and county court, and each multi-judge division of the court of common pleas, the judges of the court or division, by a majority vote of the judges of the court or division, shall elect an administrative judge from the judges of the court or division. If the judges of a court or division are unable to elect an administrative judge, the judge of the court or division having the longest total service on the court or division shall serve as administrative judge for one term. If two or more judges have equal periods of service on the court or division, the administrative judge shall be determined by lot from the judges with equal periods of service. In the event of a continued failure to elect an administrative judge, the judges of the court or division shall rotate the position based on the order of seniority as determined by the total length of service on the court

or division.

(2) The term of the administrative judge shall be one year beginning on the first day of January. An administrative judge may be elected to consecutive terms and also may serve as presiding judge pursuant to Sup. R. 3. The administrative judge shall notify the administrative director of the Supreme Court of his or her election by the fifteenth day of January.

(3) In courts or divisions consisting of one judge, the judge shall be the administrative judge.

(B) **Powers and duties** The administrative judge shall have full responsibility and control over the administration, docket, and calendar of the court or division and shall be responsible to the Chief Justice of the Supreme Court in the discharge of the administrative judge's duties, for the observance of these rules, and for the termination of all cases in the court or division without undue delay and in accordance with the time guidelines set forth in Sup. R. 39. The actions of the administrative judge may be modified or vacated by a majority of the judges of the court or division. The administrative judge shall do all of the following:

(1) Pursuant to Sup. R. 36, assign cases to individual judges of the court or division or to panels of judges of the court in the court of appeals;

(2) In municipal and county courts, assign cases to particular sessions pursuant to Sup. R. 36;

(3) Require timely and accurate reports from each judge of the court or division concerning the status of individually assigned cases and from judges and court personnel concerning cases assigned to particular sessions;

(4) Timely file all administrative judge reports required by the Case Management Section of the Supreme Court;

(5) Develop accounting and auditing systems within the court or division and the office of the clerk of the court that ensure the accuracy and completeness of all reports required by these rules;

(6) Request, as necessary, the assignment of judges to the court or division by the Chief Justice or the presiding judge of the court;

(7) Administer personnel policies established by the court or division;

(8) Perform other duties as required by the Revised Code, the Rules of Superintendence, local rules of the court or division, or the Chief Justice;

(9) Perform any other duties in furtherance of the responsibilities of the administrative judge.

(C) **Relief from case or trial duties** By local rule of the court or division, the administrative judge may be relieved of a portion of his or her case or trial duties to manage the calendar and docket of the court or division.

History: Amended, eff 7-1-09.

NOTES TO DECISIONS

Analysis

Authority of administrative judge
Authority to assign judges

There was no error in an administrative judge's transfer of a cognovit judgment action to his docket and his entry of

judgment against the guarantor, as such entry was a mere ministerial function that did not require the administrative judge to exercise personal judgment or discretion, and there was no violation of Ohio Superintendence Ct. R. 4(B) or 36(B)(1). Ohio Carpenters' Pension Fund v. La Centre, — Ohio App. 3d —, 2006 Ohio 2214, — N.E. 2d —, 2006 Ohio App. LEXIS 2060 (May 4, 2006).

Although the docketing statement did not reflect the certificate of assignment appointing a visiting judge to hear appellant's case, the clerk of courts was in possession of a valid, time-stamped copy of the certificate of assignment issued by the state supreme court's chief justice authorizing the visiting judge to preside for the specific purpose of hearing appellant's case. Thus, the appointment of the visiting judge was proper pursuant to Ohio Const. art. IV, § 5(A)(3) and Ohio Superintendence Ct. R. 4(B)(6). Spragling v. Oriana House, — Ohio App. 3d —, 2007 Ohio 3245, — N.E. 2d —, 2007 Ohio App. LEXIS 2993 (June 27, 2007).

RULE 5.   Local Rules

(A) **Adoption of local rules**

(1) Nothing in these rules prevents the adoption of any local rule of practice that promotes the use of any device or procedure to facilitate the expeditious disposition of cases. Local rules of practice shall not be inconsistent with rules promulgated by the Supreme Court.

(2) A local rule of practice shall be adopted only after the court or division provides appropriate notice and an opportunity to comment on the proposed rule. If the court or division determines that there is an immediate need for the rule, the court or division may adopt the rule without prior notice and opportunity for comment, but promptly shall afford notice and opportunity for comment.

(3) Upon adoption, the court or division shall file a local rule of practice with its clerk and the clerk of the Supreme Court. On or before the first day of February of each year, each court or division of a court shall do one of the following:

(a) File with the clerk of the Supreme Court a complete copy of all local rules of the court or division in effect on the immediately preceding first day of January;

(b) Certify to the clerk of the Supreme Court that there were no changes in the immediately preceding calendar year to the local rules of the court or division.

(B) In addition to local rules of practice adopted pursuant to division (A)(1) of this rule and any other Rule of Superintendence, each court or division, as applicable, shall adopt the following by local rule:

(1) A case management plan for the purposes of ensuring the readiness of cases for pretrial and trial, and maintaining and improving the timely disposition of cases. In addition to any other provisions necessary to satisfy the purposes of division (B)(1) of this rule, the plan shall include provisions for an early case management conference, referral to appropriate and available alternative dispute resolution programs, establishment of a binding case management schedule, and a pretrial conference in cases where the trial judge determines a conference is necessary and appropriate. A municipal or county court may establish separate provisions or

exceptions from the plan for small claims, traffic, and other types of cases that the court determines would not benefit from the case management plan.

(2) A jury management plan for purposes of ensuring the efficient and effective use and management of jury resources. In addition to any other provisions necessary to satisfy the purposes of division (B)(2) of this rule, the plan shall address the provisions of the Ohio Trial Court Jury Use and Management Standards adopted by the Supreme Court of Ohio on August 16, 1993.

NOTES TO DECISIONS

ANALYSIS

Invalidity of local rule
Unwritten local rules

Probate court erred in denying a named executor's application to open his deceased father's probate estate due to the failure of the executor to have retained local counsel, as the executor was a licensed attorney in the State of Maryland and there was no statutory requirement under RC § 2109.03 that required retention of local counsel. The probate court's claim that it was an unwritten local rule that local counsel was to have been retained had no merit, as there was no provision for purely oral local rules under Ohio Superintendence R. 5(A)(1). In re Estate of Usiak, 172 Ohio App. 3d 262, 2007 Ohio 3038, 874 N.E.2d 838, 2007 Ohio App. LEXIS 2880 (2007).

Probate court could not rely on unwritten local rules in conducting its affairs: In re Estate of Usiak, 172 Ohio App. 3d 262, 2007 Ohio 3038, 874 N.E.2d 838, 2007 Ohio App. LEXIS 2880 (2007).

RULE 6. Attorney Registration Number

Each court shall require an attorney to include the attorney registration number issued by the Supreme Court of Ohio on all documents filed with the court. Each court shall use the attorney registration number issued by the Supreme Court of Ohio as the exclusive number or code to identify attorneys who file documents with the court.

RULE 7. Filing of Judgment Entries

(A) The judgment entry specified in Civil Rule 58 and in Criminal Rule 32 shall be filed and journalized within thirty days of the verdict, decree, or decision. If the entry is not prepared and presented by counsel, it shall be prepared and filed by the court.

(B) Approval of a judgment entry by a counsel or party indicates that the entry correctly sets forth the verdict, decree, or decision of the court and does not waive any objection or assignment of error for appeal.

NOTES TO DECISIONS

ANALYSIS

Filing and entry of judgments

As defendant received a copy of a judgment that indicated that it was filed on June 9, 2006 and journalized on June 13, 2006, although the court appearance docket indicated that the judgment was both filed and journalized on June 9, 2006,

defendant was deemed to have timely appealed under Ohio R. App. P. 4(A) and Ohio R. Crim. P. 32(C) by filing his notice of appeal on July 11, 2006, as he had no way of knowing that his copy of the judgment might have been inaccurate regarding the date of judgment entry. The court clerk was not required to journalize a judgment the day that it was filed, and the judgment herein was within the time constraints for entry under Ohio Superintendence R. 7. State v. Ulis, — Ohio App. 3d —, 2006 Ohio 3987, — N.E. 2d —, 2006 Ohio App. LEXIS 3962 (Aug. 2, 2006).

RULE 8. Court Appointments

(A) As used in this rule:

(1) "Appointment" means the selection by a court of any person or entity designated pursuant to constitutional or statutory authority, rule of court, or the inherent authority of the court to represent, act on behalf or in the interests of another, or perform any services in a court proceeding.

(2) "Appointee" means any person, other than a court employee, receiving a court appointment who is selected by the court. "Appointee" does not include a person or entity who is selected by someone other than the court.

(B) Each court or division of a court shall adopt a local rule of court governing appointments made by the court or division. The local rule shall include all of the following:

(1) A procedure for selecting appointees from a list maintained by the court or division of persons qualified to serve in the capacity designated by the court or division. The procedure shall ensure an equitable distribution of appointments among all persons on the appointment list. The court may consider the skill and expertise of the appointee in the designated area of the appointment and the management by the appointee of his or her current caseload. The court or division may maintain separate lists for different types of appointments.

(2) A procedure by which all appointments made by the court or division are reviewed periodically to ensure the equitable distribution of appointments among persons on each list maintained by the court or division.

(3) The manner of compensation and rate at which persons appointed will be compensated for services provided as a result of the appointment, including, if applicable, a fee schedule.

(C) The local rule required by division (B) of this rule may include qualifications established by the court or division for inclusion on the appointment list, the process by which persons are added to or removed from the appointment list, and other provisions considered appropriate by the court or division.

(D) If a party or other person is required to pay all or a portion of the fees payable to an appointee, the appointee promptly shall notify that party or person of the appointment and the applicable fee schedule. The court or division shall require the appointee to file with the court or division and serve upon either the party or other person required to pay all or a portion of the fees itemized fee and expense statements on a regular basis as determined by the court or division. If the party or other person required to pay all or a portion of the fees claims that the fees are excessive or unreasonable, the burden of proving the reasonableness of the fees is on the appointee.

RULE 9.   Court Security Plans

(A) **Court Security Plan** For purposes of ensuring security in court facilities, each court shall develop and implement a court security plan. If more than one court occupies a court facility, the courts shall collectively develop and implement a single court security plan. In addition to any other provisions necessary to satisfy the purposes of this rule, the plan shall address the provisions of the Ohio court security standards adopted by the Supreme Court and as set forth in Appendix C to this rule.

(B) **Public Access** For purposes of ensuring security in court facilities, a court security plan, including any security policy and procedures manual, emergency preparedness manual, and continuity of operations manual adopted as part of the court security plan, shall not be available for public access.

History: Amended, eff 5-12-98; 1-30-01, 3/1/09.

RULE 10.   Notifying Law Enforcement Agencies of Criminal or Civil Protection Orders

(A) Upon issuance of a civil or criminal protection order by a court pursuant to section 2151.34, 2903.213, 2903.214, division (E)(2) of 2919.26, or 3113.31 of the Revised Code, the court shall complete "Form 10-A." "Form 10-A" and a copy of the order shall be filed by the court with the local enforcement agency for entry in the "National Crime Information Center" database and nationwide dissemination. To accommodate local court or law enforcement procedures, the format of "Form 10-A" may be modified, provided the modification does not affect the substantive content of "Form 10-A."

(B) A court shall follow the instructions in "Form 10-B" for thorough and accurate completion of "Form 10-A" and to facilitate correct entry of criminal or civil protection orders in the "National Crime Information Center" database.

FORM 10-A: PROTECTION ORDER NOTICE TO NCIC
(Required fields appear in bold print)

☐ Initial NCIC Form
☐ Modification of Previous Form

_____ of _____ Pages

SUBJECT NAME _____
(LAST)   (FIRST)   (M.I.)

ADDRESS _____
(STREET)   (CITY)   (STATE)   (ZIP)

PHYSICAL   HGT ____ WGT _____ HAIR _____ EYES _____ **RACE** _____ **SEX** _____
DESCRIPTION:

NUMERICAL IDENTIFIER (NOTE: Only ONE of the 4 numerical identifiers is needed.)
1.   SSN ____ / ____ / ____   2.   DOB ____ / ____ / ____
3.*   DRIVER'S LIC. NO. _____ STATE ____ EXPIRATION YR. ____
4.*   VEHICLE LIC. NO. _____ STATE ____ EXPIRATION YR. ____ LIC. TYPE _____
(* If #3 or #4 is used as a numerical identifier, entire line MUST be completed.)

BRADY DISQUALIFIERS:
(Pursuant to 18 U.S.C. 922(g)(8), a "yes" response to all three Brady questions disqualifies the subject from purchasing or possessing any firearms, including a rifle, pistol, revolver, or ammunition.)
- Does Order protect an intimate partner or child(ren)?   ☐ YES   ☐ NO
- Did subject have opportunity to participate in hearing regarding Order?   ☐ YES   ☐ NO
- Does Order find subject a credible threat or explicitly prohibit physical force?   ☐ YES   ☐ NO

CASE / ORDER NO. _____ (15 DIGIT MAXIMUM)

COURT ORIGINATING AGENCY IDENTIFIER _____ (9 DIGIT ORI ASSIGNED BY NCIC)

☐ R.C. 2903.213   ☐ R.C. 2903.214   ☐ R.C. 2151.34   NAME OF JUDGE _____
☐ R.C. 2919.26   ☐ R.C. 3113.31

DATE OF ORDER ____ / ____ / ____   **EXPIRATION OF ORDER** ____ / ____ / ____
(IN R.C. 2919.26 CASES, "NONEXP" MAY BE USED)

TERMS AND CONDITIONS OF ORDER (Mark all that are applicable):
☐ 01 The subject is restrained from assaulting, threatening, abusing, harassing, following, interfering, or stalking the protected person and/or the child(ren) of the protected person.
☐ 02 The subject shall not threaten a member of the protected person's family or household.
☐ 03 The protected person is granted exclusive possession of the residence or household.
☐ 04 The subject is required to stay away from the residence, property, school, or place of employment of the protected person or other family or household member.
☐ 05 The subject is restrained from making any communication with the protected person, including but not limited to, personal, written, or telephone contact, or their employer, employees, or fellow workers, or others with whom the communication would be likely to cause annoyance or alarm the victim.
☐ 06 The subject has visitation or custody rights of the children named in this Order.
☐ 07 The subject is prohibited from possessing and/or purchasing a firearm or other weapon.
☐ 08 See the Miscellaneous Field for comments regarding the specific terms and conditions of this Order.
Miscellaneous comments: _____

OHP DATA ONLY #EPO

☐ 09 The protected person is awarded temporary exclusive custody of the children named.

LIST ALL PROTECTED PERSONS (Total of 9 allowed, may attach additional forms; SSN is NOT necessary if DOB is given):
PROTECTED PERSON _____
(LAST)   (FIRST)   (M.I.)
DOB ____ / ____ / ____ SSN ____ / ____ / ____ RACE ____ SEX ____

PROTECTED PERSON _____
(LAST)   (FIRST)   (M.I.)
DOB ____ / ____ / ____ SSN ____ / ____ / ____ RACE ____ SEX ____

MIS/

PROTECTED PERSON _____
(LAST)   (FIRST)   (M.I.)
DOB ____ / ____ / ____ SSN ____ / ____ / ____ RACE ____ SEX ____

Authorized by (signature): _____ Date ____
Judge/Magistrate (circle one)

FORM 10-A: PROTECTION NOTICE TO NCIC

Amended: July 1, 2010
Discard all previous versions of this form

FORM 10-B: HOW TO COMPLETE A PROTECTION NOTICE TO NCIC

These instructions are intended to assist the court in the proper completion of Form 10-A, Protection Notice to NCIC, in compliance with requirements of Ohio and federal law. Thorough and accurate completion of Form 10-A is critical, as this form is the sole method used to enter the terms and conditions of the protection orders issued by the court into the computerized index of criminal justice information maintained by the National Crime Information Center ("NCIC"). Inaccurate or inconsistent information in Form 10-A will result in delay in entering the protection order into the NCIC index and enforcing the order. Form 10-A must be completed each time the court approves, issues, modifies, renews, or terminates a protection order or consent agreement, regardless of whether it is an *ex parte* or full hearing order.

ELEMENTS OF FORM 10-A

(A)   The required fields in Form 10-A appear in **BOLD.**

(B)   Form 10-A is the primary method used to inform law enforcement of the terms and conditions of the protection order. The court should be cautious to mark the appropriate box in the upper right corner of the form. The court must check the box next to "Initial NCIC Form" anytime the court is issuing a protection order out of the same set of facts for the first time, i.e., an *ex parte* order or a full hearing order where an *ex parte* order was not issued. The court must check the box next to "Modification of Previous NCIC" anytime the court has already issued a protection order arising out of the same facts and is now modifying or terminating the order or is making a clerical or orthographical correction to the form.

(C)   **SUBJECT'S NAME, RACE, & SEX.**   The subject's full name, including first and last name, race and sex, are mandatory identifiers that the court must provide to have the form accepted by NCIC. The other identifiers under physical description, i.e., height ("HGT"), weight ("WGT"), hair, and eyes, are not mandatory, yet they are helpful information to ensure the correct person is identified if a violation of the order occurs. Similarly, the address is not mandatory information.

(D)   **NUMERICAL IDENTIFIER.**   The FBI requires the court to provide certain numerical identifiers to properly identify the person subject to the protection order. While completion of all the numerical identifiers is very useful, the FBI mandates that only **one** of the following numerical identifiers be entered to have the form accepted by NCIC:

   1.   SOCIAL SECURITY NUMBER ("SSN");

   2.   DATE OF BIRTH ("DOB");

   3.   DRIVER'S LICENSE NUMBER ("DRIVER'S LIC. NO."): In the instance the driver's license number is to be provided, the state that issued the driver's license and the expiration date of the driver's license must also be included for this entry to be accepted by NCIC;

   4.   VEHICLE LICENSE NUMBER ("VEHICLE LIC. NO."): In the instance the vehicle's license plate is to be provided, the state that issued the license plate and the expiration date of the license plate must also be included for this entry to be accepted by NCIC.

(E)   **BRADY DISQUALIFIERS.**   Federal law makes it illegal for certain persons subject to a protection order to purchase or possess a firearm, including a rifle, pistol or revolver, or ammunition. This section guides the court in properly identifying those persons subject to a protection order that are also Brady disqualified. An affirmative response to all three questions on Form 10-A results in disqualifying the person subject to a protection order from purchasing or possessing firearms pursuant to 18 U.S.C. 922(g)(8).

   Generally, a person subject to a protection order is Brady disqualified under 18 U.S.C. 922(g)(8) when the protected party is a spouse, former spouse, person living or who lived as a spouse, a child of the person subject to the protection order or a child of a spouse, former spouse, or person living or who lived as a spouse. The court must afford the person

[Page 2 of Form 10-B]

subject to the protection order an opportunity to be heard and, after evaluating all the evidence, find that the person subject to the order poses a credible threat of harm to the protected party.

(F)   CASE/ORDER NO. The case/order number of the protection order is a required element. It is particularly relevant when the court modifies, renews, or terminates a protection order. Law enforcement and NCIC will use the case/order number to cross-reference the appropriate order. In addition, law enforcement also uses this information to verify the currency of an order.

(G)   COURT ORIGINATING AGENCY IDENTIFIER. To accept a Form 10-A entry into the federal protection order database, NCIC mandates the court issuing the protection order to include its agency identifier. The agency identifier is a unique nine digit alphabetic and/or numeric series issued by the FBI that easily allows identification of the court issuing the order. Although the "Name of Judge" is not a mandatory field, it is prudent to include the name of the judicial officer issuing the protection order. Similarly, NCIC does not require a court to indicate under which Revised Code section the order is being issued. However, this information is useful for law enforcement to quickly determine the relationship between the parties and determine how to assess risk if the order is violated.

(H)   DATE OF ORDER AND EXPIRATION OF ORDER. The court must note on the form the date the protection order was issued and the date when it will expire. The protection order database will automatically purge the orders on their expiration date. If a protection order is terminated before the original expiration, it is critical the court explicitly indicate on Form 10-A the new expiration date to allow proper removal of the order from the database.

(I)   TERMS AND CONDITIONS OF ORDER. The court must check every box that corresponds to all provisions of the protection order as ordered by the court. Note the numbering next to each term and condition in Form 10-A does not correspond to the sequence of the remedies listed in the protection orders. However, the remedies in the protection order forms cross-reference, by number, the terms and conditions listed in Form 10-A.

The court should submit a modified Form 10-A to the appropriate law enforcement reporting agency in every instance that any court order, i.e., divorce decree or custody order, results in the modification of a term or a protected party in a protection order.

(J)   LIST ALL PROTECTED PERSONS. The court must provide the full name and date of birth for all persons who are protected by the protection order. The protected person's social security number, race, and gender are not required entry in Form 10-A.

(K)   AUTHORIZED SIGNATURE. The judge or magistrate who issued the protection order must sign and date Form 10-A.

FORM 10-B: HOW TO COMPLETE A PROTECTION NOTICE TO NCIC

Effective Date: July 1, 2010

History: Amended, eff 3-24-98; 3-1-00; 6-1-02; 5-1-07; 7-1-10.

RULE 10.01. Standard Civil Protection Order Forms—Domestic Relations Division

(A) The domestic relations division of a court of common pleas shall distribute, upon request, a forms and instructions packet for use in civil protection order proceedings under section 3113.31 of the Revised Code. The packet shall include, at a minimum, forms and instructions that are substantially similar to "Forms 10.01-A through 10.01-H."

(B) An action for a civil protection order pursuant to section 3113.31 of the Revised Code shall be commenced by filing a petition form that is substantially similar to "Form 10.01-D."

(C) In every case in which the domestic relations division of a court of common pleas issues or approves an ex parte civil protection order, a full hearing civil protection order, or a consent agreement pursuant to section 3113.31 of the Revised Code, the court shall use, as applicable, forms that are substantially similar to "Forms 10.01-H through 10.01-J."

(D) Every ex parte civil protection order, full hearing civil protection order, and consent agreement that the domestic relations division of a court of common pleas issues or approves pursuant to section 3113.31 of the Revised Code shall include a cover sheet that is substantially similar to "Form 10.01-G."

(E) In every case in which the domestic relations division of a court of common pleas modifies the terms of a full hearing civil protection order or a consent agreement pursuant to section 3113.31 of the Revised Code, it shall use the applicable forms that are substantially similar to "Forms 10.01-L and 10.01-M."

(F) In every case in which the domestic relations division of a court of common pleas terminates a full hearing civil protection order or a consent agreement before its original expiration date pursuant to section 3113.31 of the Revised Code, it shall use the applicable form that is substantially similar to "Form 10.01-L."

Form 10.01-A

FORM 10.01-A: GENERAL INFORMATION ABOUT DOMESTIC VIOLENCE PROTECTION ORDERS

DEFINITIONS YOU NEED TO KNOW

Domestic violence is when a family or household member uses physical violence, threats, intimidation, and/or emotional, sexual, and economic abuse to maintain power and control over the other person, usually within an intimate relationship. Domestic violence is most often a combination of psychological and physical actions; the physical results are just the most visible. Domestic violence is a pattern of conduct in which one intimate partner uses force or threats of force to control the other person.

State law has determined that some forms of abuse do not constitute criminal behavior or behavior requiring the Court's intervention. For example, psychological battering, economic abuse, or verbal harassment without evidence of threats or physical harm are not recognized by Ohio law as domestic violence that allows a petitioner to obtain a protection order or request that criminal charges be filed.

When a family or household member tries to cause you bodily harm by hitting, pushing, beating, or physically hurting you, that is domestic violence. When a family or household member makes you afraid that you will be harmed, that is domestic violence. When a family or household member stalks, commits sexually oriented offenses against you, or forces sexual relations on you, that is domestic violence. When a family or household member abuses your children, that is domestic violence.

IN A **CIVIL** DOMESTIC VIOLENCE CASE:

> **Petition for Domestic Violence Civil Protection Order ("CPO")** is the document a domestic violence victim, the victim's parent, or an adult household member of the victim must file with the domestic relations division of the Court to obtain a civil protection order against an alleged offender.

> **Domestic Violence Civil Protection Order ("CPO")** *Ex Parte* is an emergency order the Court issues in response to the Petition for a Civil Protection Order after an *ex parte* hearing. The *ex parte* hearing is described in this form on page 3.

> **Domestic Violence Civil Protection Order ("CPO") Full Hearing** is the final order the Court issues after a full hearing. The full hearing is described in this form on page 3. The full hearing CPO replaces the *ex parte* CPO. Sometimes the final order issued by the Court is a **Consent Agreement and Domestic Violence Civil Protection Order**, Form 10.01-J, upon terms agreed to by the parties.

> **Petitioner** is the person asking or "petitioning" the Court for protection. By filing the Petition for a CPO, YOU are the Petitioner.

> **Respondent** is the alleged domestic violence offender. Petitioner seeks protection from the Respondent by filing for a CPO.

IN A **CRIMINAL** DOMESTIC VIOLENCE CASE:

> **Motion for a Domestic Violence Criminal Temporary Protection Order ("DVTPO")** is the document that must be filed in a criminal case if a victim of domestic violence or victim of a sexually oriented offense wishes to obtain a protection order against an alleged offender, who is a family or household member. The criminal case must allege the offender committed negligent assault, criminal damaging or endangering, criminal mischief, burglary, aggravated trespass, endangering children, any offense of violence, or any sexually oriented offense against a family or household member. The prosecutor has a form for this purpose.

> **Domestic Violence Temporary Protection Order ("DVTPO")** is the order the Court issues in response to the Motion for Temporary Protection Order. The DVTPO requires the offender to stop abusing and to stay away from the victim(s) named in the Motion for Temporary Protection Order. A DVTPO expires when the alleged offender's criminal case ends or when a new CPO is issued based on the same facts.

> **Alleged Victim** is the person asking the Court for protection in the Motion for a DVTPO.

> **Defendant** is the person the Motion for a DVTPO is filed against. The Defendant is the person accused of the crimes of negligent assault, criminal damaging or endangering, criminal mischief, burglary, aggravated trespass, endangering children, any sexually oriented offense, or any offense of violence against a family or household member.

FORM 10.01-A: GENERAL INFORMATION ABOUT DOMESTIC VIOLENCE PROTECTION ORDERS

Amended: July 1, 2010
Discard all previous versions of this form

[Page 2 of Form 10.01-A]

FEES

UNDER FEDERAL AND STATE LAW YOU CANNOT BE CHARGED ANY COSTS OR FEES FOR OBTAINING A PROTECTION ORDER.

CIVIL PROTECTION ORDERS

What is a Domestic Violence Civil Protection Order ("CPO")?

A CPO is issued by a domestic relations division of the Court to protect a victim of domestic violence. A CPO is intended to prevent further domestic violence. It orders someone who has been abusive to do or not do certain things in the future. You may want to consider getting a CPO even if you have a DVTPO from a criminal court because a CPO lasts longer and provides more benefits – such as child custody and support orders. Domestic violence includes the commission of sexually oriented offenses.

Violating a CPO is a crime. If the Respondent violates the CPO, he or she may be arrested, jailed, and fined for disobeying the CPO. A CPO can remain in effect for up to five years. If the Respondent violates the CPO, you can call the police, go back to the domestic relations division of the Court to file a contempt charge, and go to the prosecutor's office to have the Respondent charged with the crime of violating the CPO.

Why get a Domestic Violence Civil Protection Order?

If you are a victim of domestic violence, a CPO may help you. Once domestic violence starts, the violence often happens more often and gets increasingly severe. A CPO may stop this cycle of violence because the Court orders the Respondent to stop hurting or threatening you and your family or household members. The Court can use a CPO to order the Respondent to stay away from you for up to five years. A CPO can give you time to "sort things out" and decide what you want to do next without having to be afraid all of the time. If your children have seen domestic violence, a CPO may give all of you a chance to get some help so that you and your children are safe.

Domestic violence is a crime. A CPO tells the Respondent you and the Court are serious about requiring the Respondent to stop his or her abusive behavior and not to hurt or threaten you again.

A CPO sets some "rules" that the Respondent must obey while the CPO is in effect. These rules may require the Respondent to pay child or spousal support; give up possession of a home or car; and/or obey the Court's orders about visitation.

A CPO issued by a domestic relations division of the Court may last longer than a DVTPO issued by a criminal court and can provide more kinds of help. You should know that if you get a CPO based upon the same facts as the DVTPO, the DVTPO from the criminal court will automatically end, even if the criminal case continues.

Who can get a Domestic Violence Civil Protection Order?

You can apply for a CPO if you are related to the Respondent by blood or marriage AND have lived with Respondent at any time; OR you are living with or have lived with the Respondent during the past five years; OR you used to be married to the Respondent; OR you have a child with the Respondent, whether or not you ever married or lived together.

You can also get a CPO for any member of your household.

You may be able to get a CPO if you have been dating the Respondent; if you share family or financial responsibilities with the Respondent; AND you have an intimate relationship with the Respondent.

Remember that a CPO has limits. If you suspect that the Respondent will not obey the terms of a CPO, contact your local domestic violence program or the Ohio Domestic Violence Network at 800-934-9840.

FORM 10.01-A: GENERAL INFORMATION ABOUT DOMESTIC VIOLENCE PROTECTION ORDERS

Amended: July 1, 2010
Discard all previous versions of this form

[Page 3 of Form 10.01-A]

Do I need an attorney for me to obtain a Domestic Violence Civil Protection Order?

No, but you are often better off having legal representation in your CPO proceeding. Neither the Clerk of Court nor other Court employees can give you legal advice. Having an attorney represent you is especially helpful when your case involves contested custody and visitation and/or when an attorney represents the Respondent. If you cannot afford an attorney, contact your local legal aid office at 866-LAWOHIO (toll free), bar association, or Ohio State Legal Services (800-589-5888) for information on low cost or free legal representation.

Must there be a court hearing for me to obtain a Domestic Violence Civil Protection Order?

Yes. There are two hearings involved in a CPO case: the *ex parte* hearing and the full hearing.

***Ex Parte* Hearing:** At this hearing only you are present. The Respondent is not present.

An *ex parte* hearing is held the same day a Petition for Civil Protection Order is filed. If a Petition for a CPO is filed early enough in the day, an *ex parte* hearing is held that same day. At the *ex parte* hearing, you take an oath to tell the truth and a judge or magistrate hears your statement of what happened. If the judge or magistrate finds that the events you described meet the requirements of the law, the Court will issue an *Ex Parte* CPO and schedule a full hearing. If the Respondent is asked to vacate the home in which you live, there will be a full hearing within seven business days. Otherwise, a full hearing will be set within ten business days. The Court can hold a full hearing only after the Respondent has been served with the *Ex Parte* CPO. You may need to fill out forms for the Clerk of Court to cause service.

Full Hearing: The full hearing is the final hearing.

At this hearing, both you and the Respondent can testify. You must be present at the full hearing. You should bring any witnesses and other evidence to support your case. If the Court issues a Full Hearing CPO, it remains in force until the date indicated in the CPO, with five years being the maximum.

If the Respondent does not show up for the full hearing, you can still obtain a final CPO. However, if the Respondent is not served with the *Ex Parte* CPO before the full hearing, the Court postpones the full hearing until the Respondent is served. If the full hearing is postponed, the *Ex Parte* CPO remains in effect until the full hearing is held.

You may bring an advocate with you to the *ex parte* and full hearings for support. Some domestic violence shelters and victim assistance programs can provide advocates to go with you to these hearings. Contact your local domestic violence program or the Ohio Domestic Violence Network, 800-934-9840, for program and shelter information.

DOMESTIC VIOLENCE CRIMINAL TEMPORARY PROTECTION ORDERS

Your local criminal court grants a DVTPO. You ask the Court for a DVTPO when a criminal complaint is filed alleging someone has committed domestic violence or a sexually oriented offense against you. The DVTPO orders someone who has abused you to do or stop doing certain things in the future. Violating a DVTPO is a crime. If the Defendant violates the DVTPO, the Defendant may be arrested, jailed, and fined for disobeying the DVTPO. Violating a DVTPO is also a reason for the Court to revoke the Defendant's bail. A DVTPO lasts only until the criminal case is ended or a CPO, based on the same facts, is issued by a domestic relations division of the Court.

RESOURCES

You can find information about Domestic Violence Civil Protection Orders in R.C. 3113.31 and information about Domestic Violence Temporary Protection Orders in R.C. 2919.26.

You may be able to find additional information about domestic violence at the following Websites:

Ohio Domestic Violence Network	www.odvn.org
Ohio State Legal Services Association's DV Resource Center	www.ohiodvresources.org
National Resource Center on Domestic Violence	www.nrcdv.org

PLEASE NOTE: Computer use can be monitored. It is impossible to completely clear all website footprints. If you are in danger, please use a safer computer that your abuser cannot access directly or remotely. For example, computers at a public library, internet café, domestic violence shelter, or community technology center, which can be found through www.ctcnet.org, would be safer computers.

FORM 10.01-A: GENERAL INFORMATION ABOUT DOMESTIC VIOLENCE PROTECTION ORDERS

Amended: July 1, 2010
Discard all previous versions of this form

Form 10.01-B

FORM 10.01-B: HOW TO OBTAIN A DOMESTIC VIOLENCE CIVIL PROTECTION ORDER ("CPO")

FORMS TO FILL OUT FOR A DOMESTIC VIOLENCE CPO

To obtain a CPO, you need the following documents. You can get all of these documents from the Clerk of Court's office:

1. Petition for Domestic Violence Civil Protection Order, Form 10.01-D.

2. Domestic Violence Civil Protection Order *Ex Parte*, Form 10.01-H.

3. If you are requesting temporary custody of a child, Information for Parenting Proceeding Affidavit, Form 10.01-F.

4. If you request financial support, you <u>might</u> need to fill out additional forms that the Clerk of Court's office will provide you.

Complete the Petition for a CPO form. Complete additional forms if applicable. Take these documents to the Clerk of Court's office.

FILING THE PETITION FOR A DOMESTIC VIOLENCE CPO FORM

Present your completed forms to the filing window/counter of the Clerk of Court's office for filing. Do **NOT** file the *Ex Parte* CPO form at this time.

A Clerk of Court's office employee helps you file your documents. You should know that neither the Clerk of Court nor other Court employees can provide you with legal advice.

There is **NO FEE** for filing the Petition for a CPO form.

Ask a Clerk of Court's office employee or your local domestic violence assistance group about local Court procedures.

VICTIM ADVOCATE

State law permits you to have a victim advocate with you at all times in court during protection order proceedings. "Victim advocate" means a person who provides support and assistance for a victim of an offense during Court proceedings. Contact your local victim assistance program, local domestic violence program, or the Ohio Domestic Violence Network, 800-934-9840, for advocate information.

ATTENDING THE *EX PARTE* COURT HEARING

You must appear in front of a judge or magistrate for the *ex parte* hearing. The judge or magistrate listens to your testimony.

You should tell the judge or magistrate what the Respondent did to make you fear that you or a family member may be in danger. Tell the judge or magistrate if the Respondent injured you, attempted to injure you, or threatened you.

Tell the judge or magistrate what you would like the Court to do to help keep you and other family members safe and to protect the children. For example, you might ask the judge or magistrate to:

1. Order the Respondent to stay away from you;

2. Order the Respondent to be removed from your home;

3. Order the Respondent to get counseling;

4. Award you custody of any children;

5. Order the Respondent to have visitation only under conditions that will keep you and the children safe;

6. Order the Respondent to pay you child support and/or spousal support (alimony);

7. Order the Respondent to be prohibited from having any weapons;

8. Award you possession of a car for your use;

9. Award you possession of your personal property and the children's personal property.

FORM 10.01-B: PROCEDURES FOR OBTAINING A DOMESTIC VIOLENCE CIVIL PROTECTION ORDER

Amended: July 1, 2010
Discard all previous versions of this form

If the judge or magistrate determines that you or your family or household members are in danger of domestic violence, the judge and/or magistrate signs an *Ex Parte* CPO.

The judge or magistrate then sets a second hearing (called a "full hearing") within seven to ten business days to give the Respondent a chance to be heard. You must appear at the full hearing. Some issues, such as support, may be postponed until this second hearing.

Take the signed *Ex Parte* CPO to the Clerk of Court's office and have it filed. Tell the Clerk's office where law enforcement officers can find the Respondent to serve him or her with the *Ex Parte* CPO and other necessary papers.

YOU MUST ATTEND THE FULL HEARING

The full hearing on the Petition for a CPO will be set within seven to ten business days after the *ex parte* hearing. You **must** attend the full hearing. You may have an attorney present with you at the full hearing.

At the full hearing you must tell what happened again. This time you tell what happened in more detail. Bring with you any witnesses and evidence you have, such as photographs, answering machine tapes, other audio and video recordings, papers such as police reports, hospital records, etc, and any other evidence that will help you prove that the Respondent committed domestic violence against you or another family or household member. Tell the judge or magistrate why you fear the Respondent. You may call the Respondent as a witness to help you prove your case. Tell the judge or magistrate again what you want the Court to do to help keep you and your family members safe.

The Respondent may have an attorney. You may want to ask for a continuance in order to get an attorney. The Respondent may also present evidence and call you as a witness. You may be asked questions by the Respondent or the Respondent's attorney.

After the hearing, if the judge or magistrate decides you are entitled to a CPO, the Court issues a new CPO called a "Domestic Violence Civil Protection Order 'CPO' Full Hearing." This CPO is usually more detailed than the *Ex Parte* CPO issued after the first hearing. The judge or magistrate could also deny your Petition for a CPO if the Court decides you are not entitled to a CPO. The law does not allow the Court to issue a protection order against you, unless the Respondent has filed a separate action against you.

At the full hearing, you and the Respondent can decide to enter into a Consent Agreement instead of having a hearing in front of the judge or magistrate. If you decide to enter into a Consent Agreement, give the judge or magistrate the Consent Agreement and Domestic Violence Civil Protection Order Form 10.01-J contained in the "How to Get a Domestic Violence Protection Order" packet. The Court should also have a Consent Agreement and Domestic Violence Civil Protection Order form available.

ENFORCING YOUR CPO

Your CPO remains in effect for five years, unless the Court sets a different expiration date.

Violating a CPO is a crime. If the Respondent violates the CPO, it is a crime. Immediately contact the police.

You may also bring a contempt action in domestic relations division of the Court for CPO violations. A contempt action is brought because the Respondent is disregarding the Court's order. You must complete and file a contempt motion with the Clerk of Court's office to begin a contempt action against the Respondent.

CRIMINAL COURT

In addition to the *ex parte* hearing and full hearing in domestic relations division of the Court, you should attend all meetings and hearings as requested by the prosecutor and the Court related to any criminal case filed against the Respondent.

Tell the domestic relations division of the Court about any pending criminal cases. Tell the criminal court about any pending domestic relations division of the Court cases.

Any Domestic Violence Temporary Protection Order ("DVTPO") issued by a criminal court expires as soon as the criminal case is ended. A DVTPO issued by a criminal court also expires when a CPO is issued by the domestic relations division of the Court based upon the same facts.

FORM 10.01-B: PROCEDURES FOR OBTAINING A DOMESTIC VIOLENCE CIVIL PROTECTION ORDER

Amended: July 1, 2010
Discard all previous versions of this form

Form 10.01-C

FORM 10.01-C: HOW TO COMPLETE A PETITION FOR A DOMESTIC VIOLENCE CIVIL PROTECTION ORDER

These instructions will help you to prepare the Petition for Domestic Violence Civil Protection Order. Only the domestic relations division of the Court in your county hears a Petition for a Domestic Violence Civil Protection Order. **Throughout the Petition, you are called** *Petitioner* and the person you are filing this Petition against (the alleged domestic violence offender) is called *Respondent.*

SOME HINTS BEFORE YOU BEGIN

- All forms must be typed or printed.
- When you write your name on the Petition, use the same name you use when you write your signature.
- Write your name and Respondent's name the same way throughout the Petition.
- Fill out the Petition as completely and accurately as possible.
- If you have any questions about completing the Petition, ask the Clerk of Court's office for assistance or contact your local victim assistance program, domestic violence program, or the Ohio Domestic Violence Network at 800-934-9840.
- Under federal and state law you **cannot be charged any fees** to obtain a protection order.

FILLING OUT THE PETITION: Mark each instruction below after you read and complete it

- [ ] **On the front page, leave the "Case No." line and "Judge" lines BLANK.** The Clerk of Court's office fills in this information.
- [ ] **On the top left-hand side of the front page, fill in the requested information about yourself.** If you do not want your present address to be known, write "confidential" in the space for your address. Do not write your address anywhere on the Petition if you want it to be confidential. However, you must include someone's mailing address on the Petition to allow the Court to send you legal notices concerning your case.
- [ ] **On the top left-hand side of the front page, fill in the requested information about Respondent as best you can.** You may use Respondent's work address if you do not know Respondent's home address. If you do not know Respondent's date of birth, leave that line blank. Do not attempt to obtain this information unless it is safe to do so.
- [ ] **Paragraph 1:** If you are filing the Petition to protect yourself, mark the first box and the box that describes your relationship to Respondent.
- [ ] **Paragraph 2:** If you are filing the Petition to protect a family or household member, mark the box and fill in their name(s) and the other information requested in the chart. You may attach additional pages if you need more room.
- [ ] **Paragraph 3:** State the date(s) of the incident(s) that caused you to file the Petition. Provide a brief description of what happened. You may attach additional pages if you need more room to complete your description. You may attach an affidavit instead of or in addition to the written description.
- [ ] **Paragraph 4:** Indicate what action you want the Court to take by marking the boxes next to the numbered paragraphs that apply to your situation.
- [ ] **Paragraph 4(b):** Provide the address of the residence that you want Respondent to stay away from. If you do not want your present address known, write "address confidential." Do not write your address anywhere on the Petition if you want it to be confidential.
- [ ] **Paragraphs 4(d) and (e):** If you want temporary custody of your minor children or want the Court to establish temporary visitation rights, list the names and birth dates of the children. If you have children whose custody or visitation will be at issue in this domestic violence case, you must also complete and file a Parenting Proceeding Affidavit, Form 10.01-F. There is a separate form and instructions for the Parenting Proceeding Affidavit, Form 10.01-E and Form 10.01-F.
- [ ] **Paragraph 4(i):** If you want the Court to grant you use of a motor vehicle, describe that vehicle.
- [ ] **Paragraph 4(j):** Write any special court orders you believe would help ensure you and your family or household members' safety and protection.
- [ ] **Paragraph 5:** If you need an emergency ("*ex parte*") protection order mark the box next to Paragraph 5.
- [ ] **Paragraph 9:** List ALL present court cases and pertinent past court cases or investigations that involve you or a household member that may be related to you, your children, your family, or household members. This list should include all civil, criminal, divorce, juvenile, custody, visitation, and bankruptcy cases. Write the case name, the court, the case number, if known, the type of case, and the result of the case. If the case is not over, write "pending." You may attach additional pages if you need more room.

SIGNING THE PETITION: Try to fill out the Petition before you go to the courthouse. AFTER YOU HAVE FILLED OUT THE PETITION, TAKE IT TO A NOTARY PUBLIC TO HAVE YOUR SIGNATURE NOTARIZED. *DO NOT SIGN THE PETITION UNLESS YOU ARE IN FRONT OF A NOTARY PUBLIC.* **An employee of the Clerk of Court's office may be available to take your oath.**

FILING THE PETITION: After you have your signature notarized, file your Petition at the Clerk of Court's office. The Clerk of Court's office will tell you when and where your *ex parte* hearing will take place. **There is no filing fee for a Petition for a CPO.**

FORM 10.01-C: HOW TO COMPLETE A PETITION FOR A DOMESTIC VIOLENCE CIVIL PROTECTION ORDER

Amended: July 1, 2010
Discard all previous versions of this form

Form 10.01-D

FORM 10.01-D: PETITION FOR DOMESTIC VIOLENCE CIVIL PROTECTION ORDER

IN THE _____ COURT

_____ COUNTY, OHIO

Petitioner _____	Case No. _____
Address _____	Judge _____
City, State, Zip Code _____	
Date of Birth: _____	**PETITION FOR DOMESTIC VIOLENCE CIVIL PROTECTION ORDER (R.C. 3113.31)**
v.	
_____	**Notice to Petitioner:** Throughout this form, check every ☐ that applies.
Respondent	
Address _____	**DO NOT WRITE YOUR ADDRESS ON THIS FORM IF YOU ARE REQUESTING CONFIDENTIALITY. PLEASE PROVIDE AN ADDRESS WHERE YOU CAN RECEIVE NOTICES FROM THE COURT.**
City, State, Zip Code _____	
Date of Birth: _____	

☐ 1. Petitioner is a family or household member of Respondent and a victim of domestic violence and seeks relief on Petitioner's own behalf. The relationship of Petitioner to Respondent is that of:

☐ Spouse of Respondent
☐ Former spouse of Respondent
☐ The natural parent of Respondent's child
☐ Other relative (by blood or marriage) of Respondent/ Petitioner who has lived with Respondent at any time

☐ Child of Respondent
☐ Parent of Respondent
☐ Foster Parent
☐ Person "living as a spouse of Respondent" defined as:
  • now cohabiting;
  • or cohabited within five years before the alleged act of domestic violence

☐ 2. Petitioner seeks relief on behalf of the following family or household members:

NAME	DATE OF BIRTH	HOW RELATED TO PETITIONER	HOW RELATED TO RESPONDENT	RESIDES WITH

3. Respondent has engaged in the following act(s) of domestic violence (describe the acts as fully as possible, add additional pages if necessary): _____
_____
_____

FORM 10.01-D: PETITION FOR DOMESTIC VIOLENCE CIVIL PROTECTION ORDER

Amended: July 1, 2010
Discard all previous versions of this form

[Page 2 of Form 10.01-D]

4. Petitioner requests that the Court grant relief under R.C. 3113.31 to protect the Petitioner and or the family or household members named in this Petition from domestic violence by granting a civil protection order that:

    ☐ (a) Directs Respondent not to abuse Petitioner and the family or household members named in this Petition by harming, attempting to harm, threatening, following, stalking, harassing, forcing sexual relations upon them, or by committing sexually oriented offenses against them.

    ☐ (b) Requires Respondent to leave and not return to or interfere with the following residence and grants Petitioner exclusive possession of the residence: _____

    _____

    ☐ (c) Divides household and family personal property and directs Respondent not to remove, damage, hide, or dispose of any property or funds that Petitioner owns or possesses.

    ☐ (d) Temporarily allocates parental rights and responsibilities for the care of the following minor children and suspends Respondent's visitation rights until a full hearing is held (include names and birth dates of the minor children): _____

    _____

    _____

    _____

    ☐ (e) Establishes temporary visitation rights with the following minor children and requires visitation to be supervised or occur under such conditions that the Court determines will insure the safety of Petitioner and the minor children (include names and birth dates of the minor children): _____

    _____

    _____

    _____

    _____

    ☐ (f) Requires Respondent to provide financial support for Petitioner and the other family or household members named in this Petition.

    ☐ (g) Requires Respondent to complete batterer counseling, substance abuse counseling, or other counseling as determined necessary by the Court.

    ☐ (h) Requires Respondent to refrain from entering, approaching, or contacting (including contact by telephone, fax, e-mail, and voice mail) the residence, school, business, and place of employment of Petitioner and the family or household members named in this Petition.

    ☐ (i) Requires Respondent to permit Petitioner or other family or household member to have exclusive use of the following motor vehicle: _____

    ☐ (j) Includes the following additional provisions: _____

    _____

☐ 5. Petitioner further requests that the Court issue an *ex parte* (emergency) protection order under R.C. 3113.31(D) and (E) and this Petition.

6. Petitioner further requests that the Court issue no mutual protection orders or other orders against Petitioner unless all of the conditions of R.C. 3113.31(E)(4) are met.

7. Petitioner further requests that if Petitioner has a victim advocate, the Court permit the victim advocate to accompany Petitioner at all stages of these proceedings as required by R.C. 3113.31(M).

FORM 10.01-D: PETITION FOR DOMESTIC VIOLENCE CIVIL PROTECTION ORDER

Amended: July 1, 2010
Discard all previous versions of this form

8. Petitioner further requests that the Court grant such other relief as the Court considers equitable and fair.

9. Petitioner lists here all present court cases and pertinent past court cases (including civil, criminal, divorce, juvenile, custody, visitation, and bankruptcy cases) that relate to the Respondent, you, your children, your family, or your household members:

CASE NAME	CASE NUMBER	COURT/COUNTY	TYPE OF CASE	RESULT OF CASE

I hereby swear or affirm that the answers above are true, complete, and accurate to the best of my knowledge. I understand that falsification of this document may result in a contempt of court finding against me which could result in a jail sentence and fine, and that falsification of this document may also subject me to criminal penalties for perjury under R.C. 2921.11.

Sworn to and subscribed before me on this _____ day of _____ , _____ .

_____
SIGNATURE OF PETITIONER

DO NOT WRITE YOUR ADDRESS BELOW IF YOU ARE REQUESTING CONFIDENTIALITY. PLEASE PROVIDE AN ADDRESS WHERE YOU CAN RECEIVE NOTICES FROM THE COURT.

_____
NOTARY PUBLIC

_____

_____
Signature of Attorney for Petitioner (if applicable)

_____
Name

_____
Address

_____
Attorney Registration Number

_____
Phone Number

FORM 10.01-D: PETITION FOR DOMESTIC VIOLENCE CIVIL PROTECTION ORDER

Amended: July 1, 2010
Discard all previous versions of this form

Form 10.01-E

FORM 10.01-E: HOW TO COMPLETE THE INFORMATION FOR PARENTING PROCEEDING AFFIDAVIT

These instructions will help you prepare the Information for Parenting Proceeding Affidavit. The Affidavit must be filed if you are requesting a parenting (custody) order in a Petition for a Domestic Violence Civil Protection Order. **IF ANOTHER COURT IS ADDRESSING OR HAS ADDRESSED CUSTODY ISSUES INVOLVING THE CHILDREN, CUSTODY ISSUES WILL BE HANDLED IN THAT CASE, NOT THE DOMESTIC VIOLENCE CASE.**

FILLING OUT THE FORM: Check each instruction below after you read and complete it

---

☐ **Print or type only.** Attach an additional page to the Affidavit for your answers if you need more room.

☐ **At the top of the front page, fill in the names.** YOU are the "Petitioner." The person you want protection from is the "Respondent." Leave the Case No. and Judge lines blank for the Clerk of Court to complete.

☐ **First Paragraph.** Fill in your legal name in the blank line.

☐ **Paragraph 1:** Check this box if you wish your current address to remain confidential.

☐ **Paragraph 2:** On the blank line fill in the number of children that are subject to this court case. For each table at the top write in the child's name, place of birth, date of birth, sex, and address unless confidential. As you write on each line going across the table start with the length of time, the address unless confidential, the adult the child lived with at that time, and the relationship of that adult to the child. There are three tables. If you have more than three children that are subject to this court case, attach additional pages containing the requested information for each of those additional children.

☐ **Paragraph 3:** Mark the box showing whether or not you have participated as party, witness, or in any capacity concerning any civil or criminal case regarding custody or visitation of any of the children that are subject to this court case. If you have been involved in such a case fill in the details requested in lines a, b, c, and d.

☐ **Paragraph 4:** Mark the box showing whether or not you have any information concerning any case that could affect the current case including any case relating to custody, domestic violence and or protection orders, dependency, neglect, or abuse allegations or adoptions other than those listed in paragraph 3. If you do have such information, fill in the details requested in lines a, b, c, and d.

☐ **Paragraph 5:** List the criminal background and history of yourself and members of your household including any convictions or guilty pleas of any offense resulting in a child being an abused or neglected child, any offense that is a violation of R.C. 2919.25, any sexually oriented offense defined by R.C. 2950.01, and any offense involving a victim who was a family or household member at the time of the offense and caused physical harm to the victim during the commission of the offense.

☐ **Paragraph 6:** Check the first box if you do not know of any person not a party to this case who has physical custody or claims to have custody or visitation rights with respect to any child subject to this case. Check the second box if you do know anyone who is not a party to this case who has physical custody or claims to have custody or visitation rights with respect to any child subject to this case. If you check the second box you will fill in the required information for each person that you know who is not a party to this case who has physical custody or claims to have custody or visitation rights with respect to any child subject to this case.

Paragraph 7: You have an on-going duty to notify the Court of any custody, visitation, parenting time, divorce, dissolution of marriage, separation, neglect, abuse, dependency, guardianship, parentage, termination of parental rights, or domestic violence case concerning the children that are subject to this case.

SIGNING THE FORM: AFTER YOU HAVE FILLED OUT THE FORM, TAKE THE FORM TO THE CLERK OF COURT'S OFFICE OR TO A NOTARY PUBLIC TO HAVE YOUR SIGNATURE NOTARIZED. *DO NOT SIGN THE FORM UNLESS YOU ARE IN FRONT OF A NOTARY PUBLIC.*

FORM 10.01-E: HOW TO COMPLETE THE INFORMATION FOR PARENTING PROCEEDING AFFIDAVIT

Amended: July 1, 2010
Discard all previous versions of this form

Form 10.01-F

FORM 10.01-F: INFORMATION FOR PARENTING PROCEEDING AFFIDAVIT

IN THE _____ COURT

_____ COUNTY, OHIO

_____	:	Case No. _____
Petitioner	:	
	:	**Judge:** _____
v.	:	
	:	**INFORMATION FOR PARENTING PROCEEDING AFFIDAVIT (R.C. 3127.23(A))**
_____	:	
Respondent	:	**(Filed with Petition for Domestic Violence Civil Protection Order)**

NOTE: By law, an affidavit **must** be filed and served with the first pleading filed by each party in every parenting (custody/visitation) proceeding in this Court, including a Petition for a Domestic Violence Civil Protection Order. Each party has a continuing duty while this case is pending to inform the Court of any parenting proceeding concerning the child(ren) in any other court in this or any other state. **If more space is needed, attach an additional page.**

I (full legal name) _____, being sworn according to law, certify these cases involve the custody of a child or children and the following statements are true:

1. ☐ I am requesting the Court to not disclose my current address or that of the child(ren). My address is confidential pursuant to R.C. 3127.23(D) and should be placed under seal in that the health, safety, or liberty of myself and/or the child(ren) would be jeopardized by the disclosure of the identifying information.

2. **(Number):** _____ **Minor child(ren) are subject to this case as follows:**

   (Insert the information requested below. The residence information must be given for the last FIVE years.)

a. Child's name		Place of birth	Date of birth	Sex
Period of residence	☐ Address Confidential	Person child lived with (name & address)		Relationship
to present	☐ Address Confidential			
to	☐ Address Confidential			
to	☐ Address Confidential			
to	☐ Address Confidential			

FORM 10.01-F: INFORMATION FOR PARENTING PROCEEDING AFFIDAVIT

Amended: July 1, 2010
Discard all previous versions of this form

[Page 2 of Form 10.01-F]

Case No._____

b. Child's name		Place of birth	Date of birth	Sex
Period of residence	☐ Address Confidential	Person child lived with (name & address)	Relationship	
to present	☐ Address Confidential			
to	☐ Address Confidential			
to	☐ Address Confidential			
to	☐ Address Confidential			

c. Child's name		Place of birth	Date of birth	Sex
Period of residence	☐ Address Confidential	Person child lived with (name & address)	Relationship	
to present	☐ Address Confidential			
to	☐ Address Confidential			
to	☐ Address Confidential			
to	☐ Address Confidential			

e. Additional children are listed on Attachment 2(d). (Provide requested information for additional children on an attachment labeled 2d.)

3.   **Participation in custody case(s): (only one)**

    ☐   I **HAVE NOT** participated as a party, witness, or in any capacity in any other case, in this or any other state, concerning the custody of or visitation (parenting time) with any child subject to this case.

    ☐   I **HAVE** participated as a party, witness, or in any capacity in any other case, in this or any other state, concerning the custody of or visitation (parenting time) with any child subject to this case. Explain:

    a. Name of each child _____

    b. Type of case _____

    c. Court and State _____

    d. Date and court order or judgment (if any): _____

FORM 10.01-F: INFORMATION FOR PARENTING PROCEEDING AFFIDAVIT

Amended: July 1, 2010
Discard all previous versions of this form

[Page 3 of Form 10.01-F]

Case No._____

4.   **Information about custody case(s): (only one)**

☐   **I HAVE NO INFORMATION** of any cases that could affect the current case, any cases relating to custody, domestic violence or protection orders, dependency, neglect or abuse allegations or adoptions concerning any child subject to this case.

☐   **I HAVE THE FOLLOWING INFORMATION** concerning cases that could affect the current case, including any cases relating to custody, domestic violence or protection orders, dependency, neglect or abuse allegations or adoptions concerning any child subject to this case, other than listed in Paragraph 3. Explain:

     a.   Name of each child _____

     b.   Type of case _____

     c.   Court and state _____

     d.   Date of court order or judgment (if any): _____

5.   List all of the criminal convictions including guilty pleas for you and the members of your household for the following offenses: any criminal offense involving acts that resulted in a child being abused or neglected; any offense that is a violation of R.C. 2919.25; any sexually oriented offense as defined in R.C. 2950.01; and any offense involving a victim who was a family or household member at the time of the offense and caused physical harm to the victim during the commission of the offense.

NAME	CASE NUMBER	COURT/STATE/COUNTY	CHARGE

6.   **Persons not a party to this case: (only one)**

☐   **I DO NOT KNOW OF ANY PERSON** not a party to this case who has physical custody or claims to have custody or visitation rights with respect to any child subject to this case.

☐   **I KNOW THAT THE FOLLOWING NAMED PERSON(S)** not a party to this case has/have physical custody or claim(s) to have custody or visitation rights with respect to any child subject to this case:

   a.   Name and address of person _____

     ☐ has physical custody   ☐ claims custody rights   ☐ claims visitation rights

     Name of each child _____

   b.   Name and address of person _____

     ☐ has physical custody   ☐ claims custody rights   ☐ claims visitation rights

     Name of each child _____

   c.   Name and address of person _____

     ☐ has physical custody   ☐ claims custody rights   ☐ claims visitation rights

     Name of each child _____

FORM 10.01-F: INFORMATION FOR PARENTING PROCEEDING AFFIDAVIT

Amended: July 1, 2010
Discard all previous versions of this form

[Page 4 of Form 10.01-F]

Case No._____

7.   I understand that I have a continuing duty to advise this Court of any custody, visitation, parenting time, divorce, dissolution of marriage, separation, neglect, abuse, dependency, guardianship, parentage, termination of parental rights, or protection from domestic violence case concerning the child(ren) in this state or any other state about which information is obtained during this case.

OATH OF AFFIANT

I hereby swear or affirm that the answers above are true, complete, and accurate to the best of my knowledge. I understand that falsification of this document may result in a contempt of court finding against me which could result in a jail sentence and fine, and that falsification of this document may also subject me to criminal penalties for perjury under R.C. 2921.11.

_____

AFFIANT

Sworn to and subscribed before me on this _____ day of _____ , _____

_____

NOTARY PUBLIC

Form 10.01-G

FORM 10.01-G: WARNING CONCERNING THE ATTACHED DOMESTIC VIOLENCE PROTECTION ORDER

NOTE: Rules 10.01 and 10.02 of the Rules of Superintendence for the Courts of Ohio require this Warning to be attached to the FRONT of all civil and criminal domestic violence protection orders issued by the courts of the State of Ohio. TO BE USED WITH FORMS 10.01-H, 10.01-I, 10.01-J, 10.01-M, and 10.02-A.

WARNING TO RESPONDENT / DEFENDANT

Violating the attached Protection Order is a crime, punishable by imprisonment or fine or both, and can cause your bond to be revoked or result in a contempt of court citation against you.

This Protection Order is enforceable in all 50 states, the District of Columbia, tribal lands, and U.S. Territories pursuant to the Violence Against Women Act, 18 U.S.C. 2265. Violating this Protection Order may subject you to federal charges and punishment.

As a result of this Order or Consent Agreement, it may be unlawful for you to possess or purchase a firearm, including a rifle, pistol, or revolver, or ammunition pursuant to federal law under 18 U.S.C. 922(g)(8). If you have any questions whether these laws make it illegal for you to possess or purchase a firearm, you should consult an attorney.

Only the Court can change this Order. The Petitioner/Alleged Victim cannot give you legal permission to change this Order. If you go near the Petitioner/Alleged Victim, even with the Petitioner's/Alleged Victim's consent, you may be arrested. If you and the Petitioner/Alleged Victim want to resume your relationship you must ask the Court to modify or terminate this Protection Order. Unless the Court modifies or terminates this Order, you can be arrested for violating this Protection Order. You act at your own risk if you disregard this WARNING.

WARNING TO PETITIONER / ALLEGED VICTIM

You **cannot** change the terms of this Order by your words or actions. Only the Court can allow the Respondent/Defendant to contact you or return to your residence. This Order **cannot** be changed by either party without obtaining a written court order.

NOTICE TO ALL LAW ENFORCEMENT AGENCIES AND OFFICERS

The attached Protection Order is enforceable in all jurisdictions. Violation of this Protection Order, regardless of whether it is a criminal or civil Protection Order, is a crime under R.C. 2919.27. Law enforcement officers with powers to arrest under R.C. 2935.03 for violations of the Ohio Revised Code must enforce the terms of this Protection Order as required by R.C. 2919.26, 2919.27 and 3113.31. If you have reasonable grounds to believe that Respondent/Defendant has violated this Protection Order, it is the preferred course of action in Ohio under R.C. 2935.03 to arrest and detain Respondent/Defendant until a warrant can be obtained. Federal and state law prohibit charging a fee for service of this Order.

FORM 10.01-G: WARNING CONCERNING THE ATTACHED DOMESTIC VIOLENCE CIVIL PROTECTION ORDER

Amended: July 1, 2010
Discard all previous versions of this form

Form 10.01-H

FORM 10.01-H: DOMESTIC VIOLENCE CIVIL PROTECTION ORDER (CPO) EX PARTE

IN THE COURT OF COMMON PLEAS
_____ COUNTY, OHIO

Order of Protection

Per R.C. 3113.31(F)(3), this Order is indexed at

_____

LAW ENFORCEMENT AGENCY WHERE INDEXED

(   )   – _____

PHONE NUMBER

Case No.

Judge

County | State | **OHIO**

DOMESTIC VIOLENCE CIVIL PROTECTION ORDER (CPO) *EX PARTE* (R.C. 3113.31)

PETITIONER:

| First | Middle | Last |

v.

PERSON(S) PROTECTED BY THIS ORDER:

Petitioner: _____ DOB: _____

Petitioner's Family or Household Member(s) (May attach additional forms):

_____ DOB: _____
_____ DOB: _____
_____ DOB: _____
_____ DOB: _____

RESPONDENT:

| First | Middle | Last |

Relationship to Petitioner: _____

Address where Respondent can be found:

_____

RESPONDENT IDENTIFIERS

SEX	RACE	HT	WT
EYES	HAIR	DATE OF BIRTH	
DRIVER'S LIC. NO.	EXP. DATE	STATE	

Distinguishing features: _____

☐ **WARNING TO LAW ENFORCEMENT: RESPONDENT HAS FIREARMS ACCESS – PROCEED WITH CAUTION**

(Violence Against Women Act, 18 U.S.C. 2265, Federal Full Faith & Credit Declaration: Registration of this Order is not required for enforcement.)

THE COURT HEREBY FINDS:
That it has jurisdiction over the parties and subject matter, and the Respondent will be provided with reasonable notice and opportunity to be heard within the time required by Ohio law. **Additional findings of this Order are set forth below.**

THE COURT HEREBY ORDERS:
That the above named Respondent be restrained from committing acts of abuse or threats of abuse against the Petitioner and other protected persons named in this Order, as set forth below. Additional terms of this Order are set forth below.

The terms of this Order shall be effective until _____ / _____ / _____ (DATE CERTAIN).

WARNING TO RESPONDENT: See the warning page attached to the front of this Order.

FORM 10.01-H: DOMESTIC VIOLENCE CIVIL PROTECTION ORDER (CPO) EX PARTE

Amended: July 1, 2010
Discard all previous versions of this form

Case No._____

This proceeding came on for an *ex parte* hearing on _____ (Respondent not being present), upon the filing of a Petition by Petitioner for a domestic violence civil protection order (CPO) against the Respondent, pursuant to R.C. 3113.31. In accordance with R.C. 3113.31(D)(1), the Court held an *ex parte* hearing on the same day that the Petition was filed.

The Court finds that the protected persons herein are in immediate and present danger of domestic violence and for good cause shown, the following temporary orders are necessary to protect the persons named in this Order from domestic violence.

ALL OF THE PROVISIONS CHECKED BELOW APPLY TO THE RESPONDENT

☐ **1. RESPONDENT SHALL NOT ABUSE** the protected persons named in this Order by harming, attempting to harm, threatening, following, stalking, harassing, forcing sexual relations upon them, or by committing sexually oriented offenses against them. [NCIC 01 and 02]

☐ **2. RESPONDENT SHALL IMMEDIATELY VACATE** the following residence: _____

_____

☐ **3. EXCLUSIVE POSSESSION OF THE RESIDENCE** located at: _____

is granted to: _____. Respondent shall not interfere with this individual's right

to occupy the residence including, but not limited to canceling utilities or insurance, interrupting telephone service, mail delivery, or the delivery of any other documents or items. [NCIC 03]

☐ **4. RESPONDENT SHALL SURRENDER** all keys and garage door openers to the above residence at the earliest possible opportunity after service of this Order to the law enforcement agency that serves Respondent with this Order or as follows: _____

_____

_____

☐ **5. RESPONDENT SHALL NOT ENTER** or interfere with the residence, school, business, place of employment, day care centers, or child care providers of the protected persons named in this Order, including the buildings, grounds, and parking lots at those locations. Respondent may not violate this Order **even with the permission of a protected person**. [NCIC 04]

☐ **6. RESPONDENT SHALL STAY AWAY FROM PETITIONER** and all other protected persons named in this Order, and not be present within 500 feet or _____ (distance) of any protected persons wherever those protected persons may be found, or any place the Respondent knows or should know the protected persons are likely to be, **even with Petitioner's permission.** If Respondent accidentally comes in contact with protected persons in any public or private place, Respondent must depart *immediately*. This Order includes encounters on public and private roads, highways, and thoroughfares. [NCIC 04]

☐ **7. RESPONDENT SHALL NOT INITIATE OR HAVE ANY CONTACT** with the protected persons named in this Order or their residences, businesses, places of employment, schools, day care centers, or child care providers. Contact includes, but is not limited to, telephone, fax, e-mail, voice mail, delivery service, writings, or communications by any other means in person or through another person. Respondent may not violate this Order **even with the permission of a protected person**. [NCIC 05]

☐ **8. RESPONDENT SHALL IMMEDIATELY SURRENDER POSSESSION OF ALL KEYS TO THE FOLLOWING MOTOR VEHICLE:** _____ to the law enforcement agency that served Respondent with the Order or as follows _____

and Petitioner is granted exclusive use of this motor vehicle.

FORM 10.01-H: DOMESTIC VIOLENCE CIVIL PROTECTION ORDER (CPO) EX PARTE

Amended: July 1, 2010
Discard all previous versions of this form

[Page 3 of Form 10.01-H]

Case No._____

☐ 9. **RESPONDENT SHALL NOT REMOVE, DAMAGE, HIDE, OR DISPOSE OF ANY PROPERTY OR PETS** owned or possessed by the protected persons named in this Order. Personal property shall be apportioned as follows:

_____

_____

_____

☐ 10. **RESPONDENT SHALL NOT CAUSE OR ENCOURAGE ANY PERSON** to do any act prohibited by this Order.

☐ 11. **RESPONDENT SHALL NOT POSSESS, USE, CARRY, OR OBTAIN ANY DEADLY WEAPON.** Respondent shall turn over all deadly weapons in Respondent's possession to the law enforcement agency that serves Respondent with this Order or as follows: _____

_____

Any law enforcement agency is authorized to take possession of deadly weapons pursuant to this paragraph and hold them in protective custody until further Court order [NCIC 07]

☐ 12. **PARENTAL RIGHTS AND RESPONSIBILITIES ARE TEMPORARILY ALLOCATED AS FOLLOWS: [NCIC 09]**

_____

_____

This Order applies to the following child(ren): _____

_____

☐ 13. **VISITATION ORDERS DO NOT PERMIT RESPONDENT TO VIOLATE THE TERMS OF THIS ORDER.**

     ☐ (A)   Respondent's visitation rights are suspended; or

     ☐ (B)   As a limited exception to paragraphs 6 and 7, temporary visitation rights are established as follows: [NCIC 06]

     _____

     _____

     _____

     _____

     _____

     This Order applies to the following child(ren): _____

     _____

☐ 14. **LAW ENFORCEMENT AGENCIES,** including but not limited to, _____

are ordered to assist Petitioner in gaining physical custody of the child(ren) if necessary.

☐ 15. **RESPONDENT SHALL SUPPORT** the protected persons named in this Order as follows: _____

_____

_____

☐ 16. **RESPONDENT MAY PICK UP CLOTHING** and personal items from the above residence only in the company of a uniformed law enforcement officer within seven days of the filing of this Order. Arrangements may be made by contacting: _____

☐ 17. **RESPONDENT SHALL NOT USE OR POSSESS** alcohol or illegal drugs.

FORM 10.01-H: DOMESTIC VIOLENCE CIVIL PROTECTION ORDER (CPO) EX PARTE

Amended: July 1, 2010
Discard all previous versions of this form

[Page 4 of Form 10.01-H]

Case No._____

☐ **18. IT IS FURTHER ORDERED:** [NCIC 08]   _____

_____

_____

_____

_____

19.   **IT IS FURTHER ORDERED** that the Clerk of Court shall cause a copy of the Petition and this Order to be delivered to the Respondent as required by law. The Clerk of Court shall also provide certified copies of the Petition and this Order to Petitioner upon request. This Order is granted without bond. Under federal and state law, the Clerk shall not charge any fees for filing, issuing, registering, or serving this protection order.

20.   **ALL OF THE TERMS OF THIS ORDER SHALL REMAIN IN FULL FORCE AND EFFECT UNTIL**
_____ , _____ unless earlier modified by or dismissed by order of this Court. Except for paragraphs 12, 13, 14, and 15 above, this Order survives a divorce, dissolution of marriage, or legal separation.

   IT IS SO ORDERED.

_____   _____
MAGISTRATE   **JUDGE**

NOTICE TO RESPONDENT: THE PERSONS PROTECTED BY THIS ORDER CANNOT GIVE YOU LEGAL PERMISSION TO CHANGE OR VIOLATE THIS ORDER. IF YOU VIOLATE ANY TERMS OF THIS ORDER EVEN WITH THE PROTECTED PERSON'S PERMISSION, YOU MAY BE ARRESTED. ONLY THE COURT CAN CHANGE THIS ORDER. IF THERE IS ANY REASON WHY THIS ORDER SHOULD BE CHANGED, YOU MUST ASK THE COURT TO CHANGE IT. YOU ACT AT YOUR OWN RISK IF YOU DISREGARD THIS WARNING.

A FULL HEARING on this Order, and on all other issues raised by the Petition, shall be held	**TO THE CLERK** **COPIES OF THIS ORDER SHALL BE DELIVERED TO:**
before Judge _____ or Magistrate _____ on the _____ day of _____ , 20 _____ at _____ a.m./p.m. at the following location: _____ _____	☐ Petitioner ☐ Respondent (by personal service) ☐ Police Department Where Petitioner Resides: _____ ☐ The _____ County Sheriff's Office ☐ Police Department Where Petitioner Works: _____ ☐ Other: _____

FORM 10.01-H: DOMESTIC VIOLENCE CIVIL PROTECTION ORDER (CPO) EX PARTE

Amended: July 1, 2010
Discard all previous versions of this form

Form 10.01-I

FORM 10.01-I: DOMESTIC VIOLENCE CIVIL PROTECTION ORDER (CPO) FULL HEARING

IN THE COURT OF COMMON PLEAS
_____ COUNTY, OHIO

Order of Protection

Per R.C. 3113.31(F)(3), this Order is indexed at

_____

LAW ENFORCEMENT AGENCY WHERE INDEXED
(_____) _____ - _____
PHONE NUMBER

Case No.	
Judge	
County	State **OHIO**

DOMESTIC VIOLENCE CIVIL PROTECTION ORDER (CPO) FULL HEARING (R.C. 3113.31)
☐ **WITH SUPPORT ORDER**

PETITIONER:

First	Middle	Last

v.

RESPONDENT:

First	Middle	Last

Relationship to Petitioner: _____
Address where Respondent can be found:
_____
_____

PERSON(S) PROTECTED BY THIS ORDER:

Petitioner: _____ DOB: _____
Petitioner's Family or Household Member(s) (May attach additional form):

_____ DOB: _____
_____ DOB: _____
_____ DOB: _____
_____ DOB: _____

RESPONDENT IDENTIFIERS

SEX	RACE	HT	WT
EYES	HAIR	DATE OF BIRTH	

DRIVER'S LIC. NO.	EXP. DATE	STATE

Distinguishing features: _____

☐ **WARNING TO LAW ENFORCEMENT: RESPONDENT HAS FIREARMS ACCESS – PROCEED WITH CAUTION**

(Violence Against Women Act, 18 U.S.C. 2265, Federal Full Faith & Credit Declaration: Registration of this Order is not required for enforcement.)

THE COURT HEREBY FINDS:

That it has jurisdiction over the parties and subject matter, and the Respondent was provided with reasonable notice and opportunity to be heard within the time required by Ohio law. **Additional findings of this Order are set forth below.**

THE COURT HEREBY ORDERS:

That the above named Respondent be restrained from committing further acts of abuse or threats of abuse against the Petitioner and other protected persons named in this Order, as set forth below. Additional terms of this Order are set forth below.

The terms of this Order shall be effective until _____ / _____ / _____ (DATE CERTAIN – FIVE YEARS MAXIMUM)

WARNING TO RESPONDENT: See the warning page attached to the front of this Order.

FORM 10.01-I: DOMESTIC VIOLENCE CIVIL PROTECTION ORDER (CPO) FULL HEARING

Amended: July 1, 2010
Discard all previous versions of this form

[Page 2 of Form 10.01-I]

Case No._____

This proceeding came on for a hearing on _____ before the Court and the *Ex Parte* Order filed on
_____. The following individuals were present: _____
_____.

The Court hereby makes the following findings of fact: _____
_____
_____
_____
_____
_____

The Court further finds by a preponderance of the evidence: 1) that the Petitioner or Petitioner's family or household member(s) are in danger of or have been a victim of domestic violence or sexually oriented offenses as defined in R.C. 3113.31(A) committed by Respondent; and 2) the following orders are equitable, fair, and necessary to protect the persons named in this Order from domestic violence.

ALL OF THE PROVISIONS CHECKED BELOW APPLY TO THE RESPONDENT

☐ 1.   **RESPONDENT SHALL NOT ABUSE** the protected persons named in this Order by harming, attempting to harm, threatening, following, stalking, harassing, forcing sexual relations upon them, or by committing sexually oriented offenses against them. [NCIC 01 and 02]

☐ 2.   **RESPONDENT SHALL IMMEDIATELY VACATE** the following residence: _____
_____

☐ 3.   **EXCLUSIVE POSSESSION OF THE RESIDENCE** located at: _____
is granted to: _____ . Respondent shall not interfere with this individual's right to occupy the residence including, but not limited to canceling utilities or insurance, interrupting telephone service, mail delivery, or the delivery of any other documents or items. [NCIC 03]

☐ 4.   **RESPONDENT SHALL SURRENDER** all keys and garage door openers to the above residence at the earliest possible opportunity after service of this Order to the law enforcement agency that serves Respondent with this Order or as follows: _____
_____

☐ 5.   **RESPONDENT SHALL NOT ENTER** or interfere with the residence, school, business, place of employment, day care centers, or child care providers of the protected persons named in this Order, including the buildings, grounds, and parking lots at those locations. Respondent may not violate this Order **even with the permission of a protected person**. [NCIC 04]

☐ 6.   **RESPONDENT SHALL STAY AWAY FROM PETITIONER** and all other protected persons named in this Order and not be present within 500 feet or _____ (distance) of any protected persons wherever those protected persons may be found, or any place the Respondent knows or should know the protected persons are likely to be, **even with Petitioner's permission**. If Respondent accidentally comes in contact with protected persons in any public or private place, Respondent must depart *immediately*. This Order includes encounters on public and private roads, highways, and thoroughfares. [NCIC 04]

☐ 7.   **RESPONDENT SHALL NOT INITIATE OR HAVE ANY CONTACT** with the protected persons named in this Order or their residences, businesses, places of employment, schools, day care centers, or child care providers. Contact includes, but is not limited to, telephone, fax, e-mail, voice mail, delivery service, writings, or communications by any other means in person or through another person. Respondent may not violate this Order **even with the permission of protected person**. [NCIC 05]

FORM 10.01-I: DOMESTIC VIOLENCE CIVIL PROTECTION ORDER (CPO) FULL HEARING

Amended: July 1, 2010
Discard all previous versions of this form

[Page 3 of Form 10.01-I]

Case No._____

☐ 8. **RESPONDENT SHALL IMMEDIATELY SURRENDER POSSESSION OF ALL KEYS TO THE FOLLOWING MOTOR VEHICLE,** _____ , to the law enforcement agency that served Respondent with the Order or as follows _____
and Petitioner is granted exclusive use of this motor vehicle.

☐ 9. **RESPONDENT SHALL NOT REMOVE, DAMAGE, HIDE, OR DISPOSE OF ANY PROPERTY OR PETS** owned or possessed by the protected persons named in this Order. Personal property shall be apportioned as follows:
_____
_____

☐ 10. **RESPONDENT SHALL NOT CAUSE OR ENCOURAGE ANY PERSON** to do any act prohibited by this Order.

☐ 11. **RESPONDENT SHALL NOT POSSESS, USE, CARRY, OR OBTAIN ANY DEADLY WEAPON.** Respondent shall turn over all deadly weapons in Respondent's possession to the law enforcement agency that serves Respondent with this Order or as follows: _____
_____
_____

Any law enforcement agency is authorized to take possession of deadly weapons pursuant to this paragraph and hold them in protective custody until further Court order. [NCIC 07]

☐ 12. **PARENTAL RIGHTS AND RESPONSIBILITIES ARE TEMPORARILY ALLOCATED AS FOLLOWS:** [NCIC 09]
_____
_____

This Order applies to the following child(ren): _____
_____

☐ 13. **VISITATION ORDERS DO NOT PERMIT RESPONDENT TO VIOLATE THE TERMS OF THIS ORDER.**

     ☐ (A) Respondent's visitation rights are suspended; or

     ☐ (B) As a limited exception to paragraphs 6 and 7, temporary visitation rights are established as follows: [NCIC 06]
_____
_____
_____
_____

This Order applies to the following child(ren): _____
_____

☐ 14. **LAW ENFORCEMENT AGENCIES** including but not limited to _____
are ordered to assist Petitioner in gaining physical custody of the child(ren) if necessary.

☐ 15. **RESPONDENT SHALL SUPPORT** the protected persons named in this Order as follows: _____
_____
_____

☐ 16. **RESPONDENT MAY PICK UP CLOTHING** and personal items from the above residence only in the company of a uniformed law enforcement officer within seven days of the filing of this Order. Arrangements may be made by contacting: _____

☐ 17. **RESPONDENT SHALL NOT USE OR POSSESS** alcohol or illegal drugs.

FORM 10.01-I: DOMESTIC VIOLENCE CIVIL PROTECTION ORDER (CPO) FULL HEARING

Amended: July 1, 2010
Discard all previous versions of this form

[Page 4 of Form 10.01- I]

Case No. _____

☐ **18. IT IS FURTHER ORDERED:** [NCIC 08] _____

_____

_____

_____

☐ **19. RESPONDENT SHALL COMPLETE THE FOLLOWING COUNSELING PROGRAM:** _____

_____

Respondent shall contact this program within _____ **days after receiving this Order and immediately arrange for an initial appointment.** The counseling program is requested to provide the Court a written notice when Respondent attends the initial appointment, if the Respondent fails to attend or is discharged, and when Respondent completes the program. Respondent is required to sign all necessary waivers to allow the Court to receive information from the counseling program.

☐ **Respondent is ordered to appear before Judge** _____ **or Magistrate** _____ ,

on _____ **at** _____ **a.m. / p.m., to review Respondent's compliance with this counseling order. Respondent is warned: If you fail to attend the counseling program you may be held in contempt of court. If you fail to appear at this hearing, the Court may issue a warrant for your arrest.**

20. IT IS FURTHER ORDERED that the Clerk of Court shall cause a copy of this Order to be delivered to the Respondent as required by law. The Clerk of Court shall also provide certified copies of this Order to Petitioner upon request. This Order is granted without bond. Under federal and state law, the Clerk shall not charge any fees for filing, issuing, registering, or serving this Protection Order.

21. ALL OF THE TERMS OF THIS ORDER SHALL REMAIN IN FULL FORCE AND EFFECT FOR A PERIOD OF FIVE YEARS FROM ISSUANCE, OR UNTIL _____ unless earlier modified or terminated by order of this Court. Except for paragraphs 12, 13, 14, and 15 above, this Order survives a divorce, dissolution of marriage, or legal separation. Until this Order is delivered to Respondent, the terms of the *ex parte* CPO remain in effect.

IT IS SO ORDERED.   **APPROVED and ADOPTED by:**

_____   _____
    MAGISTRATE   **JUDGE**

NOTICE TO RESPONDENT: THE PERSONS PROTECTED BY THIS ORDER CANNOT GIVE YOU LEGAL PERMISSION TO CHANGE OR VIOLATE THIS ORDER. IF YOU VIOLATE ANY TERMS OF THIS ORDER, EVEN WITH THE PROTECTED PERSON'S PERMISSION, YOU MAY BE ARRESTED. ONLY THE COURT CAN CHANGE THIS ORDER. IF THERE IS ANY REASON WHY THIS ORDER SHOULD BE CHANGED, YOU MUST ASK THE COURT TO CHANGE IT. YOU ACT AT YOUR OWN RISK IF YOU DISREGARD THIS WARNING.

NOTICE OF FINAL APPEALABLE ORDER	**TO THE CLERK:**
Copies of the foregoing Order, which is a final appealable order, were mailed by ordinary U.S. mail or hand-delivered to the parties indicated on the _____ day of _____ , 20 _____ . By: _____ CLERK OF COURT	**COPIES OF THIS ORDER SHALL BE DELIVERED TO** ☐ Petitioner ☐ Attorney for Petitioner ☐ Respondent ☐ Attorney for Respondent ☐ Counseling Program: _____ ☐ The _____ County Sheriff's Office ☐ Police Department Where Petitioner Resides: _____ ☐ Police Department Where Petitioner Works: _____ ☐ CSEA ☐ Other: _____

FORM 10.01-I: DOMESTIC VIOLENCE CIVIL PROTECTION ORDER (CPO) FULL HEARING

Amended: July 1, 2010
Discard all previous versions of this form

Form 10.01-J

FORM 10.01-J: CONSENT AGREEMENT AND DOMESTIC VIOLENCE CIVIL PROTECTION ORDER

IN THE COURT OF COMMON PLEAS
_____ COUNTY, OHIO

# Order of Protection Per R.C. 3113.31(F)(3), this Order is indexed at _____ **LAW ENFORCEMENT AGENCY WHERE INDEXED** ( ) - **PHONE NUMBER**	Case No. [ ] Judge County [ ] State [**OHIO**] **CONSENT AGREEMENT AND DOMESTIC VIOLENCE CIVIL PROTECTION ORDER (R.C. 3113.31)** ☐ **WITH SUPPORT ORDER**

PETITIONER:

```
_____
First      Middle        Last

          v.
```

PERSON(S) PROTECTED BY THIS ORDER:

Petitioner: _____ DOB _____
Petitioner's Family or Household Member(s)(May attach additional forms):

_____	DOB _____
_____	DOB _____
_____	DOB _____
_____	DOB _____

RESPONDENT:

```
_____
First      Middle        Last
```

Relationship to Petitioner: _____
Address where Respondent can be found:
_____
_____

RESPONDENT IDENTIFIERS

SEX	RACE	HT	WT
EYES	HAIR	DATE OF BIRTH	
DRIVER'S LIC. NO.	EXP. DATE	STATE	

Distinguishing Features: _____
_____

☐ **WARNING TO LAW ENFORCEMENT: RESPONDENT HAS FIREARMS ACCESS – PROCEED WITH CAUTION**

(Violence Against Women Act, 18 U.S.C. 2265, Federal Full Faith & Credit Declaration: Registration of this Order is not required for enforcement.)

THE COURT HEREBY FINDS:
That it has jurisdiction over the parties and subject matter, and the Respondent was provided with reasonable notice and opportunity to be heard within the time required by Ohio law. **Additional findings of this Order are set forth below.**

THE COURT HEREBY ORDERS:
That the above named Respondent be restrained from committing acts of abuse or threats of abuse against the Petitioner and other protected persons named in this Order, as set forth below. Additional terms of this Order are set forth below.

The terms of this Order shall be effective until _____ / _____ / _____ (DATE CERTAIN – FIVE YEARS MAXIMUM)

WARNING TO RESPONDENT: See the warning page attached to the front of this Order.

FORM 10.01-J: CONSENT AGREEMENT AND DOMESTIC VIOLENCE CIVIL PROTECTION ORDER

Amended: July 1, 2010
Discard all previous versions of this form

[Page 2 of Form 10.01-J]

Case No._____

This proceeding came on for a hearing on _____ before the Court and the *Ex Parte* Order filed on
_____. The following individuals were present: _____

_____

The parties agree to waive their notice and hearing rights and their rights under Civ. R. 53, including the right to request findings of fact and conclusions of law and to file objections to the Magistrate's Decision in this matter.

ALL OF THE PROVISIONS CHECKED BELOW APPLY TO THE RESPONDENT.

☐ **1.   RESPONDENT SHALL NOT ABUSE** the protected persons named in this Order by harming, attempting to harm, threatening, following, stalking, harassing, forcing sexual relations upon them, or by committing sexually oriented offenses against them. [NCIC 01 and 02]

☐ **2.   RESPONDENT SHALL IMMEDIATELY VACATE** the following residence: _____

_____

☐ **3.   EXCLUSIVE POSSESSION OF THE RESIDENCE** located at: _____
is granted to: _____. Respondent shall not interfere with this individual's right to occupy the residence including, but not limited to canceling utilities or insurance, interrupting telephone service, mail delivery, or the delivery of any other documents or items. [NCIC 03]

☐ **4.   RESPONDENT SHALL SURRENDER** all keys and garage door openers to the above residence at the earliest possible opportunity after service of this Order to the law enforcement agency that serves Respondent with this Order or as follows: _____

☐ **5.   RESPONDENT SHALL NOT ENTER** or interfere with the residence, school, business, place of employment, day care center, or child care providers of the protected persons named in this Order, including the buildings, grounds, and parking lots at those locations. Respondent may not violate this Order **even with the permission of a protected person**. [NCIC 04]

☐ **6.   RESPONDENT SHALL STAY AWAY FROM PETITIONER** and all other protected persons named in this Order and not be present within 500 feet or _____ (distance) of any protected persons, wherever those protected persons may be found, or any place the Respondent knows or should know the protected persons are likely to be, **even with Petitioner's permission**. If Respondent accidentally comes in contact with protected persons in any public or private place, Respondent must depart *immediately*. This Order includes encounters on public and private roads, highways, and thoroughfares. [NCIC 04]

☐ **7.   RESPONDENT SHALL NOT INITIATE OR HAVE ANY CONTACT** with the protected persons named in this Order or their residences, businesses, places of employment, schools, day care centers, or child care providers. Contact includes, but is not limited to, telephone, fax, e-mail, voice mail, delivery service, writings, or communications by any other means in person or through another person. Respondent may not violate this Order **even with the permission of a protected person**. [NCIC 05]

☐ **8.   RESPONDENT SHALL IMMEDIATELY SURRENDER POSSESSION OF ALL KEYS TO THE FOLLOWING MOTOR VEHICLE,** _____ , to the law enforcement agency that served Respondent with the Order or as follows _____
and Petitioner is granted exclusive use of this motor vehicle.

☐ **9.   RESPONDENT SHALL NOT REMOVE, DAMAGE, HIDE, OR DISPOSE OF ANY PROPERTY OR PETS** owned or possessed by the protected persons named in this Order. Personal property shall be apportioned as follows:

_____

☐ **10. RESPONDENT SHALL NOT CAUSE OR ENCOURAGE ANY PERSON** to do any act prohibited by this Order.

FORM 10.01-J: CONSENT AGREEMENT AND DOMESTIC VIOLENCE CIVIL PROTECTION ORDER

Amended: July 1, 2010
Discard all previous versions of this form

[Page 3 of Form 10.01-J]

Case No._____

☐ **11. RESPONDENT SHALL NOT POSSESS, USE, CARRY, OR OBTAIN ANY DEADLY WEAPON.** Respondent shall turn over all deadly weapons in Respondent's possession to the law enforcement agency that serves Respondent with this Order or as follows: _____

_____

Any law enforcement agency is authorized to take possession of deadly weapons pursuant to this paragraph and hold them in protective custody until further Court order. [NCIC 07]

☐ **12. PARENTAL RIGHTS AND RESPONSIBILITIES ARE TEMPORARILY ALLOCATED AS FOLLOWS: [NCIC 09]**

_____

_____

This Order applies to the following child(ren): _____

_____

☐ **13. VISITATION ORDERS DO NOT PERMIT RESPONDENT TO VIOLATE THE TERMS OF THIS ORDER.**

   ☐ (A) Respondent's visitation rights are suspended; or

   ☐ (B) As a limited exception to paragraphs 6 and 7, temporary visitation rights are established as follows: [NCIC 06]

_____

_____

This Order applies to the following child(ren): _____

_____

☐ **14. LAW ENFORCEMENT AGENCIES,** including, but not limited to, _____
are ordered to assist Petitioner in gaining physical custody of the child(ren) if necessary.

☐ **15. RESPONDENT SHALL SUPPORT** the protected persons named in this Order as follows: _____

_____

☐ **16. RESPONDENT MAY PICK UP CLOTHING** and personal items from the above residence only in the company of a uniformed law enforcement officer within seven days of the filing of this Order. Arrangements may be made by contacting: _____

_____

☐ **17. RESPONDENT SHALL NOT USE OR POSSESS** alcohol or illegal drugs.

☐ **18. IT IS FURTHER ORDERED:** [NCIC 08] _____

_____

_____

☐ **19. RESPONDENT SHALL COMPLETE THE FOLLOWING COUNSELING PROGRAM:** _____

_____

Respondent shall contact this program within _____ **days after receiving this Order and immediately arrange for an initial appointment.** The counseling program is requested to provide the Court a written notice when Respondent attends the initial appointment, if the Respondent fails to attend or is discharged, and when Respondent completes the program. Respondent is required to sign all necessary waivers to allow the Court to receive information from the counseling program.

   ☐ **Respondent is ordered to appear before Judge** _____

or Magistrate _____ **on** _____ **at** _____ **a.m. / p.m, to review Respondent's compliance with the counseling order. Respondent is warned: If you fail to attend the counseling program you may be held in contempt of court. If you fail to appear at this hearing, the Court may issue a warrant for your arrest.**

[Page 4 of Form 10.01-J]

Case No. _____

20.   **IT IS FURTHER ORDERED** that the Clerk of Court shall cause a copy of the Petition and this Order to be delivered to the Respondent as required by law. The Clerk of Court shall also provide certified copies of the Petition and this Order to Petitioner upon request. This Order is granted without bond. Under federal and state law the Clerk shall not charge any fees for filing, issuing, registering, or serving this Protection Order.

21.   **ALL OF THE TERMS OF THIS ORDER REMAIN IN FULL FORCE AND EFFECT FOR A PERIOD OF FIVE YEARS FROM ISSUANCE, OR UNTIL** _____ unless earlier modified or terminated by order of this Court. Except for paragraphs 12, 13, 14, and 15 above, this Order survives a divorce, dissolution of marriage, or legal separation. Until this Order is delivered to Respondent, the terms of the *Ex Parte* CPO remain in effect.

IT IS SO ORDERED.   **APPROVED and ADOPTED by:**

_____   _____

MAGISTRATE   **JUDGE**

<u>**NOTICE TO RESPONDENT:**</u> **THE PERSONS PROTECTED BY THIS ORDER CANNOT GIVE YOU LEGAL PERMISSION TO CHANGE OR VIOLATE THIS ORDER. IF YOU VIOLATE ANY TERMS OF THIS ORDER, EVEN WITH THE PROTECTED PERSON'S PERMISSION, YOU MAY BE ARRESTED. ONLY THE COURT CAN CHANGE THIS ORDER. IF THERE IS ANY REASON WHY THIS ORDER SHOULD BE CHANGED, YOU MUST ASK THE COURT TO CHANGE IT. <u>YOU ACT AT YOUR OWN RISK IF YOU DISREGARD THIS WARNING.</u>**

I have read this Consent Agreement and Civil Protection Order and agree to its terms.   *I have read this Consent Agreement and Civil Protection Order and agree to its terms.*

_____   _____

SIGNATURE OF PETITIONER   **SIGNATURE OF RESPONDENT**

_____   _____

Address of Petitioner   Address of Respondent

_____   _____

Signature of Attorney for Petitioner   Signature of Attorney for Respondent

_____   _____

Address of Attorney for Petitioner   Address of Attorney for Respondent

---

NOTICE OF FINAL APPEALABLE ORDER

Copies of the foregoing Order, which is a final appealable order, were mailed by ordinary U.S. mail or hand-delivered to the parties indicated on the

_____ day of _____ , 20 _____ .

By: _____
           CLERK OF COURT

TO THE CLERK
COPIES OF THIS ORDER SHALL BE DELIVERED TO:

☐ Petitioner   ☐ Attorney for Petitioner
☐ Respondent   ☐ Attorney for Respondent
☐ Counseling Program: _____
☐ The _____ County Sheriff's Office
☐ Police Department Where Petitioner Resides:
_____
☐ Police Department Where Petitioner Works:
_____
☐ CSEA
☐ Other: _____

FORM 10.01-J: CONSENT AGREEMENT AND DOMESTIC VIOLENCE CIVIL PROTECTION ORDER

Amended: July 1, 2010
Discard all previous versions of this form

Form 10.01-K

FORM 10.01-K: MOTION TO MODIFY OR TERMINATE DOMESTIC VIOLENCE CIVIL PROTECTION ORDER OR CONSENT AGREEMENT

IN THE COURT OF COMMON PLEAS
_____ COUNTY, OHIO

_____ :   Case No. _____

Petitioner
   :
_____   Judge _____

Address
   :

_____
City, State, Zip Code   :

   :
      v.   :   **MOTION TO MODIFY OR TERMINATE DOMESTIC VIOLENCE CIVIL PROTECTION ORDER OR CONSENT AGREEMENT**
   :

_____
Respondent   :   **DO NOT WRITE YOUR ADDRESS ON THIS FORM IF YOU ARE REQUESTING CONFIDENTIALITY. PLEASE PROVIDE AN ADDRESS WHERE YOU CAN RECEIVE NOTICES FROM THE COURT.**
   :

_____
Address   :

_____
City, State, Zip Code   :

     Petitioner/Respondent moves this Court to modify or terminate the Domestic Violence Civil Protection Order or Consent Agreement issued on _____. In the original proceeding, I was the ☐ Petitioner ☐ Respondent.

     The terms of the civil protection order or consent agreement to be modified or terminated are: _____
_____
_____
_____

     The reasons for the modification or termination are: _____
_____
_____
_____

     If you are the Petitioner, you cannot be assessed court fees or other costs for filing a Motion to Modify or Terminate Domestic Violence Civil Protection Order or Consent Agreement.

Respectfully submitted,

_____
SIGNATURE OF PETITIONER/RESPONDENT

FORM 10.01-K: MOTION TO MODIFY OR TERMINATE DOMESTIC VIOLENCE CIVIL PROTECTION ORDER OR CONSENT AGREEMENT

Effective Date: July 1, 2010

[Page 2 of Form 10.01-K]

Case No._____

Address where Petitioner/Respondent can be contacted:

_____

_____

_____

DO NOT WRITE your address on this form if you are requesting confidentiality. Please provide an address where you can receive notices from the Court.

_____
Signature of Attorney for Petitioner/Respondent (if applicable)

_____
Name

_____

_____
Address

_____
Attorney Registration Number

_____
Telephone Number

_____
Fax Number

_____
Email

REQUEST FOR SERVICE

Please serve a copy of the foregoing Motion upon _____

by certified mail or personal service at the following address: _____

_____

FORM 10.01-K: MOTION TO MODIFY OR TERMINATE DOMESTIC VIOLENCE CIVIL PROTECTION ORDER OR CONSENT AGREEMENT

Effective Date: July 1, 2010

Form 10.01-L

FORM 10.01-L: JUDGMENT ENTRY ON MOTION TO MODIFY/TERMINATE DOMESTIC VIOLENCE CIVIL PROTECTION ORDER OR CONSENT AGREEMENT

IN THE COURT OF COMMON PLEAS
_____ COUNTY, OHIO

Petitioner	Case No. _____
Date of Birth: _____	
	Judge _____
	JUDGMENT ENTRY ON MOTION TO MODIFY/TERMINATE DOMESTIC VIOLENCE CIVIL PROTECTION ORDER OR CONSENT AGREEMENT
v.	
Respondent	
Date of Birth: _____	

Upon the motion of ☐ Petitioner ☐ Respondent, this proceeding came on for a hearing on _____ before the Court to modify/terminate the Domestic Violence Civil Protection Order or Consent Agreement issued on

_____ .

☐ The Petitioner was present.

☐ The Petitioner was not present, but had reasonable notice and opportunity to be heard.

☐ The Respondent was present.

☐ The Respondent was not present, but had reasonable notice and opportunity to be heard.

The Court has considered the following factors:

1. Petitioner ☐ consents ☐ does not consent to the ☐ modification ☐ termination of the Domestic Violence Civil Protection Order or Consent Agreement.

2. Petitioner ☐ continues to fear ☐ does not fear the Respondent.

3. The current nature of the relationship between the Petitioner and Respondent is as follows: _____
_____

4. Relative proximity of the Petitioner's and Respondent's workplaces and residences.

5. Petitioner and Respondent ☐ have ☐ do not have minor children together.

6. Respondent has ☐ complied ☐ failed to comply with the terms and conditions of the original civil protection order or consent agreement.

7. Respondent ☐ has ☐ does not have a continuing involvement with illegal drugs or alcohol.

FORM 10.01-L: JUDGMENT ENTRY ON MOTION TO MODIFY/TERMINATE DOMESTIC VIOLENCE CIVIL PROTECTION ORDER CONSENT AGREEMENT

Effective Date: July 1, 2010

[Page 2 of Form 10.01-L]

Case No._____

8. Respondent ☐ has been ☐ has not been convicted of or pleaded guilty to an offense of violence since the protection order was issued or the consent agreement was approved.

9. Other protection orders, consent agreements, restraining orders, or no contact orders ☐ have been ☐ have not been issued against the Respondent pursuant to R.C. 3113.31 or 2919.26, any other provision of state law, or the law of any other state.

10. Respondent ☐ participated ☐ has not participated in a domestic violence treatment, intervention program, or other counseling addressing domestic violence.

11. Respondent ☐ completed ☐ has not completed the domestic violence treatment, intervention program, or other counseling addressing domestic violence.

12. _____ (time) has elapsed since the protection order was issued or the consent agreement was approved.

13. The age and health of the Respondent is as follows: _____
_____

14. The last incident of abuse, threat of harm, or commission of a sexually oriented offense occurred on:
_____
_____

15. Other information considered concerning the safety and protection of the Petitioner or other protected parties:
_____
_____

Based on all relevant factors, including those set in R.C. 3113.31(E)(8), the Court finds:

☐ The terms of the original civil protection order or consent agreement are no longer appropriate. The Order shall be **modified** as follows: _____
_____
_____
_____

☐ The civil protection order or consent agreement is no longer needed. The Order is **terminated**.

☐ The civil protection order or consent agreement remains in full force and effect. The motion is **denied**.

A new Protection Notice to NCIC, Form 10-A, has been prepared to show the modification or termination of the prior order. In the event of modification, a Modified Domestic Violence Civil Protection Order (Form10.01-M) has been filed with this entry.

The costs of this action are ☐ assessed against the Respondent ☐ waived.

IT IS SO ORDERED.   **APPROVED and ADOPTED by:**

_____   _____
MAGISTRATE   **JUDGE**

FORM 10.01-L: JUDGMENT ENTRY ON MOTION TO MODIFY/TERMINATE DOMESTIC VIOLENCE CIVIL PROTECTION ORDER CONSENT AGREEMENT

Effective Date: July 1, 2010

Form 10.01-M

FORM 10.01-M: MODIFIED DOMESTIC VIOLENCE CIVIL PROTECTION ORDER

IN THE COURT OF COMMON PLEAS

_____ COUNTY, OHIO

Order of Protection

Per section R.C. 3113.31(E)(8), this Order is indexed at

Case No.	
Judge	

_____

LAW ENFORCEMENT AGENCY WHERE INDEXED

(   )   -

PHONE NUMBER

County		State	**OHIO**

MODIFIED DOMESTIC VIOLENCE CIVIL PROTECTION ORDER (R.C. 3113.31)

PETITIONER:

First	Middle	Last

v.

PERSON(S) PROTECTED BY THIS ORDER:

Petitioner: _____ DOB: _____

Petitioner's Family or Household Member(s)(May attach additional forms):

_____ DOB: _____

_____ DOB: _____

_____ DOB: _____

_____ DOB: _____

RESPONDENT:

First	Middle	Last

Relationship to Petitioner: _____

Address where Respondent can be found:

_____

_____

RESPONDENT IDENTIFIERS

SEX	RACE	HT	WT
EYES	HAIR	DATE OF BIRTH	
DRIVER'S LIC. NO	EXP. DATE	STATE	

Distinguishing Features: _____

☐ **WARNING TO LAW ENFORCEMENT: RESPONDENT HAS FIREARMS ACCESS – PROCEED WITH CAUTION**

(Violence Against Women Act, 18 U.S.C. 2265, Federal Full Faith & Credit Declaration: Registration of this Order is not required for enforcement.)

THE COURT HEREBY FINDS:

That it has jurisdiction over the parties and subject matter, and the Petitioner and Respondent were provided with reasonable notice and opportunity to be heard within the time required by Ohio law. **Additional findings of this Order are set forth in the companion judgment entry.**

THE COURT HEREBY ORDERS:

That the above named Respondent be restrained from committing acts of abuse or threats of abuse against the Petitioner and other protected persons named in this Order. Additional terms of this Order are set forth below.

The terms of this Order shall be effective until ____ / ___ / _____ **(SHALL BE SAME EXPIRATION DATE AS IN CIVIL PROTECTION ORDER OR CONSENT AGREEMENT)**

WARNING TO RESPONDENT: See the warning page attached to the front of this Order.

FORM 10.01-M: MODIFIED DOMESTIC VIOLENCE CIVIL PROTECTION ORDER

Effective Date: July 1, 2010

Case No. _____

This proceeding came on for a hearing on _____. Based on the evidence presented and consideration of factors set forth in R.C. 3113.31(E)(8), the Court finds that the motion to modify the prior Domestic Violence Civil Protection Order issued on _____ is well taken.

ALL OF THE PROVISIONS CHECKED BELOW APPLY TO THE RESPONDENT

☐ 1. **RESPONDENT SHALL NOT ABUSE** the protected persons named in this Order by harming, attempting to harm, threatening, following, stalking, harassing, forcing sexual relations upon them, or by committing sexually oriented offenses against them. [NCIC 01 and 02]

☐ 2. **RESPONDENT SHALL IMMEDIATELY VACATE** the following residence: _____
_____

☐ 3. **EXCLUSIVE POSSESSION OF THE RESIDENCE** located at: _____
       is granted to: _____ . Respondent shall not interfere with this individual's right to occupy the residence including, but not limited to canceling utilities or insurance, interrupting telephone service, mail delivery, or the delivery of any other documents or items. [NCIC 03]

☐ 4. **RESPONDENT SHALL SURRENDER** all keys and garage door openers to the above residence at the earliest possible opportunity after service of this Order to the law enforcement agency that serves Respondent with this Order or as follows: _____
_____

☐ 5. **RESPONDENT SHALL NOT ENTER** or interfere with the residence, school, business, place of employment, day care centers, or child care providers of the protected persons named in this Order, including the buildings, grounds, and parking lots at those locations. Respondent may not violate this Order **even with the permission of a protected person**. [NCIC 04]

☐ 6. **RESPONDENT SHALL STAY AWAY FROM PETITIONER** and all other protected persons named in this Order, and not be present within 500 feet or _____ (distance) of any protected persons wherever those protected persons may be found, or any place the Respondent knows or should know the protected persons are likely to be, **even with Petitioner's permission**. If Respondent accidentally comes in contact with protected persons in any public or private place, Respondent must depart *immediately*. This Order includes encounters on public and private roads, highways, and thoroughfares. [NCIC 04]

☐ 7. **RESPONDENT SHALL NOT INITIATE OR HAVE ANY CONTACT** with the protected persons named in this Order or their residences, businesses, places of employment, schools, day care centers, or child care providers. Contact includes, but is not limited to, telephone, fax, e-mail, voice mail, delivery service, writings, or communications by any other means in person or through another person. Respondent may not violate this Order **even with the permission of protected person**. [NCIC 05]

☐ 8. **RESPONDENT SHALL IMMEDIATELY SURRENDER POSSESSION OF ALL KEYS TO THE FOLLOWING MOTOR VEHICLE** _____ to the law enforcement agency that served Respondent with the Order or as follows _____
       and Petitioner is granted exclusive use of this motor vehicle.

☐ 9. **RESPONDENT SHALL NOT REMOVE, DAMAGE, HIDE, OR DISPOSE OF ANY PROPERTY OR PETS** owned or possessed by the protected persons named in this Order. Personal property shall be apportioned as follows:
_____
_____

☐ 10. **RESPONDENT SHALL NOT CAUSE OR ENCOURAGE ANY PERSON** to do any act prohibited by this Order.

FORM 10.01-M: MODIFIED DOMESTIC VIOLENCE CIVIL PROTECTION ORDER

Effective Date: July 1, 2010

[Page 3 of Form 10.01-M]

Case No. _____

☐ **11. RESPONDENT SHALL NOT POSSESS, USE, CARRY, OR OBTAIN ANY DEADLY WEAPON.** Respondent shall turn over all deadly weapons in Respondent's possession to the law enforcement agency that serves Respondent with this Order or as follows: _____

_____

Any law enforcement agency is authorized to take possession of deadly weapons pursuant to this paragraph and hold them in protective custody until further Court order. [NCIC 07]

☐ **12. PARENTAL RIGHTS AND RESPONSIBILITIES ARE TEMPORARILY ALLOCATED AS FOLLOWS:** [NCIC 09]

_____

_____

_____

This Order applies to the following child(ren): _____

_____

_____

☐ **13. VISITATION ORDERS DO NOT PERMIT RESPONDENT TO VIOLATE THE TERMS OF THIS ORDER.**

   ☐ (A) Respondent's visitation rights are suspended; or

   ☐ (B) As a limited exception to paragraphs 6 and 7, Respondent's visitation rights are established as follows:
   [NCIC 06]

_____

_____

_____

This Order applies to the following child(ren): _____

_____

☐ **14. LAW ENFORCEMENT AGENCIES** including but not limited to _____ are ordered to assist Petitioner in gaining physical custody of the child(ren) if necessary.

☐ **15. RESPONDENT SHALL SUPPORT** the protected persons named in this Order as follows: _____

_____

_____

_____

☐ **16. RESPONDENT MAY PICK UP CLOTHING** and personal items from the above residence only in the company of a uniformed law enforcement officer within seven days of the filing of this Order. Arrangements may be made by contacting: _____

_____

☐ **17. RESPONDENT SHALL NOT USE OR POSSESS** alcohol or illegal drugs.

☐ **18. IT IS FURTHER ORDERED:** [NCIC 08] _____

_____

_____

_____

_____

_____

_____

_____

FORM 10.01-M: MODIFIED DOMESTIC VIOLENCE CIVIL PROTECTION ORDER

Effective Date: July 1, 2010

Case No. _____

☐ **19. RESPONDENT SHALL COMPLETE THE FOLLOWING COUNSELING PROGRAM:** _____

_____

Respondent shall contact this program within _____ **days after receiving this Order and immediately arrange for an initial appointment.** The counseling program is requested to provide the Court a written notice when Respondent attends the initial appointment, if the Respondent fails to attend or is discharged, and when Respondent completes the program. Respondent is required to sign all necessary waivers to allow the Court to receive information from the counseling program.

☐ **Respondent is ordered to appear before Judge** _____ **or Magistrate** _____

on _____ **at** _____ **a.m. / p.m., to review Respondent's compliance with this counseling Order. Respondent is warned: If you fail to attend the counseling program you may be held in contempt of court. If you fail to appear at this hearing, the Court may issue a warrant for your arrest.**

20.   **IT IS FURTHER ORDERED** that the Clerk of Court shall cause a copy this Order to be delivered to the Respondent as required by law. The Clerk of Court shall also provide certified copies of this Order to Petitioner upon request. This Order is granted without bond. Under federal and state law, the Clerk shall not charge any fees for filing, issuing, registering, or serving this Protection Order to the Petitioner.

21.   **ALL OF THE TERMS OF THIS ORDER SHALL REMAIN IN FULL FORCE AND EFFECT FOR A PERIOD OF NOT TO EXCEED THE DATE SET IN THE PRIOR ORDER OR UNTIL** _____ / _____ / _____ unless earlier modified or terminated by order of this Court. Except for paragraphs 12, 13, 14, and 15 above, this Order survives a divorce, dissolution of marriage, or legal separation. Until this Order is delivered to Respondent, the terms of the prior Domestic Violence Civil Protection Order remain in effect.

IT IS SO ORDERED.   **APPROVED and ADOPTED by:**

_____   _____
MAGISTRATE   **JUDGE**

NOTICE TO RESPONDENT: THE PERSONS PROTECTED BY THIS ORDER CANNOT GIVE YOU LEGAL PERMISSION TO CHANGE OR VIOLATE THIS ORDER. IF YOU VIOLATE ANY TERMS OF THIS ORDER, EVEN WITH THE PROTECTED PERSON'S PERMISSION, YOU MAY BE ARRESTED. ONLY THE COURT CAN CHANGE THIS ORDER. IF THERE IS ANY REASON WHY THIS ORDER SHOULD BE CHANGED, YOU MUST ASK THE COURT TO CHANGE IT. YOU ACT AT YOUR OWN RISK IF YOU DISREGARD THIS WARNING.

NOTICE OF FINAL APPEALABLE ORDER	**TO THE CLERK:** **COPIES OF THIS ORDER SHALL BE DELIVERED TO**
Copies of the foregoing Order, which is a final appealable order, were mailed by ordinary U.S. mail or hand-delivered to the parties indicated on the _____ day of _____ , 20 _____ . By: _____ CLERK OF COURT	☐ Petitioner ☐ Attorney for Petitioner ☐ Respondent ☐ Attorney for Respondent ☐ Counseling Program: _____ ☐ The _____ County Sheriff's Office ☐ Police Department Where Petitioner Resides: _____ ☐ Police Department Where Petitioner Works: _____ ☐ CSEA ☐ Other: _____

Form 10.01-N

FORM 10.01-N: HOW TO COMPLETE A MOTION FOR CONTEMPT FOR VIOLATING A DOMESTIC VIOLENCE CIVIL PROTECTION ORDER

ENFORCING YOUR CIVIL PROTECTION ORDER

Violating a Domestic Violence Civil Protection Order ("CPO") is a crime. If the Order is violated, call the police or prosecutor. You may also bring a contempt action in the Court that issued your CPO if the other party is not obeying the Order. You may hire an attorney to assist you. You must file a contempt motion with the Clerk of Court to begin a contempt action.

SOME HINTS BEFORE YOU BEGIN

- All forms must be typed or printed.
- When you write your name on the Motion for Contempt of a Domestic Violence Civil Protection Order, use the same name that is on your CPO.
- Fill out the Motion as completely and accurately as possible.

FORM YOU WILL NEED

You can get the Motion from the Clerk of Court. Complete the Motion as explained below:

☐ Fill in the name of the Court, the case number and the judge's last name.

☐ **If you obtained the CPO, you are the Petitioner.** Fill in your name and address. If you want your address to be confidential, do not write your address anywhere on the Motion. However, you must include someone's mailing address to allow the Court to send you legal notices about your case.

☐ **If the Court issued the CPO against you, you are the Respondent.** Fill in your name and address.

☐ Fill in the other party's name and address.

☐ Complete the first paragraph.

☐ In the numbered paragraphs, check every box that applies. There is space at the end of the Motion for any facts or explanations that you want to tell the Court. Attach additional pages, if needed.

☐ **Signing the Motion:** Try to fill out the Motion before you go to the courthouse. AFTER YOU HAVE FILLED OUT THE MOTION, TAKE IT TO A NOTARY PUBLIC TO HAVE YOUR SIGNATURE NOTARIZED. *DO NOT SIGN THE MOTION UNLESS YOU ARE IN FRONT OF A NOTARY PUBLIC.* **An employee of the Clerk of Court may be available to notarize your Motion.**

☐ Complete the Instructions for Service at the end of the Motion. This tells the Clerk of Court how you want the Motion delivered.

FILING THE MOTION FOR CONTEMPT OF A DOMESTIC VIOLENCE CPO

- Present your completed Motion to the filing window/counter of the Clerk of Court's office for filing.
- A Clerk of Court's office employee helps you file the Motion.
- The Court shall not charge a fee for filing a contempt motion to you if the CPO was issued for your protection.
- Ask a Clerk of Court's office employee or your local domestic violence assistance provider about your local court procedures.

[Page 2 of Form 10.01-N]

VICTIM ADVOCATE

State law permits you to have a victim advocate with you at all times in Court during protection order proceedings. Victim advocate means a person who provides support and assistance for a victim of an offense during Court proceedings. Contact your local victim assistance program, local domestic violence program, or the Ohio Domestic Violence Network, 800-934-9840, for advocate information.

ATTENDING THE CONTEMPT HEARING

At the hearing, you should tell the judge or magistrate what the other party did to fail to obey the CPO. If you have any physical evidence (photographs, documents, broken property, etc), bring it to this hearing. If you have any witnesses to the violations, bring them to this hearing. If you want the Court to order any witness to appear at the hearing, you can ask the Clerk of Court to issue a subpoena. This needs to be done as far in advance of the hearing as possible.

The Court will give each party the opportunity to present evidence and witnesses.

After all the evidence is presented at the contempt hearing, the Court may find that the Respondent or Petitioner has failed to comply with the CPO. If so, the Court may order the offending party to do or stop certain acts to comply with the terms of the CPO. The Court can also order the offending party to serve time in jail, pay a fine, or both.

Form 10.01-O

FORM 10.01-O: MOTION FOR CONTEMPT OF A DOMESTIC VIOLENCE CIVIL PROTECTION ORDER

IN THE COURT OF COMMON PLEAS

_____ **COUNTY, OHIO**

Petitioner	: Case No. _____
	:
Address	: Judge _____
	:
City, State, Zip Code	: **MOTION FOR CONTEMPT OF A DOMESTIC**
v.	**VIOLENCE CIVIL PROTECTION ORDER**
	: **Notice: Throughout this form, check every ☐ that applies**
	:
Respondent	: **DO NOT WRITE YOUR ADDRESS ON THIS FORM IF YOU ARE REQUESTING CONFIDENTIALITY. PLEASE PROVIDE AN ADDRESS WHERE YOU CAN RECEIVE NOTICES FROM THE COURT.**
Address	:
	:
City, State, Zip Code	:

☐ Petitioner ☐ Respondent moves this Court to find _____
in contempt of this Court's Civil Protection Order dated _____ for the reasons below.

For any item that needs additional explanation, you may use paragraph 18 and/or attach additional pages as needed.

1.   ☐   Respondent violated the Civil Protection Order by engaging in one or more of the following acts against me and/or another protected person:

         ☐   Harmed or attempted to harm
         ☐   Threatened
         ☐   Followed
         ☐   Stalked
         ☐   Harassed
         ☐   Forced sexual relations upon
         ☐   Committed a sexually oriented offense
         ☐   Other _____

2.   ☐   Respondent failed to vacate the residence at _____

3.   ☐   Respondent interfered with the exclusive possession of the residence located at _____

       Furthermore, Respondent interfered with my right to occupy the residence by
       ☐   Canceling utilities
       ☐   Canceling insurance
       ☐   Interrupted telephone service
       ☐   Interrupted mail delivery
       ☐   Interrupted delivery of any other documents or items

FORM 10.01-O: MOTION FOR CONTEMPT OF A DOMESTIC VIOLENCE CIVIL PROTECTION ORDER

Effective Date: July 1, 2010

[Page 2 of Form 10.01-O]

Case No._____

4. ☐ Respondent failed to surrender keys and/or garage door openers to the residence for which exclusive use was ordered in the Civil Protection Order.

5. ☐ Respondent entered or interfered with the residence, school, business, place or employment, day care center, or child care provider of the protected persons.

6. ☐ Respondent violated the stay away provision of the Civil Protection Order.

7. ☐ Respondent violated the no contact provision of the Civil Protection Order.

8. ☐ Respondent failed to surrender the keys to the motor vehicle for which exclusive use was granted to the Petitioner in the Civil Protection Order.

9. ☐ Respondent removed, damaged, hid or disposed of personal property or pets in violation of the Civil Protection Order.

10. ☐ Respondent caused or encouraged another person to do acts prohibited by the Civil Protection Order.

11. ☐ Respondent violated the Civil Protection Order by possessing, using, carrying, obtaining or failing to turn over a deadly weapon.

12. ☐ ☐ Petitioner ☐ Respondent violated the temporary allocation of parental rights and responsibilities (custody).

13. ☐ ☐ Petitioner ☐ Respondent violated the visitation order.

14. ☐ ☐ Petitioner ☐ Respondent violated the support provision of the Civil Protection Order.

15. ☐ Respondent used or possessed alcohol and/or illegal drugs in violation of the Civil Protection Order.

16. ☐ ☐ Petitioner ☐ Respondent failed to attend the ordered counseling program.

17. ☐ List other violations of the Civil Protection Order here: _____
_____
_____
_____
_____

18. ☐ Additional explanation here: _____
_____
_____
_____
_____
_____

I hereby swear or affirm that the statements above are true, complete, and accurate to the best of my knowledge. I understand that falsification of this document may result in a contempt of court finding against me which could result in a jail sentence and fine, and that falsification of this document may also subject me to criminal penalties for perjury under R.C. 2921.11.

_____
SIGNATURE OF PETITIONER/RESPONDENT

FORM 10.01-O: MOTION FOR CONTEMPT OF A DOMESTIC VIOLENCE CIVIL PROTECTION ORDER

Effective Date: July 1, 2010

[Page 3 of Form 10.01-O]

Case No._____

**DO NOT WRITE YOUR ADDRESS BELOW IF YOU ARE
REQUESTING CONFIDENTIALITY. PLEASE PROVIDE
AN ADDRESS WHERE YOU CAN RECEIVE NOTICES
FROM THE COURT.**

Sworn to and subscribed before me on this _____
day of _____ , _____ .

_____
Address

NOTARY PUBLIC

_____
Signature of Attorney (if applicable)

_____
Name

_____
Address

_____
Attorney Registration Number

_____
Phone Number

INSTRUCTIONS FOR SERVICE

Please serve a copy of the foregoing Motion upon _____
by ☐ personal service or ☐ certified mail, return receipt requested at the following address: _____

_____

FORM 10.01-O: MOTION FOR CONTEMPT OF A DOMESTIC VIOLENCE CIVIL PROTECTION ORDER

Effective Date: July 1, 2010

History: Effective 1-1-98; amended, eff 6-1-00; 6-1-02; 7-1-10.

RULE 10.02.   Standard Criminal Temporary Protection Order Forms

(A) A court that has jurisdiction to issue a temporary protection order pursuant to section 2919.26 of the Revised Code shall distribute upon request a forms and instructions packet for use in domestic violence temporary protection order proceedings. The packet shall include, at a minimum, forms and instructions that are substantially similar to Forms 10.01-A, 10.01-B,

10.01-G, 10.02-A, and the motion for temporary protection order form set forth in section 2919.26 of the Revised Code.

(B) In every case in which the court issues a temporary protection order pursuant to section 2919.26 of the Revised Code, it shall use a form that is substantially similar to Form 10.02-A.

(C) Every temporary protection order that the court issues pursuant to section 2919.26 of the Revised Code shall include a cover sheet that is substantially similar to Form 10.01-G.

Form 10.02-A

FORM 10.02-A: DOMESTIC VIOLENCE TEMPORARY PROTECTION ORDER (DVTPO)

IN THE _____ COURT

_____ COUNTY, OHIO

Order of Protection

Per R.C. 2919.26(G)(3), this Order is indexed at

Case No. _____

Judge _____

County [_____]   State **OHIO**

LAW ENFORCEMENT AGENCY WHERE INDEXED

(___) ___ - ___

PHONE NUMBER

STATE OF OHIO/CITY OF _____

v.

_____

DEFENDANT

DOMESTIC VIOLENCE TEMPORARY PROTECTION ORDER (DVTPO) (R.C. 2919.26)

☐ New Order   ☐ Modification of Previous Order

ALLEGED VICTIM:

First   Middle   Last

PERSON(S) PROTECTED BY THIS ORDER:

Alleged Victim _____ DOB: _____

Alleged Victim's Family or Household Member(s):

_____ DOB: _____

_____ DOB: _____

_____ DOB: _____

_____ DOB: _____

DEFENDANT:

First   Middle   Last

Address where Defendant can be found:

_____

_____

_____

DEFENDANT IDENTIFIERS

SEX	RACE	HT	WT
EYES	HAIR	DATE OF BIRTH	
DRIVER'S LIC. NO.	EXP. DATE	STATE	

Distinguishing Features: _____

☐ **WARNING TO LAW ENFORCEMENT: RESPONDENT HAS FIREARMS ACCESS – PROCEED WITH CAUTION**

☐ *Ex Parte* DVTPO Granted: _____ **(Date)**

☐ DVTPO Granted: _____ **(Date)**

(Violence Against Women Act, 18 U.S.C. 2265, Federal Full Faith & Credit Declaration: Registration of this Order is not required for enforcement.)

THE COURT HEREBY FINDS:

That it has jurisdiction over the parties and subject matter, and the Defendant has been or will be provided with reasonable notice and opportunity to be heard within the time required by Ohio law. **Additional findings of this Order are set forth below.**

THE COURT HEREBY ORDERS:

That the above named Defendant be restrained from committing acts of abuse or threats of abuse against the Alleged Victim and other protected persons named in this Order, as set forth below. Additional terms of this Order are set forth below.

WARNING TO DEFENDANT: See the warning page attached to the front of this Order.

FORM 10.02-A: DOMESTIC VIOLENCE TEMPORARY PROTECTION ORDER (DVTPO)

Amended: July 1, 2010
Discard all previous versions of this form

[Page 2 of Form 10.02-A]

Case No._____

(Ex Parte DVTPO)   (DVTPO)

Upon a hearing held on _____ OR _____ the Court finds
that the Motion for a Domestic Violence Temporary Protection Order is well taken. The Court finds that the safety and
protection of protected persons named in this Order may be impaired by the continued presence of Defendant. Therefore, the
following orders, which are designed to ensure the safety and protection of protected persons named in this Order, are issued
to Defendant as pretrial conditions in addition to any bail set under Crim. R. 46.

ALL OF THE PROVISIONS CHECKED BELOW APPLY TO THE DEFENDANT

☐ 1. **DEFENDANT SHALL NOT ABUSE** protected persons named in this Order by harming, attempting to harm,
threatening, following, stalking, harassing, forcing sexual relations upon them, or by committing sexually oriented
offenses against them. [NCIC 01 and 02]

☐ 2. **DEFENDANT SHALL NOT ENTER** the residence, school, business, place of employment, day care centers, or child
care providers of the protected persons named in this Order, including the buildings, grounds, and parking lots at those
locations. Defendant may not violate this Order **even with the permission of a protected person.** [NCIC 04]

☐ 3. **DEFENDANT SHALL NOT INTERFERE** with protected persons' right to occupy any residence by canceling utilities or
insurance and interrupting telephone service, mail delivery, or the delivery of any other documents or items. [NCIC 03]

☐ 4. **DEFENDANT SHALL SURRENDER** all keys and garage door openers to the following residence: _____

at the earliest possible opportunity after service of this Order to the law enforcement agency that serves Defendant
with this Order or as follows: _____
_____
_____

☐ 5. **DEFENDANT SHALL STAY AWAY FROM PROTECTED PERSONS NAMED IN THIS ORDER**, and shall not be
present within 500 feet or _____ (distance) of any protected persons wherever those protected
persons may be found, or any place the Defendant knows or should know the protected persons are likely to be, **even
with the protected persons' permission**. If Defendant accidentally comes in contact with protected persons in any
public or private place, Defendant must depart *immediately*. This Order includes encounters on public and private
roads, highways, and thoroughfares. [NCIC 04]

☐ 6. **DEFENDANT SHALL NOT INITIATE OR HAVE ANY CONTACT** with the protected persons named in this Order at
their residences, businesses, places of employment, schools, day care centers, or child care providers. Contact
includes, but is not limited to, telephone, fax, e-mail, voice mail, delivery service, writings, or communications by any
other means in person or through another person. Defendant may not violate this Order **even with the permission of
a protected person**. [NCIC 05]

☐ 7. **DEFENDANT SHALL NOT REMOVE, DAMAGE, HIDE, OR DISPOSE OF ANY PROPERTY OR PETS** owned or
possessed by the protected persons named in this Order.

☐ 8. **DEFENDANT SHALL NOT CAUSE OR ENCOURAGE ANY OTHER PERSON** to do any act prohibited by this Order.

☐ 9. **DEFENDANT SHALL NOT POSSESS, USE, CARRY, OR OBTAIN ANY DEADLY WEAPON.** Defendant shall turn
over all deadly weapons in Defendant's possession to the law enforcement agency that serves Defendant with this
Order as follows: _____
_____

Any law enforcement agency is authorized to take possession of deadly weapons pursuant to this paragraph and hold
them in protective custody until further Court order. [NCIC 07]

☐ 10. **DEFENDANT MAY PICK UP CLOTHING** and personal items from the following residence: _____
_____ only in the company of a uniformed law enforcement
officer within seven days of the filing of this Order or the date of Defendant's release on bond in connection with
this charge, whichever is later. Arrangements may be made by contacting: _____
_____

FORM 10.02-A: DOMESTIC VIOLENCE TEMPORARY PROTECTION ORDER (DVTPO)

Amended: July 1, 2010
Discard all previous versions of this form

[Page 3 of Form 10.02-A]

Case No._____

☐ **11. DEFENDANT SHALL NOT USE OR POSSESS** alcohol or illegal drugs.

☐ **12. IT IS FURTHER ORDERED:** [NCIC 08] _____

_____

_____

☐ **13. DEFENDANT IS ADVISED THAT VISITATION ORDERS DO NOT PERMIT DEFENDANT TO VIOLATE ANY OF THE TERMS OF THIS ORDER.**

14. IT IS FURTHER ORDERED that a copy of this Order shall be delivered to Defendant on the same day that the Order is entered.

15. THIS ORDER REMAINS IN EFFECT: (1) until modified by this Court; or (2) until the criminal proceeding arising out of the complaint upon which these orders were issued is disposed by this Court or by the court of common pleas to which the defendant is bound over for prosecution; or (3) until a Court issues a Domestic Violence Civil Protection Order ("CPO") arising out of the same activities as those that were the basis of the complaint filed in this action.

IT IS SO ORDERED.

_____   _____
MAGISTRATE – DATE OF *EX PARTE* **DVTPO**   **JUDGE – DATE OF** *EX PARTE* **DVTPO**

_____   _____
MAGISTRATE – DATE OF DVTPO   **JUDGE– DATE OF DVTPO**

NOTICE TO DEFENDANT: THE PERSONS PROTECTED BY THIS ORDER CANNOT GIVE YOU LEGAL PERMISSION TO CHANGE OR VIOLATE THIS ORDER. IF YOU VIOLATE ANY TERMS OF THIS ORDER EVEN WITH THE PROTECTED PERSON'S PERMISSION, YOU MAY BE ARRESTED. ONLY THE COURT CAN CHANGE THIS ORDER. IF THERE IS ANY REASON WHY THIS ORDER SHOULD BE CHANGED, YOU MUST ASK THE COURT TO CHANGE IT. YOU ACT AT YOUR OWN RISK IF YOU DISREGARD THIS WARNING.

A HEARING on this Order shall be held before Judge _____ or Magistrate _____ on _____ , at _____ a.m./p.m., (the next court day) at the following location: _____ _____	**TO THE CLERK:** **COPIES OF THIS ORDER SHALL BE DELIVERED TO:** ☐ Prosecutor ☐ Alleged Victim ☐ Defendant (by personal service) ☐ Attorney for Defendant ☐ Police Department Where Alleged Victim Resides: _____ ☐ Police Department Where Alleged Victim Works: _____ ☐ The _____ County Sheriff's Office ☐ Other _____

Service acknowledged: _____   _____
                        Defendant Signature   **Date**

WAIVER OF HEARING

I HAVE BEEN ADVISED OF MY RIGHT TO HAVE A HEARING ON THE MOTION FOR A DOMESTIC VIOLENCE TEMPORARY PROTECTION ORDER AND HEREBY KNOWINGLY AND VOLUNTARILY WAIVE THE HEARING ON THE MOTION AND AGREE TO BE BOUND BY THE TERMS OF THIS ORDER.

DEFENDANT: _____   DATE: _____

FORM 10.02-A: DOMESTIC VIOLENCE TEMPORARY PROTECTION ORDER (DVTPO)

Amended: July 1, 2010
Discard all previous versions of this form

History: Effective 1-1-98; amended, eff 6-1-02; 5-1-07.

RULE 10.03. Standard Criminal Protection Order Forms and Standard Civil Stalking Protection Order or Civil Sexually Oriented Offense Protection Order Forms

(A) A court that has jurisdiction to issue a criminal protection order pursuant to section 2903.213 of the Revised Code shall distribute, upon request, a form packet for use in criminal protection order proceedings. The packet shall include, at a minimum, a form that is substantially similar to "Form10.03-A."

(B) A court that has jurisdiction to issue a civil stalking protection order or civil sexually oriented offense protection order pursuant to section 2903.214 of the Revised Code shall distribute, upon request, a forms and instructions packet for use in civil stalking protection order or civil sexually oriented offense protection order proceedings. The packet shall include, at a minimum, forms and instructions that are substantially similar to "Forms 10.03-D, 10.03-E, and 10.03-G."

(C) In every case in which a court issues a criminal protection order pursuant to section 2903.213 of the Revised Code, it shall use the applicable form that is substantially similar to "Form 10.03-B" and a cover sheet that is substantially similar to "Form 10.03-H."

(D) In every case in which a court issues a civil stalking protection order or civil sexually oriented offense protection order pursuant to section 2903.214 of the Revised Code, it shall use the applicable form that is substantially similar to "Form 10.03-E or 10.03-F" and a cover sheet that is substantially similar to "Form 10.03-H."

Form 10.03-A

FORM 10.03-A: MOTION FOR CRIMINAL PROTECTION ORDER (CRPO)

IN THE _____ COURT
_____ COUNTY, OHIO

STATE OF OHIO/CITY OF

_____ : Case No. _____

:

v. : Judge _____

:

_____ :
DEFENDANT : **MOTION FOR CRIMINAL PROTECTION ORDER (CRPO) (R.C. 2903.213)**

_____ (Name of person), moves the Court to issue a protection order containing terms designed to ensure the safety and protection of the complainant or the alleged victim in the above captioned case, in relation to the named defendant, pursuant to its authority to issue a protection order under R.C. 2903.213.

A complaint, a copy of which has been attached to this motion, has been filed in this Court charging the named defendant with a violation of R.C. 2903.11 (*Felonious Assault*), 2903.12 (*Aggravated Assault*), 2903.13 (*Assault*), 2903.21 (*Aggravated Menacing*), 2903.211 (*Menacing by Stalking*), 2903.22 (*Menacing*), or 2911.211 (*Aggravated Trespass*) or a violation of a municipal ordinance substantially similar to R.C. 2903.13, 2903.21, 2903.211, 2903.22, or 2911.211, or the commission of sexually oriented offenses as defined in R.C. 2950.01.

I understand that I must appear before the Court, at a time set by the Court not later than the next day that the Court is in session after the filing of this motion, for a hearing on the motion, and that any protection order granted pursuant to this motion is a pretrial condition of release and is effective only until the disposition of the criminal proceeding arising out of the attached complaint or until the issuance under R.C. 2903.214 of a protection order arising out of the same activities as those that were the basis in the attached complaint.

_____
Signature of Alleged Victim

_____

_____
Address of Alleged Victim

NOTES: (1) This form must be provided by the Clerk of Court, per R.C. 2903.213(B).

(2) By its own definitions [see R.C. 2903.213(A)], this statute does not apply to a complaint that involves a person who is a family or household member. In those cases where the Alleged Victim is a family or household member of the defendant, use Domestic Violence Temporary Protection Order (DVTPO) forms and procedures under R.C. 2919.26, and/or Civil Protection Order (CPO) forms and procedures under R.C. 3113.31.

FORM 10.03-A: MOTION FOR CRIMINAL PROTECTION ORDER (CRPO)

Amended: July 1, 2010
Discard all previous versions of this form

Form 10.03-B

FORM 10.03-B: CRIMINAL PROTECTION ORDER (CRPO)

IN THE _____ COURT

_____ COUNTY, OHIO

Order of Protection Per R.C. 2903.213(G)(2), this Order is indexed at	Case No.
	Judge
_____ LAW ENFORCEMENT AGENCY WHERE INDEXED	County _____ State **OHIO**
(___) _____ - _____ PHONE NUMBER	
STATE OF OHIO/CITY OF _____	**CRIMINAL PROTECTION ORDER (CRPO)** **(R.C. 2903.213)**
v.	☐ New Order ☐ Modification of Previous Order
DEFENDANT	

ALLEGED VICTIM	**PERSON(S) PROTECTED BY THIS ORDER:**
	Alleged Victim _____ DOB: _____ Alleged Victim's Family or Household Member(s) (May attach additional form):
First Middle Last	_____ DOB: _____ _____ DOB: _____ _____ DOB: _____ _____ DOB: _____

DEFENDANT:

DEFENDANT IDENTIFIERS

SEX	RACE	HT	WT
EYES	HAIR	DATE OF BIRTH	

First   Middle   Last

Address where Defendant can be found:

DRIVER'S LIC. NO.	EXP. DATE	STATE

Distinguishing Features: _____

☐ **WARNING TO LAW ENFORCEMENT: DEFENDANT HAS FIREARMS ACCESS – PROCEED WITH CAUTION**
☐ *Ex Parte* CRPO Granted: _____ **(Date)**
☐ CRPO Granted: _____ **(Date)**

(Violence Against Women Act, 18 U.S.C. 2265, Federal Full Faith & Credit Declaration: Registration of this Order is not required for enforcement.)

THE COURT HEREBY FINDS:
That it has jurisdiction over the parties and subject matter, and the Defendant has been provided with reasonable notice and the opportunity to be heard within the time required by Ohio law. **Additional findings of this Order are set forth below.**

THE COURT HEREBY ORDERS:
That the above named Defendant be restrained from committing acts of abuse or threats of abuse against and contacting the Alleged Victim and other protected persons named in this Order, as set forth below. Additional terms of this Order are set forth below.
WARNING TO DEFENDANT: See the warning page attached to the front of this Order.

FORM 10.03-B: CRIMINAL PROTECTION ORDER (CRPO)

Amended: July 1, 2010
Discard all previous versions of this form

[Page 2 of Form 10.03-B]

Case No._____

This matter came before the Court on _____ for hearing on Alleged Victim's Motion for Criminal Protection Order. The Court finds the Motion of the Alleged Victim for a Criminal Protection Order is well taken. The Court finds that the safety and protection of the Alleged Victim and protected persons named in this Order may be impaired unless the Court acts. The following provisions of this Order are designed to enhance the safety of those covered by its terms. They are issued to the Defendant as pretrial conditions, in addition to any bail.

ALL OF THE PROVISIONS CHECKED BELOW APPLY TO THE DEFENDANT

☐ 1. **DEFENDANT SHALL NOT ABUSE** the protected persons named in this Order by harming, attempting to harm, threatening, following, stalking, harassing, contacting, forcing sexual relations upon them, or by committing sexually oriented offenses against them. [NCIC 01 and 02]

☐ 2. **DEFENDANT SHALL NOT ENTER** the residence, school, business, place of employment, day care centers, or child care providers of the protected persons named in this Order, including the buildings, grounds, and parking lots at those locations. Defendant may not violate this Order **even with the permission of a protected person.** [NCIC 04]

☐ 3. **DEFENDANT SHALL NOT INTERFERE** with protected persons' right to occupy the residence including, but not limited to canceling utilities, insurance, interrupting telephone service, mail delivery, or the delivery of any other documents or items. [NCIC 03]

☐ 4. **DEFENDANT SHALL SURRENDER** all keys and garage door openers to the following residence: _____
_____
at the earliest possible opportunity after service of this Order to the law enforcement agency that serves Defendant with this Order or as follows: _____
_____

☐ 5. **DEFENDANT SHALL STAY AWAY** from protected persons named in this Order, and shall not be present within 500 feet or _____ (distance) of any protected persons, wherever those protected persons may be found, or any place the Defendant knows or should know the protected persons are likely to be, **even with protected persons' permission.** If Defendant accidentally comes in contact with protected persons in any public or private place, Defendant must depart *immediately.* This Order includes encounters on public and private roads, highways, and thoroughfares. [NCIC 04]

☐ 6. **DEFENDANT SHALL NOT REMOVE, DAMAGE, HIDE, OR DISPOSE OF ANY PROPERTY OR PETS** owned or possessed by the protected persons named in this Order.

☐ 7. **DEFENDANT SHALL NOT INITIATE OR HAVE ANY CONTACT** with the protected persons named in this Order at their residences, businesses, places of employment, schools, day care centers, or child care providers. Contact includes, but is not limited to, telephone, fax, e-mail, voice mail, delivery service, writings, or communications by any other means in person or through another person. Defendant may not violate this Order **even with the permission of a protected person.** [NCIC 05]

☐ 8. **DEFENDANT SHALL NOT CAUSE OR ENCOURAGE ANY OTHER PERSON** to do any act prohibited by this Order.

☐ 9. **DEFENDANT SHALL NOT POSSESS, USE, CARRY, OR OBTAIN ANY DEADLY WEAPON.** Defendant shall turn over all deadly weapons in Defendant's possession to the law enforcement agency that serves Defendant with this Order or as follows: _____
_____
Any law enforcement agency is authorized to take possession of deadly weapons pursuant to this paragraph and hold them in protective custody until further Court order. [NCIC 07]

☐ 10. **IT IS FURTHER ORDERED:** [NCIC 08] _____
_____
_____
_____

FORM 10.03-B: CRIMINAL PROTECTION ORDER (CRPO)

Amended: July 1, 2010
Discard all previous versions of this form

[Page 3 of Form 10.03-B]

Case No._____

11. **IT IS FURTHER ORDERED** that a copy of this Order shall be delivered to Defendant on the same day that the Order is entered.

12. **THIS ORDER REMAINS IN EFFECT:** (1) until modified by this Court; or (2) until the criminal proceeding arising out of the complaint upon which these orders were issued is disposed by this Court or by the court of common pleas to which the Defendant is bound over for prosecution; or (3) until the Court issues a Civil Stalking Protection Order ("CSPO") or Civil Sexually Oriented Offense Protection Order ("CSOOPO") arising out of the same activities as those that were the basis of the complaint filed in this action.

IT IS SO ORDERED.

_____
MAGISTRATE – DATE OF *EX PARTE* CRPO

_____
JUDGE – DATE OF *EX PARTE* CRPO

_____
MAGISTRATE – DATE OF CRPO

_____
JUDGE– DATE OF CRPO

NOTICE TO DEFENDANT: THE PERSONS PROTECTED BY THIS ORDER CANNOT GIVE YOU LEGAL PERMISSION TO CHANGE OR VIOLATE THIS ORDER. IF YOU VIOLATE ANY TERMS OF THIS ORDER, EVEN WITH THE PROTECTED PERSON'S PERMISSION, YOU MAY BE ARRESTED. ONLY THE COURT CAN CHANGE THIS ORDER. IF THERE IS ANY REASON WHY THIS ORDER SHOULD BE CHANGED, YOU MUST ASK THE COURT TO CHANGE IT. YOU ACT AT YOUR OWN RISK IF YOU DISREGARD THIS WARNING.

NOTES: By its own definitions [see R.C. 2903.213(A)], this statute does not apply to a complaint that involves a person who is a family or household member. In those cases where the Alleged Victim is a family or household member of the Defendant, use the Domestic Violence Temporary Protection Order ("DVTPO") forms and procedures under R.C. 2919.26, and/or Domestic Violence Civil Protection Order ("DVCPO") forms and procedures under R.C. 3113.31.

A HEARING on this Order shall be held before

Judge _____

or Magistrate _____

on _____ , at _____ a.m./p.m.

(the next court day) at the following location:

_____

_____

TO THE CLERK

COPIES OF THIS ORDER SHALL BE DELIVERED TO:

☐ Prosecutor
☐ Alleged Victim
☐ Defendant (by personal service)
☐ Attorney for Defendant
☐ Police Department Where Alleged Victim Resides:
_____
☐ Police Department Where Alleged Victim Works:
_____
☐ The _____ County Sheriff's Office
☐ Other: _____

Service acknowledged: _____

Defendant Signature   **Date**

WAIVER OF HEARING

I HAVE BEEN ADVISED OF MY RIGHT TO HAVE A HEARING ON THE MOTION FOR A CRIMINAL PROTECTION ORDER AND HEREBY KNOWINGLY AND VOLUNTARILY WAIVE THE HEARING ON THE MOTION AND AGREE TO BE BOUND BY THE TERMS OF THIS ORDER.

DEFENDANT: _____ DATE: _____

FORM 10.03-B: CRIMINAL PROTECTION ORDER (CRPO)

Amended: July 1, 2010
Discard all previous versions of this form

Form 10.03-D

FORM 10.03-D: PETITION FOR CIVIL STALKING PROTECTION ORDER OR CIVIL SEXUALLY ORIENTED OFFENSE PROTECTION ORDER

IN THE COURT OF COMMON PLEAS
_____ COUNTY, OHIO

Petitioner _____	:	Case No. _____
Address _____	:	Judge _____
City, State, Zip Code _____	:	PETITION FOR CIVIL STALKING PROTECTION ORDER OR CIVIL SEXUALLY ORIENTED OFFENSE PROTECTION ORDER (R.C. 2903.214)
Date of Birth: _____	:	
v.	:	Notice to Petitioner: Check every ☐ that applies.
	:	**DO NOT WRITE YOUR ADDRESS ON THIS FORM IF YOU ARE REQUESTING CONFIDENTIALITY. PLEASE PROVIDE ANOTHER ADDRESS WHERE YOU CAN RECEIVE NOTICES FROM THE COURT.**
Respondent _____	:	
Address _____	:	
City, State, Zip Code _____	:	**The Respondent does NOT have to be related to Petitioner in any way for Petitioner to be eligible for relief.**
Date of Birth: _____	:	

☐ 1. Petitioner seeks relief on Petitioner's own behalf.

☐ 2. Petitioner seeks relief on behalf of the following family or household members:

NAME	DATE OF BIRTH	HOW RELATED TO PETITIONER

Ohio law defines "Menacing by Stalking" as follows:

"No person by engaging in a pattern of conduct shall knowingly cause another person to believe that the offender will cause physical harm to the other person or cause mental distress to the other person." R.C. 2903.211(A)(1).

"No person, through the use of any electronic method of remotely transferring information, including, but not limited to, any computer, computer network, computer program, or computer system, shall post a message with purpose to urge or incite another to commit a violation of division (A)(1) of this section (above)" R.C. 2903.211-(A)(2).

"Sexually oriented offenses" are defined in R.C. 2950.01.

FORM 10.03-D: PETITION FOR CIVIL STALKING PROTECTION ORDER OR CIVIL SEXUALLY ORIENTED OFFENSE PROTECTION ORDER

Amended: July 1, 2010
Discard all previous versions of this form

[Page 2 of 10.03-D]

Case No._____

3.   Petitioner states that Respondent has engaged in the following act(s) which create an immediate and present danger. For (a), (b), or (c) below, attach additional paper if you need more room.

☐ (a)   For a civil stalking protection order due to menacing by stalking, describe the nature and extent of the pattern of conduct that causes you to believe that Respondent will cause you physical harm or causes (or has caused) mental distress. Also describe any previous convictions of Respondent for the crime of Menacing by Stalking, if known.

_____

_____

_____

_____

_____

☐ (b)   For a civil sexually oriented offense protection order due to a sexually oriented offense, describe the acts of Respondent as fully as possible. You do not need to include any pattern of conduct information for a protection order due to a sexually oriented offense.

_____

_____

_____

_____

_____

_____

_____

☐ (c)   For electronic monitoring of the Respondent, describe the nature and extent of the Respondent's conduct before the filing of this Petition that puts you or your family or household members' health, welfare, or safety at risk. Also describe how the Respondent presents a continuing danger to you or your family or household members.

_____

_____

_____

_____

_____

4.   Petitioner requests the Court grant relief under R.C. 2903.214 for the Petitioner and the family or household members named in this Petition by granting a Civil Stalking Protection Order or Civil Sexually Oriented Offense Protection Order that:

☐ (a)   Requires Respondent not to abuse the Petitioner and the family or household members named in this Petition by harming, attempting to harm, threatening, following, stalking, harassing, contacting, forcing sexual relations upon them, or by committing sexually oriented offenses against them.

☐ (b)   Requires Respondent to refrain from entering the residence, school, business, place of employment, child care providers, or day care centers of Petitioner and the family or household members named in this Petition, including the buildings, grounds, and parking lots at those locations.

☐ (c)   Requires Respondent not to interfere with Petitioner's right to occupy the residence including, but not limited to canceling any utilities, insurance, interrupting phone service, mail delivery, or the delivery of any other documents or items.

FORM 10.03-D: PETITION FOR CIVIL STALKING PROTECTION ORDER OR CIVIL SEXUALLY ORIENTED OFFENSE PROTECTION ORDER

Amended: July 1, 2010
Discard all previous versions of this form

[Page 3 of 10.03-D]

Case No._____

☐ (d)   Requires Respondent not to remove, damage, hide, or dispose of any property or pets owned or possessed by the Petitioner and Petitioner's family or household members named in this Petition.

☐ (e)   Requires Respondent not to possess, use, carry, or obtain any deadly weapon.

☐ (f)   Requires Respondent to be electronically monitored.

☐ (g)   Includes the following additional provisions: _____
_____

☐ 5.   Petitioner further requests that the Court issue an *ex parte* (emergency) protection order under R.C. 2903.214(D) and this Petition.

☐ 6.   Petitioner further requests that the Court not issue any mutual protection orders or other orders against Petitioner unless all of the conditions of R.C. 2903.214(E)(3) are met.

☐ 7.   Petitioner further requests that if Petitioner has a victim advocate, the Court permit the victim advocate to accompany Petitioner at all stages of these proceedings as required by R.C. 2903.214(L).

☐ 8.   Petitioner further requests that the Court grant such other relief as the Court considers equitable and fair.

☐ 9.   The following is a list of all present and past court cases involving Respondent, that Petitioner knows of:

CASE NAME	CASE NUMBER	COURT/COUNTY	OUTCOME OF CASE

I hereby swear or affirm that the answers above are true, complete, and accurate to the best of my knowledge. I understand that falsifying this document may result in a contempt of court finding against me which could result in a jail sentence and fine, and that falsifying this document may also subject me to criminal penalties for perjury under R.C. 2921.11.

_____

SIGNATURE OF PETITIONER

Sworn to and subscribed before me on this _____ day of _____ , _____ .

_____

NOTARY PUBLIC

FORM 10.03-D: PETITION FOR CIVIL STALKING PROTECTION ORDER OR CIVIL SEXUALLY ORIENTED OFFENSE PROTECTION ORDER

Amended: July 1, 2010
Discard all previous versions of this form

[Page 4 of 10.03-D]

Case No._____

DO NOT WRITE YOUR ADDRESS BELOW IF YOU ARE REQUESTING CONFIDENTIALITY. PLEASE PROVIDE ANOTHER ADDRESS WHERE YOU CAN RECEIVE NOTICES FROM THE COURT.

_____

_____

_____

_____
Signature of Attorney for Petitioner (if applicable)

_____
Name

_____
Address

_____
City, State, Zip Code

_____
Attorney Registration Number

_____
Telephone Number

_____
Fax

_____
Email

FORM 10.03-D: PETITION FOR CIVIL STALKING PROTECTION ORDER OR CIVIL SEXUALLY ORIENTED OFFENSE PROTECTION ORDER

Amended: July 1, 2010
Discard all previous versions of this form

Form 10.03-E

FORM 10.03-E: CIVIL STALKING PROTECTION ORDER OR CIVIL SEXUALLY ORIENTED OFFENSE PROTECTION ORDER *EX PARTE*

IN THE COURT OF COMMON PLEAS
_____ COUNTY, OHIO

Order of Protection
Per R.C. 2903.214(F)(3), this Order is indexed at

_____
LAW ENFORCEMENT AGENCY WHERE INDEXED

(_____)_____
PHONE NUMBER

Case No.

Judge

County [_____]   State   **OHIO**

☐ CIVIL STALKING PROTECTION ORDER *EX PARTE* (R.C. 2903.214)

☐ CIVIL SEXUALLY ORIENTED OFFENSE PROTECTION ORDER *EX PARTE* (R.C. 2903.214)

PETITIONER:

First   Middle   Last

v.

RESPONDENT:

First   Middle   Last

Address where Respondent can be found:
_____
_____

PERSON(S) PROTECTED BY THIS ORDER:
Petitioner: _____ DOB: _____
Petitioner's Family or Household Member(s):
_____ DOB: _____
_____ DOB: _____
_____ DOB: _____
_____ DOB: _____

RESPONDENT IDENTIFIERS

SEX	RACE	HT	WT
EYES	HAIR	DATE OF BIRTH	
DRIVER'S LIC. NO.	EXP. DATE	STATE	

Distinguishing Features: _____

☐ **WARNING TO LAW ENFORCEMENT: RESPONDENT HAS FIREARMS ACCESS – PROCEED WITH CAUTION**

(Violence Against Women Act, 18 U.S.C. 2265, Federal Full Faith & Credit Declaration: Registration of this Order is not required for enforcement.)

THE COURT HEREBY FINDS:
That it has jurisdiction over the parties and subject matter, and the Respondent will be provided with reasonable notice and opportunity to be heard within the time required by Ohio law. **Additional findings of this Order are set forth below.**

THE COURT HEREBY ORDERS:
That the above named Respondent be restrained from committing acts of abuse or threats of abuse against the Petitioner and other protected persons named in this Order, as set forth below. Additional terms of this Order are set forth below.

The terms of this Order shall be effective until _____ / _____ / _____ (DATE CERTAIN).

WARNING TO RESPONDENT: See the warning page attached to the front of this Order.

FORM 10.03-E: CIVIL STALKING PROTECTION ORDER OR CIVIL SEXUALLY ORIENTED OFFENSE PROTECTION ORDER *EX PARTE*

Amended: July 1, 2010
Discard all previous versions of this form

Case No._____

This proceeding came on for an *ex parte* hearing on _____ , _____ (Respondent not being present), upon the filing of a Petition by Petitioner for a civil stalking protection order or civil sexually oriented offense protection order against the Respondent, pursuant to R.C. 2903.214. In accordance with R.C. 2903.214(D)(1), the Court held an *ex parte* hearing not later than the next day that the Court was in session after the Petition was filed.

The Court finds that the protected persons named herein are in immediate and present danger and, for good cause shown, the following temporary orders are necessary to protect the persons named in this Order.

ALL OF THE PROVISIONS CHECKED BELOW APPLY TO THE RESPONDENT

☐ 1. **RESPONDENT SHALL NOT ABUSE** the protected persons named in this Order by harming, attempting to harm, threatening, following, stalking, harassing, forcing sexual relations upon them, or by committing sexually oriented offenses against them. [NCIC 01 and 02]

☐ 2. **RESPONDENT SHALL NOT ENTER** the residence, school, business, place of employment, day care centers, or child care providers of the protected persons named in this Order, including the buildings, grounds and parking lots at those locations. Respondent may not violate this Order **even with the permission of a protected person.** [NCIC 04]

☐ 3. **RESPONDENT SHALL NOT INTERFERE** with protected persons' right to occupy the residence including, but not limited to canceling utilities, insurance, interrupting telephone service, mail delivery, or the delivery of any other documents or items.

☐ 4. **RESPONDENT SHALL SURRENDER** all keys and garage door openers to the following residence:

_____

at the earliest possible opportunity after service of this Order to the law enforcement agency that serves Respondent with this Order or as follows: _____

_____

☐ 5. **RESPONDENT SHALL STAY AWAY FROM** protected persons named in this Order, and shall not be present within 500 feet or _____ (distance) of any protected persons wherever those protected persons may be found, or any place the Respondent knows or should know the protected persons are likely to be, **even with protected persons' permission.** If Respondent accidentally comes in contact with protected persons in any public or private place, Respondent must depart *immediately*. This Order includes encounters on public and private roads, highways, and thoroughfares. [NCIC 04]

☐ 6. **RESPONDENT SHALL NOT REMOVE, DAMAGE, HIDE, OR DISPOSE OF ANY PROPERTY OR PETS** owned or possessed by the protected persons named in this Order.

☐ 7. **RESPONDENT SHALL NOT INITIATE OR HAVE ANY CONTACT** with the protected persons named in this Order at their residences, businesses, places of employment, schools, day care centers, or child care providers. Contact includes, but is not limited to, telephone, fax, e-mail, voice mail, delivery service, writings, or communications by any other means in person or through another person. Respondent may not violate this Order **even with the permission of a protected person**. [NCIC 05]

☐ 8. **RESPONDENT SHALL NOT CAUSE OR ENCOURAGE ANY OTHER PERSON** to do any act prohibited by this Order.

☐ 9. **RESPONDENT SHALL NOT POSSESS, USE, CARRY, OR OBTAIN ANY DEADLY WEAPON.** Respondent shall turn over all deadly weapons in Respondent's possession to the law enforcement agency that serves Respondent with this Order or as follows: _____

_____

Any law enforcement agency is authorized to take possession of deadly weapons pursuant to this paragraph and hold them in protective custody until further Court order. [NCIC 07]

FORM 10.03-E: CIVIL STALKING PROTECTION ORDER OR CIVIL SEXUALLY ORIENTED OFFENSE PROTECTION ORDER *EX PARTE*

Amended: July 1, 2010
Discard all previous versions of this form

[Page 3 of Form 10.03-E]

Case No._____

☐ **10. IT IS FURTHER ORDERED:** [NCIC 08]   _____

_____

_____

_____

11.   **IT IS FURTHER ORDERED** that the Clerk of Court shall cause a copy of the Petition and this Order to be delivered to the Respondent as required by law. The Clerk of Court shall also provide certified copies of the Petition and this Order to Petitioner upon request. This Order is granted without bond. Under federal and state law, the Clerk shall not charge any fees for filing, issuing, registering, or serving this Protection Order.

12.   **ALL OF THE TERMS OF THIS ORDER REMAIN IN FULL FORCE AND EFFECT UNTIL**

_____ , _____ .

    IT IS SO ORDERED.

_____   _____
MAGISTRATE   **JUDGE**

NOTICE TO RESPONDENT: THE PERSONS PROTECTED BY THIS ORDER CANNOT GIVE YOU LEGAL PERMISSION TO CHANGE OR VIOLATE THIS ORDER. IF YOU VIOLATE ANY TERMS OF THIS ORDER, EVEN WITH THE PROTECTED PERSON'S PERMISSION, YOU MAY BE ARRESTED. ONLY THE COURT CAN CHANGE THIS ORDER. IF THERE IS ANY REASON WHY THIS ORDER SHOULD BE CHANGED, YOU MUST ASK THE COURT TO CHANGE IT. YOU ACT AT YOUR OWN RISK IF YOU DISREGARD THIS WARNING.

A FULL HEARING on this Order shall be held before Judge _____ or Magistrate _____ on _____ , at _____ a.m./p.m. at the following location: _____ _____	**TO THE CLERK:** **COPIES OF THIS ORDER SHALL BE DELIVERED TO:** ☐ Petitioner ☐ Respondent (by personal service) ☐ Police Department Where Petitioner Resides: _____ ☐ Police Department Where Petitioner Works: _____ ☐ The _____ County Sheriff's Office ☐ Other: _____

FORM 10.03-E: CIVIL STALKING PROTECTION ORDER OR CIVIL SEXUALLY ORIENTED OFFENSE PROTECTION ORDER *EX PARTE*

Amended: July 1, 2010
Discard all previous versions of this form

Form 10.03-F

FORM 10.03-F: CIVIL STALKING PROTECTION ORDER OR CIVIL SEXUALLY ORIENTED OFFENSE PROTECTION ORDER FULL HEARING

IN THE COURT OF COMMON PLEAS
_____ COUNTY, OHIO

Order of Protection Per R.C. 2903.214(F)(3), this Order is indexed at	Case No. _____ Judge _____ County _____ State **OHIO**

_____
LAW ENFORCEMENT AGENCY WHERE INDEXED

(___) _____ - _____
PHONE NUMBER

☐ CIVIL STALKING PROTECTION ORDER FULL HEARING (R.C. 2903.214)

☐ CIVIL SEXUALLY ORIENTED OFFENSE PROTECTION ORDER FULL HEARING (R.C. 2903.214)

PETITIONER:

_____

First   Middle   Last

v.

PERSON(S) PROTECTED BY THIS ORDER:

Petitioner: _____ DOB: _____
Petitioner's Family or Household Member(s):
_____ DOB: _____
_____ DOB: _____
_____ DOB: _____
_____ DOB: _____

RESPONDENT:

_____

First   Middle   Last

Address where Respondent can be found:

_____
_____

RESPONDENT IDENTIFIERS

SEX	RACE	HT	WT

EYES	HAIR	DATE OF BIRTH

DRIVER'S LIC. NO.	EXP. DATE	STATE

Distinguishing Features: _____

☐ **WARNING TO LAW ENFORCEMENT: RESPONDENT HAS FIREARMS ACCESS – PROCEED WITH CAUTION**

(Violence Against Women Act, 18 U.S.C. 2265, Federal Full Faith & Credit Declaration: Registration of this Order is not required for enforcement.)

THE COURT HEREBY FINDS:
That it has jurisdiction over the parties and subject matter, and the Respondent was provided with reasonable notice and opportunity to be heard within the time required by Ohio law. **Additional findings of this Order are set forth below.**

THE COURT HEREBY ORDERS:
That the above named Respondent be restrained from committing acts of abuse or threats of abuse against the Petitioner and other protected persons named in this Order, as set forth below. Additional terms of this Order are set forth below.

The terms of this Order shall be effective until _____ / _____ / _____ (DATE CERTAIN – FIVE YEARS MAXIMUM).

WARNING TO RESPONDENT: See the warning page attached to the front of this Order.

FORM 10.03-F: CIVIL STALKING PROTECTION ORDER OR CIVIL SEXUALLY ORIENTED OFFENSE PROTECTION ORDER FULL HEARING

Amended: July 1, 2010
Discard all previous versions of this form

[Page 2 of Form 10.03-F]

Case No._____

This proceeding came on for a hearing on _____ before the Court and the Civil Stalking Protection Order *Ex Parte* or Civil Sexually Oriented Offense Protection Order *Ex Parte* filed on _____ all in accordance with R.C. 2903.214. The following individuals were present: _____

_____

The Court hereby makes the following findings of fact: _____

_____
_____
_____
_____
_____

☐   The Court finds by a preponderance of the evidence that 1) the Respondent has knowingly engaged in a pattern of conduct that caused Petitioner to believe that the Respondent will cause physical harm or cause or has caused mental distress; and 2) the following orders are equitable, fair, and necessary to protect the persons named in this Order from stalking offenses.

☐   The Court finds by a preponderance of the evidence that 1) the Petitioner or Petitioner's family or household member(s) are in danger of or have been a victim of a sexually oriented offense as defined in R.C. 2950.01, committed by Respondent; and 2) the following orders are equitable, fair, and necessary to protect the persons named in this Order from sexually oriented offenses.

☐   The Court finds by clear and convincing evidence that 1) the Petitioner or Petitioner's family or household member reasonably believed the Respondent's conduct before the filing of the Petition endangered the health, welfare, or safety of the Petitioner or Petitioner's family or household member(s); 2) the Respondent presents a continuing danger to the Petitioner or Petitioner's family or household member(s); and 3) the following orders are equitable, fair, and necessary to protect the person(s) named in this Order.

ALL OF THE PROVISIONS CHECKED BELOW APPLY TO THE RESPONDENT

☐ **1. RESPONDENT SHALL NOT ABUSE** the protected persons named in this Order by harming, attempting to harm, threatening, following, stalking, harassing, forcing sexual relations upon them, or by committing sexually oriented offenses against them. [NCIC 01 and 02]

☐ **2. RESPONDENT SHALL NOT ENTER** the residence, school, business, place of employment, day care centers, or child care providers of the protected persons named in this Order, including the buildings, grounds, and parking lots at those locations. Respondent may not violate this Order **even with the permission of a protected person**. [NCIC 03]

☐ **3. RESPONDENT SHALL NOT INTERFERE** with protected persons' right to occupy the residence including, but not limited to canceling utilities, insurance, interrupting telephone service, mail delivery, or the delivery of any other documents or items.

☐ **4. RESPONDENT SHALL SURRENDER** all keys and garage door openers to the following residence:

_____

at the earliest possible opportunity after service of this Order to the law enforcement agency that serves Respondent with this Order or as follows: _____

_____

☐ **5. RESPONDENT SHALL STAY AWAY** from protected persons named in this Order, and shall not be present within 500 feet or _____ (distance) of any protected persons, wherever those protected persons may be found, or any place the Respondent knows or should know the protected persons are likely to be, **even with protected persons' permission**. If Respondent accidentally comes in contact with protected persons in any public or private place, Respondent must depart *immediately*. This Order includes encounters on public and private roads, highways, and thoroughfares. [NCIC 04]

FORM 10.03-F: CIVIL STALKING PROTECTION ORDER OR CIVIL SEXUALLY ORIENTED OFFENSE PROTECTION ORDER FULL HEARING

Amended: July 1, 2010
Discard all previous versions of this form

Case No._____

☐ 6. **RESPONDENT SHALL NOT REMOVE, DAMAGE, HIDE, OR DISPOSE OF ANY PROPERTY OR PETS** owned or possessed by the protected persons named in this Order.

☐ 7. **RESPONDENT SHALL NOT INITIATE OR HAVE ANY CONTACT** with the protected persons named in this Order at their residences, businesses, places of employment, schools, day care centers, or child care providers. Contact includes, but is not limited to, telephone, fax, e-mail, voice mail, delivery service, writings, or communications by any other means in person or through another person. Respondent may not violate this Order **even with the permission of a protected person.** [NCIC 05]

☐ 8. **RESPONDENT SHALL NOT CAUSE OR ENCOURAGE ANY OTHER PERSON** to do any act prohibited by this Order.

☐ 9. **RESPONDENT SHALL NOT POSSESS, USE, CARRY, OR OBTAIN ANY DEADLY WEAPON.** Respondent shall turn over all deadly weapons in Respondent's possession to the law enforcement agency that serves Respondent with this Order or as follows: _____

Any law enforcement agency is authorized to take possession of deadly weapons pursuant to this paragraph and hold them in protective custody until further Court order. [NCIC 07]

☐ 10. **IT IS FURTHER ORDERED:** [NCIC 08] _____
_____
_____
_____

☐ 11. **RESPONDENT IS ORDERED TO COMPLETE** the following counseling program: _____
_____

Respondent shall contact this program within seven days after receiving this Order and immediately arrange for an initial appointment. The counseling program is requested to provide the Court a written notice when Respondent attends the initial appointment, if the Respondent fails to attend or is discharged, and when Respondent completes the program. Respondent is required to sign all necessary waivers to allow the Court to receive information from the counseling program.

☐ **Respondent is ordered to appear before Judge** _____ or **Magistrate** _____
on _____ **at** _____ **a.m. / p.m., to review Respondent's compliance with this Counseling Order. Respondent is warned: If you fail to attend the program you may be held in contempt of court. If you fail to appear at this hearing, the Court may issue a warrant for your arrest.**

☐ 12. **RESPONDENT SHALL NOT USE OR POSSESS** alcohol or illegal drugs.

☐ 13. **RESPONDENT SHALL BE SUBJECT TO ELECTRONIC MONITORING.** Respondent is ordered to report to _____ for the placement of a global positioning system for the purpose of electronic monitoring for the duration of this Order or until _____ , whichever expires first. The Court further imposes the following terms and conditions: _____
_____
_____

14. **IT IS FURTHER ORDERED** that the Clerk of Court shall cause a copy of the Petition and this Order to be delivered to the Respondent as required by law. The Clerk of Court shall also provide certified copies of the Petition and this Order to Petitioner upon request. This Order is granted without bond. Under federal and state law, the Clerk shall not charge any fees for filing, issuing, registering, or serving this Protection Order.

[Page 4 of Form 10.03-F]

Case No._____

15.   ALL OF THE TERMS OF THIS ORDER REMAIN IN FULL FORCE AND EFFECT FOR A PERIOD OF FIVE YEARS FROM ISSUANCE, OR UNTIL _____

     IT IS SO ORDERED.   APPROVED and ADOPTED by:

_____   _____
MAGISTRATE   **JUDGE**

NOTICE TO RESPONDENT: THE PERSONS PROTECTED BY THIS ORDER CANNOT GIVE YOU LEGAL PERMISSION TO CHANGE OR VIOLATE THIS ORDER. IF YOU VIOLATE ANY TERMS OF THIS ORDER, EVEN WITH THE PROTECTED PERSON'S PERMISSION, YOU MAY BE ARRESTED. ONLY THE COURT CAN CHANGE THIS ORDER. IF THERE IS ANY REASON WHY THIS ORDER SHOULD BE CHANGED, YOU MUST ASK THE COURT TO CHANGE IT. <u>YOU ACT AT YOUR OWN RISK IF YOU DISREGARD THIS WARNING.</u>

NOTICE OF FINAL APPEALABLE ORDER	TO THE CLERK

Copies of the foregoing Order, which is a final appealable order, were mailed by ordinary U.S. mail or hand-delivered to the parties indicated on the following date:
 	
_____ , _____
 	
By: _____
       CLERK OF COURT
	COPIES OF THIS ORDER SHALL BE DELIVERED TO:
	☐ Petitioner ☐ Attorney for Petitioner
	☐ Respondent ☐ Attorney for Respondent
	☐ Police Department Where Petitioner Resides:
	    _____
	☐ Police Department Where Petitioner Works:
	    _____
	☐ The _____ County Sheriff's Office
	☐ Other: _____

WAIVER

I, _____, understand that I have the right to a full hearing on the Petition for Civil Stalking Protection Order or Civil Sexually Oriented Offense Protection Order, and acknowledge each of the following:

    1. I waive the right to have a full hearing on this Protection Order;

    2. I waive the right to cross-examine witnesses and review evidence submitted in support of this Protection Order;

    3. I waive the right to present witnesses and evidence on my own behalf;

    4. I waive the right to request specific factual findings from the Court concerning the issuance of this Protection Order.

I understand that based on the foregoing waivers a Protection Order will be entered against me.

RESPONDENT: _____   DATE: _____

Form 10.03-G

FORM 10.03-G: HOW TO OBTAIN A CIVIL STALKING PROTECTION ORDER OR CIVIL SEXUALLY ORIENTED OFFENSE PROTECTION ORDER

These instructions are intended to assist you in preparing the Petition for a Civil Stalking Protection Order or Sexually Oriented Offense Protection Order, which can only be heard by the court of common pleas in your county. **Throughout the Petition you are called** *Petitioner* **and the person you are filing this Petition against is called** *Respondent.*

SOME HINTS BEFORE YOU BEGIN

- All forms must be typed or printed.
- When you print your name on the Petition, use the same name you use when you write your signature.
- Write your name and Respondent's name the same way throughout the Petition.
- Fill out the Petition as completely and accurately as possible.
- If you have any questions about completing the Petition, ask the Clerk of Court's office for assistance or contact your local domestic violence program or the Ohio Domestic Violence Network at 800-934-9840.
- Under federal and state law no fees may be charged to obtain a protection order.

FILLING OUT THE PETITION: Mark each instruction below after you read and complete it

☐ **On the front page, leave the "Case No." line and "Judge" lines blank.** The Clerk of Court's office will fill in this information.

☐ **On the top left-hand side of the front page, fill in the requested information about yourself.** If you do not want your present address to be known, write "confidential" in the space for your address, but list someone else's address where you can receive notices from the Court.

☐ **Also on the top left-hand side of the front page, fill in the requested information about Respondent as best you can.** You may use Respondent's work address if you do not know Respondent's home address. If you do not know Respondent's date of birth, leave that line blank. <u>Do not attempt to obtain this information unless it is safe to do so.</u>

☐ **Paragraph 1:** If you are filing the Petition on behalf of yourself, mark the first box.

☐ **Paragraph 2:** If you are filing the Petition on behalf of a family or household member, mark the box and fill in their name(s) and the other information requested in the chart. You may attach additional pages if you need more room.

☐ **Paragraph 3(a):** State the date(s) of the incident(s) that caused you to file the Petition. Exact date(s) is not necessary; approximate time frame may be sufficient. If you are requesting a civil stalking protection order due to stalking, provide a brief description of the pattern of conduct (two or more instances) that caused you to believe that the Respondent will cause physical harm or cause mental distress to you or another family member. (NOTE: Petitioner and/or Respondent need not be related in any way for Petitioner to obtain the protection order.) If you are aware of·any prior convictions of the Respondent for menacing by stalking or similar offenses, or prior convictions of Respondent for any sexually oriented offenses, list what information you know about those convictions. You may attach additional pages if you need more room to complete your description.

☐ **Paragraph 3(b):** State the date(s) of the incident(s) that caused you to file the Petition. Exact date(s) is not necessary; approximate timeframe may be sufficient. If you are requesting a civil sexually oriented offense protection order due to a sexually oriented offense, you do not have to provide a description of a pattern of conduct. A brief description of what happened that caused you to request the protection order will be enough. (NOTE: Petitioner and/or Respondent need not be related in any way for Petitioner to obtain the protection order.) If you are aware of any prior convictions of the Respondent for menacing by stalking or similar offenses, or prior convictions of Respondent for any sexually oriented offenses, list what information you know about those convictions. You may attach additional pages if you need more room to complete your description.

☐ **Paragraph 3(c):** State the date(s) of the incident(s) that caused you to file the Petition and request electronic monitoring of the Respondent. Exact date(s) is not necessary; approximate timeframe may be sufficient. If you are requesting electronic monitoring of the Respondent, describe the nature and extent of the Respondent's conduct before the filing of this Petition that puts you or your family or household members' health, welfare, or safety at risk. Also describe how the Respondent presents a continuing danger to you or your family or household members.

☐ **Paragraph 4:** Indicate the action you want the Court to take by marking the boxes next to the numbered paragraphs that apply to your situation.

FORM 10.03-G: HOW TO OBTAIN A CIVIL STALKING PROTECTION ORDER OR CIVIL SEXUALLY ORIENTED OFFENSE PROTECTION ORDER

Amended: July 1, 2010
Discard all previous versions of this form

☐ **Paragraph 4(f):** Write any special court orders you believe would help protect you and your family or household members.

☐ **Paragraph 5:** Be sure to mark the box next to Paragraph 5 if you need an emergency ("*ex parte*") protection order.

☐ **Paragraph 9:** List ALL present or past court cases or investigations that involve Respondent. This includes all criminal, divorce, custody, visitation, and any other case that may have a bearing on the safety of you or your family or household members. Write the case name, the court, the case number, and the outcome of the case, if known. You may attach additional pages if you need more room.

SIGNING THE PETITION

Try to fill out the Petition before you go to the courthouse. AFTER YOU HAVE FILLED OUT THE PETITION, TAKE IT TO A NOTARY PUBLIC TO HAVE YOUR SIGNATURE NOTARIZED. *DO NOT SIGN THE PETITION UNLESS YOU ARE IN FRONT OF A NOTARY PUBLIC.* An employee of the Clerk of Court's office may be available to take your oath.

FILING THE PETITION

After you have your signature notarized, file your Petition at the Clerk of Court's office. The Clerk of Court's office will tell you when and where your *ex parte* hearing will take place.

FEES

Under federal and state law, you cannot be charged any costs or fees for filing and obtaining a protection order.

FORM 10.03-G: HOW TO OBTAIN A CIVIL STALKING PROTECTION ORDER OR CIVIL SEXUALLY ORIENTED OFFENSE PROTECTION ORDER

Amended: July 1, 2010
Discard all previous versions of this form

Form 10.03-H

FORM 10.03-H: WARNING CONCERNING THE ATTACHED PROTECTION ORDER

NOTE: *Rule 10.03 of the Rules of Superintendence for the Courts of Ohio requires this Warning to be attached to the FRONT of all protection orders issued pursuant to R.C. 2903.213 and 2903.214 by the courts of the State of Ohio. TO BE USED WITH FORMS 10.03-B, 10.03-E, and 10.03-F.*

WARNING TO RESPONDENT/ DEFENDANT

Violating the attached Protection Order is a crime, punishable by imprisonment or fine or both, and can cause your bond to be revoked or result in a contempt of court citation against you.

This Protection Order is enforceable in all 50 states, the District of Columbia, tribal lands, and U.S. Territories pursuant to the Violence Against Women Act, 18 U.S.C. 2265. Violating this Protection Order may subject you to federal charges and punishment.

As a result of this Order, it may be unlawful for you to possess or purchase a firearm, including a rifle, pistol, or revolver, or ammunition pursuant to federal law under 18 U.S.C. 922(g)(8). If you have any questions whether these laws make it illegal for you to possess or purchase a firearm, you should consult an attorney.

Only the Court can change this Order. The Petitioner/Alleged Victim cannot give you permission to violate this order. If you go near the Petitioner or other protected persons, even with their consent, you may be arrested. You act at your own risk if you disregard this WARNING. If you want to change the Order you must ask the Court.

WARNING TO PETITIONER / ALLEGED VICTIM

You cannot change the terms of this Order by your words or actions. This Order **cannot** be changed by either party without obtaining a written court order.

NOTICE TO ALL LAW ENFORCEMENT AGENCIES AND OFFICERS

The attached Protection Order is enforceable in all jurisdictions. Violating this Protection Order, whether it is a criminal or civil Protection Order, is a crime under R.C. 2919.27. Law enforcement officers with powers to arrest for violations of the Ohio Revised Code must enforce the terms of this Protection Order as required by R.C. 2919.27, 2903.213, and 2903.214. If you have reasonable grounds to believe that Respondent/Defendant has violated this Protection Order, in Ohio under R.C. 2935.03, you should arrest and detain Respondent/Defendant until you can obtain a warrant. Federal and state laws prohibit charging a fee for service of this order.

History: Effective 3-1-00; amended, eff. 6-1-02; 5-1-07; 2-1-09; 7-1-10.

RULE 10.04. Standard Notice Concerning Possession or Purchase of a Firearm

(A) A court that has jurisdiction to convict a person of a misdemeanor offense of violence against a family or household member shall provide notice to the defendant pursuant to section 2943.033 of the Revised Code.

(B) In every case prior to accepting a guilty plea or plea of no contest to an indictment, information, or complaint that charges a person with a misdemeanor offense of violence against a family or household member, the court shall use a form that is substantially similar to Form 10.04-A unless the court provides oral notice to the defendant.

Form 10.04-A

FORM 10.04-A: NOTICE CONCERNING POSSESSION OR PURCHASE OF FIREARMS

NOTE: Rule 10.04 of the Rules of Superintendence for the Courts of Ohio requires notice of possible firearm restrictions be provided to the Defendant before entering a guilty plea or plea of no contest to a misdemeanor crime of violence against a family or household member.

Pursuant to R.C. 2943.033, you are advised that if you enter a guilty plea or plea of no contest to a misdemeanor crime involving violence where you are or were any of the following:

- A spouse, person living as a spouse, former spouse of the Alleged Victim;

- A parent or child of the Alleged Victim;

- A parent or child of a spouse, person living as a spouse, or former spouse of the Alleged Victim;

- The natural parent of any child of whom the Alleged Victim is the other natural parent or the putative natural parent

it may be unlawful for you to ship, transport, purchase, or possess a firearm or ammunition as a result of any conviction for a misdemeanor offense of violence pursuant to federal law under 18 U.S.C. 922(g)(9).

If you have any questions whether this law makes it illegal for you to ship, transport, purchase, or possess a firearm or ammunition, you should consult an attorney.

FORM 10.04-A: NOTICE CONCERNING THE POSSESSION OR PURCHASE OF FIREARMS

Amended: July 1, 2010
Discard all previous versions of this form

History: Effective 2-1-09.

RULE 11. Recording of Proceedings

(A) **Recording devices** Proceedings before any court and discovery proceedings may be recorded by stenographic means, phonogramic means, photographic means, audio electronic recording devices, or video recording systems. The administrative judge may order the use of any method of recording authorized by this rule.

(B) **Appeal** Transcripts of proceedings in electronic media shall be prepared in accordance with Rule 9(A) of the Rules of Appellate Procedure.

(C) **Custody** Electronically recorded transcripts of proceedings shall be maintained and transcribed in the manner directed by the trial court.

(D) **Inspection of electronically recorded transcripts of proceedings** A party may request a copy of an electronically recorded transcript of proceedings, or a portion of the transcript. The court may permit a party to view or hear the transcript of proceedings on file with the court.

(E) **Reference to electronically recorded transcripts of proceedings** Reference to a particular portion of an electronically recorded transcript of proceedings shall be to the event, the number of the reel of tape on which it was recorded and the elapsed time counter reading.

(F) **Expense of electronically recorded transcripts of proceedings** The expense of copies of electronically recorded transcripts of proceedings or such portions as are considered necessary by a party shall be borne by the requesting party or as provided by law. The expense of viewing or hearing an electronically recorded transcript of proceedings under division (D) of this rule shall be borne by the requesting party. All other expenses of electronically recorded transcripts of proceedings shall be costs in the action.

RULE 12. Conditions for Broadcasting and Photographing Court Proceedings

(A) **Presiding judge** The judge assigned to the trial or hearing shall permit the broadcasting or recording by electronic means and the taking of photographs in court proceedings that are open to the public as provided by Ohio law. After consultation with the media, the judge shall specify the place or places in the courtroom where the operators and equipment are to be positioned. Requests for permission for the broadcasting, televising, recording, or taking of photographs in the courtroom shall be in writing and the written order of the judge shall be made a part of the record of the proceedings.

(B) **Permissible equipment and operators**

(1) Use of more than one portable television, videotape, or movie camera with one operator shall be allowed only with the permission of the judge.

(2) Not more than one still photographer shall be permitted to photograph trial proceedings without permission of the judge. Still photographers shall be limited to two cameras with two lenses for each camera.

(3) For radio broadcast purposes, not more than one audio system shall be permitted in court. Where available and suitable, existing audio pickup systems in the court facility shall be used by the media. If existing audio pickup systems are not available, microphones and other electronic equipment necessary for the audio pickup shall be as inconspicuous as possible but shall be visible.

(4) Visible audio recording equipment may be used by news media reporters with the prior permission of the judge.

(5) Arrangements between or among media for "pooling" of equipment shall be the responsibility of the media representative authorized to cover the proceeding. "Pooling" arrangements are to be made outside the courtroom and without imposing on the judge or court personnel. If disputes arise over arrangements between or among media representatives, the judge may exclude all contesting representatives from the proceedings.

(6) The judge shall prohibit the use of electronic or photographic equipment that produces distracting sound or light. No artificial lighting other than that normally used in the courtroom shall be employed, provided that, if the normal lighting in the courtroom can be improved without becoming obtrusive, the judge may permit modification.

(7) Still photographers and television and radio representatives shall be afforded a clear view but shall not be permitted to move about in the courtroom during court proceedings from the places where they have been positioned by the judge, except to leave or enter the courtroom.

(C) **Limitations**

(1) There shall be no audio pickup or broadcast of conferences conducted in a court facility between attorneys and clients or co-counsel or of conferences conducted at the bench between counsel and the judge.

(2) The judge shall inform victims and witnesses of their right to object to being filmed, videotaped, recorded, or photographed.

(3) This rule shall not be construed to grant media representatives any greater rights than permitted by law.

(4) Media representatives shall not be permitted to transmit or record anything other than the court proceedings from the courtroom while the court is in session.

(D) **Revocation of permission** Upon the failure of any media representative to comply with the conditions prescribed by this rule or the judge, the judge may revoke the permission to broadcast or photograph the trial or hearing.

NOTES TO DECISIONS

ANALYSIS

Juvenile courts
Trial court's orders without a hearing

Because SupR 12(A) requires judges to permit the taking of photographs in court proceedings that are open to the public as provided by law, and the juvenile court did not hear evidence and argument and make the requisite findings in accordance with the applicable law before preventing photographs of the alleged juvenile delinquent's face, prohibition will issue to prevent enforcement of the order: State ex rel. Dispatch Printing Co. v. Geer, 114 Ohio St. 3d 511, 2007 Ohio 4643, 873 N.E.2d 314, 2007 Ohio LEXIS 2219 (2007).

Because Superintendence Ct. R. 12(A) required the judge to permit the taking of photographs in court proceedings that were open to the public as provided by law, and the juvenile court did not hear evidence and argument or make the requisite findings in accordance with the applicable law before preventing photographs of the alleged juvenile delinquent's face, the writ of prohibition was granted for the newspaper. Even though the judge's order did not prevent public access, since it did not totally ban the photographing of the proceedings or ban the photographing of the juvenile entirely, but merely prevented the photographing of the juvenile's face, it was based upon unsupported findings; at the very least, all parties affected had to have the opportunity to respond to the possibility of any restriction. State ex rel. Dispatch Printing Co. v. Geer, 114 Ohio St. 3d 511, 2007 Ohio 4643, 873 N.E.2d 314, 2007 Ohio LEXIS 2219 (2007).

RULE 13. Videotaped Testimony and Evidence

(A) **Videotape depositions**

(1) **Authority** Videotape depositions are authorized by Civil Rule 30(B)(3).

(2) **Notice** The notice requirements of Civil Rule 30(B)(3) regarding the manner of recording, preserving, and filing depositions apply to videotape depositions. Notice is sufficient if it specifies that the videotape deposition is to be taken pursuant to the provisions of this rule.

(3) **Persons authorized to take depositions** The officer before whom a videotape deposition is taken shall be one of those persons enumerated in Civil Rule 28.

(4) **Date and time recording** A date and time generator shall be used to superimpose the year, month, day, hour, minute, and second over the video portion of the recording during the taking of the deposition. The total deposition time shall be noted on the outside of the videotape.

(5) **Objections** The officer shall keep a log of objections referenced to the time of making each objection as superimposed on the video portion of the recording. If the deposition is transcribed, the log shall include the page of the transcript on which each objection occurs.

(6) **Copies of the deposition** Upon the request of a party, the officer shall provide an audio cassette recording of the deposition at the conclusion of its taking. Upon the request of a party, the officer shall provide a copy of the deposition in the medium of videotape or a written transcript of the deposition within a reasonable period of time. The requesting party shall bear the cost of the copy requested.

(7) **Submission to witness** After a videotape deposition is taken, the videotape shall be shown immediately to the witness for his examination, unless the examination is waived by the witness and the parties.

(8) **Certification of original videotape deposi-tion** The officer before whom the videotape deposition is taken shall cause a written certification to be attached to the original videotape. The certification shall state that the witness was fully sworn or affirmed by the officer and that the videotape is a true record of the testimony given by the witness. If the witness has not waived his or her right to a showing and examination of the videotape deposition, the witness shall also sign the certification.

When an officer makes a copy or a transcription of the videotape deposition in any medium, he or she shall attach a written certification to the copy or transcription. The certification shall state that the copy is a true record of the videotape testimony of the witness.

(9) **Certification of edited videetape depositions** The officer who edits the original videotape deposition shall attach a written certification to the edited copy of the videotape deposition. The certification shall state that the editing complies with the rulings of the court and that the original videotape deposition has not been affected by the editing process.

(10) **Filing where objections not made** Where objections are not made by a party or witness during the deposition and, if pursuant to Civil Rule 30(F)(1) a party requests, or the court orders, that the deposition be filed with the court, the officer shall file the deposition with the clerk of the court.

(11) **Filings where objections made** When a deposition containing objections is filed with the court pursuant to Civil Rule 30(F)(1), it shall be accompanied by the officer's log of objections. A party may request that the court rule upon the objections within fourteen days of the filing of the deposition or within a reasonable time as stipulated by the parties. In ruling upon objections, the court may view the videotape recording in its entirety or view only those parts of the videotape recording pertinent to the objections made. If the parties are not present at the time the court's rulings are made, the court shall provide the parties with copies of its rulings on the objections and his instructions as to editing.

(12) **Editing alternatives** The original videotape shall not be affected by any editing process.

(a) In its order and editing instructions the court may do any of the following:

(i) Release the videotape to the officer with instructions to keep the original videotape intact and make an edited copy of the videotape that deletes all references to objections and objectionable material;

(ii) Order the person showing the original videotape at trial to suppress the objectionable audio portions of the videotape;

(iii) Order the person showing the original videotape at trial to suppress the objectionable audio and video portions of the videotape.

(b) If the court uses alternative in division (A)(12)(a)(i) of this rule, the officer shall cause both the original videotape recording and the edited videotape recording, each clearly identified, to be filed with the clerk of the court. If the court uses the alternative in division (A)(12)(a)(ii) of this rule, it shall, in jury trials, instruct the jury to disregard the video portions of the presentation when the audio portion is suppressed. If the court uses the alternative in division (A)(12)(a)(iii) of this rule, it shall, in jury trials, instruct the jury to disregard any deletions apparent in the playing of the videotape.

(13) **Storage** Each court shall provide secure and adequate facilities for the storage of videotape recordings.

(14) **Inspection or viewing** Except upon order of the court and upon such terms as it may provide, the videotape recordings on file with the clerk of the court shall not be available for inspection or viewing after filing and prior to use at trial or disposition in accordance with this rule. Upon the request of a party under division (A)(3) of this rule, the clerk, without court order, may release the videotape to the officer to allow the making of a copy of the videotape.

(15) **Objections at trial** Objections should be made prior to trial, and all objections shall be made before actual presentation of the videotape at trial. If an objection is made at trial that has not been waived pursuant to Civil Rule 32(D)(3) or previously raised and ruled upon, the objection shall be made before the videotape deposition is presented. The trial judge shall rule on objections prior to the presentation of the videotape. If an objection is sustained, that portion of the videotape containing the objectionable testimony shall not be presented.

(B) **Videotape trials**

(1) **Authority** Videotape trials are authorized by Civil Rule 40. In videotape trials, videotape is the exclusive medium of presenting testimony irrespective of the availability of the individual witness to testify in person. All testimony is recorded on videotape and the limitations of Civil Rule 32 upon the use of depositions shall not apply.

(2) **Initiation of videtape trial** By agreement of the parties and with the consent of the trial judge all or a portion of testimony and appropriate evidence may be presented by videotape. The trial judge may order the recording of all or a portion of testimony and evidence on videotape in an appropriate case. In determining whether to order a videotape trial, the trial judge, after consultation with counsel, shall consider the costs involved, the nature of the action, and the nature and amount of testimony.

(3) **Procedure** Divisions (A)(3) to (13) and (D) apply to videotape trials. The sequence of taking the testimony of individual witnesses and the sequence of presentation of that testimony shall be at the option of the proponent. In ordering or consenting to the recording of all of the testimony on videotape, the trial judge shall fix a date prior to the date of trial by which all recorded testimony shall be filed with the clerk of the court.

(4) **Objections** All objections shall be made and ruled upon in advance of the trial. Objections may not be made during the presentation of the videotape evidence.

(5) **Presence of counsel and trial judge** In jury trials, counsel for the parties and the trial judge are not required to be present in the courtroom when the videotape testimony is played to the jury. If the trial judge leaves the courtroom during the playing of the videotape, the judge shall admonish the jurors regarding their duties and responsibilities. In the absence of the judge, a responsible officer of the court shall remain with the jury. The trial judge shall remain within such proximity to the courtroom that he or she can be readily summoned.

(C) **Equipment**

(1) **Standard** There are several recording format standards used in the trial courts of this state. Proponents of videotape testimony or evidence shall determine the format utilized by the trial court in which the videotape is to be filed and shall make the videotape recording on the appropriate format machine. If a party records testimony or evidence on videotape that is not compatible with the trial court equipment, the party shall be responsible for the furnishing of reproduction equipment of institutional quality or for the conversion of the videotape to the standards used in trial court equipment, all of which shall be at the cost of the party and not chargeable as costs of the action.

Each court shall provide for the availability of playback equipment. As may be appropriate, the court may purchase or lease equipment or make contract for the equipment on occasions of need. The court shall provide for the adequate training of an operator from the personnel of the court or for the services of a competent operator to operate the equipment when videotape testimony or evidence is presented in court.

(2) **Minimum equipment** At a minimum, facilities for playback at trial shall consist of a videotape player and one monitor, having at least a fourteen-inch screen. Color facilities are not required.

(3) **Maintenance** The trial court shall take reasonable steps to ensure that the equipment is maintained within operating tolerances. The trial court shall provide for competent regular maintenance of equipment that is owned or leased by the court.

(D) **Costs; videotape depositions**

(1) The expense of videotape as a material shall be borne by the proponent.

(2) The reasonable expense of recording testimony on videotape, the expense of playing the videotape recording at trial, and the expense of playing the videotape recording for the purpose of ruling upon objections shall be allocated as costs in the proceeding in accordance with Civil Rule 54.

(3) The expense of producing the edited version of the videotape recording shall be costs in the action, provided that the expense of the videotape, as a material, shall be borne by the proponent of the testimony.

(4) The expense of a copy of the videotape recording and the expense of an audio tape recording of the videotape sound track shall be borne by the party requesting the copy.

(E) **Disposition of videotape filed with the court**

(1) **Ownership** Videotape used in recording testimony shall remain the property of the proponent of the testimony. Videotape may be reused, but the proponent is responsible for submitting a recording of acceptable quality.

(2) **Release of videotape recordings**

(a) The court may authorize the clerk of the court to release the original videotape recording and the edited videotape recording to the owner of the videotape upon any of the following:

(i) The final disposition of the cause where no trial occurs;

(ii) The expiration of the appeal period following trial, if no appeal is taken;

(iii) The final determination of the cause, if an appeal is taken.

If the testimony is recorded stenographically by a court reporter during the playing of the videotape at trial, the videotape may be returned to the proponent upon disposition of the cause following the trial.

(b) The court shall order release by journal entry.

NOTES TO DECISIONS

ANALYSIS

Costs of videotaped depositions
Objections

Driver who was awarded a judgment in his favor, arising from a motor vehicle accident with a motorist, was not entitled to costs for a court reporter's services to attend the deposition of the driver's medical expert pursuant to RC §§ 2319.27 and 2303.21, although the expense of procuring the transcript of the expert's videotaped deposition was possibly recoverable under RC § 2303.21; although the reasonable expenses of recording the testimony on a videotape and playing it at trial were possibly recoverable under Ohio Superintendence Ct. R. 13(D)(2), the cost of the videotape itself was not a recoverable cost under Ohio R. Civ. P. 54(D). Naples v. Kinczel, — Ohio App. 3d —, 2007 Ohio 4851, — N.E. 2d —, 2007 Ohio App. LEXIS 4332 (Sept. 20, 2007).

Trial court's award of costs to a motorist in his personal injury action, arising from a vehicular collision, was proper under Ohio R. Civ. P. 54(D), as the requisite costs associated with the videotaped deposition of an expert witness were awarded pursuant to Ohio Superintendence R. 13(D), there was no authority to award costs for a court reporter, subpoena expenses, or filing fees pursuant to RC § 2303.20, and costs for medical records were properly not included. Wingfield v. Howe, — Ohio App. 3d —, 2006 Ohio 276, — N.E. 2d —, 2006 Ohio App. LEXIS 245 (Jan. 26, 2006).

After a trial court ordered, pursuant to Ohio Superintendence Ct. R. 13, Lorain County, Ohio, Ct. C.P. R. 23, and Ohio R. Civ. P. 40, ordered that trial in a personal injury case would be conducted by videotape, it was an abuse of discretion for the trial court to deny the request of the alleged injured party to testify in person at the trial and then to grant the party's request to allow a third party to read a physician's deposition at the trial, without providing an explanation for the different orders, as the trial court did not consult counsel or consider the factors required by Ohio Superintendence Ct. R. 13(B) in issuing its orders. Armbruster v. Hampton, — Ohio App. 3d —, 2006 Ohio 4530, — N.E. 2d —, 2006 Ohio App. LEXIS 4518 (Sept. 5, 2006).

RULE 14.   Administration of Courts During Civil Disorder

(A) **Authority of Chief Justice** During a judicial emergency, the Chief Justice or the acting Chief Justice shall have authority to suspend the operation of any local court rule, promulgate temporary rules of court, and do and direct to be done all things necessary to ensure the orderly and efficient administration of justice for the duration of the emergency. In case of the absence or disability of the Chief Justice, the justice, who is not absent or disabled, having the period of longest total service upon the Court shall be the acting Chief Justice within the meaning of this rule.

(B) **Assignment of judges** The Chief Justice or acting Chief Justice may assign and transfer to emergency judicial duties judges of any court of record in the state, including retired judges within the meaning of Article IV, Section 6(C) of the Ohio Constitution.

(C) **Consultation among Justices** The Chief Justice or the acting Chief Justice, whenever possible under the circumstances, shall consult with and report to the other justices any actions contemplated or taken in accordance with this rule.

(D) **Assigned judges; remuneration** Statutes and rules governing payment and reimbursement of expenses of assigned judges in effect at the time of a judicial emergency shall apply to judges assigned under this rule.

RULE 15.   Arbitration

(A) **Arbitration in civil cases**

(1) The judge or judges of general divisions of courts of common pleas, of municipal courts, or of county courts shall consider, and may adopt, a plan for the mandatory arbitration of civil cases. The plan shall specify the amount in controversy that will require submission of the case to arbitration and arbitration shall be required in cases where the amount in controversy does not exceed that specified sum. Arbitration shall be permitted in cases where the amount in controversy exceeds the sum specified in the plan for mandatory arbitration where all parties to the action agree to arbitration. The court shall determine at an appropriate pre-trial stage whether a case is to be referred to mandatory arbitration.

(2) Every plan for the mandatory arbitration of civil cases adopted pursuant to this rule shall be filed with the Supreme Court and shall include the following basic principles:

(a) **Actions excluded** Actions involving title to real estate, equitable relief and appeals shall be excluded.

(b) **Arbitrators** The court shall establish a list of qualified attorneys who have consented to serve as arbitrators. The court shall appoint from the list an arbitrator who has no interest in the determination of the case or relationship with the parties or their counsel that would interfere with an impartial consideration of the case. Upon written request of a party, the court shall appoint a board of three arbitrators in the same manner as a single arbitrator is appointed.

(c) **Report and award** Within thirty days after the hearing, the board or the single arbitrator shall file a report and award with the clerk of the court and forward copies to all parties or their counsel. The report and award, unless appealed, shall be final and have the legal effect of a verdict upon which judgment shall be entered by the court.

(d) **Appeals** Any party may appeal the award to the court if, within thirty days after the filing of the award with the clerk of court, the party does both of the following:

(i) Files a notice of appeal with the clerk of courts and serves a copy on the adverse party or parties accompanied by an affidavit that the appeal is not being taken for delay;

(ii) Reimburses the county or municipal corporation for all fees paid to the arbitrator or arbitrators in the case or pays the fees directly to the arbitrator or arbitrators, unless otherwise directed by the court.

All appeals shall be de novo proceedings at which members of the deciding board or the single arbitrator are barred as witnesses.

Exceptions to the decision of the board or single arbitrator based on either misconduct or corruption of the board or single arbitrator may also be filed by any party within thirty days after the filing of the report, and, if sustained, the report shall be vacated.

(B) **Arbitration in juvenile and domestic relations cases**

(1) The judge or judges of a division of a court of common pleas having domestic relations or juvenile jurisdiction may, at the request of all parties, refer a case or a designated issue to arbitration.

(2) The parties shall propose an arbitrator to the court and identify all issues to be resolved by the arbitrator. The arbitrator shall consent to serve and shall have no interest in the determination of the case or relationship with the parties or their counsel that would interfere with the impartial consideration of the case. An arbitrator selected pursuant to this section is not required to be an attorney.

(3) The request for arbitration submitted by the parties shall provide for the manner of payment of the arbitrator.

(4) The arbitrator shall file a report and award pursuant to division (A)(2)(c) of this rule.

(5) Any party may appeal the report and award pursuant to division (A)(2)(d) of this rule.

NOTES TO DECISIONS

Analysis

Local court rules

Pursuant to Ohio Superintendence R. 15 and Ohio Const. art. IV, § 5(B), there was nothing unconstitutional about Cuyahoga County, Ohio, Ct. C.P. R. 59, as it furthered the orderly administration of justice and set procedures to be followed for appeals of arbitrations. Cavalry Invs., LLC v. Dzilinski, — Ohio App. 3d —, 2007 Ohio 3767, — N.E. 2d —, 2007 Ohio App. LEXIS 3435 (July 26, 2007).

RULE 16. Mediation

(A) **General Provisions** A division of the court of common pleas, municipal court, and county court shall consider, and may adopt, a local rule providing for mediation.

(B) **Content of Mediation Rule** A local rule providing for mediation shall include the applicable pro-

visions set forth in this division, in addition to such other provisions as the court or division considers necessary and appropriate.

(1) **Required provisions for all mediation rules** A local mediation rule shall include all of the following provisions:

(a) Procedures for ensuring that parties are allowed to participate in mediation, and if the parties wish, that their attorneys and other individuals they designate are allowed to accompany them and participate in mediation.

(b) Procedures for screening for domestic violence both before and during mediation.

(c) Procedures for encouraging appropriate referrals to legal counsel and other support services for all parties, including victims of and suspected victims of domestic violence.

(d) Procedures for prohibiting the use of mediation in any of the following:

(1) As an alternative to the prosecution or adjudication of domestic violence;

(2) In determining whether to grant, modify or terminate a protection order;

(3) In determining the terms and conditions of a protection order; and

(4) In determining the penalty for violation of a protection order.

Nothing in division (B)(1)(d) of this rule shall prohibit the use of mediation in a subsequent divorce or custody case even though that case may result in the termination of the provisions of a protection order.

(2) **Required provisions for domestic relations and juvenile court mediation rules** A local rule for mediation of allocation of parental rights and responsibilities or the care of, or visitation with, minor children or delinquency or status offense cases shall include the provisions of division (B)(1) of this rule. The mediation rule shall include provisions that allow mediation to proceed, when violence or fear of violence is alleged, suspected, or present, only if the mediator has specialized training set forth in division (C)(2) of this rule and all of the following conditions are satisfied:

(a) The person who is or may be the victim of domestic violence is fully informed, both orally and in writing, about the mediation process, his or her right to decline participation in the mediation process, and his or her option to have a support person present at mediation sessions.

(b) The parties have the capacity to mediate without fear of coercion or control.

(c) Appropriate procedures are in place to provide for the safety of the person who is or may be the victim of domestic violence and all other persons present at the mediation.

(d) Procedures are in place for the mediator to terminate mediation if he or she believes there is continued threat of domestic violence or coercion between the parties.

(e) Procedures are in place for issuing written findings of fact, as required by R.C. 3109.052, to refer certain cases involving domestic violence to mediation.

(3) **Required provisions for child abuse, ne-**

glect, or dependency mediation rules A local rule for mediation in child abuse, neglect, or dependency cases shall include the provisions of division (B)(1) and (B)(2) of this rule and all of the following:

(a) A provision that allows mediation to proceed only if the mediator has specialized training set forth in division (C)(1), (C)(2), and (C)(3) of this rule.

(b) Procedures for ensuring that parties who are not represented by counsel attend mediation only if they have waived the right to counsel in open court, and that parties represented by counsel attend mediation without counsel only where the right to have counsel present at the mediation has been specifically waived. Waivers can be rescinded at any time.

(c) Procedures for the selection and referral of a case to mediation at any point after the case is filed.

(d) Procedures for notifying the parties and nonparty participants of the mediation.

(C) **Qualification and Training for Domestic Relations and Juvenile Mediators** Each domestic relations and juvenile division of the court of common pleas that adopts a local rule providing for mediation shall include the following applicable provisions for the qualification and training of mediators.

(1) **General qualifications and training** A mediator employed by the division or to whom the division makes referrals for mediation of allocation of parental rights and responsibilities, the care of, or visitation with, minor children, abuse, neglect, and dependency, or juvenile perpetrated domestic violence cases shall satisfy all of the following:

(a) Possess a bachelor's degree, or equivalent education experience as is satisfactory to the division, and at least two years of professional experience with families. "Professional experience with families"' includes mediation, counseling, casework, legal representation in family law matters, or such other equivalent experience satisfactory to the division.

(b) Complete at least twelve hours of basic mediation training or equivalent experience as a mediator that is satisfactory to the division.

(c) After completing the training required by division (C)(1)(b) of this rule, complete at least forty hours of specialized family or divorce mediation training that is provided by a training program approved by the Dispute Resolution Section in accordance with standards established by the Supreme Court Advisory Committee on Dispute Resolution.

(2) **Specific qualifications and training; domestic abuse** A mediator employed by the division or to whom the division makes referrals for mediation of any case shall complete at least fourteen hours of specialized training in domestic abuse and mediation through a training program approved by the Dispute Resolution Section in accordance with standards established by the Supreme Court Advisory Committee on Dispute Resolution. A mediator who has not completed this specialized training may mediate these cases only if he/she co-mediates with a mediator who has completed the specialized training.

(3) **Specific qualifications and training; abuse, neglect, and dependency cases** In addition to satisfying the requirements of division (C)(1) and (C)(2) of this rule, a mediator employed by the division or to

whom the division makes referrals for mediation of abuse, neglect, or dependency cases shall satisfy both of the following:

(a) Possess significant experience in mediating family disputes;

(b) Complete at least thirty-two hours of specialized child protection mediation training through either a formal training session or through a mentoring program approved by the Dispute Resolution Section in accordance with standards established by the Supreme Court Advisory Committee on Dispute Resolution.

(D) **Aspirational Standards** Each division that adopts a local rule providing for mediation of family cases shall encourage mediators to comply with the Model Standards of Practice for Family and Divorce Mediation as set forth in Appendix F and the Special Policy Considerations for State Regulation of Family Mediators and Court Affiliated Programs as set forth in Appendix G to this rule. Wherever a conflict exists between the Model Standards of Practice for Family and Divorce Mediation set forth in Appendix F and the Special Policy Considerations for State Regulation of Family Mediators and Court Affiliated Programs in Appendix G and this rule, this rule shall control.

History: Amended, eff 11-24-97; eff 1-1-07

RULE 17. Assignment of Judges—Municipal and County Courts

(A) **Definitions** As used in this rule:

(1) "Retired judge" means a person who left service on the applicable court either voluntarily by reason of resignation or retirement or involuntarily by reason of Article IV, Section 6(C) of the Ohio Constitution. "Retired judge" does not include either of the following:

(a) A person who was removed or suspended without reinstatement from service on any court of the state pursuant to the Rules for the Government of the Judiciary or resigned or retired from service on any court of the state while a complaint was pending against the person under those rules;

(b) A person who is engaged in the practice of law.

(2) "Sitting judge" means a person who currently holds judicial office by reason of election or gubernatorial appointment.

(B) **Assignment** The Chief Justice or acting Chief Justice of the Supreme Court may assign any of the following persons who consent to temporarily serve as a judge on any municipal or county court:

(1) A sitting judge of a municipal or county court;

(2) A retired judge of a municipal or county court, provided the judge was not defeated in the judge's final election for new or continued service on a municipal or county court;

(3) A sitting judge of a court of common pleas or court of appeals who formerly served as a judge of a municipal or county court, provided the judge was not defeated in the judge's final election for new or continued service on a municipal or county court;

(4) A retired judge of a court of common pleas or court of appeals who formerly served as a judge of a municipal or county court, provided the judge was not defeated in the judge's final election for new or con-

tinued service on a municipal or county court;

(5) A sitting judge of a court of common pleas who has not formerly served as a judge of a municipal or county court, but has completed an educational program established by the Supreme Court of Ohio Judicial College;

(6) A retired judge of a court of common pleas who has not formerly served as a judge of a municipal or county court, but has completed an educational program established by the Judicial College.

(C) **Compensation**

(1) While serving on assignment pursuant to this rule, a judge shall receive actual and necessary expenses, in addition to compensation for each day assigned, computed as follows:

(a) If the assigned judge is a sitting full-time judge of a municipal court, thirty dollars.

(b) If the assigned judge is a sitting part-time judge of a municipal court or a sitting judge of a county court, the greater of the following:

(i) Thirty dollars;

(ii) The per diem compensation of a full-time judge of a municipal court, less the per diem compensation of the assigned judge, each calculated on the basis of two hundred fifty working days per year.

(c) If the assigned judge is a retired judge of a municipal or county court or a court of common pleas, the established per diem compensation for a full-time judge of a municipal court calculated on the basis of two hundred fifty working days per year, in addition to any retirement benefits to which the assigned judge may be entitled;

(d) If the assigned judge is a sitting judge of the court of appeals or court of common pleas, fifty dollars.

(2) All compensation and expenses payable to an assigned judge under this rule, other than any compensation payable pursuant to division (A)(5) or (6) of section 141.04 of the Revised Code, shall be paid from the municipal treasury or, in the case of a county-operated municipal court or a county court, from the county treasury. Payment by and reimbursement to the county treasury of any per diem compensation payable pursuant to division (A)(5) or (6) of section 141.04 of the Revised Code shall be made in the manner set forth in section 1901.121 of the Revised Code.

(D) **Construction** This rule shall not be construed to limit the operation of section 2701.031 of the Revised Code or the assignment of acting judges pursuant to sections 1901.10 or 1901.12 of the Revised Code.

(E) **Waiver** The Chief Justice may waive compliance with any requirement of this rule to assist the exercise of the Chief Justice's discretion in making temporary assignments of judges pursuant to the Ohio Constitution and the Revised Code.

History: Amended, eff. December 1, 2009.

RULE 18. Minor Misdemeanors: Violations Bureau—Municipal and County Courts

Each municipal and county court shall establish a violations bureau for minor misdemeanors utilizing the citation system and procedure set forth in Criminal Rule 4.1.

RULE 19. Magistrate – Qualifications

(A) **Eligibility** A magistrate shall have been engaged in the practice of law for at least four years and be in good standing with the Supreme Court of Ohio at the time of appointment.

(B) **Qualification; procedure** A magistrate shall have the qualifications specified in division (A) of Sup. R. 19, Civil Rule 53, and Traffic Rule 14. In civil matters, a magistrate shall act pursuant to Civil Rule 53, and in traffic matters pursuant to Traffic Rule 14.

History: Amended, eff. March 1, 2008.

RULE 19.1. Magistrate—Municipal Court

(A) **Mandatory appointment and use** All municipal courts having more than two judges shall appoint one or more magistrates who may hear the following proceedings:

(1) Default proceedings under Civil Rule 55;

(2) Forcible entry and detainer proceedings under Chapter 1923 of the Revised Code in which the right to trial by jury is waived or not demanded;

(3) Small claims proceedings under Chapter 1925 of the Revised Code;

(4) Traffic proceedings in which there is a guilty plea or written waiver by the defendant of the right to trial by a judge;

(5) Other appropriate matters referred by the court for report and recommendation.

(B) **Permissive appointment** This rule does not preclude the appointment of magistrates by courts having two or fewer judges.

RULE 20. Appointment of Counsel for Indigent Defendants in Capital Cases

I. Scope of rules

(A) Rules 20 through 20.05 of the Rules of Superintendence for the Courts of Ohio shall apply in cases where an indigent defendant has been charged with aggravated murder and the indictment includes one or more specifications of aggravating circumstances listed in division (A) of section 2929.04 of the Revised Code. These rules shall apply in cases where a juvenile defendant is indicted for a capital offense, but because of the juvenile's age, cannot be sentenced to death.

(B) The provisions for the appointment of counsel set forth in Sup. R. 20 through 20.05 apply only in cases where the defendant is indigent and counsel is not privately retained by or for the defendant.

(C) If the defendant is entitled to the appointment of counsel, the court shall appoint two attorneys certified pursuant to Sup. R. 20 through 20.05. If the defendant engages one privately retained attorney, the court shall not appoint a second attorney pursuant to this rule.

(D) The provisions of Sup. R. 20 through 20.05 apply in addition to the reporting requirements created by section 2929.021 of the Revised Code.

II. Appointment of counsel for indigent defendants in capital cases

(A) **Trial counsel** At least two attorneys shall be appointed by the court to represent an indigent defendant charged with aggravated murder and the indictment includes one or more specifications of aggravating circumstances listed in R.C. 2929.04(A). At least one of the appointed counsel shall maintain a law office in Ohio and have experience in Ohio criminal trial practice. The counsel appointed shall be designated "lead counsel" and "co-counsel" and must meet the qualifications set forth in Sup. R. 20.01.

(B) **Appellate counsel** At least two attorneys shall be appointed by the court to appeal cases where the trial court has imposed the death penalty on an indigent defendant. At least one of the appointed counsel shall maintain a law office in Ohio. Appointed counsel shall meet the qualifications for appellate counsel set forth in Sup. R. 20.01.

(C) **Exceptional circumstances** If an attorney does not satisfy the requirements of divisions (A) or (B) of this section, the attorney may be certified as lead counsel, co-counsel, or appellate counsel if it can be demonstrated to the satisfaction of the Committee on the Appointment of Counsel for Indigent Defendants in Capital Cases that competent representation will be provided to the defendant. In so determining, the committee may consider all of the factors in Sup. R. 20.01 and any other relevant considerations.

III. **Procedures for court appointments of counsel**

(A) **Appointing counsel** Only counsel who have been certified by the committee shall be appointed to represent indigent defendants charged with aggravated murder and the indictment includes one or more specifications of aggravating circumstances listed in division (A) of section 2929.04 of the Revised Code. Each court may adopt local rules establishing qualifications in addition to and not in conflict with those established by Sup. R. 20.01. Appointments of counsel for these cases should be distributed as widely as possible among the certified attorneys in the jurisdiction of the appointing court.

(B) **Workload of appointed counsel**

(1) In appointing counsel, the court shall consider the nature and volume of the workload of the prospective counsel to ensure that counsel, if appointed, could direct sufficient attention to the defense of the case and provide competent representation to the defendant.

(2) Attorneys accepting appointments shall provide each client with competent representation in accordance with constitutional and professional standards. Appointed counsel shall not accept workloads that, by reason of their excessive size, interfere with the rendering of competent representation or lead to the breach of professional obligations.

(C) **Notice to the committee**

(1) Within two weeks of appointment, the appointing court shall notify the committee secretary of the appointment on a form prescribed by the committee. The notice shall include all of the following:

(a) The court and the judge assigned to the case;

(b) The case name and number;

(c) A copy of the indictment;

(d) The names, business addresses, telephone numbers, and certification of all attorneys appointed;

(e) Any other information considered relevant by the committee or appointing court.

(2) Within two weeks of disposition, the trial court shall notify the committee secretary of the disposition of the case on a form prescribed by the committee. The notice shall include all of the following:

(a) The outcome of the case;

(b) The title and section of the Revised Code of any crimes to which the defendant pleaded or was found guilty;

(c) The date of dismissal, acquittal, or that sentence was imposed;

(d) The sentence, if any;

(e) A copy of the judgment entry reflecting the above;

(f) If the death penalty was imposed, the name of counsel appointed to represent the defendant on appeal;

(g) Any other information considered relevant by the Committee or trial court.

(D) **Support services** The appointing court shall provide appointed counsel, as required by Ohio law or the federal Constitution, federal statutes, and professional standards, with the investigator, mitigation specialists, mental health professional, and other forensic experts and other support services reasonably necessary or appropriate for counsel to prepare for and present an adequate defense at every stage of the proceedings including, but not limited to, determinations relevant to competency to stand trial, a not guilty by reason of insanity plea, cross-examination of expert witnesses called by the prosecution, disposition following conviction, and preparation for and presentation of mitigating evidence in the sentencing phase of the trial. Lead counsel bears overall responsibility for the performance of the defense team and shall allocate, direct, and supervise the work in accordance with Sup. R. 20 through 20.04 and professional standards. In addition, all counsel bear a responsibility to comply with Sup. R. 20 through 20.04 and professional standards.

(E) **Terms; vacancies** The term of office for each member shall be five years, each term beginning on the first day of January. Members shall be eligible for reappointment. Vacancies shall be filled in the same manner as original appointments. Any member appointed to fill a vacancy occurring prior to the expiration of a term shall hold office for the remainder of the term.

(F) **Election of chair** The Committee shall elect a chair and such other officers as are necessary. The officers shall serve for two years and may be reelected to additional terms.

(G) **Powers and duties of the Committee** The Committee shall do all of the following:

(1) Prepare and notify attorneys of procedures for applying for certification to be appointed counsel for indigent defendants in capital cases;

(2) Periodically provide all common pleas and appellate court judges and the Ohio Public Defender with a list of all attorneys who are certified to be appointed counsel for indigent capital defendants;

(3) Periodically review the list of certified counsel, all court appointments given to attorneys in capital cases, and the result and status of those cases;

(4) Develop criteria and procedures for retention of certification including, but not limited to, mandatory continuing legal education on the defense and appeal of capital cases;

(5) Expand, reduce, or otherwise modify the list of certified attorneys as appropriate and necessary in accord with division (G)(4) of this section;

(6) Review and approve specialized training programs on subjects that will assist counsel in the defense and appeal of capital cases;

(7) Recommend to the Supreme Court of Ohio amendments to this rule or any other rule or statute relative to the defense or appeal of capital cases.

(H) **Meetings** The Committee shall meet at the call of the chair, at the request of a majority of the members, or at the request of the Supreme Court of Ohio. A quorum consists of three members. A majority of the Committee is necessary for the Committee to elect a chair and take any other action.

(I) **Compensation** All members of the Committee shall receive equal compensation in an amount to be established by the Supreme Court of Ohio.

IV. Procedures for court appointments of counsel

(A) **Appointing counsel** Only counsel who have been certified by the Committee shall be appointed to represent indigent defendants charged with aggravated murder and the indictment includes one or more specifications of aggravating circumstances listed in R.C. 2929.04(A). Each court may adopt local rules establishing qualifications in addition to and not in conflict with those established by this rule. Appointments of counsel for these cases should be distributed as widely as possible among the certified attorneys in the jurisdiction of the appointing court.

(B) **Workload of appointed counsel**

(1) In appointing counsel, the court shall consider the nature and volume of the workload of the prospective counsel to ensure that counsel, if appointed, could direct sufficient attention to the defense of the case and provide competent representation to the defendant.

(2) Attorneys accepting appointments shall provide each client with competent representation in accordance with constitutional and professional standards. Appointed counsel shall not accept workloads that, by reason of their excessive size, interfere with the rendering of competent representation or lead to the breach of professional obligations.

(C) **Notice to the Committee**

(1) Within two weeks of appointment, the appointing court shall notify the Committee secretary of the appointment on a form prescribed by the Committee. The notice shall include all of the following:

(a) The court and the judge assigned to the case;

(b) The case name and number;

(c) A copy of the indictment;

(d) The names, business addresses, telephone numbers, and Sup. R. 20 certification of all attorneys appointed;

(e) Any other information considered relevant by the Committee or appointing court.

(2) Within two weeks of disposition, the trial court shall notify the Committee secretary of the disposition of the case on a form prescribed by the Committee.

The notice shall include all of the following:

(a) The outcome of the case;

(b) The title and section of the Revised Code of any crimes to which the defendant pleaded or was found guilty;

(c) The date of dismissal, acquittal, or that sentence was imposed;

(d) The sentence, if any;

(e) A copy of the judgment entry reflecting the above;

(f) If the death penalty was imposed, the name of counsel appointed to represent the defendant on appeal.

(g) Any other information considered relevant by the Committee or trial court.

(D) **Support services** The appointing court shall provide appointed counsel, as required by Ohio law or the federal Constitution, federal statutes, and professional standards, with the investigator, mitigation specialists, mental health professional, and other forensic experts and other support services reasonably necessary or appropriate for counsel to prepare for and present an adequate defense at every stage of the proceedings including, but not limited to, determinations relevant to competency to stand trial, a not guilty by reason of insanity plea, cross-examination of expert witnesses called by the prosecution, disposition following conviction, and preparation for and presentation of mitigating evidence in the sentencing phase of the trial.

History: Amended, eff. 1-6-03; 3-7-05; 3-1-10.

RULE 20.01. Qualifications Required for Appointment as Counsel for Indigent Defendants in Capital Cases

(A) **Generally** Every attorney representing a capital defendant shall have all of the following:

(1) Demonstrated commitment to providing high quality legal representation in the defense of capital cases;

(2) Substantial knowledge and understanding of the relevant state, federal, and international law, both procedural and substantive, governing capital cases;

(3) Skill in the management and conduct of complex negotiations and litigation;

(4) Skill in legal research, analysis, and the drafting of litigation documents;

(5) Skill in oral advocacy;

(6) Skill in the use of expert witnesses and familiarity with common areas of forensic investigation, including fingerprints, ballistics, arson, forensic pathology, and DNA evidence;

(7) Skill in the investigation, preparation, and presentation of evidence bearing upon mental status;

(8) Skill in the investigation, preparation, and presentation of mitigating evidence;

(9) Skill in the elements of trial advocacy, such as jury selection, cross-examination of witnesses, and opening and closing statements.

(B) **Lead counsel** Lead counsel shall satisfy all of the following:

(1) Be admitted to the practice of law in Ohio or admitted to practice *pro hac vice*;

(2) Have at least five years of civil or criminal

litigation or appellate experience;

(3) Have specialized training, as approved by the committee, on subjects that will assist counsel in the defense of persons accused of capital crimes in the two-year period prior to making application;

(4) Have at least one of the following qualifications:

(a) Experience as "lead counsel" for the defense in the jury trial of at least one capital case;

(b) Experience as "co-counsel" for the defense in the jury trial of at least two capital cases.

(5) Have at least one of the following qualifications:

(a) Experience as "lead counsel" in the jury trial of at least one murder or aggravated murder case;

(b) Experience as "lead counsel" in ten or more criminal or civil jury trials, at least three of which were felony jury trials;

(c) Experience as "lead counsel" in three murder or aggravated murder jury trials; one murder or aggravated murder jury trial and three felony jury trials; or three aggravated or first- or second-degree felony jury trials in a court of common pleas in the three years prior to making application.

(C) **Co-counsel** Co-counsel shall satisfy all of the following:

(1) Be admitted to the practice of law in Ohio or admitted to practice *pro hac vice*;

(2) Have at least three years of civil or criminal litigation or appellate experience;

(3) Have specialized training, as approved by the committee, on subjects that will assist counsel in the defense of persons accused of capital crimes in the two years prior to making application;

(4) Have at least one of the following qualifications:

(a) Experience as "co-counsel" in one murder or aggravated murder jury trial;

(b) Experience as "lead counsel" in one first-degree felony jury trial;

(c) Experience as "lead" or "co-counsel" in at least two felony jury or civil jury trials in a court of common pleas in the three years prior to making application.

(D) **Appellate counsel** Appellate counsel shall satisfy all of the following qualifications:

(1) Be admitted to the practice of law in Ohio or admitted to practice *pro hac vice*;

(2) Have at least three years of civil or criminal litigation or appellate experience in Ohio;

(3) Have specialized training, as approved by the committee, on subjects that will assist counsel in the appeal of cases in which the death penalty was imposed in the two years prior to making application;

(4) Have experience as counsel in the appeal of at least three felony convictions in the three years prior to making application.

(E) **Definition** As used in this rule, "trial" means a case concluded with a judgment of acquittal under Rule 29 of the Ohio Rules of Criminal Procedure or submission to the trial court or jury for decision and verdict.

History: Eff. 3-1-10.

RULE 20.02. Committee on the Appointment of Counsel for Indigent Defendants in Capital Cases

(A) **Committee creation** There shall be a Committee on the Appointment of Counsel for Indigent Defendants in Capital Cases.

(B) **Appointment of committee members** The committee shall be composed of five attorneys. Three members shall be appointed by a majority vote of all members of the Supreme Court of Ohio; one shall be appointed by the Ohio State Bar Association; and one shall be appointed by the Ohio Public Defender Commission.

(C) **Eligibility for appointment to the committee** Each member of the committee shall satisfy all of the following qualifications:

(1) Be admitted to the practice of law in Ohio;

(2) Have represented criminal defendants for not less than five years;

(3) Demonstrate a knowledge of the law and practice of capital cases;

(4) Currently not serving as a prosecuting attorney, city director of law, village solicitor, or similar officer or their assistant or employee, or an employee of any court.

(D) **Overall composition** The overall composition of the committee shall meet both of the following criteria:

(1) No more than two members shall reside in the same county;

(2) No more than one shall be a judge.

(E) **Terms; vacancies** The term of office for each member shall be five years, each term beginning on the first day of January. Members shall be eligible for reappointment. Vacancies shall be filled in the same manner as original appointments. Any member appointed to fill a vacancy occurring prior to the expiration of a term shall hold office for the remainder of the term.

(F) **Election of chairperson** The committee shall elect a chairperson and such other officers as are necessary. The officers shall serve for two years and may be reelected to additional terms.

(G) **Powers and duties of the committee** The committee shall do all of the following:

(1) Prepare and notify attorneys of procedures for applying for certification to be appointed counsel for indigent defendants in capital cases;

(2) Certify attorneys as qualified to be appointed to represent defendants in capital cases;

(3) Periodically provide all common pleas and appellate court judges and the Ohio Public Defender with a list of all attorneys who are certified to be appointed counsel for indigent capital defendants;

(4) Periodically review the list of certified counsel, all court appointments given to attorneys in capital cases, and the result and status of those cases;

(5) Develop criteria and procedures for retention of certification including, but not limited to, mandatory continuing legal education on the defense and appeal of capital cases;

(6) Monitor the performance of attorneys providing representation in capital proceedings;

(7) Investigate and maintain records concerning complaints about the performance of attorneys providing representation in capital cases and take appropriate corrective action pursuant to Rule 20.03 of the Rules of Superintendence;

(8) Expand, reduce, or otherwise modify the list of certified attorneys as appropriate and necessary;

(9) Review and approve specialized training programs on subjects that will assist counsel in the defense and appeal of capital cases;

(10) Recommend to the Supreme Court of Ohio amendments to this rule or any other rule or statute relative to the defense or appeal of capital cases;

(11) Adopt best practices for representation of indigent defendants in capital cases and disseminate those best practices appropriately.

(H) **Meetings** The committee shall meet at the call of the chairperson, at the request of a majority of the members, or at the request of the Supreme Court of Ohio. A quorum consists of three members. A majority of the committee is necessary for the committee to elect a chairperson and take any other action.

(I) **Compensation** All members of the committee shall receive equal compensation in an amount to be established by the Supreme Court of Ohio.

History: Eff. 3-1-10.

RULE 20.03. Monitoring of Counsel; Removal

(A) **Duty of court** The appointing court shall monitor the performance of all defense counsel to ensure that the client is receiving representation that is consistent with the American Bar Association's "Guidelines for the Appointment and Performance of Defense Counsel in Death Penalty Cases" and referred to herein as "high quality representation." The court, in addition to any other action it may take, shall report an attorney to the Committee on the Appointment of Counsel for Indigent Defendants in Capital Cases who has not provided high quality representation. Where there is a complaint from a judge that an attorney has not provided high quality representation, the committee shall investigate the complaint. The committee will not start an investigation while counsel is still appointed in the matter.

(B) **Investigation of complaint** The chairperson shall appoint a member of the committee or appoint an attorney qualified as lead counsel under this rule, who will investigate complaints made by a judge that defense counsel appointed pursuant to this rule failed to provide high quality representation under this rule.

(1) As part of the investigation of a complaint from a judge, the attorney shall be notified and given an opportunity to respond.

(2) After an investigation and after the attorney has been given an opportunity to respond to the factual allegations, the members of the committee, excluding the investigator and chairperson, will meet and vote whether a violation of rules 20 through 20.05 has occurred and whether the violation requires removal

from the list of qualified attorneys.

Before taking action making an attorney ineligible to receive additional appointments, the committee shall provide written notice that such action is being contemplated, and give the attorney an opportunity to respond. If there is no apparent merit to the allegation the complainant will be advised and the matter will be closed.

(3) If an attorney is deemed ineligible to remain on the list of attorneys qualified to accept appointments, the attorney may appeal the decision of the committee to the chairperson. Upon appeal, the chairperson will review all applicable allegations, findings, and responses and determine whether a violation has occurred and whether appropriate action was taken and issue a decision. The decision of the chairperson is final.

(C) **Revocation** An attorney whose certification has been revoked pursuant to this rule shall be restored to the roster only in exceptional circumstances. The findings made by the committee are not related to or part of the grievance process governing all attorneys in Ohio and the findings made by the committee are only for the purpose of determining continued eligibility for appointment.

History: Eff. 3-1-10.

RULE 20.04. Programs for Specialized Training

(A) **Programs for specialized training in the defense of persons charged with a capital offense**

(1) Attorneys seeking to qualify to receive appointments shall be required to satisfactorily complete a comprehensive training program, approved by the Committee on the Appointment of Counsel for Indigent Defendants in Capital Cases, in the defense of capital cases. To be approved a program should include, but not be limited to, presentations and training in the following areas:

(a) Relevant state, federal, and international law;

(b) Pleading and motion practice;

(c) Pretrial investigation, preparation, and theory development regarding trial and sentencing;

(d) Jury selection;

(e) Trial preparation and presentation, including the use of experts;

(f) Ethical considerations particular to capital defense representation;

(g) Preservation of the record and of issues for post-conviction review;

(h) Counsel's relationship with the client and his family;

(i) Post-conviction litigation in state and federal courts;

(j) The presentation and rebuttal of scientific evidence, and developments in mental health fields and other relevant areas of forensic and biological science;

(k) The unique issues relating to the defense of those charged with committing capital offenses when under the age of eighteen;

(l) The best practices for representing an indigent capital defendant adopted by the committee pursuant to division (G)(11) of Rule 20.02 of the Rules of

Superintendence for the Courts of Ohio;

(m) Death penalty appellate and post-conviction litigation in state and federal courts.

(B) **Programs for specialized training in the appeal of cases in which the death penalty has been imposed**

(1) To be approved by the committee, a death penalty appeals seminar shall include instruction devoted to the appeal of a case in which the death penalty has been imposed.

(2) The curriculum for an approved death penalty appeal seminar should include, but is not limited to, specialized training in the following areas:

(a) An overview of current developments in death penalty law;

(b) Completion, correction, and supplementation of the record on appeal;

(c) Reviewing the record for unique death penalty issues;

(d) Motion practice for death penalty appeals;

(e) Preservation and presentation of constitutional issues;

(f) Preparing and presenting oral argument;

(g) Unique aspects of death penalty practice in the courts of appeals, the Supreme Court of Ohio, and the United States Supreme Court;

(h) The relationship of counsel with the appellant and the appellant's family during the course of the appeals;

(i) Procedure and practice in collateral litigation, extraordinary remedies, state post-conviction litigation, and federal habeas corpus litigation;

(j) The best practices for representing an indigent capital defendant adopted by the committee pursuant to Sup. R. 20.02(G)(11).

(C) **Application for training approval** The sponsor of a program for specialized training under division (A) or (B) of this rule shall apply for approval from the committee at least sixty days before the date of the proposed seminar. An application for approval shall include the curriculum for the seminar and include biographical information of each member of the seminar faculty.

(D) **Verification of attendance** The committee shall obtain a list of attendees from the Supreme Court Commission on Continuing Legal Education that shall be used to verify attendance and grant credit for each committee-approved seminar. Credit for purposes of this rule shall be granted to instructors using the same ratio provided in Rule X of the Supreme Court Rules for the Government of the Bar of Ohio.

(E) **Accreditation of other programs** The committee may accredit programs other than those approved pursuant to divisions (A) and (B) of this rule. To receive accreditation, the program shall include instructions in all areas set forth in divisions (A) and (B) of this rule. Application for accreditation of an in-state program may be made by the program sponsor or a program attendee and shall be made prior to the program. Application for accreditation of an out-of-state program may be submitted by the program sponsor or a program attendee and may be made prior to or after completion of the program. The request for credit from a program sponsor shall include the program curriculum and individual faculty biographical information. The request for credit from a program attendee shall include all of the following:

(1) Program curriculum;

(2) Individual faculty biographical information;

(3) A written breakdown of sessions attended and credit hours received if the seminar held concurrent sessions;

(4) Proof of attendance.

(F) **Specialized Training for Sup. R. 20 certification**

(1) To be certified as lead or co-counsel or to retain certification, an attorney shall complete at least twelve hours of committee-approved specialized training every two years. To maintain certification as lead counsel or co-counsel, the twelve hours shall be devoted to instruction in the trial of capital cases.

(2) To be certified as appellate counsel or to retain certification as appellate counsel, an attorney shall complete at least twelve hours of committee-approved training every two years. At least six of the twelve hours shall be devoted to instruction in the appeal of capital cases.

(3) On or before the last day of December, each certified counsel shall complete the applicable specialized training requirements of divisions (A) and (B) of this rule. The committee shall review the list of certified counsel for the prior two years and revoke the certification of any attorney who has not complied with the specialized training requirements of this rule. An attorney whose certification has been revoked shall not be eligible to accept future appointment as counsel for an indigent defendant charged with or convicted of an offense for which the death penalty can be or has been imposed.

(4) The committee may accredit an out-of-state program that provides specialized instruction devoted to the investigation, preparation, and presentation of a death penalty trial or specialized instruction devoted to the appeal of a case in which the defendant received the death penalty, or both. Requests for credit for an out-of-state program may be submitted by the seminar sponsor or a seminar attendee. The request for credit from a program sponsor shall include the program curriculum and individual faculty biographical information. The request for credit from a program attendee shall include all of the following:

(a) Program curriculum;

(b) Individual faculty biographical information;

(c) A written breakdown of sessions attended and credit hours received if the seminar held concurrent sessions;

(d) Proof of attendance.

(5) An attorney who has previously been certified but whose certification has been revoked for failure to comply with the specialized training requirements of this rule must, in order to regain certification, submit a new application that demonstrates that the attorney has completed twelve hours of committee approved specialized training in the two year period prior to making application for recertification.

History: Eff. 3-1-10.

RULE 20.05. Effective dates

(A) The effective date of this rule shall be October 1, 1987.

(B) The amendments to Section II(A)(5)(b), Section III(B)(2), and to the Subcommittee Comments following Section II of this Rule adopted by the Supreme Court of Ohio on June 28, 1989, shall be effective on July 1, 1989.

(C) The amendments to Sections I(A)(2), I(A)(3), I(B), and II, and the addition of Sections I(C) and IV, adopted by the Supreme Court of Ohio on December 11, 1990, shall be effective on January 1, 1991.

(D) The amendments to this rule adopted by the Supreme Court of Ohio on April 19, 1995, shall take effect on July 1, 1995.

(E) The amendment to Sup. R. 20 adopted by the Supreme Court on December 4, 2002, shall take effect on January 6, 2003.

(F) The amendment to Sup. R. 20 adopted by the Supreme Court on February 1, 2005, shall take effect on March 7, 2005.

(G) On January 12, 2010, former Rule 20 and Rule 21 of the Rules of Superintendence for the Courts of Ohio was repealed by the Supreme Court and Rules 20 through 20.05 were adopted. Rules 20 through 20.05 are effective March 1, 2010.

History: Eff. 3-1-10.

RULE 21. Repealed

RULE 22. Verification of Indigency

Where required by law to appoint counsel to represent indigent defendants in cases for which the county will apply to the Ohio Public Defender Commission for reimbursement of costs, the court shall require the applicant to complete the financial disclosure form. The court shall follow rules promulgated by the Commission pursuant to division (B)(1) of section 120.03 of the Revised Code as guidelines to determine indigency and standards of indigency.

RULE 23. Juvenile Court Procedures — Complaint for Abortion Without Parental Notification

(A) **Complaint — sealing identifying information** All actions pursuant to section 2151.85 of the Revised Code shall be commenced by filing a complaint on Form 23-A issued by the clerk of the Supreme Court of Ohio. A certified copy of the second page, with the case number noted on it, shall be given to the complainant after she signs it. The original second page shall be removed from the file jacket and filed under seal in a safe or other secure place where access is limited to essential court personnel. All index records shall be under, "In the Matter of Jane Doe."

Minors seeking to file an action under section 2151.85 of the Revised Code shall be given prompt assistance by the clerk in a private, confidential setting. Assistance shall include performing the notary services necessary to file the complaint and affidavits described in Sup. R. 23 and 24.

The complaint shall be filed promptly upon the request of the minor. The complaint and other forms described in these rules shall be provided without cost to the minor. No filing fees or court costs shall be imposed on the minor in connection with these proceedings or any notice of appeal filed in connection with these proceedings.

(B) **Appointment of counsel** Upon the filing of the complaint, the court shall appoint an attorney to represent the complainant if she is not represented by an attorney. Court-appointed attorneys shall be paid by the court without expense to the complainant.

(C) **Appointment of guardian ad litem** Upon the filing of the complaint the court shall also appoint a guardian ad litem. The court may appoint the same individual to serve as both the attorney and the guardian ad litem. If the court appoints an individual who volunteers to serve as a guardian for the complainant, that individual need not be paid. Other guardians shall be paid by the court without expense to the complainant.

(D) **Hearing** A hearing shall be conducted promptly after the filing of the complaint, if possible within twenty-four hours. In no event shall the hearing be held later than five business days after the filing of the complaint. The court shall accommodate school hours if at all possible. The hearing shall be conducted by a judge and shall not be heard by a magistrate. Hearings must be closed to the public and exclude all persons except witnesses on behalf of the complainant, her attorney, her guardian ad litem, and essential court personnel. The hearing shall be conducted in a manner that will preserve the anonymity of the complainant. The complainant's name shall not appear on the record.

If both maturity and either abuse or best interest are alleged in the complaint, or if maturity, abuse, and best interest are alleged in the complaint, the court shall rule on the issue of maturity first. If the court finds against the complainant on the issue of maturity, it then shall determine the other issues alleged in the complaint.

(E) **Judgment** The court shall enter judgment immediately after the conclusion of the hearing and a copy of the judgment shall be immediately provided to the complainant. If the court finds by clear and convincing evidence either that the complainant is sufficiently mature and well enough informed to decide intelligently; or that there is evidence of a pattern of physical, sexual, or emotional abuse by one or both of her parents, guardian, or custodian; or that notification is not in the best interest of the complainant, the court shall issue an order on Form 23-B authorizing the complainant to consent to the performance of an abortion without notice to a parent, guardian, or custodian.

If the court determines that the complainant has not established the allegations of the complaint by clear and convincing evidence, the court shall dismiss the complaint and notify the complainant that she has a right to appeal under section 2505.073 of the Revised Code. In that event the complainant shall be provided with a copy of the notice of appeal, Form 23-C.

(F) **Appeals**

(1) Immediately after the notice of appeal has been filed by the complainant, the clerk of the juvenile court shall notify the court of appeals. Within four days after the notice of appeal is filed in the juvenile court, the clerk of the juvenile court shall deliver a copy of the notice of appeal and the record, except page two of the complaint, to the clerk of the court of appeals who immediately shall place the appeal on the docket of the court of appeals.

(2) The juvenile court shall prepare a written transcript if possible. However, if a transcript cannot be prepared timely and if the testimony is on audio tape, the tape may be forwarded as part of the record in the case to the court of appeals without prior transcription and the court of appeals shall accept the audio tape as the transcript in the case without prior transcription. The juvenile court shall ensure that the court of appeals has the necessary equipment to listen to the audio tape.

(G) **General rule of expedition** If a complainant files her notice of appeal on the same day as the dismissal of her complaint, the entire court process, including the juvenile court hearing, appeal, and decision, shall be completed in sixteen calendar days from the time the complaint was filed.

(H) **Confidentiality** The court shall not notify the parents, guardian, or custodian of the complainant that she is pregnant, that she wants to have an abortion, or that the complaint was filed. All court papers and records that pertain to the action shall be kept confidential and are not public records under section 149.43 of the Revised Code.

(I) **Verification notice** Upon request of the complainant or her attorney, the clerk shall verify on Form 28-D the date the complaint was filed and whether a hearing has been held within five business days after the filing of the complaint. The form shall be filed and included as part of the record and a date-stamped copy shall be provided to the complainant or her attorney.

**Form 23-A. Complaint for an Order Authorizing
Consent to an Abortion Without Notification of a
Parent, Guardian, or Custodian**

FORM 23-A. COMPLAINT FOR AN ORDER AUTHORIZING
CONSENT TO AN ABORTION WITHOUT NOTIFICATION
OF A PARENT, GUARDIAN, OR CUSTODIAN

JUVENILE COURT

_____COUNTY, OHIO

In re complaint of Jane Doe   Case No. _____

COMPLAINT

Promulgated by the Clerk of the Supreme Court
of Ohio pursuant to R.C. 2151.85(G)

I swear or affirm that:

1. I am pregnant.

2. I am unmarried, under 18 years of age, and unemancipated.

3. I wish to have an abortion without notification of my parent, guardian, or custodian.

4. This complaint is being filed in the juvenile court of the county where I reside or have a legal settlement, in a county bordering the county where I reside or have a legal settlement, or in the county where the abortion will be performed.

[CHECK <u>ONE OR MORE</u> OF THE FOLLOWING STATEMENTS.]

5. ___ I am sufficiently mature and well enough informed to intelligently decide whether to have an abortion without the notification of my parent, guardian, or custodian.

    ___ One or both of my parents, my guardian, or my custodian has engaged in a pattern of physical, sexual, or emotional abuse against me.

    ___ Notification of my parent, guardian, or custodian of my desire to have an abortion is not in my best interest.

[CHECK <u>ONE</u> OF THE FOLLOWING STATEMENTS.]

6. ___ I do not have a lawyer.

    ___ I have a lawyer. The name, address, and telephone number of my lawyer are:

    Lawyer's Name: _____
    Lawyer's Address: _____
                          _____
    Lawyer's Phone No: _____

    THEREFORE, I request that this Court issue an order authorizing me to consent to an abortion without the notification of my parent, guardian, or custodian.

Page 2 of the complaint.   Case no. _____
THIS PAGE OF THE ORIGINAL MUST BE REMOVED
AND PLACED UNDER SEAL IN A SAFE OR OTHER
SECURE PLACE AS REQUIRED BY RULE 23(A) OF THE
RULES OF SUPERINTENDENCE FOR OHIO COURTS.

    I swear or affirm that the information in the attached complaint is true and accurate to the best of my knowledge and belief.

_____
Signature

Sworn to or affirmed in my presence this _____ day of _____, 19__.

_____
Notary Public

* *

PLEASE NOTE:

    If you do <u>not</u> have a lawyer, please provide in the spaces below any address and phone number where the Court may contact you until a lawyer is appointed to represent you. You do <u>not</u> need to use your home address and phone number.

_____
Address

_____

_____
Phone

Form 23-A
Revised 11/92

COMPLAINT FOR AN ORDER AUTHORIZING CONSENT TO
AN ABORTION WITHOUT NOTIFICATION OF A PARENT,
GUARDIAN, OR CUSTODIAN

INSTRUCTIONS

If you are pregnant, unmarried, under eighteen years old and unemancipated, and want to have an abortion without telling your parent, guardian, or custodian, you may ask a court for permission. The court will then decide whether your parent, guardian, or custodian must be told before you may have an abortion. The attached form, called a complaint, should be used to ask a court to let you have an abortion without telling your parent, guardian, or custodian.

If you are under 18 and not married, you are "unemancipated" if:

1.   You have not entered the armed services of the United States or

2.   You do not have a job and support yourself or

3.   You are under the care and control of your parent, guardian, or custodian.

By law, you do not have to pay a filing fee or any court costs. If you do not have a lawyer, the court will appoint one for you free of charge.

The court is not allowed to tell your parent, guardian, or custodian that you are pregnant or that you want to have an abortion. The court must keep the complaint and all other papers in your case confidential.

The complaint must be filed in a juvenile court in the county where the abortion would be performed, in the county where you reside or have a legal settlement, or in any county that borders the county where you reside or have a legal settlement.

HOW TO FILL OUT THE FORM

Completing Statement #5: Check one or more of the statements. If you check the first statement, the court will first consider if you are mature enough and well enough informed to intelligently decide whether to have an abortion without telling your parent, guardian, or custodian. If the court does not find that you are sufficiently mature and well enough informed to make the decision, and you have checked either or both of the remaining statements, the court will then consider:

--   whether there is a pattern of physical, sexual, or emotional abuse of you by your parent, guardian, or custodian, or,

--   whether telling your parent, guardian, or custodian is not in your best interest.

Completing Statement #6: Check the statement that applies to you. If you have a lawyer, fill in the name, address and telephone number of your lawyer.

Completing the Top of Page 2: The law requires that the statements in the complaint be made under oath. This part of the form must be completed in the presence of a person who is allowed to administer oaths, such as a notary public, a lawyer, or a judge. After you sign your name on the signature line, that person should notarize the form.

Completing the Bottom of Page 2: Fill out the bottom of Page 2 only if you do not have a lawyer. Provide any address and phone number where you may be contacted about this matter. When the court appoints a lawyer for you, the lawyer will reach you at the address or phone number you provide. You do not have to complete the bottom of Page 2 until after the notary public signs the top of Page 2.

[Revised 11/92]

Form 23-B. Judgment

FORM 23-B. JUDGMENT

JUVENILE COURT
_____COUNTY, OHIO

In re complaint of Jane Doe   Case No._____

JUDGMENT

    This matter came on for hearing on the _____ day of_____, 19___. Based upon the testimony and evidence presented, this court finds:

1.   The complainant is an unemancipated minor.

2.   The complainant is pregnant and she wishes to obtain an abortion.

3.   No parent, legal guardian, or custodian of the complainant has been notified that she is seeking an abortion.

4.   That clear and convincing evidence has been presented to support the following: [decide maturity issue first if pleaded]

    ____ Complainant is sufficiently mature and well enough informed to decide intelligently whether to have an abortion without notifying a parent, guardian, or custodian.

    ____ There is evidence of a pattern of physical, sexual, or emotional abuse of the complainant by one or both of her parents, her guardian, or her custodian.

    ____ Notification of a parent, guardian, or custodian would not be in complainant's best interest.

    ____ None of the criteria set forth in paragraph 4 has been established by clear and convincing evidence.

THEREFORE, IT IS ORDERED:

    ____ The complaint is granted and the complainant is hereby authorized to consent to the performance or inducement of an abortion without the notification of a parent, guardian, or custodian.

    ____ The complaint is dismissed. The Clerk is instructed to provide the complainant with the notice of appeal form and advise her of her right to an expedited appeal.

_____, OH   _____

                                         Judge

_____, 19__

[Effective: October 5, 1990; amended effective January 1, 1992.]

Form 23-C. Notice of Appeal

JUVENILE COURT
_____COUNTY, OHIO

In re complaint of Jane Doe   Case No._____

NOTICE OF APPEAL

Promulgated by the Clerk of the Supreme
Court of Ohio pursuant to R.C. 2151.85(G)

Notice is hereby given that the complainant appeals to the Court of Appeals for _____ County from
the final order entered in the above-styled cause on_____, 19__, dismissing the complaint seeking
an abortion without notification of complainant's parents, guardian or custodian.

_____
Signature of Attorney for Complainant

_____
Attorney Name

_____
Attorney Address

_____
Attorney Phone

[Effective: October 5, 1990.]

Form 23-D. Verification

FORM 23-D. VERIFICATION

JUVENILE COURT
_____COUNTY, OHIO

In re complaint of Jane Doe   Case No._____

VERIFICATION

      This will verify that on_____, 19__, Jane Doe filed her complaint for an order authorizing consent to an abortion without notification of a parent, guardian or custodian and as of_____, 19__, which is more than five business days after the filing of the complaint, the court has not held a hearing to consider her complaint.

                                             _____
                                           Clerk

(Seal)

[Effective: October 5, 1990.]

NOTES TO DECISIONS

ANALYSIS

Dismissal of complaint

_____

Trial court did not abuse its discretion in concluding that the minor was not sufficiently mature to consent to an abortion because this was the minor's third pregnancy, indicating that she was in need of parental guidance, and her school record indicated a lack of maturity in that she had to repeat a grade and was suspended for fighting. The trial court also did not err in refusing to conclude that it was in the minor's best interest to grant the petition because, although the evidence indicated that the minor believed that her mother would be angry if she was told that her daughter was pregnant again, the minor conceded that her mother would be supportive in resolving the situation. In re Doe, — Ohio App. 3d —, 2007 Ohio 3495, — N.E. 2d —, 2007 Ohio App. LEXIS 3212 (June 13, 2007).

RULE 23.1. Juvenile Court Procedures — Application for Authorization to Consent to an Abortion or for Judicial Consent to an Abortion (R.C. 2919.121)

(A) **Petition; filing; sealing identifying information**

(1) All actions pursuant to section 2919.121 of the Revised Code shall be commenced by filing a petition on Form 23.1-A issued by the clerk of the Supreme Court of Ohio. A certified copy of the second page, with the case number noted on it, shall be given to the petitioner after the petitioner or next friend signs it. The original second page shall be removed from the file jacket and filed under seal in a safe or other secure place where access is limited to essential court personnel. All index records shall be filed under, "In re the Petition of Jane Doe."

(2) Minors seeking to file an action under section 2919.121 of the Revised Code shall be given prompt assistance by the clerk in a private, confidential setting. Assistance shall include performing the notary services necessary to file the petition and affidavits described in this rule.

(3) The petition shall be filed promptly upon the request of the petitioner. The petition and other forms described in these rules shall be provided without cost to the petitioner. No filing fees or court costs shall be imposed on the petitioner in connection with these proceedings or any notice of appeal filed in connection with these proceedings.

(B) **Appointment of counsel** Upon the filing of the petition and at least twenty-four hours before hearing scheduled pursuant to division (D) of this rule, the court shall appoint an attorney to represent the petitioner if she is not represented by an attorney. Court-appointed attorneys shall be paid by the court without expense to the petitioner.

(C) **Appointment of guardian ad litem** Upon the filing of the petition, the court shall appoint a guardian ad litem pursuant to Rule 4 of the Ohio Rules of Juvenile Procedure.

(D) **Hearing**

(1) A hearing shall be conducted promptly after the filing of the petition, if possible within twenty-four hours. In no event shall the hearing be held later than five calendar days after the filing of the petition. The court shall accommodate school hours if at all possible. The hearing shall be conducted by a judge and shall not be heard by a magistrate. Hearings shall be closed to the public and exclude all persons except witnesses on behalf of the petitioner, her attorney, her guardian ad litem, her next friend, if any, and essential court personnel. The hearing shall be conducted in a manner that will preserve the anonymity of the petitioner. The petitioner's name shall not appear on the record.

(2) If maturity and best interest are alleged in the petition, the court shall rule on the issue of maturity first. If the court finds against the petitioner on the issue of maturity, it then shall determine the issue of best interest.

(E) **Judgment**

(1) If the court finds that the petitioner is sufficiently mature and well enough informed to decide intelligently whether to consent to an abortion or that the abortion is in the best interests of the petitioner, the court shall issue an order on Form 23.1-B authorizing the petitioner to consent to the performance of an abortion or giving judicial consent to the abortion. If the court does not find that the petitioner is sufficiently mature and well enough informed to decide intelligently or that the abortion is in the best interests of the petitioner, or if the court finds that it does not have jurisdiction over the petition, the court shall issue an order on Form 23.1-B denying or dismissing the petition. The court shall enter judgment as soon as possible and no later than twenty-four hours after the conclusion of the hearing.

(2) If the judgment is entered immediately at the conclusion of the hearing, the court shall provide the petitioner and her attorney with a copy of the judgment. If the court denies or dismisses the petition, the court shall notify the petitioner that she has a right to appeal under division (C)(6) of section 2919.121 of the Revised Code and provide the petitioner and her attorney with a copy of the notice of appeal, Form 23.1-C.

(3) If the judgment is not entered immediately at the conclusion of the hearing, the court shall do all of the following:

(a) Inform the petitioner that the judgment will be entered within twenty-four hours;

(b) Inform the petitioner that the court will notify her attorney of the judgment upon its issuance;

(c) Inform the petitioner of the availability of other confidential procedures, which have been established by the court, to notify the petitioner of the court's judgment, including, but not limited to, providing the petitioner with the name of a designated court employee whom the petitioner may contact to obtain the judgment, arranging for the pick-up of the judgment at the court, or arranging for delivery of the judgment to an address designated by the petitioner;

(d) Notify the petitioner that, if the court denies or dismisses the petition, she has the right to appeal under division (D)(6) of section 2919.121 of the Revised Code;

(e) Provide the petitioner and her attorney with a copy of the notice of appeal, Form 23.1-C, and explain to the petitioner that the form may be filed only if the court denies or dismisses the petition.

(F) Appeals

(1) Immediately after the notice of appeal has been filed by the petitioner, the clerk of the juvenile court shall notify the court of appeals. Within four calendar days after the notice of appeal is filed in the juvenile court, the clerk of the juvenile court shall deliver a copy of the notice of appeal and the record, except page two of the petition, to the clerk of the court of appeals who immediately shall place the appeal on the docket of the court of appeals.

(2) The juvenile court shall prepare a written transcript if possible. If a transcript cannot be prepared timely and if the testimony is on audio tape, the tape may be forwarded as part of the record in the case to the court of appeals without prior transcription, and the court of appeals shall accept the audio tape as the transcript in the case without prior transcription. The juvenile court shall ensure that the court of appeals has the necessary equipment to listen to the audio tape.

(G) General rule of expedition

(1) If a petitioner files a notice of appeal on the same day as the denial or dismissal of her petition, the entire court process, including the juvenile court hearing, appeal, and decision, shall be completed in sixteen calendar days from the time the petition was filed.

(2) If a petitioner files a notice of appeal after the day on which the court denies or dismisses her petition, the entire court process, including the juvenile court hearing, appeal, and decision, shall be completed in sixteen calendar days from the time the petition was filed, plus the number of calendar days that elapsed between the date on which the court's decision was issued and the date on which the notice of appeal was filed.

(H) Confidentiality The court shall not notify the parents, guardian, or custodian of the petitioner that she is pregnant, that she wants to have an abortion, or that the petition was filed. All court papers and records that pertain to the action shall be kept confidential and are not public records under section 149.43 of the Revised Code.

(I) Definition As used in this rule, Sup. R. 25, and Forms 23.1-A, 23.1-B, 23.1-C, and 25, "petitioner" means the minor female who is seeking consent to have an abortion regardless of whether the minor female or a next friend filed the petition.

FORM 23.1-A. PETITION FOR AUTHORIZATION TO CONSENT TO AN ABORTION OR FOR JUDICIAL CONSENT TO AN ABORTION (R.C. 2919.121)

JUVENILE DIVISION

COURT OF COMMON PLEAS

_____COUNTY, OHIO

In re petition of Jane Doe.   Case No._____

                                           PETITION
                                           Promulgated by the Supreme Court
                                           of Ohio pursuant to R.C. 2919.121

I swear or affirm that:

1.   I am pregnant.

2.   I am unmarried, _____ years of age, and unemancipated.

3.   I wish to have an abortion and have been fully informed of the risks and   consequences of an abortion.

4.   This petition is being filed in the juvenile court of the county where I reside, in a county bordering the county where I reside, or in the county where the abortion will be performed.

[CHECK ONE OR BOTH OF THE FOLLOWING STATEMENTS.]

5.   ___   I am of sound mind and have sufficient intellectual capacity to consent to an abortion.

      ___   The court should find that an abortion is in my best interests and give judicial consent to the abortion.

[CHECK ONE OF THE FOLLOWING STATEMENTS.]

6.   ___   I do not have a lawyer and ask that the court appoint a lawyer free of charge.

      ___   I have a lawyer. The name, address, and telephone number of my lawyer are:

             Lawyer's Name: _____

Lawyer's Address: _____

_____

Lawyer's Phone No: _____

Page 2 of the petition.   Case no. _____

THIS PAGE OF THE ORIGINAL MUST BE REMOVED AND PLACED UNDER SEAL IN A
SAFE OR OTHER SECURE PLACE AS REQUIRED BY RULE 23.1 OF THE RULES OF
SUPERINTENDENCE FOR THE COURTS OF OHIO.

7.   The following is/are the name(s) and address(es) of my parent(s), guardian(s),
      custodian(s) or, if my parents are deceased and no guardian(s) is/are appointed,   any
person standing in place of my parent(s), guardian(s), or custodian(s):

      Name(s): _____

      Address(es): _____
                   _____

THEREFORE, I request that this Court appoint a lawyer if I do not already have one, appoint a
guardian *ad litem* to represent my best interests, and issue an order authorizing me to consent or
granting judicial consent to an abortion without the consent of my parent, guardian, or custodian.

I swear or affirm that the information in the attached petition is true and accurate to the best of
my knowledge and belief.

_____
Signature (Minor or Next Friend)

If this petition is being filed by a next friend on behalf of a minor, the minor's initials are:
_____.

Sworn to or affirmed in my presence this _____ day of _____, _____.

_____
Notary Public

* *

PLEASE NOTE:
If you do not have a lawyer, please provide in the spaces below any address and phone number
where the Court may contact you until a lawyer is appointed to represent you. You do not need
to use your home address and phone number.

      Address: _____
               _____

      Telephone: _____

Form 23.1-A

Effective: May 22, 2007

PETITION FOR CONSENT TO AN ABORTION OR FOR JUDICIAL CONSENT TO AN ABORTION (R.C. 2919.121).

INSTRUCTIONS

If you are pregnant, unmarried, under eighteen years old and unemancipated, and want to have an abortion without the consent of your parents, you may ask a court for permission. The court will then decide whether you are sufficiently mature and well-enough informed to decide intelligently to have an abortion or whether an abortion is in your best interests. The attached form, called a petition, should be used to ask a court to let you have an abortion without the consent of your parents.

If you are under 18 and not married, you are "unemancipated" if:

1. You have not entered the armed services of the United States or

2. You do not have a job and support yourself or

3. You are under the care and control of your parent, guardian, or custodian.

By law, you do not have to pay a filing fee or any court costs. If you do not have a lawyer, the court will appoint one for you free of charge. The court also will appoint a guardian *ad litem*, who is a person responsible for protecting your interests. The court may appoint your lawyer to be your guardian *ad litem*.

The court is not allowed to tell your parent, guardian, or custodian that you are pregnant or that you want to have an abortion. The court must keep the petition and all other papers in your case confidential.

The petition must be filed in a juvenile court in the county where the abortion would be performed, in the county where you reside, or in any county that borders the county where you reside.

HOW TO FILL OUT THE FORM

Completing Statement #5: Check one or both of the statements. If you check the first statement, the court will first consider if you are mature enough and well enough informed to intelligently decide whether to have an abortion. If the court does not find that you are sufficiently mature and well enough informed to make the decision, and you have checked the second statement, the court will then consider whether the abortion is in your best interest. If you are not sure which statement to check, you may check both and then discuss this with your lawyer.

Completing Statement #6: Check the statement that applies to you. If you have a lawyer, fill in the name, address and telephone number of your lawyer.

Completing Page 2: The law requires that the statements in the petition be made under oath. This part of the form must be completed by you or someone who is assisting you (called a "next friend") in the presence of a person who is allowed to administer oaths, such as a notary public, a lawyer, or a judge. After you or the person assisting you signs the petition, the person who administers oaths should sign the form.

Completing the Bottom of Page 2: Fill out the bottom of page 2 only if you do not have a lawyer. Provide any address and phone number where you may be contacted about this matter. When the court appoints a lawyer for you, the lawyer will reach you at the address or phone number you provide. You do not have to complete the bottom of page 2 until after the notary public signs on page 2.

Effective: May 22, 2007

Commentary May 22, 2007

Form 23.1-A was amended to reflect the decision in *Cincinnati Women's Services v. Taft*, 468 F.3d 361 (6th Cir. 2006) which ruled that the portions of the Ohio Revised Code Section 2919.121 that limit minors to one judicial-bypass petition per pregnancy place an undue burden on minors' constitutional right to an abortion.

JUVENILE COURT
_____ COUNTY, OHIO

In re petition of Jane Doe   Case No. _____

JUDGMENT

This matter came on for hearing on the _____ day of ____, ____. Based upon the testimony and evidence presented, this court finds:

1. The court:

    ____ Has jurisdiction over the petition.

    ____ Does not have jurisdiction over the petition for the following reasons:

    ____

    ____

    ____

2. _____ The petitioner is an unemancipated minor.

3. _____ The petitioner is pregnant and she wishes to obtain an abortion.

4. _____ The petitioner has been fully informed of the risks and consequences of the abortion.

5. That evidence has been presented to support the following [decide maturity issue first if pleaded]:

    a. _____ Petitioner is sufficiently mature and well informed to decide intelligently whether to have an abortion without obtaining the consent of a parent, guardian, or custodian.

    b. _____ The abortion would be in petitioner's best interest for the following reasons:

    _____

    _____

    _____

    c. ____ Neither 5a. nor 5b. has been established for the following reasons:

    _____

    _____

    _____

THEREFORE, IT IS ORDERED:

    ____ The petition is granted and the petitioner is hereby authorized to consent to the performance or inducement of an abortion.

    ____ The court finds the abortion is in the best interest of the petitioner and judicial consent is hereby authorized.

    ____ The petition is denied. The Clerk is instructed to provide the petitioner with the notice of appeal form and advise her of her right to an expedited appeal.

    ____ The petition is dismissed for lack of jurisdiction. The Clerk is instructed to provide the petitioner with the notice of appeal form and advise her of her right to an expedited appeal.

_____, Ohio _____

                 Judge

_____

Date

Form 23.1-C Notice of Appeal

JUVENILE COURT
_____ COUNTY, OHIO

In re petition of Jane Doe   Case No. _____

NOTICE OF APPEAL
Promulgated by the Supreme
Court of Ohio pursuant to R.C.
2919.121

Notice is hereby given that the petitioner appeals to the Court of Appeals for ____ County from the final order entered in the above-styled cause on ____, ____, denying or dismissing the petition seeking an abortion.

_____
Signature of Attorney for Petitioner

_____
Attorney Name

_____
Attorney Address

_____
Attorney Phone

History: Effective 10-15-01.

RULE 24. Notifying Physicians of Affidavits Alleging Abuse Under 2919.12

(A) **Filing affidavit — procedure** Pursuant to division (B)(1)(b) of section 2919.12 of the Revised Code, a minor may have notice of an intended abortion given to a specified adult instead of one of her parents, guardian, or custodian. Two affidavits must be filed with the clerk of the juvenile court by anyone seeking to invoke the notice provisions of the law. The first affidavit is executed by the minor and should be on Form 24-A. The second affidavit is executed by the specified adult and should be on Form 24-B. Anyone receiving these forms also shall be given the accompanying instruction sheet.

Upon the filing of both affidavits and upon the request of the minor, her attorney, or the person who will perform the abortion, the clerk of the juvenile court shall issue a notice on Form 24-C verifying that the affidavits have been filed with the court.

(B) **Confidentiality** All affidavits filed and notices issued pursuant to this rule shall be placed under seal in a safe or other secure place where access is limited to essential court personnel.

Persons becoming aware of the contents of any affidavits prepared pursuant to this rule or section 2919.12 of the Revised Code are exempt from reporting such contents under section 2151.421 of the Revised Code. Any reporting by court personnel would breach the duty of confidentiality and is prohibited by section 102.03 of the Revised Code.

Form 24-A. Affidavit of Minor

FORM 24-A. AFFIDAVIT OF MINOR

JUVENILE COURT
_____ COUNTY, OHIO

In re complaint of Jane Doe   Case No._____

AFFIDAVIT
R.C. 2919.12(B)(1)(b)(ii)

STATE OF OHIO   )
)
COUNTY OF   )

I, _____, being duly sworn, state as follows:

1.   I am pregnant, unmarried, under 18 years of age, and unemancipated.

2.   I wish to have an abortion without notification of a parent, guardian, or custodian.

3.   I request instead that notice of my intention to have the abortion be given to one of the following [Select One]:

    a.   _____, a brother or sister twenty-one years of
    Name   age or older or,

    b.   _____, a stepparent or grandparent.
        Name

4.   I am in fear of physical, sexual, or severe emotional abuse from a parent, guardian, or custodian who otherwise would be notified of my intention to have an abortion under section 2919.12 of the Revised Code.

5.   My fear is based on a pattern of physical, sexual, or severe emotional abuse exhibited by a parent, guardian, or custodian.

6.   I understand that upon the filing of this affidavit and an affidavit from the person specified above with the juvenile court, an officer of that court will prepare a notice verifying that the affidavits have been filed.

7.   The person who intends to perform or induce my abortion and the address of that person are as follows:

_____
Name of Abortion Provider

_____
Address

                                        _____
                                        Signature

        Before me appeared the above named person who under oath or by affirmation did sign this affidavit this _____ day of _____, 19__.

                                        _____
                                        Notary Public

Form 24-A
Revised 11/92

                            Page 2 of 2

Form 24-B. Affidavit of Recipient of Notice of Minor's Intention to Receive an Abortion

FORM 24-B. AFFIDAVIT OF RECIPIENT OF NOTICE OF MINOR'S INTENTION TO RECEIVE AN ABORTION

JUVENILE COURT
_____COUNTY, OHIO

In re complaint of Jane Doe   Case No._____

AFFIDAVIT
R.C. 2919.12(B)(1)(b)(iii)

STATE OF OHIO   )
)
COUNTY OF   ).

_____, being duly sworn, states as follows:
    (Name)

1.   I am [select appropriate one]

       _____   over twenty-one years of age and I am a brother or sister of

       _____   a stepparent or grandparent of

       _____, (hereafter, minor) who has [name of pregnant minor]
       filed an affidavit with the Juvenile Court under section 2919.12(B)(1)(b)(ii) of the Revised Code.

2.   I have been specified in the minor's affidavit as the person to receive notice of the minor's intention to receive an abortion.

3.   The minor has reason to fear physical, sexual, or severe emotional abuse from a parent, guardian, or custodian who otherwise would be notified of her intention to have an abortion under section 2919.12 of the Revised Code.

4.   Her fear is based on a pattern of physical, sexual, or severe emotional abuse exhibited by a parent, guardian, or custodian.

                                _____
                                    Signature

Before me appeared the above named person who under oath or by affirmation did sign this affidavit this _____ day of_____, 19__.

                                _____
                                    Notary Public

Revised 11/92

FORMS ALLEGING ABUSE BY PARENT AND REQUESTING THAT
NOTIFICATION OF ABORTION BE PROVIDED TO OTHER RELATIVE

INSTRUCTIONS FOR FORMS 24-A and 24-B

If you use these forms, the person performing your abortion will not be required to give notice of your abortion to a parent, guardian, or custodian. Instead, you can choose to have notice provided to a brother or sister over twenty-one years of age or a stepparent or grandparent.

These forms are called affidavits. An affidavit is a sworn statement signed before a notary public or other person, such as a judge or attorney, authorized to administer oaths. The clerk's office will provide a notary public if you want to complete the forms in the clerk's office.

These forms may be used if all of the following apply.

You are:

1. pregnant;

2. unmarried;

3. under eighteen years old;

4. unemancipated, which means that:
   you have not entered the armed forces of the United States, or
   you do not have a job and support yourself, or
   you are under the care and control of a parent, guardian, or custodian;

5. you fear, based on events that have happened in the past, physical, sexual, or severe emotional abuse if notice of the abortion is given to a parent, guardian, or custodian.

These forms will be filed with the juvenile court and kept confidential. The clerk of the juvenile court will provide notice to the abortion provider that the forms have been filed and the clerk will inform the abortion provider of the name of the person you have chosen to receive notice of your abortion. The forms will not be released by the juvenile court.

You do not have to pay any filing fee or court costs to the clerk for notarizing these forms, filing these forms, or issuing the notice to the abortion provider.

The affidavit must be filed in a juvenile court in the county where the abortion will be performed, in the county where you reside or have a legal settlement, or in any county that borders the county where you reside or have a legal settlement.

HOW TO FILL OUT THE FORMS

There are two forms. You complete one of them. The other form is completed by the person you select to receive notice of your abortion. That must be a brother or sister over twenty-one years old or a stepparent or grandparent.

Your form requires that you name the person to receive notice and provide the name and address of the person to perform the abortion.

Both of the forms must be signed in front of a notary public or other person, such as a judge or attorney, authorized to administer oaths.

WHAT TO DO AFTER FILLING OUT THE FORMS

After the forms are signed and notarized, give them to the juvenile court clerk who will file them in a confidential place within the clerk's office. Then the clerk will issue a notice that you may take to the abortion provider. With that notice the abortion provider will be authorized to provide notice of the abortion to the brother, sister, stepparent, or grandparent that you have selected.

Effective 11/92

Form 24-C. Notice

FORM 24-C. NOTICE

JUVENILE COURT
_____COUNTY, OHIO

In re complaint of Jane Doe   Case No._____

NOTICE

Notice is hereby given that on_____, 19__, (minor's name) filed affidavits pursuant to Section 2919.12(B)(1)(b)(ii) and (iii) of the Revised Code and may therefore proceed to have any notifications required by that statute issued to the following specified adult: _____.

_____
Clerk

(Seal)

RULE 25. Procedure on Appeals Under Sections 2151.85, 2919.121 and 2505.073 of the Revised Code

(A) General rule of expedition

(1) If a complainant or petitioner files her notice of appeal on the same day as the dismissal of her complaint or petition by the juvenile court, the entire court process, including the juvenile court hearing, appeal, and decision, shall be completed in sixteen calendar days from the time the original complaint or petition was filed.

(2) If a complainant or petitioner files a notice of appeal after the day on which the court denies or dismisses her complaint or petition, the entire court process, including the juvenile court hearing, appeal, and decision, shall be completed in sixteen calendar days from the time the complaint or petition was filed, plus the number of calendar days that elapsed between the date on which the court's decision was issued and the date on which the notice of appeal was filed.

(B) Processing appeal

(1) Immediately after the notice of appeal has been filed by the complainant or petitioner, the clerk of the juvenile court shall notify the court of appeals. Within four days after the notice of appeal is filed in juvenile court, the clerk of the juvenile court shall deliver a copy of the notice of appeal and the record, except page two of the complaint or petition, to the clerk of the court of appeals who immediately shall place the appeal on the docket of the court of appeals.

(2) Record of all testimony and other oral proceedings in actions pursuant to section 2151.85 or 2919.121 of the Revised Code may be made by audio recording. If the testimony is on audio tape and a transcript cannot be prepared timely, the court of appeals shall accept the audio tape as the transcript in this case without prior transcription.

(3) The appellant under this section shall file her brief within four days after the appeal is docketed. Unless waived, the oral argument shall be within five days after docketing. Oral arguments must be closed to the public and exclude all persons except the appellant, her attorney, her guardian *ad litem*, and essential court personnel.

(4) Under this rule, "days" means calendar days and includes any intervening Saturday, Sunday, or legal holiday. To provide full effect to the expedition provision of the statute, if the last day on which a judgment is required to be entered falls on a Saturday, Sunday, or legal holiday, the computation of days shall not be extended and judgment shall be made either on the last business day before the Saturday, Sunday, or legal holiday, or on the Saturday, Sunday, or legal holiday.

(C) Confidentiality

All proceedings pursuant to division (A) of section 2505.073 or 2919.121 of the Revised Code shall be conducted in a manner that will preserve the anonymity of the appellant on appeal. Except as set forth in division (E) of this rule, all papers and records that pertain to an appeal under section 2505.073 or 2919.121 of the Revised Code shall be kept confidential and are not public records under section 149.43 of the Revised Code.

(D) Judgment entry

The court of appeals shall enter judgment immediately after conclusion of oral argument or, if oral argument is waived, within five days after the appeal is docketed.

(E) Release of records

The public is entitled to secure all of the following from the records pertaining to each case filed under section 2505.073 or 2919.121 of the Revised Code:

(1) The docket number;

(2) The name of the judge;

(3) The judgment entry and, if appropriate, a properly redacted opinion.

Opinions shall set forth the reasoning in support of the decision in a way that does not directly or indirectly compromise the anonymity of the minor. Opinions written in compliance with this requirement shall be considered public records available upon request. If, in the judgment of the court, it is impossible to release an opinion without compromising the anonymity of the minor, the entry that journalizes the outcome of the case shall include a specific finding that no opinion can be written without disclosing the identity of the minor. Such finding shall be a matter of public record.

It is the obligation of the court to remove any and all information in its opinion that would directly or indirectly disclose the identity of the minor.

(F) Notice and hearing before release of opinion

After an opinion is written and before it is available for release to the public, the minor must be notified and be given the option to appear and argue at a hearing if she believes the opinion may disclose her identity. Notice may be provided by including the following language in the opinion:

If the appellant believes that this opinion may disclose her identity, appellant has a right to appear and argue at a hearing before this court. Appellant may perfect this right to a hearing by filing a motion for a hearing within fourteen days of the date of this opinion.

The clerk is instructed that this opinion is not to be made available for release until either of the following:

(1) Twenty-one days have passed since the date of the opinion and appellant has not filed a motion;

(2) If appellant has filed a motion, after this court has ruled on the motion.

Notice shall be provided by mailing a copy of the opinion to the attorney for the appellant or, if she is not represented, to the address provided by appellant for receipt of notice.

(G) Constructive order

Upon request of the appellant or her attorney in proceedings pursuant to section 2151.85 or 2505.073 of the Revised Code, the clerk shall verify on Form 25-A the date the appeal was docketed and whether a judgment has been entered within five days of that date. The completed form shall include the case number from the juvenile court and the court of appeals, and shall be filed and included as part of the record. A date-stamped copy shall be provided to the appellant or her attorney.

History: Amended, eff 10-15-01.

FORM 25-A. Verification

COURT OF APPEALS
____ COUNTY, OHIO

In re complaint of Jane Doe   Case No. ____
                                                        Juvenile Court No. ____

VERIFICATION

This will verify that on _____, _____, the appeal of Jane Doe was docketed in this court under section 2151.85 or 2505.073 of the Revised Code and as of _____, _____, which is more than five calendar days after the docketing of the appeal, the court has not rendered a judgment in the matter.

                                        _____
                                                    Clerk

(Seal) Amended, eff 10-15-01.

RULE 26. Court Records Management and Retention

(A) Applicability

(1) This rule and Sup. R. 26.01 to 26.05 are intended to provide minimum standards for the maintenance, preservation, and destruction of records within the courts and to authorize alternative electronic methods and techniques. Implementation of this rule and Sup. R. 26.01 to 26.05 is a judicial, governmental function.

(2) This rule and Sup. R. 26.01 to 26.05 shall be interpreted to allow for technological advances that improve the efficiency of the courts and simplify the maintenance, preservation, and destruction of court records.

(B) Definitions As used in this rule and Sup. R. 26.01 to 26.05:

(1) "Administrative record" means a record not related to cases of a court that documents the administrative, fiscal, personnel, or management functions of the court.

(2) "Case file" means the compendium of original documents filed in an action or proceeding in a court, including the pleadings, motions, orders, and judgments of the court on a case by case basis.

(3) "Index" means a reference record used to locate journal, docket, and case file records.

(4) "Journal" means a verbatim record of every order or judgment of a court.

(5) "OHS" means the Ohio Historical Society, State Archives Division.

(6) "Record" means any document, device, or item, regardless of physical form or characteristic, created or received by or coming under the jurisdiction of a court that serves to document the organization, functions, policies, decisions, procedures, operations, or other activities of the court.

(C) Combined records Notwithstanding any other provision of the law, a court may combine indexes, dockets, journals, and case files provided that the combination contains the components of indexes, dockets, journals, and case files as defined in this rule and Sup. R. 26.01 to 26.05. A court may replace any paper bound books with an electronic medium or microfilm in accordance with this rule.

(D) Allowable record media

(1) A court may create, maintain, record, copy, or preserve a record on traditional paper media, electronic media, including text or digital images, or microfilm, including computer output to microfilm.

(2) A court may create, maintain, record, copy, or preserve a record using any nationally accepted records and information management process, including photography, microfilm, and electronic data processing, as an alternative to paper. The process may be used in regard to the original or a copy of a record if the process produces an accurate record or copy and the process complies with American National Standards Institute ("ANSI") standards and guidelines or, in the event that ANSI standards cease to exist, other nationally accepted records and information management process standards.

(a) If a court creates, maintains, records, copies, or preserves a record using a records and information management process in accordance with division (D)(2) of this rule and the record is required to be retained in accordance with the schedules set forth in Sup. R. 26.01 to 26.05, the court shall cause a back-up copy of the record to be made at periodic and reasonable times to insure the security and continued availability of the information. If Sup. R. 26.01 to 26.05 require the record to be retained permanently, the back-up copy shall be stored in a different building than the record it secures.

(b) Records shall be maintained in conveniently accessible and secure facilities, and provisions shall be made for inspecting and copying any public records in accordance with applicable statutes and rules. Machines and equipment necessary to allow inspection and copying of public records, including public records that are created, maintained, recorded, copied, or preserved by an alternative records and information management process in accordance with division (D)(2) of this rule, shall be provided.

(c) In accordance with applicable law and purchasing requirements, a court may acquire equipment, computer software, and related supplies and services for records and information management processes authorized by division (D)(2) of this rule.

(d) Paper media may be destroyed after it is converted to other approved media in accordance with division (D) of this rule.

(E) **Destruction of records**

(1) Subject to the notification and transfer requirements of divisions (E)(2) and (3) of this rule, a record and any back-up copy of a record produced in accordance with division (D)(2) of this rule may be destroyed after the record and its back-up copy have been retained for the applicable retention period set forth in Sup. R. 26.01 to 26.05.

(2) If Sup. R. 26.01 to 26.05 set forth a retention period greater than ten years for a record, or if a record was created prior to 1960, the court shall notify the OHS in writing of the court's intention to destroy the record at least sixty days prior to the destruction of the record.

(3) After submitting a written notice in accordance with division (E)(2) of this rule, the court shall, upon request of the OHS, cause the record described in the notice to be transferred to the OHS, or to an institution or agency that meets the criteria of the OHS, in the media and format designated by the OHS.

(F) **Exhibits, depositions, and transcripts** At the conclusion of litigation, including times for direct appeal, a court or custodian of exhibits, depositions, or transcripts may destroy exhibits, depositions, and transcripts if all of the following conditions are satisfied:

(1) The court notifies the party that tendered the exhibits, depositions, or transcripts in writing that the party may retrieve the exhibits, depositions, or transcripts within sixty days from the date of the written notification;

(2) The written notification required in division (F)(1) of this rule informs the party that tendered the exhibits, depositions, or transcripts that the exhibits, depositions, or transcripts will be destroyed if not retrieved within sixty days of the notification;

(3) The written notification required in division (F)(1) of this rule informs the party that tendered the exhibits, depositions, or transcripts of the location for retrieval of the exhibits, depositions, or transcripts;

(4) The party that tendered the exhibits, depositions, or transcripts does not retrieve the exhibits, depositions, or transcripts within sixty days from the date of the written notification required in division (F)(1) of this rule.

(G) **Local rules** By local rule, a court may establish retention schedules for any records not listed in Sup. R. 26.01 to 26.05 and may extend, but not limit, the retention schedule for any record listed in Sup. R. 26.01 to 26.05. Any record that is not listed in Sup. R. 26.01 to 26.05 but is listed in a general retention schedule established pursuant to section 149.331 of the Revised Code may be retained for the period of time set by the general retention schedule and then destroyed.

(H) **Extension of retention period for individual case files** A court may order the retention period for an individual case file extended beyond the period specified in Sup. R. 26.02 to 26.05 for the case file.

History: Effective 10-1-97; amended, eff 7-1-01.

RULE 26.01. Rentention Schedule for the Administrative Records of the Courts

The following retention schedule shall apply for the administrative records of the courts:

(A) **Administrative journal** Administrative journals that consist of court entries, or a record of court entries, regarding policies and issues not related to cases shall be retained permanently.

(B) **Annual reports** Two copies of each annual report shall be retained permanently.

(C) **Bank records** Bank transaction records, whether paper or electronic, shall be retained for three years or until the issuance of an audit report by the Auditor of State, whichever is later.

(D) **Cash books** Cash books, including expense and receipt ledgers, shall be retained for three years or until the issuance of an audit report by the Auditor of State, whichever is later.

(E) **Communication records** Communication records, including routine telephone messages on any medium where official action will be recorded elsewhere, may be destroyed in the normal course of business as soon as they are considered to be of no value by the person holding the records.

(F) **Correspondence and general office records** Correspondence and general office records, including all sent and received correspondence, in any medium, may be destroyed in the normal course of business as soon as they are considered to be of no value by the person holding the records.

(G) **Drafts and informal notes** Drafts and informal notes consisting of transitory information used to prepare the official record in any other form may be destroyed in the normal course of business as soon as they are considered to be of no value by the person holding the drafts and informal notes.

(H) **Employment applications for posted positions** Employment applications for posted or advertised positions shall be retained for two years.

(I) **Employee benefit and leave records** Employee benefit and leave records, including court office copies of life and medical insurance records, shall be retained by the appropriate fiscal officer for three years or until the issuance of an audit report by the Auditor of State, whichever is later.

(J) **Employee history and discipline records** Records concerning the hiring, promotion, evaluation, attendance, medical issues, discipline, termination, and retirement of court employees shall be retained for ten years after termination of employment.

(K) **Fiscal records** Fiscal records, including copies of transactional budgeting and purchasing documents maintained by another office or agency, shall be retained for three years or until the issuance of an audit report by the Auditor of State, whichever is later.

(L) **Grant records** Records of grants made or received by a court shall be retained for three years after expiration of the grant.

(M) **Payroll records** Payroll records of personnel time and copies of payroll records maintained by another office or agency shall be retained for three years or until the issuance of an audit report by the Auditor of State, whichever is later.

(N) **Publications received** Publications received by a court may be destroyed in the normal course of business as soon as they are considered to be of no value by the person holding the publications.

(O) **Receipt records** Receipt and balancing records shall be retained for three years or until the issuance of an audit report by the Auditor of State, whichever is later.

(P) **Requests for proposals, bids, and resulting contracts** Requests for proposals, bids received in response to a request for proposal, and contracts resulting from a request for proposal shall be retained for three years after the expiration of the contract that is awarded pursuant to the request for proposal.

History: Effective 10-1-97.

RULE 26.02. Courts of Appeals — Records Retention Schedule

(A) **Definition of docket** As used in this rule, "docket" means the record where the clerk of the court of appeals enters all of the information historically included in the appearance docket, the trial docket, the journal, and the execution docket.

(B) **Required records**

(1) The court of appeals shall maintain an index, docket, journal, and case files in accordance with Sup. R. 26(B) and divisions (A) and (C) of this rule.

(2) Upon the filing of any paper or electronic entry permitted by the court of appeals, a time stamp or entry shall be placed on the paper or electronic entry to indicate the time, day, month, and year of filing.

(C) **Content of docket** The docket of the court of appeals shall be programmed to allow retrieval of orders and judgments of the court in a chronological as well as a case specific manner. Entries in the docket shall be made as events occur, shall index directly and in reverse the names of all parties to cases in the court of appeals, and shall include:

(1) Names and addresses of all parties in full;

(2) Names, addresses, and Supreme Court attorney registration numbers of all counsel;

(3) The issuance of documents for service upon a party and the return of service or lack of return;

(4) A brief description of all records and orders filed in the proceeding, the date and time filed, and a cross reference to other records as appropriate;

(5) A schedule of court proceedings for the court of appeals and its officers to use for case management purposes;

(6) All actions taken by the court of appeals to enforce orders or judgments.

(D) **Retention schedule for the index, docket, and journal** The index, docket, and journal of the court of appeals shall be retained permanently.

(E) **Retention schedule for case files**

(1) Court of appeals case files shall be retained for two years after the final order of the court, except for files of death penalty cases, which shall be retained permanently in their original form.

(2) Judge, magistrate, and clerk notes, drafts, and research prepared for the purpose of compiling a report, opinion, or other document or memorandum

may be kept separate from the case file, retained in the case file, or destroyed at the discretion of the preparer.

History: Effective 10-1-97.

RULE 26.03. General, Domestic Relations, and Juvenile Divisions of the Courts of Common Pleas — Records Retention Schedule

(A) **Definitions**

(1) As used in divisions (A) to (D) of this rule, "division" means the general, domestic relations, or juvenile division of the court of common pleas or any combination of the general, domestic relations, or juvenile divisions of the court of common pleas.

(2) As used in this rule, "docket" means the record where the clerk of the division enters all of the information historically included in the appearance docket, the trial docket, the journal, and the execution docket.

(B) **Required records**

(1) Each division shall maintain an index, docket, journal, and case files in accordance with Sup. R. 26(B) and divisions (A) and (C) of this rule.

(2) Upon the filing of any paper or electronic entry permitted by the division, a time stamp or entry shall be placed on the paper or electronic entry to indicate the time, day, month, and year of filing.

(C) **Content of docket** The docket of a division shall be programmed to allow retrieval of orders and judgments of the division in a chronological as well as a case specific manner. Entries in the docket shall be made as events occur, shall index directly and in reverse the names of all parties to cases in the division, and shall include:

(1) Names and addresses of all parties in full;

(2) Names, addresses, and Supreme Court attorney registration numbers of all counsel;

(3) The issuance of documents for service upon a party and the return of service or lack of return;

(4) A brief description of all records and orders filed in the proceeding, the time and date filed, and a cross reference to other records as appropriate;

(5) A schedule of court proceedings for the division and its officers to use for case management;

(6) All actions taken by the division to enforce orders or judgments; and

(7) Any information necessary to document the activity of the clerk of the division regarding the case.

(D) **Retention schedule for the index, docket, and journal** The index, docket, and journal of a division shall be retained permanently.

(E) **Judge, magistrate, and clerk notes, drafts, and research** Judge, magistrate, and clerk notes, drafts, and research prepared for the purpose of compiling a report, opinion, or other document or memorandum may be kept separate from the case file, retained in the case file, or destroyed at the discretion of the preparer.

(F) **Retention schedule for case files—general division of the court of common pleas**

(1) **Death penalty cases** Death penalty case files shall be retained permanently.

(2) **Real estate** Case files of matters that resulted in a final judgment determining title or interest in real

estate shall be retained permanently.

(3) **Search warrant records** Search warrant records shall be indexed and the warrants and returns retained in their original form for five years after the date of service or last service attempt.

(4) **Voluntary dismissals** Case files of matters that are voluntarily dismissed shall be retained for three years after the date of the dismissal.

(5) **Other case files** Any case file not listed in division (F) of this rule shall be retained for twelve years after the final order of the general division. Documents within a case file admissible as evidence of a prior conviction in a criminal proceeding shall be retained for fifty years after the final order of the general division.

(G) **Retention schedule for case files—domestic relations division of the court of common pleas**

(1) **Certified mail receipts in uncontested cases and post-decree motions** In new cases and cases involving post-decree motions where personal jurisdiction is established by certified mail receipt and the defendant/respondent fails to answer, enter an appearance, or otherwise defend, the certified mail receipt shall be retained for thirty years after the date of issuance and may be retained in a separate file from the case file.

(2) **Divorce or dissolution:** Minor children. Case files of divorce and dissolution that involve minor children shall be retained for twenty-five years after the date of the final order of the domestic relations division.

(3) **Divorce or dissolution:** No children. Case files of divorce and dissolution not involving minor children shall be retained for twelve years after the final order of the domestic relations division.

(4) **Domestic violence petitions** Case files of petitions for domestic violence protection orders shall be retained for one year after the expiration of any resulting protection order. If the parties to a petition for a domestic violence protection order are also parties to a petition for a domestic violence protection order are also parties to a divorce, the case file of the petition shall be retained for one year after the expiration of any resulting protection order or until the parties are divorced, whichever is later. In case files of petitions for domestic violence protection orders in which no protection order is issued, the case file shall be retained for one year from the date the petition was filed. If post-decree motions have been filed, the case filed shall be retained for one year after the adjudication of the post-decree motion or the date specified for case files of petitions for domestic violence protection orders in division (G)(4) of this rule, whichever is later.

(5) **Legal separation** Case files of legal separation shall be retained until the parties are divorced or for two years after the spousal support terminates, whichever is later, unless otherwise ordered by the court. If post-decree motions have been filed, the case file shall be retained for two years after the adjudication of the post-decree motion or the date specified for case files in division (G)(5) of this rule, whichever is later.

(6) **Real estate** Case files of matters that resulted in a final judgment determining title or interest in real estate shall be retained permanently.

(7) **Registration or adoption of foreign decree** Case files of registrations or adoptions of foreign decrees shall be retained for two years after the emancipation of all of the parties' minor children. If post-decree motions have been filed, records shall be retained for two years after the adjudication of the post-decree motion or the date specified for case files in division (G)(7) of this rule, whichever is later.

(8) **Uniform Reciprocal Enforcement of Support Act ("URESA") filings** Case files involving URESA filings shall be retained for nineteen years after the final order of the domestic relations division or for one year after transfer of the case to another jurisdiction.

(H) **Retention schedule for case files—juvenile division of the court of common pleas**

(1) **Delinquency and adult records** Delinquency and adult records shall be retained for two years after the final order of the juvenile division or one year after the issuance of an audit report by the Auditor of State, whichever is later. Documents admissible as evidence of a prior conviction in a criminal proceeding shall be retained for fifty years after the final order of the juvenile division.

(2) **Juvenile by-pass records** Juvenile by-pass records shall be maintained in two separate and secure files. The first file shall contain the first page of the form complaint and other relevant documents and the second file shall contain the second page of the form complaint bearing the signature of the complainant. Each file shall be retained for two years after the final order of the juvenile division or, if an appeal is sought, for two years after the filing of the appeal.

(3) **Permanent custody, custody, parentage, visitation, support enforcement, abuse, neglect, dependency, and URESA records** Permanent custody, custody, parentage, visitation, support enforcement, abuse, neglect, dependency, and URESA records shall be retained for two years after the child who is the subject of the case obtains the age of majority. If post-decree motions have been filed, records shall be retained for one year after the adjudication of the post-decree motion or the date specified for case files in division (H)(3) of this rule, whichever is later.

(4) **Search warrant records** Search warrant records shall be indexed and the warrants and returns retained in their original form for five years after the date of service or last service attempt.

(5) **Traffic, unruly and marriage consent records** Unruly and marriage consent records shall be retained for two years after the final order of the juvenile division or one year after the issuance of an audit report by the Auditor of State, whichever is later. Minor misdemeanor traffic records shall be retained for five years after the final order of the juvenile division. Misdemeanor traffic records shall be retained for twenty-five years after the final order of the juvenile division. All other traffic records shall be retained for fifty years after the final order of the juvenile division.

History: Amended, eff 9-23-04; 3-23-05.

RULE 26.04. Probate Divisions of the Courts of Common Pleas — Records Retention Schedule

(A) **Definitions** As used in this rule:

(1) "Docket" means a reference record that provides the dates and a summary of all hearings, pleadings, filings, orders, and other matters that are essential to an action, proceeding, or other matter in the probate division.

(2) "Probate record" means a record that pertains to the duties of the probate division including, but not limited to, adoptions, marriage licenses, name changes, birth records, orders of civil commitment, the resolution of civil actions, and the appointment and supervision of fiduciaries.

(3) "Record of documents" means a collection of single or several page documents in which each document represents the probate division's action in a single incident of the same duty of the probate division, such as the issuance of marriage licenses.

(B) **Closed probate record or case file** For purposes of this rule, a probate record or case file of an estate, trust, or other fiduciary relationship shall be considered closed when a final accounting has been filed and, if required by law at the time of the filing, the account has been approved and settled. All other probate records and case files shall be considered closed when the probate division orders the matter closed or there is a final disposition of the action or proceeding for which the probate record or case file is kept.

(C) **Required records**

(1) **Dockets**

(a) The probate division shall maintain all of the following dockets:

(i) An administration docket showing the name of the deceased;

(ii) A guardian's docket showing the name of each ward and, if the ward is a minor, the ward's age and name of the ward's parents and any limited powers or limited duration of powers;

(iii) A civil docket in which the names of the parties to actions and proceedings shall be noted;

(iv) A testamentary trust docket showing the names of the testator and trustee or trustees;

(v) A change of name docket showing the name of the petitioner and the present and proposed names of the person whose name is to be changed;

(vi) A birth registration and correction docket showing the name of the person whose birth certificate is being registered or corrected;

(vii) A civil commitment docket showing the name of the prospective patient;

(viii) A separate adoption docket, in accordance with section 3107.17 of the Revised Code, showing the name of the child as it would exist after finalization of the adoption and the name or names of the adoptive parent or parents;

(ix) A paternity docket showing the birth name of the child who is the subject of the petition, the name of the father, the name of the mother, and the name of the child after adjudication;

(x) A miscellaneous docket showing the names of parties or petitioners and the nature of the action or proceeding. The miscellaneous docket shall be limited to actions within the probate division's jurisdiction that are not kept in one of the other dockets described in division (C)(1) of this rule. If the number of filings warrants a miscellaneous docket may be subdivided or grouped into sections containing files or records of similar content.

(b) All dockets of the probate division shall contain the dates of filing or occurrence and a brief description of any bond and surety, letter of authority, and each filing, order, or record of proceeding related to the case or action, with a reference to the file or record where the bond and surety, letter of authority, filing, order, or record of proceeding is to be found, and such other information as the court considers necessary.

(2) **Records of documents**

(a) The probate division shall maintain both of the following records of documents:

(i) A record of wills, if wills are not copied and permanently retained as part of an estate case file under division (D)(2) of this rule, in which the wills proved in the court shall be recorded with a certificate of the probate of the will, and wills proved elsewhere with the certificate of probate, authenticated copies of which have been admitted to record by the court;

(ii) A marriage record, in which shall be entered licenses, the names of the parties to whom the license is issued, the names of the persons applying for a license, a brief statement of the facts sworn to by the persons applying for a license, and the returns of the person solemnizing the marriage.

(b) Records of documents of the probate division shall contain documents, applications or affidavits, either original or copies, and information pertaining to those documents, as found in division (C)(2)(a) of this rule or as considered necessary by the court.

(3) **Journal.** The probate division shall maintain a journal for orders, entries, or judgments pertaining to the business and administration of the division, and other miscellaneous orders, entries, or judgments which the court may consider necessary to journalize, including all of the following:

(a) Orders of appointment and oaths of office pursuant to section 2101.11 of the Revised Code of court personnel and other nonfiduciary appointees;

(b) Orders of reference to magistrates;

(c) Changes of the local rules of the probate division;

(d) Orders changing the hours for the opening and closing of the probate court.

(4) **Indexes.** The probate division shall maintain an index for each docket, record of documents, and journal described in division (C) of this rule. Each index shall be kept current with names or captions of proceedings in alphabetical order and references to a docket, record or documents, journal, or case file where information pertaining to those names or proceedings may be found.

(5) **Time stamp.** Upon the filing of any paper or electronic entry permitted by the probate division, a time stamp or entry shall be placed on the paper or electronic entry to indicate the time, day, month, and year of filing.

(D) Destruction and preservation of probate records

(1) The vouchers, proof, or other evidence filed with the probate division in support of the expenditures or distribution slated in an account, after review and reconciliation with the accounting and notation of reconciliation in the record or file, may be returned to the fiduciary or retained in accordance with divisions (D)(2) and (E) of this rule.

(2) All records, vouchers, inventories, accounts, pleadings, applications, petitions, records of adoptions, marriages, and mental health commitments, wills, trusts, journals, indexes, dockets, records or documents related to estate or inheritance taxes, and other papers and filings of the probate division, may be preserved using any nationally accepted records and information management process in accordance with Sup. R 26(D).

(3) In the probate division's discretion, any nonessential note, notice, letter, form, or other paper, document, or memorandum in a case file that is not essential to providing a record of the case and the judgment of the probate division may be destroyed prior to, or after, the case is closed. For purposes of division (D)(3) of this rule, evidence of service of notice of the initial complaint, petition, or application that establishes the probate division's jurisdiction is essential to providing a record of a probate case.

(4) Judge, magistrate, investigator, and clerk notes, drafts, and research prepared for the purpose of compiling a report, opinion, or other document or memorandum may be kept separate from the case file, retained in the case file, or destroyed at the discretion of the preparer.

(E) Case file and probate record retention schedule

(1) **Adoption records** Adoption records shall be retained permanently.

(2) **Birth and death registrations** Birth and death registrations dated prior to 1908 shall be retained permanently.

(3) **Civil commitment records** Civil commitment records shall be retained for three years after the case is closed.

(4) **Dockets, records of documents, journals and indexes** Dockets, records of documents, journals, and indexes shall be retained permanently.

(5) **Evidence filed in support of expenditures or distributions** Vouchers, proof, or other evidence filed in support of expenditures or distributions stated in an account shall be retained for three years after the date of filing.

(6) **Marriage license records** Marriage license records shall be retained permanently.

(7) **Trust accountings** Trust accountings shall be retained for twelve years after the date the accounting was approved.

(8) **All other records** All other records shall be retained for twelve years after the date the case, cause, proceeding, or matter is closed or completed.

(F) **Temporary estate tax orders** Divisions (D) and (E) of this rule do not apply to records of estates in which temporary estate tax orders are pending.

History: Effective 10-1-97.

RULE 26.05. Municipal and County Courts — Records Retention Schedule

(A) **Definition of docket** As used in this rule, "docket" means the record where the clerk of the municipal or county court enters all of the information historically included in the appearance docket, the trial docket, the journal, and the execution docket.

(B) **Required records**

(1) Municipal and county courts shall maintain an index, docket, journal, and case files in accordance with Sup. R. 26(B) and divisions (A) and (C) of this rule.

(2) Upon the filing of any paper or electronic entry permitted by the municipal or county court, a time stamp or entry shall be placed on the paper or electronic entry to indicate the time, day, month, and year of filing.

(C) **Content of docket**

(1) The docket shall be programmed to allow retrieval of orders or judgments of the municipal or county court in a chronological as well as a case specific manner. Entries in the docket shall be made as events occur, shall index directly and in reverse the names of all parties to cases in the municipal or county court and shall include all of the following:

(a) Names and addresses of all parties in full;

(b) Names, addresses, and Supreme Court attorney registration numbers of all counsel;

(c) The issuance of documents for service upon a party and the return of service or lack of return;

(d) A brief description of all records and orders filed in the proceeding, the date filed, and a cross reference to other records as appropriate;

(e) A schedule of court proceedings for the municipal or county court and its officers to use for case management.

(f) All actions taken by the municipal or county court to enforce orders or judgments.

(2) "Financial record" means a record that is related to the imposition of fines, costs, and other fees in cases and controversies heard in the municipal and county courts.

(D) **Retention schedule for financial records**

(1) **Auditor reports** Auditor of State reports shall be retained permanently.

(2) **Monetary records** Monetary records shall be retained for three years after the issuance of an audit report by the Auditor of State.

(3) **Rental escrow account records** Rental escrow account records shall be retained for five years after the last date of deposit with the municipal or county court.

(4) **Yearly reports** Yearly reports shall be retained permanently.

(E) **Retention schedule for the index, docket, and journal** The index, docket, and journal shall be retained for twenty-five years.

(F) **Judge, magistrate, and clerk notes, drafts, and research** Judge, magistrate, and clerk notes, drafts, and research prepared for the purpose of compiling a report, opinion, or other document or memorandum may be kept separate from the case file, retained in the case file, or destroyed at the discretion of the preparer.

(G) **Retention schedule for case files**

(1) **Civil case files** Civil case files shall be retained for two years after the issuance of an audit report by the Auditor of State.

(2) **DUI case files** Driving under the influence of alcohol or drug ("DUI") case files shall be retained for fifty years after the date of the final order of the municipal or county court.

(3) **First through fourth degree misdemeanor traffic and criminal case files** Except for DUI case files, first through fourth degree misdemeanor traffic files shall be retained for twenty-five years and criminal case files shall be retained for fifty years after the date of the final order of the municipal or county court or one year after the issuance of an audit report by the Auditor of State, whichever is later.

(4) **Minor misdemeanor traffic and minor misdemeanor criminal case files** Minor misdemeanor traffic and minor misdemeanor criminal case files shall be retained for five years after the final order of the municipal or county court or one year after the issuance of an audit report by the Auditor of State, whichever is later.

(5) **Parking ticket records** Parking ticket records shall be retained until the ticket is paid and the Auditor of State issues an audit report.

(6) **Real estate** Case files of matters that resulted in a final judgment determining title or interest in real estate shall be retained permanently.

(7) **Search warrant records** Search warrant records shall be indexed and the warrants and returns retained in their original form for five years after the date of service or last service attempt.

History: Amended, eff 9-23-04; 3-23-05.

RULE 27. Approval of Local Rules of Court Relative to Information Technology

(A) **Purpose and definitions**

(1) This rule provides a process for establishing uniform, minimum standards for the use of electronic documents and records in the courts of Ohio. This rule is intended to facilitate the sharing of information between and among Ohio courts, reduce costs and provide consistency for practitioners and the public, and provide guidance to persons who develop information systems for use by Ohio courts. This rule shall be interpreted consistent with this intent and to allow for technological enhancements that improve the efficiency of Ohio courts.

(2) As used in this rule, "electronic" and "electronic signature" have the same meaning as used in section 1306.01 of the Revised Code.

(B) **Advisory Committee** The Supreme Court Advisory Committee on Technology and the Courts shall do all of the following:

(1) Promulgate and publish regulations governing the use of information technology in the courts of Ohio, including but not limited to all of the following:

(a) Minimum, uniform standards relating to the creation, distribution, filing, and storage of and access to electronic documents;

(b) Minimum, uniform standards relating to the use of electronic signatures for electronic documents;

(c) Minimum, uniform standards for information and document systems;

(d) The process pursuant to which local rules of court are reviewed and approved by the committee pursuant to division (B) of this rule.

(2) Review local rules of court proposed pursuant to division (C) of this rule and approve those rules that satisfy the minimum, uniform standards adopted by the committee pursuant to division (B) of this rule.

(C) **Approval of local rules** Before adopting any local rule of practice that relates to the use of information technology, a court shall submit a copy of the proposed local rule to the Supreme Court Commission on Technology and the Courts for review in accordance with the process established by the Commission. A local rule of practice that relates to the use of information technology shall be considered inconsistent with this rule and of no force and effect unless the Commission determines that the local rule complies with the minimum, uniform standards adopted by the Commission.

History: Effective 7-1-01; Amended 12-1-07.

RULES 28-34

RULE 35. Case Management Section

There shall be a Case Management Section of the Supreme Court. The Case Management Section shall have the authority and responsibility to do all of the following:

(A) Receive, analyze, maintain, audit, and publish, at the direction of the Chief Justice of the Supreme Court, statistical data from the courts of Ohio, including an annual compilation of the reports required by Sup. R. 37;

(B) Assist and train judges, court administrators, clerks, and other court personnel in performing the reporting functions required by these rules;

(C) Monitor statistical reporting by conducting audits of the various courts in accordance with statistical auditing standards and procedures;

(D) Review audit results with judges and court personnel;

(E) Prepare and provide an implementation manual that contains commentary and explanatory material pertaining to these rules and the report forms required by these rules;

(F) Make ongoing recommendations regarding both of the following:

(1) Amendments to the Rules of Superintendence in order that the rules remain current with changes in the law;

(2) Auditing standards and procedures so that the Case Management Section can effectively accomplish its stated objectives.

History: Amended, eff 7-1-09.

RULE 36. Designation of Trial Attorney; Assignment System

(A) **Designation of trial attorney** In civil cases the attorney who is to try the case shall be designated as trial attorney on all pleadings. In criminal cases, except felonies, the attorney who is to try the case, upon being retained or appointed, shall notify the court that he or she is the trial attorney by filing a written statement with the clerk of the court.

(B)(1) **Individual assignment system** As used in these rules, "individual assignment system" means the system in which, upon the filing in or transfer to the court or a division of the court, a case immediately is assigned by lot to a judge of the division, who becomes primarily responsible for the determination of every issue and proceeding in the case until its termination. All preliminary matters, including requests for continuances, shall be submitted for disposition to the judge to whom the case has been assigned or, if the assigned judge is unavailable, to the administrative judge. The individual assignment system ensures all of the following:

(a) Judicial accountability for the processing of individual cases;

(b) Timely processing of cases through prompt judicial control over cases and the pace of litigation;

(c) Random assignment of cases to judges of the division through an objective and impartial system that ensures the equitable distribution of cases between or among the judges of the division.

(2) Each multi-judge general, domestic relations, and juvenile division of the court of common pleas shall adopt the individual assignment system for the assignment of all cases to judges of the division. Each multi-judge municipal or county court shall adopt the individual assignment system for the assignment of all cases to the judges of that court, except as otherwise provided in division (C) of this rule. Modifications to the individual assignment system may be adopted to provide for the redistribution of cases involving the same criminal defendant, parties, family members, or subject-matter. Any modifications shall satisfy divisions (B)(1)(a) to (c) of this rule and be adopted by local rule of court.

(C) **Assignment system** In each multi-judge municipal or county court, cases may be assigned to an individual judge or to a particular session of court pursuant to the following system:

(1) **Particular session** A particular session of court is one in which cases are assigned by subject category rather than by the individual assignment system. The following subject categories shall be disposed of by particular session:

(a) Civil cases in which a motion for default judgment is made;

(b) Criminal cases in which a plea of guilty or no contest is entered;

(c) Initial appearance in criminal cases;

(d) Preliminary hearings in criminal cases;

(e) Criminal cases in which an immediate trial is conducted upon initial appearance;

(f) Small claims cases;

(g) Forcible entry and detainer cases in which the right to trial by jury is waived or not demanded.

(h) Cases where a party has made application to, or has been accepted into, a specialized court or docket.

To guarantee a fair and equal distribution of cases, a judge who is assigned a case by subject matter pursuant to Sup. R. 36(B)(2), or by virtue of a specialized court or docket pursuant to Sup. R. 36(C)(1)(h), may request the administrative judge to reassign a similar case by lot to another judge in that multi-judge common pleas, municipal, or county court.

(2) **Assignment** Cases not subject to assignment in a particular session shall be assigned using the individual assignment system. Civil cases shall be assigned under division (C)(2) of this rule when an answer is filed or when a motion, other than one for default judgment, is filed. Criminal cases shall be assigned under division (C)(2) of this rule when a plea of not guilty is entered.

(3) **Duration of assignment to particular session** The administrative judge shall equally apportion particular session assignments among all judges. A judge shall not be assigned to a particular session of court for more than two consecutive weeks.

(D) **Assignment of refiled cases** In any instance where a previously filed and dismissed case is refiled, that case shall be reassigned to the judge originally assigned by lot to hear it unless, for good cause shown, that judge is precluded from hearing the case.

(E) **Assignment — new judicial positions** After the date of election, but prior to the first day of the term of a new judicial position, the administrative judge of a court or division through a random selection of pending cases shall equitably reassign cases pending in the court or division between or among the judges of the court or division and shall create a docket similar to a representative docket. Reassignment shall be completed in a manner consistent with this rule and may exclude criminal cases and cases scheduled for trial. Any matters arising in cases assigned to the docket for the new judicial position prior to the date on which the judge elected to that position takes office shall be resolved by the administrative judge or assigned to another judge.

NOTES TO DECISIONS

ANALYSIS

Authority of administrative judge
Mandamus
Waiver of reassignment or transfer

There was no error in an administrative judge's transfer of a cognovit judgment action to his docket and his entry of judgment against the guarantor, as such entry was a mere ministerial function that did not require the administrative judge to exercise personal judgment or discretion, and there was no violation of Ohio Superintendence Ct. R. 4(B) or 36(B)(1). Ohio Carpenters' Pension Fund v. La Centre, — Ohio App. 3d —, 2006 Ohio 2214, — N.E. 2d —, 2006 Ohio App. LEXIS 2060 (May 4, 2006).

Criminal defendant was not entitled to mandamus because the criminal defendant failed to establish that a judge had an absolute duty to find that the judge's recusal violated Ohio Superintendence Ct. R. 36(B)(1); the judge's decision to voluntarily recuse himself was a matter of judicial discretion which could not be controlled through mandamus. State ex

889 [Sup. R. 36.1]

rel. Brady v. Russo, — Ohio App. 3d —, 2007 Ohio 3277, — N.E. 2d —, 2007 Ohio App. LEXIS 3033 (June 22, 2007).

When defendant was placed on community control and told that her case would probably be reassigned to another judge, which it was, and she, at no time, stated an objection in the trial court to the reassignment of her case, she waived any objection, under Ohio Superintendence Ct. R. 36(B)(1), to the judge to whom her case was transferred imposing a sentence upon her admission that she violated the terms of her community control. State v. Sizemore, — Ohio App. 3d —, 2006 Ohio 1434, — N.E. 2d —, 2006 Ohio App. LEXIS 1302 (Mar. 27, 2006).

RULE 36.1.   Notice of Appellate Panels

No later than fourteen days prior to the date on which oral argument will be heard, the court of appeals shall make available to the parties the names of the judges assigned to the three-judge panel that will hear the case. If the parties waive oral argument, the court of appeals shall make available to the parties the names of the judges assigned to the three-judge panel that will hear the case no later than fourteen days prior to the date on which the case is submitted to the panel. If the membership of the panel changes after the names of the judges are made available to the parties pursuant to this rule, the court of appeals shall immediately make the new membership of the panel available to the parties.

History: Effective 7-1-02.

RULE 37.   Reports and Information

(A) **Report forms; responsibility for submission** Judges of the courts of appeals, courts of common pleas, municipal courts, and county courts shall submit to the Case Management Section of the Supreme Court the following report forms in the manner specified in this division no later than the fifteenth day after the close of the reporting period.

(1) **Courts of appeal** The following reports shall be prepared and submitted quarterly:

(a) The presiding or administrative judge in each appellate district shall prepare and submit a Presiding Judge Report of the status of all pending cases in the court.

(b) Each judge of a court of appeals shall prepare and submit an Appellate Judge Report of the judge's work. The report shall be submitted through the presiding or administrative judge and shall contain the signatures of the reporting judge, the presiding or administrative judge, and the preparer, if other than the reporting judge, attesting to the accuracy of the report.

(2) **Courts of common pleas** The following reports shall be prepared and submitted monthly, except that Form C shall be prepared and submitted quarterly:

(a) Each judge of a general, domestic relations, or juvenile division and each judge temporarily assigned to a division by the presiding judge is responsible for a report of the judge's work in that division. In a multi-judge general, domestic relations, or juvenile division, the reports shall be submitted through the administrative judge. In a multi-judge probate division, the judges shall sign and submit one report of the work in that division. The reports shall contain the signatures of the reporting judge, the administrative judge, and the preparer, if other than the reporting judge, attesting to the accuracy of the report.

(b) Each judge sitting by assignment of the Chief Justice of the Supreme Court shall submit a report of the judge's work. The reports shall be submitted through the administrative judge of the division to which the judge is assigned and shall contain the signatures of the reporting judge, the administrative judge, and the preparer, if other than the reporting judge, attesting to the accuracy of the report.

(3) **Municipal and county courts** The following reports shall be prepared and submitted monthly:

(a) Each administrative judge shall submit a completed Administrative Judge Report which shall be a report of all cases not individually assigned.

(b) Each judge shall submit a completed Individual Judge Report, which shall be a report of all cases assigned to the individual judge. The report shall be submitted through the administrative judge and shall contain the signatures of the reporting judge, the administrative judge, and the preparer, if other than the reporting judge, attesting to the accuracy of the report.

(c) Each judge sitting by assignment of the Chief Justice shall submit a report of the judge's work. The report shall be submitted through the administrative judge of the division to which the judge is assigned and shall contain the signatures of the reporting judge, the administrative judge, and the preparer, if other than the reporting judge, attesting to the accuracy of the report.

(4) **Reporting Standards** The following standards shall apply in completing the statistical reports required by these rules:

(a) In domestic relations cases, motions filed prior or subsequent to a final decree of divorce or dissolution shall be considered part of the original case and reported under the original case number;

(b) A motion filed in delinquency and unruly cases shall be considered part of the case in which the motion is filed unless the motion is considered a separate delinquency case under division (B) of section 2151.02 of the Revised Code;

(c) A criminal case and a traffic case arising from the same act, transaction, or series of acts or transactions shall be considered separate cases.

(B) **Capital case reporting** Each judge assigned a criminal case in which an indictment or a count in an indictment charges the defendant with aggravated murder and contains one or more specifications of aggravating circumstances listed in division (A) of section 2929.04 of the Revised Code shall include with the report submitted pursuant to division (A) of this rule notice, on a form prescribed by the Supreme Court, of any of the following events that occur during the reporting period:

(1) The assignment of the case to the judge;

(2) The defendant pleading guilty or no contest to any offense in the case or the dismissal of the indictment or any count in the indictment;

(3) The final disposition of the charges and specifications in the case. This shall include when the defendant is found guilty of capital charges and specifications, but does not receive the death penalty.

(C) **Reports available for public access when filed** All reports required by these rules shall be available for public access pursuant to Sup. R 44 through 47 upon filing with the Case Management Section. All judges and clerks shall cooperate with the Case Management Section to ensure the accuracy of the reports.

(D) **Chief Justice; requests for additional information** The Chief Justice may require additional information concerning the disposition of cases and the management of the courts in order to discharge the Chief Justice's constitutional and statutory duties. All judges, clerks, and other officers of all courts shall furnish the Chief Justice with any information requested by the Chief Justice.

History: SupR 37(A)(4)(b), (c) effective 1-1-98; 7-1-09.

RULE 38. Annual Physical Case Inventory; New Judge Inventory

(A) Except as provided in division (B) of this rule, each judge, on or before the first day of October, shall complete an annual physical inventory of all cases reported as pending on the applicable statistical report forms filed by the judge.

(B) A judge, when initially elected or appointed to the court of appeals, court of common pleas, municipal court, or county court shall complete a physical case inventory within three months of the date on which the judge first takes office. Subsequent annual physical inventories shall be completed on or before the first day of October of each ensuing year.

(C) Completion of the physical inventory required by this rule shall be documented in the appropriate space on the applicable statistical report forms.

RULE 39. Case Time Limits

(A) **Appellate and civil case time limits** The time limits for disposition of appellate and civil cases shall be as indicated on the Supreme Court report forms.

(B) **Criminal case time limits**

(1) In common pleas court, all criminal cases shall be tried within six months of the date of arraignment on an indictment or information. In municipal and county court, all criminal cases shall be tried within the time provided in Chapter 2945. of the Revised Code. Whenever a hearing or trial time is extended or shortened pursuant to section 2945.72 of the Revised Code or Criminal Rule 5 or 45, the judge shall state the reason for the change in an order and journalize the order.

(2) **Grand jury proceedings** When an accused has been bound over to a grand jury and no final action is taken by the grand jury within sixty days after the date of the bindover, the court or the administrative judge of the court shall dismiss the charge unless for good cause shown the prosecuting attorney is granted a continuance for a definite period of time.

(3) **Felony preliminary hearing** A preliminary hearing in a felony case shall be held within one month of the date of arrest or the date of issuance of the summons.

(4) **Sentencing** Provided the defendant in a criminal case is available, the court shall impose sentence or hold a sentencing hearing with all parties present within fifteen days of the verdict or finding of guilt or receipt of a completed pre-sentence investigation report. Any failure to meet this time standard shall be reported to the administrative judge, who shall take the necessary corrective action. In a single judge division, the failure shall be reported by the judge to the Case Management Section, which shall refer the matter to the Chief Justice of the Supreme Court for corrective action.

(5) **Post-conviction relief petitions; death penalty cases** All post-conviction relief petitions filed in death penalty cases shall be ruled upon within one hundred eighty days of the date of filing. In any month where a post-conviction relief petition in a death penalty case is filed, pending, or terminated, the administrative judge shall submit the Post-Conviction Relief Petition Report detailing the status of the petition.

(C) **Reporting** Any failure to comply with the time limits specified in this rule, and the reason for the failure, shall be reported immediately to the administrative judge, who shall take the necessary corrective action. In a single-judge court or division, the failure shall be reported by the judge to the Case Management Section. The Case Management Section shall report to the Chief Justice, who may take such action as may be necessary to cause the delinquent case to be tried forthwith.

History: Amended, eff 7-1-09.

NOTES TO DECISIONS

ANALYSIS

Discovery
Guidelines for judges

Trial court erred by dismissing the complaint with prejudice, based on the state's failure to provide discovery. The prosecutor's motion for a brief continuance so that defense counsel could prepare should have been granted: State v. Johnson, 169 Ohio App. 3d 552, 2006 Ohio 6227, 863 N.E.2d 1088, 2006 Ohio App. LEXIS 6196 (2006).

Superintendence Rules are guidelines for judges only and cannot be used by criminal defendants as a ground for discharge. The trial court had no obligation to dismiss the charges with prejudice based on a delay in the grand jury's indictment, and had the trial court ordered a dismissal, the State could have simply re-filed the charges, so defendant failed to demonstrate prejudice arising from alleged deficiency of counsel in not seeking a ruling on a motion to dismiss. State v. Perry, — Ohio App. 3d —, 2006 Ohio 220, — N.E. 2d —, 2006 Ohio App. LEXIS 179 (Jan. 20, 2006).

RULE 40. Review of Cases; Dismissal; Rulings on Motions and Submitted Cases

(A) Review; dismissal; rulings

(1) Each trial judge shall review, or cause to be reviewed, all cases assigned to the judge. Cases that have been on the docket for six months without any proceedings taken in the case, except cases awaiting trial assignment, shall be dismissed, after notice to counsel of record, for want of prosecution, unless good cause be shown to the contrary.

(2) All cases submitted for determination after a court trial shall be decided within ninety days from the date the case was submitted.

(3) All motions shall be ruled upon within one hundred twenty days from the date the motion was filed, except as otherwise noted on the report forms.

(4) All child support hearings involving an obligor or obligee called to active military service in the uniformed services, as defined in section 3119.77 of the Revised Code, shall be heard within thirty days from the date the court receives notice that the obligor or oblige has requested a hearing.

(B) Reporting

(1) Each judge shall report to the administrative judge decisions that have not been ruled upon within the applicable time period. The administrative judge shall confer with the judge who has motions pending beyond the applicable time period and shall determine the reasons for the delay on the rulings. If the administrative judge determines that there is no just cause for the delay, the administrative judge shall seek to rectify the delay within sixty days. If the delay is not rectified within sixty days, the administrative judge shall report the delay to the Case Management Section of the Supreme Court.

(2) In a single-judge court, if the judge has not rectified the delay, the judge shall report the delay in the rulings to the Case Management Section within one hundred eighty days from the date of the filing of the overtime motion or the submission of the case.

(3) All reports submitted to the administrative judge and the Case Management Section under this rule shall be available for public access pursuant to Sup. R. 44 through 47.

(C) Assigned judges

The provisions of this rule apply to judges sitting by assignment of the Chief Justice of the Supreme Court.

History: Amended, eff 7-1-09.

NOTES TO DECISIONS

ANALYSIS

Litigants' rights
Ruling on motions to suppress
Time limit for acting on motions

Flavoring manufacturer's action, seeking a writ of mandamus pursuant to RC § 2731.03 in order to compel a trial court judge to rule on its pending dismissal motions in an underlying negligence action filed against it, lacked merit, as the manufacturer failed to show that it had a clear legal right to have the judge rule on its pending motions prior to a discovery date cutoff and the holding of a pretrial conference; although Ohio Superintendence Ct. R. 40(A)(3) required the trial court to rule on a pending motion within 120 days, there was no corresponding right of a litigant to force the court to so rule upon expiration of that time period. Ohio Ex Rel. Givaudan v. Nadel, — Ohio App. 3d —, 2007 Ohio 5971, — N.E. 2d —, 2007 Ohio App. LEXIS 5274 (Nov. 9, 2007).

Trial court erred in denying defendant's motion to dismiss as 311 days passed between the filing of defendant's suppression motion and the filing of defendant's motion to dismiss. A reasonable time within which to rule on a motion was 120 days under Ohio Superintendence R. 40, leaving a balance of 191 days. Clearly defendant was not brought to trial on his disorderly conduct charge, which was a second-degree misdemeanor, within 90 days as required by RC § 2945.71, the Sixth Amendment, and Ohio Const. art. I, § 10. State v. Fields, — Ohio App. 3d —, 2006 Ohio 223, — N.E. 2d —, 2006 Ohio App. LEXIS 190 (Jan. 20, 2006).

Court dismissed an inmate's mandamus action pursuant to RC § 2731.04, wherein he sought to compel a judge to rule on motions to correct sentence in underlying criminal matters, as the criminal motions had not yet been pending for 120 days and accordingly, there was no unreasonable delay under Ohio Superintendence Ct. R. 40(A)(3). There was no procedural compliance by the inmate with the certified statement requirement of RC § 2969.25(C), the inclusion of party addresses as required by Ohio R. Civ. P. 10(A), and the specifications of the claim pursuant to Ohio Eighth Dist. Ct. App. R. 45, and lastly, the request lacked substantive merit because the sentences imposed were proper under RC § 2929.14(E)(1)(a). State ex rel. Smith v. Court of Common Pleas, — Ohio App. 3d —, 2007 Ohio 89, — N.E. 2d —, 2007 Ohio App. LEXIS 83 (Jan. 10, 2007).

Petitioner's mandamus or prohibition petition challenging a judge's decision to issue a bench warrant and a license and registration block was properly denied because there was no indication that the judge had refused to enter judgment on petitioner's pending motions to remove the block and set aside the warrant or that the judge had unnecessarily delayed ruling on the motions in light of the fact that, at the time that the mandamus petition was filed, the motions had been pending less than four months, and no response had been filed by the State. The direction in Ohio Superintendence Ct. R. 40(A)(3) that trial courts should rule on a pending motion within 120 days from the date that the motion was filed did not automatically entitle petitioner to a writ of mandamus as there had not been an unreasonable delay in ruling on the motions when the mandamus petition was filed. Powell v. Houser, — Ohio App. 3d —, 2007 Ohio 2866, — N.E. 2d —, 2007 Ohio App. LEXIS 2660 (June 6, 2007).

Incarcerated father was entitled to a writ of mandamus directing a trial court to rule on the motion the father filed in 2003 regarding his child support arrearage; the more than four years that had elapsed since the motion was filed was well beyond what was contemplated in Stark County, Ohio, Ct. C.P. Dom. Rel. Div. R. 13, 15 and Ohio Superintendence Ct. R. 40, the father had a clear legal right to a ruling on his motion, the trial court had a duty to provide the ruling, and the father had no adequate remedy at law and could not pursue an appeal without first obtaining a judgment from the trial court. Selway v. Court of Common Pleas Stark County, — Ohio App. 3d —, 2007 Ohio 4566, — N.E. 2d —, 2007 Ohio App. LEXIS 4086 (Sept. 4, 2007).

Where a common pleas court judge failed to rule on an inmate's timely filed motion for post-conviction relief pursuant to RC § 2953.21(E) and (G), as there was no ruling within the required 120-day period under Ohio Superintendence R. 40(A), the inmate's application for a writ of procedendo in order to compel the judge to issue the required ruling was granted. The inmate showed that he had a clear legal right to the relief requested and that there was no adequate remedy in the ordinary course of law. State ex rel. Martin v. Mannen, — Ohio App. 3d —, 2006 Ohio 3832, — N.E. 2d —, 2006 Ohio App. LEXIS 3809 (July 26, 2006).

RULE 41. Conflict of Trial Court Assignment Dates, Continuances, and Engaged Counsel

(A) **Continuances; granting of** The continuance of a scheduled trial or hearing is a matter within the sound discretion of the trial court for good cause shown.

No party shall be granted a continuance of a trial or hearing without a written motion from the party or counsel stating the reason for the continuance, endorsed in writing by the party as well as counsel, provided that the trial judge may waive this requirement upon a showing of good cause. No court shall grant a continuance to any party at any time without first setting a definite date for the trial or hearing.

When a continuance is requested by reason of the unavailability of a witness at the time scheduled for trial or hearing, the court shall consider the feasibility of resorting to the several methods of recording testimony permitted by Civil Rule 30(B) and authorized for use by Civil Rule 32(A)(3).

(B) **Conflict of trial assignment dates**

(1) When a continuance is requested for the reasons that counsel is scheduled to appear in another case assigned for trial on the same date in the same or another trial court of this state, the case which was first set for trial shall have priority and shall be tried on the date assigned. Criminal cases assigned for trial have priority over civil cases assigned for trial. The court should not consider any motion for a continuance due to a conflict of trial assignment dates unless a copy of the conflicting assignment is attached to the motion and the motion is filed not less than thirty days prior to trial.

(2) Except as provided in division (B)(3) of this rule, a continuance shall be granted, upon request, under either of the following circumstances:

(a) A party, counsel, or witness under subpoena is scheduled to appear on the same date at a hearing before the Board of Commissioners on Grievances and Discipline of the Supreme Court as a member of the Board, as a party, as counsel for a party, or as a witness under subpoena for the hearing;

(b) Counsel requesting the continuance will be unavailable to participate in the judicial proceeding because counsel is a member of the General Assembly whose attendance is required at a scheduled voting session or committee meeting of the General Assembly.

(3) In considering a continuance requested pursuant to division (B)(2)(b) of this rule, the court may require counsel to obtain the consent of the client and provide notice to all other parties to the action. The court may deny the requested continuance if either or both of the following apply:

(a) Counsel has been granted prior continuances in the same case based on attendance at scheduled voting sessions or committee meetings of the General Assembly;

(b) The court determines that further delay in the proceeding would result in substantial prejudice to a party.

(C) **Engaged counsel** If a designated trial attorney has such a number of cases assigned for trial in courts of this state so as to cause undue delay in the disposition of such cases, the administrative judge may summon such trial attorney who persistently requests continuances and extensions to warn the attorney of the possibility of sanctions and to encourage the attorney to make necessary adjustments in the management of his or her practice. Where such measures fail, restrictions may properly be imposed by the administrative judge on the number of cases in which the attorney may participate at any one time.

(D) **Continuances; reporting** Trial continuances shall be reported on a monthly basis to the administrative judge. Where a judge is persistently and unreasonably indulgent in granting continuances or extensions, the administrative judge shall investigate the reasons for the excessive continuances and take appropriate corrective action at the local level. If corrective action at the local level is unsuccessful, the administrative judge shall report that fact to the Case Management Section of the Supreme Court. If it comes to the attention of the Case Management Section that the judge of a single-judge division is persistently and unreasonably indulgent in granting continuances, it shall report the information to the Chief Justice, who shall take appropriate corrective action.

History: Amended, eff 10-1-03; 7-1-09.

NOTES TO DECISIONS

ANALYSIS

Denial of continuance
Written basis for continuances

As a trial of a lender's action against a debtor, seeking recovery for amounts due under her three defaulted loans, was continued multiple times and on the last such occasion, the trial court advised the parties that any further continuances would not be permitted, the trial court did not abuse its discretion under Franklin County, Ohio, Ct. C.P. R. 79, Ohio R. Civ. P. 5(A), and Ohio Superintendence Ct. R. 41(A) in holding the trial despite the debtor's absence and in denying her counsel's request for a continuance. Kemba Fin. Credit Union v. Fish, — Ohio App. 3d —, 2007 Ohio 43, — N.E. 2d —, 2007 Ohio App. LEXIS 33 (Jan. 9, 2007).

Trial court did not abuse its discretion under Ohio Superintendence Ct. R. 41(B)(1) where it denied a motion by counsel for appellants to continue a scheduled trial, which forced appellants to proceed unrepresented at the one-day bench trial, whereupon judgment was entered against them, as counsel was aware of a schedule conflict with another case in sufficient time to have made a timely continuance motion, but instead, he waited until two days prior to the scheduled trial date to make the motion. He failed to attach the requisite documents to the motion. Timeoni v. Ciancibelli, — Ohio App. 3d —, 2007 Ohio 2312, — N.E. 2d —, 2007 Ohio App. LEXIS 2134 (May 11, 2007).

Counsel's oral motion to continue, made on the day of the trial, failed to comply with filing requirements of motion for continuance and was properly denied. Pinson v. Lytle, — Ohio App. 3d —, 2006 Ohio 5441, — N.E. 2d —, 2006 Ohio App. LEXIS 5423 (Oct. 19, 2006).

RULE 42. Complex Litigation — Court of Common Pleas

(A) **Complex litigation determination** An attorney representing a party to an action filed in the general division of the court of common pleas may request that the case be designated as complex litigation. The attorney filing the request shall certify that the attorney has approval from his or her client to file the request. In determining whether a case shall be designated as complex litigation, the judge to whom the case is assigned shall consider all of the following:

(1) Number of parties involved;

(2) Whether a class action is involved;

(3) Whether it is a products liability case;

(4) Whether there are other related cases involving unusual multiplicity or complexity of factual or legal issues;

(5) Extent of discovery necessary to prepare the case for trial;

(6) Number or availability of parties and witnesses for trial;

(7) Any endorsement of or objections to the request from an opposing party or counsel for an opposing party.

(B) **Complex litigation determination — judicial** The judge to whom the case is assigned may designate a case as complex litigation without a request from an attorney representing a party to the action. The designation shall be made after the judge considers the factors set forth in divisions (A)(1) to (7) of this rule.

(C) **Time; reporting** A designation of a case as complex litigation pursuant to division (A) of this rule shall be made within six months of the date on which the case was filed. If a case is designated as complex litigation, the judge shall submit to the Case Management Section of the Supreme Court a report specifying the reasons for the designation of the case as complex litigation. The case shall be reported on Supreme Court Report Form A in the category of complex litigation and given thirty-six months from the date of filing to be terminated.

(D) **Authority of the Chief Justice** The Case Management Section shall periodically report the designation of cases as complex litigation to the Chief Justice of the Supreme Court, who may decide that a case should not be classified as complex litigation. If the Chief Justice determines that a case should not be classified as complex litigation, the Case Management Section shall notify the judge who shall remove the case from the complex litigation docket and notify the parties.

History: Amended, eff 7-1-09.

RULE 43. Case Numbering — Municipal and County Court

(A) **Method** When filed in the clerk's office, cases shall be categorized as civil, criminal, or traffic and serially numbered within each category on an annual basis beginning on the first day of January of each year. Cases shall be identified by year and by reference to the case type designator on the administrative judge report form. Additional identifiers may be added by local court rule.

(B) **Multiple defendants or charges in criminal cases**

(1) In criminal cases, including traffic cases, all defendants shall be assigned separate case numbers.

(2) Where a defendant is charged with a misdemeanor and a traffic offense, the defendant shall be assigned separate case numbers pursuant to Sup. R. 37(A)(4)(c). The category selected for the case number and its case type designator shall be that of the offense having the greatest potential penalty.

(3) Where as a result of the same act, transaction, or series of acts or transactions, a defendant is charged with a felony or felonies and a misdemeanor or misdemeanors, including traffic offenses, the defendant shall be assigned separate case numbers, one for the felony or felonies and one for each other type of offense pursuant to Sup. R. 37(A)(4)(c). The category selected for the case number and its case type designator shall be that of the offense having the greatest potential penalty.

History: Sup. R. 43(B)(2) effective 1-1-98.

RULE 44. Court Records - Definitions

In addition to the applicability of these rules as described in Sup. R. 1, Sup. R. 44 through 47 apply to the Supreme Court.

As used in Sup. R. 44 through 47:

(A) "Actual cost" means the cost of depleted supplies; records storage media costs; actual mailing and alternative delivery costs, or other transmitting costs; and any direct equipment operating and maintenance costs, including actual costs paid to private contractors for copying services.

(B) "Court record" means both a case document and an administrative document, regardless of physical form or characteristic, manner of creation, or method of storage.

(C)(1) "Case document" means a document and information in a document submitted to a court or filed with a clerk of court in a judicial action or proceeding, including exhibits, pleadings, motions, orders, and judgments, and any documentation prepared by the court or clerk in the judicial action or proceeding, such as journals, dockets, and indices, subject to the exclusions in division (C)(2) of this rule.

(2) The term "case document" does not include the following:

(a) A document or information in a document exempt from disclosure under state, federal, or the common law;

(b) Personal identifiers, as defined in division (H) of this rule;

(c) A document or information in a document to which public access has been restricted pursuant to division (E) of Sup. R. 45;

(d) Except as relevant to the juvenile's prosecution later as an adult, a juvenile's previous disposition in abuse, neglect, and dependency cases, juvenile civil commitment files, post-adjudicatory residential treatment facility reports, and post-adjudicatory releases of a juvenile's social history;

(e) Notes, drafts, recommendations, advice, and research of judicial officers and court staff;

(f) Forms containing personal identifiers, as defined in division (H) of this rule, submitted or filed pursuant to division (D)(2) of Sup. R. 45;

(g) Information on or obtained from the Ohio Courts Network, except that the information shall be available at the originating source if not otherwise exempt from public access.

(D) "Case file" means the compendium of case documents in a judicial action or proceeding.

(E) "File" means to deposit a document with a clerk of court, upon the occurrence of which the clerk time or date stamps and dockets the document.

(F) "Submit" means to deliver a document to the custody of a court for consideration by the court.

(G)(1) "Administrative document" means a document and information in a document created, received, or maintained by a court that serves to record the administrative, fiscal, personnel, or management functions, policies, decisions, procedures, operations, organization, or other activities of the court, subject to the exclusions in division (G)(2) of this rule.

(2) The term "administrative document" does not include the following:

(a) A document or information in a document exempt from disclosure under state, federal, or the common law, or as set forth in the Rules for the Government of the Bar;

(b) Personal identifiers, as defined in division (H) of this rule;

(c) A document or information in a document describing the type or level of security in a court facility, including a court security plan and a court security review conducted by a local court, the local court's designee, or the Supreme Court;

(d) An administrative or technical security recordkeeping document or information;

(e) Test questions, scoring keys, and licensing, certification, or court-employment examination documents before the examination is administered or if the same examination is to be administered again;

(f) Computer programs, computer codes, computer filing systems, and other software owned by a court or entrusted to it;

(g) Information on or obtained from the Ohio Courts Network, except that the information shall be available at the originating source if not otherwise exempt from public access;

(h) Data feeds by and between courts when using the Ohio Courts Network.

(H) "Personal identifiers" means social security numbers, except for the last four digits; financial account numbers, including but not limited to debit card, charge card, and credit card numbers; employer and employee identification numbers; and a juvenile's name in an abuse, neglect, or dependency case, except for the juvenile's initials or a generic abbreviation such as "CV" for "child victim."

(I) "Public access" means both direct access and remote access.

(J) "Direct access" means the ability of any person to inspect and obtain a copy of a court record at all reasonable times during regular business hours at the place where the record is made available.

(K) "Remote access" means the ability of any person to electronically search, inspect, and copy a court record at a location other than the place where the record is made available.

(L) "Bulk distribution" means the distribution of a compilation of information from more than one court record.

(M)(1) "New compilation" means a collection of information obtained through the selection, aggregation, or reformulation of information from more than one court record.

(2) The term "new compilation" does not include a collection of information produced by a computer system that is already programmed to provide the requested output.

RULE 45. Court Records - Public Access

(A) **Presumption of public access** Court records are presumed open to public access.

(B) **Direct access**

(1) A court or clerk of court shall make a court record available by direct access, promptly acknowledge any person's request for direct access, and respond to the request within a reasonable amount of time.

(2) Except for a request for bulk distribution pursuant to Sup. R. 46, a court or clerk of court shall permit a requestor to have a court record duplicated upon paper, upon the same medium upon which the court or clerk keeps it, or upon any other medium the court or clerk determines it can be reasonably duplicated as an integral part of its normal operations.

(3) A court or clerk of court shall mail, transmit, or deliver copies of a requested court record to the requestor within a reasonable time from the request, provided the court or clerk may adopt a policy allowing it to limit the number of court records it will mail, transmit, or deliver per month, unless the requestor certifies in writing that the requestor does not intend to use or forward the records, or the information contained in them, for commercial purposes. For purposes of this division, "commercial" shall be narrowly construed and does not include news reporting, the gathering of information to assist citizens in the understanding of court activities, or nonprofit educational research.

(4) A court or clerk of court may charge its actual costs incurred in responding to a request for direct access to a court record. The court or clerk may require a deposit of the estimated actual costs.

(C) **Remote access**

(1) A court or clerk of court may offer remote access to a court record. If a court or clerk offers remote access to a court record and the record is also available by direct access, the version of the record available through remote access shall be identical to the version of the record available by direct access, provided the court or clerk may exclude an exhibit or attachment

that is part of the record if the court or clerk includes notice that the exhibit or attachment exists and is available by direct access.

(2) Nothing in division (C)(1) of this rule shall be interpreted as requiring a court or clerk of court offering remote access to a case document in a case file to offer remote access to other case documents in that case file.

(3) Nothing in division (C)(1) of this rule shall be interpreted as prohibiting a court or clerk of court from making available on a website any court record that exists only in electronic form, including an on-line journal or register of actions.

(D) **Omission of personal identifiers prior to submission or filing**

(1) When submitting a case document to a court or filing a case document with a clerk of court, a party to a judicial action or proceeding shall omit personal identifiers from the document.

(2) When personal identifiers are omitted from a case document submitted to a court or filed with a clerk of court pursuant to division (D)(1) of this rule, the party shall submit or file that information on a separate form. The court or clerk may provide a standard form for parties to use. Redacted or omitted personal identifiers shall be provided to the court or clerk upon request or a party to the judicial action or proceeding upon motion.

(3) The responsibility for omitting personal identifiers from a case document submitted to a court or filed with a clerk of court pursuant to division (D)(1) of this rule shall rest solely with the party. The court or clerk is not required to review the case document to confirm that the party has omitted personal identifiers, and shall not refuse to accept or file the document on that basis.

(E) **Restricting public access to a case document**

(1) Any party to a judicial action or proceeding or other person who is the subject of information in a case document may, by written motion to the court, request that the court restrict public access to the information or, if necessary, the entire document. Additionally, the court may restrict public access to the information in the case document or, if necessary, the entire document upon its own order. The court shall give notice of the motion or order to all parties in the case. The court may schedule a hearing on the motion.

(2) A court shall restrict public access to information in a case document or, if necessary, the entire document, if it finds by clear and convincing evidence that the presumption of allowing public access is outweighed by a higher interest after considering each of the following:

(a) Whether public policy is served by restricting public access;

(b) Whether any state, federal, or common law exempts the document or information from public access;

(c) Whether factors that support restriction of public access exist, including risk of injury to persons, individual privacy rights and interests, proprietary business information, public safety, and fairness of the adjudicatory process.

(3) When restricting public access to a case document or information in a case document pursuant to this division, the court shall use the least restrictive means available, including but not limited to the following:

(a) Redacting the information rather than limiting public access to the entire document;

(b) Restricting remote access to either the document or the information while maintaining its direct access;

(c) Restricting public access to either the document or the information for a specific period of time;

(d) Using a generic title or description for the document or the information in a case management system or register of actions;

(e) Using initials or other identifier for the parties' proper names.

(4) If a court orders the redaction of information in a case document pursuant to this division, a redacted version of the document shall be filed in the case file along with a copy of the court's order. If a court orders that the entire case document be restricted from public access, a copy of the court's order shall be filed in the case file. A journal entry shall reflect the court's order. Case documents ordered restricted from public access or information in documents ordered redacted shall not be available for public access and shall be maintained separately in the case file.

(F) **Obtaining access to a case document that has been granted restricted public access**

(1) Any person, by written motion to the court, may request access to a case document or information in a case document that has been granted restricted public access pursuant to division (E) of this rule. The court shall give notice of the motion to all parties in the case and, where possible, to the non-party person who requested that public access be restricted. The court may schedule a hearing on the motion.

(2) A court may permit public access to a case document or information in a case document if it finds by clear and convincing evidence that the presumption of allowing public access is no longer outweighed by a higher interest. When making this determination, the court shall consider whether the original reason for the restriction of public access to the case document or information in the case document pursuant to division (E) of this rule no longer exists or is no longer applicable and whether any new circumstances, as set forth in that division, have arisen which would require the restriction of public access.

RULE 46.   Court Records - Bulk Distribution

(A) **Requests for bulk distribution and new compilations**

(1) Bulk distribution

(a) Any person, upon request, shall receive bulk distribution of information in court records, provided that the bulk distribution does not require creation of a new compilation. The court or clerk of court shall permit the requestor to choose that the bulk distribution be provided upon paper, upon the same medium upon which the court or clerk keeps the information, or upon any other medium the court or clerk determines it can be reasonably duplicated as an integral part of its normal operations, unless the choice requires a new compilation.

(b) The bulk distribution shall include a time or date stamp indicating the compilation date. A person who receives a bulk distribution of information in court records for redistribution shall keep the information current and delete inaccurate, sealed, or expunged information in accordance with Sup. R. 26.

(2) New compilation

(a) A court or clerk of court may create a new compilation customized for the convenience of a person who requests a bulk distribution of information in court records.

(b) In determining whether to create a new compilation, a court or clerk of court may consider if creating the new compilation is an appropriate use of its available resources and is consistent with the principles of public access.

(c) If a court or clerk of court chooses to create a new compilation, it may require personnel costs in addition to actual costs. The court or the clerk may require a deposit of the estimated actual and personnel costs to create the new compilation.

(d) A court or clerk of court shall maintain a copy and provide public access to any new compilation. After recouping the personnel costs to create the new compilation from the original requestor, the court or clerk may later assess only actual costs.

(B) **Contracts with providers of information technology support** A court or clerk of court that contracts with a provider of information technology support to gather, store, or make accessible court records shall require the provider to comply with requirements of Sup. R. 44 through 47, agree to protect the confidentiality of the records, notify the court or clerk of court of all bulk distribution and new compilation requests, including its own, and acknowledge that it has no ownership or proprietary rights to the records.

RULE 47. Court Records - Application, Remedies, and Liability

(A) **Application**

(1) The provisions of Sup. R. 44 through 47 requiring redaction or omission of information in case documents or restricting public access to case documents shall apply only to case documents in actions commenced on or after the effective date of this rule. Access to case documents in actions commenced prior to the effective date of Sup. R. 44 through 47 shall be governed by federal and state law.

(2) The provisions of Sup. R. 44 through 47 requiring omission of information in administrative documents or restricting public access to administrative documents shall apply to all documents regardless of when created.

(B) **Denial of public access - remedy** A person aggrieved by the failure of a court or clerk of court to comply with the requirements of Sup. R. 44 through 47 may pursue an action in mandamus pursuant to Chapter 2731. of the Revised Code.

(C) **Liability and immunity** Sup. R. 44 through 47 do not affect any immunity or defense to which a court, court agency, clerk of court, or their employees may be entitled under section 9.86 or Chapter 2744. of the Revised Code.

(D) **Review** Sup. R. 44 through 47 shall be subject to periodic review by the Commission on the Rules of Superintendence.

RULE 48. Guardians ad litem

(A) **Applicability** This rule shall apply in all domestic relations and juvenile cases in the courts of common pleas where a court appoints a guardian ad litem to protect and act in the best interest of a child.

(B) **Definitions** For purposes of this rule:

(1) "Guardian ad litem" means an individual appointed to assist a court in its determination of a child's best interest.

(2) "Child" means:

(a) A person under eighteen years of age, or

(b) A person who is older than eighteen years of age who is deemed a child until the person attains twenty-one years of age under section 2151.011(B)(5) or section 2152.02(C) of the Revised Code.

(c) A child under R.C. 3109.04 or a disabled child under R.C.3119.86 who falls under the jurisdiction of a domestic relations court or of a juvenile court with a paternity docket.

(C) **Appointment of guardian ad litem**

(1) Each court appointing a guardian ad litem under this rule shall enter an Order of Appointment which shall include:

(a) A statement regarding whether a person is being appointed as a guardian ad litem only or as a guardian ad litem and attorney for the child.

(b) A statement that the appointment shall remain in effect until discharged by order of the court, by the court filing a final order in the case or by court rule.

(c) A statement that the guardian ad litem shall be given notice of all hearings and proceedings and shall be provided a copy of all pleadings, motions, notices and other documents filed in the case.

(2) Whenever feasible, the same guardian ad litem shall be reappointed for a specific child in any subsequent case in any court relating to the best interest of the child.

(3) The court shall make provisions for fees and expenses in the Order.

(D) **Responsibilities of a guardian ad litem** In order to provide the court with relevant information and an informed recommendation regarding the child's best interest, a guardian ad litem shall perform, at a minimum, the responsibilities stated in this division, unless impracticable or inadvisable to do so.

(1) A guardian ad litem shall represent the best interest of the child for whom the guardian is appointed. Representation of best interest may be inconsistent with the wishes of the child whose interest the guardian ad litem represents.

(2) A guardian ad litem shall maintain independence, objectivity and fairness as well as the appearance of fairness in dealings with parties and professionals, both

in and out of the courtroom and shall have no ex parte communications with the court regarding the merits of the case.

(3) A guardian ad litem is an officer of the court and shall act with respect and courtesy to the parties at all times.

(4) A guardian ad litem shall appear and participate in any hearing for which the duties of a guardian ad litem or any issues substantially within a guardian ad litem's duties and scope of appointment are to be addressed.

(5) A non-attorney guardian ad litem must avoid engaging in conduct that constitutes the unauthorized practice of law, be vigilant in performing the guardian ad litem's duties and request that the court appoint legal counsel, or otherwise employ the services of an attorney, to undertake appropriate legal actions on behalf of the guardian ad litem in the case.

(6) A guardian ad litem who is an attorney may file pleadings, motions and other documents as appropriate under the applicable rules of procedure.

(7) When a court appoints an attorney to serve as both the guardian ad litem and attorney for a child, the attorney shall advocate for the child's best interest and the child's wishes in accord with the Rules of Professional Conduct. Attorneys who are to serve as both guardian ad litem and attorney should be aware of Rule 3.7 of the Rules of Professional Conduct and act accordingly.

(8) When a guardian ad litem determines that a conflict exists between the child's best interest and the child's wishes, the guardian ad litem shall, at the earliest practical time, request in writing that the court promptly resolve the conflict by entering appropriate orders.

(9) A guardian ad litem shall avoid any actual or apparent conflict of interest arising from any relationship or activity including, but not limited to, those of employment or business or from professional or personal contacts with parties or others involved in the case. A guardian ad litem shall avoid self-dealing or associations from which the guardian ad litem might benefit, directly or indirectly, except from compensation for services as a guardian ad litem.

(10) Upon becoming aware of any actual or apparent conflict of interest, a guardian ad litem shall immediately take action to resolve the conflict, shall advise the court and the parties of the action taken and may resign from the matter with leave of court, or seek court direction as necessary. Because a conflict of interest may arise at any time, a guardian ad litem has an ongoing duty to comply with this division.

(11) Unless excepted by statute, by court rule consistent with this rule, or by order of court pursuant to this rule, a guardian ad litem shall meet the qualifications and satisfy all training and continuing education requirements under this rule and under any local court rules governing guardians ad litem. A guardian ad litem shall meet the qualifications for guardians ad litem for each county where the guardian ad litem serves and shall promptly advise each court of any grounds for disqualification or unavailability to serve.

(12) A guardian ad litem shall be responsible for providing the court or its designee with a statement indicating compliance with all initial and continuing educational and training requirements so the court may maintain the files required in division (G) of this rule. The compliance statement shall include information detailing the date, location, contents and credit hours received for any relevant training course.

(13) A guardian ad litem shall make reasonable efforts to become informed about the facts of the case and to contact all parties. In order to provide the court with relevant information and an informed recommendation as to the child's best interest, a guardian ad litem shall, at a minimum, do the following, unless impracticable or inadvisable because of the age of the child or the specific circumstances of a particular case:

(a) Meet with and interview the child and observe the child with each parent, foster parent, guardian or physical custodian and conduct at least one interview with the child where none of these individuals is present;

(b) Visit the child at his or her residence in accordance with any standards established by the court in which the guardian ad litem is appointed;

(c) Ascertain the wishes of the child;

(d) Meet with and interview the parties, foster parents and other significant individuals who may have relevant knowledge regarding the issues of the case;

(e) Review pleadings and other relevant court documents in the case in which the guardian ad litem is appointed;

(f) Review criminal, civil, educational and administrative records pertaining to the child and, if appropriate, to the child's family or to other parties in the case;

(g) Interview school personnel, medical and mental health providers, child protective services workers and relevant court personnel and obtain copies of relevant records;

(h) Recommend that the court order psychological evaluations, mental health and/or substance abuse assessments, or other evaluations or tests of the parties as the guardian ad litem deems necessary or helpful to the court; and

(i) Perform any other investigation necessary to make an informed recommendation regarding the best interest of the child.

(14) A guardian ad litem shall immediately identify himself or herself as a guardian ad litem when contacting individuals in the course of a particular case and shall inform these individuals about the guardian ad litem's role and that documents and information obtained may become part of court proceedings.

(15) As an officer of the court, a guardian ad litem shall make no disclosures about the case or the investigation except in reports to the court or as necessary to perform the duties of a guardian ad litem. A guardian ad litem shall maintain the confidential nature of personal identifiers, as defined in Rule 44 of the Rules of Superintendence, or addresses where there are allegations of domestic violence or risk to a party's or child's safety. A guardian ad litem may recommend that the court restrict access to the report or a portion of the report, after trial, to preserve the privacy, confidentiality, or safety of the parties or the person for whom the guardian ad litem was appointed in accordance with Rule 45 of the Rules of Superintendence. The court

may, upon application, and under such conditions as may be necessary to protect the witnesses from potential harm, order disclosure of or access to the information that addresses the need to challenge the truth of the information received from the confidential source.

(16) A guardian ad litem shall perform responsibilities in a prompt and timely manner, and, if necessary, an attorney guardian ad litem may request timely court reviews and judicial intervention in writing with notice to parties or affected agencies.

(17) A guardian ad litem who is to be paid by the court or a party, shall keep accurate records of the time spent, services rendered, and expenses incurred in each case and file an itemized statement and accounting with the court and provide a copy to each party or other entity responsible for payment.

(E) **Training requirements** In order to serve as a guardian ad litem, an applicant shall have, at a minimum, the following training:

(1) Successful completion of a pre-service training course to qualify for appointment and thereafter, successful completion of continuing education training in each succeeding calendar year to qualify for continued appointment.

(2) The pre-service training course must be the six hour guardian ad litem pre-service course provided by the Supreme Court of Ohio, the Ohio CASA/GAL Association's pre-service training program, or with prior approval of the appointing court, be a course at least six hours in length that covers the topic areas in division (E) (3).

(3) To meet the requirements of this rule, the pre-service course shall include training on all the following topics:

(a) Human needs and child development including, but not limited to, stages of child development;

(b) Communication and diversity including, but not limited to, communication skills with children and adults, interviewing skills, methods of critical questioning, use of open- ended questions, understanding the perspective of the child, sensitivity, building trust, multicultural awareness, and confidentiality;

(c) Preventing child abuse and neglect including, but not limited to, assessing risk and safety;

(d) Family and child issues including, but not limited to, family dynamics, substance abuse and its effects, basic psychopathology for adults and children, domestic violence and its effects;

(e) Legal framework including, but not limited to, records checks, accessing, assessing and appropriate protocol, a guardian ad litem's role in court, local resources and service practice, report content, mediation and other types of dispute resolution.

(4) The continuing education course must be at least three hours in length and be provided by the Supreme Court of Ohio or by the Ohio CASA/GAL Association, or with prior approval of the appointing court, be a training that complies with division (5) of this rule.

(5) To meet the requirements of this rule, the three hour continuing education course shall:

(a) Be specifically designed for continuing education of guardians ad litem and not pre- service education; and

(b) Consist of advanced education related to topics identified in division (E)(3) (a)–(e) of this rule.

(6) If a guardian ad litem fails to complete a three hour continuing education course within any calendar year, that person shall not be eligible to serve as a guardian ad litem until this continuing education requirement is satisfied. If the person's gap in continuing education is three calendar years or less, the person shall qualify to serve after completing a three hour continuing education course offered under this rule. If the gap in continuing education is more than three calendar years that person must complete a six hour pre-service education course to qualify to serve.

(7) An individual who is currently serving as a guardian ad litem on the effective date of this rule, or who has served during the five years immediately preceding the effective date, shall have one year from the effective date to obtain the required six hour pre-service training in order to avoid removal from the court's list of approved guardians ad litem.

(8) Attendance at an Ohio Guardian ad Litem Training Program approved by the Supreme Court of Ohio or at an Ohio CASA/Guardian Association pre-service training program at any time prior to the effective date of this rule shall be deemed compliance with the pre-service training requirement.

(F) **Reports of guardians ad litem** A guardian ad litem shall prepare a written final report, including recommendations to the court, within the times set forth in this division. The report shall detail the activities performed, hearings attended, persons interviewed, documents reviewed, experts consulted and all other relevant information considered by the guardian ad litem in reaching the guardian ad litem's recommendations and in accomplishing the duties required by statute, by court rule, and in the court's Order of Appointment. In addition, the following provisions shall apply to guardian ad litem reports in the juvenile and domestic relations divisions of Courts of Common Pleas:

(1) In juvenile abuse, neglect, and dependency cases and actions to terminate parental rights:

(a) All reports, written or oral, shall be used by the court to ensure that the guardian ad litem has performed those responsibilities required by section 2151.281 of the Revised Code.

(b) Oral and written reports may address the substantive allegations before the court, but shall not be considered as conclusive on the issues.

(c) Unless waived by all parties or unless the due date is extended by the court, the final report shall be filed with the court and made available to the parties for inspection no less than seven days before the dispositional hearing. Written reports maybe accessed in person or by phone by the parties or their legal representatives. A copy shall be provided to the court at the hearing.

(d) A guardian ad litem shall be available to testify at the dispositional hearing and may orally supplement the final report at the conclusion of the hearing.

(e) A guardian ad litem also may file an interim report, written or oral, any time prior to the dispositional hearing and prior to hearings on actions to terminate parental rights. Written reports may be accessed in person or by phone by the parties or their legal representatives.

(f) Any written interim report shall be filed with the court and made available to the parties for inspection no less than seven days before a hearing, unless the due date is extended by the court. Written reports may be accessed in person or by phone by the parties or their legal representatives. A copy of the interim report shall be provided to the court at the hearing.

(2) In domestic relations proceedings involving the allocation of parental rights and responsibilities, the final report shall be filed with the court and made available to the parties for inspection no less than seven days before the final hearing unless the due date is extended by the court. Written reports may be accessed in person or by phone by the parties or their legal representatives. A copy of the final report shall be provided to the court at the hearing. The court shall consider the recommendation of the guardian ad litem in determining the best interest of the child only when the report or a portion of the report has been admitted as an exhibit.

(G) **Responsibilities of the court** In order to ensure that only qualified individuals perform the duties of guardians ad litem and that the requirements of this rule are met, each court appointing guardians ad litem shall do all of the following:

(1) Maintain a public list of approved guardians ad litem while maintaining individual privacy under Rules 44 through 47 of the Rules of Superintendence.

(2) Establish criteria, which include all requirements of this rule, for appointment and removal of guardians ad litem and procedures to ensure an equitable distribution of the work load among the guardians ad litem on the list.

(3) Appoint or contract with a person to coordinate the application and appointment process, keep the files and records required by this rule, maintain information regarding training opportunities, receive written comments and complaints regarding the performance of guardians ad litem practicing before that court and perform other duties as assigned by the court.

(4) Maintain files for all applicants and for individuals approved for appointment as guardians ad litem with the court. The files shall contain all records and information required by this rule, and by local rules, for the selection and service of guardians ad litem including a certificate or other satisfactory proof of compliance with training requirements.

(5) Require all applicants to submit a resume or information sheet stating the applicant's training, experience and expertise demonstrating the person's ability to successfully perform the responsibilities of a guardian ad litem.

(6) Conduct, or cause to be conducted, a criminal and civil background check and investigation of information relevant to the applicant's fitness to serve as a guardian ad litem.

(7) Conduct, at least annually, a review of its list to determine that all individuals are in compliance with the training and education requirements of this rule and local rules, that they have performed satisfactorily on all assigned cases during the preceding calendar year and are otherwise qualified to serve.

(8) Require all individuals on its list to certify annually they are unaware of any circumstances that would disqualify them from serving and to report the training they have attended to comply with division (E) of this rule.

(9) Each court shall develop a process or local rule and appoint a person for accepting and considering written comments and complaints regarding the performance of guardians ad litem practicing before that court. A copy of comments and complaints submitted to the court shall be provided to the guardian ad litem who is the subject of the complaint or comment. The person appointed may forward any comments and complaints to the administrative judge of the court for consideration and appropriate action. Dispositions by the court shall be made promptly. The court shall maintain a written record in the guardian ad litem's file regarding the nature and disposition of any comment or complaint and shall notify the person making the comment or complaint and the subject guardian ad litem of the disposition.

History: Effective March 1, 2009.

RULE 49.   [Reserved]

COURT OF COMMON PLEAS — PROBATE DIVISION

RULE 50.   Definitions

As used in Sup. R. 50 to 82 "case" means any of the following when filed in the probate division of the court of common pleas:

(A) A civil complaint, petition, or administrative appeal;

(B) A decedent's estate; a testamentary, inter vivos or wrongful death trust; a guardianship, conservatorship or request for emergency orders pursuant to division (B)(3) of 2111.02 of the Revised Code; an adoption or name change. Each beneficiary of a wrongful death trust, each ward or conservatee, each adoptee and each individual requesting a change of name in those proceedings with multiple interested parties, shall be considered a separate "case."

(C) Any other proceeding for which a case number is assigned including but not limited to the following: tax filings, filings of wills for probate or record, real estate transfers, and filings of foreign records where an estate is not opened; release from administration; minor's settlements; birth corrections; delayed birth registrations; mental retardation or tuberculosis commitments; petition for protective services; petition to compel HIV testing; an application to appoint a guardian, trustee, protector, or conservator of a mentally retarded or developmentally disabled person; acknowledgment of paternity; a petition for release of adoption information; powers of attorney including those for health care; declarations concerning life-sustaining treatment; proceedings to designate heir; applications to disinter or to oppose disinterment; and voluntary assignment for the benefit of creditors.

History: Effective 7-1-97; amended, eff 3-25-02.

RULE 51. Standard Probate Forms

(A) **Applicability** This rule prescribes the format, content, and use of standard forms for designated applications, pleadings, waivers, notices, entries, and other filings in certain proceedings in the probate division of the courts of common pleas.

Where a standard form has not been prescribed by this rule, the form used shall be that required by the Civil Rules, or prescribed or permitted by the probate division of the court of common pleas in which it is being filed.

(B) **Effective date; use of standard and non-standard forms**

(1) This rule takes effect July 1, 1977 and applies to proceedings had on and after that date, including proceedings in pending cases.

(2) The standard forms shall be used on and after January 1, 1978, and nonstandard forms shall be rejected for filing.

(C) **Modification of standard forms; pleadings and filings prepared for particular cases**

(1) A printed, blank standard form may be modified by deletion or interlineation to meet the circumstances of a particular case or proceeding, if the modification can be accomplished neatly and conveniently. No court shall require the modification of a standard form as a routine matter. If any allegation, statement, data, information, pleading, or filing is required by an appropriate local rule of court and a standard form does not make provision therefor, it shall be provided in a separate or supplemental filing.

(2) Even though a standard form is prescribed, an original instrument may be prepared for filing. Any such instrument shall be typed on eight and one-half by eleven inch paper. The caption prescribed in Sup. R. 52 shall be used, and the instrument shall follow the format prescribed for the standard forms. Any such instrument may modify the language of the standard form, omit inapplicable matter required by the standard form, and add matter not included in the standard form to the extent required by the circumstances of the particular case or proceeding.

(D) **Standard probate forms** The standard forms prescribed for use in the probate division of the courts of common pleas are as follows:

Standard probate forms follow the Rules of Superintendence.

RULE 52. Specifications for Printing Probate Forms

(A) **Applicability**

(1) The specifications in this rule govern the reproduction of blank forms intended for, or used in, the administration of decedents' estates, guardianships, and adoptions in this state, including:

(a) Standard forms prescribed in Sup. R. 51;

(b) Commercially prepared blank forms, including standard and nonstandard forms, designed for use in any aspect of the administration of decedents' estates, guardianships, and adoptions;

(c) Blank forms prescribed by local rule of court for use in situations for which no standard form is prescribed.

(2) This rule does not apply to any of the following:

(a) Any pleading, application, entry, waiver, notice, or other filing that is prepared ad hoc for use in a particular case or proceeding, or that is not reproduced in any manner for use as a blank form;

(b) Any routing slip, memorandum index, cost bill, or other form designed solely for internal administrative or clerical use;

(c) Forms intended for use in matters other than the administration of decedents' estates, guardianships, or adoptions;

(d) Estate tax returns, reports, and other forms prescribed by the Department of Taxation.

(B) **Size of forms; stock** All forms shall be on paper size eight and one-half by eleven inches, printed on twenty-four pound bond or heavier stock.

(C) **Margins** Right and left margins shall be approximately one-half to three-quarters of one inch, and shall be justified. The top margin shall be approximately seven-eighths to one and one-eighth inches, measured from the top edge of the paper to the top of the first line of the caption. The distance between the bottom of the repeat of the main heading at the foot of the first page shall be as required by division (K) of this rule.

(D) **Type styles**

(1) All type shall be sans serif. Bold face type shall be used only as required or permitted by division (D)(2) of this rule. Italics shall not be used. Except as provided in division (D)(3) of this rule, all type shall be upper and lower case.

(2) Bold face type shall be used for the main heading immediately following the caption, and for the form number and repeat of the main heading at the foot of the first page. In addition bold face type may be used for:

(a) The caption;

(b) Subheadings;

(c) Directions enclosed in brackets;

(d) Instructions or identification under a blank line, indicating what is to be inserted in the line or identifying the office or status of a signer;

(e) Column headings;

(f) Any matter not covered in division (D)(2)(a) to (e) of this rule, for which the use of bold face type is expressly indicated on a standard form in Sup. R. 51.

(3) The following shall be printed in all capital letters:

(a) The first two lines of the caption;

(b) The main heading immediately following the caption;

(c) All subheadings;

(d) The form number and repeat of the main heading at the foot of the first page;

(e) Any matter not covered in division (D)(3)(a) to (d) of this rule, for which the use of all capital letters is expressly indicated on a standard form in Sup. R. 51.

(E) **Type sizes**

(1) The following type sizes shall be used:

(a) Main headings immediately following the caption shall use sixteen-point or larger type;

(b) The first line of the caption, and all subheadings, shall use not smaller than twelve-point nor larger than sixteen-point type;

(c) The last two lines of the caption, the body, and the form number and repeat of the main heading at the foot of the first page, shall use not smaller than eight-point nor larger than twelve-point type;

(d) Instructions or identification under a blank line, indicating what is to be inserted in the line or identifying the office or status of a signer, shall use not larger than eight-point type.

(2) Whatever type size is used with the limitations of division (E)(1) of this rule:

(a) The first line of the caption and all subheadings shall use type at least two points smaller than the main heading immediately following the caption;

(b) The last two lines of the caption, the body, and the form number and repeat of the main heading at the foot of the first page, shall use type at least two points smaller than the subheadings;

(c) Instructions or identification under a blank line, indicating what is to be inserted in the line or identifying the office or status of a signer, shall use type at least two points smaller than the body.

(F) **Vertical spacing**

(1) The vertical spacing on all forms shall be in units of one pica, to conform to standard typewriter vertical spacing.

(2) In order to permit optimum placement and promote visual appeal, the main heading and any subheading may be moved up or down within the available area without regard to the vertical spacing of the rest of the form, provided the rest of the form from head to foot maintains vertical spacing in units of one pica.

(G) **Centering** The first line of the caption, the main heading, any explanatory information supplementing the main heading and appearing directly below it, subheadings, and the form number and repeat of the main heading at the foot of the first page of a form, shall be centered.

(H) **Blank lines; length; vertical spacing in series**

(1) Blanks to be filled in shall be indicated by a printed solid line. Wherever possible, such lines shall be of sufficient length to accommodate comfortably all characters included in any word, phrase, name, date, or other information that might reasonably be expected to be placed in the blank. Spaces and punctuation shall be included in counting characters. It shall be assumed that six pica will accommodate ten characters in calculating the length of a line.

(2) Wherever possible, blank lines shall be a minimum length of:

(a) Eight pica, when the name of a county is to be inserted;

(b) Eighteen pica, when a date is to be inserted;

(c) Twenty pica, when a name or signature is to be inserted;

(d) Eight pica, not counting the dollar sign, when a dollar amount is to be inserted.

(3) One, or two or more blank lines may be used for the insertion of an address. Wherever possible, such lines shall be a minimum length of:

(a) Forty pica when a single line is used;

(b) Twenty pica per line when two or more lines are used.

(4) When a series of signature lines, lines for tabulating particular information, or other blank lines in vertical series are called for in a form, then except where expressly indicated on a standard form in Sup. R. 51, the vertical spacing between lines shall be two pica. This spacing shall be maintained without regard to instructions or identification printed below a line.

(I) **Boxes to be checked**

(1) Where a form calls for a "check" or "X" to be inserted, a box shall be used for the purpose. The box shall precede the information to which it refers.

(2) When a series of "checks" or "X's" are called for in the same sentence or paragraph, each box and the information to which it refers shall be set apart visually from the preceding and following information in the same sentence or paragraph. Any device that provides visual separation and minimizes possible confusion may be used, including without limitation space-hyphen-space or a double or triple space, as in the following example:

"[check one of the following]—[ ]Decedent's will has been admitted to probate in this court—[ ]To applicant's knowledge decedent did not leave a will."

(J) **Caption**

(1) Except as provided in division (J)(3) of this rule, the following captions shall be used, respectively, on all forms for the administration of decedents' estates, guardianships, and adoptions:

PROBATE　　COURT　　OF　　_____
COUNTY, OHIO
　　ESTATE OF _____ DECEASED
　　Case No. _____;
PROBATE　　COURT　　OF　　_____
COUNTY, OHIO
　　GUARDIANSHIP OF _____
　　Case No. _____;
PROBATE　　COURT　　OF　　_____
COUNTY, OHIO

ADOPTION OF

_____
　　　　　　(Name after adoption)

Case No. _____

(2) The first line of the caption shall be centered. The second and third lines shall begin at the left margin and end at the right margin. The vertical space between the first and second lines may be two or three pica. The vertical space between the second and third lines shall be two pica.

(3) The following variations from the caption prescribed in division (J)(1) and (2) of this rule are permitted:

(a) The blank line in the first line of the caption may be replaced by the imprinted name of a particular county.

(b) The caption may be expanded to include the address of a particular court, using type of any suitable size. In such case, the blank lines intended for the court's address in the body of any form and introductory material for the address such as, "the Court is located at ____," shall be omitted.

(c) In Standard Decedents' Estates Form 5.5, and in any other decedents' estates form dealing with two or more estates, the last two lines of the caption shall be omitted.

(K) Form number and repeat of main heading

(1) The main heading of a form, which appears immediately below the caption on the first page of a form, shall be repeated at the foot of the first page. If the form is a standard form, the repeat of the main heading shall be preceded on the same line by the form number.

(2) The form number and repeat of the main heading shall be centered, and located not higher than three-eighths inch above the bottom edge of the form.

(L) Printing front and back When a standard probate form consists of more than one page, each page shall contain the case number in the upper portion of the page.

(M) Standard forms to govern; variations

(1) Matters not specifically covered in this rule are governed by the standard forms prescribed in Sup. R. 51. Overall, the format of all printed blank forms, whether standard or nonstandard, shall conform substantially to the standard forms. Except as provided in division (M)(2) of this rule, no additions to, deletions from, or changes in the form, content, or language of the standard forms are permitted when printing blank standard forms.

(2) The following variations from the standard forms in Sup. R. 51 are permitted:

(a) In any form calling for a court's address, the blank lines intended for the insertion of such information may be replaced by the imprinted information itself. If the court's address is imprinted in the caption, the blank lines in the body of the form for the address and introductory material for the address shall be omitted as provided in division (J)(3) of this rule.

(b) The name as well as the title of the probate judge may be imprinted below a judge's signature line on any form.

(c) In any form calling for the attorney's typed or printed name, address, telephone number, and attorney identification number, the blank lines intended for the insertion of such information may be replaced by the imprinted information itself. The signature line for the attorney shall be retained.

(d) In Standard Decedents' Estates Form 4.2, the portion of the form below the date line and principal's signature line, and above the repeat at the foot of the page, may be replaced by the imprinted name and address of a corporate surety, identified in some appropriate manner as the surety on the particular bond, and including a signature line for the attorney in fact. The last paragraph of the body of the form, relating to justification of personal sureties, shall be omitted.

(e) When standard forms are generated by computer, they shall conform to all specifications for standard forms stated in this rule. A court may accept for filing nonstandard computer generated forms for the receipts and disbursements attached to a standard account form or the schedule of assets attached to a standard inventory and appraisal form.

(f) All forms may include suitable coding for optical or magnetic scanning, or similar system designed to aid docketing, indexing, cost accounting, or other administrative or clerical activities.

(g) On all forms, the publisher may add its name, logotype, or other suitable identification. The size, style, and placement shall be such as not to detract from, interfere with, or overpower any part of the form.

(h) Wherever a form contains "19____" or "199____", a blank line shall be substituted to accommodate the correct year.

(N) Effective date

(1) This rule takes effect July 1, 1977.

(2) On and after January 1, 1978, any pleading, application, entry, waiver, notice, or other filing, prepared using a blank form to which this rule applies, shall not be accepted for filing by the probate division of a court of common pleas of this state unless such blank form complies with the specifications in this rule.

(3) The amendment to division M(2)(h) shall take effect on November 16, 1999.

History: Amended, eff 11-16-99; 6-12-00; 12-1-02.

RULE 53.   Hours of the Court

Each court shall establish hours for the transaction of business.

RULE 54.   Conduct in the Court

(A) Proper decorum in the court is necessary to the administration of the court's function. Any conduct that interferes or tends to interfere with the proper administration of the court's business is prohibited.

(B) No radio or television transmission, voice recording device, other than a device used by a court reporter making a record in a proceeding, or the making or taking of pictures shall be permitted without the express consent of the court in advance and pursuant to Sup. R. 12.

RULE 55.   Examination of Probate Records

(A) Records shall not be removed from the court, except when approved by the judge. Violation of this rule may result in the issuance of a citation for contempt.

(B) Copies of records may be obtained at a cost per page as authorized by the judge.

(C) Adoption, mental illness, and mental retardation proceedings are confidential. Records of those proceedings, and other records that are confidential by statute, may be accessed as authorized by the judge.

(D) A citation for contempt of court may be issued against anyone who divulges or receives information from confidential records without authorization of the judge.

RULE 56.   Continuances

(A) Motions for continuance shall be submitted in writing with the proper caption and case number.

(B) Except on motion of the court, no continuance shall be granted in the absence of proof of reasonable notice to, or consent by, the adverse party or the party's counsel. Failure to object to the continuance within a reasonable time after receiving notice shall be considered consent to the continuance.

(C) A proposed entry shall be filed with a motion for continuance, leaving the time and date blank for the court to set a new date.

RULE 57.   Filings and Judgment Entries

(A) All filings, except wills, shall be on eight and one-half by eleven inch paper, without backings, of stock that can be microfilmed.

(B) All filings shall contain the name, address, telephone number, and attorney registration number of the individual counsel representing the fiduciary and, in the absence of counsel, the name, address, and telephone number of the fiduciary. Any filing not containing the above requirements may be refused.

(C) Failure of the fiduciary to notify the court of the fiduciary's current address shall be grounds for removal. Not less than ten days written notice of the hearing to remove shall be given to the fiduciary by regular mail at the last address contained in the case file or by other method of service as the court may direct.

(D) Filings containing partially or wholly illegible signatures of counsel, parties or officers administering oaths may be refused, or, if filed, may be stricken, unless the typewritten or printed name of the person whose signature is purported to appear is clearly indicated on the filing.

(E) All pleadings, motions, or other filings are to be typed or printed in ink and correctly captioned.

(F) Unless the court otherwise directs, counsel for the party in whose favor a judgment is rendered, shall prepare the proposed judgment entry and submit the original to the court with a copy to counsel for the opposing party. The proposed judgment entry shall be submitted within seven days after the judgment is rendered. Counsel for the opposing party shall have seven days to object to the court. If the party in whose favor a judgment is rendered fails to comply with this division, the matter may be dismissed or the court may prepare and file the appropriate entry.

(G) When a pleading, motion, judgment entry or other filing consists of more than one page, each page shall contain the case number in the upper portion of the page.

History: Amended, eff 12-1-02.

RULE 58.   Deposit for Court Costs

(A) Deposits in the amount set forth in a local rule shall be required upon the filing of any action or proceeding and additional deposits may be required.

(B) The deposit may be applied as filings occur.

RULE 59.   Wills

(A) Before an application is made to admit the will to probate, to appoint an estate fiduciary, or to relieve an estate from administration, each applicant or the applicant's attorney shall examine the index of wills deposited pursuant to section 2107.07 of the Revised Code. Wills deposited pursuant to section 2107.07 of the Revised Code previous to the will offered for probate shall be filed in the estate proceedings for record purposes only.

(B) Fiduciaries appointed to administer testate estates shall file a Certificate of Service of Notice of Probate of Will (Standard Probate Form 2.4) within two months of their appointment or be subject to removal proceedings. If required by the court, proof of service shall consist of either waivers of notice of the probate of the will or original certified mail return receipt cards as provided under Civil Rule 73(E)(3), or if necessary, under Civil Rule 73(E)(4) or (5). A waiver of notice may not be signed by any minor, or on behalf of a minor sixteen or seventeen years of age. See Civil Rule 4.2.

History: Amended, eff 12-1-02.

RULE 60.   Application for Letters of Authority to Administer Estate and Notice of Appointment

(A) Notice of an application for appointment of administrator shall be served at least seven days prior to the date set for hearing. If there is no known surviving spouse or next of kin resident of the state, the notice shall be served upon persons designated by the court.

(B) The administrator shall give notice of the appointment within seven days after the appointment to all persons entitled to inherit, including persons entitled to an allowance for support, unless those persons have been provided notice of the hearing on the appointment or have waived notice.

(C) The probate court shall serve by certified mail the spousal citation and summary of rights required by R.C. 2106.02 to the surviving spouse within 7 days of the initial appointment of the administrator or executor, unless a different time is established by local court rule.

History: Amended, eff 12-1-02.

RULE 61.   Appraisers

(A) Without special application to the court, a fiduciary may allow to the appraiser as compensation for services a reasonable amount agreed upon between the fiduciary and the appraiser, provided the compensation does not exceed the amount allowed by local court rule. If no local court rule exists, the compensation shall be subject to court approval.

(B) If, by reason of the special and unusual character of the property to be appraised, the fiduciary is of the opinion that the appraisal requires the services of persons qualified in the evaluation of that property, a qualified appraiser may be appointed and allowed compensation as provided in division (A) of this rule.

RULE 62.   Claims Against Estate

(A) When a claim has been filed with the court pursuant to section 2117.06 of the Revised Code, the fiduciary shall file a copy of any rejection of the claim with the court.

(B) If the court requires a hearing on claims or the fiduciary requests a hearing on claims or insolvency, the fiduciary shall file a schedule of all claims against the estate with the court. The schedule of claims shall be filed with the fiduciary's application for hearing or within ten days after the court notifies the fiduciary of a court-initiated hearing.

RULE 63. Application to Sell Personalty

An application to sell personal property shall include an adequate description of the property. Except for good cause shown, an order of sale shall not be granted prior to the filing of the inventory.

RULE 64. Accounts

(A) The vouchers or other proofs required by section 2109.302 and 2109.303 [2109.30.2 and 2109.30.3] of the Revised Code and receipts filed or exhibited pursuant to section 2109.32(B)(1)(b) of the Revised Code, shall be referenced to the account by number, letter, or date.

(B) If land has been sold during the accounting period, the account shall show the gross amount of the proceeds and include a copy of the closing statement itemizing all of the disbursements.

(C) Receipts for distributive shares signed by persons holding power of attorney may be accepted, provided the power of attorney is recorded in the county in which the estate is being administered and a copy of the recorded power is attached to the account.

(D) **Exhibiting assets**

(1) The court may require that all assets be exhibited at the time of filing a partial account.

(2) Cash balances may be verified by exhibiting a financial institution statement, passbook, or a current letter from the financial institution in which the funds are deposited certifying the amount of funds on deposit to the credit of the fiduciary. Assets held in a safe deposit box of a fiduciary or by a surety company on a fiduciary's bond may be exhibited by filing a current inventory of the assets. The inventory shall be certified by the manager of the safe deposit box department of the financial institution leasing the safe deposit box or by a qualified officer of the surety company if the assets are held by a surety. If the assets are held by a bank, trust company, brokerage firm, or other financial insitution, exhibition may be made by proper certification as to the assets so held. For good cause shown, the court may designate a deputy clerk of the court to make an examination of the assets located in the county, not physically exhibited to the court or may appoint a commissioner for that purpose if the assets are located outside the county. The commissioner appointed shall make a written report of findings to the court.

(E) A final or distributive account shall not be approved until all court costs have been paid.

History: Amended eff. 4-8-04.

RULE 65. Land Sales — R.C. Chapter 2127

(A) In all land sale proceedings, the plaintiff, prior to the issuance of an order finding the sale necessary, shall file with the court evidence of title showing the record condition of the title to the premises described in the complaint and prepared by a title company licensed by the state of Ohio, an attorney's certificate, or other evidence of title satisfactory to the court. Evidence of title shall be to a date subsequent to the date on which the complaint was filed.

(B) The plaintiff shall give notice of the time and place of sale by regular mail at least three weeks prior to the date of a public sale to all defendants at their last known addresses. Prior to the public sale, the plaintiff shall file a certificate stating that the required notice was given to the defendants and the sale was advertised pursuant to section 2127.32 of the Revised Code.

(C) In all private land sale proceedings by civil action, the judgment entry confirming sale, ordering issuance of deed, and ordering distribution shall show the gross amount of the proceeds and include a copy of the proposed closing statement itemizing all of the proposed disbursements.

(D) The court may appoint a disinterested person, answerable to the court, who shall investigate the circumstances surrounding the proposed transaction, view the property, ascertain whether the proposed sale is justified and report findings in writing. The report shall be a part of the record. The compensation for the person performing these services shall be fixed by the court, according to the circumstances of each case, and shall be taxed as costs.

RULE 66. Guardianships

(A) All applications for the appointment of a guardian on the grounds of mental incompetency shall be accompanied by either a statement of a physician or clinical psychologist or a statement that the prospective ward has refused to submit to an examination.

(B) An Application for Authority to Expend Funds (Standard Probate Form 15.7) shall not be approved until an Inventory (Standard Probate Form 15.5) has been filed.

(C) An application for allowance of care and support of a minor shall allege, if such is the fact, that the father and mother are financially unable to provide the items for which the amount is sought.

NOTES TO DECISIONS

ANALYSIS

Application

Probate court did not err in denying an adult incompetent's motion to dismiss a guardianship proceeding, as whether the applicant for the guardianship position was the incompetent's nephew or not, which was disputed by the parties, was irrelevant because RC § 2111.02 provided that such a proceeding could be commenced by any interested party. As the incompetent did not object to the fact that the guardianship applicant had failed to attach a physician's statement with his application pursuant to Ohio Superintendence Ct. R. 66(A), the issue was waived for purposes of appeal. In re Lipford, — Ohio App. 3d —, 2007 Ohio 3527, — N.E. 2d —, 2007 Ohio App. LEXIS 3260 (July 12, 2007).

RULE 67. Estates of Minors of Not More Than Ten Thousand Dollars

(A) Each application relating to a minor shall be

submitted by the parent or parents or by the person having custody of the minor and shall be captioned in the name of the minor.

(B) Each application shall indicate the amount of money or property to which the minor is entitled and to whom such money or property shall be paid or delivered. Unless the court otherwise orders, if no guardian has been appointed for either the receipt of an estate of a minor or the receipt of a settlement for injury to a minor, the attorney representing the interests of the minor shall prepare an entry that orders all of the following:

(1) The deposit of the funds in a financial institution in the name of the minor;

(2) Impounding the principal and interest;

(3) Releasing the funds only upon an order of the court or to the minor at the age of majority.

(C) The entry shall be presented at the time the entry dispensing with appointment of a guardian or approving settlement is approved. The attorney shall be responsible for depositing the funds and for providing the financial institution with a copy of the entry. The attorney shall obtain a Verification of Receipt and Deposit (Standard Probate Form 22.3) from the financial institution and file the form with the court within seven days from the issuance of the entry.

RULE 68. Settlement of Injury Claims of Minors

(A) An application for settlement of a minor's claim shall be brought by the guardian of the estate. If there is no guardian appointed and the court dispenses with the need for a guardian, the application shall be brought by the parents of the child or the parent or other individual having custody of the child. The noncustodial parent or parents shall be entitled to seven days notice of the application to settle the minor's claim which notice may be waived. The application shall be captioned in the name of the minor.

(B) The application shall be accompanied by a current statement of an examining physician in respect to the injuries sustained, the extent of recovery, and the permanency of any injuries. The application shall state what additional consideration, if any, is being paid to persons other than the minor as a result of the incident causing the injury to the minor. The application shall state what arrangement, if any, has been made with respect to counsel fees. Counsel fees shall be subject to approval by the court.

(C) The injured minor and the applicant shall be present at the hearing.

RULE 69. Settlement of Claims of or Against Adult Wards

(A) An application for settlement of a claim in favor of or against an adult ward shall be brought by the guardian of the estate. Notice of the hearing on the application shall be given to all persons who are interested parties to the proposed settlement, as determined by the court. The court may authorize or direct the guardian of the ward's estate to compromise and settle claims as the court considers to be in the best interest of the ward. The court may dispense with notice of hearing.

(B) The application for settlement of an injury claim shall be accompanied by a current statement of the examining physician describing the injuries sustained, the extent of recovery from those injuries, and permanency of any injuries. The application shall state what additional consideration, if any, is being paid to persons other than the ward as a result of the incident causing the injury to the ward. The application shall state what arrangement, if any, has been made with respect to counsel fees. Counsel fees shall be subject to approval by the court.

RULE 70. Settlement of Wrongful Death and Survival Claims

(A) An application to approve settlement and Distribution of Wrongful Death and Survival Claims (Standard Probate Form 14.0) shall contain a statement of facts, including the amount to be allocated to the settlement of the claim and the amount, if any, to be allocated to the settlement of the survival claim. The application shall include the proposed distribution of the net proceeds allocated to the wrongful death claim.

(B) The fiduciary shall give written notice of the hearing and a copy of the application to all interested persons who have not waived notice of the hearing. Notwithstanding the waivers and consents of the interested persons, the court shall retain jurisdiction over the settlement, allocation, and distribution of the claims.

(C) The application shall state what arrangements, if any, have been made with respect to counsel fees. Counsel fees shall be subject to approval by the court.

NOTES TO DECISIONS

ANALYSIS

Relief from judgment

When a son moved for relief from judgments entered in a probate case, under Ohio R. Civ. P. 60(B), the fact that a statutory beneficiary's notice, pursuant to Ohio Superintendence Ct. R. 70(B), differed from service of process, under Ohio R. Civ. P. 4, went to the merits of the son's motion for relief from judgment rather than whether the trial court should have held an evidentiary hearing on the son's motion. In re Estate of Perez, — Ohio App. 3d —, 2006 Ohio 2841, — N.E. 2d —, 2006 Ohio App. LEXIS 2665 (June 5, 2006).

RULE 71. Counsel Fees

(A) Attorney fees in all matters shall be governed by Rule 1.5 of the Ohio Rules of Professional Conduct.

(B) Attorney fees for the administration of estates shall not be paid until the final account is prepared for filing unless otherwise approved by the court upon application and for good cause shown.

(C) Attorney fees may be allowed if there is a written application that sets forth the amount requested and will be awarded only after proper hearing, unless otherwise modified by local rule.

(D) The court may set a hearing on any application

for allowance of attorney fees regardless of the fact that the required consents of the beneficiaries have been given.

(E) Except for good cause shown, attorney fees shall not be allowed to attorneys representing fiduciaries who are delinquent in filing the accounts required by section 2109.30 of the Revised Code.

(F) If a hearing is scheduled on an application for the allowance of attorney fees, notice shall be given to all parties affected by the payment of fees, unless otherwise ordered by the court.

(G) An application shall be filed for the allowance of counsel fees for services rendered to a guardian, trustee, or other fiduciary. The application may be filed by the fiduciary or attorney. The application shall set forth a statement of the services rendered and the amount claimed in conformity with division (A) of this rule.

(H) There shall be no minimum or maximum fees that automatically will be approved by the court.

(I) Prior to a fiduciary entering into a contingent fee contract with an attorney for services, an application for authority to enter into the fee contract shall be filed with the court, unless otherwise ordered by local court rule. The contingent fee on the amount obtained shall be subject to approval by the court.

History: Amended, eff 2-1-07.

NOTES TO DECISIONS

Analysis

Generally
Contingent fee agreement
Denial of fees
Division of fees
Practice and procedure

Trial court reasonably considered the fact that mistakes by the attorney necessitated additional filings and complicated the case. It abused its discretion by ruling that requests for fees for services performed after the original request would not be considered. It abused its discretion as to the fees awarded to the previous attorney for the estate: In re Estate of Kendall, 171 Ohio App. 3d 109, 2007 Ohio 1672, 869 N.E.2d 728, 2007 Ohio App. LEXIS 1516 (2007).

Probate court's attorney fee award to a litigation attorney who defended a decedent's estate, as well as the estate executor and attorney, was reasonable pursuant to the factors under Ohio Code Prof. Resp. DR 2-106 and Ohio Superintendence R. 71, where the services were clearly delineated and clearly benefited the estate. Services that were for the exclusive personal benefit of the executor and the estate attorney were excluded for purposes of reimbursement. In re Estate of Fouras, — Ohio App. 3d —, 2006 Ohio 3461, — N.E. 2d —, 2006 Ohio App. LEXIS 3389 (July 3, 2006).

Although an attorney who unsuccessfully defended an executor in a will contest submitted a very detailed statement of the services rendered by himself and his associate, the probate court denied the fee request and held that it was unreasonable; however, as the probate court failed to provide any explanation as to what factors under Ohio Code Prof. Resp. DR 2-106 and Ohio Superintendence R. 71(A) were not met, a remand for further consideration and explanation was

required. Estate of Szczotka, 166 Ohio App. 3d 124, 2006 Ohio 1449, 849 N.E. 2d 302, 2006 Ohio App. LEXIS 1283 (Mar. 24, 2006).

Attorney fees in all matters are governed by Ohio Code Prof. Resp. DR 2-106, and a trial court's decision regarding the reasonableness of fees must be based upon the evidence of the actual services performed by the attorneys and upon the reasonable value of those services. Further, Loc. R. 24(E) of the Court of Common Pleas of Cuyahoga County's limitation of attorney fees to $850 except in contested cases where extraordinary circumstances were demonstrated, was invalid since it conflicted with RC § 5721.39, and a trial court erred in denying a buyer's request for attorney fees in excess of $850. Gls Capital Cuyahoga, Inc. v. Abuzahrieh, — Ohio App. 3d —, 2006 Ohio 298, — N.E. 2d —, 2006 Ohio App. LEXIS 248 (Jan. 26, 2006).

Attorneys' failure to file an application with the probate court for authority to enter into their respective contingent fee contracts was not fatal to their claims because the probate court addressed the reasonableness of both contingency fee agreements at the hearing and in its judgment entry. In re Stine, — Ohio App. 3d —, 2006 Ohio 6687, — N.E. 2d —, 2006 Ohio App. LEXIS 6567 (Dec. 18, 2006).

Probate court properly adopted a magistrate's decision, denying a decedent's estate executor's application for attorney fees for the estate attorney pursuant to RC § 2113.36, as the fees initially awarded to the attorney were reasonable under former Ohio Code Prof. Resp. DR 2-106 (now at Ohio Code Prof. Conduct 1.5), and additional work was caused by the attorney's own errors in failing to serve the beneficiaries with the inventory and partial account initially; further, the fact that the attorney had sought a fee award prior to the final account was not the basis for the fee denial, such that there was no error under Ohio Superintendence R. 71(B). In re Estate of Born, — Ohio App. 3d —, 2007 Ohio 5006, — N.E. 2d —, 2007 Ohio App. LEXIS 4920 (Sept. 25, 2007).

Probate court did not abuse its discretion in awarding attorney fees in the amount of $100,000 and directing that they should be apportioned $25,000 to the new attorney and $75,000 to the former attorney. The new attorney failed to demonstrate how the probate court erred, especially since he failed to offer any evidence beyond his original contingency contract to support his claim for attorney fees, and the probate court's ultimate decision regarding the award of attorney fees was supported by the record and the probate court properly considered the totality of the circumstances involved before entering judgment. In re Stine, — Ohio App. 3d —, 2006 Ohio 6687, — N.E. 2d —, 2006 Ohio App. LEXIS 6567 (Dec. 18, 2006).

Probate court did not have to wait until final judgment in order to make an attorney fee award to an attorney who defended the estate against claims that required litigation, pursuant to Ohio Superintendence R. 71(B) and RC § 2113.36. In re Estate of Fouras, — Ohio App. 3d —, 2006 Ohio 3461, — N.E. 2d —, 2006 Ohio App. LEXIS 3389 (July 3, 2006).

RULE 72. Executor's and Administrator's Commissions

(A) Additional compensation for extraordinary services may be allowed upon an application setting forth an itemized statement of the services rendered and the amount of compensation requested. The court may require the application to be set for hearing with notice given to interested persons in accordance with Civil Rule 73(E).

(B) The court may deny or reduce commissions if there is a delinquency in the filing of an inventory or an account, or if, after hearing, the court finds that the executor or administrator has not faithfully discharged the duties of the office.

(C) The commissions of co-executors or co-administrators in the aggregate shall not exceed the commissions that would have been allowed to one executor or administrator acting alone, except where the instrument under which the co-executors serve provides otherwise.

(D) Where counsel fees have been awarded for services to the estate that normally would have been performed by the executor or administrator, the executor or administrator commission, except for good cause shown, shall be reduced by the amount awarded to counsel for those services.

RULE 73.   Guardian's Compensation

(A) Guardian's compensation shall be set by local rule.

(B) Additional compensation for extraordinary services, reimbursement for expenses incurred and compensation of a guardian of a person only may be allowed upon an application setting forth an itemized statement of the services rendered and expenses incurred and the amount for which compensation is applied. The court may require the application to be set for hearing with notice given to interested persons in accordance with Civil Rule 73(E).

(C) The compensation of co-guardians in the aggregate shall not exceed the compensation that would have been allowed to one guardian acting alone.

(D) The court may deny or reduce compensation if there is a delinquency in the filing of an inventory or account, or after hearing, the court finds the guardian has not faithfully discharged the duties of the office.

RULE 74.   Trustee's Compensation

(A) Trustee's compensation shall be set by local rule.

(B) Additional compensation for extraordinary services may be allowed upon application setting forth an itemized statement of the services rendered and the amount of compensation requested. The court may require that the application be set for hearing with notice given to interested parties in accordance with Civil Rule 73(E).

(C) The compensation of co-trustees in the aggregate shall not exceed the compensation that would have been allowed to one trustee acting alone, except where the instrument under which the co-trustees are acting provides otherwise.

(D) Except for good cause shown, neither compensation for a trustee nor fees to counsel representing the trustee shall be allowed while the trustee is delinquent in the filing of an account.

(E) The court may deny or reduce compensation if there is a delinquency in the filing of an inventory or account, or after hearing, the court finds the trustee has not faithfully discharged other duties of the office.

RULE 75.   Local Rules

The local rules of the court shall be numbered to correspond with the numbering of these rules and shall incorporate the number of the rule it is intended to supplement. For example, a local rule that supplements Sup. R. 61 shall be designated County Local Rule 61.1.

RULE 76.   Exception to the Rules

Upon application, and for good cause shown, the probate division of the court of common pleas may grant exception to Sup. R. 53 to 79.

RULE 77.   Compliance

Failure to comply with these rules may result in sanctions as the court may direct.

RULE 78.   Probate Division of the Court of Common Pleas — Case Management in Decedent's Estates, Guardianship, and Trusts

(A) Each fiduciary shall adhere to the statutory or court-ordered time period for filing the inventory, account, and, if applicable, guardian's report. The citation process set forth in section 2109.31 of the Revised Code shall be utilized to ensure compliance. The attorney of record and the fiduciary shall be subject to the citation process. The court may modify or deny fiduciary commissions or attorney fees, or both, to enforce adherence to the filing time periods.

(B)(1) If a decedent's estate must remain open more than six months pursuant to R.C. 2109.301(B)(1) [R.C. 2109.30.1(B)(1)], the fiduciary shall file an application to extend administration (Standard Probate Form 13.8).

(2) An application to extend the time for filing an inventory, account, or guardian's report, shall not be granted unless the fiduciary has signed the application.

(C) The fiduciary and the attorney shall prepare, sign, and file a written status report with the court in all decedent's estates that remain open after a period of thirteen months from the date of the appointment of the fiduciary and annually thereafter. At the court's discretion, the fiduciary and the attorney shall appear for a status review.

(D) The court may issue a citation to the attorney of record for a fiduciary who is delinquent in the filing of an inventory, account, or guardian's report to show cause why the attorney should not be barred from being appointed in any new proceeding before the court or serving as attorney of record in any new estate, guardianship, or trust until all of the delinquent pleadings are filed.

(E) Upon filing of the exceptions to an inventory or to an account, the exceptor shall cause the exceptions to be set for a pretrial within thirty days. The attorneys and their clients, or individuals if not represented by an attorney, shall appear at the pretrial. The trial shall be set as soon as practical after pretrial. The court may dispense with the pretrial and proceed directly to trial.

History: Amended, eff 12-1-02.

RULE 79   is reserved for future use

RULE 80.   Definitions

As used in Rules 80 through 87 of the Rules of Superintendence for the Courts of Ohio:

(A) "Consecutive interpretation" means interpretation in which a foreign language interpreter waits until the speaker finishes an entire message rendered in a source language before rendering the message in a target language.

(B) "Consortium for Language Access in the Courts" means the multi-state partnership dedicated to developing foreign language interpreter proficiency tests, making tests available to member states, and regulating the use of the tests.

(C) "Foreign language interpreter" means an individual who, as part of any case or court function, facilitates communication between or among legal professionals and a limited English proficient or non-English speaking party or witness through consecutive interpretation, simultaneous interpretation, or sight translation.

(D) "Limited English proficient" means an individual who does not speak English as a primary language or who has a limited ability to read, speak, write, or understand English and requires the assistance of a foreign language interpreter to effectively communicate.

(E) "Program" means the Supreme Court Interpreter Services Program.

(F) "Provisionally qualified foreign language interpreter" means a foreign language interpreter who has received provisional certification from the Program pursuant to Sup. R. 81(G)(3).

(G) "Sight translation" means interpretation in which a foreign language interpreter reads aloud in a target language a written document composed in a source language.

(H) "Sign language interpreter" means an individual who, as part of any case or court function, facilitates communication between or among legal professionals and a deaf, hard of hearing, or deaf blind party, witness, or juror through the use of sign language or other manual or oral representation of a spoken language.

(I) "Simultaneous interpretation" means interpretation in which, after a brief pause to listen for or view key grammatical information, a foreign language interpreter or sign language interpreter renders in a target language the message of a person rendered in a source language as the person continues to communicate.

(J) "Supreme Court certified foreign language interpreter" means a foreign language interpreter who has received certification from the Program pursuant to Sup. R. 81.

(K) "Supreme Court certified sign language interpreter" means a sign language interpreter who has received certification from the Program pursuant to Sup. R. 82.

(L) "Translator" means an individual who, as part of any case or court function, takes written text composed in a source language and renders it into an equivalent written text of a target language.

RULE 81.   Certification for Foreign Language Interpreters

(A) **Certification** A foreign language interpreter may receive certification from the Program and be styled a "Supreme Court certified foreign language interpreter" pursuant to the requirements of this rule.

(B) **General requirements for certification** An applicant for certification as a Supreme Court certified foreign language interpreter shall satisfy each of the following requirements:

(1) Be at least eighteen years old;

(2) Be a citizen or legal resident of the United States or have the legal right to remain and work in the United States;

(3) Have not been convicted of any crime involving moral turpitude.

(C) **Application for certification** An applicant for certification as a Supreme Court certified foreign language interpreter shall file an application with the Program. The application shall include each of the following:

(1) Verification the applicant is at least eighteen years old;

(2) Verification the applicant is a legal resident or citizen of the United States or has the legal right to remain and work in the United States;

(3) A copy of a completed criminal background check showing no conviction of a crime involving moral turpitude;

(4) A nonrefundable application fee in an amount as determined by the Program.

(D) **Orientation training** An applicant shall attend an orientation training session conducted or sponsored by the Program providing an introductory course to interpreting and addressing ethics, legal procedure and terminology, modes of interpretation, and other substantive topics. The Program may waive this requirement upon demonstration by the applicant of equivalent experience or training. The Program shall charge the applicant a nonrefundable fee in an amount as determined by the Program for attendance at a Program-sponsored training session.

(E) **Written examination**

(1) An applicant for certification as a Supreme Court certified foreign language interpreter shall take the written examination of the Consortium for Language Access in the Courts. The examination shall be administered by the Program in accordance with the standards described in the test administration manuals of the Consortium.

(2) To pass the written examination of the Consortium for Language Access in the Courts, an applicant shall receive an overall score of eighty percent or better in the English language and grammar, court-related terms and usage, and professional conduct sections of the examination.

(3) An applicant who fails the written examination of the Consortium for Language Access in the Courts shall wait one year before retaking the examination.

(4) An applicant who has taken the written examination of the Consortium for Language Access in the Courts in another Consortium member state within the past twenty-four months may apply to the Program for

recognition of the score. The Program shall recognize the score if it is substantially comparable to the score required under division (E)(2) of this rule.

(F) **Post-written examination training course** Upon compliance with the written examination requirements of division (E) of this rule, an applicant for certification as a Supreme Court certified foreign language interpreter shall attend a training course sponsored by the Program focusing on simultaneous, consecutive, and sight translation modes of interpretation in English and the target language of the applicant. The Program may charge the applicant a nonrefundable fee in an amount as determined by the Program for attendance at the training course.

(G) **Oral examination**

(1) After attending the post-written examination training course pursuant to division (F) of this rule, an applicant for certification as a Supreme Court certified foreign language interpreter shall take the oral examination of the Consortium for Language Access in the Courts. The examination shall be administered by the Program in accordance with the standards described in the test administration manuals of the Consortium.

(2) To pass oral examination of the Consortium for Language Access in the Courts, an applicant shall receive a score of seventy percent or better in each of the sections of the examination.

(3) An applicant who receives a score of less than seventy percent but at least sixty percent in each of the sections of the oral examination of the Consortium for Language Access in the Courts shall receive provisional certification from the Program and be styled a "provisionally qualified foreign language interpreter." The applicant may maintain provisional certification for up to twenty-four months following the examination. If the applicant fails to receive an overall score of at least seventy percent in the sections of the examination within this time frame, the provisional certification of the applicant shall cease.

(4) An applicant who receives a score of at least seventy percent in two of the sections of the oral examination of the Consortium for Language Access in the Courts may carry forward the passing scores for up to twenty-four months or two testing cycles, whichever occurs last. If the applicant fails to successfully pass any previously failed sections of the examination during the time period which passing scores may be carried forward, the applicant shall complete all sections of the examination at a subsequent examination. An applicant may not carry forward passing scores from an examination taken in another Consortium member state.

(H) **Written and oral examination preparation** The Program shall provide materials to assist applicants for certification as Supreme Court certified foreign language interpreters in preparing for the written and oral examinations of the Consortium for Language Access in the Courts, including overviews of each examination. The Program also shall provide and coordinate training for applicants.

(I) **Reciprocity** An applicant for certification as a Supreme Court certified foreign language interpreter who has previously received certification as a foreign language interpreter may apply to the Program for certification without fulfilling the training and examination requirements of division (D) through (G) of this rule as follows:

(1) An applicant who has received certification from the federal courts shall provide proof of certification and be in good standing with the certifying body.

(2) An applicant who has received certification from another member state of the Consortium for Language Access in the Courts shall provide proof of having passed the oral examination of Consortium. The Program may verify the test score information and testing history before approving certification.

(3) An applicant who has received certification from the National Association of Judiciary Interpreters and Translators shall provide proof of having received a score on the examination of the Association substantially comparable to the scores required under divisions (E)(2) and (G)(2) of this rule. The Program may verify the test score information and testing history before approving reciprocal certification.

(4) Requests for reciprocal certification from all other applicants shall be reviewed by the Program on a case-by-case basis, taking into consideration testing criteria, reliability, and validity of the examination procedure of the certifying body. The Program shall verify the test score of the applicant after accepting the certification criteria of the certifying body.

(J) **Oath or affirmation** Each Supreme Court certified foreign language interpreter and provisionally qualified foreign language interpreter shall take an oath or affirmation under which the interpreter affirms to know, understand, and act according to the Code of Professional Conduct for Court Interpreters and Translators, as set forth in Appendix H to this rule.

RULE 82. Certification for Sign Language Interpreters

(A) **Certification** A sign language interpreter who has received a passing score on the "Specialist Certification: Legal" examination of the Registry of Interpreters for the Deaf may receive certification from the Program and be styled a "Supreme Court certified sign language interpreter" pursuant to the requirements of this rule.

(B) **General requirements for certification** An applicant for certification as a Supreme Court certified sign language interpreter shall satisfy each of the following requirements:

(1) Be at least eighteen years old;

(2) Be a citizen or legal resident of the United States or have the legal right to remain and work in the United States;

(3) Have not been convicted of any crime involving moral turpitude.

(C) **Application for certification** An applicant for certification as a Supreme Court certified sign language interpreter shall file an application with the Program. The application shall include each of the following:

(1) Verification the applicant is at least eighteen years old;

(2) Verification the applicant is a legal resident or citizen of the United States or has the legal right to remain and work in the United States;

(3) A copy of a completed criminal background check showing no conviction of a crime involving moral turpitude;

(4) Proof of having received a passing score on the "Specialist Certification: Legal" examination;

(5) A nonrefundable application fee in an amount as determined by the Program.

(D) **Oath or affirmation** Each Supreme Court certified sign language interpreter shall take an oath or affirmation under which the interpreter affirms to know, understand, and act according to the Code of Professional Conduct for Court Interpreters and Translators, as set forth in Appendix H to this rule.

RULE 83. Revocation of Certification

The Program may revoke the certification of a Supreme Court certified foreign language interpreter or a Supreme Court certified sign language interpreter or the provisional certification of a provisionally qualified foreign language interpreter for any of the following reasons:

(A) A material omission or misrepresentation in the application for certification from the interpreter;

(B) A substantial breach of the Code of Professional Conduct for Court Interpreters and Translators, as set forth in Appendix H to this rule;

(C) Noncompliance with the applicable continuing education requirements of Rule 85 of the Rules of Superintendence for the Courts of Ohio.

RULE 84. Code of Professional Conduct for Court Interpreters and Translators

Supreme Court certified foreign language interpreters, Supreme Court certified sign language interpreters, provisionally qualified foreign language interpreters, and translators shall be subject to the Code of Professional Conduct for Court Interpreters and Translators, as set forth in Appendix H to this rule.

RULE 85. Continuing Education

(A) **Requirements**

(1) Each Supreme Court certified foreign language interpreter and Supreme Court certified sign language interpreter shall complete and report, on a form provided by the Program, at least twenty-four credit hours of continuing education offered or accredited by the Program for each two-year reporting period. Six of the credit hours shall consist of ethics instruction and the remaining eighteen general credit hours shall be relevant to the work of the interpreter in the legal setting. The interpreter may carry forward a maximum of twelve general credit hours into the following biennial reporting period.

(2) Each provisionally qualified foreign language interpreter shall complete and report, on a form provided by the Program, at least twenty-four credit hours of continuing education offered or accredited by the Program within twenty-four months after the date of the last oral examination of the Consortium for Language Access in the Courts administered by the Program.

(B) **Duties of the Program** In administering the continuing education requirements of this rule, the Program shall do both of the following:

(1) Keep a record of the continuing education hours of each Supreme Court certified foreign language interpreter, Supreme Court certified sign language interpreter, and provisionally qualified foreign language interpreter, provided it shall be the responsibility of the interpreter to inform the Program of meeting the continuing education requirements;

(2) Accredit continuing education programs, activities, and sponsors and establish procedures for accreditation, provided any continuing education programs or activities offered by the Consortium for Language Access in the Courts, the National Association of Judiciary Interpreters and Translators, the Registry of Interpreters for the Deaf, and the National Interpreter Council shall not require accreditation. The Program may assess a reasonable nonrefundable application fee in an amount as determined by the Program for a sponsor submitting a program or activity for accreditation.

RULE 86. Certification Roster

The Program shall maintain a list of each Supreme Court certified foreign language interpreter, Supreme Court certified sign language interpreter, and provisionally qualified foreign language interpreter who is in compliance with the applicable continuing education requirements of Rule 85 of the Rules of Superintendence for the Courts of Ohio and shall post the list on the website of the Supreme Court.

RULE 87. Establishment of Procedures by the Program

The Program may establish procedures as needed to implement Rules 80 through 86 of the Rules of Superintendence for the Courts of Ohio.

RULES 88–98   are reserved for future use

RULE 99. Effective Date

(A) Except as otherwise provided in this rule, the Rules of Superintendence, adopted by the Supreme Court of Ohio on April 15, 1997, shall take effect on July 1, 1997. The rules govern all proceedings in actions brought on or after the effective date and to further proceedings in actions then pending, except to the extent that application in a particular pending action would not be feasible or would work an injustice, in which case the former procedure applies. Sup. R. 37(A)(4)(b) and (c) and 43(B)(2) shall take effect January 1, 1998.

(B) The amendments to Sup. R. 51 to 78, adopted by the Supreme Court of Ohio on July 7, 1997, shall take effect on October 1, 1997.

(C) Sup. R. 26 to 26.05, adopted by the Supreme Court of Ohio on July 7, 1997, shall take effect on October 1, 1997.

(D) The amendments to standard probate forms 18.0, 18.1, 18.2, 18.3, 18.4, 18.5, 18.6, 18.7, 18.8, and 18.9, adopted by the Supreme Court of Ohio on August 26, 1997, shall take effect on October 1, 1997.

(E) The amendments to Sup. R. 26.02 to 26.05 adopted by the Supreme Court of Ohio on September 9, 1997, shall take effect on October 1, 1997.

(F) Sup. R. 10.01 and 10.02 and standard domestic violence protection order forms 10.01-A to 10.01-J and 10.02-A, adopted by the Supreme Court of Ohio on October 7, 1997, shall take effect January 1, 1998.

(G) The amendments to standard domestic violence protection order form 10.02-A, adopted by the Supreme Court of Ohio on November 4, 1997, shall take effect on January 1, 1998.

(H) The amendments to Sup.R. 16 of the Rules of Superintendence for the Courts of Ohio, adopted by the Supreme Court on Sept. 9, 1997, shall take effect on Nov. 24, 1997.

(I) The amendments to Sup. R. 10 and 99 of the Rules of Superintendence for the Courts of Ohio, and Form 10-A adopted by the Supreme Court on March 24, 1998, shall take effect on March 24, 1998.

(J) The amendments to Sup. R. 9 of the Rules of Superintendence for the Courts of Ohio, adopted by the Supreme Court on May 12, 1998, shall take effect on May 12, 1998.

(K) The amendments to Sup. R. 10, 10.03 and stalking protection order forms (Forms 10.03-A to 10.03-H), adopted by the Supreme Court of Ohio on Dec. 14, 1999, shall take effect on March 1, 2000.

(L) The amendments to Sup. R. 10.01, Forms 10.01-A through 10.01-J, 10.02-A, and Form 10-A were adopted by the Supreme Court on April 10, 2000, shall take effect on June 1, 2000.

(M) The amendments [to] Sup. R. 52(L) and to standard probate form 18.2, adopted by the Supreme Court of Ohio on May 9, 2000, shall take effect June 12, 2000.

(N) The amendments to Sup. R. 26 and 27 adopted by the Supreme Court on April 24, 2001, shall take effect on July 1, 2001.

(O) The amendments to Sup. R. 23.1, Forms 23.1-A to 23.1-C, Sup. R. 25 and Form 25-A adopted by the Supreme Court on September 18, 2001, shall take effect on October 15, 2001.

(P) The amendment to Sup. R. 50(C) adopted by the Supreme Court on February 26, 2002, shall take effect on March 25, 2002.

(Q) The amendment to Sup. R. 36.1 adopted by the Supreme Court on March 26, 2002, shall take effect on July 1, 2002.

(R) The amendments to Sup. R. 52(L), 57(G), 59(B), 60(C), 78(B) and (C) and Standard Probate Forms 1.0, 20, 2.1, 2.2, 4.0, 4.4, 6.0, 8.0, 8.1, 8.2, 8.3, 8.4, 8.5, 10.4A (eliminated), 13.0, 13.3, 13.8, 13.9, and 13.10 adopted by the Supreme Court on September 17, 2002, shall take effect on December 1, 2002.

(S) The amendment to Sup. R. 20 adopted by the Supreme Court on December 4, 2002, shall take effect on January 6, 2003.

(T) The amendments to Sup. R. 41 adopted by the Supreme Court on June 24, 2003, shall take effect on October 1, 2003.

(U) The amendments to Sup. R. 64 and Standard Probate Forms 7.0 and 8.6 adopted by the Supreme Court on February 3, 2004, shall take effect on April 8, 2004.

(V) The amendments to Sup. R. 26.03 and 26.05 adopted by the Supreme Court on September 14, 2004, shall take effect on September 23, 2004.

(W) The amendments to Sup. R. 26.03 and 26.05 adopted by the Supreme Court on February 1, 2005, shall take effect on March 23, 2005.

(X) The amendments to Sup. R. 40 adopted by the Supreme Court on June 14, 2005, shall take effect on July 4, 2005.

(Y) The amendments to standard probate form 15.2, adopted by the Supreme Court of Ohio on June 14, 2005, shall take effect on July 4, 2005.

(Z) The amendments to Sup. R. 16 adopted by the Supreme Court on August 8, 2006 shall take effect on January 1, 2007.

(AA) The amendments to Sup. R. 36 adopted by the Supreme Court of Ohio on September 19, 2006, shall take effect on November 1, 2006.

(BB) The amendments to Sup. R. 71 adopted by the Supreme Court on January 23, 2007 shall take effect on February 1, 2007.

(CC) The amendments to Sup. R. 10.02, 10.03, and protection order forms 10.01-A through 10.01-J, 10.02-A, 10.03-A through 10.03-H, 10-A shall take effect on May 1, 2007.

(DD) The amendments to standard probate form 17.8, adopted by the Supreme Court of Ohio on September 18, 2007, shall take effect on October 1, 2007.

(EE) The amendment to Sup. R. 27 adopted by the Supreme Court of Ohio on November 6, 2007, shall take effect on December 1, 2007.

(FF) The amendments to Sup. R. 19 and 19.1 adopted by the Supreme Court of Ohio on February 5, 2008, shall take effect on March 1, 2008. A magistrate appointed prior to the effective date of these amendments shall be deemed in compliance with the eligibility and qualifications requirements of Sup. R. 19.

(GG) The amendments to standard probate forms 5.10, 12.0, 15.9, 16.1, 17.0, and 18.0 and adopted by the Supreme Court of Ohio on February 5, 2008, shall take effect on March 1, 2008.

(HH) The amendments to Sup. R. 10.04 and forms 10.04-A, 10.01-G, and 10.03-H adopted by the Supreme Court of Ohio on December 15, 2008, shall take effect on February 1, 2009.

(II) The amendments to Sup. R. 9 and Appendix C, adopted by the Supreme Court on November 18, 2008, shall take effect on March 1, 2009.

(JJ) The amendments to Sup. R. 48 of the Rules of Superintendence adopted by the Court on January 20, 2009 shall take effect on March 1, 2009.

(KK) The amendments to Sup. R. 44 through 47 adopted by the Supreme Court on December 15, 2008 shall take effect on July 1, 2009.

(LL) The amendments to Sup. R. 2, 4, 35, 37, 39, 40, 41, 42, and Temp Sup. R. 1.08 and 1.10 were adopted by the Supreme Court on March 9, 2009 shall take effect on July 1, 2009.

(MM) The amendments to Sup. R. 17, adopted by the Supreme Court on November 2, 2009, shall take effect on December 1, 2009.

(NN) The amendments to Sup. R. 80 through 87 and

Appendix H, adopted by the Supreme Court on November 2, 2009, shall take effect on January 1, 2010.

(OO) The amendments to standard probate forms 18.0, 18.2, 18.4, 21.5, 23.0, 23.1, 23.2, 23.3, 23.4, 23.6, and 23.7 and adopted by the Supreme Court of Ohio on November 2, 2009 shall take effect on January 1, 2010.

Temporary Rules

1.01. Definitions As used in Temporary Rules 1.01 through 1.11 of the Rules of Superintendence for the Courts of Ohio, "business entity" means a for profit or nonprofit corporation, partnership, limited liability company, limited liability partnership, professional association, business trust, joint venture, unincorporated association, or sole proprietorship.

1.02. Designation and Organization

(A) **Designation of pilot project courts** The Chief Justice of the Supreme Court shall designate up to five courts of common pleas to participate in the commercial docket pilot project pursuant to Temporary Rules 1.01 through 1.11 of the Rules of Superintendence for the Courts of Ohio. Such courts shall be styled "pilot project courts." The Supreme Court Task Force on Commercial Dockets shall recommend to the Chief Justice courts for designation as pilot project courts. The Chief Justice shall not designate a court as a pilot project court unless the court agrees to participate in the commercial docket pilot project.

(B) **Establishment of commercial docket** Notwithstanding any rule of the Rules of Superintendence for the Courts of Ohio or local rule of court to the contrary, each pilot project court is authorized to establish and maintain a commercial docket pursuant to the requirements of Temporary Rules 1.01 through 1.11 of the Rules of Superintendence for the Courts of Ohio.

(C) **Designation and training of commercial docket judges**

(1) The Chief Justice of the Supreme Court shall designate one or more sitting judges of each pilot project court to hear all cases assigned to the commercial docket. Such judges shall be styled "commercial docket judges." In the event of the death, resignation, or removal from or forfeiture of office of a commercial docket judge, the Chief Justice may designate another sitting judge of that pilot project court to serve as a commercial docket judge. The Supreme Court Task Force on Commercial Dockets shall recommend to the Chief Justice candidates for designation as commercial docket judges. The Chief Justice shall not designate a judge as a commercial docket judge unless the judge agrees to participate in the commercial docket pilot project.

(2) Each commercial docket judge shall complete an orientation and training seminar on the administration of commercial dockets to be offered or approved by the Supreme Court of Ohio Judicial College.

1.03. Scope of the Commercial Docket

(A) **Cases accepted into the commercial docket** A commercial docket judge shall accept a civil case, including any jury; non-jury; injunction, including any temporary restraining order; class action; declaratory judgment; or derivative action, into the commercial docket of the pilot project court if the case is within the statutory jurisdiction of the court and the gravamen of the case relates to any of the following:

(1) The formation, governance, dissolution, or liquidation of a business entity, as that term is defined in Temporary Rule 1.01 of the Rules of Superintendence for the Courts of Ohio;

(2) The rights or obligations between or among the owners, shareholders, partners, or members of a business entity, or rights and obligations between or among any of them and the entity;

(3) Trade secret, non-disclosure, non-compete, or employment agreements involving a business entity and an owner, sole proprietor, shareholder, partner, or member thereof;

(4) The rights, obligations, liability, or indemnity of an officer, director, manager, trustee, partner, or member of a business entity owed to or from the business entity;

(5) Disputes between or among two or more business entities or individuals as to their business or investment activities relating to contracts, transactions, or relationships between or among them, including without limitation the following:

(a) Transactions governed by the uniform commercial code, except for consumer product liability claims described in division (B)(2) of this rule;

(b) The purchase, sale, lease, or license of, or a security interest in, or the infringement or misappropriation of, patents, trademarks, service marks, copyrights, trade secrets, or other intellectual property;

(c) The purchase or sale of a business entity or the assets of a business entity;

(d) The sale of goods or services by a business entity to a business entity;

(e) Non-consumer bank or brokerage accounts, including loan, deposit, cash management, and investment accounts;

(f) Surety bonds and suretyship or guarantee obligations of individuals given in connection with business transactions;

(g) The purchase, sale, lease, or license of, or a security interest in, commercial property, whether tangible, intangible personal, or real property;

(h) Franchise or dealer relationships;

(i) Business related torts, such as claims of unfair competition, false advertising, unfair trade practices, fraud, or interference with contractual relations or prospective contractual relations;

(j) Cases relating to or arising under state or federal antitrust laws;

(k) Cases relating to securities, or relating to or arising under federal or state securities laws;

(*l*) Commercial insurance contracts, including coverage disputes.

(B) **Cases not accepted into the commercial docket** A commercial docket judge shall not accept a civil case into the commercial docket of the pilot project court if the gravamen of the case relates to any of the following:

(1) Personal injury, survivor, or wrongful death matters;

(2) Consumer claims against business entities or insurers of business entities, including product liability and personal injury cases, and cases arising under federal or state consumer protection laws;

(3) Matters involving occupational health or safety, wages or hours, workers' compensation, or unemployment compensation;

(4) Environmental claims, except those arising from a breach of contractual or legal obligations or indemnities between business entities;

(5) Matters in eminent domain;

(6) Employment law cases, except those involving owners described in division (A)(3) of this rule;

(7) Cases in which a labor organization is a party;

(8) Cases in which a governmental entity is a party;

(9) Discrimination cases based upon the United States constitution, the Ohio constitution, or the applicable statutes, rules, regulations, or ordinances of the United States, the state, or a political subdivision of the state;

(10) Administrative agency, tax, zoning, and other appeals;

(11) Petition actions in the nature of a change of name of an individual, mental health act, guardianship, or government election matters;

(12) Individual residential real estate disputes, including foreclosure actions, or non-commercial landlord-tenant disputes;

(13) Any matter subject to the jurisdiction of the domestic relations, juvenile, or probate division of the court;

(14) Any matter subject to the jurisdiction of a municipal court, county court, mayor's court, small claims division of a municipal court or county court, or any matter required by statute or other law to be heard in some other court or division of a court;

(15) Any criminal matter, other than criminal contempt in connection with a matter pending on the commercial docket of the court.

1.04. Transfer of Case to the Commercial Docket

(A) **Random assignment** A case filed with a pilot project court shall be randomly assigned to a judge in accordance with the individual assignment system adopted by the court pursuant to division (B)(2) of Rule 36 of the Rules of Superintendence for the Courts of Ohio.

(B) **Transfer procedure**

(1) If the gravamen of a case filed with a pilot project court relates to any of the topics set forth in division (A) of Temporary Rule 1.03 of the Rules of Superintendence for the Courts of Ohio, the attorney filing the case shall include with the initial pleading a motion for transfer of the case to the commercial docket.

(2) If the gravamen of the case relates to any of the topics set forth in division (A) of Temporary Rule 1.03 of the Rules of Superintendence for the Courts of Ohio, if the attorney filing the case does not file a motion for transfer of the case to the commercial docket, and if the case is assigned to a non-commercial docket judge, an attorney representing any other party shall file such a motion with that party's first responsive pleading or upon that party's initial appearance, whichever occurs first.

(3) If the gravamen of the case relates to any of the topics set forth in division (A) of Temporary Rule 1.03 of the Rules of Superintendence for the Courts of Ohio, if no attorney representing a party in the case files a motion for transfer of the case to the commercial docket, and if the case is assigned to a non-commercial docket judge, the judge shall sua sponte request the administrative judge to transfer the case to the commercial docket.

(4) If the case is assigned to the commercial docket and if the gravamen of the case does not relate to any of the topics set forth in division (A) of Temporary Rule 1.03 of the Rules of Superintendence for the Courts of Ohio, upon motion of any party or sua sponte at any time during the course of the litigation, the commercial docket judge shall remove the case from the commercial docket.

(5) Copies of a party's motion for transfer of a case to the commercial docket filed pursuant to division (B)(1) or (2) of this rule shall be delivered to the administrative judge.

(C) **Ruling or decision on transfer**

(1) A non-commercial docket judge shall rule on a party's motion for transfer of a case filed under divisions (B)(1) or (2) of this rule no later than two days after the filing of the motion. A party to the case may appeal the non-commercial docket judge's decision to the administrative judge within three days of the non-commercial docket judge's decision. The administrative judge shall decide the appeal within two days of the filing of the appeal.

(2) An administrative judge shall decide the sua sponte request of a non-commercial docket judge for transfer of a case made under division (B)(3) of this rule no later than two days after the request is made.

(D) **Review of transfer**

(1) The factors set forth in Temporary Rule 1.03 of the Rules of Superintendence for the Courts of Ohio shall be dispositive in determining whether a case shall be transferred to or removed from the commercial docket pursuant to division (B) of this rule.

(2) The decision of the administrative judge as to the transfer of a case under division (C) of this rule is final and not appealable.

(E) **Adjustment of other case assignments** To guarantee a fair and equal distribution of cases, a commercial docket judge who is assigned a commercial docket case pursuant to division (B) of this rule may request the administrative judge to reassign a similar civil case by lot to another judge in the pilot project court.

1.05. Special Masters

(A) **Appointment**

(1) With the consent of all parties in a commercial docket case, a commercial docket judge may appoint a special master to do any of the following with regard to the case:

(a) Perform duties consented to by the parties;

(b) Hold trial proceedings and make or recommend findings of fact on issues to be decided by the judge without a jury if appointment is warranted by some exceptional condition or the need to perform an accounting or resolve a difficult computation of damages;

(c) Address pretrial and post-trial matters that cannot be addressed effectively and timely by the judge.

(2) A special master shall not have a relationship to the parties, counsel, the case, or the commercial docket judge that would require disqualification of a judge under division (E) of Canon 3 of the Code of Judicial Conduct unless the parties consent with the judge's approval to appointment of a particular person after disclosure of any potential grounds for disqualification.

(3) In appointing a special master, the commercial docket judge shall consider the fairness of imposing the likely expenses on the parties and shall protect against unreasonable expense or delay.

(B) **Order appointing a special master**

(1) A commercial docket judge shall give the parties notice and an opportunity to be heard before appointing a special master. Any party may suggest candidates for appointment.

(2) An order appointing a special master shall direct the special master to proceed with all reasonable diligence and shall include each of the following:

(a) The special master's duties, including any investigation or enforcement duties, and any limits on the special master's authority under division (C) of this rule;

(b) The circumstances, if any, under which the special master may communicate ex parte with the commercial docket judge or a party;

(c) The basis, terms, and procedure for fixing the special master's compensation.

(3) A commercial docket judge may amend an order appointing a special master at any time after notice to the parties, and an opportunity to be heard.

(C) **Special master's authority** Unless the appointing order expressly directs otherwise, a special master shall have authority to regulate all proceedings and take all appropriate measures to perform fairly and efficiently the assigned duties. The special master may impose appropriate sanctions for contempt committed in the presence of the special master and may recommend a contempt sanction against a party and sanctions against a nonparty.

(D) **Evidentiary hearings** Unless the appointing order expressly directs otherwise, a special master conducting an evidentiary hearing may exercise the power of the commercial docket judge to compel, take, and record evidence.

(E) **Special master's orders** A special master who makes an order shall file the order with the clerk of the court of common pleas and promptly serve a copy on each party. The clerk shall enter the order on the docket.

(F) **Special master's reports** A special master shall report to the commercial docket judge as required by the order of appointment. The special master shall file the report and promptly serve a copy of the report on each party unless the commercial docket judge directs otherwise.

(G) **Action on special master's order, report, or recommendations**

(1) In acting on a special master's order, report, or recommendations, the commercial docket judge shall afford the parties an opportunity to be heard; may receive evidence; and may adopt or affirm, modify, wholly or partly reject or reverse, or resubmit to the special master with instructions.

(2) A party may file an objection to or a motion to adopt or modify the special master's order, report, or recommendations no later than fourteen days after a copy is served, unless the court sets a different time.

(3) The court shall decide all objections to findings of fact made or recommended by the special master in accordance with the same standards as a ruling of a magistrate under paragraph (D)(3) of Rule 53 of the Rules of Civil Procedure, unless the parties, with the commercial docket judge's approval, stipulate either of the following:

(a) The findings will be reviewed for clear error;

(b) The findings of a special master appointed under division (A)(1)(a) or (b) of this rule will be final.

(4) The commercial docket judge shall decide de novo all objections to conclusions of law made or recommended by a special master.

(5) Unless the order of appointment establishes a different standard of review, the commercial docket judge may set aside a special master's ruling on a procedural matter only for an abuse of discretion.

(H) **Compensation**

(1) The commercial docket judge shall fix the special master's compensation before or after judgment on the basis and terms stated in the order of appointment, but the judge may set a new basis and terms after notice and an opportunity to be heard.

(2) The compensation of the special master shall be paid either by a party or parties or from a fund or subject matter of the case within the commercial docket judge's control.

(3) The commercial docket judge shall allocate payment of the special master's compensation among the parties after considering the nature and amount of the controversy and the extent to which any party is more responsible

than other parties for the reference to a special master. An interim allocation may be amended to reflect a decision on the merits.

1.06. Commercial Docket Case Management Plan The Supreme Court Task Force on Commercial Dockets shall establish a model commercial docket case management pretrial order to provide for the issuance of a commercial docket case management plan tailored to the requirements of the commercial docket. A commercial docket judge may use the model commercial docket case management pretrial order. Notwithstanding any contrary provision of a case management plan adopted by a pilot project court pursuant to division (B)(1) of Rule 5 of the Rules of Superintendence for Courts of Ohio, a commercial docket case management plan issued by a commercial docket judge shall govern the litigation of each commercial docket case assigned to that judge.

1.07. Rulings on Motions and Submitted Cases

(A) **Rulings on motions**

(1) A commercial docket judge shall rule upon all motions in a commercial docket case within sixty days of the date on which the motion was filed.

(2) If a commercial docket judge fails to rule upon a motion in a commercial docket case within sixty days of the date on which the motion was filed, an attorney representing the movant shall provide the judge with written notification alerting the judge of this fact. The attorney shall provide a copy of the notification to all other parties to the case.

(B) **Submitted cases**

(1) A commercial docket judge shall issue a decision in all commercial docket cases submitted for determination after a court trial within ninety days of the date on which the case was submitted.

(2) If a commercial docket judge fails to issue a decision in a commercial docket case submitted for determination after a court trial within ninety days of the date on which the case was submitted, an attorney representing a party to the case shall provide the judge with written notification alerting the judge of this fact. The attorney shall provide a copy of the notification to all other parties to the case.

1.08. Commercial Docket Case Disposition Time Guideline

(A) **Time guideline** Except for a case designated as complex litigation pursuant to Rule 42 of the Rules of Superintendence for the Courts of Ohio, a pilot project court shall aspire to have each case assigned to a commercial docket judge to disposition within eighteen months of the date on which the case was filed. This time guideline is not mandatory, but rather is intended to serve as a benchmark and assist pilot project courts and commercial docket judges in measuring the effectiveness of their case management.

(B) **Notification of delay** If a commercial docket judge has not disposed of a commercial docket case assigned to the judge within eighteen months of the date on which the case was filed, the judge shall notify the Case Management Section of the Supreme Court as to the cause for delay for the purpose of providing the information to the Supreme Court Task Force on Commercial Dockets.

1.09. Publication of Opinions and Orders Opinions and dispositive orders of the commercial docket judges shall be promptly posted on the website of the Supreme Court.

1.10. Pilot Project Evaluation The Supreme Court Task Force on Commercial Dockets shall collect, analyze, correlate, and interpret information and data concerning the commercial docket of each pilot project court. The Task Force may request the assistance of the Case Management Section of the Supreme Court and collect additional information from pilot project courts as needed.

1.11. Term of Temporary Rules 1.01 through 1.11 Temporary Rules 1.01 through 1.11 of the Rules of Superintendence for the Courts of Ohio adopted by the Supreme Court on May 6, 2008 shall take effect on July 1, 2008 and shall remain in effect through July 1, 2012, unless extended, modified, or withdrawn by the Supreme Court prior to that date. Any commercial docket case pending after the term of these temporary rules shall continue pursuant to the requirements of the rules until final disposition thereof.

APPENDICES

APPENDIX A. STATISTICAL REPORTING FORMS

THE SUPREME COURT OF OHIO
PRESIDING JUDGE REPORT
COURT OF APPEALS

	Date of completion of most recent physical case inventory

Appellate District _____ Judge _____

Report for the quarter ending: _____ , 20 _____

	A	B	C	D	E	F	G	H	I	T
	Criminal Appeals Common Pleas	Criminal Appeals w/Death Penalty Common Pleas	Criminal Appeals Muni. & Cnty.	Original Actions	Civil Appeals Common Pleas	Domestic Rel. Probate/Juv. Common Pleas	Civil Appeals Muni. & County	Administrative Appeals	Court of Claims (10th District Only)	TOTAL

I. DISTRICT TOTALS

		Mur.		Mur.		Mur.				Mur.			
Pending beginning of period	1												1
New cases filed	2												2
Cases transferred in, reactivated, or redesignated	3												3
TOTAL (Add lines 1-3)	4												4

II. TERMINATIONS BY:

		A	B	C	D	E	F	G	H	I	T	
Decisions or Opinions	5											5
Dismissal	6											6
Bankruptcy stay	7											7
Other Terminations	8											8
TOTAL TERMINATIONS (Add Lines 5-8)	9											9
Pending end of period (Subtract line 9 from line 4)	10											10
Time guideline (Days)		210	210	210	210	210	210	180	210	210	210	210	200	210	X	
Number pending beyond time guideline	11											11

III. STATUS OF PENDING CASES

		A	B	C	D	E	F	G	H	I	T	
Number pending with no record filed	12				X							12
Time Guideline (Days)		40	40	40	40	40	40	X	40	40	40	40	30	40	X	
Number pending beyond time guideline	13				X							13
Number pending with transcript of proceedings not filed within 180 days	14				X							14
Number pending with record filed but all briefs not received	15											15
Time Guideline (Days)		50	50	50	50	50	50	60	50	50	50	50	50	50	X	
Number pending beyond time guideline	16											16
Number pending with all papers in but not argued	17											17
Time Guideline (Days)		60	60	60	60	60	60	60	60	60	60	60	60	60	X	
Number pending beyond time guideline	18											18
Number assigned but no opinion released	19											19
Opinions released but not journalized	20											20
Time Guideline (Days)		60	60	60	60	60	60	60	60	60	60	60	60	60	X	
Cases pending beyond time guideline	21											21
		A	B	C	D	E	F	G	H	I	T	

Mail to:
Court Statistical Reporting Section
Supreme Court of Ohio
65 S. Front Street, 6th Floor
Columbus, Ohio 43215-3431

_____
Presiding or Administrative Judge Signature   Date

_____
Preparer and telephone number if other than judge   Date

THE SUPREME COURT OF OHIO
APPELLATE JUDGE REPORT
COURT OF APPEALS

Appellate District: _____ Judge: _____

Report for the quarter ending: _____ 19_____

Date of completion of most recent physical case inventory

_____

☐ CHECK IF JUDGE ASSIGNED BY CHIEF JUSTICE

I. CASES PENDING, END OF PERIOD - Cases Assigned For Opinion And No Opinion Released (one case per line)

	A	B	C	D	E	F	G	H	I	Date filed	Date Assigned	Number of Days Since Assignment	
	Crim. Appeals Common Pleas	Crim. Appeals w/death penalty Common Pleas	Crim. Appeals Muni. & Cnty.	Original Actions	Civil Appeals Common Pleas	Dom. Rel./Juv. Probate Common Pleas	Civil Appeals Muni. & Cnty.	Administrative Appeals	Court of Claims (10th District only)				
1													1
2													2
3													3
4													4
5													5
6													6
7													7
8													8
9													9
10													10
11													11
12													12
13													13
14													14
15													15
16													16
17													17
18													18
Total													
	A	B	C	D	E	F	G	H	I				

II. CASES TERMINATED DURING PERIOD

	A	B	C	D	E	F	G	H	I	T
	Criminal Appeals Common Pleas	Criminal Appeals w/ Death Penalty Common Pleas	Criminal Appeals Muni. & County	Original Actions	Civil Appeals Common Pleas	Dom. Rel./Juv. Probate Common Pleas	Civil Appeals Muni. & County	Administrative Appeals	Court of Claims (10th District Only)	TOTAL
Terminated by: Decision or Opinion										
Other Terminations										

Mail to:
Court Statistical Reporting Section
Supreme Court of Ohio
30 East Broad Street
Columbus, Ohio 43266-0419

f28746

Appellate Judge _____ Date _____

Preparer and telephone number if other than judge _____ Date _____

Presiding or Administrative Judge _____ Date _____

THE SUPREME COURT OF OHIO
FORM A
GENERAL DIVISION
COURT OF COMMON PLEAS

Date of completion of most recent physical case inventory _____

County _____ Judge _____

Report for the month of _____, 20_____

	A Professional Tort	B Product Liability	C Other Torts	D Workers Compensation	E Foreclosures	F Administrative Appeal	G Complex Litigation	H Other Civil	I Criminal	T TOTAL	V Visiting Judge	
Pending beginning of period 1												1
New cases filed 2							X					2
Cases transferred in, reactivated or redesignated 3												3
TOTAL (Add lines 1-3) 4												4

TERMINATIONS BY:

	A	B	C	D	E	F	G	H	I	T	V	
Jury trial 5												5
Court trial 6												6
Settled or dismissed prior to trial 7												7
Dismissal 8												8
Dismissal for lack of speedy trial (criminal) or want of prosecution (civil) 9												9
Magistrate 10									X			10
Diversion or arbitration 11												11
Guilty or no contest plea to original charge (criminal); Default (civil) 12												12
Guilty or no contest plea to reduced charge 13	X	X	X	X	X	X	X	X				13
Unavailability of party for trial or sentencing 14												14
Transfer to another judge or court 15												15
Referral to private judge 16									X			16
Bankruptcy stay or interlocutory appeal 17												17
Other terminations 18												18
TOTAL (Add lines 5-18) 19												19
Pending end of period (Subtract line 19 from line 4) 20												20
Time Guideline (Months)	24	24	24	12	12	9	36	24	6	X	X	
Cases pending beyond time guideline 21												21
Number of months oldest case is beyond time guideline 22									X			22
Cases submitted awaiting sentencing or judgment beyond time guideline 23												23
	A	B	C	D	E	F	G	H	I	T	V	

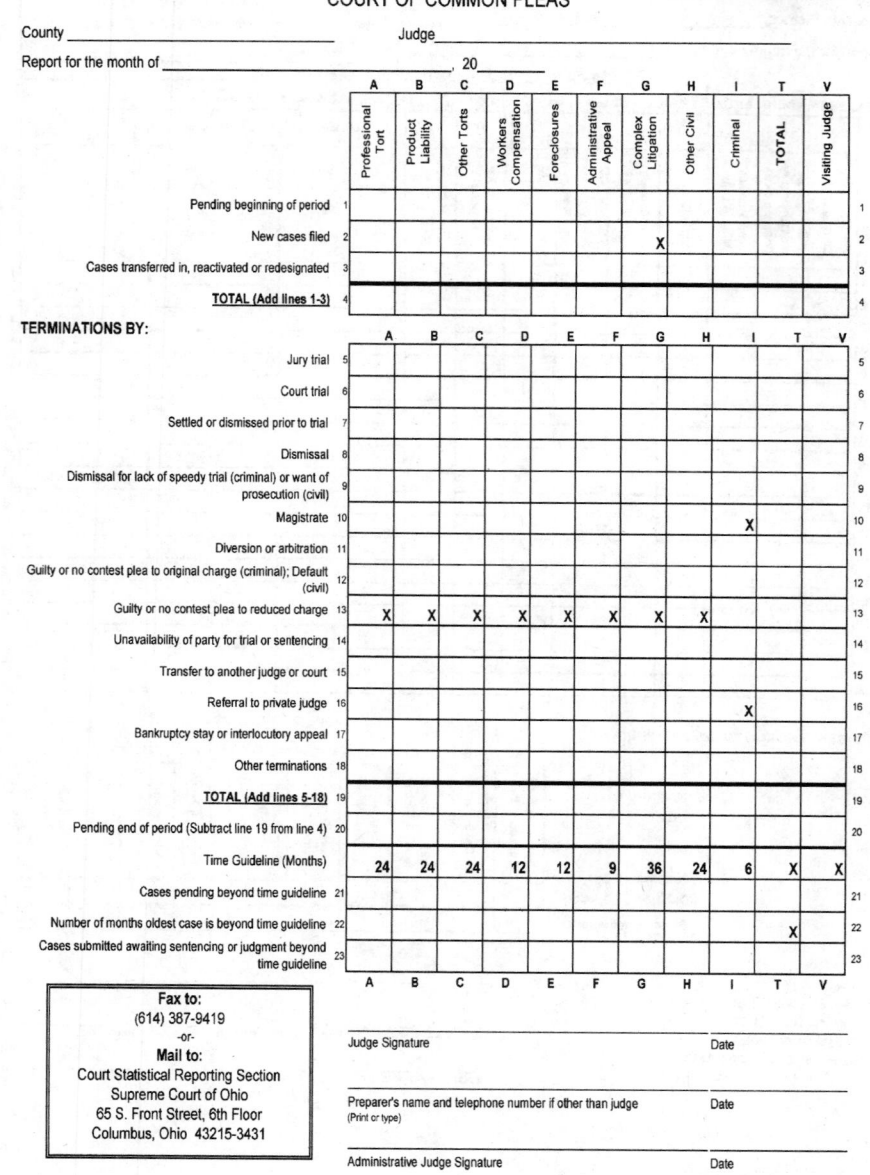

Fax to:
(614) 387-9419
-or-
Mail to:
Court Statistical Reporting Section
Supreme Court of Ohio
65 S. Front Street, 6th Floor
Columbus, Ohio 43215-3431

_____ Judge Signature   Date _____

_____ Preparer's name and telephone number if other than judge (Print or type)   Date _____

_____ Administrative Judge Signature   Date _____

THE SUPREME COURT OF OHIO
POST-CONVICTION RELIEF PETITIONS
DEATH PENALTY CASES
COURT OF COMMON PLEAS

County _____ Administrative Judge _____

Report for the month of _____, 20 _____

	A	B	C	D	E	F	G	H	I
	Case name	Case number	Date petition filed	Date terminated	Number of days pending	Time guideline (days)	Days beyond guideline	Status	Judge assigned
1						180			
2						180			
3						180			
4						180			
5						180			
6						180			
7						180			
8						180			
9						180			
10						180			
11						180			
12						180			
13						180			
14						180			
15						180			
16						180			
17						180			
18						180			
19						180			
20						180			

Include with monthly Form A and submit to:

Fax to:
(614) 387-9419
-or-
Mail to:
Court Statistical Reporting Section
Supreme Court of Ohio
65 S. Front Street, 6th Floor
Columbus, Ohio 43215-3431

_____
Administrative Judge Signature

_____
Preparer and telephone number if other than judge

THE SUPREME COURT OF OHIO
FORM B
DOMESTIC RELATIONS DIVISION
COURT OF COMMON PLEAS

Date of completion of most recent physical case inventory
_____

County _____ Judge _____

Report for the month of _____ , 20 _____

	A	B	C	D	E	F	G	H	I	J	K	T	V
	Marriage Terminations with Children	Marriage Terminations without Children	Marriage Dissolutions with Children	Marriage Dissolutions without Children	Change of Custody	Visitation Enforcement or Modification	Support Enforcement or Modification	Domestic Violence	U.I.F.S.A.	Parentage	All Others	TOTAL	Visiting Judge
Pending beginning of period 1													
New cases filed 2													
Cases transferred in, reactivated or redesignated 3													
TOTAL (Add lines 1-3) 4													

TERMINATIONS BY:

	A	B	C	D	E	F	G	H	I	J	K	T	V
Judge:Default, Uncontested, Dissolution 5													
Magistrate:Default, Uncontested, Dissolution 6													
Trial by Judge 7													
Trial by Magistrate 8													
Voluntary Dismissal 9													
Mediation or Concillation 10													
Bankruptcy stay or interlocutory appeal 11													
Transfer to another judge or court 12													
Referral to private judge 13													
Unavailability of party for trial 14													
Other terminations 15													
TOTAL (Add lines 5-15) 16													
Pending end of period (Subtract line 16 from line 4) 17													
Time Guideline (Months)	18	12	3	3	9	9	12	1	3	12	6	X	X
Cases pending beyond time guideline 18													
Number of months oldest case is beyond time guideline 19												X	
	A	B	C	D	E	F	G	H	I	J	K	T	V

Fax to:
(614) 387-9419
-or-
Mail to:
Court Statistical Reporting Section
Supreme Court of Ohio
65 S. Front Street, 6th Floor
Columbus, Ohio 43215-3431

_____ _____
Judge Signature   Date

_____ _____
Preparer's name and telephone number if other than judge (print or type)   Date

_____ _____
Administrative Judge Signature   Date

THE SUPREME COURT OF OHIO
FORM C

(page 1 of 2)

PROBATE DIVISION
COURT OF COMMON PLEAS

Date of completion of most recent physical case inventory
_____

County:_____ Judge:_____

Report for the quarter ending: _____

Visiting
Judge

Decedents' Estates

Pending at end of preceding quarter ------------------------------------ 1 _____ 1 _____
Filed during quarter --- 2 _____ 2 _____
Closed during quarter --- 3 _____ 3 _____
Pending at end of quarter --- 4 _____ 4 _____
Number in which accounts are past due ---------------------------------- 5 _____ 5 _____
Number of notices to file accounts, or citations issued ----------------- 6 _____ 6 _____

Guardianships

Guardianships of Minors

Pending at end of preceding quarter -------------------------------- 7 _____ 7 _____
Filed during quarter --- 8 _____ 8 _____
Closed during quarter -- 9 _____ 9 _____
Pending at end of quarter -- 10 _____ 10 _____

Guardianships of Incompetents

Pending at end of preceding quarter -------------------------------- 11 _____ 11 _____
Filed during quarter --- 12 _____ 12 _____
Closed during quarter -- 13 _____ 13 _____
Pending at end of quarter -- 14 _____ 14 _____

Number of Emergency, Limited, and Interim Guardians
Appointed during Quarter --- 15 _____ 15 _____

Conservatorships

Pending at end of preceding quarter -------------------------------------- 16 _____ 16 _____
Filed during quarter --- 17 _____ 17 _____
Closed during quarter --- 18 _____ 18 _____
Pending at end of quarter --- 19 _____ 19 _____

Testamentary Trusts

Pending at end of preceding quarter -------------------------------------- 20 _____ 20 _____
Filed during quarter --- 21 _____ 21 _____
Closed during quarter --- 22 _____ 22 _____
Pending at end of quarter --- 23 _____ 23 _____

Guardianships, Conservatorships, and
Testamentary Trusts

Number in which accounts are past due ----------------------------------- 24 _____ 24 _____
Number of notices to file accounts, or citations issued ------------------ 25 _____ 25 _____

Civil Actions (Include Appropriation Cases, Land Sales, Declaratory Judgments,
Will Contests, Determination of Heirs, Concealment of Assets and all other
contested civil actions)

Pending at end of preceding quarter -------------------------------------- 26 _____ 26 _____
Filed during quarter --- 27 _____ 27 _____
Closed during quarter --- 28 _____ 28 _____
Pending at end of quarter --- 29 _____ 29 _____

THE SUPREME COURT OF OHIO
FORM C
(page 2 of 2)
PROBATE DIVISION
COURT OF COMMON PLEAS

		Visiting Judge	
Adoptions			
Pending at end of preceding quarter	30 _____	30 _____	
Filed during quarter	31 _____	31 _____	
Closed during quarter	32 _____	32 _____	
Pending at end of quarter	33 _____	33 _____	
Mental Illness and Mental Retardation			
Pending at end of preceding quarter	34 _____	34 _____	
Filed during quarter	35 _____	35 _____	
Closed during quarter	36 _____	36 _____	
Pending at end of quarter	37 _____	37 _____	
Minors' Settlements			
Pending at end of preceding quarter	38 _____	38 _____	
Filed during quarter	39 _____	39 _____	
Closed during quarter	40 _____	40 _____	
Pending at end of quarter	41 _____	41 _____	
Wrongful Death (if not included with decedents' estate)			
Pending at end of preceding quarter	42 _____	42 _____	
Filed during quarter	43 _____	43 _____	
Closed during quarter	44 _____	44 _____	
Pending at end of quarter	45 _____	45 _____	
Delayed Registration of Birth and Correction of Birth			
Filed during quarter	46 _____	46 _____	
Heard and terminated during quarter	47 _____	47 _____	
Change of Name			
Filed during quarter	48 _____	48 _____	
Heard and terminated during quarter	49 _____	49 _____	
Marriage Applications			
Granted during quarter	50 _____	50 _____	

Fax to:
(614)387-9419
-or-
Mail to:
Court Statistical Reporting Section
Supreme Court of Ohio
65 S. Front Street, 6th Floor
Columbus, Ohio 43215-3431

_____ Judge   Date

_____ Preparer's name and telephone number if other than judge   Date

_____ Administrative Judge   Date

Rev. 3/01 #16678

THE SUPREME COURT OF OHIO
FORM D
JUVENILE DIVISION
COURT OF COMMON PLEAS

Date of completion of most recent physical case inventory

_____

County _____ Judge _____

Report for the month of _____, 20 _____

	A Delinquency	B Traffic	C Dependency, Neglect, or Abuse	D Unruly	E Adult Cases	F Motion for Permanent Custody	G Custody, Change of Custody, Visitation	H Support Enforcement or Modification	I Parentage	J U.I.F.S.A.	K All Others	T TOTAL	V Visiting Judge
Pending beginning of period 1													
New cases filed 2													
Cases transferred in, reactivated or redesignated 3													
TOTAL (Add lines 1-3) 4													

TERMINATIONS BY:

	A	B	C	D	E	F	G	H	I	J	K	T	V
Trial by Judge 5													
Trial by Magistrate 6													
Dismissal by party, judge, or prosecutor 7													
Admission to judge 8													
Admission to magistrate 9													
Certification/Waiver granted 10		X	X	X	X	X	X	X	X	X	X		
Unavailability of party for trial 11													
Transfer to another judge or court 12													
Referral to private judge 13	X	X	X	X	X	X							
Interlocutory appeal or order 14													
Other terminations 15													
TOTAL (Add lines 5-15) 16													
Pending end of period (Subtract line 16 from line 4) 17													
Time Guideline (Months)	6	3	3	3	6	9	9	12	12	3	6	X	X
Cases pending beyond time guideline 18													
Number of months oldest case is beyond time guideline 19												X	
Number of informal cases (all case types) 20													
	A	B	C	D	E	F	G	H	I	J	K	T	V

Fax to:
(614) 387-9419
-or-
Mail to:
Court Statistical Reporting Section
Supreme Court of Ohio
65 S. Front Street, 6th Floor
Columbus, Ohio 43215-3431

_____   _____
Judge Signature   Date

_____   _____
Preparer's name and telephone number if other than judge (print or type)   Date

_____   _____
Administrative Judge Signature   Date

THE SUPREME COURT OF OHIO
ADMINISTRATIVE JUDGE REPORT
MUNICIPAL COURT AND COUNTY COURT

Court _____ Judge _____

Report for the month of _____, 20 _____

		A Felonies	B Misdemeanors	C O.V.I.	D Other Traffic	E Personal Injury & Property Damage	F Contracts	G F.E.D.	H Other Civil	I Small Claims	T TOTAL
Pending beginning of period	1										
New cases filed	2										
Cases transferred in, reactivated or redesignated	3										
TOTAL (Add lines 1-3)	4										

TERMINATIONS BY:

		A	B	C	D	E	F	G	H	I	T
Trial/Hearing by judge (Include bindover by preliminary hearing, guilty or no contest pleas and defaults)	5										
Hearing by Magistrate (Include guilty or no contest pleas and defaults)	6	X									
Transfer (Include waivers of preliminary hearing and individual judge assignments)	7										
Dismissal for lack of speedy trial (criminal) or want of prosecution (civil)	8										
Other dismissals (Include dismissals at preliminary hearing)	9										
Violations Bureau	10	X		X		X	X	X	X	X	
Unavailability of party for trial or sentencing	11										
Bankruptcy stay or interlocutory appeal	12										
Other terminations	13										
TOTAL (Add lines 5-13)	14										
Pending end of period (Subtract line 14 from line 4)	15										
Time Guideline (Months)		1	6	6	6	24	12	12	12	6	X
Cases pending beyond time guideline	16										
Number of months oldest case is beyond time guideline	17										X

A	B	C	D	E	F	G	H	I	T

Fax to:
(614) 387-9419
-or-
Mail to:
Court Statistical Reporting Section
Supreme Court of Ohio
65 S. Front Street, 6th Floor
Columbus, Ohio 43215-3431

_____   _____
Administrative Judge Signature   Date

_____   _____
Preparer's name and telephone number if other than judge (print or type)   Date

THE SUPREME COURT OF OHIO
INDIVIDUAL JUDGE REPORT
MUNICIPAL COURT AND COUNTY COURT

Court _____ Judge _____

Report for the month of _____, 20 _____

Date of completion of most recent physical case inventory
_____

	B	C	D	E	F	G	H	T	V	
	Misdemeanors	O.V.I.	Other Traffic	Personal Injury & Property Damage	Contracts	F.E.D.	Other Civil	TOTAL	Visiting Judge	
Pending beginning of period 1										1
New cases filed 2										2
Cases transferred in, reactivated or redesignated 3										3
TOTAL (Add lines 1-3) 4										4

TERMINATIONS BY:

	B	C	D	E	F	G	H	T	V	
Jury trial 5										5
Court trial 6										6
Default 7	X	X	X							7
Guilty or no contest plea to original charge 8				X	X	X	X			8
Guilty or no contest plea to reduced charge 9				X	X	X	X			9
Dismissal for lack of speedy trial (criminal) or want of prosecution (civil) 10										10
Other Dismissals 11										11
Transfer to another judge or court 12										12
Referral to private judge 13	X	X	X							13
Unavailability of party for trial or sentencing 14										14
Bankruptcy stay or interlocutory appeal 15										15
Other terminations 16										16
TOTAL (Add lines 5-16) 17										17
Pending end of period (Subtract line 17 from line 4) 18										18
Time Guideline (Months)	6	6	6	24	12	12	12	X	X	
Cases pending beyond time guideline 19										19
Number of months oldest case is beyond time guideline 20								X		20
Cases submitted awaiting sentencing or judgment beyond time guideline 21										21
	B	C	D	E	F	G	H	T	V	

Fax to:
(614) 387-9419
-or-
Mail to:
Court Statistical Reporting Section
Supreme Court of Ohio
65 S. Front Street, 6th Floor
Columbus, Ohio 43215-3431

_____   _____
Judge Signature   Date

_____   _____
Preparer's name and telephone number if other than judge (print or type)   Date

_____   _____
Administrative Judge Signature   Date

APPENDIX B.
OHIO TRIAL COURT JURY USE AND MANAGEMENT STANDARDS

Adopted by the Supreme Court of Ohio on August 16, 1993.

STANDARD 1.   Opportunity for Service

A. The opportunity for jury service should not be denied or limited on the basis of race, national origin, gender, age, religious belief, income, occupation, disability, or any other factor that discriminates against a cognizable group in the jurisdiction.

B. Jury service is an obligation of all qualified citizens.

STANDARD 2.   Jury Source List

A. The names of potential jurors should be drawn from a jury source list compiled from one or more regularly maintained lists of persons residing in the court jurisdiction.

B. The jury source list should be representative and should be as inclusive of the adult population in the jurisdiction as is feasible.

C. The court should periodically review the jury source list for its representativeness and inclusiveness of the adult population in the jurisdiction as is feasible.

D. Should the court determine that improvement is needed in the representativeness or inclusiveness of the jury source list, appropriate corrective action should be taken.

STANDARD 3.   Random Selection Procedures

A. Random selection procedures should be used throughout the juror selection process. Any method may be used, manual or automated, that provides each eligible and available person with an equal probability of selection. These methods should be documented.

B. Random selection procedures should be employed in:

1.   Selecting persons to be summoned for jury service;

2.   Assigning prospective jurors to panels; and

3.   Calling prospective jurors for voir dire.

C. Departures from the principle of random selection are appropriate:

1.   To exclude persons ineligible for service in accordance with Standard 4;

2.   To excuse or defer prospective jurors in accordance with Standard 6;

3.   To remove prospective jurors for cause or if challenged peremptorily in accordance with Standards 8 and 9; and

4.   To provide all prospective jurors with an opportunity to be called for jury service and to be assigned to a panel in accordance with Standard 13.

STANDARD 4.   Eligibility for Jury Service

All persons should be eligible for jury service except those who:

A.   Are less than eighteen years of age;

B.   Are not citizens of the United States;

C.   Are not residents of the jurisdiction in which they have been summoned to serve;

D.   Are not able to communicate in the English language; or

E.   Have been convicted of a felony and have not had their civil rights restored.

STANDARD 5.   Term of and Availability for Jury Service

A. The time that persons are called upon to perform jury service and to be available should be the shortest period consistent with the needs of justice.

B. A term of service of one day or the completion of one trial, whichever is longer, is recommended. However, a term of one week or the completion of one trial, whichever is longer, is acceptable.

C. Persons should not be required to maintain a status of availability for jury service for longer than two weeks except in jurisdictions where it may be appropriate for persons to be available for service over a longer period of time.

STANDARD 6. Exemption, Excuse, and Deferral

A. All automatic excuses or exemptions, with the exception of statutory exemptions, from jury service should be eliminated.

B. Eligible persons who are summoned may be excused from jury service only if:

1.   Their ability to receive and evaluate information is so impaired that they are unable to perform their duties as jurors and they are excused for this reason by a judge; or

2.   They request to be excused because their service would be a continuing hardship to them or to members of the public and they are excused by a judge or a specifically authorized court official.

C. Deferrals for jury service for reasonably short periods of time may be permitted by a judge or a specifically authorized court official.

D. Requests for excuses and deferrals and their disposition should be written or otherwise made or recorded. Specific uniform guidelines for determining such requests should be adopted by the court.

STANDARD 7.   Voir Dire

A. Voir dire examination should be limited to matters relevant to determining whether to remove a juror for cause and to determine the juror's fairness and impartiality.

B. To reduce the time required for voir dire, basic background information regarding panel members should be made available to counsel in writing for each party on the day on which jury selection is to begin.

C. The trial judge should conduct a preliminary voir dire examination. Counsel shall then be permitted to question panel members for a reasonable period of time.

D. The judge should ensure that the privacy of prospective jurors is reasonably protected, and the questioning is consistent with the purpose of the voir dire process.

E. In criminal cases, the voir dire process shall be held on the record. In civil cases, the voir dire process shall be held on the record unless waived by the parties.

STANDARD 8.   Removal from the Jury Panel for Cause

If the judge determines during the voir dire process that any individual is unable or unwilling to hear the particular case at issue fairly and impartially, that individual should be removed from the panel. Such a determination may be made on motion of counsel or by the judge.

STANDARD 9.   Peremptory Challenges

A. Rules determining procedure for exercising peremptory challenges should be uniform throughout the state.

B. Peremptory challenges should be limited to a number no larger than necessary to provide reasonable assurance of obtaining an unbiased jury.

C. In civil cases, the number of peremptory challenges should not exceed three for each side. If the court finds that there is a conflict of interest between parties on the same side, the court may allow each conflicting party up to three peremptory challenges.

D. In criminal cases, the number of peremptory challenges should not exceed:

1.   Six for each side when a death sentence may be imposed upon conviction;

2.   Four for each side when a sentence of imprisonment (state institution) may be imposed upon conviction; or

3.   Three for each side in all other prosecutions. One additional peremptory challenge should be allowed for each defendant in a multi-defendant criminal proceeding.

E. In criminal and civil proceedings each side should be allowed one peremptory challenge if one or two alternate jurors are impaneled, two peremptory challenges if three or four alternates are impaneled, and three peremptory challenges if five or six alternates are impaneled. These additional peremptory challenges shall be used against an alternate juror only, and the other peremptory challenges allowed by law shall not be used against an alternate juror.

STANDARD 10.   Administration of the Jury System

A. The responsibility for administration of the jury system should be vested exclusively in the judicial branch of government.

B. All procedures concerning jury selection and service should be governed by Ohio Rules of Court.

C. Responsibility for administering the jury system should be vested in a single administrator acting under the supervision of the administrative judge of the court.

STANDARD 11.   Notification and Summoning Procedures

A. The notice summoning a person to jury service and the questionnaire eliciting essential information regarding that person should be:

1.   Combined in a single document;

2.   Phrased so as to be readily understood by an individual unfamiliar with the legal and jury systems; and

3.   Delivered by ordinary mail.

B. A summons should clearly explain how and when the recipient must respond and the consequences of a failure to respond.

C. The questionnaire should be phrased and organized so as to facilitate quick and accurate screening and should request only that information essential for:

1.   Determining whether a person meets the criteria for eligibility;

2.   Providing basic background information ordinarily sought during voir dire examination; and

3.   Efficiently managing the jury system.

D. Policies and procedures should be established for monitoring failures to respond to a summons and for enforcing a summons to report for jury service.

STANDARD 12.   Monitoring the Jury System

Courts should collect and analyze information regarding the performance of the jury system on a regular basis in order to evaluate:

A.   The representativeness and inclusiveness of the jury source list;

B.   The effectiveness of qualification and summoning procedures;

C.   The responsiveness of individual citizens to jury duty summonses;

D.   The efficient use of jurors; and

E.   The cost-effectiveness of the jury management system.

STANDARD 13.   Juror Use

A. Courts should employ the services of prospective jurors so as to achieve optimum use with a minimum of inconvenience to jurors.

B. Courts should determine the minimally sufficient number of jurors needed to accommodate trial activity. This information and appropriate management techniques should be used to adjust both the number of individuals summoned for jury duty and the number assigned to jury panels.

1.   Courts using jury pools should ensure that each prospective juror who has reported to the court is assigned for voir dire; and

2.   Courts using panels should ensure that each prospective juror who has reported to the court is assigned for voir dire.

C. Courts should coordinate jury management and

calendar management to make effective use of jurors.

STANDARD 14. Jury Facilities

A. Courts should provide an adequate and suitable environment for jurors.

B. The entrance and registration area should be clearly identified and appropriately designed to accommodate the daily flow of prospective jurors to the courthouse.

C. Jurors should be accommodated in pleasant waiting facilities furnished with suitable amenities.

D. Jury deliberation rooms should include space, furnishings, and facilities conducive to reaching a fair verdict. The safety and security of the deliberation rooms should be ensured.

E. To the extent feasible, juror facilities should be arranged to minimize contact between jurors, parties, counsel, and the public.

STANDARD 15. Juror Compensation

A. Persons called for jury service should receive a reasonable fee for their service and expenses.

B. Such fees should be paid promptly.

C. Employers shall be prohibited from discharging, laying-off, denying advancement opportunities to, or otherwise penalizing employees who miss work because of jury service.

STANDARD 16. Juror Orientation and Instruction

A. Orientation programs should be:

1. Designed to increase prospective jurors' understanding of the judicial system and prepare them to serve competently as jurors; and

2. Presented in a uniform and efficient manner using a combination of written, oral, and audiovisual materials.

B. Courts should provide some form of orientation or instructions to persons called for jury service:

1. Upon initial contact prior to service;

2. Upon first appearance at the court; and

3. Upon reporting to a courtroom for voir dire.

C. The trial judge should:

1. Give preliminary instructions to all prospective jurors.

2. Give instructions directly following impanelment of the jury to explain the jury's role, the trial procedures including notetaking and questioning by jurors, the nature of evidence and its evaluation, the issues to be addressed, and the basic relevant legal principles;

3. Prior to the commencement of deliberations, instruct the jury on the law, on the appropriate procedures to be followed during deliberations, and on the appropriate method for reporting the results of its deliberations. Such instructions should be made available to the jurors during deliberations;

4. Prepare and deliver instructions which are readily understood by individuals unfamiliar with the legal system; and

5. Recognize utilization of written instructions is preferable.

6. Before dismissing a jury at the conclusion of a case:

a. Release the jurors from their duty of confidentiality;

b. Explain their rights regarding inquiries from counsel or the press;

c. Either advise them that they are discharged from service or specify where they must report; and

d. Express appreciation to the jurors for their service, but not express approval or disapproval of the result of the deliberation.

D. All communications between the judge and members of the jury panel from the time of reporting to the courtroom for voir dire until dismissal shall be in writing or on the record in open court. Counsel for each party shall be informed of such communication and given the opportunity to be heard.

STANDARD 17. Jury Size and Unanimity of Verdict

Jury size and unanimity in civil and criminal cases shall conform with existing Ohio law.

STANDARD 18. Jury Deliberations

A. Jury deliberations should take place under conditions and pursuant to procedures that are designed to ensure impartiality and to enhance rational decision-making.

B. The judge should instruct the jury concerning appropriate procedures to be followed during deliberations in accordance with Standard 16C.

C. The deliberation room should conform to the recommendations set forth in Standard 14C.

D. The jury should not be sequestered except under the circumstances and procedures set forth in Standard 19.

E. A jury should not be required to deliberate after a reasonable hour unless the trial judge determines that evening or weekend deliberations would not impose an undue hardship upon the jurors and are required in the interest of justice.

F. Training should be provided to personnel who escort and assist jurors during deliberation.

STANDARD 19. Sequestration of Jurors

A. A jury should be sequestered only for good cause, including but not limited to insulating its members from improper information or influences.

B. During deliberations in the guilt phase and penalty phase, the jury shall be sequestered in a capital case.

C. The trial judge shall have the discretion to sequester a jury on the motion of counsel or on the judge's initiative and shall have the responsibility to oversee the conditions of sequestration.

D. Standard procedures should be promulgated to:

1. Achieve the purpose of sequestration; and

2. Minimize the inconvenience and discomfort of the sequestered jurors.

E. Training shall be provided to personnel who escort and assist jurors during sequestration.

APPENDIX C.
OHIO COURT SECURITY STANDARDS

COURT SECURITY STANDARDS

Preamble

The following Ohio Court Security Standards represent the efforts of the Supreme Court Advisory Committee on Court Security & Emergency Preparedness. The Standards were first adopted by the Supreme Court in 1994 and are now revised to reflect changes in our society affecting them.

Ohio citizens should expect all court facilities to be safe and secure for all who enter so that justice for all may be sought and not unjustly interrupted. Court facilities and each courtroom therein should have appropriate levels of security to address any foreseeable concern or emergency that may arise during the course of business. Elected officials charged with court facility authority must be proactive and sensitive to court security and emergency preparedness concerns. While the Advisory Committee understands providing a safe court facility to all carries a financial price, it is imperative that the topics discussed in the Ohio Court Security Standards be addressed.

Court security and emergency strategies and actions must be consistent with individual rights, civil liberties, and freedoms protected by the United States Constitution, the Ohio Constitution, and the rule of law. Because Ohio has a diverse population, special thought should be given to overcoming language and cultural barriers and physical disabilities when addressing security and emergency issues. However, Ohio citizens must be assured that any security practice or policy is employed in a neutral manner.

The Ohio Court Security Standards attempt to balance the diverse needs of each community. However, each locale is encouraged to promulgate policies and procedures to meet its specific needs. Special consideration should be given to defining the roles and responsibilities of the court and law enforcement officials within each local jurisdiction.

STANDARD 1.   Court Security Committee

Each court shall appoint a court security committee to meet on a periodic basis for the purpose of implementing these standards. If more than one court occupies a court facility, the courts shall collectively appoint a single committee.

STANDARD 2.   Security Policy And Procedures Manual

(A) **Adoption of manual** As part of its court security plan, each court shall adopt a written security policy and procedures manual governing security of the court and the court facility to ensure consistent, appropriate, and adequate security procedures. The manual shall include each of the following:
(1)   A physical security plan;
(2)   Routine security operations;

(3)   An emergency action plan that addresses events such as a hostage situation, an escaped prisoner, violence in the courtroom, a bomb threat, and fire;
(4)   A high risk trial plan.
(B) **Review of manual** A court shall periodically test and update its security policy and procedures manual for operational effectiveness.
(C) **Multiple courts** If more than one court occupies a court facility, the courts shall collectively adopt and review a single security policy and procedures manual.

STANDARD 3.   Emergency Preparedness Manual

(A) **Adoption of manual** As part of its court security plan, each court shall adopt a written emergency preparedness manual. The manual shall include a plan providing for the safety of all persons present within the court facility during an emergency.
(B) **Review of manual** A court shall periodically test and update its emergency preparedness manual for operational effectiveness.
(C) **Multiple courts** If more than one court occupies a court facility, the courts shall collectively adopt and review a single emergency preparedness manual.

STANDARD 4.   Continuity Of Operations Manual

(A) **Adoption of manual** As part of its court security plan, each court shall adopt a written continuity of operations manual. The manual shall include a plan that addresses each of the following:
(1)   The continued operation of the court at an alternative site should its present site be rendered inoperable due to a natural disaster, act of terrorism, security breach within the building, or other unforeseen event;
(2)   The provisions of the "Court Continuity of Operations (COOP) Plan Template" available on the website of the Supreme Court.
(B) **Review of manual** A court shall periodically test and update its continuity of operations manual for operational effectiveness.
(C) **Multiple courts** If more than one court occupies a court facility, the courts shall collectively adopt and review a single continuity of operations manual.

STANDARD 5.   Persons Subject To A Security Search

All persons entering a court facility shall be subject to a security search. A security search should occur for each visit to the court facility, regardless of the purpose or the hour.

STANDARD 6. Court Security Officers

(A) **Assignment** Uniformed court security officers should be assigned in sufficient numbers to ensure the security of each courtroom and the court facility.

(B) **Certification and training** All court security should be certified through the Ohio Peace Officers Training Council. These officers should receive specific training on court security and weapons instruction specific to the court setting.

STANDARD 7. Weapons In Court Facilities

(A) **Prohibition** No weapons should be permitted in a court facility except those carried by court security officers or as permitted under division (B)(1) of this standard. The court should establish and install adequate security measures to ensure no one will be armed with any weapon in the court facility.

(B) **Law enforcement**

(1) Each court should promulgate a local court rule governing the carrying of weapons into the court facility by law enforcement officers who are not a component of court security and are acting within the scope of their employment. If more than one court occupies a court facility, the courts shall collectively promulgate a single rule.

(2) In all cases, law enforcement officers who are parties to a judicial proceeding as a plaintiff, defendant, witness, or interested party outside of the scope of their employment should not be permitted to bring weapons into the court facility.

STANDARD 8. Prisoner Transport Within Court Facilities

(A) **Transport** Prisoners should be transported into and within a court facility through areas that are not accessible to the public. When a separate entrance is not available and public hallways must be utilized, prisoners should be handcuffed behind the back or handcuffed with use of "belly chains" to limit hand movement and always secured by leg restraints.

(B) **Carrying of firearms** During the transport of prisoners, personnel in direct contact with the prisoners should not carry firearms. However, an armed court security officer should be present.

(C) **Holding area** Once within a court facility, prisoners should be held in a secure holding area equipped with video monitoring, where practicable, while awaiting court hearings and during any recess.

STANDARD 9. Duress Alarms For Judges And Court Personnel

All courtrooms, hearing rooms, judges' chambers, clerks of courts' offices, and reception areas should be equipped with a duress alarm system connected to a central security station. The duress alarm system should include enunciation capability.

STANDARD 10. Closed-Circuit Video Surveillance

If a court utilizes closed-circuit video surveillance, the system should include the court facility parking area, entrance to the court facility, court lobby, courtroom, and all other public areas of the court facility.

STANDARD 11. Restricted Access To Offices

To ensure safe and secure work areas and to protect against inappropriate interaction between judges and participants in the judicial process, an effective secondary security perimeter should be utilized at the entrance to the office space housing judges and court personnel.

STANDARD 12. Off-Site Personal Security

As part of its court security plan, each court, in conjunction with law enforcement officers, should adopt procedures for the personal security of judges and court personnel at locations outside the court facility. If more than one court occupies a court facility, the courts shall collectively adopt procedures applicable to all judges and court personnel in the court facility.

STANDARD 13. Structural Design Of Court Facilities And Courtrooms

When designing new or remodeling old court facilities, consideration should be given to circulation patterns that govern the movement of people to, from, and in the courtroom. Judges, juries, court personnel, and prisoners should have routes to and from the courtroom separate from public routes. Waiting areas should be available to allow separation of parties, victims, and witnesses.

STANDARD 14. Security Incident Reporting

(A) **Reporting of security incidents**

(1) Every violation of law that occurs within a court facility should be reported to the law enforcement agency having jurisdiction. To facilitate reporting, all court personnel should familiarize themselves with the law enforcement agency that has jurisdiction within and around their court facility.

(2) Each court should adopt a policy for reporting court security incidents and should include the policy in the court's security policy and procedures manual. If more than one court occupies a court facility, the courts shall collectively adopt a single policy.

(3) A summary of court security incidents should be compiled annually for the court's benefit in evaluating security measures.

(B) **Periodic review of security incidents** All courts within the court facility should periodically review all court security incidents so the judges and court personnel are aware of recent events.

STANDARD 15. News Media In The Court Facility

The court security committee, along with other court officials, should consider and formulate a plan governing news media in a court facility. The plan should comply with the requirements of Rule 12 of the Rules of Superintendence for the Courts of Ohio and address both of the following:

(A) The process for news media entering and departing from the court facility in a minimally intrusive manner so other court offices are not disturbed;

(B) The safety of news media representatives in the courtroom as well as the location of their equipment so as to protect all persons in the courtroom and not create an impediment to court operations.

STANDARD 16. Information Technology Operations Security

Each court should periodically evaluate and update its security for its information technology operations and implement appropriate security controls to ensure protection of those operations.

APPENDIX D.
COURT FACILITY STANDARDS

Court Facility Standards

These standards apply to all courts of record in Ohio except as otherwise indicated. The standards represent the minimum requirements to ensure the efficient and effective administration of justice and are intended to complement federal, state, and local laws, regulations, and standards pertaining to building construction, safety, security, and access.

(A) **General considerations**   In order to maintain suitable judicial atmosphere and properly serve the public, clean, well-lighted, adequately heated and air-conditioned court facilities shall be provided and maintained.

(B) **Location**   The facilities should be located in a courthouse or county or municipal building. The location within the building should be separate from the location of non-judicial governmental agencies. Court facilities should be located in a building that is dignified and properly maintained.

(C) **Courtroom**   Every trial judge should have a separate courtroom.

The courtroom should have adequate seating capacity so that litigants and others are not required to stand or wait in hallways and areas adjacent to the courtroom.

All participants must be able to hear and to be heard. If the room acoustics are not satisfactory, an efficient public address system shall be provided.

Every courtroom should have an elevated bench. Adequate shelving should be provided adjacent to the bench for legal reference materials. United States and Ohio flags should flank the bench.

The witness chair should be near the bench, slightly elevated, and situated in an appropriate enclosure.

Desks, tables, and chairs should be provided for all court personnel regularly present in the courtroom.

Tables and chairs should be provided for parties and counsel. Tables shall be situated to enable all participants to hear and to allow private interchanges between litigants and counsel.

Each trial courtroom should be equipped with a jury box, suitable for seating jurors and alternates sufficient to meet the demands of the court. The jury box should be situated so that jurors may observe the demeanor of witnesses and hear all proceedings.

A blackboard and other necessary demonstrative aids should be readily available. Unnecessary material or equipment should not be kept in the courtroom.

Each judge should have private chambers convenient to the courtroom. Access from chambers to the courtroom should be private. Chambers should be decorated and equipped in appropriate fashion.

(D) **Library**   Each court shall be provided an adequate law library comprised of those materials, including electronic media, considered necessary by the court.

(E) **Magistrate**   Magistrates should have courtroom and office facilities similar to those of a judge.

(F) **Juror and witness facilities**   Each trial courtroom shall have a soundproof jury deliberation room located in a quiet area as near the courtroom as possible. Access from the jury deliberation room to the courtroom should be private. Private personal convenience facilities should be available for the jurors.

An adequate waiting room must be provided for jurors. Reading material of general interest, television, and telephones should be provided.

A waiting room comparable to the jurors' waiting room should be provided for witnesses.

(G) **Consultation room**   A room should be provided for use of attorneys.

(H) **Violations Bureaus and pay-in windows**   Facilities for violations bureaus and pay-in windows should be located near public parking areas.

(I) **Court staff and court-related personnel facilities**   Adequate space and equipment shall be provided for court personnel to prepare, maintain, and store necessary court records. Space and equipment should be utilized to ensure efficiency, security, and confidentiality.

Adequate restroom facilities separate from public restroom facilities should be provided for all court personnel.

(J) **Public convenience facilities**   Clean, modern restroom facilities should be available in the vicinity of the public areas of the court. Public telephones should be available and afford privacy.

APPENDIX E.
FACSIMILE FILING STANDARDS FOR OHIO COURTS

FACSIMILE FILING STANDARDS FOR OHIO COURTS

These Facsimile Filing Standards are adopted November 3, 2003 pursuant to Superintendence Rule 27, effective May 1, 2004.

Table of Contents

1.00 Definitions

1.01 "**Facsimile transmission**" means the transmission of a source document by a facsimile machine that encodes a document into signals, transmits, and reconstructs the signals to print a duplicate of the source document at the receiving end.

1.02 "**Facsimile machine**" means a machine that can send and receive a facsimile transmission either as a stand alone device or as part of a computer system.

[Commentary: E-MAILING OF FILING IS NOT CONSIDERED PART OF FAX FILING. IT WILL BE ADDRESSED IN ELECTRONIC FILING STANDARDS.]

1.03 "**Fax**" is an abbreviation for "facsimile" and refers, as indicated by the context, to facsimile transmission or to a document so transmitted.

1.04 "**Source document**" means the document transmitted to the court by facsimile machine/system.

1.05 "**Effective original document**" means the facsimile copy of the source document received by the Clerk of Court and maintained as the original document in the court's file.

1.06 "**Effective date and time of filing**" means the date and time that a facsimile filing is accepted by the Clerk of court for filing.

2.00 Applicability of local rules.

2.01 All local rules of court adopted to permit filing of facsimile documents will be deemed to permit filing of all pleadings, motions, exhibits and other documents that may be filed with the Clerk of Courts. The local rules must specify any exceptions to this permission.

[Commentary: There is not a mandate that requires a court to accept filings by FAX. Only those Courts, that choose to accept faxes, need to create local rules that meet the minimum standards set. We also created a "model rule" for those courts that are looking for more guidance. Clerks who serve in more than one location should specify all exceptions to fax filing.]

2.02 All local rules of court for facsimile filing SHALL place a requirement that the filer provide a cover page containing the following:

(I)   the caption of the case;
(II)   the case number;
(III)   the assigned judge;
(IV)   a description of the document being filed;
(V)   the date of transmission;
(VI)   the transmitting fax number; and
(VII)   an indication of the number of pages included in the transmission, including the cover page.

If a document is sent by fax to the Clerk of Court without the cover page information listed above, it may be deposited in the case jacket but need not be entered into the Case Docket and may be considered to be a nullity and thereby stricken from the record.

3.00 Place of filing

3.01 All local rules of court must specify the telephone number of the facsimile machine receiving transmission. The facsimile machine must have a dedicated telephone line and must be available to receive facsimile transmissions on the basis of 24 hours per day 7 days per week.

4.00 Time of filing

4.01 All local rules of court must specify that the date and time of ~~filing~~ receipt of any document is the date and time imprinted on the document by the facsimile machine receiving the transmission.

4.02 All local rules of court must permit receipt of facsimile transmissions on the basis of 24 hours per day 7 days per week.

4.03 All local rules of court may specify the effective date and time of filing for all documents received outside of the normal business hours of the office of the Clerk of Court and queue them in order of their receipt as documented by the date and time imprinted by the receiving facsimile machine.

4.04 The Clerk of Court may but need not acknowledge receipt of a facsimile transmission.

[Commentary: It was the intention of the committee that if for any reason the fax is not received, the burden of validating or confirming the receipt of the complete fax transmission is on the sending party. Most Fax machines are equipped with the capacity to report back to the sending party, a validation of transmission or a "failed transmission" report.]

5.00 Filing of originals

5.01 All local rules of court must provide that documents filed by facsimile are accepted as the effective original document in the court file. The source document need not be filed. However, the sending party must maintain possession of the source document and make them available for inspection by the court upon request.

[Commentary: The Standards Subcommittee recommends that local rules address the issue of retention of the source document until opportunities for the post judgment relief are exhausted.]

5.02 Documents shall be filed with a signature or notation "/s/" followed by the name of the person signing the source document. The person transmitting the document represents that the signed source document is in his/her possession.

5.03 A local rule of court may limit the number of pages that it will accept by facsimile transmission. If the document to be transmitted exceeds the page limit established by local rule, the original must be filed. All local rules of court may permit exhibits that cannot be transmitted accurately or are lengthy to be replaced by an insert page describing the exhibit. The local rules may provide that the original of such an exhibit may be filed within a specified time subsequent to the facsimile filing.

5.04 A local rule may be adopted that is not inconsistent with any standard regarding the filing of an original source document.

[Commentary: The local rule should address and define what it felt was reasonable page limit. A filing that exceeds the page limit detailed in the local rule would either require filing through other allowable channels. or as is the case with Exhibits in section 6.01 of the Model rule; if the filing has exhibit(s) that cause it to exceed the page limit, then, in the fax filing the exhibit (or other lengthy document), would be "replaced by an insert page describing the exhibit and why it is missing. Unless the court otherwise orders, the missing exhibit shall be filed with the court, as a separate document, not later than five (5) court days following the filing of the facsimile document. Failure to file the missing exhibits as required by this paragraph may result in the court striking the document and/or exhibit." This allows the local court to facilitate filing by allowing faxes without placing an unusual burden on the clerk's office.]

6.00 Filing Fees

6.01 All local rules of court must specify the effective methods of paying fees and costs for any pleading or other document requiring such a fees or costs. The local rules may provide that the Clerk of Court does not have to accept a facsimile transmission filing unless the acceptable method of payment has been paid or arranged to be paid. Local rules of court may not require premium fee schedules for facsimile filings.

[Commentary: In terms of costs associated with acceptance of fax filings, some clerks have expressed concern over related costs. In the case of FAX filing, the only substantive difference between a single original coming in over the counter and one coming in via FAX is the presentation. Section 6 specifically prohibits the charging of fees above and beyond the $3.00/$10.00 fee allowed for court technology, for accepting a FAX filing. However, if it's customary for a clerk's office to charge for copies (including service copies) or additional charges for administrative costs, mailing /postage costs, etc. ... then those fees would still apply regardless of how the original filing came in. Those additional fees would most likely fall under a separate local rule regarding fees that your court would already have in place.]

7.00 Effective Date of Local Rules

7.01 All local rules of court will become effective upon approval by the Supreme Court Committee on Technology and the Courts.

8.00 Time to Compliance

8.01 Courts which choose to offer facsimile filing shall submit local rules for approval by the Supreme Court of Ohio. Courts offering facsimile filing at the time this standard is adopted shall submit their local rule for approval within six months of the adoption of this standard.

APPENDIX

Model Facsimile Filing Rule for Ohio Courts

The Model Facsimile Rule for Ohio Courts is included for illustration. This form is expressly declared as sufficient to meet the requirements of the Facsimile Filing Standards for Ohio Courts. Departures from this form shall not void a local rule that is otherwise sufficient to meet the requirements of the aforesaid Facsimile Filing Standards for Ohio Courts.

STANDARDS SUBCOMMITTEE OF THE
SUPREME COURT ADVISORY COMMITTEE
ON TECHNOLOGY AND THE COURTS

MODEL FACSIMILE FILING RULE FOR OHIO COURTS

The provisions of this local rule are adopted under [Civ.R. 5(E)] [Civ.R. 73(J)] [Crim.R.12(B)] [Juv.R. 8] [App.R. 13(A)].

Pleadings and other papers may be filed with the Clerk of Courts by facsimile transmission to [area code and number of receiving machine] subject to the following conditions:

APPLICABILITY

1.01 These rules apply to [civil], [criminal], [small claims], [probate], [juvenile], [appellate] and [domestic relations], proceedings in the [name of court].

1.02 These rules do not apply to [civil], [criminal], [small claims], [probate], [juvenile], [appellate] and [domestic relations], proceedings. In these proceedings no facsimile transmission of documents will be accepted.

1.03 The following documents will not be accepted for fax filing: [original wills and codicils] [cognovit promissory notes], [insert other examples]

ORIGINAL FILING

2.01 A document filed by fax shall be accepted as the effective original filing. The person making a fax filing need not file any source document with the Clerk of Court but must, however, maintain in his or her records and have available for production on request by the court the source document filed by fax, with original signatures as otherwise required under the applicable rules, together with the source copy of the facsimile cover sheet used for the subject filing.

2.02 The source document filed by fax shall be maintained by the person making the **filing** until the case is closed and all opportunities for post judgment relief are exhausted.

DEFINITIONS

As used in these rules, unless the context requires otherwise:

3.01   A "facsimile transmission" means the transmission of a source document by a facsimile machine that encodes a document into optical or electrical signals, transmits and reconstructs the signals to **print** a duplicate of the source document at the receiving end.

3.02   A "facsimile machine" means a machine that can send and receive a facsimile transmission.

3.03   "Fax" is an abbreviation for "facsimile" and refers, as indicated by the context, to facsimile transmission or to a document so transmitted.

COVER PAGE

4.01   The person filing a document by fax shall also provide therewith a cover page containing the following information: [See appendix for sample cover page form.]

(I)   the name of the court;

(II)   the title of the case;

(III)   the case number;

(IV)   the assigned judge;

(V)   the title of the document being filed (e.g. Defendant Jones' Answer to Amended Complaint; Plaintiff Smith's Response to Defendants' Motion to Dismiss; Plaintiff Smith's Notice of Filing Exhibit "G" to Plaintiff Smith's Response to Defendants' Motion to Dismiss) ;

(VI)   the date of transmission;

(VII)   the transmitting fax number;

(VIII)   an indication of the number of pages included in the transmission, including the cover page;

(IX)   if a judge or case number has not been assigned, state that fact on the cover page;

(X)   the name, address, telephone number, fax number, Supreme Court registration number, if applicable, and e-mail address of the person filing the fax document if available; and

(XI)   if applicable, a statement explaining how costs are being submitted.

4.02   If a document is sent by fax to the Clerk of Court without the cover page information listed above, the Clerk may, at its discretion:

(I)   enter the document in the Case Docket and file the document; or

(II)   deposit the document in a file of failed faxed documents with a notation of the reason for the failure; in this instance, the document *shall not* be considered filed with the Clerk of Courts.

4.03   The Clerk of Court is not required to send any form of notice to the sending party of a failed fax filing. However, if practicable, the Clerk of Court may inform the sending party of a failed fax filing.

SIGNATURE

5.01   A party who wishes to file a signed source document by fax shall either:

(I)   fax a copy of the signed source document; or

(II)   fax a copy of the document without the signature but with the notation "/s/" followed by the name of the signing person where the signature appears in the signed source document.

5.02   A party who files a signed document by fax represents that the physically signed source document is in his/her possession or control.

[Commentary: 5.01 (II) addresses those instances where the fax transmission is generated by the sending party's computer and therefore the document is not printed and capable of being signed prior to transmission.]

EXHIBITS

6.01   Each exhibit to a facsimile produced document that cannot be accurately transmitted via facsimile transmission for any reason must be replaced by an insert page describing the exhibit and why it is missing. Unless the court otherwise orders, the missing exhibit shall be filed with the court, as a separate document, not later than five (5) court days following the filing of the facsimile document. Failure to file the missing exhibits as required by this paragraph may result in the court striking the document and/or exhibit.

6.02   Any exhibit filed in this manner shall be attached to a cover sheet containing the caption of the case which sets forth the name of the court, title of the case, the case number, name of the judge and the title of the exhibit being filed (e.g., Plaintiff Smith's Notice of Filing Exhibit "G" to Plaintiff Smith's Response to Defendants' Motion to Dismiss), and shall be signed and served in conformance with the rules governing the signing and service of pleadings in this court. [See appendix for sample exhibit cover sheet.]

TIME OF FILING

(OPTION I)

7.01 Subject to the provisions of these rules, all documents sent by fax and accepted by the Clerk shall be considered filed with the Clerk of Courts as of the date and time the fax transmission was received by the Clerk of Court. The office of the Clerk of Court will be deemed open to receive facsimile transmission of documents on the basis of 24 hours per day seven days per week including holidays. Each page of any document received by the Clerk will be automatically imprinted with the date and time of receipt. The date and time imprinted on the document will determine the time of filing, provided the document is deemed accepted by the Clerk.

(OPTION II)

7.01 Subject to the provisions of these rules, all documents sent by fax and accepted by the Clerk shall be considered filed with the Clerk of Courts as of the date and time the Clerk time-stamps the document received, as opposed to the date and time of the fax transmission. The office of the Clerk of Court will be deemed open to receive facsimile transmission of documents on the same days and at the same time the court is regularly open for business.

7.02 Fax filings may NOT be sent directly to the court for filing but may only be transmitted directly through the facsimile equipment operated by the Clerk of Courts.

7.03 The Clerk of Court may, but need not, acknowledge receipt of a facsimile transmission.

7.04   The risks of transmitting a document by fax to the Clerk of Courts shall be borne entirely by the sending party. Anyone using facsimile filing is urged to verify receipt of such filing by the Clerk of Court through whatever technological means are available.

FEES AND COSTS

8.01   No document filed by facsimile that requires a filing fee shall be accepted by the Clerk for filing until court cost and fees have been paid. Court cost and fees may be paid by credit or debit cards or through an escrow account established with the Clerk. The forms necessary for the authorization of payment by credit card or escrow account shall be available at the Clerk's office during normal business hours [and are accessible on-line at _____]. Documents tendered to the Clerk without payment of court cost and fees, or with incomplete information on the charge authorization or request, or which do not conform to applicable rules will not be filed. [See appendix for sample credit card payment form.]

[Commentary: Information furnished for authorization of payment by credit/debit card shall not be part of the case file.]

8.02   No additional fee shall be assessed for facsimile filings.

LENGTH OF DOCUMENT

9.01   Facsimile filings shall not exceed _____ pages in length. . The filer shall not transmit service copies by facsimile.

[Commentary: The local rule should address and define what it felt to be a reasonable page limit. The subcommittee also recommends that service copies not be sent by fax. However, this is optional, and at the discretion of the local court.]

EFFECTIVE DATE

10.01   These local rules shall be effective [insert date], and shall govern all proceedings in actions brought after they take effect and also further proceedings in pending actions, except to the extent that, in the opinion of the court, their application in a particular action pending on the effective date would not be feasible or would work an injustice, in which event, the former procedure applies.

[Commentary: Facsimile filing standards in the model rule contemplate the facsimile transmission of documents to a court by electronic means. The court receiving the facsimile

transmission will maintain its equipment to reconstruct a paper copy version of the source document to serve as the original document. These standards should be differentiated from other types of electronic filing, for which other standards will apply.]

APPENDIX

1. Sample Facsimile Filing Cover Page

2. Sample Exhibit Cover Page

3. Sample Credit Card Payment Form

FACSIMILE FILING COVER PAGE

RECIPIENT INFORMATION:

NAME OF COURT: _____

FAX NUMBER: _____

SENDING PARTY INFORMATION:

NAME: _____
SUPREME COURT
REGISTRATION NO. (if applicable): _____

OFFICE/FIRM: _____

ADDRESS: _____

TELEPHONE NO. _____

FAX NUMBER: _____

E-MAIL ADDRESS (if available): _____

CASE INFORMATION:

TITLE OF THE CASE: _____

CASE NUMBER[*]: _____

TITLE OF THE DOCUMENT: _____
_____

JUDGE[*]: _____

FILING INFORMATION:

DATE OF FAX TRANSMISSION: _____

NUMBER OF PAGES (including this page): _____

STATEMENT EXPLAINING HOW COSTS ARE BEING SUBMITTED, IF
APPLICABLE:_____
_____

_____

[*]If a judge or case number has not been assigned, please state that fact in the space provided.

IN THE COURT OF COMMON PLEAS
_____ COUNTY, OHIO

JOHN SMITH, Plaintiff,	
v.	Case No.: 1234567
BILL JONES, Defendant.	Judge _____ *(in the alternative a notation here that the case is not yet assigned)*

PLAINTIFF SMITH'S NOTICE OF FILING EXHIBIT "G"
TO
PLAINTIFF SMITH'S RESPONSE TO DEFENDANT'S MOTION TO DISMISS

Plaintiff Smith, through counsel, hereby files Exhibit "G" to Plaintiff Smith's Response to Defendant's Motion to Dismiss. The referenced pleading was filed by facsimile transmission with the Court on [date]. Exhibit "G" could not be accurately transmitted by fax and is therefore being timely filed as a separate document with the Court pursuant to Local Rule XX.X.

Respectfully Submitted,

_____
Attorney Name (Sup. Crt. Reg. No.)
Office/Firm
Address
Telephone
Facsimile
E-mail

Counsel for Plaintiff John Smith

CERTIFICATE OF SERVICE

I certify that a copy of this Notice of Filing Exhibit "G" was sent by ordinary U.S. mail on [date] to counsel for defendant Bill Jones, [name and address of recipient].

_____
Attorney Name
Counsel for Plaintiff John Smith

CREDIT / DEBIT CARD AUTHORIZATION FORM

To: Clerk, _____ County Common Pleas Court _____ Division

Fax No:_____

Regarding (if applicable):

Case Name:_____

Case Number:_____

Dear Clerk's Office Representative:

Please charge my credit / debit card in the amount of $_____ in payment of

fees for the following court costs/service(s): [Identify document to be filed or other service to be

performed by the Clerk's Office for which a fee is assessed.]_____

_____

Circle One: MasterCard   Visa

Credit / Debit Card Number: _____
Expiration Date: _____

Name of Cardholder: _____

Billing Address: _____

                              _____

Telephone No.:   _____

Fax No.:   _____

Cardholder Signature: _____

Date: _____

Name & Telephone No. of Person Submitting This form: _____

APPENDIX F.
MODEL STANDARDS OF PRACTICE FOR FAMILY AND DIVORCE MEDIATION

[Model Standards of Practice for Family and Divorce Mediation (adopted by the American Bar Association, Association of Family and Conciliation Courts and the Association for Conflict Resolution) modified to reference express provisions of Ohio law.]

Overview and Definitions

Family and divorce mediation ("family mediation" or "mediation") is a process in which a mediator, an impartial third party, facilitates the resolution of family disputes by promoting the participants' voluntary agreement. The family mediator assists communication, encourages understanding and focuses the participants on their individual and common interests. The family mediator helps the participants to explore options, make decisions and reach their own agreements.

Family mediation is neither a substitute for the need for family members to obtain independent legal advice or counseling or therapy, nor is it appropriate for all families. However, experience has established that family mediation is a valuable option for many families because it can:

(A) Increase the self-determination of participants and improve their ability to communicate;

(B) Promote the best interests of children; and

(C) Reduce the economic and emotional costs associated with the resolution of family disputes.

Effective mediation requires that the family mediator be qualified by training, experience and temperament; that the mediator be impartial; that the participants reach their decisions voluntarily; that their decisions be based on sufficient factual data; that the mediator be aware of the impact of culture and diversity issues that impact the mediation process; and that the best interests of children be taken into account. Further, the mediator should also be prepared to identify families whose history includes domestic abuse or child abuse.

These Model Standards of Practice for Family and Divorce Mediation ("Model Standards") aim to perform three major functions:

(A) To serve as a guide for the conduct of family mediators;

(B) To inform the mediating participants of what they can expect; and

(C) To promote public confidence in mediation as a process for resolving family disputes.

The Model Standards are aspirational in character. They describe good practices for family mediators. They are not intended to create legal rules or standards of liability.

The Model Standards include different levels of guidance:

Use of the term "may" in a Standard is the lowest strength of guidance and indicates a practice that the family mediator should consider adopting but which can be deviated from in the exercise of good professional judgment.

Most of the Standards employ the term "should" which indicates that the practice described in the Standard is highly desirable and should be departed from only with very strong reason.

The term "shall" in a Standard is a higher level of guidance to the family mediator, indicating that the mediator should not have discretion to depart from the practice described.

Standard I

A family mediator shall recognize that mediation is based on the principle of self-determination by the participants.

(A) Self-determination is the fundamental principle of family mediation. The mediation process relies upon the ability of participants to make their own voluntary and informed decisions.

(B) The primary role of a family mediator is to assist the participants to gain a better understanding of their own needs and interests and the needs and interests of others and to facilitate agreement among the participants.

(C) A family mediator shall inform the participants that they may seek information and advice from a variety of sources during the mediation process.

(D) A family mediator shall inform the participants that they may withdraw from family mediation at any time and are not required to reach an agreement in mediation.

(E) The family mediator's commitment shall be to the participants and the process. Pressure from outside of the mediation process shall never influence the mediator to coerce participants to settle.

Standard II

A family mediator shall be qualified by education and training to undertake the mediation.

(A) To perform the family mediator's role, a mediator should:

(1) have knowledge of family law;

(2) have knowledge of and training in the impact of family conflict on parents, children and other participants, including knowledge of child development, domestic abuse and child abuse and neglect;

(3) have education and training specific to the process of mediation; and

(4) Be able to recognize the impact of culture and diversity.

(B) Family mediators shall provide information to the participants about the mediator's relevant training, education and expertise.

Standard III

A family mediator shall facilitate the participants' understanding of what mediation is and assess their capacity to mediate before the participants reach an agreement to mediate.

(A) Before family mediation begins, a mediator shall provide the participants with an overview of the process and its purposes, including:

(1) informing the participants that reaching an agreement in family mediation is consensual in nature, that a mediator is an impartial facilitator, and that a mediator may not impose or force any settlement on the parties;

(2) distinguishing family mediation from other processes designed to address family issues and disputes;

(3) informing the participants that any agreements reached will be reviewed by the court when court approval is required;

(4) informing the participants that they may obtain independent advice from attorneys, counsel, advocates, accountants, therapists or other professionals during the mediation process;

(5) advising the participants, in appropriate cases, that they can seek the advice of religious figures, elders or other significant persons in their community whose opinions they value;

(6) discussing, if applicable, the issue of separate sessions with the participants, a description of the circumstances in which the mediator may meet alone with any of the participants, or with any third party and the conditions of confidentiality concerning these separate sessions;

(7) Informing the participants that the presence or absence of other persons at mediation, including attorneys, counselors or advocates, depends on the wishes of the participants. The mediator shall take controlling statutes or rules into consideration. The mediator may encourage the presence of another person when there is a history or threat of violence or other serious coercive activity by a participant;

(8) describing the obligations of the mediator to maintain the confidentiality of the mediation process and its results as well as any exceptions to confidentiality;

(9) Advising the participants of the circumstances under which the mediator may suspend or terminate the mediation process and that a participant has a right to suspend or terminate mediation at any time.

(B) The family mediator should have participants sign a written agreement to mediate their dispute and the terms and conditions thereof within a reasonable time after first consulting the family mediator, if they desire to mediate.

(C) The family mediator should be alert to the capacity and willingness of the participants to mediate before proceeding with the mediation and throughout the process. A mediator shall not agree to conduct the mediation if the mediator reasonably believes one or more of the participants are unable or unwilling to participate.

(D) Family mediators should not accept a dispute for mediation if they cannot satisfy the expectations of the participants concerning the timing of the process.

Standard IV

A family mediator shall conduct the mediation process in an impartial manner. A family mediator shall disclose all actual and potential grounds of bias and conflicts of interest reasonably known to the mediator. The participants shall be free to retain the mediator by an informed, written waiver of the conflict of interest. However, if a bias or conflict of interest clearly impairs a mediator's impartiality, the mediator shall withdraw regardless of the express agreement of the participants.

(A) Impartiality means freedom from favoritism or bias in word, action or appearance, and includes a commitment to assist all participants as opposed to any one individual.

(B) Conflict of interest means any relationship between the mediator, any participant or the subject matter of the dispute that compromises or appears to compromise the mediator's impartiality.

(C) A family mediator should not accept a dispute for mediation if the family mediator cannot be impartial.

(D) A family mediator shall identify and disclose potential grounds of bias or conflict of interest upon which a mediator's impartiality might reasonably be questioned. Such disclosure should be made prior to the start of mediation and in time to allow the participants to select an alternate mediator.

(E) A family mediator shall resolve all doubts in favor of disclosure. All disclosures shall be made as soon as practical after the mediator becomes aware of the bias or potential conflict of interest. The duty to disclose is a continuing duty.

(F) A family mediator shall guard against bias or partiality based on the participants' personal characteristics, background or performance at the mediation.

(G) A family mediator shall avoid conflicts of interest in recommending the services of other professionals.

(H) A family mediator shall not use information about participants obtained in mediation for personal gain or advantage.

(I) A family mediator shall withdraw pursuant to Standard XI if the mediator believes the mediator's impartiality has been compromised or a conflict of interest has been identified and has not been waived by the participants.

Standard V

A family mediator shall fully disclose and explain the basis of any compensation, fees and charges to the participants.

(A) The participants shall be provided with sufficient information about fees at the outset of mediation to determine if they wish to retain the services of the mediator.

(B) The participants' written agreement to mediate their dispute shall include a description of their fee arrangement with the mediator.

(C) A mediator shall not enter into a fee agreement that is contingent upon the results of the mediation or the amount of the settlement.

(D) A mediator shall not accept a fee for referral of a matter to another mediator or to any other person.

(E) Upon termination of mediation a mediator shall return any unearned fee to the participants.

Standard VI

A family mediator shall structure the mediation process so that the participants can make decisions based on sufficient information and knowledge.

(A) The mediator should facilitate full and accurate disclosure and the acquisition and development of information during mediation so that the participants can make informed decisions. This may be accomplished by encouraging participants to consult appropriate experts.

(B) Consistent with standards of impartiality and preserving participant selfdetermination, a mediator may provide the participants with information that the mediator is qualified by training or experience to provide. The mediator shall not provide therapy or legal advice.

(C) If the participants so desire, the mediator shall allow attorneys, counsel or advocates for the participants, or other individual designated by the participants, to be present at the mediation sessions.

(D) With the agreement of the participants, the mediator may document the participants' resolution of their dispute. The mediator should inform the participants that any agreement should be reviewed by an independent attorney before it is signed.

Standard VII

A family mediator shall maintain the confidentiality of all information acquired in the mediation process, unless the mediator is permitted or required to reveal the information by law or agreement of the participants.

(A) The mediator should discuss the participants' expectations of confidentiality with them prior to undertaking the mediation. The written agreement to mediate should include provisions concerning confidentiality.

(B) Prior to undertaking the mediation the mediator shall inform the participants of the limitations of confidentiality such as statutory, judicially or ethically mandated reporting.

(C) As permitted by law, the mediator shall disclose a participant's threat of suicide or violence against any person to the threatened person and the appropriate authorities if the mediator believes such threat is likely to be acted upon.

(D) If the mediator holds private sessions with a participant, the obligations of confidentiality concerning those sessions should be discussed and agreed upon prior to the sessions.

(E) If subpoenaed or otherwise noticed to testify or to produce documents the mediator should inform the participants immediately. The mediator shall not testify or provide documents in response to a subpoena without an order of the court that is pursuant to O.R.C. 3109.52, if the mediator reasonably believes doing so would violate an obligation of confidentiality to the participants.

Standard VIII

A family mediator shall assist participants in determining how to promote the best interests of children.

(A) The mediator should encourage the participants to explore the range of options available for separation or post divorce parenting arrangements and their respective costs and benefits. Referral to a specialist in child development may be appropriate for these purposes. The topics for discussion may include, among others:

(1) Information about community resources and programs that can help the participants and their children cope with the consequences of family reorganization and family violence;

(2) Problems that continuing conflict creates for children's development and what steps might be taken to ameliorate the effects of conflict on the children;

(3) Development of a parenting plan that covers the children's physical residence and decision-making responsibilities for the children, with appropriate levels of detail as agreed to by the participants;

(4) The possible need to revise parenting plans as the developmental needs of the children evolve over time; and

(5) Encouragement to the participants to develop appropriate dispute resolution mechanisms to facilitate future revisions of the parenting plan.

(B) The mediator shall be sensitive to the impact of culture and religion on parenting philosophy and other decisions.

(C) The mediator shall inform any court-appointed representative for the children of the mediation. If a representative for the children participates in mediation, the mediator should, at the outset, discuss the effect of that participation on the mediation process and the confidentiality of the mediation with the participants. Whether the representative of the children participates or not, the mediator shall provide the representative with the resulting agreements insofar as they relate to the children.

(D) Except in extraordinary circumstances, the children shall not participate in the mediation process without the consent of both parents and, if applicable, the children's courtappointed representative.

(E) Prior to including the children in the mediation process, the mediator shall consult with the parents and the children's court-appointed representative, if applicable, about whether the children should participate in the mediation process and the form of that participation.

(F) The mediator shall inform all concerned about the available options for the children's participation (which may include personal participation, an interview with a mental health professional, the mediator interviewing the child, or a videotaped statement by the child) and discuss the costs and benefits of each with the participants.

Standard IX

A family mediator shall take reasonable steps to ascertain a family situation involving child abuse or neglect and take appropriate steps to shape the mediation process accordingly.

(A) As used in these Standards, child abuse or neglect is defined by applicable state law.

(B) A mediator shall not undertake a mediation in which the family situation has been assessed to involve child abuse or neglect without having completed appropriate and adequate training.

(C) If the mediator has reasonable grounds to believe that a child of the participants is abused or neglected within the meaning of the jurisdiction's child abuse and neglect laws, the mediator shall comply with applicable child protection laws.

(1) The mediator should encourage the participants to explore appropriate services for the family.

(2) The mediator shall consider the appropriateness of suspending or terminating the mediation process in light of the allegations.

Standard X

A family mediator shall take reasonable steps to ascertain a family situation involving domestic abuse and take appropriate steps to shape the mediation process accordingly.

(A) As used in these Standards, domestic abuse includes domestic violence as defined by applicable state law and issues of control and intimidation.

(B) A mediator shall not undertake a mediation in which the family situation has been assessed to involve domestic abuse without having completed appropriate and adequate training.

(C) Some cases are not suitable for mediation because of safety, control or intimidation issues. A mediator shall make a reasonable effort to screen for the existence of domestic abuse prior to entering into an agreement to mediate. The mediator shall continue to assess for domestic abuse throughout the mediation process.

(D) If domestic abuse appears to be present the mediator shall consider taking measures to insure the safety of participants and the mediator including, among others:

(1) establishing appropriate security arrangements;

(2) holding separate sessions with the participants even without the agreement of all participants;

(3) allowing a friend, representative, advocate, counsel or attorney to attend the mediation sessions;

(4) encouraging the participants to be represented and or accompanied by an attorney, counsel or an advocate throughout the mediation process;

(5) referring the participants to appropriate community resources;

(6) Suspending or terminating the mediation sessions, with appropriate steps to protect the safety of the participants.

The mediator should facilitate the participants' formulation of parenting plans that protect the physical safety and psychological well being of the participants and their children.

Standard XI

A family mediator shall suspend or terminate the mediation process when the mediator reasonably believes that a participant is unable to effectively participate or for other compelling reason.

(A) Circumstances under which a mediator should consider suspending or terminating the mediation, may include, among others:

(1) the safety of a participant or well-being of a child is threatened;

(2) a participant has or is threatening to abduct a child;

(3) a participant is unable to participate due to the influence of drugs, alcohol, or physical or mental condition;

(4) the participants are about to enter into an agreement that the mediator reasonably believes to be unconscionable;

(5) a participant is using the mediation to further illegal conduct;

(6) a participant is using the mediation process to gain an unfair advantage;

(7) If the mediator believes the mediator's impartiality has been compromised in accordance with Standard IV.

(B) If the mediator does suspend or terminate the mediation, the mediator shall take all reasonable steps to minimize prejudice or inconvenience to the participants, which may result.

Standard XII

A family mediator shall be truthful in the advertisement and solicitation for mediation.

(A) Mediators should refrain from promises and guarantees of results. A mediator should not advertise statistical settlement data or settlement rates.

(B) Mediators shall accurately represent their qualifications. In an advertisement or other communication, a mediator may make reference to meeting state, national, or private organizational qualifications only if the entity referred to has a procedure for qualifying mediators and the mediator has been duly granted the requisite status.

Standard XIII

A family mediator shall acquire and maintain professional competence in mediation.

(A) Mediators should continuously improve their professional skills and abilities by, among other activities, participating in relevant continuing education programs and should regularly engage in self-assessment.

(B) Mediators should participate in programs of peer consultation and should help train and mentor the work of less experienced mediators.

(C) Mediators should continuously strive to understand the impact of culture and diversity on the mediator's practice.

APPENDIX G.
SPECIAL POLICY CONSIDERATIONS FOR STATE REGULATION OF FAMILY MEDIATORS AND COURT AFFILIATED PROGRAMS

The Model Standards recognize the National Standards for Court Connected Dispute Resolution Programs (1992). There are also state and local regulations governing such programs and family mediators. The following principles of organization and practice, however, are especially important for regulation of mediators and court-connected family mediation programs. They are worthy of separate mention.

(A) Individual states or local courts should set standards and qualifications for family mediators including procedures for evaluations and guidelines for handling grievances against mediators. In developing these standards and qualifications, regulators should consult with appropriate professional groups, including professional associations of family mediators.

(B) When family mediators are appointed by a court or other institution, the appointing agency should make reasonable efforts to insure that each mediator is qualified for the appointment. If a list of family mediators qualified for court appointment exists, the requirements for being included on the list should be made public and available to all interested persons.

(C) Confidentiality should not be construed to limit or prohibit the effective monitoring, research or evaluation of mediation programs by responsible individuals or academic institutions provided that no identifying information about any person involved in the mediation is disclosed without their prior written consent. Under appropriate circumstances, researchers may be permitted to obtain access to statistical data and, with the permission of the participants, to individual case files, observations of live mediations and interviews with participants.

APPENDIX H.
CODE OF PROFESSIONAL CONDUCT FOR COURT INTERPRETERS AND TRANSLATORS

Preamble.

Foreign language interpreters, sign language interpreters, and translators help ensure that individuals enjoy equal access to justice, including case and court functions and court support services. Foreign language interpreters, sign language interpreters, and translators are highly skilled professionals who fulfill an essential role by assisting in the pursuit of justice. They act strictly in the interest of the courts they serve and are impartial officers of those courts, with a duty to enhance the judicial process.

Definitions.

As used in this code, "provisionally qualified foreign language interpreter," "Supreme Court certified foreign language interpreter," "Supreme Court certified sign language interpreter," and "translator" have the same meanings as in Rule 80 of the Rules of Superintendence for the Courts of Ohio.

Applicability.

This code applies to Supreme Court certified foreign language interpreters, provisionally qualified foreign language interpreters, Supreme Court certified sign language interpreters, and translators. This code shall bind all agencies and organizations that administer, supervise, use, or deliver interpreting or translating services in connection with any case or court function.

A court may use this code to assist it in determining the qualifications of any individual providing services as an interpreter under Rule 702 of the Rules of Evidence.

Canon 1. **High Standards of Conduct.**

Interpreters and translators shall conduct themselves in a manner consistent with the dignity of the court and shall be as unobtrusive as possible, consistent with the ends of justice.

Canon 2. Accuracy and Completeness.

Interpreters and translators shall render a complete and accurate interpretation or translation without altering, omitting, or adding anything to what is spoken or written, and shall do so without explaining the statements of the original speaker or writer.

Canon 3. Impartiality and Avoidance of Conflicts of Interest.

Interpreters and translators shall be impartial and unbiased. Interpreters and translators shall refrain from conduct that may give the appearance of bias and shall disclose any real or perceived conflict of interest.

Canon 4. Confidentiality.

Interpreters and translators shall protect from unauthorized disclosure all privileged or other confidential communications, documents, or information they hear or obtain while acting in a professional capacity.

Canon 5. Representation of Qualifications.

Interpreters and translators shall accurately and completely represent their credentials, certifications, training, references, and pertinent experience.

Canon 6. Proficiency.

Interpreters and translators shall provide professional services only in matters in which they can proficiently perform.

Canon 7. Assessing and Reporting Impediments to Performance.

Interpreters and translators shall at all times assess their ability to perform effectively and accurately. If an interpreter or translator discovers anything impeding full compliance with the oath or affirmation of the interpreter or translator and this code, the interpreter or translator shall immediately report this information to the court.

Canon 8. Duty to Report Ethical Violations.

Interpreters and translators shall report to the court any efforts to impede their compliance with any law, this code, or other official policy governing interpreting or translating. Interpreters and translators shall promptly report to the appropriate legal or disciplinary authority if they observe another interpreter or translator improperly performing an assignment; accepting remuneration apart from authorized fees; disclosing privileged or confidential communications, documents, or information; or otherwise committing a breach of this code.

Canon 9. Scope of Practice.

Interpreters and translators shall not give legal advice, communicate their conclusions with respect to any answer, express personal opinions to individuals for whom they are interpreting or translating, or engage in any other activity that may be construed to constitute a service other than interpreting or translating while serving as an interpreter.

Canon 10. Restrictions from Public Comment.

Consistent with Canon 4 of this code, interpreters and translators shall not publicly discuss, report, or offer an opinion concerning a matter in which they are or have been engaged, even when that information is not privileged or required by law to be confidential.

STANDARD PROBATE FORMS

Decedent's Heirs—Form 1.0

PROBATE COURT OF _____ **COUNTY, OHIO**

ESTATE OF _____ **, DECEASED**

CASE NO. _____

SURVIVING SPOUSE, CHILDREN, NEXT OF KIN, LEGATEES AND DEVISEES
[R.C. 2105.06, 2106.13 and 2107.19]

**[Use with those applications or filings requiring some or all of the
information in this form, for notice or other purposes. Update as required.]**

The following are decedent's known surviving spouse, children, and the lineal descendants of deceased children. If none, the following are decedent's next of kin who are or would be entitled to inherit under the statutes of descent and distribution.

Name	Residence Address	Relationship to Decedent	Birthdate of Minor
		Surviving Spouse	

[Check whichever of the following is applicable]

☐ The surviving spouse is the natural or adoptive parent of all of the decedent's children.

☐ The surviving spouse is the natural or adoptive parent of at least one, but not all, of the decedent's children.

☐ The surviving spouse is not the natural or adoptive parent of any of the decedent's children.

☐ There are minor children of the decedent who are not the children of the surviving spouse.

☐ There are minor children of the decedent and no surviving spouse.

FORM 1.0 - SURVIVING SPOUSE, CHILDREN, NEXT OF KIN, LEGATEES AND DEVISEES   12/01/2002

[Side 2 of Form 1.0]

CASE NO. _____

The following are the vested beneficiaries named in the decedent's will:

Name	Residence Address	Birthdate of minor

[Check whichever of the following is applicable]

☐ The will contains a charitable trust or a bequest or devise to a charitable trust, subject to R.C. 109.23 to 109.41.

☐ The will is not subject to R.C. 109.23 to 109.41 relating to charitable trusts.

_____   _____
Date   Applicant (or give other title)

                                 _____

Probating The Will—Forms 2.0 To 2.4

PROBATE COURT OF _____ COUNTY, OHIO

ESTATE OF _____ , DECEASED

CASE NO. _____

APPLICATION TO PROBATE WILL
[R.C. 2107.11, 2107.18, and 2107.19]

Applicant states that decedent died on _____

Decedent's domicile was _____

Street Address

_____

City or Village, or Township if unincorporated area   County

_____

Post Office   State   Zip Code

A document purporting to be decedent's last will is attached and offered for probate, and applicant waives notice of probate of this will.

Decedent's surviving spouse, children, next of kin, and legatees and devisees, known to applicant, are listed on the attached Form 1.0.

_____   _____
Attorney for Applicant   Applicant

_____   _____
Typed or Printed Name   Typed or Printed Name

_____   _____
Address   Address

_____   _____

_____   _____
Phone Number (include area code)   Phone Number (include area code)

Attorney Registration No. _____

WAIVER OF NOTICE OF PROBATE OF WILL

The undersigned, being persons entitled to notice of the probate of this will, waive such notice. After a certificate is filed evidencing these waivers and any notices given, any action to contest the validity of this will must be filed no more than three months after the filing of the certificate for estates of decedents who die on or after January 1, 2002, and no more than four months after the filing of the certificate for estates of decedents who die before January 1, 2002.

_____   _____

_____   _____

_____   _____

_____   _____

FORM 2.0 - APPLICATION TO PROBATE WILL   12/01/2002

(Reverse of Form 2.0)

CASE NO. _____

ENTRY ADMITTING WILL TO PROBATE

The Court finds that the purported will of decedent, either on its face or from testimony of the witnesses, complies with applicable law. It is therefore admitted to probate and ordered recorded. The Court further orders that notice of the probate be given to all parties entitled to notice.

_____   _____
Date   Probate Judge

CERTIFICATE OF WAIVER OF NOTICE

The undersigned states that all persons entitled to notice:

[Check applicable boxes]

☐ Have waived notice of the application for probate of this will or of a contest as to jurisdiction.

☐ Have waived notice of this will's admission to probate. The waivers are filed herein.

☐ Have not been notified because their names or places of residence are unknown and cannot with reasonable diligence be ascertained.

_____
☐ Fiduciary
☐ Applicant for the admission of this will to probate
☐ Applicant for a release from administration
☐ Other interested person
☐ Attorney for any of the above

Attorney Registration No. _____

PROBATE COURT OF _____ COUNTY, OHIO

ESTATE OF _____, DECEASED

CASE NO. _____

WAIVER OF NOTICE OF PROBATE OF WILL
[R.C. 2107.19(A)(2)]

The undersigned, being persons entitled to notice of the probate of this will, waive such notice. After a certificate is filed evidencing these waivers and any notices given, any action to contest the validity of this will must be filed no more than three months after the filing of the certificate for estates of decedents who die on or after January 1, 2002, and no more than four months after the filing of the certificate for estates of decedents who die before January 1, 2002.

_____   _____

_____   _____

_____   _____

_____   _____

_____   _____

_____   _____

_____   _____

_____   _____

PROBATE COURT OF _____ COUNTY, OHIO

ESTATE OF _____, DECEASED

CASE NO. _____

NOTICE OF PROBATE OF WILL
[R.C. 2107.19(A)]

To: _____

         _____

         _____

You are hereby notified that the decedent died on _____, _____, that the decedent's will was admitted to probate by this Court located at _____
_____ Ohio, on _____, _____.
This notice is given to all persons who would be entitled to inherit from the decedent had the decedent died intestate and to all legatees and devisees named in this will who do not waive notice. You are receiving this notice as: [check all of the following that apply]

☐ The Surviving Spouse.

☐ A person who would be entitled to inherit from the decedent had the decedent died intestate.

☐ A legatee or devisee named in the will.

After a certificate is filed evidencing any notices given, any action to contest the validity of this will must be filed no more than three months after the filing of the certificate for estates of decedents who die on or after January 1, 2002, and no more than four months after the filing of the certificate for estates of decedents who die before January 1, 2002.

_____   _____
Date   ☐ Fiduciary
                                             ☐ Applicant for the admission of this will to probate
_____   ☐ Applicant for a release from administration
Typed or Printed Name   ☐ Other interested person
                                             ☐ Attorney for any of the above
_____
Address   Attorney Registration No. _____

_____

_____
Phone Number (include area code)

FORM 2.2 - NOTICE OF PROBATE OF WILL   12/01/2002

PROBATE COURT OF _____ COUNTY, OHIO

ESTATE OF _____, DECEASED

CASE NO. _____

ENTRY ADMITTING WILL TO PROBATE

The Court finds that the purported will of decedent, either on its face or from testimony of the witnesses, complies with the applicable law. It is therefore admitted to probate, and ordered recorded. The Court further orders that notice of the probate be given to all parties entitled to notice.

_____   _____
Date   Probate Judge

PROBATE COURT OF _____ COUNTY, OHIO

ESTATE OF _____, DECEASED

CASE NO. _____

CERTIFICATE OF SERVICE OF NOTICE OF PROBATE OF WILL
[R.C. 2107.19(A)(3)]

The undersigned states that all persons entitled to notice:

[Check all applicable boxes]

☐ Have waived notice of the admission of this will to probate. The waivers are filed herein.

☐ Have received notice of the admission of this will to probate.

☐ Have been notified of the hearing on the probate of this will or a contest as to jurisdiction.

☐ Evidence of notification is filed herein.

☐ Have not been notified because their names or places of residence are unknown and cannot with reasonable

diligence be ascertained.

_____

☐ Fiduciary
☐ Applicant for the admission of this will to probate
☐ Applicant for a release from administration
☐ Other interested person
☐ Attorney for any of the above

Attorney Registration No. _____

Appointing the Appraiser — Form 3.0

PROBATE COURT OF _____ **COUNTY, OHIO**

ESTATE OF_____**, DECEASED**

CASE NO. _____

APPOINTMENT OF APPRAISER

    The fiduciary appoints _____
to appraise those assets of decedent's estate which do not have readily ascertainable value, and asks the Court to approve the appointment. Subject to Court approval on the amount of such compensation, the fiduciary agrees to pay the appraiser reasonable compensation for his services as part of the expenses of administering the estate.

_____
Fiduciary (or applicant)

_____

ENTRY SETTING HEARING

    The Court sets _____ at _____ o'clock _____.M. as the date and time for hearing the above appointment of appraiser.

_____   _____
Date   Probate Judge

ENTRY APPROVING APPRAISER

The appointment of appraiser in the above application is hereby approved.

_____   _____
Date   Probate Judge

FORM 3.0 - APPOINTMENT OF APPRAISER

Appointing The Fiduciary — Forms 4.0 To 4.5

PROBATE COURT OF _____ COUNTY, OHIO

ESTATE OF _____, DECEASED

CASE NO. _____

APPLICATION FOR AUTHORITY TO ADMINISTER ESTATE
[R.C. 2109.02 and 2109.07]

[For Executors and all Administrators; attach supplemental
application for ancillary administration, if applicable]

Applicant states that decedent died on _____

Decedent's domicile was _____
                                                    Street Address

_____   _____
City or Village, or Township if unincorporated area   County

_____   _____
Post Office   State   Zip Code

Applicant asks to be appointed _____
of decedent's estate. **[Check whichever of the following are applicable]** - ☐ To applicant's knowledge, decedent did not leave a
Will - ☐ Decedent's Will has been admitted to probate in this Court - ☐ A supplemental application for ancillary administration
is attached.

Attached is a list of the surviving spouse, children, next of kin, and legatees and devisees, known to applicant, which list includes
those persons entitled to administer the estate.

The estimated value of the estate is:

Personal property... $ _____

Annual real property rentals.. $ _____

Subtotal, personalty and rentals.. $ _____

Real Property... $ _____

Total estimated estate.. $ _____

Applicant owes the estate... $ _____

The estate owes applicant... $ _____

    [Check one of the following four paragraphs]

☐   Applicant says that decedent's Will requests that no bond be required, and therefore asks the Court to dispense with
bond.

☐   Applicant is a trust company duly qualified in Ohio, and bond is dispensed with by law.

(Reverse of Form 4.0)

CASE NO. _____

☐   Applicant is decedent's surviving spouse and is entitled to the entire net proceeds of the estate, or applicant is the next of kin entitled to the entire net proceeds of the estate and there is no will. Bond is dispensed with by law.

☐   Applicant offers the attached bond in the amount of $ _____.

Applicant accepts the duties of fiduciary in the estate imposed by law, and such additional duties as may be required by the Court. Applicant acknowledges being subject to removal as fiduciary for failure to perform such duties as required, and also acknowledges being subject to criminal penalties for improper conversion of any property held as fiduciary.

_____	_____
Attorney for Applicant	Applicant
_____	_____
Typed or Printed Name	Typed or Printed Name
_____	_____
Address	Address
_____	_____
_____	_____
Phone Number (include area code)	Phone Number (include area code)

Attorney Registration No. _____

WAIVER OF RIGHT TO ADMINISTER
[R.C. 2113.06]

The undersigned, being persons entitled to administer decedent's estate, and whose priority of right to do so is equal or superior to that of applicant, hereby waive appointment to administer the estate.

_____	_____
_____	_____
_____	_____
_____	_____

ENTRY SETTING HEARING AND ORDERING NOTICE

The Court sets _____, at _____ o'clock _____. M. as the date and time for hearing the application for authority to administer decedent's estate. The Court orders notice to take or renounce administration to be given those persons entitled to administer decedent's estate, whose priority of right to do so is equal or superior to that of applicant, and who have not waived appointment to administer the estate.

_____	_____
Date	Probate Judge

PROBATE COURT OF _____ **COUNTY, OHIO**

ESTATE OF _____ **, DECEASED**

CASE NO. _____

SUPPLEMENTAL APPLICATION FOR ANCILLARY ADMINISTRATION

Applicant says that the decedent named in the attached application for authority to administer the estate died **[check one of the following]** - ☐ owning property in this county - ☐ having a debtor residing in this county.

Applicant is a resident of Ohio.

[Check one of the following three paragraphs]

☐   Applicant is the general executor named in decedent's Will, and is duly appointed, qualified and acting in that capacity in the state of _____. An exemplified record of the grant of his letters of authority is attached.

☐   Applicant is named in decedent's Will as executor of his Ohio estate.

☐   Applicant is a resident of this county. Decedent either died intestate, or did not designate an Ohio executor or administrator in his Will.

[Check if applicable] - ☐ An authenticated copy of decedent's Will, duly proved in another state, is attached and offered for record.

The estimated value of decedent's Ohio estate is $ _____.

_____
Applicant

FORM 4.1 - SUPPLEMENTAL APPLICATION FOR ANCILLARY ADMINISTRATION

PROBATE COURT OF _____ **COUNTY, OHIO**

ESTATE OF_____, **DECEASED**

CASE NO. _____

FIDUCIARY'S BOND

[For Executors and all Administrators]

Amount of bond $ _____

The undersigned principal, and sureties if any, are obligated to the State of Ohio in the above amount, for payment of which we bind ourselves and our successors, heirs, executors, and administrators, jointly and severally.

The principal has accepted in writing the duties of fiduciary in decedent's estate, including those imposed by law and such additional duties as may be required by the Court.

This obligation is void if the principal performs such duties as required.

This obligation remains in force if the principal fails to perform such duties, or performs them tardily, negligently, or improperly, or if the principal misuses or misappropriates estate assets or improperly converts them to his own use or the use of another.

[Check if personal sureties are involved.] ☐ The sureties certify that each of them owns real estate in this county, with a reasonable net value as stated below.

_____   _____
Date   Principal

_____   _____
Surety   Surety

by _____   by _____
   Attorney in Fact   Attorney in Fact

_____   _____
Typed or Printed Name   Typed or Printed Name

_____   _____
Address   Address

_____   _____
Net value of real estate owned in this county   Net value of real estate owned in this county

$ _____ $ _____

FORM 4.2 - FIDUCIARY'S BOND

PROBATE COURT OF _____ **COUNTY, OHIO**

ESTATE OF _____ **, DECEASED**

CASE NO. _____

WAIVER OF RIGHT TO ADMINISTER

Application of _____ for appointment
to administer decedent's estate.

The undersigned, being persons entitled to administer decedent's estate, and whose priority of right to do so is equal or
superior to that of the applicant, hereby waive appointment to administer the estate.

_____   _____

_____   _____

_____   _____

_____   _____

_____   _____

_____   _____

_____   _____

_____   _____

_____   _____

_____   _____

_____   _____

_____   _____

_____   _____

_____   _____

_____   _____

_____   _____

FORM 4.3 - WAIVER OF RIGHT TO ADMINISTER

PROBATE COURT OF _____ COUNTY, OHIO

ESTATE OF _____ **, DECEASED**

CASE NO. _____

NOTICE AND CITATION OF HEARING ON APPOINTMENT OF FIDUCIARY
[R.C. 2113.06 and 2113.07]

To the following persons:

Name	Address
Name	Address
Name	Address
Name	Address
Name	Address

_____ has filed an application in this Court, asking to be
appointed to administer decedent's estate.

The hearing on the application will be held _____
at _____ o'clock _____ M. in this Court.

The Court is located at _____

You are one of the persons entitled to administer decedent's estate, and if you wish to be considered for appointment to do so you must apply to this Court. If you do not apply, it will be considered that you renounce your right to administer the estate. The Court may appoint any suitable and competent person to administer the estate, giving due weight to relative priority of right to do so. Even if you decline appointment yourself, if you know of any reason why the above applicant is not suitable or competent, you should appear and inform the Court.

_____
Probate Judge/Deputy Clerk

FORM 4.4 - NOTICE AND CITATIN OF HEARING ON APPOINTMENT OF FIDUCIARY   12/01/2002

PROBATE COURT OF _____ COUNTY, OHIO

ESTATE OF _____, **DECEASED**

CASE NO. _____

ENTRY APPOINTING FIDUCIARY; LETTERS OF AUTHORITY

[For Executors and all Administrators]

Name and Title of Fiduciary _____
_____

On hearing in open Court the application of the above fiduciary for authority to administer decedent's estate, the Court finds that;

Decedent died **[check one of the following]** ☐ testate - ☐ intestate - on _____, domiciled in _____.

[Check one of the following] ☐ Bond is dispensed with by the Will - ☐ Bond is dispensed with by law - ☐ Applicant has executed and filed an appropriate bond, which is approved by the Court; and

Applicant is a suitable and competent person to execute the trust.

The Court therefore appoints applicant as such fiduciary, with the power conferred by law to fully administer decedent's estate. This entry of appointment constitutes the fiduciary's letters of authority.

_____   _____
Date   PROBATE JUDGE

CERTIFICATE OF APPOINTMENT AND INCUMBENCY

The above document is a true copy of the original kept by me as custodian of the records of this Court. It constitutes the appointment and letters of authority of the named fiduciary, who is qualified and acting in such capacity.

                                                    _____
                                                    Probate Judge/Clerk

                                                    by _____
[Seal]

                                                    _____
                                                    Date

FORM 4.5 - ENTRY APPOINTING FIDUCIARY; LETTERS OF AUTHORITY

Relief From Administration — Forms 5.0 To 5.11

PROBATE COURT OF _____ COUNTY, OHIO

ESTATE OF _____, DECEASED

CASE NO. _____

APPLICATION TO RELIEVE ESTATE FROM ADMINISTRATION
[R.C. 2113.03]

Applicant states that decedent died on _____

Decedent's domicile was _____

Street Address

City or Village, or Township if unincorporated area — County

Post Office — State — Zip Code

[Check one of the following]
☐ Decedent's will has been admitted to probate in this Court.
☐ To applicant's knowledge, decedent did not leave a will.

[Check one of the following]
☐ The assets are $15,000 or less and decedent died on or after January 1, 1976.
☐ The assets are $25,000 or less and decedent died on or after October 20, 1987.
☐ The assets are $35,000 or less and decedent died on or after November 9, 1994.
☐ The assets are $50,000 or less; the surviving spouse is entitled to all of the assets and the decedent died on or after April 16, 1993.
☐ The assets are $85,000 or less; the surviving spouse is entitled to all of the assets and the decedent died on or after September 14, 1993.
☐ The assets are $100,000 or less; the surviving spouse is entitled to all of the assets and the decedent died on or after March 18, 1999.

Applicant asks that the estate be relieved from administration because the assets do not exceed the statutory limits. A statement of the assets and liabilities of the estate is listed on the attached Form 5.1.

The decedent's surviving spouse, next of kin, legatees, and devisees known to applicant, are listed on the attached Form 1.0.

_____
Attorney for Applicant

_____
Typed or Printed Name

_____
Address

_____

_____
Phone Number (include area code)

Attorney Registration No. _____

_____
Applicant

_____
Typed or Printed Name

_____
Address

_____

_____
Phone Number (include area code)

FORM 5.0 - APPLICATION TO RELIEVE ESTATE FROM ADMINISTRATION

5/3/99

(Reverse of Form 5.0)

WAIVER OF NOTICE

The undersigned surviving spouse, heirs at law, legatees, devisees, and other persons entitled to notice of the filing of the application to relieve decedent's estate from administration, waive such notice.

_____   _____

_____   _____

_____   _____

_____   _____

ENTRY SETTING HEARING AND ORDERING NOTICE

The Court sets _____, at _____ o'clock _____. M., as the date and time for hearing the application to relieve decedent's estate from administration.

[Check one of the following]

☐ All notice is dispensed with as unnecessary.

☐ Notice by publication to interested parties is dispensed with as unnecessary. Written notice shall be given, as provided by law and the Rules of Civil Procedure, to those persons entitled to notice, who have not waived notice.

☐ Written notice is dispensed with as unnecessary. Notice by publication shall be given to interested parties as provided by law and the Rules of Civil Procedure.

☐ Written notice shall be given to those persons entitled to notice, who have not waived notice, and notice by publication shall be given to interested parties, as provided by law and the Rules of Civil Procedure.

_____   _____
Date   Probate Judge

PROBATE COURT OF _____ COUNTY, OHIO

ESTATE OF _____, **DECEASED**

CASE NO. _____

ASSETS AND LIABILITIES OF ESTATE TO BE RELIEVED FROM ADMINISTRATION

Following is a summary statement of the character and value of the assets in decedent's estate [Insert a check in the "Appraised" column opposite an item if it was valued by the appraiser. Leave blank if the readily ascertainable value of the item was determined by applicant. Use extra sheets if necessary.]

Automobiles distributed to surviving spouse by affidavit	Value	
First automobile selected by surviving spouse under R.C. 2106.18		
[Omit value when computing total assets] --------- Appraised value $		XXXX
Second automobile selected by surviving spouse under R.C. 2106.18		
[Omit value when computing total assets] --------- Appraised value $		XXXX
Total value [not to exceed $40,000.00]	$	XXXX

Character of asset	Appraised	Value
Real Estate, described in accompanying		
Certificate of Transfer No.		$
Other assets		$
Total Assets		$

(Reverse of Form 5.1)

Following is a list of decedent's known debts. [Use extra sheets if necessary]

Name of Creditor	Nature of Debt	Amount
		$
Total Debts		$

CERTIFICATION

The undersigned appraiser agreed to act as appraiser of decedent's estate, and to appraise the property exhibited truly, honestly, impartially, and to the best of the appraiser's knowledge and ability. The appraiser further says that those assets whose values were not readily ascertainable are indicated above by a check in the "Appraised" column opposite each such item, and that such values are correct.

The undersigned applicant determined the value of those assets whose values were readily ascertainable and were not appraised by the appraiser, and that such values are correct, and to applicant's knowledge the above list of decedent's debts is correct.

_____
Date

_____   _____
Appraiser   Applicant

PROBATE COURT OF _____ COUNTY, OHIO

ESTATE OF _____, DECEASED

CASE NO. _____

WAIVER OF NOTICE OF APPLICATION TO RELIEVE ESTATE FROM ADMINISTRATION

The undersigned surviving spouse, heirs at law, legatees, devisees, and other persons entitled to notice of the filing of the application to relieve decedent's estate from administration, waive such notice.

_____   _____
_____   _____
_____   _____
_____   _____
_____   _____
_____   _____
_____   _____
_____   _____
_____   _____
_____   _____
_____   _____
_____   _____
_____   _____
_____   _____
_____   _____
_____   _____
_____   _____

FORM 5.2 - WAIVER OF NOTICE OF APPLICATION TO RELIEVE ESTATE FROM ADMINISTRATION

PROBATE COURT OF _____ COUNTY, OHIO

ESTATE OF _____ **, DECEASED**

CASE NO. _____

NOTICE OF APPLICATION TO RELIEVE ESTATE FROM ADMINISTRATION

To the following persons:

_____	_____
Name	Address
	_____
_____	_____
Name	Address
	_____
_____	_____
Name	Address
	_____
_____	_____
Name	Address
	_____
_____	_____
Name	Address
	_____

     An application has been filed in this Court asking that decedent's estate be relieved from administration, saying that the assets in the estate do not exceed the statutory limits.

     The hearing on the application will be held _____
at _____ o'clock _____ M. in this Court.

     The Court is located at _____

_____

If you know of any reason why the application should not be granted, you should appear and inform the Court.

_____
Probate Judge/Deputy Clerk

FORM 5.3 - NOTICE OF APPLICATION TO RELIEVE ESTATE FROM ADMINISTRATION

PROBATE COURT OF _____ COUNTY, OHIO

ESTATE OF _____ **, DECEASED**

CASE NO. _____

PUBLICATION OF NOTICE

[Use when only one estate included in notice]

To: _____
Newspaper of General Circulation in the County

Please publish the following notice [check one of the following] - ☐ once - ☐ once per week for two consecutive weeks - ☐ once per week for three consecutive weeks. When publication is complete, fill out the attached proof of publication and return to the Court.

"TO ALL PERSONS INTERESTED IN THE ESTATE OF _____
Decedent's Name

DECEASED, LATE OF _____
Decedent's Address

_____ COUNTY PROBATE COURT, CASE NO. _____

An application as been filed asking to relieve the estate from administration, saying that the assets do not exceed the statutory

limits. A hearing on the application will be held _____.

at _____ o'clock ____.m. Persons knowing any reason why the application should not be granted should appear

and inform the Court. The Court is located _____

_____."

_____
Probate Judge/Deputy Clerk

FORM 5.4 - PUBLICATION OF NOTICE

(Reverse of Form 5.4)

PROOF OF PUBLICATION

As directed by the Court, the attached notice was published in the named newspaper, in editions dated

_____

The cost of publication is $ _____

_____
Editor [or give other title]

_____

[Attach copy of printed notice below]

PROBATE COURT OF _____ COUNTY, OHIO

ESTATE OF _____, **DECEASED**

CASE NO. _____

PUBLICATION OF NOTICE

[Use when multiple estates are included in same notice]

To: _____
Newspaper of General Circulation in the County

Please publish the following notice [check one of the following] - ☐ once - ☐ once per week for two consecutive weeks - ☐ once per week for three consecutive weeks. When publication is complete, fill out the attached proof of publication and return to the Court.

"TO ALL PERSONS INTERESTED IN THE FOLLOWING DECEDENT'S ESTATE PENDING IN THE _____ COUNTY PROBATE COURT. Applications have been filed asking to relieve the estates from administration, saying that the assets in each case do not exceed the statutory limits. Persons knowing any reason why any such application should not be granted should appear and inform the Court. The Court is located

_____

_____ "

The decedent's name, case number, and the date and time for hearing in each case are as follows:

Decedent's Name and Address	Case Number	Date of Hearing	Time

FORM 5.5 - PUBLICATION OF NOTICE
PROOF OF PUBLICATION

(Reverse of Form 5.5)

As directed by the Court, the attached notice was published in the named newspaper, in editions dated

_____

The cost of publication is $ _____

_____
Editor [or give other title]

_____

[Attach copy of printed notice below]

PROBATE COURT OF _____ COUNTY, OHIO

ESTATE OF _____ , DECEASED

CASE NO. _____

ENTRY RELIEVING ESTATE FROM ADMINISTRATION
[R.C. 2113.03]

Upon hearing the application to relieve decedent's estate from administration, the Court finds that:

Decedent died [check one of the following] - ☐ testate - ☐ intestate. The date of death and domicile are as stated in the application, and the Court has jurisdiction over the estate;

Notice to the surviving spouse, heirs at law, legatees, devisees, and other persons was duly effected or dispensed with by the Court as unnecessary;

The values of the several assets in the estate, given in the application do not exceed the statutory limits.

The Court therefore relieves the estate from administration, and orders [check and complete whichever of the following are applicable]:

☐ That the following personal property be sold [describe]:

_____

_____

☐ That the following debts of decedent shall be paid to the extent of assets:

_____

_____

☐ That the statutory family allowance be paid to the ☐ surviving spouse - ☐ minor children of the decedent - ☐ apportioned between the surviving spouse and minor children of the decedent who are not the children of the surviving spouse. Attach Form 7.2A if necessary.

☐ That Certificate of Transfer No. _____, attached to the application and describing decedent's real estate, issue and be preserved in the records of the Court and that authenticated copies of the certificate be delivered as required to the persons entitled to them;

☐ That the financial institutions holding accounts in decedent's name as set forth below pay the same upon proper tax release [check one of the following] - ☐ to the commissioner - ☐ to

_____

_____

_____

FORM 5.6 - ENTRY RELIEVING ESTATE FROM ADMINISTRATION

(Reverse of Form 5.6)

☐ That the remainder of the estate be distributed in cash or in kind, as follows:

Name of Distributee	Property	Value or Amount
		$

The Court appoints _____
commissioner, to receive and sell or distribute the personal property or proceeds thereof, and to execute all necessary documents of conveyance, including without limitation those necessary to transfer title to any motor vehicle, motorcycle, watercraft, or other titled personal property sold or distributed in kind. The commissioner shall complete the duties and report to the Court within sixty days of the date of this entry.

_____   _____
Date   PROBATE JUDGE

PROBATE COURT OF _____ COUNTY, OHIO
_____, JUDGE

ESTATE OF _____, **DECEASED**

CASE NO. _____

APPLICATION FOR SUMMARY RELEASE FROM ADMINISTRATION
[R.C. 2113.031]

Applicant states that decedent died on _____.

Decedent's domicile was _____.

                                         Street Address

_____   _____
City or Village, or Township if unincorporated area   County

_____   _____
Post Office   State   Zip Code

[Check one of the following]

☐   The applicant is decedent's surviving spouse entitled to one hundred percent of the allowance for support and decedent's funeral and burial expenses have been prepaid or the surviving spouse has paid or is obligated in writing to pay decedent's funeral and burial expenses and the value of the assets does not exceed the $40,000 allowance for support under R.C. 2106.13(B) plus an amount not exceeding $5,000 for decedent's funeral and burial expenses.

☐   The applicant, who is not the surviving spouse, has paid or is obligated in writing to pay decedent's funeral and burial expenses and the value of the assets is the lesser of $5,000 or the amount of decedent's funeral and burial expenses.

Attached hereto is a receipt, contract or other document that confirms the applicant's payment or obligation to pay decedent's funeral and burial expenses or if the applicant is the surviving spouse, the prepayment receipt, if applicable.

The decedent's surviving spouse, next of kin, legatees and devisees known to applicant, are listed on attached Form 1.0.

Applicant states that there are no pending proceedings for the administration of decedent's estate or relief of decedent's estate from administration under R.C. 2113.03.

All known assets with date of death values of the estate are as follows:

☐   Motor Vehicles (include year, make, model, body type, manufacturer's vehicle identification number and Certificate of Title number)

_____ $_____
_____ $_____

CASE NO._____

☐ Accounts maintained by a Financial Institution (include financial institution name and the account's complete identifying number):

_____ $_____

_____ $_____

☐ Stocks and Bonds (include for each stock or bond its serial number, the name of its issuer, the name and address of its transfer agent, and the total number of shares of stocks or bonds):

_____ $_____

_____ $_____

☐ Real estate described in accompanying Form 12.0 Application for Certificate of Transfer and Form 12.1 Certificate of Transfer and date of death value. **[Attach verification of value.]** $_____

☐ Other assets and date of death values

_____ $_____

Total Assets $_____

Applicant requests an order granting summary release.

_____   _____
Attorney for Applicant   Applicant's Signature

_____   _____
Typed or Printed Name   Applicant's Typed or Printed Name

_____   _____
Street Address   Street Address

_____   _____
City   State   Zip Code   City   State   Zip Code

_____   _____
Phone Number (include area code)   Phone Number (include area code)

Attorney Registration No. _____

Signed and acknowledged by the applicant in my presence this _____ day of

_____, _____.

_____
NotaryPublic/DeputyClerk

FORM 5.10 - APPLICATION FOR SUMMARY RELEASE FROM ADMINISTRATION

Eff. Date March 1, 2008

PROBATE COURT OF _____ COUNTY, OHIO

ESTATE OF _____, DECEASED

CASE NO. _____

ENTRY GRANTING SUMMARY RELEASE FROM ADMINISTRATION
[R.C. 2113.031]

The Court finds that the application by _____, satisfies all requirements of R.C. 2113.031 and therefore summarily releases the estate from administration and directs:

☐   The delivery to the applicant of decedent's personal property set forth in the application with the title to that property.

☐   That Certificate(s) of Transfer, attached to the application, be issued.

A certified copy of this order together with a certified copy of the application for this order constitutes sufficient authority for a financial institution, corporation or other entity or person referred to in division (A) to (F) of Section 5731.39 of the Revised Code or for a clerk of a Court of Common Pleas to transfer title to the applicant of an asset of the decedent's estate listed in the application.

This order eliminates the need for a financial institution, corporation, or other entity or person to be provided a written consent of the tax commissioner prior to the delivery, transfer, or payment to the applicant of an asset of the decedent's estate listed in the application.

This order eliminates the duty of all persons to file an Ohio Estate Tax Return exclusively for the assets listed in the application.

_____   _____
        Date   PROBATE JUDGE

FORM 5.11 - ENTRY GRANTING SUMMARY RELEASE FROM ADMINISTRATION

7/9/01

Inventory And Appraisal — Forms 6.0 To 6.3

PROBATE COURT OF _____ **COUNTY, OHIO**

ESTATE OF _____ , DECEASED

CASE NO. _____

INVENTORY AND APPRAISAL
[R.C. 2115.02 and 2115.09]

To the knowledge of the fiduciary the attached schedule of assets in decedent's estate is complete. The fiduciary determined the value of those assets whose values were readily ascertainable and which were not appraised by the appraiser, and that such values are correct.

The estate is recapitulated as follows:

Tangible personal property...$_____

Intangible personal property...$_____

Real property..$_____

Total..$_____

First automobile transferred to surviving spouse under R.C. 2106.18   value $_____
Second automobile transferred to surviving spouse under R.C. 2106.18   value $_____

Total value [not to exceed $40,000.00]... $_____

Insofar as it can be ascertained, an Ohio Estate Tax Return ☐ will ☐ will not be filed.

☐ The fiduciary is also the surviving spouse of the decedent and waives notice of the taking of the inventory.

_____   _____
Attorney   Fiduciary

Attorney Registration No. _____

APPRAISER'S CERTIFICATE

The undersigned appraiser agrees to act as appraiser of decedent's estate and to appraise the property exhibited truly, honestly, impartially, and to the best of the appraiser's knowledge and ability. The appraiser further says that those assets whose values were not readily ascertainable are indicated on the attached schedule by a check in the "Appraised" column opposite each such item, and that such values are correct.

_____
Appraiser

FORM 6.0 - INVENTORY AND APPRAISAL   12/01/2002

(Reverse of Form 6.0)

CASE NO. _____

WAIVER OF NOTICE OF TAKING OF INVENTORY
[R.C. 2115.04]

The undersigned surviving spouse hereby waives notice of the time and place of taking the inventory of decedent's estate.

_____
Surviving Spouse

WAIVER OF NOTICE OF HEARING ON INVENTORY
[Use when notice is required by the Court or deemed necessary by the fiduciary]

The undersigned, who are interested in the estate, waive notice of the hearing on the inventory.

_____   _____

_____   _____

_____   _____

_____   _____

_____   _____

_____   _____

_____   _____

ENTRY SETTING HEARING

The Court sets _____ at _____ o'clock _____ .M., as the date and time for hearing the inventory of decedent's estate.

_____   _____
Date   Probate Judge

PROBATE COURT OF _____ COUNTY, OHIO

ESTATE OF _____, DECEASED

CASE NO. _____

SCHEDULE OF ASSETS

(Attach to inventory and appraisal)

Page _____ of _____ pages.

(Insert a check in the column "Appraised" opposite an item if it was valued by the appraiser. Leave blank if the readily ascertainable value was determined by fiduciary)

Item	Appraised	Value
		$

(Reverse of Form 6.1)

Page _____ of _____ pages.

Item	Appraised	Value
		$

_____
Fiduciary

PROBATE COURT OF _____ COUNTY, OHIO

ESTATE OF _____, DECEASED

CASE NO. _____

WAIVER OF NOTICE OF HEARING ON INVENTORY

[Use when notice is required by the Court or deemed necessary by the fiduciary]

The undersigned, who are interested in the estate, waive notice of the hearing on the inventory.

_____   _____

_____   _____

_____   _____

_____   _____

_____   _____

_____   _____

_____   _____

_____   _____

_____   _____

_____   _____

_____   _____

_____   _____

_____   _____

_____   _____

FORM 6.2 - WAIVER OF NOTICE OF HEARING ON INVENTORY   3/1/96

PROBATE COURT OF _____ COUNTY, OHIO

ESTATE OF _____ **, DECEASED**

CASE NO. _____

NOTICE OF HEARING ON INVENTORY
[R.C. 2115.16]

To:

_____

_____

_____

You are hereby notified that the inventory of decedent's assets has been filed, and the hearing on the inventory will be held on
_____ at _____ o'clock _____ . M.
The Court is located at _____
_____
Exceptions to the inventory must be filed in writing at least five days prior to the date set for the hearing.

_____

Fiduciary/Attorney for Fiduciary

Attorney Registration No._____

FORM 6.3 - NOTICE OF HEARING ON INVENTORY   3/1/96

Claims Against The Estate — Forms 7.0 To 7.2

PROBATE COURT OF _____ COUNTY, OHIO

ESTATE OF _____, DECEASED

CASE NO. _____

NOTICE OF ADMINISTRATOR OF
ESTATE RECOVERY PROGRAM
[R.C. 2117.061]

The undersigned gives notice to the Administrator of the Estate Recovery Program that the decedent was fifty-five (55) years of age or older at the time of death and has been determined to have been a recipient of medical assistance under Chapter 5111 of the Revised Code.

_____

☐ Executor
☐ Administrator
☐ Commissioner
☐ Person who filed pursuant to 2113.03 of the
Revised Code for release from administration.

CERTIFICATE OF SERVICE

This is to certify a true copy of the above notice was served by certified U.S. mail, postage prepaid to the Administrator of the Estate Recovery Program, on the _____ day of _____, 20_____.

_____
Person Responsible for the Estate

_____
Typed or Printed Name

_____
Address

_____
City, State, Zip

_____
Phone Number (include area code)

FORM 7.0 – NOTICE TO ADMINISTRATOR OF ESTATE RECOVERY PROGRAM   4/8/04

PROBATE COURT OF _____ COUNTY, OHIO

ESTATE OF _____, DECEASED

CASE NO. _____

APPLICATION FOR FAMILY ALLOWANCE
[R.C. 2106.13]

The fiduciary states that there is [ ] a surviving spouse and no minor children of the decedent who are not the children of the surviving spouse; [ ] no surviving spouse and one minor child of the decedent; that the surviving spouse or minor child is entitled to receive in money or property the sum of [ ] $25,000, if decedent died prior to March 18, 1999 or [ ] $40,000, if the decedent died on or after March 18, 1999, as an allowance for support, and the fiduciary hereby moves the Court to allow the surviving spouse or minor child the following items:

Description   Appraised Value

[ ] _____   _____
Second automobile selected pursuant to R.C. 2106.18

_____ ____   _____

_____ ____   _____

_____ ____   _____

_____ ____   _____

DO NOT USE THIS FORM IF THERE ARE MINOR CHILDREN OF THE DECEDENT WHO ARE NOT THE CHILDREN OF THE SURVIVING SPOUSE, OR IF THERE IS NO SURVIVING SPOUSE AND MORE THAN ONE MINOR CHILD. USE FORM 7.2

_____
FIDUCIARY

ENTRY

The Court finds that there is [ ] a surviving spouse and no minor children of the decedent who are not the children of the surviving spouse; [ ] no surviving spouse and one minor child of the decedent; who is entitled to receive [ ] $25,000 or [ ] $40,000 in money or property as an allowance for support.

Therefore it is ORDERED that the property requested in the foregoing application be transferred to the person described in said application.

The Court further orders that the fiduciary, if not the surviving spouse, serve a copy of this Entry upon all interested persons within seven (7) days.

_____
PROBATE JUDGE

FORM 7.1 - APPLICATION FOR FAMILY ALLOWANCE   5/3/99

PROBATE COURT OF _____ COUNTY, OHIO

ESTATE OF _____ **, DECEASED**

CASE NO. _____

APPLICATION FOR APPORTIONMENT OF FAMILY ALLOWANCE
[R.C. 2106.13(B)(3) and (4)]

The fiduciary states that there is [ ] a surviving spouse and minor children of the decedent who are not the children of the surviving spouse; [ ] no surviving spouse and more than one minor child; and the fiduciary requests the Court for an Order to apportion the family allowance. The fiduciary states that the names of the surviving spouse and minor children are as follows:

SPOUSE

_____
NAME   ADDRESS

MINOR CHILDREN

1. _____
   Minor   Address   Date of Birth

   _____
   (Parent)(Custodian)   Address

2. _____
   Minor   Address   Date of Birth

   _____
   (Parent)(Custodian)   Address

3. _____
   Minor   Address   Date of Birth

   _____
   (Parent)(Custodian)   Address

4. _____
   Minor   Address   Date of Birth

   _____
   (Parent)(Custodian)   Address

5. _____
   Minor   Address   Date of Birth

   _____
   (Parent)(Custodian)

                                  _____
                                      FIDUCIARY

(Reverse of Form 7.2)

ENTRY SETTING HEARING AND ORDERING NOTICE

The Court finds that there is [ ] a surviving spouse and minor children of the decedent who are not the children of the surviving spouse; [ ] no surviving spouse and more than one minor child; and assigns this application for hearing on _____, 20____, at _____ o'clock ____.m. and orders that the fiduciary give seven (7) days notice of this hearing by certified mail to all interested parties.

_____

PROBATE JUDGE

ENTRY ON APPORTIONMENT
[R.C. 2106.13(B)(3) and (4)]

The Court finds that there is [ ] a surviving spouse and minor children of the decedent who are not the children of the surviving spouse; [ ] no surviving spouse and more than one minor child; and orders that the family allowance be apportioned as follows:

[ ]
_____
Surviving spouse - second automobile selected   Property or Amount
pursuant to R.C. 2106.18
[ ]
_____
Surviving spouse   Property or Amount

_____
Distributee   Property or Amount

_____
Distributee   Property or Amount

_____
Distributee   Property or Amount

_____
Distributee   Property or Amount

_____
Distributee   Property or Amount

The Court further orders that the fiduciary serve a copy of this Entry upon all interested persons within seven (7) days.

_____

PROBATE JUDGE

Election Of Surviving Spouse — Forms 8.0 To 8.5

PROBATE COURT OF _____ **COUNTY, OHIO**

ESTATE OF: _____

CASE NO. _____

CITATION TO SURVIVING SPOUSE TO
EXERCISE ELECTIVE RIGHTS
[R.C. 2106.01 and 2106.02]

To: _____
           Name of Surviving Spouse

_____
           Address

_____
           City, State, Zip Code

You are hereby cited to elect to exercise your rights as surviving spouse. A summary of these rights is attached and incorporated herein. These rights include the right to elect against the will. Most of the rights must be exercised within five months from the date of the initial appointment of the administrator or executor. If you do not timely elect to exercise any specific right, it will be conclusively presumed you have elected not to exercise that right and the right will be forfeited. If you have questions concerning your rights, you should consult an attorney of your choice.

The date of appointment of the administrator or executor is: _____.

The address of the probate court is: _____
_____.

The names and addresses of the executor or administrator and his or her attorney are:

_____   _____
Attorney for Applicant   Name

_____   _____
Attorney Registration No.   Title

_____   _____
Address   Address

_____   _____

_____   _____
Phone Number (include area code)   Phone Number (include area code)

                                   Probate Judge

Date: _____   By: _____
                                         Deputy Clerk

PROBATE COURT OF _____ COUNTY, OHIO

ESTATE OF _____,DECEASED

CASE NO. _____

ELECTION OF SURVIVING SPOUSE TO TAKE UNDER WILL
[R.C. 2106.05]

I, decedent's surviving spouse, elect to take under decedent's Will.

_____   _____
Date   Surviving Spouse

Approved By:

_____
Attorney for Surviving Spouse

_____
Typed or Printed Name

_____
Address

_____

_____
Phone Number (include area code)

Attorney Registration No. _____

PROBATE COURT OF _____ COUNTY, OHIO

ESTATE OF _____ , DECEASED

CASE NO. _____

ELECTION OF SURVIVING SPOUSE TO TAKE AGAINST WILL
[R.C. 2106.01 and 2106.06]

I, decedent's surviving spouse, elect to take against decedent's Will.

Decedent's Will, my rights under the Will, and my rights by electing to take against the Will have been explained to me.

_____   _____
Date   Surviving Spouse

The above election to take against decedent's Will was made by the surviving spouse in person, before me. Before accepting the election, I explained to the surviving spouse the decedent's Will, the rights under the Will, and the rights by electing to take against the Will.

                                                    _____
                                                    Probate Judge/Magistrate

Approved By:

_____
Attorney for Surviving Spouse

_____
Typed or Printed Name

_____
Address

_____

_____
Phone Number (include area code)

Attorney Registration No. _____

PROBATE COURT OF _____ COUNTY, OHIO

ESTATE OF: _____

CASE NO. _____

SUMMARY OF GENERAL RIGHTS OF SURVIVING SPOUSE
[R.C. 2106.02]

To: _____   _____
            Surviving Spouse   Address

                                          _____
                                          City, State, Zip Code

This is a summary of your general rights as surviving spouse under Chapter 2106 of the Revised Code. Many of these rights have specific time limits in which they must be exercised. If you have questions concerning your rights, you should discuss them with an attorney of your choice. The Court cannot advise you.

1.   Election to Take Under or Against the Will (R.C. 2106.01 - 2106.08)

If you elect to take against the Will, you are entitled to one-half of the decedent's net estate, unless there are two or more of the decedent's children or their lineal descendants surviving, in which case you are entitled to one-third of the decedent's net estate. You will not be entitled to receive any assets given to you under the Will.

If you elect to take under the Will, you will receive those assets given to you under the Will.

Whichever choice you make, (unless you elect to take under the Will and the Will specifically precludes you from exercising these rights), you will not be barred from your rights to purchase certain assets at the appraised value, to remain in the mansion house (the residence) for one year, to receive an allowance for support, to receive not more than two automobiles and one watercraft and one outboard motor owned by the decedent, and to such other rights as a surviving spouse may be entitled under law.

Although your election may not affect certain non-probate property, such as joint and survivorship, payable on death, and transfer on death property, it may have an effect on other types of non-probate property, including property held in trust.

Before making your election, you are entitled to file a complaint in this Court asking that the Will be construed.

If you elect to take under the Will, you may do so in writing if you wish, but you may also do so by taking no action.

If you elect to take against the Will, you must do so in person before the Probate Judge or a Magistrate. This election must be exercised within five months from the date of the initial appointment of the administrator or executor of the estate or it is forfeited.

2.   Right to Receive Mansion House (R.C. 2106.10)

Depending upon the value of the real estate, you may have the right to receive the mansion house (the residence) as part of your inheritance.

3.   Right to Place Charge on Real Estate (R.C. 2106.11)

If there is no Will and there are insufficient assets to pay the specific monetary share due to the surviving spouse pursuant to R.C. 2106.05, you have the right to place a charge (lien) on any real property included in the probate estate in the amount of the unpaid portion of the specific monetary share.

[Side 2 of Form 8.3]

CASE NO. _____

4.   Allowance for Support (R.C. 2106.13)

You may be entitled to an allowance for support. For deaths occurring after March 18, 1999, the amount is $40,000 of probate assets. If there are one or more minor children of the decedent, not the children of the surviving spouse, this Court will apportion the allowance among those children and the surviving spouse.

5.   Right to Remain in the Mansion House (R.C. 2106.15)

You have the right to remain in the mansion house (the residence), if it is a probate asset, for a period of one year from the date of death without the payment of rent to the estate. If the mansion house is sold to pay debts during this period of time, you may be entitled to the fair rental value of the mansion house. This election must be exercised within five months from the initial appointment of the administrator or executor or the right is forfeited.

6.   Right to Purchase Property (R.C. 2106.16)

You have the right to purchase assets of the probate estate at the appraised values. The application or petition to purchase the assets must be filed within one month of the approval of the inventory or the right is forfeited.

7.   Right to Automobiles (R.C. 2106.18)

You may be entitled to receive up to two automobiles, not specifically bequeathed, that would otherwise be included in the probate estate and do not exceed an aggregate value of $40,000. This right may affect the amount you may receive under the allowance for support. This right must be exercised within five months from the initial appointment of the administrator or executor or the right is forfeited.

8.   Right to Watercraft and Outboard Motor (R.C. 2106.19)

You may be entitled to receive one watercraft and one outboard motor, not specifically bequeathed, that would otherwise be included in the probate estate. This right must be exercised within five months from the initial appointment of the administrator or executor or the right is forfeited.

9.   Right to Reimbursement of Funeral Bill (R.C. 2106.20)

You may be entitled to be reimbursed for the payment of the funeral bill.

10.   Right to Challenge Antenuptial or Separation Agreement (R.C. 2106.22)

You are entitled to file an action to contest the validity of an antenuptial or separation agreement. This action must be filed within four months after the appointment of the executor or administrator or the right is forfeited.

This is a summary of your general rights. There may be additional rights to which you are entitled.

Ohio Revised Code § 2106.25 states:

Unless otherwise specified by a provision of the Revised Code or this section, a surviving spouse shall exercise all rights under Chapter 2106. of the Revised Code within five months of the initial appointment of an executor or administrator of the estate. It is conclusively presumed that a surviving spouse has waived any right not exercised within that five-month period or within any longer period of time allowed by the court pursuant to this section. Upon the filing of a motion to extend the time for exercising a right under Chapter 2106. of the Revised Code and for good cause shown, the court may allow further time for exercising the right that is the subject of the motion.

PROBATE COURT OF _____ COUNTY, OHIO

ESTATE OF: _____

CASE NO. _____

CERTIFICATE OF SERVICE AND NOTICE OF CITATION TO
SURVIVING SPOUSE TO EXERCISE ELECTIVE RIGHTS
[R.C. 2106.02]

This is to certify that a Citation to Surviving Spouse to Exercise Elective Rights and a Summary of General Rights of Surviving Spouse were mailed to the surviving spouse by certified mail, and a copy of this Certificate mailed to the administrator, executor, or the attorney for the administrator or executor, by ordinary mail, on this _____ day of _____, _____.

Probate Judge

By: _____
Deputy Clerk

PROBATE COURT OF _____ **COUNTY, OHIO**

ESTATE OF: _____

CASE NO. _____

**RETURN FOR CERTIFICATE OF SERVICE OF CITATION TO
SURVIVING SPOUSE TO EXERCISE ELECTIVE RIGHTS**
[R.C. 2106.02]

ATTACH

RETURN

RECEIPT

HERE

PROBATE COURT OF _____ COUNTY, OHIO

ESTATE OF _____ **, DECEASED**

CASE NO. _____

WAIVER OF SERVICE TO SURVIVING SPOUSE
OF THE CITATION TO ELECT
[R.C. 2106.01(A)]

The undersigned, surviving spouse of the above named decedent, being eighteen years of age or older and not under disability, waives the service of the citation required by section 2106.01(A) of the Revised Code.

I acknowledge I have received Standard Probate Form 8.3, Summary of General Rights of Surviving Spouse.

I understand that most of my rights must be exercised within five months from the date of the initial appointment of the administrator or executor. If I do not timely elect to exercise any specific right, it will be conclusively presumed I have elected not to exercise that right and the right will be forfeited.

_____
Date

_____
Signature of Surviving Spouse

_____
Typed or printed name of surviving spouse

_____
Attorney for Fiduciary

_____
Typed or Printed Name

_____
Address

_____
City, State, Zip

_____
Telephone Number (including area code)

Attorney Registration No. _____

FORM 8.6 – WAIVER OF SERVICE TO SURVIVING SPOUSE OF THE CITATION TO ELECT   4/8/04

Sale Of Personal Property — Forms 9.0 To 9.2

PROBATE COURT OF _____ COUNTY, OHIO

ESTATE OF _____, **DECEASED**

CASE NO. _____

APPLICATION TO SELL PERSONAL PROPERTY
[R.C. 2113.40, 2113.41, 2113.42, and 2113.43]

The fiduciary asks the Court to authorize the sale of the personal property of the decedent listed on the within schedule, at a public or private sale, for a fixed price or for the best price obtainable, and for cash or on terms as the Court may determine.

The fiduciary states that the sale will be in the best interests of the estate, that none of the property listed is subject to a demand for distribution in kind made by the surviving spouse or other beneficiary entitled to such distribution, and that none of the property listed is subject to a wish expressed by the decedent in the Will that it not be sold. Further, none of the property listed is specifically bequeathed; or if some or all of the property is specifically bequeathed, as noted on the schedule, either its sale is necessary to pay debts, or the persons entitled to it consented to the sale.

The fiduciary further states that: **[Check the applicable boxes]**

☐ The sale is before the expiration of the time within which the surviving spouse may elect to take at the appraised value and
☐ the surviving spouse consents to such sale or waives notice thereof ☐ the surviving spouse does not consent to such sale,
☐ the property is not perishable and the surviving spouse is entitled to notice of the sale as provided by law.

☐ The fiduciary further states that: **[Include any special allegations or information]**

_____

_____

The fiduciary further states that for a public sale, notice will be given by advertisement appearing at least three times in a newspaper of general circulation in the county during a period of fifteen days next preceding such sale and/or by advertisement posted not less than fifteen days next preceding such sale in at least five public places in the township or municipal corporation where such sale is to take place.

_____

Fiduciary

CONSENT TO SALE AND WAIVER OF NOTICE

The undersigned, being the decedent's surviving spouse or other interested persons, hereby waive notice and consent to the sale as described herein.

_____   _____
Surviving Spouse

_____   _____

_____   _____

FORM 9.0 - APPLICATION TO SELL PERSONAL PROPERTY   10/1/98

(Reverse of Form 9.0)

SCHEDULE OF PERSONAL PROPERTY FOR SALE

Item	Sale Method Public/Private	Price Fixed/Best	Payment Cash/Terms

ENTRY AUTHORIZING SALE OF PERSONAL PROPERTY

The Court finds that the sale of the personal property of the decedent as set forth herein is not prohibited by law and will be in the best interests of the estate.

It is hereby ordered: **[check the applicable boxes]**

☐ That the fiduciary is authorized to sell the personal property in accordance with the terms and conditions as set forth in the application.

☐ That the fiduciary is authorized to sell the personal property in accordance with the terms and conditions as set forth in the application, except as follows: _____

_____

_____

[Check if applicable] - ☐ The time has not expired within which the surviving spouse may elect to purchase personal property at its appraised value; the surviving spouse has not consented to the sale, and the property is not perishable. It is therefore further ordered that the fiduciary give at least ten days notice of the sale to the surviving spouse, as provided by law.

_____   _____
Date   **Probate Judge**

PROBATE COURT OF _____ COUNTY, OHIO

ESTATE OF _____ **, DECEASED**

CASE NO. _____

ENTRY AUTHORIZING SALE OF PERSONAL PROPERTY

The Court finds that the sale of the personal property of the decedent as set forth in the application is not prohibited by law and will be in the best interests of the estate.

It is hereby ordered: **[check the applicable boxes]**

☐ That the fiduciary is authorized to sell the personal property in accordance with the terms and conditions as set forth in the application.

☐ That the fiduciary is authorized to sell the personal property in accordance with the terms and conditions as set forth in the application, except as follows: _____

_____

_____

[Check if applicable] - ☐ The time has not expired within which the surviving spouse may elect to purchase personal property at its appraised value; the surviving spouse has not consented to the sale, and the property is not perishable. It is therefore ordered that the fiduciary serve at least ten days notice of the sale upon the surviving spouse, as provided by law.

_____   _____
Date   **Probate Judge**

PROBATE COURT OF _____ COUNTY, OHIO

ESTATE OF _____ **, DECEASED**

CASE NO. _____

NOTICE OF SALE OF PERSONAL PROPERTY

To: _____   _____
         Surviving Spouse   Address
                                                             _____

     This Court has approved an application to sell certain items of personal property belonging to decedent. The items to be sold, and the manner and terms of sale are as listed and described in the attached schedule.

     The sale will be held on _____ , at
                                                             Date
_____ .
                              Location

                                            _____
                                            Probate Judge

Distribution In Kind — Forms 10.0 To 10.4

PROBATE COURT OF _____ COUNTY, OHIO

ESTATE OF _____, DECEASED

CASE NO. _____

APPLICATION TO DISTRIBUTE IN KIND
[R.C. 2113.55]

The fiduciary asks the Court to authorize distribution in kind, according to the within schedule, of personal property in the estate which is not specifically bequeathed and is available for distribution.

[Check one of the following] - ☐ Decedent's known debts have been paid or secured to be paid - ☐ Sufficient assets are in hand to pay decedent's known debts.

[Check whichever of the following paragraphs are applicable]:

☐ All interested persons whose interests may be affected by the distribution have consented to the distribution as proposed in the within schedule.

☐ All interested persons whose interests may be affected by the distribution have not consented to the distribution as proposed in the within schedule. The fiduciary will give notice as required by law to all interested persons who have not consented and who are listed on the notice of hearing accompanying this application.

☐ The distribution is to satisfy part or all of the allowance for support due decedent's **[check applicable boxes]** - ☐ surviving spouse - ☐ minor children.

☐ The distribution is with the consent of the surviving spouse, and is to satisfy part or all of the specific monetary share due the surviving spouse under the Statute of Descent and Distribution **[if this paragraph is checked, the following must be completed and the surviving spouse must sign the consent form]**:

Specific monetary share due surviving spouse $_____

Less: Value of property to be distributed
      hereunder to surviving spouse $_____

      Probate assets previously received by
      surviving spouse in excess of the
      allowance for support $_____

Balance of specific monetary share remaining $_____

_____
Fiduciary

FORM 10.0 - APPLICATION TO DISTRIBUTE IN KIND   10/1/98

(Reverse of Form 10.0)

CONSENT TO DISTRIBUTION IN KIND

The undersigned, being the decedent's surviving spouse or other interested persons, hereby consent to the distribution as described herein.

_____   _____
Surviving Spouse

_____   _____

_____   _____

SCHEDULE OF PROPERTY TO BE DISTRIBUTED IN KIND

Name of Distributee	Item to be Distributed	Appraised Value
		$

JUDGMENT ENTRY

[Check the applicable boxes]

☐ The Court finds that the distribution in kind as set forth herein is not prohibited by law and will be in the best interests of the estate, and that all interested persons have consented to the proposed distribution. It is ordered that the fiduciary is authorized to distribute the personal property in accordance with the within application.

☐ The Court finds that all interested persons have not consented, and it is therefore ordered that the Application to Distribute in Kind is scheduled for hearing before the Court located at _____
_____ on
_____ at _____ o'clock _____M., and that the fiduciary shall
serve a copy of the application and notice of the hearing as required by law, upon all interested persons who have not consented.

☐ The Court further finds and orders: _____
_____

_____   _____
Date   **Probate Judge**

PROBATE COURT OF _____ COUNTY, OHIO

ESTATE OF _____ , DECEASED

CASE NO. _____

ENTRY APPROVING DISTRIBUTION IN KIND

[Check the applicable boxes]

☐ The Court finds that the distribution in kind as set forth in the application is not prohibited by law and will be in the best interests of the estate, and that all interested persons have consented to the proposed distribution. It is ordered that the fiduciary is authorized to distribute the personal property in accordance with the within application.

☐ The Court finds after hearing that the distribution in kind as set forth in the application is not prohibited by law and will be in the best interests of the estate. It is ordered that the fiduciary is authorized to distribute the personal property in accordance with the application.

☐ The Court further finds and orders: _____

_____

_____

_____ .

_____   _____

Date   **Probate Judge**

PROBATE COURT OF _____ COUNTY, OHIO

ESTATE OF _____, DECEASED

CASE NO. _____

NOTICE OF HEARING ON APPLICATION TO DISTRIBUTE IN KIND

To the following persons:

Name	Address
Name	Address
Name	Address
Name	Address
Name	Address

An application has been filed in this Court asking for authority to distribute certain personal property of decedent in kind.

The hearing on the application will be held _____
at _____ o'clock _____ M. in this Court.

The Court is located at _____
_____

You are one of those persons whose interests may be affected by the proposed distribution in kind, and if you know of any reason why such distribution should not be permitted you should appear and inform the Court.

_____
Probate Judge/Deputy Clerk

FORM 10.2 - NOTICE OF HEARING ON APPLICATION TO DISTRIBUTE IN KIND   10/1/98

Consent To Power To Sell Real Estate — Form 11.0

PROBATE COURT OF _____ COUNTY, OHIO

ESTATE OF _____, DECEASED

CASE NO. _____

CONSENT TO POWER TO SELL REAL ESTATE

The undersigned are the surviving spouse and legatees, devisees or heirs of decedent. Each declares that he is an adult.

The undersigned empower the fiduciary in the estate, at any time, to sell at public or private sale, or to grant options to buy, or to exchange or re-exchange real estate belonging to the estate, and to execute and deliver the necessary deeds or other conveyances, consistent with law and this power of sale.

Any such sale, option, exchange or re-exchange shall be on terms consistent with law and at a price of not less than eighty per cent of the appraised value of the parcel, as shown on the inventory and appraisal filed in this Court.

[Check one of the following]

☐   The power of sale consented to herein is general, and extends to all real estate in the estate.

☐   The power of sale consented to herein is limited, and applies only to the parcels of real estate particularly described below **[describe on back]**.

FORM 11.0 - CONSENT TO POWER TO SELL REAL ESTATE

(Reverse of Form 11.0)

The particular parcels of real estate in decedent's estate and to which this power of sale is limited are described as follows **[use extra sheets if necessary]:**

Transfer Of Real Estate — Forms 12.0 To 12.2

PROBATE COURT OF _____ **COUNTY, OHIO**
_____ **, JUDGE**

ESTATE OF _____ **DECEASED**

CASE NO. _____

APPLICATION FOR CERTIFICATE OF TRANSFER
[R.C. 2113.61]

Applicant states that decedent died on _____ .

Decedent's residence at death was _____
Street Address

_____
City or Village, or Township if unincorporated area   County

_____
Post Office   State   Zip Code

Decedent died owning the real property described in the accompanying Certificate of Transfer No. _____, which also lists those persons to whom the real property passed. Applicant asks the Court to issue a Certificate of Transfer so that new ownership interests may be recorded.

[Check the applicable boxes]

☐ Decedent died intestate.

☐ Decedent died testate on _____; will admitted to probate on _____.

☐ Decedent's known debts have been paid or secured to be paid.

☐ Sufficient other assets are in hand to pay decedent's known debts.

☐ Estate is insolvent and the transfer shall apply toward the allowance for support.

☐ Applicant was appointed by this court on _____ and is the qualified and acting executor or administrator of decedent's estate.

☐ Executor or administrator of decedent's estate failed to file this application before being discharged.

☐ Applicant is the executor or administrator appointed in another state. There is and has been no ancillary administration in Ohio. The real property to be transferred is located in this county.

☐ The transfer is subject to a written contract for the sale and conveyance of the real property, entered into but uncompleted by decedent before death. A copy of the contract is attached.

☐ The transfer is pursuant to decedent's Will.

☐ The transfer is pursuant to the statutes of descent and distribution.

☐ The transfer is pursuant to summary release from administration [R.C. 2113.031(D)(3)]

☐ The real property to be transferred is subject to a charge in favor of the surviving spouse in the amount of $ _____ as computed pursuant to R.C. 2106.11 on attached Exhibit A, and as shown on the accompanying Certificate of Transfer, in respect of the unpaid balance of the specific monetary share which is part of the surviving spouse's total intestate share.

FORM 12.0 – APPLICATION FOR CERTIFICATE OF TRANSFER

Eff. Date March 1, 2008

CASE NO._____

☐ The transfer is of decedent's entire interest in the mansion house to the surviving spouse, who hereby elects to take such interest as part or all of the intestate share and/or allowance for support. [If this paragraph is checked, the following must be completed, and both the surviving spouse and applicant must sign this form].

The value of the total intestate share to which decedent's surviving spouse is entitled is .... $_____

The value of the allowance for support to which decedent's surviving spouse is entitled is .... $_____

The value of decedent's entire interest in the mansion house is:

      Interest in mansion house...$ _____

      Interest in household goods in house ....$ _____

      Interest in lots or farm land adjacent to house
      and used in conjunction with it, which are
      described in certificate of transfer and which
      spouse hereby elects to include ....$ _____

    Less: Decedent's share of liens
           on any and all of above ....$ _____

          Total   ....$ _____ $ _____

_____   _____
Surviving Spouse   Applicant

                                     _____
                                     Title or status

ENTRY ISSUING CERTIFICATE OF TRANSFER

The Court finding that the above application contains the information required by statute orders that Certificate of Transfer No. _____ be filed with this Entry and a copy of the Certificate of Transfer be issued for recording.

☐ [Check if applicable] The Court further finds that the transfer is subject to a charge pursuant to R. C. 2106.11.

_____   _____
Date   Probate Judge

FORM 12.0 – APPLICATION FOR CERTIFICATE OF TRANSFER
Eff. Date March 1, 2008

PROBATE COURT OF _____ COUNTY, OHIO

ESTATE OF _____**, DECEASED**

CASE NO. _____

CERTIFICATE OF TRANSFER
NO. _____

[Check one of the following]

☐ Decedent died intestate.

☐ Decedent died testate.

Decedent died on _____ owning the real property described in this certificate. The persons to whom such real property passed by devise, descent or election are as follows:

Name	Residence Address	Transferee's share of decedent's interest

[Complete if applicable] The real property described in this certificate is subject to a charge of $ _____

in favor of decedent's surviving spouse, _____ in respect

of the unpaid balance of the specific monetary share which is part of the surviving spouse's total intestate share.

12.1 CERTIFICATE OF TRANSFER

PROBATE COURT OF _____ COUNTY, OHIO

CASE NO. _____

The legal description of decedent's interest in the real property subject to this certificate is: **[use extra sheets, if necessary].**

Prior Instrument Reference:

Parcel No:

ISSUANCE

This Certificate of Transfer is issued this _____ day of _____ , 20___ .

_____
Judge

CERTIFICATION

I certify that this document is a true copy of the original Certificate of Transfer No. _____ issued on _____ and kept by me as custodian of the official records of this Court.

_____
Date

_____
Judge

By _____
Deputy Clerk

Accounts — Forms 13.0 To 13.10

PROBATE COURT OF _____ COUNTY, OHIO

ESTATE OF _____ , DECEASED

CASE NO. _____

FIDUCIARY'S ACCOUNT
[R.C. 2109.30, 2109.301 and 2109.32]

[Executors and Administrators]

The fiduciary offers the account given below and on the attached itemized statement of receipts and disbursements. The fiduciary states that the account is correct, and asks that it be approved and settled.

[Check one of the following]

☐ This is a partial account. A statement of the assets remaining in the fiduciary's hands is attached.

☐ This is a final account. A statement of the assets remaining in the fiduciary's hands for distribution to the beneficiaries is attached.

☐ This is an account of distribution, and fiduciary asks to be discharged upon its approval and settlement.

☐ This is a final and distributive account, and the fiduciary asks to be discharged upon its approval and settlement.

☐ This is a supplemental final account.

[Complete if this is a partial account, or if one or more accounts have previously been filed in the estate] The period of this account is from _____ to _____

[Complete if applicable] Accounts previously filed in the estate, the accounting periods, and the fiduciary and attorney fees paid for each period, are as follows:

Date Filed	Accounting Period	Fiduciary Fees Paid	Attorney Fees Paid
		$	$

Note:
2117.06(K) states: "The distributee may be liable to the estate up to the value of the distribution and may be required to return all or any part of the value of the distribution if a valid claim is subsequently made against the estate within the time permitted under this section."
2109.32(C) states: "The rights of any person with a pecuniary interest in the estate are not barred by approval of an account pursuant to division (A) and (B) of this section. These rights may be barred following a hearing on the account pursuant to section 2109.33 of the Revised Code."

13.0 - FIDUCIARY'S ACCOUNT   12/01/2002

[Side 2 of Form 13.0]

Case No. _____

This account is recapitulated as follows:

RECEIPTS

Personal property not sold . . . . $_____

Proceeds from sale of personal property. . . . . _____

Real property not sold. . . . . _____

Proceeds from sale of real property. . . . . _____

Income. . . . . _____

Other receipts. . . . . _____

Total receipts . . . . $_____

DISBURSEMENTS

Fiduciary fees this accounting period . . . . $_____

Attorney fees this accounting period . . . . _____

Other administration costs and expenses. . . . . _____

Debts and claims against estate . . . . _____

Ohio and federal estate taxes . . . . _____

Personal property distributed in kind . . . . _____

Real property transferred . . . . _____

Other distributions to beneficiaries . . . . _____

Other disbursements . . . . _____

Total disbursements . . . . $_____

BALANCE REMAINING IN FIDUCIARY'S HANDS . . . . $_____

_____   _____
Attorney   Fiduciary

Attorney Registration No. _____ Date_____

ENTRY SETTING HEARING

The Court sets _____ at _____ o'clock _____ M., as the date and time for
hearing the above account.

Date_____   Probate Judge_____

PROBATE COURT OF _____ COUNTY, OHIO

ESTATE OF _____, DECEASED

CASE NO. _____

RECEIPTS AND DISBURSEMENTS

[Attach to fiduciary's account]

Page _____ of _____ pages

Following is an itemized statement of receipts and disbursements by the fiduciary in the administration of his trust.

Item	Voucher No.	Value or Amount	Value or Amount
		$	$

13.1 - RECEIPTS AND DISBURSEMENTS

(Reverse of Form 13.1)

Page _____ of _____ pages

Item	Voucher No.	Value or Amount	Value or Amount
		$	$

Fiduciary

PROBATE COURT OF _____ COUNTY, OHIO

ESTATE OF _____, DECEASED

CASE NO. _____

ASSETS REMAINING IN FIDUCIARY'S HANDS

[Attach to partial or final fiduciary's account]

Page _____ of _____ pages

The estate assets remaining in fiduciary's hands are recapitulated as follows:

Tangible personal property... $_____

Intangible personal property .... $_____

      Total Personal property .... $_____

Real Estate.. $_____

      Total assets remaining in fiduciary's hands....................................... $_____

Following is an itemized statement of estate assets remaining in the fiduciary's hands.

Item	Value or Amount	Value or Amount
	$	$

13.2 - ASSETS REMAINING IN FIDUCIARY'S HANDS

(Reverse of Form 13.2)

Page _____ of _____ pages

Item	Value or Amount	Value or Amount
	$	$

_____
Fiduciary

PROBATE COURT OF _____ COUNTY, OHIO

TRUST OF
GUARDIANSHIP OF
ESTATE OF _____

CASE NO. _____

ENTRY APPROVING AND SETTLING ACCOUNT
[R.C. 2109.32]

Upon hearing the account filed _____, the Court finds that:

[Check whichever of the following are applicable]

☐   The _____ partial account has been lawfully administered;

☐   The estate has been lawfully administered, except for final distribution to the beneficiaries;

☐   The estate has been fully and lawfully administered, and the assets have been distributed in accordance with the law or the applicable instruments governing distribution;

☐   The events have occurred after which the Court may approve and settle a final account;

☐   The events have occurred after which the Court may approve and settle a supplemental final account.

The account is therefore approved and settled.

[Check whichever of the following are applicable]

The fiduciary shall be discharged without further order of the Court twelve months following the approval of the final and distributive account unless discharged by this entry.

☐   The fiduciary is discharged herewith;

☐   The surety bond is terminated herewith.

_____   _____
Date   Probate Judge

FORM 13.3 - ENTRY APPROVING AND SETTLING ACCOUNT AND DISCHARGING   12/01/2002

PROBATE COURT OF _____ COUNTY, OHIO

ESTATE OF _____, DECEASED

CASE NO. _____

WAIVER OF PARTIAL ACCOUNT
[R.C. 2109.30(B)(2)]

Partial Account due _____

The fiduciary says that all of the decedent's legatees, devisees, or heirs have waived the above partial account. This waiver is accordingly presented in lieu of the partial account.

_____   _____
Date   Fiduciary

The undersigned legatees, devisees, or heirs of decedent not under legal disability hereby waive the filing of the above partial account by the fiduciary, and consent to the filing of this waiver in lieu thereof.

Legatees, Devisees, or Heirs:

_____   _____

_____   _____

_____   _____

_____   _____

_____   _____

_____   _____

_____   _____

_____   _____

_____   _____

_____   _____

_____   _____

_____   _____

_____   _____

FORM 13.4 - WAIVER OF PARTIAL ACCOUNT   3/1/96

PROBATE COURT OF _____ COUNTY, OHIO

ESTATE OF _____, DECEASED

CASE NO. _____

NOTICE OF HEARING ON ACCOUNT
[R.C. 2109.33]

To:

_____

_____

_____

You are hereby notified that a _____ account covering the period from _____ to _____ has been filed, and the hearing will be held on _____ at _____ o'clock ____ M. The Court is located at _____ _____.

You are required to examine the account, to inquire into the contents of the account, and into all matters that may come before the Court at the hearing on the account. Any exceptions to the account shall be filed in writing not less than five days prior to the hearing. Absent the filing of written exceptions, the account may be approved without further notice.

_____
Fiduciary/Attorney for Fiduciary

Attorney Registration No. _____

PROBATE COURT OF _____ COUNTY, OHIO

ESTATE OF _____, DECEASED

CASE NO. _____

CERTIFICATE OF TERMINATION
[R.C. 2109.30]

I certify I am the executor or administrator and the sole legatee, devisee or heir.

I further certify:

(1) all debts and claims presented to the estate have been paid in full or settled finally;

(2) an estate tax return, if required under Chapter 5731 of the Revised Code, has been filed, and any estate tax due under that chapter has been paid;

(3) all attorney fees have been [check one] ☐ waived by counsel of record, ☐ paid to counsel of record in the amount of $ _____;

(4) all fiduciary fees have been [check one] ☐ waived by the fiduciary; ☐ paid to the fiduciary in the amount of $ _____;

(5) all assets remaining after completion of the activities described above have been distributed to myself as the sole legatee, devisee or heir.

_____   _____
Attorney for Fiduciary   Fiduciary

Attorney Registration No. _____

ENTRY

Based upon the above certification it is ordered that the fiduciary and surety, if any, are discharged.

_____
Probate Judge

FORM 13.6 - CERTIFICATE OF TERMINATION   3/1/96

PROBATE COURT OF _____ COUNTY, OHIO

ESTATE OF _____ , DECEASED

CASE NO. _____

WAIVER OF NOTICE OF HEARING ON ACCOUNT
[R.C. 2109.33]

The undersigned, who are interested in the estate, waive notice of the hearing on the account.

_____   _____

_____   _____

_____   _____

_____   _____

_____   _____

_____   _____

_____   _____

_____   _____

_____   _____

_____   _____

_____   _____

_____   _____

_____   _____

_____   _____

FORM 13.7 - WAIVER OF NOTICE OF HEARING ON ACCOUNT   3/1/96

PROBATE COURT OF _____ COUNTY, OHIO

ESTATE OF _____

CASE NO. _____

APPLICATION TO EXTEND ADMINISTRATION
[R.C. 2109.301, Sup. R. 78(B) and (C)]

The undersigned fiduciary applies to extend the administration of the estate beyond six months. The fiduciary states it would be detrimental to the estate and its beneficiaries or heirs to file a final and distributive account or certificate of termination within that time for the following reasons (state with specificity):

_____

_____

_____

_____

_____

_____   _____
Attorney   Fiduciary

Attorney Registration No._____

ENTRY

Upon consideration of the Application, the Court orders:

☐ An account or certificate of termination shall be due not later than thirteen months after the appointment of the fiduciary.

☐ A final and distributive account or certificate of termination is due _____.

☐ The Application is denied.

☐ Other: _____

A status letter shall be filed with each partial account or waiver of partial account.

Probate Judge_____

FORM 13.8 - APPLICATION AND ENTRY TO EXTEND ADMINISTRATION   12/01/2002

PROBATE COURT OF _____ COUNTY, OHIO

ESTATE OF _____

CASE NO. _____

CERTIFICATE OF SERVICE OF ACCOUNT
TO HEIRS OR BENEFICIARIES
[R.C. 2109.32]

This is to certify that a true and accurate copy of the _____ account was

Type of Account

served _____ upon all beneficiaries of the estate except:

Date

☐   The following heir or beneficiary whose address is unknown: _____

_____

☐   The following beneficiary of a specific bequest or devise who has received his or her distribution
     and for which a receipt has been filed or exhibited with the Court:

_____

_____   _____
Attorney   Fiduciary

Attorney Registration No._____

PROBATE COURT OF _____ COUNTY, OHIO

ESTATE OF _____

CASE NO. _____

NOTICE TO EXTEND ADMINISTRATION
[R.C. 2109.301, Sup. R. 78(B) and (C)]

The undersigned fiduciary herby gives notice to extend the administration beyond six months for the following reason(s):

☐   An Ohio estate tax return must be filed for the estate.

☐   A proceeding contesting the validity of the decedent's will pursuant to R.C. 2107.71 has been commenced.

☐   The surviving spouse has filed an election to take against the will.

☐   The administrator or executor is a party in a civil action, Case No. _____ in _____ Court.

☐   The estate is insolvent.

An account or certificate of termination shall be due not later than thirteen months after the appointment of the fiduciary.

_____   _____
Attorney   Fiduciary

Attorney Registration No. _____

Wrongful Death Proceeds — Forms 14.0 To 14.3

PROBATE COURT OF _____ COUNTY, OHIO

ESTATE OF _____, DECEASED

CASE NO. _____

APPLICATION TO APPROVE SETTLEMENT AND DISTRIBUTION OF
WRONGFUL DEATH AND SURVIVAL CLAIMS
[R.C.2117.05, 2125.02, 2125.03, Civ. R. 19.1 and Sup. R. 70]

The fiduciary states:
[Check whichever of the following are applicable, strike inapplicable words, and incorporate all attachments into a single statement.]

☐ There is an offer of (full) (partial) settlement without suit being filed.

☐ There is an offer of (full) (partial) settlement after suit was filed. The style of the case, the court and the case number being _____.

☐ A judgment has been recovered for damages for decedent's wrongful death (and personal injury and property damage arising out of the same act and which survive the decedent).

☐ The amount of the settlement or judgment is $ _____.

☐ This is a partial settlement and therefore the estate must remain open pending final disposition of the claims.

☐ The offer includes, or the judgment sets forth separately, reasonable funeral and burial expenses in the amount of $ _____.

☐ Reasonable compensation for the fiduciary's services is $ _____ and an itemization of such services is attached.

☐ A reasonable attorney fee for the attorney's services is $ _____ and reimbursement to the attorney for case expenses is $ _____. A copy of the attorney's fee contract that (has) (has not) received prior approval of this Court, subject to modification, and an itemization of case expenses are attached.

☐ The net proceeds of $ _____ should be allocated $_____ to the wrongful death action and $ _____ to the survival action. A statement in support thereof is attached.

☐ A statement in support of the proffered settlement is attached.

☐ Supplemental forms required by local rule of court are attached.

☐ All of the beneficiaries of the wrongful death action are on an equal degree of consanguinity, are adults, and have agreed how the net proceeds are to be distributed.

☐ The beneficiaries of the wrongful death action are not on an equal degree of consanguinity, or one or more of the beneficiaries is a minor, or the beneficiaries have not agreed how the net proceeds are to be distributed.

(Reverse of Form 14.0)

☐ The surviving spouse, children, and parents of the decedent and other next of kin who have suffered damages by reason of the wrongful death are as follows and the distribution should be as follows:

Name	Residence Address	Relationship to Decedent	Birthdate of Minor	Amount

☐ The survival claim beneficiaries are as follows:

Name	Residence Address	Relationship to Decedent	Birthdate of Minor

The fiduciary requests that the Court approve the application and authorize the fiduciary to execute a (complete) (partial) release which upon payment of the settlement shall be a (complete) (partial) discharge of the claim.

_____   _____
Attorney for Fiduciary   Fiduciary

Attorney Registration No. _____

ENTRY SETTING HEARING AND ORDERING NOTICE

The Court sets _____ at _____ o'clock ____.M. as the date and time for hearing the above application and orders notice to be given by the fiduciary, as provided in the Rules of Civil Procedure, to the wrongful death and survival claim beneficiaries who have not waived notice.

_____
PROBATE JUDGE

PROBATE COURT OF _____ COUNTY, OHIO

ESTATE OF _____ **, DECEASED**

CASE NO. _____

WAIVER AND CONSENT
WRONGFUL DEATH AND SURVIVAL CLAIMS

The undersigned waive notice of the hearing and consent to and approve the settlement and distribution as set forth in Form 14.0, Application to Approve Settlement and Distribution of Wrongful Death and Survival Claims, a copy of which I have received.

_____   _____

_____   _____

_____   _____

_____   _____

_____   _____

_____   _____

_____   _____

PROBATE COURT OF _____ COUNTY, OHIO

ESTATE OF _____, DECEASED

CASE NO. _____

ENTRY APPROVING SETTLEMENT AND DISTRIBUTION OF
WRONGFUL DEATH AND SURVIVAL CLAIMS

Upon hearing the application to approve settlement and distribution of the wrongful death and survival claims, the Court:

☐ Approves the proffered settlement of $ _____.

☐ Orders payment of $ _____ to be applied to decedent's funeral and burial expenses.

☐ Orders payment of $ _____ to the fiduciary for services rendered with respect to the wrongful death and survival claims.

☐ Orders payment of $ _____ to the attorney for reimbursement of case expenses and $ _____ for attorney fees for services rendered with respect to the wrongful death and survival claims.

☐ Orders that the net proceeds of $ _____ be allocated $ _____ to the wrongful death claim and $ _____ to the survival claim. The amount allocated to the survival claim shall be considered an asset of the estate and shall be reflected in the fiduciary's account of the administration of the estate.

☐ Finds all of the beneficiaries of the wrongful death claim are on an equal degree of consanguinity, are adults, and have agreed how the net proceeds allocated to the wrongful death claim are to be distributed.

☐ Orders distribution of the net proceeds allocated to the wrongful death claim to the surviving spouse, children, parents and other next of kin, in the equitable shares shown below, fixed by the Court having due regard for the injury and loss to each beneficiary resulting from the death and for the age and condition of the beneficiaries.

Name	Residence Address	Relationship to Decedent	Birthdate of Minor	Amount

FORM 14.2 - ENTRY APPROVING SETTLEMENT AND DISTRIBUTION OF
WRONGFUL DEATH AND SURVIVAL CLAIMS   4/1/97

(Reverse of Form 14.2)

Orders that the share of:

☐ _____a minor(s) be
deposited in lieu of bond pursuant to R.C. 2111.05.

☐ _____a minor(s) be paid to
the guardian of the estate of such minor.

☐ _____a child(ren) be
deposited in a trust for the benefit of the child(ren) until twenty-five years of age.

Authorizes the fiduciary to execute a release which, upon payment, shall be a discharge of the claim.

Orders the fiduciary and the attorney to report the distribution of the proceeds within thirty days of the date of this Entry.

Further orders _____

_____

_____

_____

Approved:

_____   _____
Attorney for Fiduciary   Probate Judge

Attorney Registration No. _____   _____
                                             Date

PROBATE COURT OF _____ COUNTY, OHIO

ESTATE OF _____, DECEASED

CASE NO. _____

REPORT OF DISTRIBUTION OF
WRONGFUL DEATH AND SURVIVAL CLAIMS

Pursuant to Entry filed _____, _____, the proceeds have been paid as shown
below and on the accompanying vouchers.

Gross Proceeds	$ _____
Funeral and burial expenses	$ _____
Fiduciary fees to _____	$ _____
Reimbursement of case expenses to	
_____	$ _____
Attorney fees to _____	$ _____
Survival claim to the estate	$ _____
Total Deductions	$ _____
Net Proceeds	$ _____

Net proceeds to beneficiaries:

To: _____	$ _____
To: _____	$ _____
To: _____	$ _____
To: _____	$ _____
To: _____	$ _____
To: _____	$ _____
To: _____	$ _____
Total payments to beneficiaries	$ _____
	Balance -0-

☐ The fiduciary states that there are no other assets remaining in the estate.

☐ The fiduciary states that there are assets remaining in the estate.

_____   _____
Attorney for Fiduciary   Fiduciary

Attorney Registration No. _____

(Reverse of Form 14.3)

ENTRY

The above report of the distribution of the proceeds is hereby approved.

☐ There being no further assets to administer, the fiduciary and surety, if any, are discharged.

_____   _____
Date   PROBATE JUDGE

Guardianship — Forms 15.0 To 17.8

PROBATE COURT OF _____ COUNTY, OHIO

IN THE MATTER OF THE GUARDIANSHIP OF _____

CASE NO. _____

NEXT OF KIN OF PROPOSED WARD
[R.C. 2111.04]

(NOTE: Specify age and birthdate of each minor <u>under</u> 16 on the line containing the minor's name. List the name and
address of the minor's parent, guardian or custodian on the name and address lines following the minor's address.)

Service Waived		Relationship	Birthdate Of Minor
1. [ ]	Name _____	_____	_____
	Address _____	Zip	_____
2. [ ]	Name _____	_____	_____
	Address _____	Zip	_____
3. [ ]	Name _____	_____	_____
	Address _____	Zip	_____
4. [ ]	Name _____	_____	_____
	Address _____	Zip	_____
5. [ ]	Name _____	_____	_____
	Address _____	Zip	_____
6. [ ]	Name _____	_____	_____
	Address _____	Zip	_____
7. [ ]	Name _____	_____	_____
	Address _____	Zip	_____
8. [ ]	Name _____	_____	_____
	Address _____	Zip	_____
9. [ ]	Name _____	_____	_____
	Address _____	Zip	_____
10. [ ]	Name _____	_____	_____
	Address _____	Zip	_____

_____   _____
Date   Applicant

15.0 NEXT OF KIN OF PROPOSED WARD

PROBATE COURT OF _____ COUNTY, OHIO

IN THE MATTER OF THE GUARDIANSHIP OF

_____

CASE NO. _____

JUDGMENT ENTRY
SETTING HEARING ON APPLICATION FOR APPOINTMENT
OF GUARDIAN

This day _____ appeared in open Court, and filed an application for the

appointment of (limited) guardian of the (person and estate) of _____.

It is ordered that the _____ day of _____, 20____ at _____o'clock ___.M., be

and is hereby fixed as the time of hearing said application before this Court. It is further ordered that written

notice be served personally upon minors over fourteen years of age and in the manner as is provided by law

upon all others entitled to receive the same.

_____   _____
Date   Probate Judge

15.01 JUDGMENT ENTRY SETTING HEARING ON APPLICATION FOR APPOINTMENT OF GUARDIAN

PROBATE COURT OF _____ COUNTY, OHIO

IN THE MATTER OF THE GUARDIANSHIP OF _____

CASE NO. _____

WAIVER OF NOTICE AND CONSENT

We, the undersigned, do each of us hereby waive the issuing and service of notice, and voluntarily enter our appearance herein.

We do hereby consent to the appointment of _____.

_____   _____

_____   _____

_____   _____

_____   _____

15.1 WAIVER OF NOTICE AND CONSENT

PROBATE COURT OF _____ COUNTY, OHIO

IN THE MATTER OF THE GUARDIANSHIP OF _____

CASE NO. _____

FIDUCIARY'S ACCEPTANCE

GUARDIAN
[R.C. 2111.14]

I, the undersigned, hereby accept the duties which are required of me by law, and such additional duties as are ordered by the Court having jurisdiction.

AS GUARDIAN OF THE ESTATE, I WILL:

1. Make and file an inventory of the real and personal estate of the ward within 3 months after my appointment.
2. Deposit funds which come into my hands in a lawful depository located within this state.
3. Invest surplus funds in a lawful manner.
4. Make and file an account biennially, or as directed by the Court.
5. File a final account within 30 days after the guardianship is terminated.
6. Inventory any safe deposit box of the ward.
7. Preserve any and all Wills of the ward as directed by the Court.
8. Expend funds only upon written approval of the Court.
9. Make and file a guardian's report biennially, or as directed by the Court.

AS GUARDIAN OF THE PERSON, I WILL:

1. Protect and control the person of my ward, and make all decisions for the ward based upon the best interest of the ward.
2. Provide suitable maintenance for my ward when necessary.
3. Provide such maintenance and education for my ward as the amount of his estate justifies if the ward is a minor and has no father or mother, or has a father or mother who fails to maintain or educate him/her.
4. Make and file a guardian's report biennially, or as directed by the Court.
5. Obey all orders and judgments of the Court pertaining to the guardianship.
6. Obtain the written approval of the Court before executing a caretaker power of attorney authorized by R.C. 3109.52.

If I change my address or the ward's address, I shall immediately notify Probate Court in writing. I acknowledge that I am subject to removal as such fiduciary if I fail to perform such duties. I also acknowledge that I am subject to possible penalties for improper conversion of the property which I hold as such fiduciary.

_____   _____
Date   Fiduciary

PROBATE COURT OF _____ COUNTY, OHIO

IN THE MATTER OF THE GUARDIANSHIP OF _____

CASE NO. _____

GUARDIAN'S BOND
[R.C. 2109.04(A)(1)]

Amount of this bond $ _____

The undersigned principal, and sureties if any, are obligated to the State of Ohio in the above amount, for payment of which we bind ourselves and our successors, heirs, executors, and administrators, jointly and severally.

The principal has accepted in writing the duties of fiduciary in ward's estate, including those imposed by law and such additional duties as may be required by the Court.

This obligation is void if the principal performs such duties as required.

This obligation remains in force if the principal fails to perform such duties, or performs them tardily, negligently, or improperly, or if the principal misuses or misappropriates estate assets or improperly converts them to his own use or the use of another.

[Check if personal sureties are involved.] [ ] The sureties certify that each of them owns real estate in this county, with a reasonable net value as stated below.

_____	_____
Date	Principal
_____	_____
Surety	Surety
by _____	by _____
Attorney in Fact	Attorney in Fact
p	
_____	_____
Typed or Printed Name	Typed or Printed Name
_____	_____
Address	Address
_____	_____
Net value of real estate owned in this county	Net value of real estate owned in this county
$ _____	$ _____

15.3 GUARDIAN'S BOND

PROBATE COURT OF _____ COUNTY, OHIO

IN THE MATTER OF THE GUARDIANSHIP OF

_____

CASE NO. _____

LETTERS OF GUARDIANSHIP
[R.C. 2111.02]

_____ is appointed Guardian of

_____, an _____ Incompetent _____ Minor.

Guardian's powers are:

    All powers conferred by the laws of Ohio and rules of this Court over the ward's:

    _____ Person and Estate   _____ Person Only   _____ Estate Only

    Limited to   _____

                       _____

                       _____

                       _____

    Those guardianship powers, until revoked, are for an:

    _____ Indefinite time period

    _____ Definite time period to _____

The above named Guardian has the power conferred by law to do and perform all the duties of Guardian as described. **No expenditures shall be made without prior Court authorization.**

_____   _____

Date   PROBATE JUDGE

NOTICE TO FINANCIAL INSTITUTIONS

Funds being held in the name of the within-named Ward shall not be released to Guardian without a Court order directing release of a specific fund and amounts thereof.

CERTIFICATE OF APPOINTMENT AND INCUMBENCY

The above document is a true copy of the original kept by me as custodian of this Court. It constitutes the appointment and letters of authority of the named guardian, who is qualified and acting in such capacity.

                                    Probate Judge

                                    by_____

(Seal)   Deputy Clerk

                                    _____

                                    Date

15.4 LETTERS OF GUARDIANSHIP

PROBATE COURT OF _____ COUNTY, OHIO

IN THE MATTER OF THE GUARDIANSHIP OF _____

CASE NO. _____

GUARDIAN'S INVENTORY
[R.C. 2111.14(A)]

**of the real and personal estate of the ward with its
value and the value of the yearly rent of the real estate**

List any safe deposit box and date and location of any will. $

RECAPITULATION

Total value of Personal Estate . . . . $
_____

Total value of Real Estate . . . . $ _____

Yearly rent of Real Estate . . . . $ _____

Other Annual Income . . . . $ _____

Total . . . . $ _____

_____
Guardian

15.5 GUARDIAN'S INVENTORY

PROBATE COURT OF _____ COUNTY, OHIO

IN THE MATTER OF THE GUARDIANSHIP OF _____

CASE NO. _____

APPLICATION TO RELEASE FUNDS TO GUARDIAN

Now comes the guardian of the above named ward and makes application for authority to secure the release of the following funds of the ward.

The applicant further states that it is for the best interest of the ward that this authority be granted.

_____
Guardian

ORDER AUTHORIZING RELEASE OF FUNDS

This _____ day of _____, 20___, this cause came on to be heard upon the application of the guardian of the above named ward and the evidence, and the Court being fully advised in the premises, hereby authorized the release of the above named funds to the guardian.

_____
Probate Judge

15.6 APPLICATION TO RELEASE FUND TO GUARDIAN

PROBATE COURT OF _____ COUNTY, OHIO

IN THE MATTER OF THE GUARDIANSHIP OF _____

CASE NO. _____

APPLICATION FOR AUTHORITY TO EXPEND FUNDS

Now comes the undersigned, guardian of the estate of the above named _____ minor _____incompetent ward, and makes application for authority to expend funds for the best interest of the ward as follows: [State amount requested, nature of expenditure, and the frequency and duration of authority requested. Attach additional explanation, documentation, or estimates as needed.]

_____
Guardian

ORDER AUTHORIZING EXPENDITURE OF FUNDS

This _____day of _____, 20___, this cause came on to be heard upon the application of the guardian of the estate of the above named ward and the evidence, and the Court being fully advised in the premises, hereby authorizes the guardian to expend funds as set forth in the Application.

_____
Probate Judge

15.7 APPLICATION FOR AUTHORITY TO EXPEND FUNDS

PROBATE COURT OF _____ COUNTY, OHIO

IN THE MATTER OF THE GUARDIANSHIP OF _____

CASE NO. _____

GUARDIAN'S ACCOUNT
[R.C. 2109.30]

_____ ACCOUNT

FROM _____ TO _____

_____

20_**_**   (Balance from previous account)   Voucher $ $
                                                   No.

15.8 GUARDIAN'S ACCOUNT   3/96

(Reverse of Form 15.8)

RECAPITULATION

Total Receipts _____ $ _____

Total Disbursements _____ $ _____

Balance Remaining _____ $ _____

ITEMIZED STATEMENT OF ALL FUNDS, ASSETS AND INVESTMENTS

ITEM _____

$

_____   _____

Attorney   Guardian

Attorney Registration No. _____   _____

Typed or Printed Name

_____

Address of Guardian

_____

ENTRY SETTING HEARING

The Court sets _____ at _____ o'clock _____.M.,

as the date and time for hearing the above account.

_____   _____

Date   Probate Judge

PROBATE COURT OF _____ **COUNTY, OHIO**
_____ **, Judge**

GUARDIANSHIP OF _____

CASE NO. _____

OATH OF GUARDIAN
[R.C. 2111.02(C)]
[To be taken on Appointment of Guardian]

I, _____, Guardian of
_____, will faithfully and completely fulfill my duties as
Guardian, including the duty:

☐   To file, and continue to make diligent efforts to file, a true inventory in accordance with the Ohio Revised Code, and report all assets belonging to the estate of my ward.

☐   To file timely and accurate reports.

☐   To file timely and accurate accounts.

☐   To, at all times, protect my ward's interests and to make all decisions based on the best interest of my ward.

☐   To apply to the Court for authority to expend funds prior to so doing.

☐   To obey all orders and rules of this Court pertaining to guardianships.

_____
Guardian

The above oath was taken and signed in my presence on this _____ day of
_____, _____.

_____
Judge/Magistrate

FORM 15.9 - OATH OF GUARDIAN

Eff. Date March 1, 2008

PROBATE COURT OF _____ COUNTY, OHIO

IN THE MATTER OF THE GUARDIANSHIP OF _____

CASE NO. _____

APPLICATION FOR APPOINTMENT OF GUARDIAN
OF MINOR
[R.C. 2111.03(C)]

Applicant, a resident of _____ County, Ohio, hereby applies for the appointment of (himself) (herself) or some suitable person as guardian of the following minor and represents that the applicant is not an administrator, executor, or other fiduciary of an estate wherein the minor is interested

Name of Minor	Age	Date of Birth	Residence or Legal Settlement

Attached is a list of the next of kin of the minor. (Form 15.0)

A guardian is necessary because (R.C. 2111.06), _____

_____

TYPE OF GUARDIANSHIP APPLIED FOR IS

_____ non-limited _____ limited _____ person and estate _____ estate only _____ person only

IF THE APPLICATION IS FOR LIMITED GUARDIANSHIP,

The length (time period) of the guardianship requested is:

_____ indefinite _____ definite to _____, 20____

The limited powers requested are: _____

_____

_____

Applicant attaches affidavit pursuant to R.C. 3109.27.

Applicant represents that grounds exist for the Court to exercise its jurisdiction. (Applies to guardianship of person only. R.C. 3109.22).

The Applicant has (not) been charged with or convicted of a crime involving theft, physical violence, or sexual, alcohol or substance abuse except as follows (if applicable, state date and place of each charge or each conviction.)

_____

_____

16.0 APPLICATION FOR APPOINTMENT OF GUARDIAN OF MINOR

(Reverse of Form 16.0)

The whole estate of said minor is estimated as follows:

Personal Property .... $ _____

Real Estate .... $ _____

Annual Rents .... $ _____

Other annual income .... $ _____

Total $ _____

Applicant offers the attached bond in the amount of $ _____

     I hereby certify that all the information and statements contained in this application and attached exhibits are correct to the best of my knowledge and belief.

_____   _____
Attorney for Applicant   Applicant

_____   _____
Typed or Printed Name   Typed or Printed Name

_____   _____
Address   Address

_____   _____
City   State   Zip   City   State   Zip

_____   _____
Phone Number (include area code)   Phone Number (include area code)

_____
Supreme Court Registration Number

PROBATE COURT OF _____ COUNTY, OHIO

_____, Judge

GUARDIANSHIP OF _____

CASE NO. _____

AFFIDAVIT
[R.C. 3127.23]

State of Ohio, County of _____ s.s.

(To be filed only when guardianship of the person of a minor is sought.)

Affiant being first duly sworn, deposes and says:

1. That the child's present address, the places where the child has lived within the last five years, and the names and present addresses of the person(s) with whom the child has lived during that period are:

2. That affiant has (not) participated as a party, witness, or in any other capacity in any litigation concerning the custody of the child(ren) in this or any other state.

3. That affiant has (no) information of any custody proceeding concerning the child(ren) pending in a court of this or any other state, except _____
_____.

4. That affiant has (no) knowledge of any person not a party to the proceedings who has physical custody of the child(ren) or claims to have custody or visitation rights with respect to the child(ren).

If 2, 3, or 4 is answered in the affirmative, and the space afforded is insufficient for full explanation, please attach and incorporate herein any necessary information.

Affiant realizes that affiant has a continuing duty to inform the Court of any custody proceedings concerning the child(ren) in this or any other state of which affiant obtains information during the pendency of this proceeding.

_____

Sworn to before me and subscribed in my presence this _____ day of
_____, _____.

_____
Notary Public

FORM 16.1 - AFFIDAVIT

Eff. Date March 1, 2008

PROBATE COURT OF _____ COUNTY, OHIO

IN THE MATTER OF THE GUARDIANSHIP OF _____

CASE NO. _____

SELECTION OF GUARDIAN BY MINOR
OVER FOURTEEN YEARS OF AGE
(R.C. 2111.12)

The undersigned hereby selects _____

a resident of _____ County, Ohio, as Guardian of the (person and estate), and

respectfully asked the Court to appoint _____ Guardian.

Signature   Date of Birth

_____   _____

PROBATE COURT OF _____ COUNTY, OHIO

IN THE MATTER OF THE GUARDIANSHIP OF _____

CASE NO. _____

NOTICE OF HEARING FOR APPOINTMENT
OF GUARDIAN OF MINOR
To Minor Over Age 14
(R.C. 2111.04)

To_____

Address_____

You are hereby notified that an application was filed in the Court by _____

_____
for the appointment of a (limited) guardian for your (person and estate).

A minor over the age of fourteen years may select a guardian who shall be appointed if a suitable person. If such minor fails to select a suitable person, an appointment may be made without reference to his wishes.

The application will be for hearing before the Probate Court in _____

_____

on the _____ day of _____, 20____ at _____ o'clock ____.M.

If you are over age 14 and fail to appear in said Court on or before the time of hearing and select some suitable person to act as your guardian, the Court will appoint a guardian for you, if a guardian is found necessary.

Witness my signature and the seal of the Court,

this _____ day of _____, 20____

Probate Judge

By:_____
        Deputy Clerk

16.3 NOTICE OF HEARING FOR APPOINTMENT OF GUARDIAN OF MINOR
(TO MINOR OVER AGE 14)

(Reverse of Form 16.3)

RETURN

_____County, Ohio

_____, 20____

Received this writ on the _____ day of _____, 20___, at _____ o'clock

_____. M., and on the _____ day of _____, 20___, I served the same by

delivering a true copy thereof personally to

_____

_____   _____

_____   _____

_____   _____

_____Fees_____   _____

Service and return, 1st name $_____   _____

_____Additional names, at _____   _____

_____Miles traveled,   at _____

_____

                                                        _____
                                                        Sheriff
        Total $ _____
                                                        _____
_____   Deputy

AFFIDAVIT OF SERVICE

The State of Ohio, _____ County.

_____, being first duly sworn, says that on the

_____ day of _____, 20_____, he served the within notice by delivering a true copy

thereof personally to _____

_____

_____

Sworn to before me and signed in my presence, this _____ day of _____, 20 _____

                                                        _____

                                                        _____

PROBATE COURT OF _____ COUNTY, OHIO

IN THE MATTER OF THE GUARDIANSHIP OF _____

CASE NO. _____

NOTICE OF HEARING ON APPLICATION FOR APPOINTMENT
GUARDIAN OF MINOR
To Parent, Known Next of Kin and Person Having Custody
(R.C. 2111.04)

To _____

Address _____

To _____

Address _____

To _____

Address _____

You are hereby notified that _____ filed in this Court an

application for appointment of a (limited) guardian of the (person and estate) of the minor.

The application will be for hearing before the Probate Court in _____

_____

on the _____ day of _____, 20___ at _____o'clock ____.M.

Witness my signature and the seal of the Court,

this _____ day of _____, 20____

(Seal)   Probate Judge

By: _____
                          Deputy Clerk

16.4 NOTICE OF HEARING ON APPLICATION FOR APPOINTMENT
GUARDIAN OF MINOR
TO PARENT, KNOWN NEXT OF KIN AND PERSON HAVING CUSTODY

(Reverse of Form 16.4)

RETURN

_____ County, Ohio

_____ , 20____

Received this writ on the _____ day of _____ , 20_____ , at _____

o'clock _____.M., and on the _____ day of _____ , 20_____ , I served

the same by delivering a true copy thereof personally to _____

_____

_____

_____   _____

_____ Fees _____   _____

Service and return, 1st name $_____   _____

_____ Additional names,   at _____

_____ Miles traveled,   at _____

_____   _____
                                                         Sheriff
      Total, $_____   _____
_____   Deputy

AFFIDAVIT OF SERVICE

The State of Ohio, _____ County.

_____ , being first duly sworn, says that on the

_____ day of _____ , 20_____ , he served the within notice by delivering a true

copy thereof personally to _____

_____

_____

Sworn to before me and signed in my presence, this _____ day of _____ , 20_____

                                                         _____

                                                         _____

PROBATE COURT OF _____ COUNTY, OHIO

IN THE MATTER OF THE GUARDIANSHIP OF _____

CASE NO. _____

JUDGMENT ENTRY
APPOINTMENT OF GUARDIAN OF MINOR
[R.C 2111.02]

Upon hearing the application for appointment of guardian herein the Court finds that _____ is a minor and that a guardianship is necessary.

The Court further finds that all persons who were entitled to notice of the hearing thereon were given or waived notice thereof, that the minor is (not) over the age of fourteen years (and has (not) made selection of a guardian, whom the Court finds suitable), that the minor is a resident of this county or has legal settlement herein; that this Court has jurisdiction and that grounds exist for the Court to exercise that jurisdiction.

The Court therefore appoints _____, a suitable and competent person, (limited) guardian of the (person and estate) of_____ _____, minor, with the powers conferred as described, and limited to those powers contained in the Letters of Guardianship issued by this Court.

The Court approves the bond as filed.

The Court finds a record of the hearing was waived.

The Court orders Letters of Guardianship issued to _____ as provided by law.

_____   _____
Date   PROBATE JUDGE

PROBATE COURT OF _____ **COUNTY, OHIO**
_____ **, Judge**

GUARDIANSHIP OF _____

CASE NO. _____

APPLICATION FOR APPOINTMENT OF GUARDIAN
OF ALLEGED INCOMPETENT
[R.C. 2111.03]

Applicant represents to the Court that _____ aged _____ years,

resides or has a legal settlement at _____ in _____ County, Ohio

and that the prospective ward is incompetent by reason of (R.C. 2111.01(D)) _____

_____ .

A Statement of Expert Evaluation is attached. (Form 17.1)

A list of Next of Kin of Proposed Ward is also attached. (Form 15.0)

The whole estate of the prospective ward is estimated as follows:

　　　　　　　Personal Property...................$ _____

　　　　　　　Real Estate...........................$_____

　　　　　　　Annual Rents........................$ _____

　　　　　　　Other annual income...............$ _____

Applicant represents that the applicant is not an administrator, executor or other fiduciary of the estate wherein the alleged incompetent is interested.

Applicant offers the attached bond in the amount of $ _____.

Applicant further represents that a guardian of the alleged incompetent is necessary in order that ☐ the ward ☐ the ward's property may be taken proper care of and asks that a guardian be appointed.

TYPE OF GUARDIANSHIP APPLIED FOR IS **[check the applicable boxes]**

☐ non-limited 　 ☐ limited 　 ☐ person and estate 　 ☐ estate only 　 ☐ person only

If limited guardianship is applied for, the limited powers requested are

_____

_____ .

FORM 17.0 – APPLICATION FOR APPOINTMENT OF GUARDIAN
(AN ALLEGED INCOMPETENT)

Eff. Date March 1, 2008

CASE NO._____

The time period requested is ☐ indefinite ☐ definite to _____
_____.

Applicant's relationship to alleged incompetent is _____
_____.

The Applicant has (not) been charged with or convicted of a crime involving theft, physical violence, or sexual, alcohol or substance abuse except as follows (if applicable, state date and place of each charge or each conviction.)

_____
_____.

Attorney for Applicant	Applicant
Type or Print Name	Type or Print Name
Address	Age
City State Zip	Address
Phone number (include area code)	City State Zip
Attorney Registration Number	Phone number (include area code)

FORM 17.0 – APPLICATION FOR APPOINTMENT OF GUARDIAN
(AN ALLEGED INCOMPETENT)

Eff. Date March 1, 2008

PROBATE COURT OF _____ COUNTY, OHIO

IN THE MATTER OF THE GUARDIANSHIP OF _____

CASE NO. _____

STATEMENT OF EXPERT EVALUATION
[Sup. R. 66 & R.C. 2111.49]

Definition of Incompetent (R.C. 2111.01(D)): ""Incompetent" means any person who is so mentally impaired as a result of a mental or physical illness or disability, or mental retardation, or as a result of chronic substance abuse, that the person is incapable of taking proper care of the person's self or property or fails to provide for the person's family or other persons for whom the person is charged by law to provide, or any person confined to a correctional institution within this State."

The Statement of Evaluation does not declare the individual competent or incompetent, but is evidence to be considered by the Court. The fee for completing this evaluation **WILL NOT** be paid by the Probate Court. Each evaluator should secure payment from the Applicant/Guardian.

1. This Statement of Expert Evaluation is to be filed with or attached to:

    ☐ A. Guardianship Application: Completed by ☐ Licensed Physician or ☐ Licensed Clinical Psychologist prior to the filing and attached to the application.

    ☐ B. Guardian's Report: Completed by ☐ Licensed Physician ☐ Licensed Clinical Psychologist ☐ Licensed Independent Social Worker ☐ Licensed Professional Clinical Counselor or ☐ Mental Retardation Team.
    The evaluation or examination shall be completed within three months prior to the date of the Report. R.C. 2111.49

    ☐ C. Application for Emergency Guardian: ☐ of the person: a Licensed Physician shall complete the Supplement for Emergency Guardian, form 17.1A with specificity indicating the emergency, and why immediate action is required to prevent significant injury to the person. The Supplement shall be signed, dated, and attached as part of this completed Statement.

2. Statement completed by:

    Name & Title/Profession: _____

    Business Address: _____

    Business Telephone Number: _____

3. Date(s) of evaluation:

    _____

    Place(s) of evaluation: _____

    Amount of time spent on evaluation: _____

    Length of time the individual has been your patient:

    _____

17.1 STATEMENT OF EXPERT EVALUATION

CASE NO._____

4.   Is the individual presently under medication?   ☐ Yes   ☐ No   If yes, what is the medication, dosage, and purpose?

_____

Are there any signs of physical and/or mental impairments caused by the medications themselves? _____

_____

5.   Is the individual mentally impaired?   ☐ Yes   ☐ No   If yes, indicate the diagnosis below:

☐ Mental Retardation/Developmental Disabilities:

   ☐ Profound   ☐ Severe   ☐ Moderate   ☐ Mild

☐ Mental Illness: Type and Severity _____

_____

☐ Substance Abuse: Description _____

_____

☐ Dementia: Description _____

_____

☐ Other: Description _____

_____

Please provide additional comments and test scores if available. (Continue comments on page 4): _____

_____

6.   During the examination did you notice an impairment of the individual's:

   a) Orientation   ☐ Yes   ☐ No   ☐ Unknown
   b) Speech   ☐ Yes   ☐ No   ☐ Unknown
   c) Motor Behavior   ☐ Yes   ☐ No   ☐ Unknown
   d) Thought Process   ☐ Yes   ☐ No   ☐ Unknown
   e) Affect   ☐ Yes   ☐ No   ☐ Unknown
   f) Memory   ☐ Yes   ☐ No   ☐ Unknown
   g) Concentration and comprehension   ☐ Yes   ☐ No   ☐ Unknown
   h) Judgment   ☐ Yes   ☐ No   ☐ Unknown

7.   Please describe any impairments identified in question six. (Continue comments on page 4).

_____

CASE NO._____

8.   Is the individual physically impaired?   ☐ Yes   ☐ No   If yes: Description

_____

9.   Are there any special characteristics of the individual which should be considered in evaluating the individual for
     guardianship: ☐ Yes   ☐ No   If yes: Explain

_____

_____

10. Are there any indication of abuse, neglect or exploitation of the individual?   ☐ Yes   ☐ No
     If yes: Explain _____

     _____

11. Do you believe the individual is capable of caring for the individual's activities of daily living or making
     decisions concerning medical treatments, living arrangements and diet?   ☐ Yes   ☐ No
     If no: Explain _____

12   Do you believe this individual is capable of managing the individual's finances and property?
     ☐ Yes   ☐ No   If no: Explain

     _____

13. Prognosis:
     A.   Is the condition stabilized?   ☐ Yes   ☐ No
     B.   Is the condition reversible: ☐ Yes   ☐ No

14. In my opinion a guardianship should be:
     ☐ Established/Continued
     ☐ Denied/Terminated

I certify that I have evaluated the individual on _____ , 20
_____ .

Date: _____   _____
                                                 Signature of Evaluator

---

GUARDIAN'S REPORT ADDENDUM
(Not to be used with initial Application)

     It is my opinion, based upon a reasonable degree of medical or psychological certainty, that the mental capacity of
this ward will not improve.

Date _____   _____
                                                 Signature – Licensed Physician/Clinical Psychologist

CASE NO._____

ADDITIONAL COMMENTS

_____
_____
_____
_____
_____
_____
_____
_____
_____
_____
_____
_____
_____
_____
_____

Date _____   _____
                                     Signature – Licensed Physician/Clinical Psychologist

PROBATE COURT OF _____ COUNTY, OHIO

IN THE MATER OF THE GUARDIANSHIP OF_____

CASE NO. _____

SUPPLEMENT FOR EMERGENCY GUARDIAN OF PERSON
[R.C. 2111.49]

This Supplement must be completed when there is a request for Emergency Guardianship. The following questions must be answered with specificity and item 1.C, page 1 of the Statement of Expert Evaluation, Form 17.1 must be checked.

A.   Does the individual have a durable health care power of attorney?   _____   If yes, why is it not being honored?

_____

_____

B.   Exact nature of emergency: _____

_____

_____

C.   Length of time emergency has existed, and why? _____

_____

D.   Specific action required to prevent significant injury to the person: _____

_____

_____

E.   Ability of the alleged Incompetent to receive notice and give consent: _____

_____

F.   Medical prognosis in detail if immediate action, within 24 hours, is not taken: _____

_____

_____

G.   Additional statements regarding condition, family, support services, etc: _____

_____

_____

Note: Any above answers may be supplemented by attachments.

_____   _____
Date and Time of Evaluation   Licensed Physician

_____
Date of Report
                       17.1A - SUPPLEMENT FOR EMERGENCY GUARDIAN OF PERSON

PROBATE COURT OF _____ COUNTY, OHIO

IN THE MATTER OF THE GUARDIANSHIP OF _____

CASE NO. _____

NOTICE TO PROSPECTIVE WARD OF APPLICATION AND HEARING

To _____

Address _____

An application for appointment of _____ as
(limited) guardian for your (person and estate) has been filed with the Probate Court.

A hearing on that application will be held on _____ at _____ o'clock
____.M. at the Probate Court, _____. At that hearing,
Applicant must prove by clear and convincing evidence that, because of mental impairment, you are unable to handle
your own affairs.

1. You have the right to be present at the hearing to contest the application, and to be
    represented by an attorney of your choice;

2. The right to have a friend or family member of your choice present at the hearing;

3. The right to have evidence of an independent expert evaluation introduced at the
    hearing;

4. If you are indigent, upon your request, an attorney and an independent expert
    evaluator will be appointed at court expense;

5. If you are indigent, and you appeal the guardianship decision, you have the right to
    have an attorney appointed and necessary transcripts prepared at court expense.

Witness my signature and the seal of the Court,

this _____ day of _____, 20___

(Seal)   Probate Judge

By: _____
                Deputy Clerk

17.3 NOTICE TO PROSPECTIVE WARD OF APPLICATION AND HEARING

(Reverse of Form 17.3)

RETURN

_____ County, Ohio

_____ , 20____

Received this notice on the _____ day of _____ , 20_____, and on the

_____ day of _____ , 20_____, I served the same by delivering a true

copy thereof personally to _____ .

I communicated with him/her in a language or method of communication understandable to the alleged incompetent.

_____
Investigator

PROBATE COURT OF _____ COUNTY, OHIO

IN THE MATTER OF THE GUARDIANSHIP OF _____

CASE NO. _____

NOTICE OF HEARING FOR APPOINTMENT
OF GUARDIAN OF ALLEGED INCOMPETENT PERSON
To Spouse and Known Next of Kin
[R.C. 2111.04]

To _____

Address _____

To _____

Address _____

To _____

Address _____

next of kin of _____ known to reside in this state.

You are hereby notified that on the _____ day of _____, 20____,

_____ filed in the Court an application for the appointment

of a (limited) guardian of the (person and estate) of _____, an alleged

incompetent.

The application will be for hearing before the Probate Court in _____

_____, on the _____ day of _____, 20_____, at

_____ o'clock ____.M.

Witness my signature and the seal of the Court,

this _____ day of _____, 20___

(Seal)

_____
Probate Judge

By: _____
Deputy Clerk

17.4 NOTICE OF HEARING FOR APPOINTMENT OF GUARDIAN OF ALLEGED INCOMPETENT PERSON

[Reverse of Form 17.4]

RETURN

_____ County, Ohio

_____, 20____

Received this writ on the _____ day of _____, 20____, at _____ o'clock ____.M.
and on the _____ day of _____, 20____, I served the same by (insert, "delivering",
"leaving", or "sending") _____ a true copy thereof (insert, "personally to", "at the
usual place of residence", or "by certified mail to the last known address of") _____

_____

_____ FEES _____	_____
	_____
Service and return, 1st name, $ _____	_____
_____ Additional names at _____	_____
_____ Miles traveled at _____	_____
_____	_____
	Sheriff
Total $ _____	_____
_____	Deputy

AFFIDAVIT OF SERVICE

The State of Ohio, _____, County.

_____, being first duly sworn, says that on the
_____ day of _____, 20____, he served the within notice by delivering a true
copy thereof personally to _____

_____

_____

Sworn to before me and signed in my presence, this _____ day of _____, 20____

_____

_____

PROBATE COURT OF _____ COUNTY, OHIO

IN THE MATTER OF THE GUARDIANSHIP OF _____

CASE NO. _____

JUDGMENT ENTRY

APPOINTMENT OF GUARDIAN FOR INCOMPETENT PERSON
[R.C 2111.02]

Upon hearing the application for appointment of guardian herein the Court finds that
_____ is incompetent by reason of
_____ and therefore
is incapable of taking proper care of _____ self and _____ property, and that a guardianship is necessary.

The Court further finds that all persons who were entitled to notice of the hearing thereon were given or waived notice thereof; that the incompetent is a resident of this county or has legal settlement herein; and that this Court has jurisdiction.

It is therefore ordered that a (limited) guardian of the (person and estate) be appointed.

The Court therefore appoints _____ , a suitable and competent person, (limited) guardian of the (person and estate) of _____
_____ , incompetent, with the powers conferred as described, and limited to those powers contained in the Letters of Guardianship issued by this Court. This appointment is in compliance with R.C. 2111.09.

The Court approves the bond as filed.

The Court finds a record of the hearing was waived.

The Court orders Letters of Guardianship issue to _____
as provided by law.

_____   _____
Date   PROBATE JUDGE

        (Seal)

17.5 JUDGMENT ENTRY
APPOINTMENT OF GUARDIAN FOR INCOMPETENT PERSON

PROBATE COURT OF _____ COUNTY, OHIO

IN THE MATTER OF THE GUARDIANSHIP OF _____

CASE NO. _____

GUARDIAN'S REPORT
[R.C. 2111.49]

NOTE: If allotted space is inadequate to respond, write "See Exhibit" in the space and add appropriate exhibit letter sequence, then attach exhibit containing information requested for that space.

1.   This is the (circle one) 1st, 2nd, 3rd, 4th, 5th, 6th, or _____, Guardian's Report.

2.   Ward's present address: _____

City _____ State _____

Zip _____ Telephone (_____)_____

3.   Ward's living arrangements at the above address are best described as:

☐   a.   His or her own apartment or home (includes assisted living facilities.)

☐   b.   Private home or apartment of:

☐   (1) the ward's guardian

☐   (2) a relative of the ward, whose name is _____

and relationship is _____

☐   (3) a non-relative whose name is _____

☐   c.   A foster, group or boarding home.

☐   d.   A nursing home.

☐   e.   A medical facility or state institution.

☐   f.   Other (describe) _____

_____

g.   If **c, d, e** or **f** is checked, complete the following:

(1)   The name of the home, facility or institution _____

(2)   The name of an individual at the home, facility or institution who has knowledge and is authorized

to give information to the court about the ward.

Name _____

Telephone Number (_____)_____

4.   The ward will be at the address given in Item 2:

☐   a. Indefinitely.   ☐   b. Temporarily. The new address and telephone number is:

☐   (1)   Unknown. I will provide this information when known.

☐   (2) _____

City _____ State _____

Zip _____ Telephone (_____)_____

17.7 GUARDIAN'S REPORT

[Reverse of Form 17.7]

5.   Guardian's contact with the ward.

     a.   Approximate number of times the guardian had contact with the ward during the period covered by this
          report: _____

     b.   The nature of those contacts (phone, personal, or other): _____
          _____

     c.   Date the ward was last seen by the guardian: _____

6.   Have you observed any **major** change in the ward's physical or mental condition during the period covered
     by this report?   ☐ Yes ☐ No

     If "yes" is checked, briefly describe the changes. _____
     _____
     _____

7.   The care giver to the ward is   ☐ Adequate   ☐ Not Adequate

     If "Not Adequate" is checked, explain. _____
     _____
     _____

8.   The guardianship should be   ☐ Continued   ☐ Not Continued
     If "Not Continued" is checked, explain. _____ _____
     _____
     _____

9.   During the period covered by this report, the ward ☐ has ☐ has not been seen by a physician. If the ward has been
     seen, the last date was _____ and for the purpose of
     _____

Attached is a statement by a licensed physician, a licensed clinical psychologist, a licensed social worker, or a mental retardation
team, that has evaluated or examined the ward within three months prior to the date of this report regarding the need for continuing
the guardianship. [R.C. 2111.49(A)(1)(I)](Form 17.1)

If an attorney has been consulted on this report: Date _____

_____   _____
Attorney's Signature   Guardian's Signature

_____   _____
(Type or Print Attorney's Name)   (Type or Print Guardian's Name)

_____   _____
(Street)   (Street)

_____   _____
(City, State, Zip Code)   (City, State, Zip Code)

(_____)_____ _____   (_____)_____
Telephone Number   Supreme Court Registration No.   Telephone Number

(Knowingly giving false information on a Probate document is a criminal offense)
[R.C. 2921.13(A)(11)]

PROBATE COURT OF_____COUNTY, OHIO
_____, JUDGE

GUARDIANSHIP OF:_____

CASE NO: _____

COURT INVESTIGATOR'S REPORT ON PROPOSED GUARDIANSHIP
[R.C. 2111.041]
GENERAL INFORMATION
[To be compiled by Probate Court Investigator]

Individual's age_____   Relationship to applicant_____

Individual's residence_____

Grounds for application (R.C.2111.01 (D)):

The individual is alleged to be:

☐ mentally impaired as a result of a mental illness or disability.

☐ mentally impaired as a result of a physical illness or disability.

☐ mentally impaired as a result of mental retardation.

☐ mentally impaired as a result of chronic substance abuse.

☐ any person confined to a correctional institution within this state.

so that

☐ the individual is incapable of taking proper care of the individual's self.

☐ the individual is incapable of taking proper care of the individual's property.

☐ the individual fails to provide for the individual's family or other individual for whom the person is charged by law to provide.

Documentation submitted and date of evaluation_____

Referral Source:_____

17.8 - COURT INVESTIGATOR'S REPORT ON PROPOSED GUARDIANSHIP

Eff. Date October 1, 2007

CASE NO. _____

INVESTIGATOR'S REPORT

I. **Service of Notice**
☐   Made at Individual's home
☐   Made in Hospital, Nursing Facility, or Community-Based Care Facility:

Name of Facility_____

Address of Facility_____

Administrator or representative served_____

☐Other_____

Date of Service of Notice:_____

Others present during the contact (if yes, list name and relationship)_____

_____

A. Individual's understanding of the concept of guardianship:

☐Good   ☐Fair   ☐Poor   ☐Unable to determine.
Explain: _____

_____.

B. Individual's attitude to the concept of guardianship:

☐Consenting   ☐Opposed   ☐Unable to Determine.
Explain: _____

_____.

C. Specific requests of the individual concerning enumerated rights: _____

_____.

II. Mental and Physical Conditions of Individual

A. Individual's reported mental and physical diagnosis: _____

Individual's reported medications:_____

Reported by whom: _____

CASE NO._____

B. Mental Status Observations: During interview were impairments noted in the Individual's:

	Yes	No	Unable to Determine
1. Orientation (Person, Place and Time)	☐	☐	☐
2. Speech	☐	☐	☐
3. Thought Process	☐	☐	☐
4. Affect	☐	☐	☐
5. Memory	☐	☐	☐
6. Concentration & Comprehension	☐	☐	☐
7. Judgment	☐	☐	☐

Explain further if necessary:_____
_____.

C. Describe the Physical Condition of Individual

1. Isolation_____
2. Eating Habits_____
3. Significant Weight Loss or Gain_____
4. Sleep Habits_____
5. Motor Behavior _____
Explain further if necessary:_____
_____

D. Describe the Environmental or Living Condition of the Individual:

1. Housing & Sanitation_____
2. Risk of Accidents_____
3. Physical Barriers_____
4. Resource Availability_____
Explain further if necessary:_____
_____.

III. Functional Capacities

Activities and Instrumental Activities of Daily Living

	Capable	Incapable	Unable to Determine
1. Eating	☐	☐	☐
2. Dressing	☐	☐	☐
3. Transfer from bed	☐	☐	☐
4. Toileting	☐	☐	☐
5. Bathing	☐	☐	☐

3   17.8 COURT INVESTIGATOR'S REPORT ON PROPOSED GUARDIANSHIP

CASE NO._____

6. Handling personal finances   ☐   ☐   ☐
7. Shopping   ☐   ☐   ☐
8. Driving   ☐   ☐   ☐
9. Meal preparation   ☐   ☐   ☐
10. Doing housework   ☐   ☐   ☐
11. Using telephone   ☐   ☐   ☐
12. Taking medications   ☐   ☐   ☐

Explain further if necessary:

_____

_____.

IV.   Additional Items Affecting Guardianship Plan Development

A.   Are there any indications or allegations of substance abuse by the individual or significant others that could impact the guardianship issue? Yes ☐   No ☐   Explain and recommend actions needed:

_____

_____

_____.

B. Are there any special characteristics of the individual (including aggressive, violent, or sexual behaviors, or other vulnerabilities) that pose a risk to self or others, which should be considered as guardianship decisions on living arrangements and supervision are made? Yes☐ No☐
Explain the characteristics and make recommendations: _____

_____

_____.

C.   Are there any allegations or indications of abuse, neglect, or exploitation of the individual?
Yes ☐ No ☐
Explain and recommend needed actions:_____

_____

_____.

D.   Is there a need for additional medical, psychiatric or psychological testing? Yes☐   No☐
     If yes, give specific recommendations:

_____

_____.

CASE NO._____

E. Are there inconsistencies between the Expert Evaluation and the Court Investigator's findings that need further review by the Court? Yes ☐   No ☐   If yes, identify the inconsistencies and make a recommendation(s) to the Court:_____

_____

_____.

F. Are there unresolved issues/conflicts/ differences among the parties? Yes☐ No☐
If yes, would mediation be of assistance? Yes☐ No☐
Explain:_____

_____.

G. Is there a power of attorney for financial affairs? Yes☐   No☐   Unknown☐   If yes, where is it located?

_____.

Who is the attorney-in-fact?_____

H. Is there a last will and testament? Yes☐   No☐   Unknown☐
If yes, where is it located? _____.

I. Is there a durable power of attorney for health care/living will?
Yes☐   No☐   Unknown☐
If yes, where is it located? _____.

Give name and address of attorney-in-fact:_____

J. Is there an advance directive for mental health care? Yes☐   No☐   Unknown☐   If yes, where is it located? _____.

Give name and address of attorney-in-fact:_____

K. Is the individual a veteran? Yes ☐   No ☐

CASE NO._____

V. RECOMMENDATIONS: Given the above information and Expert Evaluation(s):

A. IS A GUARDIANSHIP NECESSARY?
☐ Yes

      ☐ Person Only
      ☐ Estate Only
      ☐ Person and Estate
      ☐ Limited   List Duties_____

_____

_____

☐ No Explain and recommend a less restrictive alternative:_____

_____

_____

Are any of the mental, physical, or environmental conditions reversible?
Yes☐   No☐ Unknown☐
If yes, explain and recommend a date for the Court to review the guardianship._____

_____

B. NECESSITY FOR THE APPOINTMENT OF:

Attorney ☐   Independent Expert Evaluator ☐

Are there special urgency needs? Explain:_____

_____

_____

Remarks:

_____

_____

_____

_____

_____

_____

6   **17.8 COURT INVESTIGATOR'S REPORT ON PROPOSED GUARDIANSHIP**

Eff. Date October 1, 2007

CASE NO._____

I certify that I have served notice to the alleged incompetent as required by statute and I have communicated to the individual in a language and method best understandable by the individual the individual's right to be present at the hearing, the right to contest any application for the appointment of a guardian for his or her person, estate, or both, and the right to be represented by counsel.

_____   _____
Date   Investigator

Adoption — Forms 18.0 To 19.1

PROBATE COURT OF _____ **COUNTY, OHIO**

_____ **, JUDGE**

ADOPTION OF _____

(Name after adoption)

CASE NO. _____

PETITION FOR ADOPTION OF MINOR
[R.C. 3107.05]

The undersigned petitions to adopt _____ ,

a minor, and to change the name of the minor to _____ .

The petitioner states the following: **PETITIONER**

Full Name: _____ Age _____

Full Name: _____ Age _____

Place of Residence: _____

Street Address

City or Village or Township if unincorporated area	County

Post Office	State	Zip Code	Duration of residence

Marital Status: _____ Date and Place of Marriage: _____

Relationship   of   Minor   to   Petitioner:

_____

The petitioner has facilities and resources suitable to provide for the nurture and care of the minor and it is the desire of the petitioner to establish the relationship of parent and child with the minor.

MINOR TO BE ADOPTED

Birth Name: _____ Date of Birth: _____

Place of Birth: _____ Property and Value: _____

☐   The minor is living in the home of the petitioner, and was placed therein for adoption on the _____
day of _____ , 20_____ by _____ .

☐   The minor is not living in the home of the petitioner, and resides at_____
_____ .

☐   The minor will be an adopted person as defined in R.C. 3107.39;

☐   The minor will be an adopted person as defined in R.C. 3107.45;

A certified copy of the birth certificate of the minor is filed with this petition or is not available due to the following:
_____
_____ .

A Preliminary Estimate Accounting (Form 18.9), if required, is filed with this petition.

FORM 18.0 – PETITION FOR ADOPTION OF MINOR

Eff. Date: January 1, 2010

CASE NO._____

☐   The minor is in the permanent custody of_____
whose address is _____ .

☐   The guardian ad litem during the permanent custody proceedings was

_____
whose address is _____ .

☐   The attorney representing the minor during the permanent custody proceedings was

_____
whose address is _____ .

PERSONS OR AGENCIES WHOSE CONSENT TO THE ADOPTION IS REQUIRED

☐   Name: _____ Relationship:_____ Age, if minor _____

☐ Consent
     Address: _____
filed

☐   Name: _____ Relationship: _____ Age, if minor _____

     Address :_____ ☐ Consent filed

☐   _____ , the agency has permanent

custody of the minor filed under, _____ . _____ ☐ Consent filed
                                  Court - County   Case No.

PERSONS WHOSE CONSENT TO THE ADOPTION IS NOT REQUIRED

☐   No person has timely registered pursuant to R.C. 3107.062 as a putative father of the minor born on
or after January 1, 1997. Attached is Ohio Department of Human Services Form 1697.

A   The consent of _____
                    Name   Address   Relationship

B   The consent of _____
                    Name   Address   Relationship
     is/are not required because:

A   B
☐   ☐   The parent has failed without justifiable cause to provide more than de minimis contact with the
minor for a period of at least one year immediately preceding the filing of the adoption petition or the
placement of the minor in the home of the petitioner.
☐   ☐   The parent has failed without justifiable cause to provide for the maintenance and support of the
minor as required by law or judicial decree for a period of at least one year immediately preceding the filing of
the adoption petition or the placement of the minor in the home of the petitioner..
☐   ☐   State other grounds under R.C. 3107.07 (includes putative father of the minor born before January 1,
1997.)

_____

_____

FORM 18.0 – PETITION FOR ADOPTION OF MINOR

Eff. Date: January 1, 2010

CASE NO._____

Attorney for Petitioner

Typed or Printed Name

Street Address

City   State   Zip Code

Phone Number (include area code)

Attorney Registration No. _____

Petitioner

Typed or Printed Name

Petitioner

Typed or Printed Name

Street Address

City   State   Zip Code

Phone Number (include area code)

FORM 18.0 – PETITION FOR ADOPTION OF MINOR

Eff. Date: January 1, 2010

PROBATE COURT OF _____ **COUNTY, OHIO**

IN THE MATTER OF THE ADOPTION OF _____
                                                                                    (Name after adoption)
CASE NO. _____

JUDGMENT ENTRY
SETTING HEARING AND ORDERING NOTICE
[R.C. 3107.11]

On the _____ day of _____, 20 _____ , _____

_____

filed a petition to adopt _____

and to change the name of the minor to _____

It is ordered that the Petition For Adoption will be heard on the _____ day of _____ ,

20 _____ , at _____ o'clock _____. M. , and that notice be given as required by law.

                                                    _____
                                                                Probate Judge

PROBATE COURT OF _____ COUNTY, OHIO
_____ , JUDGE

ADOPTION OF _____
(Name after adoption)

CASE NO. _____

NOTICE OF HEARING ON PETITION FOR ADOPTION
Notice must be served not less than 20 days before the date of the hearing
[R.C. 3107.11]

To: _____
(Give Names and Addresses)

You are hereby notified that on the _____ day of _____ , 20____, _____
_____ , filed in this Court a Petition for Adoption of _____ , a
minor, whose date of birth is _____ , and for change of the name of the minor
to_____ . This Court, located at _____
_____ will hear the petition on the _____ day of _____ ,
20____, at _____ o'clock ____.M.

It is alleged in the petition, pursuant to R.C. 3107.07, that the consent of _____
is not required due to the following: (Name)

That person is a parent who has failed without justifiable cause to provide more than de minimis contact with the minor for a period of at least one year immediately preceding the filing of the adoption petition or the placement of the minor in the home of the petitioner.

That person is a parent who has failed without justifiable cause to provide for the maintenance and support of the minor as required by law or judicial decree for a period of at least one year immediately preceding the filing of the adoption petition or the placement of the minor in the home of the petitioner.

State other grounds under R.C. 3107.07 (includes putative father of the minor born prior to January 1, 1997).
_____

"A FINAL DECREE OF ADOPTION, IF GRANTED, WILL RELIEVE YOU OF ALL PARENTAL RIGHTS AND RESPONSIBILITIES, INCLUDING THE RIGHT TO CONTACT THE MINOR, AND, EXCEPT WITH RESPECT TO A SPOUSE OF THE ADOPTION PETITIONER AND RELATIVES OF THAT SPOUSE, TERMINATE ALL LEGAL RELATIONSHIPS BETWEEN THE MINOR AND YOU AND THE MINOR'S OTHER RELATIVES, SO THAT THE MINOR THEREAFTER IS A STRANGER TO YOU AND THE MINOR'S FORMER RELATIVES FOR ALL PURPOSES. IF YOU WISH TO CONTEST THE ADOPTION, YOU MUST FILE AN OBJECTION TO THE PETITION WITHIN FOURTEEN DAYS AFTER PROOF OF SERVICE OF NOTICE OF THE FILING OF THE PETITION AND OF THE TIME AND PLACE OF HEARING IS GIVEN TO YOU. IF YOU WISH TO CONTEST THE ADOPTION, YOU MUST ALSO APPEAR AT THE HEARING. A FINAL DECREE OF ADOPTION MAY BE ENTERED IF YOU FAIL TO FILE AN OBJECTION TO THE ADOPTION PETITION OR APPEAR AT THE HEARING."

_____ ,Probate Judge

By:_____
Deputy Clerk

18.2 - NOTICE OF HEARING ON PETITION FOR ADOPTION

Eff. Date: January 1, 2010

CASE NO. _____

The State of Ohio, _____ Probate Court

    I hereby certify that I caused a copy of the within notice to be mailed, by certified mail, to the last known address of
_____

At _____

_____

At _____

_____

                                      _____ ,Probate Judge

                         By: _____
                                         Deputy Clerk

RETURN

                                  _____ , County, Ohio

                                  _____ , 20 _____

    Received this writ on the _____ day of _____ , 20___ , at _____ o'clock ____ . M.,
and on the _____ day of _____ , 20___ , I served the same by delivering a true copy thereof
personally to _____

_____

FEES		
Service and return, 1st name,	$ _____	
____ Additional names, at	$ _____	
____ Miles traveled. at	$ _____	
Total	$ _____	

Sheriff _____

Deputy Sheriff _____

Name _____

Title _____

18.2 - NOTICE OF HEARING ON PETITION FOR ADOPTION

Eff. Date: January 1, 2010

PROBATE COURT OF _____ COUNTY, OHIO

IN THE MATTER OF THE ADOPTION OF _____
(Name after adoption)

CASE NO. _____

CONSENT TO ADOPTION
[R.C. 3107.06, 3107.08 & 3107.081]

The undersigned _____

[check one of the following seven capacities by which your consent is given]

Mother
Father
Putative father who has registered under R.C. 3107.062 (for a minor born on or after January 1, 1997)
Putative father (for a minor born before January 1, 1997)
Agency having permanent custody
Minor, who is more than twelve years of age (this consent must be executed in the presence of the Court)
Other _____

hereby waives notice of the hearing on the Petition For Adoption to be filed in the court, and consents to the

adoption of _____
(Name before adoption)

as proposed in the petition.

The undersigned further states that this consent is voluntarily executed irrespective of disclosure of the name or other

identification of the prospective adopting parents.

_____

Sworn to before me and signed in my presence this _____ day of _____, 20____

_____
Person authorized pursuant to R.C. Chapter 3107
to take this acknowledgement

_____
Title

18.3 - CONSENT TO ADOPTION   10/1/97

PROBATE COURT OF _____ **COUNTY, OHIO**
_____ **, JUDGE**

ADOPTION OF _____
(Name after adoption)

CASE NO. _____

JUDGMENT ENTRY FINDING CONSENT NOT REQUIRED
[R.C. 3107.07]

The Court finds all parties properly before the Court by waiver of notice or by proper service and after hearing the

testimony of witnesses, and the evidence, finds that the consent of _____

_____ is not required because;

That person is a parent who has failed without justifiable cause to provide more than de minimis contact with the minor for a period of at least one year immediately preceding the filing of the adoption petition or the placement of the minor in the home of the petitioner.

That person is a parent who has failed without justifiable cause to provide for the maintenance and support of the minor as required by law or judicial decree for a period of at least one year immediately preceding the filing of the adoption petition or the placement of the minor in the home of the petitioner.

State other grounds under R.C. 3107.07 (includes putative father of the minor born prior to January 1, 1997).

_____

_____

_____

It is ordered that the consent of the above-named person is not required.

_____ , Probate Judge

FORM 18.4 - JUDGMENT ENTRY FINDING CONSENT NOT REQUIRED

Eff. Date: January 1, 2010

PROBATE COURT OF _____ COUNTY, OHIO

IN THE MATTER OF THE ADOPTION OF _____
                                              (Name after adoption)
CASE NO. _____

INTERLOCUTORY ORDER OF ADOPTION
[R.C. 3107.14]

This day this matter came on to be heard on the petition of _____

_____ for the adoption and change of name of the minor being adopted.

The Court finds that notice has been given to all parties in interest; that all consents have been filed herein or have been found not required; that the allegations in the petition are true; that the minor has been lawfully placed in the home of the petitioner; that the minor has resided for a period of _____ in the home of the petitioner in accordance with the laws relating to the placement of children; that the best interests of the minor will be promoted by the adoption and that the accountings, as required, have been filed, reviewed and approved.

It is therefore ordered that an Interlocutory Order of Adoption is granted, and this cause is continued until the minor has lived in the home of the petitioner for at least six months.

It is further ordered that the assessor shall make and file a further assessment on or before

_____

_____   _____
Date   Probate Judge

18.5 - INTERLOCUTORY ORDER OF ADOPTION   10/1/97

PROBATE COURT OF _____ **COUNTY, OHIO**

IN THE MATTER OF THE ADOPTION OF _____
                                                              (Name after adoption)

CASE NO. _____

FINAL DECREE OF ADOPTION
(After Interlocutory Order)
[R.C. 3107.14]

The Court finds that the minor has now lived in the home of the petitioner, _____

_____ for at least six

months; that a further report of the assessor has been filed and is approved; that the adoption is in the best interest of

the minor being adopted; that the accountings, as required, have been filed, reviewed and approved; and that the

minor is an adopted person as defined in Section   3107.39 or   3107.45 of the Revised Code.

It is therefore ordered that the Petition for Adoption is granted, and that the name of the minor is changed to

_____

_____   _____
Date   Probate Judge

18.6 - FINAL DECREE OF ADOPTION
(After Interlocutory Order)   10/1/97

PROBATE COURT OF _____ **COUNTY, OHIO**

N THE MATTER OF THE ADOPTION OF _____

(Name after adoption)

CASE NO. _____

FINAL DECREE OF ADOPTION
(Without Interlocutory Order)
[R.C. 3107.13, 3107.14 & 3107.19]

This day this matter came on to be heard on the petition of _____

_____ for the adoption and change of name of the minor

being adopted.

The Court finds that notice has been given to all parties; that all consents have been filed or have been found

not required; that the allegations in the petition are true; that the minor has been lawfully placed in the home of the

petitioner; that the minor has lived in the home of the petitioner for six months as required by law; that a report of the

assessor has been filed and is approved; that the adoption is in the best interest of the minor being adopted; that the

accountings, as required, have been filed, reviewed and approved, and that the minor is an adopted person as defined

in Section   3107.39 or   3107.45 of the Revised Code.

It is therefore ordered that the Petition for Adoption is granted, and that the name of the minor is changed to

_____

_____   _____
Date   Probate Judge

18.7 - FINAL DECREE OF ADOPTION
(Without Interlocutory Order)   10/1/97

PROBATE COURT OF _____ **COUNTY, OHIO**

IN THE MATTER OF THE ADOPTION OF _____
                                              (Name after adoption)

CASE NO. _____

ADOPTION CERTIFICATE FOR PARENTS

This is to certify, that in an action pending in this Court, on a petition filed by _____

_____

to adopt _____

a minor, satisfactory evidence was submitted to prove, and the Court found, that the minor was born on the

_____ day of _____, 20_____, at _____

and that all necessary proceedings relative to an adoption were complied with; and the Court on the _____ day

of _____, 20_____, decreed that the minor is legally adopted by

_____

and the minor's name is changed to _____ in the

records of the Court.

WITNESS my signature and seal of said Court,

this _____ day of _____, 199_____

_____
Probate Judge

By: _____
            Deputy Clerk

18.8 - ADOPTION CERTIFICATE FOR PARENTS   10/1/97

PROBATE COURT OF _____ COUNTY, OHIO

IN THE MATTER OF THE ADOPTION OF _____

(Name after adoption)

CASE NO. _____

PETITIONER'S ACCOUNT
(R.C. 3107.10)

PRELIMINARY ESTIMATE ACCOUNTING
(To be filed not later than date petition filed)

FINAL ACCOUNTING
(To be filed not later than 10 days
prior to date of final hearing)

This accounting specifies all disbursements of anything of value the petitioner, a person on the petitioner's behalf, and the agency or attorney made and has agreed to make in connection with the minor's permanent surrender under division (B) of Section 5103.15 of the Revised Code, placement under Section 5103.16 of the Revised Code, and adoption under Chapter 3107. (Attach extra sheets if necessary)

DATE	NAME AND ADDRESS	DISBURSEMENTS MADE OR AGREED TO BE MADE	ACTUAL COSTS
	PHYSICIAN		
	HOSPITAL/MEDICAL FACILITY		
	ATTORNEY		
	ACTUAL COST TO THE ATTORNEY		
	AGENCY		
	ACTUAL COST TO THE AGENCY		
	MAINTENANCE AND MEDICAL CARE REQUIRED UNDER R.C. 5103.15		
	FOSTER CARE		
	GUARDIAN AD LITEM		
	COURT COSTS		
	ALL OTHER DISBURSEMENTS		
	TOTAL		

[Reverse of Form 18.9]

CERTIFICATION OF PETITIONER'S ACCOUNT

The undersigned certifies this _____ day of _____, 20___, that this accounting is true and accurate.

_____
Attorney or Agency

_____
Typed or Printed Name

_____
Address

_____
City   State

_____
Telephone Number (include area code)

The petitioner has reviewed this accounting and attests to its accuracy this _____ day of _____, 20_____.

_____
Petitioner

_____
Petitioner

PROBATE COURT OF _____ COUNTY, OHIO

IN THE MATTER OF THE ADOPTION OF _____

(Name after adoption)

CASE NO. _____

PETITION FOR ADOPTION OF ADULT

The undersigned respectfully petitions the court for permission to adopt _____,

an adult and to have the adult's name changed to

_____.

Petitioner says he may adopt the adult because the adult

☐ is totally and permanently disabled.

☐ is determined to be a mentally retarded person.

☐ had established a child-foster parent or child-stepparent relationship with the petitioner as a minor.

_____	_____
Attorney for Petitioner	Petitioner
_____	_____
Typed or Printed Name	Typed or Printed Name
_____	_____
Street Address	Street Address
_____	_____
City State Zip	City State Zip
_____	_____
Phone Number (include area code)	Phone Number (include area code)
Attorney Registration No. _____	

ENTRY

This cause is set for hearing on the _____ day of _____, 20

_____ at _____ o'clock _____.m.

_____

PROBATE JUDGE

19.0 PETITION FOR ADOPTION OF ADULT

PROBATE COURT OF _____ COUNTY, OHIO

IN THE MATTER OF THE ADOPTION OF _____

(Name after adoption)

CASE NO. _____

FINAL ORDER OF ADOPTION OF ADULT

This day this cause came on to be hear on the petition of

_____

_____

_ to adopt

_____, an

adult, and on the evidence.

On consideration thereof the Court finds (R.C. 3107.02(B)) _____

_____

_

_____

_

and that the adoption should be granted.

It is ordered that the name of the adopted adult be changed to _____

_____

_

It is therefore further ordered by a final decree of adoption be, and the same hereby is entered herein.

It is further ordered that at that time a Certificate of Adoption, certified by the Court, be forwarded to the

State Department of Health, Division of Vital Statistics at

_____. Further, that a copy of this decree be forwarded to the

Ohio State Department of Human Services for Statistical purposes.

_____   _____
Date   PROBATE JUDGE

19.1 – FINAL ORDER OF ADOPTION OF ADULT

Conservatorship — Forms 20.0 To 20.2

PROBATE COURT OF_____COUNTY, OHIO

IN THE MATTER OF THE CONSERVATORSHIP OF

CASE NO._____

APPLICATION FOR APPOINTMENT OF CONSERVATOR
(R. C. 2111.021)

I,_____, Petitioner, hereby state that I am a competent adult but am physically infirm. I request that:

1   Name of Proposed Conservator _____

Street _____

City_____, Ohio (Zip) _____ Telephone(____)

be appointed conservator of my:

[   ] Person and Estate   [   ] Person Only   [   ] Estate Only

2.   The length (time period) of the conservatorship is:

[   ] Indefinite   [   ] Definite - to_____ _____

3.   (If "Person Only" or "Person and Estate" is checked), I give the following power over my PERSON to the:

a.   Conservator:
[   ] (1) All powers that a guardian would have under the guardianship laws of Ohio.
[   ] (2) Limited to the power to_____
_____
_____

b.   Court
[   ] (1) All powers that a Court would have under the guardianship laws of Ohio.
[   ] (2) Limited to the power to _____
_____
_____

4.   (If "Estate Only" or "Person and Estate" is checked), I give the following power over my ESTATE to the:

a.   Conservator:
[   ] (1) All powers that a guardian would have under the guardianship laws of Ohio.
[   ] (2) Limited to the power to _____
_____
_____

FORM 20.0 - APPLICATION FOR APPOINTMENT OF CONSERVATOR   9/1/91

b.   Court

    [   ] (1)   All powers that a Court would have under the guardianship laws of Ohio.

    [   ] (2)   Limited to the power to _____

_____

_____

c.   The following of my property is subject to the foregoing powers:

    [   ] (1) All property. (attach description of property)

    [   ] (2) Only the property listed as follows:

_____

_____

_____

5.   If the application is for a conservatorship of the estate:

    a.   The estate to be placed under conservatorship is:

Personal Property	$ _____
Real Property	$ _____
Annual Rents	$ _____
Other Annual Income	$ _____
TOTAL	$ _____

    b.   A bond in the amount of $ _____ is attached.
        (R.C. 21 09.04(A) (1))(Form 15.3)

6.   Service of notice of the conservatorship is to be given to:

    [   ] None [   ] Same as Guardianship [   ] As Listed on Form 15.0

     Based on the foregoing information, I do hereby petition the Court to appoint a Conservator for myself, and do so freely and of my own will. I certify that all information and statements contained in this application and the attached exhibits are correct to the best of my knowledge and belief.

_____

Date

_____   _____

Attorney's Signature   Applicant's Signature

_____   _____

(Type or print Attorney's Name)   (Type or print Applicant's Name)

_____   _____

(Street)   (Street)

_____   _____

(City, State, Zip Code)   (City, State, Zip Code)

(___) _____   (___) _____

(Telephone Number   - Include Area Code)   (Telephone Number - Include Area Code)

_____

Supreme Court Registration Number

FORM 20.0 - APPLICATION FOR APPOINTMENT OF CONSERVATOR

PROBATE COURT OF _____ COUNTY, OHIO

IN THE MATTER OF THE CONSERVATORSHIP OF _____

CASE NO. _____

JUDGMENT ENTRY
APPOINTMENT OF CONSERVATOR
[R.C 2111.021]

Upon hearing the application for appointment of a Conservator herein, the Court finds that the petitioner is a resident of this County, or has legal settlement herein; that this Court has jurisdiction; and that

_____ is a competent, but physically infirm adult, who has

voluntarily petitioned for, and the Court does declare _____

as his/her Conservator, and grants to the Conservator powers fully described in the Letters of Conservatorship.

The Court further finds that powers of the Court shall be:

☐ 1.   Full powers as proscribed in the Laws of Guardianship of the State of Ohio.

☐ 2.   Limited to the following powers, but not limited to the power to set bond, and all powers in Section 2111.021 of the Revised Code.

_____

_____

_____

_____

The Court approves the bond as filed.

The Court orders Letters of Conservatorship issue to _____

as provided by law.

_____   _____
Date   Judge

PROBATE COURT OF_____**COUNTY, OHIO**

IN THE MATTER OF THE CONSERVATORSHIP OF

CASE NO. _____

LETTERS OF CONSERVATORSHIP

_____ is appointed Conservator

of_____

As Conservator, his/her powers are:

1   All powers conferred by the Guardianship laws of Ohio and the Rules of this Court over the conservatee's:

     ☐ Person and Estate   ☐ Person Only   ☐ Estate Only

2.   Those guardianship powers, until revoked, are for an:

     ☐ Indefinite time period

     ☐ Definite time period to_____

3.   The Conservator's powers are limited to:

_____

_____

_____

4.   The following property of the conservatee is subject to the above power of the conservator:

     ☐ All property.

     ☐ Only the property listed as follows:

_____

_____

_____

The above-named Conservator has the power conferred by law to do and perform all the duties of Conservator as described.

_____   _____
Date   Probate Judge

NOTE TO FINANCIAL INSTITUTIONS

Funds being held in the name of the within-named Conservatee shall not be released to Conservator without a Court Order directing release of a specific fund and amounts thereof.

FORM 20.2 - LETTERS OF CONSERVATORSHIP   9/1/91

CERTIFICATE OF APPOINTMENT AND INCUMBENCY

This document is a true copy of the original kept by me as custodian of this Court.   it constitutes the appointment and letters of authority of the named Conservator, who is qualified and acting in such capacity.

(SEAL)

(Probate Judge)
by
Deputy Clerk

(Date)

FORM 20.2 - LETTERS OF CONSERVATORSHIP

Change Of Name — Forms 21.0 To 21.5

PROBATE COURT OF _____ COUNTY, OHIO

IN RE: CHANGE OF NAME OF _____
(Present Name)

To _____
(Name Requested)

Case No. _____

APPLICATION FOR CHANGE OF NAME OF ADULT
[R.C. 2717.01]

The applicant states that the applicant is an adult and has been a bona fide resident of _____ County,

Ohio, for at least one year immediately prior to the filing of this application.

The applicant requests a change of name from _____

to _____

for the following reason: _____

_____

_____

The applicant states that the applicant will cause notice of the application to be published once in a newspaper of general circulation in this

county at least thirty (30) days before the hearing on this application.

_____	_____
Attorney for Applicant	Applicant's Signature
_____	_____
Typed or Printed Name	Typed or Printed Name
_____	_____
Address	Address
_____	_____
City State Zip	City State Zip
_____	_____
Telephone Number (include area code)	Telephone Number (include area code)

Attorney Registration No. _____

FORM 21.0 - APPLICATION FOR CHANGE OF NAME OF ADULT   11/01/00

(Reverse of Form 21.0)

JUDGMENT ENTRY SETTING HEARING AND ORDERING NOTICE

The Court orders this application set for hearing on the _____ day of _____, _____, at

_____ o'clock ____.m. The applicant is ordered to cause notice of the application to be given by one publication in a newspaper of

general circulation in this county at least thirty (30) days prior to the hearing date as required by law.

_____
Probate Judge

By: _____
         Deputy Clerk

PROBATE COURT OF _____ COUNTY, OHIO

IN RE: CHANGE OF NAME OF _____
                                                            (Present Name)

To _____
                                  (Name Requested)

Case No. _____

JUDGMENT ENTRY - CHANGE OF NAME OF ADULT

On _____ an application for change of name was heard by this Court. The Court finds that

proper notice of the application and hearing date was given by one publication in a newspaper of general circulation in this county at least

thirty days prior to the hearing on the application. The Court further finds that reasonable and proper cause exists for changing the name.

The Court finds that the applicant's complete name at birth was _____,

applicant's date of birth was _____, and the place of birth was

_____
                City   County   State

Therefore, it is **ORDERED** the name of _____

be changed to _____

_____
                              Probate Judge

CERTIFICATION OF JUDGMENT ENTRY

The above Judgment Entry - Change of Name of Adult is a true copy of the original kept by me as custodian of the records of this

Court.

_____
                              Probate Judge/Clerk

By _____
                              Deputy Clerk

_____
                              Date

FORM 21.1 - JUDGMENT ENTRY - CHANGE OF NAME OF ADULT   11/01/00

PROBATE COURT OF _____ COUNTY, OHIO

IN RE: CHANGE OF NAME OF _____
_____(Present Name)

To _____
_____(Name Requested)

Case No. _____

APPLICATION FOR CHANGE OF NAME OF MINOR
[R.C. 2717.01]

The applicant states that the applicant is the ☐ parent ☐ legal guardian ☐ guardian ad litem of the minor and that the minor has been a

bona fide resident of _____ County, Ohio, for at least one year immediately prior to the filing of this

application. A certified copy of the minor's birth certificate is attached.

☐ The applicant states that the name and address of the mother of the minor is:

_____
Name

_____
Address

_____
City   State   Zip

☐ and the name and address of the father or alleged father of the minor is:

_____
Name

_____
Address

_____
City   State   Zip

☐ Applicant states that the address of the ☐ mother ☐ father or alleged father is unknown and cannot with reasonable diligence be

ascertained.

☐ There is no person alleged to be the father of said minor.

The applicant requests a change of name of the minor from _____

to _____

for the following reason: _____

_____

_____

FORM 21.2 - APPLICATION FOR CHANGE OF NAME OF MINOR   11/01/00

(Reverse of Form 21.2)

The applicant states that the applicant will cause notice of the application to be published once in a newspaper of general circulation in this county at least thirty (30) days before the hearing on this application. In addition, notice will be given by the applicant to any non-consenting parent or alleged father, whose addresses are known, by certified mail, return receipt requested.

_____	_____
Attorney for Applicant	Applicant's Signature
_____	_____
Typed or Printed Name	Typed or Printed Name
_____	_____
Address	Address
_____	_____
City State Zip	City State Zip
_____	_____
Telephone Number (include area code)	Telephone Number (include area code)

Attorney Registration No. _____

JOURNAL ENTRY SETTING HEARING AND ORDERING NOTICE

The Court orders this application set for hearing on the _____ day of _____ , _____ , at _____ o'clock ____.m. The applicant is ordered to cause notice of the application to be given by one publication in a newspaper of general circulation in this county at least thirty (30) days prior to the hearing date, as well as certified mail service, return receipt requested, if necessary, as required by law.

_____
Probate Judge

By: _____
Deputy Clerk

PROBATE COURT OF _____ COUNTY, OHIO

IN RE: CHANGE OF NAME OF _____

(Present Name)

To _____

(Name Requested)

Case No. _____

JUDGMENT ENTRY - CHANGE OF NAME OF MINOR

On _____ an application for change of name was heard by this Court. The Court finds that

proper notice of the application and hearing date was given by one publication in a newspaper of general circulation in this county at least

thirty days prior to the hearing on the application and proper notice was given to the legal parents, known father, or alleged father, as

required by law. The Court further finds that reasonable and proper cause exists for changing the name and the name change is in the best

interest of the minor.

The Court finds the minor's complete name at birth was _____, the

minor's date of birth was _____, and the place of birth was

_____

City   County   State

Therefore, it is **ORDERED** the name of _____

be changed to _____

_____

Probate Judge

CERTIFICATION OF JUDGMENT ENTRY

The above Judgment Entry - Change of Name of Minor is a true copy of the original kept by me as custodian of the records of this

Court.

_____

Probate Judge/Clerk

By _____

Deputy Clerk

_____

Date

FORM 21.3 - JUDGMENT ENTRY - CHANGE OF NAME OF MINOR   11/01/00

PROBATE COURT OF _____ COUNTY, OHIO

IN RE: CHANGE OF NAME OF _____
                                                    (Present Name)

To _____
                                (Name Requested)

Case No. _____

CONSENT TO CHANGE OF NAME

The undersigned _____

[check one of the following 3 capacities by which your consent is given]

☐ Mother

☐ Father

☐ Alleged Father

hereby waives notice of the hearing on the Application for Change of Name and consents to the change of name of

_____

to _____

as proposed in the Application.

_____

Sworn to before me and signed in my presence this _____ day of _____, _____

_____
Deputy Clerk/Notary Public

FORM 21.4 - CONSENT TO CHANGE OF NAME   11/01/00

PROBATE COURT OF _____ COUNTY, OHIO
_____, JUDGE

IN RE: CHANGE OF NAME OF _____
                                                        (Present Name)

_____
                                                        (Name Requested)
Case No. _____

NOTICE OF HEARING ON CHANGE OF NAME
[R.C. 2717.01]

Applicant hereby gives notice to all interested persons and to _____,
                                                        (Necessary person whose address is unknown)
whose last known address is _____,

that the applicant has filed an Application for Change of Name in the Probate Court of _____

County, Ohio, requesting the change of name of _____

to _____

The hearing on the application will be held on the _____ day of _____, 20___,

at _____ o'clock ____M. in the Probate Court of _____, County, located at

_____

_____
Applicant's Signature

_____
Typed or Printed Name

_____
Address

_____
City   State   Zip

Note to Publisher: The above legal notice including the caption is to be published once in its entirety. Costs are to be paid by applicant and an Affidavit of Publication is to be furnished to applicant.

FORM 21.5 - NOTICE OF HEARING ON CHANGE OF NAME
                                                        Eff. Date: January 1, 2010

Minor Settlement — Forms 22.0 To 22.4

PROBATE COURT OF _____ COUNTY, OHIO

IN THE MATTER OF _____

CASE NO. _____

APPLICATION TO SETTLE A MINOR'S CLAIM
[R.C. 2111.05, R.C. 2111.18, SUP. R. 67 AND 68]

[Check applicable boxes, complete applicable blanks, strike inapplicable language, and attach supporting documentation.]

The applicant states that:

_____, is an unemancipated minor, born _____, _____, residing at _____ in this county who on or about _____, _____, suffered personal injury (and damage to this minor's property) by wrongful act, neglect, or default that entitles this minor to maintain an action to recover damages. A copy of the birth certificate is attached.

Attached is a narrative statement in support of the proffered settlement setting forth a description of the occurrence, the injury or damage, the treatment progress and current prognosis by the treating physicians, and other proposed or actual settlements resulting from the same occurrence being paid to persons other than this minor. Counsel will advise at the hearing as to liability and collectability.

☐ There is no legal guardian of the estate, and the Court may authorize the settlement without the appointment of a guardian.

☐ _____ is the legal guardian of the estate. Case No. _____

☐ _____ is (are) the parent__ and natural guardian__.

☐ _____ is the person by whom the minor is maintained.

☐ There is a (full) (partial) settlement offer of $ _____ without suit being filed.

☐ There is a (full) (partial) settlement offer of $ _____ after suit was filed; the style of the case, court, and case number being _____.

☐ The proffered settlement should be approved.

☐ Unreimbursed medical and other expenses of $ _____ have been incurred. Attached is a list of such expenses and proposed payees.

☐ A reasonable attorney fee for the attorney's services is $ _____ and reimbursement to the attorney for suit expenses is $ _____. A copy of the attorney's fee contract that has (has not) received prior approval of this Court, subject to modification, and an itemization of suit expenses are attached.

☐ The parent_, _____, claim $ _____ for damages on account of loss of service of this minor and that claim is included in this settlement offer.

☐ This is a structured settlement. All necessary documents, including a statement of the present value of the settlement, are filed herewith.

The applicant requests that:

☐ The Court authorize the applicant to execute a release which shall be effective upon payment of the settlement.

☐ The Court order payment of the above expenses and order that the net amount of
$ _____ for the benefit of the minor be:

    ☐ Deposited in the name of the minor with _____ _____, a financial institution, and not to be released until the minor attains the age of majority or upon further order of this Court.

    ☐ Delivered to the legal guardian.

    ☐ Delivered to _____, parent__ and natural guardian__.

    ☐ Delivered to _____, the person by whom the minor is maintained.

    ☐ Structured as set forth in the attached documents.

☐ Supplemental forms required by local rule of Court are attached.

_____
Attorney for Applicant

_____
Typed or Printed Name

_____

_____
Address

_____
Phone Number (include area code)

Attorney Registration No. _____

_____
Applicant

_____
Typed or Printed Name

_____

_____
Address

_____
Phone Number (include area code)

ENTRY SETTING HEARING AND ORDERING NOTICE

The Court sets _____, at _____ o'clock __.m. as the date and time for hearing the above application and orders notice to be given by the applicant, as provided in the Rules of Civil Procedure, to the parents who have not waived notice and (further orders that the minor and parent_ attend the hearing.)

_____
Probate Judge

PROBATE COURT OF _____ COUNTY, OHIO

IN THE MATTER OF _____

CASE NO. _____

WAIVER AND CONSENT TO SETTLE MINOR'S CLAIM

The undersigned, waive all claims for damages on account of loss of services of said minor, waive notice of the hearing, and consent to and approve the Form 22.0, Application To Settle Minor's Claim, a copy of which is attached hereto.

_____   _____

_____   _____
Typed or Printed Name   Typed or Printed Name

_____   _____

_____   _____

_____   _____

PROBATE COURT OF _____ **COUNTY, OHIO**

IN THE MATTER OF _____

CASE NO. _____

ENTRY APPROVING SETTLEMENT OF A MINOR'S CLAIM

Upon hearing the application to approve and distribute the settlement of the claim of the minor, the Court: [check whichever of the following are applicable]

☐ Approves the proffered settlement of $ _____ ;

☐ Orders payment of $ _____ for medical and other expenses, as follows:
_____
_____ ;

☐ Orders payment of $ _____ to the attorney for reimbursement of suit expenses
and $ _____ for attorney fees for service rendered with respect to this matter;

☐ Orders payment of $ _____ to the parent_, _____,
for damages on account of loss of service of this minor;

☐ Authorizes the applicant to execute a release which shall be effective upon payment of the settlement;

☐ Orders that the net amount of $ _____ , for the benefit of the minor be:

    ☐ Deposited in the name of the minor and not to be released until the minor attains the age of majority or upon further order of this Court with Form 22.3 Verification of Receipt and Deposit filed with the Court;

    ☐ Delivered to the legal guardian of the estate of this minor;

    ☐ Delivered to _____ , parent_ and natural guardian_;

    ☐ Delivered to _____ , the person by whom the minor is maintained;

    ☐ Structured as set forth in the documents attached to the application;

☐ Orders the applicant and the attorney to report on their distribution of the proceeds within thirty days of the date of this entry;

☐ Further orders _____
_____

_____   _____
Date   Probate Judge

FORM 22.2 - ENTRY APPROVING SETTLEMENT OF A MINOR'S CLAIM   10/1/98

PROBATE COURT OF _____ COUNTY, OHIO

IN THE MATTER OF _____

CASE NO. _____

VERIFICATION OF RECEIPT AND DEPOSIT

Pursuant to Court order, the sum of $_____ was deposited with

_____ on the _____ day of _____, _____,

as evidenced by Savings/Certificate of Deposit Account Number _____.

This account is held solely in the name of _____,

a minor, whose Social Security Number is _____.

By accepting said deposit for said minor, this institution agrees that said deposit, together with

accumulated interest, shall be held and no part thereof released until minor attains the age of

majority or upon further order of this Court.

_____
Financial Institution

By_____
Authorized Officer

_____
Typed or Printed Name

_____
Phone Number

_____
Date

PROBATE COURT OF _____ COUNTY, OHIO

IN THE MATTER OF _____

CASE NO. _____

REPORT OF DISTRIBUTION MINOR'S CLAIM

Pursuant to Entry filed _____, _____, the proceeds have been paid as shown below and on the accompanying vouchers.

Gross Proceeds $_____

Less:
Medical expenses $_____
Reimbursement of suit expenses to_____
_____ $_____
Attorney fees to _____ $_____
Loss of service to _____ $_____
Other: _____ $_____
Total $_____

Net Proceeds

☐ Deposited pursuant to R.C. 2109.13
   Form 22.3 attached $_____

☐ Delivered to _____,
   legal guardian of the estate $_____

☐ Delivered to _____,
   parent _ and natural guardian_ $_____

☐ Delivered to _____,
   the person by whom the minor is maintained $_____

☐ Structured - see documents previously filed $_____

   Balance $_____ - 0 - _____

_____   _____
Attorney for Applicant   Applicant

Attorney Registration No. _____

ENTRY

The above report of distribution is hereby approved and the applicant is discharged from further responsibility.

_____   _____
Date   Probate Judge

Protective Services — Forms 23.0 To 23.7

PROBATE COURT OF _____COUNTY, OHIO
_____, JUDGE

IN THE MATTER OF _____, AN ADULT

CASE NO. _____

PETITION FOR PROTECTIVE SERVICES
[R.C. 5101.65]

1.   Petitioner, _____. is an authorized provider of adult protective Services pursuant to R.C. 5101.60, *et seq.* and has received a report that the above named Adult is in need of protective services.

2.   The Adult, _____, residing at_____
_____ is _____ years of age, with a date of birth of _____
and is alleged to be an incapacitated person subject to abuse, neglect, or exploitation.

3.   The specific facts alleging the abuse, neglect, or exploitation are:
_____
_____
_____

4.   The proposed protective service plan including the least restrictive placement, if applicable, is as follows:
_____
_____
_____
_____

5.   The Adult and the following persons are required to receive notice pursuant to R.C. 5101.66:

Name	Address	Relationship to Adult

FORM 23.0 – PETITION FOR PROTECTIVE SERVICES

Eff. Date: January 1, 2010

CASE NO._____

6.   The Adult has not consented and there is no person authorized by law or court order available to give consent to the protective services.

WHEREFORE, the Petitioner requests the Court to authorize the implementation of the proposed protective services plan and for such other relief as may be equitable.

_____County Department of Job and Family Services

_____
Attorney

By:_____

_____
Address

_____
Title

_____

_____
Address

_____
Phone Number (including area code)

_____

_____
Registration No.

_____
Phone Number (including area code)

_____
E-mail

_____
E-mail

FORM 23.0 – PETITION FOR PROTECTIVE SERVICES

Eff. Date: January 1, 2010

PROBATE COURT OF _____COUNTY, OHIO
_____, JUDGE

IN THE MATTER OF _____, AN ADULT

CASE NO. _____

NOTICE OF PETITION FOR COURT ORDERED PROTECTIVE SERVICES
[R.C. 5101.66]

TO: _____
Name and Address of Adult Incapacitated Person

Name	Address	Relationship of Adult

Adult, Guardian, Legal Counsel, Caretaker, Spouse, if any, and if none of these to the Adult's Children or Next of Kin

You are hereby notified that on the _____ day of _____, 20 _____, the _____County Department of Job and Family Services filed in this Court a Petition for Court Ordered Protective Services for the above named Adult for the following reason(s): _____
_____.

This Petition for Court Ordered Protective Services shall be heard in the _____County Probate Court, _____, Ohio located at _____ on the _____ day of _____, 20 ____, at _____o'clock _____.M.

The Adult has the right to legal counsel and if indigent, legal counsel will be appointed if requested.

Witness my signature and the seal of the Court
this _____ day of _____, 20 _____.

_____
Probate Judge

By:

_____
Deputy Clerk

WAIVER OF NOTICE

We, the undersigned, whose relationship to the Adult is indicated, enter our appearance and waive notice and consent to the hearing.

Name	Relationship to the Adult

FORM 23.1 – NOTICE OF PETITION FOR COURT ORDERED PROTECTIVE SERVICES
Eff. Date: January 1, 2010

CASE NO._____

State of Ohio, _____ County Probate Court

     I hereby certify that I caused a copy of the within notice to be mailed, by certified mail, to the last known address of

_____

at _____

_____

at _____

_____, Probate Judge

By: _____
              Deputy Clerk

RETURN

_____County, Ohio

_____._____

     Received this notice on the _____ day of _____, 20_____, at _____ o'clock _____.M., and on the _____ day of _____, 20_____, I served the same by delivering a true copy thereof personally to _____
_____

FEES		
Service and return, 1st name,	$	_____
Additional names, at	$	_____
Miles traveled, at	$	_____
_____	$	_____
Total	$	_____

_____
Sheriff

_____
Deputy Sheriff/Process Server

_____
Name

_____
Title

FORM 23.1 – NOTICE OF PETITION FOR COURT ORDERED PROTECTIVE SERVICES
Eff. Date: January 1, 2010

PROBATE COURT OF _____COUNTY, OHIO
_____, JUDGE

IN THE MATTER OF _____, AN ADULT

CASE NO. _____

PETITION FOR EMERGENCY PROTECTIVE SERVICES
[R.C. 5101.69]

1.   Petitioner, _____, is an authorized provider of adult protective Services pursuant to R.C. 5101.60, *et seq.* and has received a report that the above named Adult is in need of protective services.

2.   The Adult, _____, residing at _____
_____is _____years of age, with a date of birth of
_____, is alleged to be an incapacitated person and an emergency exists.

3.   The specific facts alleging the nature of the emergency are:
_____
_____
_____

4.   The proposed emergency protective services including placement, if applicable, are:
_____
_____
_____
_____

5.   The Adult and the following persons are required to receive notice 24 hours prior to the hearing pursuant to R.C. 5101.69:

Name	Address	Relationship to Adult

FORM 23.2 – PETITION FOR EMERGENCY PROTECTIVE SERVICES

Eff. Date: January 1, 2010

CASE NO._____

6.   (Complete if applicable) Petitioner requests a waiver of the 24 hour notice requirement because:

      a.)   Immediate and irreparable physical harm to the Adult or others will result from the 24 hour delay. Explain:_____

_____
_____
_____

and

      b.)   Reasonable attempts have been made to notify the above listed individuals, if any, if their whereabouts are known. Explain:_____

_____
_____
_____

7.   The Adult has not consented and there is no person authorized by law or court order available or willing to give consent to the emergency protective services.

WHEREFORE, the Petitioner requests the Court to authorize the implementation of the proposed emergency protective services and for such other relief as may be equitable.

_____County Department of Job and Family Services

_____   By:_____
Attorney

_____   _____
Address   Title

                                                          _____
                                                          Address

_____
Phone Number (including area code)   _____

_____   _____
Registration No.   Phone Number (including area code)

_____   _____
E-mail   E-mail

FORM 23.2 – PETITION FOR EMERGENCY PROTECTIVE SERVICES
Eff. Date: January 1, 2010

PROBATE COURT OF _____**COUNTY, OHIO**
_____, **JUDGE**

IN THE MATTER OF _____, **AN ADULT**

CASE NO. _____

NOTICE OF PETITION FOR COURT ORDERED
PROTECTIVE SERVICES ON AN EMERGENCY BASIS
[R.C. 5101.69]

TO:_____
Name of Adult, spouse, if any, if no spouse, adult children or next of kin, and guardian, if any, if their whereabouts are known.

_____

You are hereby notified that on the _____ day of _____, 20 ____, the _____County Department of Job and Family Services filed a Petition for Court Ordered Protective Services to be provided for the above named Adult without the Adult's consent on the grounds that an emergency exists and that the Department has been unable to obtain the consent of the Adult for protective services to be given. A copy of the petition is attached hereto.

The Petition has been set for hearing in the _____ County Probate Court, _____, Ohio located at _____ on the _____ day of _____, 20 _____ at _____ o'clock _____.M. The Adult may appear at the hearing, may present, examine, and cross-examine witnesses, and present evidence to contest the petition. The Adult is entitled to be represented by an attorney and, if found to be indigent, the Adult may request an attorney to be appointed without cost.

Witness my signature and the seal of the Court this _____ day of _____, 20 _____.

_____
Probate Judge

By:_____
Deputy Clerk

FORM 23.3 – NOTICE OF PETITION FOR COURT ORDERED
PROTECTIVE SERVICES ON AN EMERGENCY BASIS
Eff. Date: January 1, 2010

CASE NO._____

The State of Ohio, _____ County Probate Court

      I hereby certify that I caused a copy of the within notice to be mailed, by certified mail, to the last known address of

_____

at_____

_____

at_____

                                 _____, Probate Judge

                   By:_____
                       Deputy Clerk

RETURN

                       _____County, Ohio

                       _____,_____

      Received this notice on the _____ day of _____, 20_____, at _____ o'clock _____.M., and on the _____ day of _____, _____, I served the same by delivering a true copy thereof personally to _____

_____

FEES		
Service and return, 1st name,	$ ____	
_____ Additional names, at	$ ____	
_____Miles traveled, at	$ ____	
_____	$ ____	
Total	$ ____	

Sheriff

_____

Deputy Sheriff/Process Server

_____

Name

_____

Title

FORM 23.3 – NOTICE OF PETITION FOR COURT ORDERED
PROTECTIVE SERVICES ON AN EMERGENCY BASIS

Eff. Date: January 1, 2010

PROBATE COURT OF _____**COUNTY, OHIO**
_____ **, JUDGE**

IN THE MATTER OF _____ **, AN ADULT**

CASE NO. _____

PETITION FOR TEMPORARY RESTRAINING ORDER TO PREVENT
INTERFERENCE WITH INVESTIGATION OF REPORTED ABUSE OF AN ADULT
[R.C. 5101.63]

1.   Petitioner, _____, is an authorized provider of adult protective services pursuant to R.C. 5101.60, _et seq._ and has received a report that the above named Adult is in need of protective services.

2.   The Adult, _____, residing at _____
_____ is _____ years of age, with a date of birth of _____
and is alleged to be an incapacitated person subject to abuse, neglect, or exploitation.

3.   The Respondent (Name and Address):_____
_____
denied or obstructed access by Petitioner to the residence of the Adult.

4.   Unless Respondent is restrained, Petitioner will be unable to perform its duty to investigate the report as mandated by R.C. 5101.62.

5.   An Affidavit setting forth the facts to support this petition is attached.

WHEREFORE, the Petitioner requests the Court to issue an order restraining Respondent from obstructing or in any way interfering with Petitioner's access to the residence of the Adult and further ordering access to the Adult by any Peace Officer requesting to accompany the Petitioner.

_____County Department of Job and Family Services

_____	By:_____
Attorney	
_____	_____
Address	Title
	_____
	Address
_____	_____
Phone Number (including area code)	
_____	_____
Registration No.	Phone Number (including area code)
_____	_____
E-mail	E-mail

FORM 23.4 – PETITION FOR TEMPORARY RESTRAINING ORDER TO PREVENT INTERFERENCE WITH
INVESTIGATION OF REPORTED ABUSE OF AN ADULT
Eff. Date: January 1, 2010

PROBATE COURT OF _____**COUNTY, OHIO**
_____**, JUDGE**

IN THE MATTER OF _____**, AN ADULT**

CASE NO. _____

**PETITION FOR TEMPORARY RESTRAINING ORDER TO PREVENT
INTERFERENCE WITH THE PROVISION OF PROTECTIVE SERVICES TO
AN ADULT**
[R.C. 5101.68]

1.   The above-named Adult is in need of protective services for the following reasons:
_____
_____
_____

2.   The Adult has consented to the protective services.

3.   The Respondent (Name and Address):
_____
_____

has interfered with the provision of these services in the following manner:
_____
_____
_____

4.   Unless Respondent is restrained, Petitioner will be unable to provide protective services
in accordance with Chapter 5101. of the Revised Code.

WHEREFORE, the Petitioner requests the Court to issue an order restraining Respondent from
interfering with the provision of protective services to the Adult and such further relief as may be
equitable.

_____County Department of Job and Family Services

_____	By:_____
Attorney	
_____	_____
Address	Title
_____	_____
	Address
_____	
Phone Number (including area code)	_____
_____	Phone Number (including area code)
Registration No.	_____
_____	E-mail
E-mail	

FORM 23.6 – PETITION FOR TEMPORARY RESTRAINING ORDER TO PREVENT INTERFERENCE WITH
THE PROVISION OF PROTECTIVE SERVICES TO AN ADULT
Eff. Date: January 1, 2010

PROBATE COURT OF _____ COUNTY, OHIO

_____, JUDGE

IN THE MATTER OF _____, AN ADULT

CASE NO. _____

NOTICE OF HEARING ON PETITON FOR TEMPORARY RESTRAINING ORDER
TO PREVENT INTERFERENCE WITH THE PROVISION OF SERVICES
[R.C. 5101.68]

TO:_____
        (Name of Person interfering with the provision of services)

_____
                              (Address)

The above captioned Adult has consented to the provision of adult protective services pursuant to Chapter 5101. of the Revised Code.

You hereby notified that a Petition for Temporary Restraining Order to Prevent Interference with the Provision of Services was filed with this Court pursuant to R.C. 5101.68. It is alleged in the Petition that you are interfering with the provision of protective services for the Adult, and that a temporary restraining order should be issued against you to prevent your interference. A copy of the Petition is attached hereto.

The Petition for Temporary Restraining Order to Prevent Interference with the Provision of Services shall be heard in the _____ County Probate Court, _____, Ohio located at _____ on the _____ day of _____, 20 _____ at _____ o'clock _____.M. You or any interested person is permitted to attend this hearing and give testimony or present other evidence as to why the petition for restraining order should or should not be granted.

Witness my signature and the seal of the Court
This _____ day of _____, 20 _____.

_____
Probate Judge

By:_____
        Deputy Clerk

CASE NO. _____

The State of Ohio, _____ County Probate Court

   I hereby certify that I caused a copy of the within notice to be mailed, by certified mail, to the last known address of

_____

at _____

_____

at _____

            _____, Probate Judge

      By: _____
         Deputy Clerk

RETURN

          _____County, Ohio

          _____._____

   Received this notice on the _____ day of _____, 20_____, at _____ o'clock _____.M., and on the _____ day of _____, 20_____, I served the same by delivering a true copy thereof personally to _____

_____

_____	_____
FEES	Sheriff
_____	
Service and return, 1st name, $ _____	_____
	Deputy Sheriff/Process Server
_____ Additional names, at $ _____	
_____ Miles traveled, at $ _____	_____
	Name
_____ $ _____	
	_____
Total $ _____	Title
_____	

FORM 23.7 – NOTICE OF HEARING ON PETITION FOR TEMPORARY RESTRAINING ORDER
TO PREVENT INTERFERENCE WITH THE PROVISION OF SERVICES
Eff. Date: January 1, 2010

COMMISSION ON THE RULES OF SUPERINTENDENCE FOR OHIO COURTS

Section 1. Creation of Commission. Pursuant to the powers vested in the Supreme Court of Ohio by Article IV, Section 5(A) of the Ohio Constitution regarding general superintendence over all courts in the state, and to assist the Court in the exercise of its rule-making powers, there shall be a Supreme Court Commission on the Rules of Superintendence for Ohio Courts.

Section 2. Duties of Commission. The Commission shall review all rules of superintendence for Ohio courts. The Commission shall receive and consider proposed rules and amendments, and recommend rules and amendments for adoption to the Court.

Section 3. Membership. The Commission shall consist of twenty members appointed by the Supreme Court.

(A) The Chief Justice shall appoint seven members who shall be members of the following organization and nominated by:

(1) the President of the Ohio Courts of Appeals Judges Association;

(2) the President of the Ohio Common Pleas Judges Association;

(3) the President of the Ohio Association of Probate Judges;

(4) the President of the Ohio Association of Domestic Relations Judges;

(5) the President of the Ohio Association of Juvenile Court Judges;

(6) the President of the Association of Municipal/County Court Judges of Ohio;

(7) the President of the Ohio Association of Magistrates.

(B) Six members shall be appointed by a justice of the Court other than the Chief Justice as follows:

(1) one court of appeals judge;

(2) one judge of the court of common pleas, general division;

(3) one judge of the court of common pleas with probate jurisdiction;

(4) one judge of the court of common pleas with domestic relations jurisdiction;

(5) one judge of the court of common pleas with juvenile jurisdiction;

(6) one judge of a municipal or county court.

(C) Six members appointed by the Chief Justice, including one clerk of court, one court administrator, and one attorney admitted to the practice of law in Ohio.

(D) The Administrative Director of the Supreme Court of Ohio shall serve as a non-voting, ex officio member.

(E) Initial appointments shall be made as follows:

(1) The court of appeals judge appointed by a justice, the judge of the court of common pleas with domestic relations jurisdiction appointed by a justice, the judge appointed by the Chief Justice upon the nomination of the President of the Ohio Common Pleas Judges Association, the judge appointed by the Chief Justice upon the nomination of the President of the Ohio Association of Juvenile Court Judges, the magistrate appointed by the Chief Justice upon the nomination of the President of the Ohio Association of Magistrates, and two at large appointees made by the Chief Justice shall be appointed to a term that ends on December 31, 2006.

(2) The judge of the court of common pleas with general jurisdiction appointed by a justice, the judge of the court of common pleas with juvenile jurisdiction appointed by a justice, the judge appointed by the Chief Justice upon the nomination of the President of the Ohio Association of Probate Judges, the judge appointed by the Chief Justice upon the nomination of the President of the Association of Municipal/County Court Judges of Ohio, and two at large appointees made by the Chief Justice shall be appointed to a term that ends on December 31, 2007.

(3) The judge of the court of common pleas with probate jurisdiction appointed by a justice, the judge of the municipal/county court appointed by a justice, the judge appointed by the Chief Justice upon the nomination of the President of the Ohio Court of Appeals Judges Association, the judge appointed by the Chief Justice upon the nomination of the President of the Ohio Association of Domestic Relations Judges, and two at large appointees shall be appointed to a term that ends on December 31, 2008.

Section 4. Terms. (A) Members of the Commission shall serve three year terms beginning on the first day of January. Members shall be eligible for reappointment, but shall not be eligible to serve more than two consecutive terms of three years without a six month break in service.

(B) Vacancies shall be filled in the same manner as original appointments. A member appointed to fill a vacancy occurring prior to the expiration of the term for which his or her predecessor was appointed shall hold office for the remainder of the term. If a judge member leaves office, if an attorney member no longer practices in Ohio, if the magistrate member is no longer employed as a full-time magistrate, if the clerk of court leaves office, if the court administrator is no longer employed in that capacity, the member shall be disqualified and a vacancy shall occur.

Section 5. Chair; Vice-Chair. The Court shall appoint one of the members as chair and one of the members as vice-chair. The chair and vice-chair shall serve for two years, and may be reappointed, but a member shall not serve as chair or vice-chair for more than two consecutive terms of two years.

Section 6. Compensation. Members of the Commission shall serve without compensation, but shall be reimbursed for expenses incurred in the performance of their official duties.

Section 7. Staff. The Administrative Director of the Supreme Court, or the director's designee, shall serve as staff liaison to the Commission.

Section 8. Effective Date; Transition of Membership. This rule shall take effect on January 1, 2006; amended effective October 15, 2007.

COMMISSION ON TECHNOLOGY AND THE COURTS

Effective December 1, 2007

The Supreme Court of Ohio has established the Commission on Technology and the Courts effective December 1, 2007.

Section 1. Creation of Commission Pursuant to the powers vested in the Supreme Court of Ohio by Article IV, Section 5(A) of the Ohio Constitution regarding general superintendence over all courts in the state, and to assist the Court in the exercise of its general superintendence powers in regards to statewide technology issues, there shall be a Supreme Court Commission on Technology and the Courts.

Section 2. Duties of Commission The Commission shall advise the Supreme Court of Ohio on the following:

• the promulgation of statewide rules, policies and uniform standards for the development and use of information technology systems in Ohio courts;

• the delivery of technology services to courts throughout the state including the development and implementation of educational and training programs for judges and court personnel;

• the exchange of data and information by and between Ohio courts and other justice system partners for greater efficiency of judicial administration including the development and operation of the Ohio Courts Network;

• any other issues necessary to aid and promote the orderly adoption and comprehensive use of technology in Ohio courts.

Section 3. Membership The Commission shall consist of 25 members.

(A) Eighteen members shall be appointed by the Supreme Court as follows:

(1) two members nominated by the Chief Justice of the Court of Appeals Judges Association;

(2) two members nominated by the President of the Ohio Common Pleas Judges Association;

(3) two members nominated by the President of the Ohio Association of Probate Judges;

(4) two members nominated by the President of the Ohio Association of Domestic Relations Judges;

(5) two members nominated by the President of the Ohio Association of Juvenile Court Judges;

(6) two members nominated by the President of the Ohio Association of Municipal and County Court Judges of Ohio;

(7) one member nominated by the President of the Ohio Association of Magistrates;

(8) one member nominated by the President of the Ohio Association for Court Administration;

(9) one member nominated by the President of the Ohio Clerks of Court Association;

(10) one member nominated by the President of the Ohio Association of Municipal/County Clerks;

(11) one member nominated by the President of the Ohio State Bar Association;

(12) one member nominated by the President of the Consortium of Ohio Metropolitan Bar Associations.

(B) Three members shall be appointed by the Chief Justice and shall be information technology managers for Ohio courts.

(C) Two members shall be appointed by the Chief Justice and one shall be an employee of an Ohio law enforcement agency and one shall be an employee of an office or agency that manages or operates a jail or correctional institution.

(D) Two members shall serve ex officio as follows:

(1) The Administrative Director of the Supreme Court of Ohio, who shall be a non-voting member; and

(2) The Chair of the Court Technology Committee of the Ohio Judicial Conference.

(E) Initial appointments shall be made as follows:

(1) One judge of the court of appeals, one judge of the court of common pleas with general jurisdiction, one judge of the court of common pleas with domestic relations jurisdiction, one judge of the court of common pleas with juvenile jurisdiction, the representative of the Ohio Association of Magistrates, the representative of the Ohio Association of Municipal/County Clerks, one manager of information technology of any court appointed by the Chief Justice, and one employee of a law enforcement agency appointed by the Chief Justice, shall be appointed to a term that ends on December 31, 2008.

(2) One judge of the court of appeals, one judge of the court of common pleas with probate jurisdiction, one judge of the court of common pleas with domestic relations jurisdiction, one municipal or county court judge, the representative of the Ohio Association for Court Administration, the representative of the Ohio State Bar Association, one manager of information technology of any court appointed by the Chief Justice, and the employee of an office or agency that manages or operates a jail or correctional institution appointed by the Chief Justice shall be appointed to a term that ends on December 31, 2009.

(3) One judge of the court of common pleas with general jurisdiction, one judge of the common pleas with probate jurisdiction, one judge of the court of common pleas with juvenile jurisdiction, one municipal or county court judge, the representative of the Ohio Clerks of Court Association, the representative of the Ohio Metropolitan Bar Association, and one manager of information technology of any court appointed by the Chief Justice shall be appointed to a term that ends on December 31, 2010.

Section 4. Terms (A) Members of the Commission shall serve three year terms beginning on the first day of January. Members shall be eligible for reappointment, but shall not be eligible to serve more than two consecutive terms of three years without a six month break in service.

(B) Vacancies shall be filled in the same manner as original appointments. A member appointed to fill a vacancy occurring prior to the expiration of the term for which his or her predecessor was appointed shall hold office for the remainder of the term. If a judge member leaves office, if an attorney member no longer practices in Ohio, if a clerk of court leaves office, if a court administrator is no longer employed in that capacity, if a law enforcement officer is no longer employed in that capacity, if a manager of information technology of any court is no longer employed in that capacity, the member shall be disqualified and a vacancy shall occur.

Section 5. Chair; Vice-Chair The Court shall appoint one of the members as chair and one of the members as vice-chair. The chair and vice-chair shall serve for three years, and may be reappointed, but a member shall not serve as chair or vice-chair for more than two consecutive terms of three years.

Section 6. Compensation Members of the Commission shall serve without compensation, but shall be reimbursed for expenses incurred in the performance of their official duties.

Section 7. Staff Liaison The Administrative Director of the Supreme Court or a designee shall serve as staff liaison to the Commission.

Section 8. Effective Date; Transition of Membership This rule shall take effect on December 1, 2007.

Index to Rules of Superintendence for the Court of Ohio

RULES OF PRACTICE OF THE SUPREME COURT OF OHIO

INTRODUCTION

The Supreme Court is the highest court in the State of Ohio. The Court consists of a Chief Justice and six Justices who are elected by the citizens of the State of Ohio to six-year terms. A majority of the Supreme Court is necessary to constitute a quorum or to render a judgment.

The jurisdiction of the Supreme Court is outlined in Article IV, Section 2(B) of the Ohio Constitution as summarized below.

The Supreme Court has original jurisdiction in the following:

(1) Quo warranto;

(2) Mandamus;

(3) Habeas corpus;

(4) Prohibition;

(5) Procedendo;

(6) Any cause on review as may be necessary to its complete determination;

(7) Admission to the practice of law, the discipline of persons admitted to the practice of law, and all other matters relating to the practice of law.

The Supreme Court has appellate jurisdiction in the following:

(1) Appeals from the courts of appeals as a matter of right in the following:

(a) Cases originating in the courts of appeals;

(b) Cases in which the death penalty has been affirmed by a court of appeals (for an offense committed prior to January 1, 1995);

(c) Cases involving questions arising under the constitution of the United States or of Ohio;

(2) Appeals from the courts of appeals in felony cases if leave is first obtained;

(3) Direct appeals from the courts of common pleas or other courts of record inferior to the court of appeals as a matter of right in cases in which the death penalty has been imposed (for an offense committed on or after January 1, 1995);

(4) Appeals of the proceedings of certain administrative officers or agencies as provided by statute;

(5) Cases of public or great general interest, if the Supreme Court directs a court of appeals to certify its record to the Supreme Court;

(6) Any case certified by a court of appeals to the Supreme Court pursuant to Article IV, Section 3(B)(4) of the Ohio Constitution.

The Supreme Court holds regular sessions that are open to the public. Generally, these sessions are held in the Supreme Court Courtroom on the first floor of the Ohio Judicial Center, 65 South Front Street, in Columbus, Ohio. Calendars of the Court sessions are available in the Clerk's Office and on the Supreme Court of Ohio's Web site at the following address: www.supremecourt.ohio.gov

History: Amended, eff 4-1-96; 7-1-04; 1-1-10.

SECTION 1. REQUIREMENTS FOR ATTORNEYS PRACTICING BEFORE THE SUPREME COURT

S.Ct. Prac. R. 1.1. Prerequisites to Appearance

(A) In order to file documents other than those required to perfect an appeal, or to participate in oral argument, attorneys shall be registered for active status with the Office of Attorney Services of the Supreme Court as required by Rule VI of the Supreme Court Rules for the Government of the Bar of Ohio or shall have complied with the pro hac vice requirements of Rule 1.2 of the Rules of Practice of the Supreme Court of Ohio. In addition to meeting the preceding requirements, in death penalty cases any appointed attorney shall satisfy the certification requirements of the Rules of Superintendence for the Courts of Ohio and appear on the list of attorneys certified to represent capital defendants on appeal.

(B) The first document filed by a party shall serve as the notice of appearance of counsel. Any attorney appearing in a case after the first document has been filed, shall file a notice of appearance identifying the party on whose behalf the attorney is appearing. Any attorney who withdraws representation of a party shall file a notice of withdrawal.

(C) The Supreme Court may strike documents filed by attorneys not in compliance with this rule.

S.Ct. Prac. R. 1.2.   Admission *Pro Hac Vice*

(A) The Supreme Court may permit any attorney who is admitted to practice in the highest court of a state, commonwealth, territory, or possession of the United States or the District of Columbia, or who is admitted to practice in the courts of a foreign state, to appear pro hac vice and file documents or participate in oral argument before the Supreme Court.

(B) Admission pro hac vice will be allowed only on motion of an attorney admitted to practice in Ohio and registered with the Attorney Services Division for active status. The motion shall succinctly state the qualifications of the attorney seeking admission. The motion shall be filed with the first document the attorney files. If the attorney seeks to participate in oral argument, and has not already been admitted in the case, the motion shall be filed at least thirty days before oral argument. The Supreme Court may withdraw admission pro hac vice at any time.

S.Ct. Prac. R. 1.3.   Designation of Counsel of Record

(A) The attorney representing a party shall be designated as counsel of record for that party. Where two or more attorneys represent a party, only one attorney shall be designated as counsel of record to receive notices and service on behalf of that party. The designation shall be made on the cover page of the first document filed by the party in the Supreme Court. If an attorney is not designated counsel of record, the first attorney listed for the party on the cover page of the first document filed shall be considered the counsel of record. To change a party's designation of its counsel of record, the party shall file a separate notice of change of counsel of record.

(B) The Clerk shall send notices and orders in a case to counsel of record at the office address that counsel has registered with the Office of Attorney Services under Gov. Bar R. VI. If no office address is registered, the Clerk will send notices and orders to the residence address that counsel has registered with the Office of Attorney Services. Counsel of record may request that the Clerk send notices and orders in a case to an address other than one registered with the Office of Attorney Services by filing a notice with the Clerk designating the address to be used in that case.

History: Amended, eff 4-1-96; 6-1-00; 7-1-04; 1-1-08; 1-1-10.

SECTION 2.   INSTITUTION OF APPEALS; NOTICE OF APPEAL

S.Ct. Prac. R. 2.1.   Types of Appeals

(A) **Appeals from courts of appeals**

(1) **Appeals of right** An appeal of a case in which the death penalty has been affirmed for an offense committed prior to January 1, 1995, an appeal from the decision of a court of appeals under App. R. 26(B) in a capital case, or a case that originated in the court of appeals invokes the appellate jurisdiction of the Supreme Court and shall be designated an appeal of right. The Supreme Court will render judgment after the parties are given an opportunity to brief the case on the merits in accordance with S.Ct. Prac. R. 6.1 through 6.8.

(2) **Claimed appeals of right** An appeal that claims a substantial constitutional question, including an appeal from the decision of a court of appeals under App. R. 26(B) in a noncapital case, may invoke the appellate jurisdiction of the Supreme Court and shall be designated a claimed appeal of right. In accordance with S.Ct. Prac. R. 3.6, the Supreme Court will determine whether to accept the appeal.

(3) **Discretionary appeals** An appeal that involves a felony or a question of public or great general interest invokes the discretionary jurisdiction of the Supreme Court and shall be designated a discretionary appeal. In accordance with S.Ct. Prac. R. 3.6, the Supreme Court will determine whether to accept the appeal.

(4) **Certified conflict cases** A case in which the court of appeals has issued an order certifying a conflict under Article IV, Section 3(B)(4) of the Ohio Constitution invokes the appellate jurisdiction of the Supreme Court. In accordance with S.Ct. Prac. R. 4.2, the Supreme Court will act upon the court of appeals order.

(B) **Appeals from administrative agencies: Board of Tax Appeals; Public Utilities Commission; Power Siting Board** An appeal that involves review of the action of the Board of Tax Appeals, the Public Utilities Commission, or the Power Siting Board invokes the appellate jurisdiction of the Supreme Court. The Supreme Court will render judgment after the parties are given an opportunity to brief the case on the merits in accordance with S.Ct. Prac. R. 6.1 through 6.8.

(C) **Appeals from courts of common pleas**

(1) An appeal of a case in which the death penalty has been imposed for an offense committed on or after January 1, 1995, invokes the appellate jurisdiction of the Supreme Court and shall be designated an appeal of right. The Supreme Court will render judgment after the parties are given an opportunity to brief the case on the merits in accordance with S.Ct. Prac. R. 6.1 through 6.8 and 19.6.

(2) An appeal of a case contesting an election under section 3515.15 of the Revised Code shall be designated an appeal of right. The Supreme Court will render judgment after the parties are given an opportunity to brief the case on the merits in accordance with S.Ct. Prac. R. 6.1 through 6.8.

S.Ct. Prac. R. 2.2. Institution of Appeal from Court of Appeals

(A) **Perfection of appeal**

(1)(a) To perfect an appeal from a court of appeals to the Supreme Court, other than in a certified conflict case, which is addressed in S.Ct. Prac. R. 4.1, the appellant shall file a notice of appeal in the Supreme Court within forty-five days from the entry of the judgment being appealed. The date the court of appeals filed its judgment entry for journalization with its clerk, in accordance with App. R. 22, shall be considered the date of entry of the judgment being appealed. If the appeal is a claimed appeal of right or a discretionary appeal, the appellant shall also file a memorandum in support of jurisdiction, in accordance with S.Ct. Prac. R. 3.1, at the time the notice of appeal is filed.

(b) Except as provided in divisions (A)(2), (3), (4), (5), and (6) of this rule, the time period designated in this rule for filing a notice of appeal and memorandum in support of jurisdiction is mandatory, and the appellant's failure to file within this time period shall divest the Supreme Court of jurisdiction to hear the appeal. The Clerk of the Supreme Court shall refuse to file a notice of appeal or a memorandum in support of jurisdiction that is received for filing after this time period has passed.

(2)(a) If a party timely files a notice of appeal in the Supreme Court, any other party may file a notice of appeal or cross-appeal in the Supreme Court within the later of the time prescribed by division (A)(1) of this rule or ten days after the first notice of appeal was filed.

(b) A notice of appeal shall be designated and treated as a notice of cross-appeal if it is filed both:

(i) After the original notice of appeal was filed in the case;

(ii) By a party against whom the original notice of appeal was filed.

(c) If a notice of cross-appeal is filed, a combined memorandum both in response to appellant/cross-appellee's memorandum and in support of jurisdiction for the cross-appeal shall be filed by the deadline imposed in S.Ct. Prac. R. 3.4.

(3)(a) In a claimed appeal of right or a discretionary appeal, if the appellant intends to seek from the Supreme Court an immediate stay of the court of appeals judgment that is being appealed, the appellant may file a notice of appeal in the Supreme Court without an accompanying memorandum in support of jurisdiction, provided both of the following conditions are satisfied:

(i) A motion for stay of the court of appeals judgment shall accompany the notice of appeal.

(ii) A copy of the court of appeals opinion and judgment entry being appealed shall be attached to the motion for stay.

(b) A memorandum in support of jurisdiction shall be filed no later than forty-five days from the entry of the court of appeals judgment being appealed. The Supreme Court will dismiss the appeal if the memorandum in support of jurisdiction is not timely filed pursuant to this provision.

(4)(a) In a felony case, when the time has expired for filing a notice of appeal in the Supreme Court, the appellant may seek to file a delayed appeal by filing a motion for delayed appeal and a notice of appeal. The motion shall state the date of entry of the judgment being appealed and the reasons for the delay. Facts supporting the motion shall be set forth in an affidavit. A copy of the court of appeals opinion and the judgment entry being appealed shall be attached to the motion.

(b) A memorandum in support of jurisdiction shall not be filed at the time a motion for delayed appeal is filed. If the Supreme Court grants a motion for delayed appeal, the appellant shall file a memorandum in support of jurisdiction within thirty days after the motion for delayed appeal is granted. If a memorandum in support of jurisdiction is not timely filed after a motion for delayed appeal has been granted, the Supreme Court will dismiss the appeal.

(c) The provision for delayed appeal does not apply to appeals involving postconviction-relief or appeals brought pursuant to App. R. 26(B). The Clerk shall refuse to file motions for delayed appeal involving postconviction-relief or App. R. 26(B).

(5)(a) When a party timely files an application for reconsideration in the court of appeals pursuant to App. R. 26(A)(1), the time for filing a notice of appeal from the court of appeals entry of judgment shall be tolled.

(b) If a timely application for reconsideration is filed in the court of appeals, and the appellant seeks to appeal from the court of appeals entry of judgment, the appellant shall file a notice of appeal within forty-five days of the court of appeals decision denying the application for reconsideration, or if reconsideration is granted, from the subsequent entry of judgment.

(c) To file an appeal from the court of appeals opinion and judgment entry after the court of appeals has ruled on an application for reconsideration, the appellant shall comply with the timeframe imposed by S.Ct. Prac. R. 2.2(A)(5)(b) and shall include the following:

(i) A notice of appeal that complies with the requirements of S.Ct. Prac. R. 2.2(B), and that indicates the date of the filing of the application for reconsideration, the date of the court of appeals decision on the application for reconsideration, and the date of the court of appeals opinion and judgment entry that is being appealed.

(ii) A memorandum in support of jurisdiction that complies with the requirements of S.Ct. Prac. R. 3.1, and that also has attached a date-stamped copy of the court of appeals decision denying the application for reconsideration, or if reconsideration is granted, from the subsequent entry of judgment.

(6)(a) When a party timely files an application for en banc consideration in the court of appeals pursuant to App. R. 26(A)(2), the time for filing a notice of appeal from the court of appeals entry of judgment shall be tolled.

(b) If a timely application for en banc consideration is filed in the court of appeals, and the appellant seeks to appeal from the court of appeals entry of judgment, the appellant shall file a notice of appeal within forty-five days of the court of appeals decision denying the application for en banc consideration, or if en banc consideration is granted, from the subsequent entry of judgment.

(c) To file an appeal from the court of appeals opinion and judgment entry after the court of appeals has ruled on an application for en banc consideration, the appellant shall comply with the timeframe imposed by S.Ct. Prac. R. 2.2(A)(6)(b) and shall include the following:

(i) A notice of appeal that complies with the requirements of S.Ct. Prac. R. 2.2(B), and that indicates the date of the filing of the application for en banc consideration, the date of the court of appeals decision on the application for en banc consideration, and the date of the court of appeals opinion and judgment entry that is being appealed.

(ii) A memorandum in support of jurisdiction that complies with the requirements of S.Ct. Prac. R. 3.1, and that also has attached a date-stamped copy of the court of appeals decision denying the application for en banc consideration, or if en banc consideration is granted, from the subsequent entry of judgment.

(B) **Contents of notice of appeal** *[See Appendix A for a sample notice of appeal from a court of appeals.]*

(1) The notice of appeal shall state all of the following:

(a) The name of the court of appeals whose judgment is being appealed;

(b) The case name and number assigned to the case by the court of appeals;

(c) The date of the entry of the judgment being appealed;

(d) That one or more of the following are applicable:

(i) The case involves affirmance of the death penalty;

(ii) The case originated in the court of appeals;

(iii) The case raises a substantial constitutional question;

(iv) The case involves a felony;

(v) The case is one of public or great general interest;

(vi) The case involves termination of parental rights or adoption of a minor child, or both;

(vii) The case is an appeal of a court of appeals determination under App.R. 26(B).

(2) In an appeal of right under S.Ct. Prac. R. 2.1(A)(1), a date-stamped copy of the court of appeals judgment entry that is being appealed shall be attached to the notice of appeal. For purposes of this rule, a date-stamped copy of the court of appeals judgment entry shall mean a copy bearing the file stamp of the clerk of the court of appeals and reflecting the date the court of appeals filed its judgment entry for journalization with its clerk under App. R. 22. If the opinion of the court of appeals serves as its judgment entry, a date-stamped copy of the opinion shall be attached.

(3) In a discretionary appeal or claimed appeal of right, if a party has timely moved the court of appeals to certify a conflict under App. R. 25, the notice of appeal shall be accompanied by a notice of pending motion to certify a conflict, in accordance with S.Ct. Prac. R. 4.4(A), that a motion to certify a conflict is pending with the court of appeals.

(C) **Notice to the court of appeals** The Clerk of the Supreme Court shall send a copy of any notice of appeal or cross-appeal to the clerk of the court of

appeals whose judgment is being appealed.

(D) **Jurisdiction of court of appeals after appeal to Supreme Court is perfected**

(1) After an appeal is perfected from a court of appeals to the Supreme Court, the court of appeals is divested of jurisdiction, except to take action in aid of the appeal, to rule on an application timely filed with the court of appeals pursuant to App. R. 26, or to rule on a motion to certify a conflict under Article IV, Section 3(B)(4) of the Ohio Constitution.

(2) In all appeals from a court of appeals, the court of appeals retains jurisdiction to appoint counsel to represent indigent parties before the Supreme Court where a judgment of the court of appeals is being defended by a defendant or upon order of the Supreme Court that counsel be appointed in a particular case.

S.Ct. Prac. R. 2.3. Institution of Appeal from Administrative Agency

(A) **Appeal from the Board of Tax Appeals**

(1) A notice of appeal from the Board of Tax Appeals shall be filed with the Supreme Court and the Board within thirty days from the date of the entry of the decision of the Board, include a copy of the decision being appealed, set forth the claimed errors, comply with the service requirements of S.Ct. Prac. R. 14.2(B)(2), and otherwise be in conformance with section 5717.04 of the Revised Code.

(2) If a party timely files a notice of appeal in the Supreme Court, any other party may file a notice of appeal pursuant to section 5717.04 of the Revised Code.

(B) **Appeal from the Public Utilities Commission**

(1) A notice of appeal from the Public Utilities Commission shall be filed with the Supreme Court and with the Commission within the time specified in and in conformance with sections 4903.11 and 4903.13 of the Revised Code and sections 4901-1-02(A) and 4901-1-36 of the Ohio Administrative Code.

(2) If a party files a notice of appeal in the Supreme Court, any other party may file a notice of cross-appeal pursuant to section 4903.13 of the Revised Code. The notice of cross-appeal shall be filed within the later of the time prescribed by section 4903.11 of the Revised Code or ten days after the first notice of appeal was filed.

(C) **Appeal from the Power Siting Board** A notice of appeal or cross-appeal from the Power Siting Board shall be filed with the Supreme Court and the Board in accordance with division (B) of this rule and pursuant to section 4906.12 of the Revised Code.

S.Ct. Prac. R. 2.4. Filing of Joint Notice of Appeal

Where there are multiple parties appealing from the same decision of a court of appeals or an administrative agency, appellants may join in the filing of a single notice of appeal.

S.Ct. Prac. R. 2.5. Name of Case on Appeal

Unless rule, statute, or the Clerk's discretion require

otherwise, an appeal shall be docketed under the case name assigned to the action in the court or agency whose decision is being appealed.

S.Ct. Prac. R. 2.6.   Request for Mediation

In any discretionary appeal or claimed appeal of right of a civil case, a party may file a motion to refer the case to mediation pursuant to S.Ct. Prac. R. 17.1. The motion should be filed no later than thirty days after the filing of the memorandum in support of jurisdiction. The Clerk shall refuse to file a motion to refer a criminal case to mediation.

History: Amended, eff 4-1-96; 4-1-00; 6-1-00; 7-1-04; 8-1-04; 1-1-08; 1-1-10; 7-1-10.

SECTION 3.   DETERMINATION OF JURISDICTION ON CLAIMED APPEALS OF RIGHT AND DISCRETIONARY APPEALS

S.Ct. Prac. R. 3.1.   Memorandum in Support of Jurisdiction

[See Appendix B following these rules for a sample memorandum.]

(A) In a claimed appeal of right or a discretionary appeal, the appellant shall file a memorandum in support of jurisdiction with the notice of appeal.

(B) A memorandum in support of jurisdiction shall contain all of the following:

(1) A table of contents, which shall include the propositions of law;

(2) A thorough explanation of why a substantial constitutional question is involved, why the case is of public or great general interest, or, in a felony case, why leave to appeal should be granted;

(3) A statement of the case and facts;

(4) A brief and concise argument in support of each proposition of law.

(C) Except in postconviction death penalty cases, a memorandum shall not exceed fifteen numbered pages, exclusive of the table of contents and the certificate of service.

(D)(1) A date-stamped copy of the court of appeals opinion and judgment entry being appealed shall be attached to the memorandum. For purposes of this rule, a date-stamped copy of the court of appeals judgment entry shall mean a copy bearing the file stamp of the clerk of the court of appeals and reflecting the date the court of appeals filed its judgment entry for journalization with its clerk under App. R. 22.

(2) In postconviction death penalty cases, the appellant shall also attach the findings of fact and conclusions of law entered by the trial court.

(3) The appellant may also attach any other judgment entries or opinions issued in the case, if relevant to the appeal. The memorandum shall not include any other attachments.

(E) Except as otherwise provided in S.Ct. Prac. R. 2.2(A), if the appellant does not tender a memorandum in support of jurisdiction for timely filing along with the notice of appeal, the Clerk shall refuse to file the notice of appeal.

S.Ct. Prac. R. 3.2.   Memorandum in Response

(A) Within thirty days after the appellant's memorandum in support of jurisdiction is filed, the appellee may file a memorandum in response. If the appeal involves termination of parental rights or adoption of a minor child, or both, any memorandum in response shall be filed within twenty days after the memorandum in support of jurisdiction is filed.

(B) Except in postconviction death penalty cases, the memorandum in response shall not exceed fifteen numbered pages, exclusive of the certificate of service; shall not include any attachments; and shall contain the following:

(1) A statement of appellee's position as to whether a substantial constitutional question is involved, whether leave to appeal in a felony case should be granted, or whether the case is of public or great general interest;

(2) A brief and concise argument in support of the appellee's position regarding each proposition of law raised in the memorandum in support of jurisdiction.

(C) The appellee shall include the Supreme Court case number on the cover page of the memorandum in response.

(D) If two or more memoranda in support of jurisdiction are filed in a case, the appellee shall file only one memorandum in response. The time specified in division (A) of this rule for filing the memorandum in response shall be calculated from the date the last memorandum in support of jurisdiction was filed in the case.

(E) The appellee may waive the filing of a memorandum in response. A waiver shall be on a form prescribed by the Clerk and shall be filed within twenty days after the memorandum in support of jurisdiction is filed.

[See Appendix C following these rules for the prescribed waiver form.]

S.Ct. Prac. R. 3.3.   Prohibition Against Supplemental and Reply Memoranda

(A) Except as provided in S.Ct. Prac. R. 8.7, jurisdictional memoranda shall not be supplemented. If a relevant authority is issued after the deadline has passed for filing a party's jurisdictional memorandum, that party may file a citation to the relevant authority but shall not file additional argument.

(B) The appellant shall not file a reply to the memorandum in response filed by the appellee under S.Ct. Prac. R. 3.2.

(C) The Clerk shall refuse to file supplemental or reply memoranda received for filing in violation of this rule and motions to waive the provisions of this rule are prohibited and shall not be filed.

S.Ct. Prac. R. 3.4.   Jurisdictional Memoranda in Case Involving Cross-Appeal

(A) In a case involving a cross-appeal, the appellee/cross-appellant shall file a combined memorandum both in response to appellant/cross-appellee's memorandum and in support of jurisdiction for the cross-appeal within thirty days of the filing of appellant/cross-appellee's memorandum in support of jurisdiction.

Except as otherwise provided by this rule, the combined memorandum shall comply with all of the requirements contained in S.Ct. Prac. R. 3.1 and 3.2; however, a date-stamped copy of the court of appeals opinion and judgment entry being appealed need not be attached to the combined memorandum. Within thirty days after the filing of appellee/cross-appellant's combined memorandum, the appellant/cross-appellee shall file the last memorandum, which shall be limited to a response to appellee/cross-appellant's arguments in support of jurisdiction for the cross-appeal.

(B) If the appeal or the cross-appeal involves termination of parental rights or adoption of a minor child, or both, the combined memorandum of appellee/cross-appellant shall be filed within twenty days after the filing of appellant/cross-appellee's memorandum in support of jurisdiction, and the last memorandum of appellant/cross-appellee shall be filed within twenty days after the filing of appellee/cross-appellant's combined memorandum.

(C) Except in postconviction death penalty cases, a memorandum filed under this rule by the appellant/cross-appellee shall not exceed fifteen numbered pages, and the memorandum filed by the appellee/cross-appellant shall not exceed thirty numbered pages.

S.Ct. Prac. R. 3.5. Jurisdictional Memorandum of *Amicus Curiae*

(A) An amicus curiae may file a jurisdictional memorandum urging the Supreme Court to accept or decline to accept a claimed appeal of right or a discretionary appeal. Leave to file an amicus memorandum is not required. An amicus memorandum shall conform to the requirements of this rule, except that a copy of the court of appeals opinion and judgment entry is not required to be attached to the amicus memorandum.

(B) An amicus memorandum in support of jurisdiction shall be filed by the appellant's deadline for perfecting an appeal to the Supreme Court or, if later, by the appellant's deadline for filing a memorandum in support of jurisdiction. An amicus memorandum in response shall be filed by the appellee's deadline for filing a memorandum in response. The Clerk shall refuse to file an amicus memorandum that is not timely received.

S.Ct. Prac. R. 3.6. Determination of Jurisdiction by the Supreme Court

(A) **Time to review**

(1) After the time for filing jurisdictional memoranda has passed, the Supreme Court will review the jurisdictional memoranda filed and determine whether to accept the appeal and decide the case on the merits. If the appeal involves termination of parental rights or adoption of a minor child, or both, the Supreme Court will expedite its review and determination.

(2) If the appellee has filed a waiver in lieu of a memorandum in response, the Supreme Court may review the memorandum in support of jurisdiction and determine whether to allow the appeal before the deadline for filing the memorandum in response. Upon review of the memorandum in support of jurisdiction

and notwithstanding the appellee's filing of a waiver, the Supreme Court may direct the appellee to file a memorandum in response before it decides whether to allow the appeal.

(3) The Supreme Court may hold its determination of jurisdiction on a claimed appeal of right or a discretionary appeal pending the outcome of any other case before the Supreme Court that may involve a dispositive issue.

(B) **Decision on jurisdiction**

(1) If the appeal is a claimed appeal of right, the Supreme Court will either:

(a) Dismiss the appeal as not involving any substantial constitutional question; or

(b) Accept the appeal, and either order the case or limited issues in the case to be briefed and heard on the merits or enter judgment summarily.

(2) If the appeal is a discretionary appeal involving a felony, the Supreme Court will either:

(a) Deny leave to appeal, refusing jurisdiction to hear the case on the merits; or

(b) Grant leave to appeal, accepting the appeal, and either order the case or limited issues in the case to be briefed and heard on the merits or enter judgment summarily.

(3) If the appeal is a discretionary appeal asserting a question of public or great general interest, the Supreme Court will either:

(a) Decline jurisdiction to decide the case on the merits; or

(b) Grant jurisdiction to hear the case on the merits, accepting the appeal, and either order the case or limited issues in the case to be briefed and heard on the merits or enter judgment summarily.

(C) **Jurisdictional memorandum from state solicitor** In any claimed appeal of right or discretionary appeal in which the state is not a party but nevertheless may have an interest, the Supreme Court may invite the state solicitor to file a jurisdictional memorandum expressing the views of the state before making its determination of jurisdiction.

S.Ct. Prac. R. 3.7. Appointment of Counsel in Felony Cases

If the Supreme Court grants leave to appeal in a discretionary appeal involving a felony and an unrepresented party to the appeal is indigent, the Supreme Court will appoint the Ohio Public Defender or other counsel to represent the indigent party or order the court of appeals to appoint counsel as provided in S.Ct. Prac. R. 2.2(D)(2).

History: Amended, eff 4-1-96; 4-1-00; 4-1-02; 6-1-03; 7-1-04; 1-1-08; 1-1-10.

SECTION 4. CERTIFICATION OF CONFLICT BY COURT OF APPEALS

S.Ct. Prac. R. 4.1. Filing of Court of Appeals Order Certifying a Conflict

When a court of appeals issues an order certifying a conflict pursuant to Article IV, Section 3(B)(4) of the

Ohio Constitution, any interested party to the proceeding may institute an appeal by filing a notice of certified conflict in the Supreme Court. The notice shall have attached a copy of the court of appeals order certifying a conflict, a copy of the certifying court's opinion, and copies of the conflicting court of appeals opinions. The party who files the order certifying a conflict shall be considered the appellant. Failure to file the court of appeals order certifying a conflict within thirty days after the date of such order shall divest the Supreme Court of jurisdiction to consider the order certifying a conflict.

S.Ct. Prac. R. 4.2.   Supreme Court Review of Court of Appeals Order Certifying a Conflict

(A) The Supreme Court will review the court of appeals order certifying a conflict. If the case involves termination of parental rights or adoption of a minor child, or both, the Supreme Court will expedite its review.

(B) If the rule of law upon which the alleged conflict exists is not clearly set forth in the order certifying a conflict, the Supreme Court may dismiss the case or remand it to the court of appeals with an order that the court of appeals clarify the issue presented.

(C) If the Supreme Court determines that a conflict does not exist, it will issue an order dismissing the case.

(D) If the Supreme Court determines that a conflict exists, it will issue an order finding a conflict, identifying those issues raised in the case that will be considered by the Supreme Court on appeal, and ordering those issues to be briefed.

S.Ct. Prac. R. 4.3.   Briefs; Supplement to the Briefs

If the Supreme Court determines that a conflict exists, the parties shall file their merit briefs in conformance with S.Ct. Prac. R. 6.1 through 6.8 and, if applicable, supplements in conformance with S.Ct. Prac. R. 7.1 and 7.2. The parties shall brief only the issues identified in the order of the Supreme Court as issues to be considered on appeal, and those issues shall be clearly identified in the table of contents, in accordance with S.Ct. Prac. R. 6.2(B)(1). In cases where an appeal from an order certifying a conflict has been consolidated with an appeal under S.Ct. Prac. R. 4.4(C), the brief shall identify the issues that have been found by the Supreme Court to be in conflict and shall distinguish those issues from any other issues being briefed in the consolidated appeal.

S.Ct. Prac. R. 4.4.   Effect of Pending Motion to Certify a Conflict upon Discretionary Appeal or Claimed Appeal of Right Filed in Supreme Court

(A) If a party has perfected a discretionary appeal or a claimed appeal of right with the Supreme Court in accordance with S.Ct. Prac. R. 2.2(A), but also has timely moved the court of appeals to certify a conflict in the case, that party shall file a notice with the Supreme Court that a motion to certify a conflict is pending in the court of appeals. The Supreme Court will stay consideration of the jurisdictional memoranda filed in the discretionary appeal or claimed appeal of right until the court of appeals has determined whether to certify a conflict in the case.

(B) If the court of appeals determines that a conflict does not exist, the party that moved the court of appeals to certify a conflict shall immediately file a notice of that determination with the Supreme Court. In accordance with S.Ct. Prac. R. 3.6, the Supreme Court will consider the jurisdictional memoranda filed in the discretionary appeal or the claimed appeal of right.

(C) If both a certified conflict and discretionary appeal or claimed appeal of right are perfected, the Supreme Court will review the court of appeals order certifying a conflict when it reviews the jurisdictional memoranda filed by the parties. In accordance with S.Ct. Prac. R. 3.6 and 4.2, the Supreme Court will issue an order determining both whether a conflict exists and whether to allow the discretionary appeal or the claimed appeal of right, and consolidating the cases if necessary.

History: Amended, eff 4-1-96; 4-1-00; 6-1-00; 7-1-04; 1-1-08; 1-1-10.

NOTES TO DECISIONS

ANALYSIS

Certification of conflicts to supreme court
Improper assignment to a judge

Certification of conflicts to supreme court

Three conditions must be met for certification of a conflict, under Ohio Const. art. III, § 3(B)(4) and Ohio Sup. Ct. Prac. R. IV; first, the certifying court must find that its judgment is in conflict with that of a court of appeals of another district and the conflict must be on the same question, second, the conflict must be on a rule of law -- not facts, and third, the journal entry or opinion of the certifying court must clearly set forth that rule of law which the certifying court contends is in conflict with the judgment on the same question of law by other district courts of appeals. State v. Davis, — Ohio App. 3d —, 2006 Ohio 4457, — N.E. 2d —, 2006 Ohio App. LEXIS 4369 (Aug. 29, 2006).

Improper assignment to a judge

Although the trial court failed to impose post-release control as required by RC § 2967.28, the judge who imposed the post-release control six years later had no authority to do so, and the order had no effect; there was nothing to indicate that the judge who imposed the order was the judge who properly succeeded the originally assigned trial judge, that the matter was transferred, or that there was consent to the order. Since defendant had completed his sentence, he could not be resentenced and he was released from post-release control. State v. Webb, — Ohio App. 3d —, 2007 Ohio 1852, — N.E. 2d —, 2007 Ohio App. LEXIS 1687 (Apr. 19, 2007).

SECTION 5.   RECORD ON APPEAL

S.Ct. Prac. R. 5.1.   Composition of the Record on Appeal

In all appeals, the record on appeal shall consist of the original papers and exhibits to those papers; the transcript of proceedings and exhibits, along with an electronic version of the transcript, if available; and certified copies of the journal entries and the docket prepared by the clerk of the court or other custodian of the original papers. Where applicable, the record on appeal shall consist of all of the above items from both the court of appeals and the trial court.

S.Ct. Prac. R. 5.2. When Record Is to Be Transmitted to Supreme Court from Court of Appeals

In every case on appeal to the Supreme Court from a court of appeals, the clerk of the court of appeals or other custodian having possession of the record shall not transmit the record to the Supreme Court unless and until the Supreme Court issues an order to the custodian to transmit the record pursuant to S.Ct. Prac. R. 5.3.

S.Ct. Prac. R. 5.3. Certification and Transmission of Record from Court of Appeals

(A) Upon order of the Supreme Court, the clerk of the court of appeals or other custodian having possession of the record shall certify and transmit the record to the Clerk of the Supreme Court. Unless otherwise ordered by the Supreme Court, the record shall be transmitted within twenty days of the order. If the case involves termination of parental rights or adoption of a minor child, or both, preparation and transmission of the record shall be expedited and given priority over preparation and transmission of the records in other cases.

(B) The record shall be transmitted along with an index that lists all items included in the record. All items and exhibits listed in the index, regardless of whether they are transmitted, shall be briefly described. The clerk of the court of appeals or other custodian transmitting the record shall send a copy of the index to all counsel of record in the case. The Clerk of the Supreme Court shall notify counsel of record when the record is filed in the Supreme Court.

S.Ct. Prac. R. 5.4. Submission of Record from Board of Tax Appeals

(A) Transmission of the record in an appeal of a decision from the Board of Tax Appeals shall be as prescribed by section 5717.04 of the Revised Code. For the purposes of filing the record with the Clerk of the Supreme Court, the Board may transmit a video or audio record of any hearing before the Board, and if a written transcript was created, it shall be included.

(B) If a written transcript of a hearing is not included, the appellant shall file a written transcript of the hearing with the Clerk of the Supreme Court when the appellant files its merit brief as provided by S.Ct. Prac. R. 6.2. The Supreme Court may dismiss an appeal where no written transcript has been provided, or sua sponte order the appellant to file a written transcript.

S.Ct. Prac. R. 5.5. Submission of Record from Public Utilities Commission

The word "forthwith" as used in section 4903.21 of

the Revised Code, providing that upon service or waiver of service of the notice of appeal the Public Utilities Commission shall forthwith transmit to the Clerk of the Supreme Court a complete transcript of the proceeding, shall mean a period of thirty days. If at the expiration of thirty days the transcript has not been filed, the appellant shall have an additional three days in which to file a complaint in the Supreme Court for a writ of mandamus to compel the Commission to file the transcript. The appeal shall be dismissed if, at the expiration of thirty-three days, neither the transcript nor a complaint for a writ of mandamus has been filed.

S.Ct. Prac. R. 5.6. Items Not to Be Transmitted with the Record

(A) The custodian of the record shall not transmit any physical exhibits unless directed to do so by the Clerk of the Supreme Court or as required by division (B) of this rule.

(B) The custodian shall transmit any audio exhibits, video exhibits, and documents such as papers, maps, or photographs.

(C) If exhibits are not transmitted pursuant to division (A) of this rule the custodian who certifies the record shall designate in the index the exhibits not being transmitted and identify the custodian of those exhibits.

S.Ct. Prac. R. 5.7. Transmission of Record in Death Penalty Appeals

(A) In cases in which the death penalty has been imposed by the court of common pleas for an offense committed before January 1, 1995, the creation, transmission, supplementation, and correction of the record shall be governed by S.Ct. Prac. R. 5.1 through 5.8.

(B) In cases in which the death penalty has been imposed by the court of common pleas for an offense committed on or after January 1, 1995, the creation, transmission, supplementation, and correction of the record shall be governed by S.Ct. Prac. R. 19.4 and 19.5.

S.Ct. Prac. R. 5.8. Supplementation of the Record

If any part of the record is not transmitted to the Supreme Court but is necessary to the Supreme Court's consideration of the questions presented on appeal, the Supreme Court, on its own initiative or on motion of a party, may direct that a supplemental record be certified and transmitted to the Clerk of the Supreme Court in accordance with S.Ct. Prac. R. 5.3(B).

S.Ct. Prac. R. 5.9. Return of Record

After the mandate has been issued in a case on appeal, the Clerk of the Supreme Court shall return the record to the clerk or custodian that transmitted the record.

History: Amended, eff 4-1-96; 4-1-00; 7-1-04; 1-1-08; 1-1-10.

SECTION 6. BRIEFS ON THE MERITS IN APPEALS

S.Ct. Prac. R. 6.1. Limitation on Application of Briefing Rules

The filing deadlines imposed by S.Ct. Prac. R. 6.2 through 6.7 do not apply to appeals involving the imposition of the death penalty for an offense committed on or after January 1, 1995, and instituted under S.Ct. Prac. R. 2.1(C)(1). Filing deadlines for briefs in those appeals are governed by S.Ct. Prac. R. 19.6.

S.Ct. Prac. R. 6.2. Appellant's Brief

[See Appendix D following these rules for a sample brief.]

(A) **Time to file**

(1) In every appeal involving termination of parental rights or adoption of a minor child, or both, the appellant shall file a merit brief with the Supreme Court within twenty days from the date the Clerk of the Supreme Court files the record from the court of appeals.

(2) In every other appeal, the appellant shall file a merit brief within forty days from the date the Clerk files the record from the court of appeals or the administrative agency. In any case, the appellant shall not file a merit brief prior to the filing of the record by the Clerk.

(B) **Contents** The appellant's brief shall contain all of the following:

(1) A table of contents listing the table of authorities cited, the statement of facts, the argument with proposition or propositions of law, and the appendix, with references to the pages of the brief where each appears.

(2) A table of the authorities cited, listing the citations for all cases or other authorities, arranged alphabetically; constitutional provisions; statutes; ordinances; and administrative rules or regulations upon which appellant relies, with references to the pages of the brief where each citation appears.

(3) A statement of the facts with page references, in parentheses, to supporting portions of both the original transcript of testimony and any supplement filed in the case pursuant to S.Ct. Prac. R. 7.1 through 7.2.

(4) An argument, headed by the proposition of law that appellant contends is applicable to the facts of the case and that could serve as a syllabus for the case if appellant prevails. If several propositions of law are presented, the argument shall be divided with each proposition set forth as a subheading.

(5) An appendix, numbered separately from the body of the brief, containing copies of all of the following:

(a) The date-stamped notice of appeal to the Supreme Court, the notice of certified conflict, or the federal court certification order, whichever is applicable;

(b) The judgment or order from which the appeal is taken;

(c) The opinion, if any, relating to the judgment or order being appealed;

(d) All judgments, orders, and opinions rendered by any court or agency in the case, if relevant to the issues on appeal;

(e) Any relevant rules or regulations of any department, board, commission, or any other agency, upon which appellant relies;

(f) Any constitutional provision, statute, or ordinance upon which appellant relies, to be construed, or otherwise involved in the case;

(g) In appeals from the Public Utilities Commission, the appellant's application for rehearing.

(C) **Page limit** Except in death penalty appeals of right, the appellant's brief shall not exceed fifty numbered pages, exclusive of the table of contents, the table of authorities cited, the certificate of service, and the appendix.

S.Ct. Prac. R. 6.3. Appellee's Brief

(A) **Time to file**

(1) In every appeal involving termination of parental rights or adoption of a minor child, or both, within twenty days after the filing of appellant's brief the appellee shall file a merit brief.

(2) In every other appeal, the appellee shall file a merit brief within thirty days after the filing of appellant's brief.

(3) If the case involves multiple appellants who file separate merit briefs, the appellee shall file only one merit brief responding to all of the appellants' merit briefs. The time for filing the appellee's brief shall be calculated from the date the last brief in support of appellant is filed.

(B) **Contents** The appellee's brief shall comply with the provisions in S.Ct. Prac. R. 6.2(B), answer the appellant's contentions, and make any other appropriate contentions as reasons for affirmance of the order or judgment from which the appeal is taken. A statement of facts may be omitted from the appellee's brief if the appellee agrees with the statement of facts given in the appellant's merit brief. The appendix need not duplicate any materials provided in the appendix of the appellant's brief.

(C) **Page limit** Except in death penalty appeals of right, the appellee's brief shall not exceed fifty numbered pages, exclusive of the table of contents, the table of authorities cited, the certificate of service, and any appendix.

S.Ct. Prac. R. 6.4. Appellant's Reply Brief

(A) **Time to file**

(1) In every appeal involving termination of parental rights or adoption of a minor child, or both, the appellant may file a reply brief within fifteen days after the filing of appellee's brief.

(2) In every other appeal, the appellant may file a reply brief within twenty days after the filing of appellee's brief.

(3) If the case involves multiple appellees who file separate merit briefs, the appellant shall file only one reply brief, if any, responding to all of the appellees' merit briefs. The time for filing the appellant's reply brief, if any, shall be calculated from the date the last brief in support of appellee is filed.

(B) **Page limit** Except in death penalty appeals of right, the reply brief shall not exceed twenty numbered pages, exclusive of the table of contents, the table of authorities cited, the certificate of service, and any appendix.

S.Ct. Prac. R. 6.5.   Merit Briefs in Case Involving Cross-Appeal

(A) **Requirements** In a case involving a cross-appeal, each of the parties shall be permitted to file two briefs, and each brief shall conform to the requirements of S.Ct. Prac. R. 6.2(B).

(B) **First brief**

(1)(a) In every appeal involving termination of parental rights or adoption of a minor child, or both, the appellant/cross-appellee shall file the first merit brief within twenty days from the date the Clerk files the record from the court of appeals.

(b) In every other appeal, the appellant/cross-appellee shall file the first merit brief within forty days from the date the Clerk files the record from the court of appeals or the administrative agency.

(2) Except in death penalty appeals of right, this first brief shall not exceed fifty numbered pages, exclusive of the table of contents, the table of authorities cited, the certificate of service, and the appendix.

(C) **Second brief**

(1)(a) In every appeal involving termination of parental rights or adoption of a minor child, or both, the appellee/cross-appellant shall file the second merit brief within twenty days after the filing of the first brief.

(b) In every other appeal, the appellee/cross-appellant shall file the second merit brief within thirty days after the filing of the first brief. The second brief shall be a combined brief containing both a response to the appellant/cross-appellee's brief and the propositions of law and arguments in support of the cross-appeal.

(2) Except in death penalty appeals of right, the second brief shall not exceed fifty numbered pages, exclusive of the table of contents, the table of authorities cited, the certificate of service, and the appendix.

(D) **Third brief**

(1)(a) In every appeal involving termination of parental rights or adoption of a minor child, or both, the appellant/cross-appellee shall file the third merit brief within twenty days after the filing of the second brief.

(b) In every other appeal, the appellant/cross-appellee shall file the third merit brief within thirty days after the filing of the second brief. If the appellant/cross-appellee elects to file a reply brief in that party's appeal, the third brief shall be a combined brief containing both a reply and a response to the arguments in the cross-appeal. Otherwise, the third brief shall include only a response in opposition to the cross-appeal.

(2) Except in death penalty appeals of right, the third brief shall not exceed fifty numbered pages, exclusive of the table of contents, the table of authorities cited, and any appendix.

(E) **Fourth brief**

(1) The fourth brief may be filed by the appellee/cross-appellant only as a reply brief in the cross-appeal.

(a) In every appeal involving termination of parental rights or adoption of a minor child, or both, if a fourth brief is filed, it shall be filed within fifteen days after the filing of the third brief.

(b) In every other appeal, if a fourth brief is filed, it shall be filed within twenty days after the filing of the third brief.

(2) Except in death penalty appeals of right, a fourth brief shall not exceed twenty numbered pages, exclusive of the table of contents, the table of authorities cited, the certificate of service, and any appendix.

S.Ct. Prac. R. 6.6.   Brief of *Amicus Curiae*

(A) An amicus curiae may file a brief urging affirmance or reversal, and leave to file an amicus brief is not required. The brief shall conform to the requirements of this rule, except that an amicus filing a brief in support of an appellant need not include the appendix required by S.Ct. Prac. R. 6.2(B)(5).

(B) The cover of an amicus brief shall identify the party on whose behalf the brief is being submitted or indicate that the brief does not expressly support the position of any parties to the appeal. If the amicus brief is in support of an appellant, the brief shall be filed within the time for filing allowed to the appellant to file a merit brief, and the amicus curiae may file a reply brief within the time allowed to the appellant to file a reply brief. If the amicus brief is in support of an appellee or does not expressly support the position of any party, the brief shall be filed within the time for filing allowed to the appellee to file a merit brief. The Clerk shall refuse to file an amicus brief that is not submitted timely.

S.Ct. Prac. R. 6.7.   Consequence of Failure to File Briefs

(A) If the appellant fails to file a merit brief within the time provided by S.Ct. Prac. R. 6.2 or as extended in accordance with S.Ct. Prac. R. 14.3, the Supreme Court may dismiss the appeal.

(B) If the appellee fails to file a merit brief within the time provided by S.Ct. Prac. R. 6.3 or as extended in accordance with S.Ct. Prac. R. 14.3, the Supreme Court may accept the appellant's statement of facts and issues as correct and reverse the judgment if appellant's brief reasonably appears to sustain reversal.

Section 8.   Prohibition Against Supplemental Briefing

Except as provided in S.Ct. Prac. R. 8.7 and S.Ct. Prac. R. 9.8 and 9.9, merit briefs shall not be supplemented. If a relevant authority is issued after the deadline has passed for filing a party's merit brief, that party may file a citation to the relevant authority but shall not file additional argument.

History: Amended, eff 4-1-96; 10-19-98; 4-1-00; 6-1-00; 7-1-04; 1-1-08; 1-1-10.

SECTION 7.   SUPPLEMENTS TO THE BRIEFS

S.Ct. Prac. R. 7.1.   Parties' Supplements and Content

(A) In every civil case on appeal to the Supreme Court from a court of appeals or an administrative agency, the appellant may prepare and file a supplement to the briefs that contains those portions of the record necessary to enable the Supreme Court to determine the questions presented. Parties to an appeal are encouraged to consult and agree on the contents of the supplement to minimize the appellee's need for filing a supplement. Documents not necessary to determine the questions presented shall not be included in the supplement. The fact that parts of the record are not included in the supplement shall not prevent the parties or the Supreme Court from relying on those parts of the record.

(B) The appellant shall file the supplement with the appellant's merit brief.

(C) The appellee may file a supplement to the merit briefs in the manner required by division (A) of this rule. The appellee's supplement shall not unnecessarily duplicate documents contained in the appellant's supplement.

(D) The appellee's supplement shall be filed with the appellee's merit brief.

S.Ct. Prac. R. 7.2.   Pagination and Indexing of Supplement

(A) The pages of the supplement shall be consecutively numbered in the bottom right-hand corner.

(B) If any portion of a transcript is included in the supplement, the original page numbering of the transcript shall be placed in parentheses.

(C) The supplement shall include an index that lists all items included in the supplement and references the page numbers at which each item can be located.

History: Amended, eff 4-1-96; 7-1-04; 1-1-08; 1-1-10.

SECTION 8.   REQUIREMENTS AS TO FORM AND NUMBER OF DOCUMENTS FILED

S.Ct. Prac. R. 8.1.   Scope of Rules

S.Ct. Prac. R. 8.1 through 8.7 set forth the requirements as to the form and number of all documents filed in Supreme Court cases.

S.Ct. Prac. R. 8.2.   Cover Page

(A) Each document filed in the Supreme Court shall contain a cover page, which shall be white. Except as provided in division (B) of this rule, the cover page shall contain only the following information:

(1) The case name and the case number assigned when the case was filed in the Supreme Court;

(2) The nature of the proceeding in the Supreme Court (e.g., appeal, original action in mandamus, etc.);

(3) If the proceeding is an appeal, the name of the court or the administrative agency from which the appeal is taken;

(4) The title of the document (e.g., notice of appeal, appellant's merit brief, memorandum in support of jurisdiction, etc.);

(5) An identification of the party on whose behalf the document is filed;

(6) The name, attorney registration number, address, telephone number, facsimile number, and e-mail address, if available, of each attorney who has filed an appearance in the case; an indication as to what party each attorney represents; and, where two or more attorneys represent a party, an indication of counsel of record in accordance with S.Ct. Prac. R. 1.3. A party who is not represented by an attorney shall indicate his or her name, address, and telephone number.

(B) The cover page of a notice of appeal shall also provide the name of each appellee in the appeal before the Supreme Court.

S.Ct. Prac. R. 8.3.   Signature

The original of every document filed in the Supreme Court shall be signed by an attorney representing the party on whose behalf the document is filed. A party who is not represented by an attorney shall sign the document being filed.

S.Ct. Prac. R. 8.4.   Mechanical Requirements

(A)(1) Every original document filed with the Supreme Court shall be single-sided, shall be typewritten or prepared by word processor or other standard typographic process, and shall comply with the requirements of this rule. A medium weight, noncondensed Roman type style is preferred, and italic type style may be used only for case citations and emphasis. The Clerk may accept a handwritten document for filing only in an emergency, provided the document is clearly legible.

(2) All documents shall be on opaque, unglazed, 20 to 22 pound weight, white paper, 8½ by 11 inches in size. The original shall not be stapled nor otherwise bound and shall not contain dividers or tabs. All margins shall be at least one inch, and the left margin shall be justified. Documents shall not be enclosed in notebooks or binders and shall not have plastic cover pages.

(3) The text of all documents shall be at least 12-point, double-spaced noncondensed type. Footnotes and quotations may be single-spaced; however, they shall also be in 12-point, noncondensed type. As used in this provision, "noncondensed type" shall refer either to Times New Roman type or to another type that has no more than eighty characters to a line of text.

(B) When these rules require that a copy of the court or agency opinion or decision being appealed be attached to a document filed with the Supreme Court, the copy shall be either of the following:

(1) A photocopy of the opinion or decision issued directly by the court or agency;

(2) An electronically generated copy that meets the requirements of division (A)(3).

(C) Any supplement to the briefs filed pursuant to S.Ct. Prac. R. 7.1 may be prepared and reproduced by photocopying the relevant documents in the record, even if those documents do not comply with the mechanical requirements of division (A), provided that the requirements as to paper size and paper type are met and each page of the supplement is clearly legible. Both sides of the paper may be used in preparing a supplement.

(D) Any document filed with the Supreme Court that exceeds two inches in thickness shall be bound and numbered in two or more parts, with each part containing a cover page.

S.Ct. Prac. R. 8.5.   Number and Form of Copies

(A) The original of a document filed in the Supreme Court shall be accompanied by an appropriate number of copies as follows, unless otherwise provided by S.Ct. Prac. R. 14.1(C)(3):

Notice of appeal	1
Notice of cross-appeal	1
Praecipe filed in death penalty appeal	1
Jurisdictional memorandum	10
Waiver of memorandum in response	0
Brief in an appeal or original action	16
List of additional authorities filed pursuant to S.Ct. Prac. R. 9.8	16
Supplement to a merit brief filed pursuant to S.Ct. Prac. R. 7.1	2
Complaint in an original action	12 — plus an additional copy for each named respondent
Evidence in an original action	12
Request for extension of time	0
Stipulation to an agreed extension of time	0
Notices related to attorney representation under S.Ct. Prac. R. 1.1 through 1.3	0
Affidavits of compliance	1
Application for dismissal	1
Any other document	10

(B) Any party wishing to receive a date-stamped copy of a document submitted for filing with the Clerk shall provide the Clerk with an extra copy of the document and an appropriately-sized, self-addressed, postage-paid envelope.

(C) Copies of documents shall be on opaque, unglazed, 20 to 22 pound weight, white paper, 8½ by 11 inches in size. All copies shall be firmly stapled or bound on the left margin and both sides of the paper may be used as long as the document is clearly legible. Copies shall not be enclosed in notebooks or binders and shall not have plastic cover pages.

S.Ct. Prac. R. 8.6.   Maintaining Privacy of Personal Identifying Numbers

[See Appendix F for a sample personal identifier form.]

(A) As indicated in S.Ct. Prac.R. 14.1(B) all documents filed with the Supreme Court shall be treated as public records.

(B)(1) To protect legitimate personal privacy interests, social security numbers and other personal identifying information shall be redacted from documents before the documents are filed with the Supreme Court in accordance with the Rules of Superintendence. The responsibility for redacting personal identifying information rests solely with the attorneys and

parties who file the documents. The Clerk will not review the documents to confirm that personal identifying information has been excluded.

(2) If personal identifying information is redacted or omitted from a document, the information shall be provided to the Court on a separate form that indicates what information has been reacted or omitted, and provides the location of the redacted or omitted information.

(C) S.Ct. Prac. R. 8.7 notwithstanding, a party may file a motion for leave to redact the original of a previously filed document if personal identifying information was not omitted or redacted when the document was initially filed.

S.Ct. Prac. R. 8.7.   Corrections or Additions to Previously Filed Documents

A party who wishes to make corrections or additions to a previously filed document shall file a revised document and copies that completely incorporate the corrections or additions. The revised document shall be filed within the time permitted by these rules for filing the original document, except that corrections or additions shall not be made to a motion if a memorandum opposing the motion has already been filed. Time permitted by these rules for filing any responsive document shall begin to run when the revised document is filed. The Clerk shall refuse to file a revised document that is not submitted in the form and within the deadlines prescribed by this rule.

History: Amended, eff 4-1-96; 6-1-00; 2-1-01; 7-1-04; 2-1-07; 1-1-08; 1-1-10.

SECTION 9.   ORAL ARGUMENT

S.Ct. Prac. R. 9.1.   Cases in Which Oral Argument Will Be Scheduled

(A) **Appeals from other courts** Oral argument in the following cases will be scheduled and heard after the case has been briefed on the merits in accordance with S.Ct. Prac. R. 6.1 through 6.8 or 19.6:

(1) If the appeal is an appeal of the affirmance of the death penalty by the court of appeals or the imposition of the death penalty by a court of common pleas;

(2) If the appeal is a discretionary appeal that is accepted by the Supreme Court pursuant to S.Ct. Prac. R. 3.6;

(3) If the appeal is a claimed appeal of right that is not determined summarily by the Supreme Court pursuant to S.Ct. Prac. R. 3.6;

(4) If the appeal is filed pursuant to S.Ct. Prac. R. 4.1 and the Supreme Court determined the existence of a conflict certified to it by a court of appeals in accordance with that rule.

(B) **Appeals from administrative agencies** In an appeal from the Board of Tax Appeals, the Public Utilities Commission, or the Power Siting Board, oral argument will be scheduled and heard after the case has been briefed on the merits in accordance with S.Ct. Prac. R. 6.1 through 6.8.

(C) **State law questions** In a certified state law case under S.Ct. Prac. R. 18.1, oral argument will be scheduled and heard after the case has been briefed on the merits in accordance with S.Ct. Prac. R. 18.7.

S.Ct. Prac. R. 9.2.   Oral Argument in Other Cases

(A) In an original action, or in an appeal that is not scheduled for oral argument pursuant to S.Ct. Prac. R. 9.1, the Supreme Court may order oral argument on the merits either sua sponte or in response to a request by any party.

(B) A request for oral argument on the merits shall be by motion and filed no later than twenty days after the filing of appellee's or respondent's merit brief.

S.Ct. Prac. R. 9.3.   Waiver of Oral Argument

(A) Any party may waive oral argument and submit the case to the Supreme Court on the briefs. A waiver of oral argument shall be in writing. It shall be filed at least seven days before the date scheduled for the oral argument; however, if a party files a waiver on the seventh day before oral argument, any other party shall have until the day before oral argument to file a waiver.

(B) Any party who fails to file a merit brief pursuant to S.Ct. Prac. R. 6.2, 6.3, or 19.6 shall be deemed to have waived oral argument.

(C) If not all parties to a case waive oral argument, the oral argument shall be heard and the party or parties not waiving shall be permitted to argue.

(D) If an appellant neither waives oral argument pursuant to this rule nor appears at the argument, the Supreme Court may dismiss the case for lack of prosecution.

S.Ct. Prac. R. 9.4.   Scheduling of Oral Argument in Certain Cases

If a case that involves termination of parental rights or adoption of a minor child, or both, is scheduled for oral argument, it shall be scheduled at the earliest practicable time.

S.Ct. Prac. R. 9.5.   Time and Procedures for Oral Argument

(A)(1) In cases involving affirmance or imposition of the death penalty, thirty minutes shall be allotted to each side for oral argument on the merits.

(2) In all other cases scheduled for oral argument, fifteen minutes shall be allotted to each side for argument on the merits. In cases where there are multiple parties per side, the parties shall share the time allotted to each side.

(B) Either sua sponte or upon motion, the Supreme Court may vary the time for oral argument permitted by this rule. Motions to vary the time for oral argument shall be filed at least seven days before the date scheduled for oral argument.

(C) The appellant shall open oral argument and may conclude oral argument by reserving time for rebuttal. In a case involving a cross-appeal, the appellee/cross-appellant may reserve time for rebuttal of the appellant/cross-appellee's argument in response to the cross-appeal.

S.Ct. Prac. R. 9.6.   Oral Argument by *Amicus Curiae*

(A) No time for oral argument shall be allotted to counsel who have filed amicus curiae briefs. However, with leave of the Supreme Court and the consent of counsel for the side whose position the amicus curiae supports, counsel for the amicus curiae may present oral argument within the time allotted to that side. If an amicus curiae wishes to participate in oral argument but either does not receive the consent of counsel for the side whose position the amicus curiae supports or does not expressly support the position of any parties to the case, the amicus curiae may seek leave from the Supreme Court to participate in oral argument, but such leave will be granted only in the most extraordinary circumstances.

(B) A motion of amicus curiae for leave to participate in oral argument shall be filed at least seven days before the date scheduled for the oral argument.

S.Ct. Prac. R. 9.7.   Reference of Certain Cases to Master Commissioner for Oral Argument

(A) Appeals from the Board of Tax Appeals shall be referred to a regular or special master commissioner for oral argument unless the parties waive the argument or the Supreme Court, sua sponte or upon motion, decides to hear the argument itself. A motion for the Supreme Court to hear oral argument shall be filed within twenty days after the filing of appellee's brief.

(B) The Supreme Court may refer any other matter scheduled for oral argument to a regular or special master commissioner for argument.

S.Ct. Prac. R. 9.8.   List of Additional Authorities Relied Upon During Oral Argument

A party who intends to rely during oral argument on authorities not cited in the merit briefs shall file a list of citations to those authorities no fewer than seven days before oral argument.

S.Ct. Prac. R. 9.9.   Supplemental Filings After Oral Argument

Unless ordered by the Supreme Court, the parties shall not tender for filing and the Clerk shall not file any additional briefs or other materials relating to the merits of the case after the case has been orally argued. If a relevant authority is issued after oral argument, a party may file a citation to the relevant authority but shall not file additional argument.

History: Amended, eff 4-1-96; 4-1-00; 2-1-01; 4-1-02; 7-1-04; 2-1-07; 1-1-08; 1-1-10.

SECTION 10.   ORIGINAL ACTIONS

S.Ct. Prac. R. 10.1.   Application of Rules

(A) S.Ct. Prac. R. 10.1 through 10.12 apply only to actions, other than habeas corpus, within the original jurisdiction of the Supreme Court under Article IV, Section 2 of the Ohio Constitution. The following Revised Code chapters also are applicable: Mandamus, R.C. Chapter 2731; Quo Warranto, R.C. Chapter 2733.

(B) Habeas corpus actions shall be brought and proceed in accordance with R.C. Chapter 2725.

S.Ct. Prac. R. 10.2.   Form and Procedure

In all original actions filed in the Supreme Court of Ohio, the Rules of Practice of the Supreme Court of Ohio shall govern the procedure and the form of documents filed in the actions. The Ohio Rules of Civil Procedure shall supplement these rules unless clearly inapplicable. Where these rules conflict with the Ohio Rules of Civil Procedure, these rules shall control.

S.Ct. Prac. R. 10.3.   Parties

The party filing an action in mandamus, prohibition, procedendo, or quo warranto shall be referred to as the relator. The party named in an original action shall be referred to as the respondent.

S.Ct. Prac. R. 10.4.   Institution of Original Action

(A) An original action shall be instituted by the filing of a complaint. The cover page of the complaint shall contain the name, title, and address of the respondent. The Clerk of the Supreme Court shall issue a summons and serve the summons and a copy of the complaint by certified mail sent to the address of the respondent as

indicated on the cover page of the complaint. The summons shall inform the respondent of the time permitted to respond to the complaint pursuant to S.Ct. Prac. R. 10.5.

(B) All complaints shall contain a specific statement of facts upon which the claim for relief is based, shall be supported by an affidavit specifying the details of the claim, and may be accompanied by a memorandum in support of the writ. The affidavit required by this division shall be made on personal knowledge, setting forth facts admissible in evidence, and showing affirmatively that the affiant is competent to testify to all matters stated in the affidavit. All relief sought, including the issuance of an alternative writ, shall be set forth in the complaint.

S.Ct. Prac. R. 10.5.   Response to Complaint; Court Action

(A) Except as provided by S.Ct. Prac. R. 10.9 and 10.10, the respondent shall file an answer to the complaint or a motion to dismiss within twenty-one days of service of the summons and complaint. If an amended complaint is filed under S.Ct. Prac. R. 8.7, and Civ. R. 15(A), the respondent shall file an answer to the amended complaint or a motion to dismiss within twenty-one days of the filing of the amended complaint.

(B) The respondent may file a motion for judgment on the pleadings at the same time an answer is filed. The relator may not file a response to an answer. The relator may file a memorandum in opposition to a motion to dismiss or a motion for judgment on the pleadings within ten days of the filing of the motion. Neither party may file a motion for summary judgment.

(C) After the time for filing an answer to the complaint or a motion to dismiss, the Supreme Court will either dismiss the case or issue an alternative or a peremptory writ, if a writ has not already been issued.

S.Ct. Prac. R. 10.6.   Alternative Writs

When an alternative writ is issued, the Supreme Court will issue a schedule for the presentation of evidence and the filing and service of briefs or other pleadings. Unless the Supreme Court orders otherwise, issuance of an alternative writ in a prohibition case stays proceedings in the action sought to be prohibited until final determination of the Supreme Court.

S.Ct. Prac. R. 10.7.   Presentation of Evidence

To facilitate the consideration and disposition of original actions, counsel, when possible, should submit an agreed statement of facts to the Supreme Court. All other evidence shall be submitted by affidavits, stipulations, depositions, and exhibits. Affidavits shall be made on personal knowledge, setting forth facts admissible in evidence, and showing affirmatively that the affiant is competent to testify to all matters stated in the affidavit. Sworn or certified copies of all papers or parts of papers referred to in an affidavit shall be attached.

S.Ct. Prac. R. 10.8.   Merit Briefs

All merit briefs shall conform to the requirements

set forth in S.Ct. Prac. R. 6.1 through 6.8 and 8.1 through 8.7, to the extent those rules are applicable.

S.Ct. Prac. R. 10.9.   Expedited Election Cases

(A) **Procedure**

(1) Because of the necessity of a prompt disposition of an original action relating to a pending election, and in order to give the Supreme Court adequate time for full consideration of the case, if the action is filed within ninety days prior to the election, the respondent shall file an answer to the complaint within five days after service of the summons.

(2) Unless otherwise ordered by the Supreme Court, original actions governed by this rule shall proceed as follows:

(a) Relator shall file any evidence and a merit brief in support of the complaint within three days after the filing of the answer or, if no answer is filed, within three days after the answer was due.

(b) Respondent shall file any evidence and a merit brief within three days after the filing of relator's merit brief, and

(c) Relator may file a reply brief within three days after the filing of respondent's merit brief.

(3) Motions to dismiss and for judgment on the pleadings shall not be filed in expedited election cases.

(B) **Reconsideration** A motion for reconsideration may be filed in an expedited election case. Any motion for reconsideration shall be filed within three days after the Supreme Court's judgment entry or order is filed with the Clerk. A memorandum in opposition may be filed within three days of the filing of the motion for reconsideration.

(C) **Service of documents** All documents in expedited election cases shall be served on the date of filing by personal service, facsimile transmission, or e-mail.

S.Ct. Prac. R. 10.10.   Expedited Adoption/Termination of Parental Rights Cases

If the original action involves termination of parental rights or adoption of a minor child, or both, the respondent shall file a response to the complaint within fifteen days after service of the summons. After the time for filing a response to the complaint, the Supreme Court will decide on an expedited basis whether to dismiss the case or issue an alternative or a peremptory writ, if a writ has not already been issued. In order to invoke these expedited procedures, the relator shall designate on the cover page of the complaint that the original action involves termination of parental rights or adoption of a minor child, or both.

S.Ct. Prac. R. 10.11.   Reference to a Master Commissioner

The Supreme Court may refer original actions to a master commissioner for hearing and argument.

S.Ct. Prac. R. 10.12.   Consequence of Failure to File Briefs

If the relator fails to file a merit brief within the time provided by this rule or as ordered by the Supreme Court, an original action shall be dismissed for want of prosecution. Unless otherwise ordered by the Supreme Court, a dismissal under this rule operates as an adjudication on the merits. If the respondent fails to file a merit brief within the time provided by this rule or as ordered by the Supreme Court, the Supreme Court may accept the relator's statement of facts and issues as correct and grant the writ if relator's brief reasonably appears to sustain the writ.

History: Amended, eff 4-1-96; 4-1-00; 8-1-02; 7-1-04; 1-1-08; 1-1-10.

NOTES TO DECISIONS

ANALYSIS

Expedited election action
Pleadings
Submitting evidence

Expedited election action

Although a candidate for a local board of education did not file her election action until 21 days after the county board of education refused to file her nominating petition, laches did not bar the candidate's claim as any delay did not prejudice the board of elections because even if the case would have been filed within a week, it would still have been an expedited election case under Ohio Sup. Ct. Prac. R. X(9) and it still would have been decided after the absentee-ballot deadline in RC § 3509.01. State Ex Rel. Brinda v. Lorain County Bd. of Elections, 115 Ohio St. 3d 299, 2007 Ohio 5228, — N.E. 2d —, 2007 Ohio LEXIS 2399 (Oct. 2, 2007).

Pleadings

In an original action filed in the Ohio Supreme Court, an affidavit of a relator's counsel does not comply with the Ohio Sup. Ct. Prac. R. X(4)(B) personal-knowledge requirement when it states that the facts in the complaint are "true and correct to the best of his knowledge." State Ex Rel. Comm. for the Charter Amendment for An Elected Law Dir. v. City of Bay Vill., — Ohio St. 3d —, 2007 Ohio 5380, — N.E. 2d —, 2007 Ohio LEXIS 2515 (Oct. 8, 2007).

Submitting evidence

City was not entitled to submit evidence in an expedited election case, under Ohio Sup. Ct. Prac. R. X(9), because the city was not allowed to intervene, and only parties were allowed to submit evidence. Hamilton County Bd. of Elections, — Ohio St. 3d —, 2007 Ohio 5379, — N.E. 2d —, 2007 Ohio LEXIS 2514 (Oct. 8, 2007).

SECTION 11.   ENTRY OF SUPREME COURT JUDGMENT; MOTIONS FOR RECONSIDERATION AND FOR REOPENING; ISSUANCE OF MANDATE

S.Ct. Prac. R. 11.1.   Entry of Judgment

The filing of a judgment entry or other order by the Supreme Court with the Clerk for journalization constitutes entry of the judgment or order. A Supreme Court judgment entry or other order is effective when it is filed with the Clerk. In every case involving termination of parental rights or adoption of a minor child, or both, the Supreme Court will expedite the filing of the judgment entry or other orders for journalization.

S.Ct. Prac. R. 11.2.   Motion for Reconsideration

(A) Except as provided in S.Ct. Prac. R. 10.9(B), any motion for reconsideration must be filed within ten days after the Supreme Court's judgment entry or order is filed with the Clerk.

(B) A motion for reconsideration shall not constitute a reargument of the case and may be filed only with respect to the following:

(1) The Supreme Court's refusal to grant jurisdiction to hear a discretionary appeal or the dismissal of a claimed appeal of right as not involving a substantial constitutional question;

(2) The sua sponte dismissal of a case;

(3) The granting of a motion to dismiss;

(4) A decision on the merits of a case.

(C) An amicus curiae may not file a motion for reconsideration. An amicus curiae may file a memorandum in support of a motion for reconsideration within the time permitted for filing a motion for reconsideration.

(D) The Clerk shall refuse to file a motion for reconsideration that is not expressly permitted by this rule or that is not timely.

S.Ct. Prac. R. 11.3.   Memorandum Opposing Motion for Reconsideration

(A) Except as provided in S.Ct. Prac. R. 10.9(B), a party opposing reconsideration may file a memorandum opposing a motion for reconsideration within ten days of the filing of the motion.

(B) An amicus curiae may file a memorandum opposing a motion for reconsideration within ten days of the filing of the motion.

S.Ct. Prac. R. 11.4.   Issuance of Mandate

(A) After the Supreme Court has decided an appeal on the merits, the Clerk shall issue a mandate. The mandate shall be issued ten days after entry of the judgment, unless a motion for reconsideration is filed within that time in accordance with S.Ct. Prac. R. 10.9(B) or 11.2.

(1) If a motion for reconsideration is denied, the mandate shall be issued when the order denying the motion for reconsideration is filed with the Clerk.

(2) If a motion for reconsideration is granted, the mandate shall be issued ten days after the entry of the judgment is filed with the Clerk.

(B) No mandate shall be issued on the Supreme Court's refusal to grant jurisdiction to hear a discretionary appeal or the dismissal of a claimed appeal of right as not involving a substantial constitutional question.

(C) A certified copy of the judgment entry shall constitute the mandate.

S.Ct. Prac. R. 11.5.   Assessment of Costs

(A) Unless otherwise ordered by the Supreme Court, costs in an appeal shall be assessed as follows at the conclusion of the case:

(1) If an appeal is dismissed, to the appellant;

(2) If the judgment or order being appealed is affirmed, to the appellant;

(3) If the judgment or order being appealed is reversed, to the appellee.

(4) If the judgment or order being appealed is affirmed or reversed in part or is vacated, the parties shall bear their respective costs.

(B) As used in this rule, "costs" includes only the filing fee paid to initiate the appeal with the Supreme Court, unless the Court, sua sponte or upon motion, assesses additional costs.

S.Ct. Prac. R. 11.6.   Application for Reopening

(A) An appellant in a death penalty case involving an offense committed on or after January 1, 1995, may apply for reopening of the appeal from the judgment of conviction and sentence, based on a claim of ineffective assistance of appellate counsel in the Supreme Court. An application for reopening shall be filed within ninety days from the issuance of the mandate of the Supreme Court, unless the appellant shows good cause for filing at a later time.

(B) An application for reopening shall contain all of the following:

(1) The Supreme Court case number in which reopening is sought and the trial court case number or numbers from which the appeal was taken;

(2) A showing of good cause for untimely filing if the application is filed more than ninety days after entry of the judgment of the Supreme Court;

(3) One or more propositions of law or arguments in support of propositions of law that previously were not considered on the merits in the case or that were considered on an incomplete record because of the claimed ineffective representation of appellate counsel;

(4) An affidavit stating the basis for the claim that appellate counsel's representation was ineffective with respect to the propositions of law or arguments raised pursuant to S.Ct. Prac. R. 11.6(B)(3) and the manner in which the claimed deficiency prejudicially affected the outcome of the appeal, which affidavit may include citations to applicable authorities and references to the record;

(5) Any relevant parts of the record available to the applicant and all supplemental affidavits upon which the applicant relies.

(C) Within thirty days from the filing of the application, the attorney for the prosecution may file and serve affidavits, parts of the record, and a memorandum of law in opposition to the application.

(D) An application for reopening and an opposing memorandum shall not exceed ten pages, exclusive of affidavits and parts of the record.

(E) An application for reopening shall be granted if there is a genuine issue as to whether the applicant was deprived of the effective assistance of counsel on appeal.

(F) If the Supreme Court grants the application, the Clerk shall serve notice on the clerk of the trial court, and the Supreme Court will do both of the following:

(1) Appoint counsel to represent the applicant if the applicant is indigent and not currently represented;

(2) Impose conditions, if any, necessary to preserve the status quo during the pendency of the reopened appeal.

(G) If the application is granted, the case shall proceed as on an initial appeal in accordance with these rules except that the Supreme Court may limit its review to those propositions of law and arguments not previously considered. The time limits for preparation and transmission of the record pursuant to S.Ct. Prac. R. 19.5 shall run from entry of the order granting the application. The parties shall address in their briefs the claim that representation by prior appellate counsel was deficient and that the applicant was prejudiced by that deficiency.

(H) If the Supreme Court determines that an evidentiary hearing is necessary, the evidentiary hearing may be conducted by the Supreme Court or referred to a master commissioner.

(I) If the Supreme Court finds that the performance of appellate counsel was deficient and the applicant was prejudiced by that deficiency, the Supreme Court shall vacate its prior judgment and enter the appropriate judgment. If the Supreme Court does not so find, it shall issue an order confirming its prior judgment.

History: Amended, eff 4-1-96; 4-1-00; 7-1-04; 1-1-08; 1-1-10.

SECTION 12. DISPOSITION OF APPEALS IMPROVIDENTLY ACCEPTED OR CERTIFIED; SUMMARY DISPOSITION OF APPEALS

S.Ct. Prac. R. 12.1. Improvidently Accepted Appeals

When a case has been accepted for determination on the merits pursuant to S.Ct. Prac. R. 3.6, the Supreme Court may later find that there is no substantial constitutional question or question of public or great general interest, or that the same question has been raised and passed upon in a prior appeal. Accordingly, the Supreme Court may sua sponte dismiss the case as having been improvidently accepted, or summarily reverse or affirm on the basis of precedent.

S.Ct. Prac. R. 12.2. Improvidently Certified Conflicts

When the Supreme Court finds a conflict pursuant to S.Ct. Prac. R. 4.2, it may later find that there is no conflict or that the same question has been raised and passed upon in a prior appeal. Accordingly, the Supreme Court may sua sponte dismiss the case as having been improvidently certified, or summarily reverse or affirm on the basis of precedent.

History: Amended, eff 4-1-96; 7-1-04; 1-1-08; 1-1-10.

SECTION 13. PETITION CHALLENGES; ELECTION CONTESTS

S.Ct. Prac. R. 13.1. Petition Challenges

(A) To invoke the original jurisdiction of the Supreme Court pursuant to Article II, Section 1g of the Ohio Constitution, for the purpose of challenging an initiative, supplementary, or referendum petition or the signatures upon such petition, a party shall file a challenge with the Clerk of the Supreme Court. The challenge shall designate on the cover page that it challenges an initiative, supplementary, or referendum petition pursuant to Article II, Section 1g. The challenge shall contain a statement of the reasons for the challenge and a specific statement of facts upon which the challenge is based. The party filing a challenge shall be referred to as the relator. The party submitting the petition that is the subject of the challenge shall be referred to as the respondent.

(B) The relator shall have the burden of demonstrating by a preponderance of the evidence that the petition or signatures thereon do not comply with applicable law.

(C) In all challenge proceedings filed under this rule, these rules shall govern the procedure and the form of all documents. The Ohio Rules of Civil Procedure and the Ohio Rules of Evidence, including those related to depositions, interrogatories, requests for production of documents, and subpoenas, shall supplement these rules unless clearly inapplicable. Where these rules conflict with the Ohio Rules of Civil Procedure or the Ohio Rules of Evidence, these rules shall control.

(D) The Supreme Court may refer challenge actions to a master commissioner for any purpose including resolution of discovery disputes, and to conduct a hearing for the presentation of evidence. The Supreme Court may also order oral argument before the Court.

(E) In a challenge to an initiative, supplementary, or referendum petition brought under Article II, Section 1g of the Ohio Constitution, the Supreme Court may do all things necessary for an efficient and timely ruling on the challenge. The Supreme Court may sua sponte, or on motion by a party, issue a procedural order to govern the receipt of evidence, filing of briefs, conduct of hearings, and manner for ruling on any challenges.

(F) All documents filed under this Rule, including the challenge, shall be served by the parties on the date of filing by personal service, facsimile transmission, or e-mail.

S.Ct. Prac. R. 13.2. Contest of an Election

Contests of an election brought pursuant to R.C. 3515.08 shall proceed in accordance with the applicable provisions of R.C. Chapter 3515.

History: Eff 1-1-10.

SECTION 14. GENERAL PROVISIONS

S.Ct. Prac. R. 14.1. Filing with the Supreme Court

(A) **Filing defined**

(1) Filing with the Supreme Court shall be made by submitting the documents to the Clerk of the Supreme Court during the regular business hours of the Clerk's Office. Only documents that are timely received and in compliance with these rules shall be filed by the Clerk. Documents may be submitted for filing in person, by delivery service, or by mail addressed to the Clerk, The Supreme Court of Ohio, 65 S. Front St., 8th Floor, Columbus, Ohio 43215-3431.

(2) Documents submitted by mail or delivery service shall not be considered for filing until received in the Clerk's Office. Documents received in the Clerk's Office after 5:00 p.m. shall not be considered for filing until the next business day. Confirmation of delivery by any source other than the Clerk's Office does not verify actual receipt by the Clerk's Office. The alteration of hours or procedures by any delivery service, including but not limited to the United States Postal Service, shall not affect the filing deadlines and requirements imposed by these rules.

(B) **Filings treated as public records** Documents filed with the Supreme Court shall be treated as public records unless they have been sealed pursuant to a court order or are the subject of a motion to seal pending in the Supreme Court.

(C) **Filing by facsimile transmission**

(1) The following documents may be filed by facsimile transmission to the Clerk:

(a) A request for extension of time or a stipulation to an agreed extension of time that complies with S.Ct. Prac. R. 14.3;

(b) A list of additional authorities filed under S.Ct. Prac. R. 6.8 or 9.8;

(c) An application for dismissal filed by an appellant or a relator;

(d) A waiver of oral argument filed under S.Ct. Prac. R. 9.3;

(e) A notice related to attorney representation filed under S.Ct. Prac. R. 1.3;

(f) A notice of a court of appeals determination of no conflict filed under S.Ct. Prac. R. 4.4(B);

(g) A waiver of a memorandum in response under S.Ct. Prac. R. 3.2(E).

(2) Each facsimile transmission shall be accompanied by a cover page requesting that the document be filed and providing the name, telephone number, and facsimile number of the person transmitting the document.

(3) Only one copy of the document shall be transmitted. The Clerk shall provide any additional copies required to be filed by these rules. The person filing a document by facsimile transmission shall retain the original document and make it available upon request of the Supreme Court.

(4) Documents transmitted by facsimile transmission and received in the Clerk's Office on a Saturday, Sunday, or other day the Clerk's Office is closed to the public, or after 5:00 p.m. on a business day, shall be considered for filing on the next business day.

(D) **Prohibition against untimely filings** No document may be filed after the filing deadlines imposed by these rules, set by Court order, or as extended in accordance with S.Ct. Prac. R. 14.3(B)(2) or with S.Ct. Prac. R. 19.5(C). The Clerk shall refuse to file a document that is not timely received in accordance with S.Ct. Prac. R. 14.1(A). Motions to waive this rule are prohibited and shall not be filed.

(E) **Rejection of noncomplying documents** The Clerk may reject documents unless they are legible and comply with the requirements of these rules.

S.Ct. Prac. R. 14.2. Service of Documents; No-

tice When Documents Are Rejected for Filing

(A) **Service requirement**

(1) When a party or an amicus curiae files any document with the Clerk, except a complaint filed to institute an original action or a form containing omitted personal identifiers as required by the Rules of Superintendence for the Courts of Ohio, that party or amicus curiae shall also serve a copy of the document on all parties to the case. Service on a party represented by counsel shall be made on counsel of record.

(2) Service of a copy of a notice of appeal from a decision of the Public Utilities Commission or the Power Siting Board shall be made pursuant to section 4903.13 of the Revised Code. In an appeal or a cross-appeal from the Public Utilities Commission or the Power Siting Board, a copy of the notice of appeal or cross-appeal shall also be served upon all parties to the proceeding before the Public Utilities Commission or the Power Siting Board that is the subject of the appeal or cross-appeal.

(3) In a case involving a felony, when a county prosecutor files a notice of appeal under S.Ct. Prac. R. 2.2 or 2.3 or an order certifying a conflict under S.Ct. Prac. R. 4.1, the county prosecutor shall also serve a copy of the notice or order on the Ohio Public Defender.

(B) **Manner of service**

(1) Except as otherwise provided by this rule, service may be personal or by delivery service, mail, e-mail, or facsimile transmission. Except as provided in division (A), personal service includes delivery of the copy to counsel or to a responsible person at the office of counsel and is effected upon delivery. Service by delivery service is effected by depositing the copy with the delivery service. Service by mail is effected by depositing the copy with the United States Postal Service for mailing. Service by e-mail is effected upon the successful electronic transmission of the copy. Service by facsimile transmission is effected upon the successful electronic transmission of the copy by facsimile process.

(2) In appeals from the Board of Tax Appeals under S.Ct. Prac. R. 2.3(A), service of a notice of appeal or cross-appeal shall be made by certified mail.

(3) In expedited election cases under S.Ct. Prac. R. 10.9, service of all documents, except the complaint filed to institute the original action, shall be personal, by e-mail, or by facsimile transmission.

(C) **Certificate of service; certificate of filing**

(1) Unless a document is filed jointly and is signed by all parties to the case, all documents presented for filing with the Clerk, except complaints filed to institute an original action or a form containing omitted personal identifiers as required by the Rules of Superintendence for the Courts of Ohio, shall contain a certificate of service. The certificate of service shall state the date and manner of service, identify the names of the persons served, and be signed by the party or the amicus curiae who files the document. The certificate of service for a document served by facsimile transmission shall also state the facsimile number of the person to whom the document was transmitted. The

Clerk shall refuse to accept for filing any document that does not contain a certificate of service, unless these rules require that the document is served by the Clerk.

(2) In an appeal from the Public Utilities Commission or the Power Siting Board, the notice of appeal shall also contain a certificate of filing to evidence that the appellant filed a notice of appeal with the docketing division of the Public Utilities Commission in accordance with sections 4901-1-02(A) and 4901-1-36 of the Ohio Administrative Code.

(D) **Failure to provide service**

(1) When a party or amicus curiae fails to provide service upon a party or parties to the case in accordance with S.Ct. Prac. R. 14.2(A), any party adversely affected may file a motion to strike the document that was not served. Within ten days after a motion to strike is filed, the party or amicus curiae against whom the motion is filed may file a memorandum opposing the motion.

(2) If the Supreme Court determines that service was not made as required by this rule, it may strike the document or, if the interests of justice warrant, order that the document be served and impose a new deadline for filing any responsive document. If the Supreme Court determines that service was made as required by this rule or that service was not made but the movant was not adversely affected, it may deny the motion.

(E) **Notice to other parties when document is rejected for filing** If a document presented for filing is rejected by the Clerk under these rules, the party or amicus curiae who presented the document for filing shall promptly notify all of the parties served with a copy of the document that the document was not filed in the case.

S.Ct. Prac. R. 14.3. Computation and Extension of Time

(A) **Computation of time**

(1) In computing any period of time prescribed or allowed by these rules or by an order of the Supreme Court, the day of the act from which the designated period of time begins to run shall not be included and the last day of the period shall be included. If the last day of the period is a Saturday, Sunday, or legal holiday, the period runs until the end of the next day that is not a Saturday, Sunday, or legal holiday.

(2) Notwithstanding Civ. R. 6(A), when the period of time prescribed or allowed is less than seven days, as in expedited election cases under S.Ct. Prac. R. 10.9, intermediate Saturdays, Sundays, and legal holidays shall be included in the computation.

(3) When the Clerk's Office of the Supreme Court is closed to the public for the entire day that constitutes the last day for doing an act, or before the usual closing time on that day, then that act may be performed on the next day that is not a Saturday, Sunday, or legal holiday.

(B) **Extension of time**

(1) **General prohibition against extensions of time** Except as provided in division (B)(2), the Supreme Court will not extend the time for filing a

document as prescribed by these rules or by Court order, and the Clerk shall refuse to file requests for extension of time.

(2) **Extension of Time to File Certain Documents**

(a) Except in expedited election cases under S.Ct. Prac. R. 10.9, parties may stipulate to extensions of time to file merit briefs, including reply briefs, under S.Ct. Prac. R. 6.2 through 6.5; merit briefs, including reply briefs, under S.Ct. Prac. R. 19.6; or the response to a complaint or evidence under S.Ct. Prac. R. 10.5 and 10.6. Each party may obtain in a case only one agreed extension of time not to exceed twenty days, provided the party has not previously obtained an extension of time from the Supreme Court under division B(2)(b). An agreed extension of time shall be effective only if a stipulation to the agreed extension of time is filed with the Clerk within the time prescribed by these rules for filing the brief or other document that is the subject of the agreement. The stipulation shall state affirmatively the new date for filing agreed to by the parties. The Clerk shall refuse to file a stipulation to an agreed extension of time that is not tendered timely in accordance with this rule, or if a request for extension of time has already been granted under division (B)(2)(b) to the party filing the stipulation.

(b) In an expedited election case or any other case where a stipulation to an agreed extension of time cannot be obtained under S.Ct. Prac. R. 14.3(B)(2)(a), a party may file a request for extension of time to file a brief, the response to a complaint, or evidence. The Supreme Court will grant a party only one extension of time, not to exceed ten days, provided the request for extension of time states good cause for an extension and is filed with the Clerk within the time prescribed by the rules for filing the brief or other document that is the subject of the request. The Clerk shall refuse to file a request for extension of time that is not tendered timely in accordance with this rule, or if a stipulation to an agreed extension of time has already been filed under division (B)(2)(a) by the party filing the request.

(3) **Effect of extension of time upon other parties on the same side** When one party receives an extension of time under division (B)(2), the extension shall apply to all other parties on that side.

S.Ct. Prac. R. 14.4. Motions; Responses

(A) Unless otherwise prohibited by these rules, an application for an order or other relief shall be made by filing a motion for the order or relief. The motion shall state with particularity the grounds on which it is based. A motion to stay a lower court's decision pending appeal shall include relevant information regarding bond. A copy of the lower court's decision and any applicable opinion shall be attached.

(B) If a party files a motion with the Supreme Court, any other party may file a memorandum opposing the motion within ten days from the date the motion is filed, unless otherwise provided in these rules. A reply to a memorandum opposing a motion shall not be filed by the moving party. The Clerk shall refuse to file a reply to a memorandum opposing a motion, and motions to waive this rule are prohibited and shall not be filed.

(C) The Supreme Court may act upon a motion before the deadline for filing a memorandum opposing the motion if the interests of justice warrant immediate consideration by the Supreme Court. Any party adversely affected by the action of the Supreme Court may file a motion to vacate the action.

S.Ct. Prac. R. 14.5.   Frivolous Actions; Sanctions; Vexatious Litigators

(A) If the Supreme Court, sua sponte or on motion by a party, determines that an appeal or other action is frivolous or is prosecuted for delay, harassment, or any other improper purpose, it may impose, on the person who signed the appeal or action, a represented party, or both, appropriate sanctions. The sanctions may include an award to the opposing party of reasonable expenses, reasonable attorney fees, costs or double costs, or any other sanction the Supreme Court considers just. An appeal or other action shall be considered frivolous if it is not reasonably well-grounded in fact or warranted by existing law or a good faith argument for the extension, modification, or reversal of existing law.

(B) If a party habitually, persistently, and without reasonable cause engages in frivolous conduct under division (A), the Supreme Court may, sua sponte or on motion by a party, find the party to be a vexatious litigator. If the Supreme Court determines that a party is a vexatious litigator under this rule, the Court may impose filing restrictions on the party. The restrictions may include prohibiting the party from continuing or instituting legal proceedings in the Supreme Court without first obtaining leave, prohibiting the filing of actions in the Supreme Court without the filing fee or security for costs required by S.Ct. Prac. R. 15.1 and 15.2, or any other restriction the Supreme Court considers just.

History: Amended, eff 4-1-96; 4-28-97; 7-12-99; 7-1-04; 10-1-05; 1-1-08; 1-1-10.

SECTION 15.   FILING FEES AND SECURITY DEPOSITS

S.Ct. Prac. R. 15.1.   Filing Fees to Institute a Case

The following filing fees are imposed by section 2503.17 of the Revised Code and shall be paid before a case is filed:

For filing a notice of appeal	$100.00
For filing a notice of cross-appeal	$100.00
For filing an order of a court of appeals certifying a conflict	$100.00
For instituting an original action	$100.00

S.Ct. Prac. R. 15.2.   Security Deposits in Original Actions

Original actions also require a deposit in the amount of one hundred dollars as security for costs. The security deposit shall be paid before the case is filed. In extraordinary circumstances, the Supreme Court may require an additional security deposit at any time during the action.

S.Ct. Prac. R. 15.3.   Affidavit of Indigency or Entry of Appointment of Counsel in Lieu of Fees

[See Appendix E following these rules for an affidavit of indigency form.]

(A) An affidavit of indigency may be filed in lieu of filing fees or security deposits. The affidavit shall be executed within six months prior to being filed in the Supreme Court by the party on whose behalf it is filed. The affidavit shall state the specific reasons the party does not have sufficient funds to pay the filing fees or the security deposit. The Clerk shall refuse to file an affidavit of indigency that does not comply with this rule.

(B) Where counsel has been appointed by a trial or appellate court to represent an indigent party, a copy of the entry of appointment may be filed in lieu of an affidavit of indigency.

History: Amended, eff 4-1-96; 7-1-04; 1-1-08; 10-16-09; 1-1-10.

SECTION 16.   PRESERVATION OF RECORDS AND FILES

S.Ct. Prac. R. 16.1.   Custodian of Documents

The Clerk of the Supreme Court is the custodian of all documents and other items filed in Supreme Court cases, and they shall not be taken from the Clerk's custody unless by order of the Supreme Court. The Supreme Court may direct that any records may be reproduced as set forth in section 9.01 of the Revised Code.

History: Amended, eff 6-1-94; 4-1-96; 1-1-10.

SECTION 17.   MEDIATION PROCEEDINGS

S.Ct. Prac. R. 17.1.   Referral of Cases for Mediation

(A) **Referral** The Supreme Court may, sua sponte or on motion by a party, refer to its mediator for mediation any case that originated in the court of appeals, any appeal from an administrative agency, any original action, or pursuant to S.Ct. Prac. R. 2.6 any civil case that the Supreme Court deems appropriate. The mediator may conduct mediation conferences at which the parties shall explore settling the case, simplifying the issues, and expediting the procedure, and may consider any other matter that might aid in resolving the case. Unless otherwise provided by Court order, referral of a case for mediation does not alter the filing deadlines prescribed by these rules.

(B) **Statements**

(1) Any party seeking a monetary settlement shall prepare a statement setting forth the amount of the demand and a detailed explanation for it. Such party shall submit this statement to the opposing parties and to the mediator ten days prior to the scheduled mediation. This statement will not be filed in the case.

(2) Parties may submit to the mediator a confidential statement analyzing the settlement potential of the case. The mediation counsel will not disclose this statement to the other parties, unless the submitting party consents to disclosure. This statement will not be filed in the case.

(C) **Attendance**

(1) If a case is referred for mediation, each party to the case, or the representative of each party who has full settlement authority, and the attorney for each party shall attend the mediation conferences, unless excused by the mediator. If a party or its representative is excused from a conference, the party or its representative must provide its attorney authority beyond initial mediation positions, and the party or its representative must be available for consultation during the course of the mediation.

(2) If a party or an attorney fails to attend the mediation conference without being excused, the Supreme Court may assess the party or the attorney reasonable expenses caused by the failure, including reasonable attorney fees or all or a part of the expenses of the other party. The Supreme Court may also dismiss the action, strike documents filed by the offending party, or impose any other appropriate penalty.

(D) **Extension of time to file briefs or other documents** Notwithstanding S.Ct. Prac. R. 14.3(B), the Supreme Court, sua sponte or upon motion by a party, may extend filing deadlines or stay the case referred under this rule, if the extension or stay will facilitate mediation. A request for an extension of time shall be filed with the Clerk within the time prescribed by the rules for filing the brief or other document that is the subject of the request.

(E) **Supreme Court orders** The Supreme Court may issue orders to supervise mediation. At the conclusion of the mediation, the Supreme Court will enter an appropriate order.

S.Ct. Prac. R. 17.2. Privileges and Confidentiality

The definitions contained in section 2710.01 of the Revised Code apply to Supreme Court mediation. The privileges contained in section 2710.03 of the Revised Code and the exceptions contained in section 2710.05 of the Revised Code apply to mediation communications. The privileges may be waived under section 2710.04 of the Revised Code. Mediation communications are confidential, and no one shall disclose any of these communications unless all parties and the mediator consent to disclosure. The Supreme Court may impose penalties for any improper disclosures made in violation of this rule.

History: Eff 1-1-10.

SECTION 18. CERTIFICATION OF QUESTIONS OF STATE LAW FROM FEDERAL COURTS

S.Ct. Prac. R. 18.1. When a State Law Question May Be Certified

The Supreme Court may answer a question of law certified to it by a court of the United States. This rule may be invoked when the certifying court, in a proceeding before it, issues a certification order finding there is a question of Ohio law that may be determinative of the proceeding and for which there is no controlling precedent in the decisions of this Supreme Court.

S.Ct. Prac. R. 18.2. Contents of Certification Order

The certification order shall contain all of the following:

(A) The name of the case;

(B) A statement of facts showing the nature of the case, the circumstances from which the question of law arises, the question of law to be answered, and any other information the certifying court considers relevant to the question of law to be answered;

(C) The name of each of the parties;

(D) The names, addresses, and telephone numbers of counsel for each party;

(E) A designation of one of the parties as the moving party.

S.Ct. Prac. R. 18.3. Preparation of Certification Order; Notice of Filing

The certification order shall be signed by any justice or judge presiding over the cause or by a magistrate judge presiding over the cause pursuant to 28 U.S.C. Section 636(c). The clerk of the certifying court shall serve copies of the certification order upon all parties or their counsel of record and file with the Clerk of the Supreme Court the certification order under seal of the certifying court.

S.Ct. Prac. R. 18.4. Record

The Supreme Court may request that copies of all or any portion of the record before the certifying court be transmitted to the Clerk of the Supreme Court.

S.Ct. Prac. R. 18.5. Parties

The party designated by the certifying court as the moving party shall be referred to as the petitioner. The party adverse to the petitioner shall be referred to as the respondent.

S.Ct. Prac. R. 18.6. Preliminary Memoranda; Court Determination of Whether to Answer Question Certified

Within twenty days after a certification order is filed with the Supreme Court, each party shall file a memorandum, not to exceed fifteen pages in length, addressing all questions of law certified to the Supreme Court. An amicus curiae may file a memorandum conforming to the requirements of this rule and supporting either party within twenty days after a certification order is filed with the Supreme Court. The Supreme Court will review the memoranda and issue an order identifying the question or questions it will answer or decline to answer. The Clerk of the Supreme Court shall send a copy of the order to the certifying court and to all parties or their counsel.

S.Ct. Prac. R. 18.7.   Merit Briefs

If the Supreme Court decides to answer any of the questions certified to it, the parties shall brief the merits of the issue certified in accordance with S.Ct. Prac. R. 6.2 through 6.4. The petitioner shall proceed under the provisions of S.Ct. Prac. R. 6.2 through 6.4 that are applicable to an appellant and the respondent shall proceed under the provisions applicable to an appellee.

S.Ct. Prac. R. 18.8.   Opinion

If the Supreme Court decides to answer a question or questions certified to it, it will issue a written opinion stating the law governing the question or questions certified. The Clerk shall send a copy of the opinion to the certifying court and to the parties or their counsel.

History: Amended, eff 6-1-94; 4-1-96; 7-1-04; 1-1-08; 1-1-10.

SECTION 19.   DEATH PENALTY APPEALS

S.Ct. Prac. R. 19.1.   Scope of Rules

S.Ct. Prac. R. 19.1 through 19.6 apply only to death penalty appeals from the courts of common pleas for offenses committed on or after January 1, 1995.

S.Ct. Prac. R. 19.2.   Institution of Appeal

(A) **Perfection of appeal**

(1) To perfect an appeal of a case in which the death penalty has been imposed for an offense committed on or after January 1, 1995, the appellant shall file a notice of appeal in the Supreme Court within forty-five days from the journalization of the entry of the judgment being appealed or the filing of the trial court opinion pursuant to section 2929.03(F) of the Revised Code, whichever is later.

(2) If the appellant timely files in the trial court a motion for a new trial, or for arrest of judgment, the time for filing a notice of appeal begins to run after the order denying the motion is entered. However, a motion for a new trial on the ground of newly discovered evidence extends the time for filing the notice of appeal only if the motion is made before the expiration of the time for filing a motion for a new trial on grounds other than newly discovered evidence.

(3) When the time has expired for filing a notice of appeal in the Supreme Court, the appellant may seek to file a delayed appeal by filing a motion for delayed appeal and a notice of appeal. The motion shall state the date of the journalization of the entry of the

judgment being appealed, the date of the filing of the trial court opinion pursuant to section 2929.03(F) of the Revised Code, and adequate reasons for the delay. Facts supporting the motion shall be set forth in an affidavit.

(B) **Copy of the praecipe to court reporter** The notice of appeal shall be accompanied by a copy of the praecipe that was served by the appellant on the court reporter pursuant to S.Ct. Prac. R. 19.4(B)(2). The appellant shall certify on this copy the date the praecipe was served on the reporter.

(C) **Notice to the common pleas court** The Clerk of the Supreme Court shall send a date-stamped copy of the notice of appeal to the clerk of the court of common pleas whose judgment is being appealed.

(D) **Jurisdiction of common pleas court after appeal to Supreme Court is perfected** After an appeal is perfected from a court of common pleas to the Supreme Court, the court of common pleas is divested of jurisdiction, except to take action in aid of the appeal, to grant a stay of execution if the Supreme Court has not set an execution date, or to appoint counsel.

S.Ct. Prac. R. 19.3.   Appointment of Counsel

If a capital appellant is unrepresented and is indigent, the Supreme Court will appoint the Ohio Public Defender or other counsel qualified pursuant to the Rules of Superintendence to represent the appellant, or order the trial court to appoint qualified counsel.

S.Ct. Prac. R. 19.4.   Record on Appeal

(A) **Composition of the record to be transmitted**

(1) Unless otherwise ordered by the Court, the record to be transmitted on appeal shall consist of the original papers filed in the trial court; the transcript of proceedings, an electronic version of the transcript, if available; and a certified copy of the docket and journal entries prepared by the clerk of the trial court.

(2) The custodian of the record shall not transmit any physical exhibits unless directed to do so by the Clerk of the Supreme Court or as provided by S.Ct. Prac. R. 19.4(A)(3).

(3) The custodian shall transmit any audio exhibits, video exhibits, and documents such as papers, maps, or photographs.

(4) If exhibits are not transmitted pursuant to subdivision (2), the custodian who certifies the record shall designate in the index the exhibits not being transmitted and identify the custodian of those exhibits.

(B) **The transcript of proceedings; duty of appellant to order**

(1) The transcript of proceedings shall be prepared by the court reporter appointed by the trial court to transcribe the proceedings for the trial court. The reporter shall transcribe into written form all of the trial court proceedings, including pre-trial, trial, hearing, and other proceedings.

(2) Before filing a notice of appeal in the Supreme Court, the appellant shall, by written praecipe, order from the reporter a complete transcript of the proceedings.

(3) A transcript prepared by a reporter under this rule shall be in the following form:

(a) The transcript shall include a front and back cover; the front cover shall bear the case name and number and the name of the court in which the proceedings occurred;

(b) The transcript shall be firmly bound on the left side;

(c) The first page inside the front cover shall set forth the nature of the proceedings, the date or dates of the proceedings, and the judge or judges who presided;

(d) The transcript shall be prepared on white paper, 8 ½ by 11 inches in size, with the lines of each page numbered and the pages sequentially numbered;

(e) An index of witnesses shall be included in the front of each volume of the transcript and shall contain page and line references to direct, cross, re-direct, and re-cross examination;

(f) An index to exhibits, whether admitted or rejected, briefly identifying each exhibit, shall be included in each volume following the index of witnesses and shall reflect page and line references where each exhibit was identified and offered into evidence, was admitted or rejected, and if any objection was interposed;

(g) No volume of a transcript shall exceed two hundred fifty pages in length, except it may be enlarged to three hundred pages, if necessary, to complete a part of the voir dire, opening statements, closing arguments, or jury instructions. When it is necessary to prepare more than one volume, each volume shall contain the number and name of the case and be numbered sequentially and consecutively from the previous volume, and the separate volumes shall be approximately equal in length.

(4) The reporter shall certify that the transcript is correct and complete.

(C) **Statement of the evidence or proceedings when no report was made or when the transcript is unavailable** If no report of the evidence or proceedings at a hearing or trial was made, or if a transcript is unavailable, the appellant may prepare a statement of the evidence or proceedings from the best available means, including the appellant's recollection. The statement shall be served on the appellee no later than twenty days prior to the time for transmission of the record pursuant to S.Ct. Prac. R. 19.5. The appellee may serve objections or proposed amendments to the statement within ten days after service. The statement and any objections or proposed amendments shall be forthwith submitted to the trial court for settlement and approval. The trial court shall act prior to the time for transmission of the record pursuant to S.Ct. Prac. R. 19.5, and, as settled and approved, the statement shall be included by the clerk of the trial court in the record on appeal.

(D) **Correction or modification of the record** If any difference arises as to whether the record truly discloses what occurred in the trial court, the difference shall be submitted to and settled by that court and the record made to conform to the truth. If anything material to either party is omitted from the record by error or accident or is misstated in the record, the parties by stipulation, or the trial court, either before or

after the record is transmitted to the Supreme Court, or the Supreme Court, sua sponte or upon motion, may direct that the omission or misstatement be corrected, and if necessary that a supplemental record be certified and transmitted. All other questions as to the form and content of the record shall be presented to the Supreme Court.

S.Ct. Prac. R. 19.5. Transmission of the Record

(A) **Time for transmission; duty of appellant**

(1) The clerk of the trial court shall prepare a certified copy of the docket and journal entries, assemble the original papers, and transmit the record on appeal to the Clerk of the Supreme Court within ninety days after the date the notice of appeal is filed in the Supreme Court, unless an extension of time is granted under division (I).

(2) The appellant shall take any action necessary to enable the clerk to assemble and transmit the record, including, if required, filing a motion for an extension of time for transmission of the record under division (C).

(B) **Duty of trial court and Supreme Court clerks**

(1) Before transmitting the record to the Supreme Court, the clerk of the trial court shall number the documents, transcripts, and exhibits comprising the record. The clerk of the trial court shall prepare an index of the documents, transcripts, and exhibits, correspondingly numbered and identified. All exhibits listed in the index shall be briefly described. If applicable, a separate index shall be prepared identifying any exhibits that are part of the record, but which have not been transmitted under division (B)(3). The clerk of the trial court shall send a copy of each index to all counsel of record in the case and transmit each index with the record to the Clerk of the Supreme Court.

(2) Documentary exhibits offered at trial whose admission was denied shall be included with the record and transmitted in a separate envelope with a notation that they were not admitted.

(3) Transmission of the record is effected when the Clerk of the Supreme Court files the record. The Clerk of the Supreme Court shall notify counsel of record and the clerk of the trial court when the record is filed in the Supreme Court.

(C) **Extension of time for transmission of the record**

(1) The Supreme Court may extend the time for transmitting the record or, notwithstanding the provisions of S.Ct. Prac. R. 14.1, may permit the record to be transmitted after the expiration of the time prescribed by this rule or set by order of the Supreme Court.

(2) A request for extension of time to transmit the record shall be made by motion, stating good cause for the extension and accompanied by one or more affidavits setting forth facts to demonstrate good cause. The motion shall be filed within the time originally prescribed for transmission of the record or within the time permitted by a previously granted extension.

(3) A request for extension of time to transmit the record shall be accompanied by an affidavit of the court

reporter if the extension is necessitated by the court reporter's inability to transcribe the proceedings in a timely manner.

(D) **Retention of copy of the record in the trial court**

(1) Before transmitting the record to the Clerk of the Supreme Court, the clerk of the trial court shall make a copy of the record. A copy of the original papers, transcript of proceedings, and any documentary exhibits shall be made by photocopying the original papers, transcript of proceedings, and documentary exhibits. A copy of any physical exhibits may be made by either photographing or videotaping the physical exhibits. A copy of a video, audio, or other electronic recording that is part of the record shall be made by making a duplicate recording.

(2) The clerk of the trial court shall retain the copy of the record for use in any postconviction proceeding authorized by section 2953.21 of the Revised Code or for any other proceeding authorized by these rules.

S.Ct. Prac. R. 19.6.   Briefs on the Merits

(A) The appellant shall file a merit brief with the Supreme Court within one hundred eighty days from the date the Clerk of the Supreme Court files the record from the trial court.

(B) Within one hundred twenty days after the filing of appellant's brief, the appellee shall file a merit brief.

(C) The appellant may file a reply brief within forty-five days after the filing of appellee's brief.

(D) The form of the briefs shall comply with the provisions of S.Ct. Prac. R. 6.1 through 6.8.

(E) A party may obtain one extension of time to file a merit brief in accordance with the provisions of S.Ct. Prac. R. 14.3(B)(2).

History: Amended, eff 6-1-94; 4-1-96; 6-1-98; 6-1-00; 7-1-04; 10-1-05; 1-1-08; 1-1-10.

SECTION 20.   [RESERVED.]

SECTION 21.   TITLE

S.Ct. Prac. R. 21.1.   Title

These rules shall be known as the Rules of Practice of the Supreme Court of Ohio and shall be cited as "S.Ct. Prac. R. _____".

History: Amended, eff 6-1-94; 1-1-10.

APPENDICES

Note: Some of the following samples include material taken from actual Supreme Court cases. However, the material has been edited to conform to the requirements of the current rules. Fictitious attorney names and related data have also been used.

The authorities cited in the samples are cited in accordance with the Manual of the Forms of Citation used in the Ohio Official Reports, Interim Edition (July 1, 1992, revised July 12, 2002), issued by the Reporter of the Supreme Court. However, conformance to the Reporter's style manual is not required, provided citations conform to another generally recognized and accepted style manual. See, for example, A Uniform System of Citation (current edition) ("Blue Book"); University of Chicago Manual of Legal Citation (current edition) ("Maroon Book"); Association of Legal Writers and Directors Citation Manual (current edition) ("ALWD Citation Manual"); and Judicial Opinion Writing Manual (current edition) ("ABA Manual").

APPENDIX A. NOTICE OF APPEAL FROM A COURT OF APPEALS

IN THE SUPREME COURT OF OHIO

John B. DeVennish,	:	On Appeal from the Franklin
Appellant,	:	County Court of Appeals,
v.	:	Tenth Appellate District
City of Columbus, Division	:	Appellate District
of Public Safety, et al.,	:	Court of Appeals
Appellees.	:	Case No. 02AP-433

NOTICE OF APPEAL OF APPELLANT JOHN B. DEVENNISH

John Miller (1234567) (COUNSEL OF RECORD)
Susan Smith (7654321)
Miller, Miller & Smith
100 South High Street, Suite 100
Columbus, Ohio 43215
(614) 233-1111
Fax No. (614) 233-2222
jmiller@e-mail

COUNSEL FOR APPELLANT, JOHN B. DEVENNISH

Jane Doe (0909090)
Columbus City Attorney
Peter Jones (0999999) (COUNSEL OF RECORD)
Chief Labor Attorney
City of Columbus Dept. of Law
90 West Broad Street
Columbus, Ohio 43215
(614) 222-3456
pjones@e-mail
COUNSEL FOR APPELLEES, CITY OF
COLUMBUS AND COLUMBUS MUNICIPAL
CIVIL SERVICE COMMISSION

Notice of Appeal of Appellant John B. DeVennish

Appellant John B. DeVennish hereby gives notice of appeal to the Supreme Court of Ohio from the judgment of the Franklin County Court of Appeals, Tenth Appellate District, entered in Court of Appeals case No. 02AP-433 on October 24, 2003.

This case raises a substantial constitutional question and is one of public or great general interest.

Respectfully submitted,

By: _____
    John Miller, Counsel of Record

By: _____
    Susan Smith

COUNSEL FOR APPELLANT,
JOHN B. DEVENNISH

Certificate of Service

I certify that a copy of this Notice of Appeal was sent by ordinary U.S. mail to counsel for appellees, Jane Doe, Columbus City Attorney, and Peter Jones, Chief Labor Attorney, City of Columbus Dept. of Law, 90 West Broad Street, Columbus, Ohio 43215 on November 22, 2003.

Susan Smith

COUNSEL FOR APPELLANT,
JOHN B. DEVENNISH

APPENDIX B. MEMORANDUM IN SUPPORT OF JURISDICTION

IN THE SUPREME COURT OF OHIO

John B. DeVennish,   :

           :

      Appellant,   :   On Appeal from the

           :   Franklin County Court

      v.   :   of Appeals, Tenth

           :   Appellate District

City of Columbus, Division   :

of Public Safety, et al.,   :   Court of Appeals

           :   Case No. 02AP-433

      Appellees.   :

MEMORANDUM IN SUPPORT OF JURISDICTION
OF APPELLANT JOHN B. DEVENNISH

John Miller (1234567) (COUNSEL OF RECORD)
Susan Smith (7654321)
Miller, Miller & Smith
100 South High Street, Suite 100
Columbus, Ohio 43215
(614) 233-1111
Fax No. (614) 233-2222
jmiller@e-mail

COUNSEL FOR APPELLANT, JOHN B. DEVENNISH

Jane Doe (0909090)
Columbus City Attorney
Peter Jones (0999999) (COUNSEL OF RECORD)
Chief Labor Attorney
City of Columbus Dept. of Law
90 West Broad Street
Columbus, Ohio 43215
(614) 222-3456
pjones@e-mail

COUNSEL FOR APPELLEES, CITY OF
COLUMBUS AND COLUMBUS MUNICIPAL
CIVIL SERVICE COMMISSION

1

TABLE OF CONTENTS

EXPLANATION OF WHY THIS CASE IS A CASE OF
PUBLIC OR GREAT GENERAL INTEREST AND
INVOLVES A SUBSTANTIAL CONSTITUTIONAL QUESTION

This cause presents two critical issues for the future of public employee collective bargaining in Ohio: (1) whether promotions are a mandatory subject of collective bargaining under R.C. Chapter 4117, the Public Employees' Collective Bargaining Act; and (2) whether a city may disclaim the legal identity between itself and its civil service commission in order to evade municipal obligations under a public employee collective bargaining agreement.

In this case, the court of appeals excluded promotions from the mandatory topics of collective bargaining and concluded, therefore, that the promotional provisions of a collective bargaining agreement could not supersede an existing civil service regulation. The court of appeals also ruled that, under the Home-Rule provisions of the Ohio Constitution, a civil service commission is not bound by the collective bargaining agreement entered into by the public employer but instead is entitled to enforce its own rules and regulations.

The decision of the court of appeals threatens the structure of public employees' collective bargaining created by the General Assembly in R.C. Chapter 4117. By its ruling, the court of appeals undermines legislative intent, ignores the plain meaning of the Act, and creates its own unsupported view of public employee collective bargaining. Moreover, the court of appeals' decision establishes the illogical and untenable rule that a city can ignore its collective bargaining agreement by delegating labor matters to a municipal agency that can violate the agreement with impunity. Finally, the decision of the court of appeals elevates the Home-Rule provisions of the Ohio Constitution over the authority of the General Assembly to enact employee welfare legislation pursuant to Section 34, Article II of the Ohio Constitution. These unprecedented inroads into the scope of the Public Employees' Collective Bargaining Act offend the plain

- 1 -

language of the Act and the principles of constitutional governance. They urgently need correction by this court.

The implications of the decision of the court of appeals affect every governmental entity in Ohio, and touch the lives of tens of thousands of public employees in the state. The public's interest in the orderly operation of government is profoundly affected by a holding that the agreements of municipalities are not binding on agencies of the municipality. Such a rule would sabotage the integrity of governmental contracts, and undermine the fundamental principle that the rule of law constrains governments as well as citizens. Similarly, the public interest is affected if the plain meaning of a statute duly adopted by the General Assembly can be judicially altered to subvert the legislature's intent that the labor relations of governmental units throughout the state be controlled by certain uniform principles.

Apart from these governmental considerations, which make this case one of great public interest, the decision of the court of appeals has broad general significance. Thousands and thousands of citizens of Ohio are public employees who perform the essential work of governance. The General Assembly has recognized their right to bargain collectively over the terms and conditions of their employment, and has codified a clear and orderly process for that bargaining. Under this codification, public employees can, through bargaining, determine the terms and conditions of their employment. The resulting collective bargaining agreement represents the product of a time-honored process by which employers and employees mutually agree on matters that jointly affect them.

The decision of the court of appeals sets a precedent that would exclude an entire subject matter—promotions—from collective bargaining by public employees. Under this rule, public employees would be denied the right to bargain over one of the most significant terms and conditions of employment affecting their career paths. The result of this rule would be

- 2 -

preposterous. Employee representatives would bargain with the municipalities' representatives about the full range of terms and conditions that affect their employment, but would see the central issue of promotions relegated to the unilateral determinations of civil service commissions, which would be unconstrained by any agreement of the city.

Not surprisingly, the conclusion of the court of appeals is contrary both to the statutory scheme of R.C. Chapter 4117 and to all legal authority. Courts and public employment boards throughout the country, as well as the National Labor Relations Board, have endorsed the proposition that promotions are mandatorily subject to collective bargaining laws. Similarly, the State Employee Relations Board has recognized the mandatory bargaining nature of promotions.

The judgment of the court of appeals has great general significance also because it undermines collective bargaining by permitting cities to circumvent their collective bargaining agreements. If civil service commissions had exclusive jurisdiction over promotional matters, despite contrary provisions of collective bargaining agreements, the force and value of agreements and the objectives of the Act would be severely compromised. Municipal administrative agencies, such as civil service commissions, could negate at will agreements made under the Act. Such a prospect is contrary to current case law and the stated purpose of the Act.

Finally, this case involves a substantial constitutional question. The decision offends Ohio's constitutional scheme by elevating the Home-Rule powers of municipalities, granted by the Ohio Constitution, Section 3, Article XVIII, over the constitutional power of the General Assembly to enact employee welfare legislation pursuant to Section 34, Article II of the Ohio Constitution. Such a constitutional imbalance is contrary to this court's holding in *Rocky River v. State Emp. Relations Bd.* (1989), 43 Ohio St.3d 1, 539 N.E.2d 103.

Contrary to the holding in *Rocky River*, the lower court's interpretation of R.C. 4117.08(B) impairs the functioning of the Act. The decision would invite a return to pre-collective bargaining

- 3 -

days. This court rejected such a regression in *Kettering v. State Emp. Relations Bd.* (1986), 26

Ohio St.3d 50, 56, 26 OBR 42, 496 N.E.2d 983:

> "A myopic insistence on returning a significant portion of Ohio's public
> employee labor relations to the pre-Act *ad hoc* 'system,' under the rubric of
> local self-government powers, only invites a return to the very litigation and
> controversy which had prompted the General Assembly to address that
> distressing state of affairs. * * *" (Footnote omitted.) See also, *Dublin v. State,*
> 118 Ohio Misc.2d 18, 2002-Ohio-2431, 769 N.E.2d 436; *Sanders v. Summit
> Cty. Veterans' Serv. Comm.*, Summit App. No. 20800, 2002-Ohio-2653, at ¶ 20.

If allowed to stand, the decision of the court of appeals would ravage the Public

Employees' Collective Bargaining Act. Under the decision, the collective bargaining process

would be chaotic and uncertain, and would lack finality. Municipal collective bargaining

agreements would be subject to interference and rejection by municipal agencies, whose actions

would undermine not only individual agreements, but also the general framework of public labor

relations intended by the legislative branch. The entire process of collective bargaining under R.C.

Chapter 4117, designed to result in enforceable contractual relationships and coherent public labor

relations, would be frustrated if the decision of the court of appeals is permitted to stand.

In sum, this case puts in issue the essence of public employee collective bargaining and the

fate of public labor relations, thereby affecting every governmental entity and employee in Ohio.

To promote the purposes and preserve the integrity of the Public Employees' Collective

Bargaining Act, to assure uniform application of the Act, to promote orderly and constructive

negotiations between employers and their public employees, and to remove impediments to the

collective bargaining process, this court must grant jurisdiction to hear this case and review the

erroneous and dangerous decision of the court of appeals.

STATEMENT OF THE CASE AND FACTS

The case arises from the attempt of appellant John B. DeVennish ("DeVennish") to attain the rank of sergeant in the Columbus Police Department. The Columbus Municipal Civil Service Commission (the "commission") ruled that DeVennish was not eligible to take the necessary promotional examination because, under the rules and regulations of the commission, he did not meet the minimum requirement of three years of continuous accredited service as a permanent employee immediately prior to the date of the examination.

The commission's "continuous-service" requirement was in obvious conflict with the provisions of the existing collective bargaining agreement ("agreement") between the appellee city of Columbus (the "city") and the Fraternal Order of Police, Capital City Lodge No. 9 (the "FOP"). Article 15 of the agreement requires an applicant for the sergeant's examination to have at least three years of service; however, the agreement does not mandate that the service be continuous or be immediately prior to the examination. DeVennish met the requirement as established by the collective bargaining agreement. The commission, however, refused to honor the provisions of the agreement and found that DeVennish did not meet the minimum qualifications to take the promotional examination.

The appellant appealed to the Franklin County Common Pleas Court and, upon the affirmance of the commission's decision, appealed to the Franklin County Court of Appeals. The court of appeals affirmed the judgment of the court of common pleas and found that: (1) Section E, Article 15 of the agreement addresses matters that are not appropriate subjects of bargaining under R.C. 4117.08(B) and, therefore, the promotional provisions of the collective bargaining agreement could not supersede the existing civil service regulation; and (2) the commission was an entity separate from the city and, under the Home-Rule provisions of the Ohio Constitution, was entitled to enforce its own rules and regulations.

- 5 -

The court of appeals erred in ruling that the Public Employees' Collective Bargaining Act

excludes promotions from the mandatory topics of collective bargaining. The court of appeals

also erred in failing to recognize that a municipality binds its civil service commission when it

enters into a collective bargaining agreement with a public employee union.

In support of its position on these issues, the appellant presents the following argument.

ARGUMENT IN SUPPORT OF PROPOSITIONS OF LAW

**Proposition of Law No. I: Promotions are a mandatory subject of
collective bargaining pursuant to R.C. 4117.08.**

Matters dealing with promotion are mandatory subjects for bargaining under the Ohio

Public Employees' Collective Bargaining Act ("Act"), R.C. Chapter 4117. The statutory scheme

of the Act makes this clear.

R.C. 4117.08(A) sets forth the matters that are subject to collective bargaining between a

public employer and the exclusive representative of a public employee bargaining unit. Under that

statute, "[a]ll matters pertaining to wages, hours, or terms and other conditions of employment * *

* are subject to collective bargaining" unless otherwise specified in the statute. The few statutory

exclusions from this broad mandate are set out in R.C. 4117.08(B), which provides:

> "The conduct and grading of civil service examinations, the rating of
> candidates, the establishment of eligible lists from the examinations, and the
> *original appointments from the eligible lists* are not appropriate subjects for
> collective bargaining." (Emphasis added.)

This provision excludes from collective bargaining only lists for *original* appointments, not

promotional appointments. This statute codifies a distinction widely accepted in traditional private

sector labor law: original hiring practices are left to the employer's discretion and are not

appropriate subjects of collective bargaining; promotions, in contrast, are proper subjects of

- 6 -

collective bargaining. See, e.g., *Ford Motor Co. v. Huffman* (1953), 345 U.S. 330, 341-342, 73

S.Ct. 681, 97 L.E. 1048; *Amalgamated Transit Union Internatl., AFL-CIO v. Donovan*

(C.A.D.C.1985), 767 F.2d 939; *Houston Chapter, Associated Gen. Contrs. of Am., Inc.* (1963),

143 N.L.R.B. 409.

This plain meaning of the narrow exclusion embodied in R.C. 4117.08(B) is supported by

the language of the section that immediately follows it. R.C. 4117.08(C) provides as follows:

> "Unless a public employer agrees otherwise in a collective bargaining
> agreement, nothing in Chapter 4117. of the Revised Code impairs the right and
> responsibility of each public employer to:
>
> " * * *
>
> "(5)   * * * promote * * * employees."

This section expressly permits a public employer to address promotional matters in a

collective bargaining agreement. More forcefully, the final provision of R.C. 4117.08(C) requires

an employer to bargain on subjects that affect "wages, hours, [and] terms and conditions of

employment." Promotions obviously are such a subject; they inherently affect wages, hours and

terms or conditions of employment.

The court of appeals held that, under this clear statutory scheme, the determination of who

is eligible for a promotion, and therefore eligible for a promotional civil service examination, is a

prohibited topic for collective bargaining. This holding ignores the evident meaning of R.C.

4117.08 and improperly broadens the narrow exceptions enumerated in R.C. 4117.08(B). The

court of appeals erroneously interpreted the statutory phrase "establishment of eligible lists *from*

the examination" (emphasis added) to include the determination of an applicant's eligibility to sit

for an examination. Such a judicial expansion of a clear and carefully drafted statutory exclusion

violates the rules of statutory construction established and applied by this court. See *State ex rel.*

Keller v. Forney (1923), 108 Ohio St. 463, 141 N.E. 16; *Kroff v. Amrhein* (1916), 94 Ohio St. 282,

114 N.E. 267; *Erich v. Mayfield Village*, (July 13, 2000), Cuyahoga App. No. 76675; *Leland v.*

Lima, Allen App. No. 1-02-59, 2002-Ohio-6188, at ¶ 20-21.

> **Proposition of Law No. II:** **A civil service commission is bound by the**
> **collective bargaining agreement entered into by the public employer**
> **under R.C. Chapter 4117.**

As with any municipal agency, a civil service commission is bound by the contracts of the

municipality. Thus, a collective bargaining agreement between a city and a public employee union

binds the civil service commission.

As the State Employee Relations Board and several Ohio courts have ruled, and as the

appellee city has acknowledged in other forums, a civil service commission has no separate legal

identity or capacity apart from the city that created it. A collective bargaining agreement entered

into by a municipality, as a public employer, therefore, binds a civil service commission as well.

Furthermore, the provisions of a collective bargaining agreement entered into by a

municipality must prevail over a conflicting regulation of a civil service commission. This court

held in *Rocky River v. State Emp. Relations Bd.*, supra, 43 Ohio St.3d 1, 539 N.E.2d 103, that the

exercise by municipalities of Home-Rule powers is constitutionally limited to the exercise of

powers that do not conflict with any general law. Thus, the provisions of R.C. Chapter 4117, a

general state law, prevail over conflicting municipal enactments, such as the commission's

regulations. See *State ex rel. Dayton Fraternal Order of Police, Lodge No. 44, v. State Emp.*

Relations Bd. (1986), 22 Ohio St.3d 1, 22 OBR 1, 488 N.E.2d 181; *Kettering v. State Emp.*

Relations Bd., supra, 26 Ohio St.3d 50, 26 OBR 42, 496 N.E.2d 983; and *Dist. 1199, Health Care*

& Soc. Serv. Union, SEIU, AFL-CIO v. State Emp. Relations Bd., Franklin App. No. 02AP-391,

2003-Ohio-3436.

CONCLUSION

For the reasons discussed above, this case involves matters of public and great general interest and a substantial constitutional question. The appellant requests that this court accept jurisdiction in this case so that the important issues presented will be reviewed on the merits.

Respectfully submitted,

John Miller, Counsel of Record

_____

Susan Smith
COUNSEL FOR APPELLANT,
JOHN B. DEVENNISH

Certificate of Service

I certify that a copy of this Memorandum in Support of Jurisdiction was sent by ordinary U.S. mail to counsel for appellees, Jane Doe, Columbus City Attorney, and Peter Jones, Chief Labor Attorney, City of Columbus Dept. of Law, 90 West Broad Street, Columbus, Ohio 43215 on November 22, 2003.

_____

Susan Smith

COUNSEL FOR APPELLANT,
JOHN B. DEVENNISH

APPENDIX C. WAIVER OF MEMORANDUM IN RESPONSE

IN THE SUPREME COURT OF OHIO

_____   :
                                       :   Case No. _____
          v.   :
                                         :
_____   :

Waiver of Memorandum in Response*

I am filing this waiver pursuant to S.Ct.Prac.R. III, Section 2(E). I do not intend to file a response to the memorandum in support of jurisdiction unless one is requested by the Court.

_____   _____
Name   Address

_____   _____
Attorney Registration #   City & State

_____   _____
Phone Number   Zip Code

Please enter my appearance as follows (check one):

☐   Enter my appearance as counsel of record for all appellees.

☐   There are multiple appellees, and I do not represent all of them. Enter my appearance as counsel of record for the following appellee(s):

_____   _____

_____   _____

I certify that I am sending a copy of this form, on this date, to all other parties in compliance with S.Ct.Prac.R. XIV, Section 2(B).

                                   _____
                                   Signature

                                   _____
                                   Date

_____

Note: If a waiver is filed in lieu of a memorandum in response, it must be filed within 20 days after the memorandum in support of jurisdiction is filed. If there are multiple appellants and more than one memorandum in support of jurisdiction is filed, the appellee may file only one waiver, and it must be filed within 20 days after the filing of the last memorandum in support.

APPENDIX D. MERIT BRIEF OF APPELLANT

IN THE SUPREME COURT OF OHIO

John B. DeVennish,	:	
	:	
Appellant,	:	Case No. 02-2177
	:	
v.	:	
	:	On Appeal from the
City of Columbus, Division	:	Franklin County Court
of Public Safety, et al.,	:	of Appeals, Tenth
	:	Appellate District
Appellees.	:	

MERIT BRIEF OF APPELLANT JOHN B. DEVENNISH

John Miller (1234567) (COUNSEL OF RECORD)
Susan Smith (7654321)
Miller, Miller & Smith
100 South High Street, Suite 100
Columbus, Ohio 43215
(614) 233-1111
Fax No. (614) 233-2222
jmiller@e-mail

COUNSEL FOR APPELLANT, JOHN B. DEVENNISH

Jane Doe (0909090)
Columbus City Attorney
Peter Jones (0999999) (COUNSEL OF RECORD)
Chief Labor Attorney
City of Columbus Dept. of Law
90 West Broad Street
Columbus, Ohio 43215
(614) 222-3456
pjones@e-mail

COUNSEL FOR APPELLEES, CITY OF
COLUMBUS AND COLUMBUS MUNICIPAL
CIVIL SERVICE COMMISSION

TABLE OF CONTENTS

TABLE OF CONTENTS (Cont'd.)

TABLE OF AUTHORITIES

Page

STATEMENT OF FACTS

This case arises from the attempt of appellant John B. DeVennish ("DeVennish") to attain the rank of sergeant in the Columbus Police Department. DeVennish joined the Columbus police force on March 17, 1985. (Supp. 38.) He voluntarily resigned in good standing on April 30, 1991 to work in private industry. (Supp. 38, Tr. 15.) On October 6, 1999, DeVennish rejoined the Columbus police force and graduated first academically in his police academy class. (Supp. 38, Tr. 16.)

In 2000, DeVennish applied to take the police sergeant promotional examination. (Supp. 41.) The staff of the Columbus Municipal Civil Service Commission (the "commission"), and later the executive director of the commission, rejected the application of DeVennish on the ground that DeVennish did not meet a minimum requirement under the rules and regulations of the commission. Specifically, they found that DeVennish did not have "three years of continuous accredited service as a permanent appointee immediately prior to the date of examination." (Supp. 32, 30.)

DeVennish appealed this decision to the commission. (Supp. 31.) Pending that appeal, he was permitted to take the promotional examination. (Supp. 143.) On the posted list of test scores, DeVennish ranked twenty-first out of one hundred seventy-nine applicants. (Supp. 143.) On July 22, 2001, the commission dismissed DeVennish's appeal on the ground that he did not have three years of continuous service prior to the examination. (Appx. 18.) In so doing, the commission refused to honor the provisions of a contract, effective December 29, 1998, between the city of Columbus (the "city") and

1

the Fraternal Order of Police, Capital City Lodge No. 9 (the "FOP") pursuant to R.C.

Chapter 4117. (See Supp. 118.)

Section E, Article 15 of the collective bargaining agreement ("the agreement")

between the city and the FOP provides, in part, that:

> "The City and * * * [FOP] agree that, within 60 days of the ratification
> date of this Agreement, they shall jointly support and petition the * * *
> Commission to request that the following be included in the Civil Service
> Rules and Regulations:
>
> " * * *
>
> "(E) To be eligible for the next promotional examination, the
> applicant must have had at least 3 years as a Police Officer for the rank of
> Sergeant and at least one year in prior ranks for all other ranks. * * *"
> (Supp. 83-84.)

Despite the terms of the agreement and the effort of the FOP, the city neither

joined in a petition nor caused the commission to formally adopt the new promotional

eligibility rule. In determining the eligibility of DeVennish, the commission elected to

apply the civil service regulation instead of the standard of the agreement, a standard

DeVennish met.

Pursuant to R.C. 119.12 and Chapter 2505, DeVennish appealed to the Franklin

County Common Pleas Court. (Supp. 26.) The Franklin County Common Pleas Court

(Crawford, J.) issued its decision on February 27, 2003, affirming the decision of the

commission, and entered its judgment on March 10, 2003. (Appx. 11, 17.) DeVennish

filed his notice of appeal to the Franklin County Court of Appeals on April 10, 2003.

(Supp. 136.)

On October 24, 2003, the Franklin County Court of Appeals affirmed the

judgment of the common pleas court. (Appx. 3, 9.) The court of appeals ruled that the promotional provisions of the collective bargaining agreement did not apply to

DeVennish on grounds that: (a) Section E, Article 15 of the collective bargaining

agreement between the city and the FOP addressed a matter that was not an appropriate

subject of bargaining under R.C. 4117.08(B) and, therefore, the agreement could not

supersede the existing civil service regulation; (b) the Columbus Municipal Civil Service

Commission was an entity separate from the city of Columbus and had the right, under

the Home-Rule provisions of the Ohio Constitution, to enforce its own rules and

regulations; and (c) the commission had never formally adopted the promotional standard

set forth in the collective bargaining agreement between the city and the FOP and was not

bound by the agreement between the city and the FOP.

DeVennish filed his notice of appeal to the Supreme Court of Ohio on November

22, 2003. (Appx. 1.) On April 4, 2004, the Supreme Court granted jurisdiction to hear

the case and allowed the appeal.

ARGUMENT

Proposition of Law No. I:
Promotions are a mandatory subject of collective
bargaining pursuant to R.C. 4117.08.

R.C. 4117.08(A) provides that "[a]ll matters pertaining to wages, hours, or terms

and other conditions of employment" are mandatory subjects of collective bargaining

between public employers and exclusive representatives unless otherwise specified in the

statute. R.C. 4117.08(B) excludes only four topics from this broad mandate:

1.   The conduct and grading of civil service examinations;

2.   The rating of candidates;

3

3.   The establishment of eligible lists from examinations; and

4.   The original appointments from the eligible lists.

The court of appeals in this case ruled that the determination of a public

employee's eligibility to sit for a promotional civil service examination is "the

establishment of the eligible lists from [an] examination" and, therefore, falls within the

statutory exclusion. As a result of this conclusion, the court ruled that a collective

bargaining agreement cannot address the subject of eligibility for promotions.

The court of appeals misread the exclusionary language contained in R.C.

4117.08(B) which, in its entirety, states:

> "The conduct and grading of civil service examinations, the rating of
> candidates, the establishment of eligible lists from the examinations, and
> the *original appointments from the eligible lists* are not appropriate
> subjects for collective bargaining." (Emphasis added.)

Two provisions of this section are relevant here: (a) "the establishment of eligible

lists from the examinations"; and (b) "the original appointments from the eligible lists."

Accepted canons of statutory construction make clear that these contiguous phrases are

related. Read together, as they must be, the clauses exclude from collective bargaining

two matters: (1) determination of eligibility based on the results of examinations, and (2)

original appointments of persons determined by the examination to be eligible. This

section plainly does not exclude from collective bargaining the subjects of eligibility for

promotion or promotional appointments. The use of the term "original" makes clear the

legislature's intent to exclude only original appointments. In doing so, the General

Assembly merely codified the standard practice of labor relations under which original

hiring practices typically are left to the employer's discretion and not considered an

appropriate subject of collective bargaining.

4

The court of appeals' decision in this case would render the evident statutory scheme meaningless. Nowhere in R.C. 4117.08 did the General Assembly evince the slightest intent to exclude promotions from the broad requirement of R.C. 4117.08(A) that "terms and other conditions of employment" be subject to bargaining. Of course, had the General Assembly actually intended to exclude promotions from collective bargaining, it would have done so directly and simply—by using the word "promotion" in R.C. 4117.08(B), which defines excluded topics. That the General Assembly did not do so is conclusive evidence that it did not intend to exclude promotions. Any contrary conclusion, such as that reached by the court of appeals, violates a basic principle of statutory construction.

The court of appeals' error is compounded by its obvious misreading of the specific exclusions in the statute. The court of appeals erroneously interpreted the phrase, "the establishment of eligible lists *from* the examinations," to include the determination of an applicant's eligibility to sit *for* an examination. Such judicial expansion of a clear and carefully drafted statutory exclusion violates the rules of statutory construction established and applied by this court, and the critical constitutional concerns for separation of powers that animate those rules. In *State ex rel. Keller v. Forney* (1923), 108 Ohio St. 463, 141 N.E. 16, this court held that exceptions to a general law must be strictly construed, because of the presumption that matters not clearly excluded from the operation of the law are clearly included in the operation of the law. Similarly, in *Kroff v. Amrhein* (1916), 94 Ohio St. 282, 286, 114 N.E. 267, this court held that exceptions in a remedial statute should be strictly construed. In so ruling, the court embraced "the familiar rule that the exclusion clearly made in the exception only

5

emphasizes the inclusion of all other things germane to the statute which are not so

excluded." Id.; *Leland v. Lima*, Allen App. No. 1-02-59, 2002-Ohio-6188, at ¶ 20-21.

This plain meaning of the narrow exclusion set out in R.C. 4117.08(B) is

confirmed by the section that immediately follows it. R.C. 4117.08(C) provides in part as

follows:

> "Unless a public employer agrees otherwise in a collective
> bargaining agreement, nothing in Chapter 4117. of the Revised Code
> impairs the right and responsibility of each public employer to:
>
> " * * *
> "(5)   * * * promote * * * employees.
>
> " * * *
>
> "The employer is not required to bargain on subjects reserved to
> the management and direction of the governmental unit except as
> affect wages, hours, terms and conditions of employment, and the
> continuation, modification, or deletion of an existing provision of a
> collective bargaining agreement."

R.C. 4117.08(C) expressly contemplates that a public employer may address the

subject of promotions in a collective bargaining agreement. Otherwise, the introductory

phrase of Division (C) would be superfluous, and the term "promote" in Subdivision

(C)(5) would be pointless. Indeed, under R.C. 4117.08(C) an employer is required to

bargain with respect to those matters involving promotions. In *Lorain City Bd. of Edn. v.*

State Emp. Relations Bd. (1988), 40 Ohio St.3d 257, 533 N.E.2d 264, this court analyzed

the scope of management rights and bargaining obligations. The court held that "a public

employer must bargain with its employees regarding a management decision to the extent

that the decision 'affects wages, hours, terms and conditions of employment.'" Id. at

262, 533 N.E.2d 264. Promotions obviously affect wages and terms and conditions of

6

employment and, therefore, under the court's holding in *Lorain*, they are subject to bargaining.

That promotions are a mandatory subject of bargaining is widely established in the United States.[1] For example, the California Public Employment Relations Board held that promotional proposals must be negotiated since promotional rights bear a close relationship to virtually every subject of bargaining set forth in the California Act. *California School Emp. Assn. v. Healdsburg Union High School Dist.* (Jan. 4, 1984), Pub. Emp. Bargaining (CCH), 1983-1987 Transfer Binder (Adm. Rulings), Paragraph 43,573. Promotions are recognized as a mandatory bargaining subject in the private sector as well. *Ford Motor Co. v. Huffman* (1953), 345 U.S. 330, 73 S.Ct. 681, 97 L.Ed. 1048.

The exceptions enumerated in R.C. 4117.08(B) are the conduct and grading of civil service examinations, the establishment of eligible lists from the examination, the rating of candidates, and the original appointment from the eligible lists. The court of appeals found that the establishment of eligible lists from the examination encompasses the determination of the eligibility of an applicant to sit for the examination. The lower court's decision erroneously interprets R.C. 4117.08. The decision ignores the plain meaning of the statute, improperly broadens a narrow and clearly drafted exclusion, and offends the basic tenets of statutory construction. Not surprisingly, the decision is contrary not only to the law of Ohio, but also to the settled law throughout the United States. The court of appeals' decision must be reversed. Applying the unmistakable language of R.C. 4117.08, this court should hold that the subject of eligibility to sit for a

---

[1] *Note: This footnote contains string citations supporting appellant's statement. However, because of space limitations, these citations have been omitted from publication in the sample brief.*

promotional civil service examination is a proper subject for bargaining. As

demonstrated in the next section, once a collective bargaining agreement addresses a

subject, that agreement prevails over conflicting civil service rules. See *Rocky River v.*

State Emp. Relations Bd. (1989), 43 Ohio St.3d 1, 539 N.E.2d 103.

Proposition of Law No. II:
A civil service commission is bound by the collective
bargaining agreement entered into by the public employer
under R.C. Chapter 4117.

The city in the instant case has attempted to portray the civil service commission

as an independent entity that is exclusively responsible for promotions. This attempted

portrait is inconsistent with the statutory scheme of R.C. Chapter 4117.

R.C. 4117.01(B) defines "public employer" as including any "municipal

corporation with a population of at least five thousand." R.C. 4117.10(C) states that

"[t]he chief executive officer, or his representative, of each municipal corporation * * * is

responsible for negotiations in the collective bargaining process * * * ." Finally, and

critically, the section expressly prescribes the binding effect of agreements produced by

this process:

" * * * When the matters about which there is agreement are reduced
to writing and approved by the employee organization and the
legislative body, the agreement is binding upon the legislative body,
the employer, and the employee organization and employees covered
by the agreement."

The law provides no role for a civil service commission in the collective

bargaining process. The comprehensive legislative scheme defines who the public

employer is, who can bargain on behalf of the public employer, and the matters over

which bargaining must occur. Promotions are expressly included as a topic of

8

bargaining. This coherent process requires the conclusion that a civil service commission has no independent role regarding promotions. As with any municipal agency, the commission is bound by the contracts of the municipality, particularly those entered into pursuant to express statutory authority. Any contrary conclusion would frustrate the legislative scheme and severely disrupt governmental operations.

This court recently recognized the importance of permitting the Act to function as intended, without local interference from municipalities or their agencies. In *Rocky River v. State Emp. Relations Bd.,* supra (43 Ohio St.3d 1), this court found that R.C. Chapter 4117 is a constitutional enactment within the General Assembly's authority to enact employee welfare legislation pursuant to Section 34, Article II of the Ohio Constitution. Accordingly, the court held, at paragraph two of the syllabus, that the functioning of the Act may not be impaired, limited or negated by local enactments pursuant to the Home-Rule provision, Section 3, Article XVIII. The lower court's decision in the case now before the court threatens this critical allocation of responsibility for governmental labor relations. If allowed to stand, the court of appeals' decision will create chaos in the collective bargaining process and frustrate the essential objective of establishing an orderly and constructive relationship between the public employer and its employees.

Before the Act was adopted to promote this objective, public labor relations were characterized by wide and irrational variations among various local governmental entities relating to all manner of terms and conditions of employment. Not long ago, this court recalled that deplorable time. In *Kettering v. State Emp. Relations Bd.* (1986), 26 Ohio St.3d 50, 56, 26 OBR 42, 496 N.E.2d 983, this court stated:

> "A myopic insistence on returning a significant portion of Ohio's
> public employee labor relations to the pre-Act *ad hoc* 'system,' under

9

the rubric of local self-government powers, only invites a return to the very litigation and controversy which had prompted the General Assembly to address that distressing state of affairs. * * *" (Footnote omitted.)

The decision below represents precisely the sort of return to the pre-Act "system" that this court condemned in *Kettering*, supra. This court's holdings in *Rocky River* and *Kettering* make clear that, under the Act, a collective bargaining agreement binds the municipality and all of its agencies. No municipal agency can operate independently of that agreement; nor can it render the agreement a nullity by purporting to assume control over a term or condition of employment that is governed by the agreement.

In accordance with this important principle, the court of appeals in *State ex rel. Darvanan v. Youngstown* (Jan. 27, 1987), Mahoning App. No. 85 C.A. 131, directly addressed a conflict between a negotiated promotional procedure and municipal civil service commission control over promotions. Relying on R.C. 4117.10, the court held that bargaining under the Public Employees' Collective Bargaining Act superseded conflicting language in the Youngstown City Charter:

> "It is our conclusion that [R.C.] Chapter 4117. authorizes public employers and public employees to enter into labor agreements which agreements provide for promotions within the classified services without competitive examinations and that such a process does not conflict with the Constitution or laws of Ohio." Id. at 7.

In *Fraternal Order of Police, Capital City Lodge No. 9 v. Columbus* (June 11, 1987), Franklin C.P. No. 86CV-04-2336, the common pleas court followed this logic when it restrained the city from conducting police promotional examinations without the addition of seniority points. In ruling on a motion for equitable relief, Judge George C. Smith, in a consent decree, included the civil service commission as part of the city administration. (Supp. 177.)

10

The city itself has acknowledged that the civil service commission does not occupy any independent status. In stipulations filed by the parties in a SERB case, *State Emp. Relations Bd. v. Columbus* (Dec. 31, 1987), Docket No. 86-ULP-04-0122, 5 OPER, Paragraph 5119 (SERB Hearing Officer), Stipulation – Admission No. 15 reads as follows:

> "['] * * * The Municipal Civil Service Commission is created by Columbus City Charter §146. The Municipal Civil Service Commission acts on behalf of the City of Columbus, particularly in its rule-making capacity. City Charter §149. The Civil Service Commissioners are appointed by and pursuant to the Columbus City Charter §§146-147. They have no separate legal identity [and] cannot be considered separate and distinct from the City of Columbus. * * * [']"

CONCLUSION

The decision below is fundamentally wrong in its reasoning and dangerous in its implications for public employee collective bargaining. The decision undermines the structure and purpose of the Public Employees' Collective Bargaining Act. In place of that coherent Act, the decision below would establish a disorderly and outmoded method of governmental labor relations, a method this court condemned in *Kettering*, supra. Such a process, under which municipal agencies would be free to disregard the municipality's collective bargaining agreement, and exercise unilateral control over topics that are subject to mandatory bargaining, must be rejected.

The decision below must be reversed. A reversal will promote the exemplary purposes of the Act and preserve the unmistakable legislative intent, which this court has uniformly supported.

Respectfully submitted,

John Miller, Counsel of Record

_____

Susan Smith
COUNSEL FOR APPELLANT,
JOHN B. DEVENNISH

Certificate of Service

I certify that a copy of this Merit Brief was sent by ordinary U.S. mail to counsel of record for appellees, Peter Jones, Chief Labor Attorney, City of Columbus Dept. of Law, 90 West Broad Street, Columbus, Ohio 43215 on May 21, 2004.

_____

Susan Smith

COUNSEL FOR APPELLANT,
JOHN B. DEVENNISH

1

APPENDIX E. AFFIDAVIT OF INDIGENCY

IN THE SUPREME COURT OF OHIO

Affidavit of Indigency

I, _____, do hereby state that I am without the necessary funds to pay the costs of this action for the following reason(s):

[Note: S. Ct. Prac. R. XV, Sec. 3, requires your affidavit of indigency to state the reason(s) you are unable to pay the docket fees and/or security deposit. Failure to state specific reasons that you are unable to pay will result in your affidavit being rejected for filing by the Clerk.]

Pursuant to Rule 15.3, of the Rules of Practice of the Supreme Court of Ohio, I am requesting that the filing fee and security deposit, if applicable, be waived.

_____
Affiant

Sworn to, or affirmed, and subscribed in my presence this _____ day of _____, 20____.

_____
Notary Public

_____
My Commission Expires: _____

[Note: This affidavit must be executed not more than six months prior to being filed in the Supreme Court in order to comply with S. Ct. Prac. R. 15.3. Affidavits not in compliance with that section will be rejected for filing by the Clerk.]

PERSONAL IDENTIFIER FORM

APPENDIX F
IN THE SUPREME COURT OF OHIO
PERSONAL IDENTIFIER FORM

_____	:	Case No. _____
Appellant,	:	
Relator,	:	
Petitioner, v.	:	
_____	:	
Appellee.		
Respondent.		

Confidential Personal Identifiers Contained in Filing

(Rule 45(D) of the Rules of Superintendence for the Courts of Ohio. *Effective* July 1, 2009)

REFERENCE LIST

	COMPLETE PERSONAL IDENTIFIER	CORRESPONDING REFERENCE	LOCATION
	Use this column to list the personal identifiers that have been redacted from the document that is to be placed in the case file.	*Use this column to list the reference or abbreviation that will refer to the corresponding complete personal identifier.*	*Use this column to identify the document or documents where the reference appears in place of the personal identifier.*
1.			
2.			
3.			
4.			

☐ **Check if additional pages are attached.**

_____
Signature of person submitting the information

_____
Date

THIS IS PAGE _____ OF ____ PAGES

CREDIT CARD FILING FEE FORM

APPENDIX G
SUPREME COURT OF OHIO

CREDIT CARD FILING FEE FORM

This form provides the Clerk's Office with the necessary information to process a new appeal or new original action and charge the one-hundred ($100) dollar filing fee, and one-hundred ($100) dollar security deposit, if applicable, to the credit card you have provided. Please note that you are responsible for providing correct information that is clear and legible. Incorrect or illegible information, or rejected credit cards, may result in the Clerk's Office rejecting your notice of appeal thus divesting the Supreme Court of jurisdiction or rejection of your original action. You may wish to contact the Clerk's Office to confirm that we were able to file your original action or timely file in your appeal. The phone number is **(614) 387-9530.**

NAME AS IT APPEARS ON CREDIT CARD_____

ADDRESS_____   ZIP CODE_____

CITY_____STATE_____

EMAIL ADDRESS_____

CASE CAPTION_____

_____
(Please use the caption and prior case number as provided on the entry that you are appealing)

CREDIT CARD NUMBER_____

EXPIRATION DATE_____   CORPORATE CARD ____YES ____NO

CARD TYPE   MasterCard _____   Visa _____   American Express_____

TELEPHONE NUMBER_____
Please provide a number at which you can be reached from 8 a.m. to 5 p.m. Monday through Friday. The number will be used if the information you provided is incorrect or illegible. If we are unable to reach you and the charge is not accepted *for any reason* the appeal or original action will not be filed thus possibly divesting the Supreme Court of jurisdiction to consider your case.

_____$100 Filing Fee   OR   _____$100 Filing Fee and $100 Security Deposit

By initialing the appropriate line above and signing and dating below you authorize the Clerk's Office to deduct the specified amount required to initiate an appeal or original action with the Ohio Supreme Court from the credit card provided above.

SIGNATURE_____DATE_____

PLEASE NOTE THAT IT IS THE CLERK'S OFFICE POLICY TO DESTROY THIS FORM IMMEDIATELY UPON THE FILING OF THE CASE

COMMISSION ON THE RULES OF PRACTICE AND PROCEDURE IN OHIO COURTS

The Supreme Court of Ohio has established the Commission on the Rules of Practice and Procedure effective January 1, 2006. The Commission replaces the Supreme Court Rules Advisory Committee, formerly established in Rule XII of the Supreme Court Rules for the Government of the Bar of Ohio.

Section 1. Creation of Commission. Pursuant to the power vested in the Supreme Court of Ohio by Article IV, Section 5(B) of the Ohio Constitution regarding rules governing practice and procedure in all courts of the state, and by R.C. 2935.17 and R.C. 2937.46 regarding rules governing procedure in traffic cases, and to assist the Court in the exercise of its rule-making powers, there shall be a Supreme Court Commission on the Rules of Practice and Procedure in Ohio Courts.

Section 2. Duties of Commission. The Commission shall review all rules governing practice and procedure in the courts of Ohio, including the Rules of Civil Procedure, the Rules of Criminal Procedure, the Rules of Appellate Procedure, the Rules of Juvenile Procedure, and the Rules of Evidence. For the purpose of convenience and consistency, the Commission shall also review all rules governing procedure in traffic cases which pursuant to Article IV, Section 5(B) of the Ohio Constitution are not considered rules of practice and procedure. The Commission shall receive and consider proposed rules and amendments, and recommend rules and amendments for adoption to the Court.

Section 3. Membership. The Commission shall consist of nineteen members appointed by the Supreme Court.

(A) Ten members shall be members of the following organizations or committees and shall be nominated for appointment by:

(1) the Chair of the Civil Law and Procedure Committee of the Ohio Judicial Conference;

(2) the Chair of the Criminal Law and Procedure Committee of the Ohio Judicial Conference;

(3) the President of the Ohio Courts of Appeals Judges Association;

(4) the President of the Ohio Common Pleas Judges Association;

(5) the President of the Ohio Association of Probate Judges;

(6) the President of the Ohio Association of Domestic Relations Judges;

(7) the President of the Ohio Association of Juvenile Court Judges;

(8) the President of the Association of Municipal/County Court Judges of Ohio;

(9) the President of the Ohio Association of Magistrates;

(10) the Chair of the Judicial Administration and Legal Reform Committee of the Ohio State Bar Association.

(B) Nine members shall be appointed by the Supreme Court as follows:

(1) Five attorneys admitted to and engaged in the practice of law in Ohio;

(2) Two attorneys who are members of law faculty and are engaged in full-time legal education in Ohio law schools;

(3) One attorney admitted to the practice of law in Ohio who is employed full-time as a prosecuting attorney, city prosecutor, or city law director;

(4) One attorney admitted to the practice of law in Ohio whose practice includes the representation of persons charged with criminal offenses.

Section 4. Committees. (A) The Commission shall establish a Traffic Rules Committee. The Traffic Rules Committee shall consist of the members of the Commission as are appointed by the chair, municipal court judges appointed by the chair, a municipal court clerk of court appointed by the chair and the following *ex officio* members, or their designees:

(1) The Superintendent of the Ohio Highway Patrol;

(2) The chair of the Traffic Law Committee of the Ohio State Bar Association;

(3) The Director of the Department of Public Safety.

(B) The Chair may also establish other committees to aid the Commission in the completion of its work. These committees may include a Civil Rules Committee, Criminal Rules Committee, Appellate Rules Committee, Evidence Rules Committee and Juvenile Rules Committee. The committees shall consist of members of the Commission and others as are appointed by the chair.

Section 5. Terms. (A) Members of the Commission shall serve three year terms beginning on the first day of January. Members shall be eligible for reappointment, but shall not be eligible to serve more than two consecutive terms of three years without a six month break in service.

(B) Vacancies shall be filled in the same manner as original appointments. A member appointed to fill a vacancy occurring prior to the expiration of the term for which his or her predecessor was appointed shall hold office for the remainder of the term. If an attorney member no longer practices in Ohio, if an educator member is no longer engaged in full-time legal education in an Ohio law school, if a judge member leaves office, if the magistrate member is no longer employed as a full-time magistrate, if the prosecuting attorney, city prosecutor, or city law director member is no longer employed full-time in that capacity, or if the member whose practice includes the representation of persons charged with criminal offenses ceases such representation, the member shall be disqualified and a vacancy shall occur.

Section 6. Chair; Vice-Chair. The Court shall appoint one of the members as chair and one of the members as vice-chair. The chair and vice-chair shall serve for two years, and may be reappointed, but a member shall not serve as chair or vice-chair for more than two consecutive terms of two years.

Section 7. Compensation. Members of the Commission shall serve without compensation, but shall be reimbursed for expenses incurred in the performance of their official duties.

Section 8. Staff. The Administrative Director of the Supreme Court, or the director's designee, shall serve as staff liaison to the Commission.

Section 9. Effective Date; Transition of Membership. This rule shall take effect on January 1, 2006; amended effective November 1, 2007. Each member of the Supreme Court Rules Advisory Committee serving on the Committee as of the effective date of this rule shall continue to serve on the Commission for the balance of the term to which the member was appointed. The service of a member on the Rules Advisory Committee shall be included in determining the eligibility of the member for reappointment to the Commission pursuant to Section 4(A) of this rule.

Index to Rules of Practice of the Supreme Court of Ohio

RULES OF THE COURT OF CLAIMS OF OHIO

Effective July 1, 1975

Complete with amendments through July 1, 2010

Rule

RULE 1. Scope; Applicability; Citation

(A) **Scope; applicability** These rules, and those Civil Rules not clearly inapplicable to the special statutory procedures set forth in R.C. Chapter 2743, govern practice and procedure in the Court of Claims.

(B) **Citation** These rules shall be known as the Rules of the Court of Claims of Ohio and shall be cited as "C.C.R....."

RULE 2. Clerk's Fees

(A) **Deposit** The clerk, except as provided in subdivision (B), shall not accept a claim for filing including claims removed to the court of claims, unless such filing is accompanied by the filing fee prescribed by the court.

(B) **Poverty affidavit** The clerk shall accept for filing all claims accompanied by a poverty affidavit which states specific reasons for the inability to pay the deposit to secure costs. In a claim accompanied by a poverty affidavit, the clerk shall serve all process and pay the expense therefor from the funds of the court and tax such expenses as costs. The clerk or the court may at any time require additional information and a hearing, or both, to determine the validity of the poverty affidavit.

(C) **Fees** The clerk shall charge and collect the fees established by local rule of the court.

RULE 3. Reserved

Former C.C.R. 3 rescinded effective July 1, 1980.

RULE 4. Procedure for Removal and Remand

(A) **Petition for removal** A party who serves a counterclaim against the state or makes the state a third-party defendant in an action commenced in a court other than the court of claims shall file a petition for removal in the court of claims. The petition shall state the basis for removal, be accompanied by a copy of all process, pleadings, and other papers served upon the petitioner and shall be signed in accordance with Civil Rule 11.

(B) **Time for filing petition** A petition for removal based on a counterclaim shall be filed within twenty-eight days after service of the counterclaim of the petitioner. A petition for removal based on third-party practice shall be filed within twenty-eight days after filing of the third-party complaint of the petitioner.

(C) **Notice to parties** Within seven days after filing a petition for removal, the petitioner shall serve a copy of the petition upon all parties and the attorney general of this state, and shall file a copy of the petition with the clerk of the court in which the action was originally brought.

(D) **Adjudication and remand** The court of claims shall adjudicate all claims removed, except that the court may remand a claim to the court in which it originated upon a finding that the removal petition does not justify removal or upon a finding that the state is no longer a party.

History: Amended, eff 7-1-76.

RULE 5. Selection of Jurors

(A) **Panel of prospective jurors** In an action in the court of claims where one of the parties is entitled to a jury, the clerk of the court of claims, upon motion of the party or his own motion, shall request the jury commissioners of the court of common pleas of the county in which the action is to be tried to provide a panel of prospective jurors. The jury commissioners shall, pursuant to the request, provide such a panel at the time and place designated by the clerk of the court of claims.

(B) **Trial jurors** The trial judge or the clerk of the court of claims may order the trial jury to be selected outside the courtroom, and the trial judge may set the procedure for the examination of prospective jurors.

History: Amended, eff 7-1-76.

RULE 6. Administrative Determination of Claims by the Clerk; Duties of Claimant, Defendant, and Clerk

(A) **Initiation of administrative determination** A claim against the state which may be determined administratively pursuant to R.C. § 2743.10 shall be filed on a complaint form provided by the clerk of the court of claims. The clerk shall retain the original complaint form and send copies of the complaint form to the attorney general and the state department, board, office, commission, agency, institution, or instrumentality named as defendant in the complaint form.

The defendant shall investigate the claim and file three copies of a completed court of claims investigation form with the clerk. The investigation form and attachments shall be filed with the clerk within sixty days of receipt of the claim by the defendant. Within the sixty day period, the attorney general, by written motion, may request an extension of time for filing the investigation report, provided that he sets forth reasons for the extension. If an extension is granted, the clerk shall set a date certain for the filing of the investigation report.

The clerk shall retain one copy of the investigation report and send copies to the attorney general and the claimant. The clerk shall notify the claimant that within twenty-one days after receipt of the report, the claimant may, in person or in writing, respond to the investigation report. Within the twenty-one day period, the claimant, by written motion, may request an extension of time in which to respond to the investigation report, provided that he sets forth reasons for the extension. If an extension is granted, the clerk shall set a date certain for the filing of responses to the investigation report.

(B) **Time of administrative determination** Within forty-two days after mailing the investigation report to the claimant, or as soon thereafter as practicable, the clerk, or deputy clerk, shall administratively determine the claim.

(C) **Power of the clerk** In administrative determinations, the clerk or deputy clerk has the same power as a judge of the court of claims to regulate all proceedings before him. He may, among other things, conduct hearings, require the production of evidence, rule upon motions, determine admissibility and probative value of, evidence, require submission of briefs or memoranda, summon and compel attendance of witnesses, including parties, and call and examine them under oath.

(D) **Conduct of administrative determination** Unless otherwise ordered by the clerk, administrative determinations shall be made upon the form complaint, attachments to the form complaint, the investigation report attachments to the investigation report, claimant's written or oral responses to the investigation report and such other testimony or material that the clerk deems to have probative value.

(E) **Evidence in administrative determinations** The formal rules of evidence do not apply in administrative determinations, but all proof shall have such probative value as satisfies the clerk.

(F) **Discovery** Discovery procedures shall not be initiated in administrative determinations without the permission of the clerk.

(G) **Determination of the clerk** The clerk's determination shall be in writing and include findings of fact and conclusions of law. The clerk shall, simultaneously with the entry of the determination, send copies of the determination to the attorney general, the claimant, and the named defendant.

(H) **Appeal of determination**

(1) **Determination of the clerk final** The determination of the clerk is final unless a motion for court review is filed within thirty days of the entry of the determination. A motion for court review filed before entry of such determination shall be treated as filed after such entry and on the day thereof.

(2) **Motion for court review** A motion for review shall be in writing, specify the determination or part thereof to be reviewed, state with particularity the errors complained of and include a memorandum which sets forth movant's argument and supporting legal authorities.

(3) **Service of motion for review** A motion for review shall be served pursuant to Civil Rule 5(B).

(4) **Reply memorandum** A reply memorandum may be served and filed by the responding party within fourteen days after service of the motion for review.

(5) **Hearing on motion for review** Upon the filing of a motion for review, the clerk shall submit the entire file of the claim to a judge of the court of claims who shall review the clerk's determination. The judge may order oral argument.

(6) **Court review** Upon review of the clerk's determination, the judge shall confirm the clerk's determination and enter judgment thereon or, if there is substantial error, vacate the clerk's determination and, pursuant to R.C. § 2743.12, draft and journalize his own judgment.

History: Amended, eff 7-1-91.

RULE 7. Settlement of Claims Filed in the Court of Claims

(A) **Settlement of claim** Pursuant to R.C. § 2743.15, a claimant and the state may execute an agreement to settle a claim filed in the court of claims. A settlement agreement shall be signed by the claimant and the director or other administrative chief, or the governing body, of any department, board, office, commission, agency, institution, or other instrumentality of the state named as defendant in the action. The settlement agreement shall be approved by the attorney general and filed with the clerk of the court of claims for review by the court.

(B) **Review by the court** The court shall review the settlement agreement. If the court concurs with the terms of the settlement agreement, it shall approve and journalize the agreement. If the settlement agreement is not approved, the court may require the claimant and the state to reconsider the agreement. If the court does not approve the reconsidered agreement, the court shall assign the claim for trial.

RULE 8. Enforcement of Money Judgments

Money judgments against the state which shall include all departments, offices, bureaus, commissions, boards, agencies, institutions or instrumentalities, may be enforced only through the procedure established by R.C. § 2743.19. Other money judgments in the court of claims against parties other than the state shall be enforced pursuant to Civil Rule 69. The court of claims shall not enforce money judgments against parties other than the state. Upon written request of a party, the clerk shall issue a certificate of judgment which may be enforced pursuant to law in other courts.

RULE 9. Effective date

(A) **Effective date of rules** The rules submitted by the Supreme Court to the General Assembly on January 10, 1975, as amended by the amendments submitted to the General Assembly on April 29, 1975, shall take effect on July 1, 1975. They govern all proceedings in actions brought after they take effect and also all further proceedings in actions then pending, except to the extent that their application in a particular action pending when the amendments take effect would not be feasible or would work injustice, in which event the former procedure applies.

(B) **Effective date of amendments** The amendments submitted by the Supreme Court to the General Assembly on January 9, 1976, shall take effect on July 1, 1976. They govern all proceedings in actions brought after they take effect and also all further proceedings in actions then pending, except to the extent that their application in a particular action pending when the amendments take effect would not be feasible or would work injustice, in which event the former procedure applies.

(C) **Effective date of amendments** The amendments submitted by the Supreme Court to the General

Assembly on January 14, 1980, shall take effect on July 1, 1980. They govern all proceedings in actions brought after they take effect and also all further proceedings in actions then pending, except to the extent that their application in a particular action pending when the rules take effect would not be feasible or would work injustice, in which event the former procedure applies.

(D) **Effective date of amendments** The amendments submitted by the Supreme Court to the General Assembly on January 10, 1991, shall take effect on July 1, 1991. They govern all proceedings in actions brought after they take effect and also all further proceedings in actions then pending, except to the extent that their application in a particular action pending when the amendments take effect would not be feasible or would work injustice, in which event the former procedure applies.

History: Amended, eff 7-1-76; 7-1-80; 7-1-91.

COURT OF CLAIMS OF OHIO

Instructions For Form Complaint

The form follows these instructions

USE OF FORM COMPLAINT:

The form complaint must be used for all claims for $2,500.00 or less. All claims for $2,500.00 and less are administratively determined by the Clerk or Deputy Clerk of the Court of Claims pursuant to the statutes and the Court of Claims Administrative Determination Rule, a copy of which is attached to these instructions. Complaints for more than $2,500.00 should be drafted to conform to the requirements of the Ohio Rules of Civil Procedure. Although the form complaint may be used to commence claims for over $2,500.00, the Court may require the complaint to be redrafted to conform to the requirements of the Ohio Rules of Civil Procedure.

PROOF OF CLAIM:

There is no right of jury trial in claims against the State of Ohio. All claims against the State are determined by the Clerk, a Deputy Clerk or a Judge of the Court of Claims. As in all civil actions, the plaintiff has the burden of proof. Plaintiff must prove liability, injury and damages by a preponderance of the evidence. Plaintiff must attach two copies of all supporting documents to the complaint. The Court may require that plaintiff produce the originals. The following is a partial list of evidence that plaintiff should, if appropriate, use to prove a claim: the certificate of title for an automobile; detailed medical reports prepared and signed by plaintiff's physician or physicians; paid or unpaid bills; estimates of the cost of repair or replacement; the actual document-the contract, check, drawing, plan, memo, etc., which is the basis of the claim; sworn, signed and notarized statements from witnesses to the incident or from witnesses with knowledge of the incident; police reports; and photographs.

NUMBER OF COPIES, FILING, FILING FEE:

Plaintiff must complete and file the complaint form with the Clerk of the Court of Claims, The Ohio Judicial Center, 65 South Front Street, Third Floor, Columbus, Ohio 43215. A filing may be made by mail. The Clerk will not process the complaint unless it is accompanied by a filing fee of $25.00 in the form of a check or money order made payable to the Court of Claims. The Clerk will file and process the complaint if the plaintiff is in fact unable to pay the filing fee and files an affidavit of indigency in lieu of the filing fee.

HOW TO COMPLETE FORM:

The instructions that follow are personalized in an attempt to assist plaintiffs. Plaintiff must properly complete and file the form. Remember, this form begins a civil action in which YOU-the plaintiff-must prove your claim by a preponderance of the evidence.

Blanks (1) through (8). This information is very important. The Court must be able to contact you and must know exactly what state agency is involved so that it can send a copy of this complaint to that state agency. You must name the proper defendant agency and state the agency's complete address. If there is more than one plaintiff in an action, each plaintiff should be listed, on additional sheets if necessary, and each plaintiff should sign at Blank 21.

Blanks (9) through (11). Self-explanatory.

Blank (12). In Blank 12, tell how the incident occurred, e.g., "negligently drove his state truck into the left side of my 1981 Chevrolet Citation on 1-71 northbound, approximately 300 feet north of milepost 120north of the 1-270 interchange"; "entered into an oral contract to purchase fuel oil from me and failed to pay for 222 gallons of diesel fuel, which I delivered on February 11,1983, to the Department of Transportation Garage at Route 303 and Interstate 71 in Medina County"; "took my radio and watch during a shake-down inspection at the Southern Ohio Correctional Facility"

Blank (13). In Blank 13, state the location and extent of the injury, damage or loss, e.g., "damage to the left front door and vent window of my car"; "loss of $99.99 for 222 gallons of diesel fuel at $.45 a gallon"; "loss of one Timex electric watch valued at $45.00"; "one G.E. clock radio valued at $45.00"; and "hurt my left wrist and incurred the following expense: Riverwood Hospital emergency room $25.00, Dr. James Brown $25.00, Doc's Pharmacy $10.50." To substantiate your injury, damage, or loss you should attach two copies of each bill, receipt or statement to the complaint filed with the Court, e-g., you must make two copies of the paid bill for "Doc's Pharmacy" and attach them to the complaint.

COURT OF CLAIMS OF OHIO

Blank (14). Add all the individual items listed in Blank (12). If the amount is over $2.500.00, you should file your complaint on the form required by the Ohio Rules of Civil Procedure. You may use the form complaint to commence a claim of more than $2,500.00 but the Court may require you to redraft and refile your complaint.

Blank (15). State the names and addresses of all witnesses. If possible, obtain witness statements and attach two copies of each statement to the form complaint. If you learn of additional witnesses after you file your claim, you must promptly inform the Court of their names and addresses.

Blank (16). If you have insurance coverage circle "/have/" and complete Blanks (17) and (18). If you do not have insurance coverage, circle "/do not have/" and disregard Blanks (17) and (18).

Blank (19). If you have received payments from any source, e.g., auto insurance, hospitalization, workers' compensation, etc. as a result of the injury, damage or loss, circle "/have/" and complete Blank (20). If you have not received any payments, circle "I have not/" and disregard Blank (20). If you receive any payments for your injury, damage, or loss after you file your claim, you must inform the Court of the amount and source of the payment.

Blank (21). Your signature on Blank (21) certifies that the statements contained in the form are true. Making a false report is a crime under R.C. 2921.13 which reads in pertinent part:

> (A) no person shall knowingly make a false statement, or knowingly swear or affirm the truth of a false statement previously made, when any of the following apply:

>> (1) The statement is made in any official proceeding . . .
>> (3) The statement is made with purpose to mislead a public official in performing his official function . . .
>> (6)The statement is sworn or affirmed before a notary public or other person empowered to administer oaths . . .

In addition, if your claim is based on personal injury, your signature waives the physician-patient privilege. This means that the defendant or the Court can ask your doctor or doctors about the injury which is the basis of the claim. If plaintiff is under eighteen years of age, Blank (21) should be signed by plaintiff's father, or mother, or his legal guardian, e.g., "John Smith, father of plaintiff James F. Smith." The parent or guardian should sign all further filings which are made while the plaintiff is under eighteen years of age.

Blank (22). Civil Rule 11 applies to signatures by attorneys.

Blanks (23) through (25). Self-explanatory.

ADDITIONAL PAGES:

If this form does not provide sufficient space, you may state the information on continuation pages if you identify this information as "Continuation of Blank ( )" and then state the information, e.g., "Continuation of Blank (13): one Parker pen and pencil set valued at $28.00, five tapes having a total value of $40.00," etc.

APPEAL:

After the claim has been decided, the losing party may file a motion for court review of the Clerk's determination within thirty (30) days of the entry of that decision [see attached Rule 6(H)]. If you win your case, processing for payment cannot be initiated until this appeal period has run.

COURT COSTS:

The$25.00 filing fee required by statute is not returnable. The Clerk must charge the fees and costs required by the statutes and court rules. Thus, if you lose the case and costs are assessed against you, you will have to pay additional court costs.

If you move or change your telephone number, you must give the Court written notice of the new address or telephone number. Your case may be DISMISSED if the Court cannot contact you.

READ THE COMPLAINT AGAIN:

Have you completed every blank? Have you signed it?

Have you included two copies of the supporting documents?

Have you included the filing fee of $25.00?

COURT OF CLAIMS OF OHIO

The Ohio Judicial Center
65 South Front Street, Third Floor
Columbus, OH 43215
614. 387.9800 or 1.800.824.8263
www.cco.state.oh.us

Form Complaint

Case Number _____

for Court use only

PLAINTIFF:

(1) _____

plaintiff's name   age

(2) _____

street address

(3) _____

city   state   zip

(4) _____

telephone (business)   area code

(5) _____

telephone (home)   area code

NOTE: if you move or change telephone numbers you must give
the Court written notice of the new address or telephone number

DEFENDANT:

(6) _____

defendant state department, board, commission, etc

(7) _____

street address

(8) _____

city   state   zip

The defendant listed in (6) above through its agent(s)

(9) _____

fill in name(s) and title(s) of the agents if known, if unknown state unknown

did on or about **(10)** _____ **(11)** _____ am/pm

fill in date   state approximate hour

(12) Describe in ordinary language the basis of the claim (see instructions)

_____

_____

_____

Court of Claims of Ohio

(12) Continued

_____

_____

_____

_____

_____

_____

_____

_____

_____

_____

_____

causing plaintiff the following injury, damage or loss (13) _____

_____
                        list each item separately

_____

_____

_____

_____

for a total claim of (14)   _____

The witnesses, if any, to the injury, damage or loss are (15) _____
                                                    Fill in name and address

_____

_____

COURT OF CLAIMS OF OHIO

(16) I *(circle the appropriate word or phrase)/*have/do not have/insurance coverage for the injury, damage or loss with the

(17) _____

fill in company name and address and policy number

The policy has a (18) $ _____ deductible provision.

(19) I (circle the appropriate word or phrase)/have/have not/ received insurance payment(s) in the amount of

(20) $ _____ as a result of the incident described above. (see instructions).

I ask the Court to grant a judgment in the amount stated in blank (14).

If the amount exceeds $2,500.00 the Court may require that a civil rules complaint be filed.
Under the penalties of perjury and falsification, I state that I have read or had read to me the above complaint and that it is true. Further, I expressly waive, on behalf of myself and of any person who shall have any interest in this claim, all provisions of law forbidding any physician or other person who has heretofore attended or examined me, or who may hereafter attend or examine me from disclosing any knowledge or information which they thereby acquired.

(21) _____

signature of plaintiff (see instructions)

BE SURE TO INCLUDE FILING FEE AND TO GIVE THE COURT WRITTEN NOTICE OF ADDRESS CHANGES (see Instructions)

NOTE: Plaintiff need not have an attorney. If plaintiff files the complaint without an attorney, plaintiff completes Blank (21). If plaintiff files through an attorney, plaintiff signs Blank (21) and the attorney signs Blank (22) and completes Blanks (23) through (25).

Pursuant to Civil Rule 11, I state I have read the above complaint; that to the best of my knowledge, information, and belief there is good ground to support it; and that it is not interposed for delay.

(22) _____

signature of plaintiff's attorney

(23) _____

street address

(24) _____

city   state   zip

(25) _____

telephone   area code

Index to Rules of the Court of Claims of Ohio

RULES OF THE COURT OF CLAIMS, VICTIMS OF CRIME COMPENSATION SECTION

Effective October 17, 1983

Complete with amendments through July 1, 2010

Rule
1.   Attorney Fees

RULE 1.   Attorney Fees

(A) **Hourly rate** Reimbursement for attorney fees under R.C. 2743.65(A) shall be made on the basis of a maximum of $60 per hour up to the maximum amounts authorized by divisions (B) and (C) of this Rule.

(B) **Maximum hours; maximum amounts of reimbursement** Unless otherwise provided by division (C) of this Rule or by order of a commissioner, panel of commissioners, or judge of the Court of Claims, the following are the maximum amounts of reimbursement allowable to an attorney for services performed during certain stages of the process:

(1) Through determination by a single commissioner, $720 (12 hours @ $60);

(2) Through determination by a panel of commissioners, $1,020 (17 hours @ $60);

(3) Through determination by a judge of the Court of Claims, $1,320 (22 hours @ $60);

(4) Representation at the three commissioner panel hearing only where attorney was not involved prior to the decision by a single commissioner, $540 (9 hours @ $60);

(5) Representation at the three commissioner panel hearing and the hearing before a judge of the Court of Claims where attorney was not involved prior to the decision by a single commissioner, $840 (14 hours @ $60);

(6) Representation at a hearing before a judge of the Court of Claims only where attorney was not involved prior to the decision by a three commissioner panel, $540 (9 hours @ $60);

(7) Where counsel has represented only through part of a proceeding, reimbursement will be based upon the hourly rate mentioned in division (A) of this Rule up to the maximum authorized for the segment of the proceeding during which representation occurred.

(C) **Award below maximum amounts; requests for additional reimbursement; guardianships; expenses**

(1) A commissioner may determine that a lesser number of hours should have been required in a given case. Additional reimbursement may be made, based upon the hourly rate listed in division (A) of this rule, where the attorney demonstrates to the satisfaction of the commissioner that the nature of the particular claim required the expenditure of an amount of time in excess of that allowed by division (B) of this Rule.

(2) Attorneys may be reimbursed for fees incurred in the creation of a guardianship, if the guardianship is required in order for an individual to receive an award of reparations.

(3) Expenses that are related to the representation of a claimant, that have a direct bearing on a factual or legal issue before a commissioner, panel of commissioners, or judge of the Court of Claims, and that exceed one hundred dollars, shall be approved in advance by a commissioner, panel of commissioners, or judge. Prior to incurring the expense, counsel shall submit a written motion that details the reason the expense is necessary for representation of the claimant. For purposes of this division, "expenses" includes, but is not limited to, trial transcripts, depositions, and expert witness fees.

(D) **Unreimbursable fees** Fees that may be related to the incident giving rise to the application for reparations but that are not directly related to the claim for reparations, including, but not limited to, estate work or representation of a claimant against a collateral source, are not reimbursable under R.C. 2743.65(A). No fee will be awarded for the following:

(1) Duplication of investigative work required to be performed by the Attorney General pursuant to R.C. 2743.59;

(2) Performance of unnecessary criminal investigation of the offense;

(3) Presenting or appealing an issue that has or issues that have been repeatedly ruled upon by the highest appellate authority, unless a unique set of facts or unique issue of law exists that may distinguish it;

(4) Any fee request that is unreasonable, is not commensurate with services rendered, is violative of the Ohio Code of Professional Responsibility, or is based upon services that are determined to be frivolous.

(E) **Comments of judge and panel commissioners considered** In determining the award of attorney fees authorized by R.C. 2743.65(A) and this Rule, the commissioner shall consider the comments of the panel of commissioners and judge of the Court of Claims with respect to the representation before them.

(F) **Forwarding applications for attorney fees; contents of application** The Clerk of the Court of Claims shall forward applications for attorney fees to the applicant and the applicant's attorney upon journalizing of a reparations award order, or at any time in response to inquiries. The application for fees shall apprise the attorney of the requirements of R.C. 2743.65(A), require a verification statement comporting with Civil Rule 11 and with the law prohibiting falsification, and require an itemized fee statement. A copy of this Rule shall be forwarded to the applicant and the attorney with the application for attorney fee form. The attorney shall file the attorney fee application and serve a copy upon both the Attorney General and the applicant. Service by the attorney upon himself or herself is not service upon the applicant.

(G) **Right of Attorney General or applicant to oppose application** The applicant and the Attorney General may oppose either the initial application or a motion for reconsideration. The attorney may oppose a motion for reconsideration filed by an applicant or the Attorney General. All material filed in opposition to a motion for reconsideration or an initial application shall be received by the court within fourteen days of the filing of the motion or application. Any party filing in opposition shall serve a copy of all material filed on the other parties authorized to file by this Rule.

(H) **Motion for reconsideration**

(1) The decision with respect to an award of attorney fees shall be final ten days after the order is journalized.

(2) Prior to the expiration of the ten day period and upon presentation of new evidence, or an argument that the single commissioner has erred in applying criteria for awarding attorney fees, the attorney, applicant, or Attorney General may move for reconsideration by the single commissioner of the attorney fee award on grounds that it is insufficient or excessive. The party filing the motion for reconsideration shall serve a copy upon the other parties authorized by division (G) to file a motion. Motions for reconsideration shall require reconsideration of the entire file and fee statement, and may result in a revised award that is greater or lesser than the amount claimed or granted. The decision made by the commissioner on the motion for reconsideration is final.

(I) **Source of funds for payment of attorney fees** Attorney fees awarded under R.C. 2743.65(A) are payable from the Reparations Special Account in addition to the award of reparations, if any, made to the applicant. An attorney who represents an applicant for an award of reparations shall not charge the applicant or any other person for the services rendered in relation to that representation but shall apply to the Court of Claims for payment. Receipt of any fee in connection with an application for reparations under R.C. 2743.51 to 2743.72, other than that contemplated by R.C. 2743.65(A) and this Rule, shall constitute reason for the denial of attorney fees under R.C. 2743.65(A) and this Rule. When any instance of violation of this Rule, or R.C. 2743.65(A), comes to the attention of a commissioner, panel of commissioners, judge of the Court of Claims, the Clerk of the Court of Claims, or the staff of any of them, the matter may be referred to the Office of Disciplinary Counsel of the Supreme Court of Ohio for action under the Ohio Code of Professional Responsibility and Rule V of the Rules for the Government of the Bar of Ohio.

(J) **Citation** This Rule shall be cited as V.C.C.R. 1.

APPLICATION FOR COMPENSATION
The Ohio Victims of Crime Compensation Program
1-800-824-8263
Administered by the Court of Claims of Ohio ■ Investigated by the Ohio Attorney General

Court of Claims OFFICE USE ONLY	Court of Common Pleas OFFICE USE ONLY	Court of Common Pleas OFFICE USE ONLY
	C.P. Case #_____	
	☐ Filing Fee Paid ☐ Statement of Indigency ☐ Neither Provided	
	Clerk: Please docket and mail to Court of Claims within seven (7) business days	
Date Stamp Here		Date Stamp Here

You must file an original application, not a copy
PLEASE (1) TYPE OR PRINT CLEARLY IN INK, and (2) READ INSTRUCTIONS CAREFULLY

SECTION A. INFORMATION ABOUT THE VICTIM OF CRIME

Name of victim_____ Social Security #_____
last   first   middle

Street Address _____

City _____ County _____ State _____ Zip Code _____
Birthdate _____ Home phone number(___)_____ Work phone number (___)_____
month / day / year

Victim is/was: ☐ male ☐ female ☐ single ☐ married ☐ separated ☐ divorced ☐ widowed

Did the victim live at the above address at the time of the crime? ☐ Yes ☐ No (If no, write down address at time of crime)

Street Address _____ City _____ County _____ State _____ Zip Code

Occupation & employer of victim at time of crime _____

Please list all addresses of the victim for 10 years prior to the injury

City _____ County _____ State _____ Dates _____

City _____ County _____ State _____ Dates _____

SECTION B. INFORMATION ABOUT THE PERSON SEEKING COMPENSATION, IF HE/SHE IS NOT THE VICTIM
If the applicant is the victim, skip this section and go to Section C.

Name of this person_____ Social Security #_____

Street Address _____

City _____ County _____ State _____ Zip Code
Birthdate _____ Home phone number (___)_____ Work phone number (___)_____
month / day / year

Are you: ☐ male ☐ female ☐ single ☐ married ☐ separated ☐ divorced ☐ widowed

What is your relationship to the victim of crime? _____

Your occupation & employer (if applicant is not the victim) _____

Please list all addresses of the applicant (if the applicant is not the victim) for 10 years prior to the injury

City _____ County _____ State _____ Dates _____

City _____ County _____ State _____ Dates _____

SECTION C. CRIMINAL HISTORY

Has the VICTIM been arrested for, or convicted of, any felony within 10 years prior to the injury? Yes ☐ No ☐

Has the APPLICANT been arrested for, or convicted of, any felony within 10 years prior to the injury? Yes ☐ No ☐

ON THIS PAGE, YOU NEED TO PROVIDE INFORMATION ABOUT THE CRIME THAT HAPPENED TO YOU,
AND THE INJURIES AND EXPENSES YOU HAVE BECAUSE OF THIS CRIME.
IF YOU NEED MORE ROOM, USE ANOTHER SHEET OF PAPER AND ATTACH IT TO YOUR APPLICATION.

SECTION D. INFORMATION ABOUT THE CRIME

Type of crime: ☐ murder/homicide   ☐ assault   ☐ child physical abuse   ☐ domestic abuse
(check one)   ☐ drunk driver   ☐ sexual assault   ☐ child sexual abuse   ☐ other

Date of crime _____   Crime happened where?
              month / day / year

Time of crime _____ Address of crime _____

Date crime reported _____
                    month / day / year   City   County   State   Zip Code

Time crime reported _____   If not reported within 72 hours, write down why not and attach explanation to application

Crime reported to _____
                  name of law enforcement agency   city   zip code

Who are the offenders (if known or suspected)?

_____   _____   _____
Name   Street Address   City, State, Zip

_____   _____   _____
Name   Street Address   City, State, Zip

SECTION E. DESCRIPTION OF THE CRIME

In your own words, briefly describe what happened during the crime:

_____

_____

What were the victim's injuries?

_____

_____

Did the victim die as a result of injuries received in the crime?   Yes ☐   No ☐

SECTION F. EXPENSES AND LOSSES CAUSED BY THE CRIME: CHECK ALL THAT APPLY

I am seeking compensation for:

☐ Medical/dental/mental health expenses
   These expenses include rehabilitation, prescriptions and co-pays, mileage for transportation to appointments, etc.
☐ Loss of earnings because I couldn't work as a result of this crime
   Including loss of wages because you stayed home to care for the victim, like a husband caring for an injured wife
☐ Replacement services
   These are expenses for services the victim normally did, but due to the victim's injury or death, someone else is now
   paid to do these services. Examples of these services include child care, cleaning, home projects, errands, etc.
☐ Loss of support for dependents (please attach a list of all of the victim's dependents to this application)
   This is income that the victim can no longer provide to dependents because the victim is deceased
☐ Funeral and/or burial expenses
   These are expenses for the deceased victim, up to $5,000 (legal maximum)
☐ Loss of unemployment benefits
   These expenses include unemployment benefits you were not able to collect, because you did not meet the "able to
   work" requirement
☐ Any other expenses related to injury - please describe below

_____

_____

SECTION G. EXTENT OF INJURIES CAUSED BY THE CRIME

Did the victim miss work because of   Was the victim hospitalized because of injuries received in
injuries received in the crime?   ☐ Yes ☐ No   the crime?   ☐ Yes   ☐ No

If yes, for how long? _____   If yes, for how long? _____

                                                 Hospital name: _____

YOU ARE DONE PROVIDING INFORMATION TO FILE YOUR APPLICATION FOR COMPENSATION.
NOW PLEASE READ THE INFORMATION BELOW CAREFULLY AND SIGN WHERE NEEDED.
Your application cannot be processed unless you sign section H.

SECTION H. SUBROGATION, AUTHORIZATION AND SIGNATURE

I understand that if I get money from any other source to cover the same expenses I get compensation for, I have to reimburse the state of Ohio that amount of money.

I hereby authorize any person (including any physician, medical facility or health care provider), organization, the Ohio Department of Human Services, the appropriate county Department of Human Services, law enforcement agency or government agency, upon request, to release to the Ohio Attorney General, the Court of Claims of Ohio, or to my attorney, a copy of any report, document, record, criminal record or other information (including tax information or returns, or medical information) in any way relating to my claim for an award of reparations under the Ohio Victims of Crime Compensation Program. I understand that medical records may contain information regarding care of psychiatric/psychological conditions, drug or alcohol abuse, HIV test results, AIDS and AIDS-related conditions. I understand that disclosure of confidential information from medical records may be protected by state or federal law. If applicable, state law (R.C.3701.243) and federal regulations (42 C.F.R. part 2) prohibit the Ohio Attorney General or the Court of Claims of Ohio from making any further disclosure of confidential information without my specific written consent or as otherwise permitted by such regulations. This authorization or a copy hereof shall be valid for a period of two years without any further consent by me.

I, the applicant, hereby state under the penalties of perjury and falsification that this application of three pages has been prepared or read by me and the information given herein, including any records or certificates, is true and accurate to the best of my knowledge.

_____   _____
Date of signature   *Signature of person seeking compensation*

· VICTIM SERVICE PROVIDER:
Place Status Report code number and address below

APPLICANT:
Your application for compensation must be filed either at any county court of common pleas or at the Court of Claims of Ohio within two (2) years of the date of the crime.
You must include the $7.50 filing fee, or a statement signed by you that says you cannot afford to pay this fee.

To file at the Court of Claims,
mail this completed application to:
Ohio Victims of Crime Compensation Program
Court of Claims of Ohio
65 East State Street, Suite 1100
Columbus, Ohio, 43215

SECTION I. ATTORNEY INFORMATION (to be completed by attorney, if any)

You are not required to have an attorney help you submit your application. But if an attorney does help you, the attorney also must sign this application. **The attorney cannot charge you** for representing you. The attorney will be paid by the Court of Claims of Ohio, regardless of the outcome of your claim. The attorney's fee will not be deducted from any amount that is awarded to you, if you are given compensation.

_____   _____
Attorney name   *Attorney telephone number*

_____   _____
Attorney street address   *City*   *State*   *Zip Code*

_____   _____
Attorney registration number   *Attorney Social Security or Tax ID number*

Pursuant to Civil Rule 11, I state that I have read the application for compensation; that to the best of my knowledge, information, and belief, there is good ground to support it. I further state that I have read Section 2743.65 of the Revised Code concerning attorney fees.

_____
Attorney Signature

VC-1.   Rev. 4/99

SUPPLEMENTAL COMPENSATION APPLICATION
Court of Claims of Ohio
Victims of Crime Compensation Program

65 East State Street, Suite 1100 ▪ 1-800-824-8263 ▪ Columbus, Ohio, 43215

PLEASE NOTE:
There is no fee to file a supplemental compensation application. This application can be filed only at the Court of Claims of Ohio by mail or in person.

ADMINISTERED BY THE COURT OF CLAIMS OF OHIO
INVESTIGATED BY THE OHIO ATTORNEY GENERAL

Court of Claims
OFFICE USE ONLY

ORIGINAL COMPENSATION APPLICATION NUMBER:

V ___ ___ – ___ ___ ___ ___ ___

PLEASE (1) TYPE OR PRINT CLEARLY IN INK, and (2) READ INSTRUCTIONS CAREFULLY

SECTION A. INFORMATION ABOUT THE VICTIM OF CRIME

Name of victim _____ Social Security # _____
last   first   middle

Street Address _____ City ___ County ___ State ___ Zip Code

Birthdate _____ Home phone number ( ) ___ Work phone number ( )
month / day / year

Victim is/was: ☐ male ☐ female ☐ single ☐ married ☐ separated ☐ divorced ☐ widowed

Did the victim live at the above address at the time of the crime? ☐ Yes ☐ No (If no, write down address at time of crime)

Street Address _____ City ___ County ___ State Zip Code

Occupation & employer of victim at time of crime _____

Please list all addresses of the victim for 10 years prior to the injury

City _____ County _____ State ___ Dates _____
City _____ County _____ State ___ Dates _____
City _____ County _____ State ___ Dates _____

SECTION B. INFORMATION ABOUT THE PERSON SEEKING COMPENSATION, IF HE/SHE IS NOT THE VICTIM
If the applicant is the victim, skip this section and go to Section C.

Name of this person _____ Social Security # _____
last   first   middle

Street Address _____ City ___ County ___ State ___ Zip Code

Birthdate _____ Home phone number ( ) ___ Work phone number ( )
month / day / year

Are you: ☐ male ☐ female ☐ single ☐ married ☐ separated ☐ divorced ☐ widowed

What is your relationship to the victim of crime? _____

Your occupation & employer (if applicant is not the victim) _____

Please list all addresses of the applicant (if the applicant is not the victim) for 10 years prior to the injury

City _____ County _____ State ___ Dates _____
City _____ County _____ State ___ Dates _____
City _____ County _____ State ___ Dates _____

SECTION C. CRIMINAL HISTORY

Has the VICTIM been arrested for, or convicted of, any felony within 10 years prior to the injury or since filing the original application?
Yes ☐ No ☐

Has the APPLICANT been arrested for, or convicted of, any felony within 10 years prior to the injury or since filing the original application?
Yes ☐ No ☐

SECTION D. NEW EXPENSES SINCE ORIGINAL APPLICATION WAS FILED: CHECK ALL THAT APPLY

[ ] Medical/dental/mental health expenses
These expenses include rehabilitation, prescriptions and co-pays, mileage for transportation to appointments, etc.

[ ] Loss of earnings because I couldn't work as a result of this crime
Including loss of wages because you stayed home to care for the victim, like a husband caring for an injured wife

[ ] Replacement services
These are expenses for services the victim normally did, but due to the victim's injury or death, someone else is now paid to do these services. Examples of these services include child care, cleaning, home projects, errands, etc.

[ ] Loss of support for dependents *(please attach a list of all of the victim's dependents to this application)*
This is income that the victim can no longer provide to dependents because the victim is deceased

[ ] Funeral and/or burial expenses
These are expenses for the deceased victim

[ ] Loss of unemployment benefits
These expenses include unemployment benefits you were not able to collect, because you did not meet the "able to work" requirement

[ ] Any other expenses related to injury - please describe below

SECTION E. SUBROGATION, AUTHORIZATION AND SIGNATURE

I understand that if I get money from any other source to cover the same expenses I get compensation for, I have to reimburse the state of Ohio that amount of money.

I hereby authorize any person (including any physician, medical facility or health care provider), organization, the Ohio Department of Human Services, the appropriate county Department of Human Services, law enforcement agency or government agency, upon request, to release to the Ohio Attorney General, to the Court of Claims of Ohio, or to my attorney, a copy of any report, document, record, criminal record or other information (including tax information or returns, or medical information) in any way relating to my claim for an award of reparations under the Ohio Victims of Crime Compensation Program. I understand that medical records may contain information regarding care of psychiatric/psychological conditions, drug or alcohol abuse, HIV test results, AIDS and AIDS-related conditions. I understand that disclosure of confidential information from medical records may be protected by state or federal law. If applicable, state law (R.C.3701.243) and federal regulations (42 C.F.R. part 2) prohibit the Ohio Attorney General or the Court of Claims of Ohio from making any further disclosure of confidential information without my specific written consent or as otherwise permitted by such regulations. This authorization or a copy hereof shall be valid for a period of two years without any further consent by me.

I, the applicant, hereby state under the penalties of perjury and falsification that this application of two pages has been prepared or read by me and the information given herein, including any records or certificates, is true and accurate to the best of my knowledge.

_____   _____
Date   Signature of person seeking compensation

SECTION G. ATTORNEY INFORMATION

You are not required to have an attorney help you submit your application. But if an attorney does help you, the attorney also must sign this application. **The attorney cannot charge you** for representing you. The attorney will be paid by the Court of Claims of Ohio, regardless of the outcome of your claim. The attorney's fee will not be deducted from any amount that is awarded to you, if you are given compensation.

_____   _____
Attorney's name   Attorney's telephone number

_____   _____
Attorney's street address   City   State   Zip Code

_____   _____
Attorney's registration number   Attorney's Social Security or Tax ID number

Pursuant to Civil Rule 11, I state that I have read the supplemental compensation application; that to the best of my knowledge, information, and belief, there is good ground to support it. I further state that I have read Section 2743.65 of the Revised Code concerning attorney fees.

_____
Signature of attorney

VC-2.   Rev. 03/99.

COURT OF CLAIMS OF OHIO
Victims of Crime Division
Capitol Square Office Building
65 East State Street, Suite 1100
Columbus, Ohio 43215

INDIGENCY STATEMENT

VICTIM   _____

CLAIMANT   _____   CLAIM NO.   _____

    I, Claimant, state under the penalties of perjury and falsification that I am indigent and that payment of the $7.50 filing fee would create a financial hardship for me.

_____
Claimant's Signature

_____
Date

Under R.C. 2921.11 and R.C. 2929.11 perjury is a felony of the third degree and punishable by imprisonment for one to ten years and fine up to $5,000.00. Under R.C. 2921.13 and R.C. 2929.21 falsification is a misdemeanor of the first degree and punishable by imprisonment for six months and fine up to $1,000.00.

History: Effective 10-17-83; amended, eff 7-1-89.

Index to Rules of the Court of Claims, Victims of Crime Compensation

LOCAL RULES OF THE COURT OF CLAIMS OF OHIO

(Amended, and re-adopted as amended, effective January 1, 1984)

Complete with amendments through July 1, 2010

Rule

RULE 1. Scope; applicability; citation

(A) **Scope; authority** These rules, promulgated pursuant to Article IV, Section 5(B) of the Constitution of the State of Ohio, Civil Rule 83, and the Rules of the Court of Claims of Ohio, govern local practice and procedure in the Court of Claims.

(B) **Applicability** These rules govern all proceedings in actions brought after they take effect, and all further proceedings in actions pending when they take effect, except to the extent that their application in a particular action pending when these rules take effect would not be feasible or would work injustice, in which event the former rules apply. These rules supersede the Local Rules of the Court of Claims of Ohio effective January 1, 1975, and as amended on June 14, 1977, October 26, 1978, December 19, 1978, January 1, 1983, May 2, 1983 and July 21, 1983.

(C) **Citation** These rules shall be known as the Local Rules of the Court of Claims of Ohio and shall be cited as "L.C.C.R.____."

RULE 2. Address; court hours

(A) **Address** The court of claims shall be located at The Ohio Judicial Center, 65 South Front Street, Third Floor, Columbus, Ohio 43215. All correspondences shall be directed to the following mailing address:

Court of Claims of Ohio, The Ohio Judicial Center, 65 South Front Street, Third Floor, Columbus, Ohio 43215.

(B) **Court hours** The clerk's office of the court of claims shall be open from 8:30 A.M. to 5:00 P.M., Monday through Friday, except for legal holidays. The clerk may adjust the hours of the clerk's office as necessary.

History: Amended, eff 6-4-86; 5-12-04.

RULE 3. Fees; costs

(A) **Fees** In civil actions, the fees charged shall be as provided in R.C. § 2303.20.

(B) **Poverty affidavit** The clerk shall accept for filing all complaints accompanied by a poverty affidavit which states specific reasons for the inability to pay the filing fee. In an action in which a poverty affidavit has been filed, the clerk shall serve all process and pay the expense therefor from the funds of the court and tax such expenses as costs. The clerk or the court may at any time require additional information and a hearing, or both, to determine the validity of the poverty affidavit.

(C) **Copying fee** The clerk shall charge a fee of twenty-five cents per page for uncertified copies of pleadings, process, records, or files.

(D) **Witness fees; service of subpoena** Pursuant to R.C. § 2743.06, in civil actions in the court of claims, the party at whose instance a witness is subpoenaed or a deposition is taken shall pay the witness fees and mileage, except that the state may not pay the fees to its own employees. The witness fees and mileage shall not be taxed as costs.

Where a party requests service upon a witness who resides outside the county in which the trial will be located, the request shall, pursuant to Civil Rule 45(C), be accompanied by a check made payable to the requested witness, in the amount of one day's witness fees plus mileage. The clerk shall enter the fact of the receipt of the check, along with the request for service of the subpoena, in the docket and shall forward the subpoena and check, to be served by the sheriff of the county in which the witness resides or where service is directed by the party.

(E) **Overpayment of costs or fees** If any party, including a claimant for an award of reparations, or counsel for any party tenders payment for more than the cost or fee to be assessed, the clerk may cause the entire amount tendered to be deposited or may refuse and return the amount tendered. Refusal and return does not constitute waiver of the payment of the required fee or cost. If the amount tendered is deposited and the overpayment is two dollars or more, a refund for the excess amount shall be processed. No refund shall be made for any overpayment of fees or costs if the amount of the overpayment is less than two dollars.

History: Amended, eff 8-10-95.

RULE 4. Pleadings and motions

(A) **Form of pleadings and motions; copies of complaint** Because of filing and binding requirements, the top one and one-half inches of all pages of all papers shall be left blank.

All pleadings and motions shall be typewritten or printed on 8 ½ by 11 paper, securely bound at the top.

Recognizing that R.C. § 2743.02(E) and R.C. § 2743.13 provide that the only defendant in this court is the state but that the complaint shall name as defendant each state department, board, office, commission, agency, institution, or other instrumentality whose actions are alleged as the basis for the complaint, the caption of every complaint shall state the name and address of each plaintiff and defendant. The plaintiff shall file a sufficient number of copies of the complaint to permit the clerk to retain one copy and to serve a copy of the complaint upon each named defendant and upon the attorney general.

The caption of every motion and pleading subsequent to the complaint shall include the number of the case, the name of the first party plaintiff and the first party defendant. Each paper filed shall be identified by title and shall bear the name, Supreme Court Registration Number, address and telephone number of trial counsel. Where a paper is filed by a party without counsel, the paper shall bear the party's name, address and telephone number.

(B) **Extension of time** All extensions of time shall be made by written motion which states the specific basis of the extension and which is supported by documentation and, if appropriate, affidavit. Motions for extension of time may be determined *ex parte* in accordance with Civil Rule 6(B)(1). Motions for extensions of time shall be accompanied by a proposed order which states the duration of the extension.

(C) **Submission and hearing of motions** Unless otherwise ordered by the court, motions shall be determined without oral argument.

The movant shall serve and file with his motion a brief written statement of reasons in support of the motion and the authorities upon which he relies. If the motion requires the consideration of facts not appearing of record, the movant shall also serve and file copies of all the evidence which supports his motion.

Each party opposing the motion shall serve and file, within fourteen days after service upon him of movant's motion, a brief written statement of reasons in opposition to the motion and the authorities upon which he relies. If the motion requires the consideration of facts not appearing of record, he shall also serve and file copies of all evidence in opposition to the motion. Failure to file a written statement in opposition to the motion may be cause for the court to grant the motion as filed.

Reply briefs or additional briefs may be filed only upon a showing of the necessity therefor and with leave of court.

(D) **Motion for summary judgment, date of non-oral hearing** All motions for summary judgment filed pursuant to Civil Rule 56 are hereby set for a non-oral hearing date on the 28th day following the filing of the motion for summary judgment. Motions shall be deemed submitted to the judge for non-oral hearing on that date. Any party seeking to change the hearing date must do so by entry signed by the trial judge and served on all counsel.

(E) **Page limitations** Supporting, opposing, or memorandum briefs shall not exceed fifteen pages in length, exclusive of attachments. Reply briefs shall not exceed seven pages in length, exclusive of attachments. Applications for leave to file a long brief shall be by motion that sets forth the unusual and extraordinary circumstances which necessitate the filing of a long brief.

History: Amended, eff 6-4-86; 11-16-89; 3-31-93; 7-11-97.

RULE 4.1. Immunity determinations

Any party shall file a motion requesting that the Court of Claims make a determination, as required by R.C. 2743.02(F), as to whether the officer or employee is entitled to personal immunity under R.C. 9.86 and whether the courts of common pleas have jurisdiction over the civil action. If no motion for this determination is made, the Court of Claims may *sua sponte* set this matter down for the R.C. 2743.02(F) hearing.

History: Effective 3-31-93; amended, eff 11-27-95.

RULE 4.2. Discovery materials

(A) **Filing of discovery materials** Depositions, interrogatories, requests for production or inspection, requests for admissions, and any answers or responses thereto, shall not be filed by the clerk unless they meet the requirements of Civil Rule 5(D). Parties may, if they wish, file with the court a one-page notice of service or notice of deposition.

(B) **Interrogatories submitted for service with the complaint** The clerk shall remove and discard any interrogatories attached to the original copy of the complaint before it is placed in the case file.

(C) **Removal of erroneously filed discovery material** When previously filed discovery material is found which does not comply with this rule or Civil Rule 5(D), the clerk shall, without further order of the court, (1) prepare a notice which describes the material to be removed, (2) file and serve the notice, and (3) after 21 days, discard any material which has not been claimed.

(D) **Motion for relief** If relief is sought concerning any discovery matter, copies of only those portions of discovery material which are relevant to the dispute shall be filed with the motion for relief.

History: Effective 11-16-89; amended, eff 3-31-93.

RULE 5. Motion submitted to chief justice of the supreme court

(A) **Motion for three-judge panel**

(1) **Motion, when filed, contents** Not later than ten days after a notice of trial is served in an action filed

in or removed to the court of claims, the claimant or the state may file a written motion requesting the chief justice of the supreme court to assign, pursuant to R.C. § 2743.03(C)(1), a panel of three judges to hear and determine the action. The motion shall be accompanied by a memorandum indicating the novel or complex issues of law or fact present in the action. Two copies of the motion and memorandum shall be filed with the clerk of the court of claims. The movant shall serve all other parties pursuant to Civil Rule 5.

(2) **Response to motion, when filed, contents** Each party opposing the motion may file and serve, within fourteen days after service of the motion, a memorandum opposing the motion which shall state all reasons for opposition and authorities upon which the party relies.

(3) **Duty of the clerk** After all responses, if any, are received or the time for response has elapsed, the clerk shall forward to the chief justice of the supreme court the motion and all memoranda. The clerk of the court of claims shall journalize the decision of the chief justice and serve copies upon all parties.

(B) **Motions for change of situs of civil action**

(1) **Motion, when filed, contents** Not later than ten days after a notice of trial is served in an action in the court of claims, any party may file a written motion requesting the chief justice of the supreme court to direct, pursuant to R.C. § 2743.03(B) that the court sit in a county other than Franklin County. The motion shall be accompanied by a memorandum showing the substantial hardship which will result if the action is tried in Franklin County or why the interests of justice dictate that the situs be changed. Two copies of the motion and memorandum shall be filed with the clerk of the court of claims. The movant shall serve a copy of the motion and memorandum on all other parties pursuant to Civil Rule 5.

(2) **Response to motion, when filed, contents** Each party opposing the motion may file and serve within fourteen days after service of the motion a memorandum opposing the motion, which shall state all reasons for the opposition and authorities upon which the party relies.

(3) **Duty of clerk** After all responses are received or the time for response has elapsed, the clerk shall forward to the chief justice of the supreme court the motion and all memoranda. The clerk of the court of claims shall journalize the decision of the chief justice and serve copies upon all parties.

(C) **Request for referees**

(1) **Motion, when filed, contents** Not later than ten days after a notice of trial has been served in an action filed in the court of claims pursuant to R.C. § 153.12(C) either the state or a contractor may request that, pursuant to R.C. § 2743.03(C)(3), the chief justice of the supreme court appoint a referee or a panel of referees. The request shall be accompanied by a memorandum which shows that the requesting party is entitled to the appointment of a referee or a panel of referees pursuant to R.C. § 153.12(C) and § 2743.03(C)(3). Two copies of the motion and memorandum shall be filed with the clerk of the court of claims. The movant shall serve all other parties pursuant to Civil Rule 5.

(2) **Response to motion, when filed, contents** Each party opposing the motion may file and serve, within fourteen days after service of the motion, a memorandum opposing the motion, which shall state all reasons for the opposition and authorities upon which the party relies.

(3) **Duty of clerk** After all responses are received or the time for response has elapsed, the clerk shall forward to the chief justice of the supreme court the motion and all memoranda. The clerk of the court of claims shall journalize the decision of the chief justice and serve copies upon all parties.

(D) **Hearing on motion to chief justice** Motions submitted to the chief justice pursuant to section (A), (B), or (C) of this rule shall be determined without an oral hearing unless a hearing is ordered by the chief justice. Unless ordered by the chief justice, no reply brief on behalf of the movant shall be filed.

(E) **Affidavits of bias and prejudice** Affidavits of bias and prejudice filed against judges of the court of claims shall be processed in accordance with R.C. § 2701.03.

RULE 6.   Right to jury

(A) **Right to jury trial under R.C. § 2743.11** Pursuant to R.C. § 2743.11, a party who has filed a claim against the state is not entitled to a jury trial, but parties retain their right to jury trial in claims against parties other than the state.

(B) **Jury demand in removed actions** Removal of actions to the court of claims does not extend the time for jury demand specified in Civil Rule 38.

RULE 7.   Pretrial conference and procedure

(A) **Pretrial conference** In accordance with Civil Rule 16, after a case is at issue, the court may, on its own motion or at the request of a party, fix a date and place for a formal pretrial conference, and may also fix a date and place for one or more informal pretrial status conferences.

(B) **Pretrial statement** Not less than seven days prior to the date of the formal pretrial conference, all trial attorneys shall file with the clerk and serve upon all other trial attorneys appearing in the action, a pretrial statement which:

(1) Informs the court in detail of the factual and legal issues which the case presents;

(2) Sets forth the party's position on legal issues, including any significant evidentiary questions, and the authorities in support thereof;

(3) Includes a list of all witnesses expected to testify.

(4) Includes a list of all exhibits which are to be introduced in evidence.

(C) **Conference procedure** Trial attorneys shall be prepared and present at the pretrial conference and shall have full authorization to negotiate a settlement from the parties they represent. Upon the request of a trial attorney or upon its own motion, the court may order the parties or their respective sureties, indemnitors or insurers to be present at the pretrial conference.

(D) **Pretrial order** The court may, and at the request of a party shall, prepare, or cause to be prepared, a written order which recites the action taken at the pretrial conference. The court shall enter the order and submit copies to the trial attorneys. The order, subject to Civil Rule 60(A), shall control the subsequent course of the action, unless modified at the trial to prevent manifest injustice.

(E) **Expert witnesses** Each trial attorney shall exchange with all other trial attorneys, in advance of the trial, written reports of medical and expert witnesses expected to testify. The parties shall submit expert reports in accordance with the schedule established by the court.

A party may not call an expert witness to testify unless a written report has been procured from said witness. It is the trial attorney's responsibility to take reasonable measures, including the procurement of supplemental reports, to insure that each such report adequately sets forth the expert's opinion. However, unless good cause is shown, all supplemental reports must be supplied no later than thirty days prior to trial. The report of an expert must reflect his opinions as to each issue on which the expert will testify. An expert will not be permitted to testify or provide opinions on issues not raised in his report.

All experts must submit reports. If a party is unable to obtain a written report from an expert, counsel for the party must demonstrate that a good faith effort was made to obtain the report and must advise the court and opposing counsel of the name and address of the expert, the subject of the expert's expertise together with his qualifications and a detailed summary of his testimony. In the event the expert witness is a treating physician, the court shall have the discretion to determine whether the hospital and/or office records of that physician's treatment which have been produced satisfy the requirements of a written report. The court shall have the power to nevertheless exclude testimony of the expert if good cause is not demonstrated.

If the court finds that good cause exists for the non-production of an expert's report, the court shall assess costs of the discovery deposition of the non-complying expert against the party offering the testimony of the expert unless, by motions, the court determines such payment would result in manifest injustice. These costs may include the expert's fee, the court reporter's charges and travel costs.

If the court finds that good cause exists for the non-production of a report from a treating physician, the court shall assess costs of the discovery deposition of the physician equally between the plaintiff and the party or parties seeking discovery of the expert. These costs may include the physician's fee, the court reporter's charges and travel costs.

(F) **Failure to comply** The sanctions stated in Civil Rule 37(B)(2) may be assessed for failure to timely comply with this rule.

History: Amended, eff 6-4-86; 11-16-89; 11-27-95.

RULE 8.   Findings of fact and conclusions of law; judgments

(A) **Preparation of findings** The court may require the prevailing party to submit proposed findings of fact and conclusions of law.

(B) **Judgment of the court** The court shall trans-

mit its written judgment to the clerk for entry, and the clerk shall, simultaneously with the entry of judgment, send copies of the judgment by certified mail to the attorney general, the claimant and the named defendants.

RULE 9.   Reserved

RULE 10.   Records of the clerk

The clerk of the court of claims shall prepare and maintain the following books:

(1) A general appearance docket;
(2) A receipt book;
(3) A journal book.

In addition, the clerk shall keep a direct and reverse index to the appearance docket.

RULE 11.   Recording of proceedings; disposition of exhibits and materials; videotaped testimony and evidence

(A) **Reporting and recording services** The clerk shall appoint a court reporter or enter into a contract on behalf of the court for court reporting services including recording of proceedings pursuant to subdivision (B).

(B) **Methods of recording** Proceedings before the court may be recorded by stenographic means, by phonographic means, by photographic means, by the use of audio electronic devices, or by the use of video recording systems. The clerk may order the use of any method of recording authorized by this rule.

(C) **Payment** The party ordering a transcript of proceedings, or a copy thereof, shall pay the court reporter or reporting service the expense of such service. The reporter or the court reporting service shall not prepare transcripts of proceedings or copies thereof until satisfactory payment arrangements have been made.

(D) **Custody; disposition of recordings** Electronically recorded transcripts of proceedings shall be retained by the clerk at the conclusion of the trial or hearing. Electronically recorded transcripts of proceedings shall be maintained by the clerk until the case is finally determined. The clerk, upon order by the court, may dispose of an electronically recorded transcript of proceedings or may cause the recording medium to be erased so that it may be reused after the expiration of three years from the conclusion of all proceedings in the action or claim.

(E) **Inspection of electronically recorded transcripts of proceedings** In lieu of requesting a copy of an electronically recorded transcript of proceedings, or a portion thereof, a party may view or hear the transcript of proceedings on file with the clerk.

(F) **Disposition of exhibits and materials** Except as provided by these rules, models, diagrams, depositions, photographs, x-rays, and other exhibits and materials filed in an action in the court or offered in evidence are not considered pleadings and, unless otherwise ordered by the court, shall be withdrawn by the parties within six months after conclusion of all proceedings in the action. Upon order by the court, the clerk may dispose of all models, diagrams, depositions, photographs, x-rays and other exhibits and materials not withdrawn by the parties within the six month period provided by this rule.

(G) **Videotaped testimony and depositions** If videotaped testimony or videotaped depositions are used, the parties shall comply with the provisions of Rule 12 of the Rules of Superintendence for Courts of Common Pleas. If a trial or hearing in the action is to be held at a location other than the address stated in Rule 2 of these rules or if a motion to change the situs of the trial or hearing is pending, the party intending to use a videotape shall disclose that fact when contacting the clerk's office to determine the appropriate video-tape format.

RULE 12.   Trial scheduling

(A) **Sequence of assignments** Trial assignments, when practical, will be made based on date of filing.

(B) **Advancement for trial** A motion may be addressed to the court to advance a case for trial stating the reasons therefor.

(C) **Delay of trial** When trial or hearing assignments are made they will contain a date limitation for requesting vacation and reassignment, with related instructions. A request for reassignment submitted thereafter will ordinarily not be granted absent an emergency which could not be anticipated. No party to a claim or action shall be granted a vacation and reassignment without a written motion stating the reasons for the request, which motion shall be served upon all other parties according to Civil Rule 5. The motion shall indicate at least two alternative dates upon which all the parties and counsel would be available for trial or hearing. Unless counsel submit agreed dates when the case can be tried, if a vacation is granted a reassignment may be indefinitely postponed and the case may be dismissed for want of prosecution. The granting of a continuance is a matter within the discretion of the court or referee.

(D) **Conflict of trial assignment dates** When a continuance of a trial is requested for the reason that counsel is scheduled to appear in another case assigned for trial on the same date in another court of this state, the case which was first set for trial shall have priority and shall be tried on the date assigned. Criminal cases assigned for trial shall have priority over civil cases assigned for trial.

RULE 13.   Court files and papers

Court papers, files of the court or parts thereof shall not be removed from the custody of the clerk without the consent of the clerk.

RULE 14.   Trial procedures

(A) **Engaged counsel** If a particular attorney has such a number of actions pending in the court of claims that the disposition of the actions is unduly delayed, the trial judge may require the attorney to provide a substitute trial attorney. If the original attorney fails to provide a substitute trial attorney, the trial judge may remove him as counsel in the action.

(B) **Examination of witnesses** At a trial or hearing

where witnesses are called, only one attorney for each party may examine or cross-examine a witness unless otherwise permitted by the trial judge or referee.

RULE 15.   Review of caseload

(A) **Review of pending cases** The clerk of the court of claims shall from time to time review all causes pending in the court. In causes in which no proceedings have been undertaken within six months of the date of commencement, the court may give written notice to all counsel of record, or to a party if he has no counsel of record, that the cause will be dismissed at a time certain unless before that time has expired good cause is shown that the cause should remain pending.

(B) **Review of newly filed complaints** The clerk of the court of claims shall review newly filed complaints to determine whether: a complaint inappropriately designates a defendant state department, board, office, commission, agency, institution, or other instrumentality; a complaint names as defendant a nonstate party over which the court of claims has no jurisdiction; or a complaint contains some ambiguity or other aberration. If any of these appear on a complaint, then the clerk, prior to the issuance of summons, shall refer the complaint to a judge of the court of claims for review and, if necessary, for the issuance of an appropriate order. No unnecessary delay in processing complaints shall ensue due to this process. This process is intended to reduce confusion, time, and expense in maintaining the court's case index, appearance docket, case files, and issuance of papers. The ultimate responsibility for correctly designating an appropriate defendant and filing a complaint which is free from error or ambiguity remains with the party filing the complaint. The failure of the clerk, deputy clerk, or court to act under this rule does not alter that responsibility.

(C) **Information concerning cases, claims based on essentially the same facts** Upon the filing of an original complaint, the clerk shall serve, by ordinary mail, a request for information about connected cases or claims (hereafter referred to as "request for information") upon the plaintiff's attorney or upon the plaintiff where plaintiff has no attorney. This division (C) does not apply to actions which must be determined administratively in accordance with R.C. § 2743.10. The request for information shall, inter alia, require the plaintiff to state whether a case, claim, application, etc., based on essentially the same facts as the complaint or petition for removal filed in the court of claims, is pending in any court or any bureau, board, commission or agency. The clerk shall draft the request for information form and all necessary instructions for such form.

The plaintiff's attorney or the plaintiff shall complete the request for information form and file it with the court within twenty-eight days after the date the form was mailed by the clerk. The plaintiff's attorney or the plaintiff shall serve a copy of the completed form upon the attorney general and all other parties pursuant to Civil Rule 5. All other parties have the continuing duty to immediately inform the court in writing where the information stated in a request for information form is incorrect or incomplete and where there is a change in the status of the case, claim, application, etc., noted in a request for information form, or an additional case, claim, application, etc., based on essentially the same facts as the complaint or petition for removal filed in the court of claims, is filed with any court or any bureau, board, commission or agency. The sanctions stated in Civil Rule 37(B)(2) may be assessed for failure to timely comply with this rule.

History: Amended, eff 11-16-89.

RULE 16. Assignments of awards of reparations

Assignments of awards of reparations in claims based on criminally injurious conduct which occurred prior to March 18, 1983 shall not be recognized by a single commissioner, a panel of commissioners, or the court. Assignments of awards of reparations in claims based upon criminally injurious conduct which occurred on or after March 18, 1983 shall be recognized only as provided by R.C. § 2743.66.

RULE 17. Attorneys not admitted to the practice of law in Ohio

(A) **Nonresident attorney, request for leave to represent applicant for award of reparations, contents of request** A nonresident attorney who is not admitted to the practice of law in Ohio may request leave to represent an applicant for an award of reparations before the court of claims.

The request must be made at the earliest opportunity in the proceedings. The request shall certify that the attorney is admitted to the practice of law in the highest court of another state or in the District of Columbia and that the attorney is not a resident of this state. The request must be cosigned by an attorney admitted to the practice of law in this state and registered under Rule VI of the Rules for the Government of the Bar of Ohio.

(B) **Duty of court upon filing of request** A judge of the court of claims may grant or deny the request, and may reconsider and deny a request which was granted at an earlier stage in the proceedings. An attorney, who is a resident of this state, not admitted to the practice of law in this state or not registered under Rule VI of the Rules of the Government of the Bar of Ohio, shall not be granted leave under this rule.

(C) **Duty of resident attorney; service of papers; attorney fees** Where leave has been granted under this rule, the attorney at law of this state shall examine and cosign all motions, pleadings and other papers prepared by the nonresident attorney. The nonresident attorney shall not appear at oral hearings in the absence of the attorney at law of this state.

Service of orders, motions, pleadings and any other papers upon the nonresident attorney shall be upon the attorney at law of this state.

Any award of attorney fees pursuant to R.C. § 2743.65(A) shall be made payable only to the attorney at law of this state.

(D) **Failure to comply, claim not affected** The filing and processing of an applicant's claim for repa-rations shall not be affected or prejudiced by the failure of a nonresident attorney to comply with this rule.

RULE 18. Conditions for broadcasting and photographing court of claims proceedings

(A) **Permission for broadcasting, recording by electronic means or photographing** Except as supplemented by this rule, the provisions of Rule 11 of the Rules of Superintendence for Courts of Common Pleas shall be applicable to requests for permission to broadcast, record by electronic means or photograph proceedings in the court of claims.

(B) **Administration**

(1) **Requests for permission; when and where filed** Requests for permission to broadcast, televise, record or photograph in the courtroom shall be in writing to the clerk as far in advance as reasonably practical, but in no event later than one work day prior to the courtroom session to be broadcast or photographed unless otherwise permitted by the trial judge. Request forms may be obtained from the clerk's office.

(2) **Duty of clerk upon receipt; duty of court** The clerk shall immediately inform the trial judge of the request. The trial judge shall grant the request in writing consistent with Canon 3A(7) of the Code of Judicial Conduct, Superintendence Rule 11, and this local rule. Written permission shall be made a part of the record of the proceeding.

(C) **Pooling** Arrangements shall be made between or among media for pooling equipment and personnel authorized by this rule to cover the court sessions. Such arrangements are to be made outside the courtroom and without imposing on the trial judge or court personnel to mediate any dispute as to the appropriate media "pool" representative or equipment authorized to cover a particular session. In the event disputes arise between or among media representatives, the trial judge may exclude all contesting representatives from the proceeding.

(D) **Equipment and personnel**

(1) **Television, videotape or movie equipment and personnel** Not more than one portable camera (television, videotape or movie), operated by not more than one in-court camera person, shall be permitted without authorization of the trial judge.

(2) **Photographic equipment and personnel** Not more than one still photographer, utilizing not more than two still cameras of professional quality with not more than two lenses for each camera, shall be permitted without authorization of the trial judge.

(3) **Radio equipment** Not more than one audio system for radio broadcast purposes shall be permitted without authorization of the trial judge.

(4) **Audio tape equipment** If audio arrangements cannot be reasonably made in advance, the trial judge may permit one audio portable tape recorder at the bench which will be activated prior to commencement of the courtroom session. Audio portable tape recorders may not be used without prior permission of the trial judge.

(E) **Light and sound criteria**

(1) **Distracting equipment** Only professional quality telephonic, photographic and audio equipment

which does not produce distracting sound or light shall be employed to cover courtroom sessions. No motor driven still cameras shall be permitted.

(2) **Artificial light** No artificial lighting device other than that normally used in the courtroom shall be employed. However, if the normal lighting in the courtroom can be improved without becoming obtrusive, the trial judge may permit modification.

(3) **Audio pickup** Audio pickup by microphone for all media purposes shall be accomplished from existing audio systems present in the courtroom. If no technically suitable audio system exists in the courtroom, microphones and related wiring essential for all media purposes shall be unobtrusive and located in places designated by the trial judge, in advance of any session.

(F) **Location of equipment and personnel**

(1) **Location of equipment** Court of Claims trials to be heard in Franklin County where media coverage is requested pursuant to this rule shall, to the extent possible, be held in Court Room 1 of the Court of Claims. In the event that the subject trial is a jury trial, one television camera shall be positioned on a tripod in the northwest corner of the courtroom, but shall not interfere with the jury's access to the jury room. If the subject trial is not a jury trial, one television camera shall be positioned on a tripod in the southeast corner of the jury box. Videotape recording equipment or other technical equipment which is not a component part of an in-court television or broadcasting unit shall be located in a room adjacent to or outside of the courtroom.

(2) **Conduct of operators** The television, broadcast and still camera operators shall position themselves in a location in the courtroom as directed by the trial judge, either standing or sitting, and shall assume a fixed position within that area. Having established themselves in a shooting position, they shall act so as not to call attention to themselves through further movement. Sudden moves, pans, tilts or zooms by any camera operators are prohibited. Operators shall not be permitted to move about in order to obtain photographs or broadcasts of courtroom sessions, but only to leave or enter the courtroom.

(3) **Time for placing or removing equipment** Television cameras, microphones and taping equipment shall not be placed in, moved about or removed from the courtroom except prior to commencement or after adjournment of the session (the trial judge has not gaveled the proceeding to order or adjournment), or during a recess. Neither television film magazines, rolls or lenses, still camera film, nor audio portable tape cassettes shall be changed within a courtroom except during a recess.

(G) **Miscellaneous** Proper courtroom decorum shall be maintained by all media pool participants. All media representatives shall be properly attired, in a manner that reflects positively upon the journalistic profession.

(H) **Limitations**

(1) **Audio pickup of conferences** There shall be no audio pickup or broadcast of conferences conducted in a courtroom between counsel and clients, co-counsel, or the trial judge and counsel.

(2) **Jurors; witnesses** The photographing, filming, videotaping, televising or recording of any juror shall not be permitted. The trial judge shall inform victims and witnesses of their right to object to being photographed, filmed, videotaped, televised or recorded and shall prohibit the photographing, filming, videotaping, televising or recording of any victim or witness who does object.

(I) **Revocation of permission** Upon the failure of any media representative to comply with the conditions prescribed by the trial judge, the Rules of Superintendence of the Supreme Court, or this rule, the trial judge may revoke the permission to broadcast, photograph or record the trial or hearing.

RULE 19.   Substitution or withdrawal of trial counsel

The substitution or withdrawal of trial counsel shall be permitted only (1) upon filing with the Court, with service on all other parties, a notice of substitution of trial counsel signed by withdrawing trial counsel, the client and substitute trial counsel. (The client's signature is not required if trial counsel is a member of the same law firm as substitute trial counsel and if it is affirmatively stated that the substitution is made with the client's knowledge and consent), or (2) upon written application served upon the client, showing good cause for substitution or withdrawal of trial counsel. Unless otherwise ordered, trial counsel shall not be permitted to withdraw from an action at any time later than twenty days in advance of trial or the setting of a hearing on any motion for judgment or dismissal. Substitution of trial counsel shall not in and of itself be sufficient cause for the granting of a postponement of any trial or hearing.

History: Effective 6-5-92.

RULE 20.   Security plan

The clerk shall develop and implement a court security policy and procedures plan in accordance with the Ohio Court Security Standards adopted by the Supreme Court of Ohio on October 17, 1994, and they may be amended.

History: Effective 6-22-95.

RULE 21.   Records management and retention

(A) **Applicability**

(1) This rule is intended to provide minimum standards for the production, maintenance, preservation, and destruction of records within the court and to authorize alternative electronic methods and techniques.

(2) This rule shall be interpreted to allow for technological enhancements that improve the efficiency of the court and simplify the production, maintenance, preservation, and destruction of court records.

(B) **Definitions** As used in this rule:

(1) "Administrative record" means a record not related to cases of the court that documents the administrative, fiscal, personnel, or management functions of the court.

(2) "Case file" means the compendium of original documents filed in an action or proceeding in the court, including the pleadings, motions, orders, and judgments of the court on a case by case basis.

(3) "Docket" means the official summary of the proceedings in a case that is maintained by the clerk of the court and contains basic information regarding the case, including the case number and case type, the parties to the case, the attorneys of record, and the chronological list of all documents filed in the case, action taken by the court, and writs and processes issued in the case.

(4) "Index" means a reference record used to locate journal, docket, and case file records.

(5) "Journal" means a verbatim record of every order or judgment of the court.

(6) "OHS" means the Ohio Historical Society, State Archives Division.

(7) "Record" means any document, device, or item, regardless of physical form or characteristic, created or received by or coming under the jurisdiction of the court that serves to document the organization, functions, policies, decisions, procedures, operations, or other activities of the court.

(C) **Combined records** Notwithstanding any other provision of the law, the court may combined indexes, dockets, journals, and case files provided that the combination contains the components of indexes, dockets, journals, and case files as defined in this rule. The court may replace any paper bound books with an electronic medium or microfilm in accordance with this rule.

(D) **Allowable record media**

(1) The court may create, maintain, receive, record, copy, or preserve a record on traditional paper media, electronic media, including text or digital images, or microfilm, including computer output to microfilm.

(2) The court may create, maintain, receive, record, copy, or preserve a record using any nationally accepted records and information management process, including photography, microfilm, and electronic data processing, as an alternative to paper. The process may be used in regard to the original or a copy of a record if the process produces an accurate record or copy and the process complies with American National Standards Institute ("ANSI") standards and guidelines or, in the event that ANSI standards cease to exist, other nationally accepted records and information management process standards.

(a) If the court creates, maintains, receives, records, copies, or preserves a record using a records and information management process in accordance with division (D)(2) of this rule and the record is required to be retained in accordance with the schedules set forth in this rule, the court shall cause a back-up copy of the record to be made at periodic and reasonable times to insure the security and continued availability of the information. If this rule requires the record to be retained permanently, the back-up copy shall be stored in a different building than the record it secures.

(b) Records shall be maintained in conveniently accessible and secure facilities, and provisions shall be made for inspecting and copying any public records in accordance with applicable statutes and rules. Ma-

chines and equipment necessary to allow inspection and copying of public records, including public records that are created, maintained, received, recorded, copied, or preserved by an alternative records and information management process in accordance with division (D)(2) of this rule, shall be provided.

(c) In accordance with applicable law and purchasing requirements, the court may acquire equipment, computer software, and related supplies and services for records and information management processes authorized by division (D)(2) of this rule.

(d) Paper media may be destroyed after it is converted to other approved media in accordance with division (D) of this rule.

(E) **Destruction of records**

(1) Subject to the notification and transfer requirements of divisions (E)(2) and (3) of this rule, a record and any back-up copy of a record produced in accordance with division (D)(2) of this rule may be destroyed after the record and its back-up copy have been retained for the applicable retention period set forth in this rule.

(2) If this rule sets forth a retention period greater than ten years for a record, or if a record was created prior to 1960, the court shall notify the OHS in writing of the court's intention to destroy the record at least sixty days prior to the destruction of the record.

(3) After submitting a written notice in accordance with division (E)(2) of this rule, the court shall, upon request of the OHS, cause the record described in the notice to be transferred to the OHS, or to an institution or agency that meets the criteria of the OHS, in the media and format designated by the OHS.

(F) **Exhibits, depositions, and transcripts** At the conclusion of litigation, including times for direct appeal, the court or custodian of exhibits, depositions, or transcripts may destroy exhibits, depositions, and transcripts if all of the following conditions are satisfied:

(1) The court notifies the party that tendered the exhibits, depositions, or transcripts in writing that the party may retrieve the exhibits, depositions, and transcripts within sixty days from the date of the written notification;

(2) The written notification required in division (F)(1) of this rule informs the party that tendered the exhibits, depositions, or transcripts that the exhibits, depositions, or transcripts will be destroyed if not retrieved within sixty days of the notification;

(3) The written notification required in division (F)(1) of this rule informs the party that tendered the exhibits, depositions, or transcripts of the location for retrieval of the exhibits, depositions, or transcripts;

(4) The party that tendered the exhibits, depositions, or transcripts does not retrieve the exhibits, depositions, or transcripts within sixty days from the date of the written notification required in division (F)(1) of this rule.

(G) **Other records** Any record that is not listed in this rule but is listed in a general retention schedule established pursuant to section 149.331 of the Revised Code may be retained for the period of time set by the general retention schedule and then destroyed.

(H) **Extension of retention period for indi-**

vidual case files The court may order the retention period for an individual case file extended beyond the period specified in this rule for the case file.

(I) **Retention schedule for the administrative records of the court** The following retention schedule shall apply for the administrative records of the court:

(1) **Administrative journal** Administrative journals that consist of court entries, or a record of court entries, regarding policies and issues not related to cases shall be retained permanently.

(2) **Annual reports** Two copies of each annual report shall be retained permanently.

(3) **Bank records** Bank transaction records, whether paper or electronic, shall be retained for three years or until the issuance of an audit report by the Auditor of State, whichever is later.

(4) **Cash books** Cash books, including expense and receipt ledgers, shall be retained for three years or until the issuance of an audit report by the Auditor of State, whichever is later.

(5) **Communication records** Communication records, including routine telephone messages on any medium where official action will be recorded elsewhere, may be destroyed in the normal course of business as soon as they are considered to be of no value by the person holding the records.

(6) **Copies and Duplicates** Copies and duplicates that are used for informational purposes and for which the official record is located elsewhere may be destroyed in the normal course of business as soon as they are considered to be no value by the person holding the copies and duplicates.

(7) **Correspondence and general office records** Correspondence and general office records, including all sent and received correspondence, in any medium, may be destroyed in the normal course of business as soon as they are considered to be of no value by the person holding the records.

(8) **Drafts and informal notes** Drafts and informal notes consisting of transitory information used to prepare the official record in any other form may be destroyed in the normal course of business as soon as they are considered to be of no value by the person holding the drafts and informal notes.

(9) **Employment applications for posted positions** Employment applications for posted or advertised positions shall be retained for two years.

(10) **Employee benefit and leave records** Employee benefit and leave records, including court office copies of life and medical insurance records, shall be retained for three years or until the issuance of an audit report by the Auditor of State, whichever is later.

(11) **Employee history and discipline records** Records concerning the hiring, promotion, evaluation, attendance, medical issues, discipline, termination, and retirement of court employees shall be retained for ten years after termination of employment.

(12) **Fiscal records** Fiscal records, including copies of transactional budgeting and purchasing documents, shall be retained for three years or until the issuance of an audit report by the Auditor of State, whichever is later.

(13) **Grant records** Records of grants made or received by the court shall be retained for three years after expiration of the grant.

(14) **Informational materials about the victims of crime reparations program** Informational materials about the victims of crime reparations program may be destroyed as soon as they are considered to be of no value by the person holding the materials.

(15) **Payroll records** Payroll records of personnel time and copies of payroll records maintained by another office or agency shall be retained for three years or until the issuance of an audit report by the Auditor of State, whichever is later.

(16) **Publications received** Publications received by the court may be destroyed in the normal course of business as soon as they are considered to be of no value by the person holding the publications.

(17) **Receipt records** Receipt and balancing records shall be retained for three years or until the issuance of an audit report by the Auditor of State, whichever is later.

(18) **Requests for proposals, bids, and resulting contracts** Requests for proposals, bids received in response to a request for proposal, and contracts resulting from a request for proposal shall be retained for three years after the expiration of the contract that is awarded pursuant to the request for proposal.

(J) **Required records**
(1) The court shall maintain an index, docket, journal, and case files in accordance with this rule.

(2) Upon the filing of any paper or electronic entry permitted by the court, a stamp or entry shall be placed on the paper or electronic entry to indicate the day, month, and year of filing.

(K) **Retention schedule for the index, docket, and journal** The index, docket, and journal of the court shall be retained permanently.

(L) **Retention schedule for case files**
(1) **Civil actions** All case files of civil actions shall be retained for three years after dismissal or final order.

(2) **Claims for reparations**
(a) Case files of claims for reparations filed on behalf of a minor victim shall be retained for at least three years after the minor reaches the age of majority.

(b) Case files of claims for reparations filed with respect to deceased victims shall be retained for at least twenty-two years after the date of the death of the victim.

(c) All other case files of claims for reparations shall be retained for six years after the last court award or order.

(3) **Judge and clerk notes, drafts, and research** Judge and clerk notes, drafts, and research prepared for the purpose of compiling a report, opinion, or other document or memorandum may be kept separate from the case file, retained in the case file, or destroyed at the discretion of the preparer.

History: Effective 8-15-97.

RULE 22.   Mediation

(A) **Referral to mediation** At an initial conference with the parties, the judge shall determine whether a civil case is appropriate for mediation, and if it is referred to mediation, set the time limits within which mediation will occur.

At the request of a party or upon the court's own motion, the court may at any time refer a civil case to mediation.

(B) **Discovery** Mediation shall not stay discovery, which may continue throughout the mediation process in accordance with the Rules of Civil Procedure.

(C) **Statements of evidence** Statements made during mediation are subject to Evid. R. 408.

(D) **Mediators** The court may appoint one or more mediators who shall serve at the pleasure of the court and may receive compensation as described in R.C. 2743.03(C)(3).

History: Effective 10-1-98.

RULE 23. Victims of Crime Division Assigned Counsel Appointments

(A) **Assigned Counsel Appointment Review Board** Members of the assigned counsel appointment review board shall be designated by the court and shall include a judge of the court of claims, two panel commissioners, a magistrate, and the clerk or his designee. The assigned counsel review board shall:

(1) Set and publish qualifications of counsel eligible for appointment to represent claimants who have filed an appeal in the court of claims victims of crime division;

(2) Approve an application form and process to be utilized by applicants seeking appointment;

(3) Approve applications for appointment;

(4) Create a master appointment list of counsel eligible for appointment;

(5) Evaluate the performance of appointed counsel representing claimants in the court of claims victims of crime division;

(6) Remove counsel, if necessary, from the master appointment list;

(7) Establish the requirements for reinstatement to the master appointment list.

(B) **Appointment of Assigned Counsel** A judge or a panel of commissioners may appoint assigned counsel to represent a claimant if the interests of justice require the appointment. Assigned counsel shall be selected from the master appointment list maintained by the assigned counsel appointment review board. Unless otherwise ordered, assigned counsel shall continue to represent the claimant through all remaining proceedings in the court of claims.

(C) **Compensation of Assigned Counsel** Assigned counsel shall be compensated pursuant to R.C. 2743.65.

History: Effective 3-11-05.

RULE 24. Reparations appeals

(A) **Appeals from decisions of the attorney general**

(1) An appeal pursuant to R.C. 2743.61(B) shall be taken by filing a notice of appeal with the clerk of the court of claims within the time allowed under R.C. 2743.61. The notice of appeal shall be filed on a notice of appeal form prescribed by the clerk of the court of claims and provided to the claimant by the attorney general.

(2) The clerk of the court of claims shall serve a copy of the notice of appeal upon the attorney general and upon appellant and appellant's counsel, if any. The clerk shall note on the copy of the notice of appeal the date on which it was filed.

(3) If a party attempts to file a notice of appeal by delivering it to the attorney general instead of the court of claims, the attorney general shall forward the notice of appeal to the clerk of the court of claims within three days and the date of filing of the appeal shall, in the interests of justice, be deemed to be not later than the date the notice was received by the attorney general.

(4) Pursuant to R.C. 2743.61(B), the attorney general shall file the record with the clerk of the court of claims within fourteen days after the appeal is filed. The appeal shall be heard within ninety days of receiving a fully completed notice of appeal form.

(5) A notice of appeal filed prior to the final decision of the attorney general shall be treated as filed immediately after such final decision.

(B) **Appeals from orders of the panel of commissioners**

(1) An appeal pursuant to R.C. 2743.61(C) shall be taken by filing a notice of appeal with the clerk of the court of claims within the time allowed under R.C. 2743.61. The notice of appeal shall be filed on a notice of appeal form provided by the clerk of the court of claims.

(2) The clerk of the court of claims shall serve notice of the filing of a notice of appeal by forwarding a copy to counsel of record of each party other than the appellant, or, if a party is not represented by counsel, to the party at the party's last known address. The clerk of the court of claims shall note on each copy served the date on which the notice of appeal was filed. The clerk shall make a record of the parties served, the date served, and the means of service.

History: Effective 4-30-01.

RULE 25. Effective date

(A) **Effective date of rules** These rules shall take effect on January 1, 1984. These rules govern all proceedings in actions brought after they take effect, and all further proceedings in actions pending when they take effect, except to the extent that their application in a particular action pending when these rules take effect would not be feasible or would work injustice, in which event the former rules apply. These rules supersede the Local Rules of the Court of Claims of Ohio effective January 1, 1975, and as amended on June 14, 1977, October 26, 1978, December 19, 1978, January 1, 1983, May 2, 1983 and July 21, 1983.

(B) **Effective date of amendments** The amendments to these rules journalized on June 4, 1986, shall be effective on that date and shall govern all proceedings taken on and after the effective date.

(C) **Effective date of amendments** The amendments to these rules journalized on November 16,

1989, shall be effective on that date and shall govern all proceedings taken on and after the effective date.

(D) **Effective date of amendment** The amendment to these rules journalized on June 5, 1992, shall be effective on that date and shall govern all proceedings taken on and after the effective date.

(E) **Effective date of amendments** The amendments to these rules journalized on March 31, 1993, shall be effective on that date and shall govern all proceedings taken on and after the effective date.

(F) **Effective date of amendments** The amendments to these rules journalized on June 22, 1995, shall be effective on that date and shall govern all proceedings taken on and after the effective date.

(G) **Effective date of amendments** The amendments to these rules journalized on August 10, 1995, shall be effective on that date and shall govern all proceedings taken on and after the effective date.

(H) **Effective date of amendments** The amendments to these rules journalized on November 27, 1995, shall be effective on that date and shall govern all proceedings taken on and after the effective date.

(I) **Effective date of amendments** The amendments to these rules journalized on July 11, 1997, shall be effective on that date and shall govern all proceedings taken on and after the effective date.

(J) **Effective date of amendments** The amendments to these rules journalized on August 15, 1997, shall be effective on that date and shall govern all proceedings taken on and after the effective date.

(K) **Effective date of amendments** The amendments to these rules journalized on October 1, 1998, shall be effective on that date and shall govern all proceedings taken on and after the effective date.

(L) **Effective date of amendments** The amendments to these rules journalized on June 28, 2000, shall be effective on that date and shall govern all proceedings taken on and after the effective date.

(M) **Effective date of amendments** The amendments to these rules journalized on April 12, 2001, shall be effective on April 30, 2001 and shall govern all proceedings taken on and after the effective date.

(N) **Effective date of amendments** The amendments to these rules journalized on May 2, 2002, shall be effective on that date and shall govern all proceedings taken on and after the effective date.

(O) **Effective date of amendments** The amendments to these rules journalized on May 12, 2004, shall be effective on that date and shall govern all proceedings taken on and after the effective date.

(P) **Effective date of amendments** The amendments to these rules journalized on March 11, 2005, shall be effective on March 11, 2005 and shall govern all proceedings taken on and after the effective date.

History: Amended, eff 6-4-86; 11-16-89; 6-5-92; 3-31-93; 6-22-95; 8-10-95; 11-27-95; 7-11-97; 8-15-97; 10-1-98; 6-28-00; 4-30-01; 5-2-02; 05-12-04; 3-11-05.

Index to Local Rules of the Court of Claims of Ohio

SUPREME COURT RULES FOR THE GOVERNMENT OF THE BAR OF OHIO

RULE I.

ADMISSION TO THE PRACTICE OF LAW

SECTION 1. General Requirements

To be admitted to the practice of law in Ohio, an applicant shall satisfy all of the following requirements:

(A) Be at least twenty-one years of age;

(B) Have earned a bachelor's degree from an accredited college or university in accordance with any of the following:

(1) Prior to admission to law school;

(2) Subsequent to admission to law school, through completion of courses and credits other than those received in law school, if the applicant has made a record of academic achievement that is satisfactory to the Court and receives Court approval;

(3) From participation in a joint bachelor's/law degree program that has been reviewed and approved by the Court, requires at least seven years of full-time study, and results in the award of both a bachelor's degree and a law degree;

(C) Have earned a J.D. or an L.L.B. degree from a law school that was approved by the American Bar Association at the time the degree was earned or, if not located in the United States, from a law school evaluated and approved in accordance with Section 2(C) or Section 9(C)(13) of this rule;

(D) Prior to taking the Ohio bar examination or being admitted without examination pursuant to Section 9 of this rule, have demonstrated that the applicant possesses the requisite character, fitness, and moral qualifications for admission to the practice of law and have been approved as to character, fitness, and moral qualifications under procedures provided in this rule;

(E) Have passed both the Ohio bar examination and the Multistate Professional Responsibility Examination, or have been approved for admission without examination pursuant to Section 9 of this rule;

(F) Have taken the oath of office pursuant to Section 8(A) of this rule.

As used in this section, "accredited college or university" means a college or university approved by one of the following accrediting associations or, if not located in the United States, a college or university evaluated and approved in accordance with Section 2(C) or Section 9(C)(13) of this rule: Middle States Association of Colleges and Schools/Commission on Higher Education; New England Association of Schools and Colleges--Commission on Institutions of Higher Education; North Central Association of Colleges and Schools; Northwest Association of Schools and Colleges; Southern Association of Colleges and Schools--Commission on Colleges; Western Association of Schools and Colleges--Accrediting Commission for Senior Colleges.

SECTION 2. Preliminary Registration Requirements

(A) Every applicant who intends to take the Ohio bar examination shall file with the Office of Bar Admissions of the Supreme Court an Application to Register as a Candidate for Admission to the Practice of Law. The applicant shall file the registration application by the fifteenth day of November in the applicant's second year of law school.

(B) The registration application shall be on forms furnished by the Office of Bar Admissions and shall include all of the following:

(1) A certificate from the dean of the law school the applicant is attending, certifying that the applicant has begun the study of law;

(2) A properly authenticated transcript of college credits or any other documentation deemed necessary by the Office of Bar Admissions to show compliance

with Section 1(B) of this rule;

(3) Fingerprint identification taken by a sheriff, deputy sheriff, municipal police officer, or state highway patrol officer;

(4) A registration fee of seventy-five dollars;

(5) A fee in the amount charged by the National Conference of Bar Examiners for its character investigation and report;

(6) A completed character questionnaire, in duplicate, in the form prescribed by the Board of Commissioners on Character and Fitness;

(7) Authorization and release forms in the number required by the Office of Bar Admissions.

(C) If the applicant's undergraduate or legal education was not received in the United States, an additional fee of one hundred fifty dollars shall accompany the application for the evaluation of the applicant's education. If the applicant's legal education was not received in the United States, the registration application shall not be processed until the applicant's legal education is approved by the Court.

(D) If an applicant does not file a complete registration application on or before the fifteenth day of November in the applicant's second year of law school, the applicant shall pay an additional late fee of two hundred dollars.

(E) An applicant may not apply to take the February Ohio bar examination unless the applicant has filed a complete registration application by the fifteenth day of August immediately preceding the February examination. An applicant may not apply to take the July Ohio bar examination unless the applicant has filed a complete registration application by the fifteenth day of January immediately preceding the July examination.

(F) Until admitted to the practice of law in Ohio, the applicant is under a continuing duty to update the information contained in the registration application, including the character questionnaire, and to report promptly to the Office of Bar Admissions all changes or additions to information in the application.

(G) Unless the Board of Commissioners on Character and Fitness grants an extension to the applicant, a registration application shall be deemed withdrawn, and the applicant shall no longer be considered a candidate for admission, if either of the following occurs:

(1) The applicant fails to take the Ohio bar examination within four years after filing the registration application;

(2) The applicant takes but fails the Ohio bar examination and does not retake one of the four immediately ensuing bar examinations.

SECTION 3. Application for Ohio Bar Examination; Updating Character and Fitness Information after the Examination

(A) An applicant who has filed a registration application pursuant to Section 2 of this rule and who seeks to take the Ohio bar examination shall file with the Office of Bar Admissions of the Supreme Court an Application to Take the Bar Examination. An application to take the February examination shall be filed by the first day of November immediately preceding the examination. An application to take the July examination shall be filed by the first day of April immediately preceding the examination.

(B) The examination application shall be on forms furnished by the Office of Bar Admissions and shall include all of the following:

(1) An affidavit that the applicant has read and studied the Rules for the Government of the Bar of Ohio, the Ohio Rules of Professional Conduct, and the Code of Judicial Conduct adopted by the Court;

(2) An affidavit that the applicant has not engaged in the unauthorized practice of law;

(3) A certificate signed by the dean or associate dean of the applicant's law school certifying that the signatory does not have knowledge of any information that would cause signatory to doubt the applicant's character, fitness, and moral qualifications to practice law;

(4) A completed supplemental character questionnaire, in duplicate, in the form prescribed by the Board of Commissioners on Character and Fitness, updating the information on the applicant's character, fitness, and moral qualifications furnished on the applicant's registration application pursuant to Section 2 of this rule;

(5) A fee in the amount charged by the National Conference of Bar Examiners for the Multistate Performance Test items;

(6) A fee of three hundred thirty dollars if the examination application is filed on or before the dates set forth in division (A) of this section. The fee shall be four hundred thirty dollars if either of the following applies:

(a) An examination application for the February examination is filed after the first day of November but on or before the tenth day of December;

(b) An examination application for the July examination is filed after the first day of April but on or before the tenth day of May.

(C) The Office of Bar Admissions shall refer the examination application to the regional or local bar association admissions committee in accordance with Section 11 of this rule. The admissions committee shall review the examination application, conduct further investigation and interviews under Section 11 of this rule if appropriate or necessary, and report its final recommendation regarding the applicant's character, fitness, and moral qualifications to the Board of Commissioners on Character and Fitness on a form prescribed by the Board. The Board shall make a final determination regarding the applicant's character, fitness, and moral qualifications to practice.

(D) Notwithstanding an applicant's timely filing of an Application to Register as a Candidate for Admission to the Practice of Law and an Application to Take the Bar Examination, an applicant may not take the Ohio bar examination unless the Board of Commissioners on Character and Fitness has issued a final approval of the applicant's character, fitness, and moral qualifications at least three weeks prior to the examination.

(E) At least thirty days before the date fixed for the examination, the applicant shall submit both of the following:

(1) A certificate signed by the dean or associate dean of the applicant's law school certifying that the appli-

cant has received a law degree, has sufficient knowledge and ability to discharge the duties of an attorney at law, and has successfully completed a course of not fewer than ten classroom hours of instruction in legal ethics;

(2) A certificate from a law school or a continuing legal education sponsor, certifying that the applicant has received at least one hour of instruction on substance abuse, including causes, prevention, detection, and treatment alternatives. Substance abuse instruction that is provided by a continuing legal education sponsor qualifies under this section only if it has been accredited by the Commission on Continuing Legal Education as an approved substance abuse activity under Gov. Bar R. X.

(F) The applicant is under a continuing duty to update the information contained in the examination application, including the supplemental character questionnaire, and to report promptly to the Office of Bar Admissions all changes or additions to information in the application that occur prior to the applicant's admission to practice.

(G) If an applicant passes the Ohio bar examination but is not admitted to practice within twelve months following that bar examination, the applicant shall file another supplemental character questionnaire with the Office of Bar Admissions. The supplemental character questionnaire shall supplement the information on the applicant's character, fitness, and moral qualifications furnished in the applicant's examination application. The Office of Bar Admissions shall refer the supplemental character questionnaire to a regional or local bar association admissions committee in accordance with Section 11 of this rule. The admissions committee shall review the supplemental character questionnaire, conduct further investigation and interviews pursuant to Section 11 of this rule, if appropriate and necessary, and report to the Board its recommendation regarding the applicant's character, fitness, and moral qualifications to practice law. The applicant shall not be admitted to the practice of law unless the Board reissues a final approval of the applicant's character, fitness, and moral qualifications no fewer than six months before the applicant's admission.

SECTION 4. Bar Examiners; Readers

(A) The Board of Bar Examiners shall be appointed by the Court and shall consist of eighteen members of the bar of Ohio in good standing. The term of office of each bar examiner shall be five years, beginning the first day of April immediately following the appointment. Each bar examiner shall be appointed six months before the start of the term and shall serve an internship for those six months. During the internship, the intern shall attend Board meetings, Board training, and question review sessions and may assist in drafting essay questions. Vacancies for any cause shall be filled by appointment by the Court for the unexpired term. Each year, the Court shall designate one bar examiner as Chair of the Board and one bar examiner as Vice-Chair of the Board. The Director of Attorney Services or his or her designee shall serve as secretary of the Board.

(B) The Board shall be responsible for examination of applicants for admission to the practice of law in Ohio. Subject to the Court's approval, the Board may promulgate rules and adopt procedures to aid in the administration and conduct of the examination.

(C)(1) A bar examiner shall devote the time necessary to perform the duties of the office.

(2) A bar examiner shall be conscientious, studious, thorough, and diligent in considering, developing, and implementing sound testing and grading procedures; in preparing bar examination questions; and in seeking to improve the examination and its administration. Before an essay question prepared by a bar examiner is accepted for use in a bar examination, the question shall be analyzed and approved by the Board or a committee of the Board.

(3) A bar examiner shall be just and impartial in performing the duties of the office.

(4) A bar examiner should not have adverse interests, conflicting duties, or inconsistent obligations that will in any way interfere or appear to interfere with the proper administration of the bar examiner's duties. A bar examiner shall not participate directly or indirectly in courses for the preparation of applicants for bar admission or act as a trustee, administrator, professor, adjunct professor, or instructor for a law school or for a university of which a law school is a part, or with which a law school is affiliated. No bar examiner shall be an employee or consultant of a trade association in the field of Board interest. The conduct of a bar examiner shall be such that there may be no suspicion that the bar examiner's judgment may be swayed by improper considerations.

(D) The Court will select readers to assist with grading the written portion of the Ohio bar examination. Readers shall be members of the bar of Ohio in good standing and satisfy the same standards of conduct as those required of bar examiners, to the extent those standards are applicable to readers. The Board shall train and supervise the readers.

SECTION 5. Ohio Bar Examination

(A) Two Ohio bar examinations shall be held each year in Columbus, one commencing in February and one commencing in July. The examinations shall be scheduled consistent with the dates designated by the National Conference of Bar Examiners for administration of the Multistate Bar Examination (MBE) and the Multistate Performance Test (MPT). Each examination shall consist of five half-day sessions over a period of two and one-half days.

(1) Two of the half-day sessions of each examination shall consist of the MBE prepared by the National Conference of Bar Examiners.

(2) One of the half-day sessions of each examination shall consist of two MPT items prepared by the National Conference of Bar Examiners.

(3)(a) Two of the half-day sessions of each examination shall consist of twelve essay questions prepared by the Board of Bar Examiners.

(b) The essay portion of each examination shall consist of at least one question, and no more than two questions, in each of the following subjects:

Business Associations (including Agency, Partner-

ships, and Corporations)
    Civil Procedure
    Commercial Transactions
    Constitutional Law
    Contracts
    Criminal Law
    Evidence
    Legal Ethics
    Property (Real and Personal)
    Torts
    Wills

(c) The subject matter of the essay questions shall not be designated or labeled on the examination.

(B)(1) The MBE shall be graded by the National Conference of Bar Examiners or its agent. An applicant's MBE scaled score shall be used in computing the applicant's Ohio bar examination score.

(2) All answers to the written portion of the examination, which shall consist of both the essay questions and the MPT items, shall be graded under the direction of the Board. The Board shall adopt rules for grading that are consistent with sound testing practices. The rules shall include a provision for scaling raw scores on the written portion of an examination to the MBE range of scores for that examination using the mean and standard deviation method. The rules also shall include a provision for regrading of the written portion of the examination for any applicant whose total examination score after scaling falls within one point below the minimum passing score.

(3) In the calculation of an applicant's total examination score, the applicant's scaled score on the written portion of the examination shall be weighed twice as much as the applicant's scaled MBE score. Subject to the Court's approval, the Board shall determine and publish the total score necessary to pass the examination.

(4) Except where a mathematical or clerical error has been made, scores determined in accordance with this section and Board rules shall be final and shall not be subject to appeal.

(C) Within a reasonable time following the announcement of examination results, the Board shall publish the essay questions used on the examination. The Board may publish a selection of applicant answers to the written portion of the examination. For a reasonable fee, applicants who did not pass the examination may obtain copies of their answers to the written portion of the examination. All other examination and Board materials shall not be considered public information.

(D) Information regarding whether an applicant has taken or passed a particular bar examination shall be public information. An applicant's bar examination scores shall not be public information.

SECTION 6. Multistate Professional Responsibility Examination

(A) Before being admitted to the practice of law in Ohio by examination, an applicant shall take and pass the Multistate Professional Responsibility Examination (MPRE) prepared and administered by the National Conference of Bar Examiners. An applicant may take the MPRE at any time before or after taking the Ohio bar examination.

(B) An applicant shall make arrangements for taking the MPRE directly with the National Conference of Bar Examiners and shall pay the fee for the MPRE to the Conference.

(C) Subject to the Court's approval, the Board of Bar Examiners shall determine and publish the scaled score necessary to pass the MPRE.

SECTION 7. Application for Re-Examination

(A) An applicant who seeks to retake an Ohio bar examination shall file with the Clerk of the Supreme Court an Application for Re-examination. An Application for Re-examination at a February examination shall be filed by the first day of November immediately preceding the examination. An Application for Re-examination at a July examination shall be filed by the first day of April immediately preceding the examination. The Clerk may set a later filing deadline for applicants for re-examination who have taken a bar examination, the results of which have not been released prior to the filing deadlines referred to above.

(B) The application shall be on forms furnished by the Court and shall include all of the following:

(1) an affidavit that the applicant has not engaged in the unauthorized practice of law;

(2) a completed supplemental re-examination character questionnaire, in duplicate, in the form prescribed by the Board of Commissioners on Character and Fitness, updating the previously furnished information on the applicant's character, fitness, and moral qualifications;

(3) a non-refundable fee of $275, by certified check or money order;

(4) a non-refundable fee in the amount charged by the National Conference of Bar Examiners for the Multistate Performance Test items.

(C) The Clerk shall refer the application to the regional or local bar association admissions committee in accordance with Section 11 of this Rule. The admissions committee shall review the application, conduct further investigation and interviews under Section 11 of this Rule if appropriate or necessary, and report its recommendation regarding the applicant's character, fitness, and moral qualifications to the Board on a form prescribed by the Board.

(D) Notwithstanding an applicant's timely filing of an Application for Re-examination, an applicant may not take an Ohio bar examination unless the Board of Commissioners on Character and Fitness has reissued a final approval of the applicant's character, fitness, and moral qualifications at least three weeks prior to the examination.

(E) Applicants for re-examination shall be admitted to the February examination only, provided, however, that applicants for re-examination may be admitted to the July examination if the physical limitations of the examination hall permit after all applicants for examination have been admitted. If all applicants for re-examination cannot be admitted to the July examination because of the physical limitations of the examination hall, then such applicants shall be admitted in the order in which their applications were received by the Clerk.

(F) The applicant is under a continuing duty to update the information contained in the Application for Re-examination, including the supplemental re-examination character questionnaire, and to report promptly to the Admissions Office all changes or additions to the information in the application that occur prior to the applicant's admission to practice.

SECTION 8. Induction to the Bar

(A) Each applicant accepted for admission to the practice of law in Ohio shall take the following oath of office:

I, ____, hereby (swear or affirm) that I will support the Constitution and the laws of the United States and the Constitution and the laws of Ohio, and I will abide by the Ohio Rules of Professional Conduct.

In my capacity as an attorney and officer of the Court, I will conduct myself with dignity and civility and show respect toward judges, court staff, clients, fellow professionals, and all other persons.

I will honestly, faithfully, and competently discharge the duties of an attorney at law. (So help me God.)

(B) An applicant's statement of the oath shall indicate that the applicant either swears or affirms to be bound by the oath.

(C) Following administration of the oath, the Court shall present the applicant with a certificate of admission. A duplicate certificate shall not be issued by the Court unless the original certificate is lost or destroyed. A replacement certificate may be issued to a licensed attorney who has had a legal change of name.

SECTION 9. Admission Without Examination

(A) An applicant may apply for admission to the practice of law in Ohio without examination if all of the following apply:

(1) The applicant has taken and passed a bar examination and has been admitted as an attorney at law in the highest court of another state or in the District of Columbia, which jurisdiction shall be considered the jurisdiction from which the applicant seeks admission;

(2) The applicant has engaged in the practice of law, provided, however, that the practice of law:

(a) Was engaged in subsequent to the applicant's admission as an attorney at law in another jurisdiction;

(b) Occurred for at least five full years out of the last ten years prior to the applicant's submission of an application pursuant to division (C) of this section; and

(c) Was engaged in on a fulltime basis;

(3) The applicant has not taken and failed an Ohio bar examination;

(4) The applicant has not engaged in the unauthorized practice of law;

(5) The applicant is a citizen or a resident alien of the United States;

(6) The applicant intends to engage in the practice of law in Ohio actively on a continuing basis;

(7) The applicant satisfies the general admission requirements of Section 1(A) to (C) of this rule;

(8) If applicable, the applicant has registered pursuant to Gov. Bar R. VI, Section 4.

(B) For purposes of this section, "practice of law" shall mean any one or more of the following:

(1) Private practice as a sole practitioner or for a law firm, legal services office, legal clinic, or similar entity, provided such practice was performed in a jurisdiction in which the applicant was admitted or in a jurisdiction that affirmatively permitted such practice by a lawyer not admitted to practice in that jurisdiction;

(2) Practice as an attorney for a corporation, partnership, trust, individual, or other entity, provided such practice was performed in a jurisdiction in which the applicant was admitted or in a jurisdiction that affirmatively permitted such practice by a lawyer not admitted to practice in that jurisdiction and involved the primary duties of furnishing legal counsel, drafting legal documents and pleadings, interpreting and giving advice regarding the law, or preparing, trying, or presenting cases before courts, tribunals, executive departments, administrative bureaus, or agencies;

(3) Practice as an attorney for the federal government, a branch of the United States military, or a state or local government with the same primary duties as described in division (B)(2) of this section;

(4) Employment as a judge, magistrate, referee, or similar official for the federal or a state or local government, provided that such employment is available only to attorneys;

(5) Fulltime employment as a teacher of law at a law school approved by the American Bar Association.

(C) An applicant for admission to the practice of law in Ohio without examination shall file with the Office of Bar Admissions an Application for Admission to the Practice of Law Without Examination. The application shall include all of the following:

(1) An affidavit stating all of the following:

(a) That the applicant has not engaged in the unauthorized practice of law;

(b) That the applicant has studied the Rules for the Government of the Bar of Ohio, the Ohio Rules of Professional Conduct, and the Code of Judicial Conduct, all as adopted by the Court;

(c) That the applicant is a citizen or a resident alien of the United States;

(d) That the applicant intends to engage in the practice of law in Ohio actively on a continuing basis;

(2) A certificate from the admissions authority in the jurisdiction from which the applicant seeks admission, demonstrating that the applicant has taken and passed a bar examination and has been admitted to the practice of law in that jurisdiction;

(3) A certificate of good standing from each jurisdiction in which the applicant is admitted to practice law, dated no earlier than sixty days prior to the submission of the application;

(4) An affidavit that demonstrates that the applicant has complied with division (A)(2) of this section and that includes a description of the applicant's practice of law, the dates of such practice, and, if applicable, a description of the applicant's employment subsequent to ceasing such practice;

(5) To confirm that the applicant has engaged in the full-time practice of law for at least five full years out of the last ten years prior to the applicant's submission of the application, an affidavit from the applicant's employer or employers verifying the applicant's full-time practice of law or, if the applicant has been self-employed, an affidavit from an attorney who is a member of the bar in the jurisdiction in which the applicant practiced and who knows the applicant, verifying the applicant's full-time practice of law. As used in division (C)(5) of this section, "full-time practice of law" means practice in which the applicant was actively and substantially engaged as a principal business or occupation;

(6) To confirm that the applicant's practice was performed in a jurisdiction that affirmatively permitted such practice by a lawyer not admitted to practice in that jurisdiction, if applicable, a rule, statute, or other authority verifying that the applicant's practice was lawful at the time the practice occurred;

(7) Such other evidence, as may be reasonably requested by the Court, demonstrating that the applicant has met the requirements of division (A) of this section;

(8) A certificate by an attorney admitted to the practice of law in Ohio and duly registered pursuant to Gov. Bar R. VI, who will present the applicant to the Court pursuant to division (F) of this section, stating that the applicant is of good moral character and recommending the applicant for admission to the practice of law in Ohio without examination;

(9) Fingerprint identification taken by a sheriff, deputy sheriff, municipal police officer, or state highway patrol officer;

(10) A questionnaire, typed and in duplicate, for use by the National Conference of Bar Examiners, the Board of Commissioners on Character and Fitness, and the regional or local bar association admissions committee in conducting a character investigation of the applicant;

(11) A fee of one thousand two hundred fifty dollars;

(12) A fee in the amount charged by the National Conference of Bar Examiners for its character investigation and report;

(13) Certificates or official transcripts evidencing compliance with Section 1(B) and (C) of this rule. If the applicant's undergraduate or legal education was not received in the United States, a one hundred fifty dollar fee shall accompany the application for evaluation of the applicant's legal education. If the applicant's legal education was not received in the United States, the application shall not be processed until the applicant's legal education is approved by the Court.

(D) The Office of Bar Admissions shall refer the application and the report of the National Conference of Bar Examiners to the regional or local bar association admissions committee in accordance with Section 11 of this rule. The applicant shall be reviewed and approved as to character, fitness, and moral qualifications in accordance with the procedures provided in Sections 11 and 12 of this rule.

(E) The applicant is under a continuing duty to update the information contained in the application, including the character questionnaire, and to report promptly to the Office of Bar Admissions all changes or additions to information in the application that occur prior to the applicant's admission to practice.

(F)(1) The Court shall review the application and in its sole discretion shall approve or disapprove the application. In reaching its decision, the Court shall consider both of the following:

(a) Whether the applicant has met the requirements of division (A) of this section;

(b) Whether the applicant's past practice of law is of such character, description and recency as shall satisfy the Court that the applicant currently possesses the legal skills deemed adequate for admission to the practice of law in Ohio without examination.

(2) The Office of Bar Admissions shall notify the applicant of the Court's determination.

(G) An applicant who has been approved for admission under this section shall be presented to the Court in regular session by an attorney at law of this State. Upon approval of the applicant for admission under this Section, the Office of Bar Admissions shall schedule the presentation and notify the applicant of the date and time of the presentation. It shall be the applicant's responsibility to notify the presenting attorney. The presentation shall be allotted two minutes and the applicant and the presenting attorney shall appear in person. The applicant shall be administered the oath of office following the presentation. An application for admission without examination shall be considered withdrawn if the applicant does not attend a presentation and take the oath of office within twelve months after the Court's approval of the application.

(H) An applicant under this section shall not engage in the practice of law in Ohio prior to the presentation of the applicant to the Court pursuant to division (G) of this section. This division does not apply to participation by an attorney not yet admitted to practice in Ohio in a cause being litigated in Ohio when such participation is with leave of the judge hearing such cause.

(I) The Court may require an attorney who was admitted to the practice of law under this section after January 1, 1989, to demonstrate that since being so admitted he or she has been actively engaged in the practice of law in Ohio on a continuing basis. If the attorney subsequently ceases to engage in the practice of law in Ohio actively on a continuing basis, the Court may revoke that attorney's license.

SECTION 10. Board of Commissioners on Character and Fitness

(A)(1) The Board of Commissioners on Character and Fitness shall be appointed by the Court and shall consist of twelve attorneys admitted to the practice of law in Ohio, one from each appellate district. The term of office of each commissioner shall be three years, beginning on the first day of January next following the appointment. Appointments shall be made prior to the eleventh day of December of the year preceding the year in which the term commences. Vacancies for any cause shall be filled by appointment by the Court for the unexpired term.

(2) Any commissioner whose term has expired and who has an uncompleted assignment as a member of a panel may continue to serve for the purpose of concluding the assignment until it is concluded before the Board. The secretary of the Board may replace the retiring panel member with any other commissioner, provided that an

evidentiary hearing has not occurred. If the retiring commissioner continues to serve on the panel, the successor commissioner shall take no part in the proceedings of the Board concerning the uncompleted assignment.

(3) Each year, the Court shall designate one commissioner as chair of the Board. The Director of Attorney Services or his or her designee shall serve as the Secretary of the Board. The chair and the secretary may execute documents on behalf of the Board and the panels.

(B) The Board shall do all of the following:

(1) Meet annually and at other times as called by the secretary or the chair of the Board.

(2) Supervise and direct the regional or local bar association admissions committees in the investigation of the character, fitness, and moral qualifications of applicants for admission to the practice of law. In furtherance of this duty, the Board may do the following:

(a) Establish rules of procedure;

(b) Promulgate, subject to the approval of the Court, standards of conduct for applicants;

(c) Develop forms to be used by applicants and admissions committees;

(d) Require that standard background checks of all applicants be made;

(e) At any time prior to an applicant's admission to the practice of law, investigate *sua sponte* the character, fitness, and moral qualifications of the applicant;

(f) Appoint special investigators;

(g) Refer any matter to a regional or local bar association admissions committee with directions for further investigation by that committee with a report to be made to the Board.

(3) Hear all appeals by applicants from recommendations of regional or local bar association admissions committees.

(4) Approve applicants who possess the requisite character, fitness, and moral qualifications for admission.

(5) Submit recommendations to the Court as to the disapproval of applicants by the Board in accordance with Section 12 of this rule, or the approval of applicants who must be reviewed by the Court under Section 11(D)(5)(c) of this rule.

(6) Investigate any matter brought to the attention of the Board after an applicant has been admitted to the practice of law and alleging that the applicant made a materially false statement in, or deliberately failed to disclose any material fact in connection with, the applicant's application for admission to the practice of law.

SECTION 11. Character Investigation by Admissions Committees

(A) The president of each local bar association shall appoint an admissions committee, provided, however, that the local bar association permits the membership of any attorney practicing within the geographic area intended to be served by that association without reference to the attorney's area of practice, special interest, or other criteria. Local bar associations may join together on a regional basis to create a regional admissions committee. Each admissions committee shall consist of three or more members, each of whom shall serve without compensation for a term of three years. One-third of the admissions committee members' terms shall expire each year. Each admissions committee shall file with the Office of Bar Admissions the following information, updated as necessary:

(1) The names, addresses, telephone numbers, and terms of all members of the admissions committee;

(2) Designation of chair of the admissions committee;

(3) The name, address, and telephone number of the admissions committee representative who shall be responsible for receipt of material forwarded by the Office of Bar Admissions under division (C) of this section.

(B) The admissions committee shall investigate the character, fitness, and moral qualifications of applicants for admission to the practice of law in the State, report its findings and recommendations to the Board of Commissioners on Character and Fitness, and obtain and offer such information as pertains to the character, fitness, and moral qualifications of the applicants at hearings conducted by the Board's duly designated panels pursuant to this rule.

(C)(1) Upon receipt of an applicant's complete Application to Register as a Candidate for Admission to the Practice of Law filed under Section 2 of this rule or Application for Admission to the Practice of Law Without Examination filed under Section 9 of this rule, the Office of Bar Admissions shall forward one copy of the applicant's character questionnaire to the National Conference of Bar Examiners for a character investigation and report. Upon receipt of this report, the Office of Bar Admissions shall forward the report and the applicant's character questionnaire to one of the following admissions committees:

(a) An admissions committee of the county in which the applicant claims permanent residence, if the applicant is a resident of Ohio;

(b) An admissions committee in the county in which the applicant is enrolled in law school;

(c) An admissions committee in the county in which the applicant intends to practice law;

(d) Such other admissions committee as the Office of Bar Admissions deems appropriate.

(2) Within thirty-five days after the admissions committee's receipt of the applicant's character questionnaire and the report of the National Conference of Bar Examiners, the admissions committee shall review the character questionnaire and the report, schedule an interview, and notify the applicant, in writing, of the date and place of the interview. The notice shall inform the applicant that the applicant's failure to cooperate in completing the interview may be grounds for disapproval of the application.

(3) At least two members of the admissions committee shall jointly conduct a personal interview of the applicant and record the results on a form prescribed by the Board. During the interview of the applicant, the admissions committee shall inquire of the applicant whether any answer on the character questionnaire should be changed or supplemented because of events occurring after the date on which the character questionnaire was originally signed by the applicant and notarized. A member of an admissions committee shall not interview an applicant or otherwise participate in an admissions committee's investigation or recommendation of an applicant if it is reasonable to expect that the member's judgment will be, or could be, affected by such member's own financial, business, property, or personal interest or other conflict of interest.

(4) The admissions committee shall ascertain, from the character questionnaire, the report of the National Conference of Bar Examiners, and the interview, whether the applicant possesses the requisite character, fitness, and moral qualifications for admission to the practice of law. If the admissions committee deems it necessary or appropriate under the circumstances, it shall conduct further investigation of the applicant before ascertaining the applicant's character, fitness, and moral qualifications.

(D)(1) The applicant has the burden to prove by clear and convincing evidence that the applicant possesses the requisite character, fitness, and moral qualifications for admission to the practice of law. An applicant's failure to provide requested information, including information regarding expungements and juvenile court proceedings, or otherwise to cooperate in proceedings before the admissions committee may be grounds for a recommendation of disapproval.

(2) The admissions committee shall determine an applicant's character, fitness, and moral qualifications in accordance with all of the following:

(a) The provisions of this rule;

(b) The applicable decisions of the Supreme Court of the United States;

(c) The applicable decisions of the Supreme Court of Ohio;

(d) Any standards of conduct promulgated by the Board and approved by the Court under Section 10(B)(2)(b) of this rule.

(3) An applicant may be approved for admission if the applicant's record of conduct justifies the trust of clients, adversaries, courts, and others with respect to the professional duties owed to them and demonstrates that the applicant satisfies the essential eligibility requirements for the practice of law as defined by the Board. A record manifesting a significant deficiency in the honesty, trustworthiness, diligence, or reliability of an applicant may constitute a basis for disapproval of the applicant. Factors to be considered carefully by the admissions committee before making a recommendation about an applicant's character, fitness, and moral qualifications shall include, but are not limited to, all of the following:

(a) Commission or conviction of a crime, subject to division (D)(5) of this section;

(b) Evidence of an existing and untreated chemical (drug or alcohol) dependency;

(c) Commission of an act constituting the unauthorized practice of law;

(d) Violation of the honor code of the applicant's law school or any other academic misconduct;

(e) Evidence of mental or psychological disorder that in any way affects or, if untreated, could affect the applicant's ability to practice law in a competent and professional manner;

(f) A pattern of disregard of the laws of this state, another state, or the United States;

(g) Failure to provide complete and accurate information concerning the applicant's past;

(h) False statements, including omissions;

(i) Acts involving dishonesty, fraud, deceit, or misrepresentation;

(j) Abuse of legal process;

(k) Neglect of financial responsibilities;

(l) Neglect of professional obligations;

(m) Violation of an order of a court;

(n) Denial of admission to the bar in another jurisdiction on character and fitness grounds;

(o) Disciplinary action by a lawyer disciplinary agency or other professional disciplinary agency of any jurisdiction.

(4) The admissions committee shall determine whether the present character, fitness, and moral qualifications of an applicant qualify the applicant for admission to the practice of law. In making this determination, the following factors shall be considered in assigning weight and significance to the applicant's prior conduct:

(a) Age of the applicant at the time of the conduct;

(b) Recency of the conduct;

(c) Reliability of the information concerning the conduct;

(d) Seriousness of the conduct;

(e) Factors underlying the conduct;

(f) Cumulative effect of the conduct;

(g) Evidence of rehabilitation;

(h) Positive social contributions of the applicant since the conduct;

(i) Candor of the applicant in the admissions process;

(j) Materiality of any omissions or misrepresentations.

(5)(a) If an applicant has been convicted of a felony under the laws of this state, the laws of the United States, or the laws of another state or territory of the United States, or adjudicated a delinquent child for conduct that, if committed by an adult, would be such a felony, the applicant shall undergo a review by the Board of Commissioners on Character and Fitness in accordance with Section 12 of this rule. In addition to considering the factors listed in (D)(3) of this Section, the Board shall consider the following:

(i) The amount of time that has passed since the applicant was convicted of the felony, but in no event may an applicant be approved before being released from parole, probation, community control, post-release control, or prison if no post-release control or parole was maintained;

(ii) If the applicant was convicted in this state, whether the rights and privileges of the applicant that were forfeited by conviction have been restored by operation of law, expungement, or pardon under the laws of Ohio; or, if the applicant was convicted under the laws of the United States or the laws of another state or territory, whether the applicant would be eligible to have his rights and privileges restored under the laws of Ohio if convicted in this state for the same offense;

(iii) Whether the applicant is disqualified by law from holding an office of public trust;

(iv) How an approval of the applicant would impact the public's perception of, or confidence in, the legal profession.

(b) If the applicant's conviction or delinquency adjudication was for aggravated murder, murder, or any first or second degree felony under Ohio law, and the Board votes to approve the applicant in accordance with this section and Section 12 of this rule, the Board shall make a final report, with its findings of fact and recommendation of approval, for the Supreme Court's review. The Board shall file the report and the record with the Clerk of the Supreme Court. Consistent with the procedures established in Section 12(F) and (G) of this rule, the Court will review the applicant and make the final determination on whether the applicant shall be approved for admission.

(6) In determining an applicant's character, fitness, and moral qualifications for the practice of law, the admissions committee shall not consider factors that do not directly bear a reasonable relationship to the practice of law, including but not limited to the following impermissible factors:

(a) Age, sex, race, color, national origin, or religion of the applicant;

(b) Disability of the applicant, provided that the applicant, though disabled, is able to satisfy the essential eligibility requirements for the practice of law.

(E) After reviewing the character questionnaire and the report of the National Conference of Bar Examiners, interviewing the applicant, and conducting any further investigation, the admissions committee shall file with the Office of Bar Admissions a written report with its recommendations on a form prescribed by the Board.

(F)(1) An admissions committee recommendation other than an unqualified approval shall be deemed a recommendation that the applicant not be admitted to the practice of law, in which case the written report shall enumerate the specific reasons for such recommendation with relation to the standards set forth in divisions (D)(3) and (4) of this section, and the matter shall proceed as provided in Section 12 of this rule.

(2) An admissions committee recommendation of unqualified approval shall be submitted to the Board, and the Board shall determine whether the applicant has the requisite character, fitness, and moral qualifications for admission to the practice of law. The Office of Bar Admissions shall notify the applicant in writing of the Board's determination.

(G) An admissions committee may establish bylaws or procedures, not inconsistent with this rule, for the conduct of its proceedings. The functions of an admissions committee under this rule may be delegated to a subcommittee or subcommittees thereof.

SECTION 12. Appeal to Board of Commissioners on Character and Fitness

(A) If an admissions committee makes a recommendation other than an unqualified approval, or if the Board of Commissioners on Character and Fitness is required to review the applicant pursuant to Section 11(D)(5)(a) of this rule, the Office of Bar Admissions shall forward a copy of the report required under Section 11(E) of this rule by certified mail to the applicant, and the applicant may file a written notice of appeal with the secretary of the Board. The report shall be sent by certified mail to the address listed on the application or as supplemented by the applicant. If the certified mail is returned as unclaimed, refused, or otherwise undeliverable, the Office of Bar Admissions shall send the report to the applicant by regular mail.

(B) The applicant's notice of appeal shall be filed within thirty days of the applicant's receipt, by certified mail, of the admissions committee report or within thirty days of the date the Office of Bar Admissions mailed the report to the applicant by ordinary mail if the certified mail was returned as unclaimed, refused, or otherwise undeliverable. The applicant shall serve a copy of the notice of appeal on the admissions committee. If the applicant files a timely notice of appeal, the admissions committee shall appoint counsel to represent it before the Board and notify the applicant and the secretary of the name and address of counsel. If the applicant does not file a timely notice of appeal, the application shall be considered withdrawn.

(C)(1) Upon receipt of a notice of appeal that has been timely filed, the secretary shall, by entry, appoint a panel consisting of three commissioners and designate one of them chair of the panel. No commissioner appointed to the panel shall be from the appellate district in which the admissions committee that made the recommendation is located. Except with the consent of the applicant, a commissioner shall not sit as a member of a hearing panel or otherwise participate in the Board's investigation or recommendation of an applicant if it is reasonable to expect that the commissioner's judgment will be, or could be, affected by such commissioner's financial, business, property, or personal interest. The secretary shall serve a copy of the entry appointing the panel on the applicant, the admissions committee, and all counsel of record.

(2) After reasonable written notice to the applicant, and the admissions committee, and all counsel of record, the panel shall conduct a hearing at a place designated by the panel chair and otherwise inquire into the character, fitness, and moral qualifications of the applicant. At such hearing, the admissions committee and the applicant shall offer such information as bears upon the character, fitness, and moral qualifications of the applicant. The applicant shall be entitled to be represented by counsel of the applicant's choice, at the applicant's expense.

(3) The panel may take and hear testimony in person or by deposition, administer oaths, and compel by subpoena the attendance of witnesses and the production of books, papers, documents, records, and materials. The panel shall report its findings, together with the stenographic record of the proceedings, to the Board for its consideration and decision.

(4) The chair of the Board, the chair of the panel, and the secretary of the Board shall have authority to issue subpoenas, which shall be issued in the name and under the Seal of the Supreme Court and signed by the chair of the Board, the chair of the panel, or the secretary of the Board. In order to preserve confidentiality consistent with Section 13 of this rule, subpoenas shall bear the case number but not the name of the applicant. The party calling or subpoenaing a witness

shall inform the witness of the purpose of the hearing and of the confidentiality provisions of this rule. All witnesses, whether or not subpoenaed, are bound by the confidentiality provisions of this rule. The refusal or neglect of the person subpoenaed or called as a witness to obey a subpoena, attend the hearing, be sworn or affirm, answer any proper question, or abide by the confidentiality provisions of this rule shall be deemed to be contempt of the Supreme Court and may be punished accordingly.

(5) All relevant evidence as determined by the panel shall be considered by the panel. The parties and their counsel shall cooperate with the panel and shall not keep relevant information from the panel.

(6) The burden of proof in such hearings shall be on the applicant to establish by clear and convincing evidence the applicant's present character, fitness, and moral qualifications for admission to the practice of law in Ohio. An applicant's failure to provide requested information, including information regarding expungements and juvenile court proceedings, or otherwise to cooperate in proceedings before the Board may be grounds for a recommendation of disapproval.

(7) The hearing may be waived upon agreement of the parties and the panel, and the Board or panel may proceed with its own investigation of the applicant, and base its recommendation on the results.

(8) The Board may remand any matter on appeal to a local or regional admissions committee with directions for further investigation by that committee with a report to the Board.

(D) An applicant reviewed by the Board will be approved only if the applicant receives a vote in favor of approval from not fewer than seven commissioners. If the applicant is approved by such vote, the Board shall forthwith notify the applicant, the admissions committee, and all counsel of record.

(E) If the applicant is not approved, the Board shall make a final report of the proceedings, with its findings of fact and recommendation, and shall file its report and the record with the Clerk of the Supreme Court. The Board shall recommend that the applicant not be permitted to reapply for admission to the practice of law or that the applicant be permitted to re-apply only after a specified period of time.

(F)(1) On the filing of the Board's report and record with the Clerk of the Supreme Court, the Court shall issue an order to show cause why the report should not be confirmed and why the Board's recommendation should not be adopted. The Clerk shall send a copy of the show cause order and a copy of the Board's report, by both ordinary and certified mail, to the applicant at the address listed in the application or as supplemented by the applicant, to the admissions committee, and to all counsel of record.

(2) Within thirty days after issuance of the show cause order, the applicant and the admissions committee may file objections to the findings or recommendation of the Board. The objections shall be accompanied by the original and eighteen copies of a brief in support of the objections.

(3) The original and eighteen copies of an answer brief may be filed within fifteen days after the objections have been filed with the Clerk.

(4) Unless clearly inapplicable, the Rules of Practice of the Supreme Court of Ohio shall apply to proceedings filed in the Supreme Court under this division. Service of briefs and other documents shall be made upon the applicant, the admissions committee, and all counsel of record.

(G) After a hearing on objections or if objections are not filed within the prescribed time, the Court shall enter such order as it may find proper. Upon the entry of any order pursuant to this rule, the Clerk shall send by ordinary mail certified copies of the order to the applicant at the address listed in the application or as supplemented by the applicant, to the admissions committee, and to all counsel of record.

SECTION 13. Confidentiality of Character and Fitness Matters

(A) All information, proceedings, or documents relating to the character and fitness investigation of an applicant for admission, including all character questionnaires submitted pursuant to this rule, shall be confidential, and no person shall disclose any information, proceedings and documents except for any of the following purposes:

(1) To further any character and fitness investigation of the applicant under this rule;

(2) In connection with investigations of the applicant under Gov. Bar R. V;

(3) Pursuant to a written release of the applicant in connection with the applicant's application for admission to the practice of law in another jurisdiction;

(4) To file a final report with the Court pursuant to Sections 11(D)(5)(c) or 12(E) of this rule;

(5) Pursuant to divisions (C) and (D) of this section.

(B) This section applies to members, employees, and agents of the Supreme Court; members, employees, and agents of the Board of Commissioners on Character and Fitness; members and employees of local and regional admissions committees and the employees of the members of such committees; employees of local or regional bar associations; court reporters retained for character and fitness hearings or proceedings; witnesses; and attorneys representing applicants.

(C) A record filed with the Clerk of the Supreme Court pursuant to Section 12(E) of this rule shall be filed under seal. After sixty days, the record shall become public unless the Supreme Court, on motion by the applicant or sua sponte, orders that the record or portions of the record remain confidential.

(D) Information or documents otherwise confidential pursuant to division (A) of this section may be released to an appropriate governing board, law enforcement agency, or other authority having jurisdiction to investigate a violation of a rule of the Supreme Court or of a state or federal statute, if all of the following apply:

(1) During the course of the character and fitness investigation of an applicant under this rule, an attorney who is licensed to practice law in Ohio learns of a violation of a rule of the Supreme Court or of a state or federal statute;

(2) The attorney obtains the consent of the Board to release the otherwise confidential information or documents in order to report the violation to the appropriate governing board, law enforcement agency, or other authority having jurisdiction to investigate the violation;

(3) The attorney reveals only such information or documents as are necessary for the authority to investigate the violation.

(E) The failure of any person to abide by these confidentiality provisions and any confidentiality procedures established by the Board shall be deemed to be contempt of the Supreme Court and may be punished accordingly.

SECTION 14. Admissions Fund

(A) The fees collected under this rule, the fees charged and collected by the Court for admissions-related services, and the fees collected under Rules II, IX, and XI of the Supreme Court Rules for the Government of the Bar shall constitute the Admissions Fund. All application fees assessed under this rule and Gov. Bar R. II, IX, and XI shall be nonrefundable and payable to the Supreme Court of Ohio by certified check or money order.

(B) The Admissions Fund shall be used for matters approved by the Court and relating to the admission of applicants to the practice of law or relating to the certification of Foreign Legal Consultants, and for the administration and operation of all of the following:

(1) The Board of Bar Examiners;

(2) The Board of Commissioners on Character and Fitness, including the fees and expenses of special investigators appointed by the Board under Section 10(B)(2)(f) of this rule;

(3) The admissions committees, provided, however, that such use of the Admissions Fund shall be limited to reimbursing admissions committees for costs incurred in conducting investigations under Section 11 of this rule.

(C) Parties shall bear their own costs in proceedings brought under Section 12 of this rule before the Board of Commissioners on Character and Fitness and the Court.

(D) In addition to the purposes set forth in division (B) of this section, moneys in the Admissions Fund may be placed in the custody of the Treasurer of State pursuant to division (B) of section 113.05 of the Revised Code or transferred to the credit of the Supreme Court Admissions Fund in the state treasury. Investment earnings on moneys placed in the custody of the Treasurer shall be credited to the custodial account and investment earnings on moneys transferred to the Supreme Court Admissions Fund in the state treasury shall be credited to that Fund.

SECTION 15. Publication of List of Applicants for Admission

At least twice yearly, the Court shall publish in the *Ohio Official Reports Advance Sheets* a list of the names, cities, and counties or states of residence of those persons who have applied for admission to the practice of law in Ohio since the list was last published.

The Court shall distribute copies of the list to all regional and local bar association admissions committees.

History: Effective 2-28-72; amended eff 10-30-72; 11-27-72; 3-19-73; 11-12-73; 3-1-74; 7-8-74; 4-26-76; 1-24-77; 3-9-77; 8-1-77; 1-1-82; 3-9-83; 7-1-83; 5-7-84; 5-28-84; 12-31-84; 4-1-87; 5-6-87; 1-1-89; 7-1-89; 1-1-91; 2-1-91; 10-1-91; 2-1-92; 5-1-92; 7-1-92; 8-1-92; 1-1-93; 9-15-93; 1-1-95; 5-1-97; 8-3-98; 6-1-00; 10-1-00; 2-1-03; 10-1-03; 2-1-07; 5–1–07; 10–1–07; 01–01–08, 2/1/09.

NOTES TO DECISIONS

ANALYSIS

Admission pro hac vice
Disapproval of application

Admission pro hac vice

Trial court did not abuse its discretion by denying a motion for admission pro hac vice where admission would have been inconvenient to the proceeding and denial was not prejudicial to the moving parties: LMC Weight Loss, Inc. v. Victory Mgmt., 182 Ohio App. 3d 228, 2009 Ohio 2287, 912 N.E.2d 175, 2009 Ohio App. LEXIS 1932 (2009).

Trial court order denying pro hac vice status to Pennsylvania counsel in a probate matter was arbitrary. The trial court provided no reason whatsoever for overruling a well-supported and unopposed pro hac vice motion, and it did not appear that the trial court actually considered the totality of the motion, which revealed that the client seeking the pro hac vice admission had a long relationship with the out-of-state counsel and that counsel had appeared on behalf of the client in multiple cases in Ohio, including cases that ended up before the appellate court. In re Estate of Ramun, — Ohio App. 3d —, 2007 Ohio 3150, — N.E. 2d —, 2007 Ohio App. LEXIS 2913 (June 22, 2007).

Trial court's denial of defendant's request to have a Georgia attorney admitted pro hac vice to serve as co-counsel in her drug posssession trial pursuant to Ohio Sup. Ct. R. Gov't Bar I(9)((H) was an abuse of discretion and violated defendant's rights under U.S. Const. amend. VI and Ohio Const. art. I, § 10, as defendant's motion was made months before trial, she provided counsel's qualifications and reasons for the need for his representation, and the State did not oppose the representation. Defendant was found in possession of Khat, a little-known substance from Somali which contained controlled substances, however, those substances deteriorated when not kept in particular conditions, and the Georgia attorney had unique experience in representing criminal defendants who were charged with drug possession of Khat. State v. Roble, — Ohio App. 3d —, 2006 Ohio 328, — N.E. 2d —, 2006 Ohio App. LEXIS 288 (Jan. 27, 2006).

Disapproval of application

Financial irresponsibility alone is enough to disapprove a bar candidacy or bar exam application, as is an applicant's failure to provide requested information. In re Application of Stewart, 112 Ohio St. 3d 415, 2006 Ohio 6579, 860 N.E.2d 729, 2006 Ohio LEXIS 3540 (2006).

RULE II.

LIMITED PRACTICE OF LAW BY A LEGAL INTERN

SECTION 1. Definitions

As used in this rule:

(A) "Legal intern" means a person who holds a valid legal intern certificate issued pursuant to this rule.

(B) "Supervising attorney" means an attorney who satisfies all of the following:

(1) Has been admitted to practice law in Ohio pursuant to Gov. Bar R. I or has been temporarily certified to practice law in Ohio pursuant to Gov. Bar R. IX;

(2) Is in good standing in each jurisdiction in which the attorney is admitted to practice law;

(3) Is either employed by or associated with a law school clinic, legal aid bureau, public defender's office, or other legal services organization that provides legal assistance primarily to financially needy individuals, or is responsible for handling civil cases or prosecuting criminal cases for the state of Ohio or a municipal corporation.

SECTION 2. Eligibility

To be eligible for a legal intern certificate, an applicant shall satisfy all of the following:

(A) Be enrolled in a law school approved by the American Bar Association;

(B) Have received at least two-thirds of the total hourly academic credits required for graduation;

(C) Be approved for a legal intern certificate by the dean of the law school in which the applicant is enrolled;

(D) Have read and agreed to be bound by this rule, Gov. Bar R. IV, and the Ohio Rules of Professional Conduct as adopted by the Supreme Court.

SECTION 3. Application

An applicant for a legal intern certificate shall file an application with the Office of Bar Admissions of the Supreme Court. The application shall be on forms provided by the Office of Bar Admissions and shall include all of the following:

(A) A certificate from the dean of the law school in which the applicant is enrolled, certifying both of the following:

(1) That the applicant satisfies Sections 2(A) and (B) of this rule and has met all of the academic and ethical standards of the law school;

(2) That the dean does not have knowledge of any information that would cause the dean to doubt the applicant's character, fitness, and moral qualifications to practice law;

(B) A certificate from the applicant's supervising attorney, certifying that the supervising attorney will perform all duties required pursuant to Section 7 of this rule;

(C) A written oath, signed by the applicant, swearing or affirming that the applicant has read and agrees to be bound by this rule, Gov. Bar R. IV, and the Ohio Rules of Professional Conduct as adopted by the Supreme Court;

(D) A fee of twenty-five dollars;

(E) Any other information considered necessary or appropriate by the Office of Bar Admissions.

SECTION 4. Issuance and Duration of Certificate

(A) The Office of Bar Admissions shall issue a legal intern certificate to an applicant who satisfies Sections

2 and 3 of this rule. Unless revoked earlier pursuant to division (B) of this section, the legal intern certificate shall automatically expire upon the occurrence of one of the following:

(1) On the date, prior to graduation, the legal intern is no longer enrolled in a law school approved by the American Bar Association;

(2) On the date the legal intern graduates from law school, if the legal intern has not applied to take the first Ohio bar examination following graduation;

(3) On the Monday after distribution of the results of the first Ohio bar examination following the legal intern's graduation from law school. If the legal intern passes that bar examination, the legal intern's certificate shall continue in effect until the legal intern is admitted to the practice of law in Ohio so long as the legal intern is admitted to practice within twelve months following that bar examination. If the legal intern is not admitted to the practice of law in Ohio within twelve months following that bar examination, the legal intern certificate shall automatically expire.

(B) A legal intern certificate may be revoked, prior to its expiration and without hearing or statement of cause, by either of the following:

(1) The Supreme Court, *sua sponte*, on notification to the legal intern, the legal intern's supervising attorney, and the dean of the law school in which the legal intern is enrolled;

(2) The dean of the law school in which the legal intern is enrolled, on written notification to the Office of Bar Admissions and to the intern. The dean promptly shall revoke the legal intern's certificate if the legal intern ceases to meet all of the academic and ethical standards of the law school.

(C) Upon revocation of a legal intern certificate, the legal intern promptly shall return the certificate to the Office of Bar Admissions.

(D) A legal intern certificate that expires or is revoked shall not be renewed or reissued.

SECTION 5. Scope of Authority

(A) A legal intern may represent either of the following:

(1) Any person who qualifies for legal services at a law school clinic, legal aid bureau, public defender's office, or other legal services organization that provides legal assistance primarily to financially needy individuals, provided the person obtaining legal assistance from the legal intern consents in writing to the legal intern's representation;

(2) The state of Ohio or any municipal corporation, with the consent of the official charged with the responsibility of handling or prosecuting the matters or cases that are referred to the legal intern.

(B) Any entity supervising a legal intern pursuant to Section 5(A) must provide professional liability insurance coverage for the legal intern.

(C) A legal intern may provide representation in civil and administrative actions, misdemeanor and felony cases, or juvenile matters, including those juvenile matters involving an alleged offense that would be a felony if committed by an adult.

(D) When a legal intern prepares and signs, in whole or in part, any correspondence, legal documents, pleadings, or other papers, the legal intern's signature shall be followed by the designation "legal intern."

(E) A legal intern shall not appear before any court or administrative board or agency in the absence of a supervising attorney, unless the supervising attorney and the client consent in writing or on the record, and the absence of the supervising attorney is approved by the judge, referee, magistrate, or hearing officer hearing the matter. In the representation of a criminal defendant charged with a felony of the fourth or fifth degree or a juvenile charged with an offense that would be a felony of the fourth or fifth degree if committed by an adult, the supervising attorney shall be present throughout all court proceedings. In the representation of a criminal defendant charged with a felony of the first, second, or third degree or a juvenile charged with an offense that would be a felony of the first, second, or third degree if committed by an adult, the supervising attorney shall act as co-counsel throughout all court proceedings.

(F) The communications of the client to the legal intern shall be privileged under the same rules that govern the attorney-client privilege.

SECTION 6. Compensation

A legal intern shall not ask for or receive any compensation or remuneration of any kind from a financially needy client on whose behalf services are rendered. However, the law school clinic, legal aid bureau, public defender's office, or other legal services organization may be awarded attorney fees for services rendered by the legal intern consistent with the Ohio Rules of Professional Conduct and as provided by law. A law school clinic, legal aid bureau, public defender's office, or other legal services organization, the state, or any municipal corporation may pay compensation to the legal intern.

SECTION 7. Duties of Supervising Attorney

(A) A supervising attorney shall assume professional responsibility for each case, client, or matter assigned to the legal intern by that supervising attorney. The supervising attorney shall read and cosign all correspondence, legal documents, pleadings, and other papers prepared, in whole or in part, by the intern relating to any matter assigned to the legal intern by that supervising attorney. In any matter before a court or administrative board or agency in which a legal intern participates upon assignment by the supervising attorney, the supervising attorney shall ensure that the judge, referee, magistrate, or hearing officer is informed of the legal intern's status as a legal intern and shall be present with the legal intern in court or before the administrative board or agency, except as provided by Section 5(E) of this rule.

(B) The supervising attorney shall provide the legal intern with the opportunity to engage in and observe the practice of law, shall discuss and counsel the intern regarding matters of professional responsibility that arise, and shall train and supervise the legal intern on matters assigned to the intern by that supervising attorney to the extent necessary to properly protect the interests of the client and to properly advance and promote the intern's training.

(C) The supervising attorney shall cooperate with the legal intern's law school on any reporting or evaluation requirements regarding an award of academic credit to the legal intern.

History: Effective 2-28-72; amended eff. 2-12-73; 1-1-79; 7-1-83; 1-1-92; 10-1-00; 2-1-07, 5-1-07, 8-1-09.

RULE III.

PRACTICE OF LAW — FIRM ORGANIZA- TION; NAME; ETHICS; FINANCIAL RESPON- SIBILITY

SECTION 1. Firm Organization

An attorney who is otherwise authorized to practice as an active attorney under Gov. Bar. R. VI may practice law in Ohio, to the same extent as individuals and groups of individuals, through a legal professional association, corporation, or legal clinic, formed under Chapters 1701. or 1785. or licensed under Chapter 1703. of the Revised Code, a limited liability company, formed or registered under Chapter 1705. of the Revised Code, or a partnership having limited liability, registered under Chapter 1775. of the Revised Code.

SECTION 2. Name

The name of a legal professional association, corporation, legal clinic, limited liability company, or registered partnership shall comply with Rule 7.5 of the Ohio Rules of Professional Conduct. The name of a legal professional association or legal clinic shall end with the legend, "Co., L pa" or shall have immediately below it, in legible form, the words "A Legal Professional Association." The name of a corporation, limited liability company, or registered partnership shall include a descriptive designation as required under sections 1701.05(A), 1705.05(A), or 1775.62, respectively, of the Revised Code.

SECTION 3. Ethics and Discipline

(A) Participation in a legal professional association, corporation, legal clinic, limited liability company, or registered partnership shall not relieve an attorney of or diminish any obligation under the Ohio Rules of Professional Conduct or under these rules.

(B) An attorney shall not use a legal professional association, corporation, legal clinic, limited liability company, or registered partnership to share legal fees with a person not authorized to practice law in Ohio or elsewhere, except as permitted by Rule 5.4 of the Ohio Rules of Professional Conduct. An attorney shall not participate in a legal professional association, corporation, legal clinic, limited liability company, or registered partnership in which a member, partner, or other equity holder is a person not authorized to practice law in Ohio or elsewhere, except as permitted by Rule 5.4

of the Ohio Rules of Professional Conduct.

(C) An attorney shall not use a legal professional association, corporation, legal clinic, limited liability company, or registered partnership to attempt to limit liability for his or her personal malpractice in violation of Rule 1.8 of the Ohio Rules of Professional Conduct.

(D) A legal professional association, corporation, legal clinic, limited liability company, or registered partnership in which an attorney is an officer, director, agent, employee, manager, member, partner, or equity holder shall be considered the attorney's firm for purposes of the Ohio Rules of Professional Conduct and these rules.

SECTION 4. Financial Responsibility

(A) A legal professional association, corporation, legal clinic, limited liability company, or registered partnership shall maintain adequate professional liability insurance or other form of adequate financial responsibility for any liability of the firm arising from acts or omissions in the rendering of legal services by an officer, director, agent, employee, manager, member, partner, or equity holder.

(1) "Adequate professional liability insurance" means one or more policies of attorneys' professional liability insurance that insure the legal professional association, corporation, legal clinic, limited liability company, or registered partnership both:

(a) in an amount for each claim, in excess of any deductible, of at least fifty thousand dollars multiplied by the number of attorneys practicing with the firm, and

(b) an amount of one hundred thousand dollars for all claims during the policy year, multiplied by the number of attorneys practicing with the firm. No firm shall be required to carry insurance of more than five million dollars per claim, in excess of any deductible, or more than ten million dollars for all claims during the policy year, in excess of any deductible.

(2) "Other form of adequate financial responsibility" means funds, in an amount not less than the amount of professional liability insurance applicable to a firm under Section 4(A)(1) of this rule for all claims during the policy year, available to satisfy any liability of the firm arising from acts or omissions in the rendering of legal services by an officer, director, agent, employee, manager, member, partner, or equity holder. The funds shall be available in the form of a deposit in trust of cash, bank certificate of deposit, or United States Treasury obligation, a bank letter of credit, or a surety bond.

(B) Each member, partner, or other equity holder of a legal professional association, corporation, legal clinic, limited liability company, or registered partnership shall be jointly and severally liable for any liability of the firm based upon a claim arising from acts or omissions in the rendering of legal services while he or she was a member, partner, or equity holder, in an amount not to exceed the aggregate of both of the following:

(1) The per claim amount of professional liability insurance applicable to the firm under this rule, but only to the extent that the firm fails to have the professional liability insurance or other form of adequate financial responsibility required by this rule;

(2) The deductible amount of the professional liability insurance applicable to the claim.

The joint and several liability of the member, partner, or other equity holder shall be reduced to the extent that the liability of the firm has been satisfied by the assets of the firm.

(C) Each officer, director, agent, employee, manager, member, partner or equity holder of a legal professional association, corporation, legal clinic, limited liability company, or registered partnership shall be liable for his or her own acts or omissions as provided by law, without prejudice to any contractual or other right that the person may be entitled to assert against a firm, an insurance carrier, or other third party.

History: Effective 2-28-72; amended eff. 6-11-79; 3-30-80; 7-1-83; 1-1-93; 11-1-95; 2-1-07.

NOTES TO DECISIONS

ANALYSIS

Malpractice

Malpractice

Law firm does not engage in the practice of law and therefore cannot directly commit legal malpractice. A law firm may be vicariously liable for legal malpractice only when one or more of its principals or associates are liable for legal malpractice: Nat'l Union Fire Ins. Co. v. Wuerth, 122 Ohio St. 3d 594, 2009 Ohio 3601, 913 N.E.2d 939, 2009 Ohio LEXIS 1957 (2009).

RULE IV.
PROFESSIONAL RESPONSIBILITY

SECTION 1. Applicability

The Ohio Rules of Professional Conduct, effective February 1, 2007, as amended, shall be binding upon all persons admitted to practice law in Ohio. The willful breach of the Rules shall be punished by reprimand, suspension, disbarment, or probation as provided in Gov. Bar R. V.

SECTION 2. Duty of Lawyers

It is the duty of the lawyer to maintain a respectful attitude toward the courts, not for the sake of the temporary incumbent of the judicial office, but for the maintenance of its supreme importance. Judges and Justices, not being wholly free to defend themselves, are peculiarly entitled to receive the support of lawyers against unjust criticism and clamor. Whenever there is proper ground for serious complaint of a judicial officer, it is the right and duty of the lawyer to submit a grievance to proper authorities. These charges should be encouraged and the person making them should be protected.

History: Effective 2-28-72; amended eff. 7-15-74; 7-1-83; 1-1-93; 2-1-07.

RULE V.
DISCIPLINARY PROCEDURE

SECTION 1. Creation of Board of Commissioners on Grievances and Discipline of the Supreme Court

(A) **Composition** There shall be a Board of Commissioners on Grievances and Discipline of the Supreme Court consisting of twenty-eight members as follows: seventeen attorneys admitted to the practice of law in Ohio, seven active or voluntarily retired judges of the state of Ohio or judges retired pursuant to Article IV, Section 6 of the Ohio Constitution, and four nonattorney members.

(B) **Distribution** The attorney members of the Board shall be appointed from Ohio appellate districts as follows: First District, two members; Second District, one member; Third District, one member; Fourth District, one member; Fifth District, one member; Sixth District, two members; Seventh District, one member; Eighth District, three members; Ninth District, one member; Tenth District, two members; Eleventh District, one member; and Twelfth District, one member. The active and retired judge members shall be members at large appointed from separate appellate districts, and the nonattorney members of the Board shall be members at large appointed from separate appellate districts.

(C) **Term of Office** The term of office of each member of the Board shall be three years, beginning on the first day of January next following the member's appointment. Any member of the Board whose term has expired and who has an uncompleted assignment as a member of a panel may continue to serve for the purpose of the assignment until it is concluded before the Board. The successor member shall take no part in the proceedings of the Board concerning the assignment.

(D) **Appointments** The Chief Justice and Justices of the Supreme Court each shall appoint members of the Board. Appointments to terms commencing the first day of January of any year shall be made prior to the first day of December of the preceding year. Vacancies for any cause shall be filled for the unexpired term by the Justice who appointed the person causing the vacancy or by the successor of that Justice. A member appointed to a term of fewer than three years may be reappointed to not more than three, three-year terms. No person may be appointed to more than three, three-year terms on the Board. Three-year terms served prior to April 1, 2008 shall be included when determining whether a person is eligible for appointment or reappointment to the Board.

(E) **Chair and Vice-chair** The Board shall each year elect a judge or attorney member as chair and vice-chair. The chair, vice-chair, and Secretary each may execute journal entries on behalf of the Board and of panels of the Board. The chair and vice-chair shall serve in that capacity for no longer than two years.

(F) **Meetings** The Board shall meet in Columbus at least six times each year. The chair, vice-chair, or Secretary may call additional meetings of the Board when necessary.

(G) **Campaign Contributions** Members and employees of the Board, the Disciplinary Counsel, or employees of the Office of Disciplinary Counsel shall not make any contribution to, or for the benefit of, or take part in the campaign of, or campaign for or against, any justice, judge, or judicial candidate in this state. A Board member who is a candidate for a judicial office or for reelection to a judicial office may contribute to, may make a contribution for the benefit of, or take part in his or her own campaign.

SECTION 2. Jurisdiction and Powers of the Board

(A) **Exclusive Jurisdiction** All grievances involving alleged misconduct by justices, judges, or attorneys, all proceedings with regard to mental illness, all proceedings for the discipline of justices, judges, attorneys, persons under suspension, probation, or disbarred from the practice of law, and all proceedings for the reinstatement as an attorney shall be brought, conducted, and disposed of in accordance with the provisions of this rule.

(B) **Powers** The Board shall receive evidence, preserve the record, make findings, and submit recommendations to the Supreme Court as follows:

(1) Concerning complaints of misconduct that are alleged to have been committed by a judge, an attorney, a person under suspension from the practice of law, or a person on probation;

(2) Concerning the mental illness of any judge or attorney;

(3) Relating to petitions for reinstatement as an attorney;

(4) Upon reference by the Supreme Court of conduct by a judge or an attorney affecting any proceeding under this rule, where the acts allegedly constitute a contempt of the Supreme Court or a breach of these rules but did not take place in the presence of the Supreme Court or a member of the Supreme Court, whether by willful disobedience of any order or judgment of the Supreme Court or the Board, by interference with any officer of the Supreme Court in the prosecution of any duty, or otherwise. This rule shall not limit or affect the plenary power of the Supreme Court to impose punishment for either contempt or breach of these rules committed in its presence, or the plenary power of any other court for contempt committed in its presence.

(C) **Advisory Opinions** The Board may issue informal, nonbinding advisory opinion letters in response to prospective or hypothetical questions directed to the Board regarding the application of the Supreme Court Rules for the Government of the Bar of Ohio, the Supreme Court Rules for the Government of the Judiciary of Ohio, the Ohio Rules of Professional Conduct, the Code of Judicial Conduct, or the Attorney's Oath of Office. Subject to the approval of the Supreme Court, the Board shall adopt regulations for the issuance of advisory opinions.

SECTION 3. Secretary; Disciplinary Counsel; Certified Grievance Committees; Administration

(A) **Secretary** There shall be a Secretary of the Board, which shall be a full-time position. The Secretary shall be an attorney admitted to the practice of law in Ohio, shall be appointed by a majority of the Board, and shall serve at the pleasure of the Board.

(1) **Responsibilities** The Secretary shall have the overall scheduling, administrative, and fiscal responsibility of the Board. The Secretary shall schedule all hearings for the Board and panels of the Board; keep a docket of each complaint and of all proceedings on each complaint, which shall be retained permanently as a part of the records of the Board; execute journal entries for extensions of time where appropriate; maintain the records for the receipt and expenditure of money; prepare financial reports and budgets as required by the Supreme Court Rules for the Government of the Bar of Ohio, the Supreme Court Rules for the Government of the Judiciary of Ohio, and when requested by the Board; assist the Board in preparing opinion letters pursuant to Section 2(C) of this rule; take all necessary steps to see that office facilities, furnishings, stationery, equipment, and office supplies are available as needed; and any other action consistent with the Secretary's position as chief administrative and fiscal officer and not otherwise inconsistent with the Supreme Court Rules for the Government of the Bar of Ohio and the Supreme Court Rules for the Government of the Judiciary of Ohio.

(2) **Personnel** The Secretary shall employ personnel as are reasonably necessary to discharge the responsibilities set forth in this rule and shall establish the salaries of personnel, subject to approval by the Board. The Secretary and staff shall not be employed by any court.

(3) **Annual Reports** The Secretary shall file annually with the Supreme Court a report of the activities and expenses of the Board.

(B) **Disciplinary Counsel** With the approval of the Supreme Court, the Board, by majority vote, shall appoint a Disciplinary Counsel who shall investigate allegations of misconduct by judges or attorneys and allegations of mental illness affecting judges or attorneys, initiate complaints as a result of investigations under the provisions of this rule, and certify bar counsel designated by Certified Grievance Committees.

(1) **Appointment; Removal** The Disciplinary Counsel shall be appointed for a term of four years and shall be removed only for just cause. Removal for just cause shall be instituted by the filing, with the Chief Justice, of a written petition by the chair, acting by authority of a two-thirds vote of the Board. Upon receipt of the petition, the Chief Justice shall cause it to be served on the Disciplinary Counsel for response. Thereafter, the Chief Justice shall schedule a hearing before the Supreme Court, which shall determine whether there is just cause for the removal of the Disciplinary Counsel. The Disciplinary Counsel shall be removed upon the affirmative vote of five or more members of the Supreme Court.

(2) **Assistants; Staff** Assistant Disciplinary Counsel and staff in the Office of Disciplinary Counsel shall serve at the pleasure of the Disciplinary Counsel. The Disciplinary Counsel may appoint assistants as necessary who shall be attorneys admitted to the practice of law in Ohio and who shall not engage in the private

practice of law while serving in that capacity. The Disciplinary Counsel shall appoint staff as required to satisfactorily fulfill the duties of the Office of Disciplinary Counsel. The Disciplinary Counsel shall retain one or more parttime investigators who may be assigned by the Disciplinary Counsel to assist Certified Grievance Committees in the investigation of grievances.

(3) **Compensation; Supplies; Annual Report** The compensation of the Disciplinary Counsel shall be fixed by the Supreme Court. The compensation of personnel employed by the Disciplinary Counsel, including any Assistant Disciplinary Counsel, shall be fixed by the Disciplinary Counsel with the approval of the Supreme Court. The Supreme Court shall provide office facilities, furnishings, stationery, equipment, and office supplies for the Disciplinary Counsel. The Disciplinary Counsel shall file annually with the Supreme Court and the Board a report of the activities and expenses of the office.

(4) **Quarterly Report** By the fifteenth day of January, April, July, and October of each year, the Disciplinary Counsel shall file with the Supreme Court and the Board a report of the number of grievances made to the Disciplinary Counsel during the preceding quarter. The report shall specify the types of grievances filed, including commingling of funds, conviction of crime, failure to file income tax returns, failure to protect the interests of a client, soliciting, embezzlement, conversion, failure to account, excessive fees, mental illness, and any other type of grievance not set forth in this rule. The report shall indicate the number of grievances filed, the number pending in each category, and the number terminated by action of the Disciplinary Counsel during the reporting period.

(C) **Certified Grievance Committee** A Certified Grievance Committee shall be an organized committee of the Ohio State Bar Association or of one or more local bar associations in Ohio that permits the membership of any attorney practicing within the geographic area served by that association without reference to the attorney's area of practice, special interest, or other criteria. Except in Cuyahoga county, there shall be only one Certified Grievance Committee in each county. Two or more bar associations may establish a joint Certified Grievance Committee. Membership on a joint Certified Grievance Committee shall be in proportion to the number of attorneys employed in the geographic area served by each bar association establishing the joint Committee. Upon designation by a bar association or bar associations and satisfaction of the standards set forth in division (C)(1) of this section, a grievance committee shall be certified by the Board to investigate allegations of misconduct by judges or attorneys and mental illness affecting judges or attorneys and initiate complaints as a result of investigations under the provisions of these rules. A Certified Grievance Committee shall not have the authority to investigate allegations of misconduct against an attorney who is a member of any Certified Grievance Committee in the county and shall refer those allegations to the Secretary of the Board. A Certified Grievance Committee may adopt and utilize written procedures for handling allegations of client dissatisfaction that do not constitute disciplinary violations, to include mediation,

office practice monitoring, and other Alternative Dispute Resolution (ADR) methods. Only ADR procedures developed by the Board shall be used by Certified Grievance Committees. The procedures shall provide that mediators and ADR facilitators shall not be members of or subject to the jurisdiction of the Certified Grievance Committee.

(1) **Minimum Standards** To obtain and retain certification, each grievance committee shall satisfy all of the following minimum standards:

(a) Consist of no fewer than fifteen persons, including a chair who shall not serve as chair for more than two consecutive years. On or after January 1, 2000, both of the following shall apply:

(i) A majority of the members of the Certified Grievance Committee shall consist of attorneys admitted to the practice of law in Ohio;

(ii) At least three members or ten percent of the Certified Grievance Committee, whichever is greater, shall consist of persons who are not admitted to the practice of law in Ohio or any other state.

(b) Meet at least once every third month.

(c) Maintain a full-time, permanent office that is open during regular business hours, has a listed telephone number, and is staffed by a minimum of one full-time employee to process grievances received by the grievance committee.

(d) Designate bar counsel, who shall be certified by the Disciplinary Counsel, to supervise the receipt, investigation, and prosecution of grievances. Bar counsel may be a volunteer or paid for his or her services by the Certified Grievance Committee.

(e) Maintain permanent files and records of proceedings, and be sufficiently funded by the sponsoring bar association or associations to perform the duties imposed by these rules.

(f) Establish written procedures filed with the Board for the processing of grievances that conform to standard regulations promulgated by the Board. The written procedures shall provide a method for notifying potential grievants that they have the option to file a grievance with the Disciplinary Counsel rather than with the Certified Grievance Committee.

(g) File quarterly reports similar to those required of the Disciplinary Counsel under Section 3(B)(4) of this rule. Each Certified Grievance Committee shall include in the report the results of cases referred to Board-approved ADR methods along with recommendations for further action, including discontinuance or amendment of ADR procedures.

(2) **Chair** The president of each bar association having a Certified Grievance Committee shall report annually and in writing the name of the chair of the Certified Grievance Committee to the Board and the Disciplinary Counsel.

(3) **Continuing Education** Each certified committee shall encourage its members to attend continuing education programs and activities on subjects related to legal and judicial ethics.

(4) **Annual Publication** At least once a year in a local newspaper with the largest general circulation in its jurisdiction, the Certified Grievance Committee shall publish an announcement containing the address and telephone number of its office and a brief descrip-

tion of its functions. The announcement shall be published in the legal notice section in a style and size commensurate with legal advertisements.

(5) **Decertification** The Board may decertify a Certified Grievance Committee, at the request of one or more of its sponsoring local bar associations or *sua sponte*, if the committee fails to maintain the minimum standards set forth in division (C)(1) of this section and regulations adopted by the Board, or substantially fails to conform to these rules. A Certified Grievance Committee may be decertified only by majority vote of the Board. Prior to decertifying a Certified Grievance Committee, the Board shall hold a hearing before three commissioners, chosen by lot, who do not reside in the same appellate district where the Certified Grievance Committee is located. If the panel of commissioners recommends decertification, it shall issue findings setting forth all of the following:

(a) The reasons for decertification;

(b) All of the Certified Grievance Committee's pending matters;

(c) Any special circumstances by reason of which the committee should not be required to discharge its remaining responsibilities in any or all pending matters.

In the absence of special circumstances, the Board shall not decertify a Certified Grievance Committee before the committee has discharged to the Board's satisfaction the committee's remaining responsibilities in its then-pending matters.

(D) **Funding and Budgets** Funds for the operation of the Board and the Disciplinary Counsel and development and distribution of materials describing the disciplinary process shall be provided from the Attorney Services Fund.

(1) **Budget** At the request of the Administrative Director of the Supreme Court, the Board and the Disciplinary Counsel shall prepare and submit a proposed annual budget for approval by the Supreme Court.

(2) **Reimbursement for Expenses** Certified Grievance Committees may be reimbursed from the Attorney Services Fund for expenses incurred by the committees in performing the obligations imposed on them by these rules. Reimbursement is not permitted for costs associated with compliance with the standards contained in division (C)(1) of this section, except for the costs listed in division (D)(2)(b) of this section.

(a) **Reimbursement of Direct Expenses** A Certified Grievance Committee may be reimbursed for direct expenses incurred in performing the obligations imposed by this rule. Reimbursement shall be limited to costs for depositions, transcripts, copies of documents, necessary travel expenses for witnesses and volunteer attorneys, witness fees, costs of subpoenas and the service of subpoenas, and compensation of investigators and expert witnesses authorized in advance by the Board. There shall be no reimbursement for the costs of the time of other bar association personnel or attorneys in discharging these obligations. Reimbursement shall be made upon submission to the Secretary of the Board of proof of expenditures. Upon approval by the Board, reimbursement shall be made from the Attorney Services Fund.

(b) **Annual Reimbursement of Indirect Ex-**

penses Certified Grievance Committees may apply to the Board prior to the first day of February each year for partial reimbursement of other expenses necessarily and reasonably incurred during the preceding calendar year in performing their obligations under these rules. The Board shall establish criteria for determining whether expenses under divisions (D)(2)(b) and (c) of this section are necessary and reasonable. The Board shall deny reimbursement for any expense for which a Certified Grievance Committee seeks reimbursement on or after the first day of May of the year immediately following the calendar year in which the expense was incurred. Expenses eligible for reimbursement are those specifically relating to professional responsibility enforcement and include all of the following:

(i) The personnel costs for the portion of an employee's work that is dedicated to this area;

(ii) The costs of bar counsel who is retained pursuant to written agreement with or employed by the Certified Grievance Committee;

(iii) Postal and delivery charges;

(iv) Long distance telephone charges;

(v) Local telephone charges and other appropriate line charges including, but not limited to, per call charges;

(vi) The cost of dedicated telephone lines;

(vii) Subscriptions to professional journals, law books, and other legal research services and materials related to professional responsibility;

(viii) Organizational dues and educational expenses relating to professional responsibility enforcement;

(ix) All costs of defending grievance and disciplinary-related law suits and that portion of professional liability insurance premiums directly attributable to the operation of the committees in performing their obligations under this rule;

(x) The percentage of rent, insurance premiums not reimbursed pursuant to division(D)(2)(b)(ix) of this section, supplies and equipment, accounting costs, occupancy, utilities, office expenses, repair and maintenance, and other overhead expenses directly attributable to the operation of the committees in performing their obligations under this rule, as determined by the Board and provided that no Certified Grievance Committee shall be reimbursed in excess of thirty thousand dollars per calendar year for such expenses. Reimbursement shall not be made for the costs of the time of other bar association personnel, volunteer attorneys, depreciation, or amortization. No expense reimbursed under division (D)(2)(a) of this section is eligible for reimbursement under division (D)(2)(b) of this section.

(c) **Quarterly Reimbursement of Certain Indirect Expenses** In addition to applying annually for reimbursement pursuant to division (D)(2)(b) of this section, a Certified Grievance Committee may apply quarterly to the Board for reimbursement of the expenses set forth in divisions (D)(2)(b)(i) and (ii) of this section that were necessarily and reasonably incurred during the preceding calendar quarter. Quarterly reimbursement shall be submitted in accordance with the following schedule:

Reimbursement for the months of:	Due by:
January, February, and March	May 1
April, May, and June	August 1
July, August, and September	November 1
October, November, and December	February 1 (with annual reimbursement request)

Any expense that is eligible for quarterly reimbursement, but that is not submitted on a quarterly reimbursement application, shall be submitted no later than the appropriate annual reimbursement application pursuant to division (D)(2)(b) of this section and shall be denied by the Board if not timely submitted. The application for quarterly reimbursement shall include an affidavit with documentation demonstrating that the Certified Grievance Committee incurred the expenses set forth in divisions (D)(2)(b)(i) and (ii) of this section.

(3) **Audit** Expenses incurred by Certified Grievance Committees and reimbursed under division (D)(2) of this section may be audited at the discretion of the Board or the Supreme Court and paid out of the Attorney Services Fund.

(4) **Availability of Funds** Reimbursement under division (D)(2) of this section is subject to the availability of moneys in the Attorney Services Fund.

(E) **Public Records** Except as provided in Section 11(E) of this rule and by state and federal law, documents and records of the Board, the Secretary, and the Disciplinary Counsel, including budgets, reports, and records of income and expenditures, shall be made available for inspection to any member of the general public at reasonable times during regular business hours. Upon request, a person responsible for the records shall make copies available at cost, within a reasonable period of time. The records shall be maintained in a manner that they can be made available for inspection.

SECTION 4. Investigation and Filing of Complaints

(A) **Referral by Board** The Board may refer to a Certified Grievance Committee or the Disciplinary Counsel any matter filed with it for investigation as provided in this section.

(B) **Referral by Certified Grievance Committee** If a Certified Grievance Committee determines in the course of a disciplinary investigation that the matters of alleged misconduct under investigation are sufficiently serious and complex as to require the assistance of the Disciplinary Counsel, the chair of the Certified Grievance Committee may direct a written request for assistance to the Disciplinary Counsel. The Disciplinary Counsel shall investigate all matters contained in the request and report the results of the investigation to the committee that requested it.

(C) **Power and Duty to Investigate** The investigation of grievances involving alleged misconduct by justices, judges, and attorneys and grievances with regard to mental illness shall be conducted by the Disciplinary Counsel or a Certified Grievance Committee. The Disciplinary Counsel and a Certified Grievance Committee shall investigate any matter filed with it or that comes to its attention and may file a complaint pursuant to this rule in cases where it finds probable cause to believe that misconduct has occurred or that a condition of mental illness exists.

(D) **Time for Investigation** The investigation of grievances by Disciplinary Counsel or a Certified Grievance Committee shall be concluded within sixty days from the date of the receipt of the grievance. A decision as to the disposition of the grievance shall be made within thirty days after conclusion of the investigation.

(1) **Extensions of Time** Extensions of time for completion of the investigation may be granted by the Secretary of the Board upon written request and for good cause shown. Investigations for which an extension is granted shall be completed within one hundred fifty days from the date of receipt of the grievance. Time may be extended when all parties voluntarily enter into an alternative dispute resolution method for resolving fee disputes sponsored by the Ohio State Bar Association or a local bar association.

(2) **Extension Limits** The chair or Secretary of the Board may extend time limits beyond one hundred fifty days from the date of filing in the event of pending litigation, appeals, unusually complex investigations, including the investigation of multiple grievances, time delays in obtaining evidence or testimony of witnesses, or for other good cause shown. If an investigation is not completed within one hundred fifty days from the date of filing the grievance or a good cause extension of that time, the Secretary may refer the matter either to a geographically appropriate Certified Grievance Committee or the Disciplinary Counsel. The investigation shall be completed within sixty days after referral. No investigation shall be extended beyond one year from the date of the filing of the grievance.

(3) **Time Limits not Jurisdictional** Time limits set forth in this rule are not jurisdictional. No grievance filed shall be dismissed unless it appears that there has been an unreasonable delay and that the rights of the respondent to have a fair hearing have been violated. Investigations that extend beyond one year from the date of filing are prima facie evidence of unreasonable delay.

(E) **Retaining Outside Experts** A particular investigation may benefit from the services of an independent investigator, auditor, examiner, assessor, or other expert. A Certified Grievance Committee may retain the services of an expert in accordance with the Board regulations.

(F) **Cooperation with Clients' Security Fund** Upon the receipt of any grievance presenting facts that may be the basis for an award from the Clients' Security Fund under Gov. Bar R. VIII, the Disciplinary Counsel or a Certified Grievance Committee shall notify the grievant of the potential right to an award from the Fund and provide the grievant with the forms necessary to initiate a claim with the Clients' Security Fund. The Disciplinary Counsel, a Certified Grievance Committee, and the Board shall provide the Board of Commissioners of the Clients' Security Fund with findings from investigations, grievances, or any other records it requests in connection with an investigation under Gov. Bar R. VIII. The transmittal of confidential information may be delayed pending the termination of the disciplinary investigation or proceedings.

(G) **Duty to Cooperate** The Board, the Disciplinary Counsel, and president, secretary, or chair of a Certified Grievance Committee may call upon any justice, judge, or attorney to assist in an investigation or testify in a hearing before the Board or a panel for which provision is made in this rule, including mediation and ADR procedures, as to any matter that he or she would not be bound to claim privilege as an attorney at law. No justice, judge, or attorney shall neglect or refuse to assist or testify in an investigation or hearing.

(H) **Referral of Procedural Questions to Board** In the course of an investigation, the chair of a Certified Grievance Committee, the president of a bar association, or the Disciplinary Counsel may direct a written inquiry regarding a procedural question to the chair of the Board of Commissioners. The written inquiry shall be filed with the Secretary of the Board. Upon receipt of a written inquiry, the chair of the Board and the Secretary shall consult and direct a response.

(I) **Requirements for Filing a Complaint**

(1) **Definition** "Complaint" means a formal written allegation of misconduct or mental illness of a person designated as the respondent.

(2) **Notice of Intent to File** No investigation conducted by the Disciplinary Counsel or a Certified Grievance Committee shall be completed, and no complaint shall be filed with the Board, without first giving the judge or attorney who is the subject of the grievance or investigation notice of each allegation and the opportunity to respond to each allegation.

(3) **Majority Vote Required** No complaint shall be filed by a Certified Grievance Committee unless a majority of a quorum of that committee determines the complaint is warranted.

(4) **Notice of Intent not to File** If, upon investigation of a grievance, a Certified Grievance Committee or the Disciplinary Counsel determines that the filing of a complaint with the Board is not warranted, the grievant and the judge or attorney shall be notified in writing of that determination, with a brief statement of the reasons that a complaint was not filed with the Board. Upon request, a Certified Grievance Committee or the Disciplinary Counsel shall provide the judge or attorney with a copy of the grievance.

(5) **Appeal** A grievant who is dissatisfied with a determination by a Certified Grievance Committee not to file a complaint may secure a review of the determination by filing a written request with the Secretary of the Board within fourteen days after the grievant is notified of the determination. The Secretary shall refer the request for review to the Disciplinary Counsel. The review shall be considered promptly by the Disciplinary Counsel, a decision made within thirty days, and the grievant notified. Extensions of time for completion of the review may be granted by the Secretary for good cause shown. No further review or appeal by a grievant

shall be authorized. If the original determination is not affirmed, any further proceedings shall be handled by the Disciplinary Counsel.

(6) **Attachments to Complaint** Sufficient investigatory materials to demonstrate probable cause shall be submitted with the complaint. The materials shall include any response filed by or on behalf of the respondent pursuant to division (I)(2) of this section and may include investigation reports, summaries, depositions, statements, the response of the respondent, and any other relevant material.

(7) **Complaint Filed by Certified Grievance Committee** Six copies of all complaints shall be filed with the Secretary of the Board. Complaints filed by a Certified Grievance Committee shall be filed in the name of the committee as relator. The complaint shall not be accepted for filing unless signed by one or more attorneys admitted to the practice of law in Ohio, who shall be counsel for the relator. The complaint shall be accompanied by a written certification, signed by the president, secretary, or chair of the Certified Grievance Committee, that the counsel are authorized to represent the relator in the action and have accepted the responsibility of prosecuting the complaint to conclusion. The certification shall constitute the authorization of the counsel to represent the relator in the action as fully and completely as if designated and appointed by order of the Supreme Court with all the privileges and immunities of an officer of the Supreme Court. The complaint also may be signed by the grievant.

(8) **Complaint Filed by Disciplinary Counsel** Six copies of all complaints shall be filed with the Secretary of the Board. Complaints filed by the Disciplinary Counsel shall be filed in the name of the Disciplinary Counsel as relator.

(9) **Service** Upon the filing of a complaint with the Secretary of the Board, the relator shall forward a copy of the complaint to the Disciplinary Counsel, the Certified Grievance Committee of the Ohio State Bar Association, the local bar association, and any Certified Grievance Committee serving the county or counties in which the respondent resides and maintains an office and for the county from which the complaint arose.

SECTION 5. Interim Suspension from the Practice of Law for a Felony Conviction or Default under a Child Support Order

(A)(1) **Interim Suspension** A justice, judge, or an attorney admitted to the practice of law in Ohio shall be subject to an interim suspension under either of the following circumstances:

(a) The justice, judge, or attorney is convicted in Ohio of a felony or of an equivalent offense under the laws of any other state or federal jurisdiction;

(b) A final and enforceable determination has been made pursuant to Chapter 3123. of the Revised Code that the justice, judge, or attorney is in default under a child support order.

(2) A certified copy of the judgment entry of conviction of a justice, judge, or an attorney of a felony offense shall be transmitted by the judge entering the judgment to the Secretary of the Board and to the Disciplinary Counsel or the president, secretary, or chair of the geographically appropriate Certified Griev-

ance Committee. A certified copy of the court or child support enforcement agency determination that a justice, judge, or attorney is in default under a child support order shall be transmitted as provided in division (B) of section 4705.021 of the Revised Code.

(3) Upon receipt from any source of a certified copy of the judgment entry of conviction or of the determination of default under a child support order, the Secretary promptly shall submit the entry or determination to the Supreme Court. The entry shall be submitted whether the conviction resulted from a plea of guilty or nolo contendere, from a verdict after trial, or otherwise and regardless of the pendency of an appeal.

(4) The Supreme Court may enter an order as it considers appropriate, including an order immediately suspending the justice, judge, or attorney from the practice of law pending further proceedings pursuant to these rules.

(B) **Conclusive Evidence** A certified copy of a judgment entry of conviction of an offense or of a determination of default under a child support order shall be conclusive evidence of the commission of that offense or of the default in any disciplinary proceedings instituted against a justice, judge, or an attorney based upon the conviction or default.

(C) **Time for Hearing** Any disciplinary proceeding instituted against a justice, judge, or an attorney based on a conviction of an offense or on default under a child support order shall not be brought to hearing until all appeals from the conviction or proceedings directly related to the default determination are concluded.

(D)(1) **Reinstatement** A justice, judge, or an attorney suspended under this rule or Rule II of the Supreme Court Rules for the Government of the Judiciary of Ohio shall be reinstated by the Supreme Court upon the filing with and submission to the Supreme Court by the Secretary of any of the following:

(a) A certified copy of a judgment entry reversing the conviction of the offense;

(b) A certified copy of a judgment entry reversing the determination of default under a child support order;

(c) A notice from a court or child support enforcement agency that the justice, judge, or attorney is no longer in default under a child support order or is subject to a withholding or deduction notice or a new or modified child support order to collect current support or any arrearage due under the child support order that was in default and is complying with that notice or order.

(2) Reinstatement shall not terminate any pending disciplinary proceeding.

(E) **Duty of Clerk on Entering Order** Upon the entry of an order suspending or reinstating a justice, judge, or an attorney pursuant to this section, the Clerk of the Supreme Court shall mail certified copies of the order as provided in Section 8(D)(1) of this rule.

SECTION 5A. Interim Remedial Suspension

(A)(1) **Motion; Response** Upon receipt of substantial, credible evidence demonstrating that a Justice, judge, or attorney has committed a violation of the Code of Judicial Conduct or Ohio Rules of Professional Conduct and poses a substantial threat of serious harm to the public, the Disciplinary Counsel or appropriate Certified Grievance Committee, which shall be referred to as the relator, shall do both of the following:

(a) Prior to filing a motion for an interim remedial suspension, make a reasonable attempt to provide the Justice, judge, or attorney, who shall be referred to as the respondent, with notice, which may include notice by telephone, that a motion requesting an order for an interim remedial suspension will be filed with the Supreme Court.

(b) File a motion with the Supreme Court requesting that the Court order an interim remedial suspension. The Disciplinary Counsel or appropriate Certified Grievance Committee shall include, in its motion, proposed findings of fact, proposed conclusions of law, and other information in support of the requested order. Evidence relevant to the requested order shall be attached to or filed with the motion. The motion may include a request for an immediate, interim remedial suspension pursuant to Rule XIV, Section 4(C) of the Rules of Practice of the Supreme Court of Ohio. The motion shall include a certificate detailing the attempts made by the relator to provide advance notice to the respondent of the relator's intent to file the motion. The motion also shall include a certificate of service on the respondent at the most recent address provided by the respondent to the attorney registration office and at the last address of the respondent known to the relator, if different.

(2) After the filing of a motion for an interim remedial suspension, the respondent may file a memorandum opposing the motion in accordance with Rule XIV, Section 4 of the Rules of Practice of the Supreme Court of Ohio. The respondent shall attach to or file with the memorandum any rebuttal evidence.

(B) **Order** Upon consideration of the motion and any memorandum opposing the motion, the Supreme Court may enter an interim remedial order immediately suspending the respondent, pending final disposition of disciplinary proceedings predicated on the conduct threatening the serious harm or may order other action as the Court considers appropriate. If requested by the relator, the Supreme Court may order an immediate interim remedial suspension, prior to receipt of a memorandum opposing the relator's motion, pursuant to Rule XIV, Section 4(C) of the Rules of Practice of the Supreme Court of Ohio. If an order is entered pursuant to this division, an attorney may be appointed pursuant to Section 8(F) of this rule to protect the interest of the suspended attorney's clients.

(C)(1) **Motion for Dissolution or Modification of the Suspension** The respondent may request dissolution or modification of the order of suspension by filing a motion with the Supreme Court. The motion shall be filed within thirty days of entry of the order imposing the suspension, unless the respondent first obtains leave of the Supreme Court to file a motion beyond that time. The motion shall include a statement and all available evidence as to why the respondent no longer poses a substantial threat of serious harm to the public. A copy of the motion shall be served by the respondent on the relator. The relator shall have ten days from the date the motion is filed to file a response to the motion. The Supreme Court promptly shall review the motion after a response has been filed or after the time for filing a response has passed.

(2) In addition to the motion allowed by division (C)(1) of this section, the respondent may file a motion requesting dissolution of the interim remedial suspension order, alleging that one hundred eighty days have elapsed since the entry of the order and the relator has failed to file with the Board a formal complaint predicated on the conduct that was the basis of the order. A copy of the motion shall be served by the respondent on the relator. The relator shall have ten days from the date the motion is filed to file a response to the motion. The Supreme Court promptly shall review the motion after a response has been filed or after the time for filing a response has passed.

(D) **Procedure** The Rules of Practice of the Supreme Court of Ohio shall apply to interim remedial suspension proceedings filed pursuant to this section.

(E) **Duty of Clerk on Entering Order** Upon the entry of an order suspending or reinstating the respondent pursuant to this section, the Clerk of the Supreme Court shall mail certified copies of the order as provided in Section 8(D)(1) of this rule.

SECTION 6. Proceedings of the Board after Filing of the Complaint

(A) **Definitions**

(1) **Misconduct** "Misconduct" means any violation by a justice, judge, or an attorney of any provision of the oath of office taken upon admission to the practice of law in this state or any violation of the Ohio Rules of Professional Conduct or the Code of Judicial Conduct, disobedience of these rules or of the terms of an order imposing probation or a suspension from the practice of law, or the commission or conviction of a crime involving moral turpitude.

(2) **Probable Cause** "Probable cause" means there is substantial, credible evidence that misconduct, as defined in division (A)(1) of this section, has been committed.

(B) **Manner of Discipline** Any justice, judge, or attorney found guilty of misconduct shall be disciplined as follows:

(1) Disbarment from the practice of law;

(2) Suspension from the practice of law for an indefinite period subject to reinstatement as provided in Section 10 of this rule;

(3) Suspension from the practice of law for a period of six months to two years subject to a stay in whole or in part;

(4) Probation for a period of time upon conditions as the Supreme Court determines, but only in conjunction with a suspension ordered pursuant to division (B)(3) of this section;

(5) Public reprimand.

(C) **Effect of Discipline; Enhancement** A person who is disbarred or who voluntarily has surrendered his or her license to practice shall not be readmitted to the practice of law in Ohio. Prior disciplinary offenses shall be considered as a factor that may justify an increase in the degree of discipline to be imposed for subsequent misconduct.

(D) **Probable Cause Determination; Appointment of Hearing Panel**

(1) **Probable Cause Determination** Upon receipt of a complaint, the Secretary shall direct the complaint and investigatory materials to a probable cause panel for review. Each panel shall be composed of three members of the Board, chosen by the chair, who shall designate one attorney or judge member as chair of the panel. Upon review solely of the complaint and investigation materials, the probable cause panel shall make an independent determination of whether probable cause exists for the filing of a complaint. The panel shall issue an order certifying the complaint to the Board or dismissing the complaint and investigation. The determination of the panel shall be sent by certified mail to the Disciplinary Counsel, to the appropriate Certified Grievance Committee, and to the respondent.

(2) **Dismissal for Lack of Probable Cause** Within seven days of receipt of the decision of the probable cause panel to dismiss the complaint, the Disciplinary Counsel or Certified Grievance Committee may appeal the decision to the full Board by filing a written appeal with the Secretary of the Board. The Board shall review the investigation and make an independent determination as to whether probable cause exists for the filing of a complaint. The Board shall issue an order certifying the complaint or dismissing it and send a copy of its decision to the parties by certified mail. There shall be no appeal from the decision of the Board.

(3) **Appointment of Hearing Panel** After the respondent has filed an answer or the time for filing an answer has elapsed, the Secretary shall appoint a hearing panel consisting of three members of the Board chosen by lot from members who did not serve on the probable cause panel. The Secretary shall designate one attorney or judge member of the panel to serve as chair of the panel. No member of the hearing panel shall be a resident of the appellate district from which the complaint originated. Not more than one nonattorney shall serve on any hearing panel. A majority of the panel shall constitute a quorum. The panel chair shall rule on all motions and interlocutory matters, and no ruling by the panel chair on motions and interlocutory matters may be appealed prior to entry of the final order.

(E) **Notice to Respondent upon Filing of the Complaint** The Secretary of the Board shall send a copy of the complaint by certified mail to the respondent with a notice requiring the respondent to file, within twenty days after the mailing of the notice, six copies of his or her answer and serve copies of the answer on counsel of record named in the complaint. Extensions of time for the filing of the answer may be granted by the Secretary for good cause shown.

(F) **Default** If the respondent has not filed an answer within twenty days of the answer date set forth in the notice to respondent of the filing of the complaint or any extension of the answer date, the relator shall file a motion for default. Prior to filing a motion for default, relator shall make reasonable efforts to contact the respondent.

(1) **Motion** A motion for default shall contain all of the following:

(a) A statement of the effort made to contact the respondent and the result;

(b) Sworn or certified documentary prima facie evidence in support of the allegations made;

(c) The recommendation of the relator for sanction;

(d) A statement of any mitigating factors of which the relator is aware;

(e) A certificate of service of the motion on respondent at the address shown for the respondent on the records of the Supreme Court and at the last address known to the relator, if different.

(2) **Disposition** The secretary of the Board may refer the motion for default to a judge or attorney member of the Board or master commissioner who shall rule on the motion. If a motion is granted, the Board member or master commissioner shall prepare a certified report for review by the Board pursuant to division (J) of this section. If a motion is denied, a hearing panel shall proceed with a formal hearing pursuant to division (G) of this section. For good cause shown, the chair of the Board may set aside a default entry and order a panel hearing at any time before the report and recommendation of the Board are certified to the Supreme Court.

(G) **Hearing** Upon reasonable notice and at a time and location set by the panel chair pursuant to the hearing procedures and guidelines of the Board, the panel shall hold a formal hearing on the complaint. Requests for continuances may be granted by the panel chair for good cause shown. All hearings shall be recorded by a court reporter provided by the Board and a transcript filed with the Secretary.

(H) **Authority of Hearing Panel; Dismissal** If, at the end of the evidence presented by the relator or of all evidence, a unanimous hearing panel finds that the evidence is insufficient to support a charge or count of misconduct, the panel may order that the complaint or count be dismissed. The panel chair shall give written notice of the action taken to the Board, the respondent, all counsel of record, the Disciplinary Counsel, the Certified Grievance Committee for and the local bar association of the county or counties in which the respondent resides and maintains his or her office and the county from which the complaint arose, and the Ohio State Bar Association.

(I) **Referral by Panel** In the alternative, if the hearing panel determines that findings of fact and recommendations for dismissal should be referred to the Board for review and action by the full Board, the panel may submit its findings of fact to the Board and may recommend dismissal in the same manner as provided in this rule with respect to public reprimand, probation, suspension, or disbarment.

(J) **Public Reprimand, Probation, Suspension, or Disbarment; Duty of Hearing Panel** If the hearing panel determines, by clear and convincing evidence, that respondent is guilty of misconduct and that public reprimand, suspension for a period of six months to two years, probation, suspension for an indefinite period, or disbarment is merited, the hearing panel shall file its certified report of the proceedings, its finding of facts and recommendations, including any recommendations as to probation and the conditions of probation, with the Secretary. The report shall include the transcript of testimony taken and an itemized statement of the actual and necessary expenses incurred in connection with the proceedings.

(K) **Review by Entire Board** After review, the Board may refer the matter to the hearing panel for further hearing, order a further hearing before the Board, or proceed on the certified report of the prior proceedings before the hearing panel. After the final review, the Board may dismiss the complaint or find that the respondent is guilty of misconduct. If the complaint is dismissed, the dismissal shall be reported to the Secretary of the Board, who shall notify the same persons and organizations that would have received notice if the complaint had been dismissed by the hearing panel.

(L) **Public Reprimand; Probation, Suspension, or Disbarment; Duty of Board after Review** If the Board determines that a public reprimand, suspension for a period of six months to two years, probation, suspension for an indefinite period, or disbarment is merited, the Board shall file a final certified report of its proceedings, including its findings of fact and recommendations, with the Clerk of the Supreme Court. The report shall include the transcript of testimony taken and an itemized statement of the actual and necessary expenses incurred in connection with the proceedings. The Board forthwith shall notify the respondent and all counsel of record of the action, enclosing with the notice a copy of the findings of fact and recommendations and a copy of the statement of the actual and necessary expenses incurred.

SECTION 7. Mental Illness Suspension; Standard; Findings; Examination; Duty of Clerk; Termination

(A) **Definition** "Mental illness" has the same meaning as in division (A) of section 5122.01 of the Revised Code.

(B) **Mental Illness Suspension**

(1) After an answer has been filed or the time for answer has elapsed, the Board forthwith shall certify a complaint to the Supreme Court if either of the following applies:

(a) The complaint, answer, or other subsequent pleading alleges mental illness that substantially impairs the ability of the attorney to practice law and is supported by a certified copy of a journal entry of a court of competent jurisdiction adjudicating mental illness:

(b) After an examination as provided in division (C) of this section, the Board finds an existing mental illness that substantially impairs the ability of the attorney to practice law.

(2) Upon receipt of a certified complaint pursuant to division (B)(1) of this section, the Supreme Court may suspend the respondent from the practice of law.

(C) **Examination**

(1) The Board or hearing panel, on its own motion or motion of either party, may order a medical or psychiatric examination of the respondent if either of the following applies:

(a) The complaint, answer, or any subsequent pleading alleges existing mental illness that substantially impairs the ability of the attorney to practice law but is unsupported by a journal entry of a court of competent jurisdiction;

(b) Mental illness that substantially impairs the ability of the attorney to practice law otherwise is placed in issue.

(2) The medical or psychiatric examination of respondent shall be conducted by one or more physicians designated by the Board or hearing panel. The findings of the physician or physicians shall be presented to the Board or hearing panel as evidence and made available to both parties. If the results of the examination are contested, the hearing panel shall submit its findings of fact and conclusions to the Board.

(D) **Board Review** If, after reviewing the report of the hearing panel, the Board concludes the record establishes that the respondent suffers from mental illness that substantially impairs the ability of the attorney to practice law, the Board forthwith shall certify the complaint to the Supreme Court. The Supreme Court may suspend the respondent from the practice of law.

(E) **Duty of Clerk on Entering Order** Upon the entry of an order suspending respondent for mental illness that substantially impairs the ability of the attorney to practice law, the Clerk of the Supreme Court shall mail certified copies of the order as provided in Section 8(D)(1) of this rule. The order shall not be published but shall be a matter of public record.

(F) **Termination** A suspension under this section may be terminated on application of the respondent to the Board and a showing of removal of the cause for the suspension. The termination of the suspension shall be certified by the Board to, and affirmed by, the Supreme Court.

SECTION 8. Review by Supreme Court; Orders; Costs; Publication; Duties of Disqualified or Resigned Attorney

(A) **Show Cause Order** After the filing of a final report of the Board, the Supreme Court shall issue the respondent an order to show cause why the report of the Board shall not be confirmed and a disciplinary order entered. Notice of the order to show cause shall be served by the Clerk of the Supreme Court on the respondent and all counsel of record personally or by certified mail.

(B) **Response to Show Cause Order** Within twenty days after the issuance of an order to show cause, the respondent or relator may file objections to the findings or recommendations of the Board and to the entry of a disciplinary order or to the confirmation of the report on which the order to show cause was issued. The objections shall be accompanied by a brief in support of the objections and proof of service of copies of the objections and the brief on the Secretary of the Board and all counsel of record. Objections and briefs shall be filed in the number and form required for original actions by the Rules of Practice of the Supreme Court of Ohio.

(C) **Answer Briefs** Answer briefs and proof of service shall be filed within fifteen days after briefs in support of objections have been filed. All briefs shall be filed in the number and form required for original actions by the Rules of Practice of the Supreme Court of Ohio.

(D) **Supreme Court Proceedings** After a hearing on objections, or if objections are not filed within the prescribed time, the Supreme Court shall enter an order as it finds proper. If the Court rejects the sanction contained in a certified report submitted pursuant to Section 11 of the Rules and Regulations Governing Procedure on Complaints and Hearings Before the Board of Commissioners on Grievances and Discipline, the Court shall remand the matter to the board for a hearing. Unless otherwise ordered by the court, any disciplinary order or order accepting resignation shall be effective on the date that the order is announced by the court. The order may provide for reimbursement of costs and expenses incurred by the Board or panels. An order imposing a suspension for an indefinite period or for a period of six months to two years may allow full or partial credit for any period of suspension imposed under Section 5 of this rule.

(1) Notice. Upon the entry of any disciplinary order pursuant to this rule or the acceptance of a resignation from the practice of law, the Clerk of the Supreme Court shall mail certified copies of the entry or acceptance to counsel of record, to the Board, to respondent at his or her last known address, to the Disciplinary Counsel, to the Certified Grievance Committee for and the local bar association of the county or counties in which the respondent resides and maintains his or her office, and the county or counties from which the complaint arose, to the Ohio State Bar Association, to the administrative judge of the court of common pleas for each county in which the respondent resides or maintains an office, and to the chief judges of the United States District Courts in Ohio, the United States Court of Appeals for the Sixth Circuit, and to the Supreme Court of the United States.

(2) Publication. The Supreme Court Reporter shall publish any disciplinary order or acceptance of a resignation from the practice of law entered by the Supreme Court under this rule in the Ohio Official Reports, the Ohio State Bar Association Report, and in a publication, if any, of the local bar association. The publication shall include the citation of the case in which the disciplinary order or the acceptance of a resignation was issued. Publication also shall be made in a local newspaper having the largest general circulation in the county or counties designated by the Board. This publication shall be in the form of a paid legal advertisement, in a style and size commensurate with legal advertisements, and shall be published three times within the thirty days following the order of the Supreme Court. Publication fees shall be assessed against the respondent as part of the costs.

(E) **Duties of a Disbarred or Suspended Attorney**

(1) In its order disbarring or suspending an attorney or in any order pertaining to the resignation of an attorney, the Supreme Court shall include a time limit, not to exceed thirty days, within which the disqualified attorney shall do all of the following:

(a) Notify all clients being represented in pending matters and any co-counsel of his or her disbarment, suspension, or resignation and consequent disqualification to act as an attorney after the effective date of the order, and, in the absence of co-counsel, notify the clients to seek legal service elsewhere, calling attention to any urgency in seeking the substitution of another attorney in his or her place;

(b) Regardless of any fees or expenses due the attorney, deliver to all clients being represented in pending matters any papers or other property pertaining to the client, or notify the clients or co-counsel, if any, of a suitable time and place where the papers or other property may be obtained, calling attention to any urgency for obtaining the papers or other property;

(c) Refund any part of any fees or expenses paid in advance that are unearned or not paid, and account for any trust money or property in his or her possession or control;

(d) Notify opposing counsel in pending litigation or, in the absence of counsel, the adverse parties, of his or her disqualification or resignation to act as an attorney after the effective date of the disqualification order, and file a notice of disqualification of counsel with the court or agency before which the litigation is pending for inclusion in the respective file or files.

(2) All notices required by a disciplinary order of the Supreme Court shall be sent by certified mail and contain a return address where communications may be directed to the disqualified attorney.

(3) Within the time limit prescribed by the Supreme Court, the disqualified attorney shall file with the Clerk of the Supreme Court and the Disciplinary Counsel an affidavit showing compliance with the order entered pursuant to this rule and proof of service of notices required by the order. The affidavit also shall set forth the address where the affiant may receive communications and the disqualified attorney shall inform the Clerk and the Disciplinary Counsel of any subsequent change in address.

(4) A disqualified attorney shall maintain a record of the various steps taken pursuant to the order entered by the Supreme Court so that, in any subsequent proceeding, proof of compliance with the order will be available for receipt in evidence.

(F) **Appointed Attorney to Inventory and Protect Clients** Whenever an attorney is suspended for mental illness or pursuant to Section 5a of this rule, cannot be found in the jurisdiction for a period of sixty days or more or such shorter time as ordered by the Supreme Court, dies, refuses to meet or work with a significant number of clients for a period of sixty days or more, or fails to comply with division (E) of this section, and no partner, executor, or other responsible party capable of conducting the attorney's affairs is available and willing to assume appropriate responsibility, the Disciplinary Counsel or chair of a Certified Grievance Committee may appoint an attorney or attorneys to inventory the files of the attorney and take action, including action set forth in division (E) of this section, as is necessary to protect the interest of clients of the attorney. Upon approval by the Secretary of the Board, reasonable fees may be paid to the appointed attorney or attorneys from the Attorney Registration Fund. Except as necessary to carry out the order of appointment by the Disciplinary Counsel or chair of a

Certified Grievance Committee, the appointed attorney or attorneys shall not disclose any information contained in inventoried files without the written consent of the client to whom the files relate. An appointed attorney may not represent that client.

(G)(1) **Employment of a Disqualified or Suspended Attorney.** A disqualified or suspended attorney subject to division (G) of this rule shall not do either of the following:

(a) Have any direct client contact, other than serving as an observer in any meeting, hearing or interaction between an attorney and a client;

(b) Receive, disburse, or otherwise handle client trust funds or property.

(2) On or after September 1, 2008, a disqualified attorney subject to division (G) of this rule shall not enter into an employment, contractual, or consulting relationship with an attorney or law firm with which the disqualified attorney was associated as a partner, shareholder, member, or employee at the time the attorney engaged in misconduct that resulted in his or her disqualification from the practice of law.

(3) An attorney or law firm seeking to enter into an employment, contractual, or consulting relationship with a disqualified or suspended attorney shall register the employment, contractual, or consulting relationship with the Office of Disciplinary Counsel. The registration shall be on a form provided by the Office of Disciplinary Counsel and shall include all of the following:

(a) The name of and contact information for the disqualified or suspended attorney;

(b) The name of and contact information for the attorney or law firm seeking to enter into the relationship with the disqualified or suspended attorney;

(c) The name of and contact information for the attorney responsible for directly supervising the disqualified or suspended attorney, if different than the attorney identified in division (G)(3)(b) of this section;

(d) The capacity in which the disqualified or suspended attorney will be employed, including a description of duties to be performed or services to be provided;

(e) An affidavit executed by either the attorney filing the registration or the supervising attorney indicating that the attorney has read the Supreme Court's order disbarring, accepting the resignation of, or suspending the attorney to be employed and understands the limitations contained in that order;

(f) Any other information considered necessary by the Office of Disciplinary Counsel.

(4) Upon receipt of a completed registration form, the Office of Disciplinary Counsel shall send a written acknowledgement to the attorney or law firm that filed the registration form and any supervising attorney identified on the form. Upon receipt of the written acknowledgement, the employment, contractual, or consulting relationship may commence.

(5) An attorney who registers the employment of a disqualified or suspended attorney shall file an amended registration form with the Office of Disciplinary Counsel when there is any material change in the information provided on a prior registration form and

shall notify the Office of Disciplinary Counsel upon termination of the employment, contractual, or consulting relationship.

(6) If a disqualified or suspended attorney will perform work or provide services in connection with any client matter, the employing attorney or law firm shall inform the client of the status of the disqualified or suspended attorney. The notice shall be in writing and provided to the client before the disqualified or suspended attorney performs any work or provides any services in connection with the client matter.

(H) **Definition** As used in this section, "disqualified attorney" means a former attorney who has been disbarred or who has resigned with discipline pending.

SECTION 9. Probation Procedures

(A) **Supervision** If the disciplinary order entered by the Supreme Court imposes a term of probation, the relator shall do all of the following:

(1) Supervise the term and conditions of probation;

(2) Maintain the probation file;

(3) Appoint, in any manner it considers appropriate, one or more monitoring attorneys who are admitted to the practice of law in Ohio and in good standing and are not members of a Certified Grievance Committee or counsel for the relator and select one or more replacement monitoring attorneys, if necessary;

(4) Receive reports from the monitoring attorneys;

(5) Investigate reports of probation violations.

(6) If the probation involves recovery from substance abuse, select as one of the monitoring attorneys a person designated by a committee or subcommittee of a bar association, or by a non-profit corporation established by a bar association, designed to assist lawyers with substance abuse problems, which person shall satisfy the requirements of division (A)(3) of this section and who shall monitor compliance with only that portion of the term of probation involving recovery from substance abuse.

(B) **Monitoring** The monitoring attorney shall, with respect to those aspects of the terms of probation assigned to that attorney, do all of the following:

(1) Monitor compliance by the respondent with the conditions of probation imposed by the Supreme Court;

(2) File with the relator, at least quarterly or as otherwise determined by the relator, written, certified reports regarding the status of the respondent and compliance with the conditions of probation;

(3) Immediately report to the relator any violations by the respondent of the conditions of probation.

(C) Duties of Respondent. The respondent shall do all of the following:

(1) Have a personal meeting with the monitoring attorneys at least once each month during the first year of probation, and at least quarterly thereafter, unless the monitoring attorneys require more frequent meetings;

(2) Provide the monitoring attorneys with a written release or waiver, on a form approved by the Board, for use in verifying compliance regarding medical, psychological, substance abuse, or other treatment and attendance at self-help programs;

(3) Cooperate fully with the efforts of each monitor-

ing attorney to monitor the respondent's compliance.

(D) **Termination of Probation** At the expiration of the probation period, the respondent shall apply for termination of probation. The application shall be in writing and filed with the Clerk of the Supreme Court. The application shall indicate the date probation was ordered, include an affidavit by respondent stating that the respondent has complied with the conditions of probation, indicate whether any formal disciplinary proceedings are pending against the respondent, and request termination of probation. The Supreme Court shall order the termination of probation if all costs of the proceedings as ordered by the Supreme Court have been paid, the respondent has complied with the conditions of probation, and no formal disciplinary proceedings are pending against the respondent. The Clerk of the Supreme Court shall provide notice of the termination of probation to all persons and organizations who received copies of the disciplinary order pursuant to Section 8(D)(1) of this rule.

(E) **Violation of Probation; Authority and Duty of Relator** The relator immediately shall investigate any report of a violation of the conditions of probation by the respondent. If it finds probable cause to believe that a significant or continuing violation of the conditions of probation has occurred, it shall notify the respondent of the report of probation violation and provide an opportunity to respond to the report. Thereafter, if warranted, the relator shall file a petition for the revocation of probation, reinstatement of any stayed suspension, and citation for contempt with the Secretary of the Board within thirty days after its receipt of the report, in the same manner as provided in Section 4(I)(8) of this rule. If, upon investigation of a report of a violation of probation, the relator determines that the filing of a petition for revocation of probation with the Secretary of the Board is not warranted, the person reporting the alleged violation of probation shall be notified in writing of that determination.

(F) **Duty of the Board upon Filing of Petition** Upon receipt of a petition for revocation of probation, the Secretary of the Board shall send a copy of the petition by certified mail to the respondent with a notice requiring the respondent to file, within ten days after the mailing of the notice, six copies of the respondent's answer and serve copies on counsel of record. Extensions of time for the filing of the answer may be granted by the Secretary of the Board for good cause shown.

(G) **Hearing by Panel; Motion for Default**

(1) After the respondent has filed an answer, a formal hearing shall be held by a panel of three members of the Board appointed in the same manner as provided in Section 6(D)(3) of this rule. The panel shall conduct a hearing only on the issue of probation violation within thirty days after the answer date set forth in the notice to the respondent of the filing of the petition or any extension of the answer date.

(2) If no answer has been filed by the respondent within ten days after the answer date set forth in the notice to the respondent of the filing of the petition or any extension of the answer date, relator shall file a motion for default in accordance with Section 6(F) of

this rule. If a motion for default is granted, the panel forthwith shall make its certified report to the Supreme Court, pursuant to division (H) of this section.

(H) **Certification of Panel Report** If the panel determines by clear and convincing evidence that the respondent is guilty of a significant or continuing violation of the conditions of probation, the panel shall make a certified report of the proceedings before it, including findings of fact and recommendations, and shall file the report, together with the transcript of testimony taken or, in the case of a default, the documentary evidence received, and an itemized statement of the actual and necessary expenses incurred in connection with the proceedings, with the Clerk of the Supreme Court. The panel promptly shall notify the respondent and all counsel of record of its action, enclosing with the notice a copy of the findings of fact and recommendations and a copy of the statement of the actual and necessary expenses incurred. If the panel finds that the evidence is insufficient to support a charge of a violation of probation, the panel shall order that the petition for revocation of probation be dismissed. The panel shall report its action to the Secretary of the Board who shall give written notice of the action taken to those persons and organizations identified in Section 6(H) of this rule.

(I) **Reinstatement of Stayed Suspension** On the filing of the final certified report by the panel, the Supreme Court may issue to the respondent an order reinstating any period of suspension previously stayed by the Supreme Court, pending the entry of a final order by the Supreme Court. Notice of an order reinstating any period of suspension previously stayed shall be served personally or by certified mail by the Clerk of the Supreme Court on the respondent and all counsel of record.

(J) **Show Cause Order; Objections; Answer Briefs** On the filing of the final certified report of the panel, the Supreme Court shall issue to the respondent an order to show cause in accordance with Section 8(A) of this rule. Any response or objections to the order to show cause, and any answer briefs, shall be filed in accordance with Sections 8(B) and (C) of this rule.

(K) **Review by Court** After a hearing on objections, or if objections are not filed within the prescribed time, the Supreme Court shall enter an order as it finds proper in accordance with Section 8(D) of this rule. If the Supreme Court finds that the respondent has not violated the conditions of probation, the Supreme Court shall issue an order that does all of the following:

(1) Dismisses the matter;

(2) Reinstates the respondent to the practice of law, if the Supreme Court suspended the respondent pursuant to division (I) of this section;

(3) Reinstates any remaining period of probation, subject to any full or partial credit allowed by the Supreme Court for any period of suspension imposed under division (I) of this section.

(L) **Reimbursement of Expenses** A monitoring attorney may be reimbursed from the Attorney Registration Fund for direct expenses incurred by the monitoring attorney in performing the obligations imposed on the monitoring attorney by this section. Reimbursement shall be limited to necessary costs for copies of documents, travel expenses, postage, and long distance telephone charges. No reimbursement shall be allowed for the cost of the time of the monitoring attorney or other personnel in discharging these obligations. Reimbursement shall be made on submission to the Secretary of the Board of proof of expenditures.

SECTION 10. Reinstatement Proceedings

(A) **Suspension; Reinstatement** Upon dissolution of an interim remedial suspension imposed pursuant to Section 5a of this rule or expiration of a suspension for a period of six months to two years, including any period that the order of the Supreme Court has allowed as a credit for a suspension imposed under Section 5 of this rule, the respondent may apply for reinstatement to the practice of law. The application shall be in writing and twelve copies shall be filed with the Clerk of the Supreme Court. The application shall include the date the suspension was ordered and a request for reinstatement. The application shall be accompanied by an affidavit executed by the respondent indicating whether any formal disciplinary proceedings are pending against the respondent and whether the respondent has complied with the continuing legal education requirements of Gov. Bar R. X, Section 3(G). The Supreme Court shall order the respondent reinstated if all of the following conditions are satisfied:

(1) All costs of the proceedings as ordered by the Supreme Court have been paid;

(2) The respondent has complied with the order of suspension;

(3) The respondent has complied with the continuing legal education requirements of Gov. Bar R. X, Section 3(G);

(4) No formal disciplinary proceedings are pending against the respondent.

The Clerk of the Supreme Court shall provide notice of the reinstatement to all persons or organizations who receive copies of the Supreme Court disciplinary order of suspension.

(B) Petition for Reinstatement. No petition for reinstatement to the practice of law may be filed or entertained by the Supreme Court within two years of either of the following:

(1) The entry of an order suspending the petitioner from the practice of law for an indefinite period, including any period that the order of the Supreme Court imposing the suspension has allowed as a credit for a suspension imposed under Section 5 of this rule;

(2) The denial of a petition for reinstatement to the practice of law filed by the petitioner.

(C) **Contents of Petition for Reinstatement** Except as provided in division (B) of this section, a person who has been suspended from the practice of law for an indefinite period and who wishes to be reinstated may file a verified petition and twenty copies of the petition with the Clerk of the Supreme Court. The petition shall include all of the following:

(1) The date on which the suspension was ordered and, if there was a reported opinion, the volume and page of the *Ohio Official Reports* where the opinion appears;

(2) The dates on which all prior petitions for rein-

statement were filed and denied or granted;

(3) The names of all persons and organizations, except the petitioner and the Board, who were or would be entitled under this rule to receive from the Clerk of the Supreme Court certified copies of the disciplinary order of the Supreme Court against petitioner resulting in his or her suspension, the name of the bar association of the county or counties in which he or she resides at the time of the filing of the petition and of each county in which he or she proposes to maintain an office if reinstated, and the Ohio State Bar Association;

(4) A statement that the petitioner has complied with the continuing legal education requirements of Gov. Bar R. X, Section 3(G);

(5) The facts upon which the petitioner relies to establish by clear and convincing evidence that he or she possesses all the mental, educational, and moral qualifications that were required of an applicant for admission to the practice of law in Ohio at the time of his or her original admission and that he or she is now a proper person to be readmitted to the practice of law in Ohio, notwithstanding the previous disciplinary action.

(D) **Costs to be Deposited with Petition for Reinstatement** A petition for reinstatement shall be accompanied by a deposit, in an amount fixed by the Clerk, for probable costs and expenses to be incurred in connection with the proceedings. The costs shall include any amounts unpaid under any prior order of the Supreme Court and any amounts owed to the Clients' Security Fund of Ohio for reimbursement of an award made pursuant to Gov. Bar R. VIII as the result of petitioner's misconduct.

(E) **Requisites for Reinstatement** The petitioner shall not be reinstated unless he or she establishes all of the following by clear and convincing evidence to the satisfaction of the panel hearing the petition for reinstatement:

(1) That the petitioner has made appropriate restitution to the persons who were harmed by his or her misconduct;

(2) That the petitioner possesses all of the mental, educational, and moral qualifications that were required of an applicant for admission to the practice of law in Ohio at the time of his or her original admission;

(3) That the petitioner has complied with the continuing legal education requirements of Gov. Bar R. X, Section 3(F);

(4) That the petitioner is now a proper person to be readmitted to the practice of law in Ohio, notwithstanding the previous disciplinary action.

The order of reinstatement may be subject to conditions the Supreme Court considers appropriate including, but not limited to, requiring the petitioner to serve a period of probation on conditions the Supreme Court determines and requiring the petitioner to subsequently take and pass a regular bar examination of the Supreme Court and take the oath of office.

(F) **Petition for Reinstatement Referred to Board** Unless denied forthwith for insufficiency in form or substance, the Clerk shall forward five copies of the petition to the Secretary of the Board. The Board shall conduct a hearing or hearings and take and report evidence relevant to the rehabilitation of the petitioner and his or her possession of all the mental, educational, and moral qualifications required of an applicant for admission to the practice of law in Ohio at the time of his or her original admission.

(G) **Hearing of Petition; Appeal**

(1) Appointment of Panel. The Secretary, by lot, shall appoint a hearing panel of three board members, none of whom shall be a resident of the appellate district in which the petitioner resides or of the appellate district in which the petitioner resided at the time of suspension. The Secretary shall appoint an attorney or judge member as chair and the panel shall conduct a hearing or hearings upon the petition.

(2) Notice; Hearing. The Board shall provide reasonable notice of any hearing to the petitioner or counsel for the petitioner and to all persons or organizations referred to in division (C)(3) of this section. Hearings shall be public and any interested person, member of the bar, and the Disciplinary Counsel may appear before the hearing panel in support of or opposition to the petition.

(3) Referral to Disciplinary Counsel. If a Certified Grievance Committee of a bar association referred to in division (C)(3) of this section determines that matters relating to petitioner's qualifications for reinstatement are sufficiently serious and complex as to require the assistance of Disciplinary Counsel, the chair of the committee shall direct a written request for assistance to the Disciplinary Counsel. The Disciplinary Counsel shall investigate all referred matters and report the results of the investigation to the committee that requested it.

(4) Panel Report. The hearing panel shall make and certify a report to the Board of the proceedings before it, including its findings of fact and recommendations. All proceedings before the panel and the Board, whenever appropriate, shall be governed by the provisions of this rule governing disciplinary proceedings, including proceedings in the Supreme Court for an issuance of an order to show cause why the final report of the Board should not be confirmed.

(5) Conditional Grant; Denial; Appeal. The Board may recommend that the petitioner be required to take and pass a regular bar examination of the Supreme Court as a condition to readmission. If the final report recommends denial of the petition, the petitioner shall have ten days from receipt of notice of the date of filing the report to file objections and a brief in support of the objections.

(6) Grant of Petition; Appeal. If the final report recommends granting the petition, any person or organization referred to in division (C)(3) of this section shall have ten days from the receipt of notice of filing of the report to file objections to the recommendations and a brief in support of the objections. The Supreme Court shall enter an appropriate order, which may include provisions for reimbursement of the costs and expenses incurred in connection with the proceedings.

SECTION 11. Applicability of Rules; Regulations; Special Service; Contempt; Confidentiality; Reciprocal Discipline

(A) Applicability of Rules; Regulations of Board

(1) The Board and hearing panels shall follow the Ohio Rules of Civil Procedure and the Ohio Rules of Evidence wherever practicable unless a specific provision of this rule or Board hearing procedures and guidelines provides otherwise.

(2) With the prior approval of the Supreme Court, the Board may adopt regulations consistent with this rule.

(3) With the prior approval of the Supreme Court, the Board shall adopt regulations that contain all of the following:

(a) Procedures for regularly reviewing the performance of Certified Grievance Committees, identifying Certified Grievance Committees that are not in compliance with the standards set forth in this rule, and for decertifying a Certified Grievance Committee that fails to improve its performance after being notified of noncompliance;

(b) Time guidelines for the processing of disciplinary cases pending before the Board and panels of the Board;

(c) Procedures to allow the Board to make a recommendation of discipline, other than an indefinite suspension or disbarment, where the Disciplinary Counsel or Certified Grievance Committee and the respondent enter into a written agreement in which the respondent admits to the existence of a disciplinary violation.

(B) Clerk is Agent for Service of Notices on Nonresident Justice, Judge, or Attorney Any nonresident of this state, having been admitted as an attorney by the rules of the Supreme Court, or any resident of this state, having been admitted as an attorney by the rules of the Supreme Court, who subsequently becomes a nonresident or conceals his or her whereabouts, by such admission to the practice of law within this state makes the Clerk of the Supreme Court his or her agent for the service of any notice provided for in any proceeding instituted against such justice, judge, or attorney, pursuant to this rule.

(C) Effect of Refusal to Testify The refusal or neglect of a person subpoenaed as a witness to obey a subpoena, to attend, to be sworn or to affirm, or to answer any proper question shall be considered a contempt of the Supreme Court and shall be punishable accordingly.

(D) Rule to be Liberally Construed The process and procedure under this rule and regulations approved by the Supreme Court shall be as summary as reasonably may be. Amendments to any complaint, notice, answer, objections, report, or order to show cause may be made at any time prior to final order of the Supreme Court. The party affected by an amendment shall be given reasonable opportunity to meet any new matter presented. No investigation or procedure shall be held to be invalid by reason of any nonprejudicial irregularity or for any error not resulting in a miscarriage of justice. This rule and regulations relating to investigation and proceedings involving complaints of misconduct and petitions for reinstatement shall be construed liberally for the protection of the public, the courts, and the legal profession and shall apply to all pending investigations and complaints so far as may be practicable and to all future investigations, complaints, and petitions whether the conduct involved occurred prior or subsequent to the amendment of this rule. To the extent that application of this amended rule to pending proceedings may not be practicable, the regulations in force at the time this amended rule became effective shall continue to apply.

(E) Proceedings Private; Public

(1) All proceedings and documents relating to review and investigation of grievances made under these rules shall be private except as follows:

(a) Where the respondent requests in writing that they be public;

(b) Where the respondent voluntarily waives privacy of the proceedings.

(c) Where the proceedings reveal reasonable cause to believe that respondent is or may be addicted to alcohol or other chemicals, is abusing the use of alcohol or other chemicals, or may be experiencing a mental health condition or problem that is substantially impairing the respondent's ability to practice law, the information giving rise to this belief shall be communicated to a committee or subcommittee of a bar association, or to an executive officer or employee of a nonprofit corporation established by a bar association, designed to assist lawyers with substance abuse or mental health problems.

(d) Where, in the course of an investigation by the Office of Disciplinary Counsel or a certified grievance committee, it is found that a person involved in the investigation may have violated federal or state criminal statutes, the entity conducting the investigation shall notify the appropriate law enforcement or prosecutorial authority of the alleged criminal violation.

(2)(a) From the time a complaint has been certified to the Secretary of the Board by a probable cause panel, the complaint and all subsequent proceedings in connection with the complaint shall be public; except that deliberations by the panel and deliberations by the Board shall be confidential and the recommendations of the Board shall be private until filed with the Supreme Court. The Board-approved ADR process shall be confidential. Any knowledge obtained by a mediator or facilitator shall be privileged for all purposes under Rule 8.3 of the Ohio Rules of Professional Conduct, provided the knowledge was obtained while the mediator or facilitator was acting as a mediator or facilitator.

(b) Proceedings by a Certified Grievance Committee and Disciplinary Counsel shall be private until certified by a probable cause panel; except that deliberations by a Certified Grievance Committee, Disciplinary Counsel, panel, or Board, shall be confidential.

(c) As used in Section 11 of this rule, the terms "private" and "confidential" shall have the following meanings:

(i) "Private" acknowledges the right of the respondent to the right of privacy as to the proceedings relative to an uncertified complaint, which may be waived by the respondent as provided in Section 11(E)(1) of this rule;

(ii) "Confidential" acknowledges the oath of office of section 11(e)(4) of this rule, acknowledges the necessity of confidentiality in the deliberations stage of the proceedings of the Certified Grievance Committee, Disciplinary Counsel, panel, and Board, and applies to members and employees of the Certified Grievance Committee, Disciplinary Counsel, panel, and Board, such that deliberations cannot be disclosed or waived by anyone for any reason.

(3) Notwithstanding the other provisions of this rule, the respondent's reply to the grievance, made during the course of an investigation by Disciplinary Counsel or a Certified Grievance Committee, shall be furnished to the grievant without waiving any other right to privacy or confidentiality provided by this rule. If the respondent specifically requests, in writing, to the Disciplinary Counsel or Certified Grievance Committee that the reply not be furnished to the grievant, the Disciplinary Counsel or Certified Grievance Committee shall not furnish the reply to the grievant. Release to the grievant of the respondent's reply is, nevertheless, encouraged and consistent with the liberal construction of this rule for the protection of the public stated in Section 11(D) of this rule.

(4) Prior to taking office, all members and employees of the Board, all members of any Certified Grievance Committee, the Disciplinary Counsel, and all employees of the Office of Disciplinary Counsel shall swear or affirm that they will abide by these rules and protect the privacy of the proceedings, documents, and confidentiality of the deliberations, relating to those proceedings.

(F) Reciprocal Discipline

(1) **Notification of Disciplinary Action** Within thirty days of the issuance of a disciplinary order in another jurisdiction, an attorney admitted to the practice of law in Ohio shall provide written notification to the Disciplinary Counsel and the Clerk of the Supreme Court of the action. Upon receiving notice from the attorney or another party that an attorney admitted to the practice of law in Ohio has been subjected to discipline in another jurisdiction, the Disciplinary Counsel shall obtain a certified copy of the disciplinary order and file the copy with the Clerk of the Supreme Court.

(2) **Show Cause Order** Upon receipt of a certified copy of an order demonstrating that an attorney admitted to the practice of law in Ohio has been subjected to discipline in another jurisdiction, the Supreme Court shall issue a notice directed to the attorney containing both of the following:

(a) A copy of the order from the other jurisdiction;

(b) An order directing that the attorney notify the Supreme Court, within twenty days from the service of notice, of any claim by the attorney predicated upon the grounds set forth in division (F)(4) of this section that the imposition of the identical or comparable discipline in Ohio would be unwarranted and the reasons for that claim.

(3) **Deferral** If the discipline imposed in the other jurisdiction has been stayed, any reciprocal discipline imposed in Ohio shall be deferred until the stay expires.

(4) **Disposition**

(a) Thirty days after service of the notice issued pursuant to division (F)(2) of this section, the Supreme Court shall impose the identical or comparable discipline imposed in the other jurisdiction, unless the attorney proves either of the following by clear and convincing evidence:

(i) A lack of jurisdiction or fraud in the other jurisdiction's disciplinary proceeding;

(ii) That the misconduct established warrants substantially different discipline in Ohio.

(b) Reciprocal discipline may be imposed even if the term of the attorney's discipline in the other jurisdiction has expired. In determining whether to impose reciprocal discipline after the attorney's discipline in the other jurisdiction has expired, the Supreme Court may consider whether the attorney provided timely written notification pursuant to division (F)(1) of this section and, if the attorney delayed in providing written notification, whether the delay in notification was caused by factors beyond the attorney's control.

(c) Reciprocal discipline shall be effective on the date it is announced by the Supreme Court.

(5) **Res Judicata** In all other respects, a final adjudication in another jurisdiction that an attorney has been subjected to discipline shall establish conclusively the misconduct for purposes of a disciplinary proceeding in Ohio.

(6) **Enhancement of Sanction** If an attorney fails to report to the Disciplinary Counsel and to the Clerk of the Supreme Court that he or she has been subjected to discipline in another jurisdiction, the Supreme Court may enhance the sanction that it would have imposed had the attorney complied with division (F)(1) of this section.

(7) **Court Discretion** The Supreme Court may make its determination under this section from the pleadings filed, or may permit or require briefs or a hearing or both.

(G) **Note:** Gov. Bar R. V, Section 11(G) [Resignation from the Practice of Law] is repealed in its entirety, effective September 1, 2007. The provisions of former Gov. Bar R. V, Section 11(G) have been replaced by Gov. Bar R. VI, Section 6 [Retirement or Resignation from the Practice of Law], effective September 1, 2007.

Existing Gov. Bar R. V, Sections 12 to 50, are repealed.

History: Amended, eff 10-1-86; 9-1-87; 1-1-88; 3-16-88; 7-27-88; 1-1-89; 10-11-89; 11-8-89; 12-5-89; 9-1-90; 7-1-92; 9-1-95; 11-1-95; 7-1-96; 9-1-96; 4-21-97; 10-1-97; 11-3-97; 1-20-98; 11-2-98; 9-1-99; 5-8-00; 5-1-01; 2-1-03; 1-12-04; 2-1-07, 09/01/07; 01/01/08; 04/01/08, 09/01/08.

NOTES TO DECISIONS

ANALYSIS

Failure to cooperate with investigation
Felony conviction
Jurisdiction
Resignation with disciplinary action pending

Failure to cooperate with investigation

Attorney was suspended from the practice of law for six months based on findings that he neglected a client's case, attempted to cover up the neglect, failed to return the client's file on request, and failed to cooperate in the ensuing disciplinary investigation, in violation of former Ohio Code Prof. Resp. 9-102(B)(4), 6-101(A)(3), and 1-102(A)(4), and Ohio Sup. Ct. R. Gov't Bar V(4)(G), because the record amply justified the conclusions that the attorney neglected to appropriately advise his client of the proceedings in its case and then fabricated one or more letters to conceal his neglect. The mitigating factors did not outweigh the aggravating effect of having submitted false evidence and having acted out of self-interest in trying to cover up his misconduct. Disciplinary Counsel v. Broeren, — Ohio St. 3d —, 2007 Ohio 5251, — N.E. 2d —, 2007 Ohio LEXIS 2525 (Oct. 10, 2007).

Felony conviction

Attorney who was convicted of a felony conviction was suspended from the practice of law in Ohio pursuant to Ohio Sup. Ct. R. Gov't Bar V(5)(A)(4), he was instructed to complete continuing legal education under Ohio Sup. Ct. R. Gov't Bar X(3)(G), and he was directed as to how to handle clients, fees, files, and opposing counsel. In re Howard, 114 Ohio St. 3d 1515, — Ohio App. 3d —, 2007 Ohio 4425, 872 N.E. 2d 955, 2007 Ohio LEXIS 2163 (Aug. 30, 2007).

Jurisdiction

As the Ohio Board of Commissioners on Grievances and Discipline of the Supreme Court had jurisdiction over the alleged misconduct of judges pursuant to Ohio Sup. Ct. R. Gov't Bar V, §§ 1, 2, an inmate's claim in his civil action that the judge violated various canons of judicial conduct and that he violated local court rules lacked merit for purposes of an appeal of the dismissal of the inmate's action for failure to prosecute. Brown v. Weidner, — Ohio App. 3d —, 2006 Ohio 6852, — N.E. 2d —, 2006 Ohio App. LEXIS 6765 (Dec. 26, 2006).

Resignation with disciplinary action pending

Upon an attorney's affidavit of resignation and waiver pursuant to Ohio Sup. Ct. R. Gov't Bar V(11)(G)(1), the Ohio Supreme Court accepted the resignation with disciplinary action pending, and it directed the attorney regarding the return of client files, property, and funds, and the notification to clients and counsel of his status. In re Schnitkey, 115 Ohio St. 3d 1201, 2007 Ohio 4841, 873 N.E. 2d 894, 2007 Ohio LEXIS 2223 (Aug. 30, 2007).

RULE VI.
REGISTRATION OF ATTORNEYS

SECTION 1. Certificate of Registration and Registration Fee; Active Attorneys

(A) On or before the first day of September in each odd-numbered year, each attorney who is admitted to the practice of law in Ohio shall file with the Office of Attorney Services of the Supreme Court a Certificate of Registration furnished by the Office of Attorney Services together with a registration fee of three hundred fifty dollars. An attorney who registers and pays the fee required under this section shall be granted active status.

(B) An attorney admitted to the practice of law in Ohio during the first twelve months of a biennial registration period shall file a Certificate of Registration within thirty days of the date of admission and pay the three hundred fifty dollar registration fee. An attorney admitted to the practice of law in Ohio during the second twelve months of a biennial registration period and prior to the first day of May of an odd-numbered year shall file a Certificate of Registration

within thirty days of the date of admission and pay a registration fee of one hundred seventy-five dollars. An attorney admitted to the practice of law in Ohio on or after the first day of May of an odd-numbered year shall file a Certificate of Registration within thirty days of the date of admission but shall not be required to pay a registration fee for the biennial registration period in which admission occurs.

(C) Each attorney who is admitted to the practice of law in Ohio shall keep informed of the registration requirements, deadlines, and fees. Failure to receive notice that the registration and the fee are due or notice of noncompliance shall not affect any action taken under this rule.

(D) Each attorney who is registered for active status shall keep the Office of Attorney Services apprised of the attorney's current residence address and office address and office telephone number and shall notify the Office of Attorney Services of any change in the information on the Certificate of Registration.

(E) For the purpose of compiling demographic data regarding attorneys registered in Ohio, the Office of Attorney Services, at the Court's direction, may require each attorney to provide additional identifying information, including gender, race, and ethnicity, for the attorney's registration record. This information may be requested in the Certificate of Registration or on a separate form.

(F)(1) For the purpose of compiling information regarding interest-bearing trust accounts established pursuant to section 3953.231 or 4705.09 of the Revised Code, the Office of Attorney Services shall require each attorney to provide the following information on the Certificate of Registration:

(a) The number of each trust or escrow account established by the attorney and the name and location of the financial institution with which each account is established;

(b) If the attorney is affiliated with a law firm, legal professional association, corporation, legal clinic, limited liability company, or registered partnership having limited liability, or owns, operates, or owns an interest in a business that provides a law-related service, the number of each trust or escrow account established by the attorney and the name and location of the financial institution with which each account is established;

(c) If the attorney is not required to maintain an interest-bearing trust or escrow account, information as to the basis for the exemption.

(2) The Office of Attorney Services shall forward the information required by division (F) of this section to the Ohio Legal Assistance Foundation, which shall maintain the information consistent with division (B) of section 4705.10 of the Revised Code and the rules of the Foundation.

(G) Except for residence addresses, residence telephone numbers, e-mail addresses, and social security numbers, information maintained by the Office of Attorney Services, provided to another office of the Supreme Court, or provided to the Ohio Legal Assistance Foundation pursuant to division (F) of this section shall be a public record. The residence address of an attorney shall be considered a public record if the attorney has not provided a valid office address to the Office of Attorney Services.

SECTION 2. Inactive Attorneys

(A) An attorney who is admitted to the practice of law in Ohio may be granted inactive status by registering as inactive with the Office of Attorney Services. Until the attorney requests and is granted reinstatement of active status, an inactive attorney shall not be entitled to practice law in Ohio; hold himself or herself out as authorized to practice law in Ohio; hold nonfederal judicial office in Ohio; occupy a nonfederal position in this state in which the attorney is called upon to give legal advice or counsel or to examine the law or pass upon the legal effect of any act, document, or law; be employed in the Ohio judicial system in a position required to be held by an attorney; or practice before any nonfederal court or agency in this state on behalf of any person except himself or herself.

(B) An attorney who is registered for inactive status is not required to file a biennial Certificate of Registration but shall keep the Office of Attorney Services apprised of the attorney's current residence and office address and office telephone number and notify the Office of Attorney Services of any change in the information provided on the most recent Certificate of Registration filed by the attorney.

(C) A law firm may include the name of an inactive attorney on its letterhead if the name was included prior to the time the attorney registered for inactive status, provided the attorney is not suspended from the practice of law and the letterhead includes a designation that the attorney is "inactive." An inactive attorney shall not be listed as "of counsel" or otherwise be represented as being able to engage in the practice of law.

SECTION 3. Attorneys not Admitted in Ohio

(A) An attorney who is admitted to the practice of law in another state or in the District of Columbia, but not in Ohio, and who is employed full-time by a nongovernmental Ohio employer may register for corporate status by filing a Certificate of Registration and paying the fee as required by Section 1 of this rule. The Office of Attorney Services may require additional information and documents, including a certificate of admission and good standing from the jurisdiction in which the attorney is admitted, from an attorney who registers for corporate status. An attorney who is registered for corporate status may perform legal services in Ohio solely for a nongovernmental Ohio employer, as long as the attorney is a full-time employee of that employer. Registration under this section shall be effective and may be renewed biennially only as long as the attorney is so employed. An attorney who is granted corporate status shall promptly notify the Office of Attorney Services in writing upon termination of fulltime employment with the Ohio employer.

(B) An attorney who is registered for corporate status may not practice before any court or agency of this state on behalf of the attorney's employer or any person except himself or herself, unless granted leave by the court or agency.

(C) An attorney who is admitted to the practice of law in another state or in the District of Columbia, but not in Ohio, and who performs legal services in Ohio for his or her employer, but fails to register in compliance with this section or does not qualify to register under this section, may be referred for investigation of the unauthorized practice of law under Gov. Bar R. VII and shall be precluded from applying for admission without examination under Gov. Bar R. I.

(D) Division (A) of this section shall not apply to an attorney who is admitted to the practice of law in another state or in the District of Columbia, but not in Ohio, and who is employed by, associated with, or a partner in an Ohio law firm. Until the attorney is admitted to the practice of law in Ohio, the attorney may not practice law in Ohio, hold himself or herself out as authorized to practice law in Ohio, or practice before any nonfederal court or agency in this state on behalf of any person except himself or herself, unless granted leave by the court or agency. The law firm may include the name of the attorney on its letterhead only if the letterhead includes a designation that the attorney is not admitted in Ohio.

SECTION 4. Exemptions

The following persons are exempt from the requirements of this rule:

(A) A person certified to practice law temporarily in Ohio under Gov. Bar R. IX;

(B) A Foreign Legal Consultant registered under Gov. Bar R. XI.

SECTION 5. Failure to Register; Late Registration Fee; Summary Suspension; Reinstatement

(A) An attorney who fails to file a Certificate of Registration and pay the fee required by this rule on or before the date on which it becomes due, but does so within sixty days of that date, shall be assessed a late registration fee of fifty dollars. The late registration fee shall be in addition to the applicable registration fee.

(B) An attorney who fails to file a Certificate of Registration and pay the fees required by this rule either on a timely basis or within the late registration period provided for in division (A) of this section shall be notified of apparent noncompliance by the Office of Attorney Services. The Office of Attorney Services shall send the notice of apparent noncompliance by regular mail to the attorney at the most recent address provided by the attorney to the Office of Attorney Services. The notice shall inform the attorney that he or she will be summarily suspended from the practice of law in Ohio and not entitled to practice law in Ohio unless, on or before the date set forth in the notice, the attorney either files evidence of compliance with the requirements of this rule or comes into compliance. If the attorney does not file evidence of compliance or come into compliance on or before the date set forth in the notice, the attorney shall be summarily suspended from the practice of law in Ohio. The Office of Attorney Services shall record the suspension on the roll of attorneys and send notice of the suspension by certified mail to the attorney at the most recent address provided by the attorney to the Office of Attorney

Services. The Supreme Court Reporter shall publish notice of the suspension in the *Ohio Official Reports* and the *Ohio State Bar Association Report.*

(C) An attorney who is summarily suspended under this section shall not practice law in Ohio; hold himself or herself out as authorized to practice law in Ohio; hold nonfederal judicial office in Ohio; occupy a nonfederal position in this state in which the attorney is called upon to give legal advice or counsel or to examine the law or pass upon the legal effect of any act, document, or law; be employed in the Ohio judicial system in a position required to be held by an attorney; or practice before any nonfederal court or agency in this state on behalf of any person except himself or herself. A summarily suspended attorney who fails to comply with this provision may be referred for investigation of the unauthorized practice of law under Gov. Bar R. VII.

(D) An attorney who is summarily suspended under this section may be reinstated to the practice of law by applying for reinstatement with the Office of Attorney Services, complying with the requirements of Section 1 of this rule, including payment of the applicable registration fee, and paying a reinstatement fee of three hundred dollars. The Office of Attorney Services shall send notice of reinstatement to an attorney who meets the conditions for reinstatement and shall record the reinstatement on the roll of attorneys. The Supreme Court Reporter shall publish notice of the reinstatement in the *Ohio Official Reports* and the *Ohio State Bar Association Report.*

SECTION 6. Retirement or Resignation from the Practice of Law

(A) An attorney who wishes to retire or resign from the practice of law shall file an application with the Office of Attorney Services. The application shall be on a form furnished by the Office of Attorney Services and contain both of the following:

(1) A notarized affidavit setting forth the attorney's full name, attorney registration number, date of birth, mailing address, and all other jurisdictions and registration numbers under which the attorney practices. The affidavit shall state all of the following:

(a) The attorney wishes to retire or resign from the practice of law in the State of Ohio;

(b) The attorney fully understands that the retirement or resignation completely divests him or her of the privilege of engaging in the practice of law, and of each, any and all of the rights, privileges, and prerogatives appurtenant to the office of attorney and counselor at law;

(c) The attorney fully understands that the retirement or resignation is unconditional, final, and irrevocable.

(2) A written waiver allowing Disciplinary Counsel to review all proceedings and documents relating to review and investigation of grievances made against the attorney under the Rules for the Government of the Bar of Ohio and the Rules for the Government of the Judiciary of Ohio, and to disclose to the Supreme Court any information it deems appropriate, including, but not limited to, information that otherwise would be private pursuant to Gov. Bar R. V.

(B) The Office of Attorney Services shall refer the application to Disciplinary Counsel. Upon receipt of the referral, Disciplinary Counsel shall determine whether any disciplinary proceedings are pending against the attorney. After completing this inquiry, Disciplinary Counsel shall submit to the Office of Attorney Services a confidential report, under seal, recommending whether the application should be accepted, denied, or delayed. If Disciplinary Counsel recommends that the application be accepted, the report shall indicate whether the attorney should be designated as retired or designated as resigned with disciplinary action pending. If Disciplinary Counsel recommends that the application be denied or delayed, the report shall provide reasons for the recommendation. Upon receipt of the report from Disciplinary Counsel, the Office of Attorney Services shall do one of the following:

(1) Accept the application and designate the attorney as retired if the report recommends such acceptance and designation;

(2) File the application and the report with the Clerk of the Supreme Court if the report recommends acceptance of the application with a designation of resigned with discipline pending or the denial or deferral of the application.

(C) Upon receipt and consideration of an application filed pursuant to division (B)(2) of this section, the Supreme Court shall enter an order it deems appropriate. An order accepting an application to resign from the practice of law shall indicate that the attorney be designated as resigned with disciplinary action pending. The Clerk of the Supreme Court shall serve copies of the order as provided in Gov. Bar R. V, Section 8(D)(1).

(D) A retired attorney may be designated as "retired" on law firm letterhead if the attorney's name was included on the letterhead prior to the time that the attorney's retirement was accepted by the Supreme Court. A retired attorney shall not be listed as "of counsel" or otherwise be represented as able to engage in the practice of law in Ohio.

SECTION 7. Attorney Services Fund

(A) Except as otherwise provided in the Rules for the Government of the Bar of Ohio, all fees collected pursuant to the Rules for the Government of the Bar of Ohio shall be deposited in the Attorney Services Fund. Moneys in the fund shall be used for the following purposes:

(1) The investigation of complaints of alleged misconduct pursuant to Gov. Bar R. V or Rule II of the Supreme Court Rules for the Government of the Judiciary of Ohio and the investigation of the alleged unauthorized practice of law pursuant to Gov. Bar R. VII;

(2) To support the activities of the Clients' Security Fund established under Gov. Bar R. VIII;

(3) To support the activities of the Commission on Continuing Legal Education pursuant to Gov. Bar R. X;

(4) Any other purposes considered necessary by the Supreme Court for the government of the bar and of the judiciary of Ohio;

(5) To support any other activities related to the administration of justice considered necessary by the Supreme Court of Ohio.

(B) In addition to the purposes set forth in division (A) of this section, moneys in the Attorney Services Fund may be placed in the custody of the Treasurer of State pursuant to division (B) of section 113.05 of the Revised Code or transferred to the credit of the Supreme Court Attorney Services Fund in the state treasury. Investment earnings on moneys placed in the custody of the Treasurer shall be credited to the custodial account and investment earnings on moneys transferred to the Supreme Court Attorney Services Fund in the state treasury shall be credited to that fund.

(C) On or before the first day of November each year, the Administrative Director of the Supreme Court shall prepare and publish a report on the activity of the Attorney Services Fund.

History: Not analogous to former Rule VI, effective 2-28-72; amended, eff 1-1-81; 11-17-82; 7-1-83; 5-13-85; 7-1-86; 1-1-89; 7-1-91; 9-1-91; 1-1-92; 7-1-92; 7-1-93; 1-1-95; 7-1-95; 11-1-95; 7-1-97; 7-1-99; 11-28-00; 6-1-02; 8-19-02; 11-1-02; 7-1-03; 7-1-05; 9-1-05; 7-1-07; 9-1-07; 01-01-08; 5-1-09.

RULE VII.

UNAUTHORIZED PRACTICE OF LAW

SECTION 1. Board on the Unauthorized Practice of Law

(A) There shall be a Board on the Unauthorized Practice of Law of the Supreme Court consisting of twelve commissioners appointed by this Court. Eleven commissioners shall be attorneys admitted to the practice of law in Ohio and one commissioner shall be a person who is not admitted to the practice of law in any state. The term of office of each commissioner shall be three years, beginning on the first day of January next following the commissioner's appointment. Appointments to terms commencing on the first day of January of any year shall be made prior to the first day of December of the preceding year. A commissioner whose term has expired and who has an uncompleted assignment as a commissioner shall continue to serve for the purpose of that assignment until the assignment is concluded before the Board, and the successor commissioner shall take no part in the proceedings of the Board concerning the assignment. No commissioner shall be appointed for more than two consecutive three-year terms. Vacancies for any cause shall be filled for the unexpired term by the Justice who appointed the commissioner causing the vacancy or by the successor of that Justice. A commissioner appointed to a term of fewer than three years to fill a vacancy may be reappointed to not more than two consecutive three-year terms.

(B) Annually, the Court shall designate one commissioner as chair of the Board. A commissioner may be reappointed as chair, but shall not serve as chair for more than three consecutive one-year terms. The Administrative Director or his or her designee shall serve as the Secretary of the Board. The chair or the

Secretary may execute administrative documents on behalf of the Board. The Secretary may execute any other documents at the direction of the chair.

(C) Commissioners shall be reimbursed for expenses incurred in the performance of their official duties. Reimbursement shall be paid from the Attorney Registration Fund.

(D) Initial appointments for terms beginning January 1, 2005, shall be as follows:

(1) One attorney and one nonattorney shall be appointed for terms ending December 31, 2005. Commissioners appointed pursuant to this division shall be eligible for reappointment to two consecutive three-year terms.

(2) Two attorneys shall be appointed for terms ending December 31, 2006. Commissioners appointed pursuant to this division shall be eligible for reappointment to two consecutive three-year terms.

(3) One attorney shall be appointed for a term ending December 31, 2007. A commissioner appointed pursuant to this division shall be eligible for reappointment to one three-year term.

(4) Thereafter, appointments shall be made pursuant to division (A) of this section.

SECTION 2. Jurisdiction of Board

(A) The unauthorized practice of law is the rendering of legal services for another person by any person not admitted to practice in Ohio under Rule I and not granted active status under Rule VI, or certified under Rule II, Rule IX, or Rule XI of the Supreme Court Rules for the Government of the Bar of Ohio.

(B) The Board shall receive evidence, preserve the record, make findings, and submit recommendations concerning complaints of unauthorized practice of law.

(C) The Board may issue informal, nonbinding advisory opinions to any regularly organized bar association in this state, or Disciplinary Counsel in response to prospective or hypothetical questions of public or great general interest regarding the application of Gov. Bar R. VII and the unauthorized practice of law. The Board shall not issue advisory opinions in response to requests concerning a question that is pending before a court or a question of interest only to the person initiating the request. All requests for advisory opinions shall be submitted, in writing, to the Secretary of the Board with information and details sufficient to enable adequate consideration and determination of eligibility under these rules.

The Secretary shall acknowledge the receipt of each request for an advisory opinion and forward copies of each request to the commissioners. The Board shall select those requests that shall receive an advisory opinion. The Board may decline to issue an advisory opinion and the Secretary promptly shall notify the requesting party. An advisory opinion approved by the Board shall be issued to the requesting party over the signature of the Secretary.

Advisory opinions shall be public and distributed by the Board.

(D) **Referral of Procedural Questions to Board** In the course of an investigation, the chair of the unauthorized practice of law committee of a bar association or Disciplinary Counsel may direct a written inquiry regarding a procedural question to the chair of the Board. The inquiry shall be sent to the Secretary of the Board. The chair and the Secretary shall consult and direct a response.

SECTION 3. Referral for Investigation

The Board of Commissioners may refer to the unauthorized practice of law committee of the appropriate bar association or to Disciplinary Counsel any matters coming to its attention for investigation as provided in this rule.

SECTION 4. Application of Rule

(A) All proceedings arising out of complaints of the unauthorized practice of law shall be brought, conducted, and disposed of in accordance with the provisions of this rule. A bar association that permits the membership of any attorney practicing within the geographic area served by that association without reference to the attorney's area of practice, special interest, or other criteria and that satisfies other criteria that may be established by Board regulations may establish an unauthorized practice of law committee. Members of bar association unauthorized practice of law committees shall be attorneys admitted to the practice of law in Ohio. Unauthorized practice of law committees and Disciplinary Counsel may share information with each other regarding investigations and prosecutions. Such discussions shall be confidential and not subject to discovery or subpoena. Unauthorized practice of law committees may conduct joint investigations and prosecutions of unauthorized practice of law matters with each other and with Disciplinary Counsel.

(B) The unauthorized practice of law committee of a bar association or Disciplinary Counsel shall investigate any matter referred to it or that comes to its attention and may file a complaint pursuant to this rule. The Board, Disciplinary Counsel, and the president, secretary, or chair of the unauthorized practice of law committee of a bar association may call upon an attorney or judge in Ohio to assist in any investigation or to testify in any hearing before the Board as to any matter as to which he or she would not be bound to claim privilege as an attorney. No attorney or judge shall neglect or refuse to assist in any investigation or to testify.

(C) By the thirty-first day of January of each year, each bar association and Disciplinary Counsel shall file with the Board, on a form provided by the Board, a report of its activity on unauthorized practice of law complaints, investigations, and other matters requested by the Board. The report shall include all activity for the preceding calendar year.

(D) For complaints filed more than sixty days prior to the close of the report period on which a disposition has not been made, the report shall include an expected date of disposition and a statement of the reasons why the investigation has not been concluded.

SECTION 5. The Complaint; Where Filed; By Whom Signed

(A) A complaint shall be a formal written complaint alleging the unauthorized practice of law by one who shall be designated as the Respondent. The original complaint shall be filed in the office of the Secretary of the Board and shall be accompanied by thirteen copies plus two copies for each respondent named in the complaint. A complaint shall not be accepted for filing unless it is signed by one or more attorneys admitted to the practice of law in Ohio, who shall be counsel for the Relator. The complaint shall be accompanied by a certificate in writing signed by the president, secretary or chair of the unauthorized practice of law committee of any regularly organized bar association or Disciplinary Counsel, who shall be the Relator, certifying that counsel are authorized to represent relator and have accepted the responsibility of prosecuting the complaint to conclusion. The certification shall constitute a representation that, after investigation, relator believes probable cause exists to warrant a hearing on the complaint and shall constitute the authorization of counsel to represent relator in the action as fully and completely as if designated by order of the Supreme Court of Ohio with all the privileges and immunities of an officer of this Court.

(B) Upon the filing of a complaint with the Secretary of the Board, the relator shall forward a copy of the complaint to Disciplinary Counsel, the unauthorized practice of law committee of the Ohio State Bar Association, and any local bar association serving the county or counties from which the complaint emanated, except that the relator need not forward a copy of the complaint to itself.

SECTION 5A. Interim Cease and Desist Order

(A)(1) Upon receipt of substantial, credible evidence demonstrating that an individual or entity has engaged in the unauthorized practice of law and poses a substantial threat of serious harm to the public, the Disciplinary Counsel or unauthorized practice of law committee of any regularly organized bar association, which shall be referred to as the relator, shall do both of the following:

(a) Prior to filing a motion for an interim cease and desist order, make a reasonable attempt to provide the individual or entity, who shall be referred to as respondent, with notice, which may include notice by telephone, that a motion requesting an interim order that the respondent cease and desist engaging in the unauthorized practice of law will be filed with the Supreme Court and the Board on the Unauthorized Practice of Law.

(b) Simultaneously file a motion with the Supreme Court and the Board on the Unauthorized Practice of Law requesting that the Court order respondent to immediately cease and desist engaging in the unauthorized practice of law. The relator shall include, in its motion, proposed findings of fact, proposed conclusions of law, and other information in support of the requested order. Evidence relevant to the requested order shall be attached to or filed with the motion. The motion shall include a certificate detailing the attempts made by relator to provide advance notice to the respondent of relator's intent to file the motion. The motion also shall include a certificate of service on the respondent at the most recent address of the respondent known to the relator. Upon the filing of a motion with the Court and the Board, proceedings before the Court shall be automatically stayed and the matter shall be deemed to have been referred by the Court to the Board for application of this rule.

(2) After the filing of a motion for an interim cease and desist order the respondent may file a memorandum opposing the motion in accordance with Rule XIV of the Rules of Practice of the Supreme Court of Ohio. The respondent shall attach or file with the memorandum any rebuttal evidence and simultaneously file a copy with the Board on the Unauthorized Practice of Law. If a memorandum in opposition to the motion is not filed the stay of proceedings before the Court shall be automatically lifted and the Court shall rule on the motion pursuant to division (C).

(B) Upon the filing of a memorandum opposing the motion for interim cease and desist, the Chair of the Board on the Unauthorized Practice of Law or the Chair's designee ("Commissioner") shall set the matter for hearing within seven days. A designee shall be an attorney member of the Board. Upon review of the filings of the parties, the Commissioner will determine whether an oral argument or an evidentiary hearing shall be held based upon the existence of any genuine issue of material fact. Within seven days after the close of hearing, the Commissioner shall file a Report, including the transcript of hearing and the record, with the Supreme Court recommending whether or not an interim cease and desist order should be issued. Upon the filing of the Commissioner's Report, the stay of Supreme Court proceedings shall be automatically lifted.

(C) Upon consideration of the Commissioner's Report, or if no memorandum in opposition is filed, the Supreme Court may enter an order that the respondent cease and desist engaging in the unauthorized practice of law, pending final disposition of proceedings before the Board, predicated on the conduct threatening the serious harm or may order other action as the Court considers appropriate.

(D)(1) The respondent may request dissolution or modification of the cease and desist order by filing a motion with the Supreme Court. The motion shall be filed within thirty days of entry of the cease and desist order, unless the respondent first obtains leave of the Supreme Court to file a motion beyond that time. The motion shall include a statement and all available evidence as to why the respondent no longer poses a substantial threat of serious harm to the public. A copy of the motion shall be served by the respondent on the relator. The relator shall have ten days from the date the motion is filed to file a response to the motion. The Supreme Court promptly shall review the motion after a response has been filed or after the time for filing a response has passed.

(2) In addition to the motion allowed by division (D)(1) of this section, the respondent may file a motion requesting dissolution of the interim cease and desist order, alleging that one hundred eighty days have elapsed since the entry of the order and the relator has failed to file with the Board a formal complaint predicated on the conduct that was the basis of the order. A copy of the motion shall be served by the respondent on the relator. The relator shall have ten days from the date the motion is filed to file a response to the motion. The Supreme Court promptly shall review the motion after a response has been filed or after the time for filing a response has passed.

(E) The Rules of Practice of the Supreme Court of Ohio shall apply to interim cease and desist proceedings filed pursuant to this section.

(F) Upon the entry of an interim cease and desist order or an entry of dissolution or modification of such order, the Clerk of the Supreme Court of Ohio shall mail certified copies of the order as provided in Section 19(E) of this Rule.

SECTION 5B. Settlement of Complaints; Consent Decrees

(A) As used in this section:

(1) A "settlement agreement" is a voluntary written agreement entered into between the parties without the continuing jurisdiction of the Board or Court.

(2) A "consent decree" is a voluntary written agreement entered into between the parties, approved by the Board, and approved and ordered by the Court. The consent decree is the final judgment of the Court and is enforceable through contempt proceedings before the Court.

(3) A "proposed resolution" is a proposed settlement agreement or a proposed consent decree.

(B)(1) The proposed resolution of a complaint filed pursuant to Gov. Bar R.VII, Section 5, prior to adjudication by the Board, shall not be permitted without the prior review of the Board, or the Court, or both. Parties contemplating the proposed resolution of a complaint shall file a motion with the Secretary of the Board. The voluntary dismissal of a Complaint filed pursuant to Civ.R. 41(A) in conjunction with a proposed resolution is subject to the requirements of this section.

(C) The Board shall determine whether a proposed resolution shall be considered and approved by either the Board or the Court based on the following factors:

(1) The extent the agreement is submitted in the form of a proposed consent decree;

(2) The admission of the respondent to material allegations of the unauthorized practice of law as stated in the complaint;

(3) The extent the public is protected from future harm and any substantial injury is remedied by the agreement;

(4) Any agreement by the respondent to cease and desist the alleged activities;

(5) The extent the settlement agreement resolves material allegations of the unauthorized practice of law;

(6) The extent the agreement involves public policy issues or encroaches upon the jurisdiction of the Supreme Court to regulate the practice of law;

(7) The extent the settlement agreement furthers the stated purposes of Gov. Bar R. VII;

(8) Any other relevant factors.

(D) Review by the Board

(1) Upon receipt of a proposed resolution, the Board chair shall direct the assigned hearing panel to prepare a written report setting forth its recommendation for the acceptance or rejection of the proposed resolution. The Board shall vote to accept or reject the proposed resolution. Upon a majority vote to accept a settlement agreement, an order shall be issued by the Board chair dismissing the complaint. Upon a majority vote to accept a consent decree, the Board shall prepare and file a final report with the Court in accordance with division (E)(1) of this section.

(2) The refiling of a complaint previously resolved as a settlement agreement pursuant to this section shall reference the prior settlement agreement, and proceed only on the issue of the unauthorized practice of law. The case shall be presented on the merits and any previous admissions made by the respondent to allegations of conduct may be offered into evidence.

(E) Review by the Court

(1) After approving a proposed consent decree, the Board shall file an original and twelve copies of a final report and the proposed consent decree with the Clerk of Court of the Supreme Court. A copy of the report shall be served upon all parties and counsel of record. Neither party shall be permitted to file an objection to the final report.

(2) A consent decree may be approved or rejected by the Court. If a consent decree is approved, the Court shall issue the appropriate order.

(3) A motion to show cause alleging a violation of a consent decree and any memorandum in opposition shall be filed with the both the Court and the Board. The Board, upon receipt of the motion and memorandum in opposition, by panel assignment shall conduct either an evidentiary hearing or oral argument hearing on the motion, and by a majority vote of the Board submit a final report to the Court with findings of fact, conclusions of law, and recommendations on the issue of whether the consent decree was violated. Neither party shall be permitted to file objections to the Board's report without leave of Court.

(F) Rejection of a Proposed Resolution

(1) A complaint will proceed on the merits pursuant to Gov. Bar R. VII if a proposed resolution is rejected by either the Board or the Court. Upon rejection by the Board, an order shall be issued rejecting the proposed resolution and remanding the matter to the hearing panel for further proceedings. Upon rejection by the Court, an order shall be issued remanding the matter to the Board with or without instructions.

(2) A rejected proposed resolution shall not be admissible or otherwise used in a subsequent proceeding before the Board.

(3) No objections or other appeal may be filed with the Court upon a rejection by the Board of a proposed resolution.

(4) Any panel member initially considering a proposed resolution and voting with the Board on the rejection of the proposed resolution may proceed to hear the original complaint.

(G) The parties may consult with the Board through the Secretary concerning the terms of a proposed resolution.

(H) All settlement agreements approved by the Board and all consent decrees approved by the Court shall be recorded for reference by the Board, bar association unauthorized practice of law committees, and the Office of Disciplinary Counsel.

(I) This regulation shall not apply to the resolution of matters considered by an unauthorized practice of law committee or the Office of Disciplinary Counsel before a complaint is filed pursuant to Gov. Bar R. VII, Section 5.

SECTION 6. Duty of the Board Upon Filing of the Complaint; Notice to Respondent

The Secretary of the Board shall send a copy of the complaint by certified mail to respondent at the address indicated on the complaint with a notice of the right to file, within twenty days after the mailing of the notice, an original and thirteen copies of an answer and to serve copies of the answer upon counsel of record named in the complaint. Extensions of time may be granted, for good cause shown, by the Secretary of the Board.

SECTION 7. Proceedings of the Board after Filing of the Complaint

(A) Hearing Panel

(1) After respondent's answer has been filed, or the time for filing an answer has elapsed, the Secretary shall appoint a hearing panel consisting of three commissioners chosen by lot. The Secretary shall designate one of the commissioners chair of the panel, except that a non-attorney commissioner shall not be chair of the panel. The Secretary shall serve a copy of the entry appointing the panel on the respondent, relator, and all counsel of record.

(2) A majority of the panel shall constitute a quorum. The panel chair shall rule on all motions and interlocutory matters. The panel chair shall have a transcript of the testimony taken at the hearing, and the cost of the transcript shall be paid from the Attorney Registration Fund and taxed as costs.

(3) Upon reasonable notice and at a time and location set by the panel chair, the panel shall hold a formal hearing. Requests for continuances may be granted by the panel chair for good cause. The panel may take and hear testimony in person or by deposition, administer oaths, and compel by subpoena the attendance of witnesses and the production of books, papers, documents, records, and materials.

(B) Motion for Default

If no answer has been filed within twenty days of the answer date set forth in the notice to respondent of the filing of the complaint, or any extension of the answer date, relator shall file a motion for default. Prior to filing, relator shall make reasonable efforts to contact respondent.

A motion for default shall contain at least all of the following:

(1) A statement of the effort made to contact respondent and the result;

(2) Sworn or certified documentary *prima facie* evidence in support of the allegations of the complaint;

(3) Citations of any authorities relied upon by relator;

(4) A statement of any mitigating factors or exculpatory evidence of which relator is aware;

(5) A statement of the relief sought by relator;

(6) A certificate of service of the motion on respondent at the address stated on the complaint and at the last known address, if different.

The hearing panel appointed pursuant to division (A) of this section shall rule on the motion for default. If the motion for default is granted by the panel, the panel shall prepare a report for review by the Board pursuant to division (E) of this section. If the motion is denied, the hearing panel shall proceed with a formal hearing pursuant to division (A) of this section.

The chair of the Board may set aside a default entry, for good cause shown, and order a hearing before the hearing panel at any time before the Board renders its decision pursuant to division (F) of this section.

(C) **Authority of Hearing Panel; Dismissal** If at the end of evidence presented by relator or of all evidence, the hearing panel unanimously finds that the evidence is insufficient to support a charge or count of unauthorized practice of law, or the parties agree that the charge or count should be dismissed, the panel may order that the complaint or count be dismissed. The panel chair shall give written notice of the action taken to the Board, the respondent, the relator, all counsel of record, the Disciplinary Counsel, the unauthorized practice of law committee of the Ohio State Bar Association, and the bar association serving the county or counties from which the complaint emanated.

(D) **Referral by the Panel** If the hearing panel is not unanimous in its finding that the evidence is insufficient to support a charge or count of unauthorized practice of law, the panel may refer its findings of fact and recommendations for dismissal to the Board for review and action by the full Board. The panel shall submit to the Board its findings of fact and recommendation of dismissal in the same manner as provided in this rule with respect to a finding of unauthorized practice of law pursuant to division (E) of this section.

(E) **Finding of Unauthorized Practice of Law; Duty of Hearing Panel** If the hearing panel determines, by a preponderance of the evidence, that respondent has engaged in the unauthorized practice of law, the hearing panel shall file its report of the proceedings, findings of facts and recommendations with the Secretary for review by the Board. The report shall include the transcript of testimony taken and an itemized statement of the actual and necessary expenses incurred in connection with the proceedings.

(F) **Review by Entire Board** After review, the Board may refer the matter to the hearing panel for further hearing or proceed on the report of the prior proceedings before the hearing panel. After the final review, the Board may dismiss the complaint or find that the respondent has engaged in the unauthorized practice of law. If the complaint is dismissed, the dismissal shall be reported to the Secretary, who shall notify the same persons and organizations that would have received notice if the complaint had been dismissed by the hearing panel.

(G) **Finding of Unauthorized Practice of Law; Duty of Board** If the Board determines, by a preponderance of the evidence, that the respondent has engaged in the unauthorized practice of law, the Board shall file the original and twelve copies of its final report with the Clerk of the Supreme Court, and serve a copy of the final report upon all parties and counsel of record, Disciplinary Counsel, the unauthorized practice of law committee of the Ohio State Bar Association, and the bar association of the county or counties from which the complaint emanated. The final report shall include the Board's findings, recommendations, a transcript of testimony, if any, an itemized statement of costs, recommendation for civil penalties, if any, and a certificate of service listing the names and addresses of all parties and counsel of record.

(H) **Hearing on Stipulated Facts** A stipulation of facts and waiver of notice and hearing, mutually agreed and executed by relator and respondent, or counsel, may be filed with the Board prior to the date set for formal hearing. If a stipulation and waiver are filed, the parties are not required to appear before the hearing panel for a formal hearing, and the hearing panel shall render its decision based upon the pleadings, stipulation, and other evidence admitted.

The stipulation of facts must contain sufficient information to demonstrate the specific activities in which the respondent is alleged to have engaged and to enable the Board to determine whether respondent has engaged in the unauthorized practice of law.

The waiver of notice and hearing shall specifically state that the parties waive the right to notice of and appearance at the formal hearing before the hearing panel.

SECTION 8. Costs; Civil Penalties

(A) **Costs** As used in section 7(G) of this rule, "costs" includes both of the following:

(1) The expenses of relator, as described in Section 9 of this rule, that have been reimbursed by the Board;

(2) The direct expenses incurred by the hearing panel and the Board, including, but not limited to, the expense of a court reporter and transcript of any hearing before the hearing panel.

"Costs" shall not include attorney's fees incurred by the relator.

(B) **Civil Penalties** The Board may recommend and the Court may impose civil penalties in an amount up to ten thousand dollars per offense. Any penalty shall be based on the following factors:

(1) The degree of cooperation provided by the respondent in the investigation;

(2) The number of occasions that unauthorized practice of law was committed;

(3) The flagrancy of the violation;

(4) Harm to third parties arising from the offense;

(5) Any other relevant factors.

SECTION 9. Expenses

(A) **Reimbursement of Direct Expenses** A bar association may be reimbursed for direct expenses incurred in performing the obligations imposed by this rule. Reimbursement shall be limited to costs for depositions, transcripts, copies of documents, necessary travel expenses for witnesses and volunteer attorneys, witness fees, subpoenas, the service of subpoenas, postal and delivery charges, long distance telephone charges, and compensation of investigators and expert witnesses authorized in advance by the Board. There shall be no reimbursement for the costs of the time of other bar association personnel or attorneys in discharging these obligations.

An application for reimbursement of expenses, together with proof of the expenditures, shall be filed with the Secretary of the Board. Upon approval by the Board, reimbursement shall be made from the Attorney Services Fund.

(B) **Annual Reimbursement of Indirect Expenses** A bar association may apply to the Board prior to the first day of February each year for partial reimbursement of other expenses necessarily and reasonably incurred during the preceding calendar year in performing their obligations under these rules. The Board, by regulation, shall establish criteria for determining whether expenses under this section are necessary and reasonable. The Board shall deny reimbursement for any expense for which a bar association seeks reimbursement on or after the first day of May of the year immediately following the calendar year in which the expense was incurred. Expenses eligible for reimbursement are those specifically related to unauthorized practice of law matters and include the following:

(1) The personnel costs for the portion of an employee's work that is dedicated to this area;

(2) The costs of bar counsel who is retained pursuant to a written agreement with the unauthorized practice of law committee;

(3) Postal and delivery charges;

(4) Long distance telephone charges;

(5) Local telephone charges and other appropriate line charges included, but not limited to, per call charges;

(6) The costs of dedicated telephone lines;

(7) Subscription to professional journals, law books, and other legal research services and materials related to unauthorized practice of law;

(8) Organizational dues and educational expenses related to unauthorized practice of law;

(9) All costs of defending a law suit relating to unauthorized practice of law and that portion of professional liability insurance premiums directly attributable to the operation of the committees in performing their obligations under this rule;

(10) The percentage of rent, insurance premiums not reimbursed pursuant to division(B)(9) of this section, supplies and equipment, accounting costs, occupancy, utilities, office expenses, repair and maintenance, and other overhead expenses directly attributable to the operation of the committees in performing their obligations under this rule, as determined by the Board and provided that no bar association shall be reimbursed in excess of three thousand five hundred dollars per calendar year for such expenses. Reimbursement shall not be made for the costs of the time of other bar association personnel, volunteer attorneys, depreciation, or amortization. No bar

association shall apply for reimbursement or be entitled to reimbursement for expenses that are reimbursed pursuant to Gov. Bar R. V, Sec. 3(D).

(C) **Quarterly Reimbursement of Certain Indirect Expenses** In addition to applying annually for reimbursement pursuant to Section 9(B), a bar association may apply quarterly to the Board for reimbursement of the expenses set forth in Section 9(B)(1) and (2) that were necessarily and reasonably incurred during the preceding calendar quarter. Quarterly reimbursement shall be submitted in accordance with the following schedule:

Reimbursement for the months of:	Due by:
January, February, and March	May 1
April, May, and June	August 1
July, August, and September	November 1
October, November, and December	February 1 (with annual reimbursement request)

Any expense that is eligible for quarterly reimbursement, but that is not submitted on a quarterly reimbursement application, shall be submitted no later than the appropriate annual reimbursement application pursuant to division (B) of this section and shall be denied by the Board if not timely submitted. The application for quarterly reimbursement shall include an affidavit with documentation demonstrating that the unauthorized practice of law committee incurred the expenses set forth in Section 9(B)(1) and (2).

(D) **Audit** Expenses incurred by bar associations and reimbursed under divisions (A), (B), and (C) of this section may be audited at the discretion of the Board or the Supreme Court and paid out of the Attorney Services Fund.

(E) **Availability of Funds** Reimbursement under divisions (A), (B), and (C) of this section is subject to the availability of moneys in the Attorney Services Fund.

SECTION 10. Manner of Service

Whenever provision is made for the service of any complaint, notice, order, or other document upon a respondent or relator in connection with any proceeding under this rule, service may be made upon counsel of record for the party personally or by certified mail.

If service of any document by certified mail is refused or unclaimed, the Secretary may make service by ordinary mail evidenced by a certificate of mailing. Service shall be considered complete when the fact of mailing is entered in the record, provided that the ordinary mail envelope is not returned by the postal authorities with an endorsement showing failure of delivery.

SECTION 11. Quorum of Board

A majority of the commissioners shall constitute a

quorum for all purposes and the action of a majority of those present comprising such quorum shall be the action of the Board.

SECTION 12. Power to Issue Subpoenas

In order to facilitate any investigation and proceeding under this rule, upon application by the Disciplinary Counsel, the unauthorized practice of law committee of any regularly organized bar association, respondent, or relator, the Secretary, the chair of the board, and the chair of a hearing panel may issue subpoenas and cause testimony to be taken under oath before Disciplinary Counsel, the unauthorized practice of law committee of any regularly organized bar association, a hearing panel of the Board, or the Board. All subpoenas shall be issued in the name and under the Seal of this Court and shall be signed by the Secretary, the chair of the Board, or the chair of the hearing panel and served as provided by the Rules of Civil Procedure. Fees and costs of all subpoenas shall be provided from the Attorney Registration Fund and taxed as costs.

The refusal or neglect of a person subpoenaed or called as a witness to obey a subpoena, to attend, to be sworn or to affirm, or to answer any proper question shall be deemed to be contempt of the Supreme Court and may be punished accordingly.

SECTION 13. Depositions

The Secretary, the chair of the board, and the chair of the hearing panel may order testimony of any person to be taken by deposition within or without this state in the manner prescribed for the taking of depositions in civil actions, and such depositions may be used to the same extent as permitted in civil actions.

SECTION 14. Conduct of Hearing

The hearing panel shall follow the Rules of Civil Procedure and Rules of Evidence wherever practicable, unless a provision of this rule or Board hearing procedures and guidelines provide otherwise. The panel chair shall rule on evidentiary matters. All evidence shall be taken in the presence of the hearing panel and the parties except where a party is absent, is in default, or has waived the right to be present. The hearing panel shall receive evidence by sworn testimony and may receive additional evidence as it determines proper. Any documentary evidence to be offered shall be served upon the adverse parties or their counsel and the hearing panel at least thirty days before the hearing, unless the parties or their counsel otherwise agree or the hearing panel otherwise orders. All evidence received shall be given the weight the hearing panel determines it is entitled after consideration of objections.

SECTION 15. Records

The Secretary of the Board shall maintain permanent public records of all matters processed by the Board and the disposition of those matters.

SECTION 16. Board May Prescribe Regulations

Subject to the prior approval of this Court, the Board may adopt regulations not inconsistent with this rule.

SECTION 17. Rules to be Liberally Construed

Amendments to any complaint, notice, answer, objections, or report may be made at any time prior to final order of the Board. The party affected by the amendment shall be given reasonable opportunity to meet any new matter presented by the amendment. This rule and regulations relating to investigations and proceedings involving complaints of unauthorized practice of law shall be liberally construed for the protection of the public, the courts, and the legal profession and shall apply to all pending investigations and complaints so far as may be practicable, and to all future investigations and complaints whether the conduct involved occurred prior or subsequent to the enactment or amendment of this rule.

SECTION 18. Records and Proceedings Public

All records, documents, proceedings, and hearings of the Board relating to investigations and complaints pursuant to this rule shall be public, except that deliberations by a hearing panel and the Board shall not be public.

SECTION 19. Review by Supreme Court of Ohio; Orders; Costs

(A) **Show Cause Order** After the filing of a final report of the Board, the Supreme Court shall issue to respondent an order to show cause why the report of the Board shall not be confirmed and an appropriate order granted. Notice of the order to show cause shall be served by the Clerk of the Supreme Court on all parties and counsel of record by certified mail at the address provided in the Board's report.

(B) **Response to Show Cause Order** Within twenty days after the issuance of an order to show cause, the respondent or relator may file objections to the findings or recommendations of the Board and to the entry of an order or to the confirmation of the report on which the order to show cause was issued. The objections shall be accompanied by a brief in support of the objections and proof of service of copies of the objections and the brief on the Secretary of the Board and all counsel of record. Objections and briefs shall be filed in the number and form required for original actions by the Rules of Practice of the Supreme Court of Ohio, to the extent such rules are applicable.

(C) **Answer Briefs** Answer briefs and proof of service shall be filed within fifteen days after briefs in support of objections have been filed. All briefs shall be filed in the number and form required for original actions by the Rules of Practice of the Supreme Court of Ohio, to the extent such rules are applicable.

(D) **Supreme Court Proceedings**

(1) After a hearing on objections, or if objections are not filed within the prescribed time, the Supreme Court shall enter an order as it finds proper. If the

Court finds that respondent's conduct constituted the unauthorized practice of law, the Court shall issue an order that does one or more of the following:

(a) Prohibits the respondent from engaging in any such conduct in the future;

(b) Requires the respondent to reimburse the costs and expenses incurred by the Board and the relator pursuant to this rule;

(c) Imposes a civil penalty on the respondent. The civil penalty may be imposed regardless of whether the Board recommended imposition of the penalty pursuant to Section 8(B) of this rule and may be imposed for an amount greater or less than the amount recommended by the Board, but not to exceed ten thousand dollars per offense.

(2) Payment for costs, expenses, sanctions, and penalties imposed under this rule shall be deposited in the Attorney Registration Fund established under Gov. Bar R. VI, Section 7.

(E) **Notice** Upon the entry of any order pursuant to this rule, the Clerk of the Supreme Court shall mail certified copies of the entry to all parties and counsel of record, the Board, Disciplinary Counsel, and the Ohio State Bar Association.

(F) **Publication** The Supreme Court Reporter shall publish any order entered by the Supreme Court under this rule in the *Ohio Official Reports*, the *Ohio State Bar Association Report*, and in a publication, if any, of the local bar association in the county in which the complaint arose. The publication shall include the citation of the case in which the order was issued. Publication also shall be made in a local newspaper having the largest general circulation in the county in which the complaint arose. The publication shall be in the form of a paid legal advertisement, in a style and size commensurate with legal advertisements, and shall be published three times within the thirty days following the order of the Supreme Court. Publication fees shall be assessed against the respondent as part of the costs.

History: Amended, eff 11-30-83; 6-6-88; 1-1-89; 1-1-90; 1-1-92; 1-1-93; 1-1-95; 6-16-03; 1-1-05; 11/01/07; 01/01/08, 09/01/08.

NOTES TO DECISIONS

ANALYSIS

Accountants
Jailhouse lawyers
Unauthorized practice of law

Accountants

CPA and his accounting firm engaged in the unauthorized practice of law by advising clients on how to establish and protect legal interests through incorporation and by preparing documents for filing with the secretary of state. The facts that there were numerous violations and that they produced a great benefit weighed in favor of imposing a civil penalty: Dayton Bar Ass'n v. Stewart, 116 Ohio St. 3d 289, 2007 Ohio 6461, 878 N.E.2d 628, 2007 Ohio LEXIS 3042 (2007).

Jailhouse lawyers

Legal assistance to inmates by a fellow nonlawyer inmate is not prohibited, and a charge of unauthorized practice will be dismissed, where the state fails to demonstrate the availability

of a reasonable alternative providing adequate access to courts: Disciplinary Counsel v. Cotton, 115 Ohio St. 3d 113, 2007 Ohio 4481, 873 N.E.2d 1240, 2007 Ohio LEXIS 2165 (2007).

Unauthorized practice of law

Court sua sponte struck and dismissed an application pursuant to Ohio R. App. P. 26(B) of defendant's wife to reopen an appellate judgment, which had affirmed his conviction for intimidation, as she was not a registered attorney and the fact that he had given her a durable power of attorney did not give her authority to represent him pursuant to RC § 4705.01. Her preparation of the legal papers and her management thereof constituted the unauthorized practice of law under Ohio Sup. Ct. R. Gov't Bar VII, § 4(A), which the court had an ethical duty to prohibit pursuant to Ohio Code Prof. Conduct R. 5.5(a). State v. Block, — Ohio App. 3d —, 2007 Ohio 1979, — N.E. 2d —, 2007 Ohio App. LEXIS 1830 (Apr. 20, 2007).

Respondent, who graduated from law school but never passed the bar examination, engaged in the unauthorized practice of law by holding himself out as a licensed attorney. That conduct warranted a civil penalty and an injunction against ever applying for admission to the bar: Disciplinary Counsel v. Robson, 116 Ohio St. 3d 318, 2007 Ohio 6460, 878 N.E.2d 1042, 2007 Ohio LEXIS 3055 (2007).

Enterprises in which laypersons associate with licensed practitioners in various minimally distinguishable ways as a means to superficially legitimize sales of living trust packages are engaged in the unauthorized practice of law. By facilitating such sales, licensed lawyers violate professional standards of competence and ethics, including the prohibition against aiding others in the unauthorized practice of law: Columbus Bar Ass'n v. Am. Family Prepaid Legal Corp., 123 Ohio St. 3d 353, 2009 Ohio 5336, 916 N.E.2d 784, 2009 Ohio LEXIS 2834 (2009).

Respondents engaged in the unauthorized practice of law by providing legal advice to solicited customers facing pending property foreclosures and representing the customers in negotiations to settle with their mortgagees: Cincinnati Bar Ass'n v. Foreclosure Solutions, L.L.C., 123 Ohio St. 3d 107, 2009 Ohio 4174, 914 N.E.2d 386, 2009 Ohio LEXIS 2267 (2009).

Private right of action for the unauthorized practice of law did not exist before September 15, 2004. The Supreme Court of Ohio has exclusive jurisdiction over the practice of law in Ohio, including the unauthorized practice of law: Greenspan v. Third Fed. S&L Ass'n, 122 Ohio St. 3d 455, 2009 Ohio 3508, 912 N.E.2d 567, 2009 Ohio LEXIS 1938 (2009).

RULE VIII.

CLIENTS' SECURITY FUND

SECTION 1. Establishment of Fund

(A) There shall be a Clients' Security Fund of Ohio consisting of amounts transferred to the fund pursuant to this rule and any other funds received in pursuance of the fund's objectives. The purpose of the fund is to aid in ameliorating the losses caused to clients and others by defalcating members of the bar acting as attorney or fiduciary, and this rule shall be liberally construed to effectuate that purpose. No claimant or other person shall have any legal interest in the fund or right to receive any portion of the fund, except for discretionary disbursements directed by the Board of Commissioners of the Clients' Security Fund of Ohio, all payments from the fund being a matter of grace and not right.

(B) The Supreme Court shall provide appropriate and necessary funding for the support of the Clients' Security Fund from the Attorney Registration Fund. The Clerk of the Supreme Court of Ohio shall transfer funds to the Clients' Security Fund at the direction of the Court.

SECTION 2. Board of Commissioners of the Clients' Security Fund of Ohio; Administrator; Chair

(A) **Creation; Members** There is hereby created a Board of Commissioners of the Clients' Security Fund of Ohio consisting of seven members appointed by the Supreme Court, at least one of whom shall be a person not admitted to the practice of law in Ohio or any other state. The Court shall designate one member as chair and one member as vice-chair, who shall hold such office for the length of their term. All terms shall be for a period of three years commencing on the first day of January. No member shall serve more than two consecutive three-year terms. The Board shall have its principal office in Columbus.

(B) **Administrator** There shall be an Administrator of the Board of Commissioners of the Clients' Security Fund. The Court shall appoint and fix the salary of the Administrator. If the Administrator is an attorney admitted to practice in Ohio, he or she shall not engage in the private practice of law while serving in that capacity. The Administrator shall be the secretary to the Board. The Administrator shall appoint, with the approval of the Court, staff as required to satisfactorily perform the duties imposed by this rule. The Court shall fix compensation of personnel employed by the Administrator.

(C) **Powers of the Board** The Board shall do all of the following:

(1) Investigate applications by claimants for disbursement from the fund;

(2) Conduct hearings relative to claims;

(3) Authorize and establish the amount of disbursements from the fund in accordance with this rule;

(4) Adopt rules of procedure and prescribe forms not inconsistent with this rule.

(D) **Powers of the Chair**

(1) The chair of the Board shall be the trustee of the fund and shall hold, manage, disburse, and invest the fund, or any portion of the fund, in a manner consistent with the effective administration of this rule. All investments shall be made by the chair upon the approval of a majority of the Board. Investments shall be limited to short-term insured obligations of the United States government, deposits at interest in federally insured banks or federally insured savings and loan institutions located in the state of Ohio, and in no-front-end-load money market mutual funds consisting exclusively of direct obligations of the United States Treasury, and repurchase agreements relating to direct Treasury obligations, with the interest or other income on investments becoming part of the fund. Annually and at additional times as the Supreme Court may order, the chair shall file with the Supreme Court a written report reviewing in detail the administration of the fund during the year. The fund shall be audited biennially by the Auditor of State at the same time as the Supreme

Court's regular biennial audit. The Supreme Court may order an additional audit at any time, certified by a certified public accountant licensed to practice in Ohio. Audit reports shall be filed with the Board, which shall send a copy to the Supreme Court. The report shall be open to public inspection at the offices of the Board.

(2) The chair and vice-chair of the Board shall file a bond annually with the Supreme Court in an amount fixed by the Supreme Court.

(3) The chair of the Board shall have the power and duty to render decisions on procedural matters presented by the Board and call additional meetings of the Board when necessary.

(4) The vice-chair of the Board shall exercise the duties of the chair during any absence or incapacity of the chair.

(E) **Meetings** The Board shall meet at least two times a year, in Columbus and at other times and locations as the chair designates.

(F) **Expenses** Expenses for the operation of the Board as authorized by this rule shall be paid from the fund, including bond premiums, the cost of audits, personnel, office space, supplies, equipment, travel and other expenses of Board members.

SECTION 3. Eligible Claims

For purposes of this rule, an eligible claim shall be one for the reimbursement of losses of money, property, or other things of value that meet all of the following requirements:

(A) The loss was caused by the dishonest conduct of an attorney admitted to the practice of law in Ohio when acting in any of the following capacities:

(1) As an attorney;

(2) In a fiduciary capacity customary to the practice of law;

(3) As an escrow agent or other fiduciary, having been designated as an escrow agent or fiduciary by a client in the matter or a court of this state in which the loss arose or having been selected as a result of a client-attorney relationship.

(B) The conduct was engaged in while the attorney was admitted to the practice of law in Ohio and acting in his capacity as an attorney admitted to the practice of law in Ohio, or in any capacity described in division (A) of this section.

(C) On or after the effective date of this rule, the attorney [has] been disbarred, suspended, or publicly reprimanded, has resigned, or has been convicted of embezzlement or misappropriation of money or other property and the claim is presented within one year of the occurrence or discovery of the applicable event. The taking of any affirmative action by the claimant against the attorney within the one-year period shall toll the time for filing a claim under this rule until the termination of that proceeding. In the event disciplinary or criminal proceedings, or both, cannot be prosecuted because the attorney cannot be located or is deceased, the Board may consider a timely application if the claimant has complied with the other conditions of this rule.

(D) The claim is not covered by any insurance or by any fidelity or similar bond or fund, whether of the attorney, claimant, or otherwise.

(E) The claim is made directly by or on behalf of the injured client or his personal representative or, if a corporation, by or on behalf of itself or its successors in interest.

(F) The loss was not incurred by any of the following:

(1) The spouse, children, parents, grandparents or siblings, partner, associate, employee or employer of the attorney, or a business entity controlled by the attorney. The Board may, in its discretion, recognize such a claim in cases of extreme hardship or special or unusual circumstances;

(2) An insurer, surety or bonding agency or company, or any entity controlled by any of the foregoing;

(3) Any governmental unit.

(G) A payment from the fund, by way of subrogation or otherwise, will not benefit any entity specified in division (F) of this section.

SECTION 4. Dishonest Conduct

For purposes of this rule, dishonest conduct consists of wrongful acts or omissions by an attorney in the nature of defalcation or embezzlement of money, or the wrongful taking or conversion of money, property, or other things of value.

SECTION 5. Maximum Recovery

The Board shall determine the maximum amount of reimbursement to be awarded to a claimant. No award shall exceed seventy-five thousand dollars.

SECTION 6. Conditions of Payment; Attorney Fees

(A) As a condition to payment, the claimant shall execute any interest, take any action, or enter into any agreements as the Board requires, including assignments, subrogation agreements, trust agreements, and promises to cooperate with the Board in prosecuting claims or charges against any person. Any amounts recovered by the Board through an action shall be deposited with the fund.

(B) No attorney fees may be paid from the proceeds of an award made to a claimant under authority of this rule. The Board may allow an award of attorney fees to be paid out of the fund if it determines that the attorney's services were necessary to prosecute a claim under this rule and upon other conditions as the Board may direct.

SECTION 7. Claims Procedure

(A) **Forms** The Board shall provide forms for the presentation of claims to Disciplinary Counsel, all bar associations, and to any other person upon request. The Board shall create a complaint form for the use of claimants that shall include, but not be limited to the name and address of the claimant, the name and last known address of the attorney against whom the claim is made, the date of the alleged wrongful act, a clear and simple statement describing the wrongful act, the amount of the claimed loss, and a statement as to whether other affirmative action has been taken as

described in Section 3(C) of this rule. A claim shall be considered as filed on the date the Board receives written notification of the claim, even in the absence of the prescribed form. However, completion of the formal application may subsequently be required by the Board.

(B) **Notice** Upon receipt of a claim against an attorney, the secretary of the Board shall notify the attorney by certified mail, when possible, of the fact of its filing. All parties shall be notified by any action taken by the Board with respect to a claim.

(C) **Investigation; Cooperation With Disciplinary Counsel and Local Bar Associations**

(1) The Board shall investigate or cause to be investigated all claims received under this rule.

(2) At the request of the Board, Disciplinary Counsel and local bar associations authorized to investigate attorney discipline complaints under Gov. Bar R. V shall make available to the Board all reports of investigations and records of formal proceedings in their possession with respect to any attorney whose conduct is alleged to amount to dishonest conduct under this rule. Where the information sought is the subject of a pending investigation or disciplinary proceeding required by Gov.Bar R. V to be confidential, disclosure shall not be required until the termination of the investigation or disciplinary proceeding, or both.

(3) Where the Board receives a claim that is ineligible because disciplinary proceedings have not been undertaken, the Board shall hold the claim in abeyance, forward a copy of the claim to Disciplinary Counsel for further action, and advise the claimant that these procedures have been undertaken and that disciplinary action is a prerequisite to eligibility under this rule. If filed within the time limits prescribed in Section 3(C) of the rule, the claim shall be considered timely regardless of the time it is held in abeyance pending the outcome of disciplinary proceedings. Disciplinary Counsel shall advise the Board as to the disposition of the complaint.

(D) **Hearings; Subpoenas** The Board may conduct hearings for the purpose of resolving factual issues. Upon determining that any person is a material witness to the determination of a claim made against the fund, the Board, chair, or vice-chair shall have authority to issue a subpoena requiring the person to appear and testify or produce records before the Board. All subpoenas shall be issued in the name and under the Seal of the Supreme Court, signed by the chair, vice-chair, or Administrator, and served as provided by law.

(E) **Confidentiality** All claims filed under this rule and all records obtained by the Board pursuant to this rule shall be confidential. If an award is made under this rule, the award, the name of the claimant, the name of the attorney, and the nature of the claim may be disclosed.

(F) **Consideration of Claims** The Board, in its sole discretion, but on the affirmative vote of at least four members, shall determine the eligible claims that merit reimbursement from the fund and the amount, time, manner, conditions, and order of payments of reimbursement. No award may include interest from the date of the award. In making each determination, the Board shall consider, among other factors set forth in this rule, all of the following:

(1) The amounts available and likely to become available to the fund for the payment of claims and the size and number of claims that are likely to be presented;

(2) The amount of the claimant's loss as compared with the amount of losses sustained by other eligible claimants;

(3) The degree of hardship suffered by the claimant as a result of the loss;

(4) The degree of negligence, if any, of the claimant that may have contributed to the loss.

(5) Any special or unusual circumstances.

To preserve the fund, the board may adopt rules implementing a sliding scale whereby eligible claims are compensable at fixed percentages of the total loss but not to exceed the maximum award allowed by this rule.

The determination of the Board shall be final.

History: Amended, eff 5-13-85; 7-29-87; 10-1-89; 1-1-90; 1-1-93; 12-1-96; 10-20-97; 4-13-98; 8-19-98; 8-1-03.

NOTES TO DECISIONS

ANALYSIS

Relief from judgment

Relief from judgment

When a trial court entered summary judgment in favor of the Ohio Supreme Court's Client Security Fund, when it sued a former attorney for funds it had paid to his former client, the attorney showed that he might have a meritorious defense to the judgment when he alleged that he was not notified of the client's claim against the Fund and that the claim was improperly paid, because, while the Fund did not have to notify the attorney of the client's claim, under Ohio Sup. Ct. R. Gov't Bar VIII, the attorney had to be able to defend himself in the Fund's collection case against him, and, if he could prove the client's claim was improperly paid, this would constitute a defense to the collection case, so he was entitled to relief from the judgment. State v. Potts, — Ohio App. 3d —, 2006 Ohio 7057, — N.E. 2d —, 2006 Ohio App. LEXIS 6989 (Dec. 28, 2006).

RULE IX.

TEMPORARY CERTIFICATION FOR PRACTICE IN LEGAL SERVICES, PUBLIC DEFENDER, AND LAW SCHOOL PROGRAMS

SECTION 1. Eligibility

A person not admitted to the practice of law in Ohio may become certified to temporarily practice law in this state if that person satisfies all of the following:

(A) The person has earned a degree from a law school that is accredited by the American Bar Association;

(B) The person has taken and passed a bar examination, and has been admitted and is in good standing as an attorney at law in the highest court of another state, the District of Columbia, or a territory of the United States;

(C) The person has not taken and failed the Ohio bar examination;

(D) The person has not had an application for admission in Ohio denied on character and fitness grounds pursuant to Gov. Bar R. I;

(E) The person is employed by or associated with a legal services or public defender program that provides legal services solely to indigent clients, or is employed as a supervising attorney in a criminal or poverty law and litigation program administered by an Ohio law school that is accredited by the American Bar Association. For purposes of this rule, legal services program shall mean any organization that receives financial assistance from the state public defender pursuant to section 120.53 of the Revised Code.

SECTION 2. Application

An applicant for certification under this rule shall file with the Office of Bar Admissions of the Supreme Court an Application for Temporary Certification. The application shall be on forms furnished by the Office of Bar Admissions and shall include all of the following:

(A) A certificate from the applicant's law school certifying that the applicant has received a law degree;

(B) A certificate of admission as an attorney at law from another state, the District of Columbia, or a territory of the United States;

(C) A certificate of good standing from each jurisdiction in which the applicant is admitted to practice law;

(D) An affidavit that the applicant has read, is familiar with, and agrees to be bound by the Ohio Code of Professional Responsibility and to submit to the jurisdiction of the Supreme Court for disciplinary purposes pursuant to Gov. Bar R. V;

(E) An affidavit from the director of the legal services or public defender program or the dean of the law school where the applicant is employed or associated certifying all of the following:

(1) That the applicant is employed by or associated with the legal services, public defender, or law school program;

(2) That the director or law school dean has no knowledge of information that would cause him or her to doubt the applicant's character, fitness, or moral qualifications to practice law or the applicant's ability to discharge the duties of an attorney at law;

(3) That the director or law school dean will notify the Office of Bar Admissions in writing immediately upon termination of the applicant's employment or association with the legal services, public defender, or law school program;

(F) A questionnaire, in duplicate, for use by the National Conference of Bar Examiners and the Board of Commissioners on Character and Fitness in conducting a character investigation of the applicant;

(G) A fee in the amount charged by the National Conference of Bar Examiners for its report;

(H) A fee of three hundred dollars. Fees paid under this rule may be applied toward the fees for admission under Gov. Bar R. I.

SECTION 3. Certification

Upon filing of a completed application that demonstrates the applicant's eligibility under this rule, the Office of Bar Admissions shall issue a temporary certificate to the applicant. The certificate shall be subject to the limitations imposed by Sections 4 and 5 of this rule and shall authorize the practice of law in Ohio only to the extent that practice is engaged in by the applicant as an employee or associate of a legal services, public defender, or law school program.

SECTION 4. Review by the Board of Commissioners on Character and Fitness

The Office of Bar Admissions shall forward the applicant's questionnaire to the National Conference of Bar Examiners. Upon receipt of a report from the National Conference of Bar Examiners, the Office of Bar Admissions shall submit the report and the application to the Board of Commissioners on Character and Fitness, which shall review the report and the application. The Board may request additional information or materials from the applicant and may conduct a personal interview to determine the applicant's character, fitness, and moral qualifications to practice law. The Board shall recommend that the applicant's temporary certificate either be approved or revoked. If the Board recommends revocation of the certificate, it shall file a report of its recommendation and the basis for its recommendation with the Office of Bar Admissions, who immediately shall revoke the certificate and send a copy of the report and recommendation to the applicant. An applicant whose certificate is revoked shall be entitled to review by the Supreme Court pursuant to Gov. Bar R. I, Section 11(F).

SECTION 5. Duration and Renewal of the Certificate

(A) A certificate issued pursuant to this rule shall expire one year from the date of issuance unless, prior to the date of expiration, one of the following events occurs, in which case the certificate shall expire on the date the event occurs:

(1) The applicant is admitted to the bar of Ohio;

(2) The applicant is denied admission to the practice of law under Gov. Bar R. I;

(3) The applicant receives a failing score on the Ohio bar examination;

(4) The applicant's employment or association with the legal services, public defender, or law school program is terminated and, within thirty days of the date of the notice provided for in Section 2(E)(3) of this rule, the director of a legal services or public defender program or law school dean fails to notify the Office of Bar Admissions that the applicant has become employed by or associated with another legal services, public defender, or law school program in this state.

(B) A certificate issued pursuant to this rule may be renewed once for a period of one year from the date on which the certificate would have expired. An applicant may obtain renewal by filing an application for renewal and both of the following with the Office of Bar Admissions:

(1) An affidavit from the director of the legal services or public defender program or the dean of the law school where the applicant is employed or associated

certifying the applicant's continued employment or association with the legal services, public defender, or law school program;

(2) An affidavit from the applicant stating that the applicant has not engaged in the practice of law in Ohio outside the scope of employment or association with the legal services, public defender, or law school program where the applicant is employed or associated.

(C) An applicant who is granted temporary certification under this rule is subject to all provisions of the Ohio Code of Professional Responsibility and submits to the jurisdiction of the Supreme Court for disciplinary purposes under Gov. Bar R. V. The Supreme Court, on its own initiative and at any time, may revoke a temporary certificate for disciplinary or other reasons.

SECTION 6. Effect of Temporary Certification on Applying for Admission without Examination

The practice of law engaged in pursuant to a temporary certificate issued under this rule shall not be considered in determining whether an applicant for admission without examination satisfied the practice of law requirements contained in Gov. Bar R. I, Section 9(A)(2).

SECTION 7. Repeal Date; Effect of Repeal

(A) This rule is hereby repealed effective July 2, 1991, subject to further action by the Supreme Court.

SECTION 8. Effect of Repeal on Temporary Certificates

(A) The repeal of this rule shall not affect any of the following:

(1) The validity of a temporary certificate issued pursuant to the former provisions of this rule;

(2) The ability of the Clerk to revoke a temporary certificate or the availability of an appeal from a revocation of a certificate;

(3) The expiration of a certificate;

(4) The jurisdiction of the Supreme Court over an applicant who was granted a certificate pursuant to the former provisions of this rule.

(B) Any action taken with respect to a temporary certificate or an attorney who was granted a temporary certificate shall be consistent with the provisions of this rule, as it existed on the date of repeal.

History: Not analogous to former Rule IX, effective 1-1-81; Amended eff. 7-2-90; 7-2-91; 10-1-00; 10-1-03; 2-1-07, 5–1–01; 01–01–08.

RULE X.

CONTINUING LEGAL EDUCATION

SECTION 1. Purpose; Construction

(A) The purpose of this rule is to maintain and improve the quality of legal and judicial services in Ohio by requiring continuing legal education for Ohio attorneys and regulating the provision of continuing legal education to Ohio judges.

(B) This rule and regulations adopted under authority of this rule by the Supreme Court Commission on Continuing Legal Education shall be construed liberally to accomplish the purpose of this rule.

(C) As used in this rule, "judge" includes the Chief Justice and Justices of the Supreme Court.

SECTION 2. Supreme Court Commission on Continuing Legal Education

(A)(1) There is hereby created the Supreme Court Commission on Continuing Legal Education, consisting of nineteen members appointed by the Supreme Court, as follows:

(a) Twelve attorneys licensed to practice law in Ohio, one from each appellate district;

(b) One dean or member of a law faculty engaged in full-time legal education in an Ohio law school;

(c) Five judges;

(d) One member who shall not be an attorney.

(2) Terms of office shall be three years. Members shall be eligible for reappointment, but shall not serve more than two full terms. A member appointed to fill a vacancy occurring prior to the expiration of a term shall hold office for the remainder of the unexpired term. If an attorney member no longer resides or practices in the district from which the attorney member is appointed, if the educator or dean member is no longer engaged in full-time legal education in an Ohio law school, or if a judge member leaves office, the member shall be disqualified and a vacancy shall occur.

(3) Each year, the Commission shall elect a chair, a vice-chair, and other officers as are necessary. The Commission shall meet at the call of the chair or upon written request of a majority of the members. A majority of the members duly appointed and qualified constitutes a quorum. No action shall be taken by the Commission without the concurrence of a majority of the members constituting a quorum at that meeting.

(4) Members shall serve without compensation, but shall be reimbursed for expenses incurred in the performance of their official duties.

(B)(1) The Commission shall administer the continuing legal education requirements of this rule and Rule IV of the Rules for the Government of the Judiciary of Ohio, including promulgating regulations and performing other administrative functions necessary to carry out the duties of the Commission.

(2) The Director of Attorney Services or the Director's designee shall serve as Secretary of the Commission.

(3) The Commission shall accredit continuing legal education programs, activities, and sponsors and establish procedures for accreditation. The Commission, by regulation, may assess reasonable application fees for accreditation, sponsors that submit a program or activity for accreditation, or both.

(4) The Commission shall accredit mayor's court continuing education courses and sponsors pursuant to the Mayor's Court Education and Procedure Rules and establish procedures for accreditation.

(5) The Commission shall establish procedures for awarding credits toward the completion of the continuing legal education requirements of this rule and Gov. Jud. R. IV.

(6) The Commission shall endeavor to make accredited programs and activities on a variety of subjects available at a reasonable cost to attorneys and judges in all areas of the state.

(7) The Commission shall not sponsor programs and activities for continuing legal education.

(8) The Commission shall report, at least annually, to the Supreme Court concerning the activities of the Commission and the status of continuing legal education in the state.

(C) Commission operations shall be funded by the Attorney Services Fund established pursuant to Gov. Bar R. VI. All fees collected pursuant to this rule shall be deposited in the Attorney Services Fund.

(D) At the request of the Administrative Director of the Supreme Court, the Secretary of the Commission shall prepare and submit a proposed budget for approval by the Supreme Court.

(E) Records of the Commission shall be public records.

SECTION 3. Attorney Continuing Legal Education Requirements

(A)(1) Each attorney admitted to the practice of law in this state and each attorney registered for corporate status pursuant to Gov. Bar R. VI, Section 4 shall complete and report, on a form provided by the Commission, at least twenty-four credit hours of continuing legal education for each two-year reporting period. At least two and one-half of the twenty-four credit hours of instruction shall be related to professional conduct and shall include all of the following:

(a) Thirty minutes of instruction on substance abuse, including causes, prevention, detection, and treatment alternatives;

(b) Sixty minutes of instruction related to the Ohio Rules of Professional Conduct;

(c) Sixty minutes of instruction related to professionalism (including A Lawyer's Creed and A Lawyer's Aspirational Ideals adopted by the Supreme Court).

(2) The instruction related to professional conduct required by division (A)(1) of this section may be obtained in a single program or activity or in separate programs or activities that include one or more of the subjects set forth in division (A)(1) of this section.

(B)(1) An attorney whose last name begins with a letter from A through L shall report compliance with the requirements of this rule on or before the thirty-first day of January of even-numbered years for the preceding two calendar years. An attorney whose last name begins with a letter from M through Z shall report compliance with the requirements of this rule on or before the thirty-first day of January of odd-numbered years for the preceding two calendar years. If an attorney's name changes after the attorney is admitted to the practice of law or registers for corporate status pursuant to Gov. Bar R. VI, Section 4, the attorney shall remain in the same alphabetical grouping for purposes of filing all future reports.

(2) If the Commission determines that an attorney has timely completed and timely reported more than the required number of credit hours in a reporting period the Commission may apply a maximum of twelve credit hours to the next reporting period.

(C)(1) If an attorney becomes subject to this rule during a biennial reporting period, the Commission shall adjust the requirements of this rule on a pro rata basis.

(2) An attorney newly admitted to the practice of law or registered for corporate status under Gov. Bar R. VI, Sec. 3, shall be exempt from the educational requirements of division (A) of this section during the lawyer's first biennial reporting period, except if the attorney is admitted to the practice of law or registered for corporate status during the second year of the attorney's reporting period, the attorney shall be exempt during the reporting period that follows the attorney's year of admission or year of initial corporate registration. However, such attorneys shall be required to do both the following:

(a) Complete the New Lawyers Training educational requirements in accordance with division (H) of this section by the deadline set forth in division (C)(2) of this section;

(b) File the report with the Commission required by division (B) of this section.

(3) The following newly admitted attorneys are exempted from the New Lawyers Training educational requirements, but shall otherwise comply with the applicable requirements of this rule:

(a) An attorney registered as inactive pursuant to Gov. Bar R. VI, Section 2;

(b) An attorney admitted to the practice of law in Ohio pursuant to Gov. Bar R. I, Section 9.

(4) If the attorney has been exempt because he or she has been registered as inactive and subsequently registers as active, the attorney shall complete the New Lawyers Training educational requirements of division (H) of this section by the end of the biennial reporting period in which active status is reinstated or, if the attorney's exemption ends on or after July 1 of the second year of the attorney's reporting period, by the end of the next biennial reporting period.

(5) If the attorney has been granted an exemption pursuant to division (F)(1) of this section, which exempts the attorney from completing the New Lawyers Training educational requirements, and the exemption is subsequently terminated, the attorney shall complete the New Lawyers Training educational requirements of division (H) of this section by the end of the biennial reporting period in which the exemption is terminated or, if the exemption ends on or after July 1 of the second year of the attorney's reporting period, by the end of the next reporting period.

(6) Upon registration as active, an attorney who was registered as inactive pursuant to Gov. Bar R. VI, Section 2 or as retired pursuant to former Gov. Bar R. VI, Section 3 may have his or her continuing legal education requirements prorated pursuant to CLE Regulation 305 for the reporting period in which the attorney registers as active. An attorney shall not have his or her continuing legal education requirements prorated and shall comply with all applicable requirements of this rule if the attorney was not registered as inactive or retired for at least twenty-four consecutive months immediately preceding registration as active.

(7) An attorney who is granted a military exemption pursuant to division (F) of this section and whose exemption is terminated may have his or her continu-

ing legal education requirements prorated pursuant to CLE Regulation 305 for the reporting period in which the exemption ends.

(8) An attorney who was exempt for more than two years from the requirements of this rule pursuant to division (F) of this section may have his or her continuing legal education requirements prorated pursuant to CLE Regulation 305 for the reporting period in which the exemption ends.

(D)(1) As part of the continuing legal education requirements of this rule, a magistrate appointed pursuant to Rule 53 of the Ohio Rules of Civil Procedure, Rule 40 of the Ohio Rules of Juvenile Procedure, Rule 14 of the Ohio Traffic Rules, or Rule 19 of the Ohio Rules of Criminal Procedure shall complete at least ten credit hours of continuing legal education in each reporting period that are offered by the Judicial College of the Supreme Court of Ohio and that do not consist solely of the classroom instruction related to professional conduct required by division (A)(1) of this section. A magistrate shall receive one hour of credit under this rule for each credit hour of continuing education completed by the magistrate and offered by the Judicial College of the Supreme Court of Ohio.

(2) Each magistrate shall register annually with the Secretary of the Commission on a form provided by the Commission and shall note the fact of the appointment on the biennial report form filed with the Commission.

(E)(1) As part of the continuing legal education requirements of this rule, an acting judge appointed pursuant to sections 1901.10, 1901.12, or 1907.14 of the Revised Code shall complete at least ten credit hours of continuing legal education in each reporting period that are offered by the Judicial College of the Supreme Court of Ohio and that do not consist solely of the classroom instruction on legal ethics, professional responsibility, and substance abuse required by division (A) of this section. An acting judge shall receive one hour of credit under this rule for each credit hour of continuing education completed by the acting judge and offered by the Judicial College of the Supreme Court of Ohio.

(2) Each acting judge shall register annually with the Secretary of the Commission on a form provided by the Commission and shall note the fact of the appointment on the biennial report form filed with the Commission.

(3) Divisions (E)(1) and (2) of this rule shall not apply to an acting judge who is appointed to serve during an emergency. Unless an acting judge registered pursuant to division (E)(2) of this rule or a visiting or retired assigned judge cannot be assigned, the emergency appointment shall last no longer than twenty-four hours or until the conclusion of the next day the court regularly is open if the appointment is made on a weekend, holiday, or other day on which the court is not open.

(4) As used in division (E)(3) of this rule, "emergency" means an event or circumstance that satisfies both of the following:

(a) The event or circumstance, including but not limited to a family illness or death, is unforeseen and requires the judge to be away from the court;

(b) An acting judge registered pursuant to division (E) of this rule is unavailable or the application for a visiting or retired assigned judge would be impracticable.

(F)(1) Upon approval by the Commission, the following attorneys may be exempted from the requirements of division (A) of this section, but shall be required to file the report required by this section:

(a) An attorney on full-time military duty who does not engage in the private practice of law in Ohio;

(b) An attorney suffering from severe, prolonged illness or disability preventing participation in accredited programs and activities for the duration of the illness or disability;

(c) An attorney who has demonstrated special circumstances unique to that attorney and constituting good cause to grant an exemption for a period not to exceed one year and subject to any prorated adjustment of the continuing legal education requirements.

(2) An attorney who, because of a permanent physical disability or other compelling reason, has difficulty attending programs or activities may request, and the Commission may grant, approval of a substitute program.

(3) A person certified to practice law temporarily pursuant to Gov. Bar R. IX or a foreign legal consultant registered pursuant to Gov. Bar R. XI shall be exempt from the requirements of this rule.

(4) The following attorneys are exempt from all requirements of this rule while in office:

(a) United States judges appointed to office for life pursuant to Article III of the United States Constitution.

(b) United States bankruptcy judges.

(c) United States magistrate judges.

(5) An attorney registered as inactive pursuant to Gov. Bar R. VI, Section 2 or as retired pursuant to former Gov. Bar R. VI, Section 3 shall be exempt from the requirements of this rule.

(G) An attorney against whom a definite or an indefinite suspension is imposed pursuant to Gov. Bar R. V shall complete one credit hour of continuing legal education for each month, or portion of a month, of the suspension. As part of the total credit hours of continuing legal education required under this division, the attorney shall complete one credit hour of the instruction related to professional conduct required by division (A)(1) of this section for each six months, or portion of six months, of the suspension.

(H)(1) Each attorney newly admitted to the practice of law or registered for corporate status under Gov. Bar R. VI, Sec. 3 shall complete and report, as required by division (B) of this section, at least twelve hours of New Lawyers Training instruction in the time frame set forth in division (3)(C)(2) of this section. The twelve credit hours of instruction shall include both the following:

(a) Three hours of instruction in professionalism, law office management, and client fund management consisting of sixty minutes of instruction on topics related to professional conduct, professional relationships, obligations of lawyers, or aspirational ideals of the profession; sixty minutes of instruction on topics related to

fundamental law office management practices; sixty minutes of instruction on topics related to client fund management; and

(b) Nine hours of instruction in one or more substantive law topics that focus on handling legal matters in specific practice areas.

(2) An attorney newly admitted to the practice of law may satisfy the New Lawyers Training instruction requirement by participating in and successfully completing the Supreme Court Lawyer to Lawyer Mentoring Program, provided the attorney also completes three hours of instruction as required in division (H)(1)(a) of this section.

(3) To be approved by the Commission as a New Lawyers Training activity, the activity shall satisfy the following standards, together with any other standards as established by regulation of the Commission:

(i) The activity shall consist of live instruction in a setting physically suited to the educational activity of the program;

(ii) The activity shall be a minimum of one hour in length;

(iii) The activity shall include thorough, high-quality, written materials that emphasize and include checklists of procedures to follow, practical instructions, and forms with guidance as to how they should be completed and when they should be used.

(4) An attorney subject to the provisions of division 3(C)(2) of this section who completes and timely reports more than the number of credit hours required under division (H)(1) of this section may be awarded a maximum of twelve credit hours to the next reporting period.

(5) The Commission may award one credit hour of continuing legal education for every credit hour of New Lawyers Training education completed by an attorney not subject to division (H)(1) of this section.

SECTION 4. Hours and Accreditation

(A)(1) Sixty minutes of actual instruction or other approved activity shall constitute one credit hour.

(2)(a) The Commission may allow up to three credit hours to an instructor for each credit hour taught in an approved continuing legal education program or activity the first time the program is presented by that instructor and one credit hour for each credit hour taught for subsequent presentations of the same program or activity by that instructor, with a maximum of one-half the required credit hours for teaching during the biennial reporting period.

(b) The Commission may allow one-half credit hour for each semester hour taught at a law school accredited by the American Bar Association. Prorated credit may be granted for quarter or trimester hours.

(3) The Commission may allow up to ten credit hours for the publication of an article or book personally authored by the applicant, with a maximum of ten credit hours for publications during a biennial reporting period.

(4) The Commission may allow up to six credit hours for approved self-study during a biennial reporting period.

(5) The Commission may allow three credit hours for each semester hour of a course taken at a law school accredited by the American Bar Association. Prorated credit may be granted for quarter or trimester hours.

(6) The Commission may allow one credit hour for every two credit hours of accredited mayor's court education completed by an attorney for the purpose of serving as a mayor's court magistrate pursuant to section 1905.05 of the Revised Code.

(B) In establishing standards for the granting of credit hours for programs or activities, the Commission shall consider all of the following:

(1) The program or activity shall have significant intellectual or practical content and the primary objective shall be to improve the participant's professional competence as an attorney or judge.

(2) The program or activity for attorneys shall be an organized program of learning dealing with matters directly related to the practice of law, professional responsibility or ethical obligations, law office economics, or similar subjects that will promote the purposes of this rule. The program or activity for judges shall be an organized program of learning dealing with matters directly related to the law or judicial administration that will promote the purposes of Gov. Jud. R. IV.

(3) The program or activity may consist of live instruction or other methods as approved in advance by the Commission, including the use of self-study materials, and that are prepared and conducted by an individual or a group qualified by practical or academic experience.

(4) The program or activity shall be presented in a setting physically suited to the educational activity of the program.

(5) The program or activity should include thorough, high-quality written materials.

(C)(1) The Commission shall establish and publish written procedures for accreditation.

(2) The Commission may establish the term for which the accreditation of a program or activity is effective. The Commission may renew accreditation of a program or activity.

(3) The Commission shall render a decision on an application for accreditation within forty-five days after the date the Commission receives a completed application.

(4) The Commission may require prior approval of a program or activity.

(5) The Commission may accredit programs and activities of other states or national or state legal organizations.

(6) The Commission may grant reciprocal credit for courses taken in another state that are accredited under that state's continuing legal education program.

(7) The Commission may grant automatic accreditation for programs and activities offered by established sponsors, provided that the Commission shall monitor those programs and activities.

(8) The Commission shall notify a sponsor if accreditation is not granted and explain the reasons for denial.

(9) The Commission shall maintain a calendar of accredited programs and activities, and shall make the calendar available on a regular basis.

(10) The Commission shall not accredit a program or activity, any proceeds from which are to be used to support a political party, political action committee, campaign committee of a candidate for public office, or candidate for public office.

(D) The Commission may approve continuing legal education programs or activities jointly or on a reciprocal basis with other states requiring continuing legal education.

(E)(1) The Commission shall establish procedures for evaluating programs and activities offered under this rule.

(2) Commission representatives may attend any program or activity without notice or fee to evaluate the program or activity. No credit hours shall be awarded for attendance to evaluate a program or activity.

(3) The Commission may revoke accreditation for failure to comply with the requirements of this rule, regulations adopted pursuant to this rule, or for other good cause shown. An attorney or judge who attends an accredited program or activity for which accreditation is later revoked shall receive credit provided the attendance occurred prior to notice of revocation.

SECTION 5. Sanctions for Failure to Comply

(A) An attorney or judge who fails to satisfy the applicable minimum continuing legal education requirements of this rule, except for failure to complete a New Lawyers Training Program as required by Section 3(C) of this rule or Gov. Jud. R. IV, or fails to file a biennial report shall be subject to any of the following sanctions:

(1) A late filing fee or other monetary penalty;

(2) A public reprimand;

(3) Probation;

(4) Suspension from the practice of law.

(B) An attorney who is required to complete a New Lawyers Training Program as required by Section 3(C) of this rule and who, without good cause, fails to complete the Program shall be suspended from the practice of law.

(C) A sanction imposed under this section shall not be considered in the imposition of a sanction under Gov. Bar R. V, Section 8.

(D) An attorney or judge who, without good cause, fails to timely file a biennial report or fails to file a complete report may be required to pay a late filing fee of not more than five hundred dollars.

SECTION 6. Enforcement Procedures

(A) An attorney or judge who fails to comply timely with the applicable requirements of this rule or Gov. Jud. R. IV, but does so on or before the thirtieth day of April of the reporting year, shall be assessed a late compliance fee as established by the Commission. The late compliance fee shall accompany the attorney's report of completion

(B) An attorney or judge who fails to comply with the applicable requirements of this rule or Gov. Jud. R. IV, either on a timely basis or within the late compliance period provided for by division (A) of this section, shall be notified of noncompliance by the Commission. The Commission shall send notice of noncompliance by regular mail to the attorney at the address provided by the attorney to the Office of Attorney Services. The notice shall inform the attorney that the attorney will be subject to one or more of the sanctions set forth in Section 5 of this rule unless, on or before the date set forth in the notice, the attorney either comes into compliance or files evidence of compliance that is satisfactory to the Commission. If the attorney does not come into compliance or file evidence of compliance that is satisfactory to the Commission on or before the date set forth in the notice, the Commission shall issue an order imposing a sanction authorized by Section 5 of this rule and consistent with Commission regulation. Notice of the imposition of the sanction shall be sent by certified mail to the attorney at the address provided by the attorney to the Office of Attorney Services. Service of notices in accordance with this section shall be considered effective service.

SECTION 7. Reinstatement

(A) An attorney or judge who is suspended under this rule may be reinstated to the practice of law by applying for reinstatement with the Commission. The application for reinstatement shall be on a form prescribed by the Commission and accompanied by evidence that the attorney or judge has satisfied the deficiency that was the cause of the suspension under this rule and a reinstatement fee of three hundred dollars and payment of all fees assessed for noncompliance with this rule.

(B) Upon receipt of a completed application for reinstatement and verification that the attorney has fulfilled the registration requirements of Gov. Bar R. VI, the Secretary shall issue an order of reinstatement and send notice of the reinstatement to the attorney and the Office of Attorney Services.

(C) Any sanction or reinstatement ordered by the Commission pursuant to this rule shall be published by the Supreme Court Reporter in the Ohio Official Reports and the Ohio State Bar Association Report. Certified copies of any sanction or reinstatement order entered by the Commission pursuant to this rule shall be sent to those persons or organizations named in Gov. Bar R. V, Section 8 (D)(1).

SECTION 8. Effective Date

(A) The effective date of this rule shall be July 1, 1988, except Section 3, which is effective January 1, 1989.

(B)(1) The amendments to Section 3 of this rule, adopted by the Supreme Court of Ohio on June 28, 1989, shall be effective on July 1, 1989.

(2) The amendments to Section 6 of this rule, adopted by the Supreme Court of Ohio on November 22, 1989, shall be effective on December 15, 1989.

(3) The amendments to Section 3 of this rule, adopted by the Supreme Court of Ohio on May 8, 1990, shall be effective on May 28, 1990.

(4) The amendments to Section 3 of this rule, adopted by the Supreme Court of Ohio on July 19, 1990, shall be effective on September 1, 1990 and shall apply to definite and indefinite suspensions imposed on or after that effective date.

(5) The amendments to Sections 3 and 4 of this rule, adopted by the Supreme Court of Ohio on October 16,

1990 and December 11, 1990, shall be effective January 1, 1991 and shall apply to all programs and activities conducted on or after that effective date.

(6) The amendments to Section 2 of this rule, adopted by the Supreme Court of Ohio on February 5, 1991, shall be effective on February 18, 1991.

(7) The amendments to Section 3 of this rule, adopted by the Supreme Court of Ohio on June 4, 1991, shall take effect on September 1, 1991.

(8) The amendments to Section 1 to 7 of this rule, adopted by the Supreme Court of Ohio on October 8, 1991, shall take effect January 1, 1992.

(C) The amendments to this rule adopted by the Supreme Court of Ohio on December 14, 1993 shall take effect on January 1, 1994.

(D) The amendment to Section 4 of this rule, adopted by the Supreme Court of Ohio on October 12, 1994, shall be effective on January 1, 1995.

(E) The amendments to Section 3 of this rule, adopted by the Supreme Court of Ohio on July 12, 1995, shall take effect on January 1, 1996.

(F) The amendments to Section 3 of this rule, adopted by the Supreme Court of Ohio on October 20, 1997, shall take effect on January 1, 1998.

(G) The amendments to Section 3 of this rule, adopted by the Supreme Court of Ohio on September 28, 1998, shall be effective on November 1, 1998.

(H) The amendments to Section 4 of this rule, adopted by the Supreme Court of Ohio on September 21, 1999, shall take effect on January 1, 2000.

(I) The amendment to Section 2 of this rule, adopted by the Supreme Court of Ohio on April 10, 2000, shall take effect on May 8, 2000.

(J) The amendments to Sections 3(C)(2), 3(H), and Section 5 of this Rule, adopted by the Supreme Court of Ohio on November 28, 2000 and shall be effective on July 1, 2001.

(K) The amendments to Sections 2 and 3 of this rule, adopted by the Supreme Court of Ohio on December 11, 2001, shall take effect on January 21, 2002.

(L) The amendments to Section 3(B)(2) and Section 4(B)(1) of this rule, adopted by the Supreme Court of Ohio on April 22, 2002, shall be effective on July 1, 2002.

(M) The amendments to Section 3(B)(2), Section 4(A)(4) and Section 6(C) of this rule, adopted by the Supreme Court of Ohio on July 20, 2004, shall be effective on September 1, 2004.

(N) The amendments to Section 6 (A)(1)(a) of this rule, adopted by the Supreme Court of Ohio on October 11, 2005, shall be effective on November 7, 2005.

(O) The amendments to this rule, adopted by the Supreme Court of Ohio on September 11, 2007, shall be effective on November 1, 2007, and shall apply to the 2008 reporting period and subsequent reporting periods, except that former sections 5, 6, 7, and 8 shall govern sanctions and enforcement procedures for the 2007 reporting period.

(P) The amendments to this rule adopted by the Supreme Court of Ohio on June 24, 2008, shall be effective November 1, 2008, and shall apply to attorneys admitted to the practice of law and attorneys initially registered for corporate status pursuant to Gov.

Bar R. VI, Sec. 3, on or after November 1, 2008. These amendments shall not apply to attorneys registered for corporate status pursuant to Gov. Bar R. VI, Sec. 3, prior to November 1, 2008, who are subsequently admitted to the practice of law on or after November 1, 2008. Attorneys admitted to the practice of law or registered for corporate status prior to November 1, 2008, shall comply with former Sec. 3 of this rule.

History: Effective 7-1-88; 1-1-89; amended, eff 1-1-89; 7-1-89; 12-15-89; 5-28-90; 9-1-90; 1-1-91; 2-18-91; 9-1-91; 1-1-92; 7-1-92; 1-1-94; 1-1-95; 1-1-96; 1-1-98; 11-1-98; 1-1-00; 5-8-00; 7-1-01; 1-21-02; 7-1-02; 9-1-04; 11-7-05; 11-1-07; 11-1-08.

NOTES TO DECISIONS

ANALYSIS

Suspension

Suspension

Attorney who was convicted of a felony conviction was suspended from the practice of law in Ohio pursuant to Ohio Sup. Ct. R. Gov't Bar V(5)(A)(4), he was instructed to complete continuing legal education under Ohio Sup. Ct. R. Gov't Bar X(3)(G), and he was directed as to how to handle clients, fees, files, and opposing counsel. In re Howard, 114 Ohio St. 3d 1515, — Ohio App. 3d —, 2007 Ohio 4425, 872 N.E. 2d 955, 2007 Ohio LEXIS 2163 (Aug. 30, 2007).

RULE XI.

LIMITED PRACTICE OF LAW BY FOREIGN LEGAL CONSULTANTS

SECTION 1. General Requirements

A "Foreign Legal Consultant" is a person who satisfied all of the following criteria:

(A) Has been admitted to the practice of law in a foreign country or political subdivision thereof as an attorney or counselor of law or the equivalent of that country and has been in good standing as an attorney or counselor of law or the equivalent in such foreign country for at least four of the six years immediately preceding the person's application for a Certificate of Registration as described in Section 2 of this rule;

(B) Possesses the character, fitness, and moral qualifications requisite for a member of the Bar of Ohio;

(C) Possesses the requisite documentation evidencing compliance with the immigration laws of the United States;

(D) Intends to practice as a Foreign Legal Consultant in the State of Ohio and to maintain an office in the state for such practice;

(E) Is at least twenty-one years of age;

(F) Obtains a Certificate of Registration as a Foreign Legal Consultant from the Supreme Court pursuant to the requirements set forth in this rule.

SECTION 2. Application Procedure

(A) An applicant for a Certificate of Registration as a Foreign Legal Consultant shall file all of the following with the Office of Bar Admissions of the Supreme Court:

(1) A completed application and a character questionnaire on forms furnished by the Office of Bar Admissions, accompanied by a nonrefundable fee of five hundred fifty dollars;

(2) A certificate from the authority in such foreign country having final jurisdiction over admission to the practice of law or professional discipline, certifying as to the applicant's admission to practice and the date thereof, and as to the good standing of such attorney or counselor of law or the equivalent, together with an authenticated English translation of such certificate if it is not in English;

(3) A letter of recommendation from one of the members or a responsible official of the executive body of the authority having final jurisdiction over admission to the practice of law or professional discipline, or from one of the judges of the highest law court of original jurisdiction of the foreign country, together with an authenticated English translation if it is not in English;

(4) Letters of recommendation from at least two attorneys or counselors of law or the equivalent admitted to and practicing in such foreign country, setting forth the length of time, when, and under what circumstances they have known the applicant, and their appraisal of the applicant's character, fitness, and moral qualifications, together with an authenticated English translation if it is not in English;

(5) A letter of recommendation from at least one attorney who is licensed to practice law in the State of Ohio, who is not registered as a Foreign Legal Consultant under this Rule, setting forth the length of time, when, and under what circumstances he or she has known the applicant, and his or her appraisal of the applicant's character, fitness, and moral qualifications;

(6) A copy or summary of the law and customs of the foreign country that describes the opportunity afforded to members of the Bar of Ohio to establish offices for the giving of legal advice to clients in such foreign country, together with an authenticated English translation if it is not in English;

(7) Such other evidence as to the applicant's education, professional qualifications, character, fitness, and moral qualifications as the Supreme Court may require.

(B) When the applicant has filed the documents required by division (A) of this Section, the Office of Bar Admissions shall forward a copy of the documents to the admissions committee in the county where the applicant resides or intends to practice as a Foreign Legal Consultant, or to such other admissions committee as the Office of Bar Admissions deems appropriate, in accordance with Gov. Bar R. I, Section 10. The admissions committee shall conduct an investigation of the applicant's character, fitness, and moral qualifications for registration as a Foreign Legal Consultant. In conducting its investigation, the admissions committee shall follow the standards and procedures required by Gov. Bar R. I, Section 10, except that a personal interview of the applicant shall not be required. The admissions committee shall report its recommendation in writing to the Office of Bar Admissions on a form prescribed by the Office. Any recommendation other than an unqualified approval shall be deemed a recommendation that the applicant not be issued a Certificate of Registration. An appeal from such recommendation may be taken as provided in Gov. Bar R. I, Section 11.

(C) The Supreme Court shall determine from the documents filed under division (A) of this section, the report of the admissions committee and, in those instances where it is submitted, the report and recommendation of the Board of Commissioners on Character and Fitness, whether the applicant shall be issued a Certificate of Registration as a Foreign Legal Consultant. The Office of Bar Admissions shall notify the applicant concerning the acceptance or rejection of the application.

SECTION 3. Hardship Waiver

Upon a showing that strict compliance with the provisions of Section 2(A)(2), (A)(3), or (A)(4) of this rule would cause the applicant unnecessary hardship, or upon a showing of exceptional professional qualifications to practice law as a Foreign Legal Consultant, the Supreme Court may waive or vary the application of such provisions and permit the applicant to make such other showing as is satisfactory to the Supreme Court.

SECTION 4. Reciprocity

In considering whether to issue a Certificate of Registration under this rule, the Supreme Court may consider whether a member of the Bar of Ohio would have a reasonable and practical opportunity to establish an office in the applicant's country or jurisdiction of admission for the giving of legal advice to clients. Any member of the Bar of Ohio who is seeking or has sought to establish an office in that country or jurisdiction may request the Supreme Court to consider the matter, or the Supreme Court may do so on its own initiative.

SECTION 5. Scope of Practice

A person registered as a Foreign Legal Consultant by the Supreme Court may render legal services in this state subject to the limitation that such person shall not do any of the following:

(A) Appear for a person other than himself or herself as attorney in any court, before any magistrate, referee, or other judicial officer, or before any administrative agency in this state, or prepare pleadings or any other papers or issue subpoenas in any action or proceeding brought in any such court, before any such magistrate, referee, or other judicial officer, or before any such administrative agency in this state;

(B) Prepare any of the following:

(1) Any deed, mortgage, assignment, discharge, lease, or any other instrument affecting title to real property, or statement of opinion as to the legal effect or sufficiency thereof, located in the United States;

(2) Any will or trust instrument affecting the disposition on death of any property located in the United States or owned by a resident thereof;

(3) Any instrument relating to the administration of a decedent's estate in the United States; or

(4) Any instrument with respect to marital rights, relations, or duties of a resident of the United States, or the custody or care of the children of such a resident;

(C) Otherwise render professional legal advice to or perform legal service for any person, firm, corporation, or other legal entity on the law of the State of Ohio, or the United States of America, or any other state or territory thereof, including the District of Columbia, except on the basis of advice from a person acting as counsel to such Foreign Legal Consultant (and not in his or her official capacity as a public employee) duly qualified and entitled (other than by virtue of having been licensed as a Foreign Legal Consultant under this Rule) to practice law in such jurisdiction who has been consulted in the particular matter at hand and has been identified to the client by name;

(D) In any way hold himself or herself out as a member of the Bar of Ohio.

SECTION 6. Title

A person registered as a Foreign Legal Consultant shall not use any title other than "Foreign Legal Consultant" and shall include the name of the foreign country in which he or she is admitted to practice law. A Foreign Legal Consultant may also add his or her authorized title and firm name used in the foreign country.

SECTION 7. Disciplinary Provisions

(A) Each registered Foreign Legal Consultant shall do all of the following:

(1) Be subject to regulation by the Supreme Court, and to reprimand, suspension, or revocation of his or her Certificate of Registration in accordance with the Ohio Rules of Professional Conduct set forth in Gov. Bar R. IV and with the disciplinary procedural rules applicable to members of the Bar of Ohio set forth in Gov. Bar R. V;

(2) Provide the Office of Bar Admissions with evidence of professional liability insurance or other proof of financial responsibility, in such amount as the Supreme Court may prescribe, to ensure the Foreign Legal Consultant's proper professional conduct and responsibility;

(3) Execute and file all of the following with the Office of Bar Admissions, in such form and manner as the Office may prescribe:

(a) An oath attesting that such Foreign Legal Consultant will abide by the rules and regulations applicable to such Foreign Legal Consultant;

(b) A document setting forth the Foreign Legal Consultant's address in the State of Ohio and designating the Director of Bar Admissions of the Supreme Court as agent upon whom process may be served, with like effect as if served personally upon the Foreign Legal Consultant, in any action or proceeding thereafter brought against the Foreign Legal Consultant arising out of or based upon any legal services rendered or offered to be rendered by the Foreign Legal Consultant within or to residents of the State of Ohio;

(c) The Foreign Legal Consultant's commitment to notify the Office of Bar Admissions of any resignation or revocation of the Foreign Legal Consultant's admission to practice in the foreign country of admission, of any censure, suspension, or expulsion in respect to such admission, or of any change of address within the State of Ohio.

(B) Service of process on the Director of Bar Admissions, pursuant to the designation required by division (A)(3)(b) of this section, shall be made by personally delivering to and leaving with the Director of Bar Admissions at his or her office, duplicate copies of such process together with a fee of ten dollars. Service of process shall be complete when the Director of Bar Admissions has been so served. The Director of Bar Admissions shall promptly send one of such copies to the Foreign Legal Consultant to whom the process is directed, by certified mail, return receipt requested, addressed to such Foreign Legal Consultant at the address specified by him or her.

(C) Insofar as applicable and not inconsistent with this rule, Gov. Bar R. IV and V shall apply to registered Foreign Legal Consultants. For the purpose of applying Gov. Bar R. IV and V, the terms "attorney," "attorney and counselor at law," "member of the Bar of Ohio," or other such designation in those rules shall be deemed to include registered Foreign Legal Consultants.

SECTION 8. Annual Renewal

The Certificate of Registration as a Foreign Legal Consultant shall be valid for one year, unless suspended or revoked, and may be renewed upon the filing of an annual request with the Office of Bar Admissions. The annual request shall be on a form furnished by the Office of Bar Admissions and shall be accompanied by payment of an annual renewal fee of two hundred dollars and such evidence as the Supreme Court shall deem necessary to demonstrate that all requirements for the issuance of an original certificate continue to be met.

History: Effective 1-1-89; 10-1-00; 10-1-03; 2-1-07, 5-1-07.

RULE XII.
PRO HAC VICE ADMISSION [EFFECTIVE JANUARY 1, 2011]

SECTION 1. Definitions

As used in this rule:

(A) **Tribunal:** A tribunal is defined as a court, legislative body, administrative agency, or other body acting in an adjudicative capacity. A legislative body, administrative agency, or other body acts in an adjudicative capacity when a neutral official, after the presentation of evidence or legal argument by a party or parties, will render a binding legal judgment directly affecting a party's interests in a particular matter.

(B) **Proceeding:** A proceeding is defined as an adjudicative matter pending before a tribunal.

SECTION 2. Requirements for Permission to Appear Pro Hac Vice

(A) A tribunal of this state may grant permission to appear pro hac vice to an out-of-state attorney who is admitted to practice in the highest court of a state,

commonwealth, territory, or possession of the United States or the District of Columbia, or who is admitted to practice in the courts of a foreign state and is in good standing to appear pro hac vice in a proceeding.

(1) An attorney is eligible to be granted permission to appear pro hac vice if:

(a) The attorney neither resides in nor is regularly employed at an office in this state or;

(b) The attorney is registered for corporate status in Ohio pursuant to Gov. Bar R. VI, Section 3 or;

(c) The attorney resides in this state but lawfully practices from offices in one or more other states or;

(d) The attorney maintains an office or other systematic and continuous presence in Ohio pursuant to Prof. Cond. Rule 5.5(d)(2) or;

(e) The attorney has permanently relocated to Ohio in the last 120 days and is currently an applicant pending admission under Gov. Bar R. I.

(2) A tribunal shall not grant permission to appear pro hac vice to an attorney who has taken and failed the Ohio bar examination, been denied admission without examination, or had an application for admission in Ohio denied on character and fitness grounds pursuant to Gov. Bar R. I within the last five years.

(3) Prior to being granted permission to appear pro hac vice by a tribunal, the attorney shall have applied for registration with the Supreme Court Office of Attorney Services, paid an annual registration fee of $100.00, and been issued a certificate of pro hac vice registration. The application for registration shall include the following information:

(a) The attorney's residential address, office address, and the name and address of the attorney's law firm or employer, if applicable;

(b) The jurisdictions in which the attorney has ever been licensed to practice law, including the dates of admission to practice, resignation, or retirement, and any attorney registration numbers;

(c) An affidavit stating that the attorney has never been disbarred and whether the attorney is currently under suspension or has resigned with discipline pending in any jurisdiction the attorney has ever been admitted;

(d) A statement the attorney satisfies the requirements in Section 2(A)(1)-(2);

(e) A statement that the attorney will comply with the applicable statutes, law and procedural rules of the State of Ohio, and the rules, policies, and procedures of the tribunal before which the attorney seeks to practice and will be familiar with and comply with the Ohio Rules of Professional Conduct and the Rules for the Government of the Bar.

(4) An attorney representing an amicus curiae in support of an indigent defendant in a criminal matter may file with the Office of Attorney Services an application for a waiver of the annual registration fee. The waiver shall not apply to other proceedings in which the attorney seeks permission to appear pro hac vice.

(5) An attorney may participate pro hac vice in no more than three proceedings under this rule in the same calendar year the application is filed. In the event a proceeding continues to the next or subsequent

calendar years, the proceeding will not count toward the annual limitation. An appeal from a trial court or court of appeals, an appeal of an administrative agency order or ruling, a transfer of an action to a court of competent jurisdiction, or the consolidation of two or more cases, where the attorney participated in the initial proceeding, shall not be counted toward the annual limitation. Participation for the first time by an attorney at any stage during a proceeding shall count toward the annual limitation.

(6) The attorney may file a motion for permission to appear pro hac vice accompanied by a copy of the certificate of pro hac vice registration furnished by the Office of Attorney Services, and includes the following information:

(a) The attorney's residential address, office address, and the name and address of the attorney's law firm or employer, if applicable;

(b) The jurisdictions in which the attorney has ever been licensed to practice law, including the dates of admission to practice, resignation, or retirement, and any attorney registration numbers;

(c) An affidavit stating that the attorney has never been disbarred and whether the attorney is currently under suspension or has resigned with discipline pending in any jurisdiction the attorney has ever been admitted;

(d) A statement that the attorney has not been granted permission to appear pro hac vice in more than three proceedings before Ohio tribunals in the current calendar year pursuant to Section 2(A)(5);

(e) The name and attorney registration number of an active Ohio attorney, in good standing, who has agreed to associate with the out-of-state attorney.

(B) An attorney granted permission to appear pro hac vice in a pending proceeding shall inform each tribunal in which the attorney has been granted permission to appear of any disciplinary action taken against the attorney since the date permission was granted.

(C) Any party to a proceeding may object to the motion of an attorney in a manner and method prescribed by the tribunal.

(D) A motion to be granted permission to appear pro hac vice filed with a tribunal shall be served by the filing attorney on all known parties and attorneys of record.

(E) A tribunal may order a hearing on a motion to appear pro hac vice and enter an order granting or denying the motion.

SECTION 3. Leave to File a Motion Instanter

An attorney may file a motion to be granted permission to appear pro hac vice instanter with a tribunal if the attorney has previously filed an application with the Office of Attorney Services and the attorney is required to appear in a proceeding fewer than five business days from the date of filing the application. The attorney shall attach a time stamped copy of the application to the motion to be granted permission to appear pro hac

vice instanter.

SECTION 4. Notice of Permission to Appear Pro Hac Vice

All attorneys granted permission to appear pro hac vice by a tribunal shall file a Notice of Permission to Appear Pro Hac Vice with the Office of Attorney Services within thirty days after a tribunal grants permission to appear in a proceeding. The Notice of Permission to Appear Pro Hac Vice shall include copies of the court or administrative order granting permission. Failure to file the notice within the time specified shall result in automatic exclusion from practice within this state. The Office of Attorney Services shall, by certified mail, notify all tribunals in which the attorney has appeared of the attorney's exclusion.

SECTION 5. Renewal of Registration

If an attorney continues to appear on the basis of permission to appear pro hac vice in any proceeding pending as of the first day of a new calendar year, the attorney shall pay a renewal fee equal to the annual registration fee set forth in Section 2(A)(3). This renewal fee shall be due within thirty days of the start of that calendar year and shall be tendered to the Office of Attorney Services and accompanied by an updated registration form. Failure to pay the required renewal fee and file a new registration form within the time specified shall result in automatic exclusion from practice within this state. The Office of Attorney Services shall, by certified mail, notify all tribunals in which the attorney has appeared of the attorney's exclusion. If the proceeding has concluded or if the attorney has withdrawn from the proceeding, the attorney must so notify the Office of Attorney Services by the deadline for renewal of registration.

SECTION 6. Reinstatement

An attorney automatically excluded from practice in Ohio for failing to file a Notice of Permission to Appear Pro Hac Vice under Section 4, or failing to pay a renewal registration fee required under Section 5, may file a Petition for Reinstatement with the Office of Attorney Services. The petition shall describe the circumstances that resulted in the automatic exclusion, and a list of all proceedings in which the attorney had been permitted to appear pro hac vice, and shall be accompanied by the appropriate Notice of Permission to Appear Pro Hac Vice if the exclusion is under Section 4, or a renewal registration fee if the exclusion is under Section 5. The Office of Attorney Services shall inform all tribunals where the attorney appeared by certified mail if the attorney is reinstated.

SECTION 7. Attorney Services Fund

Payment of the annual registration fee shall be deposited in the Attorney Services Fund established under Gov. Bar R. VI, Section 7.

History: Effective 1-1-11.

1303 [Gov. Bar R. XIII] RULES FOR THE GOVERNMENT OF THE BAR

RULE XIII.

[RESERVED]

(Former Rule XIII entitled Funds for Dispute Resolution Program was repealed effective Oct. 12, 2004)

RULE XIV.

CERTIFICATION OF ATTORNEYS AS SPECIALISTS

SECTION 1. Purpose

The purpose of this rule is to enhance public access to appropriate legal services by regulating the certification of lawyers as specialists.

SECTION 2. Supreme Court Commission on Certification of Attorneys as Specialists; Establishment of the Commission

(A) **Membership**

(1) There is hereby created the Supreme Court Commission on Certification of Attorneys as Specialists, consisting of seventeen members appointed by the Supreme Court, as follows:

(a) Twelve attorneys admitted to the practice of law in Ohio, one from each appellate district;

(b) Three law faculty members from separate Ohio law schools engaged in full-time legal education;

(c) Two judges.

The appellate district of each of the twelve attorneys will be determined by the location of the attorney's principal office.

(2) Except as provided in division (A)(4) of this section, members of the Commission shall serve three year terms beginning on the first day of January. Members shall be eligible for reappointment, but shall not serve more than two consecutive terms of three years.

(3) Vacancies on the commission shall be filled in the same manner as original appointments. A member appointed to fill a vacancy occurring prior to the expiration of the term for which the appointee's predecessor was serving shall hold office for the remainder of the term. If an attorney member no longer has his or her principal office in the district from which he or she was appointed, if a faculty member is no longer engaged in full-time legal education in an Ohio law school, or if a judicial member leaves office, the member shall be disqualified and a vacancy shall occur.

(4) Initial appointments to the Commission shall be as follows:

(a) Five shall be for terms beginning on the date of appointment and ending December 31, 1994;

(b) Six shall be for terms beginning on the date of appointment and ending December 31, 1995;

(c) Six shall be for terms beginning on the date of appointment and ending December 31, 1996.

(5) At its first meeting, the Commission shall elect a chair and a vice-chair, and other officers as are necessary, who shall each serve for the remainder of 1993. Thereafter, the Commission shall elect a chair, vice-chair, and other officers. The officers shall serve for two years and may be reelected, but a member shall not serve as chair or vice-chair for more than two consecu-

tive two year terms.

(6) After the first meeting, the Commission shall meet at the call of the chair or upon written request of a majority of the members. A majority of the members constitutes a quorum. No action shall be taken by the Commission without the concurrence of a majority of the members attending and constituting a quorum at that meeting.

(7) Members shall serve without compensation, but shall be reimbursed for expenses incurred in the performance of their official duties.

(B) **Secretary of the Commission** The Administrative Director of the Supreme Court, or his or her designee, shall serve as the Secretary of the Commission.

(C) **Powers and Duties of the Commission** The Commission shall approve and regulate agencies that certify lawyers practicing in Ohio as specialists and shall do the following:

(1) Recommend to the Supreme Court the fields of law subject to specialization designation on the Commission's own motion or on petition of interested parties and on the criteria as it may establish. In identifying a field of law as a specialty area, the Commission shall consider whether:

(a) The public interest would be served;

(b) There is sufficient interest manifested to warrant the designation of a specialty field and the expense of its administration;

(c) Appropriate standards of proficiency can be established for the specialty field;

(d) There is satisfactory evidence of the existence or prospect of an adequate program of continuing legal education in the specialty field;

(e) Designation of the specialty field would fulfill the objectives and further the orderly growth of specialization by lawyers in Ohio.

(2) Approve agencies as qualified to certify lawyers as specialists in a particular field of law and adopt standards that must be satisfied by certifying agencies.

(3) Adopt standards that certifying agencies shall establish in certifying attorneys as specialists, in addition to those standards set forth in Section 3 of this rule.

(4) Review and evaluate the programs of certifying agencies to ensure compliance with this rule.

(5) Deny, suspend, or revoke the approval of a certifying agency upon the Commission's determination that the agency has failed to comply with the standards established by this rule and the regulations and standards of the Commission.

(6) Maintain records of attorneys certified as specialists by agencies approved under this rule and report to the Disciplinary Counsel or a Certified Grievance Committee any attorney who the Commission believes has violated this rule.

(7) Cooperate with other organizations, boards, and agencies engaged in the field of attorney specialization.

(8) Enlist the assistance of advisory committees to advise the Commission.

(9) By the first day of January of each year, submit a report to the Supreme Court concerning the activities of the Commission and the status of attorney specialization and certification in the state.

(10) Enhance public access to appropriate legal services by informing the general public of the meaning of the certification of an attorney as a specialist.

(11) Subject to the approval of the Supreme Court, adopt regulations reasonably needed to implement this rule that are not inconsistent with this rule.

SECTION 3. Standards for Approval of Certifying Agencies

(A) A certifying agency shall be a not-for-profit organization. A majority of the governing board of a certifying agency shall include attorneys who, in the judgment of the Commission, are experts in the field of law covered by the specialty and have extensive practice or involvement in the specialty.

(B) The standards for certification of specialists of a certifying agency shall include, as a minimum, the standards required for certification set out in this rule and in the regulations and standards adopted by the Commission. The standards shall provide a reasonable basis for determining that the attorney possesses special competence in a particular field of law as demonstrated by all of the following:

(1) Substantial involvement in the specialty field during the three-year period immediately preceding application to the certifying agency, measured by the type and number of cases or matters handled, the amount of time spent practicing in the specialty field, or other appropriate criteria;

(2) Recommendations from attorneys or judges who are familiar with the competence of the attorney, none of whom are related to, or engaged in the legal practice with, the attorney;

(3) Objective evaluation of the attorney's knowledge of the substantive and procedural law in the specialty field, to be determined by examination.

(C) The certifying agency shall investigate recommendations and obtain any data that may be required to ensure the attorney is in compliance with this rule.

(D) The certifying agency shall report to the Commission all attorneys it certifies as specialists under this rule.

(E) Each certifying agency shall submit annually to the Commission reports as the Commission directs to ensure compliance with this rule.

(F) The certifying agency shall cooperate with the Commission and perform other duties as may be required by the Commission.

SECTION 4. Prerequisites for Certification of Specialists

To be certified as a specialist, an attorney shall satisfy both of the following requirements:

(A) Be registered as active pursuant to Gov. Bar R. VI;

(B) Be certified by an agency approved by the Commission.

SECTION 5. Privileges Conferred and Limitations Imposed

(A) A specialist certified under this rule may communicate the fact that he or she is certified by the certifying agency as a specialist in the field of law involved. A specialist shall not represent, expressly or impliedly, that he or she is certified by the Supreme Court or the Commission or by an entity other than the certifying agency. A specialist may represent that the certifying agency is approved by the Commission, but shall not represent that the certifying agency is approved by the Supreme Court of Ohio.

(B) This rule shall not limit the right of a certified specialist to practice in any field of law.

(C) An attorney shall not be required to be certified as a specialist in order to practice in any field of law.

(D) An attorney may be certified as a specialist in more than one field of law.

SECTION 6. Minimum Standards for Continued Certification of Specialists

(A) The period of certification as a specialist shall be set by the certifying agency, but shall be not less than three or more than seven years. During the certification period, the Commission may require directly, or through the certifying agency, evidence from the specialist of continued qualification for certification as a specialist.

(B) Application for and approval of continued certification as a specialist shall be required prior to the end of each certification period. To qualify for continued certification as a specialist, an attorney applicant must pay the required fee and satisfy the requirements for certification renewal established by the Commission and the certifying agency.

(C) In addition to the requirements of Gov. Bar R. X, a specialist shall complete twelve hours of continuing legal education every two years in each specialty area for which he or she is certified. Proof of completion shall be submitted in the manner required by Gov. Bar R. X.

SECTION 7. Fees; Miscellaneous

(A) The Commission shall establish and collect reasonable fees from the certifying agencies and certified specialists under this rule.

(B) Initial funds for the operation of the Commission shall be appropriated by the Supreme Court from the Attorney Registration Fund. Thereafter, the Commission shall be funded from the fees established pursuant to this rule.

(C) At the request of the Administrative Director of the Supreme Court, the Commission shall prepare and submit a proposed annual budget for approval by the Supreme Court.

(D) Records of the Commission shall be public records and shall be made available for inspection to any member of the general public during regular business hours. Upon request, the person responsible for such records shall make copies available at cost, within a reasonable period of time, and such records shall be maintained in such a manner that they can be made available for inspection in accordance with this rule.

SECTION 8. Effective Date

This rule shall take effect on January 1, 1993.

History: Amended, eff 11-17-93; 5-8-00.

RULE XV.

SUPREME COURT COMMISSION ON PRO-FESSIONALISM

SECTION 1. Creation of Commission; Purpose

(A) There shall be a Supreme Court Commission on Professionalism, which shall have the duties set forth in this rule.

(B) The Commission is created for the purpose of promoting professionalism among attorneys admitted to the practice of law in Ohio. Professionalism connotes adherence by attorneys in their relations with judges, colleagues, clients, employees, and the public to aspirational standards of conduct. The Commission shall devote its attention to the law as a profession and to maintaining the highest standards of integrity and honor among members of the profession.

SECTION 2. Membership of the Commission

(A) The Commission shall consist of fifteen members appointed as follows:

(1) Five judges appointed by the Supreme Court;

(2) Six attorneys admitted to the practice of law in Ohio for at least six years, three of whom shall be appointed by the Ohio Metropolitan Bar Association Consortium and three of whom shall be appointed by the Ohio State Bar Association;

(3) Two law school administrators or faculty, each of whom shall be admitted to the practice of law in Ohio for at least six years and employed full-time by a different law school in Ohio, appointed by the Supreme Court;

(4) Two persons who are not admitted to the practice of law in any state, appointed by the Supreme Court.

(B)(1) Except as provided in division (C) of this section, members of the Commission shall serve three year terms beginning on the first day of January. Members shall be eligible for reappointment, but shall not serve more than two consecutive terms of three years.

(2) Vacancies on the Commission shall be filled in the same manner as original appointments. A member appointed to fill a vacancy occurring prior to the expiration of the term for which his or her predecessor was appointed shall hold office for the remainder of the unexpired term. If an attorney member no longer practices in Ohio, if a judge member leaves office, or if a law school administrator or faculty no longer is employed full-time by a law school in Ohio, the member shall be disqualified and a vacancy shall occur.

(3) The Supreme Court shall appoint one member of the Commission as chair and one member as vice-chair. The chair and vice-chair shall serve one year terms and may be reappointed, but shall not serve more than two consecutive terms of one year.

(C) Initial attorney appointments to the Commission after the effective date of this amendment shall be made as follows:

(1) One attorney shall be appointed by the Ohio Metropolitan Bar Association Consortium to a term ending December 31, 2006;

(2) Attorney members serving on the Commission on the effective date of this amendment shall continue to serve on the Commission until the expiration of the term of office to which they were appointed and, upon expiration of their terms, may be reappointed pursuant to division (C)(2) of this rule if otherwise eligible for reappointment. Upon the first expiration of terms of office after the effective date of this amendment, appointments shall be made as follows:

(a) One attorney shall be appointed by the Ohio Metropolitan Bar Association Consortium, and one attorney shall be appointed by the Ohio State Bar Association, each member to serve a term commencing January 1, 2005 and ending December 31, 2007;

(b) One attorney shall be appointed by the Ohio Metropolitan Bar Association Consortium, and one attorney shall be appointed by the Ohio State Bar Association, each member to serve a term commencing January 1, 2006 and ending December 31, 2008;

(c) One attorney shall be appointed by the Ohio State Bar Association to a term commencing January 1, 2007 and ending December 31, 2009.

(3) If an attorney member serving on the Commission on the effective date of this amendment resigns from the Commission prior to the expiration of his or her current term of office, that member's successor shall be appointed to the balance of the unexpired term. Any appointments to fill vacancies under division (C)(3) of this rule shall be alternated by the Ohio Metropolitan Bar Association Consortium and the Ohio State Bar Association, with the Ohio State Bar Association making the first appointment to fill a vacancy.

(D) Members of the Commission shall serve without compensation, but shall be reimbursed for expenses incurred in the performance of their official duties.

SECTION 3. Duties of the Commission

(A) The Commission shall do all of the following:

(1) Monitor and coordinate professionalism efforts and activities in Ohio courts, bar associations, and law schools and by other entities;

(2) Monitor professionalism efforts and activities in jurisdictions outside Ohio;

(3) Promote and sponsor state and local activities that emphasize and enhance professionalism;

(4) Develop and make available educational materials and other information for use by judicial organizations, bar associations, law schools, and other entities in emphasizing and enhancing professionalism;

(5) Assist in the development of law school orientation programs, law school curricula, new lawyer training programs, and continuing education programs that emphasize professionalism;

(6) Make recommendations to the Supreme Court, judicial organizations, bar associations, law schools, and other entities on methods by which professionalism can be enhanced;

(7) Oversee and administer a mentoring program for attorneys newly admitted to the practice of law in Ohio as the Commission deems appropriate. This program will be reviewed by the Secretary and the Commission every three years, at which time the Commission will submit a report to the Court providing statistics about program participants, an overview of feedback received from participant evaluations, and an assessment of the

program's success.

(B) The Commission shall seek and may accept grants, contributions, and other awards to supplement funding provided by the Supreme Court.

SECTION 4. Staff and Budget

In consultation with the administrative director, the Commission may employ staff appropriate to perform the duties of the Commission. On or before the first day of May each year, the Commission shall prepare and submit to the administrative director a proposed budget for the fiscal year that begins on the ensuing first day of July. The budget shall be in the form prescribed by the administrative director, include a narrative of planned activities, and identify additional sources of funding that the Commission intends to pursue to supplement funding being requested from the Supreme Court.

History: Effective 9-1-92; amended effective 9-1-04, 11-1-08.

RULE XVI.

LAWYER REFERRAL AND INFORMATION SERVICES; LEGAL SERVICES PLANS

SECTION 1. Requirements for Lawyer Referral and Information Services

(A) A lawyer referral and information service operating in Ohio shall comply with all of the following:

(1) Operate in the public interest for the purpose of referring prospective clients to lawyers, pro bono and public service programs, and government, consumer, or other agencies who can provide the assistance the clients need in light of their financial circumstance, spoken language, any disability, geographical convenience, and the nature and complexity of their problem;

(2) Call itself a lawyer referral service or a lawyer referral and information service;

(3) Be open to all lawyers who are licensed and admitted to the practice of law in Ohio, who maintain an office in the geographical area to be served by the service, and who meet reasonable, objectively determined experience requirements established by the service, pay the reasonable registration and membership fees established by the service, and maintain in force a policy of errors and omissions insurance in an amount established by the service;

(4) Establish rules that prohibit lawyer members of the service from charging prospective clients to whom a client is referred, fees and or costs that exceed charges the client would have incurred had no lawyer referral service been involved;

(5) Establish procedures to survey periodically clients referred to determine client satisfaction with its operations and to investigate and take appropriate action with respect to client complaints against lawyer members of the service, and the service and its employees;

(6) Establish procedures for admitting, suspending, or removing lawyers from its roll of panelists and promulgate rules that prohibit the making of a fee generating referral to any lawyer who has an ownership interest in, or who operates or is employed by the lawyer referral service, or who is associated with a law firm that has an ownership interest in, or operates or is employed by the lawyer referral service;

(7) Establish subject-matter panels, eligibility for which shall be determined on the basis of experience and other substantial, objectively determinable criteria;

(8) As a condition of participation in the referral service, not place limits on the lawyer's selection of co-counsel to other lawyers listed with the referral service;

(9) Not make a fee-generating referral to any lawyer who has an ownership interest in or who operates or is employed by the lawyer referral service or who is associated with a law firm that has an ownership interest in or operates or is employed by a lawyer referral service;

(B) Ninety days before a new service begins operations, it shall register with the Supreme Court Office of Attorney Services by completing and filing a registration form prescribed by the Office. On or before the first day of March each year, the service shall file an annual report with the Supreme Court Office of Attorney Services. The report shall contain information regarding the activity of the service for the preceding calendar year and shall be filed on a form prescribed by the Office.

(C) A lawyer referral and information service operating in Ohio may require lawyers participating in the service to do one or more of the following:

(1) Pay a fee calculated as a percentage of legal fees earned by any lawyer panelist to whom the lawyer referral service has referred a matter, in addition to payment of a membership or registration fee as provided in division (A)(3) of this section. The income from the percentage fee shall be used only to pay the reasonable operating expenses of the service and to fund public service activities of the service or its sponsoring organization, including the delivery of pro bono public services;

(2) Submit any fee disputes with a referred client to mandatory fee arbitration;

(3) Participate in moderate and no-fee panels and other special panels established by the service that respond to the referral needs of the consumer public, eligibility for which shall be determined on the basis of experience and other substantial objectively determinable criteria.

SECTION 2. Conditions for Participating in a Lawyer Referral Service

(A) Each lawyer referral and information service shall include the following provisions in its application or agreement governing participation in the lawyer referral and information service:

(1) Each attorney-member of the service shall maintain professional liability insurance in the minimum amounts of one hundred thousand dollars per occurrence and three hundred thousand dollars in the aggregate. The service shall require the attorney-member to provide proof of insurance on an annual basis in the form of a copy of the current policy declarations page.

(2) An attorney-member shall be suspended from further participation in the service under any of the following circumstances:

(a) The attorney-member is disbarred or suspended from the practice of law;

(b) Any grievance proceeding against the attorney-member results in a determination of probable cause;

(c) The attorney-member is named in a criminal indictment, information, or complaint that charges a crime involving moral turpitude or dishonesty.

(3) Each attorney-member shall promptly notify the service, in writing, if the attorney-member is not in full compliance with the terms of the service's referral agreement, is notified of a probable cause determination in a grievance proceeding against the attorney-member, is named in a criminal indictment, information, or complaint that charges a crime involving moral turpitude or dishonesty, or if any information in the attorney-member's application to become a member of the service is not true and correct in any respect.

(4) Each attorney-member shall waive the right to privacy granted pursuant to Gov. Bar R. V, Section 11(E) to the extent necessary to permit the service to be informed or inquire as to the existence of any grievance proceeding against the attorney-member that results in a determination of probable cause.

(5) The service and each attorney-member shall agree to participate in arbitration or mediation in an effort to settle fee disputes that may arise between the service and attorney-member, as a result of referrals made by the service to the attorney-member. Division (A)(5) of this section shall not apply to fee disputes between an attorney-member and his or her client.

(B) The requirements set forth in this rule represent minimum standards applicable to each lawyer referral and information service. A service may impose on its attorney-members more restrictive provisions, including, but not limited to any of the following:

(1) Additional grounds for suspension from further participation in the service;

(2) Additional requirements regarding notice of pending grievance proceedings;

(3) The waiver of privacy granted pursuant to Gov. Bar R. V, Section 11(E) prior to a determination of probable cause.

(C) As used in this section, "probable cause" has the same meaning as used in Gov. Bar R. V, Section 6(A)(2).

SECTION 3. Disclosure of Information for Reporting Purposes

Each attorney participating in a lawyer referral service may give written notice to his or her client informing the client that the attorney may be required to disclose to the service that referred the client certain information regarding the client's case. The notice shall describe the information that may be reported, including, but not limited to the current status of the client's case and the amount of the attorney's fee, and indicate that the disclosure is required in order for the service to satisfy its reporting requirements to the Supreme Court Committee for Lawyer Referral and Information Services. The notice shall be similar in substance to the following:

ACKNOWLEDGEMENT OF UNDERSTANDING

Pursuant to the reporting requirements set forth by the Supreme Court of Ohio Committee for Lawyer Referral and Information Services, I understand and acknowledge that (insert Attorney's Name), my attorney, may be required to release and report to (insert name of the Lawyer Referral Service), the lawyer referral service that recommended my attorney's services to me, pertinent information regarding my case, which may include the current status of my case and the amount of the attorney's fees. I further acknowledge that by signing this document, the disclosure policy applicable to my case has been fully explained to me and that all of my questions have been answered regarding this matter.

_____
Client's Signature

SECTION 4. Application

Sections 1 to 3 of this rule shall not apply to any of the following:

(A) A plan of prepaid legal services insurance authorized to operate in Ohio or a group or prepaid legal plan, whether operated by a union, trust, mutual benefit or aid association, corporation or other entity or person, that provides unlimited or a specified amount of telephone advice or personal communications at no charge, other than a periodic membership or beneficiary fee, to the members or beneficiaries and furnishes to or pays for legal services for its members or beneficiaries;

(B) Individual, attorney-to-attorney referrals;

(C) Attorneys jointly advertising their services in a manner disclosing that the advertising is solely to solicit clients for themselves;

(D) Any pro bono legal assistance program that does not accept fees from attorneys or clients for referral.

SECTION 5. Legal Service Plans

Any bona fide organization that recommends, furnishes, or pays for legal services to its members or beneficiaries shall satisfy all of the following:

(A) The organization, including any affiliate, is organized and operated so that no profit is derived by it from the rendition of legal services by lawyers, and that, if the organization is organized for profit, the legal services are not rendered by lawyers employed, directed, supervised, or selected by it except in connection with matters where the organization bears ultimate liability of its member or beneficiary.

(B) Neither the lawyer, the lawyer's partner, associate, or any other lawyer affiliated with the lawyer or the lawyer's firm, nor any nonlawyer, shall have initiated or promoted the organization for the primary purpose of providing financial or other benefit to the lawyer, partner, associate, or affiliated lawyer.

(C) The organization is not operated for the purpose of procuring legal work or financial benefit for any lawyer as a private practitioner outside of the legal services program of the organization.

(D) The member or beneficiary to whom the legal services are furnished, and not the organization, is recognized as the client of the lawyer in the matter.

(E) Any member or beneficiary who is entitled to have legal services furnished or paid for by the organization, if such member or beneficiary so desires, may select counsel other than that furnished, selected, or approved by the organization; provided, however, that the organization shall be under no obligation to pay for the legal services furnished by the attorney selected by the beneficiary unless the terms of the legal services plan specifically provide for payment.

(F) Any member or beneficiary may assert a claim that representation by counsel furnished, selected, or approved by the organization would be unethical, improper, or inadequate under the circumstances of the matter involved. The plan shall provide for adjudication of a claim under division (E) of this section and appropriate relief through substitution of counsel or providing that the beneficiary may select counsel and the organization shall pay for the legal services rendered by selected counsel to the extent that such services are covered under the plan and in an amount equal to the cost that would have been incurred by the plan if the plan had furnished designated counsel.

(G) The lawyer does not know or have cause to know that the organization is in violation of applicable laws, rules of court, and other legal requirements that govern its operations.

(H) The organization has filed with the Supreme Court Office of Attorney Services, on or before the first day of March each year, a report with respect to its legal service plan, if any, showing its terms, its schedule of benefits, its subscription charges, agreements with counsel, and financial results of its legal service activities.

History: Effective April 16, 1996; amended effective February 1, 2007; April 30, 2007.

RULE XVII.

COMMISSION ON LEGAL EDUCATION OPPORTUNITY

SECTION 1. Creation of Committee; Purpose
There shall be a Supreme Court Commission on Legal Education Opportunity, which shall have the duties set forth in this rule. The Commission is created for the purpose of assisting minority, low income, or educationally disadvantaged college graduates in pursuing a law degree at an Ohio law school that is approved by the American Bar Association.

SECTION 2. Membership of the Commission
(A) The Commission shall consist of nine members appointed by the Supreme Court as follows:

(1) Three attorneys admitted to the practice of law in Ohio;

(2) Two judges;

(3) Two administrators or faculty members from separate Ohio law schools;

(4) Two non-attorneys who are not employed by or affiliated with an Ohio law school.

(B)(1) Except as provided in division (C) of this section, members of the Commission shall serve three-year terms, beginning on the first day of January, and shall be eligible for reappointment. Members of the Commission shall serve without compensation, but shall be reimbursed for expenses incurred in the performance of their official duties.

(2) Vacancies on the Commission shall be filled in the same manner as original appointments. A member appointed to fill a vacancy prior to the expiration of the term to which his or her predecessor was appointed shall hold office for the remainder of the unexpired term. If a member no longer satisfies the requirements of division (A) of this section under which the member was appointed, the member shall be disqualified and a vacancy shall occur.

(3) The Supreme Court shall appoint one member of the Commission to serve as chair. The chair shall serve a two-year term, unless his or her term on the Commission expires prior to the end of the term as chair, and may be reappointed. No person shall serve as chair for more than two consecutive terms of two years.

(C) Initial appointments to the Commission shall be made as follows:

(1) One judge, one attorney, and one nonattorney shall be appointed to terms ending December 31, 2006;

(2) One attorney, one law school representative, and one nonattorney shall be appointed to terms ending December 31, 2007;

(3) One attorney, one law school representative, and one judge shall be appointed to terms ending December 31, 2008.

SECTION 3. Duties of the Commission
The Commission shall do all of the following:

(A) Establish a program, consisting of the components set forth in Section 4 of this rule, that is designed to assist minority, low income, or educationally disadvantaged college graduates in pursuing a law degree at an Ohio law school that is approved by the American Bar Association.

(B) Establish criteria, in addition to those set forth in Section 4 of this rule, for eligibility to participate in the program;

(C) Select students to participate in the program from among program applicants and nominations submitted annually by Ohio law schools;

(D) Annually or biennially, select an Ohio law school to sponsor the course of study required by Section 4(A)(1) of this rule from among proposals solicited by the Commission from Ohio law schools;

(E) Develop and implement a plan to publicize availability of the program to Ohio law schools, pre-law programs in undergraduate colleges and universities inside and outside of Ohio, and other applicable institutions, organizations, and programs;

(F) Adopt regulations necessary to administer the program that are not inconsistent with this rule.

(G) Perform other duties consistent with the purpose of the Commission.

SECTION 4. Components of the Program; Eligibility

(A) The program established pursuant to Section 3(A) of this rule shall consist of all of the following:

(1) A course of study, offered annually at an Ohio law school, that is designed to assist students in preparing for the demands of a law school education through classroom discussion, instruction in legal writing, research, and analysis, and other components considered relevant by the Commission;

(2) Financial assistance, in the form of an annual tuition and living expense stipend, for students who successfully complete the course of study, become certified graduates of the program, and are admitted to and maintain good academic standing in an Ohio law school;

(3) Other components that the Commission determines are necessary to further the purpose of this rule.

(B) To be eligible to participate in the program, a student shall satisfy all of the following criteria:

(1) The student shall have earned a bachelor's degree from an accredited college or university, as defined in Gov. Bar R. I, Section 1;

(2) The student shall have applied to a law school that is located in Ohio and approved by the American Bar Association;

(3) The student shall have demonstrated an interest, motivation, and capacity to earn a law degree;

(4) The student would benefit from the course of study established by the Commission pursuant to division (A) of this section.

SECTION 5. Funding

The activities of the Commission, including all expenses associated with the program established pursuant to Section 3(A) of this rule and the compensation payable to Commission staff, shall be funded from biennial appropriations made by the Ohio General Assembly to the Supreme Court for this purpose. The availability of the course of study, financial assistance, and other components of the program shall be contingent on the receipt of funds by the Supreme Court from the General Assembly.

SECTION 6. Staff

The Administrative Director shall designate staff as may be necessary to carry out the duties of the Commission.

History: Effective 8-19-02; Amended, eff. 1-1-06.

RULE XX.

TITLE AND EFFECTIVE DATES

SECTION 1. Title

These rules shall be known as the Supreme Court Rules for the Government of the Bar of Ohio and shall be cited as "Gov. Bar R. ____."

SECTION 2. Effective Dates

(A) The Supreme Court Rules for the Government of the Bar of Ohio shall take effect on February 28, 1972.

(B) Amendments to the Supreme Court Rules for the Government of the Bar of Ohio shall take effect on January 1, 1983, November 30, 1983, May 7, 1984, May 28, 1984, December 31, 1984, May 13, 1985, January 1, 1986, July 1, 1986, October 1, 1986, April 1, 1987, May 6, 1987, July 29, 1987, September 1, 1987, January 1, 1988, March 16, 1988, June 6, 1988, July 1, 1988, July 27, 1988, January 1, 1989, and July 1, 1989.

(C)(1) Amendments to Gov. Bar R. V(1)(a) shall be effective November 8, 1989.

(2) Amendments to Gov. Bar R. V(3)(d) shall be effective October 11, 1989.

(3) Amendments to Gov. Bar R. V(44) shall be effective December 5, 1989.

(4) Amendment to Gov. Bar R. VII and VIII(8)(d) shall be effective January 1, 1990.

(D) The amendments to Gov. Bar R. IX and XX, adopted by the Supreme Court on May 29, 1990, shall take effect on July 2, 1990.

(E) The amendments to Gov. Bar R. I, Sections 4 and 5, adopted by the Supreme Court on January 22, 1991, shall take effect on February 1, 1991, and shall apply to all bar examinations conducted on or after that effective date.

(F)(1) The amendments to Gov. Bar R. IX and XX, adopted by the Supreme Court on June 4, 1991, shall take effect on July 2, 1991.

(2) The amendments to Gov. Bar R. VI, Section 7, adopted by the Supreme Court on June 4, 1991, shall take effect on July 1, 1991. The amendments to Gov. Bar R. VI, Sections 1 to 6, adopted by the Supreme Court on June 4, 1991 shall take effect on September 1, 1991.

(G) The amendments to Gov. Bar R. I, Section 4, adopted by the Supreme Court on July 17, 1991, shall take effect on October 1, 1991. The amendments to Gov. Bar R. I, Section 5, adopted by the Supreme Court on July 17, 1991, shall take effect on February 1, 1992.

(H) The amendments to Gov. Bar R. V, Section 5, adopted by the Supreme Court on September 24, 1991, shall take effect on November 1, 1991.

(I) The amendments to Gov. Bar R. VI, adopted by the Supreme Court on October 8, 1991, shall take effect on January 1, 1992. The amendments to Gov. Bar R. II, Gov. Bar R. VI and Gov. Bar R. VII, adopted by the Supreme Court on December 11, 1991, shall take effect on January 1, 1992.

(J) The amendments to Gov. Bar R. I, Sections 1, 2, 6, 8, adopted by the Supreme Court on November 5, 1991, shall take effect on May 1, 1992. The amendments to Gov. Bar R. I, Section 3, adopted by the Supreme Court on December 5, 1991, shall take effect on August 1, 1992.

(K) The amendments to Section 11 of Gov. Bar R. I, Gov. Bar R. V, Section 7 of Gov. Bar R. VI, and Section 6 of Gov. Bar R. X adopted by the Supreme Court on May 19, 1992, shall take effect on July 1, 1992.

(L) Gov. Bar R. XV, adopted by the Supreme Court on July 29, 1992, shall take effect on September 1, 1992.

(M) The amendments to Section 9 of Gov. Bar R. I, Gov. Bar R. III, Sections 1 and 2 of Gov. Bar R. IV, and Gov. Bar R. VIII adopted by the Supreme Court on

October 20, 1992, shall take effect on January 1, 1993.

(N) The amendments to Gov. Bar R. VI, Section 1, adopted by the Supreme Court of Ohio on April 27, 1993, shall take effect on July 1, 1993.

(O) The amendments to Gov. Bar R. I, adopted by the Supreme Court on November 2, 1994, shall take effect on January 1, 1995, except that amendments to Sections 1 and 6 relating to the Multistate Professional Responsibility Examination shall apply to applicants who take the July 1995 or a subsequent Ohio bar examination.

(P) The amendments to Gov. Bar R. VI, Section 1, adopted by the Supreme Court of Ohio on November 30, 1994, shall take effect on January 1, 1995.

(Q) The amendments to Gov. Bar R. VII adopted by the Supreme Court of Ohio on August 31, 1994, shall take effect on January 1, 1995.

(R) The amendments to Gov. Bar R. VI, Section 1, adopted by the Supreme Court of Ohio on November 30, 1994, shall take effect on January 1, 1995.

(S) The amendments to Gov. Bar R. VI, Section 1, adopted by the Supreme Court of Ohio on March 22, 1995, shall take effect on July 1, 1995.

(T) The amendments to Gov. Bar R. V, Sections 3(C), 4(G), 4(I), 9(A), (B), and (C), and 11(E) adopted by the Supreme Court of Ohio on June 6, 1995, shall take effect on September 1, 1995.

(U) The amendments to Gov. Bar R. III, Gov. Bar R. V, Section 4(I)(2), and Gov. Bar R. VI adopted by the Supreme Court of Ohio on September 26, 1995, shall take effect on November 1, 1995.

(V) The amendment to Gov. Bar R. V, Section 9(G)(1) adopted by the Supreme Court of Ohio on October 24, 1995, shall take effect on December 1, 1995.

(W) Gov. Bar R. XVI, adopted by the Supreme Court of Ohio on April 16, 1996, shall take effect on April 16, 1996.

(X) The amendment to Gov. Bar R. V, Section 4(I), adopted by the Supreme Court of Ohio on May 7, 1996, shall take effect on July 1, 1996.

(Y) The amendment to Gov. Bar R. V, Section 11(E)(3), adopted by the Supreme Court of Ohio on June 25, 1996, shall take effect on September 1, 1996.

(Z) The amendment to Gov. Bar R. VIII, Section 3(F)(1), adopted by the Supreme Court of Ohio on October 8, 1996, shall take effect on December 1, 1996.

(AA) The amendments to Gov. Bar R. I, adopted by the Supreme Court on February 18, 1997, shall take effect on May 1, 1997.

(BB) The amendments to Gov. Bar R. VI, Sections 1(A), 1(B), and 7, adopted by the Supreme Court of Ohio on Feb. 19, 1997 shall take effect on July 1, 1997.

(CC) The amendments to Gov. Bar R. V, Section 5, adopted by the Supreme Court of Ohio on March 19, 1997, shall take effect on April 21, 1997.

(DD) The amendments to Gov. Bar R. V, Section 3(C)(5), adopted by the Supreme Court of Ohio on August 26, 1997, shall take effect on October 1, 1997.

(EE) The amendments to Gov. Bar R. V, Section 11(F), adopted by the Supreme Court of Ohio on October 7, 1997, shall take effect on November 3, 1997.

(FF) The amendments to Gov. Bar R. VIII, Sections 5 and 7(F), adopted by the Supreme Court of Ohio on August 26, 1997, shall take effect on October 20, 1997.

(GG) The amendments to Gov. Bar R. VIII, Section 2, adopted by the Supreme Court of Ohio on March 3, 1998, shall take effect on April 13, 1998.

(HH) The amendments to Gov. Bar R. I, Sec. 9 adopted by the Supreme Court on May 26, 1998, shall take effect on August 3, 1998.

(II) The amendments to Gov. Bar R. VIII, Section 1(A), adopted by the Supreme Court of Ohio on August 19, 1998, shall take effect on August 19, 1998.

(JJ) The amendments to Gov. Bar R. V, Sections 8 and 11, adopted by the Supreme Court of Ohio on September 28, 1998, shall take effect on November 2, 1998.

(KK) The amendments to Gov. Bar R. I, Sections 3, 4, 5, and 7, adopted by the Supreme Court of Ohio on March 30, 1999, shall take effect on June 1, 2000.

(LL) The amendments to Gov. Bar R. V, Sections 3, 4, 5, 8 and 11, adopted by the Supreme Court of Ohio April 13, 1999, shall take effect on September 1, 1999.

(MM) The amendments to Gov. Bar R. VI, Section 7, adopted by the Supreme Court of Ohio on June 8, 1999, shall take effect on July 1, 1999.

(NN) The amendments to Gov. Bar R. V, Section 10, adopted by the Supreme Court of Ohio on July 28, 1999, shall take effect on August 30, 1999.

(OO) The amendments to Gov. Bar R. I, Sec. 13 adopted by the Supreme Court on March 7, 2000, shall take effect on June 1, 2000.

(PP) The amendments to Gov. Bar R. V, Section 3, Gov. Bar R. X, Section 2, and Gov. Bar R. XIV, Section 7 adopted by the Supreme Court on April 10, 2000, shall take effect on May 8, 2000.

(QQ) The amendments to Gov. Bar R. I, II, IX, and XI adopted by the Supreme Court on April 10, 2000, shall take effect on October 1, 2000.

(RR) The amendments to Gov. Bar R. VI, adopted by the Supreme Court on November 28, 2000, shall take effect on November 28, 2000.

(SS) The amendments to Gov. Bar R. V, Section 8, adopted by the Supreme Court on March 27, 2001, shall take effect on May 1, 2001.

(TT) The amendments to Gov. Bar R. VI, adopted by the Supreme Court on March 12, 2002, shall take effect on June 1, 2002.

(UU) The amendments to Gov. Bar R. VI, adopted by the Supreme Court on July 24, 2002 shall take effect on August 19, 2002.

(VV) The amendments to Gov. Bar R. XVII, adopted by the Supreme Court on July 24, 2002 shall take effect on August 19, 2002.

(WW) The amendments to Gov. Bar R. VI, adopted by the Supreme Court on August 27, 2002 shall take effect on November 1, 2002.

(XX) The amendments to Gov. Bar R. V, Sections 7 and 11(E), adopted by the Supreme Court on December 4, 2002 shall take effect on February 1, 2003.

(YY) The amendments to Gov. Bar R. I, Sections 10, 11, 12, and 13 adopted by the Supreme Court on November 13, 2002, shall take effect on February 1, 2003.

(ZZ) The amendments to Gov. Bar R. VI adopted by the Supreme Court on May 14, 2003, shall take effect on July 1, 2003.

(AAA) The amendments to Gov. Bar R. VII adopted by the Supreme Court on April 29, 2003, shall take effect on June 16, 2003.

(BBB) The amendments to Gov. Bar R. VIII adopted by the Supreme Court on June 3, 2003, shall be effective and apply to claims filed on or after August 1, 2003.

(CCC) The amendments to Gov. Bar R. I, Sections 2, 3, 7, and 9; Gov. Bar R. IX, Section 2; and Gov. Bar R. XI, Section 2, adopted by the Supreme Court on June 3, 2003, shall take effect on October 1, 2003.

(DDD) The amendments to Gov. Bar R. V, Section 5 and Section 8 adopted by the Supreme Court on January 12, 2004, shall take effect on January 12, 2004.

(EEE) The amendments to Gov. Bar R. XV, adopted by the Supreme Court on July 20, 2004, shall take effect on September 1, 2004.

(FFF) The amendments to Gov. Bar R. VII, adopted by the Supreme Court on August 17, 2004, shall take effect on January 1, 2005.

(GGG) Gov. Bar R. XIII, adopted effective September 3, 1990, was repealed effective October 12, 2004.

(HHH) The amendments to Gov. Bar R. V and VI, adopted by the Supreme Court on February 1, 2005, shall take effect on September 1, 2005.

(III) The amendments to Gov. Bar R. VI, adopted by the Supreme Court on May 10, 2005, shall take effect on July 1, 2005.

(JJJ) The amendments to Gov. Bar R. XVII, adopted by the Supreme Court on November 8, 2005, shall take effect on January 1, 2006.

(KKK) Gov. Bar R. XII, adopted effective June 1, 1990, was repealed effective January 1, 2006.

(LLL) The amendments to Gov. Bar R. I, Sections 3, 8, and 9, Gov. Bar R. II, Sections 2, 3, and 6, Gov. Bar R. III, Sections 2 and 3, Gov. Bar R. IV, Section 1, Gov. Bar R. V, Sections 2, 5a, 6, and 11, Gov. Bar R. IX, Sections 2 and 5, Gov. Bar R. XI, Section 7, and Gov. Bar R. XVI, Sections 1 and 2 adopted by the Supreme Court on January 23, 2007 shall take effect on February 1, 2007.

(MMM) The amendments to Gov. Bar R. XVI adopted by the Supreme Court on April 3, 2007 and the repeal of the Lawyer Referral and Information Services Regulations shall take effect on April 30, 2007.

(NNN) The amendments to Gov. Bar R. I, II, IX, and XI adopted by the Supreme Court on April 3, 2007 shall take effect on May 1, 2007.

(OOO) Amendments to Gov. Bar R. VI, Section 1 are effective July 1, 2007. All other amendments to Gov. Bar R. VI and the repeal of Gov. Bar R. V, Section 11(G) are effective September 1, 2007.

(PPP) The amendments to Gov. Bar R. I, Sections 2, 3, 7, and 9 adopted by the Supreme Court on September 11, 2007 shall take effect on October 1, 2007.

(QQQ) The amendments to Gov. Bar R. VII, Section 5b adopted by the Supreme Court on September 11, 2007 shall take effect on November 1, 2007.

(RRR) The amendments to Gov. Bar R. X adopted by the Supreme Court on September 11, 2007 shall take effect on November 1, 2007.

(SSS) The amendments to Gov. Bar R. I, Sect. 9, VI, Sect. 3(E), and IX, Sect. 6 adopted by the Supreme Court on December 11, 2007 shall take effect on January 1, 2008.

(TTT) The amendments to Gov. Bar R. V, Section 3(D) and Gov. Bar R. VII, Section 9(A) to (E), adopted by the Supreme Court of Ohio on March 11, 2008, shall take effect on January 1, 2008. The amendments shall apply to all reimbursements and reimbursement requests for costs incurred in calendar year 2008 and subsequent calendar years.

(UUU) The amendments to Gov. Bar R. V, Section 1(D) and Board of Commissioners on Grievances and Discipline Regulation 11, adopted by the Supreme Court of Ohio on March 11, 2008, shall take effect on April 1, 2008.

(VVV) The amendments to Gov. Bar R. VII shall take effect on September 1, 2008. The amendments shall apply to a motion for interim cease and desist filed on or after the effective date.

(WWW) The amendments to Gov. Bar R. V, Section 8(G) and (H), adopted by the Supreme Court of Ohio on July 21, 2008, shall take effect on September 1, 2008. An attorney or law firm that has entered into an employment, contractual, or consulting relationship with a disqualified or suspended attorney prior to September 1, 2008 shall register such relationship as provided in Gov. Bar R. V, Section 8(G)(3) no later than November 1, 2008.

(XXX) The amendments to Gov. Bar R. X, Sect. 3 and 8 adopted by the Supreme Court on June 24, 2008 shall take effect on November 1, 2008.

(YYY) The amendments to Gov. Bar R. XV, Section 3 adopted by the Supreme Court on January 15, 2008 shall take effect on November 1, 2008.

(ZZZ) The amendments to Gov. Bar R. I, Section 4 adopted by the Supreme Court on January 20, 2009 shall take effect on February 1, 2009.

(AAAA) The amendments to Gov. Bar R. VI adopted by the Supreme Court on March 9, 2009 shall take effect on May 1, 2009.

(BBBB) The amendments to Gov. Bar R. II, Sections 1, 2, 3, 4, 5, 6, and 7 adopted by the Supreme Court on June 1, 2009 shall take effect on August 1, 2009.

(CCCC) The amendments to Gov. Bar R. I, Section 11 adopted by the Supreme Court on March 31, 2010 shall take effect on May 1, 2010.

(CCCC) † The amendments to Gov. Bar R. XII, adopted by the Supreme Court on September 1, 2009 shall take effect on January 1, 2011.

ATTORNEY CONTINUING LEGAL EDUCATION REGULATIONS

History: Adopted by the Supreme Court Commission on Continuing Legal Education, effective January 1, 1989.

REGULATION 100: Definitions

In these Regulations, the following definitions shall apply:

(A) **Approved CLE Activity:** a CLE Activity that meets the standards set forth in Regulation 406 and either: (i) has been accredited by the Commission as provided in these Regulations; or (ii) is presented by an Established Sponsor.

(B) **Attendee:** an Attorney or Judge attending an Approved CLE Activity.

(C) **Attorney:** a person who is registered under Rule VI of the Supreme Court Rules for the Government of the Bar of Ohio.

(D) **CLE Activity:** a seminar, institute, course or other educational program of legal education as described in Regulations 401 through 405 and 407 through 412.

(E) **CLE Credit:** time earned toward meeting the CLE requirements through participation in Approved CLE Activities that is awarded by the Commission.

(F) **CLE Record:** the record of CLE Credit maintained by the Commission for each Attorney and Judge that is the basis for enforcement of the CLE Requirements.

(G) **CLE Requirements:** the educational and reporting provisions of Rule X, Section 3 or Rule IV, Sections 2 and 3, and these Regulations.

(H) **Commission:** the Supreme Court Commission on Continuing Legal Education.

(I) **Compliance:** conformity with the CLE Requirements.

(J) **Established Sponsor:** a person or organization whose entire continuing legal education program has been accredited by the Commission pursuant to Regulation 404 of these Regulations.

(K) **Exemption:** relief from the duty to meet the CLE Requirements of Rule X granted by the Commission or through the operation of Rule X, Section 3(C) or (F) or Rule IV, Section 4. An Exemption specifically requested, if granted, is for a limited time as determined by the Commission. Unless otherwise provided, the grant of an Exemption does not relieve an Attorney or Judge from the duty to report such status at the end of the biennial report period.

(L) **Good Cause:** circumstances not within the reasonable control of the Attorney or Judge and having the effect of preventing, substantially hindering, or delaying Compliance, filing or payment. Good Cause shall not include mere neglect or inadvertence. Good Cause may be taken into consideration when reviewing an attorney's or judge's failure to comply with the CLE Requirements, failure to file a report of compliance as provided by these Regulations, or failure to pay any applicable fee.

(M) **Judge:** Judicial officers subject to the Supreme Court Rules for the Government of the Judiciary. Unless otherwise provided in Rule X, or in Rule IV, Judge includes those considered full-time, part-time, or retired, eligible for assignment.

(N) **New Lawyers Training Program:** An educational course for lawyers newly admitted to the practice of law that satisfies the requirements of Rule X, Section 3(H), the requirements of Regulation 414, and is approved by the Commission pursuant to Regulation 414.

(O) **Noncompliance:** Failure to be in Compliance with the CLE Requirements.

(P) **Professional Conduct Requirement:** the legal ethics and professionalism requirement, including at least thirty minutes of instruction in sub-

stance abuse, sixty minutes of instruction on the Ohio Rules of Professional Conduct, and sixty minutes of instruction on the Lawyer's Creed and Aspirational Ideals as set forth in Rule X, Section 3 (A) and the judicial ethics and professionalism and substance abuse instruction requirement as set forth in Rule IV, Section 2 (A)(2) and Section 3 (A)(2).

(Q) **Qualified Speaker:** Sponsors may utilize videotape, motion picture, audiotape, simultaneous broadcast, computer-based education or other such systems or devices provided they meet the applicable standards of Regulation 406. If the faculty members are not available either in person or via live telecommunication, then a qualified speaker, familiar with the recorded materials, must be present to expand upon and provide supplemental commentary and to answer questions posed by Attendees. The qualified speaker must have reviewed the recorded materials in their entirety prior to the replay and must remain in the room with the Attendees the entire time.

(R) **Rule X:** Supreme Court Rules for the Government of the Bar, Rule X, Attorney Continuing Legal Education.

(S) **Rule IV:** Supreme Court Rules for the Government of the Judiciary, Rule IV, Mandatory Continuing Legal Education for Judges.

(T) **Secretary:** Secretary of the Supreme Court Commission on Continuing Legal Education.

(U) **Self-Study Activity:** a CLE Activity of individualized learning engaged in by an Attorney or Judge outside of the standard classroom or seminar setting.

(V) **Special Program:** a CLE Activity sponsored by a law firm, corporation, governmental agency, or similar entity primarily for the education of its employees, members, associates or clients.

(W) **Sponsor:** a person or organization that is responsible for the costs associated with conducting or presenting a CLE Activity.

(X) **Transcript:** a copy of the CLE Record.

History: Amended, eff 1-1-00; 5-29-00; 7-1-01; 7-1-02; 11-1-07; 11-1-08.

REGULATION 200: Administration

REGULATION 201: Secretary's Determinations and Review

201.1. The Secretary of the Commission, pursuant to these Regulations shall initially take action on all applications for accreditation of CLE Activities for CLE Credit, the award of CLE Credit, to Attorneys and Judges and Exemptions. The Secretary shall make written response to the applicant within forty-five days after the application is deemed complete. In the case of requests for the award of CLE Credit, the posting of hours to the record of an Attorney pursuant to Regulation 302.4 shall constitute the written response of the Secretary.

201.2. The action of the Secretary shall constitute the action of the Commission unless and until the

Commission shall determine otherwise. At each meeting of the Commission, the Secretary shall report to the Commission all actions taken.

201.3. All actions taken by the Secretary pursuant to these Regulations shall be subject to review and approval, disapproval or modification by the Commission, *sua sponte*, or upon written appeal by any person adversely affected thereby. Such written appeal shall be in the form directed by these Regulations or otherwise by the Commission and must be received by the Commission within thirty days after the mailing by the Secretary of the determination or interpretation appealed from.

201.4. If the Commission finds that the Secretary has incorrectly interpreted or applied Rule X, Rule IV or these Regulations, the Commission shall take such action as it deems appropriate. In such instance the Commission shall give written notice of its action to the appellant.

201.5. When any person requests review of any matter within the jurisdiction of the Commission, the Chairman may appoint a committee to consider the appeal. Such committee shall be comprised of at least three members of the Commission, shall hear the issues presented by the appeal, and shall report its findings and recommendations to the Commission. The report of the Committee, or if there is no Committee appointed, the appeal shall be heard by the Commission at its next regularly scheduled meeting. In either event, the person adversely affected by the determination appealed from may present information relevant to the appeal, to the Committee, or to the Commission, in writing, in person or both.

History: Amended, eff 5-29-00; 7-1-02; 11–1–07.

REGULATION 300: Continuing Legal Education Requirements

REGULATION 301: Requests for CLE Credit

301.1. Except as otherwise provided by these Regulations, Rule X or Rule IV, CLE Credit shall be awarded only for personal attendance at or participation in an Approved CLE Activity, for a minimum of one hour.

301.2. A written request for CLE Credit shall be submitted by or on behalf of an Attorney or Judge for each Approved CLE Activity for which credit is sought.

(A) Such requests shall be on a form that shall be made available by the Commission to Attorneys, Judges, and Sponsors of Approved CLE Activities.

(B) Each request for the award of CLE Credit shall be signed by the Attorney or Judge requesting the credit at the conclusion of the Attorney's or Judge's attendance at or participation in the CLE Activity for which the Attorney or Judge seeks the award of CLE Credit.

(C) Each request for the award of CLE Credit submitted to the Commission by an Attorney or Judge shall include the name, address, and Supreme Court of Ohio attorney registration number,

and all information requested on the appropriate form provided by the Commission as described in paragraphs (1) through (5):

(1) Requests for the award of CLE Credit earned by attendance at or participation in an Approved CLE Activity.

(2) Requests for the award of CLE Credit earned by teaching at an Approved CLE Activity.

(3) Requests for the award of CLE Credit earned by teaching a course at an ABA-accredited law school.

(4) Requests for the award of CLE Credit earned by attending a course at an ABA-accredited law school.

(5) Requests for the award of CLE Credit earned by the publication of an article or book authored by the applicant.

History: Amended, eff 5-29-00; 7-1-02; 11–1–07.

REGULATION 302: Record of CLE Credit

302.1. The Commission shall maintain a CLE Record for each Attorney and Judge. The CLE Record shall contain:

(A) A list of the Approved CLE Activities for which the Attorney or Judge has been awarded CLE Credit during the Attorney's or Judge's current biennial reporting period.

(B) The total number of CLE Credit hours earned to date with a separate notation of hours that meet the Professional Conduct Requirement and the Judicial College Requirement.

(C) The date on which the Attorney's or Judge's current biennial reporting period ends.

302.2. In any proceeding authorized by the provisions of Rule X, Rule IV or these Regulations, a Transcript of an Attorney's or Judge's record, when certified as correct by the Secretary of the Commission, is rebuttably presumed to correctly show the number of CLE Credit hours that have been awarded by the Commission to the Attorney or Judge during the applicable biennial reporting period.

302.3. The Commission may maintain the information required by Regulation 302.1 in an electronic system of record storage. Upon request, a printed Transcript shall be made available in accordance with the provisions of Rule X.

302.4. CLE Credits requested by an Attorney or Judge shall be posted by the Commission to the Attorney's or Judge's CLE Record within forty-five days following the submission of the Attorney's or Judge's request for the award and is deemed complete except:

(A) When the Commission defers the award of CLE Credit pending an investigation of a request for CLE Credit, or

(B) When the Commission denies the award of CLE Credit following an investigation of a request for CLE Credit.

302.5. The Secretary of the Commission shall notify an Attorney or Judge requesting CLE Credit of any decision denying or deferring the award of CLE Credit or granting fewer than the requested number of hours of CLE Credits within thirty days after such determination. Only that number of CLE Credit hours approved by the Commission shall be posted to an Attorney's or Judge's CLE Record.

302.6. In any case in which an Attorney is awarded fewer than the total number of CLE Credit hours requested, the request for credit in question shall be kept by the Commission for a minimum of two years following its receipt by the Commission.

History: Amended, eff 5-29-00; 7-1-02; 11–1–07.

REGULATION 303: Attorney's and Judge's Report of Compliance

303.1. Not fewer than sixty days prior to the expiration of an Attorney's or Judge's biennial reporting period, the Commission shall send the Attorney or Judge a printed Transcript showing the number of CLE Credit hours that have been awarded to the Attorney or Judge during the current biennial reporting period. The Transcript shall include a report form on which the Attorney or Judge shall verify that the Attorney or Judge has complied fully with the CLE Requirements during the current biennial reporting period.

303.2. Each Attorney or Judge receiving the Transcript and report form shall review promptly the Transcript and inform the Commission if information contained in the CLE Record is inaccurate or if information that should be contained in the record is missing.

303.3. No later than January 31 of the applicable reporting year, an Attorney or Judge shall submit to the Commission the Transcript and report form provided, bearing the Attorney's or Judge's signature verifying the information contained in the Transcript and report form and compliance with all applicable CLE Requirements. The Transcript and report form shall be submitted to the Commission by the applicable deadline, regardless of whether the Attorney or Judge has complied with all applicable CLE requirements.

303.4. In the event an Attorney or Judge fails to submit a signed report form by January 31 of the applicable reporting year, the Attorney or Judge shall be subject to the sanctions of Rule X.

303.5. Failure to file a timely report or to inform the Commission of any inaccurate or missing information, or filing a late report without the required fifty dollar late fee, shall result in the loss of carryover for the next reporting period.

History: Amended, eff 5-29-00; 7-1-02; 11–1–07.

REGULATION 304. Requests for Exemption from CLE Requirements

304.1. Persons meeting the following criteria may request Exemption by the Commission from some or all of the CLE Requirements of Rule X or Rule IV:

(A) An Attorney on full-time military duty who does not engage in the private practice of law in Ohio;

(B) An Attorney or Judge suffering from severe and prolonged illness or disability preventing participation in Approved CLE Activities pursuant to these Regulations.

304.2. The effective date for any Exemption granted under Regulation 304.1 shall be the date the Attorney or Judge files the request for Exemption, unless another effective date is warranted upon review of the Request. An Exemption granted pursuant to Regulation 304.1 shall be in effect so long as the facts and circumstances upon which the Exemption is based continue materially unchanged.

304.3. An Attorney or Judge may request an Exemption for a period not to exceed one year by filing a signed written request stating with specificity any special circumstances unique to that Attorney or Judge claimed to constitute good cause for the grant of the Exemption.

304.4. An Attorney or Judge for whom attendance at CLE activities is difficult because of a permanent physical disability or other compelling reason, may request approval of a substitute program by filing a signed request, stating with specificity the components of the proposed substitute program. A proposed substitute program may include courses of self-study or "Special Programs."

304.5. An Attorney or Judge requesting an Exemption under this Regulation from some or all of the CLE Requirements of Rule X shall file a written request on a form provided by the Commission within a reasonable time after the basis for the Exemption arises. The request, signed by the Attorney or Judge, shall state with specificity the facts and circumstances upon which the request is based, and, if applicable, the date on which it is estimated that the need for Exemption will terminate.

304.6. Upon receipt of a request for Exemption, the Commission shall consider the request, and the facts supporting it, and shall notify the Attorney or Judge submitting the request of its decision to grant, deny, or grant with modifications the relief requested.

304.7. An Attorney or Judge granted an Exemption by the Commission under this Regulation shall report and verify that fact in the space provided on the Transcript and report form, and shall file the report no later than January 31 of the applicable reporting year. Failure to file the Transcript and report form may result in termination of the Exemption and subject the Attorney or Judge to additional sanctions as provided in Rule X and these Regulations.

304.8. Regulation 305 shall apply upon the expiration or termination of any Exemption granted by the Commission or allowed under Rule X or in these regulations.

History: Amended, eff 5-29-00; 7-1-02; 11–1–07.

REGULATION 305: Proration of Credit Hour Requirements

Except as is otherwise provided by Rule X, Section 3(C) or Rule IV, the CLE Requirements for Attorneys or Judges becoming subject thereto after the commencement of a biennial reporting period shall be adjusted as follows:

(A) If the Attorney or Judge becomes subject to Rule X or Rule IV after January 1 of the first year of the biennial reporting period, but before July 1 of the first year of the reporting period, there shall be no reduction in the CLE Requirement.

(B) If the Attorney or Judge becomes subject to the CLE Requirements after July 1 of the first year of the reporting period, but before January 1 of the second year of the Attorney's or Judge's biennial reporting period, the Attorney or Judge shall be required to complete three-quarters of the required CLE Credit hours and the entire Professional Conduct Requirement during the remainder of the reporting period.

(C) If the Attorney or Judge becomes subject to the CLE Requirements after January 1 of the second year of the biennial reporting period but before July 1 of the second year of the Attorney's or Judge's biennial reporting period, the Attorney or Judge shall complete one-half the required CLE Credit hours and the entire Professional Conduct Requirement during the remainder of the reporting period. Upon timely application made to the Commission, the Commission may vary the provisions of this paragraph where prejudice would result.

History: Amended, eff 5-29-00; 7-1-02; 11–1–07.

REGULATION 306: Attorney Signature

In all cases where the signature of the Attorney or Judge is required under Rule X, Rule IV, or these Regulations, the signature shall constitute verification by the Attorney or Judge that the form has been read by the Attorney or Judge and, to the best of the Attorney's or Judge's knowledge, information and belief, the form is complete and is accurate. A signature may be any electronic symbol or process that is attached to or associated with a form or other writing required to be submitted under Rule X, Rule IV, or these regulations and that is intended to express the required verification.

History: Amended, eff 5-29-00; 7-1-02; 11–1–07.

REGULATION 400: Hours and Accreditation

REGULATION 401: Credit for Teaching

401.1. Credit for Continuing Legal Education Instruction

(A) An Attorney or Judge may receive three hours of CLE Credit for each hour taught in an Approved CLE Activity the first time the program is presented by the Attorney or Judge, and one hour of CLE Credit for each hour taught during subsequent presentations of the same CLE Activity. An Attorney or Judge may receive a maximum of one-half the required hours of CLE Credit for such teaching during a biennial reporting period.

(B) The Attorney or Judge shall submit an application for credit on a form provided by the Commission within thirty days after the last presentation of the Approved CLE Activity.

401.2. Credit for Law School Instruction

(A) An Attorney or Judge may receive one-half hour of CLE Credit for each semester hour taught at an ABA-accredited law school. Prorated credit will be granted for quarter or trimester hours.

(B) The Attorney or Judge shall submit an application for credit on a form provided by the Commission within thirty days after the last day of the course.

(C) An Attorney or Judge shall not receive CLE Credit for hours taught at any other accredited higher education institution.

401.3. Credit for Lawyer to Lawyer Mentoring Program Instruction

(A) An Attorney or Judge may receive twelve hours of CLE Credit, including two and one-half hours of instruction related to professional conduct as defined in Rule X, Section 3(A)(1)(a) through (c), by participating as a mentor in the Supreme Court Lawyer to Lawyer Mentoring Program.

History: Amended, eff 5-29-00; 7-1-02; 11–1–07; 11–1–08.

REGULATION 402: Credit for Law School Courses

(A) An Attorney or Judge may receive three hours of CLE Credit for each semester hour of a course completed at an ABA-accredited law school. Prorated credit will be granted for quarter or trimester hours.

(B) Taking an examination is not required for CLE Credit. The course may be completed on an audit (*i.e.* not for academic credit) basis.

(C) The Attorney or Judge shall submit an application for credit on a form provided by the Commission within thirty days after the last day of the course.

History: Amended, eff 5-29-00; 7-1-02; 11–1–07.

REGULATION 403: Credit for Publication

An Attorney or Judge may receive up to ten hours of CLE Credit per biennial reporting period for the publication of articles or books authored or prepared by the Attorney or Judge.

(A) The article or book shall concern matters directly related to the practice of law, judicial administration, professional conduct, ethical obligations, law office economics, or other subjects that will maintain and improve the quality of legal services in Ohio.

(B) The article or book shall be intended primarily for reading or use by an Attorney or Judge.

(C) The Attorney or Judge shall submit an application for credit on a form provided by the Commission within ninety days of publication, or by the end of the biennial reporting period, whichever is later. Credit shall be awarded for the year in which the article or book is published.

History: Amended, eff 1-1-00; 5-29-00; 7-1-02; 11–1–07.

REGULATION 404: Accreditation of Established Sponsors

404.1. The Commission may, upon submission of an application on the appropriate form provided by the Commission, designate Established Sponsors of CLE Activities.

(A) Established Sponsor status may be granted to those Sponsors that are not primarily providers of Special Programs and meet either of the following criteria:

(1) The Sponsor regularly presents programs for continuing legal education that meet the standards set forth in Regulation 406, and the Sponsor meets the provisions for approval of accredited CLE Activities in at least ten states in which continuing legal education is mandatory, or

(2) The Sponsor demonstrates to the Commission, by clear and convincing evidence, that CLE Activities offered by it have consistently met the standards set forth in Regulation 406.

(B) Designation as an Established Sponsor shall be for a term not to exceed one year, and may be renewed by the Commission annually thereafter so long as the Established Sponsor continues to meet the criteria set forth in these Regulations. Established Sponsor status may be revoked by the Commission if: (i) the annual reporting requirement set forth in Regulation 404.1(D) is not met; (ii) upon review of the CLE Activities presented, the Commission determines that the quality of those CLE Activities does not meet the standards set forth in Regulation 406; (iii) the annual fee has not been paid; or (iv) the Commission finds violations of any other applicable Regulations.

(C) CLE Activities presented by Established Sponsors (other than New Lawyers Training programs) shall be deemed to be Approved CLE Activities, and shall not individually be subject to the approval process set forth in these Regulations. However, individual activities presented by Established Sponsors may be reviewed and subject to denial if the Secretary determines they do not meet the requirements of Rule X or these Regulations.

(D) Established Sponsors shall file a written report with the Commission by March 1 of each year. Such report shall describe the CLE Activities conducted during the prior calendar year and be in such detail and form as required by the Commission.

(E) An Established Sponsor shall file an announcement of each CLE Activity on a form provided by the Commission at least thirty days prior to the first presentation of that CLE Activity. Forms for requesting the award of CLE Credit for attendance at an Approved CLE Activity shall be provided to the Established Sponsor upon receipt of that announcement.

(F) An Established Sponsor shall within thirty days after presentation by it of a CLE Activity submit to the Commission all requests for CLE Credit signed by the Attorneys or Judges in attendance. Established Sponsors shall keep a list of Attendees at each CLE Activity presented by such Established Sponsor, for at least two years following the presentation of such CLE Activity.

(G) Established Sponsors shall pay fees in connection with their designation as may from time to time be established by the Commission.

(H) Any violations of these regulations shall subject the Established Sponsor to late fees established by the Commission or other sanctions as provided in Rule X or these Regulations.

404.2. An ABA-accredited law school acting as a Sponsor of CLE Activities shall be considered an Established Sponsor under this Regulation without application so long as all other provisions of these Regulations pertaining to Established Sponsors are met. The announcement required by Regulation 404.1(E) shall be accompanied by the applicable fee.

History: Amended, eff 3-1-92; 5-29-00; 7-1-01; 7-1-02; 12-26-05; 11–1–07.

REGULATION 405: Accreditation of Programs

Any Sponsor who has not been designated as an Established Sponsor may apply to the Commission for accreditation of a CLE Activity on a form provided by the Commission. The application for accreditation shall be accompanied by the applicable fee.

(A) Application for accreditation of a CLE Activity shall be submitted at least sixty days prior to the date of presentation of the program.

(B) Any representation that the CLE Activity has been accredited is prohibited until accreditation is granted, unless prior written approval is granted by the Commission.

(C) The CLE activity must meet the standards set forth in Regulation 406.

(D) The Sponsor of a CLE Activity approved under this Regulation shall, within thirty days after presentation of the CLE Activity, submit to the Commission all requests for CLE Credit signed by the Attorneys or Judges in attendance. These forms shall be provided to the Sponsor by the Commission along with notification of approval of the program. A list of Attendees at each Approved CLE Activity shall be kept by the Sponsor for at least two years following the presentation of the CLE Activity.

(E) Any violations of these regulations shall subject the Sponsor to late fees established by the Commission or other sanctions as provided in Rule X or these Regulations.

(F) A Sponsor who violates these regulations two or more times in any six month period shall be certified to the Commission as a habitual offender.

(1) Upon certification as a habitual offender, any application for accreditation by this Sponsor shall require the approval of the Commission.

(2) Upon demonstration of a commitment to compliance and application to the Commission, the Sponsor's name will be removed from the habitual offender's status.

History: Amended, eff 5-29-00; 7-1-02; 11–1–07.

REGULATION 406: Standards for Accreditation

All CLE Activities approved for CLE Credit shall meet the following standards:

(A) The CLE Activity shall have significant intellectual or practical content, the primary objective of which is to improve the participants' professional competence as an Attorney or Judge;

(B) The CLE Activity shall be an organized program of learning dealing with matters directly related to the practice of law, professional conduct or ethical obligations, law office economics, or other subjects that will maintain and improve the quality of legal services in Ohio;

(C) The program leaders or lecturers shall be qualified by education, or have the necessary practical skill to conduct the program effectively;

(D) Before or at the time of the CLE Activity, each Attendee shall be provided with course materials in the form of written or electronic media that are of such quality and quantity to indicate that adequate time has been devoted to their preparation and that they will be of value to the participants. Upon Attendee's request the Sponsor shall make materials available in written form prior to the activity.

(E) The CLE Activity must be presented in a suitable setting, conducive to a good educational environment that provides attendees with adequate writing space or surface;

(F) The Sponsor shall submit information concerning the CLE Activity, including the brochure describing the CLE Activity and qualifications of speakers, the method or manner of presentation of materials, the agenda with time schedule and, if requested, a set of the materials;

(G) The Sponsor shall develop and implement methods to evaluate its course offerings to determine their effectiveness and the extent to which they meet the needs of Attorneys and Judges and, upon a request from the Commission, provide course evaluations by Attendees;

(H) Attendance at the CLE Activity shall be open to all Attorneys and Judges, and shall consist of a minimum of one uninterrupted hour of instruction. CLE credit shall not be awarded for breaks, opening or closing remarks, keynote speeches, meals, or presentations concurrent with the consumption of a meal. Partial hours over the minimum must be rounded to the nearest one-quarter of an hour and should be expressed as decimals.

History: Amended, eff 5-29-00; 7-1-02; 11-7-05; 11-1-07.

REGULATION 407: Accreditation of Special Programs

(A) **407.1** A law firm, a corporate legal department, or a group of Attorneys in public service (*e.g.*, the Ohio Attorney General's Office, a County Prosecuting Attorney Office, a U.S. Attorney Office, a Public Defender Office, a legal department of a State or Federal agency, a legal services program, a municipal corporation) may make application for accreditation of a Special Program pursuant to Regulation 405 and this Regulation 407.1. Sponsors shall submit an application for approval of such Special Program, on a form provided by the Commission, at least sixty days prior to the date of presentation.

(B) The Special Program shall meet the standards set forth in Regulation 406 and comply with the following requirements:

(1) A description of the subject matter of the Special Program and an outline or description of the materials to be distributed prior to or at the program shall accompany the application.

(2) A resume of the speaker or speakers and a written synopsis or outline of the presentation shall accompany the application.

(3) The date, time, and place of presentation shall be set forth in the application.

(4) Actual length of the presentation, exclusive of breaks and meals, and the number of credit hours requested for accreditation shall be set forth in the application.

(5) One or more speakers shall not be a member, partner, associate or employee of the sponsoring organization.

(6) The Special Program shall be open to Attorneys and Judges not associated with the Sponsor, who shall assure that at least one-quarter of the available seating at a Special Program is made available to attendees not associated with the Sponsor.

(7) If a fee is charged, it must be reasonably related to the total cost of the Special Program and any fee shall be disclosed on the application.

(8) If confidential information is discussed the program is not eligible for CLE credit.

(C) The Commission may, upon such terms and conditions as it deems proper, grant a variance from the provisions of this Regulation upon written application in support of such variance.

(D) The Sponsor shall agree to submit to the Commission, within thirty days after presentation of an Approved Special Program, the requests for CLE Credit on a form provided by the Commission of all Attorneys and Judges in attendance. These forms shall be provided to the Sponsor by the Commission along with notification of approval. A list of Attendees at each Approved Special Program shall be kept by the Sponsor for at least two years following the presentation.

(E) The Sponsor shall advise the Commission within thirty days after the date of the Special Program if any change was made in the program format, subject matter, or speakers, in which event accreditation of the Special Program for CLE credit may be reconsidered by the Secretary or the Commission.

(F) The Special Program shall be scheduled under circumstances so as to be reasonably free of interruption by unrelated matters.

(G) Any violations of these regulations shall subject the Sponsor to late fees established by the Commission or other sanctions as provided in Rule X or these Regulations.

407.2

Not more than twelve hours of CLE Credit for any biennial reporting period may be earned by an Attorney or Judge for attendance at Special Programs sponsored by an entity with which the Attorney or Judge is associated.

History: Amended, eff 5-29-00; 7-1-02; 11-1-07.

REGULATION 408: Sponsors and Special Methods of Instruction

408.1. Sponsors may utilize videotape, motion picture, audiotape, simultaneous broadcast including videoconferencing, teleconferencing, and audioconferencing, computer-based education, or other such systems or devices provided they meet the applicable standards of Regulation 406 and the following standards:

(A) There shall be an opportunity for Attendees to ask questions of the program faculty during or immediately following the presentation;

(B) If the faculty members are not available either in person or via live telecommunication, then a qualified speaker, familiar with the recorded materials, shall be present to expand upon and provide supplemental commentary and to answer questions posed by Attendees;

(C) If the instruction is based on previously presented materials, the materials must be current and, in any event, shall have been prepared no earlier than the calendar year immediately preceding the date the application for accreditation is filed.

(D) Presentations that do not meet the applicable standards set forth in Regulation 408.1 shall not be eligible for CLE credit except under Regulations 407 or 409.

408.2. The Commission may, upon such terms and conditions as it deems proper, grant a variance from the provisions of this regulation upon written application in support of such variance.

408.3. Any special methods of instruction that do not meet the provisions under 408.1 shall be considered self-study and will be approved for credit only when they meet the standards set forth in Regulation 409.

History: Amended, eff 1-1-00; 5-29-00; 7-1-02; 9-1-04; 11-1-07.

REGULATION 409: Self-Study

409.1. A Self-Study Activity may be approved for CLE Credit provided the following criteria are met:

(A) The Self-Study Activity shall meet the standards set forth in Regulation 406 to the extent they are applicable to a program of individualized learning;

(B) The Sponsor shall submit an application for approval on a form provided by the Commission at least sixty days prior to the date of initial availability of the Self-Study Activity, together with the applicable fee. Only Sponsors may apply for accreditation of Self-Study Activities. Attorneys and Judges may not apply on their own behalf for accreditation of Self-Study Activities.

(C) Each application shall contain the following:

(1) A description of the subject matter of the Self-Study Activity and method of instruction;

(2) A written synopsis or outline of the Self-Study Activity;

(3) How and when the Self-Study Activity can be obtained;

(4) The actual length of the Self-Study Activity and number of credit hours requested for accreditation shall be set forth in the application and the Self-Study Activity shall include a minimum of one sixty-minute hour of substantive legal education.

(5) The date on which the Self-Study Activity was produced;

(D) The Commission, upon such terms and conditions as it deems proper, may grant a variance from the provisions of this Regulation 409.1 upon written application in support of such variance;

(E) The Sponsor shall agree to submit to the Commission, on a monthly basis, a request for CLE Credit for each Attorney or Judge who has successfully completed the Self-Study Activity during the preceding thirty days. The Sponsor may use a form provided by the Commission for this purpose, or the same information may be provided on a form of the Sponsor's own design. A list of those who have successfully completed the Self-Study Activity shall be kept by the Sponsor for at least two years following the completion of such Self-Study Activity;

(F) In the event that a material change is made in the Self-Study Activity, including changing from one internet service provider to another, the Sponsor shall, within thirty days of making such change, so advise the Commission, in which event accreditation of the Self-Study Activity for CLE Credit may be reconsidered by the Secretary or the Commission;

(G) The Sponsor shall have a means by which it can identify the Attorneys or Judges actually engaged in the Self-Study Activity using at least two of the following: email address and confidential password combinations, security or challenge questions, and image and image phrases authentication or other methods acceptable to the Commission.

(H) The Sponsor shall certify that the Attorney or Judge engaged in the Self-Study Activity has obtained the minimum competency and has actively participated in the Self-Study Activity for an amount of time equivalent to the number of CLE Credit hours requested. Participation may be confirmed via polling, verification codes or other methods acceptable to the Commission;

(I) All CLE Credit approved under this Regulation is Self-Study Credit;

(J) The Sponsor of a Self-Study Activity shall provide to Attendees of Self-Study Activities mandatory evaluation forms, with evaluation data submitted to the Commission every six months, beginning six months from the date of accreditation of the Self-Study Activity;

(K) The Sponsor of each Self-Study Activity shall inform all Attendees of the six hour limitation on Self-Study CLE Credit provided in Rule X, Section 4(A)(4), and Regulation 409.2;

(L) The Sponsor of each Self-Study Activity shall provide a Certificate of Completion for each Attorney or Judge who successfully completes the Self-Study Activity. The Certificate shall include the Ohio Activity Code, the Title of the Program, the correct name of the Sponsor, and the number and type of CLE Credits earned;

(M) The Sponsor shall make the Self-Study Activity's approval status in Ohio and the correct name of the Sponsor clear to participants before they pay to take the Activity;

(N) Self study materials must be current and, in any event, shall have been prepared no earlier than the calendar year immediately preceding the date the application for accreditation is filed.

(O) Any violations of these regulations shall subject the Established Sponsor or Sponsor to late fees established by the Commission.

409.2. Not more than six hours of CLE Credit for any biennial reporting period may be earned by an Attorney or Judge under this Regulation except as provided in Regulation 304.4.

History: Amended, eff 1-1-00; 5-29-00; 8-7-00; 7-1-02; 9-1-04; 11-7-05; 11–1–07.

REGULATION 410: Post-Program Approval

410.1. An Attendee at, or a Sponsor of, an out-of-state CLE Activity may seek post-program approval if such approval is applied for within sixty days after the program is presented.

410.2. Such application shall be on a form provided by the Commission and shall be accompanied by the applicable fee. The program shall meet the standards set forth in Regulation 406.

410.3. The Sponsor shall agree to submit to the Commission, within thirty days of approval of the CLE Activity, the requests for CLE Credit of all Attorneys and Judges in attendance on a form provided by the Commission.

410.4. Any violations of these regulations shall subject the Sponsor or Attorney or Judge to late fees established by the Commission or other sanctions as provided in Rule X or these Regulations.

History: Amended, eff 5-29-00; 7-1-02; 11–1–07.

REGULATION 411: Accreditation Procedures

411.1. Applications for accreditation, whether by Sponsors or by Attendees, shall be on forms provided by the Commission and shall be deemed complete when the form, applicable fee, and all information requested by the Commission is received.

411.2. With regard to a CLE Activity that has been accredited, the Sponsor may announce, in informational brochures and registration materials: "This program has been approved by the Ohio Supreme Court Commission on Continuing Legal Education for ____ hours of CLE Credit."

History: Amended, eff 5-29-00; 7-1-02; 11–1–07.

REGULATION 412: Monitoring of Programs

The Commission shall have authority to monitor any program for which CLE Credit is to be granted to Ohio Attorneys or Judges by sending an autho-

rized representative to attend the program, or any part thereof, without charge. Advance notice of such attendance need not be given.

History: Amended, eff 5-29-00; 11–1–07.

REGULATION 413: Reciprocity with Other States

The Commission may establish a system of reciprocity with other states requiring continuing legal education so that Attorneys or Judges attending accredited programs outside of Ohio may receive appropriate credit. Until such reciprocal arrangements are made, all Sponsors of programs in other states must conform to these Regulations in order to qualify programs for CLE Credit for Attorneys or Judges.

History: Amended, eff 5-29-00; 11–1–07.

REGULATION 414: Accreditation of New Lawyers Training Courses

414.1. An Established Sponsor may apply for accreditation of a New Lawyers Training course to be presented by the Established Sponsor on a form provided by the Commission. The application for accreditation shall be accompanied by a nonrefundable fee of twenty-five dollars.

414.2. Application for accreditation of a New Lawyers Training course shall be submitted at least sixty days prior to the date of the first presentation. Upon approval by the Commission, the course shall be considered as an accredited New Lawyers Training course for a period of one calendar year following the approval by the Commission. For each presentation of an accredited New Lawyers Training course after the first presentation, the Established Sponsor shall file an announcement of the presentation on a form provided by the Commission at least sixty days prior to the presentation of the course.

414.3. Within thirty days after presentation of a New Lawyers Training course, Established Sponsors shall submit to the Commission all requests for CLE credit required by the Attorneys in attendance. A list of attendees of each presentation of a New Lawyers Training course shall be retained by the Sponsor for at least two years following the presentation of the course.

414.4. To be accredited by the Commission, a New Lawyers Training course shall satisfy the requirements of Gov. Bar R. X, Section 3(H) and comply with all of the following standards:

(A) The course shall satisfy the standards of Regulation 406.

(B) Instruction shall be live. Sponsors are encouraged to use a variety of methods of instruction, including lectures, panels, workshops, and other forms of participatory or interactive learning where appropriate.

(C) The course shall be a minimum of one hour in length.

(D) The Sponsor shall assure that at least 25% of the available seating at the course is made available to attorneys subject to division (H)(1) of Section 3 of Rule X.

414.5. The Commission may revoke its accreditation of a New Lawyers Training course if it determines that the course is not in compliance with the requirements of this regulation. Revocation shall not be retroactive, but shall affect only presentations of the program occurring after the effective date of the revocation.

414.6. The Commission shall evaluate Gov. Bar R. X, Sec. 3(H) and these Regulations every five years to determine if they effectively regulate the educational training of lawyers newly admitted to the practice of law in Ohio. The first evaluation shall occur five years from the date of adoption of this regulation and every five years thereafter.

History: Effective 7-1-01; amended, eff 7-1-02; 11-1-07; 11-1-08.

REGULATION 500: Sanctions and Enforcement Procedures

REGULATION 501: Rule X Provisions

The provisions of Rule X, Sections 5, 6, and 7 shall govern all sanctions and enforcement procedures under these Regulations.

History: Amended, eff 12-15-89; 5-29-00; 11-1-07.

REGULATION 502: Commission Not Precluded

502.1. An error or inaccuracy in the CLE Record or any Transcript, or the failure by the Commission to furnish a Transcript to the Attorney or Judge, shall not preclude the Commission from enforcing Rule X, Rule IV, or these Regulations or from imposing sanctions for Noncompliance, but may be considered in making a determination of Good Cause.

502.2. An Attorney or Judge whose record is not in full compliance because of failure to pay a late filing fee, failure to file any report for which a sanction is ordered, or failure to inform the Commission of any inaccurate or missing information cannot claim Good Cause that would require the grant of carryover credit.

History: Amended, eff 12-15-89; 5-29-00; 7-1-02; 11-1-07.

REGULATION 503: Late Filing Fees; Sanctions

503.1. If the Commission finds that an Attorney or Judge is not in compliance because of a late or incomplete filing of the report required by Rule X, Section 3(B)(1), Rule IV, Section 4(A), and Regulation 303, and that the Noncompliance is not for Good Cause, it shall require payment of the applicable fee as a condition to acceptance of a complete report for filing. For purposes of this Regulation, a report shall not be considered incomplete merely because it discloses a failure by the Attorney or Judge to satisfy the CLE Requirements.

503.2.(A) If any Attorney (other than with respect to the New Lawyers Training Program) or Judge, without Good Cause, is not in Compliance, other than by reason of filing a late or incomplete report, the Commission shall impose the sanctions contained in Rule X, Section 5(A).

(B) The Commission may impose the following sanctions pursuant to Rule X, Section 5(A)(1):

(1) Failure to file the report required by Rule X, Section 3(B)(1), Rule IV, Section 4(A) and Regulation 303, $150;

(2) Failure to satisfy the legal ethics and professional conduct requirement imposed by Rule X, Section 3(A)(1) or Rule IV, Sections 2(A) and 3(A), $100;

(3) Failure to satisfy the CLE requirements, including, any applicable modifications of those requirements contained in Regulation 305:

DEFICIENCY:	RECOMMENDED SANCTION:
Six hours or less	More than $50 but not more than $90
More than six hours but not more than twelve hours	More than $90 but not more than $240
More than twelve hours but not more than eighteen hours	More than $240 but not more than $360
More than eighteen hours	More than $360 but not more than $500

(4) Failure to satisfy the Judicial College requirement imposed by Rule X, Section 3 (D)(1), Judicial Rule IV, Section 2(A)(1) or Section 3(A)(1), $100.

503.3. The recommended sanctions contained in Rule X, Section 5(A) and Regulation 503.2 shall be cumulative.

503.4. CLE credit obtained to make up a deficiency for a prior reporting period shall not be applied to satisfy the CLE requirement for the reporting period in which the Credit is obtained.

503.5. If an Attorney, without good cause, is not in compliance with Rule X or these Regulations for failure to timely complete the New Lawyers Training Program, the Commission shall impose the sanction of suspension as provided in Rule X, Section 5(B). Provided, however, if prior to the imposition of the sanction of suspension, the Attorney completes the New Lawyers Training Program and provides the Commission with satisfactory evidence thereof in compliance with Rule X and these Regulations and pays a late filing fee of three hundred dollars, the Commission shall not impose the sanction of suspension.

History: Amended, eff 12-15-89; 5-29-00; 7-1-01; 7-1-02; 11-1-07.

REGULATION 504: Enforcement Procedures

504.1. If an Attorney or Judge fails to comply with Rule X, Rule IV or these Regulations, the Commission shall send the Attorney or Judge a notice of Noncompliance. The notice shall specify the nature of the Noncompliance and state that unless the attorney comes into compliance or files evidence of compliance that is satisfactory to the Commission by the date set forth in the notice, the Commission shall issue an order imposing a sanction consistent with Commission regulation. As a condition of acceptance of late Compliance, the applicable fee shall accompany the Attorney's or Judge's report of completion.

504.2. If evidence is submitted by the date set forth in the notice that establishes timely Compliance or late Compliance by the Attorney or Judge, the notice of Noncompliance shall be withdrawn and the Commission shall so advise the Attorney or Judge.

504.3. If the Attorney or Judge does not come into compliance or file evidence of compliance that is satisfactory to the Commission by the date set forth in the notice, the Commission shall issue an order imposing a sanction consistent with Commission regulation.

History: Amended, eff 12-15-89; 5-29-00; 7-1-02; 11-1-07.

REGULATION 600: Commission Counsel; Hearing Examiners

REGULATION 601: Commission Counsel

Subject to the approval of the Supreme Court, the Commission may employ one or more Commission Counsel, on a full-time or part-time basis, to represent the Commission in all enforcement proceedings under Rule X and these Regulations. The Supreme Court shall establish the qualifications of and compensation for Attorneys employed as Commission Counsel.

History: Amended, eff 12-15-89; 5-29-00; 7-1-02.

REGULATION 602: Hearing Examiners

602.1. The Commission may appoint one or more Hearing Examiners as provided in Rule X, Section 6(A)(3) to conduct hearings under Rule X and these Regulations. Hearing Examiners shall be attorneys who have been members in good standing of the bar of Ohio for at least ten (10) years and shall have had trial experience. Hearing Examiners shall be paid $50 per hour for services performed on behalf of the Commission, not to exceed $100 per case unless approved by the Commission in advance.

602.2. No Hearing Examiner shall conduct a hearing held at the request of any Attorney or Judge who resides in or has an office in the same county as that in which the Hearing Examiner resides or has an office.

History: Amended, eff 12-15-89; 5-29-00; 7-1-02.

REGULATION 900: Fees

The Commission shall from time to time establish fees to be charged by the Commission and publish a schedule of such fees. Such fees shall bear a reasonable relation to the actual necessary costs incurred by the Commission in connection with the performance of the duties and responsibilities imposed upon it by Rule X and these Regulations.

History: Effective 7-1-02; 11-1-07.

REGULATION 1000: Effective Date

REGULATION 1001: Effective Date of Regulations

1001.1.(A) These Regulations shall be effective January 1, 1989.

(B) Regulations 500 and 600, adopted by the Supreme Court on November 22, 1989, shall take effect on December 15, 1989, and shall apply to the 1989 reporting period and subsequent reporting periods.

(C) Regulations 100, 403, 408 and 409, adopted by the Supreme Court on September 21, 1999, shall be effective January 1, 2000.

(D) Miscellaneous, nonsubstantive amendments to these Regulations correspond to amendments to Gov. Bar R. X and Gov. Jud. R. IV adopted by the Supreme Court between May 8, 1990 and October 20, 1997. These nonsubstantive amendments shall be effective May 29, 2000.

(E) Regulation 409.1(G) and (L) amended to comport with Gov. Bar R. X amendments adopted on September 21, 1999 effective August 7, 2000.

(F) Amendments to Gov. Bar R. X(3), (5) and (9) and to Attorney Continuing Legal Education Regulations 100, 404, 414 and 503 (New Lawyer Training Program) effective July 1, 2001.

(G) Amendments to Regulations 101, 201, 301, 302, 303, 304, 305, 306, 401, 402, 403, 404, 405, 406, 407, 408, 409, 410, 411, 414, 502, 503, 504, 601, 602, 900, 901 and 1001 adopted by the Supreme Court on April 22, 2002 shall be effective July 1, 2002.

(H) Amendments to Regulations 408, 409 and 1001 adopted by the Supreme Court on July 20, 2004 shall be effective September 1, 2004.

(I) Amendments to Regulations 406 and 409 adopted by the Supreme Court on October 11, 2005 shall be effective on November 7, 2005.

(J) Amendments to Regulations 404 adopted by the Supreme Court on November 29, 2005 shall be effective on December 26, 2005.

(K) Amendments to the Regulations adopted by the Supreme Court on September 11, 2007 shall be effective on November 1, 2007, and shall apply to the 2008 reporting period and subsequent reporting periods, except that former Regulations 500 and 600 shall govern sanctions and enforcement procedures for the 2007 reporting period.

(L) Amendments to the Regulations adopted by the Supreme Court on June 24, 2008, shall be effective November 1, 2008, except that programs offered to satisfy former Gov. Bar R. X, Sec. 3, shall comply with former Regulation 100(N) and former Regulation 414. Effective 1-1-89; amended, eff 12- 15-89; 5-29-00; 8-7-00; 7-1-01; 7-1-02; 9-1-04; 11-7-05; 12-26-05; 11–1–07; 11–1–08.

Schedule of Fees for Sponsors (Pursuant to Regulation 900)

Type of Sponsor	Application Fees	Late Application Fees	Late Submission of Credits	Administrative Fees (Sponsor Error)
Established Sponsors	$400 Annual Fee	$100 Submitted less than 30 days prior to presentation	$100 Submitted more than 30 days after presentation	$25 hour
Established Sponsors — ABA Accredited Law School	$25 per application not to exceed $400 annually	$100 Submitted less than 30 days prior to presentation	$100 Submitted more than 30 days after presentation	$25 hour
New Lawyer Training Programs	$25 per application (in addition to the Established Sponsor fee)	$100 Submitted less than 60 days prior to presentation	$100 Submitted more than 30 days after presentation	$25 hour
Special Program — in-House Activity	$25 per application	$100 Submitted less than 60 days prior to presentation	$100 Submitted more than 30 days after presentation	$25 hour
Sponsor Request — Ohio Program	$25 per application	$100 Submitted less than 60 days prior to presentation	$100 Submitted more than 30 days after presentation	$25 hour
Sponsor Request — Out of State Program	No Application Fee	N/A	N/A	$25 hour
Sponsor Request — Self-Study Accreditation	$25 per application (If Established Sponsor is applying this fee is in addition to the annual fee)	N/A	$50 Submitted more than 30 days after presentation	$25 hour

Schedule of Fees for Attorneys (Pursuant to Regulation 900)

Type of Sponsor	Miscellaneous Fees	Late Application Fees	Late Submission of Credits
Deposit for Costs for Appeal Hearing	$50	N/A	N/A
Individual Request for Out of State CLE Accreditation	0	$25 Submitted more than 60 days after presentation	$25 Submitted more than 60 days after presentation
Individual Request for Teaching at an Approved CLE Activity	0	N/A	$25 Submitted more than 30 days after presentation
Late Filing Fee for Final Transcript (Filed after 1/31 but no later than 4/30 of the reporting year)	$50	N/A	N/A
Publication Request	0	$25 Submitted more than 90 days after publication	N/A
Request for Credit for Law School Attendance	N/A	N/A	$25 Submitted more than 30 days after presentation

Schedule of Fees for Attorneys (Pursuant to Regulation 900)

Type of Sponsor	Miscellaneous Fees	Late Application Fees	Late Submission of Credits
Request for Credit for Law School Instruction	N/A	N/A	$25 Submitted more than 30 days after presentation
Request for Transcript	$5.00	N/A	N/A

RULES AND REGULATIONS GOVERNING PROCEDURE ON COMPLAINTS AND HEARINGS BEFORE THE BOARD OF COMMISSIONERS ON GRIEVANCES AND DISCIPLINE OF THE SUPREME COURT

Section 1. Complaint Requirements

(A) The complaint shall allege the specific misconduct detailed in Gov.Bar R. IV or Section 6(a) of Gov.Bar R. V and cite the disciplinary rule allegedly violated by the Respondent. The panel and Board shall not be limited to the citation to the disciplinary rule(s) in finding violations based on all the evidence.

(B) The Relator in the complaint shall set forth the Respondent's attorney registration number and his last known address where the Board shall serve the complaint. Effective 10-8-90.

Section 2. Pleadings and Motions

(A) Within the period of time permitted for an answer to the complaint, Respondent may file any motion appropriate under Rule 12 of the Ohio Rules of Civil Procedure, supported by a brief and affidavits if necessary. A brief and affidavits, if appropriate, in opposition to such motion may be filed within twenty days after service of such motion. No oral hearing will be granted, and rulings of the Board will be made by the Chairman of the Board or any member designated by the Secretary of the Board. All motions shall be made in accordance with this rule.

(B) The chairman or a member of the panel shall rule on all motions subsequent to the appointment of a panel.

(C) For good cause, the Chairman of the Board, or, after appointment of a panel, the chairman or member of the panel may grant extensions of time for the filing of any pleading, motion, brief or affidavit, either before or after the time permitted for filing.

(D) Every pleading after the complaint shall show proof of service. Effective 10-8-90.

Section 3. Rules of Procedure

(A) The Board and hearing panels shall follow the Ohio Rules of Civil Procedure wherever practicable unless a specific provision of Gov. Bar R. V provides otherwise.

(B) Depositions taken in Gov. Bar R. V proceedings shall be filed with the Secretary of the Board as Rule 32 of the Ohio Rules of Civil Procedure prescribes.

(C) If Relator and Respondent stipulate to facts, the chairman or member of the panel may either cancel a hearing and deem the matter submitted in writing or order that a hearing be held with all counsel and the Respondent present.

(D) Notwithstanding the agreement of Relator and Respondent on a recommended sanction for Respondent, the hearing panel and the Board are not bound by the joint recommendation and retain sole power and discretion to make a final recommendation to the Ohio Supreme Court on the appropriate sanction. Effective 10-8-90; amended, eff 6-1-00.

Section 4. Manner of Service

Whenever provision is made for the service of any notice, order, report, or other paper or copy upon any complainant, relator, respondent, petitioner, or other party, in connection with any proceeding under these rules, service may be made upon counsel of record for such complainant, relator, respondent, petitioner, or other party, either personally or by certified mail. Effective 7-1-92.

Section 5. Quorum of Panel or Board

A majority of the members of the Board of Commissioners, or a panel thereof, shall constitute a quorum for all purposes, and the action of a majority of those present comprising the quorum shall be the action of the Board of Commissioners or a panel of the Board; except for the granting of a motion for default pursuant to section 6(F) of Gov.Bar R. V, or a dismissal of the complaint at the conclusion of the hearing pursuant to section 6(H) of Gov.Bar R. V, which shall require the unanimous action of a hearing panel. Effective 7-1-92.

Section 6. Manner of Service on Clerk; Record of Such Service a Public Record

All notices shall be served by the Secretary of the Board upon the Clerk of the Supreme Court by leaving at the office of the Clerk a true and attested copy of the notice and any accompanying document and by sending to the respondent, by certified mail, postage prepaid, return receipt requested, a like, true, and attested copy, with an endorsement thereon of service, upon the Clerk of the Supreme Court, addressed to the respondent at the respondent's last known address. The receipt indicating the certified mail number shall be attached to and made a part of the return of service of such notice by the Secretary. The panel or Board or court before which there is pending any proceeding in which notice has been given as provided in this section may order a continuance as is necessary to afford the respondent reasonable opportunity to appear and defend. The Clerk of the Supreme Court shall keep a record of the day and hour of service upon the Clerk of notice and any accompanying document, which shall be a public record in the office of the Clerk. Effective 7-1-92.

Section 7. Power to Issue Subpoenas

(A) Subpoenas

In investigations and proceedings under this rule, upon application by Disciplinary Counsel, the Secretary, or chair of a Certified Grievance Committee authorized to sign a certificate under Section 4(I)(7) of Gov. Bar R. V, the Special Investigator, respondent, relator, chair of the hearing panel of the Board, and its Secretary shall have the authority to cause testimony to be taken under oath before the Special Investigator, Disciplinary Counsel, a Certified Grievance Committee, or a hearing panel of the Board. All subpoenas shall be signed and issued by the chair of the hearing panel, the chair or vice-chair of the Board, or its Secretary and served as provided by the Ohio Rules of Civil Procedure. A motion to quash a subpoena issued under this section shall be filed with the Secretary of the Board and ruled upon the chair or vice-chair of the Board.

(B) Subpoena pursuant to law of another jurisdiction

(1) A foreign disciplinary authority, pursuant to the law of that jurisdiction and where the issuance of the subpoena has been duly approved, if such approval is required by the law of that jurisdiction, may request issuance of a subpoena for use in an attorney or judicial discipline or disability proceeding. The Secretary shall issue a subpoena upon such request as provided in this rule.

(2) A subpoena issued pursuant to this rule may be issued to compel the attendance of witnesses and production of documents in the county where the witness resides, is employed or as otherwise agreed by the witness. Service, enforcement, and challenges to such subpoenas shall be as provided in these rules.

(C) Request for foreign subpoena in aid of proceeding in this jurisdiction

Disciplinary Counsel, Certified Grievance Committees, and respondents may apply for the issuance of subpoenas in other jurisdictions pursuant to the rules of those jurisdictions in the furtherance of attorney or judicial discipline or disability proceedings in the State of Ohio. The Secretary may provide assistance to facilitate these requests. [Section 7 Approved by Supreme Court of Ohio, July 1, 1992; Amended by Supreme Court of Ohio, effective, June 1, 2000; July 18, 2005.]

Section 8. Master Commissioner

(A) Appointment

With the approval of a majority of the Board of Commissioners on Grievances and Discipline, the Chair of the Board may appoint one or more master commissioners, who shall be attorneys or judges admitted to active practice in Ohio and who shall have former service as a member of the Board. At the request of a hearing panel chair, the master may assume any or all case management responsibili-

ties occurring between the appointment of a hearing panel and the formal hearing on the complaint set forth in Gov. Bar R. V, Section (6)(G). The master shall not exercise adjudicatory powers under Gov. Bar R. V.

(B) Compensation

The compensation for the services of the master shall be on the same basis as members of the Board.

(C) Proceedings and Powers

The order of reference to a master shall be signed by the chair of a hearing panel. The order of reference may specify or limit the master's powers and may direct the master to report only upon particular issues or to perform particular acts. Unless so specified or limited, the master may perform all of the following:

(1) Assist the parties and counsel in making all discovery disclosures including the use of interrogatories, depositions, and requests for admission;

(2) Conduct pre-trials with counsel and supervise the amendment of pleadings, the use of stipulations between the parties, and the preparation of witness lists and exhibits;

(3) Rule on all motions and interlocutory matters after consultation with the panel chair occurring between the time of the appointment of a hearing panel and the formal hearing on the complaint;

(4) Fix a date for the formal hearing before the hearing panel after consultation with the panel chair.

(D) Report

The master shall prepare a written report upon the matters submitted to or considered by the master after consultation with the parties and the panel chair. The master shall serve a copy of the report on each party and file the report with the Secretary of the Board. The report shall become the order of the Board unless a party files a written objection to the report within ten days of the filing with the Board. All objections shall be decided by the chair of the hearing panel as set forth in Gov. Bar R. V, Section (6)(D)(3). Effective 11-1-95.

Section 9. Time Guidelines for Pending Cases

(A) Pre-hearing Conference

(1) Within sixty days of the assignment date of a hearing panel, the panel chair shall conduct a pre-hearing conference to accomplish the following objectives:

(a) simplification of the issues;

(b) necessity of amendment to the pleadings;

(c) establishment of a discovery timetable;

(d) identification of anticipated witnesses and the exchange of reports of anticipated expert witnesses;

(e) identification and exchange of copies of anticipated exhibits;

(f) the possibility of obtaining:

(i) stipulations of fact;

(ii) stipulation of the admissibility of exhibits;

(g) such other matters as may expedite the hearing;

(h) establish a final hearing date.

At the discretion of the panel chair, a pre-hearing

conference may be held by telephone, and may be continued from day to day. The hearing date shall be no more than one hundred fifty days following the date of assignment.

The Board shall adopt a form for use in a pre-hearing conference as well as an entry setting the conference time.

(2) Continuances of the hearing date shall not thereafter be granted due to counsel's or respondent's scheduled appearance before any state court or public agency, except the Supreme Court of Ohio or this Board as set forth in Rule 41(B)(2) of the Rules of Superintendence for the Courts of Ohio.

(B) Submission of Panel Reports

(1) The report of the panel for all hearings not conducted on an expedited basis shall be submitted to the full Board within forty days of the filing of the transcript for consideration at the next regularly scheduled meeting of the Board. For good cause shown, the Secretary, at the request of the panel chair, may extend the date for the filing of the hearing panel report with the Board.

(2) To be considered at the Board meeting, the panel report should be submitted to the Secretary at least seven days prior to that date.

(C) Failure by the Board to meet the time guidelines set forth in Section 9 of this rule shall not be grounds for dismissal of the complaint.

(D) Voluntary Dismissals and Amendments

Following the filing of the complaint, the relator may not voluntarily dismiss the complaint without permission of the chair of the hearing panel. A motion to voluntarily dismiss must be accompanied by a memorandum setting forth the basis for the dismissal with supporting affidavits, depositions, or documents, if required by the panel, that support the dismissal. The panel chair may conduct a hearing on the motion to dismiss and may require the testimony of witnesses and production of documents.

The relator may not amend the complaint within thirty days of the scheduled hearing without a showing of good cause to the satisfaction of the panel chair.

(E) Probable Cause Panels

(1) Two probable cause panels will convene on the day of the Board meeting to consider all new formal complaints filed with the Board during the interim period preceding the week of the Board meeting and any other new complaints that may be otherwise pending since the Board last met.

(2) Both probable cause panels will be available to convene by telephone conference call between scheduled Board meetings if required by extraordinary circumstances. On that occasion probable cause panels would consider and decide new complaints received by the Board since the Board last met. Copies of the complaints will be sent by the Secretary and will be reviewed by the panel members prior to the scheduled conference call. Effective 6-1-00.

Section 10. Guidelines for Imposing Lawyer Sanctions

(A) Each disciplinary case involves unique facts and circumstances. In striving for fair disciplinary standards, consideration will be given to specific professional misconduct and to the existence of aggravating or mitigating factors.

(B) In determining the appropriate sanction, the Board shall consider all relevant factors; precedent established by the Supreme Court of Ohio; and the following:

(1) Aggravation. The following shall not control the Board's discretion, but may be considered in favor of recommending a more severe sanction:

(a) prior disciplinary offenses;

(b) dishonest or selfish motive;

(c) a pattern of misconduct;

(d) multiple offenses;

(e) lack of cooperation in the disciplinary process;

(f) submission of false evidence, false statements, or other deceptive practices during the disciplinary process;

(g) refusal to acknowledge wrongful nature of conduct;

(h) vulnerability of and resulting harm to victims of the misconduct;

(i) failure to make restitution.

(2) Mitigation. The following shall not control the Board's discretion, but may be considered in favor of recommending a less severe sanction:

(a) absence of a prior disciplinary record;

(b) absence of a dishonest or selfish motive;

(c) timely good faith effort to make restitution or to rectify consequences of misconduct;

(d) full and free disclosure to disciplinary Board or cooperative attitude toward proceedings;

(e) character or reputation;

(f) imposition of other penalties or sanctions;

(g) chemical dependency or mental disability when there has been all of the following:

(i) A diagnosis of a chemical dependency or mental disability by a qualified health care professional or alcohol/substance abuse counselor;

(ii) A determination that the chemical dependency or mental disability contributed to cause the misconduct;

(iii) In the event of chemical dependency, a certification of successful completion of an approved treatment program or in the event of mental disability, a sustained period of successful treatment;

(iv) A prognosis from a qualified health care professional or alcohol/substance abuse counselor that the attorney will be able to return to competent, ethical professional practice under specified conditions.

(h) other interim rehabilitation. Effective 6-1-00; amended, eff. 2-1-03.

Section 11.   Consent to Discipline

(A) As used in this section:

(1) "Misconduct" has the same meaning as used in Gov. Bar R. V, Section 6(A)(1);

(2) "Sanction" means any of the sanctions listed in Gov. Bar R. V, Section 6(B)(3), (4), or (5).

(B) Pursuant to Gov. Bar R. V, Section 11(A)(3)(c), the relator and respondent may enter into a written agreement wherein the respondent admits to alleged misconduct and the relator and respondent agree upon a sanction to be imposed for that misconduct. The written agreement may be entered into after a complaint is certified by the Board, but no later than sixty days after appointment of a hearing panel. For good cause shown, the chair of the hearing panel or the Board chair may extend the time for the parties to file a written agreement by an additional thirty days. The written agreement shall be signed by the respondent, respondent's counsel, if the respondent is represented by counsel, and relator, and shall include all of the following:

(1) An admission by the respondent, conditioned upon acceptance of the agreement by the Board, that the respondent committed the misconduct listed in the agreement;

(2) The sanction agreed upon by the relator and respondent for the misconduct admitted by the respondent;

(3) Any aggravating and mitigating factors, including but not limited to those listed in Section 10, that are applicable to the misconduct and agreed sanction;

(4) An affidavit of the respondent that includes all of the following statements:

(a) That the respondent admits to having committed the misconduct listed in the agreement, that grounds exist for imposition of a sanction against the respondent for the misconduct, and that the agreement sets forth all grounds for discipline currently pending before the Board;

(b) That the respondent admits to the truth of the material facts relevant to the misconduct listed in the agreement;

(c) That the respondent agrees to the sanction to be recommended to the Board;

(d) That the respondent's admissions and agreement are freely and voluntarily given, without coercion or duress, and that the respondent is fully aware of the implications of the admissions and agreement on his or her ability to practice law in Ohio.

(e) That the respondent understands that the Supreme Court of Ohio has the final authority to determine the appropriate sanction for the misconduct admitted by the respondent.

(C) The agreement shall be filed with the Secretary of the Board and submitted either to the hearing panel or a master commissioner appointed pursuant to Section 8. Relator and respondent may file a brief in support of the agreement. If the hearing panel, by majority vote, or master commissioner recommends acceptance of the agreement and concurs in the agreed sanction, the matter shall be scheduled for consideration by the Board in accordance with Section 9. If the agreement is not accepted by the hearing panel or master commissioner, the matter shall be set for hearing in accordance with Section 9.

(D) If the agreement is submitted to the Board, the Board, by majority vote, may accept or reject the agreement. If the board accepts the agreement, the

agreement shall form the basis for the certified report submitted to the Supreme Court pursuant to Gov. Bar R. V, Section 6(L). If the Board rejects the agreement, the matter shall be returned to the hearing panel and set for a hearing in accordance with Section 9.

(E) If the agreement is not accepted by the hearing panel or the Board, the agreement shall not be admissible or otherwise used in subsequent disciplinary proceedings.

(F) Nothing in this section shall prevent the relator and respondent from entering into stipulations and a recommended sanction against the respondent pursuant to Section 3.

(G) Nothing in this section shall affect the jurisdiction of the Supreme Court of Ohio to determine the appropriate sanction for the misconduct admitted by the respondent in accordance with Gov. Bar R. V, Section 8. Effective 5-1-01; amended effective 4-1-08.

Sections 12-19. [Reserved]

Section 20. Regulation for the Issuance of Advisory Opinions

(A) Procedure for Issuance

(1) Pursuant to Section 2(C) of Rule V of the Supreme Court Rules for the Government of the Bar of Ohio, the Board of Commissioners on Grievances and Discipline of the Supreme Court of Ohio issues informal, nonbinding advisory opinion letters to members of the Bar and the Judiciary in response to prospective or hypothetical questions regarding the application of the Supreme Court Rules for the Government of the Bar of Ohio, the Supreme Court Rules for the Government of the Judiciary of Ohio, the Ohio Rules of Professional Conduct, the Code of Professional Responsibility, the Code of Judicial Conduct, or the Attorney's Oath of Office. Pursuant to Section 102.08 of the Ohio Revised Code and in a manner consistent with Rule V and these regulations, the Board issues advisory opinions regarding the application of Chapter 102. or section 2921.42 or 2921.43 of the Ohio Revised Code.

(2) The Chair of the Board shall appoint five or more members of the Board to serve on an Advisory Opinion Subcommittee. The Advisory Opinion Subcommittee is a regular standing subcommittee of the Board. The subcommittee shall meet prior to each regularly scheduled Board meeting. The Chair shall appoint one subcommittee member to serve as Chair of the Advisory Opinion Subcommittee. Each subcommittee member shall serve for a period of one year from the date of appointment and shall be eligible for reappointment by the Chair.

(3) Requests for advisory opinion shall be submitted in writing to the Secretary of the Board or staff attorney. A letter acknowledging the receipt of the request will be sent to the requester.

(4) The Advisory Opinion Subcommittee reviews requests for advisory opinions. Within its discretion, the subcommittee may accept or decline a request for an advisory opinion. In making such determination the subcommittee strives to select prospective or hypothetical questions of broad interest or impor-

tance to the Bar or Judiciary of Ohio and to avoid questions involving the proposed conduct of someone other than the person requesting the opinion, questions regarding completed conduct, questions of law, questions pending before a court, questions that are too broad, questions that lack sufficient information, or questions of narrow interest.

(5) The requester of an advisory opinion will be notified of the subcommittee's determination to accept or decline a request.

(6) As an alternative to selecting or declining a request, the subcommittee may direct the staff attorney to provide guidance in a staff letter. The staff letter may be based upon past opinions of the Board, the subcommittee's views, and or other relevant information. A staff letter will contain language to indicate that it is a nonbinding staff letter not an advisory opinion of the Board.

(7) Draft opinions will be researched and prepared by the Board's legal staff.

(8) Draft opinions will be forwarded to the subcommittee for review approximately three weeks before a Board meeting. The subcommittee will review the draft, make comments or suggestions, and by majority decision approve or disapprove of the draft.

(9) The subcommittee and legal staff will complete the process of researching, drafting, and review as expeditiously as possible, preferably within two to six months after selection of the request.

(10) Each draft opinion approved by the subcommittee will be sent to Board members for review approximately two weeks prior to a Board meeting. Upon review, Board members may direct comments, suggestions, or objections to the Board's Staff Attorney.

(11) If objections are received, the draft opinion will be placed on the agenda for discussion at the Board meeting. If no objections are received, the draft opinion will be adopted without discussion by majority vote of the Board at the Board meeting. Minor or non-substantive changes are not considered as objections to a draft opinion.

(12) A copy of an adopted opinion will be issued to the requester. Copies of issued opinions will be submitted for publication in the ABA/BNA Lawyers' Manual on Professional Conduct, the Ohio State Bar Association Report, and other publications or electronic communications as the Board deems appropriate. Copies of issued opinions will be forwarded to the Law Library of the Supreme Court of Ohio, County Law Libraries, Office of Disciplinary Counsel, and local and state bar associations with certified grievance committees. In addition, copies of opinions relating to judges will be forwarded to the Ohio Ethics Commission, Ohio Elections Commission, Ohio Judicial Conference, Ohio Judicial College, Secretary of State of Ohio, and the American Judicature Society.

(13) Issued opinions shall not bear the name of the requester and shall not include the request letter. However, the requester's name and the request letter are not private and will be made available to the bar, the judiciary, or the public upon request.

(B) Procedure for Maintenance

(1) A copy of each advisory opinion will be kept in the Board's offices.

(2) An advisory opinion that becomes withdrawn, modified, not current, or affected by other significant changes will be marked with an appropriate designation to indicate the status of the opinion.

(3) The designation "Withdrawn" will be used when an opinion has been withdrawn by majority vote of the Board. The designation indicates that an opinion no longer represents the advice of the Board.

(4) The designation "Modified" will be used when an opinion has been modified by majority vote of the Board. The designation indicates that an opinion has been modified by a subsequent opinion.

(5) The designation "Not Current" will be used at the discretion of the Board's attorney staff to indicate that an opinion is not current in its entirety. The designation that an opinion is no longer current in its entirety may be used to indicate a variety of reasons such as subsequent amendments to rules or statutes, or developments in case law.

(6) The designation "CPR Opinion" will be used when an opinion provides guidance under the Ohio Code of Professional Responsibility that is superseded by the Ohio Rules of Professional Conduct, effective February 1, 2007. The designation indicates that the opinion provides guidance regarding the Board's advice under the superseded Code.

(7) The designation "Former CJC Opinion" will be used when an opinion provides guidance under the former Ohio Code of Judicial Conduct that is superseded by the Ohio Code of Judicial Conduct, effective March 1, 2009. The designation indicates that the opinion provides guidance regarding the Board's advice under the superseded Code.

(8) Other designations, as needed, may be used by majority vote of the Board.

(8) The Advisory Opinion Index will include a status list identifying the opinions and the designations. Effective 3-1-97; amended, eff 6-1-00; 2-1-07; 1-1-10.

Appendix III.
RULES OF THE
OHIO BOARD OF BAR EXAMINERS

EFFECTIVE JUNE 1, 2000

RULE   I.   GRADING   OF   OHIO   BAR EXAMINATION

Section 1.   Grading by and Calibration of Bar Examiners and Readers

With the assistance of readers selected by the Court pursuant to Gov. Bar R. I, Sec. 4(D), the Board of Bar Examiners shall grade applicant answers from the written portion of the Ohio bar examination, which shall consist of both the essay questions and the Multistate Performance Test (MPT) items. Before answers are graded, each bar examiner shall participate in a training and calibration session with those readers who will be assisting the bar examiner in grading answers to the same essay question or MPT item.

Section 2. Raw and Scaled Scores

(A) Scores assigned to individual answers on the written portion of the examination may range from 0 to 7 points.

(B) Scores assigned to MPT answers shall be weighted by multiplying them by 1.5.

(C) An applicant's raw score on the written portion of the examination shall be the total of the applicant's 12 essay scores plus the applicant's two weighted MPT scores.

(D) Raw scores on the written portion of an examination shall be scaled to the MBE range of scores for the examination using the mean and standard deviation scores.

Section 3. Passing Examination Score

(A) An applicant's total examination score shall be determined by the following formula:

Total score = (scaled score on written portion of examination x 2) + (MBE scaled score)

(B) An applicant shall pass the examination if the applicant achieves a total score of at least 405 points.

Section 4. Automatic Regrade of Written Answers

Applicants who achieve total scores one point or a fraction of one point less than the minimum passing score shall have their answers to the written portion of the examination regraded. Before the announcement of examination results, the Clerk shall submit the written answers of those applicants, along with a random sampling of answers written by passing applicants, to the bar examiners for regrading. The bar examiners shall not be given the original scores assigned to the essay answers they receive for regrading.

After regrading, final total scores shall be calculated for those applicants who are entitled to have their written answers regraded. For each applicant entitled to have his or her written answers regraded, the applicant's original written raw score shall be averaged with the written raw score assigned to the applicant during regrading. This average score shall be the applicant's final written raw score. The final written raw score shall be scaled and combined with the applicant's MBE scaled score, in accordance with the formula in Section 3 of this rule, to obtain the applicant's final total score.

RULE II. MULTISTATE PROFESSIONAL RESPONSIBILITY EXAMINATION

A scaled score of at least 85 points shall be required to pass the Multistate Professional Responsibility Examination.

RULE III. EFFECTIVE DATES

The Rules of the Ohio Board of Bar Examiners approved by the Supreme Court November 2, 1994, shall become effective January 1, 1995. The amend-

ments to the Rules of the Ohio Board of Bar Examiners approved by the Supreme Court June 4, 1996, shall become effective July 1, 1996. The amendments to the Rules of the Ohio Board of Bar Examiners approved by the Supreme Court March 30, 1999, shall become

effective June 1, 2000.Ohio Board Of Bar Examiners Policy On Applicants With Disabilities Approved September 26, 1995

I. POLICY

It is the policy of the Ohio Board of Bar Examiners ('Board') to administer the bar examination in a manner that does not discriminate, on the basis of a disability, against a qualified applicant with a disability. An applicant who is otherwise eligible to take the Ohio bar examination may file a request for special testing accommodations if, by virtue of a disability, the applicant cannot demonstrate, under standard testing conditions, that the applicant possesses the essential skills and aptitudes that the Supreme Court of Ohio and the Board have determined are appropriate to require admission to the practice of law in Ohio.

II. DEFINITIONS

For the purpose of this policy, the following definitions shall apply:

A. "Disability" shall mean any of the following:

1. a physical or mental impairment that substantially limits one of more of the major life activities of the applicant, under the standard testing conditions, that the applicant possesses the essential skills and aptitudes that the Supreme Court of Ohio and the Board have determined are appropriate to require the admission to the practice of law in Ohio;

2. a record of having such an impairment;

3. being regarded as having such an impairment.

B. "Physical impairment" shall mean any physiological disorder or condition, cosmetic disfigurement, or anatomical loss affecting one or more of the following body systems: neurological, musculoskeletal, special sense organ, respiratory (including speech organs), cardiovascular, reproductive, digestive, genitourinary, hemic and lymphatic, skin, and endocrine.

C. "Mental impairment" shall mean any mental or psychological disorder, such as mental retardation, organic brain syndrome, emotional or mental illness, and specific learning disabilities.

D. "Qualified applicant with a disability" shall mean an applicant with a disability who, with or without reasonable modifications to rules, policies, or practices; the removal or architectural, communication, or transportation barriers; or the provision of auxiliary aids and services, meets the essential eligibility requirements for admission to the practice of law in Ohio.

E. "Reasonable accommodation" shall mean an adjustment or modification of the standard testing conditions that ameliorates the impact of the applicant's disability without doing any of the following:

1. fundamentally altering the nature of the examination or the Board's ability to determine through

the bar examination whether the applicant possesses the essential skills and aptitudes that the Supreme Court of Ohio and the Board have determined are appropriate to require for admission to the practice of law in Ohio;

2. imposing an undue burden on the Board;

3. compromising the security of the examination;

4. compromising the integrity, the reliability, or the validity of the examination.

III. REQUESTS FOR SPECIAL TESTING ACCOMMODATIONS

A. Regular Requests

1. A regular request for special testing accommodations shall be on forms prescribed by the Board and shall consist of the following:

a. A statement of the applicant, including a description of the applicant's disability and the special accommodations requested;

b. a certificate of the applicant's medical or psychological authority;

c. a certificate from any educational institution or employer that provided special accommodations to the applicant while the applicant attended the educational institution or was employed by the employer.

The applicant may file any additional documentation in support of the request. Upon request, the applicant shall submit an authorization for release of records from the medical and/or psychological authorities who completed certificates submitted with the request if the Board reasonably determines whether an applicant's conditions meets the criteria for a disability set forth in this policy.

2. A request fro special testing accommodations for an examination shall be filed with the applicant's Application to Take the Bar Examination and by the deadline on Gov. Bar R. 1, Sec. 3, for filing that application.

B. Emergency Requests

1. An applicant may file an emergency request for special testing accommodations after the time prescribed in Part III(A)(2) of this policy if all of the following conditions are met:

a. the applicant's Application to Take the Bar Examination or Application for Re-examination was timely files and complete in all other aspects;

b. at the time of filing the Application to Take the Bar Examination of the Application for Re-examination, the applicant did not have the disability;

c. after acquiring the disability, the applicant promptly submits both of the following:

i. an emergency request on a form prescribed by the Board, providing the date and circumstance under which the disability arose;

iii. a complete request for special testing accommodations.

2. An emergency request shall not be filed fewer than 7 days preceding the scheduled bar examination.

C. Availability of Request Forms

All forms necessary to complete a regular or emergency request for special testing accommodations shall be available at no charge from the Supreme Court Admissions Office.

IV. BOARD DECISIONS

A. Procedures for Review of Requests

1. The Board shall review all requests for special testing accommodations that are properly filed in accordance with this policy. Requests that are not timely filed, that are incomplete, or that otherwise do not comply with the requirements of this policy may be rejected for consideration by the Board. The Board may request an applicant to submit additional information in support of the applicant's request. The Board may seek the assistance of a medical, psychological, or other authority of the Board's choosing in reviewing a request.

2. In reviewing a regular request, the Board shall comply with the following procedures.

a. The Board shall make a determination, and the Secretary of the Board shall send notification of the determination to the applicant, no fewer than 40 days before the examination.

b. The Board's denial of a request shall be in writing and sent to the applicant by certified mail to the address provided by the applicant on the request. The Board's denial shall include a statement of the Board's reasons for denial. The Board shall also provide the applicant with a copy of the written report any expert it consulted in reviewing the request.

c. The applicant may appeal the denial of a request to the Chair of the Board. The appeal shall be filed within 10 days of the applicant's receipt of the notice of denial. The appeal shall be conducted on the basis of the record compiled before the Board, and the applicant shall be limited to a written argument in support of the appeal.

d. Within 5 days of the filing of an appeal, the Chair shall affirm, reverse, or modify the decision of the Board and prepare a written ruling with reasons for the decision.

The Secretary of the Board shall send a copy of the ruling to the applicant at the address provided by the applicant on the request The Chair's decision on the appeal shall be final.

3. In reviewing an emergency request, the Board shall comply with the following procedures.

a. Before deciding on the merits of an emergency request, the Board shall first determine whether the request qualifies as an emergency request under this policy. If it does not qualify as an emergency, the Board may deny the request.

b. The Board may deny an emergency request if it is not practicable in the time remaining before the examination:

i. to arrange special accommodations that would provide testing conditions that are reasonable and comparable to those conditions provided to other applicants; or

ii. for the Board to take all steps reasonable and necessary for it to reach a fair determination, as soon as is reasonable but not later than 24 hours before the examination.

c. The Board shall make a determination on the emergency request, and the Secretary of the Board shall notify the applicant of the determination, as soon as is possible but no later than 24 hours before the examination.

d. The Board's decision on an emergency request shall be final and is not appealable.

4. The Board may delegate to a committee of bar examiners its authority to review and rule upon requests pursuant to this policy.

5. The Board shall incur the costs of all accommodations that it grants and that are provided to the applicant by the Board.

B. Standards for Decision on the Merits

1. The Board shall grant a request and provide special testing accommodations to an applicant if it finds all of the following:

a. the applicant is a qualified applicant with a disability who is otherwise eligible to take the bar examination;

b. the special testing accommodations are necessary to ameliorate the impact of an applicant's disability;

c. the special testing accommodations are reasonable accommodations.

2. The Board shall determine, based on the information available to it, what special testing accommodations are reasonable accommodations. The Board may provide accommodations different from those requested by the applicant if the Board determines that the accommodations provided will effectively ameliorate the impact of the applicant's disability.

3. No special testing accommodations granted pursuant to this policy shall serve to alter in any manner the limitation otherwise imposed on the length of an applicant's answers.

4. If an applicant is permitted to dictate answers to the essay portion of the examination, those answers shall be transcribed by personnel selected solely by the Board for that purpose.

V. CONFIDENTIALITY

All requests for special testing accommodations, supporting documentation, and information developed by the Board with respect to the requests shall remain confidential.

Appendix IV.
STANDARDS FOR ACCREDITATION OF SPECIALTY CERTIFICATION PROGRAMS FOR LAWYERS EFFECTIVE NOVEMBER 14, 1995

SUPREME COURT OF OHIO COMMISSION ON CERTIFICATION OF ATTORNEYS AS SPECIALISTS

SECTION 1.   Policy Statement

1.01. This document establishes standards by which the Supreme Court of Ohio Commission on Certification of Attorneys as Specialists will accredit specialty certification programs for lawyers in particular fields of law. The Standards require that an accredited organization demonstrate that lawyers certified by it possess an enhanced level of skill and expertise as well as substantial involvement in the specialty area of certification and that accredited organizations foster professional development. The Standards are designed to enable the Commission to evaluate thoroughly the objectives, standards, and procedures of Applicants and to facilitate public access to appropriate legal services.

SECTION 2.   Definitions

2.01. As used in these Standards:

(A) "Accredited Organization" means an entity that is accredited by the Supreme Court of Ohio Commission on Certification of Attorneys as Specialists to certify lawyers as specialists.

(B) "Applicant" means a certifying organization that applies to the Supreme Court of Ohio Commission on Certification of Attorneys as Specialists for accreditation or re-accreditation under these Standards.

(C) "Certifying Organization" means an entity that certifies or intends to certify lawyers as specialists.

(D) "Commission" means the Supreme Court Commission on Certification of Attorneys as Specialists.

(E) "Review Panel" means three or more members of the Supreme Court of Ohio Commission on Certification of Attorneys as Specialists designated by the Chair of the Commission, taking into consideration the expertise of the Commission members, to review the application of a Certifying Organization and make a recommendation to the full Commission as to whether that application should be approved or denied, or to review and make recommendation to the full Commission on whether a Certifying Organization should have its accreditation revoked.

(F) "Standards" means the Supreme Court Commission on Certification of Attorneys as Specialists Standards for Accreditation of Specialty Certification Programs for Lawyers.

SECTION 3.   Authority

3.01. Consistent with Gov. Bar R. XIV and these Standards, the Commission, by majority vote, may do any or all of the following:

(A) Interpret these Standards;

(B) Adopt an appropriate fee schedule to administer these Standards;

(C) Grant and withdraw accreditation and grant re-accreditation to Certifying Organizations.

3.02. Consistent with Gov. Bar R. XIV and these Standards, the Review Panel by majority vote may do any or all of the following:

(A) Consider applications by any Certifying Organization for accreditation or re-accreditation under these Standards;

(B) Evaluate applications by any Certifying Organization for accreditation or re-accreditation under these Standards;

(C) Recommend approval by the Commission of applications by any Certifying Organization for accreditation or re-accreditation under these Standards when the Review Panel determines that the organization has met the requirements of these Standards;

(D) Recommend disapproval by the Commission of applications by any Certifying Organization for accreditation or re-accreditation under these Standards when the Review Panel determines that the organization has not met the requirements of these Standards.

(E) Recommend revocation of accreditation of any Certifying Organization that ceases to meet the requirements of these Standards.

SECTION 4. Accreditation of Certifying Organizations

4.01. The accreditation process is designed to compare an Applicant's organizational features, operational methods, and certification standards against the requirements of the Standards. In conducting this comparison, the Commission and Review Panel utilizes the criteria specified below to make the examination of the Applicant as objective and fair as possible.

4.02. In order to obtain accreditation by the Commission for a specialty certification program, and Applicant shall demonstrate that the program operates in accordance with the following standards:

(A) **Purpose of Organization** The Applicant shall demonstrate that its primary purpose includes the identification of lawyers who possess an enhanced level of skill and expertise in the area of law or practice for which specialist's certification is being issued. The Applicant also shall show that its certification program has a goal of developing and improving the professional competence of lawyers. The Applicant shall be a not-for-profit organization.

(B) **Organizational Capabilities** Any program designed to certify lawyers as specialists must have a continuing responsibility to those it certifies to maintain the integrity and the value of the specialty designation. An Applicant seeking accreditation shall establish that it possesses and will continue to maintain the governance and organizational structures, a reliable source of adequate financial resources, and the established administrative processes needed to carry out a certification program in an unbiased, professional, and ethically responsible manner. The primary criteria that will be used in determining organizational capabilities are:

1. A history of adequate financing during the three years preceding the filing of the application. If the Applicant is newly formed, this criteria will be applied to a parent or sponsoring organization or to the individual founders, if no founding organization is involved;

2. The existence of a budget and financial plan for three years following a grant of accreditation should it be made;

3. The presence of persons retained by or on the governing board, evaluation committees, or staff of the organization who are qualified by experience, education, and background to carry out the program of certification operated by the Applicant, including persons with a background in evaluating the validity and reliability of examinations and experienced practitioners in the areas of law in which the organization conducts certification programs;

4. The existence of management, administrative, and business practices that allow the Applicant to operate its certification program effectively and provide efficient service to lawyers who submit applications for certification. The processes and procedures used in the certification process should include safeguards to ensure unbiased consideration of lawyers seeking certification;

5. The existence of a handbook, guide, or manual that outlines the standards, policies, procedures, guides for self-study, and application procedures.

(C) **Decision Makers** The Standards require that a majority of any Applicant's governing board be composed of lawyers who, in the judgment of the Commission, are experts in the field of law covered by the specialty and have extensive practice or involvement in the specialty. For the purpose of this criterion, a person meets the "extensive practice or involvement" requirement if he or she meets the qualifications set out in the Standards.

(D) **Uniform Applicability of Certification Requirements and Non-Discrimination** The Applicant's documents and records submitted in conjunction with its application for accreditation will be examined to ensure that the requirements for granting certification are clearly stated and that any applying lawyer who meets the requirements is granted certification.

1. The materials published by the Applicant shall not state or imply that membership in, or the completion of education programs offered by, any specific organization are required for certification. This paragraph does not apply to requirements relating to the practice of law that are set out in statutes, rules, and regulations promulgated by the government of the United States, by the government of any state or political subdivision thereof, or by any agency or instrumentality of any of the foregoing.

2. The description of the program shall indicate that the Applicant does not discriminate against lawyers seeking certification on the basis of race, color, national origin, religion, gender, sexual orientation, disability, or age. Experience requirements for lawyers seeking certification or re-certification that may indirectly have an effect on a particular age group shall be reasonable.

3. Every Certifying Agency shall develop and administer a full certification program that includes its measurement of extensive practice or involve-

ment, its own peer review, its own written examination, and its requirements regarding education experience, as those criteria are described in the Standards.

(E) Definition and Number of Specialty Areas An Applicant specifically shall define the specialty area or areas in which it proposes to certify lawyers as specialists.

1. Each specialty area in which certification is offered shall be an area in which significant numbers of lawyers regularly practice. Specialty areas shall be named and described in terms that are understandable to the potential users of legal services and in terms that will not lead to confusion with other specialty areas.

2. An Applicant may seek accreditation to certify lawyers in more than one specialty area. The organization shall be evaluated separately with respect to each specialty program.

3. An Applicant shall propose to the Commission a specific definition of each specialty area in which it seeks accreditation to certify lawyers as specialists. The Commission shall approve, modify, or reject any proposed definition and promptly shall notify the Applicant of its actions.

4. The Commission shall recommend to and secure the approval of the Supreme Court of Ohio for the fields of law subject to specialization designation.

(F) Substantial Involvement The Applicant shall require that a lawyer seeking certification make a satisfactory showing of experience through substantial involvement in the specialty area during the three-year period immediately preceding application to the Certifying Organization. Substantial involvement includes, but is not limited to, the type and number of cases or matters handled and the amount of time spent practicing in the specialty area. In order to meet this Standard, the Applicant's certification criteria shall require that the time spent practicing the specialty be at least twenty-five percent of the total practice of a lawyer engaged in a normal full-time practice throughout the three-year period immediately preceding the lawyer's application.

(G) Peer Review The Applicant shall require that a lawyer seeking certification submit the names of at least five references from attorneys or judges who are knowledgeable regarding the practice area and are familiar with the competence of the lawyer.

1. The Applicant's procedures shall provide that the Applicant, not the lawyer seeking certification, sends the reference forms to potential references.

2. The reference forms shall inquire into the respondent's areas of practice, the respondent's familiarity with both the specialty area and with the lawyer seeking certification, and the length of time that the respondent has been practicing law and has known the lawyer seeking certification. The form also shall inquire about the qualifications of the lawyer seeking certification in various aspects of the practice and, as appropriate, that lawyer's dealings with judges and opposing counsel.

3. The materials provided to a lawyer seeking certification shall specify that the lawyer may not submit as a reference the name of any lawyer or judge who is related to the lawyer seeking certification or currently engaged in legal practice with that lawyer.

4. The Applicant shall reserve the right to seek and consider references from persons of the applicant's own choosing.

(H) Written Examination The Applicant shall require that a lawyer seeking certification pass a written examination of suitable length and complexity. The examination shall test the knowledge and skills of the substantive and procedural law in the specialty area, substantially consist of questions not previously used on other examinations used by the Applicant for certification of lawyers, and include professional responsibility and ethics as it relates to the particular specialty. The following factors shall be used to judge the suitability of the examination used by the Applicant:

1. Evidence that the method by which pass/fail levels are established is reasonable;

2. Evidence of both reliability and validity for each form of the examination. Reliability is the consistency or replicability of test results. Validity requires that the content and emphasis of the examination proportionally reflect the knowledge and skills needed for an enhanced level of skill and expertise in the specialty area;

3. Evidence of periodic review of the examination to ensure relevance to knowledge and skills needed in the specialty area as the law and practice methods develop over time;

4. Evidence that the law of Ohio, when different from the general law, is a part of the examination;

5. Evidence that effective measures are taken to protect the security of all examinations.

(I) Educational Experience The Applicant shall require that a lawyer seeking certification has completed a minimum of thirty-six hours of participation in continuing legal education in the specialty area in the three-year period preceding the lawyer's application for certification. The Applicant shall impose requirements that are satisfactory to the Commission and permit the continuing legal education requirement to be met through the following means:

1. Attending programs of continuing legal education which are approved by the Certifying Organization as appropriate for credit toward the continuing legal education requirement in the specialty area. The Certifying Organization shall not refuse to approve a program solely because it is offered by an organization other than the Certifying Organization.

2. Teaching or participating as a panelist, speaker, or workshop leader in a continuing legal education course approved by the Certifying Organization. In cases considered appropriate by the Certifying Organization, three hours credit may be awarded for each hour of actual teaching or presentation time under this subparagraph. Additional credit shall not be awarded for subsequent presentations of substantially the same material.

3. Teaching at a law school that is approved by the American Bar Association. Up to eight hours of credit per year may be awarded for the teaching of a course or seminar in the specialty area as a faculty or adjunct faculty member in a law school approved by the American Bar Association.

4. Writing a book or [substantial] law review article. Up to eight hours credit may be awarded for writing a book or a [substantial] law review article in the specialty area. Credit shall be awarded for the year in which the book or article actually appears in print.

5. Taking courses at a law school that is approved by the American Bar Association. Credit hours may be awarded for courses taken at a law school approved by the American Bar Association consistent with Gov. Bar. R. X and Regulation 402 adopted by the Supreme Court Commission on Continuing Legal Education.

The Applicant shall require a lawyer seeking clarification to provide evidence that the programs, courses, seminars, conferences, and publications listed above contain sufficient intellectual and practical content so to increase a lawyer's knowledge and ability in the specialty area.

(J) **Good Standing** The Applicant shall require that a lawyer seeking certification furnish satisfactory evidence of:

1. The lawyer is active and in good standing pursuant to Gov. Bar R. VI of the Supreme Court of Ohio, and the lawyer's fitness to practice is not in question by virtue of disciplinary action in another state;

2. Coverage by professional liability insurance continually maintained through a reputable company in an amount not less than Five Hundred Thousand Dollars per loss;

3. The lawyer has demonstrated the ability to pay all claims that fall within the deductible amount selected by the attorney under the insurance policy;

4. Professional liability insurance in an amount of not less than Five Hundred Thousand Dollars ($500,000.00 US), shall be required for all lawyers seeking certification, with the exception of the following lawyers who can demonstrate to the Applicant's (Certifying Organization) satisfaction that their employment relationship as a lawyer will fully cover any professional liability claim or provide immunity therefrom:

(a) Counsel employed by an entity, other than a law firm, whose sole professional practice is for that entity;

(b) Counsel employed by a governmental entity which would be immune from liability claims.

5. The lawyer shall notify the Applicant immediately of any cancellation or change in the coverage.

6. The Applicant and Certifying Organization shall require each attorney who is or makes application to become certified by the organization to sign and submit an Attorney Certification and Acknowledgment, on a form promulgated by the Commission. This form and all documents required to be submit-

ted by the attorney, therewith (a) shall be collected by the organization from each attorney not less frequently than annually, and (b) shall be stored and maintained by the organization for not less than seven years. Any Applicant or Certifying Organization which complies with this Standard, shall be presumed by the Commission to be in compliance with section 4.02(J)(1) through (5).

ATTORNEY CERTIFICATION AND ACKNOWLEDGMENT

As an attorney certified as a specialist by ____[1] , I expressly recognize and acknowledge that the Supreme Court of Ohio ["Supreme Court"] and the Commission on Certification of Attorneys as Specialists in the State of Ohio ["Commission"] do not and shall not be construed to make any implied or expressed representation or warranty regarding the process by which I was certified or my abilities as a certified attorney.

I further understand that responsibility, obligation and liability in any way arising from my certification and holding myself out to the public and to other attorneys as a certified attorney are expressly disclaimed by the Supreme Court and the Commission. Furthermore, I knowingly accept this disclaimer as a condition of my certification as a specialist by _____.

I expressly understand and acknowledge that as an attorney specialist certified under Gov. Bar R. XIV of Ohio I may communicate the fact that I am certified by ____ as a specialist in the field of law involved. However, as a specialist I agree that I shall not represent, expressly or impliedly, that I am certified by the Supreme Court or the Commission or by an entity other than ____. However, I understand and acknowledge that as a certified attorney I may represent that is approved by the Commission, but I shall not represent that ____ is approved by the Supreme Court.

Furthermore, in compliance with Sec. 4.02(J) of the Commission's Standards for Accreditation of Specialty Certification ["Standards"], I hereby certify that currently, and at all times during which I will hold myself out as a certified attorney specialist, the following information is and will be true:

(a) I am, and will be, an active lawyer and in good standing pursuant to Gov. Bar R. VI of the Supreme Court;

(b) My fitness to practice is not, and will not be, in question by virtre of disciplinary action in another state other than Ohio;

(c) I have and will continuously maintain coverage by professional liability insurance through a reputable company in an amount not less than Five Hundred Thousand Dollars per loss,

OR

my practice relationship with my clients will fully cover any professional liability claim made against me in an amount not less than Five Hundred Thousand per loss;

[1] The full name of the certifying agency must be inserted in each location where a "blank" space is shown on this document.

(d) I have and will maintain the financial ability to pay all claims that fall within the deductible amount of my professional liability policy;

I fully understand that as a certified attorney in Ohio it is my obligation to immediately report to ____ any change in my status which is otherwise required by (a), (b), (c) or (d) hereinabove, including but not limited to any cancellation or change in my insurance coverage.

As further proof to ____ of my compliance with the Sec. 4.02(J) of the Standards I have attached hereto a copy of (1) a Certificate of Good Standing from the Supreme Court, and (2) my current insurance policy declaration page or a notarized letter or letters demonstrating that my practice relationship with my clients will fully cover any professional liability claim made against me in an amount not less than Five Hundred Thousand Dollars per loss. Furthermore, I acknowledge that in order to continue to be certified by ____, it is my responsibility to sign this form and provide current copies of each of these two documents to ____ not less frequently than annually or as ____ shall require, and that my failure to fulfill this obligation will cause failure to comply with these requirements. I also understand that my failure in this regard may result in disciplinary action by the Supreme Court.

_____
Signature of Attorney Applicant

Date Signed

CCAS Form 6

(K) Impartial Review The Applicant shall provide evidence that it maintains and publishes a policy providing an appeal procedure for a lawyer seeking certification to challenge the decision of the persons who review and pass upon the applications of lawyers seeking certification. The policy shall provide a lawyer seeking certification with the opportunity to present his or her case to an impartial decision maker in the event of denial of eligibility or denial of certification. Impartial decision makers may include persons associated with the Applicant.

(L) Requirements for Recertification The period of certification shall be set by the Applicant but shall be not less than three or more that seven years, after which time lawyers who have been certified must apply for recertification. Recertification shall satisfy the minimum standards set forth in Gov. Bar R. XIV Section 6 and shall require similar evidence of competence as that required for initial certification in the areas of substantial involvement, peer review, educational experience, and evidence of good standing. The Applicant shall have in existence or be in the process of developing a plan for periodic recertification at the time of application for accreditation.

1. The plan for periodic recertification shall be designed to measure continued competence and enhance the continued competence of certified lawyers.

2. Application for and approval of continued certification as specialists shall be required prior to the end of each certification period. To qualify for continued certification as a specialist, an attorney seeking recertification shall pay the required fee and satisfy the requirements for certification renewal established by the Commission and the Certifying Organization.

3. In addition to the requirements of Gov. Bar R. X, a specialist shall complete twelve hours of continuing legal education every two years in each specialty area for which he or she is certified. Proof of completion shall be submitted in the manner required by Gov. Bar R. X.

(M) Revocation of Certification The Applicant shall maintain a procedure for revocation of certification, including a requirement that a certified lawyer report his or her disbarment or suspension from the practice of law in any jurisdiction to the Applicant.

4.03. The Commission will consider an Applicant's prior approval for accreditation by the American Bar Association consistent with the following;

(A) Applicants If the specialty certification program of an applicant has been previously accredited by the American Bar Association (ABA) and if the requirements of the ABA are substantially identical to the requirements of the Commission, the Commission shall consider the accreditation in determining whether the applicant satisfies these Standards. In those areas where the requirements are not substantially identical, the Applicant shall meet those requirements of the Commission in the same manner as any other Applicant not having received ABA accreditation. The determination of the Commission with respect to "substantially identical" shall be final and binding.

(B) Ohio Law Requirements Certain specialty areas require substantial expertise in Ohio law as opposed to general national law. The Commission shall provide for additional or separate requirements for Applicants in those specialty areas.

(C) Time Periods for Accreditation and Reaccreditation If an Applicant has been granted approval of certain requirements of the Standards of the Commission based on prior accreditation by the ABA, the period of initial accreditation of the Certifying Organization by the Commission shall be the time remaining in the time period of current accreditation by the ABA. Thereafter, the Certifying Organization shall be required to seek reaccreditation by the Commission at the same time as that organization seeks reaccreditation by the ABA.

(D) Fees If prior accreditation by the ABA reduces the requirements of the Applicant to be reviewed, the Commission may impose a reduced fee for the Applicant.

History: Amended, eff 1-1-97; eff 7-1-05.

SECTION 5. Accreditation and Reaccred- itation Periods

5.01. Initial accreditation by the Commission of any Applicant will be granted for not less than three or more than seven years.

5.02. To retain Commission accreditation, an Accredited Organization shall be required to apply for reaccreditation, prior to the end of its initial accreditation period and at the end of the reaccreditation period. The Accredited Organization shall be granted reaccreditation upon a showing of continued compliance with these Standards.

SECTION 6.   Revocation of Accreditation

6.01 Grounds for Revocation of Accreditation The Commission may revoke an Accredited Organization's accreditation upon a determination that the organization has ceased to exist, has failed to operate its certification program in compliance with these Standards, or has materially changed its structure, operating standards, guidelines, or criteria for certification or recertification without giving prior notice to the Commission as required by these Standards.

6.02 Hearing The Commission, on its own or acting upon a complaint from a third party, may determine that reasonable grounds exist for considering the revocation of accreditation of an Accredited Organization. The Commission shall schedule the matter for deliberation at one of the Commission's regularly scheduled meetings and promptly shall provide the Accredited Organization with written notice of the meeting and an opportunity to be heard at that meeting.

6.03 New Application for Accreditation A Certifying Organization whose accreditation has been revoked may reapply, for accreditation.

6.04 Voluntary Withdrawal from Accredited Status An Accredited Organization may request that its accreditation by the Commission be withdrawn by providing written notice to the Secretary of the Commission.

SECTION   7. Accreditation   Program Components

7.01 Commission The Commission grants, denies, and revokes accreditation and reaccreditation.

7.02 Review Panel The Review Panel appointed by the Chair of the Commission for each Applicant shall submit its recommendation to the Commission to grant or deny accreditation or reaccreditation to the Certifying or Accredited Organization. Upon a finding that an Accredited Organization has ceased to exist or has failed to operate its certification program in compliance with the Standards, the Review Panel may recommend to the Commission that the accreditation of the Accredited Organization be revoked. The Review Panel also is responsible for conducting an independent evaluation of the qualifications of Applicants for accreditation and reaccreditation in accordance with Gov. R. XIV and these Standards and recommending any action to be taken by the Commission on applications for accreditation.

7.03 Pre-Application Advisory Services An entity considering filing an application for accreditation of a program to certify lawyers as specialists may obtain information [and advice] from the Commission prior to filing a formal application. Inquiries shall be addressed to the Secretary of the Commission, who shall supply a copy of these Standards, fee schedules, and other pertinent data, and may respond to questions regarding the establishment of a lawyer specialty certification program and accreditation by the Commission.

7.04 Notice of Intent to Apply for Accreditation Prior to making a formal application for accreditation, an Applicant shall file with the Commission a notice of intent to apply for accreditation form and, pay a non-refundable pre-application fee. The notice shall specify each definition of specialty for which accreditation is sought. Upon receipt of the form and fee by The Commission, and upon preliminary approval of the definition of the specialty, the Secretary shall send the Applicant an official application packet containing the forms and instructions to be used in filing the application. This requirement serves the purpose of providing basic information about the Applicant to the Commission in advance to expedite processing of the formal application when it is submitted.

7.05 Application for Accreditation Subject to the notice of intent to file requirement described above, an Applicant may file a formal application for accreditation with the Commission at any time on forms provided by the Commission, together with payment of a basic application fee and a certificate fee for each specialty certificate issued by the Applicant.

(A) Time Guidelines The Commission is not bound to any specific schedule in processing, evaluating, or deciding on the application of an Applicant for accreditation. Applications and the evaluation process will be handled as expeditiously as possible.

(B) Supporting Documents The application for accreditation shall be accompanied by all of the following supporting documents:

1. The Applicant's governing documents, including articles of incorporation, bylaws, and resolutions of the governing bodies of the Applicant or any parent organization that relate to the standards, procedures, guidelines, or practices of the Applicant's certification program;

2. Financial information about the Applicant and any supporting parent organization as specified on forms provided by the Commission;

3. Biographical summaries of members of the governing board, senior staff, and members of advisory panels, including specific information concerning the degree of involvement in the specialty area of persons who review and pass upon applications for certification;

4. Materials furnished to lawyers seeking certification, application forms, booklets or pamphlets describing the certification program, peer reference forms, rules and procedures, and evaluation guides;

5. Copies of examinations given in the past two years, or in the case of a new organization, copies of proposed examinations, or in those cases in which an agency accepts examination by another entity, copies of such examinations, with evidence

of their validity and reliability, such as written examination procedures, including a description of how examinations are developed, conducted, and reviewed; a description of the grading standards used; and the names of persons responsible for determining pass/fail standards. Actual or proposed written examinations shall be made available on a confidential basis for review by a person designated by the Commission, with the understanding that the Applicant may rule the person who reviews the examination ineligible for certification by the Applicant for a period of three years from the time of the designation;

6. The definition of the specialty or specialties in which the Applicant certifies specialists;

7. Other materials or information considered necessary by the Review Panel or the Commission.

7.06 **Preliminary Review by Staff Designee** Upon receipt of a notice of intent to apply or an application for accreditation, the Commission staff shall review all materials submitted by the Applicant for completeness and conformance with the basic requirements of these Standards.

(A) If omissions are noted or clarification of responses is needed, the staff designee shall contact the Applicant and request additional information. The staff designee's request will be followed up by written confirmation. The staff designee shall notify the Applicant once the materials are considered complete.

(B) Applications that are not accompanied by all of the supporting documents specified in these Standards shall not be processed. The staff designee promptly shall notify the Applicant of the omissions. The Applicant shall have sixty days from the receipt of the notice to submit the required materials or request an extension. If the required materials are not submitted within this period and a request for extension has not been granted, the application shall be considered lapsed and ineligible for consideration. The Applicant will receive a refund in the amount of fifty percent of the basic application fee.

(C) If the staff designee notes any obvious deficiencies in the Applicant's program or capabilities as compared with these Standards, the staff designee shall notify the Applicant and discuss possible modifications in the Applicant's program that may remedy the noted deficiencies.

(D) An Applicant who is notified during preliminary review about apparent deficiencies in its program may do either of the following:

1. Request that its application, without modification, be given full review;

2. Withdraw the application without prejudice either permanently or for the purpose of making suggested modifications in its program.

(E) An Applicant's request that consideration of its application be suspended pending modification of its program may cause presentation of a recommendation for accreditation to the Commission to be deferred until a later meeting.

(F) An application shall be considered lapsed and ineligible for consideration, and the applicant will receive a refund of fifty percent of the application fee if the applicant does either of the following:

1. Withdraws its application permanently;

2. Withdraws its application for the purpose of making modifications and does not file an amended application form within one hundred twenty days of the filing of the original application.

(G) Withdrawal of an application does not preclude a subsequent application.

7.07 **Evaluation by Review Panel** After the receipt of a completed application for accreditation, the Chair of the Commission shall designate a Review Panel for that application and forward the application to that Review Panel. The completed application form and supporting materials shall be divided among Review Panel members and provided to them for their independent review. The Review Panel Chair shall assign areas of review among Review Panel members so as to best utilize each Review Panel member's background and expertise. The Review Panel may seek expertise from other lawyers admitted to practice in Ohio who practice in or are knowledgeable about the specialty. The materials shall be accompanied by evaluation guidelines and checklists to aid in the analysis and provide consistency to the process of reviewing the application. Each Review Panel member shall receive a copy of a complete set of the Applicant's materials for reference.

(A) Each Review Panel member shall complete his or her review of the Applicant's materials and make a finding as to whether the Applicant meets the Standards within the scope of his or her assigned area.

(B) Members of the Review Panel shall submit the evaluation forms and supporting materials to the Commission staff. The staff shall compile these materials for distribution to all Review Panel members.

1. At the call of the Chair of the Review Panel, the Review Panel shall hold a meeting in person or via telephone conference call at which time each Review Panel member shall present his or her findings. If the Chair of the Review Panel is satisfied that the Review Panel has sufficient information to make an overall judgment concerning the extent to which the Applicant has met the Standards, the Review Panel shall develop a recommendation as to granting or denying of accreditation by the Commission.

2. If the Review Panel concludes that more information is necessary to make a recommendation concerning an application, the Chair of the Review Panel shall notify the Applicant and provide a reasonable time for the Applicant to respond. Once the response is received, the Review Panel shall meet and develop a recommendation. If the Review Panel does not receive a satisfactory response within the specified time, it may make its recommendation to the Commission at that time or grant additional time for the Applicant to respond.

3. The Review Panel Chair may authorize a site visit to the place of business of the Applicant to gather additional information. All costs associated with any site visits shall be borne by the Applicant.

(C) The Review Panel Chair, with assistance of the staff, shall prepare the draft and report to the Review Panel. The Review Panel Chair shall circulate a draft report to other members of the Review Panel for comment.

1. The final report shall be prepared by the Chair of Review Panel, incorporating comments and recommendations received from other Review Panel members.

2. A copy of the final report will be sent to the Applicant for factual verification and comment. The final report, with any Applicant comment attached, shall be sent to all members of the Review Panel.

3. Consideration of the final report of the Review Panel shall be placed on the agenda of the next meeting of the Commission, consistent with the time periods for Commission action specified below.

7.08 Commission Action on Applications The Commission shall act on applications for accreditation and hear any appeals from Applicants regarding any proposed adverse action regarding accreditation.

(A) **Receipt of Report Required** In order for the Commission to consider an application at a meeting, the Commission shall have received a final report containing the recommendation from the Review Panel at least three weeks prior to the date of that meeting.

(B) **Materials** In making a final recommendation regarding the accreditation of an Applicant, the Commission shall consider all materials relating to an application. These materials include the final report of the Review Panel, copies of the application and supporting documents originally submitted by the Applicant, and any further materials that the Applicant submits for consideration.

(C) **Decision** The Commission shall rule on applications for accreditation as follows:

1. If the Commission determines that the Applicant complies with the requirements of these Standards, the Applicant shall be granted accreditation.

2. If the Commission determines that the Applicant does not meet the requirements of these Standards, the application will be considered closed within thirty days after the decision of the Commission, unless the Applicant files a petition for reconsideration. The Applicant may reapply for accreditation without prejudice.

(D) **Notice of Decision** The Applicant shall be notified in writing of the decision of the Commission regarding an application for accreditation.

(E) Factual determinations shall be based solely upon the record presented consistant with these Standards, and not on any information extrinsic to the process specified in these Standards.

7.09 Reconsideration of Decision by Commission Any Applicant that is adversely affected by a decision of the Commission as specified below may petition the Commission for reconsideration of its action.

(A) **Decisions Subject to Reconsideration** Only the following decisions of the Commission are subject to a petition for reconsideration:

1. In the case of a program applying for accreditation, a decision not to accredit the Certifying Organization;

2. In the case of a program applying for reaccreditation, a decision not to reaccredit the Accredited Organization;

3. In the case of a program accredited, a decision to revoke the accreditation of an Accredited Organization.

(B) **Petition and Procedure** An Applicant or Accredited Organization shall file with the Commission a petition for reconsideration within thirty days after the decision of the Commission. The petition shall demonstrate that, on reconsideration, the petitioner would submit information or undertakings that have not been communicated adequately to the Commission. In his or her discretion, the Chair of the Commission shall determine whether the showing has been made, and if so, grant the petition for reconsideration.

(C) **Lapse of Application** Upon a denial of a petition for reconsideration, the application shall be considered closed. The Applicant may reapply for accreditation without prejudice.

SECTION 8.   Reporting

8.01. An Accredited Organization shall be responsible for reporting both of the following in writing to the Commission:

(A) By April 1 of each calendar year, on a form promulgated by the Commission, a report describing the current status of each accredited program, including the names and current addresses of Ohio lawyers certified or recertified as specialists;

(B) Any proposed material changes in the Accredited Organization's structure, operating standards, guidelines, or criteria for certification or recertification, at least sixty days before those changes are to become effective.

SECTION   9. Communication   of Accreditation

9.01. An Accredited Organization may state that it is "Accredited by the Supreme Court of Ohio Commission on Certification of Attorneys As Specialists to certify lawyers in the specialty area(s) of ____." under the following conditions:

(A) An Accredited Organization using this announcement or otherwise referring to its accreditation by the Commission shall provide notice to lawyers applying for certification that accreditation by the Commission indicates solely that the Accredited Organization's certification program has met the Standards.

(B) This announcement shall indicate the specialty areas in which accreditation has been granted by the Commission.

(C) An Accredited Organization shall not permit certified lawyers to state or imply that they are certified or accredited by the Commission or by the Supreme Court of Ohio. The certified lawyers may represent that the Accredited Organization is ap-

proved by the Commission but not the Supreme Court of Ohio. Accredited Organizations shall actively enforce this prohibition.

SECTION 10. Disclosure of Information

10.01. Except as provided below, the files, records, and documents submitted by an Applicant as part of the accreditation process shall be public information.

10.02. An Applicant may request that distribution of its materials by the Commission or by any person acting as a Review Panel member or advisor at the request of the Commission be limited to those persons who need the information to fulfill obligations specified in these rules. In such cases, the Commission shall take reasonable steps to honor such a request, but the Commission shall not be responsible for disclosure due to circumstances beyond its immediate control.

10.03. Notwithstanding other provisions of these Standards, actual or proposed written examinations submitted shall be kept confidential and handled in accordance with Section 7.05(B) of these Standards.

SECTION 11. Non-Compliance With Standards

11.01. An Applicant or an Accredited Organization that does not comply with these Standards may be denied accreditation or reaccreditation or may have its accreditation revoked. Non-compliance with these Standards and Rules or deadlines set out in the Standards may delay the disposition of an application for accreditation or reaccreditation.

SECTION 12. Indemnification and Hold Harmless

12.01. Accredited Organizations and Applicants shall agree to hold and save the Commission and the Supreme Court of Ohio, its member volunteers, officers, agents, and employees harmless form liability of any kind, including costs, expenses and attorney fees, for any suit or damages sustained by any person or property arising out of an Accredited Organization's or Applicant's application for accreditation by the Commission or arising out of any actions of the Accredited Organization or lawyers to whom specialization is granted or denied.

SECTION 13. Adoption and Amendment of Standards

13.01. These Standards and any subsequent amendments become effective upon their adoption by the Commission and approval by the Supreme Court of Ohio.

Appendix V.
STATEMENT ON PROFESSIONALISM, A LAWYER'S CREED AND A LAWYER'S ASPIRATIONAL IDEALS

ISSUED BY THE SUPREME COURT OF OHIO ON
FEBRUARY 3, 1997

The Court created the Supreme Court Commission on Professionalism in order to address its concerns that certain trends were developing among lawyers in Ohio and elsewhere. Those trends fostered commercialism in the practice of law and de-emphasized our historical heritage that the practice is a learned profession to be conducted with dignity, integrity, and honor dedicated to the service of clients and the public good. In order to facilitate the promotion of professionalism among Ohio's lawyers, judges and legal educators, the Court issued its Statement on Professionalism, A Lawyer's Creed, and A Lawyer's Aspirational Ideas [Ideals] on February 3, 1997. In recognition of the unique standards of professionalism required of a judge or a lawyer acting in a judicial capacity, the Court issues A Judicial Creed upon the recommendation of the Supreme Court Commission on Professionalism. It is the Court's goal by adopting this Creed to remind every judge and every lawyer acting in a judicial capacity of the high standards expected of each by the public whom they serve.

STATEMENT ON PROFESSIONALISM

The Court created the Supreme Court Commission on Professionalism in order to address its concerns that trends were developing among lawyers in Ohio and elsewhere which emphasize commercialism in the practice of law and de-emphasize our historical heritage that the practice is a learned profession to be conducted with dignity, integrity and honor as a high calling dedicated to the service of clients and the public good. Those trends have been evidenced by an emphasis on financial rewards, a diminishing of courtesy and civility among lawyers in their dealings with each other, a reduction in respect for the judiciary and our system of justice and a lessening of regard for others and commitment to the public good.

As professionals, we need to strive to meet lofty goals and ideals in order to achieve the highest standards of a learned profession. To this end, the Court issues A Lawyer's Creed and A Lawyer's Aspirational Ideals which have been adopted and recommended for the Court's issuance by the Supreme Court Commission on Professionalism. In so doing, it is not the Court's intention to regulate or to provide additional bases for discipline, but rather to facilitate the promotion of professionalism among Ohio's lawyers, judges and legal educators. It is the Court's hope that these individuals, their professional associations, law firms, and educational institutions will utilize the Creed and the Aspirational Ideals as guidelines for this purpose.

A LAWYER'S CREED

To my clients, I offer loyalty, confidentiality, competence, diligence, and my best judgment. I shall represent you as I should want to be represented and

be worthy of your trust. I shall counsel you with respect to alternative methods to resolve disputes. I shall endeavor to achieve your lawful objectives as expeditiously and economically as possible.

To the opposing parties and their counsel, I offer fairness, integrity, and civility. I shall not knowingly make misleading or untrue statements of fact or law. I shall endeavor to consult with and cooperate with you in scheduling meetings, depositions, and hearings. I shall avoid excessive and abusive discovery. I shall attempt to resolve differences and, if we fail, I shall strive to make our dispute a dignified one.

To the courts and other tribunals, and to those who assist them, I offer respect, candor, and courtesy. Where consistent with my client's interests, I shall communicate with opposing counsel in an effort to avoid or resolve litigation. I shall attempt to agree with other counsel on a voluntary exchange of information and on a plan for discovery. I shall do honor to the search for justice.

To my colleagues in the practice of law, I offer concern for your reputation and well-being. I shall extend to you the same courtesy, respect, candor, and dignity that I expect to be extended to me.

To the profession, I offer assistance in keeping it a calling in the spirit of public service, and in promoting its understanding and an appreciation for it by the public. I recognize that my actions and demeanor reflect upon our system of justice and our profession, and I shall conduct myself accordingly.

To the public and our system of justice, I offer service. I shall devote some of my time and skills to community, governmental and other activities that promote the common good. I shall strive to improve the law and our legal system and to make the law and our legal system available to all.

A LAWYER'S ASPIRATIONAL IDEALS

As to clients, I shall aspire:

(a) **To expeditious and economical achievement of all client objectives.**

(b) To fully informed client decision-making. I should:

(1) Counsel clients about all forms of dispute resolution;

(2) Counsel clients about the value of cooperation as a means toward the productive resolution of disputes;

(3) Maintain the sympathetic detachment that permits objective and independent advice to clients;

(4) Communicate promptly and clearly with clients; and

(5) Reach clear agreements with clients concerning the nature of the representation.

(c) To fair and equitable fee agreements. I should:

(1) Discuss alternative methods of charging fees with all clients;

(2) Offer fee arrangements that reflect the true value of the services rendered;

(3) Reach agreements respecting fees with clients as early in the relationship as possible;

(4) Determine the amount of fees by consideration of many factors and not just time spent; and

(5) Provide written agreements as to all fee arrangements

(d) To comply with the obligations of confidentiality and the avoidance of conflicting loyalties in a manner designed to achieve fidelity to clients.

(e) To achieve and maintain a high level of competence in my field or fields of practice.

As to opposing parties and their counsel, I shall aspire:

(a) To cooperate with opposing counsel in a manner consistent with the competent representation of my client. I should:

(1) Notify opposing counsel in a timely fashion of any canceled appearance;

(2) Grant reasonable requests for extensions or scheduling changes; and

(3) Consult with opposing counsel in the scheduling of appearances, meetings, and depositions.

(b) To treat opposing counsel in a manner consistent with his or her professional obligations and consistent with the dignity of the search for justice. I should:

(1) Not serve motions or pleadings in such a manner or at such a time as to preclude opportunity for a competent response;

(2) Be courteous and civil in all communications;

(3) Respond promptly to all requests by opposing counsel;

(4) Avoid rudeness and other acts of disrespect in all meetings, including depositions and negotiations;

(5) Prepare documents that accurately reflect the agreement of all parties; and

(6) Clearly identify all changes made in documents submitted by opposing counsel for review.

As to the courts and other tribunals, and to those who assist them, I shall aspire:

(a) To represent my clients in a manner consistent with the proper functioning of a fair, efficient, and humane system of justice. I should:

(1) Avoid non-essential litigation and non-essential pleading in litigation;

(2) Explore the possibilities of settlement of all litigated matters;

(3) Seek non-coerced agreement between the parties on procedural and discovery matters;

(4) Avoid all delays not dictated by competent representation of a client;

(5) Prevent misuses of court time by verifying the availability of key participants for scheduled appearances before the court and by being punctual; and

(6) Advise clients about the obligations of civility, courtesy, fairness, cooperation, and other proper behavior expected of those who use our system of justice.

(b) To model for others the respect due to our courts. I should:

(1) Act with complete honesty;

(2) Know court rules and procedures;

(3) Give appropriate deference to court rulings;

(4) Avoid undue familiarity with members of the judiciary;

(5) Avoid unfounded, unsubstantiated, or unjustified public criticism of members of the judiciary;

(6) Show respect by attire and demeanor;

(7) Assist the judiciary in determining the applicable law; and

(8) Give recognition to the judiciary's obligations of informed and impartial decision-making.

As to my colleagues in the practice of law, I shall aspire:

(a) To recognize and develop a professional interdependence for the benefit of our clients and the legal system;

(b) To defend you against unjust criticism; and

(c) To offer you assistance with your personal and professional needs.

As to our profession, I shall aspire:

(a) To improve the practice of law. I should:

(1) Assist in continuing legal education efforts;

(2) Assist in organized bar activities;

(3) Assist law schools in the education of our future lawyers; and

(4) Assist the judiciary in achieving objectives of A Lawyer's Creed and these Aspirational Ideals.

(b) To promote the understanding of and an appreciation for our profession by the public. I should:

(1) Use appropriate opportunities, publicly and privately, to comment upon the roles of lawyers in society and government, as well as in our system of justice; and

(2) Conduct myself always with an awareness that my actions and demeanor reflect upon our profession.

(c) To devote some of my time and skills to community, governmental and other activities that promote the common good.

As to the public and our system of justice, I shall aspire:

(a) To consider the effect of my conduct on the image of our system of justice, including the effect of advertising methods.

(b) To help provide the pro bono representation that is necessary to make our system of justice available to all.

(c) To support organizations that provide pro bono representation to indigent clients.

(d) To promote equality for all persons.

(e) To improve our laws and legal system by, for example:

(1) Serving as a public official;

(2) Assisting in the education of the public concerning our laws and legal system;

(3) Commenting publicly upon our laws; and

(4) Using other appropriate methods of effecting positive change in our laws and legal system.

STATEMENT ON JUDICIAL PROFESSIONALISM

Issued by the Supreme Court of Ohio
On July 9, 2001

The Court created the Supreme Court Commission on Professionalism in order to address its concerns that certain trends were developing among lawyers in Ohio and elsewhere. Those trends fostered commercialism in the practice of law and de-emphasized our historical heritage that the practice is a learned profession to be conducted with dignity, integrity, and honor dedicated to the service of clients and the public good. In order to facilitate the promotion of professionalism among Ohio's lawyers, judges and legal educators, the Court issued its Statement on Professionalism, A Lawyer's Creed, and A Lawyer's Aspirational Ideals on February 3, 1997. In recognition of the unique standards of professionalism required of a judge or a lawyer acting in a judicial capacity, the Court issues A Judicial Creed upon the recommendation of the Supreme Court Commission on Professionalism. It is the Court's goal by adopting this Creed to remind every judge and every lawyer acting in a judicial capacity of the high standards expected of each by the public whom they serve.

A JUDICIAL CREED

A JUDICIAL CREED

For the purpose of publicly stating my beliefs, convictions, and aspirations as a member of the Judiciary or as a lawyer acting in a judicial capacity in the State of Ohio:

I re-affirm my oath of office and acknowledge my obligations under the Canons of Judicial Ethics.

I recognize my role as a guardian of our system of jurisprudence dedicated to equal justice under law for all persons.

I believe that my role requires scholarship, diligence, personal integrity, and a dedication to the attainment of justice.

I know that I must not only be fair but also give the appearance of being fair.

I recognize that the dignity of my office requires the highest level of judicial demeanor.

I will treat all persons, including litigants, lawyers, witnesses, jurors, judicial colleagues, and court staff with dignity and courtesy and will insist that others do likewise.

I will strive to conduct my judicial responsibilities and obligations in a timely manner and will be respectful of others' time and schedules.

I will aspire every day to make the Court I serve a model of justice and truth.

Appendix VI.
FIELDS OF LAW SUBJECT TO SPECIALIZATION DESIGNATION IN OHIO

Effective July 10, 1996 the Supreme Court adopted the following fields of law subject to specialization designation in Ohio pursuant to recommendations of the Commission on Certification of Attorneys as Specialists.

On February 24, 1995, the Commission approved Workers' Compensation in Ohio as a field o flaw subject to specialization designation in Ohio. The following definition was adopted by the Commission.

"Workers' Compensation Law in Ohio is the practice of law that involves employees' rights, employers' defenses, and benefits provided for workplace accidents. The procedural scope of Ohio Workers' Compensation practice includes all activities before the Ohio Industrial Commission and Bureau of Workers' Compensation, as well as jury trials and attendant appellate practice."

On May 26, 1995, the Commission approved Family Relations Law as a field of law subject to specialization designation in Ohio. The following definition was adopted by the Commission.

"Family Relations Law is the practice of law that involves counseling clients in the resolution of disputes and with the termination of marriage by divorce, dissolution, or annulment and all related issues, such as legal separation; paternity; child support and the allocation of parental rights and responsibilities; division of property; and spousal support both in alternative dispute resolution processes and in court."

On May 26, 1995, the Commission on Certification of Attorneys as Specialists approved Criminal Law Trial Advocacy as a field of law subject to specialization designation in Ohio. The following definition was adopted by the Commission.

"Criminal Law Trial Advocacy is the practice of law that involves the defense and prosecution of misdemeanor and felony crimes in state and federal trial and appellate courts."

On September 22, 1995, the Commission on Certification of Attorneys as Specialists approved Civil Law Trial Advocacy as a field of law subject to specialization designation in Ohio. The following definition was adopted by the Commission.

"Civil Law Trial Advocacy is the practice of law that involves litigation of civil controversies in all areas of substantive law before state courts, federal courts, administrative agencies, and arbitrators. In addition to actual pretrial and trial process, 'civil law trial advocacy' includes evaluating, managing, and resolving civil controversies prior to the initiation of suit."

On February 23, 1996, the Commission on Certification of Attorneys as Specialists approved Business Bankruptcy Law as a field of law subject to specialization designation in Ohio. The following definition was adopted by the Commission.

"Business Bankruptcy Law is the practice of bankruptcy law when the debtor is a corporation, a partnership, an individual currently engaged in business, or an individual formerly engaged in business whose debts are primarily incurred for business purposes; including but not limited to business bankruptcies, reorganizations, liquidations, and the rights, obligations, and remedies of debtors and creditors."

On February 23, 1996, the Commission on Certification of Attorneys as Specialists approved Creditors' Rights/Debt Collection as a field of law subject to specialization designation in Ohio. The following definition was adopted by the Commission.

"Creditors' Rights/Debt Collection is the practice of law that involves all aspects of debt collection under state and federal law as it applies to the rights of creditors."

On February 23, 1996, the Commission on Certification of Attorneys as Specialists approved Consumer Bankruptcy Law as a field of law subject to specialization designation in Ohio. The following definition was adopted by the Commission.

"Consumer Bankruptcy Law is the practice of bankruptcy law when the debtor is an individual or husband and wife and where the debts are primarily non-business related. The matters are typically filed under Chapters 7 or 13 of the U.S. Bankruptcy Code."

Effective October 8, 1996, the Supreme Court adopted the following field of law subject to specialization designation in Ohio pursuant to recommendations of the Commission on Certification of Attorneys as Specialists.

On May 24, 1996, the Commission on Certification of Attorneys as Specialists approved Labor and Employment Law as a field of law subject to specialization designation in Ohio. The following definition was adopted by the Commission.

"Labor and Employment Law is the practice of law that involves the relationships among employers, employees, and their labor organizations, except workers' compensation. It includes all aspects of labor relations (private and public sectors), occupational safety and health, employment discrimination, wage and hour, employee benefits and employment-related torts and contracts. It further includes all forms of labor and employment litigation, arbitration, mediation, negotiation and other forms of alternative dispute resolution before all federal, state and local courts, agencies and private tribunals."

Effective August 26, 1997, the Supreme Court adopted the following fields of law subject to specialization designation in Ohio pursuant to recommendations of the Commission on Certification of Attorneys as Specialists.

On September 27, 1996, the Commission on Certification of Attorneys as Specialists approved Estate Planning, Trust and Probate Law as a specialty area in Ohio. The following definition was adopted by the Commission on May 30, 1997.

"Estate Planning, Trust and Probate Law is the practice of law that involves analysis and planning for the conservation and disposition of estates during lifetime and at death, preparing legal instruments to effectuate such planning, and counseling fiduciaries, while giving due consideration to the applicable trust, probate, and income, estate, and gift tax laws."

On March 21, 1997, the Commission on Certification of Attorneys as Specialists approved Federal Taxa-

tion Law as a specialty area in Ohio. The following definition was adopted by the Commission on May 30, 1997.

"Federal Taxation Law is the practice of law in the areas of individual, partnership, corporate, and fiduciary Federal Income Tax, estate and gift tax, tax-exempt organizations, qualified plans and other Federal taxes requiring a substantive and procedural knowledge of the Internal Revenue Code and Regulations, Internal Revenue Service Rulings, and Federal Taxation case law."

On March 21, 1997, the Commission on Certification of Attorneys as Specialists approved Elder Law as a specialty area in Ohio. The following definition was adopted by the Commission on May 30, 1997.

"Elder Law is the legal practice of counseling and representing older persons and their representatives about the legal aspects of health and long-term care planning, public benefits, surrogate decision-making, older persons' legal capacity, the conservation, disposition and administration of older persons' estates and the implementation of their decisions concerning such matters, giving due consideration to the applicable tax consequences of the action, or the need for more sophisticated tax expertise."

Effective February 3, 1998, the Supreme Court of Ohio adopted the following fields of law subject to specialization in Ohio pursuant to the recommendation of the Commission on Certification of Attorneys as Specialists.

On October 24, 1997, the Commission on Certification of Attorneys as Specialists approved Business, Commercial and Industrial Real Property Law, and Residential Real Property Law as specialty areas in Ohio. The following definitions were adopted by the Commission.

"Business, Commercial and Industrial Real Property Law is the practice of law that involves acquisition, ownership, leasing, management, financing, developing, use, transfer and disposition of investment, business, commercial and industrial real property, including title examination and determination of property rights."

"Residential Real Property Law is the practice of law that involves acquisition, ownership, leasing, financing, use, transfer and disposition of residential real property by individuals, including title examination and determination of property rights."

Effective January 24, 2006, the Supreme Court adopted the following fields of law subject to specialization designation in Ohio pursuant to recommendations of the Commission on Certification of Attorneys as Specialists.

On April 1, 2005, the Commission on Certification of Attorneys as Specialists approved Administrative Agency Law as a field of law subject to specialization designation in Ohio. The following definition was adopted by the Commission.

"Administrative Agency Law is the practice of law that involves the activities of agencies at the local, state and federal levels, including, but not limited to: licensing, regulation and government benefits. For purposes of this certification, it includes matters involving the Ohio Administrative Procedure Act (RC Chapter 119), local government administrative matters governed by RC Chapter 2506, and proceedings pursuant to the federal Administrative Procedures Act. It also includes, without limitation, the representation of clients before administrative agencies, the practice of law within those agencies, and administrative/judicial proceedings involving those agencies."

On June 24, 2005, the Commission on Certification of Attorneys as Specialists approved Appellate Law as a field of law subject to specialization designation in Ohio. The following definition was adopted by the Commission.

"**Appellate Law** deals primarily with practice before state and federal appellate courts. It is distinct from, although complementary to, trial advocacy. Appellate Law emphasizes critical analysis and written advocacy but includes oral advocacy skills as well. This discipline includes consultation regarding the identification and preservation of error at all stages of litigation, and the analysis of public policy goals and constitutional principles in the highest state and federal courts. Appellate Law embraces actions within the original jurisdiction of appellate courts, as well as those matters within the courts' appellate jurisdiction."

"**Social Security Disability Law** is the practice of law that involves representation of claimants for Social Security disability, survivors' and retirement benefits. Lawyers in this field routinely represent claimants throughout the administrative hearings and appeals process and into the federal courts."

History: Adopted effective: July 10, 1996; amended effective: October 8, 1996; August 26, 1997; February 3, 1998; January 24, 2006; November 1, 2008.

Appendix VII.
LAWYER REFERRAL AND INFORMATION SERVICES REGULATIONS

(Repealed effective April 30, 2007)

Appendix VIII.
REGULATIONS GOVERNING PROCEDURE ON COMPLAINTS AND HEARINGS BEFORE THE BOARD ON THE UNAUTHORIZED PRACTICE OF LAW

UPL REG. 100

TITLE, AUTHORITY AND APPLICATION

(**A**) These regulations shall be known as the Regulations Governing Procedure on Complaints and Hear-

ings Before the Board on the Unauthorized Practice of Law and shall be cited as "UPL Reg.____."

(**B**) The following regulations are adopted by the Board on the Unauthorized Practice of Law pursuant to Gov.Bar R. VII(16) of the Rules for the Government of the Bar of Ohio, with the prior approval of the Supreme Court of Ohio.

(**C**) Pursuant to Gov.Bar R. VII(14), the Board applies the Ohio Rules of Civil Procedure and Rules of Evidence whenever practicable, unless a provision of Gov.Bar R. VII, these regulations, or Board procedure provide otherwise. Local rules of court are not applicable to matters before the Board.

UPL REG. 200

CASE MANAGEMENT; PRACTICE AND PROCEDURE

201 Case Schedule
(A) After assignment of the Hearing Panel, the Secretary of the Board in consultation with the Panel Chair shall issue a case scheduling order to all parties or their counsel as set forth in this regulation. The case schedule shall be served upon the parties no more than seven days after the time to plead or otherwise defend the complaint has elapsed. The case schedule shall at a minimum establish deadlines for certain case events and may be adjusted by the Panel Chair or for good cause shown:

Assignment of Hearing Panel	0
Hearing Date	266 days after assignment
Initial Telephone Status Conference	30 days after assignment
Initial Disclosure of Witnesses	80 days after assignment or upon request of either party
Discovery Cut-off	60 days before hearing
Pre-Hearing Statement/Briefs	40 days before hearing

(B) At the discretion of the Panel Chair, the following events may also be established:

Dispositive Motion DeadlineMotions on Preliminary or Procedural Issues DeadlineDecisions on Motions-

Stipulations of Facts and/or LawSupplemental Disclosure of WitnessesFinal Pre-Hearing Conference

(C) Any complaint filed by an Unauthorized Practice of Law Committee or the Disciplinary Counsel shall state whether the relator is aware that an underlying complainant or individual is seeking a private remedy pursuant to R.C. 4705.07. Upon receipt of the complaint, the Secretary shall designate the case accordingly and inform the Panel Chair, who will have the discretion to accelerate the case management schedule and hearing date.

202 Motions; Dispositive Motions

(A) Upon the filing of a motion and unless ordered otherwise by the Panel Chair, any memorandum in opposition shall be filed within twenty-one days after the filing of the motion. The response shall be served upon the Secretary and all adverse parties or their counsel. Unless directed otherwise by the Panel Chair, any reply to the memorandum in opposition shall be filed within ten days of the filing of the memorandum in opposition. Three days shall be added to the prescribed time periods when the motion or responsive memoranda are served by mail.

(B) Any motion, including but not limited to a motion for summary judgment, a motion for judgment on the pleadings, and a motion to dismiss, that seeks to determine the merits of any claim or defense as to any or all parties shall be considered a dispositive motion. A voluntary dismissal under Civ.R. 41 is not a dispositive motion for purposes of this regulation. All dispositive motions shall be filed no later than the date specified in the case schedule. Pursuant to Civ.R. 56(A), leave is granted in all cases to file summary judgment motions between the time of service of the complaint and the dispositive motion date, unless the Panel Chair dictates otherwise by setting a different date. If a dispositive motion date was not established in the initial case schedule, leave of the Panel must be obtained pursuant to Civ.R. 56(A). Parties shall file their summary judgment motion at the earliest practical date during the pendency of the case.

(C) The Panel Chair may order the simultaneous filing of motions and memoranda in opposition without provision for reply.

203 Pre-hearing Procedure

203.1 Pre-hearing Statements, Motions, and Briefs

(A) In all cases pending hearing, all parties shall prepare and serve upon the Secretary, with a copy to all opposing counsel, a final pre-hearing statement forty days prior to the assigned hearing date. The final pre-hearing statement shall at a minimum contain:

(1) A brief statement of the facts and identification of claims and defenses;

(2) The factual and legal issues which the cause presents;

(3) For relator, its position on whether the facts and circumstances of the case warrant imposition of a civil penalty and if the relator seeks the imposition

of a civil penalty, the relator shall specify the amount of the civil penalty it is requesting and identify the unique facts and circumstances that it believes warrant imposition of the civil penalty requested; and,

(4) For respondent, an indication of whether there is opposition to any request for imposition of a civil penalty and the existence of evidence in mitigation;

(5) The estimated days required for hearing.

(B) Parties shall separately prepare and serve upon the Secretary, with a copy to all opposing counsel, forty days prior to the assigned hearing date:

(1) Stipulations of fact or law, if any;

(2) A listing of all witnesses with a brief summary of expected testimony; a copy of all available opinions of all persons who may be called as expert witnesses;

(3) A listing of all exhibits expected to be offered into evidence, except exhibits to be used only for impeachment, illustration, or rebuttal.

(C) Forty days prior to the hearing date, all other motions (other than dispositive motions), pleadings, filings or hearing briefs intended to be offered at the hearing shall be served upon the Secretary and opposing parties. A response to any motion, brief or other filing shall be served according to UPL Reg. 202(A). The required pre-hearing statement may be included as part of any hearing brief.

(D) All documentary evidence to be offered at hearing shall be served upon the Secretary, adverse parties or their counsel at least thirty days before hearing pursuant to Gov.Bar R. VII(14).

(E) There is reserved to each party, upon application to the Panel and for good cause shown, the right at the hearing to:

(1) offer additional exhibits, file additional pleadings;

(2) supplement the list of witnesses to be called; and,

(3) call such rebuttal witnesses as may be necessary, without prior notice to opposing parties.

204 Certificate of Registration

After filing a complaint alleging the unauthorized practice of law, relator shall produce a Certificate from the Supreme Court of Ohio, Office of Attorney Registration, indicating whether any responsive party to the complaint is not admitted to practice law in the State of Ohio, and serve a copy upon all respondents, counsel of record, and the Secretary of the Board, and the original shall be offered as an exhibit at hearing and filed with the Board by the relator at the conclusion of hearing.

205 Final Pre-hearing Conferences

(A) No later than sixty days before hearing, a party may file a request for a pre-hearing conference with the Panel. The request may be granted by the Panel Chair. The Panel Chair may also establish a pre-hearing conference date consistent with the initial case scheduling order. A pre-hearing conference with the parties shall at a minimum attempt to accomplish the following objectives:

(1) Simplification of the issues;

(2) Necessity of amendment to the pleadings;

(3) Resolution of outstanding discovery issues;

(4) Identification of anticipated witnesses;

(5) The possibility of obtaining:

(i) stipulations of fact or law;

(i) stipulations of the admissibility of exhibits;

(6) Such other matters as may expedite the hearing;

(7) Confirmation of the final hearing date and venue

(B) At the discretion of the Panel Chair, a pre-hearing conference may be held by telephone, and may be continued from day to day. Counsel and parties should be prepared to discuss the matters contained in this regulation. At the conclusion of the pre-hearing conference, the Panel Chair may enter an order setting forth the action taken and the agreements reached, which order shall govern the subsequent course of proceedings.

206 Electronic Filing
(Reserved)

207 Continuances
(A) The continuance of a hearing date is a matter within the discretion of the Panel for good cause shown. No party shall be granted a continuance of a hearing date without a written motion from the party or counsel stating the reason for the continuance. The motion shall be filed with the Secretary no later than ten days before the date set for hearing. If the motion is not granted by the Panel Chair, the cause shall proceed as originally scheduled.

(B) When a continuance is requested due to the unavailability of a witness at the time scheduled for hearing, the Panel may consider the feasibility of permitting testimony pursuant to Civ.R. 32.

208 Subpoenas and Orders for Testimony
(A) To compel the testimony of a witness at the hearing, requests for the issuance of subpoenas pursuant to Gov.Bar R. VII(12) shall be made in writing and filed with the Secretary no later than ten days before the date on which a complaint has been set for hearing.

(B) To compel the testimony of a witness whose testimony will be offered at the hearing via deposition pursuant to Civ.R. 32, requests for orders for testimony pursuant to Gov.Bar R.VII(13) or the issuance of subpoenas pursuant to Gov.Bar R. VII(12) shall be made in writing and filed with the Secretary no later than thirty days before the date on which a complaint has been set for hearing.

209 Post-hearing Procedure of the Panel and Board
(A) A Panel Report shall be submitted to the Secretary within sixty days of the filing of the transcript for consideration at the next regularly scheduled meeting of the Board. The Secretary, at the request of the Panel Chair, may extend the date for the filing of the Panel Report with the Board.

(B) The Final Report of the Board shall be filed with the Court by the Secretary no later than thirty days after the conclusion of the Board's review, approval and adoption of whole or part of the Panel's report. After consideration by the Board, the Chair may be granted the authority by the Board to prepare and file the Final Report.

(C) Failure by the Board to meet the time guidelines set forth in these regulations shall not be grounds for dismissal of the complaint.

UPL REG. 300

REGULATION FOR THE ISSUANCE OF ADVISORY OPINIONS

300.1 Procedure for Issuance

(A) Pursuant to Gov.Bar R. VII(2)(C) of the Supreme Court Rules for the Government of the Bar of Ohio, the Board on the Unauthorized Practice of Law may issue informal, non-binding Advisory Opinions in response to prospective or hypothetical questions regarding the application of the Supreme Court Rules for the Government of the Bar of Ohio regarding the unauthorized practice of law and issues implicated by R.C. 4705.01, 4705.07 and 4705.99. Requests for an Advisory Opinion may be submitted to the Board by Disciplinary Counsel or an Unauthorized Practice of Law Committee of a Local or State Bar Association.

(B) The Chair of the Board shall appoint three or more members of the Board to serve on an Advisory Opinion Subcommittee. The Advisory Opinion Subcommittee is a regular standing subcommittee of the Board. The subcommittee shall meet prior to each regularly scheduled Board meeting. The Chair will appoint one subcommittee member to serve as Chair of the Advisory Opinion Subcommittee. Each subcommittee member shall serve for a period of one year from the date of appointment and shall be eligible for re-appointment by the Chair.

(C) Requests for an Advisory Opinion shall be submitted in writing to the Secretary of the Board on the Unauthorized Practice of Law. The request for Advisory Opinion shall be in writing and state in detail to the extent practicable the operative facts upon which the request for Opinion is based, with information and detail sufficient to enable adequate consideration and determination of eligibility under these regulations. The request shall contain the name and address of the requester. A summary of the rules, opinions, statutes, case law and any other authority which the inquirer has already consulted concerning the questions raised should also be included in the request. A letter acknowledging the receipt of the request will be sent to the requester.

(D) The procedure for review of a request for Advisory Opinion shall be as follows:

(1) The Advisory Opinion Subcommittee shall review all requests for Advisory Opinion submitted by Disciplinary Counsel or an Unauthorized Prac-

tice of Law Committee of a Local or State Bar Association.

(2) The Advisory Opinion Subcommittee shall, within its discretion, accept or decline a request for an Advisory Opinion.

(3) In making such determination, the subcommittee shall be governed by Gov.Bar R. VII(2)(C) and respond only to prospective or hypothetical questions of public or great general interest regarding the application of Gov.Bar R. VII and the unauthorized practice of law. The subcommittee shall decline requests that concern a question that is pending before the Court, decided by the Court, or a question of interest only to the person initiating the request. If the subcommittee determines that adequate authority already exists to answer the inquiry posed, the requester will be advised of the applicable authority and no Opinion will be issued.

(4) If any member of the subcommittee requests the declination of the Advisory Opinion be considered by the full Board, such request will be presented to the full Board for consideration at the next business meeting. If the subcommittee unanimously declines a request for Advisory Opinion, such determination shall be final.

(E) The requester of an Advisory Opinion will be notified of the Board's determination to accept or decline a request.

(F) If a request for Advisory Opinion is accepted for consideration, the subcommittee will complete the process of researching, drafting and review as expeditiously as possible, preferably within two to six months after selection of the request. The subcommittee shall be empowered to request and accept the voluntary services of a person licensed to practice law in this state when the subcommittee deems it advisable to receive written or oral advice or assistance in research and analysis regarding the question presented by the requester.

(G) Conflict of Interest
Subcommittee members shall not participate in any matter in which they have either a material pecuniary interest that would be affected by a proposed Advisory Opinion or subcommittee recommendation or any other conflict of interest or an appearance of a conflict of interest that should prevent them from participating. However, no action of the subcommittee will be invalid where full disclosure has been made to the Chair of the Board and the Chair has not decided that the member's participation was improper.

(H) Each draft Opinion approved by majority vote of the subcommittee will be sent to the full Board on the Unauthorized Practice of Law for review approximately two weeks prior to the next Board meeting. Upon review, Board members may direct comments, suggestions, or objections to the Chair of the subcommittee.

(I) If objections are received, the draft Opinion will be placed on the agenda for discussion at the Board

meeting. If no objections are received, the draft 8 Opinion will be adopted by a majority vote of the Board at the Board meeting. Minor or non-substantive changes are not considered as objections to a draft Opinion.

(J) A copy of the Adopted Advisory Opinion will be issued to the requester. Copies of the issued Opinions will be submitted for publication in the ABA/BNA Lawyers Manual on Professional Conduct, the Ohio State Bar Association Report, and other publications or electronic communications as the Board deems appropriate. Copies of issued Opinions will be forwarded to the Law Library of the Supreme Court of Ohio, County Law Libraries, Office of Disciplinary Counsel, Local and State Bar Associations with Unauthorized Practice of Law Committees.

(K) Issued Opinions shall not bear the name of the requester and shall not include the request letter. However, the requester's name and the request letter are not confidential and will be made available to the Bar, Judiciary, or the public upon request.

300.2 Procedure for Maintenance

(A) A copy of each Advisory Opinion will be kept in the Board's offices.

(B) An Advisory Opinion that becomes withdrawn, modified, or not current will be marked with an appropriate designation to indicate the status of the opinion.

(C) The designation "Withdrawn" will be used when an Opinion has been withdrawn by the majority vote of the Board. The designation indicates that an Opinion no longer represents the advice of the Board.

(D) The designation "Modified" will be used when an Opinion has been modified by a majority vote of the Board. The designation indicates that an Opinion has been modified by a subsequent Opinion.

(E) The designation "Not Current" will be used at the discretion of the Board to indicate that an Opinion is not current in its entirety. The designation that an Opinion is no longer current in its entirety may be used to indicate a variety of reasons such as subsequent amendments to rules or statutes, or developments in case law.

(F) Other designations, as needed, may be used by majority vote of the Board.

(G) The Advisory Opinion index will include a list identifying the Opinions as "Withdrawn," "Modified," or "Not Current," and other designations as decided by the Board.

UPL REG. 400
GUIDELINES FOR IMPOSITION OF CIVIL PENALTIES

(A) Each case of unauthorized practice of law involves unique facts and circumstances.

(B) At the hearing and at the end of its case-in-chief, relator shall set forth its position on the imposition of a civil penalty. Relator shall specify the amount of the civil penalty it is requesting and identify the factors, circumstances, and aggravating factors, if any, that warrant imposition of the requested civil penalty.

(C) At the hearing respondent shall contest any request for imposition of a civil penalty. Evidence that is offered by respondent in mitigation shall be introduced as part of the respondent's case-in-chief .

(D) In determining whether to recommend the imposition of a civil penalty, the Board shall consider all relevant facts and circumstances, as well as precedent established by the Supreme Court of Ohio and the Board.

(E) In each case where the Board finds by a preponderance of the evidence that respondent has engaged in the unauthorized practice of law, the Board shall discuss in its final report to the Supreme Court any of the factors set forth in Gov.Bar R. VII(8)(B):

"(B) Civil Penalties. The Board may recommend and the Court may impose civil penalties in an amount up to ten thousand dollars per offense. Any penalty shall be based on the following factors:

(1) The degree of cooperation provided by the respondent in the investigation;

(2) The number of occasions that unauthorized practice of law was committed;

(3) The flagrancy of the violation;

(4) Harm to third parties arising from the offense;

(5) Any other relevant factors."

(F) As part of its analysis of "other relevant factors" pursuant to Gov.Bar R.VII(8)(B)(5), the Board may consider:

(1) Whether relator has sought imposition of a civil penalty and, if so, the amount sought.

(2) Whether the imposition of civil penalties would further the purposes of Gov.Bar R. VII.

(3) **Aggravation** The following factors may be considered in favor of recommending a more severe penalty:

(a) Whether respondent has previously engaged in unauthorized practice of law;

(b) Whether respondent has previously been ordered to cease engaging in the unauthorized practice of law;

(c) Whether respondent had been informed prior to engaging in the unauthorized practice of law that the conduct at issue may constitute an act of the unauthorized practice of law;

(d) Whether respondent has benefited from the unauthorized practice of law and ,if so, the extent of any such benefit;

(e) Whether respondent's unauthorized practice of law included an appearance before a court or other tribunal;

(f) Whether respondent's unauthorized practice of law included the preparation of a legal instrument for filing with a court or other governmental entity; and

(g) Whether respondent has held himself or herself out as being admitted to practice law in the State of Ohio, or whether respondent has allowed others to mistakenly believe that he or she was admitted to practice law in the State of Ohio.

(4) **Mitigation** The following factors may be considered in favor of recommending no penalty or less severe penalty:

(a) Whether respondent has ceased engaging in the conduct under review;

(b) Whether respondent has admitted or stipulated to the conduct under review;

(c) Whether respondent has admitted or stipulated that the conduct under review constitutes the unauthorized practice of law;

(d) Whether respondent has agreed or stipulated to the imposition of an injunction against future unauthorized practice of law;

(e) Whether respondent's conduct resulted from a motive other than dishonesty or personal benefit;

(f) Whether respondent has engaged in a timely good faith effort to make restitution or to rectify the consequences of the unauthorized practice of law; and

(g) Whether respondent has had other penalties imposed for the conduct at issue.

UPL REG. 500-900
(RESERVED)

UPL REG. 1000
EFFECTIVE DATE

(A) These regulations shall be effective June 1, 2006.

Index to Supreme Court Rules for the Government of the Bar of Ohio

OHIO RULES OF PROFESSIONAL CONDUCT

FORM OF CITATION, EFFECTIVE DATE, APPLICATION

A. Correlation Table Ohio Rules of Professional Conduct to Ohio Code of Professional Responsibility

B. Correlation Table Ohio Code of Professional Responsibility to Ohio Model Rules of Professional Conduct

OHIO RULES OF PROFESSIONAL CONDUCT

Effective February 1, 2007

The Supreme Court of Ohio adopted the Ohio Rules of Professional Conduct, effective February 1, 2007. These rules supersede and replace the Ohio Code of Professional Responsibility to govern the conduct of Ohio lawyers occurring on or after February 1, 2007. See the Form of Citation, Effective Date, and Application provision that follows the rules for more information regarding application of the Rules of Professional Conduct and the former Code of Professional Responsibility.

Background

In March 2003, Chief Justice Thomas J. Moyer appointed the Supreme Court Task Force on Rules of Professional Conduct to conduct a thorough review of Ohio's lawyer discipline code and recommend revisions. The recommendations were to include whether Ohio should adopt new disciplinary rules based on the Model Rules of Professional Conduct promulgated by the American Bar Association. During the ensuing two and one-half years, the Task Force voted to recommend adoption of the ABA Model Rules and proceeded to review and discuss each rule. Preliminary drafts of each proposed rules were published for comment by the Task Force in January, July, and November 2004. After reviewing the public comments, the Task Force prepared and presented its report and recommendations regarding adoption of the Ohio Rules of Professional Conduct to the Supreme Court in the Summer of 2005.

The Supreme Court published the Task Force report and recommendations for 90 days of public comment in November 2005. The Task Force reconvened in the Spring of 2006 to review and discuss the public comments and prepare additional revisions to the proposed rules. In June and July 2006, the Court considered the public comments and the additional recommendations from the Task Force. The Court revised the Task Force recommendations and adopted the new Ohio Rules of Professional Conduct, effective February 1, 2007, following a six-month implementation period recommended by the Task Force.

Published Rules

The Ohio Rules of Professional Conduct are published in final form. Readers who wish to see the changes made in the proposed rules that were published for comment in November 2005 may consult the "Additional Resources" noted below.

Portions of some rules and comments are designated as [RESERVED]. See, *e.g.,* Rule 1.2(b). This designation indicates that the Supreme Court did not adopt a particular provision that appears in the ABA Model Rules of Professional Conduct. The designation [RESERVED] allows the Ohio Rules to correspond, as closely as possible, to the format, lettering, and numbering of the ABA Model Rules.

The Supreme Court did not adopt four Model Rules [Rules 3.2, 6.3, 6.4, and 7.6] and has deferred consideration of Model Rule 6.1. Please see the Note that accompanies each rule. Model Rule 2.2 was repealed by the American

Bar Association in 2002, thus that rule number is reserved for future use in the Ohio Rules of Professional Conduct.

Each adopted rule contains four parts: (1) the text of the rule; (2) a comment; (3) a comparison of the Ohio rule to the former Ohio Code of Professional Responsibility; and (4) a comparison of the Ohio rule to the ABA Model Rules of Professional Conduct. Please see Scope at [14]-[21] for more information regarding the rules and comments. The comparisons that follow each rule have been prepared by the Task Force on Rules of Professional Conduct. Although the Supreme Court used these comparisons during its consideration of the proposed rules, the comparisons are not adopted by the Court and are not a part of the Ohio Rules of Professional Conduct. As such, they represent the views of the Task Force on Rules of Professional Conduct and not necessarily those of the Supreme Court.

Correlation Tables

Following the Ohio Rules of Professional Conduct are two tables that illustrate the manner in which individual rules correspond to provisions of the Ohio Code of Professional Responsibility.

Additional Resources

The Task Force web site [http://www.sconet.state.oh.us/Atty-Svcs/ProfConduct/default.asp] includes electronic versions of the Ohio Rules of Professional Conduct and additional resource materials:

- The October 2005 report from the Task Force on Rules of Professional Conduct. This report contains a narrative that summarizes several key provisions of the Rules of Professional Conduct. This report should be read in conjunction with the published narrative that summarizes significant revisions adopted by the Supreme Court following the public comment period.
- All written comments received by the Task Force and Supreme Court following the publication of the October 2005 report.
- A "mark-up" version of the proposed rules, as published for comment, that denotes the revisions made following the public comment period.
- Links to resource materials including the former Ohio Code of Professional Responsibility, the ABA Model Rules of Professional Conduct, and minutes of the meetings of the Task Force on Rules of Professional Conduct.

PREAMBLE: A LAWYER'S RESPONSIBILITIES

(1) As an officer of the court, a lawyer not only represents clients but has a special responsibility for the quality of justice.

(2) In representing clients, a lawyer performs various functions. As advisor, a lawyer provides a client with an informed understanding of the client's legal rights and obligations and explains their practical implications. As advocate, a lawyer asserts the client's position under the rules of the adversary system. As negotiator, a lawyer seeks a result advantageous to the client and consistent with requirements of honest dealings with others. As an evaluator, a lawyer examines a client's legal affairs and reports about them to the client or to others.

(3) In addition to these representational functions, a lawyer may serve as a third-party neutral, a nonrepresentational role helping the parties to resolve a dispute or other matter. See, *e.g.*, Rules 1.12 and 2.4. In addition, there are rules that apply to lawyers who are not active in the practice of law or to practicing lawyers even when they are acting in a nonprofessional capacity. For example, a lawyer who commits fraud in the conduct of a business is subject to discipline for engaging in conduct involving dishonesty, fraud, deceit, or misrepresentation. See Rule 8.4.

(4) In all professional functions a lawyer should be competent, prompt, diligent, and loyal. A lawyer should maintain communication with a client concerning the representation. A lawyer should keep in confidence information relating to representation of a client except so far as disclosure is required or permitted by the Ohio Rules of Professional Conduct or other law.

(5) Lawyers play a vital role in the preservation of society. A lawyer's conduct should conform to the requirements of the law, both in professional service to clients and in the lawyer's business and personal affairs. A lawyer should use the law's procedures only for legitimate purposes and not to harass or intimidate others. A lawyer should demonstrate respect for the legal system and for those who serve it, including judges, other lawyers, and public officials. Adjudicatory officials, not being wholly free to defend themselves, are entitled to receive the support of the bar against unjustified criticism. Although a lawyer, as a citizen, has a right to criticize such officials, the lawyer should do so with restraint and avoid intemperate statements that tend to lessen public confidence in the legal system. While it is a lawyer's duty, when necessary, to challenge the rectitude of official action, it is also a lawyer's duty to uphold legal process.

(6) A lawyer should seek improvement of the law, ensure access to the legal system, advance the administration of justice, and exemplify the quality of service rendered by the legal profession. As a member of a learned profession, a lawyer should cultivate knowledge of the law beyond its use for clients, employ that knowledge in reform of the law, and work to strengthen legal education. In addition, a lawyer should further the public's understanding of and confidence in the rule of law and the justice system because legal institutions in a constitutional democracy depend on popular participation and support to maintain their authority. A lawyer should be mindful of deficiencies in the administration of justice and of the fact that the poor, and sometimes persons who are not poor, cannot afford adequate legal assistance. Therefore, all lawyers should devote professional time and resources and use civic influence to ensure equal access to our system of justice for all those who because of economic or social barriers cannot afford or secure adequate legal counsel. A lawyer should aid the legal profession in pursuing these objectives and should help the bar regulate itself in the public interest.

(7) [RESERVED]

(8) [RESERVED]

(9) The Ohio Rules of Professional Conduct often prescribe rules for a lawyer's conduct. Within the framework of these rules, however, many difficult issues of professional discretion can arise. These issues must be resolved through the exercise of sensitive professional and moral judgment guided by the basic principles underlying the rules.

(10) [RESERVED]

(11) The legal profession is self-governing in that the Ohio Constitution vests in the Supreme Court of Ohio the ultimate authority to regulate the profession. To the extent that lawyers meet the obligations of their professional calling, the occasion for government regulation is obviated. Self-regulation also helps maintain the legal profession's independence from government domination. An independent legal profession is an important force in preserving government under law, for abuse of legal authority is more readily challenged by a profession whose members are not dependent on government for the right to practice.

(12) [RESERVED]

(13) [RESERVED]

SCOPE

(14) The Ohio Rules of Professional Conduct are rules of reason. They should be interpreted with reference to the purposes of legal representation and of the law itself. Some of the rules are imperatives, cast in the terms "shall" or "shall not." These define proper conduct for purposes of professional discipline. Others, generally cast in the term "may" are permissive and define areas under the rules in which the lawyer has discretion to exercise professional judgment. No disciplinary action should be taken when the lawyer chooses not to act or acts within the bounds of such discretion. Other rules define the nature of relationships between the lawyer and others. The rules are thus partly obligatory and disciplinary and partly constitutive and descriptive in that they define a lawyer's professional role. Many of the comments use the term "should." Comments do not add obligations to the rules but

provide guidance for practicing in compliance with the rules.

(15) The rules presuppose a larger legal context shaping the lawyer's role. That context includes court rules relating to matters of licensure, laws defining specific obligations of lawyers, and substantive and procedural law in general. The comments are sometimes used to alert lawyers to their responsibilities under such other law.

(16) Compliance with the rules, as with all law in an open society, depends primarily upon understanding and voluntary compliance, secondarily upon reinforcement by peer and public opinion, and finally, when necessary, upon enforcement through disciplinary proceedings. The rules do not, however, exhaust the moral and ethical considerations that should inform a lawyer, for no worthwhile human activity can be completely defined by legal rules. The rules simply provide a framework for the ethical practice of law.

(17) Furthermore, for purposes of determining the lawyer's authority and responsibility, principles of substantive law external to these rules determine whether a client-lawyer relationship exists. Most of the duties flowing from the client-lawyer relationship attach only after the client has requested the lawyer to render legal services and the lawyer has agreed to do so. But there are some duties, such as that of confidentiality under Rule 1.6, that attach when the lawyer agrees to consider whether a client-lawyer relationship shall be established. See Rule 1.18. Whether a client-lawyer relationship exists for any specific purpose can depend on the circumstances and may be a question of fact.

(18) Under various legal provisions, including constitutional, statutory, and common law, the responsibilities of government lawyers may include authority concerning legal matters that ordinarily reposes in the client in private client-lawyer relationships. For example, a lawyer for a government agency may have authority on behalf of the government to decide upon settlement or whether to appeal from an adverse judgment. Such authority in various respects is generally vested in the attorney general and the state's attorney in state government, and their federal counterparts, and the same may be true of other government law officers. Also, lawyers under the supervision of these officers may be authorized to represent several government agencies in intragovernmental legal controversies in circumstances where a private lawyer could not represent multiple private clients. These rules do not abrogate any such authority.

(19) Failure to comply with an obligation or prohibition imposed by a rule is a basis for invoking the disciplinary process. The rules presuppose that disciplinary assessment of a lawyer's conduct will be made on the basis of the facts and circumstances as they existed at the time of the conduct in question and in recognition of the fact that a lawyer often has to act upon uncertain or incomplete evidence of the situation. Moreover, the rules presuppose that whether or not discipline should be imposed for a violation, and the severity of a sanction, depend on all the circumstances,

such as the willfulness and seriousness of the violation, extenuating factors, and whether there have been previous violations.

(20) Violation of a rule should not itself give rise to a cause of action against a lawyer nor should it create any presumption in such a case that a legal duty has been breached. In addition, violation of a rule does not necessarily warrant any other nondisciplinary remedy, such as disqualification of a lawyer in pending litigation. The rules are designed to provide guidance to lawyers and to provide a structure for regulating conduct through disciplinary agencies. They are not designed to be a basis for civil liability. Furthermore, the purpose of the rules can be subverted when they are invoked by opposing parties as procedural weapons. The fact that a rule is a just basis for a lawyer's self-assessment, or for sanctioning a lawyer under the administration of a disciplinary authority, does not imply that an antagonist in a collateral proceeding or transaction has standing to seek enforcement of the rule. Nevertheless, since the rules do establish standards of conduct by lawyers, a lawyer's violation of a rule may be evidence of breach of the applicable standard of conduct.

(21) The comment accompanying each rule explains and illustrates the meaning and purpose of the rule. The Preamble and this note on Scope provide general orientation. The comments are intended as guides to interpretation, but the text of each rule is authoritative.

RULE 1.0: TERMINOLOGY

As used in these rules:

(a) "Belief" or "believes" denotes that the person involved actually supposed the fact in question to be true. A person's belief may be inferred from circumstances.

(b) "Confirmed in writing," when used in reference to the informed consent of a person, denotes informed consent that is given in writing by the person or a writing that a lawyer promptly transmits to the person confirming an oral informed consent. See division (f) for the definition of "informed consent." If it is not feasible to obtain or transmit the writing at the time the person gives informed consent, then the lawyer must obtain or transmit it within a reasonable time thereafter.

(c) "Firm" or "law firm" denotes a lawyer or lawyers in a law partnership, professional corporation, sole proprietorship, or other association authorized to practice law; or lawyers employed in a private or public legal aid or public defender organization, a legal services organization, or the legal department of a corporation or other organization.

(d) "Fraud" or "fraudulent" denotes conduct that has an intent to deceive and is either of the following:

(1) an actual or implied misrepresentation of a material fact that is made either with knowledge of its falsity or with such utter disregard and recklessness about its falsity that knowledge may be inferred;

(2) a knowing concealment of a material fact where there is a duty to disclose the material fact.

(e) "Illegal" denotes criminal conduct or a violation

of an applicable statute or administrative regulation.

(f) "Informed consent" denotes the agreement by a person to a proposed course of conduct after the lawyer has communicated adequate information and explanation about the material risks of and reasonably available alternatives to the proposed course of conduct.

(g) "Knowingly," "known," or "knows" denotes actual knowledge of the fact in question. A person's knowledge may be inferred from circumstances.

(h) "Partner" denotes a member of a partnership, a shareholder in a law firm organized as a professional corporation, or a member of an association authorized to practice law.

(i) "Reasonable" or "reasonably" when used in relation to conduct by a lawyer denotes the conduct of a reasonably prudent and competent lawyer.

(j) "Reasonable belief" or "reasonably believes" when used in reference to a lawyer denotes that the lawyer believes the matter in question and that the circumstances are such that the belief is reasonable.

(k) "Reasonably should know" when used in reference to a lawyer denotes that a lawyer of reasonable prudence and competence would ascertain the matter in question.

(l) "Screened" denotes the isolation of a lawyer from any participation in a matter through the timely imposition of procedures within a firm that are reasonably adequate under the circumstances to protect information that the isolated lawyer is obligated to protect under these rules or other law.

(m) "Substantial" when used in reference to degree or extent denotes a matter of real importance or great consequence.

(n) "Substantially related matter" denotes one that involves the same transaction or legal dispute or one in which there is a substantial risk that confidential factual information that would normally have been obtained in the prior representation of a client would materially advance the position of another client in a subsequent matter.

(o) "Tribunal" denotes a court, an arbitrator in a binding arbitration proceeding, or a legislative body, administrative agency, or other body acting in an adjudicative capacity. A legislative body, administrative agency, or other body acts in an adjudicative capacity when a neutral official, after the presentation of evidence or legal argument by a party or parties, will render a binding legal judgment directly affecting a party's interests in a particular matter.

(p) "Writing" or "written" denotes a tangible or electronic record of a communication or representation, including handwriting, typewriting, printing, photostating, photography, audio or videorecording, and e-mail. A "signed" writing includes an electronic sound, symbol, or process attached to or logically associated with a writing and executed or adopted by a person with the intent to sign the writing.

I CLIENT-LAWYER RELATIONSHIP

RULE 1.1: COMPETENCE

A lawyer shall provide competent representation to a client. Competent representation requires the legal knowledge, skill, thoroughness, and preparation *reasonably* necessary for the representation.

RULE 1.2: SCOPE OF REPRESENTATION AND ALLOCATION OF AUTHORITY BETWEEN CLIENT AND LAWYER

(a) Subject to divisions (c), (d), and (e) of this rule, a lawyer shall abide by a client's decisions concerning the objectives of representation and, as required by Rule 1.4, shall consult with the client as to the means by which they are to be pursued. A lawyer may take action on behalf of the client as is impliedly authorized to carry out the representation. A lawyer does not violate this rule by acceding to requests of opposing counsel that do not prejudice the rights of the client, being punctual in fulfilling all professional commitments, avoiding offensive tactics, and treating with courtesy and consideration all persons involved in the legal process. A lawyer shall abide by a client's decision whether to settle a matter. In a criminal case, the lawyer shall abide by the client's decision as to a plea to be entered, whether to waive a jury trial, and whether the client will testify.

(b) [RESERVED]

(c) A lawyer may limit the scope of a new or existing representation if the limitation is *reasonable* under the circumstances and communicated to the client, preferably in *writing*.

(d) A lawyer shall not counsel a client to engage, or assist a client, in conduct that the lawyer *knows* is *illegal* or *fraudulent*. A lawyer may discuss the legal consequences of any proposed course of conduct with a client and may counsel or assist a client in making a good faith effort to determine the validity, scope, meaning, or application of the law.

(e) Unless otherwise required by law, a lawyer shall not present, participate in presenting, or threaten to present criminal charges or professional misconduct allegations solely to obtain an advantage in a civil matter.

DECISIONS UNDER FORMER LAW

ANALYSIS

Access to legal representation
Contract of employment
Discharge for consulting attorney
Disqualification of attorney
Duty of attorney

Access to legal representation

When an employee, upon being told that her annual bonus income would be reduced by 50 percent, said she would consult an attorney and was discharged a week later for threatening another employee, it was error to grant summary judgment to her employer on a claim of wrongful discharge in violation of public policy on the theory that her threat to consult an attorney was distinct from an actual consultation and was not a protected activity giving rise to a claim of termination in violation of public policy because this was a distinction without a difference, and provisions in Ohio Const. art. I, § 16 and Ohio Code Prof. Resp. EC 1-1 and 2-1, encouraging employees to consult an attorney regarding possible claims that would affect an employer's business interests showed that the employer's claim that the termination was valid was a factual issue which had to be submitted to the trier of fact. Newcomb v. Hostetler Catering, Inc., — Ohio App. 3d —, 2007 Ohio 361, — N.E. 2d —, 2007 Ohio App. LEXIS 309 (Jan. 29, 2007).

When considering sources of public policy that encouraged employees to consult an attorney about possible claims that would affect an employer's business interests, the Ohio Constitution gave the Ohio Supreme Court the authority to adopt the Code of Professional Responsibility (CPR), and the CPR contained two provisions which helped to show that encouraging individuals to consult an attorney was a clear public policy in Ohio. Ohio Code Prof. Resp. EC 1-1 stated that every person in society should have ready access to the independent professional services of a lawyer of integrity and competence, and Ohio Code Prof. Resp. EC 2-1 stated that the need of members of the public for legal services was met only if they recognized their legal problems, appreciated the importance of seeking legal assistance, and were able to obtain the services of acceptable legal counsel. Important functions of the legal profession were to educate laymen to recognize their legal problems, to facilitate the process of intelligent selection of lawyers, and to assist in making legal services fully available, and it would be inappropriate to engraft upon the CPR the caveat "however, if a claim is against the potential client's employer, the attorney must advise the client that she might lose her livelihood simply for consulting the attorney." Newcomb v. Hostetler Catering, Inc., — Ohio App. 3d —, 2007 Ohio 361, — N.E. 2d —, 2007 Ohio App. LEXIS 309 (Jan. 29, 2007).

Contract of employment

Attorney's license to practice law was suspended for one year, stayed for six months on conditions of his repaying his client, based on findings of misconduct, including the neglect of a client's case and failure to account for unearned fees. The attorney violated former Ohio Code Prof. Resp. 6-101(A)(3), 7- 101(A)(2), and 9-102(B)(4) by abandoning his client and ignoring requests for her file and an accounting. Cuyahoga County Bar Ass'n v. Peto, — Ohio St. 3d —, 2007 Ohio 5250, — N.E. 2d —, 2007 Ohio LEXIS 2520 (Oct. 10, 2007).

Discharge for consulting attorney

When considering sources of public policy that encouraged employees to consult an attorney about possible claims that would affect an employer's business interests, the Ohio Constitution gave the Ohio Supreme Court the authority to adopt the Code of Professional Responsibility (CPR), and the CPR contained two provisions which helped to show that encouraging individuals to consult an attorney was a clear public policy in Ohio. Ohio Code Prof. Resp. EC 1-1 stated that every person in society should have ready access to the independent professional services of a lawyer of integrity and competence, and Ohio Code Prof. Resp. EC 2-1 stated that the need of members of the public for legal services was met only if they recognized their legal problems, appreciated the importance of seeking legal assistance, and were able to obtain the services of acceptable legal counsel. Important functions of the legal profession were to educate laymen to recognize their legal problems, to facilitate the process of intelligent selection of lawyers, and to assist in making legal services fully available, and it would be inappropriate to engraft upon the CPR the caveat "however, if a claim is against the potential client's employer, the attorney must advise the client that she might lose her livelihood simply for consulting the attorney." Newcomb v. Hostetler Catering, Inc., — Ohio App. 3d —, 2007 Ohio 361, — N.E. 2d —, 2007 Ohio App. LEXIS 309 (Jan. 29, 2007).

Disqualification of attorney

Trial court erred when it disqualified the attorneys. There was no evidence to aid the trial court in determining whether their testimony would have been admissible or whether their

testimony would have prejudiced their client such that the presumption of continued representation in Ohio Code Prof. Resp. DR 1-502(B) should not have applied. Hall v. Tucker, 169 Ohio App. 3d 520, 2006 Ohio 5895, 863 N.E.2d 1064, 2006 Ohio App. LEXIS 5833 (2006).

Duty of attorney

Attorney did not violate his professional duty as stated in Ohio Code Prof. Resp. EC 7-8 when he pursued suit against the buyers of certain property belonging to the client in the face of the client's alleged protestations to the contrary. Specific documentary evidence showed that the client assigned his interests in the property to the attorney, and this assignment provided evidence of the client's ratification of the attorney's course of conduct. Augusta v. Lemieux, — Ohio App. 3d —, 2006 Ohio 6696, — N.E. 2d —, 2006 Ohio App. LEXIS 6594 (Dec. 15, 2006).

Multiple attorneys who represented a minor passenger, a minor driver, and their respective parents in actions against each other, alleging claims of negligence and loss of consortium arising from a vehicle accident that each party blamed on the other, had ethical obligations to represent the clients' interest, as expressed by the client, pursuant to Ohio Code Prof. Resp. EC 7-7 and 7-8. There was no ethical violation found by the attorneys' conduct, as they each were acting in independent roles, and the client did not have the burden of electing which course of action to take, where such choice would have entitled abandoning either his defense or his pursuit of a claim. Jacobs v. McAllister, — Ohio App. 3d —, 2006 Ohio 123, — N.E. 2d —, 2006 Ohio App. LEXIS 94 (Jan. 13, 2006).

RULE 1.3: DILIGENCE

A lawyer shall act with *reasonable* diligence and promptness in representing a client.

ANALYSIS

Guardian ad litem

Guardian ad litem

Duty of a lawyer to his client and the duty of a guardian ad litem to his ward were not always identical and, in fact, could conflict. as the role of guardian ad litem was to investigate the ward's situation and then to ask the court to do what the guardian felt was in the ward's best interest, while the role of the attorney was to zealously represent his client within the bounds of the law, under Ohio Code Prof. Resp. DR 7-101 and DR 7-102. In re Butler, — Ohio App. 3d —, 2006 Ohio 4547, — N.E. 2d —, 2006 Ohio App. LEXIS 4510 (Sept. 5, 2006).

DECISIONS UNDER FORMER LAW

ANALYSIS

Neglect of an entrusted legal matter

Neglect of an entrusted legal matter

Attorney's license to practice law was suspended for one year, stayed for six months on conditions of his repaying his client, based on findings of misconduct, including the neglect of a client's case and failure to account for unearned fees. The attorney violated former Ohio Code Prof. Resp. 6-101(A)(3), 7- 101(A)(2), and 9-102(B)(4) by abandoning his client and ignoring requests for her file and an accounting. Cuyahoga County Bar Ass'n v. Peto, — Ohio St. 3d —, 2007 Ohio 5250, — N.E. 2d —, 2007 Ohio LEXIS 2520 (Oct. 10, 2007). Attorney was suspended from the practice of law for six months based on findings that he neglected a client's case, attempted to cover up the neglect, failed to return the client's file on request, and failed to cooperate in the ensuing disciplinary investigation, in violation of former Ohio Code Prof. Resp. 9-102(B)(4), 6-101(A)(3), and 1-102(A)(4), and Ohio Sup. Ct. R. Gov't Bar V(4)(G), because the record amply justified the conclusions that the attorney neglected to appropriately advise his client of the proceedings in its case and then fabricated one or more letters to conceal his neglect. The mitigating factors did not outweigh the aggravating effect of having submitted false evidence and having acted out of self-interest in trying to cover up his misconduct. Disciplinary Counsel v. Broeren, — Ohio St. 3d —, 2007 Ohio 5251, — N.E. 2d —, 2007 Ohio LEXIS 2525 (Oct. 10, 2007).

RULE 1.4:   COMMUNICATION

(a) A lawyer shall do all of the following:

(1) promptly inform the client of any decision or circumstance with respect to which the client's *informed consent* is required by these rules;

(2) *reasonably* consult with the client about the means by which the client's objectives are to be accomplished;

(3) keep the client *reasonably* informed about the status of the matter;

(4) comply as soon as practicable with *reasonable* requests for information from the client;

(5) consult with the client about any relevant limitation on the lawyer's conduct when the lawyer *knows* that the client expects assistance not permitted by the Ohio Rules of Professional Conduct or other law.

(b) A lawyer shall explain a matter to the extent *reasonably* necessary to permit the client to make informed decisions regarding the representation.

(c) A lawyer shall inform a client at the time of the client's engagement of the lawyer or at any time subsequent to the engagement if the lawyer does not maintain professional liability insurance in the amounts of at least one hundred thousand dollars per occurrence and three hundred thousand dollars in the aggregate or if the lawyer's professional liability insurance is terminated. The notice shall be provided to the client on a separate form set forth following this rule and shall be signed by the client.

(1) A lawyer shall maintain a copy of the notice signed by the client for five years after termination of representation of the client.

(2) A lawyer who is involved in the division of fees pursuant to Rule 1.5(e) shall inform the client as required by division (c) of this rule before the client is asked to agree to the division of fees.

(3) The notice required by division (c) of this rule shall not apply to either of the following:

(i) A lawyer who is employed by a governmental entity and renders services pursuant to that employment;

(ii) A lawyer who renders legal services to an entity that employs the lawyer as in-house counsel.

NOTICE TO CLIENT

Pursuant to Rule 1.4 of the Ohio Rules of Professional Conduct, I am required to notify you that I do not maintain professional liability (malpractice) insurance of at least $100,000 per occurrence and $300,000 in the aggregate.

_____
Attorney's Signature

CLIENT ACKNOWLEDGEMENT

I acknowledge receipt of the notice required by Rule 1.4 of the Ohio Rules of Professional Conduct that [insert attorney's name] does not maintain professional liability (malpractice) insurance of at least $100,000 per occurrence and $300,000 in the aggregate.

_____
Client's Signature

_____
Date

RULE 1.5:   FEES AND EXPENSES

(a) A lawyer shall not make an agreement for, charge, or collect an *illegal* or clearly excessive fee. A fee is clearly excessive when, after a review of the facts, a lawyer of ordinary prudence would be left with a definite and firm conviction that the fee is in excess of a *reasonable* fee. The factors to be considered in determining the reasonableness of a fee include the following:

(1) the time and labor required, the novelty and difficulty of the questions involved, and the skill requisite to perform the legal service properly;

(2) the likelihood, if apparent to the client, that the acceptance of the particular employment will preclude other employment by the lawyer;

(3) the fee customarily charged in the locality for similar legal services;

(4) the amount involved and the results obtained;

(5) the time limitations imposed by the client or by the circumstances;

(6) the nature and length of the professional relationship with the client;

(7) the experience, reputation, and ability of the lawyer or lawyers performing the services;

(8) whether the fee is fixed or contingent.

(b) The nature and scope of the representation and the basis or rate of the fee and expenses for which the client will be responsible shall be communicated to the client, preferably in *writing*, before or within a *reasonable* time after commencing the representation, unless the lawyer will charge a client whom the lawyer has regularly represented on the same basis as previously charged. Any change in the basis or rate of the fee or expenses is subject to division (a) of this rule and shall promptly be communicated to the client, preferably in *writing*.

(c) A fee may be contingent on the outcome of the matter for which the service is rendered, except in a matter in which a contingent fee is prohibited by division (d) of this rule or other law.

(1) Each contingent fee agreement shall be in a *writing* signed by the client and the lawyer and shall state the method by which the fee is to be determined, including the percentage or percentages that shall accrue to the lawyer in the event of settlement, trial, or appeal; litigation and other expenses to be deducted from the recovery; and whether such expenses are to be deducted before or after the contingent fee is calculated. The agreement shall clearly notify the client of any expenses for which the client will be liable

whether or not the client is the prevailing party.

(2) If the lawyer becomes entitled to compensation under the contingent fee agreement and the lawyer will be disbursing funds, the lawyer shall prepare a closing statement and shall provide the client with that statement at the time of or prior to the receipt of compensation under the agreement. The closing statement shall specify the manner in which the compensation was determined under the agreement, any costs and expenses deducted by the lawyer from the judgment or settlement involved, and, if applicable, the actual division of the lawyer's fees with a lawyer not in the same *firm*, as required in division (e)(3) of this rule. The closing statement shall be signed by the client and lawyer.

(d) A lawyer shall not enter into an arrangement for, charge, or collect any of the following:

(1) any fee in a domestic relations matter, the payment or amount of which is contingent upon the securing of a divorce or upon the amount of spousal or child support, or property settlement in lieu thereof;

(2) a contingent fee for representing a defendant in a criminal case;

(3) a fee denominated as "earned upon receipt," "nonrefundable," or in any similar terms, unless the client is simultaneously advised in writing that if the lawyer does not complete the representation for any reason, the client may be entitled to a refund of all or part of the fee based upon the value of the representation pursuant to division (a) of this rule.

(e) Lawyers who are not in the same *firm* may divide fees only if all of the following apply:

(1) the division of fees is in proportion to the services performed by each lawyer or each lawyer assumes joint responsibility for the representation and agrees to be available for consultation with the client;

(2) the client has given *written* consent after full disclosure of the identity of each lawyer, that the fees will be divided, and that the division of fees will be in proportion to the services to be performed by each lawyer or that each lawyer will assume joint responsibility for the representation;

(3) except where court approval of the fee division is obtained, the *written* closing statement in a case involving a contingent fee shall be signed by the client and each lawyer and shall comply with the terms of division (c)(2) of this rule;

(4) the total fee is *reasonable*.

(f) In cases of a dispute between lawyers arising under this rule, fees shall be divided in accordance with the mediation or arbitration provided by a local bar association. When a local bar association is not available or does not have procedures to resolve fee disputes between lawyers, the dispute shall be referred to the Ohio State Bar Association for mediation or arbitration.

DECISIONS UNDER FORMER LAW

Analysis

Generally

Although there was no abuse of discretion in awarding attorney fees, the award was sufficiently disproportionate to the damages obtained to raise a question as to reasonableness under RC § 5321.16(C). It could not be determined which of the Ohio Code Prof. Resp. 2-106(B) factors, if any, the trial court applied and the trial court did not provide any explanation as to why it found the requested fees to be fair and customary. The trial court entered judgment of $700 for return of the tenant's wrongfully withheld security deposit, plus an additional $700 in statutory damages, but the attorney fees awarded were eight and one-half times the amount that the realty company was determined to have wrongfully withheld, and over four times the total damages to which the tenant was entitled to collect. Whitestone Co. v. Stittsworth, — Ohio App. 3d —, 2007 Ohio 233, — N.E. 2d —, 2007 Ohio App. LEXIS 216 (Jan. 23, 2007).

Trial court's award of attorney fees to vehicle owners in their action against an automobile dealer and manufacturer, arising from fraudulent sales tactics after the owners were informed that their lemon would be exchanged for a new vehicle at no cost to them, only to then be forced to sign new loan papers at an increased interest rate, was proper where the fee amount was deemed reasonable in the circumstances, based on the number of hours reasonably expended multiplied by an hourly fee, and then modified by the factors under Ohio Code Prof. Resp. DR 2-106(B). Smith v. GMC, 168 Ohio App. 3d 336, 2006 Ohio 4283, 859 N.E.2d 1035, 2006 Ohio App. LEXIS 4197 (2006).

Attorney fees in all matters are governed by Ohio Code Prof. Resp. DR 2-106, and a trial court's decision regarding the reasonableness of fees must be based upon the evidence of the actual services performed by the attorneys and upon the reasonable value of those services. Further, Loc. R. 24(E) of the Court of Common Pleas of Cuyahoga County's limitation of attorney fees to $850 except in contested cases where extraordinary circumstances were demonstrated, was invalid since it conflicted with RC § 5721.39, and a trial court erred in denying a buyer's request for attorney fees in excess of $850. Gls Capital Cuyahoga, Inc. v. Abuzahrieh, — Ohio App. 3d —, 2006 Ohio 298, — N.E. 2d —, 2006 Ohio App. LEXIS 248 (Jan. 26, 2006).

Applicability

As Ohio R. Prof. Conduct 1.5 governed attorney ethics and not the law to be applied to determine the terms of a contract and the result of a breach with respect to the allowance of an attorney fee award, a magistrate properly refused to rely on the rule to determine the reasonableness of a fee sought in a commercial lease dispute. Yoder v. Hurst, — Ohio App. 3d —, 2007 Ohio 4861, — N.E. 2d —, 2007 Ohio App. LEXIS 4310 (Sept. 20, 2007).

Attorney fees

It was an abuse of discretion to deny an employee any attorney fees, under Ohio Code Prof. Resp. DR 2-106, in his intentional tort suit against his employer, in which he was awarded punitive damages, because the amount of the punitive damages award was inadequate to both compensate the employee for his attorney fees and accomplish the purposes of punitive damages. Maynard v. Eaton Corp., — Ohio App. 3d —, 2007 Ohio 1906, — N.E. 2d —, 2007 Ohio App. LEXIS 1742 (Apr. 23, 2007).

Claimed attorney fees were clearly excessive in the absence of any proof of legal service performed: In re Estate of

Keytack, 147 Ohio Misc. 2d 114, 2008 Ohio 3831, 892 N.E.2d 529, 2008 Ohio Misc. LEXIS 187 (2008).

Computation

In calculating an attorney fee award, the trial court was required to compute the lodestar figure and then deviate from that determination after consideration of any or all of the factors set forth in Ohio Code Prof. Resp. DR 2-106(B). The trial court's disallowance of time for researching the opponent's prior litigation history, counsel's travel time, and counsel's conferencing with his staff was error, as those were appropriate charges, and the time spent by in-house counsel prior to the filing of the complaint was also allowable, although any duplication of effort between in-house counsel and the new litigation counsel due to the change in representation was not compensable. Landmark Disposal, Ltd. v. Byler Flea Mkt., — Ohio App. 3d —, 2006 Ohio 3935, — N.E. 2d —, 2006 Ohio App. LEXIS 3888 (July 31, 2006).

When a law firm sued a former client for past due fees, and sought attorney fees in connection with that complaint, a trial court properly did not apply the lodestar method to a determination of the current fees the firm was entitled to because that method was inapplicable in cases where an attorney sues a former client for collection of unpaid attorney fees. Bringman v. Smith, — Ohio App. 3d —, 2007 Ohio 4684, — N.E. 2d —, 2007 Ohio App. LEXIS 4214 (Sept. 12, 2007).

Contingent fee agreements

When an attorney handled collection cases for a credit union on a contingent fee basis, and the credit union discharged the attorney, the attorney's fee recovery was properly limited to the one case handled by the attorney in which the credit union had actually recovered a judgment because that was the only case in which the contingency provided in the parties' contingent fee agreement had occurred, and the attorney was not entitled to recover on a quantum meruit basis for work done on other cases because the contingency of the credit union's actual recovery in those cases had not yet occurred, so the recovery of a fee would be excessive, under Ohio R. Prof. Conduct 1.5(a). Doellman v. Midfirst Credit Union, — Ohio App. 3d —, 2007 Ohio 5902, — N.E. 2d —, 2007 Ohio App. LEXIS 5178 (Nov. 5, 2007).

Contingent-fee agreement calling for hourly charges if an attorney is discharged regardless of whether the contingency occurred violates Ohio Code Prof. Conduct 1.5(a), which provides that a lawyer shall not enter into an agreement for, charge, or collect an illegal or clearly excessive fee. Doellman v. Midfirst Credit Union, — Ohio App. 3d —, 2007 Ohio 5902, — N.E. 2d —, 2007 Ohio App. LEXIS 5178 (Nov. 5, 2007).

When an attorney representing a client pursuant to a contingent-fee agreement is discharged, the attorney's basis of quantum meruit arises upon the successful occurrence of the contingency. Doellman v. Midfirst Credit Union, — Ohio App. 3d —, 2007 Ohio 5902, — N.E. 2d —, 2007 Ohio App. LEXIS 5178 (Nov. 5, 2007).

Attorney who represents a client on a contingency basis, yet is discharged prior to completing the attorney's service, does not have a cause of action for a fee recovery in quantum meruit until the contingency has occurred, so the discharged attorney is not compensated if the client recovers nothing. Doellman v. Midfirst Credit Union, — Ohio App. 3d —, 2007 Ohio 5902, — N.E. 2d —, 2007 Ohio App. LEXIS 5178 (Nov. 5, 2007).

Division of fees

Probate court did not abuse its discretion in awarding attorney fees in the amount of $100,000 and directing that they should be apportioned $25,000 to the new attorney and $75,000 to the former attorney. The new attorney failed to demonstrate how the probate court erred, especially since he failed to offer any evidence beyond his original contingency contract to support his claim for attorney fees, and the probate

court's ultimate decision regarding the award of attorney fees was supported by the record and the probate court properly considered the totality of the circumstances involved before entering judgment. In re Stine, — Ohio App. 3d —, 2006 Ohio 6687, — N.E. 2d —, 2006 Ohio App. LEXIS 6567 (Dec. 18, 2006).

Excessive fee

Trial court's enhancement of an award of attorney fees to a boat purchaser pursuant to RC § 1345.09(F) was an abuse of discretion, as the trial court gave great weight to the fact that the purchaser's counsel took a "risk" by entering into a contingency fee agreement, which "risk" was not supported by the record. The trial court's determination to double the amount that was deemed a risk for purposes of calculating the total attorney fee award was not reasonable under Ohio Code Prof. Resp. DR 2-106(B)(8). Borror v. Marinemax of Ohio, Inc., — Ohio App. 3d —, 2007 Ohio 562, — N.E. 2d —, 2007 Ohio App. LEXIS 525 (Feb. 9, 2007).

Fee amount

Although a trial court properly determined that automobile owners were entitled to an award of attorney fees under Ohio Rev. Code Ann. § 1345.09(F)(2) upon judgment being entered on their claims against an automobile restorer under the Ohio Consumer Sales Practices Act, Ohio Rev. Code Ann. § 1345.01 et seq., the trial court erred in awarding the fees incurred on more than claims under the Act, as other claims initially asserted had been dismissed by the owners prior to the trial. The trial court failed to indicate which factors under Ohio Code Prof. Resp. DR 2-106(B) it considered in making its award, which was necessary for proper appellate review. Grieselding v. Krischak, — Ohio App. 3d —, 2007 Ohio 2668, — N.E. 2d —, 2007 Ohio App. LEXIS 2489 (June 1, 2007).

Reasonable fee amount

Trial court erred in determining a reasonable amount of attorneys fees arising from bailees' refusal to allow a bailor to complete the removal of its property stored by the bailees because the trial court did not make an explicit finding of "bad faith" and simply accepted the amount of attorneys fees calculated by the bailor's trial counsel without ascertaining the reasonableness of the amount of those fees by addressing the factors in former Ohio Code Prof. Resp. DR 2-106. Camp-Out, Inc. v. Adkins, — Ohio App. 3d —, 2007 Ohio 3946, — N.E. 2d —, 2007 Ohio App. LEXIS 3613 (Aug. 3, 2007).

Reasonable fee amount in probate

Probate court's determination regarding the fiduciary nature of certain attorney services was not unreasonable or arbitrary and it also did not err in determining that the attorney was entitled to compensation for the 42.5 hours of routine fiduciary services at a reduced rate of $75 per hour. The probate court's determination regarding the unproductive nature of certain services was not unreasonable or arbitrary. It did not err determining that the attorney was entitled to compensation for the 32.4 hours of unproductive time at a reduced rate of $60 per hour. Re Estate of Brady, — Ohio App. 3d —, 2007 Ohio 1005, — N.E. 2d —, 2007 Ohio App. LEXIS 933 (Mar. 8, 2007).

Probate court's attorney fee award to a litigation attorney who defended a decedent's estate, as well as the estate executor and attorney, was reasonable pursuant to the factors under Ohio Code Prof. Resp. DR 2-106 and Ohio Superintendence R. 71, where the services were clearly delineated and clearly benefited the estate. Services that were for the exclusive personal benefit of the executor and the estate attorney were excluded for purposes of reimbursement. In re Estate of Fouras, — Ohio App. 3d —, 2006 Ohio 3461, — N.E. 2d —, 2006 Ohio App. LEXIS 3389 (July 3, 2006).

Trial court's fee award to a union in an action to collect a debt owed by a union member for violations of union documents was not an abuse its discretion where the trial court properly considered the factors under Ohio Code Prof. Resp. DR 2-106 in reaching the reasonable amount of fees in the circumstances. The amount sought was not large, the questions presented were not difficult, and the trial court reduced to one-quarter the amount originally sought for a fee award. IBEW, Local Union No. 8 v. Hyder, — Ohio App. 3d —, 2006 Ohio 3177, — N.E. 2d —, 2006 Ohio App. LEXIS 3096 (June 23, 2006).

Although an attorney who unsuccessfully defended an executor in a will contest submitted a very detailed statement of the services rendered by himself and his associate, the probate court denied the fee request and held that it was unreasonable; however, as the probate court failed to provide any explanation as to what factors under Ohio Code Prof. Resp. DR 2-106 and Ohio Superintendence R. 71(A) were not met, a remand for further consideration and explanation was required. Estate of Szczotka, 166 Ohio App. 3d 124, 2006 Ohio 1449, 849 N.E. 2d 302, 2006 Ohio App. LEXIS 1283 (Mar. 24, 2006).

Suspension

Attorney's license to practice law was suspended for one year, stayed for six months on conditions of his repaying his client, based on findings of misconduct, including the neglect of a client's case and failure to account for unearned fees. The attorney violated former Ohio Code Prof. Resp. 6-101(A)(3), 7- 101(A)(2), and 9-102(B)(4) by abandoning his client and ignoring requests for her file and an accounting. Cuyahoga County Bar Ass'n v. Peto, — Ohio St. 3d —, 2007 Ohio 5250, — N.E. 2d —, 2007 Ohio LEXIS 2520 (Oct. 10, 2007).

RULE 1.6: CONFIDENTIALITY OF INFORMATION

(a) A lawyer shall not reveal information relating to the representation of a client, including information protected by the attorney-client privilege under applicable law, unless the client gives *informed consent*, the disclosure is impliedly authorized in order to carry out the representation, or the disclosure is permitted by division (b) or required by division (c) of this rule.

(b) A lawyer may reveal information relating to the representation of a client, including information protected by the attorney-client privilege under applicable law, to the extent the lawyer *reasonably* believes necessary for any of the following purposes:

(1) to prevent reasonably certain death or substantial bodily harm;

(2) to prevent the commission of a crime by the client or other person;

(3) to mitigate *substantial* injury to the financial interests or property of another that has resulted from the client's commission of an *illegal* or *fraudulent* act, in furtherance of which the client has used the lawyer's services;

(4) to secure legal advice about the lawyer's compliance with these rules;

(5) to establish a claim or defense on behalf of the lawyer in a controversy between the lawyer and the client, to establish a defense to a criminal charge or civil claim against the lawyer based upon conduct in which the client was involved, or to respond to allegations in any proceeding, including any disciplinary matter, concerning the lawyer's representation of the client;

(6) to comply with other law or a court order.

(c) A lawyer shall reveal information relating to the representation of a client, including information protected by the attorney-client privilege under applicable law, to the extent the lawyer *reasonably believes* necessary to comply with Rule 3.3 or 4.1.

RULE 1.7: CONFLICT OF INTEREST: CURRENT CLIENTS

(a) A lawyer's acceptance or continuation of representation of a client creates a conflict of interest if either of the following applies:

(1) the representation of that client will be directly adverse to another current client;

(2) there is a *substantial* risk that the lawyer's ability to consider, recommend, or carry out an appropriate course of action for that client will be materially limited by the lawyer's responsibilities to another client, a former client, or a third person or by the lawyer's own personal interests.

(b) A lawyer shall not accept or continue the representation of a client if a conflict of interest would be created pursuant to division (a) of this rule, unless all of the following apply:

(1) the lawyer will be able to provide competent and diligent representation to each affected client;

(2) each affected client gives *informed consent, confirmed in writing*;

(3) the representation is not precluded by division (c) of this rule.

(c) Even if each affected client consents, the lawyer shall not accept or continue the representation if either of the following applies:

(1) the representation is prohibited by law;

(2) the representation would involve the assertion of a claim by one client against another client represented by the lawyer in the same proceeding.

DECISIONS UNDER FORMER LAW

ANALYSIS

Conflict

Conflict

Children who were not parties to a custody battle between their parents were not entitled to private counsel to represent their interests, and the payment by a third party of fees of an attorney engaged to represent the interests of the children created a conflict and was violative of Ohio Code Prof. Resp. DR 7-101 and 5-107(A)(1). Curie v. Curie, — Ohio App. 3d —, 2006 Ohio 6098, — N.E. 2d —, 2006 Ohio App. LEXIS 6058 (Nov. 17, 2006).

RULE 1.8: CONFLICT OF INTEREST: CURRENT CLIENTS: SPECIFIC RULES

(a) A lawyer shall not enter into a business transaction with a client or *knowingly* acquire an ownership, possessory, security, or other pecuniary interest adverse to a client unless all of the following apply:

(1) the transaction and terms on which the lawyer acquires the interest are fair and *reasonable* to the client and are fully disclosed to the client in writing in a manner that can be *reasonably* understood by the client;

(2) the client is advised in writing of the desirability of seeking and is given a *reasonable* opportunity to seek the advice of independent legal counsel on the transaction;

(3) the client gives *informed consent*, in a *writing* signed by the client, to the essential terms of the transaction and the lawyer's role in the transaction, including whether the lawyer is representing the client in the transaction.

(b) Except as permitted or required by these rules, a lawyer shall not use information relating to representation of a client to the disadvantage of the client unless the client gives informed consent.

(c) A lawyer shall not solicit any *substantial* gift from a client. A lawyer shall not prepare on behalf of a client an instrument giving the lawyer, the lawyer's *partner*, associate, paralegal, law clerk, or other employee of the lawyer's *firm*, a lawyer acting "of counsel" in the lawyer's *firm*, or a person related to the lawyer any gift unless the lawyer or other recipient of the gift is related to the client. For purposes of division (c) of this rule:

(1) "person related to the lawyer" includes a spouse, child, grandchild, parent, grandparent, sibling, or other relative or individual with whom the lawyer or the client maintains a close, familial relationship;

(2) "gift" includes a testamentary gift.

(d) Prior to the conclusion of representation of a client, a lawyer shall not make or negotiate an agreement giving the lawyer literary or media rights to a portrayal or account based in substantial part on information relating to the representation.

(e) A lawyer shall not provide financial assistance to a client in connection with pending or contemplated litigation, except that a lawyer may do either of the following:

(1) a lawyer may advance court costs and expenses of litigation, the repayment of which may be contingent on the outcome of the matter;

(2) a lawyer representing an indigent client may pay court costs and expenses of litigation on behalf of the client.

(f) A lawyer shall not accept compensation for representing a client from someone other than the client unless divisions (f)(1) to (3) and, if applicable, division (f)(4) apply:

(1) the client gives *informed consent*;

(2) there is no interference with the lawyer's independence of professional judgment or with the client-lawyer relationship;

(3) information relating to representation of a client is protected as required by Rule 1.6;

(4) if the lawyer is compensated by an insurer to represent an insured, the lawyer delivers a copy of the following Statement of Insured Client's Rights to the client in person at the first meeting or by mail within ten days after the lawyer receives notice of retention by the insurer:

STATEMENT OF INSURED CLIENT'S RIGHTS

An insurance company has retained a lawyer to defend a lawsuit or claim against you. This Statement of Insured Client's Rights is being given to you to assure that you are aware of your rights regarding your legal representation.

(1) Your Lawyer: Your lawyer has been retained by the insurance company under the terms of your policy. If you have questions about the selection of the lawyer, you should discuss the matter with the insurance company or the lawyer.

(2) Directing the Lawyer: Your policy may provide that the insurance company can reasonably control the defense of the lawsuit. In addition, your insurance company may establish guidelines governing how lawyers are to proceed in defending you—guidelines that you are entitled to know. However, the lawyer cannot act on the insurance company's instructions when they are contrary to your interest.

(3) Communications: Your lawyer should keep you informed about your case and respond to your reasonable requests for information.

(4) Confidentiality: Lawyers have a duty to keep secret the confidential information a client provides, subject to limited exceptions. However, the lawyer chosen to represent you also may have duty to share with the insurance company information relating to the defense or settlement of the claim. Whenever a waiver of lawyer-client confidentiality is needed, your lawyer has a duty to consult with you and obtain your informed consent.

(5) Release of Information for Audits: Some insurance companies retain auditing companies to review the billing and files of the lawyers they hire to represent policyholders. If the lawyer believes an audit, bill review, or other action initiated by the insurance company may release confidential information in a manner that may be contrary to your interest, the lawyer must advise you regarding the matter and provide an explanation of the purpose of the audit and the procedure involved. Your written consent must be given in order for an audit to be conducted. If you withhold your consent, the audit shall not be conducted.

(6) Conflicts of Interest: The lawyer is responsible for identifying conflicts of interest and advising you of them. If at any time you have a concern about a conflict of interest in your case, you should discuss your concern with the lawyer. If a conflict of interest exists that cannot be resolved, the insurance company may be required to provide you with another lawyer.

(7) Settlement: Many insurance policies state that the insurance company alone may make a decision regarding settlement of a claim. Some policies, however, require your consent. You should discuss with your lawyer your rights under the policy regarding settlement. No settlement requiring you to pay money in excess of your policy limits can be reached without your agreement.

(8) Fees and Costs: As provided in your insurance policy, the insurance company usually pays all of the fees and costs of defending the claim. If you are responsible for paying the lawyer any fees and costs, your lawyer must promptly inform you of that.

(9) Hiring your own Lawyer: The lawyer hired by the insurance company is only representing you in defend-

ing the claim brought against you. If you desire to pursue a claim against someone, you will need to hire your own lawyer. You may also wish to hire your own lawyer if there is a risk that there might be a judgment entered against you for more than the amount of your insurance. Your lawyer has a duty to inform you of this risk and other reasonably foreseeable adverse results.

(g) A lawyer who represents two or more clients shall not participate in making an aggregate settlement of the claims of or against the clients, or in a criminal case an aggregated agreement as to guilty or nolo contendere pleas, unless the settlement or agreement is subject to court approval or each client gives informed consent, in a *writing* signed by the client. The lawyer's disclosure shall include the existence and nature of all the claims or pleas involved and of the participation of each person in the settlement or agreement.

(h) A lawyer shall not do any of the following:

(1) make an agreement prospectively limiting the lawyer's liability to a client for malpractice or requiring arbitration of a claim against the lawyer unless the client is independently represented in making the agreement;

(2) settle a claim or potential claim for such liability unless all of the following apply:

(i) the settlement is not unconscionable, inequitable, or unfair;

(ii) the client or former client is advised in *writing* of the desirability of seeking and is given a *reasonable* opportunity to seek the advice of independent legal counsel in connection therewith;

(iii) the client or former client gives *informed consent*.

(i) A lawyer shall not acquire a proprietary interest in the cause of action or subject matter of litigation the lawyer is conducting for a client, except that the lawyer may do either of the following:

(1) acquire a lien authorized by law to secure the lawyer's fee or expenses;

(2) contract with a client for a *reasonable* contingent fee in a civil case.

(j) A lawyer shall not solicit or engage in sexual activity with a client unless a consensual sexual relationship existed between them when the client-lawyer relationship commenced.

(k) While lawyers are associated in a *firm*, a prohibition in divisions (a) to (i) of this rule that applies to any one of them shall apply to all of them.

DECISIONS UNDER FORMER LAW

Analysis

Attorney as witness
Attorney-client relationship

Attorney as witness

Trial court properly disqualified an attorney from continuing to represent the attorney's clients/co-defendants in litigation alleging the attorney's fraudulent statements on behalf of the attorney's clients/co-defendants because (1) the contractor bringing suit said the contractor intended to call the attorney to testify about allegations of fraud, (2) the attorney's testimony could be prejudicial to the attorney's clients/co-defendants, (3) the attorney's affidavit that the clients/co-defendants

did not intend to call the attorney to testify was irrelevant, because the threshold inquiry was whether the attorney ought to be called to testify, and (4) none of the exceptions in Ohio Code Prof. Resp. DR 5-101(B)(4), allowing the attorney to testify and represent the clients/co-defendants, applied. Quigley v. Telsat Inc., — Ohio App. 3d —, 2007 Ohio 2884, — N.E. 2d —, 2007 Ohio App. LEXIS 2684 (June 13, 2007).

Attorney-client relationship

Children who were not parties to a custody battle between their parents were not entitled to private counsel to represent their interests, and the payment by a third party of fees of an attorney engaged to represent the interests of the children created a conflict and was violative of Ohio Code Prof. Resp. DR 7-101 and 5-107(A)(1). Curie v. Curie, — Ohio App. 3d —, 2006 Ohio 6098, — N.E. 2d —, 2006 Ohio App. LEXIS 6058 (Nov. 17, 2006).

RULE 1.9: DUTIES TO FORMER CLIENTS

(a) Unless the former client gives *informed consent, confirmed in writing*, a lawyer who has formerly represented a client in a matter shall not thereafter represent another person in the same or a *substantially related matter* in which that person's interests are materially adverse to the interests of the former client.

(b) Unless the former client gives *informed consent, confirmed in writing*, a lawyer shall not *knowingly* represent a person in the same or a *substantially related matter* in which a *firm* with which the lawyer formerly was associated had previously represented a client where both of the following apply:

(1) the interests of the client are materially adverse to that person;

(2) the lawyer had acquired information about the client that is protected by Rules 1.6 and 1.9(c) and material to the matter.

(c) A lawyer who has formerly represented a client in a matter or whose present or former *firm* has formerly represented a client in a matter shall not thereafter do either of the following:

(1) use information relating to the representation to the disadvantage of the former client except as these rules would permit or require with respect to a client or when the information has become generally *known*;

(2) reveal information relating to the representation except as these rules would permit or require with respect to a client.

DECISIONS UNDER FORMER LAW

Analysis

Disqualification

Disqualification

Attorney and her new law firm were properly disqualified pursuant to ProfCondR 1.9 and 1.10 where the presumption of shared confidences arising from her work at the previous law firm was not rebutted: Litig. Mgmt. v. Bourgeois, 182 Ohio App. 3d 742, 2009 Ohio 2266, 915 N.E.2d 342, 2009 Ohio App. LEXIS 1913 (2009).

RULE 1.10: IMPUTATION OF CONFLICTS OF INTEREST: GENERAL RULE

(a) While lawyers are associated in a *firm*, none of them shall represent a client when the lawyer *knows or reasonably should know* that any one of them practicing alone would be prohibited from doing so by Rule 1.7 or 1.9, unless the prohibition is based on a personal interest of the prohibited lawyer and does not present a significant risk of materially limiting the representation of the client by the remaining lawyers in the *firm*.

(b) When a lawyer is no longer associated with a *firm*, no lawyer in that *firm* shall thereafter represent a person with interests materially adverse to those of a client represented by the formerly associated lawyer and not currently represented by the *firm*, if the lawyer knows or *reasonably should know* that either of the following applies:

(1) the formerly associated lawyer represented the client in the same or a substantially related matter;

(2) any lawyer remaining in the *firm* has information protected by Rules 1.6 and 1.9(c) that is material to the matter.

(c) When a lawyer has had *substantial* responsibility in a matter for a former client and becomes associated with a new *firm*, no lawyer in the new *firm* shall *knowingly* represent, in the same matter, a person whose interests are materially adverse to the interests of the former client.

(d) In circumstances other than those covered by Rule 1.10(c), when a lawyer becomes associated with a new *firm*, no lawyer in the new *firm* shall *knowingly* represent a person in a matter in which the lawyer is personally disqualified under Rule 1.9 unless both of the following apply:

(1) the new *firm* timely screens the personally disqualified lawyer from any participation in the matter and that lawyer is apportioned no part of the fee from that matter;

(2) *written* notice is given as soon as practicable to any affected former client.

(e) A disqualification required by this rule may be waived by the affected client under the conditions stated in Rule 1.7.

(f) The disqualification of lawyers associated in a *firm* with former or current government lawyers is governed by Rule 1.11.

NOTES TO DECISIONS

ANALYSIS

Disqualification

Disqualification

Attorney and her new law firm were properly disqualified pursuant to ProfCondR 1.9 and 1.10 where the presumption of shared confidences arising from her work at the previous law firm was not rebutted: Litig. Mgmt. v. Bourgeois, 182 Ohio App. 3d 742, 2009 Ohio 2266, 915 N.E.2d 342, 2009 Ohio App. LEXIS 1913 (2009).

RULE 1.11: SPECIAL CONFLICTS OF INTEREST FOR FORMER AND CURRENT GOVERNMENT OFFICERS AND EMPLOYEES

(a) A lawyer who has formerly served as a public officer or employee of the government shall comply with both of the following:

(1) all applicable laws and Rule 1.9(c) regarding conflicts of interest;

(2) not otherwise represent a client in connection with a matter in which the lawyer participated personally and *substantially* as a public officer or employee, unless the appropriate government agency gives its *informed consent, confirmed in writing,* to the representation.

(b) When a lawyer is disqualified from representation under division (a), no lawyer in a *firm* with which that lawyer is associated may *knowingly* undertake or continue representation in such a matter unless both of the following apply:

(1) the disqualified lawyer is timely *screened* from any participation in the matter and is apportioned no part of the fee therefrom;

(2) *written* notice is given as soon as practicable to the appropriate government agency to enable it to ascertain compliance with the provisions of this rule.

(c) Except as law may otherwise expressly permit, a lawyer having information that the lawyer *knows* is confidential government information about a person acquired when the lawyer was a public officer or employee, may not represent a private client whose interests are adverse to that person in a matter in which the information could be used to the material disadvantage of that person. As used in this rule, the term "confidential government information" means information that has been obtained under governmental authority and that, at the time this rule is applied, the government is prohibited by law from disclosing to the public or has a legal privilege not to disclose and that is not otherwise available to the public. A *firm* with which that lawyer is associated may undertake or continue representation in the matter only if the disqualified lawyer is timely *screened* from any participation in the matter and is apportioned no part of the fee therefrom.

(d) Except as law may otherwise expressly permit, a lawyer currently serving as a public officer or employee shall comply with both of the following:

(1) Rules 1.7 and 1.9;

(2) shall not do either of the following:

(i) participate in a matter in which the lawyer participated personally and *substantially* while in private practice or nongovernmental employment, unless the appropriate government agency gives its informed consent, confirmed in writing;

(ii) negotiate for private employment with any person who is involved as a party or as lawyer for a party in a matter in which the lawyer is participating personally and *substantially*, except that a lawyer serving as a law clerk to a judge, other adjudicative officer or arbitrator may negotiate for private employment as permitted by Rule 1.12(b) and subject to the conditions stated in Rule 1.12(b).

(e) As used in this rule, the term "matter" includes both of the following:

(1) any judicial or other proceeding, application, request for a ruling or other determination, contract, claim, controversy, investigation, charge, accusation, arrest, or other particular matter involving a specific party or parties;

(2) any other matter covered by the conflict of interest rules of the appropriate government agency.

RULE 1.12: FORMER JUDGE, ARBITRATOR, MEDIATOR, OR OTHER THIRD-PARTY NEUTRAL

(a) Except as stated in division (d), a lawyer shall not represent anyone in connection with a matter in which the lawyer participated personally and substantially as a judge or other adjudicative officer or law clerk to such a person or as an arbitrator, mediator, or other third-party neutral, unless all parties to the proceeding give informed consent, confirmed in writing.

(b) A lawyer shall not negotiate for employment with any person who is involved as a party or as lawyer for a party in a matter in which the lawyer is participating personally and substantially as a judge or other adjudicative officer or as an arbitrator, mediator, or other third-party neutral. A lawyer serving as a law clerk to a judge or other adjudicative officer may negotiate for employment with a party or lawyer involved in a matter in which the clerk is participating personally and substantially, but only after the lawyer has notified the judge or other adjudicative officer.

(c) If a lawyer is disqualified by division (a), no lawyer in a firm with which that lawyer is associated may knowingly undertake or continue representation in the matter unless both of the following apply:

(1) the disqualified lawyer is timely screened from any participation in the matter and is apportioned no part of the fee therefrom;

(2) written notice is promptly given to the parties and any appropriate tribunal to enable them to ascertain compliance with the provisions of this rule.

(d) An arbitrator selected as a partisan of a party in a multimember arbitration panel is not prohibited from subsequently representing that party.

RULE 1.13: ORGANIZATION AS CLIENT

(a) A lawyer employed or retained by an organization represents the organization acting through its constituents. A lawyer employed or retained by an organization owes allegiance to the organization and not to any constituent or other person connected with the organization. The constituents of an organization include its owners and its duly authorized officers, directors, trustees, and employees.

(b) If a lawyer for an organization *knows or reasonably should know* that its constituent's action, intended action, or refusal to act (1) violates a legal obligation to the organization, or (2) is a violation of law that *reasonably* might be imputed to the organization and that is likely to result in *substantial* injury to the organization, then the lawyer shall proceed as is necessary in the best interest of the organization. When it is necessary to enable the organization to address the matter in a timely and appropriate manner, the lawyer shall refer the matter to higher authority, including, if warranted by the circumstances, the highest authority that can act on behalf of the organization under applicable law.

(c) The discretion or duty of a lawyer for an organization to reveal information relating to the representation outside the organization is governed by Rule 1.6(b) and (c).

(d) In dealing with an organization's directors, offic-ers, employees, members, shareholders, or other constituents, a lawyer shall explain the identity of the client when the lawyer *knows or reasonably should know* that the organization's interests are adverse to those of the constituents with whom the lawyer is dealing.

(e) A lawyer representing an organization may also represent any of its directors, officers, employees, members, shareholders, or other constituents, subject to the provisions of Rule 1.7. If the organization's *written* consent to the dual representation is required by Rule 1.7, the consent shall be given by an appropriate official of the organization, other than the individual who is to be represented, or by the shareholders.

RULE 1.14: CLIENT WITH DIMINISHED CAPACITY

(a) When a client's capacity to make adequately considered decisions in connection with a representation is diminished, whether because of minority, mental impairment or for some other reason, the lawyer shall, as far as *reasonably* possible, maintain a normal client-lawyer relationship with the client.

(b) When the lawyer *reasonably believes* that the client has diminished capacity, is at risk of *substantial* physical, financial, or other harm unless action is taken, and cannot adequately act in the client's own interest, the lawyer may take *reasonably* necessary protective action, including consulting with individuals or entities that have the ability to take action to protect the client and, in appropriate cases, seeking the appointment of a guardian *ad litem*, conservator, or guardian.

(c) Information relating to the representation of a client with diminished capacity is protected by Rule 1.6. When taking protective action pursuant to division (b), the lawyer is impliedly authorized under Rule 1.6(a) to reveal information about the client, but only to the extent *reasonably* necessary to protect the client's interests.

RULE 1.15: SAFEKEEPING FUNDS AND PROPERTY

(a) A lawyer shall hold property of clients or third persons that is in a lawyer's possession in connection with a representation separate from the lawyer's own property. Funds shall be kept in a separate interest-bearing account in a financial institution authorized to do business in Ohio and maintained in the state where the lawyer's office is situated. The account shall be designated as a "client trust account," "IOLTA account," or with a clearly identifiable fiduciary title. Other property shall be identified as such and appropriately safeguarded. Records of such account funds and other property shall be kept by the lawyer and shall be preserved for a period of seven years after termination of the representation or the appropriate disbursement of such funds or property, whichever comes first. For other property, the lawyer shall maintain a record that identifies the property, the date received, the person on whose behalf the property was held, and the date of distribution. For funds, the lawyer shall do all of the following:

(1) maintain a copy of the fee agreement with each client;

(2) maintain a record for each client on whose behalf funds are held that sets forth all of the following:

(i) the name of the client;

(ii) the date, amount, and source of all funds received on behalf of such client;

(iii) the date, amount, payee, and purpose of each disbursement made on behalf of such client;

(iv) the current balance for such client.

(3) maintain a record for each bank account that sets forth all of the following:

(i) the name of such account;

(ii) the date, amount, and client affected by each credit and debit;

(iii) the balance in the account.

(4) maintain all bank statements, deposit slips, and cancelled checks, if provided by the bank, for each bank account;

(5) perform and retain a monthly reconciliation of the items contained in divisions (a)(2), (3), and (4) of this rule.

(b) A lawyer may deposit the lawyer's own funds in a client trust account for the sole purpose of paying or obtaining a waiver of bank service charges on that account, but only in an amount necessary for that purpose.

(c) A lawyer shall deposit into a client trust account legal fees and expenses that have been paid in advance, to be withdrawn by the lawyer only as fees are earned or expenses incurred.

(d) Upon receiving funds or other property in which a client or third person has a lawful interest, a lawyer shall promptly notify the client or third person. For purposes of this rule, the third person's interest shall be one of which the lawyer has actual knowledge and shall be limited to a statutory lien, a final judgment addressing disposition of the funds or property, or a written agreement by the client or the lawyer on behalf of the client guaranteeing payment from the specific funds or property. Except as stated in this rule or otherwise permitted by law or by agreement with the client or a third person, *confirmed in writing*, a lawyer shall promptly deliver to the client or third person any funds or other property that the client or third person is entitled to receive. Upon request by the client or third person, the lawyer shall promptly render a full accounting regarding such funds or other property.

(e) When in the course of representation a lawyer is in possession of funds or other property in which two or more persons, one of whom may be the lawyer, claim interests, the lawyer shall hold the funds or other property pursuant to division (a) of this rule until the dispute is resolved. The lawyer shall promptly distribute all portions of the funds or other property as to which the interests are not in dispute.

(f) Upon dissolution of any *law firm*, the former partners, managing partners, or supervisory lawyers shall promptly account for all client funds and shall make appropriate arrangements for one of them to maintain all records generated under division (a) of this rule.

(g) A lawyer, *law firm*, or estate of a deceased lawyer who sells a law practice shall account for and transfer all funds held pursuant to this rule to the lawyer or law firm purchasing the law practice at the time client files are transferred.

(h) A lawyer, a lawyer in the lawyer's *firm*, or a *firm* that owns an interest in a business that provides a law-related service shall:

(1) maintain funds of clients or third persons that cannot earn any net income for the clients or third persons in an interest-bearing trust account that is established in an eligible depository institution as required by sections 3953.231, 4705.09, and 4705.10 of the Revised Code or any rules adopted by the Ohio Legal Assistance Foundation pursuant to section 120.52 of the Revised Code.

(2) notify the Ohio Legal Assistance Foundation, in a manner required by rules adopted by the Ohio Legal Assistance Foundation pursuant to section 120.52 of the Revised Code, of the existence of an interest-bearing trust account;

(3) comply with the reporting requirement contained in Gov. Bar R. VI, Section 1(F).

DECISIONS UNDER FORMER LAW

ANALYSIS

Attorney-client relationship
Reprimand
Return of funds
Suspension

Attorney-client relationship

Court of appeals erred in granting board of election employees' request for a writ of mandamus to compel the county prosecutor to turn over his files with respect to a general election and a recount thereof, which records were to be used by the employees in defending themselves against criminal charges arising from the election, as they did not show that they were entitled to the relief under Ohio Rev. Code Ann. § 2731.03 because their subpoena in the criminal action for the records had been quashed by the exercise of the trial court's discretion; further, the employees had an adequate remedy at law through discovery in the criminal proceeding or a separate action based on their reliance of the election board's waiver of the attorney-client privilege pursuant to Ohio Code Prof. Resp. DR 9-102(B)(4) (now at Ohio R. Prof. Conduct 1.15), as the prosecutor had been the board's legal advisor under Ohio Rev. Code Ann. § 309.09(A). State Ex Rel. Dreamer v. Mason, 115 Ohio St. 3d 190, 2007 Ohio 4789, 874 N.E. 2d 510, 2007 Ohio LEXIS 2216 (Sept. 20, 2007).

Reprimand

Attorney was publicly reprimanded for violating Ohio Code Prof. Resp. DR 9-102(A) because the attorney, inter alia, authorized an associate attorney not listed as a signatory to write checks from an Interest on Lawyer Trust Account (IOLTA) in the attorney's name and failed to keep track of deposits and withdrawals from the IOLTA; in mitigation, the attorney had an accountant audit the IOLTA, reconciled all the IOLTA irregularities, and stopped his associate's use of the account. Medina County Bar Ass'n v. Piszczek, 115 Ohio St. 3d 228, 2007 Ohio 4946, 874 N.E. 2d 783, 2007 Ohio LEXIS 2224 (Sept. 27, 2007).

Return of funds

Based on an attorney's representation of friends and a friend's son while he was indefinitely suspended from the practice of law, his failure to inform his clients of his status, and his failure to refund money to a client upon her request, he violated Ohio Code Prof. Resp. DR 1-102(A)(4), 3-101(B), and 9-102(B)(4); as he had a prior disciplinary history, he was permanently disbarred from practicing law. Cleveland Bar Ass'n v. Rubino, 115 Ohio St. 3d 199, 2007 Ohio 4797, 874 N.E. 2d 519, 2007 Ohio LEXIS 2214 (Sept. 20, 2007).

Suspension

Attorney was suspended from the practice of law for six months based on findings that he neglected a client's case, attempted to cover up the neglect, failed to return the client's file on request, and failed to cooperate in the ensuing disciplinary investigation, in violation of former Ohio Code Prof. Resp. 9-102(B)(4), 6-101(A)(3), and 1-102(A)(4), and Ohio Sup. Ct. R. Gov't Bar V(4)(G), because the record amply justified the conclusions that the attorney neglected to appropriately advise his client of the proceedings in its case and then fabricated one or more letters to conceal his neglect. The mitigating factors did not outweigh the aggravating effect of having submitted false evidence and having acted out of self-interest in trying to cover up his misconduct. Disciplinary Counsel v. Broeren, — Ohio St. 3d —, 2007 Ohio 5251, — N.E. 2d —, 2007 Ohio LEXIS 2525 (Oct. 10, 2007).

RULE 1.16: DECLINING OR TERMINATING REPRESENTATION

(a) Subject to divisions (c), (d), and (e) of this rule, a lawyer shall not represent a client or, where representation has commenced, shall withdraw from the representation of a client if any of the following applies:

(1) the representation will result in violation of the Ohio Rules of Professional Conduct or other law;

(2) the lawyer's physical or mental condition materially impairs the lawyer's ability to represent the client;

(3) the lawyer is discharged.

(b) Subject to divisions (c), (d), and (e) of this rule, a lawyer may withdraw from the representation of a client if any of the following applies:

(1) withdrawal can be accomplished without material adverse effect on the interests of the client;

(2) the client persists in a course of action involving the lawyer's services that the lawyer *reasonably believes* is *illegal or fraudulent*;

(3) the client has used the lawyer's services to perpetrate a crime or *fraud*;

(4) the client insists upon taking action that the lawyer considers repugnant or with which the lawyer has a fundamental disagreement;

(5) the client fails *substantially* to fulfill an obligation, financial or otherwise, to the lawyer regarding the lawyer's services and has been given *reasonable* warning that the lawyer will withdraw unless the obligation is fulfilled;

(6) the representation will result in an unreasonable financial burden on the lawyer or has been rendered unreasonably difficult by the client;

(7) the client gives *informed consent* to termination of the representation;

(8) the lawyer sells the law practice in accordance with Rule 1.17;

(9) other good cause for withdrawal exists.

(c) If permission for withdrawal from employment is required by the rules of a *tribunal*, a lawyer shall not withdraw from employment in a proceeding before that tribunal without its permission.

(d) As part of the termination of representation, a lawyer shall take steps, to the extent *reasonably* prac-

ticable, to protect a client's interest. The steps include giving due notice to the client, allowing *reasonable* time for employment of other counsel, delivering to the client all papers and property to which the client is entitled, and complying with applicable laws and rules. Client papers and property shall be promptly delivered to the client. "Client papers and property" may include correspondence, pleadings, deposition transcripts, exhibits, physical evidence, expert reports, and other items *reasonably* necessary to the client's representation.

(e) A lawyer who withdraws from employment shall refund promptly any part of a fee paid in advance that has not been earned, except when withdrawal is pursuant to Rule 1.17.

DECISIONS UNDER FORMER LAW

ANALYSIS

Withdrawal of counsel

Withdrawal of counsel

In a permanent custody matter by a county social service agency, a mother received ineffective assistance of counsel when the trial court granted counsel's oral motion to withdraw at the hearings without prior notice to the mother; such violated Cuyahoga County, Ohio, Ct. C.P. Juv. Div. R. 7 and Ohio Code Prof. Resp. DR 2-110(A)(2) (now at Ohio Code Prof. Conduct 1.16), and she was prejudiced thereby where she had no one to represent her at the hearings and to present evidence on her behalf. In re J.Z., — Ohio App. 3d —, 2007 Ohio 5334, — N.E. 2d —, 2007 Ohio App. LEXIS 4670 (Oct. 4, 2007).

RULE 1.17: SALE OF LAW PRACTICE

(a) Subject to the provisions of this rule, a lawyer or *law firm* may sell or purchase a law practice, including the good will of the practice. The law practice shall be sold in its entirety, except where a conflict of interest is present that prevents the transfer of representation of a client or class of clients. This rule shall not permit the sale or purchase of a law practice where the purchasing lawyer is buying the practice for the sole or primary purpose of reselling the practice to another lawyer or *law firm*.

(b) As used in this rule:

(1) "Purchasing lawyer" means either an individual lawyer or a *law firm*;

(2) "Selling lawyer" means an individual lawyer, a *law firm*, the estate of a deceased lawyer, or the representatives of a disabled or disappeared lawyer.

(c) The selling lawyer and the prospective purchasing lawyer may engage in general discussions regarding the possible sale of a law practice. Before the selling lawyer may provide the prospective purchasing lawyer with information relative to client representation or confidential material contained in client files, the selling lawyer shall require the prospective purchasing lawyer to execute a confidentiality agreement. The confidentiality agreement shall bind the prospective purchasing lawyer to preserve information relating to the representation of the clients of the selling lawyer, consistent with Rule 1.6, as if those clients were clients of the prospective purchasing lawyer.

(d) The selling lawyer and the purchasing lawyer may negotiate the terms of the sale of a law practice, subject to all of the following:

(1) The sale agreement shall include a statement by selling lawyer and purchasing lawyer that the purchasing lawyer is purchasing the law practice in good faith and with the intention of delivering legal services to clients of the selling lawyer and others in need of legal services.

(2) The sale agreement shall provide that the purchasing lawyer will honor any fee agreements between the selling lawyer and the clients of the selling lawyer relative to legal representation that is ongoing at the time of the sale. The purchasing lawyer may negotiate fees with clients of the selling lawyer for legal representation that is commenced after the date of the sale.

(3) The sale agreement may include terms that reasonably limit the ability of the selling lawyer to reenter the practice of law, including, but not limited to, the ability of the selling lawyer to reenter the practice of law for a specific period of time or to practice in a specific geographic area. The sale agreement shall not include terms limiting the ability of the selling lawyer to practice law or reenter the practice of law if the selling lawyer is selling his or her law practice to enter academic, government, or public service or to serve as in-house counsel to a business.

(e) Prior to completing the sale, the selling lawyer and purchasing lawyer shall provide *written* notice of the sale to the clients of the selling lawyer. For purposes of this rule, clients of the selling lawyer include all current clients of the selling lawyer and any closed files that the selling lawyer and purchasing lawyer agree to make subject of the sale. The *written* notice shall include all of the following:

(1) The anticipated effective date of the proposed sale;

(2) A statement that the purchasing lawyer will honor all existing fee agreements for legal representation that is ongoing at the time of sale and that fees for legal representation commenced after the date of sale will be negotiated by the purchasing lawyer and client;

(3) The client's right to retain other counsel or take possession of case files;

(4) The fact that the client's consent to the sale will be presumed if the client does not take action or otherwise object within ninety days of the receipt of the notice;

(5) Biographical information relative to the professional qualifications of the purchasing lawyer, including but not limited to applicable information consistent with Rule 7.2, information regarding any disciplinary action taken against the purchasing lawyer, and information regarding the existence, nature, and status of any pending disciplinary complaint certified by a probable cause panel pursuant to Gov. Bar R. V, Section 6(D)(1).

(f) If the seller is the estate of a deceased lawyer or the representative of a disabled or disappeared lawyer, the purchasing lawyer shall provide the written notice required by division (e) of this rule, and the purchasing lawyer shall obtain written consent from each client to act on the client's behalf. The client's consent shall be presumed if no response is received from the client

within ninety days of the date the notice was sent to the client at the client's last known address as shown on the records of the seller or the client's rights would be prejudiced by a failure to act during the ninety day period.

(g) If a client cannot be given the notice required by division (e) of this rule, the representation of that client may be transferred to the purchaser only after the selling lawyer and purchasing lawyer have caused notice of the sale to be made by at least one publication in a newspaper of general circulation in the county in which the sale will occur or in an adjoining county if no newspaper is published in the county in which the sale will occur. Upon completion of the publication, the client's consent to the sale is presumed.

(h) The *written* notice to clients required by division (e) and (f) of this rule shall be provided by certified mail, return receipt requested. In lieu of providing notice by certified mail, either the selling lawyer or purchasing lawyer, or both, may personally deliver the notice to a client. In the case of personal delivery, the lawyer providing the notice shall obtain written acknowledgement of the delivery from the client.

(i) Neither the selling lawyer nor the purchasing lawyer shall attempt to exonerate the lawyer or *law firm* from or limit liability to the former or prospective client for any malpractice or other professional negligence. The provisions of Rule 1.8(h) shall be incorporated in all agreements for the sale or purchase of a law practice. The selling lawyer or the purchasing lawyer, or both, may agree to provide for the indemnification or other contribution arising from any claim or action in malpractice or other professional negligence.

RULE 1.18: DUTIES TO PROSPECTIVE CLIENT

(a) A person who discusses with a lawyer the possibility of forming a client-lawyer relationship with respect to a matter is a prospective client.

(b) Even when no client-lawyer relationship ensues, a lawyer who has had discussions with a prospective client shall not use or reveal information learned in the consultation, except as Rule 1.9 would permit with respect to information of a former client.

(c) A lawyer subject to division (b) shall not represent a client with interests materially adverse to those of a prospective client in the same or a *substantially related matter* if the lawyer received information from the prospective client that could be significantly harmful to that person in the matter, except as provided in division (d). If a lawyer is disqualified from representation under this paragraph, no lawyer in a *firm* with which that lawyer is associated may *knowingly* undertake or continue representation in such a matter, except as provided in division (d).

(d) When the lawyer has received disqualifying information as defined in division (c), representation is permissible if either of the following applies:

(1) both the affected client and the prospective client have given *informed consent, confirmed in writing;*

(2) the lawyer who received the information took reasonable measures to avoid exposure to more dis-

qualifying information than was reasonably necessary to determine whether to represent the prospective client, and both of the following apply:

(i) the disqualified lawyer is timely screened from any participation in the matter and is apportioned no part of the fee therefrom;

(ii) *written* notice is promptly given to the prospective client.

II. COUNSELOR

RULE 2.1: ADVISOR

In representing a client, a lawyer shall exercise independent professional judgment and render candid advice. In rendering advice, a lawyer may refer not only to law but to other considerations, such as moral, economic, social, and political factors, that may be relevant to the client's situation.

RULE 2.2: [RESERVED FOR FUTURE USE; NO CORRESPONDING ABA MODEL RULE]

RULE 2.3: EVALUATION FOR USE BY THIRD PERSONS

(a) A lawyer may agree to provide an evaluation of a matter affecting a client for the use of someone other than the client if the lawyer *reasonably believes* that making the evaluation is compatible with other aspects of the lawyer's relationship with the client.

(b) When the lawyer *knows or reasonably should know* that the evaluation is likely to affect the client's interests materially and adversely, the lawyer shall not provide the evaluation unless the client gives *informed consent*.

(c) Except as disclosure is authorized in connection with a report of an evaluation, information relating to the evaluation is otherwise protected by Rule 1.6.

RULE 2.4: LAWYER SERVING AS ARBITRATOR, MEDIATOR, OR THIRD-PARTY NEUTRAL

(a) A lawyer serves as a third-party neutral when the lawyer assists two or more persons who are not clients of the lawyer to reach a resolution of a dispute or other matter that has arisen between them. Service as a third-party neutral may include service as an arbitrator, a mediator, or in such other capacity as will enable the lawyer to assist the parties to resolve the matter.

(b) A lawyer serving as a third-party neutral shall inform unrepresented parties that the lawyer is not representing them. When the lawyer knows or reasonably should know that a party does not understand the lawyer's role in the matter, the lawyer shall explain the difference between the lawyer's role as a third-party neutral and a lawyer's role as one who represents a client.

III. ADVOCATE

RULE 3.1: MERITORIOUS CLAIMS AND CONTENTIONS

A lawyer shall not bring or defend a proceeding, or assert or controvert an issue in a proceeding, unless there is a basis in law and fact for doing so that is not frivolous, which includes a good faith argument for an extension, modification, or reversal of existing law. A lawyer for the defendant in a criminal proceeding, or the respondent in a proceeding that could result in incarceration, may nevertheless so defend the proceeding as to require that every element of the case be established.

RULE 3.2: EXPEDITING LITIGATION

RULE 3.3: CANDOR TOWARD THE TRIBUNAL

(a) A lawyer shall not *knowingly* do any of the following:

(1) make a false statement of fact or law to a tribunal or fail to correct a false statement of material fact or law previously made to the *tribunal* by the lawyer;

(2) fail to disclose to the *tribunal* legal authority in the controlling jurisdiction *known* to the lawyer to be directly adverse to the position of the client and not disclosed by opposing counsel;

(3) offer evidence that the lawyer *knows* to be false. If a lawyer, the lawyer's client, or a witness called by the lawyer has offered material evidence and the lawyer comes to *know* of its falsity, the lawyer shall take *reasonable* measures to remedy the situation, including, if necessary, disclosure to the *tribunal*. A lawyer may refuse to offer evidence, other than the testimony of a defendant in a criminal matter, that the lawyer *reasonably believes* is false.

(b) A lawyer who represents a client in an adjudicative proceeding and who *knows* that a person, including the client, intends to engage, is engaging, or has engaged in criminal or *fraudulent* conduct related to the proceeding shall take *reasonable* measures to remedy the situation, including, if necessary, disclosure to the *tribunal*.

(c) The duties stated in divisions (a) and (b) of this rule continue until the issue to which the duty relates is determined by the highest *tribunal* that may consider the issue, or the time has expired for such determination, and apply even if compliance requires disclosure of information otherwise protected by Rule 1.6.

(d) In an *ex parte* proceeding, a lawyer shall inform the *tribunal* of all material facts *known* to the lawyer that will enable the *tribunal* to make an informed decision, whether or not the facts are adverse.

RULE 3.4: FAIRNESS TO OPPOSING PARTY AND COUNSEL

A lawyer shall not do any of the following:

(a) unlawfully obstruct another party's access to evidence; unlawfully alter, destroy, or conceal a document or other material having potential evidentiary value; or counsel or assist another person to do any such act;

(b) falsify evidence, counsel or assist a witness to testify falsely, or offer an inducement to a witness that is prohibited by law;

(c) *knowingly* disobey an obligation under the rules

of a *tribunal*, except for an open refusal based on a good faith assertion that no valid obligation exists;

(d) in pretrial procedure, intentionally or habitually make a frivolous motion or discovery request or fail to make *reasonably* diligent effort to comply with a legally proper discovery request by an opposing party;

(e) in trial, allude to any matter that the lawyer does not *reasonably* believe is relevant or that will not be supported by admissible evidence or by a good-faith belief that such evidence may exist, assert personal *knowledge* of facts in issue except when testifying as a witness, or state a personal opinion as to the justness of a cause, the credibility of a witness, the culpability of a civil litigant, or the guilt or innocence of an accused;

(f) [RESERVED]

(g) advise or cause a person to hide or to leave the jurisdiction of a tribunal for the purpose of becoming unavailable as a witness.

DECISIONS UNDER FORMER LAW

ANALYSIS

Prosecutorial misconduct

Prosecutorial misconduct

Defendant failed to show that he was substantially prejudiced by alleged prosecutorial misconduct during his criminal trial under a plain error standard of review pursuant to Ohio R. Crim. P. 52(B), based on his failure to object thereto during the trial, as there was no indication of alleged non-verbal references in the record for purposes of review, and other instances asserted were either based on a misreading of the trial transcript or were within the prosecutor's "degree of latitude" and did not violate Ohio Code Prof. Resp. DR 7-106(C)(1). Defendant did not show that but for the alleged prosecutorial misconduct, he would not have been convicted. State v. Lininger, — Ohio App. 3d —, 2006 Ohio 4136, — N.E. 2d —, 2006 Ohio App. LEXIS 4085 (Aug. 11, 2006).

RULE 3.5: IMPARTIALITY AND DECORUM OF THE TRIBUNAL

(a) A lawyer shall not do any of the following:

(1) seek to influence a judicial officer, juror, prospective juror, or other official by means prohibited by law;

(2) lend anything of value or give anything of more than de minimis value to a judicial officer, official, or employee of a *tribunal*;

(3) communicate *ex parte* with either of the following:

(i) a judicial officer or other official as to the merits of the case during the proceeding unless authorized to do so by law or court order;

(ii) a juror or prospective juror during the proceeding unless otherwise authorized to do so by law or court order.

(4) communicate with a juror or prospective juror after discharge of the jury if any of the following applies:

(i) the communication is prohibited by law or court order;

(ii) the juror has made known to the lawyer a desire not to communicate;

(iii) the communication involves misrepresentation,

coercion, duress, or harassment;

(5) engage in conduct intended to disrupt a *tribunal*;

(6) engage in undignified or discourteous conduct that is degrading to a *tribunal*.

(b) A lawyer shall reveal promptly to the *tribunal* improper conduct by a juror or prospective juror, or by another toward a juror, prospective juror, or family member of a juror or prospective juror, of which the lawyer has *knowledge*.

NOTES TO DECISIONS

ANALYSIS

Substance abuse.

Substance abuse

Attorney violated Ohio Code Prof. Resp. DR 7-106(C)(6) (now Ohio R. Prof. Conduct 3.5(a)) because the attorney consulted with clients and communicated with judicial, law enforcement, and law library personnel while the attorney was intoxicated, violating the attorney's duties to competently represent clients and assist in the administration of justice and embarrassing the legal profession, but his two-year suspension was stayed on conditions because he showed that (1) he was diagnosed with alcoholism, (2) his alcoholism contributed to his misconduct, (3) he was successfully treated, and (4) a qualified professional released him to return to the practice of law. Disciplinary Counsel v. Scurry, 115 Ohio St. 3d 201, 2007 Ohio 4796, 874 N.E. 2d 521, 2007 Ohio LEXIS 2215 (Sept. 20, 2007).

RULE 3.6: TRIAL PUBLICITY

(a) A lawyer who is participating or has participated in the investigation or litigation of a matter shall not make an extrajudicial statement that the lawyer *knows or reasonably should know* will be disseminated by means of public communication and will have a *substantial* likelihood of materially prejudicing an adjudicative proceeding in the matter.

(b) Notwithstanding division (a) of this rule and if permitted by Rule 1.6, a lawyer may state any of the following:

(1) the claim, offense, or defense involved and, except when prohibited by law, the identity of the persons involved;

(2) information contained in a public record;

(3) that an investigation of a matter is in progress;

(4) the scheduling or result of any step in litigation;

(5) a request for assistance in obtaining evidence and information necessary thereto;

(6) a warning of danger concerning the behavior of a person involved when there is reason to *believe* that there exists the likelihood of *substantial* harm to an individual or to the public interest;

(7) in a criminal case, in addition to divisions (b)(1) to (6) of this rule, any of the following:

(i) the identity, residence, occupation, and family status of the accused;

(ii) if the accused has not been apprehended, information necessary to aid in apprehension of that person;

(iii) the fact, time, and place of arrest;

(iv) the identity of investigating and arresting officers or agencies and the length of the investigation.

(c) Notwithstanding division (a) of this rule, a lawyer may make a statement that a *reasonable* lawyer would *believe* is required to protect a client from the *substantial* undue prejudicial effect of recent publicity not initiated by the lawyer or the lawyer's client. A statement made pursuant to this division shall be limited to information necessary to mitigate the recent adverse publicity.

(d) No lawyer associated in a firm or government agency with a lawyer subject to division (a) of this rule shall make a statement prohibited by division (a) of this rule.

RULE 3.7: LAWYER AS WITNESS

(a) A lawyer shall not act as an advocate at a trial in which the lawyer is likely to be a necessary witness unless one or more of the following applies:

(1) the testimony relates to an uncontested issue;

(2) the testimony relates to the nature and value of legal services rendered in the case;

(3) the disqualification of the lawyer would work *substantial* hardship on the client.

(b) A lawyer may act as an advocate in a trial in which another lawyer in the lawyer's *firm* is likely to be called as a witness unless precluded from doing so by Rule 1.7 or 1.9.

(c) A government lawyer participating in a case shall not testify or offer the testimony of another lawyer in the same government agency, except where division (a) applies or where permitted by law.

DECISIONS UNDER FORMER LAW

ANALYSIS

Generally
Applicability
Attorney as witness
Disqualification of attorney
Self-representation

Generally

Proper procedure for a trial court to follow in determining whether to disqualify an attorney who has been called to testify by an opposing party is for the court to determine whether the attorney's testimony is admissible and necessary. If it is, the court must determine whether any of the exceptions under ProfCondR 3.7 apply: Brown v. Spectrum Networks, Inc., 180 Ohio App. 3d 99, 2008 Ohio 6687, 904 N.E.2d 576, 2008 Ohio App. LEXIS 5585 (2008).

Applicability

As a trial court's disqualification of an attorney was made after the effective date of the Ohio Rules of Professional Conduct, which was February 1, 2007, and the conduct at issue that gave rise to the disqualification involved ongoing litigation, the new rule under Ohio R. Prof. Conduct 3.7 was applicable. Horen v. Bd. of Educ., 174 Ohio App. 3d 317, 2007 Ohio 6883, 882 N.E. 2d 14, 2007 Ohio App. LEXIS 6008 (Dec. 21, 2007).

Attorney as witness

Trial court did not err in refusing to allow defendant's attorney to "clarify" defendant's interpreter's translation of defendant's testimony, as the attorney was required to avoid becoming a witness in a case on which he was employed pursuant to Ohio Code Prof. Resp. DR 5-102, and the

attorney could have corrected the perceived misstatement on redirect examination if she felt that her client was prejudiced thereby. State v. Vazquez, — Ohio App. 3d —, 2006 Ohio 4142, — N.E. 2d —, 2006 Ohio App. LEXIS 4087 (Aug. 11, 2006).

Disqualification of attorney

Trial court abused its discretion when it disqualified an attorney and his firm from representing debtors in an action by a creditor, seeking repayment of a loan and foreclosure of the pledged collateral, as the fact that the attorney had drafted the parties' loan agreement did not necessarily require his disqualification because the proper procedure for making such a determination was not followed by the trial court; there was insufficient evidence to determine if the attorney "ought to testify," if such testimony would be admissible under Ohio R. Evid. 403(A), and if admissible, if the testimony was subject to any exceptions or would cause prejudice to the attorney's client pursuant to considerations under Ohio Code Prof. Resp. DR 5-101(B) and 5-102(A) and (B). A.B.B. Sanitec West, Inc. v. Weinsten, — Ohio App. 3d —, 2007 Ohio 2116, — N.E. 2d —, 2007 Ohio App. LEXIS 1981 (May 3, 2007).

Trial court abused its discretion by disqualifying the attorneys in the absence of any evidence tending to demonstrate that their testimony would be prejudicial to their client. Before the court could disqualify counsel, it was required to conduct some form of hearing: Hall v. Tucker, 169 Ohio App. 3d 520, 2006 Ohio 5895, 863 N.E.2d 1064, 2006 Ohio App. LEXIS 5833 (2006).

Used car dealer failed to meet his burden of showing under Ohio Code Prof. Resp. DR 5-102(B) (now at Ohio R. Prof. Conduct 3.7) that it was apparent that an attorney would be a necessary witness and that he would give testimony that was prejudicial to his client, a car purchaser, in the purchaser's multi-count action, arising from the dealer's alleged fraudulent conduct, such that the disqualification of the attorney was an abuse of discretion by the trial court. Quiros v. Morales, — Ohio App. 3d —, 2007 Ohio 5442, — N.E. 2d —, 2007 Ohio App. LEXIS 4769 (Oct. 11, 2007).

Trial court did not abuse its discretion by disqualifying an attorney as counsel for her family members in a case where she was likely to be called as a witness where there was no evidence that the attorney had any unique legal expertise that required her participation as counsel. However, the attorney was entitled to represent herself in a case where she was named as a plaintiff: Horen v. Bd. of Educ., 174 Ohio App. 3d 317, 2007 Ohio 6883, 882 N.E. 2d 14, 2007 Ohio App. LEXIS 6008 (Dec. 21, 2007).

As there was no showing that a mother who was acting as co-counsel on behalf of herself and her family in a discrimination action against a city and a school district had unique legal expertise that required her participation in the case as counsel, there was no basis for the trial court to have found that disqualification of her in her representative capacity would have caused substantial hardship for the family; the trial court did not abuse its discretion in disqualifying her from further representation of her family. Horen v. Bd. of Educ., 174 Ohio App. 3d 317, 2007 Ohio 6883, 882 N.E. 2d 14, 2007 Ohio App. LEXIS 6008 (Dec. 21, 2007).

Self-representation

Mother who was acting as co-counsel on behalf of herself and her family in a discrimination action against a city and a school district was entitled to represent herself, although she was properly disqualified from representing her family pursuant to Ohio R. Prof. Conduct 3.7, as she had a right to self-representation. Horen v. Bd. of Educ., 174 Ohio App. 3d 317, 2007 Ohio 6883, 882 N.E. 2d 14, 2007 Ohio App. LEXIS 6008 (Dec. 21, 2007).

RULE 3.8: SPECIAL RESPONSIBILITIES OF A PROSECUTOR

prosecutor in a criminal case shall not do any of the following:

(a) pursue or prosecute a charge that the prosecutor *knows* is not supported by probable cause;

(b) [RESERVED]

(c) [RESERVED]

(d) fail to make timely disclosure to the defense of all evidence or information *known* to the prosecutor that tends to negate the guilt of the accused or mitigates the offense, and, in connection with sentencing, fail to disclose to the defense all unprivileged mitigating information *known* to the prosecutor, except when the prosecutor is relieved of this responsibility by an order of the *tribunal*;

(e) subpoena a lawyer in a grand jury or other criminal proceeding to present evidence about a past or present client unless the prosecutor *reasonably believes* all of the following apply:

(1) the information sought is not protected from disclosure by any applicable privilege;

(2) the evidence sought is essential to the successful completion of an ongoing investigation or prosecution;

(3) there is no other feasible alternative to obtain the information.

(f) [RESERVED]

RULE 3.9: ADVOCATE IN NONADJUDICATIVE PROCEEDINGS

A lawyer representing a client before a legislative body or administrative agency in a nonadjudicative proceeding shall disclose that the appearance is in a representative capacity and shall conform to the provisions of Rules 3.3(a) to (c), 3.4(a) to (c), and 3.5.

IV. TRANSACTIONS WITH PERSONS OTHER THAN CLIENTS

NOTES TO DECISIONS

ANALYSIS

Substance abuse.

Substance abuse

Attorney violated Ohio Sup. Ct. R. Gov't Bar IV(2) because the attorney consulted with clients and communicated with judicial, law enforcement, and law library personnel while the attorney was intoxicated, violating the attorney's duties to competently represent clients and assist in the administration of justice and embarrassing the legal profession, but his two-year suspension was stayed on conditions because he showed that (1) he was diagnosed with alcoholism, (2) his alcoholism contributed to his misconduct, (3) he was successfully treated, and (4) a qualified professional released him to return to the practice of law. Disciplinary Counsel v. Scurry, 115 Ohio St. 3d 201, 2007 Ohio 4796, 874 N.E. 2d 521, 2007 Ohio LEXIS 2215 (Sept. 20, 2007).

RULE 4.1: TRUTHFULNESS IN STATEMENTS TO OTHERS

In the course of representing a client a lawyer shall not *knowingly* do either of the following:

(a) make a false statement of material fact or law to a third person;

(b) fail to disclose a material fact when disclosure is necessary to avoid assisting an *illegal or fraudulent* act by a client.

RULE 4.2: COMMUNICATION WITH PERSON REPRESENTED BY COUNSEL

In representing a client, a lawyer shall not communicate about the subject of the representation with a person the lawyer *knows* to be represented by another lawyer in the matter, unless the lawyer has the consent of the other lawyer or is authorized to do so by law or a court order.

DECISIONS UNDER FORMER LAW

ANALYSIS

Criminal witness

Criminal witness

Trial court erred in allowing the State to call defendant's son as a witness to testify regarding the criminal incident that defendant was on trial for, as it was aware that the son intended to invoke his Fifth Amendment privilege because he was charged with disposing of the gun in that incident, and his claim of privilege placed an air of criminality upon his and defendant's actions. The State consciously and flagrantly built its case on the unfavorable inferences that arose therefrom, which was violative of the prosecutor's obligation under Ohio Code Prof. Resp. DR 7-104(A)(1). State v. Oldham, — Ohio App. 3d —, 2007 Ohio 3907, — N.E. 2d —, 2007 Ohio App. LEXIS 3549 (Aug. 2, 2007).

RULE 4.3: DEALING WITH UNREPRESENTED PERSON

In dealing on behalf of a client with a person who is not represented by counsel, a lawyer shall not state or imply that the lawyer is disinterested. When the lawyer *knows or reasonably should know* that the unrepresented person misunderstands the lawyer's role in the matter, the lawyer shall make *reasonable* efforts to correct the misunderstanding. The lawyer shall not give legal advice to an unrepresented person, other than the advice to secure counsel, if the lawyer *knows or reasonably should know* that the interests of such a person are or have a *reasonable* possibility of being in conflict with the interests of the client.

RULE 4.4: RESPECT FOR RIGHTS OF THIRD PERSONS

(a) In representing a client, a lawyer shall not use means that have no substantial purpose other than to embarrass, harass, delay, or burden a third person, or use methods of obtaining evidence that violate the legal rights of such a person.

(b) A lawyer who receives a document relating to the representation of the lawyer's client and *knows or reasonably should know* that the document was inadvertently sent shall promptly notify the sender.

V. LAW FIRMS AND ASSOCIATIONS

RULE 5.1 RESPONSIBILITIES OF PARTNERS, MANAGERS, AND SUPERVISORY LAWYERS

(a) [RESERVED]

(b) [RESERVED]

(c) A lawyer shall be responsible for another lawyer's violation of the Ohio Rules of Professional Conduct if either of the following applies:

(1) the lawyer orders or, with *knowledge* of the specific conduct, ratifies the conduct involved;

(2) the lawyer is a partner or has comparable managerial authority in the *law firm* or government agency in which the other lawyer practices, or has direct supervisory authority over the other lawyer, and *knows* of the conduct at a time when its consequences can be avoided or mitigated but fails to take reasonable remedial action.

RULE 5.2 RESPONSIBILITIES OF A SUBORDINATE LAWYER

(a) A lawyer is bound by the Ohio Rules of Professional Conduct notwithstanding that the lawyer acted at the direction of another person.

(b) A subordinate lawyer does not violate the Ohio Rules of Professional Conduct if that lawyer acts in accordance with a supervisory lawyer's *reasonable* resolution of a question of professional duty.

RULE 5.3 RESPONSIBILITIES REGARDING NONLAWYER ASSISTANTS

With respect to a nonlawyer employed by, retained by, or associated with a lawyer, all of the following apply:

(a) a lawyer who individually or together with other lawyers possesses managerial authority in a *law firm* or government agency shall make reasonable efforts to ensure that the *firm* or government agency has in effect measures giving reasonable assurance that the person's conduct is compatible with the professional obligations of the lawyer;

(b) a lawyer having direct supervisory authority over the nonlawyer shall make *reasonable* efforts to ensure that the person's conduct is compatible with the professional obligations of the lawyer;

(c) a lawyer shall be responsible for conduct of such a person that would be a violation of the Ohio Rules of Professional Conduct if engaged in by a lawyer if either of the following applies:

(1) the lawyer orders or, with the *knowledge* of the specific conduct, ratifies the conduct involved;

(2) the lawyer has managerial authority in the *law firm* or government agency in which the person is employed, or has direct supervisory authority over the person, and *knows* of the conduct at a time when its consequences can be avoided or mitigated but fails to take reasonable remedial action.

RULE 5.4 PROFESSIONAL INDEPENDENCE OF A LAWYER

(a) A lawyer or *law firm* shall not share legal fees with a nonlawyer, except in any of the following circumstances:

(1) an agreement by a lawyer with the lawyer's *firm, partner,* or associate may provide for the payment of money, over a *reasonable* period of time after the lawyer's death, to the lawyer's estate or to one or more specified persons;

(2) a lawyer who purchases the practice of a deceased, disabled, or disappeared lawyer may, pursuant to the provisions of Rule 1.17, pay to the estate or other representative of that lawyer the agreed-upon purchase price;

(3) a lawyer or *law firm* may include nonlawyer employees in a compensation or retirement plan, even though the plan is based in whole or in part on a profit-sharing arrangement;

(4) a lawyer may share court-awarded legal fees with a nonprofit organization that employed or retained the lawyer in the matter;

(5) a lawyer may share legal fees with a nonprofit organization that recommended employment of the lawyer in the matter, if the nonprofit organization complies with Rule XVI of the Supreme Court Rules for the Government of the Bar of Ohio.

(b) A lawyer shall not form a partnership with a nonlawyer if any of the activities of the partnership consist of the practice of law.

(c) A lawyer shall not permit a person who recommends, employs, or pays the lawyer to render legal services for another to direct or regulate the lawyer's professional judgment in rendering such legal services.

(d) A lawyer shall not practice with or in the form of a professional corporation or association authorized to practice law for a profit, if any of the following applies:

(1) a nonlawyer owns any interest therein, except that a fiduciary representative of the estate of a lawyer may hold the stock or interest of the lawyer for a *reasonable* time during administration;

(2) a nonlawyer is a corporate director or officer thereof or occupies the position of similar responsibility in any form of association other than a corporation;

(3) a nonlawyer has the right to direct or control the professional judgment of a lawyer.

RULE 5.5 UNAUTHORIZED PRACTICE OF LAW; MULTIJURISDICTIONAL PRACTICE OF LAW

(a) A lawyer shall not practice law in a jurisdiction in violation of the regulation of the legal profession in that jurisdiction, or assist another in doing so.

(b) A lawyer who is not admitted to practice in this jurisdiction shall not do either of the following:

(1) except as authorized by these rules or other law, establish an office or other systematic and continuous presence in this jurisdiction for the practice of law;

(2) hold out to the public or otherwise represent that the lawyer is admitted to practice law in this jurisdiction.

(c) A lawyer who is admitted in another United States jurisdiction, is in good standing in the jurisdiction in which the lawyer is admitted, and regularly practices law may provide legal services on a temporary basis in this jurisdiction if one or more of the following apply:

(1) the services are undertaken in association with a lawyer who is admitted to practice in this jurisdiction and who actively participates in the matter;

(2) the services are *reasonably* related to a pending or potential proceeding before a *tribunal* in this or another jurisdiction, if the lawyer, or a person the lawyer is assisting, is authorized by law or order to appear in such proceeding or *reasonably* expects to be so authorized;

(3) the services are *reasonably* related to a pending or potential arbitration, mediation, or other alternative dispute resolution proceeding in this or another jurisdiction, if the services arise out of or are *reasonably* related to the lawyer's practice in a jurisdiction in which the lawyer is admitted to practice and are not services for which the forum requires *pro hac vice* admission;

(4) the lawyer engages in negotiations, investigations, or other nonlitigation activities that arise out of or are *reasonably* related to the lawyer's practice in a jurisdiction in which the lawyer is admitted to practice.

(d) A lawyer admitted and in good standing in another United States jurisdiction may provide legal services in this jurisdiction in either of the following circumstances:

(1) the lawyer is registered in compliance with Gov. Bar R. VI, Section 3 and is providing services to the employer or its organizational affiliates for which the permission of a *tribunal* to appear *pro hac vice* is not required;

(2) the lawyer is providing services that the lawyer is authorized to provide by federal or Ohio law.

DECISIONS UNDER FORMER LAW
ANALYSIS

Lawyer under suspension

Lawyer under suspension
Based on an attorney's representation of friends and a friend's son while he was indefinitely suspended from the practice of law, his failure to inform his clients of his status, and his failure to refund money to a client upon her request, he violated Ohio Code Prof. Resp. DR 1-102(A)(4), 3-101(B), and 9-102(B)(4); as he had a prior disciplinary history, he was permanently disbarred from practicing law. Cleveland Bar Ass'n v. Rubino, 115 Ohio St. 3d 199, 2007 Ohio 4797, 874 N.E. 2d 519, 2007 Ohio LEXIS 2214 (Sept. 20, 2007).

RULE 5.6   RESTRICTIONS ON RIGHT TO PRACTICE

A lawyer shall not participate in offering or making either of the following:

(a) a partnership, shareholders, operating, employment, or other similar type of agreement that restricts the right of a lawyer to practice after termination of the relationship, except an agreement concerning benefits upon retirement;

(b) an agreement in which a restriction on the lawyer's right to practice is part of the settlement of a claim or controversy.

RULE 5.7   RESPONSIBILITIES REGARDING LAW RELATED SERVICES

(a) A lawyer shall be subject to the Ohio Rules of Professional Conduct with respect to the provision of law related services, as defined in division (e) of this rule, if the law related services are provided in either of the following circumstances:

(1) by the lawyer in circumstances that are not distinct from the lawyer's provision of legal services to clients;

(2) in other circumstances by an entity controlled or owned by the lawyer individually or with others, unless the lawyer takes *reasonable* measures to ensure that a person obtaining the law-related services *knows* that the services are not legal services and that the protections of the client-lawyer relationship do not exist.

(b) A lawyer who controls or owns an interest in a business that provides a law-related service shall not require any customer of that business to agree to legal representation by the lawyer as a condition of the engagement of that business. A lawyer who controls or owns an interest in a business that provides law-related services shall disclose the interest to a customer of that business, and the fact that the customer may obtain legal services elsewhere, before performing legal services for the customer.

(c) A lawyer who controls or owns an interest in a business that provides a law-related service shall not require the lawyer's client to agree to use that business as a condition of the engagement for legal services. A lawyer who controls or owns an interest in a business that provides a law-related service shall disclose the interest to the client, and the fact that the client may obtain the law-related services elsewhere, before providing the law-related services to the client.

(d) Limitations or obligations imposed by this rule on a lawyer shall apply to both of the following:

(1) every lawyer in a *firm* who knows that another lawyer in his or her *firm* controls or owns an interest in a business that provides a law-related service;

(2) every lawyer in a *firm* that controls or owns an interest in a business that provides a law-related service.

(e) The term "law-related services" denotes services that might reasonably be performed in conjunction with the provision of legal services and that are not prohibited as unauthorized practice of law when provided by a nonlawyer.

VI. PUBLIC SERVICE

RULE 6.1: VOLUNTARY PRO BONO PUBLICO SERVICE

RULE 6.2: ACCEPTING APPOINTMENTS

A lawyer shall not seek to avoid appointment by a court to represent a person except for good cause, such as either of the following:

(a) representing the client is likely to result in violation of the Ohio Rules of Professional Conduct or other law;

(b) representing the client is likely to result in an unreasonable financial burden on the lawyer.

RULE 6.3: MEMBERSHIP IN LEGAL SERVICES ORGANIZATION

RULE 6.4: LAW REFORM ACTIVITIES AFFECTING CLIENT INTERESTS

RULE 6.5: NONPROFIT AND COURT-ANNEXED LIMITED LEGAL SERVICES PROGRAMS

(a) A lawyer who, under the auspices of a program sponsored by a nonprofit organization or court, provides short-term limited legal services to a client without expectation by either the lawyer or the client that the lawyer will provide continuing representation in the matter is subject to both of the following:

(1) Rules 1.7 and 1.9(a) only if the lawyer knows that the representation of the client involves a conflict of interest;

(2) Rule 1.10 only if the lawyer knows that another lawyer associated with the lawyer in a *law firm* is disqualified by Rule 1.7 or 1.9(a) with respect to the matter.

(b) Except as provided in division (a)(2) of this rule, Rule 1.10 is inapplicable to a representation governed by this rule.

VII. INFORMATION ABOUT LEGAL SERVICES

RULE 7.1: COMMUNICATIONS CONCERNING A LAWYER'S SERVICES

A lawyer shall not make or use a false, misleading, or nonverifiable communication about the lawyer or the lawyer's services. A communication is false or misleading if it contains a material misrepresentation of fact or law or omits a fact necessary to make the statement considered as a whole not materially misleading.

RULE 7.2: ADVERTISING AND RECOMMENDATION OF PROFESSIONAL EMPLOYMENT

(a) Subject to the requirements of Rules 7.1 and 7.3, a lawyer may advertise services through *written*, recorded, or electronic communication, including public media.

(b) A lawyer shall not give anything of value to a person for recommending the lawyer's services except that a lawyer may pay any of the following:

(1) the *reasonable* costs of advertisements or communications permitted by this rule;

(2) the usual charges of a legal service plan;

(3) the usual charges for a nonprofit or lawyer referral service that complies with Rule XVI of the Supreme Court Rules for the Government of the Bar of Ohio;

(4) for a law practice in accordance with Rule 1.17.

(c) Any communication made pursuant to this rule shall include the name and office address of at least one lawyer or *law firm* responsible for its content.

(d) A lawyer shall not seek employment in connection with a matter in which the lawyer or *law firm* does not intend to participate actively in the representation, but that the lawyer or *law firm* intends to refer to other counsel. This provision shall not apply to organizations listed in Rules 7.2(b)(2) or (3) or if the advertisement is in furtherance of a transaction permitted by Rule 1.17.

RULE 7.3: DIRECT CONTACT WITH PROSPECTIVE CLIENTS

(a) A lawyer shall not by in-person, live telephone, or real-time electronic contact solicit professional employment from a prospective client when a significant motive for the lawyer's doing so is the lawyer's pecuniary gain, unless either of the following applies:

(1) the person contacted is a lawyer;

(2) the person contacted has a family, close personal, or prior professional relationship with the lawyer.

(b) A lawyer shall not solicit professional employment from a prospective client by *written*, recorded, or electronic communication or by in-person, telephone, or real-time electronic contact even when not otherwise prohibited by division (a), if either of the following applies:

(1) the prospective client has made known to the lawyer a desire not to be solicited by the lawyer;

(2) the solicitation involves coercion, duress, or harassment.

(c) Unless the recipient of the communication is a person specified in division (a)(1) or (2) of this rule, every *written*, recorded, or electronic communication from a lawyer soliciting professional employment from a prospective client whom the lawyer reasonably *believes* to be in need of legal services in a particular matter shall comply with all of the following:

(1) Disclose accurately and fully the manner in which the lawyer or *law firm* became aware of the identity and specific legal need of the addressee;

(2) Disclaim or refrain from expressing any predetermined evaluation of the merits of the addressee's case;

(3) Conspicuously include in its text and on the outside envelope, if any, and at the beginning and ending of any recorded or electronic communication the recital - "ADVERTISING MATERIAL" or "ADVERTISEMENT ONLY."

(d) Prior to making a communication soliciting professional employment from a prospective client pursuant to division (c) of this rule to a party who has been named as a defendant in a civil action, a lawyer or *law firm* shall verify that the party has been served with notice of the action filed against that party. Service shall be verified by consulting the docket of the court in which the action was filed to determine whether mail, personal, or residence service has been perfected or whether service by publication has been completed. Division (d) of this rule shall not apply to the solicitation of a debtor regarding representation of the debtor in a potential or actual bankruptcy action.

(e) If a communication soliciting professional employment from a prospective client or a relative of a prospective client is sent within thirty days of an accident or disaster that gives rise to a potential claim for personal injury or wrongful death, the following "Understanding Your Rights" shall be included with the communication.

UNDERSTANDING YOUR RIGHTS°

If you have been in an accident, or a family member has been injured or killed in a crash or some other incident, you have many important decisions to make. It is important for you to consider the following:

1. Make and keep records - If your situation involves a motor vehicle crash, regardless of who may be at fault, it is helpful to obtain a copy of the police report, learn the identity of any witnesses, and obtain photographs of the scene, vehicles, and any visible injuries. Keep copies of receipts of all your expenses and medical care related to the incident.

2. You do not have to sign anything - You may not want to give an interview or recorded statement without first consulting with an attorney, because the statement can be used against you. If you may be at fault or have been charged with a traffic or other offense, it may be advisable to consult an attorney right away. However, if you have insurance, your insurance policy probably requires you to cooperate with your insurance company and to provide a statement to the company. If you fail to cooperate with your insurance company, it may void your coverage.

3. Your interests versus interests of insurance company - Your interests and those of the other person's insurance company are in conflict. Your interests may also be in conflict with your own insurance company. Even if you are not sure who is at fault, you should contact your own insurance company and advise the company of the incident to protect your insurance coverage.

4. There is a time limit to file an insurance claim - Legal rights, including filing a lawsuit, are subject to time limits. You should ask what time limits apply to your claim. You may need to act immediately to protect your rights.

5. Get it in *writing* - You may want to request that any offer of settlement from anyone be put in *writing*, including a *written* explanation of the type of damages which they are willing to cover.

6. Legal assistance may be appropriate - You may consult with an attorney before you sign any document or release of claims. A release may cut off all future rights against others, obligate you to repay past medical bills or disability benefits, or jeopardize future benefits. If your interests conflict with your own insurance company, you always have the right to discuss the matter with an attorney of your choice, which may be at your own expense.

7. How to find an attorney - If you need professional advice about a legal problem but do not know an attorney, you may wish to check with relatives, friends, neighbors, your employer, or co-workers who may be able to recommend an attorney. Your local bar association may have a lawyer referral service that can be found in the Yellow Pages or on the Internet.

8. Check a lawyer's qualifications - Before hiring any lawyer, you have the right to know the lawyer's background, training, and experience in dealing with cases similar to yours.

9. How much will it cost? - In deciding whether to hire a particular lawyer, you should discuss, and the lawyer's written fee agreement should reflect:

a. How is the lawyer to be paid? If you already have a settlement offer, how will that affect a contingent fee arrangement?

b. How are the expenses involved in your case, such as telephone calls, deposition costs, and fees for expert witnesses, to be paid? Will these costs be advanced by the lawyer or charged to you as they are incurred? Since you are obligated to pay all expenses even if you lose your case, how will payment be arranged?

c. Who will handle your case? If the case goes to trial, who will be the trial attorney?

This information is not intended as a complete description of your legal rights, but as a checklist of some of the important issues you should consider.

°THE SUPREME COURT OF OHIO, WHICH GOVERNS THE CONDUCT OF LAWYERS IN THE STATE OF OHIO, NEITHER PROMOTES NOR PROHIBITS THE DIRECT SOLICITATION OF PERSONAL INJURY VICTIMS. THE COURT DOES REQUIRE THAT, IF SUCH A SOLICITATION IS MADE, IT MUST INCLUDE THE ABOVE DISCLOSURE.

(f) Notwithstanding the prohibitions in division (a) of this rule, a lawyer may participate with a prepaid or group legal service plan operated by an organization not owned or directed by the lawyer that uses in-person or telephone contact to solicit memberships or subscriptions for the plan from persons who are not *known* to need legal services in a particular matter covered by the plan.

RULE 7.4: COMMUNICATION OF FIELDS OF PRACTICE AND SPECIALIZATION

(a) A lawyer may communicate the fact that the lawyer does or does not practice in particular fields of law or limits his or her practice to or concentrates in particular fields of law.

(b) A lawyer admitted to engage in patent practice before the United States Patent and Trademark Office may use the designation "Patent Attorney" or a *substantially* similar designation.

(c) A lawyer engaged in trademark practice may use the designation "Trademarks," "Trademark Attorney," or a *substantially* similar designation.

(d) A lawyer engaged in Admiralty practice may use the designation "Admiralty," "Proctor in Admiralty," or a *substantially* similar designation.

(e) A lawyer shall not state or imply that a lawyer is a specialist in a particular field of law, unless both of the following apply:

(1) the lawyer has been certified as a specialist by an organization approved by the Supreme Court Commission on Certification of Attorneys as Specialists;

(2) the name of the certifying organization is clearly identified in the communication.

Amended effective April 1, 2009.

RULE 7.5: FIRM NAMES AND LETTERHEADS

(a) A lawyer shall not use a *firm* name, letterhead or other professional designation that violates Rule 7.1. A lawyer in private practice shall not practice under a trade name, a name that is misleading as to the identity of the lawyer or lawyers practicing under the name, or a firm name containing names other than those of one or more of the lawyers in the *firm*, except that the name of a professional corporation or association, legal clinic, limited liability company, or registered partnership shall contain symbols indicating the nature of the organization as required by Gov. Bar R. III. If otherwise lawful, a firm may use as, or continue to include in, its name the name or names of one or more deceased or retired members of the *firm* or of a predecessor firm in a continuing line of succession.

(b) A *law firm* with offices in more than one jurisdiction that lists attorneys associated with the firm shall indicate the jurisdictional limitations on those not licensed to practice in Ohio.

(c) The name of a lawyer holding a public office shall not be used in the name of a *law firm*, or in communications on its behalf, during any substantial period in which the lawyer is not actively and regularly practicing with the *firm*.

(d) Lawyers may state or imply that they practice in a partnership or other organization only when that is the fact.

RULE 7.6: POLITICAL CONTRIBUTIONS TO OBTAIN GOVERNMENT LEGAL ENGAGEMENTS OR APPOINTMENTS BY JUDGES

VIII. MAINTAINING THE INTEGRITY OF THE PROFESSION

RULE 8.1: BAR ADMISSION AND DISCIPLINARY MATTERS

In connection with a bar admission application or in connection with a disciplinary matter, a lawyer shall not do any of the following:

(a) *knowingly* make a false statement of material fact;

(b) in response to a demand for information from an admissions or disciplinary authority, fail to disclose a material fact or *knowingly* fail to respond, except that this rule does not require disclosure of information otherwise protected by Rule 1.6.

RULE 8.2: JUDICIAL OFFICIALS

(a) A lawyer shall not make a statement that the lawyer *knows* to be false or with reckless disregard as to its truth or falsity concerning the qualifications or integrity of a judicial officer, or candidate for election or appointment to judicial office.

(b) A lawyer who is a candidate for judicial office shall not violate the provisions of the Ohio Code of Judicial Conduct applicable to judicial candidates.

RULE 8.3: REPORTING PROFESSIONAL MISCONDUCT

(a) A lawyer who possesses unprivileged knowledge of a violation of the Ohio Rules of Professional Conduct that raises a question as to any lawyer's honesty, trustworthiness, or fitness as a lawyer in other respects, shall inform a disciplinary authority empowered to investigate or act upon such a violation.

(b) A lawyer who possesses unprivileged knowledge that a judge has committed a violation of the Ohio Rules of Professional Conduct or applicable rules of judicial conduct shall inform the appropriate authority.

(c) Any information obtained by a member of a committee or subcommittee of a bar association, or by a member, employee, or agent of a nonprofit corporation established by a bar association, designed to assist lawyers with substance abuse or mental health problems, provided the information was obtained while the member, employee, or agent was performing duties as a member, employee, or agent of the committee, subcommittee, or nonprofit corporation, shall be privileged for all purposes under this rule.

NOTES TO DECISIONS

Analysis

Conduct prejudicial to justice

Conduct prejudicial to justice

Employee's claim that members of the law firm that employed her were committing violations of the Ohio Code of Professional Responsibility did not provide a basis for her claim of wrongful discharge in violation of public policy, as she had no knowledge of the Code and no legal duty to report alleged violations thereof, and further, the attorneys themselves had an obligation to report any misconduct pursuant to Ohio Code Prof. Resp. DR 1-103(A). Accordingly, summary judgment for the employer on the employee's public policy violation claim was proper, as she did not establish the jeopardy element of her claim. Urda v. Buckingham, Doolittle, & Burroughs, — Ohio App. 3d —, 2006 Ohio 6915, — N.E. 2d —, 2006 Ohio App. LEXIS 6816 (Dec. 27, 2006).

RULE 8.4: MISCONDUCT

It is professional misconduct for a lawyer to do any of the following:

(a) violate or attempt to violate the Ohio Rules of Professional Conduct, *knowingly* assist or induce another to do so, or do so through the acts of another;

(b) commit an *illegal* act that reflects adversely on the lawyer's honesty or trustworthiness;

(c) engage in conduct involving dishonesty, *fraud*, deceit, or misrepresentation;

(d) engage in conduct that is prejudicial to the administration of justice;

(e) state or imply an ability to influence improperly a government agency or official or to achieve results by means that violate the Ohio Rules of Professional Conduct or other law;

(f) *knowingly* assist a judge or judicial officer in conduct that is a violation of the Ohio Rules of Professional Conduct, the applicable rules of judicial conduct, or other law;

(g) engage, in a professional capacity, in conduct involving discrimination prohibited by law because of race, color, religion, age, gender, sexual orientation, national origin, marital status, or disability;

(h) engage in any other conduct that adversely reflects on the lawyer's fitness to practice law.

DECISIONS UNDER FORMER LAW

ANALYSIS

Conduct adversely reflecting on fitness to practice
Criminal conviction
Misrepresentation to client
Notarization
Suspension

Conduct adversely reflecting on fitness to practice

Attorney violated Ohio Code Prof. Resp. DR 1-102(A)(6) (now Ohio R. Prof. Conduct 8.4(h)) because the attorney consulted with clients and communicated with judicial, law enforcement, and law library personnel while the attorney was intoxicated, violating the attorney's duties to competently represent clients and assist in the administration of justice and embarrassing the legal profession, but his two-year suspension was stayed on conditions because he showed that (1) he was diagnosed with alcoholism, (2) his alcoholism contributed to his misconduct, (3) he was successfully treated, and (4) a qualified professional released him to return to the practice of law. Disciplinary Counsel v. Scurry, 115 Ohio St. 3d 201, 2007 Ohio 4796, 874 N.E. 2d 521, 2007 Ohio LEXIS 2215 (Sept. 20, 2007).

Criminal conviction

Attorney was suspended from the practice of law for two years because the attorney's conviction for identity theft manifested violations of Ohio Code Prof. Resp. 1-102(A)(3) and (4). The attorney had no prior disciplinary record, had made full restitution, had cooperated fully in the disciplinary proceedings, and expressed genuine remorse. Because the mitigating factors outweighed the single aggravating factor, that he had acted dishonestly and out of self-interest, disbarment was not required; there was concern, however, that the attorney carefully executed a plan that compromised bank customers until he was caught. Cincinnati Bar Ass'n v. Zins, — Ohio St. 3d —, 2007 Ohio 5263, — N.E. 2d —, 2007 Ohio LEXIS 2518 (Oct. 10, 2007).

Misrepresentation to client

Based on an attorney's representation of friends and a friend's son while he was indefinitely suspended from the practice of law, his failure to inform his clients of his status, and his failure to refund money to a client upon her request, he violated Ohio Code Prof. Resp. DR 1-102(A)(4), 3-101(B), and 9-102(B)(4); as he had a prior disciplinary history, he was permanently disbarred from practicing law. Cleveland Bar Ass'n v. Rubino, 115 Ohio St. 3d 199, 2007 Ohio 4797, 874 N.E. 2d 519, 2007 Ohio LEXIS 2214 (Sept. 20, 2007).

Notarization

Attorney who notarized a signature without the signatory having been present violated Ohio Code Prof. Resp. DR 1-102(A)(4) (now at Ohio R. Prof. Conduct 8.4); as the attorney had no prior disciplinary record, the misconduct was not committed for his own benefit, and he cooperated in the disciplinary process, a public reprimand was imposed as the appropriate sanction. Cincinnati Bar Ass'n v. Gottesman, 115 Ohio St. 3d 222, 2007 Ohio 4791, — N.E. 2d —, 2007 Ohio LEXIS 2208 (Sept. 20, 2007).

Suspension

Attorney was suspended from the practice of law for six months based on findings that he neglected a client's case, attempted to cover up the neglect, failed to return the client's file on request, and failed to cooperate in the ensuing disciplinary investigation, in violation of former Ohio Code Prof. Resp. 9-102(B)(4), 6-101(A)(3), and 1-102(A)(4), and Ohio Sup. Ct. R. Gov't Bar V(4)(G), because the record amply justified the conclusions that the attorney neglected to appropriately advise his client of the proceedings in its case and then fabricated one or more letters to conceal his neglect. The mitigating factors did not outweigh the aggravating effect of having submitted false evidence and having acted out of self-interest in trying to cover up his misconduct. Disciplinary Counsel v. Broeren, — Ohio St. 3d —, 2007 Ohio 5251, — N.E. 2d —, 2007 Ohio LEXIS 2525 (Oct. 10, 2007).

RULE 8.5: DISCIPLINARY AUTHORITY; CHOICE OF LAW

(a) **Disciplinary Authority** A lawyer admitted to practice in Ohio is subject to the disciplinary authority of Ohio, regardless of where the lawyer's conduct occurs. A lawyer not admitted in Ohio is also subject to the disciplinary authority of Ohio if the lawyer provides or offers to provide any legal services in Ohio. A lawyer may be subject to the disciplinary authority of both Ohio and another jurisdiction for the same conduct.

(b) **Choice of Law** In any exercise of the disciplinary authority of Ohio, the rules of professional conduct to be applied shall be as follows:

(1) for conduct in connection with a matter pending before a tribunal, the rules of the jurisdiction in which the *tribunal* sits, unless the rules of the *tribunal* provide otherwise;

(2) for any other conduct, the rules of the jurisdiction in which the lawyer's conduct occurred, or, if the predominant effect of the conduct is in a different jurisdiction, the rules of that jurisdiction shall be applied to the conduct. A lawyer shall not be subject to discipline if the lawyer's conduct conforms to the rules of a jurisdiction in which the lawyer *reasonably believes* the predominant effect of the lawyer's conduct will occur.

FORM OF CITATION, EFFECTIVE DATE, APPLICATION

(a) These rules shall be known as the Ohio Rules of Professional Conduct and cited as "Prof. Cond. Rule ____."

(b) The Ohio Rules of Professional Conduct shall take effect February 1, 2007, at which time the Ohio Rules of Professional Conduct shall supersede and replace the Ohio Code of Professional Responsibility to govern the conduct of lawyers occurring on or after that effective date. The Ohio Code of Professional Responsibility shall continue to apply to govern conduct occurring prior to February 1, 2007 and shall apply to all disciplinary investigations and prosecutions relating to conduct that occurred prior to February 1, 2007.

(c) The Supreme Court of Ohio adopted amendments to Prof. Cond. Rule 5.5(d) and Comment [17] of the Ohio Rules of Professional Conduct effective September 1, 2007.

(d) The Supreme Court of Ohio adopted amendments to Prof. Cond. Rule 7.4 of the Ohio Rules of Professional Conduct effective April 1, 2009.

(e) The Supreme Court of Ohio adopted amendments to Prof. Cond. Rule 1.15 of the Ohio Rules of Professional Conduct effective January 1, 2010.

APPENDIX A

CORRELATION TABLE
OHIO RULES OF PROFESSIONAL CONDUCT TO
OHIO CODE OF PROFESSIONAL RESPONSIBILITY

The following is a numerical listing of the Ohio Rules of Professional Conduct with cross-references to provisions of the Ohio Code of Professional Responsibility or other Ohio law that address substantially similar subject-matter. A cross-reference does not indicate that a provision of the Ohio Code of Professional Responsibility or other Ohio law has been incorporated in the Ohio Rules of Professional Conduct. Please consult the code comparisons that follow each rule for a more detailed treatment of corresponding provisions.

Ohio Rules of Professional Conduct	Ohio Code of Professional Responsibility or Other Law
Rule 1.1 Competence	DR 6-101(A)(1) & (2)
Rule 1.2 Scope of Representation and Allocation of Authority	
Rule 1.2(a)	DR 7-101(A)(1), EC 7-7, 7-8, 7-10
Rule 1.2(c)	None
Rule 1.2(d)	DR 7-102(A)(7); EC 7-4
Rule 1.2(e)	DR 7-105
Rule 1.3 Diligence	DR 6-101(A)(3), 7-101(A)(1)
Rule 1.4 Communication	
Rule 1.4(a) & (b)	EC 7-8, 9-2
Rule 1.4(c)	DR 1-104
Rule 1.5 Fees and Expenses	
Rule 1.5(a)	DR 2-106(A) & (B)
Rule 1.5(b)	EC 2-18
Rule 1.5(c)	EC 2-18; R.C. 4705.15
Rule 1.5(d)	DR 2-106(C); EC 2-19
Rule 1.5(e) & (f)	DR 2-107
Rule 1.6 Confidentiality	
Rule 1.6(a)	DR 4-101(A), (B), & (C)(1)
Rule 1.6(b)(1)	None
Rule 1.6(b)(2)	DR 4-101(C)(3)
Rule 1.6(b)(3)	DR 7-102(B)(1)
Rule 1.6(b)(4)	None
Rule 1.6(b)(5)	DR 4-101(C)(4)

Rule 1.6(b)(6)	DR 4-101(C)(2)
Rule 1.6(c)	None
Rule 1.7 Conflict of Interest: **Current Clients**	DR 5-101(A)(1), 5-105(A), (B), & (C)
Rule 1.8 Conflict of Interest: **Current Clients: Specific Rules**	
Rule 1.8(a)	DR 5-104(A); *Cincinnati Bar Assn v.* *Hartke* (1993), 67 Ohio St.3d 65
Rule 1.8(b)	DR 4-101(B)(2)
Rule 1.8(c)	DR 5-101(A)(2) & (3)
Rule 1.8(d)	DR 5-104(B)
Rule 1.8(e)	DR 5-103(B)
Rule 1.8(f)(1), (2), & (3)	DR 5-107(A) & (B)
Rule 1.8(f)(4)	None
Rule 1.8(g)	DR 5-106
Rule 1.8(h)	DR 6-102; *Disciplinary Counsel v.* *Clavner* (1997), 77 Ohio St.3d 431
Rule 1.8(i)	DR 5-103(A)
Rule 1.8(j)	*Cleveland Bar Assn v. Feneli* (1996), 86 Ohio St. 3d 102 & *Disciplinary* *Counsel v. Moore* (2004), 101 Ohio St.3d 261
Rule 1.8(k)	DR 5-105(D)
Rule 1.9 Duties to Former Clients	DR 4-101(B); *Kala v. Aluminum* *Smelting & Refining Co.* (1998), 81 Ohio St. 3d 1
Rule 1.10 Imputation of Conflicts **of Interest: General Rule**	DR 5-105(D); *Kala v. Aluminum* *Smelting & Refining Co.* (1998), 81 Ohio St. 3d 1
Rule 1.11 Special Conflicts of **Interest for Former and Current** **Governmental Employees**	DR 9-101(B)
Rule 1.12 Former Judge, Arbitrator, **Mediator, or Other Third Party** **Neutral**	DR 9-101(A) & (B); EC 5-21
Rule 1.13 Organization as Client	EC 5-19
Rule 1.14 Client With Diminished **Capacity**	EC 7-11 & 7-12

Rule 1.15 Safekeeping Property
  Rule 1.15(a)   DR 9-102
  Rule 1.15(b)   DR 9-102(A)(1)
  Rule 1.15(c)   DR 9-102(A)
  Rule 1.15(d), (e), (f), & (g) None
  Rule 1.15(h)   DR 9-102(D) & (E)

Rule 1.16 Terminating
Representation
  Rule 1.16(a)   DR 2-110(B)
  Rule 1.16(b)   DR 2-110(A)(2), (C)(1), (C)(2), (C)(5),
                                (C)(6), & (C)(7)
  Rule 1.16(c)   DR 2-110(A)(1)
  Rule 1.16(d)   DR 2-110(A)(2)
  Rule 1.16(e)   DR 2-110(A)(3)

Rule 1.17 Sale of Law Practice   DR 2-111

Rule 1.18 Duties to Prospective EC 4-1; *Cuyahoga Cty Bar Assn v.*
Client   *Hardiman* (2003), 100 Ohio St.3d 260

Rule 2.1 Advisor   EC 7-8

Rule 2.3 Evaluation for Use by None
Third Persons

Rule 2.4 Lawyer Serving as   EC 5-21
Arbitrator, Mediator, or Third-
Party Neutral

Rule 3.1 Meritorious Claims and DR 7-102(A)(2); EC 7-25
Contentions

Rule 3.3 Candor Toward the
Tribunal
  Rule 3.3(a)   DR 7-102(A)(1), (4), & (5) &
                                  7-106(B)(1)
  Rule 3.3(b)   DR 7-102(B)
  Rule 3.3(c)   DR 7-106(B)
  Rule 3.3(d)   None

Rule 3.4 Fairness to Opposing
Party and Counsel
  Rule 3.4(a)   DR 7-102(A)(8) & 7-109(A); EC 7-27

Rule 3.4(b)	DR 7-102(A)(6) & 7-109(C); EC 7-26 & 7-28
Rule 3.4(c)	DR 7-106(A)
Rule 3.4(d)	DR 7-106(C)(7); EC 7-25
Rule 3.4(e)	DR 7-106(C)(1) & (4); EC 7-24
Rule 3.4(g)	DR 7-109(B); EC 7-27

Rule 3.5 Impartiality and Decorum of the Tribunal

Rule 3.5(a)	DR 7-106(C)(6), 7-108(A) & (B), & 7-110
Rule 3.5(b)	DR 7-108(G)

Rule 3.6 Trial Publicity   DR 7-107

Rule 3.7 Lawyer as Witness   DR 5-101(B) & 5-102

Rule 3.8 Special Responsibilities of Prosecutor

Rule 3.8(a)	DR 7-103(A)
Rule 3.8(d)	DR 7-103(B), EC 7-13
Rule 3.8(e)	None
Rule 3.8(g)	None

Rule 3.9 Advocate in Nonadjudicative Proceedings   None

Rule 4.1 Truthfulness in Statements to Others

Rule 4.1(a)	DR 7-102(A)(5)
Rule 4.1(b)	DR 7-102(A)(3) & 7-102(B)(1)

Rule 4.2 Communication with Person Represented by Counsel   DR 7-104(A)(1)

Rule 4.3 Dealing with Unrepresented Persons   DR 7-104(A)(2)

Rule 4.4 Respect for Rights of Third Persons

Rule 4.4(a)	DR 7-102(A)(1), 7-106(C)(2), & 7-108(D) & (E)
Rule 4.4(b)	None

Rule 5.1 Responsibilities of Partners and Supervisory Lawyers   None

Rule 5.2 Responsibilities of a Subordinate Lawyer   None

Rule 5.3 Responsibilities Regarding Nonlawyer Assistants   DR 4-101(D); EC 4-2; *Disciplinary Counsel v. Ball* (1993), 67 Ohio St. 3d 401 & *Mahoning Cty. Bar Assn v. Lavelle* (2005), 107 Ohio St.3d 92

Rule 5.4 Professional Independence of a Lawyer
Rule 5.4(a)   DR 3-102(A)
Rule 5.4(b)   DR 3-103
Rule 5.4(c)   DR 5-107(B)
Rule 5.4(d)   DR 5-107(C)

Rule 5.5 Unauthorized Practice of Law
Rule 5.5(a)   DR 3-101
Rule 5.5(b)   None
Rule 5.5(c)   None
Rule 5.5(d)   None

Rule 5.6 Restrictions on Right to Practice
Rule 5.6(a)   DR 2-108(A)
Rule 5.6(b)   DR 2-108(B)

Rule 5.7 Responsibilities Regarding Law-Related Services   None

Rule 6.2 Accepting Appointments   EC 2-25, 2-26, 2-27, 2-28, 2-29, 2-30, 2-31, & 2-32

Rule 6.5 Non-Profit and Court Annexed Limited Legal Service Programs   None

Rule 7.1 Communications Concerning a Lawyer's Services   DR 2-101

Rule 7.2 Advertising and Recommendation of Professional Employment	DR 2-101, 2-103, & 2-104(B)
Rule 7.3 Direct Contact with Prospective Clients	DR 2-104(A)
Rule 7.3(a)	DR 2-101(F)(1)
Rule 7.3(b)	None
Rule 7.3(c)	DR 2-101(F)(2)
Rule 7.3(d)	DR 2-101(F)(4)
Rule 7.3(e)	DR 2-101(H)
Rule 7.3(f)	DR 2-103(D)(4)
Rule 7.4 Communication of Fields of Practice and Specialization	DR 2-105
Rule 7.5 Firm Names and Letterheads	DR 2-102
Rule 8.1 Bar Admission and Disciplinary Matters	DR 1-101
Rule 8.2 Judicial Officials	
Rule 8.2(a)	DR 8-102
Rule 8.2(b)	DR 2-102(A)(1)
Rule 8.3 Reporting Professional Misconduct	DR 1-103
Rule 8.4 Misconduct	
Rule 8.4(a)	DR 1-102(A)(1) & (2)
Rule 8.4(b)	DR 1-102(A)(3)
Rule 8.4(c)	DR 1-102(A)(4)
Rule 8.4(d)	DR 1-102(A)(5)
Rule 8.4(e)	DR 1-102(A)(5) & 9-101(C)
Rule 8.4(f)	DR 1-102(A)(5)
Rule 8.4(g)	DR 1-102(B)
Rule 8.4(h)	DR 1-102(A)(6)
Rule 8.5 Disciplinary Authority, Choice of Law	None

APPENDIX B

CORRELATION TABLE
OHIO CODE OF PROFESSIONAL RESPONSIBILITY TO
OHIO MODEL RULES OF PROFESSIONAL CONDUCT

The following is a numerical listing of the Ohio Code of Professional Responsibility with cross-references to provisions of the Ohio Rules of Professional Conduct that address substantially similar subject-matter. A cross-reference does not indicate that a provision of the Ohio Code of Professional Responsibility has been incorporated in the Ohio Rules of Professional Conduct. Please consult the code comparisons that follow each rule for a more detailed treatment of corresponding provisions.

Ohio Code of Professional Responsibility	Ohio Rules of Professional Conduct
CANON 1	
DR 1-101 Maintaining Integrity and Competence of the Legal Profession	Rule 8.1
DR 1-102 Misconduct	
DR 1-102(A)(1)	Rules 8.2(b) & 8.4(a)
DR 1-102(A)(2)	Rule 8.4(a)
DR 1-102(A)(3)	Rule 8.4(b)
DR 1-102(A)(4)	Rule 8.4(c)
DR 1-102(A)(5)	Rules 8.4(d), (e), & (f)
DR 1-102(A)(6)	Rule 8.4(h)
DR 1-102(B)	Rule 8.4(g)
DR 1-103 Disclosure of Information to Authorities	Rule 8.3
DR 1-104 Disclosure of Information to the Clients	Rule 1.4(c)
CANON 2	
DR 2-101 Publicity	Rules 7.1, 7.2(a), (c), & (d), & 7.3(a), (c), (d), & (e)
DR 2-102 Professional Notices, Letterheads, and Offices	Rules 7.5 & 8.2(b)
DR 2-103 Recommendation of Professional Employment	Rules 7.2 & 7.3(f)

DR 2-104 Suggestion of Need of Legal Services

DR 2-104(A)	Rule 7.3
DR 2-104(B)	Rule 7.2

DR 2-105 Limitation of Practice Rule 7.4

DR 2-106 Fees for Legal Services

DR 2-106(A) & (B)	Rule 1.5(a)
DR 2-106(C)	Rule 1.5(d)

DR 2-107 Division of Fees Among Lawyers Rules 1.5(e) &

DR 2-108 Agreements Restricting the Practice of a Lawyer Rule 5.6

DR 2-109 Acceptance of Employment None

DR 2-110 Withdrawal from Employment Rule 1.16

DR 2-111 Sale of Law Practice Rule 1.17

CANON 3

DR 3-101 Aiding Unauthorized Practice of Law Rule 5.5(a)

DR 3-102 Dividing Legal Fees with a Nonlawyer Rule 5.4(a)

DR 3-103 Forming a Partnership with a Nonlawyer Rule 5.4(b)

CANON 4

DR 4-101 Preservation of Confidences and Secrets of a Client

DR 4-101(A), (B), & (C)(1)	Rule 1.6(a)
DR 4-101(B)	Rule 1.9
DR 4-101(B)(2)	Rule 1.8(b)
DR 4-101(C)(2)	Rule 1.6(b)(6)
DR 4-101(C)(3)	Rule 1.6(b)(2)
DR 4-101(C)(4)	Rule 1.6(b)(5)
DR 4-101(D)	Rule 5.3

CANON 5

**DR 5-101 Refusing Employment
When the Interests of the Lawyer
May Impair the Lawyer's Independent
Professional Judgment**
DR 5-101(A)(1)   Rule 1.7
DR 5-101(A)(2) & (3)   Rule 1.8(c)
DR 5-101(B)   Rule 3.7

DR 5-102 Withdrawal as Counsel When the   Rule 3.7
Lawyer Becomes a Witness

**DR 5-103 Avoiding Acquisition of
Interest in Litigation**
DR 5-103(A)   Rule 1.8(i)
DR 5-103(B)   Rule 1.8(e)

**DR 5-104 Limiting Business Relations
with a Client**
DR 5-104(A)   Rule 1.8(a)
DR 5-104(B)   Rule 1.8(d)

**DR 5-105 Refusing to Accept or Continue
Employment if the Interests of Another
Client May Impair the Independent
Professional Judgment of the Lawyer**
DR 5-105(A), (B), & (C)   Rule 1.7
DR 5-105(D)   Rules 1.8(k) & 1.10

DR 5-106 Settling Similar Claims of Clients   Rule 1.8(g)

**DR 5-107 Avoiding Influence by Others
Than the Client**
DR 5-107(A) & (B)   Rule 1.8(f)(1), (2), & (3)
DR 5-107(B) & (C)   Rule 5.4(c) & (d)

CANON 6

DR 6-101 Failing to Act Competently
DR 6-101(A)(1) & (2)   Rule 1.1
DR 6-101(A)(3)   Rule 1.3

DR 6-102 Limiting Liability to Client   Rule 1.8(h)

CANON 7

DR 7-101 Representing a Client Zealously
DR 7-101(A)(1)   Rules 1.2(a) & 1.3

**DR 7-102 Representing a Client Within
the Bounds of the Law**
DR 7-102(A)(1)   Rules 3.3(a)(3) & 4.4(a)
DR 7-102(A)(2)   Rule 3.1
DR 7-102(A)(3), (4), & (5)   Rules 3.3 & 4.1
DR 7-102(A)(4) & (6)   Rule 3.3(a)
DR 7-102(A)(6)   Rule 3.4(b)
DR 7-102(A)(7)   Rule 1.2(d)
DR 7-102(A)(8)   Rule 3.4(a)
DR 7-102(B)   Rules 1.6(b)(3), 3.3(b), & 4.1

DR 7-103 Performing the Duty of Public   Rule 3.8
Prosecutor or Other Government Lawyer

**DR 7-104 Communicating With One of
Adverse Interest**
DR 7-104(A)(1)   Rule 4.2
DR 7-104(A)(2)   Rule 4.3

DR 7-105 Threatening Criminal   Rule 1.2(e)
Prosecution

DR 7-106 Trial Conduct
DR 7-106(A)   Rule 3.4(c)
DR 7-106(B)(1)   Rule 3.3(a) & (c)
DR 7-106(C)(1) & (4)   Rule 3.4(e)
DR 7-106(C)(2)   Rule 4.4(a)
DR 7-106(C)(6)   Rule 3.5(a)(6)
DR 7-106(C)(7)   Rule 3.4(d)

DR 7-107 Trial Publicity   Rule 3.6

**DR 7-108 Communication With or
Investigation of Jurors**
DR 7-108(A) & (B)   Rule 3.5(a)
DR 7-108(D) & (E)   Rule 4.4(a)
DR 7-108(G)   Rule 3.5(b)

OHIO ETHICAL CONSIDERATIONS ADDRESSED IN OHIO RULES OF PROFESSIONAL CONDUCT

EC 2-18 Agreement with Client with Respect to Fees	Rules 1.5(b) & (c)
EC 2-19 Contingent Fee Arrangements	Rule 1.5(d)(1)
EC 2-25 – 2-32 Acceptance and Retention of Employment	Rule 6.2
EC 4-1 Confidences and Secrets	Rule 1.18
EC 4-2 Confidences and Secrets	Rule 5.3
EC 5-19 Organizational Clients	Rule 1.13
EC 5-21 Arbitrator or Mediator	Rules 1.12 & 2.4
EC 7-4 Construction of Law; Frivolous Conduct	Rule 1.2(d)
EC 7-7 Decision-Making Authority	Rule 1.2(a)
EC 7-8 Informing Client of Relevant Considerations; Withdrawal from Employment	Rules 1.2(a), 1.4(a) & (b), and 2.1
EC 7-10 Zealous Advocacy	Rule 1.2(a)
EC 7-11 Varying Responsibilities Dependent Upon Client	Rule 1.14
EC 7-12 Incompetent Client	Rule 1.14
EC 7-13 Responsibility of Prosecutor	Rule 3.8
EC 7-24 Expression by Attorney of Personal Opinion in Court	Rule 3.4
EC 7-25 Adherence to Procedural Rules	Rules 3.1 & 3.4
EC 7-26 False Testimony	Rule 3.4
EC 7-27 Suppression of Evidence	Rule 3.4
EC 7-28 Fees to Witnesses	Rule 3.4

EC 9-2 Promoting Public Confidence   Rules 1.4(a) & (b)
   in Legal Profession

Index to Code of Professional Conduct

SUPREME COURT RULES FOR THE GOVERNMENT OF THE JUDICIARY OF OHIO

RULE I
PROFESSIONAL RESPONSIBILITY AND JUDICIAL ETHICS

Section 1. Applicability

The Ohio Rules of Professional Conduct, effective February 1, 2007, as amended, shall be binding upon all persons admitted to practice law in Ohio. The willful breach of the Rules by a Justice, judge, or candidate for judicial office shall be punished by reprimand, suspension, disbarment, or probation as provided in Gov. Jud. R. II and Gov. Bar R. V. The Code of Judicial Conduct, as adopted by the Supreme Court, effective December 20, 1973, and set forth in 36 Ohio State 2d Reports, as amended, shall be binding upon all judicial officers of this state and candidates for judicial office. The willful breach of the Code shall be punished by reprimand, suspension, disbarment, or probation as provided in Gov. Jud. R. II and Gov. Bar R. V, or by retirement, removal, or suspension from office, as provided in Gov. Jud. R. III.

Section 2. Duty of Lawyers

It is the duty of the lawyer to maintain towards the courts a respectful attitude, not for the sake of the temporary incumbent of the judicial office, but for the maintenance of its supreme importance. Justices and judges, not being wholly free to defend themselves, are peculiarly entitled to receive the support of lawyers against unjust criticism and clamor. Whenever there is proper ground for serious complaint of a judicial officer, it is the right and duty of the lawyer to submit a grievance to the proper authorities. These charges should be encouraged and the person making them should be protected.

History: Amended effective October 1, 1986; January 1, 1988; January 1, 1993, February 1, 2007.

RULE II
DISCIPLINARY PROCEDURE

Section 1. Board of Commissioners on Grievances and Discipline of the Supreme Court

There is created under Rule V of the Supreme Court Rules for the Government of the Bar of Ohio a Board of Commissioners on Grievances and Discipline of the Supreme Court. The Board shall receive evidence, preserve the record, make findings, and submit recommendations to the Supreme Court as follows:

(A) Concerning complaints of misconduct that are alleged to have been committed by a justice, judge, or candidate for judicial office;

(B) Concerning allegations that a justice or judge is unable to discharge the duties of judicial office by virtue of a mental or physical disability;

(C) Upon reference by the Supreme Court of conduct by a justice, judge, or candidate for judicial office affecting any proceeding under these rules or the Supreme Court Rules for the Government of the Bar of Ohio, where the acts allegedly constitute a contempt of the Supreme Court or a breach of these rules but did not take place in the presence of the Supreme Court or a member of the Supreme Court, whether by willful disobedience of any order or judgment of the Supreme Court or an order or subpoena issued by the Board of Commissioners, by interference with any officer of the Supreme Court in the prosecution of any duty, or otherwise. Nothing in this section shall be construed as limiting or affecting the plenary power of the Supreme Court to impose punishment with reference either to contempts or breaches of these rules committed in its presence or the plenary power of any other court with reference to contempts committed in its presence.

Section 2. Authority and Duty of Disciplinary Counsel and Certified Grievance Committees

(A) Except as provided in Section 5 of this rule, a grievance alleging misconduct of a judge or candidate for judicial office, or alleging that a judge is unable to discharge the duties of judicial office by virtue of a mental or physical disability, shall be filed with Disciplinary Counsel or with a Grievance Committee certified pursuant to Gov. Bar R. V. Disciplinary Counsel and Certified Grievance Committees shall have authority to investigate grievances, file formal complaints with the Board, and prosecute formal complaints filed with the Board.

(B) Except as provided in Section 5 and 6 of this rule, a grievance alleging misconduct of the Chief Justice or a justice of the Supreme Court, or alleging that the Chief Justice or a justice of the Supreme Court is unable to discharge the duties of judicial office by virtue of a mental or physical disability, shall be filed with Disciplinary Counsel. Disciplinary Counsel shall review the grievance to determine whether an ethical violation is alleged. If the grievance alleges an ethical violation, Disciplinary Counsel promptly shall forward the grievance to the Chief Justice of the Courts of Appeals, elected pursuant to section 2501.03 of the Revised Code, for further proceedings in accordance with Section 4 of this rule. A grievance alleging misconduct by a former Chief Justice or justice of the Supreme Court shall proceed pursuant to Gov. Bar R. V or division (A) of this section.

Section 3. Application of Rule

A grievance or complaint involving alleged misconduct by a justice, judge, or judicial candidate; all proceedings for the discipline of a justice, judge, or judicial candidate; and all proceedings with regard to the alleged inability of a justice or judge to discharge the duties of judicial office by virtue of a mental or physical disability shall be brought, conducted, and disposed of in accordance with the provisions of this rule and Gov. Bar R. V. Sections 4 and 6 of this rule contain provisions for adjudicating grievances and complaints against a justice of or candidate for the Supreme Court. Section 5 of this rule contains provisions for adjudicating campaign grievances and complaints against a candidate for a trial court or court of appeals.

Section 4. Grievances Against Supreme Court Justices

(A) Initial review

(1) Upon receipt of a grievance from Disciplinary Counsel, the Chief Justice of the Courts of Appeals shall select, by lot, a three-member review panel from among the judges designated pursuant to division (A)(3) of this section. The review panel shall contact the justice named in the grievance for a written response within fourteen days to the allegations contained in the grievance. Upon request, the review panel may grant a reasonable extension of time for the justice to provide a response.

(2) Upon receipt of the response, or if no response is received, the review panel shall review the grievance and any response to determine whether good cause exists for further investigation of the grievance. The review panel shall report its determination in writing to the Chief Justice of the Courts of Appeals. If the review panel determines that good cause does not exist for further investigation, the Chief Justice of the Courts of Appeals shall notify the grievant of the determination and of the dismissal of the grievance.

(3) In January each year, the administrative judge of each appellate district shall designate one appellate judge from the district, other than the presiding judge, to be eligible for service on a review panel pursuant to division (A)(1) of this section. The administrative judge shall advise the Chief Justice of the Courts of Appeals, in writing, of the designation. Appointments shall be for a calendar year, and a judge may be reappointed to subsequent terms on the review panels.

(B) Appointment of special disciplinary counsel; time limits

(1)(a) If the review panel determines that good cause exists for further investigation, the Chief Justice of the

Courts of Appeals shall appoint a special disciplinary counsel to conduct further investigation of the allegations contained in the grievance and any other misconduct discovered during the course of investigating the grievance. The special disciplinary counsel shall possess the qualifications set forth in division (B)(3)(a) of this section and may be appointed from the list maintained by the Office of Disciplinary Counsel pursuant to division (B)(3)(c) of this section.

(b) The investigation of a grievance by special disciplinary counsel shall be concluded within sixty days from the date the grievance is transmitted to special disciplinary counsel, and a decision on disposition of the grievance shall be made within thirty days after the conclusion of the investigation. Extensions of time for completion of the investigation may be granted by the Chief Justice of the Courts of Appeals upon written request and for good cause shown, provided that an investigation for which one or more extensions are granted shall be completed within one hundred fifty days from the date the grievance is transmitted to special disciplinary counsel. Extensions beyond one hundred fifty days may be granted by the Chief Justice of the Courts of Appeals in the event of pending litigation or appeals, an unusually complex investigation, including the investigation of multiple grievances, time delays in obtaining evidence or testimony of witnesses, or for other good cause shown. No investigation shall extend more than one year from the date the grievance is transmitted to special disciplinary counsel.

(c) The time limits set forth in this rule are not jurisdictional. No grievance filed shall be dismissed unless it appears that there has been an unreasonable delay and that the rights of the respondent to a fair hearing have been violated. An investigation that extends beyond one year from the date the grievance is transmitted to special disciplinary counsel is prima facie evidence of unreasonable delay.

(2)(a) Upon completion of the investigation, special disciplinary counsel shall either report to the Chief Justice of the Courts of Appeals that the grievance should be dismissed or prepare and file a formal complaint with the Chief Justice of the Courts of Appeals, in the name of special disciplinary counsel as relator, alleging that substantial, credible evidence exists to believe that the justice named in the grievance engaged in misconduct. The complaint shall be submitted with investigatory materials sufficient to demonstrate the existence of substantial, credible evidence to support the allegations of the complaint. The materials shall include any response filed by or on behalf of the respondent and may include other reports, summaries, depositions, statements, exhibits, or any other relevant material.

(b) If the special disciplinary counsel recommends the grievance be dismissed, the Chief Justice of the Courts of Appeals shall notify the grievant and the justice named in the grievance of such determination in writing.

(c) Unless the justice against whom the grievance has been filed agrees otherwise, the matter shall remain private unless and until a formal complaint is filed.

(3)(a) The special disciplinary counsel shall be an attorney admitted to the practice of law in Ohio, or an attorney licensed and in good standing in any other state and admitted pro hac vice by the Chief Justice of the Courts of Appeals. The special disciplinary counsel shall not be an employee or appointee of the Supreme Court or have any interest in a case pending before the Supreme Court while serving as the special disciplinary counsel. The special disciplinary counsel shall have the power to issue subpoenas and cause testimony to be taken under oath.

(b) The special disciplinary counsel shall be paid expenses and reasonable compensation, upon approval of the Chief Justice of the Courts of Appeals, from the Attorney Services Fund. The Chief Justice of the Courts of Appeals may authorize the special disciplinary counsel to employ support staff as necessary to assist in the investigation and any subsequent proceedings and may authorize payment of fees, compensation, and expenses from the Fund.

(c) The Office of Disciplinary Counsel shall maintain and provide to the Chief Justice of the Courts of Appeals in January each year a list of attorneys who satisfy the qualifications for appointment as special disciplinary counsel and who are otherwise available to accept such appointment.

(C) **Appointment of hearing panel; proceedings on the formal complaint**

(1) Upon receipt of a formal complaint filed by the special disciplinary counsel, the Chief Justice of the Courts of Appeals shall do both of the following:

(a) Appoint a hearing panel of three fulltime trial court judges selected, by lot, from the list of judges developed and maintained pursuant to division (C)(5) of this section. The judges chosen shall be from separate appellate districts and shall not be from the district in which the respondent resides. The Chief Justice of the Courts of Appeals shall designate one of the judges to serve as the chair of the hearing panel.

(b) Immediately forward the formal complaint to the Secretary of the Board of Commissioners, who shall send a copy of the formal complaint by certified mail to the respondent. The complaint shall be accompanied by a notice requiring the respondent to file, within twenty days after the mailing of the complaint, six copies of the respondent's answer and serve copies of the answer on special disciplinary counsel and the Chief Justice of the Courts of Appeals. For good cause shown, the Chief Justice of the Courts of Appeals may grant an extension of time to file the answer.

(2) With reasonable notice to the parties, the hearing panel shall hold a hearing on the complaint. The hearing panel chair may grant requests for continuances for good cause shown. All hearings shall be recorded by a court reporter and a transcript included in the record of the proceedings.

(3) If at the end of the evidence presented by the relator, a unanimous hearing panel finds that the evidence is insufficient to support a charge or count of misconduct or a finding of disability, the panel may order the complaint or count be dismissed. If at the end of all evidence, a majority of the hearing panel finds that the evidence is insufficient to support a charge or count of misconduct, the panel may order the

complaint or count be dismissed. The hearing panel chair shall give written notice of the action taken to the Secretary who shall notify the Chief Justice of the Courts of Appeals, relator, and respondent. There shall be no appeal from an order dismissing the complaint or count of misconduct.

(4) If a majority of the hearing panel determines, by clear and convincing evidence, that the respondent is guilty of misconduct and a disciplinary sanction is merited or that the respondent has a mental or physical disability that makes the respondent unable to discharge the duties of office, the hearing panel shall file a certified report of the proceedings, its findings of fact, conclusions of law and recommended sanction with the Secretary. The report shall include the transcript of testimony taken and an itemized statement of the actual and necessary expenses incurred in connection with the proceedings. The Secretary shall send a copy of the hearing panel's report and recommendations to the Chief Justice of the Courts of Appeals and serve a copy of the report and recommendations, by certified mail, on the relator and respondent. At the conclusion of all proceedings before the hearing panel, the Secretary shall file the record of such proceedings with the Clerk of the Supreme Court as provided in division (E)(1) of this section.

(5) In January each year, the administrative judge of each appellate district shall designate two fulltime trial judges from within the appellate district to be eligible to serve on a hearing panel appointed pursuant to division (C)(1)(a) of this section. In selecting the trial judges who shall be eligible for appointment to hearing panels, the administrative judge shall consider legal and judicial experience, gender, race, ethnicity, and other relevant factors. Before designating a judge as eligible for selection to serve on a hearing panel, the administrative judge shall contact the judge to determine the judge's availability for potential service. The administrative judge shall advise the Chief Justice of the Courts of Appeals, in writing, of the designations.

(D) **Appointment of adjudicatory panel; proceedings before the panel**

(1) Upon receipt of the hearing panel's report and recommendations, the Chief Justice of the Courts of Appeals shall convene an adjudicatory panel of thirteen appellate judges to review the report and recommendations. The adjudicatory panel shall consist of the Chief Justice of the Courts of Appeals, who shall serve as chair of the panel, and the presiding judge of each appellate district. If a presiding judge of an appellate district is unavailable to serve on the adjudicatory panel, the appellate judge of the district who is senior in service on the court of appeals shall replace the presiding judge.

(2) The adjudicatory panel shall issue the respondent an order to show cause why the report and recommendation of the hearing panel shall not be confirmed and a disciplinary order entered. The Clerk shall serve notice of the show cause order by certified mail on relator and respondent.

(3) Within twenty days after issuance of the show cause order, the respondent or relator may file objections to the report or recommendations of the hearing panel with the Clerk. The objections shall be accom-

panied by a brief in support of the objections and proof of service of copies of the objections and the brief on all counsel of record. Twelve copies of the objections and brief in support shall be filed. Answer briefs and proof of service shall be filed within fifteen days after briefs in support of objections have been filed. Twelve copies of the answer briefs shall be filed.

(4) If objections are filed, the adjudicatory panel shall promptly schedule oral argument on objections. After the hearing on objections, or if no objections are filed, the adjudicatory panel shall issue an order as it finds proper. Unless otherwise ordered, any disciplinary order or order related to the respondent's mental or physical disability shall be effective on the date the order is announced. The order may provide for reimbursement to the Attorney Services Fund of costs and expenses incurred by special disciplinary counsel, the panels appointed pursuant to this section, or the Secretary.

(5) The Clerk shall mail certified copies of the order to the parties. The Supreme Court Reporter shall publish the disciplinary order in the *Ohio Official Reports and the Ohio State Bar Association Report.*

(E) **Miscellaneous provisions**

(1) Upon the filing of a formal complaint, the Secretary of the Board of Commissioners on Grievances and Discipline shall serve as clerk for the Chief Justice of the Courts of Appeals and the hearing panel. The relator and respondent shall file all pleadings, motions, documents, and other material with the Secretary, who shall transmit the documents and materials to the Chief Justice of the Courts of Appeals and the appropriate panel. The Chief Justice of the Courts of Appeals and panels shall transmit all orders, opinions, and other materials to the Secretary for service on or distribution to the parties. The Secretary shall maintain a complete record of the proceedings and, upon conclusion of the proceedings before the hearing panel, certify the record, including exhibits, to the Clerk of the Supreme Court who shall maintain the certified record. The Clerk shall serve as clerk for any adjudicatory panel appointed pursuant to division (D) of this section, and all proceedings before the adjudicatory panel shall be conducted as provided in this section and the Rules of Practice of the Supreme Court of Ohio. Upon request, the Secretary and Clerk shall assist the Chief Justice of the Courts of Appeals, hearing panel, and adjudicatory panel with ministerial matters such as scheduling a location for hearings and securing a court reporter.

(2) Any matter, a procedure for which is not specifically set forth in this rule, shall be handled in the manner set forth in Gov. Bar. R. V.

(3) If a judge selected to serve on any panel appointed pursuant to Section 4 of this rule is unable to serve because of the existence of a disqualifying factor, the judge shall notify the Chief Justice of the Courts of Appeals and provide written justification of the grounds for disqualification.

(4) The Chief Justice of the Courts of Appeals and any judge appointed to serve in any capacity pursuant to Section 4 of this rule shall continue to serve in the appointed capacity until the conclusion of the matter as long as the judge continues to hold judicial office. If the Chief Justice of the Courts of Appeals leaves judicial office while a matter commenced under this rule during his or her tenure remains pending, the successor Chief Justice of the Courts of Appeals shall assume responsibility for that matter. If a judge appointed to serve in any capacity under this rule leaves judicial office while a matter to which the judge was assigned under this rule remains pending, the Chief Justice of the Courts of Appeals shall designate a judge to replace the former judge in the same manner as the original appointment was made.

(5) A party may allege the existence of bias, prejudice, or other disqualifying factor on the part of a judge appointed to serve on a panel pursuant to Section 4 of this rule by filing a timely motion with the Chief Justice of the Courts of Appeals. If the Chief Justice of the Courts of Appeals finds the existence of bias, prejudice, or other disqualifying factor, the judge named in the motion shall be disqualified, and the Chief Justice of the Courts of Appeals shall designate a judge to replace the disqualified judge in the same manner as the original appointment was made.

(6) Any judge selected to serve on any panel appointed pursuant to Section 4 of this rule shall be reimbursed from the Attorney Services Fund for travel expenses incurred in association with the judge's service on the panel. Reimbursement for travel expenses shall be made as provided in the Supreme Court Guidelines for Travel by Court Appointees. A judge shall request reimbursement by submitting a signed Travel Expense Report form and required receipts to the Chief Justice of the Courts of Appeals. The Chief Justice of the Courts of Appeals shall indicate approval of the reimbursement request and submit the approved form to the Administrative Director of the Supreme Court.

Section 5. Campaign Conduct; Enforcement and Sanctions

Notwithstanding Section 2 of this rule, a grievance that alleges a violation by a judicial candidate of Canon 4 of the Code of Judicial Conduct during the course of a campaign for judicial office shall be brought, conducted, and disposed of in accordance with this rule and Gov. Bar R. V, as modified by this section. All other grievances shall be brought, conducted, and disposed of in accordance with this rule and Gov. Bar R. V.

(A) **Filing of grievance; preliminary review; referral**

(1) A grievance that alleges a violation by a judicial candidate of Canon 4 of the Code of Judicial Conduct during the course of a campaign for judicial office shall be filed with the secretary of the Board of Commissioners on Grievances and Discipline. Within two days of receiving the grievance, the secretary shall conduct a preliminary review. If the secretary is unable to conduct the preliminary review because of a conflict of interest, he or she immediately shall forward the grievance to the chair of the Board who shall conduct the preliminary review. If the chair has a conflict of interest or is unavailable, the secretary immediately shall forward the grievance to the vice-chair of the Board who shall conduct the preliminary review.

(2) If a judicial candidate files a grievance alleging a violation by his or her opponent of Canon 4 of the Code of Judicial Conduct and the judicial candidate and his or her opponent have signed an agreement with a voluntarily organized judicial election monitoring committee that provides for expedited consideration of alleged violations of Canon 4 of the Code of Judicial Conduct, the secretary may refer the grievance to the monitoring committee for consideration. The secretary shall not refer the grievance to the monitoring committee if the judicial candidate has exhausted the remedies provided for under the agreement.

(3) The secretary, chair, or vice-chair may refer a grievance to the Disciplinary Counsel under any of the following circumstances:

(a) The probable cause panel fails to find probable cause that a violation of Canon 4 has occurred;

(b) Secretary, chair, or vice-chair determines that it is unnecessary to handle the grievance on an expedited basis;

(c) The complainant withdraws the grievance or fails to prosecute the complaint before the Board hearing panel, five-judge commission, or Supreme Court.

(B) **Probable cause panel; filing of formal complaint** If, after reviewing the grievance, the secretary, chair, or vice-chair determines that the grievance is facially valid, that the Board has jurisdiction over the matters raised in the grievance, and that the grievance should be considered on an expedited basis, the secretary immediately shall appoint three members of the Board to determine whether there is probable cause that a violation of Canon 4 has occurred. No member of the probable cause panel shall be a resident of the judicial district from which the grievance arose. The probable cause panel shall determine probable cause within five days after the grievance was filed and may conduct a hearing to facilitate the determination of probable cause. If the probable cause panel finds probable cause that a violation of Canon 4 has occurred, the panel shall notify the secretary who shall prepare a formal complaint based on instructions from the probable cause panel.

(C) **Appointment of hearing panel; proceedings on the formal complaint**

(1) Within three days of the probable cause determination, the chair shall appoint three members of the Board to conduct a formal hearing on the complaint. One member of the hearing panel shall be a nonattorney member of the Board, and no member of the hearing panel shall be a resident of the judicial district in which the complaint arose. The secretary shall forward a copy of the complaint to each member of the hearing panel, the complainant, and the respondent.

(2) The chair or secretary may designate former members of the Board to serve on probable cause and hearing panels appointed pursuant to divisions (B) and (C)(1) of this section.

(3) Within five days of its appointment, the hearing panel shall conduct a formal hearing limited to the allegations contained in the complaint. The complainant and respondent shall be notified of the hearing. Within five days after conclusion of the hearing, the hearing panel shall issue a report of its findings and recommendations. If the hearing panel determines by clear and convincing evidence that a violation of Canon 4 has occurred, the hearing panel's report and the record of the proceeding shall be certified to the Supreme Court, together with a recommendation as to whether the complaint should be considered on an expedited basis and whether the five-judge commission appointed pursuant to division (D) of this section should issue a cease and desist order pursuant to division (D)(2) of this section. If the hearing panel determines by clear and convincing evidence that a violation of Canon 4 has occurred, the hearing panel shall determine whether the respondent previously has been found to have violated Canon 4 and include the determination in its report.

(D) **Appointment of five-judge commission; proceedings before the commission**

(1) Within five days of receiving the report, the Supreme Court shall appoint a commission of five judges as provided in section 2701.11 of the Revised Code and Gov. Jud. R. III. The commission shall expedite its consideration of the report and may make its determination from the report of the hearing panel, permit or require the filing of briefs, conduct oral argument, or order the hearing panel to take additional evidence. If the commission concludes the record supports the hearing panel's finding that a violation of Canon 4 has occurred and there has been no abuse of discretion by the hearing panel, the commission may enter an order that includes one or more of the following:

(a) A disciplinary sanction against the respondent;

(b) An order enforceable by contempt of court that the respondent cease and desist from engaging in the conduct that was found to be in violation of Canon 4;

(c) A fine imposed against the respondent;

(d) An assessment against the respondent of the costs of the proceeding;

(e) An assessment against the respondent of the reasonable and necessary attorneys fees incurred by the complainant in prosecuting the grievance.

(2) Upon recommendation of the hearing panel, motion of the complainant or *sua sponte*, the commission may enter an interim cease and desist order as it finds reasonable and necessary prior to making the determination required by division (D)(1) of this section. The interim order shall be based on the commission's preliminary review of the report and recommendation of the hearing panel and any record made before the commission.

(3) A party may allege the existence of bias, prejudice, or other disqualifying factor on the part of a judge appointed by the Supreme Court to serve on a commission of five judges by filing a motion with the Chief Justice of the Supreme Court. The motion shall be filed within three days of the date the party receives notice of the appointment of the commission. If the Chief Justice finds the existence of bias, prejudice, or other disqualifying factor, the judge named in the motion shall be disqualified, and the Supreme Court shall appoint a substitute judge.

(E) **Appeal of sanction** The respondent may appeal a sanction issued by the commission to the Supreme Court. Notice of appeal shall be given by the respondent to the secretary of the commission and the

Supreme Court within twenty days after the respondent's receipt by certified mail of the commission's order. After receipt of the notice of appeal, the Court may issue a briefing order and other appropriate orders.

Section 6. Campaign Conduct; Enforcement and Sanctions; Justices and Candidates for the Supreme Court

A grievance that alleges a violation by a judicial candidate for the Supreme Court of Canon 4 of the Code of Judicial Conduct during the course of a campaign for judicial office shall be brought, conducted, and disposed of in accordance with this section.

(A) **Initial review**

(1) The grievance shall be filed with the Secretary of the Board of Commissioners on Grievances and Discipline. The Secretary shall promptly forward the grievance and any supporting documentation to the Chief Justice of the Courts of Appeals, elected pursuant to section 2501.03 of the Revised Code. Within two days of receiving the grievance, the Chief Justice of the Courts of Appeals shall review the grievance to determine whether the grievance alleges a violation of Canon 4 by a judicial candidate for the Supreme Court and whether the grievance should be considered on an expedited basis. If the Chief Justice of the Courts of Appeals determines that no Canon 4 violation is alleged or that the grievance should not be considered on an expedited basis, he or she may dismiss the grievance and notify the grievant of such determination or proceed with a review of the grievance pursuant to Section 4 of this rule.

(2) If the Chief Justice of the Courts of Appeals determines that the grievance alleges a violation of Canon 4 by a judicial candidate for the Supreme Court and that the grievance should be considered on an expedited basis, the Chief Justice of the Courts of Appeals shall immediately refer the grievance to a three-member review panel selected, by lot, from among the judges designated pursuant to Section 4(A)(3) of this rule. The review panel shall contact the judicial candidate named in the grievance for a written response, and determine from the grievance and the response whether probable cause exists that a violation of Canon 4 occurred. The review panel may conduct a hearing to facilitate the determination of probable cause. The probable cause determination shall be made within five days after the grievance was received by the Chief Justice of the Courts of Appeals.

(3) The review panel shall notify the Chief Justice of the Courts of Appeals of its probable cause determination and, if applicable, instructions regarding the preparation of a formal complaint. If the review panel finds no probable cause, the Chief Justice of the Courts of Appeals shall dismiss the grievance and notify the grievant. If the review panel finds probable cause, the Chief Justice of the Courts of Appeals shall instruct the Secretary of the Board of Commissioners on Grievances and Discipline to prepare a formal complaint in accordance with the instructions of the probable cause panel and in the name of the grievant as relator. Upon preparation of the formal complaint, the Secretary shall serve a copy of the formal complaint on the relator and respondent and transmit a copy to the Chief Justice of the Courts of Appeal.

(B) **Appointment of hearing panel; proceedings on the formal complaint**

(1) Within three days of a determination that probable cause exists to support the preparation and prosecution of a formal complaint, the Chief Justice of the Courts of Appeals shall appoint a hearing panel of three fulltime trial court judges selected, by lot, from the list of judges developed and maintained pursuant to Section 4(C)(5) of this rule. The judges chosen shall be from separate appellate districts and shall not be from the district in which the respondent resides. The Chief Justice of the Courts of Appeals shall designate one of the judges to serve as the chair of the hearing panel.

(2) Within five days of appointment and with notice to the parties, the hearing panel shall hold a hearing on the complaint. All hearings shall be recorded by a court reporter and a transcript included in the record of the proceedings.

(3) Within five days of the conclusion of the hearing, the hearing panel shall prepare and issue a report of its findings and recommendations. If the panel finds, by clear and convincing evidence, that the respondent violated Canon 4 of the Code of Judicial Conduct and that a sanction for such violation is warranted, the hearing panel's report and the record of the proceedings shall be certified to the Secretary, together with a recommendation as to whether the complaint should be considered on an expedited basis and whether the five-judge commission appointed pursuant to division (C) of this section should issue a cease and desist order pursuant to division (C)(2) of this section. If the hearing panel determines, by clear and convincing evidence, that a violation of Canon 4 has occurred, the hearing panel shall determine whether the respondent previously has been found to have violated Canon 4 and include the determination in its report. The Secretary shall provide a copy of the hearing panel's report to the Chief Justice of the Courts of Appeals and send a copy of the hearing panel's report to the relator and respondent by certified mail.

(C) **Appointment of five-judge commission; proceedings before the commission**

(1) Within five days of the issuance of the hearing panel's report, the Chief Justice of the Courts of Appeals shall appoint a commission of five appellate judges, chosen by lot from separate appellate districts. The Chief Justice of the Courts of Appeals shall designate one of the judges to serve as chair of the panel. No appellate judge who served on the panel that reviewed the allegations for probable cause shall be appointed to serve on the commission.

(2) Unless otherwise recommended by the hearing panel, the commission shall expedite its consideration of the report and may make its determination from the report of the hearing panel, permit or require the filing of briefs, conduct oral argument, or order the hearing panel to take additional evidence. If the commission concludes the record supports the hearing panel's finding that a violation of Canon 4 has occurred and there has been no abuse of discretion by the hearing panel, the commission may enter an order that includes

one or more of the sanctions set forth in Section 5(D)(1) of this rule. Upon recommendation of the hearing panel or sua sponte, the commission may enter an interim cease and desist order as it finds reasonable and necessary prior to making a determination on the hearing panel's report. The interim order shall be based on the commission's preliminary review of the report and recommendation of the hearing panel and any record made before the commission.

(3) The commission's determination and any cease and desist order shall be sent to the Secretary who shall provide a copy to the Chief Justice of the Courts of Appeals and serve a copy on the respondent and relator by certified mail. At the conclusion of all proceedings before the hearing panel, the Secretary shall file the record of such proceedings with the Clerk of the Supreme Court as provided in division (F)(1) of this section.

(D) **Appeal of sanction**

(1) The respondent may appeal a sanction issued by the commission. The notice of appeal shall be filed by the respondent with the Clerk of the Supreme Court within twenty days after the receipt by certified mail of the commission's order. The Clerk shall provide a copy of the notice of appeal to the Chief Justice of the Courts of Appeals and send a copy to the relator by certified mail.

(2) Within five days of receipt of the notice of appeal, the Chief Justice of the Courts of Appeals shall convene an adjudicatory panel of thirteen appellate judges. The adjudicatory panel shall consist of the Chief Justice of the Courts of Appeals, who shall preside over the panel, and the presiding judge of each appellate district. No appellate judge who served on the panel that reviewed the allegations for probable cause or who served on the commission to review the report of the hearing panel shall be appointed to serve on the adjudicatory panel. If a presiding judge of an appellate district is unavailable to serve on the adjudicatory panel, the appellate judge of the district who is senior in service on the court of appeals shall replace the presiding judge.

(3) The adjudicatory panel may establish a briefing schedule and make other appropriate orders. All orders of the adjudicatory panel shall be issued upon instructions from the panel by the Clerk who shall send the orders by certified mail.

(E) **Failure to prosecute** If, after probable cause has been found, the relator attempts to withdraw the grievance or otherwise fails to prosecute the formal complaint, the Chief Justice of the Courts of Appeals shall appoint a special disciplinary counsel who possesses the qualifications set forth in Section 4(B)(3) of this rule. Upon appointment, the special disciplinary counsel shall act as relator in the pending matter.

(F) **Miscellaneous provisions**

(1) Upon the filing of a formal complaint, the Secretary of the Board of Commissioners on Grievances and Discipline shall serve as clerk for the Chief Justice of the Courts of Appeals, the hearing panel, and the five-judge commission. The relator and respondent shall file all pleadings, motions, documents, and other material with the Secretary, who shall transmit the documents and materials to the Chief Justice of the

Courts of Appeals and the appropriate panel. The Chief Justice of the Courts of Appeals, the panel, and the five-judge commission shall transmit all orders, opinions, and other materials to the Secretary for service on or distribution to the parties. The Secretary shall maintain a complete record of the proceedings and, upon conclusion of the proceedings before the hearing panel and five-judge commission, certify the record, including exhibits, to the Clerk of the Supreme Court who shall maintain the certified record. The Clerk shall serve as clerk for the adjudicatory panel, and all proceedings before the adjudicatory panel shall be conducted as provided in this section and the Rules of Practice of the Supreme Court of Ohio. Upon request, the Secretary and Clerk shall assist the Chief Justice of the Courts of Appeals, hearing panel, five-judge commission, and adjudicatory panel with ministerial matters such as scheduling a location for hearings and securing a court reporter.

(2) If a judge selected to serve on any panel appointed pursuant to Section 6 of this rule is unable to serve because of the existence of a disqualifying factor, the judge shall notify the Chief Justice of the Courts of Appeals and provide written justification of the grounds for disqualification.

(3) The Chief Justice of the Courts of Appeals and any judge appointed to serve in any capacity pursuant to Section 6 of this rule shall continue to serve in the appointed capacity until the conclusion of the matter as long as the judge continues to hold judicial office. If the Chief Justice of the Courts of Appeals leaves judicial office while a matter commenced under this rule during his or her tenure remains pending, the successor Chief Justice of the Courts of Appeals shall assume responsibility for that matter. If a judge appointed to serve in any capacity under this rule leaves judicial office while a matter to which the judge was assigned under this rule remains pending, the Chief Justice of the Courts of Appeals shall designate a judge to replace the former judge in the same manner as the original appointment was made.

(4) A party may allege the existence of bias, prejudice, or other disqualifying factor on the part of a judge appointed to serve on a panel or commission pursuant to Section 6 of this rule by filing a motion with the Chief Justice of the Courts of Appeals. The motion shall be filed within three days of the date the party receives notice of the appointment of the panel or commission. If the Chief Justice of the Courts of Appeals finds the existence of bias, prejudice, or other disqualifying factor, the judge named in the motion shall be disqualified, and the Chief Justice of the Courts of Appeals shall designate a judge to replace the disqualified judge in the same manner as the original appointment was made.

Section 7. Miscellaneous Provisions

The following provisions apply to proceedings under Sections 5 and 6 of this rule.

(A) Unless the justice, judge, or judicial candidate against whom a grievance has been filed agrees otherwise, the grievance shall remain private until the probable cause panel has made a determination of probable cause. After a determination of probable cause has been made, the grievance, formal complaint, report of the hearing panel, order of the five-judge commission of five judges, record of the proceedings, and all hearings shall be public.

(B) If any panel or commission of judges determines that the grievance was frivolous or filed solely for the purpose of obtaining an advantage for a judicial candidate, the panel or commission, in addition to any other order considered proper, may assess against the complainant the costs of the proceeding and any reasonable and necessary attorney fees incurred by the respondent in defending the grievance.

(C) In recommending, imposing, or reviewing a sanction for a violation of Canon 4, the panel or commission of judges shall consider any prior violations by the respondent and may increase the severity of the sanction recommended or imposed for the violation pending before the panel or commission.

(D) Any sanction imposed by the five-judge commission or adjudicatory panel shall be published by the Supreme Court Reporter in the manner prescribed in Rule V, Section 8 of the Supreme Court Rules for the Government of the Bar of Ohio and noted in the public records maintained by the Supreme Court Office of Attorney Services.

(E) The Board may adopt regulations to facilitate and implement the expeditious consideration of grievances and complaints filed under Sections 5 and 6 of this rule. A panel may extend the time requirements contained in Sections 5 and 6 of this rule on its own motion, on agreement of the parties, or on motion of a party for good cause shown. In considering an extension of the time requirements, the panel shall consider all of the following:

(1) The immediacy of the alleged violation;

(2) The complexity of the complaint;

(3) When the parties received notice of the hearing;

(4) Whether a weekend or legal holiday intervenes to shorten the applicable time period;

(5) The parties' difficulty in obtaining documentation or witnesses, or both, to prove or defend an allegation.

(F) Any judge selected to serve on a commission appointed pursuant to Section 5 of this rule or to a panel or commission appointed pursuant to Section 6 of this rule shall be reimbursed from the Attorney Services Fund for travel expenses incurred in association with the judge's service on the panel or commission. Reimbursement for travel expenses shall be made as provided in the Supreme Court Guidelines for Travel by Court Appointees. A judge appointed to a commission pursuant to Section 5 of this rule shall request reimbursement by submitting a signed Travel Expense Report form and required receipts to the Administrative Director of the Supreme Court. A judge appointed to a panel or commission pursuant to Section 6 of this rule shall request reimbursement by submitting a signed Travel Expense Report form and required receipts to the Chief Justice of the Courts of Appeals. The Chief Justice of the Courts of Appeals shall indicate approval of the reimbursement request and submit the approved form to the Administrative Director of the Supreme Court.

Section 8. Definitions

As used in this rule:

(A) "Complaint," "probable cause," and "misconduct" have the same meanings as in Gov. Bar R. V;

(B) "Costs" means expenses incurred by the Board of Commissioners on Grievances and Discipline, the Supreme Court, and any panel or commission of judges in conducting proceedings under this rule;

(C) "Disciplinary sanction" means any of the sanctions set forth in Gov. Bar R. V, Section 6, removal, or suspension from office;

(D) "Good cause," for purposes of Sections 4(A) and (B)(1) of this rule, means that, based on a review of a grievance and any response received, there exists an articulable legal and factual basis to warrant further investigation of the allegations contained in the grievance;

(E) "Judicial candidate" has the same meaning as in Rule 4.6 of the Code of Judicial Conduct.

History: Amended, eff 1-1-86; 10-1-86; 9-1-87; 1-1-88; 1-1-93; 7-1-95; 9-1-95; 1-1-96; 6-1-97; 11-1-99; 1-1-04; 1-1-10.

RULE III
RETIREMENT, REMOVAL, OR SUSPENSION OF JUDGES

The following rule is adopted pursuant to sections 2701.11 and 2701.12 of the Revised Code.

Section 1. Complaint

(A)(1) Six copies of the written and sworn complaint required by section 2701.11 of the Revised Code shall be filed with the Secretary of the Board of Commissioners on Grievances and Discipline of the Supreme Court when it is determined by Disciplinary Counsel or a Certified Grievance Committee after investigation pursuant to Gov. Jud. R. II that probable cause exists for the filing of a complaint. The Secretary shall transmit the complaint to the Chair of the Board. The complaint shall set forth specifically the grounds claimed to be cause for retirement, removal, or suspension of the Justice or judge from office and the time and place the acts or omissions occurred that are alleged to be cause for such retirement, removal, or suspension under section 2701.12 of the Revised Code. The filing of a complaint by Disciplinary Counsel or by the President, Secretary, or Chair of a Certified Grievance Committee shall constitute a representation that, after investigation, Disciplinary Counsel or a Certified Grievance Committee has determined that probable cause exists to warrant a hearing on the complaint. Complaints shall be filed in the name of Disciplinary Counsel or a Certified Grievance Committee as relator.

(2) At the time the written and sworn complaint is filed with the Secretary of the Board, the written and sworn complaint and all proceedings in connection with the complaint shall be public.

(B) In addition to the causes for removal or suspension of a Justice or judge, as provided in section 2701.12 of the Revised Code, a Justice or judge may be removed or suspended from office for any of the following:

(1) The willful and persistent failure to perform judicial duties;

(2) Habitual intemperance;

(3) Engaging in conduct prejudicial to the administration of justice or that would bring the judicial office into disrepute;

(4) Suspension from the practice of law for a period of six months to two years, probation, indefinite suspension from the practice of law, permanent disbarment, or resignation from the practice of law in Ohio.

(C) Cases involving the retirement, removal, or suspension of a Justice or Chief Justice of the Supreme Court shall be heard and decided by a panel as provided in Gov. Jud. R. II, Section 2(B).

Section 2. Action on the Complaint

(A)(1) Upon receipt of a written and sworn complaint, the Chair of the Board shall convene the Board and present the complaint. The Secretary of the Board shall send a copy of the complaint to the judge against whom the complaint is made. The Board shall then review the investigation made by the Disciplinary Counsel or a Certified Grievance Committee. If, after review of the investigation, two-thirds of the members of the Board determine that there is substantial credible evidence in support of the complaint, the Secretary of the Board shall certify to the Supreme Court the result of the investigation.

(2) The report of the Board of Commissioners shall be sent by certified mail to the judge against whom the complaint is made at the same time it is sent to the Supreme Court.

(B)(1) If the report finds there is substantial credible evidence in support of the complaint, the Supreme Court shall appoint within a reasonable time after its receipt a commission of five judges, as provided in section 2701.11 of the Revised Code.

The chair of the commission appointed to determine the question of retirement, removal, or suspension of a judge shall be designated by the Supreme Court. After receipt of the notice of appointment and the receipt of the complaint, the chair promptly shall fix a day, time, and place for the hearing.

(2) If the commission determines by majority vote that grounds for retirement, removal, or suspension without pay have been established by clear and convincing evidence as alleged in the complaint or as provided in section 2701.12 of the Revised Code, the commission shall make the necessary and proper order. Notice of any order shall be sent by certified mail with return receipt to the judge against whom the finding has been made and to the Supreme Court.

(3) As used in this rule:

(a) "Mental disability" means the condition defined in division (A) of section 5122.01 of the Revised Code that presently prevents the proper discharge of the judge's duties.

(b) "Physical disability" means the impairment of the faculties of a Justice or judge that has prevented the proper discharge of judicial duties for more than six months. Failure to be present in court or to perform usual judicial functions for six months or more shall raise a presumption of physical disability.

(4) The commission shall make the determination of disability based upon the testimony adduced before it. Expert medical testimony may be received by the commission, and, with the consent of the respondent, it may name medical experts to examine the Respondent.

Section 3. **Appeal** Any judge retired, removed, or suspended by the commission may appeal the action to the Supreme Court on the record made before the commission. Notice of the appeal shall be given by the judge to the commission and the Supreme Court within twenty days after the judge's receipt by certified mail of the findings made by the commission. After a notice of appeal is given, the time for filing a transcript of testimony, briefs, and the conduct of a hearing shall be as provided in Gov.Bar R. V.

Section 4. **Reinstatement** A Justice or judge who has been suspended by reason of physical or mental disability may apply for reinstatement by filing a petition with the Board setting forth the facts supporting the alleged restoration of health. The petition shall be processed in the same manner as a complaint.

Section 5. Procedure

(A) The commission may take testimony in any manner prescribed by Ohio law. All rules of evidence shall be observed in the conduct of hearings before the commission. Respondent may be represented by counsel.

(B) The commission shall issue subpoenas for witnesses under the seal of the Supreme Court, signed by a member of the commission or the Secretary of the Board. The refusal or neglect of a person subpoenaed as a witness to obey a subpoena, to attend, to be sworn or to affirm, or to answer any proper question shall be considered contempt of the Supreme Court, and the person shall be punished accordingly.

(C) Costs and expenses incurred by the Board and the commission shall be paid from the Attorney Registration Fund. The Supreme Court may order that the fund be reimbursed by the respondent if the proceeding terminates in retirement, removal, or suspension without pay.

(D) This rule and regulations relating to investigations and proceedings involving complaints and petitions for reinstatement shall be liberally construed for the protection of the public and the courts and shall apply to all pending investigations and complaints so far as may be practicable, and to all future investigations, complaints, and petitions whether the conduct involved occurred prior or subsequent to the adoption of this rule.

Section 6. Disqualification or Suspension without Pay; Criminal Charge or Conviction

(A) A Justice or judge is disqualified from acting as a Justice or judge while there is pending an indictment or an information charging the Justice or judge with a crime punishable as a felony under state or federal law.

(B) A Justice or judge shall be suspended from judicial office without pay if the Justice or judge pleads guilty or no contest to or is found guilty of a crime punishable as a felony under state or federal law.

(C)(1) The judge presiding over a case that satisfies the circumstances described in division (B) of this section shall prepare a certified notice of a verdict of guilty, a judicial finding of guilty, or a guilty or no contest plea. The judge shall transmit the certified notice to the Secretary of the Board of Commissioners on Grievances and Discipline and to either the Disciplinary Counsel or the president, secretary, or chair of the geographically appropriate Certified Grievance Committee. Upon receipt from any source of the certified notice, the Secretary promptly shall submit the certified notice to the Supreme Court. The Secretary shall submit the certified notice regardless of the pendency of an appeal.

(2) Upon receipt of the certified notice, the Supreme Court shall enter an order immediately suspending the Justice or judge from judicial office without pay pending further proceedings pursuant to these rules. There shall be no appeal of a suspension from judicial office without pay imposed pursuant to this section.

(D) Suspension of a Justice or judge from judicial office without pay shall remain in effect until any of the following occurs:

(1) The conviction resulting from a plea of guilty or no contest, verdict of guilty, or judicial finding of guilt is reversed;

(2) A final decision on a complaint filed pursuant to Section 1 of this rule is issued by a five-judge commission appointed pursuant to Section 2 of this rule or by the Supreme Court;

(3) A disciplinary order is entered by the Supreme Court pursuant to Rule V of the Rules for the Government of the Bar of Ohio that suspends or disbars the Justice or judge from the practice of law;

(4) A final order is issued by a court removing the Justice or judge from judicial office.

Section 7. **Suspension without Pay; Disciplinary Sanction**

(A) A disciplinary order entered by the Supreme Court pursuant to Rule V of the Rules for the Government of the Bar of Ohio that suspends a Justice or judge from the practice of law shall include a provision immediately suspending the Justice or judge from judicial office without pay for the term of the suspension, pending further proceedings pursuant to law. There shall be no appeal of a suspension from judicial office without pay imposed pursuant to this section.

(B) Suspension of a Justice or judge from judicial office without pay shall remain in effect until any of the following occurs:

(1) The Justice or judge is reinstated to the practice of law;

(2) A final decision on a complaint filed pursuant to Section 1 of this rule is issued by a five-judge commission appointed pursuant to Section 2 of this rule or by the Supreme Court;

(3) A final order is issued by a court removing the Justice or judge from judicial office.

Section 8. **Definition** As used in this rule, "pay" means all salary payable and benefits available to the Justice or judge as a result of his or her service in judicial office.

History: Amended, eff 10-1-86; 1-1-88; 1-1-93; 6-22-98.

RULE IV
MANDATORY CONTINUING LEGAL EDUCATION FOR THE JUDICIARY

Section 1. Purpose

(A) To serve the public interest that mandates the competent performance of the duties of judicial office in Ohio, each Ohio judge shall participate in continuing legal education programs in compliance with this rule and Rule X of the Supreme Court Rules for the Government of the Bar of Ohio.

(B) As used in this rule, "judge" includes the Chief Justice and Justices of the Supreme Court.

Section 2. Judicial Continuing Legal Education Requirements

(A) Full-time judges, part-time judges, and retired judges eligible for assignment to active duty pursuant to Section 6(C), Article IV of the Ohio Constitution shall complete and report a minimum of forty hours of instruction every two years on subjects devoted to the law and judicial administration.

(B) As part of the required forty hours of instruction, full-time, part-time, and retired judges shall complete at least ten hours of instruction offered by the Supreme Court of Ohio Judicial College, including at least two hours on access to justice and fairness in the courts and how these issues impact the public's trust and confidence in the judicial system and the perception of justice in Ohio. Judges may receive instruction on access to justice and fairness in the courts on one or any combination of the following topics:

(1) Self-represented litigants;

(2) Pro bono representation;

(3) Foreign language interpretation;

(4) Race, ethnicity, and foreign origin;

(5) Gender;

(6) Disability;

(7) Sexual orientation.

(C) As an additional part of the required forty hours of instruction, full-time, part-time, and retired judges shall complete at least two hours of instruction on judicial ethics and professionalism, which shall be broadly defined to cover material designed to instill in judges the importance of ethics and professionalism within the judiciary. Judges may receive instruction on judicial ethics and professionalism on one or any combination of the following topics:

(1) Ohio Ethics Law;

(2) Ohio Code of Judicial Conduct;

(3) Judicial Creed;

(4) Ohio Rules of Professional Conduct;

(5) The role of judges in facilitating legal ethics and professionalism among attorneys by encouraging and facilitating compliance with the requirements of the Ohio Rules of Professional Conduct, A Lawyer's Creed, A Lawyer's Aspirational Ideals, and a Statement on Pro Bono Activity by Lawyers Adopted by the Supreme Court;

(6) Alcoholism, substance abuse, and mental health issues, and their causes, prevention, detection, and treatment alternatives.

(D) When the Commission determines that a judge has timely completed and timely reported more than the required number of credit hours in a reporting period the Commission may apply a maximum of twenty credit hours to the next reporting period.

Section 3. Reports and Exemptions

(A) A judge whose last name begins with a letter from A through L shall report compliance with the requirements of this rule by the thirty-first day of January of even-numbered years for the preceding two calendar years. A judge whose last name begins with a letter from M through Z shall report compliance with the requirements of this rule by the thirty-first day of January of odd numbered years for the preceding two calendar years. If a judge's name changes after the judge is admitted to the practice of law, the judge shall remain in the same alphabetical grouping for purposes of filing all future reports. Reports shall be filed with the Supreme Court Commission on Continuing Legal Education on forms provided by the Commission.

(B) If a judge becomes subject to this rule during a reporting period, the Commission shall adjust the requirements of this rule on a pro rata basis.

(C) The Commission may grant a temporary exemption from the continuing legal education requirements of this rule under the following circumstances:

(1) A judge suffering from severe, prolonged illness or disability preventing participation in accredited programs and activities for the duration of the illness or disability;

(2) A judge, who has demonstrated special circumstances unique to that judge constituting good cause to grant an exemption not to exceed one year and subject to any prorated adjustment of the credit hour requirements.

(D) A judge who, because of a permanent physical disability or other compelling reason, has difficulty attending programs or activities may request, and the Commission may grant, approval of a substitute program.

Section 4. Administration of Continuing Legal Education for Judges

The Commission shall be responsible for administration of the continuing legal education requirements established by this rule. The Commission shall accredit continuing legal education programs, activities, and sponsors for judges, maintain records of continuing legal education credit for judges, issue transcripts and reports to judges, enforce and determine compliance with the provisions of this rule and Gov. Bar R. X, recommend sanctions for judges who fail to comply with the requirements of this rule or Gov. Bar R. X, and perform other functions necessary to carry out the duties of the Commission and facilitate the purpose of this rule.

Section 5. Judicial orientation

(A) A person who, after January 1, 2007, is appointed by the governor or elected to a judgeship and who has not completed the Supreme Court of Ohio Judicial College Judicial Orientation for that jurisdiction shall attend the Judicial Orientation Program developed and accredited by the Supreme Court of Ohio Judicial College. With the exception of Section 5(B)(3), this provision does not apply to any person reelected to the same judicial position.

(B) The Judicial Orientation Program shall consist of four parts:

(1) Part I consists of a general and specific curriculum applicable to the jurisdictions of the attendees. The Supreme Court of Ohio Judicial College shall conduct Part I each year after the November election but before the commencement of judicial terms in the following year.

(2) Part II consists of a general and specific curriculum applicable to the jurisdiction of the attendees. The Supreme Court of Ohio Judicial College conducts Part II within six months after the conclusion of Part I.

(3) Part III consists of a capital case seminar offered or approved by the Supreme Court of Ohio Judicial College and must be completed by a judge of the common pleas court in the general division who is elected or appointed to the bench. The seminar shall be completed within twenty-four months of assuming the bench. All judges in divisions of the common pleas court other than the general division may take the capital case seminar. Judges in divisions of the common pleas court other than the general division who take the capital case seminar shall be eligible to preside over a capital case or participate in a capital case as a member of the three judge panel.

(4) Part IV is the Supreme Court of Ohio Judicial College Mentor Program. The Mentor Program pairs a newly elected or appointed judge with an experienced judge-mentor within the same subject matter jurisdiction. Each judge required by this rule to participate in the mentor program must have regular contact with the mentoring judge for at least one year. This program does not apply to Supreme Court justices.

(C) A person elected or appointed to the Supreme Court of Ohio shall complete only those portions of Parts I and II that are relevant to appellate or Supreme Court jurisdiction.

(D) Any judge appointed after the conclusion of Part I but before the beginning of Part II must attend Part II.

(E) A sitting judge who changes jurisdictions shall be required to complete only the portions of Parts I and II of the program that are specifically designed for the new jurisdiction.

(F) The Supreme Court of Ohio Judicial College shall not charge tuition for participation in Parts I and II and, pursuant to Supreme Court guidelines, shall pay or reimburse the participating judge for the costs of mileage, lodging, and meals while attending Parts I and II.

(G) For good cause, the Executive Committee of the Supreme Court of Ohio Judicial College Board of Trustees may delay or excuse participation in Part I or Part II, but not both.

(H) Failure to comply with this rule shall result in sanctions as set forth in Section 4 of this rule, but shall not affect the force or validity of any order entered by a judge.

Section 6. Compliance

Any trial judge with capital case jurisdiction shall comply with Section 5(B)(3) within twenty-four months of the effective date of this rule. Any retired judge shall comply with Section 5(B)(3) before accepting assignment to a capital case. The Chief Justice of the Supreme Court may delay or excuse compliance with Section 6.

Section 7. Effective Dates

(A) The effective date of this rule shall be January 1, 1981.

(B) The amendments to this rule adopted by the Supreme Court of Ohio on June 28, 1989, shall be effective on July 1, 1989.

(C) The amendments to this rule adopted by the Supreme Court of Ohio on March 27, 1990, shall be effective on April 16, 1990.

(D) The amendments to this rule adopted by the Supreme Court of Ohio on October 23, 1990 shall take effect on January 1, 1991.

(E) The amendments to this rule, adopted by the Supreme Court of Ohio on October 8, 1991, shall take effect on January 1, 1992.

(F) The amendments to this rule adopted by the Supreme Court of Ohio on October 20, 1992, shall take effect on January 1, 1993.

(G) The amendments to this rule adopted by the Supreme Court of Ohio on December 14, 1993 shall take effect on January 1, 1994. All matters relating to reporting and administration of judicial continuing education requirements for calendar year 1993 shall be governed by this rule as it existed prior to January 1, 1994.

(H) The amendments to this rule adopted by the Supreme Court of Ohio on October 27, 1998, shall take effect on January 1, 1999.

(I) The amendments to Sections 2(B), 3(B) and 6(I) of this rule, adopted by the Supreme Court on April 22, 2002 and shall take effect on July 1, 2002.

(J) The amendments to Sections 2(B), 3(B) and 6 (J) of this rule, adopted by the Supreme Court on July 20, 2004, shall take effect on September 1, 2004.

(K) The amendments to Sections 6, 7, and 8 of this rule, adopted by the Supreme Court on March 14, 2008, shall take effect on January 1, 2007.

(L) The amendments to Sections 4 and 5 of this rule, adopted by the Supreme Court on September 11, 2007, shall take effect on November 1, 2007.

(M) The amendments to this rule adopted by the Supreme Court of Ohio on February 5, 2008 shall take effect on March 1, 2008.

(N) The amendments to this rule adopted by the Supreme Court on March 9, 2009 shall take effect on May 1, 2009 and first apply to a judge whose last name begins with a letter from M through Z and reports compliance with the requirements of this rule by the thirty-first day of January 2011.

RULE V
JUDICIAL COLLEGE

Section 1. Purpose; Duties; Construction

(A) The purpose of this rule is to establish and maintain the Supreme Court of Ohio Judicial College and provide for its governance.

(B) The Supreme Court of Ohio Judicial College, in cooperation with the Ohio Judicial Conference, the state judicial associations, and the associations of court personnel, shall do all of the following:

(1) Foster awareness that judicial training and education are necessary to maintain professional competence;

(2) Provide a comprehensive program of continuing education for the judges, and court personnel of this state;

(3) Create standards and curricula for education and training programs that will provide quality education and training in procedural and substantive law of Ohio, incorporating national standards and trends;

(4) Provide training and education in professional ethics and substance abuse.

(C) This rule and bylaws adopted under authority of this rule shall be construed liberally to accomplish the goals and purposes of this rule.

Section 2. Board of Trustees

(A) There is hereby created the board of trustees of the Supreme Court of Ohio Judicial College consisting of ten members appointed as follows:

(1) One judge appointed by the Ohio Judicial Conference;

(2) One judge appointed by the Association of Municipal and County Judges of Ohio;

(3) One judge appointed by the Ohio Common Pleas Judges Association;

(4) One judge appointed by the Ohio Courts of Appeals Judges Association;

(5) One judge appointed by the Ohio Association of Probate Judges;

(6) One judge appointed by the Ohio Association of Juvenile and Family Court Judges;

(7) One judge appointed by the Ohio Association of Domestic Relations Judges;

(8) One magistrate appointed by the Ohio Association of Magistrates;

(9) Two judges appointed by the Chief Justice of the Supreme Court.

The initial appointment of a trustee by the Ohio Association of Domestic Relations Judges pursuant to division (A)(7) of this section shall be made for a term beginning January 1, 1995 and ending December 31, 1997. The initial appointment of a trustee by the Ohio Association of Magistrates pursuant to division (A)(8) of this section shall be made for a term beginning January 15, 1995 and ending December 31, 1997.

(B)(1) Terms of office for trustees shall be three years. Trustees shall be eligible for reappointment, but shall not serve more than two consecutive full terms. A trustee appointed to fill a vacancy occurring prior to the expiration of the term for which the trustee's predecessor was appointed shall hold office for the remainder of the unexpired term.

(2) To be eligible for the position of trustee, an individual shall be a sitting judge or magistrate as appropriate under this rule. If a trustee leaves judicial office, the trustee shall be disqualified and a vacancy shall occur. A change in judicial position shall not disqualify a member. Vacancies shall be filled by the original appointing authority within sixty days of receiving notice of the vacancy and, if the appointing authority does not act within that time, by the board.

(C) Except for the annual meeting, the board shall meet at the call of the chair, or upon the written request of a majority of the trustees. Five trustees shall constitute a quorum. No action shall be taken by the board without the concurrence of a majority of the trustees constituting a quorum at that meeting.

(D) Trustees shall serve without compensation, but shall be reimbursed for expenses incurred in the performance of their official duties.

(E) At its first meeting each year, the board shall elect from its membership a chair, vice-chair, and secretary as the officers of the Supreme Court of Ohio Judicial College. The officers shall be elected for a term of one year beginning on the day of their election and shall serve until their successors have assumed office. No person shall serve more than three consecutive one-year terms in any office.

(F) There shall be an annual meeting of the board in September.

(G) The executive committee shall consist of the officers of the board and shall exercise the duties, powers, privileges, and prerogatives of the board, consistent with the policies of the board, between meetings of the board. The executive committee shall carry out all other duties as may be prescribed by the board.

(H) The board may adopt bylaws consistent with this rule.

Section 3. Powers of the Board of Trustees

(A) The board shall file with the Supreme Court of Ohio a proposed budget for the year beginning the ensuing first day of July for approval by the Supreme Court. The budget shall be a public record.

(B) The board shall recommend for appointment, with the advice and consent of the Supreme Court, employees necessary to carry out the duties of the Supreme Court of Ohio Judicial College and upon terms and conditions as the board shall determine.

(C) Facilities for the Supreme Court of Ohio Judicial College shall be provided by the Supreme Court.

(D) The Supreme Court of Ohio Judicial College may receive, administer, distribute, and account for any bequest, devise, grant, or gift consistent with the purpose and goals of the Supreme Court of Ohio Judicial College.

Section 4. Effective Dates

(A) The effective date of this rule shall be July 1, 1989.

(B) The amendments to Section 1 of this rule adopted by the Supreme Court of Ohio on October 23, 1990 shall take effect on January 1, 1991.

(C) The amendments to Sections 1, 2, and 3 of this rule, adopted by the Supreme Court of Ohio on October 22, 1991, shall take effect on January 1, 1992.

(D) The amendments to Section 2 of this rule, adopted by the Supreme Court of Ohio on December 14, 1993, shall take effect on January 1, 1995.

(E) The amendments to Section 2 of this rule, adopted by the Supreme Court of Ohio on January 11, 1995, shall take effect on January 15, 1995.

(F) The amendments to this rule adopted by the Supreme Court of Ohio on February 5, 2008 shall take effect on March 1, 2008.

RULE VI
REFERENCE OF CIVIL ACTION PURSUANT TO SECTION 2701.10 OF THE REVISED CODE

Section 1. Authority; Registration; Eligibility

(A) Parties to a civil action or proceeding pending in a court of common pleas, municipal court, or county court who agree to have their action or proceeding referred or issue or question submitted to a voluntarily retired judge pursuant to section 2701.10 of the Revised Code shall refer the action or proceeding or submit the issue or question according to the provisions of this rule and that section.

(B) To be eligible for the referral of actions or proceedings or submission of issues or questions, a retired judge shall register with the appropriate clerk of courts in accordance with section 2701.10 of the Revised Code and shall file a retired judge registration form with the Supreme Court.

(C)(1) A voluntarily retired judge or a judge retired under Article IV, Section 6(C) of the Ohio Constitution may register pursuant to section 2701.10 of the Revised Code.

(2) As used in this rule, "voluntarily retired judge" means any person who was elected or appointed to and served on an Ohio court without being defeated in an election for new or continued service on that court. "Voluntarily retired judge" does not include either of the following:

(a) A judge who has been removed or suspended without reinstatement from service on any Ohio court pursuant to the Supreme Court Rules for the Government of the Judiciary or who has resigned or retired from service while a complaint was pending under those rules;

(b) A judge who has resigned from office between the date of defeat in an election for further service on that court and the end of his or her term.

(D) A retired judge who registers and is selected to receive referrals and submissions pursuant to section 2701.10 of the Revised Code may accept assignments from the Chief Justice of the Supreme Court pursuant to Article IV, Section 6(C) of the Ohio Constitution.

Section 2. Reference Procedure

(A) Upon the consent of all parties to a civil action or proceeding pending in any court of common pleas, municipal court, or county court, the parties shall notify the court of their agreement to have the action or proceeding referred for adjudication or have any specific issues or questions of fact or law in the action or proceeding submitted for determination to a retired judge of their choosing who is eligible to accept referrals or submissions. The parties shall file with the clerk of courts in which the action or proceeding was pending a copy of the written agreement and exchange copies between or among themselves. The agreement shall comply with the requirements of section 2701.10 of the Revised Code and serves as the notice of the intention of the parties to refer the action or proceeding, or submit an issue or question in the action or proceeding, to a retired judge pursuant to that section.

(B) After the agreement is filed with the clerk, the judge before whom the action or proceeding is pending shall order the referral or submission in accordance with the agreement or any amendment to the agreement.

Section 3. Trial Procedure

(A) The Ohio Rules of Civil Procedure and the Ohio Rules of Evidence apply to actions or proceedings referred or issues or questions submitted to a retired judge pursuant to section 2701.10 of the Revised Code.

(B) Within a reasonable time after accepting the referral or submission, the judge shall schedule a pretrial conference. An order shall be filed with the clerk of courts that includes all of the following:

(1) The issues to be decided by the judge;

(2) A determination as to whether the case shall be submitted entirely on documentary evidence or if oral testimony is required;

(3) A date for completion of discovery;

(4) A trial date or, if the case is to be submitted to the judge on documentary evidence alone, a date for submission;

(5) Any other matters agreed upon by the parties at the pretrial conference;

(6) Any other matters resolved before trial.

(C) At the conclusion of the trial or after submission on documentary evidence, the judge may direct the parties to file post-trial memoranda. The judge shall decide the case promptly.

(D) The decision of the judge shall be in writing and contain separate findings of fact and conclusions of law. The judge shall file a copy of the decision and a judgment entry with the clerk of courts and direct the clerk to serve copies of the decision and judgment entry on all the parties.

(E) If the judge dies or becomes incapacitated before filing a decision and judgment entry in a case with the appropriate clerk of courts, the parties shall notify the court in which the action or proceeding was pending and the clerk shall return the action or proceeding to the regular docket of the judge to whom it originally was assigned.

Section 4. Authority of Chief Justice; Code of Judicial Conduct

(A) The Chief Justice of the Supreme Court shall have the same authority over actions or proceedings referred or issues or questions submitted pursuant to section 2701.10 of the Revised Code and this rule as in all other cases.

(B) A judge selected pursuant to section 2701.10 of the Revised Code shall comply with the Code of Judicial Conduct.

Section 5. Appendix of Forms

The following forms are intended for illustration only. Substantial compliance with the prescribed forms is sufficient. Minor departures that do not negate substantial compliance shall not render void forms that are otherwise sufficient, and the forms may be varied when necessary to meet the facts of a particular case.

FORM 1. RETIRED JUDGE REGISTRATION FORM

(1)
INDEX OF RETIRED JUDGES REGISTRATION FORM*
R.C. 2701.10

IN THE _____ COURT OF _____ COUNTY:

Name: _____

Address: _____

Telephone Number: _____

Attorney Registration Number: _____

    I, _____, hereby place my name on the index of retired judges in this court. In doing so, I state that I have registered with the Supreme Court of Ohio as a retired judge and I am eligible for service as a retired judge under the Constitution and laws of Ohio. I further state that, upon removing my name from registration with the Supreme Court of Ohio, I shall notify this court in writing.

_____
Signature

_____
Date

*TO BE FILED WITH THE APPROPRIATE LOCAL CLERK OF COURT.

FORM 2. REGISTRATION OF RETIRED JUDGE

(2)

THE SUPREME COURT OF OHIO
65 South Front Street
Columbus, Ohio 43215

REGISTRATION OF RETIRED JUDGE*
R.C. 2701.10

Name: _____

Address: _____

_____

Telephone Number: _____

Attorney Registration Number: _____

Date of Birth: _____

Undergraduate and graduate education (include schools, graduation date(s) and degree(s) conferred):_____

_____

Law school education (include graduation date):_____

_____

Judicial experience (include administrative experience): _____

_____

Date of retirement from judicial service: _____

_____

Area(s) of expertise (based upon legal and judicial experience, other career experience, and scholarly pursuits):_____

_____

Publications:_____

_____

I state that the information contained on this form is correct.

_____   _____
Signature   Date

* TO BE FILED WITH THE SUPREME COURT OF OHIO

FORM 3. AGREEMENT FOR REFERRAL OR SUBMISSION TO RETIRED JUDGE

(3)

IN THE COURT OF COMMON PLEAS

_____ COUNTY, OHIO

A.B.	)	CASE NO. _____
Plaintiff(s)	)	ASSIGNED JUDGE _____
v.	)	AGREEMENT FOR REFERRAL
	)	OR SUBMISSION TO RETIRED
C.D.	)	JUDGE PURSUANT TO R.C.
Defendant(s)	)	2701.10

1.   Plaintiff(s) _____ and _____ and defendant(s) _____ and _____ do hereby agree that this case shall be transferred to _____, a Retired Judge, who shall: (check appropriate item)

( )   a.   Hear and determine all issues of law and fact which may hereafter arise in this case, receive evidence, and render a judgment adjudicating the action or proceeding in its entirety, including all post-trial proceedings, if any.

( )   b.   Hear and determine issues of law and fact, receive evidence, and render a decision with respect to the following specific issue(s) or question(s) only:

_____

_____

_____

2.   The parties hereto agree to assume the responsibility for providing all facilities, equipment, and personnel reasonably deemed necessary by the Retired Judge during his or her consideration of the action or proceeding referred, or the issue(s) or question(s) submitted, and that they will pay all costs arising out of the provision of the facilities, equipment, and personnel.

3.   The parties hereto agree to pay the sum of $ ___(per diem) or $ ___(per hour) plus all reasonable expenses incurred incident to the conduct of the proceedings. Payment of all amounts due and owing to the Retired Judge for his or her services shall be made at such times and in such amounts as the parties hereto and the Retired Judge may find mutually agreeable.

4.   If any different or additional terms and conditions are desired by the parties hereto and the Retired Judge, the same will be appended hereto and signed by the parties and the Retired Judge.

THIS AGREEMENT entered into this _____ day of _____, 20__.

Plaintiff(s): _____

Defendant(s): _____

Retired Judge: _____

FORM 4. ORDER OF REFERRAL OR SUBMISSION TO RETIRED JUDGE

(4)
IN THE COURT OF COMMON PLEAS
_____ COUNTY, OHIO

A.B.	)	CASE NO. _____
Plaintiff(s)	)	ASSIGNED JUDGE _____
	)	
v.	)	AGREEMENT FOR REFERRAL
	)	OR SUBMISSION TO RETIRED
C.D.	)	JUDGE PURSUANT TO R.C.
Defendant(s)	)	2701.10

The parties having elected to have _____ a duly registered Retired Judge (act as an adjudicator of the action between them in its entirety, including all post-trial proceedings, if any) (decide the particular issue(s) of fact and/or law which they have set forth in their agreement); and it appearing that they and the Retired Judge have filed their written agreement concerning this (referral) (submission) with this Court:

IT IS HEREBY ORDERED that this case is transferred, pursuant to R.C. 2701.10, to _____, a duly registered Retired Judge, as provided in their agreement. Should the Retired Judge become unable, for any reason, to fulfill the agreement, this case will revert to the docket of this Court for further proceeding.

The Clerk of this Court is hereby ordered to deliver to _____, the Retired Judge, a complete copy of the court file in this case, including copies of all documents filed as of the date of this order. Henceforth, copies of all documents filed with this Court shall also be served upon the Retired Judge at an address he or she shall provide to the parties.

Signature: _____
                Judge of the Court of Common Pleas

Dated: _____

History: Amended, eff 1-1-89; 11-2-92; 02/02/09.

RULE XX
TITLE

These Rules shall be known as the Supreme Court Rules for the Government of the Judiciary of Ohio and shall be referred to and cited as "Gov.Jud.R. ____."

History: Effective 7-1-89.

Index to Supreme Court Rules for the Government of the Judiciary of Ohio

———

CODE OF JUDICIAL CONDUCT

The Supreme Court adopted a revised Code of Judicial Conduct, effective March 1, 2009. The new Code supersedes and replaces the former Code of Judicial Conduct and governs the conduct of Ohio judges occurring on or after March 1, 2009. See the Form of Citation, Effective Date, and Application provision that follows the Code for more information regarding application of the new Code of Judicial Conduct.

Background

In August 2007, Chief Justice Thomas J. Moyer appointed the Supreme Court Task Force on the Code of Judicial Conduct to conduct a comprehensive review of the Ohio Code of Judicial Conduct in light of revisions to the Model Code of Judicial Conduct approved by the American Bar Association in February 2007. In the ensuing months, the Task Force conducted numerous telephone conferences and met in person on five occasions to prepare a preliminary draft of a new Code of Judicial Conduct. This preliminary draft was circulated by the Task Force for public comment in February 2008.

The Task Force reconvened after the public comment period, approved further revisions to the proposed Code of Judicial Conduct, and voted to forward a report and recommendations to the Supreme Court of Ohio. In July 2008, the Supreme Court reviewed the Task Force report and recommendations and approved the publication of the proposed Code for public comment. Following the end of the public comment period in October 2008, the Task Force reconvened to review the comments and refine its recommendations to the Supreme Court. The Court reviewed and revised the Task Force recommendations and adopted a new Code of Judicial Conduct, effective March 1, 2009.

Published Rules

The 2009 Ohio Code of Judicial Conduct is published in final form. Information regarding changes to the proposed Code that was published for comment in August 2008 may be found at www.sconet.state.oh.us/boards/JudConductTF/default.asp

Portions of some rules and comments are designated as [RESERVED]. See, e.g., Rule 3.15. This designation indicates that the Supreme Court did not adopt a particular provision that appears in the ABA Model Code of Judicial Conduct. In addition, certain comments carry a numerical designation followed by the letter "A." See, e.g., Rule 2.9, Comment [4A]. These designations reflect departures from the ABA Model Code while allowing the Ohio Code to correspond, as closely as possible, to the format, lettering, and numbering of the ABA Model Code.

Each adopted rule consists of four parts: (1) the text of the rule; (2) a comment or comments; (3) a comparison of the new rule to the former Ohio Code of Judicial Conduct; and (4) a comparison of the new rule to the ABA Model Code. Please see the Scope section of the Code for more information regarding the interplay between the rules and comments. The compari-

sons that follow each rule have been prepared by the Task Force on the Code of Judicial Conduct. Although these comparisons may have been used by the Supreme Court in consideration of the proposed Code, the comparisons have not been adopted by the Court and are not part of the Code of Judicial Conduct. As such, they represent the views of the Task Force on the Code of Judicial Conduct and not necessarily those of the Supreme Court.

Correlation Tables

The 2009 Code of Judicial Conduct is followed by two tables that illustrate the manner in which individual rules in the 2009 Code correspond to the Ohio Code of Judicial Conduct.

Rule

Form of Citation, Effective Date, Application

A. Correlation Table

B. Correlation Table

PREAMBLE

[1] An independent, fair, and impartial judiciary is indispensable to our system of justice. The United States legal system is based upon the principle that an independent, impartial, and competent judiciary, composed of men and women of integrity, will interpret and apply the law that governs our society. Thus, the judiciary plays a central role in preserving the principles of justice and the rule of law. Inherent in all the rules contained in this code are the precepts that judges, individually and collectively, must respect and honor the judicial office as a public trust and strive to maintain and enhance confidence in the legal system.

[2] Judges should maintain the dignity of judicial office at all times and avoid both impropriety and the appearance of impropriety in their professional and personal lives. They should aspire at all times to conduct that ensures the greatest possible public confidence in their independence, impartiality, integrity, and competence.

[3] The Ohio Code of Judicial Conduct establishes standards for the ethical conduct of judges and judicial candidates. The code is not intended as an exhaustive guide for the conduct of judges and judicial candidates, who are governed in their judicial and personal conduct by general ethical standards as well as by the code. The code is intended, however, to provide guidance and assist judges in maintaining the highest standards of judicial and personal conduct and to provide a basis for regulating their conduct through disciplinary agencies.

Scope

[1] The Ohio Code of Judicial Conduct consists of four canons, numbered rules under each canon, and comments that generally follow and explain each rule. Scope and Terminology sections provide additional guidance in interpreting and applying the code. The Application section establishes when the various rules apply to a judge or judicial candidate.

[2] The canons state overarching principles of judicial ethics that all judges must observe. Although a judge may be disciplined only for violating a rule, the canons provide important guidance in interpreting the rules. Where a rule contains a permissive term, such as "may" or "should," the conduct being addressed is committed to the personal and professional discretion of the judge or candidate in question, and no disciplinary action should be taken for action or inaction within

the bounds of such discretion.

[3] The comments that accompany the rules serve two functions. First, they provide guidance regarding the purpose, meaning, and proper application of the rules. They contain explanatory material and, in some instances, provide examples of permitted or prohibited conduct. Comments neither add to nor subtract from the binding obligations set forth in the rules. Therefore, when a comment contains the term "must," it does not mean that the comment itself is binding or enforceable; it signifies that the rule in question, properly understood, is obligatory as to the conduct at issue.

[4] Second, the comments identify aspirational goals for judges. To implement fully the principles of this code as articulated in the canons, judges should strive to exceed the standards of conduct established by the rules, holding themselves to the highest ethical standards and seeking to achieve those aspirational goals, thereby enhancing the dignity of the judicial office.

[5] The rules of the Ohio Code of Judicial Conduct are rules of reason that should be applied consistent with constitutional requirements, statutes, other court rules, and decisional law, and with due regard for all relevant circumstances. The rules should not be interpreted to impinge upon the essential independence of judges in making judicial decisions.

[6] Although the black letter of the rules is binding and enforceable, it is not contemplated that every transgression will result in the imposition of discipline. Whether discipline should be imposed should be determined through a reasonable and reasoned application of the rules and should depend upon factors such as the seriousness of the transgression, the facts and circumstances that existed at the time of the transgression, the extent of any pattern of improper activity, whether there have been previous violations, and the effect of the improper activity upon the judicial system or others.

[7] The code is not designed or intended as a basis for civil or criminal liability. Neither is it intended to be the basis for litigants to seek collateral remedies against each other or to obtain tactical advantages in proceedings before a court.

Application

The Application section establishes how and when the various rules apply to a judge or judicial candidate.

I. **Applicability of this Code** (A) This code applies to all fulltime judges. The Application section identifies provisions that do not apply to distinct categories of judges. Canon 4 applies to judicial candidates.

(B) A judge, within the meaning of this code, is a lawyer who is authorized to perform judicial functions within a court, including an officer such as a magistrate, court commissioner, or special master.

II. **Retired Judge Subject to Recall** This code applies to a retired judge subject to recall for service, who by law is not permitted to practice law, except that a retired judge is not required to comply with either of the following:

(A) Rule 3.9, except while serving as a judge;

(B) Rule 3.8, at any time.

III. **Parttime Judge** (A) This code applies to a judge who serves repeatedly on a parttime basis by election or appointment, except that a parttime judge is not required to comply with Rules 3.4, 3.8, 3.9, 3.10, and 3.11(A) and (B), at any time.

(B) A parttime judge shall not practice law in the court on which the judge serves or in any court subject to the appellate jurisdiction of the court on which the judge serves, and shall not act as a lawyer in a proceeding in which the judge has served as a judge or in any other related proceeding.

IV. **[RESERVED]**

V. **Acting Judge** This code applies to an acting judge who serves or expects to serve once or only sporadically on a parttime basis by appointment made pursuant to R.C. 1901.10, 1901.12, or 1907.14, except that an acting judge is not required to comply with any of the following:

(A) Rules 1.2, 2.4, 2.10, 3.2, 3.12, or 3.13, except while serving as an acting judge;

(B) Rules 3.4, 3.7, 3.8, 3.9, 3.10, 3.11, 3.15, 4.1, 4.2, 4.3, 4.4, 4.5, and 4.6, at any time.

VI. **Time for Compliance** A person to whom this code becomes applicable shall comply immediately with its provisions, except as otherwise provided in Rules 3.8 and 3.11.

TERMINOLOGY

As used in Canons 1 to 3 of this Code:

"Appropriate authority" means the authority having responsibility for initiation of disciplinary process in connection with the violation to be reported. See Rule 2.15.

"Contribution" means both financial and in-kind contributions, such as goods, professional or volunteer services, advertising, and other types of assistance, which, if obtained by the recipient otherwise, would require a financial expenditure. See Rule 3.7.

"De *minimis*," in the context of interests pertaining to disqualification of a judge, means an insignificant interest that could not raise a reasonable question regarding the judge's impartiality. See Rule 2.11.

"Domestic partner" means a person with whom another person maintains a household and an intimate relationship, other than a person to whom he or she is legally married. See Rules 2.11, 3.13, and 3.14.

"Economic interest" means ownership of more than a de minimis legal or equitable interest. Except for situations in which the judge participates in the management of such a legal or equitable interest or the interest could be substantially affected by the outcome of a proceeding before a judge, "economic interest" does not include any of the following:

(1) An interest in the individual holdings within a mutual or common investment fund;

(2) An interest in securities held by an educational, religious, charitable, fraternal, or civic organization in which the judge or the judge's spouse, domestic partner, parent, or child serves as a director, an officer, an advisor, or other participant;

(3) A deposit in a financial institution or deposits or proprietary interests the judge may maintain as a member of a mutual savings association or credit union, or similar proprietary interests;

(4) An interest in the issuer of government securities held by the judge.

See Rules 1.3, 2.11, and 3.2.

"Ex parte communication" means a communication, concerning a pending or impending matter, between counsel or an unrepresented party and the court when opposing counsel or an unrepresented party is not present or any other communication made to the judge outside the presence of the parties or their lawyers. See Rule 2.9.

"Fiduciary" includes relationships such as executor, administrator, trustee, or guardian. See Rules 2.11, 3.2, and 3.8.

"Impartial," "impartiality," and "impartially" mean absence of bias or prejudice in favor of, or against, particular parties or classes of parties, as well as maintenance of an open mind in considering issues that may come before a judge. See Canons 1 and 2 and Rules 1.2, 2.2, 2.10, 2.11, 2.13, 3.1, 3.7, 3.12, 3.13, and 3.14.

"Impending" references a matter or proceeding that is imminent or expected to occur in the near future. See Rules 2.9, 2.10, and 3.13.

"Impropriety" includes conduct that violates the law, court rules, or provisions of this code, and conduct that undermines a judge's independence, integrity, or impartiality. See Canon 1 and Rule 1.2.

"Independence" means a judge's freedom from influence or controls other than those established by law. See Canon 1 and Rules 1.2, 3.1, 3.7, 3.12, 3.13, and 3.14

"Integrity" means probity, fairness, honesty, uprightness, and soundness of character. See Canon 1 and Rules 1.2, 3.1, 3.7, 3.12, 3.13, and 3.14.

"Judicial candidate" has the same meaning as in Rule 4.6. See Rule 2.11.

"Knowingly," "knowledge," "known," and "knows" mean actual knowledge of the fact in question. A person's knowledge may be inferred from circumstances. See Rules 2.11, 2.15, 2.16, 3.5, and 3.6.

"Law" encompasses court rules, including this code and the Ohio Rules of Professional Conduct, statutes, constitutional provisions, and decisional law. See Rules 1.1, 2.1, 2.2, 2.6, 2.7, 2.9, 3.1, 3.2, 3.4, 3.7, 3.9, 3.12, and 3.13.

"Member of the judge's family" means a spouse, domestic partner, child, grandchild, parent, grandparent, or other relative or person with whom the judge maintains a close familial relationship. See Rules 3.7, 3.8, 3.10, and 3.11.

"Member of a judge's family residing in the judge's household" means any relative of a judge by blood or marriage, or a person treated by a judge as a member of the judge's family, who resides in the judge's household. See Rules 2.11 and 3.13.

"Nonpublic information" means information that is not available to the public. Nonpublic information may include, but is not limited to, information that is sealed by statute or court order or impounded or communicated in camera, and information offered in grand jury proceedings, presentencing reports, dependency cases, or psychiatric reports. See Rule 3.5.

"Pending" references a matter or proceeding that has commenced. A matter continues to be pending through any appellate process until final disposition. See Rules 2.9, 2.10, and 3.13.

"Specialized docket" means a docket or court specifically created by statute or pursuant to the authority of the Rules of Superintendence of the Courts of Ohio to address similar cases and parties. "Specialized docket" includes, but is not limited to, drug courts, mental health courts, domestic violence courts, child support enforcement courts, sex offender courts, OMVI/DUI courts, reentry courts, housing courts, and environmental courts. Courts created in the Ohio Constitution or Revised Code, including appellate courts, common pleas courts and divisions of a common pleas court, municipal courts, and county courts are not, without more, a specialized docket. See Rule 2.9.

"Third degree of relationship" includes the following persons: great-grandparent, grandparent, parent, uncle, aunt, brother, sister, child, grandchild, great-grandchild, nephew, and niece. See Rule 2.11.

Comparison to Ohio Code of Judicial Conduct

The words and phrases defined in the Terminology section are comparable to those found in the corresponding section of the Ohio Code, with the following exceptions:

"Appropriate authority," "contribution," "domestic partner," "*ex parte* communication," "impartial," "impending matter," "impropriety," "independence," "integrity," "judicial candidate," "pending matter," and "specialized docket" are newly defined terms• "Appropriate authority," "contribution," "domestic partner," "ex parte communication," "impartial," "impending matter," "impropriety," "independence," "integrity," "judicial candidate," "pending matter," and "specialized docket" are newly defined terms;

The Ohio Code definition of "court personnel" is not included in the Terminology section.

Comparison to ABA Model Code of Judicial Conduct

The following modifications are made to the ABA Terminology section:

The definition of "aggregate" is stricken, due to the deletion of Rule 2.11(A)(4), and moved to Rule 4.6;

The definition of "judicial candidate" is modified to reference the definition in Rule 4.6;

The definition of "law" is modified to reference specifically the Ohio Code of Judicial Conduct and the Ohio Rules of Professional Conduct;

The definitions of "member of the candidate's family," "personally solicit," "political organization," and "public election" are stricken because those terms are not used in Canons 1-3;

Definitions of "*ex parte* communication" and "specialized docket" are added to correspond to modifications made to Rules 2.9 and 2.11.

CANON 1 A judge shall uphold and promote the *independence, integrity, and impartiality* of the judiciary, and shall avoid *impropriety* and the appearance of *impropriety*.

RULE 1.1 Compliance with the Law

A judge shall comply with the *law*.

RULE 1.2 Promoting Confidence in the Judiciary

A judge shall act at all times in a manner that promotes public confidence in the *independence, integrity, and impartiality* of the judiciary, and shall avoid *impropriety* and the appearance of *impropriety*.

RULE 1.3 Avoiding Abuse of the Prestige of Judicial Office

A judge shall not abuse the prestige of judicial office to advance the personal or *economic interests* of the judge or others, or allow others to do so.

CANON 2 A judge shall perform the duties of judicial office impartially, competently, and diligently.

RULE 2.1 Giving Precedence to the Duties of Judicial Office

The duties of judicial office, as prescribed by law, shall take precedence over all of a judge's other activities.

RULE 2.2 Impartiality and Fairness

A judge shall uphold and apply the *law*, and shall perform all duties of judicial office fairly and *impartially*.

RULE 2.3 Bias, Prejudice, and Harrassment

(A) A judge shall perform the duties of judicial office, including administrative duties, without bias or prejudice.

(B) A judge shall not, in the performance of judicial duties, by words or conduct manifest bias or prejudice, or engage in harassment, including but not limited to bias, prejudice, or harassment based upon race, sex, gender, religion, national origin, ethnicity, disability, age, sexual orientation, marital status, socioeconomic status, or political affiliation, and shall not permit court staff, court officials, or others subject to the judge's direction and control to do so.

(C) A judge shall require lawyers in proceedings before the court to refrain from manifesting bias or prejudice, or engaging in harassment, based upon attributes including but not limited to race, sex, gender, religion, national origin, ethnicity, disability, age, sexual orientation, marital status, socioeconomic status, or political affiliation, against parties, witnesses, lawyers, or others.

(D) The restrictions of divisions (B) and (C) of this rule do not preclude judges or lawyers from making legitimate reference to the listed factors, or similar factors, when they are relevant to an issue in a proceeding.

RULE 2.4 External Influences on Judicial Conduct

(A) A judge shall not be swayed by public clamor or fear of criticism.

(B) A judge shall not permit family, social, political, financial, or other interests or relationships to influence the judge's judicial conduct or judgment.

(C) A judge shall not convey or permit others to convey the impression that any person or organization is in a position to influence the judge.

RULE 2.5   Competence, Diligence, and Cooperation

(A) A judge shall perform judicial and administrative duties competently and diligently and shall comply with guidelines set forth in the Rules of Superintendence for the Courts of Ohio.

(B) A judge shall cooperate with other judges and court officials in the administration of court business.

RULE 2.6   Ensuring the Right to be Heard

(A) A judge shall accord to every person who has a legal interest in a proceeding, or that person's lawyer, the right to be heard according to *law*.

(B) A judge may encourage parties to a proceeding and their lawyers to settle matters in dispute but shall not act in a manner that coerces any party into settlement.

RULE 2.7   Responsibility to Decide

A judge shall hear and decide matters assigned to the judge, except when disqualification is required by Rule 2.11 or other *law*.

RULE 2.8   Decorum, Demeanor, and Communication with Jurors

(A) A judge shall require order and decorum in proceedings before the court.

(B) A judge shall be patient, dignified, and courteous to litigants, jurors, witnesses, lawyers, court staff, court officials, and others with whom the judge deals in an official capacity, and shall require similar conduct of lawyers, court staff, court officials, and others subject to the judge's direction and control.

(C) A judge shall not commend or criticize jurors for their verdict other than in a court order or opinion in a proceeding.

RULE 2.9   *Ex Parte* Contacts and Communications with Others

(A) A judge shall not initiate, receive, permit, or consider ex parte communications, except as follows:

(1) When circumstances require it, an ex parte communication for scheduling, administrative, or emergency purposes, that does not address substantive matters or issues on the merits, is permitted, provided the judge reasonably believes that no party will gain a procedural, substantive, or tactical advantage as a result of the *ex parte* communication;

(2) A judge may obtain the advice of a disinterested expert on the *law* applicable to a proceeding before the judge, if the judge gives notice to the parties of the person consulted and the subject-matter of the advice solicited, and affords the parties a reasonable opportunity to object or respond to the advice received;

(3) A judge may consult with court staff and court officials whose functions are to aid the judge in carrying out the judge's adjudicative responsibilities, or with other judges, provided the judge makes reasonable efforts to avoid receiving factual information that is not part of the record and does not abrogate the responsibility personally to decide the matter;

(4) A judge, with the consent of the parties, may confer separately with the parties and their lawyers in an effort to settle matters pending before the judge;

(5) A judge may initiate, receive, permit, or consider an *ex parte* communication when expressly authorized by *law* to do so;

(6) A judge may initiate, receive, permit, or consider an ex parte communication when administering a *specialized docket*, provided the judge reasonably believes that no party will gain a procedural, substantive, or tactical advantage while in the specialized docket program as a result of the ex parte communication.

(B) If a judge receives an unauthorized *ex parte* communication bearing upon the substance of a matter, the judge shall make provision promptly to notify the parties of the substance of the communication and provide the parties with an opportunity to respond.

(C) A judge shall not investigate facts in a matter independently, and shall consider only the evidence presented and any facts that may properly be judicially noticed.

(D) A judge shall make reasonable efforts, including providing appropriate supervision, to ensure that this rule is not violated by court staff, court officials, and others subject to the judge's direction and control.

RULE 2.10   Judicial Statements on Pending and Impending Cases

(A) A judge shall not make any public statement that might reasonably be expected to affect the outcome or impair the fairness of a matter *pending or impending* in any court, or make any nonpublic statement that might substantially interfere with a fair trial or hearing.

(B) A judge shall not, in connection with cases, controversies, or issues that are likely to come before the court, make pledges, promises, or commitments that are inconsistent with the *impartial* performance of the adjudicative duties of judicial office.

(C) A judge shall require court staff, court officials, and others subject to the judge's direction and control to refrain from making statements that the judge would be prohibited from making by divisions (A) and (B) of this rule.

(D) Notwithstanding the restrictions in division (A) of this rule, a judge may make public statements in the course of official duties, may explain court procedures, and may comment on any proceeding in which the judge is a litigant in a personal, nonjudicial capacity.

(E) Subject to the requirements of division (A) of this rule, a judge may respond directly or through a third-party to allegations in the media or elsewhere concerning the judge's conduct in a matter.

RULE 2.11   Disqualification

(A) A judge shall disqualify himself or herself in any

proceeding in which the judge's *impartiality* might reasonably be questioned, including but not limited to the following circumstances:

(1) The judge has a personal bias or prejudice concerning a party or a party's lawyer, or personal *knowledge* of facts that are in dispute in the proceeding.

(2) The judge *knows* that the judge, the judge's spouse or *domestic partner*, or a person within the *third degree of relationship* to either of them, or the spouse or *domestic partner* of such a person is any of the following:

(a) A party to the proceeding, or an officer, director, general partner, managing member, or trustee of a party;

(b) Acting as a lawyer in the proceeding;

(c) Has more than a *de minimis* interest that could be substantially affected by the proceeding;

(d) Likely to be a material witness in the proceeding.

(3) The judge knows that he or she, individually or as a *fiduciary*, or the judge's spouse, *domestic partner*, parent, or child, or any other member of the *judge's family residing in the judge's household*, has an *economic interest* in the subject matter in controversy or in a party to the proceeding.

(4) [RESERVED]

(5) The judge, while a judge or a *judicial candidate*, has made a public statement, other than in a court proceeding, judicial decision, or opinion, that commits or appears to commit the judge to reach a particular result or rule in a particular way in the proceeding or controversy.

(6) The judge *knows* that the judge's spouse or *domestic partner*, or a person within the *third degree of relationship* to either of them, or the spouse or domestic partner of such a person has acted as a judge in the proceeding.

(7) The judge meets any of the following criteria:

(a) The judge served as a lawyer in the matter in controversy or was associated with a lawyer who participated substantially as a lawyer in the matter during such association;

(b) The judge served in governmental employment, and in such capacity participated personally and substantially as a lawyer or public official concerning the particular matter, or has publicly expressed in such capacity an opinion concerning the merits of the particular matter in controversy;

(c) The judge was a material witness concerning the matter;

(d) The judge previously presided as a judge over the matter in another court.

(B) A judge shall keep informed about the judge's personal and *fiduciary economic interests*, and make a reasonable effort to keep informed about the personal economic interests of the judge's spouse or *domestic partner* and minor children residing in the judge's household.

(C) A judge subject to disqualification under this rule, other than for personal bias or prejudice under division (A)(1) of this rule, may disclose on the record the basis of the judge's disqualification and may ask the parties and their lawyers to consider, outside the presence of the judge and court personnel, whether to waive disqualification. If, following the disclosure, the parties and lawyers agree, without participation by the judge or court personnel, that the judge should not be disqualified, the judge may participate in the proceeding. The agreement shall be incorporated into the record of the proceeding.

RULE 2.12   Supervisory Duties

(A) A judge shall require court staff, court officials, and others subject to the judge's direction and control to act in a manner consistent with the judge's obligations under this code.

(B) A judge with supervisory authority for the performance of other judges shall take reasonable measures to ensure that those judges properly discharge their judicial responsibilities, including the prompt disposition of matters before them.

RULE 2.13   Administrative Appointments

(A) In making administrative appointments, a judge shall do both of the following:

(1) Exercise the power of appointment impartially and on the basis of merit;

(2) Avoid nepotism, favoritism, and unnecessary appointments.

(B) [RESERVED]

(C) A judge shall not approve compensation of appointees beyond the fair value of services rendered.

RULE 2.14   Disability and Impairment

(A) A judge having a reasonable belief that the performance of a lawyer or another judge is impaired by drugs or alcohol, or by a mental, emotional, or physical condition, shall take appropriate action, which may include a confidential referral to a lawyer or judicial assistance program.

(B) Any information obtained by a member or agent of a committee or subcommittee of a bar or judicial association or by a member, employee, or agent of a nonprofit corporation established by a bar association, designed to assist lawyers and judges with substance abuse or mental health problems, shall be privileged for all purposes under this rule, provided the information was obtained while the member, employee, or agent was performing duties as a member, employee, or agent of the committee, subcommittee, or nonprofit corporation.

RULE 2.15   Responding to Judicial and Lawyer Misconduct

(A) A judge having *knowledge* that another judge has committed a violation of this Code that raises a question regarding the judge's honesty, trustworthiness, or fitness as a judge in other respects shall inform the *appropriate authority*.

(B) A judge having *knowledge* that a lawyer has committed a violation of the Ohio Rules of Professional Conduct that raises a question regarding the lawyer's honesty, trustworthiness, or fitness as a lawyer in other respects shall inform the *appropriate authority*.

(C) [RESERVED]

(D) [RESERVED]

RULE 2.16 Cooperation with Disciplinary Authorities

(A) A judge shall cooperate and be candid and honest with judicial and lawyer disciplinary agencies.

(B) A judge shall not retaliate, directly or indirectly, against a person *known* or suspected to have assisted or cooperated with an investigation of a judge or a lawyer.

CANON 3 A judge shall conduct the judge's personal and extrajudicial activities so as to minimize the risk of conflict with the obligations of judicial office.

RULE 3.1 Extrajudicial Activities in General

A judge may engage in extrajudicial activities, except as prohibited by law. However, when engaging in extrajudicial activities, a judge shall not do any of the following:

(A) Participate in activities that will interfere with the proper performance of the judge's judicial duties;

(B) Participate in activities that will lead to frequent disqualification of the judge;

(C) Participate in activities that would appear to a reasonable person to undermine the judge's *independence, integrity, or impartiality;*

(D) Engage in conduct that would appear to a reasonable person to be coercive;

(E) Make use of court premises, staff, stationery, equipment, or other resources, except for incidental use for extrajudicial activities permitted by *law*.

RULE 3.2 Appearances before Governmental Bodies and Consultation with Government Officials

A judge shall not appear voluntarily at a public hearing before, or otherwise consult with, an executive or a legislative body or official, except as follows:

(A) In connection with matters concerning the law, the legal system, or the administration of justice;

(B) In connection with matters about which the judge acquired knowledge or expertise in the course of the judge's judicial duties;

(C) When the judge is acting *pro se* in a matter involving the judge's legal or *economic interests*, or when the judge is acting in a *fiduciary* capacity.

RULE 3.3 Testifying as a Character Witness

A judge shall not testify as a character witness in a judicial, administrative, or other adjudicatory proceeding or otherwise vouch for the character of a person in a legal proceeding, except when duly summoned.

RULE 3.4 Appointments to Governmental Positions

A judge shall not accept appointment to a governmental committee, board, commission, or other governmental position, unless it is one that concerns the law, the legal system, or the administration of justice.

RULE 3.5 Use of Nonpublic Information

A judge shall not *knowingly* disclose or use *nonpublic information* acquired in a judicial capacity for any purpose unrelated to the judge's judicial duties.

RULE 3.6 Affiliation with Discriminatory Organizations

(A) A judge shall not hold membership in any organization that practices invidious discrimination on the basis of race, sex, gender, religion, national origin, ethnicity, or sexual orientation.

(B) A judge shall not use the benefits or facilities of an organization if the judge *knows* or should know that the organization practices invidious discrimination on one or more of the bases identified in division (A) of this rule. A judge's attendance at an event in a facility of an organization that the judge is not permitted to join is not a violation of this rule when the judge's attendance is an isolated event that could not reasonably be perceived as an endorsement of the organization's practices.

RULE 3.7 Participation in Educational, Religious, Charitable, Fraternal, or Civic Organizations and Activities

(A) Subject to the requirements of Rule 3.1, a judge may participate in activities sponsored by organizations or governmental entities concerned with the law, the legal system, or the administration of justice, and those sponsored by or on behalf of educational, religious, charitable, fraternal, or civic organizations not conducted for profit, including but not limited to the following activities:

(1) Assisting such an organization or entity in planning related to fundraising, and participating in the management and investment of the organization's or entity's funds;

(2) Soliciting *contributions* for such an organization or entity, but only from *members of the judge's family*, or from judges over whom the judge does not exercise supervisory or appellate authority;

(3) Participating in but not soliciting funds for *de minimis* fundraising activities that are directed at a broad range of the community and that may be performed by other volunteers who do not hold judicial office;

(4) Soliciting membership for such an organization or entity, even though the membership dues or fees generated may be used to support the objectives of the organization or entity, but only if the organization or entity is concerned with the *law*, the legal system, or the administration of justice;

(5) Appearing or speaking at, receiving an award or other recognition at, being featured on the program of, and permitting his or her title to be used in connection with an event of such an organization or entity, provided the participation does not reflect adversely on the judge's *independence, integrity, or impartiality;*

(6) Making recommendations to such a public or private fund-granting organization or entity in connection with its programs and activities, but only if the organization or entity is concerned with the law, the

legal system, or the administration of justice;

(7) Serving as an officer, director, trustee, or nonlegal advisor of such an organization or entity, unless it is likely that the organization or entity will be engaged in either of the following:

(a) Proceedings that would ordinarily come before the judge;

(b) Frequently in adversary proceedings in the court of which the judge is a member, or in any court subject to the appellate jurisdiction of the court of which the judge is a member.

(B) A judge may encourage lawyers to provide pro bono publico legal services.

RULE 3.8   Appointments to Fiduciary Positions

(A) A judge shall not accept appointment to serve in a *fiduciary* position, such as executor, administrator, trustee, guardian, attorney in fact, or other personal representative, except for the estate, trust, or person of a *member of the judge's family*, and then only if such service will not interfere with the proper performance of judicial duties.

(B) A judge shall not serve in a *fiduciary* position if the judge as fiduciary will likely be engaged in proceedings that would ordinarily come before the judge, or if the estate, trust, or ward becomes involved in adversary proceedings in the court on which the judge serves, or one under its appellate jurisdiction.

(C) A judge acting in a *fiduciary* capacity shall be subject to the same restrictions on engaging in financial activities that apply to a judge personally.

(D) If a person who is serving in a *fiduciary* position becomes a judge, he or she must comply with this rule as soon as reasonably practicable, but in no event later than six months after becoming a judge.

RULE 3.9   Service as Arbitrator or Mediator

A judge shall not act as an arbitrator or a mediator or perform other judicial functions apart from the judge's official duties unless expressly authorized by *law*.

RULE 3.10   Practice of Law

A judge shall not practice law. A judge may act *pro se* and may, without compensation, give legal advice to and draft or review documents for a *member of the judge's family*, but is prohibited from serving as the family member's lawyer in any forum.

RULE 3.11   Financial, Business, or Remunerative Activities

(A) A judge may hold and manage investments of the judge and *members of the judge's family.*

(B) A judge shall not serve as an officer, director, manager, general partner, advisor, or employee of or independent contractor for any business entity except that a judge may do any of the following:

(1) Manage or participate in a business closely held by the judge or *members of the judge's family;*

(2) Manage or participate in a business entity primarily engaged in investment of the financial resources of the judge or *members of the judge's family;*

(3) Write or teach.

(C) A judge shall not engage in financial activities permitted under divisions (A) and (B) of this rule if they will do any of the following:

(1) Interfere with the proper performance of judicial duties;

(2) Lead to frequent disqualification of the judge;

(3) Involve the judge in frequent transactions or continuing business relationships with lawyers or other persons likely to come before the court on which the judge serves;

(4) Result in violation of other provisions of this code.

(D) As soon as practicable without serious financial detriment, the judge shall divest himself or herself of investments and other financial interests that might require frequent disqualification or otherwise violate this rule.

RULE 3.12   Compensation for Extrajudicial Activities

A judge may accept compensation for extrajudicial activities permitted by *law* unless such acceptance would appear to a reasonable person to undermine the judge's *independence, integrity, or impartiality.* The compensation shall be reasonable and commensurate to the task performed.

RULE 3.13   Acceptance and Reporting of Gifts, Loans, Bequests, Benefits, or Other Things of Value

(A) A judge shall not accept, and shall urge the judge's spouse, *domestic partner*, and other *members of the judge's family residing in the judge's household* not to accept, any gifts, loans, bequests, benefits, or other things of value, except as follows:

(1) Items with little intrinsic value, such as plaques, certificates, trophies, and greeting cards;

(2) Gifts, loans, bequests, benefits, or other things of value from friends, relatives, or other persons, including lawyers, whose appearance or interest in a proceeding *pending or impending* before the judge would in any event require disqualification of the judge under Rule 2.11;

(3) Ordinary social hospitality;

(4) Commercial or financial opportunities and benefits, including special pricing and discounts, and loans from lending institutions in their regular course of business, if the same opportunities and benefits or loans are made available on the same terms to similarly situated persons who are not judges;

(5) Rewards and prizes given to competitors or participants in random drawings, contests, or other events that are open to persons who are not judges;

(6) Scholarships, fellowships, and similar benefits or awards, if they are available to similarly situated persons who are not judges, based upon the same terms and criteria;

(7) Books, magazines, journals, audiovisual materials, and other resource materials supplied by publishers on a complimentary basis for official use;

(8) Gifts, awards, or benefits associated with the business, profession, or other separate activity of a

spouse, a *domestic partner,* or other *member of the judge's family residing in the judge's household,* but that incidentally benefit the judge, provided the gift, award, or benefit does not give the appearance of influencing the judge in his or her judicial duties or otherwise appear to a reasonable person to undermine the judge's *independence, integrity, or impartiality;*

(9) A gift from a relative or friend for a social occasion, such as a wedding, anniversary, or birthday, if the gift is commensurate with the relationship and occasion;

(10) A gift incident to a public testimonial;

(11) An invitation to the judge and the judge's spouse, *domestic partner,* or guest to attend without charge either of the following:

(a) An event associated with a bar-related function or other activity related to the *law,* the legal system, or the administration of justice;

(b) An event associated with any of the judge's educational, religious, charitable, fraternal, or civic activities permitted by this code, if the same invitation is offered to nonjudges who are engaged in similar ways in the activity as is the judge.

(12) Any other thing of value, if the donor is neither of the following:

(a) A party or other person who has come or is likely to come or whose interests have come or are likely to come before the judge;

(b) A person who is doing or seeking to do business with the court.

(B) A judge shall report the acceptance of any gift, loan, bequest, benefit, or other thing of value as required by Rule 3.15.

RULE 3.14 Reimbursement of Expenses and Waivers of Fees or Charges

(A) A judge may accept reimbursement of necessary and reasonable expenses for travel, food, lodging, or other incidental expenses, or a waiver or partial waiver of fees or charges for registration, tuition, and similar items if both of the following apply:

(1) The expenses or charges are associated with the judge's participation in activities permitted by this code;

(2) The source of the reimbursement or waiver does not give the appearance of influencing the judge in his or her judicial duties or otherwise appear to a reasonable person to undermine the judge's *independence, integrity, or impartiality.*

(B) Reimbursement of expenses for necessary travel, food, lodging, or other incidental expenses shall be limited to the actual costs reasonably incurred by the judge and, when appropriate to the occasion, by the judge's spouse, *domestic partner,* or guest. Any reimbursement in excess of actual cost is compensation and shall be publicly reported as required by Rule 3.15.

(C) A judge who accepts reimbursement of expenses or waivers or partial waivers of fees or charges on behalf of the judge or the judge's spouse, *domestic partner,* or guest shall publicly report such acceptance as required by Rule 3.15.

RULE 3.15 Reporting Requirements

A judge shall file annually the disclosure statement required by R.C. 102.02 with the secretary of the Board of Commissioners on Grievances and Discipline of the Supreme Court of Ohio. The completion and filing of the annual disclosure statement fulfills the reporting requirements set forth in Rules 3.12, 3.13, and 3.14.

(B) [RESERVED]

(C) [RESERVED]

(D) [RESERVED]

NOTES TO DECISIONS

ANALYSIS

Disqualification
Ex parte communication
Failure to timely decide cases
Magistrates and referees
Recusal

Disqualification

Fact that a judge sought the appointment of a special prosecutor concerning a matter that the county prosecuting attorney chose not to present to a grand jury did not warrant disqualification. The prosecuting attorney's desire to call the judge as a witness if there was a hearing on the appointment of a special prosecutor did not compel disqualification: In re Betleski, 113 Ohio St. 3d 1229, 2006 Ohio 7232, 863 N.E.2d 631, 2006 Ohio LEXIS 3684 (2007).

In a case where a judge has already testified as a material witness for the prosecution at a suppression hearing and where the judge has acknowledged holding ex parte discussions with the prosecutor about his testimony, a reasonable and objective observer familiar with these facts might harbor serious doubts about the judge's impartiality. Canon 3 (E)(1) of the Code of Judicial Conduct directs judges to step aside from any proceedings in which their impartiality might reasonably be questioned: State v. Marler (In re Rastatter), 113 Ohio St. 3d 1218, 2006 Ohio 7226, 863 N.E.2d 623, 2006 Ohio LEXIS 3685 (2007).

There were no cognizable grounds under Ohio Code Jud. Conduct Canon 3 under which the trial court would have been required to disqualify the magistrate to heard a mother's legal custody matter, and thus, the trial court did not abuse its discretion by overruling the mother's objections on the basis that the magistrate had been exposed to circumstances which may have required him to be a witness in a potential criminal case against her. The grounds for disqualification in Ohio Code Jud. Conduct Canon 3 are limited to those situations in which a magistrate would be a material witness to the proceeding being heard before him, rather than a separate criminal proceeding which may result from incidents which happen to occur within the courtroom. In re Memic, — Ohio App. 3d —, 2006 Ohio 6346, — N.E. 2d —, 2006 Ohio App. LEXIS 6302 (Dec. 1, 2006).

Where a challenge to the transfer of a divorce matter was not made by a husband until well after the final entry of divorce and the completion of the appeal, the potential disqualification of the judge under Ohio Jud. Conduct Canon 3(E)(1) could not be used as grounds to challenge the correctness of the trial court's divorce decree on the merits. Rahawangi v. Alsamman, — Ohio App. 3d —, 2006 Ohio 3163, — N.E. 2d —, 2006 Ohio App. LEXIS 3034 (June 22, 2006).

Ex parte communication

Trial court's denial of a tenant's motion for a continuance pursuant to Ohio R. Civ. P. 41(A) in a small claims matter initiated by a landlord, seeking recovery of unpaid rent, was an abuse of the trial court's discretion, as the trial court's indication that medical documentation of the tenant's illness was required was error where there was only short notice of the situation, the trial court engaged in ex parte communications in violation of Ohio Code Jud. Conduct Canon 3(B) in making its determination, and there was no pressing need to expedite the matter; there had been no prior continuances, the landlord was not represented by counsel whose schedule would be inconvenienced, and the original trial date was set outside of the time limits under RC § 1925.04(B). Frampton v. Mike & Betty Sekula, — Ohio App. 3d —, 2007 Ohio 5039, — N.E. 2d —, 2007 Ohio App. LEXIS 4461 (Sept. 20, 2007).

Failure to timely decide cases

Judge's failure to decide cases in a timely manner constituted a violation of Canon 3: Disciplinary Counsel v. Sargeant, 118 Ohio St. 3d 322, 2008 Ohio 2330, 889 N.E.2d 96, 2008 Ohio LEXIS 1333 (2008).

Magistrates and referees

There was no abuse of discretion in a trial court's denial of a motion to recuse a magistrate who was presiding over a breach of contract action, as the judge had merely expressed dissatisfaction with attorneys' tactics, and although more decorum could have been used in the magistrate's choice of words pursuant to Ohio Code Jud. Conduct Canon 3(B)(4) and (5), there was no finding of bias, prejudice, or impartiality, and the magistrate expressed willingness to hear the evidence and decide the matter fairly. Rejas Invs. v. National City Bank, — Ohio App. 3d —, 2006 Ohio 5586, — N.E. 2d —, 2006 Ohio App. LEXIS 5614 (Oct. 20, 2006).

Recusal

Defendant failed to demonstrate any improper conduct or prejudice warranting recusal, pursuant to Ohio Code Jud. Conduct Canon 3(C)(1)(a); it was clear from the record that the trial judge was not prejudiced against defendant for exercising his right to trial. The trial judge, after listening to defendant's in-artfully phrased complaints, slowly and deliberately explained the trial process to him and then explained his own thought process with respect to sentencing and that he would make no decisions on sentencing until a verdict was rendered by the jury. State v. Arrone, — Ohio App. 3d —, 2006 Ohio 4144, — N.E. 2d —, 2006 Ohio App. LEXIS 4125 (Aug. 11, 2006).

CANON 4 A judge or *judicial candidate* shall not engage in political or campaign activity that is inconsistent with the *independence, integrity, or impartiality* of the judiciary.

RULE 4.1 Political and Campaign Activities of Judges and Judicial Candidates

(A) A judge or *judicial candidate* shall not do any of the following:

(1) Act as a leader of, or hold an office in, a *political party;*

(2) Make speeches on behalf of a *political party* or another candidate for public office;

(3) Publicly endorse or oppose a candidate for another public office;

(4) Solicit funds for or make a *contribution* or expenditure of campaign funds to a *political party* or a candidate for public office, except as permitted by division (B)(2) or (3) of this rule;

(5) Comment on any substantive matter relating to a specific case pending on the docket of any judge;

(6) Make any statement that would reasonably be expected to affect the outcome or impair the fairness of a matter pending or impending in any court;

(7) In connection with cases, controversies, or issues that are likely to come before the court, make pledges, promises, or commitments that are inconsistent with the *impartial* performance of the adjudicative duties of judicial office.

(B) A judge or judicial candidate may do any of the following, subject to limitations set forth in this canon:

(1) Attend or speak to a political gathering;

(2) Make a *contribution* or expenditure of campaign funds to purchase a ticket to attend a social or fundraising event held by or on behalf of another public official or candidate for public office;

(3) Make a *contribution* or expenditure of campaign funds to a *political party* or to purchase a ticket to attend a social event sponsored by a *political party*, provided the *contribution* or expenditure will be used for any of the purposes set forth in R.C. 3517.18(A) and will not be used for any of the purposes set forth in R.C. 3517.18(B).

RULE 4.2 Political and Campaign Activities of Judicial Candidates

(A) A *judicial candidate* shall be responsible for all of the following:

(1) Acting at all times in a manner consistent with the *independence, integrity, and impartiality* of the judiciary;

(2) Reviewing and approving the content of all campaign statements and materials produced by the *judicial candidate* or his or her campaign committee before their dissemination;

(3) The content of any statement communicated in any medium by his or her campaign committee and for compliance by his or her campaign committee with the limitations on campaign solicitations and *contributions* contained in Rule 4.4, if the candidate knew of the statement, solicitation, or *contribution;*

(4) No earlier than one year prior to or no later than thirty days after certification of his or her candidacy by the election authority, completing a two-hour course in campaign practices, finance, and ethics accredited by the Commission on Continuing Legal Education and certifying such completion within five days of the date of the course to the Board of Commissioners on Grievances and Discipline.

(B) A *judicial candidate* shall not do any of the following:

(1) Jointly raise funds with a candidate for nonjudicial office, except as permitted by division (C) of this rule;

(2) Appear in a joint campaign advertisement with a candidate for nonjudicial office, except as permitted by division (C) of this rule;

(3) Expend funds in a judicial campaign that have been contributed to the *judicial candidate* to promote his or her candidacy for a nonjudicial office;

(4) After the day of the primary election, identify himself or herself in advertising as a member of or affiliated with a political party.

(C) A *judicial candidate* may do any of the following:

(1) Conduct joint fundraising activities with other *judicial candidates;*

(2) Appear in joint campaign advertisements with other *judicial candidates;*

(3) Participate with *judicial* and nonjudicial *candidates* in fundraising activities organized or sponsored by a *political party;*

(4) Appear with other candidates for public office on slate cards, sample ballots, and other publications of a *political party* that identify all of the candidates endorsed by the party in an election;

(5) Seek, accept, or use endorsements from any person or *organization;*

(6) State in person or in advertising that he or she is a nominee of or endorsed by a *political party;*

(7) From the day on which he or she becomes a judicial candidate through the day of the primary election, identify himself or herself in person or in advertising as a member of or affiliated with a political party.

RULE 4.3   Campaign Standards and Communications

During the course of any campaign for nomination or election to judicial office, a *judicial candidate,* by means of campaign materials, including sample ballots, advertisements on radio or television or in a newspaper or periodical, electronic communications, a public speech, press release, or otherwise, shall not *knowingly* or with reckless disregard do any of the following:

(A) Post, publish, broadcast, transmit, circulate, or distribute information concerning the *judicial candidate* or an opponent, either *knowing* the information to be false or with a reckless disregard of whether or not it was false or, if true, that would be deceiving or misleading to a reasonable person;

(B) Manifest bias or prejudice toward an opponent based on race, sex, religion, national origin, disability, age, sexual orientation, or socioeconomic status;

(C) Use the title of an office not currently held by a *judicial candidate* in a manner that implies that the *judicial candidate* does currently hold that office;

(D) Use the term "judge" when the *judicial candidate* is not a judge unless that term appears after or below the name of the *judicial candidate* and is accompanied by either or both of the following:

(1) The words "elect" or "vote," in prominent lettering, before the *judicial candidate's* name;

(2) The word "for," in prominent lettering, between the name of the *judicial candidate* and the term "judge;"

(E) Use the term "re-elect" in either of the following circumstances:

(1) When the *judicial candidate* has never been elected at a general or special election to the office for which he or she is a *judicial candidate;*

(2) When the *judicial candidate* is not the current occupant of the office for which he or she is a *judicial candidate;*

(F) Misrepresent his or her identity, qualifications, present position, or other fact or the identity, qualifications, present position, or other fact of an opponent;

(G) Make a false statement concerning the formal schooling or training completed or attempted by a *judicial candidate;* a degree, diploma, certificate, scholarship, grant, award, prize of honor received, earned, or held by a *judicial candidate;* or the period of time during which a *judicial candidate* attended any school, college, community technical school, or institution;

(H) Make a false statement concerning the professional, occupational, or vocational licenses held by a *judicial candidate,* or concerning any position a *judicial candidate* held for which he or she received a salary or wages;

(I) Make a false statement that a *judicial candidate* has been arrested, indicted, or convicted of a crime;

(J) Make a statement that a *judicial candidate* has been arrested, indicted, or convicted of any crime without disclosing the outcome of all pending or concluded legal proceedings resulting from the arrest, indictment, or conviction;

(K) Make a false statement that a *judicial candidate* has a record of treatment or confinement for mental disorder;

(L) Make a false statement that a *judicial candidate* has been subjected to military discipline for criminal misconduct or dishonorably discharged from the armed services;

(M) Falsely identify the source of a statement, issue statements under the name of another person without authorization, or falsely state the endorsement of or opposition to a *judicial candidate* by a person, *organization, political party,* or publication.

RULE 4.4   Campaign Solicitations and Contributions

(A) A *judicial candidate* shall not personally solicit or receive campaign *contributions.* A *judicial candidate* may establish a campaign committee to manage and conduct a campaign for the candidate, subject to the provisions of this Code. The judicial candidate is responsible for ensuring that his or her campaign committee complies with applicable provisions of this Code and other applicable *law.*

(B) A *judicial candidate* shall prohibit public employees subject to his or her direction or control from soliciting or receiving campaign *contributions.*

(C) The campaign committee of a *judicial candidate* shall not *knowingly* solicit or receive, directly or indirectly, for any political or personal purpose any of the following:

(1) A *contribution* from any employee of the court or person who does business with the court in the form of a contractual or other arrangement in which the person, in the current year or any of the previous six calendar years, received as payment for goods or services aggregate funds or fees regardless of the source in excess of two hundred fifty dollars. The committee may receive campaign *contributions* from lawyers who are not employees of the court or doing business with the court in the form of a contractual or other arrangement.

(2) A *contribution* from any appointee of the court unless the campaign committee, on its campaign *contribution* and expenditure statement, reports the name, address, occupation, and employer of the appointee,

identifies the person as an appointee of the court, and indicates whether the appointee, in the current year or in any of the previous six calendar years, received *aggregate* compensation from court appointments in excess of two hundred fifty dollars.

(3) A *contribution* from a *political party* unless the contribution is made from a separate fund established by the *political party* solely to receive donations for *judicial candidates* and the *political party* reports on the *contribution* and expenditure statements filed by the party the name, address, occupation, and employer of each person who contributed to the separate fund established by the *political party*.

(D) As used in division (C) of this rule:

(1) "Appointee" does not include a person whose appointment is approved, ratified, or made by the court based on an intention expressed in a document such as a will, trust, agreement, or contract.

(2) "Court" means the court for which the *judicial candidate* is seeking election and, if applicable, the court on which he or she currently serves. If the *judicial candidate* is seeking election to a division of a court of common pleas or a municipal court, "court" means the division of the court for which the *judicial candidate* is seeking election and, if applicable, the court or division of the court on which he or she currently serves.

(3) "Division" means any of the following whether separate or in combination: general division of the court of common pleas; domestic relations division of the court of common pleas; juvenile division of the court of common pleas; probate division of the court of common pleas; housing or environmental division of the municipal court.

(4) "Compensation" does not include reasonable reimbursement for travel, meals, and other expenses received by an appointee who serves in a volunteer capacity.

(E) A *judicial candidate* shall not participate in or receive campaign *contributions* from a judicial fundraising event that categorizes or identifies participants by the amount of the *contribution* made to the event.

(F) The campaign committee of a *judicial candidate* may begin soliciting and receiving *contributions* no earlier than one hundred twenty days before the first Tuesday after the first Monday in May of the year in which the general election is held. If the general election is held in 2000 or any fourth year thereafter, the campaign committee of a *judicial candidate* may begin soliciting and receiving contributions no earlier than one hundred twenty days before the first Tuesday after the first Monday in March of the year in which the general election is held. Except as provided in divisions (G) and (H) of this rule, the solicitation and receipt of *contributions* may continue until one hundred twenty days after the general election.

(G) If the candidate is defeated prior to the general election, the solicitation and receipt of *contributions* may continue until such time as the *contributions* solicited are sufficient to pay the campaign debts and obligations of the *judicial candidate* incurred on or before the date of the primary election, plus the costs of solicitation incurred after the date of the primary election, but in no event shall the solicitation or receipt

of *contributions* continue beyond one hundred twenty days after the date of the election at which the defeat occurred. Notwithstanding division (K) of this rule, the limits on *contributions* in a primary election period shall apply to any *contributions* solicited or received by the campaign committee of the defeated *judicial candidate* after the date of the primary election.

(H) In the case of the death or withdrawal of a *judicial candidate,* the solicitation and receipt of *contributions* may continue until such time as the *contributions* solicited are sufficient to pay the campaign debts and obligations of the *judicial candidate* incurred on or before the date of death or withdrawal, plus the costs of solicitation incurred after the date of death or withdrawal, but in no event shall the solicitation or receipt of *contributions* continue beyond one hundred twenty days after the date of death or withdrawal.

(I) Notwithstanding any provision of division (F) of this rule to the contrary, a judicial candidate may do either or both of the following:

(1) Not more than ninety days prior to the commencement of the one hundred twenty-day fundraising period described in division (F) of this rule, contribute personal funds to his or her campaign committee;

(2) After the conclusion of the applicable fundraising period described in division (F), (G), or (H) of this rule, contribute personal funds to his or her campaign committee for the express purpose of satisfying any campaign debt that was incurred during the applicable fundraising period and that remains unpaid at the conclusion of the applicable fundraising period. The name of the individual or entity to whom the debt is owed, the amount of the debt, and the date on which the debt was incurred shall be clearly noted on the appropriate campaign contribution and expenditure statement.

(J) Except as otherwise provided in division (K) of this rule, the campaign committee of a *judicial candidate* shall not directly or indirectly solicit or receive in the fundraising period allowed by division (F), (G), or (H) of this rule a campaign *contribution aggregating* more than the following:

(1) From an individual other than the *judicial candidate* or a member of his or her *immediate family,* three thousand four hundred fifty dollars in the case of a judicial candidate for chief justice or justice of the Supreme Court, one thousand one hundred fifty dollars in the case of a *judicial candidate* for the court of appeals, or five hundred seventy-five dollars in the case of a *judicial candidate* for the court of common pleas, municipal court, or county court.

(2) From any *organization,* six thousand three hundred twenty-five dollars in the case of a judicial candidate for chief justice or justice of the Supreme Court or three thousand four hundred fifty dollars in the case of all other *judicial candidates.*

(3) From a *political party:*

(a) Three hundred sixteen thousand two hundred fifty dollars in the case of a *judicial candidate* for chief justice or justice of the Supreme Court;

(b) Sixty-nine thousand dollars in the case of a *judicial candidate* for the court of appeals;

(c) Sixty-nine thousand dollars in the case of a *judicial candidate* for a court of common pleas, municipal court, or county court that serves a territorial jurisdiction with a population of more than seven hundred fifty thousand;

(d) Fifty-seven thousand five hundred dollars in the case of a *judicial candidate* for a court of common pleas, municipal court, or county court that serves a territorial jurisdiction with a population of seven hundred fifty thousand or less;

(K) If a *judicial candidate* is opposed in a primary election, the campaign committee of that *judicial candidate* shall not directly or indirectly solicit or receive either of the following:

(1) A campaign *contribution* from an individual or an organization aggregating more than the applicable limitation contained in division (J)(1) or (2) of this rule in a primary election period or in a general election period;

(2) A campaign *contribution* from a *political party* aggregating more than the applicable limitation contained in division (J)(3) of this rule in a general election period or aggregating more than the following during a primary election period:

(a) One hundred seventy-two thousand five hundred dollars in the case of a *judicial candidate* for chief justice or justice of the Supreme Court;

(b) Thirty-four thousand five hundred dollars in the case of a *judicial candidate* for the court of appeals;

(c) Thirty-four thousand five hundred dollars in the case of a *judicial candidate* for a court of common pleas, municipal court, or county court that serves a territorial jurisdiction with a population of more than seven hundred fifty thousand;

(d) Twenty-eight thousand seven hundred fifty dollars in the case of a *judicial candidate* for a court of common pleas, municipal court, or county court that serves a territorial jurisdiction with a population of seven hundred fifty thousand or less.

(L) As used in division (K) of this rule, "primary election period" begins on the first day on which *contributions* may be solicited and received pursuant to division (F) of this rule and ends on the day of the primary election, and "general election period" begins on the day after the primary election and ends on the last day on which *contributions* may be solicited or received pursuant to division (F) of this rule.

(M) For purposes of division (J), (K), and (L) of this rule:

(1) *Contributions* received from *political action committees* that are established, financed, maintained, or controlled by the same corporation, nonprofit corporation, partnership, limited liability company, association, professional association, continuing association, estate, trust, business trust, or other entity, including any parent, subsidiary, local, division, or department of that same corporation, nonprofit corporation, partnership, limited liability company, association, professional association, continuing association, estate, trust, business trust, or other entity, shall be considered to have been received from a single *political action committee*.

(2) All *contributions* received by a *judicial candidate* from a national, state, or county *political party* shall be combined in applying the limits set forth in division (J)(3) of this rule.

(3) *In-kind contributions* consisting of goods and compensated services shall be assigned a fair market value by the campaign committee and shall be subject to the same limitations and reporting requirements as other *contributions*.

(4) A *loan* made to a campaign committee by a person other than the *judicial candidate* or a member of his or her *immediate family* shall not exceed an amount equal to two times the applicable *contribution* limit, and amounts in excess of the applicable *contribution* limit shall be repaid within the fundraising period allowed by division (F) of this rule. A debt remaining at the end of the fundraising period shall be treated as a *contribution* and subject to the applicable *contribution* limit.

(5) A debt incurred by a judge or *judicial candidate* in a previous campaign for public office and forgiven by the individual, *organization, or political party* to whom the debt is owed shall not be considered a campaign *contribution*.

(N) In applying the *contribution* limits contained in division (J) and (K) of this rule, the *contributions* of an individual or organization to a *judicial candidate* fund established by a *political party* shall not be *aggregated* with other *contributions* from the same individual or *organization* made directly to the campaign committee of a judicial candidate unless the campaign committee of the *judicial candidate* directly or indirectly solicited the contribution to the *judicial candidate* fund.

(O) On or before the first day of December beginning in 2008 and every four years thereafter, the secretary of the Board of Commissioners on Grievances and Discipline shall determine the percentage change over the preceding forty-eight months in the Consumer Price Index for All Urban Consumers, or its successive equivalent, as determined by the United States Department of Labor, Bureau of Labor Statistics, or its successor in responsibility, for all items, Series A. The secretary shall apply that percentage change to the *contribution* limitations then in effect and notify the Supreme Court of the results of that calculation. The Supreme Court may adopt revised *contribution* limitations based on the secretary's calculation or other factors that the Court considers appropriate.

RULE 4.5 Activities of a Judge Who Becomes a Candidate for Nonjudicial Office

Upon becoming a candidate in a primary or general election for a nonjudicial elective office, a judge shall resign from judicial office. A judge may continue to hold judicial office while he or she is a candidate for election to or serving as a delegate in a state constitutional convention, if the judge is otherwise permitted by law to do so.

RULE 4.6 Definitions

As used in Canon 4:

(A) "Aggregate" means not only contributions in cash or in-kind made directly to a candidate's campaign committee, but also all contributions made indirectly with the understanding that they will be used to support the election of a candidate or to oppose the election of the candidate's opponent.

(B) "Contribution" has the same meaning as in R.C. 3517.01 and includes an in-kind contribution.

(C) "Immediate family" means a spouse or domestic partner or any of the following who are related by blood or marriage to the judicial candidate:

(1) Parent;

(2) Child;

(3) Brother or sister;

(4) Grandparent;

(5) Grandchild;

(6) Uncle or aunt;

(7) Nephew or niece;

(8) Great-grandparent;

(9) First cousin.

(D) "Independence," "integrity," "impartiality," "impending," and "pending" have the same meaning as in the Terminology section of this code.

(E) "In-kind contribution" has the same meaning as in R.C. 3517.01.

(F) "Judicial candidate" means a person who has made a public announcement of candidacy for judicial office, declared or filed as a candidate for judicial office with the election authority, or authorized the solicitation or receipt of contributions or support for judicial office, whichever occurred first.

(G) "Knowingly" means actual knowledge of the fact in question. A person's knowledge may be inferred from circumstances.

(H) "Law firm" means a lawyer or lawyers in a law partnership, professional corporation, sole proprietorship, or other association authorized to practice law or lawyers engaged in a private or public legal aid or public defender organization, a legal services organization, the legal department of a corporation or other organization, or the attorney general, prosecuting attorney, law director, or other public office.

(I) "Loan" means an advance of money with an absolute promise to pay, with or without interest, and includes loan guarantees.

(J) "Organization" means any entity or combination of two or more persons, other than a political party, including, but not limited to, a corporation, nonprofit corporation, partnership, limited liability company, association, professional association, continuing association, estate, trust, business trust, political action committee as defined in R.C. 3517.01, law firm, organization affiliated with a political party, labor organization, campaign committee of another candidate for public office, or caucus campaign committee.

(K) "Organization affiliated with a political party" means a combination of two or more persons, other than a political party or an organization, that is identified by its name or association with a national, state, or county political party or expressly promotes the interests, philosophy, or candidates of a political party.

(L) "Political action committee" has the same meaning as in R.C. 3517.01.

(M) "Political party" has the same meaning as in R.C. 3517.01 and includes any national, state, or county political party.

Form of Citation, Effective Date, Application

(A) These rules shall be known as the Ohio Code of Judicial Conduct and cited as "Jud. Cond. Rule _____."

(B) The Ohio Code of Judicial Conduct shall take effect March 1, 2009, at which time the Code shall supersede and replace the Ohio Code of Judicial Conduct, in effect prior to March 1, 2009, to govern the conduct of judges occurring on or after that effective date. The former Ohio Code of Judicial Conduct shall continue to apply to govern conduct occurring prior to March 1, 2009 and shall apply to all disciplinary investigations and prosecutions relating to conduct that occurred prior to March 1, 2009.

APPENDIX A

CORRELATION TABLE
2009 OHIO CODE OF JUDICIAL CONDUCT TO
FORMER OHIO CODE OF JUDICIAL CONDUCT

The following is a numerical listing of the 2009 Ohio Code of Judicial Conduct with cross-references to substantially similar provisions of the former Ohio Code of Judicial Conduct. Please consult the code comparisons that follow each rule for a more detailed treatment of corresponding provisions.

2009 OHIO CODE OF JUDICIAL CONDUCT	FORMER OHIO CODE OF JUDICIAL CONDUCT
Preamble and Scope	Preamble
Application	Compliance
Terminology	Terminology
CANON 1	
Rule 1.1 Compliance with the Law	Canon 2
Rule 1.2 Promoting Confidence in the Judiciary	Canons 1 and 2
Rule 1.3 Avoiding Abuse of the Prestige of Judicial Office	Canon 4(A)
CANON 2	
Rule 2.1 Giving Precedence to Duties of Judicial Office	Canon 3(A)
Rule 2.2 Impartiality and Fairness	Canons 3(B)(2) & (B)(5)
Rule 2.3 Bias, Prejudice, and Harassment	
Rule 2.3(A)	Canon 3(B)(5), 1st sentence
Rule 2.3(B)	Canon 3(B)(5), 2nd sentence
Rule 2.3(C)	Canon 3(B)(6)
Rule 2.3(D)	cf. Canon 3(B)(6)

Rule 2.4 External Influences on Judicial Conduct

Rule 2.4(A)	Canon 3(B)(2)
Rule 2.4(B)	Canon 4(A)
Rule 2.4(C)	Canon 4(A)

Rule 2.5 Competence, Diligence, and Cooperation

Rule 2.5(A)	Canon 3(B)(8)
Rule 2.5(B)	Canon 3(C)(1)

Rule 2.6 Ensuring the Right to be Heard

None

Rule 2.7 Responsibility to Decide

Canon 3(B)(1)

Rule 2.8 Decorum, Demeanor, and Communication with Jurors

Rule 2.8(A)	Canon 3(B)(3)
Rule 2.8(B)	Canon 3(B)(4)
Rule 2.8(C)	Canon 3(B)(10)

Rule 2.9 *Ex Parte* Contacts and Communications with Others

Rule 2.9(A)(1)	Canon 3(B)(7)(a)
Rule 2.9(A)(2)	Canon 3(B)(7)(b)
Rule 2.9(A)(3)	Canon 3(B)(7)(c)
Rule 2.9(A)(4)	None
Rule 2.9(A)(5)	Canon 3(B)(7)(d)
Rule 2.9(A)(6)	None
Rule 2.9(B)	None
Rule 2.9(C)	None
Rule 2.9(D)	None

Rule 2.10 Judicial Statements on Pending and Impending Cases

Rule 2.10(A)	Canon 3(B)(9) and Canon 7(B)(2)(e)
Rule 2.10(B)	Canons 7(B)(2)(c) & (d)
Rule 2.10(C)	Canon 3(B)(9)
Rule 2.10(D)	Canon 3(B)(9)
Rule 2.10(E)	None

Rule 2.11 Disqualification
Rule 2.11(A)(1)   Canon 3(E)(1)(a)
Rule 2.11(A)(2)   Canon 3(E)(1)(d) [part]
Rule 2.11(A)(3)   Canon 3(E)(1)(c)
Rule 2.11(A)(5)   None
Rule 2.11(A)(6)   Canon 3(E)(1)(d)(iii)
Rule 2.11(A)(7)   Canon 3(E)(1)(b) [part]
Rule 2.11(B)   Canon 3(E)(2)
Rule 2.11(C)   Canon 3(F)

Rule 2.12 Supervisory Duties
Rule 2.12(A)   Canon 3(C)(2)
Rule 2.12(B)   Canon 3(C)(3)

Rule 2.13 Administrative Appointments
Rule 2.13(A)   Canon 3(C)(4), 1st three sentences
Rule 2.13(C)   Canon 3(C)(4), last sentence

Rule 2.14 Disability and Impairment
Rule 2.14(A)   None
Rule 2.14(B)   Canon 3(D)(4)

Rule 2.15 Responding to Judicial and Lawyer Misconduct
Rule 2.15(A)   Canon 3(D)(1)
Rule 2.15(B)   Canon 3(D)(2)

Rule 2.16 Cooperation with Disciplinary Authorities
cf. Canon 3(D)(3)

CANON 3

Rule 3.1 Extrajudicial Activities in General
Rule 3.1(A)   None
Rule 3.1(B)   Canon 2(A)
Rule 3.1(C)   Canon 2(A)
Rule 3.1(D)   None
Rule 3.1(E)   None

Rule 3.2 Appearances Before Governmental Bodies and Consultation with Government Officials	
Rule 3.2(A)	Canon 2(A)(2)
Rule 3.2(B)	None
Rule 3.2(C)	Canon 4(C)(1)
Rule 3.3 Testifying as a Character Witness	Canon 4(A), last sentence
Rule 3.4 Appointments to Governmental Positions	Canon 4(C)(2)
Rule 3.5 Use of Nonpublic Information	None
Rule 3.6 Affiliation with Discriminatory Organizations	
	Canon 4(B)
Rule 3.6(A)	
Rule 3.6(B)	None
Rule 3.7 Participation in Educational, Religious, Charitable, Fraternal, or Civic Organizations and Activities	
Rule 3.7(A)	Canon 2(B), 1st paragraph
Rule 3.7(A)(1)	Canon 2(B)(2)(a)
Rule 3.7(A)(2)	Canon 2(B)(2)(a)(i)
Rule 3.7(A)(3)	Canon 2(B)(2)(a)(ii)
Rule 3.7(A)(4)	Canon 2(B)(2)(c)
Rule 3.7(A)(5)	Canons 2(B)(2)(a) & (d)
Rule 3.7(A)(6)	Canon 2(B)(2)(b)
Rule 3.7(A)(7)	Canon 2(B)(1)
Rule 3.7(B)	None
Rule 3.8 Appointments to Fiduciary Positions	
Rule 3.8(A)	Canon 4(D)(1)
Rule 3.8(B)	Canon 4(D)(2)
Rule 3.8(C)	Canon 4(D)(3)
Rule 3.8(D)	None

Rule 3.9 Service as Arbitrator or Mediator   Canon 4(E)

Rule 3.10 Practice of Law   Canon 4(F)

Rule 3.11 Financial, Business, or Remunerative Activities
Rule 3.11(A)   Canon 2(C)(2)
Rule 3.11(B)   Canon 2(C)(3)
Rule 3.11(C)   Canons 2(C)(1) & (4), first sentence
Rule 3.11(D)   Canon 2(C)(4), second sentence

Rule 3.12 Compensation for Extrajudicial Activities   Canon 2(D)

Rule 3.13 Acceptance and Reporting of Gifts, Loans, Bequests, Benefits, or Other Things of Value
Rule 3.13(A)   Canon 2(C)(5)
Rule 3.13(A)(1)   None
Rule 3.13(A)(2)   Canon 2(C)(5)(e)
Rule 3.13(A)(3)   Canon 2(C)(5)(c)
Rule 3.13(A)(4)   Canon 2(C)(5)(f)
Rule 3.13(A)(5)   None
Rule 3.13(A)(6)   Canon 2(C)(5)(g)
Rule 3.13(A)(7)   Canon 2(C)(5)(a)
Rule 3.13(A)(8)   Canon 2(C)(5)(b)
Rule 3.13(A)(9)   Canon 2(C)(5)(d)
Rule 3.13(A)(10)   Canon 2(C)(5)(a)
Rule 3.13(A)(11)(a)   Canon 2(C)(5)(a)
Rule 3.13(A)(11)(b)   None
Rule 3.13(A)(12)   Canon 2(C)(5)(h); R.C. 102.03
Rule 3.13(C)   Canon 2(D)(3)

Rule 3.14 Reimbursement of Expenses and Waivers of Fees or Charges

Rule 3.14(A)   Canons 2(D) & (D)(1)
Rule 3.14(B)   Canon 2(D)(2)
Rule 3.14 (C)   Canon 2(D)(3)

Rule 3.15 Reporting Requirements   Canon 2(D)(3); R.C. 102.02

CANON 4

Rule 4.1 Political and Campaign Activities of Judges and Judicial Candidates

Rule 4.1(A)(1)	Canon 7(B)(2)(a)
Rule 4.1(A)(2)	Canon 7(B)(2)(b)
Rule 4.1(A)(3)	Canon 7(B)(2)(b)
Rule 4.1(A)(4)	Canons 7(C)(7)(b) & (c)
Rule 4.1(A)(5)	Canon 7(B)(2)(e)
Rule 4.1(A)(6)	cf. Canons 3(B)(9) & Canon 7(B)(2)(e)
Rule 4.1(A)(7)	Canons 7(B)(2)(c) & (d)
Rule 4.1(B)(1)	Canons 7(B)(3)(a)(i) & (ii)
Rule 4.1(B)(2)	Canons 7(C)(7)(b) & (c)
Rule 4.1(B)(3)	Canons 7(C)(7)(b) & (c)

Rule 4.2 Political and Campaign Activities of Judicial Candidates

Rule 4.2(A)(1)	Canon 7(B)(1)
Rule 4.2(A)(2)	Canon 7(F)
Rule 4.2(A)(3)	Canon 7(F)
Rule 4.2(A)(4)	Canon 7(B)(5)
Rule 4.2(B)(1)	Canon 7(B)(2)(g)
Rule 4.2(B)(2)	Canon 7(B)(3)(g)
Rule 4.2(B)(3)	Canon 7(C)(7)(a)
Rule 4.2(C)(1)	Canon 7(B)(3)(g)
Rule 4.2(C)(2)	Canon 7(B)(3)(g)
Rule 4.2(C)(3)	Canon 7(B)(3)(g)
Rule 4.2(C)(4)	Canon 7(B)(3)(g)
Rule 4.2(C)(5)	None
Rule 4.2(C)(6)	Canons 7(B)(3)(a)(iii) & (iv) and 7(B)(3)(b)

Rule 4.3 Campaign Standards and Communications

Rule 4.3(A)	Canon 7(E)(1)
Rule 4.3(B)	Canon 7(E)(2)
Rule 4.3(C)	Canon 7(D)(1)
Rule 4.3(D)	Canon 7(D)(3)
Rule 4.3(E)	Canon 7(D)(4)
Rule 4.3(F)	Canon 7(B)(2)(f)
Rule 4.3(G)	Canon 7(D)(5)

Rule 4.3(H)	Canon 7(D)(6)
Rule 4.3(I)	Canon 7(D)(7)
Rule 4.3(J)	Canon 7(D)(8)
Rule 4.3(K)	Canon 7(D)(9)
Rule 4.3(L)	Canon 7(D)(10)
Rule 4.3(M)	Canon 7(D)(11)

Rule 4.4 Campaign Solicitations and Contributions

Rule 4.4(A)	Canon 7(C)(2)(a)
Rule 4.4(B)	Canon 7(C)(1)
Rule 4.4(C)	Canons 7(C)(2)(a) (i) to (iii)
Rule 4.4(D)	Canon 7(C)(2)(b)
Rule 4.4(E)	Canon 7(C)(3)
Rule 4.4(F)	Canon 7(C)(4)(a)
Rule 4.4(G)	Canon 7(C)(4)(b)
Rule 4.4(H)	Canon 7(C)(4)(c)
Rule 4.4(I)	Canon 7(C)(4)(d)
Rule 4.4(J)	Canon 7(C)(5)(a)
Rule 4.4(K)	Canon 7(C)(5)(b)
Rule 4.4(L)	Canon 7(C)(5)(c)
Rule 4.4(M)	Canon 7(C)(5)(d)
Rule 4.4(N)	Canon 7(C)(5)(e)
Rule 4.4(O)	Canon 7(C)(6)

Rule 4.5 Activities of a Judge Who Becomes a Candidate for Nonjudicial Office   Canon 7(B)(4)

Rule 4.6. Definitions

Rule 4.6(A)	None
Rule 4.6(B)	Canon 7(A)(3)
Rule 4.6(C)	Canon 7(A)(11)
Rule 4.6(D)	None
Rule 4.6(E)	Canon 7(A)(4)
Rule 4.6(F)	Canon 7(A)(1)
Rule 4.6(G)	None
Rule 4.6(H)	Canon 7(A)(9)
Rule 4.6(I)	Canon 7(A)(5)
Rule 4.6(J)	Canon 7(A)(7)
Rule 4.6(K)	Canon 7(A)(10)
Rule 4.6(L)	Canon 7(A)(8)
Rule 4.6(M)	Canon 7(A)(6)

APPENDIX B

CORRELATION TABLE
FORMER OHIO CODE OF JUDICIAL CONDUCT TO
2009 OHIO CODE OF JUDICIAL CONDUCT

The following is a numerical listing of the former Ohio Code of Judicial Conduct with cross-references to provisions of 2009 Ohio Code of Judicial Conduct that address substantially similar subject-matter. Please consult the code comparisons that follow each rule for a more detailed treatment of corresponding provisions.

FORMER OHIO CODE OF JUDICIAL CONDUCT	2009 OHIO CODE OF JUDICIAL CONDUCT
CANON 1 A Judge Shall Uphold the Integrity and Independence of the Judiciary	Rule 1.2
CANON 2 A Judge Shall Respect and Comply with the Law and Shall Act in a Manner that Promotes Public Confidence in the Integrity and Impartiality of the Judiciary	Rules 1.1 and 1.2
Canon 2(A)(1) and (2)	Rules 3.1(B) & (C) and 3.2(A)
Canon 2(B)(1)(a)	Rules 3.7(A) & (A)(7)
Canon 2(B)(1)(b)	
Canon 2(B)(2)(a)	Rules 3.7(A)(1), (2), (3), & (5)
Canon 2(B)(2)(b)	Rule 3.7(A)(6)
Canon 2(B)(2)(c)	Rule 3.7(A)(4)
Canon 2(B)(2)(d)	Rule 3.7(A)(5)
Canon 2(C)(1)	Rule 3.11(C)
Canon 2(C)(2)	Rule 3.11(A)
Canon 2(C)(3)	Rule 3.11(B)
Canon 2(C)(4)	Rules 3.11(C) & (D)
Canon 2(C)(5)	Rule 3.13(A)
Canon 2(C)(5)(a)	Rules 3.13(A)(7), (10) & (11)(a)
Canon 2(C)(5)(b)	Rule 3.13(A)(8)
Canon 2(C)(5)(c)	Rule 3.13(A)(3)
Canon 2(C)(5)(d)	Rule 3.13(A)(9)
Canon 2(C)(5)(e)	Rule 3.13(A)(2)
Canon 2(C)(5)(f)	Rule 3.13(A)(4)
Canon 2(C)(5)(g)	Rule 3.13(A)(6)
Canon 2(C)(5)(h)	Rule 3.13(A)(12)

Canon 2(D)	Rule 3.12
Canon 2(D)(1)	Rule 3.14(A)
Canon 2(D)(2)	Rule 3.14(B)
Canon 2(D)(3)	Rules 3.13(C), 3.14(C), and 3.15

CANON 3 A Judge Shall Perform the Duties of Judicial Office Impartially and Diligently

Canon 3(A)	Rule 2.1
Canon 3(B)(1)	Rule 2.7
Canon 3(B)(2)	Rules 2.2 and 2.4(A)
Canon 3(B)(3)	Rule 2.8(A)
Canon 3(B)(4)	Rule 2.8(B)
Canon 3(B)(5)	Rules 2.2 and 2.3(A) & (B)
Canon 3(B)(6)	Rule 2.3(C) & (D)
Canon 3(B)(7)(a)	Rule 2.9(A)(1)
Canon 3(B)(7)(b)	Rule 2.9(A)(2)
Canon 3(B)(7)(c)	Rule 2.9(A)(3)
Canon 3(B)(7)(d)	Rule 2.9(A)(5)
Canon 3(B)(8)	Rule 2.5(A)
Canon 3(B)(9)	Rules 2.10(A), (C), & (D) and 4.1(
Canon 3(B)(10)	Rule 2.8(C)
Canon 3(B)(11)	Rule 3.5, Comments [1A], [3], & [4
Canon 3(C)(1)	Rule 2.5(B)
Canon 3(C)(2)	Rule 2.12(A)
Canon 3(C)(3)	Rule 2.12(B)
Canon 3(C)(4)	Rules 2.13(A) & (C)
Canon 3(D)(1)	Rule 2.15(A)
Canon 3(D)(2)	Rule 2.15(B)
Canon 3(D)(3)	cf. Rule 2.16
Canon 3(D)(4)	Rule 2.14(B)
Canon 3(E)(1)(a)	Rule 2.11(A)(1)
Canon 3(E)(1)(b)	Rule 2.11(A)(7)(a)
Canon 3(E)(1)(c)	Rule 2.11(A)(3)
Canon 3(E)(1)(d)	Rules 2.11(A)(2) & (A)(6)
Canon 3(E)(2)	Rule 2.11(B)
Canon 3(F)	Rule 2.11(C)
Canon 3(G)	
Canon 3(H)	

CANON 4 A Judge Shall Avoid Impropriety and the Appearance of Impropriety in All of the Judge's Activities

Canon 4(A)	Rules 1.3, 2.4 (B) & (C) and 3.3

Canon 4(B)	Rule 3.6(A)
Canon 4(C)(1)	Rule 3.2(C)
Canon 4(C)(2)	Rule 3.4
Canon 4(D)(1)	Rule 3.8(A)
Canon 4(D)(2)	Rule 3.8(B)
Canon 4(D)(3)	Rule 3.8(C)
Canon 4(E)	Rule 3.9
Canon 4(F)	Rule 3.10

CANON 7 Judges and Judicial Candidates Should Refrain from Political Activity Inappropriate to Judicial Office

Canon 7(A)	Rule 4.6
Canon 7(B)(1)	Rule 4.2(A)(1)
Canon 7(B)(2)(a)	Rule 4.1(A)(1)
Canon 7(B)(2)(b)	Rules 4.1(A)(2) & (3)
Canon 7(B)(2)(c) and (d)	Rules 2.10(B) and 4.1(A)(6) & (A)
Canon 7(B)(2)(e)	Rule 4.1(A)(5)
Canon 7(B)(2)(f)	Rule 4.3(F)
Canon 7(B)(2)(g)	Rules 4.2(B)(1) & (2) and (C)(1) to
Canon 7(B)(3)(a) and (b)	Rules 4.1(B)(1) and 4.2(C)(6)
Canon 7(B)(4)	Rule 4.5
Canon 7(B)(5)	Rule 4.2(A)(4)
Canon 7(C)(1)	Rule 4.4(B)
Canon 7(C)(2)	Rule 4.4(A)
Canon 7(C)(2)(a)(i) to (iii)	Rule 4.4(C)
Canon 7(C)(2)(b)	Rule 4.4(D)
Canon 7(C)(3)	Rule 4.4(E)
Canon 7(C)(4)(a) and (b)	Rules 4.4(F) & (G)
Canon 7(C)(4)(c)	Rule 4.4(H)
Canon 7(C)(4)(d)	Rule 4.4(I)
Canon 7(C)(5)(a)	Rule 4.4(J)
Canon 7(C)(5)(b)	Rule 4.4(K)
Canon 7(C)(5)(c)	Rule 4.4(L)
Canon 7(C)(5)(d)	Rule 4.4(M)
Canon 7(C)(5)(e)	Rule 4.4(N)
Canon 7(C)(6)	Rule 4.4(O)
Canon 7(C)(7)(a)	Rule 4.2(B)(3)
Canon 7(C)(7)(b) & (c)	Rules 4.1(A)(4), (B)(2), & (B)(3)
Canon 7(C)(8)	None
Canon 7(D)(1)	Rule 4.3(C)
Canon 7(D)(2)	Rule 4.3, Comment [2]
Canon 7(D)(3)	Rule 4.3(D)
Canon 7(D)(4)	Rule 4.3(E)
Canon 7(D)(5)	Rule 4.3(G)

Canon 7(D)(6)	Rule 4.3(H)
Canon 7(D)(7)	Rule 4.3(I)
Canon 7(D)(8)	Rule 4.3(J)
Canon 7(D)(9)	Rule 4.3(K)
Canon 7(D)(10)	Rule 4.3(L)
Canon 7(D)(11)	Rule 4.3(M)
Canon 7(E)(1)	Rule 4.3(A)
Canon 7(E)(2)	Rule 4.3(B)
Canon 7(F)	Rules 4.2(A)(2) & (3)

Index to Code of Judicial Conduct

SUPREME COURT RULES FOR THE REPORTING OF OPINIONS

Effective May 1, 2002

Complete with amendments through July 1, 2010

RULE 1. Opinions and Syllabus of the Supreme Court; Syllabus of Opinions by Courts Other Than the Supreme Court; Numbering or Lettering of Paragraphs of Text and of Footnotes

(A) All opinions of the Supreme Court shall be reported in the advance sheets and bound volumes of the Ohio Official Reports and posted to the Supreme Court website.

(B)(1) The law stated in a Supreme Court opinion is contained within its syllabus (if one is provided), and its text, including footnotes.

(2) If there is disharmony between the syllabus of an opinion and its text or footnotes, the syllabus controls.

(3) A Supreme Court opinion may be signed by a justice, with or without a syllabus, or be *per curiam,* with or without a syllabus. *"Per curiam"* means "by a majority of the Court."

(C) A syllabus of an opinion, or a summary under Rules 6(C) and 10(C) of these rules by a court other than the Supreme Court, is not the controlling statement of the points of law decided, but is merely a research and indexing aid.

(D) All opinions of the Supreme Court shall have paragraphs of text and footnotes consecutively numbered or lettered to assist in the "pinpoint" citation of specific portions of the opinion in electronic format. Numbering and lettering shall exclude paragraphs of the syllabus and editorial content from legal publishers. In all respects, the format of opinions shall conform to the conventions adopted by the Supreme Court Reporter.

History: Effective 5-1-02.

NOTES TO DECISIONS

ANALYSIS

Interpreting text and syllabus

Interpreting text and syllabus

Trial court did not err in ordering defendant's misdemeanor sentence to run consecutively to an unrelated felony sentence because this was authorized by RC § 2929.41(B). While the text of the Supreme Court of Ohio's State v. Foster opinion held that § 2929.41 was excised in its entirety, the syllabus of the opinion held that only § 2929.41(A) was excised, and pursuant to Ohio Sup. Ct. R. Rep. Ops. 1(B)(2), the rule of law in the syllabus controlled over a conflicting statement in the opinion. State v. Terry, — Ohio App. 3d —, 2007 Ohio 1096, — N.E. 2d —, 2007 Ohio App. LEXIS 1018 (Mar. 12, 2007).

RULE 2. Opinions Shall Be Promptly Published and Posted

Opinions shall be published in the Ohio Official Reports and posted to the Supreme Court website as promptly as reasonably possible after their announcement. Posting and publication of opinions shall not be delayed by the filing of motions for reconsideration or by pending appeals.

History: Effective 5-1-02.

RULE 3. Opinions of the Courts of Appeals

(A) For purposes of these rules, opinions of the courts of appeals do not include orders on procedural matters, orders without opinions, memorandum decisions, and judgment entries under Rule 11.1(E) of the Rules of Appellate Procedure.

(B) All court of appeals opinions shall be posted to the Supreme Court website. A representative selection of those opinions meeting the criteria in Rule 5 of these rules shall be designated for print-publication and printed in the advance sheets and bound volumes of the Ohio Official Reports. No opinion (or part thereof) of a court of appeals shall be designated for print-publication unless both the following apply:

(1) It is so designated by the Supreme Court Reporter;

(2) The majority of the court of appeals panel deciding the case agrees.

(C) In lieu of the provisions of division (B) of this rule, a court of appeals may determine by local rule that all of its opinions be sent to the Supreme Court Reporter, who will determine whether the opinions shall be designated for print-publication and printed in the advance sheets and bound volumes of the Ohio Official Reports.

History: Effective 5-1-02.

RULE 4. "Controlling" and "Persuasive" Designations Based on Form of Publication Abolished; Use of Opinions

(A) Notwithstanding the prior versions of these rules, designations of, and distinctions between, "controlling" and "persuasive" opinions of the courts of appeals based merely upon whether they have been published in the Ohio Official Reports are abolished.

(B) All court of appeals opinions issued after the effective date of these rules may be cited as legal authority and weighted as deemed appropriate by the courts.

(C) Unless otherwise ordered by the Supreme Court, court of appeals opinions may always be cited and relied upon for any of the following purposes:

(1) Seeking certification to the Supreme Court of Ohio of a conflict question within the provisions of sections 2(B)(2)(f) and 3(B)(4) of Article IV of the Ohio Constitution;

(2) Demonstrating to an appellate court that the decision, or a later decision addressing the same point of law, is of recurring importance or for other reasons warrants further judicial review;

(3) Establishing *res judicata,* estoppel, double jeopardy, the law of the case, notice, or sanctionable conduct;

(4) Any other proper purpose between the parties, or those otherwise directly affected by a decision.

History: Effective 5-1-02.

RULE 5. Criteria for Designation For Print-Publication

In designating court of appeals and trial court opinions for print-publication, the Supreme Court Reporter and the judiciary shall be guided by the following criteria:

(A) Does the opinion construe, apply, or clarify recently enacted statutory law or administrative rules?

(B) Does the opinion explain, modify, criticize, or overrule an existing rule of law?

(C) Does the opinion apply an established rule of law to facts significantly different from those in previously published decisions?

(D) Does the opinion otherwise contribute significantly to the development of the law?

History: Effective 5-1-02.

RULE 6. Form of Opinions of the Courts of Appeals

(A) Court of appeals opinions shall indicate the number and caption of the case, the character of the proceeding (*e.g.,* mandamus, habeas corpus, criminal appeal from common pleas court, civil appeal from municipal court), the court deciding the case, the counsel for all parties, and the date the judgment was journalized.

(B) The Supreme Court Reporter may consult with the court that issued an opinion designated for print-publication about shortening it, or making other editorial changes. Opinion posted to the Supreme Court website may also be subject to such editing.

(C) All court of appeals opinions shall be formatted in accordance with Rule 1(D) of these rules, and be accompanied by a standardized information sheet and a succinct summary of the legal issues decided for use on the Supreme Court website.

History: Effective 5-1-02.

RULE 7. Form of Citation

(A) Opinions shall be cited in accordance with the Manual of Citations adopted by the Supreme Court Reporter.

(B) A citation to an opinion found only in electronic format shall indicate the status of any appeal, or any disposition by a superior court, known after diligent search.

(C) Unless otherwise directed by local rule, those citing an opinion found only in electronic format shall attach a legible copy of the opinion to the brief in which it is first cited. Briefs referencing an electronic opinion filed subsequently, while the case remains pending before the same court, need not attach additional copies of it.

History: Effective 5-1-02.

RULE 8. Failure to Print-Publish an Opinion in the Ohio Official Reports; Failure to Allow A Discretionary Appeal

(A) The failure of the Supreme Court Reporter or a court to designate an opinion for print-publication shall not be considered a statement as to the merits of the law stated in the opinion.

(B) The refusal of the Supreme Court to accept any case for review shall not be considered a statement of opinion as to the merits of the law stated by the trial or appellate court.

History: Effective 5-1-02.

RULE 9. Posting Trial and Appellate Court Opinions on the Supreme Court Website

(A) Beginning May 1, 2002, court of appeals and trial court opinions will be posted on the Supreme Court website pursuant to a protocol to be developed by the Court. Thereafter, opinions posted to the Supreme Court website pursuant to this rule shall be kept permanently on the website for access by the public.

(B) Effective May 1, 2002, opinions should be cited to both the Supreme Court website citation and Official Reports citation where both are available.

(C) Should the Supreme Court cease publication of the Ohio Appellate Reports and the Ohio Miscellaneous Reports in a paper medium (which event shall not occur prior to July 1, 2006), the Supreme Court website may be designated the Ohio Official Reports for those opinions.

History: Effective 5-1-02.

RULE 10. Opinions of the Trial Courts

(A) The Supreme Court Reporter shall designate for print-publication and posting to the Supreme Court website opinions of the trial courts, including the Court of Claims, that are selected by the author and which, in the Reporter's discretion, meet the criteria in Rule 5 of these rules.

(B) Trial courts, including the Court of Claims, should consider designating for print-publication and posting to the Supreme Court website opinions that reflect disposition of matters before them not routinely addressed by higher courts, such as rulings on evidence, pretrial discovery, and administrative appeals.

(C) Opinions designated for posting or print-publication pursuant to this rule shall be formatted in accordance with Rule 1(D) of these rules, and be accompanied by a standardized information sheet and a succinct summary of the legal issues decided in the opinion for use on the Supreme Court website.

(D) These rules otherwise apply to the opinions of all trial courts except to the extent that these rules would, by their nature, be clearly inapplicable.

History: Effective 5-1-02.

RULE 11. Accuracy

All opinions reported in the bound volumes of the Ohio Official Reports control as to accuracy over the same opinions as reported in any advance sheets, or posted to the Supreme Court website or any other electronic database. All publishers of opinions shall conform to paragraph numbering and footnote lettering used by the courts in the actual opinion and shall include editorial revision, if any, by the Supreme Court Reporter as found on the Supreme Court website.

History: Effective 5-1-02.

RULE 12. Effective Date

These rules shall be effective on and after May 1, 2002.

History: Effective 5-1-02.

Index to Supreme Court Rules for the Reporting of Opinions

MAYOR'S COURT EDUCATION AND PROCEDURE RULES

APPENDIX OF SUGGESTED FORMS

RULE 1. Authority and Purpose; Citation

(A) Pursuant to sections 1905.03 and 1905.031 of the Revised Code and Section 6 of Amended Substitute Senate Bill 131 of the 118th General Assembly, and to serve the public interest that mandates the fair, competent, and efficient operation of mayor's courts throughout Ohio, the Supreme Court of Ohio hereby adopts the following Mayor's Court Education and Procedure Rules. Each mayor of a municipal corporation who is authorized to conduct a mayor's court pursuant to Chapter 1905. of the Revised Code and who wishes to exercise the jurisdiction and authority granted pursuant to Chapter 1905. of the Revised Code shall comply with these rules.

(B) These rules shall be known as the Mayor's Court Education and Procedure Rules and shall be cited as "May.R. _____."

History: Amended, eff 8-1-91.

RULE 2. Definitions

As used in these rules:

(A) "Alcohol or drug related traffic offense" means all of the following, subject to the limitation contained in division (B)(2) of section 1905.01 of the Revised Code:

(1) A violation of section 4511.19 of the Revised Code;

(2) A violation of any ordinance of a municipal corporation relating to the operation of a vehicle while under the influence of alcohol, a drug of abuse, or alcohol and a drug of abuse;

(3) A violation of any ordinance of a municipal corporation relating to the operation of a vehicle with a prohibited concentration of alcohol in the blood, breath, or urine.

(B) "Mayor" means a duly elected or appointed executive of a municipal corporation and includes a municipal official who is authorized by statute, charter, or municipal ordinance to conduct mayor's court in the absence of the mayor, and a magistrate appointed pursuant to section 1905.05 of the Revised Code.

RULE 3. Initial and Continuing Education Requirements for Mayors; Alcohol or Drug Related Traffic Offenses

(A)(1) Prior to July 1, 1991, a mayor of a municipal corporation who is authorized to conduct a mayor's court and who, from July 1, 1991 to December 31, 1992, wishes to exercise the jurisdiction granted by section 1905.01 of the Revised Code over prosecutions involving an alcohol or drug related traffic offense shall obtain a minimum of six hours of classroom instruction related to all of the following:

(a) The general principles of law applicable to the hearing and determination of the prosecution of alcohol or drug related traffic offenses, including, but not limited to, the elements required to establish the existence of an alcohol or drug related traffic offense, and arrest, due process, and other constitutional issues presented in the hearing and determination of the prosecution of alcohol or drug related traffic offenses;

(b) The procedural requirements applicable to the hearing and determination of prosecutions of alcohol or drug related traffic offenses, including, but not limited to, all of the following;

(i) Use of the Ohio Uniform Traffic Ticket, as prescribed in the Ohio Traffic Rules, as the complaint and summons for alcohol or drug related traffic offenses;

(ii) Requirements relative to the initial appearance of the defendant, including the requirement that defendant be informed of his constitutional and statutory rights;

(iii) Consideration and disposition of pretrial motions, including motions to suppress evidence;

(iv) Applicable discovery rules;

(v) Procedures for the pretrial suspension of the operator's license of the defendant.

(c) Defenses that may be raised by defendants charged with alcohol or drug related traffic offenses;

(d) Evidentiary issues presented in the hearing and determination of prosecutions of alcohol or drug related traffic offenses, including, but not limited to, the admissibility of breath, blood, and urine test results and the admissibility of field test results and other evidence;

(e) Considerations relative to the sentencing of persons convicted of alcohol or drug related traffic offenses, including, but not limited to, the sanctions required and allowed to be imposed under state law or local ordinance, the disposition of fines and costs imposed under state law or local ordinance, and the procedures required to ensure the proper reporting of violations to the Ohio Bureau of Motor Vehicles;

(f) Ethical considerations relative to the hearing and determination of prosecutions involving alcohol or drug related traffic offenses.

(2) A mayor who satisfies the education requirements of division (A)(1) of this rule may exercise jurisdiction pursuant to section 1905.01 of the Revised Code over prosecutions involving alcohol or drug related traffic offenses through December 31, 1992.

(B)(1) A newly elected or newly appointed mayor of a municipal corporation who is authorized to conduct a mayor's court and who wishes to exercise the jurisdiction granted by section 1905.01 of the Revised Code over prosecutions involving an alcohol or drug related traffic offense shall obtain, within sixty days of first assuming office, a minimum of six hours of classroom instruction related to all of the subjects listed in divisions (A)(1)(a) to (A)(1)(f) of this rule. A mayor who satisfies the education requirements of division (B)(1) of this rule may exercise jurisdiction pursuant to section 1905.01 of the Revised Code over prosecutions involving alcohol or drug related traffic offenses through the thirty-first day of December of the year immediately following the year in which the education was completed.

(2) A mayor of a municipal corporation who, after assuming office in a municipal corporation that does not operate or that has suspended operation of a mayor's court, subsequently is required or subsequently chooses to conduct a mayor's court and who wishes to exercise the jurisdiction granted by section 1905.01 of the Revised Code over prosecutions involving alcohol or drug related traffic offenses, shall obtain, prior to first exercising that jurisdiction, a minimum of six hours of classroom instruction related to all of the subjects listed in divisions (A)(1)(a) to (A)(1)(f) of this rule. A mayor who satisfies the education requirements of division (B)(2) of this rule may exercise jurisdiction pursuant to section 1905.01 of the Revised Code over prosecutions involving alcohol or drug related traffic offenses through the thirty-first day of December of the year immediately following the year in which the education was completed.

(C) After complying with the initial education requirements of division (A) or (B) of this rule, a mayor who wishes to continue to exercise the jurisdiction granted by section 1905.01 of the Revised Code over prosecutions involving an alcohol or drug related traffic offense shall obtain a minimum of three hours of continuing education annually on one or more of the subjects listed in divisions (A)(1)(a) to (A)(1)(f) of this rule. The continuing education required by this division shall be obtained on or before the thirty-first day of December in each year, beginning in the year immediately following the year in which the mayor complied with division (A) or (B) of this rule. A mayor who satisfies the education requirements of this division may exercise jurisdiction pursuant to section 1905.01 of the Revised Code over prosecutions involving alcohol or drug related traffic offenses through the thirty-first day of December of the year immediately following the year in which the education was completed.

(D) The education requirements of this rule shall not apply to a mayor or mayor's court magistrate appointed pursuant to section 1905.05 of the Revised Code who, during the term of his or her appointment, is either of the following:

(1) A retired judge who is eligible for assignment by the Chief Justice of the Supreme Court of Ohio to active duty in the general division of the court of common pleas, a municipal court, or a county court;

(2) A court magistrate who serves on a fulltime or parttime basis in the general division of the court of common pleas, a municipal court, or a county court pursuant to the Rules of Criminal or Civil Procedure or the Ohio Traffic Rules.

History: Amended 3-1-00.

RULE 4. Initial and Continuing Education Requirements for Mayors; Offenses Other Than Alcohol and Drug Related Traffic Offenses

(A)(1) Prior to July 1, 1992, a mayor of a municipal corporation who is authorized to conduct a mayor's court and who, from July 1, 1992 to December 31, 1993, wishes to exercise the jurisdiction granted by section 1905.01 of the Revised Code over prosecutions, other than prosecutions of alcohol or drug related traffic offenses, shall obtain a minimum of six hours of classroom instruction related to all of the following:

(a) The structure of the Ohio judicial system, the statutory and implied powers of mayor's courts, and the sources of law in Ohio, including the Ohio Constitution, Ohio Revised Code, municipal charters and ordinances, the Rules of Criminal Procedure, the Rules of Evidence, the Ohio Traffic Rules, the Mayor's Court Education and Procedure Rules, and the Code of Judicial Conduct;

(b) The general principles of law applicable to the hearing and determination of prosecutions, other than prosecutions of alcohol or drug related traffic offenses, including, but not limited to the elements and burden of proof required to establish the existence of an offense, appointment and waiver of counsel, and arrest, due process, and other constitutional issues;

(c) The procedural requirements applicable to the hearing and determination of prosecutions, other than prosecutions of alcohol or drug related traffic offenses, including, but not limited to, all of the following:

(i) Use of the Ohio Uniform Traffic Ticket, as prescribed in the Ohio Traffic Rules, as the complaint and summons for traffic offenses;

(ii) Requirements relative to the initial appearance of the defendant, including the requirement that defendant be informed of his constitutional and statutory rights, and requirements relative to acceptance of guilty and no contest pleas;

(iii) Consideration and disposition of pretrial motions, including motions to suppress evidence;

(iv) Applicable discovery rules;

(v) The requirements relative to the transfer of cases pursuant to section 1905.032 of the Revised Code;

(vi) The procedure for appeals from mayor's courts to municipal or county courts pursuant to sections 1905.22 to 1905.25 of the Revised Code.

(d) Defenses that may be raised by defendants charged with an offense, other than an alcohol or drug related traffic offense;

(e) Evidentiary issues presented in the hearing and determination of prosecutions, other than prosecutions of alcohol or drug related traffic offenses, including, but not limited to, hearsay, relevancy, the competency of the arresting officer and other witnesses to testify, the admissibility of evidence relating to speed measured by radar or other electrical or mechanical timing devices, and the documentation of violations of state law or municipal ordinance relative to driving under suspension;

(f) Considerations relative to the sentencing of persons convicted of offenses, other than alcohol or drug related traffic offenses, including, but not limited to, the sanctions required and allowed to be imposed under state law or municipal ordinance, appropriate and available alternative sanctions, the defendant's right to be heard in mitigation, presentence investigations, probation, the disposition of fines and costs imposed under state law or local ordinance, and the procedures required to ensure the proper reporting of violations to the Ohio Bureau of Motor Vehicles;

(g) Record keeping and reporting requirements applicable to mayor's courts including, but not limited to, maintenance of a docket, establishment of fine and bail schedules, and the reporting of violations to the Ohio Bureau of Motor Vehicles;

(h) Ethical considerations relative to the hearing and determination of prosecutions, other than prosecutions of alcohol or drug related traffic offenses, including, but not limited to, the requirement that a mayor who conducts mayor's court serve as a neutral and detached magistrate, situations in which the mayor must disqualify himself from a proceeding or should disqualify himself from a proceeding to avoid the appearance of impropriety, and the requirement that a mayor not engage in ex parte communications with persons appearing before him.

(2) A mayor who satisfies the education requirements of division (A)(1) of this rule may exercise jurisdiction pursuant to section 1905.01 of the Revised Code over prosecutions, other than prosecutions of alcohol or drug related traffic offenses, through December 31, 1993.

(B)(1) A newly elected or newly appointed mayor of a municipal corporation who is authorized to conduct a mayor's court and who wishes to exercise the jurisdiction granted by section 1905.01 of the Revised Code over prosecutions, other than prosecutions of alcohol or drug related traffic offenses, shall obtain, within sixty days of first assuming office, a minimum of six hours of classroom instruction related to all of the subjects listed in divisions (A)(1)(a) to (A)(1)(h) of this rule. A mayor who satisfies the education requirements of division (B)(1) of this rule may exercise jurisdiction pursuant to section 1905.01 of the Revised Code over prosecutions, other than prosecutions of alcohol or drug related traffic offenses, through the thirty-first day of December of the year immediately following the year in which the education was completed.

(2) A mayor of a municipal corporation who, after assuming office in a municipal corporation that does not operate or that has suspended operation of a mayor's court, subsequently is required or subsequently chooses to conduct a mayor's court and who

wishes to exercise the jurisdiction granted by section 1905.01 of the Revised Code over prosecutions, other than prosecutions of alcohol or drug related traffic offenses, shall obtain, prior to first exercising that jurisdiction, a minimum of six hours of classroom instruction related to all of the subjects listed in divisions (A)(1)(a) to (A)(1)(h) of this rule. A mayor who satisfies the education requirements of division (B)(2) of this rule may exercise jurisdiction pursuant to section 1905.01 of the Revised Code over prosecutions, other than prosecutions of alcohol or drug related traffic offenses, through the thirty-first day of December of the year immediately following the year in which the education was completed.

(C) After complying with the initial education requirements of division (A) or (B) of this rule, a mayor who wishes to continue to exercise the jurisdiction granted by section 1905.01 of the Revised Code over prosecutions, other than prosecutions of alcohol or drug related traffic offenses, shall obtain a minimum of three hours of continuing education annually on one or more of the subjects listed in divisions (A)(1)(a) to (A)(1)(h) of this rule. The continuing education required by this division shall be obtained on or before the thirty-first day of December in each year, beginning in the year immediately following the year in which the mayor complies with division (A) or (B) of this rule. A mayor who satisfies the education requirements of this division may exercise jurisdiction pursuant to section 1905.01 of the Revised Code over prosecutions, other than prosecutions of alcohol or drug related traffic offenses, through the thirty-first day of December of the year immediately following the year in which education was completed.

(D) The education requirements of this rule shall not apply to a mayor or mayor's court magistrate appointed pursuant to section 1905.05 of the Revised Code who, during the term of his or her appointment, is either of the following:

(1) A retired judge who is eligible for assignment by the Chief Justice of the Supreme Court of Ohio to active duty in the general division of the court of common pleas, a municipal court, or a county court;

(2) A court magistrate who serves on a fulltime or parttime basis in the general division of the court of common pleas, a municipal court, or a county court pursuant to the Rules of Criminal or Civil Procedure or the Ohio Traffic Rules.

History: Amended, eff 8-1-91; 3-1-00.

RULE 5.   Certification of Course Attendance; Content of the Certificate

A mayor who successfully completes an accredited education program required by these rules shall receive, from the sponsor of the course, a certificate attesting to the mayor's satisfactory completion of the course. The certificate shall include all of the following:

(A) The name of the mayor to whom the certificate is issued and the name of the municipal corporation of which he serves as mayor;

(B) The title and sponsor of the course;

(C) The date on which the course was held;

(D) The number of hours of classroom instruction received at the course and whether those hours of instruction satisfy the initial education requirements of May.R. 3(A) or (B) or the continuing education requirements of May.R. 3(C);

(E) The date on which the certificate expires, which shall be the thirty-first day of December of the year immediately following the year in which the education program was completed.

History: Amended, eff 8-1-91.

RULE 6.   Accreditation of Education Courses

(A) Courses offered and completed to satisfy the education requirements of these rules shall be accredited, prior to being offered, by the Commission on Continuing Legal Education established by Rule X of the Rules for the Government of the Bar of Ohio. Each course offered and completed for the purposes of May.R. 3 or 4 shall consist of a single-day session that includes the minimum number of hours of actual instruction required by the applicable Mayor's Court Education and Procedure Rules and that is devoted to the topics required by the applicable Mayor's Court Education and Procedure Rules. Courses offered and completed for the purposes of May.R. 3(C) or 4(C) may be offered and completed jointly in a single-day, six hour session.

(B) In evaluating education programs required by these rules, the Commission shall consider the purposes of these rules, the required content of courses completed to satisfy the education requirements of these rules, the standards for accreditation set forth in Gov. Bar R. X, Section 4(B)(1) and (B)(3) to (5), and the applicable regulations adopted pursuant to Gov. Bar R. X. Time guidelines for accreditation courses completed to satisfy the education required by this rule shall be identical to those applicable to courses submitted for accreditation pursuant to Gov. Bar R. X, except that a course offered prior to July 1, 1991 may be submitted for accreditation thirty days prior to the date on which the course will be offered. Each course submitted for accreditation pursuant to this rule clearly shall be denoted as a mayor's court education course.

History: Amended, eff 8-1-91.

RULE 7.   Attendance by Mayor's Court Personnel

Mayors should require mayor's court personnel, including clerks of mayor's courts, and should encourage other persons involved in the operation of the mayor's court, to attend the education courses required of mayors pursuant to these rules.

RULES 8.   to 10 are reserved

RULE 11.   Mayor's Court Facility Standards; Courtroom Conduct

(A) In order to maintain an appropriate and dignified atmosphere and to serve the public properly, the mayor's court should be located in a municipal building or other facility that is readily accessible to the public. The facility shall be clean, properly maintained, well-lighted, and adequately heated and ventilated. The facility should have adequate seating capacity so that litigants and other members of the public are not required to stand in hallways and areas adjacent to the room in which mayor's court is conducted.

(B)(1) The room in which mayor's court is conducted should have an elevated bench or a separate table from which the mayor presides that is flanked by the United States and Ohio flags. Adequate shelving or other storage facility should be provided near the bench or table for necessary legal reference materials, including the Revised Code, the rules governing the courts of Ohio, and the ordinances of the municipal corporation.

(2) All participants must be able to hear and be heard. If the room acoustics are unsatisfactory, an efficient public address system shall be provided. An audio system to record mayor's court proceedings should be provided and tapes of proceedings should be maintained in accordance with established records retention schedules. A blackboard or other demonstrative aid should be available. Unnecessary material or equipment should not be stored in the room in which mayor's court is conducted.

(3) Desks, tables, and chairs should be provided for all mayor's court personnel regularly present during a mayor's court session. Tables and chairs for all parties and counsel and a lectern should be provided. Tables shall be situated to allow all participants to hear. If the tables are not situated to allow private exchanges between a party and counsel, a separate consultation room should be provided.

(4) Fines should be collected by court personnel in a room separate from the room in which mayor's court is conducted. If it is not possible to collect fines in a separate room, a separate area of the room in which mayor's court is conducted, away from the bench or table from which the mayor presides, should be designated as the area in which fines are collected.

(5) Security necessary for the protection of the mayor, mayor's court personnel, and the public should be provided.

(C)(1) In conducting mayor's court, the mayor shall wear clothing appropriate to demonstrate the dignity of the office and of the proceeding. Mayor's court personnel shall wear clothing appropriate to demonstrate the dignity of the proceeding.

(2) All persons appearing before a mayor's court should wear respectful clothing. Litigants and other members of the public shall refrain from talking during the proceeding, except when addressing the mayor, testifying, or conferring with counsel. All persons participating in the proceeding shall refrain from using foul or abusive language. Smoking, eating, and other activities that detract from the proceeding shall be prohibited in the room in which mayor's court is conducted.

(D) The mayor and mayor's court personnel should act in an appropriate and dignified manner when addressing parties, counsel, witnesses, and members of the public appearing in the mayor's court. First names and nicknames should not be used. Mayor's court personnel shall treat all persons appearing before the mayor's court in a fair and impartial manner. Mayor's court personnel shall refrain from offering legal advise or suggesting to a defendant or counsel the manner in which a particular case may be decided.

History: Effective 8-1-91.

RULE 12.   Mayor's Court Operation

(A)(1) It is the duty of the mayor to ensure that each defendant understands the nature of the proceeding and the charges against the defendant. Each defendant shall be provided with a written list of rights, as outlined in Rule 10 of the Ohio Rules of Criminal Procedure and Rule 8 of the Ohio Traffic Rules, or shall have those rights read to him, or both. The mayor shall inquire of each defendant whether the defendant understands these rights and may ask the defendant to sign a form declaring that the defendant has read and understands these rights.

(2) Interpreters shall be provided for persons who do not speak or understand the English language.

(3) If a defendant is charged with an offense that carries the potential for incarceration and is unable to afford to retain counsel, the mayor is responsible for appointing counsel unless the case is transferred to the court of common pleas or municipal or county court pursuant to section 1905.032 of the Revised Code.

(B) The mayor shall give each defendant the opportunity to address the court prior to making a finding of guilt or innocence and shall give each defendant the opportunity to address the court prior to imposing sentence. The mayor shall not take into consideration any prior convictions of the defendant before making a determination of guilt or innocence.

(C) The mayor shall determine whether a defendant is able to pay any fine imposed. This finding shall be signed by the mayor and journalized on the record.

(D) The mayor shall make a judgment or journal entry with regard to each case of which the mayor disposes. The entry shall indicate a finding of guilt, innocence, or dismissal without a finding, the disposition of the case, and other required information. The entry shall be signed by the mayor and journalized on the record.

History: Effective 8-1-91.

RULE 13.   Mayor's Court Personnel; Absence of the Mayor

(A) The mayor is responsible for the fair, dignified, and orderly operation of the mayor's court. The mayor may delegate authority for conducting certain nonadjudicatory functions to the appropriate personnel and should administer an oath of office to all mayor's court personnel.

(B) A mayor's court should have a clerk who, in addition to those duties delegated by the mayor, should be responsible for processing and maintaining all documents filed with the mayor's court, maintaining the docket of the court, administering the traffic violations bureau, collecting and distributing to the proper sources all fines and costs imposed by the court, and submitting abstracts of the court record and other information required by the Ohio Bureau of Motor Vehicles.

(C) A mayor's court should have a court officer or bailiff who, in addition to those duties delegated by the mayor, should be responsible for serving warrants and capiases, transporting defendants to and from jail facilities, and assisting the mayor during mayor's court.

(D) Each mayor who conducts a mayor's court shall prepare and maintain written procedures regarding the conduct of mayor's court. The procedures shall identify the individual who, pursuant to the Revised Code, municipal charter, or municipal ordinance, presides over mayor's court in the absence of the mayor and any other information considered necessary by the mayor.

History: Effective 8-1-91.

RULE 14.   Forms

The forms contained in the Appendix of Suggested Forms are illustrative and not mandatory.

History: Effective 8-1-91.

RULE 15.   Mayor's Court Registration and Reporting Requirements

(A) Each mayor of a municipal corporation that operates a mayor's court shall submit to the Court Statistical Reporting Section of the Supreme Court the following reports on a form prescribed by the Section:

(1) A Mayor's Court Registration on or before the fifteenth day of January of each year or not less than fifteen days prior to conducting mayor's court, whichever is later.

(2) A Mayor's Court Report no later than the fifteenth day of January, April, July and October of each year reflecting the work of the mayor's court for the calendar quarter immediately preceding the filing date.

(B) A mayor shall prepare and submit a report to the Bureau of Criminal Identification and Investigation of every conviction that is a misdemeanor on a first offense and a felony on any subsequent offense upon entry of the judgment of conviction.

History: Effective 1-1-04.

RULES 16 TO 19   are reserved

RULE 20.   Effective Date

(A) The Mayor's Court Education and Procedure Rules adopted by the Supreme Court of Ohio on February 5, 1991, shall be effective on February 18, 1991.

(B) The amendments to Rules 1, 4, 5, and 6 of the Mayor's Court Education and Procedure Rules, new Rules 11, 12, 13, and 14, and the Appendix of Suggested Forms, adopted by the Supreme Court of Ohio on June 26, 1991, shall be effective on August 1, 1991.

(C) The amendments to Rules 3(D) and 4(D) of the Mayor's Court Education and Procedure Rules adopted by the Supreme Court of Ohio on January 25, 2000, shall be effective on March 1, 2000.

(D) The amendments to May. R. 15 adopted by the Supreme Court of Ohio on June 24, 2003, shall be effective on January 1, 2004.

History: Amended, eff 1-1-04.

APPENDIX OF SUGGESTED FORMS

The following forms are for purposes of illustration only. The forms are limited in number and are not intended to constitute a complete manual of forms for use in mayor's courts.

Departure from the suggested forms is permitted and shall not void papers that otherwise are sufficient. Forms may be varied when necessary under the facts of a particular case.

FORM A

STATEMENT OF RIGHTS
WAIVER OF RIGHTS
PLEA OF GUILTY OR NO CONTEST

Defendant's Name: _____

In the _____ Mayor's Court, _____, Ohio

Case No. _____ Charge(s)_____

I am present in Court today and have been told:

(1) The law requires this Court to bring me to trial within thirty days of the date I was charged.

(2) I have a right to have a lawyer here at any time, and I may have my case continued to get a lawyers.

(3) If the charge I am facing carries a possible jail sentence, the Court will appoint a lawyer at no cost to me if I cannot afford to hire one.

(4) If the charge I am facing carries a possible jail sentence, I have the right to a jury trial.

(5) I have a right to remain silent. Anything I say can be used against me.

(6) The maximum penalty I can receive if I am convicted. If this is a traffic case, I also may lose the right to drive for some time and have points added to my driving record.

(7) If I am not a United States citizen, that a conviction could result in my deportation or denial of citizenship according to the laws of the United States.

(8) I have the right to remain free on a reasonable bail while my case is awaiting trial.

I HAVE READ THIS STATEMENT AND I UNDERSTAND IT. I WAS GIVEN THE CHANCE TO ASK QUESTIONS AND THEY WERE ANSWERED.

I have decided on my own to waive my rights and proceed today. I do not want a continuance to talk to a lawyer.

I plead: ☐ **Guilty**   ☐ **No Contest**

Signed: _____   Date _____

Witnessed by: _____   Date _____

FORM B

JUDGMENT ENTRY

Defendant's Name: _____

In the _____ Mayor's Court, _____Ohio

Case No. _____Charge(s) _____

The Defendant was advised of chares against him/her and possible maximum penalty. After fully explaining his/her rights and the consequences of the pleas and after determining that the defendant knowingly, voluntarily, and intelligently waived his/her rights, the Court accepts the plea.

Plea: _____ Finding: _____

Trial held. Finding of: _____

Other: _____

• •

Minor Misdemeanor: $_____   Fine and Court Costs $_____

Ability to pay: _____   Due: _____

$_____ of fine will be suspended.

First to fourth degree misdemeanor: Your sentence is as follows: _____ days in jail. $_____ fine

and Court Costs of $_____. ____ days will be suspended and $_____ fine will be suspended.

Ability of pay: _____   Due: _____

Probation of _____ months or _____ years.

(When applicable: Drivers license suspension for _____ months. Proof of FRA: _____

Fine Due: _____ Enforcement of Days: _____)

In addition of abiding to all rules and regulations of probation, special conditions are as follows: (check if ordered)

☐ Alcohol counseling or treatment as determined by probation.
☐ Pay all fines and costs.
☐ _____ hours of community service.
☐ Restitution
☐ No same or similar violations.
☐ Other _____

_____

Mayor _____   Date _____

Court Number (issued by Bureau of Motor Vehicles _____

FORM C

DEMAND FOR TRIAL

Defendant's Name: _____

In the _____Mayor's Court, _____, Ohio

Case No. _____Charge(s) _____

The Defendant demands a trial and states the following:

☐ I have been informed of the offense(s) with which I am charged and given a copy of the complaint.

☐ I plead NOT GUILTY.

☐ I give up my right to a trial by jury.

Check one of the following:

☐ I want my case tried within the time provided by law. (Thirty days from date of arrest or service of summons. Each day I am held in jail is counted as three days from the date of arrest.

☐ I am giving up my right to be tried within the time set by law, and I request that the Court notify me when my case will be set for trial.

Date of arrest or service of summons: _____

Days in jail before release on bail: _____

Arraignment date: _____ Trial date: _____

New counsel: ☐ Yes   ☐ No

_____   _____
Defendant's Signature   Attorney's Signature

_____   _____
Defendant's Name   Attorney's Name

_____   _____
Defendant's Address   Attorney's Registration Number

_____   _____
Defendant's Telephone Number   Attorney's Telephone Number

FORM D

MOTION AND ENTRY FOR CONTINUANCE

Defendant's Name: _____

In the _____Mayor's Court, _____, Ohio

Case No. _____Charge(s) _____

    The _____ moves for a continuance of the _____

scheduled for _____
                                     (arraignment/trial)

for the following reason: _____
_____

    Therefore, the case is continued to _____ at _____m.

Date case filed: _____

Date last in court: _____

Time waived nor not waived: _____

Prior number of continuances granted: _____

Mayor: _____   Date: _____

APPROVED:

_____   Date: _____
Counsel for _____

_____   Date: _____
Defendant/Counsel for defendant

Note: A copy of this Entry must be filed with the Clerk's office and served on opposing counsel or party.

FORM E

HEARING TO REVIEW PAYMENT
OF FINES AND COST

Defendant's Name: _____

In the _____Mayor's Court, _____, Ohio

Case No. _____Charge(s) _____

The Defendant appeared in court on _____, 20_____. The status of the payment of defendant's obligation was reviewed by the Court and the following information was provided by the Defendant:

_____

_____

_____

_____

Based on the foregoing information, the Court finds:

☐   The Defendant doe not have a present ability to pay.

     The case will be reviewed again

     _____

     _____

☐   The Defendant is employed and has agreed to make payments as follows:

     _____

     _____

☐   The Defendant willfully has failed to abide by the order of the Court while having an ability to do so. Sentence previously given or amended is to be enforced as follows:

     _____

     _____

Mayor _____   Date _____

Index to Mayor's Court Education and Procedure Rules

GUIDELINES FOR ASSIGNMENT OF JUDGES

The following guidelines for the assignment of judges were issued by the Chief Justice of the Supreme Court of Ohio, effective July 1, 2005.

The Guidelines for Assignment of Judges, adopted May 24, 1988, were revised on Feb. 25, 1994, March 25, 1994, March 1, 2002 and July 1, 2005. The July 1, 2005 revisions apply to assignment requests made on or after July 1, 2005 and to compensation reports submitted for work performed on or after July 1, 2005. The Guidelines have not been adopted as rules pursuant to Article IV, Section 5 of the Ohio Constitution.

GENERAL GUIDELINES

REQUIREMENTS AND PROCEDURES

FACTORS IN SELECTING JUDGES

REIMBURSEMENT AND COMPENSATION

MISCELLANEOUS

General Guidelines

The Ohio Constitution and the Ohio Revised Code vest the Chief Justice with the authority to make temporary assignments of judges to serve in any court in Ohio as established by law in whatever circumstances the Chief Justice deems appropriate.

These guidelines are intended to establish consistent standards and procedures in implementing this authority. While these guidelines may impose specific duties upon other persons, the Chief Justice may waive compliance with any guidelines to assist the exercise of that discretion.

These guidelines have not been adopted as rules pursuant to Article IV, Section 5 of the Ohio Constitution, and should not be construed as requiring adoption.

REQUIREMENTS AND PROCEDURES

1. **Reasons for Assignment of Judges** The administrative judge of any court or division of a court may request the Chief Justice to temporarily assign a sitting or retired judge to hold court pursuant to the guidelines set forth herein and for any of the following reasons:

(A) **Overburdened docket/extended trial** A judge may be assigned if the court or division that is in need of the assigned judge has an overburdened docket or anticipates an extended trial that will disrupt its docket.

(B) **Recusals for conflict of interest** A judge may be assigned if a sitting judge recuses from one or more specific cases because of a conflict of interest involving a litigant, counsel, or the subject of the case. The fact that a local attorney is a litigant should not cause the sitting judge to recuse unless the relationship of the sitting judge with the attorney justifies recusal.

(C) **Illness, emergency, vacation, and continu-**ing education A judge may be assigned if a sitting judge will be temporarily absent for one or more of the following reasons:

• The sitting judge is ill or unable to attend to judicial duties.

• The sitting judge is experiencing a personal or family emergency that interferes with the performance of judicial duties.

• The sitting judge plans to take a reasonable vacation or attend a continuing legal education conference, seminar, or workshop and the sitting judge cannot reasonably schedule his or her docket to eliminate the need for a replacement during the absence.

(D) **Extraordinary circumstance** A judge may be assigned for any extraordinary circumstance approved by the Chief Justice.

2. **Type and Length of Assignment** (A) **Type of assignment** A judge may be temporarily assigned by the Chief Justice to one or more specific cases, for a specific period of time, or in a special circumstance (e.g., the convening or deliberation of a grand jury, appointment of a special prosecutor, consideration of a particular type of docket, etc.).

(B) **Length of assignment** A judge assigned for a specific period of time will not ordinarily be continued in service in the same court, or have the length of the assignment extended beyond the original term, without the agreement of the administrative judge of that court, except as noted in Guideline 11(B) (Assignment for specific period of time).

A sitting judge will not ordinarily be assigned for a specific period of time exceeding six months and a retired judge will not ordinarily be assigned for a specific period of time exceeding three months.

3. **Requirements Before Requesting Assignment** Before requesting the Chief Justice to assign a judge to a court, the administrative judge of that court shall proceed as follows:

(A) **Other judge of the court** The administrative judge shall attempt to arrange for another sitting judge of that court to perform the duties of the judge who is in need of a replacement.

(B) **Other judges of division in common pleas court** The administrative judge of a division of the court of common pleas shall request the presiding judge of that court to assign a sitting judge from another division of that court to perform any unanticipated emergency duties of a temporarily absent judge if the temporarily absent judge has no hearings or trials scheduled for the time of that absence.

(C) **Certification by administrative judge** The administrative judge who requests an assigned judge may cause the sitting judge who requests a replacement to satisfy the first two requirements of this guideline, but the administrative judge shall certify that it has been satisfied.

(D) **Affidavits of disqualification** If a judge of a multiple-judge division of a court of common pleas is disqualified pursuant to an affidavit of disqualification, the administrative judge of that division shall assign another sitting judge as provided in R.C. 2101.39 and 2701.03. In other situations, including where all judges of a court or division are disqualified, the Chief Justice shall designate an assigned judge.

4. **Procedure for Requesting Assignment** The administrative judge shall make the request for an assigned judge on behalf of the court, division, or any of its judges, and the request shall meet the following requirements:

(A) **Written request to Chief Justice** The request shall be written and addressed to the Chief Justice. If unexpected circumstances preclude a written request, the administrative judge may request an assigned judge by telephone or other means, provided the administrative judge promptly confirms the request in writing.

(B) **Statement of reason for request** The request shall state the reason the court requires the assistance of an assigned judge, pursuant to Guideline 1 (Assignment of Judges). The Chief Justice may deny any request for an assigned judge that does not contain the reason for the request.

(C) **Type and length of assignment requested** The request shall state whether the assignment should be for one or more specific cases, for a specific period of time, or for a special circumstance, pursuant to Guideline 2 (Type and Length of Assignment), and, if for a specific period of time, it shall state the length of assignment requested.

(D) **Certification** If the court is a multiple-judge or multiple-division court, the request shall certify compliance with Guideline 3 (Requirements Before Requesting Assignment).

5. **Request for Specific Judge** The administrative judge may request the Chief Justice to assign a specific sitting or retired judge who has expressed a willingness to accept assignments. If the administrative judge has recused from a case, the administrative judge may not request a specific judge to be assigned to that case.

FACTORS IN SELECTING JUDGES

6. **General Factors in Selecting Judges for Assignment** In considering a request for assignment, the Chief Justice may consider the following factors regarding the sitting or retired judge to be assigned:

(A) **Status of docket** The Chief Justice may consider the status of the docket of the judge to be assigned, including a comparison of the docket of the judge with the docket of other judges on the same court as the judge to be assigned, and other similar courts. The Chief Justice may also consider the number of cases pending before the judge to be assigned with the number of cases the judge has pending beyond the guidelines provided by the Rules of Superintendence for the Courts of Ohio, and the extent to which the judge or court upon which the judge sits has requested assigned judges for their court.

(B) **Competence** The Chief Justice may consider the competence of the judge to be assigned for the prospective duties.

(C) **Experience** The Chief Justice may consider the experience of the judge to be assigned serving on courts of the level requesting the assignment. The Chief Justice will not ordinarily assign a sitting judge who has not completed at least one full year of judicial service as a judge on the level of court on which the judge currently serves.

(D) **Proximity** The Chief Justice may consider the proximity of the judge to be assigned to the court making the request. Whenever feasible, an assigned judge from a nearby county should be designated in order to economize on travel time as well as to eliminate or minimize overnight expenses.

(E) **Infirmities** The Chief Justice may consider the infirmities, if any, of the judge to be assigned.

7. **Additional Factors in Selecting Retired Judges for Assignment** In addition to the general factors listed in Guideline 6 (General Factors in Selecting Judges for Assignment), the Chief Justice shall consider the following factors in deciding whether to assign a retired judge:

(A) **Practice of law** A retired judge shall not be assigned while the judge is engaged in the full-time or part-time practice of law in any state.

(B) **Judicial education requirements** A retired judge shall not be assigned unless the judge has completed and properly reported his or her judicial education requirements pursuant to the Rules for the Government of the Judiciary.

(C) **Resident of state** A retired judge shall not be assigned unless the judge is a resident or elector of Ohio.

(D) **Good standing** A retired judge shall not be assigned unless the judge has paid all current attorney registration fees and otherwise is in good standing as a member of the bar.

(E) **Age** A retired judge shall not be assigned after December 31 st of the year in which the judge turns 80 years of age. However in the interest of judicial economy, a retired judge may complete after this deadline any matters to which he or she had been previously assigned.

(F) **Serving as a paid expert witness in Ohio** A retired judge shall not be assigned if the judge is serving or has served in the preceding twelve months as an expert witness for which he or she has received compensation from a party in a proceeding in any federal or state court in Ohio.

(G) **Arbitration, mediation, and private judging** A retired judge who engages in alternative dispute resolution such as arbitration, mediation, and private judging pursuant to R.C. 2701.10, is not prohibited from being assigned per se, but the level of the judge's activity in this regard, including the status of his or her arbitration, mediation, or private judging docket may limit the opportunity for assignments under these Guidelines.

LEVELS OF ASSIGNMENT

8. **Levels of Assignment of Sitting Judges** A sitting judge may be assigned by the Chief Justice to serve in other courts, subject to constitutional and statutory limitations, as follows:

(A) **Municipal and county court judge** A sitting full-time or part-time municipal or county court judge may serve on another municipal court or county court.

(B) **Court of common pleas judge** A sitting court of common pleas judge may serve on another court of common pleas, the Court of Claims, or a court of appeals.

(C) **Court of appeals judge** A sitting court of appeals judge may serve on a court of common pleas, the Court of Claims, a court of appeals, or the Supreme Court.

(D) **Supreme Court justice** A sitting Supreme Court justice may serve on any court of record as deemed necessary.

9. **Levels of Assignment of Retired Judges** A retired judge may be assigned by the Chief Justice to serve in other courts, subject to constitutional, statutory, and rule limitations as follows:

(A) **Municipal and county court judge** A retired full-time or part-time municipal or county court judge may serve on a municipal court or a county court.

(B) **Court of common pleas judge** A retired court of common pleas judge may serve on a court of common pleas or the Court of Claims.

(C) **Court of appeals judge** A retired court of appeals judge may serve on a court of common pleas, the Court of Claims, or a court of appeals.

(D) **Supreme Court justice** A retired Supreme Court justice may serve on any court of record as deemed necessary.

CERTIFICATES AND RESPONSIBILITIES ON ASSIGNMENT

10. **Certificates of Assignment** A Certificate of Assignment shall be issued by the Chief Justice for each assignment made, as follows:

(A) **Specific case** If the assignment is for a specific case, the Certificate of Assignment shall state the case caption and case number, with no more than one certificate issued per case.

(B) **Specific period of time** If the assignment is for a specific period of time, the Certificate of Assignment shall state the dates that the assignment shall be in effect.

The administrative judge of the court requesting the assignment, shall direct that the original Certificate of Assignment be filed with the clerk of the court to which the judge has been assigned and entered upon the miscellaneous journal of the court. The administrative judge shall further direct that photocopies of the file-stamped certificate be placed in the case file of every matter considered by the assigned judge pursuant to the certificate.

(C) **Special circumstances** If the assignment is for a special circumstance not covered by a specific case or for a specific period of time, the Certificate of Assignment shall state the special circumstance.

The administrative judge of the court requesting the assignment shall direct the original Certificate of Assignment to be filed with the clerk of the court to which the judge has been assigned and entered upon the miscellaneous journal of the court. The administrative judge shall further direct that photocopies of the file-stamped certificate be placed in the case file of every matter considered by the assigned judge pursuant to the certificate.

11. **Responsibility for Cases on Assignment**

(A) **Assignment for specific case** When a judge is assigned to a court for a specific case, the assignment shall continue until the conclusion of the case, including any post-judgment proceedings, unless and until the case is reassigned.

(B) **Assignment for specific period of time** When a judge is assigned to a court for a specific period of time, the temporarily absent sitting judge shall retain responsibility for cases in which the sitting judge has resolved or presided over substantial preliminary matters. The assigned judge shall assume responsibility for cases in which the temporarily absent sitting judge has had the least involvement when the assignment occurs.

When a judge is assigned to a court for specific period of time, all matters pending before the assigned judge should be concluded by the end of the period. Any matter presented to the assigned judge that is not concluded by the end of the period may be extended beyond the end of the period, to allow the assigned judge an opportunity to conclude the matter, not to exceed three months. If the matter continues for more than three months after the end of the specified period, the administrative judge shall review the request and submit a request for continuation of the assignment, if appropriate.

(C) **Assignment for special circumstance** When a judge is assigned to a court for a special circumstance, the assignment shall continue until the conclusion of the matter including any post-judgment proceedings, unless and until the case is reassigned.

When an assigned judge arrives at a court on assignment on a special circumstance, the assigned judge may not exercise other judicial duties in that court until the conclusion of the special circumstance, unless the administrative judge of the court or division specifically requests the Chief Justice to designate the assigned judge for that additional purpose by following the requirements of Guideline 4 (Procedure for Requesting Assignment).

12. **Responsibilities of Requesting Court** In addition to any other responsibilities noted herein, the court to which a judge is assigned shall also meet the following duties and responsibilities:

(A) **Notification of counsel and parties** The court to which a judge is assigned shall notify counsel of the assignment once it is made by the Chief Justice. If the parties are not represented by counsel, the parties shall be notified.

(B) **Facilities and staff support** The court to which a judge is assigned shall provide sufficient facilities and staff support to enable the assigned judge to execute the responsibilities of the assignment properly and expeditiously. Support staff should include the services of a bailiff, court reporter, secretary, or law clerk as may be necessary and appropriate for the assignment.

(C) **Reporting of case statistics** The court to which a judge is assigned shall report the work performed by the judge in the manner required by the Rules of Superintendence for the Courts of Ohio. No sitting judge shall report that he or she disposed of any case or conducted any jury or non-jury trial if the activity was performed by an assigned judge.

REIMBURSEMENT AND COMPENSATION

13. **Reimbursement for Travel Expenses** (A) **Appellate courts** Reimbursement of travel expenses incurred by judges who are assigned to duty in the Supreme Court or a court of appeals shall be governed by the Supreme Court *Guidelines for Reimbursement of Travel and Education Expenses for Appellate Judges.*

(B) **Trial courts** Reimbursement of travel expenses incurred by sitting and retired judges who are assigned to duty in a court of common pleas, municipal court, or county court is the responsibility of the applicable county or municipal funding authority and is governed by the policies adopted by such authority.

14. **Compensation of Assigned Judge** (A) **Sitting judge** If the assigned judge is a sitting judge, all requests for compensation should be forwarded as appropriate to the Supreme Court or local funding authority for payment as follows:

• if sitting with the Supreme Court, the payment of compensation is governed by R.C. 141.11, and all requests for compensation shall be submitted to the Supreme Court using its prescribed compensation form.

• if sitting with a court of common pleas, the payment of compensation is governed by R.C. 141.07.

• if sitting with a municipal or county court, the payment of compensation is governed by R.C. 1901.10 and Sup. R. 17.

(B) **Retired judge sitting on court of common pleas or court of appeals** If the assigned judge is a retired judge sitting on a court of common pleas or a court of appeals, all requests for compensation should be forwarded to the Supreme Court as follows:

• A retired judge shall request compensation for work performed while serving on assignment by submitting a monthly compensation report on a form prescribed by the Supreme Court. The report shall be submitted after the retired judge performs such work, but not later than the end of the month that immediately follows the month in which the work was performed.

• In accounting for work performed while serving on assignment, a retired judge shall specifically note the type of work performed, as required by the instructions accompanying the monthly compensation report.

• The compensation paid to a retired judge for work performed each day shall be computed by multiplying the number of hours worked that day times one-eighth of the per diem associated with that assignment, not to exceed the full per diem associated with that assignment. A retired judge shall not be entitled to more than one full per diem for each calendar day worked, regardless of the number of hours worked in a particular day.

• The aggregate annual compensation paid to a retired judge as a result of all assignments shall not exceed the annual compensation payable to a judge serving on the highest level of court to which the retired judge has been assigned during the calendar year.

• The Chief Justice reserves the right not to assign a retired judge who fails to submit monthly compensation reports in accordance with this guideline, and to order the reimbursement of compensation paid to a retired judge who through mistake, inadvertence, or error submits an inaccurate report.

(C) **Retired judge sitting on municipal court or county court** If the assigned judge is a retired judge sitting on a municipal court or county court, all requests for compensation should be forwarded to the applicable local funding authority for payment.

MISCELLANEOUS

15. **Definitions** Unless otherwise limited by the context, the following definitions apply to terms used in the Guidelines:

(A) **"Administrative judge"** means the administrative judge of a court as defined at Sup. R. 4.

(B) **"Assigned judge"** means either of the following:

• Any sitting judge whom the Chief Justice assigns to serve temporarily on any Ohio court other than the court on which the sitting judge serves;

• Any retired judge whom the Chief Justice assigns to serve temporarily on any Ohio court.

(C) **"Chief Justice"** means the Chief Justice of the Supreme Court or a designee authorized by the Chief Justice.

(D) **"Retired judge"** means any person who voluntarily retired from judicial service on any Ohio court, including any person who served as a sitting judge under either of the following circumstances:

• Until the judge was ineligible to seek continued service by reason of constitutional or statutory age limitations;

• Without being defeated in an election for new service on that court or continued service on that court.

"Retired judge" does not include any person who has either been removed or suspended without reinstatement from service on any Ohio court pursuant to the Supreme Court Rules for the Government of the Judiciary, or who has resigned or retired from service while a complaint was pending against that person under those Rules.

"Retired judge" also does not include any person who has resigned his or her office between the date of defeat in an election for further service on that court and the end of his or her term. The defeat of a judge for new or continued service on a court makes the defeated judge ineligible for assignment to any court that has the same subject-matter jurisdiction as the court for which the defeated judge was seeking election.

(E) **"Sitting judge"** means any person who holds office by reason of election or gubernatorial appointment on the Supreme Court, Courts of Appeals, Courts of Common Pleas, Municipal Courts, or County Courts of Ohio.

16. **Effective Date** These Guidelines for Assignment of Judges are effective July 1, 2005.

History: Adopted 5-24-88; Revised 2-25-94; 3-25-94; 3-1-02; 7-1-05.

Index to Guidelines for Assignment of Judges